BERGIN AND GARFIELD'S

HANDBOOK *of* PSYCHOTHERAPY *and* BEHAVIOR CHANGE

50ᵀᴴ ANNIVERSARY EDITION

EDITED BY

Michael Barkham
Wolfgang Lutz
Louis G Castonguay

WILEY

This edition first published 2021

© 2021 John Wiley & Sons, Inc.

Edition History

John Wiley & Sons, Inc. (6e, 2013); John Wiley & Sons, Inc. (5e, 2003); John Wiley & Sons, Inc. (4e, 1993); John Wiley & Sons, Inc. (3e, 1986); John Wiley & Soncs, Inc. (2e, 1978); John Wiley & Sons, Inc. (1e, 1971)

Registered Office

John Wiley & Sons, Inc., 111 River Street, Hoboken, NJ 07030, USA

Editorial Office

111 River Street, Hoboken, NJ 07030, USA

For details of our global editorial offices, customer services, and more information about Wiley products visit us at www.wiley.com.

Wiley also publishes its books in a variety of electronic formats and by print-on-demand. Some content that appears in standard print versions of this book may not be available in other formats.

Library of Congress Cataloging-in-Publication Data is Available:

ISBN 9781119536581 (hardback)
ISBN 9781119536512 (epdf)
ISBN 9781119536567 (epub)

Cover Design: Wiley
Cover Image: © The Beach by Patricia Santoso

Set in 9.5/11.5 pt of Janson Text LT Std by Straive, Chennai, India

SKY10029279_082321

We dedicate this 50th anniversary edition of the Handbook *to the vision and scholarship of Allen E Bergin and Sol L Garfield.*

CONTENTS

LIST OF CONTRIBUTORS

W Stewart Agras, MD, is a professor emeritus of psychiatry at the Stanford University School of Medicine, Stanford, California, USA. His research is focused on the efficacy, effectiveness, and mechanisms of evidence-based psychotherapies for the treatment of eating disorders in both adolescents and adults and in the implementation of variants of evidence-based treatments in community settings.

Gerhard Andersson, PhD, is a professor of clinical psychology at Linköping University, Sweden. His research focuses on internet interventions for a range of psychiatric and somatic disorders and conditions. He is also active as a clinician and researcher in the field of audiology/hearing disorders.

Paul W Andrews, PhD, is an associate professor in the Department of Psychology, Neuroscience, and Behaviour at McMaster University, Hamilton, Ontario, Canada. His research on depression as an evolved adaptation to promote rumination has been published in prominent psychology and neuroscience journals and received widespread media attention, including *The New York Times*.

Joanna J Arch, PhD, is an associate professor of psychology and neuroscience at the University of Colorado Boulder, USA. Her research focuses on developing and evaluating interventions designed to address anxiety disorders as well as to improve well-being among anxious adults with cancer, with a focus on mindfulness and acceptance-based interventions.

Scott A Baldwin, PhD, is a professor of psychology at Brigham Young University, Provo, Utah, USA. His research focuses on methodological and statistical issues in psychotherapy research and related fields. His primary substantive interest is in therapist effects and improving psychotherapy outcomes.

Jacques P Barber, PhD, is a professor and dean of the Derner School of Psychology at Adelphi University, New York, USA, and a professor at the University of Pennsylvania and adjunct professor of psychiatry at NYU Medical School. His research focuses on the efficacy and processes of change of dynamic and cognitive psychotherapies for various disorders.

Michael Barkham, PhD, is a professor of clinical psychology at the University of Sheffield, England. He is a member of the PEARLS Research Lab, and his research focuses on conducting pragmatic trials and analyzing very large practice-based datasets to enhance treatment effectiveness and understand patient and therapist variability.

Thomas Berger, PhD, is a professor of clinical psychology and psychotherapy at the University of Bern, Switzerland. His research focuses on internet-based interventions, psychotherapy process and outcome research, training of therapists, psychotherapy integration, and transdiagnostic vulnerability factors.

James F Boswell, PhD, is an associate professor of clinical psychology at the University at Albany, SUNY, New York, USA, where he directs the Practice Oriented Research Lab. His research focuses on psychotherapy process and outcome, practice-research integration, and measurement-based care.

Jonathan B Bricker, PhD, is a professor of public health at the Fred Hutchinson Cancer Research Center and affiliate professor of psychology at the University of Washington, Seattle, USA. He leads the NIH-funded Health and Behavioral Innovations in Technology (HABIT) research lab, which focuses on developing, testing, and disseminating theory-based behavioral interventions for health behavior change.

Gary M Burlingame, PhD, is Warren & Wilson Dusenberry professor and chair of psychology at Brigham Young University, Provo, Utah, USA. He is the incoming president of the American Group Psychotherapy Association and past president of APA Society of Group Psychology and Psychotherapy. His research focuses on measurement and small group treatments.

Louis G Castonguay, PhD, is a liberal arts professor of psychology at Penn State University, University Park, Pennsylvania, USA. His research focuses on the process and outcome of psychotherapy, as well as on practice-research networks and practice-based evidence.

Zachary D Cohen, PhD, is a clinical psychology researcher at University of California–Los Angeles, USA, and is currently leading an effort within UCLA's Depression Grand Challenge to develop and disseminate personalized digital therapies for depression, anxiety, trauma, and sleep problems. His work focuses on developing data-driven approaches to treatment selection and personalization.

Mary Beth Connolly Gibbons, PhD, is an associate professor of psychiatry at the Perelman School of Medicine, University of Pennsylvania, Philadelphia, USA, where she is director of the Center for Psychotherapy Research. Her studies evaluate the comparative effectiveness of treatments for depression and the effectiveness of a therapist feedback system in community settings.

Michael J Constantino, PhD, is a professor of clinical psychology at the University of Massachusetts–Amherst, USA, where he directs the Psychotherapy Research Lab. His research centers on patient, therapist, and dyadic factors in psychosocial treatments; pantheoretical principles of clinical change (common factors); therapist effects and responsivity; and measurement-based care.

Alice E Coyne, MS, is a graduate student at the University of Massachusetts–Amherst, USA, where she is a member of the Psychotherapy Research Lab. Her research aims to identify, and to develop ways to capitalize on, patient, dyadic, and therapist characteristics and processes that can enhance the efficacy of psychotherapy.

Paul Crits-Christoph, PhD, is a professor of psychiatry at the Perelman School of Medicine, University of Pennsylvania, Philadelphia, USA. His recent research has focused on the process of psychotherapies for diverse disorders and patient preferences for different treatments.

Kim de Jong, PhD, is an assistant professor of clinical psychology at Leiden University, South Holland, the Netherlands, and chair of the International Network Supporting Psychotherapy Innovation and Research into Effectiveness (INSPIRE). Her research combines basic science and practice-based methods to improve outcomes for patients and therapists in routine mental health care.

Jaime Delgadillo, PhD, is a senior lecturer in clinical psychology and a member of the PEARLS Research Lab in the Psychology Department at the University of Sheffield, England. His research focuses on outcome monitoring, prediction, and feedback in routine mental health care.

Robert J DeRubeis, PhD, is a professor of psychology and director of clinical training at the University of Pennsylvania, Philadelphia, USA. He has conducted comparative clinical trials of treatments for major depression and has made empirical and methodological contributions to the prediction and understanding of the processes of therapeutic change and the maintenance of gains made in therapy.

Gary M Diamond, PhD, professor, Department of Psychology, Ben-Gurion University of the Negev, Beersheba, Israel, has developed and tested family-based treatments for depressed and suicidal adolescents, and for sexual and gender minority young adults and their non-accepting parents. His research focuses on change mechanisms, such as the therapeutic alliance, emotional processing, and parental acceptance.

Robert Elliott, PhD, is a professor of counseling at the University of Strathclyde, Glasgow, Scotland. A psychotherapy research methodologist, his research focuses on outcomes and change processes in emotion-focused and other humanistic experiential psychotherapies. He is a fellow in the Divisions of Psychotherapy and Humanistic Psychology of the American Psychological Association.

Catherine F Eubanks, PhD, is an associate professor of clinical psychology at the Ferkauf Graduate School of Psychology of Yeshiva University, New York City, New York, USA, and associate director of the Mount Sinai-Beth Israel Brief Psychotherapy Research Program. Her research focuses on alliance ruptures, alliance-focused training, and therapist skills across theoretical orientations.

Evan M Forman, PhD, is the director of the Center for Weight Eating and Lifestyle Science and professor of psychology at Drexel University, Philadelphia, Pennsylvania, USA. He conducts NIH-supported research developing innovative technological and behavioral approaches to health behavior change, and is the author of *Effective Weight Loss: An Acceptance-Based Behavioral Approach*.

Myrna L Friedlander, PhD, professor, Department of Educational and Counseling Psychology at the University at Albany/SUNY, USA, teaches doctoral seminars on psychotherapy processes and outcomes. Her research focuses on therapeutic change processes, particularly the working alliance, within individual psychodynamic, couple and family therapies, and relational processes in psychotherapy supervision.

Brandon A Gaudiano, PhD, is a professor of psychiatry and public health at Brown University, Providence, Rhode Island, USA. He is primary faculty at the Brown Mindfulness Center, and his work centers on developing and testing transitions of care and acceptance- and mindfulness-based interventions for individuals with severe mental illness.

Simon B Goldberg, PhD, is an assistant professor of counseling psychology at the University of Wisconsin–Madison, USA. His research focuses on psychological interventions to promote well-being. His primary interests include meditation-based interventions and improving psychotherapy outcomes through augmenting transtheoretical factors.

David A F Haaga, PhD, is a professor of psychology at American University, Washington, DC, USA, where he teaches a cognitive behavior therapy practicum for doctoral students. His research interests include assessment, cigarette smoking cessation, and treatment of trichotillomania.

Laurie Heatherington, PhD, is Edward Dorr Griffin professor of psychology at Williams College, Williamstown, Massachusetts, USA, where she teaches clinical psychology courses and conducts research on the family therapy alliance, cognition and other change processes in family therapy, and therapeutic interventions in community and global mental health settings.

Clara E Hill, PhD, is a professor at the University of Maryland, College Park, Maryland, USA, and has been president of the Society for Psychotherapy Research and Society for the Advancement of Psychotherapy, as well as editor of *Journal of Counseling Psychology* and *Psychotherapy Research*. Major research interests are helping skills, psychotherapy process and outcome, training and supervision, meaning in life, qualitative research, and dream work.

Steven D Hollon, PhD, is the Gertrude Conaway Vanderbilt professor of psychology at Vanderbilt University, Nashville, Tennessee, USA. His research focuses on the nature and treatment of depression with an emphasis on enduring effects of the cognitive behavioral interventions. He has over 350 publications and has mentored more than 20 doctoral and postdoctoral advisees.

Rachel L Horn, BA, is a doctoral candidate in clinical psychology at Harvard University, Cambridge, Massachusetts, USA. Her research uses machine learning to generate individualized estimates of treatment outcome, creating models that may be used to assist clinicians with treatment assignment.

Shigeru Iwakabe, PhD, is a professor of clinical psychology at Ochanomizu University, Bunkyō-ku, Tokyo, Japan. His research focuses on the process and outcome of affect-oriented integrative psychotherapy as well as cultural issues associated with practice and training of psychotherapy.

Robin B Jarrett, PhD, is a professor of psychiatry and holds the Elizabeth H. Penn Professorship in Clinical Psychology at the University of Texas Southwestern Medical Center, Dallas, Texas, where her laboratory evaluates the role of psychosocial factors and interventions on the course of health in mood and related disorders.

Adrienne S Juarascio, PhD, is an assistant professor at the Center for Weight Eating and Lifestyle Science and Department of Psychology at Drexel University, Philadelphia, Pennsylvania, USA. Her work is focused on developing and evaluating new treatment approaches for eating disorders with an emphasis on the use of mindfulness and acceptance-based treatments.

Alan E Kazdin, PhD, ABPP, is Sterling professor of psychology and child psychiatry at Yale University, New Haven, Connecticut, USA. His 800+ publications include 50 books that focus on psychosocial interventions, parenting and child rearing, interpersonal violence, and research methodology. In 2008, he was president of the American Psychological Association.

John (Jack) R Keefe, PhD, is a research fellow at Albert Einstein College of Medicine in the Bronx, New York, USA. His research interests involve using information about individual patients to improve treatment of treatment-resistant mental illness by adapting treatments or matching patients to therapies, and LGBTQ mental health.

Matthew C Keller, PhD, is a professor of psychology and neuroscience at the University of Colorado at Boulder, USA, and a faculty fellow of the Institute for Behavioral Genetics. His work examines the genetic architecture of psychiatric disorders and other complex traits.

Sarah Knox, PhD, is a professor in the Department of Counselor Education and Counseling Psychology, in the College of Education at Marquette University, Milwaukee, Wisconsin, USA. She currently serves as Co-Editor-in-Chief of *Counselling Psychology Quarterly*. Her research interests focus on supervision and training, the therapy process and relationship, and qualitative research.

Mariane Krause, PhD, is a professor at Pontificia Universidad Católica de Chile's School of Psychology, Chile, where she is currently the dean of the Faculty for Social Sciences. Her areas of research are change processes in psychotherapy, depression, and the interaction between sociocultural conditions and mental health.

Michael J Lambert, PhD, is a professor emeritus of psychology at Brigham Young University, Provo, Utah, USA. His research has emphasized psychotherapy outcome, process, and the measurement of change. He was a developer of the OQ-45 and editor of the fifth and sixth editions of *Bergin and Garfield's Handbook of Psychotherapy and Behavior Change*.

Heidi M Levitt, PhD, is a professor of psychology at the University of Massachusetts, Boston, USA. She is a past-president of the Society for Qualitative Inquiry in Psychology. She chaired the American Psychological Association's task force on Journal Article Reporting Standards for qualitative and mixed methods research for their *Publication Manual*.

Wolfgang Lutz, PhD, is a professor of clinical psychology and psychotherapy and director of the psychotherapy research and training program at the University of Trier, Trier, Germany. His research focuses on classifying different trajectories of treatment change and illustrating how empirically derived clinical recommendations can be applied to personalize mental health care.

Marta M Maslej, PhD, is a postdoctoral fellow with the Krembil Centre for Neuroinformatics at the Centre for Addiction and Mental Health, Toronto, Canada. Her current research explores psychosocial and cognitive factors contributing to treatment outcomes in depression using methods from machine learning and natural language processing.

John McLeod, PhD, is a professor emeritus of counseling at Abertay University, Dundee, Scotland. He is the author of books and articles on case study and qualitative methods in psychotherapy research, and has been involved in the development of a collaborative, flexible, pluralistic framework for therapy practice.

Kevin S McCarthy, PhD, is associate professor of psychology at Chestnut Hill College, Philadelphia, Pennsylvania, USA, and director of Psychotherapy Curriculum in the Psychiatry Residency Program in the Perelman School of Medicine at the University of Pennsylvania. His research focuses on processes of change in psychotherapy.

J Christopher Muran, PhD, is an associate dean and professor at the Gordon F. Derner School of Psychology, Adelphi University, New York, USA. He is also principal investigator, Mount Sinai Beth Israel Psychotherapy Research Program, and on faculty at Icahn School of Medicine at Mount Sinai. His research has focused on alliance rupture repair.

Benoit H Mulsant, MD, is a professor and the Labatt Family Chair of the Department of Psychiatry, University of Toronto, Ontario, Canada, and a senior scientist at the Centre for Addiction and Mental Health (Toronto). The overarching goal of his work is to improve the treatment of persons with severe mental illness.

Michelle G Newman, PhD, is a professor of psychology and psychiatry at Penn State University, University Park, Pennsylvania, USA. Her research focuses on the nature and treatment of anxiety and mood disorders, including the etiology and classification, individual predictors of psychotherapy outcome, and impact of brief psychotherapy with respect to these disorders.

Mei Yi Ng, PhD, is an assistant professor of clinical psychology at Florida International University, Miami Florida, USA. She directs the Mechanisms Underlying Treatment Technologies (MUTT) Lab at the Center for Children and Families. Her research focuses on examining change mechanisms and processes of evidence-based psychotherapies and personalizing interventions for depressed adolescents.

Jesse Owen, PhD, is a professor in the Counseling Psychology Department at the University of Denver, Denver, Colorado, USA. He is also the senior research advisor at SonderMind. His research focuses on promoting therapists' expertise and multicultural orientation, as well as examining processes and outcomes of couple/relationship interventions.

Andrew C Page, PhD, is a professor of psychological science and pro vice-chancellor, research, at the University of Western Australia, Perth, Australia. His research aims to improve the efficiency and effectiveness in routine clinical practice, most recently by predicting self-harm and suicide. This has often been conducted in collaboration with Perth Clinic.

Shireen L Rizvi, PhD, ABPP, is a professor of clinical psychology at Rutgers University, New Brunswick, New Jersey, USA. She received her doctorate from the University of Washington under the mentorship of Dr. Marsha Linehan. She has published widely in the areas of dialectical behaviour therapy, borderline personality disorder, and suicidal behaviors.

Julian A Rubel, PhD, is an assistant professor of psychotherapy research at Justus Liebig University Giessen, Hesse, Germany. His research focuses on the development of empirically supported tools to prevent treatment failure and premature termination.

Jessica L Schleider, PhD, is an assistant professor of psychology at Stony Brook University, Stony Brook, New York, USA, where she directs the Lab for Scalable Mental Health. The objective of her research is to develop brief, accessible interventions for youth depression and anxiety; identify change mechanisms underlying their effects; and test novel approaches to dissemination.

Zindel V Segal, PhD, is distinguished professor of psychology in mood disorders at the University of Toronto, Scarborough, Canada. His program of research characterizes psychological markers of relapse vulnerability in affective disorder which, in turn, provide an empirical rationale for offering training in mindfulness meditation to recurrently depressed patients in recovery.

Jason Sharbanee, PhD, is a lecturer in clinical psychology at Edith Cowan University, Joondalup, Australia. His research focuses on the process of change in emotion-focused and experiential therapies. He is the director of the Western Australian Institute of Emotion Focused Therapy, and maintains a small private practice at Cygnet Clinic.

Daisy R Singla, PhD, is a clinician scientist and assistant professor at the Center of Addiction and Mental Health and in the Department of Psychiatry at the University of Toronto, Ontario, Canada. As a clinical psychologist by training and global health researcher at heart, her primary research interests involve scaling up evidence-based psychological interventions for depression and anxiety.

William B Stiles, PhD, is a professor emeritus of psychology at Miami University, Oxford, Ohio, USA, adjunct research professor of psychology at Appalachian State University, Boone, North Carolina, USA, and senior research fellow at Metanoia Institute, London, UK. He has written about psychotherapy process and outcome, verbal interaction, and research methods.

Bernhard Strauss, PhD, is a full professor of psychotherapy and medical psychology, head of the Institute of Psychosocial Medicine, Psychotherapy, and Psycho-Oncology at Friedrich-Schiller-University Jena, Thuringia, Germany, and is past president of the German College of Psychosomatic Medicine, German Society for Medical Psychology, and the Society for Psychotherapy Research. His research focuses on (group) psychotherapy, attachment, and psychological interventions in medicine.

Ladislav Timulak, PhD, is associate professor at Trinity College Dublin, Ireland. He is course director of the Doctorate in Counseling Psychology. His main research interest is the development of emotion-focused therapy. He currently is adapting this form of therapy as a transdiagnostic treatment for depression, anxiety and related disorders.

Kevin E Vowles, PhD, is a professor of clinical health psychology at Queen's University, Belfast, Northern Ireland. His work has examined treatment effectiveness, clinical significance, and mechanisms of change. Recent work has concentrated on identifying distinctive characteristics of effective pain rehabilitation and differentiating problematic from non-problematic opioid use.

Bruce E Wampold, PhD, is senior researcher at the Institute at Modum Bad Psychiatric Center and professor emeritus of counseling psychology at the University of Wisconsin in Madison, Wisconsin, USA. Currently his work involves understanding psychotherapy from empirical, historical, and anthropological perspectives.

Jeanne C Watson, PhD, is professor in the Department of Applied Psychology and Human Development at the University of Toronto, Ontario, Canada, and APA fellow in the Division of Psychotherapy. A major exponent of emotion-focused therapy (EFT), she has co-authored nine books and conducts research on EFT, cognitive behavioral therapy and humanistic psychotherapies.

John R Weisz, PhD, ABPP, grew up in Mississippi, got his BA from Mississippi College, Clinton, Mississippi, and his MS and PhD from Yale University, New Haven, Connecticut. He is a professor of psychology at Harvard University, Cambridge, Massachusetts, USA. He leads the Harvard Lab for Youth Mental Health, and with his colleagues and students develops and tests mental health interventions for children and adolescents.

Soo Jeong Youn, PhD, is the director of evaluation at Community Psychiatry PRIDE at Massachusetts General Hospital, and an assistant professor in psychiatry at Harvard Medical School, Boston, Massachusetts, USA. Her research focuses on psychotherapy process/outcome, community-based participatory research, and implementation science to address the access to care problem in mental health.

Sigal Zilcha-Mano, PhD, is a professor of clinical psychology and the head of the Psychotherapy Research Lab in the Department of Psychology, University of Haifa, Israel. Her research focuses on improving mental health through the personalization of treatment by facilitating change in individual-specific therapeutic mechanisms.

FOREWORD

This Foreword is addressed particularly to the younger generation of researchers, clinicians, and professors in the many parts of the world where this *Handbook* may be useful. I recall vividly my experience in 1967, as a young 33-year-old professor in the Clinical Psychology Doctoral Program at Teachers College, Columbia University in New York. It seemed that the evidence to support then-current therapeutic interventions was unclear. A systematic summary of data was needed to guide our work and to stimulate innovation or remediation where needed. I thus began to assemble every bit of solid evidence pertinent to our clinical work.

Fortuitously, working as a clinical psychologist within an educational institution brought me in contact with a path-breaking volume on the efficacy of educational methods edited by Nathaniel Gage, titled *Handbook of Research on Teaching*. Reading that book prompted the thought that something similar could and should be done for "psychotherapy," another applied intervention method, with techniques similar to the educational process.

I thus began to assemble every bit of good evidence I could find regarding the efficacy and safety of psychotherapy techniques. Even in those early days, it became obvious that there was a research literature more abundant than one person could master in a reasonable time-period. Consequently, I asked a senior colleague and director of our Doctoral Program, Sol L. Garfield, to assist me in the effort. As an established leader in the field and an accomplished writer, he provided the wisdom, encouragement, and contacts that were essential to the project. He became a treasured friend and collaborator. With his kind and competent reassurance, *The Handbook* became much more than it would have been through my effort alone.

The first edition appeared in 1971, published by the prominent international book company John Wiley and Sons, which had also printed the *Handbook of Research on Teaching*. Both books have gone through multiple editions. The *Bergin & Garfield Handbook* appeared in 1971, 1978, 1986, and 1994, followed by 5th and 6th editions edited by our younger colleague, Michael J. Lambert, in 2004 and 2013. Michael's labors and that of the contributors he recruited have extended and expanded the influence of good research on clinical practice and human welfare. These six volumes now grace the study in my and my wife, Marian's, retirement home in St George, Utah – a place near the Arizona border where the sun shines all year and keeps my aging brain alive.

The gratifying *Handbook* odyssey now continues under the leadership of new editors who reflect the international presence and value of empirically validated therapeutic interventions. This 7th edition, managed by Michael Barkham in England, Wolfgang Lutz in Germany, and Louis Castonguay in the United States, will appear in 2021, marking a most fitting 50th anniversary since the beginning in New York in 1971. I extend my good wishes to them and my gratitude to all of the fine contributors over the past five decades. May the labors of so many careful researchers whose efforts are documented therein continue to improve clinical treatments and bless the lives of the general public who rely on us for competent, effective, and safe techniques.

Allen E Bergin, PhD
Professor Emeritus, Brigham Young University

PREFACE

Like so many researchers in the field of psychotherapy research, we have each been brought up on a combination of successive editions of the *Handbook*, some now quite tattered, along with many years of collaboration and dialogue with colleagues in the Society for Psychotherapy Research (SPR). Among those who has been hugely influential for each of us is Michael Lambert, editor of the previous two editions of the *Handbook* and who, in the summer of 2017, approached MB about interest in editing the 7e, and who in turn approached WL and LGC as collaborators, having worked together previously on a chapter in the 6e.

From the very beginning of our collaboration, it was obvious that this edition would fall close to the 50th anniversary of the first edition published in 1971. And so it was agreed from the outset that the planned publication date would coincide with the 50th anniversary in 2021. With that decision made, and with a broader international editorship, we brainstormed a combination of the best researchers and scholars in the field who would capture the present state of psychotherapy research as well as having an eye to the future. Our choices were influenced by what we felt were the key areas for which there was a solid evidence-base associated with world leaders in the field.

The two defining hallmarks of the *Handbook* over the past 50 years have been its depth of content and its scholarship. In terms of its content, the *Handbook* tries to cover the key areas in the field of psychotherapy research without espousing any one particular theory or psychological approach over another. Therefore, the new edition broadly follows the structure of the 6e, although it remains more within the field of the psychological therapies rather than moving into health behaviors in the latter chapters. It is divided into six sections as follows: (1) history and methods; (2) measuring and evidencing change in efficacy and practice-based research; (5) therapeutic ingredients; (4) therapeutic approaches and formats; (5) increasing precision and scale; and (6) epilogue.

We have balanced tradition with some new elements. In the current edition, we now have two chapters focusing on qualitative research and new chapters on mindfulness and acceptance-based treatments, internet therapy, and personalized treatment approaches. And significantly, the final substantive chapter (bar the Epilogue) focuses on models of psychological therapy delivery. We also tried to include a broader international perspective and authorship, given that the *Handbook* has been influential in many countries around the world. As with all choices, some folk will ask why there isn't a chapter on this or on that, but we hope we have captured the main topic areas of interest to the majority of people within the limits of the space allowed.

And in terms of scholarship, the 23 chapters comprise a combination of updates by the same authors, updates by the same lead authors with new co-authors, updates by new authors, or new chapters by new authors. Our collective of scholars comprises 67 researchers from over 10 countries (the precise number depends on definitions), of whom a majority will be recognized as contributors to SPR. But, notwithstanding the rich tradition of research that is synonymous with SPR, we also extended the invitation to scholars in the broad field of the psychological therapies, as we are keen to collaborate with and learn from all scientist-practitioners committed to working in and promoting bona fide interventions aimed at alleviating distress for people in need and improving the quality of their lives.

In order to give greater recognition to each author and to aid new readers in becoming more familiar with these scholars, we asked each author to provide a 50-word summary of their major research interests, and these are listed at the front of the *Handbook*. As readers will see, there are many luminaries. However, on this 50th anniversary, we wanted in particular to acknowledge those who have contributed on multiple occasions (3+) to editions of the *Handbook* and in that sense have helped set the standard with which it is known internationally. Hence, our special thanks to Aaron Beck, Allen Bergin, Larry Beutler, Gary Burlingame, Robert Elliott, Paul Emmelkamp, Sol Garfield, Les Greenberg, Clara Hill, Steve Hollon, Alan Kazdin, Michael Lambert, David Orlinsky, Timothy Smith, and Bernhard Strauss. And, to be historically complete, in the initial four editions there were successive contributions from Richard Bednar, Theodore Kaul, Mary Koss, and Joseph Matarazzo. As a tribute to all contributors, we have compiled a schematic summary of the chapter titles and authors from all editions of the *Handbook* in the Appendix.

In terms of the process of producing the chapters, although we did not set out with a clear plan regarding how we would review chapters, we found a natural process whereby all three of us reviewed each chapter and fed back together to the lead authors, with all chapters running through two review cycles. All chapter leads were responsive in their revisions, which made our task so much easier. As a standard, we asked all authors to be mindful and inclusive of two points. First, to be inclusive of cultural and diversity issues relating to their chapter content. We took the decision to integrate these issues into chapters rather than focus on them as a specific topic. Second, we asked authors to avoid the use of presumptive pronouns. Beyond that, our overarching aim was to support authors in delivering the best scholarship possible. In addition, we have introduced several enhancements. First, each chapter starts with an abstract and outline and also contains a glossary of abbreviations. Second, we migrated to APA 7e referencing style, which means that the body of the text no longer has long strings of author names and all references contain author names up to 20 (plus last) rather than just 6 (plus last) and also have doi numbers where they exist, thereby making the reference lists a valuable resource in themselves. And, in order to retain the extent of references used by authors without consuming a disproportionate number of printed pages, we took the decision to reduce their font size.

The experience of editing the *Handbook* has been unique. It has been a privilege to work with so many influential scholars and creative minds from multiple regions of the world as well as to have access to a vast amount of empirical knowledge – both in terms of breadth and depth. We are grateful for this opportunity, and we also hope that the pleasure we have derived from working together has found its way into the final product that we have shepherded for close to four years.

We have also shared a deep sense of gratitude for Allen Bergin's genuine and enthusiastic support in helping us carry the torch that he and his colleague Sol Garfield started 50 years ago, before passing it on to Michael Lambert, who has been with us in spirit throughout and for whom we wish to note our special thanks.

We are grateful to all lead and co-authors for their excellent work and time given freely. We would especially like to thank Monica Rogers at Wiley, who has been the key person throughout and who, together with Kerstin Nasdeo, has calmly managed pulling the *Handbook* together. And our thanks to Cheryl Ferguson who copyedited all the material, to Suthan Raj for overseeing the production, and Christina Weyrauch and the design team for their creative contributions to the cover design. We also thank Ann-Kathrin Deisenhofer, Kate Duffy, Rebecca Janis, Ryan Kilcullen, Kaitlyn Poster, and Jana Wasserheß for their supporting work. Last, but not least, we thank Patricia Santoso for her artwork that is the cover image for this edition, a cover that captures the integration of rich traditions of knowledge that the *Handbook* has been striving toward for five decades.

Finally, we hope that this *Handbook* will be the lodestar – thank you Irene Elkin – for all psychotherapy researchers in our collective quest to deliver quality therapies and psychological interventions for all people seeking help, regardless of their personal, social, or economic circumstances.

Michael Barkham – Sheffield, UK

Wolfgang Lutz – Trier, Germany

Louis G Castonguay – State College, USA

June 2021

PART I

HISTORY
AND METHODS

•

TRADITIONS AND NEW BEGINNINGS: HISTORICAL AND CURRENT PERSPECTIVES ON RESEARCH IN PSYCHOTHERAPY AND BEHAVIOR CHANGE

WOLFGANG LUTZ, LOUIS G CASTONGUAY, MICHAEL J LAMBERT, AND MICHAEL BARKHAM

Abstract

This introductory chapter to the seventh and 50-year anniversary edition of *Bergin and Garfield's Handbook of Psychotherapy and Behavior Change* provides a context for current research activity by framing psychotherapy research since the 1950s as a series of research "generations." Each of these generations adopted specific research strategies to investigate a question that was key at the time. Reflecting the development of the field, these key questions have been addressed over the course of the previous six editions of the *Handbook*. Importantly, these questions remain relevant today. They have also been refreshed by new themes and topics that represent, to a large extent, the background of this new edition. Among them are developments pertaining to standardization and replication, evidence-based practice and practice-based evidence, process and qualitative research, methodological and technological developments, as well as issues related to theoretical integration, diversity, dissemination, psychometric feedback, and personalized mental health. This introduction concludes by providing a short overview of the chapters in this new edition of the *Handbook*.

OVERVIEW

INTRODUCTION

This seventh edition of *Bergin and Garfield's Handbook of Psychotherapy and Behavior Change* is a milestone that deserves to be celebrated as it marks the 50th anniversary of its first edition (Bergin & Garfield, 1971). Since its inception, the *Handbook* has been a cornerstone of psychotherapy research, a standard reference book that has been hugely influential in providing the scientific base for establishing psychological and mental health services in many countries around the world.

The past 50 years have seen tremendous activity in psychotherapy research. For example, searching the term *psychotherapy research* on Google Scholar between 1970 and 1995 (i.e., the 25-year time period corresponding to the first four editions of the *Handbook*) reveals approximately 384,000 publications. In contrast, the last 25-year period (i.e., 1996–2020) has seen over twice the number of publications (approximately 825,000) on the topic of psychotherapy research. The task of the past six editions has been to summarize the quintessence of empirical publications and to capture new findings (see Bergin & Garfield, 1971, 1994; Garfield & Bergin, 1978, 1986; Lambert, 2004, 2013a). The current anniversary edition continues this tradition by distilling the central findings of both current developments and emerging advances in the field.

Throughout its history, the *Handbook* has had a strong connection with the international Society for Psychotherapy Research (SPR). Allen E. Bergin, Sol L. Garfield, and Michael J. Lambert – the three previous editors – as well as the three current editors, were or are still active members of SPR. As a multidisciplinary scientific association, SPR's aim is to foster research and worldwide communication of findings in order to improve the understanding, effectiveness, and social value of psychotherapy (e.g., Orlinsky, 1995). This is fully consistent with the primary goals of this *Handbook*, which are to provide an overview of the main empirical findings in psychotherapy (about its outcomes, processes, and participants), as well as to identify implications for both clinical and research practice. By doing this over many years, the *Handbook* has not only generated broad international interest, but has become increasingly international itself by including more authors from around the world.

One of the factors that explains the impact of the *Handbook* has been its broad and integrative focus. From its first edition, it has featured empirical findings from diverse theories of psychological change and approaches to psychotherapeutic interventions, as well as from various methodological perspectives. This seventh edition is no exception. To set up the context for this edition, we provide a short overview of the history and current trends of psychotherapy research before ending with an overview of the *Handbook* chapters and their content.

A SHORT HISTORY OF PSYCHOTHERAPY RESEARCH

Psychotherapy research primarily pursues two central goals or traditions, which are not wholly independent of one another. One line of research investigates questions related to the impact of psychological therapies – *outcome research* – while the second line of research – *process research* – aims to identify the components of such therapies that facilitate or interfere with change. Both research traditions have been central to this *Handbook* from its beginning (Bergin & Garfield, 1971).

Table 1.1 and Table 1.2 display central research questions, methodologies as well as representative and highly cited publications over the history of six research generations and editions of this *Handbook*. Of course, these central questions and the chosen papers represent the authors' evaluations and selection, and other scholars with different backgrounds would likely have chosen somewhat different questions and examples (although, we hope, with some degree of overlap). Different accounts can be found, for example, in Muran et al. (2010), Orlinsky (1995), Russell and Orlinsky (1996), and Strupp and Howard (1992).

Within the framework of outcome research, randomized controlled trials (RCTs), quasi-experimental designs, and meta-analyses have been adopted to evaluate the efficacy and effectiveness of various psychotherapy approaches, interventions and techniques. In addition, outcome research includes studies on quality assurance or routine outcome monitoring (ROM), the implementation of empirically based feedback, the effect of routine clinical practice and health care systems, as well as cost and cost–benefit analyses of psychological therapies (e.g., Lambert, 2013a).

Process research, on the other hand, has focused on how psychotherapy works, by investigating various aspects of therapist and client experiences, actions, and interactions, as well as by identifying mediators and change mechanisms that are (causally) linked to treatment outcome (e.g., Crits-Christoph et al., 2013). As with outcome research, both quantitative and qualitative analyses are used to describe and understand what is taking place during (and between) therapy sessions. In both outcome and process research, attention has been given to patient and therapist characteristics that could predict or moderate how therapy may unfold and how it may have an impact – characteristics that could also have consequences for clinical training (see Chapters 5, 7, 8, 9, and 10).

Research Generations

The history of central questions addressed by psychotherapy research can be viewed as historical phases or research generations, which can be marked by the first six editions of this *Handbook*. These generations and the research questions at their respective core are set out in Table 1.1. Notably, although each research generation has a starting date, the themes have been ongoing, with researchers adopting increasingly innovative assessment and statistical tools, as well as larger databases, in order to pursue the most rigorous and robust evidence-based knowledge.

The development of research on psychotherapy – more recently referred to as the *psychological therapies* to capture the plurality of differing theoretical approaches – has been closely linked to the development of the practice of psychotherapy, and more specifically, to the development of a diversity of psychological interventions to treat behavioral and mental health problems. As Urban and Ford (1971) pointed out in the introduction to the first edition, the development of psychotherapy practice did not happen in a continuous way. After the field emerged at the end of the 19th century with the introduction of Breuer and Freud's first psychological interventions, the course of development was not a simple linear progression toward a more precise delineation and research of effective psychological procedures and change strategies. Rather, development was lateral, meaning that many different variants of psychotherapeutic treatments or treatment orientations were introduced. Wampold (2001) counted over 250 distinct psychotherapeutic approaches, and on Wikipedia, a search for the term "list of psychotherapies" provides a certainly incomplete list of 171 variants. Of course, psychotherapy research is carried out on only a small proportion of approaches and variants. In the following, we give a short overview of milestones and landmarks of this development and how psychotherapy research has emerged and developed in this context.

The Early Phase

The early phase of psychotherapy addressed the question, "What is psychotherapy?" It was characterized by well-known founders of psychotherapy schools and their comprehensive psychotherapy models but limited research endeavors. Theoretical debates about causes of mental illness and core interventions have been a central issue throughout the history of psychotherapy practice and research (Lambert, 2013b). Here is not the place to describe these numerous developments, but the *Handbook* covers research on the four main theoretical orientations (psychodynamic, humanistic, cognitive–behavioral, and systemic treatments, including variations and modifications within these broad orientations, see Chapters 12, 13, 14, 15, and 16). It also covers modalities and settings (individual,

TABLE 1.1 Summary of psychotherapy research generations

	Research Generations					
	I	II	III	IV	V	VI
Handbook editions	Handbook 1e (Bergin & Garfield, 1971)	Handbook 2e (Garfield & Bergin, 1978)	Handbook 3e (Garfield & Bergin, 1986)	Handbook 4e (Bergin & Garfield, 1994)	Bergin & Garfield's Handbook 5e (Lambert, 2004)	Bergin & Garfield's Handbook 6e (Lambert, 2013)
Time frame	1950s – 1970s onwards	1960s – 1980s onwards	1970s – 1990s onwards	1980s – 2000s onwards	1990s – 2010s onwards	2000s – 2020s onwards
Theme	Justification	Specificity	Efficacy & cost effectiveness	Effectiveness & clinical significance	Evidence-based practice	Practice-based evidence
Thematic question	Is psychotherapy effective?	Which psychotherapy is more effective?	How can treatments be made more (cost) effective?	How can research findings be transferred into clinical practice?	How can the quality of treatment delivery (by clinical guidelines) be improved?	How can treatment outcome be improved?
Methodologies	Control group comparisons; effect sizes; meta-analyses	Randomized control trial; factorial design; placebo group	Probit analysis; growth curves; structural modelling; power analyses	Clinical significance; meta-analyses	Meta-analyses; predictive modeling; patient-focused research	Patient-focused research; meta-analyses; predictive modeling; large (multisite) trials
Key issues	Efficacy; spontaneous remission	What treatment, by whom, is most effective for this individual with that specific problem, and under which set of circumstances?	Dose-response; medical offset; health economics; evidence-based medicine; low-cost interventions	User perspectives; evidence-based practice; practice guidelines; treatment gap	Evidence-based practice; empirically validated treatments; routine outcomes monitoring; good enough level of change	Patterns of change; routine outcomes monitoring; patient feedback; practice-oriented research; low-cost interventions; therapist effects

OUTCOMES

(Continued)

TABLE 1.1 (CONTINUED)

Research Generations

	I	II	III	IV	V	VI
Handbook editions	Handbook 1e (Bergin & Garfield, 1971)	Handbook 2e (Garfield & Bergin, 1978)	Handbook 3e (Garfield & Bergin, 1986)	Handbook 4e (Bergin & Garfield, 1994)	Bergin & Garfield's Handbook 5e (Lambert, 2004)	Bergin & Garfield's Handbook 6e (Lambert, 2013)
Time frame	1950s – 1970s onwards	1960s – 1980s onwards	1970s – 1990s onwards	1980s – 2000s onwards	1990s – 2010s onwards	2000s – 2020s onwards
Thematic question	Are there objective methods for evaluating process?	What components are related to outcome?	How does change occur (via a quantitative approach)?	How does change occur (via a qualitative approach)?	How to disentangle common and specific factors of change?	How to identify moderators, mediators and mechanisms of change?
Methodologies	Random sampling of sections of therapy; 'uniformity myth' assumed; therapist patient post-session evaluations	Single-case methodologies; sampling 5-minute sections of therapy	Taxonomies; linking process to outcomes	Qualitative methods; narrative approach; discourse analysis; descriptive studies; theory development	Additive and dismantling trials; factorial designs; shared components	Moderator, mediator analysis; Between and within patient process outcome relations
Key issues	Verbal & speech behaviours	Rogerian facilitative conditions (e.g., empathy)	Therapeutic alliance; verbal response modes	Events paradigm; single case approach; qualitative methods	Common factors; specific factors	Moderators; mediators; sudden gains; mechanisms of change

PROCESSES

Note: This table is an updated and substantially extended version of content previously published in Barkham, M. (2007). Methods, outcomes and processes in the psychological therapies across successive research generations. In W. Dryden (Ed.), *Dryden's handbook of individual therapy* (5th ed. pp. 451–514). Sage.

TABLE 1.2 Representative and highly cited publications over the history of research generations

Research Generations

	I	II	III	IV	V	VI
Handbook editions	Handbook 1e (Bergin & Garfield, 1971)	Handbook 2e (Garfield & Bergin, 1978)	Handbook 3e (Garfield & Bergin, 1986)	Handbook 4e (Bergin & Garfield, 1994)	Bergin & Garfield Handbook 5e (Lambert, 2004)	Bergin & Garfield Handbook 6e (Lambert, 2013)
Examples of representative texts on outcome	Eysenck (1952); Cohen (1977); Frank (1961); Kiesler (1966); Melzoff & Kornreich (1970); Sloane et al. (1975); Waskow & Parloff (1975)	Cohen (1988); Gurman & Razin (1977); Hollon & Beck (1978); Paul (1967); Smith, Glass, & Miller (1980); Stiles, Shapiro, & Elliott (1986)	Crits-Christoph et al. (1991); Horowitz et al. (1988); Roth & Fonagy (1996)	Barlow et al. (1994); Howard et al. (1996); Jacobson et al. (1984, 1991); Strupp et al. (1997)	Barkham et al. (2006); Borkovec et al. (2001); DeRubeis & Crits-Christoph (1998); Lambert (2007); Lutz et al. (1999); Wampold (2001)	Barkham et al. (2010); Clark (2018); Cuijpers (2017); Holmes et al. (2018); Kazdin (2008); Lambert (2013c); Lutz et al. (2006); Wampold & Imel (2015)
Examples of representative texts on processes	Rogers (1957); Rogers & Dymond (1954); Rogers & Gendlin (1967); Orlinsky & Howard (1967); Whitehorn & Betz (1954)	Benjamin (1974); Bordin (1979); Howard & Orlinsky (1972); Stiles (1979); Strupp (1980)	Greenberg & Pinsoff (1986); Horvath & Greenberg (1994); Goldfried (1980); Rice & Greenberg (1984); Russell & Stiles (1979)	Elliott et al. (1999); Hill et al. (1997); Orlinsky et al. (1994); Jones & Pulus (1993); Toukmanian & Rennie (1992); Safran et al. (1990); Stiles et al. (1998)	Barber et al., (1996); Castonguay & Beutler (2006); Norcross (2002); Safran & Muran (2000); Tang & DeRubeis (1999); Wampold (2001)	Crits-Christoph et al. (2011); DeRubeis et al. (2014b); Kazdin (2007); Norcross (2011)
Examples of highly cited/influential articles	Luborsky et al. (1971); Smith & Glass (1977); Strupp & Hadley (1979)	Luborsky et al. (1975); Prochaska & Di Clemente (1983); Rush et al. (1977)	Elkin et al. (1989); Howard et al. (1986); Keller et al. (1987); Prochaska & Di Clemente (1992)	Bateman & Fonagy (1999); Chambless & Hollon (1998); Horvath (1991); Linehan et al. (1991); Lipsey & Wilson (1993); Seligman (1995)	Butler et al. (2006); Chambless & Ollendick (2001); Hayes et al. (2006); Hill et al. (2005); Martin et al. (2000); Seligman (2005)	Hofmann et al. (2010); Horvath (2011); Insel (2014); Richards & Richardson (2012)

couple and family, group interventions, adults, children and adolescents, internet treatments; see Chapters 6, 16, 17, and 18) that are linked to these traditions.

Psychotherapy began with the psychoanalytic (today often termed *dynamic* or *psychodynamic*) tradition (e.g., Freud, Adler, Horney, Sullivan), with a central focus on unconscious motivations, early life experiences, repressed conflicts, interpretations, and defense mechanisms (see Chapter 12). It was the predominant orientation from the early years of the 20th century until the 1960s. From a research perspective, extensive case and preliminary outcome studies had already been conducted in this early period.

During the 1940s, however, the humanistic approaches emerged (e.g., Rogers, Frankl, Perls, Moreno), with a departure from Freudian views, the rejection of interpretations and the expert role of the therapist, and an emphasis on the self-healing process by providing a respectful, warm, and empathic therapeutic environment to the client. This new development, and especially Rogers's work (e.g., Rogers, 1957; Rogers & Dymond, 1954), also marked the beginning of psychotherapy process research through recordings of treatment sessions and their analyses (Chapter 13).

Even before the advent of the humanistic movement, laboratory experiments set the foundations of the behavioral orientation in the 1920s (e.g., Watson, Jones, Mowrer & Mowrer), which gained greater impact as a psychological therapy after the publication of Wolpe's work on the concept of reciprocal inhibition in the late 1950s (Wolpe, 1958). Defined by learning-based strategies, this approach was characterized by the therapist's directive interventions aimed at changing patient behavior and its environmental determinants (Chapter 14). Both new orientations (humanistic and behavioral) were associated with an emphasis on briefer treatments and a formal evaluation of treatment effects (Lambert, 2013b).

With the 1960s and 1970s came an expansion of the behavioral orientation with the adoption of cognitive constructs (such as automatic thoughts, schemas, and self-efficacy) and the use of interventions to change them (e.g., Beck, Ellis, Lazarus, Bandura). Along with these conceptual and clinical developments, the cognitive-behavioral approach (CBT) emphasized the systematic evaluation of treatment outcome for specific disorders and cost-effective short-term treatments (Chapters 14 and 15). More recently, a third or new wave of treatments has appeared under the CBT umbrella (e.g., Linehan, Hayes, Hofmann, Segal), with a focus on concepts such as mindfulness, acceptance and transtheoretical processes (see Chapter 15).

Yet another major treatment orientation surfaced in the 1970s, which has been labeled as the systemic approach (e.g., Minuchin, Watzlawick, Palazzoli, de Shazer). This orientation focused on family systems and the interaction of members of such a system (Chapter 16). Although its roots can be traced back to the 1930s, the 1980s saw the crystallization of an integrative movement (within and between treatment orientations), based in part on the findings that many therapists do not identify with only one approach, but rather combine elements from different orientations and then tailor them to their patients (e.g., Beutler, Garfield, Goldfried, Grawe, Prochaska, & DiClemente). All of these approaches have developed into several variations and modifications and continue to develop today.

Generations of Outcome Research

Amid the early theoretical phase and its limited research base, Eysenck (1952) criticized the lack of outcome research, comparing the effects of psychotherapy to spontaneous remission and challenging the effectiveness of psychotherapy. This event put psychotherapy outcome research and the key question "Is psychotherapy effective?" at the top of the field's priority list (see Table 1.1, research generation I). Since that time, research has convincingly demonstrated the effectiveness of psychotherapy in reducing psychological conditions and problems as well as its efficiency (positive cost–benefit ratio) for a broad spectrum of treatment concepts and psychological disorders. This has been achieved in numerous individual clinical-experimental studies and summary meta-analyses, starting with the landmark Smith, Glass, and Miller (1980) meta-analysis (for an overview, see Lambert, 2013c and Chapter 5). The effectiveness of psychological interventions has also been shown under routine conditions, as well as in comparison to psychopharmacological treatments and in severely distressed patients such as patients with personality disorders or psychosis (e.g., Lambert, 2013c; Hollon et al., 2019; see also Chapters 4, 5, 6, 9, and 20). Because of these efforts, psychotherapy has become an established treatment for psychological disorders in the health care systems of many (but unfortunately not yet all) countries around the world.

Nevertheless, the pressure to demonstrate legitimacy has never completely disappeared and is significantly stronger than, for example, somatic treatments in all health service systems. Nor has the question of "What is psychotherapy?" (as core psychological interventions) disappeared, while numerous new developments continue to take place today. It is therefore not surprising that from the beginning, the various therapeutic orientations competed with each other. Hence, starting in the 1960s, the question, "Which psychotherapy is more effective?" became more central in the research community (see Table 1.1, research generation II; e.g., Luborsky et al., 1976; Stiles, Shapiro & Elliott, 1986; Wittmann & Matt, 1986). Therefore, the second edition of the *Handbook* from 1978 introduced a chapter on the comparison between psychological therapies and psychopharmacological interventions and a discussion of the effects of potential combinations (Hollon & Beck, 1978). This research question resulted in the landmark National Institute of Mental Health Treatment of Depression Collaborative Research Program study (NIMH TDCRP; Elkin et al., 1989; 2004), which then took place in the 1980s. In this large, multicenter randomized controlled trial with 250 patients, the outcomes of four 16-week treatment conditions were compared: interpersonal psychotherapy, cognitive behavioral therapy, placebo plus clinical management, and imipramine hydrochloride plus clinical management. The data has been shared between different research groups and used for a large number of process and outcome evaluations. Today, over 30 years later, the data are still used and over 100 publications have resulted from this study (e.g., Elkin et al., 2006). The NIMH

TDCRP study was also one of the first studies to measure competence and adherence to treatment protocols (see Chapter 2).

Paul (1967) introduced a finer-grained research goal to investigate differential treatment effects and inter-individual differences by reframing the question of the optimal psychological therapy into: "*What* treatment, by *whom*, is most effective for *this* individual with *that* specific problem, and under *which* set of circumstances?" (pp. 111; see Table 1.1, research generation II). One example of an approach shaped by this question is the systematic treatment selection model (Beutler et al., 1991; 2018), an empirically derived set of guidelines to match psychotherapy practice to patients' characteristics. The idea was, and still is, to empirically identify the optimal treatment concept or intervention for the specific needs of the individual patient. This research question can be tracked to today's debate and research on empirically based personalization in psychotherapy (see Chapters 4, 18, 19, and 20).

While investigating these first two research questions further, a subsequent research generation (III in Table 1.1) and *Handbook* edition saw a broader investigation of the optimal dosage and cost-effectiveness of treatments ("How can treatments be made more cost effective?"). During this phase, Howard et al. (1986) produced a classic study on the dose–effect model. By summarizing 15 studies in a probit-analysis, the authors found that an increasing number of sessions was associated with diminishing returns regarding the percentage of improvement (see Chapters 4 and 5). This dosage research has been further developed by Lambert's group using stricter criteria (e.g., Kadera, 1996) and later extended by Barkham et al. (2006) by introducing the good-enough level model, demonstrating that patients stay in treatment (if it is not restricted by arbitrary service or clinic regulations) until they have reached a satisfying level of change.

In the next two research generations – IV and V – the scope of psychotherapy research questions broadened again, dealing with, for example, "How can research findings be transferred into clinical practice?" and how the scientist-practitioner gap in the field can be reduced. The research community tackled questions related to the development, evaluation, training, and implementation of disorder-specific manuals in order to produce best evidence for clinical guidelines and to improve treatment delivery (e.g., Chambless & Hollon, 1998; DeRubeis & Crits-Christoph, 1998). Starting in the 1990s and gaining importance in the 2000s, the question of practice-based evidence (see Table 1.1, research generation VI) and the immediate improvement of individual patients' treatments through psychometric feedback (termed *patient-focused research*; Howard et al., 1996; Lambert, 2001) became a major research topic. This area has also remained a highly relevant research topic to this day (see Chapters 4 and 6; Lambert, 2007; Lambert et al., 2018).

Generations of Process Research

From the beginning, this history of outcome research has been supplemented by research on the processes (events in treatment sessions that correlated with outcome) and mechanisms of change (hypothesized causal relations to outcome; see Chapters 7 and 8). Systematic process research began with

Rogers' assessment of sound recordings from treatment sessions and their attempt to identify process correlates of personality change and treatment outcome (e.g., Rogers & Diamond, 1954). About a decade later, the first session reports were developed (Orlinsky & Howard, 1967) to operationalize process variables including therapeutic actions and experiences related to outcome during psychotherapy sessions or longer-term outcomes in the daily lives of patients (see Table 1.1, research generation I, processes). Starting in the 1960s, these two research strategies developed and further research strategies such as single case methodologies were added (see Table 1.1, research generation II, processes). In the 1970s, the measurement of therapeutic alliance and verbal response modes gained research attention as well as the first empirically based taxonomies and/or categorizations summarizing process-outcome relations identified in individual studies (e.g., Orlinsky & Howard, 1978; Russell & Stiles, 1979). From this time on, this topic has remained a central focus of process research, while the statistical methods used to investigate process-outcome relations have become more sophisticated over the years (e.g., Castonguay & Beutler, 2006; Castonguay et al., 2019; Crits-Christoph et al., 2013; Greenberg & Pinsof, 1986; Norcross & Lambert 2019; Stiles et al., 1998). These developments have been accompanied by qualitative research methods and narrative descriptions of processes, which gained attention in the research community in the 1980s (e.g., Rice & Greenberg, 1984; see Chapters 3 and 11). In the 1990s, additive and dismantling trials as well as factorial designs were increasingly used to investigate variables and processes specific to treatment orientations, but also common factors (shared components between different treatment orientations) and therapist effects (see Chapter 9). In the 21st century, more statistically sophisticated investigations of change processes have become possible by using multilevel modeling of within and between patient variations across treatments (e.g., Crits-Christoph et al., 2011; Kazdin, 2007; see Chapters 7 and 8).

CURRENT TRENDS AND DEVELOPMENTS

As described above, psychotherapy has been established as an efficacious and a cost-effective treatment. Its effectiveness has been demonstrated under experimental conditions, in routine care, as well as in comparison to psychopharmacological or somatic treatments (Cuijpers et al., 2013, 2019; Lambert, 2013c, see Chapters 4, 5, 6, 9, 17, and 20). This statement remains valid even when taking relapses and more strict success criteria into account (e.g., Lambert, 2013c). However, even well-examined treatment packages are based on results of average effectiveness and do not provide any guarantee of success for an individual case. It is therefore necessary to increase our understanding of those patients who do and do not benefit from treatment and to further improve psychological therapies for cases at risk of drop out, less than optimal response, and treatment failure. There is also a large degree of heterogeneity regarding treatment variants, settings, and dosages provided around the world, making a future focus on cross-cultural and dissemination issues a necessity. Furthermore, although the standardization of findings in psychotherapy research has improved over the years, several measurement problems remain, and a clear definition and identification of key processes of change are still high on the research agenda.

In response to these issues and knowledge gaps, several new developments in psychotherapy research have taken place in the last decade or so. To begin with, the core thematic question of the new, now seventh, research generation might be captured as follows: "How can the evidence base of treatment personalization be strengthened, both in controlled settings and in clinical practice?" This differential question reflects a movement toward *precision mental health* that is taking hold in many contexts (see Chapters 4, 5, 6, 18, 19, and 20). Other research advances could also move the field forward in the future. For example, data analytic tools have recently been developed to analyze data sets that could potentially include hundreds of thousands of patients (machine learning), as well as to conduct intensive longitudinal assessments that could potentially involve hundreds of measurement points per person (dynamic complexity; see Chapters 2, 4, and 19). New digital technologies and models for the assessment of outcome and psychopathology have also emerged (e.g., the Research Domain Criteria; e.g., Insel, 2014). In addition, diverse modalities of treatment delivery and stratified services, including low-intensity and internet interventions, have been investigated. Moreover, higher-quality replications and better use of open science models in the field have been advocated. Along with several research topics that have guided previous research generations, these new developments are briefly summarized in the following sections and are then elaborated throughout the current edition of the *Handbook*.

Maturation of the Field: Standardization and Replication

Measuring change has been a fundamental issue in psychotherapy research from its beginning. In the early days of psychotherapy as a field of research, the fundamental question was whether change in psychotherapy could be measured at all, such that unstandardized, written reports were used to measure treatment outcome. Over time, the field has moved forward to the application of standardized outcome measures, including a multidimensional perspective on change. In recent years, the focus has shifted to how change measurement can be improved by more-intensive measures over the course of treatment and an optimal use of change measures in routine clinical practice (see Chapters 2 and 4). Measuring and tracking change has become a part of best practices in many health care systems and training programs (see Chapters 2, 4, 6, 10, and 17). This development is supported by new advances in technology (e.g., outcome tracking, feedback and clinical support tools, including wearable devices, experience sampling, software, biomarkers, and neurocognitive measures), making outcome measurement and monitoring easier to implement in practice while providing more rigorous evidence of the change process.

Nevertheless, several measurement and replication problems remain (Chapter 2). For example, although the standardization of change measurement has improved over the years, and

despite the visionary efforts to devise a core outcome battery, first by Waskow (1975) and later by Strupp, Horowitz, and Lambert (1997), there is neither agreement on core outcome nor process measurement instruments available for mental health, specific psychological disorders, or change mechanisms (Chevance et al., 2020; see Chapter 4). There is also no agreement on the definition of change (e.g., pre–post differences or rate of change) as well as a lack of standards on data sharing (although this has improved in recent years). Furthermore, as in psychology and science as a whole, the replication crisis has had an impact on psychotherapy research and demands new approaches to improve the rigor of findings and the implementation of open science practices (see Chapter 2).

Methodological and Technological Developments

Despite early critical and insightful input (e.g., Newman & Howard, 1991), psychotherapy research has predominantly been premised on investigating average differences between two groups using pre–post change measures in relatively small samples of patients. Within this context, the advances in statistical methods and the possibility of generating large datasets between and within patients – *big data* – stands out as notable advances in psychotherapy research in the last two decades (see Chapters 2, 4, 5, 6, 8, 9, and 18). These statistical advances allow researchers to conduct detailed analyses of change on several conceptual levels (e.g., sessions, patients, treatments) and levels of variation (e.g., within- and between-patient variation or between-therapist variation). Complementing these statistical advances are novel measurement options (alternatives to self-report) available via new technologies (e.g., various wearable devices of digital phenotypes, biomarkers and neurocognitive measures, advanced video analysis of emotions, gesture, movement and speech of patients and therapists; see Chapters 2, 4, 9, 21, and 22). Together, these developments have improved the investigation of longitudinal change, causal networks, and therapist effects. Technological advances are also facilitating the use of e-mental health concepts such as internet treatments, chatbots, and the potential to blend e-mental health and face-to-face therapy (see Chapters 21 and 22).

In the midst of such advancements, however, an important caveat is warranted by several methodological problems that have yet to be fully addressed in psychotherapy research (see also Chapter 2). These include (1) nonoptimal planning of studies due to the aim of supporting the effect of a favored clinical concept or approach; (2) nonoptimal operationalization of constructs with limited theoretical and/or empirical bases to support them; (3) underpowered designs; and (4) range restrictions of measures. And, importantly, enticing though more advanced statistical models are, they do not necessarily guarantee or lead to more valid results. The quality hallmark of psychotherapy research must be the clarity and the relevance of the research question(s), the rigor of the design and its implementation, as well as the psychometric value and conceptual coherence of the measures.

From Evidence-Based Practice to Practice-Based Evidence

Many conclusions in this *Handbook* are based on findings derived from research designs commonly applied to evaluate treatment orientations or packages (e.g., RCTs, meta-analyses). There are, however, many limitations to clinical conclusions that are based exclusively on RCTs and meta-analyses (see Chapters 2, 4, 5, and 6). For example, as Baldwin and Imel (2020) recently pointed out, categorization of different variants or orientations of psychotherapy is difficult (in comparison, for example, to most somatic treatments), and often leads to arbitrary decisions about where treatment boundaries are, and which specific mechanisms are actually fostered.

At the core of the criticisms leveled against traditional RCTs is their limited external validity. As a complementary alternative, practice-oriented research is aimed at investigating the impacts and processes of psychotherapy as it is conducted in day-to-day practice (see Chapters 4, 5, and 6) and comprises various activities, including patient-focused research, practice-based evidence, and practice-research networks. This research paradigm is based on the idea of an ongoing collaboration between practitioners and scientists to make immediate use of research results to describe and improve clinical practice (e.g., Howard et al., 1996; Lambert, 2001). In effect, research becomes embedded (i.e., rooted) in routine care with a primary focus on understanding the variability in patient outcomes as a function of their individual characteristics, treatment modalities and interventions, therapists, and clinics/services (e.g., Pybis et al., 2017). Within the context of patient-focused research, for example, therapists deliver treatment and simultaneously collect data by assessing patients' progress over the course of treatment (Lutz et al., 2019). The aggregated data can serve to gather practice-based evidence on superordinate levels in order to benchmark services, investigate dosage of treatment, or to assess therapist effects (e.g., Saxon & Barkham, 2012, see Chapters 4, 5, 6, and 9). Researchers can also use large databases and new statistical tools (e.g., machine learning algorithms) to develop clinical decision systems, allowing therapists not only to track progress on an individual level but also to improve treatment with additional clinical support tools, especially for patients with an early negative treatment course (Lambert et al., 2018; see Chapters 4, 17, and 18). In combination with the above-described technological innovations, these developments are particularly important, as they can facilitate the development of large scientist-practitioner infrastructures, which in the long term can provide data on thousands of patients and therapists (Chapters 4, 5, 6, and 9). The potential for national systems of data collection with public data accessible to independent research already exists, as exemplified by the Improving Access to Psychological Therapies initiative in England (see Clark et al., 2018).

In the context of practice research networks (PRNs), clinicians (and other stakeholders) can be involved in the selection, design, implementation, and dissemination of research. The activities within PRNs aim to investigate questions of interest to the clinicians, such as:

- What did my client and I find helpful and hindering in the session that just ended?
- What interventions did I use during the past session, and what impact did they have on my client?
- What are the benefits that I might gain from participating in peer supervision with other early career practitioners?

Because such studies are grounded in everyday practice, they are designed to add limited burden to routine care and have the goal of confounding the distinction between science and practice (e.g., Castonguay et al., 2013; see Chapter 6).

New Ways to Model Therapeutic Processes

Recently, conceptual and methodological advancements have also taken place in the investigation of processes and mechanisms of change. This empirical tradition began in the 1950s, and although the therapeutic alliance has received the most attention (Crits-Christoph et al., 2013), a wide range of constructs has been examined, such as therapist adherence and competence (Barber et al., 1996) and client cognitive change (Lorenzo-Luaces et al., 2015; Tang & DeRubeis, 1998). Several large meta-analyses have been conducted, providing evidence for the role of process variables in clinical practice and training (e.g., Flückiger et al., 2018; Norcross & Lambert, 2019; see Chapters 7, 8, and 10). However, progress in this line of research has often been hampered by the unknown directionality of the process–outcome relationship (e.g., is the alliance causing improvement or vice versa?), lack of consideration of client and therapist mutual influence in such a relationship, measurement problems, as well as frequent failures to account for the nested nature of psychotherapy data.

Among the methodological advances that have been made to address these issues are the analyses of both within-patient variations and client–therapist dyadic processes over the course of treatment (Chapters 2, 4, 6, 7, 8, and 9). The multilevel modeling of such factors at the session, patient, and therapist levels allows the disentanglement of variance components, the identification of potential causal relations, and the specification of the source or level of effects. Findings from these methods can lead to new and more precise clinical and training recommendations (Chapters 8, 9, and 10). At a conceptual level, process and mechanisms research is likely to be improved via methodological (e.g., intensive longitudinal analyses) and technological (e.g., computer-based evaluations of behavior and emotion) developments previously described, thereby helping researchers find more detailed answers to an old but still crucially relevant question: "What are the ingredients and mechanisms that make psychological interventions work?"

Qualitative Developments

In the last decade, modern qualitative research in psychotherapy has gained increasing prevalence and depth and has complemented and enriched quantitative research findings within the field of psychotherapy research and behavior change. Guided by a diversity (and combination) of epistemological perspectives, many methodological approaches (e.g., grounded theory, conversation analysis, task analysis, qualitative case studies) have been developed to serve various purposes, such as theory-building, fact gathering, testing, as well as enriching and deepening of knowledge (Chapters 3 and 11). Their use has provided contextualized and fine-grained understanding of various phenomena, including the internal experiences of patients and therapists, critical events in clinical practice, and specific patterns of interventions that lead to change. In addition, qualitative research has contributed to the construction and refinement of models of change (e.g., assimilation model), the evaluation of treatment outcome, and the understanding of therapist training and development (Chapters 3, 10, and 11). Recent years have seen increased prevalence of research designs involving mixed qualitative and quantitative methods (e.g., convergent, explanatory sequential, exploratory sequential), as well as the emergence of meta-analyses of qualitative studies in psychotherapy. Further, new sets of recommendations have been developed to assess and evaluate the integrity of qualitative analyses with regard to design, reporting, and review standards (Chapter 3).

Transtheoretical Integration in Clinical Practice and Theory Building

As described above, the *Handbook* has had an integrative focus from the start, including empirical findings from different and sometimes even competing theoretical orientations (Bergin & Garfield, 1971; Garfield & Bergin, 1978). The finding that a treatment concept or package works does not necessarily imply its theoretical validity or the correctness of its theoretical assumptions related to psychopathology or psychological change (Rosenzweig, 1938). Also emphasized in early editions of the *Handbook* was the potential role played by factors that are common to many treatments, as well as the fact that many therapists use and combine techniques from divergent theoretical perspectives (Garfield & Kurz, 1977).

The *Handbook's* tradition of developing a common ground between different groups identifying with differing models of psychological change based on research has also found broader support within the clinical and research communities in recent years. For example, several new concepts of psychopathology have been introduced to the field, such as the Research Domain Criteria (RDoC; Insel, 2014) or the multivariate Hierarchical Taxonomy of Psychopathology (HiTop; e.g., Conway et al., 2019). The idea behind these developments has been to move past a traditional view of categorical diagnosis (as emphasized in the *Diagnostic and Statistical Manual of Mental Disorders*) to include transdiagnostic perspectives on psychopathology and change measurement, and develop theoretically broader concepts of psychopathology. Besides these developments, other transtheoretical efforts have emerged, including modular and transdiagnostic treatments, principles or process-based approaches or perspectives, and integrative models of psychopathology and psychotherapy. Cutting across these efforts is the combination of elements within or between different treatment orientations based on empirical research and with the goal of tailoring these modules to specific patient problems and needs (e.g., Caspar, 2019; Castonguay & Beutler, 2006; Castonguay et al., 2019; Fernández-Alvarez et al.,

2015; Goldfried, 2019; Grawe, 2004; Hofmann & Hayes, 2019; Norcross & Lambert, 2019; e.g., Chapters 4, 5, 7, 8, 9, 11, and 23). Such transdiagnostic and transtheoretical approaches are likely to be further developed in the future.

In combination with adaptations to specific patient populations (e.g., ethnic, sexual, gender minorities), varying session frequencies, the integration of basic science findings, and tools from e-mental health, such developments may lead to more personalized and improved treatments, especially for patients at risk for treatment failure (see Chapters 4, 17, 18, and 19).

Diversity and Dissemination

As can be seen in the list of all chapters of the editions of this *Handbook*, the author lists have become increasingly international and cross-cultural over the years. This represents a welcome growth in the field of psychotherapy research as a whole. SPR, for example, which began as a US organization and expanded to Europe in the 1980s following its first international meeting outside North America in 1979 (Oxford, UK), now counts 51 member countries and all continents with the exception of Antarctica. However, some parts of the world remain underrepresented, and internationalization efforts are an ongoing agenda.

Furthermore, there are large cross-cultural differences and little convergence between countries regarding the frequencies and average durations of different variants of psychological treatments (Flückiger et al., 2020). A priority of the field should be the fostering of cross-cultural and international research, as well as the integration of such research into the scientific basis of psychotherapy. Increasing the comparability and practical relevance of findings across diverse communities, within and between countries, may help address the sobering problem of dissemination. This problem refers to the large gap between the number of people in need of psychological treatment and the number of people who actually receive it (Kazdin, 2018; see Chapter 22). In the US and across the globe, most people in need do *not* have access to psychological services at all. This calls for a more extensive adoption of a range of delivery services at scale including modular and transdiagnostic treatments, strategic use of lower-intensity interventions (i.e., psychoeducational), and internet-based treatments (see Chapters 18, 21, and 22). In addition to these fairly new solutions to reach out to more people in need, small group research has been a focus of the *Handbook* from its inception and empirical evidence has increased in recent years (Burlingame et al., 2013; Strauß et al., 2008; Chapter 17).

Precision Mental Health and Clinical Navigation Systems

Several new developments have emerged within the tradition of outcome monitoring and patient-focused research based on concepts from precision mental health research and precision medicine (e.g., Delgadillo & Lutz, 2020; DeRubeis et al., 2014a; Huibers et al., 2015; Chapters 4, 17, 18, and 19). The main goal has been to move beyond average differences between treatment protocols toward tailoring treatments to the individual patient – a move toward personalization research that is consistent with most therapists' individualization of their treatment based on their own clinical training and practical experience (e.g., Bickman, 2020; Page et al., 2019; Zilcha-Mano, 2021). These developments rely on the combination of treatment prediction and selection research with research on computer-based feedback, decision-making, and clinical problem solving to generate a new field of evidence-based personalization research and potential clinical practice. For instance, machine learning techniques have been applied to large datasets to develop prognostic indicators and personalized predictions for patients regarding their optimal treatment, treatment strategy, or therapist (e.g., Cohen & DeRubeis, 2018; Delgadillo et al., 2020; Fisher & Boswell, 2016; Chapter 9). As a new step, adaptive feedback tools have been used during treatment to identify patients at risk for treatment failure, dropout or self-harm, and to provide clinical problem-solving tools aimed at minimizing such risks (Lutz et al., 2019). To date, the successful implementation of such clinical navigation and stratification systems has been limited (e.g., Wilkinson et al., 2020). However, this new field of research is gaining increased attention, recently augmented by tools from e-mental health and intensive longitudinal assessments. In the future, it has the potential to translate research directly into clinical practice (see Chapters 4, 18, and 19).

Current and Future Developments: A Synopsis

Several developments and research trends have emerged in the last decade that we believe already have improved our knowledge and will continue to do so in the years to come. From the advancements presented above, the following key areas of work and impact can be delineated:

1. Greater adoption of standardized, freely available and easy-to-apply psychological measures that capture the diversity of patients' concerns.
2. Further efforts to strengthen the principles of replication.
3. Further improvement of measures tapping processes and outcomes, including new digital tools and biomarkers.
4. Further improvements in statistical methods to analyze large datasets and intensive longitudinal assessments, including idiographic approaches.
5. Greater emphasis on research conducted in routine clinical practice and on therapist effects.
6. Improved quantitative and qualitative research of processes and mechanisms of change.
7. A better integration of research findings into transdiagnostic as well as transtheoretical clinical models and concepts and their broader implementation in health service systems.
8. Improved dissemination of psychological therapies including internet services and interventions (e-mental health).
9. Further cross-cultural adaptation and dissemination of psychological therapies and research topics.
10. A better implementation of outcome monitoring and clinical navigation systems into personalized as well as evidence-based clinical services and training.

Given these new developments and prospects, we are excited and optimistic about the future advances in psychotherapy research that are likely to occur in the foreseeable future. However, we are also mindful of the challenges faced by the field in general in ensuring that we find a balance between producing the highest-quality research possible and also striving to support the practical delivery of better psychological interventions to those most in need, regardless of their social, cultural, or economic context.

OVERVIEW OF THE SEVENTH EDITION OF THIS *HANDBOOK*

We conclude this introductory chapter with a brief overview of the six sections and 23 chapters comprising the current edition of the *Handbook*.

Section 1 provides a summary of key frameworks and procedures that underpin the empirical investigation of psychotherapy and behavior change. *Chapter 1* (i.e., this chapter) has identified historical milestones from the inception of the *Handbook* in 1971 to recent trends in psychotherapy research. *Chapter 2* (Baldwin & Goldberg) covers methodological foundations and innovations in psychotherapy research. The chapter sets out core assumptions underlying high-quality quantitative psychotherapy research and introduces new methodologies and debates (e.g., about replication and transparency) that are highly relevant to psychotherapy researchers. *Chapter 3* (Levitt, Stiles, & McLeod) provides an overview of strategies and methodological issues in qualitative research. The chapter focuses on qualitative methods that have been providing additional insight into psychotherapy outcome and processes in recent years.

Section 2 addresses the topics of measuring and evidencing change in trials conducted in controlled settings, as well as in practice-oriented research. It provides a review of approaches to change and their yield in the meta-analytic literature as well as in data from routine practice settings. *Chapter 4* (Lutz, de Jong, Rubel, & Delgadillo) addresses the fundamental issue of change, how to measure, monitor, and predict change, and how to provide feedback on treatment outcomes. It also includes the application of advanced analytical procedures to large datasets and clinical navigation systems. *Chapter 5* (Barkham & Lambert) provides a state-of-the-art summary of the efficacy and effectiveness of psychological therapies. It deals with questions central to practitioners and the impact of clinical practice by drawing on findings from (network) meta-analytic studies, randomized controlled trials, other well-designed studies, and studies drawn from routine practice. *Chapter 6* (Castonguay, Barkham, Youn, & Page) complements and extends the previous chapter by providing an overview of recent practice-oriented research. It draws on the increasing evidence from routine practice that reflects how therapies are delivered in everyday situations, their impact, and factors that are associated with change in a diversity of naturalistic settings.

Section 3 focuses on therapeutic ingredients across treatment approaches and provides a detailed coverage of factors linked to the impact of psychotherapy. *Chapter 7* (Constantino, Boswell, & Coyne) focuses on patient, therapist, and relational factors as correlates of psychotherapy outcomes. *Chapter 8* (Crits-Christoph & Connolly Gibbons) covers process–outcome research, with an emphasis on studies that have attempted to examine the causal relationship between processes variables (specific to one orientation and common to all treatments) and patient change. *Chapter 9* (Wampold & Owen) focuses on therapist effects by presenting the statistical methods required to assess these effects, and by summarizing the current findings – both in terms of the magnitude of therapist differential effectiveness and the characteristics that are displayed by more as opposed to less effective therapists. *Chapter 10* (Knox & Hill) focuses on training and supervision, offering a review of current evidence for activities that provide the foundation and continuing support to high-quality practice across theoretical orientations. *Chapter 11* (McLeod, Stiles, & Levitt) covers contributions that have been made by qualitative research with regard to how psychotherapy works and its impact on patients. This second chapter on qualitative research (alongside Chapter 2) recognizes the increasing importance and advances of such methods in recent years.

Section 4 examines therapeutic approaches and formats. The chapters deliver state-of-the-art reviews of the main theoretical approaches and treatment modalities of psychological therapies. Covering both process and outcome, all but one of them (Chapter 15, which is new) are updated versions of chapters appearing in the previous edition. *Chapter 12* (Barber, Muran, McCarthy, Keefe, & Zilcha-Mano) focuses on psychodynamic therapies, *Chapter 13* (Elliott, Watson, Timulak, & Sharbane) focuses on the humanistic and experiential therapies, *Chapter 14* (Newman, Jarrett, Haaga, & Agras) focuses on behavioral therapies and cognitive-behavioral therapies, *Chapter 15* (Forman, Arch, Bricker, Gaudiano, Jurasico, Rizvi, Segal, & Vowles) attends to mindfulness and acceptance-based treatments often described as "third wave" behavioral treatments, *Chapter 16* (Friedlander, Heatherington, & Diamond) focuses on systemic and family approaches, *Chapter 17* (Burlingame & Strauss) covers small group interventions, and *Chapter 18* (Ng, Schleider, Horn, & Weisz) focuses on treatments for children and adolescents.

Section 5 addresses the personalization and/or delivery of psychological therapies at scale by covering new and well-established research areas. Reflecting a more recent innovative research strand, *Chapter 19* (Cohen, Delgadillo, & DeRubeis) is a new chapter that focuses on personalized treatment approaches. It covers new methodological (e.g., machine learning) and clinical approaches to provide innovative answers to the old question, "What works for whom?" *Chapter 20* (Hollon, Andrews, Keller, Singla, Maslej, & Mulsant) sets out the evidence regarding offering therapies alone versus in combination with medication. The chapter addresses a long-term debate in the field, covering new empirical ground and showing that psychosocial interventions work at least as well as medications and are often more enduring for nonpsychotic disorders. *Chapter 21* (Andersson & Berger) is a new chapter that addresses the considerable growth over the past 10 years in internet approaches, a format of treatment that is likely to foster the dissemination of psychotherapy. *Chapter 22* (Kazdin) discusses new ways and models of therapy delivery. This chapter is also new to the seventh edition and highlights current and promising concepts and strategies to scale up the provision

of mental health services in order to better address unmet needs around the world.

Finally, *Section 6* comprises an epilogue within its single chapter – *Chapter 23*. This chapter summarizes the current state of psychotherapy and makes both predictions and recommendations about psychotherapy research, practice, and training from an international perspective as represented by its eight authors (Castonguay, Eubanks, Iwakabe, Krause, Page, Zilcha-Mano, Lutz, & Barkham) from seven countries (Australia, Chile, Germany, Israel, Japan, UK, USA) and five continents (Asia, Australia, Europe, North America, and South America).

All chapters in this anniversary edition have been written by experts in their specific field and have the same goal as all previous chapters and editions of the *Handbook*. That is, they try to update students, clinical trainees, experienced therapists as well as early career and experienced psychotherapy researchers on the latest findings in psychotherapy research in order to improve clinical services for patients around the world.

ABBREVIATIONS

CBT	cognitive behavioral therapy
HiTop	Hierarchical Taxonomy of Psychopathology
NIMH TDCRP	National Institute of Mental Health Treatment of Depression Collaborative Research Program
PRNs	practice research networks
RCTs	randomized controlled trials
RDoC	research domain criteria
ROM	routine outcome monitoring
SPR	Society for Psychotherapy Research

REFERENCES

Baldwin, S. A., & Imel, Z. E. (2013). Therapist effects: Findings and methods. In M. J. Lambert (Ed.), *Bergin and Garfield's handbook of psychotherapy and behavior change* (6th ed., pp. 258–297). Wiley.

Baldwin, S. A., & Imel, Z. E. (2020). Studying specificity in psychotherapy with meta-analysis is hard. *Psychotherapy Research, 30*(3), 294–296. https://doi.org/10.1080/10503307.2019.1679403

Barber, J. P., Crits-Christoph, P., & Luborsky, L. (1996). Effects of therapist adherence and competence on patient outcome in brief dynamic therapy. *Journal of Consulting and Clinical Psychology, 64*(3), 619–622. doi: 10.1037/0022-006X.64.3.619

Barkham, M. (2007). Methods, outcomes and processes in the psychological therapies across successive research generations. In W. Dryden (Ed.), *Dryden's handbook of individual therapy* (5th ed. pp. 451–514). Sage.

Barkham, M., Connell, J., Stiles, W. B., Miles, J. N. V., Margison, F., Evans, C., & Mellor-Clark, J. (2006). Dose-effect relations and responsive regulation of treatment duration: The good enough level. *Journal of Consulting and Clinical Psychology, 74*(1), 160–167. https://doi.org/10.1037/0022-006X.74.1.160

Barkham, M., Hardy, G. E., & J. Mellor-Clark (Eds.) (2010). *Developing and delivering practice-based evidence*. Wiley. https://doi.org/10.1002/9780470687994

Barlow, D. H., Brown, T. A., & Craske, M. G. (1994). Definitions of panic attack and panic disorder in DSM-IV: Implications for research. *Journal of Abnormal Psychology*, *103*, 553–564. doi:10.1037//0021-843x.103.3.553

Bateman, A., & Fonagy, P. (1999). Effectiveness of partial hospitalization in the treatment of borderline personality disorder: A randomized controlled trial. *The American Journal of Psychiatry*, *156*(10), 1563–1569. https://doi.org/10.1176/ajp.156.10.1563

Benjamin, L.S. (1974). Structural analysis of social behavior (SASB). *Psychological Review*, *81*, 392–425. https://doi.org/10.1037/h0037024

Bergin, A. E., & Garfield, S. L. (Eds.). (1971). *Handbook of psychotherapy and behavior change*. Wiley.

Bergin, A. E., & Garfield, S. L. (Eds.). (1994). *Handbook of psychotherapy and behavior change*. (4th. ed.). Wiley.

Beutler, L. E., Edwards, C., & Someah, K. (2018). Adapting psychotherapy to patient reactance level: A meta-analytic review. *Journal of Clinical Psychology*, *74*(11), 1952–1963. https://doi.org/10.1002/jclp.22682

Beutler, L. E., Mohr, D. C., Grawe, K., Engle, D., & MacDonald, R. (1991). Looking for differential treatment effects: Cross-cultural predictors of differential psychotherapy efficacy. *Journal of Psychotherapy Integration*, *1*(2), 121.https://doi.org/10.1037/h0101223

Bickman, L. (2020). Improving mental health services: A 50-year journey from randomized experiments to artificial intelligence and precision mental health. *Administration and Policy in Mental Health*, *47*, 795–843. https://doi.org/10.1007/s10488-020-01065-8

Bordin, E. S. (1979). The generalizability of the psychoanalytic concept of the working alliance. *Psychotherapy: Theory, Research & Practice*, *16*(3), 252–260.https://doi.org/10.1037/h0085885

Borkovec, T. D., Echemendia, R. J., Ragusea, S. A., & Ruiz, M. (2001). The Pennsylvania Practice Research Network and future possibilities for clinically meaningful and scientifically rigorous psychotherapy effectiveness research. *Clinical Psychology: Science and Practice*, *8*(2), 155–167.https://doi.org/10.1093/clipsy.8.2.155

Burlingame, G. M., Strauss, B., & Joyce, A. (2013). Change mechanisms and effectiveness of small group treatments. In M. J. Lambert (Ed.), *Bergin and Garfield's handbook of psychotherapy and behavior change* (6th ed., pp. 640–689). Wiley.

Butler, A. C., Chapman, J. E., Forman, E. M., & Beck, A. T. (2006). The empirical status of cognitive-behavioral therapy: A review of meta-analyses. *Clinical Psychology Review*, *26*(1), 17–31. https://doi.org/10.1016/j.cpr.2005.07.003

Caspar, F. (2019). Plan Analysis and the Motive-Oriented Therapeutic Relationship. In U. Kramer (Ed.), *Case formulation for personality disorders: Tailoring psychotherapy to the individual client* (pp. 265–288). Elsevier.

Castonguay, L. G., Barkham, M., Lutz, W., & McAleavey, A. A. (2013). Practice-oriented research: Approaches and applications. In M. J. Lambert (Ed.), *Bergin and Garfield's handbook of psychotherapy and behavior change* (6th ed., pp. 85–133).Wiley.

Castonguay, L. G., & Beutler, L. E. (Eds.). (2006). *Principles of therapeutic change that work*. Oxford Series in Clinical Psychology, OUP.

Castonguay, L. G., Constantino, M. J., & Beutler, L. E. (Eds.). (2019). *Principles of change. How psychotherapists implement research in practice*. Oxford Series in Clinical Psychology, OUP.

Chambless, D. L., & Hollon, S. D. (1998). Defining empirically supported therapies.*Journal of Consulting and Clinical Psychology*,*66*(1), 7–18. https://doi.org/10.1037/0022-006X.66.1.7

Chambless, D. L., & Ollendick, T. H. (2001). Empirically supported psychological interventions: Controversies and evidence. *Annual Review of Psychology*, *52*, 685–716. https://doi.org/10.1146/annurev.psych.52.1.685

Chevance, A. M., Tran, V. T., Ravaud, P., Tomlinson, A., Le Berre, C., Teufer, B., Touboul, S., Fried, E. I., Gartlehner, G., Cipriani, A., & Tran, V. T. (2020). Identifying outcomes for depression that matter to patients, informal caregivers and healthcare professionals: qualitative content analysis of a large international online survey. *The Lancet Psychiatry*, *7*(8), 692–702.https://doi.org/10.1016/S2215-0366 (20)30191-7

Clark, D. M., Canvin, L., Green, J., Layard, R., Pilling, S., & Janecka, M. (2018). Transparency about the outcomes of mental health services (IAPT approach): An analysis of public data. *The Lancet*, *391* (10121), 679–686. https://doi.org/10.1016/S0140-6736 (17)32133-5

Cohen, J. (1977). *Statistical power analysis for the behavioral sciences (revised Edn.)*. Academic Press.

Cohen, J. (1988). *Statistical power analysis for the behavioral sciences* (2nd ed.). Erlbaum.

Cohen, Z. D., & DeRubeis, R. J. (2018). Treatment selection in depression. *Annual Review of Clinical Psychology*, *14*(1), 209–236. https://doi.org/10.1146/annurev-clinpsy-050817-084746.

Conway, C. C., Forbes, M. K., Forbush, K. T., Fried, E. I., Hallquist, M. N., Kotov, R., Mullins-Sweatt, S. N., Shackman, A. J., Skodol, A. E., South, S. C., Sunderland, M., Waszczuk, M. A., Zald, D. H., Afzali, M. H., Bornovalova, M. A., Carragher, N., Docherty, A. R.,Jonas, K. G., Krueger, R. F., ... Eaton, N. R. (2019). A hierarchical taxonomy of psychopathology can transform mental health research. *Perspectives on Psychological Science*, *14*(3), 419–436. https://doi.org/10.1177/1745691618810696

Crits-Christoph, P., Baranackie, K., Kurcias, J., Beck, A., Caroll, K., Perry, K., Luborsky, L. McLellan, A., Woody, G., Thompson, L., Gallagher, D. & Zitrin, C. (1991) Meta-analysis of therapist effects in psychotherapy outcome studies. *Psychotherapy Research*, *1*(2), 81–91. https://doi.org/10.1080/10503309112331335511

Crits-Christoph, P., Gibbons, M. B. C., Hamilton, J., Ring-Kurtz, S., & Gallop, R. (2011). The dependability of alliance assessments: The alliance–outcome correlation is larger than you might think. *Journal of Consulting and Clinical Psychology*, *79*(3), 267–278. https://doi.org/10.1037/a0023668

Crits-Christoph, P., Gibbons, M. C., & Mukherjee, D. (2013). Psychotherapy process-outcome research. In M. J. Lambert (Ed.), *Bergin and Garfield's handbook of psychotherapy and behavior change* (6th ed., pp. 298–340). Wiley.

Cuijpers, P. (2017). Four decades of outcome research on psychotherapies for adult depression: An overview of a series of meta-analyses. *Canadian Psychology/psychologie Canadienne*, *58*(1), 7–19. https://doi.org/10.1037/cap0000096

Cuijpers, P., Berking, M., Andersson, G., Quigley, L., Kleiboer, A., & Dobson, K. S. (2013). A meta-analysis of cognitive-behavioural therapy for adult depression, alone and in comparison with other treatments. *The Canadian Journal of Psychiatry*, *58*(7), 376–385. https://doi.org/10.1177/070674371305800702

Cuijpers, P., M. Reijnders, & Huibers, M. (2019). The role of common factors in psychotherapy outcomes. *Annual Review of Clinical Psychology*, *15*(1), 207–231. https://doi.org/10.1146/annurev-clinpsy-050718-095424

Delgadillo, J., & Lutz, W. (2020). A development pathway towards precision mental health care. *JAMA Psychiatry*. https://doi.org/10.1001/jamapsychiatry.2020.1048

Delgadillo, J., Rubel, J., & Barkham, M. (2020). Towards personalized allocation of patients to therapists. *Journal of Consulting and Clinical Psychology*, *88*(9), 799–808. https://doi.org/10.1037/ccp0000507

DeRubeis, R. J., Cohen, Z. D., Forand, N. R., Fournier, J. C., Gelfand, L. A., & Lorenzo-Luaces, L. (2014a). The Personalized Advantage Index: Translating research on prediction into individualized treatment recommendations. A demonstration. *PLoS ONE*, *9*(1), e83875. https://doi.org/10.1371/journal.pone.0083875

DeRubeis, R. J., & Crits-Christoph, P. (1998). Empirically supported individual and group psychological treatments for adult mental disorders. *Journal of Consulting and Clinical Psychology*, *66*(1), 37–52.https://doi.org/10.1037/0022-006X.66.1.37

DeRubeis, R. J., Gelfand, L. A., German, R. E., Fournier, J. C., & Forand, N. R. (2014b). Understanding processes of change: How some patients reveal more than others-and some groups of therapists less-about what matters in psychotherapy. *Psychotherapy Research*, *24*(3), 419–428. https://doi.org/10.1080/10503307.2013.838654

Elliott, R., Fischer, C. T., & Rennie, D. L. (1999). Evolving guidelines for publication of qualitative research studies in psychology and related fields. *British Journal of Clinical Psychology*, *38*(3), 215–229. https://doi.org/10.1348/014466599162782

Elkin, I. (1994). The NIMH treatment of depression collaborative research program: Where we began and where we are. In A. E. Bergin & S. L. Garfield (Eds.), *Handbook of psychotherapy and behavior change* (4th ed., pp. 114–139). Wiley.

Elkin, I., Falconnier, L., Martinovich, Z., & Mahoney, C. (2006). Therapist effects in the National Institute of Mental Health Treatment of Depression Collaborative Research Program. *Psychotherapy Research*, *16*(2), 144–160. https://doi.org/10.1080/10503300500268540

Elkin, I., Shea M. T., Watkins, J. T., Imber, S. D., Sotsky, S. M., Collins, J. F., Glass, D. R., Pilkonis, P. A., Leber, W. R., Docherty, J. P., Fiester, S. J., &. Parloff, M. B. (1989). National Institute of Mental Health Treatment of Depression Collaborative Research Program. *Archives of General Psychiatry, 46*(11), 971–982. https://doi.org/10.1001/archpsyc.1989.01810110013002

Eysenck, H. J. (1952). The effects of psychotherapy: an evaluation. *Journal of Consulting Psychology, 16*(5), 319–324.https://doi.org/10.1037/h0063633

Fernández-Alvarez, H., Gómez, B. & García, F. (2015) Bridging the gap between research and practice in a clinical and training network: Aigle's Program, *Psychotherapy Research, 25*(1), 84–94. https://doi/10.1080/10503307 .2013.856047

Fisher, A. J., & Boswell, J. F. (2016). Enhancing the personalization of psychotherapy with dynamic assessment and modeling. *Assessment, 23*(4), 496–506. https://doi.org/10.1177/1073191116638735

Flückiger, C., Del Re, A. C., Wampold, B. E., & Horvath, A. O. (2018). The alliance in adult psychotherapy: A meta-analytic synthesis. *Psychotherapy, 55*(4), 316–340. http://dx.doi.org/10.1037/pst0000172

Flückiger C, Wampold B, E, Delgadillo J, Rubel J, Vîslă A, Lutz W (2020). Is there an evidence-based number of sessions in outpatient psychotherapy? – A comparison of naturalistic conditions across countries. *Psychotherapy and Psychosomatics,* https://doi.org/10.1159/000507793

Frank, J. D. (1961). *Persuasion and healing: A comparative study of psychotherapy.* Johns Hopkins Press.

Garfield, S. L. & Bergin, A. E., (Eds.). (1978). *Handbook of psychotherapy and behavior change.* (2nd Ed.). Wiley.

Garfield, S. L. & Bergin, A. E. (Eds.). (1986). *Handbook of psychotherapy and behavior change.* (3rd. Ed.). Wiley.

Garfield, S. L., & Kurtz, R. (1977). A study of eclectic views. *Journal of Consulting and Clinical Psychology, 45,* 78–83. https://doi.org/10.1037/0022-006X.45.1.78

Goldfried, M. R. (1980). Toward the delineation of therapeutic change principles. *American Psychologist, 35*(11), 991–999.https://doi.org/10.1037/0003-066X.35.11.991

Goldfried, M. R. (2019). Obtaining consensus in psychotherapy: What holds us back? *American Psychologist, 74*(4), 484–496. https://doi.org/10.1037/amp0000365

Grawe, K. (2004). *Psychological therapy.* Seattle: Hogrefe.

Greenberg, L. S., & Pinsof, W. M. (Eds.). (1986). *Guilford clinical psychology and psychotherapy series. The psychotherapeutic process: A research handbook.* Guilford Press.

Gurman, A. S., & Razin, A. M. (1977). *Effective psychotherapy: A handbook of research* (Vol. 70). Pergamon.

Hayes, S. C., Luoma, J. B., Bond, F. W., Masuda, A., & Lillis, J. (2006). Acceptance and commitment therapy: Model, processes and outcomes. *Behaviour Research and Therapy, 44*(1), 1–25. https://doi.org/10.1016/j.brat.2005.06.006

Hill, C. E., Knox, S., Thompson, B. J., Williams, E. N., Hess, S. A., & Ladany, N. (2005). Consensual qualitative research: An update. *Journal of Counseling Psychology, 52*(2), 196–205.https://doi.org/10.1037/0022-0167.52.2.196

Hill, C. E., Thompson, B. J., & Williams, E. N. (1997). A guide to conducting consensual qualitative research. *The Counseling Psychologist, 25*(4), 517–572. https://doi.org/10.1177/0011000097254001

Hofmann, S. G., & Hayes, S. C. (2019). The future of intervention science: Process-based therapy. *Clinical Psychological Science, 7*(1), 37–50. https://doi.org/10.1177/2167702618772296

Hofmann, S. G., Sawyer, A. T., Witt, A. A., & Oh, D. (2010). The effect of mindfulness-based therapy on anxiety and depression: A meta-analytic review. *Journal of Consulting and Clinical Psychology, 78*(2), 169–183. https://doi.org/10.1037/a0018555

Hollon, S. D., & Beck, A. T. (1978). Psychotherapy and drug therapy: Comparisons and combinations. In S. L. Garfield & A. E. Bergin (Eds.), *Handbook of psychotherapy and behavior change: An empirical analysis* (2nd ed., pp. 437–490). Wiley.

Hollon, S. D., Cohen, Z. D., Singla, D. R., & Andrews, P. W. (2019). Recent developments in the treatment of depression. *Behavior Therapy, 50*(2), 257–269. https://doi.org/10.1016/j.beth.2019.01.002

Holmes, E. A., Ghaderi, A., Harmer, C. J., Ramchandani, P. G., Cuijpers, P., Morrison, A. P., Roiser, J. P., Bockting, C., O'Connor, R. C., Shafran, R., Moulds, M. L., & Craske, M. G. (2018). The Lancet Psychiatry Commission on psychological treatments research in tomorrow's science. *The Lancet Psychiatry, 5*(3), 237–286. https://doi.org/10.1016/S2215-0366 (17)30513-8

Horowitz, L. M., Rosenberg, S. E., Baer, B. A., Ureño, G., & Villaseñor, V. S. (1988). Inventory of interpersonal problems: psychometric properties and clinical applications. *Journal of Consulting and Clinical Psychology, 56*(6), 885. https://doi.org/10.1037/0022-006X.56.6.885

Horvath, A. O., Del Re, A. C., Flückiger, C., & Symonds, D. (2011). Alliance in individual psychotherapy. *Psychotherapy: Theory, Research, Practice, Training, 48*(1), 9–16. https://doi.org/10.1037/a0022186

Horvath, A. O., & Greenberg, L. S. (Eds.). (1994). *Wiley series on personality processes. The working alliance: Theory, research, and practice.* Wiley.

Horvath, A. O., & Symonds, B. D. (1991). Relation between working alliance and outcome in psychotherapy: A meta-analysis. *Journal of Counseling Psychology, 38*(2), 139–149. https://doi.org/10.1037/0022-0167.38.2 .139

Howard, K. I., Kopta, S. M., Krause, M. S., & Orlinsky, D. E. (1986). The dose-effect relationship in psychotherapy. *American Psychologist, 41*(2), 159–164.

Howard, K. I., Moras, K., Brill, P. L., Martinovich, Z., & Lutz, W. (1996). Evaluation of psychotherapy: Efficacy, effectiveness, and patient progress. *American Psychologist, 51*(10), 1059–1064.

Howard, K. I., & Orlinsky, D. E. (1972). Psychotherapeutic processes. *Annual Review of Psychology, 23,* 615–668. https://doi.org/10.1146/annurev .ps.23.020172.003151

Huibers, M. J., Cohen, Z. D., Lemmens, L. H., Arntz, A., Peeters, F. P., Cuijpers, P., & DeRubeis, R. J. (2015). Predicting optimal outcomes in cognitive therapy or interpersonal psychotherapy for depressed individuals using the personalized advantage index approach. *PloS one, 10*(11). https://doi.org/ 10.1371/journal.pone.0140771

Insel, T. R. (2014). The NIMH research domain criteria (RDoC) project: precision medicine for psychiatry. *American Journal of Psychiatry, 171*(4), 395–397. https://doi.org/10.1176/appi.ajp.2014.14020138

Jacobson, N. S., Follette, W. C., & Revenstorf, D. (1984). Psychotherapy outcome research: Methods for reporting variability and evaluating clinical significance. *Behavior Therapy, 15*(4), 336–352. https://doi.org/10.1016/ S0005-7894 (84)80002-7

Jacobson, N. S., & Truax, P. (1991). Clinical significance: A statistical approach to defining meaningful change in psychotherapy research. *Journal of Consulting and Clinical Psychology, 59*(1), 12–19. https://doi.org/ 10.1037/0022-006X.59.1.12

Jones, E. E., & Pulos, S. M. (1993). Comparing the process in psychodynamic and cognitive-behavioral therapies. *Journal of Consulting and Clinical Psychology, 61*(2), 306. https://doi.org/10.1037/0022-006X .61.2.306

Kadera, S. W., Lambert, M. J., & Andrews, A. A. (1996). How much therapy is really enough? A session-by-session analysis of the psychotherapy dose-effect relationship. *Journal of Psychotherapy Practice and Research, 5*(2), 132.

Kazdin, A. E. (2007). Mediators and mechanisms of change in psychotherapy research. *Annual Review of Clinical Psychology, 3,* 1–27. https://doi.org/ 10.1146/annurev.clinpsy.3.022806.091432

Kazdin, A. E. (2008). Evidence-based treatment and practice: New opportunities to bridge clinical research and practice, enhance the knowledge base, and improve patient care. *American Psychologist, 63*(3), 146–159. https:// doi.org/10.1037/0003-066X.63.3.146

Kazdin, A.E. (2018). *Innovations in psychosocial interventions and their delivery: Leveraging cutting-edge science to improve the world's mental health.* Oxford University Press.

Keller, M. B., Lavori, P. W., Friedman, B., Nielsen, E., Endicott, J., McDonald-Scott, P., & Andreasen, N. C. (1987). The longitudinal interval follow-up evaluation: A comprehensive method for assessing outcome in prospective longitudinal studies. *Archives of General Psychiatry, 44* (6), 540–548. https://doi.org/10.1001/archpsyc.1987.01800180050009

Kiesler, D. J. (1966). Some myths of psychotherapy research and the search for a paradigm. *Psychological Bulletin, 65*(2), 110. https://doi.org/10.1037/ h0022911

Lambert, M. J. (Ed.) (2004). *Bergin and Garfield's handbook of psychotherapy and behavior change* (5th ed.). Wiley.

Lambert, M. (2007). Presidential address: What we have learned from a decade of research aimed at improving psychotherapy outcome in routine care. *Psychotherapy Research, 17*(1), 1–14. https://doi.org/ 10.1080/10503300601032506

Lambert, M. J. (Ed.) (2013a). *Bergin and Garfield's handbook of psychotherapy and behavior change* (6th ed.). Wiley.

Lambert, M. J. (2013b). Introduction and historical overview. In M. J. Lambert (Ed.), *Bergin and Garfield's handbook of psychotherapy and behavior change* (6th ed., pp. 169–218). Wiley.

Lambert, M. J. (2013c). The efficacy and effectiveness of psychotherapy. In M. J. Lambert (Ed.), *Bergin and Garfield's handbook of psychotherapy and behavior change* (6th ed., pp. 169–218). Wiley.

Lambert, M. J., Hansen, N. B., & Finch, A. E. (2001). Patient-focused research: Using patient outcome data to enhance treatment effects. *Journal of Consulting and Clinical Psychology*, 69(2), 159–172. https://doi.org/10.1037/0022-006X.69.2.159

Lambert, M. J., Whipple, J. L., & Kleinstäuber, M. (2018). Collecting and delivering progress feedback: A meta-analysis of routine outcome monitoring. *Psychotherapy*, 55(4), 520–537. https://doi.org/10.1037/pst0000167

Linehan, M. M., Armstrong, H. E., Suarez, A., Allmon, D., & Heard, H. L. (1991). Cognitive-behavioral treatment of chronically parasuicidal borderline patients. *Archives of General Psychiatry*, 48(12), 1060–1064. https://doi.org/10.1001/archpsyc.1991.01810360024003

Linehan, M. M., Comtois, K. A., Murray, A. M., Brown, M. Z., Gallop, R. J., Heard, H. L., Korslund, K. E., Tutek, D. A., Reynolds, S. K., & Lindenboim, N. (2006). Two-year randomized controlled trial and follow-up of dialectical behavior therapy vs. therapy by experts for suicidal behaviors and borderline personality disorder. *Archives of General Psychiatry*, 63(7), 757–766. https://doi.org/10.1001/archpsyc.63.7.757

Lipsey, M. W., & Wilson, D. B. (1993). The efficacy of psychological, educational, and behavioral treatment: Confirmation from meta-analysis. *American Psychologist*, 48(12), 1181–1209. https://doi.org/10.1037/0003-066X.48.12.1181

Lorenzo-Luaces, L., German, R. E., & DeRubeis, R. J. (2015). It's complicated: The relation between cognitive change procedures, cognitive change, and symptom change in cognitive therapy for depression. *Clinical Psychology Review*, 41, 3–15. https://doi.org/10.1016/j.cpr.2014.12.003

Luborsky, L., Chandler, M., Auerbach, A. H., Cohen, J., & Bachrach, H. M. (1971). Factors influencing the outcome of psychotherapy: A review of quantitative research. *Psychological Bulletin*, 75(3), 145–185. https://doi.org/10.1037/h0030480

Luborsky, L., Singer, B., & Luborsky, L. (1975). Comparative studies of psychotherapies: Is it true that everyone has won and all must have prizes? *Archives of General Psychiatry*, 32 (8), 995–1008. https://doi.org/10.1001/archpsyc.1975.01760260059004

Lutz, W., Martinovich, Z., & Howard, K. I. (1999). Patient profiling: An application of random coefficient regression models to depicting the response of a patient to outpatient psychotherapy. *Journal of Consulting and Clinical Psychology*, 67(4), 571–577. https://doi.org/10.1037/0022-006X.67.4.571

Lutz, W., Rubel, J. A., Schwartz, B., Schilling, V., & Deisenhofer, A.-K. (2019). Towards integrating personalized feedback research into clinical practice: Development of the Trier Treatment Navigator (TTN). *Behaviour Research and Therapy*, 120, https://doi.org/10.1016/j.brat.2019.103438

Lutz, W., Saunders, S. M., Leon, S. C., Martinovich, Z., Kosfelder, J., Schulte, D., Grawe, K., & Tholen, S. (2006). Empirically and clinically useful decision making in psychotherapy: Differential predictions with treatment response models. *Psychological Assessment*, 18(2), 133–141. https://doi.org/10.1037/1040-3590.18.2.133

Martin, D. J., Garske, J. P., & Davis, M. K. (2000). Relation of the therapeutic alliance with outcome and other variables: A meta-analytic review. *Journal of Consulting and Clinical Psychology*, 68(3), 438–450. https://doi.org/10.1037/0022-006X.68.3.438

Meltzoff, J., & Kornreich, M. (1970). *Research in psychotherapy*. Atherom Press.

Muran, J.C., Castonguay, L.G., & Strauss, B. (2010). A brief introduction to psychotherapy research. In L.G. Castonguay, J.C. Muran, L., Angus, J. H. Hayes, N. Ladany & T. Anderson, (Eds) *Bringing psychotherapy research to life: Understanding change through the work of leading clinical researchers. Legacies from the Society for Psychotherapy* Research. Washington, DC: American Psychological Association Press.

Newman, F. L., & Howard, K. I. (1991). Introduction to the special section on seeking new clinical research methods. *Journal of Consulting and Clinical Psychology*, 59(1), 8–11. https://doi.org/10.1037/h0092573

Norcross, J. C. (Ed.) (2002). *Psychotherapy relationships that work: Therapist contributions and responsiveness to patients.* Oxford University Press.

Norcross, J. C. (Ed.). (2011). *Psychotherapy relationships that work: Evidence-based responsiveness* (2nd ed.). Oxford University Press. https://doi.org/10.1093/acprof:oso/9780199737208.001.0001

Norcross, J. C., & Lambert, M. J. (Eds.). (2019). *Psychotherapy relationships that work: Volume 1: Evidence-based therapist contributions.* Oxford University Press. https://doi.org/10.1093/med-psych/9780190843953.001.0001

Orlinsky, D. (1995). The graying and greening of SPR: A personal memoir on forming the Society for Psychotherapy Research. *Psychotherapy Research*, 5(4), 343–350. *https://doi.org/10.1080/10500330951233133145*

Orlinsky, D. E., Grawe, K., & Parks, B. K. (1994). Process and outcome in psychotherapy – Noch einmal. In A. Bergin & J. S. Garfield (Eds.), *Handbook of psychotherapy and behavior change* (4th edition, pp. 270–378). Wiley.

Orlinsky, D. E, Howard, K. I. (1967). The good therapy hour. Experiential correlates of patients' and therapists' evaluations of therapy sessions. *Archives of General Psychiatry*, 16, 621–632. doi:10.1001/archpsyc.1967.01730230105013

Orlinsky, D. E., & Howard, K. I. (1978). The relation of process to outcome in psychotherapy. In A. E Bergin & S. L. Garfield (Eds.), *Handbook of psychotherapy and behavior change*. Wiley.

Page, A. C., Camacho, K. S., & Page, J. T. (2019). Delivering cognitive behaviour therapy informed by a contemporary framework of psychotherapy treatment selection and adaptation. *Psychotherapy Research*, 29(8), 971–973. https://doi.org/10.1080/10503307.2019.1662510

Paul, G. L. (1967). Strategy of outcome research in psychotherapy. *Journal of Consulting Psychology*, 31(2), 109–118. https://doi.org/10.1037/h0024436

Prochaska, J. O., & DiClemente, C. C. (1983). Stages and processes of self-change of smoking: toward an integrative model of change. *Journal of Consulting and Clinical Psychology*, 51(3), 390. https://doi.org/10.1037/0022-006X.51.3.390

Prochaska, J. O., & DiClemente, C. C. (1992). Stages of change in the modification of problem behaviors. *Progress in Behavior Modification*, 28, 183–218.

Pybis, J., Saxon, D., Hill, A., & Barkham, M. (2017). The comparative effectiveness and efficiency of cognitive behaviour therapy and generic counselling in the treatment of depression: evidence from the 2nd UK National Audit of psychological therapies. *BMC Psychiatry*, 17(1), 215. https://doi.org/10.1186/s12888-017-1370-7

Richards, D., & Richardson, T. (2012). Computer-based psychological treatments for depression: A systematic review and meta-analysis. *Clinical Psychology Review*, 32(4), 329–342. https://doi.org/10.1016/j.cpr.2012.02.004

Rice, L. N., & Greenberg, L. S. (Eds.) (1984). *Patterns of change: Intensive analysis of psychotherapy process*. Guilford Press.

Rogers, C. R. (1957). The necessary and sufficient conditions of therapeutic personality change. *Journal of Consulting Psychology*, 21, 95–103.

Rogers, C. R., & Dymond, R. F. (Eds.) (1954). *Psychotherapy and personality change*. University of Chicago Press.

Rogers, C. R. & Gendlin, E. T. (1967). *The therapeutic relationship and its impact: A study of psychotherapy with schizophrenics*: University of Wisconsin Press.

Roth, A., & Fonagy, P. (2006). *What works for whom?: A critical review of psychotherapy research*. Guilford Press.

Rush, A. J., Beck, A. T., Kovacs, M., & Hollon, S. (1977). Comparative efficacy of cognitive therapy and pharmacotherapy in the treatment of depressed outpatients. *Cognitive Therapy and Research*, 1(1), 17–37. https://doi.org/10.1007/BF01173502

Russell, R.L. & Orlinsky, D.E. (1996). Psychotherapy research in historical perspective. Implications for mental health care policy. *Archives of General Psychiatry*, 53(8), 708–715. doi:10.1001/archpsyc.1996.01830080060010

Russell, R. L., & Stiles, W. B. (1979). Categories for classifying language in psychotherapy. *Psychological Bulletin*, 86(2), 404–419. https://doi.org/10.1037/0033-2909.86.2.404

Rosenzweig, S. (1938). A dynamic interpretation of psychotherapy oriented towards research. *Psychiatry*, 1, 521–526. https://doi.org/10.1080/00332747.1938.11022213

Safran, J. D., Crocker, P., McMain, S., & Murray, P. (1990). Therapeutic alliance rupture as a therapy event for empirical investigation. *Psychotherapy: Theory, Research, Practice, Training*, 27(2), 154–165. https://doi.org/10.1037/0033-3204.27.2.154

Safran, J. D., & Muran, J. C. (2000). *Negotiating the therapeutic alliance: A relational treatment guide*. Guilford Press.

Saxon, D., & Barkham, M. (2012). Patterns of therapist variability: Therapist effects and the contribution of patient severity and risk. *Journal of Consulting and Clinical Psychology, 80*(4), 535–546.https://doi.org/10.1037/a0028898

Seligman, M. E. P. (1995). The effectiveness of psychotherapy: The Consumer Reports study. *American Psychologist, 50*(12), 965–974. https://doi.org/10.1037/0003-066X.50.12.965

Seligman, M. E. P., Steen, T. A., Park, N., & Peterson, C. (2005). Positive psychology progress: Empirical validation of interventions. *American Psychologist, 60*(5), 410–421. https://doi.org/10.1037/0003-066X.60.5.410

Sloane, R. B., Staples F. R., Magurn, R. S, Yorkston N. J., Whipple, K. (1975). *Psychotherapy versus behavior therapy.* Harvard University Press.

Smith, M. L., & Glass, G. V. (1977). Meta-analysis of psychotherapy outcome studies. *American Psychologist, 32*(9), 752–760. https://doi.org/10.1037/0003-066X.32.9.752

Smith, M. L., Glass, G. V., & Miller, T. I. (1980). *The benefits of psychotherapy.* The John Hopkins University Press.

Stiles, W. B. (1979). Verbal response modes and psychotherapeutic technique. *Psychiatry, 42*(1), 49–62. https://doi.org/10.1080/00332747.1979.11024006

Stiles, W. B., Agnew-Davies, R., Hardy, G. E., Barkham, M., & Shapiro, D. A. (1998). Relations of the alliance with psychotherapy outcome: Findings in the second Sheffield Psychotherapy Project. *Journal of Consulting and Clinical Psychology, 66*(5), 791–802. https://doi.org/10.1037/0022-006X.66.5.791

Stiles, W. B., Shapiro, D. A., & Elliott, R. (1986). Are all psychotherapies equivalent? *American Psychologist, 41*(2), 165–180. https://doi.org/10.1037/0003-066X.41.2.165

Strauss, B., Burlingame, G. M., & Bormann, B. (2008). Using the CORE Battery-R in Group Psychotherapy. *Journal of Clinical Psychology, 64,* 1225–1237. https://doi.org/10.1002/jclp.20535

Strupp, H. H. (1980). Success and failure in time-limited psychotherapy: A systematic comparison of two cases: Comparison 1. *Archives of General Psychiatry, 37*(5), 595–596. https://doi.org/10.1001/archpsyc.1980.01780180109014

Strupp, H. H. (1997). Research, practice, and managed care. *Psychotherapy: Theory, Research, Practice, Training, 34*(1), 91–94. https://doi.org/10.1037/h0087780

Strupp, H. H., & Hadley, S. W. (1979). Specific vs nonspecific factors in psychotherapy: A controlled study of outcome. *Archives of General Psychiatry, 36*(10), 1125–1136. https://doi.org/10.1001/archpsyc.1979.01780100095009

Strupp, H. H. Horowitz, L. & Lambert, M. J. (1997) (Eds.). *Measuring patient changes in mood, anxiety, and personality disorders: Toward a core battery.* American Psychological Association.

Strupp, H. H., & Howard, K I. (1992). A brief history of psychotherapy research. In D. K. Freedheim (Ed.), *History of psychotherapy: A century of change.* Washington, DC: American Psychological Association.

Tang, T. Z., & DeRubeis, R. J. (1999). Sudden gains and critical sessions in cognitive-behavioral therapy for depression. *Journal of Consulting and Clinical Psychology, 67*(6), 894–904. https://doi.org/10.1037//0022-006x.67.6.894

Toukmanian, S. G., & Rennie, D. L. (Eds.). (1992). *Psychotherapy process research: Paradigmatic and narrative approaches.* Sage Publications, Inc.

Urban, H. B., & Ford, D. H. (1971). Some historical and conceptual perspectives on psychotherapy and behavior change. In A. E. Bergin & S. L. Garfield (Eds.), *Handbook of psychotherapy and behavior change.* Wiley.

Wampold, B. E. (2001). *The great psychotherapy debate: Models, methods and findings.* Lawrence Erlbaum, Publishers.

Wampold, B. E., & Imel, Z. E. (2015). *The great psychotherapy debate: The evidence for what makes psychotherapy work* (2nd ed.). Routledge/Taylor & Francis Group.

Waskow, I. E., & Parloff, M. B. (Eds.). (1975). *Psychotherapy change measures: Report of the clinical research branch outcome measures project.* Washington, DC: Government Printing Office.

Whitehorn, J. C., & Betz, B. J. (1954). A study of psychotherapeutic relationships between physicians and schizophrenic patients. *The American Journal of Psychiatry, 111*(5), 321–331. https://doi.org/10.1176/ajp.111.5.321

Wilkinson, J., Arnold, K. F., Murray, E. J., van Smeden, M., Carr, K., Sippy, R., de Kamps, M, Beam, A., Konigorski, Lippert, C., & Gilthorpe, M. S. (2020). Time to reality check the promises of machine learning-powered precision medicine. *The Lancet Digital Health.* https://doi.org/10.1016/S2589-7500(20)30200-4

Wittmann, W. W., & Matt, G. E. (1986). Meta-Analyse als Integration von Forschungsergebnissen am Beispiel deutschsprachiger Arbeiten zur Effektivität von Psychotherapie. [Meta-analysis as a method for integrating psychotherapy studies in German-speaking countries]. *Psychologische Rundschau, 37*(1), 20–40.

Wolpe, J. (1958). *Psychotherapy by reciprocal inhibition.* Stanford University Press.

Zilcha-Mano, S. (2021). Toward personalized psychotherapy: The importance of the trait-like/state-like distinction for understanding therapeutic change. *American Psychologist, 76*(3), 516–528. https://doi.org/10.1037/amp0000629

METHODOLOGICAL FOUNDATIONS AND INNOVATIONS IN QUANTITATIVE PSYCHOTHERAPY RESEARCH

SCOTT A BALDWIN AND SIMON B GOLDBERG

Abstract

There have been ongoing developments in research methodology since the previous edition of this text. This chapter highlights key advancements while also discussing areas of perennial importance for a robust science of psychotherapy. This discussion is contextualized within the current replication crisis within psychology. We provide several suggestions for ways to increase rigor in psychotherapy research, including a commitment to open science practices. Foundational concepts and recent innovations are reviewed in the areas of measurement, research designs commonly used to test treatment packages (e.g., clinical trials, meta-analysis), and techniques for examining the process of change (e.g., mediation, moderation). We highlight both areas of budding promise (e.g., alternatives to self-report measures) and areas of ongoing weakness (e.g., range restriction in process measures like the therapeutic alliance, underpowered designs). This chapter is designed to introduce key methodological concepts to those new to psychotherapy research as well as highlight areas of active debate for more experienced readers.

OVERVIEW

INTRODUCTION

Our experience suggests that most psychotherapists and psychotherapy researchers did not choose their profession to study research design and statistics. Nevertheless, our ability to maximize our help to patients, effect change in policy, and maintain credibility as a profession rests on our commitment to engage in transparent and rigorous study of our interventions and the theories that ground them. One way to maintain transparency and rigor is to use study designs and statistical analysis approaches that are appropriate for our research and policy questions and that allow others to check and replicate our findings. We must also understand the design and analysis issues well enough to communicate our findings accurately to patients, professionals, and policy makers. Consequently, we cannot avoid studying methods.

This chapter reviews foundational methods (e.g., measurement, power analysis, randomized designs) as well as methodological innovations (e.g., growth mixture models, between–within analysis) germane to psychotherapy research. In the most recent version of this chapter in the 6th edition of the *Handbook*, Comer and Kendall (2013) described two principles that guided their discussion of methodology in psychotherapy research: "(1) the role of the scientific practitioner in psychotherapy research and practice, and (2) the importance of empirically supported treatments" (p. 21). We echo a commitment to scientist-practitioner model and the use of empirically supported treatments and refer readers to Comer and Kendall's chapter for detailed discussion of those principles. However, we add a third guiding principle to our discussion, one which we suspect was an unstated principle in previous editions of this chapter. Specifically, we add a commitment to open, transparent, and replicable research practices.

We begin with a review of (a) foundational ideas in measurement, (b) methods and challenges for establishing the efficacy of treatment packages, (c) approaches for understanding mechanisms of change, (d) statistical power, (e) methods for modeling change, and (f) methods for summarizing literatures. Given space limitations, we do not provide step-by-step instructions or a tutorial for implementing the methods. Where relevant we provide references to resources for further study.

Following the discussion of specific methodological and statistical approaches, we discuss concerns about replication and trustworthiness of scientific results that have grown since the publication of the last edition of the *Handbook*. We believe this is critical context for learning methods because it reminds us that the hallmark of science is not using a particular design or statistical analysis nor is it getting results published. Rather, we argue that the hallmark of science is transparency of methods, open communication regarding results, and thoughtful criticism of results pre- and post-publication. These features allow scientists to correct problems, revise theories, and improve their studies. In the case of psychotherapy research, we hope that transparency and rigor ultimately lead to better patient care.

MEASUREMENT

Measurement is foundational for psychotherapy research. In science generally, measurement can be defined as "the assignment of numerals to objects or events according to rules" (Stevens, 1946, p. 677). Within psychology, measurement involves assigning scores to individuals with the belief that the scores represent a characteristic of those individuals. Despite the importance of measurement, it is too often neglected and not prioritized, both in graduate methods training as well as in the design and reporting of research studies. This is unfortunate,

as measurement can have a huge impact on research findings. Good measurement is a hallmark of good research, regardless of the scope (e.g., nomothetic versus idiographic research) or design (e.g., controlled versus observational) of the study. Indeed, no amount of statistical analyses or clever design features make up for poor measurement – one might even go so far as to say that without good measurement, research would be useless.

This section highlights several key topics in the area of measure development and evaluation (e.g., reliability and validity) as well as more recent advances in measurement methodology (e.g., item response theory, ecological momentary assessment), particularly as they pertain to measurement in psychotherapy research. Measurement-related topics with which some readers may be familiar (e.g., reliability and validity) are discussed more briefly, with references provided for more in-depth reading.

Developing Scales

Scale development is an often lengthy, multistep process. Crocker and Algina (2008) identify 10 steps for constructing a new test (e.g., identifying the test's purpose, defining of behaviors that represent the construct intended to be measured). Thorough discussion of the nuances of test construction are beyond the scope of this chapter, and many excellent resources are available for psychotherapy researchers interested in developing measures (Clark & Watson, 2019; Crocker & Algina, 2008). However, two key characteristics for consideration in scale development are discussed here – reliability and validity – due to the significant influence these factors can have on the strength of evidence a given measure can provide.

Establishing Reliability

Within the context of measurement, reliability can be defined as consistency of scores provided by a given measure. Or, more accurately, the degree to which a measure is free from measurement error (Mokkink et al., 2010). Though reliability does not address whether a measure assesses the intended construct (see validity below), a measure must first demonstrate reliability. Reliability can be established in several ways, each of which provides a slightly different perspective. The four classical forms of reliability include test–retest, alternate forms, internal consistency, and interrater. Test–retest reliability involves administering a measure repeatedly and evaluating the degree to which assessment at one time point corresponds to a second time point and is used to evaluate consistency of measurement across time (McDonald, 1999, pp. 69–70). Alternate or parallel forms reliability involves the administration of two similar but nonoverlapping versions of the same test (McDonald, 1999, pp. 70–72). Internal consistency reliability examines the degree to which items on a measure provide similar information about the test-taker (McDonald, 1999, Ch. 6). Finally, interrater reliability (Fleiss et al., 2013) establishes consistency in test scores for measures where the score is provided by an independent rater (e.g., parent, teacher, clinician).

Establishing Validity

In order for a measure to function properly, it must be reliable, whether across time, forms, items, or raters. However, a reliable measure is not necessarily a good measure. It is possible for a measure to be consistent and not provide information about the construct of interest. Thus, reliability does not equal validity, where validity means that a measure assesses what it is designed to assess. There are several aspects of validity to consider when evaluating scores from a measure, with construct and criterion validity being perhaps the most relevant to psychotherapy research. Construct validity is defined as the degree to which a measure assesses constructs as defined by a theory (Cronbach & Meehl, 1955). Key methods for establishing construct validity involve demonstrating that a measure is associated with theoretically similar constructs (i.e., convergent validity) and is not associated with measures of theoretically dissimilar constructs (i.e., discriminant or divergent validity). Criterion validity, sometimes referred to as predictive validity, is the extent to which a measure – the predictor – is related to an outcome – the criterion (Nunnally & Bernstein, 1994). Possible criteria that could be predicted in psychotherapy include response to treatment, dropout, adherence to treatment, and need for another dose of therapy. Increasingly, the need for thorough assessment of cross-cultural validity has been recognized (e.g., Zhou et al., 2019).

Factor Analytic Methods

One statistical approach that is commonly used in the development and validation of measures in psychotherapy is factor analysis. Factor analysis involves expressing patterns of association among observed variables (e.g., items on a self-report measure) as a function of a smaller number of unobserved (i.e., latent) variables called factors (Bartholomew et al., 2008). Factor analysis can be exploratory, in the case of a measure with unknown factor structure, or confirmatory, when seeking to validate a previously established structure. A primary goal of factor analysis in psychotherapy research is to investigate a measure's factorial or structural validity. Factorial or structural validity is the degree to which the empirical relationships among items on a measure are consistent with the proposed structure of the measure. For example, factor analysis could establish the presence of bond, task, and goal elements within the construct of working alliance (Horvath & Greenberg, 1989) or establish clinically meaningful subscales within a symptom measure (e.g., hyperarousal, re-experiencing, etc. for the PTSD Checklist 5; Weathers et al., 2013). Thus, factor analysis contributes evidence regarding construct validity (Nunnally & Bernstein, 1994).

Factor analysis is a powerful method. One of the major constraints for its use in psychotherapy research is the requirement of large samples for reliable estimates of factor structure. Large samples, though present in some psychotherapy research, can be difficult to obtain when working with specific disorders. Various recommendations have been offered for the recommended overall sample size (e.g., ≥300; Comrey & Lee, 1992) or number of sample size per number of items (e.g., 10:1; Everett, 1975). A rule-of-thumb sample size has not been agreed on for factor analysis because the necessary sample size is dependent on specific details regarding the study. For example, simulation studies indicate that the requisite sample size is related to not only the number of items on a given measure but also the degree of association or communality among the variables. For items that have higher communality, factor structure can be more easily established and can be reliably identified with a smaller sample size (MacCallum et al., 1999). Readers wanting a thorough introduction to factor analysis in applied settings can consult Brown (2015).

Item Response Theory

Although not a new methodology, item response theory (IRT) has become increasingly popular with increased computing power. IRT encompasses a suite of psychometric models including the Rasch and two-parameter models for binary items; the graded response, rating scale, and partial credit models for ordinal items; and the nominal response model for unordered categorical items (see Raykov and Marcoulides, 2018). Unlike classical test theory, which views test scores as a combination of true score variance and error variance, IRT views responses to test items as a mathematical combination of person and item characteristics (Embretson, 1996; Embretson & Reise, 2000). IRT theorizes that responses reflect an underlying trait that is not equally represented across all potential items. That is, some items may provide more information about the underlying trait (e.g., depression) than another item. IRT calculates the difficulty of a given item (i.e., the likelihood that individuals will respond in a given way) to create item characteristic curves that are used for scaling.

IRT has been widely embraced in contemporary test construction. IRT is a foundational technique for the development of standardized tests of academic abilities (e.g., Graduate Record Examinations; Embretson & Reise, 2000). IRT has also allowed the development of computerized adaptive tests that adjust the presentation of items based on an individual's responses. Computerized adaptive tests may have many advantages over traditional measures in the context of psychotherapy, including the ability to draw from large item banks (≥1,000 items) assessing all facets of an underlying disorder, optimizing item presentation based on patient severity, reduction of practice effects or measurement reactivity, and reduction in the necessary number of items for obtaining reliable and valid test scores (Beiser et al., 2016). Use of IRT has begun to appear in the psychotherapy literature (e.g., developing brief scales for measurement-based care; Weisz et al., 2019). However, by and large, the potential of IRT has not been realized in psychotherapy research. This is likely due to a number of factors (e.g., more complex scoring requirements, different scale development procedures). Nonetheless, IRT may play an increasingly central role in psychotherapy research in decades to come. Readers wanting a thorough introduction to IRT can consult Embretson and Reise (2000) and Raykov and Marcoulides (2018).

Alternative Measurement Methodologies

The bulk of psychotherapy research has relied on self-report measures, historically administered at the beginning and end of a course of treatment. Increasingly, session-by-session measurement occurs (Barkham, 2016), which has notable advantages (e.g., increased reliability, opportunities for modeling finer grained processes). From one perspective, a heavy reliance on self-report measures is reasonable, given the inherently internal experience of most psychological constructs being targeted and assessed in the context of psychotherapy (e.g., depression, anxiety, distress). Nonetheless, self-report is just one perspective on constructs of interest and can be subject to important biases (e.g., social desirability; Heppner et al., 2016). Concerns regarding the validity of self-report measures have encouraged the development of various alternative assessment methodologies. These include the use of ecological momentary assessment (EMA), passive or personal sensing, observer-rated measures, and psychophysiological measures.

Ecological Momentary Assessment (EMA)

EMA, or experience sampling, has been defined as "repeated sampling of subjects' current behaviors and experiences in real time, in subjects' natural environment" (Shiffman et al., 2008, p. 1). EMA data can be collected using a variety of technologies, such as electronic diaries completed on computers or smartphones, telephone calls, or even paper-and-pencil forms (e.g., responses recorded when individuals are alerted via a mobile beeper; Shiffman et al., 2008). Although clearly a more resource intensive measurement paradigm than pre–post assessment, EMA has several potential advantages. Data suggest that EMA reports minimize some reporting biases (e.g., recall bias; Bradburn et al., 1987), maximize aspects of validity (e.g., ecological validity), and allow assessment of moment-to-moment microprocesses that may influence behavior in patients' actual day-to-day lives (Shiffman et al., 2008). EMA has been employed to understand the dynamics of a variety of behaviors and psychological processes, including smoking relapse (Shiffman et al., 2002), binge eating (Haedt-Matt & Keel, 2011), and psychosis (Myin-Germeys & van Os, 2007). Recent studies have begun using EMA in the context of psychotherapy research as well (e.g., Geschwind et al., 2011; Lutz et al., 2018). As it appears that the technology for implementing EMA is available and both feasible and acceptable to patients and providers (see Goldberg, Buck, et al., 2018, for a review of studies measuring psychiatric symptoms remotely), we hope to see it increasingly used in the future.

Passive or Personal Sensing

EMA provides rich data regarding patients' symptoms and functioning, but it is also a time-intensive measurement strategy that relies on patients' compliance with the assessment paradigm. Passive or personal sensing can reduce measurement burden. Personal sensing involves "collecting and analyzing data from sensors embedded in the context of daily life with the aim of identifying human behaviors, thoughts,

feelings, and traits" (Mohr et al., 2017, p. 23). Advances in mobile technologies have contributed to increased feasibility of collecting personal sensing data. Modern data analytic techniques, most notably machine learning, have allowed the processing of low-level sensor input to derive psychologically meaningful outcomes. Machine learning involves statistical algorithms capable of learning model parameters rather than being programmed *a priori* by a human (Dwyer et al., 2018). Ubiquitous devices, such as smartphones, contain sensors capable of detecting various streams of data (e.g., location, movement, light, sound, in-phone communication) that can be converted (perhaps through machine learning models) into psychologically relevant constructs such as activity, fatigue, concentration, sleep patterns, mood, and social interaction (Mohr et al., 2017).

Observer-Rated Measures

Psychotherapy research has a long history of observer-rated measures. Observer ratings involve "evaluations of one person (the target) by another person (the rater or observer)" (Hoyt & Kerns, 1999, p. 403). Observer-rated measures have been developed and widely used for assessing a variety of psychotherapy outcomes (e.g., Hamilton Rating Scale of Depression; Hamilton, 1960) and processes (e.g., working alliance, treatment adherence, therapist interpersonal skill; Anderson et al., 2009; Moyers et al., 2005; Raue et al., 1991), as well as basic psychological and interpersonal constructs (e.g., interpersonal style; Goldberg & Hoyt, 2015). Although observer ratings have their own sources of bias (see Hoyt, 2000), they are less prone to some potentially pernicious biases in psychotherapy research (e.g., social desirability; Heppner et al., 2016).

Arguably the main drawback for observer-rated measures is that these methods have historically been highly resource intensive. Human-based coding takes time to train raters to reliably code source material. Recent advances in automated speech recognition, natural language processing, and machine learning could vastly decrease the time and resources necessary for coding source material from psychotherapy (e.g., text, speech). This is an area of active research, but preliminary results using automated coding of psychotherapy content are promising. Currently, various forms of computer-augmented speech and language processing have predicted therapist empathy (Imel et al., 2014; Lord et al., 2015), type of psychotherapy (Imel et al., 2015), motivational interviewing treatment fidelity (Atkins et al., 2014), therapeutic alliance (Goldberg et al., 2020), and factors associated with treatment success (e.g., adaptability, dealing with ambiguity; Althoff et al., 2016). We anticipate an increase in studies employing these technologies in the years to come.

Psychophysiological Measures

A final category of alternative measurement methodologies is psychophysiological measures. The world of human psychobiology is vast and complex, and clearly beyond the scope of this chapter. Nonetheless, measures of psychophysiology have high potential relevance to psychotherapy, due to their capacity to capture non-self-report metrics of key treatment processes and outcomes. Furthermore, psychophysiological measures have their own utility, often being associated with physical health morbidity and mortality (e.g., Kumari et al., 2011). Within medicine and psychology broadly, commonly assessed psychophysiological parameters include measures of brain structure and function (e.g., magnetic resonance imaging); measures of stress physiology, autonomic arousal and regulation (e.g., cortisol, skin conductance, heart rate, heart rate variability, muscle potentials, respiratory sinus arrhythmia); and measures of inflammation (e.g., interleukin-6), cellular aging (e.g., telomeres), and immune response (e.g., antibody count; Black & Slavich, 2016).

Despite links between biological and both psychological and social processes, relatively little psychotherapy research has used these measures, despite the recent emphasis on the biological bases of behavior within funding agencies (e.g., Research Domain Criteria initiative of the National Institute of Mental Health; Insel et al., 2010) and longstanding interest in the inclusion of psychophysiology in psychotherapy research (Cacioppo et al., 1991; Lacey, 1959). Some exceptions to this trend include research investigating psychophysiological concordance as a metric of empathy (Marci et al., 2007) and the use of biomarkers as indicators of treatment outcome (Olff et al., 2007) and process (e.g., alliance; Zilcha-Mano et al., 2018). The effects of some psychological interventions have included greater assessment of psychophysiology, with considerable neuroscientific and psychophysiological research on mindfulness-based interventions (Black & Slavich, 2016; Wielgosz et al., 2019).

Part of the limited uptake of psychophysiological measures in psychotherapy research is likely due to the complexity involved in collecting and analyzing these data and the lack of a tradition of collaboration with health psychologists and medical professionals. However, with increasingly common interdisciplinary collaboration (Hall et al. 2018), these barriers may be less relevant to future psychotherapy research endeavors.

EFFICACY OF TREATMENT PACKAGES

Much of psychotherapy research has been focused on evaluating treatment efficacy. Typically, this work involves testing the effects of a specific treatment package (e.g., prolonged exposure for post-traumatic stress disorder; Foa et al., 1991; Resick et al., 2002). This section reviews various designs and design-related concerns pertaining to the study of treatment effects. We discuss commonly used design elements and the ramifications of these design decisions.

Randomized Versus Nonrandomized Trials

A common initial question that arises in the design of a psychotherapy trial is whether to use a randomized controlled design. Nonrandomized designs are often used, particularly in the initial stages of treatment development. In the interest of feasibility and in the context of scarce resources, a researcher may choose to conduct a pre–post single-group assessment of a novel intervention, allowing study participants to function as

their own controls. Such a design can be useful when piloting a new intervention that lacks established feasibility and acceptability (e.g., within an underserved population; Maura et al., 2018). Data collected in this way can be critical for planning a large-scale study (i.e., as in the case of a true pilot study; Eldridge et al., 2016). However, outside of assessing feasibility and acceptability and piloting methodological features for planning a future study, there is little reason to use a pre–post single group design. Even if significant effects are observed from pre- to post-treatment, there are a variety of threats to internal validity (i.e., confidence in inferring a causal relationship between a treatment and observed effects; Heppner et al., 2016; Shadish et al., 2002) that limit the value of this research. Notable threats include maturation (i.e., normal developmental changes), testing (i.e., effects due to repeated assessment), and regression to the mean (i.e., particularly when elevated symptoms are required for inclusion).

Nonrandomized controlled designs provide a partial, but still unsatisfying solution to these threats to internal validity. Nonrandomized controlled designs include a control group, but individuals in the study do not have an equal chance of being assigned to either the intervention or control condition, thereby weakening the strength of causal inferences that can be drawn from study results. In the absence of randomization (and, at times even in the presence of randomization), groups may differ at baseline making post-treatment differences difficult to interpret. Nonrandomized controlled designs may, however, be necessary when randomization is deemed unethical or infeasible (e.g., in military settings; Jha et al., 2010). Ultimately, the randomized controlled design provides an excellent foundation for inferring causality. This is particularly the case if comparisons are designed to isolate characteristics of specific scientific interest (e.g., testing basic questions regarding psychological problems and change mechanisms through component studies as discussed below; Borkovec & Castonguay, 1998).

Types of Comparison Condition

Not all comparison conditions are created equally. Indeed, the type of comparison group strongly impacts the kinds of scientific questions that can be answered using a randomized controlled design. Perhaps the most common control group involves no treatment or delayed treatment (as in the case of a waitlist control group). This is generally viewed as the weakest control condition, allowing a researcher to assess the experimental effects of the intervention relative to no intervention. No-treatment control groups cannot, however, establish the specificity of a given therapy for a given disorder (Wampold et al., 2005).

In pharmacotherapy research, a second-tier comparison condition is the placebo control. The double-blind placebo-controlled design is the gold standard in pharmacology research, intended to account for incidental and treatment nonspecific factors that may influence outcomes (e.g., expectancy effects; Wampold et al., 2005). A double-blind placebo-controlled design includes blinding for both those receiving (i.e., the patient) and those providing (i.e., the clinician) a given treatment. It has been argued persuasively that such a design is not possible in the context of psychotherapy. At the very least, a clinician providing a so-called psychotherapy placebo would presumably be aware of the status of this treatment arm (Wampold, 2001).

Nonetheless, psychotherapy studies often include a variety of control groups that are intended to account for treatment nonspecific factors that may influence outcome. Such control groups may be called various things, including treatment-as-usual, supportive counseling, common factors psychotherapy, or attentional controls (Wampold et al., 2011; Wampold & Imel, 2015; Zautra et al., 2012). Accurate codification of these groups is an area of ongoing research, and meta-analytic evidence suggests that some terms may be used to represent a heterogeneous group of comparison types (e.g., treatment-as-usual; Wampold et al., 2011). Concerns regarding heterogeneity aside, this class of comparison condition is theoretically intended to allow researchers to evaluate the specific effects of an intervention above and beyond those due to intervention nonspecific factors.

The most rigorous comparison type would be another actual therapy. Wampold et al. (1997) define a *bona fide* psychotherapy as treatments that are (a) delivered by trained therapists, (b) based on psychological principles, and (c) offered as viable treatments to the psychotherapy community. *Bona fide* treatments can be delivered as a complete package or as a treatment containing components of a *bona fide* therapy. The use of a *bona fide* comparison group provides the strongest test of psychotherapeutic efficacy, demonstrating, for example, how a new treatment compares with frontline, evidence-based treatments (e.g., mindfulness-based interventions versus evidence-based treatments recommended by the American Psychological Association's Society of Clinical Psychology; Goldberg, Tucker, et al., 2018). Of course, such a comparison is a high bar for establishing superiority, and meta-analyses of psychotherapy trials commonly report a lack of differences between *bona fide* treatments (Baardseth et al., 2013; Wampold et al., 2017).

Trial Design

The type of comparison condition used directly relates to the broader topic of trial design. Various trial designs have been used within psychotherapy research, often to contrast forms of psychotherapy with each other and/or with pharmacotherapy (e.g., for a classic example, see Elkin et al., 1989). The three most widely implemented trial designs are discussed here, namely superiority, equivalence, and noninferiority designs. These designs differ both in the question they are intended to answer as well as the statistical procedures involved in their analysis.

The superiority design, as its name implies, aims at establishing the superiority of one condition over a competitor (Lesaffre, 2008). This design is often used to establish the superiority of a treatment of interest (e.g., cognitive behavioral therapy for depression) over an inert treatment (e.g., placebo; Cipriani et al., 2009). As has been discussed extensively (e.g., Wampold et al., 2005; Wampold & Imel, 2015), implementing a psychological placebo in psychotherapy research is not straightforward. However, researchers commonly use

interventions that lack a strong treatment rationale as a control for nonspecific factors (e.g., time, therapist attention, see Nidich et al.'s [2018] use of a health education group). Regardless of the specific comparator used, this trial evaluates the null hypothesis that the two treatments are equivalent and aims at establishing one treatment as preferable to another. Generally speaking, superiority trials require smaller sample sizes than noninferiority or equivalence designs (Leon, 2011, p. 1347), as these designs are predicated on the assumption that one treatment will show a larger treatment effect than a comparator (and thus the effect size to be detected is typically larger than the prespecified equivalence or noninferiority margin discussed next).

The classic error in logic made in the interpretation of superiority trials occurs when no difference is detected. While one may be tempted to conclude that this indicates the two treatments are equivalent, this is decidedly not the case (Leon, 2011). Indeed, a host of alternative explanations (most notably insufficient power) could produce this pattern of findings in the presence of true differences. Equivalence and noninferiority designs are the proper approach for directly examining the possibility that two treatments do not differ (or that one is not inferior to the other).

Both equivalence and noninferiority designs are similar in that they specify *a priori* a range of difference beyond which two treatments could not be considered equivalent (or the one could not be considered not inferior to the other). Once this margin is established, the sample size is planned accordingly to allow detection of a difference of that magnitude. Equivalence designs are more commonly seen in pharmacotherapy, for example where the pharmacokinetics of a generic drug is compared with a commercial drug to show that the generic produces the same effects (Lesaffre, 2008). The null hypothesis in this design is that the observed difference between treatments (e.g., generic and commercial) is larger than the prespecified magnitude. Thus, a rejection of the null indicates that the observed difference is not in fact larger, in other words, that the treatments are equivalent. Notably, this difference could be larger due to either of the two treatments performing particularly better than the other. The noninferiority design is quite similar to the equivalence design. The key difference is the null hypothesis is directional, specifying that the novel treatment is more than a prespecified amount worse than an established treatment. Thus, a rejection of the null occurs when the difference is within the prespecified range.

A recent RCT compared a novel treatment (non-trauma-focused meditation) with both an established, evidence-based treatment (prolonged exposure) and an attentional control (health education) in the treatment of post-traumatic stress disorder (PTSD) (Nidich et al., 2018). The trial was explicitly identified as a noninferiority trial and the authors specified a noninferiority margin of 10 points on the Clinician-Administered PTSD Scale (Blake et al., 1995). The authors report a power analysis, noting that the target sample size (70 participants in each group) would provide 90% power for the noninferiority comparison (meditation vs. exposure) and 85% power for the superiority comparison (meditation vs. health education, exposure vs. health education). Pre–post PTSD symptoms changed in the expected direction in the meditation and exposure groups (standardized mean difference $d = 0.90$ and $d = 0.63$, respectively) but not in the health education groups ($d = 0.14$). The authors found that both meditation and exposure were superior to health education ($d = 0.82$ and $d = 0.49$, respectively) and that meditation was not inferior to exposure ($d = 0.33$).

The Importance of Follow-Up Assessment

Along with decisions regarding control conditions, decisions regarding the schedule of assessment can significantly impact conclusions that can be drawn from a given study. One important consideration is whether a study includes assessment of treatment effects following the end of treatment. Follow-up assessment is common in largescale psychotherapy trials (e.g., Elkin et al., 1989), although such assessments are costly and may not be feasible for smaller-scale studies. Follow-up assessments allow researchers to evaluate the persistence of observed effects, which is highly relevant for determining the potential public health benefits of a given intervention. In recent years, longitudinal meta-analyses have been conducted aggregating findings from psychotherapy trials that included follow-up assessment. These studies have allowed evaluation of claims of sustained or improved efficacy in post-treatment periods (e.g., for psychodynamic psychotherapy; Kivlighan et al., 2015).

Establishing Fidelity and Adherence to Treatment

In contrast to pharmacotherapy, the presumed active ingredients in psychotherapy are not neatly packaged into uniform pills. Psychotherapy typically involves the interaction between two or more individuals, with treatment traditionally implemented through the therapist's behaviors and relationship with the patient, which in turn influences the patient's behaviors. However, evaluation of the efficacy of a given psychotherapy (e.g., Prolonged Exposure for PTSD) is predicated on the assumption that a purported course of treatment includes the theoretically defined ingredients (e.g., exposure).

Fidelity is important for confirming that the independent variable in a psychotherapy trial (i.e., the treatment) was manipulated as planned. Treatment fidelity can be viewed as including both treatment integrity, "the degree to which a treatment condition is implemented as intended" (Moncher & Prinz, 1991, p. 247), and treatment differentiation, "whether treatment conditions differ from one another in the intended manner" (Moncher & Prinz, 1991, p. 248). Considerable efforts have been devoted to developing measures and assessing the degree to which therapists deliver treatments with integrity. From the perspective of measurement, scales can assess therapist adherence, "the degree to which therapists are delivering the theory-specified techniques or methods of the intervention" (Webb et al., 2010, p. 201), and therapist competence, "the skill with which these techniques or methods are implemented" (Webb et al., 2010, p. 201). The Collaborative Study Psychotherapy Rating Scale (CSPRS; Hollon et al., 1988) is a prototypical adherence measure that was used in the landmark Treatment of Depression Collaborative Research Program (TDCRP; Elkin et al., 1989). The Cognitive Therapy Scale (CTS; J. Young & Beck, 1980) is a prototypical competence measure often used to assess competence delivering components of cognitive therapy.

Treatment fidelity and integrity are important scientifically. Interestingly, their link with treatment outcome has not been consistently established. In a meta-analysis of 32 adherence–outcome and 17 competence–outcome associations, Webb et al. (2010) failed to find a relationship between either adherence or competence and outcome ($r = 0.02$ and $r = 0.07$, for adherence and competence, respectively). However, effect sizes were heterogeneous, and varied systematically. Namely, a larger competence–outcome association was detected for studies that targeted depression or did not control for therapeutic alliance. An important potential caveat is that much of the research on adherence and competence has used RCTs, which very likely show less variability in adherence and competence due to therapist selection and supervision than naturalistic psychotherapy. Innovative technologies (e.g., natural language processing and machine learning; Atkins et al., 2014) could significantly reduce barriers to routine implementation of fidelity assessment, which may allow more definitive conclusions regarding if and when fidelity relates to treatment outcome, including within naturalistic settings.

Therapist and Group Effects

A final topic related to evaluating the efficacy of treatment packages is consideration of the influence of therapist and group factors. Psychotherapy is typically implemented in dyads or groups (although this may shift with the rise of online and mobile-based interventions). As has been discussed extensively (Baldwin et al., 2005, 2011; Baldwin & Imel, 2013), multiple individual patients being treated by the same therapist or seen within the same psychotherapy group creates statistical dependencies that violate assumptions of independence underlying most traditional analytic approaches (e.g., analysis of variance, multiple regression). Data of these kind can be viewed as nested (i.e., patients nested within the same therapist or therapy group) and ignoring dependencies within nested data tends to artificially increase the likelihood of statistical significance and inflate Type I error rates (Baldwin et al., 2005). Multilevel models, available in many statistical packages (e.g., Bates et al., 2015; Rabe-Hesketh & Skrondal, 2012a, 2012b; Raudenbush & Bryk, 2001) allow researchers to appropriately model these dependencies.

The intraclass correlation coefficient (ICC) is a standardized metric of the degree of dependency among individuals drawn from the same higher-level sampling unit (i.e., seen by the same therapist, treated in the same therapy group; Snijders & Bosker, 2012). ICCs are computed as the proportion of variance in patient outcome associated with the therapist:

$$ICC = \frac{\sigma_t^2}{\sigma_t^2 + \sigma_e^2}$$

where σ_t^2 is the variance in outcome associated with therapist (i.e., between-therapist variance) and σ_e^2 is the residual variance (i.e., within-therapist variance). ICCs, defined in this manner, range from zero to one, with zero indicating no association between individuals drawn from the same higher-level sampling unit and one indicating perfect similarity between individuals drawn from the same higher-level sampling unit. The degree of similarity (i.e., the ICC) directly reflects the impact of ignoring nested data.

How large are dependencies within therapists and therapy groups? Dependencies within therapists have now been widely studied, with a growing literature documenting the presence of what have been termed therapist effects. A meta-analysis (number of studies $k = 46$) of the magnitude of differences between therapists (or dependencies within therapists) found widely variable therapist effects estimates, ranging from .00 to .55. The weighted average therapist ICC was .05, indicating that 5% of the variance in patients' outcome were explained at the therapist level. ICCs were larger in naturalistic studies (ICC = 0.07) than efficacy studies (ICC = 0.03) but differed significantly from zero across both types (Baldwin & Imel, 2013). Another recent meta-analysis ($k = 20$) also reported variation in the magnitude of therapist effects across settings and indicated that therapist effects may be larger with increased patient severity (Johns et al., 2019). Research is ongoing to better understand what therapist factors explain differences in outcomes (e.g., Nissen-Lie et al., 2013; Pereira et al., 2017). From a methodological standpoint, therapist effects are well-established enough that they should not be ignored in studies testing the efficacy of treatment packages.

Similar to therapist effects, studies have documented the presence of group effects (Imel et al., 2008). And, similar to therapist effects, general consensus is that it is no longer acceptable to ignore the nested nature of data when patients are treated within psychotherapy groups (Baldwin et al., 2005). However, unlike therapist effects, to our knowledge there is currently no meta-analytically derived estimate of the average magnitude of group effects. Nonetheless, researchers should be encouraged to evaluate the degree of dependency among individuals treated within the same psychotherapy groups (i.e., report the group ICC) and employ appropriate multilevel models that can account for these dependencies.

While therapist and group effects are important to consider, a few final caveats are worth highlighting. First, it should be noted that meta-analytic estimates of both therapist and group effects may be inflated. As ICCs are defined as the proportion of variance associated with therapists or groups, they have a lower bound of zero. In the long run, this fact will lead to an upward bias (Baldwin & Imel, 2013), though this is less of a problem with large studies. A second factor that may contribute to upwardly biased estimates is publication bias. Null therapist or group effect findings may be more likely to be omitted from published reports than statistically significant (or larger) ICCs. However, Baldwin and Imel's (2013) assessment of publication bias did not indicate this was a concern in their meta-analytic sample. A third concern relates to biases introduced through sample size, either of the number of therapists (or groups) or the number of patients per therapist (or group). A study using simulated resampling in a large, multisite dataset indicated that therapist effects may be overestimated when a small number of patients (e.g., less than four) per therapist are included (Schiefele et al., 2017). Thus, advances in better understanding differences between therapists (or therapy groups) may need to rely on large-scale data collection efforts.

STUDYING THE PROCESS OF CHANGE

Randomized trials are typically used to evaluate the efficacy of a treatment package, such as cognitive behavioral therapy (CBT) or psychodynamic therapy. Randomized trials do not, however, provide much insight into why a treatment is effective. Comparing CBT to wait-list control in a randomized trial tells us about the effects of all the parts of CBT as a whole compared to no treatment. We do not learn anything about which parts of CBT are particularly important; we do not know if changes come about from behavioral tasks, cognitive tasks, the therapeutic relationship, or all three. One task of psychotherapy process research is to unpack which treatment components are effective at facilitating change. Identifying components that are most important in treatment can help researchers develop new treatments and refine existing ones. This research is commonly called mechanism of change research.

In this section, we discuss the two most common quantitative frameworks used in process of change research – (a) experimental component research and (b) observational process–outcome research. We also discuss how lack of variability in treatment processes within a study negatively affects the conclusions we draw from process studies. We introduce mediation models as well as multilevel models that distinguish between process–outcome relationships at the therapist-level and at the patient-level or between relationships at the session-level and the patient-level.

Component Studies

As noted previously, comparing CBT (or any treatment package) to a comparison group does not reveal how CBT works because the CBT and comparison group differ by a number of constructs. CBT may contain unique treatment elements, therapists may be better trained in the CBT condition, therapists (or the researchers themselves) may align more with CBT than the comparison treatment, or CBT may provide a higher dose. Thus, if CBT outperforms the comparison, these differences are confounded, and we cannot conclude that CBT works due to its unique treatment elements (Shadish et al., 2002).

Concerns about confounding have been central to the debates about the efficacy of Eye Movement Desensitization and Reprocessing (EMDR) in the treatment of PTSD. EMDR includes unique elements – for example, patients' eyes following therapists' finger movements – as well as elements common to other treatments for PTSD – for example, exposure. Although some studies have shown that EMDR can lead to reduction in PTSD symptoms, critics of EMDR have pointed out that there is not sufficient evidence for the efficacy of the unique parts of EMDR to judge it to be an efficacious treatment (cf. Cahill et al., 1999; McNally, 1999).

To address these types of mechanism questions, researchers have used what are called component studies. Component studies compare conditions that vary with respect to only one aspect of treatment. If a treatment package contains three main pieces, a component study could compare a condition with all three pieces to a condition with just two pieces. If the full treatment condition outperforms the modified treatment, then we have more confidence that the piece unique to the full treatment is a critical treatment mechanism.

For example, in their classic study, Jacobson et al. (1996) were interested in whether cognitive therapy for depression worked by altering cognitive structures as had been proposed. They noted that cognitive therapy consisted of multiple parts: behavioral activation, coping strategies, and schema work. Consequently, the fact that cognitive therapy might outperform control groups does not provide insight into how the treatment works.

Jacobson et al. (1996) designed a study that compared parts, or components, of cognitive therapy to see which part produced the most change in depressive symptoms. Specifically, they randomly assigned participants to receive behavioral activation, behavioral activation + thought modification, and full cognitive therapy, which include behavioral activation, thought modification, and schema work. If schema work is essential, then it should outperform both other conditions. Likewise, if thought modification is essential but schema work is ancillary, then two conditions involving thought modification should be better than behavioral activation alone. Finally, if behavioral activation is the primary mechanism of change, then all three treatments should produce the same outcomes.

Jacobson et al. (1996) found that treatments did not differ with respect to depressive symptoms after 20 sessions nor at a six-month follow-up, consistent with the notion that behavioral activation is the key component in cognitive therapy (though power was low for treatment contrasts, see Power Section). Other component studies have compared: (a) cognitive therapy, progressive muscle relaxation, and their combination in the treatment of generalized anxiety disorder (Barlow et al., 1992); (b) cognitive behavioral therapy with and without religious content in the treatment of depression among religious patients (Propst et al., 1992); (c) EMDR and eye fixation exposure and reprocessing in the treatment of panic disorder (Feske & Goldstein, 1997); see Ahn and Wampold (2001) for a review and other examples.

Component studies are not without problems, however. First and foremost is that nearly all component studies are underpowered to detect differences between active treatments. Jacobson et al. (1996) averaged 50 patients per condition, which is insufficient to detect differences between active treatments where the effect size is likely quite small. An alternative is to design an equivalence study, where the purpose is to evaluate equivalence between two treatment conditions (cf. Lakens, 2017).

Second, component studies can suffer from therapist and researcher allegiance (cf. Luborsky et al., 1999; Munder et al., 2013). Researchers and therapists often have strong beliefs about how treatments work and what is an essential part of treatment. This is understandable and even desirable in clinical settings. Patients have a right to expect that their therapists believe in what they are doing and know what aspects of treatment to emphasize and when. Strong beliefs can be problematic in research settings because it may mean that some treatments in a component study are not provided with fidelity. If, prior to the implementation of the Jacobson et al. (1996) study, the researchers and the therapists believed that behavioral activation was the only useful part of cognitive therapy, then perhaps the therapists did not adequately challenge automatic thoughts or competently work on schemas. Consequently, the trial would not be fair and does not allow for high-quality inferences about treatment mechanisms.

A solution to allegiance effects, which are likely inevitable, is to balance allegiance by including researchers and therapists who align with each of the conditions. For example, researchers aligned with behavioral activation as the primary mechanism of change can train and supervise clinicians in the behavioral activation condition whereas those aligned with schema work as the primary mechanisms of change can train and supervise clinicians in the full cognitive therapy condition. Thus, each treatment has a higher probability of being delivered with fidelity and competence than if allegiance to only one treatment is represented in the design (Luborsky et al., 1999).

A third problem in component studies is treatment diffusion (Shadish et al., 2002). Treatment diffusion occurs when the treatments provided in each condition are not kept separate. For example, in the Jacobson et al. (1996) study, treatment diffusion could occur if therapists in the behavioral activation condition taught patients how to challenge thoughts. Treatment diffusion does not only mean that therapists in the behavioral activation condition formally taught patients to challenge automatic thoughts. It also includes situations where therapists unintentionally helped patients challenge automatic thoughts and become more flexible in their thinking. Even the most structured therapies are still free-flowing and dependent on give-and-take between patient and therapist. Treatment may be focused on behavioral activation, but if patients are consistently talking about their negative thoughts and assumptions, it will be difficult to avoid teaching the skills to become more flexible in their thinking. Consequently, although it may be reasonably straightforward to keep therapists from formally teaching methods for challenging thoughts, it can be difficult to keep treatments pure due to the natural flow of therapy.

Observational Process Studies

Although component studies are elegant and, when done well, can provide clear inferences about processes of change, they are not common. It is not clear that designing well-powered component studies will bear fruit commensurate with the cost (cf. Ahn & Wampold, 2001), making it difficult to recommend component studies as a practical way forward for the field. A more practical approach (and one that is more common) are nonexperimental process–outcome studies. The general structure of these studies is to measure a key therapeutic process and correlate the process with an outcome. Likewise, studies may measure key processes and see whether those processes change more in some conditions versus others (e.g., more change in cognitions for cognitive therapy as compared to antidepressants; Simons et al., 1984). Therapeutic processes common to many treatments that have been studied include the alliance (Flückiger et al., 2018) and adherence (Webb et al., 2010).

Processes specific to treatment packages include acceptance and thought action fusion in acceptance and commitment therapy (Twohig et al., 2006, 2010) and cognitions in cognitive therapy (DeRubeis et al., 1990), among many others.

Though common, observational process studies are challenging to interpret for at least two reasons. First, it can be difficult to establish whether a process variable causes change in the outcome or vice versa. The alliance–outcome correlation is probably the most studied process–outcome relationship in psychotherapy research. However, most of the research is unable to untangle whether the alliance causes change in the outcome or if the alliance is a byproduct of good outcomes (DeRubeis et al., 2005). A common design is to measure outcome prior to treatment and immediately following treatment (cf. Baldwin et al., 2007) and to measure the alliance early in treatment (e.g., session four). The researcher then correlates alliance with outcome, perhaps controlling for pretreatment outcome. The challenge with this analysis is that we cannot rule out the possibility that improvements prior to the alliance assessment caused the alliance to be high (or lack of improvement caused it to be low). In other words, the alliance measure could be a proxy for early change in psychotherapy and the alliance–outcome correlation could really be a correlation between two outcome measures.

We can improve our inferences by assessing both outcome and alliance more frequently and model changes in both measures. For example, if alliance and outcome were measured at each session, one could use a lagged multilevel model to examine whether outcome at the current session is predicted by alliance at the previous session and vice-versa (Crits-Christoph et al., 2011; Falkenström et al., 2013). Likewise, a cross-lagged path model can be used to estimate the reciprocal relationships simultaneously. Tasca and Lampard (2012) examined the reciprocal relationship between alliance and restricted eating in group psychotherapy for eating disorders using a combination of latent-growth curve modeling (Bollen & Curran, 2006) and latent change score modeling (Mcardle & Grimm, 2010). Although these models improve on the bivariate or partial correlation methods described previously, they remain observational methods and care is still required in making causal inferences. Repeated measures and sophisticated statistical methods do not, in-and-of-themselves, ensure improved causal inference.

The second problem in interpreting observational process studies, is getting a sample with sufficient variability in the process to obtain an accurate picture of the mechanism–outcome relationship. For example, a meta-analysis of the treatment adherence–outcome correlation suggests that there is little-to-no relationship between adherence and outcome ($r = 0.02$ from 32 studies; Webb et al., 2010). As noted above, a major limitation of this literature is that adherence is assessed primarily in clinical trials where adherence is tightly controlled and kept within a small range. This is not an ideal situation for studying the importance of treatment adherence because we do not observe the whole range, or even a substantial portion, of adherence. Variability in adherence in these studies may simply be noise or trivial fluctuations in adherence.

Lack of variability in process data can also occur due to problems in measurement (cf. DeRubeis et al., 2013). Alliance

data are typically skewed toward positive ratings (Tryon et al., 2008). For example, items on the working alliance inventory have response options that range from 1 to 7. It is common to see datasets where the average rating is near 6 and the majority of ratings at or above 5 (cf. Baldwin et al., 2007). This range in the data could occur because the construct of alliance does not vary much at all or at least in the population sampled. This range can also occur if the alliance measure does not discriminate between high and low alliances well. Given the emphasis psychotherapy researchers place on the alliance and dealing with ruptures in the therapeutic alliance, we believe that alliance measures may not be sufficiently sensitive to discriminate variability in the alliance.

Regardless of the source of restricted range, little variability in the process measure is a major challenge in establishing process–outcome relationships. This is not a controversial statement as the restriction of range problem in psychometrics is well known and developed (Nunnally & Bernstein, 1994). We can use a simulation to illustrate the problem. Imagine that the population correlation between the therapeutic alliance and outcome is $\rho = 0.5$. Further, patients in the population vary in the strength of their alliance. We study the alliance–outcome relationship using a fictional alliance questionnaire. In the simulation, the alliance questionnaire does not discriminate well between high and low alliance and most patients rate their alliance as high. Thus, our sample, which was based on our population assumptions, varies with respect to the alliance but our measure does not make the discrimination.

To simulate this process, we created 10,000 datasets, each with 1,000 patients, where the population alliance–outcome relationship was $\rho = 0.5$. We used 1,000 patients so that we observed the full variability in the alliance and outcome. We then computed two correlations for each dataset. First, we computed the correlation on patients 1.5 standard deviations above the mean on the alliance. This represented the fact that patients rate their alliance highly on the alliance questionnaire. Second, we computed a correlation on a random sample (from the 1,000 observations) of the same size as the first correlation. This represented a sample of patients measured on an alliance measure that does a good job tapping the entire range.

Figure 2.1 shows the consequence of this range restriction due to a poorly performing measure. The dark bins are correlations from the truncated correlation and the light bins are from the random sample. Both correlations show variability due to sampling error. However, the correlations based on a random sample from the entire distribution of the alliance are centered right at the population mean ($\rho = 0.5$). The correlations based on the truncated alliance were more variable and considerably smaller (average $\rho = 0.2$).

This simulation emphasizes that we need to attend to measurement in our process research. If we are correct that many alliance measures are skewed toward positive values, then alliance–outcome correlations are underestimated. Likewise, if our process measures are drawn from studies where the primary goal of the study is to limit the variability of the measure, like treatment adherence in a clinical trial, then the process–outcome correlations will be underestimated. Consequently, it is likely that progress in this area will not

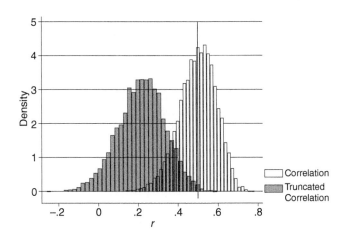

FIGURE 2.1 Simulated distribution of correlations.

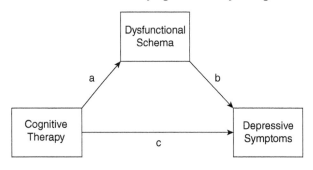

FIGURE 2.2 Mediation example as a path model.

occur unless we have more studies of therapist adherence and competence, and similar process measures, where adherence and competence are allowed to vary naturally.

Mediation and Moderation

Questions about the process of change and therapy process are typically questions about mediation. That is, stating the process of change is to state a theory about how treatment works: cognitive therapy is delivered → dysfunctional schema change → depression is reduced. In this example model for how cognitive therapy works, change in dysfunctional schema mediates the causal path from treatment to outcome – change in dysfunctional schema explains why (at least partially) cognitive therapy has a causal effect on depression symptoms.

Lachowicz et al. (2018) provide a general definition of mediation: "Mediation analysis is the study of potential pathways through which a predictor (independent) variable has an effect on an outcome (dependent) variable. These pathways can transmit the effect to the dependent variable at least partially through intervening variables called mediators" (p. 244–245). Methods for quantifying the influence of a mediating variable have been developed and refined considerably in the last 30 years. These include formal, mathematical definitions for mediation (Imai et al., 2010), multilevel mediation (Preacher et al., 2010), binary and non-normal mediators (Imai et al., 2010), and moderated mediation (Preacher et al., 2007). The goal of this section is to provide an introductory overview of mediation for treatment research, connecting it to process–outcome research, and to provide interested readers sources to learn more.

To illustrate the concepts of mediation, we continue the example of changing dysfunctional schema in cognitive therapy. A simple mediation model, depicted as a path diagram, is show in Figure 2.2.

The path diagram can be represented by two regression equations (often estimated simultaneously as a structural equation model; Lachowicz et al., 2018). The first is for the mediator (dysfunctional schema) predicted by the independent variable (cognitive therapy versus no treatment).

$$\text{Schema} = \text{Intercept} + a \times \text{Cognitive} + \text{Error}$$

The second is the dependent variable (depressive symptoms) predicted by both the mediator and independent variable.

$$\text{Depression} = \text{Intercept} + b \times \text{Schema} + c \times \text{Cognitive} + \text{Error}$$

In these equations, a is the relationship between cognitive therapy (vs. control) and dysfunctional schema (this presumably would be negative), b is the relationship between dysfunctional schema and depressive symptoms, holding treatment constant (this presumably would be positive), and c is the relationship between cognitive therapy and depressive symptoms, holding dysfunctional schema constant (this presumably would be negative).

The relationship between treatment and depressive symptoms (c), holding the mediator constant, is called the *direct effect* – the effect of treatment on depressive symptoms independent of schema. The relationship between treatment and depressive symptoms via the mediator is the *indirect effect*. The indirect effect is estimated as the product of a and b (for a proof, see Imai et al., 2010). Finally, the sum of the direct and indirect effects is the *total effect* and represents the total relationship between treatment and depressive symptoms.

The direct and indirect effects are interpreted just like any other regression coefficient. For example, suppose the measure of depressive symptoms was standardized and treatment was an indicator variable coded as 1 for cognitive therapy and 0 for control. An indirect effect of $ab = -0.25$ indicates that patients in the cognitive therapy condition are expected to have one quarter of a standard deviation fewer depressive symptoms as compared to control via change in dysfunctional schema and controlling for the direct effect of treatment condition on depressive symptoms. A direct effect of $c = -0.1$ indicates that patients in the cognitive therapy condition are expected to have one tenth of a standard deviation fewer depressive symptoms as compared to the control condition, controlling for the indirect effect.

A challenge with indirect effects involves computing the standard error (MacKinnon et al., 1995). Most approaches to computing standard errors assume the sampling distribution is normally distributed. This is not necessarily the case with an indirect effect because it is the product of two estimates. To overcome this, researchers have proposed constructing confidence intervals based on alternative methods that do not assume a normally distributed sampling distribution, such as parametric and nonparametric bootstrapping (Bauer et al., 2006; Shrout & Bolger, 2002) and Bayesian methods (Yuan & MacKinnon, 2009). Many mediational analyses are performed using structural equation modeling software, such as Mplus (Muthén & Muthén, 2017). Fortunately, obtaining appropriate standard errors for indirect effects, such as bootstrapped standard errors, is fairly straightforward in many structural equation modeling software packages. Further, Bayesian analyses are rapidly becoming more accessible and available (Stan Development Team, 2019), allowing more researchers to adequately address mediation in their research.

Lachowicz et al. (2018) reviewed proposed effect sizes for indirect effects. They noted that the most commonly used effect size is the ratio of the indirect effect to the total effect. The logic of this effect size is that the greater the proportion of the total effect that is accounted for by the indirect effect, the bigger the mediational effect is. A ratio of 1 indicates that the total effect is completely accounted for by the indirect effect whereas a ratio of 0.5 indicates that the indirect effect accounts for half of the total effect. Lachowicz et al. (2018) recommend against the use this ratio due to poor performance in simulation studies. They also reviewed several other effect size measures but argued against their use because they have limited-use cases (e.g., only relevant when the independent variable is binary).

As an alternative, Lachowicz et al. (2018) proposed a general effect size for indirect effects that is widely applicable, easy to interpret, and performs well in simulations. The effect size v is defined as

$$v = \left(\hat{B}_{MX}^2 - \hat{\sigma}_{MX}^2 \right) \left(\hat{B}_{YM.X}^2 - \hat{\sigma}_{YM.X}^2 \right) \left(\hat{\sigma}_X^2 / \hat{\sigma}_Y^2 \right)$$

Here $\hat{B}_{MX}^2$ and $\hat{B}_{YM.X}^2$ are the squared coefficients for the a and b paths of Figure 2.2, respectively; $\hat{\sigma}_{MX}^2$ and $\hat{\sigma}_{YM.X}^2$ are the variance (i.e., squared standard error) of the a and b paths, respectively; and $\hat{\sigma}_X^2$ and $\hat{\sigma}_Y^2$ are the variance of the independent and dependent variables, respectively (see Lachowicz et al., 2018, p. 251). v is interpreted as the variance in the dependent variable accounted for by the independent variable via the mediator. In the context of the cognitive therapy and depression example, v would be interpreted as the variance accounted for in depressive symptoms by cognitive therapy via dysfunctional symptoms.

The methodological concept of moderation is often discussed along with mediation (cf. Comer & Kendall, 2013). In the context of psychotherapy research, mediation aims to explain the process of change – why therapy works. In contrast, moderation aims to explain under what conditions therapy works (or is enhanced or diminished). Moderation is about the context of change and includes variables such as patient diagnosis, patient motivation, treatment setting, treatment delivery (face-to-face vs. online), and therapist training. We might predict that therapy will be most effective when patients are highly motivated – thus, the treatment effect is moderated by patient motivation.

Moderation is statistically tested via an interaction term. For example, in a study comparing cognitive therapy to control for depression, we could use a model that includes depression as the outcome with treatment condition, patient motivation, and their interaction as predictors. In that model, the interaction coefficient indicates how much the treatment effect varies as a function of patient motivation.

Moderation and mediation can be included in the same model if we believe that the size of the indirect effect is moderated by a third variable or a moderating effect is mediated by another variable (Baron & Kenny, 1986; Muller et al., 2005). The former is called moderated mediation and latter is called mediated moderation (Muller et al., 2005). Extending the mediation example above, we might predict that the indirect effect of cognitive therapy on depressive symptoms via dysfunctional schema is larger for highly verbal patients. Thus, patients' verbal abilities moderate the mediational path (i.e., moderated mediation). We could also predict that cognitive therapy works better for highly verbal patients and that the mediating variable for highly verbal patients is dysfunctional schema (i.e., mediated moderation). Methodologists have developed methods for examine both types of mediation models in both single level and multilevel models (Muller et al., 2005; Preacher et al., 2010).

Because moderated mediation and mediated moderation are conceptually appealing and are exciting to researchers who enjoy complex statistical models, we offer a caution. The number of possible moderators and mediators in psychotherapy are legion, and it can be easy to start building complex models before theories and the empirical evidence support them. We believe a cautious, deliberate approach to studying both mediation and moderation will likely benefit the field more than diving headlong into these models. As we have seen, power is low in many psychotherapy studies and the problem only gets worse as models become more complex.

Between- and Within-Cluster Relationships

The multilevel nature of psychotherapy data has methodological – measurement, design, and analysis – implications as well as conceptual implications for process–outcome studies (cf. Baldwin et al., 2007). As noted above, psychotherapy data are multilevel in the sense that patients (Level 1) are clustered within therapists (Level 2) in individual therapy, patients (Level 1) are clustered within groups (Level 2) in group therapy, and patients (Level 1) are clustered within dyads (Level 2) in couple therapy. Even more complicated designs are possible (Baldwin et al., 2011). These data structures raise the possibility that process and outcome variables are influenced more heavily at some levels than others and even that process variables and outcomes have different relationships at the distinct levels.

DeRubeis et al. (2005) described the potential impact of therapist- and patient-level variability for the alliance–outcome relationship. They note: "Aside from measurement error, there are at least four possible sources: the therapist, the client, their interaction (in the statistical sense), and symptom improvement. The theoretical implications, or our understanding of the alliance, will be very different depending on which of these causes one focuses on" (p. 178). If most of the variability in the alliance is at the patient-level, that indicates that variables such as patients' attachment style or motivation to change account for the strength of the alliance. If most of the variability in the alliance is at the therapist-level, that indicates that variables such as therapists' empathy, flexibility, and collaborative style is the most important. Finally, if the variability is due to the interaction between patient and therapist, then variables that characterize the dyad, such as mutual understanding and trust, are critical.

To further illustrate the conceptual importance of separating variability across levels, consider the measurement of group cohesion in group psychotherapy. An intraclass correlation for cohesion indicates the proportion of variability in cohesion that is associated with the specific group a patient is in. If the intraclass correlation is high, then cohesion is largely a function of the particular group and variability in group dynamics across groups could explain variability in cohesion. In contrast, if the intraclass correlation is low, then cohesion is more a function of patient-level variables and more likely to be accounted for by patient traits or states (e.g., neuroticism).

We often take for granted that scores on group cohesion measures or the therapeutic alliance measures describe something about the group or therapeutic dyad because the theories that motivated the measure or even how we named the measures. However, our measures may not actually reflect the group dynamics or therapist-patient relationships. Rather, the measures may better represent individual differences among patients – we may not be studying group dynamics or the therapeutic relationship at all. Whether that is a theoretical or measurement problem (or both) is not our concern here. Instead, we simply want to underscore the potential challenges in interpreting process and outcome measures due to the multilevel nature of the data.

In addition to separating a measure into its between-cluster (e.g., therapist-level) and within-cluster (e.g., patient-level) components, we can also use multilevel modeling to examine process–outcome relationships at the between-cluster and the within-cluster levels (Raudenbush & Bryk, 2001). For example, Baldwin et al. (2007) distinguished between the therapist-level alliance–outcome correlation and the patient-level alliance–outcome correlation. The therapist-level (i.e., between-cluster) correlation indicates how therapists' average alliance score across their entire caseload is related to their average outcome. Specifically, variability in therapist average alliance is used to predict patient outcome. The patient-level (i.e., within-cluster) correlation indicates how variability in alliance score among *patients of the same therapist* is related to outcome. Baldwin et al. (2007) state: "The within-therapist correlation tests whether patients who report a high alliance also report better outcomes than patients of the same therapist who report a low alliance" (p. 843).

The therapist- and patient-level relationships can be estimated in a single multilevel model (for an introduction to multilevel modeling see Atkins, 2005; Rabe-Hesketh & Skrondal, 2012b; Tasca & Gallop, 2009):

Outcome is the outcome score for patient i seen by therapist j; b_0 is the intercept; b_1 is the between-therapist coefficient; b_2 is the within-therapist coefficient; u_j is a random effect for therapist j; and e_{ij} is the residual. A key to this model is how the alliance variable is constructed. The variable associated with b_1 is the mean alliance score for a given therapist ($\overline{alliance}_j$). Variability among these means represents the between-therapist, or therapist-level, variability in the alliance. Likewise, the variable associated with b_2 is the deviation between patients' alliance score and their specific therapist's mean. Patients with positive deviations have an alliance score above their therapist's mean and patients with a negative deviation below their therapist's mean. Variability among the deviations represents within-therapist, or patient-level, variability in the alliance.

An analysis that does not partition the alliance into the between- and within-therapist portions, such a zero-order correlation, assumes that the between-therapist (b_1) and within-therapist (b_2) coefficients are equal. We can test that assumption directly using a post-estimation contrast[1] that tests whether b_1 and b_2 are equal. Using a model similar to those described, Baldwin et al. (2007) found that the alliance was significantly related to outcome at the therapist-level but not the patient-level. Furthermore, the between-therapist and within-therapist coefficients were significantly different from one another, indicating that it may be therapists' ability to form alliances with patients from across their caseload that is important for outcomes. See Rabe-Hesketh and Skrondal (2012b), Rabe-Hesketh, Baldwin (2019), and Baldwin et al. (2007) for more details on estimating and interpreting these models.

Of course, the distinction among between- and within-therapist alliance–outcome relationships is just one example of separating process–outcome relationships into between- and within-cluster components. These multilevel models can be extended to other process variables such as therapist adherence to a treatment manual, therapist competence in using techniques, and expressed empathy. For example, Baldwin and Imel (2013) described nine combinations of between- and within-therapist adherence–outcome relationships. For example, it is possible for adherence to matter at the therapist level (i.e., it is critical to have therapists who generally adhere to a treatment model), but variations within a caseload in adherence are not related to outcome. Or it could be that what is critical is not the average adherence for any given therapist, but how much that therapist adheres with that particular patient. Of course, the between- and within-therapist adherence–outcome relationship may be equal and the distinction is not critical.

Additional examples of separating between- and within-cluster relationships include process variables in group psychotherapy such as cohesion, readiness for group, and group member attachment styles. Finally, between-within relationships can be examined in factor analytic models, wherein the factor structure of a measure is allowed to differ at the between-cluster and within-cluster levels (Goldberg, Baldwin, et al., 2019) and structural equation modeling generally.

---

[1] Alternatively, we can respecify the model by dropping the within-therapist deviations and including the raw alliance scores. The coefficient is identical to the post-estimation contrast.

$$Outcome_{ij} = b_0 + b_1\left(\overline{alliance}_j\right) + b_2\left(alliance_{ij} - \overline{alliance}_j\right) + u_j + e_{ij}$$

STATISTICAL POWER

The debates about replication and rigor have underscored what is essentially a truism about psychological studies, including psychotherapy: Many studies are too small and use designs that are not sufficiently powered to detect the effects we care about. Small studies have been the norm across psychology and related fields for years (Button et al., 2013; Cohen, 1962) and psychotherapy research is no different (Kazdin & Bass, 1989). Reporting details of power and sample-size calculations have been the exception, not the rule (Larson & Carbine, 2017). It may be that researchers are performing power analyses but not reporting them. However, it is just as likely that researchers are not using power analyses at all.

Baldwin (2019) noted that researchers generally use three methods for settling on a sample size. First, researchers base their sample size on what published studies have used. The logic goes something like the following: given that this study similar to ours used 30 participants and was published, we will also use 30 participants as that will be sufficient for publication. Second, researchers recruit as many participants as they can afford. Third, researchers conduct a formal sample-size calculation. The problem with basing sample size on previous research is twofold. First, the justification is based not on scientific or statistical considerations but just on whether the sample size is sufficient to get a study published. That is, it is equates publication with rigor.[2] Second, as the problems with reproducibility has shown, the published literature can have serious methodological problems.

Budgetary constraints are nearly always relevant when determining sample sizes. However, determining sample size based on budgetary constraints can be misleading when it comes to the inferences we draw from studies. In psychotherapy research, stable results depend on good measurement and solid sample sizes. Statistical methods do not care that patients were difficult to recruit or that training was expensive. Although expense may account for why our sample size is small, it does not make our results precise or even useful. We are not so alone in these difficulties: The quality of results of fMRI, which is an expensive methodology, and other neuroscience research has come under scrutiny because of the small samples (Button et al., 2013). Similar critiques are likely germane to many psychotherapy process and outcome studies. Consequently, we strongly urge psychotherapy researchers to use formal power analyses that are informed by their budget. This section aims to provide a brief introduction to sample size/power calculations.

Definitions

We use the following definitions and concepts throughout the rest of this section.

- *Type I error rate.* The probability of rejecting the null hypothesis, if the null hypothesis is true. The type I error rate is equal to α and is commonly set to 0.05 (5%).

- *Type II error rate.* The probability of failing to reject the null hypothesis, if the null hypothesis false. The type II error rate is equal to β and is commonly set to 0.2 (20%) or 0.1 (10%).

- *Power.* The probability of rejecting the null hypothesis, if the null hypothesis is false. Power is equal to $1 - \beta$ and is commonly set to 0.8 (80%) or 0.9 (90%).

- *Effect size.* Statistic describing the relationship examined in the statistical model. Examples include difference between two groups or the correlation between two variables. Though not required for power calculations, effect sizes are commonly standardized. For between-group comparisons, common effect sizes are Cohen's d, Cohen's f, and η^2. For correlational designs, a correlation coefficient is typical. For studies using binary outcomes, odds ratios are typical.

Providing a thorough tutorial on power calculations is beyond the scope of this chapter. Those wanting an in-depth introduction and tutorial can consult Baldwin (2019), Cohen (1988), and Murray et al. (2007).

Power for Group Comparisons and Correlations

Designs involving group comparisons are a staple of psychotherapy research, whether the groups are different treatment conditions, diagnostic groups, or patient types. Although the specific statistical models used can vary considerably for these designs – for example, *t*-tests, analysis of variance (ANOVA), multilevel models, or structural equation models – at the end of the day, the key statistical tests are comparisons between two groups. That is, if a study compares cognitive therapy, mindfulness, and medication, the key tests typically involve comparing outcomes between pairs of treatments (e.g., cognitive therapy vs. mindfulness). Consequently, when using group comparison designs, we recommend identifying the two group contrasts that are of most importance and designing the study based on those comparisons.

Suppose we choose to compare cognitive therapy to a wait-list control on a depression measure and we want to know how many patients it will take to achieve 80% power, assuming $\alpha = 0.05$. The null hypothesis is that difference between the two conditions is 0 ($\delta = 0$). To understand power, we have to understand the notion of a null sampling distribution and alternative sampling distribution. The left-hand sampling distribution in Figure 2.3 is the null distribution and is centered at the null hypothesis. The dark solid bars are the critical values of the null distribution. If our observed results exceed the critical values in either direction, we reject the null hypothesis.[3]

The right-hand side of Figure 2.3 is the alternative sampling distribution, which is centered at a real effect of $\delta = 0.5$. Although we chose a real effect of $\delta = 0.5$, the alternative hypothesis can be centered at any value but the null hypothesis value (0 in this case). That being said, power can only be specified for a specific real effect or range of real effects. So, 80 patients may provide

---

[2] Of course, publication status and rigor are not necessarily unrelated. However, they are also not the same thing.

[3] Readers unfamiliar with null hypothesis testing and sampling distributions can consult an introductory statistics text (e.g., Pagano, 2013).

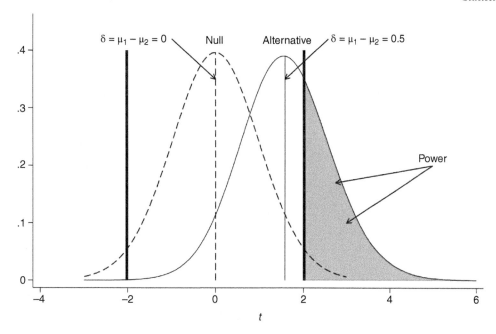

Figure 2.3 Null and alternative sampling distributions. Reproduced by permission of the publisher from S. Baldwin, *Psychological Statistics and Psychometrics Using Stata* (College Station, TX: Stata Press, 2019), fig. 8.1, copyright 2019 by StataCorp LLC.

adequate power for an effect of δ = 0.8, but be horribly underpowered for an effect of δ = 0.2. Thus, a design is neither adequately powered or inadequately powered per se.

Recall that power is the probability that we will reject the null hypothesis if the null hypothesis is false. Thus, power is equal to the proportion of the alternative distribution – we use the alternative distribution here because the null is false – that exceeds the critical values of the null distribution. In Figure 2.3, about 40% of the alternative distribution exceeds the critical value and thus power is 40%. Considering possible changes to Figure 2.3 illustrates how to increase power. Specifically, power increases if (a) the effect size is larger because this moves the alternative distribution farther to the right, (b) α is increased because this moves the critical values closer to mean of the null distribution, and (c) sample sizes increase because this makes both sampling distributions more narrow.

Figure 2.4 shows the required sample sizes for a two-group comparison to maintain 80% or 90% power for common values of Cohen's d. Published effect sizes for psychotherapy versus wait-list control are often near d = 0.8, whereas treatment versus treatment effects are near d = 0.2. Given that nearly 800 patients are needed for 80% power if the effect size we want to detect is d = 0.2 or larger, treatment comparison studies are almost always too small. Treatment versus wait-list comparisons require 52 patients (26 per condition) for 80% power, if the effect size we want to detect is d = 0.8 or larger. However, we may care about treatment versus wait-list differences smaller than d = 0.8, meaning that we would need to recruit more than 52 patients.

The upshot is that simple rules like 50 patients are good enough for treatment versus wait-list miss the mark. Necessary sample sizes given a specific power level and α are determined by the effect size of interest, which varies across content areas and

context. Small differences among treatments may matter theoretically as we try to unpack what accounts for change in psychotherapy. However, those same differences may not matter practically when we consider patient outcomes and management of a treatment facility. Therefore, researchers should consider the types of inferences they would like to make from their results as they determine plausible and interesting effect sizes.

Psychotherapy process research often focuses on the relationship between two variables, such as therapeutic alliance and outcome, treatment competence and alliance, and treatment completion and outcome. Statistical analyses used for these kinds of comparisons include correlations, regression, multilevel models, and structural equation modeling. Though it is possible to compute power using the specific parameters in these models, we find it most instructive to start with power for

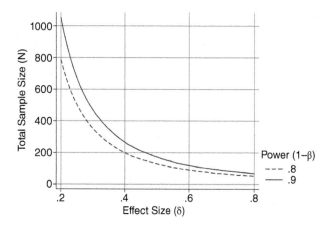

Figure 2.4 Sample size requirements for a range of effect sizes.

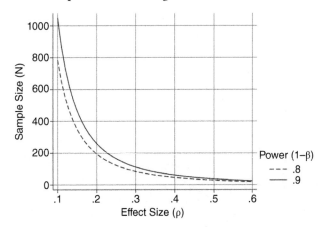

FIGURE 2.5 Power curve for a correlation.

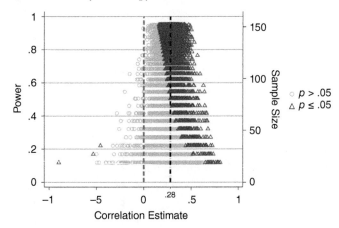

FIGURE 2.6 Illustration of type S and type M errors.

a correlation. Once the sample sizes for correlations are established, we can then move to more specific power calculations as needed.

Figure 2.5 shows the required sample sizes for a correlation between two variables to maintain 80% or 90% power for common values of r. The pattern is similar to Figure 2.4, where required sample sizes for large correlations ($r > 0.5$) are modest, but required sample sizes for small correlations ($r < 0.2$) are far larger than commonly used in psychotherapy process research. Meta-analytic evidence suggests that the alliance–outcome correlation, which is one of the most studied process–outcome relationships, is about $r = 0.28$ (Flückiger et al., 2018).

Problems With Underpowered Designs

Power is most often associated with null hypothesis testing, but it can also be instructive to consider how power affects the precision of estimates (Baldwin, 2019; Gelman & Carlin, 2014). Here, precision refers to the variability of estimates from study to study. Gelman and Carlin (2014) note that when sample sizes are small, estimates can have the wrong sign (negative when it should be positive), called a type S (Sign) error, or estimates can be exaggerated, called a type M (Magnitude) error. Furthermore, when we use statistical significance as a filter for publication, then type S and type M errors are even more pernicious (see Button et al., 2013).

To illustrate this point, we simulated 200 correlation estimates for a study of a given power, where power ranged from 0.1 to 0.95. Thus, we obtained 200 correlation estimates assuming power was 0.1 and we repeated that for power values up to 0.95. We assumed a population correlation of $\rho = 0.28$, which is the average correlation among alliance–outcome studies (Flückiger et al., 2018). Figure 2.6 is a funnel plot visualizing the simulation. Power is on the left-hand y-axis, the correlation value is on the x-axis, and sample size on the right-hand y-axis. We included vertical lines at 0.28 (the population value) and at 0 for reference.

The funnel plot shows that when power is low (20% or lower), estimates range widely ($rs = -0.9$ to 0.8). Significant correlations are typically more than double the population value. There are also a large number of negative estimates,

which are rare in the published literature (Flückiger et al., 2018). Further, when power is below 0.4 (sample size of about 65), statistically significant effects all exceed the population value. When power is above 80%, estimates are less variable and estimates above and below the population value are statistically significant.

One might argue that meta-analysis can help solve the problem of underpowered analyses. We agree in principle, but not in practice because we still use statistical significance as a filter for whether a study is publishable. That is, the common practice of filtering results via statistical significance (either journals being unwilling to publish null results or authors never submitting null results; Greenwald, 1975) can lead to substantial exaggeration of correlations in the literature.

MODELING CHANGE

Fundamentally, psychotherapy involves change. Therefore, questions regarding how best to model change are foundational to psychotherapy research. This section discusses modeling change in the context of three research designs used in psychotherapy studies (randomized designs, naturalistic datasets, intensive longitudinal data). We also address three specific modeling strategies (regression-based models, growth-mixture modeling, multivariate models) that can contribute in different ways to understanding what occurs over the course of treatment. Finally, we briefly discuss single-case designs

Change in Randomized Designs

As discussed above, randomized controlled trials provide gold standard evidence for the causal effects of a given psychotherapeutic intervention. However, even after deciding to use a randomized design, researchers still have methodological choices to make. One fundamental choice is when and how often to measure outcomes or processes of interest. Measures may be collected only at pre-, post-, and follow-up (which may be appropriate for resource intensive assessments such as clinician-rated outcomes) or assessed ongoingly (e.g., through routine outcome monitoring systems; Wampold, 2015). In deciding on a measurement schedule, researchers weigh competing factors, including participant burden, cost, and potential impact of practice effects or repeated measurement (e.g., reactivity to the experimental situation or Hawthorne effect; Adair, 1984). Although more intensive sampling paradigms may provide a richer depiction of patient change, more frequent assessment has drawbacks as well.

One potential source of bias in measurement within randomized controlled trials is having assessment occur only during study visits. Not capturing patients' symptoms in the wild of their lives outside of the research setting may miss more important aspects of how treatment may or may not be impacting their presenting concerns. Assessment within the clinical setting may be unduly influenced by response biases such as social desirability or reactivity to the experimental situation (Heppner et al., 2016). Experience sampling and ecological momentary assessment (EMA) methods discussed previously may provide an alternative approach that addresses this concern.

Naturalistic Datasets

A fair amount of psychotherapy research has relied on data drawn from naturalistic settings. These datasets often have several advantages, including the availability of large samples of patients and therapists, potentially high external validity (i.e., generalizability), and minimal cost for data collection (e.g., when data are being collected as a normal part of routine care; Boswell et al., 2015; Kraus et al., 2016). Nevertheless, naturalistic datasets pose unique challenges that can limit their utility for answering certain kinds of research questions.

One difficulty in naturalistic datasets is the problem of uneven measurement. Though uniform data collection procedures may be in place in a given clinic (e.g., assessment prior to each individual session), data are commonly missing, typically due to nonrandom reasons (e.g., patient termination of treatment). Researchers using naturalistic datasets may be required to make uncomfortable assumptions about missing data (e.g., data were missing at random, a brief course of treatment indicates dropout) that can impact the strength of conclusions.

A second common drawback is that data collection is typically outside of researchers' control. Although a researcher may have a relationship with a particular clinic, it is likely that the clinical partner has made decisions about what and how many measures can feasibly be collected. Research in naturalistic settings may involve a difficult compromise between obtaining a small number of measures on a large sample of patients and therapists.

Intensive Longitudinal Data

Through technological innovations described in greater depth elsewhere in this chapter, psychotherapy researchers may be involved in analyzing large amounts of intensive longitudinal data. For example, daily (or more frequent) assessments of mood may be collected using experience sampling/EMA technologies (Lutz et al., 2018) or passive/personal sensing (Mohr et al., 2017). Though intensive sampling of this kind is far from the norm in psychotherapy research, these data could provide an informative, granular view of psychotherapy process and outcome in future research. As noted previously, technologies

are now available for assessing psychiatric symptoms remotely that appear both feasible and acceptable to patients and therapists (Goldberg, Buck, et al., 2018). Studies using intensive longitudinal data may be valuable for informing the course of treatment through monitoring symptom change (e.g., in schizophrenia Wang et al., 2016) and predicting treatment process and outcome (e.g., treatment dropout; Lutz et al., 2018). Primary disadvantages include sacrificing breadth of assessment to prevent overburdening patients, costs of repeated assessments and the technology required, and patients not taking it seriously and responding in an invalid way simply because they are responding to the same questions repeatedly. For more information on this topic, see Chapter 4.

Regression-Based Models for Analyzing Change

Having collected data, whether using a randomized design or data drawn from a naturalistic setting, researchers must make decisions regarding how best to characterize change that may have occurred over the course of treatment. A host of statistical methods are available for this purpose. ANOVA has historically been the most common statistical method used for the analysis of randomized controlled trial data. The interaction between assessment time period and intervention group (i.e., time x group interaction) can be used to determine whether changes in one group outpaced those observed in another. Statistically, this approach is akin to using a one-way ANOVA with intervention group as a predictor of the difference between pre- and post-treatment scores. Analysis of covariance (ANCOVA) is a related approach but uses posttreatment scores as the outcome, while covarying scores at baseline (i.e., residualized gain score). Though less common, some psychotherapy studies have been conducted using posttest only, although this method is at risk for bias due to unmeasured differences at baseline. More recently, researchers have begun using multilevel modeling approaches for analyzing randomized controlled trials (e.g., Delgadillo et al., 2018) which are also well-equipped for capturing change over time. For more information on this topic, see Chapter 4.

Growth-Mixture Modeling

Multilevel models (i.e., random coefficient models) can allow for variability in the change rate across individuals through the inclusion of random slope terms (Snijders & Bosker, 2012). However, there may be clusters or populations of people who change in a particular way that is masked using multilevel modeling techniques. Growth mixture modeling (and latent class growth analysis on which it is based) involves identification of discrete groups of individuals who follow similar patterns of change over time (Muthén & Muthén, 2000). Growth mixture modeling has the additional benefit of allowing individual variation around growth curves for a given class (i.e., estimation of growth factor variances). Numerous recent studies have employed growth mixture modeling to identify patient subgroupings based on symptom change trajectories over the course of psychotherapy (e.g., Owen et al., 2015; Stulz et al., 2007; Thibodeau et al., 2015). As these approaches become more commonplace, it may be valuable to assess the degree to which patterns of findings are replicable across samples. For a recent example of replication, see Slutz et al. (2007) and Norberg et al. (2014). For more information on this topic, see Chapter 4.

Multivariate Models

A final analytical approach is the use of multivariate models. Multivariate models are relevant in instances where a study includes multiple outcome measures (Baldwin et al., 2014). Although most studies include multiple outcomes, few employ multivariate data analytic techniques. Multivariate models have several potential advantages. The most obvious is their ability to assess omnibus effects on multiple outcomes of interest (e.g., clinician- and patient-rated measures of depression; depression and quality of life). Multivariate models can also address research questions that are not easily examined using traditional regression-based approaches. For example, multivariate models can be used to assess whether change in one outcome is related to change in another (e.g., do changes in depression predict changes in quality of life; Baldwin et al., 2014). Although another methodological approach far from the norm in psychotherapy research, increased adoption of multivariate models may enhance future psychotherapy research.

Single-Case Designs

The designs we have discussed thus far are group-based designs. Another tradition in psychotherapy research is single-case designs. Hallmarks of single-case designs in psychotherapy research include (a) small number of patients, (b) tight control of the intervention and context, and (c) repeated measurement (Horner & Odom, 2014). Participants are assessed across time and researchers examine the patients' response when the intervention is added and removed. The effectiveness of an intervention is established if the outcome variable changes in the predicted direction when the intervention is added and if the outcome variable reverses when the intervention is removed (Kazdin, 2019). Change is often assessed via graphical examination of patterns, though some have proposed using statistical methods such as multilevel models (Shadish et al., 2013).

Common designs (Horner & Odom, 2014, for an introduction) include the ABAB design, where A could refer to a baseline with no intervention and B represents when the intervention is present. Thus, patients' responding is observed as the treatment is introduced and removed. If a treatment reduces the outcome, then outcome ought to come down during the B phase, increase some when the A phase is reintroduced, and then decrease again. Multiple baseline designs, as most commonly implemented, require obtaining a baseline assessment for multiple patients (e.g., 3–4). The baseline ends when the intervention is introduced. The key to this design is that the time of the intervention varies across patients, which means some patients have longer baseline periods than others. Consequently, if the outcome improves and it is due to the intervention, we should be able to tie it to the specific time that the intervention is introduced across participants.

Single-case designs have a strong history in child psychotherapy as well as behavior therapy generally (Kazdin, 2011). A special issue of *Behaviour Research and Therapy* describes many possibilities of applying single-case designs in psychotherapy research (Persons & Boswell, 2019). We suspect the use of single-case designs in child and behavior therapy is due to the nature of the outcomes in child psychotherapy (e.g., tantrums, disruptive behavior) and behavior therapy (e.g., subject distress during an exposure, avoidance behaviors in anxiety). Kazdin (2019) notes that outcome measures used in group-based research can be used in single-case designs. Though we agree in principle, a challenge involves whether the outcome measures are sufficiently sensitive to tie the change in the outcome to intervention. The longer the time frame between the intervention being introduced and the change in the measure, the less confidence we can have that intervention actually produced the change. Nonetheless, it may be that single-case designs are an untapped resource for psychotherapy researchers.

META-ANALYSIS

There has been remarkable accumulation of psychotherapy treatment research in the past several decades (Laska et al., 2014). How is a psychotherapy researcher or clinician to make sense of the increasingly dizzying accumulation of research findings? One methodological solution is using meta-analysis.

In brief, meta-analysis involves the aggregation of results across multiple studies, typically with weights applied to give larger studies a stronger pull in the aggregate (or omnibus) result. Modern meta-analysis is often traced back to the work of Gene Glass and Mary Lee Smith, with the first large-scale illustration of meta-analysis involving the aggregation of psychotherapy trials ($k = 375$ studies; Smith & Glass, 1977). As motivation for meta-analysis, Glass cites the Education Resources Information Center (ERIC) being inundated with over 2 million document requests yearly. How much more inundated is the modern researcher with hundreds of millions of scholarly publications accessible from the comfort of their own couch or smartphone (e.g., 160 million on Google Scholar in 2014; Orduna-Malea et al., 2015)? How much more is the modern researcher apt to wonder, as Glass (1976), invoking T.S. Eliot, points out, "[W]here is the knowledge we have lost in information?" (Eliot, 1971, p. 96).

A Cornerstone of Psychotherapy Research

Since its inception, meta-analysis has played a vital role in providing a robust scientific evidence base for psychotherapy. Smith and Glass (1977) conducted their groundbreaking meta-analysis within a moment in psychotherapy history marked by "tendentious diatribes" (p. 752) questioning the effectiveness of treatment (e.g., Eysenck, 1952). Their aim was ambitious: identifying and collecting all studies that tested the effects of counseling and psychotherapy. They also sought to examine what are known in meta-analysis as *moderators*, that is characteristics that vary across studies that may explain variation in observed treatment effects.

The methodological innovation represented in Smith and Glass (1977) is rivaled only by the anxiolytic effect their results had on the psychotherapy community: at last, definitive evidence for the superiority of psychotherapy over no treatment. Indeed, the standardized effect size they report (what we now call Cohen's (1988) *d*) of 0.68 is remarkably similar to current estimates of the overall effectiveness of psychotherapy vis-à-vis no treatment (*d* = 0.8; Wampold & Imel, 2015).

Beyond demonstrating the value of psychotherapy, meta-analysis has been essential for addressing many of the key debates within psychotherapy research. In addition to reporting an overall effect size of 0.68, Smith and Glass (1977) were also the first to demonstrate empirically the notion that various forms of psychotherapy tend to work about equally well (see Rosenzweig, 1936, for early intimations of this possibility). The question of relative efficacy – how the effectiveness of one form of psychotherapy compares to others (Wampold & Imel, 2015) – has been examined meta-analytically in hundreds if not thousands of meta-analyses since Smith and Glass. And, of course, meta-analysis is not restricted to aggregations of treatment effects; meta-analysis has been used to aggregate findings relevant to numerous key process and outcome questions in psychotherapy (e.g., the alliance–outcome relationship; the relationship between competence and adherence with outcome; Flückiger et al., 2018; Webb et al., 2010).

Meta-Analysis Basics

Numerous accessible and advanced treatments of meta-analysis have been published previously (Borenstein et al., 2009; Cooper et al., 2009). Nonetheless, we briefly review several basic concepts here. At a fundamental level, meta-analysis is designed to address the issue of aggregation, although meta-analysis can also serve explanatory functions (e.g., through tests of moderation). Based on the reality of sampling error alone, it is necessarily true that when multiple studies are conducted examining the same question, they will yield nonequivalent results. Of course, results may be fairly similar – for example, *d*s = 0.74 vs. 0.81 for the efficacy of mindfulness-based cognitive therapy vs. no treatment for depressive symptoms in adults (Goldberg, Tucker, et al., 2019). But, even when that occurs, which estimate is to be trusted as the true estimate? In reality, results are typically much more disparate, and readers are left to draw their own conclusions (perhaps based on highlighting the methodological flaws of studies with conclusions that contradict one's own position or work; Glass, 1976). Meta-analysis can, in theory, provide an unbiased estimate of a body of research literature.

The first step in meta-analysis involves formulating a research question, and identifying the population, intervention, comparison, and outcome of interest (PICO; Moher et al., 2015). Having clearly identified the target population of studies, a comprehensive search of the literature is conducted. Once a sample of studies meeting the prespecified inclusion have been identified, authors code the studies in order to extract information necessary for computing standardized effect sizes (e.g., *d*s, *r*s, odd ratios) as well as study features hypothesized to explain variation in effect sizes across the studies (i.e.,

moderators). While simple to describe, the translation of reported data into standardized effect sizes can be difficult when nontraditional methods are used for reporting and analysis in the original studies (i.e., when means and standard deviations are not available). Assuming meta-analysts pass the effect size gauntlet, they are now ready to aggregate across studies. For this step, the inverse of the variance of the effect size is used to weight larger studies more heavily. Modern meta-analytic software (e.g., MAd, metafor, RevMan; Del Re & Hoyt, 2014; *Review Manager (RevMan)*, 2014; Viechtbauer, 2010) make the final steps of aggregation straightforward, and provide an omnibus effect size and accompanying confidence interval, as well as estimates of heterogeneity across the included studies (e.g., I^2, Q-statistic)[4]. A variety of methods can be used for aggregation, including maximum likelihood as well as Bayesian approaches (Sterne, 2009).

Much of the meta-analytic literature in psychotherapy research has focused on the aggregating function of meta-analysis, such as establishing the absolute efficacy of psychotherapy or the strength of the alliance–outcome association (e.g., Flückiger et al., 2018; Smith & Glass, 1977). But meta-analysis can serve important explanatory functions as well. Meta-regression techniques (akin to other weighted regression models) are commonly used to assess for moderators. Moderators in meta-analysis are study characteristics that may explain systematic variation across studies. For example, Yulish et al. (2017) coded the degree to which treatments for anxiety were problem focused, finding that anxiety treatments that were focused more on addressing patients' symptoms were more effective than less focused treatments. Zoogman et al. (2015) found that mindfulness-based interventions for youth were more effective in clinical samples than nonclinical samples.

The ability to test for moderators in meta-analysis is a significant strength of the approach, supporting contributions of meta-analysis to theory building within psychotherapy research. However, it is important to note that meta-analyses, just like primary studies, may be underpowered. Tests of moderation are frequently underpowered, making moderator tests that yield null findings difficult to interpret. Thus, it is important to consider issues of statistical power when planning and evaluating meta-analyses (Baldwin & Shadish, 2011; Hedges & Pigott, 2001, 2004).

There are many useful and complex extensions of the basic principles of aggregation and tests of moderation. One of the most relevant for psychotherapy research is network meta-analysis (Li et al., 2011). In contrast to traditional meta-analysis that requires treatments to be compared directly (e.g., CBT vs. psychodynamic psychotherapy for depression), network meta-analyses allow aggregation across indirect comparisons based on a common comparator. For example, studies included in a network meta-analysis may compare CBT with psychodynamic psychotherapy and CBT with behavioral activation.

---

[4] I^2 reflects the ratio between true heterogeneity and total observed variation (Borenstein et al., 2009). Commonly used benchmarks for the interpretation of I^2 include 25% (low), 50% (moderate), and 75% (high; Higgins et al., 2003). The Q-statistic provides a formal significance test of the degree to which observer heterogeneity exceeds that expected by chance alone.

Through the technique of network meta-analysis, an estimate of the relative efficacy of psychodynamic therapy and behavioral activation could be made. This methodology is relatively new and has limitations, for example, related to the heterogeneity of treatment implementation within psychotherapy trials (in contrast to medication trials using a more tightly controlled experimental methods and more highly standardized treatments, for which network meta-analyses have been used extensively, e.g., Del Re et al., 2013). Nonetheless, it may prove a valuable technique for psychotherapy research.

Meta-Analysis Pitfalls

While an immensely powerful technique for aggregating a vast body of scientific literature, meta-analysis is not without its potential difficulties. Some of these are within the power of the meta-analyst to address while others are related to the research literature itself. Again, a thorough treatment of these dangers has been provided elsewhere (Cooper et al., 2009) but we highlight several here as instructive and important case examples.

Publication Bias

Perhaps the most pernicious source of bias in meta-analysis is not due to the *included studies* but those studies *not included*. The omission of potentially relevant studies is most commonly due to the file drawer problem (Rosenthal, 1979). Rosenthal (1979) first coined the term to highlight the possibility that the published literature is overrepresented with statistically significant findings. In particular, studies with null findings were likely to be relegated to "file drawers back at the lab" (p. 638) instead of appearing in a searchable, peer-reviewed journals. Other sources of publication bias may be less innocent (e.g., unwillingness to publish studies disconfirming one's hypothesis or the effectiveness of one's intervention/medication). Whatever the reason for omission from the published literature, results from meta-analysis are only as definitive and representative as the studies that comprise them.

A variety of sophisticated methods have been developed for detecting and attempting to address publication bias in meta-analysis. Funnel plots provide one solution (e.g., Peters et al., 2008; Sterne & Egger, 2001). These graphical representations of meta-analytic findings display individual study effect sizes on the x-axis and standard errors (in reverse numeric order) on the y-axis. The resultant plot is then examined for the presence of asymmetry, typically the absence of small null or negative findings that would be presumably more difficult to publish due to a lack of statistical power (and therefore statistical significance). Trim-and-fill analyses are designed to account for this asymmetry and adjust effect sizes accordingly (Duval & Tweedie, 2000). Other solutions can include a thorough search of the unpublished or gray literature (e.g., dissertations, through contacting research groups who may have unpublished results) and, more recently, review of clinical trial registries (e.g., ClinicalTrials.gov).

Garbage In, Garbage Out

Publication bias leads to systematic bias in meta-analysis (i.e., inflated omnibus estimates) due to patterns of dissemination of trial results. But bias can also be introduced at the level the individual trial. This issue has been termed "garbage in, garbage out" (Egger et al., 2001, p. 478). Individual trials are at risk for a wide range of biases, including selection bias (e.g., baseline differences between patient groups in a clinical trial), detection bias (e.g., bias related to assessment of outcomes), and attrition bias (e.g., differential attrition between groups). Researchers are increasingly encouraged to evaluate the individual studies included in a meta-analysis for these and other potential sources of bias (Guyatt et al., 2011; Higgins et al., 2011). Further, researchers may evaluate the risk of bias associated with an aggregated body of research. It is important to note that the available risk of bias assessment tools may or may not be sensitive to more invisible sources of bias discussed below (e.g., p-hacking). While assessing risk of bias offers a partial solution for addressing concerns of meta-analyzing "garbage," a more promising longer-term solution is increasing the quality and transparency of primary research.

Combining Apples and Oranges

Meta-analyses have also been criticized for inappropriate aggregation. The ability to combine studies is, of course, the strength of meta-analysis, but one that can be misused if not guided by theory. The onus for determining that studies are theoretically similar enough to warrant aggregation ultimately rests on the meta-analyst (although the peer review process should help with this). For example, key considerations for whether intervention studies should be combined could include the type of treatment and control conditions (e.g., waitlist and active control conditions), outcome measures (e.g., measures of depression, high school graduation), and samples (e.g., drawn from clinical vs. nonclinical populations). There are pros and cons to aggregating or not aggregating, but the decision is impactful and should be done thoughtfully.

Researcher Allegiance

Psychotherapy RCTs are prone to numerous sources of bias (e.g., lack of patient, therapist, and assessor blinding, p-hacking and selective reporting of results, inadequate randomization; Baskin et al., 2003; Cuijpers et al., 2010; Head et al., 2015) that can impact meta-analytic results. We chose to highlight researcher allegiance as one potential source of bias in original studies due to its potentially invisible and implicit nature. Research allegiance has been defined as the researcher's "belief in the superiority of a treatment [and]. . .the superior validity of the theory of change that is associated with the treatment" (Leykin & DeRubeis, 2009, p. 55).

Like other characteristics that vary systematically across studies, researcher allegiance has been examined as a potential moderator of treatment effects. Researcher allegiance has been operationalized in a variety of ways, although it is typically assessed by coding published results for indications of authors' allegiance to one treatment over another (e.g., one treatment is given an extensive description while the other is not; Gaffan et al., 1995). Self- and colleague-ratings of allegiance have also been used (Luborsky et al., 1999). It has now been demonstrated (through meta-analysis, or more specifically a meta-meta-analysis aggregating results across multiple meta-analyses) that researcher allegiance exerts a substantial influence of study findings, correlating with outcome at $r = 0.26$ (Munder et al., 2013). Still more humbling for the meta-analyst or consumer of meta-analyses, Munder et al. (2013) demonstrated researcher allegiance bias *within meta-analyses* of researcher bias. Authors with allegiance toward the allegiance bias hypothesis (i.e., that allegiance influences outcomes) showed a larger allegiance–outcome relationship in their meta-analyses than authors without allegiance toward the allegiance bias hypothesis ($r = 0.39$ vs. 0.18).

As with other systematic variations across studies (e.g., strength of the comparison condition), one method for addressing bias due to researcher allegiance is coding and modeling this study characteristic. Of course, the influence of allegiance can be hard to detect.

Variation in Meta-Analytic Methodology

A final potential pitfall is variation across meta-analysts in their methodology. The actual process of meta-analysis can be opaque to the consumer of published meta-analyses, and authors make countless decisions along the process of conducting a meta-analysis. As Munder et al. (2013) demonstrated, these decisions can impact on results. Perhaps the most impactful methodological variation is the decision whether a given study meets inclusion criteria. Whether a treatment arm can be considered a *bona fide* treatment (i.e., includes ingredients purported to be therapeutic; Wampold et al., 1997) can significantly alter important conclusions drawn in meta-analysis (e.g., the superiority of CBT; Wampold et al., 2017). Other methodological decisions, such as whether to focus on disorder-specific symptoms or include other measures of psychological functioning and how treatment classes are identified (e.g., is Eye Movement Desensitization and Reprocessing a form of CBT?; Baardseth et al., 2013) can similarly influence conclusions drawn from meta-analysis (Wampold et al., 2017).

The Meta-Analytic Future Is Now: Open Science and Meta-Analysis

Like the publication of psychotherapy RCTs, the publication of psychotherapy meta-analyses is also accumulating (Wampold & Imel, 2015), and for good reason: meta-analyses remain our best methodology for drawing reliable conclusions about a body of quantitative research. Several innovations have occurred in recent years that may address some of the pitfalls highlighted above.

The most promising innovation for addressing publication bias (and other sources of bias, e.g., meta-analyst allegiance bias; Munder et al., 2013) is a movement within psychology and scientific research generally toward open science. Preregistration of clinical trials is now required for publication of RCTs in certain outlets and preregistration of meta-analyses has also been recommended (Moher et al., 2015).

Increasing transparency of reporting in original studies as well as efforts to make study data available will likely dramatically change meta-analysis in psychotherapy and the strength of the conclusions that can be drawn. Baldwin and Del Re

(2016) also have proposed that psychotherapy meta-analyses should move toward an open science model as well, through increased transparency and sharing of data and data analysis scripts.

A related innovation is the possibility of conducting meta-analysis using integrative data analysis (i.e., combining raw datasets). Studies using this approach are appearing in the literature (e.g., Kuyken et al., 2016). This approach may become increasingly viable with a movement toward increased transparency and sharing of primary study data. The availability of individual patient data for conducting meta-analysis can address several thorny methodological issues in meta-analysis including increasing low statistical power for tests of moderation. With available individual-level data, individual-level moderators (e.g., depression severity as a moderator of the efficacy of mindfulness-based cognitive therapy; Kuyken et al., 2016) can be tested directly, rather than coded at the study level. The ability to combine data sets may also be facilitated by attempts to standardize measurement (e.g., National Institutes of Health Patient-Reported Outcomes Measurement Information System [PROMIS]; Cella et al., 2007).

REPLICATION AND TRANSPARENCY

Since the publication of the 6th edition of the *Handbook*, psychology, specifically, and science, generally, have had to face concerns about replication and quality of results. Within psychology, these concerns have stemmed from multiple sources including (a) the publication of controversial papers in major journals, such as Bem's (2011) work on extra-sensory perception (see Wagenmakers et al., 2011, for a criticism of Bem [2011]); (b) cases of academic misconduct, plagiarism, and fraud (e.g., McCook, 2018; Oransky, 2018; Palus, 2015); and (c) methodological work demonstrating major problems in the literature, such as unreasonably low statistical power (Button et al., 2013), questionable research practices (QRP) such as undisclosed methodological and statistical flexibility (e.g., *p*-hacking, failing to disclose all measures in a study; Simmons et al., 2011), and presenting research as confirmatory when it is not (HARKing = Hypothesizing After the Results Are Known; Kerr, 1998). Furthermore, efforts to replicate psychological studies have often failed (O'Donnell et al., 2018; Open Science Collaboration, 2015).

The difficulties with problematic flexibility, inadequate statistical power, multiple comparisons, and lack of transparency have been acknowledged for a long time. So why do we engage in them? The incentives in science seem to support them (Ioannidis, 2014; Nosek et al., 2012; Young et al., 2008) – scientists are rewarded for getting papers published and obtaining grants more than getting things right. Hiring, tenure, and grant committees seek highly productive scholars who publish frequently, place their work in the best journals, and secure grant money (Ioannidis, 2014; Lilienfeld, 2017). Journal editors and reviewers tend to privilege exciting, novel findings and often will not consider null results and replication studies. Grant reviewers want to see positive results in preliminary studies.

Ironically, when we teach new scientists how to do science, such as in a research methods class or in a chapter like this one, we teach the methods and logic of science. The assumption being that the methods and logic of science will produce interpretable results about our subject matter. We do not emphasize spinning results for publication or grants or how to mine data for publications. Nevertheless, when push comes to shove, we sometimes play the game to get work published even when the choices we make operate against the scientific logic we affirm. Hence, some have termed the incentives provided to researchers as *perverse incentives* (Edwards & Roy, 2016).

Few discussions about replication and rigor have been specifically about clinical and psychotherapy research. This can make it seem like psychotherapy research is somehow in a better position than other fields or simply more rigorous – or that replication is just a problem in social psychological and neuroscience. We know of no reason to believe that psychotherapy research is in a special position in this regard. Rather, many, if not all, of the problems that lead to replication issues are present in psychotherapy research. HARKing, *p*-hacking, failure to disclose all measures, underpowered studies, inadequate methodologies, inattention to measurement/psychometrics, and fuzzy theories are all active in psychotherapy research.

Tackett et al. (2017) sought to broaden the discussion about replicability to include clinical research, including psychotherapy research. They suggest that clinical research may not have been included in the conversations about replicability due to key methodological and cultural differences between social/cognitive/neuropsychology and clinical research. These differences include a larger focus on correlational research, studying large effects (e.g., some treatment effects), and the difficulty and cost of participant recruitment (e.g., many disorders are rare). Though we concur that there are some differences, perhaps important differences, between clinical research and other domains, we suspect the primary reason for the lack of attention on clinical research is that replications are more challenging. Running a replication on a social psychology experiment that used an undergraduate sample is relatively simple compared to repeating a randomized psychotherapy trial or psychotherapy process study involving coding of sessions. Thus, data on replication of psychotherapy and other clinical studies is minimal.

The fact that conversation about replication and rigor is just beginning in psychotherapy research means just that – the conversation is just beginning. It does not mean that replication is just a problem for other fields. The conversation for psychotherapy researchers may differ from the conversation for social psychologists in critical ways. Nevertheless, the themes will remain the same. For example, it is true that the high cost and effort required to collect clinical data can make it difficult to conduct replication studies or make researchers reluctant to make the data open (Tackett et al., 2017). The high cost of data collection can also increase the incentive to make sure that there is something, perhaps many things, that are publishable from a dataset. Otherwise, all that work would be of no use to hiring, tenure, and grant committees. Thus, there are strong incentives to use questionable research practices to make the results publishable.

One could argue that the professional incentives that affect scientists are the biggest reason for issues with replication and data quality (cf. Ioannidis, 2014). Psychotherapy researchers are exposed to the same professional pressures and incentives to publish as other scientists. Graduate students are taught to "Alter your perspective so that you derive your professional self-respect entirely from what is on that document [i.e., your vita]" (Lord, 2004, p. 10). Early career researchers must publish or fail to get grants, postdoctoral positions, and tenure track jobs. Once they have jobs, they must continue to publish or fail to keep their job. Hiring and tenure committees enforce these incentives by attending to whether researchers publish enough and in the right outlets. Given these incentives, it is not surprising that researchers can get focused on whether a result is publishable rather than whether a result is trustworthy.

A key source of questionable research practices (QRPs) involves problematic flexibility in design and analysis decisions. Though the term flexibility usually has a positive connotation, here flexibility is not desired because it can lead to exaggeration of effects (Gelman & Carlin, 2014), type I errors (Luck & Gaspelin, 2017), and the illusion of certainty (Ioannidis, 2005). We suspect that the vast majority of researchers do not intentionally make choices aimed at deceiving their readers (with some notable exceptions; Crocker & Cooper, 2011). Rather, the choices are a product of the research process and we aim to encourage transparency and openness regarding the decisions. Examples of *problematic flexibility* in psychotherapy research include the following:

1. *Absence of agreed definition(s) of change in outcome or process studies.* We do not, as a field, have strict and consistently followed definitions of change. This opens up the possibility of testing multiple definitions (e.g., pre–post difference, rate of change in a multilevel model, etc.) and presenting the model with the best results. This may be especially problematic in naturalistic studies where methodological conventions are not as defined as they are in controlled studies. Well-designed clinical trials often avoid this problem by transparently defining outcomes prior to data analyses (e.g., registering the trial).

2. *Failing to define inclusion/exclusion criteria prior to analyzing the data or failing to disclose changes to inclusion/exclusion criteria.* In a naturalistic study, where data come from practice records, there are so many ways to decide who to include. Participants vary with respect to (a) diagnosis (which may be unreliably defined), (b) number of sessions attended (which may be different from number of outcome measures), (c) which treatment episode this is (episodes are not strictly defined), (d) time in between sessions (how many days between sessions before we conclude that a new treatment episode has occurred), and so on. In a clinical trial, many of these inclusion/exclusion criteria are better defined, but can be adjusted along the way, which can sometimes be a problem. If recruitment is taking too long, then requirements about comorbidity or previous treatment might be loosened. If therapists cannot continue in the study, then random assignment might not be strictly adhered to or additional therapists with unique qualifications may have to be added. If these changes are not disclosed, it is difficult to trust the conclusions.

3. *Inappropriately adding, dropping, or changing outcomes.* The definition and scoring of outcomes can be a source of problematic flexibility. Perhaps some outcomes get turned into categorical variables or otherwise transformed (e.g., log-transformation) because the continuous version was not statistically significant. Outcomes may be dropped or added after having seen results. Likewise, researchers may drop some timepoints to support a particular result.

4. *Testing unplanned interactions.* This can be a problem when interactions are used to explore treatment effects (or any relationship) that are not significant for the whole sample. For example, one might split the sample into men and women or into severe and mild depression and rerun the models.

5. *Basing choices about missing data on how they affect the results.* Researchers might decide to ignore missing data because the results are statistically significant when they do so or researchers may use imputation techniques because results were null.

We include the discussion of replication and rigor because we believe that studying and implementing the methods discussed in this chapter, though important, cannot help advance our understanding of psychotherapy research if we engage in questionable research practices. Randomized trials that report a subset of outcomes based on significance or naturalistic studies that change inclusion criteria based on the results are not trustworthy. As noted previously, we believe that there are multiple opportunities in any study for researchers to make questionable decisions and psychotherapy researchers have the same incentives as other scientists. Consequently, we believe we would be remiss to not discuss potential problems and proposed solutions.

One might argue that some findings in psychotherapy research, such as the consistency of effect sizes for active treatment versus control (Wampold & Imel, 2015) and the consistency of the therapeutic alliance and outcome correlation (Flückiger et al., 2018), suggest that the problems of replicability may not be as prevalent in psychotherapy research as they are in other disciplines. We agree that these findings might indeed be robust and not biased by QRPs and lack of transparency. The difficulty is that QRPs have been the norm in many disciplines for years and one of the reasons they are pernicious is that they are not disclosed or are simply overlooked. Consistency of effects in-and-of-themselves do not provide evidence of replicability and trustworthiness because problems with the published literature can make effects look more consistent than they really are.

Indeed, another explanation of these robust findings is that some of these effects are contaminated by QRP, such as selective reporting and interpreting of results. For example, Baldwin et al. (2005) reviewed the statistical analyses of studies used to support the original list of empirically supported treatments published by the Division 12 of the American Psychological Association (Task Force 1995, 1998). They found that across the 33 studies reviewed, authors had conducted 602 statistical tests of treatment effects (average 18.2). That is a lot of tests on average per study and these are just the

tests that were reported. It is plausible that other additional analyses (e.g., subgroup tests or interactions) that were not reported. Large numbers of tests, if done without corrections for multiple comparisons, inflate type I error rates.

Likewise, Vassar et al. (2019) examined selective reporting in clinical trials for the treatment of addiction. They compared the trial registration, which was completed prior to the trial, with the published report of the completed trial and found that 47 of 162 trials had discrepancies (e.g., changing the primary outcome measure) between the registration and published report. Most literatures outside of clinical trials do not require preregistration making it impossible to determine whether such discrepancies are common outside of trials. Nevertheless, when considering other literatures, such as the alliance–outcome literature, it is not difficult to imagine authors only submitting significant correlations for publication or only reporting correlations involving some of the outcome measures (although recent meta-analytic reviews suggest the alliance–outcome literature may not be influenced by some forms of publication bias; Horvath et al., 2011; Flückiger et al., 2018).

Unfortunately, meta-analysis and systematic reviews are not necessarily able to correct or deal with these kinds of reporting issues and other QRPs. Reviews of literatures are only as good as the information reported – if primary study authors use QRPs, even unintentionally, using those primary studies biases the meta-analysis. Whether problems with QRPs are a problem for psychotherapy research is an unanswered question and time will tell whether key findings hold up as researchers are held more accountable in measurement, design, analysis, and reporting.

Fortunately, various solutions have been proposed to increase confidence in studies. Methods for improving rigor and replication typically involve improving transparency and openness. Most of the QRPs involve decisions that are not disclosed and thus not subject to peer review. By making more of the research process public, psychotherapy researchers can better justify their results and consumers of their research can better evaluate it. The following are four examples of increased transparency:

1. *Enhancing collaboration.* Academic incentives continue to prioritize many publications emerging out of a single lab directed by a scientist. However, as we discuss in the power section, it is challenging and often beyond the reach of a single lab to design studies that are sufficiently large to obtain sufficient power and precision. Embracing collaboration as an alternative allows us to pool our resources and ideas, which may improve our studies.

2. *Making data and other study materials available for review.* Sharing data (sometimes referred to as data sharing agreements) and study materials with researchers independent of the original research group facilitates the evaluation of evidence and helps promote corrections to the literature when mistakes have been made. It can also help researchers build on previous work by allowing for precise replications as well as develop new extensions. Sharing data and materials is also consistent with the ethos of openness and transparency central to scientific reform. Many journals make it

possible to include data as part of the publication. Because journals change their storage and hosting procedures, a better choice is to use the Open Science Framework (https://osf.io) which provides web hosting for data.

3. *Preregistration.* Preregistration involves documenting and publicly posting key research decisions *prior to collecting data* or *prior to the end of data collection*. If the study is a secondary data-analysis, then preregistration occurs *prior to analyzing the data*. Preregistration can include posting about (a) hypotheses, (b) participant recruitment, (c) inclusion/exclusion criteria, (d) methods for dealing with attrition, (e) measures (including scoring), (f) power analyses, and (g) data analysis plans. Given that it is hard to predict everything in advance, changes to the plan can be made and documented. The Open Science Framework (https://osf.io) provides a free service for recording pre-registrations. Likewise, journals such as *Trials* publish protocols for clinical trials and the website *PROSPERO* (https://www.crd.york.ac.uk/PROSPERO/) is a service for the preregistration of systematic reviews, thereby extending these principles to reviews and meta-analyses.

4. *Registered reports.* Registered reports are studies where the introduction and methods are submitted to a journal prior to conducting the study. The proposal is peer reviewed and, if the proposal is accepted, the journal agrees to publish the study regardless of the results as long as the study followed the proposed methods. Thus, peer reviewers can judge the study's merits by evaluating the justification for the research question and the methodology used to study it prior to knowing the results. Registered reports are similar to dissertation proposals wherein the proposal is accepted and students can graduate provided they complete the study as proposed. The journal *Psychology and Psychotherapy: Theory, Research, and Practice* currently accepts registered reports as do many other journals across many fields (https://cos.io/rr/).

None of these solutions is perfect nor applicable to all research designs. It is critical to not "let perfect be the enemy of good." If it is true that our research has problems and that we are unduly influenced by perverse incentives, then continuing with the status quo because there is not a perfect solution, furthers the problem. Attending to the limitations of the solutions is critical, both when considering the results of our studies as well as for helping better tailor the solutions our specific designs.

CONCLUSION

We have covered some key topics in measurement, research design, and statistical analysis and our coverage has only scratched the surface of possible topics. Psychotherapy researchers need to be familiar with a vast array of methodological areas, both when conducting and consuming research. Of course, expertise in all areas is not required, and is most likely impossible. Further, the demands of contemporary psychotherapy research likely require collaboration with methodological experts as research questions and data become more complex.

Indeed, the chapters in this *Handbook* along with the articles in psychotherapy journals indicate that psychotherapy research is evolving. A common theme throughout the history of psychotherapy research has been what treatments work and for whom (Paul, 1967) and this question is often seen as synonymous with psychotherapy research. Though some researchers still focus on questions involving what treatments work for which disorders, many others now focus on disseminating treatments, improving access to therapy, studying novel forms of delivery, and improving outcomes within health care systems (e.g., Boswell et al., 2015; Goldberg, Simpson, et al., 2019; Lee-Tauler et al., 2018). These types of research questions require adapting our tried-and-true methods, developing new approaches, and collaborating across disciplines. The principles of (a) transparent, open, and replicable research, (b) the role of the scientist-practitioner, and (c) a commitment to evidence-based practice (both from trials methodology and from observing naturally occurring psychotherapy) can help frame and guide our evolution as a field and help ensure the quality of our results and conclusions.

As noted, we have only covered a few topics in measurement, design, and analysis. Other topics we have not covered, but are worth the time to study include: (a) attrition and missing data (Enders, 2010), (b) the analysis of non-normal outcomes (Long & Freese, 2014), (c) Bayesian modeling (Kruschke, 2015; McElreath, 2016), (d) qualitative methods (Denzin & Lincoln, 2011, see also Chapters 3 and 11 in this *Handbook*), (e) machine learning (Alpaydin, 2009), and (f) causal inference (Gelman & Hill, 2007). All these topics, and likely others, are highly relevant to psychotherapy research.

Recommendations

We offer five recommendations regarding methodology in psychotherapy research:

1. *Return to an emphasis on measurement.* Clinical psychology as a discipline started as an assessment field. Focusing on improving measurement and ensuring the highest quality data in our studies is a fundamental requirement to good science. No amount of methodological sophistication can overcome poor measurement.

2. *Commit to additional methodological training in graduate school and beyond.* Because our field is evolving, the methodological training we receive as graduate students is generally not sufficient (Aiken et al., 2008). Students may only be required to take courses in ANOVA and regression. There is a good chance they will not be exposed to structural equation modeling, psychometrics, multilevel models, machine learning, meta-analysis, analysis of non-normal data, and computer programming (and so many other things). It will be increasingly difficult to conduct and understand the research literature without exposure to these topics. Collaboration will help, but practitioners and researchers will need some familiarity with these advanced methods. Requiring more coursework during graduate school as well as providing more continuing education credits for methodology could help.

3. *Take recommendations about statistical power seriously.* Concerns about statistical power have been expressed for a long time (Cohen, 1962). It appears that when faced with these criticisms, the field has collectively shrugged its shoulders and proceeded without attending to these problems. The broader research community has talked at length regarding incentives for researchers (cf. Ioannidis, 2014). A general theme of this discussion has been the need to change incentives regarding publications. If journal editors will publish small studies and promotion committees reward small studies, then researchers will continue to conduct small studies.

4. *Beware the siren call of statistical or design sophistication.* We are psychotherapy researchers with an interest in methodology and it can be fun to learn a new statistical approach or research design and find a way to apply it. We believe this can lead to interesting ideas and potentially important findings. Nevertheless, we also believe we can sometimes fool ourselves into thinking that the results are important because we used an advanced statistical technique or a complicated longitudinal design. Sometimes that is true and sometimes not. In the end, it is more important to have a good research question and good measurement than complicated analyses.

5. *Commit to open-science practices.* As noted previously, lack of transparency in research practices and incentives to use QRPs have reduced the quality of the scientific literature. Though psychotherapy research has not faced the same scrutiny as other fields, we do not believe that is because psychotherapy research is immune to the problems. Committing to improving the culture and incentives around open-science within psychotherapy research will help improve the quality of our results. Examples of this commitment could include (a) improving data sharing practices, (b) journal editors incentivizing open-science practices, and (c) preregistration of studies.

We hope that this chapter serves as a useful reference and starting point for learning methodology and improving psychotherapy research. Methodology can illuminate and it can obscure. Hopefully, as psychotherapy researchers, we develop a thorough understanding and command of our methods so that our data can ultimately assist with patient care and improve mental health outcomes.

ABBREVIATIONS

ANCOVA	analysis of covariance
ANOVA	analysis of variance
CBT	cognitive behavioral therapy
CSPRS	Collaborative Study Psychotherapy Rating Scale
CTS	Cognitive Therapy Scale
EMA	Ecological Momentary Assessment
EMDR	Eye Movement Desensitization Reprocessing
fMRI	functional magnetic resonance imaging
HARKing	hypothesizing after the results are known
ICC	intraclass correlation coefficient
IRT	item response theory
PTSD	posttraumatic stress disorder
QRP	questionable research practices
RCT	randomized controlled trial
TDCRP	Treatment of Depression Collaborative Research Program

REFERENCES

Adair, J. G. (1984). The Hawthorne effect: A reconsideration of the methodological artifact. *Journal of Applied Psychology, 69*(2), 334–345. https://doi.org/10.1037/0021-9010.69.2.334

Ahn, H., & Wampold, B. E. (2001). Where oh where are the specific ingredients? A meta-analysis of component studies in counseling and psychotherapy. *Journal of Counseling Psychology, 48*(3), 251–257. https://doi.org/10.1037/0022-0167.48.3.251

Aiken, L. S., West, S. G., & Millsap, R. E. (2008). Doctoral training in statistics, measurement, and methodology in psychology: Replication and extension of Aiken, West, Sechrest, and Reno's (1990) survey of PhD programs in North America. *American Psychologist, 63*(1), 32–50. https://doi.org/10.1037/0003-066X.63.1.32

Alpaydin, E. (2009). *Introduction to machine learning*. MIT Press.

Althoff, T., Clark, K., & Leskovec, J. (2016). Large-scale analysis of counseling conversations: An application of natural language processing to mental health. *Transactions of the Association of Computational Linguistics, 4*, 463–476. https://doi.org/10.1162/tacl_a_00111

Anderson, T., Ogles, B. M., Patterson, C. L., Lambert, M. J., & Vermeersch, D. A. (2009). Therapist effects: Facilitative interpersonal skills as a predictor of therapist success. *Journal of Clinical Psychology, 65*(7), 755–768. https://doi.org/10.1002/jclp.20583

Atkins, D. C. (2005). Using multilevel models to analyze couple and family treatment data: Basic and advanced issues. *Journal of Family Psychology, 19*(1), 98–110. https://doi.org/10.1037/0893-3200.19.1.98

Atkins, D. C., Steyvers, M., Imel, Z. E., & Smyth, P. (2014). Scaling up the evaluation of psychotherapy: Evaluating motivational interviewing fidelity via statistical text classification. *Implementation Science, 9*, 1–11. https://doi.org/10.1186/1748-5908-9-49

Baardseth, T. P., Goldberg, S. B., Pace, B. T., Wislocki, A. P., Frost, N. D., Siddiqui, J. R., Lindermann, A. M., Kivlighan, D. M., III, Laska, K. M., Del Re, L. C., Minami, T., & Wampold, B. E. (2013). Cognitive-behavioral therapy versus other therapies: Redux. *Clinical Psychology Review, 33*(3), 395–405. https://doi.org/10.1016/j.cpr.2013.01.004

Baldwin, S. A. (2019). *Psychological statistics and psychometrics using Stata*. Stata Press.

Baldwin, S. A., Bauer, D. J., Stice, E., & Rohde, P. (2011). Evaluating models for partially clustered designs. *Psychological Methods, 16*(2), 149–165. https://doi.org/10.1037/a0023464

Baldwin, S. A., & Del Re, A. C. (2016). Open access meta-analysis for psychotherapy research. *Journal of Counseling Psychology, 63*(3), 249–260. https://doi.org/10.1037/cou0000091

Baldwin, S. A., & Imel, Z. E. (2013). Therapist effects: Findings and methods. In *Bergin and Garfield's handbook of psychotherapy and behavior change* (6th ed.) (pp. 258–297). Wiley.

Baldwin, S. A., Imel, Z. E., Braithwaite, S. R., & Atkins, D. C. (2014). Analyzing multiple outcomes in clinical research using multivariate multilevel models. *Journal of Consulting and Clinical Psychology*, 82(5), 920–930. https://doi.org/10.1037/a0035628

Baldwin, S. A., Murray, D. M., & Shadish, W. R. (2005). Empirically supported treatments or type I errors? Problems with the analysis of data from group-administered treatments. *Journal of Consulting and Clinical Psychology*, 73(5), 924–935. https://doi.org/10.1037/0022-006X.73.5.924

Baldwin, S. A., & Shadish, W. (2011). A Primer on meta-analysis in clinical psychology. *Journal of Experimental Psychopathology*, 2, 294–317. https://doi.org/10.5127/jep.009610

Baldwin, S. A., Wampold, B. E., & Imel, Z. E. (2007). Untangling the alliance-outcome correlation: Exploring the relative importance of therapist and patient variability in the alliance. *Journal of Consulting and Clinical Psychology*, 75(6), 842–852. https://doi.org/10.1037/0022-006X.75.6.842

Barkham, M. (2016). Patient centered assessment in psychotherapy: Towards a greater bandwidth of evidence. *Clinical Psychology: Science and Practice*, 23(3), 284–287. https://doi.org/10.1111/cpsp.12163

Barlow, D. H., Rapee, R. M., & Brown, T. A. (1992). Behavioral treatment of generalized anxiety disorder. *Behavior Therapy*, 23(4), 551–570. https://doi.org/10.1016/S0005-7894(05)80221-7

Baron, R. M., & Kenny, D. A. (1986). The moderator-mediator variable distinction in social psychological research: Conceptual, strategic, and statistical considerations. *Journal of Personality and Social Psychology*, 51(6), 1173–1182. https://doi.org/10.1037/0022-3514.51.6.1173

Baskin, T. W., Tierney, S. C., Minami, T., & Wampold, B. E. (2003). Establishing specificity in psychotherapy: A meta-analysis of structural equivalence of placebo controls. *Journal of Consulting and Clinical Psychology*, 71(6), 973–979. https://doi.org/10.1037/0022-006X.71.6.973

Bates, D., Mächler, M., Bolker, B., & Walker, S. (2015). Fitting linear mixed-effects models using lme4. *Journal of Statistical Software*, 67(1), 1–48. https://doi.org/10.18637/jss.v067.i01

Bauer, D. J., Preacher, K. J., & Gil, K. M. (2006). Conceptualizing and testing random indirect effects and moderated mediation in multilevel models: New procedures and recommendations. *Psychological Methods*, 11(2), 142–163. https://doi.org/10.1037/1082-989X.11.2.142

Bem, D. J. (2011). Feeling the future: Experimental evidence for anomalous retroactive influences on cognition and affect. *Journal of Personality and Social Psychology*, 100(3), 407–425. https://doi.org/10.1037/a0021524

Black, D. S., & Slavich, G. M. (2016). Mindfulness meditation and the immune system: A systematic review of randomized controlled trials. *Annals of the New York Academy of Sciences*, 1373(1), 13–24. https://doi.org/10.1111/nyas.12998

Blake, D. D., Weathers, F. W., Nagy, L. M., Kaloupek, D. G., Gusman, F. D., Charney, D. S., & Keane, T. M. (1995). The development of a clinician-administered PTSD scale. *Journal of Traumatic Stress*, 8(1), 75–90. https://doi.org/10.1002/jts.2490080106

Bollen, K. A., & Curran, P. J. (2006). Latent curve models: A structural equation perspective (Vol. 467). John Wiley & Sons. https://doi.org/10.1002/0471746096

Borenstein, M., Hedges, L. V., Higgins, J. P. T., & Rothstein, H. (2009). *Introduction to meta-analysis*. Wiley. https://doi.org/10.1002/9780470743386

Borkovec, T. D., & Castonguay, L. G. (1998). What is the scientific meaning of empirically supported therapy? *Journal of Consulting and Clinical Psychology*, 66(1), 136–142. https://doi.org/10.1037/0022-006X.66.1.136

Boswell, J. F., Kraus, D. R., Miller, S. D., & Lambert, M. J. (2015). Implementing routine outcome monitoring in clinical practice: Benefits, challenges, and solutions. *Psychotherapy Research*, 25(1), 6–19. https://doi.org/10.1080/10503307.2013.817696

Bradburn, N. M., Rips, L. J., & Shevell, S. K. (1987). Answering autobiographical questions: The impact of memory and inference on surveys. *Science*, 236(4798), 157–161. https://doi.org/10.1126/science.3563494

Brown, T. A. (2015). *Confirmatory factor analysis for applied research* (2ed ed.). Guilford Press.

Button, K. S., Ioannidis, J. P. A., Mokrysz, C., Nosek, B. A., Flint, J., Robinson, E. S. J., & Munafò, M. R. (2013). Power failure: Why small sample size undermines the reliability of neuroscience. *Nature Reviews. Neuroscience*, 14, 365–376. https://doi.org/10.1038/nrn3475

Cacioppo, J. T., Berntson, G. G., & Andersen, B. L. (1991). Psychophysiological approaches to the evaluation of psychotherapeutic process and outcome, 1991: Contributions from social psychophysiology. *Psychological Assessment*, 3(3), 321–336. https://doi.org/10.1037/1040-3590.3.3.321

Cahill, S. P., Carrigan, M. H., & Frueh, B. C. (1999). Does EMDR work? And if so, why?: A critical review of controlled outcome and dismantling research. *Journal of Anxiety Disorders*, 13(1-2), 5–33. https://doi.org/10.1016/S0887-6185(98)00039-5

Cipriani, A., Girlanda, F., & Barbui, C. (2009). Superiority, equivalence or non-inferiority? *Epidemiology and Psychiatric Sciences*, 18(4), 311–313. https://doi.org/10.1017/S1121189X00000269

Clark, L. A., & Watson, D. (2019). Constructing validity: New developments in creating objective measuring instruments. *Psychological Assessment*, 31(12), 1412–1427. https://doi.org/10.1037/pas0000626

Cohen, J. (1962). The statistical power of abnormal-social psychological research: A review. *The Journal of Abnormal and Social Psychology*, 65(3), 145–153. https://doi.org/10.1037/h0045186

Cohen, J. (1988). *Statistical power analysis for the behavioral sciences* (2nd ed.). Erlbaum.

Comer, J. S., & Kendall, P. C. (2013). Methodology, design, and evaluation in psychotherapy research. In M. J. Lambert (Ed.) *Bergin and Garfield's handbook of psychotherapy and behavior change* (p. 21–48). Wiley.

Cooper, H. M., Hedges, L. V., & Valentine, J. C. (2009). *The handbook of research synthesis and meta-analysis* (2nd ed.). Russell Sage Foundation.

Crits-Christoph, P., Gibbons, M. B. C., Hamilton, J., Ring-Kurtz, S., & Gallop, R. (2011). The dependability of alliance assessments: The alliance-outcome correlation is larger than you might think. *Journal of Consulting and Clinical Psychology*, 79(3), 267–278. https://doi.org/10.1037/a0023668

Crocker, J., & Cooper, M. L. (2011). Addressing scientific fraud. *Science*, 334(6060), 1182–1182. https://doi.org/10.1126/science.1216775

Crocker, L., & Algina, J. (2008). *Introduction to classical and modern test theory*. Cengage Learning.

Cronbach, L. J., & Meehl, P. E. (1955). Construct validity in psychological tests. *Psychological Bulletin*, 52(4), 281–302. https://doi.org/10.1037/h0040957

Cuijpers, P., Straten, A. van, Bohlmeijer, E., Hollon, S. D., & Andersson, G. (2010). The effects of psychotherapy for adult depression are overestimated: A meta-analysis of study quality and effect size. *Psychological Medicine*, 40(2), 211–223. https://doi.org/10.1017/S0033291709006114

Del Re, A. C., & Hoyt, W. T. (2014). MAd: Meta-analysis with mean differences (Version 0.8-2) [R package]. http://CRAN.R-project.org/package=MAd

Del Re, A. C., Spielmans, G. I., Flückiger, C., & Wampold, B. E. (2013). Efficacy of new generation antidepressants: Differences Seem Illusory. *PLoS ONE*, 8(6), e63509. https://doi.org/10.1371/journal.pone.0063509

Delgadillo, J., de Jong, K., Lucock, M., Lutz, W., Rubel, J., Gilbody, S., Ali, S., Aguirre, E., Appleton, M., Nevin, J., O'Hayon, H., Patel, U., Sainty, A., Spencer, P., & McMillan, D. (2018). Feedback-informed treatment versus usual psychological treatment for depression and anxiety: a multisite, open-label, cluster randomised controlled trial. *The Lancet Psychiatry*, 5(7), 564–572. https://doi.org/10.1016/S2215-0366(18)30162-7

Denzin, N. K., & Lincoln, Y. S. (2011). *The Sage handbook of qualitative research*. Sage.

DeRubeis, R. J., Brotman, M. A., & Gibbons, C. J. (2005). A conceptual and methodological analysis of the nonspecifics argument. *Clinical Psychology: Science and Practice*, 12(2), 174–183. https://doi.org/10.1093/clipsy.bpi022

DeRubeis, R. J., Evans, M. D., Hollon, S. D., Garvey, M. J., Grove, W. M., & Tuason, V. B. (1990). How does cognitive therapy work? Cognitive change and symptom change in cognitive therapy and pharmacotherapy for depression. *Journal of Consulting and Clinical Psychology*, 58(6), 862–869. https://doi.org/10.1037/0022-006X.58.6.862

DeRubeis, R. J, Gelfand, L. A., German, R. E., Fournier, J. C., & Forand, N. R. (2013). Understanding processes of change: How some patients reveal more than others-And some groups of therapists less-About what matters in psychotherapy. *Psychotherapy Research*, 24(3), 419–428. https://doi.org/10.1080/10503307.2013.838654

Duval, S., & Tweedie, R. (2000). Trim and Fill: A simple funnel-plot-based method of testing and adjusting for publication bias in meta-analysis. *Biometrics*, 56(2), 455–463. https://doi.org/10.1111/j.0006-341X.2000.00455.x

Dwyer, D. B., Falkai, P., & Koutsouleris, N. (2018). Machine learning approaches for clinical psychology and psychiatry. *Annual Review of Clinical Psychology*, *14*, 91–118. https://doi.org/10.1146/annurev-clinpsy-032816-045037

Edwards, M. A., & Roy, S. (2016). Academic research in the 21st Century: Maintaining scientific integrity in a climate of perverse incentives and hypercompetition. *Environmental Engineering Science*, *34*(1), ees.2016.0223. https://doi.org/10.1089/ees.2016.0223

Egger, M., Smith, G. D., & Sterne, J. A. C. (2001). Uses and abuses of meta-analysis. *Clinical Medicine*, *1*(6), 478–484. https://doi.org/10.7861/clinmedicine.1-6-478

Eldridge, S. M., Lancaster, G. A., Campbell, M. J., Thabane, L., Hopewell, S., Coleman, C. L., & Bond, C. M. (2016). Defining feasibility and pilot studies in preparation for randomised controlled trials: development of a conceptual framework. *PloS ONE*, *11*(3), e0150205. https://doi.org/10.1371/journal.pone.0150205

Eliot, T. S. (1971). *Complete poems and plays: 1909-1950*. Harcourt Brace & Company.

Elkin, I., Shea, M. T., Watkins, J. T., Imber, S. D., Sotsky, S. M., Collins, J. F., Glass, D. R., Pilkonis, P. A., Leber, W. R., Docherty, J. P., Fiester, S. J., & Parloff, M. B. (1989). National Institute of Mental Health Treatment of Depression Collaborative Research Program: General effectiveness of treatments. *Archives of General Psychiatry*, *46*(11), 971–982. https://doi.org/10.1001/archpsyc.1989.01810110013002

Embretson, S. E. (1996). The new rules of measurement. *Psychological Assessment*, *8*(4), 341–349. https://doi.org/10.1037/1040-3590.8.4.341

Embretson, S. E., & Reise, S. P. (2000). *Item response theory for psychologists*. Lawrence Erlbaum Associates, Inc.

Enders, C. K. (2010). *Applied missing data analysis*. The Guilford Press.

Eysenck, H. J. (1952). The effects of psychotherapy: An evaluation. *Journal of Consulting Psychology*, *16*(5), 319–324. https://doi.org/10.1037/h0063633

Falkenström, F., Granström, F., & Holmqvist, R. (2013). Therapeutic alliance predicts symptomatic improvement session by session. *Journal of Counseling Psychology*, *60*(3), 317–328. https://doi.org/10.1037/a0032258

Feske, U., & Goldstein, A. J. (1997). Eye movement desensitization and reprocessing treatment for panic disorder: A controlled outcome and partial dismantling study. *Journal of Consulting and Clinical Psychology*, *65*(6), 1026–1035. https://doi.org/10.1037/0022-006X.65.6.1026

Fleiss, J. L., Levin, B., & Paik, M. C. (2013). *Statistical methods for rates and proportions*. John Wiley & Sons.

Flückiger, C., Del Re, A. C., Wampold, B. E., & Horvath, A. O. (2018). The alliance in adult psychotherapy: A meta-analytic synthesis. *Psychotherapy*, *55*(4), 316. https://doi.org/10.1037/pst0000172

Foa, E. B., Rothbaum, B. O., Riggs, D. S., & Murdock, T. B. (1991). Treatment of posttraumatic stress disorder in rape victims: A comparison between cognitive-behavioral procedures and counseling. *Journal of Consulting and Clinical Psychology*, *59*(5), 715–723. https://doi.org/10.1037/0022-006X.59.5.715

Gaffan, E. A., Tsaousis, J., & Kemp-Wheeler, S. M. (1995). Researcher allegiance and meta-analysis: The case of cognitive therapy for depression. *Journal of Consulting and Clinical Psychology*, *63*(6), 966–980. https://doi.org/10.1037/0022-006X.63.6.966

Gelman, A., & Carlin, J. (2014). Beyond power calculations assessing Type S (Sign) and Type M (Magnitude) errors. *Perspectives on Psychological Science*, *9*(6), 641–651. https://doi.org/10.1177/1745691614551642

Gelman, A., & Hill, J. (2007). *Data analysis using regression and multilevel/hierarchical models*. Cambridge University Press. https://doi.org/10.1017/CBO9780511790942

Geschwind, N., Peeters, F., Drukker, M., van Os, J., & Wichers, M. (2011). Mindfulness training increases momentary positive emotions and reward experience in adults vulnerable to depression: A randomized controlled trial. *Journal of Consulting and Clinical Psychology*, *79*(5), 618–628. https://doi.org/10.1037/a0024595

Glass, G. V. (1976). Primary, secondary, and meta-analysis of research. *Educational Researcher*, *5*(10), 3–8. https://doi.org/10.3102/0013189X005010003

Goldberg, S. B., Baldwin, S. A., Merced, K., Caperton, D., Imel, Z. E., Atkins, D. C., & Creed, T. (2019). The structure of competence: Evaluating the factor structure of the Cognitive Therapy Rating Scale. *Behavior Therapy*, *51*(1), 113–122. https://doi.org/10.1016/j.beth.2019.05.008

Goldberg, S. B., Buck, B., Raphaely, S., & Fortney, J. C. (2018). Measuring psychiatric symptoms remotely: A systematic review of remote measurement-based care. *Current Psychiatry Reports*, *20*, 1–12. https://doi.org/10.1007/s11920-018-0958-z

Goldberg, S. B., Flemotomos, N., Martinez, V. R., Tanana, M., Kuo, P., Pace, B. T., Villatte, J. L., Georgiou, P., Van Epps, J., Imel, Z. E., Narayanan, S., & Atkins, D. C. (2020). Machine learning and natural language processing in psychotherapy research: Alliance as example use case. *Journal of Counseling Psychology*, *67*(4), 438–448. doi: 10.1037/cou0000382.

Goldberg, S. B., & Hoyt, W. T. (2015). Group as social microcosm: Within-group interpersonal style is congruent with outside group relational tendencies. *Psychotherapy*, *52*(2), 195–204. https://doi.org/10.1037/a0038808

Goldberg, S. B., Simpson, T. L., Lehavot, K., Katon, J. G., Chen, J. A., Glass, J. E., Schnurr, P. P., Sayer, N. A., & Fortney, J. C. (2019). Mental health treatment delay: A comparison among civilians and veterans of different service eras. *Psychiatric Services*, *70*(5), 358–366. https://doi.org/10.1176/appi.ps.201800444

Goldberg, S. B., Tucker, R. P., Greene, P. A., Davidson, R. J., Kearney, D. J., & Simpson, T. L. (2019). Mindfulness-based cognitive therapy for the treatment of current depressive symptoms: A meta-analysis. *Cognitive Behaviour Therapy*, *48*(6), 445–462. https://doi.org/10.1080/16506073.2018.1556330

Goldberg, S. B., Tucker, R. P., Greene, P. A., Davidson, R. J., Wampold, B. E., Kearney, D. J., & Simpson, T. L. (2018). Mindfulness-based interventions for psychiatric disorders: A systematic review and meta-analysis. *Clinical Psychology Review*, *59*, 52–60. https://doi.org/10.1016/j.cpr.2017.10.011

Greenwald, A. G. (1975). Consequences of prejudice against the null hypothesis. *Psychological Bulletin*, *82*(1), 1–20. https://doi.org/10.1037/h0076157

Haedt-Matt, A. A., & Keel, P. K. (2011). Revisiting the affect regulation model of binge eating: A meta-analysis of studies using ecological momentary assessment. *Psychological Bulletin*, *137*(4), 660–681. https://doi.org/10.1037/a0023660

Hall, K. L., Vogel, A. L., Huang, G. C., Serrano, K. J., Rice, E. L., Tsakraklides, S. P., & Fiore, S. M. (2018). The science of team science: A review of the empirical evidence and research gaps on collaboration in science. *American Psychologist*, *73*(4), 532–548. https://doi.org/10.1037/amp0000319

Hamilton, M. (1960). A rating scale for depression. *Journal of Neurology, Neurosurgery, and Psychiatry*, *23*(1), 56–62. https://doi.org/10.1136/jnnp.23.1.56

Head, M. L., Holman, L., Lanfear, R., Kahn, A. T., & Jennions, M. D. (2015). The extent and consequences of P-Hacking in science. *PLOS Biology*, *13*(3), e1002106. https://doi.org/10.1371/journal.pbio.1002106

Hedges, L. V., & Pigott, T. D. (2001). The power of statistical tests in meta-analysis. *Psychological Methods*, *6*(3), 203–217. https://doi.org/10.1037/1082-989X.6.3.203

Hedges, L. V., & Pigott, T. D. (2004). The power of statistical tests for moderators in meta-analysis. *Psychological Methods*, *9*(4), 426–445. https://doi.org/10.1037/1082-989X.9.4.426

Heppner, P. P., Wampold, B. E., Owen, J., Thompson, M. N., & Wang, K. (2016). *Research design in counseling* (4th ed.). Cengage Learning.

Hollon, S. D., Evans, M. D., Auerbach, A., DeRubeis, R. J., Elkin, I., Lowery, A., Kriss, M. Grove, W., Tuason, V. B., & Piasecki, J. (1988). *Development of a system for rating therapies for depression: Differentiating cognitive therapy, interpersonal psychotherapy, and clinical management pharmacotherapy*. Unpublished Manuscript.

Horner, R. H., & Odom, S. L. (2014). Constructing single-case research designs: Logic and options. In Kratochwill, T. R., & Levin, J. R. (Eds.) *Single-case intervention research: Methodological and statistical advances*. (pp. 27–51). American Psychological Association. https://doi.org/10.1037/14376-002

Horvath, A. O. Del Re, A. C. Flückiger, C., & Symonds, D. (2011). Alliance in individual psychotherapy. *Psychotherapy*, *48*(1), 9–16. https://doi.org/10.1037/a0022186

Hoyt, W. T. (2000). Rater bias in psychological research: When is it a problem and what can we do about it? *Psychological Methods*, *5*(1), 64–86. https://doi.org/10.1037/1082-989X.5.1.64

Hoyt, W. T., & Kerns, M.-D. (1999). Magnitude and moderators of bias in observer ratings: A meta-analysis. *Psychological Methods*, *4*(4), 403–424. https://doi.org/10.1037/1082-989X.4.4.403

Imai, K., Keele, L., & Tingley, D. (2010). A general approach to causal mediation analysis. *Psychological Methods*, *15*(4), 309–334. https://doi.org/10.1037/a0020761

Imel, Z., Baldwin, S., Bonus, K., & MacCoon, D. (2008). Beyond the individual: Group effects in mindfulness-based stress reduction. *Psychotherapy Research*, *18*(6), 735–742. https://doi.org/10.1080/10503300802326038

Imel, Z. E., Barco, J. S., Brown, H. J., Baucom, B. R., Kircher, J. C., Baer, J. S., & Atkins, D. C. (2014). The association of therapist empathy and synchrony in vocally encoded arousal. *Journal of Counseling Psychology*, *61*(1), 146–153. https://doi.org/10.1037/a0034943

Imel, Z. E., Steyvers, M., & Atkins, D. C. (2015). Computational psychotherapy research: Scaling up the evaluation of patient-provider interactions. *Psychotherapy*, *52*(1), 19–30. https://doi.org/10.1037/a0036841

Insel, T., Cuthbert, B., Garvey, M., Heinssen, R., Pine, D. S., Quinn, K., Sanislow, C, & Wang, P. (2010). Research Domain Criteria (RDoC): Toward a new classification framework for research on mental disorders. *The American Journal of Psychiatry*, *167*(7), 748–751. https://doi.org/10.1176/appi.ajp.2010.09091379

Ioannidis, J. P. A. (2005). Why most published research findings are false. *PLoS Medicine*, *2*, e124. https://doi.org/10.1371/journal.pmed.0020124

Ioannidis, J. P. A. (2014). How to make more published research true. *PLoS Medicine*, *11*, e1001747. https://doi.org/10.1371/journal.pmed.1001747

Jacobson, N. S., Dobson, K. S., Truax, P. A., Addis, M. E., Koerner, K., Gollan, J. K., Gortner, E., & Prince, S. E. (1996). A component analysis of cognitive-behavioral treatment for depression. *Journal of Consulting and Clinical Psychology*, *64*(2), 295–304. https://doi.org/10.1037/0022-006X.64.2.295

Jha, A. P., Stanley, E. A., Kiyonaga, A., Wong, L., & Gelfand, L. (2010). Examining the protective effects of mindfulness training on working memory capacity and affective experience. *Emotion*, *10*(1), 54–64. https://doi.org/10.1037/a0018438

Johns, R. G., Barkham, M., Kellett, S., & Saxon, D. (2019). A systematic review of therapist effects: A critical narrative update and refinement to Baldwin and Imel's (2013) review. *Clinical Psychology Review*, *67*, 78–93. https://doi.org/10.1016/j.cpr.2018.08.004

Kazdin, A. E. (2011). *Single-case research designs: Methods for clinical and applied settings* (2nd ed.). Oxford University Press.

Kazdin, A. E. (2019). Single-case experimental design. Evaluating intervention in research and clinical practice. *Behaviour Research and Therapy*, *117*, 3–17. https://doi.org/10.1016/j.brat.2018.11.015

Kazdin, A. E., & Bass, D. (1989). Power to detect differences between alternative treatments in comparative psychotherapy outcome research. *Journal of Consulting and Clinical Psychology*, *57*(1), 138–147. https://doi.org/10.1037/0022-006X.57.1.138

Kerr, N. L. (1998). HARKing: Hypothesizing after the results are known. *Personality and Social Psychology Review*, *2*(3), 196–217. https://doi.org/10.1207/s15327957pspr0203_4

Kivlighan, D. M., III, Goldberg, S. B., Abbas, M., Pace, B. T., Yulish, N. E., Thomas, J. G., Cullen, M. M., Flückiger, C., & Wampold, B. E. (2015). The enduring effects of psychodynamic treatments vis-à-vis alternative treatments: A multilevel longitudinal meta-analysis. *Clinical Psychology Review*, *40*, 1–14. https://doi.org/10.1016/j.cpr.2015.05.003

Kraus, D. R., Bentley, J. H., Alexander, P. C., Boswell, J. F., Constantino, M. J., Baxter, E. E., & Castonguay, L. G. (2016). Predicting therapist effectiveness from their own practice-based evidence. *Journal of Consulting and Clinical Psychology*, *84*(6), 473–483. https://doi.org/10.1037/ccp0000083

Kruschke, J. (2015). *Doing Bayesian data analysis*. Academic Press.

Kumari, M., Shipley, M., Stafford, M., & Kivimaki, M. (2011). Association of diurnal patterns in salivary cortisol with all-cause and cardiovascular mortality: Findings from the Whitehall II Study. *The Journal of Clinical Endocrinology & Metabolism*, *96*(5), 1478–1485. https://doi.org/10.1210/jc.2010-2137

Lacey, J. I. (1959). Psychophysiological approaches to the evaluation of psychotherapeutic process and outcome. In E. A. Rubinstein & M. B. Parloff (Eds.), *Research in psychotherapy* (pp. 160–208). American Psychological Association. https://doi.org/10.1037/10036-010

Lachowicz, M. J., Preacher, K. J., & Kelley, K. (2018). A novel measure of effect size for mediation analysis. *Psychological Methods*, *23*(2), 244–261. https://doi.org/10.1037/met0000165

Lakens, D. (2017). Equivalence tests: A practical primer for t tests, correlations, and meta-analyses. *Social Psychological and Personality Science*, *8*(4), 355–362. https://doi.org/10.1177/1948550617697177

Larson, M. J., & Carbine, K. A. (2017). Sample size calculations in human electrophysiology (EEG and ERP) studies: A systematic review and recommendations for increased rigor. *International Journal of Psychophysiology*, *111*, 33–41. https://doi.org/10.1016/j.ijpsycho.2016.06.015

Laska, K. M., Gurman, A. S., & Wampold, B. E. (2014). Expanding the lens of evidence-based practice in psychotherapy: A common factors perspective. *Psychotherapy*, *51*(4), 467–481. https://doi.org/10.1037/a0034332

Lee-Tauler, S. Y., Eun, J., Corbett, D., & Collins, P. Y. (2018). A systematic review of interventions to improve initiation of mental health care among racial-ethnic minority groups. *Psychiatric Services*, *69*(6), 628–647. https://doi.org/10.1176/appi.ps.201700382

Leon, A. C. (2011). Comparative effectiveness clinical trials in psychiatry: Superiority, non-inferiority and the role of active comparators. *Journal of Clinical Psychiatry*, *72*(3), 331–340. https://doi.org/10.4088/JCP.10r06669

Lesaffre, E. (2008). Superiority, equivalence, and non-inferiority trials. *Bulletin of the NYU Hospital for Joint Diseases*, *66*(2), 150–154.

Leykin, Y., & DeRubeis, R. J. (2009). Allegiance in psychotherapy outcome research: Separating association from bias. *Clinical Psychology: Science and Practice*, *16*(1), 54–65. https://doi.org/10.1111/j.1468-2850.2009.01143.x

Li, T., Puhan, M. A., Vedula, S. S., Singh, S., Dickersin, K., & The Ad Hoc Network Meta-analysis Methods Meeting Working Group. (2011). Network meta-analysis-highly attractive but more methodological research is needed. *BMC Medicine*, *9*, 79. https://doi.org/10.1186/1741-7015-9-79

Lilienfeld, S. O. (2017). Psychology's replication crisis and the grant culture: Righting the ship. *Perspectives on Psychological Science*, *12*(4), 660–664. https://doi.org/10.1177/1745691616687745

Long, J. S., & Freese, J. (2014). *Regression models for categorical dependent variables using Stata* (3rd ed). Stata Press.

Lord, C. G. (2004). A guide to PhD graduate school: How they keep score in the big leagues. In J. M. Darley, M. P. Zanna, & H. L. Roediger III (Eds.), *The complete academic: A career guide* (pp. 3–16). American Psychological Association.

Lord, S. P., Sheng, E., Imel, Z. E., Baer, J., & Atkins, D. C. (2015). More than reflections: Empathy in motivational interviewing includes language style synchrony between therapist and client. *Behavior Therapy*, *46*(3), 296–303. https://doi.org/10.1016/j.beth.2014.11.002

Luborsky, L., Diguer, L., Seligman, D. A., Rosenthal, R., Krause, E. D., Johnson, S., Halperin, G., Bishop, M., Berman, J. S., & Schweizer, E. (1999). The researcher's own therapy allegiances: A "wild card" in comparisons of treatment efficacy. *Clinical Psychology: Science and Practice*, *6*(1), 95–106. https://doi.org/10.1093/clipsy.6.1.95

Luck, S. J., & Gaspelin, N. (2017). How to get statistically significant effects in any ERP experiment (and why you shouldn't). *Psychophysiology*, *54*(1), 146–157. https://doi.org/10.1111/psyp.12639

Lutz, W., Schwartz, B., Hofmann, S. G., Fisher, A. J., Husen, K., & Rubel, J. A. (2018). Using network analysis for the prediction of treatment dropout in patients with mood and anxiety disorders: A methodological proof-of-concept study. *Scientific Reports*, *8*, 7819. https://doi.org/10.1038/s41598-018-25953-0

MacCallum, R. C., Widaman, K. F., Zhang, S., & Hong, S. (1999). Sample size in factor analysis. *Psychological Methods*, *4*(1), 84–99. https://doi.org/10.1037/1082-989X.4.1.84

MacKinnon, D. P., Warsi, G., & Dwyer, J. H. (1995). A simulation study of mediated effect measures. *Multivariate Behavioral Research*, *30*(1), 41–62. https://doi.org/10.1207/s15327906mbr3001_3

Marci, C. D., Ham, J., Moran, E., & Orr, S. P. (2007). Physiologic correlates of perceived therapist empathy and social-emotional process during psychotherapy: *The Journal of Nervous and Mental Disease*, *195*(2), 103–111. https://doi.org/10.1097/01.nmd.0000253731.71025.fc

Maura, J., & Weisman de Mamani, A. (2018). The feasibility of a culturally informed group therapy for patients with schizophrenia and their family members. *Psychotherapy*, *55*(1), 27–38. https://doi.org/10.1037/pst0000109

McArdle, J. J., & Grimm, K. J. (2010). Five steps in latent curve and latent change score modeling with longitudinal data. *Longitudinal Research with Latent Variables*, 1–29. https://doi.org/10.1007/978-3-642-11760-2_8

McCook, A. A. (2018, August 31). Prominent video game-violence researcher loses another paper to retraction. Retraction Watch. https://retraction watch.com/2018/08/31/prominent-video-game-violence-researcher-loses-another-paper-to-retraction/

McDonald, R. P. (1999). *Test theory: A unified approach*. Lawrence Erlbaum Associates.

McElreath, R. (2016). *Statistical rethinking*. CRC Press.

McNally, R. J. (1999). EMDR and mesmerism: A comparative historical analysis. *Journal of Anxiety Disorders, 13*(1-2), 225–236. https://doi.org/10.1016/S0887-6185(98)00049-8

Moher, D., Shamseer, L., Clarke, M., Ghersi, D., Liberati, A., Petticrew, M., Shekelle, P., & Stewart, L. A., & PRISMA-P Group. (2015). Preferred reporting items for systematic review and meta-analysis protocols (PRISMA-P) 2015 statement. *Systematic Reviews, 4*(1), 1–9. https://doi.org/10.1186/2046-4053-4-1

Mohr, D. C., Zhang, M., & Schueller, S. M. (2017). Personal sensing: Understanding mental health using ubiquitous sensors and machine learning. *Annual Review of Clinical Psychology, 13*, 23–47. https://doi.org/10.1146/annurev-clinpsy-032816-044949

Moncher, F. J., & Prinz, R. J. (1991). Treatment fidelity in outcome studies. *Clinical Psychology Review, 11*(3), 247–266. https://doi.org/10.1016/0272-7358(91)90103-2

Moyers, T. B., Miller, W. R., & Hendrickson, S. M. L. (2005). How does motivational interviewing work? Therapist interpersonal skill predicts client involvement within motivational interviewing sessions. *Journal of Consulting and Clinical Psychology, 73*(4), 590–598. https://doi.org/10.1037/0022-006X.73.4.590

Muller, D., Judd, C. M., & Yzerbyt, V. Y. (2005). When moderation is mediated and mediation is moderated. *Journal of Personality and Social Psychology, 89*(6), 852–863. https://doi.org/10.1037/0022-3514.89.6.852

Munder, T., Brütsch, O., Leonhart, R., Gerger, H., & Barth, J. (2013). Researcher allegiance in psychotherapy outcome research: An overview of reviews. *Clinical Psychology Review, 33*(4), 501–511. https://doi.org/10.1016/j.cpr.2013.02.002

Murray, D. M., Blitstein, J. L., Hannan, P. J., Baker, W. L., & Lytle, L. A. (2007). Sizing a trial to alter the trajectory of health behaviours: Methods, parameter estimates, and their application. *Statistics in Medicine, 26*(11), 2297–2316. https://doi.org/10.1002/sim.2714

Muthén, B., & Muthén, L. K. (2000). Integrating person-centered and variable-centered analyses: Growth mixture modeling with latent trajectory classes. *Alcoholism: Clinical and Experimental Research, 24*(6), 882–891. https://doi.org/10.1111/j.1530-0277.2000.tb02070.x

Muthén, L. K., & Muthén, B. O. (2017). Mplus user's guide (Version 8). Muthén & Muthén.

Myin-Germeys, I., & van Os, J. (2007). Stress-reactivity in psychosis: Evidence for an affective pathway to psychosis. *Clinical Psychology Review, 27*(4), 409–424. https://doi.org/10.1016/j.cpr.2006.09.005

Nidich, S., Mills, P. J., Rainforth, M., Heppner, P., Schneider, R. H., Rosenthal, N. E., Salerno, J., Gaylord-King, C., & Rutledge, T. (2018). Non-trauma-focused meditation versus exposure therapy in veterans with post-traumatic stress disorder: A randomised controlled trial. *The Lancet Psychiatry, 5*(12), 975–986. https://doi.org/10.1016/S2215-0366(18)30384-5

Nissen-Lie, H. A., Monsen, J. T., Ulleberg, P., & Rønnestad, M. H. (2013). Psychotherapists' self-reports of their interpersonal functioning and difficulties in practice as predictors of patient outcome. *Psychotherapy Research, 23*(1), 86–104. https://doi.org/10.1080/10503307.2012.735775

Nosek, B. A., Spies, J. R., & Motyl, M. (2012). Scientific utopia II. Restructuring incentives and practices to promote truth over publishability. *Perspectives on Psychological Science, 7*(6), 615–631. https://doi.org/10.1177/1745691612459058

Nunnally, J. C., & Bernstein, I. H. (1994). *Psychometric theory* (3rd ed.). McGraw-Hill.

O'Donnell, M., Nelson, L. D., Ackermann, E., Aczel, B., Akhtar, A., Aldrovandi, S., Alshaif, N., Andringa, R., Aveyard, M., Babincak, P., Balatekin, N., Baldwin, S. A., Banik, G., Baskin, E., Bell, R., Białobrzeska, O., Birt, A. R., Boot, W. R., Braithwaite, S. R., Briggs, J. C., . . . Zrubka, M. (2018). Registered Replication Report: Dijksterhuis and van Knippenberg (1998). *Perspectives on Psychological Science, 13*(2), 268–294. https://doi.org/10.1177/1745691618755704

Olff, M., de Vries, G.-J., Güzelcan, Y., Assies, J., & Gersons, B. P. R. (2007). Changes in cortisol and DHEA plasma levels after psychotherapy for PTSD. *Psychoneuroendocrinology, 32*(6), 619–626. https://doi.org/10.1016/j.psyneuen.2007.04.001

Open Science Collaboration. (2015). Estimating the reproducibility of psychological science. *Science, 349*(6251), aac4716–aac4716. https://doi.org/10.1126/science.aac4716

Oransky, A. I. (2018, September 21). Wansink admits mistakes, but says there was "no fraud, no intentional misreporting." Retraction Watch. https://retractionwatch.com/2018/09/21/wansink-admits-mistakes-but-says-there-was-no-fraud-no-intentional-misreporting/

Orduna-Malea, E., Ayllón, J. M., Martín-Martín, A., & Delgado López-Cózar, E. (2015). Methods for estimating the size of Google Scholar. *Scientometrics, 104*, 931–949. https://doi.org/10.1007/s11192-015-1614-6

Owen, J., Adelson, J., Budge, S., Wampold, B. E., Kopta, M., Minami, T., & Miller, S. (2015). Trajectories of change in psychotherapy. *Journal of Clinical Psychology, 71*(9), 817–827. https://doi.org/10.1002/jclp.22191

Pagano, R. R. (2013). *Understanding statistics in the behavioral sciences*. Wadsworth.

Palus, A. S. (2015, December 8). Diederik Stapel now has 58 retractions. Retraction Watch. https://retractionwatch.com/2015/12/08/diederik-stapel-now-has-58-retractions/

Paul, G. L. (1967). Strategy of outcome research in psychotherapy. *Journal of Consulting Psychology, 31*(2), 109–118. https://doi.org/10.1037/h0024436

Pereira, J.-A., Barkham, M., Kellett, S., & Saxon, D. (2017). The role of practitioner resilience and mindfulness in effective practice: A practice-based feasibility study. *Administration and Policy in Mental Health and Mental Health Services Research, 44*, 691–704. https://doi.org/10.1007/s10488-016-0747-0

Persons, J. P., & Boswell, J. F. (2019). Single case and idiographic research: Introduction to the special issue. *Behaviour Research and Therapy, 117*, 1–2. https://doi.org/10.1016/j.brat.2019.03.007

Peters, J. L., Sutton, A. J., Jones, D. R., Abrams, K. R., & Rushton, L. (2008). Contour-enhanced meta-analysis funnel plots help distinguish publication bias from other causes of asymmetry. *Journal of Clinical Epidemiology, 61*(10), 991–996. https://doi.org/10.1016/j.jclinepi.2007.11.010

Preacher, K. J., Rucker, D. D., & Hayes, A. F. (2007). Addressing moderated mediation hypotheses: Theory, methods, and prescriptions. *Multivariate Behavioral Research, 42*(1), 185–227. https://doi.org/10.1080/00273170701341316

Preacher, K. J., Zyphur, M. J., & Zhang, Z. (2010). A general multilevel SEM framework for assessing multilevel mediation. *Psychological Methods, 15*(3), 209–233. https://doi.org/10.1037/a0020141

Propst, L. R., Ostrom, R., Watkins, P., Dean, T., & Mashburn, D. (1992). Comparative efficacy of religious and nonreligious cognitive-behavioral therapy for the treatment of clinical depression in religious individuals. *Journal of Consulting and Clinical Psychology, 60*(1), 94–103. https://doi.org/10.1037/0022-006X.60.1.94

Rabe-Hesketh, S., & Skrondal, A. (2012a). *Multilevel and longitudinal modeling using Stata, Volume II: Categorical responses, counts, and survival*. Stata Press.

Rabe-Hesketh, S., & Skrondal, A. (2012b). *Multilevel and longitudinal modeling using Stata, Volume I: Continuous responses* (3rd ed.). Stata Press.

Raudenbush, S. W., & Bryk, A. S. (2001). *Hierarchical linear models: Applications and data analysis methods* (2nd edition). SAGE Publications, Inc.

Raue, P. J., Castonguay, L. G., Newman, M., Gaus Binkley, V., Shearer, D., & Goldfried, M. R. (1991). *Guidelines for the Working Alliance Inventory-Observer Form (WAI-O)*. State University of New York at Stony Brook.

Raykov, T., & Marcoulides, G. A. (2018). *A course in item response theory and modeling with Stata*. Stata Press.

Resick, P. A., Nishith, P., Weaver, T. L., Astin, M. C., & Feuer, C. A. (2002). A comparison of cognitive-processing therapy with prolonged exposure and a waiting condition for the treatment of chronic posttraumatic stress disorder in female rape victims. *Journal of Consulting and Clinical Psychology, 70*(4), 867–879. https://doi.org/10.1037/0022-006X.70.4.867

Review Manager (RevMan) (Version 5.3). (2014). [Computer software]. The Nordic Cochrane Centre, The Cochrane Collaboration.

Rosenthal, R. (1979). The "File Drawer Problem" and tolerance for null results. *86*(3), 638–641. https://doi.org/10.1037/0033-2909.86.3.638

Rosenzweig, S. (1936). Some implicit common factors in diverse methods of psychotherapy. *American Journal of Orthopsychiatry*, *6*(3), 412–415. https://doi.org/10.1111/j.1939-0025.1936.tb05248.x

Schiefele, A.-K., Lutz, W., Barkham, M., Rubel, J., Böhnke, J., Delgadillo, J., Kopta, M., Schulte, D., Saxon, D., Neilsen, S. L., & Lambert, M. J. (2017). Reliability of therapist effects in practice-based psychotherapy research: A guide for the planning of future studies. *Administration and Policy in Mental Health and Mental Health Services Research*, *44*, 598–613. https://doi.org/10.1007/s10488-016-0736-3

Shadish, W. R., Cook, T. D., & Campbell, D. T. (2002). *Experimental and quasi-experimental designs for generalized causal inference*. Houghton Mifflin.

Shadish, W. R., Kyse, E. N., & Rindskopf, D. M. (2013). Analyzing data from single-case designs using multilevel models: new applications and some agenda items for future research. *Psychological Methods*, *18*(3), 385–405. https://doi.org/10.1037/a0032964

Shiffman, S., Gwaltney, C. J., Balabanis, M. H., Liu, K. S., Paty, J. A., Kassel, J. D., Hickcox, M., & Gnys, M. (2002). Immediate antecedents of cigarette smoking: An analysis from ecological momentary assessment. *Journal of Abnormal Psychology*, *111*(4), 531–545. https://doi.org/10.1037/0021-843X.111.4.531

Shiffman, S., Stone, A. A., & Hufford, M. R. (2008). Ecological momentary assessment. *Annual Review of Clinical Psychology*, *4*, 1–32. https://doi.org/10.1146/annurev.clinpsy.3.022806.091415

Shrout, P. E., & Bolger, N. (2002). Mediation in experimental and non-experimental studies: New procedures and recommendations. *Psychological Methods*, *7*(4), 422–445.s https://doi.org/10.1037/1082-989X.7.4.422

Simmons, J. P., Nelson, L. D., & Simonsohn, U. (2011). False-positive psychology: Undisclosed flexibility in data collection and analysis allows presenting anything as significant. *Psychological Science*, *22*(11), 1359–1366. https://doi.org/10.1177/0956797611417632

Simons, A. D., Garfield, S. L., & Murphy, G. E. (1984). The process of change in cognitive therapy and pharmacotherapy for depression: Changes in mood and cognition. *Archives of General Psychiatry*, *41*(1), 45–51. https://doi.org/10.1001/archpsyc.1984.01790120049007

Smith, M. L., & Glass, G. V. (1977). Meta-analysis of psychotherapy outcome studies. *American Psychologist*, *32*(9), 752–760. https://doi.org/10.1037/0003-066X.32.9.752

Snijders, T. A., & Bosker, R. J. (2012). *Multilevel analysis: An introduction to basic and advance multilevel modeling* (2nd ed.). Sage.

Stan Development Team. (2019). Stan user's guide (Version 2.19) [Computer software]. https://mc-stan.org

Sterne, J. A. C. (Ed.). (2009). Meta-analysis in Stata: An updated collection from the Stata Journal. Stata Press.

Sterne, J. A. C., & Egger, M. (2001). Funnel plots for detecting bias in meta-analysis: Guidelines on choice of axis. *Journal of Clinical Epidemiology*, *54*(10), 1046–1055. https://doi.org/10.1016/S0895-4356(01)00377-8

Stevens, S. S. (1946). On the theory of scales of measurement. *Science*, *103*(2684), 677–680. https://doi.org/10.1126/science.103.2684.677

Stokols, D., Hall, K. L., Taylor, B. K., & Moser, R. P. (2008). The science of team science: Overview of the field and introduction to the supplement. *American Journal of Preventive Medicine*, *35*(2, Supplement), S77–S89. https://doi.org/10.1016/j.amepre.2008.05.002

Stulz, N., Lutz, W., Leach, C., Lucock, M., & Barkham, M. (2007). Shapes of early change in psychotherapy under routine outpatient conditions. *Journal of Consulting and Clinical Psychology*, *75*(6), 864–874. https://doi.org/10.1037/0022-006X.75.6.864

Tackett, J. L., Lilienfeld, S. O., Patrick, C. J., Johnson, S. L., Krueger, R. F., Miller, J. D., Oltmanns, T. S. & Shrout, P. E. (2017). It's time to broaden the replicability conversation: Thoughts for and from clinical psychological science. *Perspectives on Psychological Science*, *12*(5), 742–756. https://doi.org/10.1177/1745691617690042

Tasca, G. A., & Gallop, R. (2009). Multilevel modeling of longitudinal data for psychotherapy researchers: I. The basics. *Psychotherapy Research*, *19*(4-5), 429–437. https://doi.org/10.1080/10503300802641444

Tasca, G. A., & Lampard, A. M. (2012). Reciprocal influence of alliance to the group and outcome in day treatment for eating disorders. *Journal of Counseling Psychology*, *59*(4), 507–517. https://doi.org/10.1037/a0029947

Task Force on Promotion and Dissemination of Psychological Procedures. (1995). Training in and dissemination of empirically-validated psychological treatments: Report and recommendations. *Clinical Psychologist*, *48*(1), 3–23.

Task Force on Promotion and Dissemination of Psychological Procedures. (1998). Update on empirically supported therapies II. *Clinical Psychologist*, *51*(1), 3–16.

Thibodeau, M. A., Quilty, L. C., Fruyt, F. D., Bolle, M. D., Rouillon, F., & Bagby, R. M. (2015). Latent classes of nonresponders, rapid responders, and gradual responders in depressed outpatients receiving antidepressant medication and psychotherapy. *Depression and Anxiety*, *32*(3), 213–220. https://doi.org/10.1002/da.22293

Twohig, M. P., Hayes, S. C., & Masuda, A. (2006). Increasing willingness to experience obsessions: Acceptance and commitment therapy as a treatment for obsessive-compulsive disorder. *Behavior Therapy*, *37*(1), 3–13. https://doi.org/10.1016/j.beth.2005.02.001

Twohig, M. P., Hayes, S. C., Plumb, J. C., Pruitt, L. D., Collins, A. B., Hazlett-Stevens, H., & Woidneck, M. R. (2010). A randomized clinical trial of acceptance and commitment therapy versus progressive relaxation training for obsessive-compulsive disorder. *Journal of Consulting and Clinical Psychology*, *78*(5), 705–716. https://doi.org/10.1037/a0020508

Vassar, M., Roberts, W., Cooper, C. M., Wayant, C., & Bibens, M. (2019). Evaluation of selective outcome reporting and trial registration practices among addiction clinical trials. *Addiction*, *115*(6), 1172–1179. https://doi.org/10.1111/add.14902

Viechtbauer, W. (2010). Conducting meta-analyses in R with the metafor package. *Journal of Statistical Software*, *36*(1), 1–48. https://doi.org/10.18637/jss.v036.i03

Wagenmakers, E.-J., Wetzels, R., Borsboom, D., & van der Maas, H. L. J. (2011). Why psychologists must change the way they analyze their data: The case of psi: Comment on Bem (2011). *Journal of Personality and Social Psychology*, *100*(3), 426–432. https://doi.org/10.1037/a0022790

Wampold, B. E. (2001). *The great psychotherapy debate: Models, methods, and findings*. Routledge.

Wampold, B. E. (2015). Routine outcome monitoring: Coming of age-With the usual developmental challenges. *Psychotherapy*, *52*(4), 458–462. https://doi.org/10.1037/pst0000037

Wampold, B. E., Budge, S. L., Laska, K. M., Del Re, A. C., Baardseth, T. P., Flückiger, C., Minami, T., Kivlighan 2nd, D. M., III, & Gunn, W. (2011). Evidence-based treatments for depression and anxiety versus treatment-as-usual: A meta-analysis of direct comparisons. *Clinical Psychology Review*, *31*, 1304–1312. https://doi.org/10.1016/j.cpr.2011.07.012

Wampold, B. E., Flückiger, C., Re, A. C. D., Yulish, N. E., Frost, N. D., Pace, B. T., Goldberg, S. B., Miller, S. D., Baardseth, T. P., Laska, K. M., & Hilsenroth, M. J. (2017). In pursuit of truth: A critical examination of meta-analyses of cognitive behavior therapy. *Psychotherapy Research*, *27*(1), 14–32. https://doi.org/10.1080/10503307.2016.1249433

Wampold, B. E., & Imel, Z. E. (2015). *The great psychotherapy debate: The evidence for what makes psychotherapy work* (2nd ed). Routledge. https://doi.org/10.4324/9780203582015

Wampold, B. E., Minami, T., Tierney, S. C., Baskin, T. W., & Bhati, K. S. (2005). The placebo is powerful: Estimating placebo effects in medicine and psychotherapy from randomized clinical trials. *Journal of Clinical Psychology*, *61*(7), 835–854. https://doi.org/10.1002/jclp.20129

Wampold, B. E., Mondin, G. W., Moody, M., Stich, F., Benson, K., & Ahn, H. (1997). A meta-analysis of outcome studies comparing bona fide psychotherapies: Empiricially, "all must have prizes." *Psychological Bulletin*, *122*(3), 203–215. https://doi.org/10.1037/0033-2909.122.3.203

Wang, R., Aung, M. S. H., Abdullah, S., Brian, R., Campbell, A. T., Choudhury, T., Hauser, M., Kane, J., Merrill, Scherer, E. A., Tseng, V. W. S., & Ben-Zeev, D. (2016). CrossCheck: Toward passive sensing and detection of mental health changes in people with schizophrenia. *Proceedings of the 2016 ACM International Joint Conference on Pervasive and Ubiquitous Computing*, 886–897. https://doi.org/10.1145/2971648.2971740

Webb, C. A., DeRubeis, R. J., & Barber, J. P. (2010). Therapist adherence/competence and treatment outcome: A meta-analytic review. *Journal of Consulting and Clinical Psychology*, *78*(2), 200–211. https://doi.org/10.1037/a0018912

Weisz, J. R., Vaughn-Coaxum, R. A., Evans, S. C., Thomassin, K., Hersh, J., Ng, M. Y., Lau, N., Raftery-Helmer, J. N., & Mair, P. (2020). Efficient monitoring of treatment response during youth psychotherapy: the Behavior and Feelings Survey. *Journal of Clinical Child & Adolescent Psychology*, *49*(6), 737–751. https://doi.org/10.1080/15374416.2018.1547973

Wielgosz, J., Goldberg, S. B., Kral, T. R. A., Dunne, J. D., & Davidson, R. J. (2019). Mindfulness, mediation and psychopathology. *Annual Review of Clinical Psychology*, *15*, 285–316. https://doi.org/10.1146/annurev-clinpsy-021815-093423

Young, J., & Beck, A. T. (1980). *Cognitive therapy scale: Rating manual*. University of Pennsylvania. https://doi.org/10.1037/t00834-000

Young, N. S., Ioannidis, J. P. A., & Al-Ubaydli, O. (2008). Why current publication practices may distort science. *PLOS Medicine*, *5*(10), e201. https://doi.org/10.1371/journal.pmed.0050201

Yuan, Y., & MacKinnon, D. P. (2009). Bayesian mediation analysis. *Psychological Methods*, *14*(4), 301–322. https://doi.org/10.1037/a0016972

Yulish, N. E., Goldberg, S. B., Frost, N. D., Abbas, M., Oleen-Junk, N. A., Kring, M., Chin, M. Y., Raines, C. R., Soma, C. S., & Wampold, B. E. (2017). The importance of problem-focused treatments: A meta-analysis of anxiety treatments. *Psychotherapy*, *54*(4), 321–338. https://doi.org/10.1037/pst0000144

Zautra, A. J., Davis, M. C., Reich, J. W., Sturgeon, J. A., Arewasikporn, A., & Tennen, H. (2012). Phone-based interventions with automated mindfulness and mastery messages improve the daily functioning for depressed middle-aged community residents. *Journal of Psychotherapy Integration*, *22*(3), 206–228. https://doi.org/10.1037/a0029573

Zhou, Y., Lemmer, G., Xu, J., & Rief, W. (2019). Cross-cultural measurement invariance of scales assessing stigma and attitude to seeking professional psychological help. *Frontiers in Psychology*, *10*, 1249. https://doi.org/10.3389/fpsyg.2019.01249

Zilcha-Mano, S., Porat, Y., Dolev, T., & Shamay-Tsoory, S. (2018). Oxytocin as a neurobiological marker of ruptures in the working alliance. *Psychotherapy and Psychosomatics*, *87*(2), 126–128. https://doi.org/10.1159/000487190

Zoogman, S., Goldberg, S. B., Hoyt, W. T., & Miller, L. (2015). Mindfulness interventions with youth: A meta-analysis. *Mindfulness*, *6*, 290–302. https://doi.org/10.1007/s12671-013-0260-4

THE CONCEPTUALIZATION, DESIGN, AND EVALUATION OF QUALITATIVE METHODS IN RESEARCH ON PSYCHOTHERAPY

HEIDI M LEVITT, JOHN MCLEOD, AND WILLIAM B STILES

Abstract

Qualitative research methods permit the exploration of lived experiences of therapists and clients and the tracking of change processes in sessions to develop contextualized descriptions and understandings that can guide the development of theory, policy and practice. The field of qualitative inquiry encompasses a wide range of epistemological perspectives, methodological traditions, and practices. The aim of this chapter is to describe the key features of these approaches, and how they can be engaged and adapted to develop research into the process and outcome of psychotherapy. Findings from these methods are especially apt for building theory that encompasses the complexity of psychotherapy process and outcome, and for developing a contextualized understanding of the internal experiences in psychotherapy, the influence of psychotherapy processes, and patterns of interventions that lead to change. They produce insights and principles to guide attuned training, therapy relationship development and maintenance, and responsive in-session moment-to-moment decision-making. The chapter also considers ethical issues arising from this type of research, criteria for evaluating the methodological integrity of qualitative findings, and emerging issues in this area.

OVERVIEW

INTRODUCTION

The use of qualitative methods in psychology has been increasing gradually over time, with psychotherapy researchers being among early adopters of these approaches (see reviews of this history in Faulkner et al., 2002; Hays et al., 2016; Ponterotto, et al., 2008). Within the field, growth in the number of published qualitative studies on psychotherapy has been accompanied by developments over the last decade that have centralized qualitative methods. These strides include the methods division of the *American Psychological Association* (APA), which was *Evaluation, Measurement and Statistics*, changing its name to *Quantitative and Qualitative Methods*. Within the *British Psychological Society* (BPS), the *Qualitative Methods in Psychology* section (QMiP), created in 2006, has grown rapidly to become its largest section. Although qualitative approaches comprised fewer than 10% of published studies within a 10-year review of 15 top psychotherapy journals (2003–2013), and were cited less frequently than quantitative articles, a strong positive trend was found suggesting a striking increase in qualitative research over time (Gelo et al., 2019). Also, the recent edition of the *Publication Manual of the APA* (American Psychological Association, 2020) has included reporting standards for qualitative and mixed methods for the first time (Levitt et al., 2018), acknowledging that these approaches are squarely within the canon of psychological methods.

The 6th edition of this *Handbook* was the first to carry a chapter on qualitative research (McLeod, 2013). The growing importance of qualitative methodologies is marked by the inclusion of two chapters in the current edition focusing on qualitative approaches, with this one addressing methodological issues and Chapter 11 addressing findings from qualitative studies.

In psychology, the term *qualitative methods* refers to scientific practices directed to producing knowledge about human experience and action (Fine, 2012; Morrow, 2005). These methods collect and analyze non-numeric data, including natural language and other forms of human expression. They typically use an iterative process of analysis in which data are analyzed and meanings are generated recursively, alongside reflexive self-examination of investigators' own subjective assumptions (Osbeck, 2014; Rennie, 2012; Wertz, 1999). Characteristically, qualitative inquiry pursues such goals as producing knowledge about psychological experiences that positions human beings as agentic, purposeful, and existing within a social and relational context. These inquiries may investigate a wide range of topics, including experiences of relationships, inanimate objects, or social systems. While drawing on relevant literature from other disciplines and other fields of psychology, the focus of this chapter is primarily on the use of qualitative methods in psychotherapy research.

Psychotherapy researchers have been at the vanguard of the qualitative research movement in psychology, reflecting therapists' interest in the internal experience of their clients, as well as their interest in conceptualizing the intentions that guide their own in-session decision making (Rennie & Frommer, 2015). Qualitative methods may be viewed as consistent with the types of meaning making that come naturally for many therapists (McLeod, 2011). There exist similarities between the process in therapy of slowly deepening client and therapist understanding, and the process of analysis in qualitative methods, in which researchers empathically engage with people's descriptions of their lives and identify patterns (Rennie, 2007). For these reasons, qualitative methods are particularly appropriate for the exploration of psychotherapy.

For some psychotherapy researchers, however, engagement with qualitative methods may be limited by the need for greater education on these epistemological perspectives and procedures (Rubin et al., 2018). The aim of this chapter is to provide guidance on this front, by reviewing the conceptual foundations of qualitative research, common qualitative research designs, processes for evaluating their methodological integrity, and newly emerging issues.

UNDERLYING PHILOSOPHICAL AND CONCEPTUAL FOUNDATIONS OF QUALITATIVE RESEARCH

To understand what qualitative researchers are trying to achieve and how they operate, it is necessary to consider the philosophical assumptions that underpin mainstream quantitative research, on the one hand, and qualitative inquiry, on the other. The act of measurement is part of a long tradition in human society. However, from around the 17th century, the concept of *science* began to evolve based on an assumption of an objective physical reality (e.g., atoms, molecules) that could be observed, measured and experimentally manipulated (Wootton, 2015). This shift led to the realization that mathematical analysis of patterns within these numbers would yield theories or models that could be used to develop new technologies (e.g., machines, drugs) of value to human well-being.

The act of making sense of the meaning of words or texts – the core process in much of qualitative research – is also part of a long tradition in human society. The mythology or wisdom of social groups initially were conveyed through an oral tradition of stories and myths, then later through religious texts and other writings. But the meaning of these linguistic objects was not always clear – a different kind of human science needed to be developed, focusing on the interpretation of texts in order to establish the potential truths inherent within them (Dilthey, 1989/1883; Packer & Addison, 1989; Taylor, 1971).

These alternative (and sometimes competing) knowledge-generating structures continue to exist in contemporary society, and findings from these alternative approaches can complement and strengthen each other. Although the natural science paradigm has enjoyed a dominant position within industrialized societies, in relation to public funding and influence over decision making, it is clear that interpretive forms of inquiry play a significant role in cultural life. Bruner (1986) characterized these traditions as constituting discrete *ways of knowing*: a *paradigmatic* form of knowing that seeks to explain events in terms of abstract laws, and a *narrative* form of knowing that seeks to understand events in terms of contextualized, concrete stories. The field of psychotherapy represents a domain of practical knowledge that calls for clinicians and researchers to embrace both paradigmatic and narrative ways of knowing (Madill & Gough, 2008; McLeod, 2011). For example, a female client who seeks therapy to deal with her postnatal depression may wish to explore the effects of causal/paradigmatic factors such as hormonal changes and sleep deprivation, alongside interpretive/narrative themes such as the meaning of motherhood and the renegotiation of roles within her marriage.

The implication of this kind of everyday clinical scenario is that therapists (and therapy researchers) tend to find ways to integrate knowledge and understanding from apparently quite different ontological and epistemological paradigms or traditions. As a result, psychotherapy research has moved consistently in the direction of methodological pluralism (Howard, 1983; Slife & Gantt, 1999) as it has matured as a field of inquiry in its own right and increasingly incorporated qualitative and case study methodologies alongside established large *N* statistical approaches. While the initial entry point for qualitative methods in psychotherapy research was primarily within humanistic and psychodynamic traditions (Angus et al., 2015; Giorgi, 2009; Levitt, 2016; Messer, 2011; Rennie, 2007, 2012), qualitative methods have come to be used by researchers across all theoretical orientations. The capacity to undertake rigorous qualitative research, or to be an informed user or consumer of qualitative findings, requires an understanding of the underlying conceptual foundations of qualitative research.

The philosophies underpinning science can provide insight into what qualitative researchers (or any researchers) are trying to achieve. For example, basic philosophical concepts such as ontology and epistemology have important implications for research practice. *Ontology* refers to our understanding of the fundamental nature of reality. For example, many people take the view that reality is objective and material, comprising atoms and molecules. Others believe that the ultimate nature of reality is transcendental or spiritual, animated by a Supreme Being or other life force. Alternatively, it is possible to understand reality in terms of a humanistic vision, as socially constructed and consisting of a dense net of language, ritual and meaning. The concept of *epistemology* refers to how we gain knowledge of reality and the methods of knowledge-seeking that considered to be valid. It is possible to know the world through many methods, including rigorous observation, measurement and experimentation, reflective in-dwelling, social critique, or through an interpersonal process of dialogue. Even this highly simplified account of the concepts of ontology and epistemology makes clear that there may never be rational agreement around which ontological or epistemological stance is in some sense "correct." Instead, at this philosophical level, knowledge can be regarded as an ongoing conversation between different positions (Rorty, 1980), each of which may have more purchase for specific purposes and in specific contexts.

In practical terms, it is unlikely that most researchers and clinicians in psychology will immerse themselves in philosophical debates. Fortunately, the work of translating and conveying the take-home messages of foundational philosophical ideas has been very effectively undertaken in influential reviews by Morrow (2005) and Ponterotto (2005). Their suggestion is that, for the purpose of conducting qualitative research, philosophical stances around the nature of knowledge can be regarded as reflecting clusters of idea and practices that have come to be referred to as paradigms. Although there can be exchange between these paradigms and the boundaries may blur, a discussion of some central philosophies drawn upon by qualitative researchers in psychology can serve to orient novice qualitative researchers.

This section presents an overview of the multiple conceptual traditions and paradigms that provide guiding principles for contemporary qualitative research. These include the realist/postpositivist paradigm, the constructivist paradigm, and the critical paradigm.

The Realist/Postpositivist Paradigm

During its formative stage, psychology was influenced heavily by the positivist philosophy movement, which emphasized the value of viewing human experience as observable and measurable, so that it could be examined within experimental models (Danziger, 1990) and allowed psychology to be seen as scientific. Positivist ideals advanced the vision of a psychology that reflected the key principles of natural science, a position that helped to shape the identity of the fledgling profession (Krauss, 2017). The postpositivist approaches that are adopted commonly among contemporary psychologists share many of the assumptions of positivism, while taking account of the huge challenge of ever accomplishing a true rendering of objective reality. The term *postpositivist* has been used (e.g., Morrow, 2005; Ponterotto, 2005) as a general rubric to group together researchers who might describe themselves using a variety of terms, such as realists or scientific realists as well as postpositivists. Or they might not attend to these philosophical distinctions because realism is a culturally dominant position and they assume that this is how psychologists think.

The concept of *critical realism*, based on the ideas of the philosopher Roy Bhaskar (Pilgrim, 2019), has been widely espoused as a means of making sense of the goals of scientific inquiry (Emmel et al., 2018; Pawson & Tilley, 1997). Although realism represents a heterogeneous range of positions (Maxwell, 2012), its common core meaning can be summarized in the following terms:

> Metaphysically, [scientific] realism is committed to the mind-independent existence of the world investigated by the sciences. . . . [T]he scientific realist holds that science aims to produce true descriptions of things in the world (or approximately true descriptions. . .) (Chakravartty, 2017).

Truth here can be understood as a correspondence between people's experience of the theoretical descriptions and their experience of systematic observations of the world (Stiles, 1981).

Contemporary scientific realism is not naïve, in the sense of believing that the true nature of reality is readily accessible. For example, it may acknowledge that people have only indirect and selective access to the world. People's access is though sensory receptors and brains, sometimes mediated by additional instruments, which have particular mechanical and biological properties that determine and limit what can be perceived. At best people can construct theories that describe the experiences produced by their brains and instruments, as shaped by personal history and culture, rather than a veridical representation of the real world. For this and other reasons, scientists can never be sure that their theories are accurate or complete, and a critical sensibility is essential. Nevertheless, the foundational tenet that a mind-independent real world exists offers assurance that continuing observations and logical reconciliation can yield incremental improvements the accuracy of a theoretical account.

Realism comprises a means of resolving tensions between qualitative and quantitative approaches to research (Emmel et al., 2018). From a realist perspective, both qualitative and quantitative sources of evidence are equally valuable sources of information that can feed into accurate descriptions of things in the world (Chakravartty, 2017).

The dominant approach to quantitative research in psychology is currently a realist one. In their review of 10 popular psychology methods textbooks, Eagly and Riger (2014) found that the authors' realist/postpositivist assumptions were implicit throughout the consideration of methods. Indeed, their review identified only one discussion of epistemology, leading to their recommendation that epistemological diversity be a subject of focused attention in our research education. By contrast, at the present time the majority of published qualitative studies in psychotherapy reflect a constructivist paradigm. However, the potential value of a realist perspective has received increased attention within the qualitative research community as a whole (Maxwell, 2009; 2012). Among qualitative psychotherapy researchers, those whose research purposes are what Stiles (2015, 2017, 2020) has called theory-building, fact-gathering, or product-testing (see later subsection) would predominantly endorse scientific realism as their primary perspective.

The Constructivist Paradigm

Another set of ideas that is described in many systems categorizing epistemological perspectives (e.g., Denzin & Lincoln, 2000; Morrow, 2005; Ponterotto, 2005) falls under the rubric of *constructivist* qualitative research. This rubric is used to group together traditions that might be described by such terms as social constructivist or interpretivist. Constructivism is grounded in the idea that the real nature of things is not observable, and that human life is organized around an active process of co-construction that involves attributing meaning to experience, and continually revising these meanings through collaboration and conflict between individuals and groups. From a constructivist perspective, the concepts and theories held by individuals do not comprise a mirror to nature, but instead can be regarded as comprising an ongoing conversation about how to make sense of the way that the natural and social worlds are experienced (Rorty, 1980). A version of constructivism that has been particularly influential for some qualitative researchers is *social constructionism*, which places particular emphasis on the role of talk and language as the primary means through which processes of construction takes place (Gergen & Gergen, 2003; Lock & Strong, 2010).

Constructivist and social constructionist ways of thinking imply a degree of uncertainty – there may be several valid answers to one question, depending on the perspective one takes. For instance, therapist and client may attribute distinct meanings to the same interaction and both may be valid. This work is not entirely relativistic, however, as qualitative researchers strive to maintain a balance between realism and relativism (Rennie, 2000) by keeping their interpretive process grounded in the specificities of data.

Because constructivists see the role of interpretation as central in their work, rather than trying to minimize it, they routinely engage in procedures and reporting that make their own perspectives transparent so as to limit their undue influence on the analysis. For example, a constructivist stance may entail commitment to dialogue between members of a research team, and/or between researcher and informants, so that findings can be produced that take account of, and do justice to, different ways of understanding a particular topic. By including vivid examples, in the form of cases, quotes from informants, or segments of therapy text, qualitative research attempts to show as well as tell, thus creating a space within which the reader has the possibility of arriving at his or her own interpretation of the material.

A central aspect of constructivism is the concept of the *hermeneutic circle*, which refers to the notion that any interpretation of reality, or story, can itself be reinterpreted or retold from a different viewpoint. Each piece of data can shed new light on the understanding of the whole phenomenon, just as an overall understanding can shift how one instance is perceived. There is therefore always a sense in which constructivist research recounts the history of a phenomenon or topic (Gergen, 1973) and emphasizes the interactions and contexts within which dynamics take place. A powerful interpretive account of a phenomenon can be regarded as creating a temporary "clearing," within which certain features of the terrain and associated meanings can be clearly seen (Heidegger, 1962). As these understandings become assimilated into the everyday, taken-for-granted understanding of participants in social life, that initial moment of clarity may become overlaid with layers of further meaning. As a result, constructivist qualitative research is always, to some extent, a discovery-oriented activity. Constructivist research tends to develop theories that focus on concepts that are thought to be socially constructed and describe the ways meanings are developed interpersonally (e.g., Charmaz, 2006; Levitt, 2021).

The Critical Paradigm

A critical paradigm seeks to promote awareness about how power differentials function within multiple levels of society, including cultural, economic, psychological, and political domains. A primary focus of critical social scientists, around methodological issues, has been to draw attention to the social role of science, and in particular to the ways in which science might appear to produce valid value-free knowledge but in reality often supports the interests of elites at the expense of the marginalized.

Founding influences on critical qualitative researchers include philosophical figures and social theorists including members and disciples of the Frankfurt School, such as Jurgen Habermas (1972; Kincheloe & McLaren, 2005), Michel Foucault (1972; Flyvbjerg, 2001) and Klaus Holzkamp (1992; Teo, 1998; Tolman, 2009). Within psychology, the ideas of these thinkers have found expression in the field of critical psychology (Austin & Prilleltensky, 2001). Research traditions that often are grouped under the umbrella of critical psychology include feminist research, indigenous research, queer research, multicultural research, disability research, and social constructionist research (Teo, 2015). Critical researchers use theoretical understandings from these traditions to sensitize themselves to often invisible dynamics and increase their perspicacity (i.e., perceptiveness) while engaging in their research.

There are four main strategies that critical researchers use to accomplish their aims:

1. *Give voice to marginalized experiences.* Critical qualitative research tends to focus on experiences of people whose stories are not reflected in most quantitative psychological research, which tends to focus on average experiences. Critical researchers often draw from feminist standpoint theory (Harding, 2009), arguing that it is the position of the marginalized (versus the average) person that is most revealing of how a system functions. As a result, critical qualitative researchers tend to position their work from the perspectives of people who experience oppression in order to legitimize their experiences and to learn about the weaknesses of the systems they study.

2. *Raise consciousness about power.* Critical researchers shed light on how social power influences societal assumptions and norms, especially those related to the production of knowledge. Social power operates both consciously and unconsciously to structure social dynamics so that people come to expect to be treated and to treat others in relation to their social position (e.g., often as indicated by their gender, race, ethnicity, ability status, and age). Because these expectations are so woven into the fabric of our society, the injustices that they support can be difficult to recognize – especially for people who are not suffering from them (Foucault, 1972). Critical researchers work to raise awareness of these dynamics by viewing the research subject as situated within intersecting forms of social power and by overtly considering the effects of these forces (Moradi & Grzanka, 2017). They tend to use methods, such as mapping techniques (e.g., Clarke, 2005), that shed light on the systems and mechanisms that create disparities in relation to resources, identities, discourses, and social positions.

3. *Share researcher power using participatory methods.* Critical researchers are sharply aware of the power that they hold by virtue of their positions as researchers (Parker, 2015), typically setting the goals of the research, deciding on the research design, naming phenomena, and designing applications of findings. They consider the influence of their own privileged and marginalized perspectives and how it might limit their abilities to fully understand the experiences of participants. Moreover, they often seek collaborators from differing social positions, in order to deliberately broaden the perspectives and deepen the knowledge brought to bear in the analyses (Fine, 2012). Other participatory methods include focus groups to help shape a project, or participant feedback to guide the interpretation or application of findings.

4. *Disrupt oppressive systems and promote liberation.* The purpose of critical research often goes beyond unmasking and theorizing about the impact of oppression. It aims to disrupt privilege, power, and oppression and to create liberation, transformation, and social change. Critical psychologists have called for the prioritization of research on the causes of health inequity in order to dismantle the structural inequalities that maintain it (Bowleg, 2017). Researchers use their findings in conjunction with understandings of power

dynamics and social systems to suggest alternate practices to empower marginalized groups and resolve disparities (e.g., Wendt & Gone, 2016) and suggest ways to transform institutions (e.g., Fine, 2012).

Beyond Paradigms

By explaining the philosophical approaches and aims of varied paradigms, qualitative researchers made accessible an understanding of central values underlying approaches to qualitative methods (Denzin & Lincoln, 2000; Morrow, 2005; Ponterotto, 2005), but these categories should not be understood as comprehensive. For instance, qualitative psychotherapy researchers may use a variety of theories, outside of critical theories, to guide their analyses, such as psychoanalytic theories. It is important to note that not all qualitative methods fit neatly into these paradigms. And they may be categorized in ways other than epistemological paradigms.

Although the paradigm approach usefully identifies commonalities in researchers' conceptual foundations, qualitative methods may be deeply rooted within epistemological perspectives that are much more detailed and elaborated than these general rubrics. Alternatively, epistemological perspectives may be thought to be a property of the researcher (i.e., a set of value commitments) or may be determined in connection with research project aims. They also may be used outside of any philosophical perspectives. Qualitative researchers may find it to be beneficial to draw on multiple perspectives when conducting their research. And, there are frameworks that have been developed to support researchers to combine epistemological perspectives in their work, such as Levitt's (2021) approach to critical-constructivist grounded theory that guides researchers to develop research designs and strategies that coherently integrate approaches. We describe these issues for further consideration in this section.

Use and Reporting of Epistemological Perspectives

A number of studies have examined the ways that qualitative researchers use and report on their epistemological perspectives. Within a review of 109 qualitative research studies on clients' self-described experiences of psychotherapy (Levitt et al., 2016), only 22 (20.2%) were found to include clear statements regarding the researchers' epistemological perspective and 56 (51.4%) included any language that implied an epistemological perspective. Of these, seven articles (12.5%) were based explicitly in a postpositivist perspective. However, only three appeared to draw solely from that paradigm and four also drew from constructivist perspectives as well (e.g., consensual qualitative approaches, Hill, 2012). Six articles (10.7%) described using a critical perspective. In contrast, 43 articles (76.8%) reported a constructivist approach in their research reporting – this figure was even higher (85.7%) when counting constructivist approaches used in connection with postpositivist (4) or critical approaches (1) or (85.7%). It appeared from the review that constructivist perspectives were the dominant approach reported by qualitative psychotherapy researchers, however, for half of these articles the perspective of the authors was unclear. Authors were urged to specify their perspectives going forward.

Another study found many areas of overlap and synergistic possibilities between paradigms. In a survey of qualitative studies in central–eastern European countries, with a focus on social psychology, Kovács et al. (2019) also found that constructivist approaches were dominant, that pure positivist articles were rare, and that methods often were unspecified. In addition, they found that most articles drew on a combination of postpositivist and constructivist-interpretivist perspectives. These findings suggest that, in relation to contemporary practice in qualitative research in psychology and psychotherapy, investigators appear to operate in a flexible manner, if necessary drawing on contrasting philosophical paradigms as required by the aims of their study. As APA reporting standards (2020) have encouraged clarity in research reporting, future reports may describe more thoroughly the philosophical bases and methods used.

Phenomenology: An Influential Cross-Paradigm Perspective

Phenomenology, an important school of thought within European philosophy initially developed by Edmund Husserl (1859–1938), has had a significant influence on many branches of psychology. There exist widely used approaches to qualitative research that identify as being explicitly phenomenological in intent. These include descriptive phenomenology, which espouses a mainly realist stance (Giorgi, 2009), alongside other phenomenological methods that adopt a primarily constructivist and interpretive style of data analysis (Finlay, 2008; Smith, Flowers & Larkin, 2009; Wertz, 2015).

Descriptive phenomenology (Giorgi, 2009) seeks to attain true knowledge by systematically bracketing-off everyday assumptions (natural attitude) concerning the meaning of an experience. The aim of phenomenological inquiry is to describe the phenomenon in as much detail as possible and arrive at an appreciation of its essence. The process of bracketing-off focuses the researcher's attention on the object of study (rather than preconceptions of the object) to allow a nuanced complexity to emerge and the essential quality of the object to be grasped. The principles and practices of phenomenology have proved to be enormously useful for qualitative researchers aiming to move beyond surface or taken for granted understandings of the meaning of qualitative data and to achieve a deeper and more comprehensive appreciation of the layers of meaning in verbal accounts of experience.

In contrast, interpretive phenomenology was developed by a different set of researchers (Smith et al., 2009) and does not engage in bracketing in this manner and tends not to focus on seeking essences that hold across instances of a phenomenon. Instead of seeking to produce descriptions of phenomena, it develops interpretations, with a focus on the interpretive process. The procedures used reflect the philosophical foundations of the tradition from which a method derives and of the researchers themselves. For this reason, it is helpful when researchers articulate their epistemological positions, although page limits may need to be extended to accommodate this description.

A Pragmatic Perspective

A vision of psychotherapy research that has been influential in recent years draws on a *pragmatic* image of knowledge as a basis for reasoned and responsible professional action (Fishman, 1999) that can be traced back to the ideas of William James, one of the founding figures of modern psychology, among others. A pragmatic perspective is associated with the view that there is no single source of truth to which all knowledge claims can be reduced. Instead, all sources of knowledge are both of potential value and open to critical scrutiny. Rather than beginning research with a specific epistemological paradigm or perspective, pragmatic researchers tend to be focused on problem solving and engaging whatever tools (e.g., qualitative or quantitative) best address the issue at hand. Abbott (2004) argued that breakthrough research is often associated with heuristic improvisation, combination, and inversion of standard methodological procedures. Qualitative researchers who espouse a pragmatic perspective view philosophical insights by regarding them as resources that may be deployed to heighten awareness of key aspects of the inquiry process (Abbott, 2004; Maxwell, 2009; McLeod, 2011). This approach regards researchers as *bricoleurs* who must use all means at their disposal in order to unpack the complex nature of social life.

Categories of Qualitative Research Purposes

The preceding sections have examined some of the ways in which underlying philosophical concepts and traditions function as guiding principles for the conduct of qualitative research in psychotherapy. Another approach involves categorizing qualitative research (and other research) around four broad research purposes or goals: theory-building, fact-gathering, product testing, and enriching (Stiles, 2015, 2017, 2020). In principle, any method could be used to serve any of these purposes, though in practice some methods are used mostly for particular purposes. In practice, the purposes tend to overlap with the previously described philosophical paradigms. Theory-building research is usually conducted within the realist paradigm. Fact-gathering and product-testing are usually conduced within the realist or pragmatic paradigm. Enriching research is usually conduced within the constructivist or critical paradigm. However, particular researchers may diverge from these trends.

First, in *theory-building*, research serves as quality control on a guiding theory. The research aims to test and improve that particular theory, increasing its generality, precision, and realism (Levins, 1968). A theory, in this context, is a semiotic construction, that is, an account of something (e.g., psychotherapy or some aspect of it) that is made of words, numbers, diagrams, images or other signs.

A theory-building researcher's task is to make observations, compare them with theoretical tenets or derivations, and assess their correspondence. Whereas statistical hypothesis-testing research examines only one or a few theory-derived hypotheses at a time, qualitative theory-building research can examine many theory-relevant aspects in the same study. It does this by describing the material (e.g., case study, interview) in theory-relevant terms and explicitly or implicitly assessing how well the theory describes details of the material (Stiles, 2009, 2017). Correspondence between details of the theory and detailed observations strengthens the theory, lending an increment of confidence to it. Campbell (1979) suggested that the multiple theoretically relevant observations on different aspects of the theory are analogous to degrees of freedom in statistical hypothesis-testing research.

Lack of correspondence indicates some problem. Often, the problem is with the observational methods or interpretations, so these must be checked. But if the discrepancy remains, the theory must be changed to accommodate the observations. At worst, the theory may be rejected. Usually, however, ways can be found to modify, elaborate, or extend the theory so that it corresponds to the observations, an operation called *abduction* (Rennie, 2012). Abductions are always tentative, but they justify further observations guided by the modified theory. For example, in task analysis, which has been used to build the theory underlying emotion-focused therapy (Greenberg, 2007; Rice & Greenberg, 1984), models of task steps based on one set of task instances are systematically assessed in new instances, as reviewed later. Similarly, intensive qualitative case studies have been used to build the assimilation model (Stiles, 2011; Stiles & Angus, 2001), reviewed elsewhere in this volume (McLeod, Levitt, & Stiles, 2020, Chapter 11).

Theory-building research offers a straightforward way to aggregate and synthesize qualitative observations across studies: New research observations and interpretations are integrated into the theory, as in the natural sciences. The adjusted theory must remain internally consistent, and it must continue to explain the observations it explained previously while accommodating the new ones. This involves adjusting confidence in the theory depending on how well the observations fit the theory as well as adjusting the theory to fit the new observations. Theoretical work of this sort appears in the introductions and discussions of theory-building empirical studies (qualitative or quantitative) as well as in broader synthetic reviews. For example, a series of studies on setbacks in therapy done within the assimilation model (Caro Gabalda & Stiles, 2009, 2013; Caro Gabalda et al., 2016, Mendes et al., 2016) were summarized in a synthetic review (Caro & Stiles, 2018).

Second, in *fact-gathering research*, the focus is on finding and verifying facts rather than interpreting them within a theoretical framework. Kuhn (1970) suggested that fact-gathering is what scientists do when they don't have a theory, perhaps with an implicit hope that the facts may eventually be organized into a theory. Within qualitative research, a variety of methods can be used simply to describe what happens, with a minimum of inference or interpretation; examples include consensual qualitative research (Hill, 2012; Hill, Thompson, & Williams, 1997) and conversation analysis (Peräkylä, 2013, 2019; Peräkylä et al., 2008, reviewed later).

Third, *product-testing* research aims to evaluate the effectiveness of a particular treatment approach, which is much like testing the quality of other consumer products (Stiles, 2017, 2020). In many circles, the randomized clinical trial, a quantitative strategy, is still regarded as the preferred methodology for evaluating psychotherapy approaches.

However, the hermeneutic single-case efficacy design approach (Elliott, 2002; Elliott et al., 2009; see also Bohart et al., 2011; Miller et al., 2011) offers an example of how a qualitative evaluation strategy can operate in relation to single psychotherapy cases.

Fourth, *enriching* qualitative research seeks to deepen and enrich people's appreciation or understanding of a phenomenon or experience by considering it from alternative perspectives and unpacking the history, the narrative, and the explicit and implicit meanings involved. Whereas theory-building research is guided by a particular theory and focuses on assessing and improving it, enriching research may consider many theories and propose new ones as alternative, potentially useful viewpoints. The enriching purpose is to enrich *people*, in the sense of enhancing the awareness, sensitivity and responsiveness of the readers, investigators, and participants, rather than testing and improving a semiotic construction (i.e., the guiding theory, Stiles, 2015). Insofar as enriching research is characterized by the absence of many conventional research restrictions, investigators may consider that they are doing all of the above, that is, theory-building, fact-gathering, and product-testing, as well as distinctively enriching activities. Most of the qualitative methods reviewed in this chapter have been used mainly for enriching purposes (exceptions include conversation analysis and task analysis, as noted earlier).

Clarity about these alternative research aims is important, as there is much mutual incomprehension. Readers who expect a study addressed to one purpose but encounter research addressed to a different purpose are likely to find it confusing or wrongheaded. For example, readers expecting a theory-building study are likely to find an enriching study confused and unfocused, while readers expecting an enriching study are likely to find a theory-building study narrow and restricted.

QUALITATIVE RESEARCH DESIGNS

The previous section describes philosophical foundations that have shaped the understanding of methods and research designs that are described in this section. Although early approaches to qualitative inquiry tended not to be formalized and were shaped by researchers individually to investigate specific topics (Wertz, 2014), approaches to method with step-by-step guidelines on how to engage in inquiry have been proliferating since the 1960s. Because they were accessible and detailed methodological procedures, they were more easily adopted and have increased in use since that time. Within psychotherapy research, the use of these methods has been growing steadily since the late 1980s.

Most of the methods that will be discussed in this chapter have been advanced by more than one researcher and have multiple forms. The variations may be located in epistemological frameworks, procedures, and language that are distinctive. For instance, the founders of grounded theory research, Glaser and Strauss (1967), each went on to develop their own approaches to the method (Glaser, 1992; Strauss & Corbin, 1990). Then, constructivist (Charmaz, 2006), critical realist (Rennie, 2000), and realist versions (Lo, 2014), and critical-constructivist (Levitt, 2021) versions of grounded theory methods were developed as well. So while we describe central components of each methods in this overview chapter, researchers and reviewers will wish to keep in mind that each of these qualitative methods has forms adapted for specific perspectives and purposes with distinctive characteristics.

Also, it is important to note that, although proponents of each design have described their approaches by outlining procedural steps, the successful adoption of these methods typically requires tailoring of those procedures with an eye toward the specific research aims and characteristics of a given study (see the section on evaluating methodological integrity). And, successful returns across all these methods are based on strong data collection, which in qualitative psychotherapy research often rests on the development of interviewing skills, including the development of attuned listening and facilitative skills (see Josselson, 2013).

In addition to these formalized approaches to method that we review, we wish to note that qualitative researchers also may describe their method procedurally, without reference to an established method at all. This approach to research is in keeping with the notion of the qualitative researcher as a bricoleur who selects tools that will best fit for the specific research situation (Denzin &, Lincoln, 2000; McLeod, 2011). Also, a generic approach to qualitative research has been put forward recently by Elliott and Timulak (2021) that synthesizes many of common categorizing procedures with the aim of generating interpretations and descriptions of phenomena. Still, the description of established qualitative methods is instructive in understanding the range of processes that fall under the rubric of qualitative methods. In the following subsections, distinctions across qualitative methods are highlighted as well as their application in psychotherapy research (see Table 3.1).

Qualitative Approaches Based on Categorizing Content

The most commonly used methods within contemporary qualitative psychotherapy research (Levitt, Pomerville et al., 2017) have a number of procedural similarities, and so in this section we are considering them together.

Categorizing Methods

Because of a commonality in how they organize data within the analytic process, Timulak and Elliott (2018) have referred to these approaches as categorizing qualitative approaches. They include phenomenology, grounded theory, consensual qualitative research, thematic analysis, content analysis, and narrative analysis. We discuss each briefly to indicate some unique elements associated with each method and then we consider procedural commonalities across them.

Phenomenology. One of the earliest qualitative methods to be applied to psychotherapy research was descriptive phenomenology (e.g., Fessler, 1978). Descriptive phenomenologists have a longstanding tradition of advancing qualitative methods in psychology, centered on Duquesne University's program and beginning in the 1960s (Giorgi, 2009). These researchers assume a transcendental attitude of inquiry, using processes such as bracketing (which is the setting aside of their own assumptions or judgments), so that they can empathically understand their participants' experiences without distortion. By engaging in the process of imaginative variation (i.e., eidetic analysis), researchers examine their data to determine which aspects of an experience vary and which appear to be essential aspects of a subject matter, allowing for insight into the definitional features of that topic.

Interpretative phenomenology derived from a separate school of thought (e.g., Smith et al., 2009). Instead of trying to place them aside, these researchers seek to use their preconceptions deliberately by working with participants in co-developing interpretations of their process of understanding. Despite their distinctive approaches, both methods shed light on the content and process of internal experiences and are well suited for studying psychotherapy.

Grounded Theory. David Rennie's introduction of grounded theory into psychotherapy research (Rennie et al., 1988) stimulated some of the most commonly used qualitative methods in North American psychotherapy research today. Using this method, researchers seem to develop findings that are empirically rooted in the data under analysis. The analytic process began with a close analysis of text (e.g., interview transcripts) and the creation of initial units which each are compared to each other, using a process called constant comparison, leading to the formation of categories that capture commonalities within. These categories are then grouped into higher-level categories, which in turn are grouped into higher levels until they arrive at a core category, which helps identify a central meaning in the hierarchy of categories. Two distinctive procedures introduced by grounded theory researchers are *theoretical sampling*, which is the process of examining the evolving findings to identify participants to recruit who can shed light on gaps in understanding, and *saturation*, which occurs when data analysis no longer leads to changes in the hierarchy, indicating that the analysis is comprehensive and data collection can be stopped (Glaser & Strauss, 1967).

The method was influential in the development of two other important approaches to psychotherapy research. Robert Elliott (Elliott et al., 1994) developed comprehensive process analysis (which evolved into hermeneutic single-case efficacy design; Elliott, 2015). His approach added a criterion of research group consensus to the method and incorporated quantitative measures. In turn, Clara Hill (2012) further developed this process of consensus in the method of consensual qualitative research, which has become especially influential within counseling psychology research. These methods have both been helpful in shedding light on dynamics that unfold within and across psychotherapy sessions.

Thematic, Content, and Narrative Analysis. There are other qualitative approaches that have not evolved in relation to the use of grounded theory or phenomenology within the psychotherapy research community, but that utilize many similar procedures. These include methods such as thematic analyses (e.g., Braun & Clarke, 2006), content analysis (Egberg Thyme et al., 2013), and forms of narrative analyses that identify themes generated from patterns of meaning in text (Angus & McLeod, 1999). The methods differ in that thematic and content analysts understand the units of text under analysis (i.e., themes or content) as in relation to their specific study aim (e.g., answering a

TABLE 3.1   Descriptions of Common Qualitative Methods

Method	Typical aims of the method	Perspectives of researcher	Participant/Data characteristics	Central procedures	Central citations for variants of method
Phenomenology	To develop a description or an understanding of a lived experience.	In *descriptive phenomenology (DP)*, researchers will use bracketing and the epoché, that is, the suspension of researchers' beliefs. In *interpretive phenomenological analysis (IPA)*, researchers emphasize owning their perspectives and their influence through the research process.	Typically, participants or data sources need to be descriptive and reflective about internal experiences.	DP: Using imaginative variation of psychological meanings of units to grasp essential meanings. IPA: Identifying connections between themes that reflect participants' experiences.	DP: Giorgi, 2009 IPA: Smith, Flowers, & Larkin, 2009
Grounded theory (GT)	To develop a theory or an understanding of a research topic that is grounded in data.	Varied. In the initial approach, researchers were cautioned to avoid reading research literature to minimize bias, but now many researchers find that this helps to sensitize them to their phenomenon. Approaches to ground theory analysis exist from across epistemological perspectives.	Typically, participants and data sources need to be descriptive about the research topic.	Developing a hierarchy of categories that were originally developed through a constant comparison of incidents in the data; using theoretical sampling; seeking saturation.	Original GT approaches: Glaser & Strauss, 1967; Glaser 1992; Strauss & Corbin, 1992 Constructivist GT: Charmaz, 2006 Critical-constructivist GT: Levitt, 2021
Narrative methods	To examine the formulation, effects, or structure of stories, or identify the themes associated with the research topic.	Varied. Some theory-driven approaches. Approaches to narrative analysis exist from across epistemological perspectives.	Typically, participants and data sources need to convey a story or stories about the research topic for analysis.	Examining the structure, function and evolution of narratives in relation to contextual features.	Angus & McLeod, 2004; Bamberg, 2012 (each review multiple narrative approaches)
Conversation analysis	To examine the moment-by-moment evolution of talk and its organization as it functions in relationships, social systems, and institutions.	Varied. Approaches to conversation analysis exist from across epistemological perspectives.	Data are collected from across a specific type of conversation for analysis (e.g., type of psychotherapy, form of intervention).	Analyzing how each statement indicates how a prior statement was understood. Describing the function within a pattern of interaction.	Sidnell, 2013); Peräkylä, 2013 (review common procedures) Critical discourse analysis: Potter & Wetherell, 1995

(Continued)

TABLE 3.1 (CONTINUED)

Method	Typical aims of the method	Perspectives of researcher	Participant/Data characteristics	Central procedures	Central citations for variants of method
Ethnographic & auto-ethnographic analysis	To identify cultural themes and processes in every-day life experiences of a specified individual or group.	Typically approaches are from within constructivist and critical perspectives in psychology.	Data are typically collected by researchers living within a culture or a situation over a period of time. Diaries, cultural artefacts, and field notes are often used.	Ethnography (E): Collecting and analyzing patterns in observations to identify the functions of cultural activities and processes. Autoethnography (AE): Fusing autobiographical and ethnographic methods.	E: Hammersley & Atkinson, 2019 AE: Ellis et al., 2011; Jones, Adams, & Ellis, 2013
Task analysis	To identify the steps or stages via which tasks are performed successfully.	Research is grounded in a model of dialectical constructivism in which researchers begin with a theoretical rational model that is then transformed through empirical analysis.	Data comprise successful and unsuccessful tasks that can be subjected to analysis.	The initial model is assessed using qualitative analyses to develop a new empirical model, which is turn validated using quantitative analyses.	Greenberg, 2007; Pascual-Leone & Greenberg, 2009
Case studies	To examine a case to develop an understanding of a person or episode, or to disprove an extant theory.	Approaches to case studies exist from across epistemological perspectives.	Data must provide detailed description of a case and its context.	Methods have varied forms, such as narrative, pragmatic, outcome-oriented, theory-building, and quasi-judicial case studies.	McLeod, 2010; Stiles, 2009; Rabinovich & Kacen, 2009

research question) rather than in relation to a theory of meaning-making (i.e., narrative theory). In contrast, narrative researchers often view narratives as rhetorical devices through which people represent themselves to both themselves and others. Qualitative narrative psychotherapy research can analyze entire life stories, stories told within or about people's lives, or stories related to specific topics or concerns in sessions. Narratives can be studied in isolation, as they evolve across sessions, as patterns across narratives (e.g., transference analyses), or as indications of their historical and cultural context.

Procedural Elements Common to Categorizing Qualitative Approaches

Although these varieties of qualitative methods each have brand-specific elements, their commonalities can provide an understanding of how they function to develop descriptions and interpretations of psychotherapy processes and outcomes. They guide researchers to engage in a bottom-up process of analysis intended to organize meanings, typically from interview transcripts, into a categorical framework.

Developing Researcher Capacity for Reflexivity. Throughout the course of their research – through the design, data collection, analysis, and writeup – researchers using these approaches work to adopt an attitude of both self-awareness and openness so that their own expectations will not prevent them from hearing the experiences of their participants. There are a variety of process that have been recommended across the approaches in this camp for developing this attitude.

An analytic strategy, borrowed from phenomenology, is to work to enter a state of *epoché* in which the researcher seeks to suspend their judgment and adopt an attitude of curiosity, and then will *bracket* assumptions in order to maximize their potential to hear their interviewee (Giorgi, 2009). In contrast, hermeneutic researchers tend not to believe that researchers cannot set aside their beliefs, because many are unconscious or ingrained in our thought processes, cultures, and languages, and so instead they recommend that researchers deliberately develop awareness of how their assumptions might influence research and engage in focused exploration of alternatives theories (e.g., Elliott, 2015). Grounded theory researchers have had varied stances on the extent to which researchers should become familiar with existing theories and literature, with some being concerned to avoid bias (Glaser & Strauss, 1967) and others arguing that it can increase sensitivity in coding (Charmaz, 2006). Also, some grounded theory researchers will encourage engaging in bracketing while being aware of its limitations (see Rennie, 2000 on fallible bracketing).

Researchers have a variety of ways in which to structure this process of self-reflection. Some engage in research journaling, field notes, or memoing (e.g., Glaser & Strauss, 1967) and some will hold discussions within their teams to consider their assumptive frameworks (e.g., Hill, 2012). Across these approaches to qualitative methods, however, researchers seek ways to manage their expectations and desires about findings in order to limit their undue influence on the research process. Further discussion around the nature of researcher reflexivity can be found in a later section on challenges associated with qualitative research.

Developing Units to Identify Meanings. Although it is possible to apply these categorizing methods of analysis to recordings or observations, typically they are applied to transcripts of sessions or interviews with therapists or clients. In any case, the dataset is divided into units that capture the meanings expressed within the data for closer analysis. There are two main steps in this process: the identification of units and the labeling of meanings therein. The process of unitizing centers around the identification and labeling of context that answers the research question. For instance, when creating meaning units, phenomenologists divide the text so that each unit contains one meaning that answers the question at hand (Giorgi, 2009). In this way, each of these meanings is subjected to focused analysis. Depending on the specific method in use, these meanings might be conceptualized as themes, narrative elements, descriptions, or interpretations, which can influence the analytic process.

As the units are created, they are assigned a label, which condenses the amount of text with which analysts have to work and makes the analysis more efficient. Researchers often attempt to create labels grounded in the language of the participants to closely capture their experiences, although sometimes the researcher may develop phrases that can summarize a section of text with great fidelity as well. For instance, a client may tell a long story to describe a transferential reaction without using that term, but a researcher might find it more efficient to use that label as it is more concise and describes the dynamics at hand.

The label should be developed so that it summarizes the meaning in such a way that it answers the question at hand. For instance, consider the following section of an interview in which a client describes the therapeutic experience of recovering from grief:

> *Client:* My mother died about a year ago in July and I have been struggling since with feelings of depression. What was most important was that my therapist was able to allow me to talk about my anger toward my mother and support those feelings that I can't talk about with others. Typically, people expect that when a parent dies, the children should be in mourning and there is a great deal of social pressure to experience sadness, and guilt if you don't. But my mother was abusive and narcissistic, and I mostly felt angry at how she treated members of our family and relief that we wouldn't have to deal with that in the future.

When creating units, researchers will want to hold in mind that the research question is how therapists work with complicated grief in therapy. The first sentence in the unit, although useful for contextualizing the description and containing discrete information, does not provide any guidance for the therapist, so it would be included within the first unit, rather than becoming a unit itself. In thinking about labeling this unit, researchers also should be careful about creating units that are so small that they do not capture what is psychologically meaningful. For instance, a unit like, "Clients in grief desire therapists' support" would be accurate but it would miss most of the rich meaning in this text. In contrast, a longer label can capture the dynamic of concern: "Clients need support to process grief-related anger, which is not socially acceptable and can lead to guilt." This label orients therapists to a specific client issue, suggests an in-session response, and tells them how to conceptualize underlying processes. If the labels do not capture the meanings in the data, the insight that can be developed from the analysis is limited.

Developing Themes or Categories. Across the methodological approaches in the categorizing traditions, researchers examine the labels that they have assigned to their units in order to identify patterns. In this process, researchers group together units that share similar meanings, patterns, and processes. Sometimes researchers will organize the data into domains that represent their main questions before they begin the process of identifying patterns in the answers (e.g., consensual qualitative analysis), but in other categorizing methods (e.g., grounded theory, phenomenology), researchers will look across all the data to create categories of shared meanings.

By examining units together, researchers identify trends in the data and represent experiences that cross participants. For instance, the example meaning unit above might be placed into a category of similar other units called "Focused support from therapists may be required to help clients accept emotions that are not socially condoned." By comparing each of the units to one another a list of categories is created that further reduces the amount of data under consideration.

Sometimes the analysis will stop there because these initial categories provide a rich enough answer for the question at hand (e.g., content analysis). In many categorizing methods, however, after researchers identify these initial categories they continue to examine them and begin to organize the initial descriptions, themes, or categories in order to reach a higher level of conceptualizations. This process moves the analysis to a more abstract level so it describes commonalities across the initial categories. For instance, the preceding initial category might be organized into a category with other grief reactions that are problematic for clients. The title of this category may read "Grief therapy addresses social harms by creating recognition for aspects of self that are marginalized." Most categorical approaches to qualitative research will stop at this level (e.g., phenomenological, narrative, thematic, consensual qualitative approaches), but grounded theory analysis usually will continue to organize categories until a hierarchy is developed with a core category that captures a central meaning – in this case, maybe commenting on the how therapy subverts the socially constructed moral code for grief.

The epistemological assumptions used would influence the objectives of the study and the that categorization would take as well. The categorization process described here might be typical of a constructivist researcher who is interested in examining how meaning evolves in therapy. In contrast, a realist researcher might seek to develop categories that could be reliably coded by others, perhaps en route to developing a process measure specific to complicated grief that identified the degrees to which aspects of grief were assimilated (e.g., Wilson et al., submitted). A critical researcher might seek to develop categories that explicate the social mechanisms that distort experiences of grief – perhaps connecting social expectations to dominant religious beliefs or cultural filial expectations.

When creating labels for categories, researchers carefully work to represent the experiences of their participants. Qualities that strengthen category labels include: evocatively representing the lived experience of the phenomenon, using language that is precise enough to be useful, highlighting participants' agency, and contextualizing the finding to show its boundaries (Levitt, McLeod et al., 2020). Category labels should be written to answer the questions being asked by the researchers, rather than duplicate those questions. (For instance, a study on how clients develop alliances should not have categories called, "Ways clients develop alliances" or "Reasons for having a good alliance," but instead they should explicate the ways alliance develops and articulate those reasons).

There are three reasons why this set of methods might be dominant in psychotherapy research:

1. The production of a system of categories gives the findings flexibility in terms of their application as they identify a number of the central experiences or components of a phenomenon. This can be helpful, for instance, when researchers are describing the aspects of a phenomenon, developing a treatment with multi-components, a training program with modules, or a measure with subscales.

2. Also, methods that identify layers of categories allow researchers to describe the evolution of the higher order findings by referencing the lower layers. They lead to understandings and explanations that can be easily justified in reporting and peer review because it is evident how they are grounded in the data.

3. These approaches to qualitative research are typically conducted based upon interview data and inquire into the internal experience of clients and therapists. This means that they use a type of data and allow a form of meaning-making that is similar to the processes of understanding naturally used by therapists (Rennie, 2007).

In selecting between categorizing approaches to qualitative methods, researchers may wish to consider the fit with their project question and values and how the form of the findings produced (e.g., essential meanings, narrative themes, a hierarchy of categories) will serve their goals.

Conversation Analysis

Conversation analysis studies the moment-by-moment evolution of talk, seeking to describe how it is organized as sequences of actions, such as turn-taking, preferred sequences, placement of silences, and conversational rupture and repair (Schegloff, 2007). It has been applied in research on psychotherapy (Labov & Fanshell, 1977; Madill, 2015; Peräkylä et al., 2008; Smoliak & Strong, 2018) as well as on many other sorts of conversations (Sidnell & Stivers, 2013).

Conversation analysis is a relatively circumscribed research tradition within a broader range of approaches that has been called discourse analysis or, as applied in psychology, discursive psychology (Glynos et al., 2009; Strong & Smoliak, 2018). These generally qualitative approaches explicitly approach psychology through language and associated expression. Phenomena treated as mental processes by most psychological theories of psychology are understood as constituted through discourse. Within the range of discursive approaches, conversation analysis tends to take a more micro-perspective, focusing descriptively on the details of talk, in contrast with, for example, critical discourse analysis (e.g., Potter & Wetherell 1987, 1995), which takes a relatively macro-perspective, attending to the role of talk in social structure, institutions, and power relations. However, the methods and foci of discursive approaches overlap in their close, descriptive attention to the patterns in what people actually say and do when they interact.

Peräkylä (2013) organized conversation analysis research on psychotherapy into research topics concerning sequentially organized therapeutic *practices* and topics concerning aspects of *the client-therapist relationship*, as realized through their interaction. The practices included (a) formulations, in which the therapist suggests a meaning of what the client has said, (b) interpretations, arguably a subset of formulations, focused specifically on placing the client's experience into a theoretical or therapeutic frame of reference – along with responses to the interpretation, and (c) questions, which included work on question-driven therapies, in which, to a large extent, therapeutic interventions are framed as grammatical questions. The relationship-focused topics included the conversational manifestations of (d) resistance, (e) affiliation, and (f) emotion. Each of these topics can be considered both in relation to regularities in the sequences observed and the therapeutic work thereby performed (Peräkylä, 2019).

Conversation analysis seeks to describe participants' actions and practices in a particular sort of interaction, such as emotion-focused therapy or diagnostic interviews. The actions are usually speech acts – asking, telling, requesting, offering, inviting, complaining, and so forth, while the practices refer to the conversational tasks that the actions are meant to perform. For example, asking questions (action) may be part of such therapy practices as gathering information, displaying interest, or suggesting an alternative way of viewing an experience. The analysis involves identifying and characterizing practices by describing the sequences of actions involved.

Many of the conversational patterns that conversation analyses study, such as the cues that permit smooth turn-taking, occur without participants noticing. Many are too routine, components of social skills, practiced without thinking, and some are too subtle or too brief to permit participants to simultaneously do them and attend to them. Consequently, asking people what they did in a conversation is not a useful approach. It is necessary to observe what people actually do moment-by-moment by intensively studying the nuances of talk, moving back and forth between examining the details of particular instances and an overview of the practice under study. To this end, from its beginnings, conversation analysis has sought precision by using recordings that can be repeatedly replayed and by developing highly detailed systems of transcription (Sacks et al., 1974). The transcriptions seek to represent not only the lexical elements, but also the paralinguistic parts of talk – pauses, emphasis, timing, inbreaths, disfluencies, overtalk, and much else, on the now-well-supported assumption that they often constitute essential parts of the conversation.

Conversation analysts emphasize the importance of grounding their analysis of practices in observations. They are helped by a bit of reasoning that has been called the *next-turn proof procedure*. The recipient's response to an action shows how he or she understood the prior turn, and this can be used to ground the analysis. Of course, not all recipients respond as expected. But deviant cases often provide the strongest evidence for the analysis because they show participants' understanding of the practice most clearly. For example, the recipient of a question may not answer it but may nevertheless show in the actual response that he or she should have answered (Sidnell, 2013).

Sidnell (2013) organized the typical conversation analysis procedure into three steps. (Strictly speaking, there must be a prior, very important step of selecting what material to study.)

Step 1. Observation. Like many qualitative approaches, conversation analysis begins with a familiarization step. For conversation analysis, this typically involves reviewing recordings and transcripts of one or more interactions, usually of a particular type, such as psychotherapy sessions. Typically, this is more intensive than extensive, for example replaying recordings and re-reading transcripts many times.

During this initial observation, investigators are meant to be open to alternative possibilities to let interesting phenomena emerge from the material, as figure emerges from ground. This step is meant to be open-ended, though it is of course guided by the interests that informed the choice of what material to observe, by an orientation to fine-grained details of the talk and associated behaviors (e.g., paralinguistic vocalizations, gesture, gaze, posture), by an interest in identifying recurrent or stable patterns at a fine-grained scale, and by a vocabulary and repertoire of analytic tools acquired during the analyst's training and socialization (e.g., see Schegloff, 2007). The vocabulary (e.g., adjacency pairs, preferred sequences, lexical substitution, local editing) are not organized into a unified theory but draw on the conversation analysis lore and literature. These influences tend to make the observations germane to the discipline, but they also leave plenty of room for novelty and creativity. A key experience of this observation takes the form of *I've seen that before*. Fostering this emergence of figure from ground demands immersion in the data. And it forms the basis for the next step.

Step 2. Identifying and collecting a phenomenon. The second step moves from observing something interesting in one or a few fragments of conversation to identifying a phenomenon to study and collecting instances. Gaete Silva et al. (2018) identified what they called reflexive questions, utterances that are grammatically questions but also indirectly advance a therapeutic interpretation or advice, for example, "If you did raise these worries with her, do you think she would take it as a lack of trust? . . . As an intrusion into her privacy? . . . Or as an indication of your caring as a parent?" Ekberg et al. (2013) studied question-answer-response sequences in cognitive behavioral therapy that was conducted online via chat. They focused on the therapist's third position actions, that is, what the therapist did after the client answered the therapist's question. In each case, having identified a phenomenon, the investigators gathered a corpus of instances from session recordings and analyzed these in the third step.

Step 3. Describing a practice. The final step is describing the use and function of the identified phenomenon, as manifested in the collected corpus of instances. Typically, the phenomenon of interest can be shown to function within a pattern of interaction that in turn serves (or sometimes fails to serve) the purposes of the conversation.

For example, the analysis of reflexive questions by Gaete Silva et al. (2018) showed how these questions enact both the power relationships between therapist and client and the delicate negotiation about therapeutic interpretations. By carrying their interpretive or directive message, reflexive questions redirect the client's understanding and thus exercise the therapist's power. On the other hand, the question form places the message in a less presumptuous package than a bald interpretation or directive would, so it allows more leeway for negotiation and may have less potential for offense.

In their study of the therapist's third position responses, Ekberg et al. (2013) differentiated three types of actions: *thanking*, *commiseration*, and *emotional inference*. Their analysis suggested that the choice among these depended on the level of emotion in the client's answer. Therapists could respond to less emotional answers with a nonemotional thank you, whereas the more emotional answers required the other types of responses. Client answers that included a first-person emotion description called for commiseration, whereas answers that conveyed the emotion indirectly called for emotional inference. It is challenging to use any brief example, however, to capture conversation analyses, given their focus on the context, richness, and variety of conversation.

A distinctive practice that serves conversation analysis as a method of analysis and of dissemination is the data session. An investigator meets with a group, which may be a research team or a group of interested colleagues (data sessions are given program time at conversation analysis conferences). In a typical data session, the investigator selects a stretch of talk (based on having taken the three steps listed above), such as part of a dinner table conversation or a psychotherapy session, provides a detailed transcript, and plays the recording repeatedly for the group. After several repetitions, the group selects a brief segment (perhaps a minute or less) to focus on. This segment is then played several times, and the group is then given time to make notes of their impressions – what is happening and what is interesting. There may be requests for further repetitions. After this, group members take turns describing their impressions, the investigation taking the last turn. There may then be a more general discussion and synthesis. Investigators use this process both to gather ideas for their analysis and synthesis and to share their work with colleagues.

Ethnographic and Autoethnographic Research

The *ethnographic* methods represent a long-established alternative tradition in qualitative inquiry to the analysis of data from interviews and session transcripts. Ethnography is based on the assumption that, in order to develop a full appreciation of the meaning of an experience for an individual or group of people, it is necessary not only to listen to what they say but also to observe what they do. The technique of participant observation, also known as ethnographic fieldwork, involves the researcher getting close to the lives and experiences of those being studied, by

spending time with them in everyday contexts (Hammersley & Atkinson, 2019). Ethnography is a methodological approach that aims to identify cultural themes and processes in everyday life experience, using analysis of researcher personal participation in and observation of everyday activities, researcher and informant diaries, cultural artifacts such as personal and official documents, objects, images and music, and informal interviews. To do justice to the wealth of descriptive detail that is collected, ethnographic studies are typically published in monograph or book formats.

Although ethnographic methods have been widely used in disciplines such as social anthropology, social work, and education, they have been rarely deployed in psychotherapy research, primarily because of ethical concerns arising from the private nature of the therapy encounter, and because they are highly time-consuming. Calls for wider use of ethnographic methodologies in counseling and psychotherapy research have been made by Bartholomew and Brown (2019) and Suzuki et al. (2005). Published ethnographic studies of psychotherapy include explorations of clinics (Larsen, 2001; McKinney, 2007; Waldram, 2007a,b), and studies of experiences of clients (Dreier, 2008; Mackrill, 2007) and therapists (Craciun, 2016, 2017, 2018).

An important methodological turn within the field of social anthropology was triggered by appreciation of a realization that participant observation could never be a purely detached process. Instead, it became clear that many of the most significant insights generated by ethnographers arose from reflection on the personal meaning and impact of immersion in a different cultural milieu. This notion resulted in the development of autoethnography – the fusion of autobiography and ethnography for the purpose of generating intensely personal narrative understanding of specific cultural and social contexts (Chang, 2008; Ellis et al., 2011; Jones, Adams, & Ellis, 2013; McLeod, 2015). Although other approaches to the study of personal experience have been developed, such as mindful inquiry (Bentz & Shapiro 1998), reflexive action research (Lees 2001), transpersonal research (Braud & Anderson 1998), dialogical research (Halling et al., 2006), heuristic inquiry (Douglass & Moustakas 1985; Moustakas 1990), and narrative inquiry (Etherington, 2002), autoethnography has emerged as the most influential and widely used methodology within this tradition.

Autoethnographic data are generated though activities such as both stream-of-consciousness and reflective writing, interviewing significant others within one's life, being interviewed, and analysis of personal diaries, photographs and creative art work. Such data are typically presented in terms of vivid first-person narrative accounts of autobiographical scenes or episodes that are relevant to the topic of the study: a key principle in the reporting of autobiographical analyses is to "show" as well as "tell." The value of an autoethnographic study depends to a large extent on the courage and willingness of the researcher to reflect critically and honestly on their own experience. Autoethnographic research can also be conducted by pairs or groups of researchers (Bright et al., 2012; Sawyer, & Norris, 2012). Autoethnographic studies in psychotherapy include accounts of various aspects of what it is like to be a client (Brooks, 2011; Fox, 2014; McKenzie, 2015, or a therapist (Grant, 2006, 2010a, 2010b; Hills et al., 2018; Moxnes, 2006;

McIlveen, 2007; Meekums, 2008; Olson, 2015; Råbu et al., in press; Rober, & Rosenblatt, 2017; Speciale et al., 2015), or to work together in therapy (Etherington, 2000; McMillan, & Ramirez, 2016).

Compared to other forms of qualitative therapy research, the distinctive features of ethnographic and autoethnographic studies are that they provide richly described accounts of areas of experience that are beyond the scope of other methodologies. Such approaches have been viewed as possessing a unique *heuristic* function (Moustakas, 1990), through intentionally seeking to stimulate new ways of understanding that will in turn function as catalysts for action.

Task Analysis

Task analysis emerged as an area of research that seeks to develop a deeper understanding of the nature of successful task-completion in therapy. Task analysis has a history in industrial settings and in cognitive psychology that predate its use in psychotherapy research (see Greenberg, 1984, 2007; Rice & Greenberg, 1984). Although early task analysis studies in psychotherapy were based on quantitative measures (Wiseman & Rice, 1989), its subsequent application to psychotherapy research was informed by an appreciation on the part of Laura Rice and Leslie S. Greenberg of the limitations of trying to describe the psychological change process using quantitative sequential analysis process measures:

> . . .we found that sequential analysis . . . failed to capture some of the more qualitative and contextually significant aspects of the change phenomena we were observing. . . . We, therefore, moved to a more intensive, observational method, . . . which relied on identifying and describing key change events (Rice & Greenberg, 1984). We conceptualized therapy as consisting of events composed of markers and tasks and developed task analysis to study the performance of the client changes in these key change events. (Greenberg, 2007, p. 16)

Task analysis, as developed for research on psychotherapy by this group, employs an observational, inductive and iterative strategy, in which investigators use observations of individuals performing tasks to progressively improve descriptions of how the task can best be performed. It is a qualitative method aimed at describing, step-by-step how therapists and clients go about resolving problems that emerge in therapy, such as unfinished business with significant others or ruptures in the alliance. The descriptions of the method specify a sequence of procedural steps for clinician-investigators engaging in the task of task analysis. The number and names of the steps in the procedure have differed in detail in various tellings (e.g., Benítez-Ortega & Garrido-Fernández 2016; Greenberg, 1984, 2007; Greenberg & Foerster, 1996; Pascual-Leone & Greenberg, 2009; Rice & Greenberg, 1984), but they converge on a core iterative process. The procedure begins by selecting a type of problem-solving task, such as resolving unfinished business with a significant other, and identifying in-session markers of the problem.

Using all available information, including available literature, personal clinical experience, and talking with expert therapists, the clinician-investigator then constructs a *rational model*, that is, an analysis of how the problem might be solved. The rational model tries to describe how the task can be accomplished as a series of steps, from recognizing clinical markers of the problem through to successful completion. Next the investigator conducts an empirical (qualitative) study of actual problem-solving in successful instances of the task drawn from recordings and transcripts of therapy sessions, describing what actually happens in a sort of reverse engineering of the performance. This is called the *empirical model*. The investigator then compares the empirical model with the rational model and adjusts the latter to fit the former, so that an integrated model develops that is consistent with both accounts. The product is called the *rational-empirical model*.

The rational-empirical model is then refined by alternating empirical analysis of further successful (and contrasting unsuccessful) recordings of instances with reconciliation of the results with the previous rational-empirical model. When saturation is reached – that is, when analysis of further instances no longer leads to changes, as described earlier in the section on grounded theory – the final model can be verified by comparing instances of successful and unsuccessful task completions to see if they follow the described steps. The outcomes of clients who have been successful or unsuccessful with the task can be also be compared.

Conducting a task analysis requires an understanding of the therapeutic process. Investigators must have the expertise to construct a clinically sensitive rational model of solving clinical tasks and then to refine it in light of observations of clinical performances. Thus, task analysis is best done by clinician-investigators rather than by nonclinicians. An important emphasis of all versions of task analytic instructions has been the need to explicitly identify markers and measurement criteria for the problems and steps in task resolution. These are meant to be framed in a way that they can be used both by investigators and by therapists trying to resolve these problems with their own clients.

Qualitative Case Studies

Most qualitative research is case-based or interview-based, and often these overlap. Even research on multiple cases involves intensive analysis of data from small samples. Qualitative case study researchers look closely at one case at a time and report sufficient narrative detail for the reader to get a sense of the specific person, or therapy episode (Flyvbjerg, 2001). For example, identifying themes within an interview transcript requires the researcher to make sense of informant statements in the context of previous and subsequent statements while taking account of both the settings described and the interview setting. Thus, a considerable amount of interpretive meaning-making occurs before an analytic code is formulated. The eventual list of themes or categories from a sample of informants – often regarded as the core findings of a qualitative study – requires the researcher to engage with the complexity and uniqueness of each participant in the study.

Qualitative research represents an "analyze then aggregate" knowledge-generation strategy, in contrast to the "aggregate-then-analyze" approach used in statistically based studies (Eells, 2010). Perhaps as a result, case-based approaches often yield findings that differ from statistically based investigations of the same topic (Eells, 2010). Recent work in philosophy of science suggests that analysis of single cases is more appropriate than analysis of average effects for generating knowledge about causation (Anjum, & Mumford, 2018; Maxwell, 2012).

Historically, analyzing clinical cases has been central to the development of theories of therapy. However, traditional clinical case studies that are written by the therapist solely on the basis of personal recall and scrutiny of case notes are open to criticism on the grounds that what is reported in filtered through the preexisting ideas and theory of the therapist, with little scope for independent external scrutiny. Qualitative and mixed-method (i.e., quantitative and qualitative) approaches to collecting and analyzing case data have helped make case study analyses more credible and methodologically robust. As a result, in recent years there has been a steady growth in the number of case studies published in leading psychotherapy research journals (e.g., *Psychotherapy Research*; *Journal of Counseling Psychology*).

Four Types of Case Study

We distinguish four types of therapy case study: *narrative*, *pragmatic*, *outcome-oriented*, and *theory-building* (McLeod, 2010). *Narrative* case studies aim to tell the story of the therapy from the perspective of the client and/or therapist, using thematic analysis of interview data. For example, Wendt and Gone (2016) carried out a series of interviews with a young American Indian man around his use of psychotherapy to rediscover and apply indigenous healing practices as a means of overcoming his depression. The findings arising from these interviews were presented as narrative accounts of therapy episodes that were viewed by the informant as having been particularly meaningful for him. Procedures for collecting and analyzing data were reported in a narrative style, and emergent themes were discussed in relation to previous research.

Pragmatic case studies document how a specific model of therapy was applied in a particular case (Fishman, 1999). They are usually grounded in therapist notes and observations, supplemented by other available data such as verbatim or transcribed session content, and process/outcome measures. For example, Pass (2012) described how she combined psychodynamic techniques and expressive writing with a client who had experienced single-incident trauma. Readers were told how the guiding conceptual principles and professional knowledge of the therapist were implemented, and produced specific effects. Studies using the pragmatic case study protocol differ from traditional clinical case studies in their comprehensive documentation and their standard format for analysis and presentation.

Outcome-oriented case studies aim to determine the extent to which the case can be considered to have a good outcome. By contrast with the enriching purpose of narrative and pragmatic case studies, outcome-oriented case studies have a product-testing purpose. Outcome-oriented case studies can help establish the potential effectiveness of new interventions, established

interventions with new client groups, or integrative/hybrid approaches. We note two main approaches to outcome-focused therapy case study: One approach is the $n = 1$ or single subject design method, widely applied in research on behavioral interventions. This is based in time-series analysis of quantitative symptom or behavioral measures, so it is not an example of qualitative research. The other outcome-oriented case study approach is a set of mixed-method, quasi-judicial methodologies, of which the best established is the Hermeneutic Single-Case Efficacy Design (HSCED; Elliott, 2002) approach. In an HSCED study, rich case data are collected, including process and outcome measures administered throughout therapy, and the client is interviewed. This information is assembled into a case book, which is subjected to critical interpretive analysis from two contrasting perspectives. An affirmative position constructs an interpretation to support the conclusion that the client benefited from therapy. By contrast, the sceptic position constructs an interpretation to support the conclusion that either the client did not benefit from therapy or that any observed gains could be attributed to non-therapy factors such as life events. These competing interpretations are developed by separate research teams, who then seek to rebut each other's arguments. Finally, the affirmative and sceptic briefs, rebuttals, and rejoinders are passed to expert judges, who assess the confidence with which it can be concluded that the case had a good- or a poor-outcome. For a good example of the HSCED approach, see Elliott et al. (2009).

The fourth distinctive genre of case study research comprises *theory-building* case studies, in which existing theories are tested, and if necessary further articulated, in the light of how adequately they are supported by case data (Stiles, 2009). The use of this kind of iterative case-based theory development has a long history within psychoanalytic theory (e.g., Freud, 1953/1905) and been a central aspect of critical debate within psychoanalysis and psychodynamic psychotherapy. It has continuing importance in, for example, attachment theory (e.g., Wiseman & Atzil-Slonim, 2018), assimilation theory (e.g., Brinegar et al., 2006; Caro Gabalda et al., 2016; Wilson et al., submitted), and rupture-repair theory (e.g., Safran & Muran, 1996). A comprehensive program of qualitative theory-building case study research has been used to develop the assimilation model of therapeutic change (Stiles, 2011; for an example, see Brinegar et al., 2006). Another example of theory-building case study research comprises a series of cases that aimed to develop a theory of therapist immediacy (Hill et al., 2008; Kasper et al., 2008; Mayotte-Blum et al., 2012). In theory-building case-study research, the intention is to collect case data that is explicitly relevant to the guiding theory, and to use an interpretive qualitative approach to explore the degree to which the existing conceptualization is consistent with what has been observed in the case, or needs to be altered or adjusted in some way.

Some therapy case studies may serve more than one of these purposes. For example, Quinn et al. (2012) carried out a series of narrative case studies based on therapist and client accounts of their work together around using therapy to come to terms with psychogenic seizures. As well as producing richly described stories of what happened in these therapies, this study also yielded a theoretical model that was then further explored through later studies. Somewhat similarly, Halvorsen et al. (2016) used a narrative case study to develop a conceptualization of what had been helpful in long-term therapy with a highly suicidal client.

Methodological Innovations from Case Studies

Qualitative analysis of data from therapy cases has been associated with a number of significant areas of methodological innovation. In addition, principles drawn from the methodological literature of many social science disciplines (Byrne & Ragin, 2009; George & Bennett, 2005; Yin, 2018) have influenced qualitative and mixed-methods case study research in psychotherapy in such matters as case selection, the collection of rich case data, time-series analysis/process tracing, use of team-based data analysis, and adoption of standardized reporting formats (McLeod, 2010).

A distinctive aspect of qualitative analysis of case-based data, in comparison with data produced through interviews, is the need to take account of processes that unfold over time. Therapy case studies need to tell the story of what happened across sessions, often from the start of therapy to the end. The researcher must undertake some form of qualitative time-series or process tracing analysis and consider potential causal links. How were later events in therapy shaped by earlier events? One of two main sources of evidence for sequences has been the analysis of observed shifts between one time period and the next – for instance, a shift in the answers that the client gives on a depression scale, or a change in the way they talk in the session. Another source has been client (or therapist) attributions for observed changes. For example, if the client is invited to tell the story of turning points in their therapy, or of what they believe may have brought about gains in an appropriate way, their narrative can convey their sense of what changed and what actions brought about the change. Researchers have developed new tools for collecting such information on sequences, such as the Client Change Interview protocol (Rodgers & Elliott, 2015).

A further methodological innovation within case study research is a quasi-judicial approach to data analysis (Bohart et al., 2011; Bohart et al., 2011; Elliott, 2002; McLeod, 2010; Miller et al., 2011). This approach notes that, as in legal cases, the interpretation of therapy cases is likely to be influenced by personal values and beliefs. Observers may deal with case complexity and ambiguity by focusing on certain evidence and disregarding other evidence. Legal systems have, over many centuries, devised ways of handling these factors through case law and lore regarding the admissibility or weighting given to different types of evidence, standardized procedures for presenting arguments and rebuttals, and adjudication through an independent judge and jury. Adapting these principles and procedures to clinical case studies helps address criticisms of bias and selective reporting. The HSCED approach represents the most fully articulated application of this quasi-judicial principles to case study research (Benelli, Biffi, De Carlo, & McLeod, 2015; Elliott, 2002; Elliott and Widdowson, 2017; Wall et al., 2017).

Other team-based data analysis procedures have also been developed to make use of observers' differing perspectives, including Consensual Qualitative Case Analysis (Jackson, Chui, & Hill, 2012) and the Ward method (Schielke et al., 2009; Smith et al., 2014). However, the quasi-judicial procedures such as HSCED systematically enforce a diversity and creativity of interpretive perspectives by assigning investigators to "affirmative" and "skeptic" teams (see, for example, the appendices to Elliott et al., 2009). The striking capacity for generating opposing but plausible data interpretations by teams of researchers who generally share the same ideas and professional socialization experiences deserves continued exploration.

Psychotherapy case study researchers have also developed mixed methods approaches to research, that is, ways to combine qualitative and qualitative methods (see also the following section on mixed methods). As one example, quantitative measures completed on a regular schedule (e.g., at each session), provide a basis for time-series analysis and identification of significant change events. These forms of statistical data can then be triangulated against qualitative information from therapy transcripts, open-ended instruments such as the Helpful Aspects of Therapy (HAT) forms (Llewelyn, 1988), and interviews. Such approaches invite attention to paradoxical findings, where qualitative and quantitative data support different conclusions, as well as convergence across data sources (Desmet, 2018). Interpretive frameworks such as HSCED (Elliott, 2002) have been developed to handle mixed methods data. Quantitative information from process and symptom measures on large groups of clients, for example in clinical trials, makes it possible to locate a particular case within a broader population of clients. For example, contrasting good- and poor-outcome cases from a large-scale outcome study can be subjected to qualitative case analysis, to explore the meaning quantitative findings and to communicate findings in a form that is accessible to clinicians (Fishman et al., 2017).

The increasing number of published therapy case studies has opened up possibilities for meta-analysis (Iwakabe, & Gazzola, 2009). Examples of case study meta-analysis include Rabinovich and Kacen (2009) and Willemsen et al. (2015); see also the later section on qualitative meta-analysis. Theory-building case studies can also be aggregated and synthesized within the guiding theory, as described earlier. Such work is facilitated by development of a comprehensive on-line archive of therapy case studies, at the University of Ghent, Belgium (Desmet et al., 2013).

Mixed Methods

As qualitative research has risen in use within psychology, so has mixed method research (Creswell & Plano Clark, 2011; Tashakkori, & Teddlie, 2010). In these approaches to research, quantitative and qualitative methods both are used within the same research design to strengthen the returns of each analysis. (The term *multimethods* tends to be used to describe the use of multiple methods within either quantitative or qualitative methods; Hesse-Biber & Johnson, 2015.) These approaches require researchers to design both qualitative and quantitative research elements that are rigorous and advance knowledge in their area of inquiry. The evaluation of these designs hinges not only on the evaluation of both sets of methods but also on how they are incorporated to advance the research program (Tashakkori & Teddlie, 2010).

One motivation for the growth in these methods has been the interest shown by the US National Institute of Health (see http://sigs.nih.gov/cultural/Pages/default.aspx, November 7, 2013). The Office of Behavioral and Social Science Research commissioned a report on best practices for mixed-methods research to provide guidance for developing competitive applications, evaluating these proposals, and for the office when selecting reviewers, setting priorities and establishing new initiatives (Creswell et al., 2011). This report described types of mixed-method designs, strategies to develop infrastructure and teamwork for these designs, and ways to plan and review applications.

Creswell and Plano Clark (2011) described three basic mixed-methods designs that distinguish the sequencing of the qualitative and quantitative methods. Within *convergent* (or *concurrent*) designs, the qualitative and quantitative data are collected and analyzed over the same period of time – sometimes they are analyzed iteratively so the emerging results from both methods inform each other. Within *explanatory sequential* designs researchers first collect and analyze quantitative data and these findings guide the following qualitative data. This design is especially useful when researchers seek qualitative findings to guide the interpretation or application of findings from within an initial quantitative study (e.g., O'Keeffe et al., 2019). *Exploratory sequential designs* have the reverse order and qualitative data and analysis informs the design of later quantitative research. These studies use qualitative research to empirically determine the hypotheses that would be best to explore further within a later phase of quantitative research on topic, leading to greater attunement within experiments from the start. This attunement can allow researchers to examine factors that are missed within quantitative assessments of clinical significance because of their lack of nuance. For example, De Smet et al. (2020) interrogated how *good outcome* is understood by performing a grounded theory analysis of patients in a randomized control trial of depression. They found that the patient narratives were more complex and multidimensional than their quantitative measures of outcome would have suggested, leading to recommendations that statistical indications of clinical meaningful change should be interpreted warily and ideally be contextualized by qualitative research.

Fetters et al. (2013) described how the integration of findings occur within four processes that can occur across these designs. These include *connecting*, when the participants from one method (e.g., qualitative participants) are identified from the recruitment process of another method (e.g., from a quantitative survey); integration through *building* occurs when the data collection of one method informs the other; *merging* leads to integration through the analysis and comparison of the two databases; and *embedding* indicates that data collection and analysis are integrated at multiple points – potentially involving combinations of the methods of integration. The hallmark of a successful mixed-methods study is the demonstration, not only of the use of qualitative and quantitative methods but, of the integration of findings in such a way that the methods become superior to the separate application of each approach.

A task force of the Mixed Methods International Research Association (Mertens et al., 2016) issued a report on the future of mixed methods. In this report they called for the inclusion of clinicians within these research designs in order to enhance both the interpretation and application of findings. They also described the need to use clinicians' own discourses in findings in order to bridge the practice-research gap and encouraged researchers to take up projects related to social inequalities and social injustices. These recommendations appear useful for qualitative psychotherapy researchers as a whole.

Qualitative Meta-Analysis

Qualitative meta-analytic methods allow researchers to synthesize or aggregate findings from primary research studies. They have goals that are similar to quantitative meta-analyses, such as developing a summary of findings across a literature, developing empirically informed theory, evaluating the methods used in an area of research, forming a foundation to guide measure development, and crafting principles to guide practice.

This area is relatively new in psychotherapy research. It was largely spearheaded by Ladislav Timulak who has contributed a number of early reviews to the field (Timulak, 2007 on helpful processes; Timulak & McElvaney 2013 on insight events). Other research teams have followed his example, but the number of qualitative meta-analyses that have been conducted in this area is still quite small. They include studies of the experience of psychotherapy for deaf and hard of hearing people (Gill & Fox, 2012), self-reflection in CBT (Gale & Schröder, 2014), computerized psychotherapy (Knowles et al., 2014), the training of psychotherapists (McGillivray et al., 2015), master therapists (Jennings et al., 2016), clients experiences of psychotherapy (Levitt et al., 2016), mutuality in psychotherapy (Cornelius-White et al., 2018); alliance formation in first sessions (Lavik et al., 2018), mandated personal psychotherapy during training (Murphy et al., 2018), and trauma focused CBT for youth (Neelakantan et al., 2018), and clients' formation of alliances (Noyce & Simpson, 2018). We expect that this will be a growing area in qualitative research as literatures come to contain enough primary research to support meta-analyses.

Qualitative Meta-Analytic Methods and Procedures

There are many forms of qualitative meta-analytic methods (e.g., meta-ethnography, Noblit & Hare, 1988; meta-study, Paterson et al., 2001; meta-summary, Sandelowski & Barroso, 2003) and they have varied sets of procedures and serve different purposes. These include emphasizing cataloging findings, re-analyzing and developing new findings, conducting a critical analysis of findings, and assessing the quality of findings (see Barnett-Page & Thomas, 2009; Timulak & Creaner, 2013 for detailed reviews). In addition to these established forms of meta-analysis, many primary qualitative methods can be adapted to generate a meta-analytic approach by using primary findings in place of raw data.

Qualitative meta-analyses can be used to further the goals of the original research. For instance, qualitative theory-building studies can be aggregated and synthesized within the guiding theory, as in the natural sciences. Or, a meta-analysis of constructivist studies could develop a theory or an overarching understanding of the ways that meanings are formed interpersonally. There are a number of detailed articles with guidance for conducting qualitative meta-analyses tailored for psychotherapy researchers (Levitt, 2018; Timulak, 2009; Timulak & Creaner, 2013). In this section, we describe some of the major approaches to meta-analysis and central steps.

Identifying Studies. The process of locating the primary literature for review is quite similar to the process in quantitative meta-analyses. Researchers typically will enter keywords and terms into electronic databases (e.g., PsycINFO) to locate the primary studies. They will identify in their reports the databases searched, the time period searched, the keywords used, and the languages of studies reviewed. Flow diagrams often are used to describe the process of identifying studies (e.g., Moher et al., 2009; see Swift & Wampold, 2018 for a discussion of this process in quantitative meta-analyses).

Researchers will want to develop a set of inclusion and exclusion criteria for the selection of articles that enables them to focus on their question of interest, but that enables them to locate enough articles to warrant a meta-analysis. These criteria and the process of selecting articles will be reported in the methods section. In terms of quality control, we support Timulak's (2009) suggestion to use studies that have been published. We have not found external criteria proposed for evaluating the quality of primary qualitative research to be useful (e.g., Critical Appraisal Skills Programme, 2017; Paterson et al., 2001), as it either sets too low a bar for quality and assesses only basic issues of design, or it is based on features that are hard to assess given the level of detail provided in most articles (Joanna Briggs Institute, 2007).

Conducting the Meta-Analysis. Since the qualitative meta-analyses in psychotherapy dominantly use categorizing meta-methods, we describe the process of meta-analysis in reference to those approaches. The central steps in a meta-analysis are quite similar to those of a primary analysis but the units of analysis are the findings from the primary studies. Often it may be possible to develop unit labels for a meta-analysis that reflect the labels that were given to findings within the primary studies (e.g., themes, category titles). Some elaboration may be needed to capture the meanings of the findings however (especially when category titles are poorly constructed or when the focus of the meta-analysis extends beyond that of the primary articles). For articles that present their findings in a narrative style, qualitative meta-analysts will need to read through these descriptions to draw out, unitize, and label the central findings.

To facilitate analysis, it is helpful to be as specific as possible about the common psychotherapeutic processes in use rather than to use brand names of orientations or interventions within unit labels. For instance, describing that "clients became aware of their self-criticism" will allow commonalities to be seen that might not be evident if the units were labelled "engaged in cognitive restructuring," "engaged in self-critical chairing," or "discussed the influence of the superego." It may be useful to a broader range of clinicians.

Meta-analysts will work with the units to create categories in much the same way as they would in primary analyses (see prior section on categorizing methods). Researchers will want to be certain that their category titles reflect the central question of the meta-analysis, rather than the questions of the studies that are under analysis, which might be more focused only on an aspect of the larger question. Category names should be long enough to usefully contextualize the findings and to bring to life the experiences conveyed. When there are conflicts within the units, it can be helpful to consider both how best to represent the pattern of differences within the findings (e.g., result happens only when X occurs; result X usually occurs, except for Y; result X is dependent on Y) and how differences in the perspectives of the researchers might have structured their findings, leading them to focus on specific ideas at the exclusion of others. The development of coherence across the findings by explicating patterns within findings will help readers to know how and when to apply them, and to understand which perspectives led to what findings.

Features Specific to Qualitative Meta-Analytic Methods

One way that qualitative meta-analyses may be distinctive from quantitative ones is that researchers may not need to review the entire literature to meet their goals. For quantitative analyses, the analysis of an entire literature is ideal as every effect size can continue to influence the final results of the study. This may not be the case in a qualitative meta-analysis, however.

The numbers of primary studies in these analyses can vary widely (from 2 to over 100, with 12 being an average number; Timulak, 2009). If the goal of the meta-analysis is to develop a new understanding, researchers may conduct analyses of the literature and stop once their analysis has saturated. Saturation is the point at which analyzing new data does not lead to new categories or findings being developed; it indicates that the findings are comprehensive and that data analyses can be halted. To provide an example, in our omnibus review of 109 studies of clients' experiences (Levitt et al., 2016), saturation was reached at 47 studies, with the last 20 studies not creating new categories. (Although we could have halted our review at this point, we continued the review, switching from grounded theory to a content analytic method to make this review possible, because we had an additional goal of assessing the state of the literature.) The success of a meta-analysis should be assessed in relation to its aims.

Another way that these methods are distinctive is that their reporting includes a consideration not only of the meta-analysts' expectations and positionality, but examines these characteristics of the primary researchers as well. There are a variety of ways in which meta-analysts can obtain this information. Most qualitative psychotherapy research articles have been found to include some reflexive statement in which the authors describe their positions or attitudes (80.7% of the literature on clients' experiences of therapy; Levitt, Pomerville et al., 2017), so meta-analysts can look for patterns in those statements. In addition, they can look at authors' other writings to identify their allegiance to certain perspectives and describe their situation in a field.

Researchers also can consider the forms of questions that were asked (and those that were not asked) in the literature under review. For instance, in an analysis of clients' experiences of psychotherapy (Levitt et al., 2016), most researchers were found to have focused either on issues related to multicultural power or on professional power, with very few researchers developing findings focused on the joint influence of both forms of power – so a principle was developed to guide researchers and clinicians to focus on that intersection.

The proliferation of qualitative, qualitative meta-analytic, and mixed methods used in psychotherapy research has been exciting. It has allowed psychotherapy researchers to investigate new questions and to increase the rigor of their programs of research by permitting a deeper understanding of the issues and experiences that they study. This expansion has led to questions about how these methods can be strengthened in research design and how their quality should be evaluated, as we consider in the following section.

EVALUATING THE METHODOLOGICAL INTEGRITY OF QUALITATIVE STUDIES

There has been a long tradition of qualitative researchers working to articulate criteria for evaluating rigor in qualitative methods. Many excellent guidelines have been put forward for the application of single qualitative designs (e.g., Fassinger, 2005; Fine, 2006; Giorgi, 2009; Hoshmand, 2005; Hill, 2012). In addition, sets of criteria have been developed that are particular for epistemological approaches (e.g., Guba & Lincoln, 2005; Morrow, 2005). A smaller set of articles have been developed to identify desirable procedures across qualitative methods (e.g., Elliott et al., 1999; Levitt et al., 2018; Parker, 2004; Stiles, 1993). These papers advanced qualitative methods by noting the procedures that undergirded research quality writ large, shifting the field to consider the distinct logic and common sets of procedures that advance these methods. The identification of these criteria is important because, although graduate programs increasingly offer training in qualitative methods, these courses were not available when most current editors and reviewers were in graduate training.

As qualitative methods advanced in the field, so did a focus on the procedural distinctions between methods rather than the logic underpinning them. This focus was helpful when learning qualitative methods but led to a situation in which journals began to require authors to inflexibly use the sets of procedures initially proposed by the methods' authors, rather than supporting the evaluation of methods and their adaptation in the context of a given study.

In the following section two sets of recommendations for qualitative research are discussed that were developed to address this issue – the latter building upon the former set (Levitt, Motulsky et al., 2017; Levitt et al., 2018). They have been developed to provide guidance for the review, design and reporting of a broad range of qualitative methods and approaches to inquiry. They have been favorably reviewed by qualitative researchers across varied regions and disciplines, having been incorporated into the *American Psychological Association*'s journal article reporting standards (Levitt et al., 2018), endorsed by the *British Journal of Public Health* (Shaw et al., 2019), and recommended to the field of social work in an invited article of the *Journal of Evidence-Based Social Work* (White et al., 2019).

Methodological Integrity in Design and Reviewing

To counter the growing trend in which reviewers were evaluating qualitative methods as fixed sets of procedures (also commented upon by Timulak & Elliott, 2018), a task force of the *Society for Qualitative Inquiry in Psychology* (SQIP) set out to articulate a unified set of principles that would work to evaluate the scientific credibility of the many varied approaches to qualitative research.

Common Inferential Cycles

To address the question of whether there is a sufficient basis of shared similarity to warrant a unified understanding of rigor, the researchers considered the fundamental processes of inquiry. Specifically, they considered the works of methodologists who had considered iterative processes of inferences across qualitative methods.

Across these writings (Osbeck, 2014; Rennie, 2012; Wertz et al., 2011), qualitative researchers were found to analyze data by identifying patterns that initially are rooted in certain instances or sets of data (e.g., units from an interview or data source) and then comparing initial findings to other instances or datasets. They develop a sense of the whole phenomenon as informed by those patterns and through the incremental analysis of new instances. The continued identification of patterns across the analysis of a phenomenon can shift the way the instances are understood, just as the analysis of new instances can shift the way the whole phenomenon is understood. In this way, these writers have theorized that this process, called a *hermeneutic circle*, contains fundamental inferential processes within qualitative inquiry.

It is important to note that this bottom-up cycle of analysis is self-correcting. As new instances are analyzed, their analysis corrects and refines the existing findings, and this continues until the analysis stabilizes. These understandings supported the idea that a unified approach to assessing rigor was possible across the many distinctive qualitative methods and epistemological frameworks.

Defining Methodological Integrity

Across qualitative methods, the concept of *trustworthy* put forward by Lincoln and Guba (1985) had come to signal the worthiness of the research as assessed by readers' faith in its findings. The goal of the task force was to identify the methodological basis of trustworthiness – the method-related aspects lead to the belief that a set of claims is warranted. Instead of identifying the procedural basis for this confidence, however, the task force sought to identify the principles that led to rigorous design decisions so as to support authors to adapt procedures to their specific studies. In consultation with qualitative researchers across a wide variety of approaches to inquiry and research topics in psychology, as well as the board of the *Society of Qualitative Inquiry in Psychology*, the task force put forward a white paper that developed the concept of methodological integrity (Levitt, Motulsky et al., 2017).

Methodological integrity is established when research procedures and designs act to support the goals of specific research projects (i.e., the research questions or aims); respect the approach to inquiry in use (i.e., epistemological framework); and are tailored for the characteristics of the subject matter (e.g., the complexity of the subject and the ability of data sources/participants to participate in research and be insightful) and the investigators (e.g., their identities, lived experiences, resources). Methodological integrity can be evaluated by the consideration of fidelity and utility, as will be described.

Fidelity to the subject matter occurs when researchers use procedures that develop and maintain allegiance to their topic of investigation. The idea is to have the study findings truly reflect the qualities of the subject under study. It should describe those qualities as they are conceived within the researchers' approach to inquiry. For instance, if researchers consider a subject to be socially constructed, their findings should describe how it is constructed and represent that construction faithfully. There are four concepts that can be used to evaluate fidelity – two focused on data collection and two upon data analysis. Fidelity is enhanced via *data adequacy* (i.e., when researchers collect data that shed light upon variations in the research topic that are relevant to the research goals, rather than variations in a population); *perspective management in data collection* (i.e., when researchers recognize and are transparent about the influence of their own perspectives and appropriately limit that influence within data collection); *perspective management in data analysis* (i.e., when they consider and are transparent about how these perspectives influenced or guided their analytic process in order to enhance their perceptiveness); and *groundedness* (i.e., when findings are rooted in data that support them).

Utility in achieving research goals is obtained when researchers select procedures that usefully answer their research questions and address their aims. In qualitative analyses, study objectives can vary widely and so need to be articulated clearly. They may include developing theory, deepening understanding, raising critical consciousness, identifying social practices, forming conceptual frameworks, and developing local knowledge. There are four concepts that can be used to evaluate utility, again with two being relevant for data collection and two for analysis. Utility is strengthened by the *contextualization of data* (i.e., when the presentation of data and contextual features of data collection are made explicit – for instance, their time, location, and cultural situation); by data that can act as a *catalyst for insight* (i.e., when data are collected that provide rich grounds for analyses); by *meaningful contributions* (i.e., when analyses lead to findings that meaningfully advance the analytic goals); and by *coherence among the findings* (i.e., when differences within a set of findings are explained).

Because their assessment is tied to the study aims and approach to inquiry, fidelity and utility always need to be assessed in relation to an individual research project to see if the methods were adapted to meet its goals and increase confidence in the findings developed. Fidelity and utility function independently. A study can represent its subject well but not meet its research aims or produce new insights (having high fidelity but low utility). For instance, a research study that finds

that the psychotherapeutic relationship is important may have high fidelity but not offer much specific guidance for therapists. Or, a study can contribute a potential solution but on the basis of a misrepresentation of the subject (having low fidelity but high utility). Fidelity and utility are both necessary for a study to have methodological integrity.

This concept of methodological integrity was intended to articulate a rationale for researchers to adapt the procedures within the methods they employ so as to strengthen the quality of their research. In the face of a climate in which reviewers have problematically used adherence to the procedural elements of a method as a sort of evaluative checklist (as noted by Levitt, Motulsky et al., 2017; Timulak & Elliott, 2018), researchers can use this concept to support the tailoring of methods to strengthen their work. To provide an example, in a grounded theory study of silences in psychotherapy (Levitt, 2001), it became clear that psychotherapy clients have discrete experiences of productive, neutral, and obstructive silences that need to be rated separately. Forcing the analysis to end in a singular core category, as was typical in grounded theory analyses, would not have supported the fidelity of the research. So, instead of forming a core category that would have compromised fidelity, a process measure to identify silences was formed to enhance its utility. Methods should be adapted to best support the investigation and reporting of the topics they are studying.

Researchers can use the formulation of methodological integrity to help reviewers understand the unique features of qualitative research and reviewers can use it to learn how these features relate to rigor. To provide a few examples, if reviewers question the number of participants within a study, authors can describe the concept of adequacy of data and describe how it uses a distinctive process to determine the number of participants that are required to enhance fidelity. (Also, they can cite that the average number of participants within a meta-method study of qualitative psychotherapy research has been found to be 13; Levitt, Pomerville et al., 2017.) If reviewers wonder why qualitative researchers include a description of their preconceptions, authors can describe how perspective management strengthens utility. Or, when reviewers are seeking to understand generalization in qualitative research, they can describe how fidelity and utility bolsters that process (Levitt, 2021b; see later section in this chapter on generalization).

The framework of methodological integrity is meant to guide researchers, reviewers, and editors from across epistemological perspectives and methods to understand shared criteria for rigor. It is not intended to replace methods but to guide how they should be adapted to individual studies to maximize their returns. The central advancement of this approach is the structure for evaluating methods in relation to the aims and epistemological perspectives of particular researchers and the recognition that these legitimately vary across the field.

Reporting Standards to Support the Evaluation of Methodological Integrity

The *Publication Manual of the American Psychological Association* (APA, 2020) provides guidance on research reporting standards for journals through psychology and is the dominant guide for publishing in the social sciences broadly so its impact is considerable. The development of Journal Article Reporting Standards (JARS) for Qualitative Research (Levitt et al., 2018) was a historic moment because, previously, the APA standards for reporting had only focused on quantitative methods – forcing many qualitative researchers to be asked to align their work with inappropriate standards.

Their inclusion of the qualitative JARS in the APA publication manual communicated to the field that qualitative methods are in the cannon of psychological methods and the expectation that psychological researchers should be familiar with their procedures and premises. The task force developed separate modules for primary qualitative research, qualitative meta-analysis, and mixed methods reporting (Levitt et al., 2018). They obtained feedback from APA Council of Editors, the International Committee of the SQIP, and the APA Publications and Communications Board. In this section, we review the distinctive features of the JARS-Qual.

Representation of Process over Section Demarcations

There are qualitative research traditions in which researchers do not use the standard sections headings (e.g., introduction, methods, results, discussion) to structure the story of their research. Researchers might engage a narrative style and organize their process chronologically or thematically. The method and results sections might be combined or the results and discussion. This reporting style may be more representative of their process, especially when qualitative researchers collect data and conduct analyses in waves and may adjust their data collection based upon the returns from initial analyses. Also, they may use approaches (e.g., critical approach) in which results should be evaluated in terms of their potential for social impact and so their discussion of the implications of findings might be best presented alongside the findings. As a result, the JARS-Qual emphasizes that researchers can present their research using the headings that are typical of quantitative papers or in another format that supports the communication of their research – so long as all the information needed to evaluate the manuscript is presented.

First-Person Rhetorical Style and Transparency

To limit their undue effect upon their analysis and to describe how they may deliberately use theoretical perspectives to strengthen their analyses, qualitative researchers engage in varied activities to become aware of their assumptions about their research topic and expectations for their findings. For this reason, they write explicitly in their reports about their perspectives and positions and how they managed them through the research process. Indeed, it has been found that the inclusion of statements of researcher self-reflection is the norm in qualitative psychotherapy research reporting (Levitt, Pomerville et al., 2017). To facilitate this communication, first-person writing styles facilitate their reporting as they tend not to mask the role of the researcher within the research process (as it typical in objectivist reporting styles; Rennie & Frommer, 2015).

The JARS-Qual guidelines recommend that researchers include a description both about their assumptions, recognizing their own social standpoint and positionality in relation to their topic (e.g., Harding, 2009), and about how those expectations were managed in the research process. Also, they recommend that authors state, where relevant, the relationship between the researchers and participants, considering how any prior relationships might have impacted the research process (e.g., Were there ethical consideration? Did the prior relationship enhance the disclosure?). This practice demonstrates researchers' commitment to transparency and situates the study for the reader.

Contextualization

A strength of qualitative research is its ability to develop findings that are sensitive to variations of many kinds in their context. Qualitative research typically does not aim to produce laws that hold rigidly across time and place, but to produce contextualized understandings that can be adjusted to fit the particularities of a situation. For this reason, researchers are careful to describe not only their own context, but the context of their participants and research project. For instance, a study on the expectations for psychotherapy in the United States might not be expected to have the same findings as a study in a country where this field is less established or viewed with skepticism. Also, providing contextual information when presenting quoted material to exemplify findings can allow readers to better understand the perspective of the speaker. The elaboration of contextual features can instruct readers on how to apply the findings being described and will improve the utility of the study.

Manuscript Length

To provide the information necessary for an adequate review of a qualitative study, manuscripts typically require more pages than quantitative manuscripts and an extension of manuscript page limits has been recommended (APA, 2020; Levitt et al., 2018). This extra length is necessary because there are a variety of features unique to the reporting of qualitative methods that are required for the adequate evaluation of a manuscript.

These features include: (a) justification for why a qualitative method was used, as the use of these methods may not be well-understood; (b) description of qualitative methods require detailed elaborations because they are typically adapted for each study; (c) the situation of qualitative research within an epistemological framework and an explanation of how this framework guided the analysis may be needed to understand the study aims and analytic procedure; (d) description of how established methods were adapted to the project to bolster methodological integrity; (e) exemplification of the analytic process to provide a basis for evaluation – typically through the use of quoted material from transcripts or sessions – is necessary to demonstrate the fidelity of analyses in qualitative psychotherapy research; and (f) description of researchers' assumptive framework and positionality and how that was managed through the process of data collection and analysis is needed to increase transparency and utility.

Inappropriate length requirements for qualitative manuscripts results in an inefficient process in which authors need to remove important information that is needed for the paper's evaluation only to have reviewers need to request that this necessary information be added back in so the manuscript can be evaluated properly (if it is not rejected immediately because of the absence of this material). Because reviewers differ in their understanding of this problem and have varied opinions on which aspects are most central in an initial submission, authors have little guidance on which aspects they should omit when preparing a manuscript. These limitations place unnecessary burden both on editors and reviewers as many reviews may be required just to request the information needed to evaluate the manuscript. This process can lead to the rejection of high-quality research and the acceptance of papers with thin findings that can be presented in a short manuscript and so editors have been seeking solutions.

Some journals have acted to remedy this problem by indicating flexibility on page lengths in their submission guidelines or by allotting extra pages for qualitative research. Following the practice of the *Journal of Counseling Psychology*, the JARS-Qual task force and the SQIP task force both recommended an extension of at least 10 pages to provide the material necessary for adequate review (Levitt, Motulsky et al., 2017; Levitt et al., 2018). Rather than requiring authors to submit incomplete manuscripts, it is preferable for a manuscript to be reviewed with the information necessary for its evaluation and *then* for editors and reviewers to make suggestions on which material to remove, or (better) to place online as supplementary material, as it allows for a more efficient and fair process of review. Given the switch toward the electronic distribution of journals, the manuscript length should be less of a concern going forward, making this practice less economically taxing for journals.

Recommendations for Editors and Reviewers

The two task-force papers (Levitt, Motulsky et al., 2017; Levitt et al., 2018) both encourage editors and reviewers to familiarize themselves with the distinctive features of qualitative design and reporting. The SQIP paper explicates a set of specific principles for reviewing qualitative research (Levitt, Motulsky et al., 2017) and an APA film has been made freely available on how to review qualitative manuscripts (www.apa.org/pubs/journals/resources/how-to-review-manuscripts). In addition, specific guidance has been developed for designing and reviewing psychotherapy and counseling research (Levitt et al., 2019) and for critical counseling research (Levitt, Morrill, et al., in press).

Even when a reviewer is familiar with one version of a method, it can be important to keep in mind that there are legitimate variations of most of the central qualitative methods and that the alteration of procedures is recommended when it acts to improve methodological integrity. When reviewers do not have expertise in a method, approach to inquiry, or the ways to adapt qualitative procedures to studies to increase their methodological integrity, they are encouraged to be aware of the limits of their competency. They should refrain from commenting on aspects that are unfamiliar to them. They should indicate in the review the aspects that they feel confident to review and where they feel more uncertain (e.g., qualitative methods as a whole, a specific version of a method, or an epistemological context) so that the editor has a better sense of how to reconcile differences among reviewers.

In addition to extending page lengths for qualitative manuscripts, the JARS-Qual guidelines encourage journal editors who do not have specific expertise in qualitative methods to appoint action editors who have that expertise. It is still common that reviewers offer recommendations for manuscripts that are ill-fitting with qualitative approaches and sometimes the problems with the recommendations are subtle. Someone with expertise in these methods is necessary to weigh conflicting reviews and offer direction that is appropriate for the research approach in use.

CRITICAL ISSUES AND CONTEMPORARY CHALLENGES

The field of qualitative research has always been characterized by a high level of methodological debate and innovation. Earlier sections of this chapter have demonstrated the vitality and resourcefulness of the qualitative research community, in relation to its capacity to construct solutions to methodological issues associated with the application of qualitative approaches to psychotherapy topics. The following sections outline some of the current ongoing challenges being faced by qualitative researchers in psychotherapy.

Ethical Challenges

Research in psychology and psychotherapy is regulated by ethical guidelines and Institutional Review Boards/Ethics Committees, on the basis of well-defined ethical principles. While qualitative research operates within these existing protocols, it is widely recognized that it also involves distinct ethical challenges (Haverkamp, 2005; Miller et al., 2012; Sieber & Tolich, 2013; Thompson & Russo, 2012; Van den Hoonard, 2002). A key ethical dimension of qualitative research concerns the fact that, in most qualitative studies of psychotherapy, research participants or informants are disclosing meaningful and sensitive personal information in the form of narratives and statements about aspects of their personal experience. These data are not coded numerically: instead, research reports incorporate actual informant statements. This means that, compared to statistical research, informants are more likely to be identifiable, particularly by others who are already familiar with their story. In addition, the experience of reading one's own words in a research article may trigger personal reflection on the part of informants – reflection that almost certainly takes place in a situation in which support or clarification is not readily available. In qualitative research, the process of generating data – for instance, taking part in an interview – may itself be meaningful for a participant. Questions about topics such as what was helpful or unhelpful in therapy, may evoke emotions and memories around such areas as life events that lead to entering therapy, disappointments and missed opportunities within therapy sessions, and other personal issues.

These aspects of the process of qualitative data collection and analysis mean that ethically relevant moments (Guillemin & Gillam, 2004), for example an informant getting upset, may occur at any time, requiring the researcher to make a decision in the moment, about what is the appropriate thing to do at that point in time. In response to such challenges, an important ethical strategy in qualitative research has involved implementing the principle of *process consent*: commitment to on-going dialogue and shared decision making between researcher and participants over the whole course of a project (Cutcliffe & Ramcharan, 2002; Haverkamp, 2005; Miller & Boulton, 2007; Speer & Stokoe, 2014). The researcher also needs to anticipate, plan for, and be trained to deal with, the likelihood that a research interview may be an emotionally powerful experience for either party. This includes allowing for time to honor whatever an interview might bring up for a research participant. Painful emotions may be triggered by talking about sensitive experiences. When dealt with appropriately, these moments may function as a unique and valued opportunity for reflection and meaning making. Similar reactions may occur within the interviewer and may require support or individual processing (Coles et al., 2014; Granek, 2017). Taken together, these issues underscore the importance of adopting a researcher stance based in relational as well as procedural ethics (Gabriel, 2009), and developing approaches to psychotherapy researcher training that enable the development of ethical maturity (Carroll & Shaw, 2012).

In addition to ethical challenges arising from personal and relational dimensions of qualitative research, there are further ethical issues associated with the social context within which qualitative research takes place. As discussed in an earlier section of this chapter, the social justice values and critical theory perspective that underpin much qualitative research, emphasize the importance of using research to empower participants and creating a more equal society. Although this stance is particularly salient in participatory, collaborative and action research approaches (Baum et al., 2006; Borg et al., 2012), it pervades all qualitative research to a greater or lesser extent (Natvik & Moltu, 2016). It has therefore not been easy for qualitative researchers to hear members of politically and economically oppressed groups testify that they regard much qualitative research as fulfilling a colonizing function of controlling those who are powerless and commodifying their stories and experiences to further researcher academic careers (Tuhiwai Smith,1999). Gorski and Goodman (2015) argue that, in much academic work, the assumptions of those with social power and status are applied in a downward direction, and used to categorize and control those with less power (e.g., members of disadvantaged communities). Gorski and Goodman (2015) suggest that it is necessary to develop a *decolonizing* viewpoint that invites researchers and research participants to gaze *up* the power hierarchy, to shine a light on (and change) the social systems and structures that privilege the few at the expense of the many. For qualitative researchers, one of the tangible ways that has been proposed in order to support this aim is to pay particular attention to the significance of

situations in which research participants refuse to take part in studies, or refuse to have their words included in published reports (Tuck & Yang, 2014a,b).

Another ethically problematic facet of the relationship between qualitative research and with wider social issues concerns the issue of data sharing. Secondary analysis refers to the situations in which qualitative data from a single study, or combined data from similar studies, are reanalyzed to enable closer focus on particular themes or to seek replication (Heaton, 2008). An example of secondary analysis includes the work of Nadal et al. (2015) in which data from a series of studies of the experience of microaggression in members of specific groups (e.g., ethnic identity, gender, sexual orientation) were combined in order to make it possible to analyze intersectional microaggression (e.g., when the informant belonged to more than one group). Another example can be found in Percival et al. (2017) who analyzed what patients valued in their relationship with clinicians, across pooled data from studies of patient experience of a range of treatments for depression.

The secondary analyses by Nadal et al. (2015) and Percival et al. (2017) involved direct communication between the research teams responsible for the separate studies. These negotiations included agreement over how to handle ethical issues around informant confidentiality, thus respecting the initial duty of care between primary researcher and informants. In recent years, such examples of negotiated data sharing have been subsumed into a broader movement within psychology and social science to build secure depositories into which research data would be routinely lodged. The motivation for the creation of such depositories includes not only an appreciation of the value of secondary analysis, but also considerations around historical archiving, availability of techniques for analyzing large data sets, and the possibility of combatting scientific fraud by checking the data authenticity and auditing data analysis.

Some qualitative researchers have expressed concerns about sharing qualitative research data within such depositories (Antes et al., 2018; DuBois et al., 2018; Feldman & Shaw, 2019; Guishard, 2018; Mannay, 2014). Although there is not yet consensus on how to navigate this issue, it is clear that there exist important ethical barriers that contraindicate this kind of data sharing (as detailed in the statement expressing concern about requiring data sharing for qualitative research by APA, 2020). The obligation to protect participants' confidentiality can present special ethical issues for qualitative data sharing. For instance, raw data from a qualitative study involving multiple detailed stories about participants' lives may contain details that are necessary to exemplify a finding but that can be revealing in compromising ways when read in their entirety. Qualitative research also may involve intensive case studies of people who were selected because of their unique attributes. Even when data are masked, it may not be possible to retain what is meaningful and necessary to evaluate an analysis and, at the same time, protect participants' confidentiality if the complete data set is shared. However, if only fragments are shared, it may be insufficient to conduct a secondary analysis or a check on a prior analysis.

It cannot be assumed that participants who give consent to participate in a study to a specific group of researchers wish to extend that consent to other researchers. This assumption may be especially problematic with communities or those at risk for social marginalization and it may directly counter the reason that consent was originally given. For instance, transgender participants may consent to have their data analyzed by researchers who are in their community and who are developing research to document injustices and support their rights, but that consent would not apply to other researchers with different motivations. Likewise, some individuals and communities require researchers to spend time developing trust with a community prior to consenting to have them collect and analyze data, and they would not extend that trust to other groups of researchers. Communities may be owners or co-owners of the data themselves and may need to be consulted prior to each individual decision to share data, rather than being willing to share data openly with any interested researcher (Tuck & Yang, 2014). As a result, the relationship between the researchers and the participants is an important ethical consideration and one that may contraindicate data sharing.

Finally, in many traditions of qualitative research (e.g., critical research, ethnographic research), researchers' own histories and epistemological perspectives are viewed as a legitimate influence on the process of inquiry (e.g., researchers may deliberately seek engagement with a community, a phenomenon, or a theoretical perspective to prepare them for the analysis in order to increase their perspicacity and attunement to data). Researchers should be reflective and explicit about this influence when considering data sharing. If they do not have a similar history and perspectives, similar findings may not be expected. These cautions need to be balanced by an acknowledgement that at least for some informants in qualitative studies, such as individuals with a condition or problem that they believe is not taken sufficiently seriously by service providers, participation in new forms of research may be seen as an opportunity to tell their story to as wide an audience as possible.

Training in Qualitative Methods

Although the publication of qualitative methods has been increasing gradually (Hays et al., 2016), it is challenging to assess changes in training students in qualitative methods because studies over time have not used the same questions or surveyed the same types of programs. For instance, in a survey conducted of US counseling psychology doctoral training programs (with the inclusion of one Canadian program; Ponterotto, 2005), with a 79% return rate, all of the programs were found to have qualitative courses that students could take, either within their programs or a neighboring program. Most of this training was through electives, however, as only 10% required qualitative training.

Of programs surveyed, 95% accepted qualitative dissertations and only 5% required quantitative or mixed methods dissertations. The average number of qualitative dissertations was estimated at 15.6%, but nearly doubled in programs in which students had required qualitative methods classes (29.7%). This number appears to represent an increase from 3.6%, found by assessing dissertation abstracts in 1985, although that study examined clinical psychology dissertations (Keeley et al., 1988).

In a SQIP white paper on qualitative education, Rubin et al. (2018) surveyed 340 PhD training programs in a variety of subdisciplines that historically have used qualitative methods (e.g., developmental psychology rather than neuropsychology). They reported a 42% return rate and found that 13% of the programs had required courses in qualitative methods. Of the respondents, 39% said that their department had offered a qualitative course in the last five years – although the survey did not ask whether students also obtained qualitative training through neighboring programs. The participants estimated that, on average, 14.7% of the dissertations were qualitative. Although these numbers are challenging to compare because of differences in the questions and programs surveyed, they provide a variety of baseline figures that could be used in the future.

In the UK, the uptake of qualitative methods has appeared more rapid. This may be in part because of a governmental quality assurance benchmark that required undergraduate psychology courses to include education on qualitative methods (Gibson & Sullivan, 2018). Harper (2012) compared a 1992 survey results with those from a 2005–2006 survey. In that time the number of programs that offered qualitative methods training rose from 81% to 100% and the number of dissertations was found to be at 42% in the later survey (but was not asked about in 1992).

This said, there are many indices that recognition of the advantages of training students in qualitative and mixed approaches to methods is increasing. Rubin et al. (2018) documented some of these changes. The National Science Foundation has called for increased support to qualitative dissertations (Lamont & White, 2010) in addition to an NIH report to support the use mixed methods (Creswell et al., 2011). The APA's commission on accreditation has endorsed the inclusion of qualitative methods in graduate training (although the breadth of this instruction remains unspecified). Student membership and committees within qualitative sections of SQIP and QMiP have grown as well. Also, there has been a flourishing of writing about teaching qualitative methods.

This writing focuses in a number of areas. First, papers describe why coursework in this area is needed and should become more accessible and required (e.g., Bogard & Wertz, 2006; Halbesleben, 2011; McMullen & Winston-Proctor, 2018). Reasons include developing students with more flexibility in creating research questions, developing capable journal manuscript reviewers, learning from experts while in graduate school rather than have to do so individually later, preventing students from having to learn these methods only through their dissertation work, and varying the methods researchers can use to build and evaluate theories and conduct research. These arguments are in keeping with epistemological perspectives such as critical multiplism (Shadish, 1986), which holds that the ideal strategy for scientific programs of research is to generate results from across varied methods so as to overcome the specific biases and limitations that are endemic to every method.

Also, there is a growing literature on strategies for teaching qualitative methods at both the graduate (e.g., Rennie, 1996) and undergraduate levels (e.g., McMullen & Winston-Proctor, 2018). They feature experiential exercises, engaged class projects, apprenticeships, or computerized learning (e.g.,

Neal Kimball & Turner, 2018; Levitt et al., 2013; Stadtlander & Giles, 2010). Yet another stream of writing focuses on the challenges of teaching qualitative research within a discipline in which students often are taught to devalue these approaches and within contexts that do not orient students to embrace an epistemologically pluralistic perspective (e.g., Stoppard, 2007). At the same time, there is recognition that this context is changing and that qualitative methods are being embraced, in part due to educational efforts to demystify them and shifts in the field to understand the value of diverse epistemological approaches to inquiry.

Generalizability and Transferability

There has been considerable debate among qualitative researchers about whether, and in what manner, findings in qualitative research are generalizable. This question has led to a wide variety of responses, a few of which will be described here. Influential theorists Lincoln and Guba (1985) argued that strong qualitative findings are not generalizable to a population but instead are transferable. Whereas generalization refers to the application of findings from a sample to a population, transferability refers to the ability of readers to learn about the contexts of findings and then decide how best to apply those findings in their own context.

This conceptualization places the activity of applying findings solely in the hands of the readers. Transferable enriching research deepens and broadens the practical, empathic, aesthetic, historical understanding of those who read or hear about the research or participate in it. It is successful to the extent that readers can see implications in their own lives and can apply it in their own practice. What is transferred may vary from person to person; people may understand the work differently and may apply it in varied, even contradictory ways. Many other researchers, however, do conceptualize processes of generalization as endemic to qualitative methods themselves, potentially along with the process of transferability.

The alternative purposes of qualitative research are associated with different concepts of generality (Stiles, 2015). Whereas the concept of transferability applies to enriching research, theory-building research can use the natural-science concept of generality. In theory-building research, generality is a property of a theory, not of particular research results. Each theory specifies its own degree of generality, that is, the circumstances under which it is to be applied. A particular study's results or observations are not meant to be generalized themselves; instead, they are meant to add (or subtract) an increment of confidence to the theory. When findings support the theory, confidence in the theory is increased and when findings conflict, the theory may require revision to maintain confidence in the theory's generality. Both transferability and the generality of a theory should be distinguished from external validity (Campbell, 1957), a concept applicable in qualitative as well as quantitative fact-gathering research. External validity represents a judgment of how commonly a result might apply beyond the material actually studied. Thus, it treats generality as loosely analogous to the statistical principle of generalizing to a population from which a random sample was drawn. For example, in the results of consensual qualitative research, the categories of content are classed as general, typical, variant, depending on how frequently they were found to appear (e.g., how many of the interviews with clients about their therapy termination in the study by Knox et al., 2011).

Taking another tack, Maxwell (2012) argued that qualitative research can be generalizable to populations because findings are based on identification of causal processes. While postpositivist theories of causality focused on regularity of causality, as detected through the use of statistical methods, qualitative methods are seen as best at establishing other forms of causality, such as causal processes, causal meanings (e.g., internal motivations), and the causal influence of contexts. Once causal explanations are established, these are thought to be generalized beyond the scope of a study.

Descriptive phenomenologists, in contrast, have long used processes of identifying the underlying essences that are constant within an experience under study (Wertz, 2015). In their analysis, researchers intuit the unvarying features of a phenomenon. Roald et al. (2021) drew on this understanding and implied that the identification of constancy within a subject matter creates a unified foundation for generalization across methods.

Finally, Levitt (2021b) argued that it is not consistent with the logic inherent in qualitative methods to seek to generalize to a population, because qualitative methods do not typically use probability sampling theory, so we should reconceptualize the functioning of variation in qualitative methods. While statistical generalization is based on efforts to *match the variability in a sample to the population under study*, she put forward that qualitative generalization is based upon an attempt to *match the variation in the data with the experience and practice of the phenomenon under study*. She argued that qualitative research engages a process of gradually mirroring variation by engaging the hermeneutic cycle of inferences (described earlier), which allows for self-correcting, emergent meanings based on the empirical analysis (rather than having tautological hypotheses determined at the beginning of a study). Through the iterative process of analysis, guided by deliberate attention to patterns of variation within the research topic, findings grow closer and closer to the larger experience and practice of the phenomenon and readers develop confidence in their generalization to similar contexts. This understanding was seen as congruent with existing practices used in qualitative methods such as saturation and theoretical sampling (also described earlier) and with reasoning intrinsic to qualitative methods. In any case, there seem to be multiple strong arguments that there is both a basis in qualitative research for a process of qualitative generalization as well as transferability of findings.

Handling Researcher Reflexivity

It is widely acknowledged in qualitative research that personal characteristics of a researcher influence data collection and analysis. This realization has resulted in considerable attention to the phenomenon of researcher *reflexivity* (also referred to as transparency, or positioning within a study; Tuval-Mashiach, 2017). There has been considerable attention to ways in which findings of qualitative studies can be enhanced through reflection around such topics as the personal meaning of the research, their pre-assumptions and expectations (both sensitizing and bias-producing) regarding the potential findings of the study, the influence of their gender, social class, professional background and personal style on how informants respond to them, and their emotional reactions to participants (Berger, 2005; Finlay, 2002, 2012; Finlay & Gough, 2003). An important theme within this literature has been a focus on the significance of researcher emotional responses, both during interviews and within the work of data analysis, as sources of insight into tacit or emergent dimensions of meaning regarding the topic of a study (Hubbard et al., 2001; Granek, 2017; Rennie & Fergus, 2006). Some researchers have sought to make sense of these occurrences in terms of the psychoanalytic concept of countertransference (Elliott et al., 2012; Hollway, & Jefferson, 2013; Holmes, 2014, 2017; Stänicke et al., 2015; Strømme et al., 2010).

A key area of challenge for qualitative research in psychotherapy is to develop standards of good practice, and training opportunities, around both reflexivity procedures, and formats for reporting reflexive material within publications. An additional challenge is represented by a need to address the relative absence of reflexive accounts within therapy case study research. Within quantitative research, the existence of researcher allegiance effects continues to create difficulties in interpreting findings of psychotherapy outcome research, despite more than two decades of attention to this issue (Dragioti et al., 2015; Manea, et al., 2017; Yoder et al., 2019). It is possible that there could be some value in consideration of the reciprocal relevance of reflexivity and researcher allegiance across these contrasting methodological traditions.

As the field of qualitative psychotherapy research continues to grow, practices are established and new understandings develop. These advances can lead to a future in which qualitative methods are not just employed regularly in psychotherapy research, but where the logic underpinning these approaches is understood and a truly pluralistic science is embraced.

CONCLUSIONS AND FUTURE DIRECTIONS

The growing enthusiasm for qualitative psychotherapy research seems to fit both with the needs of the field and the directions of its leaders. In a compendium of reflections of presidents of the international *Society for Psychotherapy Research* (Strauss et al., 2015), the call for expanding epistemological and methodical approaches recurred over and over again, and was described as one of the central visions of the future of psychotherapy research by its editors. As the productive returns from these methods is evident (see McLeod et al., 2020, Chapter 11 for a description of central findings from qualitative psychotherapy research), the demand for qualitative and mixed methods approaches is high.

This chapter has provided a review of the philosophical and conceptual foundations for qualitative psychotherapy research and relevant research methods and designs. It has provided a description of how to evaluate qualitative research and consider methodological integrity in the design process. We have considered critical issues and challenges that face

contemporary qualitative psychotherapy researchers, including ethical challenges that occur when the nature of qualitative research is not understood, the need for graduate-level training in these methods internationally, and systematic approaches to understanding qualitative generalization and the use of researchers' reflexivity. Under the following two headings, we describe two emergent methods and a research focus that we see as holding promise for qualitative psychotherapy researchers.

The Development of Art-Informed Research Practice

There is a growing interest within the field of qualitative research in the use of art-making activities and ways of thinking within research in psychology, education, health, and other social science disciplines (Bhattacharya & Payne, 2016; Carless, & Douglas, 2016; Douglas & Carless, 2018; Kara, 2015; Leavy, 2019). Creative media can be an adjunct to interviews within data collection, for instance, through informant engagement with taking photographs (Sandhu et al., 2017; Sitter, 2017; Woodgate et al., 2017), generating metaphoric language (Shinebourne & Smith, 2010), making art works (Rouse et al., 2015), drawing (Guillemin, 2004; Shinebourne & Smith, 2011), life space mapping (Rodgers, 2006), body-mapping (de Jager et al., 2016), and digital storytelling (de Jager et al., 2017). Findings of qualitative research have been disseminated through theater performance (Lieblich, 2006; Michalak et al., 2014; Råbu et al., 2020; Willis et al., 2014). In addition to their capacity to help research participants provide richer narratives of their lived experience, Mannay (2010) has argued that art-based methods function to "make the familiar strange" – a valuable contribution in relation to the discovery-oriented, critical goals of qualitative inquiry. It is likely that these creative methods will be more widely adopted by qualitative therapy researchers in future.

Participatory Research in Collaboration with Clients and Service Users

In connection with the development of critical paradigm qualitative approaches to inquiry within research practices discussed previously, a highly significant shift within health-care systems in industrialized democratic societies, over recent decades, has occurred. There has been an increasing expectation on the part of policy makers and managers, that, as far as possible, treatment decisions will be based on collaborative, shared decision-making between clinician and client, and that service users will be consulted around the design, conduct and dissemination of research. Although there is evidence that the use of critical perspectives is increasing (Levitt et al., 2021), the use of participatory research methods is still rare in psychotherapy research. Research by Morrow and Smith (1995; Morrow, 2006) into recovery in women survivors of sexual abuse, and Veseth et al. (2012) into recovery from bipolar disorder, highlight the possibilities arising from client active engagement in the research process. Qualitative researchers in other fields have documented the beneficial practical and societal impact of this methodological tradition (Torre et al., 2012).

Evaluating the Impact of Qualitative Research in Psychotherapy

Despite a steady growth in the proportion of qualitative studies being published, little is known about the extent to which this evidence source has an influence on individual practitioners or policy makers. Research into how therapists make use of research findings, reviewed by McLeod (2016), did not unearth any examples of clinician testimony that reading qualitative research articles had changed their practice.

On the other hand, Granek and Nakash (2016) provide convincing examples of how real-world knowledge translation, in the form of talks and workshops by researchers on the clinical implications of qualitative findings, could have a powerful impact on front-line practitioners. A potentially significant contributory factor in relation to this issue relates to the ways in which qualitative findings are presented, and the reading habits of clinicians. For example, therapists whose research training has focused mainly on quantitative methods, may have learned to expect that the findings of a study could be meaningfully conveyed in a brief headline news statement in the abstract of an article. By contrast, it seems likely that meaningful learning from a qualitative study requires engagement with detailed sections within an article. In addition, although it is clear that many of those who conduct and read qualitative research as part of therapy training regard this experience as enriching and enlightening, and that researchers find it helpful for a variety of purposes, little is known about the factors that lead to sustained use of qualitative research to inform practice across the course of a career.

Overall, qualitative approaches have particular significance for research on psychotherapy, where they provide windows into the internal experiences of clients and therapists. The returns from these methods allow for context-sensitive formulations of therapy process that can guide therapists to better support clients to make change – not through behavioral prescriptions of interventions, but through developing a deeper understanding of the dynamics at play in each moment. Findings can identify causal processes in psychotherapeutic exchanges, shed light on unspoken or hidden experiences, and reveal intentions that guide both therapist and clients. They teach therapists to be responsive to the interplay of dialogue and the variations that exist within human experience. They help therapists develop clinical wisdom and so are foundational to the conceptualization, explanation, and understanding of psychotherapeutic change.

ABBREVIATIONS

APA	American Psychiatric Association
BPS	British Psychological Society
CBT	cognitive behavioral therapy
HAT	helpful aspects of therapy
HSCED	hermeneutic single-case efficacy design
JARS	Journal Article Reporting Standards
NIH	National Institute of Health
QMiP	Qualitative Methods in Psychology
SQIP	Society for Qualitative Inquiry in Psychology

REFERENCES

American Psychological Association (2020). *Publication Manual of the American Psychological Association* (7th Edition), Washington, DC: American Psychological Association.

Angus, L. E., & McLeod, J. (2004). *The handbook of narrative and psychotherapy: Practice, theory, and research*. (L. E. Angus & J. McLeod, Eds.). Thousand Oaks, CA: Sage. https://doi.org/10.4135/9781412973496

Angus, L., Watson, J. C., Elliott, R., Schneider, K., & Timulak, L. (2015). Humanistic psychotherapy research 1990–2015: From methodological innovation to evidence-supported treatment outcomes and beyond. *Psychotherapy Research, 25*(3), 330–347. https://doi.org/10.1080/10503307.2014.989290

Anjum, R.L., & Mumford, S. (2018). *Causation in science and the methods of scientific discovery*. New York: Oxford University Press. https://doi.org/10.1093/oso/9780198733669.001.0001

Antes, A. L., Walsh, H. A., Strait, M., Hudson-Vitale, C. R., & DuBois, J. M. (2018). Examining data repository guidelines for qualitative data sharing. *Journal of Empirical Research on Human Research Ethics, 13*(1), 61–73. https://doi.org/10.1177/1556264617744121

Austin, S., & Prilleltensky, I. (2001). Contemporary debates in critical psychology: Dialectics and syntheses. *Australian Psychologist, 36*(1), 75–80. https://doi.org/10.1080/00050060108259634

Bantry White, E., Hurley, M., & Ó Súilleabháin, F. (2019). The journal article reporting standards for qualitative primary, qualitative meta-analytic and mixed methods research: Applying the standards to social work research. *Journal of Evidence-Based Social Work, 16*(5), 469–477. https://doi.org/10.1080/26408066.2019.1650317

Barnett-Page, E., Thomas, J. (2009). Methods for the synthesis of qualitative research: A critical review. *BMC Medical Research Methodology, 9*, 59–67. https://doi.org/10.1186/1471-2288-9-59

Bartholomew, T. T., & Brown, J. R. (2019). Entering the ethnographic mind: A grounded theory of using ethnography in psychological research. *Qualitative Research in Psychology*, 1-30. https://doi.org/10.1080/14780887.2019.1604927

Baum, F., MacDougall, C., & Smith, D. (2006). Participatory action research. *Journal of Epidemiology & Community Health, 60*(10), 854–857. https://doi.org/10.1136/jech.2004.028662

Benelli, E., Biffi, D., De Carlo, A., & McLeod, J. (2015). Hermeneutic single case efficacy design: a systematic review of published research and current standards. *TPM: Testing, Psychometrics, Methodology in Applied Psychology, 22*(1).

Benítez-Ortega, J. y Garrido-Fernández, M. 2016. Review of task analysis research of significant events in psychotherapy. *Revista de Psicoterapia, 27*, 99–122. https://doi.org/10.33898/rdp.v27i105.147

Berger, R. (2015). Now I see it, now I don't: Researcher's position and reflexivity in qualitative research. *Qualitative Research, 15*(2), 219–234. https://doi.org/10.1177/1468794112468475

Bhattacharya, K., & Payne, R. (2016). Mixing mediums, mixing selves: Arts-based contemplative approaches to border crossings. *International Journal of Qualitative Studies in Education, 29*(9), 1100–1117. https://doi.org/10.1080/09518398.2016.1201163

Bogard, K., & Wertz, F. J. (2006). The introduction of a qualitative perspective in advanced psychological research training: Narrative of a mixed methods doctoral dissertation. *The Humanistic Psychologist, 34*(4), 369–398. https://doi.org/10.1207/s15473333thp3404_6

Bohart, A. C., Berry, M. C., & Wicks, C. L. (2011). Developing a systematic framework for utilizing discrete types of qualitative data as therapy research evidence. *Pragmatic Case Studies in Psychotherapy, 7*(1), 145–155. https://doi.org/10.14713/pcsp.v7i1.1076

Bohart, A. C., Tallman, K., Byock, G., & Mackrill, T. (2011). The "research jury method": The application of the jury trial model to evaluating the validity of descriptive and causal statements about psychotherapy process and outcome. *Pragmatic Case Studies in Psychotherapy*, *7(1)*, 101–144. https://doi.org/10.14713/pcsp.v7i1.1075

Borg, M., Karlsson, B., Kim, H. S., & McCormack, B. (2012). Opening up for many voices in knowledge construction. *Forum Qualitative Sozialforschung/Forum: Qualitative Social Research*, 13, 1.

Bowleg, L. (2017). Towards a critical health equity research stance: Why epistemology and methodology matter more than qualitative methods. *Health Education & Behavior*, *44*(5), 677–684. https://doi.org/10.1177/1090198117728760

Braud, W., & Anderson, R. (Eds) (1998). *Transpersonal research methods for the social sciences: Honoring human experience.* Thousand Oaks, CA: Sage.

Braun, V., & Clarke, V. (2006). Using thematic analysis in psychology. *Qualitative Research in Psychology*, 3, 77–101. https://doi.org/10.1191/1478088706qp063oa

Bright, F. A.S., Boland, P., Rutherford, S. J., Kayes, N. M., & McPherson, K. M. (2012). Implementing a client-centred approach in rehabilitation: an autoethnography, *Disability and Rehabilitation*, *34*(12), 997–1004. https://doi.org/10.3109/09638288.2011.629712

Brinegar, M. G., Salvi, L. M., Stiles, W. B., & Greenberg, L. S. (2006). Building a meaning bridge: Therapeutic progress from problem formulation to understanding. *Journal of Counseling Psychology*, *53*, 165–180. https://doi.org/10.1037/0022-0167.53.2.165

Brooks C. (2011). Social performance and secret ritual: Battling against obsessive-compulsive disorder. *Qualitative Health Research*, *21*(2), 249–261. https://doi.org/10.1177/1049732310381387

Budge, S. L. (2015). Psychotherapists as gatekeepers: An evidence-based case study highlighting the role and process of letter writing for transgender clients. *Psychotherapy*, *52*(3), 287–297. https://doi.org/10.1037/pst0000034

Byrne, D. and Ragin, C. (Eds) (2009). *The SAGE handbook of case-based methods.* Thousand Oaks, CA: Sage. https://doi.org/10.4135/9781446249413

Campbell, D. T. (1957). Factors relevant to the validity of experiments in social settings, *Psychological Bulletin 54*, 297–312. https://doi.org/10.1037/h0040950

Campbell, D. T. (1979). "Degrees of freedom" and the case study. In T. D. Cook & C. S. Reichardt (Eds.), *Qualitative and quantitative methods in evaluation research* (pp. 49–67). Beverley Hills, CA: Sage.

Carless, D., & Douglas, K. (2016). Arts-based research: radical or conventional? *The Psychologist*, *29*, 350–353.

Caro Gabalda, I., & Stiles, W. B. (2009). Retrocessos no contexto de terapia linguística de avaliação [Setbacks in the context of linguistic therapy of evaluation]. *Análise Psicológica*, 27, 199–212. https://doi.org/10.14417/ap.205

Caro Gabalda, I., & Stiles, W. B. (2013). Irregular assimilation progress: Reasons for setbacks in the context of linguistic therapy of evaluation. *Psychotherapy Research*, *23*, 35–53. https://doi.org/10.1080/10503307.2012.721938

Caro Gabalda, I., & Stiles, W. B. (2018). Assimilation setbacks as switching strands: A theoretical and methodological conceptualization. *Journal of Contemporary Psychotherapy*, *48*, 205–214. https://doi.org/10.1007/s10879-018-9385-z

Caro Gabalda, I., & Stiles, W. B. (2019). Therapist activities preceding therapy setbacks in a poor-outcome case. *Counselling Psychology Quarterly*, *32*, 18–38. https://doi.org/10.1080/09515070.2017.1355295

Caro Gabalda, I., Stiles, W. B., & Pérez Ruiz, S. (2016). Therapist activities preceding setbacks in the assimilation process. *Psychotherapy Research*, *26*, 653–664. https://doi.org/10.1080/10503307.2015.1104422

Carroll, M., & Shaw, E. (2012) *Ethical maturity in the helping professions.* Making difficult life and work decisions. Melbourne: PsychOz Publications.

Castonguay, L. G., Nelson, D. L., Boutselis, M. A., Chiswick, N. R., Damer, D. D., Hemmelstein, N. A., Jackson, J. S., Morford, M., Ragusea, S. A., Roper, J. G., Spayd, C., Weiszer, T., & Borkovec, T. D. (2010). Psychotherapists, researchers, or both? A qualitative analysis of psychotherapists' experiences in a practice research network. *Psychotherapy: Theory, Research, Practice, Training*, *47*(3), 345–354. https://doi.org/10.1037/a0021165

Chakravartty, A. "Scientific Realism", The Stanford Encyclopedia of Philosophy (Summer 2017 Edition), Edward N. Zalta (ed.), URL = <https://plato.stanford.edu/archives/sum2017/entries/scientific-realism/>. (downloaded 1 May 2019)

Chang, D. F., & Yoon, P. (2011). Ethnic minority clients' perceptions of the significance of race in cross-racial therapy relationships. *Psychotherapy Research*, *21*(5), 567–582. https://doi.org/10.1080/10503307.2011.592549

Charmaz, K. (2006). Constructing grounded theory. A practical guide through qualitative analysis. Thousand Oaks, CA: Sage.

Clarke, A. E. (2005). *Situational analysis: Grounded theory after the postmodernist turn.* Thousand Oaks, CA: Sage. https://doi.org/10.4135/9781412985833

Cornelius-White, J. H. D., Kanamori, Y., Murphy, D., & Tickle, E. (2018). Mutuality in psychotherapy: A meta-analysis and meta-synthesis. *Journal of Psychotherapy Integration*, *28*(4), 489–504. https://doi.org/10.1037/int0000134

Craciun, M. (2016). The cultural work of office charisma: maintaining professional power in psychotherapy. *Theory and Society*, *45*(4), 361–383. https://doi.org/10.1007/s11186-016-9273-z

Craciun, M. (2017). Time, knowledge, and power in psychotherapy: a comparison of psychodynamic and cognitive behavioral practices. *Qualitative Sociology*, *20*(2), 165–190. https://doi.org/10.1007/s11133-017-9355-x

Craciun, M. (2018). Emotions and knowledge in expert work: A comparison of two psychotherapies. *American Journal of Sociology*, *123*(4), 959–1003. https://doi.org/10.1086/695682

Creswell, J. W., & Plano Clark, V. L. (2011). *Designing and conducting mixed methods research* (2nd ed.). Thousand Oaks, CA: Sage.

Creswell, J.W., Klassen, A.C., Plano Clark, V.L., & Smith, K.C. (2011). *Best practices for mixed methods research in the health sciences.* (For the Office of Behavioral and Social Sciences Research.) Washington, DC: National Institutes of Health. https://doi.org/10.1037/e566732013-001

Critical Appraisal Skills Programme. (2017). CASP Qualitative Checklist. [online] Available at: http://www.casp-uk.net/checklists.

Cutcliffe, J. R., & Ramcharan, P. (2002). Leveling the playing field? Exploring the merits of the ethics-as-process approach for judging qualitative research proposals. *Qualitative Health Research*, *12*(7), 1000–1010. https://doi.org/10.1177/104973202129120313

Danziger, K. (1990). *Constructing the subject: Historical origins of psychological research.* New York: Cambridge University Press. https://doi.org/10.1017/CBO9780511524059

de Jager, A., Fogarty, A., Tewson, A., Lenette, C., & Boydell, K. M. (2017). Digital storytelling in research: A systematic review. *The Qualitative Report*, *22*(10), 2548–2582.

de Jager, A., Tewson, A., Ludlow, B., & Boydell, K. (2016). Embodied ways of storying the self: A systematic review of body-mapping. *Forum Qualitative Sozialforschung/Forum: Qualitative Social Research*, 17, 2.

Denzin, N. K. & Lincoln, Y. S. (2000). Paradigms and perspectives in transition. In N. K. Denzin, & Y. S. Lincoln (Eds.), *Handbook of qualitative research* (2nd ed.) (pp. 155–162). Thousand Oaks: Sage.

De Smet, M. M., Meganck, R., De Geest, R., Norman, U. A., Truijens, F., & Desmet, M. (2020). What "good outcome" means to patients: Understanding recovery and improvement in psychotherapy for major depression from a mixed-methods perspective. *Journal of Counseling Psychology*, *67*(1), 25–39. https://doi.org/10.1037/cou0000362

De Smet, M., Meganck, R., Seybert, C., Willemsen, J., Van Camp, I., Geerardyn, F., Dedercq, F., Inslegers, R., Treason, E., Vanheule, S., Kirschner, L., Schindler, I., & Kächele, H. (2013). "Psychoanalytic single cases published in ISI-ranked journals: The construction of an online archive": Erratum. *Psychotherapy and Psychosomatics*, *82*(2), 120–121. https://doi.org/10.1159/000342019

Dilthey, W. (1989/1883). Introduction to the human sciences. In R A. Makkreel & F. Rodi (eds.). *Wilhelm Dilthey: Selected works: Volume 1* (pp. 170–245). Cambridge: Cambridge University Press.

Douglas, K. & Carless, D. (2018). Engaging with arts-based research: A story in three parts. *Qualitative Research in Psychology*, 15, 156–172. https://doi.org/10.1080/14780887.2018.1429843

Douglass, B.G., & Moustakas, C. (1985). Heuristic inquiry: The internal search to know, *Journal of Humanistic Psychology*, *25*, 39–55. https://doi.org/10.1177/0022167885253004

Dragioti, E., Dimoliatis, I., & Evangelou, E. (2015). Disclosure of researcher allegiance in meta-analyses and randomised controlled trials of psychotherapy: a systematic appraisal. *BMJ Open*, *5*, e007206. https://doi.org/10.1136/bmjopen-2014-007206

DuBois, J. M., Strait, M., & Walsh, H. (2018). Is it time to share qualitative research data? *Qualitative Psychology, 5*(3), 380–393. https://doi .org/10.1037/qup0000076

Eells, T. D. (2010). The unfolding case formulation: The interplay of description and inference. *Pragmatic Case Studies in Psychotherapy, 6*(4). https:// doi.org/10.14713/pcsp.v6i4.1046

Egberg Thyme, K., Wiberg, B., Lundman, B., & Graneheim, U. H. (2013). Qualitative content analysis in art psychotherapy research: Concepts, procedures, and measures to reveal the latent meaning in pictures and the words attached to the pictures. *The Arts in Psychotherapy, 40*(1), 101–107. https://doi.org/10.1016/j.aip.2012.11.007

Ekberg, S., Barnes, R., Kessler, D., Malpass, A., & Shaw, A. (2013). Managing the therapeutic relationship in online cognitive behavioural therapy for depression: Therapists' treatment of clients' contributions. *Language@ Internet, 10,* article 4.

Elliott, H., Ryan, J., & Hollway, W. (2012). Research encounters, reflexivity and supervision. *International Journal of Social Research Methodology, 15*(5), 433–444. https://doi.org/10.1080/13645579.2011.610157

Elliott, R. (2002). Hermeneutic single-case efficacy design. *Psychotherapy Research, 12*(1), 1–21.https://doi.org/10.1080/713869614

Elliott, R. (2015). Hermeneutic single-case efficacy design: An overview. In K. J. Schneider, J. F. Pierson, & J. F. T. Bugental (Eds.), *The handbook of humanistic psychology: Theory, research, and practice., 2nd ed.* (pp. 351–360). Thousand Oaks, CA: Sage.https://doi.org/10.4135/9781483387864.n25

Elliott, R., Fischer, C. T., & Rennie, D. L. (1999). Evolving guidelines for publication of qualitative research studies in psychology and related fields. *British Journal of Clinical Psychology, 38,* 215–229.https://doi .org/10.1348/014466599162782

Elliott, R., Partyka, R., Wagner, J., Alperin,R., Dobrenski, R., Messer, S.B., Watson, J.C. and Castonguay, L.G. (2009) An adjudicated Hermeneutic Single Case Efficacy Design study of experiential therapy for panic/phobia. *Psychotherapy Research,* 19. 543–557. [Appendices available at: http:// www.informaworld.com/smpp/content~content=a914761426~db=all~tab =multimedia] https://doi.org/10.1080/10503300902905947

Elliott, R. & Timulak, L. (2021). *Essentials of descriptive-interpretive qualitative research.* American Psychological Association.

Elliott, R. & Widdowson, M. (2017). Hermeneutic single case efficacy design for counselling psychology. In D. Murphy (Ed.). *Counselling psychology: A textbook for study and practice.* (pp. 425–438). Chichester: Wiley.

Ellis, C., Adams, T. E., & Bochner, A. P. (2011). Autoethnography: An overview. *Historical Social Research/Historische Sozialforschung, 36*(4), 273–290.

Etherington, K. (2000) *Narrative approaches to working with adult male survivors of child sexual abuse: The clients, the counsellors and the researchers Story.* London: Jessica Kingsley.

Etherington, K. (2002). Working together: Editing a book as narrative research methodology. *Counselling and Psychotherapy Research, 2,* 167–176. https:// doi.org/10.1080/14733140212331384795

Fassinger, R. E. (2005). Paradigms, praxis, problems, and promise: Grounded theory in counseling psychology research. *Journal of Counseling Psychology, 52,* 156–166. https://doi.org/10.1037/0022-0167.52.2.156

Faulkner, R. A., Klock, K., & Gale, J. E. (2002). Qualitative research in family therapy: Publication trends from 1980 to 1999. *Journal of Marital and Family Therapy, 28*(1), 69–74. https://doi.org/10.1111/j.1752-0606.2002.tb01174.x

Feldman, S., & Shaw, L. (2019). The epistemological and ethical challenges of archiving and sharing qualitative data. *American Behavioral Scientist, 63*(6), 699–721. https://doi.org/10.1177/0002764218796084

Fessler, R. (1978). A phenomenological investigation of psychotherapeutic interpretation. *Dissertation Abstracts International,* 39, 2981–82.

Fetters, M. D., Curry, L. A., & Creswell, J. W. (2013). Achieving integration in mixed methods designs-Principles and practices. *Health Services Research, 48*(6, Pt2), 2134–2156. https://doi.org/10.1111/1475-6773.12117

Fine, M. (2006). Bearing witness: methods for researching oppression and resistance: A textbook for critical research. *Social Justice Research, 19*(1), 83–108.

Fine, M. (2012). Resuscitating critical psychology for "revolting" times. *Journal of Social Issues, 68*(2), 416–438. https://doi.org/10.1111/j.1540-4560.2012 .01756.x

Finlay, L. (2002). Negotiating the swamp: the opportunity and challenge of reflexivity in research practice. *Qualitative Research, 2*(2), 209–230. https:// doi.org/10.1177/146879410200200205

Finlay, L. (2008). A dance between the reduction and reflexivity: Explicating the "phenomenological psychological attitude." *Journal of Phenomenological Psychology, 39*(1), 1–32. https://doi.org/10.1163/156916208X311601

Finlay, L. (2012). Five lenses for the reflexive interviewer. In J. F. Gubrium, J. A. Holstein, A. B. Marvasti, & K. D. McKinney (Eds). *The SAGE handbook of interview research: The complexity of the craft.* (pp. 317–333). Thousand Oaks, CA: Sage. https://doi.org/10.4135/9781452218403.n23

Finlay, L., & Gough, B. (Eds.) (2003). *Reflexivity. A practical guide for researchers in health and social sciences.* Oxford: Blackwell. https://doi.org/10.1002/ 9780470776094

Fishman, D. B. (1999) *The case for a pragmatic psychology.* New York: NYU Press.

Fishman, D., Messer, S. D., Edwards, D. J. A., & Dattilio, F. M. (2017). *Case studies within psychotherapy trials: integrating qualitative and quantitative methods.* New York, NY: Oxford University Press. https://doi.org/10.1093/med: psych/9780199344635.001.0001

Flyvbjerg, B. (2001). *Making social science matter. Why social inquiry fails and how it can succeed again.* New York: Cambridge University Press. https://doi .org/10.1017/CBO9780511810503

Foucault, M. (1972) *The archaeology of knowledge and the discourse on language.* Translated from the French by A. M. Sheridan Smith. Pantheon Books, New York.

Fox, R. (2014). Are those germs in your pocket, or am I just crazy to see you? An autoethnographic consideration of obsessive-compulsive disorder. *Qualitative Inquiry, 20*(8), 966–975. https://doi.org/10.1177/ 1077800413513732

Frantzich, K. & Fels, L. (2018). Embodied theater ecology: Illuminating the gap through bridging depth psychology's encounter with performative inquiry. *British Journal of Guidance & Counselling, 46*(3), 272–281. https:// doi.org/10.1080/03069885.2017.1371668

Freud, S. (1912). The dynamics of transference. In P. Rieff, ed.; J. Riviere, trans., *Therapy and technique,* (pp. 77–87). New York: Collier Books.

Freud, S. (1953). Fragment of an analysis of a case of hysteria. In J. Strachey (Ed. and Trans.), *The standard edition of the complete psychological works of Sigmund Freud* (Vol. 7, pp. 15–22). London: Hogarth Press. (Original work published 1905)

Gabriel. L. (2009) Exploring the researcher-contributor research alliance. *In L. Gabriel and R. Casemore (Eds.) Relational ethics in practice: Narratives from counselling and psychotherapy. London: Routledge.* https://doi.org/10 .4324/9780203883143

Gaete Silva, J., Smoliak, O., & Couture, S. (2018). Reflexive questions as constructive interventions: A discursive perspective. In O. Smoliak & T. Strong (Eds.), *Therapy as discourse: Practice and research.* Basingstoke, UK: Palgrave Macmillan. https://doi.org/10.1007/978-3-319-93067-1_6

Gale, C., & Schröder, T. (2014). Experiences of self-practice/self-reflection in cognitive behavioural therapy: A meta-synthesis of qualitative studies. *Psychology and Psychotherapy: Theory, Research and Practice, 87*(4), 373–392. https://doi.org/10.1111/papt.12026 https://doi.org/10.1111/papt.12026

Gelo, O. C. G., Lagetto, G., Dinoi, C., Belfiore, E., Lombi, E., Blasi, S., Aria, M., & Ciavolino, E. (2019). Which methodological practice(s) for psychotherapy science? A systematic review and a proposal. *Integrative Psychological & Behavioral Science.* https://doi.org/10.1007/s12124-019-09494-3

George, A. L. & Bennett, A. (2005). *Case studies and theory development.* Cambridge, MA: MIT Press.

Gergen, K. J. (1973). Social psychology as history. *Journal of Personality and Social Psychology, 26*(2), 309–320. https://doi.org/10.1037/h0034436

Gergen, M., & Gergen, K. J. (2003). Marriage as a relational engagement. *Feminism & Psychology, 13*(4), 469–474. https://doi.org/10.1177/ 09593535030134012

Gibson, S., & Sullivan, C. (2018). A changing culture? Qualitative methods teaching in UK psychology. *Qualitative Psychology, 5*(2), 197–206. https:// doi.org/10.1037/qup0000100

Gill, I. J., & Fox, J. R. E. (2012). A qualitative meta-synthesis on the experience of psychotherapy for deaf and hard-of-hearing people. *Mental Health, Religion & Culture, 15*(6), 637–651. https://doi.org/10.1080/13674676 .2011.609161

Giorgi, A. (2009). *The descriptive phenomenological method in psychology: A modified Husserlian approach.* Pittsburgh, PA: Duquesne University Press.

Glaser, B. (1992). *Basics of grounded theory analysis.* Mill Valley, CA: Sociology Press.

Glaser, B., & Strauss, A. L. (1967). *The discovery of grounded theory strategies for qualitative research*. Chicago: Aldine. https://doi.org/10.1097/00006199-196807000-00014

Glynos, J. Howarth, D., Norval, A., & Speed, E. (2009). *Discourse analysis: Varieties and methods*. ESRC National Centre for Research Methods Review paper

Goldstein, T., Gray, J., Salisbury, J. & Snell, P. (2014). When qualitative research meets theatre: The complexities of performed ethnography and research-informed theatre project design. *Qualitative Inquiry, 20*, 674–685 https://doi.org/10.1177/1077800413513738

Granek, L. (2017). Emotional aspects of conducting qualitative research on psychological topics. *Qualitative Psychology, 4*(3), 281–286. https://doi.org/10.1037/qup0000086

Granek, L., & Nakash, O. (2016). The impact of qualitative research on the "real world" knowledge translation as education, policy, clinical training, and clinical practice. *Journal of Humanistic Psychology, 56*(4), 414–435. https://doi.org/10.1177/0022167815574623

Grant, A. (2006). Testimony: God and aeroplanes: My experience of breakdown and recovery. *Journal of Psychiatric & Mental Health Nursing, 13*, 456–457. https://doi.org/10.1111/j.1365-2850.2006.01004.x

Grant, A. (2010). Autoethnographic ethics and rewriting the fragmented self. *Journal of Psychiatric & Mental Health Nursing,17*, 111–116. https://doi.org/10.1111/j.1365-2850.2009.01478.x

Greenberg, L. S. (1984). A task analysis of intrapersonal conflict resolution. In L. N. Rice & L. S. Greenberg (eds.). *Patterns of change: Intensive analysis of psychotherapy process* (pp. 67–123). New York: Guilford Press

Greenberg, L. S. (2007). A guide to conducting a task analysis of psychotherapeutic change. *Psychotherapy Research, 17*(1), 15–30 https://doi.org/10.1080/10503300600720390

Greenberg, L. S. & Foerster, F. S. (1996). Task analysis exemplified: the process of resolving unfinished business. *Journal of Consulting and Clinical Psychology, 64*, 439–446. https://doi.org/10.1037/0022-006X.64.3.439

Guillemin, M. (2004). Understanding illness: Using drawings as a research method. *Qualitative Health Research, 14*(2), 272–289. https://doi.org/10.1177/1049732303260445

Guillemin, M., & Gillam, L. (2004). Ethics, reflexivity and "ethically important moments" in research. *Qualitative Inquiry, 10*, 261–280. https://doi.org/10.1177/1077800403262360

Guishard, M. A. (2018). Now's not the time! Qualitative data repositories on tricky ground: Comment on Dubois et al. (2018). *Qualitative Psychology, 5*(3), 402–408. https://doi.org/10.1037/qup0000085

Habermas, J. (1972). *Knowledge and human interests*. Boston: Beacon Press

Halbesleben, J. R. B. (2011). A plea for more training opportunities in qualitative methods. *Journal of Occupational and Organizational Psychology, 84*(4), 661–665. https://doi.org/10.1111/j.2044-8325.2011.02040.x

Halling, S., Leifer, M., & Rowe, J. O. (2006). Emergence of the dialogal approach: Forgiving another. In C. T. Fischer (Ed.), *Qualitative research methods for psychologists: Introduction through empirical examples*. New York: Academic Press. https://doi.org/10.1016/B978-012088470-4/50012-0

Halvorsen, M. S., Benum, K., Haavind, H., & McLeod, J. (2016). A life-saving therapy: The theory-building case of "Cora". *Pragmatic Case Studies in Psychotherapy, 12*(3), 158–193. https://doi.org/10.14713/pcsp.v12i3.1975

Hammersley, M., & Atkinson, P. (2019). *Ethnography: principles in practice*. 4th edn. London: Routledge. https://doi.org/10.4324/9781315146027

Harding, S. (2009). "Standpoint theories: Productively controversial", *Hypatia, 24*, 192–200. https://doi.org/10.1111/j.1527-2001.2009.01067.x

Harper, D. J. (2012). Surveying qualitative research teaching on British clinical psychology training programmes 1992–2006: A changing relationship? *Qualitative Research in Psychology, 9*(1), 5–12. https://doi.org/10.1080/14780887.2012.630626

Haverkamp, B. E. (2005). Ethical perspectives on qualitative research in applied psychology. *Journal of Counseling Psychology, 52*(2), 146–155. https://doi.org/10.1037/0022-0167.52.2.146

Hays, D. G., Wood, C., Dahl, H., & Kirk, J. A. (2016). Methodological rigor in Journal of Counseling & Development qualitative research articles: A 15-year review. *Journal of Counseling & Development, 94*(2), 172–183. https://doi.org/10.1002/jcad.12074

Heaton, J. (2008). Secondary analysis of qualitative data: an overview. *Historical Social Research, 33*(3), 33–45.

Heidegger, M. (1962). *Being and time* (J. Macquarrie, & E. Robinson, Trans.). Oxford, UK & Cambridge, USA: Blackwell Publishers Ltd

Hesse-Biber, S., & Johnson, R. B. (Eds.). (2015). *The Oxford handbook of multimethod and mixed methods research inquiry*. Oxford, England: Oxford University Press. https://doi.org/10.1093/oxfordhb/9780199933624.001.0001

Hill, C. E. (2012). *Consensual qualitative research: A practical resource for investigating social science phenomena*. (C. E. Hill, Ed.). Washington, DC: American Psychological Association.

Hill, C.E., Sim, W.E., Spangler, P., Stahl, J., Sullivan, T., & Teyber, E. (2008). Therapist immediacy in brief psychotherapy: Case Study 2. *Psychotherapy: Theory, Research, Practice and Training, 45*, 298–315. https://doi.org/10.1037/a0013306

Hill, C. E., Thompson, B. J., & Williams, E. N. (1997). A guide to conducting consensual qualitative research. *The Counseling Psychologist, 25*, 517–572. https://doi.org/10.1177/0011000097254001

Hills, J., Lees, J., Freshwater, D., & Cahill, J. (2018). Psychosoma in crisis: an autoethnographic study of medically unexplained symptoms and their diverse contexts. *British Journal of Guidance & Counselling, 46*(2), 135–147. https://doi.org/10.1080/03069885.2016.1172201

Hollway, W., & Jefferson, T. (2013). *Doing qualitative research differently: Free association, narrative and the interview method*, 2nd edn. London: Sage. https://doi.org/10.4135/9781526402233

Holmes, J. (2014). Countertransference in qualitative research: A critical appraisal. *Qualitative Research, 14*(2), 166–183. https://doi.org/10.1177/1468794112468473

Holmes, J. (2017). Reverie-informed research interviewing. *The International Journal of Psychoanalysis, 98*(3), 709–728. https://doi.org/10.1111/1745-8315.12581

Holzkamp, K. (1992). On doing psychology critically. *Theory & Psychology, 2*(2), 193–204. https://doi.org/10.1177/0959354392022007

Hoshmand,L.T.(2005).Narratology,culturalpsychology,andcounselingresearch. *Journal of Counseling Psychology, 52*, 178–186 https://doi.org/10.1037/0022-0167.52.2.178

Howard, G. S. (1983). Toward methodological pluralism. *Journal of Counseling Psychology, 30*(1), 19–21. https://doi.org/10.1037/0022-0167.30.1.19

Hubbard, G., Backett-Milburn, K., & Kemmer, D. (2001). Working with emotion: issues for the researcher in fieldwork and teamwork. *International Journal of Social Research Methodology, 4*(2), 119–137. https://doi.org/10.1080/13645570116992

Iwakabe, S., & Gazzola, N. (2009). From single-case studies to practice-based knowledge: Aggregating and synthesizing case studies. *Psychotherapy Research, 19*(4), 601–611. https://doi.org/10.1080/10503300802688494

Jackson, J.L., Chui, H.T., & Hill, C.E. (2012). *The modification of consensual qualitative research for case study research: an introduction to CQR-C*.

Jennings, L., & Skovholt, T. M. (2016). *Expertise in counseling and psychotherapy: Master therapist studies from around the world*. (L. Jennings & T. M. Skovholt, Eds.). New York, NY: Oxford University Press. https://doi.org/10.1093/med:psych/9780190222505.001.0001

Joanna Briggs Institute. (2007). *SUMARI: The Joanna Briggs Institute system for the unified management, assessment and review of information*. Adelaide, Australia: Author. Retrieved from http://www.joannabriggs.edu.au/services/sumari.php

Jones, S.H., Adams, T.E., & Ellis, C. (Eds)(2013). *Handbook of autoethnography*. New York: Routledge.

Josselson, R. (2013). *Interviewing for qualitative inquiry: A relational approach*. New York, NY: The Guilford Press.

Kara, H. (2015). *Creative research methods in the social sciences: A practical guide*. Bristol, UK: Policy Press. https://doi.org/10.2307/j.ctt1t88xn4

Kasper, L. B., Hill, C. E., & Kivlighan Jr, D. M. (2008). Therapist immediacy in brief psychotherapy: Case study I. *Psychotherapy: Theory, Research, Practice, Training, 45*(3), 281. https://doi.org/10.1037/a0013305

Keeley, S. M., Shemberg, K. M., & Zaynor, L. (1988). Dissertation research in clinical psychology: Beyond positivism? *Professional Psychology: Research and Practice, 19*(2), 216–222. https://doi.org/10.1037/0735-7028.19.2.216

Kincheloe, J. L., & McLaren, P. (2005). Rethinking critical theory and qualitative research. In N. K. Denzin & Y. S. Lincoln (Eds.), *The Sage handbook of qualitative research., 3rd ed. (pp. 303–342)*. Sage Publications Ltd.

Knowles, S. E., Toms, G., Sanders, C., Bee, P., Lovell, K., Rennick-Egglestone, S., Coyle, D., Kennedy, C. M., Littlewood, E., Kessler, D., Gilbody, S., & Bower, P. (2014). Qualitative meta-synthesis of user experience of computerised therapy for depression and anxiety. *PLoS ONE, 9*(1). https://doi.org/10.1371/journal.pone.0084323

Knox, S., Adrians, N., Everson, E., Shirley Hess, S., Hill, C., & Crook-Lyon, R. (2011) Clients' perspectives on therapy termination, *Psychotherapy Research, 21,* 154–167. https://doi.org/10.1080/10503307.2010.534509

Kovács, A., Kiss, D., Kassai, S., Pados, E., Kaló, Z., & Rácz, J. (2019). Mapping qualitative research in psychology across five Central-Eastern European countries: Contemporary trends: A paradigm analysis. *Qualitative Research in Psychology, 16*(3), 354–374. https://doi.org/10.1080/14780887.2019.1605271

Krauss, C. R. (2017). Back to the origins of the repudiation of Wundt: Oswald Külpe and Richard Avenarius. *Journal of the History of the Behavioral Sciences, 53*(1), 28–47. https://doi.org/10.1002/jhbs.21833

Kuhn, T. S. (1970). *The structure of scientific revolutions.* Chicago: University of Chicago Press.

Labov, W., & Fanshel, D. (1977). *Therapeutic discourse: Psychotherapy as conversation.* New York: Academic Press.

Lamont, M. & White, P. (2010). *Report from workshop on interdisciplinary standards for systematic qualitative research.* Washington, DC: National Science Foundation.

Lavik, K. O., Frøysa, H., Brattebø, K. F., McLeod, J., & Moltu, C. (2018). The first sessions of psychotherapy: A qualitative meta-analysis of alliance formation processes. *Journal of Psychotherapy Integration, 28*(3), 348–366. https://doi.org/10.1037/int0000101

Leavy, P. (Ed.) (2019). *Handbook of arts-based research.* New York: Guilford Press.

Levins, R. (1968). *Evolution in changing environments: Some theoretical explorations.* Princeton, NJ: Princeton University Press. https://doi.org/10.1515/9780691209418

Levitt, H. M. (2001). Sounds of silence in psychotherapy: The categorization of clients' pauses. *Psychotherapy Research, 11*(3), 295–309. https://doi.org/10.1080/713663985

Levitt, H. M. (2016). Qualitative research and humanistic psychotherapy. In D. J. Cain, K. Keenan, & S. Rubin (Eds.), *Humanistic psychotherapies: Handbook of research and practice., 2nd ed. (pp. 81–113).* Washington, DC: American Psychological Association. https://doi.org/10.1037/14775-004

Levitt, H. M. (2018). How to conduct a qualitative meta-analysis: Tailoring methods to enhance methodological integrity. *Psychotherapy Research, 28*(3), 367–378. https://doi.org/10.1080/10503307.2018.1447708

Levitt, H. M. (2019). A psychosocial genealogy of LGBTQ+ gender: An empirically based theory of gender and gender identity cultures. *Psychology of Women Quarterly, 43*(3), 275–297. https://doi.org/10.1177/0361684319834641

Levitt, H. M. (2021a). *Essentials of critical-constructivist grounded theory research.* American Psychological Association.

Levitt, H. M. (2021b). Qualitative generalization, not to the population but to the phenomenon: Reconceptualizing variation in qualitative research. *Qualitative Psychology, 8*(1), 95–110. https://doi-org.ezproxy.lib.umb.edu/10.1037/qup0000184)

Levitt, H. M., Bamberg, M., Creswell, J. W., Frost, D., Josselson, R., & Suárez-Orozco, Carola. (2018). Journal article reporting standards for qualitative research in psychology: The APA Publications and Communications Board Task Force report. *American Psychologist, 73*(1), 26–46. https://doi.org/10.1037/amp0000151

Levitt, H. M., Kannan, D., & Ippolito, M. R. (2013). Teaching qualitative methods using a research team approach: Publishing grounded theory projects with your class. *Qualitative Research in Psychology, 10*(2), 119–139. https://doi.org/10.1080/14780887.2011.586101

Levitt, H. M., McLeod, J. M., & Oddli, H. W. (2020). *Maximising the impact of qualitative research findings in psychotherapy: Formulating meaningful and evocative category/theme labels.* Unpublished manuscript. University of Massachusetts Boston, Boston, MA.

Levitt, H. M., Morrill, Z., & Collins, K. M. (2019). Considering methodological integrity in counselling and psychotherapy research. *Counselling & Psychotherapy Research.* https://doi.org/10.1002/capr.12284

Levitt, H. M., Morrill, Z., Collins, K. M., & Rizo, J. L. (2021). The methodological integrity of critical research. *Journal of Counseling Psychology, 68*(3), 357–370. https://doi.org/10.1037/cou0000523

Levitt, H. M., Motulsky, S. L., Wertz, F. J., Morrow, S. L., & Ponterotto, J. G. (2017). Recommendations for designing and reviewing qualitative research in psychology: Promoting methodological integrity. *Qualitative Psychology, 4*(1), 2–22. https://doi.org/10.1037/qup0000082

Levitt, H. M., Pomerville, A., & Surace, F. I. (2016). A qualitative meta-analysis examining clients' experiences of psychotherapy: A new agenda. *Psychological Bulletin, 142*(8), 801–830. https://doi.org/10.1037/bul0000057

Levitt, H. M., Pomerville, A., Surace, F. I., & Grabowski, L. M. (2017). Metamethod study of qualitative psychotherapy research on clients' experiences: Review and recommendations. *Journal of Counseling Psychology, 64*(6), 626–644. https://doi.org/10.1037/cou0000222

Lieblich, A. (2006). Vicissitudes: a study, a book, a play: lessons from the work of a narrative scholar. *Qualitative Inquiry, 12,* 60–80. https://doi.org/10.1177/1077800405282795

Lincoln, Y S. & Guba, E G. (1985). *Naturalistic inquiry.* Newbury Park, CA: Sage. https://doi.org/10.1016/0147-1767(85)90062-8

Lincoln, Y. S., & Guba, E. G. (1990). Judging the quality of case study reports. *Qualitative Studies in Education, 3,* 53–59. https://doi.org/10.1080/0951839900030105

Llewelyn, S. (1988). Psychological therapy as viewed by clients and therapists. *British Journal of Clinical Psychology, 27,* 223–238. https://doi.org/10.1111/j.2044-8260.1988.tb00779.x

Lo, C. O. (2014). Enhancing groundedness in realist grounded theory research. *Qualitative Psychology, 1*(1), 61–76. https://doi.org/10.1037/qup0000001

Lock, A., & Strong, T. (2010). *Social constructionism: Sources and stirrings in theory and practice.* Cambridge University Press. https://doi.org/10.1017/CBO9780511815454

Luborsky, L., & Crits-Christoph, P. (1989). A relationship pattern measure: The core conflictual relationship theme. *Psychiatry: Interpersonal and Biological Processes, 52*(3), 250–259. https://doi.org/10.1080/00332747.1989.11024448

Madill, A. (2015). Conversation analysis and psychotherapy process research. In O. Gelo, A. Pritz, & B. Rieken (eds.), *Psychotherapy research* (pp. 501–515). Vienna: Springer. https://doi.org/10.1007/978-3-7091-1382-0_24

Madill, A., & Gough, B. (2008). Qualitative research and its place in psychological science. *Psychological Methods, 13*(3), 254–271. https://doi.org/10.1037/a0013220

Manea, L., Boehnke, J. R., Gilbody, S., Moriarty, A. S., & McMillan, D. (2017). Are there researcher allegiance effects in diagnostic validation studies of the PHQ-9? A systematic review and meta-analysis. *BMJ Open, 7*(9), e015247. https://doi.org/10.1136/bmjopen-2016-015247

Mannay, D. (2010). Making the familiar strange: Can visual research methods render the familiar setting more perceptible? *Qualitative Research, 10*(1), 91–111. https://doi.org/10.1177/1468794109348684

Mannay, D. (2014). Storytelling beyond the academy: Exploring roles, responsibilities and regulations in the Open Access dissemination of research outputs and visual data. *Journal of Corporate Citizenship, 54,* 109–116. https://doi.org/10.9774/GLEAF.4700.2014.ju.00010

Maxwell, J. A. (2012). The importance of qualitative research for causal explanation in education. *Qualitative Inquiry, 18*(8), 655–661. https://doi.org/10.1177/1077800412452856

Mayotte-Blum, J., Slavin-Mulford, J., Lehmann, M., Pesale, F., Becker-Matero, N., & Hilsenroth, M. (2012). Therapeutic immediacy across long-term psychodynamic psychotherapy: An evidence-based case study. *Journal of Counseling Psychology, 59*(1), 27–40. https://doi.org/10.1037/a0026087

McGillivray, J., Gurtman, C., Boganin, C., & Sheen, J. (2015). Self-practice and self-reflection in training of psychological interventions and therapist skills development: A qualitative meta-synthesis review. *Australian Psychologist, 50*(6), 434–444. https://doi.org/10.1111/ap.12158

McIlveen, P. (2007). The genuine scientist-practitioner in vocational psychology: an autoethnography. *Qualitative Research in Psychology, 4,* 295–311. https://doi.org/10.1080/14780880701522403

McKenzie, E. A. (2015). An autoethnographic inquiry into the experience of grief after traumatic loss. *Illness, Crisis & Loss, 23*(2), 93–109. https://doi.org/10.1177/1054137315576620

McLeod, J. (2010). *Case study research in counselling and psychotherapy*. London: Sage. https://doi.org/10.4135/9781446287897

McLeod, J. (2011). *Qualitative research in counselling and psychotherapy* (2nd ed.). London, UK: Sage.

McLeod, J. (2013) Qualitative research: methods and contributions. In M. J. Lambert (ed.) *Bergin and Garfield's handbook of psychotherapy and behavior change*, 5th ed. (pp. 49–84). New York: Wiley.

McLeod, J. (2015). *Doing research in counselling and psychotherapy*. London: Sage.

McLeod, J., Levitt, H. M., & Stiles, W. B. (2021). Qualitative research: Contributions to theory, policy and practice. In M. Barkham, W. Lutz, & L. G. Castonguay (Eds.), *Bergin and Garfield's handbook of psychotherapy and behavior change*, 7th Edition. New York: Wiley.

McMillan, C., & Ramirez, H. E. (2016). Autoethnography as therapy for trauma. *Women & Therapy*, 39(3–4), 432–458. https://doi.org/10.1080/02703149.2016.1117278

McMullen, L. M., & Winston-Proctor, C. E. (2018). Qualitative inquiry in undergraduate psychology curricula and research training: Contexts and practices for transforming the optional into the obligatory. *Qualitative Psychology*, 5(2), 191–196. https://doi.org/10.1037/qup0000123

Meekums, B. (2008). Embodied narratives in becoming a counselling trainer: an autoethnographic study. *British Journal of Guidance & Counselling*, 36(3), 287–301. https://doi.org/10.1080/03069880802088952

Mendes, I., Rosa, C., Stiles, W. B., Caro Gabalda, I., Gomes, P., Basto, I., & Salgado, J. (2016). Setbacks in the process of assimilation of problematic experiences in two cases of emotion-focused therapy for depression. *Psychotherapy Research*, 26, 638–652. https://doi.org/10.1080/10503307.2015.1136443

Mertens, D. M., Bazeley, P., Bowleg, L., Fielding, N., Maxwell, J., Molina-Azorin, J. F., & Niglas, K. (2016). Expanding thinking through a kaleidoscopic look into the future: Implications of the mixed methods international research association's task force report on the future of mixed methods. *Journal of Mixed Methods Research*, 10(3), 221–227. https://doi.org/10.1177/1558689816649719

Messer, S. B. (2011). Theory development via single cases: A case study of the therapeutic relationship in psychodynamic therapy. *Pragmatic Case Studies in Psychotherapy*, 7(4), 440–448. https://doi.org/10.14713/pcsp.v7i4.1112

Michalak, E. E., Livingston, J. D., Maxwell, V., Hole, R., Hawke, L. D., & Parikh, S. V. (2014). Using theatre to address mental illness stigma: a knowledge translation study in bipolar disorder. *International Journal of Bipolar Disorders*, 2(1), 1. https://doi.org/10.1186/2194-7511-2-1

Miller, R. B., Kessler, M.C., Bauer, M., Howell, S., Kreiling, K., and Miller, M. (2011). Findings of the panel of psychological inquiry convened at Saint Michael's College, May 13, 2008: the case of "Anna." *Pragmatic Case Studies in Psychotherapy*, 7(1). https://doi.org/10.14713/pcsp.v7i1.1074

Miller, T., Birch, M., Mauthner, M., & Jessop, J. (Eds.). (2012). *Ethics in qualitative research*. 2nd edn. Thousand Oaks, CA: Sage. https://doi.org/10.4135/9781473913912

Miller, T., & Boulton, M. (2007). Changing constructions of informed consent: Qualitative research and complex social worlds. *Social Science & Medicine*, 65(11), 2199–2211. https://doi.org/10.1016/j.socscimed.2007.08.009

Moher, D., Liberati, A., Tetzlaff, J., & Altman, D. G. (2009). Preferred reporting items for systematic reviews and meta-analyses: The PRISMA statement. *Journal of Clinical Epidemiology*, 62, 1006–1012. https://doi.org/10.1016/j.jclinepi.2009.06.005

Moradi, B., & Grzanka, P. R. (2017). Using intersectionality responsibly: Toward critical epistemology, structural analysis, and social justice activism. *Journal of Counseling Psychology*, 64(5), 500–513. https://doi.org/10.1037/cou0000203

Morrow, S. L. (2005a). Quality and trustworthiness in qualitative research in counseling psychology. *Journal of Counseling Psychology*, 52, 250–260. https://doi.org/10.1037/0022-0167.52.2.250

Morrow, S. L. (2005b). Quality and trustworthiness in qualitative research in counseling psychology. *Journal of Counseling Psychology*, 52, 250–260. https://doi.org/10.1037/0022-0167.52.2.250

Morrow, S. (2006). Honor and respect: feminist collaborative research with sexually abused women. In C. T. Fischer (Ed.), *Qualitative research methods for psychologists: Introduction through empirical examples*. New York: Academic Press. https://doi.org/10.1016/B978-012088470-4/50009-0

Morrow, S. L., & Smith, M. L. (1995). Constructions of survival and coping by women who have survived childhood sexual abuse. *Journal of Counseling Psychology*, 42(1), 24–33. https://doi.org/10.1037/0022-0167.42.1.24

Moxnes, P. (2006). Group therapy as self-management training: A personal experience. *Group Analysis*, 39, 215–234. https://doi.org/10.1177/0533316406064076

Muntigl, P., & Horvath, A. O. (2014). The therapeutic relationship in action: How therapists and clients comanage relational disaffiliation. *Psychotherapy Research*, 24, 327–345. https://doi.org/10.1080/10503307.2013.807525

Murphy, D., Irfan, N., Barnett, H., Castledine, E., & Enescu, L. (2018). A systematic review and meta-synthesis of qualitative research into mandatory personal psychotherapy during training. *Counselling & Psychotherapy Research*. https://doi.org/10.1002/capr.12162

Nadal, K. L., Davidoff, K. C., Davis, L. S., Wong, Y., Marshall, D., & McKenzie, V. (2015). A qualitative approach to intersectional microaggressions: Understanding influences of race, ethnicity, gender, sexuality, and religion. *Qualitative Psychology*, 2(2), 147–163. https://doi.org/10.1037/qup0000026

Natvik, E. & Moltu, C. (2016) Just experiences? Ethical contributions of phenomenologically-oriented research. *Scandinavian Psychologist*, 3, e17. https://doi.org/10.15714/scandpsychol.3.e17

Neal Kimball, C., & Turner, S. (2018). Nurturing the apprentice: An immersion training in qualitative research. *Qualitative Psychology*, 5(2), 290–299. https://doi.org/10.1037/qup0000105

Neelakantan, L., Hetrick, S., & Michelson, D. (2018). Users' experiences of trauma-focused cognitive behavioural therapy for children and adolescents: A systematic review and metasynthesis of qualitative research. *European Child & Adolescent Psychiatry*, 28(7), 877–897. https://doi.org/10.1007/s00787-018-1150-z

Noblit, G. W., & Hare, R. D. (1988). *Meta-ethnography: Synthesizing qualitative studies*. Newbury Park, CA: Sage. https://doi.org/10.4135/9781412985000

Noyce, R., & Simpson, J. (2018). The experience of forming a therapeutic relationship from the client's perspective: A metasynthesis. *Psychotherapy Research*, 28(2), 281–296. https://doi.org/10.1080/10503307.2016.1208373

O'Keeffe, S., Martin, P., Target, M., & Midgley, N. (2019). 'I just stopped going': A mixed methods investigation into types of therapy dropout in adolescents with depression. *Frontiers in Psychology*, 10. https://doi.org/10.3389/fpsyg.2019.00075

Olson, M. (2015). An auto-ethnographic study of "open dialogue": The illumination of snow. *Family Process*, 54(4), 716–729. https://doi.org/10.1111/famp.12160

Osbeck, L. M. (2014). Scientific reasoning as sense making: Implications for qualitative inquiry. *Qualitative Psychology*, 1, 34–46. https://doi.org/10.1037/qup0000004

Packer, M. J., & Addison, R. B. (1989). *Entering the circle: Hermeneutic investigation in psychology* (M. J. Packer & R. B. Addison (Eds.)). State University of New York Press.

Parker, I. (2004). Criteria for qualitative research in psychology. *Qualitative Research in Psychology*, 1, 95–106. https://doi.org/10.1191/1478088704qp010oa

Parker, I. (2015). Politics and "applied psychology"? Theoretical concepts that question the disciplinary community. *Theory & Psychology*, 25(6), 719–734. https://doi.org/10.1177/0959354315592173

Pascual-Leone, A., Greenberg, L. S., & Pascual-Leone, J. (2009). Developments in task analysis: New methods to study change. *Psychotherapy Research*, 19(4–5), 527–542. https://doi.org/10.1080/10503300902897797

Pass, E. R. (2012). Combining expressive writing with an affect- and attachment-focused psychotherapeutic approach in the treatment of a single-incident trauma survivor: the case of" Grace". *Pragmatic Case Studies in Psychotherapy*, 8(2), 60–112. https://doi.org/10.14713/pcsp.v8i2.1492

Paterson, B. L., Thorne, S. E., Canam, C., & Jillings, C. (2001). *Meta-study of qualitative health research: A practical guide to meta-analysis and meta-synthesis*. Thousand Oaks, CA: Sage. https://doi.org/10.4135/9781412985017

Peräkylä, A. (2013). Conversation analysis in psychotherapy. In J. Sidnell & T. Stivers (Eds.), *Handbook of conversation analysis* (pp. 551–574). Oxford: Blackwell. https://doi.org/10.1002/9781118325001.ch27

Peräkylä, A. (2019). Conversation analysis and psychotherapy: Identifying transformative sequences. *Research on Language and Social Interaction*, 52, 257–280. https://doi.org/10.1080/08351813.2019.1631044

Peräkylä, A. Antaki, C. Vehviläinen, S. & Leudar, I. (Eds.) (2008). *Conversation analysis and psychotherapy*. Cambridge University Press. https://doi.org/10.1017/CBO9780511490002

Percival, J., Donovan, J., Kessler, D., & Turner, K. (2017). 'She believed in me'. What patients with depression value in their relationship with practitioners. *A secondary analysis of multiple qualitative data sets. Health Expectations, 20*(1), 85–97. https://doi.org/10.1111/hex.12436

Pierce, C. S. (1985). The proper treatment of hypotheses: A preliminary chapter, toward an examination of Hume's argument against miracles, in its logic and in its history. In C. Eisele (Ed.), *Historical perspectives on Peirce's Logic of Science. A history of science*, Vol. 2. Berlin: Mouton Publishers.

Pilgrim, D. (2019). *Critical realism for psychologists*. London: Routledge. https://doi.org/10.4324/9780429274497

Ponterotto, J. G. (2005). Qualitative research training in counseling psychology: A survey of directors of training. *Teaching of Psychology, 32*(1), 60–62.

Ponterotto, J. G. (2010). Qualitative research in multicultural psychology: Philosophical underpinnings, popular approaches, and ethical considerations. *Cultural Diversity and Ethnic Minority Psychology, 16*(4), 581–589. https://doi.org/10.1037/a0012051

Ponterotto, J. G., Mendelowitz, D. E., & Collabolletta, E. A. (2008). Promoting multicultural personality development: A strengths-based, positive psychology worldview for schools. *Professional School Counseling, 12*(2), 93–99. https://doi.org/10.5330/PSC.n.2010-12.93

Potter, J. & Wetherell, M. (1987). *Discourse and social psychology: Beyond attitudes and behaviour*. London: Sage.

Potter, J. & Wetherell, M. (1995). 'Discourse Analysis' in J. A. Smith, R. Harre, & L. van Langenhove (eds.) *Rethinking psychology*. London: Sage.

Quinn, M. C., Schofield, M. J., & Middleton, W. (2012). Successful psychotherapy for psychogenic seizures in men. *Psychotherapy Research, 22*(6), 682–698. https://doi.org/10.1080/10503307.2012.704085

Rabinovich, M., & Kacen, L. (2009). Let's look at the elephant: Metasynthesis of transference case studies for psychodynamic and cognitive psychotherapy integration. *Psychology and Psychotherapy: Theory, Research and Practice, 82*(4), 427–447. https://doi.org/10.1348/147608309X459662

Råbu, M., McLeod, J., Haavind, H., Bernhardt, I. S., Nissen-Lie, H., & Moltu, C. (2021) How psychotherapists make use of their experiences from being a client: Lessons from a collective autoethnography, *Counselling Psychology Quarterly, 34*(1), 109–128, https://doi.org/10.1080/09515070.2019.1671319

Rennie, D. L. (1996). Fifteen years of doing qualitative research on psychotherapy. *British Journal of Guidance & Counselling, 24*(3), 317–327. https://doi.org/10.1080/03069889600760291

Rennie, D. L. (2000). Grounded theory methodology as methodical hermeneutics: Reconciling realism and relativism. *Theory & Psychology, 10*(4), 481–501. https://doi.org/10.1177/0959354300104003

Rennie, D. L. (2007). Methodical hermeneutics and humanistic psychology. *The Humanistic Psychologist, 35*(1), 1–14. https://doi.org/10.1080/08873260709336693

Rennie, D. L. (2012). Qualitative research as methodical hermeneutics. *Psychological Methods, 17*(3), 385–398. https://doi.org/10.1037/a0029250

Rennie, D. L., & Fergus, K. D. (2006). Embodied categorizing in the grounded theory method: Methodical hermeneutics in action. *Theory & Psychology, 16*(4), 483–503. https://doi.org/10.1177/0959354306066202

Rennie, D. L., & Frommer, J. (2015). Applications of qualitative and mixed-methods counseling and psychotherapy research. In O. C. G. Gelo, A. Pritz, & B. Rieken (Eds.), *Psychotherapy research: Foundations, process, and outcome*. (pp. 429–454). New York, NY: Springer-Verlag Publishing. https://doi.org/10.1007/978-3-7091-1382-0_21

Rennie, D. L., Phillips, J. R., & Quartaro, G. K. (1988). Grounded theory: A promising approach to conceptualization in psychology? *Canadian Psychology/Psychologie Canadienne, 29*(2), 139–150. https://doi.org/10.1037/h0079765

Rice, L. N. & Greenberg, L. S. (1984) *Patterns of change: intensive analysis of psychotherapy process*. New York: Guilford.

Roald, T., Køppe, S., Bechmann Jensen, T., Moeskjær Hansen, J., & Levin, K. (2021). Why do we always generalize in qualitative research? *Qualitative Psychology, 8*(1), 69–81. https://doi-org.ezproxy.lib.umb.edu/10.1037/qup0000138

Rober, P., & Rosenblatt, P. C. (2017). Silence and memories of war: An autoethnographic exploration of family secrecy. *Family Process, 56*(1), 250–261. https://doi.org/10.1111/famp.12174

Rodgers, B. (2006). Life space mapping: Preliminary results from the development of a new method for investigating counselling outcomes. *Counselling and Psychotherapy Research, 6*(4), 227–232. https://doi.org/10.1080/14733140601045437

Rodgers, B. & Elliott, R. (2015). Qualitative methods in psychotherapy outcome research. In O.C.G. Gelo, A. Pritz, & B. Rieken (Eds). *Psychotherapy research: Foundations, process and outcome*. (pp. 559–578). Vienna: Springer-Verlag. https://doi.org/10.1007/978-3-7091-1382-0_27

Rorty, R. (1980). *Philosophy and the mirror of nature*. Princeton, New Jersey: Princeton University Press.

Rouse, A., Armstrong, J., & McLeod, J. (2015). Enabling connections: Counsellor creativity and therapeutic practice. *Counselling and Psychotherapy Research, 15*(3), 171–179.

Rubin, J. D., Bell, S., & McClelland, S. I. (2018). Graduate education in qualitative methods in US psychology: Current trends and recommendations for the future. *Qualitative Research in Psychology, 15*(1), 29–50. https://doi.org/10.1080/14780887.2017.1392668

Sacks, H., Schegloff, E. A., & Jefferson, G. A. (1974). A simplest systematics for the organization of turn-taking in dyadic conversation. *Language, 50*, 697–735. https://doi.org/10.1353/lan.1974.0010

Safran, J.D. & Muran, J.C. (1996). The resolution of ruptures in the therapeutic alliance. *Journal of Consulting and Clinical Psychology, 64*, 447–458. https://doi.org/10.1037/0022-006X.64.3.447

Sandelowski, M., & Barroso, J. (2003). Creating metasummaries of qualitative findings. *Nursing Research, 52*, 226–233. https://doi.org/10.1097/00006199-200307000-00004

Sandhu, A., Ives, J., Birchwood, M., & Upthegrove, R. (2013). The subjective experience and phenomenology of depression following first episode psychosis: A qualitative study using photo-elicitation. *Journal of Affective Disorders, 149*(1–3), 166–174. https://doi.org/10.1016/j.jad.2013.01.018

Sawyer, R.D. & Norris, J. (2012). *Duoethnography*. Oxford: Oxford University Press. https://doi.org/10.1093/acprof:osobl/9780199757404.001.0001

Schegloff, E. A. (2007). *Sequence organization in interaction*. New York: Cambridge University Press. https://doi.org/10.1017/CBO9780511791208

Schielke, H.J., Fishman, J.L., Osatuke, K., & Stiles, W. B. (2009). Creative consensus on interpretations of qualitative data: The Ward method. *Psychotherapy Research, 19*(4–5), 558–565. https://doi.org/10.1080/10503300802621180

Shadish, W. R. (1986). Planned critical multiplism: Some elaborations. *Behavioral Assessment, 8*, 75–103.

Shaw, R. L., Bishop, F. L., Horwood, J., Chilcot, J., & Arden, M. A. (2019). Enhancing the quality and transparency of qualitative research methods in health psychology. *British Journal of Health Psychology, 24*(4), 739–745. https://doi.org/10.1111/bjhp.12393

Shelton, K., & Delgado-Romero, E. A. (2011). Sexual orientation microaggressions: The experience of lesbian, gay, bisexual, and queer clients in psychotherapy. *Journal of Counseling Psychology, 58*(2), 210–221. https://doi.org/10.1037/a0022251

Shinebourne, P., & Smith, J. A. (2010). The communicative power of metaphors: An analysis and interpretation of metaphors in accounts of the experience of addiction. *Psychology and Psychotherapy: Theory, Research and Practice, 83*(1), 59–73. https://doi.org/10.1348/147608309X468077

Shinebourne, P., & Smith, J. A. (2011). Images of addiction and recovery: An interpretative phenomenological analysis of the experience of addiction and recovery as expressed in visual images. *Drugs: Education, Prevention and Policy, 18*(5), 313–322. https://doi.org/10.3109/09687637.2010.514621

Sidnell, J. (2013). Basic conversation analytic methods. In J. Sidnell & T. Stivers (Eds.), *Handbook of conversation analysis* (pp. 77–99). Oxford: Blackwell. https://doi.org/10.1002/9781118325001.ch5

Sidnell, J. & Stivers, T. (eds.) (2013). *Handbook of conversation analysis. Oxford: Blackwell*. https://doi.org/10.1002/9781118325001

Sieber, J. E. and Tolich, M. B. (2013) *Planning ethically responsible research*. 2nd edn. Thousand Oaks, CA: Sage. https://doi.org/10.4135/9781506335162

Sitter, K.C. (2017). Taking a closer look at photovoice as a participatory action research method. *Journal of Progressive Human Services, 28*(1), 36–48. https://doi.org/10.1080/10428232.2017.1249243

Slife, B. D., & Gantt, E. E. (1999). Methodological pluralism: A framework for psychotherapy research. *Journal of Clinical Psychology, 55*(12), 1453–1465. https://doi.org/10.1002/(SICI)1097-4679(199912)55:12<1453::AID-JCLP4>3.0.CO;2-C

Smith, J. A., Flowers, P., & Larkin, M. (2009). *Interpretative phenomenological analysis: Theory, method and research*. London, UK: Sage.

Smith, K., Shoemark, A., McLeod, J., & McLeod, J. (2014). Moving on: A case analysis of process and outcome in person-centred psychotherapy for health anxiety. *Person-Centered & Experiential Psychotherapies, 13*(2), 111–127. https://doi.org/10.1080/14779757.2014.886080

Smoliak, O., & Strong, T. (Eds) (2018). *Therapy as discourse: Practice and research*. Basingstoke, UK: Palgrave Macmillan. https://doi.org/10.1007/978-3-319-93067-1

Speciale, M., Hess, J., & Speedlin, S. (2015). You don't look like a lesbian: A coautoethnography of intersectional identities in counselor education. *Journal of LGBT Issues in Counseling, 9*(4), 256–272. https://doi.org/10.1080/15538605.2015.1103678

Speer, S. A., & Stokoe, E. (2014). Ethics in action: Consent-gaining interactions and implications for research practice. *British Journal of Social Psychology, 53*(1), 54–73. https://doi.org/10.1111/bjso.12009

Stadtlander, L. M., & Giles, M. J. (2010). Virtual instruction: A qualitative research laboratory course. *Teaching of Psychology, 37*(4), 281–286. https://doi.org/10.1080/00986283.2010.510971

Stänicke, E., Strømme, H., Killingmo, B., & Gullestad, S. E. (2015). Analytic change: Assessing ways of being in a psychoanalytic follow-up interview. *The International Journal of Psychoanalysis, 96*(3), 797–815. https://doi.org/10.1111/1745-8315.12145

Stiles, W. B. (1981). Science, experience, and truth: A conversation with myself. *Teaching of Psychology, 8*, 227–230. https://doi.org/10.1207/s15328023top0804_11

Stiles, W. B. (1993). Quality control in qualitative research. *Clinical Psychology Review, 13*, 593–618. https://doi.org/10.1016/0272-7358(93)90048-Q

Stiles, W. B. (1999). Signs and voices in psychotherapy. *Psychotherapy Research, 9*, 1–21. https://doi.org/10.1080/10503309912331332561

Stiles, W. B. (2002). Assimilation of problematic experiences. In J. C. Norcross (Ed.), *Psychotherapy relationships that work: Therapist contributions and responsiveness to patients* (pp. 357–365). New York: Oxford University Press.

Stiles, W. B. (2006). Numbers can be enriching. *New Ideas in Psychology, 24*, 252–262. https://doi.org/10.1016/j.newideapsych.2006.10.003

Stiles, W. B. (2009). Logical operations in theory-building case studies. *Pragmatic Case Studies in Psychotherapy, 5*(3), 9–22. https://doi.org/10.14713/pcsp.v5i3.973

Stiles, W. B. (2011). Coming to terms. *Psychotherapy Research, 21*, 367–384. https://doi.org/10.1080/10503307.2011.582186

Stiles, W. B. (2015). Theory-building, enriching, and fact-gathering: Alternative purposes of psychotherapy research. In O. Gelo, A. Pritz, & B. Rieken (Eds), *Psychotherapy research: General issues, process, and outcome* (pp. 159–179). New York: Springer-Verlag. https://doi.org/10.1007/978-3-7091-1382-0_8

Stiles, W. B. (2017). Theory-building case studies. In D. Murphy (Ed.), *Counselling psychology: A textbook for study and practice* (pp. 439–452). Chichester, UK: Wiley.

Stiles, W. B. (in press). Bricoleurs and theory-building qualitative research: Responses to responsiveness. In T. G. Lindstad, E. Stänicke, & J. Valsiner (Eds), *Respect for thought: Jan Smedslund's legacy for psychology* (pp.). New York: Springer.

Stiles, W. B., & Angus, L. (2001). Qualitative research on clients' assimilation of problematic experiences in psychotherapy. In J. Frommer & D. L. Rennie (Eds), *Qualitative psychotherapy research: Methods and methodology* (pp. 112–127). Lengerich, Germany: Pabst Science Publishers. Also published in *Psychologische Beiträge, 43*, 570–585.

Stiles, W. B., Caro Gabalda, I., & Ribeiro, E. (2016). Exceeding the therapeutic zone of proximal development as a clinical error. *Psychotherapy, 53*, 268–272. https://doi.org/10.1037/pst0000061

Stoppard, J. (2002). Navigating the hazards of orthodoxy: Introducing a graduate course on qualitative methods into the psychology curriculum. *Canadian Psychology/Psychologie Canadienne, 43*(3), 143–153. https://doi.org/10.1037/h0086911

Strauss, A. L. & Corbin, J. (1990). *Basics of qualitative research: Grounded theory procedures and techniques*, Thousand Oaks, CA: Sage.

Strauss, B. M., Barber, J. P., & Castonguay, L. G. (2015). *Visions in psychotherapy research and practice: Reflections from presidents of the Society for Psychotherapy Research*. (B. M. Strauss, J. P. Barber, & L. G. Castonguay, Eds.).

New York, NY: Routledge/Taylor & Francis. https://doi.org/10.4324/9780203126714

Strømme, H., Gullestad, S.E., Stänicke, E., & Killingmo, B. (2010). A widened scope on therapist development: designing a research interview informed by psychoanalysis. *Qualitative Research in Psychology, 7*(3), 214–232. https://doi.org/10.1080/14780880802659542

Strong, T., & Smoliak, O. (2018). Introduction to discursive research and discursive therapies. In O. Smoliak & T. Strong (Eds.), *Therapy as discourse: Practice and research*. Basingstoke, UK: Palgrave Macmillan. https://doi.org/10.1007/978-3-319-93067-1

Suzuki, L. A., Ahluwalia, M. K., Mattis, J. S., & Quizon, C. A. (2005). Ethnography in counseling psychology research: Possibilities for application. *Journal of Counseling Psychology, 52*(2), 206–214. https://doi.org/10.1037/0022-0167.52.2.206

Swift, J. K., & Wampold, B. E. (2018). Inclusion and exclusion strategies for conducting meta-analyses. *Psychotherapy Research. 28*(3), 356–366. https://doi.org/10.1080/10503307.2017.1405169

Tashakkori, A., & Teddlie, C. (Eds.). (2010). *Handbook of mixed methods in social and behavioral research* (2nd ed.). Thousand Oaks, CA: Sage. https://doi.org/10.4135/9781506335193

Taylor, C. (1971). Interpretation and the sciences of man. *Review of Metaphysics, 25*, 3–51

Teo, T. (1998). Klaus Holzkamp and the rise and decline of German critical psychology. *History of Psychology, 1*(3), 235–253. https://doi.org/10.1037/1093-4510.1.3.235

Teo, T. (2015). Critical psychology: A geography of intellectual engagement and resistance. *American Psychologist, 70*(3), 243–254. https://doi.org/10.1037/a0038727

Tuck, E., & Yang, K. W. (2014b). R-words: Refusing research. In D. Paris & M. T. Winn (Eds.), *Humanizing research: Decolonizing qualitative inquiry with youth and communities*. (pp. 223–248). Thousand Oaks, CA: SAGE. https://doi.org/10.4135/9781544329611.n12

Thompson, A.R., & Russo, K. (2012) Ethical dilemmas for clinical psychologists in conducting qualitative research. *Qualitative Research in Psychology, 9*(1), 32–46. https://doi.org/10.1080/14780887.2012.630636

Timulak, L. (2007). Identifying core categories of client identified impact of helpful events in psychotherapy: A qualitative metaanalysis. *Psychotherapy Research, 17*, 310–320. https://doi.org/10.1080/10503300600608116

Timulak, L. (2009). Meta-analysis of qualitative studies: A tool for reviewing qualitative research findings in psychotherapy. *Psychotherapy Research, 19*(4–5), 591–600. https://doi.org/10.1080/10503300802477989

Timulak, L., & Creaner, M. (2013). Experiences of conducting qualitative meta-analysis. *Counselling Psychology Review, 28*(4), 94–104.

Timulak, L., & Elliott, R. (2018). Taking stock of descriptive-interpretative qualitative psychotherapy research: Issues and observations from the front line. *Counselling & Psychotherapy Research.* https://doi.org/10.1002/capr.12197

Timulak, L., & McElvaney, R. (2013). Qualitative meta-analysis of insight events in psychotherapy. *Counselling Psychology Quarterly, 26*(2), 131–150. https://doi.org/10.1080/09515070.2013.792997

Tolman, C. W. (2009). Holzkamp's critical psychology as a science from the standpoint of the human subject. *Theory & Psychology, 19*(2), 149–160. https://doi.org/10.1177/0959354309103535

Torre, M. E., Fine, M., Stoudt, B. G., & Fox, M. (2012). Critical participatory action research as public science. In H. Cooper, P. M. Camic, D. L. Long, A. T. Panter, D. Rindskopf, & K. J. Sher (Eds.), *APA handbook of research methods in psychology, Vol. 2. Research designs: Quantitative, qualitative, neuropsychological, and biological* (pp. 171–184). Washington, DC, US: American Psychological Association. https://doi.org/10.1037/13620-011

Tuck, E., & Yang, K. W. (2014). Unbecoming claims: Pedagogies of refusal in qualitative research. *Qualitative Inquiry, 20*(6), 811–818. https://doi.org/10.1177/1077800414553026

Tuhiwai Smith, L. (1999). *Decolonizing methodologies: Research and indigenous peoples*. Dunedin, NZ: Zed Books.

Tuval-Mashiach, R. (2017). Raising the curtain: The importance of transparency in qualitative research. *Qualitative Psychology, 4*(2), 126–138. https://doi.org/10.1037/qup0000062

Van den Hoonard, W.C. (2002) *Walking the tightrope: ethical issues for qualitative researchers*. Toronto: University of Toronto Press. https://doi.org/10.3138/9781442683204

Veseth, M., Binder, P. E., Borg, M., & Davidson, L. (2012). Toward caring for oneself in a life of intense ups and downs: A reflexive-collaborative exploration of recovery in bipolar disorder. *Qualitative Health Research*, 22(1), 119–133. https://doi.org/10.1177/1049732311411487

Wall, J. M., Kwee, J. L., Hu, M., & McDonald, M. J. (2017). Enhancing the hermeneutic single-case efficacy design: Bridging the research-practice gap. *Psychotherapy Research*, 27(5), 539–548. https://doi.org/10.1080/10503307.2015.1136441

Wendt, D. C., & Gone, J. P. (2016). Integrating professional and indigenous therapies: an urban American Indian narrative clinical case study. *The Counseling Psychologist*, 44(5), 695–729. https://doi.org/10.1177/0011000016638741

Wertz, F. J. (1999). Multiple methods in psychology: Epistemological grounding and the possibility of unity. *Journal of Theoretical and Philosophical Psychology*, 19, 131–166. https://doi.org/10.1037/h0091173

Wertz, F. J. (2014). Qualitative inquiry in the history of psychology. *Qualitative Psychology*, 1, 4–16. https://doi.org/10.1037/qup0000007

Wertz, F. J. (2015). Phenomenology: Methods, historical development, and applications in psychology. In J. Martin, J. Sugarman, & K. L. Slaney (Eds.), *The Wiley handbook of theoretical and philosophical psychology: Methods, approaches, and new directions for social sciences.* (pp. 85–101). Wiley-Blackwell. https://doi.org/10.1002/9781118748213.ch6

Wertz, F. J., Charmaz, K., McMullen, L., Josselson, R., Anderson, R., & McSpadden, E. (2011). *Five ways of doing qualitative analysis: Phenomenological psychology, grounded theory, discourse analysis, narrative research, and intuitive inquiry.* New York, NY: Guilford.

Willemsen, J., Inslegers, R., Meganck, R., Geerardyn, F., Desmet, M., & Vanheule, S. (2015). A metasynthesis of published case studies through Lacan's l-schema: Transference in perversion. *The International Journal of Psychoanalysis*, 96(3), 773–795. https://doi.org/10.1111/1745-8315.12179

Willis, A., Bondi, L., Burgess, M.C., Miller, G. & Fergusson, D. (2014) Engaging with a history of counselling, spirituality and faith in Scotland: a readers' theatre script. *British Journal of Guidance & Counselling*, 42(5), 525–543. https://doi.org/10.1080/03069885.2014.928667

Wilson, J., Gabriel, L., & Stiles, W. B. 2025 (submitted). Assimilation in bereavement: Charting the process of grief recovery in the case of Sophie. Manuscript submitted for publication.

Wiseman, H., & Atzil-Slonim, D. (2018). Closeness and distance dynamics in the therapeutic relationship. In O. Tishby & H. Wiseman (Eds.), *Developing the therapeutic relationship: Integrating case studies, research, and practice.* American Psychological Association. https://doi.org/10.1037/0000093-005

Wiseman, H., & Rice, L. N. (1989). Sequential analyses of therapist-client interaction during change events: A task-focused approach. *Journal of Consulting and Clinical Psychology*, 57(2), 281–286. https://doi.org/10.1037/0022-006X.57.2.281

Woodgate, R.L., Zurba, M., & Tennent, P. (2017). A day in the life of a young person with anxiety: arts-based boundary objects used to communicate the results of health research. *Forum: Qualitative Social Research*, 18(3), 17

Wootton, D. (2015). *The invention of science: a new history of the scientific revolution.* London: Penguin.

Yin, R.K. (2018). *Case study research and applications: Design and methods.* 6th edn. Thousand Oaks, CA: Sage.

Yoder, W. R., Karyotaki, E., Cristea, I. A., Van Duin, D., & Cuijpers, P. (2019). Researcher allegiance in research on psychosocial interventions: Meta-research study protocol and pilot study. *BMJ Open*, 9(2), e024622. https://doi.org/10.1136/bmjopen-2018-024622

PART II

Measuring and Evidencing Change in Efficacy and Practice-Based Research

•

CHAPTER 4

MEASURING, PREDICTING, AND TRACKING CHANGE IN PSYCHOTHERAPY

WOLFGANG LUTZ, KIM DE JONG, JULIAN A RUBEL, AND JAIME DELGADILLO

Abstract

This chapter addresses fundamental issues of change in psychotherapy: how to measure, monitor, predict change, and provide feedback on treatment outcome. The chapter starts with a historical overview, covering several approaches applied to measure change in psychotherapy research. We proceed with a description of classical concepts to evaluate change such as effect sizes, meta-analysis and clinical significance. Next, central concepts to study treatment dosage, attrition, follow-up, as well as the handling of missing data are presented. We then cover new ways to measure and to model change including item response models, multilevel and mixed models, ecological momentary assessment and new biological and technical measures. We discuss the core questions of how to optimally measure outcomes, how often to measure change during therapy, and how therapists can use measurements to improve clinical practice. In addition, the need for further improvements in measurement precision are debated. Furthermore, the chapter discusses predictors and moderators of change, rational and empirical decision-making models, as well as methods to identify patterns of early response. We explore processes and mechanisms of change including sections on between- and within-patient variation and dyadic models. In the final section, we review the evidence base for feedback-informed treatment and the application of evidence-based personalization in clinical practice. Such new developments allow the inclusion of individually tailored problem-solving strategies for treatment selection and adaptation, especially for those patients at risk of treatment failure. The development of change measurement in psychotherapy has evolved considerably in recent decades, making it an integral part of clinical practice and training.

OVERVIEW

INTRODUCTION[1]

Measuring change is one of the most fundamental issues in psychotherapy research and has been at its heart since the inception of the field over a hundred years ago. This was already recognized in the first edition of the *Handbook of Psychotherapy and Behavior Change* (Bergin & Garfield, 1971). This chapter offers an update on advances in the field, and should be seen as a companion to the comprehensive chapters on this topic found in the 5th and 6th editions of the *Handbook of Psychotherapy and Behavior Change* (Hill & Lambert, 2004; Ogles, 2013). The chapter discusses various methodologies that researchers have proposed to tackle questions of how to measure and predict change, and how to provide feedback on treatment outcomes to patients and therapists, whereas Chapter 2 discusses research designs (e.g., clinical trials, meta-analysis, examining processes) and measurement issues.

Several quantitative and qualitative perspectives on the assessment of change are applied in the psychotherapy literature, although individual researchers typically tend to prefer one method over the other. Qualitative methods are covered extensively in Chapters 3 and 9 in this volume. Therefore, this chapter will focus on the measurement of change from a quantitative and statistical perspective. This perspective reflects the most widely used paradigm in psychotherapy research since its inception and corresponds to the tradition of seeing it as belonging to the natural and social sciences.

This chapter is intended to be used as a practical guide to support the measurement of change in clinical practice, to inform the design of new studies, and also as a didactic overview of methodological developments in this field. As such, it is aimed at psychotherapy students, practitioners, and experienced researchers. To fulfill these goals, the chapter covers six broad areas. In the first two sections, definitions of psychological change, statistical measurement criteria, and solutions to deal with measurement problems are covered. The next two sections deal with methodological approaches to the prediction and understanding of change. Subsequent sections describe applications of the described methodologies in psychotherapy practice and provide an update on the evidence base for routine outcome monitoring and feedback approaches. In the concluding section, practical recommendations for future advances in this field are outlined.

QUANTIFYING CHANGE

The history of science is characterized, at least in part, by efforts to develop and calibrate measures of change processes in natural phenomena. Similar developments are evident in psychotherapy research. In the early days of the profession, clinical approaches to understanding therapeutic change

[1]The authors are most thankful for the tremendously helpful proofreading by Kaitlyn Boyle (University of Trier) as well as the extremely valuable comments and literature suggestions from Jan Böhnke (University of Dundee). We also thank Ann-Kathrin Deisenhofer, Brian Schwartz, Alice Arndt, Steffen Eberhardt, and Julia Giesemann (University of Trier) for their helpful comments, supporting figure design, and compiling the reference list.

were mostly developed based on case reports, where outcomes were assessed by expert clinical judgment (e.g., Ellis, 1957). Several decades later, considerable progress has been made in terms of standardization of change measurement. The following section deals with the most important issues and new developments with regard to measuring and modeling change in the context of psychological interventions, including perspectives on group-level and single-case level analyses.

Psychometric Issues

Several important assumptions apply to the measurement of change in psychotherapy. First, any instrument used to assess treatment outcomes should actually measure what it is intended to measure (*validity*). It should also be feasible to use in routine clinical practice (*clinical utility*). An instrument used repeatedly to assess clinical outcomes over time should consistently measure a construct in the same way (*reliability*), and clinically meaningful changes should be adequately indexed by the instrument (*sensitivity to change*). The concepts of *reliability* and *validity* have already been covered in Chapter 2 of this volume. Here, we will briefly describe current perspectives on taxonomies of measurement targets, sensitivity to change, multidimensionality, psychometric developments, and clinical utility.

Taxonomies

What should be measured to assess clinically important change in psychotherapy? Over the years, several taxonomies have been developed to conceptualize and capture the different aspects of change induced by psychological interventions. One commonly applied taxonomy was introduced and refined by Lambert and colleagues (e.g., Lambert & Hill, 1994). It includes five partially overlapping dimensions of change: *content, social level, source, technology,* and *time orientation*:

1. *Content dimension.* The content dimension includes a decision by the researcher as to whether behavioral (e.g., physiological), affective, and/or cognitive content measures are included.
2. *Social dimension.* The social level refers to the inclusion of intrapersonal (e.g., symptoms) versus interpersonal (e.g., interpersonal problems) constructs.
3. *Source dimension.* This dimension is related to the different sources of assessment that might be used to generate multiple dimensions of outcome information: (a) patient/client self-report; (b) therapist ratings; (c) other raters (e.g., spouse, family members, colleagues); (d) trained observers/judges; (e) institutional information (e.g., public or insurance company records).
4. *Technology dimension.* The technology or format dimension refers to the technology or format used to assess the information. This includes, for example, whether the outcome assessment is based on global change ratings at the end of treatment (direct change or retrospective measurement) or on pre–post measures of patient symptoms at the beginning and end of treatment (indirect change measurement). Retrospective assessment and pre–post change measures

correlate only moderately with each other. Pre–post measures represent the more common research practice, and retrospective measures are affected by recall effects that lead to higher effect sizes (e.g., Flückiger et al., 2007). Some debate centers around the question of whether to use standardized (e.g., SCL-90-R or BSI) and/or individualized measures (e.g., a specific problem or goal defined by the patient). For example, using Goal Attainment Scaling (GAS; Kiresuk & Sherman, 1968), in which therapists and patients define treatment goals together at the beginning of treatment. After the termination of treatment, the patient uses a Likert scale to rate to what degree the goals were reached. This approach has good face validity with patients and therapists, although reviews of the empirical literature raise questions about the validity and reliability of GAS as well as other idiosyncratic measures of patients' self-defined problems or targets (Lloyd et al., 2019). This makes their use as a general means of assessing treatment outcome and their comparability with standardized measures difficult. However, they are potentially complementary to nomothetic measures, helping to fit the assessment strategy to the individual patient (Lloyd et al., 2019).

5. *Time dimension.* Howard et al. (1993) provide another taxonomy, which focuses specifically on the *time orientation*, and which is informed by the *phase model* of change. The phase model postulates that three sequentially dependent dimensions constitute the therapeutic recovery process, with each further step needing more therapeutic investment (sessions) to be changed: (a) remoralization – the enhancement of hope and positive expectations; (b) remediation – the achievement of symptomatic relief; and (c) rehabilitation – the reduction of maladaptive behavior, affective and cognitive patterns, and interpersonal problems that interfere with current life functioning (Stulz & Lutz, 2007). Some newer studies on psychotherapeutic change have also compared the extent of change in individual items or patterns of symptomatology over the course of treatment (e.g., Mullarkey et al., 2018; Sembill et al., 2017). Recently, studies in the fields of clinical and personality psychology have revisited the question about whether some aspects of personality may change differentially over therapy (e.g., Roberts et al., 2017).

In recent years, several taxonomic developments based on new concepts of nosology have also been introduced into the field. The idea here was to extend the unidimensional (common cause or latent variable model) perspective to include multidimensional and transdiagnostic perspectives into psychopathology and change measurement. For example, the National Institute of Mental Health (NIMH) introduced Research Domain Criteria (RDoC; Insel, 2014) as an alternative nosology and research framework focusing on five domains (negative and positive valence, social function, cognition, and arousal) in order to move past the classic concept of diagnosis as a categorical entity with one supposed common cause (e.g., emphasized in the *Diagnostic and Statistical Manual of Mental Disorders*). The multivariate Hierarchical Taxonomy of Psychopathology (HiTop), based on factor analysis research, also focuses on transdiagnostic dimensions, but frames them in

a hierarchical order: symptoms (level 1) nested within traits (level 2), nested within factors (level 3), and broader clusters (level 4) of psychopathological conditions (e.g., internalizing, externalizing, thought disorders, detachment; e.g., Conway et al., 2019).

Such taxonomies reflect the decisions that researchers need to make about which measures (e.g., behavioral, physiological, affective, cognitive, interpersonal, psychotherapy process), which data source (e.g., patient, therapist, others), which technology (e.g., questionnaires, diary methods, assessments via wearables or smart phones), and how many assessment points to use (e.g., retrospective change ratings at the end of treatment, pre–post measurement of intended outcome measures, or continuous, daily or weekly outcome measurement). Furthermore, contemporary studies on expected treatment response show that measuring several pretreatment individual differences is useful to gain a better understanding of each patient's likely prognosis during and after therapy. Hence, psychometric and measurement considerations also extend to features of the patient's clinical, personality, and demographic profile. Clearly, researchers and therapists seeking to understand and measure change are faced with the difficult task of deciding which domains to select and measure at different possible time points. Figure 4.1 depicts these various domains and measurement targets.

Sensitivity to Change

When selecting a target construct or a series of measures, the question of sensitivity to change is of central importance. An instrument with low sensitivity to change (or low responsiveness) substantially reduces the detectability of the true effect size of an intervention. As a result, instruments with a higher sensitivity to change have often been treated as superior to other instruments. However, this judgment relies heavily on the assumption that the most responsive instrument is also the one that provides the most valid measure of patient improvement (Fried, 2016), which may not necessarily be true.

In psychotherapy research, an instrument's sensitivity to change is often estimated based on repeated assessments (e.g., pre- and posttreatment) and change scores (or effect sizes) between assessments. An anchor-based method is then used to examine the degree to which change is indexed by an instrument in comparison to another well-established instrument (e.g., Ogles, 2013; Youn et al., 2018). Examples of effect sizes and correlations between several outcome measures are depicted in the Supplement A at the end of this chapter. The tables show that the most commonly used instruments are strongly (though not perfectly) correlated and have similar, but varying change sensitivity (effect sizes[2]). An alternative estimation of the responsiveness of an instrument may be achieved by

---

[2] For example, in a sample of 521 patients from the outpatient center at the University of Trier, the disorder specific instruments had a pre–post effect size of: BDI-II = 1.2, PHQ-9 = 1.1, GAD-7=1.1; whereas the global instruments had effect sizes of: Brief Symptom Inventory (BSI) General Symptom Index (GSI) = 0.88, the Outcome Questionnaire (OQ) = 1.32; the Questionnaire for the Evaluation of Psychotherapeutic Progress (QEP) = 1.14. The BSI-GSI correlated with the disorder specific instruments: BDI-II = 0.71; PHQ-9 = 0.78; GAD-7 = 0.70 and with the global instruments: OQ = 0.77, FEP = 0.76. A more detailed table can be found in the Supplemental Materials at the end of this chapter.

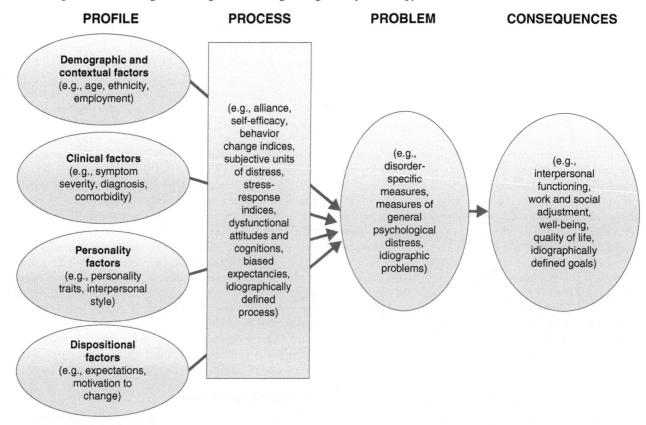

FIGURE 4.1 Potential measurement domains and targets.

calculating the intraclass correlation for slope in a growth model and to compare instruments based on that change index. It indicates how much of the total variance in the outcomes measured by the instrument (e.g., symptoms) is explained by the change in scores between time 1 and time 2 (Fok & Henry, 2015). Fok and Henry (2015) also discuss several ways by which the sensitivity to change of an instrument can be improved (e.g., eliminating redundant items).

Unidimensional versus Multidimensional

Although many studies of psychological interventions focus on psychological symptom change as the most important outcome dimension, most researchers agree that change or outcome in psychotherapy is not unidimensional. Psychological disorders are not homogeneous, but rather, multidimensional constructs that include varying content dimensions and levels of measurement. Psychological problems or disorders are often comorbid, meaning that patients seeking psychological treatment do not only have *one* symptom or disorder. Many patients show a relatively high degree of comorbidity of psychological problems (e.g., Lambert, 2013). Of course, this is a conceptual and psychometric challenge for intervention research attempting to provide both appropriate and standardized descriptions of the investigated psychological problems or disorders. One corresponding issue is the question of whether to measure symptoms using unidimensional/disorder-specific (e.g., GAD-7; PHQ-9)

or multidimensional symptom scales (e.g., OQ-45). The advantage of multidimensional scales is that they cover a wider range of problems and are especially useful when patients are not homogeneous, as is common in clinical studies (Hill & Lambert, 2004). These measures include a range of symptoms (e.g., depression, anxiety), covering not only a single dimension or specific symptoms of a disorder but also symptoms relevant to other or related disorders.

There has been a long debate about the conceptualization of psychological disorders as transdiagnostic, multidimensional, or as one general factor, rather than as specific distinct categories of disorders (see above). Nevertheless, so far, in many studies, only unidimensional scales are used to assess the most relevant symptoms related to a specific diagnosis. Unidimensional scales have the advantage of being relatively short and therefore easy to administer several times over the course of treatment. One problem is that these measures are not as distinctive as their names or labels may suggest. For example, depression and anxiety scales are often correlated (see Supplement A). There is also a debate about whether measures with the same label measure the same construct (Böhnke & Croudace, 2016; Fried, 2017). For example, Fried (2017) found substantial heterogeneity of symptoms and low overlap among common depression scales. Furthermore, different assessment sources of the same construct (e.g., self-report vs. interview-based assessments) do not necessarily result in overlapping findings (Georgi et al., 2018).

New Psychometric Developments

Lately, three new psychometric strategies have emerged, which attempt to deal with the problems posed by the heterogeneity of psychological problems or disorders. One area of psychometric investigation is related to measurement concordance. In this context, new longitudinal multi-trait-multi-method (MTMM) approaches are used to study the overlap between various sources of change (e.g., the relationship between self-report and psychophysiological data or direct and indirect change measures). These approaches allow for a better investigation of the differential impact of trait, time, and method effects on reliability, convergent, and discriminant validity, as well as measurement specificity (e.g., Eid et al., 2013; van Montfort et al., 2018). The second new area of investigation in psychometrics relates to the application of modern item response theory (IRT) or factor analytic models (e.g., bifactor models). The third recent development in psychometrics attempts to go beyond traditional scales and summary scores and instead to focus on individual items and networks of symptoms. Instead of using sum scores to study change, individual symptom networks and their change over time are investigated (e.g., Borsboom, 2017; see section on Ecological Momentary Assessment and Modeling Intensive Longitudinal Data).

Clinical Utility

Although technically not a psychometric property, when one is interested in measuring change in psychotherapy, especially in routine practice, the clinical utility of an instrument is an important factor to consider. Ogles (2013) recommends that instruments should be "reasonably priced, require little time of the therapist and patient, and be quickly and easily administered" (p. 141). Instruments that are easy to score and interpret, and short to administer, are more likely to be used in clinical practice and a range of instruments have been specifically developed with these criteria in mind, such as the Outcome Questionnaire (OQ-45; Lambert, 2015) and the Clinical Outcomes in Routine Evaluation (CORE) suite of measures (e.g., CORE-OM/CORE-10; Barkham et al., 2010). For several instruments, shorter versions were developed to enhance their clinical utility such as the Brief Symptom Inventory (BSI; Derogatis & Melisaratos, 1983; short version of Symptom Checklist-90 [SCL-90-R; Derogatis, 1977]), the Counseling Center Assessment – 34-item version (CCAPS-34; Locke et al., 2012), and the Patient Health Questionnaire – 9-item version (Kroenke et al., 2001). Note that brief versions of instruments are not always equally well assessed for psychometric properties as the original versions (Kazdin, 2017). On the positive side, well-developed shorter versions tend to correlate highly (e.g., above .80 for the SCL-90-R and its short forms and .78 with the PHQ-9) with the original instruments (e.g., Böhnke et al., 2014 and see also footnote 2). There is a similar issue with instruments that have been translated into new languages, where new language versions must also be assessed for psychometric properties as the original instrument and might require adaptations of the instrument to the cultural context.

Statistical Significance, Effect Size, and Meta-Analysis

The efficacy of psychotherapy has traditionally been evaluated in randomized controlled trials (RCTs), comparing an active treatment with no treatment, a control group (e.g., supportive listening), or another active treatment. Outcomes of interventions are then compared based on significance testing, which tests the probability of obtaining the expected result under the specified statistical model against a preset significance level (α). Most often, the results of clinical trials are examined using standardized and psychometrically robust measures that correspond to the *problem* and *consequences* domains described in Figure 4.1.

In the late 1980s, a debate emerged regarding the use of significance testing and statistical power (see Chapter 2 of this volume), as the binary nature of the test results provided little information about the magnitude or importance of the obtained differences. Furthermore, this approach fails to guide therapists on the question of which intervention works best for individual patients (e.g., Rosnow & Rosenthal, 1989).

Additionally, nonsignificant findings often remain unpublished, both because researchers may not be motivated to invest time in publishing such results (the *file-drawer problem*; Scargle, 1999) and because journal editors prefer to publish studies yielding significant findings (*publication bias*; Easterbrook et al., 1991). Moreover, there are typically many defensible approaches to statistical analyses, providing researchers with the possibility of presenting the version that is most likely to confirm their own ideas (*researcher degrees of freedom*; Simmons et al., 2011). Finally, researchers often also search for effects beyond the main study hypothesis, and when this is conducted in a very liberal manner and with insufficient attention to type I errors, it can verge on *p-hacking* (Wicherts et al., 2016). Ioannidis (2005) stated that as a result of these and other biases, published results may not represent clinical reality. In response to the criticisms surrounding significance testing, a range of alternative approaches to interpreting research results have been developed (for an overview, see Nuzzo, 2014).

Whereas significance testing only answers the question of whether a difference is statistically significant (e.g., highly probable to be the correct interpretation of a hypothesis), effect sizes provide information on the magnitude of the difference. Additionally, effect sizes are standardized scores, allowing for direct comparisons between studies, even if different outcome instruments have been used across different studies. There are multiple ways to calculate effect sizes. For instance, effect sizes can be calculated to quantify the magnitude of change that has occurred during treatment (*pre-post*, *within-group effect size*), or in order to characterize the magnitude of the difference between two treatments (*between-group effect size*). The most common metric for effect size is the standardized mean difference (SMD), which constitutes the *d*-family (e.g., Cohen's *d* or Hedges' *g*) and is calculated by dividing the mean difference (between pre- and post-treatment, or between two treatment arms) by a standard deviation of either the pretreatment score (for pre–post comparisons), or a pooled standard deviation (for comparisons between treatment groups).

One problem with the d-family effect sizes is that the magnitude of the effect is highly dependent on the distribution properties of the sample (Cohen, 1992). In particular, in the situation in which pre–post treatment differences are quantified, the effect size can be very large, even when little change has occurred. All it takes is for there to be low variability in the distributions of scores at pre- and post-treatment. Similar issues affect the interpretation of between-group effect sizes (de Jong & DeRubeis, 2018). Furthermore, effect sizes are standardized mean differences and do not control for initial impairment (at least not without adjustment). This can lead to false conclusions about effect size differences, for example when patient groups with varying initial symptom impairment are compared across studies or within a study. This can easily happen, for example, when comparing effect size differences between naturalistic settings and RCTs (Lutz et al., 2016).

Effect sizes in the d-family are typically interpreted based on recommendations by Cohen (1992) that a value of 0.20 or less is negligible, values between 0.20 and 0.49 are small effects, 0.50 to 0.79 correspond to medium-sized effects, and values of 0.80 and higher denote large effects. Most active treatments have a medium to large effect size compared to waitlist control groups and a small or negligible effect size compared to other treatments (see Chapter 5 in this volume).

Effect sizes from different studies are often synthesized using meta-analysis, which aggregates the effect sizes of original studies resulting in a pooled effect size (see Chapter 2 of this volume). The magnitude of an effect can be statistically expressed in different ways (e.g., Cohen's d, Hedges' g, correlations, odds ratios, number needed to treat [NNT]), and it is possible to convert one metric to another (e.g., Kazdin, 2017). In Table 4.1, we compare the effectiveness of psychotherapy with different effect size indices found in meta-analyses of common interventions in medicine. The comparison demonstrates that the effect sizes of psychotherapy are at least as good and often better than those found in medical interventions for common illnesses.

Clinical Significance

Effect sizes do not necessarily allow conclusions of the clinical relevance of an intervention for individual patients. Several authors have devised methods to address this issue. For example, Kazdin (2017) presented nine different methods to evaluate the clinical significance of change in intervention studies. These methods include: no longer meeting diagnostic criteria or the problem is no longer present, falling in the range of a nonclinical group at posttreatment, a large improvement between pre- and post-treatment on outcome measures,

TABLE 4.1   Effect Size Indices for Various Psychological and Medical Treatments

Treatment	Effect size SMD	Point biserial correlation r (r^2)	NNT	Probability of superiority	Odds ratio
Psychotherapy overall[1] (Wampold & Imel, 2015)	.75–.85	.35–.39 (.12) – (.15)	3.4–3.9	70.21–72.61%	3.9–4.7
Psychotherapy for depression[2] (Cuijpers et al., 2021)	.65	.31 (.10)	4.5	67.77%	3.3
Corticosteroid treatment of chronic asthma[3] (Leucht et al., 2015)	.56	.27 (.07)	5.4	65.39%	2.8
Aspirin for prevention of vascular disease[3] (Leucht et al., 2015)	.12	.06 (.004)	29.2	53.38%	1.2
Etanercept treatment of rheumatoid arthritis[3] (Kristensen et al., 2007)	.64	.31 (.09)	4.6	67.46%	3.2
Copaxone treatment of relapsing-remitting multiple sclerosis[3] (Freedman et al., 2008)	.16	.08 (.006)	21.6	54.50%	1.3
Oesophageal cancer: Chemoradiotherapy plus surgery vs. only surgery (Fiorica et al., 2004)	.35	.17 (.03)	9.2	59.77%	1.9

[1] Waitlist controls, treatment-as-usual or placebo used in the control group (see Chapter 5 for a debate on effect sizes in different control groups)
[2] Average SMD of psychological therapies with significant effects compared to pill placebo control (Cuijpers et al., 2021)
[3] Placebo controls
SMD = standardized mean difference; r = point biserial correlation; r^2 = explained variance (Rosenthal et al., 1994).
Odds ratio = A measure that quantifies the odds of an event (e.g., positive treatment outcome) occurring in one group (e.g., clinical intervention) to the odds of it occurring in another group (e.g., control group). An odds ratio of 1 indicates that the investigated event (e.g., positive outcome) is equally likely to occur in both groups. An odds ratio greater than 1 indicates that the event (positive outcome) is more likely to occur in the first group (clinical intervention). Also, a ratio less than 1 would indicate that a positive outcome is less likely to occur in the intervention group than in the control group.
NNT = The number needed to treat (NNT) is the number of patients that need to be treated to have one additional positive outcome (Furukawa & Leucht, 2011). The NNT calculation assumes a success rate of 19% in the control group (Cuijpers et al., 2019).
Probability of superiority = The probability of superiority is the probability that a randomly selected patient from the treatment group has a better outcome than a randomly selected patient from the control group. This probability-based effect measure is also called common language effect size (CL). The nonparametric version is related to the area under the curve (AUC), the Wilcoxon Rank Sum, and the Mann-Whitney U nonparametric test statistics, and it can be calculated from d or r (Ruscio, 2008).

retrospective evaluations by the patient, as well as the social impact in daily life.

A frequently used method in psychotherapy research is a method referred to as *reliable and clinically significant change* (Jacobson & Truax, 1991). This method defines clinical significance as returning to normal functioning. The criteria are twofold: (a) the magnitude of change must be statistically reliable; and (b) the patient must complete treatment with a score indistinguishable from scores of people who are not in need of treatment.

Criterion (a) is defined via the reliable change index (RCI). The RCI is the minimum amount of change that must occur to be greater than the measurement error of the outcome instrument and is a function of the specific instrument's reliability and variability in the clinical population. Criterion (b), the cutoff point, is defined based on the norms of the outcome instrument, which serve to differentiate between individuals that are more or less likely to meet criteria for a clinically significant psychological condition or problem.

The method works best when adequate norms are available for both the patient population, referred to as the dysfunctional population, and the population that is not in need of treatment, referred to as the functional population. Jacobson and Truax (1991) provide three methods to calculate the cut-off point for normal functioning: a score of functioning (a) two standard deviations above the patient population mean; (b) two standard deviations below the normal population mean; or (c) at the intersection of the dysfunctional and functional population curves. Methods (a) and (b) can be used when information is only available for one population, or when the population curves are nonoverlapping. Method (c) is the most commonly used method. Within this method, if reliable change has occurred and symptoms reduce below the cut-off point for clinical significance, this can be referred to as a *reliable and clinically significant improvement* (RCSI). If the cut-off point is not crossed, but reliable change was achieved, this can be classified as *reliable improvement*. If reliable change occurs in a negative direction, this can be classified as *reliable deterioration*. Patients are considered non-responders if they neither improve nor deteriorate (Jacobson & Truax, 1991).

There are some limitations to defining clinically significant change in this way and many authors have criticized the method and suggested alternatives (de Jong & DeRubeis, 2018; Hiller et al., 2012; Lambert & Ogles, 2004). Usually, functional norms also include scores from patients with psychological impairment and the method is vulnerable to regression to the mean, with highly symptomatic patients having higher chances of achieving reliable change, if not controlled for (Lambert & Ogles, 2004).

Treatment Dosage

The measurement of change in psychotherapy is deeply related to our understanding of how change occurs over time. The debate about the optimal treatment dosage in psychotherapy has been influenced by pharmacological research investigating the dose of, for example, a drug treatment (measured by the quantity and/or concentration of the active pharmaceutical agent) to improve the health status of patients with a given disease (e.g., Howard et al., 1986; Lambert, 2013). In psychotherapy, dosage is usually defined as the number of treatment sessions delivered, including the frequency (e.g., one or more times per week) and total number of sessions. This relatively broad definition has been criticized and the stability of the amount of active ingredients or clinical change agents across sessions has been questioned (e.g., Cuijpers et al., 2019; Stiles et al., 1998). Furthermore, making recommendations for an optimal dose in psychotherapy is challenging in view of the diverse outcome measures, patient samples, clinical settings, and psychotherapeutic protocols that are applied across studies (Robinson et al., 2020). Nevertheless, the number of sessions has been widely applied as a practically useful definition of dosage in psychotherapy research.

RCTs and Dosage

In the RCT research tradition, dosage is usually decided a priori by specifying a set number of sessions (e.g., 8, 16, 24) in treatment protocols. For example, in a classic study comparing different treatment lengths, the Second Sheffield Psychotherapy Project (SPP2; Shapiro et al., 1994), 117 patients were assigned to 8–16 sessions of either cognitive behavioral or psychodynamic interpersonal therapy. Interestingly, an advantage of 16 over eight sessions was only present for severely depressed patients. In this study as well as other newer RCTs, the protocol defines the number of sessions and therefore the length of treatment (except for pragmatic trials where dosage mirrors routine practice). Cuijpers et al. (2013) conducted a meta-regression analysis of 70 RCTs comprising 5,403 patients in individual therapy for adult depression with a control group design (e.g., waiting list, care-as-usual). Results showed no correlation between the number of sessions and outcome (controlling for study characteristics). However, the authors found a correlation between the number of sessions per week and treatment effect sizes, showing that the increase from one session per week to two sessions per week, while keeping the overall number of treatment sessions constant, significantly increased the effect size. This conclusion is supported by an RCT that compared the post-treatment outcomes of patients who were either randomized to once versus twice-weekly sessions of psychotherapy for depression (Bruijniks et al., 2020).

Nevertheless, evidence supporting the notion that shorter treatments and longer treatments result in similar overall effects has also been reported in other studies (including internet interventions) investigating several mental health problems. It remains unclear whether this holds for all patients and settings, especially for patients with more chronic and severe mental health disorders and long-term outcomes (i.e., follow-up assessments; e.g., Robinson et al., 2020). Further studies are needed that prospectively compare once-weekly versus twice-weekly sessions and other dosage and setting regimes. There is a further problem with conclusions related to RCTs and dosage. In RCTs, the differences between treatments with a specific amount of sessions do not necessarily generalize to (especially small) differences between the same treatment provided with differing numbers of session, which would make an almost endless number of studies necessary to determine optimal length. As a result, another research tradition emerged investigating dosage in naturalistic settings.

Dose-Effect and Good-Enough Level Models

In a seminal study on dose-effect relations in psychotherapy, Howard et al. (1986) integrated data from 15 studies to determine the number of improved patients dependent on the number of sessions provided. Conducting a probit analysis, the authors found that an increasing number of sessions were associated with diminishing returns regarding the percentage of improvement. This negatively accelerating (e.g., log-linear) pattern is termed the *dose-response* or *dose-effect model* of psychotherapy (Howard et al., 1986; Kadera et al., 1996). It reflects a pattern of dose-response relations often found in pharmaceutical studies and draws on the idea that the total effect of psychotherapy decreases with an increasing number of sessions over time. Change occurs relatively quickly (for some patients) during the initial stages of therapy, but later reaches a plateau where little symptomatic change is observed over the course of additional sessions.

Using more rigorous clinically significant change criteria and session-by-session data, Kadera et al. (1996) and Hansen et al. (2002) found a similar log-linear pattern of diminishing returns for later sessions. Using the stricter change criteria, 50% of patients starting treatment in the dysfunctional range required 21 sessions to meet clinically significant change criteria. However, for 70% of patients to meet these criteria, more than 35 sessions were necessary. Numerous other studies in different countries have replicated this dose-response pattern, despite the application of different outcome measures and analytic approaches (Barkham et al., 1996). The log-linear shape of the response trajectory seems to be found in most patients, while some patients (probably less than 20%) follow a linear trend (e.g., Owen et al., 2015; Stulz et al., 2013). There is evidence that the optimal duration of therapy varies according to treatment settings and the severity/complexity of clinical samples (see review by Robinson et al., 2020).

These findings have often been used to inform recommendations of the optimal dose (i.e., number of sessions) of psychotherapy, while they have not necessarily been realized in all service systems, often leading to lower improvement rates in naturalistic settings (e.g., Hansen et al., 2002). In contrast, other studies suggest that treatments under naturalistic conditions can indeed show effects comparable to RCTs (e.g., Barkham et al., 2008; McAleavey et al., 2019). For example, Lutz et al. (2016) showed that the effects of naturalistic CBT for depression are equal to those reported in the CBT group of the National Institute of Mental Health Treatment of Depression Collaborative Research Program (NIMH TDCRP; Elkin et al., 1989), when patient samples are comparable. The authors used propensity score matching based on several patient intake characteristics (e.g., symptom severity, socio-demographics). However, to reach similar depression outcome scores, CBT in controlled settings needed about 17 sessions, while about 35 sessions were necessary in naturalistic settings. It remains unclear whether the RCT treatment resulted in faster improvements or whether the naturalistic treatment was just longer, because of the particularities of the service system.

While the dose-response model focuses on a general causal link between the number of sessions (dosage) and improvement, the *good-enough level model* (GEL, Barkham et al., 2006; Stiles et al., 2008) is more concerned with the differential responsiveness of patients. According to the GEL model, patients stay in treatment (if this is allowed and not restricted by arbitrary treatment durations) until they have reached a level of change that they perceive to be *good enough*. The GEL model interprets the diminishing returns of successive sessions (negatively accelerated or log-linear shape) as the result of aggregating patients with varying amounts of treatment sessions, and argues that the individual trajectories might be linear rather than log-linear for some patients (Barkham et al., 2006). This explanation fits better with findings showing that the number of sessions is not always positively related to the degree of improvement, assuming that patients change at different rates and early responders may leave treatment early under naturalistic conditions (cf. Baldwin et al., 2009; Owen et al., 2015).

Taken together, the findings support the notion that the dose-effect and GEL models are not as contradictory as originally thought. Importantly, there seems to be no uniform optimal dose of treatment for all patients. The dose-effect association depends on specific patient responsiveness and individual characteristics such as impairment, comorbidity or treatment target. Therefore, defining expected dose-response parameters for more clinically homogeneous groups is necessary to yield sensible recommendations. In practice, dosage is usually defined by clinical service systems, varying by country and region (and funding) and often not based on research (Flückiger et al., 2020). The routine and longitudinal monitoring of patient progress over the course of treatment would allow for a more patient-specific adaptation of treatment duration in different service settings.

Attrition and Follow-up

Related to treatment dosage and longitudinal outcome measurement is the issue of attrition (dropout). While not all patients who end treatment prematurely have a negative treatment outcome, overall, patients who drop out of treatment have poorer treatment effects, higher hospitalization rates, reduced work productivity, and higher social costs than patients who do not (e.g., Delgadillo et al., 2014; Swift & Greenberg, 2012). Clearly, missing data due to attrition is highly problematic for outcome measurement. It is well known that only analyzing data from treatment completers yields biased and unrealistically optimistic effect sizes. Hence, understanding dropout and dealing with missing data are essential.

Definition of Dropout and Empirical Findings

Swift and Greenberg (2012) conducted a meta-analysis on rates of dropout comprising 83,834 patients from 669 studies. The mean dropout rate was 19.7% for a diverse range of settings (17% in efficacy and 26% in effectiveness). However, dropout rates reported by individual studies ranged between 0 and 74.2%. This large variance is primarily due to a lack of consensus on the definition of attrition. Definitions include, for example, therapist judgment of the appropriateness of termination, attrition before a predefined number of sessions or missing final outcome assessments (e.g., Maher et al., 2010; Zimmermann et al., 2017). Furthermore, dropout definitions are related to the study design. While predefined definitions of the number of sessions according to a treatment protocol are the standard in RCTs, this is less often the case under naturalistic conditions. Defining dropout as not completing a predefined number of sessions may lead to early treatment response and termination being falsely evaluated as dropout. In any case, the interpretation of study results needs always to take the dropout definition into account and the field would profit from a more standardized definition and clearer operationalization of dropout.

Predictors of Dropout

Several studies have also investigated potential predictors of dropout. High initial impairment, low global functioning, younger age, lower level of education, having a personality disorder, and negative treatment expectations have been shown to be significant predictors (Ogrodniczuk et al., 2008; Swift & Greenberg, 2012; Zimmermann et al., 2017). Firth, Delgadillo et al. (2019) found that patients who were more sociodemographically different compared to most other members of their CBT psychoeducation group were less likely to attend and complete all treatment sessions. This effect was heightened in patients from socioeconomically deprived backgrounds.

Furthermore, therapist effects related to dropout have also been found (e.g., Xiao et al., 2017). For example, Saxon et al. (2017) investigated a sample of 10,521 patients treated by 85 therapists and found therapist effects on dropout (12.6%) and patient deterioration (10.1%). Interestingly, these therapist effects did not correlate. Lutz et al. (2015) and Zimmermann et al. (2017) also found no correlation between therapist effects on outcome, treatment length and dropout. Figure 4.2 shows standardized individual effect sizes of 42 different therapists (each treated at least five patients, N = 458) from the outpatient center at the University of Trier with respect to dropout, outcome and treatment length (case mix controlled). For example, therapist A in Figure 4.2, seems to have a high dropout rate

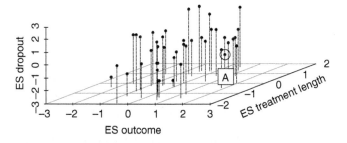

FIGURE 4.2 Therapist effects in terms of standardized effect sizes of outcome (BSI), treatment length (number of sessions), and dropout (higher ES scores represent better outcomes, less treatment sessions, and lower dropout rates).

(ES = −0.83), as well as a high treatment outcome (ES = 1.43), and an average treatment length (ES = 0.15). Taken together, therapist effects on treatment dropout, treatment length (dosage), and outcome seem not to be correlated, but can be seen as important indicators of individual therapist performance.

Follow-up

Clearly, attrition is even more of a problem in follow-up studies. Kazdin (2017) describes important issues that need to be considered in follow-up studies with the overall aim of reducing attrition rate to obtain the information necessary to evaluate the stability of treatment effects (e.g., the length of the measure, frequency and way of contacting patients). It is also important to decide how long the follow-up period after treatment should be. Most studies use follow-up periods of between six months and three years. However, psychotherapy effects have been shown to be relatively stable up to nine years and longer (Brachel et al., 2019; Lambert, 2013; McCarthy et al., 2018). This even holds when more strict clinical significance criteria are applied, although not all patients improve and a substantial number of patients do not respond or relapse (Brachel et al., 2019). However, results of psychotherapy seem to be more stable than those of psychopharmacological treatments after the intervention has ended (e.g., for depression, see Chapter 20 in this volume).

Dealing with Missing Data

Missing data and premature termination pose major challenges to the analysis of change and can seriously bias study results and interpretation (e.g., Brody, 2016). When dealing with missing data, it is important to think about the potential causes or mechanisms that are responsible for it. Typically, three types of missing data patterns are distinguished: (a) missing at random (MAR) describes a situation in which missingness may depend on observed (i.e., measured) data, but are unrelated to unobserved data (i.e., variables not measured); (b) missing completely at random (MCAR) describes missing data that are unrelated to both observed and unobserved data; and (c) missing not at random (MNAR), where missing data are related to unobserved data (e.g., Graham, 2009).

As a consequence, MCAR and MAR result in decreased power, but not necessarily in biased estimates (in the case of MAR, bias free estimates can be obtained if the variables associated with missingness are controlled for). As a result, several imputation strategies have been developed to deal with MCAR and MAR. However, if scores are MNAR, biased estimates are difficult to avoid. Traditional imputation approaches in which missing data points are imputed with one specific observed score (also called nonstochastic methods) can be differentiated from more complex predictive models in which imputation is regularly repeated several times (also called stochastic methods).

Observed Score Imputations

Replacing missing values with a mean score, best scores, worst scores, or the last observation carried forward (LOCF) are widely applied approaches. The LOCF approach uses the last available assessment for each patient in the study and replaces potential missing assessments with it (e.g., Brody, 2016). A general observation is that effect sizes from formal pre–post measures are usually higher than those obtained from pre-last available score (LOCF). Therefore, LOCF results in more conservative effect estimates. Another traditional approach to deal with missing data is listwise deletion in which all cases that have at least one missing data point on any of the variables of interest are deleted (i.e., completer analyses). Bias can be small in completer analyses if the percentage of deleted cases is lower than 5%. However, even in these scenarios, it is recommended to use one of the modern imputation strategies described below (Graham, 2009). Importantly, completers are usually very different from those who drop out. Therefore, it is recommended to compare these two groups with regard to the other observed variables. Those variables that are significantly different between the two groups should be included in the analysis as covariates (referred to as *case-mix adjustment*). Also, it is recommended to compare the results of completer analysis with intention-to-treat analyses (i.e., all patients randomized to treatment; ITT). As completers have a higher potential for a positive effect estimate, this patient group is compared to the ITT group, which has a more conservative effect estimate, to avoid overestimation of treatment effects.

Predictive Models

Multiple imputation (MI) and machine-learning approaches are two modern and commonly recommended imputation techniques. MI can be used to address missing data in both independent and dependent variables and restores the dataset to its full size. The basic principle of MI is the repeated estimation of missing values using random sections of the available data. The newly created datasets (e.g., 1000) are all used to perform the analyses of interest. Consequently, performing MI provides many (e.g., 1000) estimates and standard errors (SE). These estimates and SE are averaged and used for the final model. Many authors have illustrated that multiple imputation provides better results in statistical analyses than listwise deletion (e.g., Little & Rubin, 2002; Schlomer et al., 2010). This technique decreases estimation bias in both the parameters and the standard errors. When the imputation model is correct and the data are missing at random, the precision of the parameter estimates will approach the precision that would have been achieved with complete data (Huang et al., 2009). Commonly recommended and robust MI methods include Multivariate Imputation by Chained Equations (MICE; van Buuren & Groothuis-Oudshoorn, 2010), Expectation-Maximization (EM; Do & Batzoglou, 2008), and the Monte Carlo Markov Chain method (MCMC; Gilks, 1995).

MI performs well with continuous, categorical, and mixed-type (i.e., datasets with continuous and categorical variables) data (e.g., Graham, 2009). However, MI requires distributional assumptions to be made about the data *a priori*. This might pose problems in situations in which these distributional assumptions are not met. Supervised machine learning imputation techniques have been introduced, as they require fewer assumptions about the data and are therefore able to deal with any type of variable. For example, the MissForest approach is based on Random Forests (RF; Breiman, 2001), a nonparametric method that allows for interactive and nonlinear effects. MissForest has been shown to perform well compared to other imputation approaches and is implemented in an R package (*missForest*; Stekhoven, 2011). Overall, comparisons of several approaches to handle missing data indicate that the EM and RF-based approaches are robust and comparable in performance (e.g., see Twala, 2009).

It is important to acknowledge that modern imputation approaches also have limitations. Technically, it is possible to impute variables independently of the percentage of missing values. However, the effects of variables for which a large number of scores have been imputed are associated with a relatively large degree of uncertainty and thus cannot be trusted. As a general recommendation, some authors propose that no more than 50% of data points of a given variable should be imputed (e.g., Steyerberg, 2019).

Imputation of Nested Data

Another aspect that is often neglected in missing data imputation approaches is the hierarchical nature of psychotherapy data (e.g., patients nested within therapists). While taking the multilevel data structure into account is more or less standard in contemporary data analysis, it is almost never accounted for in data preprocessing steps such as missing data imputation. This is problematic, as simulation studies show that ignoring data clustering can result in increased type I error, especially in situations with higher intra-class correlations (ICC; Taljaard et al., 2008). Only recently, accessible software and R packages have been developed that account for this aspect when imputing missing data (e.g., Speidel et al., 2018).

Systematic Bias in Missing Data

When data is MNAR, bias is difficult to avoid. However, there are several approaches that help to better understand the pattern of missingness and even to reduce bias in these situations. Pattern-mixture models can help to identify subgroups of typical missing patterns in the data (Little & Rubin, 2002). Recent extensions of this model are able to combine information on change and information on dropout to identify typical change-dropout patterns (e.g., Arndt et al., 2019; Muthén et al., 2011). Graham (2009) provides an accessible overview of methods available to reduce bias in MNAR situations.

Summary: From Chaos to Coherence

The taxonomies and new psychometric developments to measure psychopathology and change described above provide a conceptual framework on how to systematize change measures in psychotherapy research. An important accompanying movement is the development of freely available instruments, which enable the use of frequent assessments in clinical practice.

There is still heterogeneity and debate in the field about the optimal way to assess processes, outcomes, and meaningful change. For example, a debate about a core measurement battery has pushed the field toward more standardized measures, but has yet to result in a generally accepted measurement battery used in all or most studies (see Ogles, 2013). However, (a) the measurement of multidimensional predictors and facets of psychological change (including *profile*, *process*, *problem*, and *consequence* domains); (b) the use of standardized, psychometrically robust, and comparable measures; and (c) briefer self-report questionnaires that are feasible, freely available and acceptable for intensive repeated measurements have enabled considerable advances in the field.

Similarly, debates on the usefulness of research results for clinical practice have led to a number of developments, including the use of outcome classifications that are more intuitive and easier for therapists and patients to understand and the use of practice-based research methods, the results of which are more easily generalizable to routine practice. In part, advancements of statistical approaches in dealing with complex data, such as better ways of handling missing data and modeling change, have enabled these developments.

NEW WAYS TO MEASURE AND MODEL CHANGE

There have been several recent developments in the measurement and modeling of change in psychotherapy. The first section here describes the application of item response theory (IRT) to guide the improvement of psychometric properties of items and scales. The second and third sections deal with more fine-grained assessments of change as well as nested data structures. The fourth section deals with new technological and psychobiological measures.

Application of Item Response Theory

Over the years, several approaches have been developed to enhance measurement precision. One is item response theory (see e.g., Doucette & Wolf, 2015). In this section, we review a number of applications in which IRT has shown its potential to improve measurement in psychotherapy research.

Common Metrics and Item Banks

One of the most prevalent problems of measurement in psychotherapy is the fact that several competing instruments exist to measure the same construct. IRT provides one way of addressing this problem by enabling the development of *common metrics* (e.g., Fischer et al., 2011). For example, Wahl et al. (2014) linked several datasets with different depression scales in order to develop a common metric for different depression measures. To define a general metric, so-called bifactor models are used. In this procedure, all items of several instruments are factor-analyzed to load on one general factor as well as on instrument-specific factors (e.g., Reise, 2012). The loadings can be used to estimate a patient's position on the general factor, even when only one of the instruments included in the model is available. For example, Böhnke et al. (2014) used this method to analyze three different instruments completed by the same clinical sample (PHQ-9 depression scale, GAD-7 anxiety scale, WSAS functional impairment scale) and found a general underlying factor of negative affectivity (NA). Based on this model, it is possible to estimate a patient's NA (i.e.,

underlying factor) score, as soon as they provide scores on any of these three measures.

These items that have been calibrated for a specific construct can also be used in so-called *item banks*. These item banks comprise a collection of items that all measure the same construct. Using these item banks, it is possible to adaptively select test items for an individual. That is, instead of an a priori fixed set, items are selected based on the respondent's answers to previous items. This more targeted form of testing allows a focus on questions in the relevant severity range. Thus, *theta* (i.e., the latent severity in the construct of interest) can be estimated more reliably with fewer items. These kinds of adaptive tests commonly use computer-based presentation (computerized adaptive testing, CAT). A prominent example of this research endeavor is the Patient Reported Outcome Measurement Information System – PROMIS® of the National Institute of Health (Cella et al., 2007). PROMIS® has developed a number of different item banks to measure multiple mental as well as physical and social health domains.

Definition of Reliable Change via IRT

As described above, the reliable change index (RCI) is based on the standard error (SE) of the respective measure. However, SEs can be misleading. For example, it is often falsely assumed that SEs apply to the whole range of scores. Brouwer et al. (2013) introduced an IRT-based variant, the Z-test, and compared this metric to the classic RCI. The Z-test uses the difference between the latent *theta* scores at two time-points and tests this difference against zero, using the respective estimation standard errors. Overall, the correlation between the latent *theta* change scores and the raw change scores was very high ($r = 0.98$). However, using the IRT-based Z-test statistic resulted in a different classification for 7.7% ($n = 8$) of the 103 patients compared to the RCI method. The difference between methods was most prominent in the lower range of depression scores. For some patients, the IRT-based statistic was more sensitive to significant changes than the conventional RCI method.

Short Test Versions

Another typical application of IRT is the development of short versions of existing measures. An advantage of IRT is the provision of the *information function* for each item. This function summarizes how precisely an item measures the latent trait (e.g., depression) for each value of the respective trait (Reise & Haviland, 2005). If assessments are aimed at measuring specific ranges of the trait, items can be selected that provide the most information on this specific range of trait values. The individual information functions can be aggregated to evaluate the measurement precision of group items. Based on this aggregate score, it is possible to determine the number of items needed to reach a prespecified level of precision (e.g., Choi et al., 2010). For example, Böhnke and Lutz (2014) used item information functions to develop two short versions of a 40-item measure. For example, one of these versions was designed for screening purposes. As such, this version was optimized to have especially high precision close to the cut-off that discriminates a clinical from a nonclinical sample. Outside of this "region of interest," precision was less important for this version. Using the item information functions of IRT allowed for this screening version to be reduced to five items, while achieving an a priori set reliability of 0.80.

Response Formats

IRT enables researchers to reconsider the response categories of questionnaires. For example, based on an IRT analysis of the WAI-SR, Hatcher and Gillaspy (2006) found that patients have difficulty discriminating between the levels of the original seven-point scale. As a consequence, these authors suggested collapsing the first three categories into one and the middle two categories into another one, resulting in a four-point scale. However, they decided to use a five-point scale anchored by a low point, as they considered this easier to use.

Measurement Invariance

IRT opens up possibilities to test whether different items have the same meaning for different groups of people and across time (i.e., cross-sectional and longitudinal measurement invariance). For example, people from different ethnic backgrounds may understand and answer items differently (e.g., Wetzel & Böhnke, 2017). In order to measure true change with sufficient certainty, we must rule out the possibility that an observed change is due to a shift in how the patient understands the questions. A patient who learns to talk about their emotions and thoughts in therapy may develop a more differentiated concept of terms like sadness or thoughts of failure. Fokkema et al. (2013) tested the longitudinal measurement invariance of the Beck Depression Inventory (BDI) from pre- to post-treatment in the sample from the NIMH TDCRP–study (Elkin et al., 1989). They found that a response shift did take place from pre- to post-treatment. After treatment, item scores seemed to overestimate depressive symptom severity, measurement error was smaller, and associations between the different constructs were stronger. These shifts were more pronounced for patients who received psychotherapy than for those treated with medication.

Multilevel and Mixture Models

Over the last decade, longitudinal mixture and multilevel models have become standard analytical tools in psychotherapy research. Common to all such models is their ability to handle the multilevel structure of psychotherapeutic change (e.g., Gallop & Tasca, 2014). Psychotherapy is an endeavor with several analytic levels of nested data, such as sessions over time nested within patients, whereas patients are nested within therapists, treatment groups, or treatment services (e.g., Baldwin & Imel, 2013; Firth, Saxon et al., 2019; Kenny & Hoyt, 2014; Voelkle et al., 2018).

Multilevel Models (MLM)

Models that handle such nested data structures have been discussed in the literature under several names: multilevel models (MLM), hierarchical linear models (HLM), mixed-effect models, random coefficient models, random regression models, or growth models (e.g., Raudenbush & Bryk, 2010; Singer & Willett, 2003). Models with similar structures, but expressed in the formal language of structural equation models (SEM) have been termed latent growth curve models (e.g., Muthén et al., 2011; Voelkle et al., 2018).

Two-Level Models

In MLM, modeling of the nested data structure is handled by interlaced regressions between different levels. In a two-level longitudinal model, for example, repeatedly assessed outcome scores of each patient are modeled as the dependent variable. In that case, a time-related variable (e.g., the number of sessions) must be included to model individual change (level 1). Patients are then located on level 2, meaning this level comprises between-patient differences in change. Therefore, individual growth variation is captured by two regression parameters (intercept and slopes), representing random coefficients that vary across individuals. The first level can also be termed the level of intra-individual (within person) change (Hamaker & Wichers, 2017; Singer & Willett, 2003; see next section). The second level captures the variation in individual growth parameters across the patient sample. This variation can be related to potential predictors of change (e.g., patient intake characteristics) by treating the individual growth parameters as the dependent variable at the between-group level. However, a reduced (missing or unequally spaced assessments) data structure potentially makes a more complex covariance structure of the model necessary (Singer & Willett, 2003).

In the literature, models with predictors of either inter-individual intercept or slope variance on the between-group level are termed conditional models, while models without predictors are referred to as unconditional models. Besides the above described two-level longitudinal model, pre–post designs with patients on level 1 and therapists on level 2 have also been applied in psychotherapy research. In order to examine multiple outcome measures within one analytic framework, Baldwin et al. (2014) extended univariate to multivariate MLMs.

Three-Level Models

Some studies have extended the above described two-level model to include a third level (Elkin et al., 2006; Firth, et al., 2019). This third level represents the between-therapist or between-service variation under the assumption that sessions are nested within patients and patients are nested within therapists and/or services (e.g., Ali et al., 2014; Lutz et al., 2007).

Each patient's symptom intensity can be modeled as a (e.g., log-linear) function of treatment sessions at level 1 (the session or within-patient level), resulting in two patient-specific estimated parameters: the intercept (representing the patient's impairment score at the first session) and slope (the expected change in outcome per session number). At level 2 (the patient level), patient characteristics of these individual intercept and slope parameters can be included in the model as predictors (e.g., patient symptom intensity, prior psychotherapy, chronicity, and treatment expectations). This means that estimated level 1 coefficients can be treated as dependent variables. The inclusion of these predictors results in the adjustment of therapist differences for case-mix. Based on variance components estimated at each level, the therapist effect can be estimated by dividing the therapist variance (level 3) by the total variance of all three levels.

To summarize, this approach makes it possible to generate estimates of patient and therapist contributions to change, unaffected by session-to-session variation within patients. It should be mentioned, however, that in conducting these analyses power and sample size issues at different levels must be considered (Schiefele et al., 2017).

Missing Data in MLM

An additional advantage of MLMs is their ability to handle missing data as well as irregularly spaced assessments over the course of treatment. In the above-described models, session number was treated as a random variable, which means that patients differed regarding their number and frequency of assessments. Missing data can lead to less reliable patient-specific coefficient estimates, which, in turn, results in estimates biased toward the grand mean by the maximum-likelihood algorithm. As a consequence, listwise deletion of cases or imputation of data for missing values is not advisable or necessary. Cases with some missing data can be included in MLM if two assumptions are met:

1. Data are missing at random.
2. The observed change process continues during the unobserved time points (e.g., Singer & Willett, 2003).

However, in psychotherapy research, one of the most common reasons for missing data is attrition. The reasons for attrition can be manifold and are not necessarily random. Some patients may terminate therapy because they felt their improvement was sufficient, whereas others might terminate therapy because they felt therapy was not helping. This results in varying treatment lengths, especially in naturalistic studies (e.g., Stiles et al., 2008). Therefore, Baldwin et al. (2009) recommend including an interaction term between the session variable and treatment length in order to control for the dependency of growth on treatment length.

Growth-Mixture Models

The models described above assume one underlying population with a single change pattern. In many applications in psychotherapy research (e.g., the investigation of early change patterns) this assumption is not met. Instead, investigators are sometimes interested in a potentially unknown number of (latent) classes of change patterns corresponding to subpopulations of patients. These patient subpopulations might differ regarding their mean change parameters (intercepts and slopes in the case of a linear model) and subpopulation-specific variations around these parameters. To deal with this issue, another group of change models, growth mixture models (GMM), have been developed and applied in psychotherapy research (see e.g., section on patterns of change).

In GMMs, an additional categorical variable is included in the growth model that accounts for heterogeneity in growth parameters within a given sample. This allows heterogeneity in change to be captured by the different average slopes per latent class or subpopulation. At the same time, it forces the estimation algorithm to be more sensitive to patterns of change than to differences in initial impairment scores. Such models can either allow variances of all parameters to be fixed to zero (latent class growth models; Nagin, 1999) or to be freely estimated, while hybrid versions of these models are also possible (see e.g., Hunter et al., 2010; Lutz et al., 2014, 2017). Often, variances around class-specific slopes are set to zero, while intercept variances are freely estimated, but constrained to be constant between class or subpopulation values.

Several fit indices have been developed to detect the optimal number of latent trajectory classes within a dataset (e.g., Bayesian Information Criterion (BIC); Bootstrapped Likelihood Ratio Test (BLRT); e.g., Tofighi & Enders, 2007). Furthermore, GMMs allow the optimal fitting function of the time variable (e.g., sessions) to be tested, if, for example, a log-linear, quadratic or cubic model might produce a better fit than a linear function (e.g., Muthén et al., 2011; Stulz et al., 2013). Recently, Arndt et al. (2019) used an extended version of GMM, the Muthen-Roy model, to investigate dropout (categorical outcome) in combination with change patterns (dimensional outcome). In addition, Paul et al. (2019) combined GMMs with machine learning (random forest) to detect treatment response classes in patients with major depressive disorder ($N = 809$), as well as the optimal set of clinical predictors of those classes.

Modeling Change with GMMs

The use of GMMs in psychotherapy research has recently also been criticized. For example, Krause (2018) criticized the linearity assumption and the handling of measurement error as not appropriate for the data structure in psychotherapy research for all of the above models. Furthermore, a related debate about overextraction and simpler models has taken place. Bauer and Curran (2004) pointed out that GMMs are exploratory tools, and there is a risk of overextraction of latent groups, given that the estimation algorithm seeks to transform a potentially dimensional into a categorical variable to find latent classes. Koffmann (2018) and Flood et al. (2018) compared GMMs to less statistically complex indices to study early change and came to the conclusion that GMMs did not add information to simpler models. In contrast, Rubel et al. (2015) found that GMMs showed a higher specificity than simpler criteria, such as the reliable change index.

Ecological Momentary Assessment and Modeling Intensive Longitudinal Data

In the last 15 years, ecological momentary assessment (EMA)[3] has received burgeoning interest for its ability to directly assess

---

[3] Different expressions have been used to describe assessments in people's daily lives; such as experience sampling method, ambulatory assessment, and diary methods. These expressions have been suggested in different contexts and some are preferred over others depending on the specific application. In this section, we use EMA as a broad term with which we refer to all kinds of repeated assessments in people's daily lives.

life as it is lived (Bolger et al., 2003). EMA describes the repeated assessment of self-report variables or other indicators of actual experiences (e.g., activity). This development is well aligned with a call for more idiographic research (e.g., Hofmann & Hayes, 2019). Several authors have argued theoretically (e.g., Kordy, 1982; Molenaar, 2004) and empirically (e.g., Fisher et al., 2018; Hamaker, 2012) that group statistics cannot be validly transferred to intra-individual associations. As such, EMA provides the potential for a new depth of data that enables more reliable intra-individual research.

Designing EMA Studies

EMA might overcome retrospective biases associated with classic measurements by providing better descriptions of within-person processes at a higher resolution (e.g., Ebner-Priemer & Trull, 2009). However, to date there are no agreed-upon standards regarding the optimal design of EMA studies. Several choices must be made a priori: Which and how many items or scales should be included in the measure? Should the questions refer to a certain time period or to the current moment? How many days/weeks/months should the assessment run? How often per day should participants be assessed? Should the measurement schedule be fixed, random, or contingent on certain events? How much delay is acceptable for participants to answer the questions? How can we prevent missing data? Janssens et al. (2018) conducted a study surveying 47 EMA researchers to identify practical recommendations for future research. The authors concluded that there is no gold standard and the choices should depend on the research question and the respective variables involved in the study. Interestingly, the surveyed researcher reported to have rarely used a design twice. Despite this heterogeneity, the authors provide some practical recommendations on how to enhance the reliability of the obtained data (e.g., easy wording of the items and reference to the respective moment), to increase feasibility for participants (e.g., the use of short questionnaires with about six items and the use of electronic diaries), and to increase statistical possibilities (e.g., the use of fixed equidistant designs with at least four assessments per day to ensure enough data points). These recommendations might also help to overcome one of the most crucial problems of EMA studies, which is noncompliance resulting in many missing values throughout the data collection.

Analyzing EMA Data

The special type of data provided by EMA, that is, intensive longitudinal data, requires specific statistical approaches. These can be clustered into two broad categories. The first approach refers to methods originally applied for idiographic n = 1 designs. In the case of $n > 1$ designs, results from these person-specific analyses can be aggregated to investigate inter-individual commonalities and differences (e.g., Hamaker & Wichers, 2017). Time series panel analysis (TSPA; Ramseyer et al., 2014) and group iterative multiple model estimation (GIMME; Gates & Molenaar, 2012) fall into this category, for example. Second, MLMs can be used to model within-person processes at level 1 and between-person differences in these at level 2 (see previous section on multilevel modeling). For example, Bringmann et al. (2013) introduced the multilevel vector-autoregressive model (ML-VAR). This model combines VAR, in which variables are regressed on past versions of themselves and other variables (normally lag-1 associations; that is, t regressed on $t - 1$), with MLMs (time points nested within persons). Given this combination, ML-VAR is able to estimate overall associations between the variables over time, as well as person-specific differences.

Network Analyses of EMA Data

Lately, network models have been used to visualize and quantify associations in time series data collected in EMA studies (e.g., Borsboom, 2017; Epskamp et al., 2012). These networks are built of *nodes*, each representing a different symptom and directed (i.e., unidirectional associations on the basis of lagged analyses) or undirected *edges* (i.e., bi-directional associations based on contemporaneous measurements) between the symptoms representing the strength and direction of influence. Symptom networks have been proposed to offer a better approach to describe psychological disorders and their comorbidity, in contrast to the predominant common cause or latent variable model (e.g., Borsboom, 2017; Hofmann et al., 2016).[4]

Several indices can be estimated by network analyses, which characterize either global characteristics of the network or the role of individual nodes. The most frequently used global network indicator is *density* (e.g., Newman, 2018). Density describes the overall connectivity between all symptoms in the network. Denser networks consist of nodes that are more strongly connected than in less dense networks. To quantify the relative importance of symptoms in a network, a number of centrality measures have been discussed (e.g., Newman, 2018). The three most commonly used centrality measures are node *strength*, indicating the average direct connection between a node and other nodes, *closeness*, indicating the average relative distance of a node from other directly and indirectly connected nodes (i.e., the speed with which one node influences others), and *betweenness*, indicating how often a node lies on the shortest pathway between two other nodes (e.g., Costantini et al., 2015; Newman, 2018). However, the use of centrality indices as a measure of variable importance in psychopathology networks has recently been questioned (e.g., Bringmann et al., 2019). The concerns around centrality indices mainly stem from the fact that these indices were originally developed for social networks in which nodes represent persons and edges their contact. Furthermore, *closeness* and *betweenness* have been shown to be unstable under several circumstances (e.g.,

---

[4]The assumption of the common cause model, that covariations between symptoms are explained by an underlying common cause seems to fit for physical conditions, where for example, an infection is the common cause of symptoms (sore throat, coughing, fever, etc.). Once the infection is treated, a remission of symptoms is observed. However, the common cause model might not fit certain psychological conditions (e.g., depression). Symptoms of psychological disorders might be causally interrelated (e.g., sleep problems lead to fatigue and problems concentrating). Under a common cause assumption, such interrelations are not allowed. All covariations between symptoms are assumed to result directly from the common cause (i.e., the depressive disorder) and not from causal relations with other symptoms.

Bringmann et al., 2019; Epskamp et al., 2018). Finally, it is important to keep in mind that centrality measures do not provide information on the absolute scores of the variables. As such, variables on which patients always score very highly, likely show low centrality due to low variability, but still can be of high importance to the patient.

An important assumption of the models described above is stationarity of the processes involved. That is, it is assumed that, first, the variables and, second, the associations between these variables do not change systematically over time. To address the first issue, variables are often detrended. That is, the raw scores are subtracted from a linear (or other) time slope. The resulting scores are called residuals and are adjusted for the respective time trend. However, by doing so, information about this time trend is eliminated from the data and can no longer be systematically investigated. To address the second aspect of nonstationarity, models are needed which are capable of taking these time-varying effects into account (e.g., Bringmann et al., 2017). These methods are able to estimate how the association between variables develops over time.

EMA as Predictor of Treatment Response and Dropout

EMA obtained from patients waiting for treatment can provide a new depth to pre-treatment assessments. To date, two pilot studies have tested intensive longitudinal data as an additional predictor of treatment response and dropout (Husen et al., 2016; Lutz et al., 2018). Both studies used data from a sample of 58 outpatients who participated in a two-week EMA period with four daily assessments of affective states and symptoms before treatment. Husen et al. (2016) investigated the incremental validity of EMA variables for the prediction of early treatment response over the first five sessions. The authors found the ratio of positive over negative affect and fluctuations in negative affect over the two-week period to be associated with early response above and beyond baseline symptom impairment. More positive compared to negative affect predicted steeper and more fluctuations in negative affect predicted flatter response trajectories. While symptom impairment explained 16.1% of the variation, the EMA variables explained an additional 21.73% of the variance in early response. Lutz et al. (2018) found a differential pattern of pretreatment longitudinal symptom associations for patients who terminate treatment prematurely compared to patients who complete treatment. While intake predictors (initial impairment, and sex) explained 6% of the variation in dropout, centrality scores from longitudinal network analysis explained an additional 26% of the variance. Both of these studies showed that intensive longitudinal data hold promise as an additional predictor above and beyond patient intake characteristics.

EMA as an Alternative Outcome Measure

To date, a few studies have tested indices generated from EMA data as a measure of psychopathology. For example, Pe et al. (2015) used the density in emotion networks to differentiate between 53 healthy control individuals and 53 individuals

diagnosed with major depressive disorder. In a seven-day experience sampling study with eight daily assessments they found that networks of persons with major depressive disorder were characterized by higher overall connectivity than those of healthy individuals. The authors interpreted this finding as evidence for higher network density being an indicator of resistance to change.

Snippe et al. (2017) could not find evidence connecting higher network density to decreased change. These authors used two datasets in which depressed patients participated in EMA (10 assessments per day) for six days before and after treatment with either six weeks of imipramine vs. pill placebo or eight weeks of mindfulness-based cognitive therapy vs. waitlist control. Despite marked pre–post changes in depressive symptoms over time, only a few pre–post changes in specific (e.g., strength of specific edges) and overall network connections (e.g., network density) were observed in these groups. Some of these differed between the Imipramine and pill-placebo groups, while no differences were observed between the mindfulness-based cognitive therapy and waitlist control groups.

Identifying Personalized Treatment Targets

Intensive longitudinal data has also been used to identify symptoms that, when changed, might have strong effects on other symptoms and thus may be treated as a priority (e.g., Fisher & Boswell, 2016). There are varying suggestions on how to translate these differential symptom influences into recommendations for interventions that could be delivered as a priority (e.g., Rubel, Fisher et al., 2018). However, a large international project revealed large heterogeneity regarding the applied methods and the resulting treatment recommendations (Bastiaansen et al., 2019). Given this heterogeneity, clinical trials are necessary to determine which of these algorithms result in the best recommendations (e.g., Fisher et al., 2019).

Biological and Technological Measures

Several new biological (e.g., genetic, epigenetic, inflammatory, brain imaging) and technological measures have also been tested as indicators of change in psychotherapy research and are summarized in this section.

Biomarkers

A recent systematic review by Cristea et al. (2019) on biomarkers and psychotherapy included a total of 51 RCTs with 5,123 patients diagnosed with depression and treated with behavioral activation, CBT, IPT, or mindfulness.[5] These studies either investigated the impact of psychotherapy on biological markers (43 studies), or the predictive power of biological markers (9 studies) on psychotherapy outcomes. Results at the end of treatment and follow-up were mixed and often inconclusive. The authors found that neither the use of glycaemic control

---

[5] 35 trials included further specifications on the investigated population such as e.g., diabetes, HIV, cardiovascular disorders/risk, autoimmune diseases, hypertension, or metastatic cancer.

(hemoglobin A1c test, HbA1c), immunological markers, inflammatory markers, cortisol concentration, blood pressure, nor blood lipids produced reliable associations. However, the authors concluded that only neuroimaging markers delivered promising results. Overall, the findings seem inconclusive regarding the predictive impact of biological or genetic markers on psychotherapeutic outcome, because of poor standardization, small sample sizes, use of multiple comparisons, and procedural discrepancies assessing the same biological index. Tabak et al. (2019) came to a similar conclusion regarding (intranasal) oxytocin and vasopressin administration on human social processes.

Future studies might provide more clarity, especially when biomarkers are assessed several times over the course of psychological treatments. For example, in a promising application, Zilcha-Mano et al. (2018) collected a total of 172 oxytocin saliva samples before and after sessions 4, 8, 12, and 16 for 22 patients diagnosed with major depressive disorder. The authors were able to show that oxytocin changed significantly over the course of sessions, converging with self-report and behavioral coding, depending on a positive or a disruptive working alliance during the respective sessions.

fMRI and EEG

Various imagery technologies have been tested (e.g., positron emission tomography; PET), with functional magnetic resonance imaging (fMRI) and electroencephalography (EEG) being the most widely applied in psychotherapy research (Carrig et al., 2014; Cristea et al., 2019). fMRI measures patterns of brain activity in different regions of the brain while conducting a specific task or behavior (Boccia et al., 2016; Carrig et al., 2014). It is a noninvasive adaptation of structural magnetic resonance imaging (MRI) that uses magnetic fields and radio waves to measure oxygen utilization change (blood-oxygen-level-dependent imaging or BOLD-contrast imaging), while assuming that this change corresponds to changes in brain activation. Applications of fMRI in psychological research have been improved in terms of data preprocessing (e.g., distortion correction, head motion correction, slice timing correction, correction for multiple comparisons, defining a region of interest, and task selection). Good validity and reliability are essential to the interpretation of functional associations between mental activities and brain activation patterns. However, studies assessing the quality of imagery measures (e.g., reliability) have often only had small sample sizes (e.g., Carrig et al., 2014).

Several investigators have used fMRI or EEG to study or predict change in psychological interventions (e.g., Cristea et al., 2019; Siegle et al., 2006). In the above mentioned review by Cristea et al. (2019), varying imagery markers were used in five RCTs: MRI/fMRI, EEG, single-photon emission computed tomography, and brain neurochemistry with PET. Several outcome differences in brain areas could be identified. However, findings remain inconclusive. Neuroimaging markers have also been investigated as predictors or moderators of treatment outcome and some are considered to have high potential (e.g., the impact of the subgenual cortex; e.g., Luber

et al., 2017). However, findings also remain limited as they are based on small studies, low power, and a lack of reporting standards (Cristea et al., 2019).

New Technologies

A recent overview has shown fMRI-based neurofeedback to be promising, although a further standardization of intervention guidelines and measurements of neuromodulation seems necessary (Barreiros et al., 2019; Young et al., 2017). In another line of research, Zaunmüller et al. (2014) applied a micro-intervention (a discrete, time-limited application of a psychotherapeutic technique – in this case, a 90-minute cognitive restructuring session) in a controlled experimental design to investigate whether and how cognitive restructuring contributes to the efficacy of CBT ($N = 92$). In the restructuring and control groups, an increase in positive and decrease in negative affect could be shown after the intervention. However, control and intervention groups differed significantly regarding EEG-based event-related potentials (ERPs). Such studies might be able to provide a bridge between RCTs investigating the efficacy of complex treatment modalities (e.g., CBT) and mechanism research by focusing on time-limited treatment techniques under experimental conditions (Strauman, 2017; Zaunmüller et al., 2014).

Some new technology-based measures allow continuous assessments over time and make a more fine-grained and dimensional analysis of time possible (e.g., Voelkle et al., 2018). Several investigators have recently used mobile phones, wearables, electronic health records or measures of digital screen engagement to track and predict changes in psychological distress (e.g., Jacobson et al., 2019; McCoy Jr et al., 2018). Such technologies that passively collect data on patients (e.g., steps, sleep-duration or internet use via Facebook likes), especially in specific problem areas (e.g., sleep pattern and depression), bear potential as indicators or predictors of change. Furthermore, several new tools have been developed to investigate change via automated coding of videos from psychotherapeutic sessions (Imel et al., 2015). Such systems assess, for example, movement (Motion Energy Analysis; e.g., Ramseyer & Tschacher, 2011; Schoenherr et al., 2019), emotional arousal and valence (e.g., Bryan et al., 2018), psychophysiological synchrony (e.g., Bar-Kalifa et al., 2019), and speech and dialogue analysis (e.g., Gaume et al., 2019).

Summary: The Future of Change Measurement

The development of new measures and modeling tools is an important future step to improve psychotherapy research. Especially the measurement and identification of change mechanisms, and related to this, the identification of differential response patterns has great potential for future research. A more precise operationalization of key change mechanisms could be achieved by increasing measurement precision. Furthermore, precise differences in mechanisms or outcomes between treatment models are often difficult to detect, and it is unclear if this is related to the limitations of our measures, which mostly rely on patient-reported questionnaires. New methodological developments and measurement technologies may help to elucidate greater specificity that has been covered in past research. Although it has yet to be applied in psychotherapy research more widely, recent trends developments in the field of psychometrics (e.g., item-response theory, network analysis, EMA, etc.) reflect this renewed interest in increasing measurement precision. The focus of psychotherapy research is shifting toward investigating change with greater granularity (e.g., using item-level data, intensive time-series data or personalized change models), as well as the development of more distinctive and simultaneously more homogeneous measures.

Multilevel and mixture models arrived in the field about 20 years ago and have now become the new standard to model change in psychotherapy research. The increased use of this methodology began at about the same time as a tremendous increase in sample sizes and the number of longitudinal measurements per patient in psychotherapy research. This methodology provides optimized data analytic options to disentangle variance components attributable to different levels of change (session, patient, therapist, and clinic). It improves data analysis in large patient groups as well as large patient-per-therapist and session-by-session assessments. Furthermore, biological and technological measures using, for example, wristbands to track patient change parameters (e.g., heart rate variability or sleep patterns) as well as automated analysis of patient video information, are new measurement options. All this leads to more fine-grained longitudinal and cross-sectional study options. Taken together, these various new measurement and methodological options could bring important advances in the field once standardized forms of assessment and data analytic protocols are elaborated in the future.

PREDICTORS AND MODERATORS OF CHANGE

It has long been recognized by psychotherapists and researchers that even if two patients have the same diagnosis or presenting problem, they may differ in other important ways, which can result in markedly different responses to treatment. This observation has propelled investigators to seek to understand the potential sources of heterogeneity that influence psychological outcomes. Such questions have guided numerous studies focusing on predictors and moderators of change, which are discussed in the following section.

Predictors, Moderators, and Variable Selection

Predictors, in the broadest sense, are variables that are statistically associated with an outcome of interest. In psychotherapy, these could be variables that predict poorer response to treatment, such as initial impairment, chronicity of the problems, treatment expectations or personality disorders (e.g., Beutler et al., 2018; DeRubeis et al., 2014; Kessler et al., 2017). These could also be factors that are associated with increased risk of relapse after completing psychological treatment, such as prior episodes of depression and the presence of residual symptoms at the end of therapy (Bockting et al., 2015). A comprehensive understanding of prognostic markers for mental health would ideally map these across a developmental trajectory covering risk factors for the onset of psychological problems, predictors of treatment response and future recurrence. Our field has not yet advanced sufficiently to provide replicated evidence covering the full developmental trajectory. However, the growing outcome research literature has enabled us to gain a more coherent understanding of potential predictors of acute-phase treatment outcomes, which can be summarized in four broad categories: *patient factors*, *therapist factors*, *therapy processes*, and *contextual factors* (see Figure 4.3).

In summary, a myriad of predictors of treatment outcome have been identified to date and it is plausible that such features have a cumulative effect. Patients with multiple features that are statistically associated with poor outcomes tend to have a poorer prognosis compared to cases with fewer of these features (e.g., Beutler et al., 2018; Delgadillo et al., 2016, 2017). It is also plausible that changes in some of these variables may determine the extent to which therapy

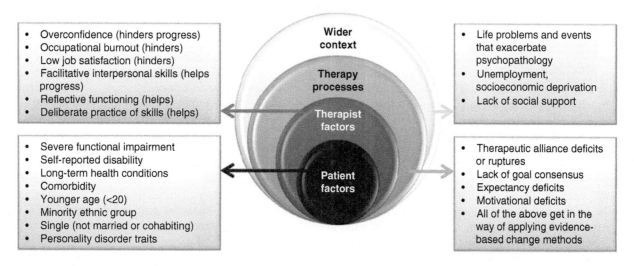

FIGURE 4.3 The concentric circles model: common predictors of psychotherapy outcome.

will work in specific cases, or may fully or partially explain the effect of therapy.

Some predictors not only have a prognostic but also a prescriptive or moderating character. For example, baseline symptom severity generally predicts poorer depression treatment response, and this severity-outcome relationship appears to be much the same in CBT and pharmacotherapy (e.g., Weitz et al., 2015). In other words, baseline depression severity is a general predictor that does not appear to moderate the relationship between different types of treatments and clinical outcomes. *Moderators* are variables that specify for whom or under which circumstances different treatments will work (Baron & Kenny, 1986). Conceptually, moderators identify subgroups/subtypes of a clinical population who respond differentially to alternative treatments (e.g., psychotherapy vs. pharmacotherapy) or circumstances (e.g., inpatient vs. outpatient setting). Methodologically, basic requirements to identify a moderator are that this variable should (a) be measured prior to treatment and (b) have a statistically significant interaction with the treatment or grouping variable. Furthermore, interactions could be disordinal, ordinal, or nonlinear (Smith & Sechrest, 1991). A disordinal interaction would indicate that the moderator (e.g., severe interpersonal problems) could be associated with better treatment outcomes in treatment A, but poorer treatment outcomes in treatment B. An ordinal interaction would indicate that the moderator could have a similar influence on treatment outcomes in both treatments (e.g., mild interpersonal problems generally associated with better treatment outcomes), but the magnitude of this effect could be significantly larger in one treatment compared to the other. A nonlinear interaction would indicate more complex relationships, such that different levels of the moderator (e.g., mild – moderate – severe interpersonal problems) may influence the magnitude and direction of effects when comparing treatments A vs. B.

Variable selection is a crucial and challenging step in the development of prediction models. Problems of statistical power and overfitting (i.e., estimations that capitalize too much on the specifics of the current dataset and are thus not replicable in other data) might complicate this task, especially when we have a large set of predictor variables. Besides classic approaches to predictor selection (i.e., a priori selection informed by prior evidence or theory), variable selection based on methods such as stepwise and univariate preselection have been criticized for leading to unstable models and biased estimates, overly relying on *p*-values, and resulting in worse models than the full model without any variable selection (e.g., Steyerberg, 2019). For these reasons, modern variable selection methods use resampling approaches like bootstrapping or *k*-fold cross-validation to determine important variables via Bayesian model averaging, or shrinkage of near-zero regression coefficients to zero (e.g., Steyerberg, 2019). All of these approaches have their respective pros and cons, which have been reviewed by several authors (e.g., Cohen & DeRubeis, 2018; Steyerberg, 2019). So far, there is no single best way to statistically select important variables to build a prediction model, and often specific characteristics of the data at hand need to be taken into consideration (see also Chapter 19 of this volume). Variable selection is a complicated problem,

and the optimal solution varies according to parameters such as sample size, the ratio of predictors-to-cases, the types of measures collected, the distribution of data in the specific sample (e.g., balanced vs. imbalanced classes; linear vs. nonlinear relationships), the target outcomes (e.g., binary, multinomial, continuous), and the context (e.g., the magnitude of variability in outcomes may vary across outpatient vs. inpatient care).

Expected Treatment Response and Decision Rules

One key application of prediction in psychotherapy research has been the development of patient-specific response curves and decision rules for outcome monitoring and progress feedback. Often, *rationally derived* models based on clinical significance criteria (Jacobson & Truax, 1991) are used to support routine outcome monitoring. For example, in the English IAPT program (Clark, 2018), patients complete standardized depression and anxiety questionnaires on a session-to-session basis and therapists apply conventional diagnostic cut-off scores to assess response to treatment. A reduction of both outcome measures below clinical cut-offs is seen as indicative of recovery from symptoms.

Another option is to develop *empirically derived* decision rules based on prediction models. These can be used to compare patients' expected (i.e., predicted) and actual treatment progress, and thus identify patients at risk of treatment failure (see section on patient-focused research). For example, expected treatment response (ETR) models generate empirically derived decision rules for outcome monitoring (Howard et al., 1996; Lambert et al., 2002; Lutz et al., 1999). In this approach, first introduced by Lutz et al. (1999), weekly routine outcome monitoring data from large groups of patients are analyzed using growth curve modeling to model expected trajectories of change. In an early application of the ETR concept, Finch et al. (2001) modeled 80% tolerance intervals around the ETR curve, which enabled therapists to identify the 10% of outlier cases that tend to deteriorate, that is, those whose symptoms fell outside the upper tolerance bound – referred to as a *failure boundary*. Cases whose symptoms are consistently contained within the lower and upper ETR boundaries are considered to be *on track* (OT; responding to treatment as expected) and those whose symptoms are more severe that the upper *failure boundary* are classified as *not on track* (NOT). This model is intended to alert therapists to NOT cases in a timely fashion, prompting them to identify and address obstacles to improvement, thus constituting a quality control mechanism to prevent treatment failure (Lambert et al., 2002).

Different approaches to modeling trajectories of change have been proposed based on the ETR concept. Influenced by evidence that response patterns of individuals can substantially deviate from aggregated group trends (e.g., Krause et al., 1998), Lutz et al. (1999) combined growth curve modeling with multivariable information available on each patient's well-being, symptoms, life functioning, past use of therapy, problem duration, treatment expectations, and the therapist's global assessment of functioning. However, the validity of such predictions rests on the assumption that the individual whose trajectory is being predicted is a representative member of the reference group used to set regression weights for patient-level predictors. To address this issue, further refinements were introduced by Lutz et al. (2005), who modeled trajectories of change for patients using their *nearest neighbors* (NN) as a reference group: a subset of (*N* = 10 to 50) patients with similar characteristics (demographics and pretreatment symptom measures). Predicted trajectories using the combined NN + ETR model were significantly more accurate than the conventional ETR model, and the predictive accuracy further increased when information from patients' previous treatment sessions and current progress was included in the NN clustering approach. In newer applications, the failure boundary of the ETR model for an individual was also recalculated dynamically on the basis of information from previous treatment sessions and current progress (e.g., Bone et al., 2021; Lutz et al., 2019; see section on evidence-based personalization).

Other variations of the ETR model include systems that model ETR norms for subgroups of cases clustered by type of diagnosis or treatment. For example, Lutz (2006) calibrated ETR norms for patients accessing different types of treatments in a study comparing CBT and an integrative CBT and IPT treatment; while Crits-Christoph et al. (2012) calibrated ETR norms in a sample of patients in treatment for substance use disorders. Other related ETR or rationally derived models have been developed to continuously monitor progress and provide feedback. For example, methods have been developed to provide therapists with feedback on common factors such as the alliance (Errázuriz & Zilcha-Mano, 2018; Janis et al., 2018; McClintock et al., 2017), outcome expectations, and empathy (McClintock et al., 2017). Schuckard et al. (2017) have demonstrated the adaptation of the ETR model for use with visual analog scales. Hooke et al. (2018) demonstrated the advantage of providing patients with feedback based on ETRs, by comparison to simple outcome monitoring graphs as a method to identify patients at risk of treatment failure. Other domains of feedback include outcomes specific to clients in university counseling centers (Castonguay et al., 2011; Nordberg et al., 2016). In line with these developments, recent studies have applied machine learning methods and multivariable prediction models to support psychological treatment selection (e.g., see review by Cohen & DeRubeis, 2018). An implementation of such a treatment selection algorithm can be found below in the section on evidence-based personalization.

Patterns of Change and Early Response

Early response refers to symptomatic improvements that occur during the initial phase of treatment (usually the first four sessions). Early response is often conceptualized applying the concepts of reliable and/or clinically significant change (Jacobson & Truax, 1991), but several studies have defined this concept using latent growth trajectories (e.g., GMM) early in treatment to predict treatment outcomes (e.g., Kyron et al., 2019; Lutz et al., 2014; Nordberg et al., 2014).

Several studies have investigated the prognostic value of early response to therapy in specific conditions such as major depressive disorder, panic disorder, generalized anxiety disorder, eating disorders, and in samples of patients presenting with heterogeneous problems as well as internet interventions (e.g., Crits-Christoph et al., 2001; Delgadillo et al., 2014; Lutz et al., 2017; Nordberg et al., 2014; Owen et al., 2015; Paul et al., 2019). A systematic review of this literature examined 25 studies and pooled available data from 15 studies in a random effects meta-analysis (Beard & Delgadillo, 2019). The authors reported a large pooled effect size (g = 0.87), indicating that early responders had significantly better post-treatment outcomes compared to cases without early response. This effect was larger for anxiety (g = 1.37) than depression (g = 0.76) measures. Early response was consistently observed in studies that applied a variety of treatment models, such as CBT, Cognitive Behavioral Analysis System of Psychotherapy (CBASP), behavioral activation, interpersonal psychotherapy (IPT), psychodynamic therapy, guided self-help, internet-based CBT, and others.

Summary: Prognosis in Psychotherapy

Several investigations of predictors of psychological treatment outcomes have accumulated over the years, and a more coherent pattern of features has emerged (see Figure 4.3). This growing literature has enabled us to better understand the multiple sources of heterogeneity that are likely to explain why some patients respond to treatment remarkably well, while others are at risk of chronic distress or even deterioration. Furthermore, the examination of differential patterns of change in psychotherapy has shown that early response to treatment, as well as nonlinear phenomena such as sudden gains and sudden losses (see next section), incrementally improve predictions of outcome beyond patient intake characteristics. These insights about differential response to treatment, together with measurement and data analytic developments described in this chapter, are paving the way for reliable prognostic assessments in psychotherapy. In the not-so-distant future, mainstream psychological services will be able to estimate an individual patient's likely prognosis before they start a specific treatment, with a specific therapist, in a specific clinical context. Such developments are likely to minimize the need for trial-and-error approaches and may enable the field to attain greater precision in its goal to improve patients' mental health.

EXPLORING PROCESSES AND MECHANISMS OF CHANGE

The study of psychotherapy process-outcome relations aims at understanding how therapy works. Following Orlinsky et al. (2004), process variables comprise actions, experiences, and relatedness during psychotherapy sessions or in the daily lives of the participants if they are referring to one another. One group of process variables that has received considerable attention over the last decades are change mechanisms. As defined by Crits-Cristoph and Connolly Gibbons in this volume, these refer to "changes occurring within the patient over the course of psychotherapy that are hypothesized to have a causal relation with treatment outcome." (see Chapter 8) Statistically, variables through which treatments may exert their effects on distress, symptoms or other outcomes of interest are called *mediators*. To be considered a mediator, a variable should measure some event or change that occurs as a result of a specific treatment, and which is associated with treatment outcomes (Kraemer et al., 2002). As such, mediators are best examined within the context of randomized controlled trials, where a psychological treatment is compared to inactive control conditions such as waitlist or usual care, so that any changes in the purported mediator can be reliably attributed to the action of psychotherapy. However, many putative change agents cannot be manipulated (often due to ethical and conceptual reasons). Thus, regularly only non-experimental data is available to investigate questions of process–outcome relations (see Chapters 7 and 8 in this volume; Crits-Christoph et al., 2013). Therefore, in recent years, new methods have been introduced that help reduce biases inherent in this kind of data and thus allow the approximation of causal inferences. One pillar of these kinds of analyses is the repeated assessment of the variables of interest over the course of therapy (e.g., session-by-session). New methodological developments in this area are reviewed in the following section.

Disentangling Within- from Between-Patient Variation

Clinical theories implicitly or explicitly refer to the within-patient level of change. For example, according to CBT theory, changing a depressed patient's dysfunctional cognitions should lead to changes in symptoms. However, session-to-session process and outcome variables capture information about both within- and between-patient variation. Drawing conclusions for within-patient associations based on between-patient associations can lead to misinterpretations, especially in cases in which the between- and within-patient associations go in different directions. This problem has been illustrated by Hamaker (2012) in an example about the relation between typing speed and typos. If the analysis to investigate this relationship only focuses on between-person differences on the aggregate level, it would likely result in a counterintuitive negative relationship between the number of words typed per minute and the percentage of typing mistakes (i.e., people who type faster make less mistakes). The reason would probably be that people who type faster are more experienced, which also results in better typing skills (i.e., less mistakes). However, this does not apply on the individual level. For the individual, in most cases it is true that a higher typing speed will result in more typos. This means that, in this case, the relationship at the individual or within-person level is opposite to the relationship between persons on the aggregated level (Hamaker, 2012).

In circumstances in which it is possible to randomize individuals to conditions, between which all potentially relevant factors are equally balanced, we assume that a transfer of findings from the between- to the within-person level is valid. Under these conditions, no known or unknown person characteristics should bias the effect due to randomization. However, psychotherapy process research often relies on observational data, as randomization to conditions with differing levels of, for example, alliance quality, is ethically problematic (Crits-Christoph et al., 2013). Again, it is crucial to decide on a specific measurement schedule that enables the researcher to detect the effect of the respective process of interest. Depending on this decision and on the number of treatment sessions provided, longitudinal panel data of varying lengths is collected.

Person-Mean Centering or Detrending

Longitudinal data allow a proper disentanglement of between- and within-patient associations. However, a number of decisions made by the analyst can substantially influence the results. The first decision concerns the specific method of disentangling within- and between-patient variation. Broadly, there are two sets of approaches.

The first approach uses the person-specific average score in the process-variable and centers each session score around this person-specific average. This is called *person-mean centering* (PMC). The second set of approaches consider that process variables are likely to change over time and argue that associations that occur due to this overall trend should be removed from the estimation of within-patient effects. Therefore, in these approaches, called *detrending*, the session-specific scores are not centered around the person-mean but around the scores that would be expected at the respective time points, given the person-specific average change in these variables. For example, a regression is estimated separately for each patient with time (e.g., session) as a predictor and the process variable as outcome. These individual regressions can then be used to calculate the expected scores at the respective time points. In a last step, the residuals are calculated by taking the difference of the expected and observed scores. These residuals are used in subsequent analyses to represent the within-patient variation in the process-variable. The same effect can be achieved by including the time/session variable as an additional predictor in the models (i.e., time as covariate model; Wang & Maxwell, 2015).

There is an ongoing debate about whether to detrend or PMC data for within-patient analyses (e.g., Wang & Maxwell, 2015). Those who argue for detrending the data warn about risking spurious associations that result from a shared trend in the process- and outcome-variable. Advocates of PMC warn against removing effects of the treatment itself along with the time trend. For example, it is assumed to be part of treatment to establish a good alliance. Removing the average increase in alliance by detrending the data seems to "throw out the baby with the bathwater," as a considerable part of the treatment itself is removed. In line with Wang and Maxwell (2015), Falkenström et al. (2017) recommended detrending only if there is a risk that time trends represent unmeasured confounding variables. If theoretically, this is not the case and the trends are expected as a result of the treatment itself, PMC is preferable. However, even in this case detrended analyses can make sense in terms of a sensitivity analysis.

Modern Cross-Lagged Panel Models

One approach that has been specifically introduced for the analysis of within-person effects in longitudinal panel data (i.e., longitudinal data of a number of individuals) is the random-intercept–cross-lagged panel model (RI–CLPM; Hamaker et al., 2015). This model is an extension of the classic cross-lagged panel model (CLPM). The CLPM includes autoregressive as well as cross-lagged associations between two variables of interest. However, the effects estimated in a CLPM do not consider the hierarchical nature of the data and thus do not properly disentangle within- from between-person effects. The RI–CLPM includes two latent variables that capture between-person variance in the investigated variables, leaving only the within-person variation for the estimation of the cross-lagged effects.

For example, Solomonov et al. (2020) used the RI–CLPM in a sample of 161 patients who received either 12-weeks of CBT or panic-focused psychodynamic therapy to investigate the within-patient effects of the quality of the working alliance on change in panic-specific reflective functioning. Both working alliance and panic-specific reflective functioning were assessed three times over the course of the treatment (alliance: week 1, week 3, week 5; reflective functioning: week 1, week 5, and week 12). Interestingly, on the within-patient level higher alliance quality in week 5 was related to decreased reflective functioning at week 12 for CBT patients, whereas higher alliance levels in weeks 3 and 5 were followed by an increase in reflective functioning in weeks 5 and 12, respectively, for patients treated with panic-focused psychodynamic therapy.

Zyphur et al. (2019) build on the RI–CLPM and provide a generalized framework to dynamic panel data. This framework includes the latent between-person variables introduced in the RI–CLPM, but also a number of other new parameters that have yet to be tested in psychotherapy research.

In the context of psychotherapy process–outcome research, where time series are usually rather short (either by design or the length of the treatment), these SEM-based models are most often applicable. However, if we have longer time series with, for example, $T > 15$, matrices often become too large and classical SEM-based methods are no longer applicable. For these kinds of data, which are more similar to intensive longitudinal data, dynamic structural equation modeling (Asparouhov et al., 2018; Rubel et al., 2019) is a viable alternative.

Standardization

Independent of the actual method used to estimate within-patient effects, the optimal standardization procedure must also be considered (e.g., Schuurman et al., 2016; Wang et al., 2019). Generally, to standardize a coefficient, the standard deviations (SD) of the predictor and dependent variable are used. However, in multilevel analysis, there are SDs at multiple levels and there is no agreed-on standard regarding which SD should be used in the standardization procedure. Generally speaking, there are two options. First, the sample's global parameters can be used. That is, the average mean and SD averaged over all individuals (called global standardization).

Second, the respective person-specific parameters can be applied. That is, each person's average score and SD (within-person standardization). Recently, it has been argued that the standardization of within-person effects should be performed using within-person standardization for both theoretical (Schuurman et al., 2016) and statistical reasons (Wang et al., 2019).

Confounders of Within-Patient Associations

It is important to note that within-patient analyses rule out any patient-specific or therapist-specific confounders of the associations (Curran & Bauer, 2011). That is, we can rule out stable patient characteristics (e.g., interpersonal problems) as alternative explanations of within-patient alliance–outcome associations. However, time-varying covariates cannot be ruled out as confounders of the association. For example, if less session-specific coping experiences lead to lower alliance scores in the same session as well as higher symptoms in the subsequent session, we could erroneously attribute increased symptomatology to the lower alliance scores. Therefore, it is important to assess all hypothetically relevant time-varying predictors in order to maximize the validity of within-patient estimates (cf. Rubel et al., 2017).

However, new developments of methods for the analysis of observational data to draw causal inference have shown that caution should be exercised in the choice of variables included in causal models (e.g., Pearl & Mackenzie, 2018). While it is important to appropriately control confounding variables (i.e., variables that are associated with the assumed cause), there are types of variables that may be mistaken as confounders but induce biased effects when included in the models. The identification of the variables that should be controlled for and those that, when included, induce bias, can be achieved with the use of directed acyclic graphs (DAGs). A DAG is a graphical representation of the assumed causal associations. The software DAGitty.net provides an accessible interface that assists users in the construction of DAGs and helps them identify which variables should and should not be controlled for. For an in-depth discussion of DAGs and their use for causal inference with observational data, refer to Pearl and Mackenzie (2018).

Cross-Level Interactions

Another important nuance is that although no higher level variables can artificially create a within-patient effect (such as patient or therapist characteristics). They can, however, moderate it (e.g., Zilcha-Mano & Errázuriz, 2015). As such, stable patient and therapist characteristics can attenuate or reduce the size of a within-patient effect. These moderations can be tested in so-called cross-level interactions.

Nonlinear Processes: Sudden Gains, Sudden Losses, and Alliance Ruptures

The fine-grained investigation of session-level processes also allows the identification of nonlinear phenomena (e.g., Hayes et al., 2007). One prominent example of these phenomena are large intersession changes (i.e., sudden gains and sudden losses;

Lutz et al., 2013; Tang & DeRubeis, 1999). For example, in the seminal study by Tang and DeRubeis (1999), 39% in a sample of depressed patients experienced at least one sudden gain during their treatment. Importantly, within the subgroup of patients with a positive outcome, this number increased to 79%. This underlines the role such sudden symptom improvements can have for ultimate treatment outcome. While sudden gains have been widely studied, research focusing on sudden losses is scarce (e.g., Krüger et al., 2014; Lutz et al., 2013). From these studies, some preliminary observations can be made: First, sudden losses seem to be less frequent than sudden gains. Second, while sudden gains take place predominantly in early sessions, sudden losses are more or less equally distributed over the course of treatment. In terms of their association with treatment outcome, patients who only perceive losses seem to have higher symptom scores after treatment than patients who have no sudden shifts, gains, or gains and losses. Patients who experience gains and losses during their treatment seem to have improved less with regard to interpersonal problems.

Another nonlinear phenomenon that has been shown to be related to sudden losses are ruptures in the therapeutic alliance (e.g., Eubanks et al., 2018). These so-called *alliance ruptures* represent impasses in the therapeutic alliance that, if successfully repaired, can be an important and helpful event for patients. However, if not recognized and resolved appropriately, these ruptures can have detrimental effects on treatment outcome (e.g., Muran et al., 2009; Rubel, Zilcha-Mano et al., 2018).

Dyadic Models

The process of psychotherapy is inherently dyadic. The complex interactions between patients and therapists and their role in the change process cannot be comprehensively described if we only focus on one of the two perspectives. This has also been recognized in contemporary psychotherapy research. Applications considering the dyadic nature of psychotherapy investigate the overlap/divergence of the patients' and therapists' perspectives on some aspect of therapy and its effects on outcome. The predominant process investigated so far is the therapeutic alliance. Therefore, the provided examples mainly deal with this variable. The present section focuses on those methods that have already been used in psychotherapy process studies: (a) the truth and bias model (T&B model; West & Kenny, 2011), (b) response surface analysis (RSA; e.g., Shanock et al., 2010), and (c) the actor-partner interdependence model (APIM; Cook & Kenny, 2005). Of course, the described methods are by no means an exhaustive list of all the models available to study dynamic interactions (see Gates & Liu, 2016).

Truth and Bias Model

When investigating the overlap or agreement between two perspectives, the most straightforward approach seems to be the use of difference scores. That is, for example, the difference between the alliance assessment of the patient and that of the therapist. However, difference scores have been criticized for various reasons (e.g., Cronbach & Furby, 1970), which is why their use as a measure of overlap is questionable.

Therefore, West and Kenny (2011) introduced the T&B model that estimates two aspects of overlap, *accuracy* and *bias*. Accuracy is a measure of the temporal correlation between the therapist and patient ratings and bias is an indicator of the average difference between the perspectives across all sessions. In this multilevel model, one perspective (e.g., therapist alliance ratings) is used as the dependent variable and the other perspective (e.g., patient alliance ratings) as the predictor. The estimated intercept constitutes the *bias* and the coefficient of the predictor is the *temporal accuracy*.

So far, several studies have used this model to investigate the alliance and its association with outcome. On average, therapists rate the alliance less positively than their patients (i.e., negative directional bias), but are also temporally accurate in their ratings (i.e., therapists do recognize fluctuations in the alliance similarly to their patients; e.g., Atzil-Slonim et al., 2015). Interestingly, those therapists who on average have a larger negative bias (i.e., rate the alliance more negatively than their patients compared to other therapists) show higher temporal accuracy over the course of treatment. Higher temporal accuracy has been shown to be associated with better outcomes in both therapeutic bond and functioning ratings (Bar-Kalifa et al., 2016; Rubel, Bar-Kalifa et al., 2018), while higher levels of bias in bond ratings (i.e., absolute scores) were generally associated with worse outcomes. Furthermore, it has been repeatedly shown that the directional bias decreases over the course of therapy. That is, therapist and patient ratings become more similar over time (e.g., Atzil-Slonim et al., 2015; Kivlighan & Shaughnessy, 1995). In the literature, this phenomenon has been called *convergence* and has been shown to be associated with treatment outcome in generalized anxiety disorder (Coyne et al., 2018) and follow-up scores in chronic depression (more convergence associated with better outcomes/follow-up scores; Laws et al., 2017).

Response Surface Analysis (RSA)

While the T&B model provides global indicators of the average difference between the two perspectives as well as their temporal congruence, it cannot estimate the session-to-session effects of this overlap on a third variable (e.g., symptoms in the subsequent session). To answer these kinds of questions, polynomial regression and RSA (e.g., Shanock et al., 2010) can be used.

RSA is especially apt to investigate the association between two predictor variables, such as patient and therapist alliance ratings, and a dependent variable (e.g., next session symptom impairment). Additionally, it can be used to examine whether agreement has a beneficial effect on the criterion variable. Specifically, in our example, symptoms in session t would be the dependent variable and patient and therapist alliance ratings in session $t - 1$ would be the predictor variables. Additionally, the interaction of the predictors as well as their quadratic transformations are included in the regression/multilevel model. Based on these coefficients, it is possible to draw a three-dimensional response surface and calculate certain characteristics. That is, indices that quantify the effect of higher/lower patient/therapist-rated alliance scores given agreement or disagreement of their ratings. Moreover, it quantifies the effect that higher levels of disagreement have on subsequent symptoms.

For example, Rubel, Bar-Kalifa et al. (2018) investigated the session-to-session effects of agreement in therapeutic bond ratings on subsequent symptoms in a naturalistic sample of 580 patients. If patient and therapist bond ratings were in agreement, higher bond scores were associated with lower symptom impairment in subsequent sessions, when controlling for symptoms in the current session. If patients and their therapists perceived the bond differently, next session symptoms were less severe when the therapist rated the bond more positively than when the patient rated the bond more positively. The authors did not find a positive effect of agreement in itself on subsequent symptoms. That is, it was more beneficial if there was a disagreement in the sense that therapists perceived the bond to be strong, while their patients perceived it less positive, instead of both parties agreeing on a person-specific average bond level (Rubel et al., 2018). This finding might hint to the possibility that therapists provide more immediately helpful interventions when they perceive the bond more positively than their patients (maybe in an effort to offer the patient short-term improvements). However, given that this primacy of the therapists' perspective stood in contrast to the authors' hypotheses, they caution against generalizing beyond this result until replication in other datasets.

Actor–Partner Interdependence Model (APIM)

Another model that has been recently applied to session-to-session psychotherapy data is the APIM (Cook & Kenny, 2003). The APIM is especially apt if therapist and patient data are available for two variables, a process variable and an outcome variable. As two dependent variables are investigated, the APIM is a multivariate model that can either be estimated within an SEM or a multilevel framework (e.g., Baldwin et al., 2014). In this model, four types of effects are differentiated: two actor effects and two partner effects. Using the alliance–outcome association as an example, the patient actor effect would be the effect of patient-rated alliance on patient-rated outcome and the therapist actor effect would be the effect of therapist-rated alliance on therapist-rated outcome. The patient partner effect would be the effect of patient-rated alliance on therapist-rated outcome and the therapist partner effect would be the effect of therapist-rated alliance on patient-rated outcome.

Recently, the APIM has been combined with the analysis of within-patient effects (see previous section). Zilcha-Mano et al. (2016) investigated within- and between-patients actor and partner effects between the working alliance and session outcome in a sample of 241 patients treated with either CBT or alliance-focused therapy. Overall, all actor effects were significantly positive. That is, within- and between-patient effects indicated that higher alliance ratings were associated with more problem reduction over the course of treatment. The within-patient therapist actor effect was moderated by treatment condition and stronger in the alliance-focused than in the CBT condition. Of the partner effects, only the within-patient patient partner effect was significant. That is, higher within-patient patient-rated alliance scores in one session were associated with greater therapist-rated problem reduction in the subsequent session.

Summary: Understanding Change

Investigating the processes and mechanisms of change in psychotherapy is a complex task. Often it is not possible to conduct rigorous experimental studies in which the processes of interest are systematically manipulated. As such, it is difficult to draw firm causal conclusions about process-outcome associations. Two major developments have recently led to the use of more appropriate methods for the study of mechanisms of change in observational data. First, the proper disentanglement of within- and between-patient variation in longitudinal data enables the exclusion of a set of potentially confounding variables (i.e., stable patient variables) and thus allows firmer conclusions about the investigated associations. Second, several methods have been introduced that take the dyadic nature of the therapeutic process into account and are thus better suited to study the complex interactions and joint effects of multiple perspectives (e.g., patients and therapists). Besides these developments, there is an increasing interest in nonlinear phenomena such as sudden symptom gains and losses as well as alliance ruptures. These sudden changes in symptoms or the alliance can direct researchers toward important sessions that warrant a more fine-grained, within-session investigation. The methodological developments described in this section will likely help the field to better answer the question "how does therapy work?" and thus to form a solid base from which to improve treatments for the individual patient.

PATIENT-FOCUSED RESEARCH AND ROUTINE OUTCOME MONITORING

The implementation of outcome measures as part of routine clinical practice and training can be seen as one of the most successful developments in psychotherapy research over the last two decades. This development was already summarized in the last edition of the Handbook (Castonguay et al., 2013) as a core component of practice-oriented research, but has gained a large amount of further research interest since the last edition. Practice-oriented research is discussed in Chapter 6 of this volume.

Over 50 years of accumulated research has shown that clinical intuition is error-prone, and is often outperformed by data-driven classification and prognostic models (e.g., Ægisdóttir et al., 2006; Meehl, 1973). In order to support and improve clinical decision-making, several research concepts have been developed, such as routine outcome monitoring (ROM), measurement-based care, and *patient-focused research*. Patient-focused research includes routine outcome measurement as well as psychometric feedback to either therapists or patients over the course of treatment. This development has considerably influenced the implementation of outcome measures in psychotherapy, as described in the last edition of this *Handbook* (Lambert, 2013).

More than 20 years ago, patient-focused research was introduced as a new research concept and an effort to establish a clinically meaningful research strategy narrowing the so-called scientist-practitioner gap (Howard et al., 1996). The time-lag from initial publication of research findings to their eventual implementation in clinical practice can easily take up to 10 years or longer. Therefore, from the start, patient-focused research has been concerned with research that is directly applicable in the form of real-time feedback of clinical progress over the course of treatment to therapists. Propelled by Michael Lambert and his research group with several large randomized controlled trials (RCTs, e.g., Lambert, Hansen et al., 2001), this research agenda has become a broad international endeavor and one of the most prolific and cited areas within psychotherapy research over the last two decades (Bickman, 2020; Lambert et al., 2018; Muran & Lutz, 2015).

This research paradigm seeks to improve the outcomes of individual patients encountered in routine practice. It is therefore complementary to, but distinctive from, paradigms applied in effectiveness and efficacy research, which investigate average treatment effects for groups of patients in controlled or naturalistic contexts (Castonguay et al., 2013). Patient-focused research seeks to derive insights and tools from clinical population data, which may help to guide treatment decisions applied to the individual, thus informing practice through scientific methods. The pursuit of answers to these questions has led to the development of rationally derived models and empirically derived statistical models, which aim to enable psychotherapists to monitor treatment progress, feed it back to therapists and patients, and to adjust psychotherapy in order to improve treatment outcomes. In this regard, this research paradigm offers an elegant bridge between nomothetic and idiographic approaches to psychological assessment and intervention and has much in common with contemporary notions of precision and personalized medicine (National Research Council, 2011).

Evidence of Feedback Effects

Ideally, outcomes should be measured frequently throughout treatment, and should enable therapists and patients to assess if the treatment approach is working, or if it should be modified. This use of ROM is referred to as progress feedback. Different types of progress feedback exist, ranging from feeding back the raw scores of an outcome instrument, to providing clinical information based on systems that apply expected treatment response (ETR) models to determine whether a patient is progressing as expected (on track; OT), or stagnating or worsening (not on track; NOT). More advanced systems have been developed to supplement ETR feedback with clinical support tools (e.g., Lutz et al., 2019; Whipple et al., 2003). These tools provide assessments of issues related to the treatment process (e.g., alliance ruptures, motivation deficits), as well as suggestions on how to best handle problems based on the scientific literature on these topics. They are predominantly used in NOT cases to provide the clinician with additional ideas on how to adapt treatment in order to prevent negative treatment outcomes such as deterioration and dropout.

To date, the effectiveness of providing clinicians and/or clients with progress feedback as part of patient-focused research has been assessed in more than fifty studies (see Supplement B at the end of this chapter for an overview of studies per country). The results of these studies have been summarized in nine meta-analyses (see Table 4.2), six of which examined adult psychotherapy, two on youth psychotherapy (Bergman et al., 2018; Tam & Ronan, 2017), and one which combined both adult and youth psychotherapy (de Jong et al., 2021). Table 4.2 outlines the results of these meta-analyses. The effect sizes of psychotherapy with feedback compared to psychotherapy without feedback range from small ($g = 0.07$) to medium ($d = 0.40$). While these effect sizes may appear small compared to studies that compare psychotherapies with control conditions, it should be noted that feedback is a relatively simple intervention provided *in addition to* psychotherapy, which already has quite large effects (see Table 4.1 and Wampold & Imel, 2015). Thus, feedback offers added value over and above the general effectiveness of psychotherapy – in other words, using feedback methods potentiates the effectiveness of therapy by a small degree. Somewhat higher effect sizes have been reported for NOT cases (see Table 4.2). The hypothesis is that feedback effects are more pronounced in NOT cases, as these cases present a greater opportunity to adapt the treatment approach based on feedback. Three meta-analyses have assessed the effects of clinical support tools (CSTs) feedback compared to no-feedback controls in NOT cases and have found effect sizes ranging from 0.36 to 0.53 (de Jong et al., 2021; Lambert et al., 2018; Shimokawa et al., 2010).

In addition to the effects of feedback on symptom reduction, meta-analyses have assessed the effects of feedback on the odds of treatment success, the odds of dropout, and treatment duration. Lambert and colleagues (2018) found that feedback nearly doubled clinically significant/reliable change rates in NOT cases when CSTs were included (OR = 2.40 versus OR = 1.89 without CSTs; Lambert, et al., 2018). Kendrick et al. (2016) assessed the effect of feedback on treatment duration and found that in the full sample feedback did not have an effect on the number of sessions attended ($g = -0.02$, 95% CI [-0.39, 0.42]), but did find that OT cases received on average 0.69 sessions fewer when feedback was provided, while NOT cases received 0.73 sessions more when feedback was provided. These results are in line with earlier findings by Lambert et al. (2003). Finally, de Jong et al. (2021) reported an effect of feedback on dropout. When feedback was provided, dropout was reduced by 20% compared to when no feedback was provided.

While meta-analyses are useful to get an overall idea of the effectiveness of feedback interventions, most of the mentioned analyses have been conducted on a relatively small number of studies (see Table 4.2). In addition, many implementation problems (see next section) potentially dilute the effect of feedback. To illustrate these issues, it is useful to highlight a few individual studies. The pioneering studies by Michael Lambert and his research group (e.g., Lambert et al., 2002; Lambert, Whipple et al., 2001) with the OQ Analyst System can be considered a demonstration of the magnitude of the effect that feedback can have, if it is well

TABLE 4.2   Results of Meta-Analyses on the Effect of Progress Feedback on Symptom Reduction

Meta-analysis	N	# of studies	Sample	Author's conclusion	ES (95% CI) full sample	ES (95% CI) NOT cases
Lambert et al., 2003	2,605	3	College counseling center in the USA	A medium effect of feedback in NOT cases	n.r.	0.39 [n.r.]
Knaup et al., 2009	4,540	12	Outpatients, inpatients and day patients in the USA, UK, and Germany	A small effect of feedback on short-term outcomes (9 weeks after intake)[1]	n.r.	n.r.
Shimokawa et al., 2010	6,151	6	College counseling center and outpatient clinic in the USA	A small-to-medium effect of feedback in NOT cases; stronger for CST feedback 0.70 [0.52, 0.88]	n.r.	0.53 [0.28, 0.78]
Kendrick et al., 2016	3,696	12	Outpatient clinics in the USA and Europe; common mental disorders	No overall effect of feedback; a small effect in NOT cases	0.07 [−0.01, 0.16]	0.22 [0.09, 0.35]
Tam & Ronan, 2017	3,804	10	Youth mental health care settings in the USA, Australia, the UK, and Ireland	A small-to-medium overall effect size of feedback. Within-patient effects were larger than between-patient effects.	0.28 [0.01, 0.55]	n.r.
Bergman et al., 2018	858	5	Youth mental health care settings in the USA and Israel	Too much heterogeneity to pool results.	n.r.	n.r.
Lambert et al., 2018		24	Outpatients in the USA, Europe, and Australia	Small overall effect of feedback for OQ-45, medium for PCOMS; medium effect in NOT cases for OQ, stronger for CST feedback (0.49, [0.25,0.73])		
- OQ	7,509				0.14 [0.08, 0.20]	0.33 [0.25, 0.41]
- PCOMS	2,113				0.40 [0.29, 0.51]	n.r. −
Østergård et al.,2018	2,910	18	Studies using PCOMS in counseling and psychiatric settings in the USA and Europe		0.27 [0.14, 0.41]	0.21 [−0.11, 0.53]
De Jong et al., 2021	22,699	58	Outpatient, day patients, and inpatients in the USA, Europe, and Australia; all diagnoses except SMI	Small effects of feedback in both full sample and NOT cases; a significant reduction of dropout in feedback conditions	0.15 [0.10, 0.20]	0.17 [0.11, 0.22]

Note. Reported effect sizes are Hedges' *g*, except for both Lambert et al. articles and de Jong et al. ES = effect size; 95% CI = 95% confidence interval; NOT = not on track; CCC = college counseling center; OQ = Outcome Questionnaire; PCOMS = Partners for Change Outcome Management System; CST = clinical support tools; SMI = severe mental illness; n.r. = not reported; N/A = not applicable.

implemented. The majority of studies by their group have been conducted in the same college counseling center in the US. While this may restrict generalizability to other settings, it also assures that the therapists are well trained and accustomed to utilizing feedback. What can be seen in the studies conducted in this setting over the years is that the effects of feedback seem to increase over time, although this is partially due to technical and conceptual innovations in the feedback.

In addition to Lambert's investigations, two additional studies shed light on current directions of research. These large-scale studies have conducted feedback trials in settings where outcome measurements were already routinely collected. In a cohort study, Janse et al. (2017) collected data on 1,006 patients receiving manualized cognitive behavioral therapy (CBT), using sessional feedback based on the Partners for Change Outcome Management System (PCOMS; Miller et al., 2005). In the control group, feedback on the SCL-90 was provided every five sessions as part of usual treatment. Adding PCOMS feedback resulted in significantly fewer sessions, thereby improving the efficiency of the CBT. Feedback also resulted in a larger symptom reduction on the SCL-90 for depressed patients ($d = 0.38$). Delgadillo et al. (2018) conducted the largest randomized controlled trial of feedback to date, and collected data on 2,233 patients with depression and anxiety who were treated within IAPT services in the UK. Session-by-session measurements on the Patient Health Questionnaire (PHQ-9) and the Generalized Anxiety Disorder questionnaire (GAD-7) were routinely conducted in the participating services to monitor response to treatment. During the study, in the feedback condition, ETR curves with warning signals for therapists were implemented into the electronic patient record in order to assess if patients were on track or NOT. Therapists were trained to use clinical troubleshooting skills with NOT cases and instructed to prioritize these cases for discussion in clinical supervision meetings. At the end of treatment, NOT cases in the feedback condition had less severe symptoms than NOT cases in the control group, and NOT cases in the control group had increased odds of deterioration (OR = 1.73 [1.18, 2.54]).

In conclusion, it seems like feedback has a small-to-medium effect on symptom reduction. It also shows potential benefits with regard to treatment duration, the odds of recovery and dropout rates, although further research is needed to establish the effects of feedback on the latter outcomes. For NOT cases, feedback supplemented with CSTs is found to have stronger effects than feedback alone. However, only a few studies have examined moderators of feedback effects; for example, implementation issues, the feedback system used, therapists' attitudes toward and handling of feedback, or its mechanisms of action (see next section).

Implementation Issues

Numerous case studies and reviews have discussed known barriers to the implementation and effective use of routine outcome measurement and psychometric feedback (e.g., Boswell et al., 2015; de Jong, 2016; Douglas et al., 2016). Several studies have shown that feedback effects are dependent on implementation issues, such as therapist behavior, attitudes, application and commitment to feedback (e.g., Brattland et al., 2018; de Jong et al., 2012; Lutz et al., 2015; Simon et al., 2012). Successful implementations of patient-focused research can lead to change in clinical interventions and services. For example, in a patient-focused research study (Lutz et al., 2015) where therapists were asked about their attitudes toward and use of feedback, in approximately 70% of occasions, when therapists received psychometric feedback, they made some use of it (e.g., by discussing results with patients or trying to adjust their interventions). Furthermore, outcome evaluation is acceptable to patients. For example, when patients in the study by Lutz et al. (2015) were asked whether they found it important to monitor the results of psychotherapeutic treatments, more than 90% agreed or partially agreed.

There are also successful and large-scale implementations of routine outcome measurement across the world. Some examples of well-established systems have already been summarized in the last edition of this *Handbook* (Castonguay et al., 2013). Measurement-based care across numerous countries and settings include inpatient, community-based, and university-based psychological services (see Supplement B and Chapter 6 in this volume). Successful implementation requires a detailed understanding of barriers and enablers, which are commonly grouped according to broad themes, such as *organizational, technological, practical, attitudinal,* and *competency-related* barriers.

Organizational obstacles arise in contexts where service policies, culture, and resources are poorly aligned with the adoption of measurements. For example, some organizations may adhere to a particular theoretical position that is at odds with outcome measurement. Similarly, particular service policies or the imposition of high caseloads and reduced administrative time available to therapists could impede the effective use of outcome measures.

Technological obstacles include the lack of modern information technology systems, but may also refer to limitations inherent to a specific system (e.g., a user interface that is overly complicated or has low face validity), or the choice of psychometric measures applied (e.g., excessively lengthy questionnaires).

Practical obstacles include inadequate procedures or support (e.g., lack of time, lack of administrative support). To some extent, overcoming these organizational and practical barriers relies on economic resources, effective project management, and committed leadership that can support financial and policy-level changes.

Attitudinal barriers and resistance to the use of outcome measurement can arise in different groups of stakeholders, including managers, therapists, and patients. If the use of data is not seen as a priority by managers, and if an organization lacks systems to incentivize its application (e.g., as part of clinical supervision), therapists are less likely to effectively implement it. Practitioner barriers include biased attitudes (e.g., prioritizing clinical judgment over measurement) and concerns about the negative consequences of measurement (burdening patients, straining the therapeutic relationship, being judged or penalized by supervisors or managers). Patients' attitudinal barriers are commonly associated with literacy, language, and cognitive problems that might make completing questionnaires burdensome or time-consuming, as well as a lack of understanding for the rationale of completing such measures.

Closely related to therapist *attitudinal* barriers are *competency-related* barriers, which can be seen as deficits in knowledge and skills that support the effective use of outcome measures. A frequent objection raised by therapists is the perceived lack of validity or relevance of psychometric tests for an individual's problems (e.g., Wolpert et al., 2016). This is a common educational deficit reflecting a lack of knowledge about psychometrics, about other measures that could be selected, or about alternative practices, such as idiographic measures and single-case experimental designs. Such attitudinal issues, knowledge gaps, and skills deficits can be improved with training and continually developed via outcome-oriented clinical supervision in mental health services (e.g., Edbrooke-Childs et al., 2016). For example, studies have shown that educational interventions informed by the theory of planned behavior effectively help to influence mental health practitioners' attitudes and behaviors (e.g., Casper, 2007). Thus, attitudinal barriers and skills deficits can be addressed by training, which should ideally be embedded in the curriculum of psychotherapy and clinical psychology programs.

In view of these multiple barriers to implementation, no single strategy is likely to succeed, and there is broad consensus that multifaceted strategies tailored to address locally relevant obstacles are necessary for successful adoption. Strategies drawn from implementation science (e.g., Nilsen, 2015) have been described by several authors: Mellor-Clark et al. (2016) recommend assessing the host setting by creating a preimplementation plan and service profile survey (listing known and expected obstacles and enablers). Boswell et al. (2015) recommend a continuous dialogue between different stakeholders, such as patients, therapists, administrators, policymakers, and researchers, for successful large-scale implementation of routine outcome measurement. Lewis et al. (2019) make several recommendations to enhance the *technological* aspects of the measurement system itself, such as harmonizing the terminology used in such systems for maximal face validity, using brief and psychometrically robust measures, using algorithms that aid interpretability (e.g., prognostic feedback signals), and incentivizing the timely use of such technologies in-session to maximize integration into routine psychological treatments.

From a wider health-care system perspective, the American Psychological Association (APA) Mental and Behavioral Health Registry Initiative proposed six key recommendations to enable psychological services to adopt outcome measurements (Wright et al., 2019):

1. Patient-reported outcome measures should be central to ensure person-centered care.
2. Measures that are relevant across a wide group of individuals receiving care should be prioritized.
3. Such measures should have rigorously established psychometric properties.
4. Such measures should be used to support continuous quality improvement initiatives, in line with the principles of a learning health system.
5. Implementation should be supported by high-quality training.
6. Regulatory and professional bodies – such as the APA – should lead the development of measures and the establishment of training standards for practicing psychologists.

Without such systemwide strategies adopted by leading professional organizations, measurement-based care is unlikely to become a fully adopted and routine aspect of psychological care.

Summary: Feedback-Informed Treatment

Measurement-based care is increasingly seen as a means of improving the effectiveness and transparency of mental health care, in line with the scientist-practitioner approach. The clinical benefits of measurement-based care are exemplified by the literature on feedback-informed treatment, which now counts with empirical support from over 40 randomized controlled trials and several meta-analyses. Integrating feedback into clinical practice can improve treatment outcomes, can help to prevent dropout, and can help to rapidly identify and resolve problems. Despite this evidence base and the adoption of feedback systems in several specialist clinics across the world, feedback-informed treatment is not yet a mainstream aspect of psychotherapy practice. Numerous barriers outlined above stand in the way of widescale adoption. In particular, policymakers, health-care leaders, and clinical educators have an important role to play in facilitating the adoption of routine outcome measures and the use of feedback as a core aspect of treatment delivery.

EVIDENCE-BASED PERSONALIZATION IN CLINICAL PRACTICE

The use of measurement in routine care has also substantially changed the way psychotherapy is thought about as an applied science. In the last decade, several new developments have emerged in the field of psychotherapy research that advance the tradition of patient-focused research with concepts from precision mental health research and precision medicine.

In clinical practice, most therapists individualize their approach based on their clinical training, continuous education, and their clinical experience. However, this also means that personalization is hardly based on empirical findings, but rather on intuition, and is conducted unsystematically in clinical practice. Therefore, the combination of treatment selection research and psychometric feedback is opening up a new field of evidence-based personalization research and practice (Page et al., 2019). This endeavor can be broadly categorized into two areas: personalized pretreatment recommendations and personalized adaptive recommendations during treatment (see also Chapters 18 and 19 in this volume).

Personalized Pretreatment Recommendations

Precision medicine or mental health research seeks to tailor treatment decisions to an individual or group of individuals with similar characteristics (i.e., phenotypes). The goal of this approach is described in the *Precision Medicine Initiative of the White House* as follows: "Until now, most medical treatments have been designed for the 'average patient.' As a result of this 'one-size-fits-all' approach, treatments can be very successful for some patients, but not for others. *Precision medicine* refers to the tailoring of medical treatment to the individual characteristics of each patient" (The White House, Precision Medicine Initiative. Barack Obama, January 30, 2015).

Personalized pre-treatment recommendations can be seen as a form of precision mental health care, attempting to forecast the most promising treatment approach or strategy given specific patient pretreatment characteristics (see section on predictors and moderators). Recent developments of multi-variable statistical algorithms, so-called machine-learning approaches, are used to identify the best sets and weighting of patient characteristics to inform these selection decisions (e.g., Kessler et al., 2017). Several machine-learning approaches (e.g., regularization, genetic regression, random forest and other decision-tree methods, Bayesian classifiers, support vector machines, k-nearest neighbors, etc.) have been applied to develop models that predict patients' expected response to treatment options of equivalent intensity and cost, such as CBT vs. EMDR (Deisenhofer et al., 2018), CBT vs. low-intensity therapy (Lorenzo-Luaces et al., 2017); CBT vs. IPT (Huibers et al., 2015), and CBT vs. psychodynamic therapy (Cohen et al., 2019; Schwartz et al., 2020).

One example is the nearest-neighbor approach, which has a good human-to-machine decision-making ratio compared to other machine-learning techniques. This allows it to remain clinically comprehensible and communicable (Beam & Kohane, 2018). Other research groups have developed different strategies, for example the Personalized Advantage Index (PAI) or network meta-regression, to select the best predictors of response to specific treatment options (e.g., DeRubeis et al., 2014; Furukawa et al., 2018).

So far, most studies have attempted to identify the most promising treatment protocol for each patient. However, personalized decision-making can go beyond treatment selection. From the perspective of a therapist who is often only trained in one treatment approach, recommendations regarding the most promising treatment techniques or strategies within their theoretical model may be especially helpful to personalize treatment. This information could aid therapists to better predict, whether the specific techniques they are planning are actually effective for the incoming patient. This personalized information at the onset of treatment may help to move from a diagnosis-specific application of clinical interventions to a more transdiagnostic and individualized form of treatment (e.g., Castonguay et al., 2013; Hofmann & Hayes, 2019; Norcross & Wampold, 2019). Several new research initiatives have therefore begun to investigate combinations of nomothetic and idiographic concepts as well as statistics that provide recommendations for clinical strategies and techniques or risk estimates for attrition, all within one treatment protocol (Fisher & Boswell, 2016; Lutz et al., 2019; Rubel, Fisher et al., 2018).

Most studies in this area of research share the limitation that treatment selection methods were retrospectively applied to study data to identify the optimal treatment protocol post-hoc, while prospective RCTs under real-world conditions are rare. Although these analyses of large archival datasets are important steps along a development pathway for precision mental health care, prospective field-tests and controlled trials are necessary to advance this field (Delgadillo & Lutz, 2020).

In one prospective study including 538 patients, optimal pre-treatment recommendations for three treatment strategies (problem-solving, motivation-oriented, or mixed strategies) were evaluated (Lutz et al., 2021). Nearest-neighbor predictions successfully selected optimal treatment strategies for individual patients at the beginning of treatment, resulting in an effect size advantage of about 0.3 (patients who received their optimal strategy vs. those who did not) over the first eight sessions.

Personalized Adaptive Recommendations

Even after the selection of a personalized treatment strategy or protocol, not all patients will benefit from treatment. Some patients will not improve as expected and have an increased risk of treatment failure at the end of treatment. Therefore, adaptive clinical recommendations during treatment are necessary and can be seen as the second part of a comprehensive personalization process. This area of investigation is traditionally called *progress feedback* (described above). Here, monitoring patient progress in real time over the course of treatment and feeding this psychometric information back to the therapist and/or patient is the basis for the second, so-called adaptive or dynamic, decision-making process. Newer psychotherapy monitoring systems include dynamic prediction algorithms that work similarly to other dynamic prediction systems, generating their results in real time (e.g., satellite navigation systems, weather or avalanche forecasting systems; for example, Bone et al., 2021; Lutz et al., 2019).

Using such psychometric feedback during the course of treatment has been shown to be an effective tool to draw therapists' attention to difficulties that might prevent treatment progress. Problem-solving and clinical support tools (CSTs) build on feedback signals by further detailing in which clinical areas treatment adaptations may be needed to improve outcomes of patients at risk of treatment failure (e.g., Whipple et al., 2003). As discussed above, CSTs seem to improve the effect of feedback and treatment monitoring.

Such systems can be used as navigation tools during treatment to improve therapy for patients at risk of treatment failure as well as to monitor treatment length. For example, Lutz et al. (2019) have recently presented such a navigation system developed using a sample of 1,234 outpatient psychotherapy patients. This system includes a dynamic failure boundary adapted session-by-session over the course of treatment that is based on pretreatment information as well as patients' individual change. In this navigation system, the therapist receives graphical feedback (see Figure 4.4) displaying patient-specific symptomatic progress (A, Figure 4.4). As soon as the dynamic failure boundary of the expected treatment response curve is crossed (B & C, Figure 4.4), the therapist receives a warning signal (D, see Figure 4.4), which activates clinical problem-solving tools that can be directly applied in clinical practice (CST, E, Figure 4.4).

The clinical problem-solving tools comprise the following problem areas: (1) risk/suicidality, (2) motivation/therapy goals, (3) therapeutic alliance, (4) social support and critical life events, and (5) emotion regulation/self-regulation. When the system indicates a risk for a negative treatment outcome as well

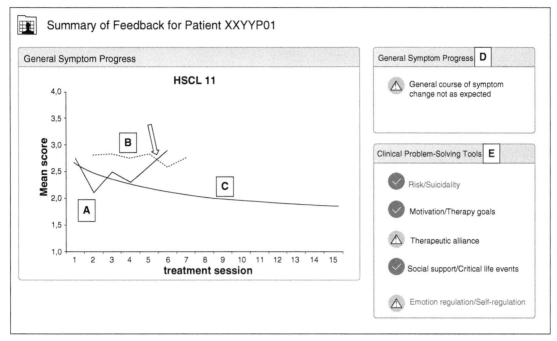

FIGURE 4.4 Screenshot of a patient-specific adaptive recommendation as it is displayed to therapists.

as a problem in a specific area (e.g., treatment motivation), the tools provide text and video-based recommendations for interventions that can help the therapist resolve the problem. In the above-mentioned prospective study on 538 outpatients, the attitude toward and confidence in using the navigation system as well as therapist symptom awareness had a significant impact on treatment outcome. Therapist-rated usefulness of recommendations was a significant moderator of effects (Lutz et al., 2021).

Summary: Change Measurement in Clinical Practice

Tailoring psychological treatments to the individual patient is not new. In fact, most therapists individualize their approach based on their clinical experience with similar patients. However, in clinical practice, personalization is mainly conducted unsystematically and has not been the focus of past research, which has tended to be dominated by the development and validation of new treatment protocols. This research focus has recently shifted. A new research paradigm has emerged, which combines advanced computer-based feedback with decision-making and clinical problem-solving tools. Machine learning techniques are applied to large datasets to develop prediction algorithms. These new methods enable the

identification of prognostic indicators and typical patterns of change, which can be translated into decision-support tools. The resulting tools help to provide personalized predictions for each new patient regarding their optimal treatment, treatment strategy, or therapist. Further, adaptive-feedback tools are not only used to identify patients at risk of treatment failure during treatment but also to estimate the risk of other events such as dropout or self-harm, and to provide clinical problem-solving tools to minimize these risks. Researchers and clinicians need to address several implementation issues that are typical when such expert systems are integrated into clinical practice and training.

CONCLUSIONS AND FUTURE DIRECTIONS

The measurement of change in psychotherapy has developed considerably in the last few decades. In the early days of psychotherapy research, the main question was whether change in psychotherapy *could* be quantitatively measured or scientifically investigated at all. Later, in the earliest studies, unstandardized and global ratings based on written case notes were used. Today, the field has advanced toward the routine application of standardized measures, taking a multidimensional perspective on change. The main questions now concern how change can be *optimally* measured, *how often* it should be measured during the therapy process, and how therapists can *make the best use* of change measures in clinical practice. Tracking change has shifted away from being seen as a questionable burden for therapists and patients and has become an integral part of best practice, health-care systems, and training programs. Similar to the measurement of blood pressure, body temperature, and many other measures used by physicians on a daily basis to identify a medical problem, to make a diagnosis, and to track improvement, psychometric measures are now often used in psychotherapeutic practice to identify and track psychological problems in order to optimize and individualize treatments. This development was and continues to be supported by new advances in technology (e.g., feedback tools, passive sensing devices, experience sampling, software, biomarkers, and neurocognitive measures), making outcome monitoring easy to implement in practice. It also makes blending e-mental health and face-to-face therapy possible.

The routine implementation of measures in clinical practice has allowed another development to emerge: research on patients at risk of treatment failure or negative treatment outcomes. For a long time, the development of new treatment concepts focused on improving average treatment outcomes for all patients with a given diagnosis. However, the more fine-grained use of measurements over the course of treatment allows the focus to be shifted to those patients who are not responding well to treatment and who may benefit most from adaptations. The use of measurement and feedback enables therapists to identify these patients and thus adapt or personalize their approach to their specific needs. Instead of new treatment approaches or models, this perspective calls for the development of specific interventions for patients at risk of treatment failure, the consideration of therapist effects, and the implementation of outcome monitoring as an essential part of clinical training.

Over the years, the practical implementation of measurement has advanced, but also the statistical models have become better able to handle such measurements. Novel methods are now able to handle large and complex datasets, which have become increasingly more extensive due to the inclusion of more measures and time series per patient to describe the course of change. About 25 years ago, researchers were pleased when they were able to investigate the average difference between two groups using only prepost change measures in a small sample of patients, as critically discussed at the time by Beutler and Howard (1998) and Newman and Howard (1991). Since that time, many advances have been made, not only in statistics but also regarding the implementation of longitudinal, causal network, and time-series research designs. These advances allow us to perform more sophisticated analyses of change patterns on several conceptual levels (e.g., sessions, patients, treatments), as well as levels of variation (e.g., within- and between-patient variation or between-therapist variation). These methodological developments are particularly important, as they have led to the development of scientist-practitioner or services research networks, which provide data on thousands of patients. Furthermore, hundreds of therapists are involved in these developments, participating in new research endeavors,

helping to move scientific knowledge within the field forward and attempting to close the scientist-practitioner gap that has hampered the field for so long.

The contemporary literature concerning measurement in psychotherapy points to some fairly clear methodological and practical recommendations for researchers and clinicians. First, measuring change in psychotherapy is a central problem of psychotherapy research, and it is best approached from a multidimensional perspective. Well-being, symptoms, functioning and interpersonal problems are common domains that have face-validity to patients and that have practical implications for routine clinical care. Of course, other process (e.g., alliance) and/or outcome (e.g., quality of life, idiographic goals) measures are valuable to practice and research, though the above domains could be seen as a basic foundation. Second, selected measures should meet the minimum requirements of psychometric validity, reliability as well as sensitivity to change and cultural adaptation if they are to be employed to develop clinical norms and decision-making tools. Third, measurements should be frequent enough to enable more reliable longitudinal data analyses, routine outcome monitoring, but measurement frequency should be balanced against potential response burden. Many studies show that weekly measurement is both acceptable and clinically useful to support feedback-informed treatment. Furthermore, without weekly measurement, valuable information about early response is neglected and there is a missed opportunity to monitor progress in cases that drop out within a few sessions of starting therapy. Fourth, prognostic estimations about the likely outcomes of treatment using psychometric data are not only possible but are indeed more accurate than clinical judgment. Training new generations of psychotherapists in principles of outcome measurement, monitoring, and prognostic assessment is essential to improve the effectiveness of treatment and to embed science at the heart of psychotherapy practice.

To conclude, we are optimistic about the future development of change measurement and its application in psychotherapy. We think that all three positive trends that have resulted from recent years' work will continue to develop and improve. That is, (a) the development of standardized, freely available, and easy-to-apply measures; (b) further developments of new statistical methods to handle large datasets and intensive longitudinal assessments; and (c) a better implementation of outcome navigation systems (including treatment/intervention recommendations, monitoring, feedback, and problem-solving tools) into clinical services and training.

ABBREVIATIONS

APA	American Psychological Association
APIM	Actor-Partner Interdependence Model
AUC	Area Under the Curve
BDI	Beck Depression Inventory
BLRT	Bootstrapped Likelihood Ratio Test

BOLD	blood oxygen level dependent
BSI	Brief Symptom Inventory
CAT	computerized adaptive testing
CBASP	Cognitive Behavioral Analysis System of Psychotherapy
CBT	cognitive behavioral therapy
CCAPS	Counseling Center Assessment of Psychological Symptoms
CL	common language effect size
CLPM	cross lagged panel model
CORE-OM	Clinical Outcomes in Routine Evaluation – Outcome Measure
CST	clinical support tools
DAG	directed acyclic graph
EEG	electroencephalography
EM	expectation-maximization
EMA	ecological momentary assessment
EMDR	eye-movement desensitization and reprocessing
ERP	event-related potentials
ETR	expected treatment response
FEP	Fragebogen zur Evaluation von Psychotherapieverläufen [Questionaire for the Evaluation of Psychotherapy]
fMRI	functional magnetic resonance imaging
GAD	Generalized Anxiety Disorder Questionnaire
GAS	goal attainment scaling
GEL	good-enough-level
GIMME	Group Iterative Multiple Model Estimation
GMM	growth mixture models
GSI	general symptom index
HiTop	Hierarchical Taxonomy of Psychopathology
HLM	hierarchical linear models
IAPT	improving access to psychological therapies
ICC	intra-class correlation
IPT	interpersonal psychotherapy
IRT	item response theory
ITT	intention to treat
LOCF	last observation carried forward
MAR	missing at random
MCAR	missing completely at random
MCMC	Monte Carlo Markov chain
MI	multiple imputation
MICE	multiple imputation by chained equations
ML-VAR	multilevel vector-autoregressive model
MLM	multilevel models
MNAR	missing not at random
MRI	magnetic resonance imaging
MTMM	multitrait-multimethod
NA	negative affect
NIMH	National Institute of Mental Health
NN	nearest neighbors
NNT	number needed to treat
NOT	not on track
OQ	outcome questionnaire
OT	on track
PAI	personalized advantage index
PCOMS	Partners for Change Outcome Management System
PET	positron emission tomography
PHQ	Patient Health Questionnaire
PMC	person-mean centering
PROMIS	Patient Reported Outcome Measurement Information System
QEP	Questionnaire for the Evaluation of Psychotherapeutic Progress
RCI	reliable change index
RCSI	reliable and clinically significant improvement
RCT	randomized controlled trials
RDoC	research domain criteria
RF	random forest
RI-CLPM	random intercept-cross lagged panel model
ROM	routine outcome monitoring
RSA	response surface analysis
SCL	symptom checklist
SD	standard deviation
SE	standard error
SEM	structural equation models
SMD	standardized mean difference
T&B	truth and bias
TDCRP	treatment of depression collaborative research program
TSPA	Time Series Panel Analysis
WAI-SR	Working Alliance Inventory – short revised version

REFERENCES

Ægisdóttir, S., White, M. J., Spengler, P. M., Maugherman, A. S., Anderson, L. A., Cook, R. S., Nichols, C. N., Lampropoulos, G. K., Walker, B. S., Cohen, G., & Rush, J. D. (2016). The meta-analysis of clinical judgment project: Fifty-six years of accumulated research on clinical versus statistical prediction. *The Counseling Psychologist*, 34(3), 341–382. https://doi.org/10.1177/0011000005285875

Ali, S., Littlewood, E., McMillan, D., Delgadillo, J., Miranda, A., Croudace, T., & Gilbody, S. (2014). Heterogeneity in patient-reported outcomes following low-intensity mental health interventions: A multilevel analysis. *PLoS ONE*, 9(9), e99658. https://doi.org/10.1371/journal.pone.0099658

Arndt, A., Lutz, W., Rubel, J., Berger, T., Meyer, B., Schröder, J., Späth, C., Hautzinger, M., Fuhr, K., Rose, M., Hohagen, F., Klein, J. P., & Moritz, S. (2020). Identifying change-dropout patterns during an Internet-based intervention for depression by applying the Muthen-Roy model. *Cognitive Behaviour Therapy*, 49(1), 22–40. https://doi.org/10.1080/16506073.2018.1556331

Asparouhov, T., Hamaker, E. L., & Muthén, B. (2018). Dynamic structural equation models. *Structural Equation Modeling: A Multidisciplinary Journal*, 25(3), 359–388. https://doi.org/10.1080/10705511.2017.1406803

Atzil-Slonim, D., Bar-Kalifa, E., Rafaeli, E., Lutz, W., Rubel, J., Schiefele, A.-K., & Peri, T. (2015). Therapeutic bond judgments: Congruence and incongruence. *Journal of Consulting and Clinical Psychology*, 83(4), 773–784. https://doi.org/10.1037/ccp0000015

Baldwin, S. A., Berkeljon, A., Atkins, D. C., Olsen, J. A., & Nielsen, S. L. (2009). Rates of change in naturalistic psychotherapy: Contrasting dose–effect and good-enough level models of change. *Journal of Consulting and Clinical Psychology*, 77(2), 203–211. https://doi.org/10.1037/a0015235

Baldwin, S. A., & Imel, Z. E. (2013). Therapist effects: Findings and methods. In M. J. Lambert (Ed.), *Bergin and Garfield's handbook of psychotherapy and behavior change* (6th ed., pp. 258–297). Wiley.

Baldwin, S. A., Imel, Z. E., Braithwaite, S. R., & Atkins, D. C. (2014). Analyzing multiple outcomes in clinical research using multivariate multilevel models. *Journal of Consulting and Clinical Psychology*, 82(5), 920–930. https://doi.org/10.1037/a0035628

Bar-Kalifa, E., Atzil-Slonim, D., Rafaeli, E., Peri, T., Rubel, J., & Lutz, W. (2016). Therapist–client agreement in assessments of clients' functioning. *Journal of Consulting and Clinical Psychology*, 84(12), 1127–1134. https://doi.org/10.1037/ccp0000157

Bar-Kalifa, E., Prinz, J. N., Atzil-Slonim, D., Rubel, J. A., Lutz, W., & Rafaeli, E. (2019). Physiological synchrony and therapeutic alliance in an imagery-based treatment. *Journal of Counseling Psychology*, 66(4), 508–517. https://doi.org/10.1037/cou0000358

Barkham, M., Connell, J., Stiles, W. B., Miles, J. N. V., Margison, F., Evans, C., & Mellor-Clark, J. (2006). Dose-effect relations and responsive regulation of treatment duration: The good enough level. *Journal of Consulting and Clinical Psychology*, 74(1), 160–167. https://doi.org/10.1037/0022-006X.74.1.160

Barkham, M., Rees, A., Stiles, W. B., Shapiro, D. A., Hardy, G. E., & Reynolds, S. (1996). Dose–effect relations in time-limited psychotherapy for depression. *Journal of Consulting and Clinical Psychology*, 64(5), 927–935. https://doi.org/10.1037/0022-006X.64.5.927

Barkham, M., Stiles, W. B., Connell, J., Twigg, E., Leach, C., Lucock, M., Mellor-Clark, J., Bower, P., King, M., Shapiro, D. A., Hardy, G. E., Greenberg, L., & Angus, L. (2008). Effects of psychological therapies in randomized trials and practice-based studies. *British Journal of Clinical Psychology*, 47(4), 397–415. https://doi.org/10.1348/014466508X311713

Barkham, M., Stiles, W. B., Lambert, M. J., & Mellor-Clark, J. (2010). Building a rigorous and relevant knowledge base for the psychological therapies. In M. Barkham, G. E. Hardy, & J. Mellor-Clark (Eds.), *Developing and delivering practice-based evidence* (pp. 21–61). John Wiley & Sons, Ltd. https://doi.org/10.1002/9780470687994.ch2

Baron, R. M., & Kenny, D. A. (1986). The moderator–mediator variable distinction in social psychological research: Conceptual, strategic, and statistical considerations. *Journal of Personality and Social Psychology*, 51(6), 1173–1182. https://doi.org/10.1037/0022-3514.51.6.1173

Barreiros, A. R., Almeida, I., Baía, B. C., & Castelo-Branco, M. (2019). Amygdala modulation during emotion regulation training with fMRI-based neurofeedback. *Frontiers in Human Neuroscience*, 13, 1–23. https://doi.org/10.3389/fnhum.2019.00089

Bastiaansen, J. A., Kunkels, Y. K., Blaauw, F., Boker, S. M., Ceulemans, E., Chen, M., Chow, S.-M., Jonge, P. de, Emerencia, A. C., Epskamp, S., Fisher, A. J., Hamaker, E., Kuppens, P., Lutz, W., Meyer, M. J., Moulder, R. G., Oravecz, Z., Riese, H., Rubel, J., ... Bringmann, L. F. (2019). Time to get personal? The impact of researchers' choices on the selection of treatment targets using the experience sampling methodology. Advance online publication. https://doi.org/10.31234/osf.io/c8vp7

Bauer, D. J., & Curran, P. J. (2004). The integration of continuous and discrete latent variable models: Potential problems and promising opportunities. *Psychological Methods*, 9(1), 3–29. https://doi.org/10.1037/1082-989X.9.1.3

Beam, A. L., & Kohane, I. S. (2018). Big data and machine learning in health care. *JAMA*, 319(13), 1317–1318. https://doi.org/10.1001/jama.2017.18391

Beard, J. I. L., & Delgadillo, J. (2019). Early response to psychological therapy as a predictor of depression and anxiety treatment outcomes: A systematic review and meta-analysis. *Depression and Anxiety*, 36(9), 866–878. https://doi.org/10.1002/da.22931

Bergin, A. E., & Garfield, S. L. (Eds.). (1971). *Handbook of psychotherapy and behavior change*. New York, NY: John Wiley & Sons, Inc.

Bergman, H., Kornør, H., Nikolakopoulou, A., Hanssen-Bauer, K., Soares-Weiser, K., Tollefsen, T. K., & Bjørndal, A. (2018). Client feedback in psychological therapy for children and adolescents with mental health problems. *Cochrane Database of Systematic Reviews. Advance online publication*. https://doi.org/10.1002/14651858.CD011729.pub2

Beutler, L. E., Edwards, C., & Someah, K. (2018). Adapting psychotherapy to patient reactance level: A meta-analytic review. *Journal of Clinical Psychology*, 74(11), 1952–1963. https://doi.org/10.1002/jclp.22682

Beutler, L. E., & Howard, K. I. (1998). Clinical utility research: An introduction. *Journal of Clinical Psychology*, 54(3), 297–301. https://doi.org/10.1002/(SICI)1097-4679(199804)54:3

Bickman, L. (2020). Improving mental health services: A 50-year journey from randomized experiments to artificial intelligence and precision mental health. *Administration and Policy in Mental Health and Mental Health Service Research*, 47, 795–843. https://doi.org/10.1007/s10488-020-01065-8

Boccia, M., Piccardi, L., & Guariglia, P. (2016). How treatment affects the brain: meta-analysis evidence of neural substrates underpinning drug therapy and psychotherapy in major depression. *Brain Imaging and Behavior*, 10(2), 619–627. https://doi.org/10.1007/s11682-015-9429-x

Bockting, C. L., Hollon, S. D., Jarrett, R. B., Kuyken, W., & Dobson, K. (2015). A lifetime approach to major depressive disorder: The contributions of psychological interventions in preventing relapse and recurrence. *Clinical Psychology Review*, 41, 16–26. https://doi.org/10.1016/j.cpr.2015.02.003

Böhnke, J. R., & Croudace, T. J. (2016). Calibrating well-being, quality of life and common mental disorder items: Psychometric epidemiology in public mental health research. *British Journal of Psychiatry*, 209(2), 162–168. https://doi.org/10.1192/bjp.bp.115.165530

Böhnke, J. R., & Lutz, W. (2014). Using item and test information to optimize targeted assessments of psychological distress. *Assessment*, 21(6), 679–693. https://doi.org/10.1177/1073191114529152

Böhnke, J. R., Lutz, W., & Delgadillo, J. (2014). Negative affectivity as a transdiagnostic factor in patients with common mental disorders. *Journal of Affective Disorders*, 166, 270–278. https://doi.org/10.1016/j.jad.2014.05.023

Bolger, N., Davis, A., & Rafaeli, E. (2003). Diary methods: Capturing life as it is lived. *Annual Review of Psychology*, 54(1), 579–616. https://doi.org/10.1146/annurev.psych.54.101601.145030

Bone, C., Simmonds-Buckley, M., Thwaites, R., Sandford, D., Merzhvynska, M., Rubel, J., Deisenhofer, A. -K., Lutz, W., & Delgadillo, J. (2021). Dynamic prediction of psychological treatment outcomes: development and validation of a prediction model using routinely collected symptom data. *The Lancet Digital Health*, 3(4), e231–e240. https://doi.org/10.1016/S2589-7500(21)00018-2.

Borsboom, D. (2017). A network theory of mental disorders. *World Psychiatry*, 16(1), 5–13. https://doi.org/10.1002/wps.20375

Boswell, J. F., Kraus, D. R., Miller, S. D., & Lambert, M. J. (2015). Implementing routine outcome monitoring in clinical practice: Benefits, challenges, and solutions. *Psychotherapy Research*, 25(1), 6–19. https://doi.org/10.1080/10503307.2013.817696

Brattland, H., Koksvik, J. M., Burkeland, O., Gråwe, R. W., Klöckner, C., Linaker, O. M., Ryum, T., Wampold, B., Lara-Cabrera, M. L., & Iversen, V. C. (2018). The effects of routine outcome monitoring (ROM) on therapy outcomes in the course of an implementation process:

A randomized clinical trial. *Journal of Counseling Psychology, 65*(5), 641–652. https://doi.org/10.1037/cou0000286

Breiman, L. (2001). Random forests. *Machine Learning, 45*(1), 5–32. https://doi.org/10.1023/A:1010933404324

Bringmann, L. F., Elmer, T., Epskamp, S., Krause, R. W., Schoch, D., Wichers, M., Wigman, J. T. W., & Snippe, E. (2019). What do centrality measures measure in psychological networks? *Journal of Abnormal Psychology, 128*(8), 892–903. https://doi.org/10.1037/abn0000446

Bringmann, L. F., Hamaker, E. L., Vigo, D. E., Aubert, A., Borsboom, D., & Tuerlinckx, F. (2017). Changing dynamics: Time-varying autoregressive models using generalized additive modeling. *Psychological Methods, 22*(3), 409–425. https://doi.org/10.1037/met0000085

Bringmann, L. F., Vissers, N., Wichers, M., Geschwind, N., Kuppens, P., Peeters, F., Borsboom, D., & Tuerlinckx, F. (2013). A network approach to psychopathology: New insights into clinical longitudinal data. *PLoS ONE, 8*(4), e60188. https://doi.org/10.1371/journal.pone.0060188

Brody, T. (2016). *Clinical trials: Study design, endpoints and biomarkers, drug safety, and FDA and ICH guidelines.* Academic Press. http://gbv.eblib.com/patron/FullRecord.aspx?p=441719

Brouwer, D., Meijer, R. R., & Zevalkink, J. (2013). Measuring individual significant change on the Beck Depression Inventory-II through IRT-based statistics. *Psychotherapy Research, 23*(5), 489–501. https://doi.org/10.1080/10503307.2013.794400

Bruijniks, S. J. E., Lemmens, L. H. J. M., Hollon, S. D., Peeters, F. P. M. L., Cuijpers, P., Arntz, A., Dingemanse, P., Willems, L., van Oppen, P., Twisk, J. W. R., van den Boogaard, M., Spijker, J., Bosmans, J., & Huibers, M. J. H. (2020). The effects of once- versus twice-weekly sessions on psychotherapy outcomes in depressed patients. *The British Journal of Psychiatry, 216*(4), 222–230. https://doi.org/10.1192/bjp.2019.265

Bryan, C. J., Baucom, B. R., Crenshaw, A. O., Imel, Z., Atkins, D. C., Clemans, T. A., Leeson, B., Burch, T. S., Mintz, J., & Rudd, M. D. (2018). Associations of patient-rated emotional bond and vocally encoded emotional arousal among clinicians and acutely suicidal military personnel. *Journal of Consulting and Clinical Psychology, 86*(4), 372–383. https://doi.org/10.1037/ccp0000295

Carrig, M. M., Kolden, G. G., & Strauman, T. J. (2014). Using functional magnetic resonance imaging in psychotherapy research. In W. Lutz & S. Knox (Eds.), *Quantitative and qualitative methods in psychotherapy research* (pp. 72–84). Routledge. https://doi.org/10.4324/9780203386071-5

Casper, E. S. (2007). The theory of planned behavior applied to continuing education for mental health professionals. *Psychiatric Services, 58*(10), 1324–1329. https://doi.org/10.1176/ps.2007.58.10.1324

Castonguay, L. G., Barkham, M., Lutz, W., & McAleavey, A. A. (2013). Practice-oriented research: Approaches and applications. In M. J. Lambert (Ed.), *Bergin and Garfield's handbook of psychotherapy and behavior change* (6th ed., pp. 85–133). Wiley.

Castonguay, L. G., Locke, B. D., & Hayes, J. A. (2011). The Center for Collegiate Mental Health: An example of a practice-research network in university counseling centers. *Journal of College Student Psychotherapy, 25*(2), 105–119. https://doi.org/10.1080/87568225.2011.556929

Cella, D., Yount, S., Rothrock, N., Gershon, R., Cook, K., Reeve, B., Ader, D., Fries, J. F., Bruce, B., & Rose, M. (2007). The patient-reported outcomes measurement information system (PROMIS): Progress of an NIH Roadmap cooperative group during its first two years. *Medical Care, 45*(5 Suppl 1), S3-S11. https://doi.org/10.1097/01.mlr.0000258615.42478.55

Choi, S. W., Reise, S. P., Pilkonis, P. A., Hays, R. D., & Cella, D. (2010). Efficiency of static and computer adaptive short forms compared to full-length measures of depressive symptoms. *Quality of Life Research, 19*(1), 125–136. https://doi.org/10.1007/s11136-009-9560-5

Clark, D. M. (2018). Realizing the mass public benefit of evidence-based psychological therapies: The IAPT program. *Annual Review of Clinical Psychology, 14*(1), 159–183. https://doi.org/10.1146/annurev-clinpsy-050817-084833

Cohen, J. (1992). A power primer. *Psychological Bulletin, 112*(1), 155–159. https://doi.org/10.1037/0033-2909.112.1.155

Cohen, Z. D., & DeRubeis, R. J. (2018). Treatment selection in depression. *Annual Review of Clinical Psychology, 14*(1), 209–236. https://doi.org/10.1146/annurev-clinpsy-050817-084746

Cohen, Z. D., Kim, T. T., Van, H. L., Dekker, J. J. M., & Driessen, E. (2020). A demonstration of a multi-method variable selection approach for treatment selection: Recommending cognitive–behavioral versus psychodynamic

therapy for mild to moderate adult depression. *Psychotherapy Research, 30*(2), 137–150. https://doi.org/10.1080/10503307.2018.1563312

Conway, C. C., Forbes, M. K., Forbush, K. T., Fried, E. I., Hallquist, M. N., Kotov, R., Mullins-Sweatt, S. N., Shackman, A. J., Skodol, A. E., South, S. C., Sunderland, M., Waszczuk, M. A., Zald, D. H., Afzali, M. H., Bornovalova, M. A., Carragher, N., Docherty, A. R., Jonas, K. G., Krueger, R. F., . . . Eaton, N. R. (2019). A hierarchical taxonomy of psychopathology can transform mental health research. *Perspectives on Psychological Science, 14*(3), 419–436. https://doi.org/10.1177/1745691618810696

Cook, W. L., & Kenny, D. A. (2005). The Actor–Partner Interdependence Model: A model of bidirectional effects in developmental studies. *International Journal of Behavioral Development, 29*(2), 101–109. https://doi.org/10.1080/01650250444000405

Costantini, G., Epskamp, S., Borsboom, D., Perugini, M., Mõttus, R., Waldorp, L. J., & Cramer, A. O.J. (2015). State of the art personality research: A tutorial on network analysis of personality data in R. *Journal of Research in Personality, 54*, 13–29. https://doi.org/10.1016/j.jrp.2014.07.003

Coyne, A. E., Constantino, M. J., Laws, H. B., Westra, H. A., & Antony, M. M. (2018). Patient–therapist convergence in alliance ratings as a predictor of outcome in psychotherapy for generalized anxiety disorder. *Psychotherapy Research, 28*(6), 969–984. https://doi.org/10.1080/10503307.2017.1303209

Cristea, I. A., Karyotaki, E., Hollon, S. D., Cuijpers, P., & Gentili, C. (2019). Biological markers evaluated in randomized trials of psychological treatments for depression: a systematic review and meta-analysis. *Neuroscience & Biobehavioral Reviews, 101*, 32–44. https://doi.org/10.1016/j.neubiorev.2019.03.022

Crits-Christoph, P., Connolly, M. B., Gallop, R., Barber, J. P., Tu, X., Gladis, M., & Siqueland, L. (2001). Early improvement during manual-guided cognitive and dynamic psychotherapies predicts 16-week remission status. *The Journal of Psychotherapy Practice and Research, 10*(3), 145–154.

Crits-Christoph, P., Gibbons, M. C., & Mukherjee, D. (2013). Psychotherapy process-outcome research. In M. J. Lambert (Ed.), *Bergin and Garfield's handbook of psychotherapy and behavior change* (6th ed., pp. 298–340). Wiley.

Crits-Christoph, P., Ring-Kurtz, S., Hamilton, J. L., Lambert, M. J., Gallop, R., McClure, B., Kulaga, A., & Rotrosen, J. (2012). A preliminary study of the effects of individual patient-level feedback in outpatient substance abuse treatment programs. *Journal of Substance Abuse Treatment, 42*(3), 301–309. https://doi.org/10.1016/j.jsat.2011.09.003

Cronbach, L. J., & Furby, L. (1970). How we should measure "change": Or should we? *Psychological Bulletin, 74*(1), 68–80. https://doi.org/10.1037/h0029382

Cuijpers, P., Huibers, M., Ebert, D. D., Koole, S. L., & Andersson, G. (2013). How much psychotherapy is needed to treat depression? A metaregression analysis. *Journal of Affective Disorders, 149*(1-3), 1–13. https://doi.org/10.1016/j.jad.2013.02.030

Cuijpers, P., Karyotaki, E., de Wit, L., & Ebert, D. D. (2019). The effects of fifteen evidence-supported therapies for adult depression: A meta-analytic review. *Psychotherapy Research, 30*(3), 279–293. https://doi.org/10.1080/10503307.2019.1649732

Cuijpers, P., Quero, S., Noma, H., Ciharova, M., Miguel, C., Karyotaki, E., Cipriani, A., Cristea, I. A., & Furukawa, T. A. (2021). Psychotherapies for depression: A network meta-analysis covering efficacy, acceptability and long-term outcomes of all main treatment types. *World Psychiatry, 20*(2), 283–293. https://doi.org/10.1002/wps.20860

Cuijpers, P., Reijnders, M., & Huibers, M. J. H. (2019). The role of common factors in psychotherapy outcomes. *Annual Review of Clinical Psychology, 15*, 207–231. https://doi.org/10.1146/annurev-clinpsy-050718-095424

Curran, P. J., & Bauer, D. J. (2011). The disaggregation of within-person and between-person effects in longitudinal models of change. *Annual Review of Psychology, 62*(1), 583–619. https://doi.org/10.1146/annurev.psych.093008.100356

Deisenhofer, A.-K., Delgadillo, J., Rubel, J. A., Böhnke, J. R., Zimmermann, D., Schwartz, B., & Lutz, W. (2018). Individual treatment selection for patients with posttraumatic stress disorder. *Depression and Anxiety, 35*(6), 541–550. https://doi.org/10.1002/da.22755

De Jong, K. (2016). Deriving implementation strategies for outcome monitoring feedback from theory, research and practice. *Administration and Policy in Mental Health, 43*(3), 292–296. https://doi.org/10.1007/s10488-014-0589-6

De Jong, K., Conijn, J. M., Gallagher, R. A., Reshetnikova, A. S., Heij, M., & Lutz, M. C. (2021). Using progress feedback to improve outcomes and reduce drop-out, treatment duration, and deterioration: A multilevel meta-analysis. *Clinical Psychology Review*, *85*, 102002. https://doi.org/10.1016/j.cpr.2021.102002

De Jong, K., & DeRubeis, R. J. (2018). Effectiveness of psychotherapy. In J. N. Butcher (Ed.), *APA handbook of psychopathology: Psychopathology: Understanding, assessing, and treating adult mental disorders* (pp. 705–725). Washington: American Psychological Association. https://doi.org/10.1037/0000064-029

De Jong, K., van Sluis, P., Nugter, M. A., Heiser, W. J., & Spinhoven, P. (2012). Understanding the differential impact of outcome monitoring: Therapist variables that moderate feedback effects in a randomized clinical trial. *Psychotherapy Research*, *22*(4), 464–474. https://doi.org/10.1080/10503307.2012.673023

Delgadillo, J., Huey, D., Bennett, H., & McMillan, D. (2017). Case complexity as a guide for psychological treatment selection. *Journal of Consulting and Clinical Psychology*, *85*(9), 835–853. https://doi.org/10.1037/ccp0000231

Delgadillo, J., Jong, K. de, Lucock, M., Lutz, W., Rubel, J., Gilbody, S., Ali, S., Aguirre, E., Appleton, M., Nevin, J., O'Hayon, H., Patel, U., Sainty, A., Spencer, P., & McMillan, D. (2018). Feedback-informed treatment versus usual psychological treatment for depression and anxiety: a multisite, open-label, cluster randomised controlled trial. *The Lancet Psychiatry*, *5*(7), 564–572. https://doi.org/10.1016/S2215-0366(18)30162-7

Delgadillo, J. & Lutz, W. (2020). A development pathway towards precision mental healthcare. *JAMA Psychiatry*. https://doi.org/10.1001/jamapsychiatry.2020.1048

Delgadillo, J., McMillan, D., Lucock, M., Leach, C., Ali, S., & Gilbody, S. (2014). Early changes, attrition, and dose-response in low intensity psychological interventions. *British Journal of Clinical Psychology*, *53*(1), 114–130. https://doi.org/10.1111/bjc.12031

Delgadillo, J., Moreea, O., & Lutz, W. (2016). Different people respond differently to therapy: A demonstration using patient profiling and risk stratification. *Behaviour Research and Therapy*, *79*, 15–22. https://doi.org/10.1016/j.brat.2016.02.003

Derogatis, L. R. (1977). *SCL-90-R: Administration, scoring and procedures manual.* Baltimore: Clinical Psychometric Research.

Derogatis, L. R., & Melisaratos, N. (1983). The Brief Symptom Inventory: an introductory report. *Psychological Medicine*, *13*(3), 595–605. https://doi.org/10.1017/S0033291700048017

DeRubeis, R. J., Cohen, Z. D., Forand, N. R., Fournier, J. C., Gelfand, L. A., & Lorenzo-Luaces, L. (2014). The Personalized Advantage Index: Translating research on prediction into individualized treatment recommendations. A demonstration. *PLoS ONE*, *9*(1), e83875. https://doi.org/10.1371/journal.pone.0083875

Do, C. B., & Batzoglou, S. (2008). What is the expectation maximization algorithm? *Nature Biotechnology*, *26*(8), 897–899. https://doi.org/10.1038/nbt1406

Doucette, A., & Wolf, A. W. (2015). Increasing measurement precision in psychotherapy research: Item Response Theory and bifactor models. In W. Lutz & S. Knox (Eds.), *Quantitative and qualitative methods in psychotherapy research* (pp. 9–43). London, New York: Routledge Taylor & Francis Group.

Douglas, S., Button, S., & Casey, S. E. (2016). Implementing for sustainability: promoting use of a measurement feedback system for innovation and quality improvement. *Administration and Policy in Mental Health and Mental Health Services Research*, *43*(3), 286–291. https://doi.org/10.1007/s10488-014-0607-8

Easterbrook, P.J., Gopalan, R., Berlin, J.A., & Matthews, D.R. (1991). Publication bias in clinical research. *The Lancet*, *337*(8746), 867–872. https://doi.org/10.1016/0140-6736(91)90201-Y

Ebner-Priemer, U. W., & Trull, T. J. (2009). Ambulatory assessment. *European Psychologist*, *14*(2), 109–119. https://doi.org/10.1027/1016-9040.14.2.109

Edbrooke-Childs, J., Wolpert, M., & Deighton, J. (2016). Using patient reported outcome measures to improve service effectiveness (UPROMISE): Training clinicians to use outcome measures in child mental health. *Administration and Policy in Mental Health and Mental Health Services Research*, *43*(3), 302–308. https://doi.org/10.1007/s10488-014-0600-2

Eid, M., Gollwitzer, M., & Schmitt, M. (2013). *Statistik und Forschungsmethoden: Lehrbuch [Statistic and research methods: A textbook].* Weinheim: Beltz. https://sfbs.tu-dortmund.de/handle/sfbs/1006

Elkin, I., Falconnier, L., Martinovich, Z., & Mahoney, C. (2006). Therapist effects in the National Institute of Mental Health Treatment of Depression Collaborative Research Program. *Psychotherapy Research*, *16*(2), 144–160. https://doi.org/10.1080/10503300500268540

Elkin, I., Shea M. T., Watkins, J. T., Imber, S. D., Sotsky, S. M., Collins, J. F., Glass, D. R., Pilkonis, P. A., Leber, W. R., Docherty, J. P., Fiester, S. J., & Parloff, M. B. (1989). National Institute of Mental Health Treatment of Depression Collaborative Research Program. *Archives of General Psychiatry*, *46*(11), 971–982. https://doi.org/10.1001/archpsyc.1989.01810110013002

Ellis, A. (1957). Rational psychotherapy and individual psychology. *Journal of Individual Psychology*, *13*, 38–44.

Epskamp, S., Borsboom, D., & Fried, E. I. (2018). Estimating psychological networks and their accuracy: A tutorial paper. *Behavior Research Methods*, *50*(1), 195–212. https://doi.org/10.3758/s13428-017-0862-1

Epskamp, S., Cramer, A. O. J., Waldorp, L. J., Schmittmann, V. D., & Borsboom, D. (2012). qgraph: Network visualizations of relationships in psychometric data. *Journal of Statistical Software*, *48*(4), 1–18. https://doi.org/10.18637/jss.v048.i04

Errázuriz, P., & Zilcha-Mano, S. (2018). In psychotherapy with severe patients discouraging news may be worse than no news: The impact of providing feedback to therapists on psychotherapy outcome, session attendance, and the alliance. *Journal of Consulting and Clinical Psychology*, *86*(2), 125–139. https://doi.org/10.1037/ccp0000277

Eubanks, C. F., Muran, J. C., & Safran, J. D. (2018). Alliance rupture repair: A meta-analysis. *Psychotherapy*, *55*(4), 508–519. https://doi.org/10.1037/pst0000185

Falkenström, F., Ekeblad, A., & Holmqvist, R. (2016). Improvement of the working alliance in one treatment session predicts improvement of depressive symptoms by the next session. *Journal of Consulting and Clinical Psychology*, *84*(8), 738–751. https://doi.org/10.1037/ccp0000119

Falkenström, F., Finkel, S., Sandell, R., Rubel, J. A., & Holmqvist, R. (2017). Dynamic models of individual change in psychotherapy process research. *Journal of Consulting and Clinical Psychology*, *85*(6), 537–549. https://doi.org/10.1037/ccp0000203

Finch, A. E., Lambert, M. J., & Schaalje, B. G. (2001). Psychotherapy quality control: the statistical generation of expected recovery curves for integration into an early warning system. *Clinical Psychology & Psychotherapy*, *8*(4), 231–242. https://doi.org/10.1002/cpp.286

Fiorica, F. (2004). Preoperative chemoradiotherapy for oesophageal cancer: a systematic review and meta-analysis. *Gut*, *53*(7), 925–930. https://doi.org/10.1136/gut.2003.025080

Firth, N., Delgadillo, J., Kellett, S., & Lucock, M. (2020). The influence of sociodemographic similarity and difference on adequate attendance of group psychoeducational cognitive behavioural therapy. *Psychotherapy Research*, *30*(3), 362–374. https://doi.org/10.1080/10503307.2019.1589652

Firth, N., Saxon, D., Stiles, W. B., & Barkham, M. (2019). Therapist and clinic effects in psychotherapy: A three-level model of outcome variability. *Journal of Consulting and Clinical Psychology*, *87*(4), 345–356. https://doi.org/10.1037/ccp0000388

Fischer, H. F., Tritt, K., Klapp, B. F., & Fliege, H. (2011). How to compare scores from different depression scales: equating the Patient Health Questionnaire (PHQ) and the ICD-10-Symptom Rating (ISR) using Item Response Theory. *International Journal of Methods in Psychiatric Research*, *20*(4), 203–214. https://doi.org/10.1002/mpr.350

Fisher, A. J., Bosley, H. G., Fernandez, K. C., Reeves, J. W., Soyster, P. D., Diamond, A. E., & Barkin, J. (2019). Open trial of a personalized modular treatment for mood and anxiety. *Behaviour Research and Therapy*, *116*, 69–79. https://doi.org/10.1016/j.brat.2019.01.010

Fisher, A. J., & Boswell, J. F. (2016). Enhancing the personalization of psychotherapy with dynamic assessment and modeling. *Assessment*, *23*(4), 496–506. https://doi.org/10.1177/1073191116638735

Fisher, A. J., Medaglia, J. D., & Jeronimus, B. F. (2018). Lack of group-to-individual generalizability is a threat to human subjects research. *Proceedings of the National Academy of Sciences*, *115*(27), E6106-E6115. https://doi.org/10.1073/pnas.1711978115

Flood, N., Page, A., & Hooke, G. (2019). A comparison between the clinical significance and growth mixture modelling early change methods at predicting negative outcomes. *Psychotherapy Research*, *29*(7), 947–958. https://doi.org/10.1080/10503307.2018.1469803

Flückiger, C., Regli, D., Grawe, K., & Lutz, W. (2007). Similarities and differences between retrospective and pre–post measurements of outcome. *Psychotherapy Research*, *17*(3), 359–364. https://doi.org/10.1080/10503300600830728

Flückiger, C., Wampold, B. E., Delgadillo, J., Rubel, J., Vîslă, A., & Lutz, W. (2020). Is there an evidence-based number of sessions in outpatient psychotherapy? – A comparison of naturalistic conditions across countries. *Psychotherapy and Psychosomatics*, 89(5), 333–335. https://doi .org/10.1159/000507793

Fok, C. C. T., & Henry, D. (2015). Increasing the sensitivity of measures to change. *Prevention Science*, 16(7), 978–986. https://doi.org/10.1007/ s11121-015-0545-z

Fokkema, M., Smits, N., Kelderman, H., & Cuijpers, P. (2013). Response shifts in mental health interventions: An illustration of longitudinal measurement invariance. *Psychological Assessment*, 25(2), 520–531. https:// doi.org/10.1037/a0031669

Freedman, M. S., Hughes, B., Mikol, D. D., Bennett, R., Cuffel, B., Divan, V., LaVallee, N., & AL-Sabbagh, A. (2008). Efficacy of disease-modifying therapies in relapsing remitting multiple sclerosis: A systematic comparison. *European Neurology*, 60(1), 1–11. https://doi.org/10.1159/0001 27972

Fried, E. I. (2016). Are more responsive depression scales really superior depression scales? *Journal of Clinical Epidemiology*, 77, 4–6. https://doi.org/ 10.1016/j.jclinepi.2016.05.004

Fried, E. I. (2017). The 52 symptoms of major depression: Lack of content overlap among seven common depression scales. *Journal of Affective Disorders*, 208, 191–197. https://doi.org/10.1016/j.jad.2016.10.019

Furukawa, T. A., Efthimiou, O., Weitz, E. S., Cipriani, A., Keller, M. B., Kocsis, J. H., Klein, D. N., Michalak, J., Salanti, G., Cuijpers, P., & Schramm, E. (2018). Cognitive-Behavioral Analysis System of Psychotherapy, drug, or their combination for persistent depressive disorder: Personalizing the treatment choice using individual participant data network metaregression. *Psychotherapy and Psychosomatics*, 87(3), 140–153. https://doi.org/ 10.1159/000489227

Furukawa, T. A., & Leucht, S. (2011). How to obtain NNT from Cohen's d: Comparison of two methods. *PLoS ONE*, 6(4), e19070. https://doi .org/10.1371/journal.pone.0019070

Gallop, R., & Tasca, G. A. (2014). Multilevel modeling of longitudinal data for psychotherapy researchers: 2. The Complexities. In W. Lutz & S. Knox (Eds.), *Quantitative and qualitative methods in psychotherapy research (pp. 117–141)*. Routledge.

Gates, K. M., & Liu, S. (2016). Methods for quantifying patterns of dynamic interactions in dyads. *Assessment*, 23(4), 459–471. https://doi.org/10 .1177/1073191116641508

Gates, K. M., & Molenaar, P. C.M. (2012). Group search algorithm recovers effective connectivity maps for individuals in homogeneous and heterogeneous samples. *NeuroImage*, 63(1), 310–319. https://doi.org/10.1016/ j.neuroimage.2012.06.026

Gaume, J., Hallgren, K. A., Clair, C., Schmid Mast, M., Carrard, V., & Atkins, D. C. (2019). Modeling empathy as synchrony in clinician and patient vocally encoded emotional arousal: A failure to replicate. *Journal of Counseling Psychology*, 66(3), 341–350. https://doi.org/10.1037/cou0000322

Georgi, H. S., Vlckova, K. H., Lukavsky, J., Kopecek, M., & Bares, M. (2018). Beck Depression Inventory-II: Self-report or interview-based administrations show different results in older persons. *International Psychogeriatrics*, 1–8.

Gilks, W. R., Richardson, S., & Spiegelhalter, D. (1995). *Markov Chain Monte Carlo in practice*. Chapman and Hall/CRC. https://doi.org/10.1201/ b14835

Graham, J. W. (2009). Missing data analysis: making it work in the real world. *Annual Review of Psychology*, 60(1), 549–576. https://doi.org/10.1146/ annurev.psych.58.110405.085530

Hamaker, E. L. (2012). Why researchers should think "within-person": A paradigmatic rationale. In M. R. Mehl & T. S. Conner (Eds.), *Handbook of research methods for studying daily life (pp. 43–61)*. New York, NY: Guilford Publications.

Hamaker, E. L., Kuiper, R. M., & Grasman, R. P. P. P. (2015). A critique of the cross-lagged panel model. *Psychological Methods*, 20(1), 102–116. https:// doi.org/10.1037/a0038889

Hamaker, E. L., & Wichers, M. (2017). No time like the present. *Current Directions in Psychological Science*, 26(1), 10–15. https://doi.org/ 10.1177/0963721416666518

Hansen, N. B., Lambert, M. J., & Forman, E. M. (2002). The psychotherapy dose-response effect and its implications for treatment delivery services.

Clinical Psychology: Science and Practice, 9(3), 329–343. https://doi.org/ 10.1093/clipsy.9.3.329

Hatcher, R. L., & Gillaspy, J. A. (2006). Development and validation of a revised short version of the working alliance inventory. *Psychotherapy Research*, 16(1), 12–25. https://doi.org/10.1080/10503300500352500

Hayes, A. M., Laurenceau, J.-P., Feldman, G., Strauss, J. L., & Cardaciotto, L. (2007). Change is not always linear: The study of nonlinear and discontinuous patterns of change in psychotherapy. *Clinical Psychology Review*, 27(6), 715–723. https://doi.org/10.1016/j.cpr.2007.01.008

Hill, C. E., & Lambert, M. J. (2004). Methodological issues in studying psychotherapy processes and outcomes. In M. J. Lambert (Ed.), *Bergin and Garfield's handbook of psychotherapy and behavior change: (5th ed.)*. New York, NY: Wiley.

Hiller, W., Schindler, A. C., & Lambert, M. J. (2012). Defining response and remission in psychotherapy research: A comparison of the RCI and the method of percent improvement. *Psychotherapy Research*, 22(1), 1–11. https://doi.org/10.1080/10503307.2011.616237

Hofmann, S. G., Curtiss, J., & McNally, R. J. (2016). A complex network perspective on clinical science. *Perspectives on Psychological Science*, 11(5), 597–605. https://doi.org/10.1177/1745691616639283

Hofmann, S. G., & Hayes, S. C. (2019). The future of intervention science: Process-based therapy. *Clinical Psychological Science*, 7(1), 37–50. https:// doi.org/10.1177/2167702618772296

Hooke, G. R., Sng, A. A. H., Cunningham, N. K., & Page, A. C. (2018). Methods of delivering progress feedback to optimise patient outcomes: The Value of Expected Treatment Trajectories. *Cognitive Therapy and Research*, 42(2), 204–211. https://doi.org/10.1007/s10608-017-9851-z

Howard, K. I., Kopta, S. M., Krause, M. S., & Orlinsky, D. E. (1986). The dose-effect relationship in psychotherapy. *American Psychologist*, 41(2), 159–164.

Howard, K. I., Moras, K., Brill, P. L., Martinovich, Z., & Lutz, W. (1996). Evaluation of psychotherapy: Efficacy, effectiveness, and patient progress. *American Psychologist*, 51(10), 1059–1064. https://doi.org/10.1037/ 0003-066X.51.10.1059

Huang, L., Li, Y., Singleton, A. B., Hardy, J. A., Abecasis, G., Rosenberg, N. A., & Scheet, P. (2009). Genotype-Imputation accuracy across worldwide human populations. *The American Journal of Human Genetics*, 84(2), 235–250. https://doi.org/10.1016/j.ajhg.2009.01.013

Huibers, M. J. H., Cohen, Z. D., Lemmens, Lotte H. J. M., Arntz, A., Peeters, F. P. M. L., Cuijpers, P., & DeRubeis, R. J. (2015). Predicting optimal outcomes in cognitive therapy or interpersonal psychotherapy for depressed individuals using the personalized advantage index approach. *PLoS One*, 10(11), e0140771. https://doi.org/10.1371/journal.pone.0140771

Hunter, A. M., Muthén, B. O., Cook, I. A., & Leuchter, A. F. (2010). Antidepressant response trajectories and quantitative electroencephalography (QEEG) biomarkers in major depressive disorder. *Journal of Psychiatric Research*, 44(2), 90–98. https://doi.org/10.1016/j.jpsychires.2009.06.006

Husen, K., Rafaeli, E., Rubel, J. A., Bar-Kalifa, E., & Lutz, W. (2016). Daily affect dynamics predict early response in CBT: Feasibility and predictive validity of EMA for outpatient psychotherapy. *Journal of Affective Disorders*, 206, 305–314. https://doi.org/10.1016/j.jad.2016.08 .025

Imel, Z. E., Steyvers, M., & Atkins, D. C. (2015). Computational psychotherapy research: Scaling up the evaluation of patient–provider interactions. *Psychotherapy*, 52(1), 19–30. https://doi.org/10.1037/ a0036841

Insel, T. R. (2014). The NIMH Research Domain Criteria (RDoC) project: Precision medicine for psychiatry. *American Journal of Psychiatry*, 171(4), 395–397. https://doi.org/10.1176/appi.ajp.2014.14020138

Ioannidis, J. P. A. (2005). Why most published research findings are false. *PLoS Medicine*, 2(8), e124. https://doi.org/10.1371/journal.pmed.0020124

Jacobson, N. C., Weingarden, H., & Wilhelm, S. (2019). Digital biomarkers of mood disorders and symptom change. *Npj Digital Medicine*, 2(1). https:// doi.org/10.1038/s41746-019-0078-0

Jacobson, N. S., & Truax, P. (1991). Clinical significance: A statistical approach to defining meaningful change in psychotherapy research. *Journal of Consulting and Clinical Psychology*, 59(1), 12–19. https://doi.org/ 10.1037//0022-006x.59.1.12

Janis, R. A., Burlingame, G. M., & Olsen, J. A. (2018). Developing a therapeutic relationship monitoring system for group treatment. *Psychotherapy*, 55(2), 105–115. https://doi.org/10.1037/pst0000139

Janse, P. D., Jong, K. de, van Dijk, M. K., Hutschemaekers, G. J. M., & Verbraak, M. J. P. M. (2017). Improving the efficiency of cognitive-behavioural therapy by using formal client feedback. *Psychotherapy Research, 27*(5), 525–538. https://doi.org/10.1080/10503307.2016.1152408

Janssens, K. A. M., Bos, E. H., Rosmalen, J. G. M., Wichers, M. C., & Riese, H. (2018). A qualitative approach to guide choices for designing a diary study. *BMC Medical Research Methodology, 18*(1). https://doi.org/10.1186/s12874-018-0579-6

Kadera, S. W., Lambert, M. J., & Andrews, A. A. (1996). How much therapy is really enough? : A session-by-session analysis of the psychotherapy dose-effect relationship. *The Journal of Psychotherapy Practice and Research, 5*(2), 132–151.

Kazdin, A. E. (2017). *Research design in clinical psychology* (Fifth edition). Boston: Pearson.

Kendrick, T., El-Gohary, M., Stuart, B., Gilbody, S., Churchill, R., Aiken, L., Bhattacharya, A., Gimson, A., Brütt, A. L., Jong, K. de, & Moore, M. (2016). Routine use of patient reported outcome measures (PROMs) for improving treatment of common mental health disorders in adults. *Cochrane Database of Systematic Reviews, 7*(7), CD011119. https://doi.org/10.1002/14651858.CD011119.pub2

Kenny, D. A., & Hoyt, W. (2014). Multiple levels of analysis in psychotherapy research. In W. Lutz & S. Knox (Eds.), *Quantitative and qualitative methods in psychotherapy research (p. 157–167).* Routledge.

Kessler, R. C., van Loo, H. M., Wardenaar, K. J., Bossarte, R. M., Brenner, L. A., Ebert, D. D., Jonge, P. de, Nierenberg, A. A., Rosellini, A. J., Sampson, N. A., Schoevers, R. A., Wilcox, M. A., & Zaslavsky, A. M. (2017). Using patient self-reports to study heterogeneity of treatment effects in major depressive disorder. *Epidemiology and Psychiatric Sciences, 26*(1), 22–36. https://doi.org/10.1017/S2045796016000020

Kiresuk, T. J., & Sherman, R. E. (1968). Goal attainment scaling: A general method for evaluating comprehensive community mental health programs. *Community Mental Health Journal, 4*(6), 443–453. https://doi.org/10.1007/BF01530764

Kivlighan, D. M., Jr. & Shaughnessy, P. (1995). Analysis of the development of the working alliance using hierarchical linear modeling. *Journal of Counseling Psychology, 42*(3), 338–349. https://doi.org/10.1037/0022-0167.42.3.338

Knaup, C., Koesters, M., Schoefer, D., Becker, T., & Puschner, B. (2009). Effect of feedback of treatment outcome in specialist mental healthcare: meta-analysis. *British Journal of Psychiatry, 195*(1), 15–22. https://doi.org/10.1192/bjp.bp.108.053967

Kordy, H. (1982). Probleme der Gruppenstatistik und Einzelfallforschung [Problems of group statistics and single case research]. *Zeitschrift für Differentielle und Diagnostische Psychologie, 3*(3), 231–239.

Krause, M. S. (2018). Associational versus correlational research study design and data analysis. *Quality & Quantity, 52*(6), 2691–2707. https://doi.org/10.1007/s11135-018-0687-8

Krause, M. S., Howard, K. I., & Lutz, W. (1998). Exploring individual change. *Journal of Consulting and Clinical Psychology, 66*(5), 838–845. https://doi.org/10.1037/0022-006X.66.5.838

Kristensen, L. E., Christensen, R., Bliddal, H., Geborek, P., Danneskiold-Samsøe, B., & Saxne, T. (2007). The number needed to treat for adalimumab, etanercept, and infliximab based on ACR50 response in three randomized controlled trials on established rheumatoid arthritis: a systematic literature review. *Scandinavian Journal of Rheumatology, 36*(6), 411–417. https://doi.org/10.1080/03009740701607067

Kroenke, K., Spitzer, R. L., & Williams, J. B. W. (2001). The PHQ-9: Validity of a brief depression severity measure. *Journal of General Internal Medicine, 16*(9), 606–613. https://doi.org/10.1046/j.1525-1497.2001.016009606.x

Krüger, A., Ehring, T., Priebe, K., Dyer, A. S., Steil, R., & Bohus, M. (2014). Sudden losses and sudden gains during a DBT-PTSD treatment for post-traumatic stress disorder following childhood sexual abuse. *European Journal of Psychotraumatology, 5*(1), 24470. https://doi.org/10.3402/ejpt.v5.24470

Kyron, M. J., Hooke, G. R., & Page, A. C. (2019). Assessing interpersonal and mood factors to predict trajectories of suicidal ideation within an inpatient setting. *Journal of Affective Disorders, 252*, 315–324. https://doi.org/10.1016/j.jad.2019.04.029

Lambert, M. J. (2013). The efficacy and effectiveness of psychotherapy. In M. J. Lambert (Ed.), *Bergin and Garfield's handbook of psychotherapy and behavior change* (6th ed., pp. 169–218). Wiley.

Lambert, M. J. (2015). Progress feedback and the OQ-system: The past and the future. *Psychotherapy, 52*(4), 381–390. https://doi.org/10.1037/pst0000027

Lambert, M. J., Hansen, N. B., & Finch, A. E. (2001). Patient-focused research: Using patient outcome data to enhance treatment effects. *Journal of Consulting and Clinical Psychology, 69*(2), 159–172. https://doi.org/10.1037/0022-006X.69.2.159

Lambert, M. J., & Hill, C. E. (1994). Assessing psychotherapy outcomes and processes. In A. E. Bergin & S. L. Garfield (Eds.), *Handbook of psychotherapy and behavior change* (4th ed., pp. 72–113). Oxford, England: John Wiley & Sons.

Lambert, M. J., & Ogles, B. M. (2004). The efficacy and effectiveness of psychotherapy. In M. J. Lambert (Ed.), *Bergin and Garfield's handbook of psychotherapy and behavior change* (pp. 139–193). Hoboken, NY: Wiley.

Lambert, M. J., Whipple, J. L., Bishop, M. J., Vermeersch, D. A., Gray, G. V., & Finch, A. E. (2002). Comparison of empirically-derived and rationally-derived methods for identifying patients at risk for treatment failure. *Clinical Psychology & Psychotherapy, 9*(3), 149–164. https://doi.org/10.1002/cpp.333

Lambert, M. J., Whipple, J. L., & Kleinstäuber, M. (2018). Collecting and delivering progress feedback: A meta-analysis of routine outcome monitoring. *Psychotherapy, 55*(4), 520–537. https://doi.org/10.1037/pst0000167

Lambert, M. J., Whipple, J. L., Smart, D. W., Vermeersch, D. A., Nielsen, S. L., & Hawkins, E. J. (2001). The effects of providing therapists with feedback on patient progress during psychotherapy: Are outcomes enhanced? *Psychotherapy Research, 11*(1), 49–68. https://doi.org/10.1080/713663852

Laws, H. B., Constantino, M. J., Sayer, A. G., Klein, D. N., Kocsis, J. H., Manber, R., Markowitz, J. C., Rothbaum, B. O., Steidtmann, D., Thase, M. E., & Arnow, B. A. (2017). Convergence in patient–therapist therapeutic alliance ratings and its relation to outcome in chronic depression treatment. *Psychotherapy Research, 27*(4), 410–424. https://doi.org/10.1080/10503307.2015.1114687

Leucht, S., Helfer, B., Gartlehner, G., & Davis, J. M. (2015). How effective are common medications: a perspective based on meta-analyses of major drugs. *BMC Medicine, 13*(1). https://doi.org/10.1186/s12916-015-0494-1

Lewis, C. C., Boyd, M., Puspitasari, A., Navarro, E., Howard, J., Kassab, H., Hoffman, M., Scott, K., Lyon, A., Douglas, S., Simon, G., & Kroenke, K. (2019). Implementing measurement-based care in behavioral health. *JAMA Psychiatry, 76*(3), 324–335. https://doi.org/10.1001/jamapsychiatry.2018.3329

Little, R. J. A., & Rubin, D. B. (2002). *Statistical analysis with missing data.* John Wiley & Sons, Inc. https://doi.org/10.1002/9781119013563

Lloyd, C. E. M., Duncan, C., & Cooper, M. (2019). Goal measures for psychotherapy: A systematic review of self-report, idiographic instruments. *Clinical Psychology: Science and Practice, 26*(3). https://doi.org/10.1111/cpsp.12281

Lorenzo-Luaces, L., DeRubeis, R. J., van Straten, A., & Tiemens, B. (2017). A prognostic index (PI) as a moderator of outcomes in the treatment of depression: A proof of concept combining multiple variables to inform risk-stratified stepped care models. *Journal of Affective Disorders, 213*, 78–85. https://doi.org/10.1016/j.jad.2017.02.010

Luber, B. M., Davis, S., Bernhardt, E., Neacsiu, A., Kwapil, L., Lisanby, S. H., & Strauman, T. J. (2017). Reprint of "Using neuroimaging to individualize TMS treatment for depression: Toward a new paradigm for imaging-guided intervention". *NeuroImage, 151*, 65–71. https://doi.org/10.1016/j.neuroimage.2017.03.049

Lutz, W., Arndt, A., Rubel, J., Berger, T., Schröder, J., Späth, C., Meyer, B., Greiner, W., Gräfe, V., Hautzinger, M., Fuhr, K., Rose, M., Nolte, S., Löwe, B., Hohagen, F., Klein, J. P., & Moritz, S. (2017). Defining and predicting patterns of early response in a web-based intervention for depression. *Journal of Medical Internet Research, 19*(6), e206. https://doi.org/10.2196/jmir.7367

Lutz, W., Deisenhofer, A.-K., Rubel, J., Bennemann, B., Giesemann, J., Poster, K., & Schwartz, B. (2021). Prospective evaluation of a clinical decision support system in psychological therapy. *Journal of Consulting and Clinical Psychology.* https://doi.org/10.1037/ccp0000642

Lutz, W., Ehrlich, T., Rubel, J., Hallwachs, N., Röttger, M.-A., Jorasz, C., Mocanu, S., Vocks, S., Schulte, D., & Tschitsaz-Stucki, A. (2013). The ups and downs of psychotherapy: Sudden gains and sudden losses identified with session reports. *Psychotherapy Research, 23*(1), 14–24. https://doi.org/10.1080/10503307.2012.693837

Lutz, W., Hofmann, S. G., Rubel, J., Boswell, J. F., Shear, M. K., Gorman, J. M., Woods, S. W., & Barlow, D. H. (2014). Patterns of early change and their relationship to outcome and early treatment termination in patients with panic disorder. *Journal of Consulting and Clinical Psychology, 82*(2), 287–297. https://doi.org/10.1037/a0035535

Lutz, W., Leach, C., Barkham, M., Lucock, M., Stiles, W. B., Evans, C., Noble, R., & Iveson, S. (2005). Predicting change for individual psychotherapy clients on the basis of their nearest neighbors. *Journal of Consulting and Clinical Psychology, 73*(5), 904–913. https://doi.org/10.1037/0022-006X.73.5.904

Lutz, W., Leon, S. C., Martinovich, Z., Lyons, J. S., & Stiles, W. B. (2007). Therapist effects in outpatient psychotherapy: A three-level growth curve approach. *Journal of Counseling Psychology, 54*(1), 32–39. https://doi.org/10.1037/0022-0167.54.1.32

Lutz, W., Martinovich, Z., & Howard, K. I. (1999). Patient profiling: An application of random coefficient regression models to depicting the response of a patient to outpatient psychotherapy. *Journal of Consulting and Clinical Psychology, 67*(4), 571–577. https://doi.org/10.1037/0022-006X.67.4.571

Lutz, W., Rubel, J., Schiefele, A.-K., Zimmermann, D., Böhnke, J. R., & Wittmann, W. W. (2015). Feedback and therapist effects in the context of treatment outcome and treatment length. *Psychotherapy Research, 25*(6), 647–660. https://doi.org/10.1080/10503307.2015.1053553

Lutz, W., Rubel, J. A., Schwartz, B., Schilling, V., & Deisenhofer, A.-K. (2019). Towards integrating personalized feedback research into clinical practice: Development of the Trier Treatment Navigator (TTN). *Behaviour Research and Therapy, 120*, 103438. https://doi.org/10.1016/j.brat.2019.103438

Lutz, W., Saunders, S. M., Leon, S. C., Martinovich, Z., Kosfelder, J., Schulte, D., Grawe, K., & Tholen, S. (2006). Empirically and clinically useful decision making in psychotherapy: Differential predictions with treatment response models. *Psychological Assessment, 18*(2), 133–141. https://doi.org/10.1037/1040-3590.18.2.133

Lutz, W., Schiefele, A.-K., Wucherpfennig, F., Rubel, J., & Stulz, N. (2016). Clinical effectiveness of cognitive behavioral therapy for depression in routine care: A propensity score based comparison between randomized controlled trials and clinical practice. *Journal of Affective Disorders, 189*, 150–158. https://doi.org/10.1016/j.jad.2015.08.072

Lutz, W., Schwartz, B., Hofmann, S. G., Fisher, A. J., Husen, K., & Rubel, J. A. (2018). Using network analysis for the prediction of treatment dropout in patients with mood and anxiety disorders: A methodological proof-of-concept study. *Scientific Reports, 8*(1). https://doi.org/10.1038/s41598-018-25953-0

Maher, M. J., Huppert, J. D., Chen, H., Duan, N., Foa, E. B., Liebowitz, M. R., & Simpson, H. B. (2010). Moderators and predictors of response to cognitive-behavioral therapy augmentation of pharmacotherapy in obsessive–compulsive disorder. *Psychological Medicine, 40*(12), 2013–2023. https://doi.org/10.1017/S0033291710000620

McAleavey, A. A., Youn, S. J., Xiao, H., Castonguay, L. G., Hayes, J. A., & Locke, B. D. (2019). Effectiveness of routine psychotherapy: Method matters. *Psychotherapy Research, 29*(2), 139–156. https://doi.org/10.1080/10503307.2017.1395921

McCarthy, K. S., Chambless, D. L., Solomonov, N., Milrod, B., & Barber, J. P. (2018). Twelve-Month outcomes following successful panic-focused psychodynamic psychotherapy, cognitive-behavioral therapy, or applied relaxation training for panic disorder. *The Journal of Clinical Psychiatry, 79*(5). https://doi.org/10.4088/JCP.17m11807

McClintock, A. S., Perlman, M. R., McCarrick, S. M., Anderson, T., & Himawan, L. (2017). Enhancing psychotherapy process with common factors feedback: A randomized, clinical trial. *Journal of Counseling Psychology, 64*(3), 247–260. https://doi.org/10.1037/cou0000188

McCoy, T. H., Yu, S., Hart, K. L., Castro, V. M., Brown, H. E., Rosenquist, J. N., Doyle, A. E., Vuijk, P. J., Cai, T., & Perlis, R. H. (2018). High throughput phenotyping for dimensional psychopathology in electronic health records. *Biological Psychiatry, 83*(12), 997–1004. https://doi.org/10.1016/j.biopsych.2018.01.011

Meehl, P. E. (1973). *Psychodiagnosis: Selected papers.* University of Minnesota Press.

Mellor-Clark, J., Cross, S., Macdonald, J., & Skjulsvik, T. (2016). Leading horses to water: Lessons from a decade of helping psychological therapy services use routine outcome measurement to improve practice. *Administration and Policy in Mental Health and Mental Health Services Research, 43*(3), 279–285. https://doi.org/10.1007/s10488-014-0587-8

Miller, S. D., Duncan, B. L., Sorrell, R., & Brown, G. S. (2005). The partners for change outcome management system. *Journal of Clinical Psychology, 61*(2), 199–208. https://doi.org/10.1002/jclp.20111

Molenaar, P. C. M. (2004). A manifesto on psychology as idiographic science: Bringing the person back into scientific psychology, this time forever.

Measurement: Interdisciplinary Research & Perspective, 2(4), 201–218. https://doi.org/10.1207/s15366359mea0204_1

Mullarkey, M. C., Marchetti, I., & Beevers, C. G. (2019). Using network analysis to identify central symptoms of adolescent depression. *Journal of Clinical Child and Adolescent Psychology, 48*(4), 656–668. https://doi.org/10.1080/15374416.2018.1437735

Muran, J. C., & Lutz, W. (2015). A train of thought: 25 years of Psychotherapy Research. *Psychotherapy Research, 25*(3), 277–281. https://doi.org/10.1080/10503307.2015.1025483

Muran, J. C., Safran, J. D., Gorman, B. S., Samstag, L. W., Eubanks-Carter, C., & Winston, A. (2009). The relationship of early alliance ruptures and their resolution to process and outcome in three time-limited psychotherapies for personality disorders. *Psychotherapy: Theory, Research, Practice, Training, 46*(2), 233–248. https://doi.org/10.1037/a0016085

Muthén, B., Asparouhov, T., Hunter, A. M., & Leuchter, A. F. (2011). Growth modeling with nonignorable dropout: Alternative analyses of the STAR*D antidepressant trial. *Psychological Methods, 16*(1), 17–33. https://doi.org/10.1037/a0022634

Nagin, D. S. (1999). Analyzing developmental trajectories: A semiparametric, group-based approach. *Psychological Methods, 4*(2), 139–157. https://doi.org/10.1037/1082-989X.4.2.139

Newman, F. L., & Howard, K. I. (1991). Introduction to the special section on seeking new clinical research methods. *Journal of Consulting and Clinical Psychology, 59*(1), 8–11. https://doi.org/10.1037/h0092573

Nickell, S. (1981). Biases in dynamic models with fixed effects. *Econometrica, 49*(6), 1417–1426. https://doi.org/10.2307/1911408

Nilsen, P. (2015). Making sense of implementation theories, models and frameworks. *Implementation Science, 10*(1). https://doi.org/10.1186/s13012-015-0242-0

Norcross, J. C., & Wampold, B. E. (2019). Relationships and responsiveness in the psychological treatment of trauma: The tragedy of the APA Clinical Practice Guideline. *Psychotherapy, 56*(3), 391–399. https://doi.org/10.1037/pst0000228

Nordberg, S. S., Castonguay, L. G., Fisher, A. J., Boswell, J. F., & Kraus, D. (2014). Validating the rapid responder construct within a practice research network. *Journal of Clinical Psychology, 70*(9), 886–903. https://doi.org/10.1002/jclp.22077

Nordberg, S. S., Castonguay, L. G., McAleavey, A. A., Locke, B. D., & Hayes, J. A. (2016). Enhancing feedback for clinical use: Creating and evaluating profiles of clients seeking counseling. *Journal of Counseling Psychology, 63*(3), 278–293. https://doi.org/10.1037/cou0000147

Nuzzo, R. (2014). Scientific method: Statistical errors. *Nature, 506*(7487), 150–152. https://doi.org/10.1038/506150a

Ogles, B. M. (2013). Measuring change in psychotherapy research. In M. J. Lambert (Ed.), *Bergin and Garfield's handbook of psychotherapy and behavior change* (6th ed.). Wiley.

Ogrodniczuk, J. S., Joyce, A. S., Lynd, L. D., Piper, W. E., Steinberg, P. I., & Richardson, K. (2008). Predictors of premature termination of day treatment for personality disorder. *Psychotherapy and Psychosomatics, 77*(6), 365–371. https://doi.org/10.1159/000151390

Østergård, O. K., Randa, H., & Hougaard, E. (2020). The effect of using the Partners for Change Outcome Management System as feedback tool in psychotherapy – A systematic review and meta-analysis. *Psychotherapy Research, 30*(2), 195–212. https://doi.org/10.1080/10503307.2018.1517949

Owen, J., Adelson, J., Budge, S., Wampold, B., Kopta, M., Minami, T., & Miller, S. (2015). Trajectories of change in psychotherapy. *Journal of Clinical Psychology, 71*(9), 817–827. https://doi.org/10.1002/jclp.22191

Page, A. C., Camacho, K. S., & Page, J. T. (2019). Delivering cognitive behaviour therapy informed by a contemporary framework of psychotherapy treatment selection and adaptation. *Psychotherapy Research, 29*(8), 971–973. https://doi.org/10.1080/10503307.2019.1662510

Paul, R., Andlauer, T. F. M., Czamara, D., Hoehn, D., Lucae, S., Pütz, B., Lewis, C. M., Uher, R., Müller-Myhsok, B., Ising, M., & Sämann, P. G. (2019). Treatment response classes in major depressive disorder identified by model-based clustering and validated by clinical prediction models. *Translational Psychiatry, 9*(1). https://doi.org/10.1038/s41398-019-0524-4

Pe, M. L., Kircanski, K., Thompson, R. J., Bringmann, L. F., Tuerlinckx, F., Mestdagh, M., Mata, J., Jaeggi, S. M., Buschkuehl, M., Jonides, J., Kuppens, P., & Gotlib, I. H. (2015). Emotion-network density in major depressive disorder. *Clinical Psychological Science, 3*(2), 292–300. https://doi.org/10.1177/2167702614540645

Pearl, J., & Mackenzie, D. (2018). *The book of why: The new science of cause and effect*. New York: Basic Books. https://doi.org/10.1126/science.aau9731

Ramseyer, F., Kupper, Z., Caspar, F., Znoj, H., & Tschacher, W. (2014). Time-series panel analysis (TSPA): Multivariate modeling of temporal associations in psychotherapy process. *Journal of Consulting and Clinical Psychology*, *82*(5), 828–838. https://doi.org/10.1037/a0037168

Ramseyer, F., & Tschacher, W. (2011). Nonverbal synchrony in psychotherapy: Coordinated body movement reflects relationship quality and outcome. *Journal of Consulting and Clinical Psychology*, *79*(3), 284–295. https://doi.org/10.1037/a0023419

Raudenbush, S. W., & Bryk, A. S. (2010). *Hierarchical linear models: Applications and data analysis methods* (2. ed.). Advanced quantitative techniques in the social sciences: Vol. 1. Thousand Oaks, Calif.: Sage Publ.

Reise, S. P. (2012). The rediscovery of bifactor measurement models. *Multivariate Behavioral Research*, *47*(5), 667–696. https://doi.org/10.1080/00273171.2012.715555

Reise, S. P., & Haviland, M. G. (2005). Item response theory and the measurement of clinical change. *Journal of Personality Assessment*, *84*(3), 228–238. https://doi.org/10.1207/s15327752jpa8403_02

Roberts, B. W., Luo, J., Briley, D. A., Chow, P. I., Su, R., & Hill, P. L. (2017). A systematic review of personality trait change through intervention. *Psychological Bulletin*, *143*(2), 117–141. https://doi.org/10.1037/bul0000088

Robinson, L., Delgadillo, J., & Kellett, S. (2020). The dose-response effect in routinely delivered psychological therapies: A systematic review. *Psychotherapy Research*, *30*(1), 79–96. https://doi.org/10.1080/10503307.2019.1566676

Rosenthal, R. (1994). Parametric measures of effect size. In H. Copper & L. V. Hedges (Eds.), *The handbook of research synthesis* (pp. 231–244). New York: Russell Sage Foundation.

Rosnow, R. L., & Rosenthal, R. (1989). Statistical procedures and the justification of knowledge in psychological science. *American Psychologist*, *44*(10), 1276–1284. https://doi.org/10.1037/0003-066X.44.10.1276

Rubel, J. A., Bar-Kalifa, E., Atzil-Slonim, D., Schmidt, S., & Lutz, W. (2018a). Congruence of therapeutic bond perceptions and its relation to treatment outcome: Within- and between-dyad effects. *Journal of Consulting and Clinical Psychology*, *86*(4), 341–353. https://doi.org/10.1037/ccp0000280

Rubel, J. A., Fisher, A. J., Husen, K., & Lutz, W. (2018b). Translating person-specific network models into personalized treatments: Development and demonstration of the Dynamic Assessment Treatment Algorithm for Individual Networks (DATA-IN). *Psychotherapy and Psychosomatics*, *87*(4), 249–251. https://doi.org/10.1159/000487769

Rubel, J. A., Hilpert, P., Wolfer, C., Held, J., Vîslă, A., & Flückiger, C. (2019). The working alliance in manualized CBT for generalized anxiety disorder: Does it lead to change and does the effect vary depending on manual implementation flexibility? *Journal of Consulting and Clinical Psychology*, *87*(11), 989–1002. https://doi.org/10.1037/ccp0000433

Rubel, J., Lutz, W., Kopta, S. M., Köck, K., Minami, T., Zimmermann, D., & Saunders, S. M. (2015). Defining early positive response to psychotherapy: An empirical comparison between clinically significant change criteria and growth mixture modeling. *Psychological Assessment*, *27*(2), 478–488. https://doi.org/10.1037/pas0000060

Rubel, J. A., Rosenbaum, D., & Lutz, W. (2017). Patients' in-session experiences and symptom change: Session-to-session effects on a within- and between-patient level. *Behaviour Research and Therapy*, *90*, 58–66. https://doi.org/10.1016/j.brat.2016.12.007

Rubel, J. A., Zilcha-Mano, S., Feils-Klaus, V., & Lutz, W. (2018c). Session-to-session effects of alliance ruptures in outpatient CBT: Within- and between-patient associations. *Journal of Consulting and Clinical Psychology*, *86*(4), 354–366. https://doi.org/10.1037/ccp0000286

Ruscio, J. (2008). A probability-based measure of effect size: Robustness to base rates and other factors. *Psychological Methods*, *13*(1), 19–30. https://doi.org/10.1037/1082-989X.13.1.19

Salkind, N. (Ed.). (2007). *Encyclopedia of measurement and statistics*. Sage Publications, Inc. https://doi.org/10.4135/9781412952644

Saxon, D., Barkham, M., Foster, A., & Parry, G. (2017). The contribution of therapist effects to patient dropout and deterioration in the psychological therapies. *Clinical Psychology & Psychotherapy*, *24*(3), 575–588. https://doi.org/10.1002/cpp.2028

Scargle, J. D. (1999, September 17). *Publication Bias (The "File-Drawer Problem") in Scientific Inference*. Retrieved from http://arxiv.org/pdf/physics/9909033v1

Schiefele, A.-K., Lutz, W., Barkham, M., Rubel, J., Böhnke, J., Delgadillo, J., Kopta, M., Schulte, D., Saxon, D., Nielsen, S. L., & Lambert, M. J. (2017). Reliability of therapist effects in practice-based psychotherapy research: A guide for the planning of future studies. *Administration and Policy in Mental Health and Mental Health Services Research*, *44*(5), 598–613. https://doi.org/10.1007/s10488-016-0736-3

Schlomer, G. L., Bauman, S., & Card, N. A. (2010). Best practices for missing data management in counseling psychology. *Journal of Counseling Psychology*, *57*(1), 1–10. https://doi.org/10.1037/a0018082

Schoenherr, D., Paulick, J., Strauss, B. M., Deisenhofer, A.-K., Schwartz, B., Rubel, J. A., Lutz, W., Stangier, U., & Altmann, U. (2019). Identification of movement synchrony: Validation of windowed cross-lagged correlation and -regression with peak-picking algorithm. *PLOS ONE*, *14*(2), e0211494. https://doi.org/10.1371/journal.pone.0211494

Schuckard, E., Miller, S. D., & Hubble, M. A. (2017). Feedback informed treatment: Historical and empirical implications. In D. S. Prescott, C. L. Maeschalck, & S. D. Miller (Eds.), *Feedback-informed treatment in clinical practice: Reaching for excellence* (pp. 13–35). Washington: American Psychological Association.

Schuurman, N. K., Ferrer, E., Boer-Sonnenschein, M. de, & Hamaker, E. L. (2016). How to compare cross-lagged associations in a multilevel autoregressive model. *Psychological Methods*, *21*(2), 206–221. https://doi.org/10.1037/met0000062

Schwartz, B., Cohen, Z. D., Rubel, J. A., Zimmermann, D., Wittmann, W. W., & Lutz, W. (2020). Personalized treatment selection in routine care: Integrating machine learning and statistical algorithms to recommend cognitive behavioral or psychodynamic therapy. *Psychotherapy Research*, *33*(1), 33–51. https://doi.org/10.1080/10503307.2020.1769219

Sembill, A., Vocks, S., Kosfelder, J., & Schöttke, H. (2019). The phase model of psychotherapy outcome: Domain-specific trajectories of change in outpatient treatment. *Psychotherapy Research*, *29*(4), 541–552. https://doi.org/10.1080/10503307.2017.1405170

Shanock, L. R., Baran, B. E., Gentry, W. A., Pattison, S. C., & Heggestad, E. D. (2010). Polynomial regression with response surface analysis: A powerful approach for examining moderation and overcoming limitations of difference scores. *Journal of Business and Psychology*, *25*(4), 543–554. https://doi.org/10.1007/s10869-010-9183-4

Shapiro, D. A., Barkham, M., Rees, A., Hardy, G. E., Reynolds, S., & Startup, M. (1994). Effects of treatment duration and severity of depression on the effectiveness of cognitive-behavioral and psychodynamic-interpersonal psychotherapy. *Journal of Consulting and Clinical Psychology*, *62*(3), 522–534. https://doi.org/10.1037/0022-006X.62.3.522

Shimokawa, K., Lambert, M. J., & Smart, D. W. (2010). Enhancing treatment outcome of patients at risk of treatment failure: Meta-analytic and mega-analytic review of a psychotherapy quality assurance system. *Journal of Consulting and Clinical Psychology*, *78*(3), 298–311. https://doi.org/10.1037/a0019247

Siegle, G. (2006). Use of fMRI to predict recovery from unipolar depression with cognitive behavior therapy. *American Journal of Psychiatry*, *163*(4), 735–738. https://doi.org/10.1176/appi.ajp.163.4.735

Simmons, J. P., Nelson, L. D., & Simonsohn, U. (2011). False-positive psychology. *Psychological Science*, *22*(11), 1359–1366. https://doi.org/10.1177/0956797611417632

Simon, W., Lambert, M. J., Harris, M. W., Busath, G., & Vazquez, A. (2012). Providing patient progress information and clinical support tools to therapists: Effects on patients at risk of treatment failure. *Psychotherapy Research*, *22*(6), 638–647. https://doi.org/10.1080/10503307.2012.698918

Singer, J. D., & Willett, J. B. (2003). *Applied longitudinal data analysis: Modeling change and event occurrence*. New York: Oxford University Press. https://doi.org/10.1093/acprof:oso/9780195152968.001.0001

Smith, B., & Sechrest, L. (1991). Treatment of aptitude × treatment interactions. *Journal of Consulting and Clinical Psychology*, *59*(2), 233–244. https://doi.org/10.1037/0022-006X.59.2.233

Snippe, E., Viechtbauer, W., Geschwind, N., Klippel, A., Jonge, P. de, & Wichers, M. (2017). The impact of treatments for depression on the dynamic network structure of mental states: Two randomized controlled trials. *Scientific Reports*, *7*(1). https://doi.org/10.1038/srep46523

Solomonov, N., Falkenström, F., Gorman, B. S., McCarthy, K. S., Milrod, B., Rudden, M. G., Chambless, D. L., & Barber, J. P. (2020). Differential effects of alliance and techniques on Panic-Specific Reflective Function and misinterpretation of bodily sensations in two treatments for panic. *Psychotherapy Research*, *30*(1), 97–111. https://doi.org/10.1080/10503307.2019.1585591

Speidel, M., Drechsler, J., & Jolani, S. (2018). R package hmi: a convenient tool for hierarchical multiple imputation and beyond. *IAB-Discussion Paper.* (16/2018).

Stekhoven, D. J. (2011). Using the missForest package. *R package,* 1–11.

Steyerberg, E. W. (2019). *Clinical prediction models: A practical approach to development, validation, and updating.* Springer Nature; Springer. https://doi.org/10.1007/978-3-030-16399-0

Stiles, W. B., Barkham, M., Connell, J., & Mellor-Clark, J. (2008). Responsive regulation of treatment duration in routine practice in United Kingdom primary care settings: Replication in a larger sample. *Journal of Consulting and Clinical Psychology,* 76(2), 298–305. https://doi.org/10.1037/0022-006X.76.2.298

Stiles, W. B., Honos-Webb, L., & Surko, M. (1998). Responsiveness in psychotherapy. *Clinical Psychology: Science and Practice,* 5(4), 439–458. https://doi.org/10.1111/j.1468-2850.1998.tb00166.x

Strauman, T. J. (2017). Self-regulation and psychopathology: Toward an integrative translational research paradigm. *Annual Review of Clinical Psychology,* 13(1), 497–523. https://doi.org/10.1146/annurev-clinpsy-032816-045012

Stulz, N., & Lutz, W. (2007). Multidimensional patterns of change in outpatient psychotherapy: The phase model revisited. *Journal of Clinical Psychology,* 63(9), 817–833. https://doi.org/10.1002/jclp.20397

Stulz, N., Lutz, W., Kopta, S. M., Minami, T., & Saunders, S. M. (2013). Dose-effect relationship in routine outpatient psychotherapy: Does treatment duration matter? *Journal of Counseling Psychology,* 60(4), 593–600. https://doi.org/10.1037/a0033589

Swift, J. K., & Greenberg, R. P. (2012). Premature discontinuation in adult psychotherapy: A meta-analysis. *Journal of Consulting and Clinical Psychology,* 80(4), 547–559. https://doi.org/10.1037/a0028226

Tabak, B. A., Teed, A. R., Castle, E., Dutcher, J. M., Meyer, M. L., Bryan, R., Irwin, M. R., Lieberman, M. D., & Eisenberger, N. I. (2019). Null results of oxytocin and vasopressin administration across a range of social cognitive and behavioral paradigms: Evidence from a randomized controlled trial. *Psychoneuroendocrinology,* 107, 124–132. https://doi.org/10.1016/j.psyneuen.2019.04.019

Taljaard, M., Donner, A., & Klar, N. (2008). Imputation strategies for missing continuous outcomes in cluster randomized trials. *Biometrical Journal,* 50(3), 329–345. https://doi.org/10.1002/bimj.200710423

Tam, H. E., & Ronan, K. (2017). The application of a feedback-informed approach in psychological service with youth: Systematic review and meta-analysis. *Clinical Psychology Review,* 55, 41–55. https://doi.org/10.1016/j.cpr.2017.04.005

Tang, T. Z., & DeRubeis, R. J. (1999). Sudden gains and critical sessions in cognitive-behavioral therapy for depression. *Journal of Consulting and Clinical Psychology,* 67(6), 894–904. https://doi.org/10.1037//0022-006X.67.6.894

Tofighi, D., & Enders, C. K. (2007). Identifying the correct number of classes in growth mixture models. *Information Age,* 317–341.

Twala, B. (2009). An empirical comparison of techniques for handling incomplete data using decision trees. *Applied Artificial Intelligence,* 23(5), 373–405. https://doi.org/10.1080/08839510902872223

van Buuren, S., & Groothuis-Oudshoorn, K. (2011). Mice: Multivariate imputation by chained equations in R. *Journal of Statistical Software,* 45(3). https://doi.org/10.18637/jss.v045.i03

van Montfort, K., Oud, J. H. L., & Voelkle, M. C. (2018). *Continuous time modeling in the behavioral and related sciences.* Springer International Publishing. https://doi.org/10.1007/978-3-319-77219-6

Voelkle, M. C., Gische, C., Driver, C. C., & Lindenberger, U. (2018). The role of time in the quest for understanding psychological mechanisms. *Multivariate Behavioral Research,* 53(6), 782–805. https://doi.org/10.1080/00273171.2018.1496813

von Brachel, R., Hirschfeld, G., Berner, A., Willutzki, U., Teismann, T., Cwik, J. C., Velten, J., Schulte, D., & Margraf, J. (2019). Long-term effectiveness of cognitive behavioral therapy in routine outpatient care: A 5- to 20-year follow-up study. *Psychotherapy and Psychosomatics,* 88(4), 225–235. https://doi.org/10.1159/000500188

Wahl, I., Löwe, B., Bjorner, J. B., Fischer, F., Langs, G., Voderholzer, U., Aita, S. A., Bergemann, N., Brähler, E., & Rose, M. (2014). Standardization of depression measurement: A common metric was developed for 11 self-report depression measures. *Journal of Clinical Epidemiology,* 67(1), 73–86. https://doi.org/10.1016/j.jclinepi.2013.04.019

Wampold, B. E., & Imel, Z. E. (2015). *The great psychotherapy debate: The evidence for what makes psychotherapy work (Second edition).* New York: Routledge Taylor & Francis. https://doi.org/10.4324/9780203582015

Wang, L., & Maxwell, S. E. (2015). On disaggregating between-person and within-person effects with longitudinal data using multilevel models. *Psychological Methods,* 20(1), 63–83. https://doi.org/10.1037/met0000030

Wang, L., Zhang, Q., Maxwell, S. E., & Bergeman, C. S. (2019). On standardizing within-person effects: Potential problems of global standardization. *Multivariate Behavioral Research,* 54(3), 382–403. https://doi.org/10.1080/00273171.2018.1532280

Weitz, E. S., Hollon, S. D., Twisk, J., van Straten, A., Huibers, M. J. H., David, D., DeRubeis, R. J., Dimidjian, S., Dunlop, B. W., Cristea, I. A., Faramarzi, M., Hegerl, U., Jarrett, R. B., Kheirkhah, F., Kennedy, S. H., Mergl, R., Miranda, J., Mohr, D. C., Rush, A. J., . . . Cuijpers, P. (2015). Baseline depression severity as moderator of depression outcomes between cognitive behavioral therapy vs pharmacotherapy. *JAMA Psychiatry,* 72(11), 1102. https://doi.org/10.1001/jamapsychiatry.2015.1516

West, T. V., & Kenny, D. A. (2011). The truth and bias model of judgment. *Psychological Review,* 118(2), 357–378. https://doi.org/10.1037/a0022936

Whipple, J. L., Lambert, M. J., Vermeersch, D. A., Smart, D. W., Nielsen, S. L., & Hawkins, E. J. (2003). Improving the effects of psychotherapy: The use of early identification of treatment and problem-solving strategies in routine practice. *Journal of Counseling Psychology,* 50(1), 59–68. https://doi.org/10.1037/0022-0167.50.1.59

Wicherts, J. M., Veldkamp, C. L. S., Augusteijn, H. E. M., Bakker, M., van Aert, R. C. M., & van Assen, M. A. L. M. (2016). Degrees of freedom in planning, running, analyzing, and reporting psychological studies: A checklist to avoid p-hacking. *Frontiers in Psychology,* 7, 1–12. https://doi.org/10.3389/fpsyg.2016.01832

Wolpert, M., Curtis-Tyler, K., & Edbrooke-Childs, J. (2016). A qualitative exploration of patient and clinician views on patient reported outcome measures in child mental health and diabetes services. *Administration and Policy in Mental Health and Mental Health Services Research,* 43(3), 309–315. https://doi.org/10.1007/s10488-014-0586-9

Wright, C. V., Goodheart, C., Bard, D., Bobbitt, B. L., Butt, Z., Lysell, K., McKay, D., & Stephens, K. (2019). Promoting measurement-based care and quality measure development: The APA mental and behavioral health registry initiative. *Psychological Services,* 17(3), 262–270. https://doi.org/10.1037/ser0000347

Xiao, H., Hayes, J. A., Castonguay, L. G., McAleavey, A. A., & Locke, B. D. (2017). Therapist effects and the impacts of therapy nonattendance. *Psychotherapy,* 54(1), 58–65. https://doi.org/10.1037/pst0000103

Youn, S. J., Castonguay, L. G., McAleavey, A. A., Nordberg, S. S., Hayes, J. A., & Locke, B. D. (2020). Sensitivity to change of the counseling center assessment of psychological symptoms-34. *Measurement and Evaluation in Counseling and Development,* 53(2), 75–88. https://doi.org/10.1080/07481756.2019.1691459

Young, K. D., Siegle, G. J., Zotev, V., Phillips, R., Misaki, M., Yuan, H., Drevets, W. C., & Bodurka, J. (2017). Randomized clinical trial of real-time fMRI amygdala neurofeedback for major depressive disorder: Effects on symptoms and autobiographical memory recall. *American Journal of Psychiatry,* 174(8), 748–755. https://doi.org/10.1176/appi.ajp.2017.16060637

Zaunmüller, L., Lutz, W., & Strauman, T. J. (2014). Affective impact and electrocortical correlates of a psychotherapeutic microintervention: An ERP study of cognitive restructuring. *Psychotherapy Research,* 24(5), 550–564. https://doi.org/10.1080/10503307.2013.847986

Zilcha-Mano, S., & Errázuriz, P. (2015). One size does not fit all: Examining heterogeneity and identifying moderators of the alliance–outcome association. *Journal of Counseling Psychology,* 62(4), 579–591. https://doi.org/10.1037/cou0000103

Zilcha-Mano, S., Muran, J. C., Hungr, C., Eubanks, C. F., Safran, J. D., & Winston, A. (2016). The relationship between alliance and outcome: Analysis of a two-person perspective on alliance and session outcome. *Journal of Consulting and Clinical Psychology,* 84(6), 484–496. https://doi.org/10.1037/ccp0000058

Zilcha-Mano, S., Porat, Y., Dolev, T., & Shamay-Tsoory, S. (2018). Oxytocin as a neurobiological marker of ruptures in the working alliance. *Psychotherapy and Psychosomatics,* 87(2), 126–127. https://doi.org/10.1159/000487190

Zimmermann, D., Rubel, J., Page, A. C., & Lutz, W. (2017). Therapist effects on and predictors of non-consensual dropout in psychotherapy. *Clinical Psychology & Psychotherapy,* 24(2), 312–321. https://doi.org/10.1002/cpp.2022

Zyphur, M. J., Allison, P. D., Tay, L., Voelkle, M. C., Preacher, K. J., Zhang, Z., Hamaker, E. L., Shamsollahi, A., Pierides, D. C., Koval, P., & Diener, E. (2019). From data to causes I: Building a general cross-lagged panel model (GCLM). *Organizational Research Methods,* 109442811984727. https://doi.org/10.1177/1094428119847278

SUPPLEMENTAL MATERIALS

SUPPLEMENT A. CORRELATIONS AND EFFECT SIZES FOR DIFFERENT OUTCOME MEASURES

The 521 outpatients in the analysis for the tables below (Tables A1–A3) were an average of 37.45 years of age (Md = 34, SD = 13.68, minimum = 16, maximum = 74) and the majority was female (*n* = 330; 63.3%). Patients were diagnosed at a university outpatient clinic using the Structured Clinical Interview for Axis I DSM-IV Disorders-Patient Edition (SCID-I; First, Spitzer, Gibbon, & Williams, 1995) and the International Diagnostic Checklist for Personality Disorders (IDCL-P; Bronisch, Hiller, Mombour, & Zaudig, 1996). Most patients suffered from affective disorders as their primary diagnosis (*n* = 290; 55.7%), followed by anxiety disorders (*n* = 58; 11.1%). Other primary diagnoses included adjustment disorder (*n* = 44; 8.4%), posttraumatic stress disorder (*n* = 43; 8.3%), somatoform disorders (*n* = 14; 2.7%), eating disorders (*n* = 12; 2.3%), and obsessive-compulsive disorder (*n* = 9; 1.7%). Of the 521 patients, 129 (24.8%) had a suspected or confirmed personality disorder, or a personality accentuation.

TABLE A1   Correlations Between Pre-treatment Outcome Measures (*N* = 521)

Measure	OQ-30	QEP-2	BSI – depression	BSI – anxiety	BSI – GSI	PHQ-9	GAD-7	BDI-II	HSCL-11	Well-being 1	Well-being 2	ORS total
OQ-30	1	.848**	.762**	.566**	.769**	.798**	.683**	.739**	.776**	.601**	.559**	.560**
QEP-2		1	.790**	.581**	.764**	.774**	.688**	.714**	.791**	.626**	.540**	.559**
BSI – depression			1	.565**	.821**	.786**	.597**	.704**	.908**	.544**	.492**	.523**
BSI – anxiety				1	.810**	.587**	.672**	.517**	.815**	.403**	.355**	.370**
BSI – GSI					1	.776**	.703**	.713**	.914**	.503**	.464**	.506**
PHQ-9						1	.675**	.737**	.807**	.630**	.536**	.541**
GAD-7							1	.548**	.715**	.549**	.472**	.413**
BDI-II								1	.699**	.472**	.453**	.552**
HSCL-11									1	.569**	.512**	.522**
Well-being 1										1	.638**	.508**
Well-being 2											1	.493**
ORS total												1

*Note.*** = *p* ≤ .01. OQ-30 = short-form of the Outcome Questionnaire (Ellsworth, Lambert, & Johnson, 2006), QEP-2 = Questionnaire for the Evaluation of Psychotherapeutic Progress-2 (Lutz et al., 2009), BSI = Brief Symptom Inventory (Derogatis & Melisaratos, 1983), PHQ-9 = Patient Health Questionnaire 9 (Kroenke, Spitzer, & Williams, 2001), GAD-7 = Generalized Anxiety Disorder 7 (Spitzer, Kroenke, Williams, & Löwe, 2006), BDI-II = Beck Depression Inventory (Beck, Steer, & Carbin, 1988), HSCL-11 = Hopkins Symptom Checklist – Short Form (Lutz, Tholen, Schürch, & Berking, 2006), well-being 1 = "How well do you feel you are getting along emotionally and psychologically?" on a scale from 1 ("Quite poorly; I can barely manage to deal with things") to 5 ("Quite well; I have no important complaints"), reverse coded (Howard, Moras, Brill, Martinovich, & Lutz, 1996), well-being 2 = "How well do you feel you are getting along emotionally and psychologically?" on a visual analogue scale from 1 ("Quite poorly") to 100 ("Quite well"), reverse coded, ORS total = total score of the Outcome Rating Scale, reverse coded (Miller, Duncan, Sorrell, & Brown, 2005). *N* = 521 for all analyses.

TABLE A2 Correlations Between Pre–Post-Effect Sizes of Several Outcome Measures ($N = 521$)

Measure	OQ-30	QEP-2	BSI – depression	BSI – anxiety	BSI – GSI	PHQ-9	GAD-7	BDI-II	HSCL-11	Well-being 1	Well-being 2	ORS total
OQ-30	1	.827**	.673**	.532**	.692**	.738**	.649**	.672**	.512**	.583**	.601**	.480**
QEP-2		1	.715**	.567**	.732**	.765**	.709**	.654**	.565**	.653**	.619**	.476**
BSI – depression			1	.568**	.833**	.777**	.569**	.627**	.719**	.522**	.516**	.427**
BSI – anxiety				1	.770**	.578**	.604**	.455**	.611**	.458**	.415**	.333**
BSI – GSI					1	.774**	.651**	.628**	.705**	.548**	.518**	.430**
PHQ-9						1	.653**	.678**	.599**	.644**	.583**	.485**
GAD-7							1	.501**	.503**	.546**	.513**	.402**
BDI-II								1	.452**	.492**	.495**	.455**
HSCL-11									1	.418**	.403**	.482**
Well-being 1										1	.643**	.435**
Well-being 2											1	.488**
ORS total												1

Note. ** = $p \leq .01$. OQ-30 = short-form of the Outcome Questionnaire (Ellsworth, Lambert, & Johnson, 2006), QEP-2 = Questionnaire for the Evaluation of Psychotherapeutic Progress–2 (Lutz et al., 2009), BSI = Brief Symptom Inventory (Derogatis & Melisaratos, 1983), PHQ-9 = Patient Health Questionnaire 9 (Kroenke, Spitzer, & Williams, 2001), GAD-7 = Generalized Anxiety Disorder 7 (Spitzer, Kroenke, Williams, & Löwe, 2006), BDI-II = Beck Depression Inventory (Beck, Steer, & Carbin, 1988), HSCL-11 = Hopkins Symptom Checklist – Short Form (Lutz, Tholen, Schürch, & Berking, 2006), well-being 1 = "How well do you feel you are getting along emotionally and psychologically?" on a scale from 1 ("Quite poorly; I have no important complaints"), reverse coded, to 5 ("Quite well; I have no important complaints"), well-being 2 = "How well do you feel you are getting along emotionally and psychologically?" on a visual analogue scale from 1 ("Quite poorly") to 100 ("Quite well"), reverse coded (Howard, Moras, Brill, Martinovich, & Lutz, 1996), ORS total = total score of the Outcome Rating Scale, reverse coded (Miller, Duncan, Sorrell, & Brown, 2005). Pre–post-effect sizes for individual i were calculated as (pre-treatment_i − posttreatment_i)/standard deviation (pretreatment). $N = 521$ for all analyses.

TABLE A3   **Effect Sizes of Different Outcome Measures ($N = 521$)**

Measure	Effect size
OQ-30	1.320
QEP-2	1.144
BSI – depression	0.861
BSI – anxiety	0.672
BSI – GSI	0.879
PHQ-9	1.064
GAD-7	1.084
BDI-II	1.217
HSCL-11	0.892
Well-being 1	1.086
Well-being 2	1.469
ORS total	1.180

Note. OQ-30 = short-form of the Outcome Questionnaire (Ellsworth, Lambert, & Johnson, 2006), QEP-2 = Questionnaire for the Evaluation of Psychotherapeutic Progress-2 (Lutz et al., 2009), BSI = Brief Symptom Inventory (Derogatis & Melisaratos, 1983), PHQ-9 = Patient Health Questionnaire 9 (Kroenke, Spitzer, & Williams, 2001), GAD-7 = Generalized Anxiety Disorder 7 (Spitzer, Kroenke, Williams, & Löwe, 2006), BDI-II = Beck Depression Inventory (Beck, Steer, & Carbin, 1988), HSCL-11 = Hopkins Symptom Checklist – Short Form (Lutz, Tholen, Schürch, & Berking, 2006), well-being 1 = "How well do you feel you are getting along emotionally and psychologically?" on a scale from 1 ("Quite poorly; I can barely manage to deal with things") to 5 ('Quite well; I have no important complaints'), reverse coded (Howard, Moras, Brill, Martinovich, & Lutz, 1996), well-being 2 = "How well do you feel you are getting along emotionally and psychologically?" on a visual analogue scale from 1 ("Quite poorly") to 100 ("Quite well"), reverse coded, ORS total = total score of the Outcome Rating Scale, reverse coded (Miller, Duncan, Sorrell, & Brown, 2005). Pre-post-effect sizes were calculated as (pretreatment$_i$ – posttreatment$_i$)/ standard deviation (pretreatment). $N = 521$ for all analyses.

SUPPLEMENT B. OVERVIEW OF PUBLISHED FEEDBACK STUDIES

TABLE B1   **Published Randomized Controlled Trials and Cohort Studies with Country and Setting**

Study	Country	Setting
Amble et al. (2015, 2016)	Norway	Inpatients and outpatients
Anker et al. (2009)	Norway	Outpatients: family counseling center
Berking et al. (2006)	Germany	Inpatients
Bickman et al. (2011)	USA	Private behavioral health: home-based treatment; youth
Bickman et al. (2016)	USA	Outpatients; youth
Brattland et al. (2018)	Norway	Outpatients
Burlingame et al. (2018)	USA	Outpatients; group
Connolly Gibbons et al. (2015)	USA	Outpatients: community mental health
Crits-Christoph et al. (2012)	USA	Outpatients: community mental health service
Davidsen et al. (2017)	Denmark	Outpatients; group
De Jong et al. (2012, 2014)	Netherlands	Outpatients
De Jong et al. (2017)	Netherlands	Inpatients
Delgadillo et al. (2017, 2018)	UK	Outpatients: primary care
Errazuriz & Zilcha-Mano (2018)	Chile	Outpatients

Study	Country	Setting
Grizzell et al. (2016)	USA	Outpatients; group
Hansen et al. (2015)	Australia	Outpatients; youth
Hansson et al. (2013)	Sweden	Outpatients
Harmon et al. (2007)	USA	Outpatients: college counseling center
Hawkins et al. (2004)	USA	Outpatients: hospital-based clinic
Janse et al. (2017, 2020)	Netherlands	Outpatients
Koementas et al. (2018)	Netherlands	Outpatients; group
Lambert et al. (2001, 2002)	USA	Outpatients: college counseling center
Lucock et al. (2015)	UK	Outpatients: secondary care
Lutz et al. (2015)	Germany	Outpatients
McClintock et al. (2017)	USA	Outpatients: training clinic
Metz et al. (2019)	Netherlands	Outpatients: secondary care
Murphy et al. (2012)	Ireland	Outpatients: college counseling center
Newnham et al. (2010)	Australia	Inpatients and day patients; group
Probst et al. (2013, 2014)	Germany	Inpatients; psychosomatic clinics
Puschner et al. (2009)	Germany	Inpatients
Reese et al. (2009)	USA	Outpatients: college counseling center
Reese et al. (2010)	USA	Outpatients; couples
Rise et al. (2012)	Norway	Outpatients; mental health hospital
Schmidt et al. (2006)	UK	Outpatients: eating disorders clinic
Schöttke et al. (2019)	Germany	Outpatients

Study	Country	Setting
Schuman et al. (2015)	USA	Outpatients: military; group
She et al. (2018)	China	Outpatients: college counseling center
Simon et al. (2012)	USA	Outpatient: hospital-based clinic
Simon et al. (2013)	USA	Inpatients
Slade et al. (2008)	USA	Outpatients: college counseling center
Slone et al. (2015)	USA	Outpatients: college counseling center; group
Tilden et al. (2020)	Norway	Outpatients: couples and family therapy centers
Tzur Bitan et al. (2019)	Israel	Outpatients: community mental health
Van Oenen et al. (2016)	Netherlands	Outpatients: psychiatric emergency center
Whipple et al. (2003)	USA	Outpatients: college counseling center

Note. This overview includes studies published in peer-reviewed journals by the end of 2020.

REFERENCES

Amble, I., Gude, T., Stubdal, S., Andersen, B. J., & Wampold, B. E. (2015). The effect of implementing the Outcome Questionnaire-45.2 feedback system in Norway: A multisite randomized clinical trial in a naturalistic setting. *Psychotherapy Research, 25*(6), 669–677. https://doi.org/10.1080/10503307.2014.928756

Amble, I., Gude, T., Ulvenes, P., Stubdal, S., & Wampold, B. E. (2016). How and when feedback works in psychotherapy: Is it the signal? *Psychotherapy Research, 26*(5), 545–555. https://doi.org/10.1080/10503307.2015.1053552

Anker, M. G., Duncan, B. L., & Sparks, J. A. (2009). Using client feedback to improve couple therapy outcomes: A randomized clinical trial in a naturalistic setting. *Journal of Consulting and Clinical Psychology, 77*(4), 693. https://doi.org/10.1037/a0016062

Beck, A. T., Steer, R. A., & Carbin, M. G. (1988). Psychometric properties of the Beck Depression Inventory: Twenty-five years of evaluation. *Clinical Psychology Review, 8*(1), 77–100. https://doi.org/10.1016/0272-7358(88)90050-5

Berking, M., Orth, U., & Lutz, W. (2006). How effective is systematic feedback of treatment progress to the therapist? An empirical study in a cognitive-behavioural-oriented inpatient setting. *Zeitschrift für Klinische Psychologie und Psychotherapie: Forschung und Praxis, 35*, 21–29. https://doi.org/10.1026/1616-3443.35.1.21

Bickman, L., Douglas Kelley, S., Breda, C., De Andrade, A. R., & Riemer, M. (2011). Effects of routine feedback to clinicians on youth mental health outcomes: A randomized cluster design. *Psychiatric Services, 62,* 1423–1429. https://doi.org/10.1176/appi.ps.002052011

Bickman, L., Douglas, S. R., De Andrade, A. R. V., Tomlinson, M., Gleacher, A., Olin, S., & Hoagwood, K. (2016). Implementing a measurement feedback system: A tale of two sites. *Administration and Policy in Mental Health and Mental Health Services Research, 43*(3), 410–425. https://doi.org/10.1007/s10488-015-0647-8

Brattland, H., Koksvik, J. M., Burkeland, O., Gråwe, R. W., Klöckner, C., Linaker, O. M., Ryum, T., Wampold, B., Lara-Cabrera, M. L., & Iversen, V. C. (2018). The effects of routine outcome monitoring (ROM) on therapy outcomes in the course of an implementation process: A randomized clinical trial. *Journal of Counseling Psychology, 65*(5), 641–652. https://doi.org/10.1037/cou0000286

Bronisch, T., Hiller, W., Mombour, W., & Zaudig, M. (1996). *International Diagnostic Checklists for Personality Disorders According to ICD-10 and DSM–IV-IDCL-P.* Seattle, WA: Hogrefe and Huber Publishers.

Burlingame, G. M., Whitcomb, K. E., Woodland, S. C., Olsen, J. A., Beecher, M., & Gleave, R. (2018). The effects of relationship and progress feedback in group psychotherapy using the Group Questionnaire and Outcome Questionnaire–45: A randomized clinical trial. *Psychotherapy, 55*(2), 116. https://doi.org/10.1037/pst0000133

Connolly Gibbons, M. B., Kurtz, J. E., Thompson, D. L., Mack, R. A., Lee, J. K., Rothbard, A., Eisen, S. V., Gallop, R., & Crits-Christoph, P. (2015). The effectiveness of clinician feedback in the treatment of depression in the community mental health system. *Journal of Consulting and Clinical Psychology, 83*(4), 748–759. https://doi.org/10.1037/a0039302

Crits-Christoph, P., Ring-Kurtz, S., Hamilton, J. L., Lambert, M. J., Gallop, R., McClure, B., Kulaga, A., & Rotrosen, J. (2012). A preliminary study of the effects of individual patient-level feedback in outpatient substance abuse treatment programs. *Journal of Substance Abuse Treatment, 42*(3), 301–309. https://doi.org/10.1016/j.jsat.2011.09.003

Davidsen, A. H., Poulsen, S., Lindschou, J., Winkel, P., Tróndarson, M. F., Waaddegaard, M., & Lau, M. (2017). Feedback in group psychotherapy for eating disorders: A randomized clinical trial. *Journal of Consulting and Clinical Psychology, 85*(5), 484–494. https://doi.org/10.1037/ccp0000173

De Jong, K., Segaar, J., Ingenhoven, T., van Busschbach, J., & Timman, R. (2017). Adverse effects of outcome monitoring feedback in patients with personality disorders: A randomized controlled trial in day treatment and inpatient settings. *Journal of Personality Disorders, 32*(3), 1–21. https://doi.org/10.1521/pedi_2017_31_297

De Jong, K., Timman, R., Hakkaart-Van Roijen, L., Vermeulen, P., Kooiman, K., Passchier, J., & Busschbach, J. V. (2014). The effect of outcome monitoring feedback to clinicians and patients in short and long-term psychotherapy: A randomized controlled trial. *Psychotherapy Research, 24*(6), 629–639. https://doi.org/10.1080/10503307.2013.871079

De Jong, K., van Sluis, P., Nugter, M. A., Heiser, W. J., & Spinhoven, P. (2012). Understanding the differential impact of outcome monitoring: Therapist variables that moderate feedback effects in a randomized clinical trial. *Psychotherapy Research, 22*(4), 464–474. https://doi.org/10.1080/10503307.2012.673023.

Delgadillo, J., de Jong, K., Lucock, M., Lutz, W., Rubel, J., Gilbody, S., Ali, S., Aguirre, E., Appleton, M., Nevin, J., O'Hayon, H., Patel, U., Sainty, A., Spencer, P., & McMillan, D. (2018). Feedback-informed treatment versus usual psychological treatment for depression and anxiety: a multisite, open-label, cluster randomised controlled trial. *The Lancet Psychiatry, 5*(7), 564–572. https://doi.org/10.1016/S2215-0366(18)30162-7

Delgadillo, J., Overend, K., Lucock, M., Groom, M., Kirby, N., McMillan, D., Gilbody, S., Rubel, J., Lutz, W., & de Jong, K. (2017). Improving the efficiency of psychological treatment using outcome feedback technology. *Behaviour Research and Therapy, 99,* 89–97. https://doi.org/10.1016/j.brat.2017.09.011

Derogatis, L. R., & Melisaratos, N. (1983). The Brief Symptom Inventory: an introductory report. *Psychological Medicine, 13*(3), 595–605. https://doi.org/10.1017/S0033291700048017

Ellsworth, J. R., Lambert, M. J., & Johnson, J. (2006). A comparison of the Outcome Questionnaire-45 and Outcome Questionnaire-30 in classification and prediction of treatment outcome. *Clinical Psychology & Psychotherapy, 13*(6), 380–391. https://doi.org/10.1002/cpp.503

Errázuriz, P., & Zilcha-Mano, S. (2018). In psychotherapy with severe patients discouraging news may be worse than no news: The impact of providing

feedback to therapists on psychotherapy outcome, session attendance, and the alliance. *Journal of Consulting and Clinical Psychology, 86*(2), 125–139. https://doi.org/10.1037/ccp0000277

First, M. B., Spitzer, R. L., Gibbon, M., & Williams, J. B. W. (1995). *Structured Clinical Interview for Axis I DSM–IV Disorders-Patient ed. (SCID-I/P).* Biometrics Research Department, NY State Psychiatric Institute.

Grizzell, S., Smart, J., Lambert, M. J., & Fargo, J. (2016). The use of feedback in group counseling in a state vocational rehabilitation setting. *Journal of Applied Rehabilitation Counseling, 47*(4), 10–19. https://doi.org/10.1891/0047-2220.47.4.10

Hannan, C., Lambert, M. J., Harmon, C., Nielsen, S. L., Smart, D. W., Shimokawa, K., & Sutton, S. W. (2005). A lab test and algorithms for identifying clients at risk for treatment failure. *Journal of Clinical Psychology, 61*(2), 155–163. https://doi.org/10.1002/jclp.20108

Hansen, B., Howe, A., Sutton, P., & Ronan, K. (2015). Impact of client feedback on clinical outcomes for young people using public mental health services: A pilot study. *Psychiatry Research, 229*(1), 617–619. https://doi.org/10.1016/j.psychres.2015.05.007

Hansson, H., Rundberg, J., Österling, A., Öjehagen, A., & Berglund, M. (2013). Intervention with feedback using Outcome Questionnaire 45 (OQ-45) in a Swedish psychiatric outpatient population. A randomized controlled trial. *Nordic Journal of Psychiatry, 67*(4), 274–281. https://doi.org/10.3109/08039488.2012.736534

Harmon, C. S., Lambert, M. J., Smart, D. M., Hawkins, E., Nielsen, S. L., Slade, K., & Lutz, W. (2007). Enhancing outcome for potential treatment failures: Therapist-client feedback and clinical support tools. *Psychotherapy Research, 17*(4), 379–392. https://doi.org/10.1080/10503300600702331

Hawkins, E. J., Lambert, M. J., Vermeersch, D. A., Slade, K. L., & Tuttle, K. C. (2004). The therapeutic effects of providing patient progress information to therapists and patients. *Psychotherapy Research, 14*(3), 308–327. https://doi.org/10.1093/ptr/kph027

Howard, K. I., Moras, K., Brill, P. L., Martinovich, Z., & Lutz, W. (1996). Evaluation of psychotherapy: Efficacy, effectiveness, and patient progress. *American Psychologist, 51*(10), 1059–1064. https://doi.org/10.1037/0003-066X.51.10.1059

Janse, P. D., de Jong, K., Van Dijk, M. K., Hutschemaekers, G. J. M., & Verbraak, M. J. P. M. (2017). Improving the efficiency of cognitive-behavioural therapy by using formal client feedback. *Psychotherapy Research, 27*(5), 525–538. https://doi.org/10.1080/10503307.2016.1152408

Janse, P. D., de Jong, K., Veerkamp, C., van Dijk, M. K., Hutschemaekers, G. J. M., & Verbraak, M. J. P. M. (2020). The effect of feedback-informed cognitive behavioral therapy on treatment outcome: A randomized controlled trial. *Journal of Consulting and Clinical Psychology, 88*(9), 818–828. https://doi.org/10.1037/ccp0000549

Kroenke, K., Spitzer, R. L., & Williams, J. B. (2001). The PHQ-9: validity of a brief depression severity measure. *Journal of General Internal Medicine, 16*(9), 606–613. https://doi.org/10.1046/j.1525-1497.2001.016009606.x

Koementas-de Vos, M. M., Nugter, M. A., Engelsbel, F., & de Jong, K. (2018). Does progress feedback enhance the outcome of group psychotherapy? *Psychotherapy, 55*(2), 151. https://doi.org/10.1037/pst0000164

Lambert, M. J., Hansen, N. B., & Finch, A. E. (2001). Patient-focused research: using patient outcome data to enhance treatment effects. *Journal of Consulting and Clinical Psychology, 69*(2), 159–172. https://doi.org/10.1037/0022-006X.69.2.159

Lambert, M. J., Whipple, J. L., Bishop, M. J., Vermeersch, D. A., Gray, G. V., & Finch, A. E. (2002). Comparison of empirically-derived and rationally-derived methods for identifying patients at risk for treatment failure. *Clinical Psychology & Psychotherapy, 9,* 149–164. https://doi.org/10.1002/cpp.333

Lucock, M., Halstead, J., Leach, C., Barkham, M., Tucker, S., Randal, C., Middleton, J., Khan, W., Catlow, H., Waters, E. (2015). A mixed-method investigation of patient monitoring and enhanced feedback in routine practice: Barriers and facilitators. *Psychotherapy Research, 25*(6), 633–646. https://doi.org/10.1080/10503307.2015.1051163

Lutz, W., Rubel, J. A., Schiefele, A.-K., Zimmermann, D., Böhnke, J. R., & Wittmann, W. W. (2015). Feedback and therapist effects in the context of treatment outcome and treatment length. *Psychotherapy Research, 25*(6), 647–660. https://doi.org/10.1080/10503307.2015.1053553

Lutz, W., Schürch, E., Stulz, N., Böhnke, J.R., Schöttke, H., Rogner, J., & Wiedl, K. H. (2009). Entwicklung und psychometrische Kennwerte des Fragebogens zur Evaluation von Psychotherapieverläufen (FEP) [Development and psychometric properties of the „Questionnaire for the Evaluation of Psychotherapy"]. *Diagnostica, 55*, 106–116. https://doi .org/10.1026/0012-1924.55.2.106

Lutz, W., Tholen, S., Schürch, E., & Berking, M. (2006). Die Entwicklung, Validität und Reliabilität von Kurzformen gängiger psychometrischer Instrumente zur Evaluation des therapeutischen Fortschrittes in Psychotherapie und Psychiatrie [Development, validity and reliability of short-forms of widespread instruments to evaluate psychotherapy]. *Diagnostica, 52*, 11–25. https://doi.org/10.1026/0012-1924.52.1.11

McClintock, A. S., Perlman, M. R., McCarrick, S. M., Anderson, T., & Himawan, L. (2017). Enhancing psychotherapy process with common factors feedback: A randomized, clinical trial. *Journal of Counseling Psychology, 64*(3), 247–260. https://doi.org/10.1037/cou0000188

Metz, M. J., Veerbeek, M. A., Twisk, J. W., van der Feltz-Cornelis, C. M., de Beurs, E., & Beekman, A. T. (2019). Shared decision-making in mental health care using routine outcome monitoring: results of a cluster randomised-controlled trial. *Social Psychiatry and Psychiatric Epidemiology, 54*(2), 209–219. https://doi.org/10.1007/s00127-018-1589-8

Miller, S. D., Duncan, B. L., Sorrell, R., & Brown, G. S. (2005). The partners for change outcome management system. *Journal of Clinical Psychology: In Session, 61*(2), 199–208. https://doi.org/10.1002/jclp.20111

Murphy, K. P., Rashleigh, C. M., & Timulak, L. (2012). The relationship between progress feedback and therapeutic outcome in student counselling: A randomized controlled trial. *Counselling Psychology Quarterly, 25*, 1–18. https://doi.org/10.1080/09515070.2012.662349

Newnham, E. A., Hooke, G. R., & Page, A. C. (2010). Progress monitoring and feedback in psychiatric care reduces depressive symptoms. *Journal of Affective Disorders, 127*(1–3), 139–146. https://doi.org/10.1016/ j.jad.2010.05.003

Probst, T., Lambert, M. J., Dahlbender, R. W., Loew, T. H., & Tritt, K. (2014). Providing patient progress feedback and clinical support tools to therapists: Is the therapeutic process of patients on-track to recovery enhanced in psychosomatic in-patient therapy under the conditions of routine practice? *Journal of Psychosomatic Research, 76*(6), 477–484. https://doi .org/10.1016/j.jpsychores.2014.03.010

Probst, T., Lambert, M. J., Loew, T. H., Dahlbender, R. W., Göllner, R., & Tritt, K. (2013). Feedback on patient progress and clinical support tools for therapists: Improved outcome for patients at risk of treatment failure in psychosomatic in-patient therapy under the conditions of routine practice. *Journal of Psychosomatic Research, 75*(3), 255–261. https://doi .org/10.1016/j.jpsychores.2013.07.003

Puschner, B., Schöfer, D., Knaup, C., & Becker, T. (2009). Outcome management in in-patient psychiatric care. *Acta Psychiatrica Scandinavica, 120*(4), 308–319. https://doi.org/10.1111/j.1600-0447.2009.01397.x

Reese, R. J., Norsworthy, L. A., & Rowlands, S. R. (2009). Does a continuous feedback system improve psychotherapy outcome? *Psychotherapy: Theory, Research, Practice, Training, 46*(4), 418–431. https://doi.org/10.1037/ a0017901

Reese, R. J., Toland, M. D., Slone, N. C., & Norsworthy, L. A. (2010). Effect of client feedback on couple psychotherapy outcomes. *Psychotherapy: Theory, Research, Practice, Training, 47*(4), 616–630. doi:10.1037/ a0021182

Rise, M. B., Eriksen, L., Grimstad, H., & Steinsbekk, A. (2012). The short-term effect on alliance and satisfaction of using patient feedback scales in mental health out-patient treatment. A randomised controlled trial. *BMC Health Services Research, 12*(1), 1–12. https://doi.org/10.1186/1472-6963- 12-348

Schmidt, U., Landau, S., Pombo-Carril, M. G., Bara-Carril, N., Reid, Y., Murray, K., Treasure, J., & Katzman, M. (2006). Does personalized feedback improve the outcome of cognitive-behavioural guided self-care in bulimia nervosa? A preliminary randomized controlled trial. *British Journal of Clinical Psychology, 45*(Pt 1), 111–121. https://doi.org/ 10.1348/014466505X29143

Schöttke, H., Unrath, M., & Uhlmann, C. (2019). Einfluss von Verlaufsfeedback auf die Behandlungseffektivität ambulanter Psychotherapien. *Verhaltenstherapie, 30*(3), 222–233. https://doi.org/10.1159/000501176

Schuman, D. L., Slone, N. C., Reese, R. J., & Duncan, B. (2015). Efficacy of client feedback in group psychotherapy with soldiers referred for substance abuse treatment. *Psychotherapy Research, 25*(4), 396–407. https://doi.org/ 10.1080/10503307.2014.900875

She, Z., Duncan, B. L., Reese, R. J., Sun, Q., Shi, Y., Jiang, G., Wu, C., & Clements, A. L. (2018). Client feedback in China: A randomized clinical trial in a college counseling center. *Journal of Counseling Psychology, 65*(6), 727–737. https://doi.org/10.1037/cou0000300

Simon, W., Lambert, M. J., Busath, G., Vazquez, A., Berkeljon, A., Hyer, K., Granley, M., & Berrett, M. (2013). Effects of providing patient progress feedback and clinical support tools to psychotherapists in an inpatient eating disorders treatment program: A randomized controlled study. *Psychotherapy Research, 23*(3), 287–300. https://doi.org/10.1080/10503307 .2013.787497

Simon, W., Lambert, M. J., Harris, M. W., Busath, G., & Vazquez, A. (2012). Providing patient progress information and clinical support tools to therapists: Effects on patients at risk of treatment failure. *Psychotherapy Research, 22*(6), 638–647. https://doi.org/10.1080/10503307.2012.698918

Slone, N. C., Reese, R. J., Mathews-Duvall, S., & Kodet, J. (2015). Evaluating the efficacy of client feedback in group psychotherapy. *Group Dynamics: Theory, Research, and Practice, 19*(2), 122. https://doi.org/10.1037/ gdn0000026

Spitzer, R. L., Kroenke, K., Williams, J. B., & Löwe, B. (2006). A brief measure for assessing generalized anxiety disorder: the GAD-7. *Archives of Internal Medicine, 166*(10), 1092–1097. https://doi.org/10.1001/ archinte.166.10.1092

Tilden, T., Wampold, B. E., Ulvenes, P., Zahl-Olsen, R., Hoffart, A., Barstad, B., Olsen, I. A., Gude, T., Pinsof, W. M., Zinbarg, R. E., Nilssen, H. H., & Håland, Å. T. (2020). Feedback in couple and family therapy: A randomized clinical trial. *Family Process, 59*(1), 36–51. https://doi.org/10.1111/ famp.12485

Tzur Bitan, D., Kivity, Y., Ganor, O., Biran, L., Grossman-Giron, A., & Bloch, Y. (2019). The effect of process and outcome feedback in highly distressed outpatients: A randomized controlled trial. *Psychotherapy Research, 30*(3), 1–12. https://doi.org/10.1080/10503307 .2019.1627014

van Oenen, F. J., Schipper, S., Van, R., Schoevers, R., Visch, I., Peen, J., & Dekker, J. (2016). Feedback-informed treatment in emergency psychiatry; a randomised controlled trial. *BMC Psychiatry, 16*(1), 1–11. https:// doi.org/10.1186/s12888-016-0811-z

Whipple, J. L., Lambert, M. J., Vermeersch, D. A., Smart, D. W., Nielsen, S. L., & Hawkins, E. J. (2003). Improving the effects of psychotherapy: The use of early identification of treatment and problem-solving strategies in routine practice. *Journal of Counseling Psychology, 50*(1), 59–68. https://doi.org/10.1037/0022-0167.50.1.59

THE EFFICACY AND EFFECTIVENESS OF PSYCHOLOGICAL THERAPIES

MICHAEL BARKHAM AND MICHAEL J LAMBERT

Abstract

This chapter sets out the current status of the evidence-base for the efficacy and effectiveness of psychological therapies. First, methods for eliciting and synthesizing evidence on efficacy and effectiveness are briefly outlined. We then address questions pertaining to the general and specific efficacy and effectiveness of psychological therapies compared with pharmacotherapy, with contrasting therapies, and with a range of presenting conditions, as well as studies of cost-effectiveness. We then consider key issues in the delivery of psychological therapies, namely matching patients with therapies, the role of individual therapists, the most appropriate dosage of therapy, and whether therapies reach the cultural and ethnic diversity of patients in need. We then move to a focus on the impact on individual clients, in terms of the significance of change, negative impacts, and longer-term gains and maintenance. We conclude with a series of observations on the status of research in general and on major issues of research design and the impact on individuals and raise questions as to how we can move outcomes research forward and also find ways to deliver the benefits of the psychological therapies at scale.

OVERVIEW

INTRODUCTION

Research on the outcomes of psychological therapies across 80 years from the 1930s through to 2010 has been summarized in the six previous editions of this chapter, listed here chronologically: Bergin (1971); Bergin and Lambert (1978); Lambert, Shapiro, and Bergin (1986); Lambert and Bergin (1994); Lambert and Ogles (2004); and Lambert (2013). Consistent with these accounts, the current chapter utilizes and complements the Lambert (2013) review but does not replace it and readers are encouraged to revisit Lambert's (2013) chapter as it contains unparalleled breadth as a review of the literature at that time. In the chapter for this edition, we have tilted the balance more to a focus on the activity of research with the view that maximizing the yield with respect to the efficacy and effectiveness of the psychological therapies is dependent on designing and conducting high-quality research. In that respect, it complements the chapter in the previous edition. And, in terms of the broad topic area, in this revision we have adopted the term *psychological therapies* in preference to *psychotherapy* in order to make clear we are addressing the plurality of practice that comprises the spectrum of bona fide psychological therapies and not a focus on a single practice that might explicitly be referred to as psychotherapy. We also use the terms client and patient interchangeably.

The evidence presented in this chapter draws heavily on the paradigm of evidence-based practice, namely reporting the yield from meta-analyses (including network meta-analyses) and randomized controlled trials (RCTs). But it also reports findings from other well-designed studies within an effectiveness as well as a practice-based paradigm that address key questions of interest to researchers and practitioners in the field. Chapter 6, which follows, summarizes evidence drawn solely from routine practice and in which there is no attempt to devise a control or comparator condition (see Barkham et al., 2010). Therefore, both this and the following chapter together provide an expanded account of therapy outcomes and should be read together in order to achieve a comprehensive appreciation of the range of evidence relating to the outcomes of the psychological therapies.

In this chapter, we consider the status and standing of psychological therapies, predominantly with adult outpatients, as the topic of psychological therapies for child and adolescence is addressed comprehensively in Chapter 18. We consider the evidence regarding various theoretical models of the therapies and their cost-effectiveness as well as comparisons with pharmacotherapy. And we also focus on the delivery of the therapies, including cultural adaptations, and the role of therapists, and on the impact the therapies have on individual people who seek support. A full cataloging of all studies and reviews in the area of behavior change is not possible. Literature was identified through employing systematic search terms of electronic databases and that we considered either central, representative, or illustrative. More comprehensive accounts of the major approaches to therapy – namely, behavioral, cognitive behavioral, acceptance and mindfulness-based, psychodynamic, humanistic, systemic, group, as well as internet approaches – are addressed in Chapters 12 to 17 and 21, respectively. In contrast, this chapter provides an overview and comparison of outcome research, along with issues of central importance, that will be relevant to anyone interested in the efficacy and effectiveness of the psychological therapies. However, before doing so, we briefly set out the main apparatus used for reviewing, assessing, and summarizing the literature together with useful aids for readers in the interpretation of results. More seasoned researchers and scholars will be familiar with this content, but for others it may provide both context and clarity.

METHODS FOR SUMMARIZING AND SYNTHESIZING EVIDENCE

Whether readers are contributors to the evidence (e.g., researchers) or consumers of it (e.g., practitioners, students, service users, etc.), how we understand and use such evidence depends on an appreciation of how material is summarized and synthesized. As such, various methods have been adopted, most notably meta-analysis, more latterly network meta-analysis, and what has often been a standard bearer for quantifying the impact of therapies, effect sizes.

Meta-Analysis

The historical controversy regarding the effects of psychological therapies compared to no treatment and to placebo controls (e.g., Bergin, 1971; Bergin & Lambert, 1978; Eysenck, 1952; Rachman & Wilson, 1980) has been addressed largely through the use of meta-analyses. Meta-analyses provide efficient and replicable integrative summaries of primary studies and apply the methods and principles of empirical research to the process of reviewing literature. While meta-analysis is not the only method for summarizing the literature, it carries the benefits of being both cumulative and comparative. That is, it shows effects over time and thereby addresses questions of stability and consistency in the literature. And it summarizes the impact of therapies relative to each other or some other benchmark. Borrowed from the field of education and applied for the first time in psychotherapy research in the classic study by Smith and Glass (1977; see also Smith, Glass, & Miller, 1980), meta-analysis has become the mainstay for determining the efficacy and effectiveness of the psychological therapies. And in the same way that meta-analysis brought rigor to the quantification of effects, a parallel effort has been made in raising the bar in relation to systematic reviews of the literature where the standard practice now is for search criteria to be preregistered on PROSPERO (Prospective Register of Ongoing Systematic Reviews; PLoS Medicine Editors, 2011). And in both meta-analyses and systematic reviews, there is far greater attention to issues of quality and bias.

The method of meta-analysis is detailed in Chapter 2 and so will not be expanded on here. But it is clear that the use of meta-analysis to summarize efficacy literature is critical for the field. That being said, meta-analyses are just as prone to poor methods and misinterpretation as other methods of research with three main threats to their validity: (i) the *file drawer* problem (the tendency for studies with small or no effects not to be published); (ii) the *apples and oranges* problem (combining studies of very different phenomena); and (iii) the *garbage in, garbage out* problem (mixing poor-quality and high-quality studies). The various levels of quality of the studies included in a meta-analysis is in part responsible for the heterogeneity of effect sizes frequently observed and statistical methods can be employed to adjust effect size estimates, such as calculating Q or I^2 to understand the heterogeneity of effect sizes (Sharpe, 1997).

Network Meta-Analysis

More recently researchers have been adopting the additional procedure of network meta-analysis (NMA; for an introduction, see Rouse et al., 2017). NMA was not evident in the literature at the time of the Lambert (2013) review and the first application of NMA in the psychological therapies was published in the same year (Barth et al., 2013). Since the publication of the sixth edition, there has been a steady growth in the use of NMA in the psychological therapy literature, with in excess of 100 publications as of early 2021. Stated simply, NMA is a logical extension of standard pairwise meta-analysis by including multiple pairwise comparisons across a range of interventions in order to address the comparative effectiveness of multiple treatment alternatives. Crucially, NMA allows both direct and indirect comparisons to be made regarding the relative efficacy of psychosocial interventions. Hence, in a context where meta-analysis has become the norm, providing a powerful method for synthesizing evidence and enabling indirect comparisons to be made is an important step in terms of informing national clinical guidelines (e.g., the UK's National Institute for Health and Care Excellence [NICE]) for decision-making by practitioners. Examples of its application include psychological and pharmacological interventions for social anxiety (Mayo-Wilson et al., 2014) – which derived from the NICE guideline on social anxiety – and comparisons of psychological therapy models of depression (Cuijpers et al., 2021), as well as a comparison between the psychological therapies and pharmacotherapy (Cuijpers, Noma et al., 2020).

The field of research evidence and synthesis is an increasingly important one in relation to systematic reviews, umbrella reviews, meta-analyses, and network meta-analyses (e.g., see Ioannidis, 2009, 2016). However, notwithstanding the advances offered by NMA, several commentators, including advocates, have stated that primacy should still be placed on securing direct evidence (Kanters, 2016; Molloy et al., 2018), a view expressed previously in the early days of meta-analysis by Shapiro and Shapiro (1982) in their calls for "same experiment data."

Effect Sizes and Confidence Intervals

Following a systematic search of the literature to locate studies meeting predefined inclusion criteria, the findings of individual studies are quantified using a common metric such as an effect size statistic, usually Hedges' *g* or Cohen's *d*, which can be read as the standardized difference between the mean of groups. The aim of *d* and related statistics is to describe the magnitude of treatment response. Since effect size can be understood in terms of the percent of patients responding to treatment, it provides an easy way to estimate the magnitude of effects a treatment has had and is not influenced by sample size.

Table 5.1 displays the meanings of various effect sizes that might be reported in studies and summed in meta-analytic reviews. Effect size (ES) is a very easy metric to use and it can also be used to determine the effect of a single intervention with no comparison group. The pre–post ES will obviously be comparatively larger than when comparing between treatments as the effect is capturing the whole extent of change rather than the difference between two conditions (see Chapter 4). Although part of the appeal of ESs is that they do not depend on statistical power, it is important to appreciate that they are very much a function of the size of the denominator (i.e., the variance in the sample). Collecting data with a restricted range will likely lead to a higher ES. Hence, ESs in trial data are invariably greater than those in practice-based data, partly because of the restricted variance arising from trials setting minimum and, on occasions, maximum thresholds for intake (e.g., restrictions on suicidality). An additional effect size, an odds ratio (OR), summarizes the probability or odds of an association between a given condition and a binary outcome (e.g., dropout).

A companion statistic is confidence intervals (CIs). If a study was repeated an infinite number of times and, on each occasion, a 95% confidence interval was calculated, then 95% of these intervals would contain the true effect. Hence, the specific relevance of CIs is that they are an indicator of precision. The tighter the CIs, then the greater the precision of the results. But, precision is not synonymous with accuracy. Very large (or wide) CIs will be more accurate in that they are more likely to contain the true value, but they do not help in determining precision. On a practical level, while ESs provide information on the magnitude of an effect, which for the evaluation of psychological therapies is crucial, CIs provide information on the precision of the results. Moreover, the span of the CIs indicates whether the effect is significant and the direction of that effect in terms of traditional *p*-values by whether or not the span includes the value 0 (i.e., to be significant, the CIs need to be one side or the other of the value 0).

These methods and tools for summarizing efficacy and effectiveness outcomes should be read in conjunction with Chapters 2 and 4 and provide the means for describing the efficacy and effectiveness of the psychological therapies as reported in this chapter. Having signposted the methods for collating and summarizing the literature, we now turn to presenting the evidence.

Key Themes that Capture Questions of Interest to Scientist-Practitioners

A large body of literature has been generated by examining the benefits of the psychological therapies. To provide a framework for organizing this body of literature, we considered key themes driven by Paul's (1967) central litany: "What treatment, by whom, is most effective for this individual with that specific problem, under which set of circumstances, and how does it

TABLE 5.1 Effect Sizes with Various Interpretations

Cohen's designation and d	Proportion of treated persons above (better than) the mean of untreated persons	Correlation (r)	Proportion of variability in outcomes due to treatment (R²)	Success rate of treated persons (BESD)	Success rate of untreated persons (BESD)	Numbers needs to treat (NNT)
Small						
0.0	.50	.00	.00	.500	.500	∞
0.1	.54	.05	>.01	.525	.475	18
0.2	.58	.10	.01	.550	.450	9
Medium						
0.3	.62	.15	.02	.574	.426	6
0.4	.66	.20	.04	.598	.402	5
0.5	.69	.24	.06	.621	.379	4
0.6	.73	.29	.08	.644	.356	4
0.7	.76	.33	.11	.665	.335	3
Large						
0.8	.79	.37	.14	.686	.314	3
0.9	.82	.41	.17	.705	.295	3
1.0	.84	.45	.20	.724	.276	2

Note: d = between group effect size, Cohen's (1988) designation, proportion or success is the proportion of patients receiving treatment who would be better off than the average patient with the alternative; r = correlation coefficient; R^2 = proportion of variance accounted for by factor; BESD = Binomial Effect Size Display (see Rosenthal & Rubin, 1982); NNT = number needed to treat. Wampold (2001). Adapted with permission.

come about?" (p. 111). The three specific themes selected in this Chapter focus on (i) the evidence-base for the psychological therapies; (ii) the allocation and delivery of therapy to client populations; and (iii) the therapeutic impact on individual clients. In focusing on efficacy and effectiveness, we have touched only briefly on the question of "How does it come about?" as this is addressed fully in subsequent chapters (e.g., Chapters 7 and 8). Within each of the three stated themes, we focus on specific questions of relevance to scientist-practitioners.

EVIDENCE BASE FOR THE PSYCHOLOGICAL THERAPIES

In this section, we review and update evidence relating to five questions:

1. Are psychological therapies, in general, efficacious?
2. Are psychological therapies more effective when combined with pharmacotherapy?
3. Is any one psychological therapy consistently more effective than another?

4. Are some psychological therapies more effective than others with specific conditions?
5. Are psychological therapies cost-effective?

Are Psychological Therapies Generally Efficacious?

Foundational Meta-Analytic Studies

Early applications of meta-analysis to psychotherapy outcomes (Smith & Glass, 1977; Smith, Glass, & Miller, 1980) addressed the overall question of the extent of benefit associated with psychotherapy as evidenced in the literature as a whole, compared the outcomes of different treatments, and examined the impact of methodological features of studies on the reported effectiveness of treatments. Smith et al. (1980) found an aggregate effect size of 0.85 standard deviation units over 475 studies comparing treated and untreated groups. Such an effect is equivalent to the average treated person being better off than about 80% of an untreated sample (see Table 5.1; column 2), accounting for approximately 15% of variability in outcome (see column 4), with the remaining variance due to client variables such as degree of disturbance, measurement error, etc.). The percent of successful clients treated is approximately 70% compared with 30% for the untreated clients (columns 5 and 6) and yielding a number needed to treat (NNT) value of 3.

Further meta-analytic reviews included both critical replications using the same database as Smith et al. (1980) (e.g., Andrews & Harvey, 1991; Landman & Dawes, 1982) and independent analyses of other large samples of studies (Shapiro & Shapiro, 1982). These studies substantiated the effect of treatment as opposed to no-treatment controls. Lipsey and Wilson (1993) summarized the results of 302 meta-analyses of psychological, educational, and behavioral treatments. The authors examined a subset of these meta-analytic studies using stringent inclusion criteria restricted to designs comprising control or comparison groups and excluding pre–post designs and estimates based only on published studies. This yielded 156 meta-analyses, 9,400 effectiveness studies and included in excess of one million individual participants. They found the average treatment effect for this restricted sample was 0.47 and 83% of the mean effect sizes to be 0.20 or more. In sum, although their resulting effect size was smaller than that reported in earlier studies based on the psychotherapy literature (i.e., 0.47 vs. 0.85), they still concluded that psychological, educational, and behavioral treatments have positive effects.

Meta-Analyses of the General Effects of Psychological Therapies

The observation regarding an overestimation of effects was noted in the previous edition of this chapter (Lambert, 2013) and more recent analyses have continued this viewpoint, focusing on the quality of studies, potential biases, and advising greater caution in estimates of the overall size of effect. For example, Cuijpers, Smit et al. (2010), when controlling for the quality of studies, estimated that the average effect size of treatments for depression should be adjusted down from 0.67 to 0.42 (across 51 studies). Such a trend was also reported across 115 RCTs for depression, in which, although the overall mean effect size of all comparisons was 0.68 (95% CI 0.60, 0.76), this estimate reduced to 0.22 for the 11 studies deemed to be of higher quality (Cuijpers, van Straten, Bohlmeijer et al., 2010).

In response to concerns about biases in published research as well as the observation that the effects for psychological therapies appeared greater than for other forms of intervention, Dragioti et al. (2017) published an umbrella review in which they conducted a meta-analysis of all forms of psychotherapy that included a minimum of 10 studies. The supplementary material shows 17 common therapies and 22 other specific approaches. They identified 173 eligible studies comprising 247 meta-analyses that synthesized data from 5157 randomized controlled trials (RCTs). Results showed 199 meta-analyses were significant and almost all (*n* = 196) favored psychotherapy. Large and very large heterogeneity was observed in 130 meta-analyses. However, when the authors devised a set of criteria for selecting only the highest-quality studies, only 16 (7%) studies provided robust evidence. In sum, the authors concluded that

while 79% of trials reported a nominally statistically significant finding favoring psychotherapy over the control condition, only a small proportion provided convincing evidence without biases. However, neither from the article nor the supplementary material is it possible to identify the 16 studies.

In a more recent study, Cuijpers, Karyotaki et al. (2019) revisited Eysenck's (1952) claim that psychotherapies are not effective in the treatment of mental disorders by reexamining the impact of type of control condition, risk of bias, and publication bias in studies of depression. At a conceptual level, the specific focus of the selected control condition was to test Eysenck's proposition of the effects of therapy vs. spontaneous remission. Crucially, these authors excluded wait-list comparisons in their meta-analysis on the basis that it yielded a significantly superior ES (0.89; 95% CI [0.80, 0.98]) compared with care as usual (0.61; 95% CI [0.53, 0.68]) and other control conditions (0.51; 95% CI [0.40, 0.62]). Excluding studies from non-Western countries, the ES (*k* = 325) was 0.63 (95% CI [0.58, 0.68]). Excluding wait-list controls reduced the ES (*k* = 179) to 0.51 (95% CI [0.45, 0.58]). And when taking account of risk of bias (*k* = 71) and publication bias (*k* = 84), the ESs further reduced to 0.38 (95% CI [0.32, 0.44]) and 0.31 (95% CI [0.24, 0.38]), respectively. The results of this analysis highlight the potential concerns around biases and the issue of control conditions. The data was then reanalyzed by Munder et al. (2019) in which the authors removed outliers and adjusted for bias, focused on studies of psychological therapies only, and, crucially, included wait-list controls. The results are shown in Figure 5.1, which yields an estimate closer to the original findings reported by Smith and Glass (1977).

Following on from the above, Cuijpers, Karyotaki, de Wit et al. (2020) carried out a meta-analytic study employing 309 RCTs yielding 385 comparisons between 15 types of psychological therapy and a control condition. They analyzed the data according to generic classes of therapy and also for specific forms and these results are considered later in this chapter. Of note here are the comparisons between psychological therapies as a single class and the control conditions of wait list, care as usual, and other (unspecified). Pooling all control conditions, the overall ES was $g = 0.72$ (95% CI [0.67, 0.78]), yielding an NNT of 4.04, rounded to 5 with high heterogeneity ($I^2 = 81\%$). But the ES changed as a function of the control condition – wait list: $g = 0.73$ (95% CI [0.69, 0.77]); care as usual: $g = 0.63$ (95% CI [0.55, 0.70]); and other: $g = 0.57$ (95% CI [0.43, 0.70]). However, all 95% CIs overlapped and there was a significant association between ES and risk of bias. Focusing on those studies rated as low risk (*n* = 103), the ES was $g = 0.48$ (95% CI [0.42, 0.55]), yielding an NNT of 6.44, (rounded to 7) while the adjusted ES was $g = 0.36$ (95% CI [0.29, 0.44]). For a subsequent network meta-analysis on a similar range of psychological therapies, see Cuijpers et al. (2021).

In sum, addressing the question of the overall effectiveness of the psychological therapies has yielded an overriding pattern of results showing that, as a class of interventions, they are effective. However, key factors impact on the point estimate of effectiveness, including risk of bias, researcher allegiance, and crucially the control condition selected, a topic we turn to next.

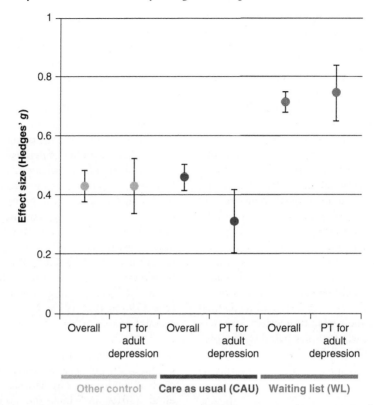

FIGURE 5.1   Effect Sizes for Psychological Interventions for Depression
Munder, T., Flückiger, C., Leichsenring, F., Abbass, A. A., Hilsenroth, M. J., Luyten, P., Rabung, S., Steinert, C., & Wampold, B. E. (2019). Is psychotherapy effective? A re-analysis of treatments for depression. *Epidemiology and Psychiatric Sciences, 28*(3), 268–274. Reproduced with permission.

Selecting the Appropriate Control Condition

While it might appear logical for most of the research effort to focus on the active treatment component, determining a point estimate for its efficacy depends crucially on the nature of the comparator arm in any trial or study. Indeed, "control conditions remain dark matter, exerting effects that are unseen, ill-defined, and for the most part unquantified" (Mohr et al., 2009, p.282). In response to such concern, Mohr and colleagues called for guidelines in the adoption of control conditions, specifically in the field of depression but the principle can be applied to all presenting conditions. Multiple factors inform the choice concerning type of control condition and at its core is the issue of construct validity (see Chapter 2).

Consistent with the above view, there have been increasing concerns expressed about pooling diverse control conditions to yield a single point estimate. Focusing on depression, Mohr et al. (2014) identified 125 trials yielding 188 comparisons using a range of control conditions: no-treatment control, wait-list control, treatment as usual, nonspecific factors component, specific factor component, active comparator, pill placebo, and minimal treatment control. The authors also considered seven additional implementation features: manualization, therapist training, therapist supervision, fidelity, experience, expertise, and crossed vs. nested. Table 5.2 presents effect sizes from 188 comparisons investigating the topic of depression with results falling into three groups: large effects (wait list; treatment as usual), moderate (no treatment, pill placebo, and specific factor

TABLE 5.2   Effect Sizes for Eight Different Control Conditions Derived from 188 Comparisons in 125 Psychotherapy Trials of Depression

Control condition	N (%)	g	95% CI
Wait list	42 (22)	0.95	0.74, 1.16
Treatment as usual	34 (18)	0.93	0.72, 1.15
No treatment	13 (7)	0.56	0.22, 0.90
Pill placebo	10 (5)	0.48	0.10, 0.86
Specific factor	31 (16)	0.35	0.11, 0.58
Non-specific factor	*37 (19)*	*0.18*	*-0.04, 0.40*
Active comparator	*16 (9)*	*0.09*	*-0.23, 0.40*
Minimal treatment	*5 (3)*	*-0.13*	*-0.75, 0.49*
All control conditions	188	0.54	0.45, 0.64

Note: Italics denotes not significant. Data extracted from Table 1 in Mohr, D. C., Ho, J., Hart, T. L., Baron, K. G., Berendsen, M., Beckner, V., Cai, X., Cuijpers, P., Spring, B., Kinsinger, S. W., Schroder, K. E., & Duffecy, J. (2014). Control condition design and implementation features in controlled trials: a meta-analysis of trials evaluating psychotherapy for depression. *Translational Behavioral Medicine, 4*(4), 407–423. Adapted with permission.

components), and nonsignificant effects (nonspecific factors, active comparator, and minimal intervention), the latter being in italics with the 95% CIs containing zero. Results showed outcomes vary as a function of the control condition, and smaller significant effects were obtained for the implementation components of manualization, therapist training and supervision, and treatment fidelity monitoring.

In general, wait-list controls are seen to be the weakest comparisons, appearing to control for the absence of a treatment, a finding endorsed by a recent meta-analysis (Michopoulos et al., 2021). Evidence has grown suggesting that the waitlist condition has the potential for creating a *nocebo* effect – that is, a person or participant-related response to an inert treatment (Kennedy, 1961; for a review, see Colloca & Barsky, 2020). In effect, this is the opposite of a placebo effect and is a factor to consider in relation to non-active control conditions. Treatment as usual has also drawn commentary with some ambiguity as to whether it is viewed as an active or inactive control (for a considered discussion on this topic, see Kazdin, 2015). Hence, a resulting issue concerns the extent of heterogeneity within treatment as usual when adopted as a control condition.

Returning to Mohr et al.'s (2009) call for guidelines informing the adoption of control conditions, Gold et al. (2017) devised a decision framework for choosing a control condition as a function of three components: (i) the phase of the trial; (ii) the level of participation risk for the patient (low, intermediate, high); and (iii) the resources required (low, intermediate, high), together with the associated sample size and effect size (both ranging from small to large). For example, a wait-list control design would be deemed suitable for early phase trials, for patients at low risk regarding their participation, and requiring a relatively low level of resource, and by their nature needing smaller sample sizes and yielding moderate-to-large effect sizes. By contrast, designs using an active comparator or patient choice are appropriate for later phase trials, for patients at potentially higher risk regarding their participation, requiring a higher level of resource, needing a large sample size and, therefore, yielding small effect sizes. Amongst a number of recommendations by the authors was the need for study investigators to justify the use of wait list in terms of ethics and specified criteria. But they went further to state that behavioral interventions should not be included in guidelines if only supported by evidence, either from trials or meta-analyses based on them, using wait-list comparisons.

A study that captured both the variability in control condition comparisons and a possible nocebo effect was a network meta-analysis conducted by Furukawa et al. (2014) in which cognitive behavioral therapy (CBT) was compared with wait list, no treatment, and psychological placebo. The odds ratios (OR) for response compared with CBT differed as a function of the control condition: psychological placebo, OR = 1.60 (95% CI [0.95, 2.67]); no treatment, OR = 2.07 (95% CI [1.35, 3.18]); and wait list, OR = 3.99 (95% CI [2.76, 5.77]). The ES for the wait-list condition was substantially greater than for no treatment, although the CIs for no treatment and wait list overlapped. However, the consequence was that the wait-list comparison appeared to elevate the effects of treatment due to

a greater differential effect. The argument goes that (some) patients on wait lists do not do anything to help themselves because they know that treatment will be forthcoming while for others, the expectation of a forthcoming treatment may yield a more positive effect. Either way, by contrast, patients in a no-treatment condition have to find other support. However, there are various caveats to the Furukawa et al. (2014) study. For example, only a quarter of the included studies were rated as having a low risk of bias and small study effects (i.e., small studies having systematically different effects to large studies) were notable, particularly in the comparison between CBT and wait list. Indeed, when Furukawa and colleagues ran sensitivity analyses to statistically adjust for such biases through meta-regression, they found the odds ratio of no treatment over wait list was no longer statistically significant in the better fitting of the two hypothesized models used.

Notwithstanding these caveats, Cuijpers, Karyotaki et al. (2019) omitted the wait-list control in their meta-analysis, yielding considerably reduced effect sizes for the impact of therapies. The Cuijpers et al. analysis was critiqued and countered in the re-analysis by Munder et al. (2019) referred to earlier, which was in turn responded to by Cristea (2019). Munder et al. (2019) argued that a no treatment condition is unethical so is, in effect, not a viable comparator, while care-as-usual is, in effect, an active control condition and so could not provide an estimate of spontaneous remission. By contrast, wait list is a best available estimate of the effect of waiting for a treatment, which would be most akin to the situation for the majority of people seeking help for a felt need. And a more sanguine view of the findings was endorsed by Cuijpers, Quero et al.'s (2019) meta-analysis of care-as-usual conditions in which they analyzed 140 studies yielding 158 comparisons in which 24 studies (17.1%) used a no-treatment condition. They reported no difference between care-as-usual in primary care settings, specialized mental health, and with no treatment. Across all care-as-usual categories, the overall ES for all 158 comparisons with psychotherapy was $g = 0.61$ (95% CI [0.52, 0.70]), although there was high heterogeneity ($I^2 = 78\%$; CI 74%, 81%). As a commentary, it has been suggested that the term *treatment as usual* be reframed as *best available and approved treatment* so as to mitigate any negative perceptions of being assigned to a standard treatment (Enck & Zipfel, 2019).

A further related topic concerns the placebo control condition. Current outcome studies of the psychological therapies seldom use the placebo term, preferring instead to control for all factors that are common to all treatments, not just expectancy effects. Others have suggested the term *common factors* in recognition that many therapies have ingredients that are not unique to a specific treatment but contribute to the process of change. Thus, research on placebo effects might be better conceptualized as research on common factors versus the specific effects of a particular technique. Common factors are those dimensions of the treatment setting (e.g., therapist belief in treatment, a confidential, legally protected activity, client expectations of a positive outcome) that are not specific to any particular theoretically based approach. The important point is that those factors common to most therapies (such as expectation for improvement, installation of hope, persuasion, warmth and attention, understanding, encouragement, and the like) should not be viewed as theoretically inert. Indeed, these factors are central to psychological interventions in both theory and practice and play an active role in patient improvement.

Returning to the view that control conditions relate directly to issues of construct validity, each comparison controls for specific components addressing specific questions and that, when considered across the range of conditions, introduces considerable heterogeneity. The error is in combining different control conditions. Put simply, the nature of the control condition determines the ES for therapy and hence ESs need to be paired with specific control conditions. And in relation to the relative impact that control conditions have on the ES, reiterating Gold et al.'s (2017) decision framework, it has been recommended that early-phase trials use weaker controls (i.e., wait list) while later-stage trials (i.e., confirmatory) use stronger controls (i.e., placebo) (Michopoulos et al., 2021), a view also aired by Guidi et al. (2018), who provide a helpful overview of the pros and cons regarding different control conditions in trials of the psychological therapies.

Summary

In considering the general effectiveness of the psychological therapies, our conclusions are similar to those made in the previous edition. First, the general index of efficacy has not improved in the time since the original work of Smith and Glass (1977). That is, when considered against a liberal comparator (i.e., wait-list control), the efforts of more than 40 years have not yielded a discernible improvement in the overall effectiveness of psychological therapies. And second, when more stringent quality criteria are applied to the re-analyses of older reviews or when newer meta-analytic reviews are published, the results have tended to produce somewhat smaller effect sizes than the original estimates or as compared with Smith and Glass. The application of greater stringency to analyses in the form of reducing biases (i.e., reducing risk of bias) is consistent with promoting more rigorous science, and there is a clear steer from commentators to be judicious in defining the limits of generalizability as determined by the specific control condition employed.

In taking an overview of the status of the psychological therapies, we conclude that the nature of the comparator condition is crucial – the point estimate of the effect is a function of the nature of the comparator. And the point estimate ranges from 0.80 (compared with wait list) to 0.40 (compared with active placebo), with the respective NNT being 3 and 5 (see Table 5.1). As Lambert (2013) stated: "Even if the effect size between treated and untreated individuals is as small as $d = 0.40$, this would still lead to an estimate of the success rate in treated persons of 60% compared to that of 40% for untreated persons" (p.172). But an NNT of 5 is on a par with a range of medical interventions noted by Wampold and Imel (2015, p.72): for example, "gastroenterology (e.g., proton pump inhibitors for bleeding peptic ulcers vis-à-vis placebo, NNT = 6), orthopedics (e.g., active treatment of whiplash vs. treatment-as-usual, NNT = 5)." See Chapter 4 for further comparisons between patient effects and medical treatments.

Considering these data in the round and when set against the Smith and Glass findings of 40 years ago, it is not so much a matter of the psychological therapies not improving or being less effective, but rather that our research methods and activities have become more exacting and precise, as should be the case over a 40-year period. And this assumes that both the complexity and severity of patients' presenting conditions have not increased over the same time period, which is likely questionable. Accordingly, we endorse the conclusion of Lambert (2013) that the psychological therapies are generally efficacious.

Are Psychological Therapies More Effective Than Pharmacotherapy (Alone or Combined)?

The issue of psychological therapies and pharmacotherapy alone or in combination has been an ongoing focus of empirical studies and reviews (e.g., Gartlehner et al., 2017). In the previous edition of the *Handbook*, Lambert (2013) concluded that in relation to depression, the effects of both psychotherapy and pharmacotherapy were broadly comparable at termination. Here we consider whether this conclusion still holds.

While presented as monotherapies, each format has its drawbacks, primarily relating to unwanted side effects from antidepressant medication and demoralization if no improvement is made from psychotherapies. Specifically, attention has focused on findings that the remission rate for depression is in the region of 30–40%, with a high rate of relapse. Medication can prevent depression symptom relapse as long as medication is not discontinued (Hollon et al., 2005). Craighead and Dunlop (2014) reviewed combination treatments for depression and considered evidence-based psychotherapies and antidepressant medication to be, on average, equally efficacious. And in the chapter focusing on combination treatments in the previous edition, Forand et al. (2013) concluded that there was clear evidence to support combined treatments for people presenting with chronic but not for mild or moderate depression.

The finding suggesting a specific benefit of combined treatment for more chronic presentations is exemplified in Hollon et al.'s (2014) RCT comparing antidepressant medication alone or combined with cognitive therapy ($N = 452$) with treatment continuing up to 42 months and using survival analysis to map treatment outcomes. Not only was this a large trial carried out at three sites, but it also allowed clinicians to adjust treatment up to 19 months in order to achieve remission and subsequently up to 42 months in order to secure the best likelihood of preventing relapse. And with the sample size, the study was powered to detect interactions as well as main effects. On the face of it, the results appeared consistent with previous findings – namely, that combination treatment yielded more favorable outcomes (i.e., more likely to recover). In addition, they were less likely to drop out of the study and reported fewer adverse effects. However, the advantage to combined treatment was small – an advantage of approximately 10% (75.2% vs. 65.6%). The more salient finding was the effect of severity (nonsignificant) and chronicity (significant) that resulted in a clear advantage for combined treatment with severe, nonchronic patients (84.7% vs. 57.7%), yielding an NNT of 4. Indeed, distinct subgroups of patients responded differentially such that, in addition, nonchronic patients who were not severely depressed responded well on antidepressant medication alone without the addition of cognitive therapy while those deemed to have chronic depression irrespective of level of severity showed no beneficial effect from adding cognitive therapy.

These findings flag a key issue in relation to questions regarding one treatment vs. another, namely the tendency of main effects to mask moderating effects. This was a central thread in observations made by Hollon (2016) regarding therapies in general; that several bona fide therapies are as effective as medication, providing they are delivered to a sufficiently competent standard, and that differential effects are most likely more noticeable in more severe levels of depression. Indeed, when considering less severe patients, Hollon (2016) concluded: "For less severe depressions, something works better than nothing and nothing works better than anything else, drug or psychotherapy" (p. 295).

Extending beyond depression alone, Cuijpers, Sijbrandij et al. (2013) reported on a meta-analysis of 40 studies focusing on depressive disorders and 27 focusing on anxiety disorders. Overall, there was no significant difference between psychotherapy and pharmacotherapy for all disorders ($g = 0.02$, 95% CI [−0.07, 0.10]), although there were exceptions. Subsequently, Cuijpers, Sijbrandij, Koole, Andersson et al. (2014) reported data from a meta-analysis comprising 32 studies of depression and 21 of anxiety showing an advantage to combination treatments ($g = 0.43$, 95% CI [0.31, 0.56]). And beyond both depression and anxiety, Huhn et al. (2014) carried out a review comprising 61 meta-analyses of 21 psychiatric disorders and considered three comparisons: psychotherapy or pharmacotherapy compared with placebo or no treatment, head-to-head comparisons of pharmacotherapies and psychotherapies, and the combination of both treatments. They found the effect sizes, expressed as standard mean differences (SMD), for acute-phase psychotherapy tended to be larger (SMD = 0.58, 95% CI [0.40, 0.76]) than for pharmacotherapy (SMD = 0.40, 95% CI [0.28, 0.52]). The effects for combining medication with psychotherapy and vice versa tended to favor combined treatments, but it was only for depression and bulimia that the effect was significant regardless of whether medication was added to psychotherapy or vice versa. In an attempt to provide an overview of this topic, Cuijpers, Noma et al. (2020) carried out a network meta-analysis comparing psychotherapy, pharmacotherapy, and both in combination. The sample comprised 101 studies with a total of 11,910 participants. The overall results showed greater benefit for combined treatments compared with psychotherapy and pharmacotherapy and no difference between the treatments alone.

However, there are cautionary points worthy of note. Generally, as identified by Gold et al. (2017), comparisons between psychological therapy and pharmacotherapy conditions are inherently difficult due to the differential impact of blinding of participants – that is, participants receiving psychological therapies know what they are receiving (i.e., are unblinded) whereas those receiving pharmacotherapy do not know whether they are receiving the active or placebo agent. And in the meta-analysis by Huhn et al. (2014), pharmacotherapy trials had almost a tenfold number of participants compared with those for psychotherapy. In addition, the authors noted significant differences in the risks of bias between pharmacotherapy and psychological therapy studies. Gold et al. (2017) argued that comparisons need to be made within the same trial between patients and therapists who are unmasked in relation to all conditions. Hence, Gold et al. argue that evidence from network analyses should not supersede evidence from individual head-to-head trials in the development of, for example, treatment guidelines.

Summary

A considerable body of meta-analyses appear to suggest that there is little difference between psychological therapies and pharmacotherapy when delivered as monotherapies but that they yield more favorable outcomes when combined. However, the literature is not always consistent and, importantly, commentators have advised caution in the interpretation of comparisons derived from meta-analytic studies. We also note comments espousing same experiment comparisons due to blinding issues and that these studies should have primacy. In particular, we point to the need for a greater focus on trials following the exemplar of Hollon et al. (2014) as a way forward in understanding the crucial impact of moderators. In addition, Hollon et al. (2019) have pointed out the possibility that medications in, for example, depression may act to prolong the episode and impact detrimentally on relapse (see Chapter 20). Finally, in terms of recommendations, in an informative and balanced position article, Ormel et al. (2020) carried out a critical analysis and synthesis of pertinent literature relating to antidepressants and, amongst a number of recommendations, advised that the first line treatment should be psychological therapies.

Is Any One Psychological Therapy Consistently More Effective Than Another?

A subsequent question, following on from the general effectiveness of the psychological therapies and their comparisons with pharmacotherapy, is whether any form of psychotherapy is *consistently* more effective than others. The literature reviewed by Lambert (2013) balanced two viewpoints:

1. Such differences between therapies as can be detected are at best small, of questionable clinical significance, and therefore different modalities are better viewed as being broadly equivalent.
2. Where differences do occur, they invariably show cognitive behavioral therapies to yield better outcomes in a majority of comparisons.

Here we consider both these accounts.

Equivalence

The view that therapies are broadly similar in their outcomes has been embodied in the litany coined by Rosenzweig (1936) in which the Dodo bird from *Alice's Adventures in Wonderland* declares: "Everyone has won and all must have prizes." This caricature of psychotherapy outcomes has been stated and restated since the 1970s (e.g., Luborsky et al., 1975), and has received considered reviews both conceptually (Stiles et al., 1986) and empirically (e.g., Elliott et al., 1993). Various meta-analyses supporting the general effectiveness of psychological therapies (i.e., treatment outcomes) also yielded contrasts between treatments (comparative outcomes), and it is the latter that are relevant to the current question. Commentators (e.g., Hunsley & Di Giulio, 2002) have noted that the meta-analysis of Smith and colleagues (1980) shows differences between specific therapies but not at the level of classes of therapies. One plausible reason is that cognitive therapy was classed as a verbal therapy rather than a behavioral therapy, thereby lessening the difference between behavioral and verbal therapies. Similarly, Shapiro and Shapiro (1982), in their replication and refinement of the Smith et al. meta-analysis, found an "undeniable superiority of behavioural and cognitive methods and a corresponding relative inferiority of dynamic and humanistic (verbal) methods, *in the results of simultaneous controlled comparisons*" (p. 596; italics added). While the overall effect size (N = 1,818) was 0.93, the differential ESs were notable: behavioral and cognitive, 1.10 and 0.97, respectively; dynamic/humanistic, 0.35. As noted by Lambert (2013), when differences were found they often favored, even if marginally, cognitive or behavioral approaches across a variety of patient diagnostic categories.

The issue was revisited by Wampold et al. (1997), drawing in part on the summary of comparative studies in an earlier version of the *Handbook* (Lambert et al., 1986). This meta-analysis differed from earlier comparisons between treatments in several ways. First, only studies that directly compared two or more treatments were included in the meta-analysis. This eliminated the potential confounds associated with comparing treatments administered in different studies (Shadish & Sweeney, 1991). Second, the treatments were not divided into general types or categories. Third, only "bona fide" treatments were included in the meta-analysis. Thus, studies in which a viable treatment was compared to an alternative therapy that was "credible" to participants in the study but not intended to be "therapeutic" were excluded. To test whether one treatment was superior to another, effect sizes calculated comparing two treatments were randomly given a positive or negative sign. The distribution of effects was then tested to see if variability in effects was homogeneously centered around zero. Using several databases with different numbers of effect sizes – "none of the databases yielded effects that vaguely approached the heterogeneity expected if there were true differences among bona fide psychotherapies" (Wampold et al., 1997, p. 205). Further analyses also indicated that more sophisticated methods associated with more recent studies were not related to increased differences between treatments and theoretically dissimilar treatments did not produce larger effect sizes. While these findings provided additional evidence for the equivalence of bona fide treatments, at a conceptual level, a majority of the comparisons were within the class of cognitive therapies (Crits-Christoph, 1997) and at a methodological level, it has been argued that it is the absolute differences that are important rather than the signed differences (Howard et al., 1997).

Small Differences

In contrast to Wampold's approach, Tolin (2010) analyzed 26 studies and adopted a different method whereby all therapies

were compared to a single comparator, namely CBT. The author reported significantly greater effects for CBT overall when compared to the other classes of therapy at posttherapy (d = 0.22, 95% CI [0.09, 0.35]), six-month follow-up (d = 0.47, 95% CI [0.29, 0.66]), and one-year follow-up (d = 0.34, 95% CI [0.06, 0.62]). At each of these three assessment times, across all conditions, CBT showed a consistently significant greater effect compared with psychodynamic therapy as follows: d = 0.28 (95% CI [0.12, 0.44]); d = 0.50 (95% CI [0.29, 0.71]); and d = 0.55 (95% CI [0.30, 0.81]), respectively. At the overall level, Tolin acknowledged that the ESs were small to medium but, invoking Rosenthal and Rubin's (1982) binomial effect size display, showed the posttherapy d value of 0.22 to equate to an 11% difference between treatments, which Tolin argued was not trivial. Baardseth et al. (2013) reanalyzed the data and reported broadly similar results for the omnibus test: g = 0.19 (95% CI [0.06, 0.31]) together with a finding of greater between-study heterogeneity in effect size than would be expected by chance alone. However, in an additional analysis of non-disorder-specific symptom outcomes for all studies that reported such measures (k = 18, n = 1359), the omnibus ES was not significant: g = 0.05 (95% CI [–0.07, 0.17]).

In a study in which the authors adopted a strategy of adversarial collaboration (i.e., co-authors included CBT as well as psychodynamic researchers), Steinert et al. (2017) drew on data from 23 RCTs (N = 2,751) with the majority (i.e., 16) focusing on contrasts between psychodynamic and CBT and with 12 of the studies focusing on depression or anxiety. They set an equivalence interval value for g of –0.25 to 0.25. For target symptoms, analyses at posttreatment yielded g = –0.15 (90% equivalence CI [–0.23, –0.08]) and at follow-up g = –0.05 (90% equivalence CI [–0.14, 0.04]). Following the logic of equivalence and noninferiority trials, given that the CIs did not cross the prespecified +/– 0.25 boundary, they argued for equivalence. Notwithstanding the logic of the difference being within the prespecified tolerances, it can also be viewed that the findings reflect the consistent finding of non-CBT therapies yielding marginally inferior outcomes. In effect, findings are consistent with the overriding view that differences are small and that those differences, where they occur, tend to favor CBT-aligned therapies.

Dismantling and Additive Studies

Among the most rigorous designs for evaluating causative mechanisms are studies that take an effective treatment and break it down into its various components (i.e., they subtract treatment elements and thereby dismantle it) or studies that add elements to an existing treatment and then contrast the outcomes. In general, the results from comparative, dismantling, and component analysis studies suggest the general equivalence of treatments based on different theories and techniques. Ahn and Wampold (2001) examined component analyses conducted over an 18-year period and found that adding or removing components of a treatment did not change the effects of the core treatment. Wampold (2001) believes that the lack of findings within these dismantling and constructive designs suggests that "there is little evidence that specific ingredients are necessary to produce psychotherapeutic change" (p. 126). It appears that subtracting elements that are considered essential to the success of a treatment does not lessen its effectiveness. Bell et al. (2013) also conducted a meta-analysis of both dismantling (*k* = 30) and additive (*k* = 36) studies but, unlike Ahn and Wampold's study, analyzed the results separately. A small effect (*d* = 0.14) was found for the treatment with the additional component in the additive studies but no effect was found for the dismantling studies (*d* = 0.10).

Crucially, however, altering a component of a treatment either by addition or omission would require anticipating a small effect size (i.e., the two treatments would have more common than not) and to be adequately powered to test for such an effect would, according to Cohen's (1992) sampling tables, require a total sample size in the region of 800, a view also arrived at by Bell et al. (2013) in their conclusion. Indeed, they were pessimistic about the yield of such studies given the statistical power required. In light of these parameters, conclusions from dismantling or additive studies that fall well short of these indicative sample sizes and yield nonsignificant findings should be eschewed. A more general conclusion was reached by Cuijpers (2016) in relation to comparisons between any two treatments as he argued that evidence for differential effects are, at best small, and that virtually all studies have been underpowered statistically, thereby questioning any claim by any therapy to show an advantage.

Accounting for Similarities and Differences

In focusing on the efficacy and effectiveness of highly diverse psychological therapies, the general finding of, at most, little difference in the outcomes requires explanation, and there are a number of credible accounts. It is possible that the research strategies, methods, and the measures (of both outcomes and processes) used are not sufficiently sensitive to differences between the therapies. Indeed, the most parsimonious explanation for a no difference finding is lack of power (i.e., a Type II error). It is also possible that different therapies achieve similar goals through different processes. Each school of therapy purports and promotes differing techniques and emphasizes differing procedures that are overtly distinguishable in content and yet yield similar outcomes (i.e., different pathways). Or, that different therapies embody a set of factors that are common to all therapies. These common factors may facilitate (i.e., enable) change or they may be curative in themselves. It is likely that any of the above accounts could be advocated and defended because of the ambiguity of the data or because there is not enough evidence available to rule out alternative explanations. Suggestions for different research strategies have been made (e.g., Watkins & Newbold, 2020) and informed conceptual reviews of possible explanations provided (see Stiles et al., 1986).

One possibility noted above is that different therapies share various common factors. Lambert (2013) presented a listing of common factors (see Table 5.3), which organizes

TABLE 5.3   Sequential Listing of Common Factors Present Across Psychotherapies

Support factors	Learning factors	Action factors
Catharsis/release of tension	Advice	Facing fears
Mitigation of isolation	Affective re-experiencing	Cognitive mastery
Structure/organization	Assimilating problematic experiences	Encouragement of experimenting with new behaviors
Positive relationship	Cognitive learning	Taking risks
Reassurance	Corrective emotional experience	Mastery efforts
Safe environment	Feedback	Modeling
Identification with therapist	Insight	Practice
Therapeutic alliance	Rationale	Reality testing
Therapist/client active participation	Exploration of internal frame of reference	Success experiences
Recognition of therapist expertness	Changing expectations of personal effectiveness	Working through
Therapist warmth, respect, empathy, acceptance, genuineness	Reframing of self-perceptions	Behavioral/emotional regulation
Trust/open exploration		

Lambert, M. J. (2013). The efficacy and effectiveness of psychotherapy. In M. J. Lambert (Ed.), *Bergin and Garfield's handbook of psychotherapy and behavior change* (6th ed., pp. 169–218). New York: Wiley. Reprinted with permission.

these into three groupings that might represent a possible sequence presumed to operate in psychological therapies, namely support, learning, and action. Together, they point to the possibility that all therapies provide a cooperative working endeavor in which a client's increased sense of trust, security, and safety, along with decreases in tension, threat, and anxiety, lead to changes in conceptualizing their problems and ultimately in acting differently by reframing fears, taking risks, and working through problems.

The developmental sequence is assumed to be at least partially mediated through factors common across therapies. The developmental nature of this sequence presumes that the supportive functions precede changes in beliefs and attitudes, which precede the therapist's attempts to encourage patient action. Table 5.3 lists a variety of common factors attributable to the therapist, therapy procedures, and the client.

Since the last edition of this chapter, there have been a number of key contributions to this area. First, Wampold (2015) provided a summary of the estimates of the differing components associated with common and specific factors set within a contextual (in contrast to a medical) model of therapy. It was argued that the evidence showed greater association between outcome and common factors than with specific factors. The estimates of the differing components associated with common factors within a contextual model are shown in Figure 5.2 in which factors associated with common factors are on the left and specific factors on the right. Factors are ordered according to their effect size (i.e., height) as

determined by meta-analytic studies and the extent of studies (i.e., evidence) according to their width. The effect sizes are primarily drawn from the 2011 *Relationships that Work* series of articles. Second, Norcross and Lambert (2018) published an update to their text on psychotherapy relationships that work. As an example, in an updated meta-analysis on the alliance, they identified 105 new studies since 2010, thereby providing 295 independent studies in total. Results yielded an ES of 0.58 when combined with studies from the earlier reviews (Flückiger et al., 2018). Hence, the finding appears to be robust and held regardless of the assessor perspective taken, specific alliance and outcome measures, treatment approaches, patient characteristics, and country in which the study was conducted. Of course, the nature of this and such studies is correlational, which does not advance our understanding of causality. Third, Cuijpers, Reijnders et al. (2019) provided a review of common factors and were critical of the *Evidence-Based Therapy Relationships* work: "The complexities involved in examining how therapies work make this an overly optimistic summary of the literature" (p. 222). For their part, Cuijpers et al. provide a more sobering account, concluding that after 30 years of mediational research, it is not clear whether the factors that lead to therapeutic change are specific, common, or both.

Set against these perspectives, we are encouraged by more novel research combining insightful conceptual work and intensive data sampling. For example, recent work on the alliance has proposed a two-component model involving a

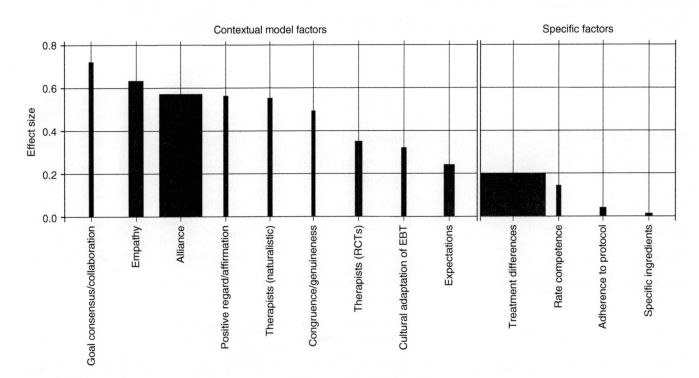

FIGURE 5.2 Effect Sizes for Common Factors of the Contextual Model and Specific Factors

Note: Width of bars is proportional to number of studies on which effect is based. RCTs – randomized controlled trials; EBT – evidence-based treatments. Wampold B. E. (2015). How important are the common factors in psychotherapy? An update. *World Psychiatry, 14*(3), 270–277. Reprinted with permission.

distinction between trait-like and state-like alliance in which the trait-like component determines a client's ability to form a strong alliance with their therapist and thereby enables other active ingredients to operate (Zilcho-Mano, 2017). By contrast, it is the state-like component that develops across therapy that is potentially curative and it is these within-client changes in state-like alliances across the course of therapy that should become the focus of research. And it is the increasing adoption of session-by-session measurement that opens up new horizons for moving from a single snapshot of a process variable to a dependable measure with the ability to show temporal relationships between process variables and client outcomes.

Summary

The foregoing meta-analyses that examine the comparative effectiveness of differing theories of psychotherapy or modalities of psychological therapies reveal a mixed picture. There is a strong trend toward no differences between techniques or modalities in the amount of change produced as realized in terms of small effect sizes (either Cohen's *d* or Hedges' *g*). This, in turn, is counterbalanced by indications that, under some circumstances, certain methods (generally cognitive behavioral) yield some advantage. In relation to comparisons between therapy modalities, Wampold et al. (1997) raised the valid question as to why researchers pursue treatment differences that are known to be small in the context of other areas such as therapist effects (see Chapter 9). And this is an argument for redressing the balance and focusing not only on treatments but on other salient proximal factors (e.g., therapists) as well as more distal factors (e.g., social context). But it is not, in itself, an argument for ignoring small effects where they occur, particularly with some consistency. The danger is that the labeling of a *d* value of 0.20 as small relegates investigations into accounting for such differences. Cohen acknowledged that labelling an effect of *d* = 0.20 as small was arbitrary. A more pragmatic as well as applicable approach would be to ask what the meaning or clinical implications are of any given effect, particularly when it comes to delivering psychological therapies at scale. In such a situation, a small difference on a large (i.e., population) scale can matter. Sanders and Hunsley (2018) provide an example of an ES of 0.2, which equates to an NNT of 9 (see Table 5.1), meaning that if two treatments are available, then 18 patients would need to be seen for there to be one additional gain. Transposed into a setting of a large clinic, a health care system, or a national program (e.g., the English Improving Access to Psychological Therapies [IAPT] program), the number of patients who could potentially benefit from being assigned to an alternative treatment with a small effect advantage would be considerable. Hence, as we strive both to improve outcomes and to deliver psychological therapies at scale, there may be an argument for being more responsive to (consistent) differences of any size in relation to treatments and the contexts in which they are delivered. This is not an argument for seeking to identify a dominant therapy, but rather to seek a greater understanding of effects that, at a population level, might enhance the outcomes for people seeking help.

Are Some Psychological Therapies More Effective Than Others With Specific Conditions?

Estimates of treatment effects, based on studies of specific disorders with well-defined psychotherapies, provide a more refined baseline for average treatment effects. In the following section, treatment effects are reviewed in relation to two broad classes of clinical presentations: (i) common mental health conditions, namely mood disorders (depression, chronic/persistent depression, bipolar disorder), anxiety disorders (i.e., generalized anxiety disorder [GAD], panic disorder, social anxiety), and obsessive-compulsive and related disorders (i.e., obsessive-compulsive disorder [OCD] and post-traumatic stress disorder [PTSD]); and (ii) personality disorders. Importantly, the reported studies do not act as a thorough review, but rather are illustrative of recent literature.

Mood Disorders

At the time of the last *Handbook* edition (2013), Hollon and Ponniah (2010) provided a summary overview in which they reviewed 125 studies evaluating empirically supported treatments for mood disorders. They reported that for major depressive disorder, including more severely depressed patients, interpersonal therapy (IPT), CBT – in particular, cognitive therapy (CT) – as well as behavioral activation (BA) and problem-solving therapy (PST) were as efficacious as medications. They declared the results for dynamic and humanistic-experiential therapies to be mixed and noted that marital and family therapies were not frequently tested. They found that CT and mindfulness-based cognitive therapy (MBCT) have enduring effects with the potential for reducing rates of recurrence. For dysthymia, their review was not encouraging with the exception of IPT which was considered possibly efficacious. And for bipolar, they noted that psychoeducation, interpersonal social rhythm therapy, CBT, and family-focused therapy showed promise as adjuncts to medication in the treatment of bipolar. Interestingly, in relation to dynamic and humanistic approaches, the authors considered themselves to be more positive about dynamic and experiential approaches although they acknowledged that, at the time, more research evidence was needed. And on a strategic point, the authors stated a preference for the approach using the minimum number of positive studies in contrast to meta-analysis due to the issues with the quality of implementation of many interventions. In particular, they considered that leaving the accrual of evidence for dynamic and humanistic approaches to advocates of alternate approaches has not been helpful for these specific approaches and espoused the RCT as the method to show efficacy, sounding a clarion call: "Advocates for the more traditional interventions avoid their [RCTs] use at the peril of their preferred interventions" (p. 926).

Since that review and the last edition of this chapter, Cuijpers (2017) reviewed 40 years of research on depression. On the basis of evidence from meta-analyses comprising a minimum of 10 studies per modality compared with control conditions, Cuijpers reported evidence supporting a range of therapies listed as follows with their associated *g* values (95% CI): CBT, 0.71 (0.62, 0.79); BA, 0.74 (0.56, 0.91); IPT, 0.60 (0.45, 0.75); problem-solving therapy, 0.83 (0.45, 1.21), nondirective supportive therapy, 0.58 (0.45, 0.72); and short-term psychodynamic therapy, 0.61 (0.33, 0.88). When these results are translated into numbers needed to treat (NNT), all the modalities obtain an NNT of 3 except for problem-solving, for which the NNT is 2. And in a wide-ranging review of CBT, Hofmann et al. (2012) reviewed 269 studies spanning 17 disorder/population categories, of which 35 were depression/dysthymia and 10 bipolar disorder. While CBT was superior (yielding medium effects) compared with passive control conditions, comparisons with active treatments yielded equivocal results.

Network meta-analysis of 91 studies of CBT was used by López-López et al. (2019) who classified mode of delivery as either face-to-face CBT, multimedia CBT, or hybrid CBT (defined as multimedia CBT with one or more face-to-face sessions). There was strong evidence for the superiority of CBT compared with treatment as usual for the treatment of depression: face-to-face CBT with a standardized difference in mean change (and 95% credible intervals) of –1.11 (95% CrI [–1.62, –0.60]) but with more uncertainty for hybrid CBT –1.06 (95% CrI [–2.05, –0.08]) and multimedia CBT of –0.59 (95% CrI [–1.20, 0.02]). By contrast, waitlist controls showed detrimental effects equivalent to a standardized difference in mean change of 0.72 (0.09, 1.35). However, they noted that treatment as usual is a highly heterogeneous grouping as a standard comparator and hence yields higher levels of uncertainty. Hence, while these findings are evidence for the overall effectiveness of CBT as a class of intervention in the treatment of depression, no evidence was found in support of any specific effects for components of CBT. Hence, the call is still for more exacting research on which components in what circumstances yield the best outcomes for patients.

One argument that has been espoused since the last edition of this review is that the effectiveness of CBT has reduced since the time of the Smith and Glass meta-analysis. Johnsen and Friborg (2015) analyzed 70 eligible studies utilizing CBT in the treatment of depression from 1977 to 2014. Their main finding was that the treatment effect of CBT showed a declining trend across time for both the Beck Depression Inventory (BDI) and Hamilton Rating Scale for Depression (HRSD). The authors concluded that contemporary clinical treatment trials appear to be less effective than the therapies conducted decades ago. Reanalyses by others (Ljótsson et al., 2017) and extensions to the database (Cristea, Hollon et al., 2017) resulted in a rebuttal (Friborg & Johnsen, 2017). Notwithstanding the minutiae of countering statistical arguments, Dobson (2016) commented that the nature of trials themselves has changed over the years, with greater attention to fidelity in earlier years giving way to a relaxation of many exclusion criteria in later years, as well as greater subsequent use of treatment as usual comparisons. The argument put forward was that the art and science of research (trials) changes over time and, as such, provides a timely reminder that in an increasingly multicultural world, care should be taken in extrapolating from historical studies.

Set against the continuing evidence for the efficacy of CBT in the treatment of mood disorders, a notable advance since the Lambert (2013) review – and a response to Hollon and Ponniah's (2010) call – has been the growing evidence in support of alternate therapy modalities. For example, a study of short-term psychodynamic psychotherapy (STPP) for depression by Driessen et al. (2015) reported STPP to be effective in the treatment of depression in adults. The study comprised 54 comparisons from 33 RCTs (*N* = 3,946 participants) with results showing STPP to be significantly more effective than a cluster of differing types of control conditions at posttreatment on measures of depression, general psychopathology and quality of life measures (*d*s = 0.49 to 0.69). Pre- to posttreatment changes (*d*s = 0.57 to 1.18) showed significant improvements on all outcome measures, which either maintained or significantly improved further at follow-up (*d*s = 0.20 to 1.04). No significant differences were found between individual STPP and other psychotherapies at posttreatment (*d* = –0.14) or follow-up (*d* = –0.06). Importantly, these analyses were adequately powered to detect a clinically relevant difference. Although more high-quality studies are needed, particularly to assess the efficacy of STPP compared to specific control conditions and at follow-up as well as to antidepressants, these findings add to the evidence-base of short-term psychodynamic psychotherapy in the treatment for depression.

At a superordinate level, a meta-analysis by Cuijpers, Karyotaki, de Wit et al. (2020) considered eight generic classes of psychological therapies for the treatment of depression and 15 therapy-specific formats across three control conditions: wait list, care as usual, and other (not specified). The unadjusted ESs in the form of *d* values, together with their 95% CIs, for the eight classes in comparison with wait list, care as usual, and other control conditions are summarized in Table 5.4. At an overall level, when outliers (*g* > 2) were removed, the ES showed wait list to yield the largest effect with the 95% CIs nonoverlapping with the other two control conditions. In terms of therapies, in none of the three control condition comparisons did CBT yield the largest ES. Moreover, inspection of Table 5.4 and focusing on the seven main theoretical models (i.e., excluding Life review and Other) shows the 95% CIs for CBT to overlap with the CIs for the other main approaches within each of the three control conditions, indicative of there being no clear evidence of a superiority of CBT, or any other therapy. However, this is in large part due to the small numbers of studies in most comparisons leading to wide confidence intervals for specific therapy classes other than CBT.

In addition to debates about the nature and appropriateness of differing control conditions, the Cuijpers, Karyotaki, de Wit et al. (2020) meta-analysis raises two key issues that have bedeviled attempts to determine the effects of psychological therapies: (i) pooling therapies into classes; and (ii) issues arising from making between-study comparisons as opposed to within-study comparisons (see Baldwin & Imel, 2020). Regarding the former, put simply, what is included in, for example CBT, may differ across studies, thereby making the entity of CBT different in different meta-analyses. And, with the continual advancements in clinical techniques, the content of a therapy in the 1980s may well – some might say, ought to – be different in some form from that utilized in more recent trials. Hence, it cannot be assumed that the class of therapy named as CBT in one meta-analysis matches the same label in another study. And in relation to the second issue, it has been argued earlier that attention is better paid to same experiment data – that is, within-study comparisons due to the inherent unreliability of assuming like-for-like comparisons between studies when referring to a supposed specific brand of therapy (see Shapiro & Shapiro, 1982).

Dysthymia, Chronic Depression, and Bipolar Disorder. In contrast to meta-analyses on major depression, there are a limited number of meta-analyses that examine the effects of psychotherapy on chronic depression and dysthymia. Compared with a range of control groups (placebo, care-as-usual, nonspecific control, or waiting list), psychological therapy has a small but significant effect ($d = 0.23$ (95% CI [0.06, 0.41]), which corresponds to an NNT of 8 (Cuijpers, van Straten, Schuurmans et al., 2010). When the effects of psychological treatments were directly compared with those of pharmacotherapy in 10 comparisons, the mean effect size was $d = -0.31$ (95% CI [-0.53, -0.09]), indicating a superior effect of pharmacotherapy (NNT = 6). The authors recommended a minimum of 18 sessions for psychological therapies to be effective. And in a network meta-analysis for persistent depression, Kriston et al. (2014) reported interpersonal psychotherapy with medication to outperform

medication alone in chronic major depression but not in dysthymia.

In relation to bipolar disorder, for several decades, lithium was overwhelmingly the most widespread treatment and has been shown to be more effective than placebo in preventing manic relapse (Geddes et al., 2004; Perlis et al., 2006). Adding psychotherapies to a mood stabilizer regimen has been shown to reduce rates of relapse over one to two years (Miklowitz & Scott, 2009). More recently, Ye et al. (2016) analyzed nine randomized controlled trials with 520 bipolar I or II disorder patients and found CBT did not significantly reduce the relapse rate of bipolar disorder or improve the mania, depression, and mixed episodes. While subgroup analyses showed that CBT had short-term efficacy in reducing relapse rate of BD (at six month follow-up), there was no effect of CBT on level of depression in bipolar disorder.

Across the Lifespan. Mindful that the focus in this chapter is predominantly on adults, it is important to locate the effects of the psychological therapies across the full life-span. In one of the largest meta-analyses to date, Cuijpers, Karyotaki, Eckshtain et al. (2020) pooled data from 366 trials ($N = 36,702$) to consider the effect of the psychological therapies versus a control condition for children (13 years and younger), adolescents (≥13–18 years), young adults (≥18–24 years), middle-aged adults (≥24–55 years), older adults (≥55–75 years) and older old

TABLE 5.4 Summary Table Showing Non-adjusted ESs for Eight Generic Therapy Classes in Three Control Comparisons for Depression

	Waiting list			Care-as-usual			Other (not specified)		
	N	g	95% CI	N	g	95% CI	N	g	95% CI
All comparisons	157	0.73	0.69, 0.77	165	0.63	0.55, 0.70	63	0.57	0.43, 0.70
Excluding outliers	140	0.73	0.66, 0.79	160	0.57	0.50, 0.63	61	0.47	0.37, 0.57
Therapy class									
Cognitive behavioral therapy	90	0.96	0.83, 1.08	86	0.59	0.50, 0.69	28	0.54	0.35, 0.73
Behavioral activation therapy	10	**1.42**	**0.91, 1.93**	8	0.85	0.53, 1.18	3	0.67	0.34, 0.99
3rd wave cognitive behavioral therapy	13	0.87	0.59, 1.16	4	0.93	0.49, 1.38	2	0.71	0.25, 1.16
Problem-solving therapy	16	0.80	0.52, 1.08	8	**0.99**	**0.43, 1.54**	6	0.27	-0.03, 0.57
Interpersonal therapy	2	0.88	0.24, 1.52	19	0.63	0.29, 0.97	6	0.35	0.09, 0.61
Psychodynamic therapy	1	1.09	0.19, 1.99	8	0.32	0.08, 0.55	3	0.38	-0.34, 1.09
Non-directive therapy	4	1.11	0.32, 1.91	13	0.42	0.30, 0.54	2	**0.97**	**0.52, 1.42**
Life review therapy	4	0.61	0.29, 0.93	5	0.83	0.44, 1.22	5	1.74	0.62, 2.86
Other therapy	21	0.61	0.49, 0.72	18	0.70	0.51, 0.88	13	0.73	0.32, 1.18

Note: Bold signifies largest effect size within control condition. Data extracted from Cuijpers, P., Karyotaki, E., de Wit, L., & Ebert, D. D. (2020). The effects of fifteen evidence-supported therapies for adult depression: A meta-analytic review. *Psychotherapy Research, 30*(3), 279–293. Adapted with permission.

adults (75 years and older). While the overall ES for all aged groups was $g = 0.75$ (95% CI [0.67, 0.82], the equivalent ES for children was low ($g = 0.35$; 95% CI [0.15, 0.55]) and for young adults was high ($g = 0.98$; 95% CI [0.79, 1.16]). The authors reported no significant difference between older adults ($g = 0.66$; 95% CI [0.51, 0.82]) and older old adults ($g = 0.97$; 95% CI [0.42, 1.52]). The suggestion is that the psychological therapies are less effective with children and they reported no significant difference across the adult age groups. However, the authors advised caution due to the high level of heterogeneity ($I^2 = 80\%$). The finding for older adults was very similar to an earlier study in which Cuijpers, Karyotaki et al. (2014) conducted a meta-analysis comprising 44 studies with participants aged 50 or more and compared psychological therapies to control groups, other therapies, or pharmacotherapy. The overall effect size indicating the difference between therapy and control groups was $g = 0.64$ (95% CI [0.47, 0.80]), which corresponds to an NNT of 3. Evidence was stronger for CBT and problem-solving therapy.

Notwithstanding the effectiveness of the psychological therapies for substantial portions of people across the lifespan, delivery of any therapy needs to be context dependent. For example, in a systematic review of 27 qualitative studies, Frost et al. (2019) found evidence of limited time in consultations and the complexity of needs in later life meant physical health was often prioritized over mental health, particularly in people with frailty. Good management of late-life depression appeared to depend more on the skills and interest of individual General/Family Practitioners and nurses than on any structured approach.

Guidelines and Choice. In considering the available evidence, the American Psychological Association (APA) guidelines for depression (APA, 2019) recommended either second generation antidepressants or one of various forms of psychological therapy, for which they determined there to be similar levels of effectiveness and therefore not able to recommend any specific monotherapy for initial treatment. Their list comprised the following: behavioral therapy, cognitive, cognitive behavioral (CBT), and mindfulness-based cognitive-therapy (MBCT), interpersonal psychotherapy (IPT), psychodynamic therapies, and supportive therapy. Importantly, these interventions are listed in the context of shared decision making and offer individuals choice, although such choice will always be a function of availability and access.

Summary

In summary, Lambert (2013) previously concluded that individuals in receipt of psychological therapies for mood disorders can expect considerable relief, although the extent will be determined by its type and chronicity. Our observations now are that the range of bona fide psychological therapies available offers individuals choice within the context of no definitive evidence of the superiority of one approach over another. That said, guideline review bodies, as is their function, revisit and seek new data to support specific therapies. As such, we reiterate Hollon and Ponniah's (2010) call referenced earlier in this section in order to ensure that there is a continuing source of evidence for the broad range of bona fide psychological therapies in the treatment of mood disorders.

Anxiety Disorders: Multiple Conditions

Since the previous edition of the *Handbook*, the taxonomy of anxiety disorders within DSM-5 has been revised (e.g., Craske et al., 2017). Accordingly, this section addresses the cluster comprising generalized anxiety disorder (GAD), panic disorder (PD), and social anxiety disorder (SAD), while the now-differentiated classifications of obsessive-compulsive and related disorders (i.e., OCD) and trauma- and stressor-related disorders (i.e., PTSD) are addressed subsequently. Notwithstanding these distinctions, many research outputs have addressed multiple conditions from the above listing, and such studies are documented first before presenting selected studies on specific conditions.

In an updated and extended study originally conducted by Hofmann and Smits (2008), Carpenter et al. (2018) analyzed 41 studies comparing CBT treatments to placebos for a range of anxiety-related conditions (acute stress disorder, GAD, PD, & SAD) as well as for PTSD and OCD. The between-group effect sizes for continuous measures of target disorder symptoms from pre- to posttreatment were in the medium range (Hedges' $g = 0.56$, 95% CI [0.44, 0.69]). Accordingly, the authors concluded that CBT was a moderately efficacious treatment for this cluster of conditions when compared with a placebo with specific diagnostic groups showing effects to be highest (large) for OCD ($g = 1.13$ [0.58, 1.68]) and GAD ($g = 1.01$ [0.44, 1.57]) and lower (medium) for PTSD ($g = 0.48$ [0.26, 0.71]), SAD ($g = 0.41$ [0.26, 0.57]), and PD ($g = 0.39$ [0.12, 0.65]). Just less than half the studies (22) reported follow-up data for an average of 5.5 months yielding an effect size for target disorder symptoms of $g = 0.47$ (95% CI [0.30, 0.64]). Hence it appears that, overall, sufficient benefit remains at around six months from gains made in the course of therapy.

Cuijpers, Cristea et al. (2016) carried out a meta-analysis comparing CBT with wait list, care as usual, or pill placebo for GAD, PD, and SAD, as well as for major depressive disorder. The study yielded a total of 144 trials and 184 comparisons with large ESs for GAD, $g = 0.80$ (95% CI [0.67, 0.93]), PD, $g = 0.81$ (95% CI [0.59, 1.04]), SAD, $g = 0.88$ (95% CI [0.74, 1.03]), and major depressive disorder, $g = 0.75$ (95% CI [0.64, 0.97]). However, two caveats need to be made. First, these ESs are averages of a mix of comparator conditions and, as has already been noted, the effect size is a function of the type of control comparison used; and second, only 17.4% of trials were deemed to be high quality. Crucially, findings were larger when comparisons were made with a wait-list condition (>80% of trials) and small to moderate when compared with care as usual or pill placebo. Specific details of each of these four conditions is considered later in this section.

A metric that has more direct relevance to clinical practice is that of remission rates and these have been investigated in relation to CBT and anxiety disorders by Springer et al. (2018) who reported an overall remission rate of 51% (95% CI [47.8%, 54.2%]). For patients completing treatment, studies of PTSD yielded the highest remission rates (62.8%), followed by GAD (56.3%), PD (and/or agoraphobia) (55.5%), SAD

(40.4%), and OCD (45.2%). The overall remission rate across anxiety disorders for intent-to-treat (ITT) samples was 47.9% at posttreatment and 53.0% at follow-up, while the remission rate for completer samples was, understandably, slightly higher at 53.6% for posttreatment and 56.1% for follow-up. As previously noted, these results suggest posttreatment gains are sustained at follow-up. In addition, as might be expected, analyses of completer samples yield better rates than ITT samples where the latter comprises all patients randomized to treatments regardless of whether they completed the course of treatment. However, implications from this work are that the rates leave considerable room for improvement with the corollary that research efforts need to move from focusing on efficacy at the end of treatment to enhancing and maintaining remission rates, a focus akin to greater attention on longer-term effects of therapy.

Longer-Term Outcomes. The issue of longer-term effects generally is considered at the end of this chapter, but more immediately regarding longer-term treatment effects of CBT for the anxiety disorders, van Dis et al. (2020) sampled 69 randomized clinical trials (N = 4118) that were mainly of low quality. They found CBT compared with control conditions to be associated with improved outcomes after treatment completion. Their analyses established Hedges' g effect sizes for three occasions: posttreatment, 1–6 months follow-up, and 6–12 months follow-up. Across these three occasions, the ES for panic disorder was small and was highest at 6–12 months (g = 0.35), with GAD showing a similar pattern but with the highest at posttreatment and 6–12 months (g = 0.39 and 0.40, respectively), while g = 0.60 was the highest ES for SAD. The specific phobias, PTSD, and OCD returned consistently higher ESs (medium to large) with the highest for specific phobia being at 1–6 months (g = 0.72), for PTSD at posttreatment (g = 0.72), and for OCD at 1–6 months (g = 0.85). In addition to these three assessment occasions, beyond 12 months the data was more limited and the ESs for only three conditions were still significant: GAD (g = 0.22), SAD (g = 0.42), and PTSD (g = 0.84). The conclusion was that the gains from CBT for the anxiety disorders as well as PTSD and OCD are moderate up to 12 months with strongest outcomes for PTSD beyond 12 months. Indeed, the authors identified the need for longer-term follow-up studies beyond 12 months.

Longer-term (enduring) impacts is one of two areas where an extension to the data traditionally collected in studies would be informative, with the other area being impacts on quality of life. Regarding the former, longer-term effects have been investigated by Bandelow et al. (2018) who found that gains with psychological therapies were maintained for up to two years with a significant improvement over time showing for CBT, while a medication group remained stable during the treatment-free period. Patients in a placebo condition did not deteriorate but showed worse outcomes than those in receipt of CBT. And in relation to the impact on quality of life of CBT for anxiety disorders, Hofmann et al. (2014) reported medium effects for both pre–post within-group (g = 0.54, 95% CI [0.45, 0.63]) and pre-post controlled effect sizes (g = 0.56, 95% CI [0.32, 0.80]). The impact was particularly strong in the physical and psychological domains and provided evidence that CBT

has a beneficial effect on quality of life, especially when CBT is conducted over a longer course of time and person-to-person.

Self-Help Interventions. A major development over the past 20 years has been the growth of self-help interventions that have had a natural fit with anxiety disorders. Haug et al. (2012) reported a large ES g = 0.78 (95% CI [0.67, 0.90]) when comparing self-help with wait list or placebo controls, but also found a small effect favoring person-to-person over self-help interventions, g = –0.20 (–0.37, 0.02). Other research on the effectiveness of internet interventions for GAD has been reported to be on a par with person-to-person interventions (Richards et al., 2015), while Andersson et al. (2019) reported on an umbrella review of recent meta-analyses of internet-delivered CBT (iCBT) and concluded it to be as effective as person-to-person CBT. Meta-analytic findings from Grist and Cavanagh (2013) yielded an overall ES of g = 0.77 (95% CI [0.59, 0.95]) in favor of computerized CBT interventions compared with control conditions and argued the results were comparable to the average effect size of person-to-person CBT interventions for common mental health disorders (d = 0.68, Haby et al., 2006). This finding corroborates those of previous meta-analyses that have typically found medium to large effect sizes in favor of the effectiveness of computerized CBT in comparison to control conditions (Andersson & Cuijpers, 2009; Barak et al., 2008; Spek et al., 2007).

However, O'Kearney et al. (2019) concluded that, based on evidence from head-to-head RCTs, it is premature to suggest that the treatment effects of CBT for anxiety disorders delivered by the internet or computer are equivalent to or not less than those of therapist-delivered CBT, or that internet CBT with minimal therapist contact is an equivalent first-line treatment to in-person CBT (Andersson et al., 2014; Andrews, Basu et al., 2018; Andrews, Bell et al., 2018; Carlbring et al., 2018). They considered that, with one exception (i.e., Hedman et al., 2011), this comparison has not been addressed in properly conducted noninferiority RCTs of CBT for anxiety disorders, PTSD, or OCD. Similarly, Gilbody et al. (2015), in a large pragmatic RCT comprising 691 patients, found that neither a commercially available nor a free computerized CBT package yielded better outcomes in depression than standard general practitioner care either in the short term or long term (i.e., 24 months).

Non-CBT therapies. In contrast to the mood disorders, cognitive models of anxiety disorders have had considerable success over the years, which has made the development of CBT-oriented interventions a natural consequence. However, attention in recent years has also focused on non-CBT therapies for anxiety and related conditions. Keefe et al. (2014) analyzed 14 studies of psychodynamic therapies for a range of anxiety disorders. The pre–post effect size was g = 1.06 (95% CI [0.79, 1.33]) with an overall effect of g = 0.64 (95% CI [0.35, 0.94]) with no differential effects when compared with other active treatments (g = 0.02, 95% CI [–0.21, 0.26]). The authors concluded that psychodynamic therapy did not differ in its effectiveness from other psychological interventions for anxiety, with results obtaining for primary and secondary measures as well as at follow-up. With data on dropout rates being no different from other active treatments, the authors concluded that psychodynamic therapy for anxiety disorders as delivered in RCTs is well tolerated. But there was a suggestion that larger studies may show potentially true differences in treatment effects. The issue of ensuring that trials are adequately powered is crucial. And a noteworthy conclusion emphasized the point that no single treatment is going to be effective for all patients, suggesting therefore that there should be a particular focus on identifying those subgroups of patients for whom psychodynamic therapy is particularly efficacious.

Taking a slightly different perspective, Fonagy (2015) provided a wide-ranging review of the effectiveness of psychodynamic therapies for mental health conditions. Of note, and mirroring the earlier point made by Hollon and Ponniah (2013), Fonagy focused on selective individual studies rather than meta-analytic studies, arguing that there is a benefit in considering quality trials reporting individual patient data as opposed to pooled effects. Social anxiety, as well as, likely, general anxiety and panic disorder, were identified as being amenable to a generic psychodynamic approach but was clear on the lack of supporting evidence for PTSD and OCD, the two conditions differentiated from the anxiety disorders in DSM-5 and the two that yielded predominantly large differential effects in the van Dis et al. (2020) meta-analysis focusing on CBT.

Psychodynamic therapies more generally have been reviewed by Leichsenring and Klein (2014) and, in the area of anxiety disorders, they reported evidence of no differences for certain conditions although the Ns for the study samples were small, making such studies vulnerable to Type II errors. But in a general perspective on treatments for mental health conditions generally, Leichsenring and Steinert (2017) presented challenges to the view that CBT is the main (or only) approach to the treatment of common mental health conditions. Arguments included the relative paucity of high-quality comparisons; variability in the type of control condition, with the majority using a wait-list comparison that is inferred to be weaker; the effects of uncontrolled researcher allegiance; the attribution of change in CBT to cognitive mechanisms; and findings where CBT does not yield superior outcomes. The authors acknowledged that CBT is the most researched therapy but challenged that it is, de facto, the gold standard and, in contrast, espoused a position of plurality both in research and treatment in the context of no treatment being suitable for all patients.

Summary

Studies addressing clusters of anxiety disorders have found effects ranging from medium to large, with evidence that gains achieved in treatment are likely to last at least six months. The differentiated classifications of OCD and PTSD appear to yield larger effects, which may endorse their separation from the anxiety disorders of GAD, PD, and SAD although the separation is contentious and not uniformly accepted. Of note is the practice of combining differing control conditions when drawing comparisons and also questions about the quality of many of the individual studies that contribute to a meta-analysis.

Anxiety Disorders: Specific Conditions

While reports, as represented by those above, have addressed multiple anxiety and related disorders, others have focused on specific disorders for anxiety. The previous edition of this chapter provided broad-brush summaries of specific anxiety disorders (Lambert, 2013). In this edition, we highlight primarily key (network or pairwise) meta-analytic studies published since the previous edition. But we also refer to specific trials that provide promise in relation to the provision of choice for people seeking treatment relating to each of the specific anxiety disorders as well as with passing comment on methodological advances and issues. Accordingly, in this section, we summarize selected studies that focus on discrete anxiety and related conditions. In order to provide an overview of the selected studies in this section, we have summarized in Table 5.5 what we consider to be robust evidence derived from meta-analyses in which the control condition was defined and not combined with other control conditions and for which there was a minimum of five studies contributing to the resulting effect size. We accept these criteria may be viewed as somewhat arbitrary, but in our reading of the literature, there was a tendency for contrasts using very small numbers of trials to yield results at the outer ranges of effects and we therefore excluded such contrasts.

Generalized Anxiety Disorder (GAD). A cluster of meta-analyses by Cuijpers and colleagues has yielded largely consistent results in terms of the effects of psychological therapies as an effective treatment for GAD. Cuijpers, Sijbrandij, Kool, Huibers et al. (2014) analyzed 41 studies focusing on GAD from which they were able to establish effects of psychological therapies with control groups in 38 comparisons from 28 studies. The overall effect was $g = 0.84$ (95% CI [0.71, 0.97]), with low to moderate but significant heterogeneity ($I^2 = 33\%$), corresponding to an NNT of 3. One key finding from this meta-analysis was the large effect on depression ($g = 0.71$, 95% CI [0.59, 0.82]). Cuijpers, Cristea et al.'s (2016) finding of a 0.80 effect size for psychological therapies reported earlier showed a difference between comparisons using wait list ($g = 0.85$, 95% CI [0.72, 0.99]) versus care as usual ($g = 0.45$, 95% CI [0.26, 0.64]). From a research perspective, only 9 of the 31 studies (29%) were deemed to be high-quality. Interestingly, however, when only high-quality studies were considered, the ESs remained very similar: 0.88 and 0.45 for wait list and care as usual comparisons, respectively. An updated meta-analysis was conducted by Carl et al. (2020) for GAD comprising 39 comparisons between psychological therapies and control conditions yielding a large ES ($g = 0.76$, 95% CI [0.61, 0.91]). By contrast, 43 comparisons between pharmacotherapy and control conditions yielded a small effect for medication ($g = 0.38$, 95% CI [0.30, 0.47]). This study also yielded differing effect sizes as a function of the control condition: wait-list controls ($n = 22$, $g = 0.90$, 95% CI [0.73, 1.08]), psychological placebo ($n = 10$, $g = 0.47$, 95% CI [0.25, 0.69]), and treatment as usual ($n = 5$, $g = 0.38$, 95% CI [0.05, 0.71]).

In sum, studies focusing on GAD show evidence-based psychological therapies to be effective, more so than medication or psychological placebo (see Table 5.5). But there are issues concerning the quality of the studies included in these meta-analyses.

Social Anxiety Disorder. Returning to the Cuijpers, Cristea et al. (2016) meta-analysis, this study yielded a large ES for CBT compared with predominantly wait-list controls (*g* = 0.88, 95% CI [0.74, 1.03]). But again, the size of the effect was a function of the control condition: wait list, *g* = 0.98 (95% CI [0.83, 1.14]); pill placebo, *g* = 0.47 (95% CI [0.24, 0.70]); and care as usual, *g* = 0.44 (95% CI [0.12, 0.77]). And of the 48 studies in total, only 8 (17%) were deemed to be of high quality. In a separate systematic review and meta-analysis, Guo et al. (2020) investigated social anxiety and found internet-CBT to be more effective than a wait-list control (*g* = −0.79; 95% CI [−0.92, −0.67]) and broadly equivalent with in-person CBT (*g* = −0.18; 95% CI [−0.45, 0.09]). Importantly, the effects appeared to be maintained at 6- and 12-month follow-up.

Network meta-analysis has been applied to the literature on SAD published between 1988 and 2013 from which 101 trials were sourced (Mayo-Wilson et al., 2014). Results showed various classes of psychological interventions to be effective when compared with a wait list: individual CBT (SMD −1.19, 95% CrI [−1.56, −0.81]), group CBT (−0.92, [−1.33, −0.51]), exposure and social skills (−0.86, [−1.42, −0.29]), self-help with support (−0.86, [−1.36, −0.36]), self-help without support (−0.75, [−1.25, −0.26]), and psychodynamic psychotherapy (−0.62, [−0.93, −0.31]). In addition, there was evidence of a differential effect in favor of individual CBT having a greater effect than both psychodynamic psychotherapy (SMD −0.56, 95% CrI [−1.03, −0.11]) and a class of other therapies that comprised interpersonal psychotherapy, mindfulness, and supportive therapy (−0.82, [−1.41, −0.24]). This dataset was further utilized by Mavranezouli et al. (2015) who reported the rankings of interventions according to the probability of recovery. These showed individual CBT based on the Clark and Wells (1995) model to be highest (*M* = 0.62; 95% CrI: [0.16, 0.95]), ahead of individual CBT (*M* = 0.47; 95% CrI: [0.08, 0.90]). Overall, the various forms of individual CBT showed high probabilities of recovery (range of mean probabilities of recovery from 0.39 to 0.62), while other individually delivered psychological therapies were less effective (mean probabilities of recovery varying from 0.16 to 0.26).

In sum, a range of interventions for SAD have been shown to be more effective than control conditions and comparisons between treatments appear to favor CBT or cognitive models and there is evidence that internet-based CBT can be effective. Table 5.5 shows broadly similar ESs to those for GAD for comparisons between psychological therapies and both placebo and wait-list controls.

Panic Disorder. The findings from a Cochrane review of psychological treatments for panic disorder concluded that there was no high-quality and unequivocal evidence lending support to one form of intervention over another for panic disorder with or without agoraphobia (Pompoli et al., 2016). The quantitative component of the review included 54 studies (3021 patients) and considered the primary outcome to be short-term remission. Two comparisons yielded 10 or more studies, namely CBT versus wait list yielding a superiority to CBT (OR = 7.7, 95% CI [4.5, 14.3]), and CBT versus behavioral therapy, which also favored CBT (OR = 2.09, 95% CI [1.10, 3.97]). The authors concluded that behavioral therapy did not appear to be a valid alternative to CBT.

Notwithstanding results favoring CBT, albeit they were small effects, the authors flagged promise for psychodynamic therapies on the basis of two included studies (Beutal et al., 2013; Milrod et al., 2007). More recently, Milrod et al. (2016) compared CBT, panic-focused psychodynamic psychotherapy (PFPP), and applied relaxation training (ART) for panic disorder in a trial conducted at two sites (Cornell University and University of Pennsylvania). Results favored both CBT and panic-focused psychodynamic psychotherapy in comparison to applied relaxation training although CBT was the more consistent treatment modality given that there was a significant treatment-by-site interaction. The overall response rates for CBT and panic-focused psychodynamic psychotherapy were 63% and 59%, respectively. However, considering the two sites separately, applied relaxation training was numerically best at one site (63.2%) and significantly worse at the other (30%). Even though both treatments were delivered equally at both sites, the treatment-by-site interaction flags up the potential perils of multi-center trials (see Chapter 20 for a comment by Hollon et al.). Notwithstanding this issue, the study is noteworthy in promoting comparative analyses in which a treatment with promise (i.e., panic-focused psychodynamic psychotherapy) was compared with a leading intervention (CBT) and followed up with investigations aimed at understanding the processes of therapeutic change in these two active treatments (Barber et al., 2020).

Relatedly, the question as to the effect of giving patients a choice between CBT or panic-focused psychodynamic psychotherapy on therapy outcomes was addressed by Svensson et al. (2020) in a comparison between panic control therapy and panic-focused psychodynamic psychotherapy. While there was no difference between these two treatments during or at follow-up, a differential effect did occur when panic severity was the index, with results favoring panic control therapy during treatment (SMD = −0.64, 95% CI [−1.02, −0.25]) and panic-focused psychodynamic psychotherapy during follow-up (SMD = 0.62, 95% CI [0.27, 0.98]). Hence, the provision of choice of treatment to patients appeared to confer no advantage in outcomes over randomization. From the perspective of research methodology, one notable feature of this study was the double randomization schedule in which participants were initially randomized to the randomized or choice arms and then, within the former, randomized again. By contrast, the choice arm participants selected their treatment. As such, double randomization is an aspired standard for the design of patient preference trials. However, the yield from patient preference trials is questionable and the processes involved in how patients make choices are unclear.

In sum, studies focusing on panic disorder appear to suggest no clear lead for any particular intervention, although CBT appears to yield better outcomes than behavioral therapy and there are promising results from studies of panic-focused psychodynamic therapy. The listed studies reported in

Table 5.5 show the same stepped effect between comparisons with placebo and those of wait lists.

Obsessive-Compulsive and Trauma- and Stressor-Related Disorders

We now consider OCD and PTSD and have grouped them separately from the anxiety disorders to reflect current diagnostic classification. The results are summarized in Table 5.5.

Obsessive-Compulsive Disorder (OCD). Öst et al. (2015) carried out a systematic review and meta-analysis of CBT for the period 1993–2014. The effect sizes for comparisons of CBT with wait list, $d = 1.31$ (95% CI [1.08, 1.55]), and placebo conditions, $d = 1.33$ (95% CI [0.91, 1.76]) were very large, whereas those for comparisons between individual versus group treatment, $d = 0.17$ (95% CI [–0.06, 0.40]), and exposure and response prevention versus cognitive therapy, $d = 0.07$ (95% CI [–0.15, 0.30]) were small and nonsignificant. CBT was significantly better than antidepressant medication, $d = 0.55$ (95% CI [0.05, 1.04]). However, Öst et al. noted that 37% of studies employed only one or two therapists, thereby introducing a fair degree of confounding.

The results were complemented by a network meta-analysis of psychological and pharmacological interventions conducted on 54 trials with 6652 participants (Skapinakis et al., 2016). Results showed all active psychological therapies had greater effects than drug placebo. However, somewhat unexpectedly, they found CBT to have a smaller effect than cognitive therapy or behavioral therapy, but such differences disappeared once wait-list controls were excluded and the authors' conclusion was that there was no real difference between these three psychological therapies (i.e., CT, CBT, and BT) for the treatment of OCD. But they also observed that many patients in psychological therapy trials are also on stable regimes of medication. Hence, they concluded that their results were limited to individuals on stable medication and, as such, lending support to evidence for the combined treatment of medication and psychological therapy, particularly when delivered to patients presenting with a more severe form of OCD.

Using a different methodology, Fisher et al. (2020) conducted an individual patient data meta-analysis with data available for 24 ($N = 1626$) of 43 eligible RCTs with results showing that treatment efficacy was moderated by treatment type. The most efficacious treatment was individual CT followed by group CT plus exposure and response prevention (ERP) and, to a lesser extent, individual ERP. Amongst these treatments, recovery rates of 55%, 42%, and 41%, respectively, were found at posttreatment, while asymptomatic rates of 41%, 24%, and 20%, respectively, were found at posttreatment. Of particular interest was the adoption of clinical significance as an indication of the actual benefit of psychological treatment. This showed that 32% of treated patients recovered posttreatment compared with 3% of controls, rising to 38% and falling to 21%, respectively, after three to six months. In addition, only 18% of treated patients were asymptomatic at posttreatment, although this was a higher percentage compared to controls at 4%. And at follow-up, only around 20% of patients were asymptomatic regardless of whether they were allocated to treatment or control conditions. Deterioration rates were very low (0–1%) and did not differ between treated and control patients at either posttreatment or at follow-up.

These studies focusing on OCD raise a number of research-related issues that mean some of the treatment effect may be confounded with therapist and/or medication effects. And while the overall effects appear particularly large in comparison to placebo (compared with other anxiety conditions), one estimate is that only approximately one-third of patients meet a criterion of clinically significant improvement posttreatment.

Post-Traumatic Stress Disorder (PTSD). Recently, two substantial reviews – one pairwise and one network meta-analysis – have provided results at the level of specific therapy models for PTSD (Lewis et al., 2020; Mavranezouli et al., 2020). The meta-analysis by Lewis et al. (2020) comprised 114 RCTs with 8171 participants yielding a total of 23 treatment comparisons with wait list or treatment as usual, along with 27 comparisons between treatments. They set thresholds for the effects of an intervention to be determined as being clinically important: > 0.80 for wait-list control comparisons, > 0.5 for attention control comparisons, > 0.4 for placebo control comparisons, and > 0.2 for any active treatment control comparisons. Using these criteria, they confirmed, as a class of interventions, support for therapies termed as CBT-T (trauma) as well as eye movement desensitization and reprocessing (EMDR). For the former, these specifically identified prolonged exposure, cognitive therapy, and cognitive processing therapy. However, somewhat alarmingly, of the 23 comparisons with control conditions, 21 were rated as low or very low-quality evidence, while all of the 27 comparisons with active treatments were rated as low or very low-quality evidence.

Applying network meta-analysis to the literature, Mavranezouli et al. (2020) analyzed 90 trials comprising 6560 individuals and 22 interventions focused on psychological interventions for PTSD. In comparisons with wait list, a range of interventions were effective, including EMDR (SMD = –2.07; 95% CrI: [–2.70, –1.44]), combined somatic/cognitive therapies (SMD = –1.69; 95% CrI: [–2.66, –0.73]), trauma-focused CBT (SMD = –1.46; 95% CrI [–1.87, –1.05]), and self-help with support (SMD = –1.46; 95% CrI [–2.33, –0.59]). Both EMDR and trauma-focused-CBT showed sustained effects at one- to four-month follow-up while EMDR, trauma-focused-CBT, self-help with support and counseling improved remission rates posttreatment. Results for other interventions were either inconclusive or based on limited evidence. However, the evidence was of moderate-to-low quality and there was a call for evidence of longer-term comparative effectiveness.

These studies provide strong support for CBT-based trauma therapies as well as EMDR for the treatment of PTSD. As shown in Table 5.5, whereas the placebo comparison is equivalent to other conditions reported here, as are the non-CBT and CBT-based psychological therapies, the ES for EMDR is at the upper limits of reported ranges for all conditions. However, the consistently lower quality of studies across these two analyses should be a concern.

TABLE 5.5   Summary Effect Sizes (95% CIs) for Anxiety Disorders, Obsessive-Compulsive and Related Disorders, and Trauma- and Stressor-Related Disorders: Illustrative Meta-Analytic Studies (2014–2020) of Psychological Therapies across a Range of Clinical Settings and Populations for Distinct Control Conditions and Effects Derived from a Minimum of Five Comparisons

Condition	Modality	Distinct control condition(s)	Effect sizes (Hedges' *g*/ SMD)	Source	Total *N* of studies
Generalized anxiety disorder	EBPs	TAU	*g* = 0.38 (0.05, 0.71)	Carl et al. (2020)	5
	EBPs	Psychological placebo	*g* = 0.47 (0.25, 0.69)	Carl et al. (2020)	10
	CBT/EBPs	WL	*g* = 0.85 (0.72, 0.99) to 0.90 (0.73, 1.08)	Cuijpers, Cristea et al. (2016)/Carl et al. (2020)	46
Social anxiety disorder	CBT	Pill placebo	*g* = 0.47 (0.24, 070)	Cuijpers, Cristea et al. (2016)	5
	CBT	Psychological/ pill placebo	*g* = 0.48 (0.26, 0.71)	Carpenter et al. (2018)	10
	Range of therapies (not CBT)	WL	*g* = –0.75 (–1.26, 0.26) to –0.86 (–1.42, –0.29)	Mayo-Wilson et al. (2014)/ Guo et al. (2020)	49
	group CBT	WL	*g* = –0.92 (–1.33, 0.51)	Mayo-Wilson et al. (2014)	28
	CBT	WL	*g* = 0.98 (0.83, 1.14) to –1.19 (–1.56, 0.81)	Cuijpers, Cristea et al. (2016)/ Mayo-Wilson et al. (2014)	55
Panic disorder	CBT	Pill placebo	*g* = 0.28 (0.03, 0.54)	Cuijpers, Cristea et al. (2016)	5
	CBT	WL	*g* = 0.96 (0.70, 1.23)	Cuijpers, Cristea et al. (2016)	33
Obsessive-compulsive disorder	CBT	Psychological placebo	*g* = 1.29 (0.76, 1.81)	Öst et al. (2015)	6
	CBT	WL	*g* = 1.31 (1.08, 1.55)	Öst et al. (2015)	15
Post-traumatic stress disorder	CBT	Psychological/ pill placebo	*g* = 0.41 (0.26, 0.57)	Carpenter et al. (2018)	14
	Non-CBT therapies	WL	SMD = –0.73 to –1.46	Mavranezouli et al. (2020)	25
	TF CBT/ Non-TF CBT	WL	SMD = –1.22 to 1.46	Mavranezouli et al. (2020)	36
	EMDR	WL	SMD = –2.07 (–2.70, –1.44)	Mavranezouli et al. (2020)	11

Note: CBT = cognitive behavioral therapy; EBPs = evidence-based psychotherapies; EMDR = eye movement desensitization and reprocessing; TF CBT = trauma focused cognitive behavioral therapy; TAU = treatment as usual; WL = wait list; SMD = standardized mean difference.

Personality Disorders

In concluding this section on specific disorders, we briefly summarize the current status regarding personality disorders. We do so in order to reflect the continuum of more complex, chronic, and enduring conditions in view of the high rates of comorbidity or coincidence of personality disorders with, in particular, mood disorders. However, we acknowledge the inherent problems regarding the validity, reliability, and clinical utility of Axis II diagnoses. As an example, data from a naturalistic cohort study within a UK urban Improving Access to Psychological Therapies (IAPT) service found 69% of patients, the majority of whom were assigned to high-intensity treatments (e.g., CBT), to be at high risk of meeting criteria for a personality disorder (Hepgul et al., 2016; see also Lamph et al., 2020). Also, based on a sample of 3,689 adults receiving community-based treatments within the IAPT program, Mars et al. (2021) reported that those with three or more difficulties as determined by the Standardised Assessment of Personality–Abbreviated Scale (Moran et al., 2003) were more than 30% less likely to recover or reliably improve. A meta-analysis of 122 empirical articles focusing on comorbid personality disorders in mood disorders concluded that although common in mood disorders, they were highest in dysthymic disorders (Friborg et al., 2013). In terms of psychological interventions, Budge et al. (2013) analyzed 30 studies comparing evidence-based treatments (EBTs) with treatment as usual for personality disorders and reported an overall effect of $d = 0.40$ in favor of EBTs. Of the 12 studies making direct comparisons between EBTs, while there was an overall effect, $d = 0.32$ (95% CI [0.13, 0.50]), much of the effect was attributable to two studies focusing on mentalization-based treatments (Bateman & Fonagy, 2010) and schema-focused therapy (Giesen-Bloo et al., 2006).

Focusing on borderline personality disorder, a Cochrane Review concluded that while there is some support for dialectical behavior therapy (DBT), the overall evidence is not particularly robust (Stoffers et al., 2012). A similar conclusion regarding DBT as the preferred choice of treatment for women with borderline personality disorder and co-occurring substance abuse was proposed from a systematic review of 10 studies in service of developing the Australian Clinical Practice Guideline for the Management of Borderline Personality Disorder (Lee et al., 2015). The authors concluded that DBT was the preferred option due to its better evidence base for women without substance abuse disorder.

Remaining with borderline personality disorder and based on 17 trials, Cristea, Gentili et al. (2017) reported an overall effect of $g = 0.32$ (95% CI [0.14, 0.51]) based on borderline symptoms, self-harm and parasuicidal behavior, and suicide, in standalone trials. Importantly, subgroup analyses showed DBT ($n = 9$) and psychodynamic approaches ($n = 7$) to be effective: DBT, $g = 0.34$ (95% CI [0.15, 0.53]); psychodynamic approaches, $g = 0.41$ (95% CI [0.12, 0.69]). These were the only psychological therapy formats to be more effective than control interventions. The authors of a subsequent meta-analysis (Oud et al., 2018) reported what they considered an enhancement on the Cristea et al. study by focusing on specialized psychological therapies, namely DBT, mentalization-based treatment, transference-focused therapy, and schema therapy (formerly schema-focused therapy). Overall, these specialized therapies were found to be more effective, as determined by a reduction in the severity of borderline personality disorder, than community-based treatments as usually delivered by experts: SMD = –0.59 (95% CI [–0.90, –0.28]).

In contrast to a focus on specialized interventions, Finch et al. (2019) carried out a meta-analysis of the treatment as usual arms of 11 trials and found, based on the primary outcome of reduced borderline symptoms, a small to medium improvement: $g = 0.37$ (95% CI [0.25, 0.50]). The authors concluded that, in the absence of specialized care, standard treatment is a practical option. Finally, Spong et al. (2021) reviewed 27 studies of briefer psychological therapies for borderline personality disorder and found interventions that included additional support to yield the largest symptom reductions, $g = -1.23$ (95% CI [–2.13, –0.33]). Results suggested that interventions delivered in addition to ongoing support were more effective than in their absence but, overall, there appeared to be no evidence showing brief interventions to have an advantage over regular or structured support.

In sum, personality disorders, however they are defined or measured, appear to be prevalent and an additional obstacle to recovery. For borderline personality disorder, DBT appears to be a leading contender, as are other specialized treatments but, if not available, standard care has been suggested to be a practical option.

Summary

We have cited larger illustrative studies published since the last edition and summarized the main findings when compared with control conditions (see Tables 5.4 and 5.5). From a clinical perspective, a range of psychological interventions are supported by the evidence and, when comparisons are made between therapies, these either show no differences or tend to favor CBT or its derivatives. However, there are also credible alternatives. However, it behooves researchers committed to non-CBT therapies in particular to deliver high-quality research to underpin the evidence base. The delivery of these effective interventions then depends on there being sufficient resources (i.e., trained practitioners) available to deliver them. From a research perspective, we note the clear pattern of stepped-down effects in relation to the size of ESs ranging from large (with wait list) to moderate (placebo). Comparisons with treatment as usual are problematic as it can be both a passive and active control (see Kazdin, 2015). However, our main observation concerns the large numbers of low- (and very-low-) quality studies that are included. Larger trials and longer-term outcomes are also necessary in order to deliver cost-effectiveness analyses that are increasingly necessary in delivering services within national fiscal constraints. Accordingly, the question as to whether psychological therapies are cost-effective is one we turn to next.

Are Psychological Therapies Cost-Effective?

In the previous edition (Lambert, 2013), the topic of cost offset was addressed in the context of extending the evidence for the clinical meaning of gains made by clients, providing further evidence for the impact of the psychological therapies. In this edition, we have reframed and relocated a consideration of cost and economic issues as part of the overall evaluation of psychological therapies on the following basis. First, cost issues are likely to be matters for policy makers and commissioners of services and to be a high-level consideration as to whether a particular therapy is delivered or not at a national or local level. Hence, it seems appropriate to consider these issues here. Second, the concept of cost offset has been viewed as somewhat narrow and imposing a standard on psychotherapy (i.e., to show savings against other medical care) that is not required for other medical care (see Sledge et al., 2010). Accordingly, here we have broadened the scope of this topic under the general heading of the cost-effectiveness of psychological therapies within which we address *cost-effectiveness* (the direct comparison between two or more interventions), *cost–benefit* (focusing on a socially desirable outcome), and *cost–utility* (set against a standard such as the quality-adjusted life years [QALYs]). In general, cost-effectiveness implies a relative cost saving in comparison with an alternative intervention. However, it is also possible for a cost-effectiveness study to show that a treatment does not save money, but, rather, provides a better yield in terms of effectiveness per monetary unit (e.g., dollar) spent and invokes an upper limit that is deemed to reflect society's willingness to pay for any such treatment (e.g., in the US this is $50,000 per QALY; in the UK it is £30,000 per QALY).

Evidence from Cost-Effectiveness, Cost–Benefit, and Cost–Utility Studies

A selective review and meta-analysis of methodologically rigorous studies (Gabbard et al., 1997) found that 8 of 10 trials sampled and all 8 nontrials sampled suggested that psychotherapy reduces total costs. This held particularly for patients with schizophrenia, bipolar affective disorder, and borderline personality disorder where there was improved work functioning and a decrease in hospitalizations. In an edited text, Lazar (2010) documented a comprehensive review of the cost-effectiveness of psychological therapies for a range of conditions in the adult population, including depression, anxiety, PTSD, schizophrenia, substance abuse, associated medical conditions, long-term and intensive psychotherapy, but also for children and adolescents. Overall, the thrust of the text argued that sufficient evidence was present to support the cost-effectiveness of psychological therapies. However, their conclusion was that "the decision to support a particular treatment should be made based on a delicate balance of considering both the scientific evidence that supports it and the values of the society in which it is offered (Sledge et al., 2010; p. 313).

In relation to depression, Lazar (2010) reviewed 28 cost-effectiveness studies with many supporting either directly or indirectly the cost-effectiveness of psychological therapies. However, there were exceptions (e.g., Bosmans et al. 2007;

Friedli et al. 2000; Scott & Freeman 1992) where investigators suggested that a longer course of treatment and a more comprehensive account of the depression-related societal costs might have yielded a different conclusion. More recently, Brettschneider et al. (2015) carried out a systematic review of 22 studies comprising cost-utility analyses of CBT for depression published between 2004–2012, of which 15 sampled adults and 7 sampled children or adolescents with sample sizes ranging from 94 to 1,356 participants. As a stand-alone treatment or in combination with medication, CBT for adults was found to be cost-effective in comparison to usual care, bibliotherapy, and referral to community services and was found not to be inferior to medication. Evidence appeared to support group CBT for adults while findings regarding computerized CBT were inconsistent, showing computerized CBT to be less costly but also less effective than usual care. Using CBT for maintenance and prevention tended to be cost-effective. Importantly, findings differentiated between adults as compared with children and adolescents, showing CBT in the adult population to be cost-effective but not in children and adolescents. Notwithstanding these results, two key issues are highlighted. First, the time frame for cost-effective studies is relatively short with few extending beyond two years. And second, there are inconsistencies across studies as to what is included within the pool of indirect costs.

The cost-effectiveness of CBT has been evaluated against second-generation antidepressant medication and yielded a short-term advantage (at one year) but a longer-term (five-year) advantage in terms of cost-effectiveness to CBT (Ross et al., 2019). Given such findings, the authors argued that there should be shared decision-making between patients and providers accounting for the values and preferences of patients. From an economic perspective, they made a conservative estimate that adopting a model based on patients' preferences for CBT could save in excess of $1.5 billion after five years (notwithstanding initial outlay costs due to geographical accessibility and initial higher costs). However, the levels of uncertainty around costings appear to focus on the higher relapse rate for CBT compared with second generation antidepressants.

In relation to anxiety, a systematic review of the cost-effectiveness of psychological and pharmacotherapy interventions identified 42 studies up to 2016 that met inclusion criteria, of which the majority (38) targeted adults (Ophuis et al., 2017). Psychological interventions were more cost-effective than pharmacological interventions and, when comparing psychological interventions with other psychological interventions, individual CBT appeared to be cost-effective in comparison with family CBT for children aged 8–18 years (Bodden, Dirksen et al., 2008). CBT and psychodynamic therapy appeared to be cost-effective in comparison with a wait-list condition (Egger et al., 2015) and internet CBT (iCBT) was cost-effective in comparison with all control conditions consisting of group CBT and inactive treatment (Andersson et al., 2015; Hedman et al., 2011, 2014). Ophuis and colleagues concluded that psychological interventions might be more cost-effective in comparison with pharmacological interventions, while iCBT in particular appeared to be cost-effective in comparison with control conditions. However, this latter result contrasts with findings from a review by Arnberg et al. (2014) that was unable to establish evidence of the cost-effectiveness of iCBT.

At a national level, cost–benefit analyses have been employed by Layard et al. (2007) to underpin the argument for creating a new psychological therapies program in England – Improving Access to Psychological Therapies (IAPT). In brief, the argument was made on the basis of existing economic data that the cost of devising and delivering an evidence-based therapy (focused on CBT at the time and involving the creation of a new low-intensity workforce of psychological well-being practitioners) with a focus on improved access by patients could be cost-neutral within two years. This was an estimated time frame to enable sufficient people to access therapy and benefit sufficiently such that they could return to work (i.e., generate income and pay taxes) and thereby cease claiming invalidity benefits from the government. Hence, the initiative would potentially be cost neutral and also deliver benefits to society beyond those experienced by the service users themselves. Such a vision could not, however, have foreseen the financial crisis of 2008 that led to a global economic downturn. Even so, a cost-effectiveness study of the pilot IAPT sites suggested that the program was cost-effective compared with comparator (pre-IAPT implementation) sites with a cost per QALY gained of £29,500 (Mukuria et al., 2013). The cost of achieving reliable and clinically significant improvement was £9440 per patient.

While the original IAPT program focused on depression and anxiety, it has extended the population served to those presenting with severe mental illness. Zala et al. (2019) studied six sites focused on severe mental illness for psychosis or bipolar disorder, and for personality disorder. Data suggested that although IAPT costs more overall, it saves substantial nonpsychological treatment costs over 12 months, particularly regarding acute secondary care costs. It suggested the program could improve functional impairment in patients with psychosis or bipolar disorder, and also reduce harmful behaviors in patients with personality disorders.

In terms of comparisons between the prominent models of CBT and IPT, Gajic-Veljanoski et al. (2018) conducted a systematic review of the cost-effectiveness of treating depression and anxiety and identified 15 studies (14 CBT, 1 IPT). With the exception of one study, they found CBT alone or in combination with pharmacotherapy represented good value for money compared with usual care at a range of country-specific willingness-to-pay thresholds (e.g., £30,000 per QALY in the UK). The probability of cost-effectiveness was especially high (>96%) for severe depression. The single study for IPT (Bosmans et al., 2007) suggested this modality was not cost-effective at thresholds specific to the Netherlands.

From a European perspective, Brettschneider et al. (2020) reported on a cost-effectiveness analysis comparing a four-level stepped care model recommended by the German National Clinical Practice Guideline with treatment-as-usual utilizing a prospective cluster-randomized trial ($N = 737$). Using quality-adjusted life years (QALYs), they found no evidence to support the cost-effectiveness of the recommended treatment. Indeed, for severe patients, the treatment as usual condition was more cost-effective. It is noteworthy that this study was well powered, which is crucial for cost-effectiveness studies even more so than in determining clinical effectiveness. And Baumann et al. (2020) showed that in a simulation of internet CBT versus face-to-face CBT, internet CBT saved €2536 per patient compared to person-to-person CBT. The implication of such a study is that it provides an evidence base for the planning of effective services to patients that enables, for example, more severe or complex cases to be treated person-to-person.

In contrast to costs arising from more prevalent conditions (e.g., depression, anxiety), significant costs also arise from those people presenting with conditions that have a low prevalence but high economic costs. For example, Kraiss et al. (2020) reported a systematic review of bipolar disorder and found that of eight economic evaluation studies, all yielded improved clinical outcomes and five of them reported decreased costs. A key conclusion made by the authors was the need to increase cost-effectiveness studies of BD and to encourage researchers to adopt quality of life measures, which include traditional measures (e.g., EQ-5D or SF-12) but also more recently developed ones (e.g., Recovering Quality of Life [ReQoL]; Keetharuth et al., 2018). But while cost-effectiveness studies or their components may not appear directly essential to psychotherapy researchers, there are ways in which they can be incorporated at no or minimal additional burden. For example, Wickramasekera and Tubeuf (2020) reported using the CORE-6D (Mavranezouli et al., 2013), comprising six items contained in the Clinical Outcomes in Routine Evalualuation-Outcome Measure (CORE-OM), and found it to be a reliable and valid cost-effectiveness tool in a primary care sample. Similarly, a walk-across table has been devised for translating between Patient Health Questionnaire-9 (PHQ-9) scores and QALYs (see Furukawa et al., 2021). Being able to derive such information from a generic measure of psychological distress means that the information already exists in many routinely collected datasets. Reducing the gap between psychological therapy studies and cost-effectiveness studies would be a valuable advance.

Summary

Overall, the evidence from cost-effectiveness studies is broadly supportive of the range of psychological therapies, but it is not always the case that novel interventions deliver savings over standard treatments. And from a methodological perspective, the levels of uncertainty around the costs are invariably considerable. Realizing cost-effectiveness data as a part of standard data collection is possible, particularly as it can be based on the use of quality-of-life measures and could thereby yield valuable cumulative information to support the funding and delivery of the psychological therapies and evidence its impact beyond the realms of defined symptomatology.

Overall Summary of Evidence-Based Psychological Therapies

In the previous edition, Lambert (2013) concluded that both in terms of broad summaries of the field and the outcomes for specific treatments for specific disorders, the psychological therapies had been shown to be highly beneficial.

The consistent finding of positive *psychotherapy* effects – across decades, thousands of studies and hundreds of meta-analyses, examining diverse disorders and therapies – is clear. More apparent in the current review is the observation that the issue focuses now more on how the relative size of the effect alters as a function of the comparator condition (as well as aspects of bias). And if the effect size span, depending on the comparator, ranges from 0.40 to 0.80, this equates to 60–69% of treated patients having a positive outcome, in contrast to the relative comparator condition for the same time period (see Table 5.1; columns 1 and 5, respectively).

In terms of therapy approaches, where one psychological intervention is pitted against another, results most often show no significant difference. However, where differences do occur, they tend to favor CBT, although there is strong evidence for alternative treatments for certain conditions, which are essential in order to provide people with a choice from the rich spectrum of evidence-based therapies. However, we conclude our summary comments expressing concern about the all-to-often observation that too many individual studies included in meta-analyses are of low or lower quality and underpowered. We return to these issues in the concluding section of this chapter.

DELIVERING PSYCHOLOGICAL THERAPIES

In the previous section, we set out the evidence for the efficacy and effectiveness of psychological therapies. Here we focus on the delivery of effective therapies and address four key questions:

1. Can we allocate patients to therapies that give them the best possible outcome?
2. What is the contribution of the individual therapist?
3. How much therapy is necessary?
4. Do psychological therapies reach culturally and diverse client populations?

Can We Allocate Patients to Therapies That Give Them the Best Possible Outcome?

The evidence base for the psychological therapies attests to there being numerous bona fide treatments but also that the overall effectiveness has not been enhanced since Smith and Glass' (1977) meta-analysis. This is the case even in light of the development of newer models of therapy, although it may be possible to fine-tune therapies if and when their key mechanisms of change have been determined. A different approach to improving outcomes has been to focus on the point at which treatment decision-making takes place – namely, in allocating or assigning a person to a specific therapy model. The question of best or most appropriate allocation is an attempt to address two key positions within the psychological therapies: (i) at the aggregate level, in many settings, there is very little difference in the outcomes between contrasting bona fide therapy approaches; and (ii) at the individual level there is considerable variability such that some clients do well in certain therapies and others not so well. Hence, frontline treatment choices can often be based on severity (e.g., NICE) and, while this may be a reasonable fit for many clients, aggregate level decision-making will always mismatch a significant proportion of clients.

Personalized Treatments

In light of a research tradition showing that decisions based on actuarial data are more reliable than those based on clinical hunches (see Hannan et al., 2005; Meehl, 1954), there has been research activity in pursuit of better prediction modeling regarding patient outcomes. Early attempts to use data-driven models to generate case-specific outcome predictions have been applied using a nearest neighbor strategy (see Lutz et al., 2005) and extended to predict expected treatment response in differing treatments (e.g., Lutz et al., 2006). Such a data-analytic strategy was a precursor to the adoption of computer algorithms that adapt in light of new data and that has become central to the field of personalized medicine, an area that has taken root since the last review (Lambert, 2013) and is the focus of Chapter 19.

In pursuit of generating prediction models to aid allocation of patients between different treatments, and building on earlier work of Barber and Munez (1996), DeRubeis et al. (2014) used baseline data (i.e., not including any patient self-report measures based on sessions administered) from an existing trial comparing CBT with antidepressant medication to develop point predictions of symptom severity at posttreatment for each individual in each of these two interventions. The comparison between the two estimates yielded an index – the *personalized advantage index* (PAI) – to indicate which of the two treatments would be better and by how much on the basis of a cluster of multiple predictors. When they applied this metric to the sample as a whole, a comparison between those randomized to their optimal versus nonoptimal treatment showed an average difference of 1.8 points on the Hamilton Rating Scale for Depression (HRSD) and was not significant (see left portion of Figure 5.3). But while the differential prediction for 40% of the whole sample indicated that it would not make a clinically meaningful difference (i.e., a score of less than 3 points on the HRSD), when the analysis was rerun on the 60% of cases for which a difference of greater than 3 points was predicted, the results showed an average difference of 3.6 points on the HRSD and are shown in the right portion of Figure 5.3. Importantly, although this was a retrospective test, as any given individual's data was omitted from the predictions regarding their treatment, the test approximated a prospective test. The authors argued that if this procedure had actually been used prospectively, the difference would have approximated those derived from comparisons between an active and control conditions.

Similar results have been reported in a number of other studies. For example, in a trial comparing sertraline versus placebo, 31% of trial participants were identified as likely to show a clinically better outcome score if assigned to sertraline (Webb et al., 2019). While the overall ES difference for the whole contrast was $d = 0.15$, the identified group who would benefit most from the active medication showed an ES of $d = 0.58$ compared with placebo. And testing has been extended to comparisons between CBT and IPT (Huibers et al., 2015), while, more recently, in a comparison of data drawn from a trial between these two therapy modalities, patients receiving the treatment predicted by an algorithm were less depressed at posttreatment and follow-up compared to those receiving their nonindicated treatment (van Bronswijk, Lemmens et al., 2021). However, in a test of the generalizability of the PAI to clinical practice, a cross-trial test of the PAI in which predictions derived from each of two trials were tested on the other (STEPd: *n* = 151 and FreqMech: *n* = 200) yielded modest results (van Bronswijk, Bruijniks et al., 2021). The authors flagged the need for greater validation of the PAI prior to adoption in clinical practice.

Such studies have moved beyond RCTs to use practice-based datasets comparing person-centered experiential therapy and CBT. In this comparison, Delgadillo and Gonzalez Salas Duhne (2020) reported equivalent outcomes at an aggregated level but identified a subgroup of clients – approximately 30% – showing differential responses to these treatments. The authors used machine learning to determine which treatment was a better predictor of outcome and found that patients assigned to their optimal treatment had a significantly higher reliable and clinically significant improvement rate (62.5%) compared to those who received their suboptimal treatment (41.7%).

While such studies signal promise, they are retrospective in nature. Addressing this issue, Delgadillo et al. (submitted) report the results of a prospective study testing the clinical and cost-effectiveness of stratified care (i.e., selecting the intensity of treatment based on each patient's expected prognosis) versus stepped care. The sample comprised 951 eligible patients within England's IAPT stepped care program who received either stratified (*n* = 583) or stepped (*n* = 368) care. While all patients received the same structured interview, therapists in the stratified care group received a personalized treatment recommendation for each patient – generated by a prognostic machine learning algorithm. A significantly higher proportion of stratified care patients attained remission of depression symptoms relative to stepped care patients; 52.3% vs. 45.1%, OR = 1.40, 95% CI [1.04, 1.87]. The additional cost-effectiveness component showed that although stratified care was associated with a higher cost, this yielded a 7.9% increase in the likelihood of reliable improvement. And Lutz et al. (2021) have also reported results from a prospective study in which therapist–patient dyads in a CBT outpatient clinic were randomized to either having access to a decision support system (intervention group; *n* = 335) or not (treatment as usual; *n* = 203). Results showed a small differential effect size (*d* = 0.28), yielding a reliable improvement rate of 61.7% (compared with 47.6%) when therapists followed the recommended treatment strategy in the first 10 sessions. Worthy of note is that both these studies employed sample sizes that are more in line with the larger-scale studies required to progress effective strategies for fine-tuning psychological therapies.

Summary

At present, the body of literature is relatively small but it captures an area of research that goes to the heart of Paul's litany of "which treatment for which patient" and is underpinned by cutting-edge research methodology offering the possibility of enhancing outcomes for a significant proportion of patients. Clearly, more prospective studies are needed that could be coupled with feedback research (see Chapter 4; also, see de Jong et al., 2021). As such, it is providing considerable potential for identifying a route to improving the match between client and therapy (for a detailed account, see Chapter 19). However, importantly, this approach is not a panacea but, akin to the provision of feedback, and also other areas to be discussed, may impact on a portion of sufficient patients such as to raise overall improvement rates in terms of the effectiveness of

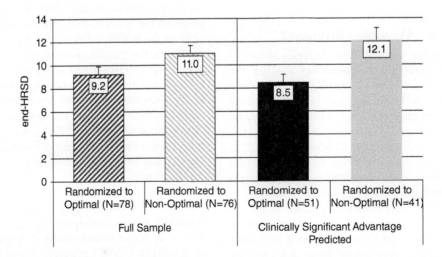

FIGURE 5.3 Comparison of Mean End-HRSD Scores for Patients Randomly Assigned to Their Optimal Treatment Versus Those Assigned to Their Non-Optimal Treatment
DeRubeis, R. J., Cohen, Z. D., Forand, N. R., Fournier, J. C., Gelfand, L. A., & Lorenzo-Luaces, L. (2014). The Personalized Advantage Index: translating research on prediction into individualized treatment recommendations. A demonstration. *PloS One, 9*(1), e83875. https://doi.org/10.1371/journal.pone.0083875. Reprinted according to permissions granted by Creative Commons BY 4.0 license.

the psychological therapies. And it is consistent with a focus away from the global question of whether one therapy modality is better than another, instead focusing on how to ensure that each person receives the most appropriate therapy modality for their issues at this particular time. And in a similar vein, another factor that can impact on the outcomes for specific groups of patients is the role of the therapist, an issue to which we now turn.

Is One Therapist More Effective Than Another?

In terms of the major activities of psychotherapy research, most attention has focused on treatments (therapies) and patients in terms of presenting conditions. By contrast, relatively little attention, until recently, has focused on therapists. The previous edition of the *Handbook* set a clear marker in replacing longstanding chapters investigating therapist variables with a chapter specifically on therapist effects (Baldwin & Imel, 2013) and has been continued and expanded in this edition (see Chapter 9).

Therapist Effects

It is important at the outset to define the term *therapist effects* as it is conceptually different from *therapist effectiveness*. Therapist effectiveness refers to the actual level of effectiveness and it may be that, in a clinic, all therapists are very effective such that there is little, if any, difference between them, and hence no therapist effect. That is, there is little or no variability such that a patient's outcome would not be affected by the therapist to which they were allocated. The same would be true if all the therapists were equally ineffective – there would be no variability and hence no therapist effect. But, as with most human activities, people vary in their abilities, so there is inevitable variability in the outcomes of therapists – hence, there are, in most situations, therapist effects. Put another way, the outcomes of patients for therapist A are likely to be correlated with each other and different from the outcome of patients seen by therapist B.

Pioneering studies investigating therapist effects were summarized in the previous version of this chapter (see Lambert, 2013). These include studies by Orlinsky and Howard (1980), Luborsky et al. (1985), Crits-Christoph and Mintz (1991), Crits-Christoph et al. (1991), and Blatt et al. (1996). All these studies pointed to the contribution that therapists make to client outcomes. And further, analyses of data from routine care settings where the selection, training, and supervision of therapists are less controlled, the number of clients per therapist is much larger, and length of treatment is variable, have provided a unique window into the phenomenon of therapist effects. Two landmark studies carried out by Okiishi et al. (2003, 2006) examined routine care outcomes by therapists. Outcome by therapist showed considerable variability, with the most effective therapist's patients showing both rapid and substantial treatment response, while the least effective therapist's patients showed an average worsening in functioning. One of the more dramatic findings was that a typical client seeing the most efficient therapist would need between six and seven sessions of treatment to recover, while the average client seeing the least efficient therapist would need 94 sessions, (i.e., nearly two years of weekly treatment). The most effective therapists yielded a rate of change over three times greater than that of the less-effective therapists and overall change that was twice as much. Bottom-ranked therapists had deterioration rates (11%) twice as high as top-ranked therapists (5%).

In the previous edition of the *Handbook*, Baldwin and Imel (2013) captured such variability by determining an overall assessment of the extent of therapist effects and concluded it accounted for approximately 5% of the outcome variance and argued that, although small in absolute terms, it was as important as, for example, the therapeutic alliance and of greater import than, for example, adherence to treatment protocols. Building on this account, there has been a growth in publications in this area with literature searches showing more than a fourfold increase in articles published 2011–2020 compared with 2001–2010 as well as several brief introductions to the topic (e.g., Adelson & Owen, 2012; Barkham et al., 2017). And the extent of therapist effects has been confirmed in an update of Baldwin and Imel's review, which affirmed a therapist effect of 5% (Johns et al., 2019). However, there is a strong suggestion that the extent of the effect is not uniform across settings, being substantially less in universities and workplace counseling settings compared with community outpatient settings (Firth et al., 2020).

One explanation for this finding may relate to the moderating impact of patient severity. Indeed, this impact was a finding in one of the largest therapist effect studies at the time comprising 119 therapists and yielding a therapist effect of 6.8% (Saxon & Barkham, 2012). The authors displayed how the 95% CIs for 29% of therapists were consistently (i.e., reliably) either above or below the average outcome for therapists in the sample (see also Chapter 9; Figure 9.2). In effect, therapists who were consistently above average were twice as effective as therapists consistently below the average therapist. In addition, however, the therapist effect increased as a function of initial patient severity. In other words, the higher the patient's presenting severity at intake, the more it mattered which therapist saw the patient. Following a similar approach, Saxon et al. (2017) used data from an IAPT service and grouped the 61 therapists into three categories with a mean, *M*, and range of patient recovery rates: below average (*M* = 25.6%, range = 16.0–37.1%), average (*M* = 46.4%, range 21.9–71.4%), and above average (*M* = 63.7%; range = 49.6–75.8%). Similar to the earlier study, the 13% of therapists who were significantly more effective than average had recovery rates that were more than twice those of the 16% of therapists identified as significantly less effective than average.

Data such as these have immediate relevance to service delivery and have raised the specter of performance-based retention of therapists, a strategy that Imel et al. (2015) proposed could improve the quality of psychotherapy in health systems by increasing the average response rate and decreasing the probability that a patient will be treated by a therapist who consistently has poor outcomes. And in a sample of 3,540 clients treated in naturalistic settings by a sample of 59 therapists,

Kraus et al. (2016) demonstrated that therapist effectiveness was relatively stable, although somewhat domain specific. Therapists classified as exceptional were significantly more likely to remain above average with future cases, suggesting that a therapist's past performance is an important predictor of their future performance.

A different approach has focused on the impact of therapist effects and treatment duration. Goldberg et al. (2018) found that for clients attending four sessions of therapy, there was relatively little difference in the pre–post change scores between a higher and lower performing therapist (i.e., the top and bottom 10% of the sample of therapists) as shown by *d* values of 1.00 and 0.73, respectively. But at 16 sessions, the gain was identical for lower-performing therapists (*d* = 0.73) but greater for higher-performing therapists (*d* = 1.42). However, caution needs to be taken concerning some of the findings due to their being drawn from college or university samples.

Importantly, attention has focused on the impact of therapist effects and race and ethnic minorities (REMs). Kivlighan et al. (2018) investigated whether some therapists are more culturally effective than others and found differential therapist effectiveness to be related to clients' race-ethnicity. Additionally, they found that therapist effectiveness differed based on the intersectionality of clients' race-ethnicity and gender. On average, the rates of change did not significantly differ between Men of Color, Women of Color, White Women, and White Men. One of the strengths of this study was its use of a longitudinal design to operationalize therapist effects in contrast to the majority of studies testing therapist effects with REM clients that operationalize therapist effectiveness as pre-post changes (e.g., Hayes et al., 2015, 2016; Imel et al., 2011). And it adopted an intersectionality approach to study therapist effectiveness with Women of Color, Men of Color, White Women, and White Men, advancing our understanding of therapist effects in terms of clients' cultural identities of race and gender.

In the same way that procedures are being developed to better assign patients to treatments, a parallel approach has been applied to assigning patients to therapists. Delgadillo et al. (2020) employed a sample of 4,849 patients and 68 therapists over a two-year period and developed models from year one data to predict the outcomes of the same therapists in year two. While the base rate of reliable and clinically significant improvement (RCSI) was 40%, they found the matching of specific groups of therapists with specific patients showed rates of improvement to range from 10.5% (for one group of therapists with unemployed patients) to 74.2% (for another group of therapists with patients who were employed with intake PHQ-9 scores between 14 and 16). Notably, there were three therapists who were effective with all patients they saw (i.e., there was no interaction with patient variables) yielding a RCSI rate of 69.9%. Like many such datasets, there was no available information on therapist characteristics, but it flags the need to move toward being able to identify what features characterize an effective therapist.

While a focus on therapists appears all too obvious, research on this topic carries with it specific methodological issues of which two are primary. The first relates to statistical power, both at an overall study level and at the level of numbers of patients per therapist. The review by Johns et al. (2019) recommended the collection of multiple measures on a sufficient number of therapists (e.g., minimum of 50), although ideally numbers in excess of 100 should be the target. In addition, Schiefele et al. (2017) provided a guide to planning the numbers of patients and therapists and concluded that the key component was a patient sample size of 1200 comprising, for example, at least 4 patients per therapist with 300 therapists, or at least 30 patients per therapist with 40 therapists. The second issue is that many of the studies have drawn data from college or university settings and samples; we advise caution in extrapolating from these settings to community samples.

Effective Therapists

Since the Lambert (2013) review, there has been a considerable growth in innovative attempts to determine the characteristics of effective therapists (see Wampold et al., 2017). Nissen-Lie (2013) characterized effective therapists as being people who were kind to themselves but carried an air of tentativeness about their professional expertise, as captured in the phrase "love yourself as a person, doubt yourself as a therapist." This work was followed by a review of the professional and personal characteristics of effective therapists (Heinonen & Nissen-Lie, 2020). Importantly, these authors gave greater emphasis to studies where patients rated the outcomes, where valid measures were used, and the analyses took account of the nested nature of the data. They considered key characteristics under the headings of professional and personal attributes and found that those most associated with patient outcomes could be identified as professional, namely factors more related to carrying out therapy. They concluded that effective therapists "are characterized by interpersonal capacities that are professionally cultivated but likely rooted in their personal lives and attachment history – such as empathy, verbal and nonverbal communication skills, and capacity to form and repair alliances – especially with interpersonally challenging clients" (p. 429). The topic of effective therapists is address in detail in Chapter 9.

Heinonen and Nissen-Lie (2020) also identified one of the most promising therapist-level predictors of client outcomes as being the Facilitative Interpersonal Skills (FIS) Performance Task (Anderson et al., 2019; for an overview of the method, see Anderson et al., 2020). The FIS is defined as a set of qualities that correspond to a person's ability to perceive, understand, and communicate a wide range of interpersonal messages, as well as a person's ability to persuade others with personal problems to apply suggested solutions to their problems and abandon maladaptive patterns. The performance task was designed as a means of measuring therapists' abilities to respond to *challenging* therapy situations based on viewing video recordings. Four problematic therapy process segments were selected from the videotaped archives of a study that focused on problematic interpersonal interactions between patients and therapists (Strupp, 1993). In addition, four unique interpersonal patient styles were selected to represent a range of challenging interpersonal patterns, including (i) a confrontational and angry patient ("You can't help me"); (ii) a passive, silent, and withdrawn patient ("I don't know what to talk about"); (iii) a confused and yielding patient (only the therapist's opinion matters); and (iv) a controlling and blaming patient (implies that others, including the therapist, are not worthy of them). Thus, two cases were designed to include patients who were highly self-focused, negative, and self-effacing, and the remaining two cases were designed to be highly other-focused, friendly, but highly dependent clients. Therapist responses are rated across eight interpersonal "skills": verbal fluency, emotional expression, persuasiveness, hopefulness, warmth, empathy, alliance-bond capacity, and problem focus.

In a quasi-therapeutic trial employing doctoral candidates as therapists and non-help-seeking students as clients, Anderson, Crowley et al. (2016) found that therapists previously identified as scoring high on the FIS realized better outcomes for their clients on multiple outcome measures (e.g., Outcome Questionnaire-45 [OQ-45], Inventory of Interpersonal Problems-64 [IIP-64]) compared with therapists scoring low on the FIS. In addition, the rate of change over the course of therapy, as measured by sessional OQ-45, was significantly greater for the high as compared with the low FIS group. The study design also included a no-treatment control group, and results showed near equivalence between the low FIS group and the control group on some outcome measures. Unsurprisingly, the high FIS therapists had higher client ratings of alliance from the initial session. Overall, the study promotes the role of facilitative interpersonal skills as impacting on outcomes although it is not clear whether the dyads as generated in this study are representative of therapist–patient dyads within community or primary-care clinical settings. And in another study using clinical trainees, Anderson, McClintock et al. (2016) found that FIS ratings at the beginning of training predicted patient outcomes at one year later such that therapists with initially higher FIS scores were subsequently more effective. However, this effect only obtained for durations up to eight sessions; thereafter, there was no difference. A possible explanation by the authors for this seemingly counterintuitive qualifier was the proposition that those patients remaining in therapy beyond eight sessions might reflect a greater portion of harder-to-treat patients who have not reached a sufficient level of improvement as predicted by the good enough level (GEL) (Barkham et al., 2006), a topic addressed in the next section. Overall, however, a focus on interpersonal aspects of therapists and also on their ability to respond to challenges and conflicts may turn out to be a key component of the effective therapist.

Summary

In the context where evidence of differences between treatments is, at best, small, some of the differences between therapists are considerable. Specific research strands have focused heavily on technique factors as being the key ones accounting for therapeutic change and, from this perspective, differences in effectiveness between therapists are likely to be attributed to variability in technical skill rather than personal qualities or dynamic elements of the interaction between patient and therapist. As argued by Lambert (2013), in order to advance causal mechanisms, there needs to be monitoring in outcome studies of individual therapist

variation in skill (and personal qualities like empathic attunement or flexibility). There is certainly an argument for greater focus on therapists as persons and in their interaction with techniques, as well as with patient characteristics. Since Lambert's (2013) review, there has been a consolidation regarding research attesting to therapist effects as well as to characteristics that are displayed by more-effective therapists. The field has moved on from a focus on therapist variables to attention on more interpersonal and dynamic qualities. However, it is still the case that much of the work on therapists is secondary and not arising from bona fide studies focusing on therapists per se. Notwithstanding the need for a specific focus on therapists, greater attention needs to be given to reporting information on therapists and also on the assignments of patients to therapists.

How Much Therapy Is Necessary?

Beyond the choice of specific treatments and allocation of therapists, an important issue for patients, policy makers, and psychotherapists is the optimal dosage of therapy needed to reduce impairment and increase positive life functioning. Attempts at determining the relationship between dosage and treatment length have yielded two viable models: the dose–effect model and the good enough level model.

Dose–Effect and Good Enough Level (GEL) Models

In a classic study, Howard et al. (1986) reported a meta-analysis on 2,431 patients from published research covering a 30-year period. Their analysis showed a stable pattern across studies reflecting the relationship of amount of therapy to patient improvement. They concluded that the relationship between the number of sessions and client improvement took a form similar to that evidenced by many medications – namely, a negatively accelerating curve leading to diminishing returns at higher doses. Their analysis of the data indicated that 14% of clients improved before attending the initial session, 53% were improved following 8 weekly sessions, 75% by 26 sessions, and 83% after 52 sessions. The Howard et al. study supported findings indicating that treatment produces a benefit that surpasses spontaneous remission rates by demonstrating that clients receiving treatments make substantial gains early in treatment. However, a limitation of the Howard et al. study was their reliance on pre–post estimates of patient improvement to model change over time, rather than session-by-session ratings of improvement. Later studies did adopt session-by-session mental health ratings, and follow-up data (e.g., Anderson & Lambert, 2001; Kadera et al., 1996) suggested that the review by Howard et al. (1986) overestimated the speed of recovery and indicated that 50% of patients needed 13 sessions of therapy before they reached criteria for clinically significant change while 75% of patients met criteria after more than 50 sessions. This finding was partially replicated in an Australian population, where 50% of clients at two university training clinics were estimated to recover after 14 sessions and 70% required 23 sessions (Harnett et al., 2010).

However, research now suggests some modification to the idea that more therapy will necessarily lead to better outcomes (also see Chapter 4, this *Handbook*). The earlier research in this area combined data across patients who varied in their total dose of therapy and assumed that the rate of change during therapy is constant across different doses. In contrast, Barkham et al. (2006) and Stiles et al. (2008) suggested that there is a "good enough" dose of therapy and that the rate of change will be related to the total dose of therapy. In other words, rather than a negatively accelerating curve, where a session of therapy incrementally contributes to change, individual rate of change determines the dose, rather than the number of sessions predicting recovery. Barkham et al. (2006) theorized that the speed of recovery would predict the number of sessions. This model was termed the *good enough level* (GEL) model. The key differences between the dose–effect and GEL models are listed by Bone et al. (2021) and presented in Table 5.6.

Empirical Studies, Systematic Reviews, and Meta-Analyses

Baldwin et al. (2009) evaluated the competing predictions proposed by these two models by examining the relationship between rate of change and total dose in 4,676 psychotherapy patients who received individual psychotherapy. The initial aggregate model replicated the negative accelerating curve described in the dose–effect literature. When the sample was stratified by number of sessions, however, the model indicated that although patients improved during treatment, patients' rate of change varied as a function of total dose of treatment. Small doses of treatment were related to relatively fast rates of change, whereas large doses of treatment were related to slower rates of change, as illustrated in Figure 5.4. Interestingly, this suggests that equal amounts of change occur over the course of therapy but at different rates for different patients. Some clients require only four sessions to achieve recovery, and others more than 20. A statistically significant

TABLE 5.6   Differences between Dose–Response and Good Enough Level Models

Dose–response model	Good enough level model
Curvilinear response is an average of multiple individual curvilinear responses	Curvilinear response is an artefact of aggregating people, where faster remitters end therapy earlier (the GEL model does not prescribe any particular shape of change)
Rate of change does not vary with total sessions	Rate of change does vary with total sessions
Improvement is associated with total sessions	Improvement is not associated (or negatively) with total sessions
Therapy length determines progress	Progress determines therapy length

Bone, C., Delgadillo, J., & Barkham, M. (2021). A systematic review and meta-analysis of the good-enough level (GEL) literature. *Journal of Counseling Psychology*. Reprinted with permission.

dose–response relationship was found, as the early research suggested, but this relationship was slight and detected only in the first eight sessions. As the dosage increased beyond that limit, the dose response relationship became insignificant. This phenomenon is depicted in Figure 5.4 as well, where it can be seen that the expected percentage of patients recovering depends on response more than dose. Overall, these findings

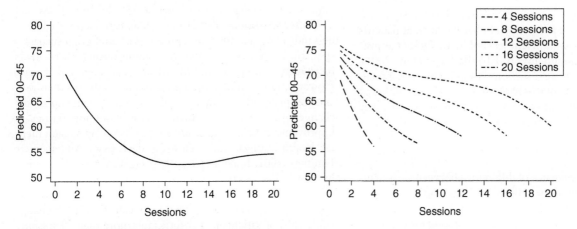

FIGURE 5.4   Predicted Rate of Change in Outcome Questionnaire-45 (OQ-45) Scores Across Sessions in Treatment
The top panel represents the aggregate model, which averaged the rate of change across all patients, ignoring the number of sessions they attended. The bottom panel represents the stratified model, which stratified rate of change across the total number of sessions patients attended. Baldwin, S. A., Berkeljon, A., Atkins, D. C., Olsen, J. A., & Nielsen, S. L. (2009). Rates of change in naturalistic psychotherapy: Contrasting dose-effect and good-enough level models of change. *Journal of Consulting and Clinical Psychology*, 77(2), 203–211. Reprinted with permission of the American Psychological Association.

indicate that the GEL model of psychotherapy change – where patients remain in therapy until they recover – is possibly a better description of the relationship between dose and individual patient recovery than earlier dose–response models.

Since Lambert's (2013) review, there have been a number of studies investigating the dose–effect and GEL models. Stulz et al. (2013), utilizing a dataset comprising 6375 outpatients, found supporting evidence for both the dose–effect and the GEL models of change. They found the expected course of improvement in psychotherapy to follow a negatively accelerated pattern, irrespective of the duration of the treatment – that is, consistent with the dose–effect model. However, they argued that this did not imply that the rate of negative acceleration is constant across all treatment lengths. Given that the rate of change varies as a function of treatment duration, it was no longer plausible to argue for a consistent relationship between the expected effect of treatment and number of sessions across clients (e.g., a 75% chance of improvement after 26 sessions of treatment for every client). As proposed by the GEL model, people seem to remain in therapy until they reach a good enough level, leading to termination. This level of improvement, however, is typically reached by a log-linear rather than by a linear and steady pattern of change.

Falkenström et al. (2016) sampled two datasets from Sweden, one community-based primary care and one psychiatric care. Irrespective of whether data were analyzed at an aggregate level or stratified by treatment length, the dose–response pattern did not follow a negatively accelerating curve in either sample and reported greater RCSI in therapies up to 13 sessions, after which further gains diminished.

A recent systematic review of the dose–effect literature identified 26 studies, of which 14 (54%) sampled US university counseling centers while 5 (19%) studies sampled primary care settings (Robinson et al., 2020). Within university counseling center samples, the optimal dose across studies appeared to range between 4 and 24 sessions for those with common mental health problems, although up to 30 sessions may be indicated for cases with more severe mental health problems (e.g., psychosis). Of the five studies examining primary care samples (four from the UK; one from Sweden), two of them focused on low-intensity psychological therapies (e.g., guided self-help) for depression and anxiety in the UK IAPT service model (Delgadillo et al., 2014, 2016). Stiles et al. (2008) and Stiles et al. (2015) sampled high-intensity psychological therapies in the UK and found a trend for diminishing RCSI rates with lengthier therapies, but, consistent with the GEL model philosophy, did not recommend an optimal dose. Viewing the data from high intensity primary care, for patients presenting with more severe symptomatology, they suggested upward of 13 sessions in order to meet the criteria of reliable and clinically significant improvement. However, these estimates are considerably less than those previously noted in Lambert (2013), and more than half of the studies on this topic were carried out using university/college counseling samples. We advise caution in placing estimates on numbers of sessions, for two reasons. First, as indicated, there is at least a reasonable suggestion that time in

therapy is determined by each patient's individual rate of change, thereby providing considerable levels of uncertainty around any estimates. And second, to the extent that national context plays a part, differing models of delivery in different countries are likely to vary in their impact, making any notion of universal treatment lengths unhelpful or misleading.

Robinson et al. (2020) concluded that there was consistent evidence for a curvilinear relationship between the number of sessions and the probability of treatment response, yielding diminishing returns with longer treatments. However, they also found consistent support for the GEL model assumption that different subgroups of patients yield different rates of improvement, indicating that treatment duration is a function of therapeutic responsiveness. They argued that patients with differing levels of severity use a differential number of sessions necessary to improve, but usually do so within predictable boundaries, operationalized as an optimal dose. A parallel systematic review and meta-analysis of the GEL literature considered 15 studies of which 10 contributed to a meta-analysis (Bone et al., 2021). The authors found support for the GEL model in that there was no overall association between treatment duration and patient outcomes ($r = -0.24, 95\%$ CI [$-0.70, 0.36$]). In addition, longer treatments were associated with higher baseline symptom scores ($r = 0.15, 95\%$ CI [$0.08, 0.22$]) as well as slower rates of change.

Overall, the research focusing on the dose–response and GEL models yields intriguing findings that suggest a single model does not provide a clear account on all occasions. And it may be that each model is focusing on and appealing to a different level whereby the dose–response model addresses a population level while the GEL model focuses more at the level of the individual patient and their responsiveness to the therapeutic process. In general, universal treatment lengths appear to be suspect and the GEL model challenges the notion that predetermined fixed treatment lengths are appropriate for all patients.

Sudden Gains and Their Prediction

Other important questions related to the dose–effect relationship have come into their own as the practice of monitoring patient treatment response has become more widespread. One particularly intriguing phenomenon in contrast to gradual session-by-session change is what can be described as a dramatic between-session response, namely sudden gains. Tang and DeRubeis (1999) introduced the concept of sudden gains as sudden, substantial, and stable improvements that occur in one between-session interval. Three criteria were required: (i) a reduction of seven or more BDI points (i.e., the gain is large in absolute terms); (ii) the reduction is ≥25% of the preceding score (i.e., the reduction is large in relative terms); and (iii) a significant difference on an independent *t*-test comparing the mean BDI score for the three preceding sessions with the mean score for the three post-gain sessions (i.e., the gain is stable). By definition, this excluded sudden gains from occurring very early in therapy. Using this definition, evidence of sudden gains was found in 39% of clients in the Tang and DeRubeis (1999) study.

Since the Lambert (2013) review, two major meta-analyses have been reported on sudden gains (Aderka et al., 2012; Shalom & Aderka, 2020). Aderka et al. (2012) reported on 16 studies and found that sudden gains were associated with greater pre-posttreatment change as compared with those individuals not experiencing sudden gains, with moderate effect sizes at posttreatment (g = 0.62, 95% CI [0.43, 0.80]) and follow-up at an average of 4.4 months (g = 0.56, 95% CI [0.36, 0.75]). They argued that these results showed sudden gains to represent a significant impact on treatment outcome. Moreover, they noted that the effect, originally observed in studies of depression, was apparent across the anxiety disorders. In addition, the effect was found to be greater in CBT (g = 0.75, 95% CI [0.53, 0.91]) than non-CBT (g = 0.23, 95% CI [–0.02, 0.48]) therapies. Interestingly, no actual difference in the features of the sudden gains themselves (e.g., the size or frequency of the gain) was found and it was therefore argued that sudden gains may impact on further cognitive changes and hence lead to an upward spiral of change in CBT (Tang & DeRubeis, 1999). A subsequent meta-analysis comprising 50 studies (N = 6,355) reported the average occurrence rate of sudden gains to be approximately 35% with a median occurrence at the fifth session (Shalom & Aderka, 2020). The average extent of the sudden gain was approximately 1.5 SDs of pretreatment severity levels. However, approximately one-third (31.5%) of sudden gains were reversed during the course of therapy. The meta-analysis largely confirmed and extended the results from the earlier 2012 meta-analysis by finding an association at posttreatment with secondary measures. The authors concluded that sudden gains are a ubiquitous phenomenon in the psychological therapies.

One observation about sudden gains is whether it is possible to predict their occurrence rather than their being viewed as unpredictable events that then subsequently yield high predictive value regarding patient outcomes. However, no consistent predictors of sudden gains appear to have been reported in the literature. A different and maybe more dynamic approach to sudden gains focuses on the concept of variability in viewing sudden gains as one, perhaps the most extreme, form of fluctuation in symptom levels during the course of therapy (e.g., Stiles et al., 2003). Accordingly, variability in symptoms becomes a potential predictor of sudden gains. Shalom et al. (2018) took this notion and tested the intra-individual variability of symptoms for patients in three independent RCTs investigating differing psychological conditions (prolonged exposure, CBT, and psychodynamic therapy) in children and adults. Their index of variability was the absolute extent of change scores between sessions 1 and 2 and between sessions 2 and 3. By ignoring the direction of the change, it guarded against opposite directions cancelling each other out. They found that such an index of individual symptom variability correctly predicted 81.0%, 69.2%, and 76.9% of individuals as experiencing sudden gain or non-sudden gain status in each of the three trials, respectively. Subsequently, it was shown that intra-variability both during but also prior to therapy predicted over 80% of sudden gains (Shalom et al., 2020). This approach appears both promising in its predictive potential but also in its relative simplicity of using existing or routinely collected patient monitoring data. Indeed, Aderka and Shalom (2021) have proposed a revised model of sudden gains whereby they are construed as the result of a combination of symptom fluctuation allied with a reduction in level of symptoms over the course of treatment. Hence, the model proposes that treatment facilitates rather than causes sudden gains.

Overall, research on sudden gains provides a focus on what happens during psychotherapy that can lead to such lasting changes (for about a third of patients). Many patients who respond to therapy make gains early on and these gains precede rather than follow the specific techniques deemed to be essential by many theories of psychotherapeutic intervention. Such findings call for additional research into these change processes, but also encourage weekly routine monitoring of patient treatment response (Lambert, 2010). This would allow therapists (and systems of care) to end therapy with such patients sooner, freeing up capacity and resources for patients that have been placed on a wait list.

Summary

For both policy makers and therapists, as well as patients themselves as recipients of therapy, the dose response literature has important implications for routine care. Research has provided two models for understanding the relationship between dose and effect with many studies finding support for aspects of both models. However, it is not clear that patients are best served by having, within reason, limits placed on courses of treatment and it would seem sensible to build into any service delivery system the fact that different individuals move (i.e., improve) at differing rates. Standard, fixed, low doses of treatment are not justified for the majority of individuals who enter treatment, although a minority do respond. Rather, there is an argument for the "implementation of individualized intervention lengths" (Evans et al., 2017; p. 399). These findings have implications for research trials and for clinical practice. For both, they suggest that prespecified treatment lengths may not be a meaningful route to maximizing the effectiveness of psychological therapies. And for research it would suggest the adoption of pragmatic trials in which treatment length is not prespecified although, perhaps, within a limited maximum. Since the last review (Lambert, 2013), the take-up of routine outcome monitoring (ROM), as well as increasingly sophisticated statistical modeling of data, provide the opportunity to go beyond an overdependence on baseline severity and move toward the dynamic use of information gained from successive sessions (see Chapter 4). In addition, multivariable prognostic indices must assist in determining possible intensity of treatment, particularly for more severe or complex cases (e.g., Lorenzo-Luaces et al., 2017).

Do Psychological Therapies Reach Culturally Diverse Populations?

From the findings reported to date, there is a wealth of evidence in support of psychological therapies and how they can best be delivered, but it is apparent that the evidence derives from a restricted sampling in terms of geography and populations. A key question focuses on whether evidence-based therapies are delivered and responsive to the diversity of client populations in need. The broader topic of delivery models is addressed in Chapter 22. However, the focus here is on two aspects of what might be viewed as central to the issue of the reach of the psychological therapies: (i) the degree of inclusivity and responsiveness regarding culturally diverse client groups within the current evidence base (see Forehand & Kotchick, 2016); and (ii) socioeconomic barriers to accessing and utilizing psychological therapies.

The psychological therapies are situated within differing societies that each place a greater or lesser value on the psychological health of individuals. Indeed, it has been argued that psychological therapies are culturally bound practices that are created from and dedicated to specific cultural contexts (Wampold, 2007). One index of such values is the scope and reach of psychological support provided and the relative ease with which people in need can access support. Hence, the primary issues here are those of reach and access for all sections of society who have a need. The issue (and challenge) is that currently, conventional psychotherapy is a practice that is that is mostly focused on dominant cultural groups within developed countries but that is also likely unaffordable and culturally incongruent with the values and worldviews of ethnic and racial minority groups (e.g., Sue et al., 1992), as well as being virtually unattainable for people in developing countries (Patel et al., 2011).

Ethnic Minorities and Culturally Adapted Therapies

In a major review of therapies with ethnically diverse populations, Huey et al. (2014) concluded that minority-focused therapies appear to be effective across a wide range of presenting conditions. The authors analyzed data from 140 trials and established effect sizes (d) ranging from 0.37 for smoking through 0.46 for depression and to 0.74 and 0.76 for anxiety and schizophrenia, respectively. While such evidence is supportive in general, a key issue is whether there are differential effects as a function of ethnicity such that there is ethnic disparity – poorer outcomes for ethnic minorities – rather than ethnic invariance, where there is no difference as a result of ethnicity. When considering evidence from various meta-analyses that comprised both youth and adults, the authors found a majority of studies (just over 60%) showed ethnic invariance. And of the remainder, it was broadly evenly split between an advantage to White or to ethnic minorities.

However, Huey and colleagues argued that such ethnic invariance might be due to the therapies being culturally tailored (i.e., adapted) in response to differing cultures. Griner and Smith (2006) conducted a meta-analysis of culturally adapted psychotherapy comprising 76 published and unpublished studies and concluded that culturally adapted treatment resulted in moderate effects (d = 0.45) and produced significant results when provided to racially homogeneous client groups or when conducted in clients' preferred language (d = 0.49). In a further study, Huey and Polo (2008) examined evidence-based treatments for ethnic and racial minority youth and, although limited by a relatively small number of controlled

studies to satisfy evidence-based treatment standards, derived an effect size of d = 0.58 for culturally adapted treatments compared to no treatment and d = 0.22 compared to treatment as usual. The relative efficacy of culturally adapted psychotherapy versus unadapted, bona fide psychotherapy was addressed by Benish et al. (2011) who, drawing on 21 studies, found that culturally adapted psychotherapy produced superior outcomes for ethnic and racial minority clients over conventional psychotherapy (d = 0.32, 95% CI [0.21, 0.43]). Unlike previous studies, culturally adapted therapy was compared with bona fide therapies rather than a heterogeneous collection, which may account for the slightly reduced effect.

More recently, in a meta-analysis comprising 78 studies, Hall, Ibaraki et al. (2016) found an overall ES of g = 0.67 (95% CI [0.49, 0.86]) in favor of culturally adapted interventions over no interventions or other interventions and g = 0.52 (95% CI [0.15, 0.90]) when compared with the same but unadapted intervention (n = 9). For studies that reported remission rates (n = 16), culturally adapted interventions had close to five times greater odds (4.7) of yielding remission than unadapted interventions. And in a meta-analysis of treatments for Asian American, Huey and Tilley (2018) reported a large effect (d = 0.75) for the pooled studies, over 90% of which were culturally adapted.

Hence, there is consistent evidence that culturally adapted therapies are effective. However, there is a debate in terms of the tensions between employing a top-down approach to adapting or modifying existing therapies from that of a bottom-up approach in which therapies are developed within the specific cultural context. In this situation, comparisons are not made back to the original reference group (Hall, Yip et al., 2016). There is clearly a need to find a balance between fit (to cultural specificity) and fidelity (to the evidence-based intervention) in this important area in which people in need reflect increasing diversity in terms of ethnicity and culture.

Therapist Multicultural Competency and Orientation

Parallel to developments in adapting treatments, there has been a significant focus on therapist competencies in relation to multicultural aspects. The key components of therapist multicultural competence comprise a specific set of knowledge, skills, beliefs, and attitudes (Sue et al., 1992). These competencies can be identified in therapists who continuously work toward (i) expanding their knowledge of their clients' cultural background and worldview; (ii) developing and utilizing culturally relevant interventions and treatment strategies that are appropriate to clients; (iii) gaining awareness of one's own assumptions, beliefs, and values and how they can impact on interactions with clients or perceptions of the presenting issue; and (iv) including a provider's ability to recognize how the merging of heritage or personal backgrounds influence their own and their clients' behaviors (Sue et al., 2009; Whaley & Davis, 2007).

Tao et al. (2015) summarized the extant literature as showing multicultural competencies to be associated with client satisfaction and session impact while the effects regarding the working alliance varied and the association with outcomes appeared smaller compared with process variables. And in their subsequent meta-analysis of 18 studies yielding 53 effects, the authors established that the percentage of variance accounted for by client ratings of their therapists' multicultural competence was approximately 37% in working alliance, 52% in client satisfaction, 38% in general counseling competence, and 34% in session depth. By contrast, it accounted for approximately 8% of variance in therapy outcomes. Notwithstanding the important role of multicultural competencies, especially concerning process variables, the vast majority of studies comprised university counseling students and it is important to acknowledge that findings may not generalize to primary or community-based populations.

However, the notion of competencies itself has been challenged, and it has been argued that a more appropriate model is one of adopting a multicultural *orientation*, of which the principle component is cultural humility, which in turn leads to cultural opportunities and comfort (Davis et al., 2018). The process comprises the orienting virtue and attitude of the therapist (cultural humility), together with the context-specific behaviors involved in exploring a client's salient identities (cultural opportunities), leading to the therapist's ability to self-regulate in the situation (cultural comfort). Initial evidence provides some support for the role of these factors. For example, Owen et al. (2016) found that cultural humility predicted better therapy outcome and moderated the association between perceived missed opportunities and poorer outcomes in therapy.

Impact of Ethnicity and Socioeconomic Factors

Beyond a consideration of adapting therapies and identifying therapist competencies as responsive to increased diversity, research has focused on the impacts of therapies in more diverse populations. Hayes et al. (2015) sampled 36 therapists and 228 clients seen at a university training clinic to investigate whether differences in therapist effectiveness were a function of client ethnicity. Applying multilevel modeling analyses to OQ-45 data collected at each session showed no difference in the outcomes between racial and ethnic minority (REM) and non-REM clients. Moreover, some therapists produced better outcomes than others, and this variability was due in part to client REM status. These findings are consistent with those of Owen et al. (2012), who found that therapists differed in their dropout rates among REM clients, as well as Larrison & Schopplerey (2011), who found that therapist effects were associated with client race in reducing psychological symptoms. A substantially larger study by Hayes et al. (2016) investigated whether treatment outcomes differed between REM and White clients. Although outcomes were similar for REM and White clients, there was evidence that some therapists enabled better outcomes than other therapists with their REM clients. Similar to calls within the therapist effects literature, the authors called for future investigations to focus on proximal rather than distal variables in order to further our understanding of working more effectively with clients from culturally diverse and ethnic minorities.

In a study carried out in the US, Zeber et al. (2017) utilized a large database (N = 242,765) from six service providers within a mental health research network to investigate potential factors affecting patient return rates. They found that patients from racial and ethnic minorities were less likely to attend for a subsequent visit in the 45 days following their initial visit. Using a non-Hispanic White group as a referent, the odds ratios (ORs) for all ethnic minorities were lower, ranging from 0.8 to 0.9: for example; non-Hispanic black, OR = 0.81 (95% CI [0.78, 0.84]), and Asian, OR = 0.85 (95% CI [0.82, 0.89]). The authors argued that efforts should be made to reduce barriers for returning to therapy by considering areas such as the therapeutic alliance, better tailoring of therapy to patients, cultural competencies, the potential for unconscious bias, organizational culture as well as standard procedures such as appointment reminders.

Questions as to whether mental health problems have been sufficiently described in terms of sample characteristics such as the ethnic/racial, linguistic, socioeconomic, and immigrant backgrounds of participants have been addressed by Polo et al. (2019). They reviewed trials over a 36-year period (1981 to 2016; N = 342) and concluded that reporting for ethnicity and socioeconomic indicators have improved over time. However, they were not able to endorse the view that findings from trials evaluating the psychosocial interventions could be reliably applied to groups not represented in such research. For example, they found that trials were far more likely to exclude, rather than include, linguistic minorities, and had not enrolled meaningful numbers of Asian American, Native Hawaiian/Pacific Islander, Native American/Native Alaskan, and multiethnic participants. Important to note is that although the review was considering diversity, the sampling of the trial data was limited to the US only.

An additional key factor is socioeconomic status. Rojas-Garcia et al. (2015) characterized and analyzed the short- and long-term effectiveness of health-care interventions for depressive disorders in low socioeconomic status populations. They conducted two meta-analyses for assessing both the short (n = 11) and long-term effectiveness (n = 12) of interventions and reported a statistically significant reduction in overall depressive symptoms (SMD = –0.58, 95% CI [–0.74, –0.42]) at short-term (up to three months after the intervention), and a slightly decreased effect at long-term (SMD = –0.42, 95% CI [–0.63, –0.21]). Interventions that included culturally specific training for providers and booster sessions appeared more effective in reducing depressive disorders both at short- and long-term assessments. They concluded that health-care interventions are effective in decreasing clinically significant depressive disorders in low socioeconomic status populations.

Because of the potential for economics or finances to be an obstacle to seeking support, evidence from countries where costs are not a barrier are of particular value. Epping et al. (2017) reported data from Germany and found that where finance was not an obstacle to accessing support due to insurance cover, there was an underutilization by people from lower socioeconomic groups resulting in those people at highest risk of psychological difficulties having the lowest utilization rate. The major factor influencing access was education and the authors suggested that education and public health policy are crucial in ensuring a viable and open gateway to psychological support for people.

In the final analysis, the ability of countries to respond to the psychological needs of their population depends, in part, on fiscal constraints. From an economic perspective, Patel et al. (2016) identified a key role to be played at the health-care level platform in which the two most relevant delivery channels impacting on public health are self-management (e.g., web-based psychological therapies for depression and anxiety) and primary care and community outreach (e.g., nonspecialist health workers delivering psychological management for specific conditions). Relatedly, it was calculated that the costs of providing a significantly scaled-up package of specified cost-effective interventions for key psychological (and other) disorders in low-income and lower-middle-income countries would be approximately $US3-4 per head of population per year.

Summary

In a world that is, by definition, multicultural and with huge discrepancies in the economic welfare of continents, countries, and regions, it is logical that no single format of any single therapy modality could meet such needs. Cultural adaptations appear to be effective and yet there is a debate as to whether they are modified via a top-down or bottom-up process. Of note is the positioning toward cultural humility, mirroring an evidence stream arising from research into effective therapists. Our collective ability to respond to the needs of so many people across the spectrum of available economic resources is likely to be one of the biggest challenges facing the psychological therapies going forward and one we return to in the final section.

THERAPEUTIC IMPACT ON INDIVIDUAL CLIENTS

In the previous section we focused on service or clinic-level questions of implementation and reach and considered research more at a population level. Here we move to a focus that is more centered on individual clients and address three questions:

1. Do clients receiving therapy make clinically meaningful changes?
2. Do some patients get worse?
3. Do clients maintain their gains?

Do Patients Make Clinically Meaningful Changes?

The scientific study of the efficacy of the psychological therapies has focused primarily on testing whether a group of patients who received treatment has a better outcome than a group who did not receive an optimal treatment. As we have discussed, an effect size is a statistic that is derived from efficacy study estimates of change expressed in standardized units. But presenting change in this way obscures whether the change made by a patient is clinically important. Cuijpers, Turner et al. (2014) built on the concept of minimal important difference by using calculations regarding health utilities to estimate that an effect size of 0.24 captured a clinically relevant change in the treatment of depression. However, at a group level, this is a point estimate and it would require the lowest 95% CI of this value to exceed this estimate to have confidence that the true

value met a minimal important difference criterion. Considerable attention has focused on group comparisons, and many researchers have supplemented statistical comparisons between groups and the use of the effect size statistics with additional analyses that investigate the clinical significance of changes that occur as a result of psychological therapy.

Indices of Response and Recovery (Nomothetic and Idiographic)

Two indices have been used in trials methodology: response and recovery. Treatment *response* is usually taken as a 50% fall from the patient's intake score, while *recovery* is determined by a posttreatment score being below a prespecified cut-off score denoting not-caseness. These two elements capture what might be termed *extent* and *status of change*, the two criteria utilized in Jacobson and Truax's (1991) index of reliable and clinically significant change. One crucial advance of their method was that the index of reliable change was derived from the specific psychometric properties of any given measure. Hence, better reliability yields reduced measurement error and a more precise estimate of whether the change can be attributed to therapy (i.e., not to chance). As a consequence, Lambert and Ogles (2009) argued strongly for the adoption of Jacobson and Truax's method within all psychotherapy studies, including the reporting of percentage of patients reliably deteriorating. In addition, a general review of methods has been reported by Lambert and Bailey (2012), providing an overview of the Jacobson and Truax method as well as a range of variants and highlight the value of this method in capturing within group variability.

The Jacobson and Truax method, with its intrinsic clinical relevance and relative ease in calculation, has made this approach highly appealing, particularly to clinical practice. For example, the Improving Access to Psychological Therapies initiative, the largest national program in England, has adopted the principles of the Jacobson and Truax approach in all but name to capture, in addition to deterioration, three outcome indices tapping improvement: reliable improvement, recovery (i.e., not caseness), and reliable recovery (i.e., equivalent to reliable and clinically significant improvement) (NHS Digital, 2020). A crucial issue, however, is equating statistical recovery with clinical recovery as the method is still derived from statistical premises such that it cannot be known if a patient making reliable and clinically significant improvement on a specific measure actually experiences the psychological benefits of recovery. Hence, use of the term *reliably recovered* should be used with caution.

In a study investigating the meaning underpinning good outcomes for patients who met the Jacobson and Truax criteria of either improvement or recovery, De Smet et al. (2020) drew on the reported experiences of 28 recovered and 19 improvement patients, so categorized according to their posttreatment scores meeting the respective Jacobson and Truax criteria. Of the 47 patients, 27 had received CBT and 20 psychodynamic therapy. Using grounded theory, recovered patients referred to experiencing significant changes but residual issues still remained. For improved patients, there was greater variability (ranging from feeling better to not doing very well). Of course, greater variability of experience for improvement is natural as, unlike the criterion of recovery, improvement is not anchored to any absolute score: the change is all relative to the individual's pretherapy score. Hence, greater homogeneity of experience would be expected from recovery while those patients reporting improvement indicated greater instability regarding their gains and more heterogeneity in their experiences. However, in both groups three themes emerged from the analyses: empowerment (including increased self-confidence, putting themselves more to the fore, and realizing new coping skills); personal balance (comprising more positive aspects in terms of relationships, insight and self-understanding, and feeling calmer); and ongoing struggle (involving unresolved or recurring problems). The first two themes are similar to those that have been derived from analyses of helpful events in therapy (see Timulak, 2007, 2010). Such studies are useful in giving greater personal meaning to the categories employed in research and act as a caution against the reifying of recovery labels.

Notwithstanding the contribution that the Jacobson and Truax procedure has made to determining and categorizing clinical change at an individual level, it derives from measures premised largely on nomothetic assumptions in which the items are invariant. An alternative or complementary approach to capturing meaningful change data is to ensure that the individual items have immediate and specific relevance to an individual via the adoption of idiographic measures. Again, this work aims to provide personal meaning to an index of improvement or recovery. Idiographic measurement has a rich history in the psychological therapies (see Hobson & Shapiro, 1970; Shapiro, 1961) and, in a systematic review of individualized assessment tools used in psychotherapeutic practice and research, Sales and Alves (2016) identified two problem-focused outcome measures – the Simplified Personal Questionnaire (PQ; Elliott et al., 2016) and the Psychological Outcome Profiles (PSYCHLOPS; Ashworth et al., 2005) – and a goal-focused outcome measure, Goal Attainment Scaling (Kiresuk et al., 1994). Elliott et al. (2016) provided psychometric data supporting the utility of Personal Questionnaire (PQ) methodology, making the argument that the derivation of such items from individual people infuses them with both specificity and personal meaning, thereby mirroring both cognitive-behavioral and humanistic approaches, as well as providing the basis for case formulation as reflected by the interrelationship between generated items. And in a study comparing patients' responses using patient-generated items in PSYCHLOPS compared with nomothetic measures (PHQ-9 and CORE-OM), Sales et al. (2018) reported that 95% and 71% of patients reported an item whose content was not contained in the PHQ-9 or CORE-OM, respectively. However, rather than a criticism of nomothetic methods, it is simply testimony to the differential yield of contrasting methods and their underlying assumptions.

Summary

Although the effect size statistic overestimates the proportion of individuals who experience clinically meaningful changes, there is substantial evidence that the psychotherapies also produce outcomes that are clinically meaningful. Both primary studies and meta-analytic reviews find that many clients improve to levels that might be considered a full recovery. However, we also know that meeting a criterion of statistical recovery does not necessarily mean that a client is clinically recovered. Tapping both nomothetic and idiographic approaches to the measurement of change is likely to yield greater clinical information although also likely to be statistically more challenging.

Do Some Patients Get Worse?

Although negative effects are difficult, if not impossible, to study in an experimentally controlled way, research clearly indicates that some patients are worse at the time therapy is terminated than when they started. Framed as deterioration, this issue was raised in the seminal work of Bergin (1963, 1966). Bergin's conceptualization of the deterioration effect captured the greater variability in outcomes within the treatment condition compared with the control condition in seven studies for which there appeared to be no apparent difference in outcomes. It is likely that the drive for overall effects with the emphasis on group means has masked the individual variability within which fall cases of deterioration. On this basis, Barlow (2010) called for the greater adoption of idiographic approaches to data analysis in trials such that data observation was more akin to clinical practice using repeated administration of measures contributing to large practice-based datasets.

Negative Impacts

In reviewing the general question of negative impacts, we consider three distinct but overlapping concepts in the literature that capture differing aspects of this phenomenon – harm, adverse effects, and deterioration – with the common impact that they have a negative impact on the patient. A recent commentary concluded that "Negative effects of psychotherapy are multifaceted, warranting careful considerations in order for them to be monitored and reported in research settings and routine care" (Rozental, 2018, p.307). The difficulty in progressing this topic reflects an element of reluctance at one level, but also the slowness in adopting agreed-upon definitions. Since the last edition of this *Handbook* (Lambert, 2013), various calls have been made for clearer definitions, and better monitoring and reporting of negative effects (e.g., Linden & Schermuly-Haupt, 2013; Scott & Young, 2016). In addition, Linden (2013) published a detailed account of such definitions for a range of themes pertinent to negative effects: unwanted events, treatment-emergent reactions, adverse treatment reactions, malpractice reactions, treatment nonresponse, deterioration of illness, therapeutic risks, and contraindications.

Harm. Dimidjian and Hollon (2010) focused on harm – that is, where the treatment causally made a person worse, thereby making a distinction with treatments (and by implication, therapists) that are unhelpful or ineffective. Hence, not all instances of worsening are the product of therapy. Some cases may be on a progressive decline that no therapist effort can stop. Other cases may experience highly negative life events that therapy is unable to protect them from (such as a new medical condition or loss of a loved one). The extent or rate of such negative change or of "spontaneous" deterioration in untreated groups has never been determined, so there is no baseline from which to judge deterioration rates observed in treated groups.

Randomized controlled trials provide a specific source of information relating to the methodology for collecting, reporting, and responding to issues of harm. Jonsson et al. (2014) identified 132 published studies in the calendar year 2010, of which only 28 (21%) provided information noting that monitoring of potential harms was carried out. Of these 28, 4 reported adverse events and a method for their detection and reporting, 5 reported adverse events but no method, 4 reported no adverse events, and 15 reported information only on deterioration. Reporting of a method for monitoring adverse events was associated with the impact factor of the journal. When analyzed according to the mental health condition reported in the trial, the percentage of studies with reported procedures for reactions to severe stress/adjustment disorders (e.g., PTSD) was, at 50%, twice that of any other condition. From such data, it is a general recommendation that there needs to be more active and regular monitoring of potential harms and the reporting of reliable deterioration should be standard. The CONSORT for trials requires all important harms and unintended events to be reported and is consistent with a policy of transparency in reporting the outcomes of the psychotherapies whether delivered in trials or routine practice.

Adverse Effects. In terms of adverse effects, survey methods have identified possible rates. User-perspectives were sought by Crawford et al. (2016) who employed a cross-sectional survey of people in receipt of psychological therapies from 184 services in England and Wales as part of an audit of the delivery and impact of the IAPT program. They were asked whether they had experienced lasting bad effects from treatment. Of 14,587 respondents, 763 (5.2%) reported experiencing lasting bad effects. People aged over 65 were less likely to report such effects whereas sexual and ethnic minorities were more likely to report them. People who were unsure what type of therapy they received were more likely to report negative effects and those that stated that they were given enough information about therapy before it started were less likely to report them.

Taking a different perspective, it appears that therapists underestimate negative incidents. Schermuly-Haupt et al. (2018) screened 100 CBT therapists for side effects of therapy using the Unwanted Events-Adverse Treatment Reactions Checklist (Linden 2013), which comprises 17 domains of possible unwanted events. While 74% of therapists reported no side effects when asked for a spontaneous response, only 2% claimed this to be the case following the in-depth interview from which 372 unwanted events were derived. Although the majority of side effects were rated as mild or moderate (59.6%) and transient (89.6%), 15.3% were deemed to be definitely related to treatment and 8.8% rated as having persistent (i.e., ongoing) effects in a patient's life.

Deterioration. In relation to deterioration, for depression, Cuijpers, Reijnders et al. (2018) identified 18 studies (23 comparisons) comparing therapy with a control group and found patients in the therapy conditions to have a 61% lower chance of deterioration. The deterioration rates in the psychotherapy groups ranged from 0 to 25% (Median 4%) compared with a range of 1% to 44% (Median 11%) in the control groups. The authors suggested that one possibility that may account for low reporting rate in trials is that, because of the low base rate, there is rarely a significant difference in adverse events between conditions. However, this is to miss the key point of the first principle of any trial (or intervention): *primum non nocere* (first, do no harm). For OCD, Moritz et al. (2015), based on a sample of 85 participants, found a substantial subgroup complained about new symptoms (e.g., after exposure treatment). Approximately 1 in 4 patients mentioned fear of treatment stigma, adaptation problems after therapy, and relationship problems due to treatment. True side effects of psychotherapy were negatively correlated with patient-perceived positive effects of treatment.

Overall, in the past decade there has been an appropriate engagement by research into the phenomenon of negative or side effects in the psychological therapies. Having a better understanding of the contributions of treatments and therapists to this phenomenon will help to protect more vulnerable patients and also enhance effectiveness.

Do Patients Maintain Their Gains?

Although early outcome research focused primarily on the immediate posttreatment status of patients who participated in therapy, hundreds of studies have now considered the maintenance of treatment gains. Similarly, many meta-analytic reviews consider outcome immediately following treatment and at follow-up. There is no reason to believe that a single course of psychotherapy (especially as practiced in the United States where average doses hover around 4 to 5 sessions in routine care; or 4 to 20 sessions in an RCT; Hansen et al., 2002), should inoculate a person forever from relapse and the development of new symptoms. Yet, many patients who undergo therapy achieve healthy adjustment for long periods of time. This is true even though some have had a long history of recurrent problems. At the same time, there is clear evidence that a portion of patients who are improved at termination do relapse and continue to seek help from a variety of mental health providers, including their former therapists.

Relapse

Lambert (2013) drew out the distinction between the relapse rates for people who complete a course of treatment from those who drop out. For the former, examples of more high-end estimates have been in the region of 42% (Koppers et al., 2011) to 49% after five years (Jarrett et al., 2001). This compares with estimates of 83% for people experiencing a depressive episode and not completing their treatment course (Jarrett et al., 2001). Delgadillo et al. (2018) reported a relapse recurrence rate of 65.8% for low intensity CBT at 24 months. And the risk of relapse increases with each successive relapse (Solomon et al., 2000; ten Doesschate, 2010). Using data from a 10-year prospective multicenter study, Solomon and colleagues (2000) estimated the risk of relapse to increase 16% with each subsequent depressive episode. On the other hand, risk of relapse progressively decreases as recovery length increases, such that the probability of relapse diminishes from 20% within the first six months following a depressive episode to 9% after three years of maintaining gains (Solomon et al., 2000). And in a review focused on predictors of relapse and recurrence, Buckman et al. (2018) identified a series of strong predictors for risk of recurrence, namely childhood maltreatment, residual symptoms, history of recurrence, a history or current comorbid anxiety disorders, and ruminations.

Biesheuvel-Leliefeld et al. (2015) carried out a meta-analysis and meta-regression of trial literature comprising 25 studies and found preventive psychological interventions to be superior to treatment-as-usual in reducing the risk of relapse or recurrence (RR = 0.64, 95% CI: [0.53, 0.76]). Perhaps most noteworthy was the finding that within any given trial, the effectiveness of preventative interventions was greater for those patients who had received any psychological or pharmacological (or both) intervention during the acute phase, thereby suggesting that preventative interventions after remission should become an integral component of a comprehensive treatment plan. Clarke et al. (2015) also carried out a similar systematic review and meta-analysis of 29 studies and found, at 12-months, that CBT, mindfulness-based cognitive therapy (MBCT), and interpersonal therapy (IPT) yielded a 22% (95% CI [15%, 29%]) reduction in relapse compared with controls. For CBT, the effect was maintained at 24 months, but not for IPT and there was no available data for MBCT. A limitation noted was that MBCT tended to be used following medication, making the need for more evidence following psychological interventions. And, in a narrative review, Bockting et al. (2015) arrived at a similar conclusion stating that cognitive-behavioral interventions appear to bestow an enduring effect against relapse posttreatment. Moreover, cognitive therapy and possibly IPT as a continuation treatment can further reduce the risk of relapse. They also advocated the adoption of continuation and preventative approaches following remission due to the recurrent nature of depression. Noteworthy, they pointed to the need for national health policies to take account of relapse and recurrence due to the high economic burden arising from depression.

Wojnarowski et al. (2019) reviewed relapse and recurrence specifically in relation to depression and CBT, drawing on 13 articles, of which 5 contributed to a meta-analysis. Overall, the authors reported a relapse rate of 33.4%. Seven categories of events were identified from the literature: residual depressive symptoms; prior episodes of depression; cognitive reactivity; stressful life events; personality factors; clinical/diagnostic factors; and demographics. However, the meta-analysis indicated that only residual depressive symptoms ($r = 0.34$, 95% CI [0.10, 0.54]) and prior episodes ($r = 0.19$, 95% CI [0.07, 0.30]) were statistically significant predictors of relapse or recurrence. In a separate systematic review focusing on CBT and anxiety, a relapse rate of 23.4% was established (Lorimer et al., 2021). The phenomenon of residual symptoms was also identified in a sample of 494 patients whose depressive symptoms remitted following a nine-week course of pharmacological treatment for depression (Akechi et al., 2019). Investigating predictors of 71

people (14.4%) who relapsed at 25 weeks showed the only significant predictor to be residual symptoms at posttreatment. Similarly, Ali et al. (2017) investigated the relapse rates in the IAPT program for patients 12 months after completing low-intensity CBT with 439 completers who were in remission providing PHQ-9 and Generalized Anxiety Disorder-7 (GAD-7) scores each month for one year. The authors reported a relapse rate of 53% with the majority occurring within the initial six months and those with residual symptoms having a higher risk of relapse (Hazard Ratio [HR] =1.90).

The continual finding relating to the predictive potential of residual symptoms has also been captured in the application of network analysis. Lorimer et al. (2020) found that although the network of PHQ-9 residual symptoms at baseline and post-therapy were broadly similar, there were noteworthy differences in key symptom items between patients who remitted versus those who relapsed. They found that the item focusing on "trouble concentrating" became more central in the relapse network as compared with the remission network where "trouble relaxing" was the most central symptom. The search for greater specificity in residual symptoms as possible flags for targeting subsequent integrated continuation and maintenance support may be a potential tool that has significant research and clinical utility. Indeed, it may prove to be useful in predictive modeling approaches given its proximity to the time when plans for continuation or maintenance interventions for patients need to be made.

Interventions to Reduce Relapse and Maximize Maintenance

Efforts to address the phenomenon of relapse (and also recurrence) was a primary rationale for the development of mindfulness-based cognitive therapy (MBCT; Segal et al., 2002). In a review of the literature, Beshai et al. (2011) reported risk ratios from 24 studies representing the probability of relapse between cognitive therapy (CT; range of risk ratios = 0.25–1.32), mindfulness-based cognitive therapy (MBCT; range of risk ratios = 0.29–1.80), and interpersonal therapy (IPT; range of risk ratios = 0.51–1.23). The authors suggested that MBCT had a significant preventive effect in recurrent depression, relative to treatment as usual, but the observed differences between therapy type appear to be small. Notably, however, this effect was only found for patients with a more chronic course of depression, defined as having had three or more episodes of depression. The authors also concluded that initial evidence suggested IPT to have a prophylactic effect regarding recurrent depression. Interestingly, it was suggested that IPT, in contrast to CBT, may be better able to address recurrence arising from negative life events.

Research on MBCT has been captured in a number of systematic reviews and meta-analyses. Kuyken et al. (2016) conducted an individual patient data meta-analysis comprising 1329 patients. At 60 weeks, patients in receipt of MBCT had a reduced risk of relapse compared with patients who did not receive MBCT; HR = 0.69 (95% CI [0.58, 0.82]). Data from four studies showed MBCT also to be superior to antidepressant medication; HR = 0.77 (95% CI [0.60, 0.98]). In addition, its effects did not appear to be a function of patient age, educational level, marital status, or sex, suggesting the wider utility of the intervention. They found that the treatment effect of MBCT was greater for those patients with higher levels of depression symptoms at baseline, a finding that links with earlier findings pointing to the potential vulnerability of levels of residual symptomatology. These findings also equate with results from a meta-analysis of the effect of MBCT for patients with recurrent depression reported by Goldberg et al. (2019). They found MBCT to be superior to nonspecific control conditions, d = 0.71 (95% CI [0.47, 0.96]) but no difference between MBCT and active control conditions, which comprised studies of a range of interventions, including psychoeducation, CBT, Cognitive Behavioral Analysis System of Psychotherapy, and a Health Education Program, d = 0.002 (95% CI [–0.43, 0.44]). And another meta-analysis involved 16 studies including databases from China (Zhang et al., 2018) in which results showed CBT to be superior to control conditions in terms of risk reduction for patients in remission; HR = 0.50 (95% CI [0.35, 0.72]). The results for MBCT showed it also to be superior to control conditions, but only for individuals with three or more prior episodes; HR = 0.46 (95% CI [0.31, 0.70]).

Most recently, a systematic review and network meta-analysis of MBCT considered relapse of depression and time to relapse (McCarthy et al., 2021). For relapse of depression, analyses showed statistically significant advantages for MBCT over treatment as usual for relapse of depression (RR = 0.73, 95% CI [0.54, 0.98]). And for time to relapse for depression, MBCT was also superior to treatment as usual and placebo (MBCT vs. TAU: HR = 0.57, 95% CI [0.37, 0.88]; MBCT vs. placebo: HR = 0.23, 95% CI [0.08, 0.67]). Interestingly, no difference was found in the risk of relapse between those patients who had more or less than three previous episodes. This result counters UK NICE guidance that stipulates that MBCT is only recommended for people experiencing three or more previous episodes.

Longer-Term Outcomes

Under the final heading in this section, we consider what might be viewed as the most salient perspective on the efficacy and effectiveness of the psychological therapies, namely their longer-term outcomes – that is, their enduring effects.

Since the Lambert (2013) review, there have been a number of studies reporting longer-term outcomes. For example, Steinert et al. (2014) investigated the longer-term effectiveness of psychotherapy for depression and carried out two meta-analyses focusing on overall rates of relapse two-years beyond treatment in a comparison with pharmacotherapy or treatment as usual over a similar time period. From their review, they reported that upwards of 89% of people were recovered at the time of follow-up but that a lower percentage, between 35% and 60% of people, experienced a stable recovery during the follow-up period, meaning that they did not experience a further episode during the follow-up period. And psychological therapies resulted in significantly less relapses than comparison treatments (53.1% vs. 71.1%; OR 0.51; 95% CI [0.32,

0.82]). The authors concluded that even though the relapse rate was relatively high, the evidence showed the rate to be significantly lower compared with nonpsychotherapeutic approaches.

The enduring effects, albeit over a relatively short time frame, were investigated by Flückiger et al. (2014), who found small to moderate effect size differences in favor of evidence-based psychotherapies, although the effects decreased over time such that at 12- to 18-month assessments, the effect was g = 0.20, (95% CI [0.08, 0.31]). The authors concluded that there was no support to show that evidence-based psychotherapies generally enhance their efficacy at the follow-up assessments relative to treatment as usual. So, the small effect sizes found in favor of therapies at follow-up assessments confirmed findings from an earlier meta-analysis showing a positive effect of evidence-based psychotherapies versus treatment as usual for acute depression and anxiety disorders at treatment termination (Wampold et al., 2011). However, Flückiger and colleagues were sanguine about the cost and effort of investing in such evidence-based therapies over and above treatment as usual in light of the lack of evidence for their enhanced impacts beyond treatment termination.

A meta-analysis on short-term psychodynamic psychotherapy (STPP; Driessen et al., 2015) was presented earlier in this chapter. Pertinent here are results considering changes at follow-up. In terms of presenting conditions, changes from posttreatment to follow-up greater than six months yielded mean pooled effect sizes of 0.04 (95% CI [–0.08, 0.17] for depression, 0.27 (95% CI –0.00, 0.54]) for anxiety, 0.16 (95% CI [–0.08, 0.41]) for general psychopathology, and 0.11 (95% CI [–0.09, 0.32]) for interpersonal functioning measures, all indicating nonsignificant changes from posttreatment to follow-up. At follow-up greater than six months, no significant differences between STPP and other psychotherapies were found on measures of depression; d = –0.08 (95% CI [–0.32, 0.17]). However, the mean pooled effect size of four studies assessing symptoms of anxiety at follow-up indicated a significant superiority of STPP over a collection of other psychotherapies including brief supportive psychotherapy, CBT, behavior therapy, and art therapy (d = 0.76; 95% CI [0.23, 1.28], NNT = 2.44). The mean pooled effect size of five studies assessing general psychopathology at follow-up indicated a small advantage of STPP over the other psychotherapies while for outcomes of interpersonal functioning there were no differences between STPP and other psychotherapies at follow-up. These results support the efficacy of STPP for depression beyond the end of treatment with effects showing in measures of general and interpersonal domains.

Several studies have focused on IPT and comparisons particularly with CBT. In one such study, Karyotaki et al. (2016) investigated long-term effects and found that treatment gains were maintained through six months or longer post-randomization for IPT, CBT, and problem-solving therapy but not for nondirective supportive treatment, which was found to be less efficacious. It was also the case that in the longer-term, psychotherapy resulted in higher effects compared to control groups when it was provided with additional booster sessions, or when it was exclusively targeted at adults with major depressive disorder. Results indicated that as the follow-up time progressively increased, the effects of psychotherapy versus control decreased. The evidence points to greater gains being made earlier with bona-fide therapies which, for patients, converts into better quality of life for periods beyond the end of therapy.

In another study, Lemmens et al. (2018) reported comparative outcomes of patients receiving either IPT or CBT for depression at 7 months (end of treatment; $n = 134$) and treatment responders at 24 months (follow-up; $n = 85$). The study reported on the follow-up phase as a sequel to the finding of no difference between the two active therapies at end of treatment and at 5-month follow-up (i.e., at 12 months) (Lemmens et al., 2015). The predictions were that there would be broad maintenance of gains with relapse rates of around 30% and that CBT might perform slightly better. Indeed, the change effect sizes across the follow-up period were small and there was no difference between the two therapy conditions. The relapse rates in both conditions were low and were not significantly different: 13 (28.9%) for CBT and 15 (37.5%) for IPT. And the period of time to relapse was slightly shorter for IPT than for CBT (54.1 weeks and 69.8 weeks, respectively). On the basis of these results, the authors held out the possibility of enduring effects of IPT. In a similar vein, Mulder et al. (2017) reported findings suggesting CBT to be more effective than IPT in reducing symptoms of depression at 10 months as it acted more quickly but found no differential predictors in terms of response to either treatment.

For treatment-resistant depression (Li et al., 2018) identified two RCTs reporting outcomes after 12 months. The pooled SMD was –0.29 (95% CI [–0.43, –0.16]), indicating that CBT had a longer-term effect on reducing depression symptoms. At 12 months, of the sample of patients in these two trials, 61% of CBT participants were deemed to have responded compared with 35% of control participants. The pooled RR was 1.73 (95% CI = 1.42, 2.11), supporting the longer-term efficacy of CBT with treatment-resistant depression. Remission rates showed 26% of CBT participants and 14% of control participants to have remitted with a pooled RR of 2.01 (95% CI = 1.54, 2.62), thereby supporting the comparative efficiency of CBT. And in a further RCT on treatment-resistant depression, Wiles et al. (2016) carried out a follow-up study over an average of 46 months evaluating CBT as an adjunct to usual care. Gains made at 6 months were largely maintained in both CBT and usual care conditions at both 12 and 46 months such that the small advantage to CBT largely remained, albeit very slightly reduced.

Summary

The findings from this body of literature yield both promise in the stable gains retained by some patients but also cause for concern in terms of the rates of relapse, particularly for certain conditions such as depression. There is a clear need for research efforts to shift focus to a longer-term view of outcomes, with perhaps a more granular focus on within-therapy predictors that will enable maintenance and follow-up strategies to be developed and integrated into treatment plans. This area of

impact and research may be one bridge toward encompassing a model of ongoing health monitoring that interfaces with population health, a shift we identity in the next and final section of this chapter.

RESEARCHING, ENHANCING, AND EXTENDING EFFICACY AND EFFECTIVENESS

In the final section of this chapter, we draw out key points from this review of efficacy and effectiveness and consider their implications for the practice of research in the psychological therapies and thereby for practice itself in this field. This chapter overlaps with, complements, and updates the equivalent chapter in the previous edition (see Lambert, 2013). The conclusions for practice remain broadly the same and, as such, readers should refer to that text for a fuller account. Here we update them but have focused more on implications for research as these lay the foundations for the evidence that arises and the subsequent implications for practice. To put it another way – unless we get the practice of research right, we will not provide the right research to underpin and inform practice. On this basis, we have also tried to make observations aimed at moving the field forward for the next decade of psychological therapies research.

Meta-Analysis, Trials, and Variability

The past 40 years have yielded a wealth of evidence attesting to the absolute and relative efficacy of a range of psychological therapies with the source of much of this evidence deriving from meta-analytic studies (Wampold & Imel, 2015). The landmark publication of Smith and Glass' (1977) meta-analysis was a watershed – it marked a stepped change in the method by which data was analyzed and reported. Over 40 years later, meta-analyses are commonplace and have become the currency for guideline development along with their cousin, network meta-analyses. We know that bona fide psychotherapies are effective, yielding improvements based on conservative estimates of, on average, between 60% and upward of 70% of patients. However, in reviewing the literature cited in this chapter (and more), what has been striking has been the oft-made comment by authors and commentators about both the quality of the evidence underpinning meta-analytic studies and the procedures employed in making between study comparisons (e.g., Baldwin & Imel, 2020).

Hence, we consider there is merit in focusing on same experiment data that is drawn from trials that, rather than being isolated from everyday practice, are in fact embedded within larger state or nationally mandated psychological therapy programs (e.g., England's IAPT program). Such nested designs provide considerable potential for bridging the values underpinning efficacy and effectiveness research. More specifically, embedding efficacy trials within larger programs can provide tests of the validity of results arising from routine settings, thereby providing a connection between the evidence derived from trials and routine practice (i.e., data archives).

For example, Barkham et al. (2021) reported the outcomes of a large RCT comparing person-centered experiential therapy (PCET) with CBT nested within the English IAPT program. They found PCET to be noninferior to CBT at 6 months postrandomization or end of treatment but to favor CBT at 12 months, particularly for more severe patients. Hence, the trial results both corroborated reports of the shorter-term outcomes from routine (practice-based) data showing no meaningful difference between modalities, but also extended the understanding of where differences may subsequently occur (see Chapter 13). More generally, comparisons can be made between trial patients and those within the normal service and also with those people who were offered but declined participation in the trial. The strategic aim should be to utilize available quantitative and qualitative data from pragmatic trials, together with that from practice-based datasets to enhance the scientific connectedness between these two paradigms and thereby provide a richer source of knowledge to enhance the quality of psychological therapies and their delivery for patients.

Crucially, such trials would be larger and hence more inclusive, thereby including greater variability in terms of breadth and diversity of participants and therefore enable better understanding of cases where interventions may be more challenged or do not work as well (Dimidjian & Hollon, 2011). This would include greater attention to negative or side effects, adverse events, and also deterioration. And in addition to inter-individual variability, concerns about capturing intra-individual variability could build on the increased interest in idiographic measurement (Molenaar, 2004; see also Fisher et al., 2018). Greater inclusivity will extend the reach of trials so that they become living laboratories for research in the psychological therapies.

And in terms of meta-analyses, previously, Lambert (2013) concluded that it was not a panacea and had not reduced controversies, and this still appears to be the case. In terms of the yield of meta-analytic studies, we posit two thought challenges. The first is that rather than viewing meta-analyses as the culmination of a research process, as is often the case in guideline development, we might be better viewing it as the beginning of the conversation and not the end (Hollon, 2021; personal communication; 7th February, 2021). For example, initial components of such a conversation could focus on what such analyses tell us about when therapy does not work and for whom, and from a methodological perspective to improve the quality of the trials such that subsequent meta-analytic studies (and systematic reviews) are informed by higher-quality and larger studies. And the second thought returns to an observation by one of the original authors in the field of meta-analysis, Gene Glass, who has argued more recently that a focus on meta-analytic studies reflects a less effective and efficient research process (Glass, 2015). Glass contends that few physicists talk about their latest study and suggests that rather than focusing on "publishing 'studies,'" we need to be "contributing to data archives," a position from which he concludes: "Then there will be no need for meta-analysis" (p. 230). Visions of living labs with pragmatic trials nested within routine settings running extended sequential trials may be some way off. But in the meantime, the field might benefit from ensuring there is a balance between the march of meta-analytic studies and a focus

on designing and delivering higher-quality inclusive head-to-head (i.e., same experiment) comparisons embedded in routine services.

And in pursuant of higher quality trials, we note, as others have done, that many trials are still underpowered, some woefully (Cuijpers, 2016). We should be looking to find cost-efficient ways of generating larger pragmatic trials with the starting point for any trial being Cohen (e.g., 1988, 1992) and its modern morph, G*Power. Comparisons between active psychological therapies are always likely to need to be powered to detect an effect size (d) of 0.2. And if the argument about the role of common factors is correct, then differing therapies have much in common. So, if credible therapies are being implemented in practice, it would seem questionable to be doing so on the basis of any power calculation premised on anything other than a small effect difference between them.

And an observation on the issue of small effects is worth noting. It is questionable what further gain there is in assigning small effects to the Dodo bird verdict. Labeling differences as small disincentivizes research effort and interest aimed at understanding such differences. And when they occur consistently, we are likely to be missing something that could be important. The problem is that a small effect is viewed as an absolute – that is, it is not important, irrespective of any other factor or consideration. But, context is crucial such that a small effect occurring at a population level (e.g., in a national delivery program) will have implications for thousands of people. Hence, it might be better to consider the importance of any effects in terms of their *impact* on specific groups of people or at a population level rather than continuing to categorize effect sizes only in absolute terms (i.e., small, medium, or large).

Controls, Comparators, and Contrasts

Reviewing the literature in this chapter has shown clearly that the nature of the control or comparator condition has a defining impact on the reported effect size. Use of well-designed placebos or comparative treatments, where they are feasible, may yield more exacting evidence (see Guidi et al., 2018). Indeed, if we are aiming to move research on the psychological therapies forward, then it might be that an appropriate comparator condition is CBT as the standard benchmark. Our designs are not then ones of superiority over a wait list and its associated ethical concerns, unless there is good scientific reason to test for expectancy effects, but rather of comparative effectiveness that reflects choices in the real world via pragmatic trials embedded in routine practice and therefore have the potential for directly informing clinical practice. And if comparative trials are not premised on the assumption of superiority, then concerns about noninferiority trials need to be addressed so that the practical question as to the comparative effectiveness of, for example, humanistic therapies and other non-CBT therapies versus CBT can be addressed.

In relation to identifying the effective components of therapies, there are calls for dismantling and additive studies. These seem logical designs in moving toward considering what are the essential components of therapeutic change. However, such studies require considerable statistical power to detect what are likely to be, by definition, smaller effects; for example, Cuijpers (2016) estimated a sample size of 548 was required to detect a minimally important difference indicated by an ES of 0.24. Hence, dismantling studies that are underpowered and find no difference between treatments will be prone to Type II errors and therefore would appear questionable and probably a misleading basis for informing clinical practice.

Comparative trials, pitting one therapy against another, yield few differences although, as we have acknowledged, these exist at the group level and it is crucial that analyses report the variability in the data to capture those for whom an intervention is not working. But, the finding that interventions are similar in their outcomes is important in terms of patient choice and ensuring that the best resource of professional therapists and practitioners are available to meet demand. Hence, there need to be viable choices of evidence-based therapies with the aim of maximizing the outcomes of specific therapies through better allocation and the use of predictive modeling. It has been commented that, whatever benchmark is taken, the absolute effectiveness of the psychological therapies has not improved over the past 40 years, with the question being asked as to where the breakthroughs will come (e.g., Prochaska et al., 2020). Developing new psychological therapies does not seem to have achieved any such breakthrough, although greater choice of bona fide and evidence-based therapies is an asset in terms of patient choice. Indeed, it may be that the enhancement regarding specific models of therapy is more about fine-tuning via detailed process research and combinations of dynamic adjustments adopting predictive modeling and feedback rather than via developing any new models of therapy.

The one nascent area that could have promise lies in the area of transdiagnostic approaches to mental health, with some specific models being well promoted (e.g., Barlow's Unified Protocol; Barlow et al., 2017). The critical comparisons are with diagnostic-specific treatments and findings for anxiety and depression are promising albeit comprising small numbers of studies (e.g., Newby et al., 2015). A less favourable review has appeared (Fusar-Poli et al., 2019) although it received critical reactions (e.g., McGorry & Nelson, 2019). Set against this background, Dalgleish et al. (2020) have provided a considered narrative review of the current status and future directions of this field and flag the associated need for more innovative and fit-for-purpose research designs in place of superiority trials for evaluating transdiagnostic interventions.

Cost-Effectiveness and Outcome Measurement

In terms of cost-effectiveness, psychological therapies appear cost effective – but much depends on the values placed on them by society in terms of a willingness to pay. However, cost-effectiveness components are not commonplace in studies, and the degrees of uncertainty returned by most studies that include this element are considerable. In reality, the numbers needed for a true cost-effectiveness study are large. But, notwithstanding this point, all psychological interventions carry a monetary cost, and whether the funding of treatment is through insurance or a national health service, fiscal constraints will come to bear at some point or time. It might be shrewd for researchers to adopt a cost-effectiveness measure so that outcomes can at least speak to this agenda, particularly as this information can be derived from specific items within an increasing number of standard psychological measures of distress.

In terms of measurement in general, our measurement of outcomes has improved over the past 20 years with better outcome measures available. There is, however, a tension between a focus on mono-symptomatic measures and broader measures of psychological distress. Arguments for the former are that they provide more precise answers to questions regarding the impact of psychological therapies on a given condition. But in practice, for individuals, there is often a broader context whereby the areas of functioning, relationships, and quality of life are of equal, if not greater, importance. We need to ensure that there is a balance such that our measurement tools reflect the bandwidth of people's lives by adopting broader measures of their presentations, their functioning, quality of life and relationships and not just specific symptoms of a given disorder (Barkham, 2021). And a stepped change toward the adoption of session-by-session measurement has made available richer datasets to researchers, as well as to practitioners.

Therapist Effects, Severity, and Personalized Approaches

The focus on treatments and their differences (or not) has been understandable but it has come at the expense of a balanced focus on other aspects of the helping process, not least that of therapists and on the allocation of patients to therapies. In terms of both therapists and the form of psychological therapy, research suggests that for many individuals, their assignment to a modality of therapy and a particular therapist will not be a major factor in determining their, more than likely, successful outcome. But for a significant minority it will matter. And we know that in routine practice, the higher the severity of presenting problem, the more it likely matters who an individual sees for therapy. And research has shown that in routine practice, some therapists are consistently twice as effective as others. There is, however, a question to be asked of the value and variability of reported therapist effects derived from RCTs given their highly controlled environment (e.g., see Johns et al., 2019). Certainly, in routine practice, we need to know more about therapists and the dynamic relationship with clients and, in that spirit, it would be timely to move toward a more balanced policy whereby we collect more information on therapists (given the extent of information collected on patients) and also, therefore, provide more information in written reports on therapists and also the distribution (n) of patients assigned to specific therapists. A combination of underpowered trials with few therapists and imbalanced assignment of patients to therapists will do little to advance the field.

Similar to the finding that some therapists yield improvement rates twice those of other therapists with specific patient groups, similar sized differential effects between patient outcomes have been reported when considering subsamples of patients who received their model-indicated treatment (i.e., the one they would be predicted to do best in) versus those who didn't. This line of research is likely to be transformed by developments in and applications of machine learning (e.g., see Chekroud et al., 2021). And findings from feedback research also show an impact on improving outcomes for patients (see de Jong et al., 2021). With the adoption of dynamic systems of prescription and feedback, together with learning from consistently effective therapists, we are likely to enhance the outcomes for a sufficient number of patients so as to improve the overall rates of recovery.

Sufficient Therapy and Reaching Diverse Populations

A key decision in securing effective therapy is ensuring that individuals receive a sufficient dose. Two models have been developed from data to account for treatment length – the dose–effect and the good enough level – with different results supporting each model. However, there is growing evidence that setting session limits, within reason, on treatment duration may not be the most helpful strategy (e.g., Lee et al., 2021). In addition, differing funding models occur in different countries and the culture of what is deemed appropriate will vary. Indeed, a recent review concluded that there was considerable variability across countries and the authors "urge[d] researchers and clinicians to exercise caution when generalizing conclusions regarding the optimal number of sessions across countries" (Flückiger et al., 2020; p. 335). Accordingly, it may be more appropriate to focus on research efforts investigating those factors that moderate treatment duration, together with continuing efforts to determine under what conditions the dose–response and GEL models each provide the better explanation for treatment duration.

Clearly, whatever the amount of therapy is, it needs to reach and be accessible to diverse populations. That is, we need to ensure that findings from research studies have wider clinical applicability such that results are generalizable to the breadth of the clinical population. In this respect, there is a priority for research to encompass individuals from ethnic minorities and to work toward samples being reflective of cultural diversity. Culturally adapted psychotherapies are effective but there is a tension as to the extent to which in their adaptations they move away from the evidence base. At the other end of the spectrum, some areas of research are likely overrepresented by samples drawn from college settings and a similar issue arises about the extent of generalizability.

Research efforts moving forward need to ensure there is a balance across the life span and establish the validity of generalizations to wider clinical populations. Intersecting with this issue is that of the severity of presenting problems. There is evidence that differential effects, whether it be in relation to therapies or therapists, are more pronounced in subgroups of more severe patient symptomatology. This makes clinical sense. It is likely that there is less differential response to different therapies and therapists by individuals experiencing lower levels of psychological distress. Put another way, the assignment to a specific therapy or therapist may matter more for people experiencing higher levels of a presenting condition.

Maintaining Gains and Longer-Term Follow-up

Beyond what index we select to capture improvement or changes in psychological state, research designs need to capture longer-term follow-up as part of a strategy of repeated measurement. In the same way that there is now an increasing adoption of session-by-session measurement, there would be benefits in extending measurement beyond the end of therapy with, for example, monthly collection of data via smart phone technology that is broader and more inclusive than a single symptom (e.g., depression or anxiety).

A clear and constant plea in the discussion of study results is the need for longer-term follow-up. Adoption of 6- and 12-month follow-up should be standard and working toward 18- and 24-month follow-up assessments should become the aspiration of trial designs. Extending routine measurement beyond trial termination would appear to be a natural extension of the practice of routine outcome monitoring and, with the current use of smart phones and apps, data collection could be made relatively easy. A further strategy is to follow-up trial participants by linkage to subsequent routinely collected health-related data (see Fitzpatrick et al., 2018). Such data might comprise subsequent episodes, re-referral, and service utilization. It might also include outcome measurement if that is a mandatory component of the service delivery model (e.g., IAPT). This agenda would meet a central focus on relapse and recurrence rates that addresses the enduring effects of psychological therapies. While there is a rightful wish to focus on questions of mechanisms of effective treatments, it would seem that there is still much basic research to be carried out in relation to obtaining longer-term follow-up, reducing relapse rates, and securing lasting impact of the psychological therapies.

Delivering Efficacy and Effectiveness at Scale

Finally, there is the task of delivering psychological therapies and/or psychologically informed interventions at scale (Kazdin, 2018). This poses a challenge for the psychological therapies as it encompasses an agenda dovetailing with that of population health. Crucial to this agenda is the concept of *impact*. If we have effective therapies of whatever name and yet they reach but a fraction of people in need, we might wish to revisit our activities and consider whether the research questions we are asking and the foci of our research efforts can be made more relevant, inclusive, and impactful. Here, we give two examples of psychological therapy programs that are aimed at improving access in developed countries, one framed as an RCT and the other as an effectiveness program. The first example is a large-scale ($N = 1368$) noninferiority pragmatic RCT carried out in North America for the treatment of perinatal depression – Scaling Up Maternal Mental healthcare by Increasing access to Treatment (SUMMIT) Trial (Singla et al., 2021). The trial compares two delivery modes of a brief, evidence-based, behavioral activation intervention for depressive symptoms (telemedicine vs. in-person) provided by two different delivery agents – mental health specialists vs. trained nonspecialist providers. The second example is a national implementation program in England, the Improving Access to Psychological Therapies (IAPT) program (Clark, 2018). This initiative has involved training a new workforce to deliver a quick access service where the interventions are based on psychoeducation and coaching with mandated measures taken at every session that are used to monitor and, if necessary, step up a patient to a number of approved high-intensity psychological therapies. The outcomes are reported nationally and top-level improvement rates for services are publicly available. That is, the data and outcomes of individual services are transparent.

Both these initiatives are rooted in the psychological therapies and have adapted the therapies and systems with the central aim of making psychological interventions more accessible. Of course, both examples are situated in high-income countries and the agenda is to reach low- and middle-income countries. In this respect, trials by Patel et al. (e.g., 2017) have been examples of extending psychological support beyond high-income countries. And as an indicator of one direction of travel, we note trials utilizing the common elements treatment approach (CETA), which comprise modular, flexible, multi-problem transdiagnostic psychological interventions, aimed at scaling up to deliver in low- and middle-income countries (Murray et al., 2020). These examples point to an agenda for the psychological therapies that is both larger-scale and driven by principles of equity and access. Such an agenda needs to be responsive to the wider social context and the presence of social and economic deprivation that are barriers to the availability of effective treatments to the majority of people in need.

Conclusion

In this chapter, we have covered a range of topics that, in our view, underpin and affect the delivery of effective psychological therapies. As stated, the conclusions drawn in this chapter have emphasized research methods as the foundation for delivering evidence-based interventions. And although we have identified shortcomings as well as identifying ways to improve research, it is clear that bona fide psychological therapies are effective for a majority of people who are fortunate enough to be offered access to such interventions. And from where we stand at present, it would appear that the need for psychological therapies and psychological support in general has never been greater. In that sense, there is a responsibility to deliver such evidence-based interventions beyond selective or privileged populations. As such, the challenge for the future lies in devising and packaging the evidence-based interventions we have and delivering them to appropriately targeted groups at scale, mindful of cultural differences, and with the element of actual patient choice, by therapists and practitioners who are engaged in ongoing monitoring of and learning from their own practice and that of others. At one level, this is about utilizing all the skills we have learned as research methodologists and professional practitioners. At another, it is about moving beyond our comfort zone into the realms of population health and realizing that the psychological therapies and the components that constitute them have a central contribution to make on this global stage.

ABBREVIATIONS

ADM	antidepressant medication
APA	American Psychological Association
BD	bipolar disorder
BDI	Beck Depression Inventory
CBT	cognitive behavioral therapy
CBT-T	cognitive behavioral therapy-trauma
CETA	common elements treatment approach
CI	confidence interval
CONSORT	Consolidated Standards of Reporting Trials
CORE-6D	Clinical Outcomes in Routine Evaluation-6D
CORE-OM	Clinical Outcomes in Routine Evaluation-Outcome Measure
CrI	credible interval
CT	cognitive therapy
DBT	dialectical behavior therapy
DSM-5	*Diagnostic and Statistical Manual-5*
EBPs	evidence-based psychotherapies
EBTs	evidence-based therapies
EMDR	eye movement desensitization and reprocessing
ERP	exposure and response prevention
ES	effect size
FIS	facilitative interpersonal skills
GAD	generalized anxiety disorder
GAD-7	generalized anxiety disorder-7
GEL	good enough level
HR	hazard ratio
HRSD	Hamilton Rating Scale for Depression
IAPT	Improving Access to Psychological Therapies
iCBT	internet cognitive behavioral therapy
IIP-64	Inventory of Interpersonal Problems-64
IPT	interpersonal psychotherapy
MBCT	mindfulness-based cognitive therapy
MDD	major depressive disorder
NICE	National Institute for Health and Care Excellence
NMA	network meta-analysis
NNT	numbers needed to treat
OCD	obsessive-compulsive disorder
OQ-45	Outcome Questionnaire-45
OR	odds ratio
PAI	patient advantage index
PD	panic disorder
PHQ-9	Patient Health Questionnaire-9
PROSPERO	Prospective Register of Ongoing Systematic Reviews
PST	problem solving therapy
PSYCHLOPS	Psychological Outcomes Profiles
PTSD	post-traumatic stress disorder
QALY	quality-adjusted life years
RCSI	reliable and clinically significant improvement
RCT	randomized controlled trial
REM	race and ethnic minority
ReQoL	Recovering Quality of Life
ROM	routine outcome monitoring

RR	relative risk
SAD	social anxiety disorder
SMD	standardized mean difference
STPP	short-term psychodynamic psychotherapy
SUMMIT	Scaling Up Maternal Mental healthcare by Increasing access to Treatment
TAU	treatment as usual
WL	wait list

REFERENCES

Adelson, J. L., & Owen, J. (2012). Bringing the psychotherapist back: Basic concepts for reading articles examining therapist effects using multi-level modeling. *Psychotherapy, 49*(2), 152–162. https://doi.org/10.1037/a0023990

Aderka, I. M., Nickerson, A., Bøe, H. J., & Hofmann, S. G. (2012). Sudden gains during psychological treatments of anxiety and depression: a meta-analysis. *Journal of Consulting and Clinical Psychology, 80*(1), 93–101. https://doi.org/10.1037/a0026455

Aderka, I. M., & Shalom, J. G. (2021). A revised theory of sudden gains in psychological treatments. *Behaviour Research and Therapy, 139*, 103830. https://doi.org/10.1016/j.brat.2021.103830

Ahn, H., & Wampold, B. E. (2001). Where oh where are the specific ingredients? A meta-analysis of component studies in counseling and psychotherapy. *Journal of Counseling Psychology, 48*(3), 251–257. https://doi.org/10.1037/0022-0167.48.3.251

Akechi, T., Mantani, A., Kurata, K., Hirota, S., Shimodera, S., Yamada, M., Inagaki, M., Watanabe, N., Kato, T., Furukawa, T. A., & SUND Investigators (2019). Predicting relapse in major depression after successful initial pharmacological treatment. *Journal of Affective Disorders, 250*, 108–113. https://doi.org/10.1016/j.jad.2019.03.004

Ali, S., Rhodes, L., Moreea, O., McMillan, D., Gilbody, S., Leach, C., Lucock, M., Lutz, W., & Delgadillo, J. (2017). How durable is the effect of low intensity CBT for depression and anxiety? Remission and relapse in a longitudinal cohort study. *Behaviour Research and Therapy, 94*, 1–8. https://doi.org/10.1016/j.brat.2017.04.006

American Psychological Association (2019). Clinical practice guideline for the treatment of depression across three age cohorts. American Psychological Association guideline development panel for the treatment of depressive disorders. Adopted as APA Policy Feb. 16, 2019.

Anderson, E. M., & Lambert, M. J. (2001). A survival analysis of clinically significant change in outpatient psychotherapy. *Journal of Clinical Psychology, 57*(7), 875–888. https://doi.org/10.1002/jclp.1056

Anderson, T., Crowley, M. E., Himawan, L., Holmberg, J. K., & Uhlin, B. D. (2016). Therapist facilitative interpersonal skills and training status: A randomized clinical trial on alliance and outcome. *Psychotherapy Research, 26*(5), 511–529. https://doi.org/10.1080/10503307.2015.1049671

Anderson, T., Finkelstein, J. D., & Horvath, S. A. (2020). The facilitative interpersonal skills method: Difficult psychotherapy moments and appropriate therapist responsiveness. *Counselling and Psychotherapy Research, 20*(3), 463–469. https://doi.org/10.1002/capr.12302

Anderson, T., McClintock, A. S., Himawan, L., Song, X., & Patterson, C. L. (2016). A prospective study of therapist facilitative interpersonal skills as a predictor of treatment outcome. *Journal of Consulting and Clinical Psychology, 84*(1), 57–66. https://doi.org/10.1037/ccp0000060

Anderson, T., Patterson, C., McClintock, A. S., McCarrick, S. M., Song, X., & The Psychotherapy and Interpersonal Lab Team. (2019). Facilitative Interpersonal Skills Task and Rating Manual. Ohio University, Athens, Ohio.

Andersson, E., Hedman, E., Ljótsson, B., Wikström, M., Elveling, E., Lindefors, N., Andersson, G., Kaldo, V., & Rück, C. (2015). Cost-effectiveness of internet-based cognitive behavior therapy for obsessive-compulsive disorder: Results from a randomized controlled trial. *Journal of Obsessive-Compulsive and Related. Disorders. 4*, 47–53. https://doi.org/10.1016/j.jocrd.2014.12.004

Andersson, G., Carlbring, P., Titov, N., & Lindefors, N. (2019). Internet interventions for adults with anxiety and mood disorders: A narrative umbrella review of recent meta-analyses. *Canadian Journal of Psychiatry, 64*(7), 465–470. https://doi.org/10.1177/0706743719839381

Andersson, G., & Cuijpers, P. (2009). Internet-based and other computerized psychological treatments for adult depression: a meta-analysis. *Cognitive Behaviour Therapy, 38*(4), 196–205. https://doi.org/10.1080/16506070903318960

Andersson, G., Cuijpers, P., Carlberg, P., Riper, H., & Hedman, E. (2014). Guided internet-based vs. face-to-face cognitive behaviour therapy for psychiatric and somatic disorders: A systematic review and meta-analysis. *World Psychiatry 13*(3), 288–295. https://doi.org/10.1002/wps.20151

Andrews, G., Basu, A., Cuijpers, P., Craske, M. G., McEvoy, P., English, C. L., & Newby, J. M. (2018). Computer therapy for the anxiety and depression disorders is effective, acceptable and practical health care: An updated meta-analysis. *Journal of Anxiety Disorders, 55*, 70–78. https://doi.org/10.1016/j.janxdis.2018.01.001

Andrews, G., Bell, C., Boyce, P., Gale, C., Lampe, L., Marwat, O., Rapee, R., & Wilkins, G. (2018). Royal Australian and New Zealand College of Psychiatrists clinical practice guidelines for the treatment of panic disorder, social anxiety disorder and generalised anxiety disorder. *Australian & New Zealand Journal of Psychiatry, 52*(12), 1109–1172. https://doi.org/10.1177/0004867418799453

Andrews, G., & Harvey, R. (1981). Does psychotherapy benefit neurotic patients: A re-analysis of the Smith, Glass, & Miller data. *Archives of General Psychiatry, 38*(11), 1203–1208. https://doi.org/10.1001/archpsyc.1981.01780360019001

Arnberg, F. K., Linton, S. J., Hultcrantz, M., Heintz, E., & Jonsson, U. (2014). Internet-delivered psychological treatments for mood and anxiety disorders: a systematic review of their efficacy, safety, and cost-effectiveness. *PLoS one, 9*(5), e98118. https://doi.org/10.1371/journal.pone.0098118

Ashworth, M., Robinson, S. I., Godfrey, E., Shepherd, M., Evans, C., Seed, P., Parmentier, H. & Tylee, A. (2005). Measuring mental health outcomes in primary care: The psychometric properties of a new patient-generated outcome measure, "PSYCHLOPS" ("psychological outcome profiles"). *Primary Care Mental Health, 3*(4), 261–270.

Baardseth, T. P., Goldberg, S. B., Pace, B. T., Wislocki, A. P., Frost, N. D., Siddiqui, J. R., Lindemann, A. M., Kivlighan, D. M., III, Laska, K. M., Del Re, A. C., Minami, T., & Wampold, B. E. (2013). Cognitive-behavioral therapy versus other therapies: redux. *Clinical Psychology Review, 33*(3), 395–405. https://doi.org/10.1016/j.cpr.2013.01.004

Baldwin, S. A., Berkeljon, A., Atkins, D. C., Olsen, J. A., & Nielsen, S. L. (2009). Rates of change in naturalistic psychotherapy: Contrasting dose-effect and good-enough level models of change. *Journal of Consulting and Clinical Psychology, 77*(2), 203–211. https://doi.org/10.1037/a0015235

Baldwin, S., A., & Imel, Z. (2013). Therapist effects: Findings and methods. In M. J. Lambert (Ed.), *Bergin and Garfield's handbook of psychotherapy and behavior change.* 6th Edition Wiley.

Baldwin, S. A., & Imel, Z. E. (2020). Studying specificity in psychotherapy with meta-analysis is hard. *Psychotherapy Research, 30*(3), 294–296. https://doi.org/10.1080/10503307.2019.1679403

Bandelow, B., Sagebiel, A., Belz, M., Görlich, Y., Michaelis, S., & Wedekind, D. (2018). Enduring effects of psychological treatments for anxiety disorders: Meta-analysis of follow-up studies. *The British Journal of Psychiatry, 212*(6), 333–338. https://doi.org/10.1192/bjp.2018.49

Barak, A., Hen, L., Boniel-Nissim, M., & Shapira, N. (2008). A comprehensive review and a meta-analysis of the effectiveness of Internet-based psychotherapeutic interventions. *Journal of Technology in Human Services, 26*(2-4), 109–160. https://doi.org/10.1080/15228830802094429

Barber, J. P., Milrod, B., Gallop, R., Solomonov, N., Rudden, M. G., McCarthy, K. S., & Chambless, D. L. (2020). Processes of therapeutic change: Results from the Cornell-Penn Study of Psychotherapies for panic disorder. *Journal of Counseling Psychology, 67*(2), 222–231. https://doi.org/10.1037/cou0000417

Barber, J. P., & Muenz, L. R. (1996). The role of avoidance and obsessiveness in matching patients to cognitive and interpersonal psychotherapy: Empirical findings from the Treatment for Depression Collaborative Research Program.

Journal of Consulting and Clinical Psychology, 64(5), 951–958. https://doi.org/10.1037//0022-006x.64.5.951

Barkham, M. (2021). Towards greater bandwidth for standardised outcome measures. *The Lancet Psychiatry, 8*(1), 17. https://doi.org/10.1016/S2215-0366(20)30488-0

Barkham, M., Connell, J., Stiles, W. B., Miles, J. N. V., Margison, J., Evans, C., & Mellor-Clark, J. (2006). Dose-effect relations and responsive regulation of treatment duration: The good enough level. *Journal of Consulting and Clinical Psychology, 74*(1), 160–167. https://doi.org/10.1037/0022-006X.74.1.160

Barkham, M., Hardy, G. E., & Mellor-Clark, J. (Eds.) (2010). *Developing and delivering practice-based evidence: A guide for the psychological therapies.* Chichester: Wiley.

Barkham, M., Lutz, W., Lambert, M. J., Saxon, D. (2017). Therapist effects, effective therapists, and the law of variability. In L. G. Castonguay & C. E. Hill (Eds.), *Therapist effects: Toward understanding how and why some therapists are better than others* (pp. 13–36). Washington: American Psychological Association.

Barkham, M., Saxon, D., Hardy, G. E., Bradburn, M., Galloway, D., Wickramasekera, N., Keetharuth, A. D., Bower, P., King, M., Elliott, R., Gabriel, L., Kellett, S., Shaw, S., Wilkinson, T., Connell, J., Harrison, P., Ardern, K., Bishop-Edwards, L., Ashley, K., . . . Brazier, J. E. (2021). Clinical and cost-effectiveness of person-centred experiential therapy vs. cognitive behavioural therapy for moderate and severe depression as delivered in the English Improving Access to Psychological Therapies (IAPT) national programme: A pragmatic randomised non-inferiority trial [PRaCTICED]. *The Lancet Psychiatry. 8*(6), 487–499. https://doi.org/10.1016/S2215-0366(21)00083-3

Barlow D. H. (2010). Negative effects from psychological treatments: a perspective. *American Psychologist, 65*(1), 13–20. https://doi.org/10.1037/a0015643

Barlow, D. H., Farchione, T. J., Bullis, J. R., Gallagher, M. W., Murray-Latin, H., Sauer-Zavala, S., Bentley, K. H., Thompson-Hollands, J., Conklin, L. R., Boswell, J. F., Ametaj, A., Carl, J. R., Boettcher, H. T., & Cassiello-Robbins, C. (2017). The Unified Protocol for transdiagnostic treatment of emotional disorders compared with diagnosis-specific protocols for anxiety disorders: A randomized clinical trial. *JAMA Psychiatry, 74*(9), 875–884. https://doi.org/10.1001/jamapsychiatry.2017.2164

Barth, J., Munder, T., Gerger, H., Nüesch, E., Trelle, S., Znoj, H., Jüni, P., & Cuijpers, P. (2013). Comparative efficacy of seven psychotherapeutic interventions for patients with depression: A network meta-analysis. *PLoS Medicine, 10*(5), e1001454. https://doi.org/10.1371/journal.pmed.1001454

Bateman, A., & Fonagy, P. (2010). Mentalization based treatment for borderline personality disorder. *World Psychiatry, 9*(1), 11–15. https://doi.org/10.1002/j.2051-5545.2010.tb00255.x

Baumann, M., Stargardt, T., & Frey, S. (2020). Cost-utility of internet-based cognitive behavioral therapy in unipolar depression: A Markov Model simulation. *Applied Health Economics and Health Policy, 18*(4), 567–578. https://doi.org/10.1007/s40258-019-00551-x

Bell, E. C., Marcus, D. K., & Goodlad, J. K. (2013). Are the parts as good as the whole? A meta-analysis of component treatment studies. *Journal of Consulting and Clinical Psychology, 81*(4), 722–736. https://doi.org/10.1037/a0033004

Benish, S. G., Quintana, S., & Wampold, B. E. (2011). Culturally adapted psychotherapy and the legitimacy of myth: A direct-comparison meta-analysis. *Journal of Counseling Psychology, 58*(3), 279–289. https://doi.org/10.1037/a0023626

Bergin, A. E. (1963). The empirical emphasis in psychotherapy: A symposium. The effects of psychotherapy: Negative results revisited. *Journal of Counseling Psychology, 10*(3), 244–250. https://doi.org/10.1037/h0043353

Bergin A. E. (1966). Some implications of psychotherapy research for therapeutic practice. *Journal of Abnormal Psychology, 71*(4), 235–246. https://doi.org/10.1037/h0023577

Bergin, A. E. (1971). The evaluation of therapeutic outcomes. In A. E. Bergin & S. L. Garfield (Eds.), *Handbook of psychotherapy and behavior change* (pp. 217–270). New York, NY: Wiley.

Bergin, A. E., & Lambert, M. J. (1978). The effectiveness of psychotherapy. In S. L. Garfield & A. E. Bergin (Eds.), *Handbook of psychotherapy and behavior change* (2nd ed.) (pp. 139–190). New York, NY: Wiley.

Beshai, S., Dobson, K. S., Bockting, C. L. H., & Quigley, C. (2011). Relapse and recurrence prevention in depression: Current research and future

prospects. *Clinical Psychology Review, 31*(8), 1349–1360. https://doi.org/10.1016/j.cpr.2011.09.003

Beutel, M. E., Scheurich, V., Knebel, A., Michal, M., Wiltink, J., Graf-Morgenstern, M., Tschan, R., Milrod, B., Wellek, S., & Subic-Wrana, C. (2013). Implementing panic-focused psychodynamic psychotherapy into clinical practice. *Canadian Journal of Psychiatry, 58*(6), 326–334. https://doi.org/10.1177/070674371305800604

Biesheuvel-Leliefeld, K. E., Kok, G. D., Bockting, C. L., Cuijpers, P., Hollon, S. D., van Marwijk, H. W., & Smit, F. (2015). Effectiveness of psychological interventions in preventing recurrence of depressive disorder: meta-analysis and meta-regression. *Journal of Affective Disorders, 174*, 400–410. https://doi.org/10.1016/j.jad.2014.12.016

Blatt, S. J., Sanislow, C. A., Zuroff, D. C., & Pilkonis, P. A. (1996). Characteristics of effective therapists: Further analyses of data from the National Institute of Mental Health Treatment of Depression Collaborative Research Program. *Journal of Consulting and Clinical Psychology, 64*(6), 1276–1284. https://doi.org/10.1037/0022- 006X.64.6.1276

Bockting, C. L., Hollon, S. D., Jarrett, R. B., Kuyken, W., & Dobson, K. (2015). A lifetime approach to major depressive disorder: The contributions of psychological interventions in preventing relapse and recurrence. *Clinical Psychology Review, 41*, 16–26. https://doi.org/10.1016/j.cpr.2015.02.003

Bodden, D. H., Dirksen, C. D., & Bögels, S. M. (2008). Societal burden of clinically anxious youth referred for treatment: a cost-of-illness study. *Journal of Abnormal Child Psychology, 36*(4), 487–497. https://doi.org/10.1007/s10802-007-9194-4

Bone, C., Delgadillo, J., & Barkham, M. (2021). A systematic review and meta-analysis of the Good-Enough Level (GEL) literature. *Journal of Counseling Psychology, 68*(2), 219–231. https://doi,org/10.1037/cou0000521

Bosmans, J. E., van Schaik, D. J., Heymans, M. W., van Marwijk, H. W., van Hout, H. P., & de Bruijne, M. C. (2007). Cost-effectiveness of interpersonal psychotherapy for elderly primary care patients with major depression. *International Journal of Technology Assessment in Health Care, 23*(4), 480–487. https://doi.org/10.1017/S0266462307070572

Brettschneider, C., Djadran, H., Härter, M., Löwe, B., Riedel-Heller, S., & König, H.-H. (2015). Cost-utility analyses of cognitive-behavioural therapy of depression: A systematic review. *Psychotherapy and Psychosomatics, 84*(1), 6–21. https://doi.org/10.1159/000365150

Brettschneider, C., Heddaeus, D., Steinmann, M., Härter, M., Watzke, B., & König, H.-H. (2020). Cost-effectiveness of guideline-based stepped and collaborative care versus treatment as usual for patients with depression - a cluster-randomized trial. *BMC Psychiatry, 20*(1), 427. https://doi.org/10.1186/s12888-020-02829-0

Buckman, J., Underwood, A., Clarke, K., Saunders, R., Hollon, S. D., Fearon, P., & Pilling, S. (2018). Risk factors for relapse and recurrence of depression in adults and how they operate: A four-phase systematic review and meta-synthesis. *Clinical Psychology Review, 64*, 13–38. https://doi.org/10.1016/j.cpr.2018.07.005

Budge, S. L., Moore, J. T., Del Re, A. C., Wampold, B. E., Baardseth, T. P., & Nienhuis, J. B. (2013). The effectiveness of evidence-based treatments for personality disorders when comparing treatment-as-usual and bona fide treatments. *Clinical Psychology Review, 33*(8), 1057–1066. https://doi.org/10.1016/j.cpr.2013.08.003

Carl, E., Witcraft, S. M., Kauffman, B. Y., Gillespie, E. M., Becker, E. S., Cuijpers, P., Van Ameringen, M., Smits, J., & Powers, M. B. (2020). Psychological and pharmacological treatments for generalized anxiety disorder (GAD): A meta-analysis of randomized controlled trials. *Cognitive Behaviour Therapy, 49*(1), 1–21. https://doi.org/10.1080/16506073.2018.1560358

Carlbring, P., Andersson, G., Cuijpers, P., Riper, H., & Hedman-Lagerlöf, E. (2018). Internet-based vs. face-to-face cognitive behavior therapy for psychiatric and somatic disorders: An updated systematic review and meta-analysis. *Cognitive Behaviour Therapy, 47*(1), 1–18. https://doi.org/10.1080/16506073.2017.1401115

Carpenter, J. K., Andrews, L. A., Witcraft, S. M., Powers, M. B., Smits, J., & Hofmann, S. G. (2018). Cognitive behavioral therapy for anxiety and related disorders: A meta-analysis of randomized placebo-controlled trials. *Depression and Anxiety, 35*(6), 502–514. https://doi.org/10.1002/da.22728

Chekroud, A.M., Bondar, J., Delgadillo, J., Doherty, G., Wasil, A., Fokkema, M., Cohen, Z., Belgrave, D., DeRubeis, R., Iniesta, R., Dwyer, D. and Choi, K. (2021), The promise of machine learning in predicting treatment outcomes in psychiatry. *World Psychiatry, 20,* 154–170. https://doi.org/10.1002/wps.20882

Clark, D. M., Canvin, L., Green, J., Layard, R., Pilling, S., & Janecka, M. (2018). Transparency about the outcomes of mental health services (IAPT approach): An analysis of public data. *The Lancet, 391*(10121), 679–686. https://doi.org/10.1016/S0140-6736(17)32133-5

Clark, D. M., & Wells, A. (1995). A cognitive model of social phobia. In R. G. Heimberg, M. R. Liebowitz, D. A. Hope, & F. R. Schneier (Eds.), *Social phobia: Diagnosis, assessment, and treatment* (p. 69–93). The Guilford Press.

Clarke, K., Mayo-Wilson, E., Kenny, J., & Pilling, S. (2015). Can non-pharmacological interventions prevent relapse in adults who have recovered from depression? A systematic review and meta-analysis of ran-domised controlled trials. *Clinical Psychology Review, 39,* 58–70. https://doi.org/10.1016/j.cpr.2015.04.002

Cohen, J. (1988). *Statistical power analysis for the behavioral sciences* (2ⁿᵈ ed.). Hillsdale NJ: Erlbaum.

Cohen J. (1992). A power primer. *Psychological Bulletin, 112*(1), 155–159. https://doi.org/10.1037//0033-2909.112.1.155

Colloca, L., & Barsky, A. J. (2020). Placebo and nocebo effects. *The New England Journal of Medicine, 382*(6), 554–561. https://doi.org/10.1056/NEJMra1907805

Craighead, W. E., & Dunlop, B. W. (2014). Combination psychotherapy and antidepressant medication treatment for depression: for whom, when, and how. *Annual Review of Psychology, 65,* 267–300. https://doi.org/10.1146/annurev.psych.121208.131653

Craske, M. G., Stein, M. B., Eley, T. C., Milad, M. R., Holmes, A., Rapee, R. M., & Wittchen, H. U. (2017). Anxiety disorders. *Nature Reviews: Disease Primers, 3,* 17024. https://doi.org/10.1038/nrdp.2017.24

Crawford, M. J., Thana, L., Farquharson, L., Palmer, L., Hancock, E., Bassett, P., Clarke, J., & Parry, G. D. (2016). Patient experience of negative effects of psychological treatment: Results of a national survey. *The British Journal of Psychiatry, 208*(3), 260–265. https://doi.org/10.1192/bjp.bp.114.162628

Cristea I. A. (2019). The waiting list is an inadequate benchmark for esti-mating the effectiveness of psychotherapy for depression. *Epidemiology and Psychiatric Sciences, 28*(3), 278–279. https://doi.org/10.1017/S2045796018000665

Cristea, I. A., Gentili, C., Cotet, C. D., Palomba, D., Barbui, C., & Cuijpers, P. (2017). Efficacy of psychotherapies for borderline personality disorder: A systematic review and meta-analysis. *JAMA Psychiatry, 74*(4), 319–328. https://doi.org/10.1001/jamapsychiatry.2016.4287

Cristea, I. A., Hollon, S. D., David, D., Karyotaki, E., Cuijpers, P., & Stefan, S. I. (2017). The effects of cognitive behavioral therapy are not sys-tematically falling: a revision of Johnsen & Friborg. *Psychological Bulletin, 143*(3), 326-340. https://doi.org/10.1037/bul0000062

Crits-Christoph, P. (1997). Limitations of the dodo bird verdict and the role of clinical trials in psychotherapy research: Comment on Wampold et al. (1997). *Psychological Bulletin, 122*(3), 216–220. https://doi.org/10.1037/0033-2909.122.3.216

Crits-Christoph, P., Baranackie, K., Kurcias, J. S., Beck, A. T., Carroll, K., Perry, K., Luborsky, L., McLellan, A., Woody, G., Thompson, L., Gallagher, D., & Zitrin, C. (1991). Meta-analysis of therapist effects in psychotherapy outcome studies. *Psychotherapy Research, 1*(2), 81–91. https://doi.org/10.1080/10503309112331335511

Crits-Christoph, P., & Mintz, J. (1991). Implications of therapist effects for the design and analysis of comparative studies of psychotherapies. *Journal of Consulting and Clinical Psychology, 59*(1), 20–26. https://doi.org/10.1037/0022-006X.59.1.20

Cuijpers P. (2016). Are all psychotherapies equally effective in the treatment of adult depression? The lack of statistical power of comparative out-come studies. *Evidence-based Mental Health, 19*(2), 39–42. https://doi.org/10.1136/eb-2016-102341

Cuijpers, P. (2017). Four decades of outcome research on psychotherapies for adult depression: An overview of a series of meta-analyses. *Canadian Psychology/Psychologie Canadienne, 58*(1), 7–19. https://doi.org/10.1037/cap0000096

Cuijpers, P., Cristea, I. A., Karyotaki, E., Reijnders, M., & Huibers, M. J. (2016). How effective are cognitive behavior therapies for major depression and anxiety disorders? A meta-analytic update of the evidence. *World Psychiatry, 15*(3), 245–258. https://doi.org/10.1002/wps.20346

Cuijpers, P., Karyotaki, E., de Wit, L., & Ebert, D. D. (2020). The effects of fifteen evidence-supported therapies for adult depression: A meta-analytic review. *Psychotherapy Research, 30*(3), 279–293. https://doi.org/10.1080/10503307.2019.1649732

Cuijpers, P., Karyotaki, E., Eckshtain, D., Ng, M. Y., Corteselli, K. A., Noma, H., Quero, S., & Weisz, J. R. (2020). Psychotherapy for depression across different age groups: A systematic review and meta-analysis. *JAMA Psychiatry, 77*(7), 694-702. https://doi.org/10.1001/jamapsychiatry.2020.0164

Cuijpers, P., Karyotaki, E., Pot, A. M., Park, M., & Reynolds, C. F., 3rd (2014). Managing depression in older age: Psychological interventions. *Maturitas, 79*(2), 160–169. https://doi.org/10.1016/j.maturitas.2014.05.027

Cuijpers, P., Karyotaki, E., Reijnders, M., & Ebert, D. D. (2019). Was Eysenck right after all? A reassessment of the effects of psychotherapy for adult depression. *Epidemiology and Psychiatric Sciences, 28*(1), 21–30. https://doi.org/10.1017/S2045796018000057

Cuijpers, P., Noma, H., Karyotaki, E., Vinkers, C. H., Cipriani, A., & Furukawa, T. A. (2020). A network meta-analysis of the effects of psychotherapies, pharmacotherapies and their combination in the treatment of adult depression. *World Psychiatry, 19*(1), 92–107. https://doi.org/10.1002/wps.20701

Cuijpers, P., Quero, S., Noma, H., Ciharova, M., Miguel, C., Karyotaki, E., Cipriani, A., Cristea, I.A., & Furukawa, T. A. (2021). Psychotherapies for depression: a network meta-analysis covering efficacy, acceptability and long-term outcomes of all main treatment types. *World Psychiatry, 20*(2), 283–293. https://doi.org/10.1002/wps.20860

Cuijpers, P., Quero, S., Papola, D., Cristea, I. A., & Karyotaki, E. (2019). Care-as-usual control groups across different settings in randomized trials on psychotherapy for adult depression: a meta-analysis. *Psychological Medicine,* 1–11. https://doi.org/10.1017/S0033291719003581

Cuijpers, P., Reijnders, M., & Huibers, M. J. H. (2019). The role of common factors in psychotherapy outcomes. *Annual Review of Clinical Psychology, 15,* 207-231. https://doi.org/10.1146/annurev-clinpsy-050718-095424

Cuijpers, P., Reijnders, M., Karyotaki, E., de Wit, L., & Ebert, D. D. (2018). Negative effects of psychotherapies for adult depression: A meta-analysis of deterioration rates. *Journal of Affective Disorders, 239,* 138–145. https://doi.org/10.1016/j.jad.2018.05.050

Cuijpers, P., Sijbrandij, M., Koole, S. L., Andersson, G., Beekman, A. T., & Reynolds, C. F., 3rd (2013). The efficacy of psychotherapy and pharma-cotherapy in treating depressive and anxiety disorders: a meta-analysis of direct comparisons. *World Psychiatry, 12*(2), 137–148. https://doi.org/10.1002/wps.20038

Cuijpers, P., Sijbrandij, M., Koole, S. L., Andersson, G., Beekman, A. T., & Reynolds, C. F., 3rd (2014). Adding psychotherapy to antidepressant medication in depression and anxiety disorders: a meta-analysis. *World Psychiatry, 13*(1), 56–67. https://doi.org/10.1002/wps.20089

Cuijpers, P., Sijbrandij, M., Koole, S., Huibers, M., Berking, M., & Andersson, G. (2014). Psychological treatment of generalized anxiety disorder: a meta-analysis. *Clinical Psychology Review, 34*(2), 130–140. https://doi.org/10.1016/j.cpr.2014.01.002

Cuijpers, P., Smit, F., Bohlmeijer, E., Hollon, S. D., & Andersson, G. (2010). Efficacy of cognitive-behavioral therapy and other psychological treat-ments for adult depression: Meta-analytic study of publication bias. *The British Journal of Psychiatry, 196*(3), 173–178. https://doi.org/10.1192/bjp.bp.109.066001

Cuijpers, P., Turner, E. H., Koole, S. L., van Dijke, A., & Smit, F. (2014). What is the threshold for a clinically relevant effect? The case of major depressive disorders. *Depression and Anxiety, 31*(5), 374–378. https://doi.org/10.1002/da.22249

Cuijpers, P., van Straten, A. A., Bohlmeijer, E. E., Hollon, S. D., & Andersson, G. G. (2010). The effects of psychotherapy for adult depression are over-estimated: A meta-analysis of study quality and effect size. *Psychological Medicine, 40*(2), 211–223. https://doi.org/10.1017/S0033291709006114

Cuijpers, P., van Straten, A., Schuurmans, J., van Oppen, P., Hollon, S., & Andersson, G. (2010). Psychotherapy for chronic major depression and dysthymia: A meta-analysis. *Clinical Psychology Review, 30,* 51–62. https://doi.org/10.1016/j.cpr.2009.09.003

Dalgleish, T., Black, M., Johnston, D., & Bevan, A. (2020). Transdiagnostic approaches to mental health problems: Current status and future direc-tions. *Journal of Consulting and Clinical Psychology, 88*(3), 179–195. https://doi.org/10.1037/ccp0000482

Davis, D. E., DeBlaere, C., Owen, J., Hook, J. N., Rivera, D. P., Choe, E., Van Tongeren, D. R., Worthington, E. L., & Placeres, V. (2018). The multicultural orientation framework: A narrative review. *Psychotherapy, 55*(1), 89–100. https://doi.org/10.1037/pst0000160

de Jong, K., Conijn, J. M., Gallagher, R. A. V., Reshetnikova, A. S., Heij, M., & Lutz, M. C. (2021). Using progress feedback to improve outcomes and reduce drop-out, treatment duration, and deterioration: A multilevel meta-analysis. *Clinical Psychology Review, 85*, 102002. https://doi.org/10.1016/j.cpr.2021.102002

De Smet, M. M., Meganck, R., Truijens, F., De Geest, R., Cornelis, S., Norman, U. A., & Desmet, M. (2020). Change processes underlying "good outcome": A qualitative study on recovered and improved patients' experiences in psychotherapy for major depression. *Psychotherapy Research, 30*(7), 948–964. https://doi.org/10.1080/10503307.2020.1722329

Delgadillo, J., Ali, S., Fleck, K., Agnew, C., Southgate, A., Parkhouse, L., Adam, V., Cohen, Z. D., DeRubeis, R. J., & Barkham, M. (submitted). StratCare: A pragmatic, multi-site, single-blind, cluster randomised controlled trial of stratified care for depression.

Delgadillo, J., & Gonzalez Salas Duhne, P. (2020). Targeted prescription of cognitive–behavioral therapy versus person-centered counseling for depression using a machine learning approach. *Journal of Consulting and Clinical Psychology, 88*, 14–24. https://doi.org/10.1037/ccp0000476

Delgadillo, J., McMillan, D., Lucock, M., Leach, C., Ali, S., & Gilbody, S. (2014). Early changes, attrition, and dose-response in low intensity psychological interventions. *British Journal of Clinical Psychology, 53*(1), 114–130. https://doi.org/10.1111/bjc.12031

Delgadillo, J., Moreea, O., & Lutz, W. (2016). Different people respond differently to therapy: A demonstration using patient profiling and risk stratification. *Behaviour Research and Therapy, 79*, 15–22. https://doi.org/10.1016/j.brat.2016.02.003

Delgadillo, J., Rhodes, L., Moreea, O., McMillan, D., Gilbody, S., Leach, C., Lucock, M., Lutz, W. & Ali, S. (2018). Relapse and recurrence of common mental health problems after low intensity cognitive behavioural therapy: The WYLOW Longitudinal Cohort Study. *Psychotherapy and Psychosomatics. 8*7(2), 116–17.

Delgadillo, J., Rubel, J., & Barkham, M. (2020). Towards personalized allocation of patients to therapists. *Journal of Consulting and Clinical Psychology, 88*(9), 799–808. https://doi.org/10.1037/ccp0000507

DeRubeis, R. J., Cohen, Z. D., Forand, N. R., Fournier, J. C., Gelfand, L. A., & Lorenzo-Luaces, L. (2014). The Personalized Advantage Index: translating research on prediction into individualized treatment recommendations. A demonstration. *PloS One, 9*(1), e83875. https://doi.org/10.1371/journal.pone.0083875

Dimidjian, S., & Hollon, S. D. (2010). How would we know if psychotherapy were harmful? *American Psychologist, 65*(1), 21–33. https://doi.org/10.1037/a0017299

Dimidjian, S., & Hollon, S. D. (2011). What can be learned when empirically supported treatments fail? *Cognitive and Behavioral Practice, 18*(3), 303–305. https://doi.org/10.1016/j.cbpra.2011.02.001

Dobson, K. S. (2016). The efficacy of cognitive-behavioral therapy for depression: Reflections on a critical discussion. *Clinical Psychology: Science and Practice, 23*(2), 123–125. https://doi.org/10.1111/cpsp.12151

Dragioti, E., Karathanos, V., Gerdle, B., & Evangelou, E. (2017). Does psychotherapy work? An umbrella review of meta-analyses of randomized controlled trials. *Acta Psychiatrica Scandinavica, 136*(3), 236–246. https://doi.org/10.1111/acps.12713

Driessen, E., Hegelmaier, L. M., Abbass, A. A., Barber, J. P., Dekker, J. J., Van, H. L., Jansma, E. P., & Cuijpers, P. (2015). The efficacy of short-term psychodynamic psychotherapy for depression: A meta-analysis update. *Clinical Psychology Review, 42*, 1–15. https://doi.org/10.1016/j.cpr.2015.07.004

Egger, N., Konnopka, A., Beutel, M. E., Herpertz, S., Hiller, W., Hoyer, J., Salzer, S., Stangier, U., Strauss, B., Willutzki, U., Wiltink, J., Leichsenring, F., Leibing, E., Konig, H.H. (2015). Short-term cost-effectiveness of psychodynamic therapy and cognitive-behavioral therapy in social anxiety disorder: results from the SOPHO- NET trial. *Journal of Affective Disorders, 180*, 21–28. https://doi.org/10.1016/j.jad.2015.03.037

Elliott, R., Stiles, W. B., & Shapiro, D. A. (1993) Are some psychotherapies more equivalent than others? In T. R. Giles (Ed.) *Handbook of effective psychotherapy*. Springer. (pp. 455–479). https://doi.org/10.1007/978-1-4615-2914-9_19

Elliott, R., Wagner, J., Sales, C., Rodgers, B., Alves, P., & Café, M. J. (2016). Psychometrics of the Personal Questionnaire: A client-generated outcome measure. *Psychological Assessment, 28*(3), 263–278. https://doi.org/10.1037/pas0000174

Enck, P., & Zipfel, S. (2019). Placebo effects in psychotherapy: A framework. *Frontiers in Psychiatry, 10*, 456. https://doi.org/10.3389/fpsyt.2019.00456

Epping, J., Muschik, D., & Geyer, S. (2017). Social inequalities in the utilization of outpatient psychotherapy: analyses of registry data from German statutory health insurance. *International Journal for Equity in Health, 16*(1), 147. https://doi.org/10.1186/s12939-017-0644-5

Evans, L. J., Beck, A., & Burdett, M. (2017). The effect of length, duration, and intensity of psychological therapy on CORE global distress scores. *Psychology and Psychotherapy, 90*(3), 389–400. https://doi.org/10.1111/papt.12120

Eysenck, H. J. (1952). The effects of psychotherapy: an evaluation. *Journal of Consulting Psychology, 16*(5), 319–324. https://doi.org/10.1037/h0063633

Falkenström, F., Josefsson, A., Berggren, T., & Holmqvist, R. (2016). How much therapy is enough? Comparing dose-effect and good-enough models in two different settings. *Psychotherapy, 53*(1), 130–139. https://doi.org/10.1037/pst0000039

Finch, E. F., Iliakis, E. A., Masland, S. R., & Choi-Kain, L. W. (2019). A meta-analysis of treatment as usual for borderline personality disorder. *Personality Disorders: Theory, Research, and Treatment, 10*(6), 491–499. https://doi.org/10.1037/per0000353

Firth, N., Saxon, D., Stiles, W. B., & Barkham, M. (2020). Therapist effects vary significantly across psychological treatment care sectors. *Clinical Psychology and Psychotherapy*, 1–9. https://doi.org/10.1002/cpp.2461

Fisher, A. J., Medaglia, J. D., & Jeronimus, B. F. (2018). Lack of group-to-individual generalizability is a threat to human subjects research. *Proceedings of the National Academy of Sciences of the United States of America, 115*(27), E6106–E6115. https://doi.org/10.1073/pnas.1711978115

Fisher, P. L., Cherry, M. G., Stuart, T., Rigby, J. W., & Temple, J. (2020). People with obsessive-compulsive disorder often remain symptomatic following psychological treatment: A clinical significance analysis of manualised psychological interventions. *Journal of Affective Disorders, 275*, 94–108. https://doi.org/10.1016/j.jad.2020.06.019

Fitzpatrick, T., Perrier, L., Shakik, S., Cairncross, Z., Tricco, A. C., Lix, L., Zwarenstein, M., Rosella, L., & Henry, D. (2018). Assessment of long-term follow-up of randomized trial participants by linkage to routinely collected data: A scoping review and analysis. *JAMA Network Open, 1*(8), e186019. https://doi.org/10.1001/jamanetworkopen.2018.6019

Flückiger, C., Del Re, A. C., Munder, T., Heer, S., & Wampold, B. E. (2014). Enduring effects of evidence-based psychotherapies in acute depression and anxiety disorders versus treatment as usual at follow-up--a longitudinal meta-analysis. *Clinical Psychology Review, 34*(5), 367–375. https://doi.org/10.1016/j.cpr.2014.05.001

Flückiger, C., Del Re, A. C., Wampold, B. E., & Horvath, A. O. (2018). The alliance in adult psychotherapy: A meta-analytic synthesis. *Psychotherapy, 55*(4), 316–340. http://dx.doi.org/10.1037/pst0000172

Flückiger, C., Wampold, B. E., Delgadillo, J., Rubel, J., Vîslă, A., & Lutz, W. (2020). Is there an evidence-based number of sessions in outpatient psychotherapy? – A comparison of naturalistic conditions across countries. *Psychotherapy and Psychosomatics, 89*, 333–335. https://doi.org/10.1159/000507793

Fonagy P. (2015). The effectiveness of psychodynamic psychotherapies: An update. *World Psychiatry, 14*(2), 137–150. https://doi.org/10.1002/wps.20235

Forand, N. R., DeRubeis, R. J., & Amsterdam, J. D. (2013). Combining medication and psychotherapy in the treatment of major mental disorders. In M. J. Lambert (Ed.), *Bergin and Garfield's handbook of psychotherapy and behavior change*, 6th edition. (pp. 735-774). Wiley.

Forehand, R., & Kotchick, B. A. (2016). Cultural diversity: A wake-up call for parent training - Republished Article. *Behavior Therapy, 47*(6), 981–992. https://doi.org/10.1016/j.beth.2016.11.010

Friborg, O., & Johnsen, T. J. (2017). The effect of cognitive–behavioral therapy as an antidepressive treatment is falling: Reply to Ljòtsson et al. (2017) and Cristea et al. (2017). *Psychological Bulletin, 143*(3), 341–345. https://doi.org/10.1037/bul0000090

Friborg, O., Martinussen, M., Kaiser, S., Overgård, K. T., & Rosenvinge, J. H. (2013). Comorbidity of personality disorders in anxiety disorders: a meta-analysis of

30 years of research. *Journal of Affective Disorders, 145*(2), 143–155. https://doi.org/10.1016/j.jad.2012.07.004

Friedli, K., King, M. B., & Lloyd, M. (2000). The economics of employing a counsellor in general practice: analysis of data from a randomised controlled trial. *The British Journal of General Practice, 50*(453), 276–283.

Frost, R., Beattie, A., Bhanu, C., Walters, K., & Ben-Shlomo, Y. (2019). Management of depression and referral of older people to psychological therapies: a systematic review of qualitative studies. *The British Journal of General Practice, 69*(680), e171–e181. https://doi.org/10.3399/bjgp19X701297

Furukawa, T. A., Levine, S. Z., Buntrock, C., Ebert, D. D., Gilbody, S., Brabyn, S., Kessler, D., Björkelund, C., Eriksson, M., Kleiboer, A., van Straten, A., Riper, H., Montero-Marin, J., Garcia-Campayo, J., Phillips, R., Schneider, J., Cuijpers, P., & Karyotaki, E. (2021). How can we estimate QALYs based on PHQ-9 scores? Equipercentile linking analysis of PHQ-9 and EQ-5D. *Evidence-based Mental Health*, ebmental-2020-300240. Advance online publication. https://doi.org/10.1136/ebmental-2020-300240

Furukawa, T. A., Noma, H., Caldwell, D. M., Honyashiki, M., Shinohara, K., Imai, H., Chen, P., Hunot, V., & Churchill, R. (2014). Waiting list may be a nocebo condition in psychotherapy trials: a contribution from network meta-analysis. *Acta Psychiatrica Scandinavica, 130*(3), 181–192. https://doi.org/10.1111/acps.12275

Fusar-Poli, P., Solmi, M., Brondino, N., Davies, C., Chae, C., Politi, P., Borgwardt, S., Lawrie, S. M., Parnas, J. & McGuire, P. (2019). Transdiagnostic psychiatry: a systematic review. *World Psychiatry, 18*(2), 192–207. https://doi.org/10.1002/wps.20631

Gabbard, G. O., Lazar, S. G., Hornberger, J., & Spiegel, D. (1997). The economic impact of psychotherapy: A review. *The American Journal of Psychiatry, 154*(2), 147–155. https://doi.org/10.1176/ajp.154.2.147

Gajic-Veljanoski, O., Sanyal, C., McMartin, K., Xie, X., Walter, M., Higgins, C., Sikich, N., Dhalla, I. A., & Ng, V. (2018). Economic evaluations of commonly used structured psychotherapies for major depressive disorder and generalized anxiety disorder: A systematic review. *Canadian Psychology/Psychologie Canadienne, 59*(4), 301–314. https://doi.org/10.1037/cap0000155

Gartlehner, G., Wagner, G., Matyas, N., Titscher, V., Greimel, J., Lux, L., Gaynes, B. N., Viswanathan, M., Patel, S., & Lohr, K. N (2017). Pharmacological and non-pharmacological treatments for major depressive disorder: review of systematic reviews. *BMJ Open, 7*(6), e014912. https://doi.org/10.1136/bmjopen-2016-014912

Geddes, J. R., Burgess, S., Hawton, K., Jamison, K., & Goodwin, G. M. (2004). Long-term lithium therapy for bipolar disorder: systematic review and meta-analysis of randomized controlled trials. *The American Journal of Psychiatry, 161*(2), 217–222. https://doi.org/10.1176/appi.ajp.161.2.217

Giesen-Bloo, J., van Dyck, R., Spinhoven, P., van Tilburg, W., Dirksen, C., van Asselt, T., Kremers, I., Nadort, M., & Arntz, A. (2006). Outpatient psychotherapy for borderline personality disorder: randomized trial of schema-focused therapy vs. transference-focused psychotherapy. *Archives of General Psychiatry, 63*(6), 649–658. https://doi.org/10.1001/archpsyc.63.6.649

Gilbody, S., Littlewood, E., Hewitt, C., Brierley, G., Tharmanathan, P., Araya, R., Barkham, M., Bower, P., Cooper, C., Gask, L., Kessler, D., Lester, H., Lovell, K., Parry, G., Richards, D. A., Andersen, P., Brabyn, S., Knowles, S., Shepherd, C., Tallon, D., . . . REEACT Team (2015). Computerised cognitive behaviour therapy (cCBT) as treatment for depression in primary care (REEACT trial): large scale pragmatic randomised controlled trial. *BMJ, 351*, h5627. https://doi.org/10.1136/bmj.h5627

Glass, G. V. (2015). Meta-analysis at middle age: a personal history. *Research Synthesis Methods, 6*, 221–331. https://doi.org/10.1002/jrsm.1133

Gold, S. M., Enck, P., Hasselmann, H., Friede, T., Hegerl, U., Mohr, D. C., & Otte, C. (2017). Control conditions for randomised trials of behavioural interventions in psychiatry: a decision framework. *The Lancet Psychiatry, 4*, 725–732. https://doi.org/10.1016/ S2215-0366(17)30153-0

Goldberg, S. B., Hoyt, W. T., Nissen-Lie, H. A., Nielsen, S. L., & Wampold, B. E. (2018). Unpacking the therapist effect: Impact of treatment length differs for high- and low-performing therapists. *Psychotherapy Research, 28*(4), 532–544. https://doi.org/10.1080/10503307.2016.1216625

Goldberg, S. B., Tucker, R. P., Greene, P. A., Davidson, R. J., Kearney, D. J., & Simpson, T. L. (2019). Mindfulness-based cognitive therapy for the treatment of current depressive symptoms: a meta-analysis. *Cognitive*

Behaviour Therapy, 48(6), 445–462. https://doi.org/10.1080/16506073.2018.1556330

Griner, D., & Smith, T. B. (2006). Culturally adapted mental health intervention: A meta-analytic review. *Psychotherapy: Theory, Research, Practice, Training, 43*(4), 531–548. https://doi.org/10.1037/0033-3204.43.4.531

Grist, R., & Cavanagh, K. (2013). Computerised cognitive behavioural therapy for common mental health disorders, what works, for whom under what circumstances? A systematic review and meta-analysis. *Journal of Contemporary Psychotherapy, 43*(4), 243–251. https://doi.org/10.1007/s10879-013-9243-y

Guidi, J., Brakemeier, E. L., Bockting, C., Cosci, F., Cuijpers, P., Jarrett, R. B., Linden, M., Marks, I., Peretti, C. S., Rafanelli, C., Rief, W., Schneider, S., Schnyder, U., Sensky, T., Tomba, E., Vazquez, C., Vieta, E., Zipfel, S., Wright, J. H., & Fava, G. A. (2018). Methodological recommendations for trials of psychological interventions. *Psychotherapy and Psychosomatics, 87*(5), 276–284. https://doi.org/10.1159/000490574

Guo, S., Deng, W., Wang, H., Liu, J., Liu, X., Yang, X., He, C., Zhang, Q., Liu, B., Dong, X., Yang, Z., Li, Z., & Li, X. (2020). The efficacy of internet-based cognitive behavioural therapy for social anxiety disorder: A systematic review and meta-analysis. *Clinical Psychology & Psychotherapy*, 1–13. https://doi.org/10.1002/cpp.2528

Haby, M. M., Donnelly, M., Corry, J., & Vos, T. (2006). Cognitive behavioral therapy for depression, panic disorder and generalized anxiety disorder: A metaregression of factors that may predict outcome. *Australian and New Zealand Journal of Psychiatry, 40*(1), 9–19. https://doi.org/10.1080/j.1440-1614.2006.01736.x

Hall, G. C. N., Ibaraki, A. Y., Huang, E. R., Marti, C. N., & Stice, E. (2016). A meta-analysis of cultural adaptations of psychological interventions. *Behavior Therapy, 47*(6), 993–1014. https://doi.org/10.1016/j.beth.2016.09.005

Hall, G. C. N., Yip, T., & Zárate, M. A. (2016). On becoming multicultural in a monocultural research world: A conceptual approach to studying ethnocultural diversity. *American Psychologist, 71*, 40–51. http://dx.doi.org/10.1037/a0039734

Hannan, C., Lambert, M. J., Harmon, C., Nielsen, S. L., Smart, D. W., Shimokawa, K., & Sutton, S. W. (2005). A lab test and algorithms for identifying clients at risk for treatment failure. *Journal of Clinical Psychology, 61*(2), 155–163. https://doi.org/10.1002/jclp.20108

Hansen, N., Lambert, M. J., & Forman, E. M. (2002). The psychotherapy dose-response effect and its implication for treatment delivery services. *Clinical Psychology: Science and Practice, 9*, 329–343. https://doi.org/10.1093/clipsy.9.3.329

Harnett, P., O'Donovan, A., & Lambert, M. J. (2010). The dose response relationship in psychotherapy: Implications for social policy. *Clinical Psychologist, 14*(2), 39–44. https://doi.org/10.1080/13284207.2010.500309

Haug, T., Nordgreen, T., Öst, L. G., & Havik, O. E. (2012). Self-help treatment of anxiety disorders: a meta-analysis and meta-regression of effects and potential moderators. *Clinical Psychology Review, 32*(5), 425–445. https://doi.org/10.1016/j.cpr.2012.04.002

Hayes, J. A., McAleavey, A. A., Castonguay, L. G., & Locke, B. D. (2016). Psychotherapists' outcomes with White and racial/ethnic minority clients: First, the good news. *Journal of Counseling Psychology, 63*(3), 261–268. https://doi.org/10.1037/cou0000098

Hayes, J. A., Owen, J., & Bieschke, K. J. (2015). Therapist differences in symptom change with racial/ethnic minority clients. *Psychotherapy, 52*(3), 308–314. https://doi.org/10.1037/a0037957

Hedman, E., Andersson, E., Ljotsson, B., Andersson, G., Ruck, C., & Lindefors, N. (2011). Cost-effectiveness of Internet-based cognitive behavior therapy vs. cognitive behavioral group therapy for social anxiety disorder: Results from a randomized controlled trial. *Behaviour Research and Therapy, 49*(11), 729–736. https://doi.org/10.1016/j.brat.2011.07.009

Hedman, E., El Alaoui, S., Lindefors, N., Andersson, E., Ruck, C., Ghaderi, A., Kaldo, V., Lekander, M., Andersson, G., & Ljotsson, B. (2014). Clinical effectiveness and cost-effectiveness of Internet-vs. group-based cognitive behavior therapy for social anxiety disorder: 4-year follow-up of a randomized trial. *Behaviour Research and Therapy, 59*, 20–29. https://doi.org/10.1016/j.brat.2014.05.010

Heinonen, E., & Nissen-Lie, H. A. (2020). The professional and personal characteristics of effective psychotherapists: a systematic review. *Psychotherapy*

Research, *30*(4), 417–432. https://doi.org/10.1080/10503307.2019.162 0366

Hepgul, N., King, S., Amarasinghe, M., Breen, G., Grant, N., Grey, N., Hotopf, M., Moran, P., Pariante, C. M., Tylee, A., Wingrove, J., Young. A. H., & Cleare, A. J. (2016). Clinical characteristics of patients assessed within an Improving Access to Psychological Therapies (IAPT) service: results from a naturalistic cohort study (Predicting Outcome Following Psychological Therapy; PROMPT). *BMC Psychiatry,16*, 52. https://doi.org/10.1186/ s12888-016-0736-6

Hobson, R., & Shapiro, D. A. (1970). The Personal Questionnaire as a method of assessing change during psychotherapy. *The British Journal of Psychiatry*, *117*(541), 623–626. https://doi.org/10.1192/bjp.117.541.623

Hofmann, S. G., Asnaani, A., Vonk, I. J., Sawyer, A. T., & Fang, A. (2012). The efficacy of cognitive behavioural therapy: A review of meta-analyses. *Cognitive Therapy and Research*, *36*(5), 427–440. https://doi.org/10.1007/ s10608-012-9476-1

Hofmann, S. G., & Smits, J. A. (2008). Cognitive-behavioral therapy for adult anxiety disorders: a meta-analysis of randomized placebo-controlled trials. *Journal of Clinical Psychiatry*, *69*(4), 621–632. https://doi.org/10.4088/ jcp.v69n0415

Hofmann, S. G., Wu, J. Q., & Boettcher, H. (2014). Effect of cognitive-behavioral therapy for anxiety disorders on quality of life: a meta-analysis. *Journal of Consulting and Clinical Psychology*, *82*(3), 375–391. https://doi .org/10.1037/a0035491

Hollon, S. D. (2016). The efficacy and acceptability of psychological interventions for depression: where we are now and where we are going. *Epidemiology and Psychiatric Sciences*, *25*(4), 295–300. https://doi .org/10.1017/S2045796015000748

Hollon, S. D., Cohen, Z. D., Singla, D. R., & Andrews, P. W. (2019). Recent developments in the treatment of depression. *Behavior Therapy*, *50*(2), 257–269. https://doi.org/10.1016/j.beth.2019.01.002

Hollon, S. D., DeRubeis, R. J., Fawcett, J., Amsterdam, J. D., Shelton, R. C., Zajecka, J., Young, P. R., & Gallop, R. (2014). Effect of cognitive therapy with antidepressant medications vs. antidepressants alone on the rate of recovery in major depressive disorder: A randomized clinical trial. *JAMA Psychiatry*, *71*(10), 1157–1164. https://doi.org/10.1001/ jamapsychiatry.2014.1054

Hollon, S. D., DeRubeis, R. J., Shelton, R. C., Amsterdam, J. D., Salomon, R. M., O'Reardon, J. P., Lovett, M. L., Young, P. R., Haman, K. L., Freeman, B. B., & Gallop, R. (2005). Prevention of relapse following cognitive therapy vs. medications in moderate to severe depression. *Archives of General Psychiatry*, *62*(4), 417–422. https://doi.org/10.1001/archpsyc.62.4.417

Hollon, S. D., & Ponniah, K. (2010). A review of empirically supported psychological therapies for mood disorders in adults. *Depression and Anxiety*, *27*, 891–932. https://doi.org/10.1002/da.20741

Howard, K. I., Kopta, S. M., Krause, M. S., & Orlinsky, D. E. (1986). The dose-effect relationship in psychotherapy. *American Psychologist*, *41*(2), 159–164. https://doi.org/10.1037/0003-066X.41.2.159

Howard, K. I., Krause, M. S., Saunders, S. M., & Kopta, S. M. (1997). Trials and tribulations in the meta-analysis of treatment differences: Comment on Wampold et al. (1997). *Psychological Bulletin*, *122*(3), 221–225. https://doi .org/10.1037/0033-2909.122.3.221

Huey, S. J., Jr, & Polo, A. J. (2008). Evidence-based psychosocial treatments for ethnic minority youth. *Journal of Clinical Child and Adolescent Psychology*, *37*(1), 262–301. https://doi.org/10.1080/15374410701820174

Huey, S. J., Jr., & Tilley, J. L. (2018). Effects of mental health interventions with Asian Americans: A review and meta-analysis. *Journal of Consulting and Clinical Psychology*, *86*(11), 915–930. https://doi.org/10.1037/ccp0000346

Huey, S. J., Jr, Tilley, J. L., Jones, E. O., & Smith, C. A. (2014). The contribution of cultural competence to evidence-based care for ethnically diverse populations. *Annual Review of Clinical Psychology*, *10*, 305–338. https://doi .org/10.1146/annurev-clinpsy-032813-153729

Huhn, M., Tardy, M., Spineli, L. M., Kissling, W., Förstl, H., Pitschel-Walz, G., Leucht, C., Samara, M., Dold, M., Davis, J. M., & Leucht, S. (2014). Efficacy of pharmacotherapy and psychotherapy for adult psychiatric disorders: a systematic overview of meta-analyses. *JAMA Psychiatry*, *71*(6), 706–715. https://doi.org/10.1001/jamapsychiatry.2014.112

Huibers, M. J., Cohen, Z. D., Lemmens, L. H., Arntz, A., Peeters, F. P., Cuijpers, P., & DeRubeis, R. J. (2015). Predicting optimal outcomes in cognitive therapy or interpersonal psychotherapy for depressed individuals using the Personalized Advantage Index approach. *PloS One*, *10*(11), e0140771. https://doi.org/10.1371/journal.pone.0140771

Hunsley, J., & Di Giulio, G. (2002). Dodo bird, phoenix, or urban legend? The question of psychotherapy equivalence. *Scientific Review of Mental Health Practice*, *1*, 11–22.

Imel, Z. E., Baldwin, S. A., Atkins, D., Owen, J., Baardseth, T., & Wampold, B. E. (2011). Racial/ethnic disparities in therapist effectiveness: A conceptualization and initial study of cultural competence. *Journal of Counseling Psychology*, *58*(3), 290–298. https://doi.org/10.1037/a0023284

Imel, Z. E., Sheng, E., Baldwin, S. A., & Atkins, D. C. (2015). Removing very low-performing therapists: A simulation of performance-based retention in psychotherapy. *Psychotherapy*, *52*(3), 329–336. http://dx.doi .org/10.1037/pst0000023

Ioannidis, J. P. (2009). Integration of evidence from multiple meta-analyses: a primer on umbrella reviews, treatment networks and multiple treatments meta- analyses. *CMAJ*, *181*, 488–493.

Ioannidis, J. P. (2016). The mass production of redundant, misleading, and conflicted systematic reviews and meta-analyses. *Milbank Quarterly*, *94*, 485–514.

Jacobson, N. S., & Truax, P. (1991). Clinical significance: A statistical approach to defining meaningful change in psychotherapy research. *Journal of Consulting and Clinical Psychology*, *59*(1), 12–19. https://doi .org/10.1037//0022-006x.59.1.12

Jarrett, R. B., Kraft, D., Doyle, J., Foster, B. M., Eaves, G. G., & Silver, P. C. (2001). Preventing recurrent depression using cognitive therapy with and without a continuation phase: a randomized clinical trial. *Archives of General Psychiatry*, *58*(4), 381–388. https://doi.org/10.1001/archpsyc.58.4 .381

Johns, R., Barkham, M., Kellett, S., & Saxon, D. (2019). A systematic review of therapist effects: A critical narrative update and refinement to Baldwin and Imel's (2013) review. *Clinical Psychology Review*, *67*, 78–93. https://doi .org/10.1016/j.cpr.2018.08.004

Johnsen, T. J., & Friborg, O. (2015). The effects of cognitive behavioral therapy as an anti-depressive treatment is falling: A meta-analysis. *Psychological Bulletin*, *141*(4), 747–768. https://doi.org/10.1037/bul0000015

Jonsson, U., Alaie, I., Parling, T., & Arnberg, F. K. (2014). Reporting of harms in randomized controlled trials of psychological interventions for mental and behavioral disorders: A review of current practice. *Contemporary Clinical Trials*, *38*(1), 1–8. https://doi.org/10.1016/j.cct.2014.02 .005

Kadera, S. W., Lambert, M. J., & Andrews, A. A. (1996). How much therapy is really enough? A session-by-session analysis of the psychotherapy dose-effect relationship. *Psychotherapy: Research and Practice*, *5*(2), 1–21.

Kanters, S., Ford, N., Druyts, E., Thorlund, K., Mills, E. J., & Bansback, N. (2016). *Bulletin of the World Health Organization*, *94*, 782–784. http:// dx.doi.org/10.2471/BLT.16.174326

Karyotaki, E., Smit, Y., Holdt Henningsen, K., Huibers, M. J. H., Robayse, J., de Beurs, D., & Cuijpers, P. (2016). Combining pharmacotherapy and psychotherapy or monotherapy for major depression? A meta-analysis on the long-term effects. *Journal of Affective Disorders*, *194*(1), 144–152. https:// doi.org/10.1016/j.jad.2016.01.036

Kazdin A. E. (2015). Treatment as usual and routine care in research and clinical practice. *Clinical Psychology Review*, *42*, 168–178. https://doi.org/10.1016/ j.cpr.2015.08.006

Kazdin, A. E. (2018). *Innovations in psychosocial interventions and their delivery: Leveraging cutting-edge science to improve the world's mental health*. New York: Oxford University Press.

Keefe, J. R., McCarthy, K. S., Dinger, U., Zilcha-Mano, S., & Barber, J. P. (2014). A meta-analytic review of psychodynamic therapies for anxiety disorders. *Clinical Psychology Review*, *34*(4), 309–323. https://doi.org/10.1016/ j.cpr.2014.03.004

Keetharuth, A. D., Brazier, J, Connell, J., Bjorner, J. B., Carlton, J., Taylor Buck, E., Ricketts, T., McKendrick, K., Browne, J., Croudace, T., & Barkham, M. on behalf of the ReQoL Scientific Group. (2018). Recovering Quality of Life (ReQoL): a new generic self-reported outcome measure for use with people experiencing mental health difficulties. *The British Journal of Psychiatry*, *212*, 42–49. https://doi.org/10.1192/bjp.2017.10

Kennedy, W. P. (1961). The nocebo reaction. *Medical World*, *95*, 203–205.

Kiresuk, T. J., Smith, A., & Cardillo, J. E. (Eds.). (1994). *Goal attainment scaling: Applications, theory, and measurement*. Lawrence Erlbaum Associates, Inc.

Kivlighan, D. M. III, & Chapman, N. A. (2018). Extending the multicultural orientation (MCO) framework to group psychotherapy: A clinical illustration. *Psychotherapy*, *55*(1), 39–44. http://dx.doi.org/10.1037/pst0000142

Koppers, D. D., Peen, J. J., Niekerken, S. S., Van, R. R., & Dekker, J. J. (2011). Prevalence and risk factors for recurrence of depression five years after short term psychodynamic therapy. *Journal of Affective Disorders*, *134*(1–3), 468–472. http://dx.doi.org/10.1016/j.jad.2011.05.027

Kraiss, J. T., Wijnen, B., Kupka, R. W., Bohlmeijer, E. T., & Lokkerbol, J. (2020). Economic evaluations of non-pharmacological interventions and cost-of-illness studies in bipolar disorder: A systematic review. *Journal of Affective Disorders*, *276*, 388–401. https://doi.org/10.1016/j.jad.2020.06.064

Kraus, D. R., Bentley, J. H., Alexander, P. C., Boswell, J. F., Constantino, M. J., Baxter, E. E., & Castonguay, L. G. (2016). Predicting therapist effectiveness from their own practice-based evidence. *Journal of Consulting and Clinical Psychology*, *84*(6), 473–483. https://doi.org/10.1037/ccp0000083

Kriston, L., von Wolff, A., Westphal, A., Hölzel, L. P., & Härter, M. (2014). Efficacy and acceptability of acute treatments for persistent depressive disorder: A network meta-analysis. *Depression and Anxiety*, *31*(8), 621–630. https://doi.org/10.1002/da.22236

Kuyken, W., Warren, F. C., Taylor, R. S., Whalley, B., Crane, C., Bondolfi, G., Hayes, R., Huijbers, M., Ma, H., Schweizer, S., Segal, Z., Speckens, A., Teasdale, J. D., Van Heeringen, K., Williams, M., Byford, S., Byng, R., & Dalgleish, T. (2016). Efficacy of mindfulness-based cognitive therapy in prevention of depressive relapse: An individual patient data meta-analysis from randomized trials. *JAMA Psychiatry*, *73*(6), 565–574. https://doi.org/10.1001/jamapsychiatry.2016.0076

Lambert, M. J. (2010). *Prevention of treatment failure: The use of measuring, monitoring, & feedback in clinical practice*. Washington, DC: American Psychological Association Press.

Lambert, M. J. (2013). The efficacy and effectiveness of psychotherapy. In M. J. Lambert (Ed.), *Bergin and Garfield's handbook of psychotherapy and behavior change* (6th ed., pp. 169–218). New York, NY: Wiley.

Lambert, M. J., & Bailey, R. J. (2012). Measures of clinically significant change. In H. Cooper, P. M. Camic, D. L. Long, A. T. Panter, D. Rindskopf, & K. J. Sher (Eds.), *APA handbook of research methods in psychology, Vol. 3. Data analysis and research publication* (p. 147–160). American Psychological Association. https://doi.org/10.1037/13621-007

Lambert, M. J., & Bergin, A. E. (1994). The effectiveness of psychotherapy. In A. E. Bergin & S. L. Garfield (Eds.), *Handbook of psychotherapy and behavior change* (4th ed., pp. 143–189). New York, NY: Wiley.

Lambert, M. J., & Ogles, B. M. (2004). The efficacy and effectiveness of psychotherapy. In M. J. Lambert (Ed.), *Bergin and Garfield's handbook of psychotherapy and behavior change* (5th ed., pp. 139–193). Hoboken, NJ: Wiley.

Lambert, M. J., & Ogles, B. M. (2009). Using clinical significance in psychotherapy outcome research: the need for a common procedure and validity data. *Psychotherapy Research*, *19*(4-5), 493–501. https://doi.org/10.1080/10503300902849483

Lambert, M. J., Shapiro, D. A., & Bergin, A. E. (1986). The effectiveness of psychotherapy. In S. L. Garfield & A. E. Bergin (Eds.), *Handbook of psychotherapy and behavior change* (3rd ed., pp. 157–211). New York, NY: Wiley.

Lamph, G., Baker, J., Dickinson, T., & Lovell, K. (2020). Personality disorder co-morbidity in primary care 'Improving Access to Psychological Therapy' (IAPT) services: A qualitative study exploring patient perspectives on treatment experience. *Behavioural and Cognitive Psychotherapy*, 1–15. https://doi.org/10.1017/S1352465820000594

Landman, J. T., & Dawes, R. M. (1982). Smith and Glass' conclusions stand up under scrutiny. *American Psychologist*, *37*(5), 504–516. https://doi.org/10.1037/0003-066X.37.5.504

Larrison, C. R., & Schoppelrey, S. L. (2011). Therapist effects on disparities experienced by minorities receiving services for mental illness. *Research on Social Work Practice*, *21*(6), 727–736. https://doi.org/10.1177/1049731511410989

Layard, R., Clark, D., Knapp, M., & Mayraz, G. (2007). Cost–benefit analysis of psychological therapy. *National Institute Economic Review*, *202*(1), 90–98. https://doi.org/10.1177/0027950107086171

Lazar, S. G. (Ed.) (2010). *Psychotherapy is worth it: A comprehensive review of its cost-effectiveness*. Arlington, VA: American Psychiatric Press.

Lee, A. A., Sripada, R. K, Hale, A. C., Ganoczy, D., Trivedi, R. B., Arnow, B., & Pfeiffer, P. N. (2021). Psychotherapy and depressive symptom trajectories among VA patients: Comparing dose-effect and good-enough level models. *Journal of Consulting and Clinical Psychology*, *89*(5), 379–392. https://doi.org/10.1037/ccp0000645

Lee, N. K., Cameron, J., & Jenner, L. (2015). A systematic review of interventions for co-occurring substance use and borderline personality disorders. *Drug and Alcohol Review*, *34*(6), 663–672. https://doi.org/10.1111/dar.12267

Leichsenring, F., & Klein, S. (2014). Evidence for psychodynamic psychotherapy in specific mental disorders: A systematic review. *Psychoanalytic Psychotherapy*, *28*(1), 4–32. https://doi.org/10.1080/02668734.2013.865428

Leichsenring, F., & Steinert, C. (2017). Is cognitive behavioral therapy the gold standard for psychotherapy?: The need for plurality in treatment and research. *JAMA*, *318*(14), 1323–1324. https://doi.org/10.1001/jama.2017.13737

Lemmens, L. H., Arntz, A., Peeters, F., Hollon, S. D., Roefs, A., & Huibers, M. J. (2015). Clinical effectiveness of cognitive therapy v. interpersonal psychotherapy for depression: results of a randomized controlled trial. *Psychological Medicine*, *45*(10), 2095–2110. https://doi.org/10.1017/S0033291715000033

Lemmens, L. H. J. M., van Bronswijk, S. C., Peeters, F., Arntz, A., Hollon, S. D., & Huibers, M. J. H. (2018). Long-term outcomes of acute treatment with cognitive therapy v. interpersonal psychotherapy for adult depression: Follow-up of a randomized controlled trial. *Psychological Medicine*, *49*(3), 465–473. https://doi.org/10.1017/S0033291718001083.

Lewis, C., Roberts, N. P., Andrew, M., Starling, E., & Bisson, J. I. (2020). Psychological therapies for post-traumatic stress disorder in adults: systematic review and meta-analysis. *European Journal of Psychotraumatology*, *11*(1), 1729633. https://doi.org/10.1080/20008198.2020.1729633

Li, J. M., Zhang, Y., Su, W. J., Liu, L. L., Gong, H., Peng, W., & Jiang, C. L. (2018). Cognitive behavioral therapy for treatment-resistant depression: A systematic review and meta-analysis. *Psychiatry Research*, *268*, 243–250. https://doi.org/10.1016/j.psychres.2018.07.020

Linden M. (2013). How to define, find and classify side effects in psychotherapy: From unwanted events to adverse treatment reactions. *Clinical Psychology & Psychotherapy*, *20*(4), 286–296. https://doi.org/10.1002/cpp.1765

Linden, M., & Schermuly-Haupt, M. L. (2014). Definition, assessment and rate of psychotherapy side effects. *World Psychiatry*, *13*(3), 306–309. https://doi.org/10.1002/wps.20153

Lipsey, M. W., & Wilson, D. B. (1993). The efficacy of psychological, educational, and behavioral treatment: Confirmation from meta-analysis. *American Psychologist*, *48*(12), 1181–1209. https://doi.org/10.1037//0003-066x.48.12.1181

Ljótsson, B., Hedman, E., Mattsson, S., & Andersson, E. (2017). The effects of cognitive–behavioral therapy for depression are not falling: A re-analysis of Johnsen and Friborg (2015). *Psychological Bulletin*, *143*(3), 321–325. https://doi.org/10.1037/bul0000055

López-López, J. A., Davies, S. R., Caldwell, D. M., Churchill, R., Peters, T. J., Tallon, D., Dawson, S., Wu, Q., Li, J., Taylor, A., Lewis, G., Kessler, D. S., Wiles, N., & Welton, N. J. (2019). The process and delivery of CBT for depression in adults: A systematic review and network meta-analysis. *Psychological Medicine*, *49*(12), 1937-1947. https://doi.org/10.1017/S003329171900120X

Lorenzo-Luaces, L., DeRubeis, R. J., van Straten, A., & Tiemens, B. (2017). A prognostic index (PI) as a moderator of outcomes in the treatment of depression: A proof of concept combining multiple variables to inform risk-stratified stepped care models. *Journal of Affective Disorders*, *213*, 78–85. https://doi.org/10.1016/j.jad.2017.02.010

Lorimer, B., Delgadillo, J., Kellett, S. & Brown, G. (2020). Exploring relapse through a network analysis of residual depression and anxiety symptoms after cognitive behavioural therapy: A proof-of-concept study. *Psychotherapy Research*, *30*(5), 650–661. https://doi.org/10.1080/10503307.2019.1650980

Lorimer, B., Kellett, S., Nye, A., & Delgadillo, J. (2021) Predictors of relapse and recurrence following cognitive behavioural therapy for anxiety-related disorders: a systematic review, *Cognitive Behaviour Therapy*, *50*(1), 1–18, https://doi.org/10.1080/16506073.2020.1812709

Luborsky, L., McClellan, A. T., Woody, G. E., O'Brien, C. P., & Auerbach, A. (1985). Therapist success and its determinants. *Archives of General Psychiatry*, *42*(6), 602–611. https://doi.org/10.1001/archpsyc.1985.01790290084010

Luborsky, L., Singer, J., & Luborsky, L. (1975). Comparative studies of psychotherapy. *Archives of General Psychiatry, 32*(8), 995–1008. https://doi.org/10.1001/archpsyc.1975.01760260059004

Lutz, W., Deisenhofer, A-K., Rubel, J., Bennemann, B., Giesemann, J., Poster, K., & Schwartz, B. (2021). Prospective evaluation of a clinical decision support system in psychological therapy. *Journal of Consulting and Clinical Psychology.* Advance online publication. https://doi.org/10.1037/ccp0000642

Lutz, W., Leach, C., Barkham, M., Lucock, M., Stiles, W. B., Evans, C., Noble, R., & Iveson, S. (2005). Predicting change for individual psychotherapy clients on the basis of their nearest neighbors. *Journal of Consulting and Clinical Psychology, 73*(5), 904–913. https://doi.org/10.1037/0022-006X.73.5.904

Lutz, W., Saunders, S. M., Leon, S. C., Martinovich, Z., Kosfelder, J., Schulte, D., Grawe, K., & Tholen, S. (2006). Empirically and clinically useful decision making in psychotherapy: Differential predictions with treatment response models. *Psychological Assessment, 18*(2), 133–141. https://doi.org/10.1037/1040-3590.18.2.133

Mars, B., Gibson, J., Dunn, B. D., Gordon, C., Heron, J., Kessler, D., Wiles, N., & Moran, P. (2021). Personality difficulties and response to community-based psychological treatment for anxiety and depression. *Journal of Affective Disorders, 279,* 266–273. https://doi.org/10.1016/j.jad.2020.09.115

Mavranezouli, I., Brazier, J., Rowan, D., & Barkham, M. (2013). Estimating a preference-based index from the Clinical Outcomes in Routine Evaluation—Outcome Measure (CORE-OM): valuation of CORE-6D. *Medical Decision Making, 33,* 381–395. https://doi.org/10.1177/0272989X12464431

Mavranezouli, I., Mayo-Wilson, E., Dias, S., Kew, K., Clark, D. M., Ades, A. E., & Pilling, S. (2015). The cost effectiveness of psychological and pharmacological interventions for social anxiety disorder: A model-based economic analysis. *PloS One, 10*(10), e0140704. https://doi.org/10.1371/journal.pone.0140704

Mavranezouli, I., Megnin-Viggars, O., Daly, C., Dias, S., Welton, N. J., Stockton, S., Bhutani, G., Grey, N., Leach, J., Greenberg, N., Katona, C., El-Leithy, S., & Pilling, S. (2020). Psychological treatments for post-traumatic stress disorder in adults: a network meta-analysis. *Psychological Medicine, 50*(4), 542–555. https://doi.org/10.1017/S0033291720000070

Mayo-Wilson, E., Dias, S., Mavranezouli, I., Kew, K., Clark, D. M., Ades, A. E., & Pilling, S. (2014). Psychological and pharmacological interventions for social anxiety disorder in adults: A systematic review and network meta-analysis. *The Lancet Psychiatry, 1*(5), 368–376. https://doi.org/10.1016/S2215-0366(14)70329-3

McCartney, M., Nevitt, S., Lloyd, A., Hill, R., White, R., & Duarte, R. (2021). Mindfulness-based cognitive therapy for prevention and time to depressive relapse: Systematic review and network meta-analysis. *Acta Psychiatrica Scandinavica, 143,* 6–21. https://doi.org/10.1111/acps.13242

McGorry, P. D., & Nelson, B. (2019). Transdiagnostic psychiatry: premature closure on a crucial pathway to clinical utility for psychiatric diagnosis. *World Psychiatry, 18*(3), 359–360. https://doi.org/10.1002/wps.20679

Meehl, P. E. (1954). *Clinical versus statistical prediction: A theoretical analysis and a review of the evidence.* University of Minnesota Press. https://doi.org/10.1037/11281-000

Michopoulos, I., Furukawa, T. A., Noma, H., Kishimoto, S., Onishi, A., Ostinelli, E. G., Ciharova, M., Miguel, C., Karyotaki, E., & Cuijpers, P. (2021). Different control conditions can produce different effect estimates in psychotherapy trials for depression. *Journal of Clinical Epidemiology, 132,* 59–70. https://doi.org/10.1016/j.jclinepi.2020.12.012.

Miklowitz, D. J., & Scott, J. (2009). Psychosocial treatments for bipolar disorder: cost-effectiveness, mediating mechanisms, and future directions. *Bipolar Disorders, 11*(Suppl 2), 110–122. https://doi.org/10.1111/j.1399-5618.2009.00715.x

Milrod, B., Chambless, D. L., Gallop, R., Busch, F. N., Schwalberg, M., McCarthy, K. S., Gross, C., Sharpless, B. A., Leon, A. C., & Barber, J. P. (2016). Psychotherapies for panic disorder: A tale of two sites. *The Journal of Clinical Psychiatry, 77*(7), 927–935. https://doi.org/10.4088/JCP.14m09507

Milrod, B., Leon, A. C., Busch, F., Rudden, M., Schwalberg, M., Clarkin, J., Aronson, A., Singer, M., Turchin, W., Klass, E. T., Graf, E., Teres, J. J., & Shear, M. K. (2007). A randomized controlled clinical trial of psychoanalytic psychotherapy for panic disorder. *The American Journal of Psychiatry, 164*(2), 265–272. https://doi.org/10.1176/ajp.2007.164.2.265

Mohr, D. C., Ho, J., Hart, T. L., Baron, K. G., Berendsen, M., Beckner, V., Cai, X., Cuijpers, P., Spring, B., Kinsinger, S. W., Schroder, K. E., & Duffecy, J. (2014). Control condition design and implementation features in controlled trials: a meta-analysis of trials evaluating psychotherapy for depression. *Translational Behavioral Medicine, 4*(4), 407–423. https://doi.org/10.1007/s13142-014-0262-3

Mohr, D. C., Spring, B., Freedland, K. E., Beckner, V., Arean, P., Hollon, S. D., Ockene, J., & Kaplan, R. (2009). The selection and design of control conditions for randomized controlled trials of psychological interventions. *Psychotherapy and Psychosomatics, 78*(5), 275–284. https://doi.org/10.1159/000228248

Molenaar, P. C. M. (2004). A manifesto on psychology as idiographic science: Bringing the person back into scientific psychology, this time forever. *Measurement: Interdisciplinary Research and Perspectives, 2*(4), 201–218. https://doi.org/10.1207/s15366359mea0204_1

Molloy, G. J., Noone, C., Caldwell, D., Welton, N. J., & Newell, J. (2018). Network meta-analysis in health psychology and behavioural medicine: A primer. *Health Psychology Review, 12*(3), 254–270. https://doi.org/10.1080/17437199.2018.1457449

Moran, P., Leese, M., Lee, T., Walters, P., Thornicroft, G., & Mann, A. (2003). Standardised Assessment of Personality – Abbreviated Scale (SAPAS): Preliminary validation of a brief screen for personality disorder. *The British Journal of Psychiatry, 183*(3), 228–232. doi:10.1192/bjp.183.3.228

Moritz, S., Fieker, M., Hottenrott, B., Seeralan, T., Cludius, B., Kolbeck, K., Gallinat, J., & Nestoriuc, Y. (2015). No pain, no gain? Adverse effects of psychotherapy in obsessive-compulsive disorder and its relationship to treatment gains. *Journal of Obsessive-Compulsive and Related Disorders, 5,* 61–66. https://doi.org/10.1016/j.jocrd.2015.02.002

Mukuria, C., Brazier, J., Barkham, M., Connell, J., Hardy, G., Hutten, R., Saxon, D., Dent-Brown, K., & Parry, G. (2013). Cost-effectiveness of an improving access to psychological therapies service. *The British Journal of Psychiatry, 202*(3), 220–227. https://doi.org/10.1192/bjp.bp.111.107888

Mulder, R., Boden, J., Carter, J., Luty, S., & Joyce, P. (2017). Ten month outcome of cognitive behavioural therapy v. interpersonal psychotherapy in patients with major depression: a randomised trial of acute and maintenance psychotherapy. *Psychological Medicine, 47*(14), 2540–2547. https://doi.org/10.1017/S0033291717001106

Munder, T., Flückiger, C., Leichsenring, F., Abbass, A. A., Hilsenroth, M. J., Luyten, P., Rabung, S., Steinert, C., & Wampold, B. E. (2019). Is psychotherapy effective? A re-analysis of treatments for depression. *Epidemiology and Psychiatric Sciences, 28*(3), 268–274. https://doi.org/10.1017/S2045796018000355

Murray, L. K., Haroz, E, Dorsey, S., Kane, J., Bolton, P. A., & Pullmann, M. D. (2020). Understanding mechanisms of change: An unpacking study of the evidence-based common-elements treatment approach (CETA) in low and middle income countries. *Behaviour Research and Therapy, 130,* 103430. https://doi.org/10.1016/j.brat.2019.103430.

Newby, J. M., McKinnon, A., Kuyken, W., Gilbody, S., & Dalgleish, T. (2015). Systematic review and meta-analysis of transdiagnostic psychological treatments for anxiety and depressive disorders in adulthood. *Clinical Psychology Review, 40,* 91–110. https://doi.org/10.1016/j.cpr.2015.06.002

NHS Digital (2020). https://digital.nhs.uk/data-and-information/publications/statistical/psychological-therapies-annual-reports-on-the-use-of-iapt-services/annual-report-2019-20.2020

Nissen-Lie, H. A., Havik, O. E., Høglend, P. A., Monsen, J. T., & Rønnestad, M. H. (2013). The contribution of the quality of therapists' personal lives to the development of the working alliance. *Journal of Counseling Psychology, 60*(4), 483–495. https://doi.org/10.1037/a0033643

Norcross, J. C., & Lambert, M. J. (2018). Psychotherapy relationships that work III. *Psychotherapy, 55*(4), 303–315. http://dx.doi.org/10.1037/pst0000193

O'Kearney, R., Kim, S., Dawson, R. L., & Calear, A. L. (2019). Are claims of non-inferiority of Internet and computer-based cognitive-behavioural therapy compared with in-person cognitive-behavioural therapy for adults with anxiety disorders supported by the evidence from head-to-head randomised controlled trials? A systematic review. *The Australian and New Zealand Journal of Psychiatry, 53*(9), 851–865. https://doi.org/10.1177/0004867419864433

Okiishi, J. C., Lambert, M. J., Eggett, D., Nielsen, L., Dayton, D. D., & Vermeersch, D. A. (2006). An analysis of therapist treatment effects: Toward providing feedback to individual therapists on their clients' psychotherapy outcome. *Journal of Clinical Psychology, 62*(9), 1157–1172. https://doi.org/10.1002/jclp.20272

Okiishi, J., Lambert, M. J., Nielsen, S. L., & Ogles, B. M. (2003). Waiting for super shrink: An empirical analysis of therapist effects. *Clinical Psychology & Psychotherapy, 10*(6), 361–373. https://doi.org/10.1002/cpp.383

Ophuis, R. H., Lokkerbol, J., Heemskerk, S. C., van Balkom, A. J., Hiligsmann, M., & Evers, S. M. (2017). Cost-effectiveness of interventions for treating anxiety disorders: A systematic review. *Journal of Affective Disorders, 210*, 1–13. https://doi.org/10.1016/j.jad.2016.12.005

Orlinsky, D. E., & Howard, K. I. (1980). Gender and psychotherapeutic outcome. In A. M. Brodsky & R. T. Hare-Mustin (Eds.), *Women and psychotherapy* (pp. 3–34). New York, NY: Guilford Press.

Ormel, J., Spinhoven, P., de Vries, Y. A., Cramer, A., Siegle, G. J., Bockting, C., & Hollon, S. D. (2020). The antidepressant standoff: why it continues and how to resolve it. *Psychological Medicine, 50*(2), 177–186. https://doi.org/10.1017/S0033291719003295

Öst, L. G., Havnen, A., Hansen, B., & Kvale, G. (2015). Cognitive behavioral treatments of obsessive-compulsive disorder. A systematic review and meta-analysis of studies published 1993-2014. *Clinical Psychological Review, 40*, 156–169. https://doi.org/10.1016/j.cpr.2015.06.003

Oud, M., Arntz, A., Hermens, M. L., Verhoef, R., & Kendall, T. (2018). Specialized psychotherapies for adults with borderline personality disorder: A systematic review and meta-analysis. *The Australian and New Zealand Journal of Psychiatry, 52*(10), 949–961. https://doi.org/10.1177/0004867418791257

Owen, J., Imel, Z., Adelson, J., & Rodolfa, E. (2012). 'No-show': therapist racial/ethnic disparities in client unilateral termination. *Journal of Counseling Psychology, 59*(2), 314–320. https://doi.org/10.1037/a0027091

Owen, J., Tao, K. W., Drinane, J. M., Hook, J., Davis, D. E., & Kune, N. F. (2016). Client perceptions of therapists' multicultural orientation: Cultural (missed) opportunities and cultural humility. *Professional Psychology: Research and Practice, 47*(1), 30–37. https://doi.org/10.1037/pro0000046

Patel, V., Chisholm, D., Parikh, R., Charlson, F. J., Degenhardt, L., Dua, T., Ferrari, A. J., Hyman, S., Laxminarayan, R., Levin, C., Lund, C., Medina Mora, M. E., Petersen, I., Scott, J., Shidhaye, R., Vijayakumar, L., Thornicroft, G., Whiteford, H., & DCP MNS Author Group (2016). Addressing the burden of mental, neurological, and substance use disorders: key messages from Disease Control Priorities, 3rd edition. *The Lancet, 387*(10028), 1672–1685. https://doi.org/10.1016/S0140-6736(15)00390-6

Patel, V., Chowdhary, N., Rahman, A., & Verdeli, H. (2011). Improving access to psychological treatments: lessons from developing countries. *Behaviour Research and Therapy, 49*(9), 523-528. https://doi.org/10.1016/j.brat.2011.06.012

Patel, V., Weobong, B., Weiss, H. A., Anand, A., Bhat, B., Katti, B., Dimidjian, S., Araya, R., Hollon, S. D., King, M., Vijayakumar, L., Park, A. L., McDaid, D., Wilson, T., Velleman, R., Kirkwood, B. R., & Fairburn, C. G. (2017). The Healthy Activity Program (HAP), a lay counsellor-delivered brief psychological treatment for severe depression, in primary care in India: a randomised controlled trial. *The Lancet, 389*(10065), 176–185. https://doi.org/10.1016/S0140-6736(16)31589-6

Paul, G. L. (1967). Strategy of outcome research in psychotherapy. *Journal of Consulting Psychology, 31*(2), 109–118. https://doi.org/10.1037/h0024436

Perlis, R. H., Welge, J. A., Vornik, L. A., Hirschfeld, R. M., & Keck, P. E., Jr. (2006). Atypical antipsychotics in the treatment of mania: A meta-analysis of randomized, placebo-controlled trials. *Journal of Clinical Psychiatry, 67*(4), 509–516.

PLoS Medicine Editors (2011). Best practice in systematic reviews: The importance of protocols and registration. *PLoS Medicine.* February 22, 201. https://doi.org/10.1371/journal.pmed.1001009

Polo, A. J., Makol, B. A., Castro, A. S., Colón-Quintana, N., Wagstaff, A. E., & Guo, S. (2019). Diversity in randomized clinical trials of depression: A 36-year review. *Clinical Psychology Review, 67*, 22–35. https://doi.org/10.1016/j.cpr.2018.09.004

Pompoli, A., Furukawa, T. A., Imai, H., Tajika, A., Efthimiou, O., & Salanti, G. (2016). Psychological therapies for panic disorder with or without agoraphobia in adults: A network meta-analysis. *The Cochrane Database of Systematic Reviews, 4*(4), CD011004. https://doi.org/10.1002/14651858.CD011004.pub2

Prochaska, J. O., Norcross, J. C., & Saul, S. F. (2020). Generating psychotherapy breakthroughs: Transtheoretical strategies from population health psychology. *American Psychologist, 75*(7), 996–1010. https://doi.org/10.1037/amp0000568

Rachman, S. J., & Wilson, G. T. (1980). *The effects of psychological therapy* (2nd ed.). New York: Pergamon.

Richards D., Richardson T., Timulak L., & McElvaney J. (2015). The efficacy of internet-delivered treatment for generalized anxiety disorder: a systematic review and meta-analysis. *Internet Interventions, 2*(3), 272–282. https://doi.org/10.1016/j.invent.2015.07.003

Robinson, L., Delgadillo, J., & Kellett, S. (2020). The dose-response effect in routinely delivered psychological therapies: A systematic review. *Psychotherapy Research, 30*(1), 79–96. https://doi.org/10.1080/10503307.2019.1566676

Rojas-García, A., Ruiz-Perez, I., Rodríguez-Barranco, M., Gonçalves Bradley, D. C., Pastor-Moreno, G., & Ricci-Cabello, I. (2015). Healthcare interventions for depression in low socioeconomic status populations: A systematic review and meta-analysis. *Clinical Psychology Review, 38*, 65–78. https://doi.org/10.1016/j.cpr.2015.03.001

Rosenthal, R., & Rubin, D. B. (1982). A simple, general purpose display of magnitude of experimental effect. *Journal of Educational Psychology, 74*(2), 166–169. https://doi.org/10.1037/0022-0663.74.2.166

Rosenzweig, S. (1936). Some implicit common factors in diverse methods of psychotherapy. *American Journal of Orthopsychiatry, 6*(3), 412–415. https://doi.org/10.1111/j.1939-0025.1936.tb05248.x

Ross, E. L., Vijan, S., Miller, E. M., Valenstein, M., & Zivin, K. (2019). The cost-effectiveness of cognitive behavioral therapy versus second-generation antidepressants for initial treatment of major depressive disorder in the United States: A decision analytic model. *Annals of Internal Medicine, 171*(11), 785–795. https://doi.org/10.7326/M18-1480

Rouse, B., Chaimani, A., & Li, T. (2017). Network meta-analysis: an introduction for clinicians. *Internal and Emergency Medicine, 12*(1), 103–111. https://doi.org/10.1007/s11739-016-1583-7

Rozental, A., Castonguay, L., Dimidjian, S., Lambert, M., Shafran, R., Andersson, G., & Carlbring, P. (2018). Negative effects in psychotherapy: Commentary and recommendations for future research and clinical practice. *BJPsych Open, 4*(4), 307–312. https://doi.org/10.1192/bjo.2018.42

Sales, C. M. D., & Alves, P. C. G. (2016). Patient-centered assessment in psychotherapy: A review of individualized tools. *Clinical Psychology Science and Practice, 23*, 265–283. https://doi.org/10.1111/cpsp.12162

Sales, C. M. D., Neves, I. T., Alves, P. G., & Ashworth, M. (2018). Capturing and missing the patient's story through outcome measures: A thematic comparison of patient-generated items in PSYCHLOPS with CORE-OM and PHQ-9. *Health Expectations, 21*(3), 615–619. https://doi.org/10.1111/hex.12652

Sanders, S. G., & Hunsley, J. (2018). The new Caucus-race: Methodological considerations for meta-analyses of psychotherapy outcome. *Canadian Psychology/Psychologie canadienne, 59*(4), 387–398. https://doi.org/10.1037/cap0000164

Saxon, D., & Barkham, M. (2012). Patterns of therapist variability: Therapist effects and the contribution of patient severity and risk. *Journal of Consulting and Clinical Psychology, 80*(4), 535–546. https://doi.org/10.1037/a0028898

Saxon, D., Firth, N., & Barkham, M. (2017). The relationship between therapist effects and therapy delivery factors: Therapy modality, dosage, and non-completion. *Administration and Policy in Mental Health, 44*(5), 705–715. https://doi.org/10.1007/s10488-016-0750-5

Schermuly-Haupt, M. L., Linden, M. & Rush, A. J. (2018). Unwanted events and side effects in cognitive behavior therapy. *Cognitive Therapy and Research, 42*(3), 219–229. https://doi.org/10.1007/s10608-018-9904-y

Schiefele, A-K., Lutz, W., Barkham, M., Rubel, J., Böhnke, J., Delgadillo, J., Kopta, M. Schulte, D., Saxon, D., Neilsen, S. L., & Lambert, M. (2017). Reliability of therapist effects in practice-based psychotherapy research: A guide for the planning of future studies. *Administration and Policy in Mental Health, 44*, 598–613. https://doi.org/10.1007/s10488-016-0736-3

Scott, A. I., & Freeman, C. P. (1992). Edinburgh primary care depression study: treatment outcome, patient satisfaction, and cost after 16 weeks. *BMJ, 304*(6831), 883–887. https://doi.org/10.1136/bmj.304.6831.883

Scott, J., & Young, A. (2016). Psychotherapies should be assessed for both benefit and harm. *The British Journal of Psychiatry*, 208(3), 208–209. https://doi.org/10.1192/bjp.bp.115.169060

Segal, Z. V., Williams, J. M. G., & Teasdale, J. D. (2002). *Mindfulness-based cognitive therapy for depression: A new approach to preventing relapse*. Guilford Press.

Shadish, W. R., & Sweeney, R. B. (1991). Mediators and moderators in meta-analysis: There's a reason we don't let dodo birds tell us which psychotherapies should have prizes. *Journal of Consulting and Clinical Psychology*, 59(6), 883–893. https://doi.org/10.1037/0022-006X.59.6.883

Shalom, J. G., & Aderka, I. M. (2020). A meta-analysis of sudden gains in psychotherapy: Outcome and moderators. *Clinical Psychology Review*, 76, 101827. https://doi.org/10.1016/j.cpr.2020.101827

Shalom, J. G., Gilboa-Schechtman, E., Atzil-Slonim, D., Bar-Kalifa, E., Hasson-Ohayon, I., van Oppen, P., van Balkom, A. J. L. M., & Aderka, I. M. (2018). Intraindividual variability in symptoms consistently predicts sudden gains: An examination of three independent datasets. *Journal of Consulting and Clinical Psychology*, 86(11), 892–902. https://doi.org/10.1037/ccp0000344

Shapiro, D. A., & Shapiro, D. (1982). Meta-analysis of comparative therapy outcome studies: A replication and refinement. *Psychological Bulletin*, 92(3), 581–604. https://doi.org/10.1037/0033-2909.92.3.581

Shapiro, M. B. (1961). The single case in fundamental clinical psychological research. *British Journal of Medical Psychology*, 34, 255–262. https://doi.org/10.1111/j.2044-8341.1961.tb00949.x

Sharpe, D. (1997). Of apples and oranges, file drawers and garbage: Why validity issues in meta-analysis will not go away. *Clinical Psychology Review*, 17, 881–901.

Singla, D. R., Meltzer-Brody, S. E., Silver, R. K., Vigod, S. N., Kim, J. J., La Porte, L. M., Ravitz, P., Schiller, C. E., Schoueri-Mychasiw, N., Hollon, S. D., Kiss, A., Clark, D., Dalfen, A. K., Dimidjian, S., Gaynes, B. N., Katz, S. R., Lawson, A., Leszcz, M., Maunder, R. G., Mulsant, B. H., … Patel, V. (2021). Scaling Up Maternal Mental healthcare by Increasing access to Treatment (SUMMIT) through non-specialist providers and telemedicine: a study protocol for a non-inferiority randomized controlled trial. *Trials*, 22(1), 186. https://doi.org/10.1186/s13063-021-05075-1

Skapinakis, P., Caldwell, D. M., Hollingworth, W., Bryden, P., Fineberg, N. A., Salkovskis, P., Welton, N. J., Baxter, H., Kessler, D., Churchill, R., & Lewis, G. (2016). Pharmacological and psychotherapeutic interventions for management of obsessive-compulsive disorder in adults: a systematic review and network meta-analysis. *The Lancet Psychiatry*, 3(8), 730–739. https://doi.org/10.1016/S2215-0366(16)30069-4

Sledge, W. H., Lazar, S. G., & Waldinger, R. J. (2010). Epilogue. In Lazar, S. G. (Ed.). *Psychotherapy is worth it: A comprehensive review of its cost-effectiveness* (pp. 311–314). Arlington, VA: American Psychiatric Press.

Smith, M. L., & Glass, G. V. (1977). Meta-analysis of psychotherapy outcome studies. *American Psychologist*, 32, 752–760.

Smith, M. L., Glass, G. V., & Miller, T. I. (1980). *The benefits of psychotherapy*. Baltimore, MD: Johns Hopkins University Press.

Solomon, D. A., Keller, M. B., Leon, A. C., Mueller, T. I., Lavori, P. W., Shea, M. T., Coryell, W., Warshaw, M., Turvey, C., Maser, J. D., & Endicott, J. (2000). Multiple recurrences of major depressive disorder. *The American Journal of Psychiatry*, 157(2), 229–233. https://doi.org/10.1176/appi.ajp.157.2.229

Spek, V., Cuijpers, P., Nyklícek, I., Riper, H., Keyzer, J., & Pop, V. (2007). Internet-based cognitive behaviour therapy for symptoms of depression and anxiety: a meta-analysis. *Psychological Medicine*, 37(3), 319–328. https://doi.org/10.1017/S0033291706008944

Spong, A. J., Clare, I. C. H., Galante, J., Crawford, M. J., & Jones, P. B. (2021). Brief psychological interventions for borderline personality disorder. A systematic review and meta-analysis of randomised controlled trials, *Clinical Psychology Review*, 83, 2021, https://doi.org/10.1016/j.cpr.2020.101937

Springer, K. S., Levy, H. C., & Tolin, D. F. (2018). Remission in CBT for adult anxiety disorders: A meta-analysis. *Clinical Psychology Review*, 61, 1–8. https://doi.org/10.1016/j.cpr.2018.03.002

Steinert, C., Hofmann, M., Kruse, J., & Leichsenring, F. (2014). The prospective long-term course of adult depression in general practice and the community. A systematic literature review. *Journal of Affective Disorders*, 152–154, 65–75. https://doi.org/10.1016/j.jad.2013.10.017

Steinert, C., Munder, T., Rabung, S., Hoyer, J., & Leichsenring, F. (2017). Psychodynamic therapy: As efficacious as other empirically supported treatments? A meta-analysis testing equivalence of outcomes. *The American Journal of Psychiatry*, 174(10), 943–953. https://doi.org/10.1176/appi.ajp.2017.17010057

Stiles, W. B., Barkham, M., Connell, J., & Mellor-Clark, J. (2008). Responsive regulation of treatment duration in routine practice in United Kingdom primary care settings: Replication in a larger sample. *Journal of Consulting and Clinical Psychology*, 76(2), 298–305. https://doi.org/10.1037/0022-006X.76.2.298

Stiles, W. B., Barkham, M., & Wheeler, S. (2015). Different durations of psychological therapy have similar recovery and improvement rates: Evidence from diverse UK routine practice settings. *The British Journal of Psychiatry*, 207(2), 115–122. https://doi.org/10.1192/bjp.bp.114.145565

Stiles, W. B., Leach, C., Barkham, M., Lucock, M., Iveson, S., Shapiro, D. A., & Hardy, G. E. (2003). Early sudden gains in psychotherapy under routine clinic conditions: Practice-based evidence. *Journal of Consulting and Clinical Psychology*, 71(1), 14–21. https://doi.org/10.1037/0022- 006X.71.1.14

Stiles, W. B., Shapiro, D. A., & Elliott, R. (1986). "Are all psychotherapies equivalent?" *American Psychologist*, 41(2), 165–180. https://doi.org/10.1037/0003–066X.41.2.165

Stoffers, J. M., Völlm, B. A., Rücker, G., Timmer, A., Huband, N., & Lieb, K. (2012). Psychological therapies for people with borderline personality disorder. *The Cochrane Database of Systematic Reviews*, 8, CD005652. https://doi.org/10.1002/14651858.CD005652.pub2

Strupp H. H. (1993). The Vanderbilt psychotherapy studies: synopsis. *Journal of Consulting and Clinical Psychology*, 61(3), 431–433. https://doi.org/10.1037//0022-006x.61.3.431

Stulz, N., Lutz, W., Kopta, S. M., Minami, T., & Saunders, S. M. (2013). Dose-effect relationship in routine outpatient psychotherapy: Does treatment duration matter? *Journal of Counseling Psychology*, 60(4), 593–600. https://doi.org/10.1037/a0033589

Sue, D. W., Arredondo, P., & McDavis, R. J. (1992). Multicultural counseling competencies and standards: A call to the profession. *Journal of Multicultural Counseling and Development*, 20(2), 64–88. https://doi.org/10.1002/j.2161-1912.1992.tb00563.x

Sue, S., Zane, N., Nagayama Hall, G. C., & Berger, L. K. (2009). The case for cultural competency in psychotherapeutic interventions. *Annual Review of Psychology*, 60, 525–548. https://doi.org/10.1146/annurev.psych.60.110707.163651

Svensson, M., Nilsson, T., Perrin, S., Johansson, H., Viborg, G., Falkenström, F., & Sandell, R. (2020). Panic focused psychodynamic psychotherapy versus panic control treatment for panic disorder: A doubly randomised controlled preference trial. *Psychotherapy and Psychosomatics*, 1–12. https://doi.org/10.1159/000511469

Tang, T. Z., & DeRubeis, R. J. (1999). Sudden gains and critical sessions in cognitive-behavioral therapy for depression. *Journal of Consulting and Clinical Psychology*, 67(6), 894–904. https://doi.org/10.1037/0022– 0066x.67.6.894

Tao, K. W., Owen, J., Pace, B. T., & Imel, Z. E. (2015). A meta-analysis of multicultural competencies and psychotherapy process and outcome. *Journal of Counseling Psychology*, 62(3), 337–350. https://doi.org/10.1037/cou0000086

ten Doesschate, M. C., Bockting, C. H., Koeter, M. J., & Schene, A. H. (2010). Prediction of recurrence in recurrent depression: A 5-year prospective study. *Journal of Clinical Psychiatry*, 71(8), 984–991. doi: 10.4088/JCP.08m04858blu

Timulak, L. (2007). Identifying core categories of client-identified impact of helpful events in psychotherapy: A qualitative meta-analysis. *Psychotherapy Research*, 17, 310–320. https://doi.org/10.1080/10503300600608116

Timulak, L. (2010). Significant events in psychotherapy: An update of research findings. *Psychology and Psychotherapy: Theory, Research and Practice*, 83, 421–447. https://doi.org/10.1348/147608310X499404

Tolin D. F. (2010). Is cognitive-behavioral therapy more effective than other therapies? A meta-analytic review. *Clinical Psychology Review*, 30(6), 710–720. https://doi.org/10.1016/j.cpr.2010.05.003

van Bronswijk, S. C., Bruijniks, S. J. E., Lorenzo-Luaces, L., DeRubeis, R. J., Lemmens, L. H. J. M., Peeters, F. P. M. L., & Huibers, M. J. H. (2021) Cross-trial prediction in psychotherapy: External validation of the Personalized Advantage Index using machine learning in two Dutch randomized trials comparing CBT versus IPT for depression, *Psychotherapy Research*, 31(1), 78–91. https://doi.org/10.1080/10503307.2020.1823029

van Bronswijk, S. C., Lemmens, L. H. J. M., Huibers, M. J. H, & Peeters, F. P. M. L. (2021). Selecting the optimal treatment for a depressed individual: Clinical judgment or statistical prediction? *Journal of Affective Disorders*, *279*, 149–157. https://doi.org/10.1016/j.jad.2020.09.135

van Dis, E., van Veen, S. C., Hagenaars, M. A., Batelaan, N. M., Bockting, C., van den Heuvel, R. M., Cuijpers, P., & Engelhard, I. M. (2020). Long-term outcomes of cognitive behavioral therapy for anxiety-related disorders: A systematic review and meta-analysis. *JAMA Psychiatry*, *77*(3), 265–273. https://doi.org/10.1001/jamapsychiatry.2019.3986

Wampold, B. E. (2001). *The great psychotherapy debate: Models, methods, and findings*. Mahwah: LEA.

Wampold, B. E. (2007). Psychotherapy: The humanistic (and effective) treatment. *American Psychologist*, *62*(8), 857–873. https://doi.org/10.1037/0003-066X.62.8.857

Wampold B. E. (2015). How important are the common factors in psychotherapy? An update. *World Psychiatry*, *14*(3), 270–277. https://doi.org/10.1002/wps.20238

Wampold, B. E., Baldwin, S. A., Holtforth, M. g., & Imel, Z. E. (2017). What characterizes effective therapists? In L. G. Castonguay & C. E. Hill (Eds.), *How and why are some therapists better than others?: Understanding therapist effects* (pp. 37–53). American Psychological Association.

Wampold, B. E., Budge, S.L., Laska, K. M., Del Re, A. C., Baardseth, T. P., Flückiger, C., Minami, T., Kivlighan, D. M., III, & Gunn, W. (2011). Evidence-based treatments for depression and anxiety versus treatment-as-usual: a meta-analysis of direct comparisons. *Clinical Psychology Review*, *31*(8), 1304–1312. https://doi.org/10.1016/j.cpr.2011.07.012

Wampold, B. E., & Imel, Z. E. (2015). *The great psychotherapy debate: The evidence for what makes psychotherapy work*. 2nd Edition. Routledge.

Wampold, B. E., Mondin, G. W., Moody, M., Stich, F., Benson, K., & Ahn, H.-n. (1997). A meta-analysis of outcome studies comparing bona fide psychotherapies: Empiricially, "all must have prizes." *Psychological Bulletin*, *122*(3), 203–215. https://doi.org/10.1037/0033-2909.122.3.203

Watkins, E. R., & Newbold, A. (2020). Factorial designs help to understand how psychological therapy works. *Frontiers in Psychiatry 11*, 429. https://doi.org/10.3389/fpsyt.2020.00429

Webb, C. A., Trivedi, M. H., Cohen, Z. D., Dillon, D. G., Fournier, J. C., Goer, F., Fava, M., McGrath, P. J., Weissman, M., Parsey, R., Adams, P., Trombello, J. M., Cooper, C., Deldin, P., Oquendo, M. A., McInnis, M. G., Huys, Q., Bruder, G., Kurian, B. T., Jha, M., . . . Pizzagalli, D. A. (2019). Personalized prediction of antidepressant v. placebo response: evidence from the EMBARC study. *Psychological Medicine*, *49*(7), 1118–1127. https://doi.org/10.1017/S0033291718001708

Whaley, A. L., & Davis, K. E. (2007). Cultural competence and evidence-based practice in mental health services: A complementary perspective. *American Psychologist*, *62*(6), 563–574. https://doi.org/10.1037/0003-066X.62.6.563

Wickramasekera, N., & Tubeuf, S. (2020). Measuring quality of life for people with common mental health problems. *Journal of Mental Health*, 1–8. Advance online publication. https://doi.org/10.1080/09638237.2020.1818190

Wiles, N. J., Thomas, L., Turner, N., Garfield, K., Kounali, D., Campbell, J., Kessler, D., Kuyken, W., Lewis, G., Morrison, J., Williams, C., Peters, T. J., & Hollinghurst, S. (2016). Long-term effectiveness and cost-effectiveness of cognitive behavioural therapy as an adjunct to pharmacotherapy for treatment-resistant depression in primary care: follow-up of the CoBalT randomised controlled trial. *The Lancet Psychiatry*, *3*(2), 137–144. https://doi.org/10.1016/S2215-0366(15)00495-2

Wojnarowski, C., Firth, N., Finegan, M., & Delgadillo, J. (2019). Predictors of depression relapse and recurrence after cognitive behavioural therapy: a systematic review and meta-analysis. *Behavioural and Cognitive Psychotherapy*, *47*(5), 514–529. https://doi.org/10.1017/S1352465819000080

Ye, B. Y., Jiang, Z. Y., Li, X., Cao, B., Cao, L. P., Lin, Y., Xu, G. Y., & Miao, G. D. (2016). Effectiveness of cognitive behavioral therapy in treating bipolar disorder: An updated meta-analysis with randomized controlled trials. *Psychiatry and Clinical Neurosciences*, *70*(8), 351–361. https://doi.org/10.1111/pcn.12399

Zala, D., Brabban, A., Stirzaker, A., Kartha, M. R., & McCrone, P. (2019). The cost-effectiveness of the Improving Access to Psychological Therapies (IAPT) Programme in severe mental illness: A decision analytical model using routine data. *Community Mental Health Journal*, *55*(5), 873–883. https://doi.org/10.1007/s10597-019-00390-z

Zeber, J. E., Coleman, K. J., Fischer, H., Yoon, T. K., Ahmedani, B. K., Beck, A., Hubley, S., Imel, Z. E., Rossom, R. C., Shortreed, S. M., Stewart, C., Waitzfelder, B. E., & Simon, G. E. (2017). The impact of race and ethnicity on rates of return to psychotherapy for depression. *Depression and Anxiety*, *34*(12), 1157–1163. https://doi.org/10.1002/da.22696

Zhang, Z., Zhang, L., Zhang, G., Jin, J., & Zheng, Z. (2018). The effect of CBT and its modifications for relapse prevention in major depressive disorder: a systematic review and meta-analysis. *BMC Psychiatry*, *18*(1), 50. https://doi.org/10.1186/s12888-018-1610-5

Zilcha-Mano S. (2017). Is the alliance really therapeutic? Revisiting this question in light of recent methodological advances. *American Psychologist*, *72*(4), 311–325. https://doi.org/10.1037/a0040435

CHAPTER 6

PRACTICE-BASED EVIDENCE – FINDINGS FROM ROUTINE CLINICAL SETTINGS

LOUIS G CASTONGUAY, MICHAEL BARKHAM, SOO JEONG YOUN, AND ANDREW C PAGE[1]

Abstract

The goal of this chapter is to survey practice-based evidence (PBE) in the psychological therapies that has accumulated over the last decade. PBE, or practice-oriented research (POR), is complementary to studies that are conducted in controlled settings and are predominantly guided by researchers' agenda. In contrast to the more traditional paradigm of evidence-based practice, PBE is conducted as part of clinical routine practice and some studies involve clinicians' participation in the design, implementation and/or dissemination of empirical studies. The chapter provides examples of PBE studies implemented in different clinical settings, with various clinical populations, and by researchers and clinicians from diverse parts of the world and with different theoretical orientations. The studies address several aspects of the impact (therapist effects, effectiveness of single and multiple clinics) and process (alliance, therapist interventions, therapist and client experience) of psychological therapies, as well as participants' characteristics (e.g., expectations, interpersonal/attachment issues) and contextual factors (center and neighborhood effects, training and supervision) that contribute to therapeutic change. Other initiatives that are also aimed at closing the gap between science and practice are briefly discussed, along with new developments in POR. The chapter ends with a description of features that cut across PBE studies as well as some of the challenges and limitations of these investigations, the identification of various clinical, scientific, and policy contributions of past and current investigations of routine practice, the delineation of characteristics of high-quality PBE studies, and some recommendations to facilitate the conduct and impact of future PBE studies.

OVERVIEW

Introduction
Outcomes
  Practitioner Level: Therapist Effects
  Single Clinic Level in Routine Settings
  Multiple Clinics: Effectiveness of Psychological Therapies
    in Routine Settings
  Other Impacts of Psychological Therapies
  Summary
Process
  Alliance
  Therapist Interventions
  Client and Therapist Experience
  Summary
Participants' Characteristics
  Demographics
  Level of Symptoms/Severity
  Diagnostic/Clinical Problems

Expectations and Preferences
Interpersonal/Attachment Issues
Mixed Client Variables
Client and Therapist Matching
Summary
Contextual Variables
  Center/Clinic/Service Effects
  Neighborhood Effects
  Training/Supervision
  Summary
Other Initiatives to Close the Science–Practice Gap and
    New Developments in Practice-Oriented Research
Conclusion
  Clinical, Scientific, and Policy-Making Contributions
  Recommendations for Future Research
Abbreviations
References

[1] The authors are most grateful for the tremendous help provided by Dever Carney and J. Ryan Kilcullen in preparing this chapter.

INTRODUCTION

The first edition of the *Handbook of Psychotherapy and Behavior Change* featured a chapter titled "Clinical Innovations in Research and Practice." Written by Arnold Lazarus and Gerald Davison (1971), it was guided by the conviction that "many of our greatest advances in therapeutic theory and practice come through clinical experimentation and innovation, rather than through laboratory research or controlled field trials across large samples of cases" (p. 198). However, it was not until the sixth edition that a new chapter was devoted to research investigating the work conducted by clinicians in their practice (Castonguay et al., 2013). As stated in the first chapter of this volume, the history of the *Handbook* has paralleled the development of the field. As such, it could be argued that chapters on practice-oriented research (POR), or practice-based evidence (PBE), in the previous and current editions reflect the consolidation and growth of a new paradigm. This research paradigm is complementary to traditional studies that have either been conducted in controlled settings or have been implemented in naturalistic environments, but independently from routine clinical practice. It could also be argued that the long absence of a chapter in the *Handbook* on what clinicians do in day-to-day practice is symptomatic of the gap that for decades has existed between science and practice. In the 2013 version of this chapter, we suggested that this gap has been maintained in part because many of the efforts to foster the scientific practitioner model (including the identification and promotion of empirically supported treatments [ESTs] and empirically supported therapeutic relationships) represent a top-down approach: that is, science is transmitted, and potentially adopted, via researchers informing therapists about the issues that have been studied and the lessons that can be derived from the findings. For example, in the United Kingdom some of these findings, derived from traditional RCTs and related meta-analytic studies, largely determine the national treatment guidelines to which practitioners and services/clinics are required to adhere. In this chapter, we refer to these efforts as manifestations of the paradigm of evidence-based practice. Although such efforts have and will continue to provide useful information to therapists, they are not representative of wider practice and are giving privilege to one source of expertise in determining what should be studied and how it should be investigated in order to understand and facilitate the process of change.

POR is one of the possible ways to redress this imbalance, as well as to expand the scope of empirical research. It does so by investigating psychological therapies as they are being conducted in routine practice and, in some circumstances, by having clinicians actively engaged in the design and/or implementation of research protocols – on their own or in collaboration with researchers. Having research grounded in day-to-day clinical care reflects a bottom-up approach to building and using scientific knowledge. By emerging directly from the context in which therapists are working, POR is likely to be intrinsically relevant to their concerns and can optimally confound research and practice: that is, when clinicians perform activities that are simultaneously and intrinsically serving clinical and scientific purposes. Moreover, when designed and conducted in collaboration between clinicians and researchers, POR studies can be viewed as efforts toward creating new pathways of connections between science and practice in terms of both process and outcome. By fostering a sense of shared ownership and mutual respect, such studies can build on complementary expertise, compensate for limitations of knowledge and experience, and thus foster new ways of understanding, conducting, and investigating psychological therapies.

The chapter on POR in the previous edition of the *Handbook* (Castonguay et al., 2013) described three main approaches: patient-focused research, practice-based evidence (PBE), and practice research networks (PRNs). Whereas patient-focused research examines clients' patterns of change, PBE primarily focuses on factors that foster such change (e.g., therapists, treatment approaches, and services/clinics). In contrast, research carried out in PRNs is not defined by its research focus but rather by a process of partnership between clinicians, or between practitioners, researchers, and/or other stakeholders of mental health services. In this edition, patient-focused research is addressed in Chapter 4, while this chapter combines both PBE and PRN research. While they can be differentiated in terms of the level of practitioner involvement (who are typically more active in the design and implementation of research in PRNs), what they share in common is more important than what distinguishes them. In fact, we would argue that PRNs can generally be subsumed under PBE as a general type of research that is aimed at understanding and improving psychological therapies as they are regularly conducted in a diversity of naturalistic settings.

At the core of PBE studies are three defining features: (i) the data are collected as part of clinical routine practice; (ii) what is assessed reflects everyday practice; and (iii) what is investigated does not involve researcher-imposed constraints on day-to-day practice, such as prohibition or manipulation of interventions prescribed by external contingencies (e.g., researchers requiring participants to adhere to specific protocols that are not typically part of clinical routine). As mentioned above, some PBE studies are conducted by clinicians or are based on an active collaboration between them and other stakeholders (e.g., researchers, administrators, clients) in different aspects of design, implementation, and/or dissemination of studies – albeit with diverse levels of involvement adopted by clinicians in each or all of these aspects.

As such, PBE investigations are distinct from studies that are conducted in controlled settings, or settings created specifically for empirical investigations. These involve, but are not restricted to, RCT-based efficacy studies. They are also distinct from studies in naturalistic settings that are aimed at investigating a treatment program created primarily for research purposes. For example, studies that investigate variables (participant characteristics, process, outcome) of a specific therapeutic protocol that has been created or chosen by researchers, but that does not reflect what clinicians do in clinical routine. These involve, but are not restricted to effectiveness studies – even those that have involved the partnership of different stakeholders in the design and implementation of the studies (effectiveness studies are addressed in Chapter 5 of this *Handbook*). PBE investigations are also distinct from studies carried out in naturalistic settings that require specific inclusion and exclusion criteria for research purposes. These involve, but are not restricted to, studies for which a clinical setting has been developed (as opposed to one already existing) to recruit a particular type of clinical population.

However, we would argue that PBE studies include the investigation of specific treatment protocols and/or treatment programs for a particular clinical population, as long as these have been created for clinical purposes rather than for the primary goal of conducting a limited set of studies. For example, this includes studies measuring the process and outcome of practitioners or clinics that specialized, as part of their clinical routine, in the implementation of a particular form of therapy and/or interventions for a particular clinical problem, as well as

studies investigating new interventions – interventions developed or adopted by stakeholders, tested in daily practice, and aimed, presumably, at improving routine clinical practice.

Finally, we would point out that randomization is typically not a part of PBE, unless the randomization focuses on a component that is not directly related to the delivery of the routine practice (e.g., studies involving feedback provided to clinicians and/or clients). These studies may have an impact on treatment as usual, but do not require the implementation of a researcher-imposed protocol that would prevent clinicians from conducting therapy as they regularly do. A list of characteristics that define and distinguish PBE studies from traditional efficacy studies is presented in Table 6.1.

As was the case in the previous edition, this chapter does not stand as a comprehensive review. Rather, it provides

TABLE 6.1   Characteristics of Practice-Based Evidence

	Efficacy studies	PBE studies
Setting	Controlled	Uncontrolled
Philosophical approach	Conducted externally to the clinical setting and typically initiated by researchers	Conducted in clinical setting and at times initiated by or in collaboration with clinicians
Primary focus of investigation	Interventions derived from theory and/or research program	Services delivered in actual practice
Sampling	Selective recruitment	Naturalistic
Inclusion criteria	Study-guided to control for confounds to build internal validity	Routine clinical practice to build external validity
Exclusion criteria	Present	Absent (beyond clinical practice)
Treatment contents	Specific, manualized	Adherence to usual practice
Aim of treatment protocols	Research integrity, include therapist training	Clinical consistency, rely on existing expertise and professional development
Randomization	Focused on treatment conditions	Not used or not related to routine treatment delivery
Ethics	Randomization to conditions of controls requires informed consent	Often managed through quality assurance and de-identification of data

Note. PBE = Practice-based evidence

illustrative examples of PBE studies that have been conducted in a diversity of clinical settings. Most of the investigations presented in the 2013 edition focused on the impact of psychological therapies. By contrast, in addition to covering outcome studies, this chapter provides a more extensive coverage of PBE studies by giving greater emphasis to investigations related to the process of change, participant characteristics, and contextual variables. It also briefly addresses some additional initiatives that are aimed at fostering the link between research and practice.

Despite not being comprehensive, we hope that the chapter will show that as a paradigm aimed at re-privileging the role of the practitioner as a central focus and participant in research activity (Barkham et al., 2010), PBE can yield results at two broad levels: first, at the level of the individual practitioner whether working alone in private practice or within a community of practitioners in which the aim is to use data to *improve their practice*; and second, at a collective level in which the aim is to pool data such that it can contribute to and *enhance the scientific base* of psychological therapies. With these two central aims, practice-based evidence delivers anew to the scientist-practitioner agenda.

We hasten to say that we do not view the strategies of accumulation and dissemination of empirical knowledge described in this chapter (see also Chapter 4) as being superior to those typically associated with the evidence-based practice movement. Rather, we would argue for adopting a position of equipoise between these two complementary paradigms. Although traditional RCTs are often viewed as the gold standard within a hierarchy of evidence, this position has been challenged: "The notion that evidence can be reliably placed in hierarchies is illusory. Hierarchies place RCTs on an undeserved pedestal, for ... although the technique has advantages it also has significant disadvantages" (Rawlins, 2008).[2] Also, in relation to the potential of practice-based evidence, Kazdin (2008) has written that "[W]e are letting the knowledge from practice drip through the holes of a colander." The *colander effect* is a salutary reminder of the richness of data that are potentially collectable but invariably lost every day from routine practice. A position of equipoise would advocate that neither paradigm alone—evidence-based practice or POR/PBE research—is able to yield a robust knowledge base for the psychological therapies. Furthermore, it is important to recognize that the methods typically associated with these approaches are not mutually exclusive. As we describe later, for example, RCTs have been designed and implemented within the context of PRNs. Hence, rather than viewing these two approaches as dichotomous, a robust knowledge base must be considered as a chiasmus that delivers *evidence-based practice and practice-based evidence* (Barkham & Margison, 2007).

OUTCOMES

This section provides illustrative examples of the yield of PBE in terms of the effect of psychological therapies. We first focus on symptomatic/functioning outcomes, addressing three successive levels of routine clinical practice: the level of practitioners, then at the level of single clinics or centers, and finally, multiple clinics. Then we address two other types of impact: dropout and attendance.

Practitioner Level: Therapist Effects

As described in the 2013 chapter, the investigation of therapist effects has served as one way to correct an imbalance created by the predominant attention given to treatment effects in psychotherapy research. In that chapter, the description of several studies conducted in naturalistic settings led to conclusions that (i) differences between therapists account for 5–8% of the outcome variance, and that (ii) some therapists distinguish themselves from the majority of practitioners by being particularly effective in improving client symptoms. A large number of additional studies have since been conducted in clinical routine practice on therapist effects using multilevel modeling to account for the nesting nature of therapy data. This chapter presents examples of such studies for different client populations, and for diverse targets of change or dependent variables. A more comprehensive review of therapist effects is presented in Chapter 9, including the results of meta-analyses of the magnitude of the therapist effects in both controlled and naturalistic settings and a review of studies examining variables that can account for such effects – with many of these studies having been conducted in naturalistic settings.

Therapist Effects with Particular Client Populations

Since 2013, three studies have investigated differential levels of practitioners' effectiveness in psychological treatments provided to *clients with mild-to-moderate level of symptoms* (depression or anxiety) and problem complexity (Ali, et al., 2014; Firth et al., 2015; Green et al., 2014). The treatments in all three studies were provided by psychological well-being practitioners (PWPs) of various levels of clinical training. Low-intensity interventions (e.g., psychoeducation, computerized guided CBT interventions) were prescribed to clients in routine clinical practice as part of the English Improving Access to Psychological Therapies (IAPT) program. With a sample of 1,376 clients treated in a primary care mental health service by 38 therapists, the first study found small effect sizes varying from 0% to 3% (Ali et al., 2014). The second study examined therapist effects among 21 clinicians working with 1,122 patients across six sites (Green et al., 2014) and found that therapist effects accounted for 9%–11% of outcome variance. They also found that the more effective PWPs exhibited greater self-rated resilience (ability to cope with challenges, adversity, or stressors), organizational abilities, knowledge, and confidence. With the goal of addressing methodological limitations of these first two studies (e.g., possible confounds of unmodeled center effects), as well as to examine potential moderators of therapist effects, the third study investigated the effectiveness and efficiency of 56 practitioners treating 6,111 patients within one clinical setting (Firth et al., 2015). Therapist effects accounted for approximately 7% of patient outcome variance, which was moderated by higher initial symptom

---

[2] Sir Michael Rawlins was the first chairman of the United Kingdom's National Institute for Health and Care Excellence (NICE).

severity, treatment duration, and noncompletion of treatment. There was a twofold difference between clinically effective and less effective PWPs.

Also, as part of routine clinical practice, several recent papers have examined therapist effects with *racial/ethnic minority* (REM) clients. Larrison and Schoppelrey (2011) investigated such effects in two community mental health centers in the United States. Based on a sample of 14 therapists and 98 clients they found that therapist effects explained 28.7% of the outcome diversity between White and REM clients. Therapist effects were also observed in a larger study involving 62 therapists and 551 clients recruited in 13 community mental health centers (Larrison et al., 2011). Like in the Larrison and Schoppelrey's (2011) study, client race/ethnicity did not directly predict outcome. However, the relationship between client race and outcome was moderated by therapist differential effectiveness, "indicating that outcome differences did exist between white and black patients and that those differences were linked to clinicians" (pp. 528–529). While the authors assessed several factors that could contribute to differential outcomes (including therapist gender, race/ethnicity, education, burn out), only one was significant – namely, that higher levels of positive experiences and relationships with individuals different to their own race and ethnicity decreased outcome variability.

Research addressing this issue has also been carried out in university clinic settings where two studies also revealed that REM and non-REM clients had similar outcomes but that therapists differed in their effectiveness with these clients. The first took place in a single university training clinic in the US and involved 228 clients and 36 therapists (Hayes et al., 2015). Therapist effects explained 8.7% of the outcome variance, and 19.1% of these effects were explained by client race/ethnicity – indicating that some therapists were more effective with REM clients than others. Aiming to address several problems of previous research (e.g., relatively small number of therapists, relatively few clients per therapist, and frequently implemented in only one site), the second study was conducted as part of the Center for Collegiate Mental Health (CCMH) PRN – an infrastructure regrouping university counseling centers mostly situated in the US. This second study comprised 3,825 clients and 251 therapists across 45 university counseling centers (Hayes et al., 2016). Although therapist effects explained less of the outcome variance (3.9%) than in the first study, differences in therapist effectiveness were found and part of this difference was also explained by client race/ethnicity. Both studies found that some therapists are more effective with REM than with White clients, while others are more effective with White than with REM clients. Hayes et al. (2016) also investigated whether demographic and professional factors could predict therapist outcome differences (i.e., gender, race/ethnicity, age, highest degree, professional discipline, years of experience, staff position, and theoretical orientation), but none of them were significant.

Going a step further, one study examined therapist effects on the intersectionality of client race/ethnicity and gender (Kivlighan et al., 2019). Conducted at one of CCMH counseling centers, this study included 16 therapists and 415 clients. Based on session-by-session changes of general distress, results indicate that client racial/ethnic identity, gender, and their interaction did not differ in terms of change growth during treatment. As in previous studies, therapist effects were found for client REM status. In addition, such effects were observed with respect to client REM and gender intersectionality. As noted by the authors, "this finding suggests that therapists' effectiveness significantly differed between White Men, White Women, Women of Color, and Men of Color" (p. 125). Some therapists do appear to be more effective than others when working with REM clients, but such effectiveness may well be moderated by client gender.

Therapists also appear to have an impact on other types of treatment diversity between White and REM clients. One of them is client unilateral termination, which was investigated in a single university counseling center in the US by Owen et al. (2012). Based on a sample of 44 therapists and 332 clients, they found that the therapist variable explained a significant part (7.3%) of unilateral termination in the client sample as a whole. As predicted, REM clients reported higher rates of unilateral termination than White clients. Also, as predicted, this discrepancy varied significantly between therapists. As noted by the authors, "some therapists were more likely to have their REM clients report unilateral termination as compared with their White clients (and vice versa)" (p. 318). Interestingly, these therapist effects were found even when controlling for the quality of alliance, number of sessions, client's level of well-being, and ratio of White and REM clients in therapists' caseload. In another study conducted at a US university counseling center, Owen et al. (2017) replicated their previous finding showing that therapists vary in their rates of unilateral termination for REM and White clients. Based on a sample of 23 therapists and 177 clients, they further demonstrated that these therapist effects were in part due to therapist levels of racial/ethnic comfort – their ease when engaged in sessions with clients of diverse backgrounds.

Kivlighan et al. (2019) investigated client nonattendance at therapy sessions as yet another type of impact that therapists may have on the treatment of REM clients. A significant part of clients' nonattendance (14%) was explained by therapists' variability, replicating a finding of a study described below (Xiao, Hayes et al., 2017). Within the context of one university counseling center in the US (with a sample of 21 therapists and 616 clients), the study also found a therapist effect in varying rates of nonattendance between REM and White clients. Whereas REM clients of some therapists had higher levels of nonattendance than their White clients, the pattern was reversed for other therapists – yet for other therapists, there was no racial/ethnicity disparity in nonattendance rates.

Therapist Effects with Different Targets of Change or Types of Treatment Impact

Most of the studies on therapist effects have attempted to explain outcome variance using indices of general distress, which are typically assessed after many sessions or at the end of treatment. A number of investigations conducted since the 2013 review have examined the impact of individual practitioners on other variables, such as multiple outcome domains

(Kraus et al., 2016) and early change (Erekson et al., 2018). Here we focus on two other types of treatment impact: dropout and session attendance.

Three recent studies have examined the effect of therapist on *dropout*. In a German university outpatient clinic, and with a sample of 707 clients and 66 therapists, Zimmerman et al. (2017) found that therapists explained 5.7% of the variance in premature termination. With larger samples (10,521 clients and 85 therapists) drawn from 14 counseling and clinical service sites in the UK, Saxon et al. (2017) estimated that therapists accounted for 12.6% of the variance in client dropout. Also based on a large sample of clients (10,147) but with a substantially larger number of therapists (481), Xiao, Castonguay et al. (2017) found that therapist effects accounted for 9.5% of the observed variance for premature termination across US university counseling centers as part of the CCMH PRN infrastructure. Xiao and colleagues also assessed a number of therapist demographic variables (age, gender, professional background, level of experience, and theoretical orientation) that might explain therapist differences in dropout rates, but none of them were significant. As is the case for therapist effects on outcome (Wampold et al., 2017), such variables do not appear to be a proxy for therapist characteristics and behaviors that have an impact on the process of fostering or interfering with clients' engagement in and benefit from therapy.

Saxon et al. (2017) also investigated the impact of therapist effects on client *deterioration*. With a subset of clients used for their analyses on dropout (6,405 out of 10,521), they found therapists to explain 10.1% of the variance in client deterioration. Interestingly, therapist rate of dropout and deterioration were not significantly related.

Another study conducted within the CCMH PRN focused on *nonattendance* at therapy sessions (Xiao, Hayes et al., 2017). Based on samples of 5,253 clients and 83 therapists across 22 counseling centers, the findings revealed that therapist differences explained 45.7% of the variance for nonattendance late in treatment (after session 3). As might be expected from such large effects, rates of nonattendance varied extensively, from 0% to 35.1%. Interestingly, 26 therapists had no nonattendance, with 16 of them from the same counseling center. This suggests the possibility that this specific center might have implemented a particular routine clinical practice policy that fostered client engagement in therapy.

As a whole, the studies described in this practitioner level section show that in day-to-day routine clinical practice, therapists do make a difference, not only in terms of how a diversity of clients benefit from psychosocial therapies but also with regard to various types of impact. However, it should be acknowledged that at this point in time, such a conclusion relies substantially on datasets from US college students, indicating the need for PBE studies to further investigate the effectiveness of practitioners in a wide range of clinical settings.

Single Clinic Level in Routine Settings

A focus on therapist effects, as we mentioned above, has helped the field to pay attention to factors contributing to effectiveness other than treatment protocols. Practice-based research has further broadened the evidence base of the psychological therapies by examining whether routine clinical setting(s) – single or multiple – are effective. While it is important to know what treatment approaches work and whether therapists make a difference to client improvement, it is also highly relevant (clinically, empirically, and socially) to determine whether the professional agency where clients are receiving treatment is effective. Accordingly, single clinics are addressed in this section and multiple clinics are discussed in the next section.

When reviewing single clinic studies in the 2013 edition, the focus was on benchmarking. That is, the studies, most of which were conducted in the UK, not only reported outcome findings but also compared them to the results obtained in other clinical settings or randomized clinical trials. In this chapter, we have adopted a broader perspective with the goal of reflecting a larger variety of efforts that have been made recently to document the beneficial impact of routine clinical practice. Examples presented are grouped into two categories: theoretically based services/clinics and clinics serving particular clinical problems. While some of the retained studies used benchmarking, as a whole the studies described here represent a broad set of investigations conducted across different countries.

Theoretically Based Clinics

The robust empirical support upon which CBT currently rests (see Chapter 14) is in large part due to the prominence it has been given, for over three decades, in RCTs. In contrast, while frequently used in routine clinical practice, non-CBT treatments are underrepresented in the empirical and policy agenda driven by researchers. By targeting both non-CBT and CBT approaches, PBE investigations are not only complementing traditional research, they are also expanding the scientific basis of psychological therapies in an externally valid way.

Several studies have focused on *psychodynamic-oriented therapy* in different clinical settings (e.g., DeFife et al., 2015; Falkenström, 2010; Jankowski et al., 2019; Roseborough et al., 2012; Ward et al., 2013). One of them was conducted in US community mental health clinic involving 16 clinicians and approximately 15 graduate professionals in training (Roseborough et al., 2012). Over a period of four years, 1,050 clients filled out an outcome measure at baseline and then every three months afterward (up to 15 assessment points). The findings show a significant decrease in symptoms (with an effect size of 0.34) at the end of the first year, with the sharpest improvement having taken place within the first three months. Significant improvement was not observed between the first and second year of treatment. This appears to be explained, at least in part, by the fact that a large number of clients who had improved at the end of year 1 also terminated treatment then. While most of the clients who stayed in treatments for a second year maintained their treatment gains, the percentage of clinical deterioration from baseline scores also increased after one year. For the authors, the lack of improvement after the first year could be viewed as an indication that the time might be ripe to consolidate the changes achieved or to consider terminating treatment sooner rather than later.

Falkenström (2010) assessed the outcome of a Swedish clinic delivering psychodynamic therapy to young adults. The author examined whether the inferior outcome, as compared to those in RCTs, of some naturalistic studies (e.g., Hansen et al., 2002; Hansen & Lambert, 2003) could have been due to different treatment lengths. When using an archival sample of clients (N = 416) who had at least two appointments at the clinic, the findings revealed a smaller number of sessions (mean = 7.5) and poorer outcome than those who participated in RCTs. In contrast, however, analyses conducted with a subsample (n = 101) of clients who completed assessment and began psychotherapy showed an average of 23 sessions with outcomes within the range of RCTs.

Despite its robust empirical basis, PBE researchers have not ignored the importance of measuring the effectiveness of CBT in routine clinical practice. For example, the outcome of CBT for depressive disorders in a German outpatient university training clinic has been compared with those from RCTs (Lutz et al., 2016). Specifically, the investigators matched 574 CBT clients (treated by 94 therapists) against comparable participants in the National Institute of Mental Health Treatment of Depression Collaborative Research Program (TDCRP). The results showed that when the clients in the naturalist setting were matched on inclusion/exclusion criteria of the RCT, as well as on a number of pretreatment variables potentially predictive of outcome using the nearest neighbor (NN) or caliper matching procedure, the outcomes of the two samples were comparable in terms of effect sizes (caliper matching: d = 1.44, 95% CI [1.02, 1.87]; NN matching: d = 1.72, 95% CI [1.31, 2.17] for the naturalistic sample, and d = 1.85, 95% CI [1.39, 2.40] for the RCT sample). In addition, there were no differences in recovery rates. The duration of treatment in routine care, however, was at least twice as long (i.e., 35 vs. 16 sessions).

One of the low-intensity treatments offered in the UK National Health System is a psychoeducational/self-help group CBT for anxiety disorders called *self-control*. The acceptability (via attendance rates) and effectiveness of this treatment was investigated in a sample of 2,814 clients attending a citywide IAPT service (Burns et al., 2016). The study involved 38 groups (with a mean size of 74 clients), each of them meeting for six 2-hour sessions that were facilitated by two PWPs. A total of 1,062 clients started treatment with a score above the clinical cutoff on at least one of the outcome measures, and were identified as clinical cases. The authors concluded that the treatment was acceptable and effective, with 73.3% of all clients, and 75.4% of clinical cases having attended at least three sessions, and 37% of the clinical cases recovered without receiving any other type of IAPT interventions. The findings also showed the odds of recovery increased with more sessions attended. Patients with higher pretreatment anxiety or depression showed the greatest amount of symptom change, but patients with comorbidity improved less than those with either anxiety or depression alone.

Specialized Clinics

Not surprisingly, clinics in many regions of the world have specialized in the treatment of particular psychological problems. Again, with the goal of broadening the empirical foundations of psychological therapies beyond RCT findings, examples of such clinics that have engaged in an assessment of their effectiveness are presented here. It should be noted that some of these clinics have based the provision of their services on treatment manuals previously tested in RCTs. As noted in the introduction of this chapter, the use of such manuals is not an exclusion criterion for PBE studies, as long as they, like any other structured treatment protocol, are implemented as part of the routine clinical practice (rather than for the sake of a research project that is separate from day-to-day practice).

A number of studies have focused on *eating disorders* clinics. One of them took place in a UK National Health Service that provides CBT (in line with published evidence-based manuals) as its routine treatment (Turner et al., 2015). The study comprised a sample of 203 patients and 11 therapists. Significant improvements were observed in eating disorder psychopathology (*tau* = 1.19), anxiety (*tau* = 0.63), depression (*tau* = 0.74), and general functioning (*tau* = 0.77). In addition, eating attitudes improved in the early part of therapy. Another study assessed the outcome of a transdiagnostic program for eating disorders provided in a German university affiliated center (Beintner et al., 2020). Part of regular care, the program involved three phases: (1) individual sessions devoted to assessment and treatment goals; (2) eight weeks of day treatment (involving group sessions conducted by a team of interdisciplinary practitioners with CBT, nutritional, and art therapy expertise, as well as individual therapy); and (3) follow-up outpatient individual therapy (CBT based). For this study, 148 consecutive clients who participated in the combined day treatment and follow-up individual sessions were included. The findings showed that clients significantly improved at the end of the day treatment in terms of their symptoms, as well as maladaptive cognitions and attitudes related to eating disorders. A significant increase in body mass index (BMI) was also reported for underweight clients at the end of the day treatment. Clients' improvements were maintained, on average, at 6, 12, and 26 months after the end of day treatment.

One research program has investigated the effectiveness of a treatment protocol for eating disorders delivered in a day hospital (DH) in Canada, as well as the effect of manipulating one specific aspect of this protocol (i.e., its intensity; Olmsted et al., 2013). Using a sequential cohort ABA design, data was collected from 1985–2009 to compare the same predominantly CBT interventions, provided either as a five-day weekly or four-day weekly treatment. A total of 801 patients were treated in three successive cohorts: five-day weekly, four-day weekly, and five-day weekly treatment (i.e., ABA order). While no differences between the two treatment intensities were observed with regard to BMI, the five-day weekly treatment was significantly more effective in terms of abstinence of bingeing and vomiting, body dissatisfaction, and depression. These results led the authors to conclude: "On balance, the increase benefits associated with the five-day DH outweigh the additional costs" (p. 285).

As part of a mental health stepped care program in Canada, one study assessed the effectiveness of treatments for borderline *personality disorder* (BPD) in two distinct specialized outpatient clinics (Laporte et al., 2018). Over a 15-year period, data were collected on 479 clients referred to a clinic providing short-term treatment (12 weeks), and 145 clients referred for longer treatment (6–24 months) in an extensive care clinic. Referrals were based on pretreatment level of symptoms chronicity and functioning, and both clinics offered a structured treatment integrating interventions from ESTs for BPD (e.g., dialectic behavior therapy, mentalization-based therapy). Pre- to posttreatment scores showed significant improvement in both clinics on a range of dependent variables, including measures of impulsivity, self-esteem, depression, and emotion dysregulation. Significant change in substance abuse, however, was achieved only in the extensive care clinic. Interestingly, clients in the extensive care clinic who completed the treatment in 18 or 24 months did not show higher symptomatic improvement than those who completed treatment in 6 or 12 months. As concluded by the authors, this study provides promising support for the effectiveness of short-term treatment provided as a first-step intervention in routine clinical practice for many BPD clients.

Preliminary effectiveness data was also reported for a clinic specializing in treating clients with *psychotic symptoms* (Jolley et al., 2015). The study was conducted over a period of 14 months at an IAPT service in the UK, where a CBT protocol for psychosis (designed for 16 to 30 sessions) is the routine treatment. Pre- to posttreatment findings of treatment completers revealed improvement in terms of affective ($d = .6$) and psychotic ($d = 1.0$) symptoms.

It should be noted that the evaluation of the effectiveness of single-level clinics has not been limited to those that are primarily defined by the implementation of a particular theoretical orientation or by the services provided to specific clinical populations. De la Parra and colleagues (2018), for example, described the development and evaluation of a model of care to guide the services provided at an adult psychotherapy unit attached to a University Medical Center in Chile. In another example, one clinician published the outcome data of 1,599 cases that they treated in their clinical practice over 45 years (Clement, 2013). And two studies conducted in separate university counseling centers have respectively compared the effectiveness of individual therapy, group therapy, and conjoint individual and group therapy (Burlingame et al., 2016), and examined the impact of psychological therapies on academic distress – an outcome focus that is particularly relevant to the clients served in this clinical setting (Lockard et al., 2019)

Multiple Clinics: Effectiveness of Psychological Therapies in Routine Settings

To demonstrate the impact of psychological therapies as practiced in clinical routine, it is important to show that their effectiveness extends beyond a single clinic or center. Relying on a variety of studies, from a meta-analysis to preliminary investigations in practice research networks, the 2013 edition of this chapter presented evidence that psychological therapies work across settings, that the outcome of different types of therapy are relatively equivalent, and that clients can benefit equally from treatments that differ in length. Examples of studies, again from different countries, that have addressed these three issues since the last chapter are described here. It should also be noted that the chapter in the previous edition also reviewed effectiveness studies, which investigate whether treatments found to be empirically supported in controlled environments are effective in natural settings. As mentioned above, unless the investigated treatments are implemented as part of routine clinical practice, these studies are not covered here. However, some of these studies are reviewed in Chapter 5 of this *Handbook*.

Practice-Based Studies of Treatment Outcomes in Multiple Settings

The investigation of multiple settings has been conducted in *different types of clinical services*. A recent study in Kenya assessed the effectiveness of psychological therapies delivered in two public hospitals (Kumar et al., 2018). The rationale of the study adheres to a key axiom of practice-based research, which is to assess the services that are actually provided in a particular region of the world before assuming that psychological therapies developed in another region can be transported and implemented beyond their original locale. Across the two hospitals, 345 clients who received psychotherapy or counseling by either a mental health professional (psychiatrist, clinical psychologist, psychiatric social worker, or mental health nurse) or a postgraduate intern (in mental health or nursing fields) were recruited. As part of routine clinical practice, outcome assessments were collected before each session to assess clients' improvement (along with a measure of alliance, which was collected after each session). The findings showed an improvement in general mental health, with an average reduction in CORE-OM score at each session as therapy progressed of 1.68 (95% CI [2.07, 1.30]).

Another study assessed the outcome of psychological therapies provided in primary care in two regions of Sweden (Holmqvist et al., 2014). Pre–post changes for 733 clients treated by 70 mental health professionals (social workers, psychologists, psychiatric nurses, occupational therapists) suggested that most of them benefitted from relatively short treatment (median number of sessions was 6) provided as part of routine care. While 43% showed remittance and 34% recovered, only 0.6% deteriorated.

McAleavey and colleagues (2019) examined the effectiveness of psychological therapies provided in university counseling centers across the United States. As part of the CCMH PRN infrastructure, the sample comprised 9,895 clients treated by 1,454 therapists in 108 university counseling centers. With the overall sample of clients, the results showed pre- to posttreatment on a diversity of symptoms measured in routine clinical practice with the percentage of reliable improvement ranging from 8.0% (for alcohol use) to 28.8% (for depression). In addition, the study assessed outcome change in terms of benchmarking comparisons with RCT findings and end-state normative comparisons. For clinically distressed clients, the pre–post effect sizes were equivalent to those reported in RCTs, ranging from 0.93 for eating to 1.90 for depression. However, these clients had a lower probability of completing treatment within the range of normative functioning than clients with lower initial symptoms. As pointed out by the authors, despite the effectiveness of psychological therapies provided in counseling centers, additional treatment may be required for those with higher levels of distress.

In a different type of clinical setting, and with an even larger sample, another study reported the reliable recovery rates of patients treated as part of the day-to-day practice of 24 services in the UK IAPT program (Gyani et al., 2013). Based on routine outcome measures of depression and anxiety, 19,395 clients were identified as clinical cases at pretreatment. The majority of these clients received either high-intensity therapies (e.g., CBT, counseling) or low-intensity therapies (self-help interventions, guided or not guided) in line with the UK National Institute of Health and Care Excellence (NICE) treatment guidelines. By posttreatment, 63.7% were reliably improved, 40.3% were reliably recovered, and 6.6% were found to have reliably deteriorated. Interestingly, the rate of reliable recovery was lower for clients who received other treatments than the high- or low-intensity interventions identified in the NICE guidelines. Clients who received high-intensity interventions showed higher rates of reliable recovery than those who did not.

PBE studies involving multiple settings have not only been conducted in different types of clinical environments, they have also focused on *diverse types of treatments*. As a low-intensity treatment component of the stepped-care model implemented in the English IAPT program, the effectiveness of CBT psychoeducational group was assessed in five different health services (Delgadillo, Kellett et al., 2016). In this study, 4,451 clients received up to six didactic lectures on stress control, as part of 163 groups (varying from 4 to 111 members). The results confirmed the effectiveness of the treatment reported previously in the PBE studies involving single sites (Burns et al., 2016). The findings also revealed that in four of five sites, the outcomes were equivalent to a benchmarked effect size of guided self-help therapy (another low-level intervention routinely assigned to less distress and/or less complex cases in the IAPT model); the fifth site showed a significantly smaller effect size to the other sites and the same benchmark. Interestingly, group effects explained 3.6% of outcome variance. Other studies have investigated the effectiveness of mindfulness-based cognitive therapy provided as routine care in five mental health services in the UK (Tickell et al., 2020), and the impact of an integrative treatment for bereavement provided in diverse locations of Scotland by a community-based, nonprofit organization (Newsom et al., 2017).

Practice-Based Studies of Comparative Treatment Outcomes

The effectiveness of different treatment approaches was compared in two studies conducted in Sweden. The first one compared the outcome of three approaches: cognitive–behavioral, psychodynamic, or integrative/eclectic therapy, as identified by therapists at the end of treatment (Werbart et al., 2013). Based on data collected over a three-year period, the study involved 1,498 patients treated at 13 outpatient psychiatric care services. Analysis conducted on 180 patients (treated by 75 therapists) with pre- and posttreatment data showed no significant difference between treatments on outcome measures. The within-group effect sizes ranged from $d = 0.47$ for quality of life for the patients receiving CBT to $d = 1.54$ for self-rated health for patients receiving integrative treatment, which the authors note were comparable to those reported in RCTs and naturalistic studies. Interestingly, there was no evidence of therapist effects and, consistent with the Good-Enough Level model, duration of therapy was not associated with different outcomes.

Comparisons between treatment approaches were also reported in the study conducted in Swedish primary care centers described above (Holmqvist et al., 2014). While many clients received treatments that combined different approaches, 65% received a single type of therapy (as reported by therapists at the end of therapy). Analyses combining treatment of only cognitive, behavioral and/or CBT approaches (called directive therapy) at one end, and psychodynamic and/or relational approaches (called reflective therapy) at the other end, did not reveal significant differences in terms of outcome. Both directive and reflective therapies, however, were superior to supportive therapy. It should be mentioned that therapists who reported using supportive therapy also rated clients as less motivated, as well as lower in terms of reflective and alliance ability. As the authors suggested, since therapists decided which treatment was implemented for each of their clients, it may be that supportive therapy was used with clients who were perceived as being less likely to benefit from psychotherapy.

In a study conducted in UK health system, Pybis and colleagues (2017) evaluated the effectiveness of CBT and counseling based on a sample of 33,243 patients treated in 103 IAPT sites. The two treatments showed similar pre–post effect sizes; CBT: $d = .94$ (95% CI [0.92, 0.95]); counseling: $d = 0.95$ (95% CI [0.92, 0.98]). The rates of reliable and clinically significant improvement were also similar: 46.6% of patients for CBT and 44.3% for counseling. Multilevel modeling analyses also indicated that treatment type was not a significant predictor of outcome variance. These findings have meaningful implications for the health system within which they were obtained. As noted by the authors, "Our findings strongly suggest that, despite the very different recommendations for CBT and counseling in the NICE Guidelines for Depression in Adults, it would appear that the two therapies have a very similar impact in routine practice for the treatment of depression." (p.10). Interestingly, interaction effects were found with respect to treatment type and attended sessions. While CBT showed significantly higher recovery rates than counseling when clients received 18 or 20 sessions, the reverse was found at two sessions. These results also carried important implications:

> Given that the majority of patients in IAPT are being treated in fewer than ten sessions, this finding is of some significance and warrants further investigation as it could be argued that counseling is more efficient than CBT in

treating depression. Such a finding could have positive cost implications for the NHS (p. 11).

Other Impacts of Psychological Therapies

In addition to symptom change, PBE studies have paid attention to a number of impact indices, positive and negative, that are meaningful to clinicians and other stakeholders of mental health services. Although not systematically addressed in the 2013 chapter, examples of studies examining dropout and attendance are presented here.

The rate of dropout or premature termination in routine clinical practice has varied quite substantially. A previously described study found a rate of 15.9% drop in a large PRN of university counseling centers (Xiao, Castonguay et al., 2017). A larger rate of 33.8% was reported in a study, also described above, conducted in several UK counseling and clinical services (Saxon et al., 2017). An even larger rate, above 60%, was observed in a study combining data from three university-based (associated with departments of psychology) training clinics, involving 524 clients and 75 therapists in training (Al-Jabari et al., 2019). Mixed results were also found in terms of predictors of dropout with regard to a wide range of variables across these three studies and another study previously mentioned (Zimmermann et al., 2017). These include clients' pretreatment severity, age, gender, ethnicity, and at risk of harming self or others. The different results between studies, both in terms of rates and predictors of dropout are likely to be explained by different clinical settings and populations, assessment measures, but also by different operationalizations of dropout adopted by researchers – for example, therapist judgment, nonattendance to last session, and failure to reach a specific level of symptom change (Xiao, Castonguay et al., 2017).

With regard to attendance, a previously described multiple-site study of CBT group psychoeducation treatment (involving up to six didactic lectures) found it to be associated with therapeutic change, with participants attending four to six sessions reporting the highest reduction in anxiety symptoms (Delgadillo, Kellett et al., 2016). In a study of student counseling (also described above), Xiao, Hayes et al. (2017) discriminated between two types of nonattendance – no-show appointments and cancellations – and two time points during therapy – before and after the third session. Controlling for pretreatment symptoms and length of therapy, no-shows (but not cancellation) were negatively and significantly associated with both the magnitude and the rate of symptom change as measured by the Counseling Center Assessment of Psychological Symptoms (CCAPS, Locke et al., 2011, 2012). Moreover, the negative impact, on both measures of symptom change, was substantially worse for no-shows before as compared to after the third session. It is worth noting that these findings were obtained while accounting for therapist effects.

Summary

With the goal of redressing the balance with RCTs and their primary focus on treatment effects, the 2013 edition demonstrated the contribution to outcome variance explained by therapist, as well as the effectiveness of psychological therapies

provided in routine clinical practice, within both single clinic and multiple clinics. Studies reported here, as well as in Chapter 9 of this *Handbook*, have solidified the robustness of the therapist effect within routine clinical practice, including with diverse clinical populations, and as assessed by different types of dependent variables. Our current review has also provided further evidence that clients are benefiting from psychological therapies, as it is practiced daily in different countries (e.g., Canada, Chile, Germany, Kenya, Scotland, Sweden, UK, USA), in diverse settings (e.g., hospital, out-patient clinic, university counseling center, private practice), for a variety of clinical problems (e.g., psychotic, borderline personality and eating disorders), and via multiple approaches (e.g., psychodynamic, CBT, integrative). Over the last decade, PBE investigations have also continued to accumulate increasing evidence supporting the broad equivalence of major therapeutic approaches. It should further be noted that PBE studies have been conducted on the impact of treatment length or dosage of therapy, but this question is addressed in Chapter 5 of this *Handbook*.

PROCESS

A relatively few practiced-based process studies were included in the 2013 chapter, most of them investigating empirically supported interventions within the context of PRNs. By contrast, this chapter pays more attention to different aspects of the process of change, including the alliance, therapist interventions, as well as client and therapist experiences.

Alliance

Many studies conducted in routine clinical practice have focused on the therapeutic alliance. In our review, we present illustrative examples of such studies that examine the alliance construct from new perspectives and/or via the application of more advanced statistical analyses. The studies are clustered within four themes: within-client analyses, client and therapist convergence, actor–partner analyses, and patterns of alliance.

Within-Client Analyses

A number of recent studies conducted in routine clinical practice have attempted to address a criticism that alliance is a consequence, rather than a cause, of symptom change (Falkenström et al., 2013, 2019; Fisher et al., 2016; Rubel et al., 2017; Zilcha-Mano & Errazuriz, 2015). As noted by Falkenström et al. (2013), alliance studies have typically relied on between-client statistics to assess how the variation between clients in terms of alliance rating predicts, on average, treatment outcome at the end of therapy. For these authors, such analyses fail to account for the fact that a positive correlation between alliance and outcome could be influenced by several client and therapist characteristics. They also point out that there is no guarantee that an overall positive correlation applies to a particular client. While not ruling out all potential confounds of causality (see Chapter 8 of this *Handbook*), within-client analyses can attenuate these problems by assessing how alliance for a client predicts the outcome (of the same client) measured at a later point, and vice versa. The authors used such within-client analyses by relying on repeated measures of the alliance (after each session) and symptoms (before each session). The sample comprised 646 outpatients treated by 83 therapists (mostly social workers) in routine primary care psychotherapy across two geographic regions of Sweden. The findings provided support for reciprocal causation, with alliance predicting subsequent symptom change and symptom change predicting subsequent alliance. Interestingly, the alliance continued to predict subsequent symptom change even after controlling for the effect that the previous symptom change had on the alliance. In addition, there were individual differences, with stronger alliance–symptom relationships being evident among patients with personality problems.

Within the context of a study in Kenya previously discussed in the outcome section (Kumar et al., 2018), process analyses were conducted with the first goal of examining the generalization of findings related to the working alliance outside of Western higher-income countries (Falkenström et al., 2019). A second goal was to conduct within-client analyses based on improved statistical methods. Outpatients (N = 345) receiving routine care at the two public psychiatric hospitals completed measures of outcome and alliance at each session. Similar to findings in Western samples, session changes in the working alliance predicted subsequent changes in distress, which in turn affected the working alliance, thereby pointing to a degree of cross-cultural stability of session-by-session reciprocal effects.

Other studies have used within-client analyses to address complex questions about alliance and its relationship with different factors in psychological therapies. As in Falkenström et al. (2013), these studies used repeated assessments of both process and outcome on a session-by-session basis. Conducted within the day-to-day routine of a university training clinic in Israel, one investigation primarily focused on the impact of emotional experience in psychodynamic therapy (Fisher et al., 2016). With a sample of 101 clients and 62 therapists, the findings showed, as predicted, that increased client emotional experience was related to increased improvement, and vice versa. Also, as predicted, increase in the therapeutic bond was not only associated with increased emotional experience but also was indirectly related to symptom improvement via deeper emotional deepening. As noted by the authors, the latter result points to the contextual role of the alliance as "a fertile ground promoting other change processes, such as a deeper emotional experience" (p. 113). Inconsistent with the predictions of the authors, however, changes in emotional experience were not predictive of bond change.

Both therapeutic relationship and emotional experience were investigated in another recent study, but this time as part of the routine clinical practice of a cognitive behavioral training clinic in Germany and along with the assessment of clients' acquisition of coping skills (i.e., alternative ways of seeing self and the world, as well as adaptive ways of functioning; Rubel et al., 2017). Based on a large sample comprising 1,550 clients and 150 therapists, the authors conducted both within- and between-client analyses and did so for each process variable

separately and in combination. The findings of within- and between-client analyses were largely consistent: In both cases, higher levels of alliance and coping skills separately predicted outcome, but when all three process variables were combined, only the acquisition of coping skills was positively and significantly associated with outcome.

However, while emotional involvement predicted change at the within-level analysis (indicating that when clients are more affectively engaged in one session compared to previous ones, they will subsequently experience less symptoms), increases in emotional involvement negatively predicted improvement at between-client analyses (indicating that clients who are more emotionally involved during the course of therapy will, on average, report more severe symptoms). Of note, results of between-level analyses also revealed a significant positive interaction between coping skills and emotional experience. That is, clients who experienced higher levels of coping skills showed further improvement when they also experienced higher levels of emotional involvement, suggesting that the greater level of session-by-session changes are to be expected for clients with higher levels of both coping skills and emotional engagement. Importantly, at the within-client level of analyses, the relationship between coping skills and outcome was moderated by the alliance, indicating that the learning of new cognitions and behaviors was more highly related to outcome when the alliance was stronger. As noted by the authors, the findings suggest that, at least in their clinical setting, while the alliance may not lead to improvement on its own in CBT, it does provide helpful conditions for the beneficial implementation of the interventions emphasized in this approach – or, as inferred by Fisher et al. (2016) above, it provides fertile ground for mutative action of other processes of change.

Yet another recent practice-oriented study investigated whether positive changes in the alliance predicted improvement of symptoms, using both within and between-level analyses while also controlling for previous improvement (Zilcha-Mano & Errazuriz, 2015). The authors also explored client, therapist, and treatment variables that might moderate the relationship between alliance and outcome. The study was part of an RCT conducted at an outpatient mental health care clinic in Chile involving 547 clients and 28 therapists. Without imposing significant changes to clinical practice, the RCT compared the impact of different conditions of clinical feedback provided to therapists through routine outcome monitoring. Although both within- and between-client analyses revealed a significant and mutual relationship between quality of alliance and improvement of outcome, the between-therapist analysis did not. Examining the duration of reciprocal effects, the authors found that while symptom fluctuation predicted alliance variation for one subsequent session, alliance changes predicted symptom fluctuations over two sessions. A number of significant moderator effects were also observed. Specifically, the authors found that the alliance was more predictive of symptom improvement for clients with higher levels of symptoms at pretreatment and who had more sessions. This was also the case when treatment was provided by integrative therapists in contrast with clinicians adhering to a particular orientation, and when therapists received feedback on the alliance as opposed to when they did not.

Client and Therapist Convergence

The therapeutic alliance is a construct that can be meaningfully measured by both client and therapist. Thus, by its nature, ratings of the therapeutic alliance can vary depending on the perspective on which they are based. Several recent studies conducted in naturalistic settings have used advanced statistical analyses (such as truth and bias model, and polynomial regression response surface analyses – see Rubel et al., 2018 for description) to investigate a number of questions related to this issue.

Atzil-Slonim et al. (2015) examined temporal convergence and directional discrepancy of client and therapist ratings of the therapeutic bond, as both factors fluctuate session by session. Whereas temporal convergence refers to how much ratings of the participants correlate, directional discrepancy reflects mean differences (and their directions) in the same ratings. The authors also investigated the moderating effects of symptom severity (measured at pretreatment and at every session) and a diagnostic of personality disorder (assessed at pretreatment) on the indexes of agreement/disagreement. Patients were 213 individuals treated by trainee therapists at a German University Outpatient Clinic with a cognitive behavioral focus. As predicted, the findings revealed a significant and positive temporal congruence, indicating that therapist ratings of the bond converge with, or accurately track, clients' ratings session by session. A significant directional discrepancy was also observed, which, as predicted, showed that therapist ratings were generally lower than patient ratings. Also predicted, temporal convergence was significantly and positively correlated with directional discrepancy, suggesting that therapists who have a more negative bias in rating the bond tend to track more accurately clients' views of the relationship. For the authors, this set of findings reflects a "better safe than sorry" attitude – an attitude that may allow therapists to be particularly attuned to alliance ruptures. While pretreatment severity and personality disorder did not emerge as significant moderators, session-by-session symptom severity did – whereupon higher level of symptoms experienced by clients was associated with a further decrease in both therapist ratings of the bond and congruence with their clients.

Studies examining whether congruence is linked with different types of outcome have yielded mixed results. Marmarosh and Kivlighan (2012) reported two such studies within a single paper. The first was conducted in two university counseling centers in the United States (involving 36 client-therapist dyads) and assessed whether alliance congruence was related to two measures of session impact: smoothness and depth (Stiles & Snow, 1984). The second study aggregated samples from a university-based mental health clinic and a university counseling center (with a combined sample of 63 client-therapist dyads) and explored whether alliance congruence predicted outcome (using the SCL-90-R). The findings of the two studies suggest that when therapist and client agree on the quality of the alliance at session three, a high rating of such an alliance

is a predictor of therapeutic progress, as measured in terms of smoothness (at the third session) and symptom improvement (at the of treatment). Across the two studies reported by Marmarosh and Kivlighan (2012), interesting results were also obtained when participants disagreed in their rating of the alliance. In the first study, clients scored the session as being smoother when they rated the alliance higher than their therapist, as compared to when their therapist rated the alliance higher than they did. In line with Atzil-Slonim et al. (2015), this points to the importance of therapists being aware of relationship problems experienced by clients that, unless adequately addressed, may have a negative impact on treatment. In the second study, the overall disagreement between client and therapist rating of the alliance was positively related to symptom improvement.

Another investigation examined whether client and therapist alliance congruence at the end of one session predicted symptoms a month later (Zilcha-Mano et al., 2017). Conducted within the routine clinical practice of a psychodynamic training center in the US, the study involved 127 dyads. Consistent with some of Marmarosh and Kivlighan's (2012) findings, when client and therapist agreed and the alliance ratings were high, the symptoms were lower than when therapist and client agreed and the alliance ratings were moderate. Interestingly, however, high agreement and moderate ratings were also associated with higher symptoms than high agreement and low ratings of the alliance – perhaps indicating that a mutual recognition of problems in the relationship might foster collaborative engagement to repair alliance ruptures, which may lead to later benefit. In contrast with findings from Marmarosh and Kivlighan (2012), however, disagreement between client and therapist ratings of the alliance was not related to symptom scores.

A recent study investigated the link between alliance congruence and outcome by combining several of the methodological features of the three studies above (Rubel et al., 2018). Like Atzil-Slonim et al. (2015), the authors assessed the alliance and symptoms at every session in the same training clinic but with a much larger sample (580 patients). They also used a new and sophisticated (within dyad) statistical analysis that both Marmarosh and Kivlighan (2012) and Zilcha-Mano et al. (2017) used to assess the relationship between alliance congruence and outcome. Furthermore, because discrepancies have been found between previous studies on this relationship, most of them using between-dyad analyses, they assessed it using both within- and between-dyad levels of analyses. Consistent with both Marmarosh and Kivlighan (2012) and Zilcha-Mano et al. (2017), the results showed that when therapist and client within the same dyad agreed and the bond was rated highly, the symptoms of the client decreased at the next session. The predictive value of agreement was also supported by the between-dyad analyses, which showed that on average the temporal convergence (or correlation) between clients and therapist ratings of the therapeutic bond was associated with symptom improvement at the end of treatment. Similar to findings from Atzil-Slonim et al. (2015) and Marmarosh and Kivlighan (2012), between-dyad analyses also provided support for the importance of the therapist being attentive to relationship problems – showing that moderately lower ratings of the bond by a therapist, compared to client ratings, was related to lower posttreatment symptoms.

Actor–Partner Analyses

A number of studies have investigated the client and therapist experience of the therapeutic relationship from an actor–partner interdependence model (Kenny & Cook, 1999), where the ratings of process measures from the client and the therapist perspective are linked to the rating of impact measures either by the same perspective (actor) or the other one (partner) (Kivlighan et al., 2016; Markin et al., 2014). These investigations have revealed a wide range of associations with outcome, as well as various patterns of interdependence and influence. For example, in a study conducted at two university clinics in the US (involving a total of 87 clients and 25 therapists), Markin et al. (2014) found that while clients' ratings of session quality were only predicted by their ratings of the real relationship, therapists' ratings of session quality were predicted by both their ratings and the client ratings of the real relationship. The findings were replicated in a study conducted in a department of psychology clinic (with 74 clients and 23 therapists), suggesting that therapists' assessment of a session is influenced by their view of the relationship as well as their understanding of clients' perceptions of the relationship (Kivlighan et al., 2016). Markin et al. (2014) also found that the therapist ratings of session impact were predicted by an interaction between ratings of the real relationship and session numbers. That is, both client and therapist ratings of the real relationship were significantly and positively related to the therapist rating of the session quality early in therapy but not later in therapy – suggesting that the focus of therapy might have shifted during the course of treatment, from the establishment of a good relationship to the decrease of symptoms. Interestingly, Kivlighan et al. (2016) found the opposite, with the client rating of the real relationship significantly and positively related to the therapist rating of session quality only in the middle and late part of therapy. As noted by Kivlighan et al. (2016), this discrepancy could be due to the fact that the two studies differed substantially in treatment length (mean of less than 5 sessions vs. more than 40). Clearly, more research is indicated to clarify these mixed findings.

Patterns of Alliance

While studies on alliance have typically used a single measurement point, a recent investigation has examined patterns of scores across treatment sessions. Based in a study conducted in Sweden primary care settings described previously (see Holmqvist et al., 2014), 605 clients treated by 79 therapists filled out alliance and outcome measures at every session. The authors investigated the prevalence and the linkage with clients' improvement as reflected in three specific patterns of alliance: no rupture identified during therapy, rupture(s) identified in the course of treatment but not repaired, and a course of treatment characterized by alliance rupture(s) and repair (Holmqvist, Larsson et al., 2018). The findings revealed that the first pattern (no rupture) was the most prevalent (74.5%),

and that the other two did not differ significantly from each other in terms of prevalence (10.7% and 14.7%, respectively). As predicted, the pattern of alliance rupture without repair was associated with worst outcomes. Also, as predicted, the pattern of alliance rupture and repair was associated with significantly higher improvement than the pattern of no rupture in longer treatment. These findings suggest that the repair of alliance breaches may not always have an immediate impact on client symptoms, but that when there is sufficient time for therapists and clients to work on their relationship problems, these breaches may provide corrective experiences, allowing clients to learn and benefit from resolving interpersonal difficulties. More studies are needed to investigate further how these and other patterns of alliance are related to treatment outcome.

Therapist Interventions

A wide diversity of PBE studies has investigated therapist interventions. We present illustrative examples of such studies, which we have grouped within single-skill and multiple interventions categories.

Single Skill

The complexity and therapeutic role of therapist empathic accuracy were investigated in a psychodynamic university training clinic in Israel (Atzil-Slonim et al., 2019). Clients (n = 93) filled out session-by-session measures of their symptoms, as well as their positive and negative emotions. At each session, therapists (n = 62) reported their own emotions (positive and negative) and their perception of their clients' emotions. As predicted, the results showed that while therapists correctly captured the fluctuations of clients' emotions, they tracked their negative emotions more accurately than positive emotions. Also, as predicted, therapists rated clients' negative emotions more strongly than their clients did, and rated clients' positive emotions less strongly than the client. Importantly, higher therapist accuracy of client positive emotions was associated with subsequent positive outcome. As noted by the authors, focusing on such positive emotions can be a springboard for interventions that could foster therapeutic improvement.

Multiple Interventions

Two studies investigated the use of evidence-based interventions in a PRN-based training clinic in the US. The first study examined whether the helpfulness of therapy sessions is related to complex interactions between these interventions, therapists' theoretical orientation, and their supervisors' orientation (McAleavey et al., 2014). The interventions (reported by therapists) and session helpfulness (rated by clients) were measured after each session. Based on 328 sessions (from 26 clients and 11 therapists), the results failed to confirm the authors' prediction that higher levels of helpfulness would be associated with the use of techniques that are consistent with therapists' theoretical orientation. Contrary to such a prediction, high levels of process-experiential therapy techniques were associated with less-helpful sessions when used by humanistic-oriented therapists. In addition, unexpected, high levels of psychodynamic therapy techniques were associated with less helpful sessions when therapists were supervised by psychodynamic supervisors. Adding complexity or nuance to the results, high levels of cognitive therapy techniques predicted session helpfulness, but only when the theoretical orientation of both the therapist and supervisor was cognitive therapy.

The second study, this time involving 401 sessions with 31 clients and 16 therapists, investigated whether broad types of theoretical techniques (exploratory vs. directive) are differentially related to clients' acquisition of insight (McAleavey & Castonguay, 2014). As in the previous study, unexpected and complex findings were obtained. While sessions with higher levels of exploratory or insight-oriented interventions were associated with less insight, higher levels of directive techniques were linked with more insight. Interaction effects, once again, added nuance to the findings. Therapists who reported using more directive interventions had clients reporting more insight, but only when these therapists did not report using high levels of exploratory interventions. In addition, directive interventions were linked with insight, but only when they were used in sessions with high levels of common factors or relationship-enhancing interventions.

Mindful of the complexity of the process of change, Kivlighan et al. (2019) relied on a sequential model of change to examine the degree to which symptom outcomes were affected by therapist techniques and the working alliance. Interestingly, the authors used the same measure of treatment interventions as in the two previous studies (Multitheoretical List of Therapeutic Interventions; McCarthy & Barber, 2009). However, they focused only on psychodynamic techniques and assessed them from an observer rater perspective (in contrast to a therapist self-report perspective). The study was conducted in a psychodynamic-oriented university training clinic in the US and involved 40 clients and 14 therapists, all of them having completed a measure of the alliance at each session. Therapists' use of psychodynamic techniques was assessed by independent judges on one session from the middle of treatment. As predicted by various components of their model, the results showed that the quality of the alliance was directly associated with subsequent improvement of outcome, and that higher levels of psychodynamic techniques correlated positively with subsequent alliance. In addition, higher levels of the same techniques were indirectly related to a subsequent decrease in symptoms via the mediating role of the alliance. For the authors, this suggests that therapists should pay less attention to how their interventions may have an impact on symptoms than to how they might affect the therapeutic relationship.

A programmatic series of studies related to therapist interventions has resulted from a partnership between researchers and clinicians called the Practice and Research: Advance and Collaboration (PRAC; Garland et al., 2006). Based on the active contribution of clinicians in the research design and implementation, as well as interpretation of findings, this POR program has focused on the treatment of children with disruptive behavior problems (DBP). One of the studies, involving 96 psychotherapists and 191 children/families, examined the extent to which elements of evidence-based practices (interventions common to ESTs for DBP) are present in routine clinical

practice (Garland et al., 2010). Data were collected for up to 16 months in six publicly funded outpatient clinics in the US. All treatment sessions conducted during this period of time were videotaped and 1215 of them (randomly selected from 3,241) were coded by independent judges on several clinical strategies (techniques or content focused) associated with one or more theorical approaches. Some of these strategies were identified as evidence-based interventions and some were not. The results showed that therapists used a large variety of strategies, leading the authors to argue that although relatively few of them (i.e., 25%) identified as eclectic, eclecticism prevailed in their actual practice. The results also show that while some strategies in line with evidence-based practice occur in a high percentage of the sessions, such as using positive reinforcement (83%), others were more infrequently applied, including assigning/reviewing homework (16%). On average, all strategies associated with ESTs were implemented at a low level of intensity (in terms of time spent and thoroughness of implementation).

Interestingly, however, the level of intensity of some of these evidence-based interventions related positively with parents' perceived treatment effectiveness, as measured four months after the beginning of treatment (Haine-Schlagel et al., 2014). Clinical strategies investigated by Garland et al. (2010) were aggregated into four composites of evidence-based interventions and four composites of non-evidence-based interventions. Of these eight composites, child evidence-based techniques (including positive reinforcement, role-plays, assigning/reviewing homework) was the only composite that predicted treatment effectiveness. These findings were based on the coding of 538 videotaped sessions (involving 75 therapists and 157 children/families) conducted within the first four months of treatment.

As a whole, the studies above suggest that some interventions associated with a diversity of approaches may have multiple impacts (on symptom change, but also on session helpfulness, perceived treatment effectiveness, insight, and alliance) when used as part of routine clinical practice. The potential effect of these interventions, however, is not always consistent with the model they are associated with, nor does it reflect a simple and direct relationship between treatment components and indexes of change.

Client and Therapist Experience

A great deal of emphasis in psychotherapy research has been placed on clients' experiences (emotional, cognitive, behavioral) during therapy (see Chapter 7). Particular attention has been given to such experiences in process studies that have been conducted within RCTs as attempts to examine mechanism of change (see Chapter 8). The examples of PBE studies presented here focus on perspectives that have received somewhat less empirical attention: client and therapist mutual experience and therapist experience.

Chui et al. (2016) examined therapist and client affect before sessions as well as their affect change during sessions. Data related to 1,172 sessions (conducted by 15 therapists and 51 clients) were collected as part of the nonmanualized routine of a psychodynamic-oriented training and research clinic associated with a university in the US. The findings suggest some processes of emotional matching, such as changes in therapist affect were predicted by client affect (at pre-session, as well as changes during sessions) and vice versa. Pointing to factors that may contribute to therapist effects, high quality of sessions (as measured by the clients) was associated with therapist positive affect before the sessions and positive change in therapist affect during sessions. In contrast, low quality of both sessions and alliance (also measured by clients) was associated with therapist negative affect before the sessions and negative change in therapist affect during sessions.

A more direct investigation of mutual experience has been conducted at a university training clinic in Israel, with a sample of 109 clients and 62 therapists (Atzil-Slonim et al., 2018). The study examined whether client and therapist experience similar emotions during sessions, and whether emotional congruence predicted outcome (symptoms and level of functioning wise) in subsequent sessions. As in a previously described study on the alliance (Atzil-Slonim, 2015), emotional convergence was measured in terms of temporal similarity and directional discrepancy. As predicted, temporal convergence was observed for both positive and negative emotions, indicating that clients and therapists experience similar emotions as they fluctuate across treatment sessions. In partial support of one of the authors' hypotheses, therapists experienced less-intense positive emotions than their clients (but not less intense negative emotions). Further, as predicted, lack of emotional congruency, for both positive and negative emotions, was associated with worse symptoms at the next session. Worse outcome in terms of client level of functioning was also predicted by incongruency in positive emotions but not in negative emotions.

The experience of a therapist during psychotherapy was the focus of an intensive single case study that involved both quantitative and qualitative analyses of significant therapeutic events (Krause et al., 2018). Conducted in Chile, the study was based on the treatment of a client with depression seen for 21 sessions by a systemic-oriented therapist. All sessions were videotaped and coded by independent raters on four types of significant events: episodes of change (defined as modifications of "client's subjective theory and explanatory schemes"), episodes of being stuck (characterized by "the reiteration of the problematic issues of the patient and the lack of construction of new meanings," p. 267), alliance ruptures, and repair of alliance ruptures. The videotaped events were later reviewed by the therapist and a researcher who, after each event, asked the therapist about their experience during the event, their understanding of the event, and rationale for their interventions during the event. As a final step, the therapist's responses were analyzed using grounded theory qualitative analysis. Forty-three episodes were identified throughout the therapy: 10 change episodes, 22 stuck episodes, 9 rupture episodes, and 2 resolution episodes. In their integration of the therapist's experience across significant events, the authors highlighted how therapist emotions and perceptions of client emotions (such as fear), as well as their expectations as a therapist, influenced the type of interventions they used (such as listening or avoiding reacting when they view the client as testing them or resisting treatment). They also emphasized that the emotions experienced by the client and therapist, as well as the use of interventions, were closely linked to fluctuations in the therapeutic bond over the course of treatment.

In addition to the use of two research methodologies, Krause et al.'s (2018) study is noteworthy in its actualization of crucial features of POR: The collaboration of clinician/researchers in different components of empirical investigations, as well as the simultaneous integration of research and practice activities. Providing clear examples of such actualization, the authors pointed out that the therapist involvement in the analysis of the therapeutic event allows researchers to gain feedback about the research method and the treatment progress. Reciprocally, the principal investigator provided information about the findings, with the goal of improving the clinician's practice.

Summary

Embracing and pushing forward the clinical and empirical interests of many practitioners (see Tasca et al., 2015; Young et al., 2019), recent PBE studies have investigated various facets of psychotherapy process. Such investigations have provided additional support for the direct and indirect role of the alliance in clients' improvement. In doing so, they have demonstrated how the link between alliance and outcome defies simple associations between single sets of measurement, but rather manifests itself differentially across multiple patterns of alliance development, diverse dimensions of concordance, and interdependence in client and therapist perception, as well as various types of relationship with interventions and participant variables. Recent studies based on within-client analyses have also provided some of the building blocks upon which the link between alliance and outcome can be viewed with increased confidence as one of reciprocal causality (see Chapter 8 for a more comprehensive review of such blocks of evidence). PBE investigations presented here have also revealed complex and at times unexpected associations, both positive and negative, and between treatment impact and both single and multiple technical interventions associated with different theoretical perspectives. Moreover, they have shone a light on the importance, and again complexity, of client and therapist emotional experience with regard to their congruence, link with outcome, and guide for therapeutic interventions.

PARTICIPANTS' CHARACTERISTICS

As was the case with process variables, only a limited number of findings related to participants' pretreatment characteristics were presented in the chapter from the sixth edition of the *Handbook*. Although not comprehensive, more systematic attention has been given to these variables here. First, examples of them are grouped into six clusters of clients' characteristics: demographics; level of symptoms/severity; diagnostic/clinical problems; expectations and preferences; interpersonal/attachment issues; and mixed variables.

Following the discussion of these six clusters of variables, this section presents some PBE findings related to client and therapist matching. Therapist variables have received considerable attention in the last decade, but most of them have been examined as predictors of therapist effects rather than outcome. Accordingly, these variables are reviewed in Chapter 9 of this *Handbook*.

Demographics

Although not their primary aim, some of the studies described in the previous sections reported findings related to client demographic variables. For example, an investigation of psychotherapeutic care in Kenya hospitals revealed that while most patients were young males, women experienced higher initial distress than men, and older patients showed slower levels of improvement during treatment (Kumar et al., 2018). In contrast, other PBE studies have been conducted to specifically investigate such variables. Lockard et al. (2013), for instance, examined whether racial/ethnic identity of college students was related to academic distress at intake and to the decrease of such distress during therapy. Conducted within the CCMH PRN infrastructure, the sample comprised 1,796 undergraduate students (541 African Americans, 541 European Americans, 436 Hispanics/Latinos(as), and 278 Asian Americans) who received counseling across 65 university counseling centers in the US. At intake, the authors found that Asian American clients showed a higher level of academic distress than European American and African American clients. They also found that Asian American students showed significantly less improvement than European American and Hispanics/Latino (a). The results also indicated that pre–post outcome changes were significantly predicted by treatment length and even more strongly by pretreatment level of academic distress.

Level of Symptoms/Severity

Broader measures of initial severity than academic distress have been examined in studies described above, where, for example, a higher level of symptoms was found to be associated with lower probability of reaching normative level of functioning (McAleavey et al., 2019) and lower rates of reliable recovery (Gyani et al., 2013). Contrasting with Lockard's (2013) findings, however, in both of these studies a high level of symptoms was associated with higher pre–post symptomatic change. This lack of consistency may reflect different targets of change and/or the mixed relationship generally found between outcome and initial problems when such a construct is measured in terms of symptom severity (as opposed to functional impairment or problem/symptom chronicity; see Chapter 7 this *Handbook*).

Two recent studies examined early symptoms in treatment, each of them highlighting informative facets of therapeutic change. Interestingly, while the routine care data used in these studies was collected in different clinical settings, let alone regions of the world, and from theoretically different treatments, both studies compared their findings with those obtained in controlled studies. In the first study, Persons and Thomas (2019) examined three statistical models predicting client failure to remit from cognitive therapy for depression:

1. The full model included the client BDI score at pretreatment, the change in BDI score between pre-treatment and week four of treatment, and the BDI score at week four of treatment.

2. The second model included only the rate of change in BDI score from pre- to week four of treatment.
3. The simplest model considered only the BDI score at week four.

These predictive models were tested on two samples. The first sample involved 82 clients treated by one of 18 therapists in private practice in the US, where nonmanualized CT is conducted in clinical routine. The second sample involved 158 clients who received CBT treatments within one of six RCTs. The primary difference between these two samples was that clients seen in the private practice received less treatment before and after week 4.

In both samples, the results showed that the third, most simple model was as predictive as the more complex ones, indicating that the severity of client BDI at week 4 alone is a moderate predictor of remission in CT for depression. Also, in both samples, results showed that clients in the severe range of the BDI at week 4 had a 90% or greater probability of not recovering at the end of treatment.

The second study examined whether early symptoms in treatment could predict sudden gains. Such gains refer to substantial decreases in symptoms following a specific session, which are then maintained for a number of sessions afterward. While standing as robust predictors of outcome, finding reliable predictors of sudden gains has been shown to be difficult (Shalom et al., 2018). Guided by the view that sudden gains represent extreme fluctuations of symptoms, Shalom and colleagues have demonstrated that a client's intraindividual symptom variability during the early sessions of treatment was predictive of sudden gains in three data sets. Two of these data sets were from RCTs (investigating treatments for PTSD and OCD, respectively), while the other derived from a naturalistic setting. The latter data set, involving 106 clients, was collected as part of the clinical routine of a university-based psychodynamic training clinic in Israel that has served as a source of studies previously described (e.g., Atzil-Slonim et al., 2018). As was the case for Persons and Thomas's (2019) study, the convergence of findings across research methodologies enhances the confidence that one can have toward the robustness and generalizability of observed results.

Diagnostic/Clinical Problems

Related but yet distinct from symptom severity are the clinical disorders or problems experienced by clients. Two studies investigating these constructs have been conducted in the UK IAPT health system. In a previously described study based on the clinical routine of 24 services, higher rates of reliable recovery were found for individuals diagnosed at pretreatment with an episode of depression, generalized anxiety disorder, mixed anxiety and depressive disorder, or PTSD (Gyani et al., 2013).

Linked to a single primary care service but involving 28,498 clients, the other study assessed the potential impact of long-term medical conditions (including severe mental health problems) on psychological treatment for depression and anxiety related problems (Delgadillo, Dawson et al., 2017).

Clients received routine care following the stepped-care model adopted in the IAPT system, with high- or low-intensity interventions provided to match clients' difficulties at the beginning or during treatment. Based on data collected over five years, the results showed that clients with chronic illnesses such as musculoskeletal problems, chronic obstructive pulmonary disease, diabetes, and psychotic disorders had worse post-treatment outcomes compared to patients with no long-term medical conditions. Particularly relevant to delivery and costs of services in a stepped care model, results also show that while clients with a number of chronic conditions were more likely to be provided with high-intensity interventions, such interventions were associated with a high level of symptoms at the end of treatment. As noted by the authors, this suggests that clients with long-term medical conditions did not necessarily benefit more from such treatment than from low-intensity interventions.

Expectations and Preferences

A considerable number of studies have examined whether clients' expectations (of outcome and treatment) and preferences (of activities, treatment, therapists) are predictive of outcome (see Chapter 7 of this volume). Here we present examples of PBE studies that complement this empirical literature, in terms of types of expectations/preferences and/or targets of prediction. One of these investigations focused on clients' attendance at their initial appointment (Swift et al., 2012). Recruited in two US university training clinics, the study involved a sample of 57 clients. As predicted, outcome expectations, when combined with other pretreatment variables, such as distress level before treatment, were associated with first session appointment. Interestingly, while outcome expectations did not uniquely predict attendance, other variables did (i.e., previous therapy and shorter waiting time before beginning of treatment).

Client pretreatment expectations about treatment duration and premature termination were the foci of the first study conducted in a PRN involving six training clinics associated with psychology departments in the US (Callahan et al., 2014). A combined group of 216 clients were randomly assigned within each site into either an experimental group (as part of which clients were provided before treatment with information about the average number of sessions and percentage of clients recovering in psychotherapy) or control group (in which this information was not provided). Importantly, randomization, as noted earlier, can be involved in PBE studies as long as it focuses on a component that is not *directly* related to the delivery of the routine clinical practice. No significant difference was found between the groups in terms of clients' estimates about duration of treatment (measured at pretreatment), actual treatment duration, and rate of premature termination. When all the clients were combined, however, client expectations about the length of therapy predicted the number of treatment sessions attended, as well as outcome at the end of therapy, even when controlling for pretreatment distress and actual numbers of sessions attended.

Crits-Christoph, et al. (2017) created a measure to assess clients' preferences of treatment attributes (e.g., side effects, having to share personal information) associated with pharmacotherapy and psychotherapy for depression. Recognizing the importance of their voices as stakeholders, they secured input from 99 clients in developing their measure. They then assessed client preference of 193 depressed clients seen in one of three nonprofit community mental health clinics, and obtained information about the treatment they received and its duration. Interestingly, a substantial number of clients (19.2–43.5%, depending on assessment methods) actually received a nonpreferred treatment. Contrary to the prediction, clients receiving nonpreferred treatments did not predict dropout. It was, however, associated with longer treatment duration, perhaps reflecting that when client preferences are not systematically considered, more time is required before treatment is attuned to their needs. Receiving nonpreferred medication also increased the probability of clients switching medication right after intake, as compared to receiving preferred medication.

Interpersonal/Attachment Issues

With the attention given to early relationships and maladaptive relational patterns across a client's life, it is not surprising that psychodynamic-oriented clinicians would be interested in investigating issues related to attachment and interpersonal problems. In a preliminary study mentioned above, for example, DeFife et al. (2015) found that clients with high levels of both anxious and avoidant attachment showed slow rate of change in long-term psychodynamic therapy, compared to clients with low scores on both of these insecure attachment styles. Interestingly, related constructs have been investigated in two studies conducted in a residential treatment clinic in the US that has implemented CBT interventions to specifically address hostility problems experienced by adolescent and young adult substance abusers. Both studies, which were based on the same sample of 100 clients and 15 therapists, derived from an active collaboration between clinicians, administrators, an outcome measure developer, and researchers (faculty members and graduate students).

The first study was aimed at assessing the alliance – another construct that has been historically associated with psychodynamic therapy – and its interaction with adolescent-caregiver attachment style (Zack et al., 2015). As expected from previous literature (see Chapter 8), results show that alliance significantly predicted outcome improvement at the end of treatment. As predicted, both the alliance and outcome were negatively related to clients' poor level of attachment history. The results further confirmed the authors' hypothesis that the relationship between the alliance and outcome would be moderated by client attachment. Whereas such a relationship was significant for clients with lower attachment levels at baseline, it failed to be so for clients with higher attachment levels. These findings were in line with the theory that a good alliance can play a particularly significant corrective emotional experience for adolescents who, based on their interpersonal history, are likely to have difficulty in building such an alliance.

The second study examined client current interpersonal problems, which, like attachment style, were measured at pretreatment (Boswell et al., 2017). As a first step, two types of interpersonal sub-types were identified based on the Inventory of Interpersonal Problems (IIP-64; Horowitz et al., 2000): vindictive (individuals who are overly cold and dominant with others) and exploitable (who tend to be overly warm and submissive). Analyses were conducted to investigate their relationship with alliance and outcome trajectories (linear and quadratic time effects) during treatment. For both the alliance and outcome, no main effect of IIP sub-type was found. However, significant interaction effects were observed with respect to outcome trajectories and interpersonal sub-type: whereas vindictive clients tend to change in a steady and incremental way over the course of long treatments, exploitable clients show an initial improvement that is followed by a significant decrease in gains across the course of treatment of similar duration. These latter clients, as suggested by the authors, might benefit from longer and or alternative treatments.

Clients' current interpersonal problems were also the focus on another recent study, this time conducted in a private center in Argentina (Gómez Penedo et al., 2019). Like Zack et al.'s (2015) investigation, the goal was to determine whether interpersonal difficulty serves as a moderator of the relationship between alliance issues and outcome. A total of 96 clients with emotional disorders (mood and/or anxiety disorders) were treated by eight therapists using, as part of routine clinical practice, solution-focused brief therapy – an integrative treatment based on systemic orientation. After their first session, clients filled out the IIP-64, based on which the investigators identified two profiles of interpersonal problems: cold (with limited expression of emotion and positivity toward others) and overly nurturant. Parallel to the sub-types identified by Boswell et al. (2017), those in the cold profile were more vindictive and those in the overly nurturant were more exploitable compared to each other. After each of their first four sessions, clients also filled out the Outcome Questionnaire (OQ.45, Lambert et al., 1996) and a measure of alliance negotiation approaches, which assessed the therapist and client ability to resolve alliance ruptures. Their findings revealed a moderation effect, showing that the relationship between negotiation of alliance and the rate of change over four sessions was stronger with overly nurturant clients. As noted by the authors, the expression and integration of negative experiences toward the therapist and therapeutic process may foster early change in clients who tend to be too dependent on others.

Mixed Client Variables

A number of studies presented in previous sections have examined the relationship between various client pretreatment variables and diverse types of impact. For example, as part of their investigation of long-term psychodynamic therapy in an outpatient community mental health clinic, Roseborough et al. (2012) found two moderators of outcome: client age and initial distress. Specifically, clients aged over 60 began treatment with lower level of distress, but also showed a greater level of

improvement than younger clients after one year of therapy. Clients with elevated levels of distress at baseline showed greater change, as well as stronger initial treatment response than other clients – a response that was maintained for a year during therapy. In their study conducted in multiple service sites in the UK, Saxon et al. (2017) found that both risk of harming self and unemployment were predictive of deterioration. Interestingly, however, younger clients who completed therapy were less at risk of deteriorating. In a university outpatient clinic in Germany, dropout was predicted by a number of variables such as gender (male), high level of pretreatment impairment, low level of education, and low level of expectations toward treatment (Zimmermann et al., 2017).

Other PBE studies have focused primarily on pretreatment characteristics, while also targeting different types of impacts. One of these investigations was conducted within a national PRN regrouping several US private residential treatment centers and outdoor behavioral healthcare programs (Tucker et al., 2014). The study examined whether gender, presenting problems (e.g., substance abuse, trauma history, conduct disorders, anxiety), and history of sexual abuse predicted clinically significant improvement at posttreatment. It involved 1,058 adolescents who participated in one of 15 programs. Results indicated that for outdoor programs, females were more likely to achieve clinically significant change than males. Surprisingly, while trauma history was negatively related to clinically significant improvement in residential treatments, the reverse was observed for history of sexual abuse. Although these contradictory findings may be due to measurement issues, they also point out the need for precise assessment of clients' problems in order to provide attuned treatment.

Delgadillo, Moreea et al. (2016) examined various pretreatment characteristics of 1,347 clients to predict poor response to psychological therapies, as delivered in a primary care service of the UK IAPT program. Using a cross-validation design, the authors first identified six predictors of reliable and clinically significant improvement (RCSI) – some of them demographic variables (disability, employment status, age), while others reflecting distress (functional impairment) and cognitive (outcome expectancy) factors. These predictors were then combined in different profiles to derive a risk index, the levels of which (mild, moderate, high) were found to be associated with rates of RCSI, treatment completion, posttreatment outcome, and markers (not-on-track sessions) of problematic trajectory of change and potential deterioration. As an indication of its prognostic value, the risk index predicted up to 9% of the outcome variance, even as initial severity, early response, and treatment length were controlled for. Within the context of the IAPT stepped care system, the availability of this risk index at pretreatment could provide useful information, on a case-by-case basis, to assign clients to the most appropriate levels of interventions (high vs. low intensity).

Client characteristics were investigated to predict dropout in a specialized outpatient clinic for eating disorder in Germany, which used manualized cognitive behavior therapy in routine care (Schnicker et al., 2013). The study involved 104 clients with bulimia nervosa (BN) and anorexia nervosa (AN) seen at the clinic within a period of more than five years. For clients with BN, higher level of depression and presence of comorbidity at pretreatment were predictive of premature termination. For clients with AN, dropout was predicted by drive for thinness, unemployment, and not living with a partner.

Two studies conducted within the CCMH PRN infrastructure relied on various client pretreatment variables for different purposes. The goal of the first study was to identify profiles of clients in counseling centers that could alert clinicians about the likely course of treatment (Nordberg et al., 2016). Latent-profile analyses conducted on two samples, each of 19,247 clients, led to 16 distinct and reliable profiles based on the baseline level of several types of distress (e.g., depression, eating concerns, substance use, hostility). These profiles differed in terms of demographics, psychosocial history, and diagnostic. More helpful, clinically, they also differed in terms of serious risk (suicide, self-harm, hostility toward others), as well as treatment length and outcome. These 16 profiles were then rationally grouped into nine types based on underlying clinical problems (e.g., primary eating concerns, primary substance abuse, family concerns, and hostility), highlighting similarities and differences between clients that could inform case formulations and treatment plans. For example, four profiles of eating concerns were identified, which were divided in two groups – one with and one without substance abuse. In both groups, one profile showed high level of mood symptoms and the other not. The finding suggests that what hampered the reduction of eating problems for the clients in these profiles was not the level of mood or eating disorder distress, but rather the high level of substance use.

The second study was aimed at predicting clients who, before their first session in a counseling center, are likely to return for additional therapy after the completion of their first treatment episode (Kilcullen et al., 2020). Machine learning analyses were applied to a dataset comprising 8,329 clients treated at one of 52 university counseling centers. The results showed that 30% of clients returned for one more course of treatment. Interestingly, a return to treatment was not predicted by variables related to demographics (gender, race/ethnicity, sexual orientation), problem chronicity (history of trauma, history of sexual abuse, suicidal ideation, nonsuicidal self-injuries), or prior utilization of mental health services (counseling, psychiatric medication, or psychiatric hospitalization). Perhaps even more interesting, pre-to-post changes in all (seven) types of distress that were measured failed to emerge as significant predictors. In contrast, a high level of some specific types of distress at initial treatment course either increased (social anxiety) or decreased (academic distress and alcohol use) the likelihood of further treatment. In addition, clients' perceived social support was associated with the probability of returning for additional therapy. While recognizing that different reasons can explain why some clients will or will not return to therapy, the authors argued that their findings could be used to inform decisions related to important issues in day-to-day routine clinical practice, including referral and length of treatment provided. If made actionable and retainable, such findings could be helpful to clinicians and administrators in addressing the high demand for services, severity of distress experienced by many clients, and limited resources that characterize current care in counseling centers.

Client and Therapist Matching

In a study conducted with Axis I mood disorder clients treated at a US hospital outpatient clinic, Bhati (2014) tested the hypothesis that self-identified gender matching was predictive of the quality of the alliance early in therapy – but only in the initial phase of treatment. Based on a sample of 92 dyads (49 gender matched, 43 gender nonmatched), results revealed what the author refers to as a "female effect." The alliance ratings of female clients–female therapist dyad were significantly higher, not only early in therapy but across different phases of treatment, than dyads with male therapists. In addition, the findings revealed that alliance ratings of female therapist–male client dyads were superior to male therapist–male client dyads. In a previously mentioned study, Al-Jabari et al. (2019) also found that self-identification gender matching was associated with lower rates of premature termination in three university psychological training clinics, but the effect size was very small.

Another example of a PBE study on matching did not focus on similarity between client and therapist but rather on their complementarity (Marmarosh et al., 2014). Guided by the actor–partner interdependent model (see Process section above), the investigators examined interactions between self-reported client and therapist attachment styles (anxiety and avoidant) on the alliance, as rated by both participants between sessions three and five. Specifically, they predicted that complementary (opposite) styles on both dimensions of attachment would foster the process of change early in treatment. Recruited from two routine practice sites in the US (a university-based community mental health clinic and a university counseling center), the sample included 46 client–therapist dyads. In line with authors' predictions, higher levels of alliance were associated with dyads where therapist anxiety attachment was low and client anxiety attachment was high, and lower levels of alliance were associated with therapists high in anxiety attachment working with clients also high in levels of anxiety attachment. However, these significant findings were observed only when the client rated the alliance. Furthermore, no complementarity with respect to avoidant attachment was supported. Nevertheless, the study suggests that some type of matching between client and therapist may facilitate the building of a secure base at the beginning of therapy.

Summary

Going beyond the search for treatments that work, studies conducted as part of clinical routine have examined a host of client pre- or early treatment variables that explain, sometime in combination with therapist characteristics, some impact of therapy. As in traditional RCT, these variables include symptoms, diagnostics, and demographics. While having received less empirical attention, others map onto issues that most clinicians would find relevant in developing their case formulations and treatment plans, such as chronic medical conditions, history of trauma and sexual abuse, distinct profiles of distress, risk index of poor response, past and current maladaptive patterns of relationships, various facets of treatment expectations and preferences, and moderators of alliance and outcome relationship. The studies described above have also focused on the prediction of several consequences or concomitants of therapy. In addition to pre- and post-symptom changes, these include less typical targets of inquiry such as attendance to first session, treatment duration, dropout, failure to remit, deterioration, severe risk to self and others, alliance and outcome trajectories, sudden gains, and return to future episode of treatment. Taken together, the breath of relationships between predictors and effects revealed in recent PBE studies can be viewed as a rich source of information about treatment courses and outcomes, some beneficial and some not.

CONTEXTUAL VARIABLES

Whereas there were relatively few studies on either process or participants' factors reported in the 2013 chapter, even less attention was given to contextual variables that might contribute to the effect of psychological therapies. This was due, in part, to the paucity of studies conducted on such issues. Reflecting a growing interest in organizational factors within which treatments are provided, a number of studies are presented here. They are grouped within three clusters: center/clinic/service effects, neighborhood effects, and training/supervision.

Center/Clinic/Service Effects

Several studies investigating the potential impact of services have been conducted within the UK health care system. One of them, which we previously described, examined the relationship between service characteristics and client recovery rates (Gyani et al., 2013). Based on data collected in 24 IAPT services, the study found higher rates of reliable recovery to be associated with larger services, higher number of sessions, higher proportion of clients who began treatment with low-level intensity interventions and were then stepped up to high-intensity interventions, and a larger number of experienced staff. This study, however, did not account for the nested nature of client, therapist, and center variables.

In contrast, the next three studies all used multilevel modeling analyses to account for such nesting. In a study also described above, Delgadillo, Kellett et al. (2016) examined the effectiveness of CBT group therapy delivered in five different IAPT services. In addition to group effects, the authors reported that the outcomes in one of the clinics were significantly lower than the other four. Such a difference, however, was accounted for by group (e.g., treatment length) and case mix variables (e.g., number of participants from low socioeconomic areas/neighborhoods). Service differences were examined in another previously described study that investigated the effectiveness of CBT and counseling across 103 IAPT sites (Pybis et al., 2017). The results indicated that clinic effects explained 1.8% of the outcome variance. These findings, controlling for client variables and session attended, reflect meaningful differences in clients' improvement. For instance, the mean recovery rates of the clinics that were reliably more

effective than others (approximately 15% of the clinics) was 59% compared to 43% for a similar percentage of the total clinics that were reliably less effective. Consistent with observations regarding therapist effects (see Chapter 9), the findings also showed that clinic differences were greater with higher levels of baseline severity.

Service and therapist effects were simultaneously investigated in 30 clinics, also in the UK (Firth et al., 2019). With a sample of 26,888 patients and 462 therapists, the results revealed service effects at 1.9% that were similar to those observed by Pybis and colleagues. These effects were smaller than the therapist effects (3.4%), which in turn were smaller than those that have been typically observed in naturalistic settings. As noted by the authors, this could reflect the fact that therapist effects were, in contrast to previous investigations, controlled for by service effects. The study also investigated variables that could explain services and therapist effects, as well as overall outcome variance. Differences between clinics, but not between therapists, were mostly explained by two client-level variables, namely baseline severity and employment status, and two clinic-level variables, namely sector of care provision and ethnic composition. Specifically, the finding that some clinics had lower outcomes then others was explained by the high level of severity and unemployment of the clients they served, as well as for being a secondary care service (a sector that is more likely to serve more complex cases) and for treating a smaller proportion of White clients. These, as well as other client variables (age, ethnicity, session attendance, interaction between severity and employment status), also explained a large part of the overall outcome variance. The findings further showed that initial severity was a particularly strong predictor of improvement, and that its relationship with outcome was moderated by a client's therapist.

Clinic effects and some of the factors that might explain them were examined in psychological therapies provided to university students (Carney et al., in press). Conducted within the CCMH PRN infrastructure, the study involved 58,423 clients, 2,362 therapists, and 116 university counseling centers in the US. Also relying on multilevel modeling analyses to account for data nesting, differential effectiveness of centers was assessed with respect to magnitude and rate of change, both controlling for baseline severity at the client- and center-levels. Using posttreatment outcome, an average center effect of 1.9% was found across seven measures of distress – findings that are consistent with both Pybis et al. (2017) and Firth et al. (2019). A higher average of 3.2% was found, however, when predicting clients' rate of change during treatment. Particularly relevant for student college clients, center effects were the highest for substance abuse (2.6% for posttreatment outcome and 6.9% for rate of change). In their attempt to explain clients' outcome differences, the authors examined six potentially actionable center-level factors, in terms of procedures and policy changes: presence or absence of session limits, session frequency, number of clients served annually, center provision of noncounseling services (e.g., psychiatric treatment, neuropsychological testing), center accreditation status from the American Psychological Association [APA], as well as center accreditation status from the International Accreditation of

Counseling Services. While these variables explained a substantial part of the center effects, only one of them significantly accounted for the total variance of outcomes across different types of distress. Specifically, centers where clients received more frequent sessions had better outcomes. Consistent with Firth et al. (2019), client-level baseline distress explained the largest part of the outcome variance in general.

Neighborhood Effects

As noted above, Firth et al. (2019) found that a small proportion of White clients seen at a clinic explained part of clinic effects and overall outcome variance. The authors hypothesized that these findings reflect the impact of deprivation. More direct evidence for neighborhood effects has been provided by Delgadillo, Kellett et al.'s (2016) study, which, as previously discussed, found that service effects were accounted by a number of group and client variables, including the level of deprivation of a client's neighborhood. As noted by the authors, more socioeconomically deprived areas were associated with poorer posttreatment outcomes.

Further evidence has come from data collected in IAPT services across England involving 293,400 individuals who were referred to treatment, with 110,415 of them accessing therapy and providing outcome data (Delgadillo, Asaria et al., 2016). In line with the previous results, this study showed that poorer areas in the UK were associated with lower recovery rate from treatment for depression and anxiety. Consistent with empirical evidence that poverty is linked with a higher prevalence of mental health problems, a greater level of area deprivation was also predictive of higher levels of referrals. The results further show that area level of deprivation did not predict the caseload sizes, that is the number of clients who were referred to therapy, who got access to treatment and were discharged. Reflecting crucial issues to guide the improvement of mental care in the UK and wider afield, the authors argued that this finding "could be explained by the detrimental influence of deprivation on the likelihood of starting therapy after being referred, insufficient healthcare resources in services working in poor areas, or a combination of both" (p. 430).

Training/Supervision

Early in practitioners' professional development, and sometimes at different phases of their career, psychological therapies are conducted within the structure of training and/or supervision. As such, formal mentoring, consultation, and guidance from others represent meaningful contextual variables that are aimed at improving treatment. Although training and supervision are the focus of an entire chapter in this *Handbook* (Chapter 10), we present here a few examples of PBE studies that have recently been conducted on these topics.

One study assessed clients' outcomes of therapists at different, cross-sectional, stages of training. Conducted in a single university counseling center in the US, it involved 1,318 clients treated by 64 therapists (Budge et al., 2013). These therapists were either students in beginning doctoral practicum, students in advanced doctoral practicum, predoctoral interns/postdoctoral fellows, or licensed psychologists. The findings revealed a mixed picture about the effect of training. While interns/postdoctoral fellows show greater effectiveness in terms of clients' life functioning than advanced graduate students, they were also found to be more effective than licensed psychologists with regard to life functioning and symptoms change.

Three other studies assessed the improvement of trainees using longitudinal designs. Hill et al. (2015) examined whether doctoral student trainees improved over 12 to 42 months during an externship at a US psychodynamic/interpersonal university clinic. With data collected over a period of six years, the sample comprised 23 therapists and 168 clients. Based on both quantitative and qualitative analyses, the results indicate that while trainees showed significant improvement with respect to some important clinical skills (e.g., client and therapist rated working alliance, therapists' perceived ability in case conceptualization and helping skills), they did not show significant change with regard to judge-rated use of psychodynamic techniques. Furthermore, with the exception of significant increment in clients' interpersonal functioning, no improvement was found with various types of treatment impact (dropout after intake and eight sessions, client and therapist-rated session outcome, and symptom change) during therapists' training at the clinic.

In a larger study, Owen et al. (2016) investigated the increment in effectiveness using a sample of therapists that varied in their stage of training. The study was based on 2,991 clients treated at one of 47 US university counseling centers by 114 therapists, who were either practicum students, predoctoral interns, or postdoctoral fellows when they saw their first client in the study. They found that clients' outcomes of trainees showed small but significant increases over a period of at least 12 months (mean of 45.3 months). They also found that improvement in therapist effectiveness was moderated by client initial distress: such improvement, contrary to the authors' prediction, was only significant for less-distressed clients. Also inconsistent with one of the authors' predictions, the stages of training (practicum students vs. predoctoral interns/postdoctoral fellows) was not significantly related to client outcome change over time. Supporting another of their predictions, however, therapists varied in terms of patterns of effectiveness over time: The performance of some therapists increased, decreased, or stayed the same during different periods of their training. Such variability, the authors argued, is evidence that the effect of training fails to be uniform.

The third longitudinal study assessed whether therapists improved as they moved through distinct stages of training: as doctoral students, psychology interns, postgraduate psychology residents, and licensed professional psychologists (Erekson et al., 2017). The study involved 22 therapists who treated 4,047 clients at the same university counseling center in the US for a minimum of two stages of training. With respect to magnitude of a client's change, the results showed no improvement in therapist outcome performance in later training stages. A significant effect was found, however, in terms of rate of change, with the fastest rate of changes observed at the doctoral level and the slowest at the licensed level. As noted by the authors, more training does not seem to make therapists more effective or efficient in reducing client distress.

Supervision has failed to show more merit than training in general, at least with respect to clients' improvement, in a study conducted at a private nonprofit community-based counseling clinic in Canada (Rousmaniere et al., 2016). Data collected over a period of five years led to a sample of 6,521 clients, 175 therapists in training (pre or post master's degree), and 23 supervisors (master's- or doctoral-level) with diverse theoretical orientations. As part of the day-to-day clinic routine, each trainee received one hour of individual and two hours of group supervision weekly, provided by only one supervisor at a time. Analyses accounting for the nesting data of clients, therapists and supervisors, revealed that supervision explained only a very small part of client outcome (0.04%). Moreover, no supervisor characteristics that were assessed (level of education, years of experience in providing supervision, and professional field) predicted client outcomes. In addition, the results failed to confirm the authors' hypothesis that supervision effects would be moderated by trainees' level of experience (i.e., the differential impact of supervisors on client outcomes would be stronger with pre- than with post-master's therapists).

Summary

Recent PBE studies have suggested that some aspects of the context within which psychological therapies are conducted have an impact on client outcome. The findings presented here indicate that where clients are treated – and, perhaps more importantly, where they live – matters. Relatively small, but yet robust and meaningful service/clinic/center effects have been observed in different care settings. At least some of these effects, however, may be reflective of the impact of poorer areas. Social deprivation intrinsic to such areas does appear to put at risk individuals not optimally utilizing and/or being adequately provided with therapy, and for not fully benefiting from treatment. In contrast, other contextual variables, assumed to be necessary for effective practice, have not been shown here to have a strong and reliable effect on clients' improvements. Notwithstanding results obtained with less-distressed clients, studies in this section suggest that the focus, structure, and implementation of training and supervision conducted in the real world could be improved. Considering the importance and the complexity of these issues, optimal ways to foster such improvement might call for the collaboration of many stakeholders, including clinicians, supervisors, trainees, administrators, policy makers, and clients.

OTHER INITIATIVES TO CLOSE THE SCIENCE–PRACTICE GAP AND NEW DEVELOPMENTS IN PRACTICE-ORIENTED RESEARCH

In the 2013 edition, we presented a number of efforts aimed at reducing the scientific–practice gap, efforts that are complementary to practice-based evidence accumulated via research in routine clinical practice. These efforts included recommendations, some early (e.g., Goldfried, 1984; Stricker & Teierweiler, 1995) and some more recent (e.g., Baker et al., 2009; Beck et al., 2014), to foster the integration of research in the clinical training of doctoral students. We also identified peer-reviewed journals that encouraged and are still encouraging clinicians' contributions to, and assimilation of, empirical knowledge (*Journal of Clinical Psychology: In Session*; *Pragmatic Case Studies in Psychotherapy*; *Psychotherapy*). Since then, a new section in the *Journal of Psychotherapy Integration*, has been pursuing the related goal of deriving clinical implications from basic findings in psychology.

As ways to increase the clinical relevance of research, the chapter in the previous edition mentioned attempts to give voice to clinicians about the applicability of research in day-to-day practice. This included an initiative that allowed and has continued to allow clinicians to provide input on the problems and difficulties encountered when attempting to implement ESTs in their practice (e.g., McAleavey et al., 2014). Also going beyond the view of clinicians as passive recipients of research, a recent collaborative project has enabled the exchange of distinct but complementary expertise between researchers and experienced clinicians (Castonguay et al., 2019). While the researchers provided a list of empirically based principles of change from an extensive review of literature, the clinicians described how they typically implement such principles in their day-to-day practice. With the goal of creating new directions of knowledge and action, both group of scholars then engaged in dialogues about these and other clinically derived principles of change.

The chapter in the previous edition also referred to papers describing clinicians' experiences in participating in research. This topic, however, has received extensive attention in the last decade and can be viewed as a primary focus of new developments in practice-oriented research. These developments have in common a commitment, most often in collaboration with researchers, that parallels Sullivan's therapeutic stance of participant-observer (Sullivan, 1953), where clinicians have demonstrated their willingness and/or ability to engage in research and have reflected on this engagement. One special issue of *Counseling Psychology Quarterly* (Paquin, 2017), for example, aimed at illustrating the tensions and benefits experienced, the support needed, as well as the work conducted by scholars involved in the dual tasks of being practitioners and researchers. Two other journal issues, one in *Psychotherapy* (2019, volume 56, issue 1) and one in *Psychotherapy Research* (Castonguay & Muran, 2015), have been devoted to the process of building clinician-researcher partnerships and conducting research in routine clinical practice – together with providing a pool of lessons and recommendations for future POR across a diversity of settings and regions. Similar manifestations of collaborative commitment have been the focus of yet another special issue, this one published in *Revista Argentina de Clinical Psicologica* (Fernández-Alvarez & Castonguay, 2018), where clinical scholars from Europe, Latin America, and North America joined to provide reflections about the role of practice-based evidence in building scientific knowledge about psychological therapies, to describe the development of practice-oriented infrastructures, and to present various studies conducted in routine clinical practice.

In addition to these journal issues, several single publications have described the experience of clinical researchers in collecting and making use of empirical data. For example, two recent articles have presented challenges and ways to address them, first in initiating (DeFife et al., 2015) and then in maintaining (Drill et al., 2019) research studies on long-term psychodynamic therapy, as practiced in a public hospital clinic and training site in the US. The observations and guidelines highlighted in these papers are likely to be helpful to many psychotherapists interested in contributing to scientific knowledge as they have been derived from settings where research time is not funded, where the staff and their time to conduct such research are limited, and where, to a significant extent, clinicians and researchers "are one and the same" (DeFife et al., 2015).

Other recent papers have focused on settings and/or clinical issues that are not associated with traditional territories of psychological therapies. For example, Craner et al. (2017) have described the design and development (based on guidelines of implementation science) of a data collection system in a behavioral health program that is integrated within five primary care clinics in the US. The fruits of a research partnership involving multiple stakeholders, this system has been built to serve numerous purposes (e.g., clinical decisions, program development, training, research) via the tracking of several aspects of psychological therapies, including their utilization, effectiveness, and the use of principles linked to empirical supported treatments. Sales et al. (2014) have also described the international collaboration, within a practice-based research network, of researchers and clinicians in the development and implementation in clinical practice of a personalized health measure. Addressing the need for a nonmainstream but socially crucial segment of mental care, Steen and Mellor-Clark (2019) have described the early development of a collaborative learning network aimed at promoting the value and improving the practice of third-sector organizations. These organizations (e.g., voluntary and community services, charities) provide a range of support, including for female victims of domestic violence and women on low incomes. Involving a network of six organizations in the UK, this initiative has relied on sharing and generating practice-based knowledge, mentorship support, and integration of outcome monitoring in clinical routine. The initial year of operation has provided evidence for the benefits of such collaborative partnership in terms of improved data collection, as well as better understanding of session nonattendance, unplanned ending of treatment, and outcome trajectories.

Another recent development has been the publication of surveys of clinicians that were created within three PRNs for the sake of guiding research in their respective infrastructure. Two of them asked similar questions assessing the importance or usefulness of specific topics of research for the practice of psychotherapy (Taska et al., 2015; Youn et al., 2019). Interestingly, despite the fact that these surveys assessed different groups (more than 1,000 participants, mostly Canadian clinicians practicing in a diversity of settings; more than 600 clinicians, trainees, and administrators working in university counseling centers), the most important area of research reported in studies was the process of change and/or the therapeutic relationship. Another survey asked a more fundamental question: what makes it possible for clinicians to participate in research (Thurin et al., 2012)? The survey was completed by 36 clinicians who were participating in a study focused on the outcome and process of psychotherapy in natural settings. Importantly this collaborative initiative took place in France, a country where, as noted by the authors, empirical research on psychotherapy has been faced with hostile reactions. The survey (and the discussions it generated among clinicians in the PRN) pointed out the value of a peer group, meetings to identify and address obstacles, online support, and opportunities to reflect on treatment interventions. Capturing a broader level of learning, the authors stated that the discussion of the survey findings highlighted benefits that can be derived from an engagement in research with regard to understanding of psychological therapies.

The last type of development to be briefly covered here reflects a particularly strong form of collaborative engagement within POR: The creation and development of PRN infrastructures aimed at creating empirical and actionable knowledge via the synergistic integration of multiple sources of expertise. A substantial number of PRNs were identified in the original chapter, clustered around clinician and researcher partnerships that belong to diverse professional organizations, specialize in the treatment of various clinical problems, or work in diverse clinical settings. Several of the PRNs that were described in the previous chapter have shown extensive developments (e.g., Castonguay, Pincus, et al., 2015; Garland, et al., 2015; Huet, et al., 2014; McAleavey et al., 2015; West et al., 2015). Other PRNs were not covered, some new, some not, including several already mentioned in the current chapter (e.g., Callahan et al., 2014; Sales, 2014; Tasca et al., 2015; Thurin, et al., 2012; Tucker et al., 2014). Like several initiatives described in this chapter, additional PRNs have been developed to advance knowledge within zones of practice that have received less than optimal attention, for example, spirituality (Richards et al., 2015) and systemic orientation (Vitry et al., 2020).

The initiatives presented in this section, some of them having been built on earlier work while others having opened new areas of exploration, are likely to foster the expansion of practice-base evidence and the growth of POR partnerships around the world. More broadly, they represent worthwhile efforts toward the solidification of the scientific practitioner model and the growth of the scientific basis of psychological therapies.

CONCLUSION

PBE studies are, by definition, anchored in routine clinical practice. Their aim is to understand and improve psychological therapies as they are actually conducted – not as prescribed for a primary empirical reason – and the goal of this chapter has been to provide illustrative examples of PBE studies conducted since the chapter in the previous edition. Even when combined, these two chapters fail to provide a comprehensive review of the extent and diversity of research. As a case in point, a recently published review identified more than 250 studies conducted in psychological training clinics between 1993 and 2015 (Dyason et al., 2019). It is also important to remind the readers that a large number of practice-oriented studies, under the umbrella of patient-focused research, has been covered elsewhere in Chapter 4 of this *Handbook*. Yet, the sections above give a sense of the variety of empirical investigations that have been conducted with respect to the impact and processes of therapy, as well as to the participants and contextual variables that contribute to them. This breadth is not surprising considering the complex set of factors mapping on to the realities of day-to-day practice, especially when it is investigated by researchers and clinicians working in different countries, clinical settings, with diverse clinical populations, and from different theoretical orientations. The diversity of findings presented is also not surprising considering the multiplicity of methods that have been used, including correlational and experimental designs, multilevel modeling, case study, and qualitative analyses. Some of the topics covered by PBE studies overlap with those typically harvested in RCTs, which can contribute to science by assessing the clinical validity of results observed in controlled settings and/or by increasing the robustness of findings obtained by different empirical approaches. But many of the PBE studies also investigated issues outside of well-paved routes of inquiries, conceptualization, and action.

It should be mentioned that with the conduct of PBE studies there frequently comes a number of methodological and pragmatic challenges, some of them having been briefly mentioned in the section above. An extensive description of such challenges and obstacles has been derived from the experience of 11 researcher and clinician partnerships across three continents (Castonguay, Youn et al., 2015). These include *concerns that practitioners* may have about the study's clinical value (will it provide me with helpful information?), negative impact (will it affect the therapeutic relationship?), feasibility (can the research tasks be easily integrated in my day-to-day routine?), and the use of the data collected (will it be used to assess my performance?); *problems of communication and collaboration* that are likely to emerge when professionals who speak different languages and live in different worlds are working together; *pragmatic barriers* such as lack of time and financial support; and *costs* experienced by all stakeholders (e.g., additional responsibilities, loss of income, interference with pressure to publish). Fortunately, strategies to address these challenges have also been generated across the same partnerships, such as designing research tasks that provide immediate information about a client and/or treatment; regularly collecting feedback about the applicability and relevance of protocols; recognizing and building on unique needs, expectations, and expertise of a diversity of stakeholders; and using strategies to ease the learning and remembering of research protocols. Such strategies may not only facilitate the implementation of PBE studies, they may also help researchers and clinicians to identify research goals that are directly addressing key issues in the delivery of mental health services.

As with any type of research, including RCTs, a number of limitations have been identified with studies conducted within the paradigm of practice-oriented research (see McMillen et al., 2009; Parry et al., 2010). Some of these, especially with

regard to internal validity, are not likely to be addressed in future investigations. For example, it is neither possible nor advisable for clinicians to have every prospective new client assigned to repeated and blind assessments before and after treatment so that a reliable judgment of the diagnoses of research participants can be ascertained. However, improvements have been made to address other limitations. For example, as a whole, practice-based research can be challenged for the lack of assessment of therapists' treatment adherence and competence, thereby precluding confident statements about what interventions therapists used and how well they implemented them in studies investigating or comparing different forms of therapy. However, although no doubt costly in terms of time and expertise, observer assessments of therapists' delivery of therapy have been used in some studies (e.g., Garland et al., 2010; Kivlighan et al., 2019) and should be considered in future investigations. Other POR studies have relied on the therapist reports of techniques conducted session-by-session (e.g., McAleavey & Castonguay, 2014). While subject to their own biases, self-report measures used in these studies have been shown to be predictive of session impact. Crucially, when integrated into routine clinical practice they can be actionable, thereby delivering on the confounding of research and practice activities. Clinicians could compare their assessment of the techniques they used during a session with the client's evaluation of the impact of the same session to derive information about what interventions appear to be more or less responsive to the particular needs of the client.

Beyond the limitations of specific studies, two broad limitations related to POR in general, and PBE evidence resulting from this paradigm, need to be highlighted. First, a substantial number of investigations have been conducted with university student samples. While there is evidence that this population is experiencing significant distress and impairment (Xiao, Carney et al., 2017), it cannot be assumed that findings derived from it will generalize to other populations without clear supporting evidence. What this means is that more studies need to be conducted with non-college samples and more efforts should be made to compare findings across these populations, including benchmarking studies (e.g., McAleavey et al., 2019). It is perhaps not surprising that a large portion of POR has emerged from university training clinics and counseling centers. Operating as a single site or as part of networks, these are embedded in an environment that emphasize research and frequently have the resources and expertise to conduct such research (including faculty members, graduate students, as well as statistical and technological assistance). These resources and expertise are not likely to be easily accessible in other clinical settings, especially within single sites. Fully addressing the first broad limitation of POR might thus require the creation of new organizational frameworks, such as large PRN infrastructures (similar to CCMH) and national programs (similar to IAPT), that will encourage and facilitate research in a wide range of clinical milieux, including hospitals, residential facilities, and private practice. Moreover, given that a significant proportion of evidence derives from the CCMH and IAPT sources, it is a frustration that these two data sources do not share a common measure – a hallmark of practice-based evidence. A clear challenge would be to test out the extent of the commonality between the CCMH and IAPT populations via the adoption of, for example, the key elements of the IAPT minimum dataset within a test sample in the CCMH PRN. In this way, we might then be able to both test the generalizability of CCMH data and also move to a higher-level of internationally shared data sources.

The second broad limitation is that the current status of PBE is characterized by a wide range of studies, with a limited number of them focusing on particular topics or questions (with the notable exceptions of therapist effects and the alliance). This is reflecting, at least in part, the fact that POR is driven more by a diversity of issues faced in day-to-day work and less by the strong academic pull toward accumulating knowledge to support, or disconfirm, a specific construct or method. Unfortunately, the paucity of efforts toward replication limits the possibility of deriving robust conclusions about most aspects of psychosocial therapies investigated in POR. In the spirit of setting up a further challenge to the field, we hope that enough POR studies will be generated in the next five to seven years to allow for systematic reviews and/or metanalyses on specific topics of investigation to be conducted.

Clinical, Scientific, and Policy-Making Contributions

Practice-oriented research has offered contributions to the field that are beneficial to therapists and their clients and should be recognized both by psychotherapy scholars and by policy makers. At a clinical level, the main message that should emerge from this and the chapter in the previous edition is that clinicians can learn from what they and others are doing in their clinical practice. They do not have to restrict themselves to textbooks, training in graduate school, supervision, and results of RCTs to guide their interventions. Another source of knowledge is the empirical findings that come from investigations of how therapy is actually conducted in different types of settings. Because of the external validity of these investigations, clinical implications could be derived from virtually all PBE studies. At the minimum, these implications should be directly applicable to the setting where the data has been collected. Unless the routine clinical practice changed substantially after the completion of a study, its findings can be used to improve how care is provided (e.g., see Adelman et al., 2015). Among the countless clinical implications that can be derived from the studies described in this chapter, we highlight five here:

1. *Clinicians should be aware that they may be more effective with White than with REM clients (or vice versa), and that they may be more effective than most of their colleagues when working with White or REM clients.* Until the field provides a clear picture of who is more effective, clinicians should monitor and pay attention to the outcomes (as well as dropout and session attendance) of clients of diverse ethnicities and reflect on what they may do differently if patterns of discrepancies emerge.
2. *Clinicians are likely to benefit from monitoring alliance and outcome on a session-by-session basis, using reliable and valid measures.*

Such tools may help them recognize the incidence and recurrence of alliance ruptures, which should be acted on. Tracking the fluctuation of alliance and its potential impact may also help clinicians in assessing and responsively adjusting their attempts to repair these ruptures, which, if successful, may provide their clients with experiences in how to solve interpersonal difficulties.

3. *When monitoring the alliance, therapists might find it helpful to assess and compare their clients and their own perspectives.* Higher ratings on their part may be a cause of concern, as this has been related to lower session and treatment impact – perhaps indicating a lack of proper attention to alliance problems.
4. *Clinicians may increase their effectiveness by fostering complementary processes of change.* Examples are the acquisition of coping skills when conducting CBT and the deepening of emotional change in psychodynamic treatment. Clinicians should also be aware that a strong alliance is likely to provide an optimal condition for activating the therapeutic value of these processes.
5. *A reliable and valid self-report assessment of clients' past and current interpersonal difficulties is likely to improve clinicians' case formulations and treatment plan.* The assessment of such problems can help clinicians predict not only who is likely to require longer treatment but also who is likely to benefit more from corrective experiences that a good therapeutic relationship can provide.

At a scientific and policy-making level, the studies reported in this chapter (as well as those on outcome monitoring and feedback describe in Chapter 4) set out both the yield and potential of an overarching paradigm that goes part way to redressing the balance with trials methodology as well as promoting a strategy for ensuring better capture and use of data from routine practice; that is, addressing the colander effect (Kazdin, 2008). The combination of large data sets and multi-level modeling to reflect the hierarchical structure of such data has reprivileged practitioners in demonstrating their impact with diverse client populations, such as REM clients and clients with a mild-to-moderate level of symptoms. PBE studies have also generated evidence for the effectiveness of clinics (single and multiples) varying across a rich diversity of theoretical orientations, specializations of care, and locations across multiple regions. Yet, studies involving large number of clinics have also identified a robust clinic effect: many clinics are indeed effective, but some more so than others. In addition to who the client sees and where they are seen, studies on neighborhood effects have shown that where they live matters. These factors are hardly suitable for RCT trials but they do explain meaningful parts of outcome variance. In addition, data collected in routine clinical practice can be used to address treatment delivery issues that have not been frequently investigated by, or that are not amenable to, trials methodology. For example, identifying those clients who are more likely to return to therapy can help clinicians and administrators managed services utilization. While most trials focus on one episode of therapy, a substantial number of clients come back in the setting where they were seen to receive additional treatments.

Frequently based on large amounts of data with a wide range of client populations, PBE studies have also demonstrated a unique ability to identify distinct profiles of distress and risk that are predictive of treatment course and response.

Furthermore, studies reviewed in this chapter have also shown that therapist effects are related to practitioners' abilities to retain patients rather than dropping out, as well as to keep them engaged in treatment, which may in turn be more crucial than differences between treatment orientations for those patients completing treatment. Also based on multilevel modeling methods, as well as other sophisticated statistical analyses, some PBE studies on the process of change have helped the field get closer to establishing the causal effect of the alliance on therapeutic change. Other studies have revealed the complex and clinically helpful nature of therapist and client emotional experiences, while still others have suggested that some types of interventions can have unexpected positive or negative impacts – and that such impacts may depend on the theoretical orientation of the therapists, of their supervisors, as well as the relational context within which they are being implemented.

Taken as a whole, these examples indicate that PBE studies are increasingly able to capture and analyze data that reflect the complex structure and processes involved in delivering psychological therapies in the real world. This evidence base from routine clinical practice needs to be considered in conjunction with RCT evidence by bodies informing national policies to realize the full potential from the chiasmus of evidence-based practice and practice-based evidence.

Recommendations for Future Research

More issues remain to be investigated, and further scientific, as well as clinical, advances are likely to be achieved with increased utilization of a diversity of research methods. Among the numerous recommendations that can be made for future research, a few appear particularly worthy of attention. First, practice-oriented collaborators might be encouraged to conduct more studies exploring the interaction of participant (i.e., client and therapist) characteristics, relationship variables (e.g., alliance), and technical factors (common to several forms of psychological therapy or unique to particular approaches). Further examination of the moderating and mediating roles that some of these elements may have on treatment outcome could well capture intricate details of the change processes in applied settings. Second, and complementing these advanced quantitative analyses, we would also suggest that more emphasis be given to extensive qualitative analyses of significant events or episodes during therapy.

As can be seen in other chapters of this *Handbook*, similar recommendations for future investigations have been made toward research conducted outside PBE. Such convergence should be viewed as a warning sign of a possible false dichotomy between traditional (i.e., evidence-based) and practice-oriented research paradigms. Not only do these lines of research share important goals – including, as mentioned above, the quest to

better understand and improve psychological therapies – but they can also focus on similar issues and use similar research methods, including randomized clinical trials (e.g., Callahan et al., 2014; Zilcha-Mano & Errazuriz, 2015).

As mentioned early in the chapter, some PBE studies are designed and conducted by clinicians while others are based on an active collaboration between researchers and clinicians in different aspects of research. By having practitioners involved in deciding what to investigate and how to do so, such studies can provide practitioners with an active voice in "setting the research agenda" (Zarin et al., 1997) and a vehicle for shaping the empirical evidence upon which practice could be based. Recognizing the importance and value of the clinician's voice means that the recommendations for future research mentioned above should be viewed as tentative suggestions. Yet it is important to recognize that numerous PBE studies (such as those based on IAPT datasets) use routinely collected data but are driven by researchers, with little or no input from clinicians. What is shared by these different facets of PBE, however, is the investigation of psychosocial therapy as it is being conducted in routine clinical practice.

In terms of future directions, we believe that two issues are more important than what topics need to be investigated. The first one is: What are the characteristics that define optimal PBE studies? We believe that it is time to delineate criteria of clinical relevance and scientific rigor, both to assess the quality of PBE studies and to inform the design and conduct of future studies. As a step toward the construction of a quality scale to serve these dual purposes, we are proposing a list of characteristics related to clinical helpfulness, feasibility, methodological, and statistical sophistication (see Table 6.2).

TABLE 6.2 Characteristics of Higher-Quality Practice-Oriented Studies

(A) Clinical Helpfulness

The study provides evidence of, and/or helpful information for improving the:
- impact of therapy (e.g., outcome, retention, engagement, sudden gains, reduction of deterioration)
- utilization of services
- assessment and/or case formulation, and/or treatment plan
- implementation of interventions
- establishment and development of therapeutic relationship, and/or repair of relationship problems

The study provides information to better understand the:
- effect of psychotherapy
- process of therapy
- client and/or therapist characteristics
- contextual variables impacting psychotherapy

(Continued)

TABLE 6.2   (CONTINUED)

The information provided by the study is available and actionable as the data is being collected.

(B) Feasibility
- The study does not impose drastic or substantial changes in routine clinical practice.
- The study requires minimum burden in terms of time and/or additional tasks to routine clinical practice.
- The research tasks are easily or seamlessly integrated into the clinical care.
- The research tasks are retainable as part of clinical care, even when the study is completed.

(C) Methodological and Statistical Sophistication
- The study involves a large sample of clients.
- The study involves a large sample of therapists.
- The study involves a large number of sites.
- The study involves repeated assessments of key constructs, outcome, and/or process.
- The study relies on statistical analyses to account for the nesting of the data at multiple levels, including client, therapist, center.
- The study uses within and between clients (and/or therapists) analyses.
- The study investigates moderator variables.
- The study investigates mediator variables.
- If investigating the effects of therapist, the study involves large number of therapists and large number of clients seen by each therapist.
- If investigating the effects of center, the study involves large number of centers, large number of therapists per center, and large number of clients seen by each therapist.
- If investigating the effects of therapy, the studies assess both the magnitude and the rate of change.
- If investigating the effects of therapy, the study uses methodological designs that increase internal validity of findings (e.g., randomization in clinically valid conditions; cohort design).
- If investigating the process of change, the study uses statistical or methodological designs that increase internal validity or decrease the impact of confounding factors on cause and effects relationship (e.g., assessing process and outcome, by measuring outcome change between time of assessment of a process variable and end of treatment, while controlling for change in outcome before assessment of the process variable).
- If investigating the process of change, the study allows for examination of convergence and/or complementary of client and therapist experience of process and outcome.

There is a second crucial issue regarding future directions: What can be done to generate more PBE studies and to foster their impact on the field? On this, we can only provide a glimpse of ideals that could be pursued. On a pragmatic level, it would be beneficial to foster the following initiatives:

1. *Embed practice-oriented research during training.* This could be facilitated by implementing repeated measurements and the use of feedback within clinical training and supervision (see Chapters 1, 4, and 5), as well as by providing opportunities for students to do research that is not only clinically relevant but that also interfaces with their clinical experiences.
2. *"Ask and tell" by surveying clinicians about what they want to know and what kind of study they would like to build and implement with others.* Then publish the results of these surveys to inform and stimulate the field into action. As described above, this has recently been implemented within the context of North American PRNs (Taska et al., 2015, Youn et al., 2019). Assessment of clinicians' knowledge priorities, however, should be expended and regularly repeated – just as recommendations for future research are frequently published by and for academic researchers.
3. *Encourage clinicians to conduct studies in their own work environment.* As shown in this chapter, a large number of studies can now serve as examples. There are also detailed guidelines for developing and maintaining a research program in a variety of settings, including private practice (Koerner & Castonguay, 2015), residential treatment (Adelman et al., 2015), community centers (Garland & Brookman-Frazer, 2015), practice and training clinics (Fernández-Alvarez et al., 2015), university counseling centers (McAleavey et al., 2015), and hospitals (Drill et al. 2019).
4. *Work locally but collaborate globally.* Being engaged in scientific activities can be more rewarding, process and outcome wise, when it is carried out in connection with others. For example, the creation of networks between smaller groups of clinicians and researchers collecting data on the same variables at different sites can enrich scientific projects, both in terms of diversity of expertise and sample sizes.
5. *Design studies that can lead to actionable and retainable findings.* PBE findings can even be immediately relevant to the conduct of therapy, as when the data collected simultaneously serve both research and clinical purposes – thereby seamlessly integrating or confounding science and practice.
6. *Close clinical and empirical loops.* This can be done by (a) using clinical practice to collect data; (b) changing administrative or therapeutic procedures based on the results of this data collection; and (c) testing the impact of such changes on the provision of care delivery in the clinical practice where the data have been collected.
7. *Use data that are already available – that is, archived or secondary data sets.* Many studies can be carried out by taking advantage of archival data open to researchers.

8. *Make the research for and by clinicians count.* There is a robust argument to be made to funders and policy makers to ensure that the evidence derived from practice-oriented research contributes in equal measure to the development of national, local, and professional guidelines. Methodologists within the wider discipline of public health have argued, "if the health professions and their sponsors want more widespread and consistent evidence-based practice, they will need to find ways to generate more practice-based evidence that explicitly addresses external validity and local realities" (Green & Glasgow, 2006, p. 128). We would also argue that this is a two-way street. Although it is clear that our understanding and conduct of psychological can be improved by the scientific contributions of PBE studies, clinicians are more likely to engage in designing, implementing, and disseminating studies if there is clear evidence that the merit and impact of these studies will be fairly considered and duly recognized by scholars, researchers, and policy makers.

ABBREVIATIONS

APA	American Psychological Association
BMI	body mass index
BPD	borderline personality disorder
CBT	cognitive behavioral therapy
CCAPS	Counseling Center Assessment of Psychological Symptoms
CCMH	Center for Collegiate Mental Health
DBP	disruptive behavior problems
DH	day hospital
ESTs	empirically supported treatments
IAPT:	Improving Access to Psychological Therapies
IIP	Inventory of Interpersonal Problems
NICE	National Institute of Health and Care Excellence
OQ	outcome questionnaire
PBE	practice-based evidence
POR	practice-oriented research
PRAC:	Practice and Research: Advance and Collaboration
PRNs	practice research networks
PWPs	psychological well-being practitioners
RCSI	reliable and clinically significant improvement
RCTs	randomized controlled trials
REM	racial/ethnic minority
SCL-90-R	Symptom Checklist-90-Revised
TDCRP	Treatment of Depression Collaborative Research Program
UK	United Kingdom
US	United States

REFERENCES

Adelman, R. W., Castonguay, L. G., Kraus, D. R., & Zack, S. E. (2015). Conducting research and collaborating with researchers: The experience of clinicians in a residential treatment center. *Psychotherapy Research*, *25*(1), 108–120. https://doi.org/10.1080/10503307.2014.935520

Ali, S., Littlewood, E., McMillan, D., Delgadillo, J., Miranda, A., Croudace, T., & Gilbody, S. (2014). Heterogeneity in patient-reported outcomes following low-intensity mental health interventions: A multilevel analysis. *PLoS One*, *9*(9), 1–13. https://doi.org/10.1371/journal.pone.0099658

Al-Jabari, R., Murrell, A. R., Callahan, J. L., Cox, R. J., & Lester, E. G. (2019). Do distress level and waitlists impact termination in a training clinic? *Training and Education in Professional Psychology*, *13*(2), 127–137. https://doi.org/10.1037/tep0000223

Atzil-Slonim, D., Bar-Kalifa, E., Fisher, H., Lazarus, G., Hasson-Ohayon, I., Lutz, W., Rubel, J., & Rafaeli, E. (2019). Therapists' empathic accuracy toward their clients' emotions. *Journal of Consulting and Clinical Psychology*, *87*(1), 33–45. https://doi.org/10.1037/ccp0000354

Atzil-Slonim, D., Bar-Kalifa, E., Fisher, H., Peri, T., Lutz, W., Rubel, J., & Rafaeli, E. (2018). Emotional congruence between clients and therapists and its effect on treatment outcome. *Journal of Counseling Psychology*, *65*(1), 51–64. https://doi.org/10.1037/cou0000250

Atzil-Slonim, D., Bar-Kalifa, E., Rafaeli, E., Lutz, W., Rubel, J., Schiefele, A. K., & Peri, T. (2015). Therapeutic bond judgments: Congruence and incongruence. *Journal of Consulting and Clinical Psychology*, *83*(4), 773–784. https://doi.org/10.1037/ccp0000015

Baker, T.B., McFall, R. M., & Shoham, V. (2009). Current status and future prospects of clinical psychology: Towards a scientifically principled approach to mental and behavioral health care. *Psychological Science in the Public Interest*, *9*(2), 67–103. https://doi.org/10.1111/j.1539-6053.2009.01036.x

Barkham, M., Hardy, G.E., & Mellor-Clark, J. (Eds.). (2010). *Developing and delivering practice-based evidence. A guide for the psychological therapies.* Wiley-Blackwell.

Barkham, M., & Margison, F. (2007). Practice-based evidence as a complement to evidence-based practice: From dichotomy to chiasmus. In C. Freeman & M. Power (Eds.), *Handbook of evidence-based psychotherapies: A guide for research and practice* (pp. 443–476). John Wiley & Sons.

Beck, J.G., Castonguay, L. G., Chronis-Tuscano, A., Klonsky, E. D., McGinn, L. K., & Youngstrom, E. A. (2014). Principles for training in evidence based psychology: Recommendations for the graduate curricula in clinical psychology. *Clinical Psychology: Science and Practice*, *21*(4), 410–424. https://doi.org/10.1111/cpsp.12079

Beintner, I., Hütter, K., Gramatke, K., & Jacobi, C. (2020). Combining day treatment and outpatient treatment for eating disorders: Findings from a naturalistic setting. *Eating and Weight Disorders-Studies on Anorexia, Bulimia and Obesity*, *25*(2), 519–530. https://doi.org/10.1007/s40519-019-00643-6

Bhati, K. S. (2014). Effect of client-therapist gender match on the therapeutic relationship: An exploratory analysis. *Psychological Reports*, *115*(2), 565–583.

Boswell, J. F., Cain, N. M., Oswald, J. M., McAleavey, A. A., & Adelman, R. (2017). Interpersonal pathoplasticity and trajectories of change in routine adolescent and young adult residential substance abuse treatment. *Journal of Consulting and Clinical Psychology*, *85*(7), 676–688. https://doi.org/10.1037/ccp0000219

Budge, S. L., Owen, J. J., Kopta, S. M., Minami, T., Hanson, M. R., & Hirsch, G. (2013). Differences among trainees in client outcomes associated with the phase model of change. *Psychotherapy*, *50*(2), 150–157. httsp://doi.org/10.1037/a0029565

Burlingame, G. M., Gleave, R., Erekson, D., Nelson, P. L., Olsen, J., Thayer, S., & Beecher, M. (2016). Differential effectiveness of group, individual, and conjoint treatments: An archival analysis of OQ-45 change trajectories. *Psychotherapy Research*, *26*(5), 556–572. https://doi.org/10.1080/10503307.2015.1044583

Burns, P., Kellett, S., & Donohoe, G. (2016). "Stress Control" as a large group psychoeducational intervention at Step 2 of IAPT services: Acceptability of the approach and moderators of effectiveness. *Behavioural and Cognitive Psychotherapy*, *44*(4), 431–443. https://doi.org/10.1017/S1352465815000491

Callahan, J. L., Gustafson, S. A., Misner, J. B., Paprocki, C. M., Sauer, E. M., Saules, K. K., Schwartz, J.L., Swift, J.K., Whiteside, D.M., Wierda, K.E.,

& Wise, E. H. (2014). Introducing the association of psychology training clinics' collaborative research network: A study on client expectancies. *Training and Education in Professional Psychology*, 8(2), 95–104. https://doi .org/10.1037/tep0000047

Carney, D. M., Castonguay, L. G., Janis, R. A., Scofield, B. E., Hayes, J. A., Locke, B. D. (in press). Center effects: Organizational variables as predictors of psychotherapy outcomes. *The Counseling Psychologist*.

Castonguay, L. G., Barkham, M., Lutz, W., & McAleavey, A.A. (2013). Practice-oriented research: Approaches and applications. In M. J. Lambert (Ed.), *Bergin and Garfield's handbook of psychotherapy and behavior change* (pp. 85–133). John Wiley & Sons.

Castonguay, L. G., Constantino, M. J., & Beutler, L.E. (Eds) (2019). *Principles of change: How psychotherapists implement research in practice*. Oxford University Press.

Castonguay, L. G., & Muran, C. (2015). Fostering collaboration between researchers and clinicians through building practice-oriented research: An introduction. *Psychotherapy Research*, 25(1), 1–5. https://doi.org/10 .1080/10503307.2014.966348

Castonguay, L. G., Pincus, A. L., & McAleavey, A. A. (2015). Practice research network in a psychology training clinic: Building an infrastructure to foster early attachment to the scientific-practitioner model. *Psychotherapy Research*, 25(1), 52–66. https://doi.org/10.1080/10503307.2013.856045

Castonguay, L. G., Youn, S., Xiao, H., Muran, J. C., & Barber, J. P. (2015). Building clinicians-researchers partnerships: Lessons from diverse natural settings and practice-oriented initiatives. *Psychotherapy Research*, 25(1), 166–184. https://doi.org/10.1080/10503307.2014.973923

Chui, H., Hill, C. E., Kline, K., Kuo, P., & Mohr, J. J. (2016). Are you in the mood? Therapist affect and psychotherapy process. *Journal of Counseling Psychology*, 63(4), 405–418. https://doi.org/10.1037/cou0000155

Clement, P. (2013). Practice-based evidence: 45 years of psychotherapy's effectiveness in a private practice. *American Journal of Psychotherapy*, 67(1), 23–46. https://doi.org/10.1176/appi.psychotherapy.2013.67.1.23

Craner, J. R., Sawchuk, C. N., Mack, J. D., & LeRoy, M. A. (2017). Development and implementation of a psychotherapy tracking database in primary care. *Families, Systems, & Health*, 35(2), 207–216. https://doi.org/10.1037/ fsh0000265

Crits-Christoph, P., Gallop, R., Diehl, C. K., Yin, S., & Gibbons, M. B. C. (2017). Methods for incorporating patient preferences for treatments of depression in community mental health settings. *Administration and Policy in Mental Health and Mental Health Services Research*, 44(5), 735–746. https://doi.org/10.1007/s10488-016-0746-1

DeFife, J., Drill, R., Beinashowitz, J., Ballantyne, L., Plant, D., Smith-Hansen, L., Teran, V., Werner-Larsen, L., Westerling III, T., Yang, Y., Davila, M., & Nakash, O. (2015). Practice-based psychotherapy research in a public health setting: Obstacles and opportunities. *Journal of Psychotherapy Integration*, 25(4), 299–312. https://doi.org/10.1037/a0039564

Delgadillo, J., Asaria, M., Ali, S., & Gilbody, S. (2016). On poverty, politics and psychology: The socioeconomic gradient of mental healthcare utilisation and outcomes. *The British Journal of Psychiatry*, 209(5), 429–430. https:// doi.org/10.1192/bjp.bp.115.171017

Delgadillo, J., Dawson, A., Gilbody, S., & Böhnke, J. R. (2017). Impact of long-term medical conditions on the outcomes of psychological therapy for depression and anxiety. *The British Journal of Psychiatry*, 210(1), 47–53. https://doi.org/10.1192/bjp.bp.116.189027

Delgadillo, J., Kellett, S., Ali, S., McMillan, D., Barkham, M., Saxon, D., Donohoe, G., Stonebank, H., Mullaney, S., Eschoe, P., Thwaites, R., & Lucock, M. (2016). A multi-service practice research network study of large group psychoeducational cognitive behavioural therapy. *Behaviour Research and Therapy*, 87, 155–161. https://doi.org/10.1016/ j.brat.2016.09.010

Delgadillo, J., Moreea, O., & Lutz, W. (2016). Different people respond differently to therapy: A demonstration using patient profiling and risk stratification. *Behaviour Research and Therapy*, 79, 15–22. https://doi .org/10.1016/j.brat.2016.02.003

De la Parra, G., Gómez-Barris, E., Zúñiga, A. K., Dagnino, P., & Valdés, C. (2018). From the "couch" to the outpatient clinic: A model of psychotherapy for institutions. Learning from (empirical) experience. *Revista Argentina de Clínica Psicológica*, 27(2), 182–202. https://doi .org/10.24205/03276716.2018.1057

Drill, R., Drinkwater, R., Ernst, J., Gill, A., Hunnicutt, P., McIntyre, S., Potter, C. M., Richardson, H., & Beinashowitz, J. (2019). The vicissitudes of

conducting psychodynamic research in a naturalistic setting. *Psychotherapy*, 56(1), 126–133. https://doi.org/10.1037/pst0000181

Dyason, K. M., Shanley, D. C., Hawkins, E., Morrissey, S. A., & Lambert, M. J. (2019). A systematic review of research in psychology training clinics: How far have we come? *Training and Education in Professional Psychology*, 13(1), 4–20. https://doi.org/10.1037/tep0000196

Erekson, D. M., Horner, J., & Lambert, M. J. (2018). Different lens or different picture? Comparing methods of defining dramatic change in psychotherapy. *Psychotherapy Research*, 28(5), 750–760. https://doi.org/10.1080/ 10503307.2016.1247217

Erekson, D. M., Janis, R., Bailey, R. J., Cattani, K., & Pedersen, T. R. (2017). A longitudinal investigation of the impact of psychotherapist training: Does training improve client outcomes? *Journal of Counseling Psychology*, 64(5), 514–524. https://doi.org/10.1037/cou0000252

Falkenström, F. (2010). Does psychotherapy for young adults in routine practice show similar results as therapy in randomized clinical trials? *Psychotherapy Research*, 20(2), 181–192. https://doi.org/10.1080/10503300903170954

Falkenström, F., Granström, F., & Holmqvist, R. (2013). Therapeutic alliance predicts symptomatic improvement session by session. *Journal of Counseling Psychology*, 60(3), 317–328. https://doi.org/10.1037/a0032258

Falkenström, F., Kuria, M., Othieno, C., & Kumar, M. (2019). Working alliance predicts symptomatic improvement in public hospital–delivered psychotherapy in Nairobi, Kenya. *Journal of Consulting and Clinical Psychology*, 87(1), 46–55. https://doi.org/10.1037/ccp0000363

Fernández-Alvarez, H., & Castonguay, L. G. (2018). Investigación orientada por la práctica. Avances en colaboraciones entre clínicos e investigadores. Introducción. *Revista Argentina de Clínica Psicológica*, 27(2), 107–110. https:// doi.org/10.24205/03276716.2018.1069

Fernández-Alvarez, H., Gómez, B., & Garcia, F. (2015). Bridging the gap between research and practice in a clinical and training network: Aigle's Program. *Psychotherapy Research*, 25(1), 84–94. https://doi.org/10.1080/10 503307.2013.856047

Firth, N., Barkham, M., Kellett, S., & Saxon, D. (2015). Therapist effects and moderators of effectiveness and efficiency in psychological wellbeing practitioners: A multilevel modelling analysis. *Behaviour Research and Therapy*, 69, 54–62. https://doi.org/10.1016/j.brat.2015.04.001

Firth, N., Saxon, D., Stiles, W. B., & Barkham, M. (2019). Therapist and clinic effects in psychotherapy: A three-level model of outcome variability. *Journal of Consulting and Clinical Psychology*, 87(4), 345–356. https://doi .org/10.1037/ccp0000388

Fisher, H., Atzil-Slonim, D., Bar-Kalifa, E., Rafaeli, E., & Peri, T. (2016). Emotional experience and alliance contribute to therapeutic change in psychodynamic therapy. *Psychotherapy*, 53(1), 105–116. https://doi .org/10.1037/pst0000041

Garland, A. F., & Brookman-Frazee, L. (2015). Therapists and researchers: Advancing collaboration. *Psychotherapy Research*, 25(1), 95–107. https:// doi.org/10.1080/10503307.2013.838655

Garland, A. F., Brookman-Frazee, L., Hurlburt, M. S., Accurso, E. C., Zoffness, R. J., Haine-Schlagel, R., & Ganger, W. (2010). Mental health care for children with disruptive behavior problems: A view inside therapists' offices. *Psychiatric Services*, 61(8), 788–795. https://doi.org/10.1176/ ps.2010.61.8.788

Garland, A. F., Plemmons, D., & Koontz, L. (2006). Research–practice partnership in mental health: Lessons from participants. *Administration and Policy in Mental Health and Mental Health Services Research*, 33(5), 517–528. https://doi.org/10.1007/s10488-006-0062-2

Goldfried, M. R. (1984). Training the clinician as scientist-professional. *Professional Psychology: Research and Practice*, 15(4), 477–481. https://doi. org/10.1037/0735-7028.15.4.477

Gómez Penedo, J. M., Zilcha-Mano, S., & Roussos, A. (2019). Interpersonal profiles in emotional disorders predict the importance of alliance negotiation for early treatment outcome. *Journal of Consulting and Clinical Psychology*, 87(7), 617–628. https://doi.org/10.1037/ccp0000417

Green, H., Barkham, M., Kellett, S., & Saxon, D. (2014). Therapist effects and IAPT Psychological Wellbeing Practitioners (PWPs): A multilevel modelling and mixed methods analysis. *Behaviour Research and Therapy*, 63, 43–54. https://doi.org/10.1016/j.brat.2014.08.009

Green, L. W., & Glasgow, R. E. (2006). Evaluating the relevance, generalizability, and applicability of research: Issues in external validation and translational methodology. *Evaluation & the Health Professions*, 29, 126–153. https://doi.org/10.1177/0163278705284445

Gyani, A., Shafran, R., Layard, R., & Clark, D. M. (2013). Enhancing recovery rates: Lessons from year one of IAPT. *Behaviour Research and Therapy*, *51*(9), 597–606. https://doi.org/10.1016/j.brat.2013.06.004

Haine-Schlagel, R., Fettes, D. L., Garcia, A. R., Brookman-Frazee, L., & Garland, A. F. (2014). Consistency with evidence-based treatments and perceived effectiveness of children's community-based care. *Community Mental Health Journal*, *50*(2), 158–163. https://doi.org/10.1007/10597-012-9583-1

Hansen, N. B., & Lambert, M. J. (2003). An evaluation of the dose–response relationship in naturalistic treatment settings using survival analysis. *Mental Health Services Research*, *5*(1), 1–12. https://doi.org/10.1023/A:1021751307358

Hansen, N. B., Lambert, M. J., & Forman, E. M. (2002). The psychotherapy dose-response effect and its implications for treatment delivery services. *Clinical Psychology: Science and Practice*, *9*(3), 329–343. https://doi.org/10.1093/clipsy.9.3.329

Hayes, J. A., McAleavey, A. A., Castonguay, L. G., & Locke, B. D. (2016). Psychotherapists' outcomes with White and racial/ethnic minority clients: First, the good news. *Journal of Counseling Psychology*, *63*(3), 261–268. https://doi.org/10.1037/cou0000098

Hayes, J. A., Owen, J., & Bieschke, K. J. (2015). Therapist differences in symptom change with racial/ethnic minority clients. *Psychotherapy*, *52*(3), 308–314. https://doi.org/10.1037/a0037957

Hill, C. E., Baumann, E., Shafran, N., Gupta, S., Morrison, A., Rojas, A. E. P., Perez, A. E., Spangler, P. T., Griffin, S., Pappa, L., & Gelso, C. J. (2015). Is training effective? A study of counseling psychology doctoral trainees in a psychodynamic/interpersonal training clinic. *Journal of Counseling Psychology*, *62*(2), 184–201. http://dx.doi.org/10.1037/cou0000053

Holmqvist, R., Ström, T., & Foldemo, A. (2014). The effects of psychological treatment in primary care in Sweden—A practice-based study. *Nordic Journal of Psychiatry*, *68*(3), 204–212. https://doi.org/10.3109/08039488.2013.797023

Horowitz, L. M., Alden, L. E., Wiggins, J. S., & Pincus, A. L. (2000). *Inventory of Interpersonal Problems: Manual*. The Psychological Corporation.

Huet, V., Springham, N., & Evans, C. (2014). The art therapy practice research network: Hurdles, pitfalls and achievements. *Counselling and Psychotherapy Research*, *14*(3), 174–180. https://doi.org/10.1080/14733145.2014.929416

Jankowski, P. J., Sandage, S. J., Bell, C. A., Rupert, D., Bronstein, M., & Stavros, G. S. (2019). Latent trajectories of change for clients at a psychodynamic training clinic. *Journal of Clinical Psychology*, *75*(7), 1147–1168. https://doi.org/10.1002/jclp.22769

Jolley, S., Garety, P., Peters, E., Fornells-Ambrojo, M., Onwumere, J., Harris, V., Brabban, A., & Johns, L. (2015). Opportunities and challenges in Improving Access to Psychological Therapies for people with Severe Mental Illness (IAPT-SMI): Evaluating the first operational year of the South London and Maudsley (SLaM) demonstration site for psychosis. *Behaviour Research and Therapy*, *64*, 24–30. https://doi.org/10.1016/j.brat.2014.11.006

Kazdin, A. E. (2008). Evidence-based treatment and practice: New opportunities to bridge clinical research and practice, enhance the knowledge base, and improve patient care. *American Psychologist*, *63*(3), 146–159. https://doi.org/10.1037/0003-066X.63.3.146

Kenny, D. A., & Cook, W. (1999). Partner effects in relationship research: Conceptual issues, analytic difficulties, and illustrations. *Personal Relationships*, *6*(4), 433–448. https://doi.org/10.1111/j.1475-6811.1999.tb00202.x

Kilcullen, J. R., Castonguay, L. G., Janis, R. A., Hallquist, M. N., Hayes, J. A., & Locke, B. D. (2020). Predicting future courses of psychotherapy within a grouped LASSO framework. *Psychotherapy Research*, *31*(1), 1–15. https://doi.org/10.1080/10503307.2020.1762948

Kivlighan, D. M., Jr., Hill, C. E., Gelso, C. J., & Baumann, E. (2016). Working alliance, real relationship, session quality, and client improvement in psychodynamic psychotherapy: A longitudinal actor partner interdependence model. *Journal of Counseling Psychology*, *63*(2), 149–161. https://doi.org/10.1037/cou0000134

Kivlighan, D. M., Jr., Hill, C. E., Ross, K., Kline, K., Furhmann, A., & Sauber, E. (2019). Testing a mediation model of psychotherapy process and outcome in psychodynamic psychotherapy: Previous client distress, psychodynamic techniques, dyadic working alliance, and current client distress.

Psychotherapy Research, *29*(5), 581–593. https://doi.org/10.1080/10503307.2017.1420923

Kivlighan, D. M., III, Hooley, I. W., Bruno, M. G., Ethington, L. L., Keeton, P. M., & Schreier, B. A. (2019). Examining therapist effects in relation to clients' race-ethnicity and gender: An intersectionality approach. *Journal of Counseling Psychology*, *66*(1), 122–129. https://doi.org/10.1037/cou0000316

Kivlighan, D. M., III, Jung, A. K., Berkowitz, A. B., Hammer, J. H., & Collins, N. M. (2019). 'To show or No-show'? Therapist racial-ethnic disparities in clients' nonattendance in therapy. *Journal of College Student Psychotherapy*, *33*(1), 1–13. https://doi.org/10.1080/87568225.2018.1424597

Koerner, K., & Castonguay, L. G. (2015). Practice-oriented research: What it takes to do collaborative research in private practice. *Psychotherapy Research*, *25*(1), 67–83. https://doi.org/10.1080/10503307.2014.939119

Kraus, D. R., Bentley, J. H., Alexander, P. C., Boswell, J. F., Constantino, M. J., Baxter, E. E., & Castonguay, L. G. (2016). Predicting therapist effectiveness from their own practice-based evidence. *Journal of Consulting and Clinical Psychology*, *84*(6), 473–483. https://doi.org/10.1037/ccp0000083

Krause, M., Venegas, F., Dagnino, P., & Altimir, C. (2018). Therapist's subjective experience during significant segments of psychotherapy/La Experiencia subjetiva del terapeuta durante segmentos significativos en psicoterapia. Revista *Argentina de Clínica Psicológica*, *27*(2), 250–273. https://doi.org/10.24205/03276716.2018.1065

Kumar, M., Kuria, M. W., Othieno, C. J., & Falkenström, F. (2018). Improving psychotherapies offered in public hospitals in Nairobi, Kenya: Extending practice-based research model for LMICs. *International Journal of Mental Health Systems*, *12*(1), 76–86. https://doi.org/10.1186/s13033-018-0254-7

Lambert, M. J., Burlingame, G. M., Umphress, V., Hansen, N., Vermeersch, D. A., Clouse, G. C., & Yanchar, S. C. (1996). The reliability and validity of the outcome questionnaire. *Clinical Psychology & Psychotherapy*, *3*(4), 249–258. https://doi.org/10.1002/(SICI)1099-0879(199612)3:4<249::AID-CPP106>3.0.CO;2-S

Laporte, L., Paris, J., Bergevin, T., Fraser, R., & Cardin, J. F. (2018). Clinical outcomes of a stepped care program for borderline personality disorder. *Personality and Mental Health*, *12*(3), 252–264. https://doi.org/10.1002/pmh.1421

Larrison, C. R., & Schoppelrey, S. L. (2011). Therapist effects on disparities experienced by minorities receiving services for mental illness. *Research on Social Work Practice*, *21*(6), 727–736. https://doi.org/10.1177/1049731511410989

Larrison, C. R., Schoppelrey, S. L., Hack-Ritzo, S., & Korr, W. S. (2011). Clinician factors related to outcome differences between black and white patients at CMHCs. *Psychiatric Services*, *62*(5), 525–531. https://ps.psychiatryonline.org/doi/full/10.1176/ps.62.5.pss6205_0525

Larsson, M. H., Falkenström, F., Andersson, G., & Holmqvist, R. (2018). Alliance ruptures and repairs in psychotherapy in primary care. *Psychotherapy Research*, *28*(1), 123–136. https://doi.org/10.1080/10503307.2016.1174345

Lazarus, A. A., & Davison, G. C. (1971). Clinical innovation in research and practice. In A. E. Bergin, & S. L. Garfield (Eds.), *Handbook of psychotherapy and behavior change* (pp. 196–213). John Wiley & Sons.

Lockard, A. J., Hayes, J. A., Graceffo, J. M., & Locke, B. D. (2013). Effective counseling for racial/ethnic minority clients: Examining changes using a practice research network. *Journal of College Counseling*, *16*(3), 243–257. https://doi.org/10.1002/j.2161-1882.2013.00040.x

Lockard, A. J., Hayes, J. A., Locke, B. D., Bieschke, K. J., & Castonguay, L. G. (2019). Helping those who help themselves: Does counseling enhance retention? *Journal of Counseling & Development*, *97*(2), 128–139. https://doi.org/10.1002/jcad.12244

Locke, B. D., Buzolitz, J. S., Lei, P., Boswell, J. F., McAleavey, A. A., Sevig, T. D., Dowis, J. D., & Hayes, J. A. (2011). Development of the counseling center assessment of psychological symptoms-62 (CCAPS-62). *Journal of Counseling Psychology*, *58*(1), 97–109. https://doi.org/10.1037/a0021282

Locke, B. D., McAleavey, A. A., Zhao, Y., Lei, P., Hayes, J. A., Castonguay, L. G., Li, H., Tate, R., & Lin, Y. (2012). Development and initial validation of the counseling center assessment of psychological symptoms-34. *Measurement and Evaluation in Counseling and Development*, *45*(3), 151–169. https://doi.org/10.1177/0748175611432642

Lutz, W., Schiefele, A. K., Wucherpfennig, F., Rubel, J., & Stulz, N. (2016). Clinical effectiveness of cognitive behavioral therapy for depression in routine care: A propensity score based comparison between randomized controlled trials and clinical practice. *Journal of Affective Disorders, 189,* 150–158. https://doi.org/10.1016/j.jad.2015.08.072

Markin, R. D., Kivlighan, D. M., Jr., Gelso, C. J., Hummel, A. M., & Spiegel, E. B. (2014). Clients' and therapists' real relationship and session quality in brief therapy: An actor partner interdependence analysis. *Psychotherapy, 51*(3), 413–423. https://doi.org/10.1037/a0036069

Marmarosh, C. L., & Kivlighan, D. M. Jr. (2012). Relationships among client and counselor agreement about the working alliance, session evaluations, and change in client symptoms using response surface analysis. *Journal of Counseling Psychology, 59*(3), 352–367. https://doi.org/10.1037/a0028907

Marmarosh, C. L., Kivlighan, D. M., Jr., Bieri, K., LaFauci Schutt, J. M., Barone, C., & Choi, J. (2014). The insecure psychotherapy base: Using client and therapist attachment styles to understand the early alliance. *Psychotherapy, 51*(3), 404–412. https://doi.org/10.1037/a0031989

McAleavey, A. A., & Castonguay, L. G. (2014). Insight as a common and specific impact of psychotherapy: Therapist-reported exploratory, directive, and common factor interventions. *Psychotherapy, 51*(2), 283–294. https://doi.org/10.1037/a0032410

McAleavey, A. A., Castonguay, L. G., & Goldfried, M. R. (2014). Clinical experiences in conducting cognitive-behavioral therapy for social phobia. *Behavior Therapy, 45*(1), 21–35. https://doi.org/10.1016/j.beth.2013.09.008

McAleavey, A. A., Castonguay, L. G., & Xiao, H. (2014). Therapist orientation, supervisor match, and therapeutic interventions: Implications for session quality in a psychotherapy training PRN. *Counselling and Psychotherapy Research, 14*(3), 192–200. https://doi.org/10.1080/14733145.2014.929418

McAleavey, A. A., Lockard, A. J., Castonguay, L. G., Hayes, J. A., & Locke, B. D. (2015). Building a practice research network: Obstacles faced and lessons learned at the Center for Collegiate Mental Health. *Psychotherapy Research, 25*(1), 134–151. https://doi.org/10.1080/10503307.2014.883652

McAleavey, A. A., Youn, S., Xiao, H., Castonguay, L. G., Hayes, J. A., & Locke, B. D. (2019). Effectiveness of routine psychotherapy: Method matters. *Psychotherapy Research, 29*(2), 139–156. https://doi.org/10.1080/10503307.2017.1395921

McCarthy, K. S., & Barber, J. P. (2009). The multitheoretical list of therapeutic interventions (MULTI): Initial report. *Psychotherapy Research, 19*(1), 96–113. https://doi.org/10.1080/10503300802524343

McMillen, J. C., Lenze, S. L., Hawley, K. M., & Osbourne, V. A. (2009). Revisiting practice-based research networks as a platform for mental health services research. *Administration and Policy in Mental Health, 36*(5), 308–321. https://doi.org/10.1007/s10488-009-0222-2

Newsom, C., Schut, H., Stroebe, M. S., Wilson, S., Birrell, J., Moerbeek, M., & Eisma, M. C. (2017). Effectiveness of bereavement counselling through a community-based organization: A naturalistic, controlled trial. *Clinical Psychology & Psychotherapy, 24*(6), O1512–O1523. https://doi.org/10.1002/cpp.2113

Nordberg, S. S., Castonguay, L. G., McAleavey, A. A., Locke, B. D., & Hayes, J. A. (2016). Enhancing feedback for clinical use: Creating and evaluating profiles of clients seeking counseling. *Journal of Counseling Psychology, 63*(3), 278–293. https://doi.org/10.1037/cou0000147

Olmsted, M. P., McFarlane, T., Trottier, K., & Rockert, W. (2013). Efficacy and intensity of day hospital treatment for eating disorders. *Psychotherapy Research, 23*(3), 277–286. https://doi.org/10.1080/10503307.2012.721937

Owen, J., Drinane, J., Tao, K. W., Adelson, J. L., Hook, J. N., Davis, D., & Fookune, N. (2017). Racial/ethnic disparities in client unilateral termination: The role of therapists' cultural comfort. *Psychotherapy Research, 27*(1), 102–111. https://doi.org/10.1080/10503307.2015.1078517

Owen, J., Imel, Z., Adelson, J., & Rodolfa, E. (2012). 'No-show': Therapist racial/ethnic disparities in client unilateral termination. *Journal of Counseling Psychology, 59*(2), 314–320. https://doi.org/10.1037/a0027091

Owen, J., Wampold, B. E., Kopta, M., Rousmaniere, T., & Miller, S. D. (2016). As good as it gets? Therapy outcomes of trainees over time. *Journal of Counseling Psychology, 63*(1), 12–19. https://doi.org/10.1037/cou0000112

Paquin, J. (2017). Introduction to a special issue on clinician–researchers: A career engaged in both therapy research and practice. *Counselling Psychology Quarterly, 30*(3), 225–233. https://doi.org/10.1080/09515070.2017.1350141

Parry, G., Castonguay, L. G., Borkovec, T. D., & Wolf, A. W. (2010). Practice research networks and psychological services research in the UK and USA. In M. Barkham, G. E. Hardy, & J. Mellon-Clark (Eds.), *Developing and delivering practice-based evidence: A guide for the psychological therapies* (pp. 311–325). Wiley.

Persons, J. B., & Thomas, C. (2019). Symptom severity at week 4 of cognitive-behavior therapy predicts depression remission. *Behavior Therapy, 50*(4), 791–802. https://doi.org/10.1016/j.beth.2018.12.002

Pybis, J., Saxon, D., Hill, A., & Barkham, M. (2017). The comparative effectiveness and efficiency of cognitive behaviour therapy and generic counselling in the treatment of depression: evidence from the 2nd UK National Audit of psychological therapies. *BMC Psychiatry, 17*(1), 215. https://doi.org/10.1186/s12888-017-1370-7

Rawlins, M. (2008). De testimonio: On the evidence for decisions about the use of therapeutic interventions. *The Lancet, 372*(9656), 2152–2161. https://doi.org/10.1016/S0140-6736(08)61930-3

Richards, P. S., Sanders, P. W., Lea, T., McBride, J. A., & Allen, G. E. K. (2015). Bringing spiritually oriented psychotherapies into the health care mainstream: A call for worldwide collaboration. *Spirituality in Clinical Practice, 2*(3), 169–179. https://doi.org/10.1037/scp0000082

Roseborough, D. J., McLeod, J. T., & Bradshaw, W. H. (2012). Psychodynamic psychotherapy: A quantitative, longitudinal perspective. *Research on Social Work Practice, 22*(1), 54–67. https://doi.org/10.1177/1049731511412790

Rousmaniere, T. G., Swift, J. K., Babins-Wagner, R., Whipple, J. L., & Berzins, S. (2016). Supervisor variance in psychotherapy outcome in routine practice. *Psychotherapy Research, 26*(2), 196–205. https://doi.org/10.1080/10503307.2014.963730

Rubel, J. A., Bar-Kalifa, E., Atzil-Slonim, D., Schmidt, S., & Lutz, W. (2018). Congruence of therapeutic bond perceptions and its relation to treatment outcome: Within-and between-dyad effects. *Journal of Consulting and Clinical Psychology, 86*(4), 341–353. https://doi.org/10.1037/ccp0000280

Rubel, J. A., Rosenbaum, D., & Lutz, W. (2017). Patients' in-session experiences and symptom change: Session-to-session effects on a within-and between-patient level. *Behaviour Research and Therapy, 90,* 58–66. https://doi.org/10.1016/j.brat.2016.12.007

Sales, C. M., Alves, P. C., Evans, C., Elliott, R., & On Behalf of Ipha Group. (2014). The Individualised Patient-Progress System: A decade of international collaborative networking. *Counselling and Psychotherapy Research, 14*(3), 181–191. https://doi.org/10.1080/14733145.2014.929417

Saxon, D., Barkham, M., Foster, A., & Parry, G. (2017). The contribution of therapist effects to patient dropout and deterioration in the psychological therapies. *Clinical Psychology & Psychotherapy, 24*(3), 575–588. https://doi.org/10.1002/cpp.2028

Schnicker, K., Hiller, W., & Legenbauer, T. (2013). Drop-out and treatment outcome of outpatient cognitive–behavioral therapy for anorexia nervosa and bulimia nervosa. *Comprehensive Psychiatry, 54*(7), 812–823. https://doi.org/10.1016/j.comppsych.2013.02.007

Shalom, J. G., Gilboa-Schechtman, E., Atzil-Slonim, D., Bar-Kalifa, E., Hasson-Ohayon, I., Van Oppen, P., van Balkom, A.J.L.M., & Aderka, I. M. (2018). Intraindividual variability in symptoms consistently predicts sudden gains: An examination of three independent datasets. *Journal of Consulting and Clinical Psychology, 86*(11), 892–902. https://doi.org/10.1037/ccp0000344

Steen, S., & Mellor-Clark, J. (2019). Evaluating the efficiency of a collaborative learning network in supporting third sector organizations in the UK. In S. Reddy & A. I. Tavares (Eds.), *Evaluation of Health Programs.* IntechOpen. https://doi.org/10.5772/intechopen.79149

Stiles, W. B., & Snow, J. S. (1984). Dimensions of psychotherapy session impact across sessions and across clients. *British Journal of Clinical Psychology, 23*(1), 59–63. https://doi.org/10.1111/j.2044-8260.1984.tb00627.x

Stricker, G., & Trierweiler, S. J. (1995). The local clinical scientist: A bridge between science and practice. *American Psychologist, 50*(12), 995–1002. https://doi.org/10.1037/0003-066X.50.12.995

Sullivan, H.S. (1953). *The interpersonal theory of psychiatry.* Norton

Swift, J. K., Whipple, J. L., & Sandberg, P. (2012). A prediction of initial appointment attendance and initial outcome expectations. *Psychotherapy, 49*(4), 549–556. https://doi.org/10.1037/a0029441

Tasca, G. A., Sylvestre, J., Balfour, L., Chyurlia, L., Evans, J., Fortin-Langelier, B., Francis, K., Gandhi, J., Huehn, L., Hunsley, J., Joyce, A. S., Kinley, J., Koszycki, D., Leszcz, M., Lybanon-Daigle, V., Mercer, D., Ogrodniczuk, J. S., Presniak, M., Ravitz, P., Ritchie, K., Talbot, J., & Wilson, B. (2015). What clinicians want: Findings from a psychotherapy practice research network survey. *Psychotherapy, 52*(1), 1–11. https://doi.org/10.1037/a0038252

Thurin, J. M., Thurin, M., & Midgley, N. (2012). Does participation in research lead to changes in attitudes among clinicians? Report on a survey of those involved in a French practice research network. *Counselling and Psychotherapy Research, 12*(3), 187–193. https://doi.org/10.1080/14733145.2012.696122

Tickell, A., Ball, S., Bernard, P., Kuyken, W., Marx, R., Pack, S., Strauss, C., Sweeney, T., & Crane, C. (2020). The effectiveness of Mindfulness-Based Cognitive Therapy (MBCT) in real-world healthcare services. *Mindfulness, 11*(2), 279–290. https://doi.org/10.1007/s12671-018-1087-9

Tucker, A. R., Smith, A., & Gass, M. A. (2014). How presenting problems and individual characteristics impact successful treatment outcomes in residential and wilderness treatment programs. *Residential Treatment for Children & Youth, 31*(2), 135–153. https://doi.org/10.1080/0886571X.2014.918446

Turner, H., Marshall, E., Stopa, L., & Waller, G. (2015). Cognitive-behavioural therapy for outpatients with eating disorders: Effectiveness for a transdiagnostic group in a routine clinical setting. *Behaviour Research and Therapy, 68*, 70–75. https://doi.org/10.1016/j.brat.2015.03.001

Vitry, G., Duriez, N., Lartilleux-Suberville, S., Pakrosnis, R., Beau, A., Garcia-Rivera, T., Brosseau, O., Vargas Avalos, P., Bardot, E., & Ray, W. A. (2020). Introducing SYPRENE: An International Practice Research Network for Strategic and Systemic Therapists and Researchers. *Family Process, 59*(4), 1946–1957. https://doi.org/10.1111/famp.12520

Wampold, B. E., Baldwin, S. A., Holtforth, M. G., & Imel, Z. E. (2017). What characterizes effective therapists? In L. G. Castonguay & C. E. Hill (Eds.), *How and why are some therapists better than others: Understanding therapist effects* (pp.37–53). American Psychological Association. https://doi.org/10.1037/0000034-003

Ward, A., Wood, B., & Awal, M. (2013). A naturalistic psychodynamic psychotherapy study: Evaluating outcome with a patient perspective. *British Journal of Psychotherapy, 29*(3), 292–314. https://doi.org/10.1111/bjp.12034

Werbart, A., Levin, L., Andersson, H., & Sandell, R. (2013). Everyday evidence: Outcomes of psychotherapies in Swedish public health services. *Psychotherapy, 50*(1), 119–130. https://doi.org/10.1037/a0031386

West, J. C., Mościcki, E. K., Duffy, F. F., Wilk, J. E., Countis, L., Narrow, W. E., & Regier, D. A. (2015). APIRE Practice Research Network: Accomplishments, challenges, and lessons learned. *Psychotherapy Research, 25*(1), 152–165. https://doi.org/10.1080/10503307.2013.868948

Xiao, H., Carney, D. M., Youn, S. J., Janis, R. B, Castonguay, L. G., Hayes, J. A., & Locke, B. D. (2017). Are we in crisis? National mental health and treatment trends in college counseling centers. *Psychological Services, 14*(4), 407–415. https://doi.org/10.1037/ser0000130

Xiao, H., Castonguay, L. G., Janis, R. A., Youn, S., Hayes, J. A., & Locke, B. D. (2017). Therapist effects on dropout from a college counseling center practice research network. *Journal of Counseling Psychology, 64*(4), 424–431. https://doi.org/10.1037/cou0000208

Xiao, H., Hayes, J. A., Castonguay, L. G., McAleavey, A. A., & Locke, B. D. (2017). Therapist effects and the impacts of therapy nonattendance. *Psychotherapy, 54*(1), 58–65. https://doi.org/10.1037/pst0000103

Youn, S., Xiao, H., McAleavey, A. A., Scofield, B. E., Pedersen, T. R., Castonguay, L. G., Hayes, J. A., & Locke, B. D. (2019). Assessing and investigating clinicians' research interests: Lessons on expanding practices and data collection in a large practice research network. *Psychotherapy, 56*(1), 67–82. https://doi.org/10.1037/pst0000192

Young, C., & Grassmann, H. (2019). Towards a greater understanding of science and research within body psychotherapy. *International Body Psychotherapy Journal, 18*(1), 26–60.

Zack, S. E., Castonguay, L. G., Boswell, J. F., McAleavey, A. A., Adelman, R., Kraus, D. R., & Pate, G. A. (2015). Attachment history as a moderator of the alliance outcome relationship in adolescents. *Psychotherapy, 52*(2), 258–267. httsp://doi.org/10.1037/a0037727

Zarin, D. A., Pincus, H. A., West, J. C., & McIntyre, J. S. (1997). Practice-based research in psychiatry. *American Journal of Psychiatry, 154*(9), 1199–1208. https://doi.org/10.1176/ajp.154.9.1199

Zilcha-Mano, S., & Errázuriz, P. (2015). One size does not fit all: Examining heterogeneity and identifying moderators of the alliance–outcome association. *Journal of Counseling Psychology, 62*(4), 579–591. https://doi.org/10.1037/cou0000103

Zilcha-Mano, S., Snyder, J., & Silberschatz, G. (2017). The effect of congruence in patient and therapist alliance on patient's symptomatic levels. *Psychotherapy Research, 27*(3), 371–380. https://doi.org/10.1080/10503307.2015.1126682

Zimmermann, D., Rubel, J., Page, A. C., & Lutz, W. (2017). Therapist effects on and predictors of non-consensual dropout in psychotherapy. *Clinical Psychology & Psychotherapy, 24*(2), 312–321. https://doi.org/10.1002/cpp.2022

THERAPEUTIC INGREDIENTS

•

CHAPTER 7

PATIENT, THERAPIST, AND RELATIONAL FACTORS

MICHAEL J CONSTANTINO, JAMES F BOSWELL, AND ALICE E COYNE

Abstract

This review focuses on patient factors (across the overarching classes of demographics, mental health, beliefs and preferences, intrapsychic, interpersonal, and contributions to the therapy process), therapist factors, and relational factors as correlates of psychotherapy outcomes. To avoid overlap with other chapters in this volume, our synthesis *includes*: relational factors that are not a close derivative of the therapeutic alliance construct and/or are truly measured dyadically, patient-level factor–outcome associations, effects of adapting treatments to and matching on patients' cultural identities, and adult populations (unless children and adolescents could not be differentiated in a given study or meta-analysis). Again, owing to coverage elsewhere, we *exclude* predictors that are largely theory specific vs. common, therapist adherence to or competence in delivering therapy, routine outcomes monitoring (ROM) and ROM-based feedback, therapist training, and between-therapist effects or therapist-level factor–outcome associations.

OVERVIEW

INTRODUCTION

Virtually all psychotherapies comprise at least one patient, therapist, and relationship. Not surprisingly, then, these three general factors all have a bearing on how therapy unfolds and the outcomes it yields. Underscoring this point, most chapters in this volume discuss participant and relational factors in some manner. However, in the present chapter, our review privileges these specific elements, while appreciating that therapy participants and their relationships are nested within treatments being delivered in varied contexts. As one might imagine, it is challenging to discuss patient, therapist, and relational variables without tethering them to other psychotherapy-relevant topics discussed elsewhere in this volume. Indeed, such topics do occasionally (and necessarily) come up in this chapter; however, to make our review as distinct, yet complementary, as possible, we made several decisions regarding inclusion/exclusion criteria.

As the first criterion, we focus on the three factor classes as predictors of patient outcomes, largely in the form of correlational research.[1] However, owing to their coverage in this volume's Chapter 8, Psychotherapy Process – Outcome Research, we do not address factor–outcome correlations relevant mainly to one specific type of psychotherapy; for example, exposure frequency in exposure-based therapies; level of emotional processing in humanistic-experiential therapies; and frequency/quality

---

[1] Of course, patient, therapist, and relational factors can also moderate other treatment–outcome or process/characteristic–outcome associations, or mediate other treatment, process, or characteristic effects on outcome. Although we occasionally reference such moderator or mediator results, we do so only when it helps clarify a given literature (i.e., discussion of direct associations would be notably incomplete or misleading).

of interpretations in psychodynamic or psychanalytic thera-pies.[2] Hence, we cover only independent variables that would largely be conceptualized as pantheoretical. Again, due to cov-erage in Chapter 8 of this volume, we do not review the predic-tion of outcomes from therapist adherence or competence in delivering interventions, or from therapeutic alliance quality in any treatment modality. For the same reason, we also exclude research on alliance rupture-repair, or any relationship factors that overlap substantially with the alliance construct. Instead, we limit our coverage of relational factors to those that are (a) (arguably) not a close spinoff of the alliance, and (b) truly dyadic in nature. Regarding the latter, we mean that the predic-tor variable is created by information from two or more therapy interactants, whether combined from the participants' reports or captured by observers. For example, we cover research on dyadic congruence, which is a single index that represents the degree to which a given patient and their therapist's ratings of psychotherapy experiences are similar to or discrepant from one another (which can have a unique association with outcome relative to each person's *own* individual experience).

Although certainly relevant to patient, therapist, and relational factors, we also exclude research on routine outcomes monitoring (ROM) and the effects of ROM-based feedback on treatment out-comes, as these topics are addressed in this volume's Chapter 6, Patient-Focused Research. Similarly, we do not review research on training and its effects, as this broad topic is covered in this vol-ume's Chapter 11. Finally, we leave coverage of between-therapist effects on therapy processes and outcomes, as well as therapist-level predictors of such effects, to this volume's Chapter 9.

Relatedly, as the second inclusion criterion, we focus our review on studies conducted explicitly at the *patient* level, or for which the authors implied between-patient effects through total correlations; that is, when individual differences between patients or dyads on a predictor variable explain individual dif-ferences between patients on an outcome variable. Consequently, the present chapter inherently has more cover-age of patient-level factors/predictors, as they relate directly to patient-level outcomes. For therapist factors, we limit our review to variables that can vary at the *patient* level. For some therapist factors, though, there is simply no way they can vary between patients. For example, therapists will always have the same training background for every patient they treat after training. Similarly, they will have the same experience level for each patient they treat at the time of a given study, and, for the most part, they will have consistent traits that hold across their patients at a given cross section of time (e.g., attachment style, mental health history). Although researchers have sometimes attempted to examine such variables at the patient level, these models are biased (in that scores repeat across the number of patients nested within a given provider), thereby yielding little clinically meaningful information. For such variables that can only exist at the therapist level, they can only directly relate to between-*therapist* outcomes; thus, as noted, their coverage in this volume is more appropriate for the aforementioned

chapter on between-therapist effects (Chapter 10). Finally, for relational factors, the variables are unique to each dyad; thus, although dependency may remain (when therapists see multi-ple patients), these factors can always vary at the *patient* level.

The third inclusion criterion represents an exception to our focus on factor–outcome correlations. Namely, we review *experimental* studies of *treatment* effects when the treatment manipulation was an explicit adaptation to a specific patient cultural identity (i.e., gender/gender identity, race/ethnicity, sexual orientation/identity, and religiosity/spirituality). We also review studies that examined the effects (correlational or experimental) of matching on or tailoring to these patients' cultural identities (and, in some cases, to other patient factors). Such studies inherently relate to patient (e.g., an identity), therapist (e.g., treatment-related actions), and rela-tionship (e.g., patient–therapist identity match) factors. Moreover, we believe that studies focused on tailoring or adapting treatment to a cultural identity provide more useful clinical information than the typically mixed (at best) results on simple demographic/identity–outcome correlations.

For the fourth inclusion/exclusion decision, we reviewed chapters on patient, therapist, and relational factors in prior *Handbook* editions in order to maintain some continuity. However, because this chapter has a more expansive focus than any individual chapter from previous editions, we only retained constructs (e.g., patient race/ethnicity, patient–therapist real relationship) for which the literature revealed recent systematic reviews and/or impactful original scholarship that advanced the field beyond where it stood at the time of last inclusion in a *Handbook* chapter. For topics that did not meet these criteria (e.g., patient ego strength, therapist verbal patterns of interac-tion), we still consider prior *Handbook* coverage to be the pri-mary resource for interested readers. Of course, some research on patient, therapist, and/or relational factors (e.g., patient-perceived treatment credibility, relational synchrony) is new enough that a synthesis is unique to this chapter. As one final inclusion/exclusion decision, this chapter focused predominantly on adult samples.[3] For research reviews on child and adolescent populations, see Chapter 18, Child and Adolescent Treatment.

In terms of process, we reviewed the literature for each variable and compared the yield with past *Handbook* chapter sections to determine inclusion/exclusion. The three chapter authors com-pleted these search and selection tasks in collaboration with gradu-ate and undergraduate students. All searches were conducted between December 2018 and June 2019, and they focused on stud-ies that were published after the last relevant editions of the *Handbook*; that is, Bohart and Wade (2013) for most patient and relational factors, and Beutler et al. (2004) for most therapist factors.

PATIENT FACTORS

In this section, we focus on predictors that measure something about the patient, whether assessed via self-report, therapist-report, or independent observation. As noted, this section

---

[2]We appreciate that these phenomena do occur in, and sometimes are studied in relation to, different forms of therapy. However, their origin has such a strong connection to a specific theory that most of the research and clinical narrative maintains this link to a substantive degree.

[3]The only times that we reference research on child or adolescent samples is when they were integrated with adults in meta-analyses, or when large naturalistic studies did not separately analyze children, adolescents, and adults.

includes the most factors, as such patient-level variable–outcome correlations are the most abundant in the psychotherapy research base. Namely, we cover five major classes of patient factors that are largely assessed at pretreatment or early treatment (though some of which can change over time): demographics, mental health, beliefs and preferences, intrapsychic, and interpersonal. We also include several variables that represent patient contributions to the therapy process. For the patient factor–outcome correlations we present in this section, we also provide in Table 7.1 brief narrative summaries for each; that is, we indicate the state of the literature review and the general direction of the association. We also provide a qualitative description that efficiently captures the current state of the science on the topic/factor.

Demographics

Age

Across multiple large, naturalistic samples with varied mental health problems, patients' age failed to explain significant variance in change trajectories beyond initial symptom severity (Lambert, 2010; Nordberg et al., 2014). Similarly, a meta-analysis specifically on the age-depression outcome link failed to show a significant association (Cuijpers et al., 2009). However, some studies have shown that older individuals receiving treatment for substance abuse may derive more benefit than younger individuals (see Clarkin & Levy, 2004). Perhaps the most influential age finding concerns premature termination as the outcome. In a meta-analysis, younger vs. older patients were significantly more likely to drop out, though the effect was small ($d = 0.16$; Swift & Greenberg, 2012).

Given that the patient age–outcome association is inconsistent at best, and perhaps mostly related to specific concerns (e.g., substance abuse) or specific outcomes (e.g., drop out), more research is needed to determine the conditions under which age is most clinically meaningful. Only once these conditions are reliably identified can the focus turn to *how* treatments can be adjusted for age (e.g., specifically attending to concerns unique to aging). Moreover, future research should disentangle the effect of patient chronological age from patient symptom chronicity, as these variables are typically conflated in existing research (Fournier et al., 2009), which further muddies the water in this area.

Gender/Gender Identity

In psychotherapy research, gender has largely been treated as a binary distinction between male or female; that is, the measured variable often assumes a fully cisgendered sample (Budge & Moradi, 2018). When assessed in this restricted manner, individual studies have *occasionally* found an effect. For example, in a large sample of patients receiving naturalistic therapy in a university counseling center, women were more likely than men to improve (Pertab et al., 2014). In a qualitative study focused on community-based, outpatient treatment for drug and alcohol problems, men were more likely than women to miss appointments (Coulson et al., 2009). However, when controlling for initial severity, patient sex did not predict improvement across several large, naturalistic samples (Lambert, 2010). Thus, although some information can be gleaned from

individual studies, caution is warranted before applying it widely, as research on the gender–outcome relation is, like age, inconsistent at best (Bohart & Wade, 2013; Swift & Greenberg, 2012). Moreover, the historically typical assessment of gender fails to appreciate nonbinary gender identities, as well as dimensions of power tied to traditional gender assignments.

A more recent synthesis examined research that has moved beyond the binary to assess gender *identity*, or one's own sense of self (e.g., genderqueer, male or man, female or woman; Budge & Moradi, 2018). Although initially intended to be a quantitative meta-analysis, too few eligible studies existed. Consequently, the authors conducted a content analysis of 10 quantitative or qualitative studies that mostly centered on the treatment of transgender persons. Among the themes, patients indicated that it was challenging to discuss their gender identity in therapy, and that a strong therapeutic alliance was vital (both in general, and especially when transitioning socially or medically). Patients also valued having a knowledgeable and affirming therapist who neither over- nor underemphasized the relevance of gender to treatment goals. Many patients also reported a mix of helpful and harmful experiences in psychotherapy, with all participants rejecting diagnostic classifications of gender-based diagnoses. Finally, all mental health care stakeholders endorsed the importance of practitioners competently engaging in transgender affirmative practice. As just one notable limitation of this small research base, most work was done retrospectively. Despite such limitations, Budge and Moradi (2018) provided several guidelines for improving psychotherapy by addressing gender-based systems of power and oppression. For example, therapists should consider engaging in a collaborative gender analysis with their patients in order to optimally incorporate gender into the treatment in an accurate vs. stereotyped manner (Mizock & Lundquist, 2016), adopting a social justice framework to their work with gender-oppressed individuals, staying abreast of current issues on gender and language, and adopting a humble and curious stance.

Race/Ethnicity

Although race and ethnicity are commonly conflated, the former has typically referred to socially constructed perceptions of physical attributes shared by a group of people, whereas the latter typically refers to a group of people's shared cultural values, attitudes, and behaviors (Quintana, 2007). Extending these terms, racial identity typically represents a sense of belonging that stems from a perception that one shares a heritage with a particular racial group (Helms & Cook, 1999). Ethnic identity represents a multidimensional construct that encompasses, among a particular group: shared identity; cultural values, attitudes, and behaviors; and experiences of oppression or discrimination (Phinney, 1996).

Research suggests that there are disparities both in terms of access to (e.g., Alegría et al., 2008; Harris et al., 2005) and quality of (e.g., Alegría et al., 2008; Fortuna et al., 2010) mental health care services for racial and ethnic minority (REM) patients. Some research also indicates that adult REM patients may be at greater risk for premature termination than White patients (e.g., Kearney et al., 2005), especially early in treatment (Kilmer et al., 2019). In response to these findings, some

TABLE 7.1 Patient Factors

Factor	State of literature review (MA, SR, IS)	General direction of association (positive, negative, null, inconsistent, interaction)	Narrative summary
Demographics			
Age	MA (dropout only); IS	Inconsistent	Presence/absence of association may depend on the outcome measured and the presenting problem; clearest association (positive) is with dropout.
Gender/gender identity	SR; IS	Inconsistent	Often null, though presence/absence of association may depend on how gender/gender identity is defined/measured.
Race/ethnicity (R/E)	MA; IS		
REM status		Negative	Clear disparities in terms of access to and quality of MHC services for REM vs. non-REM patients.
Patient–therapist matching		Null	Patient–therapist R/E matching generally has a minimal effect on outcome.
CATs		Positive	CATs outperform nonculturally adapted treatments.
Sexual orientation/identity	SR	Inconsistent	Limited research, though some preliminary evidence supporting LGBQ+ affirmative psychotherapies and practices.
Religiosity/spirituality (R/S)	MA	Positive	Tailoring treatment to patients' R/S outperforms nontailored approaches.
Socioeconomic status (SES)	MA; SR	Positive	Lower SES may associate with worse outcome, though the presence/absence of this association varies based on how SES is defined/measured.
Mental Health			
Patient problem severity	MA; SR	Negative	Greater severity associates with poorer outcome, though presence/absence and direction of association depends on how severity is defined/measured.
Diagnostic comorbidity	MA; IS	Inconsistent	Presence/absence and direction of association varies based on patients' primary diagnosis and how comorbidity is defined/measured.
Beliefs and Preferences			
Outcome expectation (OE)	MA; IS	Positive	More positive OE associates with greater improvement.
Treatment expectations	SR; IS	Inconsistent	Presence/absence of association depends on how treatment expectations are defined/measured; clearest association (positive) is between duration expectations and actual treatment length/dropout.

(Continued)

TABLE 7.1 (CONTINUED)

Factor	State of literature review (MA, SR, IS)	General direction of association (positive, negative, null, inconsistent, interaction)	Narrative summary
Treatment credibility	MA	Positive	Greater patient-perceived treatment credibility associates with more improvement, though more research is needed.
Treatment/therapist preferences	MA	Positive	Accommodating patients' treatment, activity, and therapist preferences associates with better outcomes.
Intrapsychic			
Locus of control	IS	Positive	Preliminary evidence suggests higher internal vs. external locus of control associates with better therapy outcomes, though more research is needed.
Coping style	MA	Interaction	Coping style may interact with therapy type such that internalizers may have better outcomes in insight-oriented treatments and externalizers may have better outcomes in symptom-focused treatments.
Anxiety sensitivity (AS)	IS	Inconsistent	Presence/absence of association may vary based on patient presenting problem and the way AS is defined/measured.
Alexithymia	IS	Negative	Greater alexithymia associates with worse outcomes, though more research is needed.
Psychological mindedness (PM)	IS	Positive	Greater PM associates with better outcomes, though more research is needed.
Perfectionism/self-criticism	MA; SR	Negative	Greater perfectionism/self-criticism associates with worse outcomes.
Motivation	IS	Positive	Greater motivation generally associates with better outcomes, though the presence/absence of this association depends on the way motivation is defined/measured.
Stages of change	MA	Positive	Patients further along the readiness for change continuum tend to have better outcomes.
Insight	MA; IS	Positive	Greater insight associates with better outcomes; increases in insight also tend to promote improvement, though more research is needed.
Problem assimilation	IS	Positive	Preliminary evidence that treater problem assimilation may associate with better outcomes, though more research is needed.
Reactance	MA	Interaction	Patients high in reactance tend to have better outcomes when therapists are less directive, whereas patients lower in reactance tend to have better outcomes when therapists are more directive.

(Continued)

TABLE 7.1 (CONTINUED)

Factor	State of literature review (MA, SR, IS)	General direction of association (positive, negative, null, inconsistent, interaction)	Narrative summary
Interpersonal			
Interpersonal problems (IPs)	SR	Negative	Greater IPs associate with poorer outcomes, though the presence/absence and direction of associations vary for specific subtypes of IPs.
Attachment style	MA	Positive	Greater attachment security associates with better outcomes, though there is some evidence it may be a proxy for overall severity; increases in secure attachment associate with improvement, though more research is needed.
Social support	MA; SR; IS	Positive	Greater social support generally associates with better outcomes.
Contributions to Therapy Process			
Engagement	MA; IS	Positive	Greater engagement relates to better outcome, though association varies based on how engagement is defined/measured.
Emotional expression (EE)	MA	Positive	Greater EE associates with better outcomes.
Resistance	IS	Negative	Greater resistance associates with worse outcomes, though more research is needed.
Interpersonal impact/behavior Submissiveness/deference	IS	Negative	Lower or decreased submissiveness tends to associate with better outcomes, though more research is needed.
Hostility		Negative	Lower or decreased hostility tends to associate with better outcomes, though more research is needed.

Note. MA = one or more quantitative meta-analyses (unless specified as qualitative); SR = one or more systematic reviews; IS = individual studies; positive = greater/presence of factor consistently relates to more adaptive outcome; negative = greater/presence of factor consistently relates to maladaptive outcome; null = factor consistently has no association with outcome; inconsistent = no clear pattern of association or lack thereof; interaction = factor has no consistent main effect, but consistently interacts with one or more variables to influence outcome; R/E = race/ethnicity; REM = racial/ethnic minority; MHC = mental health care; CATs = culturally adapted treatments; LGBQ+ = lesbian, gay, bisexual, queer; R/S = religiosity/spirituality; SES = socioeconomic status; OE = outcome expectation; AS = anxiety sensitivity; PM = psychological mindedness; IPs = interpersonal problems; EE = emotional expression; MI = motivational interviewing.

research has focused on matching patients with therapists of the same race/ethnicity in an attempt to improve outcomes. A meta-analysis of 52 studies and a median of 123 patients found that patients significantly preferred therapists of the same vs. different race/ethnicity ($d = .32$; Cabral & Smith, 2011). Moreover, another meta-analysis of 81 studies and a median of 89 patients showed that patients tended to perceive same-race/ethnicity therapists more positively than other therapists ($d = 0.32$; Cabral & Smith). However, across 53 studies and a median of 326 patients that examined treatment outcomes, the authors found minimal benefit of such matching ($d = .09$; Cabral & Smith). There was significant heterogeneity in each of the overall effects, indicating that one or more study-level moderators might explain such variability.

Indeed, patient race/ethnicity emerged as a significant moderator across all three outcomes (Cabral & Smith, 2011). Regarding preferences, African American ($d = 0.88$) and Hispanic/Latino(a) ($d = 0.62$) patients reported stronger preferences for working with a same-race/ethnicity therapist than their Asian American ($d = 0.28$) and White ($d = 0.26$) counterparts. Regarding perceptions of therapists, only African American ($d = 0.59$) and Asian American ($d = 0.56$) patients reported significantly more positive perceptions of same-race/ethnicity therapists. Finally, regarding treatment outcomes, only African American patients experienced significantly better outcomes when treated by a same-race/ethnicity therapist ($d = 0.19$). Several additional variables emerged as outcome-specific moderators; namely, preference for racial/ethnic matching was stronger in earlier vs. more recent studies, and the positive effect of matching on perceptions of the therapist was stronger in analogue vs. clinical samples. In sum, the authors concluded that although patients prefer working with a therapist of their own race/ethnicity and perceive such therapists more positively than therapists of a different race/ethnicity, actual psychotherapy improvement rates are generally unrelated to matching (with the exception of some evidence that African American patients may have better treatment outcomes when matched with African American therapists). Thus, the authors concluded that other factors (e.g., therapist multicultural competence) may be more likely to improve outcomes with diverse patients.

Supporting this view, several studies have found that the association between patient race/ethnicity and treatment outcome varies depending on the person of the therapist (i.e., the therapist as moderator). Specifically, although most studies focused on this question have found no average differences in outcome between REM vs. White patients (Hayes et al., 2015; Imel et al., 2011; Larrison et al., 2011), all of these studies have found that some therapists were significantly *less effective* when working with REM vs. White patients (Hayes et al.; Imel et al.; Larrison et al.; Owen et al., 2012). However, these studies also found that some therapists are *more* (or equally) effective when working with REM vs. White patients. Taken together, these findings suggest that it may be important to study the specific behaviors and practices of those therapists who consistently achieve the best outcomes with REM patients.

Some research has also focused on the efficacy of culturally adapted treatments (CATs), or mental health interventions that have been systematically tailored to various aspects of patients' cultural background, including their worldviews, attitudes, and values (Bernal et al., 2009). A meta-analysis of 99 studies and 13,813 patients that compared at least one CAT to a control group (e.g., treatment-as-usual, a waiting list) found that CATs significantly outperformed the controls (*d* = 0.50; Soto et al., 2018). Although there was some evidence of publication bias, CATs remained significantly more effective than other treatments or a waiting list after correcting for this bias (*d* = 0.35; Soto et al., 2018). Thus, therapists should regularly engage in a comprehensive assessment of their patients' cultural identities and consider using CATs when indicated.

Sexual Orientation/Identity

Sexual orientation represents the sex(es) and/or gender(s) to whom a person is attracted physically and/or emotionally (Moradi & Budget, 2018). Relatedly, sexual identity represents a person's description of their orientation (e.g., queer, bisexual, heterosexual), and sexual minority is an overarching term capturing all orientations and identities that are oppressed in current sociopolitical systems. Although sexual orientation and identification are most commonly assessed using somewhat limiting predetermined categories, best practices involve inviting individuals to respond to open-ended questions (Moradi & Budge).

There has long been a call to develop lesbian, gay, bisexual, queer (LBGQ+) affirmative psychotherapies, or those that involve counteracting negative LBGQ+ attitudes, enacting affirming LGBQ+ attitudes, acquiring knowledge about

LGBQ+ individuals' experiences, integrating such knowledge into therapeutic actions, and validating patients' challenges of power inequalities. Summarizing the research on these foci, a systematic review examined studies that (a) compared LGBQ+ affirmative psychotherapies vs. another form of psychotherapy or control, and (b) compared LGBQ+ patients' outcomes to heterosexual patients' outcomes when receiving any type of psychotherapy (Moradi & Budge, 2018). However, the authors noted that too few studies existed in either category to summarize empirically. Additionally, the few existing studies were too heterogeneous with regard to design and sample to draw definitive narrative conclusions about intervention efficacy. Instead, the authors spotlighted several limitations and future directions. For example, they noted a need to investigate the efficacy of LGBQ+ affirmative psychotherapies with *all* patients and for a broader range of presenting problems than the relatively narrow focus to date on reducing sexual risk behaviors and substance abuse in HIV+ populations.

Despite such limitations, Moradi and Budge (2018) provided several preliminary guidelines for conducting LGBQ+ affirmative psychotherapy. For example, therapists should use inclusive language, which has been associated with more positive views of therapists, treatment retention, and willingness to disclose sexual orientation identities among LGB individuals (Dorland & Fischer, 2001). Additionally, therapists should adopt patients' preferred language for their own sexual orientation and their relationship partners. Therapists can also take an inclusive stance, acquire accurate knowledge about LGBQ+ people's experiences, translate such knowledge into therapeutic actions that neither over- nor underemphasize the centrality of a particular patient's LGBQ+ identity to treatment goals, and engage in and affirm patients' challenges to power inequalities. Finally, therapists might also heed research on patient–therapist matching, as there is at least some evidence that LGB patients report poorer outcomes when working with male heterosexual therapists, as opposed to female heterosexual or LGB therapists (see Cooper, 2008).

Religiosity/Spirituality

Although linked, religion and spirituality (R/S) are distinguishable. Hill et al. (2000) defined religion as adherence to common beliefs, behaviors, and practices associated with a particular faith tradition and community that provides guidance. Spirituality is a broader concept describing the subjective, embodied emotional experience of closeness and connection with what is viewed as sacred or transcendent (Davis et al., 2015).

Captari et al. (2018) conducted a meta-analysis of 97 outcome studies (*N* = 7,181 patients) examining the efficacy of tailoring treatment to patients' R/S beliefs and values. Specifically, they compared the effectiveness of R/S-tailored psychotherapy for mixed diagnoses to either no treatment (*k* = 44) or alternate secular treatments (*k* = 53). R/S-adapted psychotherapy resulted in greater posttreatment improvement in patients' psychological (*g* = 0.74) and spiritual (*g* = 0.74) functioning compared with untreated patients. R/S-adapted psychotherapy also outperformed alternate treatments on both psychological (*g* = 0.33) and spiritual (*g* = 0.43) measures. In a subsample (*k* = 23) of the active treatment comparisons that included an additive design (i.e., a standard approach that did vs. did not integrate R/S elements), the treatments were equally effective at reducing psychological distress ($g = 0.13$); however, the integrative approach promoted greater spiritual wellbeing ($g = 0.34$).

In the context of their review, Captari and colleagues (2018) also examined (across studies and treatment conditions) various predictors of within-group, pre–post change effect sizes. Focusing on R/S factors, patients' level or degree of R/S affiliation, practice, or commitment did not emerge as significant predictors. However, when treatment included a general spiritual vs. Christian accommodation, it was significantly less effective on spiritual, but not psychological, outcomes.

Overall, attending to patients' R/S values and beliefs can positively influence treatment outcomes. R/S appears to be an important individual difference that practitioners should consider with regard to treatment conceptualization, goals, intervention, and interpersonal process. Notably, the importance of R/S differs among patients, so a thorough assessment is needed to determine if, when, and how this dimension is incorporated into treatment. When a patient's treatment goals include not only symptom remission, but also spiritual development, integration of R/S may be indicated (see Aten et al., 2012, for a review of evidence-informed strategies).

Socioeconomic Status

Socioeconomic status (SES) comprises several aspects of an individual's societal standing and access to resources, including income, personal and familial wealth, occupation, and education level, all of which have served as SES measures (either in isolation or some combination). The lack of consensus on best practices for measuring SES creates difficulty in synthesizing research on it as a correlate of psychotherapy outcomes. Nonetheless, Finegan and colleagues (2018) conducted a systematic review and meta-analysis of 17 cohort studies and randomized controlled trials (RCTs) that included 165,574 patients receiving treatment for anxiety and depression. Individually, the majority of studies found associations between some index of low SES and worse outcome. Notably, a formal quantitative meta-analysis was only possible for studies that used employment status as an SES proxy, for which a small, but significant association between unemployment and lower improvement emerged ($d = -0.22$). Among studies measuring SES using education level, two of nine reported that lower SES was significantly related to worse treatment outcomes, whereas the remaining studies found no association. Finegan et al. (2018) also qualitatively compared SES–outcome findings by study design. Cohort studies were more likely to find any significant relation between at least one measure of SES and treatment outcome than RCTs.

Overall, a relatively small evidence base exists linking SES to psychotherapy outcomes, and further study is needed to determine which facets of overall socioeconomic position are most important in predicting treatment success and through what mechanism(s). At a minimum, therapists should be aware of the varied aspects of their patients' SES and appreciate that they may be facilitative or risk factors for outcomes.

Mental Health

Patient Problem Severity

As a baseline predictor, patient problem severity has often been parsed into the subtypes of functional impairment, problem/symptom chronicity, and symptom severity. The first subtype, functional impairment, represents maladaptive external behaviors, such as impaired activities of daily living, disrupted work performance, and/or social maladjustment (e.g., Beutler et al., 2002). In Beutler and colleagues' box-count review of studies including various therapies for different disorders, patients with higher functional impairment had poorer treatment outcomes in 31 of 42 studies. Of the 19 studies that examined treatment type as a moderator of the functional impairment–outcome relation, the majority (12) found no interactive effect (and across the seven studies that revealed a significant interaction, there was no clear pattern that established a specific type of treatment, or treatments, in which functional impairment had a stronger or weaker influence on outcomes). Further reflecting the prognostic risk of greater functional impairment, patients with dual diagnoses (i.e., substance use disorder and another mental health disorder) who possessed higher vs. lower functional impairment had longer treatments, more sessions, and costlier care (Alimohamed-Janmohamed et al., 2010).

For the second subtype, problem/symptom chronicity, research also generally demonstrates a negative correlation between chronicity and improvement. For example, in a large sample of schizophrenic patients presenting for their first inpatient treatment, longer symptom duration prior to hospitalization was associated with worse posttreatment symptom and functioning outcomes (Bottlender et al., 2000). Similarly, in another large study centered on outpatient psychotherapy for various disorders, patient problem chronicity related to slower improvement trajectories (Lutz et al., 1999). Finally, in a meta-analysis of 28 studies ($N = 3,339$) examining the treatment of first-episode psychosis, a longer duration of untreated psychosis was associated with more severe negative symptoms at both shorter- ($r = 0.18$) and longer-term follow up ($r = 0.20$; Boonstra et al., 2012). In some individual studies, treatment type can moderate the problem/symptom chronicity–outcome associations, including changing the direction of the association. For example, longer generalized anxiety disorder (GAD) symptom duration was associated with *greater* treatment gains in applied relaxation relative to cognitive-behavioral therapy (CBT) and non-directive therapies (Newman et al., 2019).

For the third subtype, symptom severity, research has been more mixed. A meta-analysis of 16 studies ($N = 756$) testing the efficacy of CBT for children and adults with obsessive compulsive disorder (OCD) revealed no aggregate effect of severity on outcome (Olatunji et al., 2013). However, a later study of CBT for adults with OCD demonstrated that patients with higher initial symptom severity had poorer outcomes (e.g., Kyrios et al., 2015). In some cases, the link between symptom severity and outcome may be moderated by treatment type. For example, one study revealed that higher initial severity was related to poorer outcome in psychodynamic group-based treatment for borderline personality disorder, whereas symptom severity was unrelated to outcomes for patients receiving mentalization-based treatment (Kvarstein et al., 2019).

Taking a different methodological approach, some researchers have used latent profile analysis to examine the influence of problem severity (broadly defined) on patient change trajectories. For example, when separating patients into subgroups based on their scores on four problem domains (functioning, risk of harm to self or others, subjective wellbeing, and problems/symptoms) of a ROM tool, one study yielded four distinct change profiles (Uckelstam et al., 2019). The patient profile with the slowest rate of improvement was marked by low initial distress across all four domains and low deviation from the mean on all domains, whereas the profile with the fastest rate of improvement was marked by high distress across domains, but also low specific risk of harm to self and others. The authors argued that this multidimensional approach captures nuances masked by use of total scores only. In another study of using latent growth class analysis, depression and anxiety trajectories indicating treatment response vs. non-response were predicted by lower baseline severity (Saunders et al., 2019). Additionally, some studies using growth mixture modeling have demonstrated that patients with high levels of baseline symptom severity can have notably different responsive trajectories, such as steep, positive recovery, no change, or slight worsening (e.g., Lutz et al., 2009; Nordberg et al., 2014; Stulz et al., 2007). These examples again underscore some mixed results when baseline symptom severity is examined as a correlate of change patterns.

Taken together, research points to the prognostic relevance of patients' level of problem severity for treatment response. That higher vs. lower severity carries greater risk for poorer outcomes seems most consistently the case when severity is measured as functional impairment or problem/symptom chronicity. When measuring *symptom* severity only, the poorer outcome risk of higher severity is less consistent. Such inconsistent findings suggest that, in some circumstances, psychotherapy can help even the most distressed patients (Driessen et al., 2010). In fact, when measuring problem severity multidimensionally, greater problem distress can *positively* associate with improvement *if also coupled with low risk of suicide or homicide* (Uckelstam et al., 2019). Although more research is needed to replicate and extend such results, treating problem severity as a multidimensional predictor for which different constellations of problems have therapeutic relevance holds promise for moving the empirical needle forward on this patient factor (Uckelstam et al.). Additionally, future research is needed to continue to examine the influence that treatment *outcome* measurement (e.g., change scores, change trajectories, response/nonresponse status) has on the problem-severity outcome association. That is, the association can differ depending on the outcome definition applied, which has sparked some debate in the field around such measurement issues (see also Chapter 4 in the current volume).

Diagnostic Comorbidity

The prevailing approach to diagnostic classification is predominately categorical. Individuals can meet criteria for multiple current disorders, including those within the same general class (e.g., the anxiety and related disorders). The most severe or disabling disorder is often labeled as primary or principal, whereas additional diagnoses are labeled comorbid or secondary. The pervasiveness of comorbidity is so well-documented that it has become a cliché to acknowledge that comorbidity is the rule, rather than the exception (e.g., Brown et al., 2001; Hudson et al., 2007).

Research on the comorbidity-treatment outcome relation has garnered mixed results, which appear dependent on how comorbidity is defined and analyzed (e.g., presence or absence of any, degree, or specific type; Walczak et al., 2018). In one meta-analysis on patients being treated for anxiety disorders, overall comorbidity (percentage of sample having at least one comorbid disorder of any type) was generally unrelated to treatment effect size at posttreatment or follow up (Olatunji et al., 2010). However, there were significant associations for certain subgroups. Greater overall comorbidity related to worse outcome for mixed or neurotic anxiety samples, but *better* outcome for primary panic disorder (PD) and/or agoraphobia, posttraumatic stress disorder (PTSD), or sexual abuse survivors. Additional work has shown that diagnostic comorbidity can differentially influence outcome for specific anxiety disorder diagnoses. For example, one study found that although individuals with GAD and comorbid disorders entered treatment with more severe GAD symptoms than their single diagnosis counterparts, they also demonstrated greater improvement (Newman et al., 2010).

A more consistent pattern of findings has been that patients with major depressive disorder, who have (vs. do not have) a comorbid personality disorder, demonstrate worse outcomes. In a depression focused meta-analysis, such comorbidity was associated with a twofold increase in risk of poor outcome (Newton-Howes et al., 2014). Similarly, for a large sample of primary depressed and anxious patients, the presence of comorbid personality problems (operationalized by higher scores on a personality disorder screen) was associated with worse posttreatment depression, anxiety, and social functioning (Goddard et al., 2015).

For individuals in primary substance abuse treatment, comorbid psychiatric disorders are typically associated with lower treatment retention and poorer outcomes (Bradizza et al., 2006). In a large primary substance abuse treatment sample, patients with (vs. without) psychiatric comorbidity had significantly higher odds of premature termination, and this difference was more pronounced for those with primary alcohol problems (Krawczyk et al., 2017). Regarding eating disorders (EDs), the relation between comorbid personality pathology and outcome appears dependent on the nature of the personality problem. There is some evidence that Cluster B personality disorders predict poorer long-term outcomes (e.g., Wilfley et al., 2000; Thompson-Brenner et al., 2016). Conversely, the presence or absence of any personality disorder failed to predict long-term outcome in a follow-up study of patients treated for AN (Fichter et al., 2017).

Although it seems intuitive that comorbidity would be a risk factor for poorer treatment outcome, this has not been universally the case. The most consistent evidence for such risk relates to treatments for primary depression. For other problem areas, such as EDs, the impact of comorbid personality pathology on outcome seems to vary as a function of the specific personality problem. In addition, general indicators of comorbidity (e.g., presence or absence, number of comorbid diagnoses) have not reliably predicted treatment outcome; further, for certain anxiety disorders, comorbidity has been associated with greater improvement. Attempts to draw more generalized and definitive conclusions regarding the nature and impact of comorbidity are further complicated by recent trends toward transdiagnostic treatments and alternative classification systems (e.g., Kotov et al., 2017).

Beliefs and Preferences

Outcome Expectation

The most widely studied patient belief is outcome expectation (OE), or patients' forecast of the mental health consequences of participating in treatment (Constantino et al., 2011). When trending positive, OE hastens Frank's (1961) notion of *remoralization*, or becoming more hopeful that a path to improvement exists. At its root, OE is a pandiagnostic and pantheoretical variable that can be formed before having contact with a therapist and revised over time after exposure to the clinician and treatment.

In a meta-analysis of 12,722 patients from 81 independent samples, researchers found a small-to-moderate association between patients' more positive presenting or early treatment OE and their posttreatment improvement ($r = .18$; Constantino, Vîslă et al., 2018). There was significant heterogeneity in the sample effects, indicating that study-level moderators might explain such variability. Indeed, the OE–outcome association was stronger for younger vs. older patients, when researchers used psychometrically sound vs. study-specific OE measures, and when therapists followed a fully or partially manualized treatment vs. using no manual at all.

Regarding its mechanism(s), there is mounting evidence that patient OE may partly transmit its ameliorative effect on outcome by promoting a more positive therapeutic alliance (see Constantino, Vîslă et al., 2018, for a review). Moreover, across the seven independent samples for which this mediational path has been tested, the indirect effect held in a meta-mediation analysis (Goodwin et al., 2018). This path aligns with goal theory, which posits that people will devote more resources to a goal if they believe they have a reasonable chance of achieving it (Austin & Vancouver, 1996). In the present context, patients who have a more optimistic OE may be more likely to engage, and/or be more capable of engaging, in a collaborative working relationship with their therapist, which then facilitates improvement.

Although OE is a variable squarely owned by the patient, it is intimately linked to the therapist and the therapy dyad. For example, there is some evidence of a therapist effect; that is, therapists can differ from one another with regard to their average patient's OE (Constantino et al., 2020; Vîslă et al., 2019). There is also experimental research that provides preliminary information on what therapists can do specifically to cultivate positive patient OE, such as providing a clear, compelling, and moderate length rationale (Ahmed & Westra, 2009; Ametrano et al., 2017), and describing treatment as prestigious and broadly focused on affect, cognition, and behavior, using some technical jargon, and relaying examples of successful past cases (Kazdin & Krouse, 1983).

Finally, some dyadic research is emerging on OE. For example, in one study of variants of CBT for GAD, the authors found that for *both* patients and therapists, increases in one's own ratings of OE at one session were associated with increases in their own perceptions of alliance quality at the next session, which in turn related to reduced worry at the following session (Constantino et al., 2020). Moreover, a truly dyadic pathway emerged; greater *patient* OE at one session was associated with increases in *therapist*-rated alliance at the following session, which in turn was associated with lower next-session worry. Thus, patient remoralization may be contagious to the provider and their experience of relational process.

In light of the research on patient OE, clinicians should assess, address, and cultivate this empirically supported predictor of improvement within its dyadic context, and over time. Knowledge of OE states can help therapists be validating, supportive, and prudently responsive (e.g., by personalizing OE-enhancing statements throughout treatment based on patients' experiences, strengths, and past successes, or by addressing potential relationship misattunements that are brought to light). Therapists can also try to be persuasive and hope-inspiring at a treatment's outset by using the aforementioned OE-fostering strategies, as well as providing a nontechnical review of the research support for the intended treatment (for additional details on OE-related clinical practices, see Constantino, Ametrano et al., 2012; Constantino, Vîslă et al., 2018).

Treatment Expectations

Other patient belief variables fall under the category of treatment expectations, or foretelling ideas about a current or future treatment's nature and processes (Constantino et al., 2011). These expectancies can be about patients' and therapists' respective roles, the contents and/or subjective experience of the treatment, and/or a treatment's format or length. All told, research examining the association between the varied treatment expectancies and patient outcomes has been decidedly more equivocal than research on OE (see Constantino, Ametrano et al., 2012). However, at least some significant treatment expectancy–outcome associations exist.

For example, regarding role and process expectancies, patients who expected to a play a more vs. less active role in treatment demonstrated greater improvements in their interpersonal functioning (Schneider & Klauer, 2001). When patients in behavioral medicine groups expected treatment to ensue in a way that was different from the presented treatment rationale, they were more likely to drop out of treatment prematurely compared to patients whose expectancies were more rationale aligned (Davis & Addis, 2002). Similarly, patients with increasingly non-normative role expectancies at baseline (based on the range of responses to a specific expectancy measure) were more likely to terminate therapy prematurely than patients whose expectancies were in the more normative range on the measure (Aubuchon-Endsley & Callahan, 2009). Finally, for patients receiving outpatient therapy in a training clinic, those with higher expectation for their therapist's expertise (e.g., that the therapist would be active/directive, have insight, and engage in relevant self-disclosure) also had better outcomes (Patterson et al., 2014).

Regarding duration expectancies, multiple studies have indicated that the longer patients expect to stay in therapy, the longer they will actually stay engaged (e.g., Jenkins et al., 1986; Mueller & Pekarik, 2000). Moreover, in more recent experimental work, providing patients with a brief script about the typical number of sessions it takes for patients to recover was an effective means for changing patients' duration expectations, which in turn related to more sessions attended and fewer dropouts. (Swift & Callahan, 2011).

Based on the existing treatment expectation literature, clinicians should consider regularly assessing treatment expectations and potentially addressing them with pretreatment socialization strategies that emphasize expected role behaviors, present a clear treatment rationale, and highlight the importance of patients' active involvement. Moreover, as a pretreatment tactic to improve engagement, therapists can draw on the dose-response literature to inform patients on the expected length of treatment that will likely be needed to effectively address their concerns.

Treatment Credibility

Another pantheoretical and pandiagnostic patient belief variable is patient-perceived treatment credibility, or how logical, suitable, and effective a given intervention seems (Devilly & Borkovec, 2000). Constantino, Coyne et al. (2018) conducted the first meta-analysis of studies that tested the relation between patients' early-therapy perception of treatment credibility and their posttreatment outcome. The analysis included 1,504 patients from 24 independent samples, yielding a small, but significant positive effect ($r = 0.12$). There was significant heterogeneity in the effects, indicating that study-level moderators might explain such variability. However, there were no moderating effects of several patient variables: presenting diagnosis, age, and sex; or contextual variables: treatment orientation, treatment modality, research design, date of report publication, and manualized vs. nonmanualized treatment.

Although correlational data suggest that patients' early-therapy credibility perception relates to more favorable posttreatment outcomes, there remains little information on the mechanisms through which treatment credibility operates. Further, Constantino, Coyne et al.'s (2018) review found no studies that manipulated patient-perceived treatment credibility to determine its causal relation to outcome in psychotherapy for clinical samples. Conducting such RCTs in both controlled and naturalistic contexts is a pressing next wave research agenda. At present, practitioners can assess patient-perceived credibility and interpret the data as one of many predictive analytics. In response to markers of low credibility, practitioners may want to respond initially with foundational clinical skills like empathy, validation, and evocation to gain a clearer understanding of a patient's in-the-moment low credibility belief. Clinicians might then respond with credibility enhancement strategies once a patient feels heard. The exact nature of these strategies will depend on the specific cause of a patient's reduced credibility revealed through the first step.

Treatment/Therapist Preferences

Common definitions of evidence-based practice (EBP) include privileging and, whenever possible, accommodating patients' treatment preferences (American Psychological Association, 2006), or behaviors or attributes of the therapy or therapist that patients value or desire. Swift, Callahan et al. (2018) grouped preferences into three categories: *activity preferences* are the patient's desire for the psychotherapy to include specific elements and therapist behaviors/interventions; *treatment preferences* are the patient's desire for a specific type of intervention to be used, such as psychotherapy vs. medication, or CBT vs. person-centered therapy; and *therapist preferences* are the patient's desire to work with a therapist who possesses specific characteristics (e.g., a certain gender or interpersonal style).

Swift, Callahan et al. (2018) conducted a meta-analysis of over 16,000 mixed diagnosis patients from 53 studies examining the effect of accommodating patient preferences on psychotherapy dropout and/or outcome for a range of psychotherapies and modalities. Notably, this review included studies that made a direct comparison between preference match vs. non-match conditions or studies where patients were placed into a choice vs. no-choice condition. Among the 28 studies that reported dropout results, the overall preference effect was significant; patients who were not matched to their preferred treatment or were not given a choice of treatment were 1.79 times more likely to dropout than patients who were matched or given a choice. Among the 51 studies that reported outcome results, the overall preference effect on outcome was significant ($d = 0.28$); patients who *were* vs. *were not* given their preferred psychotherapy or choice of treatment experienced better outcomes. Significant heterogeneity in between-study effects was observed, indicating possible moderators.

Indeed, several moderators emerged. The preference effect was more pronounced in RCTs and correlational studies compared with partially randomized trials and studies that assigned patients to either choice or no-choice conditions. In addition, preference matching had a larger effect on treatment process and outcome measures than patient satisfaction measures. The impact of preference accommodation was also larger for midtreatment vs. posttreatment assessments. However, patient preference type (activity, treatment type, therapist), age, gender, ethnicity, and education did not moderate either the preference-dropout or preference–outcome association. Patient diagnosis also failed to moderate the preference-dropout association, but did moderate the preference effect on outcome; the beneficial effect was more pronounced for patients with anxiety disorders or depression vs. those with psychotic disorders, substance use problems, or behavioral health problems.

Although small, the positive impact of preference accommodation, including simply offering patients a choice regarding their treatment, appears to be clinically meaningful and robust. Given that the effect of preference matching was not moderated by preference type, clinicians should consider activity, therapist, *and* treatment type preferences whenever possible. Notably, the effects of preference matching appear to be relatively stronger for patients presenting with anxiety and depression. Not only are these the most common presenting patient concerns in community settings (Kessler et al., 2005), but there are many existing evidence-based treatments and activities that a clinician and patient can collaboratively consider. Relatedly, capitalizing on the preference effect is likely associated with providing patients with an understanding of the available treatment options.

Intrapsychic

Locus of Control

As an intrapsychic trait, locus of control (LOC) refers to one's orientation regarding whether personal outcomes are attributed internally to oneself (e.g., personal performance or characteristics) or externally to other factors (e.g., chance, luck, powerful others; Rotter, 1966). A large body of research consistently supports the positive impact on mental health of having a more internal vs. external LOC (Osborne et al., 2016; Shojaee & French, 2014). Although many psychotherapy studies have examined the influence of treatment on patients' LOC, relatively few have focused on LOC as a predictor/correlate of treatment outcomes. From the existing literature, one study found that patients who received computerized CBT vs. waitlist controls exhibited higher internal LOC, which in turn associated with less severe insomnia at a four-week follow-up (Vincent et al., 2010). In another study of older adults with PTSD symptoms, higher internal LOC predicted greater posttreatment improvement (Böttche et al., 2015). Similarly, a study examining CBT for tobacco dependence found that an externally focused LOC was associated with a lower likelihood of smoking abstinence (Scheffer et al., 2012).

Insofar as higher internal LOC is associated with adaptive psychotherapy outcomes, it may be important to measure and address it. For example, exploring the amount of control patients believe they have over their own outcomes might inform the nature and format of treatment, and increasing internal LOC might become an explicit treatment goal. However, replication of the few prior studies linking LOC and treatment outcomes are needed to substantiate further the clinical implications of this intrapsychic trait.

Coping Style

Coping style refers to how one characteristically manages stress and change. Clinical research generally reduces different coping styles to two broad categories: internalizing and externalizing. So-called externalizers engage in behavioral avoidance or acting out when under stress, and place responsibility for their circumstances and experiences on others or the environment. Conversely, *internalizers* have a more neurotic style (Costa & MaCrae, 1985) that involves introversion, self-criticalness, and inwardly directed blame when under stress. Coping styles are not necessarily pathological; rather, they become problematic when extremely and/or rigidly employed.

Overall, research has failed to reliably demonstrate a clear main effect of internalizing or externalizing coping styles on outcome; however, at least one replicable interaction has emerged

(Boswell et al., 2016). In a meta-analysis of 1,947 patients from 18 studies, Beutler and colleagues (2018) specifically examined the interaction between coping style (externalizing vs. internalizing) and psychotherapy type, categorized as insight-oriented vs. symptom-focused. Insight-oriented approaches (e.g., psychodynamic, humanistic) prioritize increasing self-understanding and emotional experiencing, whereas symptom-focused approaches (e.g., cognitive, behavioral) focus on changing symptoms directly through altering behaviors, cognitions, and reinforcement contingencies. The authors found a medium interactive effect on outcome ($d = .60$); specifically, internalizers evidenced better outcomes in insight-oriented treatments and externalizers evidenced better outcomes in symptom-focused treatments. Notably, only 4 of the 18 studies used a direct measure of therapy type, and the authors did not report separate effects for studies that used direct vs. indirect measures. Although the overall pattern of the coping x treatment interaction has remained relatively consistent across studies, reliance on proxy measures of each in most studies is a clear limitation.

The internalizing vs. externalizing coping style distinction is well-supported by research, yet it is important to recognize that coping style for a given patient is unlikely to be discrete or static, and heterogeneity can be observed within diagnostic categories. Coping style may best be considered a transdiagnostic patient characteristic, and it is important to assess patients' coping styles as part of an initial assessment. If an externalizing style is apparent, then clinicians might consider adopting a symptom-focused approach. Conversely, if an internalizing style is apparent, then clinicians should consider an insight-oriented approach.

Anxiety Sensitivity

Anxiety sensitivity (AS) refers to a patient's fear of experiencing anxiety-related arousal due to beliefs that such sensations will result in negative physical, social, and/or psychological consequences (Reiss et al., 1986). Individuals high in AS tend to be hypervigilant to body cues, such as increased heart rate or dizziness, and to interpret these sensations as catastrophic events, such as an imminent heart attack. Although AS is often discussed as a trait specific to patients with PD, it has gained recognition as a transdiagnostic factor (Boswell et al., 2013).

We are unaware of reviews or meta-analyses assessing the association between baseline patient AS and treatment outcomes, although this association has been evaluated in a number of individual studies. For example, in a study of CBT for OCD, higher baseline AS related to worse posttreatment symptoms, controlling for baseline symptom severity (Blakey et al., 2017). In another study of patients with anxiety, OCD, or PTSD receiving either CBT or acceptance and commitment therapy (ACT), the CBT patients with high *and* low baseline AS (compared to those with scores closer to the mean) had greater posttreatment anxiety (Wolitzky-Taylor et al., 2012). This result implied that extreme scores on an AS dimension (in either direction) may be a negative prognostic indicator. Notably, AS at any level was not associated with outcome in ACT.

Specific dimensions of AS (i.e., physical/somatic concerns, mental/cognitive concerns, and social concerns) have also been studied as potential predictors of outcome, and results have varied based on the presenting problem. For example, in patients with OCD receiving CBT, more AS physical concerns related to worse posttreatment symptoms (Katz et al., 2018). However, there were no relations between baseline AS cognitive or AS social concerns and treatment outcomes. In contrast, a different study centered on patients with PD found that higher baseline AS social concerns were associated with higher scores on posttreatment dimensions of general psychopathology, such as depression and paranoia, whereas higher baseline AS cognitive concerns predicted lower scores on several outcomes (Ino et al. (2017). In this study, AS physical concerns were not associated with any posttreatment outcomes. In a study of patients with either social anxiety disorder (SAD) or PD, different results emerged. For patients with SAD, both reductions in AS physical and social concerns predicted better posttreatment outcome, whereas for patients with PD, only changes in AS physical concerns predicted better posttreatment outcome (Nowakowski et al., 2016). Finally, Boswell et al. (2013) found that decreases in total AS scores significantly predicted decreased clinical severity at both posttreatment and six-month follow-up for patients with anxiety disorders receiving a transdiagnostic treatment.

Baseline AS has also been inconsistently associated with treatment retention. For example, higher baseline AS predicted dropout in a residential treatment program for substance use, controlling for other patient variables (Lejuez et al., 2008). However, a more recent well-powered study of primary OCD and mixed anxiety disorder patients failed to find an association between AS and retention (Kwee et al., 2019).

Given that AS may change as a result of interventions, such as interoceptive exposure (Boswell et al., 2019), several studies have evaluated AS as a mediator (i.e., candidate mechanism) of treatment effects on outcomes (Gallagher et al., 2013). For example, ACT vs. CBT led to greater improvement in AS, which in turn associated with better outcome (Arch et al., 2012). In another study for patients with comorbid anxiety and substance use disorders, patients receiving CBT + usual substance use care vs. usual care alone had greater decreases in AS that in turn promoted more improvement (Wolitzky-Taylor et al., 2018).

In sum, AS is a transdiagnostic construct that predicts outcomes. When indicated, therapists can try various interventions to decrease patients' AS, including interoceptive exposure, cognitive restructuring of catastrophic thoughts, and psychoeducation related to anxiety-related sensations (Barlow, 2002). However, patients high in AS may be more resistant to exposure exercises, and clinicians may first need to work on promoting basic arousal tolerance.

Alexithymia

Alexithymia is commonly considered a dimensional personality construct characterized by difficulty identifying and describing emotional experiences (Taylor & Bagby, 2013). Individuals high in alexithymia typically present with restricted imaginal processes, an externally oriented cognitive style, diminished capacity for empathy, and a tendency to experience emotions somatically (Cameron et al., 2014). Researchers have conceptualized this construct as a deficit in cognitive processing of emotional experience that is evident across varying physical and mental health problems, as well as within the general population (Ogrodniczuk,

Piper et al., 2011). Given the aforementioned deficits, the reliability and validity of alexithymia measurement is unclear (Cameron et al.; Taylor & Bagby). For example, depressed individuals with high negative affectivity may be highly critical of themselves, and thus overreport their perceived inability to differentiate and describe emotions (Subic-Wrana et al., 2005).

Measurement concerns aside, higher alexithymia has been associated with poorer psychotherapy outcomes (e.g., McCallum et al., 2003; Leweke et al., 2009), and this association appears to be independent of treatment type. Moreover, decreases in alexithymia over treatment have been associated with better outcomes. For example, a naturalistic group therapy study found that alexithymia decreased significantly during treatment, and such changes were associated with improvement in interpersonal functioning (Ogrudniczuk et al., 2012). Another study comparing CBT and interpersonal psychotherapy (IPT) for depression failed to find a significant relation between global alexithymia and depression level or change over the course of either treatment; however, alexithymia subdimensions did predict outcome either directly or indirectly. Greater difficulty *identifying feelings* was associated with poorer therapeutic alliances, which in turn negatively affected treatment response; in contrast, greater *externally oriented thinking* was associated with decreased depression at posttreatment (Quilty et al., 2017). These findings indicate that distinct facets of alexithymia may differentially influence clinical outcomes, although further research is needed to solidify these patterns.

The negative influence of alexithymia on the alliance may be driven, at least partly, by inaccurate therapist assumptions regarding a particular patient's awareness and ability to access emotions. If a patient struggles to communicate their experience, it may be difficult to form a collaborative treatment plan. Furthermore, higher alexithymia tends to evoke negative reactions in therapists, such as feelings of frustration or boredom, which contribute to negative outcomes (Ogrodniczuk, Piper et al., 2011; Quilty et al., 2017). Thus, to address this patient-level characteristic, therapist techniques like managing countertransference, increasing empathy, and providing psychoeducation about emotional states and associated bodily sensations have been suggested to establish effective working alliances (Cameron et al., 2014).

Taken together, the literature suggests that alexithymia is partly modifiable with psychological intervention (Cameron et al., 2014). Skills-based therapies with an exposure component may be particularly helpful in guiding patients to label what they are feeling while they experience emotional arousal. Some evidence suggests that alexithymic patients may prefer group therapy, as it provides the opportunity to observe others speaking about emotions and to receive feedback about one's own communication style (Leweke et al., 2009). Overall, effective treatment with alexithymic patients seems to entail a focus on improving awareness of, understanding, and communicating affective experiences and generalizing these experiences to the therapeutic and other interpersonal relationships.

Psychological Mindedness

Psychological mindedness (PM) is a multifaceted construct referring to the extent to which a person values and is able to engage in introspection in the service of understanding self and others (Conte et al., 1990). Psychologically minded individuals are able to consider the internal needs, thoughts, feelings, and processes that might underlie their own or another person's behavior (Conte et al.). Although PM could be considered a patient characteristic that might bear on the outcome of many psychotherapies, it was originally conceptualized within highly introspective treatments (Appelbaum, 1973). Perhaps unsurprisingly, then, most empirical investigations of the PM–outcome association have occurred in psychodynamic or insight-oriented therapies.

Most of these studies have found that greater baseline or early treatment PM is associated with a decreased likelihood of dropout and/or lower posttreatment symptomatology (e.g., Kealy et al., 2019; Ogrodniczuk, Lynd et al., 2011; Tasca et al., 1999), though several others have failed to find such an association or have found it for only one treatment arm in a comparative trial (e.g., Kronström et al., 2009; McCallum et al., 1997). Additionally, one study of patients with heterogeneous problems treated in a CBT-focused inpatient program found that greater increases in the *insight* component of PM was associated with greater improvement (Nyklíček et al., 2010).

Given the mostly consistent evidence that greater PM associates with better outcomes, therapists could consider adopting an explicit goal of increasing patients' PM. Additionally, PM could inform treatment assignment, as there is some evidence that high PM patients may be a particularly good fit for interpretive treatments (Kealy et al., 2019). However, the best evidence-based strategies for targeting PM and for treating patients who present with low PM remain largely unknown.

Perfectionism/Self-Criticism

Although specific definitions vary, perfectionism may be considered a multi-dimensional personality construct characterized by individuals (a) holding extremely high standards for their own (and sometimes other's) performance, (b) striving to reach such lofty standards, and (c) basing their self-evaluations on the extent to which they can reach these (often unattainable) standards (Frost et al., 1990). Factor analysis has identified two primary dimensions of perfectionism: a maladaptive factor focused on evaluative concerns, and a more adaptive factor related to positive strivings based on self-defined standards/goals (e.g., Cox et al., 2002). Related to the more maladaptive aspects of perfectionism, some researchers have focused specifically on self-criticism, or a conscious negative evaluation of oneself (Kannan & Levitt, 2013). When unrelenting, such negative appraisal has been termed self-critical perfectionism.

A large literature suggests that perfectionism may represent a transdiagnostic factor associated with the symptoms of varied mental health disorders (for a meta-analytic review, see Limburg et al., 2017). Moreover, in a meta-analysis of 49 studies and 3,277 patients, greater pretreatment self-criticism or self-critical perfectionism had a small-to-moderate association with worse psychotherapy outcomes ($r = -0.20$; Löw et al., 2019). There was marginally significant heterogeneity in the sample effects, indicating that study-level moderators might explain such variability. Indeed, type of patient mental health problem moderated this association, such that the negative self-criticism–outcome association was more pronounced in ED and mood disorder samples compared to mixed and anxiety disorder samples. In contrast, treatment type, treatment duration, and type of effect size did not moderate the self-criticism–outcome association. Finally, Löw et al. conducted a systematic review of seven studies that examined the association between *change* in self-criticism and psychotherapy outcomes. The results of this review were more equivocal, with four studies demonstrating a significant association between decreases in self-criticism and adaptive outcomes and three failing to find such an association (Löw et al.).

Overall, research largely suggests that maladaptive perfectionism and self-criticism may be transdiagnostic risk factors for poorer treatment response. Importantly, psychotherapy can reduce these factors (e.g., Chui et al., 2016), perhaps especially when the treatment explicitly targets them (Lloyd et al., 2015). Thus, when patients present with high perfectionism and/or self-criticism, therapists may wish to incorporate explicit strategies focused on reducing them early in treatment (Egan et al., 2011).

Motivation

Patients' motivation refers to their dynamic propensity for initiating and sustaining behavior change (Miller & Rollnick, 2013; Ryan et al., 2011). Conceptually, motivation is considered integral to psychotherapy, and it is purported to influence therapy seeking behavior, engagement with treatment once underway, treatment response, and durability of gains (Prochaska et al., 2013). Although research *generally* supports a positive association between motivation and adaptive outcomes, the findings can depend on how motivation is measured (e.g., self-report vs. observational), the clinical population, and the outcomes of interest (e.g., symptom reduction, attrition).

Regarding the relation between patient self-reported motivation and outcome, results have been inconsistent. For example, higher pretreatment patient-reported motivation was associated with lower posttreatment symptomatology in CBT for PD (Keijsers et al., 1994). However, in CBT for OCD, motivation was unrelated to posttreatment outcome (Vogel et al., 2006). In another study of CBT for PD, motivation was unrelated to symptom reduction, but higher motivation was associated with a lower likelihood of attrition (Kampman et al., 2008).

One reason for the inconsistency in the self-reported motivation–outcome association could be a failure to differentiate between the type or source of a person's motivation. For example, motivation could be autonomous (i.e., deriving from internal, personally meaningful, and freely chosen goals) or controlled (i.e., deriving from external pressures or the desire to avoid negative internal states; Carter & Kelly, 2015). Supporting the validity of this distinction, research has generally found that greater autonomous motivation (AM) associates with better outcomes, whereas greater controlled motivation (CM) tends to either relate to worse outcomes or be unrelated to outcomes. For example, in one study of CBT, IPT, or pharmacotherapy for depression, higher AM related to greater subsequent depression reduction, whereas CM was unrelated to improvement (Zuroff et al., 2007). Another study of IPT for depression found that higher AM associated with greater likelihood of remission, whereas greater CM related to a lower likelihood of remission (McBride et al., 2010). Notably, this finding held at both the between- and within-therapist levels. Relevant to the scope of this chapter, at the within level, patients who possessed more AM and less CM relative to the average levels for a given therapist had better outcomes (Zuroff et al., 2017). In addition, there is evidence that greater AM relates to better outcomes for patients with various EDs (Carter & Kelly, 2015; Mansour et al., 2012; Steiger et al., 2017; Thaler et al., 2016) and alcohol use disorders (Ryan et al., 1995).

Another reason for the inconsistency of the global self-report motivation–outcome association could be methodological. Supporting this view, the relation between *observer*-rated patient motivation and outcome has been more consistent. For example, in the context of CBT for GAD, one study found that rater-observed in-session resistance (one potential indicator of low motivation), but not self-reported motivation, was associated with worse outcome (Westra, 2011). Likewise, in studies that measured motivation via observer-coded patient motivational language (i.e., change-talk and counter change-talk), higher early-treatment motivation (change talk) was associated with greater worry reduction in variants of CBT for GAD (e.g., Goodwin et al., 2019; Poulin et al., 2019).

Though nuanced, motivation is largely a facilitative factor in psychotherapy, especially when AM is differentiated from CM. Thus, it seems important for clinicians to assess and attend to their patients' motivation (and its subtypes). Moreover, with inconsistent findings for studies assessing global motivation through patients' own self-report, and the potential shortcomings of these measures (e.g., social desirability bias, ceiling effects; Westra, 2011), it may be prudent for researchers and clinicians to pay special attention to patient motivational language and other in-session indicators of one's propensity, or lack thereof, toward change (e.g., resistance). When a patient's motivation is low or waning, clinicians should consider integrating therapy modalities developed to directly address it, such as motivational interviewing (MI).

Stages of Change

Unsurprising to any practitioner, patients vary in their preparation and/or readiness for change, and such variability can influence the outcome of psychotherapy (Krebs et al., 2018). In succession, the most commonly operationalized change stages are: precontemplation (no problem awareness or intention to change in the near future), contemplation (problem awareness and consideration of change, but no current commitment to action), preparation (intention to take steps toward change in the near future, though without explicit effective action), action (overt behavioral change steps with commitment), and maintenance (efforts to consolidate gains and prevent relapse).

In a meta-analysis that included 25,917 adolescent and adult patients from 76 studies focused on brief-to-moderate length and theoretically diverse psychotherapies, the authors found a moderate association between stage of change and outcome; patients further along the continuum at pretreatment had greater posttreatment improvement across the outcomes of substance/alcohol use, eating disorder symptoms, and mood symptoms ($d = 0.41$; Krebs et al., 2018). There was significant heterogeneity among the studies' effects, suggesting possible study-level moderators. However, for patient characteristics, there was no moderating effect of population (adolescent vs. adult), race/ethnicity, or biological sex. For treatment features, there was no moderating effect of treatment type (e.g., CBT, motivational enhancement therapy), setting (inpatient vs. outpatient), manualized vs. nonmanualized treatments, or number of sessions.

Although correlational data suggest that patients' presenting stage of change correlates with their posttreatment outcomes, there remains little information on the mechanisms through which such readiness operates on improvement. Nonetheless, understanding a patient's stage of change can help therapists adapt and individualize their approach. Such transtheoretical tailoring can improve the fit between the patient's stage and the clinician's strategy, thereby optimizing patients' movement through the stages and their ultimate psychotherapy response. As per Krebs et al. (2018), relational matches may entail "a nurturing parent stance with a precontemplator, a Socratic teacher role with contemplator [sic], an experienced coach with a patient in action, and then a consultant once into maintenance." (p. 1977). Notably, Krebs et al. reported that their review revealed no controlled studies that tested the effect of matching treatment to patients' stage of change or readiness level. This represents a pressing future direction for research centered on transtheoretical, transdiagnostic, and person-centered models of mental health care.

Insight

Although many definitions of insight exist, as do more theory-specific sister constructs like self-understanding and reflective functioning (see this volume's chapter 8), a common thread is the process of making new and explicit connections across domains of past and present experience (e.g., relational, emotional, etc.; Castonguay & Hill, 2007; Jennissen et al., 2018). Once predominantly considered a mechanism of psychodynamically relevant outcomes, research on insight has increasingly established its benefit across varied treatments. Underscoring this pantheoretical relevance, a meta-analysis of 22 studies and 1,112 patients engaged in different psychotherapies demonstrated a medium association between greater insight and better outcome ($r = 0.31$; Jennissen et al.). Although power was too low to formally assess treatment type or diagnosis as moderators, the descriptive range of study-level effects was considerably overlapping. Thus, the attainment of insight appears to have pantheoretical and pandiagnostic benefit.

Several studies have also examined the relation between *change* in patient insight over treatment and outcome, as well as insight as a potential mediator of other process–outcome associations. In one study, increased insight during CBT for psychosis associated with less severe delusional and auditory hallucinations at posttreatment (Perivoliotis et al., 2010). In another study of patients with low quality of object relations receiving dynamic psychotherapy, increased insight partially mediated the association between working with transference in sessions and improvement on both patient- and therapist-rated measures of interpersonal problems (Høglend & Hagtvet, 2019).

Taken together, the literature suggests that patient insight meaningfully facilitates adaptive treatment outcomes, and may also partly transmit the benefits of certain interventions. Although the precise *nature* of insight may vary across theoretical orientations, there may be at least some therapeutic value to gaining insight in any treatment framework (Castonguay & Hill, 2007). To date, though, most research is correlational, leaving the causal effect of insight an open question in need of experimental tests. Moreover, there remains little consensus on how best to measure levels and change in insight in psychotherapy. Moving the needle forward on such questions is a clear priority for future research.

Problem Assimilation

Patients' level of problem assimilation refers to their place along an eight-level developmental continuum that ranges from low to high integration of problematic experiences into their dominant sense of self (Stiles, 2002). The assimilation model implies a developmental sequence for successful psychotherapy outcomes. Specifically, patients gradually assimilate thoughts, feelings, perceptions, memories, desires, intentions, will, and/or actions that had previously been distressing, problematic, or avoided, which presents an opportunity to recognize, reformulate, and eventually resolve such experiences (Stiles, 2011). To measure this construct/sequence, researchers use the *Assimilation of Problematic Experiences Scale* (APES; Honos-Webb et al., 1998). The APES requires trained observers to code session dialogue. Given this labor-intensive and time-consuming task, relatively few empirical studies have examined the association between problem assimilation and outcomes. However, for the few existing small sample or case studies, a higher level of assimilation has consistently associated with more improvement.

For example, in one study, higher assimilation predicted reduced symptom severity across both emotion-focused therapy and CBT for depression (Basto et al., 2017). Similarly, in a study of eight depressed patients, good vs. poor outcome cases demonstrated higher levels of assimilation (Detert et al., 2006). Additionally, several case studies representing varied psychotherapies have also shown a link between higher assimilation and better outcomes (e.g. Basto et al., 2016; Caro Gabalda et al., 2016; Mendes et al., 2016; Ribeiro et al., 2016). Although more research is clearly needed, the consistent findings to date preliminarily suggest that assimilation may be a theory-common facilitative process. Thus, clinicians may wish to attend to such experiences and their stunted or progressing manifestation in patients' language. In fact, moving toward integration and mastery of problematic experiences could become a formal and evidence-based pantheoretical treatment goal.

Reactance

The reactance construct refers to the emotional arousal that people experience when their freedom is being stymied by another, and the resulting motivation they possess to regain that freedom (Brehm & Brehm, 1981). Unfortunately, as applied to psychotherapy, definitions of reactance vary. Early conceptualizations framed it as a state vs. trait factor, which may account for why reactance has sometimes been used interchangeably with, or viewed as a special expression of, *resistance* (Beutler et al., 2011). More recently, though, some scholars have framed reactance as a more trait-like variable, with some people exhibiting higher reactance across varied situations than others – what has been termed *reactance potential* (Beutler & Consoli, 1993) or *characterological reactance* (Dowd & Seibel, 1990). When conceived this way, the most abundant research area has centered on the interaction between a patient's presenting reactance level and the therapist's intervention style, with the idea that therapist directiveness would be a better match for patients lower in reactance, whereas therapist nondirectiveness would be a better fit for patients higher in reactance. (In keeping with this interactive notion, we review patient's state-like *resistance* as a distinct construct later in this chapter, noting that momentary resistances are not inherently tied to characterological reactance.)

In a meta-analysis of 13 controlled studies with a total of 1,208 patients, Beutler and colleagues (2018) indeed found that patients higher in reactance had better outcomes when their therapist took a less directive approach ($d = 0.79$). Conversely, as theory and correlational logic would also suggest, patients lower in reactance had better outcomes when their therapist adopted a more directive approach. However, it is important to note that there were significant between-study differences in effects, with the weighted average effect size for studies using indirect measures of reactance (e.g., patient diagnosis; $d = 0.26$) being much lower than for those using direct measures (e.g., clinician rating, personality measure; $d = 0.88$). Moreover, as the authors highlighted, specific therapy modalities were used to represent differing degrees of therapist directiveness (e.g., MI = low-directive therapy), which possibly conflated the effects on outcome of therapist directiveness vs. other possible treatment-relevant change mechanisms. One might also argue that relying on treatment type as the index of directiveness potentially obscured between-therapist differences. For example, it is plausible that therapists vary in their natural use of more and/or less directive interventions, even when ostensibly delivering the same treatment (which, in theory, may be considered to have a more or less directive orientation; Coyne et al., 2018).

Limitations notwithstanding, the meta-analytic results underscore the importance of measuring patients' presenting reactance level and potentially adjusting one's therapeutic selection, and/or overarching stance, accordingly (for specific clinical guidelines on such adjustments, see Beutler et al., 2018). Although future research is needed to better understand the interplay of patient reactance and therapist style over time (i.e., beyond a trait-general treatment fit), as well as how reactance is distinguished from other related constructs (e.g., resistance, interpersonal complementarity), the existing research highlights trait reactance as an important treatment moderating principle (Castonguay et al., 2019).

Interpersonal

Interpersonal Problems

Interpersonal problems are characterized by difficulties in social functioning and problems with forming adaptive relationships. Capturing interpersonal problems as things people do too much or too little, the *Inventory of Interpersonal Problems* (IIP; Horowitz et al., 2000) is the most commonly used self-report measure. In addition to providing a global interpersonal distress score, multiple versions of the IIP produce scores aligned with the interpersonal circumplex (e.g., IIP-C; Alden et al., 1990). The IIP-C comprises eight subscales related to specific problematic interpersonal styles, which are theorized to exist around a circle with two axes, or dimensions: communion and agency (Alden et al., 1990).

In a systematic review of treatment for depression, six of eight studies found an association between patients' higher pretreatment IIP distress and higher posttreatment depressive symptoms (McFarquhar et al., 2018). Moreover, greater *reductions* in IIP distress has been shown to correlate with reduced depression in cognitive therapy (CT; Vittengl et al., 2004), CBT (Altenstein-Yamanaka et al., 2017), and long-term psychodynamic psychotherapy (Salzer et al., 2019). Some depression studies also report results for the association between specific IIP dimensions and outcomes, with the yield being more mixed. For example, patients who reported more baseline problems of being overly agentic (i.e., too dominant) had poorer outcome in IPT and CBT for depression (Quilty et al., 2013). However, in other depression studies, more problems of being overly agentic were associated with *better* outcomes (e.g., Dinger et al., 2013). Results have been similarly mixed with regard to the prediction of outcome from baseline problems of being overly communal. For example, one study of supportive-expressive therapy and medication found that more baseline problems of being overly communal related to slower improvement (Dinger et al.). In contrast, a study of short-term psychodynamic psychotherapy found that more baseline problems of being overly communal related to better outcomes (Schauenburg et al., 2000).

In a systematic review of treatment for EDs, 9 of 12 studies reporting a statistical test found an association between patients' higher pretreatment interpersonal problems (including, but also defined more broadly than global IIP distress) and worse posttreatment outcome (Jones et al., 2015). Some ED studies also report results for the association between specific IIP dimensions (communion and agency) or specific subscales and outcomes, with the yield being more nuanced. For example, one study of inpatient and day treatments for patients with various EDs found that whereas greater baseline problems of being overly dominant were associated with poorer outcome for anorexic patients, greater baseline problems of being socially avoidant were associated with poorer outcome for bulimic patients (Hartmann et al., 2010). In another study of patients with bulimia nervosa who received either CBT or IPT, neither baseline problems of agency nor communion was

directly related to outcomes (Gomez Penedo et al., 2019). However, this study found evidence for treatment by interpersonal problem dimension interactions; specifically, patients who presented with more problems of being overly communal and/or under agentic had better outcomes in CBT vs. IPT, whereas those with more problems of being overly domineering had better outcomes in IPT vs. CBT.

It is unlikely a coincidence that the majority of studies investigating the relation between pretreatment interpersonal problems and treatment outcome have been conducted on patient populations for which interpersonal problems are often etiologically linked (e.g., depression, EDs). Notably, though, there is some evidence that links higher baseline interpersonal problems and worse outcome for patients with other conditions, such as social phobia (Cain et al., 2010) and substance use disorders (Moos et al., 2001). Moreover, in the treatment of GAD (another disorder characterized by certain interpersonal problems), one study has found a treatment by interpersonal problem dimension interaction; specifically, patients who presented with more problems of being under agentic had greater long-term improvement in an integrative vs. standard CBT, whereas outcomes were more equivalent for patients who presented with problems of being over agentic (Gomez Penedo et al., 2017).

Despite some inconsistencies, it seems fair to say that interpersonal problems, especially when measured with a patient self-report at baseline, have prognostic utility across varied psychotherapies for patients with varied problems. Namely, worse interpersonal functioning largely relates to worse outcomes, thus underscoring interpersonal functioning in extratherapy relationships (and perhaps the therapeutic relationship as both a representative of such problems and possibly a model or vehicle for change) as worthy targets of initial and ongoing assessment in psychotherapy, and relationally pointed intervention. Additionally, it is possible that different types of baseline interpersonal problems are cause for using different types of interventions, though future research is needed to verify these interactions. Moreover, additional research is needed to further differentiate different types of interpersonal problems (beyond agency and communion), to clarify when interpersonal problems reflect more of a trait vs. state factor, and to disentangle interpersonal problems as a predictor variable from interpersonal functioning that is often embedded in therapy outcome measures.

Attachment Style

People's attachment style refers to their characteristic pattern of relating to important others. This construct has its roots in the work of Bowlby (1969) and Ainsworth (1979), which focused on the quality of the emotional bond between infant and caregiver that provides a foundation for subsequent development. Bowlby identified three attachment patterns/styles: secure, avoidant, and anxious-ambivalent (or anxious-resistant). Securely attached individuals trust others, do not fear that they will be abandoned, and explore their environment in positive ways. Individuals with an avoidant attachment style suppress their desire to be close with others, whereas individuals with an anxious-ambivalent style experience distress because of difficulty predicting when and how others will respond to their needs. Consequently, they may vacillate between clinging anxiously to and withdrawing from others. Research demonstrates that attachment styles are relatively stable over time, yet are also malleable to some degree (Grossman et al., 2005).

Levy et al. (2018) conducted a meta-analysis of the adult attachment–outcome literature that included 3,158 patients across 36 studies. The authors conducted separate analyses for pretreatment attachment security/insecurity as a predictor of outcome, pretreatment attachment security/insecurity as a predictor of dropout, and change in attachment security/insecurity as a predictor change over treatment. Greater attachment security associated with better posttreatment outcomes ($d = 0.35$). This association was also examined as a function of treatment type, and the association between more attachment security and improvement was stronger in noninterpersonally oriented therapies ($d = 0.70$) than in interpersonally oriented therapies ($d = 0.30$). Notably, the effect of pretreatment attachment security/insecurity on outcome was not statistically significant in studies that controlled for pretreatment levels on the same outcome variable. The association between pretreatment attachment security/insecurity and dropout was not significant. Regarding change, an increase in secure attachment style was positively associated with global improvement over treatment ($d = 0.32$). Levy et al. also examined moderators of the association between attachment security/insecurity and outcomes, and one interaction emerged for education. Specifically, for those without vs. with a college degree, there was a significant positive association between more attachment security and improvement.

Overall, more secure attachment is positively related with better treatment outcome, and global indicators of attachment security/insecurity appear to be the most consistent predictors as compared to more specific indicators, such as avoidance. These results underscore the importance of assessing patient attachment style at the beginning of treatment to inform treatment planning and fit. For example, people higher in attachment security may derive stronger benefit from non-interpersonally oriented therapies, whereas persons lower in attachment security may do better in interpersonal therapies.

Social Support

Although definitions vary, there is some agreement that social support is an umbrella construct that can include more objective or subjective features of one's social network (Lindfors et al., 2014). For example, more objectively, social support can represent the number of supportive people one identifies. More subjectively, social support can encompass satisfaction with the quality of one's support and a general feeling of social acceptance or belonging (Fredette et al., 2016). Different measures center on these different elements of the broader construct (Fredette et al.; Leibert et al., 2011).

A meta-analysis of 27 studies and 5,549 patients found a small but significant association between greater patient-perceived social support and improvement that appeared consistent across different treatments and diagnoses (Roehrle &

Strouse, 2008). Moreover, this association was consistent across subjective and objective social support measures. More recent studies have also supported this association. For example, a systematic review of CBT for PTSD revealed that greater social support related to better outcomes in four of six studies (Fredette et al., 2016). In a study of inpatient and day treatments for depression, greater baseline social support was associated with more improvement (Zeeck et al., 2016). Similarly, in a sample of patients with varied diagnoses receiving short-term group psychodynamic therapy, lower social support was associated with a greater likelihood of nonresponse (Jensen et al., 2017). Another study found that greater social support was associated with better functional outcomes for patients with psychosis (Norman et al., 2012). Finally, a study found that gambling disorder patients who had a concerned significant other who was willing to (and did) participate in CBT had better outcomes than patients who engaged in CBT without this type of support (Jiménez-Murcia et al., 2017).

In contrast, other studies have found unexpected, nonsignificant, or context-specific social support–outcome associations. For example, one study of brief problem-oriented counseling for diverse mental health concerns found that patients with greater baseline social support experienced *less* symptom change, though the authors speculated that this finding may have resulted from patients with higher social support having lower baseline symptoms and, thus, less room to improve (Leibert et al., 2011). Another similar counseling study found no association between social support and improvement (Leibert & Dunne-Bryant, 2015). Finally, one study comparing short-term psychodynamic or solution-focused psychotherapy to long-term psychodynamic psychotherapy for anxiety and depression found that social support only influenced outcomes in long-term therapy; that is, patients with a high level of social support benefited more from long- vs. short-term therapy (at a three-year follow-up), whereas patients with lower levels of social support benefited equally from short- and long-term treatments (Lindfors et al., 2014).

In sum, research suggests that social support may be a transdiagnostic and transtheoretical factor that largely has a small, but significant, effect on treatment outcome. Thus, therapists should consider assessing patients' social support at treatment's outset to inform treatment planning, including, in some cases, therapy length and whether it might make sense to involve a supportive significant other in the plan. Moreover, when social support is low, therapists may wish to pay particular attention to the therapeutic relationship, as there is some evidence that the beneficial effect of the alliance is magnified for patients with low social support (Leibert et al., 2011).

Contributions to the Therapy Process
Engagement

Although definitions vary, psychotherapy engagement broadly refers to the extent to which patients effortfully and actively participate in treatment (Holdsworth et al., 2014; Tetley et al., 2011). Common behavioral proxies for engagement have included session attendance, homework compliance, and patient disclosure, on which we focus here.

Although the number of sessions needed to achieve clinically significant change varies, evidence generally supports an association between more sessions attended and more improvement (Reardon et al., 2002). Additionally, more frequent no-shows and cancellations have been associated with poorer patient response (Defife et al., 2010). Some research also focuses on regularity of attendance in interaction with overall treatment duration. For example, one study found that for patients attending 11 or fewer sessions, more months in treatment was associated with worse outcome, whereas treatment duration was unrelated to improvement for those attending more than 11 sessions (Reardon, et al., 2002). This finding suggests a negative effect of few sessions spread out over time (or, alternatively, a benefit to session density for time-limited treatment). Further, in at least one study, session attendance mediated the correlation between matching to patients' treatment preferences and depression reduction (Kwan et al., 2010).

Regarding between-session homework compliance, several meta-analyses indicate a positive relation between homework completion frequency and treatment outcome. In one, there was a small-to-medium sized effect ($r = 0.26$), which was robust across symptoms assessed (Mausbach et al., 2010). In another, there was a medium-to-large effect of homework compliance on outcome at posttreatment (Hedges' $g = 0.79$) and follow-up ($g = 0.51$; Kazantzis et al., 2016). In the same study, homework *quality* also had a positive association with outcome at posttreatment ($g = 0.78$) and follow up ($g = 1.07$).

The relation between the frequency of patient disclosure and therapy outcome remains inconclusive (Blanchard & Farber, 2015). The lack of a consistent linear association may partly result from the therapeutic effects of disclosure depending more on patient-perceived salience or importance of information shared rather than its quantity (Farber, 2003). In fact, a smaller discrepancy between what patients rate as important and what they disclose has related to greater improvement (Farber & Sohn, 2001).

In sum, session attendance, homework completion, and salient disclosures are behavioral indicators of patient engagement that associate with improvement. Thus, moving forward, therapists should encourage regular attendance (especially for intentionally brief treatments) and homework completion. Moreover, therapists might assess the *importance* of patient self-disclosures, as opposed to assuming that simply disclosing more personal contents is inherently beneficial. As for future research, it should continue to evaluate moderators of engagement–outcome associations, as this will help identify patients for whom attendance, homework compliance, and/or disclosures are most or least important for their treatment's success. Moreover, researchers can employ more observational methods of in-session engagement in order to help operationalize the construct more clearly, and to understand its therapeutic consequences (Holdsworth et al., 2014).

Emotional Expression

Patients' emotional expression (EE) in therapy has long been considered a means to improving their well-being. In this context, EE represents more than simply venting; rather, it involves coming into contact with previously avoided emotions and more fully articulating heretofore constricted emotions (Greenberg, 2016). Such expression is a contributor to *processing*, whereby patients reflect on, organize, and make meaning of their emotional experiences, often in the service of resolving an emotional problem (Greenberg; Teasdale, 1999). Measurement of patient emotional process tends to focus on self-reported or other-rated "expressed emotions or perceived affect in the context of a therapy session" (Peluso & Freund, 2018; p. 463).

In a meta-analysis that included 1,715 patients across 42 studies of varied theoretical orientations, there was a medium-to-large association between greater patient EE and posttreatment improvement ($r = 0.39$; Peluso & Freund, 2018). There was significant heterogeneity in sample effects, indicating the possible existence of study-level moderators. Although there was no moderating effect of patient diagnosis, theoretical orientation, outcome measure, or treatment manual usage, one significant moderator emerged: the association between patient EE and improvement was especially strong when EE was observer-rated vs. self-reported retrospectively after the session. Although self-reported emotion still correlated with improvement, the authors reasoned that its strength was less salient once the moment passed (coders, however, could capture emotional processing at its most salient peak).

Peluso and Freund (2018) highlighted the importance of therapists facilitating patient EE as a therapeutic task that can help meet the goals of meaning making and emotional resolution. To this end, therapists might consider using emotion coaching methods vs. colluding with emotional avoidance or dismissal. Peluso and Freund also articulated the importance of orienting patients toward the importance of affect, as such orientation has been shown to precipitate greater affective display (Ulvenes et al., 2014).

Resistance

Patient resistance in therapy represents behaviors that divert, oppose, or impede the direction set by a therapist and/or treatment (Westra, 2011). Such resistance can develop from a patient's ambivalence about, or low motivation for, change (Miller & Rollnick, 2013), and it can often signal that the clinician is encouraging the patient to move in directions toward which they feel unready (Westra, 2012). The research on resistance largely indicates that when it is higher vs. lower, it associates with worse treatment outcomes across varied mental health conditions and treatments.

For example, in the context of CBT-based therapies for GAD, higher levels of observer-coded midtreatment resistance related to higher worry at posttreatment (Aviram & Westra, 2011) and higher worry and GAD-prototypic interpersonal problems across a long-term follow up (Constantino, Westra et al., 2019 & Muir et al., 2021, respectively). Also, in CBT, though this time for PD, whereas overall resistance (across one early and one middle session) was unrelated to symptom reduction, openly *hostile* resistance predicted worse outcomes. Namely, such resistance at the middle session related to more panic, whereas such resistance at the early session related to higher attrition (Schwartz et al., 2018). Finally, in naturalistically delivered psychoanalytic therapy for psychosomatic disorders, patients who reported higher rates of resistance during treatment also reported worse posttreatment outcomes (Yasky et al., 2016).

Given that patient resistance detracts from good outcomes, it seems important that training methods incorporate a focus on resistance identification and strategies for responding to this disruptive clinical process. To this end, therapists could be trained to use MI as a timely and modular intervention that employs empathy, validation, and support for patients' autonomy in the service of increasing their intrinsic change motivation and experience of self-efficacy (Westra, 2012). This training strategy would be evidence-based, as research has at least preliminarily established the integration of MI in this responsive manner as a causal change mechanism (e.g., Constantino, Westra et al., 2019; Westra et al., 2016). Nevertheless, additional research is needed to further identify best practices for addressing resistance across different time points, contexts, and populations.

Interpersonal Impact and Behavior

Patients' in-session interpersonal impacts and behaviors are often assessed with interpersonal circumplex measures that rate participant actions on two general dimensions of affiliation and interdependence. For example, to assess patient impacts on their therapist, the most commonly used instrument is the *Impact Message Inventory* (IMI; Kiesler & Schmidt, 1993). The IMI draws on interpersonal theory in assuming that a person's (in this case a patient's) evoking style can be validly quantified by the relational "impact messages" that another (in this case the therapist) receives and reports after an interaction (in this case following one or more sessions). Applying the principle of complementarity (Kiesler, 1996), interpersonal behaviors pull for specific and predictable responses; namely, complementary actions tend to match on affiliation (friendly/affiliative behaviors evoke friendly/ affiliative responses; hostile/nonaffiliative behaviors evoke hostile/nonaffiliative responses) and oppose on control (controlling actions evoke deference; deferent actions evoke control). For example, if a therapist endorsed feeling as though they needed to "take charge" when working with a patient, the impact message received would represent that patient's high level of deference; that is, the patient's submission evoked the therapist's dominance.

To assess moment-to-moment exchanges between patient and therapist within sessions, the most commonly used instrument is the *Structural Analysis of Social Behavior* (SASB; Benjamin, 1996; Constantino, 2000). Capturing the reciprocal nature of interpersonal transactions, the SASB has two interpersonal surfaces. Surface 1 captures behaviors focused on others in terms of their degree of affiliation (on a continuum from attacking to loving) and interdependence (on a continuum from emancipating to controlling). Surface 2 captures behavior focused on the self (reactions) in terms of their degree of affiliation (on a continuum from recoiling to reactive love) and interdependence (on a continuum from separating to

submitting). As noted, relevant to the present section, we specifically highlight studies using circumplex indices to examine *patient* interpersonal impacts and behaviors that associate with treatment outcomes.

Regarding IMI-assessed impacts, across two studies that compared CBT and IPT for depression, patients who averaged fewer submissive impacts on their therapists over the entirety of treatment also reported less depression (Dermody et al., 2016; Quilty et al., 2013). Examining IMI *change*, one naturalistic study of depressed patients receiving varied case-formulation driven psychotherapies found that reductions in patients' submissive and hostile impacts on significant others outside of therapy were associated with more adaptive treatment outcomes (Grosse Holtforth et al., 2012). Similarly, for chronically depressed patients receiving cognitive-behavioral analysis system of psychotherapy (CBASP), greater reductions in patients' hostile submissive impacts on their therapist were associated with better outcomes (Constantino, Laws et al., 2012). Decreases in patients' submissive impacts on their therapist were also associated with greater depression reduction in IPT (Coyne et al., 2018), whereas increases in patients' friendly dominant impacts on their therapist related to better outcome in CBT-based treatments for GAD (Constantino, Romano et al., 2018). Finally, at least one study has supported the reduction in hostile submissive impacts as a partial mechanism through which higher early alliance quality relates to subsequent depression reduction in CBASP for chronic depression (Constantino et al., 2016).

Regarding SASB-rated patient interpersonal behavior codified during sessions, earlier research highlighted behaviors toward the therapist that differentiated good from poor outcomes cases. For example, in a seminal study of time-limited dynamic psychotherapy (TLDP), patients who had good vs. poor outcome demonstrated greater friendly autonomy taking (e.g., self-disclosure) and less hostile separation (e.g., avoidance; Henry et al., 1986). In another study of dynamic therapy, this time using adaptive self-concept change as the outcome variable (which can be assessed on the SASB's third surface – introjected behavior toward self in terms of the same dimensions of affiliation and interdependence), poor vs. good outcome patients demonstrated more hostility, less affiliative autonomy taking, and more extremes of control or separation (Henry et al., 1990). Additionally, these positive self-concept change patients engaged in fewer complex communications (i.e., those that simultaneously convey different and usually contradictory information) than the negative or no-change patients.

In more recent studies, several patient interpersonal behaviors also related to outcome. For example, in CBT for GAD, greater patient hostility toward their therapist was associated with worse outcome (Critchfield et al., 2007). In a study of therapy for patients with different types of personality pathology, greater patient friendly autonomy taking related to better outcomes, whereas greater patient deference (whether friendly or hostile) to the therapist, as well as active blaming of the therapist, related to worse outcomes (Muran et al., 2018). Another study revealed a contrasting and unexpected result (Thompson et al., 2018). Namely, among depressed patients receiving CT, high vs. low symptom change patients exhibited *more* hostility toward their therapist. The authors reasoned that this unexpectedly high hostility could have been a result of having established a positive, stable relationship that allowed patients the comfort and space to manifest hostility, which could have then been processed effectively.

In light of research on patients' interpersonal impacts (measured at the session level), clinicians, irrespective of their treatment model, may benefit from attending to the principle of complementarity when working with patients. To the extent that patients' hostile and/or submissive impacts on others with whom they relate may contribute to their psychological problems, therapists can consider ways to disrupt such interpersonal patterns, including through explicit use of the patient–therapist relationship, in the service of corrective relational experiences. Additionally, research on interpersonal behavior (measured at the moment-to-moment level during sessions) again points to the importance of attending to patient interpersonal process in diverse treatments. Largely speaking, when patients are affiliative and take autonomy, it promotes good outcome, whereas when they are hostile, engage in complex communications, and tend to defer, it promotes poor outcomes. However, as some research suggests that the presence of hostility is more prevalent in good vs. poor outcome cases (Thompson et al., 2018), more research is needed to better understand the conditions under which effectively dealing with patient hostility can promote improvement.

THERAPIST FACTORS

In this section, we focus on therapist factors that can vary at the *patient* level. That is, despite sometimes ignoring dependency in the data due to multiple patients being treated by the same therapist, these predictors measure something about individual therapists that can nevertheless vary between the patients they treat, whether assessed by self-report, patient-report, or independent observation. Because we exclude factors that cannot vary between patients, all included variables could be reasonably viewed as therapist *contributions to the therapy process*. Namely, we cover OE, interactive/interpersonal style, self-disclosure/immediacy, EE, countertransference and its management, multicultural competence/treatment adaptation, multicultural orientation, and flexibility/responsivity. For the therapist factor–outcome correlations we present in this section, we also provide in Table 7.2 brief narrative summaries for each.

Outcome Expectation

Although OE has historically been considered a *patient* construct, there is increasing recognition that therapists also possess their own personal OE regarding the likelihood that therapy will be successful for a given patient. Supporting this perspective, qualitative work suggests that therapists are acutely aware of their OE for a patient and view such case-specific hope as one important vehicle for change (Bartholomew et al., 2019). Moreover, although sparse, quantitative work has generally supported the notion that more optimistic *therapist*

OE (for a specific patient) is associated with better patient outcomes.

For example, two naturalistic studies of patients with varied diagnoses have found that trainee therapists' case-specific OE related to greater patient improvement (Connor & Callahan, 2015; Swift, Derthick et al., 2018). Moreover, one study of patients with varied diagnoses being treated with short-term supportive or interpretive psychotherapy also found that greater therapist OE related to better patient outcome (Joyce et al., 2003). Similarly, in a study of various treatments for depression, the authors found that more positive therapist OE was associated with more improvement (Meyer et al., 2002). Finally, a recent longitudinal study of two forms of CBT for GAD found that therapist OE associated with treatment outcome at both the within- and between-patient levels (Constantino et al., 2020). At the within-patient level, session-by-session *increases* in therapists' case-specific OE were associated with subsequent session-by-session *decreases* in patients' worry. At the between-patient level, when a given therapist's OE for a specific patient was more positive than that therapist's OE for her average patient, that patient also tended to have lower worry than that therapist's average patient. Notably, the aforementioned studies that examined both patient- and therapist-rated OE in the same model found that therapist OE for a specific case related to patient outcome over and above patient OE; in fact, both studies found that between-patient (within-therapist) differences in therapist-rated OE were a stronger predictor than between-patient differences in patient-rated OE (Constantino et al., 2020; Swift, Derthick et al., 2018).

In light of these results, therapists should consider attending to their own OE for particular cases both in general and over time, as both relate empirically to treatment outcome; that is, therapists might consider both how their OE for a given patient compares to their OE for other patients in their caseload (between-patient) and how their OE for a given patient shifts over time (within-patient). Such information can help therapists respond effectively to relatively low (at, or averaged across, a specific time) or lowered (changing across time) OE. However, given the sparse research to date on determinants of therapist OE at any level of analysis, the factors that are most likely to increase it remain largely unknown and in need of future investigation.

Interpersonal Impact and Behavior

To examine therapists' interpersonal impacts and behaviors, researchers often draw on the aforementioned IMI and SASB circumplex measures, respectively. As noted, but now in reverse compared to patient impacts, the IMI assumes a therapist's evoking style can be validly quantified by the relational impact messages that the patient receives and reports after one or more sessions. As noted, but now focused specifically on the therapist as interactant, the SASB captures the degree of affiliation and interdependence in actions toward and reactions to patients.

Regarding impacts, one study of IPT for depression found that greater within- and between-therapist differences in

TABLE 7.2 Therapist Factors

Factor	State of litera-ture review (MA, SR, IS)	General direction of association (positive, negative, null, incon-sistent, interaction)	Narrative summary
Outcome expectation (OE)	IS	Positive	More positive therapist OE for a particular case relates to better outcomes for that case, though more research is needed
Interpersonal impact/behavior Affiliation/friendliness	IS	Positive	Greater therapist friendliness and less (or no) therapist hostility relate to better outcomes, though more research is needed.
Interdependence		Inconsistent	Association between therapist interdependence and outcome may vary based on context, though more research is needed.
Self-disclosure/immediacy	MA (qualitative)	Positive	TSD and immediacy generally relate to better process and outcome, though the impact of immediacy can vary in direction (positive or negative) across contexts; more research is needed for both self-disclosure and immediacy.
Emotional expression (EE)	MA	Positive	Greater therapist EE associates with better outcomes, though more research is needed.
Countertransference and its management	MA		
Countertransference		Negative	More frequent therapist countertransference may have a negative association with improvement, though more research is needed.
Countertransference management		Positive	Successful countertransference management associates with better outcomes, though more research is needed.
Multicultural competence (MCC)	MA	Positive	Greater MCC associates with better outcomes.
Multicultural orientation	SR; IS	Positive	Greater therapist cultural humility, attention to cultural opportunities, and cultural comfort associate with better outcomes, though more research is needed.
Flexibility/responsivity	IS	Positive	Greater therapist flexibility and appropriate responsivity associate with better outcomes, though more research is needed.

Note. MA = one or more quantitative meta-analyses (unless specified as qualitative); SR = one or more systematic reviews; IS = individual studies; positive = greater/presence of factor consistently relates to more adaptive outcome; negative = greater/presence of factor consistently relates to maladaptive outcome; null = factor consistently has no association with outcome; inconsistent = no clear pattern of association or lack thereof; interaction = factor has no consistent main effect, but consistently interacts with one or more variables to influence outcome; OE = outcome expectation; EE = emotional expression; MCC = multicultural competence.

affiliation/friendliness was associated with greater within- and between-therapist AM, which, in turn, related to better within- and between-therapist outcomes (Zuroff et al., 2017). This finding suggests that certain patients may pull for more (or less) friendliness from their therapist and that certain therapists tend to be more (or less) affiliative in general, both of which affect treatment outcomes. In another study of IPT for depression, greater therapist friendly submissiveness (high affiliation and low control) was associated with greater depression reduction (Coyne et al., 2018). Coyne and colleagues argued that because depressed patients tend to present with hostile submissive interpersonal styles (e.g., Constantino et al., 2008), therapist friendly submissiveness might be an especially helpful interpersonal stance when working with them, as it would encourage (through the principle of interpersonal complementarity) patients to take an unfamiliar (though likely corrective) friendly assertive stance.

Regarding observer-rated therapist behavior, earlier studies selected known good and poor outcome cases and used the SASB to identify therapist behaviors that differentiate them largely in interpersonal or psychodynamic therapies. This work suggested that therapists exhibited more hostile and hostile controlling behaviors in poor vs. good outcome cases and more affiliative and affiliative autonomy granting behaviors in good vs. poor outcome cases (e.g., Henry et al., 1986; Henry et al., 1990). Moreover, positive vs. negative/no self-concept change patients had therapists who used fewer complex communications (Henry et al., 1990).

In more recent studies, these differences in therapist interpersonal behavior in good vs. poor outcome cases have often held. For example, in a study of naturalistic outpatient therapy, therapists engaged in more hostile controlling or distancing behavior with negative/no change vs. positive change cases (von der Lippe et al., 2008). In a study of patients receiving therapy for varied personality disorders, greater therapist friendly directiveness (high affiliation and high control) was associated with worse patient-rated session quality; however, neither therapist friendly directiveness nor any other SASB-rated therapist indices were associated with overall symptom change (Muran et al., 2018).

The Muran et al. (2018) study also reflected the mixed nature of SASB findings as they pertain to therapist behavior. For example, whereas a study of supportive expressive therapy for avoidant personality disorder demonstrated that greater therapist disaffiliation/hostility was associated with worse treatment outcomes (Schut et al., 2005), a study of psychodynamic therapy revealed no significant associations between therapists' SASB-rated interpersonal behavior during the intake assessment and outcomes (Jørgensen et al., 2000). Similarly, in another study that examined whether SASB-rated therapist behavior differentiated good and poor outcome cases, though this time in variants of CBT for GAD, the authors found only weak associations, though there was some indication that greater total hostility among therapists *and* patients was higher in the poor outcome cases (Critchfield et al., 2007).

Perhaps unsurprisingly, there is some evidence that greater therapist friendliness and less (or no) hostility associates with better treatment outcomes. Thus, therapists could default to an affiliative stance, especially in the face of negative process or relational tensions (e.g., Schut et al., 2005). As for therapist interdependence (e.g., the extent to which they are controlling vs. emancipating), the degree to which it relates to treatment outcomes is more inconsistent, suggesting that its influence may depend on context. Thus, future research could focus on uncovering specific times and/or specific populations that render the extent to which therapists are more autonomy granting vs. controlling as therapeutically salient.

Self-Disclosure/Immediacy

Recent work has differentiated between therapist self-disclosure (TSD) and immediacy. Hill and colleagues (2014; Pinto-Coelho et al., 2016) define TSD as verbal statements that reveal something personal and external to the therapy. Such disclosures can serve multiple functions, including fostering a positive alliance, normalizing a patient experience, and/or communicating empathy. In contrast, immediacy reflects within-session, here-and-now discussions about the patient–therapist interaction (Hill, 2014). In-the-moment questions and statements about the perceived nature of the relationship and the impact of a therapist action can elicit patient reflection of feeling, as well as foster alliance negotiation. As Hill et al. (2018) have noted, "TSDs tend to be brief and not generate further discussion . . . whereas immediacy tends to involve a number of interchanges . . ." (p. 446).

Although most therapists report using some self-disclosure in therapy (Edwards & Murdock, 1994), they do so relatively infrequently (Hill et al., 2002). In addition, there is rarely a significant relation between the frequency of TSD and outcome (e.g., Levitt et al., 2016), and the most controlled research on the effects of TSD and immediacy has involved analogue samples. For example, in a meta-analysis of mostly analogue studies (90%) that randomized individuals to TSD or non-disclosure conditions, patients in the TSD conditions reported a more favorable perception of the therapist ($d = 0.15$) and more openness to their own disclosure ($d = 0.14$; Henretty et al., 2014).

Hill et al. (2018) conducted a qualitative meta-analysis of 21 studies involving 184 patients receiving actual psychotherapy, with a focus on the impact of TSD and immediacy (identified by independent observers or revealed through patient or therapist interviews) on subsequent process and outcome. Five studies focused uniquely on TSD; 15 on immediacy. Across all studies, the most common influences of TSD and/or immediacy were: enhanced therapy relationship, improved patient mental health functioning, increased patient insight, and increased patient-experienced helpfulness. Negative impacts were observed or noted in up to 30% of cases, which were more likely to occur in immediacy focused studies. Nevertheless, the majority of impacts were viewed as positive. The authors further explored differences between TSD and immediacy impacts. Compared with immediacy, TSD events related to more patient improvement in functioning and relationship quality, yet less patient opening up and immediacy.

Immediacy appears to carry both reward and risk. For example, one study found that relationship-focused immediacy interventions were often viewed as either particularly helpful or particularly hindering a given session (Castonguay, Boswell, Zack et al., 2010). Hill et al. (2014) noted that cultural factors may determine the degree to which TSD or immediacy is experienced as helpful or intrusive. Nevertheless, on average, TSD and immediacy result in positive subsequent processes for patients, and therapy process and outcome are likely enhanced by a therapist's *judicious* use of both. Notably, TSD is less likely to evoke patient immediacy; thus, if therapists are aiming to evoke immediacy in their patients, it may be important to first be immediate themselves.

Emotional Expression

We previously discussed the positive association between *patients'* EE in therapy and their improvement. Importantly, *therapists* also express emotion in psychotherapy, and Peluso and Freund (2018) also conducted a meta-analysis on the therapist EE-patient outcome link. Across 13 studies ($N = 524$ patients) of varied treatments and measures, there was a medium association between greater therapist EE and patients' posttreatment improvement ($r = 0.27$). There was no significant variability in sample effects. Thus, Peluso and Freund (2018) recommended that in addition to facilitating their patients' EE as an important therapeutic task toward meaningful clinical goals in any treatment, therapists of all orientations should also consider showing their own emotions, as this expression can be helpful. However, more research is needed to determine the specific types of therapist EE that are most beneficial, as well as the specific contexts that render them more or less effective.

Countertransference and Its Management

Although its origins align with psychoanalytic thought, countertransference (CT) is viewed more contemporarily as pantheoretical. According to an integrative definition, CT represents "internal and external reactions in which unresolved conflicts of the therapist, usually but not always unconscious, are implicated" (Hayes et al., 2018; p. 497). Such unresolved conflicts can be prompted by a patient's transference reactions, though they can be prompted in other ways too (e.g., the patient's utterances, personality style). Measurement of CT reactions tends to focus on observer- or self-rated behavioral (e.g., withdrawal, overnurturance), cognitive (e.g., perceptual distortions, content recall), somatic (e.g., fatigue, headache), and/or affective (e.g., state anxiety, excitement) manifestations. As per Hayes and colleagues' framework, CT can have positive, negative, or neutral influences on therapeutic work, in large part based on the therapist's CT *management*. Measurement of such management typically focuses on supervisor- or self-rated dimensions of a therapist's self-insight, self-integration, conceptualizing ability, empathy, and anxiety management.

In one meta-analysis that included 14 studies and 983 patients receiving varied treatments for diverse problems, there was a modest, negative association between more frequent therapist CT reactions and patient improvement ($r = -0.16$; Hayes et al., 2018), suggesting that CT presence can be a hindrance. However, this finding should be interpreted with caution given evidence of publication bias. The authors also noted significant heterogeneity in the sample effects, indicating the possible existence of study-level moderators. However, the primary moderator assessed (i.e., proximal vs. distal outcome) was not significant. In a second meta-analysis that included 9 studies and 392 patients receiving varied treatments for diverse problems, there was robust, positive association between successful CT management and patient improvement ($r = 0.39$; Hayes et al.), suggesting that such attention to and management of CT can be facilitative. The authors again noted significant heterogeneity in effects; again, though, the timing of outcome assessment did not moderate.

Although more research is needed on CT, its management, and its clinical consequences, existing research suggests that it is a factor to which clinicians might attend. Specifically, there may be a benefit to clinicians heeding the inevitability of CT reactions, and thereby privileging constant self-monitoring and restraint over impulsive acting out (Hayes et al., 2018). Moreover, irrespective of theoretical orientation, the evidence highlights that clinicians' attempts to manage potentially toxic CT and harness potentially useful CT during treatment can be clinically helpful with any patient.

Multicultural Competence

Therapist multicultural competence (MCC) is commonly defined as a commitment to increasing one's knowledge of patients' cultural backgrounds, learning and implementing culturally tailored interventions, and building an understanding of one's own cultural background (and the values, beliefs, and assumptions that may stem from it) and the influence it can have on clinical interactions (Sue et al., 1992; Sue, 1998). Inherent in this definition is the notion that MCC reflects a stable therapist *proficiency* that can be clearly defined, acquired, and used to differentiate therapists who are high vs. low in MCC across their patients (Davis et al., 2018).

A meta-analysis of 15 studies and 2,640 patients examined the association between therapist MCC and premature termination and/or treatment outcome (Soto et al., 2018). Among the four studies focused on premature termination, the authors found that greater therapist MCC was associated with a lower likelihood of premature termination ($r = 0.26$; Soto et al.). Among the 11 studies focused on outcome, the authors found a moderate, positive association between greater therapist MCC and patient improvement ($r = 0.24$; Soto et al.). Significant heterogeneity in between-study effects was observed, indicating possible moderation. Indeed, when *patients* rated their therapists' MCC, it was significantly associated with better outcome ($r = 0.38$), whereas when *therapists* rated their own MCC, it was unrelated to outcome ($r = 0.06$; Soto et al.). Additionally, the positive MCC-improvement association was stronger when the MCC measure was more reliable. Patient ethnicity, gender, age, publication status, and publication year did not moderate.

Given the moderately sized positive effect of patient-perceived therapist MCC on improvement, therapists' knowledge of their patients' cultural backgrounds, ability to implement culturally tailored interventions, and understanding of their own cultural background represent essential components of EBP (Soto et al., 2018). Clinicians should consider regularly assessing their patients' cultural identities and worldviews and their salience to inform treatment adaptations. It may also be important for clinicians to build their knowledge of specific cultural groups to help culturally tailor their treatments. Additionally, therapists should strive to handle cultural dynamics sensitively, as *patient* perceptions of therapist MCC appear most important (Soto et al.). Relatedly, therapists should consider routinely assessing patient perceptions of their MCC given that their own perceptions may be inaccurate.

Multicultural Orientation

Although the MCC notion is heavily emphasized in psychotherapy training, there is some debate as to whether the MCC theory has been supported by research (Davis et al., 2018). Specifically, the notion that MCC reflects a stable therapist *proficiency* that therapists can acquire and subsequently possess has generally failed to be empirically supported (Davis et al.). For example, one study found that less than 1% of the variability in therapist MCC is accounted for by the person of the therapist, suggesting that perceptions of it are patient or dyad specific (Owen, Leach et al., 2011).

Given this finding, Owen and colleagues have proposed the multicultural orientation (MCO) framework (e.g., Owen, Tao et al., 2011; Owen, 2013). Instead of viewing MCC as a stable therapist competency, the MCO framework represents a meta orientation that provides therapists with a "way of being" with patients regardless of their general theoretical approach (Owen, 2013). Specifically, MCO is comprised of three pillars: cultural humility (i.e., a patient-oriented stance in which therapists suspend their own cultural assumptions and take an open and curious stance toward their patients' identities), cultural opportunities (i.e., in-session markers that indicate that patients' cultural beliefs and values could be explored), and cultural comfort (i.e., the extent to which therapists feel at ease working with cultural dynamics).

A systematic review of research on MCO identified nine articles (Davis et al., 2018). Consistent with MCO theory, greater therapist cultural humility has been associated with better alliances (Hook et al., 2013; Davis et al., 2016), fewer in-session microaggressions (Hook et al., 2016), and greater patient improvement (Davis et al., 2016; Owen, Jordan et al., 2014; Owen et al., 2016). Although fewer studies exist on the other MCO pillars, one demonstrated that disparities in patient-perceived therapist cultural comfort when working with REM vs. White patients predicted racial/ethnic disparities in early termination (Owen et al., 2017). Additionally, another study found that although patient-perceived missed cultural opportunities were associated with worse outcomes, this association was mitigated by therapist cultural humility (Owen et al., 2016). Although more research is needed on all three MCO pillars, the current findings support the notion that therapist cultural humility represents an important component of EBP and provide preliminary evidence that therapist attention to cultural opportunities and comfort may facilitate better outcomes.

Flexibility/Responsivity

Growing research indirectly supports the clinical importance of therapist flexibility and responsivity when delivering interventions. For example, as discussed in this volume's Chapter 8, a meta-analysis revealed that greater therapist adherence to manual-prescribed techniques was unrelated to patient outcomes (Webb et al., 2010), thereby suggesting that the prescriptive and consistent application of theory-informed interventions is not a means to therapeutic success (at least not for many patients). Further, some research has shown that rigid model adherence in the face of patient–therapist disagreement or tension may interfere with patient improvement (Castonguay et al., 1996; Piper et al., 1991), whereas purposefully moving off protocol in such moments to be more validating, relationship-focused, collaborative, and autonomy granting can outperform protocol continuation (Constantino et al., 2008; Westra et al., 2016). Thus, overly strict model delivery, even when applied with the best of therapist intentions (what education researchers have termed *overzealous transfer*; Schwartz, et al., 2012) can be ineffective, if not occasionally harmful (Castonguay, Boswell, Constantino et al., 2010).

Regarding direct research on flexibility, some studies have demonstrated that greater *within-case variability* in a therapist's adherence to orientation-specific interventions has associated positively with patient improvement. For example, when psychodynamically oriented therapists varied in their use of theory-prescribed interventions with a given patient (as rated by observers), that patient showed more improvement relative to other patients for whom their therapists more steadily used such strategies (Owen & Hilsenroth, 2014). In a similar study of psychodynamic and interpersonally oriented therapies, when therapists integrated some cognitive and behavioral interventions when working with a given patient (again as rated by observers), that patient reported better therapy outcomes than patients whose therapist was less flexible (Katz et al., 2019).

In terms of direct research on responsivity, or therapist behavior influenced by emerging context, one study used observer ratings across the initial two sessions of treatment for depression to predict patient engagement indices (Elkin et al., 2014). The researchers found that higher scores on a single item of global therapist responsivity (e.g., being attentive, caring, and affirming) associated with higher patient ratings of early relationship quality and being more likely to continue in treatment beyond four sessions. Other research demonstrates that when therapists work to develop idiographic case formulations, and then flexibly tailor their intervention to be compatible with these formulations, such *plan compatibility* correlates with better outcomes (Silberschatz, 2017). Finally, attending to therapist responsivity vis-à-vis specific process markers, Aviram and colleagues (2016) coded therapists' naturally varying MI spirit while delivering protocol-driven CBT for GAD both during moments of disagreement and in randomly selected non-disagreement moments. When therapists were more MI-like during disagreement episodes (i.e., demonstrated more untrained empathy, emotional evocation, and autonomy granting, as opposed to sticking with traditional

CBT techniques), it had 10 times the facilitative effect on symptom reduction than when they were similarly MI-like at randomly selected times.

Although research on therapist flexibility and responsivity remains in its early stages (Hatcher, 2015), existing work demonstrates that the construct can be reliably assessed in different ways and has predictive validity. When taken together with research demonstrating the null effect of therapist protocol adherence and the possible perils of perseverate adherence in the context of negative process, it seems vital for clinicians to responsively attune to their patients' needs, progress, potentially shifting case formulation and treatment goals, etc. (Constantino, Coyne et al., 2020). Moreover, it remains pressing to replicate and extend research on flexibility and responsivity in order to keep clarifying precise ways in which therapists can adapt and attune to their patients, and the specific markers that call for these actions. As this research matures, we imagine that clinicians might begin to identify less with specific orientations and more as contextual integrationists (Constantino, Goodwin et al., in press).

RELATIONAL PROCESS FACTORS

In this final research review section, we focus on predictors that measure something about the patient–therapist relationship. As noted, we limit our coverage to two classes of such relational factors. The first class includes variables that are (arguably) fully pantheoretical and not a close spinoff of the alliance construct. Our search revealed only one variable that falls under this rubric – the real relationship (a variable that is also briefly reviewed in Chapter 8 of this *Handbook*). The

second class relates to factors that are truly dyadic in nature. As noted, we operationalize this as the independent/predictor variable being derived from information from two or more therapy interactants (whether that information is combined from the participants' report of self or other, or captured by observers). Our search revealed three overarching variables that fall under this rubric: dyadic congruence, synchrony, and interpersonal complementarity. We address in turn the four factors from these two overarching classes. Table 7.3 provides brief narrative summaries for each.

Real Relationship

The real relationship is defined as the "personal relationships between therapist and patient marked by the extent to which each is genuine with the other and perceives/experiences the other in ways that befit the other" (Gelso, 2009, p. 119). Gelso et al. (2018) conducted the first meta-analysis of the real relationship as a predictor of distal treatment outcome, treatment progress, and session quality or outcome. The analysis, which included 1,502 patients from 16 studies, revealed a significant and moderate association between higher real relationship quality and outcome ($r = 0.38$). Given significant heterogeneity in the sample effects, several moderators were investigated, including outcome type and rater perspective. No significant moderators emerged.

Some studies have examined between- and within-therapist differences on the real relationship and their associations with outcome. For example, Kivlighan et al. (2014) found that between-therapist differences on the real relationship at Session 3 accounted for significant patient-reported treatment progress variance. This result did not hold at the within-therapist level.

TABLE 7.3   Relational Process Factors

Factor	State of literature review (MA, SR, IS)	General direction of association (positive, negative, null, inconsistent, interaction)	Narrative summary
Real relationship	MA	Positive	Higher-quality real relationship associates with better outcomes, though more research is needed.
Dyadic congruence	IS	Positive	Greater dyadic congruence between patients and therapists generally associates with better outcomes, though more research is needed.
Synchrony	IS	Positive	Greater patient–therapist synchrony generally associates with better outcomes, though more research is needed.
Interpersonal complementarity	IS	Positive	Greater interpersonal complementarity (especially when "positive" or characterized by reciprocal friendliness and autonomy-enhancing exchanges) generally relates to better outcome, though more research is needed.

Note. MA = one or more quantitative meta-analyses (unless specified as qualitative); SR = one or more systematic reviews; IS = individual studies; positive = greater/presence of factor consistently relates to more adaptive outcome; negative = greater/presence of factor consistently relates to maladaptive outcome; null = factor consistently has no association with outcome; inconsistent = no clear pattern of association or lack thereof; interaction = factor has no consistent main effect, but consistently interacts with one or more variables to influence outcome.

The same pattern of results was replicated in another study using the common fate model (Lederman et al., 2012) to analyze the dyadic relationship (Li et al., 2016).

It is notable, however, that research on the real relationship is still in its relative infancy. Future work is needed to replicate and extend research on between- and within-therapist effects, as well as truly dyadic analytical methods. In addition, existing evidence is based on participant self-report, rather than independent observation, potentially highlighting the distinctions between the real relationship and common definitions of the alliance. That is, the real relationship is determined from the reported subjective experience of the patient and therapist, arguably rendering external observation less relevant. Among the clinical practice implications derived by Gelso et al. (2018), therapist consistency and transparency appear to be particularly important. Therefore, it may be helpful for therapists to not only understand their *patients'* experiences, but also to understand and share their *own* internal experiences.

Dyadic Congruence

Dyadic *congruence* has been historically operationalized as the extent to which patient and therapist ratings of psychotherapy experiences/processes are similar to or discrepant from one another at one or just a few distinct points in time (e.g., Tryon et al., 2007). The majority of studies on congruence have focused on the therapeutic alliance, which, as noted, is outside of this chapter's scope. Several studies, however, have focused on congruence of other process constructs; more specifically, these works centered on *temporal congruence*, or the extent to which patients and therapists' fluctuations in a given process accurately track each other over time. In one study, greater temporal congruence between patient and therapist ratings of patients' emotional and psychological functioning was associated with better outcomes (Bar-Kalifa et al., 2016). Similarly, another study found that *lower* patient–therapist temporal emotional congruence (in terms of during-session positive and negative affect) was associated with worse outcomes (Atzil-Slonim et al., 2018). Building on this finding, another study focused on therapists' empathic accuracy, or the extent to which therapists accurately tracked their patients' during session emotional experiences (Atzil-Slonim et al., 2019). Results indicated that therapists largely tended to accurately track their patients' emotions; however, therapist *inaccuracy* in tracking their patients' positive emotions was associated with poorer outcomes (Atzil-Slonim et al. 2019).

In sum, a small, but growing, body of research underscores the potential therapeutic value of greater patient and therapist congruence, perhaps especially in the form of therapists' tracking shifts in patient perceptions of processes (temporal congruence). Such work speaks both to the importance of measuring therapy process in a genuinely dyadic manner and to tracking such dyadic process clinically. Presently, though, both the mechanisms through which congruence translates into more positive outcomes and the specific patient and therapist behaviors that promote more vs. less congruence remain largely unknown and await future research.

Synchrony

Broadly defined, interpersonal synchrony refers to the coordination or coupling of behavior among two or more individuals, and basic research demonstrates that synchrony can occur at various levels (e.g., physiological, emotional, perceptual, neural) in any social context (see Koole & Tschacher, 2016, for a review). Moreover, there is some evidence that greater synchrony is associated with positive dyadic outcomes, such as cooperation, rapport, trust, etc. (Koole & Tschacher). Given that psychotherapy involves a special type of close relationship in which such dyadic outcomes have been shown to facilitate improvement, it stands to reason that synchrony has an important place in the treatment process.

Testing this notion, several studies have examined nonverbal synchrony in patient and therapists' movements in relation to outcomes. For example, in a study of naturalistically delivered CBT for varied mental health problems, greater movement synchrony was associated with better patient-perceived relationship quality and more improvement (Ramseyer & Tschacher, 2011). Similarly, a study of CBT or psychodynamic therapy for social anxiety found that, across both treatments, lower movement synchrony was associated with a greater likelihood of premature termination (Schoenherr et al., 2019). Finally, in a study of body-oriented psychotherapy for schizophrenia, greater increases in nonverbal synchrony were marginally associated with greater reductions in negative symptoms (Galbusera et al., 2018). Adding nuance, a study of integrative CBT for patients with varied diagnoses found that moderate movement synchrony was related to the most positive outcomes; specifically, the lowest level of synchrony was found in nonimproved, dropout cases, the highest level of synchrony was found in nonimproved, consensual termination cases, and a moderate amount of synchrony was found in improved cases (Paulick et al., 2018).

Just a few studies have examined other forms of synchrony. For example, one found that greater vocal pitch synchrony was associated with lower quality alliances and worse treatment outcomes (Reich et al., 2014). Additionally, a preliminary study of one therapist working with four patients found evidence that at least some measures of respiration, heart rate, and heart rate variability synchrony were positively associated with alliance quality and session progress ratings (Tschacher & Meier, 2019).

There is a small, but growing, research base suggesting that patients and therapists experience synchrony in various processes, and, in general, greater levels of such synchrony tend to relate to more positive treatment processes and outcomes. However, there have been some contradictory findings (e.g., Reich et al., 2014), suggesting that further research is needed before definitive conclusions can be drawn. More work is also needed to understand whether synchrony can be actively facilitated in psychotherapy; that is, is synchrony simply a marker or consequence of good process, or can therapists be trained to affect it?

Interpersonal Complementarity

As previously discussed, interpersonal complementarity represents relational transactions that correspond on the dimension of affiliation and reciprocate on the dimension of interdependence. According to interpersonal theory and research, transactions high in complementarity are familiar and satisfying, and they maintain the interactants' typical sense of self and others; conversely, transactions low in complementarity are frustrated, uncomfortable, and anxiety provoking, and they will either substantively disrupt the relationship (possibly to the point of termination) or promote behavioral change in one or both participants (Benjamin, 1984; Kiesler, 1996; Sullivan, 1953). As should be evident in these principles, and inasmuch as psychotherapy is a series of interpersonal transactions, it follows that complementarity would influence treatment outcome. Indeed, there is evidence that substantiates this empirical link, with most studies drawing on the SASB to codify complementarity. These studies have largely involved relatively small samples of patient–therapist dyads and intensive micro-process analysis of their interactions in parts of one or more sessions.

For example, in the early research conducted in the context of TLDP, the authors found that the good vs. poor outcome cases were marked by significantly greater positive complementarity (i.e., reciprocal affiliative and/or autonomy-enhancing exchanges) and less negative complementarity (i.e., reciprocal hostile and/or controlling exchanges; Henry et al., 1986). Similarly, in a study of short-term anxiety-provoking therapy, greater early positive complementarity (specifically, therapist responses to patient utterances) was associated with midtreatment patient improvement, over and above therapist competence in delivering treatment (Svartberg & Stiles, 1992).

More recently, in a study of therapy for varied personality disorders, greater hostile complementarity differentiated poor from good outcomes cases, whether the exchanges were initiated by the patient or therapist (Samstag et al., 2008). In another study, the low vs. high change group was marked by greater hostile complementarity across the early and middle (but not late) phases of treatment (von der Lippe et al., 2008). In a study of brief group psychodynamic-interpersonal therapy for binge eating disorder, greater early therapist–patient complementarity in general predicted a decrease in binge frequency at posttreatment (both for patients with low or high attachment anxiety; Maxwell et al., 2012). Finally, in a study of patient–therapist dyads in CT for depression, high change dyads evidenced greater general complementarity during an early session than low change dyads (Thompson et al., 2018). In terms of *specific* complementarity sequences, these high change dyads were especially likely to exhibit sequences of transitive affirmation followed by intransitive disclosure and transitive influence/protection followed by intransitive trust/reliance, regardless of whether the patient or therapist initiated the sequence. Conversely, complementary exchanges involving therapist control and patient submission were the most likely interpersonal transactions in low-change dyads.

Although the studies reviewed typically highlight the importance of patient–therapist complementarity at specific points in time, they have rarely tested the pantheoretical notion

that therapeutic change requires a three-stage process in which complementarity plays a central role at each stage; that is, (a) high complementary interactions in the early stage (to build early rapport); (b) lower complementarity in the middle (conflict) stage (to engage the patient differently in the service of changing interpersonal patterns and the corresponding internalizations of important people); and (c) high complementarity in the late stage of therapy (but now for healthier transactions and introjections; Kiesler, 1982; Tracey, 1993; Tracey & Ray, 1984). A small, older literature supports that this high-low-high complementarity pattern associates with positive outcomes both in psychodynamic or interpersonally informed therapy (Dietzel & Abeles, 1975; Tasca & McMullen, 1992) and in CBT (Tracey et al., 1999). However, replication of these results is needed, including in the most contemporary versions of common psychotherapies.

At present, the SASB-based research on patient–therapist complementarity points to the importance of attending closely to transactional sequences. There seems to be some benefit, especially early, to patients and therapists engaging each other with matching affiliation and reciprocal interdependence. Such benefits may derive partly from the positive relational consequences of complementarity; namely, comfortable, anxiety-free exchange. However, beyond a critical period of risk for relational termination due to low complementarity, there may come a time when engaging each other in noncomplementary exchange could stimulate adaptive change. Moreover, to the extent that novel, healthy exchanges take hold, the therapeutic dyad can then use complementarity to strengthen them. Thus, therapists might consider interpersonal theory in any treatment, as such principles can be used pantheoretically to facilitate problem and goal formulation and, when complementarity is recognized and used strategically, it may stimulate change.

CONCLUSIONS AND RECOMMENDATIONS

At the risk of stating the obvious, this chapter reminds us that in psychotherapy there is always interactions among patient, therapist, dyad, and extratherapy factors, which are surrounded by treatment types, formats, and settings. This empirical review also underscores that EBP is far more nuanced than the application of treatments to patients, even when only considering patient-level variable–outcome associations (EBP is even more complex when factoring in the therapist level, cross-level interactions, nonlinear change, process contexts, responsiveness, etc.). To us, psychotherapy research, as exemplified by the work we have reviewed on patient, therapist, and relational factors, is most centrally the study of people engaged in talk-based processes; not the study of treatments as though the people who deliver/receive them are interchangeable averages. Put differently, treatments do not treat people; rather, people treat people through the medium of conversation, and the ever-growing body of research on the people and relationships of psychotherapy continues to uncover ways in which this interpersonal transaction can be grounded in science.

Given that we have integrated clinical implications and future research directions throughout, we conclude by highlighting just a few empirical themes that stand out:

1. Unsurprisingly, we will perpetually need more creative research to inform evidence-based patient-, therapist-, and relationally related clinical practices. In the past five decades since the first edition of the *Handbook*, we have been impressed at how creative scholars have become with clinical observations, tests of theory, measurement innovations, multilevel analyses, and so forth. Thus, we have immense hope that such creativity will continue, and that the nuance of scientific results will increasingly map onto the nuance of the psychotherapy encounter and human change.

2. More research is needed to understand better the mechanisms that transmit the beneficial influences of patient, therapist, and relational factors on treatment outcomes, as well as determinants of the factors themselves. That is, we need to orient both forward to uncover causal pathways to change (e.g., patient OE affecting treatment outcome through the mechanism of alliance quality) and backward to know from where people's therapy-relevant factors come (e.g., what contributes to patients' helpful or harmful level of a factor at baseline, such as OE, alexithymia, PM, etc.).

3. As noted throughout, the vast majority of research on the three factor classes herein has been correlational, leaving the causal effect of patient, therapist, and relational factors an open question in need of experimental tests.

4. Despite methodological innovations, issues can persist with regard to measurement overlap, distribution issues, change sensitivity, power, etc. Thus, future research should aim to improve the quality of the means through which we answer our psychotherapy questions.

5. We see a pressing need to study further the three factor classes in context, with an eye on when they matter most and what contextual markers signal when they most need to be responded to in some (hopefully, evidence backed) way, shape, or form.

6. We also need to study the factor classes in interaction with each other with appropriate levels and methods of analysis (e.g., dyadic models to derive truly relational factors; actor-partner models to uncover things like factor/process contagion; truth and bias models to richly reveal things like attunement and factor/process tracking; etc.).

7. We see a need to understand even more precisely how therapists can be interpersonally effective, optimally communicative, mindful of interpersonal patterns and their meaning (e.g., collusion or correction), multiculturally oriented, and pointedly flexible and responsive across all treatment types, patients, and contexts.

To us, an important present and future direction for psychotherapy involves identifying ways to flexibly tailor interventions (the what we do) to people, dyads, and moments (the who we are in context). This type of matching, aligning, and attuning would seem to hold much more promise than trying mostly to answer the question of "what (treatment) works for whom (the average patient)." Of course, we hope that readers also extract other important themes from this review or are inspired to help fill empirical gaps that remain. All told, we look forward to where clinicians, researchers, and scholars will have taken us by the next edition of this landmark volume.

ABBREVIATIONS

ACT	Acceptance and Commitment Therapy
AM	Autonomous Motivation
AN	Anorexia Nervosa
APES	Assimilation of Problematic Experiences Scale
AS	anxiety sensitivity
ASAB	Structural Analysis of Social Behavior
CAT	culturally adapted treatments
CBASP	Cognitive Behavioral Analysis System of Psychotherapy
CBT	cognitive behavioral therapy
CM	controlled motivation
CT	cognitive therapy
CT	countertransference
EBP	evidence-based practice
EDs	eating disorders
EE	emotional expression
GAD	generalized anxiety disorder
IIP	Inventory of Interpersonal Problems
IMI	Impact Message Inventory
IPT	interpersonal psychotherapy
LBGQ+	lesbian, bisexual, gay, queer
LOC	locus of control
MCC	multicultural competence
MCO	multicultural orientation
MI	motivational interviewing
OCD	obsessive compulsive disorder
OE	outcome expectation
PD	panic disorder
PM	psychological mindedness
PTSD	post-traumatic stress disorder
R/S	religion and spirituality
RCT	randomized controlled trials
REM	racial and ethnic minority
ROM	routine outcomes monitoring
SAD	social anxiety disorder
SASB	structural analysis of social behavior
SES	socioeconomic status
TLDP	time-limited dynamic psychotherapy
TSD	therapist self-disclosure

REFERENCES

Ahmed, M., & Westra, H. A. (2009). Impact of a treatment rationale on expectancy and engagement in cognitive behavioral therapy for social anxiety. *Cognitive Therapy and Research, 33*(3), 314–322. https://doi.org/10.1007/s10608-008-9182-1

Ainsworth, M.D.S. (1979). Infant-mother attachment. *American Psychologist, 34*(10), 932–937.https://doi.org/10.1037/0003-066X.34.10.932

Alden, L. E., Wiggins, J. S., & Pincus, A. L. (1990). Construction of circumplex scales for the Inventory of Interpersonal Problem. *Journal of Personality Assessment, 55*(3–4), 537–548. https://doi.org/10.1080/00223891.1990.9674088

Alegría, M., Chatterji, P., Wells, K., Cao, Z., Chen, C. N., Takeuchi, D., Jackson, J., & Meng, X. L. (2008). Disparity in depression treatment among racial and ethnic minority populations in the United States. *Psychiatric Services, 59*(11), 1264–1272. https://doi.org/10.1176/ps.2008.59.11.1264

Alimohamed-Janmohamed, S., Charvat, M., Gheytanchi, A., Beutler, L. E., & Breckenridge, J. (2010). Point of entry and functional impairment as predictors of treatment amount and cost for patients with mental illness and substance abuse disorders in Santa Barbara County Mental Health Services. *Psychological Services, 7*(1), 44–56. https://doi.org/10.1037/a0017783

Altenstein-Yamanaka, D., Zimmermann, J., Krieger, T., Dörig, N., & grosse Holtforth, M. (2017). Self-reported interpersonal problems and impact messages as perceived by significant others are differentially associated with the process and outcome of depression therapy. *Journal of Counseling Psychology, 64*(4), 410–423. https://doi.org/10.1037/cou0000221

American Psychological Association Presidential Task Force on Evidence-Based Practice (2006). Evidence-based practice in psychology. *American Psychologist, 61*(4), 271–285. https://doi.org/10.1037/0003-066X.61.4.271

Ametrano, R. M., Constantino, M. J., & Nalven, T. (2017). The influence of expectancy persuasion techniques on socially anxious analogue patients' treatment beliefs and therapeutic actions. *International Journal of Cognitive Therapy, 10*(3), 187–205. https://doi.org/10.1521/ijct.2017.10.3.187

Appelbaum, S. A. (1973). Psychological-mindedness: Word, concept and essence. *The International Journal of Psychoanalysis, 54*(1), 35–46.

Arch, J. J., Wolitzky-Taylor, K. B., Eifert, G. H., Craske, M. G. (2012). Longitudinal treatment mediation of traditional cognitive behavioral therapy and acceptance and commitment therapy for anxiety disorders. *Behaviour Research and Therapy, 50*(7–8), 469–478. https://doi.org/10.1016/j.brat.2012.04.007

Aten, J. D., O'Grady, K., & Worthington, E., Jr (2012). *The psychology of religion and spirituality for clinicians: Using research in your practice.* New York: Routledge.

Atzil-Slonim, D., Bar-Kalifa, E., Fisher, H., Lazarus, G., Hasson-Ohayon, I., Lutz, W., Rubel, J. & Rafaeli, E. (2019). Therapists' empathic accuracy toward their clients' emotions. *Journal of Consulting and Clinical Psychology, 87*(1), 33–45. https://doi.org/10.1037/ccp0000354

Atzil-Slonim, D., Bar-Kalifa, E., Fisher, H., Peri, T., Lutz, W., Rubel, J., & Rafaeli, E. (2018). Emotional congruence between clients and therapists and its effect on treatment outcome. *Journal of Counseling Psychology, 65*(1), 51–64. https://doi.org/10.1037/cou0000250

Aubuchon-Endsley, N. L., & Callahan, J. L. (2009). The hour of departure: Predicting attrition in the training clinic from role expectancies. *Training and Education in Professional Psychology, 3*(2), 120–126. https://doi.org/10.1037/a0014455

Austin, J. T., & Vancouver, J. B. (1996). Goal constructs in psychology: Structure, process, and content. *Psychological Bulletin, 120*(3), 338–375. https://doi.org/10.1037/0033-2909.120.3.338

Aviram, A., & Westra, H. A. (2011). The impact of motivational interviewing on resistance in cognitive behavioural therapy for generalized anxiety disorder. *Psychotherapy Research, 21*(6), 698–708. https://doi.org/10.1080/10503307.2011.610832

Aviram, A., Westra, H. A., Constantino, M. J., & Antony, M. M. (2016). Responsive management of early resistance in cognitive-behavioral therapy for generalized anxiety disorder. *Journal of Consulting and Clinical Psychology, 84*(9), 783–794. https://doi.org/10.1037/ccp0000100

Bar-Kalifa, E., Atzil-Slonim, D., Rafaeli, E., Peri, T., Rubel, J., & Lutz, W. (2016). Therapist-client agreement in assessments of clients' functioning. *Journal of Consulting and Clinical Psychology, 84*(12), 1127–1134. https://doi.org/10.1037/ccp0000157

Barlow, DH. *Anxiety and its disorders: The nature and treatment of anxiety and panic. 2.* New York: The Guilford Press; 2002.

Bartholomew, T. T., Gundel, B. E., Li, H., Joy, E. E., Kang, E., & Scheel, M. J. (2019). The meaning of therapist hope for their clients: A phenomenological study. *Journal of Counseling Psychology, 66*(4), 496–507. https://doi.org/10.1037/cou0000328

Basto, I., Pinheiro, P., Stiles, W. B., Rijo, D., & Salgado, J. (2017). Changes in symptom intensity and emotion valence during the process of assimilation of a problematic experience: A quantitative study of a good outcome case of cognitive-behavioral therapy. *Psychotherapy Research, 27*(4), 437–449. https://doi.org/10.1080/10503307.2015.1119325

Basto, I. M., Stiles, W. B., Rijo, D., & Salgado, J. (2018). Does assimilation of problematic experiences predict a decrease in symptom intensity? *Clinical Psychology & Psychotherapy, 25*(1), 76–84. https://doi.org/10.1002/cpp.2130

Benjamin, L. S. (1984). Principles of prediction using structural analysis of social behavior. In R. A. Zucker, J. Aronoff, & A. J. Rabin (Eds.), *Personality and the prediction of behavior* (pp. 121–173). New York: Academic Press.

Benjamin, L. S. (1996). Introduction to the special section on structural analysis of social behavior. *Journal of Consulting and Clinical Psychology, 64*(6), 1203–1212. https://doi.org/10.1037/0022-006X.64.6.1203

Bernal, G., Jiménez-Chafey, M. I., & Domenech Rodríguez, M. M. (2009). Cultural adaptation of treatments: A resource for considering culture in evidence-based practice. *Professional Psychology: Research and Practice, 40*(4), 361–368. https://doi.org/10.1037/a0016401

Beutler, L. E., & Consoli, A. J. (1993). Matching the therapist's interpersonal stance to clients' characteristics: Contributions from systematic eclectic psychotherapy. *Psychotherapy, 30*(3), 417–422. https://doi.org/10.1037/0033-3204.30.3.417

Beutler, L. E., Edwards, C., & Someah, K. (2018). Adapting psychotherapy to patient reactance level: A meta-analytic review. *Journal of Clinical Psychology, 74*(11), 1952–1963. https://doi.org/10.1002/jclp.22682

Beutler, L. E., Harwood, T. M., Alimohamed, S., & Malik, M. (2002). Functional impairment and coping style. In J. C. Norcross (Ed.), *Psychotherapy relationships that work: Therapist contributions and responsiveness to patients.* (pp. 145–170). New York, NY: Oxford University Press.

Beutler, L. E., Harwood, T. M., Michelson, A., Song, X., & Holman, J. (2011). Reactance/resistance level. In J. C. Norcross (Ed.), *Psychotherapy relationships that work: Evidence-based responsiveness* (2nd ed., pp. 261–278). New York, NY: Oxford University Press. https://doi.org/10.1093/acprof:oso/9780199737208.003.0013

Beutler, L. E., Kimpara, S., Edwards, C. J., & Miller, K. D. (2018). Fitting psychotherapy to patient coping style: A meta-analysis. *Journal of Clinical Psychology, 74*(11), 1980–1995. https://doi.org/10.1002/jclp.22684

Beutler, L. E., Malik, M., Alimohamed, S., Harwood, T. M., Talebi, H., Noble, S., & Wong, E. (2004). Therapist variables. In M. J. Lambert (Ed.), *Bergin & Garfield's handbook of psychotherapy and behavior change* (5th ed., pp. 227–306). New York, NY: Wiley.

Blakey, S. M., Abramowitz, J. S., Reuman, L., Leonard, R. C., & Riemann, B. C. (2017). Anxiety sensitivity as a predictor of outcome in the treatment of obsessive-compulsive disorder. *Journal of Behavior Therapy and Experimental Psychiatry, 57,* 113–117. https://doi.org/10.1016/j.jbtep.2017.05.003

Blanchard, M., & Farber, B. A. (2015). Lying in psychotherapy: Why and what clients don't tell their therapist about therapy. *Counselling Psychology Quarterly, 29,* 90–112. https://doi.org/10.1080/09515070.2015.1085365

Bohart, A. C., & Wade, A. G. (2013). The client in psychotherapy. In M. J. Lambert (Ed.), *Bergin & Garfield's handbook of psychotherapy and behavior change* (6th ed., pp. 219–257). New York, NY: Wiley.

Boonstra, N., Klaassen, R., Sytema, S., Marshall, M., De Haan, L., Wunderink, L., & Wiersma, D. (2012). Duration of untreated psychosis and negative symptoms-A systematic review and meta-analysis of individual patient data. *Schizophrenia Research, 142*(1–3), 12–19. https://doi.org/10.1016/j.schres.2012.08.017

Boswell, J.F., Anderson, L.M., Oswald, J.M., Reilly, E.E., Gorrell, S., & Anderson, D.A. (2019). A preliminary naturalistic clinical case series study of the feasibility and impact of interoceptive exposure for eating disorders.

Behaviour Research and Therapy, *117*, 54–64. https://doi.org/10.1016/j.brat.2019.02.004

Boswell, J. F., Constantino, M. J., & Anderson, L. M. (2016). Potential obstacles to treatment success in adults: Client characteristics. In Malztman, S. (Ed.), *The Oxford handbook of treatment processes and outcomes in psychology* (pp. 183–205). New York: Oxford University Press, Inc. https://doi.org/10.1093/oxfordhb/9780199739134.013.17

Boswell, J. F., Farchione, T.J., Sauer-Zavala, S., Murray, H. W., Fortune, M.R., & Barlow, D. H. (2013). Anxiety sensitivity and interoceptive exposure: A transdiagnostic construct and change strategy. *Behavior Therapy*, *44*(3), 417–431. https://doi.org/10.1016/j.beth.2013.03.006

Böttche, M., Kuwert, P., Pietrzak, R. H., & Knaevelsrud, C. (2016). Predictors of outcome of an Internet-based cognitive-behavioural therapy for post-traumatic stress disorder in older adults. *Psychology and Psychotherapy: Theory, Research and Practice*, *89*(1), 82–96. https://doi.org/10.1111/papt.12069

Bottlender, R., Strauß, A., & Möller, H.-J. (2000). Impact of duration of symptoms prior to first hospitalization on acute outcome in 998 schizophrenic patients. *Schizophrenia Research*, *44*(2), 145–150. https://doi.org/10.1016/S0920-9964(99)00186-3

Bowlby, J. (1969). *Attachment and loss: Vol. 1. Attachment.* New York, NY: Basic Books.

Bradizza, C.M., Stasiewicz, P.R., & Paas, N.D. (2006). Relapse to alcohol and drug use among individuals diagnosed with co-occurring mental health and substance use disorders: A review. *Clinical Psychology Review*, *26*(2), 162–178. https://doi.org/10.1016/j.cpr.2005.11.005

Brehm, J. W. & Brehm S. S. (1981). *Psychological reactance - a theory of freedom and control.* New York, NY: Academic Press.

Brown, T. A., Campbell, L. A., Lehman, C. L., Grisham, J. R., & Mancill, R. B. (2001). Current and lifetime comorbidity of the *DSM-IV* anxiety and mood disorders in a large clinical sample. *Journal of Abnormal Psychology*, *110*(4), 585–599. https://doi.org/10.1037/0021-843X.110.4.585

Budge, S. L., & Moradi, B. (2018). Attending to gender in psychotherapy: Understanding and incorporating systems of power. *Journal of Clinical Psychology*, *74*(11), 2014–2027. https://doi.org/10.1002/jclp.22686

Cabral, R. R., & Smith, T. B. (2011). Racial/ethnic matching of clients and therapists in mental health services: A meta-analytic review of preferences, perceptions, and outcomes. *Journal of Counseling Psychology*, *58*(4), 537–554. https://doi.org/10.1037/a0025266

Cain, N. M., Pincus, A. L., & Grosse Holtforth, M. (2010). Interpersonal subtypes in social phobia: Diagnostic and treatment implications. *Journal of Personality Assessment*, *92*(6), 514–527. https://doi.org/10.1080/00223891.2010.513704

Cameron, K., Ogrodniczuk, J., & Hadjipavlou, G. (2014). Changes in alexithymia following psychological intervention: a review. *Harvard Review of Psychiatry*, *22*(3), 162–178. https://doi.org/10.1097/HRP.0000000000000036

Captari, L. E., Hook, J. N., Hoyt, W., Davis, D. E., McElroy, H. S. E., & Worthington, E. L., Jr. (2018). Integrating clients' religion and spirituality within psychotherapy: A comprehensive meta-analysis. *Journal of Clinical Psychology*, *74*(11), 1938–1951. https://doi.org/10.1002/jclp.22681

Caro Gabalda, I., Stiles, W. B., & Pérez Ruiz, S. (2016). Therapist activities preceding setbacks in the assimilation process. *Psychotherapy Research*, *26*(6), 653–664. https://doi.org/10.1080/10503307.2015.1104422

Carter, J. C., & Kelly, A. C. (2015). Autonomous and controlled motivation for eating disorders treatment: Baseline predictors and relationship to treatment outcome. *British Journal of Clinical Psychology*, *54*(1), 76–90. https://doi.org/10.1111/bjc.12062

Castonguay, L. G., Boswell, J. F., Constantino, M. J., Goldfried, M. R., & Hill, C. E. (2010a). Training implications of harmful effects of psychological treatments. *American Psychologist*, *65*(1), 34–49. https://doi.org/10.1037/a0017330

Castonguay, L. G., Boswell, J. F., Zack, S. E., Baker, S., Boutselis, M.A., Chiswick, N. R., Damer, D. D., Hemmelstein, N. A., Jackson, J. S., Morford, M., Ragusea, S. A., Roper, J. G., Spayd, C., Weiszer, T., Borkovec, T. D., & Grosse Holtforth, M. (2010). Helpful and hindering events in psychotherapy: A practice research network study. *Psychotherapy*, *47*(3), 327–344. https://doi.org/10.1037/a0021164

Castonguay, L. G., Constantino, M. J., & Beutler, L. E. (Eds.) (2019). *Principles of change: How psychotherapists implement research in practice.* New York: Oxford University Press. https://doi.org/10.1093/med-psych/9780199324729.001.0001

Castonguay, L. G., Goldfried, M. R., Wiser, S., Raue, P. J., & Hayes, A. M. (1996). Predicting the effect of cognitive therapy for depression: A study of unique and common factors. *Journal of Consulting and Clinical Psychology*, *64*(3), 497–504. https://doi.org/10.1037/0022-006X.64.3.497

Castonguay, L.G., & Hill, C.E. (2007). *Insight in psychotherapy.* Washington DC: American Psychological Association. https://doi.org/10.1037/11532-000

Chui, H., Zilcha-Mano, S., Dinger, U., Barrett, M. S., & Barber, J. P. (2016). Dependency and self-criticism in treatments for depression. *Journal of Counseling Psychology*, *63*(4), 452–459. https://doi.org/10.1037/cou0000142

Clarkin, J. F., & Levy, K. N. (2004). The influence of client variables on psychotherapy. In M. J. Lambert (Ed.), *Bergin and Garfield's handbook of psychotherapy and behavior change* (5th ed., pp. 194–226). Hoboken, NJ: Wiley.

Connor, D. R., & Callahan, J. L. (2015). Impact of psychotherapist expectations on client outcomes. *Psychotherapy*, *52*(3), 351–362. https://doi.org/10.1037/a0038890

Constantino, M. J. (2000). Interpersonal process in psychotherapy through the lens of the Structural Analysis of Social Behavior. *Applied & Preventive Psychology*, *9*(3), 153–172. https://doi.org/10.1016/S0962-1849(05)80002-2

Constantino, M. J., Ametrano, R. M., & Greenberg, R. P. (2012). Clinician interventions and participant characteristics that foster adaptive patient expectations for psychotherapy and psychotherapeutic change. *Psychotherapy*, *49*(4), 557–569. https://doi.org/10.1037/a0029440

Constantino, M. J., Aviram, A., Coyne, A. E., Newkirk, K., Greenberg, R. P., Westra, H. A., & Antony, M. M. (2020). Dyadic, longitudinal associations among patient-therapist outcome expectation and alliance quality, and their indirect effects on patient outcome: A within- and between-dyad analysis. *Journal of Counseling Psychology*, *67*(1), 40–50. https://doi.org/10.1037/cou0000364

Constantino, M. J., Coyne, A. E., Boswell, J. F., Iles, B. R., & Vîslă, A. (2018). A meta-analysis of the association between patients' early perception of treatment credibility and their posttreatment outcomes. *Psychotherapy*, *55*(4), 486–495. https://doi.org/10.1037/pst0000168

Constantino, M. J., Coyne, A. E., & Muir, H. J. (2020, February 14). Evidence-based therapist responsivity to disruptive clinical process. *Cognitive and Behavioral Practice. Advanced online publication.* https://doi.org/10.1016/j.cbpra.2020.01.003

Constantino, M. J., Glass, C. R., Arnkoff, D. B., Ametrano, R. M., & Smith, J. Z. (2011). Expectations. In J. C. Norcross (Ed.), *Psychotherapy relationships that work: Evidence-based responsiveness* (2nd ed.; pp. 354–376). New York: Oxford University Press, Inc. https://doi.org/10.1093/acprof:oso/9780199737208.003.0018

Constantino, M. J., Goodwin, B. J., Muir, H. J., Coyne, A. E., & Boswell, J. F. (in press). Contextual responsivity in cognitive-behavioral therapy. To appear in J. C. Watson & H. Wiseman (Eds.), *Attuning to enhance therapist responsiveness.* Washington DC: American Psychological Association.

Constantino, M. J., Laws, H. B., Arnow, B. A., Klein, D. N., Rothbaum, B. O., & Manber, R. (2012). The relation between changes in patients' interpersonal impact messages and outcome in treatment for chronic depression. *Journal of Consulting and Clinical Psychology*, *80*(3), 354–364. https://doi.org/10.1037/a0028351

Constantino, M. J., Laws, H. B., Coyne, A. E., Greenberg, R. P., Klein, D. N., Manber, R., Rothbaum, B. O., & Arnow, B. A. (2016). Change in patients' interpersonal impacts as a mediator of the alliance–outcome association in treatment for chronic depression. *Journal of Consulting and Clinical Psychology*, *84*(12), 1135–1144. https://doi.org/10.1037/ccp0000149

Constantino, M. J., Marnell, M. E., Haile, A. J., Kanther-Sista, S. N., Wolman, K., Zappert, L., & Arnow, B. A. (2008). Integrative cognitive therapy for depression: A randomized pilot comparison. *Psychotherapy*, *45*(2), 122–134. https://doi.org/10.1037/0033-3204.45.2.122

Constantino, M. J., Romano, F. M., Coyne, A. E., Westra, H. A., & Antony, M. M. (2018). Client interpersonal impacts as mediators of long-term outcome in cognitive-behavioral therapy integrated with motivational interviewing for generalized anxiety disorder. *Psychotherapy Research*, *28*(6), 861–872. https://doi.org/10.1080/10503307.2017.1301689

Constantino, M. J., Vîslă, A., Coyne, A. E., & Boswell, J. F. (2018). A meta-analysis of the association between patients' early treatment outcome expectation and their posttreatment outcomes. *Psychotherapy*, *55*(4), 473–485. https://doi.org/10.1037/pst0000169

Constantino, M. J., Westra, H. A., Antony, M. M., & Coyne, A. E. (2019). Specific and common processes as mediators of the long-term effects of cognitive-behavioral therapy integrated with motivational interviewing for generalized anxiety disorder. *Psychotherapy Research*, 29(2), 213–225. https://doi.org/10.1080/10503307.2017.1332794

Conte, H. R., Plutchik, R., Jung, B. B., Picard, S., Karasu, T. B., & Lotterman, A. (1990). Psychological mindedness as a predictor of psychotherapy outcome: A preliminary report. *Comprehensive Psychiatry*, 31(5), 426–431. https://doi.org/10.1016/0010-440X(90)90027-P

Cooper, M. (2008). *Essential findings in counselling and psychotherapy: The facts are friendly*. Thousand Oaks, CA: Sage.

Costa, P. T., & McCrae, R. R. (1985). *The NEO Personality Inventory manual*. Odessa, FL: Psychological Assessment Resources https://doi.org/10.1037/t07564-000

Coulson, C., Ng, F., Geertsema, M., Dodd, S., & Berk, M. (2009). Client-reported reasons for non-engagement in drug and alcohol treatment. *Drug and Alcohol Review*, 28(4), 372–378. https://doi.org/10.1111/j.1465-3362.2009.00054.x

Cox, B. J., Enns, M. W., & Clara, I. P. (2002). The multidimensional structure of perfectionism in clinically distressed and college student samples. *Psychological Assessment*, 14(3), 365–373. https://doi.org/10.1037/1040-3590.14.3.365

Coyne, A. E., Constantino, M. J., Gomez Penedo, J. M., Gnall, K.E., McBride, C., & Ravitz, P. (2018). Relation of patient and therapist interpersonal impact messages to outcome in interpersonal therapy for depression. *Journal of Psychotherapy Integration*, 28(4), 475–488. https://doi.org/10.1037/int0000125

Critchfield, K. L., Henry, W. P., Castonguay, L. G., & Borkovec, T. D. (2007). Interpersonal process and outcome in variants of cognitive-behavioral psychotherapy. *Journal of Clinical Psychology*, 63(1), 31–51. https://doi.org/10.1002/jclp.20329

Cuijpers, P., van Straten, A., Smit, F., & Andersson, G. (2009). Is psychotherapy for depression equally effective in younger and older adults? A meta-regression analysis. *International Psychogeriatrics*, 21(1), 16–24. https://doi.org/10.1017/S1041610208008089

Davis, M., & Addis, M. (2002). Treatment expectations, experiences, and mental health functioning predict attrition status in behavioural medicine groups. *Irish Journal of Psychology*, 23, 37–51.

Davis, D. E., DeBlaere, C., Brubaker, K., Owen, J., Jordan, T. A., II, Hook, J. N., & Van Tongeren, D. R. (2016). Microaggressions and perceptions of cultural humility in counseling. *Journal of Counseling and Development*, 94(4), 483–493. https://doi.org/10.1002/jcad.12107

Davis, D. E., DeBlaere, C., Owen, J., Hook, J. N., Rivera, D. P., Choe, E., Van Tongeren, D. R., Worthington, E. L., Jr., & Placeres, V. (2018). The multicultural orientation framework: A narrative review. *Psychotherapy*, 55(1), 89–100. https://doi.org/10.1037/pst0000160

Davis, D. E., Rice, K., Hook, J. N., Van Tongeren, D. R., DeBlaere, C., Choe, E., & Worthington, E. L., Jr. (2015). Development of the sources of spirituality scale. *Journal of Counseling Psychology*, 62(3), 503–513. https://doi.org/10.1037/cou0000082

Defife, J. A., Conklin, C. Z., Smith, J. M., & Poole, J. (2010). Psychotherapy appointment no-shows: Rates and reasons. *Psychotherapy*, 47(3), 413–417. https://doi.org/10.1037/a0021168

Dermody, S. S., Quilty, L. C., & Bagby, R. M. (2016). Interpersonal impacts mediate the association between personality and treatment response in major depression. *Journal of Counseling Psychology*, 63(4), 396–404. https://doi.org/10.1037/cou0000144

Detert, N. B., Llewelyn, S., Hardy, G. E., Barkham, M., & Stiles, W. B. (2006). Assimilation in good- and poor-outcome cases of very brief psychotherapy for mild depression: An initial comparison. *Psychotherapy Research*, 16(4), 393–407. https://doi.org/10.1080/10503300500294728

Devilly, G., & Borkovec, T. (2000). Psychometric properties of the Credibility/Expectancy Questionnaire. *Journal of Behavior Therapy and Experimental Psychiatry*, 31(2), 73–86. https://doi.org/10.1016/S0005-7916(00)00012-4

Dietzel, C. S., & Abeles, N. (1975). Client-therapist complementarity and therapeutic outcome. *Journal of Counseling Psychology*, 22(4), 264–272. https://doi.org/10.1037/h0076731

Dinger, U., Zilcha-Mano, S., McCarthy, K. S., Barrett, M. S., & Barber, J. P. (2013). Interpersonal problems as predictors of alliance, symptomatic improvement and premature termination in treatment of depression.

Journal of Affective Disorders, 151(2), 800–803. https://doi.org/10.1016/j.jad.2013.07.003

Dorland, J. M., & Fischer, A. R. (2001). Gay, lesbian, and bisexual individuals' perceptions: An analogue study. *The Counseling Psychologist*, 29(4), 532–547. https://doi.org/10.1177/0011000001294004

Dowd, E. T., & Seibel, C. A. (1990). A cognitive theory of resistance and reactance: Implications for treatment. *Journal of Mental Health Counseling*, 12(4), 458–469.

Driessen, E., Cuijpers, P., Hollon, S. D., & Dekker, J. J. M. (2010). Does pretreatment severity moderate the efficacy of psychological treatment of adult outpatient depression? A meta-analysis. *Journal of Consulting and Clinical Psychology*, 78(5), 668–680. https://doi.org/10.1037/a0020570

Edwards, C., & Murdock, N. (1994). Characteristics of therapist self-disclosure in the counseling process. *Journal of Counseling & Development*, 72(4), 384–389. https://doi.org/10.1002/j.1556-6676.1994.tb00954.x

Egan, S. J., Wade, T. D., & Shafran, R. (2011). Perfectionism as a transdiagnostic process: A clinical review. *Clinical Psychology Review*, 31(2), 203–212. https://doi.org/10.1016/j.cpr.2010.04.009

Elkin, I., Falconnier, L., Smith, Y., Canada, K. E., Henderson, E., Brown, E. R., & McKay, B. M. (2014). Therapist responsiveness and patient engagement in therapy. *Psychotherapy Research*, 24(1), 52–66. https://doi.org/10.1080/10503307.2013.820855

Farber, B. A. (2003). Patient self-disclosure: a review of the research. *Journal of Clinical Psychology*, 59(5), 589–600. https://doi.org/10.1002/jclp.10161

Farber, B. A., & Sohn, A. (2001). *The relationship of patient disclosure to therapy outcome*. In annual conference of the Society for Psychotherapy Research. Montevideo, Uruguay.

Fichter, M.M., Qaudflieg, N., Crosby, R.D., & Koch, S. (2016). Long-term outcomes of anorexia nervosa: Results from a large clinical longitudinal study. *International Journal of Eating Disorders*, 50(9), 1018–1030. https://doi.org/10.1002/eat.22736

Finegan, M., Firth, N., Wojnarowski, C., & Delgadillo, J. (2018). Associations between socioeconomic status and psychological therapy outcomes: A systematic review and meta-analysis. *Depression and Anxiety*, 35(6), 560–573. https://doi.org/10.1002/da.22765

Fortuna, L. R., Alegria, M., & Gao, S. (2010). Retention in depression treatment among ethnic and racial minority groups in the United States. *Depression and Anxiety*, 27(5), 485–494. https://doi.org/10.1002/da.20685

Fournier, J. C., DeRubeis, R. J., Shelton, R. C., Hollon, S. D., Amsterdam, J. D., & Gallop, R. (2009). Prediction of response to medication and cognitive therapy in the treatment of moderate to severe depression. *Journal of Consulting and Clinical Psychology*, 77(4), 775–787. https://doi.org/10.1037/a0015401

Frank, J. D. (1961). *Persuasion and healing: A comparative study of psychotherapy*. Baltimore, MD: The Johns Hopkins Press.

Fredette, C., El-Baalbaki, G., Palardy, V., Rizkallah, E., & Guay, S. (2016). Social support and cognitive-behavioral therapy for posttraumatic stress disorder: A systematic review. *Traumatology*, 22(2), 131–144. https://doi.org/10.1037/trm0000070

Frost, R. O., Marten, P., Lahart, C., & Rosenblate, R. (1990). The dimensions of perfectionism. *Cognitive Therapy and Research*, 14, 449–468. https://doi.org/10.1007/BF01172967

Galbusera, L., Finn, M. T., & Fuchs, T. (2018). Interactional synchrony and negative symptoms: An outcome study of body-oriented psychotherapy for schizophrenia. *Psychotherapy Research*, 28(3), 457–469. https://doi.org/10.1080/10503307.2016.1216624

Gallagher, M. W., Payne, L. A., White, K. S., Shear, K. M., Woods, S. W., Gorman, J. M., & Barlow, D. H. (2013). Mechanisms of change in cognitive behavioral therapy for panic disorder: The unique effects of self-efficacy and anxiety sensitivity. *Behaviour Research and Therapy*, 51(11), 767–777. https://doi.org/10.1016/j.brat.2013.09.001

Gelso, C.J. (2009). The real relationship in a postmodern world: Theoretical and empirical explorations. *Psychotherapy Research*, 19(3), 253–264. https://doi.org/10.1080/10503300802389242

Gelso, C.J., Kivlighan, D.M. Jr., & Markin, R.D. (2018). The real relationship and its role in psychotherapy outcome: A meta-analysis. *Psychotherapy*, 55(4), 434–444. https://doi.org/10.1037/pst0000183

Goddard, E., Wingrove, J., & Moran, P. (2015). The impact of comorbid personality difficulties on response to IAPT treatment for depression and anxiety. *Behaviour Research and Therapy, 73,* 1–7. https://doi.org/10.1016/j.brat.2015.07.006

Gomez Penedo, J. M., Constantino, M. J., Coyne, A. E., Bernecker, S. L., & Smith-Hansen, L. (2019). Patient baseline interpersonal problems as moderators of outcome in two psychotherapies for bulimia nervosa. *Psychotherapy Research, 29*(6), 799–811. https://doi.org/10.1080/10503307.2018.1425931

Gomez Penedo, J. M., Constantino, M. J., Coyne, A. E., Westra, H. A., & Antony, M. M. (2017). Markers for context-responsiveness: Client baseline interpersonal problems moderate the efficacy of two psychotherapies for generalized anxiety disorder. *Journal of Consulting and Clinical Psychology, 85*(10), 1000–1011. https://doi.org/10.1037/ccp0000233

Goodwin, B. J., Constantino, M. J., Vîslă, A., Coyne, A. E., & Boswell, J. F. (2018, September). *A meta-analysis of the indirect effect of patient outcome expectation on treatment outcome through therapeutic alliance quality.* Paper presented at the meeting of the North American Chapter of the Society for Psychotherapy Research, Snowbird, UT.

Goodwin, B. J., Constantino, M. J., Westra, H. A., Button, M. L., & Antony, M. M. (2019). Patient motivational language as a predictor of symptom change, clinically significant response, and time to response in psychotherapy for generalized anxiety disorder. *Psychotherapy, 56*(4), 537–548. https://doi.org/10.1037/pst0000269

Greenberg, L. S. (2016). The clinical application of emotion in psychotherapy. In L. F. Barrett, M. Lewis, & J. M. Haviland-Jones (Eds.), *Handbook of emotions* (4th ed., pp. 670–684). New York, NY: Guilford Press.

Grosse Holtforth, M., Altenstein, D., Ansell, E., Schneider, C., & Caspar, F. (2012). Impact messages of depressed outpatients as perceived by their significant others: Profiles, therapeutic change, and relationship to outcome. *Journal of Clinical Psychology, 68*(3), 319–333. https://doi.org/10.1002/jclp.20854

Grossmann, K. E., Grossmann, K., & Waters, E. (2005). *Attachment from infancy to adulthood: The major longitudinal studies.* New York, NY: Guilford Press.

Harris, K. M., Edlund, M. J., & Larson, S. (2005). Racial and ethnic differences in the mental health problems and use of mental health care. *Medical Care, 43*(8), 775–784. https://doi.org/10.1097/01.mlr.0000170405.66264.23

Hartmann A., Zeeck, A., & Barrett, M. S. (2010). Interpersonal problems in eating disorders. *International Journal of Eating Disorders, 43*(7), 619–627. https://doi.org/10.1002/eat.20747

Hatcher, R. L. (2015). Interpersonal competencies: Responsiveness, technique, and training in psychotherapy. *American Psychologist, 70*(8), 747–757. https://doi.org/10.1037/a0039803

Hayes, J. A., Gelso, C. J., Goldberg, S., & Kivlighan, D. M., III. (2018). Countertransference management and effective psychotherapy: Meta-analytic findings. *Psychotherapy, 55*(4), 496–507. https://doi.org/10.1037/pst0000189

Hayes, J. A., Owen, J., & Bieschke, K. J. (2015). Therapist differences in symptom change with racial/ethnic minority clients. *Psychotherapy, 52*(3), 308–314. https://doi.org/10.1037/a0037957

Helms, J. E., & Cook, D. A. (1999). *Using race and culture in counseling and psychotherapy: Theory and process.* Boston, MA: Allyn & Bacon.

Henretty, J. R., Currier, J. M., Berman, J. S., & Levitt, H. M. (2014). The impact of counselor self-disclosure on clients: A meta-analytic review of experimental and quasi-experimental research. *Journal of Counseling Psychology, 61*(2), 191–207. https://doi.org/10.1037/a0036189

Henry, W. P., Schacht, T. E., & Strupp, H. H. (1986). Structural analysis of social behavior: Application to a study of interpersonal process in differential psychotherapeutic outcome. *Journal of Consulting and Clinical Psychology, 54*(1), 27–31. https://doi.org/10.1037/0022-006X.54.1.27

Henry, W. P., Schacht, T. E., & Strupp, H. H. (1990). Patient and therapist introject, interpersonal process, and differential psychotherapy outcome. *Journal of Consulting and Clinical Psychology, 58*(6), 768–774. https://doi.org/10.1037/0022-006X.58.6.768

Hill, C. E. (2014). *Helping skills: Facilitating exploration, insight, and action* (4th ed.). Washington, DC: American Psychological Association. https://doi.org/10.1037/14345-000

Hill, C. E., Knox, S., & Pinto-Coelho, K. G. (2018). Therapist self-disclosure and immediacy: A qualitative meta-analysis. *Psychotherapy, 55*(4), 445–460. https://doi.org/10.1037/pst0000182

Hill, P. C., Pargament, K. I., Hood, R. W., Jr., McCullough, J. M. E., Swyers, J. P., Larson, D. B., & Zinnbauer, B. J. (2000). Conceptualizing religion and spirituality: Points of commonality, points of departure. *Journal for the Theory of Social Behavior, 30*(1), 51–77. https://doi.org/10.1111/1468-5914.00119

Høglend, P., & Hagtvet, K. (2019). Change mechanisms in psychotherapy: Both improved insight and improved affective awareness are necessary. *Journal of Consulting and Clinical Psychology, 87*(4), 332–344. https://doi.org/10.1037/ccp0000381

Holdsworth, E., Bowen, E., Brown, S., & Howat, D. (2014). Client engagement in psychotherapeutic treatment and associations with client characteristics, therapist characteristics, and treatment factors. *Clinical Psychology Review, 34*(5), 428–450. https://doi.org/10.1016/j.cpr.2014.06.004

Hook, J. N., Davis, D. E., Owen, J., Worthington, E. L., Jr., & Utsey, S. O. (2013). Cultural humility: Measuring openness to culturally diverse clients. *Journal of Counseling Psychology, 60*(3), 353–366. https://doi.org/10.1037/a0032595

Hook, J. N., Farrell, J. E., Davis, D. E., DeBlaere, C., Van Tongeren, D. R., & Utsey, S. O. (2016). Cultural humility and racial microaggressions in counseling. *Journal of Counseling Psychology, 63*(3), 269–277. https://doi.org/10.1037/cou0000114

Honos-Webb, L., Surko, M., & Stiles, W. B. (1998). *Manual for rating assimilation in psychotherapy: February 1998 version.* Unpublished manuscript, Miami University-Oxford.

Horowitz, L. M., Alden, L. E., Wiggins, J. S., & Pincus, A. L. (2000). *IIP: Inventory of Interpersonal Problems manual.* San Antonio, TX: Pearson Assessment.

Hudson, J. I., Hiripi, E., Pope, H. G., & Kessler, R. C. (2007). The prevalence and correlates of eating disorders in the National Comorbidity Survey Replication. *Biological Psychiatry, 61*(3), 348–358. https://doi.org/10.1016/j.biopsych.2006.03.040

Imel, Z. E., Baldwin, S., Atkins, D. C., Owen, J., Baardseth, T., & Wampold, B. E. (2011). Racial/ethnic disparities in therapist effectiveness: A conceptualization and initial study of cultural competence. *Journal of Counseling Psychology, 58*(3), 290–298. https://doi.org/10.1037/a0023284

Imel, Z. E., Caperton, D. D., Tanana, M., & Atkins, D. C. (2017). Technology-enhanced human interaction in psychotherapy. *Journal of Counseling Psychology, 64*(4), 385–393. https://doi.org/10.1037/cou0000213

Ino, K., Ogawa, S., Kondo, M., Imai, R., Ii, T., Furukawa, T. A., & Akechi, T. (2017). Anxiety sensitivity as a predictor of broad dimensions of psychopathology after cognitive behavioral therapy for panic disorder. *Neuropsychiatric Disease and Treatment, 13,* 1835–1840. https://doi.org/10.2147/NDT.S121360

Jenkins, S. J., Fuqua, D. R., & Blum, C. R. (1986). Factors related to duration of counseling in a university counseling center. *Psychological Reports, 58*(2), 467–472. https://doi.org/10.2466/pr0.1986.58.2.467

Jennissen, S., Huber, J., Ehrenthal, J. C., Schauenburg, H., & Dinger, U. (2018). Association between insight and outcome of psychotherapy: Systematic review and meta-analysis. *The American Journal of Psychiatry, 175*(10), 961–969. https://doi.org/10.1176/appi.ajp.2018.17080847

Jensen, H. H., Mortensen, E. L., & Lotz, M. (2017). Predictors of nonresponding in short-term psychodynamic group therapy. *Nordic Psychology, 69*(4), 264–280. https://doi.org/10.1080/19012276.2017.1323664

Jiménez-Murcia, S., Tremblay, J., Stinchfield, R., Granero, R., Fernández-Aranda, F., Mestre-Bach, G., Steward, T., del Pino-Gutiérrez, A., Baño, M., Moragas, L., Aymamí, N., Gómez-Peña, M., Tárrega, S., Valenciano-Mendoza, E., Giroux, I., Sancho, M., Sánchez, I., Mallorquí-Bagué, N., González, V., & Menchón, J. M. (2017). The involvement of a concerned significant other in gambling disorder treatment outcome. *Journal of Gambling Studies, 33*(3), 937–953. https://doi.org/10.1007/s10899-016-9657-z

Jones, A., Lindekilde, N., Lübeck, M., & Clausen, L. (2015). The association between interpersonal problems and treatment outcome in the eating disorders: a systematic review. *Nordic Journal of Psychiatry, 69*(8), 563–573. https://doi.org/10.3109/08039488.2015.1019924

Jørgensen, C., Hougaard, E., Rosenbaum, B., Valbak, K., & Rehfeld, E. (2000). The dynamic assessment interview (DAI), interpersonal process measured by structural analysis of social behavior (SASB) and therapeutic outcome. *Psychotherapy Research, 10*(2), 181–195. https://doi.org/10.1093/ptr/10.2.181

Joyce, A. S., Ogrodniczuk, J. S., Piper, W. E., & McCallum, M. (2003). The alliance as mediator of expectancy effects in short-term individual therapy. *Journal of Consulting and Clinical Psychology*, 71(4), 672–679. https://doi.org/10.1037/0022-006X.71.4.672

Kampman, M., Keijsers, G. P. J., Hoogduin, C. A. L., & Hendriks, G. J. (2008). Outcome prediction of cognitive behaviour therapy for panic disorder: Initial symptom severity is predictive for treatment outcome, comorbid anxiety or depressive disorder, cluster C personality disorders and initial motivation are not. *Behavioural and Cognitive Psychotherapy*, 36(1), 99–112. https://doi.org/10.1017/S1352465807004018

Kannan, D., & Levitt, H. M. (2013). A review of client self-criticism in psychotherapy. *Journal of Psychotherapy Integration*, 23(2), 166–178. https://doi.org/10.1037/a0032355

Katz, D., Laposa, J. M., & Rector, N. A. (2018). Anxiety Sensitivity, Obsessive Beliefs, and the Prediction of CBT treatment outcome for OCD. *International Journal of Cognitive Therapy*, 11, 31–43. https://doi.org/10.1007/s41811-018-0007-z

Katz, M., Hilsenroth, M. J., Gold, J. R., Moore, M., Pitman, S. R., Levy, S. R., & Owen, J. (2019). Adherence, flexibility, and outcome in psychodynamic treatment of depression. *Journal of Counseling Psychology*, 66(1), 94–103. https://doi.org/10.1037/cou0000299

Kazantzis, N., Whittington, C., Zelencich, L., Kyrios, M., Norton, P. J., & Hofmann, S. G. (2016). Quantity and quality of homework compliance: a meta-analysis of relations with outcome in cognitive behavior therapy. *Behavior Therapy*, 47(5), 755–772. https://doi.org/10.1016/j.beth.2016.05.002

Kazdin, A. E., & Krouse, R. (1983). The impact of variations in treatment rationales on expectancies for therapeutic change. *Behavior Therapy*, 14(5), 657–671. https://doi.org/10.1016/S0005-7894(83)80058-6

Kealy, D., Piper, W. E., Ogrodniczuk, J. S., Joyce, A. S., & Weideman, R. (2019). Individual goal achievement in group psychotherapy: The roles of psychological mindedness and group process in interpretive and supportive therapy for complicated grief. *Clinical Psychology & Psychotherapy*, 26(2), 241–251. https://doi.org/10.1002/cpp.2346

Kearney, L. K., Draper, M., & Baron, A. (2005). Counseling utilization by ethnic minority college students. *Cultural Diversity and Ethnic Minority Psychology*, 11(3), 272–285. https://doi.org/10.1037/1099-9809.11.3.272

Keijsers, G. P. J., Hoogduin, C. A. L., & Schaap, C. P. D. R. (1994). Prognostic factors in the behavioral treatment of panic disorder with and without agoraphobia. *Behavior Therapy*, 25(4), 689–708. https://doi.org/10.1016/S0005-7894(05)80204-7

Kessler, R. C., Berglund, P., Demier, O., Jin, R., Merikangas, K. R., & Walters, E. E. (2005). Lifetime prevalence and age-of-onset distributions of DSM-IV disorders in the National Comorbidity Survey Replication. *Archives of General Psychiatry*, 62(6), 593–602. https://doi.org/10.1001/archpsyc.62.6.593

Kiesler, D. J. (1982). Interpersonal theory for personality and psychotherapy. In J. C. Anchin & D. J. Kiesler (Eds.), *Handbook of interpersonal psychotherapy* (pp. 3–24). New York: Pergamon Press.

Kiesler, D. J. (1996). *Contemporary interpersonal theory & research*. New York, NY: Wiley

Kiesler, D. J., & Schmidt, J. A. (1993). *The Impact Message Inventory: Form IIA Octant Scale version*. Palo Alto, CA: Mind Garden. https://doi.org/10.1037/t64697-000

Kilmer, E. D., Villarreal, C., Janis, B. M., Callahan, J. L., Ruggero, C. J., Kilmer, J. N., Love, P. K., & Cox, R. J. (2019). Differential early termination is tied to client race/ethnicity status. *Practice Innovations*, 4(2), 88–98. https://doi.org/10.1037/pri0000085

Kivlighan, D. M. Jr., Baumann, E. C., Gelso, C. J., & Hill, C. E. (2014, June). *Symptom change and between and within therapist variability in third session intercepts and linear change slopes for longitudinal ratings of alliance and real relationships*. Paper presented at the meeting of the Society for Psychotherapy Research, Copenhagen, Denmark.

Koole, S. L., & Tschacher, W. (2016). Synchrony in psychotherapy: A review and an integrative framework for the therapeutic alliance. *Frontiers in Psychology*, 7, 862. https://doi.org/10.3389/fpsyg.2016.00862

Kotov, R., Krueger, R. F., Watson, D., Achenbach, T. M., Althoff, R. R., Bagby, R. M., Brown, T. A., Carpenter, W. T., Caspi, A., Clark, L. A., Eaton, N. R., Forbes, M. K., Forbush, K. T., Goldberg, D., Hasin, D., Hyman, S. E., Ivanova, M. Y., Lynam, D. R., Markon, K., ... Zimmerman, M. (2017). The Hierarchical Taxonomy of Psychopathology (HiTOP): A dimensional

alternative to traditional nosologies. *Journal of Abnormal Psychology*, 126(4), 454–477. https://doi.org/10.1037/abn0000258

Krawczyk, N., Feder, K. A., Saloner, B., Crum, R. M., Kealhofer, M., & Mojtabai, R. (2017). The association of psychiatric comorbidity with treatment completion among clients admitted to substance use treatment programs in a U.S. national sample. *Drug and Alcohol Dependence*, 175, 157–263. https://doi.org/10.1016/j.drugalcdep.2017.02.006

Krebs, P., Norcross, J. C., Nicholson, J. M., & Prochaska, J. O. (2018). Stages of change and psychotherapy outcomes: A review and meta-analysis. *Journal of Clinical Psychology*, 74(11), 1964–1979. https://doi.org/10.1002/jclp.22683

Kronström, K., Salminen, J. K., Hietala, J., Kajande, J., Vahlberg, T., Markkula, J., Rasi-Hakala, H., & Karlss, H. (2009). Does defense style or psychological mindedness predict treatment response in major depression? *Depression and Anxiety*, 26(7), 689–695. https://doi.org/10.1002/da.20585

Kvarstein, E. H., Pedersen, G., Folmo, E., Urnes, Ø., Johansen, M. S., Hummelen, B., Wilberg, T., & Karterud, S. (2019). Mentalization-based treatment or psychodynamic treatment programmes for patients with borderline personality disorder - the impact of clinical severity. *Psychology and Psychotherapy: Theory, Research and Practice*, 92(1), 91–111. https://doi.org/10.1111/papt.12179

Kwan, B. M., Dimidjian, S., & Rizvi, S. L. (2010). Treatment preference, engagement, and clinical improvement in pharmacotherapy versus psychotherapy for depression. *Behaviour Research and Therapy*, 48(8), 799–804. https://doi.org/10.1016/j.brat.2010.04.003

Kwee, C. M. B. & van den Hout, M. A. (2019). Anxiety sensitivity does not predict treatment outcome or treatment length in obsessive-compulsive disorder and related anxiety disorders. *Journal of Obsessive-Compulsive and Related Disorders*, 21, 18–25. https://doi.org/10.1016/j.jocrd.2018.11.003

Kyrios, M., Hordern, C., & Fassnacht, D. B. (2015). Predictors of response to cognitive behaviour therapy for obsessive-compulsive disorder. *International Journal of Clinical and Health Psychology*, 15(3), 181–190. https://doi.org/10.1016/j.ijchp.2015.07.003

Lambert, M. J. (2010). *Prevention of treatment failure: The use of measuring, monitoring, and feedback in clinical practice*. Washington, DC: American Psychological Association.

Larrison, C. R., Schoppelrey, S. L., Hack-Ritzo, S., & Korr, W. S. (2011). Clinician factors related to outcome differences between Black and White patients at CMHCs. *Psychiatric Services*, 62(5), 525–531. https://doi.org/10.1176/ps.62.5.pss6205_0525

Leibert, T. W., & Dunne-Bryant, A. (2015). Do common factors account for counseling outcome? *Journal of Counseling & Development*, 93(2), 225–235. https://doi.org/10.1002/j.1556-6676.2015.00198.x

Leibert, T. W., Smith, J. B., & Agaskar, V. R. (2011). Relationship between the working alliance and social support on counseling outcome. *Journal of Clinical Psychology*, 67(7), 709–719. https://doi.org/10.1002/jclp.20800

Lejuez, C. W., Zvolensky, M. J., Daughters, S. B., Bornovalova, M. A., Paulson, A., Tull, M. T., Ettinger, K., & Otto, M. W. (2008). Anxiety sensitivity: A unique predictor of dropout among inner-city heroin and crack/cocaine users in residential substance use treatment. *Behaviour Research and Therapy*, 46(7), 811–818. https://doi.org/10.1016/j.brat.2008.03.010

Levitt, H. M., Minami, T., Greenspan, S. B., Puckett, J. A., Henretty, J. R., Reich, C. M., & Berman, J. S. (2016). How therapist self-disclosure relates to alliance and outcomes: A naturalistic study. *Counselling Psychology Quarterly*, 29(1), 7–28. https://doi.org/10.1080/09515070.2015.1090396

Levy, K. N., Kivity, Y., Johnson, B. N., & Gooch, C. V. (2018). Adult attachment as a predictor and moderator of psychotherapy outcome: A meta-analysis. *Journal of Clinical Psychology*, 74(11), 1996–2013. https://doi.org/10.1002/jclp.22685

Leweke, F., Bausch, S., Leichsenring, F., Walter, B., & Stingl, M. (2009). Alexithymia as a predictor of outcome of psychodynamically oriented inpatient treatment. *Psychotherapy Research*, 19(3), 323–331. https://doi.org/10.1080/10503300902870554

Li, X., Kivlighan, D. M. Jr., Gelso, C. J., & Hill, C. E. (2016, November). *Longitudinal relationships among the real relationship, working alliance and session outcome: A common fate model*. Paper presented at a meeting of the North American Society for Psychotherapy Research, Berkeley, California.

Limburg, K., Watson, H. J., Hagger, M. S., & Egan, S. J. (2017). The relationship between perfectionism and psychopathology: A meta-analysis. *Journal of Clinical Psychology*, 73(10), 1301–1326. https://doi.org/10.1002/jclp.22435

Lindfors, O., Ojanen, S., Jääskeläinen, T., & Knekt, P. (2014). Social support as a predictor of the outcome of depressive and anxiety disorder in short-term and long-term psychotherapy. *Psychiatry Research, 216*(1), 44–51. https://doi.org/10.1016/j.psychres.2013.12.050

Lloyd, S., Schmidt, U., Khondoker, M., & Tchanturia, K. (2015). Can psychological interventions reduce perfectionism? A systematic review and meta-analysis. *Behavioural and Cognitive Psychotherapy, 43*(6), 705–731. https://doi.org/10.1017/S1352465814000162

Löw, C. A., Schauenburg, H., & Dinger, U. (2020). Self-criticism and psychotherapy outcome: A systematic review and meta-analysis. *Clinical Psychology Review, 75*. Advance online publication. https://doi.org/10.1016/j.cpr.2019.101808

Lutz, W., Martinovich, Z., & Howard, K. I. (1999). Patient profiling: An application of random coefficient regression models to depicting the response of a patient to outpatient psychotherapy. *Journal of Consulting and Clinical Psychology, 67*(4), 571–577. https://doi.org/10.1037/0022-006X.67.4.571

Lutz, W., Stulz, N., & Kock, K. (2009). Patterns of early change and their relationship to outcome and follow-up among patients with major depressive disorders. *Journal of Affective Disorders, 118*(1–3), 60–68. https://doi.org/10.1016/j.jad.2009.01.019

Mansour, S., Bruce, K. R., Steiger, H., Zuroff, D. C., Horowitz, S., Anestin, A. S., & Sycz, L. (2012). Autonomous motivation: A predictor of treatment outcome in bulimia-spectrum eating disorders. *European Eating Disorders Review, 20*(3), e116–e122. https://doi.org/10.1002/erv.2154

Mausbach, B. T., Moore, R., Roesch, S., Cardenas, V., & Patterson, T. L. (2010). The relationship between homework compliance and therapy outcomes: An updated meta-analysis. *Cognitive Therapy and Research, 34*, 429–438. https://doi.org/10.1007/s10608-010-9297-z

Maxwell, H., Tasca, G. A., Gick, M., Ritchie, K., Balfour, L., & Bissada, H. (2012). The impact of attachment anxiety on interpersonal complementarity in early group therapy interactions among women with binge eating disorder. *Group Dynamics: Theory, Research, and Practice, 16*(4), 255–271. https://doi.org/10.1037/a0029464

McBride, C., Zuroff, D. C., Ravitz, P., Koestner, R., Moskowitz, D. S., Quilty, L., & Bagby, R. M. (2010). Autonomous and controlled motivation and interpersonal therapy for depression: Moderating role of recurrent depression. *British Journal of Clinical Psychology, 49*(4), 529–545. https://doi.org/10.1348/014466509X479186

McCallum, M., Piper, W. E., & O'Kelly, J. (1997). Predicting patient benefit from a group-oriented, evening treatment program. *International Journal of Group Psychotherapy, 47*(3), 291–314. https://doi.org/10.1080/00207284.1997.11490831

McCallum, M., Piper, W. E., Ogrodniczuk, J. S., & Joyce, A. S. (2003). Relationships among psychological mindedness, alexithymia and outcome in four forms of short-term psychotherapy. *Psychology and Psychotherapy: Theory, Research and Practice, 76*(2), 133–144. https://doi.org/10.1348/147608303765951177

McFarquhar, T., Luyten, P., & Fonagy, P. (2018). Changes in interpersonal problems in the psychotherapeutic treatment of depression as measured by the Inventory of Interpersonal Problems: A systematic review and meta-analysis. *Journal of Affective Disorders, 226*, 108–123. https://doi.org/10.1016/j.jad.2017.09.036

Mendes, I., Rosa, C., Stiles, W. B., Caro Gabalda, I., Gomes, P., Basto, I., & Salgado, J. (2016). Setbacks in the process of assimilation of problematic experiences in two cases of emotion-focused therapy for depression. *Psychotherapy Research, 26*(6), 638–652. https://doi.org/10.1080/10503307.2015.1136443

Meyer, B., Pilkonis, P. A., Krupnick, J. L., Egan, M. K., Simmens, S. J., & Sotsky, S. M. (2002). Treatment expectancies, patient alliance, and outcome: Further analyses from the National Institute of Mental Health Treatment of Depression Collaborative Research Program. *Journal of Consulting and Clinical Psychology, 70*(4), 1051–1055. https://doi.org/10.1037/0022-006X.70.4.1051

Miller, W. R., & Rollnick, S. (2013). *Motivational interviewing: Helping people change* (3rd ed.). New York, NY: Guilford Press.

Mizock, L., & Lundquist, C. (2016). Missteps in psychotherapy with transgender clients: Promoting gender sensitivity in counseling and psychological practice. *Psychology of Sexual Orientation and Gender Diversity, 3*(2), 148–155. https://doi.org/10.1037/sgd0000177

Moos, R. H., Moos, B. S., & Finney, J. W. (2001). Predictors of deterioration among patients with substance-use disorders. *Journal of Clinical Psychology, 57*(12), 1403–1419. https://doi.org/10.1002/jclp.1105

Moradi, B., & Budge, S. L. (2018). Engaging in LGBQ+ affirmative psychotherapies with all clients: Defining themes and practices. *Journal of Clinical Psychology, 74*(11), 2028–2042. https://doi.org/10.1002/jclp.22687

Mueller, M., & Pekarik, G. (2000). Treatment duration prediction: Client accuracy and its relationship to dropout, outcome, and satisfaction. *Psychotherapy, 37*(2), 117–123. https://doi.org/10.1037/h0087701

Muir, H. J., Constantino, M. J., Coyne, A. E., Westra, H. A., & Antony, M. M. (2021). Integrating responsive motivational interviewing with CBT for generalized anxiety disorder: Direct and indirect effects on interpersonal outcomes. *Journal of Psychotherapy Integration 31*(1), 54–69. https://doi.org/10.1037/int0000194

Muran, J. C., Safran, J. D., Eubanks, C. F., & Gorman, B. S. (2018). The effect of alliance-focused training on a cognitive-behavioral therapy for personality disorders. *Journal of Consulting and Clinical Psychology, 86*(4), 384–397. https://doi.org/10.1037/ccp0000284

Newman, M. G., Przworski, A., Fisher, A. J., & Borkovec, T. D. (2010). Diagnostic comorbidity in adults with generalized anxiety disorder: Impact of comorbidity on psychotherapy outcome and impact of psychotherapy on comorbid diagnoses. *Behavior Therapy, 41*(1), 59–72. https://doi.org/10.1016/j.beth.2008.12.005

Newman, M. G., Shin, K. E., & Lanza, S. T. (2019). Time-varying moderation of treatment outcomes by illness duration and comorbid depression in generalized anxiety disorder. *Journal of Consulting and Clinical Psychology, 87*(3), 282–293. https://doi.org/10.1037/ccp0000385

Newton-Howes, G., Tyrer, P., Johnson, T., Mulder, R., Kool, S., Dekker, J., & Schoevers, R. (2014). Influence of personality on the outcome of treatment in depression: Systematic review and meta-analysis. *Journal of Personality Disorders, 28*(4), 577–593. https://doi.org/10.1521/pedi_2013_27_070

Nordberg, S. S., Castonguay, L. G., Fisher, A. J., Boswell, J. F., & Kraus, D. (2014). Validating the rapid responder construct within a practice research network. *Journal of Clinical Psychology, 70*(9), 886–903. https://doi.org/10.1002/jclp.22077

Norman, R. M. G., Windell, D., Manchanda, R., Harricharan, R., & Northcott, S. (2012). Social support and functional outcomes in an early intervention program. *Schizophrenia Research, 140*(1–3), 37–40. https://doi.org/10.1016/j.schres.2012.07.003

Nowakowski, M. E., Rowa, K., Antony, M. M., & McCabe, R. (2016). Changes in anxiety sensitivity following group cognitive-behavior therapy for social anxiety disorder and panic disorder. *Cognitive Therapy and Research, 40*, 468–478. https://doi.org/10.1007/s10608-015-9750-0

Nyklíček, I., Majoor, D., & Schalken, P. A. A. M. (2010). Psychological mindedness and symptom reduction after psychotherapy in a heterogeneous psychiatric sample. *Comprehensive Psychiatry, 51*(5), 492–496. https://doi.org/10.1016/j.comppsych.2010.02.004

Ogrodniczuk, J. S., Lynd, L. D., Joyce, A. S., Grubisic, M., Piper, W. E., & Steinberg, P. I. (2011). Predicting response to day treatment for personality disorder. *The Canadian Journal of Psychiatry / La Revue Canadienne de Psychiatrie, 56*(2), 110–117. https://doi.org/10.1177/070674371105600206

Ogrodniczuk, J. S., Piper, W. E., & Joyce, A. S. (2011). Effect of alexithymia on the process and outcome of psychotherapy: A programmatic review. *Psychiatry Research, 190*(1), 43–48. https://doi.org/10.1016/j.psychres.2010.04.026

Ogrodniczuk, J. S., Sochting, I., Piper, W. E., & Joyce, A. S. (2012). A naturalistic study of alexithymia among psychiatric outpatients treated in an integrated group therapy program. *Psychology and Psychotherapy: Theory, Research and Practice, 85*(3), 278–291. https://doi.org/10.1111/j.2044-8341.2011.02032.x

Olatunji, B., Cisler, J.M., & Tolin, D.F. (2010). A meta-analysis of the influence of comorbidity on treatment outcome in the anxiety disorders. *Clinical Psychology Review, 30*(6), 642–654. https://doi.org/10.1016/j.cpr.2010.04.008

Olatunji, B. O., Davis, M. L., Powers, M. B., & Smits, J. A. J. (2013). Cognitive-behavioral therapy for obsessive-compulsive disorder: A meta-analysis of treatment outcome and moderators. *Journal of Psychiatric Research, 47*(1), 33–41. https://doi.org/10.1016/j.jpsychires.2012.08.020

Osborne, D., Milojev, P., & Sibley, C. G. (2016). Examining the indirect effects of religious orientations on well-being through personal locus of control. *European Journal of Social Psychology, 46*(4), 492–505. https://doi.org/10.1002/ejsp.2182

Owen, J. (2013). Early career perspectives on psychotherapy research and practice: Psychotherapist effects, multicultural orientation, and couple interventions. *Psychotherapy, 50*(4), 496–502. https://doi.org/10.1037/a0034617

Owen, J., Drinane, J., Tao, K. W., Adelson, J. L., Hook, J. N., Davis, D., & Fookune, N. (2017). Racial/ethnic disparities in client unilateral termination: The role of therapists' cultural comfort. *Psychotherapy Research*, 27(1), 102–111. https://doi.org/10.1080/10503307.2015.1078517

Owen, J., & Hilsenroth, M. J. (2014). Treatment adherence: The importance of therapist flexibility in relation to therapy outcomes. *Journal of Counseling Psychology*, 61(2), 280–288. https://doi.org/10.1037/a0035753

Owen, J., Imel, Z. E., Adelson, J., & Rodolfa, E. (2012). "No-show": Therapist racial/ethnic disparities in client unilateral termination. *Journal of Counseling Psychology*, 59(2), 314–320. https://doi.org/10.1037/a0027091

Owen, J., Jordan, T. A., II, Turner, D., Davis, D. E., Hook, J. N., & Leach, M. M. (2014). Therapists' multicultural orientation: Client perceptions of cultural humility, spiritual/ religious commitment, and therapy outcomes. *Journal of Psychology and Theology*, 42(1), 91–98. https://doi.org/10.1177/009164711404200110

Owen, J., Leach, M. M., Wampold, B., & Rodolfa, E. (2011). Client and therapist variability in clients' perceptions of their therapists' multicultural competencies. *Journal of Counseling Psychology*, 58(1), 1–9. https://doi.org/10.1037/a0021496

Owen, J., Tao, K. W., Drinane, J. M., Hook, J. N., Davis, D. E., & Kune, N. F. (2016). Client perceptions of therapists' multicultural orientation: Cultural (missed) opportunities and cultural humility. *Professional Psychology: Research and Practice*, 47(1), 30–37. https://doi.org/10.1037/pro0000046

Owen, J., Tao, K., Leach, M. M., & Rodolfa, E. (2011). Clients' perceptions of their psychotherapists' multicultural orientation. *Psychotherapy*, 48(3), 274–282. https://doi.org/10.1037/a0022065

Patterson, C. L., Anderson, T., & Wei, C. (2014). Clients' pretreatment role expectations, the therapeutic alliance, and clinical outcomes in outpatient therapy. *Journal of Clinical Psychology*, 70(7), 673–680. https://doi.org/10.1002/jclp.22054

Paulick, J., Deisenhofer, A.-K., Ramseyer, F., Tschacher, W., Boyle, K., Rubel, J., & Lutz, W. (2018). Nonverbal synchrony: A new approach to better understand psychotherapeutic processes and drop-out. *Journal of Psychotherapy Integration*, 28(3), 367–384 https://doi.org/10.1037/int0000099

Peluso, P. R., & Freund, R. R. (2018). Therapist and client emotional expression and psychotherapy outcomes: A meta-analysis. *Psychotherapy*, 55(4), 461–472. https://doi.org/10.1037/pst0000165

Perivoliotis, D., Grant, P. M., Peters, E. R., Ison, R., Kuipers, E., & Beck, A. T. (2010). Cognitive insight predicts favorable outcome in cognitive behavioral therapy for psychosis. *Psychosis: Psychological, Social and Integrative Approaches*, 2(1), 23–33. https://doi.org/10.1080/17522430903147520

Pertab, J., Nielsen, S. L., & Lambert, M. J. (2014). *Does client-therapist gender matching influence therapy course or outcome in psychotherapy?* Unpublished manuscript, Department of Psychology, 272 TLRB, Brigham Young University, Provo, UT.

Phinney, J. S. (1996). When we talk about American ethnic groups, what do we mean? *American Psychologist*, 51(9), 918–927. https://doi.org/10.1037/0003-066X.51.9.918

Pinto-Coelho, K., Hill, C. E., & Kivlighan, D. M., Jr. (2016). Therapist self-disclosures in Psychodynamic psychotherapy: A mixed methods investigation. *Counselling Psychology Quarterly*, 29(1), 29–52. https://doi.org/10.1080/09515070.2015.1072496

Piper, W. E., Azim, H. F., Joyce, A. S., & McCallum, M. (1991). Transference interpretations, therapeutic alliance, and outcome in short-term individual psychotherapy. *Archives of General Psychiatry*, 48(10), 946–953. https://doi.org/10.1001/archpsyc.1991.01810340078010

Poulin, L. E., Button, M. L., Westra, H. A., Constantino, M. J., & Antony, M. M. (2019). The predictive capacity of self-reported motivation vs. early observed motivational language in cognitive behavioural therapy for generalized anxiety disorder. *Cognitive Behaviour Therapy*, 48(5), 369–384. https://doi.org/10.1080/16506073.2018.1517390

Prochaska, J. O., Norcross, J. C., & DiClemente, C. C. (2013). Applying the stages of change. In G. P. Koocher, J. C. Norcross, & B. A. Greene (Eds.), *Psychologists' desk reference., 3rd ed.* (pp. 176–181). New York, NY: Oxford University Press. https://doi.org/10.1093/med:psych/9780199845491.003.0034

Quilty, L. C., Mainland, B. J., McBride, C., & Bagby, R. M. (2013). Interpersonal problems and impacts: Further evidence for the role of interpersonal functioning in treatment outcome in major depressive disorder. *Journal of Affective Disorders*, 150(2), 393–400. https://doi.org/10.1016/j.jad.2013.04.030

Quilty, L. C., Taylor, G. J., McBride, C., & Bagby, R. M. (2017). Relationships among alexithymia, therapeutic alliance, and psychotherapy outcome in major depressive disorder. *Psychiatry Research*, 254, 75–79. https://doi.org/10.1016/j.psychres.2017.04.047

Quintana, S. M. (2007). Racial and ethnic identity: Developmental perspectives and research. *Journal of Counseling Psychology*, 54(3), 259–270. https://doi.org/10.1037/0022-0167.54.3.259

Ramseyer, F., & Tschacher, W. (2011). Nonverbal synchrony in psychotherapy: Coordinated body-movement reflects relationship quality and outcome. *Journal of Consulting and Clinical Psychology*, 79(3), 284–295. https://doi.org/10.1037/a0023419

Reardon, M. L., Cukrowicz, K. C., Reeves, M. D., & Joiner, T. E. (2002). Duration and regularity of therapy attendance as predictors of treatment outcome in an adult outpatient population. *Psychotherapy Research*, 12(3), 273–285. https://doi.org/10.1080/713664390

Reich, C. M., Berman, J. S., Dale, R., & Levitt, H. M. (2014). Vocal synchrony in psychotherapy. *Journal of Social and Clinical Psychology*, 33(5), 481–494. https://doi.org/10.1521/jscp.2014.33.5.481

Reiss, S., Peterson, R. A., Gursky, D. M., McNally R. J. (1986). Anxiety sensitivity, anxiety frequency and the prediction of fearfulness. *Behaviour Research and Therapy*, 24(1), 1–8. https://doi.org/10.1016/0005-7967(86)90143-9

Ribeiro, E., Cunha, C., Teixeira, A. S., Stiles, W. B., Pires, N., Santos, B., Basto, I., & Salgado, J. (2016). Therapeutic collaboration and the assimilation of problematic experiences in emotion-focused therapy for depression: Comparison of two cases. *Psychotherapy Research*, 26(6), 665–680. https://doi.org/10.1080/10503307.2016.1208853

Robiertello, R. C., & Schonewolf, G. (1987). *101 common therapeutic blunders: Countertransference and counter-resistance in psychotherapy*. Northvale, NJ: Jason Aronson.

Roehrle, B., & Strouse, J. (2008). Influence of social support on success of therapeutic interventions: A meta-analytic review. *Psychotherapy*, 45(4), 464–476. https://doi.org/10.1037/a0014333

Rotter, J. B. (1966). Generalized expectancies for internal versus external control of reinforcement. *Psychological Monographs: General and Applied*, 80(1), 1–28. https://doi.org/10.1037/h0092976

Ryan, R. M., Lynch, M. F., Vansteenkiste, M., & Deci, E. L. (2011). Motivation and autonomy in counseling, psychotherapy, and behavior change: A look at theory and practice. *The Counseling Psychologist*, 39(2), 193–260. https://doi.org/10.1177/0011000009359313

Ryan, R. M., Plant, R. W., & O'Malley, S. (1995) Initial motivations for alcohol treatment: Relations with patient characteristics, treatment involvement, and dropout. *Addictive Behaviors*, 20(3), 279–297. https://doi.org/10.1016/0306-4603(94)00072-7

Salzer, S., Leibing, E., Jakobsen, T., Rudolf, G., Brockmann, J., Eckert, J., Huber, D., Klug, G., Henrich, G., Grande, T., Keller, W., Kreische, R., Biskup, J., Staats, H., Waras, S., & Leichsenring, F. (2010). Patterns of interpersonal problems and their improvement in depressive and anxious patients treated with psychoanalytic therapy. *Bulletin of the Menninger Clinic*, 74(4), 283–300. https://doi.org/10.1521/bumc.2010.74.4.283

Samstag, L. W., Muran, J. C., Wachtel, P. L., Slade, A., Safran, J. D., & Winston, A. (2008). Evaluating negative process: A comparison of working alliance, interpersonal behavior, and narrative coherency among three psychotherapy outcome conditions. *American Journal of Psychotherapy*, 62(2), 165–194. https://doi.org/10.1176/appi.psychotherapy.2008.62.2.165

Saunders, R., Buckman, J. E. J., Cape, J., Fearon, P., Leibowitz, J., & Pilling, S. (2019). Trajectories of depression and anxiety symptom change during psychological therapy. *Journal of Affective Disorders*, 249, 327–335. https://doi.org/10.1016/j.jad.2019.02.043

Schauenburg, H., Kuda, M., Sammet, I., & Strack, M. (2000). The influence of interpersonal problems and symptom severity on the duration and outcome of short-term psychodynamic psychotherapy. *Psychotherapy Research*, 10(2), 133–146. https://doi.org/10.1080/713663670

Schoenherr, D., Paulick, J., Strauss, B. M., Deisenhofer, A.-K., Schwartz, B., Rubel, J. A., Lutz, W., Stangier, U., & Altmann, U. (2019). Nonverbal synchrony predicts premature termination of psychotherapy for social anxiety disorder. *Psychotherapy*, 56(4), 503–513. https://doi.org/10.1037/pst0000216

Schneider, W., & Klauer, T. (2001). Symptom level, treatment motivation, and the effects of inpatient psychotherapy. *Psychotherapy Research, 11*(2), 153–167. https://doi.org/10.1080/713663888

Schut, A. J., Castonguay, L. G., Flanagan, K. M., Yamasaki, A. S., Barber, J. P., Bedics, J. D., & Smith, T. L. (2005). Therapist interpretation, patient-therapist interpersonal process, and outcome in psychodynamic psychotherapy for avoidant personality disorder. *Psychotherapy, 42*(4), 494–511. https://doi.org/10.1037/0033-3204.42.4.494

Schwartz, D. L., Chase, C. C., & Bransford, J. D. (2012). Resisting overzealous transfer: Coordinating previously successful routines with needs for new learning. *Educational Psychologist, 47*(3), 204–214. https://doi.org/10.1080/00461520.2012.696317

Schwartz, R. A., Chambless, D. L., McCarthy, K. S., Milrod, B., & Barber, J. P. (2019). Client resistance predicts outcomes in cognitive-behavioral therapy for panic disorder. *Psychotherapy Research, 29*(8), 1020–1032. https://doi.org/10.1080/10503307.2018.1504174

Sheffer, C., MacKillop, J., McGeary, J., Landes, R., Carter, L., Yi, R., Jones, B., Christensen, D., Stitzer, M., Jackson, L., & Bickel, W. (2012). Delay discounting, locus of control, and cognitive impulsiveness independently predict tobacco dependence treatment outcomes in a highly dependent, lower socioeconomic group of smokers. *The American Journal on Addictions, 21*(3), 221–232. https://doi.org/10.1111/j.1521-0391.2012.00224.x

Shojaee, M., & French, C. (2014). The relationship between mental health components and locus of control in youth. *Psychology, 5*(8), 966–978. https://doi.org/10.4236/psych.2014.58107

Silberschatz, G. (2017). Improving the yield of psychotherapy research. *Psychotherapy Research, 27*(1), 1–13. https://doi.org/10.1080/10503307.2015.1076202

Soto, A., Smith, T. B., Griner, D., Domenech Rodríguez, M., & Bernal, G. (2018). Cultural adaptations and therapist multicultural competence: Two meta-analytic reviews. *Journal of Clinical Psychology, 74*(11), 1907–1923. https://doi.org/10.1002/jclp.22679

Steiger, H., Sansfaçon, J., Thaler, L., Leonard, N., Cottier, D., Kahan, E., Fletcher, E., Rossi, E., Israel, M., & Gauvin, L. (2017). Autonomy support and autonomous motivation in the outpatient treatment of adults with an eating disorder. *International Journal of Eating Disorders, 50*(9), 1058–1066. https://doi.org/10.1002/eat.22734

Stiles, W. B. (2002). Assimilation of problematic experiences. In J. C. Norcross (Ed.), *Psychotherapy relationships that work: Therapist contributions and responsiveness to patients.* (pp. 357–365). New York, NY: Oxford University Press.

Stiles, W. B. (2011). Coming to terms. *Psychotherapy Research, 21*(4), 367–384. https://doi.org/10.1080/10503307.2011.582186

Stulz, N., Lutz, W., Leach, C., Lucock, M., & Barkham, M. (2007). Shapes of early change in psychotherapy under routine outpatient conditions. *Journal of Consulting and Clinical Psychology, 75*(6), 864–874. https://doi.org/10.1037/0022-006X.75.6.864

Subic-Wrana, C., Bruder, S., Thomas, W., Lane, R. D., & Köhle, K. (2005). Emotional awareness deficits in inpatients of a psychosomatic ward: a comparison of two different measures of alexithymia. *Psychosomatic Medicine, 67*(3), 483–489. https://doi.org/10.1097/01.psy.0000160461.19239.13

Sue, D. W., Arredondo, P., & McDavis, R. J. (1992). Multicultural counseling competencies and standards: A call to the profession. *Journal of Counseling & Development, 70*(4), 477–486. https://doi.org/10.1002/j.1556-6676.1992.tb01642.x

Sue, S. (1998). In search of cultural competence in psychotherapy and counseling. *American Psychologist, 53*(4), 440–448. https://doi.org/10.1037/0003-066X.53.4.440

Sullivan, H. S. (1953). *The interpersonal theory of psychiatry.* New York: Norton.

Svartberg, M., & Stiles, T. C. (1992). Predicting patient change from therapist competence and patient-therapist complementarity in short-term anxiety provoking psychotherapy: A pilot study. *Journal of Consulting and Clinical Psychology, 60*(2), 304–307. https://doi.org/10.1037/0022-006X.60.2.304

Swift, J. K., & Callahan, J. L. (2011). Decreasing treatment dropout by addressing expectations for treatment length. *Psychotherapy Research, 21*(2), 193–200. https://doi.org/10.1080/10503307.2010.541294

Swift, J. K., Callahan, J. L., Cooper, M., & Parkin, S. R. (2018). The impact of accommodating client preference in psychotherapy: A meta-analysis. *Journal of Clinical Psychology, 74*(11), 1924–1937. https://doi.org/10.1002/jclp.22680

Swift, J. K., Callahan, J. L., Tompkins, K. A., Connor, D. R., & Dunn, R. (2015). A delay discounting measure of preference for racial/ethnic matching in psychotherapy. *Psychotherapy, 52*(3), 315–320. https://doi.org/10.1037/pst0000019

Swift, J. K., Derthick, A. O., & Tompkins, K. A. (2018). The relationship between trainee therapists' and clients' initial expectations and actual treatment duration and outcomes. *Practice Innovations, 3*(2), 84–93. https://doi.org/10.1037/pri0000065

Swift, J. K., & Greenberg, R. P. (2012). Premature discontinuation in adult psychotherapy: A meta-analysis. *Journal of Consulting and Clinical Psychology, 80*(4), 547–559. https://doi.org/10.1037/a0028226

Tasca, G. A., Balfour, L., Bissada, H., Busby, K., Conrad, G., Cameron, P., Colletta, S., Potvin-Kent, M., & Turpin, P. (1999). Treatment completion and outcome in a partial hospitalization program: Interactions among patient variables. *Psychotherapy Research, 9*(2), 232–247. https://doi.org/10.1080/10503309912331332711

Tasca, G. A., & McMullen, L. M. (1992). Interpersonal complementarity and antithesis within a stage model of psychotherapy. *Psychotherapy, 29*(4), 515–523. https://doi.org/10.1037/0033-3204.29.4.515

Taylor, G. J., & Bagby, R. M. (2013). Psychoanalysis and empirical research: The example of alexithymia. *Journal of the American Psychoanalytic Association, 61*(1), 99–133. https://doi.org/10.1177/0003065112474066

Teasdale, J. D. (1999). Emotional processing, three modes of mind and the prevention of relapse in depression. *Behaviour Research and Therapy, 37*(S1), S53–S77. https://doi.org/10.1016/S0005-7967(99)00050-9

Tetley, A., Jinks, M., Huband, N., & Howells, K. (2011). A systematic review of measures of therapeutic engagement in psychosocial and psychological treatment. *Journal of Clinical Psychology, 67*(9), 927–941. https://doi.org/10.1002/jclp.20811

Thaler, L., Israel, M., Antunes, J. M., Sarin, S., Zuroff, D. C., & Steiger, H. (2016). An examination of the role of autonomous versus controlled motivation in predicting inpatient treatment outcome for anorexia nervosa. *International Journal of Eating Disorders, 49*(6), 626 - 629. https://doi.org/10.1002/eat.22510

Thompson, K., Schwartzman, D., D'Iuso, D., Dobson, K. S., & Drapeau, M. (2018). Complementarity patterns in cognitive therapy for major depressive disorder. *Counselling & Psychotherapy Research, 18*(3), 286–298. https://doi.org/10.1002/capr.12175

Thompson-Brenner, H., Shingleton, R. M., Thompson, D. R., Satir, D. A., Richards, L. K., Pratt, E. M., & Barlow, D. H. (2016). Focused vs. broad enhanced cognitive behavioral therapy for bulimia nervosa with comorbid borderline personality: A randomized clinical trial. *International Journal of Eating Disorders, 49*(1), 36–49. https://doi.org/10.1002/eat.22468

Tracey, T. J. (1993). An interpersonal stage model of the therapeutic process. *Journal of Counseling Psychology, 40*(4), 396–409. https://doi.org/10.1037/0022-0167.40.4.396

Tracey, T. J., & Ray, P. B. (1984). Stages of successfully time-limited counseling: An interactional examination. *Journal of Counseling Psychology, 31*(1), 13–27. https://doi.org/10.1037/0022-0167.31.1.13

Tracey, T. J. G., Sherry, P., & Albright, J. M. (1999). The interpersonal process of cognitive-behavioral therapy: An examination of complementarity over the course of treatment. *Journal of Counseling Psychology, 46*(1), 80–91. https://doi.org/10.1037/0022-0167.46.1.80

Tryon, G. S., Blackwell, S. C., & Hammel, E. F. (2007). A meta-analytic examination of client-therapist perspectives of the working alliance. *Psychotherapy Research, 17*(6), 629–642. https://doi.org/10.1080/10503300701320611

Tschacher, W., & Meier, D. (2020). Physiological synchrony in psychotherapy sessions, *Psychotherapy Research, 30*(5), 558–573. https://doi.org/10.1080/10503307.2019.1612114

Uckelstam, C.-J., Philips, B., Holmqvist, R., & Falkenström, F. (2019). Prediction of treatment outcome in psychotherapy by patient initial symptom distress profiles. *Journal of Counseling Psychology, 66*(6), 736–746. https://doi.org/10.1037/cou0000345

Ulvenes, P. G., Berggraf, L., Wampold, B. E., Hoffart, A., Stiles, T., & McCullough, L. (2014). Orienting patient to affect, sense of self, and the activation of affect over the course of psychotherapy with cluster C patients. *Journal of Counseling Psychology, 61*(3), 315–324. https://doi.org/10.1037/cou0000028

Vincent, N., Walsh, K., & Lewycky, S. (2010). Sleep locus of control and computerized cognitive-behavioral therapy (cCBT). *Behaviour Research and Therapy, 48*(8), 779–783. https://doi.org/10.1016/j.brat.2010.05.006

Vîslă, A., Flückiger, C., Constantino, M. J., Krieger, T., & grosse Holtforth, M. (2019). Patient characteristics and the therapist as predictors of depressed patients' outcome expectation over time: A multilevel analysis. *Psychotherapy Research*, *29*(6), 709–722. https://doi.org/10.1080/10503307.2018.1428379

Vittengl, J. R., Clark, L. A., & Jarrett, R. B. (2004). Improvement in social-interpersonal functioning after cognitive therapy for recurrent depression. *Psychological Medicine*, *34*(4), 643–658. https://doi.org/10.1017/S0033291703001478

Vogel, P. A., Hansen, B., Stiles, T. C., & Götestam, K. G. (2006). Treatment motivation, treatment expectancy, and helping alliance as predictors of outcome in cognitive behavioral treatment of OCD. *Journal of Behavior Therapy and Experimental Psychiatry*, *37*(3), 247–255. https://doi.org/10.1016/j.jbtep.2005.12.001

von der Lippe, A. L., Monsen, J. T., Rønnestad, M. H., & Eilertsen, D. E. (2008). Treatment failure in psychotherapy: The pull of hostility. *Psychotherapy Research*, *18*(4), 420–432. https://doi.org/10.1080/10503300701810793

Walczak, M., Ollendick, T., Ryan, S., & Hoff Esbjorn, B. (2018). Does comorbidity predict poorer treatment outcome in pediatric anxiety disorders? An updated 10–year review. *Clinical Psychology Review*, *60*, 45–61. https://doi.org/10.1016/j.cpr.2017.12.005

Webb, C. A., DeRubeis, R. J., & Barber, J. P. (2010). Therapist adherence/competence and treatment outcome: A meta-analytic review. *Journal of Consulting and Clinical Psychology*, *78*(2), 200–211. https://doi.org/10.1037/a0018912

Westra, H. A. (2011). Comparing the predictive capacity of observed in-session resistance to self-reported motivation in cognitive behavioral therapy. *Behaviour Research and Therapy*, *49*(2), 106–113. https://doi.org/10.1016/j.brat.2010.11.007

Westra, H. A. (2012). *Motivational interviewing in the treatment of anxiety*. New York, NY: Guilford Press.

Westra, H. A., Constantino, M. J., & Antony, M. M. (2016). Integrating motivational interviewing with cognitive-behavioral therapy for severe generalized anxiety disorder: An allegiance-controlled randomized clinical trial. *Journal of Consulting and Clinical Psychology*, *84*(9), 768–782. https://doi.org/10.1037/ccp0000098

Wilfley, D. E., Friedman, M. A., Zoler Dounchis, J., Stein. R. I., Welch, R. R., Friedman, M. A., & Ball, S. A. (2000). Comorbid psychopathology in binge eating disorder: Relation to eating disorder severity at baseline and following treatment. *Journal of Consulting and Clinical Psychology*, *68*(4), 641–649. https://doi.org/10.1037/0022-006X.68.4.641

Wolitzky-Taylor, K. B., Arch, J. J., Rosenfield, D., & Craske, M. G. (2012). Moderators and non-specific predictors of treatment outcome for anxiety disorders: A comparison of cognitive behavioral therapy to acceptance and commitment therapy. *Journal of Consulting and Clinical Psychology*, *80*(5), 786–799. https://doi.org/10.1037/a0029418

Wolitzky-Taylor, K., Drazdowski, T. K., Niles, A., Roy-Byrne, P., Ries, R., Rawson, R., & Craske, M. G. (2018). Change in anxiety sensitivity and substance use coping motives as putative mediators of treatment efficacy among substance users. *Behaviour Research and Therapy*, *107*, 34–41. https://doi.org/10.1016/j.brat.2018.05.010

Yasky, J., King, R., & O'Brien, T. (2016). Resistance, early engagement and outcome in psychoanalytic psychotherapy of patients with psychosomatic disorders. *Counselling & Psychotherapy Research*, *16*(4), 266–276. https://doi.org/10.1002/capr.12093

Zeeck, A., von Wietersheim, J., Weiss, H., Scheidt, C. E., Völker, A., Helesic, A., Eckhardt-Henn, A., Beutel, M., Endorf, K., Treiber, F., Rochlitz, P., & Hartmann, A. (2016). Prognostic and prescriptive predictors of improvement in a naturalistic study on inpatient and day hospital treatment of depression. *Journal of Affective Disorders*, *197*, 205–214. https://doi.org/10.1016/j.jad.2016.03.039

Zuroff, D. C., Koestner, R., Moskowitz, D. S., McBride, C., Marshall, M., & Bagby, R. M. (2007). Autonomous motivation for therapy: A new common factor in brief treatments of depression. *Psychotherapy Research*, *17*(2), 137–148. https://doi.org/10.1080/10503300600919380

Zuroff, D. C., McBride, C., Ravitz, P., Koestner, R., Moskowitz, D. S., & Bagby, R. M. (2017). Autonomous and controlled motivation for interpersonal therapy for depression: Between-therapists and within-therapist effects. *Journal of Counseling Psychology*, *64*(5), 525–537. https://doi.org/10.1037/cou0000239

PSYCHOTHERAPY PROCESS–OUTCOME RESEARCH: ADVANCES IN UNDERSTANDING CAUSAL CONNECTIONS

PAUL CRITS-CHRISTOPH AND MARY BETH CONNOLLY GIBBONS

Abstract

Several decades of research have examined the change processes (what happens during therapy sessions that might be associated with treatment outcome) and change mechanisms (changes occurring within the patient that are hypothesized to have a causal relation with treatment outcome) in multiple types of psychotherapy. Though a large number of studies have been conducted, only in more recent years has there been attention to incorporating features into the design and analysis of process–outcome studies that more clearly identify the nature of any effects and improve the likelihood that obtained associations may be causal rather than spurious. Such features include multilevel modeling of therapist vs. patient contributions, various approaches to understanding potential causality, and testing of specificity of effects. Through the lens of these methodological issues, we update here our 2013 review focusing on common and theory-specific changes processes and change mechanisms investigated within leading modes of psychotherapy. We found that there has been considerable progress in identifying possible causal connections between change processes/mechanisms and treatment outcome. However, multilevel modeling, though increasing in use, remains underutilized. There also has been little progress in examination of the specificity of mechanisms of types of psychotherapies. Nevertheless, enough progress has been made to support the following clinical recommendations based on the scientific literature: (a) clinicians should attend to the alliance, foster it, and address ruptures in the alliance as needed, (b) therapists should focus on the arousal of emotion in exposure-based behavior therapy for anxiety disorders since such arousal appears to be an essential ingredient in achieving positive outcomes, (c) fostering self-understanding should be a priority in the practice of psychodynamic therapy, (d) cognitive therapists should maintain use of the more specific (*concrete*) techniques such as agenda setting, homework, and practicing rational responses when treating patients with depression, (e) cognitive therapists should ensure that their interventions include targeting the acquisition of positive compensatory skills when treating patients with depressive symptoms, and (f) the treatment of PTSD should focus on modification of negative trauma-related beliefs. Building on these advances, future psychotherapy process–outcome research has the potential to help refine and modify existing treatments so that more patients receive maximum benefits.

INTRODUCTION

Presumably, what happens during psychotherapy sessions – termed psychotherapy process – is either directly or indirectly largely responsible for the patient improvements that result from a course of therapy. There have now been several decades of studies that have attempted to link various aspects of psychotherapy process to treatment outcome. Earlier editions of the Handbooks have provided exhaustive reviews of the large body of scientific process–outcome studies. The process–outcome chapter in the 5th edition of the *Handbook* (Orlinsky et al., 2004) focused on a generic model of psychotherapy across various psychotherapies. The generic model is a metatheoretical framework for understanding the concepts from various theories of therapy so that an integrative summary of empirical findings from different schools of therapy can be made. Thus, in the generic model, therapeutic elements that are described differently in two (or more) forms of therapy are grouped together based on the generic metatheoretical framework. We refer the reader to the 5th edition chapter for an extensive review of the literature up to that date regarding studies examined from the generic model point of view.

In the 6th edition chapter (Crits-Christoph et al., 2013), we began with a summary and update of the research literature on common process factors in relation to treatment outcome. Common factors are those therapeutic elements that are common to all or most psychotherapies, such as the therapeutic alliance. After reviewing literature on common factors, we organized the literature on process–outcome studies in the 6th edition from the perspective of the important change processes specified in major theories of psychotherapy using the language and concepts unique to each theory (rather than translating such concepts into a metatheory, as was done in the 5th edition). The current 7th edition chapter continues the structure we introduced in the 6th edition and provides an update on the empirical literature since the 2013 review.

In our view both common factors and theory-specific factors are important targets for research and are likely to be essential aspects of the process of change in different forms of psychotherapy. In fact, within the context of studies of specific psychotherapies, the investigation of common factors continues to be a productive agenda for process–outcome studies. In part, this is because processes common to many therapies, such as the therapeutic alliance, are incorporated explicitly within the theory of change described within treatment manuals for specific psychotherapies. It is also important to acknowledge that, to some degree, the classification of variables into common factors and theory-specific factors is a misleading if not false dichotomy. Common factors such as the therapeutic relationship are, in some theories, the primary theoretical variable of interest. Moreover, some technical interventions cut across multiple theories and therefore are common to some extent. In addition, common and technical interventions interact in ways that make it difficult to distinguish the two. Nevertheless, in order to summarize what we currently know about the influence of process variables and change mechanisms, we sort the variables into the categories of common factors and theory-specific factors.

Because we review here studies of the theoretical mechanisms of action of specific psychotherapies, there is some overlap between studies reviewed in the current chapter and studies reviewed in other chapters in this volume that focus on a particular psychotherapeutic modality (see chapters 13, 14, 15, 16, and 17). Our goal in the current chapter, however, is to more critically analyze relevant studies and highlight methodological issues that constrain the inferences that can currently be made from the empirical literature. In short, our aim is to draw conclusions about what we do know and what we do not know from existing process–outcome studies about the hypothesized theoretical mechanisms of action of behavioral, cognitive-behavioral, psychodynamic, experiential, and other forms of psychotherapy. By highlighting methodological issues, our hope is that we can point the way for future research to address weaknesses in existing studies, so that more definitive studies can be planned and conducted.

Prior to presenting our literature review, it is important to define what we mean by *psychotherapy process* and *process–outcome*. Here, we follow the Orlinsky et al. (2004) description of psychotherapy process as ". . .(primarily) the actions, experiences, and relatedness of patient and therapist in therapy sessions when they are physically together, and (secondarily) the actions and experiences of participants specifically referring to one another that occur outside of therapy sessions when they are not physically together" (p. 311). We also include in our definition those changes occurring within the patient over the course of psychotherapy that are hypothesized to have a causal relation with treatment outcome. These processes are described by Doss (2004) as *change mechanisms* and are differentiated from *change processes*. Because change mechanisms are patient changes that are thought to be triggered by events within therapy sessions, we view such changes as part of the overall process of psychotherapy that subsequently leads to positive treatment outcomes.

The focus of this chapter is the process of individual adult psychotherapy. Other chapters in this *Handbook* on group (chapter 18) and family psychotherapy (chapter 17) provide information on process–outcome research relevant to those formats of treatment. We also constrain our focus to studies that link psychotherapy process or change mechanisms to treatment outcome. Studies that examine what happens during psychotherapy sessions, but do not link those events and processes to treatment outcome, are not reviewed here.

In addition, single case studies, qualitative studies, microanalysis of sequential processes in session, and investigation of critical events in psychotherapy are examples of other forms of process research that, while essential building blocks to understanding the nature of psychotherapy are not our focus here. A final caveat: although we cover a wide range of studies, our review is not an exhaustive review of all available process–outcome studies. Instead, we attempt to highlight major findings that have appeared in the literature, especially as related to important models of psychotherapy, since the last version of this chapter. We encourage interested readers to look back at the 2013 review for a more detailed account of theory-relevant process–outcome and change mechanism studies up to when that chapter was published. Readers can also refer to earlier versions (e.g., Orlinsky et al., 2004) of this *Handbook* to obtain, in particular, a historical account of process–outcome research and a more detailed review of the many individual facets of the nonspecific, therapeutic relationship component of psychotherapy process in relation to outcome.

METHODOLOGICAL CONCERNS WITHIN PROCESS–OUTCOME RESEARCH

As mentioned, our goal is to describe how conclusions from process–outcome and change mechanism studies may be influenced by certain methodological issues. In addition to updating the list of studies included, what is new in this version of the chapter is the explicit identification in each study of central methodological issues that inform the meaning of the findings. There are, of course, a wide range of methodological and design issues that might influence the nature and interpretation of findings from psychotherapy process–outcome studies. Such issues include, among others, topics such as training and reliability of judges who make ratings of therapy sessions, the unit of therapy sampled (e.g., therapist or patient statement, brief segment of a session, whole sessions), and the perspective of evaluation (e.g., client report, therapist report, independent observer ratings). These issues have been explicated elsewhere (Elliott, 2010; Hill & Lambert, 2004). We focus here on several specific methodological issues that, in our view, can greatly impact the findings from a process–outcome or change mechanism study and that can affect the interpretation of any results in terms of clinical recommendations that can be made from the studies.

We recognize that there are many reasons why a given study might not address some, if not all, of the methodological topics that we focus on here. Most commonly, a process–outcome study is conducted capitalizing on data collected for another purpose (e.g., a randomized clinical trial). In these cases, the design of the study for this other purpose often did not include features, such as repeated measurement of a mechanism variable or inclusion of potential background confounding variables, that would be ideal for interpretation of process–outcome associations. Sometimes investigators do not conduct certain types of analyses (e.g., causal inference analysis, multilevel analyses) that can better address methodological concerns because of inadequate sample size. Thus, we

understand that in most cases investigators did what they could with the available data, and it is not a criticism of their research approach that certain methodological problems were not addressed. Nevertheless, to move the scientific understanding of process–outcome relations forward, it is critical to know the extent to which these important methodological issues have been addressed in research to date.

Causal Inference

A key methodological issue is that the vast majority of process–outcome studies are not randomized experiments and therefore are limited in regard to making causal inferences. These limitations relate to time precedence (does the process variable occur before the outcome variable?) and the potential influence of confounding variables. Although there have been decades of process–outcome studies, only more recently have investigators attempted to go beyond simple associations of process and outcome by using designs and statistical approaches that allow greater confidence in making causal inferences from the data. From our perspective, further studies reporting simple associations, without any attempt to address causal inference, will add little to a scientific understanding of how psychotherapy works. Ultimately, our view is that to have the strongest base for causal inferences, findings from correlational process–outcome studies should be followed by studies that experimentally manipulate key elements of the process of specific psychotherapies. But as an alternative to a randomized experiment, modern *causal inference* statistical approaches can be applied to correlational data. To encourage the use of such approaches and to highlight the limitations of failing to rule out the influence of confounding variables, we provide a discussion here of causal inference methods and in our review primarily focus on studies that use these methods.

In the context of change mechanism research, investigators have used tests of mediation to have greater confidence in causal inferences. Traditional mediational analysis as described by Baron and Kenny (1986) examines whether, in the current context, the change mechanism variable accounts (either fully or partially) for any treatment effect (i.e., difference in outcome between two treatments, or between the treatment and control group). To fully satisfy the conditions of Baron and Kenny's (1986) approach to mediation, four conditions must be met:

1. Treatment groups must differ meaningfully on outcome.
2. Treatment groups differ on change in the mediator (change mechanism) variable.
3. Change on the mediator variable is associated with outcome.
4. The treatment effect on outcome is reduced when the mediator is in the statistical model.

A revised perspective on mediation (the MacArthur model) was subsequently described by Kraemer et al. (2001) (see also: Kraemer et al., 2002). This perspective added time precedence for the mediator variable as another criterion for establishing mediation. This approach also allowed for a treatment by mediator interaction in relation to outcome (i.e., differential relation of the mediator to outcome in treatment vs. in control/alternative treatment), rather than only reduction of the treatment effect in the context of the mediator, as evidence for mediation. Note that standard mediational analysis, even if time precedence is established, does not rule out the possibility of other possible confounding variables.

Temporal precedence can be difficult to establish within the context of a process–outcome correlational study. Typically, a process–outcome study measures outcome as change from baseline to termination of treatment. The process variable is then typically measured at some point during treatment, such as session five. The process variable at session five is then correlated with change in patient symptoms or functioning from baseline to termination, and the resultant correlation is described as evidence that the process variable is an important determinant of treatment outcome. The first issue to contemplate is whether the correct time interval has been selected. In most cases, researchers do not know what the time lag is between a process or mechanism variable and its subsequent impact on outcome. Time lags are generally chosen out of convenience, defined by the timing of data collection. But another issue to consider is that the process–outcome relationship might go in the other direction: patient improvement from baseline to session five causes the process variable to change, and such early-in-treatment improvement is often highly associated with outcome at treatment termination. This early improvement then produces an artificial relationship between the process variable at session five and change in symptoms from baseline to termination (i.e., reverse causation). It is important to recognize, however, that early improvement (reverse causation) is only one of many potential confounders that might be generating a spurious association between a process variable and outcome. Methods to address potential confounding have been pursued so that greater confidence in causal relations can be made.

In order to infer causal connections, some investigators use statistical techniques, such as structural equation modeling (SEM), which disentangle the direct and indirect effects of latent and observed variables on a specified outcome. But even techniques like SEM, as commonly used, remain vulnerable to spurious findings driven by unmeasured confounders.

One method to eliminate patient and therapist characteristics that might confound a process–outcome relation is to conduct within-patient analyses. Such within-patient analyses require that the process and outcome variables are each measured repeatedly over time (at multiple sessions) and lagged analyses (change in the process variable predicting subsequent change in symptoms) is used to eliminate reverse causation. By correlating the process variable with outcome within each patient, the role of patient and therapist confounding background (i.e., pretreatment) variables is removed from influence. Although such within-patient analyses are appealing for examining the effect of process variables on next session outcomes, there remain possible unmeasured within-patient variables that confound the process variable-symptom change association (e.g., variations in therapist empathy levels over sessions that confound a within-patient alliance-symptom relation). In addition, such analyses do not focus on the outcome that is most of interest: eventual treatment outcome.

In fact, it is conceivable that those patients that demonstrate a high association between the process variable and next session symptoms actually have relatively poor eventual (end of treatment) outcomes. This could occur if a study sample included, for example, patients with borderline personality disorder (BPD) that show high reactivity to the therapist and fluctuating symptom levels from week to week, but relatively poor (compared to those without BPD) treatment outcomes. Within-patient analyses, therefore, may be useful for asking certain questions about the process of therapy, but less useful in understanding what leads to individual differences in eventual treatment outcome. Nevertheless, this statistical approach is a notable advance over prior methods because it raises confidence in possible causal connections between process and outcome.

Another approach to the causality issue with nonrandom assignment data is the use of causal inference statistical methods. The method of instrumental variables is a causal inference approach that has been widely applied to nonexperimental studies in econometrics and other fields (see, for example, Angrist & Krueger, 2001 and Earle et al., 2001), but rarely to psychotherapy studies. The method of instrumental variables is a regression-based approach that proceeds as follows: a variable (called the instrument, typically labeled Z) is identified that in theory causes the predictor variable of interest (X, e.g., the alliance), but with the constraint that Z has no independent association with the outcome (Y; e.g., a measure of symptom severity), except through the predictor variable. To illustrate: one could, in theory, identify a patient variable such as interpersonal style (e.g., desire/willingness to emotionally connect to people vs. lack of interest in connecting emotionally to other people) as an instrument (Z) that predicts alliance in therapy (X), but Z has no other association with treatment outcome (Y), other than the causal path that Z is associated with X, which subsequently is associated with Y. The method of instrumental variables would then consist of using regression analyses to isolate the part of the alliance (X) that is associated only with patient interpersonal style (Z). This part of the alliance is then correlated in a second step with outcome (Y) to determine if that isolated part of the alliance has a statistical association with treatment outcome. Because we have isolated the part of the alliance that is caused only by the instrument (patient interpersonal style), no other causal factors (measured or unmeasured) could cause outcome (except through their association with the alliance). To isolate a larger part of the alliance, the instrument can be a set of variables, not just one.

If no attempt has been made to address issues of causal direction and/or the role of third variables, any clinical recommendations would need to be made cautiously, if at all. Our focus in this chapter, therefore, is not to conduct a detailed methodological critique of each and every process–outcome study, but rather to address the question of whether the field has moved ahead in attempting to address the possibility of a causal connection between process variables and treatment outcome.

Multilevel Modeling of Therapist Effects

Another important methodological concern is related to the fact that individual psychotherapy is not based just on an individual: it is a dyadic relationship consisting of a patient and a therapist. In most studies, each therapist in the study has treated more than one patient. From a statistical point of view, such a study is therefore a *multilevel* study with patients nested within therapists. Either the patient or the therapist, or both, might be contributing to the level of a process variables measured in treatment sessions and, therefore, might be responsible for the connection between that process variable and treatment outcome. Baldwin, Wampold, and Imel (2007) illustrate how process–outcome relationships could be occurring in opposite directions at the patient and therapist levels. Ignoring the multilevel nature of the data may therefore produce misleading findings. Modern statistical techniques of multilevel modeling (Bryk & Raudenbush, 1992) can be used to sort out the therapist contribution and the patient contribution to any process–outcome correlation. This is an important issue because knowing that the patient, the therapist, or both, are contributing to a process–outcome relationship has clear implications for any clinical recommendations in terms of how best to maximize the process variable to achieve positive outcomes. Incorporating a multilevel analysis is particularly relevant to process variables that examine the therapeutic relationship (i.e., is it the patient's contribution or the therapist's contribution to the relationship that matters?), and therapist variables.

The multilevel approach to the dyadic nature of psychotherapy has been extended to examine the interaction of patient and therapist perceptions of process. If patient and therapist perceptions of the process potentially influence each other, such an interaction can be investigated using the actor–partner interdependence model of dependencies within nested dyadic data (Kenny, 1996; Ledermann & Kenny, 2012). To use this approach, both patient and therapist measures of process and outcome are needed. Using multilevel modeling, the statistical approach simultaneously estimates actor effects (the effects of the actor's process scores on their outcome scores) and partner effects (the effects of the partner's process scores on the actor's outcome scores), with patient serving as actor and therapist as partner and also vice versa. By modeling these effects, the actor–partner approach provides a window into the dyadic nature of psychotherapy process–outcome relations in a way not obtainable through other data analytic approaches.

Specificity of Effects

Another methodological issue of relevance to process–outcome and mechanism of change studies is whether research has examined if effects are specific to a particular form of psychotherapy or not. For example, cognitive therapy for depression is hypothesized to work by changing dysfunctional depressogenic cognitions. If such change in dysfunctional cognitions (and symptoms) occurs to the same degree in a different form of psychotherapy as in cognitive therapy, and such changes drive symptomatic improvements, then there would be no need to specifically recommend cognitive therapy for depression. It may be that, as proposed by Wampold and Imel (2015), psychotherapies operate mostly by general change mechanisms and common factors, rather than by treatment-specific

mechanisms. To determine if treatment-specific mechanisms do or do not exist, testing a given theoretical mechanism in more than one therapy type (preferably nonsimilar therapies) is needed.

The Limits of Process–Outcome Research

Often, researchers and other consumers of the scientific literature on psychotherapy, as well as other areas of research in psychology, are unimpressed by findings that, in terms of effect sizes, are in the range of a 0.20–0.30 correlation. DeRubeis et al. (2014), however, demonstrate that process–outcome correlations cannot be reasonably expected to be much larger than that under conditions that would typically be found. Using data simulations, DeRubeis et al. (2014) found that the expected correlation between a measure of therapy quality and outcome would be small (about 0.25) under typical conditions. When the authors modeled conditions designed to increase the likelihood that strong process–outcome relationships could be found, expected correlations were still only in the modest range (0.38–.51). There are several reasons for this. For one, patient factors interact with therapist process variables. For example, when a given level of a therapist variable (e.g., adherence, competence, empathy, etc.) is provided to patients, the same level of the therapist process variable may lead to different outcomes depending on whether the patient is pliant (i.e., their individual response to therapy will be excellent if excellent therapy is provided, poor if the therapy is poor, etc.), prone to spontaneous remission over time regardless of level of therapist process variable, challenging (i.e., the patient will respond to therapy only if a given therapist variable is at a high quality), or intractable (i.e., the patient will not respond regardless of the level of the therapist process variable). In addition to such patient variables that might moderate or attenuate the effects of a therapist variable on outcome, there are external factors (e.g., illness, death of a loved one, meeting someone and falling in love) that likely have an impact on outcome scores, thereby diluting the influence of any process variable on outcome. DeRubeis et al. (2014) also point out that confounds (discussed above, in the section on causal inferences) if not addressed can attenuate the relationship between a process variable and outcome.

Another factor that limits process–outcome relationships is therapist responsiveness (Stiles et al., 1998), defined as the session-to-session and even moment-to-moment changes in the content and style of a therapist's statements and nonverbal behaviors in response to patient verbal and nonverbal communications and states. If therapists are responsive, therapist interventions thought to be highly relevant to outcome might be most frequently used when patients are not progressing well. Further, therapists may completely avoid using certain types of interventions in the context of a patient who has already improved. In this situation, depending on when process variables are obtained, the process variable that is hypothesized to lead to good outcome might actually show no relationship, or even a negative relationship, with outcome (Stiles, 1988). Process variables that measure the overall quality of therapy, rather than counts of specific therapist interventions, might be less prone to be influenced by therapist responsiveness. Finally, the dependability (reliability) of a process variable, or outcome variable, can affect the size of a process–outcome correlation. Session-to-session variability in process variables is particularly relevant in this regard. The selection of a single session for obtaining a process variable is common but, given variability from session-to-session, a single session may be a relatively poor indicator of the levels of that process variable for each patient in a study. This problem is relevant to between-patient analyses of process in relation to outcome. Within-patient analyses actually capitalize on such session-to-session variability in relation to session-to-session outcomes. Even with within-patient analyses, however, less than perfect reliability of process measures may attenuate process–outcome correlations. Thus, process–outcome associations need to be interpreted in the context of the likely constraints that limit the size of such relationships.

COMMON FACTORS: THE THERAPEUTIC RELATIONSHIP

Table 8.1 presents results of recent meta-analyses examining the relation of one class of common factors – namely, aspects of the therapeutic relationship – to the outcome of psychotherapy. These factors include the therapeutic alliance, the real relationship, therapist empathy, therapist positive regard, and therapist genuineness.

The Alliance
Definition
The concept of therapeutic alliance originated with psychodynamic therapy, but its role in the therapeutic process has been generalized to orientations other than just psychodynamic therapy (Horvath & Symonds, 1991). There is now recognition of the role of the alliance in cognitive-behavioral therapy (Castonguay et al., 2010), a range of psychodynamically oriented therapies (Messer & Wolitzky, 2010), interpersonally oriented treatment (Benjamin & Critchfield, 2010), modern humanistic approaches (Watson & Kalogerakos, 2010), modes of family therapy (Escudero et al., 2010), couples therapy (Horvath et al., 2010), and group therapy (Piper & Ogrodniczuk, 2010).

The therapeutic alliance is most commonly defined as the collaborative and affective relationship between the therapist and the client (Bordin, 1979). The collaborative aspects of the alliance include the extent of agreement between therapist and client about commitment, the goals of therapy, and which techniques will be implemented to achieve these goals. The affective component of the alliance is the bond between the participants and includes mutual trust, liking, respect, and caring.

Meta-Analytic Results
The most recent meta-analysis of alliance–outcome studies included a total of 295 studies that involved over 30,000 adult patients (published between 1978 and 2017) and included both face-to-face and Internet-based psychotherapy (Flückiger

TABLE 8.1 Results of Meta-Analyses of Common Process Factors in Relation to Psychotherapy Outcome

Common factor construct	Authors	# of Studies	# of Patients	Effect size (r or g) with outcome	95% Confidence interval
Alliance (adults)	Flückiger et al. (2018)	295	>30,000	.28	.26, .30
Real relationship	Gelso et al. (2018)	16	1502	.38	.30, .44
Therapist empathy	Elliot et al. (2018)	82	6138	.28	.23, .33
Therapist positive regard	Farber et al. (2018)	64	3528	.36	.28, .44
Therapist genuineness	Kolden et al. (2018)	21	1192	.23	.13, .32

et al., 2018). Consistent with previous meta-analyses, the overall alliance–outcome association for face-to-face psychotherapy was $r = 0.28$ (95% CI [0.26, 0.30]) (Table 8.1). Some heterogeneity was apparent among the effect sizes, with 2% of the 295 effect sizes indicating negative correlations. The correlation for 23 studies of internet-based psychotherapy was essentially the same ($r = 0.28$). Results were generally consistent across assessor perspectives on the alliance, specific alliance and outcome measures, types of treatments, patient characteristics, and countries.

It should be noted that most of the existing alliance–outcome studies measured the alliance at one or two sessions and therefore the meta-analytic finding of $r = 0.28$ likely underestimates the strength of the relation. Crits-Christoph et al. (2011) demonstrated that measuring the alliance using multiple patients per therapist and at least four treatment sessions per patient is crucial to adequately estimate the size of the alliance–outcome relationship. This study suggested that a single early session alliance score explained 4.7% of outcome variance, but that the average of six early sessions explained 14.7% of outcome variance. Thus, it is misleading to assume, based on the $r = 0.28$ meta-analytic result of studies that often measure the alliance at only one session, that the alliance explains only 7.8% of outcome variance.

Over the course of the history of alliance studies, some researchers have minimized the importance of the therapeutic relationship. This position is based on research suggesting that technical treatment intervention factors predict outcome more strongly than the alliance, and on research indicating that the alliance does not predict outcome in cognitive therapy for depression once other variables have been controlled (DeRubeis et al., 2005; DeRubeis & Feeley, 1990; Feeley et al., 1999; Strunk, Brotman, & DeRubeis, 2010). However, another study modifies these authors' negative view of the alliance–outcome relation. In this other study, two components of the alliance, agreement on goals and agreement on tasks, were found to be significantly associated with outcome in the context of cognitive therapy (CT) for depression, but the bond component of the alliance was not significantly associated and appeared to be more of a consequence of prior improvement (Webb et al., 2011). Thus, even original critics of the alliance–outcome relation now acknowledge that some aspects of the alliance may be part of the process of change in CT for depression.

Multilevel Modeling of the Alliance–Outcome Relation and Actor–Partner Effects

One significant development in alliance–outcome research since the 2013 review has been a notable increase in the number of studies of the alliance–outcome relation that incorporate multilevel modeling. In the 6th edition chapter, we highlighted the seminal paper by Baldwin, Wampold, and Imel (2007), which presented a multilevel framework for understanding therapist and patient contributions to the alliance–outcome relation and reported results from a large naturalistic psychotherapy sample, indicating that alliance at the therapist level, but not the patient level, significantly predicted outcome. A

therapist level effect, but not a patient level effect, was also found in another study (Crits-Christoph et al., 2009) that used multilevel modeling in a community sample of substance users. This study also addressed the potential for reverse causation by controlling for improvement up to the point the alliance was measured. Overall, however, findings have been mixed. Significant effects at the therapist level, but not the patient level, have also been reported by Dinger et al. (2008), Marcus et al. (2011), and Zuroff et al. (2010), but significant effects at the patient, but not therapist, level have been found in other studies (Crits-Christoph et al., 2011; Falkenström et al., 2014; Huppert et al., 2014). The reason for the discrepancies between these studies is not clear, but it may have to do with patient variables that moderate the alliance–outcome relation. Moderators such as patient education (Constantino et al., 2017) and patient level of interpersonal problems (Zilcha-Mano & Errázuriz, 2017) may contribute to the relative importance of patient level versus therapist level effects, particularly if patients are not randomly assigned to therapists and if the number of patients per therapist is relatively low in a given study. Understanding whether the alliance–outcome association is primarily occurring at the therapist level, patient level, or both, has implications for the clinical implementation of the empirical findings. An effect at the therapist level would suggest that there might be a focus on training therapists on how to improve their average levels of alliance with patients. An effect at the patient level, but not at the therapist level, would suggest that a focus on therapist training is not critical. Rather, the alliance should be monitored as a patient variable that forecasts eventual outcome. Other treatment approaches (e.g., medication) might be considered for patients that are predicted to have relatively poor outcomes due to below average alliance levels.

Several studies have also now applied the actor–partner model to examine the impact of a positive alliance in psychotherapy. Studies by Kivlighan (2007), Kivlighan et al. (2015), and Kivlighan et al. (2016) used the actor–partner model to examine the impact of the alliance on measures of session quality (e.g., depth of session), revealing both actor and partner effects. One study (Zilcha-Mano et al., 2016) used the actor–partner model with repeated assessments of the alliance and outcome over the course of therapy (allowing for separation of within-patient and between-patient components of the alliance). This study found both actor effects (both within- and between-patient effects for both patient and therapist as actor) and significant partner effects for within-patient changes in patient-rated alliance levels on session outcome. Lagged analyses to separate out causal direction, however, were not conducted. Nevertheless, this study and those of Kivlighan (2007), Kivlighan et al. (2015), and Kivlighan et al. (2016) highlight the importance of understanding the alliance as a dyadic variable.

Causal Effect of the Alliance

Despite the large literature documenting an association between the therapeutic alliance and psychotherapy outcome, important questions remain as to whether the alliance has a causal impact on the outcome of psychotherapy, or whether the association is spurious – or even runs in the opposite direction, with change in symptoms influencing the alliance (Feeley et al., 1999; Strunk, Brotman, & DeRubeis, 2010). To address the issue of causality, in the 6th edition of the *Handbook*, we reviewed studies that examined the relation between the alliance and subsequent symptom change, with some studies also controlling for prior change. Overall, the median squared correlation between the alliance and outcome controlling for prior symptom change (or predicting subsequent change), across 11 studies was .24. This value is only slightly lower than the average effect (.28) found in the most recent meta-analysis of all alliance–outcome studies (Flückiger et al., 2018) suggesting that the alliance causes subsequent improvement.

Studies published since the 2013 review show a more mixed picture. Webb et al. (2014) reported that, for inpatient psychotherapy, treatment outcome expectancies and the alliance significantly predicted subsequent depressive symptom change. When prior symptom change was included in the model, however, the alliance–outcome association was no longer significant ($r = 0.13$). A slightly higher ($r = 0.15$), but statistically significant ($p = 0.01$), effect was found by Zilcha-Mano et al. (2014) when predicting subsequent symptom change. Similarly, Zilcha-Mano and Errázuriz (2015) reported that the alliance significantly predicted subsequent symptom change with both between-patient and within-patient significant effects. However, Xu and Tracy (2015) found clear indication of reciprocal influence: alliance predicted subsequent symptom change and prior symptom change predicted the alliance. Overall, the evidence continues to indicate that the alliance is associated with subsequent symptom change. However, disentangling the various effects (multilevel, within- and between-patient, reciprocal effects) is challenging.

Few of the 295 studies of the alliance–outcome relation reviewed by Flückiger et al. (2018) statistically controlled for other potential confounders besides early improvement. An exception is the study by Klein et al. (2003). This study did control for several covariates, including gender, chronicity of depression, comorbid anxiety, substance use, personality disorders, social functioning, and history of abuse/neglect in childhood, and found that the alliance predicted subsequent change even after controlling for this set of variables. However, other potential confounding variables were not controlled in this, or other studies, and therefore the causality issue continues to be of central interest in research on the alliance in relation to outcome.

Since the last version of this chapter, a few studies employing alternative methods for addressing potential confounders of the alliance–outcome relation have emerged. Zilcha-Mano (2017) reviewed 8 studies that used within-patient analyses to test whether a positive alliance causes next session outcomes (Crits-Christoph et al., 2011; Falkenström et al., 2013; Falkenström et al., 2016; Hoffart et al., 2013; Vrabel et al., 2015; Zilcha-Mano & Errázuriz, 2015; Zilcha-Mano et al., 2016; Zilcha-Mano et al., 2015). All eight of these studies found significant within-patient effects with the alliance predicting next session outcome. A recent study not included in the review found that higher alliance was associated with subsequent within-patient improvement in panic-specific reflection function in panic-focused psychodynamic therapy,

but worsening in CBT (Solomonov et al., 2020). A study conducted in Kenya (Falkenström et al., 2019) also disaggregated within and between-patient effects and found that there was a within-patient effect for the alliance predicting next-session psychological distress. There was also evidence for the reverse causation (symptoms impacting alliance) in this study. In the treatment of borderline personality disorder, Kivity et al. (2019) found that, using within-patient analyses, alliance rated by either patients or therapists did not predict subsequent session outcomes. One other study failed to find a within-patient effect for the alliance predicting next session outcomes in cognitive therapy for depression (Sasso et al., 2016). In summary, 10 of 12 studies using a within-patient analysis that addresses between-patient confounds and temporal precedence found evidence that the alliance may be causally related to next session outcomes.

The method of instrumental variables was recently used as a secondary analysis of the alliance–outcome relation by Crits-Christoph et al. (2018). In this study, instrumental variables were created at the patient and therapist level using baseline patient and therapist pretreatment variables. These baseline variables were selected because they predicted the alliance but were otherwise unrelated to treatment outcome other than through their effects on the alliance. Selected variables at the patient level were: (a) patient endorses the belief that the cause of their depression was repeating relationship mistakes, (b) patient had a positive attitude about talking to a therapist, and (c) patient did not find it hard to be supportive to others. At the therapist level, selected variables included: (a) length of time therapist had been working at agency, (b) the degree of comfort the therapist had in recommending the form of therapy implemented in the study to other therapists, and (c) therapist was religious (specifically, Christian). Standard multilevel mixed effects analyses in this study found a statistically significant association of the alliance with outcome at the therapist level of analysis. When the method of instrumental variables was conducted, the therapist-level effect remained statistically significant, consistent with the possibility of a causal relation between the alliance and outcome.

One previous study also used instrumental variable analysis to examine the alliance–outcome relation (Goldsmith et al., 2015). In this study, the investigators looked at the interaction between the number of sessions attended and the alliance at session 4 in relation to the outcome of 6 weeks of cognitive behavioral therapy plus routine care, supportive counselling plus routine care, or routine care alone for patients who had a first or second episode of psychosis. The result of the instrumental variable analysis was consistent with a potential causal role for the alliance interacting with number of sessions in relation to 18-month follow-up outcomes. When a positive alliance was evident, then attending more sessions caused significantly better outcomes, but when a poor alliance was evident, then attending more sessions was detrimental. A limitation of the study is that the strength of these effects was not reported by the authors. In addition, the psychotherapy treatment was very brief (six sessions), and 45% of treated patients failed to provide an alliance score. Nevertheless, it is of note that at least two studies using the method of instrumental variables now have provided some support that the alliance may have a causal role in producing better outcomes.

Ruptures in the Alliance

An approach to the role of the alliance in therapy that has gained increasing interest is to focus on ruptures in the alliance and whether or not such ruptures are repaired. Following the Bordin (1979) definition of the alliance, ruptures are identified by a disagreement between the patient and therapist on treatment goals, a lack of collaboration on therapeutic tasks, or a strain in their emotional bond. A meta-analysis of 11 studies of rupture resolution in relation to outcome yielded an average effect size of $r = 0.29$ (Eubanks et al., 2018). An additional recent study extended the within-patient approach to the study of alliance ruptures (Rubel et al., 2018). The study found that both patient and therapist-reported ruptures were significant within-patient predictors of subsequent alliance and symptom impairment.

Relationship Factors Overlapping With the Alliance Construct

Although the alliance is often thought of as the essence of the therapeutic relationship, researchers have investigated a large number of specific components of the therapeutic relationship that, though likely highly correlated with the alliance, may also be partly independent of the alliance. The process–outcome chapter in the 5th edition of this *Handbook* provides a detailed review of these factors (Orlinsky et al., 2004), and a brief update appeared in the 2013 review. These overlapping factors included personal role involvement (of both patient and therapist), interactive coordination, expressive attunement, affective attitude, and experiential congruence. In general, the literature has shown some support for these process variables in relation to outcome, though some studies have been less supportive (e.g., Hoffart et al., 2006; Swift & Callahan, 2009; Vogel et al., 2006). In addition, older studies did not attend to methodological issues (e.g., reverse causality, multilevel modeling, or specificity of effects) that can have important implications for interpreting the results of studies and the clinical usefulness of such studies. Newer studies on these constructs have been rare. One exception is a study of therapist affective attunement rated from sessions of cognitive therapy and psychodynamic therapy for cluster C personality disorders (Håvås et al., 2015). The investigators found that higher levels of nonverbal matching of patient affect by the therapist was associated with a decrease in avoidant attachment style from baseline to termination. In addition, nonverbal matching of affect and nonverbal openness and regard for the patient's experiences was associated with a decrease in ambivalent attachment style from baseline to termination. Verbal aspects of attunement did not predict the attachment outcome variables when nonverbal aspects were controlled in the analyses.

The Real Relationship

Another perspective on the patient–therapist relationship has centered on the real relationship. Whereas the alliance is

defined as the working part of relationship, the real relationship is defined as the nonwork part. As described by Gelso (2009), the real relationship is the personal relationship between patient and therapist that is evident by the extent to which each is genuine with the other and sees the other in ways that are realistic. A recent meta-analytic study found that, across 16 studies and 1,502 patients, there was a moderate association with the strength of the real relationship with outcome ($r = 0.38$, 95% CI [.30, .44]) (Gelso et al., 2018) (Table 8.1). No attempt was made, however, in this meta-analysis to specifically address temporal precedence. However, Gelso et al. (2018) review individually three studies that conducted multilevel analyses and concluded that between-therapist differences are better predictors of treatment outcome than between-patient differences in the real relationship.

Therapist Empathy, Genuineness, and Positive Regard

Related to the alliance and relationship factors in general are the therapist qualities of empathy, genuineness, and positive regard. The centrality of these qualities to successful psychotherapy of course originated with Carl Rogers (1957) but are generally recognized by many psychotherapists and psychotherapy researchers as essential ingredients of therapy. Recent meta-analyses have summarized findings to date in the literature on each of these dimensions. Regarding empathy, a meta-analysis of 82 studies (6,138 patients) indicated that empathy is a moderately strong predictor of therapy outcome with a mean $r = 0.28$, 95% CI [0.23, 0.33] (Elliot et al., 2018) (Table 8.1). The empathy–outcome relation held for different theoretical orientations and client presenting problems. A meta-analysis of 64 studies (3,528 patients) of therapist unconditional positive regard in relation to outcome found, after controlling for the repeated use of data sets and study samples within the database, a moderate effect size (Hedges' $g = 0.36$, 95% CI [0.28, 0.44]) (Farber et al., 2018). Therapist genuineness in relation to outcome has been summarized in a meta-analysis of 21 studies representing 1,192 patients (Kolden et al., 2018). An aggregate effect size (r) of 0.23 (95% CI [.13, .32]) was found across these studies.

Though addressed in separate meta-analyses, it should be noted that the constructs of therapist empathy, positive regard, and genuineness are generally relatively highly correlated and, therefore, the effects reported in the three cited meta-analyses may not be independent. These dimensions also likely overlap with other relationship variables such as the real relationship and the alliance. In addition, these meta-analyses on empathy, genuineness, and positive regard did not address the issues of temporal precedence or multilevel analyses because the individual process–outcome studies have yet to address these methodological concerns.

Common Factors: Summary and Future Directions

From the 1970s through the present, a large body of research has consistently documented that the quality of the therapeutic relationship, particularly as captured with the alliance construct, is associated with psychotherapy outcome in a wide variety of patient populations and types of treatment. Recent research supports the potential causal role that a positive therapeutic alliance plays in leading to relatively better treatment outcomes. The degree to which the alliance influences therapy outcomes is more difficult to specify with any certainty, as the size of the relationship is influenced by factors such as how many treatment sessions are sampled, which sessions are sampled (early vs. later in treatment), type of patient population, and the type of psychotherapy. On a positive note, several newer studies have used multilevel modeling to determine patient and therapist contributions to the alliance–outcome relation, though findings to date have been mixed regarding which level carries the bulk of the effect. Future research is needed to investigate the contexts in which the patient level, or the therapist level, is more important. Results of such studies will have high relevance to how research on the alliance is translated into therapist training and clinical practice.

With regard to other aspects of the therapeutic relationship (personal role investment, interactive coordination, expressive attunement, affective attitude, experiential congruence), older studies have yielded mixed results of these constructs in relation to outcome. More consistent positive relations with outcome have been found for the therapist qualities of empathy, positive regard, genuineness, and the real relationship. However, with both the relationship qualities and therapist Rogerian qualities, the majority of studies that produced these findings have not been conducted with attention to issues of reverse causality, dependability of assessments, or multilevel modeling. Some newer studies have begun to address some of the methodological issues. Hopefully, in the years to come, more studies of these variables will incorporate greater attention to methodological issues that will allow for stronger conclusions. In addition, given the overlap between the various relationship variables that have been studied, an agenda for future research is to measure the full set of relationship variables within the same study to see which dimensions carry the bulk of the effect in relation to psychotherapy outcomes.

It should also be mentioned that complementary reviews of the empirical literature are presented in other chapters of this *Handbook* with respect to the alliance and alliance ruptures (Chapters 13, 15, and 17), real relationship (Chapter 7), as well as therapist empathy, genuineness, and positive regard (Chapter 14).

THEORY-SPECIFIC FACTORS

Change Processes in Behavior Therapy and Cognitive Behavioral Therapies for Anxiety Disorders

Behavior therapy for anxiety disorders typically consists of imaginal and/or in vivo exposure techniques. A clear theory about how the process of such treatments should relate to treatment outcome was described by Foa and Kozak (1986). Their emotional processing theory hypothesizes that successful outcome requires activation of the fear structure during exposure (as assessed by physiological responses and self-report), a gradual reduction (i.e., habituation) of the degree of fear reactions after repeated presentation of fear stimuli during sessions (i.e., habituation within sessions), and a reduction in the degree of fear reactions across exposure sessions (i.e., habituation across sessions). In the 6th edition of this *Handbook*, we reviewed nine studies that examined these process variables in relation to the outcome of behavior therapy for anxiety disorders. In general, findings were mixed across studies, but we concluded that there was some support for the emotional processing theory based on process–outcome studies.

While some of the additional studies published after completion of our 2013 review have not been supportive of emotional processing theory (Culver et al., 2012; Meuret et al., 2012), two studies of exposure therapy for PTSD found between-session habituation was significantly associated with better treatment outcome, and that higher within-session fear levels were found to be unrelated to outcome or associated with relatively poorer outcome (Harned et al., 2015; Sripada & Rauch, 2015). Another study found within-session reliable change in distress was associated with lower PTSD symptoms at posttreatment (Bluett et al., 2014). One concern that remains, however, is that the methodological issues that we described at the beginning of this chapter as critical for making stronger inferences about causal connections were not addressed in the research we reviewed in the 6th edition *Handbook* chapter, or in the newer studies mentioned above. None of these process–outcome studies of exposure therapy examined whether the process variable predicted *subsequent* change in the outcome measure, controlling for prior change in the outcome measure. Thus, it is not clear from these studies that habituation across sessions causes good outcome. Rather, other therapy elements (e.g., common factors) might be causing both the ongoing fear reduction across sessions and the final fear reduction seen at treatment termination.

In part because of the mixed results of the extant literature, an alternative theory was proposed to explain the effects of exposure therapy for anxiety disorders, specifically that exposure treatment works through facilitating inhibitory learning (i.e., learning new non-threatening associations that compete with the fearful association). According to this theory, variability in fear level during exposure, rather than the gradual reduction proposed by emotional processing theory, would be critical for treatment success (Craske et al., 2012). Variability in fear levels during exposure is hypothesized to enhance retrievability of learning, given that different levels of fear are likely to occur in situations, following exposure therapy, where retrieval is required. In addition, variability in fear levels during exposure therapy may help with generalization to other contexts by facilitating learning that one can tolerate exposure to a fear situation while experiencing a range of emotions. Interest in the inhibitory learning theory was further influenced by the hypothesis that certain chemicals, notably D-cycloserine and hydrocortisone, might facilitate inhibitory learning in the context of exposure therapy for anxiety disorders.

Several process–outcome studies have examined the inhibitory learning theory of the mechanism of exposure therapy for anxiety disorder. Culver et al. (2012) found that emotional variability based on subjective ratings predicted the outcome of exposure therapy for people with public speaking anxiety ($r = 0.41$). In a study that examined D-cycloserine (versus placebo) augmentation of exposure therapy for PTSD, within-session habituation and between session habituation both significantly predicted the outcome of exposure therapy for PTSD (de Kleine et al. 2015), but not more so for the D-cycloserine group compared to the placebo group, as the inhibitory learning theory might suggest. In contrast, a study of virtual reality-augmented exposure therapy for PTSD found between-session peak distress ratings to be predictive of outcome for patients receiving D-cycloserine, but not for those receiving placebo or alprazolam augmentation (Rothbaum et al., 2014), supporting its purported effect in augmenting inhibitory learning. However, it has been argued that the use of change in subjective ratings of distress as an indicator of inhibitory learning may be problematic given that fear learning can occur without such changes (Craske et al., 2014). Comprehensive reviews of all of the evidence for the inhibitory learning theory have concluded that, while promising, the mixed results of studies as well as lack of an established way of assessing inhibitory learning directly in clinical treatment contexts has limited inhibitory learning as an explanation for the process of exposure therapy for anxiety disorders (Cooper, Clifton, & Feeny, 2017; Jacoby & Abramowitz, 2016).

Few process–outcome studies of CBT for anxiety disorders have examined therapist techniques as the process variable. In one study, Ginzburg et al. (2012) reported that ratings of therapist competence predicted the outcome of cognitive therapy for social anxiety disorder. This study is notable in that a multilevel analysis was used (patients nested within therapists). However, the sample size was relatively small ($N = 38$) and the investigators did not predict change subsequent to the assessment of competence. In a study of CBT for panic disorder, Boswell et al. (2013) found that significant between and within-therapist variability in observer ratings of adherence and competence in-session was evident, and that adherence and competence deteriorated significantly over the course of treatment. Neither adherence nor competence predicted subsequent outcome.

Solomonov et al. (2020) found that, in both cognitive behavioral (CBT) and panic-focused psychodynamic therapy, therapist focus on interpersonal relationships predicted subsequent improvement in panic-specific reflection function, though the effect was stronger in CBT, while therapist focus on thoughts and behaviors predicted worsening in panic-specific reflective functioning. Therapist focus on affect and moment-to-moment experience early in treatment in CBT (but not in psychodynamic therapy) predicted subsequent reduced misinterpretation of bodily sensations, while high focus on thoughts and cognitions predicted subsequent increase in misinterpretation. Thus, these findings were contrary to standard theories of the process of CBT treatment.

In summary, though the evidence is somewhat mixed, on balance there continues to be reasonably good support for an association of fear activation and habituation over sessions as part of the mechanism of exposure therapy for anxiety

disorders. It should be noted that the findings for activation of fear in sessions cannot be explained away as a confound between the process variable and the outcome variable, as is the case for habituation assessments, because the finding is in the opposite direction of such a confound (i.e., higher fear in sessions is associated with lowered fear at the end of treatment). However, it is not clear if activation of the specific fear is crucial (as opposed to normal fears), or whether the effects are specific to exposure therapy compared to other forms of therapy. Regardless of whether fear activation and habituation across sessions is specific to exposure therapy, we conclude that the empirical evidence is consistent with fear activation and habituation across sessions being likely important aspects of the process of change for anxiety disorders and phobias. We can therefore recommend that clinicians attend to fear activation when conducting exposure therapy with such clients. Clinical measurement of fear activation, using simple patient-report fear ratings, should be an essential aspect of any exposure treatment so that the clinician can monitor the degree of fear activation that occurs. Although we have some confidence in these recommendations, it would also be important that further studies of the role of fear activation and habituation in exposure therapies be conducted to rule out third variables and reverse causation (particularly in the case of habituation assessments).

In regard to studies of the use of theory-relevant therapist techniques in the delivery of CBT treatments for anxiety disorders, we are hesitant to draw any firm conclusion. Not enough studies have yet been conducted, and at least two of them have yielded negative findings (i.e., Boswell et al., 2013; Solomonov et al., 2020).

Change Mechanisms in Cognitive Behavioral Therapy for Anxiety Disorders

In addition to the studies reviewed above that examine change processes in exposure therapy for anxiety disorders, other studies have examined change mechanisms (Table 8.2). In the 2013 review, we described two studies (Hofmann et al., 2007; Smits et al., 2004) that found improvements in fear of fear partially mediate the outcome of exposure-based therapy for panic disorder. The cognitive variables and the outcome variables were measured only at baseline and termination of treatment and, therefore, causal direction of the effects is unclear. Another study, Vögele et al. (2010), found that change in cognitive variables were associated with the outcome of cognitive behavioral therapy for panic disorder and agoraphobia/social phobia. However, the timing of the measurement of the mediator variables again limits inferences about mediation and causation. Similarly, three studies (Foa & Rauch, 2004; Hagenaars et al., 2010; Nacasch et al., 2015) that examined the mechanism of change of exposure therapy specifically for PTSD measured the mediator variable concurrently with outcome at pre and posttherapy.

Within the context of a study comparing CBT and acceptance and commitment therapy (ACT) treatments for social anxiety disorder, Niles et al. (2014) examined change in negative cognitions (for CBT) and change in experiential avoidance

TABLE 8.2   Change Mechanisms in CBT for Anxiety Disorders

Study	Mechanism measure	Effect size (r) with outcome	Temporal precedence incorporated	Specificity to type of treatment
Hofmann et al. (2007)	Panic-related cognitions	.23	No	No
Smits et al. (2004)	Fear cognitions	.18	No	No
Vögele et al. (2010)	Cognitions about loss of control	.40	No	No
Niles et al. (2014)	Self-statements in context of public speaking	SIG	No	No
	Experiential avoidance	NOT SIG		
Strauss et al. (2019)	Cognitive reappraisal Expressive suppression	.01 .16	Yes	No
Smits et al. (2006)	Probability bias Cost bias	SIG NOT SIG	Yes	No
Huppert et al. (2018)	Social cognitions	.25	Yes	Yes
Post-traumatic Stress Disorder				
Foa & Rauch (2004)	PTSD-related cognitions	.58	No	No
Hagenaars et al. (2010)	PTSD-related cognitions	NOT SIG	Yes	No
Nascsch et al. (2015)	PTSD-related cognitions	.41	No	No
Cooper et al. (2017)	PTSD-related cognitions	.41	Yes	Yes
Kumpula et al. (2016)	PTSD-related cognitions	.26	Yes	No
McLean et al. (2015)	PTSD-related cognitions	SIG	Yes	Yes
Øktedalen et al., (2015)	Trauma-related shame and guilt	.35	Yes	No
Zalta et al. (2014)	PTSD-related cognitions	.31	Yes	No

Note. SIG = effect size could not be calculated from study results but reported as statistically significant. NOT SIG= effect size could not be calculated from study results but reported as not statistically significant. When both concurrent and temporal precedence relations were reported in a study, we include here only the temporal precedence results.

(for ACT) as mediators of outcome. Session-by-session changes in experiential avoidance was associated with pre to post treatment changes in social anxiety symptoms and anhedonic depression in ACT, but not in CBT, with a steeper decline of the experiential avoidance at the beginning of treatment predicting fewer symptoms in ACT only. Changes in negative cognitions during both treatments predicted outcome, with a steeper decline of negative cognitions at the beginning of both treatments predicting decreased social anxiety and depressive symptoms. Though this study purported to follow the MacArthur mediational model, with the mediator occurring during treatment (prior to the outcome measured at post treatment) and with an examination of differential effects across treatment groups, we note that outcome was examined as change from pre to post treatment. Thus, change in outcome subsequent to change in the mediator was not established in this study. However, this study represents an improvement over previous studies in otherwise meeting the MacArthur criteria for testing mediation and in measuring mediator variables repeatedly throughout treatment.

More recent studies have begun to incorporate temporal precedence of mechanism variables in relation to the outcome of CBT treatments for anxiety disorders. Strauss et al. (2019) examined changes in aspects of emotion dysregulation (i.e., difficulties in effectively managing one's emotions) as the change mechanism for exposure-based CBT for panic disorder with agoraphobia. Two emotion regulation strategies were measured, along with symptoms, at each treatment session: (a) the adaptive strategy of cognitive reappraisal, defined as reinterpreting emotional stimuli in less threatening ways in order to regulate negative emotions, and (b) the maladaptive strategy of expressive suppression, defined as inhibiting the expression of one's emotions. The results of the study were that reappraisal did not change until later in therapy and was not predictive of outcome. Emotional suppression did improve over the course of treatment and, in lagged analyses, decreases in emotional suppression predicted subsequent symptom levels.

In the context of CBT treatment of social anxiety, Smits et al. (2006) addressed the temporal relation of mediators and outcome. This study examined whether change in cognitions mediated change in social anxiety symptoms over the course of exposure therapy for social anxiety. The cognitive variables in this study were reduction in the tendency to associate fearful stimuli with an unrealistic high probability of harm (probability bias) and reduction in the tendency to exaggerate the negative consequences of an anticipated harmful event (cost bias). It was found that reduction in probability bias was associated with subsequent improvement in fear, but reductions in cost bias were a consequence of improvement in fear. In another study of social anxiety disorder, the role of changes in negative cognitions in relation to the outcome of exposure-based CBT was recently examined by Huppert et al. (2018). Temporal precedence of the mechanism variable was investigated in this study using lagged analyses. It was found that cognitive changes bidirectionally correlated with symptom change in lagged analyses in CBT, suggesting a reciprocal relationship between process and outcome. The same effect was not found in a therapy that focused on attentional bias modification, indicating that the cognitive change mechanism was specific to CBT.

The temporal sequencing of mediators and outcome has also now been addressed in five adult studies of the relation of belief change to subsequent change in PTSD symptoms (Cooper et al., 2017; Kumpula et al., 2017; McLean et al., 2015; Øktedalen et al., 2015; Zalta et al., 2014). Belief change was measured in four of these studies with the Posttraumatic Cognitions Inventory (PTCI; Foa et al., 1999), a self-report instrument that assesses negative trauma-related thoughts across three domains: negative beliefs about the self, the world, and self-blame. In the study (Øktedalen et al., 2015) that did not use the PTCI, patient ratings of trauma-related shame and guilt at each session were used as the mediator variable. All five studies reported significant associations of the mediator variable with subsequent change in PTSD symptoms. In three of the studies, the effect was primarily as hypothesized (belief change was associated with PTSD symptom change to a greater extent than the reverse direction). In one of the studies, there was some evidence of a reciprocal relationship (McLean et al., 2015). In the Kumpula et al. (2017) study, no reverse causation was evident for the PTCI Beliefs About the World subscale, but some evidence for reverse causation was found for the Beliefs About the Self subscale (though the effect for change in beliefs influencing subsequent outcome was stronger than the reverse for this subscale).

The specificity of these mediational effects to exposure therapy for PTSD was shown in two of these studies. Cooper et al. (2017) found a stronger association of belief change with subsequent outcome for prolonged exposure ($d = 0.93$) than for sertraline-treated patients ($d = 0.35$). Among patients with PTSD and alcohol use disorder, McLean et al. (2015) found similar strengths of association between change in beliefs and change in PTSD symptoms for patients receiving prolonged exposure plus naltrexone, prolonged exposure plus placebo, and naltrexone plus placebo, but found a smaller effect for patients that received supportive counseling and placebo.

In summary, there has been a notable increase in the number and quality of studies of change mechanisms for exposure-based studies of anxiety disorders since the 2013 review. For PTSD, five studies have now examined the temporal course of cognitive mediators of change in PTSD symptoms, and this reflects a major important methodological advance that provides greater certainty of causal effects. In these studies, changes in negative trauma-related beliefs have consistently been found to be associated with subsequent outcome, and some evidence for specificity of effects to exposure therapy is also present, though specificity relative to other forms of psychotherapy has not been examined. The generalizability of these findings to other anxiety disorders beyond PTSD is not clear given that the mediator variable in these studies is highly specific to PTSD. It may well be that exposure therapy works by different mechanisms for a complex disorder like PTSD compared to a disorder characterized simply by phobic avoidance. Full mediational studies with temporal sequencing of mediators and outcomes have rarely been carried out for other anxiety disorders and, therefore, further research on those disorders (e.g., social anxiety, panic disorder, and obsessive-compulsive disorder) is needed.

In addition to the theory-based research we have reviewed above on change processes and change mechanisms in CBT for anxiety disorders, it is important to acknowledge that other general patient process and therapist process variables, not specific to CBT theories, may affect treatment outcome. Some general factors, such as the alliance, have been investigated in the context of CBT for anxiety disorders (Huppert et al., 2014; Weiss et al., 2014). Less attention has been paid to other generic therapy factors (e.g., personal role involvement, interactive coordination, expressive attunement, affective attitude, and experiential congruence) within the context of CBT for anxiety disorders. However, one notable recent study deserves mention. In this study (Schwartz et al., 2018), hostile resistance coded in session 10 predicted subsequent symptom change ($r = 0.28$), beyond the effects of pretreatment predictors. Hostile resistance at session 2 did not predict outcome but did highly predict attrition ($r = -0.30$), even after established predictors were controlled. These studies illustrate that, in CBT treatment for anxiety disorder, general therapy process factors (not specific to CBT) likely contribute to outcome in addition to the theory-based mechanism variables. Future studies should incorporate both general factors (e.g., resistance, alliance) and theory-specific factors when attempting to more fully understand process–outcome links within CBT, as well as in other forms of therapy.

Change Processes in Cognitive Therapy for Depressive Disorders

There have been multiple studies of ratings of therapist actions, specifically therapist adherence and competence, in sessions of cognitive therapy (CT) in relation to the outcome of CT for major depressive disorder (MDD) (Table 8.3). A widely cited meta-analysis by Webb et al. (2010) reviewed CT studies up to

TABLE 8.3 Therapist Techniques Predicting Outcome of Cognitive Therapy for Depression

Study	Process measure	Effect size (r) with outcome	Temporal precedence incorporated	Therapist effects modeled	Specificity to type of treatment
Use of CT techniques					
Feeley et al. (1999)	CT concrete techniques	.36	Yes	No	No
	CT abstract techniques	.00			
DeRubeis et al. (1990)	CT concrete techniques	.28	Yes	No	No
	CT abstract techniques	.02			
Ablon & Jones (2002)	Extent to which therapy adhered to an ideal prototype of cognitive behavioral therapy	.17	No	No	Yes
Webb et al. (2012)	CT Concrete techniques Sample 1 Sample 2	.20 −.06	Yes	No	No
Strunk et al. (2012)	CT adherence: Behavioral methods/Homework	.21	Yes	No	No
Weck et al. (2013)	CT adherence CT competence	.05 −.01	Yes	No	No
Weck et al. (2015)	CT adherence	NOT SIG	No	No	No
	CT competence	NOT SIG			
Braun et al. (2015)	Socratic Questioning	.29	Yes	No	No
Sasso et al. (2016)	CT adherence: Cognitive methods	.24	Yes	No	No
Snippe et al. (2019)	CT adherence	NOT SIG	No	Yes	No
Strunk. . .DeRubeis (2010)	CT adherence: Cognitive methods Negotiating/Structuring	.44 .38	Yes	No	No
Strunk. . .Hollon (2010)	CT competence	.33	Yes	No	No
Shaw et al. (1999)	CT competence	.15	No	No	No
Trepka et al. (2004)	CT competence	.05	No	No	No

Note. A negative *r* indicates the finding was in the opposite direction from that hypothesized. Primary outcome measures selected for each study. NOT SIG= effect size could not be calculated from study results but reported as not statistically significant.

2010, as well as such studies of other psychotherapies, and concluded that correlations of adherence and competence with outcome are, on average, not significantly different from zero, and that this effect does not vary by treatment modality. In our 2013 review, we re-examined the CT for MDD studies listed in the Webb et al. (2010) review and made different decisions

concerning the extraction of results from a couple of the CT studies included in the Webb et al. (2010) review. We concluded that there was some evidence that the use of CT techniques, particularly *concrete* techniques, such as setting an agenda for the sessions, reviewing homework, and practicing rational responses, is associated with improved outcomes, and these effects are not due to the influence of prior symptomatic change. Since the 2013 review, some additional studies that attempt to address causality have been published.

One study, not included in our 2013 review, of CT competence found that CT competence rated from sessions predicted subsequent change in depressive symptoms ($r = 0.33$) (Strunk, Brotman, DeRubeis, & Hollon, 2010). In another study, Strunk et al. (2012) examined CT adherence and alliance as predictors of subsequent session-to-session symptom change within the context of 176 depressed outpatients who received combined medication and CT. Although a scale measuring adherence to CT behavioral methods and homework and the alliance significantly predicted subsequent session-to-session symptom change, in models in which patients' medication regimen and prior symptom change were covaried, only the behavioral methods and homework adherence scale remained a significant predictor of subsequent symptom change.

Using data from the CT conditions of two depression treatment outcome trials (DeRubeis et al., 2005; Dimidjian et al., 2006), Webb et al. (2012) evaluated whether therapist adherence to concrete CT techniques and the alliance predicted subsequent symptom change. The authors reported non-significant associations between CT techniques and subsequent symptom change in both samples ($rs = 0.20$ and -0.06). Weck et al. (2013) examined both therapist adherence and therapist competence during treatment as predictors of relapse following CBT treatment for recurrent depression. No significant associations were found. In a further report that combined data from the recurrent depression study with cases from a social anxiety disorder study and a hypochondriasis study, Weck et al. (2015) found that there was an interaction of CBT adherence and alliance in relation to treatment success/failure (with dropouts and nonresponders classified as failures). When the alliance was more positive, a stronger effect of adherence on treatment outcome was found. In addition, higher therapist competence was positively related to treatment outcome, though its effects were mediated by the alliance. This study was also limited in that it did not conduct prediction of outcome subsequent to the measurement of therapist adherence/competence.

Improving on previous studies, an investigation by Braun et al. (2015) disaggregated a CT technique variable (use of Socratic questioning) into within-patient and between-patient variability when investigating the relation of CT techniques to session-to-session symptom change. Within-patient Socratic questioning was significantly associated with change in depressive symptoms to the next session ($r = 0.34$). Sasso et al. (2016) also conducted both between-patient and within-patient analyses of CT adherence ratings in relation to outcome of CT for MDD. Results were that (a) between-patient variability in a scale of therapist adherence to cognitive methods and negotiating/structuring was associated with symptom change, and (b) within-patient variability in ratings of adherence to cognitive methods predicted next-session symptom change. By predicting subsequent symptom change, and by conducting within-patient analyses that removes the influence of potential between-patient confounding variables, these studies provide the most compelling data that use of CT

techniques might be causally related to outcome. In another study, Snippe et al. (2019) used multilevel modeling (patients nested within therapist) to examine the relation of CT adherence and therapist interpersonal skill to the outcome of CT or mindfulness CT for patients with diabetes and depressive symptoms and failed to find significant associations with treatment outcome.

In part, the inconsistent effects in regard to CT adherence predicting outcome might be due to moderator effects. The Webb et al. (2012) study mentioned above found some evidence that the differential effect of CT adherence in the two samples (though not significant in both) may have been due, in part, to different baseline depression severities of the sample (suggesting that adherence matters more in predicting outcome when initial depression is more severe). Sasso et al. (2015) further found that patient gender was a significant moderator of the relationship between CT adherence (use of cognitive methods) and next-session symptom change (stronger association for women compared to men). Further, pretreatment anxiety and number of prior depressive episodes were significant moderators of the relationship between use of behavioral methods/homework and next-session symptom change (greater behavioral methods/homework predicting symptom improvement more strongly among patients high in pretreatment anxiety and among patients with fewer prior depressive episodes).

Overall, the literature on CT techniques used within CT sessions in the treatment of MDD remains mixed. Some studies, however, have consistently found that the use of CT techniques is associated with improved outcomes, and that these effects are not due to the influence of prior symptomatic change or between-patient confounders. Potential moderators of the adherence–outcome association may, in part, explain the mixed effects in the literature. In addition, the assessment of adherence in too few sessions (typically only one) may be responsible for the small or nonsignificant effects in some studies. On balance, we conclude that the use of CT techniques in CT for MDD is clinically indicated. More tentatively, we also conclude that CT competence is related to treatment outcome. The extent to which scales for CT competence measure something unique to CT or capture general psychotherapy skill is not clear.

Three studies have examined the role of interpersonal/psychodynamic techniques within the context of CT for MDD. Although two studies (Hayes et al., 1996; Jones & Pulos, 1993) reported that using techniques more aligned with a psychodynamic or developmental perspective is beneficial, these studies failed to control for prior symptom change. The one study that did control for prior symptom change reported that greater interpersonal accuracy of intervention was associated with relatively poorer outcome in CT for MDD (Crits-Christoph et al., 2010). Whether the differences between the results of these studies are a function of the different process assessments, different sampling of sessions, or controlling/failing to control for prior improvement, is not known. Thus, it is difficult to draw broad conclusions or make clinical recommendations regarding the use of psychodynamic/interpersonal techniques in CT for MDD at this time.

Change Mechanisms in Cognitive Therapy for Depressive Disorders

CT for depressive disorders specifies that depressogenic cognitions contribute to the emergence of depressive symptoms. At the deepest (i.e., not readily accessible) level of cognition are depressogenic schemas, which are long-held underlying negative beliefs about the self. At a more surface level of conscious experience, depressed individuals engage in negative automatic thoughts that arise from such depressogenic schemas. At an intermediate level, it is possible to group automatic thoughts into patterns of dysfunctional attitudes. Various theoretical ideas about how cognitions change over the course of CT have been proposed, with one model hypothesizing that the core cognitions (dysfunctional attitudes or schemas) are actually modified (Hollon et al., 1990), a second model hypothesizing that core schemas are deactivated but remain intact (Ingram & Hollon, 1986), and a third model proposing that individuals learn compensatory skills that help suppress depressogenic cognitions in the context of stressful situations that would normally activate such cognitions (Hollon et al., 1990; Barber & DeRubeis, 1992). Compensatory skills emphasized in cognitive therapy include the generation of initial explanations followed by alternative explanations for negative events and thoughts as well as the creation of concrete problem-solving plans to resolve difficult situations.

Empirical tests of the mechanism of CT for MDD have generally failed to provide compelling evidence for most cognitive measures. Although the most recent meta-analysis of 26 randomized clinical trials (Cristea et al., 2015) examining studies of change mechanisms in CT for MDD found that, on average, CT results in changes in dysfunctional thinking, there was no evidence that these changes were specific to CT compared to other psychotherapies, with the exception of greater changes on the Dysfunctional Attitudes Scale (DAS; Weissman & Beck, 1978) apparent in multiple studies (e.g., Imber et al., 1990; Quilty et al., 2008). Also important to understanding the mechanism of CT for MDD are studies examining the relation of change in dysfunctional thinking to change in depressive symptoms. Garratt et al. (2007) summarized cognitive change in relation to symptom change in 31 studies of CT for MDD and concluded that, overall, there was support for such an association. Once again, however, the hypothesis that the association was specific to CT was not supported. An additional study (Quilty et al., 2008), published after the review by Garratt et al. (2007), also addressed whether cognitive changes from pre to post treatment mediated symptom change in CT. This study found evidence that CT was associated with greater dysfunctional attitude change compared with interpersonal therapy, and greater dysfunctional attitude change was associated with greater reduction in depressive symptoms. However, neither this study, nor any of the studies in the Garratt et al. (2007) review meet all of the criteria for cognitive changes mediating change in depression using the Baron and Kenny (1986) approach to establishing mediation or MacArthur (Kraemer et al., 2001; Kraemer et al., 2002) models of

mediation. The Quilty et al. (2008) study, while presented as consistent with the MacArthur mediational model, did not establish time precedence for change in the mediator variable.

Very few studies have in fact incorporated temporal precedence of changes in cognitive variables into changes in depressive symptoms. DeRubeis et al. (1990) reported that change in both dysfunctional attitudes and hopelessness from intake to mid-treatment was associated with change in depressive symptoms from mid-treatment to termination in CT but not in pharmacotherapy. Changes in automatic thoughts and attributional style did not differ significantly between CT and pharmacotherapy in terms of their ability to predict subsequent change in depressive symptoms. A larger study was conducted by Vittengl et al. (2014). For 523 patients with recurrent MDD who received CT, hopelessness and attributional style at mid-treatment (controlling for these variables at baseline and depressive symptoms at mid-treatment), the investigators found significant relations to depressive symptoms at termination. However, support for mediation of symptom reduction by cognitive content was inconsistent and weak in terms of predicting subsequent change in depressive symptoms. More recently, Quigley et al. (2018) found that both CT and antidepressant medication resulted in reductions in maladaptive cognition and depression symptoms. Cognitive content and depression symptoms were moderately correlated within measurement waves, but cross-lagged associations between the variables and indirect (i.e., mediated) treatment effects were non-significant. In a study examining CT skills as a mediator of symptom change, Jarrett et al. (2018) found that with standard acute phase CT, level of CT skills as reported by both patient and therapist at mid-treatment was associated with change in depressive symptoms from mid treatment to post treatment. However, baseline level of CT skills was not controlled in that analysis. Within the context of continuation phase CT in the Jarrett et al. (2018) study, CT skills at month 4 controlling for CT skills at month 0 (therefore measuring acquisition of skills), did not predict change in depressive symptoms from month 4 to month 8. Therefore, unlike the authors' conclusion that mediation has been demonstrated, we conclude that the study does not offer support that acquisition of CT skills is associated with subsequent improvement in depressive symptoms.

The studies reviewed above relied on self-report measures of surface cognitions or skills. Several studies have attempted to move beyond self-report to measure cognitive processes. Segal and Gemar (1997) used a modified Stroop task to assess underlying cognitive structures. The authors reported that patients successfully treated with CT experienced a shift in the organization of their underlying negative self-schemas. However, the organization of underlying self-schemas was inferred from reaction times rather than direct measurement. Dozois et al. (2009) used a computerized task designed to measure the degree of underlying schema consolidation (or interconnectedness) of self-relevant information. The investigators found that patients receiving CT plus pharmacotherapy had greater changes in cognitive organization in both positive and negative domains than those who received pharmacotherapy alone. A more recent report (Dozois et al., 2014) from the same sample as the Dozois et al. (2009) study reported results on a Redundancy Card-Sorting Task. On this measure, the combination of CT and pharmacotherapy was only associated with significantly greater cognitive restructuring in the positive interpersonal domain (no restructuring occurred in negative domains). An additional study by Quilty et al. (2014) reported that CT and pharmacotherapy were both associated with changes in positive and negative schematic structure, indicating that this mechanism may not be specific to CT.

Several studies have tested the hypothesis that CT works by increasing positive compensatory skills in depressed patients. In the first study, Barber and DeRubeis (2001) reported that improvement from baseline to week 12 in positive compensatory skills, as measured by the Ways of Responding (WOR; Barber & DeRubeis, 1992), was correlated with reduction in depressive symptoms from baseline to week 12. A second study found that change in the quality of compensatory skills on the WOR from pre- to posttreatment predicted the likelihood of relapse among patients with MDD who were treated with CT (Strunk et al., 2007). A third study reported that total compensatory skills (positive minus negative scores) was associated with change in depression and anxiety symptoms (Connolly Gibbons et al., 2009). This effect, however, was not specific to CT: there was no difference between CT and psychodynamic therapy in mean change in compensatory skills, and no difference in the relation between change in compensatory skills and change in symptoms by treatment (no significant treatment-by-mediator interaction). A fourth study (Crits-Christoph et al., 2017) used data from a study (Connolly Gibbons et al., 2016) comparing 16 sessions of cognitive and dynamic therapies for major depressive disorder in a community mental health setting. Multiple measures of potential cognitive therapy mediators of change were obtained at baseline and months 1, 2, and 5, including assessments of compensatory skills, dysfunctional attitudes, and depressogenic schemas. The results indicated that change in all three cognitive domains was associated with concurrent change in depressive symptoms. However, only improvement in positive compensatory skills was associated with subsequent change in depressive symptoms in cognitive therapy ($r = \_0.36$), but not in dynamic therapy ($r = 0.11$), thus demonstrating specificity and time precedence of a change mechanism variable.

In summary, theories of the mechanism of change in CT for depressive disorders have proposed that CT works by changing, in the patient, (a) dysfunctional attitudes, (b) underlying schemas, and/or (c) compensatory skills. We conclude that studies of dysfunctional attitudes and underlying schemas have yet to consistently demonstrate that changes in these constructs are associated with subsequent change in depressive symptoms. More compelling evidence for causality has been found for studies examining acquisition of compensatory skills in relation to subsequent symptom change. Only one study, however, has found that this association is specific to CT. Much remains to be learned, therefore, about the mechanisms of CT for MDD.

Change Mechanisms in Behavioral Activation for Depression

A behavioral treatment for depression was described in the 1970s that specified that reduced response-contingent positive reinforcement for nondepressive behavior was the causal factor in eliciting depression, and that depression could be treated by increasing such response-contingent positive reinforcement (Lewinsohn, 1974). More recently, this approach has been revised and labeled Behavioral Activation (BA) treatment (Martell et al., 2013). The major change to the treatment was to extend it to address behavioral inhibition and avoidance in addition to increasing reinforcing activities (Martell et al., 2013). A meta-analysis of 26 studies reported that BA was superior to control groups and medication in the treatment of depression (Ekers et al., 2014). Given this evidence base for BA, we review here mechanism studies of BA in the treatment of depression (no studies rating therapist techniques or other process variables in BA, in relation to outcome, have been published as yet).

The theoretical mechanism of action of BA involves increasing rewarding activities (activation) so that higher levels of positive reinforcement are received. The increasing positive reinforcement then is hypothesized to lead to decreases in depressive symptoms. Thus, the increase in positive reinforcement is thought to mediate the relationship between activation and depressive symptoms (Dimidjian et al., 2011).

A number of studies have tested the mechanism of BA treatment of depression. Two studies have reported that improvement in activation/avoidance (Christopher et al., 2009) and change in exposure to environmental rewards (Gawrysiak et al., 2009), respectively, are associated with pre-to-post change in depressive symptoms over the course of BA treatment. A study of BA for depressed breast cancer patients found that compliance with assigned activities was associated with reduction in depressive symptoms, but the specific quantity of completed activities was not related to change in depression (Ryba et al., 2013). In addition, compliance and quantity of completed activities were not associated with self-reported environmental reward and environmental reward did not mediate the relation between activation and depression. Another study found no relation between change in activities and change in functioning among older depressed African Americans receiving BA (Gitlin et al., 2014).

The above studies failed to address temporal precedence. However, in a study that found BA to be superior to treatment-as-usual (TAU) for improving depressive symptoms in pregnant women, BA also resulted in higher levels of activation ($d = 0.69$) and environmental reward ($d = 0.54$) than TAU (Dimidjian et al., 2017). Early change in activation was significantly associated with subsequent change in depressive severity ($r = 0.50$), as was early change in environmental reward ($r = 0.59$). Further, early change in both activation and environmental reward significantly mediated the between-group differences in depression outcomes between BA and TAU. Thus, this study provides strong support, establishing both temporal precedence and mediation, for the mechanism of BA. However, more studies are needed before we can make clinical recommendations based on mechanism studies of BA.

Change Mechanisms in Treatments for Borderline Personality Disorder

One study has examined acquisition of skills in the treatment of borderline personality disorder as a mediator of outcome over the course of one year of treatment (Neacsiu et al., 2010). The study used pooled data from three studies of dialectical behavior therapy (DBT) for borderline personality disorder. The self-report DBT skills measure included questions about how the patient coped with stress in the past month, such as "Counted my blessings," "Concentrated on something good that could come out of the whole thing," and "Talked to someone about how I've been feeling." Patients treated with DBT reported using three times more skills at the end of treatment than patients who received a control treatment. DBT skills use, measured at baseline and 4, 8, 12, and 16 months after baseline, was found to fully mediate the relation of time in treatment to decrease over time in suicide attempts and depression, and the increase in control of anger over time, across both DBT and control conditions. Unlike most studies, change in the mediator was assessed prior to change in the outcome measures. Thus, this study demonstrated that staying in treatment longer was associated with increased skill use and with better outcomes, that increased skill use was associated with better outcomes, and that the relation between time in treatment and outcome was reduced (i.e., mediated by) by an increase in the use of DBT skills. Although this study is one of the better studies in terms of addressing the temporal relation of change mechanism variables (the mediator) and outcome, the focus of the investigation was on the relation of time in treatment to outcome rather than the treatment effect of DBT (i.e., comparison of DBT to control groups) and, therefore, the study does not directly address the mechanism of change of DBT. Rather, skill acquisition was examined as a nonspecific variable common to multiple treatments and, indeed, the coping strategies assessed by the scale appear to be strategies that might be learned in a variety of psychotherapies. Nevertheless, the study does provide evidence that acquiring such skills is associated with treatment outcome. Whether DBT is uniquely a treatment that enhances the acquisition of such skills is a question that should be addressed in future research.

Though not a study of change mechanisms per se, the investigation by Norrie et al. (2013) is worth describing because of the use of instrumental variable regression to make causal inferences. In this study, within the group of patients who received CBT for personality disorders, the investigators used instrumental variable regression modeling to estimate the impact of quantity and quality (ratings of therapist competence) of therapy received on number of suicidal acts and inpatient psychiatric hospitalization. Results were that the estimate of the effect of CBT could be approximately two to three times greater for those receiving the right amount of therapy from a competent therapist.

Change Mechanisms in Treatments for Eating Disorders

Wilson et al. (2002) examined mediators of cognitive-behavioral and interpersonal therapies for bulimia nervosa.

The authors found that eating frequency at posttreatment was associated with change in dietary restraint from baseline to week 4, and also baseline to week 6, and that change in eating behavior self-efficacy from baseline to week 10 mediated change in binge eating frequency from baseline to post treatment (week 20). Improvement in purge frequency from baseline to post treatment was mediated by three factors: (a) change in dietary restraint from baseline to weeks 4 and 6, (b) change in affective self-efficacy from baseline to week 10, and (c) change in eating behavior self-efficacy from baseline to week 10. These meditational effects, however, did not differ for cognitive-behavioral therapy compared to interpersonal therapy. The authors also did not demonstrate that change in the mediator predicted subsequent outcome because outcome was only measured at baseline and termination. Using data from the same trial, Loeb et al. (2005) examined the relation of adherence to outcome in cognitive-behavioral therapy, and also to interpersonal therapy, in the treatment of bulimia nervosa. Adherence was rated on sessions 6, 12, and 18 of a 19-session treatment. No significant relations were found for either treatment ($r = 0.19$ for cognitive-behavioral therapy; $r = 0.05$ for interpersonal therapy; effect sizes taken from Webb et al., 2010). A review (Linardon et al., 2017) summarizing all studies of mediators of CBT treatment for eating disorders had two main conclusions:

1. Early behavioral and cognitive symptom change was consistently found to lead to better behavioral and cognitive outcomes across all eating disorder diagnoses.
2. Reducing dietary restraint throughout the course of bulimia nervosa was associated with better behavioral outcomes.

These conclusions, however, were based on a relatively small number of studies.

A recent study (Farrell et al., 2019) examined change mechanisms for exposure-based CBT treatment of eating disorders. The mechanism variables (eating-related cognitions; anxiety about eating) were measured at baseline and week 2; outcome was measured at baseline and discharge, from four to nine weeks after baseline. Path analyses revealed that decreased eating-related cognitions (feared concerns about eating) and emotions (anxiety about eating) at two weeks predicted lowered global eating disorder symptom severity at discharge (controlling for eating disorder symptoms at baseline). Reduction of body checking and avoidance behaviors from baseline to two weeks was also associated with change in eating disorder severity from baseline to discharge. Though this study is promising and the mechanism variable was measured prior to treatment discharge, outcome was only measured at baseline and discharge and, therefore, it was not possible to predict subsequent change in outcome.

Change Mechanisms in the Treatment of Alcohol and Substance Dependence

Skill acquisition has been examined as a key mechanism variable in a number of studies of alcohol dependence, with several studies suggesting that cognitive-behavioral treatments, relative to control/comparison groups, increase skills to avoid relapse and cope with cravings (e.g., Carroll et al., 1999; Chaney et al., 1978; Hawkins et al., 1986). Other studies, however, failed to detect such effects (Kadden et al., 1992; Wells et al., 1994). None of these studies on skills acquisition examined change in the mediator variable predicting subsequent change in outcome.

Crits-Christoph et al. (2003) examined mediators of the outcome of several treatments for cocaine dependence. A measure of dysfunctional beliefs about addiction was found to correlate moderately with drug use outcomes in cognitive therapy. However, beliefs about addiction improved significantly more in individual drug counseling, compared to cognitive therapy, and the correlation between improvement in beliefs about addiction and change in drug use was the same in both cognitive therapy and individual drug counseling. Moreover, analyses examining change in beliefs about addiction in relation to subsequent outcome failed to support the hypothesis that change in the mediator causes reduced cocaine use.

Two large scale studies have examined the acquisition of coping skills as a change mechanism in CBT or integrated treatments for alcohol use disorder. One study (Roos et al., 2017) used data from Project MATCH, a large multisite alcohol treatment trial in which patients, recruited in outpatient and aftercare arms, were randomized to three treatments: CBT, motivational enhancement therapy (MET) and twelve-step facilitation (TSF). Roos et al. (2017) found that, for outpatients with high baseline alcohol dependence severity, end-of-treatment coping mediated the treatment effect of CBT compared with MET and TSF on subsequent (one-year) drinking outcomes. However, the effect size was small. In addition, for those with low or moderate dependence severity, coping was not a mediator of the CBT vs. MET/TSF outcome effect. The mediational effects were also not apparent in the aftercare arm of the study.

Hartzler et al. (2011) examined mediators using data from the large-scale Project COMBINE (*N* = 1383) study (The COMBINE Study Research Group, 2003). Project COMBINE evaluated treatments for alcohol dependence including medications (naltrexone, acamprosate, and the combination of the two), pill placebo, a psychosocial intervention that was an integration of motivational interviewing, cognitive-behavioral, and 12-step facilitation approaches, and combinations of the psychosocial intervention with each of the pill treatment groups. Hartzler et al. (2011) conducted path analyses to test whether changes in self-efficacy (from baseline to termination) mediated the association between the therapeutic bond (measured early in treatment) and change in drinking from baseline to one-year follow-up. Results indicated that the association between the bond and outcome was mediated by change in self-efficacy within the psychosocial treatment only conditions, but not within treatment groups that included medications. Causal inferences in this study are limited, given that the mediator (self-efficacy change) was not measured subsequent to assessment of the bond. Moreover, self-efficacy change was not specific to the psychosocial intervention.

A more recent report from Project COMBINE used latent class mediation to examine several aspects of coping behavior as a mediator of the treatment group benefit of combined psychosocial and medication management compared to medication only (Witkiewitz et al., 2018). In this study, coping repertoire (measured at the end of treatment) was a significant mediator: receiving the combined behavioral intervention, in addition to medication management, was associated with a greater likelihood of expected classification in the broad coping repertoire latent class (i.e., having a tendency to use a broad range of skills consistently), which in turn was associated with significant improvements in drinking outcomes at the one-year follow-up. This study therefore supports the hypothesis that an integrated psychosocial treatment for alcohol use disorder that teaches coping skills works, in part, through the acquisition of a broad range of coping skills. Although in this study the mediator was measured prior to the outcome, the investigators did not predict subsequent change in outcome, and the mediator was only measured at one point in time (end of treatment).

Anxiety sensitivity and coping motives (i.e., motivations to use substances to cope with distress) were recently examined as mediators of the superior efficacy of usual care plus a brief CBT for anxiety program compared to usual care alone for patients with comorbid anxiety and substance use disorders (Wolitzky-Taylor et al., 2018). Greater improvement over time for anxiety sensitivity was found for the usual care plus CBT treatment than in the usual care group. In addition, the decreases in anxiety sensitivity mediated the effect of treatment group on alcohol use following treatment. Decreases in substance use coping motives were not observed in either group and change in coping motives did not mediate substance use after treatment.

In summary, findings from process–outcome studies of cognitive-behavioral treatments for alcohol/substance dependence are mixed, and only one study (Roos et al., 2017) in this area has provided evidence for the causal direction of change in cognitive/skill variables leading to reductions in alcohol/substance use. However, in Roos et al. (2017) the effect size was small and was only apparent for patients with high alcohol dependence severity. Change in anxiety sensitivity appears to be a promising mechanism variable in the treatment of substance use disorders, though the finding may only apply to those with comorbid anxiety disorders. In addition, this effect has only been reported in one study thus far (Wolitzky-Taylor et al., 2018). Thus, at this point in time, the evidence is not overly compelling that the theoretical notions of skill acquisition, changes in dysfunctional beliefs, or changes anxiety sensitivity are critical elements to the process of change for cognitive-behavioral treatments for alcohol or substance dependence. Adequate studies of the causal role of skill acquisition and anxiety sensitivity as mechanisms of change in CBT for substance use disorders are needed.

Change Processes in Dynamic Therapy

There have been a number of studies that have specifically evaluated the relation between specific dynamic psychotherapy change processes and treatment outcome. Scales for assessing dynamic interventions vary, with some examining the frequency of specific types of statements over a session and other scales based on rating scales such as adherence scales applied to sessions as a whole. Another set of studies examined the accuracy of specific dynamic interventions relative to independently coded patient-specific dynamic themes.

Use of Dynamic Interventions

In the 6th edition, we reviewed multiple studies that related the frequency of use of dynamic interventions such as interpretations and transference interpretations, assessed directly from therapy process ratings, to the outcome of psychodynamic psychotherapy. Our summary was that, for the proportion of dynamic interpretations in general there was a moderate average effect (mean $r = 0.50$) across two investigations demonstrating that more dynamic interpretations were associated with better treatment outcome. For transference interpretations specifically, there was a moderate effect (mean $r = 0.49$) for higher levels of transference interpretations to predict poor treatment outcome for subsets of patients. No additional studies using counts of interpretations were located since the publication of the 2013 review.

Studies examining the relation of adherence to dynamic therapy techniques to outcome are presented in Table 8.4. In a set of studies conducted at a university counseling center, various psychodynamic technique variables predicted change from pre to post therapy (DeFife et al., 2008; Katz & Hilsenroth, 2018; Kuutmann & Hilsenroth, 2012; Levy et al., 2015; Owen & Hilsenroth, 2011; Pitman et al., 2014; Pitman et al., 2017; Slavin-Mulford et al., 2011). Of note is that in the Pitman et al. (2017) study, moderator analyses demonstrated that, among patients with co-occurring Axis I and II disorders, there were positive changes in anxiety symptoms, regardless of level of psychodynamic techniques used, whereas patients without co-occurring disorders experienced more improvement when adherence to psychodynamic techniques was greater. Despite the promising results of these studies, rigid adherence to psychodynamic techniques is likely to be counterproductive. Along these lines, Owen and Hilsenroth (2014) measured therapist adherence at the third, ninth, and termination sessions of psychodynamic therapy for 70 patients. Within-case variability in adherence was significantly associated with outcome after controlling for alliance, between-case variability, and the proportion of outcome attributed to differences among therapists. The authors speculated that such session-to-session variability in adherence may reflect flexibility regarding the use of techniques. Such therapist flexibility is hypothesized to lead to better outcomes compared to therapists who are less flexible with their interventions at the individual client level. Flexibility was also investigated in a study by Katz et al. (2019), who found that flexibly incorporating a limited amount of CBT strategies early in psychodynamic therapy for depression added some benefit to the positive relationship between psychodynamic technique adherence and outcome. It should be noted that some of the newer studies reviewed in this paragraph were conducted on the same or partially overlapping samples. Thus,

some of the findings may not be independent. Moreover, like the studies reviewed in the 6th edition, temporal precedence of the process measure in relation to outcome was not established in any of these studies as outcome was only measured at pre- and posttherapy. Nevertheless, this set of studies adds to previous findings linking use of psychodynamic techniques to treatment outcomes.

A recent study by Kivlighan et al. (2018) explores a possible mechanism through which psychodynamic techniques have their effect on outcome. While the use of psychodynamic techniques failed to have a direct effect on treatment outcome in this investigation, this variable did have an indirect effect on outcome through its effect on the alliance, which in turn influenced outcome. Change in outcome subsequent to the process measures was not examined in this study.

Temporal precedence was incorporated into the study reported by McCarthy et al. (2016). In this study of psychodynamic therapy for depression, a moderate level of use of psychodynamic techniques (assessed through a quadratic term in a regression analysis; $r = 0.37$) was associated with greater change in depression, controlling for prior change up to the point the process variable was measured, compared with either high or low use of psychodynamic techniques. One recent study that examined the process of change in panic-focused psychodynamic therapy has also addressed temporal precedence. Keefe et al. (2018) found that at session 10, but not at session 2, patients who received a higher degree of panic-focused interpretations experienced greater subsequent improvement in panic symptoms ($r = 0.37$). Non-panic-focused interpretations were not predictive of outcome. Further, patients with more interpersonal distress especially benefitted from the use of panic-focused interpretations at session 10.

Overall, these results indicate that use of dynamic interventions in general is related to positive therapeutic effects in dynamic psychotherapy. Four studies (Barber et al., 1996; Connolly et al., 1999; Keefe et al., 2018; McCarthy et al., 2016) have now examined the relation of dynamic interventions to subsequent symptom course, providing stronger empirical support for the use of psychodynamic interventions. One caveat should be noted: as reviewed in the 6th edition chapter, the use of transference interpretations at particularly high levels might not be therapeutic for certain patients. These studies examining frequency of transference interpretations, however, need to be interpreted cautiously, given that measures of counts of interventions are likely influenced by therapist responsiveness. Therapists may be increasing the rate of interpretations, or transference interpretations, for patients who have not responded previously to interpretations. This can attenuate the correlations between counts of interpretations and outcome, or even produce negative correlations (i.e., more interpretations associated with poor outcome).

Therapist Competence in Delivering Dynamic Interventions

Ratings of therapist competence in utilizing dynamic interventions may be a more accurate assessment of the role of therapist interventions in the therapeutic process. Three

TABLE 8.4   Process–Outcome Effects for Use of Dynamic Interventions in Dynamic Therapy

Study	Process measures	Effect size (*r*) with outcome	Temporal precedence incorporated	Therapist effects modeled	Specificity to type of treatment
Ratings of dynamic techniques (adherence)					
Gaston et al. (1998)	Use of expressive dynamic techniques	.22	No	No	Yes
Ogrodniczuk & Piper (1999)	Adherence	−.09	No	No	No
Hilsenroth et al. (2003)	Adherence	.49	No	No	No
Connolly Gibbons et al. (2012)	Adherence	.12	No	No	No
DeFife et al. (2008)	Patient ratings of adherence	.10	No	No	No
Spektor (2008)	Adherence	.41	No	No	No
Goldman & Gregory (2009)	Adherence	.64	No	No	No
Owen & Hilsenroth (2011)	Adherence	.02	No	Yes	No
Slavin-Mulford et al. (2011)	Use of dynamic interventions	.46	No	No	No
Kuutmann & Hilsenroth (2012)	Focus on patient–therapist relationship	.30	No	No	No
Levy et al. (2015)	Early treatment interpretations	.40	No	Yes	No
Pitman et al. (2014)	Adherence to psychodynamic techniques	.46	No	No	No
Pitman et al. (2017)	Adherence to psychodynamic techniques	.29	No	No	No
Owen & Hilsenroth (2014)	Within case variability in adherence	.41	No	Yes	No
Katz & Hilsenroth (2018)	Use of psychodynamic techniques	.31	No	No	No
Katz et al. (2019)	Use of psychodynamic techniques	.59	No	Yes	No
Keefe et al. (2018)	Panic-focused interpretations	.37	Yes	No	No
Barber et al. (2008)	Adherence	.21	No	No	No
McCarthy et al. (2016)	Moderate use of dynamic techniques	.37	Yes	No	No
Therapist competence in use of dynamic interventions					
Svartberg & Stiles (1992)	Competence	.36	No	No	No
Barber et al (1996)	Competence	.53	Yes	No	No
Barber et al. (2008)	Competence	−.21	No	No	No

Note. A negative *r* indicates the finding was in the opposite direction from that hypothesized.

investigations reviewed in the 2013 version of our *Handbook* chapter specifically examined therapist competence in dynamic interventions and are summarized in Table 8.4. No additional studies on competence have been published since the previous edition of this chapter. While there is some evidence that competence to dynamic interventions is predictive of the outcome of dynamic psychotherapy, at least for anxiety and depressive disorders, the limited number of studies precludes drawing strong conclusions about specific diagnostic groups. Moreover, the Barber et al. (1996) investigation is the only study of adherence or competence to dynamic techniques to specifically address the temporal relation between symptoms and therapist technique by showing that competence in dynamic interventions predicted subsequent symptom course after controlling for prior symptom reduction.

Further research will be needed to definitively unpack the temporal relation between adherence and competence to dynamic techniques and treatment course. Finally, many studies assessed treatment adherence and competence at a single session. It is not likely that one early session is a large enough sample to provide a dependable estimate of the effect, suggesting that the relation between adherence and competence of dynamic techniques to the outcome of dynamic psychotherapy may actually be larger than suggested by these investigations.

Therapist Accuracy of Interpretations

Beyond simple frequency of interventions, it may be more important to examine the average quality of dynamic interventions in the prediction of treatment outcome. It may be that the quality or accuracy of a therapist interpretation has more impact on the course of treatment than the raw number of interpretations implemented. Several studies in our 2013 review (Crits-Christoph et al., 1988; Norville et al., 1996; Piper et al., 1993; Silberschatz et al., 1986), plus one more recent study (Silberschatz, 2017), that evaluated the quality of therapist interpretations, all suggested that higher levels of therapist accuracy in interpreting interpersonal patterns/conflicts are significantly predictive of better therapeutic outcome. However, none of these investigations were able to demonstrate a causal pathway indicating that accurate interpretations cause positive outcome, rather than the alternative explanation that cases that are improving allow therapists to provide more accurate interpretations (i.e., outcome subsequent to the measurement of the process variables was not examined).

Change Mechanisms in Dynamic Therapy
Change in Patient Self-Understanding

Given the centrality of changes in patient insight (the term *insight* is used interchangeably with *self-understanding*) in psychodynamic models of therapeutic change, it is not surprising that multiple investigations have attempted to validate this change mechanism. A broad meta-analysis of the relation of insight to psychotherapy outcome was recently published (Jennissen et al., 2018). Across 23 studies, a significant, moderate correlation ($r = 0.31$) was observed between insight and treatment outcome. Three studies (Connolly Gibbons et al., 2009; Kallestad et al., 2010; Kivlighan et al., 2000)

controlled for temporal precedence and found evidence that gains in insight predicted subsequent improvement in outcome if psychodynamic therapy. Two studies (Connolly Gibbons et al., 2009; Kallestad et al., 2010) also provided evidence that such effects were specific to dynamic therapy.

A recently published study (Høglend & Hagtvet, 2019) on insight in psychodynamic therapy contains several important methodological features that deserve comment. This article uses data from a previous outcome study (Høglend et al., 2006) that randomized 100 patients to one year of dynamic psychotherapy with a low to moderate level of transference work, or to the same type of therapy without transference work. The main outcome finding of the Høglend et al. (2006) study was that patients with more severe interpersonal difficulties benefited significantly more from therapy with transference work than therapy without transference work. Patients with mature relationships and greater psychological resources improved in both treatments. The Høglend and Hagtvet (2019) paper examined insight in relation to outcome and also evaluated affect awareness as a possible mediator of the insight-outcome relationship. The authors tested a variety of statistical models, with the best model consistent with a mediated moderation effect where the efficacy of transference work, for patients with low quality of object relations, was mediated via both change in insight and tolerance for affects. The effect of insight on outcome was significantly reduced due to an indirect effect via tolerance for affects, suggesting that the mechanism though which dynamic transference work achieves its effects is through both gains in insight and improved affect awareness.

The process through which gains in insight occur over the course of psychotherapy is not well understood. Though it would be hypothesized that exploratory interventions by therapists would lead to insight, some research does not support that model. McAleavey and Castonguay (2014), using multilevel modeling of therapist effects, found that therapists who reported using more directive interventions than their peers, on average, had patients who reported more insight after sessions only if the therapists did not also report using high levels of exploratory interventions. Further research is needed to understand how best to facilitate gains in insight.

In summary, the literature suggests that changes in self-understanding are an important part of the therapeutic process of dynamic psychotherapy. Self-understanding has been found to change across dynamic psychotherapy and these changes in self-understanding are predictive of change in symptoms. Although these results are promising in validating this important therapeutic process, there is a substantial amount that we still do not know about the role of self-understanding in the process of psychotherapy. Published studies on insight involved a variety of patient samples and mixed diagnostic groups. Patient diagnosis or other indicators of severity of pathology or quality of object relations are likely to influence the degree of change in self-understanding achievable across treatment. More research is needed to understand the process of change in self-understanding for specific patient samples across specific time frames. Further, none of the investigations reviewed specifically addressed the dependability of self-understanding assessments, with most studies including only a few assessment points, thereby decreasing the possibility of a stable estimate.

Importantly, some studies have begun to document a possible causal effect by examining the temporal course of changes in self-understanding in relation to symptom course. Repeated assessments of self-understanding and symptoms are needed to fully unpack this temporal relationship. The specificity of effects was addressed in only a few studies. With a multitude of studies indicating that different therapeutic models are equally effective at producing symptom change, identifying whether changes in self-understanding are specific to dynamic psychotherapies will help validate that it is the active ingredient in dynamic psychotherapies that is responsible for the process outcome effects demonstrated.

Change in Reflective Functioning

Reflective functioning is defined as the capacity to reflect on internal mental states such as feelings, wishes, attitudes, and goals. Our 2013 review yielded inconclusive results. Levy et al. (2006) demonstrated significant change in reflective functioning across transference focused psychotherapy and showed specificity of such changes to dynamic psychotherapy compared to dialectical behavior therapy in the treatment of borderline personality disorder. A limitation of this study is that it did not take the next step to explore the relation of changes in reflective functioning to symptom course. Two studies, however, did conduct such an analysis. Rudden et al. (2006) failed to find a significant association of change in reflective functioning with outcome over the course of psychodynamic therapy for panic disorder. Vermote et al. (2010) evaluated the relation of change in reflective function to the outcome of dynamic psychotherapy for personality disorders administered in an inpatient setting. There was no evidence that reflective functioning changed across this inpatient treatment and change in reflective functioning was not associated with change in symptoms ($r = 0.03$).

A recent study has been positive about change in reflective functioning as one mechanism variable in psychodynamic therapy. In a sample of patients with borderline personality disorder that received long-term hospitalization-based psychodynamic treatment, De Meulemeester et al. (2018) found that improvements in reflective functioning were strongly associated with the rate of decrease in symptomatic distress over time ($r = 0.89$). Despite the repeated assessments of the mechanism and outcome measures in this study, the investigators did not conduct lagged analyses to examine whether change in reflective functioning is associated with subsequent change in symptoms. Given the potential importance of this variable in helping patients to explore and unpack their impairing relationship conflicts, this construct warrants further investigations as a mechanism of dynamic psychotherapy.

Change in Defenses

Although a number of investigations have evaluated the role of baseline defensive functioning in the course of dynamic psychotherapy, we found only three investigations for our 2013 review that evaluated whether the changes in defenses

hypothesized in dynamic models of psychotherapy predict symptom course. Winston et al. (1994) evaluated changes in defenses across 40 sessions of dynamic psychotherapy for 28 patients with personality disorders. The frequency of intermediate defenses was assessed from the videotapes of four sessions sampled across the four quartiles of treatment. There was a small but significant effect for a decrease in intermediate defenses across dynamic psychotherapy to predict a composite outcome measure ($r = 0.28$). Bond and Perry (2004) also found a large effect for the relation between change in overall defensive function and decrease in depression for a sample of 53 patients with a variety of Axis I and Axis II disorders engaged in three to five years of psychoanalytic psychotherapy ($r = 0.64$). Kramer et al. (2010) found a moderately small but significant effect ($r = 0.37$) for improvements in overall defensive functioning in the predictions of change in symptoms for 32 university students treated with up to a year of therapy for adjustment disorders. Only one study since the 2013 review examined change in defensive functioning in relation to outcome. Perry and Bond (2012) reported that change in defenses across 2.5 years in psychodynamic therapy was highly associated with change from baseline to 5 years in measures of both functioning ($r = 0.60$) and symptoms ($r = 0.58$). This study did not establish temporal precedence.

The variability in effects demonstrated across these investigations may be a result of the different patient populations sampled. Large effects were demonstrated for the investigations that included patients with severe Axis I disorders and/or personality disorders, where use of less mature defenses is hypothesized to be an important part of the psychopathology. In comparison, the study that demonstrated a very small effect for change in defensive functioning included patients with adjustment disorders for whom problems with immature defenses might not be central to the presenting problem. Although four studies (Bond & Perry, 2004; Kramer et al., 2010; Perry & Bond, 2012; Winston et al., 1994) have demonstrated that changes in defensive functioning may be a very important part of the process of dynamic psychotherapy, at least for patients with personality disorders, many more studies are needed to understand the role of this therapeutic mechanism.

An important part of exploring changes in defensive functioning in the process of dynamic psychotherapy will be to unpack the temporal relation between changes in defensive functioning and symptom course. For the Bond and Perry (2004) investigation, change in defensive functioning was related to residual change in symptoms from session 20 to treatment termination since symptom course was flat across the first 20 sessions with this seriously mentally ill sample. With such samples that demonstrate change across longer periods of time, it will be important to unpack whether changes in defensive functioning proceed and predict symptom course or whether they are a result of decreased symptoms.

The Process of Experiential Therapy

Experiential therapy (see Chapter 14) is another psychotherapeutic modality that has clear views on the curative processes that occur in psychotherapy sessions. Like exposure-based behavior therapy, in experiential therapy it is important that the patient activates, attends to, and tolerates emotions during therapy sessions. However, unlike exposure-based behavior therapy, experiential therapy focuses on optimum emotional processing that involves the integration of cognition and affect. Therapists in experiential psychotherapy encourage patients to explore, reflect on, and make sense of their emotions. This process includes exploring beliefs relating to emotions, giving voice to emotional experience, and identifying needs that can motivate change in personal meanings and beliefs (Elliott et al., 2004).

In the 6th edition of this chapter, we reviewed studies that found higher levels of emotional processing were associated with better outcomes among patients in experiential therapy (e.g., Pos et al., 2003; Pos et al., 2009; Watson & Bedar, 2006) though one study found that a moderate level of emotional arousal was optimal (Carryer & Greenberg, 2010). Subsequent to our 2013 review, only a few process–outcome studies of experiential therapy had been published. These newer studies, however, go beyond the use of standard emotional processing variables to evaluate other aspects of the experience of emotions in sessions. For example, Auszra et al. (2013) operationalized the concept of optimal patient in-session emotional processing as *client emotional productivity* that included seven features: attending, symbolization, congruence, acceptance, regulation, agency and differentiation. Client emotional productivity was found in this study to be the sole independent predictor of outcome ($r = 0.58$) in a model that included the alliance and high expressed emotional arousal. Another study (Herrman et al., 2016) examined the relationship between in-session types of emotional experience and the reduction of symptoms in emotion-focused therapy (a version of experiential therapy). The results of the study revealed that both fewer secondary ($r = 0.43$) and more primary ($r = 0.58$) adaptive emotions, in the working phases of therapy, were found to significantly predict outcome. In addition, moderate levels of primary maladaptive emotion in the middle working session were associated with outcome and, further, the frequency with which patients moved from primary maladaptive to primary adaptive emotions in the middle working session predicted outcome. Neither the Auszra et al. (2013) nor the Herrman et al. (2016) study controlled for temporal precedence. In regard to therapist empathy, as mentioned in the section on common factors in this chapter, there has been consistent evidence linking empathy with treatment outcome in both experiential therapy and other therapies, with a mean $r = 0.28$ across studies (Elliott et al., 2018).

Despite evidence linking two key clinical aspects (emotional processing; therapist empathy) of the process of experiential therapy to outcome, studies of this treatment have continued to fail to address the types of methodological issues that we have raised in this chapter. In particular, no studies of the process of experiential therapy have predicted outcome subsequent to the measurement of the process variables (controlling for prior improvement), nor used multilevel modeling to separate out therapist and patient contributions to correlations with outcome. Nevertheless, a number of other types of studies not reviewed here, primarily focusing on a

microanalysis of significant events in experiential therapy, have provided some support for the important clinical constructs of experiential therapy (Elliott, 2010).

DIVERSITY AND ETHNIC MINORITIES IN PROCESS–OUTCOME RESEARCH

It is important to consider the impact of race/ethnicity, and other individual difference variables such as gender, sexual orientation, socioeconomic status, age, physical abilities, religious beliefs, and political beliefs, on process–outcome relations. Unfortunately, largely due to small sample sizes, investigators rarely examine whether process–outcome relations differ for one racial/ethnic group (or other diversity variable) compared to another. To confirm this, we inspected all of the individual studies reviewed in Tables 8.2, 8.3, and 8.4 for report of the racial/ethnic composition of the patient sample. Over half of the studies did not provide such information. Of those that did, only a few studies reported rates of African Americans/Blacks or Hispanics higher than 10% (the percent of other racial/ethnic groups were consistently very low). The following studies reported greater than 10% of Blacks in their sample: Barber et al. (2008; $n = 45$), Connolly Gibbons et al. (2012; $n = 33$), Foa and Rauch (2004; $n = 22$), Keefe et al. (2018; $n = 11$), Kumpula et al. (2017; $n = 10$), McCarthy et al. (2016; $n = 16$), McLean et al. (2015; $n = 101$), Niles et al. (2014; $n = 11$), and Zalta et al. (2014; $n = 36$). Only Niles et al. (2014) and Keefe et al. (2018) reported greater than 10% of the sample were Hispanic, and the absolute number of such participants was relatively low in these studies given the overall sample size (Hispanic ns of 9 and 8, respectively). None of these studies examined the process–outcome effects separately by race/ethnicity. Adequate statistical power for testing differences in process–outcome correlations by race/ethnicity was likely only present in the McLean et al. (2015) and the Barber et al. (2008) study (77 whites; 45 African Americans). It is clear that substantial further research is needed to understand the role of race/ethnicity, and other diversity variables, on change processes and change mechanisms in psychotherapy.

In this chapter we did not review individual studies of common factors in relation to outcome given that recent well-done meta-analyses existed for these factors as summarized in Table 8.1. However, to explore whether any studies of common factors examined the impact of race/ethnicity on process–outcome relations, we conducted a literature search. One study of the alliance did address the impact of race. This study (Walling et al., 2012) examined race/ethnicity as a predictor of change in the alliance over the course of cognitive behavioral therapy for intimate partner violence perpetrators. The authors found a significant alliance by minority status interaction predicting outcome. For Caucasian participants, alliance trajectory was unrelated to outcome; for minority participants, alliance trajectory was significantly related to outcome. Though only one study, this investigation indicates that examination of diversity variables in process–outcome studies may be critical to understanding how psychotherapy works for people of different backgrounds and beliefs.

OVERALL CONCLUSIONS AND RECOMMENDATIONS

In this section we begin with conclusions about progress regarding general trends in the research literature in terms of scientific advancements since the publication of the 6th edition *Handbook*. We then follow this with clinical recommendations that can be made based on existing process–outcome studies. A central tenet of this chapter has been that progress on important methodological issues is critical to having confidence in the findings of process–outcome studies so that clinical recommendations can be made. Thus, a summary of such methodological progress sets the stage for understanding the basis for clinical recommendations.

As we have mentioned, it is difficult to make firm clinical recommendations from correlational studies. In fact, there have been cases of serious errors in medicine occurring because of reliance on correlational studies. For example, many correlational studies appeared to show that women receiving hormone replacement therapy had relatively lower rates of coronary heart disease compared to women not receiving hormone replacement therapy. Based on these correlational data, doctors suggested to patients that hormone replacement therapy was protective against coronary heart disease. Randomized clinical trials subsequently showed the opposite: hormone replacement therapy resulted in a small increase in rates of coronary heart disease (Lawlor et al., 2004). A confounding third variable (socioeconomic status, which was correlated with the tendency to exercise and have a healthier diet) produced the artefactual correlations between use of hormone replacement therapy and lower rates of coronary heart disease. Like this example, correlational studies that find relatively higher levels of certain psychotherapy process variables associated with better or worse treatment outcome may be misleading due to unmeasured confounding variables. Because of this inherent problem in correlational studies, we have identified in the current review whether or not studies have attempted to address causality in any number of ways.

Research Recommendations

Several firm conclusions with associated recommendation can be made based on the current review. First, progress has been made in the use of methods that attempt to address causality. Although the majority of process–outcome and mechanism studies fail to incorporate time precedence or otherwise control for confounders, an increasing number of studies do address this issue in one way or another. Most prominently, we found 12 studies that have used within-patient analyses to rule out between-patient confounding variables. Most of these 12 within-patient studies also used lagged analyses that predicted subsequent change in outcome. In addition, the temporal sequencing of mediators and outcome has been addressed in five adult studies of the relation of belief change to subsequent change in PTSD symptoms Many investigators will, for practical reasons, continue to only assess outcome at pre and post treatment, or have an inadequate sample size for conducting advanced statistical tests. However, we recommend that when

possible, addressing temporal precedence and ruling out the influence of confounders be the expected standard approach to process–outcome and mechanism studies.

Second, studies addressing the dyadic nature of psychotherapy through the use of multilevel modeling, though on the increase since our 2013 review, continue to be relatively rare. Practical issues (limited sample size) often hinder the use of such multilevel models. Our recommendation is that greater attention is needed on this issue. In the case of alliance–outcome studies where multilevel models have most frequently been applied, the results to date have been conflicting, with some studies finding effects at the patient but not the therapist level, and other studies finding effects at the therapist but not the patient level. The clinical and conceptual implications of effects at the patient versus the therapist level are completely different. Thus, further research to understand the context of effects at one level or the other would be highly valuable so that more targeted clinical recommendations can be made from the research literature.

Third, there has been little progress on examination of the specificity of mechanisms of types of psychotherapies. Large-scale randomized trials in which mechanism or process variables are repeatedly assessed over the course of at least two different psychotherapies are needed to test for specificity of mechanism. The cost of such studies is large, and in recent years there has been a downturn in available grant funding for such studies. Thus, it is not surprising that few such studies exist. However, if we are to use studies of the process/mechanism of modes of psychotherapies as part of the evidence based for making decisions about whether the specific techniques contained in psychotherapy packages are needed, or not, to induce change, then more progress on testing for the specificity of psychotherapy mechanisms is needed.

Fourth, progress has been made in formulating and testing more complex models of how process variables relate to outcome. Rather than assuming that the same process leads to good outcome in all patients, investigators have begun to test for moderators of the process–outcome relation and for interactions between patient and therapist process variables that model the complexities of therapy and human interactions. Part of modeling this complexity is the recognition that both common factors (e.g., the alliance) and specific technical factors are important, and may interact with each other. With this progress, the scientific study of psychotherapy enters a new age that has the potential to go beyond investigators' and clinicians' tendencies to oversimplify therapy by focusing on a limited number of variables contained within one theory of therapy. Clearer and nontechnical definitions of constructs within each therapy are needed in order to have greater certainty regarding similarities and differences between theories of therapy. Improved methods of assessment that then target these better-defined constructs would also facilitate the advancement of research on psychotherapy process–outcome relations. A broader perspective that includes multiple patient and therapist variables may open more avenues for developing and testing integrative therapies and breaking the field out of the stranglehold that competing forms of therapy has placed on advancement of knowledge and the practice of psychotherapy. In addition, process–outcome studies need to attend to diversity variables to a much greater extent than done to date. At the moment, only exploratory findings have emerged from the few studies examining moderator of process–outcome associations and interactions between patient and therapist process variables, and diversity variables, and therefore no firm research conclusions or clinical recommendations can therefore be made at this time. Our hope is that over the next decade, studies are produced and replicated that provide a clearer roadmap for understanding the complex dyadic process of psychotherapy.

Clinical Recommendations

We can also offer several clinical recommendations based on our review. First, consistent with the widely accepted view that the alliance is an important aspect of diverse forms of therapy, the research literature suggests that clinicians should attend to the alliance, foster it, and address ruptures in the alliance as needed. While clinicians and many psychotherapy researches have emphasized the centrality of the alliance for decades, the scientific advancements in better addressing causality in process–outcome studies of the alliance through establishing temporal precedence and ruling out confounds provide a new level of certainty in the importance of the alliance. We recommend that psychotherapy training programs and clinical supervisors implement methods for regular evaluation of the alliance so that this critical aspect of therapy is a routine and accepted focus in the teaching of all psychotherapy methods.

Second, we reiterate our conclusion from the 6th edition of the *Handbook* that arousal of emotion in exposure-based behavior therapy for anxiety disorders is likely to be an essential ingredient in achieving positive outcomes. Although studies on this topic have not controlled for prior improvement, the effect sizes are large and the finding is in the opposite direction (i.e., increasing fear in sessions leads to decreases in phobic fear by treatment termination) of what might be expected if it was due to a confound of prior improvement on the process variable.

Third, we reiterate – but now with greater confidence – that psychodynamic clinicians should focus on improving self-understanding since gains in self-understanding have been found to be associated with improvements in symptoms. This finding has been replicated across studies, and change in self-understanding has been found to predict subsequent change in symptoms. The recent empirical finding that gains in insight work in tandem with improved affect awareness to lead to better outcome resonates with clinical wisdom but awaits replication before we have confidence that the science supports a more detailed and nuanced clinical recommendation regarding self-understanding (see also complementary review and conclusion in Chapter 7 of this *Handbook*).

Fourth, we now upgrade our tentative conclusion from our 2013 review that concrete techniques (e.g., set and following an agenda; reviewed homework; practiced rational responses with patient; asked patient to record thoughts) in cognitive therapy for depression lead to better outcome. Though findings from the literature have been mixed (i.e., some studies have failed to find a relation), there have been additional studies since our 2013 review that addressed causality issues and found significant relations between use of CT techniques and the outcome of CT for MDD. Thus, the scientific basis for the use of CT techniques, particularly the more concrete techniques, has improved to the extent that we can recommend more strongly the teaching and application of such techniques on empirical grounds.

Fifth, cognitive therapists should make sure that their interventions include targeting the acquisition of positive compensatory skills when treating patients with depressive symptoms. Several studies have supported this recommendation, and temporal precedence has been addressed.

Sixth, the treatment of PTSD should focus on modification of negative trauma-related beliefs. Multiple studies have established that change in such negative trauma-related beliefs is associated with subsequent improvement in PTSD symptoms. Given the replication of this finding and that temporal precedence has been addressed in multiple studies, we have reasonably strong confidence that translating this research result into clinical practice is appropriate at this time.

In addition to the above conclusions and recommendations, we can also comment on the clinical topics that have not reached our threshold for making clinical recommendations with confidence. Of particular note, despite a relatively large number of studies that have found positive associations between use of psychodynamic techniques during sessions and outcome, establishing temporal precedence and/or using other methods of ruling out confounds has only been implementing in two studies (Keefe et al., 2018; McCarthy et al., 2016), and these studies involved different population, treatment approaches, and therapist measures. Thus, we conclude that greater attention to temporal precedence and potential confounds is an important agenda for future process–outcome studies of techniques used in psychodynamic therapy. A similar conclusion can be made regarding use of experiential therapy techniques within experiential therapy.

In the 6th edition of the process–outcome chapter, we ended by stating that the evidence base for theoretical mechanisms is building, with pieces of the puzzle beginning to fall into place for several psychotherapies. At this point in time, we are pleased to conclude that more of the pieces of the puzzle have indeed been identified through rigorous process–outcome research. Though the pace of psychotherapy research is slow, the path to future discoveries has become clearer. We hope our chapter helps to point the way for future investigations to make a difference in advancing the science and ultimately helping patients benefit from a range of psychotherapies.

ABBREVIATIONS

ACT	acceptance and commitment therapy
BA	behavioral activation
BDT	dialectical behavior therapy
BPD	borderline personality disorder
CBT	cognitive behavioral therapy

CT	cognitive therapy
MDD	major depressive disorder
MET	motivational enhancement therapy
PTCI	posttraumatic cognitions inventory
PTSD	post-traumatic stress disorder
SEM	structural equation modelling
TAU	treatment-as-usual
TSF	twelve-step facilitation
WOR	ways of responding

REFERENCES

Ablon, J. S., & Jones, E. E. (2002). Validity of controlled clinical trials of psychotherapy: Findings for the NIMH treatment of depression collaborative research program. *The American Journal of Psychiatry*, *159*(5), 775–783. https://doi.org/10.1176/appi.ajp.159.5.775

Angrist, J.D., & Kruger, A.B. (2001). Instrumental variables and the search for identification: From supply and demand to natural experiments. *Journal of Economic Perspectives*, *15*(4), 69–85. https://doi.org/10.1257/jep.15.4.69

Auszra, L., Greenberg, L.S., & Herrmann, I. (2013). Client emotional productivity- optimal client in-session emotional processing in experiential therapy. *Psychotherapy Research*, *23*(6), 732–746. https://doi.org/10.1080/10503307.2013.816882

Baldwin, S. A., Wampold, B. E., & Imel, Z. E. (2007). Untangling the alliance-outcome correlation: Exploring the relative importance of therapist and patient variability in the alliance. *Journal of Consulting and Clinical Psychology*, *75*(6), 842–852. https://doi.org/10.1037/0022-006X.75.6.842

Barber, J. P., Crits-Christoph, P., & Luborsky, L. (1996). Effects of therapist adherence and competence on patient outcome in brief dynamic therapy. *Journal of Consulting and Clinical Psychology*, *64*(3), 619–622. https://doi.org/10.1037/0022-006X.64.3.619

Barber, J. P., & DeRubeis, R. J. (1992). The ways of responding: A scale to assess compensatory skills taught in cognitive therapy. *Behavioral Assessment*, *14*, 93–115.

Barber, J. P., & DeRubeis, R. J. (2001). Change in compensatory skills in cognitive therapy for depression. *Journal of Psychotherapy Practice Research*, *10*, 8–13.

Barber, J. P., Gallop, R., Crits-Christoph, P., Barrett, M. S., Klostermann, S., McCarthy, K. S., & Sharpless, B. A. (2008). The role of the alliance and techniques in predicting outcome of supportive-expressive dynamic therapy for cocaine dependence. *Psychoanalytic Psychology*, *25*(3), 461–482. https://doi.org/10.1037/0736-9735.25.3.461

Baron, R. M., & Kenny, D. A. (1986). The moderator-mediator variable distinction in social psychological research: Conceptual, strategic, and statistical considerations. *Journal of Personality and Social Psychology*, *51*(6), 1173–1182. https://doi.org/10.1037/0022-3514.51.6.1173

Benjamin, L. S. & Critchfield, K. L. (2010). An interpersonal perspective on therapy alliances and techniques. In J. C. Muran & J. P. Barber (Eds.), *The therapeutic alliance: An evidence-based approach to practice and training* (pp. 123–149). New York, NY: Guilford Press.

Bluett, E. J., Zoellner, L. A., & Feeny, N. C. (2014). Does change in distress matter? Mechanisms of change in prolonged exposure for PTSD. *Journal of Behavior Therapy and Experimental Psychiatry*, *45*(1), 97–104. https://doi.org/10.1016/j.jbtep.2013.09.003

Bond, M., & Perry, J. C. (2004). Long-term changes in defense styles with psychodynamic psychotherapy for depressive, anxiety, and personality disorders. *The American Journal of Psychiatry*, *161*(9), 1665–1671. https://doi.org/10.1176/appi.ajp.161.9.1665

Bordin, E. S. (1979). The generalizability of the psychoanalytic concept of the working alliance. *Psychotherapy: Theory, Research & Practice*, *16*(3), 252–260. https://doi.org/10.1037/h0085885

Boswell, J. F., Gallagher, M. W., Sauer-Zavala, S. E., Bullis, J., Gorman, J. M., Shear, M. K., Woods, S, & Barlow, D. H. (2013). Patient characteristics and variability in adherence and competence in cognitive-behavioral therapy for panic disorder. *Journal of Consulting and Clinical Psychology*, *81*(3), 443–454. https://doi.org/10.1037/a0031437

Braun, J. D., Strunk, D. R., Sasso, K. E., & Cooper, A. A. (2015). Therapist use of Socratic questioning predicts session-to-session symptom change in cognitive therapy for depression. *Behaviour Research and Therapy*, *70*, 32–37. https://doi.org/10.1016/j.brat.2015.05.004

Bryk, A. & Raudenbush, S. W. (1992). *Hierarchical linear modeling: Applications and data analysis methods*. Thousand Oaks, CA: Sage Publications, Inc.

Carroll, K. M., Nich, C., Frankforter, T. L., & Bisighini, R. M. (1999). Do patients change in the ways we intend? Assessing acquisition of coping skills among cocaine-dependent patients. *Psychological Assessment*, *11*(1), 77–85. https://doi.org/10.1037/1040-3590.11.1.77

Carryer, J. R., & Greenberg, L. S. (2010). Optimal levels of emotional arousal in experiential therapy of depression. *Journal of Consulting and Clinical Psychology*, *78*(2), 190–199. https://doi.org/10.1037/a0018401

Castonguay, L. G., Constantino, M.J., McAleavey, A. A., & Goldfried, M. R. (2010). The therapeutic alliance in cognitive-behavioral therapy. In J. C. Muran & J. P. Barber (Eds.), *The therapeutic alliance: An evidence-based approach to practice and training* (pp. 150–172). New York, NY: Guilford Press.

Chaney, E. F., O'Leary, M. R., & Marlatt, G. A. (1978). Skill training with alcoholics. *Journal of Consulting and Clinical Psychology*, *46*(5), 1092–1104. https://doi.org/10.1037/0022-006X.46.5.1092

Christopher, M. S., Jacob, K. L., Neuhaus, E. C., Neary, T. J., & Fiola, L. A. (2009). Cognitive and behavioral changes related to symptom improvement among patients with a mood disorder receiving intensive cognitive-behavioral therapy. *Journal of Psychiatric Practice*, *15*(2), 95–102. https://doi.org/10.1097/01.pra.0000348362.11548.5f

COMBINE Study Research Group (2003). Testing combined pharmacotherapies and behavioral interventions in alcohol dependence: rationale and methods. *Alcoholism: Clinical and Experimental Research*, *27*(7), 1107–1122. https://doi.org/10.1111/j.1530-0277.2003.tb02873.x

Connolly, M. B., Crits-Christoph, P., Shelton, R. C., Hollon, S., Kurtz, J., Barber, J. P., Butler, S. F., Baker, S., & Thase, M. E. (1999). The reliability and validity of a measure of self-understanding of interpersonal patterns. *Journal of Counseling Psychology*, *46*(4), 472–482. https://doi.org/10.1037/0022-0167.46.4.472

Connolly Gibbons, M. B., Crits-Christoph, P., Barber, J. P., Wiltsey Stirman, S., Gallop, R., Goldstein, L. A., Temes, C. M., & Ring-Kurtz, S. (2009). Unique and common mechanisms of change across cognitive and dynamic psychotherapies. *Journal of Consulting and Clinical Psychology*, *77*(5), 801–813. https://doi.org/10.1037/a0016596

Connolly Gibbons, M.B., Gallop, R., Thompson, D., Luther, D., Crits-Christoph, K., Jacobs, J., Yin, S., & Crits-Christoph, P. (2016). Comparative effectiveness of cognitive and dynamic therapies for major depressive disorder in a community mental health setting: a randomized non-inferiority trial. *JAMA Psychiatry*, *73*(9), 904–911. https://doi.org/10.1001/jamapsychiatry.2016.1720

Connolly Gibbons, M. B., Thompson, S. M., Scott, K., Schauble, L. A., Mooney, T., Thompson, D., Green, P., MacArthur, M. J., & Crits-Christoph, P. (2012). Supportive-expressive dynamic psychotherapy in the community mental health system: a pilot effectiveness trial for the treatment of depression. *Psychotherapy*, *49*(3), 303–316. https://doi.org/10.1037/a0027694

Constantino, M. J., Coyne, A. E., Luukko, E. K., Newkirk, K., Bernecker, S. L., Ravitz, P., & McBride, C. (2017). Therapeutic alliance, subsequent change, and moderators of the alliance-outcome association in interpersonal psychotherapy for depression. *Psychotherapy*, *54*(2), 125–135. https://doi.org/10.1037/pst0000101

Cooper, A. A., Clifton, E. G., & Feeny, N. C. (2017). An empirical review of potential mediators and mechanisms of prolonged exposure therapy. *Clinical Psychology Review*, *56*, 106–121. https://doi.org/10.1016/j.cpr.2017.07.003

Cooper, A. A., Zoellner, L. A., Roy-Byrne, P., Mavissakalian, M. R., & Feeny, N. C. (2017). Do changes in trauma-related beliefs predict PTSD symptom improvement in prolonged exposure and sertraline? *Journal of Consulting and Clinical Psychology*, *85*(9), 873–882. https://doi.org/10.1037/ccp0000220

Craske, M. G., Liaoa, B., Brown, L., & Vervliet, B. (2012). Role of inhibition in exposure therapy. *Journal of Experimental Psychopathology, 3*(3), 322–345. https://doi.org/10.5127/jep.026511

Craske, M. G., Treanor, M., Conway, C. C., Zbozinek, T., & Vervliet. B. (2014). Maximizing exposure therapy: An inhibitory learning approach. *Behaviour Research and Therapy, 58,* 10–23. https://doi.org/10.1016/j.brat.2014.04.006

Cristea, I. A., Huibers, M. J. H., David, D., Hollon, S. D., Andersson, G., & Cuijpers, P. (2015). The effects of cognitive behavior therapy for adult depression on dysfunctional thinking: A meta-analysis. *Clinical Psychology Review, 42*(Dec), 62–71. https://doi.org/10.1016/j.cpr.2015.08.003

Crits-Christoph, P., Connolly Gibbons, M. B., & Mukherjee, D. (2013). Psychotherapy process-outcome research. In M. Lambert (Ed.) *Bergin and Garfield's handbook of psychotherapy and behavior change* (6th ed.) (pp. 298–340). NY: John Wiley and Sons.

Crits-Christoph, P., Cooper, A., & Luborsky, L. (1988). The accuracy of therapists' interpretations and the outcome of dynamic psychotherapy. *Journal of Consulting and Clinical Psychology, 56*(4), 490–495. https://doi.org/10.1037/0022-006X.56.4.490

Crits-Christoph, P., Gallop, R., Diehl, C., Yin, S., & Connolly Gibbons, M. B. (2017). Mechanisms of change in cognitive therapy for major depressive disorder in the community mental health setting. *Journal of Consulting and Clinical Psychology, 85*(6), 550–561 https://doi.org/10.1037/ccp0000198

Crits-Christoph, P., Gallop, R., Gaines, A., Rieger, A., & Connolly Gibbons, M.B. (2020). Instrumental variable analyses for causal inference: Application to multilevel analyses of the alliance-outcome relation. *Psychotherapy Research, 30*(1), 53–67. https://doi.org/10.1080/10503307.2018.1544724

Crits-Christoph, P., Gallop, R., Temes, C. M., Woody, G., Ball, S. A., Martino, S., & Carroll, K. M. (2009). The alliance in motivational enhancement therapy and counseling as usual for substance use problems. *Journal of Consulting and Clinical Psychology, 77*(6), 1125–1135. https://doi.org/10.1037/a0017045

Crits-Christoph, P., Gibbons, M. B., Barber, J. P., Gallop, R., Beck, A. T., Mercer, D., Tu, X., Thase, M. E., Weiss, R. D., & Frank, A. (2003). Mediators of outcome of psychosocial treatments for cocaine dependence. *Journal of Consulting and Clinical Psychology, 71*(5), 918–925. https://doi.org/10.1037/0022-006X.71.5.918

Crits-Christoph, P., Gibbons, M. B. C., Hamilton, J., Ring-Kurtz, S., & Gallop, R. (2011). The dependability of alliance assessments: The alliance-outcome correlation is larger than you might think. *Journal of Consulting and Clinical Psychology, 79*(3), 267–278. https://doi.org/10.1037/a0023668

Crits-Christoph, P., Gibbons, M. B. C., Temes, C. M., Elkin, I., & Gallop, R. (2010). Interpersonal accuracy of interventions and the outcome of cognitive and interpersonal therapies for depression. *Journal of Consulting and Clinical Psychology, 78*(3), 420–428. https://doi.org/10.1037/a0019549

Culver, N., Stoyanova, M. S., & Craske, M. G. (2012). Emotional variability and sustained arousal during exposure. *Journal of Behavior Therapy and Experimental Psychiatry, 43*(2), 787–793. https://doi.org/10.1016/j.jbtep.2011.10.009

de Kleine, R. A., Smits, J. A., Hendriks, G. J., Becker, E. S., & van Minnen, A. (2015). Extinction learning as a moderator of d-cycloserine efficacy for enhancing exposure therapy in posttraumatic stress disorder. *Journal of Anxiety Disorders, 34,* 63–67. https://doi.org/10.1016/j.janxdis.2015.06.005

De Meulemeester, C., Vansteelandt, K., Luyten, P., & Lowyck, B. (2018). Mentalizing as a mechanism of change in the treatment of patients with borderline personality disorder: A parallel process growth modeling approach. *Personality Disorders: Theory, Research, and Treatment, 9*(1), 22–29. https://doi.org/10.1037/per0000256

DeFife, J. A., Hilsenroth, M. J., & Gold, J. R. (2008). Patient ratings of psychodynamic psychotherapy session activities and their relation to outcome. *Journal of Nervous and Mental Disease, 196*(7), 538–547. https://doi.org/10.1097/NMD.0b013e31817cf6d0

DeRubeis, R. J., Evans, M. D., Hollon, S. D., Garvey, M. J., Grove, W. M., & Tuason, V. B. (1990). How does cognitive therapy work? Cognitive change and symptom change in cognitive therapy and pharmacotherapy for depression. *Journal of Consulting and Clinical Psychology, 58*(6), 862–869. https://doi.org/10.1037/0022-006X.58.6.862

DeRubeis, R. J., & Feeley, M. (1990). Determinants of change in cognitive therapy for depression. *Cognitive Therapy and Research, 14,* 469–482. https://doi.org/10.1007/BF01172968

DeRubeis, R. J., Gelfand, L. A., German, R. E., Fournier, J. C., & Forand, N. R. (2014). Understanding processes of change: How some patients reveal more than others-and some groups of therapists less-about what matters in psychotherapy. *Psychotherapy Research, 24*(3), 419–428. https://doi.org/10.1080/10503307.2013.838654

DeRubeis, R. J., Hollon, S. D., Amsterdam, J. D., Shelton, R. C., Young, P. R., Salomon, R. M., O'Reardon, J. P., Lovett, M. L., Gladis, M. M., Brown, L. L. & Gallop, R. (2005). Cognitive therapy vs. medications in the treatment of moderate to severe depression. *Archives of General Psychiatry, 62*(4), 409–416. https://doi.org/10.1001/archpsyc.62.4.409

Diener, M. J., Hilsenroth, M. J., & Weinberger, J. (2007). Therapist affect focus and patient out- comes in psychodynamic psychotherapy: A meta-analysis. *The American Journal of Psychiatry, 164*(6), 936–941. https://doi.org/10.1176/ajp.2007.164.6.936

Dimidjian, S., Barrera M., Martell, C., Munoz, R.F., & Lewinsohn, P.M. (2011). The origins and current status of behavioral activation treatment for depression. *Annual Review of Clinical Psychology, 7,* 1–38 https://doi.org/10.1146/annurev-clinpsy-032210-104535

Dimidjian, S., Goodman, S.H., Sherwood, N.E., Simon, G.E., Ludman, E., Gallop, R., Welch, S.S., Boggs, J.M., Metcalf, C.A., Hubley, S., Powers, J.D., & Beck, A. (2017). A pragmatic randomized clinical trial of behavioral activation for depressed pregnant women. *Journal of Consulting and Clinical Psychology, 85*(1), 26–36. https://doi.org/10.1037/ccp0000151

Dimidjian, S., Hollon, S.D., Dobson, K. S., Schmaling, K. B., Kohlenberg, R. J., Addis, M. E., Gallop, R., McGlinchey, J. B., Markley, D. K., Gollan, J. K., Atkins, D. C., Dunner, D. L., & Jacobson, N. S. (2006). Randomized trial of behavioral activation, cognitive therapy, and antidepressant medication in the acute treatment of adults with major depression. *Journal of Consulting and Clinical Psychology, 74*(4), 658–670. https://doi.org/10.1037/0022-006X.74.4.658

Dinger, U., Strack, M., Leichsenring, F., Wilmers, F., & Schauenburg, H. (2008). Therapist effects on outcome and alliance in inpatient psychotherapy. *Journal of Clinical Psychology, 64*(3), 344–354. https://doi.org/10.1002/jclp.20443

Doss, B. D. (2004). Changing the way we study change in psychotherapy. *Clinical Psychology: Science and Practice, 11*(4), 368–386. https://doi.org/10.1093/clipsy.bph094

Dozois, D.J.A., Bieling, P.J., Evraire, L. E., Patelis-Siotis, I., Hoar, L., Chudzik, S., McCabe, K., & Westra, H. A. (2014). Changes in core beliefs (early maladaptive schemas) and self-representation in cognitive therapy and pharmacotherapy for depression. *International Journal of Cognitive Therapy, 7*(3), 217–234. https://doi.org/10.1521/ijct.2014.7.3.217

Dozois, D.J.A., Bieling, P. J., Patelis-Siotis, I., Hoar, L., Chudzik, S., McCabe, K., & Westra, H. A. (2009). Changes in self-schema structure in cognitive therapy for major depressive disorder: A randomized clinical trial. *Journal of Consulting and Clinical Psychology, 77*(6), 1078–1088. https://doi.org/10.1037/a0016886

Earle, C. C., Tsai, J. S., Gelber, R. D., Weinstein, M. C., Neumann, P. J., & Weeks, J. C. (2001). Effectiveness of chemotherapy for advanced lung cancer in the elderly: Instrumental variable and propensity analysis. *Journal of Clinical Oncology, 19*(4), 1064–1070. https://doi.org/10.1200/JCO.2001.19.4.1064

Ekers, D., Webster, L., van Straten, A., Cuijpers, P., Richards, D., & Gilbody, S. (2014). Behavioural activation for depression: An update of meta-analysis of effectiveness and subgroup analysis. *PLoS ONE, 9,* e100100 https://doi.org/10.1371/journal.pone.0100100

Elliott, R. (2010). Psychotherapy change process research: Realizing the promise. *Psychotherapy Research, 20*(2), 123–135. https://doi.org/10.1080/10503300903470743

Elliott, R., Bohart, A. C., Watson, J. C., & Murphy, D. (2018). Therapist empathy and client outcome: An updated meta-analysis. *Psychotherapy, 55*(4), 399–410. https://doi.org/10.1037/pst0000175

Elliott, R., Watson, J. C., Goldman, R. N., & Greenberg, L. S. (2004). *Learning emotion-focused therapy: The process-experiential approach to change.* Washington, DC: American Psychological Association. https://doi .org/10.1037/10725-000

Escudero, V., Heatherington, L. & Friedlander, M.L. (2010). Therapeutic alliances and alliance building in family therapy. In J. C. Muran & J. P. Barber (Eds.), *The therapeutic alliance: An evidence-based guide to practice* (pp. 240–262). New York, NY: Guilford Press.

Eubanks, C. F., Muran, J. C., & Safran, J. D. (2018). Alliance rupture repair: A meta-analysis. *Psychotherapy, 55*(4), 508–519. https://doi.org/10.1037/ pst0000185

Falkenström, F., Ekeblad, A., & Holmqvist, R. (2016). Improvement of the working alliance in one treatment session predicts improvement of depressive symptoms by the next session. *Journal of Consulting and Clinical Psychology, 84*(8), 738–751. https://doi.org/10.1037/ccp0000119

Falkenström, F., Granström, F., & Holmqvist, R. (2013). Therapeutic alliance predicts symptomatic improvement session by session. *Journal of Counseling Psychology, 60*(3), 317–328. https://doi.org/10.1037/a0032258

Falkenström, F., Granström, F., & Holmqvist, R. (2014). Working alliance predicts psychotherapy outcome even while controlling for prior symptom improvement. *Psychotherapy Research, 24*(2), 146–159. https:// doi.org/10.1080/10503307.2013.847985

Falkenström, F., Kuria, M., Othieno, C., & Kumar, M. (2019). Working alliance predicts symptomatic improvement in public hospital-delivered psychotherapy in Nairobi, Kenya. *Journal of Consulting and Clinical Psychology, 87*(1), 46–55. https://doi.org/10.1037/ccp0000363

Farber, B. A., Suzuki, J. Y., & Lynch, D. A. (2018). Positive regard and psychotherapy outcome: A meta-analytic review. *Psychotherapy, 55*(4), 411–423. https://doi.org/10.1037/pst0000171

Farrell, N. R., Brosof, L. C., Vanzhula, I. A., Christian, C., Bowie, O. R., & Levinson, C. A. (2019). Exploring mechanisms of action in exposure-based cognitive behavioral therapy for eating disorders: The role of eating-related fears and body-related safety behaviors. *Behavior Therapy, 50*(6), 1125–1135. https://doi.org/10.1016/j.beth.2019.01.008

Feeley, M., DeRubeis, R. J., & Gelfand, L. A. (1999). The temporal relation of adherence and alliance to symptom change in cognitive therapy for depression. *Journal of Consulting and Clinical Psychology, 67*(4), 578–582. https://doi.org/10.1037/0022-006X.67.4.578

Flückiger, C., Del Re, A. C., Wampold, B. E., & Horvath, A. O. (2018). The alliance in adult psychotherapy: A meta-analytic synthesis. *Psychotherapy, 55*(4), 316–340. https://doi.org/10.1037/pst0000172

Foa, E. B., Ehlers, A., Clark, D. M., Tolin, D. F., & Orsillo, S. M. (1999). The Posttraumatic Cognitions Inventory (PTCI): Development and validation. *Psychological Assessment, 11*(3), 303–314. https://doi .org/10.1037/1040-3590.11.3.303

Foa, E. B., & Kozak, M. J. (1986). Emotional processing of fear: Exposure to corrective information. *Psychological Bulletin, 99*(1), 20–35. https://doi .org/10.1037/0033-2909.99.1.20

Foa, E. B., & Rauch, S. A. (2004). Cognitive changes during prolonged exposure versus prolonged exposure plus cognitive restructuring in female assault survivors with posttraumatic stress disorder. *Journal of Consulting and Clinical Psychology, 72*(5), 879–884. https://doi .org/10.1037/0022-006X.72.5.879

Garratt, G., Ingram, R. E., Rand, K. L., & Sawalani, G. (2007). Cognitive processes in cognitive therapy: Evaluation of the mechanisms of change in the treatment of depression. *Clinical Psychology: Science and Practice, 14*(3), 224–239. https://doi.org/10.1111/j.1468-2850.2007.00081.x

Gaston, L., Thompson, L., Gallagher, D., Cournoyer, L. G., & Gagnon, R. (1998). Alliance, technique, and their interactions in predicting outcome of behavioral, cognitive, and brief dynamic therapy. *Psychotherapy Research, 8*(2), 190–209. https://doi.org/10.1080/10503309812331332307

Gawrysiak, M., Nicholas, C., & Hopko, D. R. (2009). Behavioral activation for moderately depressed university students: randomized controlled trial. *Journal of Counseling Psychology, 56*(3), 468–475. https://doi.org/10.1037/ a0016383

Gelso, C. J. (2009). The real relationship in a postmodern world: Theoretical and empirical explorations. *Psychotherapy Research, 19*(3), 253–264. https:// doi.org/10.1080/10503300802389242

Gelso, C. J., Kivlighan, D. M., Jr., & Markin, R. D. (2018). The real relationship and its role in psychotherapy outcome: A meta-analysis. *Psychotherapy, 55*(4), 434–444. https://doi.org/10.1037/pst0000183

Ginzburg, D. M., Bohn, C., Ho€fling, V., Weck, F., Clark, D. M., & Stangier, U. (2012). Treatment specific competence predicts outcome in cognitive therapy for social anxiety disorder. *Behaviour Research and Therapy, 50*(12), 747–752. https://doi.org/10.1016/j.brat.2012.09.001

Gitlin, L.N., Szanton, S.L., Huang, J., & Roth, D.L. (2014). Factors mediating the effects of a depression intervention on functional disability in older African Americans. *Journal of the American Geriatric Society, 62*(12), 2280–2287. https://doi.org/10.1111/jgs.13156

Goldman, G. A., & Gregory, R. J. (2009). Preliminary relationships between adherence and outcome in dynamic deconstructive psychotherapy. *Psychotherapy: Theory, Research, Practice, Training, 46*(4), 480–485. https:// doi.org/10.1037/a0017947

Goldsmith, L. P., Lewis, S. W., Dunn, G., & Bentall, R. P. (2015). Psychological treatments for early psychosis can be beneficial or harmful, depending on the therapeutic alliance: An instrumental variable analysis. *Psychological Medicine, 45*(11), 2365–2373. https://doi.org/10.1017/ S003329171500032X

Hagenaars, M. A., Van Minnen, A., & De Rooij, M. (2010). Cognitions in prolonged exposure therapy for posttraumatic stress disorder. *International Journal of Clinical and Health Psychology, 10*, 421–434.

Harned, M. S., Ruork, A. K., Liu, J., & Tkachuck, M. A. (2015). Emotional activation and habituation during imaginal exposure for PTSD among women with borderline personality disorder. *Journal of Traumatic Stress, 28*(3), 253–257. https://doi.org/10.1002/jts.22013

Hartzler, B., Witkiewitz, K., Villarroel, N., & Donovan, D. (2011). Self-efficacy change as a mediator of associations between therapeutic bond and one-year outcomes in treatments for alcohol dependence. *Psychology of Addictive Behaviors, 25*(2), 269–278. https://doi.org/10.1037/a0022869

Håvås, E., Svartberg, M., & Ulvenes, P. (2015). Attuning to the unspoken: the relationship between therapist nonverbal attunement and attachment security in adult psychotherapy. *Psychoanalytic Psychology, 32*(2), 235–254. https://doi.org/10.1037/a0038517

Hawkins, J. D., Catalano, R. F., & Wells, E. A. (1986). Measuring effects of a skills training intervention for drug abusers. *Journal of Consulting and Clinical Psychology, 54*(5), 661–664. https://doi.org/10.1037/0022-006X.54.5.661

Hayes, A. M., Castonguay, L. G., & Goldfried, M. R. (1996). Effectiveness of targeting the vulnerability factors of depression in cognitive therapy. *Journal of Consulting and Clinical Psychology, 64*(3), 623–627. https://doi .org/10.1037/0022-006X.64.3.623

Herrmann, I.R., Greenberg, L.S., & Auszra, L. (2016). Emotion categories and patterns of change in experiential therapy for depression. *Psychotherapy Research, 26*(2), 178–195. https://doi.org/10.1080/10503307 .2014.958597

Hill, C. E. & Lambert, M. J. (2004). Methodological issues in studying psychotherapy processes and outcomes. In M. J. Lambert, (Ed.), *Bergin and Garfield's handbook of psychotherapy and behavior change* (5th ed.) (pp. 87–135). New York: John Wiley & Sons.

Hilsenroth, M. J., Ackerman, S. J., Blagys, M. D., Baity, M. R., & Mooney, M. A. (2003). Short-term psychodynamic psychotherapy for depression: An examination of statistical, clinically significant, and technique specific change. *Journal of Nervous and Mental Disease, 191*(6), 349–357. https:// doi.org/10.1097/01.NMD.0000071582.11781.67

Hoffart, A., Hedley, L. M., Thornes, K., Larsen, S. M., & Friis, S. (2006). Therapists' emotional reactions to patients as a mediator in cognitive behavioural treatment of panic disorder with agoraphobia. *Cognitive Behaviour Therapy, 35*(3), 174–182. https://doi.org/10.1080/16506070600862518

Hoffart, A., Øktedalen, T., Langkaas, T. F., Wampold, B. E. (2013) Alliance and outcome in varying imagery procedures for PTSD: A study of within-person processes. *Journal of Counseling Psychology, 60*(4), 471–472. https:// doi.org/10.1037/a0033604

Hofmann, S. G., Meuret, A. E., Rosenfield, D., Suvak, M. K., Barlow, D. H., Gorman, J. M., Shear, M. K., & Woods, S. W. (2007). Preliminary evidence for cognitive mediation during cognitive-behavioral therapy of panic disorder. *Journal of Consulting and Clinical Psychology, 75*(3), 374–379. https://doi.org/10.1037/0022-006X.75.3.374

Høglend, P., Amlo, S., Marble, A., Bøgwald, K.-P., Sørbye, O., Sjaastad, M. C., & Heyerdahl, O. (2006). Analysis of the patient-therapist relationship in dynamic psychotherapy: An experimental study of transference interpretations. *The American Journal of Psychiatry*, 163(10), 1739–1746. https://doi.org/10.1176/ajp.2006.163.10.1739

Høglend, P., & Hagtvet, K. (2019). Change mechanisms in psychotherapy: Both improved insight and improved affective awareness are necessary. *Journal of Consulting and Clinical Psychology*, 87(4), 332–344. https://doi.org/10.1037/ccp0000381

Hollon, S. D., Evans, M. D., & DeRubeis, R. J. (1990). Cognitive mediation of relapse prevention following treatment for depression: Implications of differential risk. In R. E. Ingram (Ed.), *Contemporary psychological approaches to depression* (pp. 117–136). New York, NY: Plenum Press. https://doi.org/10.1007/978-1-4613-0649-8_8

Horvath, A. O., & Symonds, B. D. (1991). Relation between working alliance and outcome in psychotherapy: A meta-analysis. *Journal of Counseling Psychology*, 38(2), 139–149. https://doi.org/10.1037/0022-0167.38.2.139

Horvath, A. O., Symonds, D., & Tapia, L. (2010). The web of relationships: alliances in couples therapy. In J. C. Muran & J. P. Barber (Eds.), *The therapeutic alliance: An evidence-based guide to practice* (pp. 210–239). New York, NY: Guilford Press.

Huppert, J. D., Kivity, Y. Barlow, D. H., Gorman, J. M., Shear, M. K., & Woods, S. W. (2014). Therapist effects and the outcome-alliance correlation in cognitive behavioral therapy for panic disorder with agoraphobia. *Behaviour Research and Therapy*, 52, 26–34. https://doi.org/10.1016/j.brat.2013.11.001

Huppert, J. D., Kivity, Y., Cohen, L., Strauss, A. Y., Elizur, Y., & Weiss, M. (2018). A pilot randomized clinical trial of cognitive behavioral therapy versus attentional bias modification for social anxiety disorder: An examination of outcomes and theory-based mechanisms. *Journal of Anxiety Disorders*, 59, 1–9. https://doi.org/10.1016/j.janxdis.2018.08.002

Imber, S. D., Pilkonis, P. A., Sotsky, S. M., Elkin, I., Watkins, J. T., Collins, J. F., Shea, T., Leber, W. R., & Glass, D. R. (1990). Mode-specific effects among three treatments for depression. *Journal of Consulting and Clinical Psychology*, 58(3), 352–359. https://doi.org/10.1037/0022-006X.58.3.352

Ingram, R. E., & Hollon, S. D. (1986). Cognitive therapy for depression from an information processing perspective. In R. E. Ingram (Ed.), *Personality, psychopathology, and psychotherapy series. Information processing approaches to clinical psychology.* (pp. 259–281) San Diego, CA, US: Academic Press.

Jacoby, R. J., & Abramowitz, J. S. (2016). Inhibitory learning approaches to exposure therapy: A critical review and translation to obsessive-compulsive disorder. *Clinical Psychology Review*, 49, 28–40. https://doi.org/10.1016/j.cpr.2016.07.001

Jarrett, R. B., Vittengl, J. R., Clark, L. A., & Thase, M. E. (2018). Patients' comprehension and skill usage as a putative mediator of change or an engaged target in cognitive therapy: Preliminary findings. *Journal of Affective Disorders*, 226, 163–168. https://doi.org/10.1016/j.jad.2017.09.045

Jennissen, S., Huber, J., Ehrenthal, J. C., Schauenburg, H., & Dinger U. (2018). Association between insight and outcome of psychotherapy: Systematic review and meta-analysis. *The American Journal of Psychiatry*, 175(10), 961–969. https://doi.org/10.1176/appi.ajp.2018.17080847

Jones, E. E., & Pulos, S. M. (1993). Comparing the process in psychodynamic and cognitive-behavioral therapies. *Journal of Consulting and Clinical Psychology*, 61(2), 306–316. https://doi.org/10.1037/0022-006X.61.2.306

Kadden, R. M., Litt, M. D., Cooney, N. L., & Busher, D. A. (1992). Relationship between role-play measures of coping skills and alcoholism treatment outcome. *Addictive Behaviors*, 17(5), 425–437. https://doi.org/10.1016/0306-4603(92)90003-E

Kallestad, H., Valen, J., McCullough, L., Svartberg, M., Høglend, P., & Stiles, T. C. (2010). The relationship between insight gained during therapy and long-term outcome in short-term dynamic psychotherapy and cognitive therapy for cluster C personality disorders. *Psychotherapy Research*, 20(5), 526–534. https://doi.org/10.1080/10503307.2010.492807

Katz, M., & Hilsenroth, M.J. (2018). Psychodynamic technique early in treatment related to outcome for depressed patients. *Clinical Psychology and Psychotherapy*, 25(2), 348–358. https://doi.org/10.1002/cpp.2167

Katz, M., Hilsenroth, M. J., Gold, J. R., Moore, M., Pitman, S. R., Levy, S. R., & Owen, J. (2019). Adherence, flexibility, and outcome in psychodynamic

treatment of depression. *Journal of Counseling Psychology*, 66(1), 94–103. https://doi.org/10.1037/cou0000299

Keefe, J. R., Solomonov, R. J., DeRubeis, R. J., Phillips, A. C., Busch, F. N., Barber, J. P., Chambless, D. L., & Milrod, B. L. (2018). Focus is key: Panic-focused interpretations are associated with symptomatic improvement in panic-focused psychodynamic psychotherapy. *Psychotherapy Research*, 29(8), 1033–1044. https://doi.org/10.1080/10503307.2018.1464682

Kenny, D. A. (1996). Models of non-independence in dyadic research. *Journal of Social and Personal Relationships*, 13(2), 279–294. https://doi.org/10.1177/0265407596132007

Kivity, Y., Levy, K. N., Kolly, S., & Kramer, U. (2020). The therapeutic alliance over 10 sessions of therapy for borderline personality disorder: agreement and congruence analysis and relation to outcome. *Journal of Personality Disorders*, 34(1), 1–21. https://doi.org/10.1521/pedi_2019_33_376

Kivlighan, D. M., Jr. (2007). Where is the relationship in research on the alliance? Two methods for analyzing dyadic data. *Journal of Counseling Psychology*, 54(4), 423–433. https://doi.org/10.1037/0022-0167.54.4.423

Kivlighan, D. M., Jr., Gelso, C. J., Ain, S., Hummel, A. M., & Markin, R. D. (2015). The therapist, the client, and the real relationship: An actor-partner interdependence analysis of treatment outcome. *Journal of Counseling Psychology*, 62(2), 314–320. https://doi.org/10.1037/cou0000012

Kivlighan, D. M., Jr., Hill, C. E., Gelso, C. J., & Baumann, E. (2016). Working alliance, real relationship, session quality, and client improvement in psychodynamic psychotherapy: A longitudinal actor partner interdependence model. *Journal of Counseling Psychology*, 63(2), 149–161. https://doi.org/10.1037/cou0000134

Kivlighan, D. M., Jr. Hill, C. E., Ross, K., Kline, K., Furhmann, A., & Sauber, E. (2018). Testing a mediation model of psychotherapy process and outcome in psychodynamic psychotherapy: Previous client distress, psychodynamic techniques, dyadic working alliance, and current client distress. *Psychotherapy Research*, 29(5), 581–593. https://doi.org/10.1080/10503307.2017.1420923

Kivlighan, D. M., Jr., Multon, K. D., & Patton, M. J. (2000). Insight and symptom reduction in time-limited psychoanalytic counseling. *Journal of Counseling Psychology*, 47(1), 50–58. https://doi.org/10.1037/0022-0167.47.1.50

Klein, D. N., Schwartz, J. E., Santiago, N. J., Vivian, D., Vocisano, C., Castonguay, L. G., Arnow, B., Blalock, J. A., Manber, R., Markowitz, J. C., Riso, L. P., Rothbaum, B., McCullough, J. P., Thase, M. E., Borian, F. E., Miller, I. W., & Keller, M. B. (2003). Therapeutic alliance in depression treatment: Controlling for prior change and patient characteristics. *Journal of Consulting and Clinical Psychology*, 71(6), 997–1006. https://doi.org/10.1037/0022-006X.71.6.997

Kolden, G. G., Wang, C.-C., Austin, S. B., Chang, Y., & Klein, M. H. (2018). Congruence/genuineness: A meta-analysis. *Psychotherapy*, 55(4), 424–433. https://doi.org/10.1037/pst0000162

Kraemer, H. C., Stice, E., Kazdin, A., Offord, D., & Kupfer, D. (2001). How do risk factors work together? Mediators, moderators, and independent, overlapping, and proxy risk factors. *The American Journal of Psychiatry*, 158(6), 848–856. https://doi.org/10.1176/appi.ajp.158.6.848

Kraemer, H. C., Wilson, G. T., Fairburn, C. G., & Agras, W. S. (2002). Mediators and moderators of treatment effects in randomized clinical trials. *Archives of General Psychiatry*, 59(10), 877–883. https://doi.org/10.1001/archpsyc.59.10.877

Kramer, U., Despland, J.-N., Michel, L., Drapeau, M., & de Roten, Y. (2010). Change in defense mechanisms and coping over the course of short-term dynamic psychotherapy for adjustment disorder. *Journal of Clinical Psychology*, 66(12), 1232–1241. https://doi.org/10.1002/jclp.20719

Kumpula, M. J., Pentel, K. Z., Foa, E. B., LeBlanc, N. J., Bui, E., McSweeney, L. B., Knowles, K., Bosley, H., Simon, N. M., & Rauch, S. A. M. (2017). Temporal sequencing of change in posttraumatic cognitions and PTSD symptom reduction during prolonged exposure therapy. *Behavior Therapy*, 48(2), 156–165. https://doi.org/10.1016/j.beth.2016.02.008

Kuutmann, K., & Hilsenroth, M. J. (2012). Exploring in-session focus on the patient-therapist relationship: Patient characteristics, process and outcome. *Clinical Psychology and Psychotherapy*, 19(3), 187–202. https://doi.org/10.1002/cpp.743

Lawlor, D. A., Davey Smith, G., & Ebrahim, S. (2004). Commentary: The hormone replacement-coronary heart disease conundrum: Is this the death of observational epidemiology? *International Journal of Epidemiology*, 33(3), 464–467. https://doi.org/10.1093/ije/dyh124

Laws, H. B., Constantino, M. J., Sayer, A. G, Klien, D. N, Kocsis, J. H., Manber, R., Markowitz, J. C., Rothbaum, B. O., Steidtmann, D., Thase, M. E., & Arnow, B. A. (2017). Convergence in patient-therapist therapeutic alliance ratings and its relation to outcome in chronic depression treatment. *Psychotherapy Research*, 27(4), 410–424. https://doi.org/10.1080/10503307.2015.1114687

Ledermann, T., & Kenny, D. A. (2012). The common fate model for dyadic data: Variations of a theoretically important but underutilized model. *Journal of Family Psychology*, 26(1), 140–148. https://doi.org/10.1037/a0026624

Levy, K. N., Meehan, K. B., Kelly, K. M., Reynoso, J. S., Weber, M., Clarkin, J. F., & Kernberg, O. F. (2006). Change in attachment patterns and reflective function in a randomized control trial of transference-focused psychotherapy for borderline personality disorder. *Journal of Consulting and Clinical Psychology*, 74(6), 1027–1040. https://doi.org/10.1037/0022-006X.74.6.1027

Levy, S. R., Hilsenroth, M. J., & Owen, J. J. (2015). Relationship between interpretation, alliance, and outcome in psychodynamic psychotherapy: Control of therapist effects and assessment of moderator variable impact. *Journal of Nervous and Mental Disease*, 203(6), 418–424. https://doi.org/10.1097/NMD.0000000000000302

Lewinsohn, P. M. (1974). A behavioral approach to depression. In R.J. Friedman & M. M. Katz (Eds.), *The psychology of depression: Contemporary theory and research (xvii- 318)*. Oxford, England: John Wiley & Sons.

Linardon, J., de la Piedad Garcia, X., & Brennan, L. (2017). Predictors, moderators, and mediators of treatment outcome following manualised cognitive-behavioural therapy for eating disorders: A systematic review. *European Eating Disorders Review*, 25(1), 3–12. https://doi.org/10.1002/erv.2492

Loeb, K. L., Wilson, G. T., Labouvie, E., Pratt, E. M., Hayaki, J., Walsh, B. T., Agras, W. S., & Fairburn, C. G. (2005). Therapeutic alliance and treatment adherence in two interventions for bulimia nervosa: A study of process and outcome. *Journal of Consulting and Clinical Psychology*, 73(6), 1097–1107. https://doi.org/10.1037/0022-006X.73.6.1097

Marcus, D. K., Kashy, D. A., Wintersteen, M. B., & Diamond, G. S. (2011). The therapeutic alliance in adolescent substance abuse treatment: A one-with-many analysis. *Journal of Counseling Psychology*, 58(3), 449–455. https://doi.org/10.1037/a0023196

Martell, C. R., Dimidjian, S., & Herman-Dunn, R. (2013). *Behavioral activation for depression: A clinician's guide*. New York, NY: Guilford Press.

McAleavey, A.A., & Castonguay, L.G. (2014). Insight as a common and specific impact of psychotherapy: therapist-reported exploratory, directive, and common factor interventions. *Psychotherapy*, 51(2), 283–294. https://doi.org/10.1037/a0032410

McCarthy, K. S., Keefe, J. R., & Barber, J. P. (2016). Goldilocks on the couch: Moderate levels of psychodynamic and process-experiential technique predict outcome in psychodynamic therapy. *Psychotherapy Research*, 26(3), 307–317. https://doi.org/10.1080/10503307.2014.973921

McLean, C. P., Su, Y.-J., & Foa, E. B. (2015). Mechanisms of symptom reduction in a combined treatment for comorbid posttraumatic stress disorder and alcohol dependence. *Journal of Consulting and Clinical Psychology*, 83(3), 655–661. https://doi.org/10.1037/ccp0000024

Messer, S. B., & Wolitzky, D. L. (2010). A psychodynamic perspective on the therapeutic alliance. In J. C. Muran & J. P. Barber (Eds.), *The therapeutic alliance: An evidence-based approach to practice and training* (pp. 97–122). New York, NY: Guilford Press.

Meuret, A. E., Seidel, A., Rosenfield, B., Hofmann, S.G., & Rosenfield, D. (2012). Does fear reactivity during exposure predict panic symptom reduction? *Journal of Consulting and Clinical Psychology*, 80(5), 773–785. https://doi.org/10.1037/a0028032

Nacasch, N., Huppert, J. D., Su, Y. J., Kivity, Y., Dinshtein, Y., Yeh, R., & Foa, E. B. (2015). Are 60–minute prolonged exposure sessions with 20–minute imaginal exposure to traumatic memories sufficient to successfully treat PTSD? A randomized noninferiority clinical trial. *Behavior Therapy*, 46(3), 328–341. https://doi.org/10.1016/j.beth.2014.12.002

Neacsiu, A.D., Rizvi, S. L., & Linehan, M. M. (2010). Dialectical behavior therapy skills use as a mediator and outcome of treatment for borderline personality disorder. *Behaviour Research and Therapy*, 48(9), 832–839. https://doi.org/10.1016/j.brat.2010.05.017

Niles, A. N., Burklund, L. J., Arch, J. J., Lieberman, M. D., Saxbe, D., & Craske, M. G. (2014). Cognitive mediators of treatment for social anxiety disorder: Comparing acceptance and commitment therapy and cognitive-behavioral therapy. *Behavior Therapy*, 45(5), 664–677. https://doi.org/10.1016/j.beth.2014.04.006

Norrie, J., Davidson, K., Tata, P., & Gumley, A. (2013). Influence of therapist competence and quantity of cognitive behavioural therapy on suicidal behaviour and inpatient hospitalisation in a randomised controlled trial in borderline personality disorder: Further analyses of treatment effects in the BOSCOT study. *Psychology and Psychotherapy: Theory, Research and Practice*, 86(3), 280–293. https://doi.org/10.1111/papt.12004

Norville, R., Sampson, H., & Weiss, J. (1996). Accurate interpretations and brief psychotherapy outcome. *Psychotherapy Research*, 6(1), 16–29. https://doi.org/10.1080/10503309612331331548

Ogrodniczuk, J. S., & Piper, W. E. (1999). Measuring therapist technique in psychodynamic psychother- apies, development, and use of a new scale. *Journal of Psychotherapy Practice and Research*, 8, 142–154.

Øktedalen, T., Hoffart, A., & Langkaas, T. F. (2015). Trauma-related shame and guilt as time-varying predictors of posttraumatic stress disorder symptoms during imagery exposure and imagery rescripting-A randomized controlled trial. *Psychotherapy Research*, 25(5), 1–15. https://doi.org/10.1080/10503307.2014.917217

Orlinsky, D. E., Rønnestad, M. H., & Willutzki, U. (2004). Fifty years of psychotherapy process-outcome research: Continuity and change. In M. J. Lambert, (Ed.), *Bergin and Garfield's handbook of psychotherapy and behavior change* (5th ed.) (pp. 87–135). New York: John Wiley & Sons.

Owen, J., & Hilsenroth, M. J. (2011). Interaction between alliance and technique in predicting patient outcome during psychodynamic psychotherapy. *Journal of Nervous and Mental Disease*, 199(6), 384–389. https://doi.org/10.1097/NMD.0b013e31821cd28a

Owen, J., & Hilsenroth, M. J. (2014). Treatment adherence: the importance of therapist flexibility in relation to therapy outcomes. *Journal of Counseling Psychology*, 61(2), 280–288. https://doi.org/10.1037/a0035753

Perry, J. C., & Bond, M. (2012). Change in defense mechanisms during long-term dynamic psychotherapy and five-year outcome. *The American Journal of Psychiatry*, 169(9), 916–925. https://doi.org/10.1176/appi.ajp.2012.11091403

Piper, W. E., Joyce, A. S., McCallum, M., & Azim, H. F. A. (1993). Concentration and correspondence of transference interpretations in short-term psychotherapy. *Journal of Consulting and Clinical Psychology*, 61(4), 586–595. https://doi.org/10.1037/0022-006X.61.4.586

Piper, W. E., & Ogrodniczuk, J. S. (2010). The therapeutic alliance in group therapy. In J. C. Muran & J. P. Barber (Eds.), *The therapeutic alliance: An evidence-based guide to practice* (pp. 263–282). New York, NY: Guilford Press.

Pitman, S. R., Hilsenroth, M. J., Weinberger, J., Conway, F., & Owen, J. (2017). Psychotherapy technique related to changes in anxiety symptoms with a transdiagnostic sample. *Journal of Nervous and Mental Disease*, 205(6), 427–435. https://doi.org/10.1097/NMD.0000000000000689

Pitman, S., Slavin-Mulford, J., & Hilsenroth, M. (2014). Psychodynamic techniques related to outcome for anxiety disorder patients at different points in treatment. *Journal of Nervous and Mental Disease*, 202(5), 391–396. https://doi.org/10.1097/NMD.0000000000000137

Pos, A. E., Greenberg, L. S., Goldman, R. N., & Korman, L. M. (2003). Emotional processing during experiential treatment of depression. *Journal of Consulting and Clinical Psychology*, 71(6), 1007–1016. https://doi.org/10.1037/0022-006X.71.6.1007

Pos, A. E., Greenberg, L. S., & Warwar, S. H. (2009). Testing a model of change in the experiential treatment of depression. *Journal of Consulting and Clinical Psychology*, 77(6), 1055–1066. https://doi.org/10.1037/a0017059

Quigley, L., Dozois, D. J. A., Bagby, R. M., Lobo, D. S. S., Ravindran, L., & Quilty, L. C. (2019). Cognitive change in cognitive-behavioural therapy v. pharmacotherapy for adult depression: a longitudinal mediation analysis. *Psychological Medicine*, 49(15), 2626–2634. https://doi.org/10.1017/S0033291718003653

Quilty, L. C., Dozois, D. J., Lobo, D. S. S., Ravindran, L. N., & Bagby, R. M. (2014). Cognitive structure and processing during cognitive behavioral therapy vs. pharmacotherapy for depression. *International Journal of Cognitive Therapy* 7(3), 235–250. https://doi.org/10.1521/ijct.2014.7.3.235

Quilty, L. C., McBride, C., & Bagby, R. M. (2008). Evidence for the cognitive meditational model of cognitive behavioural therapy for depression. *Psychological Medicine*, 38(11), 1531–1541. https://doi.org/10.1017/S0033291708003772

Rogers, C. R. (1957). The necessary and sufficient conditions of therapeutic personality change. *Journal of Consulting Psychology, 21*(2), 95–103. https://doi.org/10.1037/h0045357

Roos, C. R., Maisto, S. A., & Witkiewitz, K. (2017). Coping mediates the effects of cognitive-behavioral therapy for alcohol use disorder among outpatient clients in Project MATCH when dependence severity is high. *Addiction, 112*(9), 1547–1557. https://doi.org/10.1111/add.13841

Rothbaum, B. O., Price, M., Jovanovic, T., Norrholm, S. D., Gerardi, M., Dunlop, B., Davis, M., Bradley, B., Duncan, E. J., Rizzo, A., & Ressler, K. J. (2014). A randomized, double-blind evaluation of D-cycloserine or alprazolam combined with virtual reality exposure therapy for posttraumatic stress disorder in Iraq and Afghanistan War veterans. *The American Journal of Psychiatry, 171*(6), 640–648. https://doi.org/10.1176/appi.ajp.2014.13121625

Rubel, J. A., Zilcha-Mano, S., Feils-Klaus, V., & Lutz, W. (2018). Session-to-session effects of alliance ruptures in outpatient CBT: Within- and between-patient associations. *Journal of Consulting and Clinical Psychology, 86*(4), 354–366. https://doi.org/10.1037/ccp0000286

Rudden, M., Milrod, B., Target, M., Ackerman, S., & Graf, E. (2006). Reflective functioning in panic disorder patients: A pilot study. *Journal of the American Psychoanalytic Association, 54*(4), 1339–1343. https://doi.org/10.1177/00030651060540040109

Ryba, M. M., Lejuez, C. W., & Hopko, D. R. (2013). Behavioral Activation for depressed breast cancer patients: the impact of therapeutic compliance and quantity of activities completed on symptom reduction. *Journal of Consulting and Clinical Psychology, 82*(2), 325–335. https://doi.org/10.1037/a0035363

Sasso, K. E., Strunk, D. R., Braun, J. D., DeRubeis, R. J., & Brotman, M. A. (2015). Identifying moderators of the adherence-outcome relation in cognitive therapy for depression. *Journal of Consulting and Clinical Psychology. 83*(5), 976–84. https://doi.org/10.1037/ccp0000045

Sasso, K. E., Strunk, D. R., Braun, J. D., DeRubeis, R. J., & Brotman, M. A. (2016). A re-examination of process-outcome relations in cognitive therapy for depression: Disaggregating within-patient and between-patient effects. *Psychotherapy Research, 26*(4), 387–398. https://doi.org/10.1080/10503307.2015.1026423

Schwartz, R. A., Chambless, D. L., McCarthy, K. S., Milrod, B., & Barber, J. P. (2018). Client resistance predicts outcomes in cognitive-behavioral therapy for panic disorder. *Psychotherapy Research, 29*(8), 1020–1032. https://doi.org/10.1080/10503307.2018.1504174

Segal, Z. V., & Gemar, M. (1997). Changes in cognitive organisation for negative self-referent material following cognitive behaviour therapy for depression: A primed stroop study. *Cognition and Emotion, 11*(5–6), 501–516. https://doi.org/10.1080/026999397379836a

Shaw, B. F., Elkin, I., Yamaguchi, J., Olmsted, M., Vallis, T. M., Dobson, K. S., Lowery, A., Sotsky, S. M., Watkins, J. T., & Imber, S. D. (1999). Therapist competence ratings in relation to clinical outcome in cognitive therapy of depression. *Journal of Consulting and Clinical Psychology, 67*(6), 837–846. https://doi.org/10.1037/0022-006X.67.6.837

Silberschatz, G. (2017). Improving the yield of psychotherapy research. *Psychotherapy Research, 27*(1), 1–13 https://doi.org/10.1080/10503307.2015.1076202

Silberschatz, G., Fretter, P. B., & Curtis, J. T. (1986). How do interpretations influence the process of psychotherapy? *Journal of Consulting and Clinical Psychology, 54*(5), 646–652. https://doi.org/10.1037/0022-006X.54.5.646

Slavin-Mulford, J., Hilsenroth, M., Weinberger, J., & Gold, J. (2011). Therapeutic interventions related to outcome in psychodynamic psychotherapy for anxiety disorder patients. *Journal of Nervous & Mental Disease, 199*(4), 214–221. https://doi.org/10.1097/NMD.0b013e3182125d60

Smits, J. A. J., Powers, M. B., Cho, Y., & Telch, M. J. (2004). Mechanism of change in cognitive-behavioral treatment of panic disorder: Evidence for the fear of fear mediational hypothesis. *Journal of Consulting and Clinical Psychology, 72*(4), 646–652. https://doi.org/10.1037/0022-006X.72.4.646

Smits, J.A. J., Rosenfield, D., McDonald, R., & Telch, M. J. (2006). Cognitive mechanisms of social anxiety reduction: an examination of specificity and temporality. *Journal of Consulting and Clinical Psychology, 74*(6), 1203–1212. https://doi.org/10.1037/0022-006X.74.6.1203

Snippe, E., Schroevers, M. J., Tovote, K. A., Sanderman, R., Emmelkamp, P. M. G., & Fleer, J. (2019). Explaining variability in therapist adherence and patient depressive symptom improvement: The role of therapist interpersonal skills and patient engagement. *Clinical Psychology and Psychotherapy, 26*(1), 84–93. https://doi.org/10.1002/cpp.2332

Solomonov, N., Falkenström, F., Gorman, B. S., McCarthy, K. S., Milrod, B., Rudden, M. G., Chambless, D. L., & Barber, J. P. (2020). Differential effects of alliance and techniques on Panic-Specific Reflective Function and misinterpretation of bodily sensations in two treatments for panic. *Psychotherapy Research, 30*(1), 97–111. https://doi.org/10.1080/10503307.2019.1585591

Spektor, D. (2008). Therapists' adherence to manualized treatments in the context of ruptures (Doctoral dissertation). *Dissertations and Theses database.* (UMI No. 3333897).

Sripada, R. K., & Rauch, S. A. (2015). Between-session and within-session habituation in Prolonged Exposure Therapy for posttraumatic stress disorder: A hierarchical linear modeling approach. *Journal of Anxiety Disorders, 30,* 81–87. https://doi.org/10.1016/j.janxdis.2015.01.002

Stiles, W. B. (1988). Psychotherapy process-outcome correlations may be misleading. *Psychotherapy: Theory, Research, Practice, Training, 25*(1), 27–35. https://doi.org/10.1037/h0085320

Stiles, W. B., Honos-Webb, L., & Surko, M. (1998). Responsiveness in psychotherapy. *Clinical Psychology: Science and Practice, 5*(4), 439–458. https://doi.org/10.1111/j.1468-2850.1998.tb00166.x

Strauss, A. Y., Kivity, Y., & Huppert, J. D. (2019). Emotion regulation strategies in cognitive behavioral therapy for panic disorder. *Behavior Therapy, 50*(3), 659–671. https://doi.org/10.1016/j.beth.2018.10.005

Strunk, D. R., Brotman, M. A., & DeRubeis, R. J. (2010). The process of change in cognitive therapy for depression: Predictors of early inter-session symptom gains. *Behavioral Research and Therapy, 48*(7), 599–606. https://doi.org/10.1016/j.brat.2010.03.011

Strunk, D. R., Brotman, M. A., DeRubeis, R. J., & Hollon, S. D. (2010). Therapist competence in cognitive therapy for depression: Predicting subsequent symptom change. *Journal of Consulting and Clinical Psychology, 78*(3), 429–437. https://doi.org/10.1037/a0019631

Strunk, D. R., Cooper, A. A., Ryan, E. T., DeRubeis, R. J., & Hollon, S. D. (2012). The process of change in cognitive therapy for depression when combined with antidepressant medication: Predictors of early inter-session symptom gains. *Journal of Consulting and Clinical Psychology, 80*(5), 730–738. https://doi.org/10.1037/a0029281

Strunk, D. R., DeRubeis, R. J., Chiu, A. W., & Alvarez, J. (2007). Patients' competence in and performance of cognitive therapy skills: Relation to the reduction of relapse risk following treatment for depression. *Journal of Consulting and Clinical Psychology, 75*(4), 523–530. https://doi.org/10.1037/0022-006X.75.4.523

Svartberg, M., & Stiles, T. C. (1992). Predicting patient change from therapist competence and patient-therapist complementarity in short-term anxiety-provoking psychotherapy: A pilot study. *Journal of Consulting and Clinical Psychology, 60*(2), 304–307. https://doi.org/10.1037/0022-006X.60.2.304

Swift, J., & Callahan, J. (2009). Early psychotherapy processes: An examination of client and trainee clinician perspective convergence. *Clinical Psychology & Psychotherapy, 16*(3), 228–236. https://doi.org/10.1002/cpp.617

Trepka, C., Rees, A., Shapiro, D. A., Hardy, G. E., & Barkham, M. (2004). Therapist competence and outcome of cognitive therapy for depression. *Cognitive Therapy and Research, 28*(2), 143–157. https://doi.org/10.1023/B:COTR.0000021536.39173.66

Vermote, R., Lowyck, B., Luyten, P., Vertommen, H., Corveleyn, J., Verhaest, Y., Stroobants, R., Vandeneede, B., Vansteelandt, K., & Peuskens, J. (2010). Process and outcome in psychodynamic hospitalization-based treatment for patients with a personality disorder. *Journal of Nervous and Mental Disease, 198*(2), 110–115. https://doi.org/10.1097/NMD.0b013e3181cc0d59

Vittengl, J. R., Clark, L. A., Thase, M. E., & Jarrett, R. B. (2014). Are improvements in cognitive content and depressive symptoms correlates or mediators during acute-phase cognitive therapy for recurrent major depressive disorder? *International Journal of Cognitive Therapy, 7*(3), 255–271. https://doi.org/10.1521/ijct.2014.7.3.251

Vogel, P. A., Hansen, B., Stiles, T.C., & Götestam, K. G. (2006). Treatment motivation, treat- ment expectancy, and helping alliance as predictors of outcome in cognitive behavioral treatment of OCD. *Journal of Behavior Therapy and Experimental Psychiatry, 37*(3), 247–255. https://doi .org/10.1016/j.jbtep.2005.12.001

Vögele, C., Ehlers, A., Meyer, A. H., Frank, M., Hahlweg, K., & Margraf, J. (2010). Cognitive mediation of clinical improvement after intensive exposure therapy of agoraphobia and social phobia. *Depression and Anxiety, 27*(3), 294–301. https://doi.org/10.1002/da.20651

Vrabel, K. R., Ulvenes, P. G. and Wampold, B. (2015). Alliance and symptom improvement in inpatient treatment for eating disorder patients: A study of within-patient processes. *International Journal of Eating Disorders, 48*(8), 1113–1121. https://doi.org/10.1002/eat.22434

Walling, S. M., Suvak, M. K., Howard, J. M., Taft, C. T., & Murphy, C. M. (2012). Race/ethnicity as a predictor of change in working alliance during cognitive behavioral therapy for intimate partner violence perpetrators. *Psychotherapy, 49*(2), 180–189. https://doi.org/10.1037/a0025751

Wampold, B. E., & Imel, Z. E. (2015). *Counseling and psychotherapy. The great psychotherapy debate: The evidence for what makes psychotherapy work (2nd ed.).* New York, NY: Routledge/Taylor & Francis Group. https://doi .org/10.4324/9780203582015

Watson, J. C., & Bedard, D. L. (2006). Clients' emotional processing in psychotherapy: A comparison between cognitive-behavioral and process-experiential therapies. *Journal of Consulting and Clinical Psychology, 74*(1), 152–159. https://doi.org/10.1037/0022-006X.74.1.152

Watson, J. C., & Kalogerakos, F. (2010). The therapeutic alliance in humanistic psychotherapy. In J. C. Muran & J. P. Barber (Eds.), *The therapeutic alliance: An evidence-based guide to practice* (pp. 191–209). New York, NY: Guilford Press.

Webb, C. A., Beard, C., Auerbach, R. P., Menninger, E., & Björgvinsson, T. (2014). The therapeutic alliance in a naturalistic psychiatric setting: Temporal relations with depressive symptom change. *Behaviour Research and Therapy, 61*, 70–77. https://doi.org/10.1016/j.brat.2014.07.015

Webb, C. A., DeRubeis, R. J., Amsterdam, J. D., Shelton, R. C., Hollon, S. D., & Dimidjian, S. (2011). Two aspects of the therapeutic alliance: differential relations with depressive symptom change. *Journal of Consulting and Clinical Psychology, 79*(3), 279–283. https://doi.org/10.1037/a0023252

Webb, C. A., DeRubeis, R. J., & Barber, J. P. (2010). Therapist adherence/competence and treatment outcome: A meta-analytic review. *Journal of Consulting and Clinical Psychology, 78*(2), 200–211. https://doi.org/10.1037/a0018912

Webb, C. A., DeRubeis, R. J., Dimidjian, S., Hollon, S. D., Amsterdam, J. D., & Shelton, R. C. (2012). Predictors of patient cognitive therapy skills and symptom change in two randomized clinical trials: The role of therapist adherence and the therapeutic alliance. *Journal of Consulting and Clinical Psychology, 80*(3), 373–381. https://doi.org/10.1037/a0027663

Weck, F., Grikscheit, F., Jakob, M., Höfling, V., & Stangier, U. (2015). Treatment failure in cognitive-behavioural therapy: Therapeutic alliance as a precondition for an adherent and competent implementation of techniques. *British Journal of Clinical Psychology, 54*(1), 91–108. https://doi .org/10.1111/bjc.12063

Weck F., Rudari, V., Hilling, C., Hautzinger, M., Heidenreich, T., Schermelleh-Engel, K., & Stangier, U. (2013). Relapses in recurrent depression 1 year after maintenance cognitive-behavioral therapy: The role of therapist adherence, competence, and the therapeutic alliance. *Psychiatry Research, 210*(1), 140–145. https://doi.org/10.1016/j.psychres.2013.05.036

Weiss, M., Kivity, Y., & Huppert, J. D. (2014). How does the therapeutic alliance develop throughout cognitive behavioral therapy for panic disorder? Sawtooth patterns, sudden gains, and stabilization. *Psychotherapy Research, 24*(3), 407–418. https://doi.org/10.1080/10503307.2013.868947

Weissman, A. N., & Beck, A. T. (1978, March). *Development and validation of the Dysfunctional Attitudes Scale.* Paper presented at the American Educational Research Association, Toronto, Ontario, Canada.

Wells, E. A., Peterson, P. L., Gainey, R. R., Hawkins, J. D., & Catalano, R. F. (1994). Outpatient treatment for cocaine abuse: A controlled comparison of relapse prevention and Twelve Step approaches. *American Journal of Drug and Alcohol Abuse, 20*(1), 1–17. https://doi .org/10.3109/00952999409084053

Wilson, G. T., Fairburn, C. G., Agras, W. S., Walsh, B. T., & Kraemer, H. C. (2002). Cognitive behavior therapy for bulimia nervosa: Time course and mechanisms of change. *Journal of Consulting and Clinical Psychology, 70*(2), 267–274. https://doi.org/10.1037/0022-006X.70.2.267

Winston, B., Samstag, L. W., Winston, A., & Muran, J. C. (1994). Patient defense/therapist interventions. *Psychotherapy: Theory, Research, Practice, Training, 31*(3), 478–491. https://doi.org/10.1037/0033-3204.31.3.478

Witkiewitz, K., Roos, C. R., Tofighi, D., & Van Horn, M. L. (2018). Broad coping repertoire mediates the effect of the combined behavioral intervention on alcohol outcomes in the COMBINE Study: An application of latent class mediation. *Journal of Studies on Alcohol and Drugs, 79*(2), 199–207. https://doi.org/10.15288/jsad.2018.79.199

Wolitzky-Taylor, K., Drazdowski, T. K., Niles, A., Roy-Byrne, P., Ries, R., Rawson, R., & Craske, M. G. (2018). Change in anxiety sensitivity and substance use coping motives as putative mediators of treatment efficacy among substance users. *Behaviour Research and Therapy, 107*, 34–41. https://doi.org/10.1016/j.brat.2018.05.010

Xu, H., & Tracey, T. J. G. (2015). Reciprocal influence model of working alliance and therapeutic outcome over individual therapy course. *Journal of Counseling Psychology, 62*(3), 351–359. https://doi.org/10.1037/cou0000089

Zalta, A. K., Gillihan, S. J., Fisher, A. J., Mintz, J., McLean, C. P., Yehuda, R., & Foa, E. B. (2014). Change in negative cognitions associated with PTSD predicts symptom reduction in prolonged exposure. *Journal of Consulting and Clinical Psychology, 82*(1), 171–175. https://doi.org/10.1037/a0034735

Zilcha-Mano, S. (2017). Is the alliance really therapeutic? Revisiting this question in light of recent methodological advances. *American Psychologist, 72*(4), 311–325. https://doi.org/10.1037/a0040435

Zilcha-Mano, S., Dinger, U., McCarthy, K. S., & Barber, J. P. (2014). Does alliance predict symptomatic change, or is it the other way around? *Journal of Consulting and Clinical Psychology, 82*(6), 931–935. https://doi.org/10.1037/a0035141

Zilcha-Mano, S., & Errázuriz, P. (2015). One size does not fit all: Examining heterogeneity and identifying moderators of the alliance- outcome association. *Journal of Counseling Psychology, 62*(4), 579–591. https://doi.org/10.1037/cou0000103

Zilcha-Mano, S., & Errázuriz, P. (2017). Early development of mechanisms of change as a predictor of subsequent change and treatment outcome: The case of working alliance. *Journal of Consulting and Clinical Psychology, 85*(5), 508–520. https://doi.org/10.1037/ccp0000192

Zilcha-Mano, S., Muran, J. C., Hungr, C., Eubanks, C. F., Safran, J. D., & Winston, A. (2016). The relationship between alliance and outcome: Analysis of a two-person perspective on alliance and session outcome. *Journal of Consulting and Clinical Psychology, 84*(6), 484–496. https://doi .org/10.1037/ccp0000058

Zilcha-Mano, S., Solomonov, N., Chui, H., McCarthy, K. S., Barrett, M. S., & Barber, J. P. (2015). Therapist-reported alliance: Is it really a predictor of outcome? *Journal of Counseling Psychology, 62*(4), 568–578. https://doi .org/10.1037/cou0000106

Zuroff, D. C., Kelly, A. C., Leybman, M. J., Blatt, S. J., & Wampold, B. E. (2010). Between-therapist and within-therapist differences in the quality of the therapeutic relationship: effects on maladjustment and self-critical perfectionism. *Journal of Clinical Psychology, 66*(7), 681–697. https://doi .org/10.1002/jclp.20683

THERAPIST EFFECTS: HISTORY, METHODS, MAGNITUDE, AND CHARACTERISTICS OF EFFECTIVE THERAPISTS

BRUCE E WAMPOLD AND JESSE OWEN

Abstract

This chapter reviews the historical and current trends in the study of therapist effects. We discuss statistical methods for investigating therapist effects, with a primary focus and suggestion to utilize multilevel modeling to properly account for and understand therapist effects. Next, we review studies of therapist effects in randomized clinical trials and naturalistic treatment settings. The overall magnitude of therapist effects tends to be slightly greater in naturalistic settings than in randomized clinical trials, but it is sizable in comparison to other effects in psychotherapy. Then, we review the characteristics and actions that typify more effective therapists. It appears that more effective therapists have a sophisticated set of interpersonal skills that is displayed in interpersonally challenging situations. Finally, we provide some conclusions for research, practice, and training.

OVERVIEW

INTRODUCTION

It is no secret that patients, therapists, and therapist trainers alike believe that some therapists are better than others. As clear as that may be, the study of therapists and what makes therapists effective is best characterized as emergent. Previous editions of the *Handbook of Psychotherapy and Behavior Change* contained chapters on therapists. In 2004 Beutler and colleagues (Beutler et al., 2004) reviewed the research to identify variables that characterized effective therapists and commented that this research was inconclusive and as well was particularly sparse. By 2013, the research on therapist effects had improved, in terms of quality and quantity, and Baldwin and Imel (2013) concluded that indeed the evidence indicated that in clinical trials and in naturalistic settings therapists differ in their effectiveness – some therapists consistently achieved better outcomes than others. However, at that time there was little evidence about what characterizes the more effective therapists.

In this chapter, we examine the history of therapist effects, discuss statistical methods for estimating the magnitude of therapist effects, review the literature to determine the size of therapist effects, and identify the characteristics and actions of effective therapists, updating and expanding on the previous chapters on therapist effects as well as other discussion and reviews of therapist effects (see particularly Barkham et al., 2017; Castonguay & Hill, 2017; Wampold et al., 2017).

The most important advancement since 2013 has been the identification of the characteristics and actions of effective therapists. What is now known about therapists is beginning to reveal how psychotherapy works and has important implications for clinical guidelines, training of therapists, and future research.

HISTORY OF THE IMPORTANCE OF THERAPISTS

Statistical Methods Needed to Investigate Therapists

The history of therapist effects in psychotherapy is imbedded in statistical, theoretical, and cultural contexts. As we will discuss at length, estimating therapist effects requires particular statistical methods, and consequently, our understanding of therapists and how they affect therapy is intertwined with the development of statistical methods. As is often the case, competing claims in many domains of interest involve differences in the application and interpretation of statistical methods (e.g., existence of a *g* factor in intelligence and the statistical literature on factor analysis), and this phenomenon is present in the area of therapist effects as well (e.g., cf., Serlin et al., 2003; Siemer & Joormann, 2003). In psychotherapy research, statistical methods must take into account the fact that therapists treat many patients and patients typically see one therapist at a time, which, in statistical terms, implies that patients are *nested* within therapists. Furthermore, typically we want to make conclusions about therapists in general, not simply the ones we have studied, and therefore we consider therapists drawn from a population of therapists, which means that we consider therapists as a *random factor* – we will discuss this at great length when we discuss methods for estimating therapist effects and making inferences about the importance of therapists.

The statistical methods we use to examine the effects of therapists on the process and outcome of psychotherapy come from two traditions. The first tradition, as discussed by Serlin et al. (2003), emanated from the development in the 1920s of the analysis of variance (ANOVA) by Sir Ronald Fisher (Fisher, 1925), who described the intraclass correlation coefficient (ICC) as the "relative importance of two groups of factors causing variation" (p. 221). In our case, the ICC will be the proportion of variance attributed to therapists compared to the total variance, which is used to estimate therapist effects and gauge the relative importance of therapists on therapy outcomes (or processes). In the 1940s, the idea of examining variability from several sources was developed by statisticians to apply ANOVA to experiments that involved a fixed factor and a random factor. For example, in a classical example, suppose rats are exposed to one of two conditions (e.g., positive and negative ionization of air molecules, as used as an example by Kirk, 1995), which is a fixed factor, but the rats are housed in cages (i.e., rats nested within cages interact with each other, which might well affect the outcome of the experiment). Here, cages constitute a nuisance factor because the experimenter is uninterested in the effect of cages and any cage in particular, so

cages is also a random factor. However, it is necessary to control for the variability in outcomes due to the cages to properly estimate the fixed factor – this is absolutely critical to understand, and we will return to this point often in this chapter. Importantly, note that random factors need not be simply nuisance – they could be of prime interest. For example, a factory supervisor wants to know how much variability in production is due to machines (a random factor) in the factory with an eye to buying more machines of the same type. However, the factory managers might consider machines to be a fixed factor, provided they wanted to know which machine in their factory was most reliable rather than having an interest in the population of machines.

In the two examples (cages and machines), each factor could either be a nuisance factor (not of interest, e.g., cages) or a factor of interest (machines). As well, depending on the inferences to be made, a factor could be random or it could be fixed (e.g., with generalization to a population of machines or inferences about particular machines). In psychotherapy, treatment (e.g., CBT versus psychodynamic) would most likely be a fixed factor, with the goal of making inferences about CBT and dynamic therapy, while therapists would be a random factor (i.e., typically not interested in the outcomes of the therapists in the study, but the desire is to generalize to a population of therapists). Therapists are also a factor of interest – we want to know if therapists differ in their effectiveness. Models with a fixed factor (e.g., treatment) and a random factor (e.g., therapists) are called *mixed models*. It is important to note here that the statistical machinery to analyze mixed models in ANOVA was completed by the 1950s and have appeared in standard introductory statistics textbooks for decades (e.g., Hays, 1963; Kirk, 1995; Maxwell & Delaney, 1990; Winer, 1971).

The second tradition comes from sociology. The origins of sociology were cultivated by the belief that social institutions influenced an individual's behavior. Émile Durkheim, one of the founders of the field of sociology, studied the effects of the religious context (Catholic versus Protestant) on suicide using quantitative means. The idea that social institutions affect outcomes became known as the *contextual effect*, and quantitative methods to detect such effects were called *contextual analysis*. Conceptually, individuals are nested within a social context or an institution, which may themselves be nested within higher-order contexts. More sophisticated methods were needed to disentangle and estimate the importance of each level and, consequently, the quantitative methods became known as multi-level analysis or hierarchical linear models. Important developments in multilevel models (MLMs) took place in the 1970s in educational research, which considered pupils nested within classrooms and classrooms nested within schools. By the 1990s, MLMs were widely used in various disciplines in the social sciences. Since that time there existed a number of books and software devoted to this method (Bryk & Raudenbush, 1992; Hox, 2010; Raudenbush et al., 2001; Snijders & Bosker, 1999).

There are a few points to be made about the two statistical traditions, mixed-model ANOVA and MLMs. The former is derived from the experimental tradition and the latter from the naturalistic tradition, but conceptually, the two approaches are compatible, and indeed, when assumptions are met and estimation procedures are the same, the results will be identical. In many ways, the situation is similar to ANOVA and regression, both of which are subsumed under the general linear model. The multilevel modeling approach offers more flexibility, particularly for the complex data obtained from psychotherapy investigations. In this chapter, we will discuss mostly the multilevel approach, although there are aspects of therapist effects that are best understood from an ANOVA perspective, as will be discussed later. Another important point is that there have been available methods for investigating therapist effects for decades – it may seem that that there was a paucity of research on therapist effects in times past because there was a lack of statistical methods to investigate this, but that is not what has happened, as the history of therapist effects will show.

Provider Effects Historically

Agriculture, Education, and Medicine

Those familiar with the history of statistics will recall that ANOVA and many other statistics were developed in the agricultural context (e.g., think of the split-plot design). So, investigations of various factors, such as plant varieties, of farming were of prime interest. Less well documented was that at about the same time, experimental design was being applied to education. The impetus came, in part, from the desire of the American Psychological Association to demonstrate the usefulness of psychology and psychological research methods. In the early 1920s, the treatment group methodology was "being sold to American school superintendents as the 'control experiment' and touted as a key element in comparing the 'efficiency' of various administrative measures" (Danziger, 1990, p. 114). In 1923, McCall (1923) published *How to Experiment in Education*, which introduced control group experimentation in education and discussed the nascent idea of randomization. An additional context for the application of design and statistics was in medicine, which contributed the placebo control group as a means to control for psychological effects when estimating the effects of pharmacological agents (Gehan & Lemak, 1994; Shapiro & Shapiro, 1997).

It is informative to examine the three domains where experimental designs were first used (viz., education, agriculture, and medicine) to determine how providers were considered in the design and analysis of experiments. In education, randomized designs were used to test the effectiveness of educational programs. The customers were educational administrators who possessed power, whereas the providers of the programs were teachers, predominantly low-paid and low-status women who were considered interchangeable (Danziger, 1990) – consequently, there was little interest in the effect that the teacher had on student achievement. In agriculture, the focus was on soils, fertilizers, and plant varieties. The farmers were presumably able to apply the agricultural practices uniformly and were ignored as a source of variability in crop yields. In medicine, the focus was on the efficacy of interventions (viz., drugs, surgeries, inoculations) and the variability in outcomes attributable to the physician was not examined. Indeed, the promotion of Western Medicine depended on convincing the public that treatments were not what was euphemistically termed *snake oil* and that

cures did not emanate from charismatic healers (e.g., Franz Anton Mesmer; see Buranelli, 1975; Shapiro & Shapiro, 1997; Wampold & Bhati, 2004). Thus, in three prominent domains that used experimental methods to examine effective practices, the providers of services were ignored, despite the existence of sophisticated methods of analysis that could have been used to examine such provider effects.

Therapist Effects in Psychotherapy

Given that providers were ignored in agriculture, education, and medicine, it would not be surprising if therapists were ignored in psychotherapy. So, let's take a look at this issue. As discussed by Baldwin and Imel (2013) in the therapist chapter in the last edition of this volume, historically there has been recognition that therapists are worthy of our attention, as reflected in a quote of from Saul Rosenzweig in 1936:

> Very closely related to such implicit factors is the indefinable effect of the therapist's personality. Though long recognized, this effect still presents an unsolved problem. Even the personal qualities of the good therapist elude description for, while the words stimulating, inspiring, etc., suggest themselves, they are far from adequate. For all this, observers seem intuitively to sense the characteristics of the good therapist time and again in particular instances, sometimes being so impressed as almost to believe that the personality of the therapist could be sufficient in itself, apart from everything else, to account for the cure of many a patient by a sort a catalytic effect. (p. 436)

Rosenzweig recognized two critical points here: (a) the particular therapist makes a difference – some are more effective than others – and (b) what makes an effective therapist is not obvious.

Despite Rosenzweig's and others' observations about therapists, the focus of psychotherapy research typically has been centered on absolute efficacy (i.e., does psychotherapy work?) and relative efficacy (i.e., what psychotherapeutic treatment is superior?). With regard to absolute efficacy, Hans Eysenck in the 1950s and 1960s made the startling conclusion that evidence suggested psychotherapy did not produce recovery at a rate greater than spontaneous remission and might even be harmful (Eysenck, 1952, 1961, 1966; Wampold, 2013). This led to a contentious debate (for a modern incarnation, see Cuijpers et al., 2019; Munder et al., 2019), but the debate spurred the age of clinical trials in an attempt to establish the efficacy of various treatments – and little effort, to say the least, was devoted to studying therapists.

Interestingly, at about the same time Eysenck was expounding about the efficacy of psychotherapy, Donald Kiesler (1966) bemoaned the state of the art of psychotherapy research: "One of the unfortunate effects of the prolific and disorganized psychotherapy research literature is that a clear-cut, methodologically sophisticated, and sufficiently general paradigm which could guide investigations in the area has not emerged" (p. 110). To address the problems in psychotherapy research, Kiesler identified several of them, which he called myths. A prominent myth on his list was the *therapist uniformity assumption*, the effects of which he described thus: ". . .an even more devastating practice in psychotherapy research has been the selecting of various therapists for a research design on the assumptions that these therapists are more alike than different. . ." (p. 112).

About a decade after Kiesler's (1966) exposition of the therapist uniformity myth, what is credited as the first study to focus on therapists' effectiveness was published. In 1974, Ricks compared the long-term outcomes of two therapists treating 28 emotionally disturbed adolescent boys. One of the therapist's outcomes were remarkable, and Ricks used the appellation *supershrink* to describe him (see Baldwin & Imel, 2013 for a more extensive discussion of this study). It could be said that the Rick's study created a small cottage industry of examining the effects of particular therapists – with the emphasis on *small*, as we shall see.

In the middle 1980s, Lester Luborsky and colleagues became interested in the differences in outcomes of therapists involved in clinical research they were conducting (Luborsky et al., 1986; Luborsky et al., 1985). After reviewing the literature on therapist effects, they concluded, "Thus, while there have been reports of variation in therapists' treatment effectiveness, there are no consistent findings and no empirical basis established for any differences found" (Luborsky et al., 1985, p. 602). And they further noted:

It is amazing to discover the virtual absence of reported research data on differences among therapists in their usual level of success with their patients. Although by 1980 more than 500 studies had compared different forms of psychotherapy with each other and with control groups, there are almost no studies in that vast assemblage that have systematically investigated the success of the therapists who carried out the different forms of treatment. (Luborsky et al., 1986, p. 502)

In the first study (viz., Luborsky et al., 1985), Luborsky and colleagues examined the outcome of nine well-trained therapists, each of whom delivered one of three treatments (viz., supportive-expressive psychotherapy, cognitive-behavioral psychotherapy, and drug counseling) and found that there were "profound differences" (p. 602) in success rates among the therapists, although the statistical method for estimating the effects of therapists was not sophisticated. They also examined patient, therapist, patient–therapist relationship, and therapy-related variables to determine their influence on outcomes, but their examination of these variables did not meet the standards for determining what characterizes effective therapists.

In the second study (viz., Luborsky et al., 1986), Luborsky and colleagues examined the outcomes of therapists in four different studies. They again found considerable differences in outcomes among the therapists and made two important conclusions: "[there was] little support for the widely held view that certain therapists are best for certain kinds of patients; and. . . variations in success rate typically have more to do with the therapist than with the type of treatment." (p. 501). Again, the methods used attenuated the validity of these conclusions, but the questions are critical ones that we will examine in this chapter. Moreover, it must be recognized that these two studies were the first to systematically examine the variability in psychotherapy outcomes attributable to therapists in the context of clinical trials.

This brief summary of the beginnings of the study of therapist effects in psychotherapy leads us the question about how important is the study of therapist effects in psychotherapy

presently. To obtain a sense of the interest in therapist effects, we compared the number of psychotherapy clinical trials that examined therapist effects to the total number of psychotherapy clinical trials. Baldwin and Imel (2013), in their meta-analysis of therapist effects, which will be discussed in more detail later, conducted a systematic search and found 29 clinical trials that calculated therapist effects as a random factor. Johns et al. (2019) updated Baldwin and Imel's review by including studies published from January 2012 to December 2016, which yielded three additional clinical trials that examined therapist effects. Consequently, these systematic searches yielded approximately 32 clinical trials published prior to 2017 that considered therapist effects to be important. That value (viz., 32) should be considered in relation to the fact that the number of psychotherapy clinical trials published from 1965 to 2013 was 12,511 (Wampold & Imel, 2015, see Figure 4.2), which means that less than *one-quarter of one percent* of clinical trials examined whether the therapists delivering the treatment made a difference, which is the reason we referred to investigations into therapist effects as a *small* cottage industry.[1] It is safe to say that studying differences among therapists is not a priority in psychotherapy research. And, as we shall see, the consequences of ignoring therapists in the design and analysis of clinical trials involve erroneous conclusions about treatments (Crits-Christoph et al., 1991; Crits-Christoph & Mintz, 1991; Martindale, 1978; Owen et al., 2015; Serlin et al., 2003; Wampold & Serlin, 2000).

We have reviewed the history of therapist effects to offer the context of the review of the evidence related to therapists and the effects they produce. Despite the fact that the statistical machinery necessary to appropriately estimate therapist effects has existed for almost a century, agriculture, education, and medicine, as well as psychotherapy, have, for the most part, ignored the contributions of the provider to the outcome of the respective practices. Simply said, for psychotherapy this is a costly mistake, in terms of understanding how psychotherapy works, determining whether one treatment is superior to another, and for improving the quality of mental health services, as we shall see.

DEFINING AND ESTIMATING THERAPIST EFFECTS

Therapist Effects – What Are They and Why Are They Important?

Therapist effects, in its most basic conceptual sense, refer to the conjecture that some therapists achieve better therapy outcomes with their patients than do other therapists. Clearly, some patients will have poorer outcomes in therapy than others, due to factors such as motivation, comorbidity, level of distress or dysfunction, context (e.g., clinic location, economic resources), race/culture/ethnicity, personality structure, and chance events (see Chapters 4, 7; Bohart & Tallman, 1999; Bohart & Wade, 2013). The degree to which these patient factors are similarly distributed across therapists remains an

---

[1] Note that most of the therapist effects studies were secondary analyses. That is, the primary report of the results of the trial did not include therapists in the analysis, which, as will be discussed, creates a bias toward finding treatment effects.

important issue in understanding therapist effects. *Nonetheless, if therapist effects exist, some therapists*, on average, *will have superior outcomes to other therapists.* But keep in mind that even if therapist effects do exist, all therapists will have some patients who experience better outcomes than others.

There are two primary questions to be addressed in this chapter:

1. *Do therapist effects exist?* That is, do some therapists, on average, achieve better therapy outcomes than other therapists? If so, under what conditions? Further, if therapist effects exist, how large is the effect, particularly compared to other effects detected in psychotherapy? If the answers to these questions reveal that there is evidence for robust therapist effects, there arises a second critical issue.
2. *What characterizes the more effective therapists?* This second question is tremendously important because if some therapists are more effective than others and we have evidence of what characterizes effective therapists, then we can use that knowledge to better select therapy trainees, design training curricula to develop the necessary therapist skills, and assist practicing therapists to improve.

Each of these questions is addressed in major sections of this chapter. Before we get to these important questions, we discuss critical statistical and methodological issues.

Definition of Therapist Effects

The basics of the statistical methods for investigating the effects of therapists can be understood by examining Figure 9.1, which is a simplified version of the model used in investigations of therapist effects. Patients are found in level 1 (bottom level) of the model and patients are nested within therapists, who constitute level 2, creating a two-level model. In this simplified model, there is variability in outcomes of the patients, roughly classified as good, average, and poor. In the top panel each therapist produces the same outcomes, as they have some patients with good outcomes, some with average outcomes, and some with relatively poor outcomes. In terms of outcomes, there is variability among the patients (within therapists) but no variability among the therapists (i.e., on average they produce the same outcome). Thus, there are no therapist effects.

In the bottom panel, the situation is much different. There is still variability among the outcomes of the patients but most of it is due to their therapist. On average, Therapist 1 has the best outcomes and Therapist 3 has the poorest outcomes. Here the variability in outcomes is due to therapist (i.e., between therapist variability) and the therapist effect is large.

The therapist effect is formally defined as a ratio of variances:

$$\rho = ICC = \frac{\sigma_t^2}{\sigma_t^2 + \sigma_e^2}$$

where ρ is the population intraclass correlation coefficient, often denoted by ICC, σ_t^2 is variance of the outcome variable due to therapists, and σ_e^2 is the error or residual variance, which is equal to the within therapist patient variability pooled

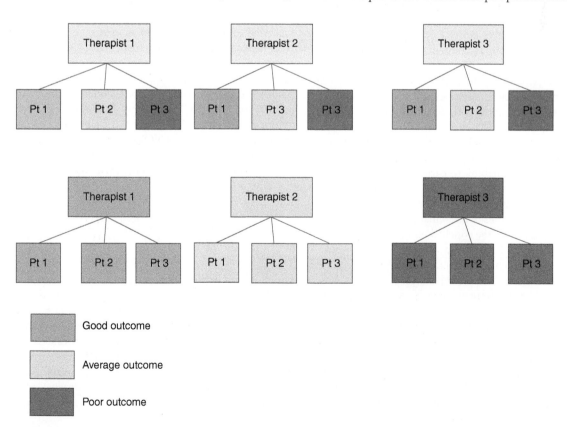

FIGURE 9.1 A simplified version of the model used in investigations of therapist effects.

over all the therapists. That is, the therapist effect is the proportion of the total variance that is associated with therapists. This ratio is intuitively appealing given outcomes depicted in Figure 9.1. In the top panel, σ_t^2 is zero and error variance (within cell variability due to patients) is relatively large and therefore the ICC is zero. In the bottom panel, σ_t^2 is relatively large and patient variability is relatively small and the ICC will be close to 1.00 (the upper bound of ρ is 1.00). Another way to think about the ICC is that if the ICC is greater than zero, then the outcomes of any two patients within the same therapist will be generally more similar than the outcomes of any two patients selected from the sample without regard for therapists. The ICC is often described as the correlation of observations within therapists. In this way, the ICC indexes the degree to which the outcomes of patients within therapists are similar to each other in their therapy outcomes.

There are some important aspects of the definition of therapist effects that are critical to understand. First, the equation is the population model – each of the parameters in this equation must be estimated, as follows, where the *caret* (often referred to as a *hat*) indicates an estimate of the parameter:

$$\hat{\rho} = I\hat{C}C = \frac{\hat{\sigma}_t^2}{\hat{\sigma}_t^2 + \hat{\sigma}_e^2}$$

The statistical procedures mentioned above (i.e., ANOVA and MLM) provide procedures to make these estimates, as well as to test whether they are nonzero (i.e., does a therapist effect exist) as mentioned earlier and discussed in more detail later. Of course, the models can become more complicated, say, for three-level longitudinal models (observations nested within patients, patients nested within therapists), which are often used. Second, valid inferences derived from the magnitude of the ICC depend on random assignment of patients to therapists. Often this is not the case and, as the case in many psychotherapy contexts, particularly naturalistic studies, scores are adjusted to attempt to account for nonrandom assignment.

A third aspect of the definition of therapist effects is central to properly understanding the implications of therapist effects. The definition of therapist effects as an intraclass correlation coefficient stipulates that therapists are considered a random factor. In psychotherapy research, at its essence, is a desire to generalize the findings to other situations. For example, in a psychotherapy randomized clinical trial (RCT) we are *not* interested in the outcomes of particular patients, per se, but rather we wish to generalize the conclusions to other patients – that is to say, we consider patients a random factor, without controversy (or even much thought). Similarly, we rarely are interested in the outcomes of particular therapists (say Chris, Pat, and Jan) but rather we want to generalize to a population of therapists (Do therapists who are similar to Chris, Pat, and Jan differ in their outcomes?). That is, do therapists in general differ in their effectiveness? Therapists as a random factor in psychotherapy research was emphasized by Martindale (1978) early on in psychotherapy research, reiterated by Crits-Christoph and colleagues (Crits-Christoph et al., 1991; Crits-Christoph & Mintz, 1991), and discussed thoroughly by others

(Serlin et al., 2003; Siemer & Joormann, 2003; Wampold & Serlin, 2000). Without going into the statistical and conceptual justification of random effects, it should be kept in mind that we are generalizing to a population of therapists with characteristics similar to the therapists in the study – or more precisely, to the population from which the sample of therapists might have been drawn (for a thorough discussion of random assignment and selection, see Serlin et al., 2003). The appearance of an ICC with regard to a therapist effect conveys that therapists were considered a random factor.

Statistical Methods for Estimating Therapist Effects

As mentioned earlier, there are two traditions for examining therapist effects, the ANOVA and MLM. We now explore these methods in more detail, beginning with ANOVA because it illustrates some critical issues.

ANOVA Analysis of Therapist Effects in Clinical Trials

To illustrate application of ANOVA to therapist effects, we take an example of two treatments ($p = 2$) with 20 patients randomly assigned to each condition (see Wampold & Serlin, 2000, for an extended discussion of this example). The ANOVA source table, ignoring therapists for this hypothetical study, is found in the top panel of Table 9.1. Here it can be seen that the two treatments are statistically significantly different ($F(1,38) = 6.60, p = .014$) and the estimate of the effect size for the fixed effect is $\hat{\omega}^2 = .124$ (ω^2 is the population treatment effect; see Hays, 1988), which is a moderate effect. However, this analysis, although it or some more sophisticated variant of it is typically used in psychotherapy research (recall, less than 0.25% of clinical trials examine therapists), is incorrect. In this study, there were five therapists in each treatment ($k = 5$), each of whom saw four patients ($n = 4$). If the ICC is nonzero, then the outcomes within a therapist are more similar than the outcomes of patients seeing different therapists, violating the independence assumption of ANOVA (Kenny & Judd, 1986; Kirk, 1995; Wampold & Serlin, 2000). For this hypothetical analysis, consider the mixed model ANOVA, with treatment as a fixed factor and therapists as a random factor, which appears in the bottom panel of Table 9.1. In the mixed model, the estimate of the ICC is given by

$$\hat{\rho} = \frac{MSTherapists - MSWithin}{MSTherapists + (n-1)MSWithin}$$

which in this hypothetical example was $\hat{\rho} = .30$; that is, 30% of the variability in outcomes was due to the therapists, which is statistically significant ($F(8,30) = 2.714, p = .022$). The correct analysis for treatment is based on the F ratio $MSTreatment/MSTherapists$, which in this case is *not* statistically significant ($F(1,8) = 3.339, p = .105$). Moreover, the correct estimate of the fixed effect is now $\hat{\omega}^2 = .100$, (that is, 10% of the variability in outcome is due to treatment), which is considerably smaller than the incorrect analysis and considerably

TABLE 9.1   Source Tables for Typical (Incorrect) Design and Proper Nested Design in ANOVA

			$\omega^2 = .1, \rho = .3, n = 4, p = 2, k = 5$			
Source	SS	df	MS	F	p	Effect size
Typical Design (Ignoring Nested Therapist Factor)						
Treatment	9.064	1	9.064	6.660	.014	$\hat{\omega}^2 = .124$
Error	51.714	38	1.361			
Total	60.778	39				
Nested Design (Correct Analysis)						
Treatment	9.064	1	9.064	3.339	.105	$\hat{\omega}^2 = .100$
Therapists	21.714	8	2.714	2.714	.022	$\hat{\rho} = .30$
WCell	30.000	30	1.000			
Total	60.778	39				

Note. ω^2 is the true population treatment effect, ρ is the true population intraclass correlation (therapist effect), n is the number of patients per therapist, p is the number of treatments, and k is the number of therapists. Adapted from "The consequences of ignoring a nested factor on measures of effect size in analysis of variance designs," by B.E. Wampold and R.C. Serlin, 2000, *Psychological Methods*, 5, p. 428. Copyright 2000 by the American Psychological Association. Reprinted with permission.

smaller than the proportion of variance due to therapists. In the correct analysis, therapist effects were statistically significant but the treatment effect was not. The untoward effects of ignoring a random factor, whether a nuisance factor or a factor of interest, have been known since the 1920s and solutions were complete by the 1950s, more than 60 years ago (Serlin et al., 2003). Ignorance is not a defense, given that Martindale introduced these considerations to the psychotherapy field in 1978.

This example illustrates critical points about psychotherapy research. Ignoring therapists has several critical consequences. The first issue is that ignoring therapists as a source of variability in outcomes replicates the pattern of medicine, agriculture, and education in that the providers of the service are thought to be unimportant and unworthy of consideration. In psychotherapy, as in the other fields, ignoring therapists assumes that therapists uniformly deliver various psychological treatments (see Imel et al., 2011). As we will see, the evidence suggests that this assumption is false – and one only has to ask patients whether they consider psychotherapists interchangeable.

The next two consequences of ignoring therapists in the design and analysis of psychotherapy clinical trials might be dismissed as statistical technicalities, but nothing is further from the truth. First, ignoring therapists inflates the error rate of the treatment fixed effect. This was seen in the example presented in Table 9.1, where there was a significant treatment effect when therapists were ignored but not when the proper analysis was conducted, as the nonindependent observations within therapists increases the size of the F statistic and the degrees of freedom – the larger the therapist effect, the larger the inflation. This is a well-known phenomenon in the

statistics literature (Barcikowski, 1981; Kenny & Judd, 1986; Kirk, 1995; Walsh, 1947) and noted in the psychotherapy literature (Baldwin & Imel, 2013; Crits-Christoph & Mintz, 1991; Martindale, 1978; Wampold & Serlin, 2000). That only .0025 or less of clinical trials examine therapist effects is a cause for concern as the remainder of the trials have an inflated error rate.[2]

However, it is not only the error rate that is inflated. The estimate of the treatment effect is also inflated (Wampold & Serlin, 2000). Again, almost all treatments effects published in the comparative clinical trial literature (i.e., the effect size between treatments) are inflated, a phenomenon perpetuated in meta-analysis of between-treatment effects (Owen et al., 2015). For instance, Owen et al. (2015) corrected between-treatment effects for the potential error rates created by ignoring therapist effects and 35–75% of significant treatment effects in meta-analyses would no longer be significant.

MLM Analysis in Naturalistic Settings

MLM is well suited to examining therapist effects in naturalistic studies. Because patients typically are not randomly assigned to therapists, it is recommended that the analyses account for differences among the patients assigned to different therapists. This case-mix analysis, at the very least, and most importantly, should account for the pretreatment score on the outcome

---

[2] Actually, most of the .0025 therapist effect studies were reanalyses, so the original analyses of these trials remain biased even though therapist effects were examined in subsequent publications.

measure. A basic model for estimating therapist effects would be as follows, following the notation of Baldwin et al. (2007):

$$Y_{ij} = \gamma_{00} + \gamma_{10}\left(x_{ij} - \bar{x}_j\right) + \gamma_{01}\left(\bar{x}_j - \bar{x}\right) + \left[\sigma_t^2 + \sigma_e^2\right]$$

where Y_{ij} is the posttreatment score for ith patient seen by the jth therapist; x_{ij} is pretreatment score of the ith patient seen by the jth therapist; $\bar{x}_j$ is the mean pretreatment score for the jth therapist (i.e., pretreatment score averaged across all of the therapist's patients); $\bar{x}$ is the pretreatment grand mean (i.e., pretreatment score averaged across all patients); γ_{00} is the intercept; γ_{10} is the within-therapist regression coefficient for pretreatment score, γ_{01} is the between-therapist regression coefficient for pretreatment score; σ_t^2 is the between-therapist variance and σ_e^2 is the within-therapist variance. In this model, γ_{00}, γ_{10}, and γ_{01} are fixed effects and σ_t^2 and σ_e^2 are random effects. The effect of pretreatment functioning on posttreatment function at both within-therapist level (i.e., γ_{10}; note the first subscript refers to a patient level predictor, i.e., patients within therapists) and the between-therapist level (i.e., γ_{01}; the second subscript refers to a therapist level predictor) is accounted for, which is an improvement over residualized gain-scores calculated ignoring therapists. The ICC is defined in the usual way as a ratio of the variance due to therapists divided by the sum of between-therapist and within-therapist variance.

This basic model can be elaborated in various ways. For one, therapists could be nested within treatments, similar to the ANOVA model presented above, in either a clinical trial or a naturalistic setting. As well, increasingly, psychotherapy researchers are measuring outcomes at each session, and in these longitudinal designs observations are nested within patients, which are nested within therapists (i.e., a three-level model; e.g., see Lutz et al., 2007). Moreover, therapists are nested within clinics, introducing a higher-order clinic level (Barkham et al., 2006; Falkenström et al., , 2018; Firth et al., 2019). Regardless of the complexity of the design, all of the cautions about ignoring therapists remain valid in these MLM models. To be clear, use of MLM in various contexts is not necessarily superior to other methods, and most importantly leads to the same inflated estimates of treatment effects if therapist effects are not modeled.

Power Issues

Before reviewing the literature to estimate therapist effects, it is helpful to know whether the studies reviewed have adequate sample size to obtain reasonable power to detect therapist effects should they exist. Determining sample size in multilevel models is complex because there are sample sizes at each level (e.g., number of therapists and number of patients per therapist). Schiefele et al. (2017) reviewed a number of guidelines suggested in the literature, including the 100/10 rule (at least 100 therapists and 10 patients per therapist) and the 50/20 rule (50 therapists and 20 patients per therapist). More patients per therapist results in more reliable estimates of effectiveness of each therapist, but having fewer therapists also reduces reliable

estimate of between therapist effects. If the goal is to estimate the ICC (i.e., the magnitude of the therapist effect) only, the requirements are smaller than if one is also attempting to model characteristics and actions of therapist effects (i.e., therapist factors that explain a portion of the therapist effects), particularly if there are cross-level interactions (therapist and patient characteristics interact to produce outcome). As well, various models will require different sample sizes (e.g., random versus fixed slopes). Schiefele et al. provide guidance with regard to sample size, but it is clear that relatively large samples, particularly of therapists, are needed.

THE MAGNITUDE OF THERAPIST EFFECTS

As mentioned several times, there are relatively few investigations of therapist effects in clinical trials, particularly when compared to the total number of trials. There have been more investigations of therapist effects in naturalistic settings. There have now been a number of meta-analyses of therapist effects in these two settings, the most recent of which was published in 2019 (viz., Johns et al., 2019). Consequently, in this section we establish the magnitude of therapist effects by reviewing the meta-analyses. However, before reviewing the meta-analyses we review a few exemplary therapist effect studies in the two contexts, as this will illustrate how therapist effects are estimated.

Therapist Effects in Clinical Trials
Exemplary Study
In the late 1980s and early 1990s, there was an interest in conducting psychotherapy clinical trials in a manner similar to multisite collaborate clinical trials in medicine. During this period, the National Institute of Mental Health (NIMH) in the United States funded such a trial, which was called the NIMH Treatment of Depression Collaborative Research Program (NIMH TDCRP, Elkin et al., 1985; Elkin et al., 1989). In three sites, depressed patients were randomly assigned to one of four conditions: cognitive-behavioral therapy (CBT), interpersonal therapy (IPT), antidepressant medication (ADM), and pill placebo (PLA). The focus here is on the two psychotherapy conditions, CBT and IPT (see McKay et al., 2006 for an analysis of psychiatrist effects in the ADM and PLA arms).

As described by Elkin and colleagues (Elkin et al., 1985; Elkin et al., 1989), 119 depressed patients were assigned to IPT (60 patients treated by 9 therapists) and CBT (59 patients treated by 8 therapists) and distress was assessed before and after treatment with four scales: Hamilton Rating Scale for Depression (HRSD), Beck Depression Inventory (BDI), Hopkins Symptom Checklist (HSCL), and the Global Assessment Scale (GAS). Kim, Wampold, and Bolt (2006) used the data from the NIMH TDCRP to estimate therapist effects.

MLM was used to estimate therapist effects, as described above. Treatment (CBT versus IPT) was considered a fixed factor, therapists within treatments as a random factor. Although patients were randomly assigned to therapists, Kim

TABLE 9.2 Kim et al. (2006) Mulitlevel Analysis of Treatment (Fixed) and Therapists (Random Slope and Fixed Intercept) Effects for NIMH TDCRP Completers

Variable	Treatment					Therapist			
	Coefficient γ_{01}	SE	t	p	$\hat{\omega}^2$	Variance component τ_o^2	p	$\hat{\rho}_t$	Error variance σ^2
HRSD	−0.903	1.432	−0.631	.537	.000	2.44	.211	.069	33.03
GAS	1.50	0.513	0.513	.615	.000	16.67	.062	.097	114.01
BDI	−3.197	1.99	−1.606	.129	.000	4.10	.293	.050	78.56
HSCL	−0.048	0.107	−0.449	.659	.000	0.018	.143	.090	0.181

Note. HRSD = Hamilton Rating Scale for Depression; GAS = Global Assessment Scale; BDI = Beck Depression Inventory; HSCL = Hopkins Symptom Checklist-90; $\hat{\omega}^2$ = estimate of the variability in outcomes due to treatment (a fixed effect, i.e., CBT vs. IPT); $\hat{\rho}_t$ = estimate of the proportion of variability due to therapists (a random effect). Adapted from "Therapist effects in psychotherapy: A random-effects modeling of the National Institute of Mental Health Treatment of Depression Collaborative Research Program data," 2006, by D.-M. Kim, B.E. Wampold, & D. M. Bolt, Psychotherapy Research, 16, p. 164. Copyright 2000 by the Society for Psychotherapy Research, Reprinted with permission.

et al. (2006) used the pretreatment assessments as a covariate. Here we report the simplest analysis for the intent-to-treat (ITT) sample, with random intercepts (therapists differ in the average outcomes) and fixed slopes (relationship between pretest and posttest is identical for all therapists, which is consistent with common practice of using residualized gain scores).

The results for the four outcome measures for the ITT sample with fixed slopes is presented in Table 10.2. Consistent with the results reported by Elkin and colleagues (Elkin et al., 1989) and the general dodo bird conclusion (Wampold & Imel, 2015), there were no significant differences between IPT and CBT; indeed, the estimate of the population effect (viz., $\hat{\omega}^2$) attributed to treatment, in this analysis that appropriately modeled therapist effects, was equal to zero for all four variables. The estimate of the therapist effects in this analysis (viz., ICC or $\hat{\rho}_I$) ranged from .032 to .087, indicating that the therapist effect account for approximately 3–8% of the variability in outcome of the two psychotherapies. However, only one of the four estimates of therapist effects was statistically significant, due to the relatively low power of this trial. Generally, letting slopes vary across therapists (random slopes) increased the magnitude of the therapist effects (.080 to .123 for completers).

A number of issues are illustrated by this study. First, the power to detect therapist effects of the magnitude observed in this study is quite low (Hox, 2010; Schiefele et al., 2017). As discussed earlier, a nonsignificant therapist effect is not a valid rationale for omitting therapists in the analysis of an RCT. It is worth mentioning that the original analysis (Elkin et al., 1989) did not consider therapists as a factor. Importantly, the conclusions differed. Elkin et al. found that IPT was superior to CBT for severely depressed patients, but when therapists were correctly modeled, there was no differences between IPT and CBT (i.e., the treatment effect $\hat{\omega}^2$ was 6% in the analysis ignoring therapists and 0% in the analysis including therapists; Wampold & Serlin, 2000). In any event, as is the case in many

RCTs, the magnitude of the therapist effect was larger than the magnitude of the fixed effect indexing the difference between treatments (Wampold & Imel, 2015).

Earlier, we discussed that conclusions about a phenomenon can differ based on the statistical procedures utilized. This was true in the present case because Elkin and colleagues (Elkin et al., 2006a) analyzed the same data and concluded that therapist effects were negligible. The arguments on either side were based largely on a critique of the statistical methods (Crits-Christoph & Gallop, 2006; Elkin et al., 2007; Elkin et al., 2006a; Elkin et al., 2006b; Kim et al., 2006; Soldz, 2006; Wampold & Bolt, 2006; Wampold & Bolt, 2007), illustrating again that many substantive debates are reducible to disagreement about statistical methods.

Meta-Analytic Findings

There are several prominent meta-analyses of therapist effects in psychotherapy trials (viz., Baldwin & Imel, 2013b; Crits-Christoph et al., 1991; Crits-Christoph & Mintz, 1991; Johns et al., 2019). We summarize the results in Table 9.3, and discuss them below.

The first reviews of therapist effects were conducted by Crits-Christoph and colleagues. Crits-Christoph and Mintz (1991) analyzed data from 10 clinical trials to estimate therapist effects, using a random effects ANOVA. Each of the studies contained multiple outcome measures. Therapist effects were reported for the outcome variable that produced the largest effect and for the arithmetic mean of the effects for all outcome variables within studies. The mean therapist effects for the average of the outcome variables across the 10 studies was 0.042 (i.e., about 4% of the variability in outcomes was due to therapists) and the mean for the outcome variable producing the largest therapist effect was 0.150. In a meta-analysis of clinical trials, Crits-Christoph and colleagues (Crits-Christoph et al., 1991) analyzed data from 15 studies (including 8 from

TABLE 9.3   Summary of Meta-Analytic Estimates of Therapist Effects in RCTs

Review	Years reviewed	# studies	ICC	SMD equivalent
Crits-Christoph & Mintz (1991)	< 1991	10	.042 to .150	0.42 to 0.85
Crits-Christoph et al. (1991)	< 1991	15	.086	0.61
Baldwin & Imel (2013)	< 2013	29	.03	0.35
Johns et al. (2019)	2012–2016	3	.082 to .174	0.60 to 0.92

Note: ICC = intraclass correlation coefficient, SMD = standardized mean difference

the previous analysis), calculated separately for 27 different treatment groups, using random effects ANOVA, averaged the effects across outcome measures within studies, and found that the aggregate therapist effect for the 15 studies was 0.086.

Baldwin and Imel (2013), in the Therapist Effects chapter in the last edition of this *Handbook*, conducted a comprehensive meta-analysis of therapist effects. Their search of the literature located 29 clinical trials for which therapist effects were estimated properly using some variant of a random effects model. For these 29 studies, the mean and range for the number of therapists and the average and range of patients per therapist *n* are found in Table 9.4. Generally speaking, the RCTs were underpowered, with relative few therapists and patients per therapist. Only 2 of the 29 RCTs had more than 10 therapists and 10 patients per therapist. Using meta-analytic methods designed to aggregate ICCs, which is methodologically more appropriate than methods used in previous reviews (viz., calculating the arithmetic mean of the ICCs), Baldwin and Imel found an aggregate ICC of 0.03 for the RCTs.

The latest meta-analysis of therapist effects in randomized clinical trials was an update, and refinement of Baldwin and Imel's (2013) review was conducted by Johns et al. (2019). Johns et al. searched the literature for RCTs (and naturalistic studies, as discussed below) that estimated therapist effects appropriately (i.e., with random effects models) between 2012

TABLE 9.4   Sample Size (Therapists and Patients/Therapist) in Baldwin and Imel (2013) and Johns et al. (2019)

Type	Mean *k*	*k* range	Mean *n*	Range *n*
Baldwin & Imel (2013)				
RCT	8.44	2–36	8.9	2.5–26.3
Naturalistic	59.02	5–581	13.38	2.2–51.1
Johns et al. (2019)				
RCT	17.0	3–38	42.0	9–65.3
Naturalistic	218.6	10–1800	52.6	6–134.6

Note: *k* = number of therapists, *n* = number of patients per therapist

and 2016, inclusive. Their search yielded only three RCTs for which there were estimates of therapist effects that met the inclusion criteria. Only 1 of 3 of the studies had more than 10 therapists and 10 patients per therapist but were remarkably better powered than the Baldwin and Imel RCTs on average.

In the Johns et al. (2019) meta-analysis, therapist effects were averaged within study across the various outcome measures used. The aggregate effect size across the three studies was calculated as a weighted average, although in this context it is not clear whether one should weight the effects by the number of patients, the number of therapists, or number of patients per therapist. When weighted by number of patients (i.e., studies with more patients had greater contribution to the aggregate), the aggregate therapist effect was 0.129; when weighted by number of therapists, the aggregate effect was 0.174; and when weighted by the number of patients per therapist, the aggregated effect was 0.082 (see Table 9.3). In this case, the effects of statistical method (i.e., what is the appropriate weighting strategy?) can be seen, but in all cases the variability of outcomes due to therapists compared to the total variability of outcomes exceeded 8 percent.

The reviews by Crits-Christoph and colleagues, Baldwin and Imel, and Johns et al. produced a range of therapist effect estimates, from .03 in Baldwin and Imel to .174 in Johns et al., when using the number of patients as the weight used in calculating a weighted average (see Table 9.3). Those desiring a point estimate of therapist effects might take the value provided by Baldwin and Imel (2013) given that it is based on the most studies and therefore the most reliable (i.e., the estimate with the smallest standard error) and used methods designed to aggregate ICCs, keeping in mind that nearly all of the individual studies were underpowered and that there remains much variability in the therapist effects estimates (Baldwin & Imel, 2013).

Are therapist effects equal to 0.03 (Baldwin & Imel, 2913) or larger important? Baldwin and Imel (2013) in the previous chapter discussed various ways to interpret ICC and their effects on outcome, a discussion that merits attention. In this chapter we make a few additional comments.

Interpretation of Therapist Effects in RCTs

Therapists effects in the range of 3% to 15% might seem quite small and unimportant. However, there are a number of considerations to keep in mind when interpreting therapist effects.

Treatments delivered in RCTs are unusual in the sense that the context in which they are delivered is quite different from the delivery of psychological treatments in practice (Wampold & Imel, 2015; Westen & Morrison, 2001; Westen et al., 2004). Patients in clinical trials typically are more homogeneous than in clinical practice; typical exclusion criteria for depression, for example, consist of suicidal ideation, use of psychotropic medication, various personality disorders, substance use, psychotic features, bipolar disorders, persistent depression, and so forth. The therapists in clinical trials are not a random sample of therapists but typically are selected for their expertise, given special training, monitored (e.g., adherence and competence), and treatment is governed by a treatment protocol, if not a manual. These operations most likely attenuate therapist effects (Crits-Christoph et al., 1991). Thus, it is not surprising that the magnitude of therapist effects in RCTs is attenuated. Another important issue is that the estimations of therapist effects in RCTs are drastically underpowered, leading to unreliable estimates of therapist effects.

To get a sense of the importance of the magnitude of therapist effects, it is informative to compare therapist effects in RCTs to coefficients derived from other factors. The standardized mean difference (SMD; either a *g* or *d* coefficient from meta-analyses) for psychotherapy versus no-treatment (e.g., waiting list controls) is in the neighborhood of 0.80 (Wampold & Imel, 2015), which is a large effect. Any within treatment factor, such as therapist effects, that approached an SMD of 0.80 would be truly remarkable. In Table 9.3, the SMD equivalents of the ICCs for the various reviews of therapist effects in RCTs are given, some of which are in the neighborhood or exceed 0.80, although the most reliable estimate of therapist effects (0.03 in Baldwin & Imel) is equivalent to a SMD of 0.35. However, an SMD of 0.35 exceeds the SMD for differences between different treatments (0.20 at most; Wampold & Imel, 2015), specific ingredients (i.e., dismantling studies of a full treatment versus treatment without critical specific ingredient; SMD = 0.0; see Ahn & Wampold, 2001; Bell et al., 2013); relation of adherence to treatment protocol and outcome in RCTs (SMD = 0.05; Webb et al., 2010); and relation of outcome and treatment specific competence ratings in RCTs (SMD = 0.14; Webb et al., 2010).

The evidence indicates that in RCTs the proportion of variability in outcomes due to the person of the therapist is modest but meaningful, particularly in comparison to other factors, including treatment differences, specific ingredients, adherence to protocols, and treatment specific competence. When therapist effects in naturalistic settings are discussed, the implications for patients will be illustrated, as this discussion is most relevant for practice.

Therapist Effects in Naturalistic Settings

Therapist effects have been investigated in naturalistic settings using MLM since around 2005 (Lutz et al., 2007; Wampold & Brown, 2005). Low power has plagued the investigation of therapist effects in RCTs, but in naturalistic settings large datasets are available from managed care or private insurance organizations, practice networks, consortia (e.g., college and university counseling centers), and national or regional governmental health services. Of course, data from naturalistic settings typically are less well controlled – patients have a variety of disorders, more comorbidity, more challenges to remaining in treatment; therapists are not selected for their expertise, do not receive training, deliver a variety of treatments, are not monitored, and receive no, or significantly less, supervision; and typically patients are not randomly assigned to therapists. It would not be surprising if therapist effects were larger in naturalistic settings than they are in RCTs.

Exemplary Study

Saxon and Barkham (2012) conducted a study to examine the characteristics of therapist effects in the United Kingdom's National Health Service (UK-NHS) primary care mental health psychotherapy services between 2000 and 2008. The study involved 10,786 patients who had received more than two sessions of face-to-face psychotherapy, had a planned ending, and completed the outcome measure (viz., the Clinical Outcomes in Routine Evaluation Outcome Measure, CORE-OM). These patients were seen by 119 therapists, which indicates that on average each therapist treated 91 patients in this study, far exceeding the sample sizes (and power) of therapist effects in RCTs and even the naturalistic studies reviewed by Baldwin and Imel (2013). In terms of sample size (number of therapists and number of patients per therapist), this study is exemplary. Another exemplary feature of this study was that patients were quasi-randomly assigned to therapists: "In most cases, patients were allocated to the next available therapist" (p.537). An MLM model was used to estimate therapist effects, using the pretreatment CORE-OM as a covariate (grand mean centered only, which creates residualized gain scores in the typical way). The CORE-OM also has risk and nonrisk items, and various models incorporated these variables into the model as well. They also used some sophisticated variations of MLM for special aspects of the data.

Therapist effects without considering risk caseload was .078; that is, almost 8% of the variability in outcomes was due to therapists. However, risk caseload accounted for some of the therapist effects (i.e., therapists with patients with more risk had slightly poorer outcomes), reducing the therapist effects to 0.066. However, therapist effects were larger for patients with greater initial nonrisk severity; for more distressed patients, therapist effects increased to 0.10.

Saxon and Barkham (2012) displayed therapist effects in an understandable way by use of a caterpillar plot, shown in Figure 9.2. In this figure, the outcomes of the 119 therapists are shown as residuals from the average outcome, ranked from least effective (negative residuals, which indicates below-average outcomes) to most effective (positive residual, which indicates above-average performance). Of course, there are errors in estimating the effectiveness of individual therapists because, as has been discussed, the outcome of individual patients is due to factors unrelated to the skill of the therapist such as various patient characteristics (n.b., Saxon & Barkham

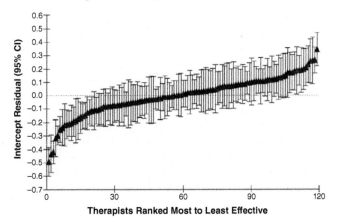

FIGURE 9.2 Intercept residuals for therapists ranked with 95% confidence intervals. From Saxon, D., & Barkham, M. (2012). Patterns of therapist variability: Therapist effects and the contribution of patient severity and risk. *Journal of Consulting and Clinical Psychology, 80,* 535–546. Reprinted with permission.

modeled some of these, including patient severity), extra-patient events (employer closes business and all employees become unemployed, a series of terrorists attacks occur geographically proximate to the patient; there is civil unrest due to an unpopular government), unreliability of measurement, and so forth. Such error generally is greatest when the number of patients per therapist is low. In Figure 9.2, the error is depicted by including the 95% confidence intervals for the estimate of each individual therapist's effectiveness. Clearly, there are sizable error of estimates here, and there is much overlap of the confidence intervals for neighboring therapists. However, the most-effective therapists are clearly superior to the less-effective therapists, a point to which we will return soon.

Meta-Analytic Findings

There are two meta-analyses of naturalistic studies of therapist effects: Baldwin and Imel (2013) and Johns et al. (2019), which also examined RCTs as discussed previously. The magnitude of the therapist effect for each meta-analysis will be reviewed briefly.

In the Baldwin and Imel (2013) meta-analysis, 17 naturalistic studies were reviewed. The mean number of therapists in these studies was approximately 59, with a mean of 13.4 patients per therapist, which is considerably larger than the sample size for RCTs (see Table 9.4). The ICCs for these studies ranged from 0.00 to 0.55, with an aggregate, using appropriate methods for ICCs, was 0.07, considerably larger than the ICC of 0.03 for RCTS found in this same meta-analysis. An ICC of 0.07 is equivalent to a SMD of 0.55, which is moderately large and impressive given that, as previously mentioned, psychotherapy versus no treatment has produced an SMD of around 0.80.

Johns et al. (2019) found an additional 17 naturalistic studies published between 2012 and 2016 inclusively that estimated therapist effects. Again, sample size was large, with a mean number of therapists in these studies of 218.6 and a mean

number of patients per therapist of 52.6 (see Table 9.4). In their meta-analysis, the estimates of therapist effects did not differ materially whether the effects were weighted by number of therapists, number of patients, or number of patients per therapist. The estimate of therapist effects for the 17 studies was 0.05, which is equivalent to an SMD of 0.46, which is a moderately large effect. Given the two studies found similar values for therapist effects (viz., 0.07 and 0.05) and the studies did not overlap, a reasonable estimate of therapist effects in naturalistic settings is 0.06.

Interpretation of Therapist Effects in Naturalistic Settings

As expected, therapist effects in naturalistic settings are larger than they are in RCTs. In RCTs, the interpretation of therapist effects was guided by comparison to other factors, many of which were investigated in RCTs. In naturalistic settings, it is important to gauge the magnitude of therapist effects by examining the implication for patient outcomes.

In the Saxon and Barkham (2012) study of 119 therapists, as described earlier, the therapist effect was about 0.07, a figure that was approximately equal to the aggregate therapist effect in Baldwin and Imel (2013). Saxon and Barkham identified 19 therapists as being least effective (as defined by their 95% CIs not containing zero). Of the 1704 patients treated by these 19 therapists, 786 recovered (a recovery rate of 46%). However, had these 1704 patients been treated by the *average* therapist – not even the most-effective therapist – an additional 265 patients would have recovered, as the average therapist produced a recovery rate of 62%. Clearly, the average therapist would have benefited these patients to a much greater extent than the least-effective therapists, demonstrating that 7% of the variability in therapists makes an important difference to patients being treated by those therapists.

As another example, consider the naturalistic study of Wampold and Brown (2005), who examined the outcomes of 6,146 patients in a managed-care network seen by 581 therapists. In this sample, the estimate of therapist effects was 0.05, about the same magnitude as that found in the Johns et al. (2019) meta-analysis. For each therapist, they examined the first half of the therapists' case load and ranked the therapists from most effective to least effective, based on their outcomes. They then examined the performance of the therapists for patients in the second half of their caseload, which constitutes a cross-validation strategy. For those therapists who had treated more than 18 patients (at least 9 in the original sample and more than 9 in the cross-validation sample), the results were quite dramatic. The effect size, in the cross-validated sample, for the top quartile of therapists was 2.5 times as great as the bottom quartile; the proportion of patients experiencing reliable change was more than 1.5 times as great for the top quartile than the bottom quartile. Keeping in mind that this is a cross-validation strategy (i.e., ability to predict therapist effectiveness in the future), a relatively modest therapist effect (5% of the variability in outcomes due to therapist) produces dramatically different outcomes when the more-effective and the less-effective therapists are compared.

There are a number of analyses in these naturalistic studies that add to and clarify the conclusion that to a large and important extent the outcomes of psychotherapy are due to the particular therapist. As mentioned earlier, Saxon and Barkham (2012) found that the variability in outcomes due to therapists was greater when initial severity was greater. In that study, therapist effects ranged from 1% to 10% based on initial non-risk severity, indicating that therapist effects are larger for more difficult patients. The effect of patient severity on therapist outcomes has been detected in studies where it has been examined (e.g., Firth et al., 2015). Not surprisingly, therapist effects increase over the course of therapy (Firth et al., 2015; Goldberg et al., 2018; Saxon et al., 2017), as the longer the therapy, the greater the magnitude of therapist effects. This effect is illustrated in Figure 9.3 that shows recovery rate for above average, average, and below average therapists conditioned on the number of sessions at discharge, as presented by Saxon et al. (2017). Clearly, as the number of sessions increases, therapist effects also increase. What is interesting – and important – is that the longer patients of the above-average therapists are treated, the greater the recovery rate. Presumably, patients who stay longer in treatment are more difficult to treat, but with the above-average therapists the patients continue to improve, whereas for the below-average therapists, the utility of additional sessions may be negative (see also Goldberg et al., 2018). It seems that the skills of effective therapists become more useful as the difficulty of the patient increases and the length of treatment increases.

There is another important implication that can be drawn from naturalistic studies in particular settings. The case has been made that therapist effects in naturalistic settings are due to the variability in the manner in which treatments are delivered (Crits-Christoph et al., 1991; Crits-Christoph & Mintz, 1991) as opposed to the relatively smaller therapist effects in RCTs, where treatment delivery is standardized. This is a reasonable conjecture, and one that has some evidence to support it (Crits-Christoph et al., 1991). However, there are a few studies of outcomes in naturalistic settings in which treatment is standardized and delivered in a manner that is comparable to that of RCTs. Laska et al. (2013) examined outcomes in a PTSD specialty clinic in which all therapists were trained to provide an evidence-based treatment (cognitive processing therapy) by two nationally recognized trainers and then were supervised by one of the trainers. Despite conditions similar to RCTs (training and supervision in an evidence-based treatment), 12% of the variability in outcomes was due to therapists. Firth et al. (2015) studied psychological well-being practitioners (PWPs) trained to provide protocol guided low-intensity treatment within England's Improved Access to Psychological Therapies (IAPT) program and found that 6–7% of the variability in outcome was due to the PWPs and that more effective PWPs "achieved almost double the change per treatment session" (p. 54). It appears that standardization of treatment and protocol adherence are not sufficient to eliminate therapist effects in naturalistic settings.

CHARACTERISTICS AND ACTIONS OF EFFECTIVE THERAPISTS

To this point, it has been well established that therapist effects exist in RCTs and in naturalistic settings. This conclusion is not much different from the previous edition chapter on Therapist Effects (viz., Baldwin & Imel, 2013). What has changed dramatically since then is that much more is known about the characteristics and actions of effective therapists. Of course, questions about the characteristics and actions of effective therapists are important because knowing what makes an effective therapist will (hopefully) lead to better training, therapist improvement, and more-effective mental health services. As was the case for therapist effects, understanding the methods for identifying the characteristics and actions of effective therapists is critical to the appropriate identification of characteristics and actions of therapists. Consequently, we begin with a methodological discussion, which illustrates the appropriate way to understand and test therapist effects.

Multilevel Models with Therapist Level Predictors

Adding Therapist-Level Predictors

To identify the characteristics and actions of effective therapists, we return to the MLM used to estimate therapist effects:

$$Y_{ij} = \gamma_{00} + \gamma_{10}\left(x_{ij} - \bar{x}_j\right) + \gamma_{01}\left(\bar{x}_j - \bar{x}\right) + \left[\sigma_t^2 + \sigma_e^2\right]$$

which predicts outcome for the ith patient of the jth therapist, adjusting for the pretreatment scores at both the patient and therapist level. For the estimate of therapist effects, we were interested in the random effects σ_t^2 and σ_e^2, which were

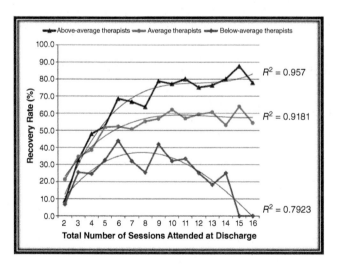

FIGURE 9.3 Statistical recovery rates for above average, average and below average therapists, for patients who attended 2–16 sessions. From Saxon, D., Firth, N., & Barkham, M. (2017). The relationship between therapist effects and therapy delivery factors: Therapy modality, dosage, and noncompletion. *Administration and Policy in Mental Health, 44*, 705–715. Reprinted with permission.

needed to calculate the ICC for therapist effects. What is needed to identify the characteristics and actions of effective therapists in this model is a term at the therapist level that would predict outcome. This term, which typically would be a fixed effect, would reflect some aspect of the therapist that would be related to outcome. Suppose that we believe that years of experience of the therapist, denoted by w_j (experience of therapist j), accounts for outcome – more experienced therapists would have better outcomes. Accordingly, the basic therapist effect MLM would be modified as follows (ignoring how w_j might be centered):

$$Y_{ij} = \gamma_{00} + \gamma_{10}\left(x_{ij} - \bar{x}_j\right) + \gamma_{01}\left(\bar{x}_j - \bar{x}\right) + \gamma_{02}w_j + \left[\sigma_t^2 + \sigma_e^2\right]$$

If the coefficient γ_{02} (subscript 02 denotes second variable at the therapist level) is positive and significantly greater than zero, then experience makes a difference in that more experienced therapists have better outcomes. Experience has been examined and we look at those results later (e.g., Goldberg, Rousmaniere et al., 2016). This strategy works appropriately for therapist variables that are measured directly, and we will review several studies that have used this strategy.

It is often the case that a process variable is measured during the course of therapy and its importance is assessed by estimating its association with outcome. The most widely studied process variable is alliance, and the association of alliance, measured relatively early in therapy, with outcome is well established (Flückiger et al., 2018; Flückiger et al., 2012; Horvath et al., 2011). However, the alliance is a dyadic construct, in the sense that it is created by therapists and patients working together (Hatcher & Barends, 2006; Horvath, 2017). That is to say, the strength of the alliance is due to the contributions of both the therapist and the patient (e.g., Mallinckrodt, 1991). The simple alliance–outcome correlation treats the alliance as the total of the therapist and patient contributions. The potency of the alliance may be due to what the therapist contributes. In this perspective, more effective therapists are able to create strong alliances with a range of patients, and their skill in forming alliances with difficult patients is what is important for outcome. In this case, it is the therapist-level variable (therapist ability to form alliances) that would be predictive of outcomes. On the other hand, it could be the patient's contribution that is important. Some patients come to therapy with reasonably good attachment styles, are motivated to collaborate and work with the therapist, and do not have personality characteristics that might complicate the relationship with the therapist. If it is these patients who are able to form a good alliance with their therapist and who make use of the alliance to produce the benefits of therapy, regardless of what the therapist does to contribute to the alliance (see Bohart & Tallman, 1999; Bohart & Wade, 2013), then the alliance–outcome association would be due to the contribution of the patient.

To determine if it is the therapist contribution to a process that is important for therapy outcomes, the therapist and patient contribution to outcomes must be disaggregated. This can be accomplished with MLM by including two additional terms, one for therapist contribution and one for patient contribution. Here we use the label z to denote the variable alliance, giving the equation for disaggregating patient and therapist contribution to the alliance (see Baldwin et al., 2007), which we will explain in some detail:

$$Y_{ij} = \gamma_{00} + \gamma_{10}\left(x_{ij} - \bar{x}_j\right) + \gamma_{01}\left(\bar{x}_j - \bar{x}\right) + \gamma_{20}\left(z_{ij} - \bar{z}_j\right) + \gamma_{02}\left(\bar{z}_j - \bar{z}\right) + \left[\sigma_t^2 + \sigma_e^2\right]$$

The two terms added to the standard therapist effect MLM equation have the coefficients γ_{20} and γ_{02}, representing the patient and therapist contributions to the alliance, respectively (the subscript 2 is used as they are the second variables at each level, the first being the pretreatment scores). The patient contribution variable is formed by taking the difference of alliance score for the ith patient of the jth therapist (i.e., z_{ij}) and the mean of the alliance scores for his or her therapist (i.e., $\bar{z}_j$); in this way, this variable represents the variability of patient alliance scores within therapists. The estimate of γ_{20} is based on pooling over all the therapists; a statistically significant estimate of γ_{20} would indicate that patients of a particular therapist with higher alliance scores than other patients of the same therapist would also have better outcomes.

The therapist contribution to the alliance is formed by taking the difference of the mean alliance score for each therapist (i.e., $\bar{z}_j$), which represents on average how high the alliance scores are for each therapist across all of his or her patients, and the grand mean of the alliance scores (i.e., $\bar{z}$). This variable represents variability among the therapists with regard to the alliance in that some therapists generally form better alliances with their patients than other therapists. A statistically significant (and positive) estimate γ_{02} would indicate that those therapists who generally produce higher alliances across their patients would also have patients with better outcomes. In that way, the therapist contribution to the alliance would characterize more effective therapists.

At this juncture, it is important to note that the identification of therapist characteristics and actions using the method described here is an association – that is, it could be revealed that some therapist characteristic is *associated* with outcomes. This logic (and language) is similar to what is used in ordinary least squares regression. Most of the evidence for characteristics and actions of effective therapists is derived from naturalistic data, but even when the data is from an RCT, the results are not experimental. Said another way, characteristics and actions of therapists are not experimentally manipulated, which limits our understanding of causality.

Example of Disaggregating Patient and Therapist Contributions

Clearly, the models that disaggregate therapist and patient contributions to a process variable are complex (and we have presented the most basic model) but are essential to identifying a therapist's contribution to various psychotherapy processes that are associated with outcome. To illustrate the therapist–patient disaggregation method, we summarize the first study that used MLM disaggregation to examine the contributions of the patient and therapist to the alliance using the method described previously. In this study, Baldwin et al. (2007) examined the outcomes of 331 patients who were treated by 80 therapists. The dataset was obtained from the Research Consortium of Counseling and Psychological Services in Higher Education. Psychological functioning was measured by the Outcome Questionnaire 45 (OQ-45) at the beginning of treatment and at the end of treatment; alliance, from the perspective of the patient, was assessed with the Working Alliance Inventory (WAI) early in therapy.

The correlation of WAI and the post-treatment OQ-45 was –0.24, which is in the neighborhood of the magnitude of the alliance–outcome correlation found in meta-analyses (Flückiger et al., 2018; Horvath et al., 2011). As expected, the pretreatment OQ scores were correlated to posttreatment scores at both the patient and therapist levels. Moreover, the ICC for this sample, adjusting for pretreatment scores, was 0.03, which is smaller than typically found for naturalistic settings (see above).

Using the MLM model described earlier, which disaggregated the patient and therapist contribution to the alliance, it was found that the therapist contribution to the alliance predicted outcome ($\gamma_{02} = -0.33, p < .01$) but the patient contribution did not ($\gamma_{20} = -0.08$, ns). In this study, it was the therapist contribution to the alliance that was important for outcome – therapists who generally were better able to form alliances with their patients generally had better outcomes, as illustrated in Figure 9.4. Interestingly, variability within therapists did not predict outcome – that is, patients with a higher alliance with their therapist did not have better outcomes than patients with a lower alliance with the same therapist. The ICC, which was 0.03 when alliance was not modeled, dropped to 0.001, suggesting that therapists' differential ability to form an alliance with their clients was responsible almost entirely for the

differential outcomes produced by the therapists. Although this is a naturalistic study, the results suggest that the ability to form an alliance across a range of patients is a skill that characterizes effective therapists.

A related way to understand therapist effects is through random slope models (Adelson & Owen, 2012). Random slope models examine whether the relationship between a predictor variable (e.g., alliance) and an outcome variable (e.g., therapy outcomes) varies across therapists. That is, in random slopes models, each therapist is considered to have their own unique regression line for the association between alliance and outcome for their clients in their caseload. In these models, the assumption is that the association between the predictor and outcome might not be consistent across therapists. In contrast, by ignoring this assumption, researchers assume that the association between the predictor and outcome is uniform across therapists. Clearly, this assumption is testable and should be examined to better contextualize the results. For instance, Owen et al. (2015) found that trainees did not generally improve in their client outcomes over the course of their training; however, there was significant variability across trainees. That is, some trainees did not change in their client outcomes, some improved and then leveled off, whereas others started to improve and then decreased. These different trajectories can be detected through a random slopes model.

Review of Therapist Studies

Now that the basics of the methods used to identify the characteristics and actions of effective therapist have been presented, we review the evidence for various factors that explain how some therapists achieve better outcomes than others. To be included in this review, it was required that the research use a multilevel approach to model therapy outcomes comprising a variable at the therapist level, as discussed earlier (or other appropriate method, as noted in Tables 9.5 to 9.10) and that considers therapists as a random factor, thereby permitting generalization. In these studies, we focused primarily on main effects, as various interactions were not predicted and were difficult to interpret. We also classified the variables examined into six categories: (a) therapist demographics/experience (Table 9.5), (b) characteristics of professional practice (Table 9.6), (c) attitudes toward practice/features of practice/therapist personality (Table 9.7), (d) therapist contribution to process variables (obtained by disaggregating therapist and patient contributions to the process) (Table 9.8), (e) relative effectiveness on variables within therapists (Table 9.9), and (f) measurement of therapist skill outside of therapy with a performance task (Table 9.10). There have been various ways to classify therapist variables (Beutler et al., 2004) and our classification made the most sense given the state of the literature but the categories are useful only in so far as they lend some organization to the presentation; in that way, the classes do not hold any particular importance theoretically. It should also be noted that the quality of the research and the presentation of the research methods vary considerably, making many conclusions tentative. As well, because of the variety of the methods and the nature of the coefficients reported, quantitative syntheses were not possible.

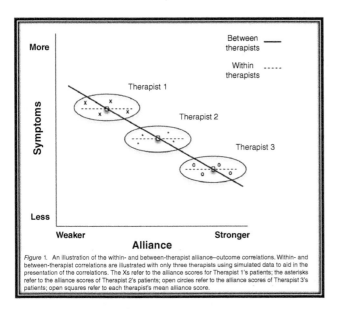

Figure 1. An illustration of the within- and between-therapist alliance–outcome correlations. Within- and between-therapist correlations are illustrated with only three therapists using simulated data to aid in the presentation of the correlations. The Xs refer to the alliance scores for Therapist 1's patients; the asterisks refer to the alliance scores of Therapist 2's patients; open circles refer to the alliance scores of Therapist 3's patients; open squares refer to each therapist's mean alliance score.

FIGURE 9.4   Alliance disaggregation.

Note: Reprinted with permission from the American Psychological Association.

Therapist Demographics/Therapist Experience

The evidence for several therapist demographic variables is presented in Table 9.5. Most of these studies entered the demographic variable at the therapist level of analysis. The age of the therapist, with one exception, did not predict the outcomes achieved by therapists. Despite a common belief that female therapists are more nurturing and consequently more effective, there is no evidence of a therapist gender effect. There is no evidence of a therapist ethnicity effect, either. Yet, even those studies that are sufficiently powered to detect an effect have not supported therapist ethnicity or client–therapist ethnic matching as having a meaningful relationship to therapy outcomes (Hayes et al., 2016; Huey et al., 2014; Maramba & Nagayama Hall, 2002).

Age and therapy experience are, of course, confounded, as older therapists usually have more experience. However, experience is a critically important variable to examine. In many domains, such as chess, musical performance, athletics, and surgery, there exist those whose performance is superior to others – that is, there are *experts* (Ericsson et al., 2018; Ericsson & Lehmann, 1996). One of the hallmarks of expertise is gradual improvement in performance over the course of one's career (Ericsson & Lehmann, 1996). Tracey et al. (2014) discussed aspects of psychotherapy that make it difficult to achieve expertise (see also Shanteau, 1992), although it seems that expertise in psychotherapy is controversial (Goodyear et al., 2017; Hill et al., 2017; Shanteau & Weiss, 2014).

Traditionally, the effects of therapist experience have been assessed cross-sectionally. In such designs, the outcomes of therapists at some point in time are assessed and therapist experience, typically expressed in number of years in therapy practice, is entered as a therapist-level variable. Cross-sectional designs ask the question of whether more experienced therapists at a given point in time have better (or poorer) outcomes than less-experienced therapists. The problem with such designs is that several confounding variables become troublesome. More experienced therapists were trained in a different era than younger therapists, and commonly more experienced therapists may assist/supervise younger therapists (Budge et al., 2013). As shown in Table 9.5, with one exception, all of

TABLE 9.5   Therapist Demographics/Therapist Experience

Therapist variable	Studies with significant results	Notes	Nonsupportive studies (null findings)	Notes
Age	Anderson et al., 2009	Older therapists had better outcomes.	Chow et al., 2015 Huppert et al., 2001 Wampold et al., 2005 Delgadillo et al., 2018	
Gender			Chow et al., 2015 Wampold et al., 2005 Anderson et al., 2009 Owen et al., 2014 Owen et al., 2009 Schöttke et al., 2017	
Experience	Goldberg, Rousmaniere et al., 2016	Longitudinal. Over time, therapist effectiveness decreased.	Chow et al., 2015	Cross-sectional
	Goldberg, Babins-Wagner et al., 2016	Longitudinal. Over time, therapists became more effective in an agency that used deliberate practice.	Erekson et al., 2017 Wampold et al., 2005	Longitudinal, mostly null findings Cross-sectional
	Owen et al., 2014	Cross-sectional; Therapists with more couple therapy experience had better outcomes in couple therapy.	Delgadillo et al., 2018 Kraus et al., 2016	Cross-sectional Cross-sectional
	Owen et al., 2016	Longitudinal; Trainees' effectiveness increased by a small amount over time, but only for nondistressed patients.	Delgadillo et al., in press	Cross-sectional
Therapist Ethnicity			Beard et al., 2019	

the cross-sectional studies showed no effect for experience. Owen et al. (2014) found that therapists with more experience in couples therapy had better outcomes in couple therapy.

In recent years, there have been several longitudinal examinations of experience in which the outcomes of therapists are examined over the course of therapists' careers. In one study that examined outcomes of therapists at a particular clinic over their careers (up to 18 years), it was found that therapists actually produced poorer outcomes over time, although the size of the effect was small (Goldberg, Rousmaniere et al., 2016). Using data from the same clinic, Erekson et al. (2017) compared outcomes of trainees over the course of their training and found that for the most part outcomes did not improve during this time, which is a quite disheartening statement about training. Similarly, Hill et al. (2015) also did not find changes in client-rated symptomology over the course of 12 to 42 months of training, but trainees did gain in other attributes (e.g., alliance, real relationship). On the other hand, Owen et al. (2016) found that trainees did improve slightly over the course of training, but only for less distressed patients. Finally, in an agency focused on improving outcomes of therapists by using deliberate practice, therapists did improve during their time at the agency (Goldberg, Babins-Wagner et al., 2016).

Neither the cross-sectional nor the longitudinal studies of therapist expertise provide compelling evidence that therapists become more effective as they gain more experience. This result challenges the field to understand why therapist experience does not lead to improved performance, a subject we address later.

Characteristics of Professional Practice

Three variables were classified as characteristics of professional practice: therapist profession (psychologist, counselor, social worker, psychiatrist), amount of supervision received, and size of therapist caseload. None of these therapist variables were predictive of therapist outcomes, as shown in Table 9.6.

Practice Characteristics/Attitudes Toward Practice/ Therapist Personality

A number of variables in the area of practice characteristics/ attitudes toward practice/therapist personality have been investigated, as shown in Table 9.7. Unfortunately, many of these variables were only examined in a single study, and many of the significant findings were not predicted (or predicted to be in the opposite direction). Consequently, we discuss only those variables that have relatively strong evidence or are theoretically or clinically important. Hopefully, by the next edition of the volume, there will be replications of several of these findings.

The first variable of importance is the theoretical orientation of the therapist. Generally, the evidence, all from naturalistic settings, is that the theoretical orientation of the therapist is not a significant predictor of outcome. This conclusion is not surprising as it is consistent with RCTs and research in naturalistic settings, which have found no differences among theoretical approaches (Wampold & Imel, 2015).

There are a series of studies examining therapist effects within the context of routine outcome monitoring and feedback (de Jong & de Goede, 2015; de Jong et al., 2012; Lutz et al., 2015). When feedback was provided to therapists, de Jong and de Goede (2015) found that more-effective therapists reported better person–organization fit and reported greater promotion focus than less-effective therapists; on the other hand, therapists who reported greater prevention focus had poorer outcomes. Two studies found that more positive therapist attitudes toward feedback were associated with better outcomes in a feedback context (de Jong et al., 2012; Lutz et al., 2015). Whereas it has been shown that feedback provides a modest improvement in outcomes, particularly for not-on-track patients (Lambert et al., 2018), the benefits seem to accrue to therapists who value and have a positive attitude toward feedback and have a better relationship with their organization.

There are a number of studies investigating constructs with different names and definitions, which might be categorized as *professional humility*, that appear to be characteristics of effective therapists. Nissen-Lie and colleagues (Nissen-Lie et al., 2013; Nissen-Lie et al., 2015) found that therapists who expressed *professional self-doubt* (PSD), a construct derived from items on a therapist questionnaire that "reflected self-questioning about professional efficacy in treating clients" (Nissen-Lie et al., 2013), predicted changes in clients' interpersonal functioning. Although the evidence for PSD is equivocal (on other outcome variables in the Nissen-Lie studies and in other studies; Odyniec et al., 2019 no effects

TABLE 9.6 Characteristics of Professional Practice

Professional characteristic	Studies with significant results	Notes	Nonsupportive studies (null findings)	Notes
Profession (e.g., psychologist, social worker, counselor)			Chow et al., 2015 Wampold et al., 2005 Kraus et al., 2016	
Amount of supervision received			Schöttke et al., 2017	
Caseload size			Chow et al., 2015 Anderson et al., 2009	

TABLE 9.7 Attitudes Toward Practice/Features of Practice/ Therapist Personality

Attitudes, feature, or personality	Studies with significant results	Notes	Nonsupportive studies (null findings)	Notes
Theoretical orientation	Schöttke et al., 2017	CBT therapists more effective than PD therapists, but only in single prediction models	Chow et al., 2015 Saxon et al., 2017 Anderson et al., 2009 Delgadillo et al., 2018	
Professional activities outside of delivering therapy	Chow et al. 2015	More-effective therapists engaged in more professional activities		
Big 5 Personality	Delgadillo et al., 2020	Psychological well-being practitioners (PWP) with above-average agreeableness had poorer outcomes. CBT therapists with above-average openness to experience had poor outcomes.	Delgadillo et al., 2020	For PWPs and CBT therapists, no other Big 5 personality factor was associated with outcome
Theoretical Integration			Chow et al., 2015	
Modesty	Ziem et al., 2019	Therapists who rate their patients less favorably had better outcomes.		
Humor style	Yonatan-Leus et al., 2018	Therapists with aggressive humor style had better outcomes.		
Honesty-humility	Yonatan-Leus et al., 2018	Therapists who reported greater honesty had poorer outcomes.		
Self-defeating humor; affiliative humor style, creativity, playfulness			Yonatan-Leus et al., 2018	
Person–organization fit	de Jong et al., 2015	Therapists with greater person–organization fit had better outcomes when feedback about patient progress was provided.		
Prevention focus	de Jong et al., 2015	Therapists with prevention focus had poorer outcomes for at-risk patients.		
Promotion focus	de Jong et al., 2015	Therapists with a promotion focus had better outcomes for at-risk patients when feedback was provided.		

(Continued)

TABLE 9.7 (CONTINUED)

Attitudes, feature, or personality	Studies with significant results	Notes	Nonsupportive studies (null findings)	Notes
Therapist expectations for long-term success	Connor et al., 2015	Therapists with greater expectations for long-term success has better outcomes.		
Therapist attitude toward feedback	Lutz et al., 2015 de Jong et al., 2012	Better attitudes toward feedback predicted better outcomes.		
Burnout–disengagement	Delgadillo et al., 2018	More burnout (disengaged type) had poorer outcomes.		
Burnout–exhaustion			Delgadillo et al., 2018	
Professional self-doubt (PSD)	Odyniec et al., 2019	In CBT, PSD was inversely related to change on interpersonal problems.	Odyniec et al., 2019	
	Nissen-Lie et al., 2013 Nissen-Lie et al., 2015	Therapist PSD predicts IIP. Interaction of PSD and self-affiliation on IIP (more change if therapist high on PSD also had self-affiliative introject).	Nissen-Lie et al., 2013	PSD does not predict GAP or GSI
Negative personal reactions (NPR)	Odyniec et al., 2019	In CBT, therapist NPR positively related to interpersonal problems.	Odyniec et al., 2019	In CBT, NPR had no effect on symptoms
	Nissen-Lie et al., 2013	Therapist NPR predicts IIP.	Nissen-Lie et al., 2013	NPR had no effect on GAF
Warm interpersonal style (WIS)			Nissen-Lie et al., 2013 Nissen-Lie et al., 2013	In CBT, WIS had no effect on symptoms WIS had no effect on GAF
Advanced relational skills (ARS)	Nissen-Lie et al., 2013	Therapist ARS predicted GAF negatively: The greater the ARS, the less change on GAF.		
	Nissen-Lie et al., 2013	Therapist ARS predicted IIP over PSD and NPR.		No effect on GSI
Attachment style	Schauenburg et al., 2010	Effect for interaction of attachment style and initial severity; better attachment security may be more beneficial for more distressed patients.	Schauenburg et al., 2010	No main effect for attachment styles
			Cologon et al., 2017	No main effect for attachment styles
Reflective functioning	Cologon et al., 2017	No main effect for attachment style but secure attachment compensated for deficit in reflective functioning.		

TABLE 9.7 (CONTINUED)

Attitudes, feature, or personality	Studies with significant results	Notes	Nonsupportive studies (null findings)	Notes
Reflective ability (understanding of theory and its relation to clinical practice)			Delgadillo et al., in press	Reflective ability, as rated by expert trainers, not associated with outcomes.
Mindfulness	Pereira et al., 2017	Therapist mindfulness was associated with better outcomes.		
Resilience	Pereira et al., 2017	When combined with mindfulness, therapist resilience was associated with outcome.		
Self-reported social skills			Anderson et al., 2009	

were found), PSD might well reflect a construct related to professional humility. There are other related constructs that have evidence from at least one study, including modesty (Ziem & Hoyer, 2019), and honesty-humility (Yonatan-Leus et al., 2018). Chow et al. (2015) found that therapists who spent more time outside of seeing patients in activities to improve performance (e.g., attending workshops, getting supervision, reviewing difficult cases) had better outcomes. It may well be that those therapists who question their ability to achieve optimal outcomes participate in activities to improve. As well, Delgadillo et al. (2018) found that therapists who were burned out in a disengaged manner (although not burnout from exhaustion) had poorer outcomes, which suggests that therapists who are not engaged to improve and who do not think about their work will have poorer outcomes. Despite professional humility as a desirable attribute, therapists who have long-term positive expectations for their patients have better outcomes (Connor & Callahan, 2015). Clearly, more consistent definitions of humility-related constructs are needed, as well as more research focused on how professional humility might lead to better outcomes, but these several studies suggest that therapists who are engaged, reflect on their practice, and seek ways to improve have better outcomes.

There is another converging finding in this area. Several studies found that various aspects of self-reported social skills or social style of the therapists did not predict the outcomes of therapists or had a complex relationship with outcome. Anderson et al. (2009) found that therapists' self-reported social skills, on a valid inventory of social skills, did not predict therapists' outcomes. Nissen-Lie et al. (2013) found that therapist self-report of a warm-interpersonal style also was not associated with outcome. Therapist report of advanced

relational skills (ARS) had a complex relationship with outcome (Nissen-Lie et al., 2013). ARS was inversely related to observer-rated global functioning (GAF) scores – the greater the therapist ARS score, the less change their patients experienced on the GAF. On the other hand, ARS predicted scores on the Inventory of Interpersonal Problems (IIP) over PSD. It appears that therapists' report of aspects of their social skills is not a reliable predictor of their outcomes.

The only other variable that has generated investigation by more than one research group is therapist attachment style. There were no main effects for this variable (Cologon et al., 2017; Schauenburg et al., 2010) but there was an interaction effect that suggested that a more secure attachment of therapists might lead to better outcomes with more distressed patients (Schauenburg et al., 2010). Given the importance of attachment styles in functioning, the lack of main effects is surprising. Delgadillo et al. (2020) investigated the effect of Big Five personality factors on outcome, but the few significant results were not predicted and were difficult to interpret. It is noteworthy that there have been so few investigations of therapist personality vis-à-vis effectiveness.

Therapist Contributions to Process Variables via Disaggregation

As discussed earlier, various process variables can be disaggregated into therapist and patient contributions. We discussed at some length Baldwin et al.'s (2007) disaggregation of the alliance, where it was found that the therapist's contribution to the alliance predicted outcome – that is, therapists who on average had better alliances with their patients also had superior outcomes. As seen in Table 9.8, there have been several studies that replicated the finding that the therapist contribution to

TABLE 9.8 Therapist Contribution to Process Variables Assessed via Disaggregation

Process variable	Studies with significant results	Notes	Nonsupportive studies (null findings)	Notes
Autonomous motivation	Zuroff et al., 2017			
Controlled motivation	Zuroff et al., 2017			
Rogerian conditions	Barnicot et al., 2014 Zuroff et al., 2010			
Alliance	Baldwin et al., 2007 Zilcha-Mano et al., 2015	For BDI	Zilcha-Mano et al., 2015	For HRSD
	Dinger et al., 2008	The influence of therapist alliance varied by therapist.	Falkenström et al., 2014	
	Crits-Christoph et al., 2018	Used instrument variable analysis.	Uckelstam et al., 2020	Used one-with-many design
	Crits-Christoph et al., 2009	Therapist contributions to alliance related to outcomes but relationship is curvilinear: Very low and very high therapist alliance associated with poorer outcomes.		
	Marcus et al., 2009	Used one-with-many design		
	Huppert et al., 2014	CBT for panic, therapist contribution to alliance was predictive only in few instances.	Huppert et al., 2014	CBT for Panic, most results did not find support for therapist contribution to alliance but no significant therapist effects on outcome or alliance was found.
	Owen et al., 2014	In couple therapy	Crits-Christoph et al., 2011	Therapist contribution to alliance not related to outcome.
	Hagen et al., 2016	Therapist contribution to task/goal dimension of alliance predicted outcome in EX/RP for OCD.	Hagen et al., 2016	Therapist contribution to bond dimension did not predict outcome.
Adherence			Boswell et al., 2013 Tschuschke et al., 2015	CBT for Panic Various forms of therapy
Rated competence			Boswell et al., 2013 Delgadillo et al., 2020	CBT for Panic CBT and psychological well-being practitioners
Cultural concealment	Drinane et al., 2018	Therapists whose clients concealed aspects of their culture had poorer outcomes.		

the alliance was associated with better outcomes, as well as a few that have failed to replicate this finding.

Interestingly, therapist effect in the alliance is one area in which a meta-analysis has been conducted. In the typical alliance-outcome studies, the correlation of the alliance and outcome does not disaggregate therapist and patient contributions. However, if there are many therapists and few patients per therapist, then this total correlation is due mostly to differences among therapists; on the other hand, if there are few therapists and many patients per therapist, then the total correlation is due mostly to differences among patients. Del Re et al. (2012; 2021) used the patient to therapist ratio (PTR) as a moderating variable in two meta-analyses and found that indeed it predicted the size of the total correlation, as would be expected if therapist contribution to the alliance was important.

Given several studies supporting the notion that therapist contribution to the alliance is associated with outcome and the meta-analyses that produced confirmatory evidence, the importance of the therapist contributions to the alliance cannot be dismissed, despite studies that have not replicated the result. However, as usual, more (and better) research is needed.

Another area in which the total correlation has been examined is adherence and competence. Webb et al. (2010) conducted a meta-analysis and found that neither adherence nor competence predicted outcome in RCTs, but again this was a total correlation (i.e., adherence and competence measured on a case-by-case basis not at the therapist level). We could only find three studies which disaggregated adherence and competence and neither found evidence of a therapist effect – that is, it was not the case that therapists who generally were more adherent or rated as more competent on average also had better outcomes (Boswell et al., 2013; Delgadillo et al., 2020; Tschuschke et al., 2015). The Boswell et al. study

was noteworthy in that it was conducted under controlled conditions in an RCT. It is interesting that in two studies (i.e., Boswell et al., 2013; Delgadillo et al., 2020), therapist rated competence was not related to outcome, tilting at our notion of what it means to be competent at therapy.

In several interesting studies (Barnicot et al., 2014; Zuroff et al., 2010; 2017) disaggregated variables related to Rogerian conditions as well as motivation (autonomous and controlled) related to relational support. In all instances, therapist contributions to the process variables predicted outcome and lend support to importance of therapist contributions to therapy processes, in particular the therapist use of Rogerian principles.

Relative Effectiveness Within Therapists

There are a few studies that have examined differences in outcomes of the same therapist with various types of patients, many of which used the random slope method discussed earlier. An important issue is whether some therapists have better or worse outcomes with racial/ethnic minority (REM) patients. If the racial/ethnic status of the patients are irrelevant to a therapist outcome but outcomes differ by therapist, it can be said that there is a general competence factor. However, if some therapists get poorer outcomes with their REM patients than with other patients, then one could say therapists have a cultural competence deficit. The methods to investigate this disparity determination are complex but several studies, as shown in Table 9.9, reveal that there are differential effects with REM patients, as some therapist have better outcomes with REM patients than their other patients and some have poorer outcomes with REM patients than with other patients (Hayes et al., 2016; Hayes et al., 2015; Imel, Baldwin, et al.,

TABLE 9.9 Relative Effectiveness Within Therapists

Effectiveness variable	Studies with significant results	Notes	Nonsupportive studies (null findings)	Notes
Psychotropic medications	Wampold et al., 2005	Patients of more effective psychotherapists had larger medication effects.		
Ethnic minority patients	Hayes et al., 2015 Imel et al., 2011 Larrison et al., 2011 Kivlighan et al., 2019 Hayes et al., 2016	Differential effects with REM patients (some therapists are more effective with REM versus other patients and some less effective with REM).		
Gender and intersectionality	Kivlighan et al., 2019	Therapist differential effects for gender and intersectionality.		
Different types of problems	Kraus et al., 2011	Some therapists had better outcome with some types of problems.	Kraus et al., 2016 Nissen-Lie et al., 2016	

2011; Kivlighan et al., 2019; Larrison et al., 2011; Owen et al., 2012). The importance of therapist cultural competence was supported by using the disaggregation method as well (Drianane et al., 2018, see Table 10.8; see also Owen et al., 2017). There is also some evidence for disparity for gender and intersectionality, as seen in Table 9.9.

An interesting question is whether some therapists obtain better outcomes with different types of problems – some therapists might have expertise in treating anxiety disorders for instance but have relatively poorer outcomes with depressive disorders. There was some evidence for this (Kraus et al., 2011) but later studies have not found such an effect (Kraus et al., 2016; Nissen-Lie et al., 2016), as shown in Table 9.9, but this is an area that needs further investigation.

Often patients have split care – psychotherapy from one clinician and psychotropic medication from a different clinician. Interestingly, there is some evidence that when the patients of more effective psychotherapists receive psychotropic medications from another clinician (primary care physician or psychiatrist), the effect of the medication is greater (Wampold & Brown, 2005), suggesting that the effective psychotherapists create positive expectations for medications.

Measurement of Therapist Skill Outside of Therapy Using a Performance Task

To this point, therapist variables have been assessed either from demographic information, therapist self-report of various characteristics of themselves, or by disaggregating process variables, which typically are derived from ratings of one of the therapy participants (e.g., an alliance measure completed by either the therapist or the patient). These strategies leave open what might at first glance seem like the most obvious way to determine what effective therapists do – observe them at work. According to this strategy, one would measure the outcomes of therapists and then observe their cases to identify the actions of the most effective therapists. As straightforward as that seems, it is problematic. What transpires in therapy is transactional in the sense that it is jointly determined by the two participants. The same therapist will appear differently with different patients – indeed, it has been shown that therapist adherence and competence are influenced to a large extent by the patient (Boswell et al., 2013; Imel, Baer et al., 2011) – an interpersonally aggressive patient will make the therapist appear less competent that he or she would have been with a motivated and agreeable patient. Of course, this is why in the disaggregation strategy process variables are averaged over all patients to yield a variable that reflects therapist skill or capacities.

One way to assess therapist skill, holding the patient constant, would be to have all the therapists in the study see the same patient. Of course, this is not feasible but Anderson and colleagues devised an ingenious way to approximate a standardized patient (Anderson et al., 2016; Anderson et al., 2016; Anderson et al., 2009). In the Anderson paradigm, therapists viewed videos of difficult patients and recorded their responses; the responses were then coded with a system that rated a set of skills, which was labeled *facilitative interpersonal skills* (FIS). The FIS included verbal fluency; hope and positive expectations; persuasiveness; emotional expression; warmth, acceptance, and understanding; empathy; alliance bond capacity; and alliance rupture-repair responsiveness. The question is whether the FIS total scores derived from the therapists' responses to the videos (averaged over all the skills and all stimulus videos) are associated with the outcomes of patients seen by the therapists.

The first study using the FIS involved a sample of 25 therapists who treated 1,141 clients in a setting where outcomes were measured with the Outcome Questionnaire-45 (Anderson et al., 2009). The FIS score for each of the 25 therapists was a statistically significant predictor of the outcomes retrospectively achieved by these therapists. This result is quite remarkable – it is the first time that therapists had been subjected to a performance task outside of therapy and found that it predicted the outcomes of the therapists.

This study was replicated in a prospective study by examining the FIS of beginning clinical psychology students and then predicting the outcomes achieved by the students more than one year in the future (Anderson et al., 2016). Replicating the previous finding, the FIS scores measured early in training predicted outcomes obtained when they began to see patients later in training. These results were also replicated in an RCT (Anderson et al., 2016).

Confirmatory evidence for interpersonal skills exhibited in a performance task was found using a very different task but a similar coding scheme. Schöttke et al. (2017) rated therapy-related interpersonal behavior (TRIB) of beginning psychotherapy trainees by using a scale that assessed the following domains: clear and positive communication; empathy and communicative attunement; respect and warmth; managing of criticism; and willingness of cooperate. TRIB was assessed in two contexts. In the first context, the trainees watched an emotionally provocative film and then discussed the film in a group (G) and the interpersonal behavior of each trainee was rated on the TRIB domains (TRIB-G). In the second context, the students participated in a structured interview (I) about clinical work and their responses were rated by experts with the same domains (TRIB-I). Scores on the TRIB-G and TRIB-I were then used to predict the outcomes of the trainees over subsequent years. The TRIB-G predicted therapist outcomes but TRIB-I did not.

The Anderson studies and the Schöttke et al. (2017) study, as well as some of the previous results, reveal something quite important. Self-reported social skills and social skills inferred from an interview show relatively little predictive validity for the outcomes of psychotherapy. On the other hand, in an interpersonally challenging situation, where affect is strong, the interpersonal skills of therapists displayed are robust predictors of outcome.

Interpretation of Evidence for Characteristic and Actions of Effective Therapists

The evidence for what characterizes effective therapists is best described as nascent. However, there are areas for which there is promising evidence. Evidence from challenge tests and disaggregation studies indicates that interpersonal skills in emotionally challenging contexts are a core feature of effective therapists. It also appears that attitudes toward professional practice that lead to efforts to improve also characterize effective therapists. Perhaps therapists with these attitudes develop the critical interpersonal skills. It seems to be that without efforts to improve, therapists do not become better therapists over the course of their careers. It is also clear that choice of theoretical orientation is not related to outcomes, although it may be the case that various therapeutic skills are implemented differently in different treatments. Particularly important is the emerging evidence that therapists' outcomes with racial/ethnic minority clients vary vis-à-vis their white clients; that is, some therapists achieve commendable outcomes with racial/ethnic minority clients but other therapists' outcomes with such clients lag behind their outcomes with white clients, creating health disparities at the therapist level (Imel et al., 2011; Hayes et al., 2016).

IMPLICATIONS FOR PSYCHOTHERAPY

Over most of the course of psychotherapy research, it was not well established that the outcomes in psychotherapy varied as a function of who delivered the psychotherapy. The estimation of therapist effects involves particular statistical methods, which although developed decades ago, have not been applied to psychotherapy research until relatively recently. At the present time, there are sufficient numbers of studies, in RCTs and in naturalistic settings, to conclude that therapist effects exist: Some therapists consistently achieve better outcomes than other therapists. In RCTs and naturalistic settings, the size of therapist effects are meaningful and important for clients and for understanding what are important factors leading to the benefits of psychotherapy.

Now that presence of therapist effects has been established, focus has turned appropriately to identifying the characteristics and actions of effective therapists. The evidence in this area is emerging, but it points to several promising areas: (a) interpersonal skills that are used in challenging interpersonal therapeutic situations, (b) professional attitudes that leads to efforts to improve, and (c) abilities to work with minority and culturally diverse clients.

The evidence derived from research on therapist effects has implications for research, practice, training, and mental health systems. We briefly discuss these areas.

Research Implications

There are two major implications of therapist effects for research. The first is that ignoring therapists in research is problematic for several reasons. Therapists are an important factor leading to the benefits of psychotherapy – many times more predictive of outcome than what type of therapy the therapist delivers, therapist adherence to the treatment protocol, or even whether the specific ingredients of the treatment are delivered. Ignoring therapist effects on outcomes is like ignoring the quality of the players on a basketball team and focusing on the style of play of the team (Wampold, 1997). Simply said, to understand how therapy works it is necessary to know what are the characteristics and actions of effective therapists. However, ignoring therapist effects also is problematic due to the fact that without a therapist factor in the model, treatment effects are overestimated and, furthermore, the effects of various process variables are not disaggregated into therapist and patient components, making interpretation of the process of psychotherapy ambiguous. The design and analysis of all psychotherapy research should include therapists.

Practice Implications

The evidence for the importance of the therapist in the practice of psychotherapy obligates the therapist to be accountable for the outcomes they achieve. Given the evidence reviewed that indicates that therapists, as a general rule, do not improve over the course of their careers, efforts need to be made to create environments that encourage improvement. First and foremost, it is impossible to know whether one is improving if the outcomes of psychotherapy are unknown – therefore, it is critical that therapists have access to information about the progress of their patients during therapy, a procedure known as routine outcome monitoring (see Chapter 4 in this volume). It appears that a mindset related to improvement characterizes more effective therapists: professional humility and a desire to improve (see Hook et al., 2017). However, the desire to improve is not sufficient. The interpersonal skills needed to produce better outcomes in therapy need to be honed over the course of one's career. Deliberate practice is an established method for achieving expertise in a number of areas (Ericsson et al., 2018; Ericsson & Lehmann, 1996), and there is preliminary evidence that therapeutic skills can be improved through the use of deliberate practice, with resulting improvement of outcomes (Chow et al., 2015; Goldberg, Babins-Wagner et al., 2016; Miller et al., 2018; Rousmaniere, 2016; Rousmaniere et al., 2017). Clearly, more knowledge about how therapists can improve their skills and achieve better outcomes is needed.

Interestingly, continuing education for therapists involves activities with little known connection to acquiring therapeutic skills (Taylor & Neimeyer, 2017). In the United States, the psychologist licensing examination (Examination for Professional Practice in Psychology) is designing and implementing a skills part in addition to the long used knowledge part (see https://www.asppb.net/page/EPPPPart2-Skills).

Lastly, there is growing evidence that mental health disparities in therapy outcomes are highly contingent on the therapist (Imel et al., 2011; Owen et al., 2012). Therapists would benefit from focusing on their level of cultural humility, especially in cases where there are value conflicts (Davis et al., 2018). Moreover, there is evidence that therapists' cultural comfort accounts for a significant proportion of variance in racial/ethnic therapy outcome disparities (Owen et al., 2017). In this case, cultural comfort is therapists' ability to be at ease and calm when discussing issues. Clearly, we need more research to better understand how to enhance therapists' multicultural orientation and how to reduce racial/ethnic (and other minority-identity based) disparities.

Training Implications

Given the evidence about the importance of interpersonal skills for producing the benefits of psychotherapy, therapist training programs should emphasize skill acquisition. Programs that primarily train therapists to follow manuals for a particular treatment approach and ignore the research that indicates that the interpersonal skills involved in delivering any treatment are critical to successful psychotherapy are not optimal. These two approaches – training therapists to deliver a treatment guided by a manual and training therapists to skillfully and strategically use interpersonal skills – are not exclusive. Indeed, they are both absolutely critical to successful therapy, and specific ingredients and common factors need to be integrated (Wampold & Ulvenes, 2019). For acquisition of interpersonal skills, deliberate practice of the skills associated with better outcomes is needed in training programs. It also appears that experience with and positive attitudes toward receiving feedback about patient progress leads to better outcomes, and consequently, therapist training should emphasize the importance of feedback.

The traditional criteria for selecting students for psychotherapy training programs, particularly those in college or university settings, involve indicators of academic performance, such as grades and scores on aptitude or achievement tests, letters of recommendation, and interviews, none of which have been shown to be related to therapeutic success. On the other hand, interpersonal skills demonstrated in challenging emotional situations, measured at the beginning of training, predicts outcomes of the trainees several years in the future (Anderson, McClintock et al., 2016; Schöttke et al., 2017), which suggests that these interpersonal skills should be used as criteria for admission into psychotherapy training programs.

Implications for Mental Health Systems

Therapists effects raises some thorny issues for managers of mental health systems and mental health policy makers. For many organizations, treatment guidelines and policy emphasize treatments – that is, particular treatments are recommended, and in some instances are mandated – despite the evidence that treatments differences are essentially nil. On the other hand, these guidelines neglect the importance of the therapeutic relationship and therapist expertise (Norcross & Wampold, 2019). Clearly, guidelines and policy should be in alignment with the research evidence on the importance of therapist effects and relationship skills.

Managers of mental health care are confronted with an issue about how to handle therapists who are underperforming. The evidence discussed in this chapter show clearly that some therapists consistently achieve poor outcomes, attenuating the overall effect of agencies and systems of care. That is to say, patients would benefit to a much greater extent if they were not assigned to those therapists evidencing poorer outcomes. Indeed, if these therapists were dismissed and new therapists were hired randomly, the average outcome of an agency would improve greatly (Imel et al., 2015). However, dismissing low-performing therapists may not be possible or even be in the best interests of the clinic or system. For example, if therapists feel that their outcomes will be used for employment decisions, morale may be jeopardized, cheating or gaming the system may occur, and burnout may be increased. However, simply providing therapists with information about their outcomes does not seem to lead to therapist improvement over time (Crits-Christoph et al., 2010; Tracey et al., 2014), and therefore information about therapist outcomes has to be used carefully to help underperforming therapists improve (Goldberg, Babins-Wagner et al., 2016).

TABLE 9.10   Measurement of Therapist Skill Outside of Therapy in a Performance Task

Therapist skill	Studies with significant results	Notes	Nonsupportive studies (null findings)	Notes
Facilitative Interpersonal Skill (FIS)	Anderson et al., 2016; Anderson et al., 2016; Anderson et al., 2009	Interpersonal skills demonstrated in response to difficult patient videos associated with outcome		
Therapy-related Interpersonal Behaviors (TRIB) in Group (TRIB-G)	Schöttke et al., 2017	Longitudinal; TRIB predicted outcomes up to 5 years after measurement, controlling for therapist gender, orientation, amount of supervision		
TRIB Assessed by Interview (TRIB-I)			Schöttke et al., 2017	

ABBREVIATIONS

ADM	antidepressant medication
ANOVA	analysis of variance
ARS	advanced relational skills
BDI	Beck Depression Inventory
CBT	cognitive behavioral therapy
CORE-OM	Clinical Outcomes in Routine Evaluation – Outcome Measure
FIS	facilitative interpersonal skills
GAF	general assessment of functioning
GAS	Global Assessment Scale
HRSD	Hamilton Rating Scale for Depression
HSCL	Hoskins Symptom Checklist
IAPT	improving access to psychological therapies
ICC	intraclass correlation
IIP	inventory of interpersonal problems
IPT	interpersonal therapy
ITT	intent to treat
MLM	multilevel models
NIMH	National Institute for Mental Health
OQ-45	Outcome Questionnaire-45
PE	prolonged exposure
PLA	pill placebo
PTSD	post-traumatic stress disorder
PWPs	psychological wellbeing practitioners
RCT	randomized clinical trial
SMD	standardized mean difference
TDCRP	Treatment of Depression Collaborative Research Project
TRIB	therapy-related interpersonal behavior
TRIB-G	therapy-related interpersonal behavior-group
TRIB-I	therapy-related interpersonal behavior-interview
UK-NHS	United Kingdom-National Health Service
WAI	Working Alliance Inventory

REFERENCES

Adelson, J. L., & Owen, J. (2012). Bringing the psychotherapist back: Basic concepts for reading articles examining therapist effects using multi-level modeling. *Psychotherapy*, 49(2), 152–162. https://doi.org/10.1037/a0023990

Ahn, H.-n., & Wampold, B. E. (2001). Where oh where are the specific ingredients? A meta-analysis of component studies in counseling and psychotherapy. *Journal of Counseling Psychology*, 48(3), 251–257. https://doi.org/10.1037/0022-0167.48.3.251

Anderson, T., Crowley, M. E. J., Himawan, L., Holmberg, J. K., & Uhlin, B. D. (2016). Therapist facilitative interpersonal skills and training status: A randomized clinical trial on alliance and outcome. *Psychotherapy Research*, 26(5), 511–529. https://doi.org/10.1080/10503307.2015.1049671

Anderson, T., McClintock, A. S., Himawan, L., Song, X., & Patterson, C. L. (2016). A prospective study of therapist facilitative interpersonal skills as a predictor of treatment outcome. *Journal of Consulting and Clinical Psychology*, 84(1), 57–66. https://doi.org/10.1037/ccp0000060

Anderson, T., Ogles, B. M., Patterson, C. L., Lambert, M. J., & Vermeersch, D. A. (2009). Therapist effects: Facilitative interpersonal skills as a predictor of therapist success. *Journal of Clinical Psychology*, 65(7), 755–768. https://doi.org/10.1002/jclp.20583

Baldwin, S. A., & Imel, Z. E. (2013). Therapist effects: Finding and methods. In M. J. Lambert (Ed.), *Bergin and Garfield's handbook of psychotherapy and behavior change* (6th ed., pp. 258–297). New York: Wiley.

Baldwin, S. A., Wampold, B. E., & Imel, Z. E. (2007). Untangling the alliance-outcome correlation: Exploring the relative importance of therapist and patient variability in the alliance. *Journal of Consulting and Clinical Psychology*, 75(6), 842–852. https://doi.org/10.1037/0022-006X.75.6.842

Barcikowski, R. S. (1981). Statistical power with group means as the unit of analysis. *Journal of Educational Statistics*, 6(3), 267–285. https://doi.org/10.3102/10769986006003267

Barkham, M., Connell, J., Stiles, W. B., Miles, J. N. V., Margison, F., Evans, C., & Mellor-Clark, J. (2006). Dose–effect relations and responsive regulation of treatment duration: The good enough level. *Journal of Consulting and Clinical Psychology*, 74(1), 160–167. https://doi.org/10.1037/0022-006X.74.1.160

Barkham, M., Lutz, W., Lambert, M. J., & Saxon, D. (2017). Therapist effects, effective therapists, and the law of variability. In L. G. Castonguay & C. E. Hill (Eds.), *How and why are some therapists better than others?: Understanding therapist effects* (pp. 13–36): American Psychological Association, Washington, DC. https://doi.org/10.1037/0000034-002

Barnicot, K., Wampold, B., & Priebe, S. (2014). The effect of core clinician interpersonal behaviours on depression. *Journal of Affective Disorders*, 167, 112–117. https://doi.org/10.1016/j.jad.2014.05.064

Bell, E. C., Marcus, D. K., & Goodlad, J. K. (2013). Are the parts as good as the whole? A meta-analysis of component treatment studies. *Journal of Consulting and Clinical Psychology*, 81(4), 722–736. https://doi.org/10.1037/a0033004

Beutler, L. E., Malik, M., Alimohamed, S., Harwood, T. M., Talebi, H., Noble, S., & Wong, E. (2004). Therapist variables. In M. J. Lambert (Ed.), *Bergin and Garfield's handbook of psychotherapy and behavior change* (5th ed., pp. 227–306). New York: Wiley.

Bohart, A. C., & Tallman, K. (1999). *How clients make therapy work: The process of active self-healing*. Washington, DC: American Psychological Association. https://doi.org/10.1037/10323-000

Bohart, A. C., & Wade, A. G. (2013). The client in psychotherapy. In M. J. Lambert (Ed.), *Bergin and Garfield's handbook of psychotherapy and behavior change* (6th ed., pp. 219–257). Hoboken, NJ: Wiley.

Boswell, J. F., Gallagher, M. W., Sauer-Zavala, S. E., Bullis, J., Gorman, J. M., Shear, M. K., Woods, S., & Barlow, D. H. (2013). Patient characteristics and variability in adherence and competence in cognitive-behavioral therapy for panic disorder. *Journal of Consulting and Clinical Psychology*, 81(3), 443–454. https://doi.org/10.1037/a0031437

Bryk, A. S., & Raudenbush, S. W. (1992). *Hierachical linear models in social and behavioral research: Applicaiton and data analysis* (1st ed.). Newbury Park, CA: Sage.

Budge, S. L., Owen, J. J., Kopta, S. M., Minami, T., Hanson, M. R., & Hirsch, G. (2013). Differences among trainees in client outcomes associated with the phase model of change. *Psychotherapy*, 50(2), 150–157. https://doi.org/10.1037/a0029565

Buranelli, V. (1975). *The wizard from Vienna: Franz Anton Mesmer*. New York: Coward, McCann & Geoghegan.

Castonguay, L. G., & Hill, C. E. (2017). *How and why are some therapists better than others?: Understanding therapist effects*. American Psychological Association. https://doi.org/10.1037/0000034-000

Chow, D. L., Miller, S. D., Seidel, J. A., Kane, R. T., Thornton, J. A., & Andrews, W. P. (2015). The role of deliberate practice in the development of highly effective psychotherapists. *Psychotherapy*, 52(3), 337–345. https://doi.org/10.1037/pst0000015

Cologon, J., Schweitzer, R. D., King, R., & Nolte, T. (2017). Therapist reflective functioning, therapist attachment style and therapist effectiveness. *Administration and Policy in Mental Health and Mental Health Services Research*, 44, 614–625. https://doi.org/10.1007/s10488-017-0790-5

Connor, D. R., & Callahan, J. L. (2015). Impact of psychotherapist expectations on client outcomes. *Psychotherapy*, 52(3), 351–362. https://doi.org/10.1037/a0038890

Crits-Christoph, P., Baranackie, K., Kurcias, J. S., Beck, A., Carroll, K., Perry, K., Luborsky, L., McLellan, T., Woody, G., Thompson, L., Gallagher, D., & Zitrin, C. (1991). Meta-analysis of therapist effects in psychotherapy outcome studies. *Psychotherapy Research*, 1(2), 81–91. https://doi.org/10.1080/10503309112331335511

Crits-Christoph, P., & Gallop, R. (2006). Therapist effects in the National Institute of Mental Health Treatment of Depression Collaborative Research Program and other psychotherapy studies. *Psychotherapy Research*, 16(2), 178–181. https://doi.org/10.1080/10503300500265025

Crits-Christoph, P., & Mintz, J. (1991). Implications of therapist effects for the design and analysis of comparative studies of psychotherapies. *Journal of Consulting and Clinical Psychology*, 59(1), 20–26. https://doi.org/10.1037/0022-006X.59.1.20

Crits-Christoph, P., Ring-Kurtz, S., McClure, B., Temes, C., Kulaga, A., Gallop, R., Foreman, R., & Rotrosen, J. (2010). A randomized controlled study of a web-based performance improvement system for substance abuse treatment providers. *Journal of Substance Abuse Treatment*, 38(3), 251–262. https://doi.org/10.1016/j.jsat.2010.01.001

Cuijpers, P., Karyotaki, E., Reijnders, M., & Ebert, D. D. (2019). Was Eysenck right after all? A reassessment of the effects of psychotherapy for adult depression. *Epidemiology and Psychiatric Sciences*, 28(1), 21–30. https://doi.org/10.1017/S2045796018000057

Danziger, K. (1990). *Constructing the subject: Historical origins of psychological research*. Cambridge, UK: Cambridge University Press. https://doi.org/10.1017/CBO9780511524059

Davis, D. E., DeBlaere, C., Owen, J., Hook, J. N., Rivera, D. P., Choe, E., Van Tongeren, D. R., Worthington, E., & Placeres, V. (2018). The multicultural orientation framework: A narrative review. *Psychotherapy*, 55(1), 89–100. https://doi.org/10.1037/pst0000160

De Jong, K., & de Goede, M. (2015). Why do some therapists not deal with outcome monitoring feedback? A feasibility study on the effect of regulatory focus and person–organization fit on attitude and outcome. *Psychotherapy Research*, 25(6), 661–668. https://doi.org/10.1080/10503307.2015.1076198

De Jong, K., van Sluis, P., Nugter, M. A., Heiser, W. J., & Spinhoven, P. (2012). Understanding the differential impact of outcome monitoring: Therapist variables that moderate feedback effects in a randomized clinical trial. *Psychotherapy Research*, 22(4), 464–474. https://doi.org/10.1080/10503307.2012.673023

Del Re, A. C., Flückiger, C., Horvath, A. O., Symonds, D., & Wampold, B. E. (2012). Therapist effects in the therapeutic alliance–outcome relationship: A restricted-maximum likelihood meta-analysis. *Clinical Psychology Review*, 32(7), 642–649. https://doi.org/10.1016/j.cpr.2012.07.002

Del Re, A. C., Flückiger, C., Horvath, A. O., & Wampold, B. E. (2021). Examining therapist effects in the alliance–outcome relationship: A multilevel meta-analysis. *Journal of Consulting and Clinical Psychology*. https://doi.org/10.1037/ccp000063710.1037/ccp0000637.supp (Supplemental)

Delgadillo, J., Branson, A., Kellett, S., Myles-Hooten, P., Hardy, G. E., & Shafran, R. (2020). Therapist personality traits as predictors of psychological treatment outcomes. *Psychotherapy Research*, 30(7), 857–870. https://doi.org/10.1002/da.22766

Delgadillo, J., Saxon, D., & Barkham, M. (2018). Associations between therapists' occupational burnout and their patients' depression and anxiety treatment outcomes. *Depression and Anxiety*, 35(9), 844–850. https://doi.org/10.1002/da.22766

Dinger, U., Strack, M., Leichsenring, F., Wilmers, F., & Schauenburg, H. (2008). Therapist effects on outcome and alliance in inpatient psychotherapy. *Journal of Clinical Psychology*, 64(3), 344–354. https://doi.org/10.1002/jclp.20443

Drinane, J., Owen, J., & Kopta, M. (2016). Racial/ethnic disparities in psychotherapy: Does the outcome matter? *Testing, Psychometrics, Methodology in Applied Psychology*, 23(4), 531–544. https://doi.org/10.4473/TPM23.4.7

Drinane, J. M., Owen, J., & Tao, K. W. (2018). Cultural concealment and therapy outcomes. *Journal of Counseling Psychology*, 65(2), 239–246. https://doi.org/10.1037/cou0000246

Elkin, I., Falconnier, L., & Martinovich, Z. (2007). Misrepresentation in Wampold and Bolt's critique of Elkin, Falconnier, Martinovich, and Mahoney's study of therapist effects. *Psychotherapy Research*, 17, 253–256. https://doi.org/10.1080/10503300500282186

Elkin, I., Falconnier, L., Martinovich, Z., & Mahoney, C. (2006b). Rejoinder to commentaries by Stephen Soldz and Paul Crits-Christoph on therapist effects. *Psychotherapy Research*, 16, 182–183. https://doi.org/10.1080/10503300500282186

Elkin, I., Falconnier, L., Martinovich, Z., & Mahoney, C. (2006a). Therapist effects in the NIMH Treatment of Depression Colloarative Research Program. *Psychotherapy Research*, 16(2), 144–160. https://doi.org/10.1080/10503300500268540

Elkin, I., Parloff, M. B., Hadley, S. W., & Autry, J. H. (1985). NIMH Treatment of Depression Collaborative Research Program: Background and research plan. *Archives of General Psychiatry*, 42(3), 305–316. https://doi.org/10.1001/archpsyc.1985.01790260103013

Elkin, I., Shea, M. T., Watkins, J. T., Imber, S. D., Sotsky, S. M., Collins, J. F., Glass, D. R., Pilkonis, P. A., Leber, W. R., Docherty, J. P., Fiester, S. J., & Parloff, M. B. (1989). National Institute of Mental Health Treatment of Depression Collaborative Research Program: General effectiveness of treatments. *Archives of General Psychiatry*, 46(11), 971–982. https://doi.org/10.1001/archpsyc.1989.01810110013002

Erekson, D. M., Janis, R., Bailey, R. J., Cattani, K., & Pedersen, T. R. (2017). A longitudinal investigation of the impact of psychotherapist training: Does training improve client outcomes? *Journal of Counseling Psychology*, 64(5), 514–524. https://doi.org/10.1037/cou0000252

Ericsson, K. A., Hoffman, R. R., Kozbelt, A., & Williams, A. M. (Eds.). (2018). *The Cambridge handbook of expertise and expert performance* (2nd ed.). New York: NY: Cambridge University Press. https://doi.org/10.1146/annurev.psych.47.1.273

Ericsson, K. A., & Lehmann, A. C. (1996). Expert and exceptional performance: Evidence of maximal adaptation to task constraints. *Annual Review of Psychology*, 47, 273–305.

Eysenck, H. J. (1952). The effects of psychotherapy: An evaluation. *Journal of Consulting Psychology*, 16(5), 319–324. https://doi.org/10.1037/h0063633

Eysenck, H. J. (1961). The effects of psychotherapy. In H. J. Eysenck (Ed.), *Handbook of abnormal psychology*. New York: Basic Books.

Eysenck, H. J. (1966). *The effects of psychotherapy*. New York: International science press.

Falkenström, F., Granström, F., & Holmqvist, R. (2014). Working alliance predicts psychotherapy outcome even while controlling for prior symptom improvement. *Psychotherapy Research*, 24(2), 146–159. https://doi.org/10.1080/10503307.2013.847985

Falkenström, F., Grant, J., & Holmqvist, R. (2018). Review of organizational effects on the outcome of mental health treatments. *Psychotherapy Research*, 28(1), 76–90. https://doi.org/10.1080/10503307.2016.1158883

Firth, N., Barkham, M., Kellett, S., & Saxon, D. (2015). Therapist effects and moderators of effectiveness and efficiency in psychological wellbeing practitioners: A multilevel modelling analysis. *Behaviour Research and Therapy*, 69, 54–62. https://doi.org/10.1016/j.brat.2015.04.001

Firth, N., Saxon, D., Stiles, W. B., & Barkham, M. (2019). Therapist and clinic effects in psychotherapy: A three-level model of outcome variability. *Journal of Consulting and Clinical Psychology*, 87(4), 345–356. https://doi.org/10.1037/ccp0000388

Fisher, R. A. (1925). *Statistical methods for research workers*. London: Oliver & Boyd.

Flückiger, C., Del Re, A. C., Wampold, B. E., & Horvath, A. O. (2018). The alliance in adult psychotherapy: A meta-analytic synthesis. *Psychotherapy*, 55(4), 316–340.

Flückiger, C., Del Re, A. C., Wampold, B. E., Symonds, D., & Horvath, A. O. (2012). How central is the alliance in psychotherapy? A multilevel longitudinal meta-analysis. *Journal of Counseling Psychology*, 59(1), 10–17. https://doi.org/10.1037/pst0000172

Gehan, E., & Lemak, N. A. (1994). *Statistics in medical research: Developments in clinical trials*. New York: Plenum Medical Book. https://doi.org/10.1007/978-1-4615-2518-9

Goldberg, S. B., Babins-Wagner, R., Rousmaniere, T., Berzins, S., Hoyt, W. T., Whipple, J. L., Miller, S.D., & Wampold, B. E. (2016). Creating a climate for therapist improvement: A case study of an agency focused on outcomes and deliberate practice. *Psychotherapy, 53*(3), 367–375. https://doi.org/10.1037/pst0000060

Goldberg, S. B., Hoyt, W. T., Nissen-Lie, H. A., Nielsen, S. L., & Wampold, B. E. (2018). Unpacking the therapist effect: Impact of treatment length differs for high- and low-performing therapists. *Psychotherapy Research, 28*(4), 532–544. https://doi.org/10.1080/10503307.2016.1216625

Goldberg, S. B., Rousmaniere, T., Miller, S. D., Whipple, J., Nielsen, S. L., Hoyt, W. T., & Wampold, B. E. (2016). Do psychotherapists improve with time and experience? A longitudinal analysis of outcomes in a clinical setting. *Journal of Counseling Psychology, 63*(1), 1–11. https://doi.org/10.1037/cou0000131

Goodyear, R. K., Wampold, B. E., Tracey, T. J. G., & Lichtenberg, J. W. (2017). Psychotherapy expertise should mean superior outcomes and demonstrable improvement over time. *The Counseling Psychologist, 45*(1), 54–65. https://doi.org/10.1177/0011000016652691

Hagen, K., Solem, S., Opstad, H. B., Vogel, P. A., Kennair, L. E. O., Kvale, G., & Hansen, B. (2016). Therapist variability in the task/goal dimension of the early working alliance predicts outcome in exposure and response prevention treatment for obsessive-compulsive disorder. *Clinical Neuropsychiatry: Journal of Treatment Evaluation, 13*, 94–99.

Hatcher, R. L., & Barends, A. W. (2006). How a return to theory could help alliance research. *Psychotherapy: Theory, Research, Practice, Training, 43*(3), 292–299. https://doi.org/10.1037/0033-3204.43.3.292

Hayes, J. A., McAleavey, A. A., Castonguay, L. G., & Locke, B. D. (2016). Psychotherapists' outcomes with White and racial/ethnic minority clients: First, the good news. *Journal of Counseling Psychology, 63*(3), 261–268. https://doi.org/10.1037/cou0000098

Hayes, J. A., Owen, J., & Bieschke, K. J. (2015). Therapist differences in symptom change with racial/ethnic minority clients. *Psychotherapy, 52*(3), 308–314. https://doi.org/10.1037/a0037957

Hays, W. L. (1963). *Statistics for psychologists*. New York City: Holt, Rinehart & Winston.

Hays, W. L. (1988). *Statistics*. New York: Holt, Rinehart, & Winston.

Hill, C. E., Baumann, E., Shafran, N., Gupta, S., Morrison, A., Rojas, A. E. P., Spangler, P. T., Griffin, S., Pappa, L., & Gelso, C. J. (2015). Is training effective? A study of counseling psychology doctoral trainees in a psychodynamic/interpersonal training clinic. *Journal of Counseling Psychology, 62*(2), 184–201. https://doi.org/10.1037/cou0000053

Hill, C. E., Spiegel, S. B., Hoffman, M. A., Kivlighan, D. M., Jr., & Gelso, C. J. (2017). Therapist expertise in psychotherapy revisited. *The Counseling Psychologist, 45*(1), 7–53. https://doi.org/10.1177/0011000016641192

Hook, D., Davis, D., Owen, J., & DeBlaere, C. (2017). *Therapists' cultural humility*. Washington, DC: American Psychological Association.

Horvath, A. O. (2017). Research on the alliance: Knowledge in search of a theory. *Psychotherapy Research, 28*(4), 499–516. https://doi.org/10.1080/10503307.2017.1373204

Horvath, A. O., Del Re, A. C., Flückiger, C., & Symonds, D. (2011). Alliance in individual psychotherapy. *Psychotherapy, 48*(1), 9–16. https://doi.org/10.1037/a0022186

Hox, J. (2010). *Multilevel analysis: Techniques and applications* (2nd ed.). London: Routledge. https://doi.org/10.4324/9780203852279

Huey, S. J., Jr., Tilley, J. L., Jones, E. O., & Smith, C. A. (2014). The contribution of cultural competence to evidence-based care for ethnically diverse populations. *Annual Review of Clinical Psychology, 10*, 305–338. https://doi.org/10.1146/annurev-clinpsy-032813-153729

Huppert, J. D., Bufka, L. F., Barlow, D. H., Gorman, J. M., Shear, M. K., & Woods, S. W. (2001). Therapists, therapists variables, and cognitive behavioral therapy outcomes in a multicenter trial for panic disorder. *Journal of Consulting and Clinical Psychology, 69*(5), 747–755. https://doi.org/10.1037/0022-006X.69.5.747

Huppert, J. D., Kivity, Y., Barlow, D. H., Gorman, J. M., Shear, M. K., & Woods, S. W. (2014). Therapist effects and the outcome – alliance correlation in cognitive behavioral therapy for panic disorder with agoraphobia. *Behaviour Research and Therapy, 52*, 26–34. https://doi.org/10.1016/j.brat.2013.11.001

Imel, Z. E., Baer, J. S., Martino, S., Ball, S. A., & Carroll, K. M. (2011). Mutual influence in therapist competence and adherence to motivational enhancement therapy. *Drug and Alcohol Dependence, 115*(3), 229–236. https://doi.org/10.1016/j.drugalcdep.2010.11.010

Imel, Z. E., Baldwin, S., Atkins, D. C., Owen, J., Baardseth, T., & Wampold, B. E. (2011). Racial/ethnic disparities in therapist effectiveness: A conceptualization and initial study of cultural competence. *Journal of Counseling Psychology, 58*(3), 290–298. https://doi.org/10.1037/a0023284

Imel, Z. E., Sheng, E., Baldwin, S. A., & Atkins, D. C. (2015). Removing very low-performing therapists: A simulation of performance-based retention in psychotherapy. *Psychotherapy, 52*(3), 329–336. https://doi.org/10.1037/pst0000023

Johns, R. J., Barkham, M., Kellett, S., & Saxon, D. (2019). A systematic review of therapist effects: A critical narrative update and refinement to review. *Clinical Psychology Review, 67*, 78–93. https://doi.org/10.1016/j.cpr.2018.08.004

Kenny, D. A., & Judd, C. M. (1986). Consequence of violating the independence assumption in analysis of variance. *Psychological Bulletin, 99*(3), 422–431. https://doi.org/10.1037/0033-2909.99.3.422

Kiesler, D. J. (1966). Some myths of psychotherapy research and the search for a paradigm. *Psychological Bulletin, 65*(2), 110–136. https://doi.org/10.1037/h0022911

Kim, D. M., Wampold, B. E., & Bolt, D. M. (2006). Therapist effects in psychotherapy: A random effects modeling of the NIMH TDCRP data. *Psychotherapy Research, 16*(2), 161–172. https://doi.org/10.1080/10503300500264911

Kirk, R. E. (1995). *Experimental design: Procedures for the behavioral sciences* (3rd ed.). Pacific Grove, CA: Brooks/Cole.

Kivlighan, D. M., III, Hooley, I. W., Bruno, M. G., Ethington, L. L., Keeton, P. M., & Schreier, B. A. (2019). Examining therapist effects in relation to clients' race-ethnicity and gender: An intersectionality approach. *Journal of Counseling Psychology, 66*(1), 122–129. https://doi.org/10.1037/cou0000316

Kraus, D. R., Bentley, J. H., Alexander, P. C., Boswell, J. F., Constantino, M. J., Baxter, E. E., & Castonguay, L. G. (2016). Predicting therapist effectiveness from their own practice-based evidence. *Journal of Consulting and Clinical Psychology, 84*(6), 473–483. https://doi.org/10.1037/ccp0000083

Kraus, D. R., Castonguay, L., Boswell, J. F., Nordberg, S. S., & Hayes, J. A. (2011). Therapist effectiveness: Implications for accountability and patient care. *Psychotherapy Research, 21*(3), 267–276. https://doi.org/10.1080/10503307.2011.563249

Lambert, M. J., Whipple, J. L., & Kleinstäuber, M. (2018). Collecting and delivering progress feedback: A meta-analysis of routine outcome monitoring. *Psychotherapy, 55*(4), 520–537. https://doi.org/10.1037/pst0000167

Larrison, C. R., Schoppelrey, S. L., Hack-Ritzo, S., & Korr, W. S. (2011). Clinician factors related to outcome differences between black and white patients at CMHCs. *Psychiatric Services, 62*(5), 525–531. https://doi.org/10.1176/ps.62.5.pss6205_0525

Laska, K. M., Smith, T. L., Wislocki, A. P., Minami, T., & Wampold, B. E. (2013). Uniformity of evidence-based treatments in practice? Therapist effects in the delivery of cognitive processing therapy for PTSD. *Journal of Counseling Psychology, 60*(1), 31–41. https://doi.org/10.1037/a0031294

Luborsky, L., Crits-Christoph, P., McLellan, A. T., Woody, G., Piper, W., Liberman, B., Imber, S., & Pilkonis, P. (1986). Do therapists vary much in their success? Findings from four outcome studies. *American Journal of Orthopsychiatry, 56*(4), 501–512. https://doi.org/10.1111/j.1939-0025.1986.tb03483.x

Luborsky, L., McLellan, A. T., Woody, G., O'Brien, C. P., & Auerbach, A. (1985). Therapist success and is determinants. *Archives of General Psychiatry, 42*(6), 602–611. https://doi.org/10.1001/archpsyc.1985.01790290084010

Lutz, W., Leon, S. C., Martinovich, Z., Lyons, J. S., & Stiles, W. B. (2007). Therapist effects in outpatient psychotherapy: A three-level growth curve approach. *Journal of Counseling Psychology, 54*(1), 32–39. https://doi.org/10.1037/0022-0167.54.1.32

Lutz, W., Rubel, J., Schiefele, A.-K., Zimmermann, D., Böhnke, J. R., & Wittmann, W. W. (2015). Feedback and therapist effects in the context of treatment outcome and treatment length. *Psychotherapy Research, 25*(6), 647–660. https://doi.org/10.1080/10503307.2015.1053553

Mallinckrodt, B. (1991). Clients' representations of childhood emotional bonds with parents, social support, and formation of the working alliance. *Journal of Counseling Psychology, 38*(4), 401–409. https://doi.org/10.1037/0022-0167.38.4.401

Maramba, G. G., & Nagayama Hall, G. C. (2002). Meta-analyses of ethnic match as a predictor of dropout, utilization, and level of functioning.

Cultural Diversity and Ethnic Minority Psychology, 8(3), 290–297. https://doi.org/10.1037/1099-9809.8.3.290

Martindale, C. (1978). The therapist-as-fixed-effect fallacy in psychotherapy research. *Journal of Consulting and Clinical Psychology, 46*(6), 1526–1530. https://doi.org/10.1037/0022-006X.46.6.1526

Maxwell, S. E., & Delaney, H. D. (1990). *Designing experiments and analyzing data: A model comparison perspective.* Mahwah, NJ: Erlbaum.

McCall, W. A. (1923). *How to experiment in education.* New York: Macmillan. https://doi.org/10.1037/13551-000

McKay, K. M., Imel, Z. E., & Wampold, B. E. (2006). Psychiatrist effects in the psychopharmacological treatment of depression. *Journal of Affective Disorders, 92*(2–3), 287–290. https://doi.org/10.1016/j.jad.2006.01.020

Miller, S. D., Hubble, M. A., & Chow, D. (2018). The question of expertise in psychotherapy. *Journal of Expertise, 1.*

Minami, T., Wampold, B. E., Serlin, R. C., Kircher, J. C., & Brown, G. S. J. (2007). Benchmarks for psychotherapy efficacy in adult major depression. *Journal of Consulting and Clinical Psychology, 75*(2), 232–243. https://doi.org/10.1037/0022-006X.75.2.232

Munder, T., Flückiger, C., Leichsenring, F., Abbass, A. A., Hilsenroth, M. J., Luyten, P., Rabung, S., Steinert, C., & Wampold, B. E. (2019). Is psychotherapy effective? A re-analysis of treatments for depression. *Epidemiology and Psychiatric Sciences, 28*(3), 268–274. https://doi.org/10.1017/S2045796018000355

Nissen-Lie, H. A., Goldberg, S. B., Hoyt, W. T., Falkenström, F., Holmqvist, R., Nielsen, S. L., & Wampold, B. E. (2016). Are therapists uniformly effective across patient outcome domains? A study on therapist effectiveness in two different treatment contexts. *Journal of Counseling Psychology, 63*(4), 367–378. https://doi.org/10.1037/cou0000151

Nissen-Lie, H. A., Monsen, J. T., Ulleberg, P., & Rønnestad, M. H. (2013). Psychotherapists' self-reports of their interpersonal functioning and difficulties in practice as predictors of patient outcome. *Psychotherapy Research, 23*(1), 86–104. https://doi.org/10.1080/10503307.2012.735775

Nissen-Lie, H. A., Rønnestad, M. H., Høglend, P. A., Havik, O. E., Solbakken, O. A., Stiles, T. C., & Monsen, J. T. (2015). Love yourself as a person, doubt yourself as a therapist? *Clinical Psychology & Psychotherapy, 24*(1), 48–60. https://doi.org/10.1002/cpp.1977

Norcross, J. C., & Wampold, B. E. (2019). Relationships and responsiveness in the psychological treatment of trauma: The tragedy of the APA Clinical Practice Guideline. *Psychotherapy, 56*(3), 391–399. https://doi.org/10.1037/pst0000228

Odyniec, P., Probst, T., Margraf, J., & Willutzki, U. (2019). Psychotherapist trainees' professional self-doubt and negative personal reaction: Changes during cognitive behavioral therapy and association with patient progress. *Psychotherapy Research, 29*(1), 123–138. https://doi.org/10.1080/10503307.2017.1315464

Owen, J., Drinane, J. M., Idigo, K. C., & Valentine, J. C. (2015). Psychotherapist effects in meta-analyses: How accurate are treatment effects? *Psychotherapy, 52*(3), 321–328. https://doi.org/10.1037/pst0000014

Owen, J., Drinane, J., Tao, K. W., Adelson, J. L., Hook, J. N., Davis, D., & Foo Kune, N. (2017). Racial/ethnic disparities in client unilateral termination: The role of therapists' cultural comfort. *Psychotherapy Research, 27*(1), 102–111. https://doi.org/10.1080/10503307.2015.1078517

Owen, J., Duncan, B., Reese, R. J., Anker, M., & Sparks, J. (2014). Accounting for therapist variability in couple therapy outcomes: What really matters? *Journal of Sex & Marital Therapy, 40*(6), 488–502. https://doi.org/10.1080/0092623X.2013.772552

Owen, J., Imel, Z., Adelson, J., & Rodolfa, E. (2012). 'No-show': Therapist racial/ethnic disparities in client unilateral termination. *Journal of Counseling Psychology, 59*(2), 314–320. https://doi.org/10.1037/a0027091

Owen, J., Wampold, B. E., Kopta, M., Rousmaniere, T., & Miller, S. D. (2016). As good as it gets? Therapy outcomes of trainees over time. *Journal of Counseling Psychology, 63*(1), 12–19. https://doi.org/10.1037/cou0000112

Owen, J., Wong, Y. J., & Rodolfa, E. (2009). Empirical search for psychotherapists' gender competence in psychotherapy. *Psychotherapy: Theory, Research, Practice, Training, 46*(4), 448–458. https://doi.org/10.1037/a0017958

Pereira, J.-A., Barkham, M., Kellett, S., & Saxon, D. (2017). The role of practitioner resilience and mindfulness in effective practice: A practice-based feasibility study. *Administration and Policy in Mental Health and Mental Health Services Research, 44*, 691–704. https://doi.org/10.1007/s10488-016-0747-0

Raudenbush, S., Bryk, A., Cheong, Y. F., & Congdon, R. (2001). *HLM 5: Hierarchical linear and nonlinear modeling.* Lincolnwood, IL: Scientific Software International.

Rousmaniere, T. (2016). *Deliberate practice for psychotherapists: A guide to improving clinical effectiveness.* New York, NY: Routledge. https://doi.org/10.4324/9781315472256

Rousmaniere, T., Goodyear, R. K., Miller, S. D., & Wampold, B. E. (Eds.). (2017). *The cycle of excellence: Using deliberate practice to improve supervision and training.* Hoboken, NJ: Wiley. https://doi.org/10.1002/9781119165590

Saxon, D., & Barkham, M. (2012). Patterns of therapist variability: Therapist effects and the contribution of patient severity and risk. *Journal of Consulting and Clinical Psychology, 80*(4), 535–546. https://doi.org/10.1037/a0028898

Saxon, D., Firth, N., & Barkham, M. (2017). The relationship between therapist effects and therapy delivery factors: Therapy modality, dosage, and non-completion. *Administration and Policy in Mental Health and Mental Health Services Research, 44*, 705–715. https://doi.org/10.1007/s10488-016-0750-5

Schauenburg, H., Buchheim, A., Beckh, K., Nolte, T., Brenk-Franz, K., Leichsenring, F., Strack, M., & Dinger, U. (2010). The influence of psychodynamically oriented therapists' attachment representations on outcome and alliance in inpatient psychotherapy. *Psychotherapy Research, 20*(2), 193–202. https://doi.org/10.1080/10503300903204043

Schiefele, A.-K., Lutz, W., Barkham, M., Rubel, J., Böhnke, J., Delgadillo, J., Kopta, M., Schulte, D., Saxon, D., Nielsen, S. L., & Lambert, M. J. (2017). Reliability of therapist effects in practice-based psychotherapy research: A guide for the planning of future studies. *Administration and Policy in Mental Health and Mental Health Services Research, 44*, 598–613. https://doi.org/10.1007/s10488-016-0736-3

Schöttke, H., Flückiger, C., Goldberg, S. B., Eversmann, J., & Lange, J. (2017). Predicting psychotherapy outcome based on therapist interpersonal skills: A five-year longitudinal study of a therapist assessment protocol. *Psychotherapy Research, 27*(6), 642–652. https://doi.org/10.1080/10503307.2015.1125546

Serlin, R. C., Wampold, B. E., & Levin, J. R. (2003). Should providers of treatment be regarded as a random factor? If it ain't broke, don't "Fix" it: A comment on Siemer and Joorman (2003). *Psychological Methods, 8*(4), 524–534. https://doi.org/10.1037/1082-989X.8.4.524

Shanteau, J. (1992). Competence in experts: The role of task characteristics. *Organizational Behavior and Human Decision Processes, 53*(2), 252–266. https://doi.org/10.1016/0749-5978(92)90064-E

Shanteau, J., & Weiss, D. J. (2014). Individual expertise versus domain expertise. *American Psychologist, 69*(7), 711–712. https://doi.org/10.1037/a0037874

Shapiro, A. K., & Shapiro, E. S. (1997). *The powerful placebo: From ancient priest to modern medicine.* Baltimore: The Johns Hopkins University Press.

Siemer, M., & Joormann, J. (2003). Power and measures of effect size in analysis variance with fixed versus random nested factors. *Psychological Methods, 8*(4), 497–517. https://doi.org/10.1037/1082-989X.8.4.497

Snijders, T., & Bosker, R. (1999). *Multilevel analysis: An introduction to basic and advanced multilevel modeling.* London, UK: Sage.

Soldz, S. (2006). Models and meanings: Therapist effects and the stories we tell. *Psychotherapy Research, 16*(2), 173–177. https://doi.org/10.1080/10503300500264937

Taylor, J. M., & Neimeyer, G. J. (2017). The ongoing evolution of continuing education: Past, present, and future. In T. Rousmaniere, R. K. Goodyear, S. D. Miller, & B. E. Wamold (Eds.), *The cycle of excellence: Using deliberate practice to improve supervision and training.* Hoboken, NJ: Wiley. https://doi.org/10.1002/9781119165590.ch11

Tracey, T. J. G., Wampold, B. E., Lichtenberg, J. W., & Goodyear, R. K. (2014). Expertise in psychotherapy: An elusive goal? *American Psychologist. 69*(3), 218–229. https://doi.org/10.1037/a0035099

Tschuschke, V., Crameri, A., Koehler, M., Berglar, J., Muth, K., Staczan, P., Von Wyl, A., Schulthess, P., & Koemeda-Lutz, M. (2015). The role of therapists' treatment adherence, professional experience, therapeutic alliance, and clients' severity of psychological problems: Prediction of treatment outcome in eight different psychotherapy approaches. Preliminary results of a naturalistic study. *Psychotherapy Research, 25*(4), 420–434. https://doi.org/10.1080/10503307.2014.896055

Uckelstam, C.-J., Holmqvist, R., Philips, B., & Falkenström, F. (2020). A relational perspective on the association between working alliance and treatment outcome. *Psychotherapy Research, 30*(1), 13–22. https://doi.org/10.1080/10503307.2018.1516306

Walsh, J. E. (1947). Concerning the effect of intraclass correlation on certain significance tests. *Annals of Mathematical Statistics, 18*(1), 88–96. https://doi.org/10.1214/aoms/1177730495

Wampold, B. E. (1997). Methodological problems in identifying efficacious psychotherapies. *Psychotherapy Research, 7*(1), 21–43. https://doi.org/10.1080/10503309712331331853

Wampold, B. E. (2013). The good, the bad, and the ugly: A 50-year perspective on the outcome problem. *Psychotherapy, 50*(1), 16–24. https://doi.org/10.1037/a0030570

Wampold, B. E., Baldwin, S. A., Holtforth, M. g., & Imel, Z. E. (2017). What characterizes effective therapists? In L. G. Castonguay & C. E. Hill (Eds.), *How and why are some therapists better than others?: Understanding therapist effects* (pp. 37–53): American Psychological Association, Washington, *DC.* https://doi.org/10.1037/0735-7028.35.6.563

Wampold, B. E., & Bhati, K. S. (2004). Attending to the omissions: A historical examination of the evidenced-based practice movement. *Professional Psychology: Research and Practice, 35*(6), 563–570. https://doi.org/10.1080/10503300500265181

Wampold, B. E., & Bolt, D. M. (2006). Therapist effects: Clever ways to make them (and everything else) disappear. *Psychotherapy Research, 16*(2), 184–187.

Wampold, B. E., & Bolt, D. M. (2007). The consequences of "anchoring" in longitudinal multilevel models: Bias in the estimation of patient variability and therapist effects. *Psychotherapy Research, 17*(5), 509–514. https://doi.org/10.1080/10503300701250339

Wampold, B. E., & Brown, G. S. (2005). Estimating therapist variability: A naturalistic study of outcomes in managed care. *Journal of Consulting and Clinical Psychology, 73*(5), 914–923. https://doi.org/10.1037/0022-006X.73.5.914

Wampold, B. E., & Imel, Z. E. (2015). *The great psychotherapy debate: The evidence for what makes psychotherapy work* (2nd ed.). New York: Routledge. https://doi.org/10.4324/9780203582015

Wampold, B. E., & Serlin, R. C. (2000). The consequences of ignoring a nested factor on measures of effect size in analysis of variance. *Psychological Methods, 5*(4), 425–433. https://doi.org/10.1037/1082-989X.5.4.425

Wampold, B. E., & Ulvenes, P. G. (2019). Integration of common factors and specific ingredients. In J. C. Norcross & M. R. Goldfried (Eds.), *Handbook of psychotherapy integration* (3rd ed., pp. 69–87).

New York City: Oxford University Press. https://doi.org/10.1093/med-psych/9780190690465.003.0003

Webb, C. A., DeRubeis, R. J., & Barber, J. P. (2010). Therapist adherence/competence and treatment outcome: A meta-analytic review. *Journal of Consulting and Clinical Psychology, 78*(2), 200–211. https://doi.org/10.1037/a0018912

Westen, D., & Morrison, K. (2001). A multidimensional meta-analysis of treatments for depression, panic, and generalized anxiety disorders: An examination of the status of empirically supported therapies. *Journal of Consulting and Clinical Psychology, 69*(6), 875–899. https://doi.org/10.1037/0022-006X.69.6.875

Westen, D., Novotny, C. M., & Thompson-Brenner, H. (2004). The empirical status of empirically supported psychotherapies: assumptions, findings, and reporting in controlled clinical trials. *Psychological Bulletin, 130*(4), 631–663.

Winer, B. J. (1971). *Statistical principles in experimental design. New York City:* McGraw Hill.

Yonatan-Leus, R., Tishby, O., Shefler, G., & Wiseman, H. (2018). Therapists' honesty, humor styles, playfulness, and creativity as outcome predictors: A retrospective study of the therapist effect. *Psychotherapy Research, 28*(5), 793–802. https://doi.org/10.1080/10503307.2017.1292067

Ziem, M., & Hoyer, J. (2020). Modest, yet progressive: Effective therapists tend to rate therapeutic change less positively than their patients. *Psychotherapy Research, 30*(4), 433–446. https://doi.org/10.1080/10503307.2019.1631502

Zilcha-Mano, S., Solomonov, N., Chui, H., McCarthy, K. S., Barrett, M. S., & Barber, J. P. (2015). Therapist-reported alliance: Is it really a predictor of outcome? *Journal of Counseling Psychology, 62*(4), 568–578. https://doi.org/10.1037/cou0000106

Zuroff, D. C., Kelly, A. C., Leybman, M. J., Blatt, S. J., & Wampold, B. E. (2010). Between-therapist and within-therapist differences in the quality of the therapeutic relationship: Effects on maladjustment and self-critical perfectionism. *Journal of Clinical Psychology, 66*(7), 681–697. https://doi.org/10.1002/jclp.20683

Zuroff, D. C., McBride, C., Ravitz, P., Koestner, R., Moskowitz, D. S., & Bagby, R. M. (2017). Autonomous and controlled motivation for interpersonal therapy for depression: Between-therapists and within-therapist effects. *Journal of Counseling Psychology, 64*(5), 525–537. https://doi.org/10.1037/cou0000239

CHAPTER 10

TRAINING AND SUPERVISION IN PSYCHOTHERAPY: WHAT WE KNOW AND WHERE WE NEED TO GO

SARAH KNOX AND CLARA E HILL

Abstract

In this chapter, we examine the literature regarding outcomes of training and individual supervision, as well as the processes associated with such outcomes in an effort to identify helpful components of training and individual supervision. In the training area, we found support for the effectiveness of the Hill model of helping skills training, particularly in terms of changes in self-efficacy, use of skills, and reduction of words spoken. We also found evidence for the effectiveness of instruction, modeling, practice, and feedback (especially for practice), as the components of training. A few studies exist for other types of training (e.g., psychodynamic, behavioral, experiential, empathy, alliance, self-awareness), but fewer studies have been conducted on these programs. In the area of individual supervision, we found that supervision yields largely positive outcomes for supervisees. As factors that may contribute to such outcomes, attachment between supervisor and supervisee, as well as a strong supervisory alliance, emerged as important, as did supervisors' use of both basic and advanced supervision skills and their providing feedback to supervisees. We close with recommendations for the field.

OVERVIEW

INTRODUCTION

In our experience, training and supervision do not follow direct paths to trainees'/supervisees' perfection and nirvana, but instead are bumpy and sometimes unpredictable processes of constant change, with exciting ups and occasionally demoralizing downs. Every trainee and supervisee brings new challenges, doubts, and insecurities, and that's when we need to reflect on our approaches and discern effective paths forward.

Because training and supervision, like psychotherapy itself, are inherently complex and human experiences, it is difficult to empirically investigate them and come to any definitive answers about their processes and associated outcomes.

Nevertheless, the centrality of both training and supervision to the activity of psychotherapy makes reviewing the empirical findings an essential task in order to see what they may tell us about these vital endeavors.

As we think about the most pivotal moments of our learning the skills to practice as psychologists, we immediately recall powerful events, both positive and negative, during our clinical training and supervision. I (SK), for instance, recall a moving experience during a training on psychodrama, one in which I connected immediately and powerfully to the client's wounding family environment. I also recall, unfortunately, a supervisor who often fell asleep in our sessions, and my not knowing what to do when that happened. Balancing that difficult experience, though, is the memory of another supervisor who helped me find my way through a period in which I questioned whether I had chosen the right profession. It is in such moments that we are not only trained and supervised but also profoundly shaped and formed into the professionals we then become.

Extension of Previous Edition Chapter

In the previous version of this chapter (Hill & Knox, 2013), we explored two fundamental questions: (1) Are training and supervision effective? And (2): If so, what contributes to making training and supervision effective? We explored these questions across the entire professional life span from undergraduate training to training experienced therapists.

With regard to the first question about whether training and supervision are effective, we offered a hesitant yes: training and supervision are effective. Based on the evidence in that chapter, we found the following:

1. Novice trainees can be trained in helping skills.
2. These trainees improve over the course of training.
3. Supervision enhances supervisees' awareness of self and others and increases their autonomy.
4. Experienced therapists can be trained to use manuals, and these training approaches can be extended to practicing therapists in the community, particularly if they continue to use the skills beyond the initial training period
5. Trainees value training and supervision.

We also found contrary evidence, however, that called into question the effectiveness of training and supervision:

1. Nonsupervised therapists performed no differently than did supervised therapists in terms of therapy alliance and client outcome.
2. Supervision sometimes led to detrimental effects on supervisees.
3. Studies involving large numbers of therapists showed no effects for therapist experience level.
4. Highly facilitative people who had no psychotherapy training were found to be as effective in helping clients as were trained therapists.

With regard to the second question about what contributes to the effectiveness of training and supervision, one major conclusion was that hands-on experience is a key component

of learning to becoming a good therapist. Therapists retrospectively stated that they learned the most from experiences with clients, and trainees indicated that practice was the most helpful component of their skills training. In addition, evidence from the helping skills literature indicated that instruction, modeling, and feedback are effective. Furthermore, supervisees noted that supervisors' openness, empathy, and supportive nurturance of supervisee growth, in the context of a safe supervision alliance, aided their development and their clinical work.

Current Chapter

Given this context, our primary goal in the current chapter was to update our prior chapter about the outcomes of training and individual supervision. These outcomes could be evidenced as changes in supervisors/trainers, supervisees/trainees, the training climate/supervision relationship, or clients. Outcomes could be "small o" (changes occurring within sessions), "medium o" (changes occurring as a result of sessions), or "big o" (changes occurring as a result of a whole training or supervision experience). Our second goal was to review literature related to processes associated with these outcomes to determine helpful components of training and supervision. Our final goal was to offer recommendations for the field based on this review.

A major difference from the 2013 chapter is that here we focused only on the empirical evidence for novices (undergraduate and graduate students) in training and supervision, whereas in the previous chapter we focused on training and supervision across the lifespan of practitioners. Doing so allowed us to examine a more focused body of literature, one that speaks directly to the type of training and supervision experiences of those preparing for careers as mental health professionals.

When referring to training, we mean structured education for groups of trainees. In contrast, we define supervision as an individualized process of one supervisor working with one trainee (supervisee) regarding specific clients. We duly acknowledge that the distinction between training and supervision is sometimes unclear, in that training programs may include a supervision element, and supervision likewise may include structured teaching or group supervision formats. Nevertheless, we present these two literatures separately, as they have been treated separately in the literature.

Although we acknowledge that group supervision is often used in graduate training, it has received minimal empirical attention. Perhaps even more importantly, group supervision seems to us to be a substantially different process and dynamic than individual supervision, which Bernard and Goodyear (2019) considered "the cornerstone of professional development" (p. 162). In addition, although extensive research has been conducted in both group and family therapy (see Chapters 17 and 18 of this handbook), space restrictions prevent us from reviewing studies related to training and supervision in these areas.

In terms of inclusion criteria, we included only empirical studies written in English. We did not include studies using analog designs, but did include studies using experimental designs, correlational data, surveys, and qualitative methods. In addition, we did not include studies focusing on training/ supervision for social justice, assessment, diagnosis, or case conceptualization; peer or group supervision; personal psychotherapy; personal relationships; basic psychology; research methods; or statistics. Narrowing our focus in this way enabled us to closely examine a body of research that addresses the core elements of therapy training and supervision for novice therapists.

To provide a comprehensive review of the evidence in this area, we started by including all of the relevant studies from the last chapter. In addition, we searched PsycINFO for articles published from 2011 to late 2018, using the search terms *counselor* or *therapist development; counseling* or *counselor* or *psychotherapy* or *therapist* or *therapy training; counseling* or *counselor* or *therapist* or *therapy supervision; helping skills training; therapist experience* or *expertise*. We also manually searched journals most likely to publish articles on training and supervision: *Clinical Supervisor, The Counseling Psychologist, Counselling Psychology Quarterly, Counselor Education and Supervision, Journal of Counseling and Professional Psychology, Journal of Counseling Psychology, Psychotherapy, Psychotherapy Research, Training and Education in Professional Psychology*. These searches yielded 106 articles published from 2011 to 2018.

Section A: Training with Novice Therapists

In this section, we address specific training programs that have been developed to train novice therapists. We also cover the effects of time and experience given that researchers have often considered these as proxies for the effects of training.

The Effects of Specific Training Programs for Novice Therapists

Many training approaches have been developed to train novice therapists. We review here the efforts to assess the effects of training in helping skills, empathy/facilitative conditions/alliance, self-awareness, theoretically specific approaches, cultural knowledge/skills/awareness, and specific situations.

Helping Skills Training for Novice Therapists

Helping skills training refers to structured programs that teach specific verbal interventions (e.g., reflections of feelings, challenges), typically to advanced undergraduate or beginning graduate students. Such instructions are based on the assumption that these skills are fundamental interventions in counseling/ psychotherapy. The origins of helping skills training trace back to Rogers (1942, 1957), who initially asserted that the facilitative conditions (empathy, warmth or unconditional positive regard, genuineness) could be taught as skills (e.g., restatements). Rogers later was concerned that the initial training programs taught skills in a simplistic way that did not take into account the clinical nuances of how to use them. Accordingly, in his seminal 1957 article, he asserted that the facilitative conditions were attitudes rather than teachable skills.

Early Research on Helping Skills Training (1950–2000)

Carkhuff's Human Relations Training (HRT; 1969) and Ivey's Microcounseling (MC; 1971), both of which focused on teaching specific verbal skills such as empathy or reflection of feeling, have received the most empirical attention. A number of narrative reviews were written about the empirical research on this early helping skills training (Ford, 1979; Kasdorf & Gustafson, 1978; Lambert et al., 1978; Matarazzo, 1971, 1978; Matarazzo & Patterson, 1986; Russell et al., 1984). For example, Matarazzo, in the first three editions of the *Handbook of Psychotherapy and Behavior Change*, concluded that warmth and empathy could be taught. More specifically, she asserted that there was sufficient evidence that Ivey's MC program could be taught in a relatively short period of time to appropriately selected students. In contrast, she dismissed the outcome studies of Carkhuff's HRT because of numerous methodological problems (e.g., skills not being operationally defined, crude and subjective assessment of skills, unspecified aspects of training, inadequate controls, using the same rating scales to assess both training and outcome, use of analog methods such as writing responses to written stimuli rather than actual interview behavior to assess outcome, inadequate training of judges for coding outcome measures, and lack of attention to the optimal sequencing of training methods). We would add that almost all studies involved only one trainer and thus trainer effects could not be estimated.

In a later meta-analytic review of Ivey's MC, Baker and Daniels (1989) reported a larger effect size (Cohen's *d*) of training for undergraduate (1.18) than graduate trainees (0.66), although Goodyear and Guzzardo (2000) argued compellingly that graduate trainees often have had more clinical experience and thus there might be a ceiling effect concerning what they can learn from a helping skills training program. Baker et al.(1990) reported a large effect (1.07) for Carkhuff's HRT and a medium effect (0.63) for Ivey's MC for graduate-level trainees. It should be noted, however, that this meta-analysis was based on a small number of studies ($k = 8$ for HRT; $k = 23$ for MC), and type and amount of training could have been confounded (HRT averaged 37 hours whereas MC averaged 19 hours).

In the above reviews, outcomes were assessed immediately after training. If training is effective, however, the results should persist over time. We found only three studies, all relatively old, that investigated whether those who had been trained for 10–40 hours maintained their skills when tested again one to nine months later. Interestingly, undergraduate trainees decreased in facilitativeness (Collingwood, 1971; Gormally et al., 1975), whereas beginning graduate trainees either maintained or increased in facilitativeness (Butler & Hansen, 1973; Gormally et al., 1975). Gormally and colleagues suggested that undergraduates were less likely to continue using the skills, given that many did not go on to graduate school or work in mental health settings, whereas graduate students continued using their skills in their professional training and so were more able to maintain and enhance their skills.

Recent Research on Helping Skills Training (2001–Present)

More recently, Hill (2004, 2009, 2014, 2020; Hill & O'Brien, 1999) developed a three-stage model (exploration, insight, action) that integrates the earlier training programs with more in-depth theorizing and empirical findings. Importantly, this training program teaches not only the skills but integrates the skills with theory, empathy, clinical nuance (e.g., timing, context), cultural considerations, self-awareness (e.g., helpers need to be aware of their own inner processing so as not to enact their problems with clients), and case conceptualization (given that clients respond differently to the various skills). In the exploration stage (Stage 1), helpers are trained to use open questions, restatements, and reflections of feelings to help clients explore their thoughts and feelings. In the insight stage (Stage 2), helpers are trained to promote client insight via open questions, challenges, interpretations, and immediacy. And in the action stage (Stage 3), helpers are trained to use questions, information, and direct guidance to help clients make changes. Trainers teach specific skills by providing theory, empirical findings, and examples, followed by practice in small groups and dyads. Notably, the Hill helping skills training typically lasts for at least one semester (about 60 hours), as compared with earlier much shorter training programs. Ridley et al. (2011), in their comparison of several training programs, concluded that Hill's program was the best in terms of coverage of skills, culture, theory, cognition and affect, integrating skills with cognition and affect, and relating skills to therapeutic change.

Given the problems noted above with the research on assessing the effectiveness of the earlier helping skills programs, Hill and colleagues developed a research program to better assess the effects of training. For example, in a key study, Hill et al. (2008) found that, compared to their pretraining performance, undergraduate students were more able to use exploration skills, were more empathic, talked less, and were evaluated by themselves and their volunteer clients as more effective in brief sessions with classmates after training in the exploration stage skills. In addition, at the end of the 15-week semester (60 hours) and after practicing all three stages, trainees had higher self-efficacy for using helping skills than at the beginning of the semester. Interestingly, based on weekly self-ratings during the semester, confidence grew steadily during training in exploration skills, declined during training in insight skills (perhaps because insight skills are more difficult to learn), and again rose during the action stage (perhaps because action skills are easier to master). Strengths of the Hill et al. (2008) study included the use of multiple perspectives of outcome, brief sessions with volunteer clients, and more than one trainer. Limitations include a lack of clear specification of the training model and the need to include more sessions per trainee to assess performance.

Several studies now exist assessing the efficacy of the Hill helping skills model, nine with undergraduate students (Chui et al., 2014; Hill, Anderson et al., 2016; Hill & Kellems, 2002; Hill et al., 2008; Jackson et al., 2014; Keum et al., 2018; Kolchakian, 2004; Lu et al., 2020; Spangler

et al., 2014), and five with master's level students (Hill, Sullivan et al., 2007 Lent et al., 2003; Lent et al., 2006; Li et al., 2018; Williams et al., 1997). We conducted separate meta-analyses (using Comprehensive Meta-Analysis version 3 with random effects) by measure and sample (undergraduate or graduate) when there were at least three studies. If there were just two studies, we averaged the effects sizes.

Across these studies, we found evidence for increases in self-efficacy/confidence for using the skills in eight quantitative studies (Chui et al., 2014; Hill et al., 2008; Hill, Anderson et al., 2016; Jackson et al., 2014; Lent et al., 2003, 2006; Spangler et al., 2014; Williams et al., 1997) and one qualitative study (Hill, Sullivan et al., 2007). A meta-analysis of the eight quantitative studies using a variety of self-efficacy measures yielded a standard mean difference of 1.25 (95% CI 0.97, 1.52). A meta-analysis of the data from three studies comprising four samples (Hill et al., 2008; Hill, Lent et al., 2016) of undergraduate students using the scales assessing self-efficacy for using exploration, insight, and action skills on the Counseling Activity Self-Efficacy Scale (CASES; Lent et al., 2003) yielded a standard mean difference of 1.59 (95% CI 1.45, 1.74). The two studies of semester-long training (part of which was focused on helping skills) with master's level students using the CASES-Total (Lent et al., 2003, 2006) found an average effect size of .90. Thus, overall there were increases in self-efficacy for using the skills and, as with earlier reviews (Baker & Daniels, 1989), undergraduate students increased more in self-efficacy than did graduate students.

We also found evidence for the increased use of the helping skills in eight studies (Chui et al., 2014; Hill, Anderson et al., 2016; Hill, Roffman et al., 2008; Hill, Sullivan et al., 2007; Hill & Kellems, 2002; Jackson et al., 2014; Li et al., 2018; Williams et al., 1997). A meta-analysis of the three studies (four samples) that used the client-rated Exploration Subscale of Helping Skills Measure (HSM; Hill & Kellems, 2002) with undergraduate samples yielded a standard mean difference of 0.60 (95% CI 0.49, 0.71. A meta-analysis of the three studies (four samples) that used the client-rated Insight Subscale of the HSM with undergraduate samples yielded a standard mean difference of 0.78 (95% CI 0.35, 1.20). A meta-analysis of the two studies (three samples) using the client-rated Action Subscale of the HSM with undergraduate samples yielded a standard mean difference of 0.15 (95% CI 0.03, 0.27). Two studies that included codings of the actual usage of exploration skills in sessions had an average effect size of 1.06. Thus, it appears that from the perspective both of client perceptions and behavioral codings, undergraduate trainees used more of the exploration and insight skills taught in the training program, but changes were modest in terms of action skills.

Furthermore, evidence was found for the reduction of words spoken in two studies with undergraduate students in brief sessions with volunteer clients (average effect size $d = .85$; Hill et al., 2008; Hill, Anderson et al., 2016). Reductions in words spoken typically reflects that the helpers are listening more.

Additional beneficial effects of training have been shown in a few studies but these cannot easily be analyzed in meta-analyses because different measures and samples were used and typically these outcomes were assessed in only one study. These outcomes include increases in self-efficacy for using specific skills (e.g., interpretations, immediacy), quality of use of specific skills (e.g., exploration, challenges), supervisor-reported use of skills, client-and helper-rated quality of sessions, empathy, self-stigma for seeking psychological help, attitudes toward seeking psychological help, working alliance, countertransference management, cohesion, catharsis, and reductions in anxiety. To highlight one recent study with undergraduate students, Lu et al. (2020) found increases in ethnocultural empathy for White students; in contrast, racial-ethnic minority female students were higher both at the beginning and end of training in ethnocultural empathy. Other possible outcomes that have been noted anecdotally but not assessed empirically include improvements in personal relationships outside of the classroom setting and improvements in personality functioning.

Follow-Up Assessment of the Effects of Skills Training

Hill, Anderson et al. (2020) followed up five years later with students from the Hill, Anderson et al. (2016) study who had taken a helping skills course. Students reported that they were continuing to use the helping skills both professionally (in jobs or further graduate training) as well as in their personal relationships. Although students had increased in self-reported self-efficacy for using the skills during training, no overall changes were reported at the follow-up. Interestingly, however, those participants who had further graduate mental health training scored higher at follow-up on self-efficacy for using the skills than did those with no further mental health education. These results supported the earlier speculation by Gormally et al. (1975) that continued exposure to and practice using the skills helps students continue to improve in their helping abilities.

Effectiveness of Components of Helping Skills Training

Most of the research on the effectiveness of components of helping skills training has been based on Bandura's (1969, 1997) social cognitive theory that instruction, modeling, practice, and feedback are the essential elements of the learning process. To facilitate learning, Bandura suggested that we first need to define what skill is to be learned and give a theoretical rationale for it, then show models of how it can be used, provide opportunities for practice, and finally offer corrective feedback about skill use.

Hill and Lent (2006) conducted a between-studies (i.e., participants came from different studies rather than being randomly assigned to training versus control) meta-analysis of Bandura's components used in helping skills studies. Across all studies, they found a large effect (0.79), indicating that the aforementioned training methods aggregated across all types were better than no training (an ES of 0.79 indicates that 69% of the trainees improved whereas only 31% of the untrained

improved). Further comparisons indicated medium to large effects for modeling (0.90), feedback (0.89), and instruction (0.63), compared to no training. Medium effects across components were found for the two most frequently used outcome measures (0.75 for judges' ratings of trainee empathy during short practice interviews; 0.62 for judges' ratings of trainee empathy in written/taped responses to written/taped analogue stimuli). Medium to large effects across components were found for both undergraduate (0.77) and graduate (0.88) trainees.

When including only those studies that compared the target variables within the same study (i.e., researchers randomly assigned participants to manipulated/experimental conditions versus control), Hill and Lent (2006) reported a medium effect size (0.67) favoring modeling over instruction and feedback, and an additive effect (0.51) indicating that using multiple methods yielded better results than using any single method. These results suggest that modeling is the most influential training component, and that using several methods is better than relying on any single method of training.

Hill and Lent (2006) noted, however, that these studies about the components of training were limited in at least nine ways:

1. Instruction typically involved only 5–10 minutes of written or taped didactic information about the definition and rationale for using a specific skill.
2. Modeling usually involved watching brief (e.g., less than 30 minutes) videotapes of expert therapists demonstrating the target skill.
3. Practice was not included in any of the studies.
4. Feedback typically involved immediate reinforcement via lights or earphones, or through a 20- to 30-minute feedback session.
5. Skills were not typically taught within the context of a training program to trainees seeking to learn skills, and participants had minimal opportunity to learn the complexities of using the interventions.
6. None of the studies involved training for more advanced or difficult skills (e.g., interpretation, immediacy) that require a foundation of empathic ability.
7. Authors were often vague about how they defined and implemented training methods.
8. Assessments of outcomes were restricted to simplistic written/oral responses to written/oral analogue vignettes.
9. There was considerable overlap between instruction and modeling (i.e., how do you model without defining what it is you are modeling?) and between practice and feedback (i.e., how can you give feedback unless it is based on something a trainee has practiced?).

Hill and colleagues have attempted to correct some of these methodological concerns in a series of studies about training in insight skills, more specifically, immediacy (Spangler et al., 2014), interpretation (Jackson et al., 2014), and challenges (Chui et al., 2014). Training for these skills was conducted within the context of complete training programs (i.e., training in insight skills occurred after training in exploration skills) (see Hill, Spangler, Chui et al., 2014; for an overview of the methods). In their review of the findings across the three studies, Hill, Spangler, Jackson et al. (2014) asserted that considerable support was found for all four methods (instruction, modeling, practice, and feedback), with students consistently reporting that practice was the most helpful method.

Prediction of Who Profits from Helping Skills Training

It is also vital to examine whether some trainees benefit more than others from training (i.e., trainee effects). In their review, Hill and Lent (2006) found five early studies that predicted outcome from trainee characteristics. However, these studies all used different predictors (e.g., gender, dominance, conceptual level, attitudes toward skills, expectations about directive versus nondirective therapy style), so Hill and Lent could not draw any conclusions about whether some types of trainees profited more than others from helping skills training.

More recently, six studies that examined predictors of who benefits from training (Chui et al., 2014; Hill et al., 2008; Hill, Anderson et al., 2016; Jackson et al., 2014; Kolchakian, 2004; Spangler et al., 2014) also found conflicting results. Initial levels of trainee-reported self-efficacy for the target skill predicted final trainee-reported self-efficacy for the target skills of immediacy and interpretation in two studies (Jackson et al., 2014; Spangler et al., 2014), although initial levels of trainee-reported self-efficacy for challenges did not predict final self-efficacy in another study (Chui et al., 2014). Similarly, trainee-reported prior helping experiences predicted outcomes of training in two studies (Jackson et al., 2014; Spangler et al., 2014) but not in two other studies (Chui et al., 2014; Hill, Anderson et al., 2016). Trainee-reported natural helping ability predicted outcomes in one study (Chui et al., 2014) but not in two others (Jackson et al., 2014; Spangler et al., 2014). Trainee performance on the Facilitative Interpersonal Skills assessment task (Anderson et al., 2009) predicted increased trainee-reported self-efficacy in the only study that included it (Hill, Anderson et al., 2016).

Characteristics that did not predict training outcomes in any studies included trainee-reported attitudes toward learning helping skills (Chui et al., 2014; Jackson et al., 2014; Spangler et al., 2014); trainee-reported empathic ability (Hill et al., 2008; Hill, Anderson et al., 2016; Kolchakian, 2004); initial grade-point average (Hill et al., 2008); client-rated perfectionism (Hill et al., 2008); trainee performance on nonverbal ability to recognize emotions (Hill, Anderson et al., 2016); trainee-reported narcissism, trainee-reported psychological mindedness, trainee-reported intuition, trainee-reported dominance, and trainee-reported problem-solving orientation (Kolchakian, 2004).

Hence, these findings provide minimal support for consistent predictors of who benefits from helping skills training. It may be that we have not yet assessed the right characteristics, that studies have been seriously limited because trainees self-select into training such that trainees who would not profit do not take the courses, or that training can be effective across trainee types.

Cultural Considerations in Learning and Using Helping Skills

Qualitative analyses have indicated that culture and gender influence trainees' ability to learn the insight skills (Chui et al., 2014; Jackson et al., 2014; Spangler et al., 2014). For example, in Spangler et al. (2014), Asian students indicated that talking about immediate feelings was discouraged in their families, whereas Jewish students indicated openness in their families to talking about feelings. Furthermore, those trainees from backgrounds that were open to using immediacy felt more able to use immediacy than did trainees from families that were not so open. Similarly, gender seemed relevant for some skills, such that female students seemed more comfortable being direct and open than did male students.

At least five years after they had taken two master's-level classes in helping skills, 13 Korean practicing therapists were interviewed about how they had modified the helping skills to fit their culture (Joo et al., 2019). The authors concluded that Korean therapists provided more education about the approach at the beginning of therapy, used more indirect than direct communication, validated the client's experiences more, worked more tentatively with emotions, were more cautious in the insight stage, and responded more to the implicit underlying communications when asking for action than they had been trained to do. We suspect (and hope) that all therapists modify the skills according to their culture, their personality, and the perceived needs of specific clients, but more research is needed to provide evidence for how to modify the training to fit the needs of trainees from different cultures.

Summary for Studies of Helping Skills Training

Although some evidence was found for the effectiveness of early training programs, serious methodological concerns limited our ability to draw conclusions. More recent research on the Hill helping skills training model suggests that there are increases in self-efficacy for using the skills, increases in the use of exploration and insight skills in brief sessions with volunteer clients, and reductions in the number of words spoken in brief sessions with volunteer clients. Although these findings are promising, we note that there have been only 15 studies of the Hill model, all conducted by Hill and colleagues. Furthermore, we should note that the reliance on self-efficacy as the major outcome, although relatively easy to assess because it is self-report, needs to be augmented by assessments of actual performance. We also note that although these recent studies have included more than one trainer, we still need to assess trainer effects.

Furthermore, some evidence from early studies was found for the effectiveness of instruction and modeling in teaching empathy and reflection of feelings. More current evidence with better methodology has yielded evidence for the effects of instruction, modeling, practice, and feedback in teaching insight skills, with the evidence for practice being most compelling. We know less, however, about the best ways to teach action skills. We also do not know much about other possible components of training, such as self-observation, self-confrontation, co-counseling, anxiety-reduction techniques, support, and transcribing and coding interventions used in sessions and receiving feedback from instructors about those interventions. In addition, we do not yet know the best sequence for the presenting the components of training. Although it makes sense that trainees first read about a skill, then learn about the skill through lecture/discussion, then see models of the skill, then practice, and then receive feedback, other sequences might be as useful, and sequences might vary for different skills. Finally, we do not know much about the role of teaching about theory in relation to teaching about skills. We are mindful of Rogers' angst about skills training being too mechanistic and encourage more thinking about how to make skills training more clinically relevant.

Given trainees' enthusiasm regarding the helpfulness of practice, we want to highlight these results, especially in light of recent theorizing (Rousmaniere, 2016, 2018) and empirical evidence about deliberate practice (Hill, Kivlighan et al., 2020). It seems to us, based on our experiences in training, that instruction and modeling provide a crucial foundation, but that trainees need extensive practice in a variety of formats (e.g., dyads, small groups, simulated vignettes), preferably with constructive feedback, to allow them to begin to master the skills. Students have commented that the skills seem easy when they read about them, but they realize how difficult they are when they begin to practice. In addition, practicing with real volunteer clients (rather than standard or trained clients) allows trainees to begin to see the clinical nuances to working with dynamic human beings. We thus suggest that helping skills training is a good example of deliberate practice training, given the focus on learning and practicing specific skills in a safe, structured setting with feedback.

In terms of proposed methods for assessing the effectiveness of the components of training, we stress that these components need to be tested within the context of a helping skills training program, especially for teaching more advanced skills. For example, early studies assessed the effects of components outside the context of programmatic training, using undergraduates who were taught a single skill (e.g., reflection of feelings) in a short period of time. In contrast, in the three studies of training insight skills (Chui et al., 2014; Jackson et al., 2014; Spangler et al., 2014), undergraduate students in semester-long helping skills courses were taught the insight skills after they had learned exploration skills. Using all the skills requires a great deal of clinical expertise, and we thus need to learn more about teaching the art of using the skills.

In terms of predicting who profits from training, we have few promising leads. Perhaps this is actually good news. Maybe there are no barriers to who can learn the skills. The qualitative studies cited above suggest, however, that cultural factors may play an important role, and thus deserve more attention.

Some hints about the influence of culture in learning helping skills come from qualitative research about cultural differences in response to learning and using insight skills (Chui et al., 2014; Jackson et al., 2014; Spangler et al., 2014), and from the Joo et al. (2019) study that Korean trainees modified the skills after training to fit their culture. Further research is needed to explore these findings in other cultures.

In addition, although the assumption is made that the skills taught in these programs are effective ingredients in counseling/psychotherapy, we have limited evidence for the efficacy of most of the skills. The exception is several studies on specific effects of therapist self-disclosure and immediacy (see review by Hill et al., 2018), interpretations vs. probes for insight (Hill, Lu et al., 2020), silence (e.g., Cuttler et al., 2019; Hill et al., 2019), restatements vs. reflections of feelings, open questions for thoughts, and open questions for feelings (Anvari et al., 2020), and advice-giving (Prass et al., in press). More research is needed to determine if skills are effective in the ways advocated by these helping skills programs (e.g., whether reflections of feelings are indeed associated client exploration of feelings, whether interpretations are indeed associated with client insight).

Now that we have some evidence for the effectiveness of training, we need to turn our attention to questions regarding what is adequate or sufficient in terms of training outcomes. Some would argue that we should develop minimum thresholds (benchmarks) of skill attainment to determine whether a student has succeeded (i.e., is competent) or failed in training. Such criteria could be used to assess the effectiveness or quality of training, just as some researchers assess the outcomes of psychotherapy by examining the number of clients who pass from the symptomatic to normal ranges of functioning. We would argue against such a trend, however, because we do not yet have enough evidence about what makes training effective. We also need a deeper evidence base regarding when and how skills should best be used in therapy before we might embark on constructing such guidelines. At this point, we believe that the goal of helping skills training is to teach students to think broadly about the skills and practice them, to learn when and how to use skills, and to observe client reactions and adjust their approach based on clients' unique needs. Every client is different, and therapists must be responsive to each client's specific needs. Thus, the goals of training are to provide therapists with an armamentarium of skills upon which they can rely, and which they can astutely use, in the inevitably dynamic and varied clinical situations they will encounter. Furthermore, we simply do not know what a skilled or competent therapist looks like post-training. In fact, there could well be a negative effect on the training process if we were to dictate exactly how trainees, or therapists, should behave with clients.

Relatedly, it also makes sense, based on our experiences and based on the cognitive psychology literature about learning and expertise (e.g., Ericsson et al., 2006; Georghiades, 2004; Hacker, 1998), that it would take two to three years for students to become relatively comfortable using the basic helping skills. Once they develop some proficiency in using the skills in an empathic, caring manner, they typically no longer focus on each individual skill (i.e., they do not think about making a reflection of feeling), but rather begin to focus more on the client and the dynamics of the therapeutic relationship (which is similar to Rogers' beliefs about attitudes). Thus, the skills become automatic and recede into the background, and other concerns (e.g., case conceptualization, session management) occupy the foreground of attention. They still use the skills, and ideally do so effectively, but no longer have to think consciously about what skill to use at which point. Thus, we need to assess changes in how skills are used over the course of training and beyond.

Training Programs in Empathy/Facilitative Conditions/Alliance for Novice Trainees

These approaches arose from Rogers' client-centered theory, with researchers seeking to teach trainees the meaning of empathy, to recognize emotions in others, to take the perspective of others, and to show empathy in social situations. Training methods typically involved experiential games and exercises, lectures, demonstrations, practice, and feedback.

In a meta-analysis of 19 randomized controlled trials (RCTs) of empathy training with 1,018 participants (Van Berkout & Malouf, 2016), studies (a) had to involve a treatment and control condition, random assignment to condition, and empathy as the main target; (b) empathy had to be measured; and (c) the article had to include enough data to determine the effect size. The overall effect of training in the meta-analysis was statistically significant ($g = 0.73$, although this lowered to 0.63 after removing an outlier). There was significant variability in the scores, however, which seemed to be because of the wide range of participants. The average g was 1.63 for the three studies with university students, and 1.04 for the four studies with medical and nursing students, suggesting that these samples gained more than did non-student samples. We note that the description of empathy training was very broad in this review and thus may not be representative of what usually occurs in graduate clinical training.

Two qualitative studies not included in the Van Berkout and Malouf (2016) meta-analysis focused specifically on empathy training for psychotherapy trainees. Nerdrum and Rønnestad (2002, 2004) found that trainees reported more empathic understanding in working with clients, more understanding of themselves as professionals, and positive effects on clients as a result of empathy training. Trainees reported that the most useful training methods were lectures about theory, role-playing, and actively participating in the training. Trainees also valued trainers' responsiveness to their individual needs, supportiveness, and being credible models of empathic functioning. All trainees also, however, commented that being vulnerable about their abilities made them anxious. In reflecting about how they changed, trainees noted the influence of new knowledge and suggested that they learned by self-observation and by observing the effects of their interventions on clients. Finally, trainees noted that both time and effort were essential for internalizing learning.

Another study not included in the above meta-analysis investigated alliance-focused training (AFT) to help doctoral student trainees work constructively with negative therapeutic processes (Safran et al., 2014). All trainees were first trained in cognitive therapy and then switched to AFT. After AFT was added, trainees were rated as displaying less controlling and more autonomy-granting and disclosing interpersonal behaviors in sessions with clients, and clients were rated as making complementary shifts in their behaviors (less friendly-submissive, more disclosing, and more asserting-separating interpersonal behaviors). In a second sample, therapists explored and reflected more about their relationships with clients after AFT was added to their training.

In summary, some evidence exists for the effectiveness of training in empathy/facilitative conditions/alliance for students. We need, however, more precise operationalizations of empathy training (alliance training was well operationalized) and examinations of how they differ from training in the exploration stage of helping skills.

Self-Awareness Training Programs for Novice Trainees

Self-awareness has been defined as "a state of being conscious of one's thoughts, feelings, beliefs, behaviors and attitudes, and knowing how these factors are shaped by important aspects of one's developmental and social history" (Pieterse et al., 2013, p. 191). Self-awareness can be either a global knowledge of one's value system and relationship processes, or a more moment-to-moment awareness of feelings and bodily sensations (Williams et al., 2003).

Many have suggested that reflecting on one's experiences and processes and gaining self-awareness are important aspects of training (e.g., Bennetts, 2003; Pieterse et al., 2013; Strawbridge & Woolfe, 2010; Williams, 2008). Likewise, a high degree of trainee openness seems crucial for making the reflection process productive (Allen, 1967; Pieterse et al., 2013). In fact, some have even suggested that experienced therapists may not continue to develop expertise because they no longer reflect enough on their clinical experiences (e.g., Nissen-Lie et al., 2017; Rousmaniere, 2016).

Trainees are thus taught in a number of training programs to reflect more deeply on what they are doing, raise their self-awareness, enhance their psychological capacity, manage countertransference, and become more mindful. The hope is that by raising awareness of inner functioning, the trainee will be less likely to act out on destructive impulses and more able to intervene effectively to help clients.

Interpersonal Process Recall (IPR; Kagan, 1984; Kagan & Kagan, 1990; Kagan et al., 1969) is perhaps the most well-known and researched program designed to strengthen self-awareness. In IPR, trainees are helped to articulate their thoughts and feelings about their interventions, under the assumption that students are blocked from effectively using their skills due to performance anxiety. A typical IPR session might involve watching and stopping the videotape of one's session at various points, with an inquirer asking about thoughts and feelings, what one imagines the client is thinking and feeling, and what one thinks the client is thinking about them.

In their meta-analysis of skills training programs including IPR ($k = 10$), Baker et al. (1990) found a small effect size of 0.20 for IPR with graduate-level trainees, although Kagan and Kagan (1990) criticized this meta-analysis for including studies that assessed skill attainment rather than more appropriate outcomes (e.g., overcoming fears of psychological intimacy, recognizing and acting on subtle messages between clients and trainees). Importantly, Kagan and Kagan noted that IPR training should logically be administered after helping skills training.

Relatedly, Meekums et al. (2016) found evidence that IPR is more valuable for developing reflectivity (i.e., self-awareness) than for developing skills (e.g., reflection of feelings, interpretations). They also suggested that reflecting teams (RT) that observe sessions and describe to therapists and clients what they have witnessed can be a good way of providing feedback. Meekums and colleagues found only one study for IPR and two studies for RT, which precludes drawing conclusions, but does support the idea of teaching reflectivity.

Furthermore, although coding intentions (Cutts, 2012), journal writing (Wright, 2005), recording sessions with clients (Gossman & Miller, 2011), and transcribing client sessions (Arthur & Gfroerer, 2002) have all been promoted as a way of helping trainees develop what is termed an *internal supervisor* so that they can reflect on their experiences, these methods have not been investigated. We also need to investigate whether training in self-awareness or reflectivity indeed decreases the probability of therapists acting out destructively or unhelpfully with clients.

Training in Theoretically Specific Approaches for Novice Trainees

Psychodynamic/Interpersonal Psychotherapy Training

In four studies, Kivlighan and colleagues (Kivlighan, 1989, 2008, 2010; Multon et al., 1996) examined changes across the course of a semester-long class in interpersonal-psychodynamic psychotherapy for master's-level trainees. Results showed a variety of changes consistent with interpersonal-psychodynamic therapy, such as changes in intentions (e.g., decreased use of assessment intentions and increased use of exploration intentions), changes in helping skills (e.g., fewer questions and minimal encouragers), and increased adherence to psychodynamic techniques, increased working alliance, and decreased verbal activity. We also note the similarity of these findings to those of the helping skills training.

In Hilsenroth et al. (2002), doctoral students who received structured clinical training in short-term psychodynamic psychotherapy had higher alliance ratings by clients and therapists after session 4 than did those who received no training. Hilsenroth et al. (2006) then investigated changes in the ability to use psychodynamic techniques within and across the first two cases seen by each of 15 clinical psychology graduate students. They found increases in psychodynamic interventions (as coded by trained judges) between sessions 3 and 9 in the first case (which could be due to experience with the client or training), but no comparable changes within the second case (which is puzzling). They also found changes across the two cases in the use of psychodynamic interventions at session 3 (which could indicate the effects of training) but not at session 9 (which is again puzzling). No differences were found within or across cases for use of cognitive-behavioral techniques, which makes sense given that these techniques were not focused on in psychodynamic training. Thus, evidence for the effects of training was somewhat mixed. Strengths of these studies include the use of data from real clients in a community-oriented clinic; limitations include the small sample of students

all trained by one trainer/supervisor, the lack of attention to dropouts, and the use of only two cases per therapist.

Experiential Psychotherapy Training

Pascual-Leone and colleagues studied the effectiveness of experiential psychotherapy training for undergraduate and graduate students (Pascual-Leone & Andreescu, 2013; Pascual-Leone et al., 2012, 2013, 2015). More specifically, this training involved exposing trainees to didactic instruction in experiential psychotherapy, watching video demonstrations of therapy, practicing sessions with peers and volunteer clients, writing weekly journals about their experiences, completing assignments meant to enhance awareness of productive therapy, coding their own personal narratives on a range of psychotherapy process measures (e.g., experiencing, narrative processes, core conflictual themes), and engaging in self-disclosure as if they were clients. A unique aspect of the training was having students rate themselves on various process measures that had been developed for research purposes. By rating themselves on these process measures, students became more aware of and reflective about their own behaviors in sessions. Results using both quantitative and qualitative methods indicated professional and personal gains after participating in such courses. Unfortunately, the effects of the specific components were not assessed.

Training for Behavioral Therapies

Freiheit and Overholser (1997) trained 40 clinical psychology students in CBT over the course of two semesters. Based on self-report, students learned CBT techniques and had more positive attitudes regarding CBT after training. Interestingly, however, a subsample of students who initially had negative evaluations of CBT did not change their evaluations.

Three studies (Kanter et al., 2013; Keng et al., 2017; Knott et al., 2019; Maitland et al., 2016) assessed the effects of training in functional analytic psychotherapy (FAP), a behavioral treatment that emphasizes the development of an intimate and intense therapy relationship as the vehicle for client change. FAP is part of the third wave of behavioral treatments focused on mindfulness, acceptance, and constructive change rather than symptom alleviation. Training is delivered either in person or online and involves a highly structured 8-week group environment that is experiential and personal, emphasizing deliberate practice and feedback. The goal is to increase therapists' awareness, courage, and love. Outcomes included improvements in self-rated FAP competency and observer-coded skill compared to a wait list (Kanter et al., 2013; Maitland et al., 2016) and increases in overall empathy, FAP skill, and treatment acceptability both after training and at a two-month follow-up (Keng et al., 2017). Thus, FAP training seems to be effective in improving empathy and FAP skills.

In a pilot study examining web-based training followed by live remote training of cognitive-behavior therapy (CBT) for anxiety disorders, Kobak et al. (2013) found a significant increase in both knowledge and skills, with user satisfaction high for both training modules; utilization of CBT also increased after training. In a similar pilot study, Puspitasari et al. (2013) found efficacy for an online training program for behavioral activation for community health providers: Participants implemented skills in actual sessions, performance was maintained at follow-up, and trainees were very satisfied with training.

Other Theoretically Specific Training Studies

Boswell et al. (2010) investigated the effects of training on 19 clinical psychology students (none of whom had prior clinical experience) in their first practicum working with community clients. Students were trained in either psychodynamic, CBT, or humanistic-interpersonal treatments (but were not randomly assigned to practica). The type of practicum had no effect on therapist post-session ratings of session process or on client-rated post-session outcome. No differences were found in how well students learned and implemented the treatment manuals. Strengths of the study include the use of real clients; limitations include a lack of attention to dropouts, the use of a small sample all from one program, and the data collection period of only one semester.

Dennhag and Ybrandt (2013) studied changes in undergraduate students after basic psychotherapy training in both CBT and psychodynamic therapy while working with their first client in one of the modalities. Over the course of 25 sessions, trainees rated themselves as having improved in technical skills, basic relational skills, and constructive coping strategies, and having decreased in perceived difficulties. Without a control group that received no training, separating out the effects of training from experience of conducting sessions was not possible. Differences between CBT and psychodynamic therapy were not investigated.

Summary of Theoretically Specific Training

Several studies of psychodynamic-interpersonal training suggest that trainees do indeed learn to use psychodynamic-interpersonal techniques. After training, trainees used more appropriate helping skills and intentions, reduced their verbal activity, and facilitated a more productive working alliance. Some evidence also exists for training in experiential and behavioral orientations. One study, however, found no differences across approaches. Given how much training is based on theoretically specific methods, we were surprised by how little evidence there is for the effectiveness of training in theory-specific methods, especially comparing different theory-specific approaches, at the undergraduate and graduate level.

Training Novice Therapists in Cultural Knowledge, Skills, and Awareness

Benuto et al. (2018) reviewed 17 outcome studies assessing the effects of training graduate psychology students in cultural competence. Although not focused on training therapists, this review is included here because training therapists to be culturally aware and humble should be a component of training programs, given changing demographics around the world and the evidence about the pervasive influence of culture (Sue et al., 2019).

Training programs in the review focused on racism and discrimination, worldviews, cultural identity, general concepts about culture, biases, information about specific cultures, and information about the therapy interaction related to culture. The authors noted, however, that descriptions of curricular content were often quite vague. The most typical curricular methods were lecture, discussion, role-play, and increased contact with diverse individuals. Time in training ranged from 2.5 to 144 hours (average = 31 hours). Outcomes were typically assessed through self-report measures of culture competency. The majority of studies found positive changes in terms of knowledge about culture, but results were mixed regarding attitudes, awareness, and skills. Clearly, more studies are needed about the inclusion of cultural components in clinical training.

Training for Specific Situations in Psychotherapy

Hess et al. (2006) provided 62 advanced doctoral student trainees with three types of brief training for managing client anger: supervisor-facilitated training (students were asked to talk about their reactions and role played responses to a vignette of an angry client to become more empathic and use more reflections of feelings and immediacy), self-training (students were asked to write about their reactions and think of what they might do differently with the client), and bibliotraining (students read an article about a treatment model for anger disorders). Students received all three types of training in a random order. Training overall was rated as very helpful, and trainees rated themselves as having higher self-efficacy for working with client anger as a result of the training. Supervisor-facilitated training appeared to be the most beneficial training method, given that trainees rated it as most helpful and used more reflections of feelings after it. Although these results are intriguing, we do not know whether they would generalize to other challenging client behaviors, or to real clinical situations, especially after such brief training.

Crook-Lyon et al. (2009) examined the effects of didactic-experiential training, individual feedback, and practice for teaching novice therapists to do dream work. Therapist self-efficacy for working with dreams and attitudes toward dreams increased after didactic training; those who received individual feedback had higher process and outcome evaluations from clients in a dream session than did those not receiving feedback; and self-efficacy, attitudes toward dreams, and perceived self-competence in dream work steadily increased across the course of conducting dream sessions with five clients. Although the sample size was small, these results support the effectiveness of didactic-experiential methods, feedback, and practice.

In summary, although many specific situations that arise in psychotherapy could be the focus of training, there is a paucity of research in this area. Other situations might include working with silence, advice-seeking, clients in crisis, and boundaries.

Deliberate Practice

Although deliberate practice is a combination of training and supervision, we include it in this section of the chapter because it is a relatively structured approach. Deliberate practice (DP) was introduced and defined by Ericsson and colleagues (Ericsson & Pool, 2016; Ericsson, Krampe, & Tesch-Römer, 1993) as "the individualized training activities specially designed by a coach or teacher to improve specific aspects of an individual's performance through repetition and successive refinement" (Ericsson & Lehmann, 1996, pp. 278–279). Binder and Henry described deliberate practice as having three components: (1) performing well-defined tasks at an appropriate difficulty level, (2) receiving immediate and informative feedback (i.e., supervision), and (3) having opportunities to repeat and correct performance errors.

DP has recently been considered as part of psychotherapy training (e.g., Caspar et al., 2004; Miller et al., 2007; Tracey et al., 2014). In psychotherapy, DP focuses on a trainee's individual skill threshold, emphasizes behavioral rehearsal for skill acquisition, aims for higher levels of sustained effort, and uses homework to advance skill acquisition (Goodyear & Rousmaniere, 2017; Rousmaniere, 2016).

Chow et al. (2015) found that self-reported, skill-focused professional development activities significantly predicted client outcome for 17 therapists working with 1,632 clients. However, Chow et al. relied on retrospective self-reports rather than evaluating DP experimentally.

Recently, Hill, Kivlighan et al. (2019) examined the effects of DP training focused on immediacy for seven doctoral student trainees. Training included an eight-hour workshop, four individual 50-minute sessions, and four individual 30-minute homework sessions. Qualitative results indicated that trainees found the DP training to be effective, especially in helping them become aware of and manage emotions and countertransference that had inhibited them from using immediacy. In addition, there was a moderate and significant effect of training on trainees' self-efficacy for using immediacy, a small and significant effect on therapist-rated working alliance, and no significant effect for client-rated working alliance. Obviously, because of the time-intensive nature of this training, it is difficult to include large numbers of participants, but we would note that future studies need to involve more trainers and trainees, additional targets of intervention, and attention to the components of the training.

INFLUENCE OF EXPERIENCE/TIME ON TRAINEE DEVELOPMENT

Time (experience) during graduate school has been used to assess the effects of training, based on the argument that if training is effective, therapists should have better outcomes at the end than at the beginning of graduate training. Of course, many other experiences (e.g., practice, maturation, personal therapy) also occur during this time, so it is not only training that is reflected in any such findings. Time/experience is thus a weak estimate of the effects of training but is included here because it has so often been used as evidence of the effects of training.

Changes in Client Outcomes

Early reviews (e.g., Beutler et al., 2004; Stein & Lambert, 1995) found modest support for the relationship between therapist experience (across the career span from graduate school to experienced therapists) and client outcomes. More recent studies, most with large numbers of clients across many therapists, and most with data on experience level ranging from graduate trainees to experienced therapists, including some longitudinal data, have shown mixed results. Positive effects were found in two studies, indicating that there were increases with experience (Hill et al., 2015; Owen et al., 2016). No effects or changes across experience level were found in two studies (Erekson et al. 2017; Okiisii et al., 2006). Negative effects, indicating decreases with experience, were found in three studies (Budge et al., 2013; Goldberg et al., 2016; Minami et al., 2009). All of the above studies, except Hill et al. (2015), included postdoctoral therapists in addition to doctoral student therapists.

Changes in Therapist Self-Efficacy

In their review of the literature, Larson and Daniels (1998) concluded that therapist self-efficacy correlated positively with developmental level, such that more experienced therapists reported higher levels of self-efficacy than did those with less experience. Self-efficacy also correlated positively with satisfaction and negatively with anxiety about conducting therapy, suggesting that it is a relevant variable for assessing changes across training. Given that self-efficacy is often used as a proxy for performance, the findings suggest that there are changes across time during training.

Changes in the Process of Psychotherapy

Several studies (Barrett-Lennard; 1962; Caracena, 1965; Mallinckrodt & Nelson, 1991) found evidence that experienced therapists provided more facilitative conditions than did graduate-student therapists. O'Donovan et al. (2005) found that one group of students who participated in a traditional graduate clinical psychology program gained more didactic knowledge than did a group who served an apprenticeship in which they obtained supervised workplace experience without organized training, but neither group changed in terms of client and observer ratings of working alliance, empathy, and dropout. Students were not randomly assigned to condition, however, and details about the training are lacking, so it is difficult to interpret these results.

In their longitudinal study of doctoral trainees over time seeing volunteer clients in brief sessions, Hill et al.'s (1981) participants increased their use of minimal encouragers; decreased their use of questions; and maintained acceptable levels of activity, anxiety, and quality of responding. Qualitatively, the students reported that graduate school was stressful but growth-producing, and that they had changed more in terms of higher-order counseling abilities (e.g., timing, appropriateness of interventions, knowledge about client dynamics, and self-confidence) than in the basic helping skills. Also, from a qualitative perspective, Williams et al. (1997) found that beginning therapists had a great deal of anxiety and insecurity about being able to use skills in a clinical situation, but that this discomfort decreased during training.

Hill et al. (2015) also examined changes in therapy process across clients over time for 23 advanced doctoral-student therapists in a psychodynamic clinic. Client- and therapist-rated working alliance and client-rated real relationship increased across clients over time. Trainees rated themselves as having improved in their ability to use some basic helping skills (e.g., reflection of feelings, interpretation, immediacy) and maintained high levels in others (approval-reassurance, self-disclosure, not interrupting). They reported substantial improvement in some advanced clinical skills (e.g., conceptualization ability, negotiating boundaries, self-awareness, presence, countertransference management, multicultural understanding). In other clinical skills (e.g., professionalism, trusting instincts, empathy, focus on clients instead of self, responsiveness to clients), they rated themselves as maintaining already-high levels. Thus, from a process perspective, trainees changed extensively during their time in the clinic, even though they began their work there as relatively advanced trainees.

In summary, four studies (Barrett-Lenard, 1962; Caracena, 1965; Hill et al., 2015; Mallinckrodt & Nelson, 1991) suggested that trainees improve in facilitativeness (e.g., empathy, warmth, working alliance) over time in graduate training. Furthermore, the studies by Hill and colleagues (Hill et al., 1981, 2015) showed a variety of ways in which doctoral student therapists changed in terms of process variables, suggesting that we need to look at process variables in addition to client outcomes to assess the effects of training.

Changes in Self-Perceptions of Professional Development

On the basis of qualitative interviews about how trainees experienced themselves over time, Skovholt and Rønnestad (1992) and Rønnestad and Skovholt (2003) described three stages of development relevant to our chapter. Prior to formal training, lay helpers typically have been involved in helping others, but offer their own solutions, engage in numerous boundary violations, strongly identify with those whom they are helping, and are not reflective or self-aware of the influence of their behaviors. At the beginning of training, trainees begin to shift to a more professional demeanor and often feel challenged, vulnerable, anxious, dependent on authorities, and in need of considerable feedback and reinforcement; skills training is particularly appropriate at this level to help trainees have something concrete to focus on. In contrast, advanced students are typically able to function at a professional level, although many feel pressured to perform perfectly and thus are more cautious and conservative than are experienced therapists. These advanced trainees have typically moved beyond rote use of skills or theory and are able to develop their own theoretical approaches to therapy, integrate their professional and personal selves, shift from an external to an internal locus of control, gain in reflective capacity, and become less anxious. These qualitative findings provide evidence that trainees think they change and also suggest specific outcomes to test in terms of actual changes in future studies.

Similarly, Carlsson and colleagues (Carlsson, Norberg, Sandell et al., 2011; Carlsson Norberg, Schubert et al., 2011)

found that trainees changed over time and felt a greater sense of freedom to use their own styles after training in psychodynamic psychotherapy. Trainees also had negative reactions to the training, perhaps because these therapists had amassed considerable clinical experience prior to their advanced training and did not feel validated for their expertise. Such findings emphasize the importance of being responsive to trainees' needs.

Summary for Effects of Time and Experiences on Trainee Development

The assumption that trainees improve (e.g., become more skilled clinically) during time in graduate training has received some support in terms of increases in therapist self-efficacy, better use of process variables, and enhanced self-perceptions, but has received mixed support in terms of client outcomes. Considerable concerns exist about this body of research, however. First, graduate training is very diverse, and researchers have seldom provided a clear description of the training. A second concern focuses on the definitions of time and experience. Some studies specified distinct levels of training (e.g., master's level, advanced doctoral, intern), but students enter training with very different levels of prior experience, and thus just examining where they are in the training process is an imprecise assessment of their experience status. Furthermore, students engage in different amounts of experience during training that a simple assessment of time or training level does not capture (e.g., some seek additional clinical practice, and thus those in their third or final year of training may have different amounts of experience). In addition, setting of training undoubtedly influences client outcomes, given that some students see clients at university counseling centers, whereas others see patients at community agencies or inpatient settings. Finally, we need to recognize that the effects of training are entangled with maturation, personal therapy, personal relationships, and work with clients. We may never be able to separate out the intertwining of these variables, and thus, discern the effects of graduate training remains a challenging endeavor.

In terms of recommendations for further research related to experience and time, we recommend the following:

- Researchers continue to assess changes across the course of graduate training, despite the inherent challenges of conducting such research. It is especially important to assess for changes using longitudinal rather than cross-sectional designs if we are to attribute any findings to the effects of training.
- Changes need to be studied across more than 1 or 2 cases per trainee (probably at least 5 to 10) to make sure that we discern true changes rather than random variation among clients.
- We need to learn more about what goes on during the time in which trainees receive training. For example: To what extent are trainees in structured training? How much personal therapy are they receiving? How many clients are they seeing (e.g., is there an optimal client load in ratio to the amount of supervision)? And how much reflection are they doing about their practice and skills?

SUMMARY AND RECOMMENDATIONS FOR RESEARCH ON TRAINING NOVICE THERAPISTS

Most of the research for novice trainees has focused on helping skills training. We suggest that this focus is prudent because trainees are learning to shift from communication that is appropriate in friendships to communication that is appropriate for therapy. Hence, they must learn to move from evenly shared conversations to listening more, interrupting less, and giving less self-disclosure and advice, all while donning the mantle of professionalism and beginning to see themselves in the professional role of therapist. It makes sense, then, to focus on these skills in safe practice situations with volunteer clients so that trainees can begin to self-reflect and observe their behaviors in a supportive environment before beginning work with actual clients.

One unresolved question, however, involves the sequencing of training. From our perspective (see also, Hill, Stahl et al., 2007), helping skills training is vital as a first exposure to the field because it allows trainees to engage in deliberate practice of the skills and focus primarily on their skills before focusing on client dynamics. Although it makes intuitive sense to provide helping skills training first, then introduce trainees to working with relatively easy clients under *in vivo* supervision, and only later train students in specific treatment approaches with more difficult clients, such sequencing of training experiences has not been investigated empirically.

In addition, we know very little about trainer effects. Undoubtedly, who the trainer is makes a difference in that some trainers inspire trainees, whereas others turn trainees off from pursuing a career as a therapist. Unfortunately, researchers have not focused on trainer effects, which we might expect to be at least as high as therapist effects in psychotherapy (e.g., 5% to 10% of the variance in client outcome; Baldwin & Imel, 2013; Castonguay & Hill, 2017; Johns et al., 2019). For adequate studies on the efficacy of training, then, we propose that researchers include at least 20 and preferably more trainers so that differences among trainers (trainer effects) can be studied. We recognize that inclusion of multiple trainers is difficult at most institutions where only one trainer is involved. Possible solutions are studying undergraduate or master's level classes at large universities where multiple courses with multiple instructors/trainers are often used, and designing multi-site studies where instructors follow a manualized training approach so that course content is similar across sites.

Based on the extant research, we offer the following suggestions for future research:

1. Continued research is needed on training in basic helping skills. We need to know which helping skills training approaches/programs are effective and what makes them effective.
2. In addition to learning the helping skills, trainers also hope that trainees become less anxious, have more self-efficacy, are better able to manage sessions, and become more self-aware. Thus, we also need to know what training approaches yield such effects for different types of trainees.
3. We need to know more about training for specific skills. As earlier noted, we have a lot of research on training for empathy/restatements/reflections of feelings, but need more research on insight skills such as interpretations, challenges, and immediacy. Relatedly, more research is needed on training in advanced skills, such as managing anger and sexual attraction, assessing for suicidality, performing intakes, developing case conceptualizations, grief counseling, and cultural competence/humility. It would also be interesting to determine whether prior training in helping skills enables trainees to learn these advanced skills more effectively.
4. We also need to know more about trainer (e.g., dogmatism, charisma) and trainee (e.g., attitudes about psychotherapy, motivations for wanting to be a therapist, tolerance for ambiguity, self-awareness) characteristics that influence training outcomes.
5. Components of training programs need to be more clearly defined.
6. We need to know more about the maintenance of skills after training. Thus, we urge others to examine empirically the assertion that continued practice using the skills helps trainees maintain their skills.
7. We need to learn more about the interaction between attitudes and skills. In other words, we need to know more about how to train students not only to learn the skills, but how to use them in a caring, empathic manner.
8. Trainers need to specify what occurs in training so that we have an adequate picture of that training. Most descriptions in the literature reviewed here were vague.
9. Ideally, trainees would be randomly assigned to training vs. comparison conditions, although we recognize the difficulty in doing so, given that most training takes place in academic settings.
10. Outcome should be assessed in a multi-method manner, such that the perspectives of helpers, helpees, and trainers are assessed, and performance should be assessed in sessions with volunteer or standard (i.e., clients taught to act in a particular way and to evaluate the skills of the helper) clients. Real volunteer clients are ideal because they present actual data and are more likely to respond naturally to trainees. Trained (or standard) clients are somewhat acceptable because comparisons can be made across time and trainees, but great care must be taken to standardize the presentation of the material so that it is consistent across trainees.
11. In the helping skills training programs, it is assumed that some skills are most effective for exploration, some for insight, and some for action, but we have minimal empirical evidence of what the actual effects of these skills are in psychotherapy. More efforts are needed to determine the effects of each of the helping skills in actual psychotherapy.
12. On the basis of initial evidence, it appears that culture influences how students learn the insight skills (Chui et al., 2014, Jackson et al., 2014; Spangler et al., 2014) and

that Korean students modify what they learned in helping skills training to fit their culture (Joo et al., 2019). We need more research on the effects of culture in helping skills training. Trainees may have preferences for different skills based on their culture, trainees from different cultures might have different reactions to learning the different skills, and trainees from different cultures might apply the skills in different ways.

SECTION B: INDIVIDUAL SUPERVISION

Supervision is required of all graduate students learning to be mental health professionals. It is also crucial to the gatekeeping function in which trainers must decide whether trainees are sufficiently competent to graduate and seek credentialing or licensure. Despite its central importance, however, we have surprisingly little evidence of its effectiveness, nor of what may lead to its effectiveness. Perhaps, then, the supervision story is more about what we do not know than what we do know, and thus we hope that this section of the chapter will inspire researchers to think about what needs to be examined.

Definition of Supervision

Psychotherapy supervision consists of a hierarchical and evaluative relationship or intervention between a supervisor and a supervisee, and seeks to promote the professional development of the supervisee through interpersonal processes, including mutual problem-solving, instruction, evaluation, mentoring, role modeling of ethical practice, and gatekeeping regarding the competence of those seeking to enter the profession. The goals of supervision include building on the supervisee's strengths, addressing weaknesses, and nurturing an environment that facilitates clinical skill development, self-efficacy, and ethical decision making, while also protecting client welfare (Bernard & Goodyear, 2019; Falender & Shafranske, 2017).

Is Supervision Effective?

To best answer the question regarding the effectiveness of supervision, researchers would need to conduct experimental studies in which they randomly assign trainees to supervision or no supervision (or a placebo), and then examine the effects on supervisee or client outcome. We found only one such investigation (Bambling et al., 2006), but this study focused on post-degree therapists and hence is not included in this review. Thus, we acknowledge in advance that insufficient evidence exists to confidently assert the causal effects of supervision. The remainder of this section, then, is a review of correlational/naturalistic studies.

Outcomes for Supervisees

Tryon (1996), in her examination of the development of doctoral students seeing clients at a university counseling center, found that supervisees reported increases in self- and other-awareness, autonomy, and motivation over the course of their practicum. Ladany, Ellis et al. (1999) found no effects of supervision for the goals, tasks, or bond of supervision; small effects for self-efficacy; and no effects for personal reactions based on

supervisees' reports of change across a semester of supervision. Cashwell and Dooley (2001) found that those who received supervision reported higher counseling self-efficacy than those who did not receive supervision. Gray et al. (2001) found that troubling events in supervision sometimes reduced supervisee self-efficacy, made supervisees less likely to disclose to supervisors, increased their fear of negative evaluation, harmed the supervision relationship, and impaired supervisees' interactions with clients. Such events also exacerbated supervisee stress and self-doubt, and stimulated questions regarding professional decisions and plans (Nelson & Friedlander, 2001).

Hill, Sullivan et al. (2007) found that novice trainees in a pre-practicum had positive feelings about their supervisors and reported that supervision helped them cope with anxieties and difficulties that arose, and supervisees seldom reported neutral and negative reactions to supervisors (e.g., lack of clear expectations, ruptures). Similarly, predoctoral trainees completing an externship in a clinic offering individual therapy to adult community-based clients (Hill et al., 2015) reported that individual supervision provided ideas about helpful interventions, elicited positive feelings (e.g., meaningful, valuable), and that their supervisors had a helpful style (e.g., provided a secure base, were supervisee-centered). Some negative effects of supervision were also reported in the Hill et al. (2015) study, including negative feelings about the supervisor's style or interventions, as well as negative transference to the supervisor. Sant and Milton (2015) reported that psychodynamic supervision provided what was termed an intense learning experience, such that supervisees praised the supervision (said it was fantastic, enjoyable, creative, spontaneous, active, stimulating, free, open), viewed supervisors as Delphic oracles, and gained clarity and insight about their work with clients (e.g., said that supervisors saw things supervisees could not yet see, and helped supervisees think about things in a new way).

Outcomes for Supervisors

We found no studies published since 2013 that examined outcomes of providing supervision for supervisors. In the 6th edition of this chapter, we did not include a review of outcomes for supervisors.

Outcomes for Clients

We found a single study that investigated the potential effect of supervision on client outcome. Callahan et al. (2009) found that supervisors were significantly related to client outcome, eliciting a moderate effect and accounting for about 16% of the outcome variance beyond that accounted for by the client's initial severity and the therapist's attributes. In our 2013 chapter, we found no studies that fit our current chapter's inclusion criteria.

Conclusions

Supervision appears to have predominantly positive effects for supervisees. Supervisees reported enhanced awareness of self and others; increased autonomy, motivation, and counseling self-efficacy; positive feelings related to supervisors and supervision; and noted that supervision provided helpful coping mechanisms and ideas about therapy and interventions, and also fostered insight and clarity about clinical work. Less frequently, neutral or negative effects were reported, including lower self-efficacy, reduced supervisee self-disclosure, fear of evaluation, difficult relationships with supervisors, impaired work with clients, increased stress and doubt, unclear expectations, ruptures, or negative feelings about the supervisor's style or interventions. In the single study we found that investigated the effects of supervision on clients, supervision also appeared to have a moderate effect on client outcome.

Limitations of these studies include the lack of control groups, lack of random assignment, use of single agencies for data collection, and having only supervisees' perspectives. An additional shortcoming is the inability to determine the source of the reported effects (e.g., individual vs. group supervision [some participants experienced both individual and group supervision], supervisors, experience of providing therapy). Relatedly, we cannot make causal assertions regarding any of these findings because there have been no experimental studies. In addition, many of the participant populations were fairly homogenous (e.g., White females). Finally, we know little about the effects of supervision on clients, and nothing about its effects on supervisors.

What Makes Supervision Effective?

Although there are many studies that examine characteristics of supervisees, supervisors, clients, and the supervisory process (e.g., supervisory alliance, supervisor interventions), few link such variables to outcome. In this section, we include only those studies that linked these variables with outcome.

Supervisee Effects

Rousmaniere et al. (2016) found that supervisees contributed to less than 1% of client outcome variance. Although these findings initially sound as if supervisee characteristics do not matter, what they mean is that there were no significant differences among supervisees in terms of client outcomes. Specific supervisee characteristics likely still influence the effects of supervision on supervisee and supervisor outcomes, especially if other types of outcomes are considered (e.g., immediate outcomes, supervisee satisfaction).

Supervisee Variables Associated with Supervision Outcomes

We found seven studies where researchers examined specific supervisee variables (i.e., characteristics of supervisees that influence the effectiveness of supervision). Only one factor was included in multiple studies (i.e., attachment), so we present those findings first.

Supervisee Attachment. Gunn and Pistole (2012) found that supervisee disclosure was increased by facilitating the security of supervisees' attachment to supervisors (as measured by their Experiences in Supervision Scale, which focuses on attachment anxiety and avoidance), which may be related to rapport in the supervision relationship. Thus, supervisors who focus solely on skill development to the exclusion of

relationship development may foster conditions that are not conducive to supervisee disclosure. Furthermore, they noted that supervisees who were more strongly attached to supervisors were likely to view supervisors as helpful to them in their journey toward becoming better therapists. Marmarosh et al. (2013) found that:

- More secure trainee attachment to supervisors was related to higher supervisory alliance but was not related to counseling self-efficacy (CSE).
- More fearful trainee attachment to supervisors was related to lower supervisory alliance and lower CSE.
- Attachment was not related to supervisory working alliance but was related to CSE.

Mesrie et al. (2018) found that supervisees had lower CSE when they demonstrated greater attachment avoidance in the supervision relationship. Supervisee level of experience did not significantly alter the relationship between attachment avoidance and CSE, nor between attachment anxiety and CSE.

Other Supervisee Variables Associated With Supervision Outcomes. Grossl et al. (2014) found that supervisees who received client feedback data during supervision reported greater satisfaction with supervision than those who did not receive such feedback, but neither supervisory alliance nor client outcome differed across feedback conditions. In an open-ended item asking supervisees to share their experience of receiving client feedback data in supervision, supervisees reported it to be a positive experience that helped them better understand their clients and better meet clients' individual needs; furthermore, receiving the feedback enabled supervisees to better assess which clients they needed to discuss in supervision. Knox et al. (2014) found that the impact of supervisees' internal representations of supervisors (supervisees carrying around the presence of supervisors when not in supervision session) was largely positive (e.g., helped supervisees navigate difficult clinical situations or feel more confident), but some negative effects were reported (e.g., increased supervisee anxiety and self-doubt). Rieck et al. (2015) found no supervisee variables (e.g., emotional intelligence, personality factors) significantly related to client outcome, but supervisee openness to experience was a significant and positive predictor of the supervisory alliance.

Summary. Integrating these supervisee effects, we see that supervisees' secure attachment to supervisors seems to be associated with increased supervisee self-disclosure, supervisors being experienced as helpful, and a stronger supervisory working alliance. Avoidant or fearful supervisee attachment to supervisors, in contrast, is associated with a poorer supervisory working alliance and weaker counselor self-efficacy. Beyond attachment, supervisees' receiving client feedback in supervision, their internal representations of their supervisors, as well as their openness to experience, all yielded positive findings (greater satisfaction, better understanding of clients and feeling more able to meet client needs, more able to navigate challenging clinical situations, stronger alliance).

Supervisor Effects

We found only one study that examined supervisor effects (i.e., the amount of outcome variance attributable to supervisors themselves, thereby addressing the question as to whether the specific supervisor makes a difference). Gerstenblith et al. (in press) found that when supervisees rated the supervisory working alliance high on average, their clients also rated the therapeutic working alliance high on average. In contrast, when supervisors rated the supervisory working alliance high on average, their supervisees' clients evaluated the sessions positively but the working alliance low on average. These results show some evidence for a triadic effect, such that what occurs in the supervisory relationship influences the therapy relationship and client outcomes.

Supervisor Variables Associated with Supervision Outcomes

We found several studies that investigated various characteristics of supervisors that may be associated with outcome.

Supervisor Personal Traits. Supervisor openness with supervisees was associated with supervisee satisfaction (Knight, 1996), normalization (Knox et al., 2011), insight (Knox et al., 2011), growth (Knight, 1996; Knox et al., 2011), heightened confidence and comfort (Knox et al., 2011), strengthened supervision relationship (Knox et al., 2011), and improved work with clients (Knox, et al., 2011). Supervisor professional and personal credibility was linked with supervisee growth and strengthened supervisory relationship (Johnston & Milne, 2012). Supervisor mindfulness predicted supervisor ratings of the facilitative conditions, the working alliance, and session depth (Daniel et al., 2015). Supervisor imparting knowledge, genuineness, collaboration, and mutual understanding was associated with supervisee satisfaction (Britt & Graves, 2011).

Supervisor Basic Skills. Supervisors' normalizing difficult reactions to clients was indeed experienced by supervisees as normalizing (Ladany et al., 1997). Likewise, supervisors' provision of instruction, support, and feedback, as well as facilitating exploration and occasionally challenging supervisees, was associated with supervisee growth (Hill, Sullivan et al., 2007). Supervisor use of self-disclosure and immediacy was associated with supervisee insight and growth, as well as heightened confidence and comfort, a strengthened supervisory relationship, and supervisee improved work with clients, but also with supervisees feeling surprised and confused/discouraged about supervision (Knox et al., 2011). Furthermore, supervisors focusing on the therapy process and exploring supervisees' feelings during gender-related events was associated with a strengthened supervisory relationship and greater supervisee self-awareness (Bertch et al., 2014). Supervisors' provision of guidance, support, and self-disclosure helped advanced doctoral student supervisees help their clients (Hill et al., 2016b).

Supervisor Advanced Skills. Supervisors' ability to establish strong boundaries (i.e., supervisors were neither unbounderied nor excessively rigid) and clear roles was related to supervisee growth and a strengthened supervisory relationship

(Johnston & Milne, 2012). Ellis et al. (2015) found: (a) tentative support for the efficacy of a supervision role induction (RI; an intervention intended to clarify supervisor and supervisee role expectations and reduce supervisee anxiety) for reducing anxiety in novice trainees, and (b) that supervisee developmental level moderated the effects of the RI on supervisee anxiety, such that the RI decreased anxiety for most novice trainees and initially decreased anxiety for interns. Supervisors' engagement in positive boundary crossings (i.e., eating/socializing with supervisees, discussing personal topics, sharing car rides) was associated with supervisee growth, a strengthened supervisory relationship, and supervisees' improved work with clients, but also with supervisees feeling discouraged or confused about supervision (Kozlowski et al., 2014). Supervisors' attending to and working on the supervisory alliance, functioning in different roles when necessary, and displaying investment and reflectivity were linked with supervisee satisfaction (Eisenhard & Muse-Burke, 2015). Supervisors' facilitating supervisees' case conceptualization, focusing on the person of the supervisee, providing feedback on supervisee performance, and helping the supervisee set realistic expectations helped supervisees assist their clients (Hill, Anderson et al., 2016a). Supervisors' use of interpersonally sensitive behaviors was associated with a strengthened supervisory relationship (Shaffer & Friedlander, 2017). Supervisors' facilitation of supervisees' work with transfer clients was linked with supervisee growth (Marmarosh et al., 2017), and their attending to parallel process was related to supervisee growth, a strengthened supervisory relationship, and supervisees' improved work with clients (Zetzer et al., 2018).

Supervisor Errors in Technique. Supervisors' lack of input in supervision was linked with supervisees feeling discouraged about supervision, experiencing negative emotions (disappointment, shame, anger, depression), and supervisees' reduced involvement in supervision (Bang & Goodyear, 2014). Additionally, supervisors' gender discrimination of supervisees has been linked with a weakened supervisory alliance (Bertsch et al., 2014). Also, supervisors' nonadherence to ethical guidelines has been related to reduced supervisee satisfaction and poorer supervisory alliance (Ladany, Lerhman-Waterman et al., 1999).

Supervisor Demographic Variables. Wrape et al. (2015) found that although supervisors' faculty status (tenured/tenure-track vs. adjunct) was not associated with client outcomes, length of time since supervisors' degree was, with more recent graduates having slightly better client outcomes. Other supervisor variables (amount of experience, field [social work vs. psychology], and level [MS vs. PhD]) did not explain a significant amount of variance in client outcome.

Dyadic Effects

In this section, we include studies whose findings were related to both supervisor and supervisee, and thus reflected the supervision dyad rather than a specific member of the dyad.

Mehr et al. (2015) found that supervisees' perceptions of a strong supervisory working alliance predicted lower supervisee anxiety and greater supervisee willingness to disclose in supervision. Relatedly, in their meta-analysis, Park et al. (2019) found that supervisees' perceived supervisory working alliance was significantly related to supervisees' self-efficacy and self-disclosure, and also to supervisors' perception of the working alliance and to the counselor–client relationship (as perceived by the supervisee).

Hill, Crowe, & Gonsalves (2016) examined supervisor/supervisee dyads completing an individual reflective practice protocol (e.g., focusing on values, intentions, thoughts, behaviors, actions, reactions) after watching a videotape of their most recent supervision session, and then sharing their reflections with each other in a second session. Their findings revealed that completing the reflective practice protocol elicited: (a) increased discussion of supervisee anxiety; (b) altered supervisory interactions (i.e., increased attention to the risks of excessive reassurance in response to supervisee anxiety); (c) discussion of supervisory roles and expectations, as well as parallels between supervision and therapy; and (d) other positive effects (e.g., more reflective practice, enhanced supervisory alliance, greater supervisee confidence). As negative impacts, participants noted that the intervention was valuable but time-consuming, and it elicited anxiety and discomfort.

Summary. In these findings, we see that some supervisors indeed established better working alliances than did other supervisors. In addition, supervisors' personal traits (openness, credibility, mindfulness) were associated with a range of positive outcomes (supervisee satisfaction, normalization, insight, growth, increased confidence/comfort, enhanced work with clients; stronger supervision relationship). Furthermore, their empathy and provision of facilitative conditions were associated with supervisee satisfaction, increased supervisee self-disclosure, reduced supervisee anxiety, and improved supervisee work with clients. Supervisors' use of basic skills (normalization, teaching, support, providing feedback, challenging supervisees, self-disclosure, immediacy, focusing on the supervisory process) was associated with mostly positive outcomes (supervisee growth, insight, normalization, enhanced confidence/comfort, improved work with clients, greater self-awareness; enhanced supervision relationship), but at times was linked with less salutary outcomes (supervisees feeling confused or discouraged). Supervisors' demonstration of more advanced skills (maintaining boundaries/roles, positive boundary crossings, interpersonal behavior, attending to parallel process, engaging in reflective practice) was associated with supervisee growth and satisfaction, stronger supervisory relationships, reduced supervisee anxiety, improved supervisee work with clients, but also with occasional supervisee confusion or discouragement. Supervisors' errors in technique (minimal input in supervision, gender discrimination, nonadherence to ethical guidelines) were linked with supervisee discouragement, negative emotions, reduced involvement and satisfaction, and weaker supervisory alliances. Finally, supervisors' demographic characteristics (faculty status, time since graduation, level of experience, professional specialization, type of degree) had minimal effect on outcome, other than supervisors who had graduated more recently having mildly better client outcomes. Dyadic effects pointed to the benefits of a strong supervisor alliance (e.g., reduced supervisee anxiety, increased supervisee self-disclosure and self-efficacy).

Client Variables Associated with Supervision Outcomes

We found no studies that examined client variables associated with supervision outcomes.

Conclusions and Recommendations for Research on Individual Supervision

In examining what may contribute to the effectiveness of supervision, a few themes emerged. First, a sound attachment of supervisee to supervisor and a strong supervisory working alliance appear vital and may provide a secure base for the inevitable struggles supervisees encounter during supervision. Likely related to this attachment and working alliance are supervisors' personal traits, empathic attunement to the supervisory alliance, and demonstration of both basic and advanced supervisory skills (the effective demonstration of such attributes and skills was associated with largely positive effects). Supervisees receiving client feedback data during supervision was also related to positive findings, suggesting that supervisees indeed benefit by receiving direct feedback regarding their clinical work. Limitations of these studies echo those noted above (e.g., no control group, only one agency for data collection in each study, only one perspective, inability to determine the source of the reported effects, no ability to make causal assertions, homogeneity of participant samples).

We also again acknowledge that we still know relatively little about the effects of supervision and its components, whether focused on supervisors, supervisees, or clients. Varied influences may well come into play in the supervision endeavor, including instruction, modeling, practice, feedback, support, challenge, and focusing on the supervision relationship, to name but a few. Echoing Watkins (2011, 2017), supervision is a complex human endeavor, one that does not lend itself to easy examination and does not willingly yield its secrets. Exacerbating this complexity are the shortcomings in the extant literature, which include overreliance on self-report and on correlational ex post facto designs, limited sample sizes, limited attention to process studies, and few psychometrically strong supervision-specific measures (Watkins, 2017). Some of these shortcomings may be inevitable artifacts of the inherent limitations of research completed in educational institutions.

Further complicating efforts to examine the effects of supervision is the reality that one supervisor may work with several supervisees, who themselves likely work with multiple clients. So, as noted by Ellis and Ladany (1997) and Goodyear and Guzzardo (2000), any effects of supervision on clients (in their view the intended target of supervision) are nested within supervisees, who are then nested within supervisors, all of which need to be examined with considerably larger samples. And all members of triads brings to it their own unique characteristics (e.g., severity of pathology, openness to feedback, awareness of parallel process, theoretical orientation), all of which introduce variability into the research endeavor. Access to understanding is no easier if we take Holloway's (1992) perspective that the focus of supervision is on supervisee development rather than just client outcome.

As an example of the complexity of this triad, consider the use of immediacy. If a supervisor uses immediacy in supervision, to what extent, if any, does the supervisee become immediate in supervision? And what influences the supervisee's response to the supervisor's use of this intervention? If the supervisee then uses immediacy with a client, to what extent, if any, does that intervention help the client become more open in therapy, and what influences the client's response to the intervention? Each person in the triad has agency: Does recommending immediacy fit with the supervisor's theoretical orientation? Is the supervisor comfortable modeling this intervention in supervision? Does the supervisee agree that this intervention might be helpful with a client, and is the supervisee willing to try immediacy with a client? Does the supervisee use immediacy at an appropriate time in therapy? And in response to the immediacy, does the client indeed become more open?

Making the endeavor even more complex is the reality that supervisors often only see or hear what supervisees choose to show or tell them. If supervisors do not have access to video- or audio-recordings of supervisees' sessions, their knowledge is quite limited. So, supervisees selectively provide the content of supervision, and may themselves not be fully aware of their struggles. Furthermore, supervisees may, or may not, implement their supervisor's suggestions; likewise, clients may or may not implement the supervisee's suggestions.

What all of this suggests is that studying supervision is not for the faint of heart. The research task is difficult, data capture is imperfect, and the concepts and processes are complex. Despite these challenges, such examinations are a worthy pursuit, for if we wish to better train supervisees and better help clients, we must increase our understanding of the supervision endeavor. We offer, then, the following recommendations for research on individual supervision:

1. Without the inclusion of control groups, we cannot discern the potential effects of supervision itself. Thus, we recommend that researchers include control groups in studies so that any potential effects of supervision may be more definitively examined.
2. Because much of the extant research relies on data collected from a single setting, we are limited in what we can infer to other settings from such findings. Thus, we urge researchers to include participants from multiple settings (e.g., agencies, academic institutions) so that the potential influence of the setting itself is tempered. Practice-research networks (PRNs; e.g., Eastern Michigan University, Western Michigan University, University of North Carolina) may be a fruitful avenue for such research efforts for they involve larger and pooled data sets that may allow the examination of client, supervisor, supervisee, and/or setting on the effects of supervision.
3. Similarly, much of the existing research has collected data from only one perspective (e.g., supervisor or supervisee). Researchers thus need to investigate multiple perspectives (e.g., supervisor, supervisee, and client) so that varied perspectives on the supervision process are examined.

4. As noted above, any effects of supervision on clients are nested within supervisees, who are themselves nested within supervisors. As such, researchers need to consider using multilevel modeling with large samples.
5. Self-reports have the potential to provide useful information, but are inherently limited, especially knowing that supervisees may be selective in what they reveal to supervisors. Thus, researchers need to also gather data from clients, supervisors, and observers.
6. Given the homogeneity of many samples in the existing research, as well as the often small samples, we encourage researchers to include more heterogeneous and larger participant samples so that findings may be more generalizable.
7. Relatedly, given that few researchers have examined cultural influences on supervision, we encourage researchers to explore how culture, broadly defined, may affect the supervision process and outcome.
8. As earlier noted, many of the existing supervision measures lack strong psychometrics, calling into question any findings based on those instruments. Thus, we recommend that researchers work to develop psychometrically sound measures to foster better research on supervision.
9. Given this section's emphasis on individual supervision, we recommend a similar examination of the effectiveness and effects of group supervision. Then we could compare such information with what we currently know about individual supervision.

CONCLUSIONS

Although more data need to be gathered to support the assertions below, here we seek to integrate the findings in this chapter and describe what we view as an ideal sequence of training and supervision. We hope that this description provides a template that can be implemented in practice and also studied empirically.

We suggest that learners begin their training experiences with a specific focus on helping skills to acquire the foundational techniques that can be useful in psychotherapy. The deliberate practice of skills at this level, along with training in empathy, self-awareness, alliance development, and case conceptualization, can prepare students to think about what interventions might be helpful under what circumstances and with which clients. Feedback at this stage could focus on nonthreateningly fostering trainees' gradual acquisition of skills, management of anxiety, and reflection on emerging strengths and growth areas. Furthermore, at this stage of development, we assert that trainees benefit from very close attention to what they say; how, when, and why they say it; as well as their physical presence and demeanor doing so (e.g., posture, facial expression, eye contact). In our years of experience training those entering the mental health professions, we have found that such an approach not only improves trainees' skills, but also enables them to build their internal sense of efficacy and confidence, both of which are essential before trainees begin to work with real clients.

Building on this foundation of helping skills training, trainees can then begin to work with volunteer clients presenting real concerns, with in vivo and postsession individual supervision and self-reflection, perhaps via interpersonal process recall (IPR) opportunities to consolidate and expand their basic helping skills. Individual supervision at this phase could focus on the helping skills, and trainees could receive intensive, but also gentle and nurturing, microsupervision on these skills (e.g., what were trainees' intentions for an intervention, how effective was the delivery of the intervention, how did the intervention affect the client, how did the identities [e.g., gender, race, age, culture] influence the delivery and receipt of the intervention?). And given that the existing research confirms the central importance of the supervision alliance, supervisors can use interpersonal skills to work toward establishing a solid supervisory process and relationship. Doing so may also encourage trainees to more freely disclose to supervisors the struggles they are encountering in their growth and development. In addition, supervision could provide space for trainees to share their thoughts and feelings as they begin to work with clients. Trainee anxiety is likely to increase at this point, so supervision could include both normalization and management of that anxiety. Supervisors can also examine how the various features of their own identity (e.g., race, ethnicity, culture, gender, age, theoretical orientation) interact with those of their supervisees and thereby influence the supervision itself.

Trainees' next steps are to see real clients under close individual supervision and to begin to refine their theoretical orientation. This step will likely take quite some time, with students completing practica, externships, and internships, and meeting expected professional standards. In this stage, supervision may well continue to address trainees' basic helping skills, for as supervisees take on more clinical responsibility and potentially more complex cases, they often need to strengthen or expand their repertoire of skills. In addition, trainees can begin to consider more macro-level dynamics such as conceptualizing cases, examining their relationships with clients, exploring countertransference, investigating what might be impeding client growth, trying different theoretical approaches to see which may be most effective for a particular client, and exploring the impact of cultural identities/contexts on therapy.

ABBREVIATIONS

AFT	alliance-focused training
CASES	Counseling Activity Self-Efficacy Scale
CBT	cognitive behavioral therapy
CI	confidence intervals
CSE	counseling self-efficacy
DP	deliberate practice
FAP	functional analytic psychotherapy
HRT	Human Relations Training
HSM	Helping Skills Measure
IPR	Interpersonal Process Recall
MC	microcounseling
PRNs	practice research networks

REFERENCES

Allen, T. W. (1967). Effectiveness of counsellor trainees as a function of psychological openness. *Journal of Counseling Psychology, 14*(1), 35–40. https://doi.org/10.1037/h0024221

Anderson, T., Ogles, B. M., Patterson, C. L., Lambert, M. J., & Veermeesch, D. A. (2009). Therapist effects: Facilitating interpersonal skills as a predictor of therapist success. *Journal of Clinical Psychology, 65*(7), 755–768. https://doi.org/10.1002/jclp.20583

Anvari, M., Hill, C. E., & Kivlighan, D. M., Jr. (2020). Therapist skills associated with client emotional expression in psychodynamic psychotherapy. *Psychotherapy Research, 30*(7), 900–911. https://doi.org/10.1080/10503307.2019.1680901

Arthur, G. L., & Gfroerer, K. P. (2002). Training and supervision through the written word: A description and intern feedback. *The Family Journal: Counseling and Therapy for Couples and Families, 10*(2), 213–219. https://doi.org/10.1177/1066480702102014

Baker, S. B., & Daniels, T. G. (1989). Integrating research on the microcounseling program: A meta-analysis. *Journal of Counseling Psychology, 36*(2), 213–222. https://doi.org/10.1037/0022-0167.36.2.213

Baker, S. B., Daniels, T. G., & Greeley, A. T. (1990). Systematic training of graduate-level therapists: Narrative and meta-analytic reviews of three major programs. *The Counseling Psychologist, 18*(3), 355–421. https://doi.org/10.1177/0011000090183001

Baldwin, S. A., & Imel, Z. E. (2013). Therapist effects: Findings and methods. In M. J. Lambert (Ed.), *Bergin and Garfield's handbook of psychotherapy and behavior change* (6th ed., pp. 258–297). Wiley.

Bambling, M., King, R., Raue, P., Schweitzer, R., & Lambert, W. (2006). Clinical supervision: Its influence on client-rated working alliance and client symptom reduction in the brief treatment of major depression. *Psychotherapy Research, 16*(3), 317–331. https://doi.org/10.1080/10503300500268524

Bandura, A. (1969). *Principles of behavior modification.* Holt, Rinehart, & Winston.

Bandura, A. (1997). *Self-efficacy: The exercise of control.* W. H. Freeman.

Bang, K., & Goodyear, R. K. (2014). South Korean supervisees' experience of and response to negative supervision events. *Counselling Psychology Quarterly, 27*(4), 353–378. https://doi.org/10.1080/09515070.2014.940851

Barrett-Lennard, G. T. (1962). Dimensions of therapist response as causal factors in therapeutic change. *Psychological Monographs: General and Applied, 76*(43), 1–36. https://doi.org/10.1037/h0093918

Bennetts, C. (2003). Self-evaluation and self-perception of student learning in person-centred Counselling training within a higher education setting. *British Journal of Guidance and Counselling, 31*, 305–323. https://doi.org/10.1080/0306988031000147901

Benuto, L. T., Casas, J., & O'Donohue, W. T. (2018). Training culturally competent psychologists: A systematic review of the training outcome literature. *Training and Education in Professional Psychology, 12*(3), 125–134. https://doi.org/10.1037/tep0000190

Bernard, J. M., & Goodyear, R. K. (2019). *Fundamentals of clinical supervision* (6th ed.). Pearson.

Bertsch, K. N., Bremer-Landau, J. D., Inman, A. G., DeBoer Kreider, E. R., Price, T. A., & DeCarlo, A. L. (2014). Evaluation of the Critical Events in Supervision Model using gender related events. *Training and Education in Professional Psychology, 8*(3), 174–181. https://doi.org/10.1037/tep0000039

Beutler, L. E., Malik, M., Alimohamed, S., Harwood, T. M., Talebi, H., Noble, S., & Wang, E. (2004). Therapist variables. In M. J. Lambert (Ed.), *Bergin and Garfield's handbook of psychotherapy and behavior change* (5th ed., pp. 227–306). Wiley.

Boswell, J. F., Castonguay, L. G., & Wasserman, R. H. (2010). Effects of psychotherapy training and intervention use on session outcome. *Journal of Consulting and Clinical Psychology, 78*(5), 717–723. https://doi.org/10.1037/a0020088

Britt, E., & Graves, D. H. (2011). Measurement and prediction of clinical psychology students' satisfaction with clinical supervision. *The Clinical Supervisor, 30*(2), 172–182. https://doi.org/10.1080/07325223.2011.604274

Budge, S. L., Owen, J. J., Kopta, S. M., Minami, T., Hanson, M. R., & Hirsch, G. (2013). Differences among trainees in counseling outcomes associated with the phase model of change. *Psychotherapy, 50*(2), 150–157. https://doi.org/10.1037/a0029565

Butler, E. R., & Hansen, J. C. (1973). Facilitative training: Acquisition, retention, and modes of assessment. *Journal of Counseling Psychology, 20*(1), 60–65. https://doi.org/10.1037/h0033989

Callahan, J. L., Almstrom, C. M., Swift, J. K., Borja, S. E., & Heath, C. J. (2009). Exploring the contribution of supervisors to intervention outcomes. *Training and Education in Professional Psychology, 3*(2), 72–77. https://doi.org/10.1037/a0014294

Caracena, P. F. (1965). Elicitation of dependency expressions in the initial stage of psychotherapy. *Journal of Counseling Psychology, 12*(3), 268–274. https://doi.org/10.1037/h0022586

Carkhuff, R. R. (1969). *Human and helping relations* (Vols. 1 & 2). Holt, Rinehart, & Winston.

Carlsson, J., Norberg, J., Sandell, R., & Schubert, J. (2011). Searching for recognition: The professional development of psychodynamic psychotherapists during training and the first few years after it. *Psychotherapy Research, 21*(2), 141–153. https://doi.org/10.1080/10503307.2010.506894

Carlsson, J., Norberg, J., Schubert, J., & Sandell, R. (2011). The development of therapeutic attitudes during and after psychotherapy training. *European Journal of Psychotherapy and Counselling, 13*(3), 213–229. https://doi.org/10.1080/13642537.2011.596722

Cashwell, T. H., & Dooley, K. (2001). The impact of supervision on counselor self-efficacy. *The Clinical Supervisor, 20*(1), 39–47. https://doi.org/10.1300/J001v20n01_03

Caspar, F., Berger, T., & Hautle, I. (2004). The right view of your patient: A computer-assisted, individualized module for psychotherapy training. *Psychotherapy: Theory, Research, Practice, Training, 41*(2), 125–135. https://doi.org/10.1037/0033-3204.41.2.125

Castonguay, L. & Hill, C. E. (Eds.) (2017). *How and why are some therapists better than others? Understanding therapist effects.* American Psychological Association.

Chow, D. L., Miller, S. D., Seidel, J. A., Kane, R. T., Thornton, J. A., & Andrews, W. P. (2015). The role of deliberate practice in the development of highly effective psychotherapists. *Psychotherapy, 52*(3), 337–345. https://doi.org/10.1037/pst0000015

Chui, H., Hill, C. E., Ain, S., Ericson, S. K., Ganginis Del Pino, H. V., Hummel, A. M., Merson, E. S., & Spangler, P. T. (2014). Training undergraduate students to use challenges. *The Counseling Psychologist, 42*(6), 758–777. https://doi.org/10.1177/0011000014542599

Collingwood, T. R. (1971). Retention and retraining of interpersonal communication skills. *Journal of Clinical Psychology, 27*(2), 294–296. https://doi.org/10.1002/1097-4679(197104)27:2<294::AID-JCLP2270270246>3.0.CO;2-S

Crook-Lyon, R. E., Hill, C. E., Hess, S., Wimmer, C., & Goates-Jones, M. K. (2009). Therapist training, feedback, and practice for dream work: A pilot study. *Psychological Reports, 105*(1), 87–98. https://doi.org/10.2466/PR0.105.1.87-98

Cuttler, E., Hill, C. E., King, S., & Kivlighan, D. M., Jr. (2019). Productive silence is golden: Predicting changes in client collaboration from process during silence and client attachment style in psychodynamic psychotherapy. *Psychotherapy, 56*(4), 568–576. https://doi.org/10.1037/pst0000260

Cutts, L. A. (2012). A case study exploring a trainee counselling psychologist's experience of coding a single session of counselling for therapeutic intentions. *Counselling Psychology Quarterly, 25*(3), 263–275. https://doi.org/10.1080/09515070.2012.716192

Daniel, L., Borders, L. D., & Willse, J. (2015). The role of supervisors' and supervisees' mindfulness in clinical supervision. *Counselor Education & Supervision, 54*(3), 221–232. https://doi.org/10.1002/ceas.12015

Dennhag, I., & Ybrandt, H. (2013). Trainee psychotherapists' development in self-rated professional qualities in training. *Psychotherapy, 50*(2), 158–166. https://doi.org/10.1037/a0033045

Eisenhard, M. L., & Muse-Burke, J. L. (2015). A comparison of individual supervision at forensic, inpatient, and college counseling internship sites. *Training and Education in Professional Psychology, 9*(1), 61–67. https://doi.org/10.1037/tep0000051

Ellis, M. V., Hutman, H., & Chapin, J. (2015). Reducing supervisee anxiety: Effects of a role induction intervention for clinical supervision. *Journal of Counseling Psychology, 62*(4), 608–620. https://doi.org/10.1037/cou0000099

Ellis, M. V., & Ladany, N. (1997). Inferences concerning supervisees and clients in clinical supervision: An integrative review. In C. E. Watkins (Ed.). *Handbook of psychotherapy supervision* (pp. 447–507). John Wiley & Sons, Inc.

Erekson, D. M., Janis, R., Bailey, R. J., Cattani, K., & Pedersen, T. R. (2017). A longitudinal investigation of the impact of psychotherapist training: Does training improve client outcomes? *Journal of Counseling Psychology, 64*(5), 514–524. https://doi.org/10.1037/cou0000252

Ericsson, K. A., Charness, N., Feltovich, P., & Hoffman, R. (2006). *Handbook of expertise and expert performance.* Cambridge University Press.

Ericsson, K. A., Krampe, R. T., & Tesch-Römer, C. (1993). The role of deliberate practice in the acquisition of expert performance. *Psychological Review, 100*(3), 363–406. http://dx.doi.org/10.1037/0033-295X.100.3.363

Ericsson, K. A., & Lehmann, A. C. (1996). Expert and exceptional performance: Evidence of maximal adaptation to task constraints. *Annual Review of Psychology, 47,* 273–305. https://doi.org/10.1146/annurev.psych.47.1.273

Ericsson, A., & Pool, R. (2016). *Peak: Secrets from the new science of expertise.* Houghton Mifflin Harcourt.

Falender, C. A., & Shafranske, E. P. (2017). *Supervision essentials for competency-based supervision.* American Psychological Association.

Ford, J. D. (1979). Research on training therapists and clinicians. *Review of Educational Research, 49*(1), 87–130.

Freiheit, S. R., & Overholser, J. C. (1997). Training issues in cognitive-behavioral psychotherapy. *Journal of Behavior Therapy and Experimental Psychiatry, 28*(2), 79–86. https://doi.org/10.1016/S0005-7916(97)00001-3

Georghiades, P. (2004). From the general to the situated: Three decades of metacognition. *International Journal of Science Education, 26*(3), 365–383. https://doi.org/10.1080/0950069032000119401

Gerstenblith, J., Kline, K., Hill, C. E., & Kivlighan, D. M., Jr. (2018). *The relationship between the supervisory and therapeutic working alliance: The supervisor's perspective.* Panel presented at the Annual Meeting of the Society for Psychotherapy Research, Amsterdam, Netherlands.

Gerstenblith, J. A., Kline, K., Hill, C. E., & Kivlighan, D. M. Jr. (in press). Triadic effect: Associations among the supervisory working alliance, therapeutic working alliance, and therapy session evaluation. *Journal of Counseling Psychology.* http://dx.doi.org/10.1037/cou0000567

Goldberg, S. B., Rousmaniere, T., Miller, S. D., Whipple, J., Nielsen, S. L., Hoyt, W. T., & Wampold, B. E. (2016). Do psychotherapists improve with time and experience? A longitudinal analysis of outcomes in a clinical setting. *Journal of Counseling Psychology, 63*(1), 1–11. https://doi.org/10.1037/cou0000131

Goodyear, R. K., & Guzzardo, C. R. (2000). Psychotherapy supervision and training. In S. Brown & R. W. Lent (Eds.), *Handbook of counseling psychology* (3rd ed., pp. 83–108). Wiley.

Goodyear, R. K. & Rousmaniere, T. (2017). Helping therapists to each day become a little better than they were the day before: The Expertise-Development Model of supervision and consultation. In T. G. Rousmaniere, R. K. Goodyear, S. D. Miller, & B. E. Wampold. *The cycle of excellence: Using deliberate practice to improve supervision and training.* Wiley Publishers.

Gormally, J., Hill, C. E., Gulanick, N., & McGovern, T. (1975). The persistence of communications skills for undergraduate and graduate trainees. *Journal of Clinical Psychology, 31*(2), 369–372. https://doi.org/10.1002/1097-4679(197504)31:2<369::AID-JCLP2270310249>3.0.CO;2-Y

Gossman, M., & Miller, J. H. (2011). "The third person in the room:" Recording the counselling interview for the purpose of counsellor training – Barrier to relationship building or effective tool for professional development? *Counselling and Psychotherapy Research, 12*(1), 25–34. https://doi.org/10.1080/14733145.2011.582649

Gray, L. A., Ladany, N., Walker, J. A., & Ancis, J. R. (2001). Psychotherapy trainees' experience of counterproductive events in supervision. *Journal of Counseling Psychology, 48*(4), 371–383. https://doi.org/10.1037/0022-0167.48.4.371

Grossl, A. B., Reese, R. J., Norsworthy, L. A., & Hopkins, N. B. (2014). Client feedback data in supervision: Effects on supervision and outcome. *Training and Education in Professional Psychology, 8*(3), 182–188. https://doi.org/10.1037/tep0000025

Gunn, J. E., & Pistole, M. C. (2012). Trainee supervisor attachment: Explaining the alliance and disclosure in supervision. *Training and Education in Professional Psychology*, 6(4), 229–237. https://doi.org/10.1037/a0030805

Hacker, D. J. (1998). Definitions and empirical foundations. In D. J. Hacker, J. Dunlosky, & A. C. Graesser (Eds.), *Metacognition in educational theory and practice* (pp. 1–23). Lawrence Erlbaum.

Hess, S., Knox, S., & Hill, C. E. (2006). Teaching graduate student trainees how to manage client anger: A comparison of three types of training. *Psychotherapy Research*, 16(3), 282–292. https://doi.org/10.1080/10503300500264838

Hill, C. E. (2004). *Helping skills: Facilitating exploration, insight, and action* (2nd ed). American Psychological Association.

Hill, C. E. (2009). *Helping skills: Facilitating exploration, insight, and action* (3rd ed). American Psychological Association.

Hill, C. E. (2014). *Helping skills: Facilitating exploration, insight, and action* (4th ed). American Psychological Association.

Hill, C. E. (2020). *Helping skills: Facilitating exploration, insight, and action* (5th ed). American Psychological Association.

Hill, C. E., Anderson, T., Gerstenblith, J. A., Kline, K. V., Gooch, C. V., & Melnick, A. (2020). A follow-up of undergraduate students five years after helping skills training. *Journal of Counseling Psychology*, 67(6), 697–705. https://doi.org/10.1037/cou0000428

Hill, C. E., Anderson, T., Kline, K., McClintock, A., Cranston, S., McCarrick, S., Petrarca, A., Himawan, L., Pérez-Rojas, A. E., Bhatia, A., Gupta, S., & Gregor, M. (2016). Helping skills training for undergraduate students: Who should we select and train? *The Counseling Psychologist*, 44(1), 50–77. https://doi.org/10.1177/0011000015613142

Hill, C. E., Baumann, E., Shafran, N., Gupta, S., Morrison, A., Rojas-Pérez, A., Spangler, P. T., Griffin, S., Pappa, L., & Gelso, C. J. (2015). Is training effective? A study of counseling psychology doctoral trainees in a psychodynamic/interpersonal training clinic. *Journal of Counseling Psychology*, 62(2), 184–201. https://doi.org/10.1037/cou0000053

Hill, C. E., Charles, C., & Reed, K. G. (1981). A longitudinal analysis of changes in counseling skills during doctoral training in counseling psychology. *Journal of Counseling Psychology*, 28(5), 428–436. https://doi.org/10.1037/0022-0167.28.5.428

Hill, C. E., & Kellems, I. S. (2002). Development and use of the helping skills measure to assess client perceptions of the effects of training and of helping skills in sessions. *Journal of Counseling Psychology*, 49(2), 264–272. https://doi.org/10.1037/0022-0167.49.2.264

Hill, C. E., Kivlighan, D. M. III, Rousmaniere, T., Kivlighan, D. M., Jr., Gerstenblith, J. A., & Hillman, J. W. (2020). Deliberate practice: Effects on doctoral student therapists and clients. *Psychotherapy*, 57(4), 587–597. https://doi.org/10.1037/pst0000247

Hill, C. E., Kline, K. V., O'Connor, S., Morales, K., Li, X., Kivlighan, D. M., Jr., & Hillman, J. (2019). Silence is golden: A mixed methods investigation of silence in one case of psychodynamic psychotherapy. *Psychotherapy*, 56(4), 577–587. https://doi.org/10.1037/pst0000196

Hill, C. E., & Knox, S. (2013). Training and supervision in psychotherapy. In Lambert, M. J. (Ed.), *Bergin and Garfield's handbook of psychotherapy and behavior change*, 6th ed. (pp. 775–811). Wiley and Sons, Inc.

Hill, C. E., Knox, S., & Pinto-Coelho, K. G. (2018). Therapist self-disclosure and immediacy: A qualitative meta-analysis. *Psychotherapy*, 55(4), 445–460. https://doi.org/10.1037/pst0000182

Hill, C. E., & Lent, R. W. (2006). A narrative and meta-analytic review of helping skills training: Time to revive a dormant area of inquiry. *Psychotherapy: Theory, Research, Practice, Training*, 43(2), 154–172.

Hill, C. E., Lent, R. W., Morrison, A., Pinto-Coelho, K., Jackson, J. J., & Kivlighan, Jr., D. M. (2016). Contribution of supervisor interventions to client change: The therapist perspective, *The Clinical Supervisor*, 35(2), 227–248. https://doi.org/10.1080/07325223.2016.1193783

Hill, C. E., Lu, Y., Gerstenblith, J. A., Kline, K. V., Wang, R. J., & Zhu, X. (2020). Facilitating client collaboration and insight through interpretations and probes for insight in psychodynamic psychotherapy: A case study of one client with three successive therapists. *Psychotherapy*, 57(2), 263–272. Advance online publication. https://doi.org/10.1037/pst0000242

Hill, C. E., & O'Brien, K. (1999). *Helping skills: Facilitating exploration, insight, and action*. American Psychological Association.

Hill, C. E., Roffman, M., Stahl, J., Friedman, S., Hummel, A., & Wallace, C. (2008). Helping skills training for undergraduates: Outcomes and prediction of outcomes. *Journal of Counseling Psychology*, 55(3), 359–370. https://doi.org/10.1037/0022-0167.55.3.359

Hill, C. E., Spangler, P. T., Chui, H., & Jackson, J. (2014). Training undergraduate students to use insight skills: Rationale, methods, and analyses. *The Counseling Psychologist*, 42(6), 702–728. https://doi.org/10.1177/0011000014542598

Hill, C. E., Spangler, P. T., Jackson, J. L., & Chui, H. (2014). Training undergraduate students to use insight skills: Integrating the results of three studies. *The Counseling Psychologist*, 42(6), 800-820. https://doi.org/10.1177/0011000014542602

Hill, C. E., Stahl, J., & Roffman, M. (2007). Training novice psychotherapists: Helping skills and beyond. *Psychotherapy: Theory, Research, Practice, Training*, 44(4), 364–370. https://doi.org/10.1037/0033-3204.44.4.364

Hill, C. E., Sullivan, C., Knox, S., & Schlosser, L. Z. (2007). Becoming psychotherapists: Experiences of novice trainees in a beginning graduate class. *Psychotherapy: Theory, Research, Practice, Training*, 44(4), 434–449. https://doi.org/10.1037/0033-3204.44.4.434

Hill, H. R., Crowe, T. P., & Gonsalvez, C. J. (2016). Reflective dialogue in clinical supervision: A pilot study involving collaborative review of supervision videos. *Psychotherapy Research*, 26(3), 263–278. https://doi.org/10.1080/10503307.2014.996795

Hilsenroth, M. J., Ackerman, S. J., Clemence, A. J., Strassle, C. G., & Handler, L. (2002). Effects of structured clinician training on patient and therapist perspectives of alliance early in psychotherapy. *Psychotherapy: Theory, Research, Practice, Training*, 39(4), 309–323. https://doi.org/10.1037/0033-3204.39.4.309

Hilsenroth, M. J., Defife, J. A., Blagys, M. D., & Ackerman, S. J. (2006). Effects of training in short-term psychodynamic psychotherapy: Changes in graduate clinician technique. *Psychotherapy Research*, 16(3), 293–305. https://doi.org/10.1080/10503300500264887

Holloway, E. L. (1992). Supervision: A way of teaching and learning. In S. D. Brown & R. W Lent (Eds.), *Handbook of counseling psychology* (2nd ed.) (pp. 177–214). Wiley.

Ivey, A. E. (1971). *Microcounseling: Innovations in interviewing training*. Charles C. Thomas.

Jackson, J., Hill, C. E., Spangler, P. T., Ericson, S., Merson, E., Liu, J., Wydra, M., & Reen, G. (2014). Training undergraduate students to use interpretation. *The Counseling Psychologist*, 42(6), 778–799. https://doi.org/10.1177/0011000014542600

Johns, R. G., Barkham, M., Kellett, S., & Saxon, D. (2019). A systematic review of therapist effects: A critical narrative update and refinement to Baldwin and Imel's (2013) review. *Clinical Psychology Review*, 67, 78–93. https://doi.org/10.1016/j.cpr.2018.08.004

Johnston, L. H., & Milne, D. L. (2012). How do supervisees learn during supervision? A grounded theory study of the perceived developmental process. *The Cognitive Behavior Therapist*, 5(1), 1–23. https://doi.org/10.1017/S1754470X12000013

Joo, E., Hill, C. E., & Kim, Y. H. (2019). Using helping skills with Korean clients: The perspectives of Korean counselors. *Psychotherapy Research*, 29(6), 812–823. https://doi.org/10.1080/10503307.2017.1397795

Kagan, N. (1984). Interpersonal process recall: Basic methods and recent research. In D. Larson (Ed.), *Teaching psychological skills: Models for giving psychology away* (pp. 229–244). Brooks/Cole.

Kagan, N. I., & Kagan, H. (1990). IPR-A validated model for the 1990s and beyond. *The Counseling Psychologist*, 18(3), 436–440. https://doi.org/10.1177/0011000090183004

Kagan, N., Schauble, P., Resnikoff, A., Danish, S. J., & Krathwohl, D. R. (1969). Interpersonal process recall. *Journal of Nervous and Mental Disease*, 148(4), 365–374. https://doi.org/10.1097/00005053-196904000-00004

Kasdorf, J., & Gustafson, L. (1978). Research related to microtraining. In A. E. Ivey & J. Authier (Eds.), *Microcounseling: Innovations in interviewing, counseling, psychotherapy, and psychoeducation* (pp. 323–376). Thomas.

Kanter, J. W., Tsai, M., Holman, G., & Koerner, K. (2013). Preliminary data from a randomized pilot study of web-based functional analytic psychotherapy therapist training. *Psychotherapy*, 50(2), 248–255. https://doi.org/10.1037/a0029814

Keng, S. L., Waddington, E., Lin, X. B., Tan, M. S. Q., Henn-Haase, C., & Kanter, J. W. (2017). Effects of functional analytic psychotherapy therapist training on therapist factors among therapist trainees in Singapore: A randomized controlled trial. *Clinical Psychology & Psychotherapy*, 24(4), 1014–1027. https://doi.org/10.1002/cpp.2064

Keum, B. T., Hill, C. E., Kivlighan, D. M., Jr., & Lu, Y. (2018). Group- and individual-level self-stigma reductions in promoting psychological help-seeking attitudes among college students in helping skills courses. *Journal of Counseling Psychology*, *65*(5), 661–668. https://doi.org/10.1037/cou0000283

Kivlighan, D. M., Jr. (1989). Changes in counselor intentions and response modes and in client reactions and session evaluation after training. *Journal of Counseling Psychology*, *36*(4), 471–476. https://doi.org/10.1037/0022-0167.36.4.471

Kivlighan, D. M., Jr. (2008). Structural changes in counselor trainee intention use and client's session evaluation. *Psychotherapy Research*, *18*(5), 560–572. https://doi.org/10.1080/10503300802010830

Kivlighan, D. M., Jr. (2010). Changes in trainees' intention use and volunteer clients' evaluations of sessions during early skills training. *Psychotherapy: Theory, Research, Practice, Training*, *47*(2), 198–210. https://doi.org/10.1037/a0019760

Knight, C. (1996). A study of MSW and BSW students' perceptions of their field instructors. *Journal of Social Work Education*, *32*(3), 399–414. https://doi.org/10.1080/10437797.1996.10778470

Knott, L. E., Wetterneck, C. T., Norwood, W., & Bistricky, S. L. (2019). The impact of training in functional analytic therapy on therapists' target behavior. *Behavior Analysis: Research and Practice*, *19*(2), 164–175. http://dx.doi.org/10.1037/bar0000097

Knox, S., Caperton, W., Phelps, D., & Pruitt, N. (2014). A qualitative study of supervisees' internal representations of supervisors. *Counselling Psychology Quarterly*, *27*(4), 334–352. https://doi.org/10.1080/09515070.2014.886999

Knox, S., Edwards, L. M., Hess, S. A., & Hill, C. E. (2011). Supervisor self-disclosure: Supervisees' experiences and perspectives. *Psychotherapy: Theory, Research, Practice, Training*, *48*(4), 336–341. https://doi.org/10.1037/a0022067

Kobak, K. A., Craske, M. G., Rose, R. D., & Wolitsky-Taylor, K. (2013). Web-based therapist training on cognitive behavior therapy for anxiety disorders: A pilot study. *Psychotherapy*, *50*(2), 235–247. https://doi.org/10.1037/a0030568

Kolchakian, M. (2004). Therapist predictors of the ability to perform helping skills. *Dissertation Abstracts International: Section B: The Sciences and Engineering*, 5788. https://www.elibrary.ru/item.asp?id=8840084

Kozlowski, J. M., Pruitt, N. T., DeWalt, T. A., & Knox, S. (2014). Can boundary crossings in clinical supervision be beneficial? *Counselling Psychology Quarterly*, *27*(2), 109–126. https://doi.org/10.1080/09515070.2013.870123

Ladany, N., Ellis, M. V., & Friedlander, M. L. (1999). The supervisory working alliance, trainee self-efficacy, and satisfaction. *Journal of Counseling and Development*, *77*(4), 447–455. https://doi.org/10.1002/j.1556-6676.1999.tb02472.x

Ladany, N., Lehrman-Waterman, D., Molinaro, M., & Wolgast, B. (1999). Psychotherapy supervisor ethical practices: Adherence to guidelines, the supervisory working alliance, and supervisee satisfaction. *The Counseling Psychologist*, *27*(3), 443–475. https://doi.org/10.1177/0011000099273008

Ladany, N., O'Brien, K. M., Hill, C. E., Melincoff, D. S., Knox, S., & Petersen, D. A. (1997). Sexual attraction toward clients, use of supervision, and prior training: A qualitative study of predoctoral psychology interns. *Journal of Counseling Psychology*, *44*(4), 413–424. https://doi.org/10.1037/0022-0167.44.4.413

Lambert, M. J., DeJulio, S. S., & Stein, D. M. (1978). Therapist interpersonal skills: Process, outcome, methodological considerations, and recommendations for future research. *Psychological Bulletin*, *85*(3), 467–489. https://doi.org/10.1037/0033-2909.85.3.467

Larson, L. M., & Daniels, J. A. (1998). Review of the counseling self-efficacy literature. *The Counseling Psychologist*, *26*(2), 179–218. https://doi.org/10.1177/0011000098262001

Lent, R. W., Hill, C. E., & Hoffman, M. A. (2003). Development and validation of the Counselor Activity Self-Efficacy Scales. *Journal of Counseling Psychology*, *50*(1), 97–108. https://doi.org/10.1037/0022-0167.50.1.97

Lent, R. W., Hoffman, M. A., Hill, C. E., Treistman, D., Mount, M., & Singley, D. (2006). Client-specific counselor self-efficacy in novice counselors: Relation to perceptions of session quality. *Journal of Counseling Psychology*, *53*(4), 453–463. https://doi.org/10.1037/0022-0167.53.4.453

Li, X., Kivlighan, D. M., Jr., Hill, C. E., Hou, J., & Xu, M. (2018). Helping skills, working alliance, and session depth in China: A multilevel analysis. *The Counseling Psychologist*, *46*(3), 379–405. https://doi.org/10.1177/0011000018763965

Lu, Y., Hill, C. E., Hancock, G., & Keum, H. B. (2020). The effectiveness of helping skills training for undergraduates: Changes in ethnocultural empathy. *Journal of Counseling Psychology*, *67*(1), 14–24. https://doi.org/10.1037/cou0000404

Maitland, D. W. M., Kanter, J. W., Tsai, M., Kuczynski, A. M., Manbeck, K. E., & Kohlenberg, R. J. (2016). Preliminary findings on the effects of online Functional Analytic training on therapist competency. *The Psychological Record*, *66*, 627–637. https://doi.org/10.1007/s40732-016-0198-8

Mallinckrodt, B., & Nelson, M. L. (1991). Counselor training level and the formation of the psychotherapeutic working alliance. *Journal of Counseling Psychology*, *38*(2), 133–138. https://doi.org/10.1037/0022-0167.38.2.133

Marmarosh, C. L., Nikityn, M., Moehringer, J., Ferraioli, L., Kahn, S., Cerkevich, A., Choi, J., & Reisch, E. (2013). Adult attachment, attachment to the supervisor, and the supervisory alliance: How they relate to novice therapists' perceived counseling self-efficacy. *Psychotherapy*, *50*(2), 178–188. https://doi.org/10.1037/a0033028

Marmarosh, C. L., Thompson, B., Hill, C., Hollman, S., & Megivern, M. (2017). Therapists-in-training experiences of working with transfer clients: One relationship terminates and another begins. *Psychotherapy*, *54*(1), 102–113. https://doi.org/10.1037/pst0000095

Matarazzo, R. G. (1971). The systematic study of learning psychotherapy skills. In A. E. Bergin & S. L. Garfield (Eds.), *Handbook of psychotherapy and behavior change* (pp. 895–924). Wiley.

Matarazzo, R. G. (1978). Research on the teaching and learning of psychotherapeutic skills. In S. L. Garfield & A. E. Bergin (Eds.), *Handbook of psychotherapy and behavior change* (2nd ed., pp. 941–966). Wiley.

Matarazzo, R. G., & Patterson, D. (1986). Research on the teaching and learning of therapeutic skills. In S. L. Garfield & A. E. Bergin (Eds.), *Handbook of psychotherapy and behavior change* (3rd ed., pp. 821–843). Wiley.

Meekums, B., Macaskie, J., & Kapur, T. (2016). Developing skills in counselling and psychotherapy: A scoping review of Interpersonal Process Recall and Reflecting Team methods in initial therapist training. *British Journal of Guidance and Counselling*, *44*(5), 504–515. https://doi.org/10.1080/03069885.2016.1143550

Mehr, K. E., Ladany, N., & Caskie, G. I. L. (2015). Factors influencing trainee willingness to disclose in supervision. *Training and Education in Professional Psychology*, *9*(1), 44–51. https://doi.org/10.1037/tep0000028

Mesrie, V., Diener, M. J., & Clark, A. (2018). Trainee attachment to supervisor and perceptions of novice psychotherapist counseling self-efficacy: The moderating role of level of experience. *Psychotherapy*, *55*(3), 216–221. https://doi.org/10.1037/pst0000191

Miller, S., Hubble, M., & Duncan, B. (2007). Supershrinks: Why do some therapists clearly stand out above the rest, consistently getting far better results than most of their colleagues? *Psychotherapy Networker*, *31*, 26.

Minami, T., Davies, D. R., Tierney, S. C., Bettmann, J. E., McAward, S. M., Averill, L. A., Huebner, L. A., Weitzman, L. M., Benbrook, A. R., Serlin, R. C., & Wampold, B. E. (2009). Preliminary evidence on the effectiveness of psychological treatments delivered at a university counseling center. *Journal of Counseling Psychology*, *56*, 309–320. https://doi.org/10.1037/a0015398

Nelson, M. L., & Friedlander, M. L. (2001). A close look at conflictual supervisory relationships: The trainee's perspective. *Journal of Counseling Psychology*, *48*(4), 384–395. https://doi.org/10.1037/0022-0167.48.4.384

Nerdrum, P., & Rønnestad, M. H. (2002). The trainees' perspective: A qualitative study of learning to empathic communication in Norway. *The Counseling Psychologist*, *30*(4), 609–629. https://doi.org/10.1177/00100002030004007

Nerdrum, P., & Rønnestad, M. H. (2004). Changes in therapists' conceptualization and practice of therapy following empathy training. *The Clinical Supervisor*, *22*(2), 37–61. https://doi.org/10.1300/J001v22n02_04

Nissen-Lie, H. A., Rønnestad, M. H., Høglend, P. A., Havik, O. E., Solbakken, O. A., Stiles, T. C., & Monsen, J. T. (2017). Love yourself as a person, doubt yourself as a therapist? *Clinical Psychology & Psychotherapy*, *24*(1), 48–60. https://doi.org/10.1002/cpp.1977.

O'Donovan, A., Bain, J. D., & Dyck, M. J. (2005). Does clinical psychology education enhance the clinical competence of practitioners? *Professional Psychology: Research and Practice*, *36*(1), 104–111. https://doi.org/10.1037/0735-7028.36.1.104

Okiishi, J. C., Lambert, M. J., Eggett, D., Nielson, L., Dayton, D. D., & Vermeersch, D. A. (2006). An analysis of therapist treatment effects: Toward providing feedback to individual therapists on their clients' psychotherapy outcome. *Journal of Clinical Psychology*, *62*(9), 1157–1172. https://doi.org/10.1002/jclp.20272

Owen, J., Wampold, B. E., Kopta, M., Rousmaniere, T., & Miller, S. D. (2016). As good as it gets? Therapy outcomes of trainees over time. *Journal of Counseling Psychology, 63*(1), 12–19. https://doi.org/10.1037/cou0000112

Park, E. H., Ha, G., Lee, S., Lee, Y. Y., & Lee, S. M. (2019). Relationship between the supervisory working alliance and outcomes: A meta-analysis. *Journal of Counseling & Development, 97*(4), 437–446. https://doi.org/10.1002/jcad.12292

Pascual-Leone, A., & Andreescu, C. (2013). Repurposing process measures to train psychotherapists: Training outcomes using a new approach. *Counselling and Psychotherapy Research, 13*(3), 210–219. https://doi.org/10.1080/14733145.2012.739633

Pascual-Leone, A., Andreescu, C., & Yeryomenko, N. (2015). Training novice psychotherapists: Comparing undergraduate and graduate students' outcomes. *Counselling and Psychotherapy Research, 15*, 137–146. https://doi.org/10.1080/14733145.2014.897360

Pascual-Leone, A., Rodriguez-Rubio, B., & Metler, S. (2013). What *else* are psychotherapy trainees learning? A qualitative model of students' personal experiences based on two populations. *Psychotherapy Research, 23*(5), 578–591. https://doi.org/10.1080/10503307.2013.807379

Pascual-Leone, A., Wolfe, B. J., & O'Connor, D. (2012). The reported impact of psychotherapy training: Undergraduate disclosures after a course in experiential psychotherapy. *Person-Centered and Experiential Psychotherapies, 11*(2), 152–168. https://doi.org/10.1080/14779757.2011.648099

Pieterse, A. L., Lee, M., Ritmeester, A., & Collins, N. (2013). Towards a model of self-awareness development four counselling and psychotherapy training. *Counselling Psychology Quarterly, 26*(2), 190–207. https://doi.org/10.1080/09515070.2013.793451

Prass, M., Ewell, A., Hill, C. E., & Kivlighan, D. M., Jr. (2021). Solicited and unsolicited therapist advice in psychodynamic psychotherapy: Is it advised?, *Counselling Psychology Quarterly, 34*(2), 253–274. https://doi.org/10.1080/09515070.2020.1723492

Puspitasari, A., Kanter, J. W., Murphy, J., Crowe, A., & Koerner, K. (2013). Developing an online, active learning training program for behavioral activation. *Psychotherapy, 50*(2), 256–265. https://doi.org/10.1037/a0030058

Ridley, C. R., Kelly, S. M., & Mollen, D. (2011). Microskills training: Evolution, reexamination, and call for reform. *The Counseling Psychologist, 39*(6), 800–824. https://doi.org/10.1177/0011000010378438

Rieck, T., Callahan, J. L., & Watkins, C. E., Jr. (2015). Clinical supervision: An exploration of possible mechanisms of action. *Training and Education in Professional Psychology, 9*(2), 187–194. https://doi.org/10.1037/tep0000080

Rogers, C. R. (1942). *Counseling and psychotherapy*. Houghton Mifflin.

Rogers, C. R. (1957). The necessary and sufficient conditions of therapeutic personality change. *Journal of Consulting Psychology, 21*(2), 95–103. https://doi.org/10.1037/h0045357

Rønnestad, M. H. & Skovholt, T. M. (2003). The journey of the counselor and therapist: Research findings and perspectives on professional development. *Journal of Career Development, 30*(1), 5–44. https://doi.org/10.1177/089484530303000102

Rousmaniere, T. G. (2016). *Deliberate practice for psychotherapists: A guide to improving clinical effectiveness*. Routledge Press (Taylor & Francis).

Rousmaniere, T. G. (2018). *Mastering the inner skills of psychotherapy: A deliberate practice handbook*. Gold Lantern Press.

Rousmaniere, T. G., Swift, J. K., Babins-Wagner, R., Whipple, J. L., & Berzins, S. (2016). Supervisor variance in psychotherapy outcome in routine practice. *Psychotherapy Research, 26*(2), 196–205. https://doi.org/10.1080/10503307.2014.963730

Russell, R. R., Crimmings, A. M., & Lent, R. W. (1984). Therapist training and supervision. In S. Brown & R. W. Lent (Eds.), *Handbook of counseling psychology* (pp. 625–681). Wiley.

Safran, J., Muran, J. C., Demaria, A., Boutwell, C., Eubanks-Carter, C., & Winston, A., (2014). Investigating the impact of alliance-focused training on interpersonal process and therapists' capacity for experiential reflection. *Psychotherapy Research, 24*(3), 269–285. https://doi.org/10.1080/10503307.2013.874054

Sant, M., & Milton, M. (2015). Trainee practitioners' experiences of the psychodynamic supervisory and supervision: A thematic analysis. *The Clinical Supervisor, 34*(2), 204–231. https://doi.org/10.1080/07325223.2015.1086917

Shaffer, K. S., & Friedlander, M. L. (2017). What do "interpersonally sensitive" supervisors do and how do supervisees experience a relational approach to supervision? *Psychotherapy Research, 27*(2), 167–178. https://doi.org/10.1080/10503307.2015.1080877

Skovholt, T. M., & Rønnestad, M. H. (1992). *The evolving professional self: Stages and themes in therapist and counselor development*. John Wiley & Sons.

Spangler, P. T., Hill, C. E., Dunn, M. G., Hummel, A, Walden, T., Liu, J., Jackson, J., Ganginis, H. V., & Salahuddin, N. (2014). Training undergraduate students to use immediacy. *The Counseling Psychologist, 42*(6), 729–757. https://doi.org/10.1177/0011000014542835

Stein, D. M., & Lambert, M. J. (1995). Graduate training in psychotherapy: Are therapy outcomes enhanced? *Journal of Consulting and Clinical Psychology, 63*(2), 182–196. https://doi.org/10.1037/0022-006X.63.2.182

Strawbridge, S., & Woolfe, R. (2010). Counselling psychology: Origins, developments and challenges. In R. Woolfe, S. Strawbridge, B. Douglas, & W. Dryden (Eds.), *Handbook of counseling psychology* (3rd ed., pp. 3–22). Sage.

Sue, D. W., Sue, D., Neville, H. A., & Smith, L. (2019). *Counseling the culturally diverse: Theory and practice* (8th ed.). Wiley,

Tracey, T. J. G., Wampold, B. E., Lichtenberg, J. W., & Goodyear, R. K. (2014). Expertise in psychotherapy: An elusive goal? *American Psychologist, 69*(3), 218–229. https://doi.org/10.1037/a0035099

Tryon, G. S. (1996). Supervisee development during the practicum year. *Counselor Education and Supervision, 35*(4), 287–294. https://doi.org/10.1002/j.1556-6978.1996.tb01929.x

Teding van Berkhout, E., & Malouff, J. M. (2016). The efficacy of empathy training: A meta-analysis of randomized controlled trials. *Journal of Counseling Psychology, 63*(1), 32–41. https://doi.org/10.1037/cou0000093

Watkins, C. E. (2011). Does psychotherapy supervision contribute to patient outcomes? Considering thirty years of research. *The Clinical Supervisor, 30*(2), 235–256. https://doi.org/10.1080/07325223.2011.619417

Watkins, C. E., Jr. (2017). How does psychotherapy supervision work? Contributions of connection, conception, allegiance, alignment, and action. *Journal of Psychotherapy Integration, 27*(2), 201–217. https://doi.org/10.1037/int0000058

Williams, E. N. (2008). A psychotherapy researcher's perspective on therapist self-awareness and self-focused attention after a decade of research. *Psychotherapy Research, 18*(2), 139–146. https://doi.org/10.1080/10503300701691656

Williams, E.N., Hurley, K., O'Brien, K., & DeGregorio, A. (2003). Development and validation of the Self-Awareness and Management Strategies (SAMS) scales for therapists, *Psychotherapy: Theory, Research, Practice, Training, 40*(4), 278–288. https://doi.org/10.1037/0033-3204.40.4.278

Williams, E., Judge, A., Hill, C. E., & Hoffman, M. A. (1997). Experiences of novice therapists in prepracticum: Trainees', clients', and supervisors' perceptions of personal reactions and management strategies. *Journal of Counseling Psychology, 44*(4), 390–399. http://dx.doi.org/10.1037/0022-0167.44.4.390

Wrape, E. R., Callahan, J. L., Ruggero, C. J., & Watkins, C. E., Jr. (2015). An exploration of faculty supervisor variables and their impact on client outcomes. *Training and Education in Professional Psychology, 9*(1), 35–43. https://doi.org/10.1037/tep0000014

Wright, J. K. (2005). "A discussion with myself on paper:" Counselling and psychotherapy masters student perceptions of keeping a learning log. *Reflective Practice, 6*(4), 507–521. https://doi.org/10.1080/14623940500300665

Zetzer, H., Hill, C. E., Hopsicker R., Krasno, A., Montojo, P. C., Plumb, E., Donahue, M., & Hoffman, M. A. (2018). *Parallel process and the supervisory and therapeutic alliance*. Panel presented at the Annual Meeting of the Society for Psychotherapy Research, Amsterdam, Netherlands.

AUTHOR NOTES

We extend our gratitude to C. Edward Watkins, Jr. and Heidi Zetzer for reviewing this manuscript. Their comments were invaluable.

CHAPTER 11

QUALITATIVE RESEARCH: CONTRIBUTIONS TO PSYCHOTHERAPY PRACTICE, THEORY, AND POLICY

JOHN MCLEOD, WILLIAM B STILES, AND HEIDI M LEVITT

Abstract

Qualitative research methodologies can be used to generate insights and evidence around core issues relating to policy and practice in psychotherapy and behavior change. A major contribution of qualitative research consists of enriched understanding and awareness of key aspects of the process of therapy and the nature of the therapeutic alliance. Qualitative inquiry can also facilitate the process of building practice-relevant theory, as well as broadening the sensitivity and relevance of evaluation of therapy outcomes. Qualitative approaches fulfill a crucial function within the array of available methodologies, by making it possible to investigate hard-to-study topics, and augmenting the interpretation of findings of randomized trials. This chapter provides critical analysis of examples of the nature and scope of currently available qualitative evidence around a range of topics, including client and therapist experience of therapy, the process of change, therapist development, and the nature of outcome. Methodological challenges associated with the use of qualitative approaches to constructing a knowledge base for therapy practice are discussed and recommendations are made regarding priorities for future research.

OVERVIEW

Introduction

How Qualitative Research Contributes to an Enriched Appreciation of the Experience of Participating in Psychotherapy

The Client's Experience of Therapy

The Therapist's Experience of Therapy

Negotiating Difference: Impact on the Process of Therapy

Conversational Strategies for Facilitating the Process of Change in Psychotherapy

How Organizational Context Shapes the Experience of Therapy

Emergent and Hard-to-Study Experiences of Therapy

Some Contributions of Qualitative Research to Theory-Building

Building the Assimilation Model

Task Analysis: Building Micro-Models of Productive Sequences of Therapeutic Interaction

Other Ways in Which Qualitative Research Can Contribute to Theory-Building

Using Qualitative Research for Fact-Gathering

Using Qualitative Research for Product Development and Testing

Qualitative Research into the Outcomes of Therapy

Clients' Perspectives on the Experience of Completing a Symptom Measure

Implications of Qualitative Research into the Process of Evaluating the Outcomes of Therapy

Other Examples of How Qualitative Research Contributes to Product Testing

Conclusions and Recommendations

Maximizing the Contribution of Qualitative Research

Integrating Qualitative Research into the Broader Research Literature

Abbreviations

References

INTRODUCTION

Culturally and historically, psychotherapy is a practical discipline. Research into the process and outcomes of psychotherapy has influenced the development of therapy theory and practice in a range of ways (McLeod, 2016). At a general level, the existence of an active research community and tradition reinforces a critical approach to practice and an ethos of accountability. For clinicians, research findings can be used to inform how to work with specific clients. At an organizational level, scientific knowledge provides a basis for decisions around service-delivery issues such as which approach to therapy is most effective for particular client conditions, how many sessions are necessary, and how to minimize client dropout. Each of these ways of using research draws on research-informed theories of therapy. Increasingly, research knowledge also is accessed by consumers of therapy as a means of supporting preferences and choices around which therapy (or other form of intervention) might be most relevant to their needs.

A complex intervention such as psychotherapy requires a knowledge strategy that embraces a plurality of methodologies (Howard, 1983). Such a strategy makes it possible to triangulate conclusions across methodologies, while at the same time using the tensions between contrasting conclusions and emphases reported by different methodologies as a means of stimulating further research and conceptual progress. Within an overall methodologically pluralist research program, the distinctive contribution made by qualitative research includes its sensitivity to client and therapist agentic involvement and meaning-making, discovery orientation and openness to emergent themes, and capacity to highlight processes associated with differences in power and status. Findings from qualitative research are also more likely to provide a case-based or micro-process level of analysis. Qualitative psychotherapy research functions both as a critical counterweight to findings and conclusions drawn from quantitative methodologies, and as a powerful evidence source in its own right.

The primary areas of focus for the present chapter are the questions: What does qualitative research tell us about the process of change? and How does knowledge from qualitative studies help us to be better therapists? These central issues are approached through an overview of how findings from qualitative studies can be used to inform the practice of psychotherapy, while also considering how such methodologies can lead to a better understanding of theoretical perspectives that guide practice, and the organizational and policy contexts within which practice takes place. For reasons of space, the chapter cannot provide a systematic or comprehensive review of current qualitative findings in respect of any of the topics that are addressed. Instead, the aim is to highlight the range of possibilities associated with qualitative research as a source of evidence for practice, and to identify key strategic directions for further research. This chapter expands on the coverage of application of qualitative research provided in the previous edition of this Handbook (McLeod, 2013). It complements Chapter 3 of the current edition (Levitt et al., 2021), on methods of qualitative research, demonstrating how different methodological approaches are applied in relation to investigation of key issues around practice, theory development and policy.

The chapter draws on a framework suggested by Stiles (2015, 2017) that distinguishes four different but complementary purposes of psychotherapy research: *enriching*, *theory-building*, *fact-gathering*, and *product testing*. The first two of these, particularly, differ in significant and often unappreciated ways.

Enriching research aims to broaden and deepen the understanding and appreciation of the target phenomenon by readers, participants (both the investigators and the investigated), and others who come in contact with the research. This particularly includes fostering insight and empathy into the experience of the research participants. Theory-building research aims to assess and improve the theory that guides the research, increasing confidence in it and enhancing its generality, precision, and realism. Whereas enriching research may draw on many theories – or devise new ones – in service of gaining a deeper, richer understanding and appreciation of a phenomenon, such as the experience of psychotherapy participants, theory-building research aims explicitly to assess, refine, and elaborate the particular theory that guided the research. Even their use of language differs. Theory-building seeks consistent definitions, striving to say the same thing to everybody across time and circumstance. Consistent meanings for terms are needed for the logical coherence of the theory, which in turn is essential so that observations on one part of the theory (e.g., a hypothesis) can affect confidence in the theory as a whole (Stiles, 2009a). (This is one reason why quantitative research is so attractive to theory builders; the meaning of numbers is more stable than the meaning of other words across time and people). In contrast, the use of language in enriching research is more like natural language, where word meanings shift with time and context. Indeed, unpacking the meanings is a central task of enriching research. In summary, whereas enriching research aims to enrich the understanding of people (readers, investigators, participants), theory-building research aims to enhance a theory, that is, a particular semiotic construction.

Fact-gathering research aims to find and verify facts, that is, observational statements that meet accepted standards of evidence. The name *fact-gathering* comes from Kuhn (1970), who described it as what scientists do when they do not have a paradigm, that is, in the absence of a comprehensive theory with associated puzzles and practices. Fact-gathering may be preliminary to theory-building, conducted in the expectation that the facts will eventually be collected and synthesized. However, the gathered facts may also be used for enriching purposes. Product-testing research focuses on the development and evaluation of some application – primarily, in psychotherapy research, a psychotherapeutic treatment or an assessment tool. Although most qualitative methods can be used to address any of the four purposes, there are some traditions that lead some methods to be more likely to be used for certain purposes.

The most extensive contributions of qualitative research considered in this chapter have been enriching, particularly research on the experience of psychotherapy participants, reviewed in the next section. Selected qualitative contributions to theory-building, fact-gathering, and product-testing research goals are reviewed later in the chapter. For reasons of space, only references to key sources and exemplar studies are provided.

How Qualitative Research Contributes to an Enriched Appreciation of the Experience of Participating in Psychotherapy

One of the major achievements of qualitative research has been its contribution to enriching our understanding of the lived experience of psychotherapy participants. The following sections seek to illustrate the practical, theoretical and policy implications of representative qualitative findings concerning a range of aspects of the experience of therapy, encompassing both client and therapist perspectives on their participation in therapy.

It is important to note that, notwithstanding the distinction between purposes, it is part of enriching research to explore alternative possibilities, and in this sense, having multiple purposes is a distinctive characteristic of enriching research. For example, enriching research often makes extensive use of theoretical concepts to inform and enrich readers' practice, their understanding of theory or treatment approaches, and their positions on matters of policy. Further, research that begins as enriching may guide the development of a new theory and in this sense serve more than one purpose (e.g., Levitt, 2019).

Similarly, there is dynamic interplay between enriching and product-testing. For example, in a later discussion, we argue that qualitative research into how clients experience the outcomes of therapy contributes to an enriched understanding of the meaning of outcome. Such research also makes it possible to develop more differentiated criteria, and more valid and reliable assessment procedures, through which therapy products, such as treatment protocols, can be evaluated.

It is also important to note that the enriching potential of a qualitative study is only minimally conveyed through brief descriptions of themes, which is typically all that is reported in review chapters such as this one. To appreciate the full enrichment potential of qualitative findings, it is necessary to read the whole of the original source article, in which the meaning of lived experience is communicated through the words and voice of research informants, framed and highlighted by interpretive reflection and explanation of context.

The Client's Experience of Therapy

Research on how clients view their therapy has a long history (e.g., Lipkin, 1954; Maluccio, 1979). More recently, influential research by David Rennie (e.g., 1994) drew attention to experiences that are not expressed to the therapist and may be deliberately hidden. Intrigued by these findings, qualitative psychotherapy researchers have developed data-gathering strategies that range from interviewing clients about their experience of their whole therapy to focusing on the processes in single sessions. An important set of studies has explored client perceptions of what has been helpful or unhelpful in their therapy (Cooper & McLeod, 2015). Qualitative methods have been used to examine client experiences of specific types of intervention, such as mindfulness training (Cairns & Murray, 2015), online therapy (Knowles et al., 2014) or shared case formulation (Redhead et al., 2015). Other studies have analyzed the meaning for clients of particular phases within therapy, such as early sessions (Lavik et al., 2018) and endings (Råbu, & Haavind, 2018).

The following sections highlight the clinical implications of research into the client's experience of therapy in three areas: (a) how clients make sense of the process of change in therapy; (b) therapy from the perspective of marginalized clients; and (c) client lived experience of diagnostic categories and patterns of emotional distress. Client experience of outcome is discussed within a later section on qualitative product-testing.

How Clients Experience the Process of Change

An omnibus qualitative meta-analysis of 109 research studies on clients' experiences of psychotherapy formulated overarching themes in terms of therapeutic principles (Levitt et al., 2016a), which can be understood as conveying clients'

understanding of how therapy works (see Levitt et al., 2006 on the rationale for principles for moment-to-moment change). The principles outlined below, which represent a condensation of 15 distinct categories of client experience, are based on support from across those studies that used diverse clients, theoretical orientations, and topic foci and so can be considered to have broad relevance for clinical practice.

Structuring Curiosity Leads to Pattern Identification. Qualitative research on clients' experiences has shed light on the process by which clients learn in session to identify the problematic patterns of functioning in which they habitually engage. These patterns included the identification of interpersonal dynamics (e.g., Binder et al., 2010), cognitive processes (Clark et al., 2004), emotional reactions (Grafanaki & McLeod, 1999), behavioral responses, and narrative re-storying. Across these types of functioning, therapists were described as guiding clients to develop a curiosity about their own experience by helping them to notice recurring patterns. After identifying characteristic ways of being, clients were able to consider whether they would like to alter these and develop new modes of being. Focused exploration of these patterns allowed clients to become more self-reflexive, to decrease defensiveness about their functioning, and to gain a sense of hope and relief as clients could see a way to change.

It might be presumed that therapists' orientations provided them with the tools and structure to help them guide clients through this process of identification. Although it may be useful for therapists to conceptualize their work as focused on one or two faculties (i.e., relationships, emotions, cognitions, behaviors), clients described experiencing change holistically. Indeed, studies of clients who received the same form of psychotherapy did not report a significantly different number of change processes when compared to studies of clients from varied approaches to treatment (Levitt et al., 2016b). With this insight in mind, regardless of the orientation in use, therapists may wish to help clients to integrate the gains they are making associated across faculties by considering how their insights are influencing their emotions, cognitions, interpersonal dynamics, behaviors and sense of self. If clients are needing support to integrate the insights into one of these areas, therapists can consider adopting an integrative or pluralistic approach to therapy to support that work (Cooper & McLeod, 2007)

Forming a Transformative Relationship Leads to the Internal and Interpersonal Safety Needed for Self-Exploration. Quantitative meta-analytic research on the relationship that has found repeatedly that the alliance accounts for more variance in client outcome than therapy orientation (Wampold & Imel, 2015). Qualitative research and meta-analytic reviews of qualitative studies of client experience of therapy complement and extend these broad-brush findings. Clients have described multiple ways in which the relationship with a therapist helped them to engage in productive change. For example, clients report that participating in a therapeutic relationship in which they feel cared for and understood permits them to lower their defensiveness, and thereby engage in increasingly vulnerable disclosure and discussion through which they are able to begin to develop self-awareness (Fitzpatrick et al., 2009). This shift occurs when clients are able to internalize the acceptance demonstrated by their therapist and to develop a more compassionate attitude toward themselves. By contrast, feeling misunderstood, unheard, or unappreciated undermined the development of such a relationship, although clients reported that overt discussion to work through differences in therapist-client perspectives was helpful to clients in these instances (Poulsen et al., 2010). In addition, when handled sensitively, the professional structure within which a therapeutic relationship exists can provide clarity and credibility. Key principles that emerged in the meta-analysis was that there are three ways that having an accepting and caring relationship permitted clients' exploration of vulnerable issues by: (a) decreasing defensiveness; (b) increasing clients' self-acceptance; and (c) internalization of the therapist as a temporary source of validation. By keeping all three dimensions in mind, therapists can develop a more responsive relational stance as they support clients to become ready to explore sensitive issues in sessions.

Discussing Differences in Both Professional Power and Culture Leads to Productive Collaboration. Issues related to power have been discussed in two contexts. In one set of studies, researchers focused on the power imbalance that is inherent in all psychotherapy relationships by virtue of the therapists' role (e.g., Bury et al., 2007; Hoener et al., 2012; Littauer et al., 2005). Therapists have power because they have expertise in the area of mental health and psychotherapeutic change. In some settings, they also may have power over patient's privileges and may be in a position to represent the patient to other health care providers or decision makers about the patient's life. Clients typically seek out therapy when they are in a state of emotional need and may feel dependent on their therapists for assistance. The central recommendation from this set of studies is that therapists should explicitly negotiate client and therapists' roles to lessen this power differential. They can transparently orient clients to the purpose of therapy, the way agenda for sessions are set, and let clients know what they can do to actively engage in their treatment.

In a second set of studies, researchers have considered how cultural identities may influence therapy by unavoidably importing into the relationship forms of power structured by positions such as gender, race, ethnicity, sexual orientation, class, religion, and disability (Chang & Yoon, 2011). Across these studies, the common theme was that it is helpful for therapists to acknowledge both cultural differences and similarities in therapy and create room to discuss them. At the same time, therapists will benefit from learning about the cultural contexts of clients while also keeping in mind that each client is an individual who may be unique in their attitudes toward or understandings of their cultural identities and positions. This literature is discussed more fully in a later section in the present chapter that explores qualitative studies of the experience of marginalized clients in therapy.

There has been a tendency for researchers to examine these two forms of power in isolation rather than considering how they intersect (Levitt et al., 2016a). There is evidence that client sensitivity to power and difference permeates all forms of therapy (Williams & Levitt, 2008). We call for research that examines how these types of power are intertwined and a clinical ethics that considers both insights from humanistic and feminist-multicultural psychology as a foundation for practice

that incorporates considerations of professional and cultural power (Comas-Diaz, 2012).

Supporting Client Self-Healing Leads to Responsive Practice. It may be natural for therapists to think about psychotherapy as a series of interventions that they deliver to their clients. However, consistent with results of meta-analytic research demonstrating that theoretical orientations account for little of the variance in client outcome, qualitative studies based in the point of view of the client draw attention to the inadequacy of conceptualizing psychotherapy as a set of interventions delivered by the therapist. Research that articulates the client's experience of therapy leads to an understanding of therapy as a context that supports clients' capacities for problem-solving. This has been described as the *self-healing paradigm* (Bohart & Tallman, 1999; Gordon, 2012).

This body of research has highlighted clients' agentic role within the therapy session, a factor common across psychotherapy orientations, and the many ways in which they influence the session and their change process. This direction may occur covertly, for instance, by deciding what to disclose, what to hide, and how to direct therapists' attention (e.g., Blanchard & Farber, 2016; Rennie, 1994). It may occur by clients deciding what homework to do and how they would like to implement suggestions made by therapists (Bohart, 2000). Instead of conceptualizing therapy as a process in which therapists produce changes in clients, the self-healing paradigm views the process as one in which clients produce change in themselves, with the support of their therapists. Client agency can be enhanced when therapists deliberately support clients to make connections in sessions and arrive at their own solutions for problems and to consider how to best implement them in their specific systemic contexts.

Therapy from the Perspective of Marginalized Clients

There is a wealth of qualitative research focused on clients who have socially marginalized identities and characteristics. This research highlights the internal experiences of clients in session related to issues of power – which are topics that can be especially difficult to discuss. Also, this research considers therapists' thoughts about how their own positionality influences their therapy and their intentions as they develop interventions with clients. In this section, we take a closer look at that literature.

Clients who embody cultural identities that are marginalized in our society (e.g., gender, race, ethnicity, religion, sexual orientation, disability, social class) have been found to have some distinctive concerns about and experience in therapy. Given that clients with marginalized experiences often experience routine minority stressors that can complicate their levels of distress and metal health (e.g., Valentine & Shipherd, 2018), the consideration of these issues is important in a therapy context. Stereotypical assumptions about clients' cultures have been reported to be damaging to their sense of the therapeutic alliance (Chang & Yoon, 2011; Shelton & Delgado-Romero, 2011). When therapists appear not to understand their cultural differences and needs, they experience this as harmful. This might be evident when therapists do not understand stressors that clients experience (e.g., related to stigma or economic strains) or are not aware of familial dynamics, cultural norms and the influence of the regional context (e.g., legislative supports or lack thereof for LGBTQ people). It was similarly described as unaffirming when therapists overidentified with clients or focused on their marginalized identity when it was not experienced as relevant. Clients have described the effects of this misunderstanding as feeling judged, stifled, offended, or invalidated and feeling that it impaired their ability to connect in therapy sessions.

Across a number of qualitative studies (e.g., Cragun & Friedlander, 2012; Thompson et al., 2012), clients have described withholding issues related to their culture from within their therapy exchanges because of the assumption that the therapist would not understand them. This nondisclosure was attributed to their own internalized sense of shame, a fear of being judged, worry about not receiving adequate empathy, or jealousy of the therapists' presumed privileged status. If therapists seemed to be open and interested in discussing the clients' culture, clients might be more likely to disclose (Pope-Davis et al., 2002). By contrast, if they failed to engage with attempts to raise these issues or could not adopt clients' frame of reference, clients were likely to stop attempting disclosure. At times, this created ruptures that could lead to the termination of therapy (Glockel, 2011).

In contrast, when therapists overtly invited discussion of cultural issues in their therapy (e.g., as part of their intake session and beyond), clients felt encouraged to raise these issues as part of their therapy (Chang & Berk, 2009). Matching therapist and client identities could be helpful in facilitating a sense of trust and shared experience, but clients also reported obstacles in these relationships, especially if clients wished to discuss experiences that differed from expectations of their culture or were viewed as shameful in their culture (e.g., sexual abuse; Chang & Yoon, 2011). When therapists acknowledged their differences and similarities with the client and the potential for issues to arise and invited discussion of differences in perspectives and cultural backgrounds, clients reported feeling more like they were allowed to be a whole person within therapy (Audet, 2011).

Client-Lived Experience of Diagnostic Categories and Patterns of Emotional Distress

Diagnosis of therapy clients in terms of psychiatric categories is widely used as a source of information that shapes clinical decision-making, as well as comprising an organizing framework for research. Studies using qualitative methodologies contribute to practice in this area in two main ways. First, qualitative research into the experience of conditions such as depression or personality disorder, opens up a wider understanding of what it is like to live with such a problem. Such research enhances the ecological validity of diagnostic categories, by making it possible to evaluate the extent to which expert-defined patterns correspond to lived experience. Second, qualitative research has investigated the meaning of receiving a diagnosis, in terms of its helpfulness (or otherwise) for clients and patients.

The diagnostic category that has received the most attention from qualitative researchers is depression. Therapy-relevant aspects of depression that have been investigated by qualitative

researchers include the experience of depression (Porr et al., 2010; Ridge & Ziebland, 2012), active steps taken by individuals to overcome depression (Kinnier et al., 2009; Villaggi et al., 2015), cultural differences in the meaning of depression (Haroz et al., 2017), and the personal meaning of taking antidepressant medication (Gibson et al., 2016; McMullen & Herman, 2009). There have also been many studies of the client experience of therapy for depression, and therapist experience of providing therapy to depressed clients. Among the general take-home messages for clinicians from qualitative research on depression are that this condition means different things to different people, and that those suffering from depression typically engage in multiple self-help activities in addition to (or instead of) psychotherapy. A further important strand of this set of studies also suggests that there are potentially important gender differences in the ways that individuals understand depression and cope with it (Seidler et al., 2016).

Qualitative methodologies have also been used to investigate the meaning and lived experience of many other mental health conditions. Typical examples of such studies include investigations of the experiences of individuals diagnosed with ADHD (Halleröd et al., 2015), avoidant personality disorder (Sørensen et al., 2019). obsessive-compulsive disorder (Brooks 2011; Fox 2014), women's perinatal mental health difficulties (Millett et al., 2019; Smith et al., 2019), post-trauma stress (Michalopoulos et al., 2020), self-harm (Stänicke et al., 2018), and social anxiety disorder (Boyle, 2019). There is also evidence from qualitative studies around the ways in which individuals respond to a psychiatric diagnosis, in terms of such themes as acceptance, ambivalence, rejection, and coping with stigma (Hundt et al., 2018).

The primary contribution of qualitative research into the experience of a diagnostic condition has been to inform policy and practice through the availability of the voices of those who are seldom heard (Ryan et al., 2017). Some of the material collected in such qualitative studies has also been put to immediate practical use, in the form of projects that disseminate online patient accounts of living with a psychiatric condition, as a public resource and an adjunct to professional education (Kidd & Ziebland, 2016). Finally, the poor fit between lived experience and psychiatric categories has stimulated the development of a more socially oriented, adversity-based model of classification of patterns of emotional distress as an alternative to medical model diagnostic systems (Johnstone et al., 2018).

The Therapist's Experience of Therapy

Clinicians inevitably reflect on their work with clients, and the experiences and insights that arise from this activity provide a potentially valuable source of knowledge about therapy. Qualitative research into therapist experience of practice can be regarded as falling into three broad categories: professional knowledge research, studies of therapist wisdom, and research that explores therapist internal experience of being in sessions with clients.

Studies of professional knowledge focus on the awareness, strategies, and learning that arise from using a particular therapy approach, or working a particular client group (McLeod, 2016). Examples of this type of therapist experience research include investigations of what it is like to work with involuntary clients (Prytz et al., 2019), disclosing aspects of personal experience to clients (Mjelve et al., 2020), engaging in therapy with autism spectrum clients (Vulcan, 2016), and having clients who "get under your skin" (Bimont & Werbart, 2015). In general, studies of therapist professional knowledge have not been considered as a discrete category within the research literature. It would be valuable, as means of highlighting the practical value of such studies, for future research, to include meta-syntheses of professional knowledge studies in specific areas (e.g., working with depressed clients) and also to address methodological issues associated with this area of inquiry, such as how to use interviews to collect information about implicit and procedural dimensions of what therapists know.

A further category of therapist experience research comprises inquiry into the nature of more general therapist wisdom that accumulates over time as a result of attempts to resolve personal and professional dilemmas arising from therapy practice (Levitt & Piazza-Bonin, 2016; Råbu, & McLeod, 2018). Both professional knowledge studies and wisdom research can be viewed as contributing to the maintenance of professional communities of practice, in which knowledge of how to conduct therapy is transmitted from one clinician to another, and from one generation to the next (Lave & Wenger, 1991). The research dimension of such communities of practice complements other ways in which such networks operate, such as through informal conversation and clinical supervision.

A third type of therapist experience research has focused on the therapists' internal experience of being in sessions with clients. Preliminary results from a qualitative meta-analysis of this literature (Levitt, Morrill & Ipecki, 2019) have revealed a variety of central topics regarding experiences of working within varied treatment approaches and implementing interventions. In this chapter, we cannot detail the results of that study, but we highlight two central clinical implications drawn from the read of this literature: learning responsive integration of theoretical orientations, and developing self-awareness and countertransference management.

Learning Responsive Integration of Theoretical Orientations

Across the studies of therapists, familiarity with psychotherapy theoretical orientations was found to aid therapists by increasing their confidence in their ability to conceptualize clients' experiences and to form interventions (Gale et al., 2015). They helped therapists to engage clients in a coherent process of change and to develop a skillset for guiding that process. At the same time, therapists described the value of responsively altering their approach to therapy in order to best fit their clients' needs (Romaiolli & Faccio, 2012). This flexibility led therapists to integrate varied therapy approaches and to deliberately retain openness to new ways of conceptualizing their work. While this set of studies provided evidence that teaching theoretical orientations was helpful for therapists, it also suggested that helping therapists to learn multiple theoretical orientations could be advantageous. Responsiveness was thought to be enhanced when therapists were familiar with not only a plurality of therapy approaches but also how to integrate them coherently and to address specific client needs.

These findings are consistent with the principle that training programs should provide overt instruction both on psychotherapy integration and on the responsive adaptation of interventions to support therapists to engage in these complex activities. Reconceptualizing interventions as requiring responsive adjustment may provide a more effective foundation for both practice and psychotherapy research when compared to attempts to validate and promote therapy orientations as whole, standardized protocols (Stiles, 2009b). It pragmatically addresses the concerns that therapists have when working with clients as well as representing a means of making sense of the repeated meta-analytic findings that psychotherapy orientation contributes little to client outcome when compared to therapist effects (Wampold & Imel, 2015). A recent qualitative meta-analysis of the therapist responsiveness literature suggested that training on responsive use of interventions tended to focus on their adaptation in relation to (a) theoretical orientations and their integration; (b) the formation and moment-to-moment maintenance of the therapeutic relationship in relation to therapy process; and (c) client needs and personal, cultural, and diagnostic characteristics (Wu & Levitt, 2020). (Please see Chapter 10 for more research on psychotherapy training).

Developing a solid basis for understanding more than one psychotherapy orientation appears to permit therapists to learn how to flexibly move between approaches, understand why separate orientations might lead to distinctive yet valid therapeutic interventions, and consider how to centralize the clients' needs in clinical decisions. In addition, it can teach therapists to appreciate the values and methods that underlie varied psychotherapy orientations' research cultures – for instance, why some approaches have historically emphasized randomized trials, and others have emphasized qualitative or process research – allowing for a more pluralistic and creative approach to research as well. These findings appear to be in synchrony with findings that therapists trained in one approach tend to become integrative in response to the demands of their practice (Rønnestad & Skovholt, 2013). They also support evidence that an integrative stance is one of the most commonly endorsed therapy approaches (Norcross & Wampold, 2011), and the views of 80% of internship and training directors who view a single orientation to be an insufficient basis for treating diverse clients (Lampropoulos & Dixon, 2007). Indeed, a survey of over 1000 therapists recently found that 85% of therapists reported using multiple orientations with a median number of four approaches (Tasca et al., 2015). A barrier to be overcome in teaching responsive therapy integration, however, is the need for clinical psychology programs to commit to building diversity in the therapeutic orientations of faculty members (Heatherington et al., 2013; Levy & Anderson, 2013).

Developing Self-Awareness and Countertransference Management

Across studies of therapists' clinical experiences, participants described emotional challenges associated with working with clients who were in crisis or who had experienced trauma (Hunter & Schofield, 2006), and relational challenges of maintaining relationships with clients who had poor relational histories (Bowen & Moore, 2014). A further struggle concerned directing diverse clients through a process of what is often arduous, gradual and fluctuating change within systems that offered limited resources (Haskayne et al., 2014). Also, therapists themselves might have had traumatic histories that complicated their own relational needs, leading them to need too much from their clients and to feel anxious (Hayes et al., 1988). Because of these impediments, processes of self-development that support therapists through their work have been found to be critical in many studies (Nanda, 2005).

Therapists' own life experiences and relationships allowed them both to develop empathic understanding and better recognize patterns in their clients as well as to form countertransferential reactions that could be problematic (Hayes et al., 2015). Problematic reactions of therapists toward their clients could prevent an accurate case conceptualization, and cause feelings of frustration, fatigue, or incompetence in the therapist – leading them to become avoidant or overly directive (Thériault & Gazzola, 2005). The main recommendation from this research is that programs seek to deliberately structure attention on developing therapist self-awareness and transferential processes within training. Even when supervision was found to be helpful and supervisors were thought to be available, therapists hesitated before reaching out for support when confronted with difficulties because they feared being judged (Bowen & Moore, 2014) and so this process of learning should be proactive. Moments that were especially susceptible to provoking difficult therapist reactions included high levels of client emotion, clients with intense need, issues that paralleled therapists' own unresolved issues (e.g., death, parenting, relationship stress; Hill et al., 1996). And so it appears helpful to include a focus on negotiating therapists' emotions within these contexts. Therapists might be guided to consider how they can learn lessons from their own relational lives so that they can maintain an experiential connection with clients without being either overwhelmed or disconnected.

How Therapists Experience the Process of Their Own Personal and Professional Development

Qualitative methods have been used to examine the meaning of being a therapist, the experience of training, and the shifts in perspective that occur over the course of a career. The Skovholt and Rønnestad (1995, 2003) model of counselor development suggested that therapists pass through six phases during their professional lifetime: lay helper; beginning student; advanced student; novice professional; experienced professional; and senior professional. Each of these phases is associated with its own distinctive set of developmental challenges. Subsequent qualitative research has explored the experiences of therapists at each of these stages. One of the practical implications of this model is that it proposes that if therapists are not successful in negotiating the challenge or challenges presented at a stage of development, he or she is likely to enter a state of stagnation, characterized by various types of withdrawal from authentic involvement in the work. By contrast, effective resolution of the challenge makes a positive contribution to therapist development, and enables the clinician to reach a higher level of expertise. Because therapists' developmental trajectories are somewhat idiosyncratic, and there exist multiple potential

challenges, such patterns are not readily detectable in studies that administer measures to large samples. By contrast, qualitative interviews that allow individual biographies to be explored, represent an effective means of identifying such phenomena.

Qualitative studies have examined the experiences of therapists in relation to formative learning experiences, such as the decision to enter training (Plchová et al., 2016), the impact of different types of training (Carlsson et al., 2011), and the challenges associated with acquiring new skills (Byrne et al., 2018). The value of qualitative methodology in relation to these topics is exemplified in a study by Carlsson (2012), which provided evidence of the ways in which trainees sought affirmation from their trainers of their preexisting ideas about therapy and the strategies they instigated to maintain these notions in the face of external challenge. This theme brings into the open an aspect of training and development that in normal circumstances participants would work hard to conceal, but that was allowed to emerge through skillful interviewing and sensitive data analysis. Other studies have highlighted the way in which training not only enables the development of professional skills but can also have a significant effect on trainee personal growth and self-awareness, including in ways that may be stressful (Kanazawa & Iwakabe, 2016). Qualitative inquiry makes it possible to study therapist stress not as a cumulative set of external pressures but as an active process in which the clinician reflects on the meaning of difficult professional experiences and agentically constructs ways of dealing with them; for example, through physical activity or involvement in art (Råbu et al., 2016), and making productive use of the tension between personal and professional areas of experience (Bernhardt et al., 2019).

There have been a large number of qualitative studies on how therapist development can be facilitated through participation in personal therapy. Reviews of this qualitative work have emphasized multiple ways in which therapists transfer learning from their experience of being a client, into their work with their own clients, as well as emphasizing the significance of choice of entering personal therapy vs. mandated therapy during training (Edwards, 2018; Murphy et al., 2018) and importance of being willing to process personal therapy experiences through on-going reflection (Wigg et al., 2011).

An increasingly influential body of qualitative research, built up over a 20-year period, has analyzed the ways in which therapy trainees engage in self-practice, defined as trying out therapy concepts and interventions in their own everyday life (Gale & Schröder, 2014). These studies have made it possible to develop a framework for making sense of how self-practice fits alongside other learning activities such as clinical supervision and personal therapy (Bennett-Levy, 2019), a set of guidelines for the facilitation of self-practice (Bennett-Levy & Finlay-Jones, 2018), and a training manual (Bennett-Levy et al., 2015).

A particularly productive strategy within qualitative research on therapist development is to focus attention on individuals whose stories and life experiences have the potential to yield theoretically significant insights. This approach has been used in a set of studies that have explored the personal characteristics of senior and master therapists, clinicians nominated by their peers as the "best of the best" – the therapists that they would recommend a family member to consult. The value of these studies lies in their capacity to use the broader perspective available to highly successful practitioners, who have survived the hazards of practice and thrived, as a means of highlighting the attitudes and strategies that are associated with excellence in the field of counseling and psychotherapy (Jennings & Skovholt, 1999; Levitt & Williams, 2010). In the first of this series of studies, Jennings and Skovholt (1999) interviewed 10 master therapists, representing a wide range of theoretical orientations. All of these therapists worked full time in private practice. The conclusions that emerged from this study were that master therapists are voracious learners who value cognitive complexity and the ambiguity of the human condition. They also seem to be psychologically healthy and mature individuals who are emotionally receptivity, self-aware, reflective, nondefensive, open to feedback, and able to use their accumulated life and professional experiences as a major resource in their work. The findings, which have been largely confirmed in later studies, suggest that the optimal therapist role might involve a high level of ongoing active commitment to use personal experience as a resource for professional learning.

Another way of focusing on theoretically interesting single cases is to use autoethnographic methods in which informants systematically engage in intensive documentation and reflection on their own personal experience of training and development (McIlveen, 2007). Powerful examples of the unique insights made available by this type of inquiry can be found in autoethnographic studies of the experiences of therapists with marginalized identities (Hargons et al., 2017; Speciale et al., 2015).

Until recently, research into therapist training and development has been dominated by quantitative studies that have endeavored to analyze the linear effects of specific training and development inputs on specific outputs. In adopting a constructivist perspective in which the person is assumed to be an active, reflective participant in learning, qualitative methods have made a major contribution to the emergence of new perspectives and practical possibilities in this field.

Negotiating Difference: Impact on the Process of Therapy

Qualitative methodologies have also been used to identify possible pathways through which client–therapist differences can influence the process of therapy. This group of studies provides a valuable illustration of the potential, and also the limitations, of qualitative research.

A useful starting point in relation to this area of inquiry is a study by Dos Santos and Dallos (2012) carried out in England, in which members of therapy dyads consisting of white therapists and clients of African-Caribbean descent were interviewed about their experiences of engaging in therapy with someone from a different culture to their own. Therapists described high levels of sensitivity to be seen to be culturally insensitive and not politically correct. This led them to avoid talking about issues around cultural difference or racism. Instead, therapists sought to identify similarities between themselves and clients, for instance around experience of being an outsider. However, this search for similarity in itself functioned to suppress exploration of cultural themes, in not

acknowledging that it was much safer for therapists to disclose such experiences, than it would be for their clients. From the point of view of the client, both their preexisting expectations about therapy, and the actions of their therapist, combined to reinforce the rule that there could be no race talk in therapy. As a consequence, clients actively implemented strategies to distance racial experiences from therapy, which meant that a wide range of significant personal issues were not discussed.

Similar findings around how the process of therapy unfolds in situations of therapist-client cultural difference have been reported a series of conversation analysis studies by Lee et al. (2019). For example, within the latter program of research, Lee and Horvath (2014) analyzed transcripts from early sessions between an experienced Canadian therapist, and a series of three minority clients (cultural origins Asia, Mexico and Arab Middle East). Segments of therapy discourse were categorized as referring to noncultural or cultural topics. Noncultural themes were explored productively, with high levels of positive therapist responses and client expressiveness. By contrast, cultural themes were marked by a fragmented conversational pattern characterized by misalignment and disengagement of both participants. The significance of these findings is underscored by evidence of their absence in studies where both client and therapist are from a minority group background (Goode-Cross, 2011; Goode-Cross & Grim, 2016).

The studies highlighted above introduce two key aspects of the process of therapy in contexts of cultural difference, that have been articulated in more detail by other researchers. One of these aspects is the experience of intersectionality. The identities of most people in modern societies comprise multiple overlapping identities that intersect with the multiple identities of others (Moradi & Grzanka, 2017). An example of how the experience of intersectionality influences therapy is a focus group study carried out with Black and Hispanic clinical social workers in the USA (Greenberg et al. 2018). Analysis of practitioner accounts of their work with therapy clients revealed complex, shifting identity negotiations that took place between them and their clients. This kind of research enables a deeper understanding of the kind of interplay of similarity and difference reported by Dos Santos and Dallos (2012).

Another significant area of focus for qualitative research on cultural difference in therapy has been around the use of language. In some therapy settings, for instance with refugee clients, interpreters are used to facilitate client–therapist communication. Qualitative studies of the experiences of therapists, clients and interpreters, in many different therapy settings and cultural contexts, have identified many ways in which elements of therapy interaction, such as empathic engagement and the expression of emotion, are altered when interpreters are involved (Pugh & Vetere, 2009; Tutani et al., 2018). Other strands of qualitative research have explored shifting patterns of language use where clients are multilingual (Rolland et al., 2017), the significance of different ways of talking about distress in different language communities (Bäärnhielm, 2012), and the effect of therapist misunderstanding of client communication difficulties (Choudhury et al., 2018).

Many therapists are aware of the challenges associated with conducting therapy with clients whose cultural identity is different from their own. Qualitative research has documented the multiple ways in which therapists have sought to overcome these challenges. Therapists use supervision to reflect on their experience in working with differences, and to identify areas for further training and private study (Apostolidou & Schweitzer, 2017). They develop their own style for using strategies such as broaching cultural difference issues with clients (Bayne & Branco, 2018). Therapists develop their own knowledge base around how to address cultural dimensions of their work (Tummala-Narra et al., 2018). This can include finding ways to incorporate indigenous healing beliefs and behaviors into their approach to therapy, such as therapists in the Pacific Islands integrating local cultural and spiritual knowledge into their practice (McRobie & Agee, 2017), or counselors in Taiwan learning to use ch'i (Liou, 2019).

Qualitative case study methods have been used to examine the ways in which therapist strategies for constructively engaging with cultural difference unfold over the course of therapy. Notable examples of this genre of research include case studies in which therapists have been responsive to the indigenous healing practices of American Indian clients (Robbins et al., 2008; Wendt & Gone, 2016) or have used an overarching social justice meta-perspective as a framework to accommodate culturally flexible and appropriate interventions (Carr & West, 2013).

The studies mentioned above are close to therapy practice, and as a result are well-placed to contribute to the enrichment of therapist awareness and competence. In some instances, such studies may confirm therapist experience in ways that help them to name, acknowledge, and reflect on difficulties. Other studies have demonstrated what is possible, with respect to more effective ways of responding to cultural difference.

Conversational Strategies for Facilitating the Process of Change in Psychotherapy

A universal aspect of psychotherapy is that it depends on the use of language and talk to facilitate personal learning and change. Historically, language has not emerged as a core topic within psychotherapy theory and research. However, different genres of qualitative research have generated important insights into aspects of how various forms of language use can contribute to therapy process. The single-most important resource in this respect is the literature in conversation analysis of therapy transcripts (Madill, 2015; Peräkylä et al., 2008). Detailed discussion of the contribution of conversation analysis is available in Chapter 3. Other qualitative studies have employed thematic or grounded theory analysis to identify patterns of productive language use in therapy; for example, hedging and vivid imagery (Oddli & Rønnestad, 2012), collaborative use of metaphor (Angus & Rennie, 1988, 1989), and linguistic strategies for maintaining control of the therapeutic agenda (Folmo et al., 2019). There also exists a rich literature on linguistic possibilities, such as language switching, occurring when therapists or clients are bi- or multilingual (Kokaliari et al., 2013; Verdinelli et al., 2013). Qualitative studies on language and talk in therapy have the potential to allow therapists to enrich their practice by critically reflecting

on their use of language and experimenting with alternative ways of talking.

How Organizational Context Shapes the Experience of Therapy

There is growing evidence that therapy clinics and agencies, and even whole treatment sectors, differ in terms of their success rates with clients, even when factors such as client symptom severity, therapist experience level and other contributory factors are partialed out (Falkenström et al., 2018; Firth et al., 2019). It seems likely that, within any therapy service, there exist a range of aspects of organizational culture and structure that come together to create an environment in which clients and staff either feel valued, or are inhibited from participating to the best of their abilities. Qualitative methodologies can be used to explore different facets of organizational context, with the eventual aim of creating a model or framework for practice around this topic.

A study by Cook et al. (2009) provides an example of the use of qualitative methods to explore the role of contextual factors in therapy. In this research, interviews were conducted with therapists in two therapy clinics within the same health care system. One of the clinics had adopted eye-movement desensitization and reprocessing (EMDR) as a favored intervention for patients with post-traumatic stress disorder, while in the other clinic this technique was not used at all. Cook et al. (2009) were able to identify the events, values, and management decision making that resulted in the dissemination (or otherwise) of EMDR in these clinics. The findings of this study were also used to generate a model of diffusion of innovation that could be applied in other settings. An example of an observational, ethnographic study of contextual aspects of therapy can be found in work of Waldram (2007), who investigated the delivery of cognitive-behavior therapy (CBT) in the context of a prison-based treatment program for sex offenders. Other qualitative studies of organizational influences on therapy include investigations of the relationship between the therapy profession and managed care organizations (Greer & Rennie, 2006), the ways in which power and status within staff teams is reflected in discourse (Altson et al., 2014), the design of offices as a means of providing safe spaces within bureaucratic systems (Fenner, 2011; Jones, 2018), and differing levels of acceptance, respect and welcoming experienced by users of different services (Bacha et al., 2019). Hannon et al. (2019) provide an analysis of how a group of counselors working in a school were able to use organizational structures and resources to augment individual therapeutic work in the process of coordinating a response to multiple student bereavements that had occurred in the school community.

Although few qualitative contextual studies of psychotherapy have been carried out, it seems clear that this type of research has the potential to make a significant contribution to policy and practice. Essentially, these studies show that the type of therapy that is delivered, and the effectiveness of that therapy, may depend less on the level of empirical support for the approach being used, or the skillfulness of the therapists who are delivering it, but on the ways in which these ideas and skills are adapted and reconstructed in the light of local conditions.

Emergent and Hard-to-Study Experiences of Therapy

Because it is flexible, does not depend on the availability of preexisting measures, and may require relatively little funding, qualitative research has the potential to identify and open up new research questions and topics. Examples of qualitative studies that have fulfilled this role include studies of informal clinical supervision (Coren & Farber, 2019) and moral injury in combat veterans (Drescher et al. 2011; Vargas et al., 2013). Qualitative studies also have laid the groundwork for future research and practice around psychotherapeutic responses to the climate change emergency. Interview-based studies have analyzed the emotional cost of climate change in front-line geographical locations such as Arctic Canada (Willox, 2013) and rural Australia (Ellis & Albrecht, 2017) and front-line occupational groups such as climate change scientists (Head & Harada, 2017). A qualitative evaluation of a community-based therapeutic intervention was carried out by MacDonald et al. (2015). In one mixed-methods study, Seaman (2016) investigated the frequency and type of client reference to climate change concerns in therapy sessions.

Qualitative research can also make a valuable contribution to knowledge around topics that are hard to study using quantitative methodologies. For example, controlled studies in interventions to reduce suicide are technically problematic because suicide is a relatively rare outcome, so the number of actual suicides in even a large-scale study is likely to be too small to be amenable to statistical analysis. Research that is based on self-report measures of suicidal intention faces the limitation that there are many reasons why therapy clients are unwilling to admit to such thoughts (Blanchard & Farber, 2020). It has therefore been valuable to augment quantitative findings on therapeutic interventions for suicide by conducting qualitative research; for instance, investigations of the professional learning of therapists with extensive experience of working with suicidal individuals (Aherne et al., 2018), the perceptions and experience of people who have known the person who committed suicide (psychological autopsies) (Rasmussen et al., 2014a, b), and the experience of suicidal clients and their therapists (Østlie et al., 2018).

SOME CONTRIBUTIONS OF QUALITATIVE RESEARCH TO THEORY-BUILDING

Psychotherapy research does not have a generally accepted paradigm in Kuhn's (1970) sense, but there are explanatory theories, such as psychoanalytic theory and attachment theory, which have associated cardinal examples, practices, and problems. Within groups who, for purposes of their research, subscribe to them, the theories serve as a paradigm. That is, the theories are treated as the best available account; they guide the research and serve as an intellectual repository for the findings. Koch (1975) called these groups *search cells*. Through the theory, the results of research can be cumulative, as observations cast in theoretical terms accumulate in the theory in the form of refinements, elaborations, and adjustments to confidence in the theory (Stiles, 2009a, 2017). We emphasize that theory-building research, in the sense used here, involves assessing and improving an existing explanatory theory, not inventing a new one.

A theory in this context is a semiotic construction – made of words, numbers, diagrams, images, or other signs. Thus, a theory is an externally observable thing, in contrast with a person's understanding of a theory – the meaning of the signs – which is experiential and thus epistemologically private.

There is extensive evidence that, in general terms, qualitative observations have an impact on psychotherapy theories. The psychoanalytic community used case studies to strengthen and modify theory right from the start. A dramatic, classic example is how observations in the Dora case (Freud, 1953/1905) led to giving the concept of transference a central place the theory. Significant shifts in psychoanalytic theory, by Davanloo, Kohut, and others, have also been based on qualitative observations. A similar process has occurred in the development of attachment theory (Slade, 2016; Wiseman & Atzil-Slonim, 2018). Probably close reading would find a similar process in many of the explanatory theories that underlie major treatment approaches. It seems reasonable to conclude that there exists a generative dynamic interplay between qualitative observations, particularly cased studies, and theory-building, through new understandings being generated through reflection on clinical practice and then disseminated though clinical case studies. What distinguishes theory-building qualitative research from the enriching qualitative research reviewed in previous sections is the focus on building a particular theory as the primary purpose of the work at the outset.

Building the Assimilation Model

A search cell researching the assimilation model (Stiles, 2011; Stiles et al., 1990) has used a mainly case-based qualitative approach. Theoretical tenets have been refined through an iterative process in which their explanatory power is tested in relation to qualitative case observations (e.g., Honos-Webb et al., 1998; Mosher et al., 2008). The assimilation model suggests that people's experiences leave traces. These traces can be reactivated by new experiences that are similar to the original experiences in some way. The traces are agentic, in the sense that when they are addressed, they act and speak, sometimes with distinguishable voice qualities (Osatuke, Gray, et al., 2004; Osatuke, Humphreys, et al., 2005). To emphasize this active, agentic nature, the traces are often characterized as *voices* (Honos-Webb & Stiles, 1998). With time and experience, the voices tend to become interlinked, or *assimilated*, a process mediated by semiotic *meaning bridges*, that is, by words and stories (Brinegar et al., 2006; Osatuke, Glick, et al., 2004) as well as by images, cultural artefacts, and other signs (Stiles, 2018; van Rijn et al., 2019).

Assimilated voices are experiential resources, but some experiences may remain unassimilated because they are painful, traumatic, unacceptable, or incompatible with the person's usual self. The voices of such problematic experiences may be suppressed or avoided. In successful therapy, however, they can be assimilated, turning problems into resources.

As a problematic experience or voice is assimilated, it seems to pass through predictable stages, summarized in the assimilation of problematic experiences sequence (APES), (0) warded off/dissociated, (1) unwanted/avoided, (2) awareness/emergence, (3) problem statement/clarification, (4) understanding/insight, (5) application/working through, (6) problem resolution, and (7) integration/mastery (Stiles, 2011; Stiles, Morrison et al., 1991). These cognitive changes are accompanied and driven by emotional changes (Basto et al., 2017; Stiles et al., 2004). Markers of the APES stages, useful for raters or for therapists, have been distinguished in session recordings and transcripts (Honos-Webb et al., 1999, 2003).

Successive qualitative case studies have refined, elaborated, and extended the assimilation model using the logical operation of *abduction*. Abduction describes the creative operation of (tentatively) modifying a theory to accommodate new observations, strongly constrained by the need for the theory to remain logically coherent and consistent with previous observations (Peirce, 1985; Rennie, 2012). An illustration of how abduction from a qualitative case study can be used to elaborate a theory comes from the case of Margaret, a 58-year-old woman seen in a clinical trial (Greenberg & Watson, 1998) of emotion-focused therapy for depression. Margaret took 9 of her 17 sessions to progress slowly and explicitly across the segment of the assimilation sequence from APES 3, problem statement, to APES 4, understanding. Brinegar et al. (2006; cf. Reid & Osatuke, 2006) used the opportunity to elaborate this segment of the APES. At APES 3, the problem is stated explicitly; the voices can recognize and name each other; the client can say what the problem is. At APES 4, the client understands the problem; the opposing voices come to an understanding with each other. Using passages from session transcripts, Brinegar et al. distinguished four intermediate substages that describe how the voices encountered each other, entered into dialogue, grew to respect each other, and eventually came to terms:

(3.2) Rapid Cross-Fire: the opposing voices seemed to interrupt each other.
(3.4) Entitlement: the problematic voice became more strident.
(3.6) Mutual Respect and Attention: the voices seemed to listened to each other
(3.8) Active Search for Understanding: the beginning of working together.

This was an abduction, an elaboration of the APES based on observations in this case. Brinegar et al. also analyzed another client, to check that the same substages could be found (they could). Of course, this abduction is tentative. Observations of other cases should be consistent with these substages. And the details will continue to be refined in future cases.

With incremental abductions from case studies, the model has been applied in a variety of disorders and problems including depression (Osatuke et al., 2007), anxiety (Gray & Stiles, 2011), post-traumatic stress disorder (Osatuke & Stiles, 2010; Varvin & Stiles, 1999), borderline personality disorder (Osatuke & Stiles, 2006), dissociative identity disorder (Humphreys et al., 2005), schizophrenia (Osatuke et al., 2011), dementia (Cheston, 2013; Lishman et al., 2016;), intellectual disability (Newman & Beail, 2002, 2005), and complex bereavement. (Wilson et al.,

submitted). Other case studies have extended the model to therapy with children (Aro et al., 2021), parental development during their child's assessment (Tikkanen et al., 2011), therapy supervision (Osatuke & Stiles, 2012), immigrants confronting their new host culture (Henry & Stiles, 2012; Henry et al., 2005, 2009, 2018), and organizational change (Moore et al., 2014). Other qualitative case studies have examined therapist contributions to APES progress (Meystre et al., 2015; Mosher & Stiles, 2009), explained setbacks and irregular APES progress (Caro Gabalda & Stiles, 2013; Mendes et al., 2016), and identified a therapeutic zone of proximal development, a current working zone within the APES that shifts with therapeutic progress (Leiman & Stiles, 2001; Stiles et al., 2016).

For example, in their extension to child therapy, Aro et al. (2021) investigated assimilation in the first year of play therapy of a severely traumatized 6-year-old girl, Lisa, who at age 3 had witnessed the murder-suicide of her mother by the mother's boyfriend and remained with the bodies for three days before she was found. Aro et al. judged that assimilation of the experience passed through APES stages 0 (warded off/dissociated) to 2 (unclear awareness/painful emergence). The study showed how meaning bridges may be constructed from the nonverbal signs in play as well as from words. It also clarified the nature of the achievement in progressing from APES 0 to APES 1 (unwanted thoughts/avoidance). For Lisa, this meant progressing from automatically warding off explicit awareness of the experience to avoiding such awareness voluntarily. Her confidence in her ability to avoid being overwhelmed with the terror was a prerequisite for subsequently allowing herself to tentatively face the painful meanings of the event for her. This explication of the achievement of APES 1 may be considered as an abduction, to be watched for in future cases. Such studies show how qualitative case research can provide the empirical observations required to assess and elaborate explanatory theories of psychotherapy.

Task Analysis: Building Micro-Models of Productive Sequences of Therapeutic Interaction

It is widely understood that effective therapy incorporates sequences of client–therapist interaction through which the client starts from a problematic state of functioning and ends up in at a more satisfactory or preferred level or way of being. One way of making sense of this process is to think about such sequences as therapeutic tasks. The idea that therapy can be considered as a matter of accomplishing tasks that represent steps toward an ultimate goal, can be found in a wide range of therapy approaches (see, for example, McGuinty et al., 2016; Meichenbaum, 2002; Omer, 1985; Worden, 2009). An important program of qualitative and mixed methods research has focused on the issue of how to develop robust knowledge about effective task sequences.

Task analysis is a method that can be used for theory-building, fact-gathering, or other purposes. But even when it is not applied to paradigm-like explanatory theories, the task analytic procedure itself is a micro-scale version of theory-building. It begins by mapping existing working models of task completion used by clinicians in their everyday practice, and using these ideas as a starting point for creating *rational-empirical* models that are supported by evidence. Methodological issues and strategies associated with task analysis are discussed in Chapter 3 of this book (Levitt et al., 2021).

One of the clearest examples of ways that task analysis has contributed to theory-building in psychotherapy can be found in the therapeutic approach originally titled process-experiential therapy (Greenberg et al., 1993), and now called emotion focused therapy (EFT; Elliott et al., 2004; Greenberg, 2002). A signal success in the use of task analysis has been to describe ways to resolve therapeutic issues conceptualized within and EFT framework. This work has been integrated into EFT practice, as the steps toward resolution have informed EFT technique. For example, Rice and Greenberg (1984) described the resolution of problematic reactions; Greenberg (1984) studied resolving indecision, understood as self-critical splits; Greenberg and Johnson (1988) described resolving conflict in couples; Greenberg and Foerster (1996) described the resolution of unfinished business events; Pascual-Leone (2005, 2009) described the resolution of states of emotional distress. These results can be understood as a form of theoretical synthesis, in which the results of multiple qualitative studies are integrated into a coherent theory – in this case, an explanatory theory with direct application in a treatment approach.

In a more recent example, Cunha et al. (2017) first constructed a rational model of self-narrative reconstruction, that is "the articulation of significant personal events into meaningful stories" (p. 693), in EFT based on previous work (e.g., Angus & Greenberg, 2011). They then conducted an empirical qualitative analysis of three successful EFT cases, from which they constructed an empirical model, compared it with their rational model and modified the latter to synthesize their rational-empirical model. An illustration of such a model is their description of successful completion of the task of self-narrative reconstruction in nine sequential steps:

> (1) Explicit recognition of differences in the present and steps in the path of change; (2) Development of a meta-perspective contrast between present self and past self; (3) Amplification of contrast in the self; (4) A positive appreciation of changes is conveyed; (5) Occurrence of feelings of empowerment, competence, and mastery; (6) Reference to difficulties still present; (7) Emphasis on the loss of centrality of the problem; (8) Perception of change as a gradual, developing process; and (9) Reference to projects, experiences of change, or elaboration of new plans. (p. 692)

Task analysis has also been applied in therapies other than EFT. For example, Agnew et al. (1994) described alliance rupture resolution in a single good-outcome case of psychodynamic interpersonal psychotherapy; Joyce et al. (1995) described receiving an interpretation in short-term dynamic therapy; Safran and Muran (1996) described the resolution of withdrawal ruptures in integrative psychotherapy; Bennett et al. (2006) described alliance-threatening transference enactments in cognitive-analytic therapy with borderline personality disorder; Aspland et al. (2008) described resolution of alliance ruptures in cognitive-behavior therapy; Meystre et al. (2015)

described interventions that facilitate assimilation progress in psychodynamic treatment of depression; Kannan et al. (2011) described task resolution in therapy for anger; and Lømo et al. (2018) identified markers and task sequences in integrative therapy for men with issues around intimate partner violence.

As an example, in their study of the pathway toward resolving anger across psychotherapies of varied theoretical orientations, Kannan et al. (2011) found that when anger was initially expressed in therapy, it tended to be resolved in one of two ways. In the first route, anger was conceptualized as a fear of being overwhelmed or losing control, leading therapists to guide clients to focus on their ability to moderate their emotional arousal and regulate the emotion. In the second route, anger was conceptualized as a fear of being hurt, leading therapists to guide clients to focus on their ability to manage interpersonal pain by either being assertive about their needs or self-protective. Both routes included a reframing of the problem with a focus on something the client could control (i.e., their emotional arousal or interpersonal actions). Also, both could end in the differentiation of anger from other emotions, metacommunications about the use of emotions, and planning for future incidents. Therapists who were more cognitive-behavioral tended to use the first pathway, whereas humanistic therapists appeared more likely to use the second pathway. In this way, task analyses can offer an understanding of the way challenging emotions are resolved across therapy orientations.

In addition, task analyses can be used to examine written change processes that are outside of the therapy dialogue. For instance, Collins and Levitt (2021) used task analysis to develop a four-stage model of how sexual minorities resolve experiences of heterosexism by through engaging in expressive writing about these experiences. The task analysis revealed how clients shifted between stages of (a) being engulfed by the pain of the experience and wishing for change; (b) becoming more self-reflective and identifying patterns of harm; (c) developing a compassionate narrative in which the self was prized; and (d) feeling empowered to advocate for themselves and their community. Results like these guide therapists by providing a map of the change process, as well as identifying obstacles that interfered with clients' ability to move between stages.

The rational-empirical models that proceed from task analyses invite further empirical investigations and abductive improvements. For example, Safran and Muran's (1996) carefully refined rational-empirical model of withdrawal ruptures was later supplemented with a further stage that involved therapists recognizing the cognitive-interpersonal cycle they and the patient are in, figuratively moving to stand outside of the cycle (Katzow & Safran, 2007; Safran & Muran, 2000). Cash et al. (2014) carried out a task analysis of alliance ruptures and resolution in cognitive behavior therapy of clients with borderline personality disorder. They began with the rational-empirical model developed by Aspland et al. (2008), applied it to good outcome cases with borderline personality disorder, and further refined the model. The Cash et al. (2014) revised rational-empirical model was similar to that of Aspland et al. (2008) but there were modifications. It did not include the step in the Aspland et al. model called *acceptance of responsibility for the therapist's own role in the rupture*. And it included a new step, which Cash et al. called *external observer*, that involved taking a reflective stance with an emphasis on collaborative inquiry. It also included a step involving the therapist's own emotional self-disclosure. These differences could reflect distinctive features of alliance ruptures in cases of borderline personality disorder. The methodological point is that the task analysis method can smoothly accommodate refinements and distinctions among types of clients and treatments.

Other Ways in Which Qualitative Research Can Contribute to Theory-Building

The work on the assimilation model and task analysis represent well-developed programs of theory-building research. However, there are other ways in which qualitative methodologies may be used to generate theoretical insights. The qualitative research literature includes many examples of studies where the potential theoretical significance of findings has not been exploited. For example, the question of how to make sense of the therapeutic relationship has been dominated by concepts such as working alliance, transference/countertransference, and the real relationship. Other ways of conceptualizing aspects of the client–therapist relationship are available within the qualitative literature. For instance, the concept of client–therapist *connection* has emerged as a useful explanatory construct in studies by Gross and Elliott (2017) and Vandenberghe et al. (2018), and *convergence of understanding* in studies by Østlie et al. (2018), and Werbart et al. (2019). A mixed-methods case study by Halvorsen et al. (2016) identified therapist and client persistence and courage as concepts that might be worthy of further investigation in subsequent studies. However, at least so far, none of these conceptual possibilities have been integrated into overarching theories of the therapy process and relationship.

Qualitative theory-building research faces significant cultural and institutional barriers to theory-building in psychotherapy. The field of psychotherapy is theoretically fragmented – concepts, models, and root metaphors associated with different schools of therapy largely exist in isolation from each other (McLeod, 2017). Because there are so many choices, investigators may find it difficult to make the sustained commitment to a specific explanatory theory or to join together to form the organized search-cells, that are required to maintain a sustained program of theory-building research. Further, unlike other disciplines, such as sociology or theoretical physics, there has never been an active tradition of critical conceptual analysis or theory construction.

A further barrier has been the view that analysis of causation requires experimental designs and is not possible within qualitative research. Theories of therapy can be regarded as comprising networks of if-then causal hypotheses. The examples of qualitative contributions to theory-building, introduced above, represent strategies for supporting existing if-then causal links and mechanisms and identifying new ones. In recent years, there has been a growth in interest around how qualitative inquiry can be used to explore causation (Emmel et al., 2018; Flyvbjerg, 2006; Maxwell, 2012). These developments have been accompanied by extensive re-appraisal, within the philosophy of science, of assumptions about the nature of

causality and how it can be investigated (see, for example, Anjum & Mumford, 2018; Rocca & Anjum, 2020).

Additionally, many of the findings of qualitative research are difficult to accommodate within current theoretical frameworks. For example, reviews of qualitative research into client perceptions of helpful aspects of therapy (Timulak, 2007) and client experience of therapy (Levitt et al., 2016) suggest that the processes described by clients typically reflect a wider range of change mechanisms than would be predicted by the approach to therapy that they received.

Finally, the feminist, multicultural, and critical tradition in qualitative research, discussed in earlier sections of this chapter, can be regarded as actively engaged with theoretical issues, but not from an explicit theory-building stance. These methods may be described as theory-driven rather than theory-building research because they are based on a range of conceptual approaches, sometimes gathered together in the term critical theory (feminist, multicultural, queer theories of oppression, etc.). They have also been used to explore the personal and societal implications of specific theoretical positions, such as psychiatric and psychotherapy theories that define individuals in terms of diagnostic categories or deny the significance of race, culture, gender, and social class.

USING QUALITATIVE RESEARCH FOR FACT-GATHERING

Fact-gathering research focuses on making and summarizing observations, to record what happens and what people report or experience under the investigated circumstances, rather than interpreting them within a guiding theoretical framework or exploring their meaning (Stiles, 2015). Facts thus obtained are then available to others who may use them for enriching or theory-building purposes. Fact-gathering comprises an underutilized but potentially valuable aspect of qualitative research.

Fact-gathering research is represented in many studies that make use of qualitative content analysis (Hsieh & Shannon, 2005; Mayring, 2001), an approach that seeks to provide a descriptive account of aspects of a topic, rather than, as in enriching studies, elucidating implicit meanings and themes. The distinction between descriptive, content-oriented analysis, and more interpretative meaning-oriented qualitative research does not take the form of a clearly defined boundary. Some approaches that are widely used in enriching studies, such as thematic analysis (Braun & Clarke, 2006) and Consensual Qualitative Research (Hill, 2012), may incorporate elements of content analysis within their analytic procedures.

Qualitative content analysis has been used to generate factual information on such topics as: the extent to which messages conveyed by advertisements for psychotherapy workshops refer to empirically validated evidence for what is being offered (Cook et al., 2008); the content of informed consent forms used in psychotherapy clinics (Talbert & Pipes, 1988); and, what clients say and create in art therapy sessions (Thyme et al., 2013). There have also been many qualitative content analyses of topics covered in therapy journals (e.g., Bedi et al., 2016). In addition, investigators who use conversation analysis often insist that their approach is strictly descriptive, rather than interpretive; in this sense their work can be seen as fact-gathering research (e.g., Peräkylä et al., 2008; see discussion of conversation analysis procedures in Chapter 3).

USING QUALITATIVE RESEARCH FOR PRODUCT DEVELOPMENT AND TESTING

The delivery of psychotherapy relies to a significant extent on the use of specific tools, packages or products. For example, therapy manuals and protocols, such as mindfulness-based CBT for depression, can be viewed as comprising packages or products that can be taken off the shelf and used in particular situations. Outcome, process and feedback measures form another substantial category of therapy product. A further important set of therapy products consists of adjunctive tools that can be applied alongside therapy as usual, for example mobile phone apps, virtual reality simulations, or instructions for writing reflective journals or forgiveness letters. There also exist products that take the form of models or frameworks for good practice in relation to a variety of topics, such as planning for therapy termination, therapist self-disclosure, use of deliberate practice to enhance therapist competence, managing risk of suicide, therapist presence on social media, or writing reports for clients undergoing gender-related medical procedures. Each of these different types of product typically requires an extensive period of initial product development, followed by evaluation of how it functions in practice, leading to further revision and refinement. This kind of iterative process generally draws on multiple sources of evidence, including expert consensus judgment, quantitative ratings, experimental studies, and qualitative reports from therapists and clients. The following sections provide an overview of the contribution of qualitative research methods to product development and testing in psychotherapy.

Qualitative Research into the Outcomes of Therapy

The single most extensive area of product-testing research consists of outcome studies of the effectiveness of treatment approaches or techniques. As will be clear from reading the other chapters in this volume, quantitative product-testing research, in the form of investment in large-scale RCTs and other kinds of outcome studies, consumes a large proportion of the global resources devoted to psychotherapy research. The product-testing function of qualitative research in relation to therapy treatment packages is less widely acknowledged. Domains of qualitative research that are relevant to product-testing the effectiveness of therapy include: intensive single-case analyses of the application of treatment approaches; qualitative and case study analyses to augment quantitative RCTs; qualitative studies of client experiences of the outcomes of therapy; and, analysis of how clients complete self-report symptom measures.

Qualitative studies can offer a more differentiated understanding of the meaning of outcome from the point of view of the client, as well as contributing to the refinement of product-testing procedures. An analogy can be made to the product testing of mattresses, a product that has been in existence for hundreds of years. At the start, mattresses were evaluated in terms of durability, comfort, and propensity to host bedbugs. Over time, other evaluation criteria have been added to this list, such as flammability, capacity for recycling, and propensity to trigger allergic reactions. Currently, therapy products, such as treatment approaches, are evaluated in terms of a relatively narrow set of criteria, such as symptom reduction and alliance scores, but there may be many other criteria that can be used to assess their value. Qualitative research, which is primarily consumer-facing, makes it possible to generate a wider set of criteria toward this end.

Evaluating Therapy Through Qualitative and Mixed Methods Single-Case Analysis

Evaluating the effectiveness of an approach to therapy can be carried out on a case by case basis. There have been many studies that have closely analyze change in single cases that are representative of a specific model of therapy, on the basis of rich process and outcome data collected through both qualitative and quantitative methods. Such case analyses make it possible to answer the question of whether, in that particular instance, changes that were observed could be attributed to therapy rather than other sources such as life events or client self-help. This approach to product testing is particularly appropriate when an innovative form of intervention is being evaluated. In such situations, it may be practically or ethically impossible to conduct an evaluation based on a large sample. The most rigorous method of single-case outcome evaluation is hermeneutic single-case efficacy design (HSCED; Elliott, 2002) that makes use of a structured quasi-judicial form of analysis to arrive at a consensus regarding whether or not the case being analyzed could be considered to represent a successful outcome. A classic example of how HSCED has been applied to analyze outcome can be found in Elliott et al. (2009). Other outcome-oriented case studies have similarly collected mixed-method process and outcome data, that has been analyzed in terms of pragmatic or narrative case study methodologies (McLeod, 2010).

Using Qualitative Research to Augment Evidence from RCTs

While RCTs of psychotherapy outcome possess wide credibility among stakeholders, this methodology has also been widely criticized in terms of its limited ecological validity and sensitivity to contextual factors (Carey & Stiles, 2016). These limitations can be mitigated by what Miller and Crabtree (2005) has described as a double-helix RCT design – wrapping enriching qualitative case studies and interview studies around the core RCT structure.

The first use of qualitative single-case analysis to deepen and extend the interpretative scope of a psychotherapy RCT occurred in the Vanderbilt I study that involved a comparison of outcomes achieved by experienced therapists and untrained college professors (Strupp, 1998). This landmark study reported minimal difference in symptom change between either condition, each of which was moderately effective. However, contrasting good- and poor-outcome narrative case analyses were used to arrive at a conceptual explanation of both similarities (e.g., the development of an authentic supportive relationship) and differences (e.g., capacity to engage in sustained therapeutic work in the face of client resistance) between these contrasting types of intervention.

A detailed rationale for incorporating case studies into RCTs has been developed by Fishman et al. (2017). Within an RCT, analysis of single cases makes it possible to identify potential causal factors not specified within the initial protocol. For example, Fishman et al. (2017) present a good-outcome and poor-outcome case drawn from a controlled outcome study of CBT for youth with anxiety disorders carried out in Denmark (Thastum et al., 2017). Case comparison revealed clear differences between the clients in terms of preferences, family involvement, attitude to therapy, and therapist flexibility. Awareness of the potential relevance of these dimensions of therapy was then able to inform the further development of the therapy protocol.

Incorporating qualitative research into an RCT makes it possible to develop a more comprehensive understanding of key aspects of both the research process and the process of therapy (O'Cathain, 2018). An example of how this works is the Improving Moods with Psychoanalytic and Cognitive Therapies (IMPACT) study, an RCT that compared the effectiveness of different psychological therapies for adolescent depression (Goodyer et al., 2017; Midgley, Ansaldo et al., 2014). The three interventions studied were: CBT, brief psychoanalytic psychotherapy, and a goal-oriented psychoeducational and psychosocial intervention that did not draw on either CBT or dynamic principles. Limited parental consultation and involvement was included within each form of intervention. Alongside the quantitative RCT analysis, this research team published qualitative studies exploring clients' feelings about taking part in the study (Midgley et al., 2016), their hopes and fears for therapy (Midgley et al., 2014), their beliefs about the causes of their depression (Midgley et al., 2017), the experience of taking antidepressant medication alongside psychotherapy (Maroun et al., 2018), their reasons for dropping out of treatment (O'Keeffe et al., 2019), and how their parents engaged with the therapy (Stapley et al., 2015; Stapley et al., 2017).

There were three main ways in which the inclusion of qualitative methodologies within the overall IMPACT trial protocol contributed to the meaningfulness of findings. First, the availability of richly described personal accounts, from clients and their parents, fulfilled an enriching function in making it possible to gain a more complete understanding of the meaning of therapy for participants. For clinicians and service managers interested in learning from the IMPACT study, the qualitative findings provided many evocative and relative points of contact between the research and their own practice contexts. Second, the qualitative findings also contributed to the interpretation of the findings of the study. Analysis of outcome measures showed no difference in efficacy between the three interventions. However, interviews with clients around their experience of participation in the study (Midgley et al., 2016), was a sense of frustration at being told that three different interventions were being evaluated, but not being allowed to choose one's preferred approach. Clients also described causal beliefs about depression that did not necessarily correspond to the underlying assumptions of the therapy approach that they were offered (Midgley et al., 2017). These qualitative themes informed the practice recommendations outlined in the main report on the findings of the study, emphasizing the importance of patient choice (Goodyer et al., 2017). A final area of learning from the qualitative studies concerned incidental findings that have potentially significant implications for practice, while not being directly linked to the objectives of the IMPACT study itself. For example, several clients reported that they experienced research interviews as more helpful than actual therapy sessions (Midgley et al., 2016), and some clients dropped out of treatment because of a lack of stability in their lives – a category of drop-out that had not previously been identified in other studies (O'Keeffe et al., 2019).

Qualitative Research into How Clients Experience the Outcomes of Therapy

Historically, product-testing studies of the outcomes of therapy have comprised the domain of therapy research that has had the most impact on practice. The adoption by governments and health-care provider organizations of service-delivery policies based on principles of evidence-based or empirically validated treatment, has created a direct link between the findings of outcome research, and the types of therapy that are offered to clients. Almost all of the evidence base for the effectiveness of psychotherapy is derived from research in which symptoms are measured before therapy and on completion of treatment (and if possible at follow-up), using client self-report measures.

Compared to the hundreds of controlled outcomes of studies of psychotherapy that have been published, relatively few qualitative outcome studies have been carried out. Nevertheless, the findings of qualitative studies have the potential to make a significant contribution to about knowledge about outcome (Binder et al., 2016; Hill et al., 2013). The following sections offer an overview of outcome-oriented qualitative research in relation to positive outcomes, negative outcomes, dropout from therapy, client experience of completing symptom measures, and implications for development and testing of therapy products.

Positive Outcomes. Findings from qualitative studies suggest that clients evaluate their therapy in ways that are not captured in analysis of changes in scores on self-report measures of symptoms such as anxiety and depression. When clients have been interviewed about how they are different at the end of therapy, compared to before they entered therapy, their accounts draw on three discursive themes: clinical, autobiographical, and agentic.

Clinical accounts of the outcomes of therapy are framed in terms of concepts and categories derived from the professional discourse associated with the therapy that has been received. For example, clients reporting on the benefits they experienced from psychodynamic psychotherapy for an eating disorder (Poulsen et al., 2010), described themselves as having fewer bingeing or purging episodes. In a study by Nilsson et al. (2007), CBT clients described themselves as being better able to cope with difficult situations, whereas psychodynamic clients viewed themselves as having changed their way of relating to others.

When asked to evaluate the therapy they have received, the starting point for many clients respond is to share relevant aspects of their life story. Autobiographical accounts of therapy outcome appraise the impact of therapy in the context of the way it has contributed to the client's narrative identity (McAdams & McLean, 2013) – their story of who they are, how they came to be this way, and who or what they aspire to become. From this perspective, therapy is judged to have been beneficial if it contributes to narrative identity repair. Several studies have found evidence for clients evaluating their therapy in terms of its relationship to an overarching life narrative (Kuhnlein, 1999; Valkonen et al., 2011). The findings of these studies suggest that there is one group of clients who view current difficulties as arising from early childhood adversity, and evaluate therapy in terms of the extent to which it enables them to come to terms with these early events. A second group of clients view themselves as generally enjoying positive psychological and emotional functioning, other than a temporary inability to cope with certain stressful events, and evaluate therapy in terms of the degree to which they have acquired coping skills. A third group of clients understand their distress as arising from a lack of meaning in their lives, and evaluate outcome in relation to what they have learned around cultivating new sources of meaning. Within each of these groups of clients, therapy was deemed helpful if it enabled them to get their lives back on track. Using therapy to cope with the experience of moral injury – for instance through being involved, as a soldier, social worker or refugee in activities that violate core moral beliefs that underpin narrative identity – can be regarded as a therapy outcome consistent with an autobiographical perspective (Schorr et al., 2018; Smith-MacDonald et al., 2019).

A contrasting type of narrative identity perspective on therapy was reported in a study by McKenna and Todd (1997), who interviewed clients who had received several episodes of therapy over the course of their lives. Participants reported that they mainly evaluated the success of their first encounter with therapy not in terms of symptom reduction or the amelioration of distress, but in terms of the extent to which they gained a sense of whether that kind of treatment might in principle be useful in resolving their problems at some point in the future. By contrast, subsequent involvement in therapy was evaluated in relation to the degree to which problems were resolved. Further therapy episodes were evaluated on the basis of whether the client was able to use treatment to maintain earlier gains. These findings suggest that at least some clients evaluate therapy in terms of when it occurs within key ongoing life projects.

A further way in which client description of change reflected a narrative identify perspective occurred in studies that highlighted the significance of *small things* (Bedi et al., 2005; Topor et al., 2018). For example, a client in a study by Bedi et al. (2005) stated that one of the things that had been important in therapy was that "the therapist walked me to the door, opened it for me, and walked out with me" (p. 348). Such small things may function as positive autobiographical memories that represented *micro-affirmations* (Topor et al., 2018), that enable the client to construct a more positive and hopeful narrative identity, in place of self-memories characterized by social exclusion and adversity.

Agentic outcome accounts described knowledge, skills and resources that the person had acquired over the course of therapy, that enabled specific action to be taken in everyday situations that in the past had been experienced as problematic or stressful. For example, in the Poulsen et al. (2010) study mentioned above, clients mentioned that therapy had helped them to learn how to pay attention to their emotions, and to limit the extent to which other people influenced or controlled them. In a study of mindfulness-based stress reduction for social anxiety disorder (Hjeltnes, et al., 2019) clients talked about the value of having learned how to be able to center themselves in the here-and-now, and develop a broader repertoire of ways of relating to others. Another resource reported in qualitative studies has been client acquisition of a benign or wise internal representation of their therapist (Knox et al., 1999; Mosher & Stiles, 2009). These clients report that, in moments of stress, they are able to recall the words of their therapists, or even to engage in internal dialogue with an imagined therapist. For some clients, an agentic accomplishment that was taken forward into life after therapy, was a capacity to make sense of difficult experiences and reactions in terms of cause-and-effect sequences (Larkings et al., 2019; Rapsey et al. 2015).

Agentic accounts of the benefits of therapy may be convey in metaphoric language, such as coming to possess new (or renewed) powers, or moving forward in an ongoing life journey. Clients report that they actively seek affirmation and feedback from significant others, regarding external verification of the reality of such changes (Multu et al., 2017). In some studies, clients who had made significant gains from their therapy emphasized that while the work that began in therapy had been valuable, it was incomplete and continued forward into their post-therapy lives, or that they had learned to live with their problem, and manage it, rather than having been able to arrive at a complete resolution of their difficulties (De Smet, Meganck, De Geest et al., 2019, 2020).

A further aspect of client accounts of the benefits of therapy comprises descriptions of therapy as having been transformational (Brooks et al., 2020; Gibson & Cartwright, 2014). Transformational outcome narratives comprise both autobiographical and agentic themes. The client has a sense that the changes that occurred represent a wide-ranging and sustained shift in their life-trajectory, accompanied by significant new powers and capabilities. Transformational change also tends to be characterized as wholly unexpected (Westra et al., 2010).

In summary, client accounts of the benefits of therapy are multifaceted and nuanced, drawing on discourses available to them within their everyday lives. By contrast, outcome estimates based on analysis of pre–post symptom measures reflect an external, expert perspective that seeks to classify outcome in relatively simple categories such as no change vs. clinically significant change. In addition, from a client perspective, psychological change may be experienced in terms of shifts from one state of being to another (e.g., unwell to well), rather than (or alongside) an incremental movement along a scalable dimension (Sandell & Wilczek, 2016).

Negative Outcomes. Negative outcome constitutes an important issue for therapy training, practice, and policy (Castonguay et al., 2010; Rozental et al., 2018). In a survey completed by more than 15,000 clients who had received therapy within the National Health Service in England and Wales, 5% reported that therapy had a lasting harmful effect on them (Crawford et al., 2016). Although routine outcome measures can provide information about the proportion of clients who have deteriorated, they are unable to determine whether worsening of symptoms was due to therapy, or to external factors such as negative life events. Qualitative research makes an important contribution to understanding negative outcome, by building an understanding of the lived experience of side-effects and harm from the perspective of the client, and the extent to which the client attributes these effects as arising from therapy or from other areas of their life.

Findings from qualitative research suggest that helpful and harmful aspects of therapy tend to coexist. It does not seem to be the case therapy is wholly beneficial or wholly harmful. Clients who complete therapy and report positive outcomes may nevertheless retain a sense of dissatisfaction and disappointment at the end of treatment because they believe that they would have done better if they had seen a different type of therapist (Nilsson et al., 2007; von Below & Werbart, 2012). In studies where interviews were conducted with clients classified as no change on the basis of pre–post measures, therapy was described as having been helpful in relation to developing insight and understanding, even though clients saw themselves as having being unable, for a variety of reasons, to take further steps in the direction of tangible behavioral change (De Smet, Meganck, Van Nieuwenhove et al., 2019; Werbart et al., 2015). Radcliffe et al. (2018) interviewed clients who self-defined as not improved, and found a pattern in which positive gains were counterbalanced by a fear of being overwhelmed and losing control whenever they were faced with the possibility of exploring painful memories and emotions.

Qualitative studies of client experience of unhelpful experiences and harm in therapy have explored the processes that lead to harmful outcomes (Bowie et al., 2016; Curran et al., 2019; Hardy et al., 2019), as well as a wide range of hindering and harmful events and processes (Burton & Thériault, 2020; Curran et al., 2019). One significant theme to emerge from these studies is betrayal (Freyd et al., 2005): hurtful therapist responses are more likely to have an enduring negative impact when they occur in the context of a preexisting supportive and facilitative relationship. A further key theme is that harmful experiences are associated with an absence of effective client–therapist collaboration. For example, Werbart et al. (2019) interviewed therapists and their clients in both good-outcome and poor-outcome dyads. Poor-outcome cases were characterized by a failure in collaboration and shared understanding, to a large extent due to a tendency for the therapist to attribute lack of progress to client factors rather than recognizing their own failure to be responsive.

As well as establishing the extent, antecedents and consequences of therapy-induced harm, it is also necessary to develop an understanding of what harm looks like. Several client self-report rating instruments have been developed, to collect data on the side-effects of therapy (Herzog et al., 2019). Typical items from one such measure include: "I feel worse" (Rheker et al., 2017). Evidence from interview-based qualitative studies add to this picture by offering a perspective on how negative effects translate into persisting outcomes. Hardy et al. (2019) identified five themes in client accounts of harmful therapy: feelings of failure, loss of hope, loss of coping skills, loss of confidence, and regret. These themes suggest that clients are able to differentiate between transient side-effects, and enduring harm. Evidence of long-term negative effects, at the level of substantial deterioration in life functioning and well-being, have been reported in qualitative case studies of clients who feel damaged by therapy (Bates, 2006; Bates & Brodsky, 1989), and interviews with clients who have been sexually exploited by their therapist (Nachmani & Somer, 2007) or have undergone sexual orientation conversion therapy (Beckstead & Morrow, 2004). Such qualitative accounts suggest that clients who have been harmed by therapy not only still need to deal with the problems for which they originally sought therapy but may also need to undo confusing ideas and counterproductive strategies that they have acquired in therapy, that make the problem even harder to address. In addition, they may need to work through feelings of self-blame associated with having allowed themselves to stay in therapy even when they knew it was not helping them. Those who pursue explanation or redress, either from a professional body or their therapist in person, may encounter a further round of negative experiences. A final dimension of enduring harm may include reluctance to seek further professional help.

An important limitation of qualitative research into harmful therapy is that it does not address the question of the existence of abusive therapists. Although this is a topic that is hard to investigate, a limited amount of evidence exists regarding the characteristics of therapists who persistently sexually violate their clients (McNulty et al., 2013; Pilgrim & Guinan, 1999). Further research is needed around the extent to which harmful therapy can be attributed to therapist effects, as well as to interactional and process factors, and whether different toxic therapist profiles can be identified.

Dropping Out of Therapy. Premature discontinuation, or dropout, from psychotherapy occurs in about 20% of cases, with higher rates in some groups of clients and in some settings (Swift & Greenberg, 2012). In addition, many clients do not attend their first scheduled session. Dropping out of therapy can result in ineffective use of therapy resources, increased wait times for clients, and lost opportunities for individuals struggling with mental health problems. A wide range of factors contributing to dropout have been identified, encompassing client, therapist, organizational and therapy process variables. Evidence-based strategies for reducing premature discontinuation (Swift et al., 2012) have had a limited impact on managing this issue. Qualitative research into the meaning for clients of early unilateral termination of therapy, and the kind of decision-process in which they engage, provides a basis for productive collaborative conversations between clients and therapists around this topic.

Interviews with clients who have dropped out of therapy consistently find that a proportion of clients stop attending because they feel they have got what they needed from therapy (O'Keeffe et al., 2019). There is some evidence that clients in this group do not understand that they might be expected to negotiate such an ending with their therapist, or inform the clinic reception (Snape et al., 2003). A central theme in client accounts of their reasons for unilateral termination of therapy is dissatisfaction with treatment (Hundt et al., 2019; O'Keeffe et al., 2019). Typically, dissatisfaction is not framed in terms of deterioration in personal symptoms, but in criticisms of specific therapy procedures and the credibility and cultural fit of the therapy approach being offered. Dissatisfaction with treatment also encompassed practical arrangements such as communication difficulties, cost, staff changes, timing of sessions, and travel to the therapy center. A third theme reflected changes to the client's living situation that made it difficult to attend (Buizza et al., 2019; O'Keeffe et al., 2019). Qualitative researchers who have interviewed clients about their reasons for staying in therapy (D'Aniello & Tambling, 2017; D'Aniello et al. 2019) have found that the decision to stay or quit, is a live issue for most clients in the early phase of therapy. An important consideration is around whether negative expectations are confirmed. For instance, one client reported that if the therapist had turned out to be young, they would not have returned. Having been allocated a therapist of an appropriate age, they decided to continue with treatment.

Qualitative studies of client reasons for dropping out, summarized above, suggest that dissatisfied clients have a wealth of suggestions for improving therapy services. It is also important to acknowledge that, From the point of view of the client, premature discontinuation of therapy is not necessarily a negative outcome. Some clients quit therapy because their problems have improved to a sufficient extent that they do not feel that they need to continue to attend. In addition, for the 5% of clients who report lasting harm from therapy (Crawford et al., 2016), dropping out of therapy as early as possible would have been a positive means of maintaining their well-being. The reasons for discontinuing therapy identified in interviews with clients are broadly similar to therapist categories for classifying drop-out, as documented in clinical notes (Bischoff et al., 2020) and surveys of therapists (Westmacott & Hunsley, 2017). Given the evidence that retention of clients in therapy is enhanced by collaborative practices that take account of client preferences (Windle et al., 2020), it would seem that in principle there exists a substantial common ground of shared understanding that can be accessed to enable termination decision-making to be mutually beneficial.

Clients' Perspectives on the Experience of Completing a Symptom Measure

While creating a credible set of criteria through which a product will be evaluated represents a crucial aspect of product testing, it is also essential to operationalize these criteria in terms of robust and valid assessment procedures. A crucial area of psychology has always comprised theory, debate and research into the nature of assessment and measurement, and the development of instruments. At the present time, data from self-report symptom measures completed by clients represent the main source of information for evaluating the effectiveness of therapy interventions. Qualitative methodologies have been used to explore client experience of responding to outcome measures.

Qualitative research into the client experience of completing a symptom measure has drawn on a broader tradition of *cognitive interviewing* within cross-cultural and survey research, in which intensive interviews are conducted with participants around their decision-making process in relation to specific test items (Miller et al., 2014). Several qualitative studies have investigated the ways in which service users make sense of, and decide how to respond to, items on outcome scales (Galasiński, & Kozłowska, 2013; Rodgers, 2018; Truijens et al., 2019). These studies have identified many ways in which responses to test items are influenced by contextual factors (McClimans, 2010; McLeod, 2001; Truijens, 2017). For example, in an intensive qualitative single-case analysis, Truijens et al. (2019) analyzed how a client with severe health anxiety and fear of hospitalization interpreted the meaning of items in standard outcome measures. Responses to items that triggered these anxieties and fears were shaped by concern over the consequences of what her answers might lead to in terms of future treatment. This high level of worry also contributed to detailed reflection on what was intended by the specific wording of items and response options (e.g., words such as "often" and "usually") in order to ensure that her answers were correct.

In addition to their deployment in product testing outcome studies, brief symptom measures also function as tools that are used within the process of therapy, in relation to routine outcome and process monitoring, and as a basis for shared decision-making. Findings from qualitative studies have formed the basis for reviews of the experience of clients and therapists around the use of these procedures (Oanes et al., 2015; Solstad et al., 2019) as well as a realist synthesis of how routine outcome monitoring functions within treatment delivery (Greenhalgh et al., 2018). A particular focus for qualitative work in this area has been around implementation of routine outcome measurement in services for young people, where studies have been carried out that have explored client, family member and clinician experiences of using different scales (Moran et al., 2012; Stasiak et al., 2013; Wolpert et al., 2016). Evidence from these, and other, qualitative studies into the experience of using feedback and monitoring tools has drawn attention to significant processes that occur within these practices. For example, the extent to which feedback tools are experienced as valuable is shaped by the perceived credibility of the instrument being used, for example whether it maps on to domains that the client believes are relevant. The extent to which use of the measure is regarded as intended to be of benefit to treatment, rather than functioning as a technique of managerial control, is also important. Other observations have been reported that are consistent with the phenomenon of question behavior effects (MacNeill et al., 2016; McCambridge, 2015) – when clients respond to a question on a measure, they are not merely reporting on their behavior or well-being but also engaging in an act of reflection that can have a therapeutic effect in itself. This process is similar to nonconscious priming, which has been shown to be capable of having an effect on client engagement in therapy (Leone et al., 2018; Marchese et al., 2018). It could be valuable to explore whether differential question behavior and priming effects are triggered by different forms of data collection in therapy, such as symptom measures, goal ratings, and interviews.

Implications of Qualitative Research into the Process of Evaluating the Outcomes of Therapy

Appraisal of the contribution of qualitative research to the development and testing of therapy protocols, and evaluation tools designed to evaluate such interventions, needs to be accompanied by notes of caution. The qualitative evidence base for therapy outcome is limited. There is a compelling need for further studies that both replicate existing studies and extend its reach into new topics, such as a wider array of therapies and a culturally more diverse set of therapy settings. There are also considerable methodological challenges associated with qualitative investigation into these topics, in respect of recruitment, and strategies for data collection analysis and data reporting (McLeod, 2011). The Client Change Interview (Elliott & Rodgers, 2008; Rodgers & Elliott, 2015) is a structured qualitative interview schedule, designed to facilitate client accurate retrospective reporting on the complex lived experience of change that can be used in both case-study research and multi-participant studies. It provides a set of questions that yield credible information about outcome, and can be supplemented by additional questions tailored to specific research goals. Wider adoption of the Client Change Interview has the potential to take qualitative outcome research to a new level, in which meta-syntheses of key important questions around implications of this line of research for policy and practice become feasible.

Notwithstanding the limitations highlighted above, it is possible to identify some significant achievements in relation to major dilemmas within the field of therapy outcome research. A persistent counterintuitive finding within this area of research has been the equivalence paradox (Luborsky et al., 1975; Stiles et al., 1986) – very different types of intervention record the same results in relation to client outcomes. A qualitative perspective suggests a possible resolution to the equivalence paradox. While interpretation of interview data from clients who have received different forms of therapy may suggest that each group may exhibit benefit in terms of a general construct such as increase agency, it is also sensitive to intervention-specific differences. For example, the psychodynamic or CBT clients studied by Nilsson et al. (2007) were equally satisfied with their therapy, but evaluated their gains in different ways, thus providing prospective clients with evidence regarding contrasting directions that each approach might take them.

The increased technical sophistication of RCTs of psychotherapy outcome is accompanied by widening concern that it is possible for savvy researchers to subtly manipulate research

designs and analytic strategies to obtain the results they want to see (Cuijpers & Cristea, 2016; Lilienfeld et al., 2014). The inclusion of controlled outcome studies of qualitative inquiry, that privileges the voices of clients, has the potential to circumvent problems related to researcher allegiance, and to communicate findings to research consumers in a more direct manner. In addition, qualitative interviews generate a more comprehensive appreciation of the multifaceted nature of therapy outcome, that incorporates but at the same time transcends a symptom change perspective. Clients generate a more balanced appraisal of therapy. When clients are provided with opportunities to evaluate outcome in their own terms, many of them describe their therapy as having been a valuable experience, but one that was only partially successful is resolving the problems in living for which they originally sought help. They also generate accounts of transformational change, that are absent from the mainstream outcome literature.

The *Clients' Experiences in Therapy Scale* (CETS; Levitt, Grabowski, Morrill & Minami, 2019) represents a innovative strategy for taking account of client perspectives. It is composed of 15 items based on the meta-analytic findings from the literature on clients' experiences of psychotherapy (Levitt et al., 2016) and indicates the quality of therapy. Its five-subscales measure the kinds of experiences that are centrally important to clients when they consider the quality of their psychotherapy (i.e., pattern identification, the development of agency, connection, transformative acceptance, and therapist responsiveness), providing a complement to symptom-based assessments of outcome. Also, because it examines the in-session processes that are descriptive of good therapy for clients across therapy orientations, it can provide feedback to therapists about the specific problematic dynamics that are unfolding in their sessions when used in outcome monitoring.

Qualitative research can enhance the use of routine outcome monitoring in many ways. Rather than starting with a researcher-defined conceptualization of what measures should assess, and what they should look like, Moltu et al. (2017, 2018) conducted qualitative interviews and focus groups with therapists and service users to co-design a feedback system that met the needs of stakeholders. Other groups of practitioners have sought to overcome the limitations of quantitative measures by developing qualitative instruments that can be used to provide a contrasting source of information around the progress of therapy (McLeod, 2017). A network of psychotherapists and mental health workers committed to the implementation of collaborative forms of practice, including use of feedback tolls, has carried out a meta-synthesis of 18 qualitative studies they have published on this topic (Sundet et al., 2020), which have formed the basis for an integrative model of therapy collaboration that is being used to inform training and service delivery (Sundet et al., 2020).

Further research is necessary in relation to all of the perspectives on therapy outcome that have emerged from qualitative studies. For example, in terms of influencing practice and policy, it would be valuable to know more about the ways that different outcome narratives are generated by clients from diverse cultural and demographic groups, or who have received different interventions. Given that quantitative outcome measures are here to stay, there is great practical utility in determining the extent to which contrasting outcome estimates produced by quantitative and qualitative analysis occur only at the margins, or whether each approach produces a substantially different overall picture of which therapy approaches are most beneficial for which problem. It is possible that qualitative and quantitative outcome judgments are generally similar, and only diverge in specific cases. In such a scenario, paradoxical outcome data would be of great interest to therapists using feedback tools to guide practice, but would be of relatively limited relevance to policy makers making judgments about which therapy to provide within a health-care system. If, on the other hand, it turns out that paradoxical outcome occur on a general and systematic basis – for example, qualitative data shows (purely hypothetically) that psychodynamic for depression is more effective while quantitative data favors CBT – then it would be necessary to conduct a fundamental revisioning of outcome assessment and recalibration of clinical guidelines. One way in which these possibilities could be investigated would be to compare client outcome profiles derived from qualitative and quantitative data, on a case-by-case basis.

It is important to take heed of developments in other fields of practice, about how to harness qualitative methodologies to enhance service delivery. Making client stories and experiences directly available to other service users – for example through online narratives and videos (Kidd & Ziebland, 2016) – has the potential to be helpful to recipients in a variety of ways, such as providing information, functioning as a source of support, reducing sense of isolation, suggesting strategies for behavior change, navigating care systems, learning how to tell one's own personal story, and visualizing one's problem (Ziebland & Wyke, 2012). Involving service users in the development of such resources can lead to greater impact (Locock et al., 2019). Making qualitative service user comments and feedback directly available to clinicians can function as a driver of quality enhancement at a local level (Locock et al., 2020; Powell et al., 2019). So far, routine outcome monitoring and feedback in psychotherapy has primarily focused on informing the actions of individual clinicians. It could be valuable for future research to examine ways in which both mixed-method feedback and service user selection of salient feedback messages could be used to enhance psychotherapy service delivery at a team or organizational level.

Other Examples of How Qualitative Research Contributes to Product Testing

The following sections briefly outline other ways, beyond a focus on outcome evaluation, in which qualitative research may play a part in product testing and development in psychotherapy.

Enhancing the Scope of Meta-Analysis

An emerging aspect of the contribution of qualitative research concerns the inclusion of qualitative findings within systematic reviews. For the most part, published reviews have tended to focus on either qualitative or quantitative studies. This separation can be attributed to the existence of contrasting procedures and criteria that have been developed for qualitative and quantitative reviews. However, strategies for overcoming methodological challenges associated with integrating both types of finding within a single review are beginning to be available. Pomerville et al. (2016) used a pragmatic approach to review both qualitative and quantitative evidence around the nature of effective therapeutic interventions for indigenous populations in Australia, Canada, New Zealand, and the United States. Wu and Levitt (2020) conducted a meta-analysis of the literature on responsiveness that integrated qualitative, quantitative, and theoretical writings. Greenhalgh et al. (2018) used realist synthesis, a mixed-methods theory-building review methodology, to analyze research into the ways in which outcome and feedback measures support clinician-patient communication and patient care. These developments are particularly relevant given the widespread dissatisfaction among clinicians regarding the practical implications of clinical guidelines based predominantly on evidence from RCTs (see, for example, McPherson et al., 2018, 2019). As the weight of qualitative and case-based outcome data expands, it seems likely that not only practitioners and policy makers but also citizen groups will increasingly expect even-handed mixed-methods reviews to be the norm.

Development of Quantitative Measures

Qualitative methods are widely used in the design and implementation of quantitative outcome and process measures. The development of a measure of therapist presence (Geller, Greenberg, & Watson, 2010) was based on a model derived from a prior qualitative interview study (Geller & Greenberg, 2002). Huber et al. (2018, 2019) synthesized evidence from a range of qualitative studies on client experience of agency in therapy, to inform the creation of a potential item pool, in the process of constructing the Therapeutic Agency Inventory. Findings from qualitative research were used in the construction of a moral injury events scale (Richardson et al., 2020).

In addition to measures of specific phenomena, process measures can develop from qualitative analyses. For instance, a process measure that identifies and categorizes seven forms of in-session silences, the Pausing Inventory Categorization System (PICS), was developed based on a qualitative analysis of clients' experiences (Levitt, 2001) to help researchers distinguish productive from obstructive forms of silence and to sensitize therapists to cues that distinguish the varied processes within silent moments. The system has high inter-rater and client-rater reliability and an empirically based sampling system that permits researchers to rate fewer units while achieving representative findings (Frankel, Levitt, Murray, Greenberg, & Angus, 2006; Stringer, Levitt, Berman & Mathews, 2010). It has been used internationally to examine silences in therapies of varied orientations to compare good and poor outcomes in RCT data, and in intensive case studies, has received cross-cultural validation (Levitt & Morrill, 2021). Its use reflects the importance of examining therapy not only as a verbal endeavor, but also as one in which the discourse reflects the rich internal world of its participants. The process of identifying internal experiences via speech and behavioral markers is typical of process measure research and what makes it so valuable as a way of understanding psychotherapy.

Outcome measures have been strengthened by a foundation in qualitative analyses as well. In developing a new brief outcome measure tailored for evaluating family therapy, Stratton et al. (2006) made extensive use of insights derived from interviews with clinicians around the way such a scale might be used in practice. In order to develop a measure of outcome that reflects how clients experience change across psychotherapy orientations, themes arising from meta-analysis of qualitative research on clients' psychotherapy experiences were used to develop a Clients' Experiences in Therapy Scale (CETS; Levitt, Grabowski, Morrill & Minami, 2019).

Collaborative Inquiry to Inform Service Delivery

There exist many well-established models of therapy that are supported by detailed accounts of how they should be implemented, procedures for training and supervision, and research evidence of effectiveness. Nevertheless, there is also broad acceptance of the need for such models to be adapted to the specific needs, worldview, and values of different groups of clients. Although this requirement has been particularly salient within the field of multicultural therapy, it has also been a feature of practice development in areas such as therapy with clients from different age groups and disabilities. Qualitative studies, in which researchers engage collaboratively actual or potential service users to identify ways of adapting an existing model of therapy to the needs of a particular client group, have made a major contribution in this area. For example, working with adolescent African American clients experiencing weight gain issues, along with their family members and community stakeholders, Cassidy et al. (2018) used thematic analysis of focus group data to build an adapted version of a preventative interpersonal therapy intervention. Naeem et al. (2015) used findings from qualitative studies that aimed to construct a culturally adapted version of cognitive behavior therapy. An international program of collaborative research has involved service users and therapists working together to use qualitative inquiry to establish a basis for more effective therapy and recovery interventions in bipolar disorder (Billsborough et al., 2014; Veseth et al., 2017). Farrand et al. (2019) describe a qualitative study to adapt CBT to treat depression in Armed Forces Veterans. These research programs illustrate the potential value of qualitative methodologies in relation to ensuring that therapy matches the needs, values, and lifestyles of clients from diverse communities. Further work of this type is necessary to expand the range of examples of collaborative service delivery projects, the ultimate effectiveness and cost-effectiveness of such initiatives, and research strategies and researcher training requirements appropriate for this field of endeavor.

Qualitative Research Techniques Used as Therapeutic Resources

The qualitative research community has devised a wide range of methods accessing and analyzing important dimensions of personal experience and meaning-making. Although their purposes differ, there exists a significant degree of overlap and synergy between the knowledge-generating functions of both qualitative research and psychotherapy. As a result, some therapy clinicians and trainers have incorporated qualitative research techniques into their practice. An example of this type of development has been around photovoice, a technique where research participants take photographs of aspects of their everyday lives and then either talk or write about the meaning of these images (Sitter, 2017). Some therapists have successfully integrated this technique into their work with clients (Smith et al., 2012). Similarly, qualitative therapy researchers have developed a range of brief, open-ended written forms through which clients and therapists can describe their experience of helpful or unhelpful aspects of each therapy session. Versions of these forms have been used as techniques for routine client outcome and feedback-monitoring purposes (McLeod, 2017). Other, so-far unpublished, examples of the practical use of qualitative techniques include adaptations of research-based diary or journal data collection tools as adjuncts to therapy, awareness training workshops for therapists based on conversation analysis and other techniques for exploring meaning-making processes in therapy transcripts, and experience of qualitative interviewing as a means of enhancing reflection and competence around interpersonal skills.

CONCLUSIONS AND RECOMMENDATIONS

Key strengths of qualitative research lie in its diversity and inclusiveness, around the kinds of questions that can be addressed, the range of individuals and organizations able to undertake this work, and the flexibility and richness of methodological options that are available. In addition, qualitative research draws on insights from across a wide spectrum of disciplines in the social sciences and humanities. As a consequence, the qualitative research community is an open system that resists centralized direction.

Despite our appreciation of the self-organizing nature of the world of qualitative inquiry, we have offered a number of suggestions for future research at various places throughout this chapter. These recommendations are made tentatively, and are based on our accumulated experience, as qualitative researchers, regarding what we consider as safe bets – projects that build on research strategies that have a clear potential to make a difference, and merely – in our view – need to be upscaled and implemented more widely. In making these recommendations, we have no intention to discount the value of other possibilities.

Maximizing the Contribution of Qualitative Research

In the following paragraphs, by contrast, we offer some general reflection on the broader intellectual and organizational agenda in relation to maximizing the contribution of qualitative research to psychotherapy practice, theory, and policy.

Articulating the Practical Implications of the Centrality of Difference and Power Within Psychotherapy Relationships

Many strands of psychotherapy theory and research converge on the notion that the client–therapist relationship underpins aspects of both the helpfulness and potential harmfulness of the psychotherapy process. A crucial achievement of qualitative research in psychotherapy has been to demonstrate the extent to which the therapy relationship reflects broader societal relationships in being characterized by the operation of processes linked to difference, status, power, and fear of the *other*. Therapy relationships are also shaped by dominant societal patterns of individualism and collectivism. Having revealed, through multiple methodological approaches, how difference and power operate in psychotherapy, qualitative (and other) psychotherapy researchers have begun the equally vital work of mapping the ways in which therapy participants use their human capacity for empathy, collaboration, shared decision-making, linguistic inventiveness, and embodied synchrony to construct situations in which therapists and clients can align with each other's goals and intentions and work meaningfully together. In an increasingly fragmented and troubled world, the understanding, acquisition, and dissemination of this kind of relational competence has important societal implications beyond the therapy room.

Conducting Qualitative Research in a Manner That More Explicitly Highlights Human Agency

One of the defining features and unique selling points of qualitative research is that it reflects a view of persons as intentional, purposeful agents engaged in collaborative action. Examples of agentic research in psychotherapy include analysis of facilitative therapist actions in early sessions (Oddli & Rønnestad, 2012) and unhelpful therapist actions in response to transgender clients (Mizock & Lundquist, 2016). Agentic qualitative research uses theme and category descriptions framed as action sequences (Sandelowski & Leeman, 2012), rather than static qualities. For example, in their meta-analysis of client experience of outcome, highlighted earlier in this chapter, Levitt et al. (2016) used category titles that were formulated from an agentic perspective, such as "Curiosity drives reflexivity, transference, and relationship pattern analysis leading to new interpersonal strategies," and "Being deeply understood and accepted helps clients engage in self-reflection nondefensively and increase their self-awareness." While the majority of qualitative studies are implicitly agentic, this aspect of both research design and findings is all too often concealed.

Using Qualitative Research to Assess, Elaborate, and Extend Our Theories

An adequate theory of psychotherapy has to accommodate the distinctive features of each case as well as the common features. Qualitative research is not restricted to phenomena that can be observed in frequencies large enough for statistical comparisons. It can accommodate distinctive features of clients and the unique contexts of their lives. This is a huge advantage for research on psychotherapy and behavior change. The distinction between theory-building and product-testing purposes of research clarifies the kind of activity that is necessary to support theoretical work. Theories such those produced by the assimilation model and task analyses apply to all forms of therapy practice. Therapy products, in the form of approaches, treatment manuals, and schools of therapy, comprise assemblages in which multiple change processes and relational processes, understood in terms of multiple theories, are bundled together. As a result, there is very limited theoretical yield from studies conducted for product-testing purposes.

Developing and Disseminating a Broader Conceptualization of the Underpinning Logic of Applied Research

A wide range of applied disciplines, including psychology, have seen a fundamental reappraisal of the ontological and epistemological basis of practical knowledge, particularly in relation to the nature of causality (Anjum et al., 2020; Cartwright & Hardie, 2012; Maxwell, 2019; Rocca & Anjum, 2020). These perspectives have led to reconsideration of the limitations of RCTs, and the potential value of qualitative research, and case study methods. Every method has strengths and weaknesses, and approaches can be used strategically to support each other, leading to a research literature in which there is a foundation for greater confidence.

Developing Institutional Supports and Expectations for the Full Integration of Qualitative Research in Psychological Science

Historically, within psychology, psychotherapy, and psychiatry, qualitative methods have had to take second place, behind the dominant quantitative-experimental tradition. This has resulted in barriers to funding of qualitative projects, hiring of faculty with expertise in qualitative methods, and access to training in qualitative research skills. In turn, a dearth of expertise in qualitative research in psychotherapy has led, at times, to unsatisfactory supervision of qualitative studies and challenges in the reviewing of qualitative manuscripts. The poor understanding of the distinctive logic within these traditions has meant that lower academic status has been attributed to qualitative research and qualitative evidence has been largely disregarded in reviews of literature. This narrowing of empirical evidence to fit the competencies of reviewing committees (rather than deliberately formulating committees with the expertise and mission to integrate research across methods and epistemological perspectives) is disadvantaging the construction of clinical guidelines that shape government policy and funding decisions and the funding of mental health grants.

Currently, a rich body of qualitative research and meta-analyses describes the contextual, intentional, and relational cues for certain interventions to be used and indicates how to conduct therapy responsively to client, cultural, and in-session dynamic. When only a limited set of evidence is consulted, the recommendations we offer as a field and our science itself is weakened. Although significant progress has been made in recent years by groups embracing and promoting qualitative methods, such as the American Psychological Association, the British Psychological Society, the Asian Qualitative Research Association, the Association for European Qualitative Researchers in Psychology, and many others, there is still much to be done (APA, 2020), to support a diversity of qualitative research traditions, there is still much to be done at all levels. The production of scientific knowledge has always depended on the existence of democratic, open systems of knowledge dissemination, research education, and critical review (Nosek & Bar-Anan, 2012; Nosek et al., 2015). This principle applies just as much to qualitative research in psychotherapy as it does to any other scientific community.

Integrating Qualitative Research into the Broader Research Literature

This chapter showcases the richness and diversity of qualitative research in psychotherapy, and describes how it has been used to inform theory, policy and practice. This chapter does not claim to be comprehensive – there are many valuable and influential qualitative studies that could not be included for reasons of space. The perspective on qualitative therapy research offered in this chapter is not intended to imply a rejection of the value of research that uses statistical techniques, large sample sizes, or experimental controls: given the complexity of what happens in therapy, it is essential to make use of all possible methodologies. It is also essential to acknowledge the limitations of the qualitative evidence base, in terms of the relatively small number of studies that have been published. In respect of any of the topics discussed in the present chapter, there is massive scope for additional research to yield valuable further insights. We believe that the studies reviewed in this chapter demonstrate that qualitative research is able to made a distinct contribution to knowledge through its power – intellectual, emotional, political – to enrich our understanding of implicit and taken-for-granted aspects of therapy outcome and process, engage constructively in the development of theory, and enhance the credibility and practical utility of attempts to evaluate the effectiveness of therapy. The main take-home message of this chapter is that the evidence base for psychotherapy is incomplete in the absence of the kind of insights that are only possible through qualitative inquiry.

This chapter used the Stiles (2015, 2017, 2020) taxonomy of purposes of psychotherapy research as a heuristic device and organizing framework. Each element of that framework invites difficult and challenging questions. For example, in respect of enriching research: Do we know how and to what extent enriching research actually enhances the awareness and responsiveness of those who engage with it? Do we know how best to communicate qualitative findings to enable their enrichment possibilities to be maximized? How do readers of qualitative studies critically assimilate this new knowledge into their existing professional schemas? These are very real questions – no study in which therapists have been interviewed about how they develop their skills, awareness, and expertise have ever reported participants indicating that reading qualitative research papers was helpful for them.

Future research should investigate how clinicians make use of knowledge from qualitative studies. Studies of the structure of professional knowledge and expertise suggest that skilled practitioners operate on the basis of complex future-oriented schemas or *clinical mindlines* that anticipate potential branching cause-and-effect sequences that may be triggered by different interventions (Gabbay & le May, 2010; Strasser, & Gruber, 2015). The literature around such mindlines and schemas suggests that, for therapists, this kind of capacity to

generate imaginative possibilities could draw on knowledge from both qualitative studies of client experience of the process and outcomes of therapy, as well as findings from studies that track sequences of change, such as task analysis and assimilation analysis. It could be instructive to carry out a psychotherapy-oriented version of the kind of ethnographic qualitative study carried out by Gabbay and le May (2010) on primary-care physicians, that investigated how they made decisions in relation to routine cases in everyday practice.

In relation to theory-building research, it seems clear that the nature of systematic theory-building in psychology and psychotherapy is not well understood, largely because the role of theoretician, and the craft of theoretical analysis, have been downplayed in the face of external demands for empirical evidence. The landscape of therapy theory comprises a fragmented mosaic of competing conceptual models and scientific "search cells." In addition, theory can be viewed as serving a complex range of functions in psychotherapy, such as providing a source of narrative meaning-making, rather than – as in mainstream physical science – operating as a framework to guide basic research (Hansen, 2006). The examples of theory-building qualitative research discussed in this chapter can be viewed as offering a glimpse of the possibilities for using qualitative methodologies to generate more differentiated and practically useful theory. However, it seems clear that further articulation of this promise will require addressing deeper ontological issues around the role of theory within the discipline of psychology as a whole.

The psychotherapy research community has currently reached a position where we know that theoretical orientation accounts for a relatively small proportion of the variance in client outcome. It is therefore a good time to take stock of how we develop hypotheses about change factors in psychotherapy, and the points of connection between hypotheses/theories and theoretical orientations/schools. Qualitative findings and analyses have mapped out a new agenda for understanding psychotherapy processes in terms of contextualized principles that are grounded in concrete real-world observations and transcend existing theoretical models (Constantino et al., 2013; Levitt et al., 2005).

The characterization, by Stiles (2017, 2020) of outcome research as product testing highlights the similarities and differences between how this kind of activity is pursued in psychotherapy, and the types of product evaluation that routinely occurs in manufacturing industries, pharmaceutical companies, and consumer organizations. In these other fields, product evaluation does not rely solely on experimental studies. Rather, massive efforts are undertaken to capture the lived experience of product usage of different groups of consumers, using ethnographic participant observation and qualitative interviews.

A distinctive feature of much qualitative research is that it is grounded in the lived experience of particular groups of people in specific contexts. This focus has meant that the qualitative literature is awash with insights from clients and therapists about what does and does not work when a therapy approach is implemented in a specific context, and how its relevance and effectiveness might be improved in that setting. This information is hard to integrate into existing therapy products, such as manuals and protocols, which tend to be compiled on the basis of assumptions that they will function as relatively static sets of procedural instructions that will need to be tested in a series of RCTs over several years, before they can be revised.

Finally, we believe that it could be valuable in future editions of this *Handbook* for contributors to integrate qualitative evidence into those chapters that review current evidence regarding therapy orientations and therapy with different client groups, critically evaluate the validity of such evidence, and discuss the ways in which absence of qualitative evidence may diminish confidence in the conclusions that can be drawn from quantitative studies alone. In similar fashion, it would be valuable for professional organizations, such as APA, to recommend that those tasked with the work of producing clinical guidelines should take qualitative evidence seriously. This kind of integration is necessary if the field is to benefit from the context-rich insights, process direction, and in-session principles generated by qualitative researchers.

ABBREVIATIONS

ADHD	Attention deficit hyperactivity disorder
APES	Assimilation of problematic experiences sequence
CBT	Cognitive behavior therapy
EFT	Emotion focused therapy
EMDR	Eye-Movement Desensitization and Reprocessing
HSCED	Hermeneutic single-case efficacy design
IMPACT	Improving Moods with Psychoanalytic and Cognitive Therapies
LGBTQ	Lesbian, gay, bisexual, transgender and questioning
PICS	Pausing Inventory Categorization System
RCT	randomized controlled trial

REFERENCES

Agnew, R. M., Harper, H., Shapiro, D. A., & Barkham, M. (1994). Resolving a challenge to the therapeutic relationship: A single case study. *British Journal of Medical Psychology*, 67(2), 155–70. https://doi.org/10.1111/j.2044-8341.1994.tb01783.x

Aherne, C., Coughlan, B., & Surgenor, P. (2018). Therapists' perspectives on suicide: A conceptual model of connectedness. *Psychotherapy Research*, 28(5), 803–19. https://doi.org/10.1080/10503307.2017.1359428

Alamo, N., Fernández, Sofía, Krause, M., & Stiles, W. B. (in preparation) Applying the assimilation model to child and adolescent psychotherapy.

Altson, C., Loewenthal, D., Gaitanidis, A., & Thomas, R. (2015). What are the perceived implications, if any, for non-IAPT therapists working in an IAPT service? *British Journal of Guidance & Counselling*, 43(4), 383–396. https://doi.org/10.1080/03069885.2014.962485

Angus, L. E., & Greenberg, L. S. (2011). *Working with narrative in emotion-focused therapy: Changing stories, healing lives*. Washington, DC: American Psychological Association. https://doi.org/10.1037/12325-000

Angus, L.E., & Rennie, D. L. (1988) Therapist participation in metaphor generation: collaborative and noncollaborative styles. *Psychotherapy*, 25(4), 552–560. https://doi.org/10.1037/h0085381

Angus, L.E., & Rennie, D. L. (1989) Envisioning the representational world: the client's experience of metaphoric expressiveness in psychotherapy. *Psychotherapy*, 26(3), 372–379. https://doi.org/10.1037/h0085448

Anjum, R.L., Copeland, S., & Rocca, E. (Eds) (2020). *Rethinking causality, complexity and evidence for the unique patient. A CauseHealth resource for health professionals and the clinical encounter*. New York: Springer. https://doi.org/10.1007/978-3-030-41239-5

Anjum, R.L., & Mumford, S. (2018). *Causation in science and the methods of scientific discovery*. New York: Oxford University Press. https://doi.org/10.1093/oso/9780198733669.001.0001

Aro, T., Kuusinen, K-L., Stiles, W. B., & Laitila, A. (2021). Progress through the early stages of assimilation in play therapy with a traumatized six-year-old girl. *Journal of Infant, Child, and Adolescent Psychotherapy*, 20(2), 119–135. https://doi.org/10.1080/15289168.2021.1916210

Asfeldt, M., & Beames, S. (2017). Trusting the journey: embracing the unpredictable and difficult to measure nature of wilderness educational expeditions. *Journal of Experiential Education*, 40(1), 72–86. https://doi.org/10.1177/1053825916676101

Aspland, H., Llewelyn, S., Hardy, G. E., Barkham, M., & Stiles, W. (2008). Alliance ruptures and rupture resolution in cognitive-behavior therapy: A preliminary task analysis. *Psychotherapy Research*, 18(6), 699–710. https://doi.org/10.1080/10503300802291463

Bäärnhielm, S. (2012). The meaning of pain: a cultural formulation of a Syrian woman in Sweden. *Transcultural Psychiatry*, 49(1), 105–120. https://doi.org/10.1177/1363461511427781

Bacha, K., Hanley, T., & Winter, L.A. (2020). 'Like a human being, I was an equal, I wasn't just a patient': service users' perspectives on their experiences of relationships with staff in mental health services. *Psychology and Psychotherapy: Theory, Research and Practice*, 93(2), 367–386. https://doi.org/10.1111/papt.12218

Basto, I., Pinheiro, P., Stiles, W. B., Rijo, D. & Salgado, J. (2017). Symptom intensity and emotion valence during the process of assimilation of a problematic experience: A quantitative study of a good outcome case in CBT. *Psychotherapy Research*, 27(4), 437–449. https://doi.org/10.1080/10503307.2015.1119325

Bayne, H. B., & Branco, S. F. (2018). A phenomenological inquiry into counselor of color broaching experiences. *Journal of Counseling & Development*, 96(1), 75–85. https://doi.org/10.1002/jcad.12179

Beckstead, A. L., & Morrow, S. L. (2004). Mormon clients' experiences of conversion therapy: The need for a new treatment approach. *The Counseling Psychologist*, 32(5), 651–690. https://doi.org/10.1177/0011000004267555

Bedi, R.P., Davis, M.D., & Williams, M. (2005). Critical incidents in the formation of the therapeutic alliance from the client's perspective. *Psychotherapy: Theory, Research, Practice, Training*, 42(3), 311–323. https://doi.org/10.1037/0033-3204.42.3.311

Bedi, R. P., Young, C. N., Davari, J. A., Springer, K. L., & Kane, D. P. (2016). A content analysis of gendered research in the Canadian Journal of Counselling and Psychotherapy. *Canadian Journal of Counselling and Psychotherapy*, 50(4), 365–383

Bennett, D., Parry, G. & Ryle, A. (2006). Resolving threats to the therapeutic alliance in cognitive analytic therapy. *Psychology & Psychotherapy*, 79(3), 395–418. https://doi.org/10.1348/147608305X58355

Bennett-Levy, J. (2019). Why therapists should walk the talk: The theoretical and empirical case for personal practice in therapist training and professional development. *Journal of Behavior Therapy and Experimental Psychiatry*, 62, 133–145. https://doi.org/10.1016/j.jbtep.2018.08.004

Bennett-Levy, J. & Finlay-Jones, A. (2018). The role of personal practice in therapist skill development: a model to guide therapists, educators, supervisors and researchers. *Cognitive Behaviour Therapy*, 47(3), 185–205. https://doi.org/10.1080/16506073.2018.1434678

Bennett-Levy, J., Thwaites, R., Haarho , B., & Perry, H. (2015). *Experiencing CBT from the inside out: A self-practice/self-reflection workbook for therapists*. New York;: Guilford.

Bernhardt, I.S., Nissen-Lie, J., Moltu, C., McLeod, J. & Råbu, M. (2019). "It's both a strength and a drawback." How therapists' personal qualities are experienced in their professional work. *Psychotherapy Research*, 29(7), 959–970. https://doi.org/10.1080/10503307.2018.1490972

Billsborough, J., Mailey, P., Hicks, A., Sayers, R., Smith, R., Clewett, N., Griffiths, C. A., & Larsen, J. (2014). 'Listen, empower us and take action now!': Reflexive-collaborative exploration of support needs in bipolar disorder when 'going up' and 'going down'. *Journal of Mental Health*, 23(1), 9–14. https://doi.org/10.3109/09638237.2013.815331

Bimont, D., & Werbart, A. (2018). "I've got you under my skin": Relational therapists' experiences of patients who occupy their inner world. *Counselling Psychology Quarterly*, 31(2), 243–268. https://doi.org/10.1080/09515070.2017.1300135

Bischoff, T., Krenicki, L., & Tambling, R. (2020). Therapist reported reasons for client termination: A content analysis of termination reports. *American Journal of Family Therapy*, 48(1), 36–52. https://doi.org/10.1080/01926187.2019.1684216

Blanchard, M., & Farber, B. A. (2016). Lying in psychotherapy: Why and what clients don't tell their therapist about therapy and their relationship. *Counselling Psychology Quarterly*, 29(1), 90–112. https://doi.org/10.1080/09515070.2015.1085365

Blanchard, M., & Farber, B.A. (2020) "It is never okay to talk about suicide": Patients' reasons for concealing suicidal ideation in psychotherapy. *Psychotherapy Research*, 30(1), 124–136. https://doi.org/10.1080/10503307.2018.1543977

Bohart, A. C. (2000). The client is the most important common factor: Clients' self-healing capacities and psychotherapy. *Journal of Psychotherapy Integration*, 10(2), 127–149. https://doi.org/10.1023/A:1009444132104

Bohart, A. C., & Tallman, K. (1999). How the active client fits in with other approaches. In *How clients make therapy work: The process of active self-healing*. (pp. 139–164). Washington, DC: American Psychological Association. https://doi.org/10.1037/10323-006

Bowen, N., & Moore, J. L., III. (2014). Common characteristics of compassionate counselors: A qualitative study. *International Journal for the Advancement of Counselling*, 36(1), 17–29. https://doi.org/10.1007/s10447-013-9187-7

Braun, V., & Clarke, V. (2006). Using thematic analysis in psychology. *Qualitative Research in Psychology*, 3(2), 77–101. https://doi.org/10.1191/1478088706qp063oa

Brinegar, M. G., Salvi, L. M., Stiles, W. B., & Greenberg, L. S. (2006). Building a meaning bridge: Therapeutic progress from problem formulation to understanding. *Journal of Counseling Psychology*, 53(2), 165–180. https://doi.org/10.1037/0022-0167.53.2.165

Brooks C. (2011). Social performance and secret ritual: Battling against obsessive-compulsive disorder. *Qualitative Health Research*, 21(2), 249–261. https://doi.org/10.1177/1049732310381387

Buizza, C., Ghilardi, A., Olivetti, E., & Costa, A. (2019). Dropouts from a university counselling service: a quantitative and qualitative study. *British Journal of Guidance & Counselling*, 47(5), 590–602. https://doi.org/10.1080/03069885.2019.1566513

Burton, L., & Thériault, A. (2020). Hindering events in psychotherapy: A retrospective account from the client's perspective. *Counselling and Psychotherapy Research*, 20(1), 116–127. https://doi.org/10.1002/capr.12268

Bury, C., Raval, H., & Lyon, L. (2007). Young people's experiences of individual psychoanalytic psychotherapy. *Psychology and Psychotherapy: Theory, Research and Practice*, 80(1), 79–96. https://doi.org/10.1348/147608306X109654

Byrne, A., Salmon, P., & Fisher, P. (2018). A case study of the challenges for an integrative practitioner learning a new psychological therapy. *Counselling and Psychotherapy Research*, 18(4), 369–376. https://doi.org/10.1002/capr.12185

Cairns, V., & Murray, C. (2015). How do the features of mindfulness-based cognitive therapy contribute to positive therapeutic change? A meta-synthesis of qualitative studies. *Behavioural and Cognitive Psychotherapy*, 43(3), 342–359. https://doi.org/10.1017/S1352465813000945

Carey, T.A. &, Stiles, W.B. (2016). Some problems with randomized controlled trials and some viable alternatives. *Clinical Psychology & Psychotherapy*, 23(1), 87–95. https://doi.org/10.1002/cpp.1942

Carlsson, J. (2012). Research on psychotherapists' professional development during and after training. *Nordic Psychology*, 64(3), 150–167. https://doi.org/10.1080/19012276.2012.731310

Caro Gabalda, I., & Stiles, W. B. (2013). Irregular assimilation progress: Reasons for setbacks in the context of linguistic therapy of evaluation. *Psychotherapy Research*, 23(1), 35–53. https://doi.org/10.1080/10503307.2012.721938

Carr, E. R., & West, L. M. (2013). Inside the therapy room: A case study for treating African American men from a multicultural/feminist perspective. *Journal of Psychotherapy Integration*, 23(2), 120–133. https://doi.org/10.1037/a0031422

Cartwright, N., & Hardie, J. (2012). *Evidence-based policy: A practical guide to doing it better*. Oxford, UK: Oxford University Press. https://doi.org/10.1093/acprof:osobl/9780199841608.001.0001

Cash, S. K., Hardy, G. E., Kellet, S., & Parry, G. (2014). Alliance ruptures and resolution during cognitive behaviour therapy with borderline personality disorder. *Psychotherapy Research*, 24(2), 132–145. https://doi.org/10.1080/10503307.2013.838652

Cassidy, O., Eichen, D.M., & Burke, N. L. (2018). Engaging African American adolescents and stakeholders to adapt interpersonal psychotherapy for weight gain prevention. *Journal of Black Psychology*, 44(2): 128–161. https://doi.org/10.1177/0095798417747142

Castonguay, L. G., Boswell, J. F., Constantino, M. J., Goldfried, M. R., & Hill, C. E. (2010). Training implications of harmful effects of psychological treatments. *American Psychologist*, 65(1), 34–49. https://doi.org/10.1037/a0017330

Chang, D. F., & Berk, A. (2009). Making cross-racial therapy work: A phenomenological study of clients' experiences of cross-racial therapy. *Journal of Counseling Psychology*, 56(4), 521–536. https://doi.org/10.1037/a0016905

Chang, D. F., & Yoon, P. (2011). Clients' perceptions of the significance and impact of race in cross-racial therapy. *Psychotherapy Research*, 21(5), 567–582. https://doi.org/10.1080/10503307.2011.592549

Cheston, R. (2013). Dementia as a problematic experience: Using the Assimilation Model as a framework for psychotherapeutic work with people with dementia. *Neurodisability and Psychotherapy*, 1(1), 70–95.

Cheston, R., Jones, K., & Gilliard, J. (2004). 'Falling into a hole': Narrative and emotional change in a psychotherapy group for people with dementia. *Dementia: The International Journal of Social Research and Practice*, 3(1), 96–109.

Chiesa, M., Drahorad, C., & Longo, S. (2000). Early termination of treatment in personality disorder treated in a psychotherapy hospital: Quantitative and qualitative study. *The British Journal of Psychiatry*, 177(2), 107–111. https://doi.org/10.1192/bjp.177.2.107

Choudhury, T. K., Stanton, K., & Balsis, S. (2018). Contextual consideration of the emergence of alexithymia: A case study highlighting cross-cultural client factors and limited English proficiency. *Psychotherapy*, 55(1), 80–88. https://doi.org/10.1037/pst0000155

Comas-Diaz, L. (2012). Humanism and multiculturalism: An evolutionary alliance. *Psychotherapy*, 49(4), 437–441. https://doi.org/10.1037/a0027126

Constantino, M. J., Boswell, J. F., Bernecker, S. L., & Castonguay, L. G. (2013). Context-responsive psychotherapy integration as a framework for a unified clinical science: Conceptual and empirical considerations. *Journal of Unified Psychotherapy and Clinical Science Volume*, 2(1), 1–20.

Cook, J. M., Weingardt, K. R., Jaszka, J., & Wiesner, M. (2008). A content analysis of advertisements for psychotherapy workshops: implications for disseminating empirically supported treatments. *Journal of Clinical Psychology*, 64(3), 296–307. https://doi.org/10.1002/jclp.20458

Cooper, M., & McLeod, J. (2007). A pluralistic framework for counselling and psychotherapy: Implications for research. *Counselling & Psychotherapy Research*, 7(3), 135–143. https://doi.org/10.1080/14733140701566282

Coren, S., & Farber, B. A. (20197). A qualitative investigation of the nature of "informal supervision" among therapists in training. *Psychotherapy Research*, 29(5), 679–690. https://doi.org/10.1080/10503307.2017.1408974

Cragun, C. L., & Friedlander, M. L. (2012). Experiences of Christian clients in secular psychotherapy: A mixed-methods investigation. *Journal of Counseling Psychology*, 59(3), 379–391. https://doi.org/10.1037/a0028283

Crawford, M. J., Thana, L., Farquharson, L., Palmer, L., Hancock, E., Bassett, P., & Parry, G. D. (2016). Patient experience of negative effects of psychological treatment: results of a national survey. *The British Journal of Psychiatry*, 208(3), 260–265. https://doi.org/10.1192/bjp.bp.114.162628

Cuijpers, P., & Cristea, I. A. (2016). How to prove that your therapy is effective, even when it is not: a guideline. *Epidemiology and Psychiatric Sciences*, 25(5), 428–435. https://doi.org/10.1017/S2045796015000864

Cunha, C., Mendes, I., Ribeiro, A. P., Angus, L., Greenberg, L. S., & Gonçalves, M. M. (2017). Self-narrative reconstruction in emotion-focused therapy: A preliminary task analysis. *Psychotherapy Research*, 27(6), 692–709. https://doi.org/10.1080/10503307.2016.1158429

Curling, L., Kellett, S., Totterdell, P., Parry, G., Hardy, G., & Berry, K. (2018). Treatment of obsessive morbid jealousy with cognitive analytic therapy: An adjudicated hermeneutic single-case efficacy design evaluation. *Psychology and Psychotherapy: Theory, Research and Practice*, 91(1), 95–116. https://doi.org/10.1111/papt.12151

Curran, J., Parry, G. D., Hardy, G., Darling, J., Mason, A. M., & Chambers, E. (2019). How does therapy harm? A model of adverse process using task analysis in the synthesis of service users' experience. *Frontiers in Psychology*, 10, 347. https://doi.org/10.3389/fpsyg.2019.00347

D'Aniello, C., Piercy, F. P., Dolbin-MacNab, M. L., & Perkins, S. N. (2019). How clients of marriage and family therapists make decisions about therapy discontinuation and persistence. *Contemporary Family Therapy*, *41*(1), 1–11. https://doi.org/10.1007/s10591-018-9469-7

D'Aniello, C., & Tambling, R. B. (2017). The effect of expectations on intention to persist in therapy. *American Journal of Family Therapy*, *45*(1), 37–50. https://doi.org/10.1080/01926187.2016.1223568

De Smet, M. M., Meganck, R., De Geest, R., Norman, U. A., Truijens, F., & Desmet, M. (2019). What "good outcome" means to patients: Understanding recovery and improvement in psychotherapy for major depression from a mixed-methods perspective. *Journal of Counseling Psychology*, *67*(1), 25–39. https://doi.org/10.1037/cou0000362

De Smet, M. M., Meganck, R., Truijens, F., De Geest, R., Cornelis, S., Norman, U. A., & Desmet, M. (2020). Change processes underlying "good outcome": A qualitative study on recovered and improved patients' experiences in psychotherapy for major depression. *Psychotherapy Research*, *30*(7), 948–964. https://doi.org/10.1080/10503307.2020.1722329

De Smet, M. M., Meganck, R., Van Nieuwenhove, K., Truijens, F. L., & Desmet, M. (2019). No change? A grounded theory analysis of depressed patients' perspectives on non-improvement in psychotherapy. *Frontiers in Psychology*, *10*, 588. https://doi.org/10.3389/fpsyg.2019.00588

Dos Santos, O., & Dallos, R. (2012). The process of cross-cultural therapy between white therapists and clients of African-Caribbean descent. *Qualitative Research in Psychology*, *9*(1), 62–74. https://doi.org/10.1080/14780887.2012.630827

Drescher, K., Foy, D., Litz, B., Kelly, C., Leshner, A., & Schutz, K. (2011). An exploration of the viability and usefulness of the construct of moral injury in war veterans. *Traumatology*, *17*(1), 8–13. https://doi.org/10.1177/1534765610395615

Edwards, J. (2018). Counseling and psychology student experiences of personal therapy: A Critical Interpretive Synthesis. *Frontiers in Psychology*, *9*, 1732. https://doi.org/10.3389/fpsyg.2018.01732

Elliott, R., & Rodgers, B. (2008). *Client change interview schedule (v5)*. Unpublished research instrument, University of Strathclyde, Glasgow.

Elliott, R., & Shapiro, D. A. (1992). Client and therapist as analysts of significant events. In S. G. Toukmanian & D. L. Rennie (Eds.), *Psychotherapy process research: Paradigmatic and narrative approaches.* (pp. 163–186). Thousand Oaks, CA: Sage

Elliott, R., Watson, J., Goldman, R., & Greenberg, L. S. (2004) *Learning emotion focused therapy*. Washington. DC: American Psychological Association Press.

Ellis, N. R., & Albrecht, G. A. (2017). Climate change threats to family farmers' sense of place and mental wellbeing: A case study from the Western Australian Wheatbelt. *Social Science & Medicine*, *175*, 161–168. https://doi.org/10.1016/j.socscimed.2017.01.009

Emmel, S., Greenhalgh, J., Manzano, A., Malkin, M., & Dalkin, S. (Eds) (2018). *Doing realist research*. London: Sage. https://doi.org/10.4135/9781526451729

Falkenström, F., Grant, J., & Holmqvist, R. (2018). Review of organizational effects on the outcome of mental health treatments. *Psychotherapy Research*, *28*(1), 76–90. https://doi.org/10.1080/10503307.2016.1158883

Farrand, P., Mullan, E., Rayson, K., Engelbrecht, A., Mead, K., & Greenberg, N. (2019). Adapting CBT to treat depression in Armed Forces Veterans: qualitative study. *Behavioural and Cognitive Psychotherapy*, *47*(5), 530–540. https://doi.org/10.1017/S1352465819000171

Fenner, P. (2011). Place, matter and meaning: Extending the relationship in psychological therapies. *Health & Place*, *17*(3), 851–857. https://doi.org/10.1016/j.healthplace.2011.03.011

Firth, N., Saxon, D., Stiles, W. B., & Barkham, M. (2019). Therapist and clinic effects in psychotherapy: a three-level model of outcome variability. *Journal of Consulting and Clinical Psychology*, *87*(4), 345–356. https://doi.org/10.1037/ccp0000388

Fishman, D., Messer, S. D., Edwards, D. J. A., & Dattilio, F. M. (2017). *Case studies within psychotherapy trials: integrating qualitative and quantitative methods*. New York;, NY: Oxford University Press. https://doi.org/10.1093/med:psych/9780199344635.001.0001

Fitzpatrick, M. R., Janzen, J., Chamodraka, M., Gamberg, S., & Blake, E. (2009). Client relationship incidents in early therapy: Doorways to collaborative engagement. *Psychotherapy Research*, *19*(6), 654–665. https://doi.org/10.1080/10503300902878235

Flyvbjerg, B. (2006). Five misunderstandings about case-study research. *Qualitative Inquiry*, *12*(2), 219–245. https://doi.org/10.1177/1077800405284363

Folmo, E. J., Karterud, S. W., Kongerslev, M. T., Kvarstein, E. H., & Stänicke, E. (2019). Battles of the comfort zone: modelling therapeutic strategy, alliance, and epistemic trust - a qualitative study of mentalization-based therapy for Borderline Personality Disorder. *Journal of Contemporary Psychotherapy*, *49*(3), 141–151. https://doi.org/10.1007/s10879-018-09414-3

Fox, R. (2014). Are those germs in your pocket, or am I just crazy to see you? An autoethnographic consideration of obsessive-compulsive disorder. *Qualitative Inquiry*, *20*(8), 966–975. https://doi.org/10.1177/1077800413513732

Frankel, Z. F., Levitt, H. M., Murray, D. M., Greenberg, L. S., & Angus, L. E. (2006). Assessing psychotherapy silences: An empirically derived categorization system and sampling strategy. *Psychotherapy Research*, *16*(5), 627–638. https://doi.org/10.1080/10503300600591635

Freud, S. (1953). Fragment of an analysis of a case of hysteria. In J. Strachey (Ed. and Trans.), *The standard edition of the complete psychological works of Sigmund Freud* (Vol. 7, pp. 15–22). London: Hogarth Press. (original work published 1905)

Freud, S. (1958). Psycho-analytic notes on an autobiographical account of a case of paranoia. In J. Strachey (Ed. And Trans.), *The standard edition of the complete psychological works of Sigmund Freud, Vol.11* (pp. 9–55). London: Hogarth Press. (original work published 1911)

Freyd, J. J., Klest, B., & Allard, C. B. (2005). Betrayal trauma: Relationship to physical health, psychological distress, and a written disclosure intervention. *Journal of Trauma & Dissociation*, *6*(3), 83 104. https://doi.org/10.1300/J229v06n03_04

Gabbay, J., & Le May, A. (2010). *Practice-based evidence for healthcare: Clinical mindlines*. Routledge. https://doi.org/10.4324/9780203839973

Galasiński, D., & Kozłowska, O. (2013). Interacting with a questionnaire: respondents' constructions of questionnaire completion. *Quality & Quantity*, *47*(6), 3509–3520. https://doi.org/10.1007/s11135-012-9733-0

Gale, C., & Schröder, T. (2014). Experiences of self-practice/self-reflection in cognitive behavioural therapy: A meta-synthesis of qualitative studies. *Psychology and Psychotherapy: Theory, Research and Practice*, *87*(4), 373–392. https://doi.org/10.1111/papt.12026

Gale, C., Schröder, T., & Gilbert, P. (2015). "Do you practice what you preach?" a qualitative exploration of therapists' personal practice of compassion focused therapy. *Clinical Psychology & Psychotherapy*, *24*(1), 171–185. https://doi.org/10.1002/cpp.1993

Geller, S. M., & Greenberg, L. S. (2002). Therapeutic presence: Therapists' experience of presence in the psychotherapeutic encounter. *Person-Centered & Experiential Psychotherapies*, *1*(1–2), 71–86. https://doi.org/10.1080/14779757.2002.9688279

Geller, S. M., Greenberg, L. S., & Watson, J. C. (2010). Therapist and client perceptions of therapeutic presence: The development of a measure. *Psychotherapy Research*, *20*(5), 599–610. https://doi.org/10.1080/10503307.2010.495957

Gibson, K. & Cartwright, C. (2014). Young clients' narratives of the purpose and outcome of counselling. *British Journal of Guidance & Counselling*, *42*(5), 511–524. https://doi.org/10.1080/03069885.2014.925084

Gibson, K., Cartwright, C., & Read, J. (2016). 'In my life antidepressants have been. . .': a qualitative analysis of users' diverse experiences with antidepressants. *BMC Psychiatry*, *16*(1), 135. https://doi.org/10.1186/s12888-016-0844-3

Gockel, A. (2011). Client perspectives on spirituality in the therapeutic relationship. *The Humanistic Psychologist*, *39*(2), 154–168. https://doi.org/10.1080/08873267.2011.564959

Goode-Cross, D. T. (2011). Same difference: Black therapists' experience of same-race therapeutic dyads. *Professional Psychology: Research and Practice*, *42*(5), 368–374. https://doi.org/10.1037/a0025520

Goode-Cross, D. T., & Grim, K. A. (2016). "An unspoken level of comfort". Black therapists' experiences working with black clients. *Journal of Black Psychology*, *42*(1), 29–53. https://doi.org/10.1177/0095798414552103

Goodyer, I. M., Reynolds, S., Barrett, B., Byford, S., Dubicka, B., Hill, J., & Senior, R. (2017). Cognitive behavioural therapy and short-term psychoanalytical psychotherapy versus a brief psychosocial intervention in adolescents with unipolar major depressive disorder (IMPACT): a multicentre, pragmatic, observer-blind, randomised controlled superiority trial. *The Lancet Psychiatry*, *4*(2), 109–119. https://doi.org/10.1016/S2215-0366(16)30378-9

Gordon, R. (2012). Where oh where are the clients? The use of client factors in counselling psychology. *Counselling Psychology Review*, 27(4), 8–17.

Grafanaki, S., & McLeod, J. (1999). Narrative processes in the construction of helpful and hindering events in experiential psychotherapy. *Psychotherapy Research*, 9(3), 289–303. https://doi.org/10.1093/ptr/9.3.289

Gray, M. A., & Stiles, W. B. (2011). Employing a case study in building an assimilation theory account of generalized anxiety disorder and its treatment with cognitive-behavioral therapy. *Pragmatic Case Studies in Psychotherapy*, 7(4), 529–557. https://doi.org/10.14713/pcsp.v7i4.1115

Greenberg L. S. (2010) *Emotion-focused therapy: Theory and practice*. Washington, D.C.; American Psychological Association.

Greenberg, J. P., Vinjamuri, M., Williams-Gray, B., & Senreich, E. (2018). Shining the light on intersectionality: The complexities of similarity and difference in the therapeutic process from the perspectives of Black and Hispanic social workers. *Smith College Studies in Social Work*, 88(1), 59–81. https://doi.org/10.1080/00377317.2018.1404563

Greenberg, L. S. (1984). Task analysis: The general approach. In L.N. Rice & L.S. Greenberg (eds.) *Patterns of change: intensive analysis of psychotherapy process*. New York: Guilford.

Greenberg, L. S. (2002). *Emotion-focused therapy: Coaching clients to work through feelings*. Washington. DC: American Psychological Association Press. https://doi.org/10.1037/10447-000

Greenberg, L. S. (2007). A guide to conducting a task analysis of psychotherapeutic change. *Psychotherapy Research*, 17(1), 15–30 https://doi.org/10.1080/10503300600720390

Greenberg, L. S. & Foerster, F. S. (1996). Task analysis exemplified: the process of resolving unfinished business. *Journal of Consulting and Clinical Psychology*, 64(3), 439–446. https://doi.org/10.1037/0022-006X.64.3.439

Greenberg, L. S., & Watson, J. (1998). Experiential therapy of depression: Differential effects of client centered relationship conditions and active experiential interventions. *Psychotherapy Research*, 8(2), 210–224. https://doi.org/10.1093/ptr/8.2.210

Greenhalgh, J., Gooding, K., Gibbons, E., Dalkin, S., Wright, J., Valderas, J., & Black, N. (2018). How do patient reported outcome measures (PROMs) support clinician-patient communication and patient care? A realist synthesis. *Journal of Patient-reported Outcomes*, 2(1), 42. https://doi.org/10.1186/s41687-018-0061-6

Gruber, H., & Harteis, C. (2018). Supporting the acquisition of expertise: fostering individual development and creating professional communities. In H. Gruber & C. Harteis. (Eds). *Individual and social influences on professional learning: Professional and practice-based learning*. (pp. 87–114). Cham, Switzerland: Springer Nature. https://doi.org/10.1007/978-3-319-97041-7_5

Halleröd, S. L. H., Anckarsäter, H., Råstam, M., & Scherman, M. H. (2015). Experienced consequences of being diagnosed with ADHD as an adult- a qualitative study. *BMC Psychiatry*, 15(1), 31. https://doi.org/10.1186/s12888-015-0410-4

Hannon, M.D., Mohabir, R.K., Cleveland, R.E., & Hunt, B. (2019). School counselors, multiple student deaths, and grief: a narrative inquiry. *Journal of Counseling and Development*, 97(1), 43–52. https://doi.org/10.1002/jcad.12234

Hansen, J. T. (2006). Counseling theories within a postmodernist epistemology: new roles for theories in counseling practice. *Journal of Counseling and Development*, 84(3), 291–297. https://doi.org/10.1002/j.1556-6678.2006.tb00408.x

Hardy, G. E., Bishop-Edwards, L., Chambers, E., Connell, J., Dent-Brown, K., Kothari, G., O'hara, R., & Parry, G. D. (2019). Risk factors for negative experiences during psychotherapy. *Psychotherapy Research*, 29(3), 403–414. https://doi.org/10.1080/10503307.2017.1393575

Haroz, E. E., Ritchey, M., Bass, J. K., Kohrt, B. A., Augustinavicius, J., Michalopoulos, L., & Bolton, P. (2017). How is depression experienced around the world? A systematic review of qualitative literature. *Social Science & Medicine*, 183, 151–162. https://doi.org/10.1016/j.socscimed.2016.12.030

Harper, H. (1989a). *Coding Guide I: Identification of confrontation challenges in exploratory therapy*. Sheffield, England: University of Sheffield.

Harper, H. (1989b). *Coding Guide II: Identification of withdrawal challenges in exploratory therapy*. Sheffield, England: University of Sheffield.

Haskayne, D., Larkin, M., & Hirschfeld, R. (2014). What are the experiences of therapeutic rupture and repair for clients and therapists within long-term psychodynamic therapy? *British Journal of Psychotherapy*, 30(1), 68–86. https://doi.org/10.1111/bjp.12061

Hayes, J. A., Nelson, D. L. B., & Fauth, J. (2015). Countertransference in successful and unsuccessful cases of psychotherapy. *Psychotherapy*, 52(1), 127–133. https://doi.org/10.1037/a0038827

Head, L., & Harada, T. (2017). Keeping the heart a long way from the brain: The emotional labour of climate scientists. *Emotion, Space and Society*, 24, 34–41. https://doi.org/10.1016/j.emospa.2017.07.005

Heatherington, L., Messer, S. B., Angus, L., Strauman, T. J., Friedlander, M. L., & Kolden, G. G. (2012). The narrowing of theoretical orientations in clinical psychology doctoral training. *Clinical Psychology: Science and Practice*, 19(4), 364–374. https://doi.org/10.1111/cpsp.12012

Henry, H. M., & Stiles, W. B. (2012). Contextual influences on acculturation: Psychological assimilation and continuing bonds for two immigrants. In M.-C. Bertau, M. Gonçalves, & P. Raggatt (Eds.), *Dialogic formations: Investigations into the origins and development of the dialogical self* (pp. 289–313). Charlotte, NC: Information Age Publishing.

Henry, H. M., Stiles, W. B., & Biran, M. W. (2005). Loss and mourning in immigration: Using the assimilation model to assess continuing bonds with native culture. *Counselling Psychology Quarterly*, 18(2), 109–119. https://doi.org/10.1080/09515070500136819

Henry, H., Stiles, W. B., & Biran, M. W. (2018). Continuing bonds with native culture: Immigrants' response to loss. In D. Klass & E. M. Steffen (Eds.), *Continuing bonds in bereavement: New directions for research and practice* (pp. 287–299). New York: Routledge. https://doi.org/10.4324/9781315202396-28

Henry, H. M., Stiles, W. B., Biran, M. W., Mosher, J. K., Brinegar, M. G., & Banerjee, P. (2009). Immigrants' continuing bonds with their native culture: Assimilation analysis of three interviews. *Transcultural Psychiatry*, 46(2), 257–284. https://doi.org/10.1177/1363461509105816

Herzog, P., Lauff, S., Rief, W., & Brakemeier, E. L. (2019). Assessing the unwanted: A systematic review of instruments used to assess negative effects of psychotherapy. *Brain and Behavior*, 9(12), e01447. https://doi.org/10.1002/brb3.1447

Hill, C. E. (Ed.). (2012). *Consensual qualitative research. A practical resource for investigating social science phenomena*. Washington, DC: American Psychological Association.

Hill, C. E., Chui, H., & Baumann, E. (2013). Revisiting and reenvisioning the outcome problem in psychotherapy: An argument to include individualized and qualitative measurement. *Psychotherapy Theory, Research, Practice, Training*, 50(1), 68–76. https://doi.org/10.1037/a0030571

Hill, C. E., Nutt-Williams, E., Heaton, K. J., Thompson, B. J., & Rhodes, R. H. (1996). Therapist retrospective recall impasses in long-term psychotherapy: A qualitative analysis. *Journal of Counseling Psychology*, 43(2), 207–217. https://doi.org/10.1037/0022-0167.43.2.207

Hoener, C., Stiles, W. B., Luka, B. J., & Gordon, R. A. (2012). Client experiences of agency in therapy. *Person-Centered & Experiential Psychotherapies*, 11(1), 64–82. https://doi.org/10.1080/14779757.2011.639460

Honos-Webb, L., Lani, J. A., & Stiles, W. B. (1999). Discovering markers of assimilation stages: The fear of losing control marker. *Journal of Clinical Psychology*, 55(12), 1441–1452. https://doi.org/10.1002/(SICI)1097-4679(199912)55:12<1441::AID-JCLP3>3.0.CO;2-K

Honos-Webb, L., & Stiles, W. B. (1998). Reformulation of assimilation analysis in terms of voices. *Psychotherapy*, 35(1), 23–33. https://doi.org/10.1037/h0087682

Honos-Webb, L., Stiles, W. B., & Greenberg, L. S. (2003). A method of rating assimilation in psychotherapy based on markers of change. *Journal of Counseling Psychology*, 50(2), 189–198. https://doi.org/10.1037/0022-0167.50.2.189

Honos-Webb, L., Stiles, W. B., Greenberg, L. S., & Goldman, R. (1998). Assimilation analysis of process-experiential psychotherapy: A comparison of two cases. *Psychotherapy Research*, 8(3), 264–286. https://doi.org/10.1093/ptr/8.3.264

Honos-Webb, L., Surko, M., Stiles, W. B., & Greenberg, L. S. (1999). Assimilation of voices in psychotherapy: The case of Jan. *Journal of Counseling Psychology*, 46(4), 448–460. https://doi.org/10.1037/0022-0167.46.4.448

Howard, G. S. (1983) Toward methodological pluralism. *Journal of Counseling Psychology*, 30(1), 19–21. https://doi.org/10.1037/0022-0167.30.1.19

Hsieh, H. F., & Shannon, S. E. (2005). Three approaches to qualitative content analysis. *Qualitative Health Research*, 15(9), 1277–1288. https://doi.org/10.1177/1049732305276687

Huber, J., Born, A. K., Claaß, C., Ehrenthal, J. C., Nikendei, C., Schauenburg, H., & Dinger, U. (2019). Therapeutic agency, in-session behavior, and patient-therapist interaction. *Journal of Clinical Psychology*, 75(1), 66–78. https://doi.org/10.1002/jclp.22700

Huber, J., Nikendei, Ehrenthal, J.C., Schauenburg, H., Mander, J. & Dinger, U. (2018). Therapeutic Agency Inventory: Development and psychometric validation of a patient self-report. *Psychotherapy Research*, 29(7), 919–934 https://doi.org/10.1080/10503307.2018.1447707

Humphreys, C. L., Rubin, J. S., Knudson, R. M., & Stiles. W. B. (2005). The assimilation of anger in a case of dissociative identity disorder. *Counselling Psychology Quarterly*, 18(2), 121–132. https://doi.org/10.1080/09515070500136488

Hundt, N. E., Ecker, A. H., Thompson, K., Helm, A., Smith, T. L., Stanley, M. A., & Cully, J. A. (2018). "It didn't fit for me:" A qualitative examination of dropout from prolonged exposure and cognitive processing therapy in veterans. *Psychological Services*. https://doi.org/10.1037/ser0000316

Hundt, N. E., Helm, A., Smith, T. L., Lamkin, J., Cully, J. A., & Stanley, M. A. (2018b). Failure to engage: A qualitative study of veterans who decline evidence-based psychotherapies for PTSD. *Psychological Services*, 15(4), 536. https://doi.org/10.1037/ser0000212

Hundt, N. E., Smith, T. L., Fortney, J. C., Cully, J. A., & Stanley, M. A. (2018). A qualitative study of veterans' mixed emotional reactions to receiving a PTSD diagnosis. *Psychological Services*. https://doi.org/10.1037/ser0000273

Hunter, S. V, & Schofield, M. J. (2006). How counsellors cope with traumatized clients: personal, professional and organizational strategies. *International Journal for the Advancement of Counselling*, 28(2), 121–138. https://doi.org/10.1007/s10447-005-9003-0

Johnstone, L. & Boyle, M. with Cromby, J., Dillon, J., Harper, D., Kinderman, P., Longden, E., Pilgrim, D. & Read, J. (2018). *The Power Threat Meaning Framework: Towards the identification of patterns in emotional distress, unusual experiences and troubled or troubling behaviour, as an alternative to functional psychiatric diagnosis*. Leicester: British Psychological Society.

Jones, J. K. (2018). A phenomenological study of the office environments of clinical social workers. *HERD: Health Environments Research & Design Journal*, 11(3), 38–48. https://doi.org/10.1177/1937586718755477

Joyce, A. S., Duncan, S. C., & Piper, W. E. (1995). Responses to dynamic interpretation in short-term individual psychotherapy. *Psychotherapy Research*, 5(1), 49–62. https://doi.org/10.1080/10503309512331331136

Kanazawa, Y., & Iwakabe, S. (2016). Learning and difficult experiences in graduate training in clinical psychology: A qualitative study of Japanese trainees' retrospective accounts. *Counselling Psychology Quarterly*, 29(3), 274–295. https://doi.org/10.1080/09515070.2015.1033383

Katzow, A. W., & Safran, J. D. (2007). Recognizing and resolving ruptures in the therapeutic alliance. In P. Gilbert & R. L. Leahy (Eds.) *The therapeutic relationship in cognitive behavioral psychotherapies*. London: Routledge.

Kidd, J., & Ziebland, S. (2016). Narratives of experience of mental health and illness on healthtalk.org. *BJPsych Bulletin*, 40(5), 273–276. https://doi.org/10.1192/pb.bp.115.052217

Kinnier, R.T., Hofsess, C., Pongratz, R., & Lambert, C. (2009). Attributions and affirmations for overcoming anxiety and depression. *Psychology and Psychotherapy: Theory, Research and Practice*, 82(2), 153–169. https://doi.org/10.1348/147608308X389418

Koch, S. (1975). Language communities, search cells, and the psychological studies. *Nebraska Symposium on Motivation*, 23 47, 7–559.

Kokaliari, E., Catanzarite, G., & Berzoff, J. (2013). It is called a mother tongue for a reason: a qualitative study of therapists' perspectives on bilingual psychotherapy-treatment implications. *Smith College Studies in Social Work*, 83(1), 97–118. https://doi.org/10.1080/00377317.2013.747396

Kuhn, T. S. (1970). *The structure of scientific revolutions*, second edition. Chicago: University of Chicago Press.

Lampropoulos, K. G., & Dixon, D. N. (2007). Psychotherapy integration in internships and counselling psychology doctoral programs. *Journal of Psychotherapy Integration*, 17(2), 185–208. https://doi.org/10.1037/1053-0479.17.2.185

Larkings, J. S., Brown, P. M., & Scholz, B. (2019). "It's often liberating": consumers discuss causal beliefs in the treatment process. *Journal of Mental Health*, 28(4), 397–403. https://doi.org/10.1080/09638237.2017.1417550

Lave, J., & Wenger, E. (1991). *Situated learning: Legitimate peripheral participation*. Cambridge: Cambridge University Press. https://doi.org/10.1017/CBO9780511815355

Lee, E., & Horvath, A. O. (2014). How a therapist responds to cultural versus noncultural dialogue in cross-cultural clinical practice. *Journal of Social Work Practice*, 28(2), 193–217. https://doi.org/10.1080/02650533.2013.821104

Lee, E., Johnstone, M., & Herschman, J. (2019). Negotiating therapy goals and tasks in cross-cultural psychotherapy. *Journal of Social Work Practice*, 33(4), 447–462. https://doi.org/10.1080/02650533.2018.1504288

Leiman, M., & Stiles, W. B. (2001). Dialogical sequence analysis and the zone of proximal development as conceptual enhancements to the assimilation model: The case of Jan revisited. *Psychotherapy Research*, 11(3), 311–330. https://doi.org/10.1080/713663986

Leone, K., Robbins, S. J., & Morrow, M. T. (2018). Using clay sculpting to prime readiness to change: an experimental analog study. *Art Therapy*, 35(3), 131–137. https://doi.org/10.1080/07421656.2018.1523652

Levitt, H. M. (2001). The sounds of silence in psychotherapy: The categorization of clients' pauses. *Psychotherapy Research*, 11(3), 295–309. https://doi.org/10.1080/713663985

Levitt, H. M. (2019). A psychosocial genealogy of LGBTQ+ gender: An empirically based theory of gender and gender identity cultures. *Psychology of Women Quarterly*, 43(3), 275–297. https://doi.org/10.1177/0361684319834641

Levitt, H. M., Bamberg, M., Creswell, J. W., Frost, D., Josselson, R., & Suárez-Orozco, C. (2018). Journal article reporting standards for qualitative research in psychology: The APA Publications and Communications Board Task Force report. *American Psychologist*, 73(1), 26–46. https://doi.org/10.1037/amp0000151

Levitt, H., Butler, M., & Hill, T. (2006). What clients find helpful in psychotherapy: Developing principles for facilitating moment-to-moment change. *Journal of Counseling Psychology*, 53(3), 314–324. https://doi.org/10.1037/0022-0167.53.3.314

Levitt, H. M., Grabowski, L., Morrill, Z., & Minami, T. (2019, September 29). Measuring psychotherapy as clients experience it: The Clients' Critical Experiences in Therapy Scale (CCETS). In J. K. Swift (chair), *Client, therapists and supervisor perspectives of change processes and outcomes*. Presented at the North American Society for Psychotherapy Research Conference, Snowbird, UT.

Levitt, H. M., McLeod, J., & Stiles, W. B. (2021). The conceptualization, design, and evaluation of qualitative methods in research on psychotherapy. In M. Barkham, W. Lutz, & L. G. Castonguay (Eds.), *Bergin and Garfield's handbook of psychotherapy and behavior change*, 7th Edition, New York Wiley.

Levitt, H. M. & Morrill, Z. (2021). Measuring silence: The pausing inventory categorization system and a review of findings (pp. 233–250). In M. Buchholz & A. Dimitrijevic (Eds.), *Silence and silencing in psychoanalysis: Cultural, clinical and research perspectives*. New York: Routledge.

Levitt, H.M., Morrill, Z. & Ipecki, B. (2019). *A qualitative meta-analysis examining therapists' experiences of guiding psychotherapy*. Unpublished manuscript. University of Massachusetts Boston, Boston, MA.

Levitt, H. M., Motulsky, S. L., Wertz, F. J., Morrow, S. L., & Ponterotto, J. G. (2017). Recommendations for designing and reviewing qualitative research in psychology: Promoting methodological integrity. *Qualitative Psychology*, 4(1), 2–22. https://doi.org/10.1037/qup0000082

Levitt, H. M., & Piazza-Bonin, E. (2015). Wisdom and psychotherapy: Studying expert therapists' clinical wisdom to explicate common processes. *Psychotherapy Research*, 26(1), 31–47. https://doi.org/10.1080/10503307.2014.937470

Levitt, H.M., Pomerville, A., & Surace, F. I. (2016a). A qualitative meta-analysis examining clients' experiences of psychotherapy: A new agenda. *Psychological Bulletin*, 142(8), 801–830. https://doi.org/10.1037/bul0000057

Levitt, H.M., Pomerville, A., & Surace, F. I. (2016b). How clients' experiences of therapy inform theories of psychotherapy integration: A meta-analysis. In H. M. Levitt (Moderator), *Qualitative methods*, Society for Psychotherapy Integration, Dublin, Ireland.

Levy, K. N., & Anderson, T. (2013). Is clinical psychology doctoral training becoming less intellectually diverse? And if so, what can be done? *Clinical Psychology: Science and Practice*, 20(2), 211–220. https://doi.org/10.1111/cpsp.12035

Lilienfeld, S. O., Ritschel, L. A., Lynn, S. J., Cautin, R. L., & Latzman, R. D. (2014). Why ineffective psychotherapies appear to work: A taxonomy of causes of spurious therapeutic effectiveness. *Perspectives on Psychological Science*, 9(4), 355–387. https://doi.org/10.1177/1745691614535216

Liou, C. P. (2019). Contemplating the unfolding of life: the lived experience of ch'i in counseling. *International Journal for the Advancement of Counselling*, 41(3), 329–338. https://doi.org/10.1007/s10447-018-9353-z

Lipkin, S. (1954). Clients' feelings and attitudes in relation to the outcome of client-centered therapy. *Psychological Monographs: General and Applied*, 68(1). https://doi.org/10.1037/h0093661

Lishman, E., Cheston, R., & Smithson, J. (2016) The paradox of dementia: Changes in assimilation after receiving a diagnosis of dementia. *Dementia*, 15(2), 181–203. https://doi.org/10.1177/1471301214520781

Littauer, H., Sexton, H., & Wynn, R. (2005). Qualities clients wish for in their therapists. *Scandinavian Journal of Caring Sciences*, 19(1), 28–31. https://doi.org/10.1111/j.1471-6712.2005.00315.x

Locock, L., Graham, C., King, J., Parkin, S., Chisholm, A., Montgomery, C., Gibbons, E., Ainley, E., Bostock, J., Gager, M., Churchill, N., Dopson, S., Greenhalgh, T., Martin, A., Powell, J., Sizmur, S., & Ziebland, S. (2020). Understanding how front-line staff use patient experience data for service improvement: an exploratory case study evaluation. *Health Services and Delivery Research*, 8, 13. https://doi.org/10.3310/hsdr08130

Locock, L., Kirkpatrick, S., Brading, L., Sturmey, G., Cornwell, J., Churchill, N., & Robert, G. (2019). Involving service users in the qualitative analysis of patient narratives to support healthcare quality improvement. *Research Involvement and Engagement*, 5(1), 1. https://doi.org/10.1186/s40900-018-0133-z

Lømo, B., Haavind, H., & Tjersland, O. A. (2018). From resistance to invitations: How men voluntarily in therapy for intimate partner violence may contribute to the development of a working alliance. *Journal of Interpersonal Violence*, 33(16), 2579–2601. https://doi.org/10.1177/0886260516628290

Luborsky, L., Singer, B., & Luborsky, L. (1975). Comparative studies of psychotherapies. *Archives of General Psychiatry*, 32(8), 995–1008. https://doi.org/10.1001/archpsyc.1975.01760260059004

MacDonald, J. P., Ford, J., Willox, A. C., & Mitchell, C. (2015). Youth-led participatory video as a strategy to enhance Inuit youth adaptive capacities for dealing with climate change. *Arctic*, 68(4), 486–499. https://doi.org/10.14430/arctic4527

MacNeill, V., Foley, M., Quirk, A., & McCambridge, J. (2016). Shedding light on research participation effects in behaviour change trials: a qualitative study examining research participant experiences. *BMC Public Health*, 16(1), 91. https://doi.org/10.1186/s12889-016-2741-6

Maluccio, A.N. (1979). *Learning from clients: Interpersonal helping as viewed by clients and social workers.* New York;: Free Press.

Marchese, M. H., Robbins, S. J., & Morrow, M. T. (2018). Nonconscious priming enhances the therapy relationship: An experimental analog study. *Psychotherapy Research*, 28(2), 183–191. https://doi.org/10.1080/10503307.2016.1158434

Marshall, D., Quinn, C., Child, S., Shenton, D., Pooler, J., Forber, S., & Byng, R. (2016). What IAPT services can learn from those who do not attend. *Journal of Mental Health*, 25(5), 410–415. https://doi.org/10.3109/09638237.2015.1101057

Maxwell, J.A. (2012). *A realist approach for qualitative research.* Thousand Oaks, CA: Sage.

Maxwell, J.A. (2019). The value of qualitative inquiry for public health. *Qualitative Inquiry.* https://doi.org/10.1177/1077800419857093

Mayring, P. (2000). Qualitative content analysis. *Forum: Qualitative Social Research*, 1(2), 20.

McAdams, D. P., & McLean, K. C. (2013). Narrative identity. *Current Directions in Psychological Science*, 22(3), 233–238. https://doi.org/10.1177/0963721413475622

McCambridge, J. (2015). From question-behaviour effects in trials to the social psychology of research participation. *Psychology & Health*, 30(1), 72–84. https://doi.org/10.1080/08870446.2014.953527

McLeod, J. (2010). *Case study research in counselling and psychotherapy.* London: Sage. https://doi.org/10.4135/9781446287897

McLeod, J. (2016). *Using research in counselling and psychotherapy.* London: Sage. https://doi.org/10.4135/9781526404084

McLeod, J. (2017a). Qualitative methods for routine outcome measurement. In T. Rousmaniere, R. K. Goodyear, S. D. Miller, & B. E. Wampold (Eds.) *The cycle of excellence: Using deliberate practice to improve supervision and training.* (pp. 99–122). New York;: Wiley-Blackwell. https://doi.org/10.1002/9781119165590.ch5

McLeod, J. (2017b). Science and psychotherapy: Developing research-based knowledge that enhances the effectiveness of practice. *Transactional Analysis Journal*, 47(2), 82–101. https://doi.org/10.1177/0362153717694885

McMullen, L. M., & Herman, J. (2009). Women's accounts of their decision to quit taking antidepressants. *Qualitative Health Research*, 19(11), 1569–1579. https://doi.org/10.1177/1049732309349936

McNulty, N., Ogden, J., & Warren, F. (2013). 'Neutralizing the patient': therapists' accounts of sexual boundary violations. *Clinical Psychology & Psychotherapy*, 20(3), 189–198. https://doi.org/10.1002/cpp.799

McPherson, S., & Beresford, P. (2019). Semantics of patient choice: how the UK national guideline for depression silences patients. *Disability & Society*, 34(3), 491–497. https://doi.org/10.1080/09687599.2019.1589757

McPherson, S., Rost, F., Town, J., & Abbass, A. (2018). Epistemological flaws in NICE review methodology and its impact on recommendations for psychodynamic psychotherapies for complex and persistent depression. *Psychoanalytic Psychotherapy*, 32(2), 102–121. https://doi.org/10.1080/02668734.2018.1458331

McRobie, S., & Agee, M. (2017). Pacific counsellors' use of indigenous values, proverbs, metaphors, symbols, and stories in their counselling practices. *New Zealand Journal of Counselling*, 37(2), 103–127. https://hdl.handle.net/2292/39223

Meichenbaum, D. (2002). Core tasks of psychotherapy: what expert therapists do. In *Brief Therapy Conference*, Orlando, FL.

Mendes, I., Rosa, C., Stiles, W. B., Caro Gabalda, I., Gomes, P., Basto, I., & Salgado, J. (2016). Setbacks in the process of assimilation of problematic experiences in two cases of emotion-focused therapy for depression. *Psychotherapy Research*, 26(6), 638–652. https://doi.org/10.1080/10503307.2015.1136443

Meystre, C., Pascual-Leone, A., de Roten, Y., Despland, J.-N., & Kramer, U. (2015). What interventions facilitate client progress through the assimilation model? A task analysis of interventions in the psychodynamic treatment of depression. *Psychotherapy Research*, 25(4), 484–502. https://doi.org/10.1080/10503307.2014.921352

Michalopoulos, L. M., Meinhart, M., Yung, J., Barton, S. M., Wang, X., Chakrabarti, U., Ritchey, M., Haroz, E., Joseph, N., Bass J, & Bolton, P. (2020). Global posttrauma symptoms: a systematic review of qualitative literature. *Trauma, Violence, & Abuse*, 21(2), 406–420. https://doi.org/10.1177/1524838018772293

Midgley, N., Ansaldo, F., & Target, M. (2014a). The meaningful assessment of therapy outcomes: Incorporating a qualitative study into a randomized controlled trial evaluating the treatment of adolescent depression. *Psychotherapy*, 51(1), 128–37. https://doi.org/10.1037/a0034179

Midgley, N., Holmes, J., Parkinson, S., Stapley, E., Eatough, V., & Target, M. (2014). "Just like talking to someone about like shit in your life and stuff, and they help you": hopes and expectations for therapy among depressed adolescents. *Psychotherapy Research*, 26(1), 11–21. https://doi.org/10.1080/10503307.2014.973922

Midgley, N., Isaacs, D., Weitkamp, K., & Target, M. (2016). The experience of adolescents participating in a randomised clinical trial in the field of mental health: A qualitative study. *Trials*, 17(1), 364. https://doi.org/10.1186/s13063-016-1474-2

Midgley, N., Parkinson, S., Holmes, J., Stapley, E., Eatough, V., & Target, M. (2016). 'Did I bring it on myself?': How adolescents referred to mental health services make sense of their own depression. *European Child and Adolescent Psychiatry*, 26(1), 25–34. https://doi.org/10.1007/s00787-016-0868-8

Midgley, N., Parkinson, S., Holmes, J., Stapley, E., Eatough, V., & Target, M. (2015). Beyond a diagnosis: The experience of depression among clinically-referred adolescents. *Journal of Adolescence*, 44, 269–279. https://doi.org/10.1016/j.adolescence.2015.08.007

Miller, K., Willson, S., Chepp, V., & Padilla, L-J. (Eds.) (2014). *Cognitive interviewing methodology.* New York;, NY: Wiley. https://doi.org/10.1002/9781118838860

Miller, S. D., Hubble, M. A., Duncan, B. L., & Wampold, B. E. (2010). Delivering what works. In B. L. Duncan, S. D. Miller, B. E. Wampold, & M. A. Hubble (Eds.), *The heart and soul of change: Delivering what works in therapy*, 2nd ed. (pp. 421–429). Washington, DC: American Psychological Association. https://doi.org/10.1037/12075-014

Millett, L., Taylor, B. L., & Howard, L. M. (2019). Experiences of Improving Access to Psychological Therapy services for perinatal mental health difficulties: a qualitative study of women's and therapists' views. *Behavioural and Cognitive Psychotherapy*, 46(4), 421–436. https://doi.org/10.1017/S1352465817000650

Mirza, M., Harrison, E. A., Chang, H. C., Salo, C. D., & Birman, D. (2017). Making sense of three-way conversations: A qualitative study of cross-cultural counseling with refugee men. *International Journal of Intercultural Relations*, 56, 52–64. https://doi.org/10.1016/j.ijintrel.2016.12.002

Mizock, L., & Lundquist, C. (2016). Missteps in psychotherapy with transgender clients: Promoting gender sensitivity in counseling and psychological practice. *Psychology of Sexual Orientation and Gender Diversity*, 3(2), 148–155. https://doi.org/10.1037/sgd0000177

Mjelve, L.H., Ulleberg, I., & Vonheim, K. (2018). "What do I share?" Personal and private experiences in educational psychological counselling. *Scandinavian Journal of Educational Research*, 64(2), 181–194. https://doi.org/10.1080/00313831.2018.1527396

Moltu, C., Binder, P., & Nielsen, G. H. (2010). Commitment under pressure: Experienced therapists' inner work during difficult therapeutic impasses. *Psychotherapy Research*, 20(3), 309–320. https://doi.org/10.1080/10503300903470610

Moltu, C., Stefansen, J., Nøtnes, J. C., Skjølberg, Å., & Veseth, M. (2017). What are "good outcomes" in public mental health settings? A qualitative exploration of clients' and therapists' experiences. *International Journal of Mental Health Systems*, 11(1), 12. https://doi.org/10.1186/s13033-017-0119-5

Moltu, C., Veseth, M., Stefansen, J., Nøtnes, J. C., Skjølberg, Å., Binder, P. E., & Nordberg, S. S. (2018). This is what I need a clinical feedback system to do for me: A qualitative inquiry into therapists' and patients' perspectives. *Psychotherapy Research*, 28(2), 250–263. https://doi.org/10.1080/10503307.2016.1189619

Moore, S. C., Osatuke, K., & Howe, S. R. (2014). Assimilation approach to measuring organizational change from pre- to post-intervention. *World Journal of Psychiatry*, 4(1), 13–29. https://doi.org/10.5498/wjp.v4.i1.13

Moradi, B., & Grzanka, P. R. (2017). Using intersectionality responsibly: Toward critical epistemology, structural analysis, and social justice activism. *Journal of Counseling Psychology*, 64(5), 500–513. https://doi.org/10.1037/cou0000203

Moran, P., Kelesidi, K., Guglani, S., Davidson, S., & Ford, T. (2012). What do parents and carers think about routine outcome measures and their use? A focus group study of CAMHS attenders. *Clinical Child Psychology and Psychiatry*, 17(1), 65–79. https://doi.org/10.1177/1359104510391859

Mosher, J. K., Goldsmith, J. Z., Stiles, W. B., & Greenberg, L. S. (2008). Assimilation of two critic voices in a person-centered therapy for depression. *Person-Centered and Experiential Psychotherapies*, 7(1), 1–19. https://doi.org/10.1080/14779757.2008.9688449

Mosher, J. K., & Stiles, W. B. (2009). Clients' assimilation of experiences of their therapists. *Psychotherapy*, 46(4), 432–447. https://doi.org/10.1037/a0017955

Murphy, D., Irfan, N., Barnett, H., Castledine, E., & Enescu. L. (2018). A systematic review and meta-synthesis of qualitative research into mandatory personal psychotherapy during training. *Counselling and Psychotherapy Research*, 18(2), 199–214. https://doi.org/10.1002/capr.12162

Nachmani, I., & Somer, E. (2007). Women sexually victimized in psychotherapy speak out: The dynamics and outcome of therapist client sex. *Women and Therapy*, 30(1), 1–17. https://doi.org/10.1300/J015v30n01_01

Naeem, F., Phiri, P., Munshi, T., Rathod, S., Ayub, M., Gobbi, M., & Kingdon, D. (2015). Using cognitive behaviour therapy with South Asian Muslims: findings from the culturally sensitive CBT project. *International Review of Psychiatry*, 27(3), 233–246. https://doi.org/10.3109/09540261.2015.1067598

Nanda, J. (2005). A phenomenological enquiry into the effect of meditation on therapeutic practice. *Counselling Psychology Review*, 20(1), 17–25.

Newman, D. W., & Beail, N. (2002). Monitoring change in psychotherapy with people with intellectual disabilities: the application of the assimilation of problematic experiences scale. *Journal of Applied Research in Intellectual Disabilities*, 15(1), 48–60. https://doi.org/10.1046/j.1360-2322.2002.00103.x

Newman, D. W., & Beail, N. (2005). Analysis of assimilation during psychotherapy with people who have mental retardation. *American Journal on Mental Retardation*, 110(5), 359–365. https://doi.org/10.1352/0895-8017(2005)110[359:AOADPW]2.0.CO;2

Norcross, J. C., & Wampold, B. E. (2011). What works for whom: Tailoring psychotherapy to the person. *Journal of Clinical Psychology*, 67(2), 127–132. https://doi.org/10.1002/jclp.20764

O'Cathain, A. (2018). *A practical guide to using qualitative research with randomized controlled trials*. Oxford: Oxford University Press. https://doi.org/10.1093/med/9780198802082.001.0001

O'Keeffe, S., Martin, P., Target, M., & Midgley, N. (2019). 'I just stopped going': A mixed methods investigation into types of therapy dropout in adolescents with depression. *Frontiers in Psychology*, 10, 75. https://doi.org/10.3389/fpsyg.2019.00075

Oanes, C. J., Anderssen, N., Karlsson, B., & Borg, M. (2015). How do therapists respond to client feedback? A critical review of the research literature. *Scandinavian Psychologist*, 2, e17. https://doi.org/10.15714/scandpsychol.2.e17 https://doi.org/10.15714/scandpsychol.2.e17

Oddli, H. W. & Rønnestad, M. H. (2012). How experienced therapists introduce the technical aspects in the initial alliance formation: Powerful decision makers supporting clients' agency. *Psychotherapy Research*, 22(2), 176–193. https://doi.org/10.1080/10503307.2011.633280

Omer, H. (1985). Fulfillment of therapeutic tasks as a precondition for acceptance in therapy. *American Journal of Psychotherapy*, 39(2), 175–186. https://doi.org/10.1176/appi.psychotherapy.1985.39.2.175

Osatuke, K., Glick, M. J., Gray, M. A., Reynolds, D. J., Jr., Humphreys, C. L., Salvi, L. M., & Stiles, W. B. (2004). Assimilation and narrative: Stories as meaning bridges. In L. Angus & J. McLeod (Eds.), *Handbook of narrative and psychotherapy: Practice, theory, and research* (pp. 193–210). Thousand Oaks, CA: Sage.

Osatuke, K., Gray, M. A., Glick, M. J., Stiles, W. B., & Barkham, M. (2004). Hearing voices: Methodological issues in measuring internal multiplicity. In H. H. Hermans & G. Dimaggio (Eds.), *The dialogical self in psychotherapy* (pp. 237–254). New York;: Brunner-Routledge. https://doi.org/10.4324/9780203314616_chapter_15

Osatuke, K., Humphreys, C. L., Glick, M. J., Graff-Reed, R. L., Mack, L. M., & Stiles, W. B. (2005). Vocal manifestations of internal multiplicity: Mary's voices. *Psychology and Psychotherapy: Theory, Research and Practice*, 78(1), 21–44. https://doi.org/10.1348/147608304X22364

Osatuke, K., Mosher, J. K., Goldsmith, J. Z., Stiles, W. B., Shapiro, D. A., Hardy, G. E., & Barkham, M. (2007). Submissive voices dominate in depression: Assimilation analysis of a helpful session. *Journal of Clinical Psychology*, 63(2), 153–164. https://doi.org/10.1002/jclp.20338

Osatuke, K., Reid, M., Stiles, W. B., Zisook, S., & Mohamed, S. (2011). Narrative evolution and assimilation of problematic experiences in a case of pharmacotherapy for schizophrenia. *Psychotherapy Research*, 21(1), 41–53. https://doi.org/10.1080/10503307.2010.508760

Osatuke, K., & Stiles, W. B. (2006). Problematic internal voices in clients with borderline features: An elaboration of the assimilation model. *Journal of Constructivist Psychology*, 19(4), 287–319. https://doi.org/10.1080/10720530600691699

Osatuke, K., & Stiles, W. B. (2010). Change in posttraumatic stress disorder: An assimilation model account. In G. Dimaggio & P. H. Lysaker (Eds.), *Metacognition and severe adult mental disorders: From research to treatment* (pp. 285–300). New York;: Brunner-Routledge.

Osatuke, K., & Stiles, W. B. (2012). Supervision as a conversation among developing voices: An assimilation model perspective. In M.-C. Bertau, M. Gonçalves, & P. Raggatt (Eds.), *Dialogic formations: Investigations into the origins and development of the dialogical self* (pp. 259–287). Charlotte, NC: Information Age Publishing.

Østlie, K., Stänicke, E., & Haavind H. (2018). A listening perspective in psychotherapy with suicidal patients: Establishing convergence in therapists' and patients' private theories on suicidality and cure. *Psychotherapy Research*, 28(1), 150–163. https://doi.org/10.1080/10503307.2016.1174347

Parry, G. D., Crawford, M. J., & Duggan, C. (2016). Iatrogenic harm from psychological therapies -time to move on. *The British Journal of Psychiatry*, 208(3), 210–212. https://doi.org/10.1192/bjp.bp.115.163618

Pascual-Leone, A. (2005). *Emotional processing in the therapeutic hour: Why the only way out is through*. Unpublished doctoral thesis, York University.

Pascual-Leone, A. (2009). Dynamic emotional processing in experiential therapy: Two steps forward, one step back. *Journal of Consulting and Clinical Psychology*, 77(1), 113–126. https://doi.org/10.1037/a0014488

Pascual-Leone, A., Greenberg, L. S., & Pascual-Leone, J. (2009). Developments in task analysis: New methods to study change. *Psychotherapy Research*, 19(4), 527–542. https://doi.org/10.1080/10503300902897797

Peräkylä, A., Antaki, C., Vehvilainen, S., & Leudar, I. (Eds.). (2008) *Conversation analysis and psychotherapy*. Cambridge, United Kingdom: Cambridge University Press. https://doi.org/10.1017/CBO9780511490002

Peirce, C. S. (1985). The proper treatment of hypotheses: A preliminary chapter, toward an examination of Hume's argument against miracles, in its logic and in its history. In C. Eisele (Ed.), *Historical perspectives on Peirce's logic of science. A history of science, Vol. 2*. Berlin: Mouton Publishers.

Pilgrim, D., & Guinan, P. (1999). From mitigation to culpability: rethinking the evidence about therapist sexual abuse. *European Journal of Psychotherapy, Counselling and Health, 2*(2), 153–168. https://doi.org/10.1080/13642539908402323

Plchová, R., Hytych, R., Řiháček, T., Roubal, J., & Vybíral, Z. (2016). How do trainees choose their first psychotherapy training? The case of training in psychotherapy integration. *British Journal of Guidance & Counselling, 44*(5), 487–503. https://doi.org/10.1080/03069885.2016.1213371

Pomerville, A., Burrage, R. L., & Gone, J. P. (2016). Empirical findings from psychotherapy research with indigenous populations: A systematic review. *Journal of Consulting and Clinical Psychology, 84*(12), 1023. https://doi.org/10.1037/ccp0000150

Pope-Davis, D. B., Toporek, R. L., Ortega-Villalobos, L., Ligiéro, D. P., Brittan-Powell, C. S., Liu, W. M., Bashshur, M. R., Codrington, J. N., & Liang, C. T. H. (2002). Client perspectives of multicultural counseling competence: A qualitative examination. *The Counseling Psychologist, 30*(3), 355–393. https://doi.org/10.1177/0011000002303001

Porr, C., Olson, K., & Hegadoren, K. (2010). Tiredness, fatigue, and exhaustion in the context of a major depressive disorder. *Qualitative Health Research, 20*(10), 1315–1326. https://doi.org/10.1177/1049732310370841

Poulsen, S., Lunn, S., & Sandros, C. (2010). Client experience of psychodynamic psychotherapy for bulimia nervosa: An interview study. *Psychotherapy: Theory, Research, Practice, Training, 47*(4), 469–483. https://doi.org/10.1037/a0021178

Prytz, M., Harkestad, K. N., Veseth, M., & Bjornestad, J. (2019). "It's not a life of war and conflict": experienced therapists' views on negotiating a therapeutic alliance in involuntary treatment. *Annals of General Psychiatry, 18*(1), 9. https://doi.org/10.1186/s12991-019-0234-6

Pugh, M.A., & Vetere, A. (2009). Lost in translation: an interpretative phenomenological analysis of mental health professionals' experiences of empathy in clinical work with an interpreter. *Psychology and Psychotherapy: Theory, Research and Practice, 82*(3), 305–321. https://doi.org/10.1348/147608308X397059

Råbu, M., & Haavind, H. (2018). Coming to terms: Client subjective experience of ending psychotherapy. *Counselling Psychology Quarterly, 31*(2), 223–242 https://doi.org/10.1080/09515070.2017.1296410

Råbu, M., & McLeod, J. (2018). Wisdom in professional knowledge: Why it can be valuable to listen to the voices of senior psychotherapists. *Psychotherapy Research, 28*(5), 776–792. https://doi.org/10.1080/10503307.2016.1265685

Råbu, M., Moltu, C., Binder, P. E., & McLeod, J. (2016). How does practising psychotherapy affect the personal life of the therapist? A qualitative inquiry of senior therapists' experiences. *Psychotherapy Research, 26*(6), 737–749. https://doi.org/10.1080/10503307.2015.1065354

Radcliffe, K., Masterson, C., & Martin, C. (2018). Clients' experience of nonresponse to psychological therapy: A qualitative analysis. *Counselling and Psychotherapy Research, 18*(2), 220–229. https://doi.org/10.1002/capr.12161

Rapsey, E. H., Burbach, F. R., & Reibstein, J. (2015). Exploring the process of family interventions for psychosis in relation to attachment, attributions and problem-maintaining cycles: an IPA study. *Journal of Family Therapy, 37*(4), 509–528. https://doi.org/10.1111/1467-6427.12085

Rasmussen, M.L., Dieserud, G., Dyregrov, K., & Haavind, H. (2014). Warning signs of suicide among young men. *Nordic Psychology, 66*(3), 153–167. https://doi.org/10.1080/19012276.2014.921576

Rasmussen, M.L., Haavind, H., Dieserud, G., & Dyregrov, K. (2014). Exploring vulnerability to suicide in the developmental history of young men: A psychological autopsy study. *Death Studies, 38*(9), 549–556. https://doi.org/10.1080/07481187.2013.780113

Redhead, S., Johnstone, L., & Nightingale, J. (2015). Clients' experiences of formulation in cognitive behaviour therapy. *Psychology and Psychotherapy: Theory, Research, and Practice, 88*(4), 453–467. https://doi.org/10.1111/papt.12054

Reid, M., & Osatuke, K. (2006). Acknowledging problematic voices: Processes occurring at early stages of conflict assimilation in patients with functional somatic disorder. *Psychology and Psychotherapy: Theory, Research and Practice, 79*(4), 539–555. https://doi.org/10.1348/147608305X90467

Rennie, D. L. (1994). Clients' deference in psychotherapy. *Journal of Counseling Psychology, 41*(4), 427–437. https://doi.org/10.1037/0022-0167.41.4.427

Rennie, D. L. (2000). Grounded theory methodology as methodical hermeneutics: Reconciling realism and relativism. *Theory & Psychology, 10*(4), 481–502. https://doi.org/10.1177/0959354300104003

Rennie, D. L. (2012). Qualitative research as methodical hermeneutics. *Psychological Methods, 17*(3), 385–398. https://doi.org/10.1037/a0029250

Rheker, J., Beisel, S., Kräling, S., & Rief, W. (2017). Rate and predictors of negative effects of psychotherapy in psychiatric and psychosomatic inpatients. *Psychiatry Research, 254*, 143–150. https://doi.org/10.1016/j.psychres.2017.04.042

Rice, L. N. & Greenberg, L. S. (1984). *Patterns of change: intensive analysis of psychotherapy process*. New York;: Guilford.

Richards D. A., Bazeley, P., Borglin, G., Craig, P., Emsley, R., Frost, J., Hill, J., Horwood, J., Hutchings, H.A., Jinks, C., & Montgomery, A. (2019). Integrating quantitative and qualitative data and findings when undertaking randomised controlled trials. *BMJ Open, 9*(11). https://doi.org/10.1136/bmjopen-2019-032081

Richards, J., Holttum, S., & Springham, N. (2016). How do "mental health professionals" who are also or have been "mental health service users" construct their identities? *Sage Open, 6*(1), 2158244015621348. https://doi.org/10.1177/2158244015621348

Richardson, C. B., Chesnut, R. P., Morgan, N. R., Bleser, J. A., Perkins, D. F., Vogt, D., Copeland, L.A., & Finley, E. (2020). Examining the factor structure of the moral injury events scale in a veteran sample. *Military Medicine, 185*(1–2), e75–e83.

Ridge, D., & Ziebland, S. (2012). Understanding depression through a 'coming out' framework. *Sociology of Health & Illness, 34*(5), 730–745. https://doi.org/10.1111/j.1467-9566.2011.01409.x

Robbins, R. R., Hill, J., & McWhirter, P. T. (2008). Conflicting epistemologies: A case study of a traditional American Indian in therapy. *Clinical Case Studies, 7*(5), 449–466. https://doi.org/10.1177/1534650108317649

Rocca, E., & Anjum, R. L. (2020). Causal evidence and dispositions in medicine and public health. *International Journal of Environmental Research and Public Health, 17*(6), 1813. https://doi.org/10.3390/ijerph17061813

Rodgers, B. (2018). More than just a measure. Exploring clients' experiences of using a standardised self-report questionnaire to evaluate counselling outcomes. *New Zealand Journal of Counselling, 38*(2), 90–112.

Rogers, C. R. (1942). *Counseling and psychotherapy*. Boston: Houghton Mifflin

Rolland, L., Dewaele, J. M., & Costa, B. (2017). Multilingualism and psychotherapy: exploring multilingual clients' experiences of language practices in psychotherapy. *International Journal of Multilingualism, 14*(1), 69–85. https://doi.org/10.1080/14790718.2017.1259009

Romaioli, D., & Faccio, E. (2012). When therapists do not know what to do: Informal types of eclecticism in psychotherapy. *Ricerca in Psicoterapia/Research in Psychotherapy: Psychopathology, Process and Outcome, 15*(1), 10–21. https://doi.org/10.4081/ripppo.2012.92

Rønnestad, M. H., & Skovholt, T. M. (2013). *The developing practitioner: Growth and stagnation of therapists and counselors*. New York, NY: Routledge/Taylor & Francis Group. https://doi.org/10.4324/9780203841402

Rozental, A., Castonguay, L., Dimidjian, S., Lambert, M., Shafran, R., Andersson, G., & Carlbring, P. (2018). Negative effects in psychotherapy: commentary and recommendations for future research and clinical practice. *BJPsych Open, 4*(4), 307–312. https://doi.org/10.1192/bjo.2018.42

Ryan, S., Hislop, J., & Ziebland, S. (2017). Do we all agree what "good health care" looks like? Views from those who are "seldom heard" in health research, policy and service improvement. *Health Expectations, 20*(5), 878–885. https://doi.org/10.1111/hex.12528

Safran, J. D., & Muran, J.C. (1996). The resolution of ruptures in the therapeutic alliance. *Journal of Consulting and Clinical Psychology, 64*(3), 447–458. https://doi.org/10.1037/0022-006X.64.3.447

Safran, J. D., & Muran, J.C. (2000). *Negotiating the therapeutic alliance: A relational treatment guide*. New York;: Guilford.

Sandell, R., & Wilczek, A. (2016). Another way to think about psychological change: experiential vs. incremental. *European Journal of Psychotherapy & Counselling, 18*(3), 228–251. https://doi.org/10.1080/13642537.2016.1214163

Sandelowski, M., & Leeman, J. (2012). Writing usable qualitative health research findings. *Qualitative Health Research*, 22(10), 1404–1413. https://doi.org/10.1177/1049732312450368

Schorr, Y., Stein, N. R., Maguen, S., Barnes, J. B., Bosch, J., & Litz, B. T. (2018). Sources of moral injury among war veterans: a qualitative evaluation. *Journal of Clinical Psychology*, 74(12), 2203–2218. https://doi.org/10.1002/jclp.22660

Seaman, E. B. (2016). Climate change on the therapist's couch: how mental health clinicians receive and respond to indirect psychological impacts of climate change in the therapeutic setting. *Dissertations, and Projects 1736*. hpps://scholarworks.smith.edu/theses/1736

Seidler, Z. E., Dawes, A. J., Rice, S. M., Oliffe, J. L., & Dhillon, H. M. (2016). The role of masculinity in men's help-seeking for depression: A systematic review. *Clinical Psychology Review*, 49, 106–118. https://doi.org/10.1016/j.cpr.2016.09.002

Sitter, K. C. (2017). Taking a closer look at photovoice as a participatory action research method. *Journal of Progressive Human Services*, 28(1), 36–48. https://doi.org/10.1080/10428232.2017.1249243

Slade, A. (2016). Attachment and adult psychotherapy: Theory, research, and practice. In J.Cassidy & P. Shaver, (Eds.), *The handbook of attachment: Theory, research, and clinical applications*, Third Edition (pp. 759–779). New York: Guilford Publications.

Smith-MacDonald, L., Raffin-Bouchal, S., Reay, G., Ewashen, C., Konnert, C., & Sinclair, S. (2020). Transitioning fractured identities: A grounded theory of veterans' experiences of operational stress injuries. *Traumatology*, 26(2), 235–245. https://doi.org/10.1037/trm0000232

Smith, M. S., Lawrence, V., & Sadler, E. (2019). Barriers to accessing mental health services for women with perinatal mental illness: systematic review and meta-synthesis of qualitative studies in the UK. *BMJ Open*, 9(1): e024803. https://doi.org/10.1136/bmjopen-2018-024803

Snape, C., Perren, S., Jones, L., & Rowland, N. (2003). Counselling-Why not? A qualitative study of people's accounts of not taking up counselling appointments. *Counselling and Psychotherapy Research*, 3(3), 239–245. https://doi.org/10.1080/14733140312331384412

Snow, K., Cheston, R., & Smart, C. (2015). 'Making sense' of dementia: Exploring the use of the MAPED to understand how couples process a dementia diagnosis. *Dementia*, 15(6), 1515–1533. https://doi.org/10.1177/1471301214564447

Solstad, S. M., Castonguay, L. G., & Moltu, C. (2019). Patients' experiences with routine outcome monitoring and clinical feedback systems: A systematic review and synthesis of qualitative empirical literature. *Psychotherapy Research*, 29(2), 157–170. https://doi.org/10.1080/10503307.2017.1326645

Sørensen, K.D., Råbu, M., & Wilberg, T. (2019). Struggling to be a person: lived experience of avoidant personality disorder. *Journal of Clinical Psychology*, 75(4), 664–680. https://doi.org/10.1002/jclp.22740

Spalding, B., Grove, J., & Rolfe, A. (2019). An exploration of Black, Asian and Minority Ethnic counsellors' experiences of working with White clients. *Counselling and Psychotherapy Research*, 19(1), 75–82. https://doi.org/10.1002/capr.12194

Speciale, M, Gess, J., & Speedlin, S. (2015). You don't look like a lesbian: A coautoethnography of intersectional identities in counselor education. *Journal of LGBT Issues in Counseling*, 9(4), 256–272. https://doi.org/10.1080/15538605.2015.1103678

Stänicke, L.I., Haavind, H., & Gullestad, S.E. (2018). How do young people understand their own self-harm? A meta-synthesis of adolescents' subjective experience of self-harm. *Adolescent Research Review*, 3, 173–191. https://doi.org/10.1007/s40894-018-0080-9

Stapley, E., Midgley, N., & Target, M. (2015). The experience of being the parent of an adolescent with a diagnosis of depression. *Journal of Child and Family Studies*, 25(2), 618–630. https://doi.org/10.1007/s10826-015-0237-0

Stapley, E., Target, M., & Midgley, N. (2017). The journey through and beyond mental health services in the UK: A typology of parents' ways of managing the crisis of their teenage child's depression. *Journal of Clinical Psychology*, 73(10), 1429–1441. https://doi.org/10.1002/jclp.22446

Stasiak, K., Parkin, A., Seymour, F., Lambie, I., Crengle, S., Pasene-Mizziebo, E., & Merry, S. (2013). Measuring outcome in child and adolescent mental health services: Consumers' views of measures. *Clinical Child Psychology & Psychiatry*, 18(4), 519–535. https://doi.org/10.1177/1359104512460860

Stiles, W. B. (2007). Theory-building case studies of counselling and psychotherapy. *Counselling and Psychotherapy Research*, 7(2), 122–127. https://doi.org/10.1080/14733140701356742

Stiles, W. B. (2009a). Logical operations in theory-building case studies. *Pragmatic Case Studies in Psychotherapy*, 5(3), 9–22. doi: 10.14713/pcsp.v5i3.973. https://doi.org/10.14713/pcsp.v5i3.973

Stiles, W. B. (2009b). Responsiveness as an obstacle for psychotherapy outcome research: It's worse than you think. *Clinical Psychology: Science and Practice*, 16(1), 86–91. https://doi.org/10.1111/j.1468-2850.2009.01148.x

Stiles, W. B. (2011). Coming to terms. *Psychotherapy Research*, 21(4), 367–384. https://doi.org/10.1080/10503307.2011.582186

Stiles, W. B. (2015). Theory-building, enriching, and fact-gathering: Alternative purposes of psychotherapy research. In O. Gelo, A. Pritz, & B. Rieken (Eds.), *Psychotherapy research: General issues, process, and outcome* (pp. 159–179). New York: Springer-Verlag. https://doi.org/10.1007/978-3-7091-1382-0_8

Stiles, W. B. (2017). Theory-building case studies. In D. Murphy (Ed.), *Counselling psychology: A textbook for study and practice* (pp. 439–452). Chichester, UK: Wiley.

Stiles, W. B. (2018). Assimilation of problematic voices and the historicity of signs: How culture enters psychotherapy. In A. Konopka, H. J. M. Hermans, & M. M. Gonçalves (Eds.) *Handbook of dialogical selftheory and psychotherapy: Bridging Psychotherapeutic and Cultural Traditions* (pp. 56–72). London: Routledge. https://doi.org/10.4324/9781315145693-5

Stiles, W. B. (2020). Bricoleurs and theory-building qualitative research: Responses to responsiveness. In T. G. Lindstad, E. Stänicke, & J. Valsiner (Eds.), *Respect for thought: Jan Smedslund's legacy for psychology* (pp. 343–359). New York: Springer.

Stiles, W. B., Caro Gabalda, I., & Ribeiro, E. (2016). Exceeding the therapeutic zone of proximal development as a clinical error. *Psychotherapy*, 53(3), 268–272. https://doi.org/10.1037/pst0000061

Stiles, W. B., Elliott, R., Llewelyn, S. P., Firth-Cozens, J. A., Margison, F. R., Shapiro, D. A., & Hardy, G. (1990). Assimilation of problematic experiences by clients in psychotherapy. *Psychotherapy*, 27(3), 411–420. https://doi.org/10.1037/0033-3204.27.3.411

Stiles, W. B., Morrison, L. A., Haw, S. K., Harper, H., Shapiro, D. A., & Firth-Cozens, J. (1991). Longitudinal study of assimilation in exploratory psychotherapy. *Psychotherapy*, 28(2), 195–206. https://doi.org/10.1037/0033-3204.28.2.195

Stiles, W. B., Osatuke, K., Glick, M. J., & Mackay, H. C. (2004). Encounters between internal voices generate emotion: An elaboration of the assimilation model. In H. H. Hermans & G. Dimaggio (Eds.), *The dialogical self in psychotherapy* (pp. 91–107). New York;: Brunner-Routledge. https://doi.org/10.4324/9780203314616_chapter_6

Stiles, W. B., Shapiro, D. A., & Elliott, R. (1986). "Are all psychotherapies equivalent?" *American Psychologist*, 41(2), 165–180. https://doi.org/10.1037/0003-066X.41.2.165

Strasser, J., & Gruber, H. (2015) Learning processes in the professional development of mental health counselors: knowledge restructuring and illness script formation. *Advances in Health Sciences Education*, 20(2), 515–530. https://doi.org/10.1007/s10459-014-9545-1

Stratton, P., McGovern, M., Wetherell, A., & Farrington, C. (2006). Family therapy practitioners researching the reactions of practitioners to an outcome measure. *Australian and New Zealand Journal of Family Therapy*, 27(4), 199–207. https://doi.org/10.1002/j.1467-8438.2006.tb00722.x

Stringer,J.V.,Levitt,H.M.,Berman,J.S.,& Mathews,S.S.(2010).A study of silent disengagement and distressing emotion in psychotherapy. *Psychotherapy Research*, 20(5), 495–510. https://doi.org/10.1080/10503301003754515

Strupp, H. (1998). The Vanderbilt I study revisited. *Psychotherapy Research*, 8(1), 17–29. https://doi.org/10.1093/ptr/8.1.17

Sundet, R., Kim, H. S. Karlsson, B. E., Borg, M., Sælør, K. T. & Ness, O. (2020b). A heuristic model for collaborative practice - Part 2: Development of the collaborative, dialogue-based clinical practice model for community mental health and substance abuse care. *International Journal of Mental Health Systems*, 14, 43. https://doi.org/10.1186/s13033-020-00377-4

Sundet, R., Kim, H. S. Karlsson, B. E., Borg, M., Sælør, K. T., & Ness, O. (2020a). A heuristic model for collaborative practice - Part 1: A meta-synthesis of empirical findings on collaborative strategies in community mental health and substance abuse practice. *International Journal of Mental Health Systems*, 14, 42. https://doi.org/10.1186/s13033-020-00376-5

Swift, J. K., & Greenberg, R. P. (2012). Premature discontinuation in adult psychotherapy: A meta-analysis. *Journal of Consulting and Clinical Psychology*, *80*(4), 547–559. https://doi.org/10.1037/a0028226

Swift, J. K., Greenberg, R. P., Whipple, J. L., & Kominiak, N. (2012). Practice recommendations for reducing premature termination in therapy. *Professional Psychology: Research and Practice*, *43*(4), 379–387. https://doi.org/10.1037/a0028291

Talbert, F. S., & Pipes, R. B. (1988). Informed consent for psychotherapy: Content analysis of selected forms. *Professional Psychology: Research and Practice*, *19*(2), 131–132. https://doi.org/10.1037/0735-7028.19.2.131

Tasca, G. A., Sylvestre, J., Balfour, L., Chyurlia, L., Evans, J., Fortin-Langelier, B., Francis, K., Gandhi, J., Huehn, L., Hunsley, J., Joyce, A. S., Kinley, J., Koszycki, D., Leszcz, M., Lybanon-Daigle, V., Mercer, D., Ogrodniczuk, J. S., Presniak, M., Ravitz, P., ... Wilson, B. (2015). What clinicians want: Findings from a psychotherapy practice research network survey. *Psychotherapy*, *52*(1), 1–11. https://doi-org.ezproxy.lib.umb.edu/10.1037/a0038252

Thériault, A., & Gazzola, N. (2006). What are the sources of feelings of incompetence in experienced therapists? *Counselling Psychology Quarterly*, *19*(4), 313–330. https://doi.org/10.1080/09515070601090113

Thompson, M. N., Cole, O. D., & Nitzarim, R. S. (2012). Recognizing social class in the psychotherapy relationship: A grounded theory exploration of low-income clients. *Journal of Counseling Psychology*, *59*(2), 208–221. https://doi.org/10.1037/a0027534

Thyme, K. E., Wiberg, B., Lundman, B., & Graneheim, U. H. (2013). Qualitative content analysis in art psychotherapy research: Concepts, procedures, and measures to reveal the latent meaning in pictures and the words attached to the pictures. *The Arts in Psychotherapy*, *40*(1), 101–107 . https://doi.org/10.1016/j.aip.2012.11.007

Tikkanen, S., Stiles, W. B., & Leiman, M. (2011). Parent development in clinical child neurological assessment process: Encounters with the assimilation model. *Psychotherapy Research*, *21*(5), 593–607. https://doi.org/10.1080/10503307.2011.594817

Topor, A., Bøe, T. D., & Larsen, I. B. (2018). Small things, micro-affirmations and helpful professionals everyday recovery-orientated practices according to persons with mental health problems. *Community Mental Health Journal*, *54*(8), 1212–1220. https://doi.org/10.1007/s10597-018-0245-9

Tormoen, M. (2019). Gaslighting: How pathological labels can harm psychotherapy clients. *Journal of Humanistic Psychology*, https://doi.org/10.1177/0022167819864258

Truijens, F. L. (2017). Do the numbers speak for themselves? A critical analysis of procedural objectivity in psychotherapeutic efficacy research. *Synthese*, *194*(12), 4721–4740. https://doi.org/10.1007/s11229-016-1188-8

Truijens, F. L., Desmet, M., De Coster, E., Uyttenhove, H., Deeren, B., & Meganck, R. (2019). When quantitative measures become a qualitative storybook: a phenomenological case analysis of validity and performativity of questionnaire administration in psychotherapy research. *Qualitative Research in Psychology*, 1–44. https://doi.org/10.1080/14780887.2019.1579287

Tummala-Narra, P., Claudius, M., Letendre, P. J., Sarbu, E., Teran, V., & Villalba, W. (2018). Psychoanalytic psychologists' conceptualizations of cultural competence in psychotherapy. *Psychoanalytic Psychology*, *35*(1), 46–59. https://doi.org/10.1037/pap0000150

Tutani, L., Eldred, C., & Sykes, C. (2018). Practitioners' experiences of working collaboratively with interpreters to provide CBT and guided self-help (GSH) in IAPT; a thematic analysis. *The Cognitive Behaviour Therapist*, 11, e3. https://doi.org/10.1017/S1754470X17000204

Valentine, S. E., & Shepherd, J. C. (2018). A systematic review of social stress and mental health among transgender and gender non-conforming people in the United States. *Clinical Psychology Review*, *66*, 24–38. https://doi.org/10.1016/j.cpr.2018.03.003

van Rijn, B., Chryssafidou, E., Falconer, C. J. & Stiles, W. B. (2019). Digital images as meaning bridges: Case study of assimilation using avatar software in counselling with a 14-year-old boy. *Counselling and Psychotherapy Research*, *19*(3), 252–263. https://doi.org/10.1002/capr.12230

Vargas, A., Hanson, T., Kraus, D., Drescher, K., & Foy, D. (2013). Moral injury themes in combat veterans' narrative responses from the National Vietnam Veterans' Readjustment Study. *Traumatology*, *19*(3), 243–250. https://doi.org/10.1177/1534765613476099

Varvin, S., & Stiles, W. B. (1999). Emergence of severe traumatic experiences: An assimilation analysis of psychoanalytic therapy with a political refugee. *Psychotherapy Research*, *9*(3), 381–404. https://doi.org/10.1093/ptr/9.3.381

Verdinelli, S., Biever, J., & Santiago-Rivera, A. (2013). Therapists' experiences of cross-ethnic therapy with Spanish-speaking Latina/o clients. *Journal of Latina/o Psychology*, *1*(4), 227–242. https://doi.org/10.1037/lat0000004

Veseth, M., Binder, P. E., & Stige, S. H. (2017). "If there's no stability around them": experienced therapists' view on the role of patients' social world in recovery in bipolar disorder. *International Journal of Mental Health Systems*, *11*(1), 55. https://doi.org/10.1186/s13033-017-0166-y

Villaggi, B., Provencher, H., Coulombe, S., Meunier, S., Radziszewski, S., Hudon, C., & Houle, J. (2015). Self-management strategies in recovery from mood and anxiety disorders. *Global Qualitative Nursing Research*, *2*, 2333393615606092. https://doi.org/10.1177/2333393615606092

Vulcan, M. (2016). "I'm a translating body": Therapists' experiences working with children diagnosed with autism spectrum disorder. *Journal of Psychotherapy Integration*, *26*(3), 326–337. https://doi.org/10.1037/int0000026

Wampold, B. E., & Imel, Z. (2015). *The great psychotherapy debate* (2nd ed.). Mahwah, NJ: Erlbaum. https://doi.org/10.4324/9780203582015

Watson, J. B., & Rayner, R. (1920). Conditioned emotional reactions. *Journal of Experimental Psychology*, *3*(1), 1–14. https://doi.org/10.1037/h0069608

Wendt, D. C., & Gone, J. P. (2016). Integrating professional and indigenous therapies: An urban American Indian narrative clinical case study. *The Counseling Psychologist*, *44*(5), 695–729. https://doi.org/10.1177/0011000016638741

Wendt, D. C., Gone, J. P., & Nagata, D. K. (2015). Potentially harmful therapy and multicultural counseling: Bridging two disciplinary discourses. *The Counseling Psychologist*, *43*(3), 334–358. https://doi.org/10.1177/0011000014548280

Werbart, A., Annevall, A., & Hillblom, J. (2019). Successful and less successful psychotherapies compared: Three therapists and their six contrasting cases. *Frontiers in Psychology*, *10*. https://doi.org/10.3389/fpsyg.2019.00816

Werbart, A., Missios, P., Waldenström, F., & Lilliengren, P. (2019). "It was hard work every session": Therapists' view of successful psychoanalytic treatments. *Psychotherapy Research*, *29*(3), 354–371. https://doi.org/10.1080/10503307.2017.1349353

Werbart, A., von Below, C., Brun, J., & Gunnarsdottir, H. (2015). "Spinning one's wheels": Nonimproved patients view their psychotherapy. *Psychotherapy Research*, *25*(5), 546–564. https://doi.org/10.1080/10503307.2014.989291

Westmacott, R., & Hunsley, J. (2017). Psychologists' perspectives on therapy termination and the use of therapy engagement/retention strategies. *Clinical Psychology & Psychotherapy*, *24*(3), 687–696. https://doi.org/10.1002/cpp.2037

Westra, H. A., Aviram, A., Barnes, M., & Angus, L. (2010). Therapy was not what I expected: Preliminary qualitative analysis of concordance between client expectations and experience of cognitive-behavioural therapy. *Psychotherapy Research*, *20*(4), 436–446. https://doi.org/10.1080/10503301003657395

Wigg, R., Cushway, D., & Neal, A. (2011). Personal therapy for therapists and trainees: A theory of reflective practice from a review of the literature. *Reflective Practice*, *12*(3), 347–359. https://doi.org/10.1080/14623943.2011.571866

Williams, D. C. & Levitt, H. M. (2007a). A qualitative investigation of eminent therapists' values within psychotherapy: Developing integrative principles for moment-to-moment psychotherapy practice. *Journal of Psychotherapy Integration*, *17*(2), 159–184. https://doi.org/10.1037/1053-0479.17.2.159

Williams, D. C. & Levitt, H. M. (2007b). Principles for facilitating agency in psychotherapy. *Psychotherapy Research*, *17*(1), 66–82. https://doi.org/10.1080/10503300500469098

Williams, D., & Levitt, H. M. (2008). Clients' experiences of difference with therapists: Sustaining faith in psychotherapy. *Psychotherapy Research*, *18*(3), 256–270. https://doi.org/10.1080/10503300701561545

Willox, A. C., Harper, S. L., Ford, J. D., Edge, V. L., Landman, K., Houle, K., Blake, S., & Wolfrey, C. (2013). Climate change and mental health: an exploratory case study from Rigolet, Nunatsiavut, Canada. *Climatic Change*, *121*(2), 255–270. https://doi.org/10.1007/s10584-013-0875-4

Wilson, J., James, H., & Gabriel, L. (2016). Making sense of loss and grief: the value of in-depth assessments. *Bereavement Care, 35*(2), 67–77. https://doi .org/10.1080/02682621.2016.1218127

Wilson, J., & Stiles, W. B. (submitted). Assimilation in bereavement: Charting the process of grief recovery in the case of Sophie. Manuscript submitted for publication.

Windle, E., Tee, H., Sabitova, A., Jovanovic, N., Priebe, S., & Carr, C. (2020). Association of patient treatment preference with dropout and clinical outcomes in adult psychosocial mental health interventions: A systematic review and meta-analysis. *JAMA Psychiatry, 77*(3), 294–302. https://doi .org/10.1001/jamapsychiatry.2019.3750

Wiseman, H., & Atzil-Slonim , D. (2018). Closeness and distance dynamics in the therapeutic relationship. In O. Tishby & H. Wiseman (Eds.), *Developing the therapeutic relationship: Integrating case studies, research, and practice.* (pp. 81–103). Washington, DC: American Psychological Association. https://doi.org/10.1037/0000093-005

Wiseman, H., & Rice, L. N. (1989). Sequential analyses of therapist-client interaction during change events: A task-focused approach. *Journal of Consulting and Clinical Psychology, 57*(2), 281–286. https://doi.org/ 10.1037/0022-006X.57.2.281

Wolpert, M., Curtis-Tyler, K., & Edbrooke-Childs, J. (2016). A qualitative exploration of patient and clinician views on patient reported outcome measures in child mental health and diabetes services. *Administration and Policy in Mental Health and Mental Health Services Research, 43*(3), 309–315. https://doi.org/10.1007/s10488-014-0586-9

Worden, J.W. (2009). *Grief counselling and grief therapy. a handbook for the mental health practitioner*, 4th edn. New York: Routledge. https://doi .org/10.1891/9780826101211

Wu, M. B., & Levitt, H. M. (2020). A qualitative meta-analytic review of the therapist responsiveness literature: Guidelines for practice and training. *Journal of Contemporary Psychotherapy.* Advance online publication. https:// doi.org/10.1007/s10879-020-09450-y

Ziebland, S. U. E., & Wyke, S. (2012). Health and illness in a connected world: how might sharing experiences on the internet affect people's health? *The Milbank Quarterly, 90*(2), 219–249. https://doi.org/ 10.1111/j.1468-0009.2012.00662.x

PART **IV**

THERAPEUTIC
APPROACHES AND FORMATS

•

CHAPTER 12

RESEARCH ON DYNAMIC THERAPIES

JACQUES P BARBER, J CHRISTOPHER MURAN, KEVIN S MCCARTHY, JOHN R KEEFE, AND SIGAL ZILCHA-MANO

Abstract

The chapter focuses on the empirical research accumulating over the years on psychodynamic treatment (PDT), especially research published since the previous edition of this book. The chapter contains meta-analyses demonstrating the efficacy of PDT across mental health disorders (depressive, anxiety, trauma, and personality disorders), and provides several examples of effective PDT implementations in the community. The chapter discusses the empirical literature on predictors and moderators of good prognosis and that on central mechanisms of change in PDT: alliance, insight, defense style and mechanisms, relationship rigidity, quality of object relations, and reflective functioning. We review the literature on the use of PDT techniques and their associations with treatment outcome. We end with clinical implications and directions for future research.

OVERVIEW

INTRODUCTION

Once psychoanalysis, or psychodynamic therapy, ruled the earth. Unlike the dinosaurs, it did not disappear but rather sprouted many variations and new offspring. Today those offspring have forgotten everything about their origins.

This chapter is a revision and an update of Barber et al. (2013) published in the 6th edition of the *Handbook*.

The main ideas behind psychodynamic therapy PDT are at the foundation of many forms of psychotherapy. Many psychotherapies evolved from psychoanalysis, including cognitive and humanistic therapies. Some of the important theorists behind these relatively newer approaches were trained as psychoanalysts (e.g., A. T. Beck, Fritz Perls, Albert Ellis) and for various reasons were dissatisfied with major aspects of psychoanalysis. It was for this reason that these influential individuals went on to make improvements to psychoanalysis and developed their own version of therapy. In their attempts to define their new approach to treatment, they emphasized what was different from psychoanalysis and perhaps minimized what was indeed borrowed from it (e.g., the importance of the therapeutic relationship, the emphasis on emotion and encouraging a more realistic view of the world). However, more relevant to the present volume is the emergence of psychodynamically oriented researchers in the past three decades. Specifically, there has been an increase in empirical evidence for the efficacy of PDTs for specific disorders as well as investigations on how and for whom PDT might be helpful and how, as we will show.

CHARACTERISTICS OF PDT

This chapter covers approaches to psychotherapy generally referred to as *psychodynamic* or *psychoanalytic*. PDT—as well as cognitive-behavior therapy (CBT) for that matter—represents a family of therapies. As in all large families, the degrees of divergence and agreement vary quite a bit. Some members of the families are not even on speaking terms and sometimes even speak different languages. Thus, by necessity, this chapter presents a narrow representation of the psychodynamic family of therapies; those that received more empirical attention. Under this large umbrella, there are many approaches, which vary in their understanding of what is the nature of "disease" or "problem" (pathology) and on how to resolve or help deal with them. Most schools of therapy derive their view of pathology and intervention from a theory of human nature that includes, among others, a theory of personality and development. We hesitate to state a view of human nature that would be acceptable to all streams of PDT. We would say that psychodynamics would involve recognizing that people are not always aware of the reasons for their behavior, that human motivations are to some extent rooted biologically, and that they are often driven by unknown motives.

Similarly, it would be wonderful if we could easily define what PDT is and what it is not. There have been several attempts to characterize psychodynamic psychotherapy (e.g., Blagys & Hilsenroth, 2000); however, it would be almost impossible to find a set of necessary and sufficient conditions to define what is psychodynamic. Nevertheless, PDT can be captured by the following characteristics: focus on unconscious processes; focus on affect, cognitions, wishes, fantasies and interpersonal relationships; lack of traditional homework; relatively less guidance, use of open-ended questions; use of interpretation and clarification; consideration of the transference and countertransference; and use of the therapeutic relationship to increase self-awareness, self-understanding, and exploration. Because it is not possible to create an unambiguous list, some treatments like Mentalization-Based Treatment (MBT, Luyten et al., 2020) may be referred to as PDT, whereas others, like the Cognitive Behavioral Analysis System of Psychotherapy (CBASP, McCullough, 2003), which also regards maladaptive interactions with significant others early in life as causing depression later in life, may not be defined as PDT.

One of the questions we need to address in writing this chapter is whether interpersonal therapy (IPT; Klerman et al., 1984), popular in the treatment of depression, is a form of PDT. IPT is similar to many PDTs because it focuses on underlying schemas and repetitive scenarios involving loss and transition, and uses empathy, exploration of painful affects, and (rarely) transference interpretations. It differs in that it is highly focused and includes a significant educational component. In fact, there is research to suggest that in practice IPT is more like CBT than PDT (e.g., Ablon & Jones, 2002). Our opinion is that depending on the training of the IPT therapists (e.g., their previous exposure to PDT or the extent of their IPT training), the differences between IPT and PDT can be elusive. Some early meta-analyses of PDT (e.g., Leichsenring 2001) included studies of IPT and showed that the overall meta-analytic results were unchanged if excluded. To be conservative, we decided not to include IPT as a form of PDT therapy, mainly due to its explicit rejection of some critical dynamic concepts.

In this chapter we cover three general aspects of PDT: its efficacy and effectiveness for symptom improvement; the therapeutic alliance and its role in PDT; and processes of change,

including mechanisms and outcome unique to PDT and the correlates of PDT techniques.

RESEARCH ON THE EFFICACY OF PDT

The Efficacy and Effectiveness of Psychodynamic Therapies

Psychodynamic therapies are effective and evidence-based treatments for many common mental disorders (Leichsenring et al., 2015). At the time of writing, there are at least 243 randomized trials of psychodynamic approaches for mental illness (Lilliengren, 2019).

Psychodynamic therapies have demonstrated efficacy compared to control groups in the treatment of mood (Driessen et al., 2015), anxiety (Keefe et al., 2014), personality (Cristea et al., 2017; Keefe et al., 2020), and somatic disorders (Abbass et al., 2009), with effects lasting into posttreatment follow-up. In the treatment of suicidality and self-harm, psychodynamic therapies are more effective than control treatments, such as treatment as usual (TAU), routine psychiatric care, enhanced usual care, placebo, or any other comparison, including with a different psychological therapy (Briggs et al., 2019). Long-term psychodynamic therapies for so-called complex or chronic disorders (e.g., borderline personality disorder; treatment-resistant depression [Leichsenring & Rabung, 2018]) and short-term psychodynamic therapies for common mental disorders (Abbass et al., 2014) have both been demonstrated to outperform active and inactive controls. A meta-analysis applying statistical equivalence criteria to trials comparing psychodynamic therapies to other gold-standard treatments found no evidence for nonequivalence between PDTs and these treatments (Steinert et al., 2017). In treatment of unipolar mood disorders, adding short-term psychodynamic therapy to psychopharmacology improves depression symptoms over medications alone ($g = 0.26$ at termination; $g = 0.50$ at follow-up; Driessen et al., 2020). There is also no evidence that trials involving PDT are on average of any different quality than those of cognitive-behavioral therapy; across trials treating depression, rated quality levels are indistinguishable (Thoma et al., 2012).

Although few studies to date have evaluated the real-world effectiveness of PDT, the findings they produced are promising. A pilot study of 40 patients indicated moderate-to-large effect sizes in favor of the dynamic psychotherapy over TAU (Connolly Gibbons et al., 2012). A larger study compared the effectiveness of PDT and CBT (Connolly Gibbons et al., 2016). In this trial, 237 adult outpatients with major depressive disorder seeking treatment at a large private, nonprofit organization were randomized to 16 sessions of either dynamic psychotherapy or cognitive therapy, delivered over five months. Findings suggest that dynamic psychotherapy is not inferior to cognitive therapy in reducing depression. Other studies focused on psychodynamic interpersonal therapy (PIT) in routine clinical practice settings, and demonstrated reliable and clinically significant change following the treatment in a sample of 62 patients (Paley et al., 2008). Although the findings based on the effectiveness trial showed less favorable improvement than generally demonstrated in efficacy trials, they were comparable with reports of the delivery of other therapies, such as CBT, in routine practice settings (Paley et al., 2008). Another study compared the effectiveness of CBT, person-centered, and PDT in a sample of 5,613 patients receiving treatment in primary-care routine practice in the UK. The findings suggest that all active treatments showed equivalent effectiveness. Similarly, in a recent study based on 147 patients, dynamic interpersonal therapy showed equivalence with CBT on most outcomes, and greater effectiveness than a low-intensity comparison treatment (Fonagy et al., 2019). Although additional studies are needed, the research reported above demonstrates the effectiveness of PDT in the community.

A common feature of psychodynamic treatments applied in clinical trials is that they are manualized within a specific psychodynamic treatment framework. For instance, transference-focused psychotherapy entails focus on interpreting paired representations of self- and other and their linked affects in the transference and other relationships (Yeomans et al., 2015), while supportive-expressive therapies organize around identifying and interpreting a patient's core conflictual relationship theme(s), which entails a wish, an expected response from the other, and one's reaction to that response (Luborsky, 1984). These formulations and the interventions derived from them often direct the therapist's attention to common dynamics or experiences surrounding particular symptoms or personalities. Panic-focused psychodynamic therapy for example encourages therapists to listen for, clarify, and interpret the links between panic symptoms and themes of separation/individuation, anger/assertion, guilt, and excitement/sexuality (Busch et al., 2012).

In the previous edition of this chapter (Barber et al., 2013), we conducted meta-analyses for psychodynamic therapies treating depressive, anxiety/trauma, and personality disorders. In the current chapter, we update the most recent meta-analysis of psychodynamic therapy for depressive disorders (Driessen et al., 2015, who should be strongly acknowledged for providing their meta-analytic data to be updated) and our meta-analysis of anxiety (Keefe et al., 2014). We also introduce a new, systematic meta-analysis of personality disorder treatments based on our previous meta-analysis for personality disorders. We updated these existing analyses with studies from the Lilliengren list of psychodynamic trials (Lilliengren, 2019). Moreover, for the personality disorders analysis we conducted a systematic search of PubMed and PsycINFO, in preparation for a separate publication (Keefe et al., 2020). Citations for studies included in the meta analyses can be found in our Supplemental References.

Methods

Random effects meta-analyses were conducted in the *R* statistical computing environment using the *R* package *metafor* (Viechtbauer, 2010). Our random effects analyses employed the Sidik-Jonkman estimator (Sidik & Jonkman, 2002) and the Knapp-Hartung adjustment to the standard errors (Hartung & Knapp, 2001), which have been suggested in tandem to produce more nominally accurate confidence intervals when including small studies and in the presence of between-study heterogeneity (IntHout et al., 2014). We analyzed a given comparison for a given outcome if at least three effect sizes were available.

We also performed sensitivity tests for leaving any one study out, for comparisons that had at least four studies. For sensitivity analyses, we note any findings changing statistical significance at $p < .05$, effect size changes ($d \geq + - 0.20$), or changes in heterogeneity (I^2 change $\geq 15\%$). Data used for final analyses can be found in the online supplemental materials.

Heterogeneity of effect sizes was described using the I^2 statistic (Higgins et al., 2003), with 0% reflecting no heterogeneity, 25% reflecting low heterogeneity, 50% reflecting moderate heterogeneity, and 75%+ reflecting high heterogeneity. Heterogeneity indicates between-study differences in effect sizes that are not attributable to within-study sampling error.

To explore common patterns of effect sizes and sample size distributions that may indicate the presence of publication bias, both Egger's regression test (Egger et al., 1997) and the Henmi and Copas method (Henmi & Copas, 2010) of detecting possible publication bias were employed. For comparisons of psychodynamic therapy with control groups, Rosenberg's variant of the fail-safe *N* was calculated (Rosenberg, 2005).

Depressive Disorders

Relative to Driessen and colleagues' (2015) meta-analysis, 10 new trials were included, of which 8 were published after 2015, summing to a total of 27 overall included studies (see Table 12.1). Trials were included if patients were considered depressed by meeting specified criteria for major depressive disorder or another mood disorder, or if they presented an elevated score on a standardized measure of depression. Outcomes used for these meta-analyses were the combination of self-report (e.g., BDI, PHQ-9) or assessor-report (e.g., HAM-D) depression measures utilized in identified trials (see Table 12.1). When continuous outcome measures were not available, diagnostic remission rates from major depression were transformed into *d*-type effect sizes.

Controlled Effect Size. PDT was superior to control conditions in improving depression symptoms with a medium effect size ($g = -0.58$ [95% CI: -0.33, -0.83], $SE = 0.11$, $p < .001$, $k = 12$), albeit with a medium-large amount of between-study heterogeneity ($I^2 = 63.19\%$). There was no evidence of publication bias.

Whether the control condition was a wait-list ($g = -1.14$ [95% CI: -1.66, -0.62], $SE = 0.23$, $p < .001$, $k = 3$) or an active control (TAU, enhanced TAU, low intensity therapy, pill placebo; $g = -0.48$ [95% CI: -0.68, -0.27], $SE = 0.09$, $p < 0.001$, $k = 9$) explained 41.9% of the between-study heterogeneity in effect sizes ($F[1,10] = 7.06$, $p = .024$). A wait-list comparison produced significantly larger effect sizes.

Active Treatment Comparisons: Termination. Psychodynamic therapies did not significantly differ from other active treatments in depression outcomes ($g = -0.01$ [95% CI: -0.34, 0.32], $SE = 0.16$, $p = .944$, $k = 20$). However, there was very large between-study heterogeneity ($I^2 = 90.05\%$) that was driven in large part by a single very large-effect outlier comparing long-term psychodynamic therapy with long-term antidepressant monotherapy (Bastos et al., 2015; $g = -2.53$ in favor of PDT; when this study is removed $g = 0.10$ [95%

TABLE 12.1   Included Studies of Depression

Study	Mood disorder	Psychodynamic therapy group(s)	Comparison groups	Follow-up (months)	Total / overall quality score
Ajilchi et al. (2013)	MDD	15 sessions ISTDP ($n = 16$)	WLC ($n = 16$)	None	10 / 1
Barber et al. (2012a)	Chronic MDD	20 sessions SE ($n = 51$)	ADP ($n = 55$), PL ($n = 50$)	None	43 / 6
Barkham et al. (1999)	Subsyndromal, dysthymia, mild MDD	2 weekly sessions then 1 session 3 months later DIT-1 ($n = 54$)	VBCBT ($n = 62$)	12	29 / 4
Bastos et al. (2015)	Moderate severity MDD	2 years LTPP ($n = 90$)	ADP ($n = 91$)	None	25 / 4
Carrington et al. (1979)	Depressive syndrome (BDI 20–40)	12 sessions BDT ($n = 10$)	12 sessions CBT ($n = 10$), WLC ($n = 10$)	None	?
Connolly Gibbons et al. (2016)	MDD	16 sessions SE ($n = 118$)	16 sessions CBT ($n = 119$)	None	38 / 6.5
Cooper et al. (2003)	Postpartum	10 sessions PIPT ($n = 45$)	CBT ($n = 42$), NDC ($n = 47$), TAU ($n = 50$)	55	37 / 5
de Roten et al. (2017)	MDD	12 sessions IBPP+TAU ($n = 76$)	TAU ($n = 73$)	9	37 / 6
Fonagy et al. (2015)	Treatment resistant MDD	60 sessions LTPP+TAU ($n = 67$)	TAU ($n = 62$)	24	40.5 / 6.5
Fonagy et al. (2019)	MDD	16 sessions DIT-2 ($n = 73$)	14 to 18 sessions CBT ($n = 20$); 9 sessions LIT ($n = 54$)	None	33.5/ 5.5
Gallagher & Thompson (1982)	Geriatric MDD	16 sessions over 12 weeks BRT ($n = 10$)	CT ($n = 10$), BT ($n = 10$)	12	27 / 4
Gallagher-Thompson & Steffen (1994)	Geriatric major, minor, or intermittent depressive disorder	16–20 sessions BDT ($n = 30$)	CBT ($n = 36$)	3	27 / 6
Hersen et al. (1984)	MDD	12 sessions BDT+PL (undefined) ($n = 22$)	SST+PL ($n = 25$), ADP ($n = 14$)	None	31 / 4
Jakobsen et al. (2014)	MDD	18 individual and 18 group mentalization-inspired therapy ($n = 20$	18 individual and 18 group mindfulness-based CBT ($n = 22$)	None	28 / 4
Knekt & Lindfors, (2004) / Knekt et al. (2008)	Depressive disorders	Avg. 18.5 sessions BDT ($n = 79$)	9.8 sessions SFT ($n = 84$)	29	36 / 5

(Continued)

TABLE 12.1 (CONTINUED)

Study	Mood disorder	Psychodynamic therapy group(s)	Comparison groups	Follow-up (months)	Total / overall quality score
Maina et al. (2005)	Dysthymia, minor depressive disorder, or adjustment disorder with depressed mood	Avg. 20 sessions BDT (*n* = 10)	SP (*n* = 10), WLC (*n* = 10)	6	22 / 3
Rosso et al. (2013)	Mild or moderate depressive disorder	Avg. 18.6 sessions BDT (*n* = 33)	Avg. 16.9 sessions SP (*n* = 55)	6	31 / 5
Salminen et al. (2008)	MDD	16 sessions BDT (*n* = 26)	ADP (*n* = 25)	None	28 / 5
Shapiro et al. (1994)	Mild, moderate, and severe MDD	8 or 16 sessions of DIT-1 (*n* = 57)	8 or 16 sessions of CBT (*n* = 59)	12	35 / 7
Thompson, Gallagher & Breckenridge (1987)	MDD	16–20 sessions BDT (*n* = 24 before wait-list integration, 30 post)	BT (*n* = 30 post wait-list), CT (*n* = 31 post wait-list), WLC (*n* = 19)	24	18 / 4
Thyme et al. (2007)	Dysthymia or subsyndromal depression	Avg. 21 sessions BDT (*n* = 21)	AT (*n* = 18)	3	17 / 3
Town et al. (2017)	Treatment resistant MDD	20 sessions ISTDP (*n* = 30)	20 sessions TAU (*n* = 30)	None	41 / 6.5
Vitriol et al. (2009)	MDD with childhood trauma	Avg. 12 sessions BDT (*n* = 44)	Enhanced TAU (*n* = 43)	3	27 / 4

ADP = antidepressant treatment; AT = art therapy; BDT = brief dynamic therapy; BT = behavior therapy; CBT = cognitive behavior therapy; CT = cognitive therapy; DIT-1 = dynamic interpersonal therapy (Shapiro model); DIT-2 = dynamic interpersonal therapy (Lemma model); IBPP = intensive brief psychodynamic psychotherapy; ISTDP = intensive short-term dynamic psychotherapy; LTPP = long-term psychodynamic psychotherapy; NDC = non-directive counseling; PIPT = parent-infant psychodynamic therapy; PL = placebo; SE = supportive-expressive psychotherapy; SFT = solution-focused therapy; SP = supportive psychotherapy; SST = social skills training; TAU = treatment as usual; VBCBT = very brief cognitive behavior therapy

CI: –0.06, 0.26], *SE* = 0.08, *p* = .211, I² = 62.44%). In this reduced sample, there was limited evidence for publication bias using Egger's regression test (*t*[17] = –1.96, *p* = .067); the trim and fill procedure estimated 3 missing studies on the left side of the estimate (toward favoring PDT), but the overall result was unaffected (*g* = –0.03 [95% CI: –0.23, 0.17, *p* = .762).

Year of study was a significant predictor of effect size, such that more recent studies reported relatively more favorable effects for PDT (*B* = –0.01 [95% CI: –0.03, –0.00], *SE* = 0.01, *p* = .014), explaining approximately 30% of between-study heterogeneity. Studies in which CBT was the comparison condition did not report reliably different effect sizes from other studies (*g* difference for CBT studies = +0.24, *p* = .132).

Active Treatment Comparisons: Follow-up. At posttreatment follow-up, there remained no significant differences between PDT and other active treatments (*g* = –0.01 [95% CI: –0.31, 0.29], *SE* = 0.13, *p* = .942, *k* = 10), albeit with a high amount of between-study heterogeneity (I² = 71.36%). One possible outlier was the Rosso et al. (2013) study of PDT versus supportive therapy, which when removed reduced heterogeneity (when removed *g* = 0.08 [95% CI: –0.14, 0.30], *SE* = 0.10, *p* = .404, I² = 49.98%).

Anxiety and Trauma Disorders

Three new trials were published since the most recent version of this meta-analysis (Keefe et al., 2014), bringing the total to 17 trials (See Table 12.2). Trials were included if patients were considered anxious by meeting specific criteria for a DSM-defined anxiety disorder, or if they presented an elevated score on a standardized measure of anxiety. For studies of anxiety disorders, effect sizes were generated from each study's primary anxiety outcome measure, giving preference to the observer-rated measure as a single effect size if multiple were specified. When no primary outcome was specified, we calculated an average effect size between all anxiety symptom measures reported in the study.

TABLE 12.2 **Included Studies of Anxiety**

Study	Anxiety disorder(s)	Psychodynamic therapy group(s)	Comparison groups	Follow-up (months)	Total / overall quality score
Alstrom et al. (1984a)	Agoraphobia	Avg. 8.5 sessions DST + 0.7 during FU (*n* = 14)	8.8 sessions ET + 5.6 during FU (*n* = 11); 9.1 sessions AR + 3.2 during FU (*n* = 17); BTC (*n* = 19)	9	20 / 3
Alstrom et al. (1984b)	Social phobias	Avg. 9.4 sessions DST + 2.6 during FU (*n* = 16)	9.1 sessions ET + 1.7 during FU (*n* = 7); 9.4 sessions AR + 1.7 during FU (*n* = 9; BTC (*n* = 10)	9	18.67 / 2.67
Beutel et al. (2013)	Panic with and without agoraphobia	24 sessions PFPP (*n* = 36)	24 sessions CBT with exposure sessions (*n* = 18)	6	35 / 5
Bögels et al. (2014)	Social anxiety	Avg. 31.1 sessions BDT (*n* = 22)	Avg. 19.8 sessions CBT (*n* = 27)	3, 12	32.67 / 5
Bressi et al. (2010)	GAD (41.0%), panic disorder (38.5%), social anxiety (20.5%)	40 sessions of BDT (*n* = 20)	ADT (*n* = 19)	None	37 / 5.67
Brom et al. (1989)	PTSD	Avg. 18.8 sessions TBDT (*n* = 26)	15 sessions TD (*n* = 28); 14.4 sessions BHT (*n* = 26); WLC (*n* = 20)	3	23 / 5
Crits-Christoph et al. (2005)	GAD	16 sessions SE therapy adapted to GAD (*n* = 14)	16 sessions SP (*n* = 14)	None	32 / 5
Durham et al. (1994) / Durham et al. (1999)	GAD	8 or 16 sessions of an unspecified model (11.86 avg) (*n* = 29)	8 sessions CT (*n* = 20); 16 session CT (*n* = 15); 8 sessions AMT (*n* = 16 at T)	6, 12	29 / 5
Knekt & Lindfors, (2004) / Knekt et al. (2008)	GAD (22.1%), Anxiety NOS (22.1%), OCD (8%), panic disorder (18.9%), social anxiety (37.9%), specific phobia (8.4%)	Avg. 18.5 sessions BDT (*n* = 50)	9.8 sessions SFT (*n* = 45)	5, 29	36 / 5
Knijnik et al. (2004)	Social anxiety	12 sessions PGT (*n* = 15)	12 sessions CGT (*n* = 15)	None	24 / 3.67
Leichsenring et al. (2009) / Salzer et al. (2011)	GAD	Avg. 29.1 sessions SE for GAD (*n* = 28)	28.8 sessions CBT (*n* = 29)	6, 12	38 / 6

(Continued)

TABLE 12.2 (CONTINUED)

Study	Anxiety disorder(s)	Psychodynamic therapy group(s)	Comparison groups	Follow-up (months)	Total / overall quality score
Leichsenring et al. (2013/2014)	Social anxiety	Avg. 25.7 sessions SE therapy adapted to social anxiety (*n* = 207)	25.8 sessions CBT (*n* = 209), WLC (*n* = 79)	6, 24	44.33 / 7
Milrod et al. (2007)	Panic disorder with and without agoraphobia	24 sessions PFPP (*n* = 26)	24 sessions AR (*n* = 23)	None	42 / 6
Milrod, Chambless et al. (2016)	Panic disorder with and without agoraphobia	24 sessions PFPP (*n* = 80)	24 sessions ART (*n* = 40); 24 sessions CBT (*n* = 80)	Only for responders	44 / 7
Moghadam et al. (2015)	Social phobia	25 sessions APT (*n* = 15)	ADT (*n* = 15); WLC = (*n* = 15)	None	16 / 2.5
Pierloot & Vinck (1978)	General anxiety (GAD-like)	Avg. 19.8 sessions FDT (*n* = 9)	Avg. 19.9 sessions SD (*n* = 13)	Mean of 3.95 months	8 / 2
Steinert et al. (2017)	PTSD	5 sessions ROT (*n* = 53)	WLC (*n* = 33)	None	30 / 5

ADT = antidepressant treatment; AMT = anxiety management training; AR = applied relaxation; BDT = brief dynamic therapy; BHT = behavioral hypnotherapy; BTC = basal therapy control; CBT = cognitive behavioral therapy; CGT = control group therapy; CT = cognitive therapy; DST = dynamic supportive therapy; ET = exposure treatment; FDT = focal dynamic therapy; PFPP = panic-focused psychodynamic psychotherapy; PGT = psychodynamic group therapy; ROT = resource activation treatment; SE = supportive-expressive psychotherapy; SFT = solution-focused therapy; SP = supportive psychotherapy; TBDT = trauma-based dynamic therapy; TD = trauma desensitization; WLC = wait-list control

Controlled Effect Size. Psychodynamic therapies outperformed control groups with a large effect size (g = −0.94 [95% CI: −1.55, −0.33], SE = 0.25, p = .009, k = 7, fail-safe n = 97), with a high amount of between-study heterogeneity (I^2 = 78.29). Much of the heterogeneity was driven by Steinert et al. (2016), a study of PDT versus wait-list for Cambodians with PTSD, the removal of which brought heterogeneity down to a medium level and a medium-to-high effect size (g = −0.72 [95% CI: −1.06, −0.37], SE = 0.13, p = .003, I^2 = 42.5%). Effect sizes did not reliably differ between studies in which the control condition included any active component versus wait-list alone (g = +0.47 for active relative to inactive, p = .401). There was no evidence of publication bias. Note that the studies contributing controlled effect sizes involved exclusively the treatment of social phobias and PTSD.

Active Treatment Comparisons: Termination. In treating core anxiety symptoms, PDT was estimated as having nearly no differences from other active treatments (g = −0.01 [95% CI: −0.21, 0.20], SE = 0.10, p = .945, k = 15), with a medium amount of between-study effect heterogeneity (I^2 = 60.49%). The only potential single-study outlier was the Milrod et al. (2007) trial comparing PDT to applied relaxation treatment, which when removed resulted in a lower amount of between-study heterogeneity (g = 0.06 [95% CI: −0.11, 0.23], SE = 0.08, p = .456, I^2 = 44.90%). There was no evidence of publication bias.

Studies comparing PDT to a form of CBT had comparable effects to studies in which the alternative treatment was not a CBT (g for CBT = +0.07, p = .757). There were no reliable differences observed between trials treating GAD (g = +0.31 relative to other disorders, p = .181), panic (g = −0.22, p = .356), or social phobias (g = +0.01, p = .977).

Remission rates for anxiety diagnoses did not significantly differ between PDT and other treatments (log odds ratio = 0.12 [95% CI: −0.76, 0.99], SE = 0.37, p = .761, k = 8), but there was a high between-study heterogeneity (I^2 = 80.09%) not driven by any single study. PDT did not significantly differ from other treatments in terms of depression outcomes (g = 0.13 [95% CI: −0.36, 0.61], SE = 0.19, p = .534, k = 6, I^2 = 80.09%). No single outlier was responsible for the heterogeneity in depression outcomes. However, 60% of the heterogeneity was accounted for by the two studies involving treatment of primary GAD (g = +0.71 relative to other studies, p = .053). Dropout from PDT was similar to that of other active treatments with moderate heterogeneity (log relative risk = −0.08 [95% CI: −0.31, 0.15], SE = 0.11, p = .475, I^2 = 44.90%).

Active Treatment Comparisons: Short-Term Follow-Up. At follow-up after treatment termination but no more than a year, PDT outcome scores did not differ from those of other active treatments (g = 0.08 [95% CI: −0.25, 0.42], SE = 0.15, p = .582, k = 10) with high between-study heterogeneity (I^2 = 73.96%). The Durham et al. (1994) trial of nonmanualized

PDT versus CT was a possible outlier in favor of CT, and when removed heterogeneity nearly halved (g = –0.03 [95% CI: –0.25, 0.19], SE = 0.10, p = .752, I² = 45.56%).

Total quality score did not significantly correlate with outcome (p = .714). Studies investigating GAD reported significantly higher effect sizes relative to other studies (g = +0.72 for studies of GAD relative to others, p = .018), accounting for 44.33% of between-study heterogeneity. This should be interpreted with caution given that the Durham et al. (1994) outlier was included in this calculation.

Active Treatment Comparisons: Long-Term Follow-Up. At over a year follow-up, PDT remained not significantly different from comparison treatments (g = 0.21 [95% CI: –0.45, 0.87], SE = 0.24, p = .431, k = 5, I² = 84.6%). The relatively high heterogeneity was almost entirely driven by the Durham et al. (1994) trial, which when removed eliminated nearly all heterogeneity (g = 0.00 [95% CI: –0.20, 0.20], SE = 0.06, p = .981, I² = 16.6%).

Personality Disorders

Sixteen trials of PDT for PD were included (see Table 12.3). Trials were included if DSM-defined PD was diagnosed using a structured interview, and the psychodynamic psychotherapy was intended to treat a personality disorder (e.g., not secondary outcomes of PD outcomes in a trial aimed at another disorder; e.g., Keefe et al., 2018). We examined several outcome domains important to PD: (a) core PD symptoms, measures encompassing the DSM-defined criteria for personality disorder, or, barring that, the averaging of the measures included to represent core PD symptoms (e.g., in Clarkin et al., 2007); (b) suicidality, encompassing measures of suicide attempt counts and the intensity of ideation from patients; (c) general psychiatric symptoms, preferencing the SCL-90 as a single effect; (d) interpersonal problems, using versions of the Inventory of Interpersonal Problems; and (e) functioning, using measures such as the global assessment of functioning (social-occupational) and the Social Adjustment Scale.

Control Group Comparisons.
Core PD Symptoms. There was a significant medium-sized effect in favor of PDT over control groups in treating core PD symptoms (g = –0.63 [95% CI: –0.87, –0.41], SE = 0.08, p = .002, fail-safe n = 25, k = 5), with no notable heterogeneity (I² =11.4%). There was no clear single outlier in this group of studies. There was no evidence of publication bias.

It was not meaningful to examine whether effects differed between studies treating Borderline Personality Disorder and otherwise, as only one study in this group did not treat BPD, nor for strength of the control condition as examples of different ratings were sparse (1 wait-list, 3 TAU, one enhanced TAU).

Suicidality. There was a significant, large effect size in favor of PDT (g = 0.79 [95% CI: 0.20, 1.38], SE = 0.21, p = .021, k = 5, fail-safe n = 47), with high heterogeneity (I² = 71.5%). Bateman & Fonagy (1999) was a positive outlier (g = 1.89) and removing the study from the analysis deflated the effect size to a medium-large effect (g = 0.67 [95% CI: 0.20, 1.13], SE = 0.15, p = .020) and strongly reduced the estimated

heterogeneity to moderate (I² = 40.1). There was no evidence of publication bias.

General Psychiatric Symptoms. PDT was reliably superior to control treatments in improving Axis-I/general psychiatric symptoms with a small-to-medium effect advantage (g = –0.47 [95% CI: –0.69, –0.25], SE = 0.09, p = .001, k = 9, I² = 34.87%).

IIP. While each individual study showed a significant advantage of PDT over control (g range = –0.69 to –2.22), the aggregate estimate was not statistically reliable in the meta-analysis due to the extremely high degree of heterogeneity introduced by a very large outlier among this small group of trials (g = –1.25 [95% CI: –3.22, 0.71], SE = 0.46, p = .111, k = 3).

Functioning. Patients significantly improved their psychosocial functioning in PDT as compared to control treatments (g = –0.66 [95% CI: –1.01, –0.32], SE = 0.14, p = .003, k = 7), with a moderate degree of heterogeneity (I² = 56.52%). Amianto et al. (2011) was potentially an outlier, reducing heterogeneity when removed (g = –0.72 [95% CI: –1.04, –0.41], SE = 0.12, p = .002, I² = 42.35%, fail-safe n = 32).

Active Treatment Comparisons: Termination.
Core PD Symptoms. PDT and other psychotherapies evidenced comparable average outcomes in terms of treating core PD symptoms (g = 0.05 [95% CI: –0.25, 0.35], SE = 0.12, p = .708, k = 7), with a moderate amount of between-study heterogeneity (I² = 54.29%). The Giesen-Bloo (2006) trial comparing TFP to schema-focused therapy was a possible outlier, reducing heterogeneity somewhat when removed (g = –0.04 [95% CI: –0.31, 0.22], SE = 0.10, p = .704, I² = 37.9%). There was no evidence for publication bias. There were no strong differences in effect (d = +0.02 for BPD, p = .953) between trials treating BPD (k = 4) and trials treating Cluster C PD (k = 3).

General Psychiatric Symptoms. In treating general psychiatric symptoms, PDT and other active treatments had almost identical outcomes (g = 0.00 [95% CI: –0.22, 0.23], SE = 0.09, p = .983, k = 7), with a low-to-moderate degree of heterogeneity (I² = 34.9%). The Hellerstein et al. (1998) trial was potentially an outlier, leading to a reduction in heterogeneity when removed but findings still remained nonsignificant (g = –0.04 [95% CI: –0.23, 0.15], SE = 0.07, p = .636, I² = 20.02%).

IIP. PDT and other active treatments had very similar outcomes on the IIP (g = –0.05 [95% CI: –0.20, 0.12], SE = 0.05, p = .439, k = 4). There was no notable heterogeneity between studies (I² = 2.34%).

Functioning. PDT and other active treatments had a comparable impact on improving psychosocial functioning (g = 0.12 [95% CI: –0.12, 0.36], SE = 0.07, p = .202, k = 4), with minimal between-study heterogeneity (I² = 2.34%).

Active Treatment Comparisons: Follow-Up.
Core PD Symptoms. PDT and other active treatments resulted in indistinguishable improvements in core PD symptoms at follow-up after treatment termination (g = 0.00 [95% CI: –0.48, 0.49], SE = 0.17, p = .996), albeit with a medium-high level of heterogeneity (I² = 63.66%). This heterogeneity was almost eliminated by removing the Emmelkamp et al. (2006) study, which resulted in a nonsignificant trend of a small advantage for PDTs at follow-up (g = –0.18 [95% CI: –0.38, 0.03], SE = 0.06, p = .072, I² = 5.08%).

TABLE 12.3 Included Studies of Personality Disorder

Study	Personality disorder(s)	Psychodynamic therapy group(s)	Comparison groups	Follow-up (months; active treatments only)	Total / overall quality score
Abbass et al. (2008)	Mixed PD	Avg. 27.7 sessions 1/wk ISTDP (*n* = 14)	WLC (*n* = 13)	N/A	27 / 4
Amianto et al. (2011)	Borderline	40 sessions 1/wk SB-APP + eTAU (*n* = 17)	eTAU (*n* = 16)	N/A	23.5 / 4
Bateman & Fonagy (1999, 2008)	Borderline	Partial hospitalization 1.5 years MBT (*n* = 19)	TAU (*n* = 19)	N/A	28 / 4.5
Bateman & Fonagy (2009)	Borderline	70 individual, 70 group 1/wk MBT (*n* = 71)	eTAU (*n* = 63)	N/A	37 / 6.5
Clarkin et al. (2007)	Borderline	1 year 2/wk TFP; 1 year 1/wk SPP (*n* = 45)	DBT (*n* = 17)	None	32 / 6.5
Doering et al. (2010)	Borderline	1 year 2/wk TFP (*n* = 52)	eTAU (*n* = 52)	N/A	35.5 / 5.5
Emmelkamp et al. (2006)	Avoidant	20 sessions 1/wk Unmanualized PDT (*n* = 23)	CBT (*n* = 18); WLC (*n* = 16)	6	17.5 / 2
Giesen-Bloo et al. (2006)	Borderline	3 years 2/wk TFP (*n* = 42)	SFT (*n* = 44)	None	34.5 / 5.5
Gregory et al. (2008; 2010)	Borderline (with alcohol use disorder)	1 year 1/wk DDP (*n* = 10)	TAU (*n* = 9)	N/A	32.5 / 4
Hellerstein et al. (1998)	Primarily Cluster C	40 sessions 1/wk STDP (*n* = 14)	ST (*n* = 12)	6	26 / 3.5
Jørgensen et al. (2013; 2014)	Borderline	2 year 1 group 1 individual/wk MBT (*n* = 42)	ST (*n* = 24)	18	28.5 / 4.5
McMain et al. (2009; 2012)	Borderline	40 sessions GPM (*n* = 90)	DBT (*n* = 90)	24	41 / 6
Muran et al. (2005)	Cluster C	30 sessions 1/wk BRT; STDP (*n* = 45)	CBT (*n* = 29)	6	29 / 3
Reneses et al. (2013)	Borderline	20 sessions 1/wk PRFP+TAU (*n* = 18)	TAU (*n* = 26)	N/A	21.5 / 3
Svartberg et al. (2004)	Cluster C	40 sessions 1/wk AFT (*n* = 25)	CBT (*n* = 25)	24	33 / 5
Winston et al. (1994)	Primarily Cluster C	40 sessions 1/wk BAP; STDP (*n* = 55)	WLC (*n* = 26)	N/A	20 / 3.5

AFT = Alliance-Focused Training; BAP = brief adaptive psychotherapy; BRT = brief relational therapy; CBT = cognitive behavioral therapy for personality disorders; DBT = dialectical behavior therapy; DDP = dynamic deconstructive therapy; eTAU = enhanced treatment as usual; GPM = general psychodynamic psychiatric management; ISTDP = intensive short-term psychodynamic psychotherapy; MBT = mentalization-based treatment; = PRFP = psychic representation focused psychotherapy; SB-APP = sequential brief adlerian psychodynamic psychotherapy; STDP = short-term psychodynamic therapy; SFT = schema-focused therapy; SP = supportive therapy; SPP = supportive psychodynamic therapy; TAU = treatment as usual; TFP = transference-focused psychotherapy; WLC = wait-list control

General Psychiatric Symptoms. General psychiatric symptom outcomes were not significantly different at follow-up between PDT and other active treatments (g = –0.14 [95% CI: –0.43, 0.16], SE = 0.11, p = .267, k = 5), with a low-to-moderate degree of heterogeneity (I² = 32.19). The Hellerstein et al. (1998) trial was potentially an outlier, leading to a reduction in heterogeneity when removed and a nonsignificant trend toward a small advantage for PDT (g = –0.20 [95% CI: –0.44, 0.05], SE = 0.08, p = .085, I² = 12.21).

IIP. Overall, PDTs did not significantly differ from other active treatments at follow-up in terms of IIP scores (g = –0.17 [95% CI: –0.42, 0.08], SE = 0.09, p = .136, k = 5), with a low amount of heterogeneity (I² = 27.33%). Removing Hellerstein et al. (1998) resulted in a lack of heterogeneity and a significant, small effect size estimate in favor of PDTs over comparison treatments (g = –0.23 [95% CI: –0.28, –0.17], SE = 0.02, p = .001, I² = 0.05%).

Conclusion and New Directions

Psychodynamic therapies do not have significantly different outcomes from other active psychiatric treatments such as CBTs and psychopharmacology in the treatment of depression, anxiety (with the possible exception of GAD), and personality disorders. These effects were maintained into post-termination follow-up. PDTs also generally outperform both active and inactive control conditions, such as treatment as usual, treatment by community experts, or low intensity therapy. Our findings converge with those of previous meta-analyses in providing evidence that PDTs are evidence-based, effective therapies for mood, anxiety, and personality disorders.

Psychodynamic therapy represents a generative and progressive program of outcome research. Current active work includes extending PDT to the DSM-5 alternative model of personality disorder (Caligor et al., 2018), separation anxiety disorder (Milrod, Altemus et al., 2016; Milrod et al., 2014), and complex PTSD resistant to CBT approaches (Busch & Milrod, 2018; Busch et al., 2019). Leichsenring and colleagues have proposed transdiagnostic models of short-term dynamic treatment for emotional disorders (Leichsenring & Steinert, 2018); panic-focused psychodynamic therapy has proposed principles to extend its treatment to anxiety and Cluster-C personality disorders generally (Busch et al., 2012) and may in fact be effective in treating other anxiety disorders (Keefe et al., 2019). Recent work has also found controlled efficacy for low-therapist contact computer-supported treatment or guided self-help from psychodynamic perspectives (Andersson et al., 2012; Johansson et al., 2012, 2013, 2017).

Another trend is that many recent, high-quality trials of PDT adopted a collaborative research stance bringing together experts in psychodynamic and other therapies (CBT, DBT) to examine efficacy and mechanisms of treatment (e.g., Leichsenring et al., 2013; McMain et al., 2009; Milrod, Chambless et al., 2016). Such collaborative approaches increase confidence in trial outcomes as they emerge from designs agreed upon by investigators from different schools, and inclusion of outcomes and mediators important to different treatment better helps us understand convergence and divergence

in mechanisms of effective psychiatric treatment. This also increases the chance that both treatments are *bona fide* and adequately conceptualized to the psychiatric problems treated in the study. Psychodynamic therapies that are less tailored to or that do not allow for the therapist to fully address core symptoms arguably often produce the most disappointing findings in psychodynamic outcome research. For instance, a nonspecific long-term psychodynamic therapy failed to treat bulimic symptoms as well as a shorter CBT targeted at eating disorders (Poulsen et al., 2014); similarly, PDT for adolescents with PTSD in which any therapist-driven discussion of trauma was verboten produced negative findings relative to CBT (Gilboa-Schechtman et al., 2010).

A critically important domain for future outcome research is identifying which patients with a particular diagnosis will benefit the most from psychodynamic approaches, given the very large degree of clinical heterogeneity recognized within diagnoses (Fisher et al., 2017). Patient characteristics may influence the degree to which they are likely to respond to psychodynamic approaches (Cohen & DeRubeis, 2018), which is difficult to explore in standard meta-analysis but may be addressed by patient-level meta-analysis (Driessen et al., 2018). Recent moderator work from randomized trials suggests that response to psychodynamic versus cognitive-behavioral therapies may be to some degree reliably predictable from patient baseline characteristics (Cohen et al., 2019; Keefe et al., 2020; Sahin et al., 2018). There is also a need to test psychodynamic approaches in patients who did not show an adequate response to other treatments, such as psychopharmacological or cognitive-behavioral therapies, as in treatment resistant depression (Fonagy et al., 2015; Town et al., 2017) and anxiety disorders comorbid with strong separation anxiety (Milrod, Altemus et al., 2016). We endorse the perspective that no treatment approach is optimal for every patient (e.g., Barber & Muenz, 1996). PDT offers a distinctive, evidence-based perspective on the treatment of psychiatric disorders that is part of the armamentarium in targeting specific treatments to specific patients. Finally, there is a need to examine the efficacy of PDT for ethnic minority and underserved populations. Some recent work in that area is promising. For example, Barber et al. (2012) reported secondary analyses from an urban, disadvantaged, chronically depressed RCT sample suggesting that SE therapy may be specifically efficacious for minority males and White females (see also Connolly Gibbons et al., 2016).

Like many psychotherapy researchers, we postulate that understanding the process of therapy will increase our ability to develop further our treatments, to make them more effective, and to perhaps individualize them better for the needs of specific individuals. We now turn to the research on those processes and begin our survey by examining a construct that has attained paramount importance in psychotherapy research, the therapeutic alliance. We discuss predictors and moderators of good prognosis in PDT, and other central mechanisms of change in PDT: insight, defense style and mechanisms, relationship rigidity, quality of object relations, and reflective functioning.

RESEARCH ON THE PROCESS OF PDT

The Therapeutic Alliance

The therapeutic alliance was first a psychodynamic construct, before it became a transtheoretical formulation (Bordin, 1979), an integrative variable (Wolfe & Goldfried, 1988), and a common factor (Wampold, 2001). The history of the construct dates back to Freud's early suggestion of the importance of making a "collaborator" of the patient in the therapeutic process, but was brought to prominence by the ego psychological tradition with its emphasis on the reality-oriented adaptation of the ego to the environment. A number of ego psychologists (see Greenson, 1967 for example) developed the alliance construct to highlight the critical importance of the real, human aspects of the therapeutic relationship, and to provide grounds for departing from the idealized therapist stance of abstinence and neutrality.

Over the years, many dynamic theorists have grappled with questions of how to conceptualize the alliance and transferential aspects of the therapeutic relationship and whether the alliance construct is meaningful and useful (e.g., Brenner, 1979). For example, criticisms have ranged from suggesting the alliance construct can lead to leaving transferential aspects unanalyzed to promoting conformity to the therapist's desires. Contemporary relational analysts have promoted an intersubjective and social constructivist take on the therapeutic relationship (e.g., Aron, 1996). From a relational take, Safran and Muran (2000, 2006) have argued that developing the alliance and resolving alliance ruptures are not prerequisite to change, but rather the very essence of the change process.

Alliance Measurement

Beginning in the 1970s, the alliance construct became the focus of the psychotherapy research community. This was due in large part to two major contributions: (1) Luborsky's (1976) development of the Penn Helping Alliance Questionnaire (HAq), which yielded measures of Perceived Helpfulness (Type I: to what extent the patient perceived the therapist to be helpful) and Collaboration or Bonding (Type II: to what degree the patient and therapist were working together); and (2) Bordin's reformulation that defined the alliance as comprised of three interdependent dimensions – Agreement on Tasks, Agreement on Goals, and the Affective Bond – which became the basis for the development of the Working Alliance Inventory (WAI; Horvath & Greenberg, 1989). These contributions spurred a proliferation of research on the alliance, as well as further measurement development. They also (Bordin's conceptualization especially) contributed to the growing interest in psychotherapy integration and the understanding of common factors that has been evident in the field since the 1980s (e.g., Goldfried, 1980).

With the development of so many alliance measures, both Hatcher (2010) and Horvath (2006) have argued that there has been a cost in the loss of definitional precision: The variety of measures has brought a variety of idiosyncratic definitions of the alliance construct and arguably a great deal of confusion about its meaning. In addition to the HAq and the WAI, other measures most often used include the Vanderbilt Psychotherapy Process Scale (VPPS; O'Malley et al., 1983) and the California Psychotherapy Alliance Scales (CALPAS; Gaston & Marmar, 1994). The VPPS has subscales measuring Patient Psychic Distress, Patient Participation, Patient Hostility, Patient Exploration, Patient Dependency, Therapist Warmth and Friendliness, Therapist Exploration, and Negative Therapist Attitude.

According to Horvath and colleagues' (2011) meta-analysis, two thirds of the studies conducted regarding the alliance-outcome relationship involved these four "core" measures,[1] which shared less than 50% of the variance. Arguably, the confusion comes from the emphasis of patient versus therapist contributions, the relation between alliance and technical intervention, and the relation between alliance and outcome. The HAq was especially criticized for conflating the quality of the relationship with outcome by its measure of Type I alliance, Perceived Helpfulness (Barber & Crits-Christoph, 1996) and was revised to address this criticism by removing several items (Luborsky et al., 1996). Trying to disentangle the alliance from these relationships, however, may be impossible: To illustrate, although the WAI emphasizes purposeful collaboration and does not include any items regarding patient or therapist contribution (unlike the CALPAS and VPPS), its emphasis on agreement on tasks and goals does suggest that technique and outcome are inherent to its conceptualization of the alliance. Nevertheless, we review the research regarding these relationships.

Alliance and Outcome

Meta-Analysis

There are now several meta-analyses on the predictive relationship between therapeutic alliance and treatment outcome in psychotherapy (e.g., Martin et al., 2000). The most recent by Flückiger et al. (2018) surveyed studies between 1978 and 2017 ($N = 30,000$ patients) and supported previous efforts demonstrating a consistent but modest relationship, with no apparent significant difference among treatment orientations. They reported an overall $r = 0.28$ (95% CI: 0.26, 0.30, $p < 0.0001$) and found an $r = 0.24$ for PDT (and an $r = 0.28$ for interpersonal therapy). In addition, they found no significant differences by treatment condition, consistent with previous meta-analyses. There is also ample evidence that weakened alliances are correlated with unilateral termination in general, and specifically in PDT (e.g., Anderson et al., 2019; Muran et al., 2009).

Temporal Precedence

There have been some noteworthy challenges to the interpretation of the alliance-outcome correlation. A number of studies have examined the relationship between early treatment gains

---

[1] These four alliance measures dominated the more recent meta-analysis by Flückiger et al. (2018; especially the WAI which was applied in 73% of 105 studies added to this meta-analysis): The authors did not find any significant differences among the effects for the different measures, although they found a great amount of variability by measure.

and alliance with some finding the former carries the predictive load. In other words, it has been suggested that the alliance itself could simply be a product of earlier changes in symptoms. Several studies have failed to demonstrate that the alliance predicts subsequent symptom change when controlling for early treatment gains (Barber et al., 1999; Barber et al., 2001; DeRubeis & Feeley, 1990; Feeley et al., 1999; Strunk et al., 2010). Several other studies, however, have still found that the alliance is predictive of outcome above and beyond the impact of early gains (e.g., Barber et al., 2000; Brottman, 2004; Constantino et al., 2005; Klein, Schwartz, et al., 2003; Strauss et al., 2006). These studies support the consideration of the alliance as a *change mechanism*, as defined by Kazdin (2007, 2009), and since, there have been a number of demonstrations of the alliance as a change mechanism in PDT, in which temporal precedence is introduced between predictor and product (e.g., Zilcha-Mano & Errázuriz, 2017; Zilcha-Mano et al., 2019, regarding an integrative therapy). Additional important support for the proposition that the alliance can serve as a change mechanism comes from studies showing that after disentangling the trait-like from the state-like components of alliance, the state-like component can still predict subsequent symptomatic change (Zilcha-Mano, 2017, 2020). These findings demonstrate that the alliance-outcome association is not merely a product of the patient's and therapist's trait-like characteristics but can also serve as an active mechanism of change. A comprehensive review of the alliance-outcome association, with emphasis on the question of temporal precedence, appears in Chapter 8 of this volume.

Alliance and Contributing Factors

Regardless of specific theoretical slant, the alliance is essentially a construct developed to understand the interaction of two people (i.e., the patient and the therapist) in the therapy context. As such, the alliance subsumes a pair of individuals' life histories, expectations, personality constellations, interpersonal and attachment styles, ways of organizing experience, and world views. These factors represent an important set of trait-like variables related to the development of the therapeutic alliance.

Patient Factors

Research has identified several important patient factors that contribute to the formation of a strong alliance. For example, patient preconceptions and expectations regarding improvement have been found to be associated with the quality of the alliance such that positive expectations are linked to stronger alliances and better overall treatment outcomes (e.g., Constantino et al., 2018; Messer & Wolitzky, 2010).

Patient personality has also been associated with the alliance: Open, agreeable, extraverted, conscientious personality traits are associated with strong alliance, whereas the presence of personality pathology strongly predicts poor early alliance (see Sharpless et al., 2010). In fact, research suggests that people with personality disorders pose the most difficulty in establishing and maintaining the therapeutic alliance (for a review, see Bender, 2005). In particular, patients with

borderline, narcissistic, antisocial, and paranoid personality features are likely to have troubled interpersonal attitudes and behaviors that will complicate, but not necessarily compromise the development of the therapeutic alliance. There is recent research demonstrating patients with personality disorders evidence more alliance ruptures (Colli et al., 2019; Tufekcioglu et al., 2013).

In addition, patients' symptom severity, interpersonal functioning, object relations, and attachment style have been associated with the alliance (see Sharpless et al., 2010, for a review; in addition, Dunster-Page et al., 2017 regarding suicidality; Dinger et al., 2017 and Tschuschke et al., 2015 regarding symptom severity). Patients with affiliative styles are more likely to manifest strong alliances than patients who are more anxious, avoidant, uncomfortable with interpersonal exchanges, and fearful of interpersonal closeness. However, there is also some evidence that poor alliances can improve with patients that have a history of interpersonal problems or those who present interpersonal challenges (see Benjamin & Critchfield, 2010, for a review; in addition, Ollila et al., 2016). Diener and Monroe's (2011) meta-analysis indicated a positive relationship between patients' attachment security and the therapeutic alliance (see also Errázuriz et. al., 2015; Smith et al., 2010).

Patients' interpersonal abilities and tendencies were found not only to predict the alliance at the beginning and throughout treatment, but also to moderate the alliance-outcome association (Piper et al., 2004). Specifically, the alliance was found to have a greater effect on treatment outcome for patients who have problems forming satisfying relationships with others outside the treatment room, especially those with greater interpersonal (Zilcha-Mano & Errázuriz, 2017) and personality problems (Falkenström et al., 2013), and those suffering from low interpersonal agency, who reported problems with submissiveness (Penedo et al., 2019).

Therapist Factors

Similar to the findings on patient variables, some therapist factors have been identified as facilitators of the alliance, whereas other qualities may impede positive alliance development. Research has generally focused on therapist attachment, personality traits, and factors that comprise technical skill and ability (see Heinonen & Nissen-Lie, 2020 for recent systematic review). Some of these variables are relatively stable, core characteristics of the therapist's person (e.g., attachment, personality), whereas other factors appear to be conducive to therapist training or remediation (e.g., technical skills).

In their review of the research, Ackerman and Hilsenroth (2003) identified several key personal qualities that support the development of a positive alliance, including professional demeanor, friendliness, empathy, flexibility, honesty, trustworthiness, confidence, genuineness, alertness, and warmth. On the other hand, therapists who are perceived by patients as rigid, uncertain, exploitive, overly critical, distant, aloof, and/or distracted tend to experience negative alliances (Ackerman & Hilsenroth, 2001). More recent research on therapist contributions to the alliance has demonstrated a predictive relation of such personality traits as agreeableness, conscientiousness, and congruence (see Chapman et al., 2009; Hersoug et al., 2009; Kolden et al., 2018; Nissen-Lie et al., 2010; Taber et al., 2011; Watson et al., 2017, regarding therapist affiliation). Studies also suggest that therapists' attachment security (i.e., low-attachment anxiety, low-attachment avoidance, greater comfort with closeness, strong interpersonal relations) predicts alliance (e.g., Black et al., 2005; Degnan et al., 2016; Schauenburg et al., 2010). And in a meta-analysis of 53 studies addressing the relevance of therapist racial/ethnic identity, there was no indication that therapist–patient match in this regard has implications for the therapeutic alliance or treatment success (Cabral & Smith, 2011).

Finally, there is research indicating that specific therapist factors such as therapist skills and abilities (as opposed to the aforementioned, nonspecific trait-based factors) make considerable contributions to the alliance. Techniques such as the appropriate use of silence, mindfulness, transference interpretation, self-disclosure and immediacy, countertransference, emotion experience (including regulation), empathy and affirmation can contribute to a strong alliance (see Crits-Christoph et al., 1993; Davis & Hayes, 2011; Elliott et al., 2019; Farber et al., 2019; Hayes et al., 2019; Hill et al., 2019; Muran, 2019; Muran et al., 2018; Peluso & Freund, 2019), whereas misdiagnosis, poor case conceptualization, and excessive or mechanical use of technique have been associated with negative alliance (Hersoug et al., 2009; Sharpless et al., 2010). With regard to ability, there is substantial evidence demonstrating that therapists' individual differences predict alliance quality and treatment success, and that some therapists are better at developing alliances, as well as achieving better outcomes (see Baldwin et al., 2007; Luborsky et al., 1986; Najavits & Strupp, 1994; Wampold & Imel, 2015).

Alliance Ruptures and Resolution
Across-Treatment

Although there is much research supporting that a strong and improving alliance predicts a positive treatment outcome (as cited earlier), there is also a growing body of research examining alliance patterns across the course of treatment and demonstrating patterns of deterioration or rupture and in cases of good outcome rupture resolution. This research was initially informed by the work of Mann (1973) and Gelso and Carter (1994), who suggested that there are identifiable patterns of alliance development: specifically, an initial high alliance when patients become mobilized and hopeful, a middle phase of low alliance when patients feel ambivalent about therapy, and then (if this phase is successfully negotiated) a high alliance indicating a working through unresolved issues. There is some empirical support for the predictive relationship of quadratic alliance growth (based on patient post-session report) to treatment outcome (Golden & Robbins, 1990; Kivlighan & Shaughnessy, 2000; Patton et al., 1997).

Stiles and colleagues (2004) initially sought to replicate Kivlighan and Shaughnessy's (2000) findings that a U-shape (high-low-high) alliance pattern was predictive of good

outcome (*n* = 79). When they were unable to replicate this finding, they shifted their focus from the global alliance pattern to the examination of discrete high-low-high, or V-shape rupture-repair episodes and found cases with such episodes had the larger treatment gains. Since their effort, there have been eight additional studies that have investigated this relationship in a larger number of cases (*N* = 1200 with Stiles et al., 2004), with prevalence rates ranging from 15 to 81% and predictive validity ranging from small to large effects (see Muran, 2019). In a recent meta-analysis that combined eight of these studies with two others that included an observer-based method to identify resolution, the aggregated correlation of rupture-repair episodes to treatment outcome indicated a medium effect of 0.29 (95% CI: 0.10, 0.47, *p* > .01) that was statistically significant (Eubanks et al., 2019).

In-Session

In contrast to the efforts mentioned above that examined patterns of postsession alliance ratings for evidence of rupture and resolution, there are a number of studies that have examined in-session evidence of ruptures and resolution. For example, Muran et al. (2009) in a clinical trial of 128 PD patients comparing a cognitive with a dynamic and an alliance-focused treatment asked patients and therapists to complete a postsession questionnaire (PSQ; Muran et al., 1992), which included a self-report measure of the alliance (WAI-12; Tracey & Kokotovic, 1989), as well as self-report indices measuring the occurrence of ruptures, rupture intensity, and the extent to which ruptures were resolved. They found that ruptures occurred frequently in the first six sessions of the three therapy treatments: Ruptures were reported by 37% of patients and 56% of therapists. Ruptures were also found to negatively predict outcome, and failure to resolve these ruptures predicted dropout. Eames and Roth (2000) also administered the WAI items and the rupture indices from the PSQ after Sessions 2 through 5 to 11 therapists and 30 of their patients receiving treatment as usual at outpatient clinics in the United Kingdom. Similar to Muran et al. (2009), they found that therapists reported ruptures more often, reporting them in 43% of sessions, while patients reported them in 19%. In addition, Sommerfeld and colleagues (2008) examined the difference between patient-report and observer-ratings of ruptures. In a study of 151 sessions from five patients in PDT, patients completed PSQs and reported ruptures in 42% of the sessions. Based on transcripts, judges identified confrontation and withdrawal ruptures using Harper's coding system (1989a, 1989b): Rupture markers were identified by observers in 77% of sessions.

Over the past 10 years, there have been a number of in-session evaluations based on observer-ratings. Eubanks-Carter et al. (2010) developed an observer-based coding system the Rupture Resolution Rating System (3RS) and compared it to patient-rated PSQs in a sample of 48 sessions from early treatment of 20 cases. They found that patients reported ruptures in 35% of sessions, observers detected withdrawal rupture markers in every session, and confrontation rupture markers in 75% of sessions. Since then, several 3RS-based studies have demonstrated the prevalence of ruptures in up to 91% of sessions (from 157 cases): withdrawal ruptures from 74% to 89%, confrontation ruptures from 43% to 66% (Coutinho et al., 2014; Eubanks, Lubitz et al., 2019; Moeseneder et al., 2019). These 3RS studies also provide some support for the predictive validity of ruptures. Colli and Lingiardi (2009) developed a method for assessing alliance ruptures and resolution, the Collaborative Interaction Scale (CIS), and applied it to a sample of 32 sessions from 16 patients and found withdrawal ruptures in 100% and confrontation ruptures in 43% of sessions. Colli et al. (2019) presented findings from a revised version of the CIS, based on 60 sessions from 30 cases, indicating withdrawal ruptures in 95% and confrontation ruptures in 33% of coded segments. The CIS has also demonstrated some promising validity data.

In sum, these studies of in-session events suggest that alliance ruptures are quite prevalent, however measured. They demonstrate that (a) patients report ruptures in 19% to 42% of sessions; (b) therapists report them in 43% to 56% of sessions; and (c) third-party raters observe ruptures anywhere from 43% to 100% of sessions. In studies that examined postsession alliance ratings across treatment to identify the prevalence of rupture–repair sequences, patients reported such sequences in 15% to 81% of cases, suggesting these are fairly common events that deserve more intensive study of what they entail. The predictive validity data is promising though limited.

Task and Qualitative Analyses

Several researchers have employed the task analytic paradigm (Rice & Greenberg, 1984), which blends qualitative and quantitative methods to study rupture resolution as a process of change. Safran, Muran, and colleagues built upon previous preliminary research (Foreman & Marmar, 1985; Harper, 1994) by undertaking an intensive examination of the process of rupture resolution in a series of small-scale studies following the task analytic paradigm (Safran & Muran, 1996; Safran, Muran, & Samstag, 1994). They compared matched resolution and nonresolution sessions from seven different cases, pulled from a pool of more than 29 cases, based on selection criteria from patient-rated PSQs, and then applied various measures of psychotherapy process to the transcribed sessions to operationalize multiple dimensions (that is, interpersonal behavior, emotional involvement, and vocal quality) of each patient and therapist position in the resolution process. They then conducted a series of lag one sequential analyses and tested the significance of transitional probabilities in order to confirm the hypothesized sequences and demonstrate a difference between resolution and nonresolution sessions.

The result of their task analysis was a stage-process model, which comprised four interactions involving patient and therapist:

1. Attending to the rupture marker
2. Exploring the rupture experience
3. Exploring the avoidance
4. Emergence of wish/need

They observed that the type of rupture marker (withdrawal or confrontation) dictated differences in the resolution process. For example, the common progression in the resolution of withdrawal ruptures consists of moving through increasingly clearer articulations of discontent to self-assertion, in which the need for agency is realized. The progression in the resolution of confrontation ruptures consists of moving through feelings of anger, to feelings of disappointment and hurt over having been failed by the therapist, to contacting vulnerability and the wish to be nurtured. Typical avoidant operations that emerge, regardless of rupture type, concern anxieties resulting from the fear of being too aggressive or too vulnerable associated with the expectation of retaliation or rejection by the therapist. In short, the result demonstrated evidence supporting the significance for the therapist and the patient to participate in a collaborative inquiry about the rupture event, including patient expression of negative feelings and therapist nondefensiveness.

There have been other task analyses of rupture resolution conducted by other researchers: Some have provided support for recognition and exploration (Agnew et al., 1994; Bennett et al., 2006; Swank & Wittenborn, 2013), others suggested the value of making extra-session links (Agnew et al., 1994; Bennett et al., 2006; Cash et al., 2014) or changing in-session tasks (Aspland et al., 2008). It is important to recognize that these studies included even smaller samples, applied different methods, and involved a variety of treatment models – from dynamic, cognitive-behavioral to humanistic-experiential. In her review of qualitative studies of negative process, Hill (2009) also promoted the value of recognition and exploration (see Lansford, 1986; Rhodes et al., 1994, for example). There have been a number of qualitative efforts that have demonstrated the complexity of negative process, including the reluctance of patients to disclose negative feelings, the difficulty for therapists to recognize these feelings, and even if aware, the challenge for therapists to address these feelings (Fuller & Hill 1985; Hill et al., 1993; Hill et al., 2003; Martin et al., 1987; Martin et al., 1986; Regan & Hill, 1992).

Alliance-Focused Training

The research reviewed thus far demonstrates both the importance of addressing ruptures and the difficulties for therapists to do so. The findings of the Vanderbilt studies by Strupp and colleagues, for example, demonstrated how difficult it can be to train therapists to resolve alliance ruptures. Accordingly, therapists may sometimes adhere to manuals in a rigid fashion that interferes with their normally supportive style (Henry et al., 1993), and there was little outcome benefit as a result of such training (Bien et al., 2000). Similarly, studies by Piper and colleagues (Piper et al., 1991; Piper et al., 1999) and Schut et al. (2005) studies of PDT have found evidence that some therapists attempt to resolve ruptures by increasing their adherence to a theoretical model (e.g., making transference interpretations in PDT). These studies found that this rigid adherence in the context of a rupture is linked to poor outcome and premature termination.

Nevertheless, there is also more recent research demonstrating that training therapists in manualized approaches that emphasize the development of an alliance and abilities to resolve ruptures may actually have a beneficial impact on treatment. For example, Bambling et al., (2006) evaluated the impact of two alliance-focused supervision conditions (alliance skill-focused and alliance process-focused supervision) versus a no-supervision condition in a brief eight-session treatment of 127 patients with major depression. In the skill-focused supervision, therapists were given explicit advice and guidance concerning the kinds of behaviors and interventions likely to enhance alliance. In the process-focused supervision, the therapists were trained to monitor implicit client feedback, changes in client anxiety level, flow of exchanges, resistance, and perceived dynamics in the relationship with the therapist. Eight sessions of supervision were provided, including one pretreatment. The results indicated a significant benefit of both supervision conditions over the no-supervision condition on working alliance, symptom change, and treatment retention, but no differences were found between supervision conditions.

In another example (a pilot study), Crits-Christoph and colleagues (2006) found support for training therapists in alliance-fostering therapy, a 16-session treatment for depression that combines psychodynamic-interpersonal interventions with alliance-focused techniques such as responding to ruptures directly by encouraging patients to express their underlying feelings and the interpersonal issues connected to them. The authors found that the training resulted in increases in alliance scores that were moderate to large in size but not statistically significant, as well as small improvements in depressive symptoms and larger improvements in quality of life.

The largest studies that have tested the effectiveness of an alliance-focused treatment have been conducted by Safran, Muran, and colleagues, who developed a short-term, alliance-focused psychotherapy treatment informed by their findings from task analytic work and principles from intersubjective psychoanalytic theories: brief relational therapy (BRT; Safran & Muran, 2000). By closely attending to ruptures, therapists and patients in BRT work collaboratively to identify the patient's core relational processes and to explore in the session with new ways of relating. The emphasis in BRT is on helping the patient to develop a generalizable skill of awareness through the use of metacommunication by which the therapist explicitly draws the patient's attention to ruptures emerging in their interactions that represent markers of core relational processes. One study compared BRT with a CBT and a PDT in a sample of 128 patients with Cluster C PDs and PD NOS (Muran et al., 2005). This study found that BRT was as effective as CBT and PDT with regard to statistical and clinical significance and was more successful than the other two treatments with respect to retention. In another study of 18 patients with PD who were identified as at risk for treatment failure from a sample of 60 patients, Safran et al. (2005) reported additional evidence that BRT successfully keeps challenging patients engaged in treatment.

In their most recent effort (Muran et al., 2018; see also Muran, 2019), a study that evaluated the impact of an Alliance-Focused Training (AFT) protocol (that was developed to support BRT and informed by research on rupture resolution,

emotion regulation, performance training) on a cognitive behavioral therapy. More specifically, the study had two phases: The first involved training novice therapists (doctoral candidates in clinical psychology) to an adherent standard in a 30-session protocol of a CBT for personality disorders. The second phase involved introducing AFT following a multiple baseline design (mixed within-subject and between-group): In this phase, AFT was introduced to one cohort of therapists after eight sessions and another after 16 sessions. The dependent variable was interpersonal process (namely, therapist and patient interpersonal behaviors). The aim by this mixed design was to try to control for variance attributable to patient, therapist and patient-therapist interactional sources. The results indicated several significant interactions between within-subject interpersonal change and between-group differences in AFT time intervals: Specifically, there were decreases in patient dependence and in therapist control (including criticism), plus increases in patient expressiveness and in therapist affirmation and expressiveness, all of which could be attributed to AFT. Additional analyses suggested increases in therapist emotional involvement attributable to AFT.

Similar efforts to integrate rupture resolution (largely informed by dynamic principles) into CT have been conducted by Castonguay and colleagues. In an effort to improve cognitive therapists' ability to respond to alliance ruptures, Castonguay developed Integrative CT for Depression (ICT; Castonguay, 1996), which primarily integrates Safran and Muran's rupture resolution strategies (Safran & Muran, 1996; Safran & Segal, 1990) into traditional CT. When ruptures are identified, the therapist breaks from the cognitive therapy protocol and addresses the rupture by inviting the patient to explore the rupture, empathizing with the patient's emotional reaction, and reducing the patient's anger or dissatisfaction by validating negative feelings or criticisms and taking at least partial responsibility for the rupture. In a pilot study ($N = 11$), Castonguay et al. (2004) found that patient symptom improvement was greater in ICT than a wait-list condition, and compared favorably to previous findings for cognitive therapy. In a randomized trial comparing ICT to CT ($N = 11$), Constantino et al. (2008) found that ICT patients had greater improvement on depression and global symptoms and more clinically significant change than CT patients. ICT also yielded better patient-rated alliance quality and therapist empathy, and there was a trend toward better patient retention in ICT than in CT. A similar effort to integrate rupture resolution strategies into CT for GAD was undertaken by Newman et al. (2008). The study ($N = 18$) found that the integrative treatment significantly decreased GAD symptoms, yielding a higher ES than the average ES of CT for GAD in the treatment literature. Participants also showed clinically significant improvements in GAD symptoms and interpersonal problems with continued gains at one-year follow-up.

In a recent meta-analysis that examined the impact of alliance-focused or rupture resolution training on patient outcome in six of the studies mentioned above (Bein et al., 2000; Constantino et al., 2008; Crits-Christoph et al., 2006; Muran et al., 2005; Newman et al., 2008), Eubanks, Muran et al. (2019) calculated group contrast ESs and found a small, insignificant between-group r of 0.11 (95% CI: –0.09, 0.30, $p = .28$); moderator analyses indicated the training was more impactful when applied to a cognitive-behavioral therapy. In a previous meta-analysis, Safran and colleagues (2011) calculated pre-post ESs and found a large, significant pre-post r for the rupture resolution training of .65 (95% CI: 0.46, 0.78, $p < .001$) based on eight studies (including Castonguay et al., 2004, and Hilsenroth et al., 2002).

Adding to the promise of alliance-focused training suggested by this meta-analysis is the body of research by Lambert and colleagues (Lambert et al., 2003) examining the impact of providing therapists feedback and clinical support tools when risk for treatment failure is indicated. A poor therapeutic alliance is one of the risk factors, and when it is indicated, a clinical support tool is triggered, which is primarily informed by principles defined by Safran and Muran (2000). In a meta-analysis of six studies ($N = 6,151$) conducted by Shimokawa and colleagues (2010), they found feedback interventions were effective in preventing treatment failure (see also Gondek et al., 2016; Lambert, 2015, for more recent reviews and future considerations); it is not evident from this research whether therapists adhered to any of the clinical support tools.

Conclusion and New Directions

The accumulated research on alliance suggests that it can consistently predict treatment outcome. Though much has been written in support of the alliance as a *change principle* or *change process* (see Castonguay, Constantino, & Beutler, 2019; Norcross & Lambert, 2019), more research is required to demonstrate its causal relationship to overall change: that is, to support it as a *change mechanism*. In addition, more is required to further understanding of various patient and therapist contributing factors to the alliance, even efforts to replicate previous findings. Research on rupture and repair (or resolution) is growing but still relatively nascent (see Eubanks, Muran et al., 2019; Muran, 2019, for critical reviews). Much work remains on operational definition and measurement development, plus clarification of patient and therapist contributing factors. More research is recommended that includes the application of mixed methods (quantitative plus qualitative) to provide a richer description and understanding of the rupture–repair processes. Research on training protocols or support tools to improve alliance and repair ruptures is even more limited, with some promising results: More definition of the construct (regarding essential elements) and replication (demonstrating impact on process and outcome) are required. Also, more research on how the implementation of therapeutic interventions are associated with change in alliance and the need to develop in greater details how relationship factors and interventions together bring about patients' improvement. In general, future research on the alliance, including rupture–repair, should aim to further clarify the relational context in which change occurs, including how patient and therapist interact in the change process. It remains an empirical challenge to go beyond just demonstrating the alliance is important to change and to show with greater detail *how so*.

PSYCHODYNAMIC PREDICTORS, MODERATORS, CHANGE MECHANISMS, AND OUTCOMES

Over the decades, many studies focused on identifying who are the patients who may benefit most from psychotherapy, irrespective of its type (prognostic variables), and from certain types of psychotherapies in particular (moderators of treatment success or prescriptive variables) (see Chapter 7 in this *Handbook*). The latter predict different outcomes depending on the type of treatment. Although at the sample level no evidence-based treatment appears to be consistently more effective than another, at the individual patient level one treatment may fit best (Cohen & DeRubeis, 2018; see also Chapter 19 in this *Handbook*). Related to the question of moderators is the issue of mechanisms of change, or what factors cause symptom improvement. Mechanisms of change occur across all treatments, like alliance, or may be unique to PDT. For a long time, PDT practitioners and researchers have considered mechanisms of change as the important targets of change in therapy in and of themselves (Lacewing, 2014, see also Chapter 8 in this *Handbook*). In this section, factors specific to PDT will first be defined and then their status as predictors, moderators, and mediators of change will be reviewed. Five unique factors to PDT are: (a) insight into unconscious conflict, (b) the use of adaptive psychological defenses, (c) flexibility (or less rigidity) in interpersonal perceptions and behaviors, (d) the quality of patients' mental representations of relationships, and (e) comprehension of patients' own and others' mental states. These unique PDT mechanisms may be outcomes in themselves or mediators by which PDT affects symptom change.

Definitions and Measurement of Unique Dynamic Factors

Insight, or self-understanding, is the awareness a person has into his or her motivations, expectations, and behaviors (Jennissen et al., 2018; see also Chapters 7 and 8 in this volume). Insight is often thought to be instilled through the therapist's interpretation of similarities between the patient's past and present experiences (Sharpless, 2019) or through the processing of the shared relationship between patient and therapist (e.g., Hill & Knox, 2009). Frequently, insight is sudden and accompanied by a sensation of discovery, or an "aha" moment (Elliott et al., 1994), although it may develop slowly over treatment (O'Connor et al., 1994). Insight may make symptoms feel more manageable through the development of a narrative as to why those symptoms occur. Alternately, self-understanding may free the individual to act in new ways by providing an emotional release (Freud, 1917/1963) or by triggering a reappraisal of the usefulness of symptom behaviors. Self-understanding may occur at an intellectual or emotional level (McCarthy et al., 2017). Intellectual insight is the cognitive recognition of the origin or purpose of symptoms. Emotional insight refers to the experience of the conflict at a new or different level. Often, emotional insight can be a different sensation of an old memory or familiar experience (a corrective emotional experience, Alexander & French, 1946; Sharpless & Barber, 2012) or a sense of mastery over a previously puzzling experience (Grenyer & Luborsky, 1996). Insight has been measured by therapist judgment (e.g., Mohr et al., 2015), observer judgment from interview (e.g., Johansson et al., 2010), or session content (e.g., Grenyer & Luborsky, 1996), and patient self-report (e.g., Connolly et al., 1999).

Psychological defenses are normative and universal mechanisms by which individuals protect themselves against anxiety arising from unconscious conflict. These mechanisms permit the expression of unacceptable feelings or behavior by the transformation of experience (e.g., denial, or refusal to admit an unpleasant experience happened). Defenses differ from coping mechanisms in that their focus is on managing the internal world of the individual, whereas coping mechanisms are patterns of handling problems in the external world (Cramer, 2015). Defenses vary in their levels of maturity, which represents their developmental appearance as well as their effectiveness in managing conflict (e.g., Cramer, 2015). Less mature defenses are seen in children and in individuals with severe mental illness. They distort perception in order to reduce anxiety, and in doing so, lead to strong inappropriate reactions or withdrawal (e.g., splitting, or when something with multiple characteristics is seen as entirely bad or good). Mature defenses are seen in healthy adults, and both express and inhibit conflict at the same time (e.g., sublimation, or turning strong desires into socially acceptable products like art or financial success). The type and frequency of defenses used are thought to be part of an individual's personality. A defensive style that employs immature defenses or that uses more mature defenses too rigidly can impair the ability to perceive and interact with the world. PDT works to increase the maturity and flexibility of defense use by pointing out the function of defenses and encouraging the use of more adaptive defenses (e.g., Summers & Barber, 2009). Measurement of defenses has been well reviewed elsewhere (Davidson & MacGregor, 1998; Perry & Ianni, 1998) and includes interview measures (e.g., Bond & Perry, 2004) and self-report instruments (e.g., Laaksonen et al., 2013). These measures describe the typical defenses employed by an individual as well as an overall maturity level of the person's defense style.

In psychodynamic theory, individuals have characteristic patterns of motivations, expectations, and reactions in their interactions with others that are learned from childhood experiences. These patterns are used later in life to interpret interpersonal information and guide behavior in new relationships (e.g., Blatt et al., 1997; Bowlby, 1988). The application of these central interpersonal patterns to new relationships is called *transference* and is generally thought to be found in all individuals to some degree. Less healthy individuals apply their relationship patterns more rigidly, adapt less to the demands of their current relationships, and experience poorer relationships and greater symptoms as a result (Kiesler, 1996). Dynamic therapists help make patients aware of their relationship patterns, perhaps through increasing insight, so that patients can more flexibly respond in their interpersonal relationships (e.g., Summers & Barber, 2009). Divergent methods have been used to estimate relationship rigidity (for a review, see McCarthy et

al., 2008), including amplitude (the distinctiveness of a single interpersonal theme in a profile of interpersonal themes; e.g., Locke & Adamic, 2012), pervasiveness (the frequency of a person's central relationship pattern in a sample of narratives; e.g., Wilczek et al., 2004), dispersion (the spread of a distribution of interpersonal themes; e.g., Atzil-Slonim et al., 2011), profile correlation (the covariance of the interpersonal themes among a patient's relationships; e.g., McCarthy et al., 2008), as well as a recent advancement in computerized detection from transcript analysis (Cohen, 2012). However, investigators rarely specify whether they measure rigidity across relationships (i.e., how similar is a person perceiving and acting in each of their relationships), within relationships (i.e., how similar is a person perceiving and acting in the same relationship), or both across and within, which may have implications for findings (see Atzil-Slonim et al., 2011, for a notable exception).

Object relations refers to the cognitive and affective representations that individuals have of their relationships and interpersonal life. Creating a schema of relationships is a developmental process that involves several tasks: populating the representation with objects (persons) derived from actual relationships; storing and organizing episodic and emotional information about these relationships; and integrating the conflicting demands within and among these relationships. These mental representations differ in quality, depending on the early experiences of the person and his or her ability to resolve specific developmental challenges. Having internal representations of relationships allows for the belief that one's own and others' personalities are stable and enduring, for soothing oneself without the direct assistance of others, and for goal-directed interactions with others. The presumed product of good quality of object relations (QOR) is long-standing, satisfying interpersonal relationships in the real world and satisfying, comforting memories of relationships past, as well as the ability to form a strong emotional bond with the therapist in PDT and to examine and grow from the strains that emerge in that relationship. QOR has been measured by clinician interview about relationships (e.g., Joyce et al., 2012; Ortigo et al., 2013) and by self-report (e.g., Huprich et al., 2017; for a review, see Huprich & Greenberg, 2003). A few studies document the concurrent validity of these measures with one another (e.g., Porcerelli et al., 2006), but there may be some interesting method effects (e.g., lower QOR scores from interview vs. written data; Fowler et al., 1996). Whereas most assessment tools describe life-long patterns of QOR, some instruments focus more on the derivatives of object relations, like current interpersonal functioning (Connolly et al., 1999).

The most prominent of the burgeoning mechanisms of change in PDT is mentalization, or reflective functioning (RF; for reviews, see Katznelson, 2014; Luyten et al., 2020). Grounded in attachment theory (Bowlby, 1988) and theory of mind (Baron-Cohen et al., 1985), RF is the ability to comprehend one's own and other's mental states and to use that information to explain and guide relationship behavior. It is considered to be a developmental achievement that occurs through the empathic mirroring behavior of early caregivers and a lack of disruptive traumatic experiences (for a review, see Katznelson, 2014). Individuals with a high degree of RF are able to contemplate their own and other's cognitive and affective states, distinguish between the implicit and explicit intentions possible in behavior, and understand how relational interactions change and develop over time. The concept of RF was initially developed to explain the experiences of patients with BPD but has been expanded to explain other conditions as well (Fonagy et al., 2011). Measurement of mentalization has largely used the Reflective Functioning Scale (RFS; Fonagy et al., 1998), which is coded from clinical interviews (e.g., Harpaz-Rotem & Blatt, 2005) or narratives told by patients in psychotherapy (e.g., Karlsson & Kermott, 2006). Additional scales to assess symptom-specific mentalization have been added to the RFS (e.g., panic, Rudden et al., 2006). Other instruments rate RF from individuals' responses to videotaped social interactions (e.g., Sharp et al., 2016). Recent validation of self-report instruments (e.g., De Meulemeester et al., 2017) and computer coding methods (e.g., Boldrini et al., 2018) have increased the convenience of RF assessment.

Predictors and Moderators of Change

A portion of this literature has focused on who may benefit most from PDT based on their characteristics before entering treatment. In general, studies that have targeted individual predictive factors not unique to PDT have yielded interesting but somewhat inconsistent results (e.g., Chambless et al., 2017; Keefe et al., 2020; see Cohen & DeRubeis, 2018 for a review). However, factors unique to dynamic therapy show more robust results.

Promising research suggests pretreatment level of maladaptive defenses is consistently linked with greater symptom levels and psychopathology (for a review, see Perry & Bond, 2017; for an exception, see Kronström et al., 2009). Possessing greater adaptive defenses at the beginning of treatment predicted a better response to PDT and other treatments (Bond & Perry, 2004; Kronström et al., 2009; Laaksonen et al., 2013). Findings further suggest that pretreatment RF may predict treatment response in PDT (for a review, see Katznelson, 2014; but see also Chambless et al., 2017; de Muelemeester et al., 2017). Furthermore, starting treatment with rigid interpersonal functioning may predispose a patient to poorer outcome in both PDT (Laaksonen et al., 2013; Mohr et al., 2015; but see Clemence & Lewis, 2018) and CBT (Laaksonen et al., 2013).

The findings regarding pretreatment quality of object relation (QOR) as predictors of PDT outcome are much less consistent (for positive examples, see Clemence & Lewis, 2018; Lindfors et al., 2014; for exceptions, see Datz et al., 2016; Høglend et al., 2006; Joyce et al., 2012). Better pretreatment QOR has also been linked to better alliance over the course of therapy (e.g., Goldman & Anderson, 2007; Hersoug et al., 2002; Van et al., 2008), which may provide a platform for PDT work (cf. Piper et al., 2004; but see Høglend et al., 2011). Higher levels of QOR have also been related to better psychological functioning, and can distinguish between clinical and nonclinical samples (e.g., Clemence & Lewis, 2018; Ortigo et al., 2013).

Finally, patients' pretreatment trait-like levels of insight have repeatedly been shown not to predict treatment outcome (Cogan & Porcerelli, 2013; Connolly et al., 1999). Perhaps

previous insights for a symptomatic patient are not presently helpful and new insight is warranted.

Recent studies implementing a machine learning approach were able to use a combination of moderators to capture more of the richness of the variability between different patients. These studies have shown that certain populations of patients may benefit more from PDT than from CBT (e.g., Cohen et al., 2020), and are at lower risk of drop out from PDT than from antidepressant medication treatment (Zilcha-Mano, Keefe et al., 2016). The studies further suggest that patients having stronger pretreatment expectations about the alliance may be at lower risk of dropping out from PDT than from antidepressant medication treatment (Zilcha-Mano, Keefe et al., 2016).

Mediators of Change

Mediators are the mechanisms within a treatment that bring about symptom change. These factors must be shown themselves to change over therapy and to be then related to subsequent symptom change. The literature on dynamic mechanisms of change documenting these associations is extensive (see for example Chapter 8 in this *Handbook*). Insight convincingly seems to increase over the course of PDT as shown in a recent meta-analysis that demonstrated a medium-sized effect of insight during treatment on symptom change in PDT (Jennissen et al., 2018). These findings are consistent with client descriptions of the importance of insight (e.g., Huang et al., 2014; Timulak & McElvaney, 2013). Smaller correlations of insight and improvement were found in other treatments (Jennissen et al., 2018), and insight may even be experienced differently by clients in therapies other than PDT (i.e., poignancy in PDT vs. empowerment in CBT; Timulak & McElvaney, 2013). Changes in self-understanding seem to precede improvement in symptoms and functioning (e.g., Høglend & Hagtvet, 2019). It is important to separate the findings based on state-like changes in insight during treatment from findings based on trait-like pretreatment levels of insight. Whereas the former demonstrate a potential role of insight as a mechanism of change, the latter yielded mostly null results, as reported above. Overall, insight is strongly implicated in the process of change in PDT. More precise definition and measurement of insight as well as an understanding of the link of insight to behavior change may increase our ability to detect who will benefit most from PDT.

Patients consistently show less reliance on immature defenses and more mature defense use over the course of PDT (for a review, Perry & Bond, 2017). Changes in the maturity of defensive functioning have been related to changes in symptom level (for a review, Perry & Bond, 2017). Whether change in defenses precedes or follows change in symptoms remains unclear and awaits further study (Hersoug et al., 2002; Kramer et al., 2013). Furthermore, improvements in defensive style may not be unique to PDT, as these changes are present and are related to symptom change in many other treatments (e.g., Kramer et al., 2013; Perry et al., 2017). In sum, defenses may be uniquely addressed by PDT but may be common to change processes in multiple forms of treatment. Further work will need to examine what factors in therapy create changes in defense style.

Rigidity has been shown to decrease in response to PDT (e.g., Atzil-Slonim et al., 2011; for exceptions, see Perry et al., 2017). The research is equivocal regarding whether changes in rigidity relate to changes in symptoms over the same period (for studies with positive relations, see Atzil-Slonim et al., 2011; Perry et al., 2017; for null relations, Wilczek et al., 2004). Recent research has shown rigidity may also change in different psychotherapies (Batista et al., 2019; Ruiz et al., 2004). Levels of relationship rigidity are seemingly independent of psychiatric problems (for a review, see McCarthy et al., 2008; for positive relations, e.g., Clemence & Lewis, 2018; Cohen, 2012 for null relations, e.g., Atzil-Slonim et al., 2011; Shell et al., 2018; for negative relations, e.g., Locke & Adamic, 2012) and may in fact share a curvilinear relation with symptoms (i.e., individuals too inflexible or too inconsistent in their relationships may experience more difficulties; Atzil-Slonim et al., 2011; McCarthy et al., 2008). The numerous operational variations in rigidity may have led to these diverse findings, but these methods are being innovatively applied in other contexts, like work on alliance ruptures (Sommerfeld et al., 2008), client and therapist attunement (Lazarus et al., 2019), therapist countertransference (Wiseman & Tishby, 2017), and supervision (Messina et al., 2018).

QOR has been shown to change across PDT in multiple studies and to be associated with symptom improvement as well (e.g., Mullin et al., 2017; Vermote et al., 2010). Change in QOR in other treatments has not been investigated and so remains an open research question. The exact role of QOR in PDT therefore remains unclear, perhaps due to its multifaceted nature (e.g., number of relationships, valence and complexity among relationships, applicability of the schema to present relationships) and the potential difficulty of capturing all of these dimensions in one score and finding a correlation with change.

Initial support for mentalization as a change factor in PDT was mixed. However, growing evidence now suggests that RF increases over PDT (for a review, see de Muelemeester et al., 2017; Katznelson, 2014; Laaksonen et al., 2013; for exceptions, see Vermote et al., 2010), and many of these more recent studies link change in RF over treatment to change in symptoms (Fischer-Kern et al., 2015; Rossouw & Fonagy, 2012; but see Vermote et al., 2010). RF did not increase in CBT (Karlsson & Kermott, 2006; but see Laaksonen et al., 2013) or in treatment as usual (Fischer-Kern et al., 2015; Roussouw & Fonagy, 2012). It improved in emotion-focused therapy (Compare et al., 2018) but significantly decreased in interpersonal psychotherapy (Karlsson & Kermott, 2006). Lower RF was associated with greater symptoms or more severe diagnoses in some studies (for a review, see Boldrini et al., 2018; Håkansson, Söderström et al., 2017) but not others (e.g., Chambless et al., 2017). As a skill, RF can be taught to trainees (Ensink et al., 2013; Scandurra et al., 2018), and higher RF in therapists may improve patient outcomes (Cologon et al., 2017). Mentalization is a process certainly linked to change in PDT, and may have a stronger relation to symptom change when it is measured for the specific disorder being examined (e.g., Rudden et al., 2006), although the overlap of symptom-specific RF and the concept of insight may need greater elaboration.

Research Contributing to Our Understanding of PDT

The findings concerning predictors and moderators of outcome in PDT, and those on mechanisms of change of PDT are together contributing to a comprehensive understanding of how PDT works and which individuals are likely to benefit most from it. Additional studies are needed to make further progress toward personalized PDT treatments. Such studies may use advanced methodological and statistical tools (e.g., machine learning approaches) to identify which subpopulations may benefit most from each of the PDT mechanisms of change detailed above, and explore how distinct mechanisms can be integrated to match the concrete needs and characteristics of subpopulations of patients. In other words, future studies should integrate questions on predictors and moderators with those on mechanisms of change to produce more personalized PDT research (Zilcha-Mano, 2019). Such research will help therapists tailor PDT treatment to diverse populations of patients.

Technique Use in PDT

One can conceptualize the two major types of PDT techniques as supportive and expressive (Luborsky, 1984; Sharpless, 2019). Supportive techniques include many of the common factors like warmth and empathy but also include ego-strengthening interventions more unique to PDT like boundary setting, gratification, and bolstering adaptive defenses. Expressive or interpretative interventions are designed to uncover or "express" the unconscious conflict behind a patient's symptoms. These interventions include exploration of affect and interpersonal themes (i.e., encouraging patients to generate affective and relationship material through free association or selectively focusing the patient's attention on these themes), clarification (i.e., drawing patients' attention to knowledge they already possess but in a new light), and interpretation (i.e., making meaningful connections between past and present relationship experiences, especially involving the therapist).

The use of PDT techniques in a session or segment of a session is often assessed for either a single class of interventions (e.g., transference interpretations) or for PDT intervention use on average. Measurement of psychodynamic techniques can be accomplished with frequency counts or percentage of total intervention use in a session (e.g., Connolly et al., 1999), or average subscale scores from intervention measures (e.g., Hilsenroth et al., 2005; McCarthy et al., 2016). A specific type of intervention measure is an adherence scale (e.g., Barber, 2009; Barber et al., 1996), which measures the degree to which a therapist followed the principles and techniques set out in a therapy manual. Adherence is often used as a manipulation check to ensure that the treatment was delivered (e.g., Spinhoven et al., 2007) but is only infrequently studied in relation to PDT process and outcome. Adherence and technique use are not synonymous (adherence is a subset of technique use), but we will not consider them separately here due to the limited number of process studies that examine the effects of PDT techniques.

Expressive interventions, when measured together on average, have demonstrated an equivocal relation with treatment outcome (for a review, see Barber, 2009; McCarthy et al., 2019; for no relation, e.g., Barber et al., 1996; Tschuschke et al., 2015; for a favorable relation, e.g., Bush & Meehan, 2011 Hilsenroth et al., 2005; for unfavorable relations, e.g., Barber et al., 2008; McAleavey et al., 2014). A comprehensive review of the literature on the relation of adherence to PDT techniques to outcome appears in Chapter 8 of this *Handbook*. Investigations of individual expressive techniques provide some additional detail to the ambiguity of these findings. Exploration of affect has been consistently linked to more positive outcomes (for a meta-analysis, see Diener et al., 2007; see also Town et al., 2017; Ulvenes et al., 2012). Exploration of interpersonal themes has also been predictive of outcome on a consistent basis (e.g., Klein et al., 2003). Confrontation was correlated with symptom change in one study (Town et al., 2012).

Interpretation is the most studied of the expressive interventions, and in contrast to other expressive interventions, is often found to be related to worse therapeutic outcomes (e.g., Høglend et al., 2006; Ryum et al., 2010; Schut et al., 2005; for a review, see Høglend, 2004). One obvious explanation of this negative association might be that interpretation has a damaging effect on patients, although this account is contradicted by the efficacy data for PDT (this chapter) as well as by clinical observation. A more subtle understanding of the negative relation between interpretation and outcome has been titled the "high risk–high gain" phenomenon (Gabbard et al., 1994). Targeted and sparing use of interpretations may lead to better outcome, but frequent use of interpretation may feel overwhelming for certain patients and therefore might temporarily increase symptoms (Strachey, 1934) or may reflect the therapists' despair at helping their patients. Some studies of the immediate in-session climate associated with interpretation support this account. For instance, interpretations are more related to symptom improvement when followed by emotion processing (McCullough et al., 1991; Milbrath et al., 1999). At the same time, interpretative work has a high probability of being perceived as disaffiliative (e.g., Klein, Milrod et al., 2003; Petraglia et al., 2015; Schut et al., 2005) and may lead to alliance ruptures and poor outcome if not handled correctly by therapists. Expressive interventions lead to change in PDT mechanisms like insight, defenses, and RF, and interpretation may have an indirect relation to symptom change through these mediators (e.g., Høglend & Hagvegt, 2019). A final explanation of the negative relation between interpretation and symptoms might be that patients unlikely to improve may receive or pull for more interpretations from their therapists (Hoglend, 2004).

Supportive interventions have largely been measured in aggregate as opposed to separately singly (e.g., Barber et al., 1996) or in relation to the expressive interventions in PDT sessions (e.g., Hendriksen et al., 2011). Surprisingly, there has been no result when supportive interventions were correlated with outcome (e.g., Barber et al., 1996, 2008; Hersoug et al., 2004; although see Bush & Meehan; 2011), even though well-provided supportive therapy is often effective (e.g., McMain et al., 2009). Supportive techniques may be essential for treatment to occur and may be helpful regardless of level. The lack of more thorough investigation of supportive techniques might be due to the greater emphasis placed on expressive techniques in PDT theory (Bush & Meehan, 2011) or due to the tendency to concentrate on the therapeutic alliance, which has been consistently shown to be a product of supportive work (Bush & Meehan, 2011; Lingiardi et al., 2011; Meystre et al., 2015; Solomonov et al., 2018).

Moderators of PDT Technique Use and Outcome

The relation between technique use and outcome in PDT has proved quite complex, although in the absence of other factors, it can be recommended that more affective and interpersonal exploration be used but only sparing interpretation. The complexity of the association between PDT interventions and outcome has caused dynamic theorists and researchers to look for how the process of therapy might influence the relation of technique use and outcome and how different methodologies might produce different findings.

Level of Intervention Use

Typical approaches correlating technique use to outcome have used a "more is better" approach (Barber, 2009; Webb et al., 2010) in which greater intervention use is hypothesized to relate to more symptom improvement. PDT researchers have begun to reimagine this association, postulating that it is flexible or adaptive use of techniques that predict best outcome (a "just right" approach) (Barber, 2009). Owen and Hilsenroth (2014) used sophisticated statistical modeling to estimate both the therapists' average level of PDT intervention use for individual patients as well as the variance in therapists' technique use for each patient across sessions. Higher average PDT intervention levels in a treatment were not related to improvement, consistent with the finding that more is not always better. However, greater within-patient variability in therapist technique use, or flexible application of PDT techniques, did correlate with later symptom change. McCarthy et al. (2016) have modeled a curvilinear relation of PDT technique to outcome in a sample of depressed patients. Moderate technique use was associated with better outcome than were very low levels (not sufficient to encourage change) or very high levels (too overwhelming or destabilizing for patients). This curvilinear relation may depend in part on the population studied, as in the PDT arm of a randomized trial for cocaine dependence, Barber and colleagues (2008) observed a curvilinear relation in the opposite direction. Very high and low levels of psychodynamic interventions, but not moderate levels, were related to greater drug abstinence. Treatment for substance use disorders may differ due to the tendency in many substance users toward externalizing behaviors (e.g., blaming, substance intake) to manage their own emotional reactions rather than verbalizing their problems more directly.

Integration of Techniques

Several recent studies have begun to document the potentially helpful effects in PDT of borrowing techniques from other therapy systems. Whereas it is nearly universal that PDT can be distinguished from other treatments based on levels of technique use, many PDT therapists will explicitly or unwittingly employ interventions from different therapy modalities (for a review, see McCarthy et al., 2019). Techniques chosen from other therapy systems tend to overlap with supportive psychotherapy (e.g., setting session goals or suggesting behavioral activation), are in response to specific patient needs (e.g., offering a cognitive reframe of a problem to a patient in distress), or are part of an integrated approach to providing psychotherapy. Empirically, incorporating CBT (Katz et al., 2019) and experiential (McCarthy et al., 2016) interventions has been shown to enhance outcomes in PDT. Individual techniques shown to be associated with outcome when added to PDT have been setting explicit goals (Goldman et al., 2013), incorporating interpersonally themed homework (Nelson & Castonguay, 2017), emotion processing (Meystre et al., 2015), and focusing on the here-and-now relationship (Hill et al., 2014).

Techniques and Alliance

PDT techniques are often assumed to influence outcome through the therapeutic alliance, but exactly how this relation works has been a matter of continued discussion. Early theorists thought that the alliance represented the rational side of the patient's unconscious which responds positively to the therapist's interpretations (Greenson, 1965). In support of this idea, technique use at one time point in therapy is often associated with higher levels of alliance at a later point (e.g., Lingiardi et al., 2011; but see Solomonov et al., 2018). Others have believed the therapeutic relationship is fostered and used differently in different treatments (e.g., Spinhoven et al., 2007, Ulvenes et al., 2012). Still others have treated the alliance as a distinct factor against which technique competes to explain the variance in outcome (e.g., Barber et al., 1996). However, many psychodynamic thinkers and researchers believe that alliance provides a context for technique use, such that greater levels of alliance permit PDT techniques to be more effective. Several studies have now documented such an interaction between alliance and expressive technique use in PDT (Barber et al., 2008; Ryum et al., 2010), showing that at high levels of alliance, expressive techniques are equal to if not superior to supportive techniques in relating to outcome, whereas at low levels of alliance supportive interventions are to be preferred (see Høglend et al., 2011, for an exception). However, there still are only a handful of studies documenting this interaction, perhaps because detecting interaction effects often requires large samples and good variability in both factors examined (McClelland & Judd, 1993), and few studies in psychotherapy research have those advantages. Finally, PDT techniques may have an indirect effect on outcome through the alliance. Kivlighan and colleagues (2019) demonstrated that higher levels of dynamic interventions were associated with greater alliances, which in turn were related to better symptom outcome.

Competence

Competency is how well a therapist implements interventions with a given patient. Competence is typically judged by individuals with recognized expertise in psychotherapy practice. Some factors entering into a judgment of a therapist's competence are: (a) the ability to formulate patient's personality organization or symptom constellation; (b) the accurate assessment of the patient's need at the moment of intervention,

including the patient's receptivity to intervention; (c) the choice of a specific intervention for a given problem, including its appropriateness for the problem; (d) the comparison of the chosen intervention to other potential interventions not selected, especially techniques proscribed for PDT; and (e) the execution of the intervention (Barber, 2009; Barber et al., 1996). A critical addition to the definition of competence in PDT consideration of the patient's relevant multicultural identifications for treatment (Tummala-Narra, 2016). Holistic judgments are common over a certain period of observation, although competence is often measured for multiple classes of interventions (e.g., Barber et al., 1996; Despland et al., 2009). Greater competence necessitates some use of PDT techniques, although the correlation found between PDT technique use or adherence to a PDT manual may be modest (Barber et al., 2007).

Competency has been shown to be related to alliance (Despland et al., 2009), however, the relation between global competence in PDT and outcome has been equivocal. A comprehensive review of the literature on the relation between competence in the delivery of PDT techniques and outcome appears in Chapter 8 in this *Handbook*. In a study of patients with depression, a positive relation between competence in expressive techniques and subsequent symptom improvement was found (Barber et al., 1996). Similarly, a positive relation between competency and outcome was observed in very brief (four-session) PDT, but only for those patients whose alliances improved over the four sessions (Despland et al., 2009). In a study of psychodynamic treatment for cocaine-dependent individuals, no relation was observed (Barber et al., 2008). Finally, competence was associated with worse outcomes in a study of short-term anxiety-provoking psychotherapy (Svartberg & Stiles, 1994). Clearly more work is needed to understand why the intuitive relation between competence and outcome is not always observed and to investigate the conditions under which competence is related to improvement. One possibility is that the breadth of judgments required to assess competence reduces not only reliability of competency estimates but also compounds the problem by multiple unreliabilities across dimensions. When dimensions of competency are examined separately, a clearer picture may emerge.

Accuracy of Interpretations

One dimension of competency in DT is how accurate a therapist's interpretations are in regard to the unconscious conflict of the patient. Accuracy has been defined as the extent to which the interpretations keep with a patient's formulation, or the theoretical understanding of the patient's problems given his or her unique history. Researchers have used experienced therapists' formulations of their patients (e.g., Castonguay et al., 2017) or observer-derived formulations (e.g., Crits-Christoph et al., 2010) as the criterion to compare the accuracy of their subsequent interpretations. There has been a strong positive correlation between accuracy and subsequent outcome (Andrusyna et al., 2006; Keefe et al., 2019). Interestingly, greater correspondence of therapists' interventions to an outside judge's formulation of a patient leads to better outcome in IPT but deleterious outcomes in CBT, providing partial evidence that interpersonal-focused psychotherapies may work in a unique and specific way through relationships (Crits-Christoph et al., 2010). Greater accuracy is associated with increased therapeutic alliance (Junod et al., 2005; Stigler et al., 2007), although interpretations that are less deep, and therefore slightly less accurate to the patient's problems, foster the strongest alliances (Hersoug et al., 2004; Petraglia et al., 2015).

Conclusion and New Directions

The findings suggest that the relation between technique use and outcome is a complex one, although interpersonal and affective exploration and sparing use of accurate interpretation appear to be generally helpful. Supportive techniques may provide a necessary backdrop for the development of alliance and delivery of other techniques. PDT techniques may produce the greatest change when alliance is high. Much exciting work concerning the PDT process remains to be done, including examining how PDT techniques relate not only to symptom change but also to change mechanisms and outcomes specific to dynamic therapy; what complex and indirect relations may exist between process variables in PDT; and how we may tailor PDT for the benefit of different individuals, especially using the lens of the patient's culture. Recent research findings and methodological advances have led to many new productive paths for investigating change in PDT.

CONCLUSION AND RECOMMENDATIONS

Accumulated findings indicate the efficacy and effectiveness of PDT in treating a variety of mental health problems. Research on PDT is becoming increasingly instrumental in exploring theory-driven predictors of PDT prognosis and mechanisms of change. These studies are beginning to shed light on which individuals are most likely to benefit from PDT, as for example, individuals with higher levels of reflective functioning and less rigid interpersonal functioning. Findings further suggest that individuals with more positive expectations about the relationship with the therapist may be less likely to drop out from PDT. Such findings can complement clinical judgment when deciding whether an individual should be referred to PDT.

Findings regarding the main mechanisms of change associated with treatment outcomes in PDT can be used in choosing the main targets of treatment, especially in short-term treatments, where cost-effective decisions are particularly needed. Among PDT mechanisms receiving the most empirical attention and support are alliance, insight, defense style, relationship rigidity, quality of object relations, and reflective functioning. Research has also focused on the use of PDT techniques that may facilitate change in these mechanisms. In the context of a strong alliance, findings indicate the advantages of targeted and sparing use of interpretations, which has been referred to as the "just right" approach, to replace the "more is better" approach. In the context of a poor alliance, therapists should be especially careful in offering interpretations. Studies have also pointed out the advantages of integrating other techniques, in addition to traditional PDT techniques, including setting explicit goals, incorporating interpersonally themed homework, and emotion processing.

Future research may focus on repeated high-resolution measurement of the process of change in PDT over the entire course of treatment, enabling close observation of the processes that occur during treatment, examining which processes precede others, and how distinct processes may interact to affect outcome. Such studies may use automated interdisciplinary approaches to measure processes of change that enable moment-to-moment assessment of the change, as it occur over the course of treatment. Future research should integrate questions concerning moderators and mechanisms of change to make progress toward personalized treatment, identifying the most effective mechanisms for each subpopulation of patients, and making possible the tailoring of PDT to diverse populations.

ABBREVIATIONS

3RS	Rupture Resolution Rating System
AFT	Alliance-Focused Training
BDI	Beck Depression Inventory
BPD	borderline personality disorder
BRT	brief relational therapy
CALPAS	California Psychotherapy Alliance Scales
CBASP	cognitive Behavioral Analysis System of Psychotherapy
CBT	cognitive-behavior therapy
CI	confidence interval
CIS	Collaborative Interaction Scale
CT	cognitive therapy
DSM	Diagnostic and Statistical Manual
ES	effect size
GAD	generalized anxiety disorder
HAM-D	Hamilton Rating Scale for Depression
HAq	Helping Alliance Questionnaire
ICT	Integrative CT for Depression
IIP	Inventory of Interpersonal Problems
IPT	interpersonal therapy
MBT	Mentalization-Based Treatment
PD	personality disorder
PD NOS	personality disorder – not otherwise specified
PDT	psychodynamic treatment
PHQ-9	Patient Health Questionnaire-9
PIT	psychodynamic interpersonal therapy
PSQ	postsession questionnaire
PTSD	post-traumatic stress disorder
QOR	quality of object relations
RF	reflective functioning
SE	standard error
TAU	treatment as usual
VPPS	Vanderbilt Psychotherapy Process Scale
WAI	Working Alliance Inventory

REFERENCES

Abbass, A. A., Kisely, S. R., & Kroenke, K. (2009). Short-term psychodynamic psychotherapy for somatic disorders: Systematic review of meta-analysis of clinical trials. *Psychotherapy and Psychosomatics, 78*(5), 265–274. https://doi.org/10.1159/000228247

Abbass, A. A., Kisely, S. R., Town, J. M., Leichsenring, F., Driessen, E., De Maat, S., Gerber, A., Dekker, J., Rabung, S., Rusalovska, S., & Crowe, E. (2014). Short-term psychodynamic psychotherapies for common mental disorders. *The Cochrane database of systematic reviews,* (7), CD004687. https://doi.org/10.1002/14651858.CD004687.pub4

Ablon, J. S., & Jones, E. E. (2002). Validity of controlled clinical trials of psychotherapy: Findings from the NIMH Treatment of Depression Collaborative Research Program. *The American Journal of Psychiatry, 159*(5), 775–783. https://doi.org/10.1176/appi.ajp.159.5.775

Ackerman, S. J., & Hilsenroth, M. J. (2001). A review of therapist characteristics and technique negatively impacting the therapeutic alliance. *Psychotherapy: Theory, Research, Practice, Training, 38*(2) 171–185. https://doi.org/10.1037/0033-3204.38.2.171

Ackerman, S., & Hilsenroth, M. (2003). A review of therapist characteristics and techniques positively impacting the therapeutic alliance. *Clinical Psychology Review, 23*(1), 1–33. https://doi.org/10.1016/S0272-7358(02)00146-0

Agnew, R. M., Harper, H., Shapiro, D. A., & Barkham, M. (1994). Resolving a challenge to the therapeutic relationship: A single-case study. *British Journal of Medical Psychology, 67*(2), 155–170. https://doi.org/10.1111/j.2044-8341.1994.tb01783.x

Alexander, F., & French, T. M. (1946). *Psychoanalytic therapy; principles and application.* Oxford, United Kingdom: Ronald Press.

Andersson, G., Paxling, B., Roch-Norlund, P., Östman, G., Norgren, A., Almlöv, J., Georén, L., Breitholtz, E., Dahlin, M., Cuijpers, P., Carlbring, P., & Silverberg, F. (2012). Internet-based psychodynamic versus cognitive behavioral guided self-help for generalized anxiety disorder: A randomized controlled trial. *Psychotherapy and Psychosomatics, 81*(6), 344–355. https://doi.org/10.1159/000339371

Andrusyna, T. P., Luborsky, L., Pham, T., & Tang, T. Z. (2006). The mechanisms of sudden gains in supportive-expressive therapy for depression. *Psychotherapy Research, 16*(5), 526–536. https://doi.org/10.1080/10503300600591379

Aron, L. (1996). *A meeting of minds: Mutuality in psychoanalysis.* (Relational perspectives book series) (Vol. 4). Hillsdale, NJ: Analytic Press.

Aspland, H., Llewelyn, S., Hardy, G. E., Barkham, M., & Stiles, W. (2008). Alliance ruptures and rupture resolution in cognitive-behavior therapy: A preliminary task analysis. *Psychotherapy Research, 18*(6), 699–710. https://doi.org/10.1080/10503300802291463

Atzil-Slonim, D., Shefler, G., Gvirsman, S. D., & Tishby, O. (2011). Changes in rigidity and symptoms among adolescents in psychodynamic psychotherapy. *Psychotherapy Research, 21*(6), 685–697. https://doi.org/10.1080/10503307.2011.602753

Baldwin, S. A., Wampold, B. E., & Imel, Z. E. (2007). Untangling the alliance-outcome correlation: Exploring the relative importance of therapist and patient variability in the alliance. *Journal of Consulting and Clinical Psychology, 75*(6), 842–852. https://doi.org/10.1037/0022-006X.75.6.842

Bambling, M., King, R., Raue, P., Schweitzer, R., & Lambert, W., (2006). Clinical supervision: Its influence on client-rated working alliance and client symptom reduction in the brief treatment of major depression. *Psychotherapy Research, 16*(3), 317–331. https://doi.org/10.1080/10503300500268524

Barber, J. P. (2009). Towards a working through of some core conflicts in psychotherapy research. *Psychotherapy Research, 19*(1), 1–12. https://doi.org/10.1080/10503300802609680

Barber, J. P., Barrett, M. S. Gallop, R., Rynn, M., & Rickels, K. (2012). Short-term dynamic therapy vs. pharmacotherapy for major depressive disorder. *Journal of Clinical Psychiatry, 73*(1), 66–73. https://doi.org/10.4088/JCP.11m06831

Barber, J. P., Connolly, M. B., Crits-Christoph, P., Gladis, L., & Siqueland, L. (2000). Alliance predicts patients' outcome beyond in-treatment change in symptoms. *Journal of Consulting and Clinical Psychology, 68*(6), 1027–1032. https://doi.org/10.1037/0022-006X.68.6.1027

Barber, J. P., Crits-Christoph, P., & Luborsky, L. (1996). Effects of therapist adherence and competence on patient outcome in brief dynamic therapy. *Journal of Consulting and Clinical Psychology, 64*(3), 619–622. https://doi.org/10.1037/0022-006X.64.3.619

Barber, J. P., Gallop, R., Crits-Christoph, P., Barrett, M. S., Klostermann, S., McCarthy, K. S., & Sharpless, B. A. (2008). The role of the alliance and techniques in predicting outcome of supportive-expressive dynamic therapy for cocaine dependence. *Psychoanalytic Psychology, 25*(3), 461–482. https://doi.org/10.1037/0736-9735.25.3.461

Barber, J. P., Luborsky, L., Crits-Christoph, P., Thase, M. E., Wiess, R., Frank, A., Onken, L., & Gallop, R. (1999). Therapeutic alliance as a predictor of outcome in treatment of cocaine dependence. *Psychotherapy Research, 9*(1), 54–73. https://doi.org/10.1093/ptr/9.1.54

Barber, J. P., Luborsky, L., Gallop, R., Crits-Christoph, P., Frank, A., Weiss, R. D., Thase, M. E., Connolly, M. B., Gladis, M., Foltz, C., & Siqueland, L. (2001). Therapeutic alliance as a predictor of outcome and retention in the National Institute on Drug Abuse Collaborative Cocaine Treatment Study. *Journal of Consulting and Clinical Psychology, 69*(1), 119–124. https://doi.org/10.1037/0022-006X.69.1.119

Barber, J. P., & Muenz, L. R. (1996). The role of avoidance and obsessiveness in matching patients to cognitive and interpersonal psychotherapy: Empirical findings from the treatment for depression collaborative research program. *Journal of Consulting and Clinical Psychology, 64*(5), 951–958. https://doi.org/10.1037/0022-006X.64.5.951

Barber, J. P., Muran, J. C., McCarthy, K. S., & Keefe, R. J. (2013). Research on psychodynamic therapies. In M. J. Lambert (Ed.). *Bergin and Garfield's handbook of psychotherapy and behavior change* (6th ed.) (pp. 443–494). New York, NY: John Wiley & Sons, Inc.

Barber, J. P., Sharpless, B. A., Klostermann, S., & McCarthy, K. S. (2007). Assessing intervention competence and its relation to therapy outcome: A selected review derived from the outcome literature. *Professional Psychology: Research and Practice, 38*(5), 493–500. https://doi.org/10.1037/0735-7028.38.5.493

Baron-Cohen, S., Leslie, A., & Frith, U. (1985). Does the autistic child have a "theory of mind?" *Cognition, 21*(1), 37–46. https://doi.org/10.1016/0010-0277(85)90022-8

Batista, J., Silva, J., Freitas, S., Alves, D., Machado, A., Sousa, I., Fernández-Navarro, P., Magalhães, C., & Gonçalves, M. M. (2019). Relational schemas as mediators of innovative moments in symptom improvement in major depression. *Psychotherapy Research, 29*(1), 58–69. https://doi.org/10.1080/10503307.2017.1359427

Bender, D. S. (2005). The therapeutic alliance in the treatment of personality disorders. *Journal of Psychiatric Practice, 11*(2), 73–87. https://doi.org/10.1097/00131746-200503000-00002

Benjamin, L. S., & Critchfield, K. L. (2010). An interpersonal perspective on therapy alliances and techniques. In J. C. Muran & J. P. Barber (Eds.), *The therapeutic alliance: An evidence-based guide to practice* (pp. 123–149). New York, NY: Guilford Press.

Bennett, D., Parry, G., & Ryle, A. (2006). Resolving threats to the therapeutic alliance in cognitive analytic therapy of borderline personality disorder: A task analysis. *Psychology and Psychotherapy: Theory, Research, and Practice, 79*(3), 395–418. https://doi.org/10.1348/147608305X58355

Bien, E., Anderson, T., Strupp, H., Henry, W., Schacht, T., Binder, J., & Butler, S. (2000). The effects of training in time-limited dynamic psychotherapy: Changes in therapeutic outcome. *Psychotherapy Research, 10*(2), 119–132. https://doi.org/10.1080/713663669

Black, S., Hardy, G., Turpin, G., & Parry, G. (2005). Self-reported attachment styles and therapeutic orientation of therapists and their relationship with reported general alliance quality and problems in therapy. *Psychology and Psychotherapy: Theory, Research and Practice, 78*(3), 363–377. https://doi.org/10.1348/147608305X43784

Blagys, M., & Hilsenroth, M. (2000). Distinctive features of short-term psychodynamic-interpersonal psychotherapy: An empirical review of the comparative psychotherapy process literature. *Clinical Psychology: Science and Practice, 7*(2), 167–188. https://doi.org/10.1093/clipsy.7.2.167

Blatt, S. J., Auerbach, J. S., & Levy, K. N. (1997). Mental representations in personality development, psychopathology, and the therapeutic process. *Review of General Psychology, 1*(4), 351–374. https://doi.org/10.1037/1089-2680.1.4.351

Boldrini, T., Nazzaro, M. P., Daminani, R., Genova, F., Gazzillo, F., & Lingiardi, V. (2018). Mentalization as a predictor of psychoanalytic outcome: An empirical study of transcribed psychoanalytic sessions through the lenses of a computerized text analysis measure of reflective functioning. *Psychoanalytic Psychology, 35*(2), 196–204. https://doi.org/10.1037/pap0000154

Bond, M., & Perry, J. C. (2004). Long-term changes in defense styles with psychodynamic psychotherapy for depressive, anxiety, and personality disorders. *The American Journal of Psychiatry, 161*(9), 1665–1671. https://doi.org/10.1176/appi.ajp.161.9.1665

Bordin, E. (1979). The generalizability of the psychoanalytic concept of the working alliance. *Psychotherapy: Theory, Research, and Practice, 16*(3), 252–260. https://doi.org/10.1037/h0085885

Bowlby, J. (1988). *A secure base.* New York, NY: Basic Books.

Brenner, C. (1979). Working alliance, therapeutic alliance, and transference. *Journal of the American Psychoanalytic Association, 27*(1) Suppl, 136–158. https://doi.org/10.1177/000306517902701S01

Briggs, S., Netuveli, G., Gould, N., Gkaravella, A., Gluckman, N. S., Kangogyere, P., Farr, R., Goldblatt, M. J., & Lindner, R. (2019). The effectiveness of psychoanalytic/psychodynamic psychotherapy for reducing suicide attempts and self-harm: Systematic review and meta-analysis. *The British Journal of Psychiatry, 214*(6), 320–328. https://doi.org/10.1192/bjp.2019.33

Brottman, M. A. (2004). *Therapeutic alliance and adherence in cognitive therapy for depression.* Unpublished doctoral dissertation, University of Pennsylvania, Philadelphia.

Busch, F. N., & Milrod, B. L. (2018). Trauma-focused psychodynamic psychotherapy. *Psychiatric Clinics, 41*(2), 277–287. https://doi.org/10.1016/j.psc.2018.01.005

Busch, F. N., Milrod, B. L., Singer, M. B., & Aronson, A. C. (2012). *Manual of panic focused psychodynamic psychotherapy – extended range* (Vol. 36). New York, NY: Routledge. https://doi.org/10.4324/9780203868560

Busch, F. N., Nehrig, N., & Milrod, B. (2019). Trauma-focused psychodynamic psychotherapy of a patient with PTSD in a Veterans Affairs setting. *American Journal of Psychotherapy, 72*(1), 24–28. https://doi.org/10.1176/appi.psychotherapy.20180019

Bush, M., & Meehan, W. (2011). Should supportive measures and relational variables be considered a part of psychoanalytic technique?: Some empirical considerations. *International Journal of Psychoanalysis, 92*(2), 377–399. https://doi.org/10.1111/j.1745-8315.2011.00403.x

Cabral, R. R., & Smith, T. B. (2011). Racial/ethnic matching of clients and therapists in mental health services: A meta-analytic review of preferences, perceptions, and outcomes. *Journal of Counseling Psychology, 58*(4), 537–554. https://doi.org/10.1037/a0025266

Caligor, E., Kernberg, O. F., Clarkin, J. F., & Yeomans, F. E. (2018). *Psychodynamic therapy for personality pathology: Treating self and interpersonal functioning.* Washington, DC: American Psychiatric Publishing. https://doi.org/10.1176/appi.books.9781615371501.lr32

Cash, S. K., Hardy, G. E., Kellett, S., & Parry, G. (2014). Alliance ruptures and resolution during cognitive behaviour therapy with patients with borderline personality disorder. *Psychotherapy Research, 24*(2), 132–145. https://doi.org/10.1080/10503307.2013.838652

Castonguay, L. G., Goldfried, M. R., Wiser, S. L., Raue, P. J. & Hayes, A. M. (1996). Predicting the effect of cognitive therapy for depression: A study of unique and common factors. *Journal of Consulting and Clinical Psychology, 64*(3), 497–504. https://doi.org/10.1037/0022-006X.64.3.497

Castonguay, L. G., Janis, R. A., Youn, S. J., Xiao, H., McAleavey, A. A., Boswell, J. F., Carney, D. M., Boutselis, M. A., Braver, M., Chiswick, N. R., Hemmelstein, N. A., Jackson, J. S., Lytle, R. A., Morford, M. E., Scott, H. S., Spayd, C. S., & Wiley, M. O. (2017). Clinicians' prediction and recall of therapeutic interventions: Practice research network study. *Counselling Psychology Quarterly, 30*(3), 308–322. https://doi.org/10.1080/09515070.2017.1334628

Castonguay, L. G., Schut, A. J., Aikins, D., Constantino, M. J., Lawrenceau, J. P., Bologh, L., & Burns, D. D. (2004). Repairing alliance ruptures in cognitive therapy: A preliminary investigation of an integrative therapy for depression. *Journal of Psychotherapy Integration, 14*(1), 4–20. https://doi.org/10.1037/1053-0479.14.1.4

Chambless, D. L., Milrod, B., Porter, E., Gallop, R., McCarthy, K. S., Graf, E., Rudden, M., Sharpless, B. A., & Barber, J. P. (2017). Prediction and moderation of improvement in cognitive-behavioral and psychodynamic psychotherapy for panic disorder. *Journal of Consulting and Clinical Psychology, 85*(8), 803–813. https://doi.org/10.1037/ccp0000224

Chapman, B. P., Talbot, N., Tatman, A. W., & Britton, P. C. (2009). Personality traits and the working alliance in psychotherapy trainees: An organizing role for the five factor model? *Journal of Social and Clinical Psychology, 28*(5), 577–596. https://doi.org/10.1521/jscp.2009.28.5.577

Clarkin, J. F., Yeomans F. E., & Kernberg O. F. (2006). *Psychotherapy for borderline personality disorder focusing on object relations.* Washington, DC: American Psychiatric.

Clemence, A. J., & Lewis, K. (2018). Flexibility and rigidity in object relational functioning: Assessing change in suicidal ideation and global psychiatric functioning using the SCORS-G. *Journal of Personality Assessment, 100*(2), 135–144. https://doi.org/10.1080/00223891.2017.1418747

Cogan, R., & Porcerelli, J. H. (2013). Validation of the Shedler-Westen Assessment Procedure Insight Scale. *The Journal of Nervous & Mental Disorder, 201*(8), 706–708. https://doi.org/10.1097/NMD.0b013e31829db5bf

Cohen, S. J. (2012). Construction and preliminary validation of a dictionary for cognitive rigidity: Linguistic markers of overconfidence and overgeneralization and their concomitant psychological distress. *Journal of Psycholinguistic Research, 41*(5), 347–370. https://doi.org/10.1007/s10936-011-9196-9

Cohen, Z. D., & DeRubeis, R. J. (2018). Treatment selection in depression. *Annual Review of Clinical Psychology, 14*(1), 209–236. https://doi.org/10.1146/annurev-clinpsy-050817-084746

Cohen, Z. D., Kim, T. T., Van, H. L., Dekker, J. J. M., & Driessen, E. (2020). A demonstration of a multi-method variable selection approach for treatment selection: Recommending cognitive-behavioral versus psychodynamic therapy for mild to moderate adult depression. *Psychotherapy Research, 30*(2), 137–150. https://doi.org/10.1080/10503307.2018.1563312

Colli, A., Gentile, D., Condino, V., & Lingiardi, V. (2019). Assessing alliance ruptures and resolutions: Reliability and validity of the Collaborative Interactions Scale-revised version. *Psychotherapy Research, 29*(3), 279–292. https://doi.org/10.1080/10503307.2017.1414331

Colli, A., & Lingiardi, V. (2009). The collaborative interactions scale: A new transcript-based method for the assessment of therapeutic alliance ruptures and resolutions in psychotherapy. *Psychotherapy Research, 19*(6), 718–734. https://doi.org/10.1080/10503300903121098

Cologon, J., Schweitzer, R. D., King, R., & Nolte, T. (2017). Therapist reflective functioning, therapist attachment style, and therapist effectiveness. *Administration and Policy in Mental Health and Mental Health Services Research, 44*(5), 614–625. https://doi.org/10.1007/s10488-017-0790-5

Compare, A., Maxwell, H., Brugnera, A., Zarbo, C., Grave, R. D., & Tasca, G. A. (2018) Change in attachment dimensions and reflective functioning following emotionally focused group therapy for binge eating disorder. *International Journal of Group Psychotherapy, 68*(3), 385–406. https://doi.org/10.1080/00207284.2018.1429928

Connolly, M. B., Crits-Christoph, P., Shelton, R. C., Hollon, S., Kurtz, J., Barber, J. P., & Thase, M. E. (1999). The reliability and validity of a measure of self-understanding of interpersonal patterns. *Journal of Counseling Psychology, 46*(4), 472–482. https://doi.org/10.1037/0022-0167.46.4.472

Constantino, M. J., Arnow, B. A., Blasey, C. & Agras, W. S. (2005). The association between patient characteristics and the therapeutic alliance in cognitive-behavioral and interpersonal therapy for bulimia nervosa. *Journal of Consulting & Clinical Psychology, 73*(2), 203–211. https://doi.org/10.1037/0022-006X.73.2.203

Constantino, M. J., Coyne, A. E., Boswell, J. F., Iles, B. R., & Vîslă, A. (2018). A meta-analysis of the association between patients' early perception of treatment credibility and their posttreatment outcomes. *Psychotherapy, 55*(4), 486–495. https://doi.org/10.1037/pst0000168

Constantino, M. J., Marnell, M. E., Haile, A. J., Kanther-Sista, S. N., Wolman, K., Zappert, L., & Arnow, B. A. (2008). Integrative cognitive therapy for depression: A randomized pilot comparison. *Psychotherapy: Theory, Research, Practice, Training, 45*(2), 122–134. https://doi.org/10.1037/0033-3204.45.2.122

Coutinho, J., Ribeiro, E., Sousa, I., & Safran, J. D. (2014). Comparing two methods of identifying alliance rupture events. *Psychotherapy, 51*(3), 434–442. https://doi.org/10.1037/a0032171

Cramer, P. (2015). Understanding defense mechanisms. *Psychodynamic Psychiatry, 43*(4), 523–552. https://doi.org/10.1521/pdps.2015.43.4.523

Cristea, I. A., Gentili, C., Cotet, C. D., Palomba, D., Barbui, C., & Cuijpers, P. (2017). Efficacy of psychotherapies for borderline personality disorder: A systematic review and meta-analysis. *JAMA Psychiatry, 74*(4), 319–328. https://doi.org/10.1001/jamapsychiatry.2016.4287

Crits-Christoph, P., Barber, J. P., & Kurcias, J. S. (1993). The accuracy of therapists' interpretations and the development of the therapeutic alliance.

Psychotherapy Research, 3(1), 25–35. https://doi.org/10.1080/10503309312 331333639

Crits-Christoph, P., & Connolly Gibbons, M. B. (2021). Psychotherapy process – outcome research: Advances in understanding causal connections. In M. Barkham, Lutz, W., & Castonguay, L. G. (Eds.), *Bergin and Garfield's handbook of psychotherapy and behavior change* (7th edition). NY: Wiley.

Crits-Christoph, P., Gibbons, M. B., Crits-Christoph, K., Narducci, J., Schamberger, M., & Gallop, R. (2006). Can therapists be trained to improve their alliances? A preliminary study of alliance-fostering psychotherapy. *Psychotherapy Research, 16*(3), 268–281. https://doi.org/10.1080/10503300500268557

Crits-Christoph, P., Gibbons, M. B. C., Temes, C. M., Elkin, I., & Gallop, R. (2010). Interpersonal accuracy of interventions and the outcome of cognitive and interpersonal therapies for depression. *Journal of Consulting and Clinical Psychology, 78*(3), 420–428. https://doi.org/10.1037/a0019549

Datz, F., Parth, K., Said, U., & Loffler-Staska, H. (2016). Countertransference triggered activity in treatment. Good, bad, or useful? *British Journal of Medicine and Medical Research, 11*(9), 1–11. https://doi.org/10.9734/BJMMR/2016/21985

Davidson, K., & MacGregor, M. W. (1998). A critical appraisal of self-report defense mechanism measures. *Journal of Personality, 66*(6), 965–992. https://doi.org/10.1111/1467–6494.00039

Davis, D. M., & Hayes, J. A. (2011). What are the benefits of mindfulness? A practice review of psychotherapy-related research. *Psychotherapy, 48*(2), 198–208. https://doi.org/10.1037/a0022062

Degnan, A., Seymour-Hyde, A., Harris, A., & Berry, K. (2016). The role of therapist attachment in alliance and outcome: A systematic literature review. *Clinical Psychology and Psychotherapy, 23*(1), 47–65. https://doi.org/10.1002/cpp.1937

De Meulemeester, C., Lowyck, B., Vermote, R., Verhaest, Y., & Luyten, P. (2017). Mentalizing and interpersonal problems in borderline personality disorder: The mediating role of identity diffusion. *Psychiatry Research, 258*, 141–144. https://doi.org/10.1016/j.psychres.2017.09.061

DeRubeis, R., & Feeley, M. (1990). Determinants of change in cognitive therapy for depression. *Cognitive Therapy and Research, 14*, 469–482. https://doi.org/10.1007/BF01172968

Despland, J.-N., de Roten, Y., Drapeau, M., Currat, T., Beretta, V., & Kramer, U. (2009). The role of alliance in the relationship between therapist competence and outcome in brief psychodynamic psychotherapy. *The Journal of Nervous & Mental Disease, 197*(5), 362–367. https://doi.org/10.1097/NMD.0b013e3181a20849

Diener, M. J., Hilsenroth, M. J., & Weinberger, J. (2007). Therapist affect focus and patient outcomes in psychodynamic psychotherapy: A meta-analysis. *The American Journal of Psychiatry, 164*(6), 936–941. https://doi.org/10.1176/ajp.2007.164.6.936

Diener, M. J., & Monroe, J. M. (2011). The relationship between adult attachment style and therapeutic alliance in individual psychotherapy: A meta-analytic review. *Psychotherapy, 48*(3), 237–248. https://doi.org/10.1037/a0022425

Dinger, U., Zimmermann, J., Masuhr, O., & Spitzer, C. (2017). Therapist effects on outcome and alliance in inpatient psychotherapy: The contribution of patients' symptom severity. *Psychotherapy, 54*(2), 167–174. https://doi.org/10.1037/pst0000059

Driessen, E., Abbass, A. A., Barber, J. P., Connolly Gibbons, M. B., Dekker, J. J. M., Fokkema, M., Fonagy, P., Hollon, S. D., Jansma, E. P., de Maat, S. C. M., Town, J. M., Twisk, J. W. R., Van, H. L., Weitz, E., & Cuijpers, P. (2018). Which patients benefit specifically from short-term psychodynamic psychotherapy (STPP) for depression? Study protocol of a systematic review and meta-analysis of individual participant data. *BMJ Open, 8*(2), e018900. https://doi.org/10.1136/bmjopen-2017–018900

Driessen, E., Dekker, J. J. M., Peen, J., Van, H. L., Maina, G., Rosso, G., Rigardetto, S., Cuniberti, F., Vitriol, V. G., Florenzano, R. U., Andreoli, A., Burnand, Y., López-Rodríguez, J., Villamil-Salcedo, V., Twisk, J. W. R., & Cuijpers, P. (2020). The efficacy of adding short-term psychodynamic psychotherapy to antidepressants in the treatment of depression: A systematic review and meta-analysis of individual participant data. *Clinical Psychology Review, 80*, 101886. https://doi.org/10.1016/j.cpr.2020.101886

Driessen, E., Hegelmaier, L. M., Abbass, A. A., Barber, J. P., Dekker, J. J. M., Van, H. L., Jansma, E. P., & Cuijpers, P. (2015). The efficacy of short-term psychodynamic psychotherapy for depression: A meta-analysis

update. *Clinical Psychology Review, 42*, 1–15. https://doi.org/10.1016/j.cpr.2015.07.004

Dunster-Page, C., Haddock, G., Wainwright, L., & Berry, K. (2017). The relationship between therapeutic alliance and patient's suicidal thoughts, self-harming behaviours and suicide attempts: A systematic review. *Journal of Affective Disorders, 223*, 165–174. https://doi.org/10.1016/j.jad.2017.07.040

Eames, V., & Roth, A. (2000). Patient attachment orientation and the early working alliance: A study of patient and therapist reports of alliance quality and ruptures. *Psychotherapy Research, 10*(4), 421–434. https://doi.org/10.1093/ptr/10.4.421

Egger, M., Davey Smith, G., Schneider, M., & Minder, C. (1997). Bias in meta-analysis detected by a simple, graphical test. *BMJ, 315*(7109), 629–634. https://doi.org/10.1136/bmj.315.7109.629

Elliott, R., Bohart, A. C., & Watson, J. C. (2019). Empathy. In J. C. Norcross, & M. J. Lambert (Eds.). *Psychotherapy relationships that work: Volume 1: Evidence-based therapist contributions* (pp. 245–287). New York, NY: Oxford University Press. https://doi.org/10.1093/med-psych/9780190843953.003.0007

Ensink, K., Maheux, J., Normandin, L., Sabourin, S., Diguer, L., Berthelot, N., & Parent, K. (2013). The impact of mentalization training on the reflective function of novice therapists: A randomized controlled trial. *Psychotherapy Research, 23*(5), 526–538. https://doi.org/10.1080/10503307.2013.800950

Errázuriz, P., Constantino, M., J., & Calvo, E. (2015). The relationship between patient object relations and the therapeutic alliance in a naturalistic psychotherapy sample. *Psychology and Psychotherapy, 88*(3), 254–269. https://doi.org/10.1111/papt.12046

Eubanks, C. F., Lubitz, J., Muran, J. C., & Safran, J. D. (2019). Rupture resolution rating system (3RS): Development and validation. *Psychotherapy Research, 29*(3), 306–319. https://doi.org/10.1080/10503307.2018.1552034

Eubanks-Carter, C., Muran, J. C., & Safran, J. D. (2010). Alliance ruptures and resolution. In J. C. Muran & J. P. Barber (Eds.), *The therapeutic alliance: An evidence-based approach to practice and training* (pp. 74–96). New York, NY: Guilford Press.

Eubanks, C. F., Muran, J. C., & Safran, J. D. (2019). Alliance rupture repair. In J. C. Norcross, & M. J. Lambert (Eds.). *Psychotherapy relationships that work: Volume 1: Evidence-based therapist contributions* (pp. 549–579). New York, NY: Oxford University Press. https://doi.org/10.1093/med-psych/9780190843953.003.0016

Falkenström, F., Granström, F., & Holmqvist, R. (2013). Therapeutic alliance predicts symptomatic improvement session by session. *Journal of Counseling Psychology, 60*(3), 317–328. https://doi.org/10.1037/a0032258

Farber, B. A., Suzuki, J. Y., & Lynch, D. A. (2019). Positive regard and affirmation. In J. C. Norcross, & M. J. Lambert (Eds.). *Psychotherapy relationships that work: Volume 1: Evidence-based therapist contributions* (pp. 288–322). New York, NY: Oxford University Press. https://doi.org/10.1093/med-psych/9780190843953.003.0008

Feeley, M., DeRubeis, R. J., & Gelfand, L. A. (1999). The temporal relation of adherence and alliance to symptom change in cognitive therapy for depression. *Journal of Consulting and Clinical Psychology, 67*(4), 578–582. https://doi.org/10.1037/0022–006X.67.4.578

Fischer-Kern, M., Doering, S., Taubner, S., Horz, S., Zimmermann, J., Rentrop, M., Schuster, P., Buchheim, P., & Buchheim, A. (2015). Transference-focused psychotherapy for borderline personality disorder: Change in reflective function. *The British Journal of Psychiatry, 207*(2), 173–174. https://doi.org/10.1192/bjp.bp.113.143842

Fisher, A. J., Reeves, J. W., Lawyer, G., Medaglia, J. D., & Rubel, J. A. (2017). Exploring the idiographic dynamics of mood and anxiety via network analysis. *Journal of Abnormal Psychology, 126*(8), 1044–1056. https://doi.org/10.1037/abn0000311

Flückiger, C., Del Re, A. C., Wampold, B. E., & Horvath, A. O. (2018). The alliance in adult psychotherapy: A meta-analytic synthesis. *Psychotherapy, 55*(4), 316–340. https://doi.org/10.1037/pst0000172

Fonagy, P., Bateman, A., & Bateman, A. (2011). The widening scope of mentalization: A discussion. *Psychology and Psychotherapy: Theory, Research and Practice, 84*(1), 98–110. https://doi.org/10.1111/j.2044–8341.2010.02005.x

Fonagy, P., Target, M., Steele, H., & Steele, M. (1998). *Reflective functioning manual* (Version 5). London, United Kingdom: University College London Psychoanalysis Unit. https://doi.org/10.1037/t03490–000

Foreman, S. A., & Marmar, C. R. (1985). Therapist actions that address initially poor therapeutic alliances in psychotherapy. *The American Journal of Psychiatry*, 142(8), 922–926. https://doi.org/10.1176/ajp.142.8.922

Fowler, C., Hilsenroth, M. J., & Handler, L. (1996). A multimethod approach to assessing dependency: The early memory dependency probe. *Journal of Personality Assessment*, 67(2), 399–413. https://doi.org/10.1207/s15327752jpa6702_13

Fuller, F., & Hill, C. E. (1985). Counselor and helpee perceptions of counselor intentions in relation to outcome in a single counseling session. *Journal of Counseling Psychology*, 32(3), 329–338. https://doi.org/10.1037/0022-0167.32.3.329

Gabbard, G. O., Horwitz, L., Allen, J. G., Frieswyk, S., Newsom, G., Colson, D. B., & Coyne, L. (1994). Transference interpretation in the psychotherapy of borderline patients: A high-risk, high-gain phenomenon. *Harvard Review of Psychiatry*, 2(2), 59–69 https://doi.org/10.3109/10673229409017119

Gaston, L., & Marmar, C. (1994). The California Psychotherapy Alliance Scales. In A. O. Horvath & L. S. Greenberg (Eds.), *The working alliance: Theory, research, & practice* (pp. 85–108). New York, NY: Wiley.

Gelso, C. J., & Carter, J. A. (1994). Components of the psychotherapy relationship: Their interaction and unfolding during treatment. *Journal of Counseling Psychology*, 41(3), 296–306. https://doi.org/10.1037/0022-0167.41.3.296

Gerber, A. J., Kocsis, J. H., Milrod, B. L., Roose, S. P., Barber, J. P., Thase, M. E., Perkins, P., & Leon, A. C. (2011). A quality-based review of randomized controlled trials of psychodynamic psychotherapy. *The American Journal of Psychiatry*, 168(1), 19–28. https://doi.org/10.1176/appi.ajp.2010.08060843

Gibbons, M. B. C., Gallop, R., Thompson, D., Luther, D., Crits-Christoph, K., Jacobs, J., Yin, S., & Crits-Christoph, P. (2016). Comparative effectiveness of cognitive therapy and dynamic psychotherapy for major depressive disorder in a community mental health setting: A randomized clinical noninferiority trial. *JAMA Psychiatry*, 73(9), 904–912. https://doi.org/10.1001/jamapsychiatry.2016.1720

Gibbons, M. B. C., Thompson, S. M., Scott, K., Schauble, L. A., Mooney, T., Thompson, D., Green, P., MacArthur, M. J., & Crits-Christoph, P. (2012). Supportive-expressive dynamic psychotherapy in the community mental health system: A pilot effectiveness trial for the treatment of depression. *Psychotherapy*, 49(3), 303–316. https://doi.org/10.1037/a0027694

Gilboa-Schechtman, E., Foa, E. B., Shafran, N., Aderka, I. M., Powers, M. B., Rachamim, L., Rosenbach, L., Yadin, E., & Apter, A. (2010). Prolonged exposure versus dynamic therapy for adolescent PTSD: A pilot randomized controlled trial. *Journal of the American Academy of Child and Adolescent Psychiatry*, 49(10), 1034–1042. https://doi.org/10.1016/j.jaac.2010.07.014

Golden, B. R., & Robbins, S. B. (1990). The working alliance within time-limited therapy. *Professional Psychology: Research and Practice*, 21(6), 476–481. https://doi.org/10.1037/0735-7028.21.6.476

Goldfried, M. R. (1980). Toward the delineation of therapeutic change principles. *American Psychologist*, 35(11), 991–999. https://doi.org/10.1037/0003-066X.35.11.991

Goldman, G. A., & Anderson, T. (2007). Quality of object relations and security of attachment as predictors of early therapeutic alliance. *Journal of Counseling Psychology*, 54(2), 111–117. https://doi.org/10.1037/0022-0167.54.2.111

Goldman, R. E., Hilsenroth, M. J., Owen, J. J., & Gold, J. R. (2013). Psychotherapy integration and alliance: Use of cognitive-behavioral techniques within a short-term psychodynamic treatment model. *Journal of Psychotherapy Integration*, 23(4), 373–385. https://doi.org/10.1037/a0034363

Gondek, D., Edbrooke-Childs, J., Fink, E., Deighton, J., & Wolpert, M. (2016). Feedback from outcome measures and treatment effectiveness, treatment efficiency, and collaborative practice: A systematic review. *Administration and Policy in Mental Health*, 43(3), 325–343. https://doi.org/10.1007/s10488-015-0710-5

Greenson, R. R. (1965). The working alliance and the transference neurosis. *Psychoanalytic Quarterly*, 34(2), 155–179. https://doi.org/10.1080/21674086.1965.11926343

Greenson, R. R. (1967). *Technique and practice of psychoanalysis*. New York, NY: International University Press.

Grenyer, B. F. S., & Luborsky, L. (1996). Dynamic change in psychotherapy: Mastery of interpersonal conflicts. *Journal of Consulting and Clinical Psychology*, 64(2), 411–416. https://doi.org/10.1037/0022-006X.64.2.411

Håkansson, U., Söderström, K., Watten, R., Skårderud, F., & Øie, M. G. (2018). Parental reflective functioning and executive functioning in mothers with substance use disorder. *Attachment and Human Development*, 20(2), 181–207. https://doi.org/10.1080/14616734.2017.1398764

Harpaz-Rotem, I., & Blatt, S. J. (2005). Changes in representations of self-designated significant other in long-term intensive inpatient treatment of seriously disturbed adolescents and young adults. *Psychiatry*, 68(3), 266–282. https://doi.org/10.1521/psyc.2005.68.3.266

Harper, H. (1989a). *Coding Guide I: Identification of confrontation challenges in exploratory therapy*. Sheffield, England: University of Sheffield.

Harper, H. (1989b). *Coding Guide II: Identification of withdrawal challenges in exploratory therapy*. Sheffield, England: University of Sheffield.

Harper, H. (1994). *The resolution of client confrontation challenges in exploratory psychotherapy: Developing the new paradigm in psychotherapy research*. Unpublished doctoral dissertation, University of Sheffield.

Hartung, J., & Knapp, G. (2001). On tests of the overall treatment effect in meta-analysis with normally distributed responses. *Statistics in Medicine*, 20(12), 1771–1782. https://doi.org/10.1002/sim.791

Hatcher, R. L. (2010). Alliance theory and measurement. In J. C. Muran & J. P. Barber (Eds.), *The therapeutic alliance: An evidence-based approach to practice and training* (pp. 7–28). New York, NY: Guilford Press.

Hayes, J. A., Gelso, C. J., Kivlighan, D. M., III & Goldberg, S. B. (2019). Managing countertransference. In J. C. Norcross, & M. J. Lambert (Eds.). *Psychotherapy relationships that work: Volume 1: Evidence-based therapist contributions* (pp. 522–548). New York, NY: Oxford University Press. https://doi.org/10.1093/med-psych/9780190843953.003.0015

Heinonen, E., & Nissen-Lie, H. A. (2020). The professional and personal characteristics of effective psychotherapists: a systematic review. *Psychotherapy Research*, 30(4), 417–432. https://doi.org/10.1080/10503307.2019.1620366

Henmi, M., & Copas, J. B. (2010). Confidence intervals for random effects meta-analysis and robustness to publication bias. *Statistics in Medicine*, 29(29), 2969–2983. https://doi.org/10.1002/sim.4029

Henry, W. P., Strupp, H. H., Butler, S. F., Schacht, T. E., & Binder, J. L. (1993). Effects of training in time-limited dynamic psychotherapy: Changes in therapist behavior. *Journal of Consulting and Clinical Psychology*, 61, 434–440. https://doi.org/10.1037/0022-006X.61.3.434

Hersoug, A. G., Høglend, P., & Bøgwald, K.-P. (2004). Is there an optimal adjustment of interpretation to the patient's level of defensive functioning? *American Journal of Psychotherapy*, 58(3), 349–361. https://doi.org/10.1176/appi.psychotherapy.2004.58.3.349

Hersoug, A. G., Høglend, P., Havik, O., von der Lippe, A., & Monsen, J. (2009). Therapist characteristics influencing the quality of alliance in long-term psychotherapy. *Clinical Psychology & Psychotherapy*, 16(2), 100–110. https://doi.org/10.1002/cpp.605

Hersoug, A. G., Monsen, J. T., Havik, O. E., & Høglend, P. (2002). Quality of early working alliance in psychotherapy: Diagnoses, relationship and intrapsychic variables as predictors. *Psychotherapy and Psychosomatic*, 71(1), 18–27. https://doi.org/10.1159/000049340

Hersoug, A. G., Sexton, H. C., & Høglend, P. (2002). Contribution of defensive functioning to the quality of working alliance and psychotherapy outcome. *American Journal of Psychotherapy*, 56(4), 539–554. https://doi.org/10.1176/appi.psychotherapy.2002.56.4.539

Higgins, J. P. T., Thompson, S. G., Deeks, J. J., & Altman, D. G. (2003). Measuring inconsistency in meta-analyses. *BMJ*, 327(7414), 557–560. https://doi.org/10.1136/bmj.327.7414.557

Hill, C. E., Gelso, C. J., Chui, H., Spangler, P. T., Hummel, A., Huang, T., Jackson, J., Jones, R. A., Palma, B., Bhatia, A., Gupta, S., Ain, S. C., Klingaman, B., Lim, R. H., Liu, J., Hui, K., Jezzi, M. M., & Miles, J. R. (2014). To be or not to be immediate with clients: The use and perceived effects of immediacy in psychodynamic/interpersonal psychotherapy. *Psychotherapy Research*, 24(3), 299–315. https://doi.org/10.1080/10503307.2013.812262

Hill, C. E., Kellems, I. S., Kolchakian, M. R., Wonnell, T. L., Davis, T. L., & Nakayama, E. Y. (2003). The therapist experience of being the target of hostile versus suspected-unasserted client anger: Factors associated with resolution. *Psychotherapy Research*, 13(4), 475–491. https://doi.org/10.1093/ptr/kpg040

Hill, C. E., & Knox, S. (2009). Processing the therapeutic relationship. *Psychotherapy Research*, *19*(1), 13–29. https://doi.org/10.1080/10503300802621206

Hill, C. E., Knox, S., & Pinto-Coelho, K. G. (2019). Self-disclosure and immediacy. In J.C. Norcross, & M.J. Lambert (Eds.). *Psychotherapy relationships that work: Volume 1: Evidence-based therapist contributions* (pp. 379–420). New York, NY: Oxford University Press. https://doi.org/10.1093/med-psych/9780190843953.003.0011

Hill, C. E., Thompson, B. J., Cogar, M. C., & Denman, D. W. (1993). Beneath the surface of long-term therapy: Therapist and client report of their own and each other's covert processes. *Journal of Counseling Psychology*, *40*(3), 278–287. https://doi.org/10.1037/0022-0167.40.3.278

Hilsenroth, M. J., Ackerman, S. J., Clemence, A. J., Strassle, C. G., & Handler, L. (2002). Effect of structured clinician training on patient and therapist perspectives of alliance early in psychotherapy. *Psychotherapy: Theory, Research, Practice, Training*, *39*(4), 309–323. https://doi.org/10.1037/0033-3204.39.4.309

Hilsenroth, M. J., Blagys, M. D. Ackerman, S. J., Bonge, D. R., & Blais, M. A. (2005). Measuring psychodynamic-interpersonal and cognitive-behavioral techniques: Development of the comparative psychotherapy process scale. *Psychotherapy: Theory, Research, Practice, Training*, *42*(3), 340–356. https://doi.org/10.1037/0033-3204.42.3.340

Hilsenroth, M. J., Callahan, K. L., & Eudell, E. M. (2003). Further reliability, convergent and discriminant validity of overall defensive functioning. *The Journal of Nervous & Mental Disease*, *191*(11), 730–737. https://doi.org/10.1097/01.nmd.0000095125.92493.e8

Høglend, P. (2004). Analysis of transference in psychodynamic psychotherapy: a review of empirical research. *Canadian Journal of Psychoanalysis*, *12*(2), 280–300.

Høglend, P., Amlo, S., Marble, A., Bogwald, K.-P., Sorbye, O., Sjaastad, M. C., & Heyerdahl, O. (2006). Analysis of the patient-therapist relationship in dynamic psychotherapy: An experimental study of transference interpretations. *The American Journal of Psychiatry*, *163*(10), 1739–1746. https://doi.org/10.1176/ajp.2006.163.10.1739

Høglend, P., & Hagtvet, K. (2019). Change mechanisms in psychotherapy: Both improved insight and improved affective awareness are necessary. *Journal of Consulting and Clinical Psychology*, *87*(4), 332–344. https://doi.org/10.1037/ccp0000381

Høglend, P., Hersoug, A. G., Bøgwald, K. P., Amlo, S., Marble, A., Sørbye, Ø., Røssberg, J. I., Ulberg, R., Gabbard, G. O., & Crits-Christoph, P. (2011). Effects of transference work in the context of therapeutic alliance and quality of object relations. *Journal of Consulting and Clinical Psychology*, *79*(5), 697–706. https://doi.org/10.1037/a0024863

Horvath, A. O. (2006). The alliance in context: Accomplishments, challenges, and future directions. *Psychotherapy: Theory, Research, Practice, Training*, *43*, 258–263. https://doi.org/10.1037/0033-3204.43.3.258

Horvath, A. O., & Greenberg, L. S. (1989). Development and validation of the working alliance inventory. *Journal of Counseling Psychology*, *36*, 223–233. https://doi.org/10.1037/0022-0167.36.2.223

Huang, T. C. C., Hill, C. E., Strauss, N., Heyman, M., & Hussain, M. (2016). Corrective relational experiences in psychodynamic-interpersonal psychotherapy: Antecedents, types, and consequences. *Journal of Counseling Psychology*, *63*(2), 183–197. https://doi.org/10.1037/cou0000132

Huprich, S. K., & Greenberg, R. P. (2003). Advances in the assessment of object relations in the 1990s. *Clinical Psychology Review*, *23*(5), 665–698. https://doi.org/10.1016/S0272-7358(03)00072-2

IntHout, J., Ioannidis, J. P., & Borm, G. F. (2014). The Hartung-Knapp-Sidik-Jonkman method for random effects meta-analysis is straightforward and considerably outperforms the standard DerSimonian-Laird method. *BMC Medical Research Methodology*, *14*(1), 25. https://doi.org/10.1186/1471-2288-14-25

Jennissen, S., Huber, J., Ehrenthal, J. C., Schauenburg, H., & Dinger, U. (2018) Association between insight and outcome of psychotherapy: Systematic review and meta-analysis. *The American Journal of Psychiatry*, *175*(10), 961–969. https://doi.org/10.1176/appi.ajp.2018.17080847

Johansson, R., Björklund, M., Hornborg, C., Karlsson, S., Hesser, H., Ljótsson, B., Rousseau, A., Frederick, R. J., & Andersson, G. (2013). Affect-focused psychodynamic psychotherapy for depression and anxiety through the Internet: a randomized controlled trial. *PeerJ*, *1*, e102. https://doi.org/10.7717/peerj.102

Johansson, R., Ekbladh, S., Hebert, A., Lindström, M., Möller, S., Petitt, E., Poysti, S., Larsson, M. H., Rousseau, A., Carlbring, P., Cuijpers, P., & Andersson, G. (2012). Psychodynamic guided self-help for adult depression through the internet: A randomised controlled trial. *PLOS ONE*, *7*(5), e38021. https://doi.org/10.1371/journal.pone.0038021

Johansson, R., Hesslow, T., Ljótsson, B., Jansson, A., Jonsson, L., Färdig, S., Karlsson, J., Hesser, H., Frederick, R. J., Lilliengren, P., Carlbring, P., & Andersson, G. (2017). Internet-based affect-focused psychodynamic therapy for social anxiety disorder: A randomized controlled trial with 2-year follow-up. *Psychotherapy*, *54*(4), 351–360. https://doi.org/10.1037/pst0000147

Johansson, P., Høglend, P., Ulberg, R., Amlo, S., Marble, A., Bogwald, K.-P., & Heyerdahl, O. (2010). The mediating role of insight for long-term improvements in psychodynamic therapy. *Journal of Consulting and Clinical Psychology*, *78*(3), 438–448. https://doi.org/10.1037/a0019245

Joyce, A. S., O'Kelly, J. G., Ogrodniczuk, J. S., Piper, W. E., & Rosie, J. S. (2012). A naturalistic trial of brief psychodynamic therapy for recurrent major depression. *Psychodynamic Psychiatry*, *40*(4), 645–672. https://doi.org/10.1521/pdps.2012.40.4.645

Junod, O., de Roten, Y., Martinez, E., Drapeau, M., & Despland, J. N. (2005). How to address patients' defences: A pilot study of the accuracy of defence interpretations and alliance. *Psychology and Psychotherapy: Theory, Research and Practice*, *78*(4), 419–430. https://doi.org/10.1348/147608305X41317

Karlsson, R., & Kermott, A. (2006). Reflective-functioning during the process in brief psychotherapies. *Psychotherapy: Theory, Research, Practice, Training*, *43*(1), 65–84. https://doi.org/10.1037/0033-3204.43.1.65

Kazdin, A.E. (2007). Mediators and mechanisms of change in psychotherapy research. *Annual Review of Clinical Psychology*, *3*, 1–27. https://doi.org/10.1146/annurev.clinpsy.3.022806.091432

Kazdin, A.E. (2009). Understanding how and why psychotherapy leads to change. *Psychotherapy Research*, *19*(4–5), 418–428. https://doi.org/10.1080/10503300802448899

Katz, M., Hilsenroth, M. J., Gold, J. R., Moore, M., Pitman, S. R., Levy, S. R., & Owen, J. (2019). Adherence, flexibility, and outcome in psychodynamic treatment. *Journal of Counseling Psychology*, *66*(1), 94–103. https://doi.org/10.1037/cou0000299

Katznelson, H. (2014). Reflective functioning: A review. *Clinical Psychology Review*, *34*(2), 107–117. https://doi.org/10.1016/j.cpr.2013.12.003

Keefe, J. R., Chambless, D. L., Barber, J. P., & Milrod, B. L. (2019). Treatment of anxiety and mood comorbidities in cognitive-behavioral and psychodynamic therapies for panic disorder. *Journal of Psychiatric Research*, *114*, 34–40. https://doi.org/10.1016/j.jpsychires.2019.04.009

Keefe, J. R., Kim, T. T., DeRubeis, R. J., Streiner, D. L., Links, P. S., & McMain, S. F. (2020). Treatment selection in borderline personality disorder between dialectical behavior therapy and psychodynamic psychiatric management. *Psychological Medicine*, 1–9. https://doi.org/10.1017/S0033291720000550

Keefe, J. R., McCarthy, K. S., Dinger, U., Zilcha-Mano, S., & Barber, J. P. (2014). A meta-analytic review of psychodynamic therapies for anxiety disorders. *Clinical Psychology Review*, *34*(4), 309–323. https://doi.org/10.1016/j.cpr.2014.03.004

Keefe, J. R., McMain, S. F., McCarthy, K. S., Zilcha-Mano, S., Dinger, U., Sahin, Z., Graham, K., & Barber, J. P. (2020). A meta-analysis of psychodynamic treatments for borderline and cluster C personality disorders. *Personality Disorders: Theory, Research, and Treatment*, *11*(3), 157–169. https://doi.org/10.1037/per0000382

Keefe, J. R., Solomonov, N., Derubeis, R. J., Phillips, A. C., Busch, F. N., Barber, J. P., Chambless, D. L., & Milrod, B. L. (2019). Focus is key: Panic-focused interpretations are associated with symptomatic improvement in panic-focused psychodynamic psychotherapy. *Psychotherapy Research*, *29*(8), 1033–1044. https://doi.org/10.1080/10503307.2018.1464682

Kiesler, D. J. (1996). *Contemporary interpersonal theory and research: Personality, psychopathology, and psychotherapy*. Oxford, United Kingdom: Wiley.

Kivlighan, D. M., Jr., Hill, C. E., Ross, K., Kline, K., Furhmann, A., & Sauber, E. (2019). Testing a mediation model of psychotherapy process and outcome in psychodynamic psychotherapy: Previous client distress, psychodynamic techniques, dyadic working alliance, and current client distress. *Psychotherapy Research*, *29*(5), 581–593. https://doi.org/10.1080/10503307.2017.1420923

Kivlighan, D. M., Jr. & Shaughnessy, P. (2000). Patterns of working alliance development: A typology of client's working alliance ratings. *Journal of Counseling Psychology*, *47*(3), 362–371. https://doi.org/10.1037/0022-0167.47.3.362

Klein, C., Milrod, B., Busch F., Levy, K., & Shapiro, T. (2003). A preliminary study of clinical process in relation to outcome in psychodynamic psychotherapy for panic disorder. *Psychoanalytic Inquiry, 23*(2), 308–331. https://doi.org/10.1080/07351692309349035

Klein, D. N., Schwartz, J. E., Santiago, N. J., Vivian, D., Vocisano, C., Castonguay, L. G., Arnow, B., Blalock, J. A., Manber, R., Markowitz, J. C., Riso, L. P., Rothbaum, B., McCullough, J. P., Thase, M. E., Borian, F. E., Miller, I. W., & Keller, M. B. (2003). Therapeutic alliance in depression treatment: Controlling for prior change and patient characteristics. *Journal of Consulting and Clinical Psychology, 71*(6), 997–1006. https://doi.org/10.1037/0022-006X.71.6.997

Klerman, G., Weissman, M., Rounsaville, B., & Chevron, E. (1984). *Interpersonal psychotherapy of depression*. New York, NY: Basic Books.

Knijnik, D. Z., Kapczinski, F., Chachamovich, E., Margis, R., & Eizirik, C. L. (2004). Psychodynamic group treatment for generalized social phobia. *Revista Brasileira de Psiquiatria, 26*, 77–81. https://doi.org/10.1590/S1516-44462004000200003

Kolden, G. G., Wang, C. C., Austin, S. B., Chang, Y., & Klein, M. H. (2018). Congruence/genuineness: A meta-analysis. *Psychotherapy, 55*(4), 424–433. https://doi.org/10.1037/pst0000162

Kramer, U., de Roten, Y., Perry, J. C., & Despland, J. N. (2013). Change in defense mechanisms and coping patterns during the course of 2–year-long psychotherapy and psychoanalysis for recurrent depression: A pilot study of a randomized controlled trial. *The Journal of Nervous and Mental Disease, 201*(7), 614–620. https://doi.org/10.1097/NMD.0b013e3182982982

Kronström, K., Salminen, J. K., Hietala, J., Kajander, J., Vahlberg, T., Markkula, J., Rasi-Hakala, H., & Karlsson, H. (2009). Does defense style or psychological mindedness predict treatment response in major depression? *Depression and Anxiety, 26*(7), 689–695. https://doi.org/10.1002/da.20585

Laaksonen, M. A., Knekt, P., Sares-Jaske, L., & Lindfors, O. (2013). Psychological predictors on the outcome of short-term psychodynamic psychotherapy and solution-focused therapy in the treatment of mood and anxiety disorder. *European Psychiatry, 28*(2), 117–124. https://doi.org/10.1016/j.eurpsy.2011.12.002

Lacewing, M. (2014). Psychodynamic psychotherapy, insight, and therapeutic action. *Clinical Psychology: Science and Practice, 21*(2), 154–171. https://doi.org/10.1111/cpsp.12065

Lambert, M. J. (2015). Progress feedback and the OQ-system: The past and the future. *Psychotherapy, 52*(4), 381–390. https://doi.org/10.1037/pst0000027

Lambert, M. J., Whipple, J. L., Hawkins, E. J., Vermeersch, D. A., Nielsen, S. L., & Smart, D. W. (2003). Is it time for clinicians to routinely track patient outcome? A meta-analysis. *Clinical Psychology: Science and Practice, 10*(3), 288–301. https://doi.org/10.1093/clipsy.bpg025

Lansford, E. (1986). Weakenings and repairs of the working alliance in short-term psychotherapy. *Professional Psychology: Research and Practice, 17*(4), 364–366. https://doi.org/10.1037/0735-7028.17.4.364

Lazarus, G., Atzil-Slonim, D., Bar-Kalifa, E., Hasson-Ohayon, I., & Rafaeli, E. (2019). Clients' emotional instability and therapists' inferential flexibility predict therapists' session-by-session empathic accuracy. *Journal of Counseling Psychology, 66*(1), 56–69. https://doi.org/10.1037/cou0000310

Leichsenring, F. (2001). Comparative effects of short-term psychodynamic psychotherapy and cognitive-behavioral therapy in depression: A meta-analytic approach. *Clinical Psychology Review, 21*(3), 401–419. https://doi.org/10.1016/S0272-7358(99)00057-4

Leichsenring, F., Luyten, P., Hilsenroth, M. J., Abbass, A., Barber, J. P., Keefe, J. R., Leweke, F., Rabung, S., & Steinert, C. (2015). Psychodynamic therapy meets evidence-based medicine: A systematic review using updated criteria. *The Lancet Psychiatry, 2*(7), 648–660. https://doi.org/10.1016/S2215-0366(15)00155-8

Leichsenring, F., & Rabung, S. (2018). Long-term psychodynamic psychotherapy in complex mental disorders: Update of a meta-analysis. *The British Journal of Psychiatry, 199*(1), 15–22. https://doi.org/10.1192/bjp.bp.110.082776

Leichsenring, F., & Steinert, C. (2018). Towards an evidence-based unified psychodynamic protocol for emotional disorders. *Journal of Affective Disorders, 232*, 400–416. https://doi.org/10.1016/j.jad.2017.11.036

Lilliengren, P. (2019, December 9). Comprehensive compilation of randomized controlled trials (RCTs) involving psychodynamic treatments and interventions. Retrieved December 9, 2019, from https://www.researchgate.net/publication/317335876_Comprehensive_compilation_of_randomized_controlled_trials_RCTs_involving_psychodynamic_treatments_and_interventions

Lindfors, O., Knekt, P., Heinonen, E., & Virtala, E. (2014). Self-concept and quality of object relations as predictors of outcome in short- and long-term psychotherapy. *Journal of Affective Disorders, 152–154*, 202–211. https://doi.org/10.1016/j.jad.2013.09.011

Lingiardi, V., Colli, A., Gentile, D., & Tanzilli, A. (2011). Exploration of session process: Relationship to depth and alliance. *Psychotherapy, 48*(4), 391–400. https://doi.org/10.1037/a0025248

Locke, K. D., & Adamic, E. J. (2012). Interpersonal circumplex vector length and interpersonal decision making. *Personality and Individual Differences, 53*(6), 764–769. https://doi.org/10.1016/j.paid.2012.06.001

Luborsky, L. (1976). Helping alliances in psychotherapy. In J. L. Cleghhorn (Ed.), *Successful psychotherapy* (pp. 92–116). New York, NY: Brunner/Mazel.

Luborsky, L. (1984). *Principles of psychoanalytic therapy*. New York, NY: Basic Books.

Luborsky, L., Barber, J. P., Siqueland, L., Johnson, S., Najavits, L. M., Frank, A., & Daley, D. (1996). The revised helping alliance questionnaire (HAQ-II): Psychometric properties. *Journal of Psychotherapy Practice and Research, 5*(3), 260–271. https://doi.org/10.1037/t07504-000

Luborsky, L., Crits-Christoph, P., McLellan, A. T., Woody, G., Piper, W., Liberman, B., Imber, S., & Pilkonis, P. (1986). Do therapists vary much in their success? Findings from four outcome studies. *American Journal of Orthopsychiatry, 56*(4), 501–512. https://doi.org/10.1111/j.1939-0025.1986.tb03483.x

Luyten, P., Campbell, C., Allison, E., & Fonagy, P. (2020). The mentalizing approach to psychopathology: State of the art and future directions. *Annual Review of Clinical Psychology, 16*, 297–325. https://doi.org/10.1146/annurev-clinpsy-071919-015355

Mann, J. (1973). *Time-limited psychotherapy*. Cambridge, MA: Harvard University Press.

Martin, D. J., Garske, J. P., & Davis, M. K. (2000). Relation of the therapeutic alliance with outcome and other variables: A meta-analytic review. *Journal of Consulting & Clinical Psychology, 68*(3), 438–450. https://doi.org/10.1037/0022-006X.68.3.438

Martin, J., Martin, W., Meyer, M., & Slemon, A. (1986). Empirical investigation of the cognitive mediational paradigm for research in counseling. *Journal of Counseling Psychology, 33*(2), 115–123. https://doi.org/10.1037/0022-0167.33.2.115

Martin, J., Martin, W., & Slemon, A. (1987). Cognitive mediation in person-centered and rational-emotive therapy. *Journal of Counseling Psychology, 34*(3), 251–260. https://doi.org/10.1037/0022-0167.34.3.251

McAleavey, A. A., Castonguay, L. G., & Xiao, H. (2014). Therapist orientation, supervisor match, and therapeutic interventions: Implications for session quality in a psychotherapy training PRN. *Counselling and Psychotherapy Research, 14*(3), 192–200. https://doi.org/10.1080/14733145.2014.929418

McCarthy, K. L., Caputi, P., & Grenyer, B. F. S. (2017) Significant change events in psychodynamic psychotherapy: Is cognition or emotion more important? *Psychology and Psychotherapy: Theory, Research, and Practice, 90*(3), 377–388. https://doi.org/10.1111/papt.12116

McCarthy, K. S., Gibbons, M. B. C., & Barber, J. P. (2008). The relation of rigidity across relationships with symptoms and functioning: An investigation with the revised central relationship questionnaire. *Journal of Counseling Psychology, 55*(3), 346–358. https://doi.org/10.1037/a0012578

McCarthy, K. S., Keefe, J. R., & Barber, J. P. (2016). Goldilocks on the couch: Moderate levels of psychodynamic and process-experiential technique predict outcome in psychodynamic therapy. *Psychotherapy Research, 26*(3), 307–317. https://doi.org/10.1080/10503307.2014.973921

McCarthy, K. S., Zilcha-Mano, S., & Barber, J. P. (2019). Process research in psychodynamic psychotherapy: Interventions and the therapeutic relationship. In D. Kealy & J. S. Ogrodniczuk (Eds.), *Contemporary psychodynamic psychotherapy: Evolving clinical practice* (pp. 75–88). London, UK: Elsevier. https://doi.org/10.1016/B978-0-12-813373-6.00005-2

McClelland, G. H., & Judd, C. M. (1993). Statistical difficulties of detecting interactions and moderator effects. *Psychological Bulletin, 114*(2), 376–390. https://doi.org/10.1037/0033-2909.114.2.376

McCullough Jr, J. P. (2003). Treatment for chronic depression: Cognitive behavioral analysis system of psychotherapy (CBASP) (Vol. 13, No. 3–4, p. 241). Educational Publishing Foundation. https://doi.org/10.1037/1053-0479.13.3-4.241

McCullough, L., Winston, H. A., Farber, B. A., Porter, F., Pollack, J., Laikin, M., Vingiano, W., & Trujillo, M. (1991). The relationship of patient-therapist interaction to the outcome in brief dynamic psychotherapy. *Psychotherapy: Theory, Practice, Research, Training, 28*(4), 525–533. https://doi.org/10.1037/0033-3204.28.4.525

McMain, S. F., Guimon, T., Streiner, D. L., Cardish, R. J., & Links, P. S. (2012). Dialectical behavior therapy compared with general psychiatric management for borderline personality disorder: Clinical outcomes and functioning over a 2–year follow-up. *The American Journal of Psychiatry, 169*(6), 650–661. https://doi.org/10.1176/appi.ajp.2012.11091416

McMain, S. F., Links, P. S., Gnam, W. H., Guimond, T., Cardish, R. J., Korman, L., & Streiner, D. L. (2009). A randomized trial of dialectical behavior therapy versus general psychiatric management for borderline personality disorder. *The American Journal of Psychiatry, 166*(12), 1365–1374. https://doi.org/10.1176/appi.ajp.2009.09010039

Messer, S. B., & Wolitzky, D. L. (2010). A psychodynamic perspective on the therapeutic alliance. In J. C. Muran & J. P. Barber (Eds.), *The therapeutic alliance: An evidence-based guide to practice* (pp. 97–122). New York, NY: Guilford Press.

Messina, I., Solina, C., Arduin, A., Frangioni, V., Sambin, M., & Gelso, C. (2018). Origins of countertransference and core conflictual relationship theme of a psychotherapist in training as emerging in clinical supervision. *Psychotherapy, 55*(3), 222–230. https://doi.org/10.1037/pst0000148

Meystre, C., Pascual-Leone, A., de Roten, Y., Despland, J.-N., & Kramer, U. (2015) What interventions facilitate client progress through the assimilation model?: A task analysis of interventions in the psychodynamic treatment of depression. *Psychotherapy Research, 25*(4), 484–502. https://doi.org/10.1080/10503307.2014.921352

Milrod, B., Altemus, M., Gross, C., Busch, F., Silver, G., Christos, P., Stieber, J., & Schneier, F. (2016). Adult separation anxiety in treatment nonresponders with anxiety disorders: Delineation of the syndrome and exploration of attachment-based psychotherapy and biomarkers. *Comprehensive Psychiatry, 66*, 139–145. https://doi.org/10.1016/j.comppsych.2016.01.004

Milrod, B., Chambless, D. L., Gallop, R., Busch, F. N., Schwalberg, M., McCarthy, K. S., Gross, C., Sharpless, B. A., Leon, A. C., & Barber, J. P. (2016). Psychotherapies for panic disorder: A tale of two sites. *Journal of Clinical Psychiatry, 77*(7), 927–935. https://doi.org/10.4088/JCP.14m09507

Milrod, B., Markowitz, J. C., Gerber, A. J., Cyranowski, J., Altemus, M., Shapiro, T., Hofer, M., & Glatt, C. (2014). Childhood separation anxiety and the pathogenesis and treatment of adult anxiety. *American Journal of Psychiatry, 171*(1), 34–43. https://doi.org/10.1176/appi.ajp.2013.13060781

Moeseneder, L., Ribeiro, E., Muran, J. C., & Caspar, F. (2019). Impact of confrontations by therapists on impairment and utilization of the therapeutic alliance, *Psychotherapy Research, 29*(3), 293–305, https://doi.org/10.1080/10503307.2018.1502897

Mohr, J. J., Fuertes, J. N., & Stracuzzi, T. I. (2015). Transference and insight in psychotherapy with gay and bisexual male clients: The role of sexual orientation identity integration. *Psychotherapy, 52*(1), 119–126. https://doi.org/10.1037/a0036510

Mullin, A. S. J., Hilsenroth, M. J., Gold, J., & Farber, B. A. (2017). Changes in object relations over the course of psychodynamic psychotherapy. *Clinical Psychology and Psychotherapy, 24*(2), 501–511. https://doi.org/10.1002/cpp.2021

Muran, J. C. (2019). Confessions of a New York rupture researcher: An insider's guide and critique. *Psychotherapy Research, 29*(1), 1–14. https://doi.org/10.1080/10503307.2017.1413261

Muran, J. C., Safran, J. D., Eubanks, C. F., & Gorman, B. S. (2018). The effect of an alliance-focused training on cognitive-behavioral therapy for personality disorders. *Journal of Consulting & Clinical Psychology, 86*(4), 384–397. https://doi.org/10.1037/ccp0000284

Muran, J. C., Safran, J. D., Gorman, B. S., Samstag, L. W., Eubanks-Carter, C., & Winston, A. (2009). The relationship of early alliance ruptures and their resolution to process and outcome in three time-limited psychotherapies for personality disorders. *Psychotherapy: Theory, Research, Practice, Training, 46*(2), 233–248. https://doi.org/10.1037/a0016085

Muran, J. C., Safran, J. D., Samstag, L. W., & Winston, A. (1992). *Patient and therapist postsession questionnaires*, Version 1992. Beth Israel Medical Center, New York.

Muris, P., & Merckelbach, H. (1996). Defence style and behaviour therapy outcome in a specific phobia. *Psychological Medicine, 26*(3), 635–639. https://doi.org/10.1017/S0033291700035704

Najavits, L. M., & Strupp, H. H. (1994). Differences in the effectiveness of psychodynamic therapists: A process-outcome study. *Psychotherapy, 31*(1), 114–123. https://doi.org/10.1037/0033-3204.31.1.114

Nelson, D. L., & Castonguay, L. G. (2017). The systematic use of homework in psychodynamic-interpersonal psychotherapy for depression: An assimilative integration approach. *Journal of Psychotherapy Integration, 27*(2), 265–281. https://doi.org/10.1037/int0000063

Newman, M. G., Castonguay, L. G., Borkovec, T. D., Fisher, A. J., & Nordberg, S. S. (2008). An open trial of integrative therapy for generalized anxiety disorder. *Psychotherapy: Theory, Research, Practice, Training, 45*(2), 135–147. https://doi.org/10.1037/0033-3204.45.2.135

Nissen-Lie, H. A., Monsen, J. T., & Rønnestad, M. H. (2010). Therapist predictors of early patient-rated working alliance: A multilevel approach. *Psychotherapy Research, 20*(6), 627–646. https://doi.org/10.1080/10503307.2010.497633

O'Connor, L. E., Edelstein, S., Berry, J. W., & Weiss, J. (1994). Changes in the patient's level of insight in brief psychotherapy: Two pilot studies. *Psychotherapy, 31*(3), 533–544. https://doi.org/10.1037/0033-3204.31.3.533

Ollila, P., Knekt, P., Heinonen, E. & Lindfors, O. (2016). Patients' pre-treatment interpersonal problems as predictors of therapeutic alliance in long-term psychodynamic psychotherapy. *Psychiatry Research, 241*, 110–117. https://doi.org/10.1016/j.psychres.2016.04.093

O'Malley, S. S., Suh, C. S., & Strupp, H. H. (1983). The Vanderbilt psychotherapy process scale: A report on the scale development and a process-outcome study. *Journal of Consulting and Clinical Psychology, 51*(4), 581–586. https://doi.org/10.1037/0022–006X.51.4.581

Ortigo, K. M., Westen, D., DeFife, J. A., & Bradley, B. (2013). Attachment, social cognition, and posttraumatic stress symptoms in a traumatized, urban population: Evidence for the mediating role of object relations. *Journal of Traumatic Stress, 26*(3), 1–8. https://doi.org/10.1002/jts.21815

Owen, J., & Hilsenroth, M. J. (2014). Treatment adherence: The importance of therapist flexibility in relation to therapy outcomes. *Journal of Counseling Psychology, 61*(2), 280–288. https://doi.org/10.1037/a0035753

Paley, G., Cahill, J., Barkham, M., Shapiro, D., Jones, J., Patrick, S., & Reid, E. (2008). The effectiveness of psychodynamic-interpersonal therapy (PIT) in routine clinical practice: A benchmarking comparison. *Psychology and Psychotherapy: Theory, Research and Practice, 81*(2), 157–175. https://doi.org/10.1348/147608307x270889

Patton, M. J., Kivlighan, D. M., Jr. & Multon, K. D. (1997). The Missouri psychoanalytic counseling research project: Relation of changes in counseling process to client outcomes. *Journal of Counseling Psychology, 44*(2), 189–208. https://doi.org/10.1037/0022–0167.44.2.189

Peluso, P. R., & Freund, R. R. (2019). Emotional expression. In J. C. Norcross, & M. J. Lambert (Eds.). *Psychotherapy relationships that work: Volume 1: Evidence-based therapist contributions* (pp. 421–460). New York, NY: Oxford University Press. https://doi.org/10.1093/med-psych/9780190843953.003.0012

Penedo, J. M. G., Babl, A., Krieger, T., Heinonen, E., Flückiger, C., & Grosse Holtforth, M. (2019). Interpersonal agency as predictor of the within-patient alliance effects on depression severity. *Journal of Consulting and Clinical Psychology, 88*(4), 338–349. https://doi.org/10.1037/ccp0000475.

Perry, J. C., & Bond, M. (2017) Addressing defenses in psychotherapy to improve adaptation. *Psychoanalytic Inquiry, 37*(3), 153–166. https://doi.org/10.1080/07351690.2017.1285185

Perry, J. C., Constantinides, P., & Simmonds, J. (2017). Dynamic conflicts in recurrent major depression: Does combined short-term psychotherapy and antidepressant medication lead to healthy dynamic functioning? *Psychoanalytic Psychology, 34*(1), 3–32. https://doi.org/10.1037/pap0000058

Perry, J. C., & Ianni, F. F. (1998). Observer-rated measures of defense mechanisms. *Journal of Personality, 66*(6), 993–1024. https://doi.org/10.1111/1467–6494.00040

Petraglia, J., Bhatia, M., de Roten, Y., Despland, J.-N., & Drapeau, M. (2015). An empirical investigation of defense interpretation depth, defense functioning and alliance strength in psychodynamic psychotherapy. *American Journal of Psychotherapy, 69*(1), 1–17. https://doi.org/10.1176/appi.psychotherapy.2015.69.1.1

Piper, W. E., McCallum, M., Joyce, A. S., Rosie, J. S., & Ogrodniczuk, J. S. (2001). Patient personality and time-limited group psychotherapy for complicated grief. *International Journal of Group Psychotherapy*, *51*(4) 525–552. https://doi.org/10.1521/ijgp.51.4.525.51307

Piper, W. E., Ogrodniczuk, J. S., & Joyce, A. S. (2004). Quality of object relations as a moderator of the relationship between pattern of alliance and outcome in short-term individual psychotherapy. *Journal of Personality Assessment*, *83*(3), 345–356. https://doi.org/10.1207/s15327752jpa8303_15

Piper, W. E., Ogrodniczuk, J. S., Joyce, A. S., McCallum, M., Rosie, J. S., O'Kelly, J. G., & Steinberg, P. I. (1999). Prediction of dropping out in time-limited, interpretive individual psychotherapy. *Psychotherapy*, *36*(2), 114–122. https://doi.org/10.1037/h0087787

Porcerelli, J. H., Shahar, G., Blatt, S. J., Ford, R. Q., Mezza, J. A., & Greenlee, L. M. (2006). Social cognition and object relations scale: Convergent validity and changes following intensive inpatient treatment. *Personality and Individual Differences*, *41*(3), 407–417. https://doi.org/10.1016/j.paid.2005.10.027

Poulsen, S., Lunn, S., Daniel, S. I., Folke, S., Mathiesen, B. B., Katznelson, H., & Fairburn, C. G. (2014). A randomized controlled trial of psychoanalytic psychotherapy or cognitive-behavioral therapy for bulimia nervosa. *The American Journal of Psychiatry*, *171*(1), 109–116. https://doi.org/10.1176/appi.ajp.2013.12121511

Regan, A. M., & Hill, C. E. (1992). An investigation of what clients and counselors do not say in brief therapy. *Journal of Counseling Psychology*, *39*(2), 168–174. https://doi.org/10.1037/0022-0167.39.2.168

Reneses, B., Galián, M., Serrano, R., Figuera, D., del Moral, A. F., López-lbor, J. J., Fuentes, M., & Trujillo, M. (2013). Una nueva Psicoterapia Breve para Trastornos Iímite de la personalidad. Resultados preliminares de un Ensayo controlado y aleatorizado [A new time limited psychotherapy for BPD: Preliminary results of a randomized and controlled trial]. *Actas Españolas de Psiquiatría*, *41*(3), 139–148.

Rhodes, R., Hill, C., Thompson, B., & Elliott, R. (1994). Client retrospective recall of resolved and unresolved misunderstanding events. *Counseling Psychology*, *41*(4), 473–483. https://doi.org/10.1037/0022-0167.41.4.473

Rice, L. N., & Greenberg, L. S. (1984). *Patterns of change: Intensive analysis of psychotherapy process*. New York, NY: Guilford Press.

Rosenberg, M. S. (2005). The file-drawer problem revisited: A general weighted method for calculating fail-safe numbers in meta-analysis. *Evolution*, *59*(2), 464–468. https://doi.org/10.1111/j.0014-3820.2005.tb01004.x

Rosso, G., Martini, B., & Maina, G. (2013). Brief dynamic therapy and depression severity: A single-blind, randomized study. *Journal of Affective Disorders*, *147*(1–3), 101–106 https://doi.org/10.1016/j.jad.2012.10.017

Rossouw, T. I., & Fonagy, P. (2012). Mentalization-based treatment for self-harm in adolescents: A randomized controlled trial. *Journal of the American Academy of Child and Adolescent Psychiatry*, *51*(12), 1304–1318. https://doi.org/10.1016/j.jaac.2012.09.018

Rudden, M., Milrod, B., Target, M., Ackerman, S., & Graf, E. (2006). Reflective functioning in panic disorder patients: A pilot study. *Journal of the American Psychoanalytic Association*, *54*(4), 1339–1343. https://doi.org/10.1177/00030651060540040109

Ruiz, M. A., Pincus, A. L., Borkovec, T. D., Echemendia, R. J., Castonguay, L. G., & Ragusea, S. A. (2004). Validity of the inventory of interpersonal problems for predicting treatment outcome: An investigation with the Pennsylvania practice research network. *Journal of Personality Assessment*, *83*(3), 213–222. https://doi.org/10.1207/s15327752jpa8303_05

Ryum, T., Stiles, T. C., Svartberg, M., & McCullough, L. (2010). The role of transference work, the therapeutic alliance, and their interaction in reducing interpersonal problems among psychotherapy patients with cluster c personality disorders. *Psychotherapy: Theory, Research, Practice, Training*, *47*(4), 442–453. https://doi.org/10.1037/a0021183

Safran, J. D., & Muran, J. C. (1996). The resolution of ruptures in the therapeutic alliance. *Journal of Consulting and Clinical Psychology*, *64*(3), 447–458. https://doi.org/10.1037/0022-006X.64.3.447

Safran, J. D., & Muran, J. C. (2000). *Negotiating the therapeutic alliance: A relational treatment guide*. New York, NY: Guilford Press.

Safran, J. D., & Muran, J. C. (2006). Has the concept of the therapeutic alliance outlived its usefulness? *Psychotherapy: Theory, Research, Practice, Training*, *43*(3), 286–291. https://doi.org/10.1037/0033-3204.43.3.286

Safran, J. D., Muran, J. C., & Eubanks-Carter, C. (2011). Repairing alliance ruptures. *Psychotherapy*, *48*(1), 80–87. https://doi.org/10.1037/a0022140

Safran, J. D., Muran, J. C., & Samstag, L. W. (1994). Resolving therapeutic alliance ruptures: a task analytic investigation. In A. O. Horvath & L. S. Greenberg (Eds.), *The working alliance: Theory, research, and practice* (pp. 225–255). New York, NY: Wiley.

Safran, J. D., Muran, J. C., Samstag, L. W., & Winston, A. (2005). Evaluating alliance-focused intervention for potential treatment failures: A feasibility study and descriptive analysis. *Psychotherapy: Theory, Research, Practice, Training*, *42*(4), 512–531. https://doi.org/10.1037/0033-3204.42.4.512

Safran, J. D., & Segal, Z. V. (1990). *Interpersonal process in cognitive therapy*. New York, NY: Basic Books.

Sahin, Z., Vinnars, B., Gorman, B. S., Wilczek, A., Åsberg, M., & Barber, J. P. (2018). Clinical severity as a moderator of outcome in psychodynamic and dialectical behavior therapies for borderline personality disorder. *Personality Disorders: Theory, Research, and Treatment*, *9*(5), 437–446. https://doi.org/10.1037/per0000276

Scandurra, C., Picariello, S., Scafaro, D., Bochicchio, V., Valerio, P., & Amodeo, A. L. (2018). Group psychodynamic counselling as a clinical training device to enhance metacognitive skills and agency in future clinical psychologists. *Europe's Journal of Psychology*, *14*(2), 444–463. https://doi.org/10.5964/ejop.v14i2.1528

Schauenburg, H., Buchheim, A., Beckh, K., Nolte, T., Brenk-Franz, K., Leichsenring, F., Strack, M., & Dinger, U. (2010). The influence of psychodynamically oriented therapists' attachment representations on outcome and alliance in inpatient psychotherapy. *Psychotherapy Research*, *20*(2), 193–202. https://doi.org/10.1080/10503300903204043

Schut, A. J., Castonguay, L. G., Flanagan, K. M., Yamasaki, A. S., Barber, J. P., Bedics, J. D., & Smith, T. L. (2005). Therapist interpretation, patient-therapist interpersonal process, and outcome in psychodynamic *Psychotherapy*, for avoidant personality disorder. *Psychotherapy: Theory, Research, Practice, Training*, *42*(4), 494–511. https://doi.org/10.1037/0033-3204.42.4.494

Sharp, C., Venta, A., Vanwoerden, S., Schramm, A., Ha, C., Newlin, E., Reddy, R., & Fonagy, P. (2016). First empirical evaluation of the link between attachment, social cognition, and borderline features in adolescents. *Comprehensive Psychiatry*, *64*, 4–11. https://doi.org/10.1016/j.comppsych.2015.07.008

Sharpless, B. (2019). *Psychodynamic therapy techniques: A guide to expressive and supportive interventions*. New York, NY: Oxford. https://doi.org/10.1093/med-psych/9780190676278.001.0001

Sharpless, B. A., & Barber, J. P. (2012). Corrective emotional experiences from a psychodynamic perspective. In L. G. Castonguay & C. Hill (Eds.), *Transformation in psychotherapy: Corrective experiences across cognitive behavioral, humanistic, and psychodynamic approaches*. Washington, DC: American Psychological Association. https://doi.org/10.1037/13747-003

Sharpless, B. A., Muran, J. C., & Barber, J. P. (2010). Coda: Recommendations for practice and training. In J. C. Muran & J. P. Barber (Eds.), *The therapeutic alliance: An evidence-based guide to practice* (pp. 341–354). New York, NY: Guilford Press.

Shimokawa, K., Lambert, M. J., & Smart, D. W. (2010). Enhancing treatment outcome of patients at risk of treatment failure: Meta-analytic and mega-analytic review of a psychotherapy quality assurance system. *Journal of Consulting and Clinical Psychology*, *78*(3), 298–311. https://doi.org/10.1037/a0019247

Sidik, K., & Jonkman, J. N. (2002). A simple confidence interval for meta-analysis. *Statistics in Medicine*, *21*(21), 3153–3159. https://doi.org/10.1002/sim.1262

Smith, A. E. M., Msetfi, R. M., & Golding, L. (2010). Client self-rated adult attachment patterns and the therapeutic alliance: A systematic review. *Clinical Psychology Review*, *30*(3), 326–337. https://doi.org/10.1016/j.cpr.2009.12.007

Solomonov, N., McCarthy, K. S., Keefe, J. R., Gorman, B. S., Blanchard, M., & Barber, J. P. (2018). Fluctuations in alliance and use of techniques over time: A bidirectional relation between use of "common factors" techniques and the development of the working alliance. *Clinical Psychology and Psychotherapy*, *25*(1), 102–111. https://doi.org/10.1002/cpp.2143

Sommerfeld, E., Orbach, I., Zim, S., & Mikulincer, M. (2008). An in-session exploration of ruptures in working alliance and their associations with clients' core conflictual relationship themes, alliance-related discourse, and clients' postsession evaluation. *Psychotherapy Research*, *18*(4), 377–388. https://doi.org/10.1080/10503300701675873

Spinhoven, P., Giesen-Bloo, J., van Dyck, R., Kooiman, K., & Arntz, A. (2007). The therapeutic alliance in schema-focused therapy and transference-focused psychotherapy for borderline personality disorder. *Journal of Consulting and Clinical Psychology*, 75(1), 104–111. https://doi.org/10.1037/0022–006X.75.1.104

Steinert, C., Munder, T., Rabung, S., Hoyer, J., & Leichsenring, F. (2017). Psychodynamic therapy: As efficacious as other empirically supported treatments? A meta-analysis testing equivalence of outcomes. *The American Journal of Psychiatry*, 174(10), 943–953. https://doi.org/10.1176/appi.ajp.2017.17010057

Steinert, C., Schauenburg, H., Dinger, U., & Leichsenring, F. (2016). Short-term psychodynamic therapy in depression-an evidence-based unified protocol. *Psychotherapie, Psychosomatik, medizinische Psychologie*, 66(1), 9–20. https://doi.org/10.1055/s-0035-1559612

Stigler, M., de Roten, Y., Drapeau, M., & Despland, J. N. (2007). Process research in psychodynamic psychotherapy: A combined measure of accuracy and conflictuality of interpretations. *Swiss Archives of Neurology and Psychiatry*, 58, 225–232. https://doi.org/10.4414/sanp.2007.01862

Stiles, W. B., Glick, M. J., Osatuke, K., Hardy, G. E., Shapiro, D. A., Agnew-Davies, R., Rees, A., & Barkham, M. (2004). Patterns of alliance development and the rupture-repair hypothesis: Are productive relationships U-shaped or V-shaped *Journal of Counseling Psychology*, 51(1), 81–92. https://doi.org/10.1037/0022-0167.51.1.81

Strachey, J. (1934). The nature of the therapeutic action of psycho-analysis. *International Journal of Psycho-Analysis*, 15, 127–159.

Strauss, J. L., Hayes, A. M., Johnson, S. L., Newman, C. F., Brown, G. K., Barber, J. P., Laurenceau, J.-P., & Beck, A. T. (2006). Early alliance, alliance ruptures, and symptom change in a nonrandomized trial of cognitive therapy for avoidant and obsessive-compulsive personality disorders. *Journal of Consulting and Clinical Psychology*, 74(2), 337–345. https://doi.org/10.1037/0022-006X.74.2.337

Strunk, D. R., Brotman, M. A., & DeRubeis, R. J. (2010). The process of change in cognitive therapy for depression: Predictors of early inter-session symptom gains. *Behaviour Research and Therapy*, 48(7), 599–606. https://doi.org/10.1016/j.brat.2010.03.011

Summers, R. J., & Barber, J. P. (2009). *Dynamic psychotherapy: A guide to evidence-based practice*. New York, NY: Guilford Press.

Svartberg, M., & Stiles, T. (1994). Therapeutic alliance, therapist competence, and client change in short-term anxiety-provoking psychotherapy. *Psychotherapy Research*, 4(1), 20–33. https://doi.org/10.1080/10503309412331333872

Swank, L. E., & Wittenborn, A. K. (2013). Repairing alliance ruptures in emotionally focused couple therapy: A preliminary task analysis. *The American Journal of Family Therapy*, 41(5), 389–402. https://doi.org/10.1080/01926187.2012.726595

Taber, B. J., Leibert, T. W., & Agaskar, V. R. (2011). Relationships among client-therapist personality congruence, working alliance, and therapeutic outcome. *Psychotherapy*, 48(4), 376–380. https://doi.org/10.1037/a0022066

Thoma, N. C., McKay, D., Gerber, A. J., Milrod, B. L., Edwards, A. R., & Kocsis, J. H. (2012). A quality-based review of randomized controlled trials of cognitive-behavioral therapy for depression: An assessment and metaregression. *The American Journal of Psychiatry*, 169(1), 22–30. https://doi.org/10.1176/appi.ajp.2011.11030433

Timulak, L., & McElvaney, R. (2013). Qualitative meta-analysis of insight events in psychotherapy. *Counselling Psychology Quarterly*, 26(2), 131–150. https://doi.org/10.1080/09515070.2013.792997

Town, J. M., Abbass, A., Stride, C., & Bernier, D. (2017). A randomised controlled trial of Intensive Short-Term Dynamic Psychotherapy for treatment resistant depression: The Halifax Depression Study. *Journal of Affective Disorders*, 214, 15–25. https://doi.org/10.1016/j.jad.2017.02.035

Town, J. M., Hardy, G. E., McCullough, L., & Stride, C. (2012). Patient affect experiencing following therapist interventions in short-term dynamic psychotherapy. *Psychotherapy Research*, 22(2), 208–219. https://doi.org/10.1080/10503307.2011.637243

Tracey, T. J., & Kokotovic, A. M. (1989). Factor structure of the Working Alliance Inventory. *Psychological Assessment*, 1(3), 207–210. https://doi.org/10.1037/1040-3590.1.3.207

Tschuschke, V., Crameri, A., Koehler, M., Berglar, J., Muth, K., Staczan, P., Von Wyl, A., Schulthess, P., & Koemeda-Lutz, M. (2015). The role of therapists' treatment adherence, professional experience, therapeutic alliance, and clients' severity of psychological problems: Prediction of treatment outcome in eight different psychotherapy approaches. Preliminary results of a naturalistic study. *Psychotherapy Research*, 25(4), 420–434. https://doi.org/10.1080/10503307.2014.896055

Tufekcioglu, S., Muran, J. C., Safran, J.D., & Winston, A. (2013), Personality disorder and early therapeutic alliance in two time-limited therapies. *Psychotherapy Research*, 23(6), 646–657. https://doi.org/10.1080/10503307.2013.843803

Tummala-Narra, P. (2016). *Psychoanalytic theory and cultural competence in psychotherapy*. Washington, DC: American Psychological Association. https://doi.org/10.1037/14800-000

Ulvenes, P. G., Berggraf, L., Hoffart, A., Stiles, T. C., Svartberg, M., McCullough, L., & Wampold, B. E. (2012). Different processes for different therapies: Therapist actions, therapeutic bond, and outcome. *Psychotherapy*, 49(3), 291–302. https://doi.org/10.1037/a0027895

Vermote, R., Lowyck, B., Luyten, P., Vertommen, H., Corveleyn, J., Verhaest, Y., & Peuskens, J. (2010). Process and outcome in psychodynamic hospitalization-based treatment for patients with a personality disorder. *The Journal of Nervous & Mental Disease*, 198(2), 110–115. https://doi.org/10.1097/NMD.0b013e3181cc0d59

Viechtbauer, W. (2010). *Conducting meta-Analyses in R with the metafor package*. 2010, 36(3), 1–48. https://doi.org/10.18637/jss.v036.i03

Wampold, B. E. (2001). *The great psychotherapy debate: Models, methods, and findings*. Mahwah, NJ: Erlbaum.

Wampold, B. E., & Imel, Z. E. (2015). *The great psychotherapy debate: The evidence for what makes psychotherapy work*. Routledge. https://doi.org/10.4324/9780203582015

Watson, R., Daffern, M., & Thomas, S. (2017). The impact of interpersonal style and interpersonal complementarity on the therapeutic alliance between therapists and offenders in sex offender treatment. *Sexual Abuse*, 29(2), 107–127. https://doi.org/10.1177/1079063215580969

Webb, C. A., DeRubeis, R. J., & Barber, J. P. (2010). Therapist adherence/competence and treatment outcome: A meta-analytic review. *Journal of Consulting and Clinical Psychology*, 78(2), 200–211. https://doi.org/10.1037/a0018912

Wilczek, A. Weinryb, R. M., Barber, J. P., Gustavsson, J. P., & Asberg, M. (2004). Change in the core conflictual relationship theme after long-term dynamic psychotherapy. *Psychotherapy Research*, 14(1), 107–125. https://doi.org/10.1093/ptr/kph007

Wiseman, H., & Tishby, O. (2017). Applying relationship anecdotes paradigm interviews to study client-therapist relationship narratives: Core conflictual relationship theme analyses. *Psychotherapy Research*, 27(3), 283–299. https://doi.org/10.1080/10503307.2016.1271958

Wolfe, B. E., & Goldfried, M. R. (1988). Research on psychotherapy integration: Recommendations and conclusions from an NIMH workshop. *Journal of Consulting and Clinical Psychology*, 56(3), 448–451. https://doi.org/10.1037/0022–006X.56.3.448

Yeomans, F. E., Clarkin, J. F., & Kernberg, O. F. (2015). *Transference-focused psychotherapy for borderline personality disorder*. Washington, DC: American Psychiatric Publishing. https://doi.org/10.1176/appi.books.9781615371006

Zilcha-Mano, S. (2017). Is alliance really therapeutic? A systematic answer based on recent methodological developments. *American Psychologist*, 72(4), 311–325. https://doi.org/10.1037/a0040435

Zilcha-Mano, S. (2019). Major developments in methods addressing for whom psychotherapy may work and why. *Psychotherapy Research*, 29(6), 693–708. https://doi.org/10.1080/10503307.2018.1429691

Zilcha-Mano, S. (2021). Toward personalized psychotherapy: The importance of the trait-like/state-like distinction for understanding therapeutic change. *American Psychologist*, 76(3), 516–528. https://doi.org/10.1037/amp0000629

Zilcha-Mano, S., & Errázuriz, P. (2015). One size does not fit all: Examining heterogeneity and identifying moderators of the alliance-outcome association. *Journal of Counseling Psychology*, 62(4), 579–591. https://doi.org/10.1037/cou0000103

Zilcha-Mano, S., & Errázuriz, P. (2017). Early development of mechanisms of change as a predictor of subsequent change and treatment outcome: The case of working alliance. *Journal of Consulting and Clinical Psychology, 85*(5), 508–520. https://doi.org/10.1037/ccp0000192

Zilcha-Mano, S., Eubanks, C. F., & Muran, J. C. (2019). Sudden gains in the alliance in cognitive behavioral therapy versus brief relational therapy. *Journal of Consulting and Clinical Psychology, 87*(6), 501–509. https://doi.org/10.1037/ccp0000397

Zilcha-Mano, S., Keefe, J. R., Chui, H., Rubin, A., Barrett, M. S., & Barber, J. P. (2016). Reducing dropout in treatment for depression: Translating dropout predictors into individualized treatment recommendations. *The Journal of Clinical Psychiatry, 77*(12), e1584–e1590. https://doi.org/10.4088/JCP.15m10081

SUPPLEMENTAL MATERIALS

REFERENCES

Abbass, A., Sheldon, A., Gyra, J., & Kalpin, A. (2008). Intensive short-term dynamic psychotherapy for DSM-IV personality disorders: A randomized controlled trial. *The Journal of Nervous and Mental Disease, 196*(3), 211–216. https://doi.org/10.1097/NMD.0b013e3181662ff0

Ajilchi, B., Ahadi, H., Najati, V., & Delavar, A. (2013). The efficacy of intensive short-term dynamic psychotherapy on attention bias in depressed patients. *European Journal of Experimental Biology, 3*(3), 492–497

Alstrom, J. E., Norlund, C. L., Persson, G., Harding, M., & Ljungqvist, C. (1984a). Effects of four treatment methods on agoraphobic women not suitable for insight-oriented psychotherapy. *Acta Psychiatrica Scandinavica, 70*(1), 1–17. https://doi.org/10.1111/j.1600-0447.1984.tb01176.x

Alstrom, J. E., Norlund, C. L., Persson, G., Harding, M., & Ljungqvist, C. (1984b). Effects of four treatment methods on social phobic patients not suitable for insight-oriented psychotherapy. *Acta Psychiatrica Scandinavica, 70*(2), 97–110. https://doi.org/10.1111/j.1600-0447.1984.tb01187.x

Amianto, F., Ferrero, A., Pierò, A., Cairo, E., Rocca, G., Simonelli, B., Fassina, S., Abbate-Daga, G., & Fassino, S. (2011). Supervised team management, with or without structured psychotherapy, in heavy users of a mental health service with borderline personality disorder: A two-year follow-up preliminary randomized study. *BMC Psychiatry, 11*(1), 181. https://bmcpsychiatry.biomedcentral.com/articles/10.1186/1471-244X-11-181

Anderson, K.N., Bautista, C. L., & Hope, D. A. (2019). Therapeutic alliance, cultural competence and minority status in premature termination of psychotherapy. *American Journal of Orthopsychiatry, 89*(1), 104–114. https://doi.org/10.1037/ort0000342

Barkham, M., Shapiro, D. A., Hardy, G. E., & Rees, A. (1999). Psychotherapy in two-plus-one sessions: Outcomes of a randomized controlled trial of cognitive-behavioral and psychodynamic-interpersonal therapy for sub-syndromal depression. *Journal of Consulting and Clinical Psychology, 67*(2), 201–211. https://doi.org/10.1037/0022-006X.67.2.201

Bastos, A. G., Guimaraes, L. S. P., & Trentini, C. M. (2015). The efficacy of long-term psychodynamic psychotherapy, fluoxetine and their combination in the outpatient treatment of depression. *Psychotherapy Research, 25*(5), 612–624. https://doi.org/10.1080/10503307.2014.935519

Bateman A. W., & Fonagy P. (1999). Effectiveness of partial hospitalization in the treatment of borderline personality disorder: A randomized controlled trial. *The American Journal of Psychiatry, 156*(10), 1563–1569. https://doi.org/10.1176/ajp.156.10.1563

Bateman, A. W., & Fonagy, P. (2008). 8-year follow-up of patients treated for borderline personality disorder: Mentalization-based treatment versus treatment as usual. *The American Journal of Psychiatry, 165*(5), 631–638. https://doi.org/10.1176/appi.ajp.2007.07040636

Bateman A. W., & Fonagy, P. (2009). Randomized controlled trial of outpatient mentalization-based treatment versus structured clinical management for borderline personality disorder. *The American Journal of Psychiatry, 166*(12), 1355–1364. https://doi.org/10.1176/appi.ajp.2009.09040539

Beutel, M. E., Scheurich, V., Knebel, A., Michal, M., Wiltink, J., Graf-Morgenstern, M., Tschan, R., Milrod, B., Wellek, S., & Subic-Wrana, C. (2013). Implementing panic-focused psychodynamic psychotherapy

into clinical practice. *The Canadian Journal of Psychiatry, 58*(6), 326–334. https://doi.org/10.1177/070674371305800604

Bögels, S. M., Wijts, P., Oort, F. J., & Sallaerts, S. J. M. (2014). Psychodynamic versus cognitive behavior therapy for social anxiety disorder: An efficacy and partial effectiveness trial. *Depression and Anxiety, 31*, 363–373. https://doi.org/10.1002/da.22246

Bressi, C., Porcellana, M., Marinaccio, P. M., Nocito, E. P., & Magri, L. (2010). Short-term psychodynamic psychotherapy versus treatment as usual for depressive and anxiety disorders: A randomized clinical trial of efficacy. *The Journal of Nervous and Mental Disease, 198*(9), 647–652. https://doi.org/10.1037/0022-006X.57.5.607

Brom, D., Kleber, R. J., & Defares, P. B. (1989). Brief psychotherapy for post-traumatic stress disorders. *Journal of Consulting and Clinical Psychology, 57*(5), 607–612. https://doi.org/10.1037/0022-006X.57.5.607

Carrington, C. H. (1979). A comparison of cognitive and analytically oriented brief treatment approaches to depression in Black women. *Dissertation Abstracts International, 40*(6–B), 2829.

Clarkin, J. F., Levy, K. M., Lenzenweger, M. F., & Kernberg, O. F. (2007). Evaluating three treatments for borderline personality disorder: A multiwave study. *The American Journal of Psychiatry, 164*(6), 922–928. https://doi.org/10.1176/ajp.2007.164.6.922

Cooper, P. J., Murray, L., Wilson, A., & Romaniuk, H. (2003). Controlled trial of the short- and longterm effect of psychological treatment of postpartum depression. 1. Impact on maternal mood. *The British Journal of Psychiatry, 182*(5), 412–419. https://doi.org/10.1192/bjp.182.5.412

Crits-Christoph, P., Gibbons, M. B. C., Narducci, J., Schamberger, M., & Gallop, R. (2005). Interpersonal problems and the outcome of interpersonally oriented psychodynamic treatment of GAD. *Psychotherapy: Theory, Research, Practice, Training, 42*(2), 211–224. https://doi.org/10.1037/0033-3204.42.2.211

De Roten, Y., Ambresin, G., Herrera, F., Fassassi, S., Fournier, N., Preisig, M., & Despland, J. N. (2017). Efficacy of an adjunctive brief psychodynamic psychotherapy to usual inpatient treatment of depression: Results of a randomized controlled trial. *Journal of Affective Disorders, 209*, 105–113. https://doi.org/10.1016/j.jad.2016.11.013

Doering, S., Hörz, S., Rentrop, M., Fischer-Kern, M., Schuster, P., Benecke, C., Buchheim, A., Martius, P., & Buchheim, P. (2010). Transference-focused psychotherapy v. treatment by community psychotherapists for borderline personality disorder: randomised controlled trial. *The British Journal of Psychiatry, 196*(5), 389–395. https://doi.org/10.1192/bjp.bp.109.070177

Durham, R. C., Fisher, P. L., Trevling, L. R., Hau, C. M., Richard, K., & Stewart, J. B. (1999). One year follow-up of cognitive therapy, analytic psychotherapy and anxiety management training for generalized anxiety disorder: Symptom change, medication usage and attitudes to treatment. *Behavioural and Cognitive Psychotherapy, 27*(1), 19–35. https://doi.org/10.1017/S1352465899271056

Durham, R. C., Murphy, T., Allan, T., Richard, K., Treliving, L. R., & Fenton, G. W. (1994). Cognitive therapy, analytic psychotherapy and anxiety management training for generalised anxiety disorder. *The British Journal of Psychiatry, 165*(3), 315–323. https://doi.org/10.1192/bjp.165.3.315

Emmelkamp, P. M. G., Benner, A., Kuipers, A., Feiertag, G. A., Koster, H. C., & van Apeldoorn, F. J. (2006). Comparison of brief dynamic and cognitive-behavioural therapies in avoidant personality disorder. *The British Journal of Psychiatry, 189*(1), 60–64. https://doi.org/10.1192/bjp.bp.105.012153

Fonagy, P., Lemma, A., Target, M., O'Keeffe, S., Constantinou, M. P., Wurman, T. V., Luyten, P., Allison, E., Roth, A., Cape, J., & Pilling, S. (2020). Dynamic interpersonal therapy for moderate to severe depression: A pilot randomized controlled and feasibility trial. *Psychological Medicine, 50*(6), 1010–1019. https://doi.org/10.1017/S0033291719000928

Fonagy, P., Rost, F., Carlyle, J. A., McPherson, S., Thomas, R., Pasco Fearon, R. M., Goldberg, D., & Taylor, D. (2015). Pragmatic randomized controlled trial of long-term psychoanalytic psychotherapy for treatment-resistant depression: the Tavistock Adult Depression Study (TADS). *World Psychiatry, 14*(3), 312–321. https://doi.org/10.1002/wps.20267

Gallagher, D. E., & Thompson, L. W. (1982). Treatment of major depressive disorder in older adult outpatients with brief psychotherapies. *Psychotherapy: Theory, Research & Practice, 19*(4), 482–490. https://doi.org/10.1037/h0088461

Gallagher-Thompson, D. & Steffen, A. M. (1994). Comparative effects of cognitive-behavioral and brief psychodynamic psychotherapies for depressed family caregivers. *Journal of Consulting and Clinical Psychology*, *62*(3), 543–549. https://doi.org/10.1037/0022-006X.62.3.543

Giesen-Bloo, J., van Dyck, R., Spinhoven, P., van Tilburg, W., Dirksen, C., van Asselt, T., Kremers, I., Nadort, M., & Arntz, A. (2006). Outpatient psychotherapy for borderline personality disorder: Randomized trial of schema-focused therapy vs transference-focused psychotherapy. *Archives of General Psychiatry*, *63*(6), 649–658. https://doi.org/10.1001/archpsyc.63.6.649

Gregory, R. J., Chlebowski, S., Kang, D., Remen, A. L., Soderberg, M. G., Stepkovitch, J., & Virk, S. (2008). A controlled trial of psychodynamic psychotherapy for co-occurring borderline personality disorder and alcohol use disorder. *Psychotherapy: Theory, Research, Practice, Training*, *45*(1), 28–41. https://doi.org/10.1037/0033-3204.45.1.28

Gregory, R. J., DeLucia-Deranja, E., & Mogle, J. A. (2010). Dynamic deconstructive psychotherapy versus optimized community care for borderline personaity disorder co-occuring with alcohol use disorders: A 30–month follow-up. *The Journal of Nervous and Mental Disease*, *198*(4), 292–298. https://doi.org/10.1097/NMD.0b013e3181d6172d

Hellerstein, D. J., Rosenthal, R. N., Pinsker, H., Samstag, L. W., Muran, J. C., & Winston, A. (1998). A randomized prospective study comparing supportive and dynamic therapies: Outcome and alliance. *Journal of Psychotherapy Practice & Research*, *7*(4), 261–271.

Hersen, M., Bellack, A. S., Himmelhoch, J. M., & Thase, M. E. (1984). Effects of social skill training, amitriptyline, and psychotherapy in unipolar depressed women. *Behavior Therapy*, *15*(1), 21–40. https://doi.org/10.1016/S0005-7894(84)80039-8

Jakobsen, J. C., Gluud, C., Kongerslev, M., Larsen, K. A., Sørensen, P., Winkel, P., Lange, T., Søgaard, U., & Simonsen, E. (2012). 'Third wave' cognitive therapy versus mentalization-based treatment for major depressive disorder. A protocol for a randomised clinical trial. *BMC Psychiatry*, *12*, 232–232. https://doi.org/10.1186/1471-244X-12-232

Jørgensen, C. R., Bøye, R., Andersen, D., Døssing Blaabjerg, A. H., Freund, C., Jordet, H., & Kjølbye, M. (2014). Eighteen months post-treatment naturalistic follow-up study of mentalization-based therapy and supportive group treatment of borderline personality disorder: Clinical outcomes and functioning. *Nordic Psychology*, *66*(4), 254–273. https://doi.org/10.1080/19012276.2014.963649

Jørgensen, C. R., Freund, C., Bøye, R., Jordet, H., Andersen, D., & Kjølbye, M. (2013). Outcome of mentalization-based and supportive psychotherapy in patients with borderline personality disorder: A randomized trial. *Acta Psychiatrica Scandinavica*, *127*(4), 305–317. https://doi.org/10.1111/j.1600-0447.2012.01923.x

Knekt, P., Lindfors, O., Laaksonen, M. A., Raitasalo, R., Haaramo, P., Järvikoski, A., & Helsinki Psychotherapy Study Group. (2008). Effectiveness of short-term and long-term psychotherapy on work ability and functional capacity-a randomized clinical trial on depressive and anxiety disorders. *Journal of Affective Disorders*, *107*(1–3), 95–106. https://doi.org/10.1016/j.jad.2007.08.005

Knekt, P., Lindfors, O., Renlund, C., Kaipainen, M., Mäkelä, P., Järvikoski, A., Maljanen, T., ; Marttunen, M. J., Raitasalo, R., Härkänen, T, Virtala, E., Rissanen, H., Laine, H., Hannula, J., & Aalberg, V. (2004). A randomized trial on the effect of four forms of psychotherapy on depressive and anxiety disorders: Design, methods and results on the effectiveness of short-term psychodynamic psychotherapy and solution focused therapy during a one-year follow-up. Helsinki: KELA, 2004. 112 p. (Sosiaali-ja terveysturvan tutkimuksia / Studies in social security and health).

Leichsenring, F., Salzer, S., Beutel, M. E., Herpertz, S., Hiller, W., Hoyer, J., Huesing, J., Joraschky, P., Nolting, B., Poehlmann, K., Ritter, V., Stangier, U., Strauss, B., Tefikow, S., Teismann, T., Willutzki, U., Wiltink, J., & Leibing, E. (2014). Long-term outcome of psychodynamic therapy and cognitive-behavioral therapy in social anxiety disorder. *The American Journal of Psychiatry*, *171*(10), 1074–1082. https://doi.org/10.1176/appi.ajp.2014.13111514

Leichsenring, F., Salzer, S., Jaeger, U., Kächele, H., Kreische, R., Leweke, F., Rüger, U., Winkelbach, C., & Leibing, E. (2009). Short-term psychodynamic psychotherapy and cognitive-behavioral therapy in generalized anxiety disorder: A randomized, controlled trial. *The American Journal of Psychiatry*, *166*(8), 875–881. https://doi.org/10.1176/appi.ajp.2009.09030441

Maina, G., Forner, F., & Bogetto, F. (2005). Randomized controlled trial comparing brief dynamic and supportive therapy with waiting list condition in minor depressive disorders. *Psychotherapy and Psychosomatics*, *74*(1), 43–50. https://doi.org/10.1159/000082026

Milrod, B., Leon, A. C., Busch, F., Rudden, M., Schwalberg, M., Clarkin, J., Aronson, A., Singer, M., Turchin, W., Klass, E. T., Graf, E., Teres, J. J., & Shear, M. K. (2007). A randomized controlled clinical trial of psychoanalytic psychotherapy for panic disorder. *The American Journal of Psychiatry*, *164*(2), 265–272. https://doi.org/10.1176/ajp.2007.164.2.265

Moghadam, M. N. M., Atef-Vahid, M. K., Asgharnejad-Farid, A. A., Shabani, A., & Lavasni, F. (2015). Short-term dynamic psychotherapy versus sertraline in treatment of social phobia. *Iranian Journal of Psychiatry and Behavioral Sciences*, *9*(2). https://doi.org/10.5812/ijpbs.228

Muran, J. C., Safran, J. D., Samstag, L. W., & Winston, A. (2005). Evaluating an alliance-focused treatment for personality disorders. *Psychotherapy: Theory, Research, Practice, Training*, *42*, 532–545. https://doi.org/10.1037/0033-3204.42.4.532

Pierloot, R., & Vinck, A. (1978). Differential outcome of short-term dynamic psychotherapy and systematic desensitizationin the treatment of anxious outpatients: A preliminary report. *Psychologica Belgica*, *18*(1), 87–98.

Salminen, J. K., Karlsson, H., Hietala, J., Kajander, J., Aalto, S., Markkula, J., Rasi-Hakala, H., & Toikka, T. (2008). Short-term psychodynamic psychotherapy and fluoxetine in major depressive disorder: A randomized comparative study. *Psychotherapy and Psychosomatics*, *77*(6), 351–357. https://doi.org/10.1159/000151388

Salzer, S., Winkelbach, C., Leweke, F., Leibing, E., & Leichsenring, F. (2011). Long-term effects of short-term psychodynamic psychotherapy and cognitive-behavioural therapy in generalized anxiety disorder: 12–month follow-up. *The Canadian Journal of Psychiatry*, *56*(8), 503–508. https://doi.org/10.1177/070674371105600809

Shapiro, D. A., Barkham, M., Rees, A., Hardy, G. E., Reynolds, S., & Startup, M. (1994). Effects of treatment duration and severity of depression on the effectiveness of cognitive-behavioral and psychodynamic-interpersonal psychotherapy. *Journal of Consulting and Clinical Psychology*, *62*(3), 522–534. https://doi.org/10.1037/0022-006X.62.3.522

Svartberg, M., Stiles, T. C., & Seltzer, M. H. (2004). Randomized, controlled trial of the effectiveness of short-term dynamic psychotherapy and cognitive therapy for cluster C personality disorders. *The American Journal of Psychiatry*, *161*(5), 810–817. https://doi.org/10.1176/appi.ajp.161.5.810

Thompson, L. W., Gallagher, D., & Breckenridge, J. S. (1987). Comparative effectiveness of psychotherapies for depressed elders. *Journal of Consulting and Clinical Psychology*, *55*(3), 385–390. https://doi.org/10.1037/0022-006X.55.3.385

Thyme, K. E., Sundin, E. C., Stahlberg, G., Lindstrom, B., Eklof, H., & Wiberg, B. (2007). The outcome of short-term psychodynamic art therapy compared to short-term psychodynamic verbal therapy for depressed women. *Psychoanalytic Psychotherapy*, *21*(3), 250–264. https://doi.org/10.1080/02668730701535610

Town, J. M., Abbass, A., Stride, C., & Bernier, D. (2017b). A randomised controlled trial of Intensive Short-Term Dynamic Psychotherapy for treatment resistant depression: The Halifax Depression Study. *Journal of Affective Disorders*, *214*, 15–25. https://doi.org/10.1016/j.jad.2017.02.035

Vitriol, V. G., Ballesteros, S. T., Florenzano, R. U., Weil, K. P., & Benadof, D. F. (2009). Evaluation of an outpatient intervention for women with severe depression and a history of childhood trauma. *Psychiatric Services*, *60*(7), 936–942. https://doi.org/10.1176/ps.2009.60.7.936

Winston, A., Laikin, M., Pollack, J., Samstag, L. W., McCullough, L., & Muran, J. C. (1994). Short-term psychotherapy of personality disorders. *The American Journal of Psychiatry*, *151*(2), 190–194. https://doi.org/10.1176/ajp.151.2.190

CHAPTER 13

RESEARCH ON HUMANISTIC-EXPERIENTIAL PSYCHOTHERAPIES: UPDATED REVIEW

ROBERT ELLIOTT, JEANNE WATSON, LADISLAV TIMULAK, AND JASON SHARBANEE

Abstract

We review recent research on humanistic-experiential psychotherapies (HEPs), which include person-centered therapy (PCT), emotion-focused therapy (EFT), gestalt, and psychodrama approaches, along with generic relationship control conditions characterized as supportive or nondirective. A key part of this review is a meta-analysis of 91 studies of the effectiveness/efficacy of HEPs, published between 2009 and 2018, which produced the following results: (1) HEPs were associated with large pre-post client change (d = .86). (2) In controlled studies, clients in HEPs generally showed large gains relative to clients who received no therapy (.88). (3) In comparative outcome studies, HEPs in general were statistically and clinically equivalent in effectiveness to other therapies (–.08). (4) Overall, CBT appeared to have an equivocal advantage over HEPs (–.26). However, these studies were overwhelmingly delivered by CBT researchers in largely non-bona fide versions of HEPs as comparison conditions. Overall, the strongest results were found for EFT, followed by PCT; generic supportive-nondirective approaches were least effective, especially when compared to CBT. HEPs appeared to be most effective with relationship/interpersonal difficulties, self-damaging activities, coping with chronic medical conditions, and psychosis. Findings were more mixed for depression and anxiety. In addition, we offer an updated meta-synthesis of the qualitative outcomes of these therapies, which fell into three main categories: appreciating experiences of self; appreciating experience of self in relationship to others; and changed view of self/others. We also provide narrative reviews of recent qualitative research on helpful and unhelpful factors in HEPs, along with quantitative process-outcome research on HEPs including process-outcome research and work on mediating processes. In an integrative summary we identify a core set of interwoven client change processes involving emotional expression, deepening and transformation, the emergence of new client narratives, and the assimilation of problematic experiences. We conclude with a set of recommendations for research, practice and mental health guideline development.

OVERVIEW

INTRODUCTION

This review covers approaches to psychotherapy generally referred to as *humanistic* or *experiential*. These therapies are part of the main tradition of humanistic psychology (see Cain et al., 2016), with major subapproaches being person-centered therapy (PCT; e.g., Rogers, 1961), gestalt (e.g., Perls et al., 1951), emotion-focused (EFT, previously referred to as process-experiential; Greenberg et al., 1993), motivational interviewing (Miller & Rollnick, 2012), psychodrama (Moreno & Moreno, 1959), focusing-oriented (Gendlin, 1996), expressive (Daldrup et al., 1988), and body-oriented (Kepner, 1993), and, in some cases, existential (e.g., Schneider & Krug, 2017; Yalom, 1980). In addition, humanistic-experiential psychotherapies (HEPs) are often used as generic relationship control conditions by researchers from other theoretical orientations under store-brand labels such as *supportive* or *nondirective* (see Table 13.1 for an overview).

Although these approaches have varied somewhat in technique and conception over the course of their historical development, in their contemporary expressions they nevertheless share several distinctive theoretical assumptions. Most important among these is the centrality of a genuinely empathic and prizing *therapeutic relationship*. In the HEPs, the therapeutic relationship is seen as potentially curative. Each person's subjective experience is of central importance, and, in an effort to grasp this experience, the therapist attempts to enter empathically into the client's world in a way that goes beyond usual relationships. Being allowed to share another person's world is viewed as a privilege, and all HEPs reject the idea that the relationship between the client and the therapist can be reduced to either a technically oriented service encounter or an unconscious repetition of previous attachments. Rather, they generally share the view of an authentic but boundaried relationship with the therapist providing the client with a new, corrective and validating emotional experience (Greenberg & Elliott, 2012).

HEPs also share a focus on promoting in-therapy client *experiencing*, defined as the holistic process of immediate, ongoing awareness that includes perceiving, sensing, feeling, thinking, and wanting/intending. Thus, methods that deepen or stimulate client emotional experiencing are used within the context of an empathic facilitative relationship. Commitment to a phenomenological approach flows directly from this central interest in experiencing. People are viewed as meaning-creating, symbolizing agents, whose subjective experience is an essential aspect of their humanity. In addition, the experiential-humanistic view of functioning emphasizes the operation of an integrative, formative or actualizing tendency, oriented toward survival, growth, and the creation of meaning. Moreover, all HEPs are united by the general principle that people are wiser than their intellect alone. Internal tacit experiencing is seen as an important guide to conscious experience, fundamentally adaptive, and potentially available to awareness when the person turns attention internally within the context of a supportive interpersonal relationship. Interpersonal safety and support are thus viewed as key elements in enhancing the amount of attention available for self-awareness and exploration. HEPs are also consistently *person-centered*. This involves genuine concern and respect for each person. The person is viewed holistically, neither as a symptom-driven case nor as a diagnosis (Pos et al., 2008).

Recent developments in the HEPs include the continuing revival of research on person-centered therapy (PCT) and expanding study of process-guiding forms of HEP, including emotion-focused therapy (EFT; Elliott et al., 2004; Greenberg & Johnson, 1988) and motivational interviewing (Miller & Rollnick, 2012). A continuing key point of contention within the humanistic-experiential psychotherapies, however, is the degree to which therapists should act as process-experts by offering ways clients can work more productively on particular types of problems (process guiding). All HEPs are process-guiding to a certain extent, but EFT, gestalt, psychodrama and MI are more so, while PCT and so-called supportive or nondirective therapies attempt to minimize process guiding. On the other hand, recently developed existential therapies such as meaning-centered psychotherapy (Breitbart & Poppito, 2014) take a more explicit content directive approach, putting them outside the purview of this review, along with compassion-focused therapy (Gilbert, 2009) and schema therapy (Young et al., 2003), which, though typically associated with CBT, have borrowed heavily from HEPs.

In this chapter we focus on research published since our previous reviews (Elliott et al., 2004; Elliott et al., 2013; Greenberg et al., 1994), which covered research published prior to 2009. A key element of the chapter is a meta-analysis of 91 studies of the effectiveness/efficacy of HEPs, published between 2009 and 2018, together with a survey of the use of the approach with different client groups. We also offer an updated meta-synthesis of qualitative research on these therapies (cf. Timulak & Creaner, 2010). Finally, we provide narrative reviews of recent quantitative process research on HEPs, including process-outcome research and work on mediating processes.

Because of space limitations and the increasing amount and range of research this survey is not exhaustive. In particular, we have not reviewed the rather sparse literature on predictors/moderators of client outcome in HEPs. Similarly, we do not review therapeutic alliance, child psychotherapy, and on measure development (but see Cooper, Watson, & Hölldampf, 2010, for reviews of these topics). In addition, we have chosen not to review research on the growing number of related integrative approaches, such as emotion-focused psychodynamic approaches (e.g., Fosha, 2000), and "emotion-friendly" forms of CBT (e.g., Gilbert, 2009; Young et al., 2003). Limitations of

TABLE 13.1   Humanistic-Experiential Psychotherapies: Main Features and Subapproaches

I. Main features:

Therapeutic relationship	Facilitative: empathy, unconditional positive regard, genuineness
Focus	Experiencing: immediate involving awareness, including perceiving, sensing, feeling, thinking, and wanting/intending
Goals	Self-awareness, growth, meaning creation
Main exclusion feature:	Major content direction: Advisement, interpretation, disagreement

II. Main subapproaches:

A. Less Process-Guiding:

Person-Centred/Client-Centred	Developed by Rogers: relatively nondirective; based on therapist empathy, unconditional positive regard, genuineness
Supportive/Nondirective	Not associated with a particular HEP subapproach; therapist empathy and/or client experiencing are central; generally used as a control condition by CBT researchers (often in non bona fide)

B. More Process-Guiding:

Emotion(ally)-Focused/ Process-Experiential/ Attachment-based	Integrates person-centered and Gestalt therapies; focused on client emotions; process-guiding; uses therapeutic tasks
Motivational Interviewing/ Motivational Enhancement Therapy	Helping client explore their ambivalence about change; focusing on desire for change
Gestalt	Developed by Perls: enacting experiments in session; spontaneity, authenticity are central
Psychodrama	Developed by Moreno: enacting experiences in group therapy context
Expressive	Emotional expression is central
Body-Oriented	Awareness of and work with body are central
Humanistic-Existential	Focused on existential themes: responsibility, isolation, meaning, mortality
Focusing-Oriented	Focus on helping clients slow down and turn attention inside to bodily experiencing

resources and the availability of other systematic reviews have also led us to limit coverage of motivational interviewing.

ARE HUMANISTIC-EXPERIENTIAL THERAPIES EFFECTIVE? 2009–2018 META-ANALYSIS UPDATE

In North America and Europe, economic pressures on mental health services and scientific-political trends toward treatment standardization have led to the continued development of guidelines calling for certain psychological treatments to be officially recognized as effective, reimbursed by insurance, and actively promoted in training courses, at the expense of other treatments

(e.g., American Psychological Association, 2019; National Collaborating Centre for Mental Health, 2009). To date, the evidence supporting the efficacy of HEPs has not found its way into mainstream guidelines, which have in effect enshrined as supposed scientific fact and health care policy widely shared preconceptions about the perceived ineffectiveness of these approaches. Although research on HEPs has rapidly expanded over the past 20 years (see previous reviews in Elliott et al., 2004; Elliott et al., 2013), they continue to be overlooked or dismissed, as in the NICE Guidelines for Depression and Schizophrenia (National Collaborating Centre for Mental Health, 2009, 2014).

Understandably, humanistic-experiential therapists (e.g., Bohart et al., 1998) have responded to these challenges with alarm. Although philosophical assumptions and methods of the evidence-based practice movement have been and continue to be challenged, our strategy here is to look instead at the research evidence, which has sometimes been neglected in the controversy. In fact, as we show, a substantial and ever-growing body of research data supports the effectiveness of HEPs.

We report here the latest in a continuing series of meta-analytic reviews of HEP quantitative outcome research, substantially updating earlier reports (Elliott, 1996, 2001; Elliott et al., 2004; Elliott et al., 2013; Greenberg et al., 1994). The present update includes 91 studies published between 2009 and 2018, and follows PRISMA guidelines for systematic reviews. These studies offer further evidence for a revival of outcome research on HEPs.

Our most recent HEP outcome meta-analysis (Elliott et al., 2013) included pre-post effectiveness effect size data from 199 different samples of clients seen in some form of HEP, drawing from 186 studies (involving a total of 14,206 clients). In terms of efficacy research, we reported on 59 controlled studies with wait-list or no-treatment conditions (62 comparisons, involving 2,149 therapy clients and 1,988 controls); 31 of these were randomized control trials (RCTs). In addition, we also analyzed results from 100 comparative studies, in which HEPs were compared to other treatments: There were 135 comparisons, involving 108 samples of clients in HEPs; 82 of the studies were RCTs (n = 6,271 HEP clients, 7,214 clients in non-HEP therapies).

Meta-Analytic Approach

Because of its history and the philosophy behind this line of meta-analyses, we have followed (and continue to follow) a set of analytic strategies at variance with the practice of much of the burgeoning field of meta-analysis. Our fundamental principle continues to be to use all available data, including pre–post effectiveness data (as opposed to post-only contrasts) and associated open clinical trial designs; studies focused on general or mixed (rather than specific) client populations; and studies of widely varying methodological quality. We have also compared analyses using all available outcome measures to those looking only at primary outcomes. In our experience, the more selective reviewers are about the studies they take into a review, the more opportunities there are for reviewer bias to creep in. Instead, we have followed Smith et al.'s (1980) strategy of taking studies of widely varying quality in order to determine which methodological factors make a difference. In our experience, the results of following these meta-analytic practices have often been surprising and at odds with widely shared conventional wisdom.

Nevertheless, the previous versions of this meta-analysis have had a couple of key limitations, which we have attempted to address in this update. First, our previous versions ignored primary outcomes and intent-to-treat (ITT) designs, making it difficult to compare our results to other meta-analyses (e.g., Cuipers et al., 2012). Second, owing to the cumulative collection of the large number of studies over time, we were unable to construct a PRISMA diagram tracing our handling of studies, now a necessity for meta-analyses.

For this update, we decided to focus on the 10 years since our previous review (2009–2018). The inclusion criteria were: treatment labeled as Client/Person-centered, (Process-) Experiential, Focusing, Gestalt, Motivational Interviewing; or described as using empathy as a key element of therapy or being centered on client experience; psychotherapy or mental health counseling carried out by mental health professional or professional-in-training; treatment of three or more sessions; sample size of 10 or more; therapy outcome study; clients aged 13 or older; effect size (standardized mean difference) could be calculated. Figure 13.1 summarizes the results of this search process and the subsequent screening of possible studies. The final sample consisted of 91 separate studies, many represented by several publications (which were combined in our analyses). (See Supplemental Material Table 13S-1 for more detail on the screening of sources; and Table 13S-2 for a summary of the characteristics of the sample.)

(See Supplemental Material, Table 13S-1 for more detail.)

Diversity Issues

For our update, we were able to locate studies from a broader range of cultures and client populations than ever before. Eleven studies came from the Middle East (especially Iran and Turkey); six were from east or south Asia (including China and India); there was one study from South Africa (Edwards & Edwards, 2009). Two studies included a majority of black clients (Foa et al., 2013; Magidson et al., 2011). Seven studies involved elderly clients; three addressed the application of HEPs for people with disabilities (head injury or autism; Moss-Morris et al., 2013; Murphy et al., 2017; Ward & Hogan, 2009).

Effectiveness Research on Humanistic-Experiential Therapies: Total Pre–Post Change

How much do clients seen in HEPs change over the course of therapy? In our previous meta-analysis (see Table 13.2, lines designated as "2013"), Hedge's g for PP-All (per protocol analyses of all outcome measures) was .93 (k = 199 study samples; 95% CI [.88, 1.04]). For the current sample, the comparable value was statistically significantly smaller but still a large effect: .73 (k = 97; 95% CI [.62, .83]). In contrast, the intent-to-treat primary outcome (ITT-PO) value for the current sample was comparable to our previous value but had a larger confidence interval: .95 (95% CI [.73, 1.16]). The increased variability can be attributed to a substantially smaller sample size (k = 35), which in turn raises issues of representativeness and possible bias in ITT-PO values. In this case, we found the per protocol primary outcome (PP-PO) value of .86 (k = 94; 95% CI [.74, .97]) to be a reasonable compromise, both more representative of the existing research and less variable, with a larger sample and smaller confidence interval, while at the same time correlating essentially perfectly with ITT-PO scores (r = .99) and strongly with PP-All scores (r = .90). Thus, we conclude that our best estimate of client pre–post change in HEPs is likely to be provided by PP-PO scores, pointing to an effect of about .86 sd, a large effect only slightly smaller than the .93 value we reported in 2013. For these reasons, we will focus on PP-PO scores for the remainder of this meta-analysis. On the other hand, this effect size figure is characterized by large

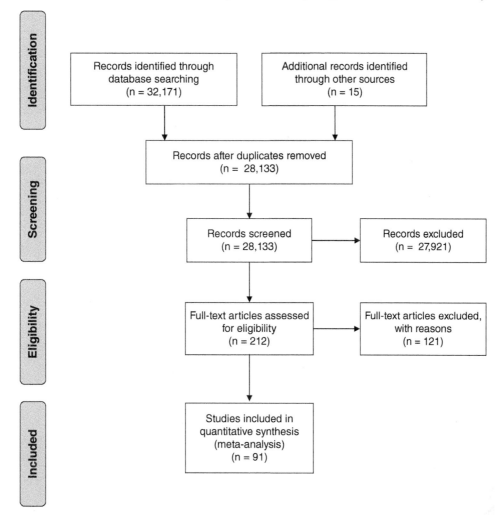

FIGURE 13.1 HEP Outcome Meta-Analysis PRISMA Diagram.

estimates of heterogenenity (Cochrane's Q of 559.5; $p < .01$; Higgins' $I^2 = 88\%$).

Next, we looked at how much change clients showed at different times following the end of therapy. In our 2013 analysis, we found that clients maintained or perhaps even increased their immediate posttreatment gains ($d = .95$) over the post-therapy period, with slightly larger effects obtained at early (1–11 months; 1.05) and late (12+ months; 1.11) follow-ups. With our current data set, at immediate post-therapy, we found weighted mean effects ranging from .73 (PP-All; $k = 91$), to .86 (PP-PO; $k = 91$), to .94 (ITT-PO; $k = 33$), all virtually identical to the overall effect. In addition, similar to the previous meta-analysis, clients generally maintained their post-therapy gains during the year following therapy ($ES_w = .88$; $k = 41$; 95% CI [.67, 1.1]) and beyond ($ES_w = .92$; $k = 15$; 95% CI [.52, 1.31]).

Controlled Efficacy Studies on Humanistic-Experiential Therapies

Pre–post effects do not tell us whether clients in HEPs fared better than untreated clients, and thus make it difficult to infer that therapy was responsible for changes made by clients. They

have also been reported to produce generally larger effects than control group comparisons (Lipsey & Wilson, 1993). Therefore, we examined control-referenced effect sizes (differences between pre-post ESs) in the 21 studies/treated groups in which HEPs were compared to wait-list or no-treatment controls. The weighted mean-controlled effect size (ES_{wc}) for these studies (Table 13.2) was .88 (95% CI [.55, 1.20]), quite similar to the overall pre–post effect reported earlier and slightly larger than the .76 controlled PP-All ES reported by Elliott et al. (2013). Breaking down the current controlled ES, we found that the average pre–post effect for clients seen in HEPs was virtually identical ($k = 20$; $ES_{wc} = .95$; 95% CI [.65, 1.26]), while participants seen in untreated control groups showed little or no change ($ES_{wc} = .09$; 95% CI [–.03, .21]). When only the randomized studies were considered ($k = 15$), the controlled effect was slightly but not significantly larger ($ES_{wc} = .98$; 95% CI [.51, 1.44]). From the pattern of results in this section, three conclusions can be drawn:

1. There is likely to be a strong causal relationship between the HEPs delivered in these studies and client change.

TABLE 13.2 Summary of Overall Pre–Post Change, Controlled, and Comparative Weighted Effect Sizes

	k	n	m	se	95% CI	Q	I^2
Pre–Post Effects in HEP Samples							
Overall (combined time periods)							
ITT Primary Outcomes	35	2430	.95	.11	.73, 1.16	329.6**	90%
Per Protocol Primary Outcomes	94	7558	.86	.06	.74, .97	559.5*	88%
Per Protocol All Outcomes	94	7376	.73	.05	.62, .83	466.7**	85%
2013: Per Protocol All Outcomes	199	14,032	.93	.04	.88, 1.04	–	–
Post (0–1 mo post)							
ITT Primary outcomes	33	1474	.94	.11	.73, 1.15	213.4**	86%
Per Protocol Primary Outcomes	91	6842	.86	.06	.75, .98	462.0**	87%
Per Protocol All Outcomes	91	6813	.73	.05	.63, .83	407.6**	83%
2013: Per Protocol All Outcomes	181	13,109	.95	.05	.86, 1.04	–	–
Early follow-up (2–11 mos.)							
Per Protocol Primary Outcomes	41	2161	.88	.11	.67, 1.10	265.4**	89%
2013: Per Protocol All Outcomes	77	2125	1.05	.07	.90, 1.20	–	–
Late follow-up (12+ mos.)							
Per Protocol Primary Outcomes	15	599	.92	.20	.52, 1.31	105.5**	90%
2013: Per Protocol All Outcomes	52	2611	1.11	.09	.93, 1.29	–	–
Type of HEP (PP-PO effects combined over time periods)							
Supportive-Nondirective	30	1564	.73	.09	.55, .92	163.3**	82%
Person-Centered	18	1258	.98	.16	.66, 1.29	138.0**	89%
EFT	18	464	1.31	.13	1.05, 1.58	47.8**	67%
Gestalt/Psychodrama	17	723	.78	.10	.57, .98	54.2**	65%
Other HEPs	11	3521	.53	.10	.32, .73	47.6**	78%
Controlled ES (HEPs vs. untreated participants)							
Controlled studies overall	21	1519	.88	.16	.55, 1.20	119.8**	87%
Controlled RCTs	14	848	.98	.24	.51, 1.44	105.6**	90%
2013 Controlled PP-All	62	4102	.76	.06	–	–	–
HEP pre–post	20	621	.95	.15	.65, 1.26	103.3**	84%
2013 HEP pre–post ES	59	2144	1.01	–	–	–	–
Untreated Control pre–post ES	20	648	.09	.06	−.03, .21	18.1**	15%
2013: Control pre–post ES	53	1958	.19	–	–	–	–

(Continued)

TABLE 13.2 (CONTINUED)

	k	n	m	se	95% CI	Q	I²
Comparative ES (HEPs vs. NonHEP treatments)							
Overall – all studies PP-PO	63	16266	–.08	.06	–.21, .04	245.8**	91%
2013 HEP comparative ES PP-All	*135*	*6097*	*.01*	*.03*	*–.05, .07*	*305.2**	*–*
RCTs only	56	6931	–.07	.07	–.21, .07	225.6**	88%
2013 RCTs only PP All	*113*	*–*	*–.01*	*.04*	*–.11, .07*	*–*	*–*
HEP pre–post PP Primary	62	5876	.76	.07	.62, .88	450.9**	91%
2013 HEP pre–post ES PP All	*124*	*6097*	*.98*	*–*	*–*	*–*	*–*
NonHEP PP Primary	62	10,262	.82	.09	.65, 1.00	693.2**	95%
2013 NonHEP pre–post ES PP All	*124*	*–*	*1.02*	*–*	*–*	*–*	*–*
HEP vs. CBT							
All Studies	36	13,785	–.26	.06	–.37, –.15	103.2**	78%
RCTs	32	4641	–.26	.05	–.36, –.16	74.8**	58%
2013 Comparative PP-All	*76*	*–*	*–.13*	*.04*	*–.21, –.06*	*–*	*–*
HEP vs. non-CBT							
Overall	27	2481	.19	.12	–.04, .43	110.3**	90%
RCTs	24	2290	.24	.14	–.03, .51	107.1**	92%
2013 Comparative PP-All	*59*	*–*	*.01*	*.03*	*–*	*–*	*–*
More vs. less intensive/ process guiding HEPS	6	640	.18	.15	–.12, .48	*–*	*–*

Note. *p < .05; **p < .01. Hedges's g used (corrects for small sample bias). Weighted effects used inverse variance based on *n* of clients in humanistic-experiential therapy conditions. Positive values indicate pro-HEP or pro-process guiding results. All values are Per Protocol-Primary Outcomes (PP-PO) unless otherwise noted. PP-All: Per Protocol-All Outcomes; ITT-PO: Intent-to-Treat-Primary Outcomes.

2. The controlled effects are roughly equivalent to the pre–post effects, which would be consistent with the idea that almost all of the pre–post gains reported for clients in HEPs can be attributed to the therapy (including both client and therapist within-therapy factors), as opposed to external or nontherapy factors.
3. These results suggest that if anything treatment effects might be stronger for RCTs than for nonrandomized controlled studies.

As in our earlier meta-analyses, randomization appeared to make little difference in the effects obtained, thus supporting the internal validity of the nonrandomized controlled studies, as well as the larger body of one-group pre–post studies. One caution: Although this body of evidence supports the internal validity efficacy of HEPs, it does not tell us what aspects of the HEPs studied might be responsible for client pre–post change.

Comparative Outcome Research on Humanistic-Experiential versus Other Therapies

While impressive, the pre–post and controlled effect-size analyses reported do not address the issue of comparative treatment effectiveness, which is central to continuing discussions about mental health policy, the effectiveness of HEPs and the sources of their effects. For this, we first examined the whole set of 63 comparisons between HEPs and other therapies (including 56 RCTs). Applying random effects model significance testing (Lipsey & Wilson, 2001) and equivalence analysis to this and other treatment comparisons made it possible to examine the statistical equivalence between HEPs and non-HEPs. These analyses are summarized in Tables 13.2 and 13.3, with equivalence analyses given in the "95% Confidence Interval," "Different from 0," and "Different from 1.41" columns. If the "Different from 0" column is "No" and the

TABLE 13.3 Equivalence Analyses: Key Comparisons Between HEPs and non-HEPs (Per Protocol Primary Variable Analyses)

	k	ES_w	SE	95% CI	Diff: 0	Diff: <|.4|	Result[a]
All HEPs							
HEP vs. non-HEP: All studies	63	−.08	.06	−.21, .04	No	Yes	Equivalent
RCTs only	56	−.07	.07	−.21, .07	No	Yes	Equivalent
HEP vs. CBT: All studies	36	−.26	.06	−.37, −.15	Yes	Yes	Equivocally worse
(allegiance-controlled)[b]		(−.26)	(.15)	(−.56, .04)	(No)	(No)	(same)
RCTs only	32	−.26	.05	−.36, −.16	Yes	Yes	Equivocally worse
(allegiance-controlled)		(.00)	(.16)	(−.31, .32)	(No)	(Yes)	(Equivalent)
HEP vs. non-CBT All studies	27	.19	.12	−.04, .43	No	No	Trivially better
(allegiance-controlled)		(.06)	(.24)	(−.41, .52)	(No)	(No)	(Equivocally better)
RCTs only	24	.24	.14	−.03, .51	No	No	Equivocally better
(allegiance-controlled)		(.05)	(.26)	(−.46, .56)	(No)	(No)	(Equivocally better)
CBT vs. Common Forms of HEP							
PCT vs. CBT: All studies	10	−.30	.13	−.55 to −.05	Yes	No	Equivocally worse
(allegiance-controlled)		(−.27)	(.21)	(−.68, .13)	(No)	(No)	(same)
RCTs only	8	−.20	.12	−.45, .04	No	No	Equivocally worse
		(.01)	(.22)	(−.42, .44)	(No)	(No)	(same)
Supportive vs. CBT: (All RCTs)	23	−.28	.06	−.40, −.16	Yes	No	Equivocally worse
Supportive vs. CBT: (Bona fide HEP)	9	−.15	.06	−.27, −.03	Yes	Yes	Equivocal

Note. ES_w: weighted comparative effect size (difference between therapies weighted by inverse variance); SE: standard error for the comparative effect sizes, random effects model; 95% CI: 95% confidential interval; Diff: 0: ES_w statistically significantly different from zero; Diff: <|.4| : ES_w statistically significantly smaller than minimum clinical practical value of .4 sd. HEP: humanistic-experiential psychotherapy; CBT: cognitive-behavioral therapy.
[a] "Result" refers to the practice implications of obtained value of mES: "Equivalent": within .1 sd of zero (greater than −.1 and less than .1); "Trivially (worse/better)": between 0.1 and 0.2 sd from zero; "Equivocally (worse/better)": between 0.2 and 0.4 sd from zero; "Clinically worse/better": at least 0.4 sd from zero.
[b] Values in parenthesized italics are results of analyses controlling for researcher allegiance, performed when uncontrolled differences had been obtained.

"Different from |.4|" column is "Yes," it means that the confidence interval includes zero but neither +.4 or −.4, indicating that the mean comparative effect demonstrated statistical equivalence. In addition, when these first two criteria didn't apply (i.e. because of small numbers of comparisons and large confidence intervals), we adopted the following conventions for interpreting the practical or clinical implications of these ambiguous results: "Equivalent": within .1 sd of zero (greater than −0.1 and less than .1); "Trivially Different": between .1 and .2 sd from zero; "Equivocal": between .2 and .4 sd from zero; "Clinically Better/Worse": at least 0.4 sd from zero.

The overall mean weighted comparative effect (ES_w) was −.08 (k = 63; 95% CI [−0.21, .04]); analyzing only the 56 RCTs produced nearly identical results (ES_{wc} = −.07; 95% CI [−.21, .07]). As indicated in Table 13.3, these results suggest that in general HEPs and other treatments (including CBT) are equivalent in effectiveness. In keeping with this conclusion, we found that for 43 (68%) of the comparisons, pre-post change for clients in HEPs vs. non-HEPs was within .4 standard deviations of each other, a value proposed as the minimum clinically interesting difference in effects (Elliott et al., 1993). This general result has been a consistent result of our earlier meta-analyses (e.g., Elliott et al., 2004; Elliott at al., 2013) and appears to be quite stable at this point. Nevertheless, this consistent statistical equivalence conceals significant variability in effects, as indicated by a Cochrane's Q of 245.8 ($p < 0.01$); the proportion of true between-study variability (I^2) was estimated at 91%, extremely high. Examination of possible moderators of comparative outcome effects is clearly called for (Lipsey & Wilson, 2001).

HEPs Versus Cognitive-Behavioral Therapies (CBTs) and Other Therapies

A significant center of continuing controversy involves widely held assumptions that HEPs are inferior to cognitive-behavioral treatments (CBT). The comparative studies analyzed above did not exclusively use CBT (36 out of 63 comparisons). Therefore, it can be argued that the effects of CBT were diluted by the inclusion of comparisons involving other types of therapy, often a mixture of ill-defined treatment as usual or integrative approaches.

To clarify this issue, we undertook a series of further equivalence analyses (see Table 13.3). For the 36 studies comparing HEPs to CBT, ES_w was –.26 (95% CI [–.37, –.15]), which is an equivocal result in favor of CBT (significantly different from both zero and |.4| and larger than .2). Results for RCTs were identical, and also best characterized as equivocally in favor of CBT (see Tables 13.2 and 13.3).

We also compared HEPs to other psychotherapies that weren't CBT in 27 studies involving a wide range of treatments, including treatment as usual. The ES_w was .19 for the whole sample ($k = 27$) and .24 ($k = 24$) for RCTs (see Table 13.3), suggesting trivially or equivocally better outcomes for HEPs.

Of considerable importance to practitioners and policy makers is the possibility that differences between active treatments may be due to researcher allegiance effects (e.g., Luborsky et al., 1999), which therefore need to be statistically controlled, as we did in previous versions of this meta-analysis. For the current sample of comparative studies, we found both: (i) a high rate of negative researcher allegiance: overall 59% but even higher in the HEP vs.CBT studies (78%); and (ii) a very large negative correlation between researcher allegiance and comparative effect size (meta-regression $r = –.56$; $n = 63$; $p < .01$), higher than reported by Elliott et al. (2013). Therefore, we ran additional analyses attempting to statistically control for researcher allegiance by removing variance in comparative ESs due to this variable. Table 13.3, where these analyses are indicated in italics and parentheses, shows mixed results, attenuating to zero (i.e. equivalence) the advantage for CBT for RCTs, but not when nonrandomized studies were included. We were able to trace this discrepancy to the presence of outliers (especially Marriott et al., 2009). Along the same line, in comparisons between HEPs and non-CBT other therapies, controlling for researcher allegiance reduced the effect to near zero, resulting in equivalence.

Thus, our data present a less clear picture than Elliott et al. (2013) were able to provide, at least when it comes to the issue of whether CBT is more effective or equivalent to HEPs. In our view, the researcher allegiance problem has gotten worse since our previous review, reaching a level that in some cases made it difficult to control for statistically.

CBT Versus HEP Subtypes

Moderator analyses for HEPs vs. CBT indicated a significant effect for type of HEP ($Q_m = 19.07$; $p < .01$). We were able to examine the two types of HEP for which there were at least 10 comparative studies: supportive-nondirective and person-centered. The results of these analyses are given in the lower part of Table 13.3. Supportive-directive therapies in this dataset were equivocally less effective than CBT. The comparative effect for CBT vs. supportive-nondirective therapies was –.29 ($k = 22$, all RCTs; 95% CI [–.42, –.16]), a result that might be due in part to the use of non--bona fide versions of the therapy that were either very generic (Kiosses et al. 2015) or in which something had been done to render the treatment less effective (e.g., "supportive emotion-focused" therapists working with traumatized clients were told not to help clients elaborate trauma memories; Ehlers et al., 2014). Further investigation of the supportive therapies revealed that in addition to being subjected to negative researcher allegiance, 59% were diluted, non–bona fide versions of person-centered therapy. Removing supportive treatments rated as non–bona fide (but not correcting for researcher allegiance) resulted in a slightly less negative effect ($ES = –.15$; $k = 9$; 95% CI [–.27, .03]), but still in the trivially worse range. We have included these here as part of our inclusive search strategy, because they meet our inclusion criteria and because they have been widely researched; however, we question their ecological validity and representativeness in clinical practice.

In contrast to our previous review, person-centered therapy (PCT) in this dataset was not equivalent in effectiveness to CBT, but instead, like supportive-nondirective therapy, was equivocally worse than CBT (all studies: –.30; $k = 10$; 95% CI [–.55, –.05]), although the effect was less negative for clients in RCTs (–.20; $k = 8$; 95% CI [–.45, .04]). The source of this difference from our previous review is not entirely clear to us: On the one hand, it is likely to be due at least in part to high levels of negative research allegiance; on the other, it is possible that in more recent research PCT has been pitted against more challenging, complex client populations outside its natural range of effectiveness, such as young people with mixed complex sexual abuse trauma and substance misuse problems (e.g., Foa et al., 2013).

Comparisons Among Types of Humanistic-Experiential Therapies

As noted at the beginning of this chapter, HEPs can be divided into different groupings, sometimes referred to as "tribes." In the current sample of studies these fall naturally into five categories (see Table 13.2): As in previous versions of this meta-analysis, person-centered therapy (PCT) was the best represented of these, with EFT close behind; gestalt therapy and psychodrama use similar methods and for convenience have been grouped here. Supportive-nondirective therapy continued to be the most common form of HEP studied, even though it appeared to be an intervention of questionable ecological validity largely constructed by CBT researchers to contrast with their approach. Finally, there was an assortment of other HEPs. In Table 13.2, we summarize the pre–post data for these five groupings. Moderator variable analysis (using R) examined the relation between type of HEP and pre–post mean ES, resulting in a statistically significant main effect $(Q_m$ [df = 7] = 19.9, $p < .01$). Unsurprisingly, given issues of negative researcher allegiance and non–bona fide treatments, supportive-nondirective therapies showed the smallest pre–post effects (.68; $k = 31$; 95% CI [.47, .89]). In contrast, clients in EFT had the largest pre–post effects ($ES = 1.31$, $k = 18$ 95% CI [1.05, 1.58]), with clients in EFT showing statistically significantly more pre–post change than clients in supportive-nondirective therapies.

None of these comparisons, however, were direct, and only six studies in our dataset involved direct comparisons between different HEPs. It was possible to code the six pairs of treatment conditions in these studies into more (i.e. EFT) vs. less (e.g., PCT) intensiveness or process-guiding, so that we could test the hypothesis that more intensive/process-guiding HEPs would produce larger pre-post effects. However, as was the case in previous versions of this meta-analysis, the difference was equivocal and only trivially in favor of more process-guiding HEPs: neither large/statistically different from zero, nor equivalent ($ES = .18$; 95% CI [.12, .48]). Unfortunately, the sample is too small and diverse to provide adequate statistical power or even to be considered particularly reliable. Clearly, more research is needed to explore this key issue.

OUTCOME FOR DIFFERENT CLIENT PROBLEMS: DIFFERENTIAL TREATMENT EFFECTS

Investigation of HEPs for specific client-presenting problems or disorders has blossomed over the past 30 years, since this series of meta-analyses began. The three lines of evidence (pre–post, controlled, and comparative studies) are summarized in Table 13.4 for six commonly studied relatively coherent types of client problem plus other populations, evaluated both relative to zero (*no* change/difference) and for benchmarking purposes to the whole sample. In brief, the largest amount of evidence and the strongest support for HEPs have been found for depression, relationship problems, coping with chronic medical problems (e.g., HIV, cancer), habitual self-damaging behaviors (substance misuse, eating disorders), and psychosis. There is also considerable, but more mixed, evidence supporting the application of these approaches with anxiety. In this section, we provide meta-analytic evidence, summarize key recent studies, and evaluate the status of HEPs as empirically supported treatments for these six particular client problems plus other client populations.

Depression
Pre–Post Effects
There were more studies of depression in our data set than any other client presenting problem, with results generally consistent but somewhat smaller than in our previous review. Within the larger dataset we included studies in which either a majority of clients had been assessed as depressed using standard diagnostic instruments, or where the mean pretreatment score

TABLE 13.4 Effect Size by Selected Client Problems/Disorders

Problem/disorder	Pre-post ES		Controlled ES		Comparative ES	
	k	$ES_w \pm$ 95% CI	k	$ES_w \pm$ 95% CI	k	$ES_w \pm$ 95% CI
Depression	30	.96 ± .16*	3	.51 ± .30*(−)	25	−.20 ± .18* (=)
Relationship/interpersonal/trauma	27	1.13 ± .20*(+)	8	1.26 ± .59*	12	−.10 ± .42
Anxiety	26	.94 ± .20*	3	.93 ± .74*	13	−.34 ± .23*(−)
Medical	28	.69 ± .22*(−)	5	.48 ± .23*(−)	26	−.07 ± .24(=)
Psychosis	5	.72 ± .54*(−)	0	−	6	.15 ± .43(+)
Self-damaging activities	8	1.00 ± .51*(+)	1	.53 ± .80(−)	8	.09 ± .35(+)
Other populations	21	.89 ± .24*	9	1.00 ± .65*	11	−.17 ± .21(=)
Total sample (used for benchmarking)	94	.86 ± .10*	21	.88 ± .32*	63	−.08 ± .12(=)

Note. *$p < .05$ in null hypothesis test against $ES = 0$; ks refer to number of client samples (pre-post ESs) or comparisons with other conditions (controlled and comparative ESs). 95% CI: 95% confidence intervals; Benchmarking results vs. total sample: (+): value is above benchmark confidence interval; (−): value is below benchmark confidence interval. (=): meets criteria for statistical equivalence (*not* significant difference from 0 and also significantly different from 1.41.

on a standard measure of depression (e.g., BDI) was in the clinical range. We identified 30 samples of clients (from 27 studies; n = 5053 clients) for whom pre–post effects could be calculated, most commonly supportive-nondirective (14 samples), EFT (7 samples), PCT (5 samples), or other HEPs/Gestalt/Psychodrama (6 samples).

The weighted mean pre–post effect size across these 30 samples was substantial but highly heterogeneous (ES = .96, 95% CI [.80, 1.12]; Q = 190.8, p < .01; I^2 = 85%). Most of these samples involved mild to moderately depressed clients (26 out of 30). Clients were generally seen in individual psychotherapy (23 samples) rated as a bona fide HEP (23 samples). Severity of depression appeared to make little difference (ES_w = .95 for mild/moderate vs. 1.00 for severe). The main effect for HEP type was significant (Q_m = 200.0; df = 5; p < .001); however, the confidence intervals for all four sets of studies all overlapped with each other and fell within the confidence interval for depression studies as a whole. The pre–post effects varied from .52 (95% CI [.20, .83]; k = 5) for PCT to 1.33 (95% CI [.85, 1.81]; k = 7) for EFT.

Controlled Effects

We found only three reasonably sized controlled studies (Cho & Chen, 2011; Grassi et al., 2009; Stice et al., 2008), in which depressed clients (total n = 157) were compared to untreated participants (total n = 204). The mean-controlled effect was relatively and consistently of medium-size across these three studies: ES_w = .51 (95% CI [.21, .81]; Q = 3.1; ns; I^2 = 35%). This effect reflects a reasonably-sized and highly consistent HEP pre–post effect (ES_w = .81; 95% CI [.58, 1.04]; Q = .4; ns; I^2 = 0%) equivalent to that reported for the whole sample. However, the effect for the untreated control group was unexpectedly large and consistent (.31; 95% CI [.12, .51]; Q = 1.9; ns; I^2 = 0%), in contrast to the mean-controlled effect of .09 for the whole sample. As the controlled effect for depression is virtually identical with what we found in our previous meta-analysis, we are inclined to hypothesize that this is a generalizable finding, possibly consistent with the idea of depression as episodic and subject to spontaneous recovery, as least on a short-term basis (Whiteford et al., 2013).

Comparative Effects

The 25 HEP versus non-HEP comparisons included 19 samples of clients, from 18 studies, n = 4679 and 8717, respectively. Most commonly CBT (18 comparisons) was compared to supportive-nondirective therapy (13 comparisons), with clients with mild to moderate depression (20 comparisons). There were also studies using person-centered therapy (9 comparisons), other HEPs or EFT (1 each). Half of the studies used modern, more rigorously designed RCTs (with ITT analyses or specified randomization methods; 12 comparisons) but researcher allegiance was overwhelmingly negative (17 comparisons). Using meta-regression, we found a clear negative research allegiance effect of r = –.42.

The overall comparative effect was –.19 (k = 25; 95% CI [–.30, –.07]), with high heterogeneity (Q = 129.8; p < .01; I^2 = 82%). Following our equivalence analysis strategy, this effect would be designated trivially worse, in contrast to the

–.02 equivalence finding reported by Elliott et al. (2013). At the individual comparison level, 17 of the effects were neutral (between –.4 and .4), but seven were substantial and negative, with very large negative effects for studies by Kiosses et al. (2010) and Koszycki et al. (2012), and one strongly positive comparative effect for McLean et al. (2013).

Breaking down the overall comparative effect, we looked first at type of HEP, the main effect for which was significant (Q_m = 12.5; df = 4; p < 05). The effect for supportive-nondirective treatments was equivocally worse (–.30; k = 14; 95% CI [–.49, –.10]); for person-centered therapy the negative effect was smaller but still in the equivocally worse range (–.20; k = 9; 95% CI [–.39, –.01]).

Next, we calculated the mean comparative effect for comparisons between HEPs and CBT: –.26 (k = 18; 95% CI [–.37, –.15]), finding that in general HEPs were equivocally less effective than CBT. However, a large majority of CBT studies were characterized by negative researcher allegiance (13 out of 18 samples); this effect was somewhat attenuated when only studies with pro-HEP or neutral researcher allegiance were analyzed separately (ES_w = –.19; k = 5; 95% CI [–.37, –.01]). On the other hand, when HEPs were compared to non-CBT therapies, the effect was in the equivalent range (ES_w =.06; k = 7; 95% CI [–.31, .44]).

One very large recent study in this data set used an HEP approach that fell into the other HEP category (because of minor directive elements) and is worth mentioning here due to the fact that it comprised 55% of the total sample for this meta-analysis. Barkham and Saxon (2018) compared 3000 clients seen in generic humanistic counseling ("Counseling for Depression," now referred to as "person-centered experiential counseling" or "person-centered experiential therapy") to almost 6000 clients who received CBT, all in primary mental health services in the UK, in a reanalysis of an earlier UK practice-based study by Pybis et al. (2017) using data from a national audit of Improving Access to Psychological Therapies (IAPT) services. In our analysis, we favored the Barkham and Saxon report over Pybis et al. because the latter included clients who had also received low-intensity CBT prior to their high-intensity CBT or supportive counseling, thus confounding their results. In their re-analysis, Barkham and Saxon looked only at clients whose treatment was limited to either high-intensity CBT or supportive counseling (coded here as other HEP rather than person-centered because of the presence of minor directive elements). Outcome was assessed using the Patient Health Questionnaire (PHQ-9), a measure of depression, on which the client pretreatment mean was in the clinical range. Clients were not assigned randomly; however, the authors reported equivalent outcome for supportive counseling and CBT with a comparative effect of –.06 (95% CI [–.11, –.01]; HEP n = 3003; CBT n = 5975). As an interesting side note, they reported that in treatments that lasted up to 11 sessions clients did better in supportive counseling than in CBT; in contrast, CBT did better in treatments of 12 sessions or more. They also reported that the HEP was equivalent to CBT in effectiveness with more severely depressed clients, concluding that: "Such a finding challenges the current NICE guideline for the management of severe depression." (p. 5)

In addition to the evidence discussed here, the PRaCTICED Trial (*not* included in this meta-analysis because it fell outside our review period and was not available when we carried out our analyses) is a large, balanced allegiance study, designed to test the clinical efficacy and cost-effectiveness of contemporary PCE therapy in comparison to CBT in a real-world clinical practice setting (Barkham et al., 2021; Saxon et al., 2017). A sample of 298 clients completed at least four sessions (PCE: 154; CBT: 144) and provided data on the primary outcome measure, the PHQ-9 (Patient Health Questionnaire-9) at the primary outcome point, six months after randomization. The pre–post effects for PCE therapy were much closer to EFT than PCT pre–post effects for our meta-analysis: ES = 1.22. Moreover, at 6 months PCT was found to be equivalent (i.e. noninferior) in outcome to CBT, using both intent-to-treatment and per protocol analyses. When we applied our meta-analysis methods to this study, we calculated a comparative effect size of 0 sd. However, CBT had better outcomes than PCE therapy 12 months post-randomization, with a negative effect size of −.48 on the primary outcome measure. In addition, more severely depressed clients did better with CBT, especially at 12 months. Pooling these two effects produces an overall result quite comparable to that found in this meta-analysis (comparative *ES*: −.20). Looking further into the data, we found that clients in PCE therapy retained their posttherapy gains, while clients who had been seen in CBT continued to improve during the posttherapy period. Although the form of PCE therapy used in this trial contained some process-guiding elements of EFT, we note that it did not include chair work. Left for future research is the question of whether EFT chair work might have led to delayed post therapy benefits comparable to those found in CBT.

Conclusions

In comparison to our previous review of research on the application of HEPs to depression, we again found large pre–post effects (current: .96 vs. 2013: 1.23) and medium-sized controlled effects (.51 vs. .42). On the other hand, comparative effects were slightly worse here (−.2 vs. −.02), reflecting either stronger negative researcher allegiance effects or more focused, effective forms of CBT in the past 10 years. Two clusters of promising studies featured in our previous review, EFT for depression (e.g., Watson et al., 2003) and person-centered therapy for perinatal depression (e.g., Cooper et al., 2003). Two key studies on these topics fell within our review period here: McLean et al. (2013) applied EFT for couples to anxious-depressed couples with a partner with metastatic cancer, with strongly positive pre–post and comparative effects relative to treatment as usual; and a major study (Morrell, Slade et al., 2009; Morrell, Warner et al., 2009) with a large sample size that showed superiority to treatment as usual and no difference in comparison to CBT. In addition, two large-sample studies in naturalistic health care settings produced results consistent with the rest of the sample, while suggesting that there is room for improvement in the outcomes of HEPs with clinically depressed clients. Pooling evidence from this review and the previous one, it appears to us that the evidence continues to meet Chambless and Hollon's (1998) criteria for efficacious and specific treatments.

Relationship and Interpersonal Difficulties
Pre-Post Effects

In our previous reviews, HEPs came out as consistently and strongly effective for clients presenting with either specific unresolved relationship issues or more general interpersonal difficulties. In this review, the largest number of the 23 studies (including 28 samples of clients, total *n* = 769) addressed specific current relationship problems (10 samples, e.g., Burgess-Moser et al., 2016) or general interpersonal difficulties, such as social anxiety (Elliott et al., 2018) or high-functioning autism (9 samples, e.g., Murphy et al., 2017). However, there were also smaller clusters of studies on single incident trauma or specific emotional injuries (4 samples, e.g., Nixon, 2012), and childhood abuse/complex trauma (4 studies, e.g., Foa et al., 2013). In contrast to our previous review, most clients in these studies were seen individually (15 samples, e.g., Marriott et al., 2009) or in groups (10 samples, e.g., Cho & Chen, 2011); only 3 studies involved couples or family therapy (e.g., Diamond et al., 2016). EFT was the most common studied therapy in the pre–post sample, with 10 studies involving 13 samples of clients: six on individual therapy (e.g., Paivio et al., 2010), three on group therapy (e.g., Hagl et al., 2015), two on couples therapy (e.g., McLean et al., 2013) and one on family therapy (Diamond et al., 2016). Person-centered therapy (e.g., Yousefi & Kiani, 2014) and gestalt/psychodrama (e.g., Karatas, 2011) each featured in 6 studies. Two studies used supportive-nondirective therapy (e.g., Hagl et al., 2015).

The weighted mean pre-post effect size was large but moderately variable (*ES* = 1.12, 95% CI [.92, 1.33]; *Q* = 88.4, *p* < .01; *I²* = 69%). Effects did not vary between individual, group or couple/family formats, ranging between 1.08 and 1.16 sd. Similarly, there was little variability in pre–post change between general interpersonal difficulties (*ES* = 1.09; *k* = 9; 95% CI [.7, 1.49]) and specific relational difficulties or conflicts (*ES* = 1.17; *k* = 10; 95% CI [.8, 1.54]). However, unexpectedly, effects for childhood abuse/complex trauma (*ES* = 1.31; *k* = 4; 95% CI [.72, 1.9]) were about .5 SD higher (but not significantly so) than for single episode trauma (*ES* = .8; *k* = 4; 95% CI [.38, 1.22]). Finally, effects for EFT (*ES* = 1.36; *k* = 13; 95% CI [1.09, 1.64]) were somewhat larger than those for person-centered therapy (*ES* = .98; *k* = 6; 95% CI [.65, 1.3]) and gestalt therapy/psychodrama (*ES* = .98; *k* = 76; 95% CI [.54, 1.43]). However, none of these differences were statistically significant.

Controlled Effects

There were 10 controlled comparisons (6 of them RCTs) in which clients seen in HEPs (*n* = 212) were compared to participants assigned to no treatment or waitlist control conditions (*n* = 320). These comparisons provided a large and highly heterogeneous weighted controlled effect (*ES* = 1.13; 95% CI [.45, 1.82]; *Q* = 58.1, *p* < .01; *I²* = 85%), with all controlled effects being substantial and positive. The controlled effect was almost identical to the uncontrolled pre–post effect, pointing to the absence of natural self-healing processes in this broad client population. (In our previous review we even found evidence of client deterioration in this population.) In spite of the heterogeneity, overall controlled effects were large for both clients seen individually (*ES* = 1.33; *k* = 3; 95% CI [.84, 1.82]; e.g.,

Cornish & Wade, 2015) and in group format (*ES* = 1.65; *k* = 4; 95% CI [.65, 2.65]; Singal, 2009). This broad between-group consistency was also the case for clients seen in EFT (*ES* = 1.13; *k* = 6; 95% CI [.45, 1.82]; e.g., Shahar et al., 2017) and in gestalt therapy/psychodrama (*ES* = 1.4; *k* = 3; 95% CI [.01, 2.8]; e.g., Cho & Chen, 2011). In terms of the kind of interpersonal difficulty, clients with general interpersonal difficulties (*ES* = 1.72; *k* = 3; 95% CI [.35, 3.1]; e.g., Karataş & Gökçakan, 2009) did better than clients with specific relational difficulties (*ES* = 1.01; *k* = 7; 95% CI [.46, 1.56]; e.g., Greenberg et al., 2010). We are not sure why more generalized interpersonal difficulties might respond better than specific relational difficulties; perhaps this is a sample difference in that the current crop of studies didn't include much in the way of couples therapy, where the two parties to a relational conflict are able to face each other and work through the difficulty. In the absence of a partner, clients are encouraged to work at a more general level on their own side of a difficulty, which could be easier to do in individual or group therapy.

Comparative Effects

There were 12 comparisons (from 10 studies) of clients seen in HEPs (*n* = 273) versus non-HEPs (*n* = 338), most commonly CBT (8 comparisons; e.g., Ford et al., 2013), but also one study with two samples of clients seen in cognitive analytic therapy (CAT; Marriott et al., 2009). The overall weighted effect was highly heterogeneous and trivially worse than non-HEPs for interpersonal difficulties (comparative ES_w = −.10; 95% CI [−.49, .27]; *Q* = 66.8, *p* < .01; I^2 = 84%). Four (involving 3 studies) of the 12 comparative effects were substantial (> |.4|) and negative, favoring the alternative treatment (Foa et al., 2013; Marriott et al., 2009; Nixon, 2012); two effects were substantial and positive (Karatas et al, 2011; McLean et al., 2013). There was a large negative correlation between researcher allegiance and comparative effect size for these 12 comparisons (*r* = −.48, *p* < .01, weighted meta-regression), with only 2 positive researcher allegiance studies included. The effect size for the negative allegiance studies was −.37 (*k* = 6; 95% CI [−.69, −.14]); the effect for pro and neutral allegiance studies combined was .21 (*k* = 6; 96% CI [−.6, 1.01]).

The typical comparative study in this dataset involved CBT (*ES* = −.46; *k* = 8; 95% CI [−.75, −.16]) compared to individual (ES_w = −.40; *k* = 9; 95% CI [−.68, −.11]) person-centered therapy (ES_w = −.41; *k* = 7; 95% CI [−.78, −.04]) for clients with general interpersonal difficulties (*ES* = −.16; *k* = 6; 95% CI [−.61, .28]). (Marriott et al., 2013, is an example of such a study.) HEPs fared most poorly when applied to clients with simple or complex trauma (*ES* = −.50; *k* = 4; 95% CI [−.95, −.06]; Foa et al., 2013). The exception to this pattern was the three comparisons using either EFT or gestalt therapy/psychodrama (*ES* = .8; *k* = 3; 95% CI [−.59, 2.18]; e.g., Karatas et al., 2011).

Conclusions

Overall, in the present review the effects of HEPs for interpersonal difficulties are lower than those we found in our previous meta-analysis, across all three lines of evidence: For pre–post and controlled studies the drop was minimal: .15 and .19 SDs respectively. However, for the comparative studies the drop was substantial and clinically important: .45 SD, from .34 (equivocally more effective than nonHEPs) to −.11 (trivially less effective than nonHEPs). The drop in comparative effectiveness for pre–post and controlled effects is consistent with the overall drop in effectiveness for the entire current dataset (−.09 SD), but the large drop in the comparative effects greatly exceeds that (−.45 SD).

What is the reason for the apparent drop in effectiveness over the intervening years? There are at least five explanations for which there is evidence in our data: First, by broadening the inclusion criteria for the client population with interpersonal difficulties, we may have diluted the evidence. In particular, in this round we have added client presentations involving social anxiety, autism, and PTSD, much of which we had included only under anxiety in our 2013 review (in this review, most of these studies are included in both interpersonal and anxiety subsets). Second, it also appears likely that since our previous review there have been shifts in the client subpopulations that are the focus of research. For example, within this client population over the past 10 years there has been a decreased interest in couples therapy, especially in comparative studies; more studies of young people (e.g., Foa et al., 2013) and the first outcome study examining HEP (person-centered therapy) for autism (Murphy, 2017).

Third, HEPs may have become less effective (either generally or because less effective versions are being studied). As noted, we have documented a slight drop in HEP pre–post effectiveness in our data, but more importantly we have noted a decrease in the amount of research on EFT for couples, especially comparative studies. While these had strongly bolstered the results of our previous analysis, here they have been replaced by individual person-centered therapy. Fourth, non-HEPs (especially CBT) may have become more effective with the advent of treatments such as Resnick's cognitive processing therapy for PTSD (cf. Foa et al., 2013, here). On the other hand, NonHEP pre–post effects also have dropped from our previous review (1.02 SD) to the present one (.8 SD). Fifth, researcher allegiance effects may have become more pronounced over time. This was certainly our impression in reading and analyzing the studies included here, an impression that is borne out by an increase in negative researcher allegiance in comparative outcome studies from 44% in our 2013 review to 58% in this review. All these explanations appear to have played some role in the results we obtained here.

We close this section on a more positive note by recalling some of our conclusions from our previous review: To begin with, we want to remind readers that in spite of its relative dearth in the present review, EFT for couples has long been included in lists of empirically supported treatments for marital distress (e.g., Baucom et al., 1998); and our previous meta-analytic review found that EFT for individuals was efficacious and specific for unresolved relationship issues, including emotional injuries (e.g., Greenberg et al., 2010) and unresolved abuse survivor issues (Paivio et al., 2001; Paivio et al., 2010). While it would be encouraging to see more recent studies on this well-established treatment, we see no reason to revise these earlier conclusions.

Anxiety

Research on HEPs for anxiety, most commonly the application of supportive therapies with PTSD, is strongest for pre–post and controlled studies and weakest for comparative studies.

Pre–Post Effects

We found 27 samples of clients from 23 studies (n = 1045 clients) for which pre–post effects could be calculated, covering a range of HEPs, most commonly supportive-nondirective (9 samples of clients), EFT (8 samples), followed by PCT and gestalt/psychodrama (4 samples each). There was a mix of researcher allegiance (15 pro vs. 11 con). Types of anxiety difficulties studied were also quite varied and included PTSD (10 samples; many more than in our previous review), mixed anxiety (8 samples), social anxiety (4 samples), medical/disease progression/ recurrence (3 samples), and generalized anxiety (2 samples). The weighted mean pre–post effect size for the 27 sets of anxious clients was .92 (95% CI [.73, 1.12]), quite near the benchmark for the entire sample of pre–post effects (see Table 13.4) and almost identical to the pre–post effect reported by Elliott et al. (2013). Although the confidence intervals mostly overlapped, pre–post effects varied significantly across type of HEP (Q_m = 15.8; p < .001), with the effect for EFT significantly larger (k = 8; ES = 1.49; 95% CI [1.17, 1.81]) than for supportive treatments (k = 9; ES = .62; 95% CI [.37, .88]). There was also a large effect for other HEPs (ES = 1.25; k = 5; 95% CI [.74, 1.76]), while gestalt/psychodrama (ES = .78; k = 4; 95% CI [.46, 1.10]) and PCT (k = 4; ES = .82; 95% CI [.26, 1.39]) fell in between. In terms of client anxiety subpopulations, the most promising applications for HEPs appear to be PTSD (ES = 1.04; k =10; 95% CI [.75, 1.34]), social anxiety (ES = 1.20; k = 4; 95% CI [.54, 1.87]), and GAD (ES = 1.48; k = 2; 95% CI [.2, 2.77]). We found substantially smaller effects for mixed anxiety populations (ES = .62; k = 7; 95% CI [.36, .88]) and medically related anxiety (ES = .38; k = 3; 95% CI [.09, .66]).

Controlled Effects

There were only three controlled studies in our dataset (n = 112 clients in HEPs; 113 participants in no treatment conditions) drawn from a range of HEPs and client anxiety subpopulations. The mean-controlled effect was large: .93 (95% CI [.21, 1.66]), the same as the uncontrolled pre–post effect and substantially larger than the controlled effect of .5 reported by Elliott et al. (2013).

Comparative Effects

Comparative studies with anxious client populations were carried out in 13 studies (n = 566 clients in HEPs vs. 607 clients in nonHEPs). Six of these studies addressed PTSD. All had high internal validity and used modern RCT designs. The great majority of these were of supportive-nondirective therapy vs. CBT (11 out of 13 studies) with a negative researcher

allegiance (10 out of 13 studies). Thus, it is not surprising that the overall mean comparative effect was negative and fairly homogeneous (ES = –.36; 95% CI [–.59, –.13]; Q = 10.2, p <.01). Five of the 13 comparative effects favored CBT by more than .4 SD, the cutoff we are using defining superior effectiveness in clinical settings. Of the 6 specific client population clusters we are reviewing for comparative effects in this chapter, HEPs fared most poorly with anxiety problems (this was also case in our 2013 review). The confounding of CBT with negative researcher allegiance made it impossible to run allegiance-corrected analyses. Digging into the data, it appears that the source of this negative effect is studies on posttraumatic stress difficulties, which we included here in spite of recent changes in DSM-5 because of the prominent place of anxiety in its presentation. In fact, the effect for CBT vs. supportive-nondirective therapy for PTSD is quite large: –.68 (k = 6; 95% CI [–1.05, –.31]). In complete contrast are the results for medically-related anxiety, the second most common client anxiety presentation in our dataset, where we found equivalence (ES = –.03; k = 4; 95% CI [–.19, .14]; Q = 1.9, NS) in a set of four studies, all on supportive-nondirective HEP vs. either CBT or treatment as usual (two studies each). Based on this, we provisionally conclude that clients seen in supportive-nondirective approaches to PTSD would probably be better served by CBT.

However, this conclusion says nothing about promising HEPs for post trauma difficulties, including EFT for complex trauma (Paivio et al., 2010) and a closely related form of gestalt therapy referred to as dialogical exposure therapy (Butollo et al., 2016). To date, there have been no studies directly comparing CBT to these more recent process-guiding HEPs. The best we could do here is to compare pre–post effect sizes for the 6 CBT/PTSD studies in our dataset (ES = 1.81; 95% CI [1.26, 2.37]) to the pre–post effects for the 10 HEP/PTSD studies included here (ES = 1.04; k =10; 95% CI .75 to 1.34]). Clearly research directly comparing these two promising approaches to PTSD and other anxiety difficulties is urgently needed.

Conclusions

Applying the adaption of the Chambless and Hollon (1998) criteria used in our previous review to specific types of anxiety difficulty, we found very large pre–post effects across multiple studies of HEPs for generalized anxiety (Brenes et al., 2015; Timulak et al., 2017), social anxiety (Elliott et al., 2018; Shahar et al., 2017), and PTSD (Butollo et al., 2016; Ehlers et al., 2014; Foa et al., 2013; Paivio et al., 2010). Thus, we conclude that the application of HEPs for these kinds of anxiety difficulties, especially EFT and newer process-guiding HEPs such as dialogical exposure therapy (e.g., Butollo et al) meet Chambless and Hollon's (1998) criteria as possibly efficacious, while also suggesting that CBT may be more specific and efficacious for PTSD when compared to supportive-nondirective therapy. As we concluded in our previous review, the apparent CBT advantage with PTSD is likely due to two possible factors: First, researcher allegiance effects were operating, and so pervasive that we were unable to control for them statistically here.

In addition, it now seems likely that anxiety difficulties may respond somewhat better to more structured, process guiding approaches including in session psychoeducation and structured therapeutic tasks such as empty chair work that share something in common with exposure work in CBT, as opposed to the predominantly nondirective forms of HEPs that have so far been studied.

A surprising result to have emerged from this set of anxiety studies came out of the studies of medically related anxiety, such as fear of disease progression or recurrence. We were surprised to find reliable statistical equivalence between supportive-nondirective HEPs and CBT or treatment as usual, in spite of negative researcher allegiance and minimal treatment development. In our view, this is a particularly promising area for further HEP treatment development and research, especially with the application of a broader range of HEPs such as EFT. (For an example, see Elliott et al., 2014.)

In our clinical experience, clients with significant anxiety difficulties frequently have a problem with the lack of structure in purely nondirective therapies, often asking directly for expert guidance. For the past 10 years, the authors of this chapter have been involved in research on the effectiveness of EFT with generalized anxiety (Watson, Timulak) and social anxiety (Elliott, Shahar). For now, our advice for humanistic-experiential therapists is to discuss the issue with clients, to consider adding process guiding elements to their therapy, and to provide information about the role of trauma or emotional processes in anxiety difficulties (e.g., Wolfe & Sigl, 1998).

Coping with Chronic Medical Conditions
Pre–Post Effects

The use of HEPs to help clients coping with chronic or life-threatening medical illnesses has continued to burgeon, with the total number of studies having doubled since our 2013 review. Our current sample turned up 28 new studies over the past 10 years (n = 1210 clients); in 2013 we reported on 29 studies (n = 1145 clients). Intervention with a broad range of medical conditions has now been investigated, the most common being cancer, both early stage/remitted (8 studies; e.g., Carlson et al., 2017) and late stage/metastatic (4 studies. e.g., Breitbart et al., 2015). Others include autoimmune disorders such as MS and rheumatoid arthritis (3 studies; e.g., Herschbach et al., 2010b) and early dementia (i.e. executive dysfunction, cognitive impairment; 3 studies: e.g., Kiosses et al., 2015); the meta-analysis also includes two studies each for gastrointestinal problems (IBS, obesity; e.g., Compare, Calugi, Marchesini, Shonin et al., 2013), pain, including ME (myalgic encephalopathy; e.g., Ward & Hogan, 2009), surgery patients (heart and hip fracture; e.g., Gambatesa et al., 2013), and infertility (e.g., Terzioğlu & Özkan, 2018). Of the studies, 15 (53%) involved group formats (e.g., Manne et al., 2016). Fifteen were also carried out by researchers with a negative researcher allegiance, and 10 (36%) utilized treatments rated as non–bona fide.

During the same period the nature of the HEPs being studied has shifted. Ten years ago, the most common form of HEP studied was supportive-expressive group therapy, an existential-experiential treatment developed by Spiegel et al., (1981) and the subject of 12 studies. In the current review, this approach was the subject of 5 studies, usually as a foil for a newer treatment, such as meaning-centered group therapy, a directive form of existential therapy. In its place we found that more than half of the identified studies used supportive-nondirective therapy (16 studies). In addition, person-centered therapy was examined in 3 studies, and EFT in 2 studies.

The overall weighted mean pre–post effect size across the 28 samples for which pre–post effects could be calculated was medium in size but highly inconsistent (ES = .70, 95% CI [.47, .92]; Q = 177.5, p < .01; I^2 = 85%). Statistically significant pre–post effects (ES), in descending order of size, were found for 6 kinds of medical condition: gastrointestinal problems/obesity (1.53; k = 2; 95% CI [1.03, 2.03]), early dementia (1.37; k = 2; 95% CI [1.13, 1.60]), infertility (1.27; k = 2; 95% CI [.7, 1.84]), pain/ME (.60; k = 2; 95% CI [13, 1.07]), early stage cancer (.37; k = 8; 95% CI [.20, .55]), and autoimmune conditions/HIV (.26; k = 3; 95% CI [.03, .50]). Three other conditions were also represented by two or more studies, but were not significantly greater than zero: patients preparing for or recovering from surgery (1.06; k = 2; 95% CI [–.18, 2.36]), metastatic/late stage cancer (.78; k = 4; 95% CI [–.07, 1.62), and diabetes (.12; k = 2; 95% CI [–.87, 1.11]).

In terms of type of HEP, we found the largest pre–post effects for active, process guiding approaches including EFT (couples and individual) or psychodrama (ES = 1.78; k = 3; 95% CI [1.45, 2.11]; Q = .35, ns). Although the three studies (Compare, Calugi, Marchesini, Molinari et al., 2013; McLean et al., 2013; Terzioğlu & Özkan, 2018) in this subset involved different modes of delivery (structured treatment program, couples' sessions, group work) and diverse client populations (obesity with binge eating disorder, metastatic cancer, and infertility), the effect sizes were quite consistent. Quite substantial effects were also found for person-centered therapy (ES = .90; k = 3; 95% CI [.12, 1.67]); while smaller effects were found for supportive-nondirective therapy (ES = .60; k = 16; 95% CI [.30, .89]) and supportive-expressive group therapy (ES = .4; k = 5; 95% CI [.11, .65]; Q = 8.6, ns; I^2 = 53%).

Group formats were used frequently with medically related presentations, but produced slightly (but not statistically significant) smaller effects (ES = .52; k = 15; 95% CI [.28, .77]) than individual treatment (ES = .86; k = 11; 95% CI [.47, 1.25]).

Controlled Effects

There were five controlled studies (e.g., van der Spek et al., 2017) versus no treatment/wait list, on diverse client populations of primarily older adults (early stage or remitted cancer, heart surgery patients, HIV, ME). There were 179 clients in HEP conditions and 213 participants in no treatment or wait-list control groups. Overall, these studies showed a highly consistent medium effect size of .48 (95% CI [.27, .69]; Q = 3.8, ns; I^2 = 0%), a value very similar to that reported by Elliott et al (2013): .53 SD. Three of the studies used some form of supportive-nondirective therapy.

Comparative Effects

There were 21 comparative studies, including 26 comparisons to non-HEPs. All but two comparisons were randomized (88%) and there was a mixture of bona fide (54%) and non–bona fide (46%) HEPs. The most common HEPs were supportive-nondirective treatments (16 comparisons; e.g., Szigethy et al., 2014), PCT (9 comparisons), and supportive-expressive groups (5 comparisons; e.g., Ho et al., 2016). Also represented were EFT (3 comparisons; e.g., Compare, Calugi, Marchesini, Molinari et al., 2013) and person-centered therapy (2 studies; Manne et al., 2016). HEPs were most often applied to helping clients cope with cancer early/remitted (9 comparisons, e.g., Carlson et al., 2013); also represented by three comparisons each were advanced/metastatic cancer (McLean et al., 2013), autoimmune diseases (e.g., Moss-Morris et al., 2013), gastrointestinal conditions/obesity (e.g., Szigethy et al., 2014), and early dementia (e.g., Arean et al., 2010). The most common non-HEP comparison treatments were CBT (12 studies; e.g., Wei et al., 2018) and treatment as usual (6 studies, e.g., Herschbach et al., 2010a). Researcher allegiances substantially favored non-HEPS, mostly CBT (con: 62%).

The overall comparative effect was a highly heterogeneous equivalence finding ($ES_w = -.08$; 95% CI [−.27, .10]; $Q = 139.7$, $p < .01$; $I^2 = 82\%$). (In the previous meta-analysis, the comparative effect was also an equivalence result: −.01 but was much more consistent.)

Five comparisons substantially (> .4) favored non-HEPs therapies, two of these from the same study (Breitbart et al, 2010; Kiosses et al., 2010; Koszycki et al., 2012; Rief et al., 2017); two comparisons substantially (>1.80) favored HEPs (Gambatesa et al., 2013; McLean et al., 2013). Nineteen effects were within .4 of each other.

Supportive-nondirective treatment, the most common HEP condition studied, was also the least effective when compared to other treatments ($ES = -33$; $k = 16$; 95% CI [−.52, −.15]). The combination of all the other HEPs (person-centered, EFT and supportive-expressive group therapy) was significantly more effective when compared to other treatments ($ES = .38$; $k = 10$; 95% CI [.04, .71]). HEPs did best when compared to mental health treatment as usual conditions (often psychoeducation, e.g., Carlson et al., 2013): $ES = .66$ ($k = 6$; 95% CI [.06, 1.25]). They did significantly less well when compared to CBT (e.g., Kiosses et al., 2010), where we found a comparative effect of −.22 ($k = 12$; 95% CI [−.4, −.03]), or when compared to other psychological treatments (most often meaning-centered group therapy, e.g., van der Spek et al., 2017; $ES = -.31$; $k = 8$; 95% CI [−.61, −.00]). Finally, we compared CBT to supportive-nondirective therapy, and found that CBT was equivocally more effective ($ES = -.30$; $k = 10$; 95% CI [−.49, −.11]; $Q = 21.7$, $p < .01$; $I^2 = 58\%$).

In contrast to Elliott et al. (2013), we did not find clear differences between different medical conditions. However, the strongest comparative effects were coping with cancer (either early or late stage, e.g., Carlson et al., 2017), where ES was .05 ($k = 12$; 95% CI [−.17, .27]), an equivalence finding. Grouping all the rest of the disparate medical conditions together, we obtained an overall equivocally worse comparative effect of −.21 ($k = 14$; 95% CI [−.50, .08]).

Researcher allegiance proved to be a very strong predictor of comparative effect size; the meta-regression r was .59 ($p < .01$). Positive researcher allegiance was associated strongly with positive comparative effects ($ES = .54$; $k = 8$; 95% CI [12, .96]) while negative researcher allegiance was associated with moderately negative comparative effects ($ES = -.34$; $k = 16$; 95% CI [−.51, −.16]).

Conclusions

Given the diversity of medical conditions and treatments studies, it is difficult to apply the Chambless and Hollon (1998) criteria to this set of studies. Nevertheless, from these data, we can conclude that in working with clients coping with a range of medical problems: (1) CBT appears to be equivocally more effective than supportive-nondirective therapy; and (2) mainstream HEPs such as person-centered, EFT and supportive-expressive group therapy appear to be efficacious treatments for helping this population of clients, based on (a) their substantial pre–post effects, (b) their superiority to no treatment control conditions; and (c) their greater effectiveness than nonHEP treatments. These optimistic recommendations need to be tempered by several cautions: First, strong researcher allegiance effects (on both sides) continue to compromise findings, along with the use of non–bona fide versions of HEPs. Second, there are still very few head-to-head comparisons between CBT and bona fide, standard HEPs (we counted two in our sample of studies), which makes it difficult to draw clear conclusions. Third, except for cancer, there are only a few studies for each kind of medical condition that has been studied. As we concluded in our previous review, this continues to be a highly promising area of the development of theory and practice for HEPs. However, much more research is needed.

Psychosis

In our 2013 review, we wrote:

> The use of HEPs for clients diagnosed with psychosis, including schizophrenia, has become controversial, particularly in the United Kingdom, where the latest version of the Department of Health's treatment guidelines (National Collaborating Centre for Mental Health [NICE], 2010) effectively banned the practice via the following negative recommendation: "Do not routinely offer counseling and supportive psychotherapy (as specific interventions) to people with schizophrenia" (Elliott et al., 2013, p. 508).

> This proclamation is still on the NICE website (see guideline 1.4.4.6 at https://www.nice.org.uk/guidance/cg178/chapter/1-Recommendations#care-across-all-phases).

When first implemented in 2009, the prohibition on the use of counseling and supportive psychotherapy had a severely damaging effect on the provision of mental health care to individuals living with psychotic processes, wiping out a longstanding tradition of offering person-centered counseling to this client population (documented by Traynor et al., 2011), and cutting off development of promising newer practices such as pretherapy contact work for restoring psychological contact with clients in psychotic states (see Dekeyser et al., 2008, for a review).

In our previous review, we also reported our reanalysis of the evidence NICE had used to ban supportive therapy for psychosis:

> The full NICE 2010 guideline includes extensive documentation from the evidence survey on which the recommendation was supposedly based. Thus, it was not difficult for us to carry out a quick, rough analysis of the evidence from the nine studies comparing the supportive treatments (defined in the document as person-centered in orientation) to CBT in the NICE 2010 evidence survey (see Appendix 16D): Contrary to the strongly negative guideline, the data reported in the evidence survey instead pointed to a trivially small superiority for CBT over supportive counseling: mean $d = -.19$; mean relative risk ratio = 1.08. In addition, these overall mean effects were characterized by large standard deviations (.59, .32 respectively), indicating substantial heterogeneity... Two possible interpretations of these data appear to fit the evidence better than that drawn by the NICE committee: First, supportive treatments are almost as effective as CBT, even without the benefit of recent focused treatment development efforts and even when carried out by researchers with an anti-HEP theoretical allegiance. Second, more conservatively, the data are too inconsistent to warrant any overall conclusions at the present moment.

We then went on to report the results of our own small meta-analysis of six studies (including five RCTs): Large pre–post effects ($ES = 1.08$; 95% CI [.51, 1.65]) and greater change in HEPs than nonHEPs ($ES_w = .39$; 95% CI [.10, .69]).

Pre–Post Effects

Given the controversy and tantalizing nature of our previous results, we were naturally curious (and more than a little apprehensive) to see the results of another 10 years of research on the use of HEPs with clients with psychotic processes. Our current meta-analysis dataset does contain pre–post effects for five studies (all RCTs), including a total of 200 clients. These clients were either diagnosed with schizophrenia (two studies; e.g., Martin et al., 2016) or showed early signs of psychosis (three studies; e.g., Stain et al., 2016). The HEPs they were seen in consisted of either supportive-nondirective therapy (three studies; e.g., Shi et al. 2017) or bodily expressive movement therapy (two studies, e.g., Priebe et al., 2016); the most common comparison nonHEP used in these studies was CBT (two studies, e.g., Addington et al., 2011); clients were seen in either individual (three studies; Shi et al., 2017) or group (two studies; e.g., Martin et al., 2016) modalities.

The weighted pre–post effect size for these five studies was .72 (95% CI [.21, 1.23]; $Q = 16.3$, $p < .01$; $I^2 = 75\%$). Although uncontrolled and highly heterogenous, these effects nevertheless demonstrate moderate to large pre–post effect sizes with this chronic and severely distressed clinical population. Consistent with effects throughout the current meta-analysis, this result is .36 *SD* smaller than the value of 1.08 we reported in 2013; however, this value is only a little less than the review-wide pre–post bench mark of .86 *SD* (see bottom row in Table 13.4), not surprising for what is considered to be a challenging client population. There were two subclusters of rather different studies, the contrast between which tells us a lot about the politics and practicalities of contemporary psychotherapy outcome research: On the one hand, two studies by pro-HEP researchers (Martin et al., 2016; Priebe et al., 2016) tested a new, bona fide group-based body-movement expressive therapy with populations of clients with long-standing psychotic conditions (diagnosed with schizophrenia); this new body-oriented HEP was compared to medication (Martin et al, 2016) and to a pilates exercise control condition (Priebe et al., 2016). The weighted mean pre–post effect for the HEP body therapy was small but highly consistent: .34 ($k = 2$; 95% CI [.11, .56]; $Q = .2$, ns: $I^2 = 0$). On the other hand, there were three studies carried out with populations judged to be at high risk for developing psychosis because of the emergence of mild psychotic symptoms. In all three studies, clients in the HEP condition received individual supportive-nondirective therapy as a control condition for new individual treatment being advocated by the researchers: new forms of CBT in two instances (Addington et al., 2011; Stain et al., 2016) and a new systemic treatment in the other study (Shi et al., 2017). In two of these studies (Shi et al., 2017; Stain et al., 2016), the HEP was judged by two raters to have failed Wampold et al.'s (1997) test for bona fideness. Nevertheless, for these three studies, the pre–post HEP effect size was very large: 1.05 (95% CI [.13, 1.98]; $Q = 8.4$, $p < .05$; $I^2 = 76\%$).

Comparative Effects

Although there were no studies comparing an HEP to a no-treatment or wait-list control condition, we did locate six comparative treatment RCTs; 265 clients were seen in HEPs and 253 in nonHEPs, bringing the total number of clients to 518, more than three times the size of the total sample reviewed by Elliott et al. (2013). To the five pre–post studies reviewed above, we were able to add a sixth (Bechdolf et al., 2012), another negative researcher allegiance study comparing a non-bona fide supportive-nondirective treatment to a new form of mostly individual cognitive remediation-based CBT aimed at preventing individuals with prodromal mild psychotic symptoms from transitioning into full psychosis. (Because this study used only survival analyses we were unable to calculate a valid pre–post effect, but were able to compare post-therapy rates of transition to psychosis.)

The mean weighted, highly heterogenous comparative effect size across the six studies was .15 (95% CI [−.25, .55]; $Q = 19.6$, $p < .01$; $I^2 = 74\%$), which can be interpreted as indicating that HEPs are trivially but equivocally more effective that nonHEPs in psychological intervention with clients on the psychotic spectrum. The six comparative effects included one that favored CBT over supportive-nondirective (Bechdolf et al., 2012) and two that favored an HEP (body movement therapy: Martin et al., 2016; or nondirective listening: Stain et al., 2016) over standard treatments (medication or CBT, respectively); the other three effects were in the neutral zone (between −.4 and +.4). We ran the same subgroup analyses of comparative effects as we had for pre-post effects. The CBT-vs.-supportive-nondirective-for-high-risk-prodromal-psychosis cluster of studies produced a moderately heterogenous mean weighted comparative effect of –.02 (k = 4; 95% CI [–.5, .47]; Q = 7.5, ns; I^2 = 60%). This result is probably best described as "equivocally equivalent": the value is near zero but the confidence interval wide enough to encompass all three critical values (–.4, 0, and +.4). The comparative effect size for the expressive-body-movement-therapy-vs-medication/exercise cluster was .45 (k = 2; 95% CI [–.52, 1.41]; Q = 8.8, p < .01; I^2 = 89%), a result than can be described as "equivocally better" because of extremely high heterogeneity and a very wide confidence interval.

Conclusions

Probably the safest thing to say about these results is that more research is needed, except that our results here replicate the results we found in our previous meta-analysis. Thus, we conclude that for psychosis, treatment guidelines (such as the NICE guidelines in the UK) that unquestioningly recommend CBT over HEPs are out of date and are hampering care for an important and vulnerable client population. We have now shown consistent results from two separate small meta-analyses that indicate the following:

1. When clients with a range of psychotic processes are seen in HEPs (whether these be nondirective or process-guiding), they generally show large pre–post improvement.
2. Those improvements are at a minimum on par with improvements seen in clients offered CBT (and possibly other nonHEPs), and in some cases have been found to be superior to nonHEPS, even under adverse conditions of negative researcher allegiance and when non–bona fide versions of supportive nondirective therapy are used.

Finally, we conclude that, based on existing evidence, HEPs appear to be, in Chambless and Hollon's (1998) terms, *efficacious and specific*, having been shown to be equivalent to and in some case superior to another established treatment (CBT). In other words, they are supported by enough evidence to make them front-line treatments. In a way, this conclusion is confirmed by recent moves in CBT toward more person- or mindfulness-based forms of CBT for schizophrenia (e.g., Chadwick, 2019).

Habitual Self-Damaging Activities

Recurrent self-damaging activities such as substance misuse and eating difficulties are the subject of an emerging body of evidence using a wide variety of HEPs. Most of these studies are on motivational interviewing (MI), which was developed by Miller in the 1980s as a person-centered humanistic alternative to behavioral approaches to alcohol abuse (Miller & Moyers, 2017). MI has been the subject of hundreds of RCTs, and in our initial search we found 183 possible MI outcome studies published between 2008 and 2018. Given the limits of our available resources and time as well as the existence of a large number of systematic reviews and meta-analyses (PubMed listed 184 as of 15 April 2020, 164 of which were published during our review period), we have decided to omit this HEP from our meta-analysis. The most recent general quantitative meta-analysis of MI for the wide range of self-damaging activities is Lundahl et al.'s (2010) review (k = 119), which reported small-sized but consistent comparative effects against wait-list or treatment as usual control groups (Hedges's g = .28; k = 88) and no difference (i.e. equivalence) results against specific, active treatments such as CBT or 12-step programs (g = .09; k = 39).

In contrast, the past 10 years has seen systematic reviews and meta-analyses of many specific applications of MI. One collection of such reviews can be found in Arkowitz et al.'s (2015) survey of applications of MI to a wide range of psychological problems, which range across all of the different client populations reviewed here. In an attempt to integrate these disparate literatures, DeClemente et al. (2017) carried out a qualitative systematic review of reviews of the application of MI to substance misuse and gambling, identifying 34 review articles. They concluded that the strongest evidence was for MI for alcohol, tobacco, and marijuana use problems, with some evidence supporting its use with gambling problems, and insufficient evidence for methamphetamine and opiate use difficulties. It is worth noting that the robustness of MI effects is all the more impressive given that it is a brief intervention typically of two to four sessions.

Pre–Post Effects

In our current review, we identified eight non-MI studies (total n = 248) of clients focusing on recurrent, self-damaging activities, most commonly eating difficulties (four studies; e.g., Compare, Calugi, Marchesini, Molinari et al., 2013) but also four studies on a range of other self-damaging activities such as substance misuse (two studies; e.g., Kay-Lambkin et al., 2011), self-injury (Cottraux et al., 2009) and oppositional/defiant behavior (Singal, 2009). A wide range of HEPs feature in these studies, with two each on person-centered (e.g., Schützmann et al., 2010), supportive-nondirective (e.g., Magidson et al., 2011), EFT (e.g., Wnuk et al., 2015), and psychodrama/expressive therapy (e.g., Boerhout et al., 2016). Half of the studies studied individual therapy, the other half group therapy. All HEPs in these studies were rated as bona fide and all except Compare, Calugi, Marchesini, Molinari et al. (2013) were RCTs.

The weighted pre–post effect was large and highly heterogenous: .99 (k = 8; 95% CI [.41, 1.58]; Q = 59.8, p < .01; I^2 = 88%), but substantially larger than the .65 effect obtained in our 2013 review. Effects were much larger for eating difficulties (ES = 1.49; k = 4; 95% CI [.82, 2.16]) than for the collection of other self-damaging activities (ES = .41; k = 4; 95% CI [.14, .69]), a difference that was statistically significant. In terms of type of HEP, the largest effects were for person-centered (ES = 1.23; k = 2; 95% CI [–.79, 3.25]) and EFT (ES = 1.23; k = 2; 95% CI [.00, 2.46]), both with very large confidence intervals. Pre–post effects about .5 SD smaller were obtained for supportive-nondirective therapy (ES = .72; k = 2; 95% CI [.27, 1.18]) and psychodrama/expressive (ES = .79; k = 2; 95% CI [.20, 1.37]). We found little or no difference in pre–post effect sizes for individual vs. group formats.

Controlled and Comparative Effects

The only controlled study was Singal's (2009) study on psychodrama for adolescents with oppositional defiant difficulties, which found no difference between the HEP and a wait-list control group.

In terms of comparative studies, we found six studies (eight comparisons of clients; HEPs: n = 221; nonHEPs: n = 365), which involved a range of HEPs (supportive and other HEP were most common) compared to other treatments, most often CBT (6 studies). The weighted comparative effect was .07 (95% CI [–.24, .38]; Q = 27.2, p < .01; I^2 = 74%), identical to what we found in out 2013 review, and a statistically significant equivalence result, indicating that HEPs and non-HEPs for habitual self-damaging difficulties were equivalent in effectiveness, although with high heterogeneity. One study favored the nonHEP by more than .4: Cottraux et al. (2009) compared supportive-nondirective therapy to CBT for self-harm in clients with borderline diagnoses (referred to as "fragile process" by HEP therapists). Two studies favored HEPs by more than .4: Boerhout et al. (2018) compared a brief six-session psychomotor therapy (an expressive, body-oriented treatment) to supportive contact (a treatment as usual) for clients with a range of eating difficulties; and Schützmann et al. (2010) compared person-centered therapy to guided behavioral self-help for clients diagnosed with bulimia. The other five studies fell into the neutral zone.

The comparisons/studies again fell into two clusters, with distinctly different results: The first cluster consisted of four comparisons from three studies (Boerhout et al., 2016; Compare, Calugi, Marchesini, Molinari et al., 2013; Schützmann et al., 2010) and focused on eating difficulties. It used a process-guiding HEP (i.e. EFT, psychomotor therapy, and a more structured person-centered therapy), generally compared the HEP to a non-CBT intervention (except in one case), and was carried out by researchers with a pro-HEP researcher allegiance. For these studies, the weighted mean comparative effect was .44 (95% CI [–.06, .94]; Q = 10.7, p < .05; I^2 = 72%), a strong effect favoring HEPs but highly heterogenous and not significantly different from zero. The second cluster consisted of the other four comparisons from three studies with negative researcher allegiance (Cottraux et al., 2009; Kay-Lambkin et al., 2011; Magidson et al., 2011). This cluster addressed the application of CBT to forms of self-harm (substance misuse, self-injury), and used a non-process-guiding HEP (supportive-nondirective or person-centered therapy) as a control condition. The comparative effect was in the equivocally negative range with low heterogeneity (ES_w = –.25; 95% CI [–.50, .00]; Q = 4.7, ns; I^2 = 36%).

Unsurprisingly, we found a very strong researcher allegiance operating in these studies, with a weighted meta-regression correlation of –.84 between researcher allegiance and comparative effect size. Comparisons with a pro-HEP researcher allegiance returned a weighted mean comparative effect of .63 (k = 3; 95% CI [.21, 1.04]); while for comparisons with an anti-HEP researcher allegiance the effect was –.23 (k = 5; 95% CI [–.42, –.03]).

Conclusions

Overall, the preponderance of the evidence reviewed here, including both pre–post and comparative treatment lines of evidence, indicates that process-guiding HEPs are *possibly efficacious* treatments for eating difficulties. They have been shown to be either equivalent to another treatment (Boerhout et al., 2016; Schützmann et al., 2010) or equivalent to an already established treatment, CBT (Compare, Calugi, Marchesini, Molinari et al., 2013). This is a turnaround from our previous meta-analysis, when the evidence for the application of HEPs to eating difficulties was weak and just emerging, and represents the recent development of robust HEP approaches for this challenging client population. On the other hand, substance misuse difficulties fared less well in this review than in the previous one (Elliott et al., 2013).

It is our continuing view that HEPs are likely to be useful and effective approaches for use with a range of self-damaging activities, including in particular substance misuse and eating difficulties, and we note the relative neglect of these difficulties by HEP practitioners and researchers. Actually, this statement is not completely accurate, indicating a common prejudice among HEP researchers, theoreticians and practitioners that motivational interviewing is not really an HEP, probably because, for political reasons it has been widely portrayed as a form of CBT. It is our view that MI, when properly practiced within "the spirit of MI" (Miller & Rollnick 2012) is just another one of the many tribes or suborientations within the broader HEP approach. HEP practitioners do themselves, the MI community, and their clients a disservice by continuing to ignore the many contributions of MI.

Other Client Populations

The six client populations that we have reviewed above accounted for about 85% of the HEP outcome studies we identified. However, 21 studies (including 22 separate samples of clients; n = 3971) did not fit readily into any one of these six client populations. These studies fell into several groups, the largest of which were studies of general or mixed client populations, roughly corresponding to what used to be referred to as "neurosis" (11 studies, 12 samples of clients; Barkham & Saxon, 2018, being the largest). Other groupings included: (i) nonclinical populations with only minor levels of distress (3 studies; i.e. masters students, nurses, psychological helpers; e.g., Fillion et al., 2009); (ii) prisoners and other individuals with violent or antisocial processes (2 studies; e.g., Ford et al., 2013); and (iii) various other client populations (5 studies: borderline personality disorder, parents, divorced individuals, people with autism). Nine of these studies had secondary foci such as depression or anxiety (e.g., Barkham & Saxon, 2018), which also led us to include them in those client populations, but 13 were included nowhere else. Although the heterogeneity of these populations meant it would be unlikely that we would be able to come to general conclusions, we include them here for the sake of completeness, and will primarily focus on the separate subgroups.

Pre–Post Effects

Overall, the weighted mean pre-post effect for this group of studies was .87 (k = 22; 95% CI [.68, 1.07]; Q = 123.2. $p < .01$; I^2 = 83%), with high heterogeneity, but very similar to the whole sample benchmark of .87 SD. The effect size for the 13 studies not included elsewhere was somewhat higher, at 1.06 (95% CI [.55, 1.21]). All of this subgroup of studies used bona fide HEPs; 10 were RCTs.

For the largest group of these studies, which used general or mixed client populations (approximating the old "neurotic" category), the mean pre–post effect was 1.03 (k = 12; 95% CI [.78, 1.28]), slightly above the overall benchmark confidence interval for the whole sample (.74 to .98). Clients from non-clinical populations showed relatively small amounts of pre-post change (ES = .41; k = 3; 95% CI [.08, .75]), as did clients in the various other populations grouping (ES = .58; k = 5; 95% CI [.22, .94]).

Controlled Effects

Controlled studies, in which HEPs for other client populations were compared to no treatment or wait-list conditions, produced nine comparisons (HEP n = 307; control n = 424), with an overall mean ES of 1.02 (95% CI [.41, 1.36]; Q = 105.0; $p < .01$; I^2 = 92%), a large but highly heterogenous effect. (For the 5 studies only in this subsample, controlled ES = .95; 95% CI [–.10, 2.0)]. All comparisons used bona fide HEPs and had a pro-HEP researcher allegiance. All but two (Leung & Khor, 2017; Pascual-Leone et al., 2011) were RCTs (ES = 1.25; 95% CI [.37, 2.13]). There was a small cluster of studies worth noting here: Three UK-based studies examined school-based humanistic counseling for young people, generally positioned as broadly person-centered (Cooper et al., 2010; McArthur et al., 2013; Pybis et al., 2015), comparing them to a wait-list control group. For these studies the controlled effect was medium-sized: .6 (95% CI [.09, 1.12]). Another apparent cluster of two studies both used process-guiding HEPs for aggression but involved such different populations and research designs and produced such divergent results that in our view no sound conclusion can be drawn (e.g., Karataş & Gokçakan, 2009; Pascual-Leone et al., 2011).

Comparative Effects

There were eight comparative studies in which HEPs were compared to other treatments, producing 11 comparisons (HEP n = 3187; nonHEP n = 6228). The overall mean weighted effect was –.19 (95% CI [–.39, .02]; Q = 24.2, $p < .01$; I^2 = 59%), which fell into the trivially worse range, but also met the criteria for statistical equivalence (see Table 13.3). In three comparisons (from two studies) CBT did better than HEP by more than the .4 standard (Cottraux et al., 2009; Marriott et al., 2009); the other eight comparisons fell into the neutral zone. There were no studies in which HEP did better than the nonHEP by at least .4 SD. A medium-sized researcher allegiance effect was operating in this data set (meta-regression r = –.36). All HEPs were judged to be bona fide and six were RCTs. HEPs did slightly better in RCTs (ES = –.05; k = 6; 95% CI [–.33, .24]) than in nonrandomized studies (ES = –.31; k = 5; 95% CI [–.65, .03]),

although the difference was not statistically significant. In 9 of the 11 comparisons, the HEP was either person-centered or supportive-nondirective. There were six general/mixed (neurotic) population comparisons (four from Marriott et al., 2009), with a comparative effect of –.22 (95% CI [–.61, .25]), equivocally worse in comparison to a nonHEP, generally (in all but one case) either CBT or cognitive analytic therapy.

QUALITATIVE RESEARCH ON HUMANISTIC-EXPERIENTIAL PSYCHOTHERAPIES

Because of its philosophical compatibility, researchers within the HEP tradition continue to favor qualitative research, including, most importantly, outcome studies (to complement the quantitative meta-analysis presented in the initial sections of this review), research change processes, and qualitative case study research.

Update on Qualitative Outcomes in Humanistic-Experiential Psychotherapies

The previous edition of this chapter reported on the qualitative meta-analysis conducted by Timulak and Creaner (2010), who analyzed qualitative descriptions by a total of 106 clients participating in a variety of HEPs. The results of that qualitative meta-analysis were summarized in 11 meta-categories of qualitative outcomes (e.g., healthier emotional processing, feeling empowered). For this chapter, we carried out a cumulative review, updating Timulak and Creaner and finding a further 9 studies reporting the views of another 71 clients on outcomes of HEPs (see Supplemental materials for more detail about the search and screening process.)

The findings of those studies were generally consistent with and helped elaborate the category system offered by Timulak and Creaner (2010; for more detail, see Supplemental Table 13S-3). We found three main categories: *appreciating experiences of self*; *appreciating experience of self in relationship to others*; and *changed view of self/others*. In terms of second-level meta-categories, our analysis (in addition to fine-tuning the wording of original meta-categories) further stresses nuances of experiences regarding the self and interpersonal changes. There were four second-level meta-categories under the first main category (appreciating experiences of self): *smoother and healthier emotional experiencing*; *self-acceptance of vulnerability* (which included *appreciating vulnerability* and *experiencing self-compassion/self-acceptance/valuing self*); *mastery/resilience of problematic experiences* (which included *experience of resilience, feeling empowered*, and *mastering symptoms*); and *enjoying change in circumstances*. The second main category (*appreciating experience of self in relationship to others*) contained two meta-categories: *feeling supported* and *being different/healthier in interpersonal encounters*. The third main category (*changed view of self/others*) had two meta-categories under it: *self-insight and self-awareness*, and *changed view of others*.

Furthermore, two studies (McElvaney & Timulak, 2013; Steinmann et al., 2017) offered interesting comparisons. McElvaney and Timulak's study looked at qualitative outcomes reported by primary care clients who quantitatively (as measured by pre–post CORE-OM) achieved successful vs. unsuccessful outcomes. Interestingly, there was a minimal difference in what these two groups reported as changes due to therapy. The only observable difference concerned increased awareness, which was more likely to be reported by clients with quantitatively poor outcomes. Although they reported increased awareness, it seemed to be an awareness of their problematic functioning. Steinmann et al.'s study looked at client-reported outcomes in individual EFT vs. attachment-based family therapy for anger directed at a parent. Although, clients in the two therapies reported roughly comparable outcomes, there were suggestions of some differences. In general, these differences were – as might perhaps be expected with clients in individual EFT reporting – more emotional processing and agency/individuation, and clients in attachment-based family therapy more likely to report changes for the better in their relationship with the parent.

In the previous edition of this chapter, we noted the lack of studies on negative outcomes of HEPs. Although we identified a few more in this follow-up study, there was sometimes an overlap between negative outcomes and unhelpful/hindering experiences of therapy process, which will be discussed later in this chapter. Steinmann at al. (2017) reported the following negative outcomes: therapy increased levels of anger; therapy made the relationship with the target parent worse; and positive changes did not last. The issue of changes not lasting was also reported in Perren et al. (2009). These add to the other negative outcomes reported in the previous edition of this chapter, such as nonresolution of the presenting issues and increase in emotional restriction/avoidance.

Qualitative Process and Case Study Research on HEPs

Our search for qualitative HEP research also yielded several new studies focusing on helpful/unhelpful aspects of therapy, significant events studies, studies focusing on clients' in-session presentations, and case studies, some of which studied a particular theoretical conceptualization coming from the HEP tradition. While the picture of what clients find helpful in HEPs was quite clear in the previous edition of this chapter, we could now identify more studies that spoke to difficulties clients may experience in HEPs.

Helpful and Difficult Aspects of HEPs

First, to summarize, many recent qualitative studies on HEPs documented the importance of clients feeling understood, listened to, supported, and validated by the therapist, (e.g., MacLeod & Elliott, 2014; MacLeod et al., 2012; McElvaney & Timulak, 2013; Smith et al., 2014; Sousa, 2018; Timulak et al., 2017). These findings also extend to a group format (Vassilopoulos & Brouzos, 2012). Studies also reported the client's agency, motivation to work, and particular personal attributes as contributing critically to the success of therapy (e.g., Perren et al., 2009; Timulak et al., 2017). Similarly, important and already mentioned in the previous edition of this chapter was client-therapist co-construction of new awareness and meaning regarding their experience (e.g.,

Balmforth & Elliott, 2012; MacLeod & Elliott, 2014; McElvaney & Timulak, 2013; Smith et al., 2014; Sousa, 2018; Stephen et al., 2011; Watson et al., 2012). In the case of group therapy, this could also include learning from co-participants (Vassilopoulos & Brouzos, 2012).

Particularly relevant were in-session emotional experiences of attending to own needs, feeling free, or having a sense of empowerment (e.g., MacLeod et al., 2012; Stephen et al., 2011; Vassilopoulos & Brouzos, 2012; Watson et al., 2012), but also expressions of vulnerability (e.g., Steinmann et al., 2017). Again, in the group format this type of experience includes shared poignant experiences with other group members (Vassilopoulos & Brouzos, 2012). Some studies captured the importance of clients opening up to the therapist in therapy (e.g., Balmforth & Elliott, 2012; Stephen et al., 2011; Timulak et al., 2017) and/or co-participants (Vassilopoulos & Brouzos, 2012). This could be also a difficult experience for clients, but beneficial in the long run.

The processing of painful emotional experiences also appeared very important (e.g., MacLeod et al., 2012; Steinmann et al., 2017; Timulak et al., 2017). Clients in experientially active therapies such as EFT reported that experiential work such as the use of empty-chair dialogues played a major and meaningful role in therapy (e.g., MacLeod et al., 2012; Steinmann et al., 2017; Stiegler et al., 2018; Timulak et al., 2017). Clients could access particularly powerful adaptive emotional experiences such as the feeling of being cared for and loved by the self or other (even God – see MacLeod et al., 2012). This process was also reported as being particularly difficult but helpful in the long run (e.g., Stiegler et al., 2018; Timulak et al., 2017). Chair work could be demanding, as enactments pushed clients outside their comfort zone (Stiegler et al. 2018), but also because they tended to bring up chronically painful emotions (Timulak et al., 2017). Experiential work also stimulated new awareness and recognition of the client's own agency (Steinmann et al., 2017; Stiegler et al., 2018) in certain experiences such as self-criticism (Stiegler et al. 2018).

Unhelpful Aspects of HEPs

In a small minority of cases, the experience could be difficult to the extent that clients did not see the benefit in it (Stiegler et al., 2018; Timulak et al., 2017). All of this points to the central role of evocative experiential exercises as used in process-guiding HEPs (e.g., EFT). While they are seen by clients as central to the main therapeutic work, they are also difficult to engage in and occasionally are not well tolerated (this may be in some respects similar to exposure in cognitive-behavioral therapy). The therapist's facilitative style and awareness of the client's potential fragility thus has to remain central when engaging in these powerful tasks.

Nevertheless, unhelpful aspects of therapy were sometimes reported as a part of negative or problematic outcomes of therapy. In the previous edition of this chapter, we mentioned a number of unhelpful aspects of therapy – for instance, nonresolution of presenting issue, feeling overwhelmed, disappointment over not being understood by the therapist, and fear of changing/increase in emotional restriction. Some of these also presented in our current search, including continuing symptoms (Timulak et al., 2017), finding experiential work overwhelming and being too exposing (Steinmann et al., 2017; Stiegler et al., 2018; Timulak et al., 2017), and misunderstandings in the therapeutic relationship (MacLeod et al. 2012). The current studies also reported as problematic shortness of therapy (MacLeod et al., 2012; Steinmann et al., 2017; Timulak et al., 2017), and the client not putting in enough work or holding back (MacLeod et al., 2012; Timulak et al., 2017).

Other Qualitative Studies

Apart from qualitative outcome studies and qualitative process studies focusing on helpful, difficult and unhelpful aspects of therapy, we located a number of other qualitative studies on HEPs. Some looked at therapists' experiences of therapy (e.g., Carrick, 2014). There were also studies using mixed-methods approaches, such as task analysis, which has a long tradition, particularly in EFT research (Greenberg, 2007). This method uses strategies that rely on an interpretive framework embedded in an HEP theory. For instance, Murphy et al. (2017) applied task analysis to explicate the therapist and client processes in worry dialogues, as used in EFT for generalized anxiety.

In a theory-guided qualitative study, O'Brien et al. (2019) examined in-session presentations of clients with generalized anxiety disorder. They used EFT theory to illustrate that although clients were preoccupied with apparently indiscriminate anxieties about what could happen in various situations, these anxieties were related to the underlying painful feelings of loneliness/loss, shame, and terror that those worried-about situations could bring. Narratively, the feared painful feelings were related to idiosyncratic client stories in which they had experienced those painful feelings in an unbearable manner.

Although not explicitly a theory-guided study, but nonetheless clearly embedded in EFT theory, Brennan et al. (2015) examined the perspectives of participants in an EFT group for patients with eating disorders. Perspectives were expressed in feedback forms and in clients' letters to their critic and eating disorder. The findings show how clients struggle with not being defined by their critic, how they recognize the destructive impact of the critic, but how they can also recognize its protective function. Clients also became aware of their needs in the face of such self-criticism and reported on the importance of self-assertion on behalf of those needs, all in the context of a group that offered an opportunity for learning from others' struggles with their own self-criticism. Another study (Toolan et al., 2019), embedded in EFT theory, examined the relationship between the worry process (in worry dialogues in EFT for generalized anxiety) and the self-critic process. Examination of recordings of worry dialogues showed that worries focus on potential situations that could trigger emotional vulnerabilities in the person, thus setting off a self-critical process.

Qualitative Case Studies

Empirical case study research has a rich tradition in the humanistic-experiential paradigm (see Elliott, 2002a;

McLeod, 2010; Stiles, 2007). The previous edition of this chapter reviewed case studies establishing efficacy of a HEP therapy as well as theory-building case studies. The period since the last edition of this *Handbook* again saw original contributions in this area. Several hermeneutic single case studies examined the efficacy of person-centered as well as EFT for conditions such as health anxiety (Smith et al., 2014) and social anxiety (MacLeod & Elliott, 2014; MacLeod et al., 2012; Stephen et al., 2011). These studies showed that these therapies can be effective with those conditions and that processing of painful emotions as well as relational validation provided by the therapist plays an important role in therapy.

Theory-building case studies also looked at extending the work of person-centered/experiential therapists to presentations or client populations not typically associated with these types of therapies. For example, Gunst and Vanhooren (2018) illustrated a powerful longing for connection in a client with an offender history. Such case studies also demonstrated their ability to shed light on theoretical aspects of humanistic therapies such as the reciprocal/mutual interaction between the relational conditions that both clients and therapists offer each other (Tickle & Murphy, 2014). As in the previous edition, we could also find at least one instance of an assimilation of problematic experiences case study, here used to examine therapeutic collaboration (Ribeiro et al., 2016).

Several studies (Dillon et al., 2018; McNally et al., 2014; Pascual-Leone et al., 2019) examined a theory of sequential emotional processing (Pascual-Leone & Greenberg, 2007; Pascual-Leone, 2018) that is becoming a central pillar of understanding the process of change in EFT and a range of other therapies. Some of those studies examined aspects of this theory, while others elaborated and built on the original formulation. The studies illustrated that in successful cases of EFT, clients move from an undifferentiated, global, symptomatic distress; through underlying core painful feelings of shame, fear and/or loneliness; to unmet needs; and eventually to a response to those unmet needs in the form of self-compassion and/or boundary-setting healthy anger. This theoretical conceptualization has not only been developed within a humanistic tradition but is very powerfully informing the therapeutic practice of EFT (Timulak & Pascual-Leone, 2015).

Qualitative Research on HEPs: Conclusions

Systematic qualitative research on HEPs has a long tradition. It is clearly a success story, as perhaps none of the other therapeutic approaches have been influenced to such an extent by qualitative studies. Its contribution is well established in informing the development of these therapies (cf. Timulak et al., 2018). Nevertheless, it is also worth noting the lack of cultural (or even clinical) diversity in the current body of qualitative research on HEPs. It appears that future research of this type should further focus on more diverse client populations, as well as adverse experiences of clients in HEPs and how to overcome them. We see potential also in theoretically informed qualitative studies, as these can further and deepen our understanding of therapeutic process and further inform development and training in HEPs.

QUANTITATIVE PROCESS RESEARCH ON HUMANISTIC-EXPERIENTIAL PSYCHOTHERAPY

Research on the process of change is foundational to HEP approaches, as research clinicians within this approach have tried to specify the therapist and client processes that contribute to successful outcomes. Historically, the focus of this research agenda has been on general therapeutic relationship conditions or attitudes as delineated by Rogers (1957) and on client experiencing (Gendlin, 1981). This has evolved over time to a more differentiated focus on therapist interventions and techniques and client processes that are related to change in psychotherapy.

Process-Outcome Research on the Therapeutic Relationship

Since Rogers (1957) first articulated his hypothesis about the necessary and sufficient conditions of therapeutic change, much evidence has accumulated. Norcross and Lambert (2019) updated the reviews for the most recent edition of *Psychotherapy Relationships that Work*. They have provided up-to-date summaries of the broad base of evidence supporting the therapist relational conditions specified by Rogers, including chapters by Elliott et al. (2019) on empathy; Farber et al. (2019) on positive regard and affirmation; Kolden et al. (2019) on congruence/genuineness, and Flückiger et al. (2019) on the therapeutic alliance in adult psychotherapy generally. The Elliott et al. meta-analysis of the relation between therapist empathy and client outcome found a weighted mean r of .28 (equivalent to d = .58), only slightly lower than their 2011 analysis (r = .31; to d = .65). As for positive regard, Farber et al. found a mean r of .18 (d = .36), clearly lower than they reported in Farber et al (2011; r = .27; d = .56). Nevertheless, both have been shown to be robust, medium-sized predictors of client outcome. Finally, Kolden et al. (2019) reported the r for congruence/genuineness as .23 (d = .46). Thus, the effect for empathy has been more consistent and slightly larger than the effect for positive regard and congruence.

The research collected and meta-analyzed in the Norcross & Lambert (2019) review volume came from a broad range of therapies, mostly not from the HEP tradition. For example, only 14 out of 82 (17%) of the studies reviewed in Elliott et al.'s (2019) empathy-outcome meta-analysis focused on HEPs. The mean weighted correlation for these eight studies was .24, statistically significant, highly consistent (I^2 = 15%) and in line with the overall value of .28 for the entire sample of 82 studies. HEPs were grouped under "other treatments" in the Farber et al. (2019) and Kolden et al. (2019) reviews of positive regard and genuineness respectively, but appear to comprise only a tiny proportion the studies reviewed.

In any case, the links between outcome, therapist empathy, and the working alliance are some of the most strongly evidenced findings in the psychotherapy research literature (Elliott et al., 2019; Norcross & Lambert, 2019). This has been found across different therapeutic approaches (Watson &

Geller, 2005). As originally formulated, Rogers specified that therapists needed to convey the relational attitudes of acceptance, empathy, congruence and prizing, and these attitudes needed to be received by clients. In a recent study investigating the role of the therapeutic relationships on outcome, Murphy and Cramer (2014) found that client progress was better if both clients and therapists rated the relationship as improving over the course of therapy.

Nevertheless, as we noted in earlier versions of this review, several methodological weaknesses have been identified in this body of quantitative process-outcome research on the impact of the relationship conditions on outcome. In an earlier, unsystematic review, Sachse and Elliott (2002) noted that the facilitative conditions did not yield consistent results for all clients and client problems, as some clients seem to benefit and others not. Other methodological problems include a failure to assess clients for incongruence (as originally proposed by Rogers, 1957); poor sampling methods; small sample sizes; different rating perspectives; inadequate levels of the therapeutic conditions; restricted range of measurement of the relationship conditions; possible nonlinear effects; low measurement reliability; third variable or reverse causation; and inconsistencies in the experience levels of the therapists (Elliott et al., 2019; Watson et al., 2010). Notwithstanding these methodological problems, the accumulated evidence to date points to a moderately strong relationship between the therapeutic conditions and outcome, although the relationship may be substantially more complex than initially thought. Chief among these complexities is the large degree of conceptual overlap between empathy, positive regard, and genuineness; indeed, Elliott et al. (2019) recently concluded that these relationship variables are so deeply interwoven that it is a mistake to treat them as distinct and to study them independently of one another.

Relationship Variable Mediator and Moderator Research

Key among the failings of traditional process-outcome research therapist-offered relational conditions is the fact that they do not tell us what mediates the relation between therapist relational conditions and outcome (Elliott et al., 2019). To address this gap in the literature, Watson and colleagues have investigated the role of different mediating variables, including attachment insecurity and negative treatment of self, e.g., criticism, neglect, and self-silencing behaviors, on the empathy-outcome relationship (Watson et al., 2014). Watson et al. investigated whether clients' self-reported experience of therapists' empathy contributed to changes in their attachment styles and treatment of self, after 16 weeks of psychotherapy for depression. There was a significant direct relationship between therapists' empathy and outcome and a significant indirect effect, showing that clients' perceptions of therapists' empathy was associated with significant improvement in attachment insecurity and significant decreases in negative self-treatment, including self-criticism and self-silencing, at the end of therapy as well as reductions on BDI, IIP, DAS and SCL-90-R, GSI, and increases on RSE. The findings suggest that clients' perception of their therapists as empathic is an important mechanism of change in psychotherapy that warrants ongoing investigation. These more recent studies continue to provide additional, more nuanced evidence and support for the role of the clients' experience of the therapeutic relationship in promoting positive outcomes in psychotherapy. In a later study, Malin and Pos (2015) continued to explore the impact of therapist empathy, the working alliance, and client emotional processing on client outcome. Using an observer measure of therapist expressed empathy in the first session, they found that therapists' empathy predicted outcome indirectly and was mediated by clients working alliance scores after the first session and the level of clients' emotional processing in the mid-phase of therapy.

Wong and Pos (2014) examined the relationships among client pretreatment characteristics, clients' and therapists' interpersonal process in the first session, and the working alliance after the first session in low- and high-alliance groups. Both clients' pretherapy interpersonal problems as measured by the IIP and clients' in-session process as measured by SASB predicted clients' first session alliance scores. Clients who were more socially inhibited had significantly lower alliances scores after the first session, while greater self-disclosure predicted higher alliance scores after session 1. Moreover, clients in the low-alliance group disclosed less during the second and third phase of the first session than those in the high-alliance group. There were significantly more asserting and separating behaviors in the low alliance group than the high-alliance one. Client disclosure significantly and uniquely predicted the bond subscale of the alliance, while social inhibition and client disclosure significantly predicted the goal subscale, although in opposite directions. Notably, therapists' loving and approaching behaviors were higher in the high-alliance group than the low-alliance group. This study highlights the impact of client pretreatment characteristics and mode of engagement from the point of initial contact on the formation of the alliance and therapist behaviors. We recommend more research like the studies we've reviewed in this section, to clarify on the role of moderator and mediator variables in the relationship between key HEP relationship variables and client outcome. (see also Chapter 8 in this volume)

Research on Specific Therapeutic Tasks

As we noted in previous versions of this review, research on specific therapeutic tasks has been an important and useful line in HEP research for deepening our understanding of the steps necessary for facilitating client change in therapy.

Two-Chair Dialogue for Conflict Splits

There is a long tradition of research on the client change processes in the two-chair dialogue task in EFT and Gestalt therapies (e.g., Greenberg, 1979; Whelton & Greenberg; 2000). Shahar and colleagues (2012) examined the efficacy of two-chair dialogue task with nine clients who were judged to be self-critical. The intervention was associated with clients becoming significantly more compassionate and reassuring toward themselves, with significant reductions in self-criticism and symptoms of depression and anxiety, which were

maintained over a six-month follow-up period. More recently, Stiegler et al. (2018) used a multiple-baseline additive design to compare person-centered therapy (=baseline) to EFT chair work for depressed-anxious clients with self-critical processes; they found that two chair work was associated with greater reductions in client anxiety and depression.

Empty Chair Work for Unfinished Business

Earlier studies found the empty chair task to be more effective in resolving unfinished business than empathy using measures of both in-session process and session outcome (Greenberg & Foerster, 1996) and clients who resolved their unfinished business reported significantly greater improvement in symptom distress, interpersonal problems, target complaints, affiliation toward self, and degree of unfinished business (Greenberg & Malcolm, 2002). Following up on this line of research, Paivio et al.'s (2010) study compared two forms of EFT for trauma. In one condition (imaginal confrontation), clients were required to use empty chair work – that is, to speak directly to the perpetrator of their abuse or important nonprotective others in the empty chair. In the other condition (empathic exploration), clients instead spoke to the therapist *about* the perpetrator/nonprotective other. Clients in both forms of EFT showed substantial pre–post gains, with those in the empty chair work condition showing more pre–post change; however, they also had a higher dropout rate (20% versus 7%), suggesting that not all clients will respond positively to this highly evocative therapeutic task, and should not be forced to use it.

Interpersonal Forgiveness in Couples

Research on specific therapeutic tasks has occurred within the context of couples' therapy, as well as individual therapy. Parallel task analytic studies have explored how forgiveness unfolds in EFT for couples (EFT-C), using cases where one member of the couple felt abandoned or betrayed by their partner (Johnson et al., 2001; Makinen & Johnson, 2006; Woldarsky Meneses, 2006; Woldarsky Meneses & Greenberg, 2011). The task analyses tracked the steps leading from markers of injury to forgiveness, using videotapes of therapy sessions.

The earliest presentations of the resolution models from the two research teams had some notable differences. The early versions of Johnson et al. (2001; Makinen & Johnson, 2006) included the injured party requesting and receiving comfort and care from the injurer as central to the change process. In contrast, Woldarsky Meneses's model (2006; Woldarsky Meneses & Greenberg, 2011) described the injurer's expressions of shame about the injury and their apology as pulling for forgiveness from the injured party, without necessarily requiring comfort and care. Subsequent refinements of the Johnson et al. model have deemphasized the role of comfort and care for the injured (e.g., Zuccarini et al., 2013), bringing the two models into closer alignment about the central elements required for resolution: (i) First, the injured party expresses their hurt and the impact of the injury; (ii) then the injurer offers non-defensive acceptance of responsibility for the emotional injury; (iii) they express shame, remorse or empathic distress about the injury; (iv) before offering a heartfelt apology. This is then followed by (v) the injured partner showing a shift in their view of the other and expressing forgiveness; (vi) after which the injurer express acceptance of the forgiveness, along with relief or contrition.

Woldarsky, Meneses, and Greenberg (2014) further related the in-session process during the interpersonal forgiveness task to outcome, based on data from 33 couples who received emotion-focused couples' therapy for an emotional injury (a betrayal; Greenberg et al., 2010). The results showed that expressed shame accounted for 33% of the outcome variance in posttherapy forgiveness. The addition of acceptance explained an additional 9%, while in-session forgiveness explained another 8%, with the final regression model accounting for 50% of the outcome variance. These findings lend support to the couples' forgiveness model (Meneses & Greenberg, 2011).

Research on Client Processes

In HEP theories of personality change (Gendlin, 1970; Greenberg, 2019; Rogers, 1959), depth of experiential self-exploration is seen as one of the pillars of psychotherapy process and client change. During the past 50 years much research has been carried out on the relationship between experiential depth and outcome. Within this context, several instruments have been constructed to measure levels of clients' involvement in an experiential process of self-exploration, the most common being the Client Experiencing Scale (Klein et al., 1986).

Depth of Experiencing and Emotion Processing

Client Experiencing. Ratings of clients' depth of experiencing have been related to good outcome consistently in HEPs, consistently showing a positive relationship: the higher the experiencing level, the better the therapy outcome (Elliott et al., 2004; Hendricks, 2002; Pascual-Leone & Yeryomenko, 2017). In particular, Pascual-Leone and Yeryomenko (2017) reported a meta-analysis of 406 clients from 10 studies that found that client experiencing was a small to medium size predictor of outcome, with $r = .19$ for self-report measures of outcome. This increased to $r = .25$ with observational measures of clients' process and outcome. Thus, although the association between client experiencing level and outcome is consistent, it is not large, suggesting that other factors play a role in fruitful therapy process. In addition, it is simplistic to hold a linear view of the stages of the experiencing scale (i.e. "the higher the score, the better the process quality of the exploration process"). Two lines of investigation of psychotherapy change process (e.g., Angus et al., 1999; Watson et al., 2007) emphasize that *all* narrative modalities, representing the full range of the client experiencing scale, are important and serve useful functions for clients in exploring their problems.

Rogers' process view (1961), however, also predicted that there would be an *increase* of experiencing level throughout the course of successful therapy. Unfortunately, this has not been confirmed in most studies, possibly due to methodological issues such as sampling problems. Most importantly, researchers typically measure experiencing levels at the beginning, middle, and end phases of therapy, but randomly select segments within and across sessions. On the other hand, several studies have revealed significant differences in the manner in which good and poor outcome clients refer to their emotional experience during the session, across different therapeutic approaches (Pos et al., 2003; Watson & Bedard, 2006). These findings suggest that processing one's bodily felt experience and deepening this in therapy may well be a core ingredient of change in psychotherapy regardless of approach. However, an alternative interpretation is that clients who enter therapy with these skills do better in short-term therapy than those who do not enter with these skills. Thus, these skills may be an indicator of clients' readiness or capacity to engage in short term therapy (Watson et al., 2007).

Depth of Experiencing, Emotional Expression, and Outcome. EFT researchers have examined the relationship between client levels of emotional arousal and outcome. These studies found that higher emotional arousal at mid-treatment, coupled with reflection on the aroused emotion and deeper emotional processing late in therapy, predicted good treatment outcomes (Pos et al, 2003; Warwar, 2003). EFT thus appears to work by enhancing a particular type of emotional processing: first helping the client experience, then accept, and finally make sense of their emotions. Pos et al. (2010) examined the role of the alliance and emotional processing across different phases of therapy and how they relate to outcome. After controlling for both the alliance and client emotional processing at the beginning of therapy, client level of experiencing during the working phase predicted reductions in depressive and general symptoms, as well as gains in self-esteem.

In another study of relations among the alliance, frequency of aroused emotional expression, and outcome, in EFT for depression, Carryer and Greenberg (2010) found that the expression of high versus low emotional arousal correlated with different types of outcome. Moderate frequency of heightened emotional arousal was found to add significantly to outcome variance predicted by the working alliance. The majority of process research studies have focused on a direct linear relationship between process and outcome; however, this study showed that a rate of 25% for moderate-to-high emotional expression predicted best outcomes. Lower rates, indicating lack of emotional involvement, represented an extension of the generally accepted relationship between low levels of expressed emotional arousal and poor outcome, while higher rates, indicating excessive amounts of highly aroused emotion, were also related to poor outcome. This suggests that having the client achieve an intense and full level of emotional expression is predictive of good outcome, as long as the client does not maintain this level of emotional expression for too long a time or too often. In addition, frequency of reaching only minimal or marginal level of arousal was found to predict poor outcome. Thus, emotional expression that does not attain a heightened level of emotional arousal, or that reflects an inability to express full arousal and possibly indicates interruption of arousal, appears undesirable, rather than a lesser but still desirable goal. This complex relationship offers a challenge to therapists in managing levels of arousal and possibly selecting clients for EFT.

For example, Paivio and Pascual Leone (2010) noted that studies of EFT for trauma (e.g., Paivio et al., 2001) have found that good client process early in therapy is important because it sets the course for therapy and allows more time to explore and process emotion related to traumatic memories.

Extending this line of inquiry, Watson et al. (2011) examined relationships among client affect regulation, in-session emotional processing, working alliance, and outcome in 66 clients who received either CBT or EFT for depression. They found that client initial level of affect regulation predicted their emotional processing during early and working phases of therapy. Moreover, the quality of client emotional processing in the session mediated the relationship between client level of affect regulation at the beginning of therapy and at termination; and client level of affect regulation at the end of therapy mediated the relationship between client level of emotional processing in therapy and final outcome, independently of the working alliance. These studies demonstrate the importance of client emotional processing in the session and suggest important ways that it can be facilitated by specific therapist interventions, for example, by facilitating client symbolization, acceptance, owning, regulation, and differentiation of key emotions.

Modeling Client Emotional Processing. Emotional processing of global distress is a meta-task in EFT, in that clients often enter therapy with either strong or partially blocked/undifferentiated feelings (i.e. feeling "upset" or "bad"). Using a model of emotional processing that identifies clients' movement through various emotional states (Pascual-Leone & Greenberg, 2007), Pascual-Leone (2009) used univariate and bootstrapping statistical methods to examine how dynamic emotional shifts accumulate moment-by-moment to produce in-session gains in emotional processing. This study found that effective emotional processing was simultaneously associated with steady improvement and increased emotional range. Good events were shown to occur in a "two-steps-forward, one-step-backward" fashion, and it was found that there were increasingly shorter emotional collapses in helpful in-session events, as compared to unhelpful in-session events where the opposite was true.

Choi et al. (2014) continued the examination of clients' emotional change process in the resolution of self-criticism as measured by changes in self-esteem at the end of therapy in a sample of nine clients, consisting of five who had improved significantly in terms of their self-esteem by the end of therapy and four who had not. They found that resolvers (who decreased self-criticism over the course of therapy) also showed drops in expression of secondary emotions and increases in expression of primary adaptive emotions, both within and across phases of therapy. Good resolvers also exhibited more sequences of EEs consistent with transformation of secondary and maladaptive emotions to adaptive emotions.

Recently, Dillon et al. (2018) examined emotional processing in using the model of sequential emotional processing for an intensive case analysis of a good outcome client's emotional processing over 15 sessions. A model of change emerged that

highlighted the important role played by accessing clients' adaptive primary emotions and expressing self-compassion and assertive anger in positive outcome in EFT.

Another focus of inquiry in EFT has been the examination of clients' optimal emotional processing in therapy and its relationship with outcome. Using a measure of Client Emotional Productivity (CEP), Auszra et al., (2013) examined whether productive processing of emotion predicted improvement at the end of therapy in clients receiving experiential therapy to treat depression. Hierarchical regression showed that clients' emotional processing during the working or middle phase of therapy predicted improvement over and above that predicted by their emotional processing in the beginning phase, working alliance and clients' emotional arousal during the working phase of therapy. The quality of clients' emotional processing during the working phase of therapy emerged as the sole predictor of improvement in depression. This suggests that improvement in experiential therapy is characterized by the activation of productive primary emotion.

Herrmann et al. (2016 continued the investigation of client in-session emotion processing as a predictor of good outcome. Using a process measure of the four types of emotion response identified in EFT theory (adaptive primary, maladaptive primary, secondary, instrumental), they studied a sample of 30 clients in EFT who were treated for depression. They found that a lower frequency of secondary emotion and a higher frequency of primary adaptive emotion in the working phase predicted outcome. In addition, it was important that clients not be overwhelmed by negative emotion, because moderate levels of primary maladaptive emotion were related to outcome and the frequency with which clients moved from primary maladaptive to primary adaptive in the working phase predicted outcome. Thus, evidence of clients moving through different stages of emotional processing and transforming maladaptive into adaptive emotions is significantly related to successful change in psychotherapy.

Narrative Processes and Assimilation

Narrative processes in humanistic and experiential psychotherapies have been investigated using several different scales, including narrative processing markers (Angus & Greenberg, 2011), as well as innovative moments and narrative shifts (Goncalves et al., 2011). Studies on client narrative sequences in EFT have revealed interesting and unique patterns associated with good outcome (Boritz et al., 2008; Boritz et al., 2011). These authors investigated the relationship of expressed emotional arousal and specific autobiographical memory in the context of early, middle, and late phase sessions drawn from the York I Depression Study (Greenberg & Watson, 1998). Hierarchical Linear Modeling analyses established that there was a significant increase in the specificity of autobiographical memories from early to late phase therapy sessions and that treatment outcome was predicted by a combination of high narrative specificity plus expressed arousal in late phase sessions. Recovered clients emotionally expressed their feelings in the context of telling specific autobiographical memory narratives to a greater degree than clients who remained depressed at treatment termination (Boritz et al, 2010). However, neither expressed emotional arousal nor narrative specificity alone was associated with complete recovery at treatment termination.

Subsequently, Angus and Greenberg (2011) developed a map of narrative indicators that have been tested in different therapeutic approaches. Boritz et al. (2017) examined narrative flexibility, defined by movement among the various indicators, in clients' narratives in CBT and EFT in relation to treatment outcome. Using logistic regression, the authors reported that the probability that client narratives would shift among different narrative markers over the course of therapy was constant for those clients who recovered but declined for those that did not change. This suggests that client narrative flexibility may be an important indicator of good outcome.

Client narrative processes have also been extensively investigated by Gonçalves and colleagues. They developed a coding system that identifies five kinds or stages of innovative moments including action, reflection, protest, reconceptualization, and performing change. In a study of innovative moments (IMs) in therapy, Gonçalves and colleagues (2011) showed that clients shift from focusing on habitual problematic narratives about self to new alternative narratives. In an exploratory study with a small sample, Mendes et al. (2011) examined the role of the two most common IMs, reflection and protest, in good and poor outcome cases. Two subtypes were identified for each of the IMs: *Reflection subtype 1* involved new understandings that created distance from the problem; it decreased across sessions in both poor and good outcome cases. On the other hand, Reflection subtype 2, which was centered on change (both changes made already and strategies going forward), increased and was highest in good outcome cases. Differences in the Protest IM subtypes were also observed: Subtype 1 involved statements of problem-oriented positions, and was stable across sessions in both outcome groups. Subtype 2 involved the emergence of self-empowerment; it was absent in the sessions of the poor outcome group and increased in the middle phase of therapy in the good outcome group.

Cunha et al. (2012) analyzed both client and therapist behaviors using the Innovative Moments scale and the Helping Skills System (HSS-Hill, 2009). A study of therapists' use of exploration, insight, and action skills and IMs in two initial, two middle, and two final sessions of three good outcome and three poor outcome cases treated with EFT for depression found that IMs occurred more often in good outcome cases than poor outcome cases. Furthermore, therapists' use of exploration and insight skills more often preceded client action, reflection, and protest IMs in the initial and middle phases of therapy in the good outcome cases than the poor outcome ones. However, in the final phase of therapy these therapist skills of exploration and insight more often preceded moments identified as reconceptualization and performing change. Therapists' use of action skills was more often associated with client innovative moments identified as action, reflection, and protest across all phases, and especially in the final phase for good outcome clients.

Expanding IM research, Cunha and associates (2017) conducted an exploratory task analysis of the consolidation phase

in EFT, which shows clients moving from an exploration of a problem to reconstructing a new view of self. The authors identified nine steps in the resolution of the task including recognition of the differences between present and past views of self; development of a meta-perspective on past and present; amplifying the contrast between past and present; expressing a positive appreciation of change; experiencing feelings of empowerment; identifying ongoing difficulties; emphasizing that the problem is no longer central; seeing change as ongoing and gradual; and referring to new projects, plans, and experience of change.

In a further examination of changes in clients' narratives, Fernández-Navarro et al. (2018) examined moments when clients reconceptualized their narratives. They identified two subtypes of reconceptualization, one when the client made a positive contrast between a present view of self and a past view and another in which the client described why and how this change occurred. In order to determine whether the global category of reconceptualization of a problem state predicted outcome as much as either single subtype alone, they analyzed 16 cases of clients treated for depression in EFT. Longitudinal regression models showed that the umbrella category of reconceptualization occurred less frequently than either of the other two did separately. However, reconceptualization was a better predictor of outcome than either of the two subtypes. Changes in clients' narratives were indicative of changes in psychotherapy and the authors suggested that these types of changes might be encouraged or consolidated by therapists asking clients to identify what has changed and what has facilitated the change.

We recognize that much of this research is exploratory and has focused on developing the Innovative Moments Rating Scale. Much of it has been based on small samples, and in some studies raters were not blind to outcome, being very familiar with the data set; there have also been challenges identifying problematic narratives.

A recent line of research has focused on the relation between narrative processes and Stiles' (2001) assimilation of problematic experiences (APES) model, a stage model of client change. Mendes et al. (2016) examined change in one good and one poor outcome case drawn from an EFT treatment study for depression using the assimilation model (APES; Stiles, 2001). They found that both clients experienced setbacks – that is, moments in the session when their ratings on the APES reverted to a lower level. However, the type of setback varied in each case.

Setbacks in the poor outcome case typically occurred when the therapist was working ahead of the client's proximal level of development (ZPD), trying to get them to move to a higher level of assimilation before they are ready. On the other hand, setbacks in the good-outcome case resulted from the use of either (i) a "balanced strategy" in which the therapist recognized client progress before redirecting the client's attention to less assimilated aspects of a problem or (ii) allowed the client to change focus to less assimilated aspects of a problem (spontaneous switches). Thus, in the good-outcome case setbacks were part of a process of capitalizing on therapeutic progress to broaden or deepen therapeutic work.

Similarly, using the assimilation model, Ribeiro et al. (2016) compared two cases drawn from the EFT arm of the York Depression Project. They observed how two different EFT therapists worked within their clients' ZPDs. Specifically, they found that the therapist of the client who achieved higher levels on APES used a balance of supportive and challenging interventions, in contrast with the therapist of the other client who used primarily supportive interventions. The authors suggested that challenging interventions that foster change may be helpful in a positive relationship in which the client feels safe, as long as the therapist stays within their client's ZPD.

Finally, Barbosa et al. (2018), using data from a good-outcome case of EFT for depression, found that lower levels of client assimilation were associated with what they referred to as *immersion*, characterized by a narrow, self-absorbed perspective on difficult experiences, which were more common early in therapy. Higher levels of assimilation, however, occurred later in therapy and involved a *distanced* perspective, in which the client took a distanced, observer perspective on their difficult experiences, pointing to an increase in client capacity to reflect on and make meaning out of emotional experience, an important outcome in EFT.

CONCLUSIONS

In this update of research on humanistic-experiential psychotherapies, we have emphasized recent outcome research, but have also updated our reviews of qualitative research on client experiences of therapy and quantitative investigations of change processes. We therefore begin by summing up what we have learned about the outcome of HEPs.

Humanistic-Experiential Psychotherapies as Evidence-Based Treatments

Current mental health politics urgently require continuing collection, integration, and dissemination of information about the rapidly expanding body of outcome evidence, to help deal with challenges to HEPs in many countries. HEP outcome research has grown rapidly, with a 50% increase in the past 10 years. This has allowed us to pursue increasingly sophisticated analytic strategies and to break down the evidence by client subpopulation and type of HEP. We believe that these analyses go a long way toward meeting the demands of the various national guideline development groups (e.g., APA Division 12 Task Force on Empirically Supported Treatments in the United States; National Institute for Health and Care Excellence [NICE] in the United Kingdom).

Looking at our current data set of 91 recent studies, together with our previous collection of nearly 200 outcome studies, we see that evidence for the effectiveness of HEPs comes from five separate lines of evidence and supports the following conclusions:

1. Overall, HEPs are associated with large *pre–post* client change. These client changes are maintained over the early posttherapy period (< 12 months), although not enough recent studies have addressed late (a year or more) outcomes.

2. In *controlled studies*, clients in HEPs generally show large gains relative to clients who receive no therapy, regardless of whether studies are randomized. This allows the causal inference that HEP, in general, causes client change; or rather, speaking from the client's perspective, we can say that clients use HEP to cause themselves to change.

3. In *comparative outcome* studies, HEPs overall are statistically and clinically equivalent in effectiveness to other therapies (especially non-CBT therapies), regardless of whether studies are randomized.

4. In the current dataset, CBT appears to have a small advantage over HEPs. However, this effect seems to be due in part to non–bona fide treatments usually labeled by researchers as *supportive* (or sometimes *nondirective*), which are generally less effective than CBT. These therapies are typically delivered when there is a negative researcher allegiance and in non–bona fide versions, and appear to be the mediator for the substantial researcher allegiance effect that we have found repeatedly. In our previous review, when the supportive treatments were removed from the sample, or when researcher allegiance was controlled for statistically, HEPs appeared to be equivalent to CBT in their effectiveness. However, levels of researcher allegiance in the current sample were so high that it proved difficult to control for them statistically, leading to an equivocal finding in favor of CBT over person-centered therapy, in contrast to the clear equivalence finding we reported in our previous review.

5. In terms of type of HEP, EFT continues to fare the best, although the number of recent controlled and comparative studies is too small to warrant a strong conclusion. There are plenty of studies of supportive-nondirective therapy, a weaker form of HEP, and these continue to do most poorly against CBT. However, it is not clear how much this is due to negative researcher allegiance effects and how much is due to this approach being less effective. In terms of effectiveness, Person-centered therapy falls in between supportive-nondirective therapies and EFT, a consistent finding across both our previous and current meta-analyses.

Going beyond these general conclusions, we have argued that there is now enough research to warrant varying positive valuations of HEP in six important client populations: depression, relationship/interpersonal problems, anxiety, coping with chronic medical conditions, psychosis, and self-damaging activities.

For *depression*, HEPs continue to be extensively researched, with large pre–post effects and medium controlled effects; for this dataset we found an equivocally negative comparative effect size, characterized by overwhelmingly negative researcher allegiance. This result is suspect because it contradicts our previous clear equivalence finding that supported the use of HEPs for depression generally, but particularly for EFT for mild to moderate depression (e.g., Goldman et al., 2006; Watson et al., 2003), and PCT for perinatal depression (e.g., Cooper et al., 2003; Holden et al., 1989). However, recent large-scale balanced allegiance studies (Barkham & Saxon, 2018; Barkham et al., 2020) suggest that there are some specific situations in which CBT may do better that PCT: for example, with more severely distressed clients seen for more sessions or tracked a year later. This, in turn, points to the possibility that when applied to depression PCT may need to be bolstered with more powerful methods, for example, EFT chair work.

For *relationship and interpersonal problems*, HEPs clearly meet criteria as an *efficacious* treatment, based on pre–post and controlled effects. Our previous review contained a substantial number of studies of couples therapy, with large pre–post, controlled and even comparative effects. However, the current review was dominated by individual therapy and included more studies of social anxiety and PTSD, which resulted in smaller comparative effects in the equivalent or trivially less-effective range.

For helping clients cope psychologically with *chronic medical conditions*, we found a large body of studies and replicated our previous finding of reasonably large pre–post effects, clear superiority to no treatment control conditions, and equivalence to other treatments including CBT. This client population continues to be a promising one for further exploration of the value of HEPs including supportive-nondirective and PCT.

For *habitual self-damaging activities*, including eating difficulties, our analysis points to the effectiveness of HEPs in general (primarily supportive and other HEPs). Although time and resources precluded including Motivational Interviewing (MI) here, our results are again comparable to those commonly reported for MI (Lundahl et al., 2010).

For *anxiety* difficulties overall, the recent evidence is as in the previous review mixed, but sufficient to warrant a general continuing verdict of possibly efficacious: We found large pre–post and very large controlled effects, but general superiority of CBT to supportive-nondirective treatments in negative researcher allegiance studies. There are at least two major comparative treatment studies (e.g., Timulak et al., 2018) pitting EFT against CBT currently in progress, but none of these have yet reported results.

For *psychotic* conditions such as schizophrenia, we replicated our previous finding of promising pre–post and comparative effects supporting the use of HEPS for this challenging client population. This directly contradicts the UK guideline contraindicating humanistic counseling for clients with this condition (National Collaborating Centre for Mental Health, 2010). In fact, the comparative evidence we have reviewed points to the possibility that HEPs may in some cases be *more* effective than the other therapies to which they have been compared. Clearly, this is an area that warrants further investigation and treatment development.

Key Change Processes in Humanistic-Experiential Psychotherapies

Our review of quantitative and qualitative change process research on HEPs shows that researchers continue to refine their understanding of the therapist and client processes that bring about change in therapy. This research uses all four of the change process research paradigms defined by Elliott (2010), including quantitative process-outcome, qualitative helpful factors, significant events, and sequential process approaches, in the context of both group designs and single case studies. Over time, the research has moved beyond global therapist facilitative processes such as empathy, positive regard, genuineness, and collaboration to more specific within-session client change processes.

Qualitative change process research, for example, reveals the complexity of clients' experiences of therapy. Clients have their own agendas, may be ambivalent about change, and may sometimes experience aspects of therapy as difficult or hindering, all of which can significantly affect the outcomes of therapy. In successful therapy, the therapist is seen as reaching out to the client in a way that promotes the client's sense of safety, but that also responds to the client's emotional pain and unmet needs with compassionate and authentic presence. These needs are affirmed by the therapist, thus facilitating the development of self-compassion and self-acceptance as well as self-empowerment grounded in awareness of key emotions and unmet needs.

Furthermore, the use of task analysis to model sequences of particular client and therapist performances has led to the development of additional models of therapeutic change processes and has broadened the range of therapist behaviors and types of interventions that have been shown to facilitate good outcome. Process-outcome research on client experiencing has been extended to productive emotion and narrative processes. Over the past 20 years much quantitative change process research has focused on central client processes such as emotional processing, including expression, deepening, transformation and regulation, the emergence of new client narratives, changes in clients' self-organizations and the assimilation of problematic experiences. These new client variables and their associated process measures are providing more fine-grained tools for understanding how client change occurs. These conceptual and research tools are generating new, more precise maps of the change process. Thus, we can see more precise answers emerging to key questions about productive therapy process:

Question 1: What is the most productive sequence of narrative exploration in therapy? Answer: Description of external events, leading to initial self-reflection, leading to access to internal experiences, leading to self-reflection on broader meaning (research by Angus and colleagues).

Question 2: How do new narratives emerge and become established in client's lives? Answer: By a spiraling movement between action and reflection, starting with attempts to change the problem, leading to reflection on the nature of the old problematic narrative, followed by active protest or working against the problem, then to emerging re-conceptualization of self and the process of change, and finally to carrying out the change in one's life (research by Gonçalves and colleagues).

Question 3: How do problematic or painful client experiences get assimilated? Answer: Via an extended sequence over time starting from warded off or painful awareness, then to problem clarification and insight, and finally to working through and mastery (research by Stiles and colleagues).

Question 4: When is client emotional expression most likely to lead to good outcome? Answer: When it is grounded in specific autobiographical memories, accompanied by deeper levels of experiencing, and becomes more regulated and differentiated as it is explored (research by Greenberg, Angus, Pascual-Leone, Auszra and Hermann, and others).

Question 5: How do stuck, symptomatic emotions get transformed into more useful, productive emotions? Answer: By helping clients move from an undifferentiated, global or secondary symptomatic distress (e.g., anxiety, depression); through underlying core painful feelings (e.g., shame/guilt, fear, brokenness); to unmet needs (e.g., for validation, safety, protection); and thence to a response to those unmet needs in the form of self-compassion or assertive anger (research by Pascual-Leone, Timulak and colleagues). The many ways in which these different lines of theory development and research run parallel to and complement one another continue to point to the possibility of a larger synthesis with many useful clinical implications, and leads to a further question:

Question 6: How can therapists most effectively facilitate these client change processes? Answer: After focusing for so long on the evolution of client change processes, more precise research is just beginning on how therapists can best facilitate this evolution. At present, several promising leads are being pursued: (i) Therapist responses within the client's zone of proximal development, that are neither too behind or too far ahead the client's current state of progress are likely to be most effective. (ii) A balance is needed between, on the one hand, supportive/ following therapist responses that provide safety and openness and, on the other hand, challenging, process-guiding responses that offer clients opportunities to move forward when they are ready to do so. Clearly, much more research on therapist facilitation of client productive processes is needed.

Recommendations for Research, Practice, and Training

It is our view that the research reviewed here has important scientific and practical implications.

First, while the field of humanistic-experiential therapy research has continued to make substantial progress during the past 10 years, more research is clearly needed, particularly with client populations where clear recommendations are not yet possible, such as different types of anxiety, psychosis, particular medical conditions, and eating difficulties, and others. At the same time, more research on well-studied client problems such as depression are also needed, in order to bolster or upgrade the existing evidence, which runs the risk of becoming obsolete as standards for research evidence shift over time (e.g., requiring larger samples, RCTs, intent-to-treat analyses, and more sophisticated meta-analysis techniques). In addition, more research on different types of HEPs is needed, particularly comparing more vs. less process-guiding HEPs. In general, however, we are heartened by the continuing flow of HEP studies being produced.

Second, from a health care policy point of view, the available outcome data (almost 300 outcome studies) clearly support the proposition that HEPs are empirically supported by multiple lines of scientific evidence, including "gold standard" RCTs and recent large RCT-equivalent practice-based studies in the UK (e.g., Barkham & Saxon, 2018). This body of research suggests that the lists of empirically supported or evidence-based psychotherapies that have been constructed in various countries—the NICE Guidelines in the United Kingdom or the list of empirically supported treatments in the United States, for example—need to be updated with the type of evidence we have reviewed. HEPs should be offered to clients in national health service contexts and other mental health settings, and paid for by health insurance, especially for the well-evidenced client populations highlighted.

Third, there are two possible lessons to be learned from the negative results we have consistently identified for often non–bona fide supportive-nondirective therapies: On the one hand, if these results are due to negative researcher allegiance, the lesson is: Don't do therapies you don't believe in. On the other hand, it is possible that in general such nonspecific, nontargeted, non-process guiding therapies are just not as effective as CBT; in this case, if the choice is between a supportive-nondirective HEP and CBT, then clients should generally receive CBT. In other words, based on the large body of evidence we've reviewed over the past 30 years, we don't recommend supportive-nondirective therapies for use in routine practice situations, especially when these have been modified to make them less effective. Even here, however, the literature is full of exceptions this rule, where supportive-nondirective and CBT failed to differ in outcome.

Fourth, for those of us in the HEP tradition, the moral of this story continues to be that we do not need to be afraid of quantitative outcome research, including RCTs. Naturally, there are many problems and limitations with RCTs, just as there are with all research methods. Nevertheless, it is imperative that as humanistic-experiential therapists we do our own outcome research—including RCTs—on bona fide versions of our therapies and that we train more HEP researchers to carry out such studies. Beyond this, it is also essential that we collaborate with researchers from other therapeutic approaches on balanced-researcher-allegiance comparative RCTs, in order to achieve the level of equipoise in our studies needed to really understand the strengths and limitations of our approach.

Fifth, as for the specific research implications of our review, it certainly seems to us to illustrate the value of using a wide range of research methods, qualitative and quantitative, group and single case, to address questions of therapeutic change processes, effectiveness and efficacy. Furthermore, going forward it will be possible to make good use of this diverse range of research methods to bear on a more diverse range of clients, including those from more different countries, minority populations, LGBTQIA clients, and neuro-atypicals. At the same time, it is worth noting that our data indicate that the current emphasis on randomization in controlled and comparative outcome studies is misplaced: In fact, we once again found that randomization made no difference whatsoever in our meta-analysis. Although randomization is a useful research tool, nonrandomized studies, especially large-scale practice-based research, also need to be given significant weight in integrating research findings.

Sixth, it now appears to us that research alone will not suffice. The development of treatment guidelines in various countries has in our experience become increasingly politicized, with powerful interest groups dominating the committees charged with reviewing the evidence. These groups determine what counts as evidence, what evidence is reviewed, and how that evidence is interpreted as a basis for formulating treatment guidelines. We are particularly disturbed by the recent trend toward using increasingly opaque methods such as network analysis, which are built on questionable assumptions such as the equivalence of client populations, versions of a treatment, and research procedures (cf. Faltinsen et al., 2018). This is often portrayed as an objective, neutral process of making straightforward inferences from research evidence to the real world of practice. According to Bayesian statistics (e.g., Lynch, 2010), however, this is an instance of the logical fallacy of the "transposed conditional" (Siegfried, 2010): The famous "null hypothesis" against which we test our results only evaluates the likelihood of hypothetical inference from practice (the "real world") to our research results, not in the opposite direction, from our results to practice, which is the inference that we (and policymakers in general) want to make. Inference from evidence to practice only becomes possible when we factor in our prior expectations, that is, our researcher and reviewer theoretical allegiances. This means that it is critically important who reviews the research evidence and what their prior expectations or allegiances are. And that means that the guideline development committees that review research evidence will only produce valid and fair guidelines if they contain a balanced representation of researchers with varied theoretical allegiances. The implication for the supporters of HEPs is that they need to put pressure on guideline development bodies for proper representation.

Finally, we conclude as we did in our previous review (Elliott et al., 2013), with training implications. The neglect of HEPs in training programs and treatment guidelines is not warranted. Humanistic-experiential therapies should generally be offered in postgraduate programs and internships as an alternative to CBT, especially as treatments for depression, interpersonal difficulties, coping with chronic medical conditions and psychosis, and self-damaging activities, and possibly also to support clients with anxiety difficulties. Like CBT, HEPs are evidence-based for a wide range of client presenting problems and therefore need to be included in the education of psychotherapists.

ABBREVIATIONS

APA	American Psychological Association
APES	Assimilation of Problematic Experiences Scale
BDI	Beck Depression Inventory
CBT	cognitive behavioral therapy
CI	confidence interval
DAS	Dyadic Adjustment Scale
EFT	emotion(ally) focused therapy
ESw	effect size weighted
ESwc	effect size weighted comparative
GSI	global severity index
HEP	humanistic experiential psychotherapies
IIP	Inventory of Interpersonal Problems
IM	innovative moments
ITT	intention to treat
ITT-PO	intention to treat–primary outcome
LGBTQIA	lesbian, gay, bisexual, transgender, queer, intersex, and asexual
MI	motivational interviewing
NICE	National Institute for Health and Care Excellence
PCT	person-centered therapy
PP-All	per protocol–all
PP-PO	per protocol–primary outcome
PRISMA	Preferred Reporting Items for Systematic Reviews and Meta-Analyses
PTSD	post-traumatic stress disorder
RSE	Rosenberg Self-esteem
SCL-90-R	Symptom Checklist-90-R
ZPD	proximal level of development

REFERENCES

*Studies in the 2009–2018 outcome meta-analysis sample
§Studies in qualitative outcome meta-analysis

*Addington, J., Epstein, I., Liu, L., French, P., Boydell, K. M., & Zipursky, R. B. (2011). A randomized controlled trial of cognitive behavioral therapy for individuals at clinical high risk of psychosis. *Schizophrenia Research*, *125*(1), 54–61. https://doi.org/10.1016/j.schres.2010.10.015

*Alexopoulos, G. S., Raue, P. J., Kiosses, D. N., Mackin, R. S., Kanellopoulos, D., McCulloch, C., & Areán, P. A. (2011). Problem-solving therapy and supportive therapy in older adults with major depression and executive dysfunction: Effect on disability. *Archives of General Psychiatry*, *68*(1), 33–41. https://doi.org/10.1001/archgenpsychiatry.2010.177

American Psychological Association. (2019). *APA Practice Guidelines*. https://www.apa.org/practice/guidelines/index

Angus, L., & Greenberg, L. (2011). *Working with narrative in emotion-focused therapy: Changing stories, healing lives.* Washington DC: American Psychological Association.

Angus, L., Levitt, H., & Hardtke, K. (1999). The narrative processes coding system: Research applications and implications for psychotherapeutic practice. *Journal of Clinical Psychology, 55*(10), 1255–1270. https://doi.org/10.1002/(SICI)1097-4679(199910)55:10<1255::AID-JCLP7>3.0.CO;2-F

*Areán, P. A., Raue, P., Mackin, R. S., Kanellopoulos, D., McCulloch, C., & Alexopoulos, G. S. (2010). Problem-solving therapy and supportive therapy in older adults with major depression and executive dysfunction. *The American Journal of Psychiatry, 167*(11), 1391–1398. https://doi.org/10.1176/appi.ajp.2010.09091327

Arkowitz, H., Miller, W.R., & Rollnick, S. (eds.) (2015). *Motivational interviewing in the treatment of psychological problems* (2nd ed.). Guilford Press.

Auszra, L., Greenberg, L. S., & Herrmann, I. (2013). Client emotional productivity—optimal client in-session emotional processing in experiential therapy. *Psychotherapy Research, 23*(6), 732–746. https://doi.org/10.1080/10503307.2013.816882

Balmforth, J., & Elliott, R. (2012). 'I never talked about, ever': A comprehensive process analysis of a significant client disclosure event in therapy. *Counselling and Psychotherapy Research, 12*(1), 2–12. https://doi.org/10.1080/14733145.2011.580353

Barbosa, E., Couto, A.B., Basto, I., Stiles, W.B., Pinto-Gouveia, J. & Salgado, J. (2018) Immersion and distancing during assimilation of problematic experiences in a good-outcome case of emotion-focused therapy, *Psychotherapy Research, 28*(2), 313–327, https://doi.org/10.1080/10503307.2016.1211347

*Barkham, M., & Saxon, D. (2018). The effectiveness of high-intensity CBT and counselling alone and following low-intensity CBT: A reanalysis of the 2nd UK National Audit of Psychological Therapies data. *BMC Psychiatry, 18*(321), 1–5. https://doi.org/10.1186/s12888-018-1899-0

Barkham, M., Saxon, D., Hardy, G.E., Bradburn, M., Galloway, D., Wickramasekera, N., Keetharuth, A.D., Bower, P., King, M., Elliott, R., Gabriel, L., Kellett, S., Shaw, S., Wilkinson, T., Connell, J., Harrison, P., Ardern, K., Bishop-Edwards, L., Ashley, K., . . . Brazier, J.E. (2021). Clinical and cost-effectiveness of person-centred experiential therapy vs. cognitive behavioural therapy delivered in the English Improving Access to Psychological Therapies national program: A pragmatic randomised non-inferiority trial [PRaCTICED]. *The Lancet Psychiatry, 8*(6), 487–499. https://doi.org/10.1016/S2215-0366(21)00083-3

Baucom, D. H., Mueser, K. T., Shoham, V., & Daiuto, A. D. (1998). Empirically supported couple and family interventions for marital distress and adult mental health problems. *Journal of Consulting and Clinical Psychology, 66*(1), 53–88. https://doi.org/10.1037//0022-006x.66.1.53

*Bechdolf, A., Wagner, M., Ruhrmann, S., Harrigan, S., Putzfeld, V., Pukrop, R., Brockhaus-Dumke, A., Berning, J., Janssen, B., Decker, P., Bottlender, R., Maurer, K., Möller, H-J., Gaebel, W., Häfner, H., Maier, W., & Klosterkötter, J. (2012). Preventing progression to first-episode psychosis in early initial prodromal states. *The British Journal of Psychiatry, 200*(1), 22–29. https://doi.org/10.1192/bjp.bp.109.066357

*Boerhout, C., Swart, M., Van Busschbach, J. T., & Hoek, H. W. (2016). Effect of aggression regulation on eating disorder pathology: RCT of a brief body and movement oriented intervention. *European Eating Disorders Review, 24*(2), 114–121. https://doi.org/10.1002/erv.2429

Bohart, A. C., O'Hara, M. & Leitner, L. M. (1998). Empirically violated treatments: Disenfranchisement of humanistic and other psychotherapies. *Psychotherapy Research, 8*(2), 141–157. https://doi.org/10.1093/ptr/8.2.141

Boritz, T. Z., Angus, L., Monette, G., & Hollis-Walker, L. (2008). An empirical analysis of autobiographical memory specificity subtypes in brief emotion-focused and client-centered treatments of depression. *Psychotherapy Research, 18*(5), 584–593. https://doi.org/10.1080/10503300802123245

Boritz, T. Z., Angus, L., Monette, G., Hollis-Walker, L., & Warwar, S. (2011). Narrative and emotion integration in psychotherapy: Investigating the relationship between autobiographical memory specificity and expressed emotional arousal in brief emotion-focused and client-centred treatments of depression. *Psychotherapy Research, 21*(1), 16–26. https://doi.org/10.1080/10503307.2010.504240

Boritz, T., Barnhart, R., Angus, L., & Constantino, M. J. (2017). Narrative flexibility in brief psychotherapy for depression. *Psychotherapy Research, 27*(6), 666–676. https://doi.org/10.1080/10503307.2016.1152410

*Bowles, T. (2012). Developing adaptive change capabilities through client-centred therapy. *Behaviour Change, 29*(4), 258–271. https://doi.org/10.1017/bec.2012.24

*Brach, M., Sabariego, C., Herschbach, P., Berg, P., Engst-Hastreiter, U., & Stucki, G. (2010). Cost-effectiveness of cognitive-behavioral group therapy for dysfunctional fear of progression in chronic arthritis patients. *Journal of Public Health, 32*(4), 547–554. https://doi.org/10.1093/pubmed/fdq022

*Breitbart, W., Rosenfeld, B., Gibson, C., Pessin, H., Poppito, S., Nelson, C., Tomarken, A., Timm, A.K., Berg, A., Jacobson, C., Sorger, B., Abbey, J. & Olden, M. (2010). Meaning-centered group psychotherapy for patients with advanced cancer: A pilot randomized controlled trial. *Psycho-Oncology, 19*(1), 21–28. https://doi.org/10.1002/pon.1556

*Breitbart, W., Rosenfeld, B., Pessin, H., Applebaum, A., Kulikowski, J., & Lichtenthal, W. G. (2015). Meaning-centered group psychotherapy: An effective intervention for improving psychological well-being in patients with advanced cancer. *Journal of Clinical Oncology, 33*(7), 749–754. https://doi.org/10.1200/JCO.2014.57.2198

Breitbart, W.S., & Poppito, S.R. (2014). *Meaning-centered group psychotherapy for patients with advanced cancer: A treatment manual.* Oxford University Press; 2014.

*Brenes, G. A., Danhauer, S. C., Lyles, M. F., Anderson, A., & Miller, M. E. (2016). Effects of telephone-delivered cognitive-behavioral therapy and nondirective supportive therapy on sleep, health-related quality of life, and disability. *The American Journal of Geriatric Psychiatry, 24*(10), 846–854. https://doi.org/10.1016/j.jagp.2016.04.002

*Brenes, G. A., Danhauer, S. C., Lyles, M. F., Anderson, A., & Miller, M. E. (2017). Long-term effects of telephone-delivered psychotherapy for late-life GAD. *The American Journal of Geriatric Psychiatry, 25*(11), 1249–1257. https://doi.org/10.1016/j.jagp.2017.05.013

*Brenes, G. A., Danhauer, S. C., Lyles, M. F., Hogan, P. E., & Miller, M. E. (2015). Telephone-delivered cognitive behavioral therapy and telephone-delivered nondirective supportive therapy for rural older adults with generalized anxiety disorder: A randomized clinical trial. *JAMA Psychiatry, 72*(10), 1012–1020. https://doi.org/10.1001/jamapsychiatry.2015.1154

Brennan, M. A., Emmerling, M. E., & Whelton, W. J. (2015). Emotion-focused group therapy: Addressing self-criticism in the treatment of eating disorders. *Counselling and Psychotherapy Research, 15*(1), 67–75. https://doi.org/10.1080/14733145.2014.914549

*Butollo, W., Karl, R., König, J., & Rosner, R. (2016). A randomized controlled clinical trial of dialogical exposure therapy versus cognitive processing therapy for adult outpatients suffering from PTSD after type I trauma in adulthood. *Psychotherapy and Psychosomatics, 85*(1), 16–26. https://doi.org/10.1159/000440726

*Brownlow, J.A., McLean, C. P., Gehrman, P. R., Harb, G. C., Ross, R.J., & Foa, E. B. (2016). Influence of sleep disturbance on global functioning after posttraumatic stress disorder treatment. *Journal of Traumatic Stress, 29*(6), 515–521. https://doi.org/10.1002/jts.22139

*Burgess Moser, M., Johnson, S. M., Dalgleish, T. L., Lafontaine, M.-F., Wiebe, S. A., & Tasca, G. A. (2016). Changes in relationship-specific attachment in emotionally focused couple therapy. *Journal of Marital and Family Therapy, 42*(2), 231–245. https://doi.org/10.1111/jmft.12139

*Butollo, W., Karl, R., König, J., & Rosner, R. (2016). A randomized controlled clinical trial of dialogical exposure therapy versus cognitive processing therapy for adult outpatients suffering from PTSD after type I trauma in adulthood. *Psychotherapy and Psychosomatics, 85*(1), 16–26. https://doi.org/10.1159/000440726

Cain, D.J., Keenen, K., & Rubin, S. (Eds.). (2016). *Humanistic psychotherapies: Handbook of research and practice* (2nd ed.). American Psychological Association.

*Carlson, L. E., Beattie, T. L., Giese-Davis, J., Faris, P., Tamagawa, R., Fick, L. J., Degelman, E.S., & Speca, M. (2015). Mindfulness-based cancer recovery and supportive-expressive therapy maintain telomere length relative to controls in distressed breast cancer survivors. *Cancer, 121*(3), 476–484. https://doi.org/10.1002/cncr.29063

*Carlson, L. E., Doll, R., Stephen, J., Faris, P., Tamagawa, R., Drysdale, E., & Speca, M. (2013). Randomized controlled trial of mindfulness-based cancer recovery versus supportive expressive group therapy for distressed survivors of breast cancer. *Journal of Clinical Oncology, 31*(25), 3119–3126. https://doi.org/10.1200/JCO.2012.47.5210

*Carlson, L. E., Rouleau, C. R., Speca, M., Robinson, J., & Bultz, B. D. (2017). Brief supportive-expressive group therapy for partners of men with early stage prostate cancer: Lessons learned from a negative randomized controlled trial. *Supportive Care in Cancer*, 25(4), 1035–1041. https://doi.org/10.1007/s00520-016-3551-1

*Carlson, L. E., Tamagawa, R., Stephen, J., Drysdale, E., Zhong, L., & Speca, M. (2016). Randomized-controlled trial of mindfulness-based cancer recovery versus supportive expressive group therapy among distressed breast cancer survivors (MINDSET): Long-term follow-up results. *Psycho-Oncology*, 25(7), 750–759. https://doi.org/10.1002/pon.4150

Carrick, L. (2014). Person-centred counsellors' experiences of working with clients in crisis: A qualitative interview study. *Counselling and Psychotherapy Research*, 14(4), 272–280. https://doi.org/10.1080/14733145.2013.819931

Carryer, J. R., & Greenberg, L. S. (2010). Optimal levels of emotional arousal in experiential therapy of depression. *Journal of Consulting and Clinical Psychology*, 78(2), 190–199. https://doi.org/10.1037/a0018401

Chadwick, P. D. J. (2019). Mindfulness for psychosis: A humanising therapeutic process. *Current Opinion in Psychology*, 28, 317–320. https://doi.org/10.1016/j.copsyc.2019.07.022

Chambless, D. L., & Hollon, S. D. (1998). Defining empirically supported therapies. *Journal of Consulting and Clinical Psychology*, 66(1), 7–18. https://doi.org/10.1037/0022-006X.66.1.7

*Cho, W.-C., & Chen, C.-S. (2011). The effects of Gestalt group therapy on college experiences parental divorced in childhood. *Chinese Journal of Guidance and Counseling*, 30(3), 69–100.

Choi, B. H., Pos, A. E., & Magnusson, M. S. (2016). Emotional change process in resolving self-criticism during experiential treatment of depression. *Psychotherapy Research*, 26(4), 484–499. https://doi.org/10.1080/10503307.2015.1041433

*Compare, A., Calugi, S., Marchesini, G., Molinari, E., & Dalle Grave, R. (2013). Emotion-focused therapy and dietary counseling for obese patients with binge eating disorder: A propensity score-adjusted study. *Psychotherapy and Psychosomatics*, 82(3), 193–194. https://doi.org/10.1159/000343209

*Compare, A., Calugi, S., Marchesini, G., Shonin, E., Grossi, E., Molinari, E., & Dalle Grave, R. (2013). Emotionally focused group therapy and dietary counseling in binge eating disorder. Effect on eating disorder psychopathology and quality of life. *Appetite*, 71, 361–368. https://doi.org/10.1016/j.appet.2013.09.007

*Cooper, M., McGinnis, S., & Carrick, L. (2014). School-based humanistic counselling for psychological distress in young people: A practice research network to address the attrition problem. *Counselling & Psychotherapy Research*, 14(3), 201–211. https://doi.org/10.1080/14733145.2014.929415

*Cooper, M., Rowland, N., McArthur, K., Pattison, S., Cromarty, K., & Richards, K. (2010). Randomised controlled trial of school-based humanistic counselling for emotional distress in young people: feasibility study and preliminary indications of efficacy. *Child and Adolescent Psychiatry and Mental Health*, 4(12). https://doi.org/10.1186/1753-2000-4-12.

Cooper, M., Watson, J. C., & Hölldampf, D. (Eds.). (2010). *Person-centred and experiential therapies work: A review of the research on counselling, psychotherapy and related practices*. PCCS Books.

Cooper, P. J., Murray, L., Wilson, A., & Romaniuk, H. (2003). Controlled trial of the short- and long-term effect of psychological treatment of post-partum depression. *The British Journal of Psychiatry*, 182(5), 412–419. https://doi.org/10.1192/bjp.182.5.412

*Cornish, M. A., & Wade, N. G. (2015). Working through past wrongdoing: Examination of a self-forgiveness counseling intervention. *Journal of Counseling Psychology*, 62(3), 521–528. https://doi.org/10.1037/cou0000080

*Cottraux, J., Note, I. D., Boutitie, F., Milliery, M., Genouihlac, V., Yao, S. N., Note, B., Mollard, E., Bonasse, F., Gaillard, S., Djamoussian, D., Guillard, C.d.M., Culem, A., & Gueyffier, F. (2009). Cognitive therapy versus Rogerian supportive therapy in borderline personality disorder. Two-year follow-up of a controlled pilot study. *Psychotherapy and Psychosomatics*, 78(5), 307–316. https://doi.org/10.1159/000229769

Cuijpers, P., Driessen, E., Hollon, S.D., van Oppen, P. Barth, J., & Andersson, G. (2012). The efficacy of non-directive supportive therapy for adult depression: A meta-analysis *Clinical Psychology Review*, 32(4), 280–291. https://doi.org/10.1016/j.cpr.2012.01.003

Cunha, C., Gonçalves, M. M., Hill, C. E., Mendes, I., Ribeiro, A. P., Sousa, I., Angus, L., & Greenberg, L. S. (2012). Therapist interventions and client innovative moments in emotion-focused therapy for depression. *Psychotherapy*, 49(4), 536–548. http://dx.doi.org/10.1037/a0028259

Cunha, C., Mendes, I., Ribeiro, A. P., Angus, L., Greenberg, L. S., & Gonçalves, M. M. (2017). Self-narrative reconstruction in emotion-focused therapy: A preliminary task analysis. *Psychotherapy Research*, 27(6), 692–709. https://doi.org/10.1080/10503307.2016.1158429

Daldrup, R., Beutler, L., Engle, D., & Greenberg, L. (1988). *Focused expressive therapy: Freeing the overcontrolled patient*. Cassell.

§Dale, P., Allen, J., & Measor, L. (1998). Counselling adults who were abused as children: Clients' perceptions of efficacy, client-counsellor communication, and dissatisfaction. *British Journal of Guidance and Counselling*, 26(2), 141–157. https://doi.org/10.1080/03069889800760151

Dekeyser, M., Prouty, G., & Elliott, R. (2008). Pre-therapy process and outcome: A review of research instruments and findings. *Person-Centered and Experiential Psychotherapies*, 7(1), 37–55. https://doi.org/10.1080/14779757.2008.9688451

*Diamond, G. M., Shahar, B., Sabo, D., & Tsvieli, N. (2016). Attachment-based family therapy and emotion-focused therapy for unresolved anger: The role of productive emotional processing. *Psychotherapy*, 53(1), 34–44. https://doi.org/10.1037/pst0000025

DiClemente, C.C., Corno, C.M., Graydon, M.M., Wiprovnick, A.E., & Knoblach, D.J. (2017). Motivational interviewing, enhancement, and brief interventions over the last decade: A review of reviews of efficacy and effectiveness. *Psychology of Addictive Behaviors*, 31(8), 862–887. https://doi.org/10.1037/adb0000318

Dillon, A., Timulak, L., & Greenberg, L. S. (2018). Transforming core emotional pain in a course of emotion-focused therapy for depression: A case study. *Psychotherapy Research*, 28(3), 406–422. https://doi.org/10.1080/10503307.2016.1233364

*Dogan, T. (2010). The effects of psychodrama on young adults' attachment styles. *The Arts in Psychotherapy*, 37(2), 112–119. https://doi.org/10.1016/j.aip.2010.02.001

*Edwards, S. D., & Edwards, D. J. (2009). Counselling for psychological well-being in persons living with HIV/AIDS. *Journal of Psychology in Africa*, 19(4), 561–564. https://doi.org/10.1080/14330237.2009.10820329

*Ehlers, A., Hackmann, A., Grey, N., Wild, J., Liness, S., Albert, I., Deale, A., Stott, R., & Clark, D. M. (2014). A randomized controlled trial of 7-day intensive and standard weekly cognitive therapy for PTSD and emotion-focused supportive therapy. *The American Journal of Psychiatry*, 171(3), 294–304. http://doi.org/10.1176/appi.ajp.2013.13040552.

Elliott, R. (1996). Are client-centered/experiential therapies effective? A meta-analysis of outcome research. In U. Esser, H. Pabst, G-W Speierer (Eds.), *The power of the Person-Centered-Approach: New challenges-perspectives-answers* (pp. 125–138). Köln, Germany: GwG Verlag.

§Elliott, R. (2002a). Hermeneutic single case efficacy design. *Psychotherapy Research*, 12(1), 1–20. https://doi.org/10.1080/713869614

§Elliott, R. (2002b). Render unto Caesar: Quantitative and qualitative knowing in research on humanistic therapies. *Person-Centered and Experiential Psychotherapies*, 1(1–2), 102–117. https://doi.org/10.1080/14779757.2002.9688281

Elliott, R. (2010). Psychotherapy change process research: Realizing the promise. *Psychotherapy Research*, 20(2), 123–135. https://doi.org/10.1080/10503300903470743

*Elliott, R. (2013). Person-centered-experiential psychotherapy for anxiety difficulties: Theory, research and practice. *Person-Centered and Experiential Psychotherapies*, 12(1), 16–32. https://doi.org/10.1080/14779757.2013.767750

Elliott, R., Bohart, A.C., Watson, J.C., & Greenberg, L.S. (2019). Empathy. In J. C. Norcross & M. J. Lambert (Eds.), *Psychotherapy relationships that work: Evidence-based therapist contributions* (3rd ed) (Volume 1, pp. 245–287). Oxford University Press.

§Elliott, R., Clark, C., Kemeny, V., Wexler, M. M., Mack, C., & Brinkerhoff, L. J. (1990). The impact of experiential therapy on depression: The first ten cases. In G. Lietaer, J. Rombauts, & R. Van Balen (Eds.), *Client-centered and experiential psychotherapy in the nineties* (pp. 549–578). Katholieke Universiteit Leuven.

Elliott, R., Greenberg, L. S., & Lietaer, G. (2004). Research on experiential psychotherapies. In M. J. Lambert (Ed.), *Bergin & Garfield's handbook of psychotherapy and behaviour change* (5th ed., pp. 493–540). Wiley.

§Elliott, R., Partyka, R., Wagner, J., Alperin, R., Dobrenski. R., Messer, S. B., Watson, J.C., & Castonguay, L. G. (2009). An adjudicated hermeneutic single-case efficacy design of experiential therapy for panic/phobia. *Psychotherapy Research*, *19*(4–5), 543–557. https://doi.org/10.1080/10503300902905947

*Elliott, R, Rodgers, B., Stephen, S., Carrock, L. Cooper, M. & Berdondini, L. (2018) *Emotion-focused and person-centred therapies for social anxiety: a pilot comparative outcome study*. Unpublished manuscript.

Elliott, R., Silva, E., & Almeida, S. (October, 2014). *Emotion-Focused Therapy for people with cancer*. Workshop presented at conference of the International Psycho-Oncology Society, Lisbon, Portugal.

Elliott, R., Stiles, W. B., & Shapiro, D. A. (1993). Are some psychotherapies more equivalent than others? In T. R. Giles (Ed.), *Handbook of effective psychotherapy* (pp. 455–479). Plenum Press.

Elliott, R., Watson, J.C., Goldman, R.N., & Greenberg, L.S. (2004). *Learning emotion-focused therapy: The process-experiential approach to change*. American Psychological Association.

Elliott, R., Watson, J., Greenberg, L.S., Timulak, L., & Freire, E. (2013). Research on humanistic-experiential psychotherapies. In M.J. Lambert (Ed.), *Bergin & Garfield's handbook of psychotherapy and behavior change* (6th ed.) (pp. 495–538). Wiley.

Ellis, L. A. (2016). Qualitative changes in recurrent PTSD nightmares after focusing-oriented dreamwork. *Dreaming*, *26*(3), 185. https://doi.org/10.1037/drm0000031

Faltinsen, E.G., Storebø, O.J., Jakobsen, J.C., Boesen, K., Lange, T., & Gluud, C. (2018). Network meta-analysis: the highest level of medical evidence? *BMJ Evidence-Based Medicine*, *23*(2), 56–59. https://doi.org/10.1136/bmjebm-2017-110887

Farber, B.A., & Doolin, E.M. (2011). Positive regard and affirmation. In J. Norcross (ed.), *Psychotherapy relationships that work* (2nd ed.) (pp. 168–186). Oxford University Press.

Farber, B.A. & Suzuki, J.Y., & Lynch, D.A. (2019) Positive regard and affirmation. In J.C. Norcross & M.J. Lambert, (Eds.), *Psychotherapy relationships that work: Evidence-based therapist contributions* (3rd ed.) (Volume 1, pp. 288–322). Oxford University Press.

Fernández-Navarro, P, Rosa, C, Sousa, I, et al. (2018). Reconceptualization innovative moments as a predictor of symptomatology improvement in treatment for depression. *Clinical Psychology & Psychotherapy*, *25*(6), 765–773. https://doi.org/10.1002/cpp.2306

*Fillion, L., Duval, S., Dumont, S., Gagnon, P., Tremblay, I., Bairati, I., & Breitbart, W. S. (2009). Impact of a meaning-centered intervention on job satisfaction and on quality of life among palliative care nurses. *Psycho-Oncology*, *18*(12), 1300–1310. https://doi.org/10.1002/pon.1513

Flückiger, C., Del Re, A.C., Wampold, B.E. & Horvath, A.O. (2019). Alliance in adult psychotherapy. In J.C. Norcross & M.J. Lambert (Eds)., *Psychotherapy relationships that work: Evidence-based therapist contributions* (3rd ed.) (Volume 1, pp. 24–78). Oxford University Press.

*Foa, E. B., McLean, C. P., Capaldi, S., & Rosenfield, D. (2013). Prolonged exposure vs. supportive counseling for sexual abuse–related PTSD in adolescent girls: A randomized clinical trial. *JAMA*, *310*(24), 2650–2657. https://doi.org/10.1001/jama.2013.282829

*Ford, J. D., Chang, R., Levine, J., & Zhang, W. (2013). Randomized clinical trial comparing affect regulation and supportive group therapies for victimization-related PTSD with incarcerated women. *Behavior Therapy*, *44*(2), 262–276. https://doi.org/10.1016/j.beth.2012.10.003

Fosha, D. (2000). *The transforming power of affect: A model of accelerated change*. Basic Books.

*Freire, E., Williams, C., Messow, C.-M., Cooper, M., Elliott, R., McConnachie, A., Walker, A., Heard, D., & Morrison, J. (2015). Counselling versus low-intensity cognitive behavioural therapy for persistent sub-threshold and mild depression (CLICD): a pilot/feasibility randomised controlled trial. *BMC Psychiatry*, *15*(197). https://doi.org/10.1186/s12888-015-0582-y

*Gambatesa, M., D'Ambrosio, A., D'Antini, D., Mirabella, L., De Capraris, A., Iuso, S., Bellomo, A., Macchiarola, A., Dambrosio, M., & Cinnella, G. (2013). Counseling, quality of life, and acute postoperative pain in elderly patients with hip fracture. *Journal of Multidisciplinary Healthcare*, *6*, 335–346. https://doi.org/10.2147/JMDH.S48240

Gendlin, E. T. (1970). A theory of personality change. In J. T. Hart & T. M. Tomlinson (Eds.), *New directions in client-centered therapy* (pp. 129–173). Houghton Mifflin.

Gendlin, E. T. (1981). *Focusing*. Bantam Books.

Gendlin, E. T. (1996). *Focusing-oriented psychotherapy: A manual of the experiential method*. Guilford Press.

Gilbert, P. (2009). *The compassionate mind*. Constable & Robinson.

Goldman, R. N., Greenberg, L. S., & Angus, L. (2006). The effects of adding emotion-focused interventions to the client-centered relationship conditions in the treatment of depression. *Psychotherapy Research*, *16*(5), 537–549. https://doi.org/10.1080/10503300600589456

Gonçalves, M. M., Ribeiro, A. P., Mendes, I., Matos, M., & Santos, A. (2011). Tracking novelties in psychotherapy process research: The innovative moments coding system. *Psychotherapy Research*, *21*(5), 497–509. https://doi.org/10.1080/10503307.2011.560207

*Grassi, L., Sabato, S., Rossi, E., Marmai, L., & Biancosino, B. (2009). Effects of supportive-expressive group therapy in breast cancer patients with affective disorders: A pilot study. *Psychotherapy and Psychosomatics*, *79*(1), 39–47. https://doi.org/10.1159/000259416

Greenberg, L. S. (1979). Resolving splits: The two-chair technique. *Psychotherapy: Theory, Research and Practice*, *16*(3), 316–324. https://doi.org/10.1037/h0085895

Greenberg, L. S. (2007). A guide to conducting a task analysis of psychotherapeutic change. *Psychotherapy Research*, *17*(1), 15–30. https://doi.org/10.1080/10503300600720390

Greenberg, L. S. (2019). Theory of functioning in emotion-focused therapy. In L. S. Greenberg & R. N. Goldman (Eds.), *Clinical handbook of emotion-focused therapy* (pp. 37–59). American Psychological Association. http://dx.doi.org/10.1037/0000112-002

Greenberg, L. S., & Elliott, R. (2012). Corrective experience from a humanistic/experiential perspective. In L. G. Castonguay & C. E. Hill (Eds.), *Transformation in psychotherapy: Corrective experiences across cognitive behavioral, humanistic, and psychodynamic approaches* (pp. 85–101). American Psychological Association.

Greenberg, L. S., Elliott, R., & Lietaer, G. (1994). Research on humanistic and experiential psychotherapies. In A. E. Bergin & S. L. Garfield (Eds.), *Handbook of psychotherapy and behavior change* (4th ed., pp. 509–539). Wiley.

Greenberg, L. S., & Foerster, F. (1996). Resolving unfinished business: The process of change. *Journal of Consulting and Clinical Psychology*, *64*(2), 439–446. https://doi.org/10.1037/0022-006X.70.2.406

Greenberg, L. S. & Johnson, S. M (1988). *Emotionally focused therapy for couples*. New York, NY: Guilford Press.

Greenberg, L. S., & Malcolm, W. (2002). Resolving unfinished business: Relating process to outcome. *Journal of Consulting and Clinical Psychology*, *70*(2), 406–416. https://doi.org/10.1037/0022-006X.70.2.406

Greenberg, L. S., Rice, L. N., & Elliott, R. (1993). *Facilitating emotional change: The moment-by-moment process*. Guilford Press.

Greenberg, L. J., Warwar, S. H., & Malcolm, W. M. (2008). Differential effects of emotion-focused therapy and psychoeducation in facilitating forgiveness and letting go of emotional injuries. *Journal of Counseling Psychology*, *55*(2), 185–196. https://doi.org/10.1037/0022-0167.55.2.185

*Greenberg, L., Warwar, S., & Malcolm, W. (2010). Emotion-focused couples therapy and the facilitation of forgiveness. *Journal of Marital and Family Therapy*, *36*(1), 28–42. https://doi.org/10.1111/j.1752–0606.2009.00185.x

Greenberg, L. S., & Watson, J. (1998). Experiential therapy of depression: Differential effects of client-centered relationship conditions and process experiential interventions. *Psychotherapy Research*, *8*(2), 210–224. https://doi.org/10.1093/ptr/8.2.210

Gunst, E., & Vanhooren, S. (2018). The destructive pattern: an experiential and existential theory-building case study. *Person-Centered & Experiential Psychotherapies*, *17*(1), 1–18. https://doi.org/10.1080/14779757.2017.1396239

*Hagl, M., Powell, S., Rosner, R., & Butollo, W. (2015). Dialogical exposure with traumatically bereaved Bosnian women: findings from a controlled trial. *Clinical Psychology & Psychotherapy*, *22*(6), 604–618. https://doi.org/10.1002/cpp.1921

*Hazrati, M., Hamid, T. A., Ibrahim, R., Hassan, S. A., Sharif, F., & Bagheri, Z. (2017). The effect of emotional focused intervention on spousal emotional abuse and marital satisfaction among elderly married couples:

A randomized controlled trial. *International Journal of Community Based Nursing and Midwifery*, 5(4), 329–334. Retrieved from cmedm. (29043279)

Hendricks, M. (2002). Focusing-oriented/experiential psychotherapy. In D. Cain & J. Seeman (Eds.), *Humanistic psychotherapies: Handbook of research and practice* (pp. 221–251). American Psychological Association.

Herrmann, I.R., Greenberg, L.S. & Auszra, L. (2016) Emotion categories and patterns of change in experiential therapy for depression, *Psychotherapy Research*, 26(2), 178–195. https://doi.org/10.1080/10503307 .2014.958597

*Herschbach, P., Berg, P., Waadt, S., Duran, G., Engst-Hastreiter, U., Henrich, G., Book, K., & Dinkel, A. (2010a). Group psychotherapy of dysfunctional fear of progression in patients with chronic arthritis or cancer. *Psychotherapy and Psychosomatics*, 79(1), 31–38. https://doi.org/10.1159/000254903

*Herschbach, P., Book, K., Dinkel, A., Berg, P., Waadt, S., Duran, G., Engst-Hastreiter, U., & Henrich, G. (2010). Evaluation of two group therapies to reduce fear of progression in cancer patients. *Supportive Care in Cancer*, 18(4), 471–479. https://doi.org/10.1007/s00520-009-0696-1

Hill, C. E. (2019). *Helping skills: Facilitating exploration, insight, and action.* (5th ed.). American Psychological Association.

*Ho, R. T. H., Fong, T. C. T., Lo, P. H. Y., Ho, S. M. Y., Lee, P. W. H., Leung, P. P. Y., Spiegel, D., & Chan, C. L. W. (2016). Randomized controlled trial of supportive-expressive group therapy and body-mind-spirit intervention for Chinese non-metastatic breast cancer patients. *Supportive Care in Cancer*, 24(12), 4929–4937. https://doi.org/10.1007/s00520-016-3350-8

Holden, J. M., Sagovsky, R., & Cox, J. L. (1989). Counselling in a general practice setting: Controlled study of health visitor intervention in treatment of postnatal depression. *British Medical Journal*, 298(6668), 223–226. https:// doi.org/10.1136/bmj.298.6668.223

Johnson, S. M., Makinen, J. A., & Millikin, J. W. (2001). Attachment injuries in couple relationships: A new perspective on impasses in couples therapy. *Journal of Marital and Family Therapy*, 27(2), 145–155. https://doi .org/10.1111/j.1752-0606.2001.tb01152.x

*Kaczkurkin, A. N., Asnaani, A., Zhong, J., & Foa, E. B. (2016). The moderating effect of state anger on treatment outcome in female adolescents with PTSD. *Journal of Traumatic Stress*, 29(4), 325–331. https://doi. org/10.1002/jts.22116

*Karataş, Z. (2011). Investigating the effects of group practice performed using psychodrama techniques on adolescents' conflict resolution skills. *Kuram ve Uygulamada Eğitim Bilimleri [Educational Sciences: Theory & Practice]*, 11(2), 609–614.

*Karataş, Z., & Gökçakan, D. Z. (2009). [The effect of group-based psychodrama therapy on decreasing the level of aggression in adolescents]. *Turk Psikiyatri Dergisi [Turkish Journal of Psychiatry]*, 20(4), 357–366.

*Kay-Lambkin, F. J., Baker, A. L., Kelly, B., & Lewin, T. J. (2011). Clinician-assisted computerised versus therapist-delivered treatment for depressive and addictive disorders: a randomised controlled trial. *The Medical Journal of Australia*, 195(3), S44–S50. https://doi.org/10.5694/j.1326-5377.2011 .tb03265.x

Kepner, J. (1993). *Body process: Working with the body in psychotherapy.* San Francisco, CA: Jossey-Bass.

*Kiosses, D. N., Arean, P. A., Teri, L., & Alexopoulos, G. S. (2010). Home-delivered problem adaptation therapy (PATH) for depressed, cognitively impaired, disabled elders: A preliminary study. *The American Journal of Geriatric Psychiatry*, 18(11), 988–998. https://doi.org/10.1097/ JGP.0b013e3181d6947d

*Kiosses, D.N., Ravdin, L. D., Gross, J.J., Raue, P., Kotbi, N., & Alexopoulos, G. S. (2015). Problem adaptation therapy for older adults with major depression and cognitive impairment: a randomized clinical trial. *JAMA Psychiatry*, 72(1), 22–30. https://doi.org/10.1001/jamapsychiatry.2014.1305

Klein, M. H., Mathieu-Coughlan, P. L., & Kiesler, D. J. (1986). The experiencing scales. In L. S. Greenberg & W. M. Pinsof (Eds.), *The psychotherapeutic process: A research handbook* (pp. 21–71). Guilford Press.

§Klein, M. J., & Elliott, R. (2006). Client accounts of personal change in process-experiential psychotherapy: A methodologically pluralistic approach. *Psychotherapy Research*, 16(1), 91–105. https://doi.org/10 .1080/10503300500090993

*Kocsis, J. H., Gelenberg, A. J., Rothbaum, B. O., Klein, D. N., Trivedi, M. H., Manber, R., Keller, M. B., Leon, A. C., Wisniewski, S. R., Arnow, B. A.,

Markowitz, J. C., & Thase, M. E. (2009). Cognitive behavioral analysis system of psychotherapy and brief supportive psychotherapy for augmentation of antidepressant nonresponse in chronic depression: The REVAMP trial. *Archives of General Psychiatry*, 66(11), 1178–1188. https:// doi.org/10.1001/archgenpsychiatry.2009.144

Kolden, G.G., Wang, C-C, Austin, S.B., Chang, Y., & Klein, M.H. (2019) Congruence / Genuineness. In J.C. Norcross & M.J. Lambert (Eds)., *Psychotherapy relationships that work: Evidence-based therapist contributions* (3rd ed.) (Volume 1, pp. 323–350). New York: Oxford University Press.

*König, J., Karl, R., Rosner, R., & Butollo, W. (2014). Sudden gains in two psychotherapies for posttraumatic stress disorder. *Behaviour Research and Therapy*, 60, 15–22. https://doi.org/10.1016/j.brat.2014.06.005

*Koszycki, D., Bisserbe, J.-C., Blier, P., Bradwejn, J., & Markowitz, J. (2012). Interpersonal psychotherapy versus brief supportive therapy for depressed infertile women: First pilot randomized controlled trial. *Archives of Women's Mental Health*, 15(3), 193–201. https://doi.org/10.1007/s00737-012-0277-z

*Kraljević, R. (2011). Neki indikatorl promjena nakon podrške roditeľjima djece s posebnim potrebama primjenom Integrativnog Gestalt pristupa. = Indicators of changes after organized integrative Gestalt support to parents of children with special needs. *Hrvatska Revija Za Rehabilitacijska Istraživanja [Croatian Journal of Rehabilitation Research]*, 47(1), 41–48. Accessed at: https://hrcak.srce.hr/63441

*Leung, G. S. M., & Khor, S. H. (2017). Gestalt intervention groups for anxious parents in Hong Kong: A quasi-experimental design. *Journal of Evidence-Informed Social Work*, 14(3), 183–200. https://doi.org/10.1080/23761407 .2017.1311814

*Leung, G. S. M., Leung, T. Y. K., & Ng, M. L. T. (2013). An outcome study of gestalt-oriented growth workshops. *International Journal of Group Psychotherapy*, 63(1), 117–125. https://doi.org/10.1521/ijgp.2013.63 .1.117

§Lipkin, S. (1954). Clients' feelings and attitudes in relation to the outcome of client-centered therapy. *Psychological Monographs*, 68(1), 1–30. https://doi .org/10.1037/h0093661

Lipsey, M. W., & Wilson, D. B. (1993). The efficacy of psychological, educational, and behavioral treatment: Confirmation from meta-analysis. *American Psychologist*, 48(12), 1181–1209. https://doi.org/10.1037//0003-066x.48.12.1181

Lipsey, M. W., & Wilson, D. B. (2001). *Practical meta-analysis.* Thousand Oaks, CA: Sage.

Luborsky, L., Diguer, L., Seligman, D. A., Rosenthal, R., Krause, E. D., Johnson, S., Halperin, G., Bishop, M., Berman, J. S., & Schweizer, E. (1999). The researcher's own therapy allegiances: A "wild card" in comparisons of treatment efficacy. *Clinical Psychology: Science and Practice*, 6(1), 95–106. https://doi.org/10.1093/clipsy.6.1.95

Lundahl, B. W., Kunz, C., Brownell, C., Tollefson, D., & Burke, B. L. (2010). A meta-analysis of motivational interviewing: Twenty-five years of empirical studies. *Research on Social Work Practice*, 20(2), 137–160. https://doi .org/10.1177/1049731509347850

Lynch, S. (2010). *Introduction to applied bayesian statistics and estimation for social scientists.* Springer.

§MacLeod, R., & Elliott, R. (2014). Nondirective Person-centered therapy for social anxiety: a hermeneutic single-case efficacy design study of a good outcome case. *Person-Centered & Experiential Psychotherapies*, 13(4), 294–311. https://doi.org/10.1080/14779757.2014.910133

§MacLeod, R., Elliott, R., & Rodgers, B. (2012). Process-experiential/emotion-focused therapy for social anxiety: A hermeneutic single-case efficacy design study. *Psychotherapy Research*, 22(1), 67–81. https://doi.org/10.1080/ 10503307.2011.626805

*Magidson, J. F., Gorka, S. M., MacPherson, L., Hopko, D. R., Blanco, C., Lejuez, C. W., & Daughters, S. B. (2011). Examining the effect of the Life Enhancement Treatment for Substance Use (LETS ACT) on residential substance abuse treatment retention. *Addictive Behaviors*, 36(6), 615–623. https://doi.org/10.1016/j.addbeh.2011.01.016

Makinen, J. A., & Johnson, S. M. (2006). Resolving attachment injuries in couples using emotionally focused therapy: Steps toward forgiveness and reconciliation. *Journal of Consulting and Clinical Psychology*, 74(6), 1055. https://doi.org/10.1037/0022-006X.74.6.1055

Malin, A.J., & Pos, A.E. (2015) The impact of early empathy on alliance building, emotional processing, and outcome during experiential treatment of depression, *Psychotherapy Research, 25*(4), 445–459. https://doi.org/10.1080/10503307.2014.901572

*Manne, S. L., Siegel, S. D., Heckman, C. J., & Kashy, D. A. (2016). A randomized clinical trial of a supportive versus a skill-based couple-focused group intervention for breast cancer patients. *Journal of Consulting and Clinical Psychology, 84*(8), 668–681. https://doi.org/10.1037/ccp0000110

*Marriott, M., & Kellett, S. (2009). Evaluating a cognitive analytic therapy service; practice-based outcomes and comparisons with person-centred and cognitive-behavioural therapies. *Psychology and Psychotherapy, 82*(1), 57–72. https://doi.org/10.1348/147608308X336100

*Martin, L.A.L., Koch, S.C., Hirjak, D., & Fuchs, T. (2016). Overcoming disembodiment: The effect of movement therapy on negative symptoms in schizophrenia: A multicenter randomized controlled trial. *Frontiers in Psychology, 7*(483), 1–14. https://doi.org/10.3389/fpsyg.2016.00483

*Masheb, R. M., Kerns, R. D., Lozano, C., Minkin, M. J., & Richman, S. (2009). A randomized clinical trial for women with vulvodynia: Cognitive-behavioral therapy vs. supportive psychotherapy. *Pain, 141*(1–2), 31–40. https://doi.org/10.1016/j.pain.2008.09.031

*McArthur, K., Cooper, M., & Berdondini, L. (2013). School-based humanistic counseling for psychological distress in young people: Pilot randomized controlled trial. *Psychotherapy Research, 23*(3), 355–365. https://doi.org/10.1080/10503307.2012.726750

§McElvaney J., & Timulak, L. (2013). Clients' experience of therapy and its outcomes in quantitatively "good outcome" and "poor outcome" psychological therapy in a primary care setting. *Counselling and Psychotherapy Research, 13*(4), 246–253. https://doi.org/10.1080/14733145.2012.761258

*McLean, L. M., Walton, T., Rodin, G., Esplen, M. J., & Jones, J. M. (2013). A couple-based intervention for patients and caregivers facing end-stage cancer: outcomes of a randomized controlled trial. *Psycho-Oncology, 22*(1), 28–38. https://doi.org/10.1002/pon.2046

McLeod, J. (2010). *Case study research in counselling and psychotherapy.* London, UK: Sage Publications.

McNally, S., Timulak, L., & Greenberg, L. S. (2014). Transforming emotion schemes in emotion focused therapy: a case study investigation. *Person-Centered & Experiential Psychotherapies, 13*(2), 128–149. https://doi.org/10.1080/14779757.2013.871573

Mendes, I., Ribeiro, A. P., Angus, L., Greenberg, L. S., Sousa, I., & Goncalves, M. M. (2011). Narrative change in emotion-focused psychotherapy: A study on the evolution of reflection and protest innovative moments. *Psychotherapy Research, 21*(3), 304–315. https://doi.org/10.1080/10503307.2011.565489

Mendes, I., Rosa, C., Stiles, W.B., Gabalda, I.C., Gomes, P., Basto, I. & Salgado, J. (2016). Setbacks in the process of assimilation of problematic experiences in two cases of emotion-focused therapy for depression. *Psychotherapy Research, 26*(6), 638–652. https://doi.org/10.1080/10503307.2015.1136443

Miller, W.R., & Moyers, T.B. (2017). Motivational interviewing and the clinical science of Carl Rogers. *Journal of Consulting & Clinical Psychology, 85*(8), 757–766. https://doi.org/10.1037/ccp0000179.

Miller, W.R., & Rollnick, S. (2012). *Motivational interviewing: Preparing people for change* (3rd ed.). New York: Guilford.

Moreno, J. L., & Moreno, Z.T. (1959). *Foundations of psychotherapy.* Beacon House.

*Morrell, C. J., Slade, P., Warner, R., Paley, G., Dixon, S., Walters, S. J., Brugha, T., Barkham, M., Parry, G.J., & Nicholl, J. (2009). Clinical effectiveness of health visitor training in psychologically informed approaches for depression in postnatal women: Pragmatic cluster randomised trial in primary care. *BMJ: British Medical Journal, 338*(7689), 1–14. https://doi.org/10.1136/bmj.a3045

*Morrell, C J, Warner, R., Slade, P., Dixon, S., Walters, S., Paley, G., & Brugha, T. (2009). Psychological interventions for postnatal depression: cluster randomised trial and economic evaluation. The PoNDER trial. *Health Technology Assessment, 13*(30), iii. https://doi.org/10.3310/hta13300

*Moss-Morris, R, Dennison, L, Landau, S, Yardley, L, Silber, E, & Chalder, T. (2013). A randomized controlled trial of cognitive behavioral therapy (CBT) for adjusting to multiple sclerosis (the saMS trial): Does CBT work and for whom does it work? *Journal of Consulting & Clinical Psychology, 81*(2), 251–262. https://doi.org/10.1037/a0029132.

*Moss-Morris, R., Dennison, L., Yardley, L., Landau, S., Roche, S., McCrone, P., & Chalder, T. (2009). Protocol for the saMS trial (supportive adjustment for multiple sclerosis): a randomized controlled trial comparing cognitive behavioral therapy to supportive listening for adjustment to multiple sclerosis. *BMC Neurology, 9*(45). https://doi.org/10.1186/1471-2377-9-45

*Motaharinasab, A., Zare Bahramabadi, M., & Ahmadi, K. (2016). The effect of emotionally focused therapy on emotional expression styles among married women. *International Journal of Mental Health and Addiction, 14*(4), 505–513. https://doi.org/10.1007/s11469-015-9614-6

Murphy, D. & Cramer, D. (2014) Mutuality of Rogers's therapeutic conditions and treatment progress in the first three psychotherapy sessions, *Psychotherapy Research, 24*(6), 651-661, https://doi.org/10.1080/10503307.2013.874051

Murphy, J., Rowell, L., McQuaid, A., Timulak, L., O'Flynn, R., & McElvaney, J. (2017). Developing a model of working with worry in emotion-focused therapy: A discovery-phase task analytic study. *Counselling and Psychotherapy Research, 17*(1), 56–70. https://doi.org/10.1002/capr.12089

*Murphy, S. M., Chowdhury, U., White, S. W., Reynolds, L., Donald, L., Gahan, H., Iqbal, Z., Kulkarni, M., Scrivener, L., Shaker-Naeeni, H., & Press, D. A. (2017). Cognitive behaviour therapy versus a counselling intervention for anxiety in young people with high-functioning autism spectrum disorders: A pilot randomised controlled trial. *Journal of Autism and Developmental Disorders, 47*(11), 3446–3457. https://doi.org/10.1007/s10803-017-3252-8

National Collaborating Centre for Mental Health. (2009). *Depression: The treatment and management of depression in adults (update) (NICE clinical guideline 90).* London, United Kingdom: National Institute for Clinical Excellence. Available from www.nice.org.uk/CG90

National Collaborating Centre for Mental Health [NICE]. (2014). *Psychosis and schizophrenia in adults: Prevention and management (clinical guideline 178).* Leicester and London, United Kingdom: British Psychological Society & Royal College of Psychiatrists.

*Nazari, S., Moradi, N., & Sadeghi Koupaei, M. T. (2014). Evaluation of the effects of psychotherapy on anxiety among mothers of children with leukemia. *Iranian Journal of Child Neurology, 8*(1), 52–57.

*Nixon, R. D. (2012). Cognitive processing therapy versus supportive counseling for acute stress disorder following assault: A randomized pilot trial. *Behavior Therapy, 43*(4), 825–836. https://doi.org/10.1016/j.beth.2012.05.001

Norcross, J., & Lambert, M.J. (Eds.) (2019) *Psychotherapy relationships that work: Evidence-based therapist contributions* (3rd ed.). New York: Oxford University Press.

O'Brien, K., O'Keeffe, N., Cullen, H., Durcan, A., Timulak, L., & McElvaney, J. (2019). Emotion-focused perspective on generalised anxiety disorder: A qualitative analysis of clients' in-session presentations. *Psychotherapy Research, 29*(4), 524–540. https://doi.org/10.1080/10503307.2017.1373206

Paivio, S. C., Hall, I. E., Holowaty, K. A. M., Jellis, J. B., & Tran, N. (2001). Imaginal confrontation for resolving child abuse issues. *Psychotherapy Research, 11*(4), 433–453. https://doi.org/10.1093/ptr/11.4.433

*Paivio, S. C., Jarry, J. L., Chagigiorgis, H., Hall, I., & Ralston, M. (2010). Efficacy of two versions of emotion-focused therapy for resolving child abuse trauma. *Psychotherapy Research, 11*(4), 353–366. https://doi.org/10.1093/ptr/11.4.433

Paivio, S. C., & Pascual-Leone, A. (2010). *Emotion-focused therapy for complex trauma: An integrative approach.* Washington, DC: American Psychological Association.

Pascual-Leone, A. (2009). Dynamic emotional processing in experiential therapy: Two steps forward, one step back. *Journal of Consulting and Clinical Psychology, 77*(1), 113–126. doi:10.1037/a0014488

Pascual-Leone, A. (2018). How clients "change emotion with emotion": A programme of research on emotional processing. *Psychotherapy Research, 28*(2), 165–182. https://doi.org/10.1080/10503307.2017.1349350

*Pascual-Leone, A., Bierman, R., Arnold, R., & Stasiak, E. (2011). Emotion-focused therapy for incarcerated offenders of intimate partner violence: a 3-year outcome using a new whole-sample matching method. *Psychotherapy Research, 21*(3), 331–347. https://doi.org/10.1080/10503307.2011.572092

Pascual-Leone, A., & Greenberg, L. S. (2007). Emotional processing in experiential therapy: Why "the only way out is through." *Journal of Consulting and Clinical Psychology, 75*(6), 875–887. https://doi.org/10.1037/0022-006X.75.6.875

Pascual-Leone, A. & Yeryomenko, N. (2017) The client "experiencing" scale as a predictor of treatment outcomes: A meta-analysis on psychotherapy process, *Psychotherapy Research, 27*(6), 653–665. https://doi.org/10.1080/10503307.2016.1152409

Pascual-Leone, A., Yeryomenko, N., Sawashima, T., & Warwar, S. (2019). Building emotional resilience over 14 sessions of emotion focused therapy: Micro-longitudinal analyses of productive emotional patterns. *Psychotherapy Research, 29*(2), 171–185. https://doi.org/10.1080/10503307.2017.1315779

*Pearce, P., Sewell, R., Cooper, M., Osman, S., Fugard, A. J. B., & Pybis, J. (2017). Effectiveness of school-based humanistic counselling for psychological distress in young people: Pilot randomized controlled trial with follow-up in an ethnically diverse sample. *Psychology and Psychotherapy, 90*(2), 138–155. https://doi.org/10.1111/papt.12102

Perls, F. S., Hefferline, R. F., & Goodman, P. (1951). *Gestalt therapy.* Julian Press.

§Perren, S., Godfrey, M., & Rowland, N. (2009). The long-term effects of counselling: The process and mechanisms that contribute to ongoing change from a user perspective. *Counselling and Psychotherapy Research, 9*(4), 241–249. https://doi.org/10.1080/14733140903150745

Pos, A., Greenberg, L.S., & Elliott, R. (2008). Experiential therapy. In J. Lebow (Ed.), *21st century psychotherapies: Contemporary approaches to theory and practice* (pp. 80–122). Wiley.

Pos, A. E., Greenberg, L. S., Goldman, R. N., & Korman, L. M. (2003). Emotional processing during experiential treatment of depression. *Journal of Consulting and Clinical Psychology, 71*(6), 1007–1016. https://doi.org/10.1037/0022-006X.71.6.1007

Pos, A. E., Greenberg, L. S., & Warwar, S. (2010). Testing a model of change for experiential treatment of depression. *Journal of Consulting and Clinical Psychology, 77*(6), 1055–1066. https://doi.org/10.1037/a0017059

*Priebe, S., Savill, M., Wykes, T., Bentall, R., Lauber, C., Reininghaus, U, McCrone, P., Mosweu, I., Bremner, S., Eldridge, S., Röhricht, F., & NESS team. (2016). Clinical effectiveness and cost-effectiveness of body psychotherapy in the treatment of negative symptoms of schizophrenia: a multicentre randomised controlled trial. *Health Technology Assessment, 20*(11), 1–100. https://doi.org/10.3310/hta20110

*Pybis, J., Cooper, M., Hill, A., Cromarty, K., Levesley, R., Murdoch, J., & Turner, N. (2015). Pilot randomised controlled trial of school-based humanistic counselling for psychological distress in young people: Outcomes and methodological reflections. *Counselling & Psychotherapy Research, 15*(4), 241–250. https://doi.org/10.1080/14733145.2014.905614

*Reuter, K., Scholl, I., Sillem, M., Hasenburg, A., & Härter, M. (2010). Implementation and benefits of psychooncological group interventions in German breast centers: A pilot study on supportive-expressive group therapy for women with primary breast cancer. *Breast Care (Basel, Switzerland), 5*(2), 91–96. https://doi.org/10.1159/000297739

Ribeiro, E., Cunha, C., Teixeira, A.S., Stiles, W.B., Pires, N., Santos, B., Basto, I., & Salgado, J. (2016). Therapeutic collaboration and the assimilation of problematic experiences in emotion-focused therapy for depression: Comparison of two cases, *Psychotherapy Research, 26*, 665–680. https://doi.org/10.1080/10503307.2016.1208853

*Rief, W, Shedden-Mora, MC, Laferton, JA, Auer, C, Petrie, KJ, Salzmann, S, Schedlowski, M, Moosdorf, R. (2017). Preoperative optimization of patient expectations improves long-term outcome in heart surgery patients: Results of the randomized controlled PSY-HEART trial. *BMC Medicine, 15*(1), 4. https://doi.org/10.1186/s12916-016-0767-3.

§Rodgers, B. (2002). Investigation into the client at the heart of therapy. *Counselling and Psychotherapy Research, 2*(3), 185–193. https://doi.org/10.1080/14733140212331384815

Rogers, C. R. (1957). The necessary and sufficient conditions of therapeutic personality change. *Journal of Consulting Psychology, 21*(2), 95–103. https://doi.org/10.1037/h0045357

Rogers, C. R. (1959). A theory of therapy, personality and interpersonal relationships as developed in the client-centered framework. In S. Koch (Ed.), *Psychology: A study of science. Vol. III, Formulations of the person and the social context* (pp. 184–256). McGraw Hill.

Rogers, C. R. (1961) *On becoming a person: A therapist's view of psychotherapy.* Constable.

*Rohde, P., Stice, E., & Gau, J. M. (2012). Effects of three depression prevention interventions on risk for depressive disorder onset in the context of depression risk factors. *Prevention Science, 13*(6), 584–593. https://doi.org/10.1007/s11121-012-0284-3

*Sabariego, C., Brach, M., Herschbach, P., Berg, P., & Stucki, G. (2011). Cost-effectiveness of cognitive-behavioral group therapy for dysfunctional fear of progression in cancer patients. *The European Journal of Health Economics, 12*(5), 489–497. https://doi.org/10.1007/s10198-010-0266-y

Sachse, R., & Elliott, R. (2002). Process-outcome research on humanistic therapy variables. In D. J. Cain & J. Seeman (Eds.), Humanistic psychotherapies. *Handbook of research and practice* (pp. 83–116). APA Books.

*Salzmann, S., Euteneuer, F., Laferton, J. A. C., Auer, C. J., Shedden-Mora, M. C., Schedlowski, M., Moosdorf, R., & Rief, W. (2017). Effects of preoperative psychological interventions on catecholamine and cortisol level after surgery in coronary artery bypass graft patients: The randomized controlled PSY-HEART trial. *Psychosomatic Medicine, 79*(7), 806–814. https://doi.org/10.1097/PSY.0000000000000483

*Savill, M., Orfanos, S., Bentall, R., Reininghaus, U., Wykes, T., & Priebe, S. (2017). The impact of gender on treatment effectiveness of body psychotherapy for negative symptoms of schizophrenia: A secondary analysis of the NESS trial data. *Psychiatry Research, 247*, 73–78. https://doi.org/10.1016/j.psychres.2016.11.020

Saxon, D., Ashley, K., Bishop-Edwards, L., Connell, J. Harrison, P., Ohlsen, S. Hardy, G.E., Kellett, S., Mukuria, C., Mank, T., Bower, P., Bradburn, M., Brazier, J. Elliott, R., Gabriel, L., King, M. Pilling, S., Shaw, S., Waller, G., & Barkham, M. (2017). A pragmatic randomized controlled trial assessing the non-inferiority of counselling for depression versus cognitive-behaviour therapy for patients in primary care meeting a diagnosis of moderate or severe depression (PRaCTICED): Study protocol for a randomized controlled trial. *Trials 18*: 93. https://doi.org/10.1186/s13063-017-1834-6

Schneider, K.J., & Krug, O.T. (2017). *Existential-humanistic therapy* (2nd ed.). Washington, DC: APA.

*Schramm, E., Kriston, L., Zobel, I., Bailer, J., Wambach, K., Backenstrass, M., Klein, J.P., Schoepf, D., Schnell, K., Gumz, A., Bausch, P., Fangmeier, T., Meister, R., Berger, M., Hautzinger, M., & Härter, M. (2017). Effect of disorder-specific vs. nonspecific psychotherapy for chronic depression: A randomized clinical trial. *JAMA Psychiatry, 74*(3), 233–242. https://doi.org/10.1001/jamapsychiatry.2016.3880

*Schulthess, P., Tschuschke, V., Koemeda-Lutz, M., von Wyl, A., & Crameri, A. (2016). Comparative naturalistic study on outpatient psychotherapeutic treatments including Gestalt therapy. In J. Roubal & J. Roubal (Ed) (Eds.), *Towards a research tradition in Gestalt therapy.* (pp. 335–355). Newcastle upon Tyne: Cambridge Scholars Publishing.

*Schützmann, K., Schützmann, M., & Eckert, J. (2010). Wirksamkeit von ambulanter Gesprachspsychotherapie bei Bulimia nervosa: Ergebnisse einer randomisiert-kontrollierten Studie [The efficacy of outpatient client-centered psychotherapy for bulimia nervosa: results of a randomised controlled trial]. *Psychotherapie, Psychosomatik, medizinische Psychologie, 60*(2), 52–63. https://doi.org/10.1055/s-0029-1234134

Sellman, J. D., Sullivan, P. F., Dore, G. M., Adamson, S. J., & MacEwan, I. (2001). A randomized controlled trial of motivational enhancement therapy (MET) for mild to moderate alcohol dependence. *Journal of Studies on Alcohol, 62*(3), 389–396. https://doi.org/10.15288/jsa.2001.62.389

*Shahar, B., Bar-Kalifa, E., & Alon, E. (2017). Emotion-focused therapy for social anxiety disorder: Results from a multiple-baseline study. *Journal of Consulting & Clinical Psychology*, 85(3), 238–249. https://doi.org/10.1037/ccp0000166

*Shahar, B., Carlin, E. R., Engle, D. E., Hegde, J., Szepsenwol, O., & Arkowitz, H. (2012). A pilot investigation of emotion-focused two-chair dialogue intervention for self-criticism. *Clinical Psychology & Psychotherapy*, 19(6), 496–507. https://doi.org/10.1002/cpp.762

*Shi, J., Wang, L., Yao, Y., Zhan, C., Su, N., & Zhao, X. (2017). Systemic therapy for youth at clinical high risk for psychosis: A pilot study. *Frontiers in Psychiatry*, 8(211). https://doi.org/10.3389/fpsyt.2017.00211

Siegfried, T. (2010, March 27). Odds are, it's wrong: Science fails to face the shortcomings of statistics. *Science News*, 26–29.

*Singal, S. (2009). *The efficacy of psychodrama in the treatment of oppositional and defiant adolescents*. (ProQuest Information & Learning). Retrieved from http://ezproxy.ecu.edu.au/login?url=http://search.ebscohost.com/login.aspx?direct=true&db=psyh&AN=2009-99120-132&site=ehost-live&scope=site

§Smith, K., Shoemark, A., McLeod, J., & McLeod, J. (2014). Moving on: A case analysis of process and outcome in person-centred psychotherapy for health anxiety. *Person-Centered & Experiential Psychotherapies*, 13(2), 111–127. https://doi.org/10.1080/14779757.2014.886080

Smith, M. L., Glass, G. V., & Miller, T. I. (1980). *The benefits of psychotherapy*. Johns Hopkins University Press.

Sousa, D., Pestana, A., & Tavares, A. (2018). Self-awareness, verbalization and new meanings as the heart and soul of significant events in existential psychotherapy. *Journal of Contemporary Psychotherapy*, 49, 161–167. https://doi.org/10.1007/s10879-018-9410-2

Spiegel, D., Bloom, J. R., & Yalom, I. (1981). Group support for patients with metastatic cancer. *Archives of General Psychiatry*, 38(5), 527–533. https://doi.org/10.1001/archpsyc.1980.01780300039004

*Stain, H. J., Bucci, S., Baker, A. L., Carr, V., Emsley, R., Halpin, S., Lewin, T., Schall, U., Clarke, V., Crittenden, K., & Startup, M. (2016). A randomised controlled trial of cognitive behaviour therapy versus non-directive reflective listening for young people at ultra-high risk of developing psychosis: The detection and evaluation of psychological therapy (DEPTh) trial. *Schizophrenia Research*, 176(2–3), 212–219. https://doi.org/10.1016/j.schres.2016.08.008

§Steinmann, R., Gat, I., Nir-Gottlieb, O., Shahar, B., & Diamond, G. M. (2017). Attachment-based family therapy and individual emotion-focused therapy for unresolved anger: Qualitative analysis of treatment outcomes and change processes. *Psychotherapy*, 54(3), 281–291. https://doi.org/10.1037/pst0000116

§Stephen, S., Elliott, R. & Macleod, R. (2011). Person-centred therapy with a client experiencing social anxiety difficulties: A hermeneutic single case efficacy design. *Counselling & Psychotherapy Research*, 11(1), 55–66. https://doi.org/10.1080/14733145.2011.546203

*Stevens, C., Stringfellow, J., Wakelin, K., & Waring, J. (2011). The UK Gestalt psychotherapy CORE research project: The findings. *British Gestalt Journal*, 20, 22–27.

*Stice, E., Rohde, P., Gau, J. M., & Wade, E. (2010). Efficacy trial of a brief cognitive–behavioral depression prevention program for high-risk adolescents: Effects at 1-and 2-year follow-up. *Journal of Consulting and Clinical Psychology*, 78(6), 856. https://doi.org/10.1037/a0020544

*Stice, E., Rohde, P., Seeley, J. R., & Gau, J. M. (2008). Brief cognitive-behavioral depression prevention program for high-risk adolescents outperforms two alternative interventions: a randomized efficacy trial. *Journal of Consulting and Clinical Psychology*, 76(4), 595. https://doi.org/10.1037/a0012645

Stiegler, J. R., Binder, P. E., Hjeltnes, A., Stige, S. H., & Schanche, E. (2018). 'It's heavy, intense, horrendous and nice': clients' experiences in two-chair dialogues. *Person-Centered & Experiential Psychotherapies*, 17(2), 139–159. https://doi.org/10.1080/14779757.2018.1472138

*Stiegler, J. R., Molde, H., & Schanche, E. (2018). Does an emotion-focused two-chair dialogue add to the therapeutic effect of the empathic attunement to affect? *Clinical Psychology & Psychotherapy*, 25(1), e86–e95. https://doi.org/10.1002/cpp.2144

Stiles, W. B. (2001). Assimilation of problematic experiences. *Psychotherapy: Theory, Research, Practice, Training*, 38(4), 462–465. https://doi.org/10.1037/0033-3204.38.4.462

Stiles, W. B. (2007). Theory-building case studies of counselling and psychotherapy. *Counselling and Psychotherapy Research*, 7(2), 122–127. https://doi.org/10.1080/14733140701356742

*Strahan, E. J., Stillar, A., Files, N., Nash, P., Scarborough, J., Connors, L., Gusella, J., Henderson, K., Mayman, S., Marchand, P., Orr, E.S., Dolhanty, J., & Lafrance, A. (2017). Increasing parental self-efficacy with emotion-focused family therapy for eating disorders: A process model. *Person-Centered and Experiential Psychotherapies*, 16(3), 256–269. https://doi.org/10.1080/14779757.2017.1330703

*Szigethy, E., Bujoreanu, S. I., Youk, A. O., Weisz, J., Benhayon, D., Fairclough, D., Ducharme, P., Gonzalez-Heydrich, J., Keljo, D., Srinath, A., Bousvaros, A., Kirshner, M., Newara, M., Kupfer, D., & DeMaso, D. R. (2014). Randomized efficacy trial of two psychotherapies for depression in youth with inflammatory bowel disease. *Journal of The American Academy of Child And Adolescent Psychiatry*, 53(7), 726–735. https://doi.org/10.1016/j.jaac.2014.04.014

*Terzioğlu, C., & Özkan, B. (2018). Psychodrama and the emotional state of women dealing with infertility. *Sexuality and Disability*, 36(1), 87–99. https://doi.org/10.1007/s11195-017-9514-8

Tickle, E., & Murphy, D. (2014). A journey to client and therapist mutuality in person-centered psychotherapy: A case study. *Person-Centered & Experiential Psychotherapies*, 13(4), 337–351. https://doi.org/10.1080/14779757.2014.927390

Timulak, L., Belicova, A., & Miler, M. (2010). Client identified significant events in a successful therapy case: The link between the significant events and outcome. *Counselling Psychology Quarterly*, 23(4), 371–386. https://doi.org/10.1080/09515070.2010.534329

Timulak, L., & Creaner, M. (2010). Qualitative meta-analysis of outcomes of person-centred/experiential therapies. In M. Cooper, J. C. Watson, & D. Hölldampf (Eds.), *Person-centred and experiential psychotherapies work*. Ross-on-Wye, United Kingdom: PCCS Books.

Timulak, L. & Iwakabe, S., & Elliott, R. (2018). Clinical implications of quantitative, qualitative and case study research on emotion-focused therapy (pp. 93–110). In L. S. Greenberg & R. N. Goldman (Eds.), *Clinical handbook of emotion-focused therapy*. Washington, DC: American Psychological Association.

Timulak, L., Keogh, D., Chigwedere, C., Wilson, C., Ward, F., Hevey, D., Griffin, P., Jacobs, L. & Irwin, B. (2018). A comparison of emotion-focused therapy and cognitive-behavioural therapy in the treatment of generalised anxiety disorder: study protocol for a randomised controlled trial. *Trials*, 19(1), 506. https://doi.org/10.1186/s13063-018-2892-0

*§Timulak, L., McElvaney, J., Keogh, D., Martin, E., Clare, P., Chepukova, E., & Greenberg, L. S. (2017). Emotion-focused therapy for generalized anxiety disorder: An exploratory study. *Psychotherapy*, 54(4), 361. https://doi.org/10.1037/pst0000128

Timulak, L., & Pascual-Leone, A. (2015). New developments for case conceptualization in emotion-focused therapy. *Clinical Psychology & Psychotherapy*, 22(6), 619–636. https://doi.org/10.1002/cpp.1922

Toolan, R., Devereux, M, Timulak, L., & Keogh, D. (2019). Relationship between self-worrying and self-critical messages in clients with generalized anxiety engaging in emotion-focused worry dialogues. *Counselling and Psychotherapy Research*, 19(3), 294–300. https://doi.org/10.1002/capr.12229

Traynor, W., Elliott, R., & Cooper, M. (2011). Helpful factors and outcomes in person-centered therapy with clients who experience psychotic processes: Therapists' perspectives. *Person-Centered and Experiential Psychotherapies*, 10(2), 89–104. https://doi.org/10.1080/14779757.2011.576557

*van der Spek, N., Vos, J., van Uden-Kraan, C. F., Breitbart, W., Cuijpers, P., Holtmaat, K., Witte, B.I., Tollenaar, R.A.E.M., & Verdonck-de Leeuw, I. M. (2017). Efficacy of meaning-centered group psychotherapy for cancer survivors: a randomized controlled trial. *Psychological Medicine*, 47(11), 1990–2001. https://doi.org/10.1017/S0033291717000447

*van Rijn, B. & Wild, C. (2013) Humanistic and integrative therapies for anxiety and depression. *Transactional Analysis Journal*, 43(2), 150–163, https://doi.org/10.1177/0362153713499545

*Vassilopoulos, S. P., & Brouzos, A. (2012). A pilot person-centred group counselling for university students: Effects on social anxiety and self-esteem. *The Hellenic Journal of Psychology, 9*(3), 222–239.

*von Humboldt, S., & Leal, I. (2013). The promotion of older adults' sense of coherence through person-centered therapy: A randomized controlled pilot study. *Interdisciplinaria Revista de Psicología y Ciencias Afines, 30*(2), 235–251. https://doi.org/10.16888/interd.2013.30.2.4

*Voseckova, A., Truhlarova, Z., Janebová, R., & Kuca, K. (2017). Activation group program for elderly diabetic patients. *Social Work in Health Care, 56*(1), 13–27. https://doi.org/10.1080/00981389.2016.1247410

*Ward, T., & Hogan, K. (2009). A trial of client-centred counselling over the telephone for persons with ME. *Counselling Psychology Review, 24*(2), 34–41.

Warwar, S. H. (2003). *Relating emotional processes to outcome in experiential psychotherapy of depression*. Unpublished doctoral dissertation, York University, Toronto, Canada.

Watson, J. C., & Bedard, D. L. (2006). Clients' emotional processing in psychotherapy: A comparison between cognitive-behavioral and process-experiential therapies. *Journal of Consulting and Clinical Psychology, 74*(1), 152–159. https://doi.org/10.1037/0022-006X.74.1.152

Watson, J. C., & Geller, S. (2005). The relation among the relationship conditions, working alliance, and outcome in both process-experiential and cognitive-behavioral psychotherapy. *Psychotherapy Research, 15*(1–2), 25–33.

Watson, J. C., Goldman, R. N., & Greenberg, L. S. (2007). *Case-studies in the experiential treatment of depression: A comparison of good and bad outcome*. APA Books.

Watson, J. C., Gordon, L. B., Stermac, L., Kalogerakos, F., & Steckley, P. (2003). Comparing the effectiveness of process-experiential with cognitive-behavioral psychotherapy in the treatment of depression. *Journal of Consulting and Clinical Psychology, 71*(4), 773–781. https://doi.org/10.1037/0022-006X.71.4.773

Watson, J. C., Greenberg, L. S., & Lietaer, G. (2010). Relating process to outcome in person-centered and experiential psychotherapies: The role of the relationship conditions and clients' experiencing. In M. Cooper, J. C. Watson & D. Hölldampf (Eds.), *Person-centred and experiential therapies work: A review of the research on counseling, psychotherapy and related practices* (pp. 132–163). PCCS Books.

Watson, J. C., McMullen, E. J., Prosser, M. C., & Bedard, D. L. (2011). An examination of the relationships among clients' affect regulation, in-session emotional processing, the working alliance, and outcome. *Psychotherapy Research, 21*(1), 86–96. https://doi.org/10.1080/10503307.2010.518637

Watson, J.C., Steckley, P.L., & McMullen, E.J. (2014) The role of empathy in promoting change. *Psychotherapy Research, 24*(3), 286–298. https://doi.org/10.1080/10503307.2013.802823

Watson, V. C., Cooper, M., McArthur, K., & McLeod, J. (2012). Helpful therapeutic processes: Client activities, therapist activities and helpful effects. *European Journal of Psychotherapy & Counselling, 14*(1), 77–89. https://doi.org/10.1080/13642537.2012.652395

*Wei, C., Allen, R. J., Tallis, P. M., Ryan, F. J., Hunt, L. P., Shield, J. P., & Crowne, E. C. (2018). Cognitive behavioural therapy stabilises glycaemic control in adolescents with type 1 diabetes-Outcomes from a randomised control trial. *Pediatric Diabetes, 19*(1), 106–113. https://doi.org/10.1111/pedi.12519

Whelton, W. J., & Greenberg, L. S. (2000). The self as a singular multiplicity: A process experiential perspective. In J. Muran (Ed.), *The self in psychotherapy*. American Psychological Association.

Whiteford, H.A., Harris, M.G., McKeon, G., Baxter, A., Pennell, C., Barendregt, J.J., & Wang, J. (2013). Estimating remission from untreated major depression: a systematic review and meta-analysis. *Psychological Medicine, 43*(8), 1569–1585. https://doi.org/10.1017/S0033291712001717.

*Wiebe, S. A., Johnson, S. M., Lafontaine, M.-F., Burgess Moser, M., Dalgleish, T. L., & Tasca, G. A. (2017). Two-year follow-up outcomes in emotionally focused couple therapy: An investigation of relationship satisfaction and attachment trajectories. *Journal of Marital and Family Therapy, 43*(2), 227–244. https://doi.org/10.1111/jmft.12206

*Wnuk, S. (2009). *Treatment development and evaluation of emotion-focused group therapy for women with symptoms of bulimia nervosa*. Unpublished Doctoral Dissertation, York University, Toronto, Canada.

*Wnuk, S. M., Greenberg, L., & Dolhanty, J. (2015). Emotion-focused group therapy for women with symptoms of bulimia nervosa. *Eating Disorders: The Journal of Treatment & Prevention, 23*(3), 253–261. https://doi.org/10.1080/10640266.2014.964612

Woldarsky Meneses, C. (2006). *A task analysis of forgiveness in Emotion-focused couple therapy*. Unpublished master's thesis, York University, Toronto, Canada.

Woldarsky Meneses, C., & Greenberg, L. S. (2011). The construction of a model of the process of couples' forgiveness in emotion-focused therapy for couples. *Journal of Marital and Family Therapy, 37*(4), 491–502. https://doi.org/10.1111/j.1752-0606.2011.00234.x

Woldarsky Meneses, C., & Greenberg, L. S. (2014). Interpersonal forgiveness in emotion-focused couples' therapy: Relating process to outcome. *Journal of Marital and Family Therapy, 40*(1), 49–67. https://doi.org/10.1111/j.1752-0606.2012.00330.x

Wolfe, B., & Sigl, P. (1998). Experiential psychotherapy of the anxiety disorders. In L. S. Greenberg, J. C. Watson, & G. Lietaer (Eds.), *Handbook of experiential psychotherapy* (pp. 272–294). Guilford Press.

Wong, K. & Pos, A.E. (2014). Interpersonal processes affecting early alliance formation in experiential therapy for depression, *Psychotherapy Research, 24*(1), 1–11. https://doi.org/10.1080/10503307.2012.708794

*Woodward, E., Hackmann, A., Wild, J., Grey, N., Clark, D. M., & Ehlers, A. (2017). Effects of psychotherapies for posttraumatic stress disorder on sleep disturbances: Results from a randomized clinical trial. *Behaviour Research and Therapy, 97*, 75–85. http://dx.doi.org/10.1016/j.brat.2017.07.001

Yalom, I. D. (1980). *Existential psychotherapy*. Basic Books.

Young, J.E., Klosko, J.S., & Weishaar, M.E. (2003). *Schema therapy: A practitioner's guide*. Guilford Press.

*Yousefi, N., & Kiani, M. A. (2014). The study of two psychotherapy approaches (Rogers self theory and Ellis rational theory) in improvement of Bowen self-differentiation and intimacy. *Iranian Journal of Psychiatry and Behavioral Sciences, 8*(1), 32–41.

*Zandberg, L., Kaczkurkin, A. N., McLean, C. P., Rescorla, L., Yadin, E., & Foa, E. B. (2016). Treatment of adolescent PTSD: The impact of prolonged exposure versus client-centered therapy on co-occurring emotional and behavioral problems. *Journal of Traumatic Stress, 29*(6), 507–514. https://doi.org/10.1002/jts.22138

Zuccarini, D., Johnson, S. M., Dalgleish, T. L., & Makinen, J. A. (2013). Forgiveness and reconciliation in emotionally focused therapy for couples: The client change process and therapist interventions. *Journal of Marital and Family Therapy, 39*(2), 148–162. https://doi.org/10.1111/j.1752-0606.2012.00287.

SUPPLEMENTAL MATERIAL

1. Quantitative Outcome Meta-Analysis Search & Analysis Process

Search Syntax

We used the EBSCO host interface engine to search PsycINFO and MEDLINE, applying the following syntax:

(TI+(humanistic+OR+experiential+OR+person-cent* +OR+client-cent*+OR+non-directive+OR+psychodrama+OR +gestalt+OR+empty-chair+OR+emotion-focused+OR+ emotionally-focused+OR+expressive+OR+existential+OR+ supportive+OR+Motivational-interviewing+OR+Motivational-Enhancement+OR+pre-therapy)+AND+(psychotherapy+OR+ therapy+OR+counseling+OR+counselling+OR+treatment+OR +intervention+OR+program)+ AND+(outcome+OR+effect+OR +efficacy+OR+effectiveness+OR+clinical-trial+OR+change+ OR+impact+OR+improvement))+OR+(AB+(humanistic+OR+ experiential+OR+person-cent*+OR+client-cent*+OR+non-directive+OR+psychodrama+OR+gestalt+OR+empty-chair

+OR+emotion-focused+OR+emotionally-focused+OR+
expressive+OR+existential+OR+supportive+OR+Motivational-
interviewing+OR+Motivational-Enhancement+OR+pre-
therapy)+ AND+(psychotherapy+OR+therapy+OR+counseling
+OR+counselling+OR+treatment+OR+intervention+OR+
program)+ AND+(outcome+OR+effect+OR+efficacy+OR+
effectiveness+OR+clinical-trial+OR+change+OR+impact
+OR+improvement)

Further Screening of Possible Sources

The need to search for supportive therapy studies generated a very large data set (*n* = 32,171 references), including more than 99% false positives. While retaining a generally inclusive approach to screening likely studies for inclusion, we applied the following additional exclusion criteria in screening these possible sources:

- Duplicate reference
- Not psychotherapy or mental health counselling (e.g., occupational health intervention, primary care, training)
- Not HEP (major content directive approach was basis of therapy, e.g., CBT or psychodynamic)
- Lacking either a clear reference to either therapist empathy or client experience; or HEP only minor part of therapy
- Not outcome research (descriptive, process, process-outcome or qualitative research;
- No pre-post analyses reported
- Review articles

Following a two-stage abstract screening process, 395 likely HEP outcome studies remained, falling into three groups: mainstream band-name HEPs (*n* = 139), "supportive" or "nondirective" approaches (*n* = 77), and motivational interviewing (*n* = 183). At this point, time and resource limitations required us to drop (at least for this review) MI studies, leaving us with 197 studies to retrieve and analyze. The remaining studies were each reviewed by two of the co-authors, who resolved disagreements by consensus. Of these, 76 were retained for analysis. However, in the process of analyzing these studies, 15 additional studies were identified from the references of the included studies, bringing the sample to 91.

Detailed PRISMA Information

The PRISMA flow diagram presented as Figure 13.1 is a simplified version of the process of screening sources. For example, the addition of records from other sources actually took place at the end of the screening process rather than at the beginning. Table 13.S-1 provides more detailed information about the screening process.

Coding of Studies

For each study, characteristics of the treatments, clients, therapists and study methods were rated in order to estimate their contribution to effect size. For example, internal validity was coded, with one-group pre–post uncontrolled open clinical trials rated as "0"; one group wait list own control designs as "1"; two group nonrandomized designs as "2"; traditional multigroup randomized controlled trials (RCTs) as "3"; and modern RCTs that used ITT analyses or specified randomization procedures as "4".

TABLE 13.S-1 PRISMA Information for HEP Outcome Meta-analysis

Stage	*N* of studies included	*N* of studies excluded	Notes
1. Search Result:	32,171		Date of search: 24 March 2018; period covered: Jan 2009 – March 2018
2. Duplicates removed	28,118	4053	
3. Initial abstract screening: Possible HEP Outcome studies	1000	27,118	
4. Second abstract screening: Likely HEP outcome studies	395	605	• Duplicates: 32 • Not HEP: 198 • Not therapy outcome research: 187 • *N* ≤ 5: 21 • Not formal psychotherapy: 40 • Children < 13: 19 • Reviews: 76 • < 3 sessions: 26 • Outside review period: 6

(Continued)

TABLE 13.S-1 (CONTINUED)

Stage	N of studies included	N of studies excluded	Notes
5. Motivational Interviewing studies dropped	212	183	Retained: • Mainstream HEPs: 139 • "Supportive therapy": 77 Client populations: • Anxiety: 25 • Medical conditions: 52 • Depression: 35 • Self-damaging: 20 • Interpersonal difficulties: 28 • Psychosis: 18 • Other/mixed: 34
6. Full text retrieval	197	15	Unable to retrieve full text
7. Met criteria after full text review by two reviewers	76	121	Failed exclusion criteria at full text review or analysis: • Not HEP: 54 • Combined with main study report: 29 • No outcome data: 14 • $n < 10$: 11 • Other reasons (e.g., duplicates): 13
8. Final data set (with added studies)	91	(15 studies added)	Added studies: Mostly from branching references

Effect Size Calculations

As in previous versions of this meta-analysis, the basic effect size (ES) unit was the standardized pre–post difference (d) calculated using standard estimation procedures (e.g., Smith, et al., 1980) and corrected for small-sample bias (Hedges's g; Hedges & Olkin, 1985). ESs were calculated for each subscale of each outcome measure used, then sample-size weighted averages were calculated across subscales within measures, using inverse variance weighting. Weighted mean ESs were calculated for both primary and all outcome measures for each post-therapy/follow-up time; amount of time from end of therapy was coded and effects grouped into three temporal phases: immediate post-therapy (0–1 month), early follow-up (2–11 months), and late follow-up (a year or longer). However, most analyses used overall inverse variance weighted averages of all available time periods.

Each HEP and nonHEP treatment in each study was represented by up to three different sets of summary statistics: First, we carried out intent-to-treat analyses of primary outcomes (ITT-PO) because this is the most common form of analysis used in contemporary meta-analysis, but is limited because many studies fail to report ITT results. Second, in order to provide backward compatibility with the previous versions of this meta-analysis, we carried out per protocol analyses of treatment completers on all outcome measures (PP-All).

Third, as a compromise between the first two, we carried out per protocol analyses of treatment completers or primary outcomes (PP-PO), which is the metric we will generally rely on. (Where primary outcomes were not specified, we designated one or two based on order of presentation, client presenting problem, or prominence in abstract or hypotheses.)

Analyses of *controlled and comparative effect sizes* compared weighted mean overall effects between HEPs and control or comparative treatment conditions, with positive values assigned where the HEP treatment showed a larger amount of change. Significance testing and estimations of overall effects used a random-effects, restricted maximum likelihood (REML) model (Lipsey & Wilson, 2001), cross-checked using both the Wilson macros (Lipsey & Wilson, 2001) and the *metaphor* package in R (Viechtbauer, 2010). As in Elliott et al. (2013), these were combined with equivalence analyses (Rogers, Howard, & Vessey, 1993) for key comparisons, using 1.41 sd as a critical value for defining the minimum clinically interesting difference. Next, we analyzed for heterogeneity of effects using Cochrane's Q, which tests for whether the overall effect estimate is compromised by significant between-study variability. Finally, we estimated the proportion of the between study variation due to true variability as opposed to random error by using the I^2 statistic (Higgins et al., 2003). (Higgins et al. recommend interpreting I^2 values of 25%, 50%, and 75%, respectively, as small, medium, and large.)

Study Characteristics

Table 13.S-2 summarizes the salient features of this sample. The 91 studies include 94 different samples of clients seen in HEPs, amounting to 7624 clients, seen for an average of about 11 sessions and assessed on an average of 4 different outcome measures, most commonly client self-report or clinician-reported measures of specific presenting symptoms (e.g., Beck Depression Inventory; Hamilton Depression Scale). Clients were typically adults (25–50 years old) seen in individual outpatient psychotherapy by therapists using manualized versions of an HEP. Clients most commonly presented with depression (30 studies), interpersonal difficulties (28 studies), coping with medical conditions (28 studies), or anxiety (27 studies). Clients most commonly received therapies labeled as supportive (29 studies), person-centered (19 studies), emotion-focused (18 studies), or gestalt/psychodrama (17 studies).

TABLE 13.S-2 Selected Study Characteristics

Parametric characteristics:	Number	M	Sd	Range
Studies	91			
Pre–post analyses				
Samples	94			
Sample Size: Clients:	7624	78.8 (mdn: 25)	309.4	7–3003
Length of therapy (sessions)	91	11.3 (mdn: 10)	7.8	4–67
Measures per study	95	4.2	2.5	1–18

Categorical characteristics:	Number	Selected categories	*n* studies
Type of HEP (pre–post effects)	95	Supportive-nondirective	30
		Person-centered	19
		Emotion-focused therapy	18
		Gestalt/psychodrama	17
		Other HEP	11
Treatment format	95	Individual	55
		Group	34
Treatment setting	95	Outpatient	79
HEP manualized	95	Yes	66
Region	95	North America	28
		Europe (not UK)	25
		UK/British Commonwealth	24
		Asia/Middle East	17
Therapist experience level	86	Master's level	30
		Recent PhD or MD	24
		10+ years' experience	23
Client presenting problem	98	Depression	30
		Interpersonal difficulties	28
		Coping with medical conditions	28
		Anxiety	27
		Habitual self-damaging activities	8
		Psychosis	5
		Other client populations	22
Client age range	94	Adults 25–50	57
Primary outcome measure type	95	Self-report: Specific symptoms	56
		Clinician rated: symptoms	21

(Continued)

TABLE 13.S-2 (CONTINUED)

Categorical characteristics:	Number	Selected categories	*n* studies
Internal validity	95	One-group pre–post	22
		One-group own control	2
		Two-group nonrandomized	12
		Traditional RCT	34
		Modern RCT	25
Researcher allegiance (pre–post)	95	Pro-HEP	55
		Neutral	5
		Con-HEP	35
Comparative studies			
Researcher allegiance	63	Pro-HEP	17
		Neutral	9
		Con-HEP	37
Comparative treatment	63	CBT	35

2. Qualitative Outcomes/Effects Meta-Analysis: Search Methods and Detailed Results

Search Methods

For the purpose of this chapter we searched literature in PsychInfo from January 2009 to January 2019 (search words: humanistic OR person-cent* OR client-cent* OR process OR experiential OR emotion-focused OR focusing OR gestalt AND [outcome OR benefits or effects] AND qualitative AND [therapy OR treatment OR intervention]). The search picked up 920 entries. We were also aware anecdotally of further studies that were not picked up by the search. In total, we found a further 9 studies (Ellis, 2016; MacLeod & Elliott, 2014; MacLeod, Elliott, & Rodgers, 2012; McElvaney & Timulak, 2013; Perren, Godfrey & Rowland, 2009; Smith, Shoemark, McLeod & McLeod, 2014; Steinmann, Gat, Nir-Gottlieb, Shahar & Diamond, 2017; Stephen, Elliott & MacLeod, 2011; Timulak et al., 2017) reporting the views of another 71 clients on outcomes of HEPs such as emotion-focused therapy, attachment-based family therapy, (integrative) person-centered counselling, or focusing-oriented dreamwork (Note: Some of these studies may have included other therapies but HEPs most likely constituted the majority of the sample). Studies conducted primarily by HEP researchers using versions of descriptive–interpretive analysis (Elliott & Timulak, 2021) were based primarily on mid-therapy, post-therapy and/or follow-up interviews (with the exception of Ellis who analyzed in session presentations of dreams across several sessions).

Detailed Results

A complete cumulative qualitative meta-analysis of HEP outcomes is given in Table S.13-3, where additions to the Timulak and Creaner (2010) original are marked in bold.

REFERENCES

Studies in qualitative outcome meta-analysis

Dale, P., Allen, J., & Measor, L. (1998). Counselling adults who were abused as children: Clients' perceptions of efficacy, client–counsellor communication, and dissatisfaction. *British Journal of Guidance & Counselling, 26*(2), 141–157. https://doi.org/10.1080/03069889800760151

Elliott, R. (2002a). Hermeneutic single case efficacy design. *Psychotherapy Research, 12*(1), 1–20. https://doi.org/10.1080/713869614

Elliott, R. (2002b). Render unto Caesar: Quantitative and qualitative knowing in research on humanistic therapies. *Person-Centered and Experiential Psychotherapies, 1*(1-2), 102–117. https://doi.org/10.1080/14779757.2002.9688281

Elliott, R., Clark, C., Kemeny, V., Wexler, M. M., Mack, C., & Brinkerhoff, L. J. (1990). The impact of experiential therapy on depression: The first ten cases. In G. Lietaer, J. Rombauts, & R. Van Balen (Eds.), *Client-centered and experiential psychotherapy in the nineties* (pp. 549–578). Leuven, Belgium: Katholieke Universiteit Leuven.

Elliott, R., Partyka, R., Wagner, J., Alperin, R., Dobrenski. R., Messer, S. B., Watson, J. C., & Castonguay, L. G. (2009). An adjudicated hermeneutic single-case efficacy design of experiential therapy for panic/phobia. *Psychotherapy Research, 19*, 543–557. https://doi.org/10.1080/10503300902905947

Elliott, R., & Timulak, L. (2021). *Essentials of descriptive-interpretive qualitative research: A generic approach.* Washington, DC: APA.

Elliott, R., Watson, J., Greenberg, L.S., Timulak, L., & Freire, E. (2013). Research on humanistic-experiential psychotherapies. In M.J. Lambert (Ed.), *Bergin & Garfield's handbook of psychotherapy and behavior change* (6th ed.) (pp. 495-538). New York: Wiley.

Ellis, L. A. (2016). Qualitative changes in recurrent PTSD nightmares after focusing-oriented dreamwork. *Dreaming, 26*(3), 185. https://doi.org/10.1037/drm0000031

Hedges, L. V., & Olkin, I. (1985). *Statistical methods for meta-analysis.* San Diego, CA: Academic Press.

Higgins, J. P. T., Thompson, S. G., Deeks, J. J., & Altman, D. G. (2003). Measuring inconsistency in meta-analyses, *British Journal of Medicine, 327,* 557–560.

Klein, M. J., & Elliott, R. (2006). Client accounts of personal change in process-experiential psychotherapy: A methodologically pluralistic approach. *Psychotherapy Research*, *16*, 91–105. https://doi.org/10.1080/10503300500090993

Lipkin, S. (1954). Clients' feelings and attitudes in relation to the outcome of client-centered therapy. *Psychological Monographs*, *68*, 1–30.

Lipsey, M. W., & Wilson, D. B. (2001). *Practical meta-analysis*. Thousand Oaks, CA: Sage.

MacLeod, R., & Elliott, R. (2014). Nondirective person-centered therapy for social anxiety: a hermeneutic single-case efficacy design study of a good outcome case. *Person-Centered & Experiential Psychotherapies*, *13*(4), 294–311. https://doi.org/10.1080/14779757.2014.910133

MacLeod, R., Elliott, R., & Rodgers, B. (2012). Process-experiential/emotion-focused therapy for social anxiety: A hermeneutic single-case efficacy design study. *Psychotherapy Research*, *22*(1), 67–81. https://doi.org/10.1080/10503307.2011.626805

McElvaney J., & Timulak, L. (2013). Clients' experience of therapy and its outcomes in quantitatively "good outcome" and "poor outcome" psychological therapy in a primary care setting. *Counselling and Psychotherapy Research*, *13*, 246–253. https://doi.org/10.1080/14733145.2012.761258

Perren, S., Godfrey, M., & Rowland, N. (2009). The long-term effects of counselling: The process and mechanisms that contribute to ongoing change from a user perspective. *Counselling and Psychotherapy Research*, *9*(4), 241–249. https://doi.org/10.1080/14733140903150745

Rodgers, B. (2002). Investigation into the client at the heart of therapy. *Counselling and Psychotherapy Research*, *2*, 185–193. https://doi.org/10.1080/14733140212331384815

Rogers, J. L., Howard, K. I., & Vessey, J. T. (1993). Using significance tests to evaluate equivalence between two experimental groups. *Psychological Bulletin*, *113*, 553–565. https://doi.org/10.1037/0033-2909.113.3.553

Smith, K., Shoemark, A., McLeod, J., & McLeod, J. (2014). Moving on: A case analysis of process and outcome in person-centred psychotherapy for health anxiety. *Person-Centered & Experiential Psychotherapies*, *13*(2), 111–127. https://doi.org/10.1080/14779757.2014.886080

Smith, M. L., Glass, G. V., & Miller, T. I. (1980). *The benefits of psychotherapy*. Baltimore, MD: Johns Hopkins University Press.

Steinmann, R., Gat, I., Nir-Gottlieb, O., Shahar, B., & Diamond, G. M. (2017). Attachment-based family therapy and individual emotion-focused therapy for unresolved anger: Qualitative analysis of treatment outcomes and change processes. *Psychotherapy*, *54*(3), 281-291. https://doi.org/10.1037/pst0000116

Stephen, S., Elliott, R. & Macleod, R. (2011). Person-centred therapy with a client experiencing social anxiety difficulties: A hermeneutic single case efficacy design. *Counselling and Psychotherapy Research*, *11*(1), 55–66. https://doi.org/10.1080/14733145.2011.546203

Timulak, L., Belicova, A., & Miler, M. (2010). Client identified significant events in a successful therapy case: The link between the significant events and outcome. *Counselling Psychology Quarterly*, *23*, 371–386. https://doi.org/10.1080/09515070.2010.534329

Timulak, L., & Creaner, M. (2010). Qualitative meta-analysis of outcomes of person-centred/experiential therapies. In M. Cooper, J. C. Watson, & D. Hölldampf (Eds.), *Person-centred and experiential psychotherapies work*. Ross-on-Wye, United Kingdom: PCCS Books.

Timulak, L., McElvaney, J., Keogh, D., Martin, E., Clare, P., Chepukova, E., & Greenberg, L. S. (2017). Emotion-focused therapy for generalized anxiety disorder: An exploratory study. *Psychotherapy*, *54*(4), 361–366. https://doi.org/10.1037/pst0000128

Viechtbauer W. (2010). Conducting meta-analyses in R with the metafor package. *Journal of Statistical Software*, *36*, 1–48.

TABLE **S.13-3**   Client-Reported Qualitative Outcomes/Effects of HEPs: Qualitative Meta-Analysis Update

Main meta-category	Meta-categories	Primary study findings
A. Appreciating experiences of self	1. Smoother and healthier emotional experiencing	**Hopefulness, peace and stability, emotional well-being, greater sense of energy (Klein & Elliott, 2006); calmer, at peace (Elliott, 2002a;** Lipkin, 1954); improved mood, optimism; general openness to own feelings (Elliott et al., 1990); ability to express and contains feelings **(Dale et al., 1998); feeling more free and easy, more light and lively** (Lipkin, 1954); less reactive to anger in relation to parents; purification/ cleaned out (Steinmann et al., 2017); smoother emotional functioning (Timulak et al., 2017); not feeling burdened by problems (Timulak et al. 2010); not so affected by things – crying less; emotions and reactions are less extreme (MacLeod & Elliott, 2014); improved emotional functioning (McElvaney & Timulak, 2013); more self-contained; better able to regulate mood (Perren et al., 2009); feeling more grounded; shift in grief for Dad – not emotionally upset; not panicking/allowing time to respond to self before others; ability to not flee from initial reaction to new events (MacLeod et al., 2012); feeling happier **(Smith et al. 2014) (14/17; 14 out of 17 studies)**
	2. Self-acceptance of vulnerability	
	2a. Appreciating vulnerability	Permission to feel the pain; transparency (dropping barriers and defenses) (Rodgers, 2002); honest with self (Rodgers, 2002; Elliott, 2002a); open to change; awareness of being old, process of grieving, grieving is undoing problematic anger/anxiety (Elliott, 2002b); self-acceptance of existential isolation (Dale et al., 1998) more tolerant of difficulties and set-backs (Elliott et al., 2009); **more aware and accepting of own difficulties opened up emotionally, able to be more vulnerable and less ashamed (Stephen et al., 2011); awareness and feelings of loss (Smith et al., 2014) (6/17)**
	2b. Experiencing self-compassion/**Self-acceptance/valuing self**	Self-esteem, self-care (Klein & Elliott, 2006), improved self-esteem (Elliott et al., 1990); engagement with self (experiencing support from within) (Rodgers, 2002); valuing self (Dale et al., 1998); giving self-credit for accomplishments, trying new things, reading (Elliott, 2002b), **more self-compassionate stance; increased self-acceptance (self-worth) (Timulak et al., 2017); greater self-acceptance (McElvaney & Timulak, 2013);** continued improvement in self-esteem (Perren et al., 2009); asking for, receiving, and/or giving help in the dream (Ellis, 2016); slowing down and becoming more aware of self; more self-accepting and less people-pleasing (MacLeod et al., 2012) (10/17)

(Continued)

TABLE S.13-3 (Continued)

Main meta-category	Meta-categories	Primary study findings
3. Mastery/resilience of problematic experiences		
	3a. Experience of resilience	Restructuring (recycling the bad things) (Rodgers, 2002); insight first painful then feeling better (Lipkin, 1954); **increased resilience (Timulak et al., 2017); increased acceptance of role in life: responsibility (McElvaney & Timulak, 2013), increased resilience (Ellis, 2016) (5/17)**
	3b. Feeling empowered	Self-confident, strength within (Rodgers, 2002; Klein & Elliott, 2006; Lipkin, 1954); newfound or improved abilities to act (Klein & Elliott, 2006); preparing to take action to deal with problems (Elliott et al., 1990); specific wishes/attitudes strengthened (Elliott et al., 1990); being able to make decision, gaining control over life (Timulak at al., 2010; Lipkin, 1954; Rodgers, 2002); able to stand up for self, more initiative instead of fear of doing things (Lipkin, 1954); agency/confidence; increased individuation (Steinmann et al., 2017); increased inner confidence (Timulak et al., 2017); **braver/stronger and more confident, with less anger; better in my job (MacLeod & Elliott, 2014); increased sense of personal power (McElvaney & Timulak, 2013); gaining maturity (Perren et al., 2009); finding one's voice, standing up for oneself (Ellis, 2016); dropping some things that had been forcing self to do; able to say no despite fear of the consequences (Stephen et al., 2011); more discerning/realize entitled to choice; belief in self (MacLeod et al., 2012); myself again, more assertive again (Smith et al., 2014) (14/17)**
	3c. Mastering symptoms	Can cross bridges, can fly (Elliott et al., 2009); symptoms went one by one, sudden relief (Lipkin, 1954); gaining control over her life (Timulak et al., 2010); improved ability to cope (Elliott et al., 1990); General sense of well-being: health, energy, activities (Klein & Elliott, 2006); improved general day-to-day coping (Dale et al., 1998); **acquired new coping strategies (Steinmann et al., 2017); less anxiety (Timulak et al., 2017); less trembling, though still nervous sometimes (MacLeod & Elliott, 2014); improved coping strategies (McElvaney & Timulak, 2013); behavior change (Perren et al., 2009); positive ending to nightmares, greater control over nightmares (Ellis, 2016); putting self into position of potentially being judged (being on show); learning/practicing/knowing old behavior/self-awareness; Christmas: not running away from it, letting it unfold, facing it head-on (MacLeod et al., 2012); symptoms of anxiety more manageable (Smith et al., 2014) (14/17)**
4. Enjoying change in circumstances		Improved nonrelationship aspects of life independent of therapy (Elliott et al., 1990; Elliott, 2002b) (2/17)

(Continued)

TABLE S.13-3 (CONTINUED)

Main meta-category	Meta-categories	Primary study findings
B. Appreciating experience of self in relationship with others	1. Feeling supported	Feeling respected by children, seeking support group (Klein & Elliott, 2006); people tell me I am a nicer person (Elliott et al., 2009); in many studies attributions to therapy/therapist as provider of support (3/17) Note. reported changes in others' view of self
	2. **Being different/healthier in** interpersonal encounters	Better interpersonal functioning (all, romantic, family) (Klein & Elliott, 2006); reordering relationships (Dale et al., 1998); being able to cope with reactions of others (Timulak at al., 2010); increased independence/assertion; increased positive openness; improved relationships (Elliott et al., 1990); better relationship with my wife, more tolerant (Elliott at al., 2009); **relationship with parents (others) changed for the better; became more compassionate/forgiving toward parents (Steinmann et al., 2017); more at ease socially (interpersonally); less socially embarrassed (more outgoing); more self-assertive; resolved interpersonal unfinished business (Timulak et al., 2017);** talking more openly and honestly with others **(MacLeod & Elliott, 2014); improved interpersonal relationships (McElvaney & Timulak, 2013);** more honest, more assertive, less critical; more appropriate in their responses to criticism (Perren et al., 2009); seeing more people socially; lasting new relationship and shift in criteria relating to what might be OK in a relationship; able to manage a relationship with difficult colleague (Stephen et al., 2011); having a sense of belonging; don't need to hide/open to invites (MacLeod et al, 2012); happier – knock on effect on family **(Smith et al., 2014)** (13/17)
C. Changed view of self/others	1. Self-insight and self-awareness	Development of meaning and understanding of abuse, learning from therapy (Dale et al., 1998; Lipkin, 1954); more aware and true of myself (Klein & Elliott, 2006); realizations about self (Elliott et al., 1990); enlightened (problem fitting in like a glove), better understanding self, seeing patterns (Lipkin, 1954; **Timulak et al., 2017); changed way I generally look at life (Steinmann et al., 2017); greater self-awareness (McElvaney & Timulak, 2013);** awareness of having choices (Perren et al. 2009); **seeing what I do/seeing the old attitude (MacLeod et al, 2012); realization that symptoms will pass; awareness I did not do anything wrong (Smith et al., 2014)** (10/17)
	2. Changed view of others	See other viewpoints (Klein & Elliott, 2006); accepting parent faults; being more interested in others (Timulak at al., 2010); changes in views and attitudes toward others (Elliott et al., 1990); **changed way I look at parents, new perspective of parents (Steinmann et al., 2017); more understanding of those who caused me pain (MacLeod & Elliott, 2014); aware of their impact on others (Perren et al., 2009)** (6/17)

Note. The wordings in bold are the new additions to the table in comparison to the previous edition based on Timulak and Creaner (2010).

CHAPTER 14

COGNITIVE, BEHAVIORAL, AND COGNITIVE BEHAVIORAL THERAPY

MICHELLE G NEWMAN, W STEWART AGRAS, DAVID A F HAAGA, AND ROBIN B JARRETT

Abstract

This chapter provides an update of Emmelkamp (2013) and Hollon and Beck (2013) from the 6th edition of this *Handbook*. We review the research and most recent meta-analyses on traditional cognitive, behavioral, and combined cognitive behavioral therapy (so called "first and second waves") for a variety of disorders in adults. The disorders we focus on include anxiety disorders, posttraumatic stress disorder, obsessive compulsive disorder, depressive disorders, eating disorders, substance use and dependence disorders with smaller focused sections on personality disorders and psychosis. For most of these disorders we summarize research on outcomes (efficacy and specificity), primary and secondary prevention (e.g., preventing first full onset of the disorder in the lifetime), predictors and moderators, mediators and mechanisms, and dissemination studies. Overall, similar to the prior 6th edition of this *Handbook*, we conclude that CBT shows strong efficacy and specificity across a wide variety of disorders as well as strong effectiveness in the real world.

OVERVIEW

INTRODUCTION

Cognitive behavioral therapy (CBT) emerged from several disciplines. Basic research on behavioral learning in the first half of the 20th century ignited purely behavioral therapy in the 1950s, and this continued on until the 1970s. Separately, in the 1960s there was a development of cognitive therapy (CT). CT progressively merged with the dominant behavioral approach, until cognitive-behavioral approaches grew to predominance in the 1980s and beyond. In this chapter, we focus on CBT and use the term broadly to include behavioral therapy, cognitive therapy, and cognitive behavioral therapy to denote initial (so-called "first and second wave") therapies that have evolved from Skinnerian (Skinner, 1963), Pavlovian (Pavlov, 1994), and social learning (Bandura, 1977) theories, and functional analyses (Ferster, 1973). The principles of change within CBT include classical conditioning, operant conditioning, reinforcement, punishment, observational, and cognitive principles of learning. We will not cover more recent developments in CBT. For that, we refer the reader to Forman et al. herein on the "third wave" approaches in CBT (e.g., dialectical behavior therapy, mindfulness, and acceptance and commitment therapy) whose research base and clinical application are growing (see Chapter 16).

Several factors distinguish CBT from other forms of therapy. CBT tends to be less focused on *etiology* (or how a problem came about) and more focused on *maintaining factors* (what keeps the problem going). These maintaining factors also play a role in the treatment targets and theories regarding how specific techniques work to change those targets. CBT is more directive than most other therapies. Given its directiveness, the therapeutic relationship is more didactic than in other approaches with the therapist acting like a teacher. In CBT, therapists actively attempt to transfer specific skills to clients.

Within CBT, therapists also tend to be more explicit about the therapeutic tasks and goals than in other approaches. Therapists tell clients what to expect, and how and why a particular technique may be effective. There is also ongoing delivery of rationales for each technique as well as efforts to help maintain clients' expectations about how techniques work, and the best way to implement strategies. Homework assigned after every session is also central to CBT. Ongoing diary self-monitoring of symptoms, environmental, and internal contingencies, and tracking and charting of daily change also distinguishes CBT from other forms of therapy, which don't typically include diary symptom and contingency tracking as central to the therapeutic approach.

This chapter will focus primarily on five types of studies: *outcome* studies, which assess efficacy, defined as whether a treatment is effective in controlled settings, and specificity, defined as whether a treatment is more effective than a nonspecific control group or to a credible alternative psychotherapy; *prevention* studies, assessing whether CBT either leads to reduced levels of subthreshold symptoms (secondary prevention) or prevents the development of a new onset of the index disorder (primary prevention); *predictor and moderator* studies, which attempt to identify individual differences that predict change, or examine whether specific interventions work better for some people when directly compared to other interventions; *mediators and mechanism* studies, which attempt to determine if changing one variable precedes and predicts change in other variables, or assess core constructs that are thought to be the central aspects of the therapy that create change; and *dissemination* studies, which measure the effectiveness of interventions implemented in naturalistic settings, and thus investigate whether CBT works in the real world outside of academic settings.

Although CBT and its components remain among the most empirically supported treatments for many disorders, a number of studies have been comparing CBT to other forms of therapy since the prior edition of this *Handbook*. Additional studies have also examined cultural adaptations of CBT. Along with more

studies examining these factors, newer statistical techniques have also emerged that account for the nesting of the data, and that can be applied to evaluate change across time within individuals as opposed to mean levels of change across time.

The prior edition of this *Handbook* included two separate chapters on behavioral therapy (Emmelkamp, 2013) and cognitive and behavioral therapies (Hollon & Beck, 2013). This chapter will focus on an update of these two chapters with respect to traditional implementation of CBT for adults. In doing so, the chapter will emphasize depressive disorders, anxiety disorders, eating disorders, substance abuse and dependence, and with smaller focused sections on personality disorders and psychosis.

DEPRESSIVE DISORDERS

Depression is a frequent global public health problem with adverse effects on society and all forms of psychosocial functioning; it impairs physical and emotional health, and has the potential to be fatal and costly based on both human and financial merits (World Health Organization, 2017). Poverty, aging, physical illness, drug and alcohol use, and being female have been linked to depression (Pratt & Brody, 2014; World Health Organization, 2017).

We use the term *depression* broadly to cover unipolar, nonpsychotic, negative affective (and related) syndromes with functional impairments, characterized by systems such as the American Psychiatric Association's *Diagnostic and Statistical Manual 5th Edition* (DSM-5; American Psychiatric Association, 2013) as major depressive disorder and *International Classification of Diseases 11th Edition* (ICD-11; World Health Organization, 2018) as depressive disorders. Although these types of diagnostic classifications have been criticized (Lilienfeld & Treadway, 2016), we use DSM/ICD referents (throughout this chapter) to organize findings and to increase their relevance to clinical practice and health systems since these tend to use diagnoses as a pathway to access CBT and health care generally.

Outcome

Numerous texts and articles (e.g., Cuijpers et al., 2013a; Driessen & Hollon, 2010; Jarrett & Vittengl, 2016), as well as a chapter in the previous edition of this text (i.e., Hollon & Beck, 2013), have documented extensively the efficacy of CBT for adults with unipolar depression; these data have been instrumental in CBT being viewed as a first-line treatment for depression. Here we will guide the reader to extensive reviews and illustrate findings evaluating efficacy and exploring therapeutic processes with CBT for depression. In doing so, we will strive to uncover gaps and highlight innovation in research and practice to inspire the next generation of scientist practitioners who focus on improving outcomes for adults with depression using CBT and its variants as we are optimistic about inevitable advances.

Acute-phase CBT reduces depressive symptoms in approximately 40–50% of adults who begin the treatment (Jarrett & Vittengl, 2016); varying rates are affected by operational definitions and sampling. Using an updated method of meta-analysis conducted with individual patient level data from trials (rather than averaged data collected from tables in journal articles), Cuijpers and international collaborators compared CBT to other treatments (Cuijpers et al., 2013a). Overall, the effect sizes for acute-phase CBT were superior to treatment as usual (TAU) ($g = 0.59$, 95% CI [0.42, 0.76], $I^2 = 66\%$), placebo ($g = 0.51$, 95% CI [0.32, 0.69], $I^2 = 53\%$) and wait list ($g = 0.83$, 95% CI [0.72, 0.94], $I^2 = 37\%$) with medium to large effect sizes. Effects tended not to differ from similar comparisons within interpersonal ($g = -0.09$, 95% CI [-0.39, 0.20], $I^2 = 42\%$), dynamic ($g = 0.25$, 95% CI [-0.07, 0.58], $I^2 = 16\%$), and supportive psychotherapy ($g = 0.1$, 95% CI [-0.06, 0.25], $I^2 = 27\%$). These effects are also similar to those achieved when adults were treated with antidepressant medications (Amick et al., 2015; Gartlehner et al., 2015; Gartlehner et al., 2016; Weitz et al., 2015), which is emphasized here as a comparator because pharmacotherapy continues to be the modal first-line treatment (Cipriani et al. (2018). For example, Cuijpers, Berking et al. (2013a) found a Hedges's g of 0.03 (95% CI [-0.13, 0.18]) when comparing CBT to pharmacotherapy. Perhaps antidepressant medication is most frequently used due to access, advertising, and perceived short-term convenience. It is noteworthy that the effects of antidepressant medications are similar to those of frequently used medications in general medicine (Leucht et al., 2012). By inference, the effects of both are also similar to those of CBT for depression. Approximately 41% of patients who receive acute-phase CBT have significantly fewer depressive symptoms post-CBT than the average patient treated in a placebo or waiting list control group; this estimate is also similar for those treated with antidepressant medication (~40% chance; Jarrett & Vittengl, 2016), based on extensions of the U statistics (Seggar et al., 2002).

Although the findings from individual patient level meta-analyses do not challenge the antidepressant effects of either CBT or pharmacotherapy (Huhn et al., 2014), they may, however, raise questions regarding identifying the extent to which there could be conditions whereby acute-phase antidepressant medications could be slightly more efficacious than CBT (Weitz et al., 2015). Differential effects have been reported with CBT improving less than half (specifically, 5) of the 12 depressive symptoms including suicidal ideation, depressed mood, guilt feelings, psychic anxiety, and general somatic symptoms (Boschloo et al., 2019). It is important to note, however, that these differential effect sizes from 17 randomized trials were quite small (0.13–0.16) and resulted from controversial network estimation techniques, which some criticize as potentially unreliable (Forbes et al., 2017). Thus, effects require cautious interpretation and replication; they are not ready for clinical application. At the same time, if antidepressant medications are hypothesized to reduce suicidal ideation in affected adults, it would be important to avoid a type II error and to evaluate the hypothesis prospectively. If the effect is replicable, there may be an opportunity to reduce the risk of fatalities by applying a moderator with prescriptive potential (e.g., treating patients with suicidal ideation with antidepressant medication instead of or combined with CBT) (see Chapter 21).

These findings were also preceded by reports that the effect sizes between psychotherapy and pill placebo tended to be larger than those between medication and pill placebo, with concurrent evidence of methodological differences (Huhn et al., 2014), as well as findings that higher-quality studies of psychotherapy, with stronger controls, have smaller effects than those of lower quality (Cuijpers et al., 2010). Nonetheless, at this time the question of the conditions under which treatment equivalency (i.e., effects of CBT do not differ from pharmacotherapy for depression) or difference occur has been reopened for rigorous investigation with well-characterized samples of adequate size. These findings lay the foundation for adequately powered, multisite randomized controlled trials of CBT alone, CBT plus pill placebo, pharmacotherapy alone, and pill placebo alone in relevant generalizable samples, followed by attempts to find moderators and to replicate. Perhaps collaboration between networks of researchers and research-ready health care providers and systems could create and sustain such opportunities.

CBT for Depression and Social Functioning

Whereas the field initially focused on depressive symptoms, as noted in the DSMs and characterized by symptom severity measures, research outcomes have broadened to include psychosocial functioning, including interpersonal and role functioning, as well as quality of life. A meta-analysis suggested that, compared to control conditions, psychotherapy for depression (which included but was not limited to CBT) showed small to moderate effects on social functioning ($g = 0.40$, 95% CI [0.25, 0.55]); null effects were found when comparing types of therapies (Renner et al., 2014).

Acute-phase CBT was associated with improvements in social functioning compared to baseline; normalization occurred only for some (Vittengl et al., 2004), and improvement was maintained for at least 32 months post-acute phase response (Vittengl et al., 2016b). Similarly, six months after acute phase, CBT (alone or combined with antidepressant medication), antidepressant medications, and standard therapy, all yielded improved work and social functioning (with medium effect sizes) with no difference between treatment modalities (Zu et al., 2014). In addition, residual impairment in social functioning after CBT has been found to predict relapse/recurrence (Vittengl et al., 2016b; Vittengl et al., 2009).

Acute-phase CBT may improve but not normalize quality of life in depressed adults (Jha et al., 2014). According to a meta-analysis, both individual CBT ($g = 0.70$, 95% CI [0.49, 0.91]) and selective serotonin reuptake inhibitors ($g = 0.79$, 95% CI [0.67, 0.91]) improved quality of life compared to baseline (Hofmann et al., 2017). In addition, effect sizes remained stable (pre to follow-up $g = 0.72$, 95% CI [0.48, 0.97]) after discontinuation of CBT but there was no data on follow-up from SSRIs. More research is needed to determine how much improvement in psychosocial functioning after CBT and other anti-depressant therapies is unique or due to improvement in depressive symptoms. Given that depressive symptoms and psychosocial functioning are highly (albeit only partially) correlated, the directionality and parameters of the relationships require further exploration.

Can CBT Be Associated with Clinically Significant, Replicable Harms?

The literature on psychotherapy, including CBT, has been criticized for failing to assess potential side effects and adverse event profiles (Schermuly-Haupt et al., 2018). A meta-analysis of randomized trials comparing CBT to pharmacotherapy showed that during and after CBT extreme deterioration and non-response were infrequent (Vittengl et al., 2016a). Deterioration, defined as symptom severity increasing from pre- to posttreatment, occurred in 5–7% of patients and extreme nonresponse, defined as severe depressive symptoms posttreatment, occurred in 4–5%.

This line of research is in its infancy, in part because the concept of adverse events or negative effects in psychotherapy is underdeveloped (Linden, 2013). It will be important to reliably and validly assess and understand the concept. Definitions need to include issues that are important to patients and are not confounded with the symptoms of mood disorders. Such routine reports and assessment of harms, as well as its associated domains and durability of symptoms and functioning are needed. Large heterogeneous samples (i.e., diverse symptom profiles and demographics) will contribute to a more comprehensive understanding of any potential and *relative* harms in candidate antidepressant treatments, including CBT and other depression specific alternatives. Including relative harms in comparative studies will give the field and patients additional merits to use in evaluating the costs and benefits of available effective treatments, as well as their modes of delivery.

Does CBT Plus Pharmacotherapy Improve Acute-Phase Outcomes?

There is some evidence that when CBT is added to pharmacotherapy, effects exceed those of either modality used alone, with significant small effect sizes (Cuijpers et al., 2013a; Cuijpers et al., 2015; Huhn et al., 2014). For example, CBT plus pharmacotherapy versus pharmacotherapy alone had a medium effect size ($g = 0.49$, 95% CI [.29, .69], $I^2 = 16\%$; Cuijpers, Berking et al., 2013). Similarly, CBT plus pharmacotherapy versus CBT alone had a small to medium effect size ($g = 0.35$, 95% CI [.12, .58], $I^2 = 49\%$; Cuijpers et al., 2015). Effect sizes were small, however, when comparing combined treatment to CBT plus pill placebo ($g = 0.24$, 95% CI [−.13, .60], $I^2 = 51\%$; Cuijpers et al., 2015). On the other hand, in a meta-analysis, Amick et al. (2015) reported no difference in the effects of second generation antidepressants for combined treatments (RR = 0.98, 95% CI [.73,1.32]) and, when present, the benefit may be limited to patients with higher severity in presenting symptoms (Hollon et al., 2014). Again, inconsistency in findings prompts the need for attempts to replicate with adequately powered samples. Because combination therapy adds fiscal and human costs, it is important to identify when, *if it all*, it is most efficacious compared to the extent to which particular sequences of monotherapies might offer lower cost alternatives for populations of affected people.

What Are the Next Steps When First-Line, Acute-Phase Treatments Are Insufficient for Optimal Short- and Long-Range Outcomes?

Replicable algorithms are needed to identify which patients are at risk for acute-phase CBT nonresponse or incomplete remission. Vittengl et al. (2019) reported that patients offered 16–20 sessions of acute-phase CBT (in the context of two clinical trials) who had no symptom improvement by session 9 (which also was about week 5, in a protocol where patients initially had two sessions a week) had ≤ 10% probability of remission and > 75% probability of nonresponse. Important for generalizability of these effects are reports replicating the effect, for example, in a sample of patients treated in private practice combined with those from randomized trials (using different variations of CBT). Persons and Thomas (2019) showed that patients who did not remit by session 5 with one session per week had a poor chance of remission.

These data highlight the robust finding that early patterns of change in depressive symptoms can signal which patients benefit from treatment switches, augmentation, and/or targeted or sequence care. For example, research has shown that depressed adults who did not achieve remission after 12 weeks of monotherapy (either pharmacotherapy or CBT) had higher remission rates when switched to pharmacotherapy plus CBT (Dunlop et al., 2019). This finding is in line with the conditional recommendation from the APA guideline panel (American Psychological Association, 2019) to add CBT, interpersonal psychotherapy or psychodynamic psychotherapy to the first-line pharmacotherapy of adults who respond partially or do not respond.

Less-than-optimal acute-phase remission requires attention because it is important both when observed and also because it forecasts an increased risk of relapse and/or recurrence. It is noteworthy that the full recommendation by APA was to switch nonresponders or partial responders from antidepressant medication (alone) to CBT (alone) or to switch to a different antidepressant medication. More research is needed to inform best practices for nonresponders and partial responders generally, and particularly with respect to incomplete CBT response. To guide treatment when acute-phase CBT fails or produces partial remission and to promote reduced relapse and recurrence, the emerging literature has been subjected to patient-level meta-analysis. In one such meta-analysis of 13 studies, Guidi et al. (2016) examined the effects of adding CBT following the acute phase of antidepressants. Findings suggested that patients evidenced significantly less relapse/recurrence when CBT was added at the time antidepressant medications were tapered or discontinued, compared to when they received continued antidepressant medications or simply clinical management (RR = 0.67, 95% CI [0.48, 0.94], $I^2 = 0\%$). In addition, there was an advantage to adding CBT to continuation of pharmacotherapy versus continuation of antidepressants alone or TAU (RR = 0.81, 95% CI [0.69, 0.96], $I^2 = 0\%$). There was no advantage found with respect to pharmacotherapy being continued versus pharmacotherapy being tapered (RR = 0.09, 95% CI [−0.10, 0.28], $I^2 = 0\%$).

With respect to relapse prevention and sequenced care using CBT as a solitary acute-phase therapy, a randomized controlled trial showed that acute-phase CBT responders who were at higher risk for relapse/recurrence due to unstable/partial remission had fewer relapses over 8 months when treated with continuation-phase CT or fluoxetine plus clinical management compared to pill placebo plus clinical management (Jarrett et al., 2013). Further, even for the responders at higher risk for relapse, 70% went on to evidence stable remission and 47% went on to recover 32 months after responding to CBT and prior to relapse, recurrence, or dropping out (Vittengl et al., 2014). These findings suggest that there are likely parametric relationships between amount, length, and spacing of CBT sessions and remission and recovery, pending further replication and further exploration of sequenced treatments, and/or varying durations. It will be important to unravel the extent to which parametric differences exist when acute phase, continuation, and maintenance-phase treatment modalities are matched or unmatched in sequential care.

CBT and Relapse

As shown by Vittengl et al. (2007), when depressed adults discontinue antidepressant medications, they relapse (i.e., experience a return of the index episode) or recur (i.e., experience a new episode following a sustained asymptomatic period) significantly more than those who discontinue CBT. These findings of the antidepressant effects of acute CBT enduring following discontinuation were replicated (Cuijpers et al., 2013b; Hollon et al., 2005). For example, Cuijpers, Hollon et al. (2013) found an odds ratio of 2.61 (95% CI [1.58, 4.31], I^2 = 0%,) when comparing relapse between discontinued pharmacotherapy versus discontinued CBT. Biesheuvel-Leliefeld et al. (2015) also found stronger maintenance effects from CBT than treatment as usual (RR = 0.68, 95% CI [0.54, 0.87], I^2 = 52%). Although these results are promising for CBT, the meta-analysis by Vittengl et al. (2007) showed that approximately 29% of CBT responders would relapse/recur one year after discontinuation, and by two years the rate grew to 54%. Another more recent meta-analysis found that the overall likelihood of relapse following CBT was 33.4% (ranging from 18.5% to 46.5%) across a maximum of three years (Wojnarowski et al., 2019). These findings highlight the need to better understand the predictors and moderators of risk, particularly their potential interactions with the protective mechanisms in CBT which could lower relapse/recurrence rates further. For example, Jarrett et al. (2016) showed that most CBT responders who achieved a stable remission during the acute phase might remain episode free for a year, compared to their counterparts with unstable remission who relapsed earlier and required some type of immediate continuation-phase treatment. Similarly, for adults with chronic depression, Cognitive Behavioral Analysis System of Psychotherapy (CBSAP) increased "well weeks" over one year more than supportive psychotherapy (Schramm et al., 2019).

Continuation-Phase CBT and Relapse

Depressive relapse (i.e., a continuation of the presenting episode) is probable and risk increases if residual symptoms are present (r = 0.34, 95% CI [0.10, 0.54], I^2 = 85%) or as number of prior episodes increase (r = 0.19, 95% CI [0.07, 0.30], I^2 = 0%; Wojnarowski et al., 2019). However, relapse reduction was shown in continuation-phase CBT for responders to acute-phase CBT, who during the continuation phase were not on antidepressant medications in either phase (Jarrett et al., 2001; Jarrett et al., 2013; Jarrett et al., 2000; Jarrett et al., 1998) Relapse reductions after acute-phase CBT with and without antidepressants have also been reported when remitted patients received eight additional weeks of CBT. Specifically, this relapse-reducing form of CBT delayed onset of relapse over 15 months, but did not reduce the severity or number of episodes (de Jonge et al., 2019), perhaps due to its shorter duration during the period of high risk. Relapse reduction effects for continuation-phase CBT alone and combined with antidepressant medications were also evident in responders or remitters to acute-phase pharmacotherapy (Bockting et al., 2015; Bockting et al., 2005; Fava, 2016; Fava et al., 2004; Paykel et al., 2005). In fact, the APA treatment guideline provided a conditional recommendation for adults who achieve remission from depression to receive psychotherapy (e.g., CBT, mindfulness-based cognitive therapy, or interpersonal psychotherapy) rather than antidepressant medication or treatment as usual in order to prevent relapse (American Psychological Association, 2019).

Maintenance-Phase CBT Studies and Recurrence

There are few studies available to determine how and when to best extend CBT into a maintenance phase to prevent recurrence (a new episode, *distinct from the presenting episode due to recovery*), which limits understanding of CBT's full potential. Promising results suggest that maintenance-phase CBT may prevent recurrence in adults whose depression had remitted in spite of a history of five or more episodes (e.g., Stangier et al., 2013). Additionally, a form of maintenance-phase CBT (alone or as an adjunctive treatment) was just as effective in reducing recurrence over two years as maintenance-phase antidepressant medication (Bockting et al., 2018). A novel finding occurred in a three-year follow-up of adults who recovered with antidepressant medication alone or combined with CBT suggested that adding antidepressants to CBT may interfere with the enduring effects of CBT (DeRubeis et al., 2020). If replicable, these findings may transform recommendations for patients who may wish to continue and discontinue medications. Nevertheless, the generalizability of these results is, largely, untested. The literature is inconsistent in the usage of the terms *relapse* and *recurrence* (as well as *response*, *remission*, and *recovery*) making careful attention to sample definition essential in comparing results. Therefore, at this time, definitive comments on the elimination or reduction of *recurrence* using maintenance-phase CBT remains premature; this topic represents a highly promising area for new research.

Prevention

There is meta-analytic evidence that psychological interventions including CBT and interpersonal psychotherapy can reduce the incidence and/or delay the onset of first cases of depression in youth, adults, and during the postpartum period. Cuijpers et al. (2008) concluded that compared to treatment as usual, such psychological interventions significantly reduced the incidence of depression by 22% based on 19 studies. van Zoonen et al. (2014) replicated this meta-analytic finding updating it with 32 studies and reporting an incidence reduction of 21%. Because preventive CBT is both feasible and effective, it shows promise in reducing the global disease burden of depression.

Predictors and Moderators

Often, studies addressing the question of which patients respond best to CBT alone or compared with other antidepressant therapies have insufficient power (i.e., inadequate sample sizes), thereby making most of the extant findings only suggestive. Higher baseline depressive symptom severity remains one of the most robust predictors of worse outcomes after CBT (Vittengl et al., 2016c; Wardenaar et al., 2015). However, baseline severity does not appear to interact with or moderate the selection of which modalities should be selected. For example, baseline severity does not help a clinician work with a patient to determine if pharmacotherapy versus CBT is the best choice (Weitz et al., 2015).

Novel research designs are needed (e.g., Kelley et al., 2018) to identify moderators of response. The literature on CBT is not based on diverse samples that reflect the global problem that depression represents. For example, a major gap in the literature of CBT for depression exists in characterizing the effective practices and processes for older adults (i.e., aged 50 or more) (Wilkinson & Izmeth, 2016). Further, exploration of the full range of variables – including but not limited to demographics, clinical characteristics, biomarkers, and genetics that may predict or moderate outcomes in CBT – is needed (see Chapter 7).

Risk Factors for Depressive Relapse and Recurrence

Identifying high-risk factors matters in antidepressant treatment selection (Bockting et al., 2015; Brouwer et al., 2019). For example, Jarrett and colleagues (2001; 2013) demonstrated that more residual symptoms and/or early age of onset were strong predictors of which patients benefited most from continuation-phase CT. Jarrett and colleagues (2016) went on to show that residual symptoms could be used prescriptively to distinguish the adult acute-phase CT responders who did and did not need continuation-phase CT or fluoxetine to reduce relapse. Only 12.4% of CT responders with fewer residual symptoms relapsed or recurred over the first year after responding to acute-phase CBT, showing that these lower risk responders did not require continuation-phase CT (Jarrett et al., 2016). Such findings, if replicable, have implications for reducing human, societal, and health care costs based on use of algorithms to guide care.

Notably, Buckman et al. (2018) reviewed the literature on the risk factors for depressive relapse and recurrence in adults. They reported that a history of childhood maltreatment or past episodes and residual symptoms are strong prognostic indicators of risk and might be indicators to use prescriptively to determine which patients need continuation/maintenance phase or prophylactic treatment. Buckman et al. reported evidence, albeit inconsistent, for neuroticism, comorbid anxiety, rumination, and early age of onset as risk markers. They highlight neurocognitive and neuroendocrine factors as potential risk markers that need more study. Interestingly, they found no evidence that a positive family history of depression increased risk and that if a patient can remain well for five or more years, that person's risk is substantially lowered. These risk factors, as well as others (e.g., genetic profiles), may relate or interact, possibly influencing depressive trajectories causally in the absence and presence of CBT and other antidepressant therapies (Bockting et al., 2015; Clarke et al., 2015).

Mediators and/or Mechanisms

Depression is associated with negative affect, impairment in thinking, social and interpersonal functioning as well as engagement in activities that maintain health (e.g., sleeping, eating, and moving). Not surprisingly, these are also the symptoms that acute-phase depression-specific therapies, including CBT and antidepressant medications, change. The early clinical theory underlying CBT for depression initially focused on the characteristically negative cognitive content adults reported in describing self, world, and future. The cognitive model has been updated to incorporate findings from disciplines such as behavioral genetics, cognitive neuroscience, personality, and social psychology (Beck, 2008). Beck and associates articulated verbal and behavioral strategies that help patients to evaluate the extent to which their cognitions and behaviors were accurate and helpful (Beck et al., 1979). Through cognitive and behavioral changes, therapists collaborate with patients to improve negative affect when the patient has explored and experimented with different (i.e., challenging) ways of thinking and behaving.

One mechanism through which CBT may produce effects is that the patient learns something new, such as compensatory skills or new assumptions about self, world, and future (Bruijniks et al., 2019; Jarrett et al., 2018; Jarrett et al., 2008). Notably, the key question within this hypothesis is what is the *something* that is learned? The traditional theory is that patients with depression have a cognitive vulnerability that is activated or intensified by stress and that what CBT teaches is an adaptive method for restructuring depressogenic cognition (Nolen-Hoeksema et al., 2008). One highly innovative corollary of this hypothesis is that the learning in CBT is akin to the process of second language acquisition and that technical aspects of CBT could be improved by using cognitive science to model how people learn new languages (Haeffel & Kaschak, 2018). Innovations in improving memory and neurocognitive functioning in depressed adults hold promise in helping depressed people process information more fully (Zieve et al., 2019) and develop and use new perspectives. For additional studies and future empirical directions on processes and mechanisms of change in CBT for depressive disorders, including the therapeutic alliance (see Chapter 8).

Collaboration with Neuroscience Provides Opportunities to Find Moderators, Mediators, and Mechanisms

When people are depressed, they have difficulties not only regulating emotion but also in processing information, which are both targets of CBT for depression. Chalah and Ayache (2018) summarized findings from neuroscience relevant to the biological effects of depression and CBT. Studies of depressed patients have implicated the dorsal network (i.e., orbitofrontal cortex, anterior cingulate cortex, prefrontal cortex [which also includes working memory, reasoning, problem solving, and self-referential processing]). Additional findings implicate the ventral limbic affective network (including the amygdala and hippocampus) in depression. Taylor et al. (2010) posit bidirectional relationships between *bottom-up emotional processes* (i.e., decreases in the activation of the amygdala-hippocampus complex) and *top-down processes* (i.e., regulating emotions through cognitive control). Further, the default mode network (i.e., prefrontal cortex, anterior cingulate cortex, posterior cingulate cortex, precuneus, inferior parietal cortex, and lateral temporal cortex) may also be related to major depressive disorder. Chalah and Ayache (2018) note that this network is activated during activities like meditation and deactivated when attention shifts toward the external environment. They hypothesize that CBT achieves its antidepressant effects through modulating both the affective and cognitive networks.

McGrath et al. (2013) have shown that the insula *hypo*metabolism was associated with CBT remission (compared to escitalopram), while *hyper*metabolism was associated with escitalopram remission (compared to CBT). They reported that the anterior insula was involved in "interoception, emotional self-awareness, decision making and cognitive control" (p. 826). Future studies may explore the conditions under which neurocognitive correlates function as independent or dependent variables in CBT. Path models may be helpful.

Fundamental CBT skills for depression target the excesses and deficits outlined above. While the literature on how CBT works is inconclusive, it is possible that attention to *affect shifts* increases emotional regulation and *logical analysis and hypothesis testing* increase cognitive control. Both basic processes in CBT are designed to reduce emotional reactivity and restructure cognition. Perhaps such shifts in affect and attention come to trigger or facilitate problem solving, logical analysis, and behavioral experiments, thereby allowing the patient to develop new perspectives and learn through natural contingencies which were previously avoided or infrequently experienced. At this time, however, these hypotheses highlight gaps in knowledge and inspire new research.

Collaborations between clinical scientists who understand how to deliver CT to typical patients and neuroscientists who use cutting edge paradigms to assess emotional regulation, information processing, and human learning hold promise for advancing knowledge. For example, it may be instructive to learn how, if at all, adjunctive Cognitive Control Therapy (Koster et al., 2017) facilitates learning and reduces depressive symptoms. We predict that as measurement of the key concepts (e.g., symptoms, moderators and mechanisms, as well as the technical aspects of CBT, including delivery platforms) become more advanced, usable knowledge will follow.

Dissemination

A criticism of CBT for depression and related disorders is that CBT is not widely accessible due to small numbers of competent and/or credentialed providers and the costs of CBT, both practically and financially. This criticism requires attention because the typical depressed adult prefers psychotherapy to antidepressant medication (McHugh et al., 2013; Olfson & Marcus, 2010).

As described below, progress has been made in the dissemination of CBT to naturalistic settings, use of nontraditional delivery modalities, and involvement of paraprofessionals and professionals with differing levels of experience. Illustrations of effective dissemination of CBT for depression to naturalistic settings can be found in public mental health care (Lopez & Basco, 2015), insured care (Karlin et al., 2019), and the Veterans Administration (Karlin et al., 2013).

With respect to delivery formats, a recent network meta-analysis (Cuijpers et al., 2019) suggests that the efficacy of CBT delivered to individuals compared to groups (SMD –0.32, 95% CI [–0.63, 0.00], $I^2 = 24\%$), telephone (CBT vs. telephone: SMD –.04, 95% CI [–0.30, 0.22], $I^2 = 16\%$), or guided self-help (CBT vs. guided self-help: SMD –0.12, 95% CI [–0.54, 0.31], $I^2 = 6\%$) was not significantly different. At the same time, all of these modalities were more efficacious than waiting list (SMDs, range 0.87, 1.02), TAU (SMDs, range 0.47, 0.72) and unguided self-help CBT (SMDs, range 0.34, 0.59). Drop-out in guided self-help was higher than wait list (RR = 0.63, 95% CI [0.52, 0.75]) and TAU (RR = 0.72, 95% CI [0.57, 0.90]), as is self-help without therapist involvement vs. wait list (RR = 0.75, 95% CI [0.62, 0.91]) vs. TAU (RR = 0.86, 95% CI [0.69, 1.08]; Cuijpers et al., 2019). If these findings continue to be replicated, they may change the way the field designs and evaluates dissemination and may propel innovative uses of these tools as adjuncts in traditional settings. Perhaps, such innovations, coupled with a focus on patient engagement, can increase access to CBT. In order for the field to disseminate CBT for mood and related disorders effectively and widely (i.e., to boost global health), we must identify which therapeutic components produce the reliable effects of CBT (from whom), and thus are candidates for dissemination, reaching patients where they are.

Summary

In considering the extent to which traditional cognitive behavioral interventions improve outcomes in adults with major depressive disorders, we conclude (as did the authors of the sixth edition of the *Handbook*) that CBT improves both short- and long-term outcomes for some adults. We add that at least half the depressed adults who start CBT improve, albeit at different levels of reduction in depressive symptoms and improvements in psychosocial functioning. Cognitive behavioral therapy appears similar to interpersonal psychotherapy, dynamic psychotherapy, and supportive psychotherapy in acute-phase antidepressant effects. The short-term effects of CBT on depressive symptoms are similar to antidepressant medications. There is some evidence that if CBT is combined with pharmacotherapy, either as a first-line treatment (perhaps reserved for patients with more severe baseline symptoms) or when pharmacotherapy fails, then outcomes might improve. These findings informed the American Psychological Association's (2019) development of guidelines for the treatment of depression, which is a new and important development since the sixth edition.

Compared to pharmacotherapy, acute-phase CBT offers the distinguishing advantage of reducing the likelihood of depressive *relapse*, and possibly *recurrence*, pending more evidence. Based on the available evidence, these enduring effects are the distinguishing feature of CBT for depression. There is compelling evidence that the continuation-phase formulations of CBT also reduce relapse and perhaps recurrence, particularly for patients at higher risk. Studies with CBT maintenance phases (alone and combined with antidepressant medication) and longer longitudinal follow-up are needed for definitive statements.

For responders to acute-phase CBT, residual symptoms and/or extent of partial remission appear to forecast which patients can benefit from immediate continuation-phase therapy to prevent relapse and which patients may not need further treatment, at least for some period of time. Some patients, however, who achieve full remission and/or recovery, appear to need a maintenance-phase treatment in order to prevent a recurrence. Identification of specific duration and intensity of CBT needed to neutralize risk of relapse/recurrence and promote normalization, in both symptoms and functioning, will be important and may be guided by the need to replicate reported interactions between risk and treatment (i.e., moderators), particularly in generalizable samples of adequate size with longitudinal follow-up. With respect to which patients should start with CBT rather than the alternative acute-phase treatments, the evidence is inconclusive. We need to learn more about potential adverse effects of CBT as a solitary treatment or when combined with antidepressant medication. Instead, we know more about which characteristics may predict adequate versus inadequate response for patients who start with CBT (e.g., early response trajectories). Cognitive behavioral therapy offers promise in preventing lifetime first onsets of depressive disorders.

ANXIETY DISORDERS, POSTTRAUMATIC STRESS DISORDER, AND OBSESSIVE-COMPULSIVE DISORDER

As with depression, anxiety disorders are costly to society in terms of medical morbidity, disability, and healthcare utilization (Newman, 2000). Thus, treatment for these problems is important.

Outcome

Below we discuss outcome of CBT for anxiety disorders in terms of overall efficacy for CBT versus placebo, efficacy of specific components of CBT, and comparison between CBT and other forms of psychotherapy and or with and without medications.

Efficacy of CBT for Specific Anxiety and Related Disorders

In a recent meta-analysis of 41 studies, compared to placebo, CBT for anxiety disorders had moderate effect sizes for acute treatment ($g = 0.56$, 95% CI [0.44, 0.69]) and follow-up ($g = 0.47$, 95% CI [0.30, 0.64]; Carpenter et al., 2018). Effect sizes were similar when comparing CBT to psychological ($g = 0.52$, 95% CI [0.38, 0.66]) or pill placebo ($g = 0.66$, 95% CI [0.36, 0.97]). There were large effect sizes of CBT versus placebo for obsessive-compulsive disorder (OCD; $g = 1.13$, 95% CI [0.58, 1.68]), generalized anxiety disorder (GAD; $g = 1.01$, 95% CI [0.44, 1.57]), and acute stress disorder (ASD; $g = 0.87$, 95% CI [0.32, 1.41]), and small to moderate effect sizes for post-traumatic stress disorder (PTSD; $g = 0.48$, 95% CI [0.26, 0.71]), social anxiety disorder (SAD; $g = 0.41$, 95% CI [0.25, 0.57]), and panic disorder (PD; $g = 0.39$, 95% CI [0.12, 0.65]). Similar conclusions regarding the strong efficacy of CBT were drawn for the treatment of youth with anxiety disorders (Higa-McMillan et al., 2016). Another meta-analysis showed a medium effect size ($g = 0.69$, 95% CI [0.47, 0.92], $I^2 = 70\%$) favoring CBT for anxiety disorders over treatment as usual (Watts et al., 2015). The latter study also examined type of usual treatment and found there were moderate effect sizes ($g = 0.57$, $I^2 = 53\%$) showing CBT to be superior to other types of psychotherapy-only treatments (included a mix of psychodynamic, interpersonal, integrative, supportive, and nondirective approaches). Not only does CBT have enduring effects, but it shows additional gains following anxiety disorder treatment termination lasting up to two years (Bandelow et al., 2018).

In terms of its effects on complete recovery, in a recent meta-analysis, remission rates across anxiety disorders were 51% on average with highest rates in PTSD (53.3% at post and 54.8% at follow-up), GAD (51.4% at post and 65% at follow-up) and PD (48% at post and 55.6% at follow-up) and lowest rates in OCD (37.9% at post and 52.3% at follow-up) and SAD (40.1% at post and 43.2% at follow-up) (Springer et al., 2018). At the same time, these results have some caveats, including that most studies did not include dropouts in their analyses and that there was a possibility of publication bias.

CBT also has shown strong efficacy for comorbid anxiety and depressive disorders (Cuijpers et al., 2016a; Cuijpers et al., 2014; Cuijpers et al., 2016b). In addition, CBT has a significant effect on quality of life ($g = 0.30$, 95% CI [0.13, 0.48], Carpenter et al., 2018). Such quality of life measures typically assessed life satisfaction regarding such things as love and relationships, work, recreation, self-esteem, and physical health. There is also emerging evidence for an effect of CBT on reduced heart rate in those with anxiety disorders, particularly for PTSD, social anxiety disorder, specific phobia, and OCD (Gonçalves et al.,

2015). Another meta-analysis showed an effect of CBT on brain function (Marwood et al., 2018), particularly with regard to decreases in anterior cingulate/paracingulate gyrus, inferior frontal gyrus and insula activation after therapy.

Efficacy of Specific Components of CBT

CBT packages or manuals for anxiety disorders vary widely both with respect to techniques included for any one disorder and across disorders. Exposure tends to be emphasized most heavily in PD, SAD, specific phobia, OCD and PTSD treatments. Nonetheless, the way exposure is delivered within each of these problems varies. Panic disorder treatments, for example, tend to focus heavily on both situational and interoceptive exposure (entailing techniques that elicit internal symptoms related to panic attacks to target fear of fear, and to ensure that individuals habituate to anxiety associated with internal cues). Interoceptive exposure tends to be unique to panic disorder treatments. Exposure for social anxiety disorder often entails a lot of role-playing within sessions in addition to situational exposure outside of sessions. For PTSD, imaginal exposure is heavily emphasized involving having individuals relive and process the traumatic event both within and between sessions in addition to situational exposure to reminders of the traumatic experience. This can take the form of having the client graphically describe the traumatic event over and over again, or even having the client write a letter to a perpetrator or imagine a conversation with a perpetrator. In OCD, exposure is paired with response prevention. This entails abstaining from engaging in a compulsion during and following exposure to the obsessive concern (e.g., touching a public door knob and abstaining from hand washing). For GAD treatments, some CBT packages have not used exposure at all (Wells, 2007), some used exposure only in cases where the client was avoiding situations or procrastinating, and instead focused on counterconditioning (i.e., pairing relaxation with worry triggers; Borkovec et al., 2002), some treatments entailed worry exposure (Hoyer et al., 2009), and some have focused on exposure to feared outcomes of worry (Zinbarg et al., 2006).

Regarding the efficacy of exposure, no recent studies have examined it as a standalone treatment. One meta-analysis of 17 prior component controlled trials (conducted between 1988 and 2004), however, found that the addition of cognitive therapy to exposure-based treatments did not enhance their efficacy (Adams et al., 2015). The combined effect sizes were not significantly different when comparing CBT to exposure alone with both having an effect size of $d = 1.23$. Consistent with this idea, Carpenter et al. (2018) found that intervention packages that contained exposure as the main treatment technique had larger effect sizes ($g = 0.78$, 95% CI [0.45, 1.10]) than primarily cognitive intervention packages ($g = 0.38$, 95% CI [0.18, 0.57]). Similarly, in a meta-analysis containing efficacy studies, therapies that contained exposure for anxiety disorders ($d = 1.40$, 95% CI [1.2, 1.59]) had significantly larger effect sizes than therapies that did not contain exposure ($d = 0.96$, 95% CI [0.75, 1.16]), particularly for PTSD (exposure: $d = 1.43$, 95% CI [1.14, 1.79] and nonexposure: $d = 0.94$, 95% CI [.59, 1.29]; Parker et al., 2018).

Another behavioral technique included within almost all cognitive and behavioral treatments for anxiety is relaxation training. However, the extent to which it is emphasized and the actual techniques used vary widely within treatment packages. For most anxiety disorder CBTs, clients receive diaphragmatic breathing, also called breathing retraining, as part of only one session. Meuret et al. (2003) have made the case that breathing retraining might be efficacious on its own for anxiety disorders, if done correctly. However, it isn't always done well or thoroughly across multiple sessions. In particular, although hyperventilation is the target of breathing retraining, few studies have examined whether the techniques used do actually target it by measuring arterial $pCo2$. These authors have tested a method of respiratory biofeedback that was shown in combination with thorough breathing retraining taught within four weekly sessions to be helpful in raising $pCo2$ and lowering panic symptoms with gains maintained at the one-year follow-up (Meuret et al., 2008; Meuret et al., 2001).

Separately, clients with anxiety disorders also typically receive at least some training in progressive muscle relaxation (PMR). However, it is rare that randomized controlled trials of CBT for anxiety disorders also include applied relaxation (Öst, 1987), which was shown in a series of studies by Öst and colleagues to be helpful for PD (Öst & Westling, 1995), and significantly better for PD than progressive relaxation alone (Öst, 1988). Whereas progressive muscle relaxation (PMR) emphasizes practicing systematic tensing and releasing of muscle groups in a quiet and convenient space, applied relaxation begins with PMR but then teaches clients to achieve rapid and cue-controlled relaxation in response to anxiety triggers and attempts to generalize that practice to clients' use of quick relaxation in their natural environments to ensure that it is portable to their daily lives. Unfortunately, this form of systematic and targeted relaxation has been rarely included in commonly used treatment packages.

When considering findings of meta-analyses that examine the efficacy of relaxation, it is important to keep in mind that they have often lumped together different approaches to relaxation training and thus may not have been done optimally. Nonetheless, in a meta-analysis, the overall effect comparing combined CBT across all anxiety disorders to relaxation training alone was small but significant and favored CBT ($g = -0.25$, 95%, CI [-0.38, -0.13], $I^2 = 53\%$). When broken down by anxiety disorder, however, relaxation was not significantly less effective than combined CBT for panic disorder ($g = -0.09$, 95% CI [-0.29, 0.11], $I^2 = 32\%$), and GAD ($g = -0.01$, 95% CI [-0.20, 0.20], $I^2 = 0\%$). At the same time, it was less efficacious than combined CBT for PTSD ($g = -0.60$, 95% CI [-0.94, -0.27], $I^2 = 0\%$), OCD ($g = -0.58$, 95% CI [-0.90, -0.27], $I^2 = 60\%$), any phobia ($g = -0.22$, 95% CI [-0.42, -0.03], $I^2 = 27\%$), and there was a trend for maintenance of gains for PD ($g = -0.31$, 95% CI [-0.56, -0.06]; Montero-Marin et al., 2018). Interestingly, however, whereas PMR alone was inferior to CBT ($g = -0.47$, 95% CI [-0.63, -0.30], $I^2 = 37\%$), there was no significant difference between applied relaxation (AR) and CBT ($g = -0.05$, 95% CI [-0.19, 0.09], $I^2 = 12\%$) consistent with the argument that AR should be employed much more than it is currently.

CBT for anxiety disorders also typically includes cognitive restructuring. As noted earlier, the addition of cognitive restructuring didn't enhance the efficacy of exposure therapy for anxiety treatments (Adams et al., 2015). At the same time, the efficacy of exposure therapy was significantly better than the efficacy of cognitive restructuring for anxiety disorders (Parker et al., 2018).

CBT versus Other Forms of Psychotherapy

Efficacy of CBT was also not significantly different from mindfulness-based therapies when using difference in standardized mean change (DSMC) as the outcome on internalizing symptoms (DSMC = 0.17, 95% CI [–0.06, 0.39], Q = 39.15) and distress (DSMC = 0.00, 95% CI [–0.47, 0.47], Q = 19.78,) but was superior to mindfulness on fear symptoms (DSMC = 0.28, 95% CI [0.1, 0.46], Q = 9.91(de Abreu Costa et al., 2018). Since fear symptoms are central targets in the treatment of most anxiety disorders, this suggests that mindfulness-based therapies may not be as good as CBT for anxiety disorder symptoms. Other meta-analyses also found larger effect sizes for CBT for anxiety disorders (Hedman-Lagerlöf et al., 2018; Newby et al., 2015). For Hedman et al. (g = –0.33, 95% CI = [–0.86, 0.19], I^2 = 60%) the comparison failed to reach significance. However, Newby et al. found that CBT had significantly larger effect sizes for anxiety outcomes (g =0 .88, 95% CI [0.77, 1.0], Q = 7.95).

Unified protocol interventions are also not more efficacious than targeted CBT (Newby et al., 2015) for primary disorders (g = 0.15, 95% CI = [–0.09, .38], I^2 = 0%; Pearl & Norton, 2017), but study quality for unified interventions is generally poor so it is difficult to draw conclusions. As noted above, there is also some evidence for the superiority of CBT to other psychotherapies when delivered in the real world (Watts et al., 2015), but that study lumped a wide variety of other therapies together so one cannot draw definitive conclusions yet about any one other therapy. The case has also been made that most randomized trials comparing CBT to other forms of therapy were underpowered and inadequate to detect a small effect size (Cuijpers, 2016). It has also been argued that meta-analyses comparing CBT to other forms of therapy have additional methodological weaknesses and thus it isn't possible to draw conclusions from them (Craske & Stein, 2017). However, as noted above, psychotherapies that included exposure as a major component of them were consistently superior to those that did not insofar as anxiety disorders were concerned. Considering that exposure is a core component of most of its protocols, and based on the substantial evidence about the efficacy of CBT as a general approach demonstrating short and long-term superiority to TAU and placebos, we believe that CBT should be considered the first line of psychotherapeutic interventions for anxiety disorders.

CBT Combined with Medication or Alone

There has been a lot of debate regarding what is the first line of treatment for anxiety disorders regarding CBT, medications, or their combination. When CBT alone was compared directly to the efficacy of medications alone for anxiety disorders, most studies found that the approaches were not significantly different from one another in their acute or short-term efficacy (e.g., d = 0.08, 95% CI = [–0.13, 0.28]) (Bandelow et al., 2007; Tolin, 2017). However, CBT termination showed significantly greater maintenance of gains than pill placebo termination, but active medication termination was not significantly different in its gain maintenance than pill placebo termination (Bandelow et al., 2018). Other meta-analyses suggested a decline when medications were terminated (Tolin, 2017) and continued gains when CBT was terminated (Bandelow et al., 2018). When comparing CBT plus medications to CBT plus pill placebo, there was a slight advantage to combined CBT with antidepressants during the acute phase (for antidepressants g = –0.28, 95% CI [0.09, 0.41], Q = 45.34; for anxiolytics: g = 0.13, 95% CI [0.10, 0.35], Q = 11.12), but this advantage was lost following treatment discontinuation (for antidepressants g = –0.17, 95% CI = [–0.38, 0.03], Q = 4.85; for anxiolytics: g = 0.07, 95% CI [–0.14, 0.28], Q = 0) (Tolin, 2017). Another meta-analysis comparing CBT versus medication for GAD found that none of the medication studies that met inclusion criteria collected follow-up data (Carl et al., 2019). Also, studies have found that medication treatments are more costly than psychotherapy (Ophuis et al., 2017). There are also theoretical reasons not to encourage concurrent medication use with CBT including concerns that clients tend to attribute any gains they might make to the medication as opposed to attributing it to their efforts during therapy resulting in a lack of investment in the therapy. Also, medications have side effects, which can lead to greater dropouts than CBT (Würz & Sungur, 2009). Overall, the suggestion has been made that for anxiety disorders, there is no reason to recommend medications as a first-line intervention over CBT or in combination with CBT. Instead, CBT should be the first-line intervention. However, medications may be beneficial in the treatment of nonresponders to CBT (Tolin, 2017).

When examining whether CBT can be enhanced with medications, it is also important to consider novel compounds that have been tested in the context of exposure for SAD, specific phobia, PD, PTSD, and OCD. These compounds are only delivered acutely and during exposure and thus do not require any long-term use. For example, D-cycloserene is a compound that enhances fear extinction in animals and a recent meta-analysis by Bürkner et al. (2017) suggested that its effects showed a small enhancement at one–month follow-up (g = –0.27, 95% CI [–0.47, –0.08]). Nonetheless, any added efficacy disappeared at three-month (g = 0.06, 95% CI [–0.08, 0.21]) and six-month follow-up (g = 0.13, 95% CI [–0.06, 0.32]). When examining acute effects by individual diagnoses, this meta-analysis found a trend for SAD (g = –0.37, 95% CI[–0.76, 0.00]), but effects failed to reach significance for specific phobia, PD, PTSD, or OCD. One possible benefit of this drug, however, might be to speed up the effects of exposure, thus requiring fewer sessions, and increasing the cost-effectiveness of CBT for SAD (Tolin, 2017). Tolin's (2017) meta-analysis found advantages of two additional agents used to enhance exposure. Both yohimbine (g = 1.40, 95% CI = [–0.78, 2.02],

I^2 = 0%) and methylene blue (*g* = 0.56, 95% CI [0.18, 0.94], I^2 = 0%) created additional gains at follow-up, despite modest effects at posttreatment (yohimbine: *g* = 0.35, 95% CI [–0.01, 0.70], I^2 = 30%; methylene blue: *g* = –0.01, 95% CI [–0.49, 0.48], I^2 = 0%). Oxytocin, which has also been tested as an exposure enhancer, showed no added benefit to date (Tolin, 2017). Thus, some of these novel agents show promise.

Prevention

A meta-analysis of CBT prevention programs found significant effect sizes overall for prevention of pathological anxiety (*g* = 0.67, 95% CI [0.50, 0.84], I^2 = 0%) with gains maintained at follow-up ranging from 4 to 157 weeks (*g* = 0.58, 95% CI [0.46, 0.69]). When divided by approach, the authors also found significant effects for CBT (*g* = 0.43, 95% CI [0.14, 0.73], I^2 = 0%), social skills training (*g* = 0.96, 95% CI [0.37, 1.54], I^2 = 0%), and relaxation based interventions (*g* = 0.69, 95% CI [0.44, 0.93], I^2 = 0%) compared to no treatment or waiting list (Conley et al., 2017). Smaller but still significant effects were found for placebo-controlled trials of CBT for targeted (*g* = 0.27, 95% CI [0.11, 0.43], *Q* = 6.26) and nontargeted outcomes (*g* = 0.16, 95% CI [0.02, 0.30], *Q* = 18.05) (Conley et al., 2017). When examined within samples free of anxiety at baseline, there were small but significant preventative effects of CBT (*g* = –0.30, 95% CI [–0.40, –0.21], I^2 = 61%) (Moreno-Peral et al., 2017). Resembling CBT for clinical levels of anxiety, individual preventative CBT (*g* = 1.08, 95% CI [0.79, 1.36]) yielded significantly larger effects than group interventions (*g* = 0.60, 95% CI [0.53, 0.68]) (Conley et al., 2017). A preventative CBT was also significantly helpful for late-life anxiety and depression (van't Veer-Tazelaar et al., 2011; van't Veer-Tazelaar et al., 2009).

Predictors, Moderators, and Mediators

Mode of therapy predicts outcome. Individual CBT for anxiety disorders leads to larger effect sizes than group CBT (Bandelow et al., 2015; Carpenter et al., 2018). For example, Carpenter et al. found that individual CBT for PTSD or SAD (*g* = 0.54, 95% CI [0.40, 0.68]) led to larger effect sizes than group CBT (*g* = 0.16, 95% CI [0.01, 0.31]) in their meta-analysis of placebo-controlled trials. Similarly, Bandelow et al. found that individual CBT was superior to wait list (*d* = 1.23, 95% CI [1.02, 1.45], I^2 = 70%), psychological placebo (*d* = 0.75, 95% CI [0.34, 1.16], I^2 = 84%), and pill placebo (*d* = 0.57, 95% CI [0.20, 0.94], I^2 = 65%). On the other hand, whereas group CBT was superior to a waiting list treatment (*d* = 1.33, 95% CI [1.06, 1.60], I^2 = 0%), it did not show better results than pill placebo (*d* = 0.12, 95% CI [–0.10, 0.35]) (Bandelow et al., 2015; Covin et al., 2008). As noted above, individual psychotherapy was also superior to group prevention interventions (Conley et al., 2017).

The presence of comorbidity has been shown to predict larger effect sizes for CBT for anxiety disorders than absence of comorbidity effects explaining 6% of variance in the model (Pearl & Norton, 2017). Thus, comorbidity does not decrease its efficacy. There is also some evidence that baseline severity predicts lower effect sizes (Haby et al., 2006; Taylor et al., 2012). For example, Haby and colleagues compared studies that made a statement about including more severe clients to studies that did not include severe clients and found that the effect size was, on average, significantly lower by 0.27 SD units in studies that included severe clients. Moreover, in a meta-analytic sample, CBT for older working adults was only marginally better than active controls at post (*g* = –0.22, 95% CI = [–0.89, 0.44], I^2 = 61.3%), and gains were no longer different at one year follow-up (*g* = 0.14, 95% CI [–0.77, 1.05], I^2 = 76%) (Gould et al., 2012). Although these authors did not compare older adults directly to younger adults they did tentatively conclude that this might suggest that older anxious adults are less responsive to CBT than younger adults.

Sudden gains are defined as at least a 25% reduction in symptoms that occurs between two sessions, following at least three pre-gain sessions where mean symptoms were significantly higher. In one meta-analysis (Aderka et al., 2012), sudden gains during CBT for anxiety disorders predicted both short (*g* = 0.68, 95% CI [0.33, 1.03]) and longer-term (*M* = 4.44 months) primary measure outcomes (*g* = 0.56, 95% CI = 0.36 to 0.75). However, they seem only to predict the symptoms targeted and not secondary measures. Interestingly, the predictive value of sudden gains was significantly greater for CBT (*g* = 0.75, 95% CI [0.53, 0.91]) compared to non-CBT (*g* = 0.23, 95% CI [0.02, 0.48]) even though such sudden gains were experienced at an equal rate across both types of psychotherapies. Whether or not a study included first session gains also had no impact on the predictive value of sudden gains. However, sudden gains in the first session tended to be more unstable and showed more losses of 50% or more during the course of treatment. At the same time, the specific timing of sudden gains was not important (Aderka et al., 2012).

Additionally, attempts to minimize or distract oneself from distress during exposure (also known as safety behaviors) tends to predict worse outcome from exposure (Blakey & Abramowitz, 2016; Meulders et al., 2016). For more studies on process and mediating variables in CBT for anxiety disorders (see Chapter 8).

Regarding moderators, PTSD studies tended to demonstrate larger dropout rates from CBT (29.0%) in comparison to placebo (17.2%), but there were no differences compared to placebo in dropout across other anxiety disorders with an average of 24% dropout across all CBT studies (Carpenter et al., 2018). With respect to CBT versus its components, we are aware of only one replicated finding showing that those with longer duration of GAD benefited more from a component treatment (in this case either purely cognitive or purely behavioral treatments) than from combined CBT, whereas those with shorter duration benefitted from combined CBT (Newman & Fisher, 2013; Newman et al., 2019). These findings were explained as suggesting the possibility that due to entrenched bad habits in those who had GAD longer, clients may require more practice with fewer skills in order to break those habits. Regarding mechanism of change for anxiety, systematic reviews have concluded that threat reappraisal and extinction of fear are the most likely mechanisms for anxiety disorder CBT (Powers et al., 2017; Smits et al., 2012).

Dissemination

As with efficacy studies, effectiveness studies support the use of CBT for anxiety disorders. CBT showed large effect sizes compared to control groups for disorder specific symptoms ($g = 1.29$, CI [0.76, 1.83]). This translates to 78% improvement from CBT versus 22% improvement in control conditions (Stewart & Chambless, 2009). Benchmarking showed that effect sizes for real world CBT were in the range of efficacy studies. Outcomes were best when therapists were trained ($d = 0.31$), therapists used treatment manuals ($d = 0.16$), when there was monitoring to make sure therapists followed manuals ($d = 0.18$), and when there was not random assignment of treatments ($d = 0.11$) (Stewart & Chambless, 2009). Gains from effectiveness studies were maintained with a trend toward further improvement during the course of a one-year follow-up (Hans & Hiller, 2013). A more recent meta-analysis conducted within a primary care environment confirmed the effectiveness of CBT, although effect sizes were smaller ($d = 0.39$) (Zhang et al., 2019). As with other meta-analyses, individual treatments were better than group treatments ($d = 0.41$). Also, only delivery using nonprimary care physicians for CBT was effective ($d = 0.39$). This may be because primary care physicians don't typically receive training in CBT or psychotherapy and because they are unlikely to deliver it with high fidelity given time constraints.

Summary

Similar to the conclusions drawn within the prior editions of this *Handbook* (Emmelkamp, 2013; Hollon & Beck, 2013), we conclude that CBT is both efficacious and specific for the treatment of anxiety disorders, PTSD, and OCD with maintenance or additional gains at follow-up. Some more recent findings show that CBT is effective in the real world and can prevent anxiety and related disorders in those at risk. Furthermore, CBT or exposure alone should be the first-line intervention for most anxiety disorders, PTSD, and OCD, and medication is recommended only in cases where patients are nonresponsive to CBT. Consistently across studies, individual CBT was more effective than group CBT.

EATING DISORDERS

In the previous edition of this *Handbook*, Hollon and Beck (2013) noted that "CBT appears to be efficacious and specific with enduring effects in the treatment of bulimia nervosa (BN) and possibly efficacious in maintaining weight in the treatment of anorexia nervosa (AN). CBT also appears to be efficacious and specific in the treatment of binge eating disorder (BED)" (p. 409). For the treatment of BN and BED these conclusions are still valid. However, the effectiveness of CBT for eating disorders has not been much improved upon in the intervening years. For AN, the treatment of adolescents with a specialized behavioral family therapy (family-based therapy-FBT) has considerably improved treatment results and may eventually lead to fewer persistent cases of AN. While improving the results of treatment remains a priority, providing improved access to treatment is emerging as an additional research priority (Kazdin, 2017). This priority arises from the realization that

evidence-based treatments such as CBT are little used in the community and that prevailing treatments will need to be modified, tested, and implemented in a variety of community contexts often in briefer form.

In this section the research on anorexia nervosa will be treated separately from that for BN and BED because the research literature is less well developed with fewer controlled outcome studies. This is partly because the incidence of AN is much lower than for BN or BED often restricting study sample size.

The three primary eating disorders – bulimia nervosa, binge eating disorder, and anorexia nervosa – differ in their clinical presentations. However, core concerns about weight and shape are shared across the syndromes and diagnostic thresholds between syndromes are often crossed. This has given rise, as the authors of the previous volume note, to a transdiagnostic approach to the eating disorders (Fairburn & Cooper, 2007). Although this conception is useful and economical in designing cognitive-behavioral therapy for all three disorders, it has drawbacks. For example, the transdiagnostic approach has changed the nature of controlled treatment trials because mixed diagnostic samples are now entered to such trials (usually excluding anorexia nervosa) rather than single syndromes. Hence, comparisons between treatment trials are difficult to interpret, especially in meta-analyses, when different proportions of diagnostic entities with different treatment outcomes are entered into the analysis.

BULIMIA NERVOSA AND BINGE EATING DISORDER

Both BN and BED are characterized by binge eating associated with a sense of loss-of-control over eating and intake of an excessive amount of food, more than would usually be eaten in similar circumstances. However, unlike individuals with BN those with BED do not purge. Because of the similarity between BN and BED, the therapeutic model is identical, and CBT can be applied without modification. However, because many patients with BED wish to lose weight, it is necessary to ensure that they do not engage in restricted eating but rather gradually move toward a healthy diet and exercise regimen that can be sustained over time.

Cognitive-behavioral therapy was first designed to treat bulimia nervosa and then adapted for BED. The original treatment was subsequently revised to an enhanced, transdiagnostic, and more personalized form, namely CBT-E (Fairburn et al., 2008). This enhanced version is based on an individualized functional analysis of factors maintaining the disorder. There are two forms of this treatment, focused and broad. The focused version is similar to the original CBT but involves a revised approach to weight and shape concerns and a treatment module for mood intolerance as a trigger for binge eating and/or purging. The broad form addresses comorbid elements that are believed to maintain the eating disorder such as perfectionism, intense mood states, and interpersonal difficulties. In the following sections, CBT will refer to the use of the originally described treatment and CBT-E to the enhanced form.

Outcome

A meta-analysis of controlled studies of CBT compared with some form of active psychotherapy concluded that CBT outperformed non-CBT interventions by a statistically significant margin at end of treatment (EOT) ($d = 0.27$, $I^2 = 0\%$), but only approached statistical significance for BN ($d = 0.24$, $I^2 = 20\%$) and BED ($d = 0.30$, $I^2 = 0\%$) when examined individually (Spielmans et al., 2013). At follow-up, comparison between CBT and non-CBT also only approached significance ($d = 0.19$, $I^2 = 0\%$). A further meta-analysis came to similar conclusions about the superiority of CBT when examining 21 eligible trials including psychological, pharmacological or combined treatments (Slade et al., 2018). However, the authors noted several design issues that may have contributed to the advantage of CBT such as site therapist allegiance to CBT, superior training and expertise for CBT versus the comparison treatment, and restrictions to the comparison therapy to avoid overlap with components of CBT.

In an interesting and important study controlling for site allegiance effects, Poulsen and colleagues compared five months of treatment with CBT-E to two years of psychoanalytic psychotherapy for BN (Poulsen et al., 2014). The study was carried out at a site with therapists who were expert in psychoanalytic psychotherapy (PP) and both treatments were supervised by the developers of each treatment. Hence, this was a strict test of the comparative efficacy of the two treatments with any existing bias directed toward PP. After five months of treatment, 42% of those treated with CBT-E were abstinent compared with 6% of those treated with psychoanalytic psychotherapy (odds ratio 13.4). At 24 months, after completion of psychoanalytic psychotherapy, 42% had recovered with CBT-E compared with 15% for PP (odds ratio 4.34). Hence, CBT-E was faster, more effective, and based on fewer sessions than PP would be less costly. One reason for the better response to CBT-E may have been therapists' focus on eating disordered behaviors in CBT-E compared to little focus on such behaviors in the case of PP (Tasca et al., 2014). This hypothesis was tested in a second comparison of PP to CBT (Stefini et al., 2017). In this study, 81 females with BN or partial BN were randomly allocated to up to 60 sessions of either CBT or psychodynamic psychotherapy over a 12-month period. It should be noted that this is far more than the usual number of sessions for CBT. There was no significant difference in remission rates between the two treatments (CBT 33%, PP 31%) at EOT or the 12-month follow-up. A symptom-focused form of psychodynamic psychotherapy was used in this study possibly accounting for the improved results. These two studies suggest that the focus of psychotherapy is an important variable to consider in evaluating treatment outcomes. It also suggests that features such as the exact treatment protocol, often overlooked in literature reviews and meta-analyses, may hide significantly different treatment processes under the same name.

Recovery rates tend to be higher in BED than BN, perhaps because the placebo response is greater in BED (Blom et al., 2014). This issue was exemplified in a meta-analysis of 27 effectiveness studies carried out in routine clinical practice (Linardon et al., 2018). The meta-analysis found an abstinence rate of 37.4% (95% CI [29.1, 46.5]) for BN compared with 50.2% (95% CI [29.4, 70.9]) for BED. In addition, treatment outcomes for CBT in clinical practice were similar to those found in controlled outcome studies, suggesting that CBT is usable and effective in routine clinical practice when implementation of the full treatment is feasible.

Is CBT-E Superior to CBT?

Given that CBT-E is an enhanced version of CBT and therefore likely, especially in the broad form, to be more effective than the original, it is surprising that there have been few controlled studies comparing the two forms of CBT. Thompson-Brenner et al. (2016) examined the relative efficacy of the focused form of CBT-E (similar to the original CBT), compared with the broad form in 50 patients with bulimia nervosa and borderline personality disorder randomly allocated to the two treatment conditions. At EOT, 55.3% of patients were remitted (abstinent from binge eating and purging) with no significant difference between treatment groups (44 vs. 40%, ES = 0.04). However, there was a statistically significant moderator effect for the severity of affective/interpersonal problems. Using a median split, those with more severe problems at baseline showed a significantly higher remission rates with the broad form of CBT-E (77.8% vs. 22.2%). A previous controlled study by Fairburn et al. (2009) reported similar findings in a post-hoc analysis, suggesting that the broad form of CBT-E performed better for participants with more severe affective and interpersonal problems than the narrow form. Evidently, more research comparing the two forms of CBT-E and also comparing CBT-E to CBT is needed. Given the added complexity of CBT-E, it is important to know if and for what it is useful.

Shortening CBT

The need to find a shorter yet effective version of CBT in order to provide treatment to a wider population is evident, given the overall lack of treatment settings that can provide full CBT. One way to shorten treatment is to provide a written guide, placing the patient in charge of recovery, and providing a therapist-coach to ensure that the patient follows the guide book – a treatment known as guided self-help (CBTgsh). Typically, CBTgsh involves fewer (8–10) and shorter (20- to 30-minute) sessions than full CBT. Controlled studies and a meta-analysis suggest that CBTgsh is superior to pure self-help, to a waiting list control condition, and to treatment as usual (Traviss-Turner et al., 2017). Overall, for reduction of global ED psychopathology guided self-help showed a medium ES of –0.46 (95% CI [–0.64, –0.28], $I^2 = 57\%$), and for abstinence from binge eating and/or purging a small ES of –0.20 (95% CI [–0.28, –0.12], $I^2 = 65\%$). There is also some evidence that CBTgsh is as effective as full CBT in treating bulimia nervosa, at least when both groups were offered medication when they were not progressing well in either of the treatments (Mitchell et al., 2011). Although there were no differences between groups posttreatment, there was a significant difference in favor of guided self-help for reduction in binge eating and purging at follow-up. A further study found that CBTgsh was as effective as IPT in reducing binge eating in participants with BED and more effective than weight loss therapy used to reduce binge eating at two-year follow-up (OR = 2.3), although a moderator analysis suggested that IPT was superior for patients with high comorbidity (Wilson et al., 2010). These findings suggest that guided self-help may be useful at least as a first step in the treatment of BN and BED followed by full CBT if the patient does not progress well. Moreover, as noted earlier CBTgsh may well be useful in disseminating CBT more widely.

Prevention

Since the publication of the previous *Handbook* there has been considerable progress in attempts to either ameliorate or prevent the onset of BN or BED. Although several prevention methods have been proposed, only two have sufficient evidence at this time to determine efficacy and effectiveness. The first is a cognitive-behavioral approach "Student Bodies" (Taylor et al., 2016) and the second a cognitive dissonance intervention (Stice et al., 2017). Prevention research has two aims: First to reduce one or more risk factors for the development of an eating disorder that have been identified in longitudinal studies, and second to reduce the onset of eating disorder cases.

Student Bodies is an eight-session program delivered face-to-face in group format or via the internet often with some form of group interaction. The program is based on a social learning cognitive-behavioral approach that includes discussion of healthy eating, cultural ideals and determinants of attractiveness, media influences on body image, and cognitive-behavioral techniques for improving body image. Overall, Student Bodies successfully reduces risk factors for eating disorders such as body image concerns with small to medium effect sizes (e.g., d = 0.2–0.42) and also reduces the onset of eating disorders (e.g., 20% vs. 42%) in those at the highest risk of developing an eating disorder (Taylor et al., 2016). Whether it is effective in reducing ED onset in broader populations is uncertain at this point. Cognitive dissonance programs consist of providing participants with skills to oppose the many social and media messages concerning weight and appearance (Stice et al., 2012). Overall, this program when targeted at a high-risk population reduces risk factors with a small to medium effect size (d = -0.32, 95% CI [-0.52, -0.13]) and probably reduces ED onset particularly in participants with higher ED psychopathology (Le et al., 2017).

Little is known about prevention of relapse for either BN or BED. It is likely, based on the studies reviewed above that treating individuals with BN or BED with comorbid severe affective and interpersonal problems with the broad form of CBT-E would likely reduce relapse rates (Fairburn et al., 2009; Thompson-Brenner et al. (2016)). (74.4% vs. 48.7%)

Predictors and Moderators

The most consistent predictor of outcome is rapid response in the first few sessions of treatment which increases the probability for successful outcome for both BN and BED (Lutz et al., 2014; Unick et al., 2014). Data from a large-scale study comparing CBT, interpersonal psychotherapy (IPT) and behavioral weight loss treatment (BWL) for BED found that rapid response predicted a favorable outcome with CBT, but not IPT or BWL, indicating specificity of treatment with CBT (Hilbert et al., 2015). There have been similar findings for the treatment of BN predicting both short- and long-term outcomes (Wilson et al., 2002). Moreover, rapid response also occurs in routine clinical treatment confirming the robustness of early rapid response (Raykos et al., 2013). Early rapid response is a marker of superior outcome and also marks those who are not responding optimally to treatment. This allows for a modified treatment approach early in treatment for those predicted to respond suboptimally and offers the opportunity to enhance the efficacy of existing treatments. Very few baseline variables predict outcome for either BN or BED and the effects vary considerably from study to study. Among reasonably consistent nonspecific predictors of poor outcome are: high comorbid psychopathology, more severe binge eating and purging, and higher weight and shape concerns. No consistent moderators of outcome for CBT have yet been identified for the treatment of either BN or BED despite numerous studies. Hence, it is not possible to determine which individuals might respond better to one treatment or another.

Mediators and Mechanisms

Given the within-group variability in outcomes in clinical trials investigating the treatment of BN and BED with CBT, it is unlikely that a single mechanism will explain the effectiveness of CBT. It is theorized that dietary restriction and concerns about body shape are key factors maintaining eating disorders (Fairburn, 1981). Hence, it would be expected that CBT would exert its effects by reducing dietary restraint and concerns about body shape. The identification of mechanisms is important because treatment effects may be strengthened by enhancing the effects of the mechanism. A recent systematic review examined mediators of CBT in BN and BED (Linardon et al., 2017). Two studies examined dietary restraint and body concerns as mediators of outcome. Both found dietary restraint to be a mediator, and neither found that body concerns mediated outcome (Spangler et al., 2004; Wilson et al., 2002). We can tentatively conclude that CBT works by reducing dietary restraint, consistent with both theory and the fact that dietary restraint is targeted early in treatment by instituting the consumption of regular meals and snacks.

ANOREXIA NERVOSA

Anorexia nervosa has one of the highest mortality rates for any psychiatric disorder due to high suicide rates and the sequelae of starvation (Arcelus et al., 2011). Thus, treatment and prevention are particularly important.

Outcome

Studies suggest that the disorder is more responsive to treatment early in the course of the illness. Hence, treatment studies in adolescence are important not only because more individuals may respond to treatment but also because successful treatment may lower the proportion of adolescents who continue to experience persistent AN as adults. Thus, it is important to distinguish between early-onset AN and persistent AN when considering treatment options and outcomes.

Persistent Anorexia Nervosa

Often termed *adult* or *chronic* AN, persistent AN responds poorly to treatment, and it is doubtful whether there is an evidence-based treatment for this syndrome despite many years of research effort (Hay et al., 2015; Zeeck et al., 2018). Moreover, because AN is a relatively rare disorder (12-month prevalence estimate of 0.05%; Udo & Grilo, 2018), sample sizes in controlled trials have often been small, limiting the conclusions that can be drawn from many studies. Add to this the high dropout rates in many of these studies that may bias the results because dropout may be a non-random event (Halmi et al., 2005). In addition, given the severity of the disorder, the use of an inactive or placebo control condition is not possible. Hence, only comparisons with other active treatments, or with the addition of a placebo condition added to standard treatment such as hospital care, are possible.

Several uncontrolled trials of CBT-E treating persistent AN have been published, suggesting, as noted in the previous edition of this handbook, that CBT-E is a potentially useful treatment (Byrne et al., 2011; Calugi et al., 2017; Fairburn et al., 2013; Frostad et al., 2018). Usually, 40 treatment sessions of CBT over a 40-week period are used to treat persistent AN, about double the number for BN or BED. Dropout rates in these preliminary studies were 35–50% and over half of those completing treatment were in remission at EOT (an overall remission rate of about 30%) with good maintenance at follow-up. More recently, controlled trials examining the relative efficacy of CBT-E compared to other active treatments have been reported. In the largest psychotherapy study of persistent AN, 242 adult patients were randomized to either CBT-E, focal psychodynamic therapy, or enhanced treatment as usual (Zipfel et al., 2014). The latter treatment included supervision by the patient's family physician and referral to a psychotherapist for supportive psychotherapy. Treatment dropout rates were low at 22%, with no difference between treatment groups. At EOT and follow-up, there were no differences between the three treatment groups on the primary outcome weight gain. CBT-E compared with treatment as usual showed ES = 0.13 posttreatment and ES = 0.08 at 12-month follow-up. At the 12-month follow-up, psychodynamic psychotherapy was superior to treatment as usual, with 35% and 13%, respectively, recovered with a small ES = 0.13.

A second multi-center trial randomly allocated 120 adults with AN to one of three treatments: CBT-E, supportive clinical management, or the Maudsley Model Anorexia Treatment (MANTRA; Byrne et al., 2017). The latter treatment is individualized targeting three maintaining factors: the person's thinking and emotional/relational style, close others' responses to the illness, and beliefs about the utility of AN in the person's life (Treasure & Schmidt, 2013). Some 40% of participants did not complete treatment, with no differences between treatments either at EOT or at 12-month follow-up. Overall, 28% of participants were in remission and 50% were at a healthy weight. Effect size for CBT-E vs. supportive clinical management was 0.21. Assessment of therapy fidelity was reported in a separate paper, demonstrating marked differences in treatment processes between the three treatments and good fidelity to each treatment (Andony et al., 2015). These results suggest that at the present time there is no evidence for the specificity of CBT-E in the treatment of persistent AN and no firm evidence that CBT-E (or any other medication or psychotherapy) is more effective than specialist clinical management in the treatment of persistent AN.

Adolescent Anorexia Nervosa

Evidence is accruing for supporting family-based therapy (FBT), a behavioral therapy, for the treatment of both adolescent BN and AN (Jewell et al., 2016). Broadly speaking, FBT focuses on enhancing parental skills in refeeding their child (Lock et al., 2013). Family-based treatment has shown specificity in at least one study (Lock et al., 2010) where it was compared with adolescent-focused individual psychotherapy (AFT) (Lock et al., 2010). In this two-site study, 121 adolescents with AN were randomly allocated to one of the two therapies (AFT or FBT) conducted over 24 sessions of outpatient therapy. Overall study dropout was low, at 14%. Using a strict definition of remission, there was no difference between treatment groups at the end of treatment. However, at follow-up, FBT was superior to AFT, with 40% and 18% of patients remitted, respectively, at 6 months and 49% and 23% at 12 months, with a medium effect (NNT = 4). Hospitalization rates during treatment were higher for AFT (37%) than for FBT (15%). This is important because of the high cost of hospitalization.

In a large-scale six-site clinical trial involving 164 adolescents with AN, FBT was compared with systemic family therapy (SyFT), which focuses on family processes rather than directly focusing on weight gain (Agras et al., 2014). There were no differences between treatments in weight gain or remission at EOT or follow-up. However, the FBT group had significantly fewer hospital days, 8.3 compared with 21 days for SyFT, resulting in significantly reduced overall direct costs of treatment for FBT compared with SyFT. A more detailed analysis revealed that hospitalizations were equal for both treatments during the first five weeks of treatment but that hospitalizations for SyFT continued after that time whereas they leveled off for FBT (Lock et al., 2016). This difference may be due to the immediate focus of FBT on eating and weight, resulting in more rapid nutritional restoration, hence avoiding later weight loss or poor weight gain leading to hospitalization.

In an interesting modification of FBT, parent-focused treatment (PFT) in which a nurse briefly saw the adolescent with therapy conducted solely with the parents was compared with FBT as usual (Le Grange et al., 2016): 107 adolescents with AN were allocated at random to one of the two 18-session treatments. At EOT remission was greater in PFT (43%) than with FBT (22%). However, there were no statistically significant differences in remission at either 6- or 12-month follow-up. An important feature of this study is that PFT does not require skilled family therapists and may therefore be more easily implemented in community clinics.

A significant gap in treatment research is the absence of controlled comparisons of CBT-E with FBT nor any controlled trial of CBT or CBT-E with adolescent AN. Hence, with nine controlled studies, FBT is recommended as a first-line effective and cost-effective treatment for adolescent AN (Jewell et al., 2016; National Institute for Health and Care Excellence, 2017).

Prevention

At this point, there have been no controlled relapse prevention studies following a psychotherapeutic treatment for anorexia nervosa.

Predictors and Moderators

As was the case with BN and BED, the most consistent predictor of favorable outcome for adolescent AN treated with FBT is early response – in this case, the amount of weight gain by the fourth treatment session (Le Grange et al., 2014). A weight gain of 4 lb (1.8 kg) or more optimally predicted a good outcome. There are few pretreatment predictors of outcome for CBT with either adolescent or adult patients. A meta-analysis including both inpatient and outpatient treatments concluded that pretreatment variables predicting outcome were weak and variable between studies (Gregertsen et al., 2019). Predictors of poor outcome found in that analysis were greater ED psychopathology and lower motivation for treatment. A further predictor of poor outcome for both adolescent and persistent AN is limited cognitive flexibility expressed through perseverative and obsessive thinking styles (Lock & LeGrange, 2018).

Mediators and Mechanisms

Family behavior therapy is hypothesized to achieve its effects via changes in parental behavior focused on refeeding their child. Hence, it is not surprising that parental self-efficacy related to refeeding partially mediates treatment outcome (Lock & Le Grange, 2019), suggesting that methods to enhance parental self-efficacy may enhance FBT outcome.

Dissemination

The need for treatment of AN far outpaces the availability of specialized centers to provide evidence-based treatments for adolescents. Enhancing therapist training with online methods is one approach to this problem, although there is no convincing research that this can be accomplished in a scalable form at present.

Summary

Although there has been considerable research in the treatment of eating disorders since the previous publication of this *Handbook*, there has been little improvement in the effectiveness of cognitive-behavioral therapy for BN or BED. It is likely that CBT-E is more effective with individuals with high comorbidity, although this conclusion rests on relatively little evidence. Nor is there any evidence that other evidence-based treatments either are superior to CBT or are useful adjunctive treatments. At this point, few mediators of outcome for CBT have been identified. This may be due to the limited sample size in many studies. The major treatment advance in the last few years has been the development of a behavioral family-based treatment for adolescent AN. Treating AN early in its development is evidently more successful that treating the persistent form of the disorder and may reduce the frequency of persistent AN.

Substance Abuse

There are a wide range of CBT approaches to treatment of substance abuse. As such, we believed that the most coherent way to present the results relating to treatment outcomes, prevention, predictors and moderators, and mediators and mechanisms of action, was to group all information pertaining to a given CBT approach together. There is a general comment on dissemination, using mainly contingency management as an illustration, at the end of the substance abuse section. It should also be noted that the prevention studies presented here are not addressing whether CBT can prevent a first episode of substance abuse or the recurrence of future ones. Rather, the focus is on relapse prevention, which is a form of treatment aimed at arming people with tools needed to cope with relapse triggers, and the central problem for any treatment of these conditions. There has been no primary prevention for substance abuse, certainly in recent years, that at all resembles the CBT methods on which this section focuses. Furthermore, a complementing review of studies on the mechanisms of change of treatments (including CBT) of substance use problems is presented in Chapter 8.

A hallmark of cognitive-behavioral approaches to substance use disorders is to treat substance abuse as a dysfunctional behavioral excess. This characterization might sound glaringly obvious, but it is distinct from some traditional conceptualizations that emphasize addictive personality traits or physiological dependence on a particular substance as explanatory factors. A corollary of treating substance abuse as behavior is that functional analysis should be useful in understanding and modifying the behavior. Consistent with this viewpoint, this section of the chapter is organized in light of a very simple ABC functional analysis (Antecedents, Behaviors, and Consequences), where the B consists of excessive use of drugs in a way that interferes with physical and/or mental health.

Acknowledging that there is considerable overlap in these approaches and that many studies implement multicomponent treatment packages drawing from more than one of them, we can nevertheless differentiate (a) interventions aimed at bolstering patients' readiness to make changes in substance use behavior (notably *motivational interviewing*); (b) interventions aimed at modifying the AB (antecedent-behavior) connection, such as *cue exposure*, with its primary focus on environmental antecedents to substance use behavior, or *cognitive therapy*, with its primary focus on internal antecedents such as negative mood or positive outcome expectancies for substance use; and (c) interventions aimed at modifying the BC (behavior-consequence) connection, especially *contingency management*, in which principles of operant conditioning are used to try to inculcate and sustain abstinence from problematic drug use. We will argue also that *behavioral couples Therapy*, which has been studied especially in the context of alcohol abuse, might be viewed as a special case of contingency management addressed to the BC connection in functional analytic terms.

Motivational Interviewing

Motivational interviewing (MI) was developed by Miller (1983) initially for treatment of alcohol problems but has subsequently been applied much more broadly. Using a nondirective style, the therapist avoids confrontation in order not to evoke resistance. Instead, the therapist uses open-ended questions and gives feedback aimed at helping the patient to develop a sense of discrepancy between the effects of substance use and the patient's aspirations. Therapists are attentive to process markers such as the occurrence of *change talk* on the part of the patient; that is, discussion of potential advantages of behavior change and disadvantages of the status quo, in contrast to *sustain talk*, which would be seen as a red flag indicative of a need to modify the therapist's line of questioning.

In the previous edition of this *Handbook*, Emmelkamp (2013) noted that MI has been used and studied as a standalone treatment at times but also can be grafted onto other interventions, typically preceding them in a logical sequence of first fostering motivation for and commitment to change before introducing specific methods of making the changes. In terms of effects of MI, Emmelkamp's (2013) review noted that in alcohol studies MI appeared to work better than a directive confrontational counseling style and was approximately equal to cognitive behavioral therapy (for a measure of drinking consequences: $d = 0.01$, 95% CI [–0.20, 0.19]) and to a 12-step facilitation condition (on drinking consequences: $d = -0.18$, 95% CI [–0.37, 0.01]) in the multisite Project MATCH trial (Project MATCH Research Group, 1997). More generally, effect sizes appeared to be in the low to moderate range for MI in treatment of alcohol abuse. With respect to drug abuse more generally, Emmelkamp (2013) concluded that MI had proven better than no treatment, with medium effect sizes, ($d = 0.56$ in the meta-analysis by Burke et al. (2003) and equivalent to other active interventions (i.e., efficacious but not specific).

A more recent review suggested that effect sizes for MI in treatment of alcohol abuse differ by time of follow-up and perhaps by age range of patients (DiClemente et al., 2017). In particular, as applied to adults, MI showed a small but significant advantage over no treatment in relation to reduction of alcohol-related problems. For alcohol use itself, MI had a large advantage relative to no treatment at posttest (standardized mean difference (SMD) = 0.79, 95% CI [0.48, 1.09]), a small advantage (SMD = 0.17, 95% CI [0.09, 0.26]) in short follow-ups up to 6 months, and a small advantage (SMD = 0.15, 95% CI [0.04, 0.25]) in follow-ups of 6–12 months. In samples of

adolescents or young adults, small effects were evident on alcohol use, with no significant effects on risky behavior or binge drinking. Results were mixed and overall nonsignificant in comparisons of MI with other active interventions for alcohol use.

Therapist effects may be important to consider in predicting response to MI and other cognitive and behavioral interventions for alcohol abuse, as research suggests that these effects can be sizable; the difficulty lies not with showing that therapists vary in effectiveness but in uncovering reliable prediction of these effects. For example, an exceptionally large study of therapist effects (80 carefully trained study therapists nested within three conditions: 12-step facilitation, motivational enhancement therapy [based on MI], and cognitive-behavioral coping skills training) detected therapist effects but no consistency across treatment conditions or clinical settings (outpatient clinic vs. aftercare), and most effects were attributable to a single outlier with highly variable client drinking outcomes (Project Match Research Group, 1998). No prediction of CBT therapist effects in particular was significant on the basis of therapist background attributes such as personality traits.

A Cochrane review (Gates et al., 2016) of RCTs testing treatment of cannabis use disorder showed similar results as for MI studies of alcohol treatment. Motivational enhancement therapy did not differ significantly (RR = 1.19, 95% CI [0.43, 3.28]) in leading to point prevalence abstinence as compared to no treatment. Longer-term outcomes and comparison with alternative interventions, were also not significant. About one quarter of participants were abstinent at final follow-up on average. Several reviews summarized by DiClemente et al. (2017) converge on the conclusion that MI has not proven superior to no treatment in relation to treatment of cocaine use disorder, underscoring the point that treatment efficacy cannot be assumed to generalize from one form of substance use to another even if the conceptual model guiding the intervention is essentially the same.

A Cochrane review of 28 randomized clinical trials of MI for cigarette-smoking cessation found small but positive effects of MI relative to brief advice or routine care, with a relative risk (of six-month point prevalence abstinence from smoking) of 1.26 (95% CI [1.16, 1.36], $I^2 = 49\%$) (Lindson-Hawley et al., 2015). Abstinence rates averaged approximately 17% in MI conditions and 14% in control conditions. Interestingly, effects were stronger for very brief MI interventions, as little as 20 minutes in one session, than for multisession MI. These results require cautious interpretation, however, in that (a) there was some evidence of possible inflation of MI effects as a function of publication bias, and (b) the dose effects result was based on cross-study comparisons, not a within-study manipulation of the length of MI intervention.

A review of the Cochrane review as well as several others found consensus on the modest but positive effects of MI for smoking abstinence, with some indication of moderator effects (DiClemente et al., 2017). In particular, MI appeared to be more effective for those with initially low levels of motivation to quit ($d = 0.34$–0.39), and appeared no better than usual care in samples of pregnant smokers. Finally, there was no clear evidence of specificity in the sense of superiority of MI to other active treatments.

In brief, MI has been tested in a wide range of settings, with varying lengths of intervention (sometimes exceptionally brief), for treating abuse of various substances. There is good evidence of efficacy relative to no treatment, albeit qualified by type of substance (no advantage in cocaine use disorder, small effects on nicotine and cannabis dependence, large effect at posttreatment in adult alcohol samples). Durability of effects is modest in nicotine and alcohol dependence, and not evident for cannabis. Specificity in the sense of superiority to other active treatments is not evident. Moderator analyses suggest that the particular advantage of MI may be for patients with low pretreatment motivation to change.

Cue Exposure

The rationale for development of cue exposure as an addiction treatment is that unreinforced presentation of drug-taking cues (conditioned stimuli) would lead to extinction of conditioned responses to those cues. In the ABC functional analytic scheme mentioned earlier, this amounts to trying to modify the AB connection by presenting environmental cues normally linked to substance use (e.g., the sight of a pack of one's favorite brand of cigarette, the smell of a preferred brand of beer, handling of drug paraphernalia, etc.) without allowing drug use to take place. In the most recent edition of this *Handbook*, Emmelkamp (2013) indicated that evidence on the effects of cue exposure for substance use disorders was mixed and inconclusive, suggesting that it might have a role only in combination with other approaches.

An early conceptual and quantitative review of cue exposure trials for substance abuse (mostly opioids, cocaine, nicotine, and alcohol) found that effect sizes for cue exposure did not differ significantly from zero and argued that improvement of the clinical efficacy of cue exposure would require refinements in procedure based on closer attention to modern animal research on conditioning of drug cues (Conklin & Tiffany, 2002). Somewhat similarly, reviewers have argued that use of virtual reality immersion would enhance the impact of cue exposure, but there was not yet sufficient evidence from clinical trials to know whether long-term abstinence rates are increased by such methods (Hone-Blanchet et al., 2014).

Subsequent reviews of cue exposure continued to paint a disappointing picture of its efficacy. For example, a review by Kantak and Nic Dhonnchadha (2011) described studies showing no incremental benefit for cue exposure as an addition to CBT for severe alcohol dependence, actual worsening of results for opiate addiction, and cigarette smoking abstinence results that were no better than comparison conditions and modest in absolute terms (9% at 12-month follow-up).

Finally, a meta-analysis of seven controlled trials of cue exposure for alcohol use disorder, in particular (four inpatient studies, three outpatient), found no significant effect ($g = -0.21$, 95% CI [-0.48, 0.06], $I^2 = 24\%$) for cue exposure on number of drinking days at six-month follow-up and no

significant effect on heavy drinking days ($g = -.02$, 95% CI [-0.38, 0.41], $I^2 = 37\%$) or on average number of drinks per day ($g = -0.16$, 95% CI [-0.52, 0.19], $I^2 = 64\%$) (Mellentin et al., 2017). Results were relatively more favorable when cue exposure was compared to relaxation or assessment-only comparison conditions rather than to other forms of CBT and were more favorable when urge-specific coping skills training was appended to cue exposure per se. Taken together with a lack of incremental benefit of cue exposure when added to CBT (Kavanagh et al., 2006), the coping skills data suggest that the efficacy of cue exposure alone is limited.

In summary, cue exposure is a compelling idea having connections to basic research on craving and appears analogous to procedures that have worked well in anxiety disorders treatment. However, its potential has not yet been translated into efficacy in treating substance use disorders.

Cognitive Therapy and Relapse Prevention

Cognitive therapy (CT or CBT) of substance use disorders (Beck et al., 2001) emphasizes teaching skills for identifying and questioning one's automatic thoughts that promote substance use. An influential framework used by many CBT therapists is the relapse prevention (RP) model introduced by Marlatt and colleagues (e.g., Marlatt & Donovan, 2005), which supplements focus on internal (e.g., mood states) determinants of substance use with consideration of external cues (e.g., high-risk situations such as places in which indirect or even direct social pressure to use drugs is present). Coping skills relevant to making it possible to manage those situations without drinking, smoking, or using illicit drugs are taught and practiced.

In the previous edition of this *Handbook*, Emmelkamp (2013) concluded that CBT based on the RP model showed strong effects in the treatment of cocaine dependence. In the context of alcohol dependence, RP was associated with small effects on alcohol use itself, with a more substantial impact on psychosocial functioning. RP treatment appeared to be effective but not specific (equivalent to 12-step facilitation) in the treatment of illicit drug use in general, with inconclusive results concerning marijuana dependence. There was little clear evidence of theory-specified mediation (e.g., the treatment specifically increasing coping skills, and reducing drug use to the extent that coping skills had improved earlier).

Since the last edition, more recent studies continue to show little robust evidence as to the mediating mechanisms of CBT effects on substance use outcomes. In particular, though, as in other areas, homework adherence is associated with favorable outcome, it is not clear that improvements in targeted cognitive and behavioral skills specifically mediate the effects of CBT (Carroll & Kiluk, 2017).

Focusing on CBT and the RP model in the prior *Handbook* edition, Hollon and Beck (2013) concluded that effects were inconsistent across studies, with no reliable indicators of moderator effects as were hypothesized, for instance, by the Project MATCH Research Group (1997). Their review concluded that RP is efficacious (small to moderate effects) but not specific in the treatment of alcohol abuse. This finding is evident again for CBT coping skills interventions in a more recent Cochrane review, which concluded that there was no significant difference between CBT and 12-step facilitation (RR = 2.38, 95% CI [0.10, 55.06]) with regard to drinking behavior among samples with comorbid illicit substance use (Klimas et al., 2018). Qualifying this conclusion, the authors depicted the dataset as being of low quality.

CBT for cocaine dependence has shown mixed results, ranging from not adding to the effectiveness of other interventions to faring better or worse than 12-step facilitation in leading to abstinence (Penberthy et al., 2010). One review suggested that, whereas contingency management approaches reliably reduced cocaine use, CBT had inconsistent effects across trials; an interesting temporal pattern suggested that CBT effects on cocaine use might be delayed and emerge only after the active treatment period, during maintenance (Farronato et al., 2013). Two randomized trials reviewed by Dugosh et al. (2016) revealed no significant advantage on use of opioids for the addition of CBT to methadone maintenance treatment.

An overview of CBT for substance use disorders in general indicated that there is consistent evidence of superiority to no treatment with a large effect size ($g = 0.80$), and a small advantage over active comparison conditions for CBT ($g = 0.13$) (Carroll & Kiluk, 2017). Generally similar results were reported in a more recent meta-analysis of 30 randomized clinical trials of CBT for alcohol and other drug use, but not cigarette smoking, disorders (Magill et al., 2019). In particular, focusing on frequency measures such as percent days abstinent, CBT exceeded the efficacy of wait list or other minimal conditions, yielding moderate effects ($g = 0.58$, 95% CI [0.15, 1.01], $I^2 = 59\%$) at early assessments of 1–6 months after posttreatment and at later assessments of 8+ months after posttreatment assessment ($g = 0.44$, 95% CI [0.02, 0.86], $I^2 = 0\%$). Comparisons with what the authors considered nonspecific interventions (treatment as usual, supportive therapy, group drug counseling) showed a significant but small ($g = 0.18$, 95% CI [0.02, 0.35], $I^2 = 45\%$) advantage for CBT at early assessments but nonsignificance ($g = 0.05$, 95% CI [–0.09, 0.19], $I^2 = 0\%$) at late assessments. Finally, CBT did not differ significantly from specific comparison treatments (contingency management, motivational interviewing) at either early ($g = -0.02$, 95% CI [–0.12, 0.08], $I^2 = 14\%$) or late ($g = -.04$, 95% CI [–0.15, 0.08], $I^2 = 15\%$) assessments. Moderator effects have been examined in a couple of ways since the last edition of the *Handbook*. With respect to race and ethnicity effects, there appears to be no significant moderation. A meta-analysis of 16 controlled trials of CBT for substance use disorders found similar effect sizes for CBT substance use outcomes in comparison to other interventions between studies consisting of predominantly (> 70%) non-Hispanic White samples ($g = -0.01$, 95% CI [–0.09, 0.10], $I^2 = 0\%$) versus predominantly (> 70%) Black or Hispanic samples ($g = 0.03$, 95% CI [–0.25, 0.31], $I^2 = 17\%$) (Windsor et al., 2015). The average effect size for substance use outcomes in this meta-analysis did not differ significantly from zero in either set of studies, indicating that CBT failed to exceed comparisons such as 12-step programs

or treatment as usual and again does not appear to be specifically effective.

A more promising place to search for moderator effects may be in the realm of comorbidity. A meta-analysis specifically focused on treatment of alcohol use disorder with comorbid major depression via the combination of CBT and motivational interviewing found that inclusion of these components as an addition to treatment as usual led to a small but significant advantage at posttreatment ($g = 0.17$, CI [0.07, 0.28], $I^2 = 16\%$) and at 6- to 12-month follow-ups ($g = 0.31$, 95% CI [0.16, 0.47]), relative to treatment as usual alone (Riper et al., 2014). A secondary analysis of this dataset detected a surprising *inverse* relation between number of treatment sessions and effect size ($\beta = -0.016$, 95% CI [–0.027, –0.005]), which seems at odds with a more typical dose-response effect. Given that length of treatment was not manipulated within trials, it is of course possible that confounds such as sample or setting characteristics might be responsible for this finding. Moreover, everyone in these studies had comorbid depression, so while the research bears on a subgroup of those in alcohol treatment it is not indicative of moderation as such.

Particularly in the area of smoking cessation, however, CBT researchers have looked specifically for moderation and, in doing so, extended the consideration of depression to the case of depression vulnerability. Vulnerability has been measured either as a history of recurrent major depression (Haas et al., 2004) or as a high score on a continuous self-rating of depression proneness (Brandon et al., 1997; Kapson & Haaga, 2010). Results are not completely consistent across studies (Brown et al., 2007) but as first reported by Hall et al. (1994) several studies find that a CBT mood-management coping skills treatment component is specifically helpful for smokers vulnerable to depression.

As an example, CBT mood management plus scheduled reduced smoking and health education led to three-month follow-up abstinence for 35% of high depression-proneness smokers, compared to 22% for a time-matched treatment lacking the CBT component, whereas results were the opposite (33% for the time-matched comparison treatment; 10% for the condition incorporating CBT mood management) for smokers low in depression proneness (Kapson & Haaga, 2010).

This moderator effect dovetails with descriptive results suggesting that depression-prone smokers lack the cognitive coping skills taught in CBT (Rabois & Haaga, 1997) but is somewhat puzzling in connection to results showing a *lack* of specific impact of CBT mood-management therapy on improving these skills (Thorndike et al., 2006).

In summary, empirical evidence concerning CBT for substance use disorders is consistent in showing efficacy, with the important exception of opioid disorders, and particularly in the area of cocaine use disorder there is promising evidence of durability of effects. Specificity may be evident only for a subset of disorders (e.g., marijuana dependence). Comorbid depression or depression vulnerability could be a moderator enabling prescription of CBT relative to alternative interventions. There is no consistent evidence as to mediating mechanisms of CBT effects.

Behavioral Couples Therapy

Behavioral couples therapy (BCT) has been adapted to the substance use context, particularly for distressed relationships in which one partner is abusing alcohol. There is a focus on substance-specific interventions such as trying to (a) decrease enabling behaviors by non-substance-using partners, that is inadvertent reinforcement of drinking (e.g., reduction of demands on the drinking partner or increased expression of sympathy or compassion), (b) decrease exposure to alcohol or drug cues, and (c) plan frequent discussions aimed at solidifying and expressing trust in one another and commitment to abstinence.

Although it is unlikely that a nondrinking partner could or would wish to administer a contingent reinforcement plan quite as systematic as would be typical of formal Contingency Management programs, we nevertheless believe that BCT interventions can be conceptualized as a form of attempt to change the contingencies operative in the drinker's natural environment for drinking behavior and for abstinence. In the sixth edition of the *Handbook*, Emmelkamp (2013) reviewed evidence indicating that BCT outperformed control conditions in reducing drinking behavior and improving relationship satisfaction.

A randomized trial with 105 women diagnosed with alcohol dependence and married or living with a male partner found that three months of weekly BCT plus weekly individual 12-step oriented counseling was significantly more effective than the same number of sessions devoted exclusively to individual counseling in terms of percentage of days abstinent over the year after treatment, yielding a small to medium effect (d = 0.33, 95% CI [0.00, 0.66]) (Schumm et al., 2014). At 12-month follow-up, on average the women in the BCT + counseling condition were abstinent on 82% of days vs. 73% in the individual-only treatment condition and vs. 26% at baseline.

Other studies have been consistent with this conclusion that BCT outperforms individual treatment in reducing alcohol use, and in increasing relationship satisfaction (McCrady et al., 2016; Ruff et al., 2010), as well as reducing intimate partner violence (O'Farrell & Clements, 2012). There is little information available on mediating mechanisms by which BCT has an impact on alcohol use disorder (Magill et al., 2015).

Contingency Management

Contingency management (CM) interventions in general are based on principles of operant conditioning and entail making reinforcement contingent on the patient's achievement of clinical goals such as remaining in treatment or providing evidence of abstinence from drug use (Higgins et al., 2018). In our ABC functional analysis scheme, they represent efforts to manipulate the BC connection such that the immediate consequences become more favorable for abstaining than for using drugs.

Higgins et al. (2018) described principles for maximizing the likelihood of success for contingency management interventions for substance use disorders, which track well with what is known about effects of reinforcers in general. Some examples of this include: communicating in advance the

consequences to be delivered and the exact way in which the desired response is defined and measured; keeping the delay from response to consequence as short as possible; keeping in mind that effects of the intervention will likely vary directly with the magnitude of reinforcer; and making the reinforcer contingent.

Contingency management has typically been used in conjunction with other interventions such as medication, motivational interviewing, or CBT, rather than on its own. Many controlled studies have used financial incentives (money or vouchers) as the contingent reinforcer, with escalating magnitude (i.e., a higher-value voucher for a third straight week of abstinence than for the first or second). As indicated also in the prior edition of this *Handbook* (Emmelkamp, 2013), the vast majority of these studies have shown evidence of efficacy for contingency management (Higgins et al., 2018) in treating cocaine dependence, alcohol use, cigarette smoking, and other substance use. It is not clear that escalation of incentives, as opposed to a fixed incentive, significantly affects efficacy (Davis et al., 2016).

In one quantitative review, Ainscough et al. (2017) analyzed 22 controlled trials of contingency management aimed at reducing nonprescribed (e.g., not methadone maintenance) substance use during treatment for opiate addiction. Overall results showed medium effect sizes favoring contingency management over control conditions for dependent measures of longest duration of abstinence (LDA: d = 0.57, 95% CI [0.42, 0.72], I^2 = 51%) and percentage of negative samples (PNS: d = 0.41, 95% CI [0.28, 0.54], I^2 = 0%). Interestingly, results varied by type of drug; there was actually no significant benefit of contingency management for nonprescribed opiate use (LDA: d = –0.10, 95% CI [–0.61, 0.41]; PNS: d = 0.18, 95% CI [0.11, 0.46]), whereas there was benefit for tobacco use (LDA: d = 1.02, 95% CI [0.37, 1.67]; PNS: d = 1.02, 95% CI [0.37, 1.67]), cocaine (LDA: d = 0.75, 95% CI [0.45, 1.04]; PNS: d = 0.40, 95% CI [0.13, 0.67]) or polysubstance use (LDA: d = 0.62, 95% CI [0.27, 0.98]; PNS: d = 0.49, 95% CI [0.23, 0.74]).

Whereas initial behavior change data are thus impressive for contingency management, continued work is needed on how best to sustain therapeutic gains in the longer term after incentives are withdrawn. One sample study illustrating the concern about maintenance of effects was reported by Rohsenow et al. (2017). They used contingency management in the context of nicotine replacement therapy plus counseling (vs. same interventions without contingency management) in attempting cigarette smoking cessation during residential treatment for other drug use. The effect of contingency management was favorable during treatment (20% vs. 5% abstinence) but dissipated by 6- and 12-month follow-ups.

A narrative review of CM for cocaine dependence treatment underscored the issue of durability of gains from contingency management interventions. CM increased efficacy of standard treatments and decreased attrition, primarily within the first 12 weeks of treatment, with less clear benefit in the longer term (Schierenberg et al., 2012).

Nonetheless, in large samples a sustained effect of contingency management may be detectable. A Cochrane review of

20 clinical trials of contingency management for smoking cessation, for instance, found a significant positive overall effect (odds ratio = 1.42, 95% CI [1.19, 1.69], I^2 = 33) at longest follow-up assessment (range = 6–24 months post-quit date) favoring contingency management (11.2% abstinence on average) over control conditions (8.4%) (Cahill et al., 2015). The review noted that making the incentive a return of money the participant had deposited in the first place was more efficacious, but less likely to stimulate joining the program in the first place, compared to incentive systems in which the participant is simply paid by the investigators.

Broadening the scope to include the full range of substance use disorders, Davis et al. (2016) found a small average effect size of $d = 0.26$ (95% CI [0.11, 0.41]) favoring CM over control conditions in follow-up evaluations, weaker than the medium average effect of $d = 0.62$ (95% CI [0.54, 0.70]) shown in the same set of trials in during-treatment evaluations but still significantly greater than zero.

Little information is available as to replicated moderator effects suggesting for which types of patients' contingency management should be used vs. alternative interventions (Rash et al., 2017). One cocaine trial reported that anhedonia may predict poor response to contingency management, but results varied across anhedonia measures (more favorable for self-report than for behavioral) and type of analyses (more favorable for Bayesian than for traditional frequentist analysis) (Wardle et al., 2017).

In summary, contingency management programs show consistent evidence of efficacy. They are usually deployed in combination with other interventions, not as alternatives to them, so the issue of specificity is less pressing than for stand-alone interventions. Durability of effects has proven challenging, but it does appear that small effects of the programs may still be detectable at follow-up assessments.

Dissemination

A long-standing concern in the substance abuse field is lack of relation, or perhaps even a negative relation, between what treatments are supported by methodologically sound studies and what treatments are commonly offered in the community (e.g., Miller et al., 2006). As seen in the previous section, studies across a range of substance use disorders show that CM interventions can be integrated with other treatment components and add to the efficacy of such programs, particularly but not solely during the treatment period itself. On the face of it, CM also seems to lend itself well to standardization and applicability in nearly any setting. At the same time, this evidence of efficacy has not been matched by a commensurate uptake of CM interventions in routine clinical practice (Rash et al., 2017).

Petry et al. (2017) analyzed in detail the apparent nature of concerns about CM that may interfere with its utilization by clinicians. The authors found little evidence consistent with the identified concerns, including ostensible incompatibility of CM with standard interventions such as 12-step programs and concern that provision of external rewards for abstinence could undermine intrinsic motivation.

Another set of challenges for dissemination of CM relates to the economics of the intervention. First, there is the basic point that the intervention is associated with unique additional costs (e.g., frequent urine testing to determine whether contingencies are met, administrative costs of running the program as an addition to usual care, actual value of the money or vouchers dispensed to patients). A possible way to reduce costs of the reinforcers is to make greater use of lottery tickets with the potential to win larger prizes, rather than vouchers offering smaller but guaranteed prizes (Schierenberg et al., 2012). One review indicated that prize lottery systems were just as effective as vouchers in relation to treatment outcome but were less costly (Rash et al., 2017).

Second, if clinics cannot be reimbursed for the incremental costs of CM programs, then these costs are incurred directly, whereas benefits (e.g., societal benefit of longer duration of abstinence on the part of substance users) do not accrue to the clinics directly. As such, fuller implementation of CM may require that steps be taken to align better the incentives for using vs. not using it.

Summary

The impact of behavioral and cognitive-behavioral therapies for substance use disorders is mixed, in terms of both the specific therapeutic approach and the specific substance being studied. Briefly, MI appears to be efficacious relative to no treatment, though effects vary by substance. It is not specific in the sense of superiority to other active treatments. Its particular advantage may be for patients with low pretreatment motivation to change. Cue exposure has not proven successful as a treatment for substance use disorders. CBT for substance use disorders is consistent in showing efficacy, with the exception of opioid disorders, and particularly in the area of cocaine use disorder there is promising evidence of durability of effects. Specificity may be evident only for a subset of disorders (e.g., marijuana dependence). Comorbid depression or depression vulnerability could be a moderator enabling prescription of CBT relative to alternative interventions. Behavioral couples therapy appears to be superior to individual treatment in reducing alcohol use, and in increasing relationship satisfaction. Contingency management programs show consistent evidence of immediate efficacy, and small effects of the programs may still be detectable at follow-up assessments.

PERSONALITY DISORDERS

In this section we will briefly describe studies to date using traditional CBT for personality disorders focusing only on outcome findings (for process findings; see Chapter 8). Many more so-called third wave studies have addressed the treatment of personality disorders (for more details; see Chapter 16).

In terms of CBT targeting cluster C personality disorders (including avoidant, obsessive-compulsive, and dependent personality disorders), there have been several studies showing promise. In particular, an intensive open trial of four-day long behavioral group treatment was helpful for avoidant personality disorder (AvPD) on a composite measure (combining measures of fear of negative evaluation, social avoidance and distress, state and trait anxiety, depression, negative self-image, assertiveness, and social adjustment; $d = 1.66$), and gains were maintained from posttreatment to one-year follow-up (Renneberg et al., 1990). Behavior therapy also led to a similar degree of improvement (significant $ds = 1.60$–4.21) in socially phobic participants with and without AvPD (Hofmann et al., 1995). Group skills training for AvPD led to significant decreases on social avoidance ($d = 5.33$) and social anxiety ($d = 7.51$) with gains maintained from pretest to three-month follow-up ($d = 5.49$ and 8.20, respectively). In addition, there was no added benefit of doing some of the skills training outside of the clinic versus in the clinic on most measures (Stravynski et al., 1994). In another study (Alden, 1989), adding group skills training did not improve on group exposure alone for AvPD, but both treatments were significantly better than no treatment ($d = 0.40$). Continued improvement occurred from pretest to one-year follow-up, ($d = 0.66$). However, those with AvPD were still not in the normative range with their mean score for social reticence significantly greater than the mean score for a normative sample at both post-assessment ($d = 2.98$) and one-year follow-up ($d = 2.83$). A more recent study found that 20 sessions of individual CBT was better than 20 sessions of individual brief dynamic therapy for AvPD on all primary outcome measures (Cohen's $d = 0.48$–0.91). At the same time, the brief dynamic therapy was not superior to the waiting list control group on any outcome measures. (Emmelkamp et al., 2006). At six-month follow-up whereas 91% of those who had received CBT no longer met criteria for AvPD, only 64% of those who received brief dynamic therapy no longer met criteria.

Also, one small open trial examined the effect of CBT for 10 patients with obsessive compulsive personality disorder (OCPD). Following three months of no treatment wherein participants showed no change, CBT led to statistically significant changes (Ng, 2005). In addition, clinically significant change was demonstrated on mean number of DSM-IV symptoms for OCPD (from 6.8 after the waiting period to an average of 3.2 at postassessment), and 90% of them no longer met full criteria for OCPD.

Studies also examined the efficacy of CBT for mixed cluster C personality disorders. Comparing 40 sessions of individual CBT versus brief dynamic therapy there were no statistical differences in efficacy at either posttreatment or two-year follow-up. Both treatments led to clinically significant change (Svartberg et al., 2004). In particular, whereas 87.5% of patients in the CBT condition had a prominent cluster C syndrome at baseline, 72% had so at termination, and 50% had this condition at two-year follow-up, with nearly identical numbers in the brief dynamic therapy condition. A follow-up analysis of the data from this study also found that the treatments did not differ in their impact on defensive functioning (using objective coders of videotapes) at post or two-year follow-up, even though brief dynamic therapy was specifically meant to target such defenses (Johansen et al., 2011). For the latter study, overall change in defensive functioning had an effect size of $d = 1.12$ in the CBT group and $d = 1.51$ in the dynamic therapy condition. In another study, inpatients with agoraphobia plus

cluster C personality problems receiving a combination of individual and group cognitive therapy for agoraphobia plus schema focused treatment did better than those assigned to psychodynamic therapy on interpersonal problem improvement ($d = 0.88$ vs. 0.55) and phobic anxiety ($d = 1.82$ vs. 0.01) at one-year follow-up (Gude & Hoffart, 2008).

CBT also shows some promise for antisocial personality disorder (AsPD). Two studies compared contingency management (CM) to standard methadone maintenance alone (MM) for participants with drug dependence and AsPD (Messina et al., 2003; Neufeld et al., 2008). In Messina and colleagues' (2008) those with AsPD in either group CBT (54%) or CM (79%) were significantly more likely than those with AsPD in the MM condition (30%) to abstain from cocaine use at posttreatment using objective measures (Messina et al., 2003). In addition, those with AsPD in the CM condition did better than those with AsPD treated with CBT or MM alone at post. A greater percentage of those with AsPD who received CM (71%) and CBT (67%) were also abstinent than those who received MM (20%) at 52-week follow-up. In the second study, individual CM led to better treatment attendance (83% vs. 53%) and less psychosocial impairment ($d = 0.58$) in those with both high and low AsPD compared to the MM condition-treatment (Neufeld et al., 2008).

Four additional studies compared CBT plus treatment as usual (TAU) to TAU alone in those with AsPD. In the first study, violent offenders with AsPD showed trends toward more change in problematic drinking and social functioning in response to individual CBT compared to TAU (Davidson et al., 2009). However, both groups showed similar decreases in incidents of verbal aggression (TAU = 15.35% reduction, CBT = 22.73% reduction) or physical aggression (TAU = 47% reduction, CBT = 56.18% reduction). Furthermore, in a nonrandomized study that examined the likelihood of re-offense in 257 adult male offenders in prison, there was a 6% reduction in reconviction ($d = 0.18$) and 50% fewer re-offenses ($d = 0.48$) in response to a CBT called *enhanced thinking skills training* compared to a matched sample of 257 prisoners receiving TAU (Sadlier, 2010). In addition, in those with AsPD, enhanced thinking skills were superior to TAU on decreasing impulsivity/aggression ($d = 0.69$), withdrawal ($d = 0.42$), anger ($d = 0.72$), and social problem-solving ($d = 0.84$) (Doyle et al., 2013). Another investigation showed efficacy of a group cognitive skills training intervention for AsPD with attention deficit hyperactivity disorder (ADHD) in improving problem-solving ability ($d = 0.38$) and emotional stability ($d = 0.47$) while reducing ADHD symptoms ($d = 0.80$), violent attitudes ($d = 0.58$), and anger problems ($d = 0.72$) in offenders at posttreatment compared to TAU (Young et al., 2013).

The majority of studies on CBT for personality disorders have focused on borderline personality disorder (BPD). Note that we are not including work on dialectical behavior therapy (DBT) here (see Chapter 16). Individual CBT for BPD led to significant improvement in an open trial on number of BPD criteria met ($d = 0.55$), suicidal ideation ($d = 0.24$), depressed mood ($d = 0.48$), and hopelessness ($d = 0.37$) from pretreatment through follow-up (Brown et al., 2004). Individual CBT was also better than individualized Rogerian therapy for BPD at retaining participants (CBT *M* = 51 days vs. Rogerian *M* = 29 days) and showed 61% greater odds of success using all available outcome information (Cottraux et al., 2009). Another study found that CBT plus TAU was better than TAU alone on reduced number of suicidal acts (mean difference of –0.91, 95% CI [–1.67, -0.15]), personality disorder schemas (mean difference –0.58, 95% CI [–1.00, -0.17]), and distress (mean difference –0.39, 95% CI [–0.66, –0.12]) (Davidson et al., 2006). These gains were generally maintained at six-year follow-up (Davidson et al., 2010). Individuals with repeated suicide attempts were also 50% less likely to re-attempt suicide after receiving CBT than TAU (*d* = 0.37) (Brown et al., 2005). In addition, behavior therapy was superior to insight-oriented therapy on suicidal attempts and ideation (Liberman & Eckman, 1981). Also, twice as many of those treated with CBT had fulltime employment at the six month and two-year follow-up than those treated with insight-oriented therapy. CBT and dialectical behavior therapy (DBT) group treatments were both equally efficacious for college students with BPD on depression and suicide reattempts. Both groups went from 100% at baseline to 0% at 32 weeks with the total sample leading to a significant reduction (Lin et al., 2019).

Manual assisted cognitive therapy (MACT) for deliberate self-harm and personality disturbance has demonstrated efficacy for BPD in several studies. Both MACT and MACT augmented with a therapeutic assessment tailored to the individual led to significant change in borderline symptoms (*d* = 0.46) and suicidal ideation (*d* values = 0.60-0.86) (Morey et al., 2010). MACT was also more efficacious and cost-effective than TAU in several studies (Byford et al., 2003; Evans et al., 1999; MacLeod et al., 1998; Weinberg et al., 2006). For example, in Byford and colleagues (2003), MACT led to significantly lower costs per patient than TAU at 6 months (–£897, 95% CI [–1747, –48]) with indications that this superiority was maintained at the 12-month follow-up. In Evans et al. (1999) the level of depression and rate of suicidal acts per month (median 0.17/month MACT vs. 0.37/month TAU, *p* = 0.11) was less than TAU in those who received MACT. In addition, MACT was 46% more cost-effective. In a third study, MACT was more efficacious in decreasing deliberate self-harm (50% fewer incidents) than TAU. In addition, those with AsPD cost about $2,962 less if they received MACT compared to TAU whereas those with BPD cost about $1,959 more in MACT than TAU (Tyrer et al., 2004). In MacLeod and colleagues (1998), MACT also led to greater improved positive future thinking in parasuicidal patients compared to TAU, and self-rated depressive symptoms also improved significantly. MACT was also significantly better than TAU at reducing deliberate self-harm frequency at post (*d* = 0.57), and both deliberate self-harm frequency (*d* = 0.34) and deliberate self-harm severity (*d* = 0.12) at 6-month follow-up (Weinberg et al., 2006).

Systems training for emotional predictability and problem solving is a group therapy skills-based approach (STEPPs) for BPD. STEPPs was effective at reducing borderline personality disorder symptoms (Cohen's *d* = 0.73) and depression (Cohen's *d* = 0.86) in women offenders in an open trial at postassessment (Black et al., 2014). In addition, STEPPs was better than TAU in leading to improvements in BPD symptoms (*d* = 0.84), and

on objectively rated overall improvement (40.0% vs. 5.1%) and self-rated improvement (58.5% vs. 22 %). Most gains were maintained at one-year follow-up including fewer emergency room visits (Blum et al., 2008). Superiority to TAU for STEPPs was replicated in a Dutch efficacy sample (*d*s = 0.53–0.96) (Bos et al., 2010) as well as an effectiveness sample (*d*s = 0.42–0.68) at both post and six-month follow-up (Bos et al., 2011). In addition, Bos and colleagues (2010) found that 58.3% STEPPs vs. 29.2% TAU showed reliable change and 70% STEPPs vs. 46.5% TAU had clinically recovered at *both* post and 6-month follow-up.

Another series of studies examined the efficacy and effectiveness of schema therapy for BPD. Combined group plus individual schema therapy was effective (Dickhaut & Arntz, 2014; Reiss et al., 2014). In Dickhaut and Arntz (2014), Cohen's *d* ranged from 1.12 to 14.03 and in Reiss and colleagues (2014) it ranged from 0.43 to 2.84. In addition, schema therapy was superior to transference focused psychotherapy (TFP; between group *d*s = 0.46–0.72) for BPD (Giesen-Bloo et al., 2006). Schema therapy also was more cost-effective, led to greater percentage recovery (52% vs. 29%; van Asselt et al., 2008) and had better therapeutic alliance than TFP (Spinhoven et al., 2007). Furthermore, schema therapy was superior to TAU for BPD at post (*d*s = 1.35–2.22) and six-month follow-up (*d*s = 2.20–3.13) (Farrell et al., 2009). Subsequent studies found that schema therapy for BPD could be successfully implemented in regular mental health care (*d*s = 0.57–1.44; Nadort et al., 2009). Oud et al. (2018) concluded that specialized therapies for BPD, including schema therapy were better than TAU.

Schema therapy has also been examined across mixed samples of personality disorders. In open trials, group schema therapy was effective on targeted symptoms when delivered to inpatients (*d* = 0.86) (Nenadic et al., 2017) and in older outpatients with mixed PDs (*d* = 0.54) (Videler et al., 2014). It also had low dropout rates (weighted mean dropout rate of 23.3%) (Gülüm, 2018), and rates lower than TAU (15% vs. 40%) (Bamelis et al., 2014). Group schema therapy also led to improvements in previously unresponsive psychiatric inpatients with personality disorders (Cohen's *d* adjusted for dropouts ranging from 0.49 to 1.52) (Schaap et al., 2016). Within opioid-dependent patients with mixed personality disorders receiving methadone maintenance, schema therapy led to faster decreases in the frequency of their use of substances over six months compared to 12-step facilitation therapy based on both therapist reports and patient reports (Ball, 2007). Schema therapy was also superior on recovery in global functioning compared to TAU (odds ratio 4.07, 95% CI [1.77, 9.35]) and compared to clarification-oriented therapy (odds ratio 2.20, 95% CI [1.04, 8.16]) for cluster C, paranoid, histrionic, or narcissistic personality disorder (Bamelis et al., 2014). Clarification-oriented psychotherapy did not differ in global functioning improvement from TAU. There were also no differences in efficacy across types of personality disorder diagnosis. In addition, after three years the proportion of recovered patients was 81.4% in schema therapy, 51.2% in clarification-oriented therapy and 51.8% in TAU. Moreover, schema therapy was more cost-effective overall for personality disorders than TAU or clarification-oriented therapy (Bamelis et al.,

2015). Preliminary results of schema therapy with forensic patients with personality disorders also showed promise compared to TAU (Bernstein et al., 2012). Problem-solving therapy also led to better problem-solving skills (*difference* = 2.09, 95% CI [1.21, 2.97]) and social functioning (*difference* –1.05, 95% CI [–1.99, –0.18]) than wait list in a mixed personality disorder effectiveness sample at post (Huband et al., 2007).

In summary, several variants of CBT have shown promise for personality disorders, particularly Cluster C, antisocial and borderline personality disorders. However, much more research is needed on traditional CBT for these problems, particularly for AvPD, OCPD, and AsPD. Also, no CBT trials exist for schizoid, or schizotypal personality disorder.

PSYCHOSIS

CBT has demonstrated strong efficacy for psychosis and schizophrenia. A recent network meta-analysis of 40 studies of moderately ill schizophrenic patients attempted to improve on the methodological problems of prior meta-analyses (Bighelli et al., 2018). These authors concluded that CBT for psychosis (CBTp) plus TAU led to significantly more reduction in positive symptoms (standardized mean difference (SMD) –0.30, 95% CI [–0.45, –0.14]), negative symptoms (SMD –0.16, 95% CI [–0.29, -0.03]), and overall symptoms (SMD –0.38, 95% CI [–0.56, –0.20]) than TAU. These findings remained when controlling for researcher allegiance and blinding of assessors. CBTp was also superior to supportive therapy on positive symptoms (SMD –0.47, 95% CI [–0.91, –0.03]). There were too few studies of other psychosocial therapies to draw any conclusions regarding their efficacy. One negative finding was that CBTp had higher dropout rates than TAU (18.8% vs. 12%; risk ratio, RR = 0.74, 95% CI [0.58, 0.95]) (Bighelli et al., 2018). However, it doesn't appear that TAU dropout in this meta-analysis accounted for nonadherence to antipsychotic medication. In other studies, nonadherence to antipsychotic medications has been estimated to be as high as 66% when measured objectively (Geretsegger et al., 2019). Another meta-analysis compared attrition in CBTp to attrition from other active psychosocial interventions and found relatively lower attrition at 14% (95% CI = 13–15%) on average (Szymczynska et al., 2017). A more recent meta-analysis of CBTp that targeted specific symptoms found that all adequately powered studies reviewed reported effect sizes (*d*) of superiority to TAU as above .4 on at least one primary outcome measure with effects maintained across follow-up periods (Lincoln & Peters, 2019). Another meta-analysis of ten controlled trials of low intensity CBT (fewer than 16 sessions) for psychosis (compared to another active intervention) found that it was promising (Hazell et al., 2016). In particular, at post assessment (*d* –0.28, 95% CI [–0.54, –0.02], Q_r = 14.11) there was greater reduction in psychotic symptoms from CBTp and these effects were maintained at follow-up (*d* –0.40, 95% CI [–0.74, –0.06], Q_r = 13.79).

Two recent studies examined CBTp for patients who chose not to take antipsychotic medication. In an open trial of 20 such patients, CBTp led to significant reduction on psychotic symptoms (*d* = 1.26, 95% CI [0.66, 1.84]) and total

psychiatric symptoms (*d* = 0.87, 95% CI [0.34, 1.37]) from pretreatment to follow-up (Morrison et al., 2012). A subsequent randomized controlled trial demonstrated the safety and acceptability of CBTp plus TAU for patients who chose not to take psychotic medication compared to TAU alone (Morrison et al., 2014). CBTp led to greater improvement than TAU on psychotic symptoms (*d* = 0.46) (Morrison et al., 2014). A secondary analysis of Morrison and colleagues (2014) found a dose-response effect of CBTp with more therapy sessions leading to better outcome (Spencer et al., 2018).

Another more recent trial randomized psychotic individuals who had not received either CBTp or antipsychotic medications in the last 3 months to CBTp, antipsychotics, or CBTp plus antipsychotics. They found that antipsychotics plus CBTp were significantly better than CBTp alone on overall symptoms (Mean difference(MD) –5.65, 95% CI [–10.37, –0.93]) with no significant difference between CBTp alone and antipsychotics alone (MD –1.13, 95% CI [–5.81, 3.55]) or between antipsychotics alone and CBTp plus antipsychotics (MD –4.52, 95% CI [–9.30, 0.26]) although the latter finding approached significance favoring the combined group over antipsychotics alone. At the same time, fewer side effects were found in the CBTp alone group compared to antipsychotics alone (MD = 3.22, 95% CI [0.58, 5.87]) or compared to the CBTp plus antipsychotic group (MD = 3.99, 95% CI [1.36, 6.64]) (Morrison et al., 2018).

In summary, CBTp is a feasible, potentially efficacious and effective option, particularly for clients who either don't want antipsychotics or who are nonresponsive to antipsychotics. Unfortunately, however, those who train psychotherapists are often unaware of the strong efficacy of CBTp. A large survey of training directors in the United States found very little awareness of the evidence for CBTp, as well as inadequate training opportunities to provide effective CBTp (Kimhy et al., 2013). Interestingly, researchers have also investigated factors that predict a more favorable outcome from CBTp. A systematic review found that being female, shorter duration of illness, older age, more clinical insight at the start of therapy, and higher educational achievement predicted the best outcome (O'Keeffe et al., 2017).

DIVERSITY CONSIDERATIONS

Recent meta-analyses of treatments for diverse samples have mostly not examined specific diagnoses separately. Therefore, we include this section to summarize what we know generally about CBT. Studies examining the efficacy of CBT generally have found that it works with those of differing races and ethnicities. CBT for anxiety in African Americans showed large pre–post effect sizes comparable to what has been shown in other samples (Gregory, 2018). CBT for anxiety was also effective for Chinese people showing a medium effect size at both short and long-term follow-up.

However, an effectiveness study of CBT found that race moderated outcome with White participants faring better than non-White participants (Zhang et al., 2019). This is consistent with recent findings suggesting that the short-term efficacy of culturally adapted CBT for any problem in Chinese individuals was superior to non-adapted CBT (Ng & Wong, 2017). Other meta-analyses conducted across cultures have also suggested that culturally tailored interventions outperformed nonculturally tailored interventions (Hall et al., 2016; Huey & Tilley, 2018). In fact, Hall and associates (2016) found that culturally adapted treatments had 4.68 times greater odds of achieving remission than nonculturally adapted CBT with larger effect sizes for intervention studies than prevention studies. Additional research suggests that faith-adapted CBT for anxiety may outperform nonfaith adapted CBT for individuals who label themselves as religious (Anderson et al., 2015).

Transdiagnostic Predictors

There are also some transdiagnostic predictors of CBT outcome. Studies have shown that both quality and quantity of homework compliance predicted outcome at post treatment (quantity: $g = 0.79$, 95% CI [0.57, 1.02], $I^2 = 80\%$; quality: $g = 0.78$, 95% CI [0.03, 1.53], $I^2 = 91\%$) and follow-up (quantity: $g = 0.51$, 95% CI [0.28, 0.74], $I^2 = 74\%$; quality: $g = 1.07$, 95% CI [0.06, 2.08], $I^2 = 94\%$) (e.g., Kazantzis et al., 2016). Both alliance and alliance rupture repair also predicted outcome from all types of psychotherapy including CBT with moderate effect sizes ($r = 0.29$, $I^2 = 82\%$) (Fluckiger et al., 2012). Similarly, both goal consensus ($r = 0.34$, 95% CI [0.23, 0.45]) and collaboration ($r = 0.33$, 95% CI [0.25, 0.42]) predicted outcome (Tryon & Winograd, 2011). Feedback provided to therapists also predicted better outcome from CBT with effect sizes ranging from $r = 0.23$ to $r = 0.33$ depending on the system used (Lambert & Shimokawa, 2011).

Concluding Remarks

Overall, this chapter summarizes strong evidence supporting the efficacy and effectiveness of CBT. In addition, we conclude as did prior versions of this chapter that CBT has strong evidence of specificity for a variety of disorders and for many of them, continues to remain the treatment of choice. As was concluded in the prior two chapters, CBT is at least as good as medication for most disorders, and for some disorders isn't enhanced with the addition of medication, whereas for others more research is needed. Furthermore, CBT shows long-term maintenance of gains and/or continued improvement when discontinued, whereas medication does not. Although most of our conclusions do not differ from those of previous versions of this chapter, the evidence has only become stronger. As a whole, the general clinical implications that can be derived from this evidence is that traditional CBT (as now defined as its first and second phase) is an empirically supported treatment that provides therapists with helpful tools for a wide range of highly distressing and impairing psychological problems. Regarding specific disorders, the following seven specific conclusions can be drawn:

1. For depressed adults, CBT reduces symptoms at least as much as antidepressant medication, interpersonal psychotherapy, dynamic psychotherapy, and supportive psychotherapy. Similarly, CBT improves psychosocial functioning and quality of life in treated adults. The hallmark of CBT for depression is that its health promoting effects endure, albeit not indefinitely, after patients discontinue formal therapy. Cognitive behavioral therapy shows promise in reducing the incidence of and/or delaying first onset of depressive disorders which has the potential to reduce global burden.

2. For anxiety and related disorders, CBT is efficacious, specific, and leads to continued gains following discontinuation. There is also new evidence that it is a preventative tool and has significant evidence for real-world effectiveness. In terms of components, exposure (especially for SAD, OCD, PTSD, phobias, and PD) and applied relaxation (especially for GAD and PD) should be emphasized in most treatment packages. Group CBT is less efficacious than individual CBT so research developing more efficacious group treatments may be important. There is also evidence for mechanisms of CBT including threat reappraisal and extinction of fear. CBT alone should be the first-line choice for treatment and medications should be considered only for nonresponders to CBT.

3. CBT continues to be the most effective treatment for BN and BED although there has been little improvement in the effectiveness of CBT over the past decade. CBT has also shown specificity in the treatment of BN but not BED. There is also evidence that CBT is as effective in community settings as in controlled trials when community facilities can support the length of treatment. There is tentative evidence that the improved version of CBT (CBT-E) may be more effective in treating BN with severe comorbid psychopathology. The situation is different in the outpatient treatment of AN. No treatment, including CBT, has been shown superior to usual care for the persistent (adult) form of AN. For adolescents with AN, a family-based behavior therapy (FBT) has shown both effectiveness and specificity in a number of controlled trials and is probably the most effective treatment for adolescent AN.

4. CBT has a mixed track record in treatment of substance use disorders. Some of the variability is a function of treatment focus; for instance, contingency management interventions appear to add substantially to the effectiveness of other treatments during the active treatment phase, whereas cue exposure treatment has not proven to be efficacious. Variability is also evident across disorders, with favorable results for alcohol, smoking, and cannabis use but not for opioid dependence. Specificity is seldom obtained, and effects are weaker at longer-term follow-ups. Mediating mechanisms are generally not established, though in a few instances moderator effects appear promising (e.g. motivational interviewing being especially useful for less motivated patients).

5. For personality disorders there is evidence for efficacy and specificity of CBT in the treatment of avoidant, antisocial, and borderline PD as well as mixed PDs.

6. For psychosis, there is a substantial amount of research that suggests that whether or not patients are willing to comply with medication, CBT is efficacious and specific. CBT can

address both positive and negative symptoms and is better than treatment as usual.

7. At the same time, we know more about predicting CBT outcomes for some of the disorders reviewed than we do about moderation, so future research should continue to examine this in representative samples.

For CBT nonresponders and/or partial responders, more research is needed to characterize efficacious treatment (e.g., through switches or augmentation [with other psychotherapy or modalities] or changes in parameters of "dosing" [e.g., session frequency, duration of session or treatment phase]). If moderators (e.g., of differential effects of single modality versus combination treatment; comparisons of treatment sequences) can be identified and replicated, these results have the potential to improve patients' lives and address the needs of demographic groups that are both understudied and underserved. As research and technology advance the classification systems used, we will also be better poised to match treatments to specific problems. Characterizing symptom profiles will be necessary in order to know which people benefit most from which interventions. Suitable and tested protocols (allowing for personalization) require development and evaluation of initial and long-term effects of all affected individuals. Next steps would include pairing replicated results with practical screening, diagnostic, and treatment algorithms.

The field is also poised to focus on mechanistic and parametric studies, as well as longer-term outcomes. It is paramount to identify the specific treatment components and their targets (i.e., mechanisms) of CBT's short- and long-term effects, not only to harness its potential effectiveness but also to simplify CBT training and delivery formats. To further identify mechanisms underlying the effectiveness of CBT, all controlled clinical trials should be powered to detect mediational effects. A speculative literature on mechanisms is just beginning to emerge but can be facilitated by improved measurement, more basic science research, and other advances.

Another very important issue is that CBT is not reaching the majority of those who might benefit from it. For example, even when people have severe depressive symptoms, only about 35% seek treatment from a mental health professional (Pratt & Brody, 2014). Most people (75%) prefer psychotherapy compared to pharmacotherapy (McHugh et al., 2013; Olfson & Marcus, 2010); yet, the majority of adults receive pharmacotherapy (Cipriani et al., 2018). Psychotherapy, including CBT, is not widely accessible to the people who need and prefer it. Barriers to any treatment can include stigma, finances, culture, and access to competent personnel who practice within an evidence-based treatment paradigm (Mohr et al., 2010; Mohr et al., 2006).

Populations that may benefit from wider dissemination of CBT include: youth, un/affected women, people at higher risk, those in rural and economically disadvantaged communities, newly diagnosed patients with life-limiting or disabling illness (as well as their caretakers), new parents, elderly people with recent physical, social, and emotional loss and/or nonpsychiatric medical illnesses, health care workers, and first responders. The perinatal period for at-risk conceiving, pregnant, and post-partum women is likely a "sensitive period" in which cognitive behavioral therapists can have a positive impact on the mental health trajectory of entire families.

While a full discussion of dissemination exceeds the scope of this chapter, suggestions are available elsewhere (see Chapter 22; also see, e.g., Goodwin et al., 2018; Kazdin & Blase, 2011; Lemmens et al., 2016; Teachman et al., 2018; Wright et al., 2018. We offer the following "emerging frontiers" as exemplars, holding promise toward improving access and addressing the public need globally. Putative candidates include but are not limited to "health apps," (which may be thought of as interactive bibliotherapy and self-help [which provides a potential baseline literature on which to build and adapt]). Although such apps to monitor and manage symptoms are available, their effectiveness needs more evaluation in order to create a valid evidence base (Hollis et al., 2015). After evaluation and approval as safe and effective, apps can be disseminated to the public (Bates et al., 2018; Weir, 2018) for initial self-help and as adjuncts to face-to-face CBT to improve symptoms, as well as skill attainment and maintenance (Warmerdam et al., 2012). Further, the field will need to better understand how to best engage participants in initial and longitudinal use of these tools to realize their full potential.

Low-intensity psychosocial interventions based on CBT are also candidates to improve access for patients who may not need a full trial of CBT due to their symptom profiles. These interventions could offer innovation in universal, secondary, and tertiary prevention. For example, the "Thinking Healthy" manual describes how community health workers can reduce perinatal depression through CBT techniques (Eappen et al., 2018; World Health Organization, 2015). Also, characterizing the most-effective methods for providing CBT in groups rather than to one individual at a time will improve access in busy health systems, community, and educational settings. Williams and Martinez (2008) promote increasing access with low- and high-intensity CBT, using a stepped-care delivery model, including self-help through individual delivery with a focus on how the person wants to learn.

High-quality, nonequivalence research designs may prove helpful. Developing and testing specific CBT protocols and technological adjuncts for high-risk patients at each point in the illness trajectory has the potential to reduce human, societal, and fiscal costs. We predict that the marriage of the fields of basic and applied psychology, neuroscience, public health, and informatics combined with insights from diverse patient and provider perspectives may hold the key to innovation in delivery methods of CBT with the potential to address the public health problem that is evident. This will require strong collaboration among basic science, technology, clinical science and practice, and public health in order to facilitate human learning involving not only patients but also providers.

Similarly, research is needed to determine the conditions under which paraprofessionals (e.g., Singla et al., 2017), teachers in all walks of life, and non-doctoral-level providers can provide preventive psychoeducation based on cognitive behavioral principles to forestall future suffering and disease expression in vulnerable populations. Studies also might match professionals with various competencies to types of clinically disordered patients within a stepped CBT approach. This might allow symptom profiles to be matched to providers with different levels of competency and experience. For example, providers in community settings with greater freedom to prescribe length and dose of therapy may be well suited to treat patients who suffer from chronic interpersonal distress and untreated trauma and/or cumulative life stress. As suggested by the United Kingdom's use of psychological well-being practitioners in the initiative to improve access to psychological therapies, provider competence may be an important moderator of outcomes (Green et al., 2014).

We note that both the popularity and the available evidence supporting CBT as a psychotherapy of viable choice is remarkable, given that its research and development have been propelled by a cottage industry initially funded largely through public monies and institutions rather than corporate industries. We observe, however, that the field may be at a "tipping point" (Gladwell, 2006) with respect to this trend, given both the opportunities and challenges that new technologies for measurement and dissemination offer. We mention this because digital health (United States Food and Drug Administration, 2017) and the types of collaboration ahead will likely rely on new combinations of funding and novel social structures (for social scientists) with the potential to introduce new conflicts of interest, financial and otherwise, to the field of psychotherapy (Cristea & Ioannidis, 2018). Such potential conflicts of interest will require safeguards and management (e.g., disclosure, identification, and, when indicated, elimination of the potential conflict of interest) to keep our field focused on the common good. Including our patients' voices and using rigorous methods to identify, manage, and/or eliminate financial and professional conflicts of interest will be essential as behavioral technology advances to practice and begins to address the global need inherent in psychological disorders.

The goal of collaborative basic and applied research is to prevent and reduce the suffering associated with these disorders. More gaps in measurement and knowledge will be identified. Advanced measurement combined with team-based, interdisciplinary collaboration (in both research and practice), which focuses on preventing initial and recurrent onsets and restoring full recovery for patients and their families over their lifetimes, has the potential to advance knowledge and begin to address the global need and societal costs.

ABBREVIATIONS

AB	antecedent-behavior
ABC	antecedents, behaviors, and consequences
ADHD	attention deficit hyperactivity disorder (ADHD)
AFT	adolescent-focused individual psychotherapy
AN	anorexia nervosa
AR	applied relaxation
ASD	acute stress disorder
AsPD	antisocial personality disorder
AvPD	avoidant personality disorder
BCT	behavioral couples therapy
BED	binge eating disorder
BN	bulimia nervosa
BPD	borderline personality disorder
BWL	behavioral weight loss
CBSAP	cognitive behavioral analysis system of psychotherapy
CBT	cognitive behavioral therapy
CBTp	cognitive behavioral therapy for psychosis
CBT-E	cognitive behavioral therapy-enhanced
CBTgsh	cognitive behavioral therapy guided self help
CI	confidence interval
CM	contingency management
CT	cognitive therapy
DBT	dialectical behavior therapy
DSMC	difference in standardized mean change
ED	eating disorder
EOT	end of treatment
FBT	family-based therapy
GAD	generalized anxiety disorder
IPT	interpersonal therapy
LDA	longest duration of abstinence
MACT	manual assisted cognitive therapy
MANTRA	Maudsley model anorexia treatment
MATCH	matching alcoholism treatment to client heterogeneity
MI	motivational interviewing
MM	methadone maintenance
OCD	obsessive compulsive disorder
OCPD	obsessive compulsive personality disorder
OR	odds ratio
pCo2	partial pressure of carbon dioxide
PD	panic disorder
PFT	parent-focused treatment
PMR	progressive muscle relaxation
PP	psychodynamic psychotherapy
PNS	percentage of negative samples
PTSD	post-traumatic stress disorder
RR	relative risk
SAD	social anxiety disorder
SMD	standardized mean difference

STEPPs	systems training for emotional predictability and problem solving
SyFT	systemic family therapy
TAU	treatment as usual
TFP	transference focused psychotherapy

REFERENCES

Adams, T. G., Brady, R. E., Lohr, J. M., & Jacobs, W. J. (2015). A meta-analysis of CBT components for anxiety disorders. *The Behavior Therapist*, *38*(4), 87–97.

Aderka, I. M., Nickerson, A., Bøe, H. J., & Hofmann, S. G. (2012). Sudden gains during psychological treatments of anxiety and depression: A meta-analysis. *Journal of Consulting and Clinical Psychology*, *80*(1), 93–101. https://doi.org/10.1037/a0026455

Agras, W. S., Lock, J., Brandt, H., Bryson, S. W., Dodge, E., Halmi, K. A., Jo, B., Johnson, C., Kaye, W., Wilfley, D., & Woodside, B. (2014). Comparison of 2 family therapies for adolescent anorexia nervosa: A randomized parallel trial. *JAMA Psychiatry*, *71*(11), 1279–1286. https://doi.org/10.1001/jamapsychiatry.2014.1025

Ainscough, T. S., McNeill, A., Strang, J., Calder, R., & Brose, L. S. (2017). Contingency management interventions for non-prescribed drug use during treatment for opiate addiction: A systematic review and meta-analysis. *Drug and Alcohol Dependence*, *178*, 318–339. https://doi.org/10.1016/j.drugalcdep.2017.05.028

Alden, L. (1989). Short-term structured treatment for avoidant personality disorder. *Journal of Consulting and Clinical Psychology*, *57*(6), 756–764. https://doi.org/10.1037/0022-006X.57.6.756

American Psychiatric Association. (2013). *Diagnostic and statistical manual of mental disorders* (DSM-5; 5th ed.). Arlington, Virginia: American Psychiatric Association. https://doi.org/10.1176/appi.books.9780890425596

American Psychological Association (2019). Clinical practice guideline for the treatment of depression across three age cohorts. Guideline development panel for depressive disorders. Retrieved from http://www.apa.org/depression-guideline/guideline.pdf

Amick, H. R., Gartlehner, G., Gaynes, B. N., Forneris, C., Asher, G. N., Morgan, L. C., Coker-Schwimmer, E., Boland, E., Lux, L. J., Gaylord, S, Bann, C., Pierl, C. B., & Lohr, K. N. (2015). Comparative benefits and harms of second generation antidepressants and cognitive behavioral therapies in initial treatment of major depressive disorder: Systematic review and meta-analysis. *BMJ*, *351*, h6019. https://doi.org/10.1136/bmj.h6019

Anderson, N., Heywood-Everett, S., Siddiqi, N., Wright, J., Meredith, J., & McMillan, D. (2015). Faith-adapted psychological therapies for depression and anxiety: Systematic review and meta-analysis. *Journal of Affective Disorders*, *176*, 183–196. https://doi.org/10.1016/j.jad.2015.01.019

Andony, L. J., Tay, E., Allen, K. L., Wade, T. D., Hay, P., Touyz, S., McIntosh, V. V., Treasure, J., Schmidt, U. H., Fairburn, C. G., Erceg-Hurn, D. M., Fursland, A., Crosby, R. D., & Byrne, S. M. (2015). Therapist adherence in the strong without anorexia nervosa (SWAN) study: A randomized controlled trial of three treatments for adults with anorexia nervosa. *International Journal of Eating Disorders*, *48*(8), 1170–1175. https://doi.org/10.1002/eat.22455

Arcelus, J., Mitchell, A. J., Wales, J., & Nielsen, S. (2011). Mortality rates in patients with anorexia nervosa and other eating disorders. A meta-analysis of 36 studies. *Archives of General Psychiatry*, *68*(7), 724–731. https://doi.org/10.1001/archgenpsychiatry.2011.74

Ball, S. A. (2007). Comparing individual therapies for personality disordered opioid dependent patients. *Journal of Personality Disorders*, *21*(3), 305–321. https://doi.org/10.1521/pedi.2007.21.3.305

Bamelis, L. L., Arntz, A., Wetzelaer, P., Verdoorn, R., & Evers, S. M. (2015). Economic evaluation of schema therapy and clarification-oriented psychotherapy for personality disorders: A multicenter, randomized controlled trial. *Journal of Clinical Psychiatry*, *76*(11), e1432–1440. https://doi.org/10.4088/JCP.14m09412

Bamelis, L. L., Evers, S. M., Spinhoven, P., & Arntz, A. (2014). Results of a multicenter randomized controlled trial of the clinical effectiveness of schema therapy for personality disorders. *The American Journal of Psychiatry*, *171*(3), 305–322. https://doi.org/10.1176/appi.ajp.2013.12040518

Bandelow, B., Reitt, M., Rover, C., Michaelis, S., Gorlich, Y., & Wedekind, D. (2015). Efficacy of treatments for anxiety disorders: A meta-analysis. *International Clinical Psychopharmacology*, *30*(4), 183–192. https://doi.org/10.1097/YIC.0000000000000078

Bandelow, B., Sagebiel, A., Belz, M., Görlich, Y., Michaelis, S., & Wedekind, D. (2018). Enduring effects of psychological treatments for anxiety disorders: Meta-analysis of follow-up studies. *The British Journal of Psychiatry*, *212*(6), 333–338. https://doi.org/10.1192/bjp.2018.49

Bandelow, B., Seidler-Brandler, U., Becker, A., Wedekind, D., & Ruther, E. (2007). Meta-analysis of randomized controlled comparisons of psychopharmacological and psychological treatments for anxiety disorders. *World Journal of Biological Psychiatry*, *8*(3), 175–187. https://doi.org/10.1080/15622970601110273

Bandura, A. (1977). Self-efficacy: Toward a unifying theory of behavioral change. *Psychological Review*, *84*(2), 191–215. https://doi.org/10.1037/0033-295X.84.2.191

Beck, A. T. (2008). The evolution of the cognitive model of depression and its neurobiological correlates. *The American Journal of Psychiatry*, *165*(8), 969–977. https://doi.org/10.1176/appi.ajp.2008.08050721

Beck, A. T., Rush, A. J., Shaw, B. F., & Emery, G. (1979). *Cognitive therapy of depression*. New York: Guilford.

Beck, A. T., Wright, F. D., Newman, C. F., & Liese, B. S. (2001). *Cognitive therapy of substance abuse*. New York: Guilford Press.

Bernstein, D. P., Nijman, H. L. I., Karos, K., Keulen-de Vos, M., de Vogel, V., & Lucker, T. P. (2012). Schema therapy for forensic patients with personality disorders: Design and preliminary findings of a multicenter randomized clinical trial in the Netherlands. *International Journal of Forensic Mental Health*, *11*(4), 312–324. https://doi.org/10.1080/14999013.2012.746757

Biesheuvel-Leliefeld, K. E., Kok, G. D., Bockting, C. L., Cuijpers, P., Hollon, S. D., van Marwijk, H. W., & Smit, F. (2015). Effectiveness of psychological interventions in preventing recurrence of depressive disorder: Meta-analysis and meta-regression. *Journal of Affective Disorders*, *174*, 400–410. https://doi.org/10.1016/j.jad.2014.12.016

Bighelli, I., Salanti, G., Huhn, M., Schneider-Thoma, J., Krause, M., Reitmeir, C., Wallis, S., Schwermann, F., Pitschel-Walz, G., Barbui, C., Furukawa, T. A., & Leucht, S. (2018). Psychological interventions to reduce positive symptoms in schizophrenia: Systematic review and network meta-analysis. *World Psychiatry*, *17*(3), 316–329. https://doi.org/10.1002/wps.20577

Black, D. W., Blum, N., Eichinger, L., McCormick, B., Allen, J., & Sieleni, B. (2014). STEPPS: Systems Training for Emotional Predictability and Problem Solving in women offenders with borderline personality disorder in prison – A pilot study. *CNS Spectrums*, *13*(10), 881–886. https://doi.org/10.1017/S1092852900016989

Blakey, S. M., & Abramowitz, J. S. (2016). The effects of safety behaviors during exposure therapy for anxiety: Critical analysis from an inhibitory learning perspective. *Clinical Psychology Review*, *49*, 1–15. https://doi.org/10.1016/j.cpr.2016.07.002

Blom, T. J., Mingione, C. J., Guerdjikova, A. I., Keck, P. E., Jr., Welge, J. A., & McElroy, S. L. (2014). Placebo response in binge eating disorder: A pooled analysis of 10 clinical trials from one research group. *European Eating Disorders Review*, *22*(2), 140–146. https://doi.org/10.1002/erv.2277

Blum, N., St John, D., Pfohl, B., Stuart, S., McCormick, B., Allen, J., Arndt, S., & Black, D. W. (2008). Systems Training for Emotional Predictability and Problem Solving (STEPPS) for outpatients with borderline personality disorder: A randomized controlled trial and 1-year follow-up. *The American Journal of Psychiatry*, *165*(4), 468–478. https://doi.org/10.1176/appi.ajp.2007.07071079

Bockting, C. L., Hollon, S. D., Jarrett, R. B., Kuyken, W., & Dobson, K. (2015). A lifetime approach to major depressive disorder: The contributions of psychological interventions in preventing relapse and recurrence. *Clinical Psychology Review*, *41*, 16–26. https://doi.org/10.1016/j.cpr.2015.02.003

Bockting, C. L. H., Klein, N. S., Elgersma, H. J., van Rijsbergen, G. D., Slofstra, C., Ormel, J., Buskens, E., Dekker, J., de Jong, P. J., Nolen, W. A., Schene, A. H., Hollon, S. D., & Burger, H. (2018). Effectiveness of preventive cognitive therapy while tapering antidepressants versus maintenance antidepressant treatment versus their combination in prevention of depressive relapse or recurrence (DRD study): A three-group, multicentre, randomised controlled trial. *The Lancet Psychiatry, 5*(5), 401–410. https://doi .org/10.1016/S2215-0366(18)30100-7

Bockting, C. L., Schene, A. H., Spinhoven, P., Koeter, M. W., Wouters, L. F., Huyser, J., & Kamphuis, J. H. (2005). Preventing relapse/recurrence in recurrent depression with cognitive therapy: A randomized controlled trial. *Journal of Consulting and Clinical Psychology, 73*(4), 647–657. https:// doi.org/10.1037/0022-006X.73.4.647

Borkovec, T. D., Newman, M. G., Pincus, A. L., & Lytle, R. (2002). A component analysis of cognitive-behavioral therapy for generalized anxiety disorder and the role of interpersonal problems. *Journal of Consulting and Clinical Psychology, 70*(2), 288–298. https://doi.org/10.1037/0022-006X.70.2.288

Bos, E. H., van Wel, E. B., Appelo, M. T., & Verbraak, M. J. (2010). A randomized controlled trial of a Dutch version of Systems Training for Emotional Predictability and Problem Solving for borderline personality disorder. *The Journal of Nervous and Mental Disease, 198*(4), 299–304. https://doi.org/10.1097/NMD.0b013e3181d619cf

Bos, E. H., van Wel, E. B., Appelo, M. T., & Verbraak, M. J. (2011). Effectiveness of Systems Training for Emotional Predictability and Problem Solving (STEPPS) for borderline personality problems in a "real-world" sample: Moderation by diagnosis or severity? *Psychotherapy and Psychosomatics, 80*(3), 173–181. https://doi.org/10.1159/000321793

Boschloo, L., Bekhuis, E., Weitz, E. S., Reijnders, M., DeRubeis, R. J., Dimidjian, S., Dunner, D. L., Dunlop, B. W., Hegerl, U., Hollon, S. D., Jarrett, R. B., Kennedy, S. H., Miranda, J., Mohr, D. C., Simons, A. D., Parker, G., Petrak, F., Herpertz, S., Quilty, L. C., John Rush, A., . . . Cuijpers, P. (2019). The symptom-specific efficacy of antidepressant medication vs. cognitive behavioral therapy in the treatment of depression: Results from an individual patient data meta-analysis. *World Psychiatry, 18*(2), 183–191. https://doi.org/10.1002/wps.20630

Brandon, T. H., Juliano, L. M., Copeland, A. L., Collins, B. N., Quinn, E. P., & Lazev, A. B. (1997). *Matching smokers to treatment based on negative affectivity.* Paper presented at the Society of Behavioral Medicine, San Francisco, CA.

Brouwer, M. E., Williams, A. D., Kennis, M., Fu, Z., Klein, N. S., Cuijpers, P., & Bockting, C. L. H. (2019). Psychological theories of depressive relapse and recurrence: A systematic review and meta-analysis of prospective studies. *Clinical Psychology Review, 74*, 101773. https://doi.org/10.1016/ j.cpr.2019.101773

Brown, G. K., Newman, C. F., Charlesworth, S. E., Crits-Christoph, P., & Beck, A. T. (2004). An open clinical trial of cognitive therapy for borderline personality disorder. *Journal of Personality Disorders, 18*(3), 257–271.

Brown, G. K., Ten Have, T., Henriques, G. R., Xie, S. X., Hollander, J. E., & Beck, A. T. (2005). Cognitive therapy for the prevention of suicide attempts: A randomized controlled trial. *Journal of the American Medical Association, 294*(5), 563–570. https://doi.org/10.1521/pedi.18.3.257.35450

Brown, R. A., Niaura, R., Lloyd-Richardson, E. E., Strong, D. R., Kahler, C. W., Abrantes, A. M., Abrams, D., & Miller, I. W. (2007). Bupropion and cognitive-behavioral treatment for depression in smoking cessation. *Nicotine and Tobacco Research, 9*(7), 721–730. https://doi.org/ 10.1080/14622200701416955

Bruijniks, S. J. E., DeRubeis, R. J., Hollon, S. D., & Huibers, M. J. H. (2019). The potential role of learning capacity in cognitive behavior therapy for depression: A systematic review of the evidence and future directions for improving therapeutic learning. *Clinical Psychological Science, 7*(4), 668–692. https://doi .org/10.1177/2167702619830391

Buckman, J. E. J., Underwood, A., Clarke, K., Saunders, R., Hollon, S. D., Fearon, P., & Pilling, S. (2018). Risk factors for relapse and recurrence of depression in adults and how they operate: A four-phase systematic review and meta-synthesis. *Clinical Psychology Review, 64*, 13–38. https:// doi.org/10.1016/j.cpr.2018.07.005

Burke, B. L., Arkowitz, H., & Menchola, M. (2003). The efficacy of motivational interviewing: A meta-analysis of controlled clinical trials. *Journal of Consulting and Clinical Psychology, 71*(5), 843–861. https://doi .org/10.1037/0022-006X.71.5.843

Bürkner, P.-C., Bittner, N., Holling, H., & Buhlmann, U. (2017). D-cycloserine augmentation of behavior therapy for anxiety and obsessive-compulsive disorders: A meta-analysis. *PLoS ONE, 12*(3), e0173660. https://doi .org/10.1371/journal.pone.0173660

Byford, S., Knapp, M., Greenshields, J., Ukoumunne, O. C., Jones, V., Thompson, S., Tyrer, P., Schmidt, U., Davidson, K., & POMACT Group

(2003). Cost-effectiveness of brief cognitive behaviour therapy versus treatment as usual in recurrent deliberate self-harm: A decision-making approach. *Psychological Medicine, 33*(6), 977–986. https://doi.org/10.1017/ S0033291703008183

Byrne, S. M., Fursland, A., Allen, K. L., & Watson, H. (2011). The effectiveness of enhanced cognitive behavioural therapy for eating disorders: An open trial. *Behaviour Research and Therapy, 49*(4), 219–226. https://doi .org/10.1016/j.brat.2011.01.006

Byrne, S., Wade, T., Hay, P., Touyz, S., Fairburn, C. G., Treasure, J., Schmidt, U., McIntosh, V., Allen, K., Fursland, A., & Crosby, R. D. (2017). A randomised controlled trial of three psychological treatments for anorexia nervosa. *Psychological Medicine, 47*(16), 2823–2833. https://doi .org/10.1017/S0033291717001349

Cahill, K., Hartmann-Boyce, J., & Perera, R. (2015). Incentives for smoking cessation. *Cochrane Database of Systematic Reviews*, CD004307. https://doi .org/10.1002/14651858.CD004307.pub5

Calugi, S., El Ghoch, M., & Dalle Grave, R. (2017). Intensive enhanced cognitive behavioural therapy for severe and enduring anorexia nervosa: A longitudinal outcome study. *Behaviour Research and Therapy, 89*, 41–48. https://doi.org/10.1016/j.brat.2016.11.006

Carl, E., Witcraft, S. M., Kauffman, B. Y., Gillespie, E. M., Becker, E. S., Cuijpers, P., Van Ameringen, M., Smits, J., & Powers, M. B. (2019). Psychological and pharmacological treatments for generalized anxiety disorder (GAD): A meta-analysis of randomized controlled trials. *Cognitive Behaviour Therapy, 49*(1), 1–21. https://doi.org/10.1080/16506073.2018.1560358

Carpenter, J. K., Andrews, L. A., Witcraft, S. M., Powers, M. B., Smits, J. A. J., & Hofmann, S. G. (2018). Cognitive behavioral therapy for anxiety and related disorders: A meta-analysis of randomized placebo-controlled trials. *Depression and Anxiety, 35*(6), 502–514. https://doi.org/10.1002/ da.22728

Carroll, K. M., & Kiluk, B. D. (2017). Cognitive behavioral interventions for alcohol and drug use disorders: Through the stage model and back again. *Psychology of Addictive Behavior, 31*(8), 847–861. https://doi.org/10.1037/ adb0000311

Chalah, M. A., & Ayache, S. S. (2018). Disentangling the neural basis of cognitive behavioral therapy in psychiatric disorders: A focus on depression. *Brain Sciences, 8*(8), 150. https://doi.org/10.3390/brainsci8080150

Cipriani, A., Furukawa, T. A., Salanti, G., Chaimani, A., Atkinson, L. Z., Ogawa, Y., Leucht, S., Ruhe, H. G., Turner, E. H., Higgins, J. P. T., Egger, M., Takeshima, N., Hayasaka, Y., Imai, H., Shinohara, K., Tajika, A., Ioannidis, J. P. A., & Geddes, J. R. (2018). Comparative efficacy and acceptability of 21 antidepressant drugs for the acute treatment of adults with major depressive disorder: A systematic review and network meta-analysis. *The Lancet, 391*, 1357–1366. https://doi.org/10.1016/S0140-6736(17)32802-7

Clarke, K., Mayo-Wilson, E., Kenny, J., & Pilling, S. (2015). Can non-pharmacological interventions prevent relapse in adults who have recovered from depression? A systematic review and meta-analysis of randomised controlled trials. *Clinical Psychology Review, 39*, 58–70. https://doi .org/10.1016/j.cpr.2015.04.002

Conklin, C. A., & Tiffany, S. T. (2002). Applying extinction research and theory to cue-exposure addiction treatments. *Addiction, 97*(2), 155–167. https:// doi.org/10.1046/j.1360-0443.2002.00014.x

Conley, C. S., Shapiro, J. B., Kirsch, A. C., & Durlak, J. A. (2017). A meta-analysis of indicated mental health prevention programs for at-risk higher education students. *Journal of Counseling Psychology, 64*(2), 121–140. https://doi .org/10.1037/cou0000190

Cottraux, J., Note, I. D., Boutitie, F., Milliery, M., Genouihlac, V., Yao, S. N., Note, B., Mollard, E., Bonasse, F., Gaillard, S., Djamoussian, D., Guillard, C., Culem, A., & Gueyffier, F. (2009). Cognitive therapy versus Rogerian supportive therapy in borderline personality disorder. Two-year follow-up of a controlled pilot study. *Psychotherapy and Psychosomatics, 78*(5), 307–316. https://doi.org/10.1159/000229769

Covin, R., Ouimet, A. J., Seeds, P. M., & Dozois, D. J. (2008). A meta-analysis of CBT for pathological worry among clients with GAD. *Journal of Anxiety Disorders, 22*(1), 108–116. https://doi.org/10.1016/j.janxdis.2007.01.002

Craske, M. G., & Stein, M. B. (2017). No psychotherapy monoculture for anxiety disorders – Authors' reply. *The Lancet, 389*(10082), 1883. https://doi .org/10.1016/S0140-6736(17)31208-4

Cuijpers, P. (2016). Are all psychotherapies equally effective in the treatment of adult depression? The lack of statistical power of comparative outcome studies. *Evidence-Based Mental Health, 19*(2), 39–42. https://doi.org/10.1136/eb-2016-102341

Cuijpers, P., Berking, M., Andersson, G., Quigley, L., Kleiboer, A., & Dobson, K. S. (2013). A meta-analysis of cognitive-behavioural therapy for adult depression, alone and in comparison with other treatments. *Canadian Journal of Psychiatry, 58*(7), 376–385. https://doi.org/10.1177/070674371305800702

Cuijpers, P., Cristea, I. A., Karyotaki, E., Reijnders, M., & Huibers, M. J. H. (2016). How effective are cognitive behavior therapies for major depression and anxiety disorders? A meta-analytic update of the evidence. *World Psychiatry, 15*(3), 245–258. https://doi.org/10.1002/wps.20346

Cuijpers, P., Cristea, I. A., Weitz, E., Gentili, C., & Berking, M. (2016). The effects of cognitive and behavioural therapies for anxiety disorders on depression: A meta-analysis. *Psychological Medicine, 46*(16), 3451–3462. https://doi.org/10.1017/S0033291716002348

Cuijpers, P., De Wit, L., Weitz, E., Andersson, G., & Huibers, M. J. H. (2015). The combination of psychotherapy and pharmacotherapy in the treatment of adult depression: A comprehensive meta-analysis. *Journal of Evidence-Based Psychotherapies, 15*(2), 147–168.

Cuijpers, P., Hollon, S. D., van Straten, A., Bockting, C., Berking, M., & Andersson, G. (2013). Does cognitive behaviour therapy have an enduring effect that is superior to keeping patients on continuation pharmacotherapy? A meta-analysis. *BMJ Open, 3*(4), e002542. https://doi.org/10.1136/bmjopen-2012-002542

Cuijpers, P., Noma, H., Karyotaki, E., Cipriani, A., & Furukawa, T. A. (2019). Effectiveness and acceptability of cognitive behavior therapy delivery formats in adults with depression: A network meta-analysis. *JAMA Psychiatry, 76*(7), 700–707. https://doi.org/10.1001/jamapsychiatry.2019.0268

Cuijpers, P., Sijbrandij, M., Koole, S., Huibers, M., Berking, M., & Andersson, G. (2014). Psychological treatment of generalized anxiety disorder: A meta-analysis. *Clinical Psychology Review, 34*(2), 130–140. https://doi.org/10.1016/j.cpr.2014.01.002

Cuijpers, P., Smit, F., Bohlmeijer, E., Hollon, S. D., & Andersson, G. (2010). Efficacy of cognitive-behavioural therapy and other psychological treatments for adult depression: Meta-analytic study of publication bias. *The British Journal of Psychiatry, 196*(3), 173–178. https://doi.org/10.1192/bjp.bp.109.066001

Cuijpers, P., van Straten, A., Smit, F., Mihalopoulos, C., & Beekman, A. (2008). Preventing the onset of depressive disorders: A meta-analytic review of psychological interventions. *The American Journal of Psychiatry, 165*(10), 1272–1280. https://doi.org/10.1176/appi.ajp.2008.07091422

Davidson, K., Norrie, J., Tyrer, P., Gumley, A., Tata, P., Murray, H., & Palmer, S. (2006). The effectiveness of cognitive behavior therapy for borderline personality disorder: Results from the borderline personality disorder study of cognitive therapy (BOSCOT) trial. *Journal of Personality Disorders, 20*(5), 450–465. https://doi.org/10.1521/pedi.2006.20.5.450

Davidson, K. M., Tyrer, P., Norrie, J., Palmer, S. J., & Tyrer, H. (2010). Cognitive therapy v. usual treatment for borderline personality disorder: Prospective 6-year follow-up. *The British Journal of Psychiatry, 197*(6), 456–462. https://doi.org/10.1192/bjp.bp.109.074286

Davidson, K. M., Tyrer, P., Tata, P., Cooke, D., Gumley, A., Ford, I., Walker, A., Bezlyak, V., Seivewright, H., Robertson, H., & Crawford, M. J. (2009). Cognitive behaviour therapy for violent men with antisocial personality disorder in the community: An exploratory randomized controlled trial. *Psychological Medicine, 39*(4), 569–577. https://doi.org/10.1017/S0033291708004066

Davis, D. R., Kurti, A. N., Skelly, J. M., Redner, R., White, T. J., & Higgins, S. T. (2016). A review of the literature on contingency management in the treatment of substance use disorders, 2009–2014. *Preventive Medicine, 92*, 36–46. https://doi.org/10.1016/j.ypmed.2016.08.008

de Abreu Costa, M., D'Alò de Oliveira, G. S., Tatton-Ramos, T., Manfro, G. G., & Salum, G. A. (2018). Anxiety and stress-related disorders and mindfulness-based interventions: A systematic review and multilevel meta-analysis and meta-regression of multiple outcomes. *Mindfulness, 10*, 996–1005. https://doi.org/10.1007/s12671-018-1058-1

de Jonge, M., Bockting, C. L. H., Kikkert, M. J., van Dijk, M. K., van Schaik, D. J. F., Peen, J., Hollon, S. D., & Dekker, J. J. M. (2019). Preventive cognitive therapy versus care as usual in cognitive behavioral therapy responders: A randomized controlled trial. *Journal of Consulting and Clinical Psychology, 87*(6), 521–529. https://doi.org/10.1037/ccp0000395

DeRubeis, R. J., Zajecka, J., Shelton, R. C., Amsterdam, J. D., Fawcett, J., Xu, C., Young, P. R., Gallop, R., & Hollon, S. D. (2020). Prevention of recurrence after recovery from a major depressive episode with antidepressant medication alone or in combination with cognitive behavioral therapy: A phase 2 randomized clinical trial. *JAMA Psychiatry, 77*(3), 237–245. https://doi.org/10.1001/jamapsychiatry.2019.3900

Dickhaut, V., & Arntz, A. (2014). Combined group and individual schema therapy for borderline personality disorder: A pilot study. *Journal of Behavior Therapy and Experimental Psychiatry, 45*(2), 242–251. https://doi.org/10.1016/j.jbtep.2013.11.004

DiClemente, C. C., Corno, C. M., Graydon, M. M., Wiprovnick, A. E., & Knoblach, D. J. (2017). Motivational interviewing, enhancement, and brief interventions over the last decade: A review of reviews of efficacy and effectiveness. *Psychology of Addictive Behavior, 31*(8), 862–887. https://doi.org/10.1037/adb0000318

Doyle, M., Khanna, T., Lennox, C., Shaw, J., Hayes, A., Taylor, J., Roberts, A., & Dolan, M. (2013). The effectiveness of an enhanced thinking skills programme in offenders with antisocial personality traits. *Journal of Forensic Psychiatry & Psychology, 24*(1), 1–15. https://doi.org/10.1080/14789949.2012.752519

Driessen, E., & Hollon, S. D. (2010). Cognitive behavioral therapy for mood disorders: Efficacy, moderators and mediators. *Psychiatric Clinics of North America, 33*(3), 537–555. https://doi.org/10.1016/j.psc.2010.04.005

Dugosh, K., Abraham, A., Seymour, B., McLoyd, K., Chalk, M., & Festinger, D. (2016). A systematic review on the use of psychosocial interventions in conjunction with medications for the treatment of opioid addiction. *Journal of Addiction Medicine, 10*(2), 93–103. https://doi.org/10.1097/ADM.0000000000000193

Dunlop, B. W., LoParo, D., Kinkead, B., Mletzko-Crowe, T., Cole, S. P., Nemeroff, C. B., Mayberg, H. S., & Craighead, W. E. (2019). Benefits of sequentially adding cognitive-behavioral therapy or antidepressant medication for adults with nonremitting depression. *The American Journal of Psychiatry, 176*(4), 275–286. https://doi.org/10.1176/appi.ajp.2018.18091075

Emmelkamp, P. M. G. (2013). Behavior therapy with adults. In M. J. Lambert (Ed.), *Bergin and Garfield's handbook of psychotherapy and behavior change* (6th ed., pp. 343–392). Hoboken, NJ: Wiley.

Emmelkamp, P. M., Benner, A., Kuipers, A., Feiertag, G. A., Koster, H. C., & van Apeldoorn, F. J. (2006). Comparison of brief dynamic and cognitive-behavioural therapies in avoidant personality disorder. *The British Journal of Psychiatry, 189*(1), 60–64. https://doi.org/10.1192/bjp.bp.105.012153

Evans, K., Tyrer, P., Catalan, J., Schmidt, U., Davidson, K., Dent, J., Tata, P., Thornton, S., Barber, J., & Thompson, S. (1999). Manual-assisted cognitive-behaviour therapy (MACT): A randomized controlled trial of a brief intervention with bibliotherapy in the treatment of recurrent deliberate self-harm. *Psychological Medicine, 29*(1), 19–25. https://doi.org/10.1017/S003329179800765X

Fairburn, C. (1981). A cognitive behavioural approach to the treatment of bulimia. *Psychological Medicine, 11*(4), 707–711. https://doi.org/10.1017/S0033291700041209

Fairburn, C. G., & Cooper, Z. (2007). Thinking afresh about the classification of eating disorders. *International Journal of Eating Disorders, 40*(S3) Suppl, S107–S110. https://doi.org/10.1002/eat.20460

Fairburn, C. G., Cooper, Z., Doll, H. A., O'Connor, M. E., Bohn, K., Hawker, D. M., Wales, J. A., & Palmer, R. L. (2009). Transdiagnostic cognitive-behavioral therapy for patients with eating disorders: A two-site trial with 60-week follow-up. *The American Journal of Psychiatry, 166*(3), 311–319. https://doi.org/10.1176/appi.ajp.2008.08040608

Fairburn, C. G., Cooper, Z., Doll, H. A., O'Connor, M. E., Palmer, R. L., & Dalle Grave, R. (2013). Enhanced cognitive behaviour therapy for adults with anorexia nervosa: A UK-Italy study. *Behaviour Research and Therapy, 51*(1), R2–R8. https://doi.org/10.1016/j.brat.2012.09.010

Fairburn, C. G., Cooper, Z., & Shafran, R. (2008). Enhanced cognitive behavior therapy for eating disorders (CBT-E): An overview. In C. G. Fairburn (Ed.), *Cognitive behavior therapy and eating disorders* (pp. 23–34). New York: Guilford Press.

Farrell, J. M., Shaw, I. A., & Webber, M. A. (2009). A schema-focused approach to group psychotherapy for outpatients with borderline personality disorder: A randomized controlled trial. *Journal of Behavior Therapy and Experimental Psychiatry, 40*(2), 317–328. https://doi.org/10.1016/j.jbtep.2009.01.002

Farronato, N. S., Dursteler-Macfarland, K. M., Wiesbeck, G. A., & Petitjean, S. A. (2013). A systematic review comparing cognitive-behavioral therapy and contingency management for cocaine dependence. *Journal of Addictive Diseases, 32*(3), 274–287. https://doi.org/10.1080/10550887.2013.824328

Fava, G. A. (2016). Well-being therapy: Current indications and emerging perspectives. *Psychotherapy and Psychosomatics, 85*, 136–145. https://doi.org/10.1159/000444114

Fava, G. A., Ruini, C., Rafanelli, C., Finos, L., Conti, S., & Grandi, S. (2004). Six-year outcome of cognitive behavior therapy for prevention of recurrent depression. *The American Journal of Psychiatry, 161*(10), 1872–1876. https://doi.org/10.1176/ajp.161.10.1872

Ferster, C. B. (1973). A functional analysis of depression. *American Psychologist, 28*(10), 857–870. https://doi.org/10.1037/h0035605

Flückiger, C., Del Re, A. C., Wampold, B. E., Symonds, D., & Horvath, A. O. (2012). How central is the alliance in psychotherapy? A multilevel longitudinal meta-analysis. *Journal of Counseling Psychology, 59*(1), 10–17. https://doi.org/10.1037/a0025749

Forbes, M. K., Wright, A. G. C., Markon, K. E., & Krueger, R. F. (2017). Evidence that psychopathology symptom networks have limited replicability. *Journal of Abnormal Psychology, 126*(7), 969–988. https://doi.org/10.1037/abn0000276

Frostad, S., Danielsen, Y. S., Rekkedal, G. A., Jevne, C., Dalle Grave, R., Ro, O., & Kessler, U. (2018). Implementation of enhanced cognitive behaviour therapy (CBT-E) for adults with anorexia nervosa in an outpatient eating-disorder unit at a public hospital. *Journal of Eating Disorders, 6*, 12. https://doi.org/10.1186/s40337-018-0198-y

Gartlehner, G., Gaynes, B. N., Amick, H. R., Asher, G., Morgan, L. C., Coker-Schwimmer, E., Forneris, C., Boland, E., Lux, L. J., Gaylord, S., Bann, C., Pierl, C. B., & Lohr, K. N. (2015). Nonpharmacological versus pharmacological treatments for adult patients with major depressive disorder. *Agency for Healthcare Research and Quality* (US). Report No.: 15(16)-EHC031–EF

Gartlehner, G., Gaynes, B. N., Amick, H. R., Asher, G. N., Morgan, L. C., Coker-Schwimmer, E., Forneris, C., Boland, E., Lux, L. J., Gaylord, S., Bann, C., Pierl, C. B., & Lohr, K. N. (2016). Comparative benefits and harms of antidepressant, psychological, complementary, and exercise treatments for major depression: An evidence report for a clinical practice guideline from the american college of physicians. *Annals of Internal Medicine, 164*(5), 331–341. https://doi.org/10.7326/M15-1813

Gates, P. J., Sabioni, P., Copeland, J., Le Foll, B., & Gowing, L. (2016). Psychosocial interventions for cannabis use disorder. *Cochrane Database of Systematic Reviews*, CD005336. https://doi.org/10.1002/14651858.CD005336.pub4

Geretsegger, C., Pichler, E. M., Gimpl, K., Aichhorn, W., Stelzig, R., Grabher-Stoeffler, G., Hiemke, C., & Zernig, G. (2019). Non-adherence to psychotropic medication assessed by plasma level in newly admitted psychiatric patients: Prevalence before acute admission. *Psychiatry and Clinical Neurosciences, 73*(4), 175–178. https://doi.org/10.1111/pcn.12809

Giesen-Bloo, J., van Dyck, R., Spinhoven, P., van Tilburg, W., Dirksen, C., van Asselt, T., Kremers, I., Nadort, M., & Arntz, A. (2006). Outpatient psychotherapy for borderline personality disorder: Randomized trial of schema-focused therapy vs transference-focused psychotherapy. *Archives of General Psychiatry, 63*(6), 649–658. https://doi.org/10.1001/archpsyc.63.6.649

Gonçalves, R., Rodrigues, H., Novaes, F., Arbol, J., Volchan, E., Coutinho, E. S. F., Figueira, I., & Ventura, P. (2015). Listening to the heart: A meta-analysis of cognitive behavior therapy impact on the heart rate of patients with anxiety disorders. *Journal of Affective Disorders, 172*, 231–240. https://doi.org/10.1016/j.jad.2014.09.058

Gould, R. L., Coulson, M. C., & Howard, R. J. (2012). Efficacy of cognitive behavioral therapy for anxiety disorders in older people: A meta-analysis and meta-regression of randomized controlled trials. *Journal of the American Geriatrics Society, 60*(2), 218–229. https://doi.org/10.1111/j.1532-5415.2011.03824.x

Gregertsen, E. C., Mandy, W., Kanakam, N., Armstrong, S., & Serpell, L. (2019). Pre-treatment patient characteristics as predictors of drop-out and treatment outcome in individual and family therapy for adolescents and adults with anorexia nervosa: A systematic review and meta-analysis. *Psychiatry Research, 271*, 484–501. https://doi.org/10.1016/j.psychres.2018.11.068

Gregory, V. L. (2018). Cognitive-behavioral therapy for anxious symptoms in persons of African descent: A meta-analysis. *Journal of Social Service Research, 45*(1), 87–101. https://doi.org/10.1080/01488376.2018.1479344

Gude, T., & Hoffart, A. (2008). Change in interpersonal problems after cognitive agoraphobia and schema-focused therapy versus psychodynamic treatment as usual of inpatients with agoraphobia and Cluster C personality disorders. *Scandinavian Journal of Psychology, 49*(2), 195–199. https://doi.org/10.1111/j.1467-9450.2008.00629.x

Guidi, J., Tomba, E., & Fava, G. A. (2016). The sequential integration of pharmacotherapy and psychotherapy in the treatment of major depressive disorder: A meta-analysis of the sequential model and a critical review of the literature. *The American Journal of Psychiatry, 173*(2), 128–137. https://doi.org/10.1176/appi.ajp.2015.15040476

Gülüm, İ. V. (2018). Dropout in schema therapy for personality disorders. *Research in Psychotherapy: Psychopathology, Process and Outcome, 21*, 116–122. https://doi.org/10.4081/ripppo.2018.314

Haas, A. L., Muñoz, R. F., Humfleet, G. L., Reus, V. I., & Hall, S. M. (2004). Influences of mood, depression history, and treatment modality on outcomes in smoking cessation. *Journal of Consulting and Clinical Psychology, 72*(4), 563–570. https://doi.org/10.1037/0022-006X.72.4.563

Haby, M. M., Donnelly, M., Corry, J., & Vos, T. (2006). Cognitive behavioural therapy for depression, panic disorder and generalized anxiety disorder: A meta-regression of factors that may predict outcome. *Australian and New Zealand Journal of Psychiatry, 40*(1), 9–19. https://doi.org/10.1080/j.1440-1614.2006.01736.x

Haeffel, G. J., & Kaschak, M. P. (2018). Rethinking how we think about cognitive interventions for depression: An example from research on second-language acquisition. *Clinical Psychological Science, 7*(1), 68–76. https://doi.org/10.1177/2167702618794157

Hall, G. C. N., Ibaraki, A. Y., Huang, E. R., Marti, C. N., & Stice, E. (2016). A meta-analysis of cultural adaptations of psychological interventions. *Behavior Therapy, 47*(6), 993–1014. https://doi.org/10.1016/j.beth.2016.09.005

Hall, S. M., Muñoz, R. F., & Reus, V. I. (1994). Cognitive-behavioral intervention increases abstinence rates for depressive-history smokers. *Journal of Consulting and Clinical Psychology, 62*(1), 141–146. https://doi.org/10.1037/0022-006X.62.1.141

Halmi, K. A., Agras, W. S., Crow, S., Mitchell, J., Wilson, G. T., Bryson, S. W., & Kraemer, H. C. (2005). Predictors of treatment acceptance and completion in anorexia nervosa: Implications for future study designs. *Archives of General Psychiatry, 62*(7), 776–781. https://doi.org/10.1001/archpsyc.62.7.776

Hans, E., & Hiller, W. (2013). A meta-analysis of nonrandomized effectiveness studies on outpatient cognitive behavioral therapy for adult anxiety disorders. *Clinical Psychology Review, 33*(8), 954–964. https://doi.org/10.1016/j.cpr.2013.07.003

Hay, P. J., Claudino, A. M., Touyz, S., & Abd Elbaky, G. (2015). Individual psychological therapy in the outpatient treatment of adults with anorexia nervosa. *Cochrane Database of Systematic Reviews, 27*, CD003909. https://doi.org/10.1002/14651858.CD003909.pub2

Hazell, C. M., Hayward, M., Cavanagh, K., & Strauss, C. (2016). A systematic review and meta-analysis of low intensity CBT for psychosis. *Clinical Psychology Review, 45*, 183–192. https://doi.org/10.1016/j.cpr.2016.03.004

Hedman-Lagerlöf, M., Hedman-Lagerlöf, E., & Öst, L.-G. (2018). The empirical support for mindfulness-based interventions for common psychiatric disorders: A systematic review and meta-analysis. *Psychological Medicine, 48*(13), 2116–2129. https://doi.org/10.1017/S0033291718000259

Higa-McMillan, C. K., Francis, S. E., Rith-Najarian, L., & Chorpita, B. F. (2016). Evidence base update: 50 years of research on treatment for child and adolescent anxiety. *Journal of Clinical Child and Adolescent Psychology, 45*(2), 91–113. https://doi.org/10.1080/15374416.2015.1046177

Higgins, S. T., Kurti, A. N., & Keith, D. R. (2018). Contingency management. In S. C. Hayes & S. G. Hofmann (Eds.), *Process-based CBT: The science and core clinical competencies of cognitive behavioral therapy* (pp. 197–209). Oakland, CA: Context Press.

Hilbert, A., Hildebrandt, T., Agras, W. S., Wilfley, D. E., & Wilson, G. T. (2015). Rapid response in psychological treatments for binge eating disorder. *Journal of Consulting and Clinical Psychology, 83*(3), 649–654. https://doi.org/10.1037/ccp0000018

Hofmann, S. G., Curtiss, J., Carpenter, J. K., & Kind, S. (2017). Effect of treatments for depression on quality of life: A meta-analysis. *Cognitive Behaviour Therapy*, *46*(4), 265–286. https://doi.org/10.1080/16506073.2017.1304445

Hofmann, S. G., Newman, M. G., Becker, E., Taylor, C. B., & Roth, W. T. (1995). Social phobia with and without avoidant personality disorder: Preliminary behavior therapy outcome findings. *Journal of Anxiety Disorders*, *9*(5), 427–438. https://doi.org/10.1016/0887-6185(95)00022-G

Hollon, S. D., & Beck, A. T. (2013). Cognitive and cognitive-behavioral therapies. In M. J. Lambert (Ed.), *Bergin and Garfield's handbook of psychotherapy and behavior change* (6th ed., pp. 393–442). Hoboken, NJ: Wiley.

Hollon, S. D., DeRubeis, R. J., Fawcett, J., Amsterdam, J. D., Shelton, R. C., Zajecka, J., Young, P. R., & Gallop, R. (2014). Effect of cognitive therapy with antidepressant medications vs antidepressants alone on the rate of recovery in major depressive disorder: A randomized clinical trial. *JAMA Psychiatry*, *71*(10), 1157–1164. https://doi.org/10.1001/jamapsychiatry.2014.1054

Hollon, S. D., DeRubeis, R. J., Shelton, R. C., Amsterdam, J. D., Salomon, R. M., O'Reardon, J. P., Lovett, M. L., Young, P. R., Haman, K. L., Freeman, B. B., & Gallop, R. (2005). Prevention of relapse following cognitive therapy vs. medications in moderate to severe depression. *Archives of General Psychiatry*, *62*(4), 417–422. https://doi.org/10.1001/jamapsychiatry.2014.1054

Hone-Blanchet, A., Wensing, T., & Fecteau, S. (2014). The use of virtual reality in craving assessment and cue-exposure therapy in substance use disorders. *Frontiers in Human Neuroscience*, *8*, 844–857. https://doi.org/10.3389/fnhum.2014.00844

Hoyer, J., Beesdo, K., Gloster, A. T., Runge, J., Hofler, M., & Becker, E. S. (2009). Worry exposure versus applied relaxation in the treatment of generalized anxiety disorder. *Psychotherapy and Psychosomatics*, *78*(2), 106–115. https://doi.org/10.1159/000201936

Huband, N., McMurran, M., Evans, C., & Duggan, C. (2007). Social problem-solving plus psychoeducation for adults with personality disorder: Pragmatic randomised controlled trial. *The British Journal of Psychiatry*, *190*, 307–313. https://doi.org/10.1192/bjp.bp.106.023341

Huey, S. J., & Tilley, J. L. (2018). Effects of mental health interventions with Asian Americans: A review and meta-analysis. *Journal of Consulting and Clinical Psychology*, *86*(11), 915–930. https://doi.org/10.1037/ccp0000346

Huhn, M., Tardy, M., Spineli, L. M., Kissling, W., Forstl, H., Pitschel-Walz, G., Leucht, C., Samara, M., Dold, M., Davis, J. M., & Leucht, S. (2014). Efficacy of pharmacotherapy and psychotherapy for adult psychiatric disorders: A systematic overview of meta-analyses. *JAMA Psychiatry*, *71*(6), 706–715. https://doi.org/10.1001/jamapsychiatry.2014.112

Jarrett, R. B., Basco, M. R., Risser, R., Ramanan, J., Marwill, M., Kraft, D., & Rush, A. J. (1998). Is there a role for continuation phase cognitive therapy for depressed outpatients? *Journal of Consulting and Clinical Psychology*, *66*(6), 1036–1040. https://doi.org/10.1037/0022-006X.66.6.1036

Jarrett, R. B., Kraft, D., Doyle, J., Foster, B. M., Eaves, G. G., & Silver, P. C. (2001). Preventing recurrent depression using cognitive therapy with and without a continuation phase. *Archives of General Psychiatry*, *58*(4), 381–388. https://doi.org/10.1001/archpsyc.58.4.381

Jarrett, R. B., Kraft, D., Schaffer, M., Witt-Browder, A., Risser, R., Atkins, D. H., & Doyle, J. (2000). Reducing relapse in depressed outpatients with atypical features: A pilot study. *Psychotherapy and Psychosomatics*, *69*(5), 232–239. https://doi.org/10.1159/000012401

Jarrett, R. B., Minhajuddin, A., Gershenfeld, H., Friedman, E. S., & Thase, M. E. (2013). Preventing depressive relapse and recurrence in higher-risk cognitive therapy responders: A randomized trial of continuation phase cognitive therapy, fluoxetine, or matched pill placebo. *JAMA Psychiatry*, *70*(11), 1152–1160. https://doi.org/10.1001/jamapsychiatry.2013.1969

Jarrett, R. B., Minhajuddin, A., Vittengl, J. R., Clark, L. A., & Thase, M. E. (2016). Quantifying and qualifying the preventive effects of acute-phase cognitive therapy: Pathways to personalizing care. *Journal of Consulting and Clinical Psychology*, *84*(4), 365–376. https://doi.org/10.1037/ccp0000069

Jarrett, R. B., & Vittengl, J. R. (2016). The efficacy of cognitive behaviour therapy for depression. In A. Wells & P. Fisher (Eds.), *Treating depression: MCT, CBT, and third wave therapies* (pp. 52–80). Chichester, UK: John Wiley & Sons, Inc. https://doi.org/10.1002/9781119114482.ch3

Jarrett, R. B., Vittengl, J. R., & Clark, L. A. (2008). Preventing recurrent depression. In M. A. Whisman (Ed.), *Adapting cognitive therapy for depression: Managing complexity and comorbidity* (pp. 132–158). New York, NY: Guilford Publications.

Jarrett, R. B., Vittengl, J. R., Clark, L. A., & Thase, M. E. (2018). Patients' comprehension and skill usage as a putative mediator of change or an engaged target in cognitive therapy: Preliminary findings. *Journal of Affective Disorders*, *226*, 163–168. https://doi.org/10.1016/j.jad.2017.09.045

Jewell, T., Blessitt, E., Stewart, C., Simic, M., & Eisler, I. (2016). Family therapy for child and adolescent eating disorders: A critical review. *Family Process*, *55*(3), 577–594. https://doi.org/10.1111/famp.12242

Jha, M. K., Minhajuddin, A., Thase, M. E., & Jarrett, R. B. (2014). Improvement in self-reported quality of life with cognitive therapy for recurrent major depressive disorder. *Journal of Affective Disorders*, *167*, 37–43. https://doi.org/10.1016/j.jad.2014.05.038

Johansen, P. Ø., Krebs, T. S., Svartberg, M., Stiles, T. C., & Holen, A. (2011). Change in defense mechanisms during short-term dynamic and cognitive therapy in patients with cluster C personality disorders. *The Journal of Nervous and Mental Disease*, *199*(9), 712–715. https://doi.org/10.1097/NMD.0b013e318229d6a7

Kantak, K. M., & Nic Dhonnchadha, B. A. (2011). Pharmacological enhancement of drug cue extinction learning: Translational challenges. *Annals of the New York Academy of Sciences*, *1216*, 122–137. https://doi.org/10.1111/j.1749-6632.2010.05899.x

Kapson, H. S., & Haaga, D. A. (2010). Depression vulnerability moderates the effects of cognitive behavior therapy in a randomized controlled trial for smoking cessation. *Behavior Therapy*, *41*(4), 447–460. https://doi.org/10.1016/j.beth.2009.10.001

Karlin, B. E., Brown, G. K., Jager-Hyman, S., Green, K. L., Wong, M., Lee, D. S., Bertagnolli, A., & Ross, T. B. (2019). Dissemination and implementation of cognitive behavioral therapy for depression in the Kaiser Permanente Health Care System: Evaluation of initial training and clinical outcomes. *Behavior Therapy*, *50*(2), 446–458. https://doi.org/10.1016/j.beth.2018.08.002

Karlin, B. E., Trockel, M., Taylor, C. B., Gimeno, J., & Manber, R. (2013). National dissemination of cognitive behavioral therapy for insomnia in veterans: Therapist- and patient-level outcomes. *Journal of Consulting and Clinical Psychology*, *81*(5), 912–917. https://doi.org/10.1037/a0032554

Kavanagh, D. J., Sitharthan, G., Young, R. M., Sitharthan, T., Saunders, J. B., Shockley, N., & Giannopoulos, V. (2006). Addition of cue exposure to cognitive-behaviour therapy for alcohol misuse: A randomized trial with dysphoric drinkers. *Addiction*, *101*(8), 1106–1116. https://doi.org/10.1111/j.1360-0443.2006.01488.x

Kazantzis, N., Whittington, C., Zelencich, L., Kyrios, M., Norton, P. J., & Hofmann, S. G. (2016). Quantity and quality of homework compliance: A meta-analysis of relations with outcome in cognitive behavior therapy. *Behavior Therapy*, *47*(5), 755–772. https://doi.org/10.1016/j.beth.2016.05.002

Kazdin, A. E. (2017). Addressing the treatment gap: A key challenge for extending evidence-based psychosocial interventions. *Behaviour Research and Therapy*, *88*, 7–18. https://doi.org/10.1016/j.brat.2016.06.004

Kelley, M. E., Dunlop, B. W., Nemeroff, C. B., Lori, A., Carrillo-Roa, T., Binder, E. B., Kutner, M. H., Rivera, V. A., Craighead, W. E., & Mayberg, H. S. (2018). Response rate profiles for major depressive disorder: Characterizing early response and longitudinal nonresponse. *Depression and Anxiety*, *35*(10), 992–1000. https://doi.org/10.1002/da.22832

Kimhy, D., Tarrier, N., Essock, S., Malaspina, D., Cabannis, D., & Beck, A. T. (2013). Cognitive behavioral therapy for psychosis — Training practices and dissemination in the United States. *Psychosis*, *5*(3), 296–305. https://doi.org/10.1080/17522439.2012.704932

Klimas, J., Tobin, H., Field, C. A., O'Gorman, C. S., Glynn, L. G., Keenan, E., Saunders, J., Bury, G., Dunne, C., & Cullen, W. (2018). Psychosocial interventions to reduce alcohol consumption in concurrent problem alcohol and illicit drug users. *Cochrane Database of Systematic Reviews*, *12*, CD009269. https://doi.org/10.1002/14651858.CD009269.pub4

Koster, E. H. W., Hoorelbeke, K., Onraedt, T., Owens, M., & Derakshan, N. (2017). Cognitive control interventions for depression: A systematic review of findings from training studies. *Clinical Psychology Review*, *53*, 79–92. https://doi.org/10.1016/j.cpr.2017.02.002

Lambert, M. J., & Shimokawa, K. (2011). Collecting client feedback. *Psychotherapy: Theory, Research, Practice, Training*, *48*(1), 72–79. https://doi.org/10.1037/a0022238

Le, L. K.-D., Barendregt, J. J., Hay, P., & Mihalopoulos, C. (2017). Prevention of eating disorders: A systematic review and meta-analysis. *Clinical Psychology Review*, *53*, 46–58. https://doi.org/10.1016/j.cpr.2017.02.001

Le Grange, D., Accurso, E. C., Lock, J., Agras, S., & Bryson, S. W. (2014). Early weight gain predicts outcome in two treatments for adolescent anorexia nervosa. *International Journal of Eating Disorders*, *47*(2), 124–129. https://doi.org/10.1002/eat.22221.

Le Grange, D., Hughes, E. K., Court, A., Yeo, M., Crosby, R. D., & Sawyer, S. M. (2016). Randomized clinical trial of parent-focused treatment and family-based treatment for adolescent anorexia nervosa. *Journal of the American Academy of Child and Adolescent Psychiatry*, *55*(8), 683–692. https://doi.org/10.1016/j.jaac.2016.05.007

Leucht, S., Hierl, S., Kissling, W., Dold, M., & Davis, J. M. (2012). Putting the efficacy of psychiatric and general medicine medication into perspective: Review of meta-analyses. *The British Journal of Psychiatry*, *200*(2), 97–106. https://doi.org/10.1192/bjp.bp.111.096594

Liberman, R. P., & Eckman, T. (1981). Behavior therapy vs insight-oriented therapy for repeated suicide attempters. *Archives of General Psychiatry*, *38*(10), 1126–1130. https://doi.org/10.1001/archpsyc.1981.01780350060007

Lilienfeld, S. O., & Treadway, M. T. (2016). Clashing diagnostic approaches: DSM-ICD versus RDoC. *Annual Review of Clinical Psychology*, *12*, 435–463. https://doi.org/10.1146/annurev-clinpsy-021815-093122

Lin, T. J., Ko, H. C., Wu, J. Y., Oei, T. P., Lane, H. Y., & Chen, C. H. (2019). The effectiveness of dialectical behavior therapy skills training group vs. cognitive therapy group on reducing depression and suicide attempts for borderline personality disorder in Taiwan. *Archives of Suicide Research*, *23*(1), 82–99. https://doi.org/10.1080/13811118.2018.1436104

Linardon, J., de la Piedad Garcia, X., & Brennan, L. (2017). Predictors, moderators, and mediators of treatment outcome following manualised cognitive-behavioural therapy for eating disorders: A systematic review. *European Eating Disorders Review*, *25*(1), 3–12. https://doi.org/10.1002/erv.2492

Linardon, J., Messer, M., & Fuller-Tyszkiewicz, M. (2018). Meta-analysis of the effects of cognitive-behavioral therapy for binge-eating-type disorders on abstinence rates in nonrandomized effectiveness studies: Comparable outcomes to randomized, controlled trials? *International Journal of Eating Disorders*, *51*(12), 1303–1311. https://doi.org/10.1002/eat.22986

Lincoln, T. M., & Peters, E. (2019). A systematic review and discussion of symptom specific cognitive behavioural approaches to delusions and hallucinations. *Schizophrenia Research*, *203*, 66–79. https://doi.org/10.1016/j.schres.2017.12.014

Linden, M. (2013). How to define, find and classify side effects in psychotherapy: From unwanted events to adverse treatment reactions. *Clinical Psychology and Psychotherapy*, *20*(4), 286–296. https://doi.org/10.1002/cpp.1765

Lindson-Hawley, N., Thompson, T. P., & Begh, R. (2015). Motivational interviewing for smoking cessation. *Cochrane Database of Systematic Reviews*, CD006936. https://doi.org/10.1002/14651858.CD006936.pub3

Lock, J., Agras, W. S., Bryson, S. W., Brandt, H., Halmi, K. A., Kaye, W., Wilfley, D., Woodside, B., Pajarito, S., & Jo, B. (2016). Does family-based treatment reduce the need for hospitalization in adolescent anorexia nervosa? *International Journal of Eating Disorders*, *49*(9), 891–894. https://doi.org/10.1002/eat.22536

Lock, J., & Le Grange, D. (2019). Family-based treatment: Where are we and where should we be going to improve recovery in child and adolescent eating disorders. *International Journal of Eating Disorders*, *52*(4), 481–487. https://doi.org/10.1002/eat.22980

Lock, J., Le Grange, D., Agras, W. S., & Dare, C. (2013). *Treatment manual for anorexia nervosa: A family-based approach*. New York, NY, US: Guilford Press.

Lock, J., Le Grange, D., Agras, W. S., Moye, A., Bryson, S. W., & Jo, B. (2010). Randomized clinical trial comparing family-based treatment with adolescent-focused individual therapy for adolescents with anorexia nervosa. *Archives of General Psychiatry*, *67*(10), 1025–1032. https://doi.org/10.1001/archgenpsychiatry.2010.128

Lopez, M. A., & Basco, M. A. (2015). Effectiveness of cognitive behavioral therapy in public mental health: Comparison to treatment as usual for treatment-resistant depression. *Administration and Policy in Mental Health*, *42*(1), 87–98. https://doi.org/10.1007/s10488-014-0546-4

Lutz, W., Hofmann, S. G., Rubel, J., Boswell, J. F., Shear, M. K., Gorman, J. M., Woods, S. W., & Barlow, D. H. (2014). Patterns of early change and their relationship to outcome and early treatment termination in patients with panic disorder. *Journal of Consulting and Clinical Psychology*, *82*(2), 287–297. https://doi.org/10.1037/a0035535

MacLeod, A. K., Tata, P., Evans, K., Tyrer, P., Schmidt, U., Davidson, K., Thornton, S., & Catalan, J. (1998). Recovery of positive future thinking within a high-risk parasuicide group: Results from a pilot randomized controlled trial. *British Journal of Clinical Psychology*, *37*(4), 371–379. https://doi.org/10.1111/j.2044-8260.1998.tb01394.x

Magill, M., Kiluk, B. D., McCrady, B. S., Tonigan, J. S., & Longabaugh, R. (2015). Active ingredients of treatment and client mechanisms of change in behavioral treatments for alcohol use disorders: Progress 10 years later. *Alcoholism, Clinical and Experimental Research*, *39*(10), 1852–1862. https://doi.org/10.1111/acer.12848

Magill, M., Ray, L., Kiluk, B., Hoadley, A., Bernstein, M., Tonigan, J. S., & Carroll, K. (2019). A meta-analysis of cognitive-behavioral therapy for alcohol or other drug use disorders: Treatment efficacy by contrast condition. *Journal of Consulting and Clinical Psychology*, *87*(12), 1093–1105. https://doi.org/10.1037/ccp0000447

Marlatt, G. A., & Donovan, D. M. (Eds.). (2005). *Relapse prevention: Maintenance strategies in the treatment of addictive behaviors*. (2nd ed.). New York: Guilford Press.

Marwood, L., Wise, T., Perkins, A. M., & Cleare, A. J. (2018). Meta-analyses of the neural mechanisms and predictors of response to psychotherapy in depression and anxiety. *Neuroscience and Biobehavioral Reviews*, *95*, 61–72. https://doi.org/10.1016/j.neubiorev.2018.09.022

McCrady, B. S., Wilson, A. D., Munoz, R. E., Fink, B. C., Fokas, K., & Borders, A. (2016). Alcohol-focused behavioral couple therapy. *Family Process*, *55*(3), 443–459. https://doi.org/10.1111/famp.12231

McGrath, C. L., Kelley, M. E., Holtzheimer, P. E., Dunlop, B. W., Craighead, W. E., Franco, A. R., Craddock, R. C., & Mayberg, H. S. (2013). Toward a neuroimaging treatment selection biomarker for major depressive disorder. *JAMA Psychiatry*, *70*(8), 821–829. https://doi.org/10.1001/jamapsychiatry.2013.143

McHugh, R. K., Whitton, S. W., Peckham, A. D., Welge, J. A., & Otto, M. W. (2013). Patient preference for psychological vs pharmacologic treatment of psychiatric disorders: A meta-analytic review. *Journal of Clinical Psychiatry*, *74*(6), 595–602. https://doi.org/10.4088/JCP.12r07757

Mellentin, A. I., Skøt, L., Nielsen, B., Schippers, G. M., Nielsen, A. S., Stenager, E., & Juhl, C. (2017). Cue exposure therapy for the treatment of alcohol use disorders: A meta-analytic review. *Clinical Psychology Review*, *57*, 195–207. https://doi.org/10.1016/j.cpr.2017.07.006

Messina, N., Farabee, D., & Rawson, R. (2003). Treatment responsivity of cocaine-dependent patients with antisocial personality disorder to cognitive-behavioral and contingency management interventions. *Journal of Consulting and Clinical Psychology*, *71*(2), 320–329. https://doi.org/10.1037/0022-006X.71.2.320

Meulders, A., Van Daele, T., Volders, S., & Vlaeyen, J. W. (2016). The use of safety-seeking behavior in exposure-based treatments for fear and anxiety: Benefit or burden? A meta-analytic review. *Clinical Psychology Review*, *45*, 144–156. https://doi.org/10.1016/j.cpr.2016.02.002

Meuret, A. E., Wilhelm, F. H., Ritz, T., & Roth, W. T. (2008). Feedback of end-tidal pCO2 as a therapeutic approach for panic disorder. *Journal of Psychiatric Research*, *42*(7), 560–568. https://doi.org/10.1016/j.jpsychires.2007.06.005

Meuret, A. E., Wilhelm, F. H., & Roth, W. T. (2001). Respiratory biofeedback-assisted therapy in panic disorder. *Behavior Modification*, *25*(4), 584–605. https://doi.org/10.1177/0145445501254006

Meuret, A. E., Wilhelm, F. H., Ritz, T., & Roth, W. T. (2003). Breathing training for treating panic disorder: Useful intervention or impediment? *Behavior Modification*, *27*(5), 731–754. https://doi.org/10.1177/0145445503256324

Miller, W. R. (1983). Motivational interviewing with problem drinkers. *Behavioural Psychotherapy*, *11*(2), 147–172. https://doi.org/10.1017/S0141347300006583

Miller, W. R., Sorensen, J. L., Selzer, J. A., & Brigham, G. S. (2006). Disseminating evidence-based practices in substance abuse treatment: A review with suggestions. *Journal of Substance Abuse Treatment*, *31*(1), 25–39. https://doi.org/10.1016/j.jsat.2006.03.005

Mitchell, J. E., Agras, S., Crow, S., Halmi, K., Fairburn, C. G., Bryson, S., & Kraemer, H. (2011). Stepped care and cognitive-behavioural therapy for bulimia nervosa: Randomised trial. *The British Journal of Psychiatry*, *198*(5), 391–397. https://doi.org/10.1192/bjp.bp.110.082172

Montero-Marin, J., Garcia-Campayo, J., Lopez-Montoyo, A., Zabaleta-Del-Olmo, E., & Cuijpers, P. (2018). Is cognitive-behavioural therapy more effective than relaxation therapy in the treatment of anxiety disorders? A meta-analysis. *Psychological Medicine*, *48*(9), 1427–1436. https://doi.org/10.1017/S0033291717003099

Moreno-Peral, P., Conejo-Cerón, S., Rubio-Valera, M., Fernández, A., Navas-Campaña, D., Rodríguez-Morejón, A., Motrico, E., Rigabert, A., Luna, J. D., Martín-Pérez, C., Rodríguez-Bayón, A., Ballesta-Rodríguez, M. I., Luciano, J. V., & Bellón, J. Á. (2017). Effectiveness of psychological and/or educational interventions in the prevention of anxiety: A systematic review, meta-analysis, and meta-regression. *JAMA Psychiatry*, *74*(10), 1021–1029. https://doi.org/10.1001/jamapsychiatry.2017.2509

Morey, L. C., Lowmaster, S. E., & Hopwood, C. J. (2010). A pilot study of manual-assisted cognitive therapy with a therapeutic assessment augmentation for borderline personality disorder. *Psychiatry Research*, *178*(3), 531–535. https://doi.org/10.1016/j.psychres.2010.04.055

Morrison, A. P., Hutton, P., Wardle, M., Spencer, H., Barratt, S., Brabban, A., Callcott, P., Christodoulides, T., Dudley, R., French, P., Lumley, V., Tai, S. J., & Turkington, D. (2012). Cognitive therapy for people with a schizophrenia spectrum diagnosis not taking antipsychotic medication: An exploratory trial. *Psychological Medicine*, *42*(5), 1049–1056. https://doi.org/10.1017/S0033291711001899

Morrison, A. P., Law, H., Carter, L., Sellers, R., Emsley, R., Pyle, M., French, P., Shiers, D., Yung, A. R., Murphy, E. K., Holden, N., Steele, A., Bowe, S. E., Palmier-Claus, J., Brooks, V., Byrne, R., Davies, L., & Haddad, P. M. (2018). Antipsychotic drugs versus cognitive behavioural therapy versus a combination of both in people with psychosis: A randomised controlled pilot and feasibility study. *The Lancet Psychiatry*, *5*(5), 411–423. https://doi.org/10.1016/S2215-0366(18)30096-8

Morrison, A. P., Turkington, D., Pyle, M., Spencer, H., Brabban, A., Dunn, G., Christodoulides, T., Dudley, R., Chapman, N., Callcott, P., Grace, T., Lumley, V., Drage, L., Tully, S., Irving, K., Cummings, A., Byrne, R., Davies, L. M., & Hutton, P. (2014). Cognitive therapy for people with schizophrenia spectrum disorders not taking antipsychotic drugs: A single-blind randomised controlled trial. *The Lancet*, *383*(9926), 1395–1403. https://doi.org/10.1016/S0140-6736(13)62246-1

Nadort, M., Arntz, A., Smit, J. H., Giesen-Bloo, J., Eikelenboom, M., Spinhoven, P., van Asselt, T., Wensing, M., & van Dyck, R. (2009). Implementation of outpatient schema therapy for borderline personality disorder with versus without crisis support by the therapist outside office hours: A randomized trial. *Behaviour Research and Therapy*, *47*, 961–973. https://doi.org/10.1016/j.brat.2009.07.013

National Institute for Health and Care Excellence. (2017). *Eating Disorders: Recognition and treatment* (NG69). London, UK: National Institute for Health and Care Excellence.

Nenadic, I., Lamberth, S., & Reiss, N. (2017). Group schema therapy for personality disorders: A pilot study for implementation in acute psychiatric in-patient settings. *Psychiatry Research*, *253*, 9–12. https://doi.org/10.1016/j.psychres.2017.01.093

Neufeld, K. J., Kidorf, M. S., Kolodner, K., King, V. L., Clark, M., & Brooner, R. K. (2008). A behavioral treatment for opioid-dependent patients with antisocial personality. *Journal of Substance Abuse Treatment*, *34*(1), 101–111. https://doi.org/10.1016/j.jsat.2007.02.009

Newby, J. M., McKinnon, A., Kuyken, W., Gilbody, S., & Dalgleish, T. (2015). Systematic review and meta-analysis of transdiagnostic psychological treatments for anxiety and depressive disorders in adulthood. *Clinical Psychology Review*, *40*, 91–110. https://doi.org/10.1016/j.cpr.2015.06.002

Newman, M. G. (2000). Recommendations for a cost-offset model of psychotherapy allocation using generalized anxiety disorder as an example. *Journal of Consulting and Clinical Psychology*, *68*(4), 549–555. https://doi.org/10.1037/0022-006X.68.4.549

Newman, M. G., & Fisher, A. J. (2013). Mediated moderation in combined cognitive behavioral therapy versus component treatments for generalized anxiety disorder. *Journal of Consulting and Clinical Psychology*, *81*(3), 405–414. https://doi.org/10.1037/a0031690

Newman, M. G., Shin, K. E., & Lanza, S. T. (2019). Time-varying moderation of treatment outcomes by illness duration and comorbid depression in generalized anxiety disorder. *Journal of Consulting and Clinical Psychology*, *87*(3), 282–293. https://doi.org/10.1037/ccp0000385

Ng, R. M. K. (2005). Cognitive therapy for obsessive-compulsive personality disorder — A pilot study in Hong Kong Chinese patients. *Hong Kong Journal of Psychiatry*, *15*(2), 50–53. https://doi.org/10.1016/S1569-1861(09)70031-2

Ng, T. K., & Wong, D. F. K. (2017). The efficacy of cognitive behavioral therapy for Chinese people: A meta-analysis. *Australian and New Zealand Journal of Psychiatry*, *52*(7), 620–637. https://doi.org/10.1177/0004867417741555

Nolen-Hoeksema, S., Wisco, B. E., & Lyubomirsky, S. (2008). Rethinking rumination. *Perspectives on Psychological Science*, *3*(5), 400–424. https://doi.org/10.1111/j.1745-6924.2008.00088.x

O'Farrell, T. J., & Clements, K. (2012). Review of outcome research on marital and family therapy in treatment for alcoholism. *Journal of Marital and Family Therapy*, *38*(1), 122–144. https://doi.org/10.1111/j.1752-0606.2011.00242.x

O'Keeffe, J., Conway, R., & McGuire, B. (2017). A systematic review examining factors predicting favourable outcome in cognitive behavioural interventions for psychosis. *Schizophrenia Research*, *183*, 22–30. https://doi.org/10.1016/j.schres.2016.11.021

Olfson, M., & Marcus, S. C. (2010). National trends in outpatient psychotherapy. *The American Journal of Psychiatry*, *167*(12), 1456–1463. https://doi.org/10.1176/appi.ajp.2010.10040570

Ophuis, R. H., Lokkerbol, J., Heemskerk, S. C., van Balkom, A. J., Hiligsmann, M., & Evers, S. M. (2017). Cost-effectiveness of interventions for treating anxiety disorders: A systematic review. *Journal of Affective Disorders*, *210*, 1–13. https://doi.org/10.1016/j.jad.2016.12.005

Öst, L. G. (1987). Applied relaxation: Description of a coping technique and review of controlled studies. *Behaviour Research and Therapy*, *25*(5), 397–409. https://doi.org/10.1016/0005-7967(87)90017-9

Öst, L. G. (1988). Applied relaxation vs progressive relaxation in the treatment of panic disorder. *Behaviour Research and Therapy*, *26*(1), 13–22. https://doi.org/10.1016/0005-7967(88)90029-0

Öst, L. G., & Westling, B. E. (1995). Applied relaxation vs cognitive behavior therapy in the treatment of panic disorder. *Behaviour Research and Therapy*, *33*(2), 145–158. https://doi.org/10.1016/0005-7967(94)E0026-F

Parker, Z. J., Waller, G., Duhne, P. G. S., & Dawson, J. (2018). The role of exposure in treatment of anxiety disorders: A meta-analysis. *International Journal of Psychology and Psychological Therapy*, *18*(1), 111–141.

Pavlov, I. P. (1994). *Psychopathology and psychiatry*. Piscataway, NJ, US: Transaction Publishers.

Paykel, E. S., Scott, J., Cornwall, P. L., Abbott, R., Crane, C., Pope, M., & Johnson, A. L. (2005). Duration of relapse prevention after cognitive therapy in residual depression: Follow-up of controlled trial. *Psychological Medicine*, *35*(1), 59–68. https://doi.org/10.1017/S003329170400282X

Pearl, S. B., & Norton, P. J. (2017). Transdiagnostic versus diagnosis specific cognitive behavioural therapies for anxiety: A meta-analysis. *Journal of Anxiety Disorders*, *46*, 11–24. https://doi.org/10.1016/j.janxdis.2016.07.004

Penberthy, J. K., Ait-Daoud, N., Vaughan, M., & Fanning, T. (2010). Review of treatment for cocaine dependence. *Current Drug Abuse Reviews*, *3*(1), 49–62. https://doi.org/10.2174/1874473711003010049

Persons, J. B., & Thomas, C. (2019). Symptom severity at week 4 of cognitive-behavior therapy predicts depression remission. *Behavior Therapy*, *50*(4), 791–802. https://doi.org/10.1016/j.beth.2018.12.002

Petry, N. M., Alessi, S. M., Olmstead, T. A., Rash, C. J., & Zajac, K. (2017). Contingency management treatment for substance use disorders: How far has it come, and where does it need to go? *Psychology of Addictive Behavior*, *31*(8), 897–906. https://doi.org/10.1037/adb0000287

Poulsen, S., Lunn, S., Daniel, S. I., Folke, S., Mathiesen, B. B., Katznelson, H., & Fairburn, C. G. (2014). A randomized controlled trial of psychoanalytic psychotherapy or cognitive-behavioral therapy for bulimia nervosa. *The American Journal of Psychiatry*, *171*(1), 109–116. https://doi.org/10.1176/appi.ajp.2013.12121511

Powers, M. B., de Kleine, R. A., & Smits, J. A. J. (2017). Core mechanisms of cognitive behavioral therapy for anxiety and depression: A review. *Psychiatric Clinics of North America*, *40*(4), 611–623. https://doi.org/10.1016/j.psc.2017.08.010

Pratt, L. A., & Brody, D. J. (2014). *Depression in the U.S. household population, 2009–2012*. National Center for Health Statistics data brief, 172, 1–8.

U.S. Department of Health & Human Services, Centers for Disease Control and Prevention. Retrieved from https://www.cdc.gov/nchs/data/databriefs/db172.pdf

Project MATCH Research Group. (1997). Matching alcoholism treatments to client heterogeneity: Project MATCH posttreatment drinking outcomes. *Journal of Studies on Alcohol, 58*(1), 7–29. https://doi.org/10.15288/jsa.1997.58.7

Project MATCH Research Group. (1998). Therapist effects in three treatments for alcohol problems. *Psychotherapy Research, 8*(4), 455–474. https://doi.org/10.1080/10503309812331332527

Rabois, D., & Haaga, D. A. F. (1997). Cognitive coping, history of depression, and cigarette smoking. *Addictive Behaviors, 22*(6), 789–796. https://doi.org/10.1016/S0306-4603(97)00062-2

Rash, C. J., Stitzer, M., & Weinstock, J. (2017). Contingency management: New directions and remaining challenges for an evidence-based intervention. *Journal of Substance Abuse Treatment, 72*, 10–18. https://doi.org/10.1016/j.jsat.2016.09.008

Raykos, B. C., Watson, H. J., Fursland, A., Byrne, S. M., & Nathan, P. (2013). Prognostic value of rapid response to enhanced cognitive behavioral therapy in a routine clinic sample of eating disorder outpatients. *International Journal of Eating Disorders, 46*(8), 764–770. https://doi.org/10.1002/eat.22169

Reiss, N., Lieb, K., Arntz, A., Shaw, I. A., & Farrell, J. (2014). Responding to the treatment challenge of patients with severe BPD: Results of three pilot studies of inpatient schema therapy. *Behavioural and Cognitive Psychotherapy, 42*(3), 355–367. https://doi.org/10.1017/S1352465813000027

Renneberg, B., Goldstein, A. J., Phillips, D., & Chambless, D. L. (1990). Intensive behavioral group treatment of avoidant personality disorder. *Behavior Therapy, 21*(3), 363–377. https://doi.org/10.1016/S0005-7894(05)80337-5

Renner, F., Cuijpers, P., & Huibers, M. J. (2014). The effect of psychotherapy for depression on improvements in social functioning: A meta-analysis. *Psychological Medicine, 44*(14), 2913–2926. https://doi.org/10.1017/S0033291713003152

Riper, H., Andersson, G., Hunter, S. B., de Wit, J., Berking, M., & Cuijpers, P. (2014). Treatment of comorbid alcohol use disorders and depression with cognitive-behavioural therapy and motivational interviewing: A meta-analysis. *Addiction, 109*(3), 394–406. https://doi.org/10.1111/add.12441

Rohsenow, D. J., Martin, R. A., Tidey, J. W., Colby, S. M., & Monti, P. M. (2017). Treating smokers in substance treatment with contingent vouchers, nicotine replacement and brief advice adapted for sobriety settings. *Journal of Substance Abuse Treatment, 72*, 72–79. https://doi.org/10.1016/j.jsat.2016.08.012

Ruff, S., McComb, J. L., Coker, C. J., & Sprenkle, D. H. (2010). Behavioral couples therapy for the treatment of substance abuse: A substantive and methodological review of O'Farrell, Fals-Stewart, and colleagues' program of research. *Family Process, 49*(4), 439–456. https://doi.org/10.1111/j.1545-5300.2010.01333.x

Sadlier, G. (2010). *Evaluation of the impact of the HM prison service enhanced thinking skills programme on reoffending outcomes of the surveying prisoner crime reduction sample.* Ministry of Justice Research Series 19/10. Retrieved from http://www.justice.gov.uk/downloads/publications/research-and-analysis/moj-research/eval-enhanced-thinking-skills-prog.pdf

Schaap, G. M., Chakhssi, F., & Westerhof, G. J. (2016). Inpatient schema therapy for nonresponsive patients with personality pathology: Changes in symptomatic distress, schemas, schema modes, coping styles, experienced parenting styles, and mental well-being. *Psychotherapy: Theory, Research, Practice, Training, 53*(4), 402–412. https://doi.org/10.1037/pst0000056

Schermuly-Haupt, M.-L., Linden, M., & Rush, A. J. (2018). Unwanted events and side effects in cognitive behavior therapy. *Cognitive Therapy and Research, 42*(3), 219–229. https://doi.org/10.1007/s10608-018-9904-y

Schierenberg, A., van Amsterdam, J., van den Brink, W., & Goudriaan, A. E. (2012). Efficacy of contingency management for cocaine dependence treatment: A review of the evidence. *Current Drug Abuse Reviews, 5*(4), 320–331. https://doi.org/10.2174/1874473711205040006

Schramm, E., Kriston, L., Elsaesser, M., Fangmeier, T., Meister, R., Bausch, P., Zobel, I., Bailer, J., Wambach, K., Backenstrass, M., Klein, J. P., Schoepf, D., Schnell, K., Gumz, A., Löwe, B., Walter, H., Wolf, M., Domschke, K., Berger, M., Hautzinger, M., . . . Härter, M. (2019). Two-year follow-up after treatment with the cognitive behavioral analysis system of psychotherapy versus supportive psychotherapy for early-onset chronic depression. *Psychotherapy and Psychosomatics, 88*(3), 154–164. https://doi.org/10.1159/000500189

Schumm, J. A., O'Farrell, T. J., Kahler, C. W., Murphy, M. M., & Muchowski, P. (2014). A randomized clinical trial of behavioral couples therapy versus individually based treatment for women with alcohol dependence. *Journal of Consulting and Clinical Psychology, 82*(6), 993–1004. https://doi.org/10.1037/a0037497

Seggar, L. B., Lambert, M. J., & Hansen, N. B. (2002). Assessing clinical significance: Application to the beck depression inventory. *Behavior Therapy, 33*(2), 253–269. https://doi.org/10.1016/S0005-7894(02)80028-4

Skinner, B. F. (1963). Operant behavior. *American Psychologist, 18*(8), 503–515. https://doi.org/10.1037/h0045185

Slade, E., Keeney, E., Mavranezouli, I., Dias, S., Fou, L., Stockton, S., Saxon, L., Waller, G., Turner, H., Serpell, L., Fairburn, C. G., & Kendall, T. (2018). Treatments for bulimia nervosa: A network meta-analysis. *Psychological Medicine, 48*(16), 2629–2636. https://doi.org/10.1017/S0033291718001071

Smits, J. A., Julian, K., Rosenfield, D., & Powers, M. B. (2012). Threat reappraisal as a mediator of symptom change in cognitive-behavioral treatment of anxiety disorders: A systematic review. *Journal of Consulting and Clinical Psychology, 80*(4), 624–635. https://doi.org/10.1037/a0028957

Spangler, D. L., Baldwin, S. A., & Agras, W. S. (2004). An examination of the mechanisms of action in cognitive behavioral therapy for bulimia nervosa. *Behavior Therapy, 35*(3), 537–560. https://doi.org/10.1016/S0005-7894(04)80031-5

Spencer, H. M., McMenamin, M., Emsley, R., Turkington, D., Dunn, G., Morrison, A. P., Brabban, A., Hutton, P., & Dudley, R. (2018). Cognitive behavioral therapy for antipsychotic-free schizophrenia spectrum disorders: Does therapy dose influence outcome? *Schizophrenia Research, 202*, 385–386. https://doi.org/10.1016/j.schres.2018.07.016

Spielmans, G. I., Benish, S. G., Marin, C., Bowman, W. M., Menster, M., & Wheeler, A. J. (2013). Specificity of psychological treatments for bulimia nervosa and binge eating disorder? A meta-analysis of direct comparisons. *Clinical Psychology Review, 33*(3), 460–469. https://doi.org/10.1016/j.cpr.2013.01.008

Spinhoven, P., Giesen-Bloo, J., van Dyck, R., Kooiman, K., & Arntz, A. (2007). The therapeutic alliance in schema-focused therapy and transference-focused psychotherapy for borderline personality disorder. *Journal of Consulting and Clinical Psychology, 75*(1), 104–115. https://doi.org/10.1037/0022-006X.75.1.104

Springer, K. S., Levy, H. C., & Tolin, D. F. (2018). Remission in CBT for adult anxiety disorders: A meta-analysis. *Clinical Psychology Review, 61*, 1–8. https://doi.org/10.1016/j.cpr.2018.03.002

Stangier, U., Hilling, C., Heidenreich, T., Risch, A. K., Barocka, A., Schlösser, R., Kronfeld, K., Ruckes, C., Berger, H., Röschke, J., Weck, F., Volk, S., Hambrecht, M., Serfling, R., Erkwoh, R., Stirn, A., Sobanski, T., & Hautzinger, M. (2013). Maintenance cognitive-behavioral therapy and manualized psychoeducation in the treatment of recurrent depression: A multicenter prospective randomized controlled trial. *The American Journal of Psychiatry, 170*(6), 624–632. https://doi.org/10.1176/appi.ajp.2013.12060734

Stefini, A., Salzer, S., Reich, G., Horn, H., Winkelmann, K., Bents, H., Rutz, U., Frost, U., von Boetticher, A., Ruhl, U., Specht, N., & Kronmüller, K. T. (2017). Cognitive-behavioral and psychodynamic therapy in female adolescents with bulimia nervosa: A randomized controlled trial. *Journal of the American Academy of Child and Adolescent Psychiatry, 56*(4), 329–335. https://doi.org/10.1016/j.jaac.2017.01.019

Stewart, R. E., & Chambless, D. L. (2009). Cognitive–behavioral therapy for adult anxiety disorders in clinical practice: A meta-analysis of effectiveness studies. *Journal of Consulting and Clinical Psychology, 77*(4), 595–606. https://doi.org/10.1037/a0016032

Stice, E., Gau, J. M., Rohde, P., & Shaw, H. (2017). Risk factors that predict future onset of each DSM-5 eating disorder: Predictive specificity in high-risk adolescent females. *Journal of Abnormal Psychology, 126*(1), 38–51. https://doi.org/10.1037/abn0000219

Stice, E., Rohde, P., & Shaw, H. (2012). *The Body Project: A dissonance-based eating disorder intervention* (2nd ed.). New York, NY: Oxford University Press. https://doi.org/10.1093/med:psych/9780199859245.003.0007

Stravynski, A., Belisle, M., Marcouiller, M., Lavallee, Y. J., & Elie, R. (1994). The treatment of avoidant personality disorder by social skills training in the clinic or in real-life settings. *Canadian Journal of Psychiatry, 39*(8), 377–383. https://doi.org/10.1177/070674379403900805

Svartberg, M., Stiles, T. C., & Seltzer, M. H. (2004). Randomized, controlled trial of the effectiveness of short-term dynamic psychotherapy and cognitive therapy for cluster C personality disorders. *The American Journal of Psychiatry, 161*(5), 810–817. https://doi.org/10.1176/appi.ajp.161.5.810

Szymczynska, P., Walsh, S., Greenberg, L., & Priebe, S. (2017). Attrition in trials evaluating complex interventions for schizophrenia: Systematic review and meta-analysis. *Journal of Psychiatric Research, 90*, 67–77. https://doi.org/10.1016/j.jpsychires.2017.02.009

Tasca, G. A., Hilsenroth, M., & Thompson-Brenner, H. (2014). Psychoanalytic psychotherapy or cognitive-behavioral therapy for bulimia nervosa. *The American Journal of Psychiatry, 171*(5), 583–584. https://doi.org/10.1176/appi.ajp.2014.13121616

Taylor, A. G., Goehler, L. E., Galper, D. I., Innes, K. E., & Bourguignon, C. (2010). Top-down and bottom-up mechanisms in mind-body medicine: Development of an integrative framework for psychophysiological research. *Explore, 6*(1), 29–41. https://doi.org/10.1016/j.explore.2009.10.004

Taylor, C. B., Kass, A. E., Trockel, M., Cunning, D., Weisman, H., Bailey, J., Sinton, M., Aspen, V., Schecthman, K., Jacobi, C., & Wilfley, D. E. (2016). Reducing eating disorder onset in a very high risk sample with significant comorbid depression: A randomized controlled trial. *Journal of Consulting and Clinical Psychology, 84*(5), 402–414. https://doi.org/10.1037/ccp0000077

Taylor, S., Abramowitz, J. S., & McKay, D. (2012). Non-adherence and non-response in the treatment of anxiety disorders. *Journal of Anxiety Disorders, 26*(5), 583–589. https://doi.org/10.1016/j.janxdis.2012.02.010

Thompson-Brenner, H., Shingleton, R. M., Thompson, D. R., Satir, D. A., Richards, L. K., Pratt, E. M., & Barlow, D. H. (2016). Focused vs. broad enhanced cognitive behavioral therapy for bulimia nervosa with comorbid borderline personality: A randomized controlled trial. *International Journal of Eating Disorders, 49*(1), 36–49. https://doi.org/10.1002/eat.22468

Thorndike, F. P., Friedman-Wheeler, D. G., & Haaga, D. A. (2006). Effect of cognitive behavior therapy on smokers' compensatory coping skills. *Addictive Behaviors, 31*(9), 1705–1710. https://doi.org/10.1016/j.addbeh.2005.12.005

Tolin, D. F. (2017). Can cognitive behavioral therapy for anxiety and depression be improved with pharmacotherapy? A meta-analysis. *Psychiatric Clinics of North America, 40*(4), 715–738. https://doi.org/10.1016/j.psc.2017.08.007

Traviss-Turner, G. D., West, R. M., & Hill, A. J. (2017). Guided self-help for eating disorders: A systematic review and metaregression. *European Eating Disorders Review, 25*(3), 148–164. https://doi.org/10.1002/erv.2507

Treasure, J., & Schmidt, U. (2013). The cognitive-interpersonal maintenance model of anorexia nervosa revisited: A summary of the evidence for cognitive, socio-emotional and interpersonal predisposing and perpetuating factors. *Journal of Eating Disorders, 1*, 13. https://doi.org/10.1186/2050-2974-1-13

Tryon, G. S., & Winograd, G. (2011). Goal consensus and collaboration. *Psychotherapy: Theory, Research, Practice, Training, 48*(1), 50–57. https://doi.org/10.1037/a0022061

Tyrer, P., Tom, B., Byford, S., Schmidt, U., Jones, V., Davidson, K., Knapp, M., MacLeod, A., Catalan, J., & POPMACT Group (2004). Differential effects of manual assisted cognitive behavior therapy in the treatment of recurrent deliberate self-harm and personality disturbance: The POPMACT study. *Journal of Personality Disorders, 18*(1), 102–116. https://doi.org/10.1521/pedi.18.1.102.32770

Udo, T., & Grilo, C. M. (2018). Prevalence and correlates of DSM–5–defined eating disorders in a nationally representative sample of U.S. adults. *Biological Psychiatry, 84*(5), 345–354. https://doi.org/10.1016/j.biopsych.2018.03.014

Unick, J. L., Hogan, P. E., Neiberg, R. H., Cheskin, L. J., Dutton, G. R., Evans-Hudnall, G., Jeffery, R., Kitabchi, A. E., Nelson, J. A., Pi-Sunyer, F. X., West, D. S., Wing, R. R., & Look AHEAD Research Group (2014). Evaluation of early weight loss thresholds for identifying nonresponders to an intensive lifestyle intervention. *Obesity, 22*(7), 1608–1616. https://doi.org/10.1002/oby.20777

van Asselt, A. D., Dirksen, C. D., Arntz, A., Giesen-Bloo, J. H., van Dyck, R., Spinhoven, P., van Tilburg, W., Kremers, I. P., Nadort, M., & Severens, J. L. (2008). Out-patient psychotherapy for borderline personality disorder: Cost-effectiveness of schema-focused therapy v. transference-focused psychotherapy. *The British Journal of Psychiatry, 192*(6), 450–457. https://doi.org/10.1192/bjp.bp.106.033597

van Zoonen, K., Buntrock, C., Ebert, D. D., Smit, F., Reynolds, C. F., 3rd, Beekman, A. T., & Cuijpers, P. (2014). Preventing the onset of major depressive disorder: A meta-analytic review of psychological interventions. *International Journal of Epidemiology, 43*(2), 318–329. https://doi.org/10.1093/ije/dyt175

van't Veer-Tazelaar, P. J., van Marwijk, H. W. J., van Oppen, P., van der Horst, H. E., Smit, F., Cuijpers, P., & Beekman, A. T. F. (2011). Prevention of late-life anxiety and depression has sustained effects over 24 months: A pragmatic randomized trial. *The American Journal of Geriatric Psychiatry, 19*(3), 230–239. https://doi.org/10.1097/JGP.0b013e3181faee4d

van't Veer-Tazelaar, P. J., van Marwijk, H. W. J., van Oppen, P., van Hout, H. P. J., van der Horst, H. E., Cuijpers, P., Smit, F., & Beekman, A. T. F. (2009). Stepped-care prevention of anxiety and depression in late life: A randomized controlled trial. *Archives of General Psychiatry, 66*(3), 297–304. https://doi.org/10.1001/archgenpsychiatry.2008.555

Videler, A. C., Rossi, G., Schoevaars, M., van der Feltz-Cornelis, C. M., & van Alphen, S. P. (2014). Effects of schema group therapy in older outpatients: A proof of concept study. *International Psychogeriatrics, 26*(10), 1709–1717. https://doi.org/10.1017/S1041610214001264

Vittengl, J. R., Clark, L. A., Dunn, T. W., & Jarrett, R. B. (2007). Reducing relapse and recurrence in unipolar depression: A comparative meta-analysis of cognitive-behavioral therapy's effects. *Journal of Consulting and Clinical Psychology, 75*(3), 475–488. https://doi.org/10.1037/0022-006X.75.3.475

Vittengl, J. R., Clark, L. A., & Jarrett, R. B. (2004). Improvement in social-interpersonal functioning after cognitive therapy for recurrent depression. *Psychological Medicine, 34*(4), 643–658. https://doi.org/10.1017/S0033291703001478

Vittengl, J. R., Clark, L. A., & Jarrett, R. B. (2009). Deterioration in psychosocial functioning predicts relapse/recurrence after cognitive therapy for depression. *Journal of Affective Disorders, 112*(1–3), 135–143. https://doi.org/10.1016/j.jad.2008.04.004

Vittengl, J. R., Clark, L. A., Thase, M. E., & Jarrett, R. B. (2014). Stable remission and recovery after acute-phase cognitive therapy for recurrent major depressive disorder. *Journal of Consulting and Clinical Psychology, 82*(6), 1049–1059. https://doi.org/10.1037/a0037401

Vittengl, J. R., Clark, L. A., Thase, M. E., & Jarrett, R. B. (2016a). Longitudinal social-interpersonal functioning among higher-risk responders to acute-phase cognitive therapy for recurrent major depressive disorder. *Journal of Affective Disorders, 199*, 148–156. https://doi.org/10.1016/j.jad.2016.04.017

Vittengl, J. R., Clark, L. A., Thase, M. E., & Jarrett, R. B. (2016b). Defined symptom-change trajectories during acute-phase cognitive therapy for depression predict better longitudinal outcomes. *Behaviour Research and Therapy, 87*, 48–57. https://doi.org/10.1016/j.brat.2016.08.008

Vittengl, J. R., Clark, L. A., Thase, M. E., & Jarrett, R. B. (2019). Estimating outcome probabilities from early symptom changes in cognitive therapy for recurrent depression. *Journal of Consulting and Clinical Psychology, 87*(6), 510–520. https://doi.org/10.1037/ccp0000409

Vittengl, J. R., Jarrett, R. B., Weitz, E., Hollon, S. D., Twisk, J., Cristea, I., David, D., DeRubeis, R. J., Dimidjian, S., Dunlop, B. W., Faramarzi, M., Hegerl, U., Kennedy, S. H., Kheirkhah, F., Mergl, R., Miranda, J., Mohr, D. C., Rush, A. J., Segal, Z. V., Siddique, J., ... Cuijpers, P. (2016). Divergent outcomes in cognitive-behavioral therapy and pharmacotherapy for adult depression. *The American Journal of Psychiatry, 173*(5), 481–490. https://doi.org/10.1176/appi.ajp.2015.15040492

Wardenaar, K. J., Monden, R., Conradi, H. J., & de Jonge, P. (2015). Symptom-specific course trajectories and their determinants in primary care patients with major depressive disorder: Evidence for two etiologically distinct prototypes. *Journal of Affective Disorders, 179*, 38–46. https://doi.org/10.1016/j.jad.2015.03.029

Wardle, M. C., Vincent, J. N., Suchting, R., Green, C. E., Lane, S. D., & Schmitz, J. M. (2017). Anhedonia is associated with poorer outcomes in contingency management for cocaine use disorder. *Journal of Substance Abuse Treatment, 72*, 32–39. https://doi.org/10.1016/j.jsat.2016.08.020

Watts, S. E., Turnell, A., Kladnitski, N., Newby, J. M., & Andrews, G. (2015). Treatment-as-usual (TAU) is anything but usual: A meta-analysis of CBT versus TAU for anxiety and depression. *Journal of Affective Disorders, 175*, 152–167. https://doi.org/10.1016/j.jad.2014.12.025

Weinberg, I., Gunderson, J. G., Hennen, J., & Cutter, C. J., Jr. (2006). Manual assisted cognitive treatment for deliberate self-harm in borderline personality disorder patients. *Journal of Personality Disorders, 20*(5), 482–492. https://doi.org/10.1521/pedi.2006.20.5.482

Weitz, E. S., Hollon, S. D., Twisk, J., van Straten, A., Huibers, M. J., David, D., DeRubeis, R. J., Dimidjian, S., Dunlop, B. W., Cristea, I. A., Faramarzi, M., Hegerl, U., Jarrett, R. B., Kheirkhah, F., Kennedy, S. H., Mergl, R., Miranda, J., Mohr, D. C., Rush, A. J., Segal, Z. V., … Cuijpers, P. (2015). Baseline depression severity as moderator of depression outcomes between cognitive behavioral therapy vs pharmacotherapy: An individual patient data meta-analysis. *JAMA Psychiatry, 72*(11), 1102–1109. https://doi.org/10.1001/jamapsychiatry.2015.1516

Wells, A. (2007). Cognition about cognition: Metacognitive therapy and change in generalized anxiety disorder and social phobia. *Cognitive and Behavioral Practice, 14*(1), 18–25. https://doi.org/10.1016/j.cbpra.2006.01.005

Wilkinson, P., & Izmeth, Z. (2016). Continuation and maintenance treatments for depression in older people. *Cochrane Database of Systematic Reviews, 9*, CD006727. https://doi.org/10.1002/14651858.CD006727.pub3

Wilson, G. T., Fairburn, C. C., Agras, W. S., Walsh, B. T., & Kraemer, H. (2002). Cognitive-behavioral therapy for bulimia nervosa: Time course and mechanisms of change. *Journal of Consulting and Clinical Psychology, 70*(2), 267–274. https://doi.org/10.1037/0022-006X.70.2.267

Wilson, G. T., Wilfley, D. E., Agras, W. S., & Bryson, S. W. (2010). Psychological treatments of binge eating disorder. *Archives of General Psychiatry, 67*(1), 94–101. https://doi.org/10.1001/archgenpsychiatry.2009.170

Windsor, L. C., Jemal, A., & Alessi, E. J. (2015). Cognitive behavioral therapy: A meta-analysis of race and substance use outcomes. *Cultural Diversity and Ethnic Minority Psychology, 21*(2), 300–313. https://doi.org/10.1037/a0037929

Wojnarowski, C., Firth, N., Finegan, M., & Delgadillo, J. (2019). Predictors of depression relapse and recurrence after cognitive behavioural therapy: A systematic review and meta-analysis. *Behavioural and Cognitive Psychotherapy, 47*(5), 514–529. https://doi.org/10.1017/S1352465819000080

World Health Organization. (2017). Depression and other common mental disorders: Global health estimates. Retrieved from https://apps.who.int/iris/bitstream/handle/10665/254610/WHO-MSD-MER-2017.2-eng.pdf

World Health Organization. (2018). *International statistical classification of diseases and related health problems* (11th Revision). Retrieved from https://icd.who.int/browse11/l-m/en

Würz, A., & Sungur, M. Z. (2009). Combining cognitive behavioural therapy and pharmacotherapy in the treatment of anxiety disorders: True gains or false hopes? *Klinik Psikofarmakoloji Bulteni, 19*(4), 436–446.

Young, S., Hopkin, G., Perkins, D., Farr, C., Doidge, A., & Gudjonsson, G. (2013). A controlled trial of a cognitive skills program for personality-disordered offenders. *Journal of Attention Disorders, 17*(7), 598–607. https://doi.org/10.1177/1087054711430333

Zeeck, A., Herpertz-Dahlmann, B., Friederich, H. C., Brockmeyer, T., Resmark, G., Hagenah, U., Ehrlich, S., Cuntz, U., Zipfel, S., & Hartmann, A. (2018). Psychotherapeutic treatment for anorexia nervosa: A systematic review and network meta-analysis. *Frontiers in Psychiatry, 9*, 158. https://doi.org/10.3389/fpsyt.2018.00158

Zhang, A., Borhneimer, L. A., Weaver, A., Franklin, C., Hai, A. H., Guz, S., & Shen, L. (2019). Cognitive behavioral therapy for primary care depression and anxiety: A secondary meta-analytic review using robust variance estimation in meta-regression. *Journal of Behavioral Medicine, 42*(6), 1117–1141. https://doi.org/10.1007/s10865-019-00046-z

Zieve, G. G., Dong, L., & Harvey, A. G. (2019). Patient memory for psychological treatment contents: Assessment, intervention, and future directions for a novel transdiagnostic mechanism of change. *Behaviour Change, 36*(1), 1–11. https://doi.org/10.1017/bec.2019.1

Zinbarg, R. E., Craske, M. G., & Barlow, D. H. (2006). *Mastery of your anxiety and worry (MAW): Therapist guide (Vol. 1)*. Oxford, UK: Oxford, University Press. https://doi.org/10.1093/med:psych/9780195300024.003.0001

Zipfel, S., Wild, B., Groß, G., Friederich, H. C., Teufel, M., Schellberg, D., Giel, K. E., de Zwaan, M., Dinkel, A., Herpertz, S., Burgmer, M., Löwe, B., Tagay, S., von Wietersheim, J., Zeeck, A., Schade-Brittinger, C., Schauenburg, H., Herzog, W., & ANTOP study group. (2014). Focal psychodynamic therapy, cognitive behaviour therapy, and optimised treatment as usual in outpatients with anorexia nervosa (ANTOP study): Randomised controlled trial. *The Lancet, 383*(9912), 127–137. https://doi.org/10.1016/S0140-6736(13)61746-8

Zu, S., Xiang, Y. T., Liu, J., Zhang, L., Wang, G., Ma, X., Kilbourne, A. M., Ungvari, G. S., Chiu, H. F., Lai, K. Y., Wong, S. Y., Yu, D. S., & Li, Z. J. (2014). A comparison of cognitive-behavioral therapy, antidepressants, their combination and standard treatment for Chinese patients with moderate-severe major depressive disorders. *Journal of Affective Disorders, 152–154*, 262–267. https://doi.org/10.1016/j.jad.2013.09.022

CHAPTER 15

MINDFULNESS AND ACCEPTANCE-BASED TREATMENTS

EVAN M FORMAN, JOANNA J ARCH, JONATHAN B BRICKER, BRANDON A GAUDIANO,
ADRIENNE S JUARASCIO, SHIREEN L RIZVI, ZINDEL V SEGAL, AND KEVIN E VOWLES

Abstract

Mindfulness and acceptance-based treatments (MABTs) combine Western cognitive and behavioral treatment approaches with Eastern-inspired concepts of mindfulness and psychological acceptance. As such, MABTs seek to train the abilities to live in the present moment; to maintain awareness of, nonreactivity to, and nonjudgment of one's internal experiences (thoughts, emotions and sensations); and to orient behaviors toward one's ultimate personal values regardless of one's internal experiences. This chapter reviews the empirical research for MABTs across a range of diagnostic and problem areas, with a focus on individual treatments that have been well-researched in each such area. Specifically, we review acceptance and commitment therapy (ACT)-inspired for anxiety and obsessive-compulsive disorder, mindfulness-based cognitive therapy (MBCT) for depression, ACT for psychosis, dialectical behavior therapy (DBT) for borderline personality disorder (BPD) and suicidality, acceptance-based treatments for eating disorders, ACT for smoking, acceptance-based treatment for obesity, and ACT for chronic pain. On the whole, MABTs have been found to be equivalently effective to gold-standard treatment approaches, with evidence in some areas (e.g., MBCT for prevention of depressive relapse and ABT for obesity) that MABTs outperform gold-standard treatments. While the evidence base for MABTs has grown considerably, there remains much to be learned, including the durability of effects, the specific mechanisms underlying MABTs, and improved methods for identifying those people for whom these treatments are best suited.

OVERVIEW

INTRODUCTION

Over the past several decades, a group of therapies gained prominence that blended traditional, Western cognitive–behavioral approaches with Eastern concepts of mindfulness and psychological acceptance. We use the umbrella term *mindfulness and acceptance-based treatments* (MABTs) to refer to these treatments, but others have used a variety of other terms. For instance, "third wave" behavioral treatments has been used to recognize that these approaches followed the first wave of conditioning-based behavior therapies developed in the 1950s, and a second wave in the 1970s that emphasized cognition (Hayes, 2004; Hayes, Villatte et al., 2011). Relative to the first two waves, MABTs deemphasize strategies to directly alter internal experience (e.g., to decrease anxiety, modify a thought, or utilize distraction) based on theoretical and empirical evidence that such change strategies have paradoxical effects of increasing distress (Najmi & Wegner, 2008; Wegner, 1994; Wegner & Zanakos, 1994). In fact, MABTs take the position that psychopathology is maintained through experiential avoidance or problematic attempts to control distressing or undesired internal experiences.

As such, MABTs promote a suite of conceptually coherent strategies designed to promote skillful responses to, and adaptive behavioral choices, in the face of challenging internal experiences (thoughts, emotions, and sensations (Keng et al., 2015; Norton et al., 2015). Mindfulness represents one core set of strategies. These strategies seek to train dimensions of mindfulness, which include living in the present moment, as well as awareness of, labeling of, nonreactivity to, and nonjudgment of internal and external stimuli (Baer et al., 2006). Similarly, MABTs promote a willingness to experience all aspects of one's present experience (acceptance) in the service of meeting one's immediate goals and ultimate personal *values* (Forman et al., 2012; Hayes, Strosahl et al., 2011; Hofmann & Asmundson, 2008). MABTs also feature metacognitive and decentering strategies that help the patient recognize, in real time, that internal experiences are simply transient neural phenomena (versus an absolute arbiter of "truth") (Hayes et al., 1999a; Teasdale et al., 2002). Most MABTs also place value on the practice of mindfulness meditation, which involves concentrated and dedicated practice in intentionally directing one's attention to one's present moment experience and to fully embracing all internal experiences that arise (Brown & Ryan, 2003; Chiesa & Serretti, 2011; Hofmann et al., 2010; Keng et al., 2011).

MABTs include a number of specific treatments components. For instance, acceptance and commitment therapy (ACT) is a therapeutic approach that uses acceptance and mindfulness processes as well as values-guided commitment and behavioral change processes to enhance psychological flexibility and valued living (Hayes et al., 1999a). ACT has six core processes, two of which are based on behavioral commitment to values (values clarity, committed action) and four of which are mindfulness and acceptance based (being present, defusion, experiential acceptance, self-as-context). ACT has also inspired several related treatments referred to as acceptance-based behavior therapy (ABBT or ABT). These treatments have behavioral treatments as their foundation and include mindfulness and acceptance components, with the goal of reducing experiential avoidance and promoting adaptive behavioral choices (Roemer & Orsillo, 2005). Mindfulness-based cognitive therapy (MBCT) teaches practices that foster acceptance and decentering from thoughts, emotions, and physical sensations. MBCT has a heavy focus on mindfulness meditation practice, during which patients are asked to turn toward and accept any discomfort that arises, but also use the cognitive strategy of decentering from these internal experiences (Segal & Teasdale, 2018). Dialectical behavior therapy (DBT) encompasses the dialectic of acceptance and change. It has four skill modules, two of which are primarily focused on acceptance (mindfulness, distress tolerance) and two of which are primarily focused on change (interpersonal effectiveness, emotion regulation) (Linehan, 1993).

In recent years, we have witnessed a rapid proliferation of MABTs across a range of psychological and behavioral medicine problem areas, along with concomitant studies of their effectiveness, mechanisms of action, and predictors of outcome. In order to keep this chapter focused, we have limited our scope to a single, representative application of an MABT for each problem area. We based our selection of treatment on which was most commonly in practice and had the most empirical study to date. In some cases, a highly related group of treatments was clustered and reviewed. As such, the chapter reviews the following: ACT (and ACT-inspired acceptance-based behavioral treatments) for anxiety and obsessive-compulsive disorder, MBCT for depression, ACT for psychosis, DBT for borderline personality disorder and suicidality, mindfulness and acceptance-based treatments for eating disorders, ACT for smoking, ABT for obesity, and ACT for chronic pain.

ACCEPTANCE-BASED TREATMENTS FOR ANXIETY DISORDERS AND OBSESSIVE-COMPULSIVE DISORDER

A body of research converged early on in suggesting that mindfulness and acceptance-based practices provided a promising approach for treating anxiety disorders and obsessive-compulsive disorder (OCD). In fact, these disorders were among the first for which high-profile theoretical papers (Roemer & Orsillo, 2002) and mindfulness- and acceptance-based treatment manuals were published (e.g., Eifert & Forsyth, 2005), and relatively large randomized trials were conducted (see Landy et al., 2014). Interestingly, anxiety disorders were also one of the first disorders to which mindfulness-based stress reduction (MBSR) research was applied (Kabat-Zinn et al., 1992).

Many different types of mindfulness and acceptance-based interventions have been tested for anxiety disorders and OCD. However, ACT and its variants appear to represent the most commonly applied mindfulness and acceptance-based psychotherapies for anxiety disorders and OCD. Thus, our focus in this section is on ACT and its variants in treating anxiety disorders, acceptance-based behavior therapy (ABBT), and mindfulness and acceptance-based group therapy (MAGT).

ACT treatments for anxiety disorders and OCD aim to reduce experiential avoidance by cultivating the ability to acknowledge, notice, and willingly experience thoughts, feelings, urges, and sensations associated with anxiety and fear (e.g., Twohig et al., 2018) and to more flexibly and objectively related to anxiety-related cognitions. ACT treatments for anxiety disorders and OCD also draw on personal values to help clients deliberately engage with feared and avoided, but valued, contexts and stimuli.

Efficacy and Effectiveness

ACT and its variants have been tested in more than a dozen randomized clinical trials for anxiety disorders and OCD (Twohig & Levin, 2017). ACT treatment trials have been reviewed in several anxiety disorder–focused papers (Swain, Hancock, Hainsworth et al., 2013; Twohig & Levin, 2017) and meta-analysis, either alone (Bluett et al., 2014) or in combination with other mindfulness- and acceptance-based interventions such as MBSR and MBCT (Vøllestad et al., 2011). In considering the efficacy of ACT for anxiety disorders and OCD, we draw on these reviews and meta-analyses, as well as on the larger randomized trials conducted in this area (Landy et al., 2014) and trials conducted since these reviews.

The Twohig and Levin (2017) descriptive review concluded that ACT for anxiety disorders and OCD is more efficacious than treatment-as-usual and wait-list conditions and largely equivalent relative to traditional (i.e., classic) CBT. This conclusion converges with quantitative evidence from their preliminary meta-analysis of ACT for anxiety disorders and OCD, which concluded that ACT was similarly effective as cognitive behavioral treatments, $g = .00$ ($k = 5$, 95% CI [–0.24, 0.25]) (Bluett et al., 2014). Similar conclusions were drawn in a subsequent meta-analysis of diverse ACT trials that showed no differences between ACT and classic CBT for anxiety outcomes, $g = .14$ ($k = 9$, 95% CI [–0.18, 0.45]) (Ruiz, 2012), and in a systematic review of 38 ACT interventions (total $N = 323$) for anxiety disorders and related symptoms (Swain, Hancock, Hainsworth et al., 2013). In summary, ACT appears to offer a treatment approach that is similar in efficacy as classic CBT.

Many of these ACT trials for anxiety disorders and OCD have been uncontrolled or use small samples (e.g., < 50 total participants randomized across two or more treatment conditions). To follow, we highlight larger randomized trials, as they are likely to reflect more stable between-group differences.

As a transdiagnostic treatment approach, ACT has often been tested in mixed or heterogeneous anxiety disorder samples, including in some of the largest trials of face-to-face ACT for anxiety disorders to date (Arch, Eifert et al., 2012; Hancock et al., 2018). Thus, we begin by reviewing the efficacy findings of ACT for heterogeneous anxiety disorders prior to reporting efficacy findings for each individual anxiety disorder.

Heterogeneous Anxiety Disorders

The largest known randomized trial of ACT for heterogeneous anxiety disorders involved 193 Australian youth age 7–17 with one or more DSM-IV anxiety disorder(s) (Hancock et al., 2018; Swain, Hancock, Dixon et al., 2013). This rigorously conducted trial randomized youth to either a 10-week ACT or CBT group or wait-list control condition. ACT and CBT group treatments produced similar outcomes and were superior to wait-list control across all outcomes. Anxiety disorder clinical severity findings slightly favored CBT over ACT, $d = .32$ (95% CI [0.02, 0.67], but these finding did not withstand statistical correction.

The second major randomized trial of ACT for heterogeneous anxiety disorders compared 12 sessions of individual ACT or CBT for adults with one more DSM-IV anxiety disorders ($n = 128$), with behavioral exposure used in both conditions (Arch, Eifert et al., 2012). This trial found similarly strong improvements in both ACT and CBT from pre- to posttreatment, with significantly steeper linear improvements during the 12-month follow-up period in ACT relative to CBT for the primary outcome of anxiety disorder severity, $d = 1.26$. On reliable change indices, both treatments showed similar treatment response rates. In summary, the Arch et al. (2012) and the Hancock et al. (2018) trials suggest that ACT offers a viable treatment approach for heterogeneous youth and adult anxiety disorders, with similar efficacy to classic CBT.

Though we focus on anxiety disorders, it is worth noting that some of the largest randomized trials of ACT for addressing mixed anxiety concerns were conducted in effectiveness trials with minimal inclusion criteria (Forman et al., 2007; Ritzert et al., 2016). These trials ranged from 101 students with elevated anxiety or depressive symptoms seeking mental health services at an urban university counseling center, randomized to ACT or classic CBT (Forman et al., 2007), to 503 adults randomized to a published ACT self-help book (Forsyth & Eifert, 2016) or wait-list control group (Ritzert et al., 2016). The Forman et al. (2007) trial showed similar outcomes for ACT and CBT from pre- to posttreatment. Outcomes at 18-month follow-up, however, favored CBT over ACT (Forman et al., 2012), suggesting advantages for CBT over ACT in this student population. In the Ritzert et al. (2016) study of 503 adults, ACT showed superior improvements on all outcomes from pre- to posttreatment compared to wait-list control, with gains maintained at follow-up. Most participants were recruited online and did not complete the assessments, reflecting the minimal-contact nature of the study. The high attrition indicates caution in interpreting study findings.

In summary, these four sizable trials (Arch, Eifert et al., 2012; Forman et al., 2007; Hancock et al., 2018; Ritzert et al., 2016) provide consistent evidence that ACT offers a viable treatment approach for heterogeneous youth and adult anxiety disorders, and for elevated anxiety symptoms. Notably, this work reflects both efficacy and effectiveness studies, suggesting the utility of ACT for anxiety disorders and symptoms across diverse treatment settings.

Generalized Anxiety Disorder (GAD)

ACT and ABBT for GAD represent one of the more active areas of research regarding the efficacy of mindfulness- and acceptance-based behavioral therapies for anxiety disorders. The two largest trials in this area (Dahlin et al., 2016; Hayes-Skelton et al., 2013) both used ABBT, which is a GAD-focused application of ACT that has a strong emphasis on cultivating mindfulness (Roemer & Orsillo, 2002, 2008). The first of these trials (Hayes-Skelton et al., 2013) randomized 81 adults with GAD to ABBT or applied relaxation, an established evidence-based intervention for GAD (Borkovec & Costello, 1993). Both interventions led to large and significant improvements for all primary outcomes (d = 1.27–1.61) with no significant differences between the two interventions, suggesting that ABBT provides a viable alternative to treating GAD. In the second trial (Dahlin et al., 2016), therapist-guided, online-delivered ABBT was compared to a wait-list control in treating 103 Swedish adults with GAD. Relative to wait-list control, ABBT showed large and superior effects on GAD symptoms (d = .70–.98), with gains maintained at six-month follow-up. Combined with meta-analytic and systematic review findings (Bluett et al., 2014; Handcock et al., 2018; Swain, Hancock, Hainsworth et al., 2013; Twohig & Levin, 2017), these two trials suggest that ABBT is similarly effective as established treatment (i.e., applied relaxation) and more effective than wait-list control for GAD.

Social Anxiety Disorder (SAD)

Three trials for SAD evaluated either individual ACT (Craske et al., 2014; Herbert et al., 2018) or MAGT, i.e., mindfulness and acceptance group therapy, a group ACT intervention adapted with enhanced mindfulness practice (Kocovski et al., 2013). Both trials compared individual ACT or MAGT to individual or group CBT, respectively, and a wait-list control condition (N = 87 and 137, respectively). The three studies found that the active treatment conditions (ACT, MAGT, CBT) led to large and significant improvements relative to the wait-list control conditions (d = .60–2.19 for SAD outcomes in Craske et al., 2014; d = 1.00–1.02 on the primary outcome for Kocovski et al., 2013; and $\eta p2$ = .25–.27 on primary outcomes for Herbert et al., 2018). Only the latter study found a significant difference between active treatment conditions, in which CBT outperformed ACT on self-reported total social anxiety symptoms, $\eta p2$ = .30, but not on blind clinician-rated diagnostic status, fear or avoidance measures, $\eta p2$ = .00–.01. A fourth rigorous trial (Kocovski et al., 2019) compared a published self-help ACT workbook for SAD (Fleming & Kocovski, 2013) to a wait-list control condition (N = 117), and found large and significant between-group differences on social anxiety outcomes (d = .74–.79). In summary, ACT interventions reflecting multiple variants of content and delivery format were shown to serve as a viable treatment for SAD, with similar or somewhat lower efficacy as classic CBT and substantially greater efficacy than wait-list control conditions.

Panic Disorder

Though only one known ACT randomized trial to date has focused exclusively on panic disorder (Gloster et al., 2015), the trial was innovative. Forty-three German adults who had previously not responded to state-of-the-art treatment for panic disorder (e.g., CBT, exposure therapy, or guideline-driven pharmacotherapy), were randomized to receive ACT immediately (eight individual sessions delivered twice per week) or after a month-long wait-list period. Treatment was an adapted version of the manual (Eifert & Forsyth, 2005) used in the Arch et al. (2012) trial, delivered by novice graduate student therapists. At post, relative to the wait-list control, the ACT condition showed medium-to-large gains in the primary outcomes (panic and agoraphobia symptoms, global improvement) and a very low attrition rate (9%), with gains continuing over the seven-month follow-up. Though modest in size, this study suggests that ACT represents a promising option for a clinically challenging population – adults with treatment-resistant panic disorder.

Obsessive-Compulsive Disorder (OCD)

The first randomized trial of ACT for OCD was conducted by Twohig et al. (2010) and compared ACT to progressive muscle relaxation (PMR), without in-session exposure, using eight sessions of each, thus representing relatively brief behavioral treatments for OCD that omitted an active treatment element (e.g., in-session exposure). ACT significantly outperformed PMR on OCD severity outcomes by a large effect (d = .84), including producing more clinically significant change (d = .62–1.10, depending on assessment point and use of imputed values for missing data), suggesting the promise of ACT as an OCD treatment approach, even without in-session exposure. A second randomized trial compared 16 sessions of exposure and response prevention (ERP; a gold standard OCD treatment) with versus without ACT for 58 adults with OCD (Twohig et al., 2018). Both treatments were highly effective (d = 2.5–2.7, within condition) but showed no significant differences in outcomes, processes of change, exposure engagement, or acceptability. Though one possibility is that ERP + ACT is a fundamentally different treatment than ERP alone, the measured processes of change – psychological flexibility and obsessive beliefs – did not distinguish them. Thus, ERP, both with and without ACT, provides a similarly efficacious treatment approach for OCD. ACT on its own, without ERP, also provides an efficacious treatment for OCD. Perhaps both treatments (ACT and ERP) function similarly by orienting individuals toward an actively approach-oriented (e.g., nonavoidant) stance toward their OCD symptoms.

Two randomized trials (N = 90 and 60, respectively) conducted in Iran found superior results for ACT or ACT plus imipramine relative to imipramine alone (Baghooli et al., 2014) and for the superiority of ACT relative to narrative therapy or time perspective therapy (Esfahani et al., 2015). These comparison conditions (imipramine, narrative therapy, time perspective therapy) had not shown good efficacy in previous OCD trials (e.g., Foa et al., 1992), if tested at all, and thus, particularly for narrative and time perspective therapy, should be characterized as active control conditions rather than as evidence-based comparison conditions. Thus, we can conclude that ACT for OCD showed good efficacy relative to both medication and psychotherapy-based active control conditions.

Processes and Moderators

The therapeutic processes and mechanisms (or mediators) of change in ACT for anxiety disorders are conceptualized as reflecting core ACT model processes, including cognitive defusion and reduced experiential avoidance (framed as the opposite of active acceptance). ACT process or mediation variables have most commonly been assessed with the Acceptance and Action Questionnaires (AAQ), either the original (Hayes et al., 2004) or the revised version (the AAQ-II; Bond et al., 2011). These measures were designed to assess experiential avoidance (Hayes et al., 1996). Meta-analytic findings demonstrate that the AAQ and AAQ-II correlate moderately and significantly with anxiety symptoms: $r = .45$, $n = 13,788$ (Bluett et al., 2014). The AAQ/AAQ-II and its disorder-specific variants have been found to mediate or predict anxiety outcomes in numerous clinical trials of ACT (Eustis et al., 2016; Kocovski et al., 2019); however, there are two caveats. First, the AAQ/AAQ-II and other ACT process measures also have been found to mediate outcomes in other non-ACT behavioral therapies for anxiety disorders, for example, in cued relaxation for GAD (Eustis et al, 2016), suggesting that the processes they reflect may be shared with other forms of behavioral therapy. Similarly, the Bluett et al. (2014) meta-analysis of ACT for anxiety found that change on the AAQ did not differ between ACT and CBT conditions; $g = .13$ ($k = 3$, 95% CI [–0.12, 0.39]). Second, the AAQ-II has been found to correlate more with distress (Wolgast, 2014) and negative affect/neuroticism (Rochefort et al., 2018) than with experiential avoidance or acceptance. That stated, other ACT-consistent measures – apart from the AAQ or AAQ-II – also have mediated ACT for anxiety disorder outcomes. For example, in the Arch et al. (2012) trial comparing ACT vs. CBT for heterogeneous anxiety disorders, it was found that session-by-session increases in cognitive defusion mediated numerous outcomes in both treatments. Thus, mediation via experiential avoidance or cognitive defusion has been evident using different measures and has been shown to predict outcomes in ACT as well as in other behavioral/cognitive behavioral therapies such as CBT.

Regarding treatment moderators, the trial of ACT for heterogeneous DSM-IV anxiety disorders comparing individual ACT vs. individual CBT (Arch, Eifert et al., 2012) conducted moderator analyses. Moderator findings showed that ACT performed better than CBT among those with comorbid mood disorders, whereas CBT outperformed ACT among those without comorbid mood disorder (Wolitzky-Taylor et al., 2012), suggesting that treatment matching may be feasible (see Niles et al., 2017 for an example). The Craske et al. trial (2014) also examined treatment moderators and found that participants with higher baseline levels of experiential avoidance or more extreme (high or low) levels of fear of negative evaluation did better in CBT than ACT.

Conclusions

Mindfulness and acceptance-based interventions for anxiety disorders (and related symptoms), and particularly ACT and its variants, represent viable treatment approaches that shows similar efficacy to classic CBT and have been successfully delivered in multiple formats (individual, group, therapist-guided online, bibliotherapy). The anxiety disorders with two or more rigorous ACT trials include GAD, SAD, and OCD, as well as mixed or heterogeneous anxiety disorders, demonstrating a growing evidence base published largely over the last decade. The number and size of trials of mindfulness and acceptance-based interventions for anxiety disorders does not yet match that of classic CBT, which has been evaluated in large trials for anxiety disorders over a significantly longer period of time. Nonetheless, we conclude that ACT provides an important treatment approach for anxiety disorders for at least three reasons, two in terms of clinical implications and one in terms of conceptual understanding of these disorders.

First, ACT provides an important behavioral option for treating anxiety disorders, one that uses a rather different therapeutic stance and approach to content than classic CBT (McGrath et al., 2010). Thus, ACT provides patients and therapists with *choice* regarding behavioral approaches to treatment anxiety disorders, as some clients and therapists may resonate more with one behavioral approach than another. Just as psychiatric medications offer multiple medications within the same medication class, which offers patients and providers a sense of choice to select one according to its particular characteristics, and options if one fails, so too do anxiety disorder and OCD patients and providers benefit from choice regarding behavioral approaches to treatment.

Second and relatedly, many people with anxiety disorders and OCD do not respond to CBT (Loerinc et al., 2015), yet most adults prefer psychotherapy over pharmacologic treatments (McHugh et al., 2013). Evidence-based psychotherapy alternatives for treating anxiety disorders are vitally needed for CBT nonresponders. ACT provides one such important alternative. Nascent evidence in panic disorder shows that adults who failed to improve after a course of CBT show significant improvement after ACT (Gloster et al., 2015), providing important initial support for this idea. Relatedly, nascent moderator evidence suggests that baseline client characteristics predict different outcomes in ACT and CBT (Craske et al., 2014; Wolitzky-Taylor et al., 2012), and that treatment matching may be possible (Niles et al., 2017). Thus, in addition to providing choice, some clients respond better to ACT than to classic CBT (or other evidence-based treatment options).

Third, the ACT theoretical model has expanded the field's understanding of the core processes involved in the development and maintenance of anxiety disorders. Specifically, theory-derived ACT processes (cognitive defusion, acceptance, experiential avoidance) have been shown to mediate outcomes from both ACT and other evidence-based behavioral therapies for anxiety disorders, including classic CBT and cued relaxation (e.g., Arch, Wolitzky-Taylor et al., 2012; Eustis et al., 2016). ACT processes also predict clinically relevant responses to anxiety in laboratory studies (e.g., Campbell-Sills et al., 2005; Eifert & Heffner, 2003), suggesting that they are likely involved in the development of anxiety disorders as well as their maintenance (Forsyth et al., 2006). In summary, mindfulness- and acceptance-based psychotherapy approaches, most prominently ACT, have made important theoretical and applied contributions to the treatment of anxiety disorders and OCD.

MINDFULNESS-BASED COGNITIVE THERAPY FOR DEPRESSION

Contemporary approaches to care for patients with a mood disorder increasingly emphasize the utility of sequential treatment algorithms that target both the acute episode and the period of clinical remission/recovery (Guidi et al, 2016). The most widely supported approach for prevention of relapse/recurrence in formerly depressed patients has been maintenance antidepressant medication (mADM) (Geddes et al., 2003), although CT delivered during the acute phase of depression has also been shown to be prophylactic (Hollon et al., 2005). A drawback associated with the ongoing use of antidepressants for preventing depressive relapse/recurrence is that the rates of treatment compliance are quite low (Samples & Mojtabai, 2015). Discontinuation of mADM leaves many formerly depressed patients "unprotected" during a period where their risk of relapse/recurrence remains elevated. It was against this backdrop that mindfulness-based cognitive therapy for depression (MBCT) was developed.

Mindfulness-based cognitive therapy (Segal et al., 2013) was designed to build metacognitive skills in formerly depressed patients in order to preempt the establishment of mood-linked depressogenic ruminative cycles (Teasdale et al., 1995). Metacognitive skills refer to the ability to be acutely aware of patterns of thinking in the moment and to observe rather, than identify with these internal experiences; this ability is believed to play a pivotal role in adaptive responses to stressors and emotion regulation more generally (Teasdale et al., 2002). Applied to relapse prevention, it was proposed that the risk of relapse and recurrence would be reduced if previously depressed patients could learn, first, to be more aware of negative thoughts and feelings when they arise (e.g., "I can't do anything right"), and, second, to view these thoughts and feelings as mental events, allowing them to disengage from ruminative depressive thinking and feelings (Nolen-Hoeksema & Morrow, 1991). Participants in this eight-session, weekly group intervention, learn both formal mindfulness meditation, such as the body scan or breath meditation along with informal mindfulness practices such as mindful eating or noting pleasant and unpleasant experiences. These practices are supplemented by CBT exercises to identify relapse triggers, with the overarching goal of all this work being to help patients observe and bring an attitude of curiosity, rather than reacting reflexively, to what gets noticed (Segal et al., 2013).

Efficacy

The earliest randomized clinical trials of MBCT were conducted to determine its effectiveness compared to usual care (Ma & Teasdale, 2004; Teasdale et al., 2000). Teasdale et al. (2000) conducted a multisite study (Toronto; Bangor, Wales; and Cambridge, UK) with participants randomized into either MBCT or treatment as usual (TAU) conditions (N = 145). The rationale here was that given the somewhat unusual proposition of featuring mindfulness meditation at the core of this intervention, it would be important to firstly establish whether there was a 'signal' before moving on to more stringent comparisons. Participants in both studies were in remission from depression and had a history of at least two previous episodes. Those in the TAU condition were instructed to seek support from their physician or community sources as they normally would. Those in the MBCT condition participated in eight weekly group sessions, plus four follow-up sessions scheduled at one-, two-, three-, and four-month intervals and

could access usual care as needed. Both groups were followed for a total of 60 weeks. Severity of depressive symptoms and relapse were evaluated with the Structured Clinical Interview for Diagnosis (SCID; First et al., 1996), and the primary outcome measure was whether and when participants experienced relapse (i.e., met criteria for a major depressive episode according to the DSM). In each condition, participants were stratified according to the number of previous episodes (two versus three or more) they had experienced. Results revealed differential treatment outcomes based on the number of prior depressive episodes. For individuals who had two past episodes, there were no differences between MBCT and TAU in terms of relapse rates at 15 months. However, in the sample of individuals with three or more previous episodes (77% of the overall sample), there was a significant benefit of MBCT. Using Intention to Treat analyses, relapse was observed in only 34% of the MBCT group, while those in the TAU condition had a relapse rate of 66%. These findings were replicated in a smaller single-site trial (N = 75) (Ma & Teasdale, 2004). It is still unclear what the cardinal differences are between these two past-episode defined groups, other than recognizing that they may come from populations with different risk profiles and that the more vulnerable patients showed greater treatment gains. Because independent replication is important for any emerging intervention, it is noteworthy that several independent trials have provided support for MBCT's prevention effects, including longer periods of inter-episode wellness, reduction in residual depressive symptoms, and lower rates of relapse (Bondolfi et al., 2010; Geschwind et al., 2011; Godfrin and van Heeringen, 2010; Kuyken et al., 2008).

With promising data suggesting MBCT's protective effects against depressive relapse, the next step in studying its efficacy was to compare it against the benefits conferred by mADM, the current standard of care. Segal et al. (2010) conducted the first placebo-controlled comparison of MBCT and mADM with 84 individuals who achieved remission via ADM and were then subsequently assigned to come off their medication and receive MBCT, receive a pill-placebo, or stay on mADM. Participants were further categorized according to the stability of their remission during the acute phase of treatment for depression, as determined by symptom elevations on the Hamilton Rating Scale for Depression (HRSD; Hamilton, 1960). Unstable remitters (51% of the sample), compared to stable remitters (49% of the sample), were those who experienced "symptom flurries," or occasional, transient symptom elevations on the HRSD. For stable remitters, ITT analyses demonstrated no difference in relapse rates across the three conditions. For unstable remitters, the MBCT (28%) and mADM (27%) conditions offered equivalent protection, with relapse rates being significantly higher in the placebo group (71%).

In a related vein, Kuyken et al. (2015) studied 24-month relapse survival rates between individuals who were supported in discontinuing their mADM and received MBCT compared to a group that continued on mADM. They reported that there was no difference between the groups (hazard ratio = 0·89, 95% CI [0.67, 1.18]) and that both interventions were associated with improved quality of life. Huijbers et al. (2015)

examined an interesting corollary of these findings, namely, if MBCT is protective for those who discontinue mADM, does it boost protection for those who choose to stay on their medication? Sixty-eight depressed patients in remission who had been on ADM for at least six months were assigned to either MBCT+mADM (*n* = 33) or mADM alone (*n* = 35) groups. Their findings indicated no significant difference between the groups over a 15-month follow-up.

Perhaps more definitively, two recent meta-analyses have examined the efficacy of MBCT's prevention effects. Kuyken et al. (2016) conducted an individual patient data (IPD) meta-analysis, drawing on nine randomized controlled trials (*N* = 1329) conducted by a variety of research groups and using a range of European and North American participants. Compared to those enrolled in other depression treatments, individuals who completed MBCT had a significantly reduced risk of depressive relapse over a 60-week follow-up period (hazard ratio = 0.69, 95% CI [0.58, 0.82]). When compared to mADM treatment alone (*N* = 637), MBCT reduced the risk of relapse (hazard ratio = 0.77, 95% CI [0.60, 0.98]).

Moving past relapse prevention as the sole clinical outcome, a meta-analysis by Goldberg et al. (2019) examined MBCT's efficacy for patients with current depressive symptoms. Data were collected from 13 studies (*N* = 1046) of MBCT for adults with depression. Comparisons were reported between specific/active control or nonspecific control conditions. Results indicated that MBCT outperformed nonspecific controls at posttreatment (*k* = 10, *d* = 0.71, 95% CI [0.47, 0.96]), although not over a follow-up interval (*k* = 2, *d* = 1.47, 95% CI [−0.71, 3.65]). MBCT was no different from other active psychological therapies at posttreatment (*k* = 6, *d* = 0.002 [−0.43, 0.44]), and follow-up (*k* = 4, *d* = 0.26, 95% CI [−0.24, 0.75]). The authors reported a trend for more methodologically sound studies to show reduced effects at posttreatment, but no evidence that effects varied by whether the level of depressive symptoms at baseline was minimal or more pronounced. Given the relatively short follow-up period (mean = 5.70-month follow-up duration), the authors suggested that the long-term effects of MBCT with this population deserved further study.

MBCT sees its basic framework being adaptable for the treatment of several other disorders with hypothetically similar underlying mechanisms. For example, rumination, avoidance, and hypervigilance to body sensations are important drivers of symptom severity in anxiety and pain disorders. A recent RCT (*N* = 182) compared a modified version of MBCT with CBT-based psychoeducation and TAU in the treatment of generalized anxiety disorder (GAD; Wong et al., 2016, see also Evans et al., 2008). This version of MBCT was widened to encompass the experience of people suffering from anxiety (e.g., discussing automatic thoughts related to anxiety; developing action plans to prevent avoidance and symptom return) and thus to enhance overall participant engagement. BAI scores at post treatment and at five-month follow-up showed a significant decline for participants receiving MBCT or psychoeducation compared to those in usual care. Similar findings have been reported for the treatment of health anxiety/hypochondriasis (McManus et al., 2012) and perinatal depression (Dimidjian et al., 2016). For example, in a recent RCT (*N* = 74) that

compared MBCT for hypochondriasis to TAU, participants who completed MBCT were significantly less likely to meet criteria for the diagnosis of hypochondriasis than those in the TAU condition (McManus et al., 2012), both immediately following treatment (50.0% vs. 78.9%) and at one-year follow-up (36.1% vs. 76.3%).

Dissemination

While MBCT has considerable empirical support, it faces several practical challenges to dissemination. At the very least, access to a trained practitioner is required. Beyond physical access, service costs and waiting lists may be prohibitive for those interested in treatment (Wang et al., 2003). Web-based treatments can offer an alternative that addresses several of these challenges (e.g., Warmerdam et al. 2010). Recently, MBCT has been adapted for online dissemination. Mindful Mood Balance (MMB; https://mindfulnoggin.com/) was developed to digitize the content of in-person MBCT into an eight-session, self-guided online program. MMB closely follows the session structure of MBCT, but utilizes a variety of learning modalities (e.g., video, audio, eLearning interactions). To simulate the group-based inquiry component of MBCT, videos of selected portions of an in-person MBCT group are provided. A quasi-experimental investigation demonstrated that MMB significantly reduced residual depression symptom severity, which was sustained over six months, and was associated with improvement in measures of rumination and mindfulness (Dimidjian et al., 2014). Segal et al. (2020) report the results of an RCT (*N* = 460) of MMB compared to a depression care pathway offered at a large HMO for participants who had an elevated PHQ-9 score (≥5 and ≤ 9; Kroenke et al., 2001). Results indicated that MMB was associated with a significant decrease in depressive symptom severity over three months and these gains were maintained one year later. As with other digital therapeutics, the larger questions of where programs such as MMB are hosted, the nature of their financial support and how they are promoted have yet to be addressed.

Predictors and Moderators

Several studies have identified potential predictors or moderators. In Kuyken et al.'s (2016) meta-analysis, the treatment effect of MBCT on risk of relapse was larger in participants who reported more severe depression at baseline, as compared with non-MBCT conditions. Consistent with the findings of Teasdale and colleagues (2000), these results suggest that MBCT may be particularly helpful for individuals with higher levels of residual depressive symptoms. And in Williams et al.'s (2014) dismantling study, when the data for individuals with a history of childhood trauma was examined, MBCT (and mindfulness training) was significantly more effective at curbing this risk of relapse than CPE and TAU (41% MBCT, 54% CPE, and 65% TAU). These results suggest that gains in mindfulness and meta-cognitive skills following MBCT may be mechanisms of change that are particularly crucial for populations that are most at risk of re-experiencing depression (e.g., individuals with a history of three or more episodes; patients with a history of childhood trauma).

Processes and Mechanisms of Change

The theoretical background behind MBCT's development specifies a number of treatment targets that, if addressed, should be associated with positive clinical outcomes (Teasdale et al., 1995). Van der Velden et al. (2015) published a systematic review of 23 studies examining the mechanisms of change underlying MBCT. Specifically, they asked whether (i) increases in mindfulness and decentering skills; (ii) reductions in rumination, worry, and low self-esteem; and (iii) cognitive reactivity were associated with heightened relapse prevention. In line with the theoretically predicted mechanisms of change, they reported that changes in mindfulness, meta-cognitive skills, as well as depressogenic cognitions predicted or mediated the effects of MBCT on treatment outcome.

Two studies utilized a dismantling strategy to examine key elements of the MBCT program. In Williams et al. (2014), two groups of remitted depressed participants were compared to treatment-as-usual (TAU): (i) A cognitive psychoeducation program (CPE) that was matched to MBCT on both nonspecific and specific factors but excluded training in mindfulness meditation, and (ii) the full MBCT program. The aim here was to isolate the contribution of one of MBCT's hypothesized therapeutic ingredients – training in mindfulness meditation – on treatment outcomes. There were no differences in relapse rates between the groups (46% MBCT group, 50% CPE group, and 53% TAU group), suggesting that mindfulness skills may not provide any additional protection against relapse.

A second relevant study conducted by Shallcross et al. (2015) compared MBCT against Health Enhancement Program, similar to Williams et al. (2014), featured psychoeducation and wellness practices to reduce stress and negative affect, but omitted training in mindfulness meditation. Survival analyses over 60 weeks indicated no difference between the groups, with 32.6% of MBCT and 30.4% of the HEP participants suffering a relapse. Both studies are important in highlighting the role played by group inclusion, normalization, and destigmatization, regardless of whether this is provided in an active or nonspecific control condition. It is unlikely, however, that these studies were adequately powered for a true noninferiority design, which may temper their conclusions regarding the centrality of mindfulness meditation in the prevention of mood disorders.

With respect to cognitive reactivity, Kuyken et al. (2010) studied whether changes in the number of depressive cognitions elicited by a dysphoric mood induction mediated the effects of MBCT on subsequent relapse risk. MBCT participants were compared to participants receiving mADM and contrary to expectations, this study found that MBCT participants demonstrated greater cognitive reactivity posttreatment compared to the mADM control group. What is important, however, is that cognitive reactivity predicted poorer outcome only for the mADM group, and not for the MBCT group. This suggests that MBCT may not so much reduce the automatic nature of cognitive reactivity in formerly depressed patients but may help prevent the elaboration of depressogenic cognitions from feeding further rumination and perpetuating depressed mood.

An additional change mechanism is MBCT's effect on the quality and frequency of positive affect in everyday life. By increasing one's ability to generate positive affect from pleasant daily life events, MBCT may build resilience in the face of negativity. Geschwind et al. (2011) found that MBCT was associated with reports of increased experience of momentary positive emotions, as well as enhanced responsiveness to (and greater appreciation for) pleasant daily-life activities. These findings remained significant even after controlling for variance in depressive symptoms, negative emotion, rumination, and worry. In a related vein, Batink et al. (2013) demonstrated that for patients with three or more previous depressive episodes, changes in positive and negative affect predominantly mediated the effect of MBCT on posttreatment symptoms of depression.

Viewed from a clinical lens, a broad implication of the research on mechanisms is that MBCT provides patients with an opportunity to disengage from depressogenic patterns of thinking. Through training in mindfulness, meditation patients learn to identify vulnerability inducing habits of thinking and how to relate to them through a meta-cognitive, present-moment orientation. MBCT is firmly rooted in the view of mindfulness as a form of attentional training that first requires familiarity with the automatic or mindless modes of cognitive processing. With consistent practice, patients can become acquainted with new modes of mind that provide flexibility in the midst of possible relapse triggers and, more widely, with life's ever-present challenges, and opportunities.

Conclusions

MBCT was developed to prevent depression relapse among individuals with recurrent depression. Research from numerous randomized control trials support the efficacy of MBCT, and preliminary research evidences novel extensions of MBCT. In addition, MBCT may be particularly suited to people experiencing higher levels of residual depressive symptoms and those more prone to relapse. Overall, the primary clinical implication that can be derived from these findings is that MBCT allows for patients to learn to disengage from depressogenic patterns of thinking, by teaching them to identify vulnerability inducing habits of thinking with the goal of relating to them through a meta-cognitive, present-moment orientation.

ACCEPTANCE AND COMMITMENT THERAPY FOR PSYCHOSIS

Acceptance and commitment therapy for psychosis (ACTp) has been adapted to address the symptoms and clinical sequelae of schizophrenia and other psychotic-spectrum disorders. Experiential avoidance, or the maladaptive attempt to avoid distressing thoughts and feelings when it impairs functioning, is understood to play a key role in psychosis, as it does in other forms of psychopathology (Hayes et al., 2006). In particular, experiential avoidance in psychosis can be understood as driving ruminative thinking patterns, tendencies to engage or resist voices, negative reinforcement mechanisms related to anxiety reduction, maladaptive attempts to maintain self-esteem, and ineffective efforts to withdraw from aversive environmental contingencies (Thomas, 2015). Although protocols vary, ACTp addresses experiential avoidance by helping individuals with psychosis take three steps:

1. Accept (i.e., willingness to contact) unavoidable psychological distress associated with psychosis without avoidance or struggle.
2. Notice psychotic experiences when they occur, without treating them as true or false (i.e., nonjudgmental awareness).
3. Identify and work toward valued goals, despite any symptoms present (Gaudiano et al., 2010).

Efficacy

Although several different types of acceptance/mindfulness-based psychotherapies have been adapted for individuals with psychosis (e.g., mindfulness-based cognitive therapy, person-based cognitive therapy for distressing psychosis, meta-cognitive therapy, compassion-focused therapy), ACTp is the most comprehensively studied of these "third-wave" approaches to date (Gaudiano, 2015). All studies conducted of these interventions have included patients being prescribed psychiatric medications in addition to receiving ACTp.

Currently, ACTp is the only acceptance/mindfulness-based therapy listed as an empirically supported treatment for psychosis by the American Psychological Association's Society of Clinical Psychology ("modest research support" designation) (Society of Clinical Psychology, 2016), which is based on the criteria originally proposed by Chambless and Hollon (1998). This designation was made based on the selective review of four individual studies that support the safety and efficacy of ACTp. Öst (2014) independently evaluated four ACTp randomized controlled trials (RCTs) and also concluded that the treatment meets APA's "modest research support" criteria. However, Atkins et al. (2017) detailed numerous systematic errors in Öst's data analysis and interpretation that could have underestimated the overall strength of ACT research in this area (and others). Newer meta-analyses are reviewed below.

Recent reviews of acceptance/mindfulness-based interventions for psychosis including RCTs of ACTp have generally concluded that these treatments are safe and efficacious for patients with psychosis (Aust & Bradshaw, 2017; Martins et al., 2017). More specifically, Wakefield et al. (2018) published a systematic review of ACTp evaluating 13 open trials and RCTs, using appropriate Preferred Reporting Items for Systematic Reviews and Meta-Analyses (PRISMA) methods (Moher et al., 2009). They noted that the intervention has been delivered in briefer formats, with individuals experiencing severe psychosis, and in those with complex comorbidities. Although Wakefield et al. did not report specific effect sizes in their review, they summarized previous ACTp studies reporting that the treatment showed statistically significant effects in reducing rehospitalization rates, improving indices of psychological flexibility, and improving psychotic and other psychiatric symptoms, as well as functioning. These effects tended to persist beyond the posttreatment period during follow-up when collected. Wakefield et al.'s assessment of the methodological characteristics of each trial revealed both strengths and weaknesses. Larger and more rigorous trials were called for based on this initial review.

More recently, Yıldız (2020) completed a systematic review limited to RCTs (*N* = 11) of ACTp. Studies were published between 2002 and 2018 in the United States and other countries (Australia, UK, Iran, Sweden, and Canada). Most of the studies used some version of treatment as usual as the control group (standard or enhanced in some way), and two studies used a time-and-attention matched "befriending" comparison condition. Sample sizes ranged from *N* = 13 for pilot studies to *N* = 96 for larger trials, and average age ranges for the samples were 27–50. The RCTs were conducted in both inpatient and outpatient samples, including those with comorbid childhood trauma and drug use disorders. Most study interventionists were trained ACT clinicians, with length of ACT treatment ranging from a few sessions over 1 week to 10 sessions over 12 months. Study follow-up periods were 3–6 months. The most commonly used symptom outcome measures included the Positive and Negative Syndrome Scale (Kay et al., 1987) and the Brief Psychiatric Rating Scale (Overall & Gorham, 1962), and 64% of studies used blind outcome raters. Results reported across the studies included small to large effect size improvements for ACTp on measures of psychotic symptoms ($d = .60$), anxiety ($d = .60$), depression ($d = .43–.93$), help-seeking ($d = .21–.43$), satisfaction ($d = .65$), and psychological flexibility ($d = 1.87$), as well as increased time to rehospitalization. Methodological quality scores for the 11 trials were rated as modest (ranging from 6 to 9 out of 10).

In addition to these reviews, a number of meta-analyses have provided evidence supporting ACTp. An early meta-analysis by Khoury et al. (2013) included 13 studies consisting of open trials and RCTs, five of which were of ACTp. Results showed that acceptance/mindfulness-based therapies had an overall moderate effect size pre–post (ES = 0.52, 95% CI [0.40, 0.64]) and relative to controls (ES = 0.41, 95% CI [0.23, 0.58]) across all clinical outcomes, which included positive, negative, and affective symptom domains. These effects tended to persist at follow-up time points. However, there was significant heterogeneity of effects given the diversity of interventions and samples included in this meta-analysis. Furthermore, specific types of interventions could not be independently investigated given the small number of studies on each approach. A subsequent meta-analysis of four RCTs of ACTp concluded that the treatment was effective for reducing negative symptom severity (SMD = 0.65, 95% CI [0.17, 1.13]) and rehospitalization rates (RR = 0.54, 95% CI [0.31, 0.95]), but not positive symptoms, relative to comparison conditions (Tonarelli et al., 2016). However, this meta-analysis was limited by the number of studies examined. Also, the authors recommended that future studies include larger samples, extended follow-ups, increased methodological rigor, and active treatment comparisons.

Several recent meta-analyses have been conducted of acceptance/mindfulness-based studies that have included trials of ACTp. Cramer et al. (2016) conducted a meta-analysis of eight RCTs of third-wave interventions for psychosis, including four studies involving ACTp. In the ACTp subanalysis conducted, the authors found significant effects for positive psychotic symptoms (SMD = −.63, 95% CI [−1.05, −0.22]) and rehospitalization rates (OR = 0.41, 95% CI [0.18, 0.95]), but not negative symptoms. It should be noted that the effect on positive symptoms reported by the authors was in contrast to those found in an earlier meta-analysis by Tonarelli et al. (2016), which noted the opposite effect (i.e., significant effects on positive, but not on negative symptoms for ACTp). However, this discrepancy may be accounted for by the fact that Tonarelli et al. (2016) and Cramer et al. (2016) examined a slightly different group of studies in their respective meta-analyses. In addition, Louise et al. (2018) conducted a meta-analysis of 10 RCTs of mindfulness, acceptance, and compassion-focused interventions for psychosis, which included four studies of ACTp. They found significant effects on overall psychotic symptom outcomes for mindfulness-based intervention studies using group therapy (g = .46) vs. ACTp studies using individual therapy (g = .08); but this effect was confounded by differences in methodology and comparison conditions in these studies. In particular, Louise et al. also failed to include several additional ACTp studies based on the restrictive study inclusion criteria used in their meta-analysis, which limited the conclusions that could be drawn.

Most recently, Wood et al. (2020) conducted a meta-analysis of 18 RCTs testing second- and third-wave cognitive-behavioral interventions for psychiatric inpatients with psychosis, including five studies of ACTp. Of note, results showed that third-wave interventions (including ACTp) had a stronger effect on total symptom outcomes compared with traditional CBTp interventions at posttreatment in these inpatient samples (SMD = −0.276, 95% CI [−0.510, −0.041] vs. SMD = −0.207, 95% CI [−0.742, 0.328], respectively). Additionally, Lincoln and Pedersen (2019) conducted a review of individual meta-analyses that have been conducted for various types of psychological interventions for psychosis. As noted above, ACTp meta-analyses conducted to date have used different collections of studies and examined various types of outcomes, leading to differences (and sometimes contradictions) in reported results. Consistent with this observation, Lincoln and Petersen concluded that acceptance/mindfulness-based interventions, including ACTp, appear to be efficacious when examined in meta-analyses, but that this conclusion is based on a relatively small number of studies analyzed to date that tend to vary based on the specific outcomes evaluated.

Dissemination

Less work has been conducted to date on the dissemination and implementation of ACTp. An implementation-focused open trial (n = 26) of ACTp for inpatients showed that the treatment was acceptable to patients and could be effectively delivered on a routine hospital unit by non-ACT specialist hospital staff (e.g., social workers, psychiatric nurses, occupational therapists) (Gaudiano et al., 2020). Results of this trial

indicated that patients' symptoms (d = .91, 95% CI [0.33, 1.47]), distress (d = .66, 95% CI [0.09, 1.21]), and mindfulness (d = −.68, 95% CI [−1.22, −0.11]) significantly improved at posttreatment through a four-month follow-up. Additional work has demonstrated that ACTp could be implemented successfully in community settings with 120 outpatients with psychosis, with results showing the intervention to be feasible, acceptable, and potentially effective as a routine frontline intervention in psychosis services (Butler et al., 2016). Recently, work has been conducted testing the dissemination of ACTp as part of mobile digital interventions to extend the reach and impact of the treatment (van Aubel et al., 2020).

Predictors and Moderators

Less work has been done to date investigating possible predictors and moderators of ACTp's treatment effects. Spidel et al. (2019) conducted an RCT including 50 participants with psychosis and childhood trauma who received an eight-week group ACTp intervention vs. treatment as usual. Overall, ACTp was found to improve symptom severity and acceptance, and treatment engagement was significantly higher in ACTp relative to the comparison group. However, trauma severity did not moderate the effectiveness of ACTp in the trial as hypothesized. Furthermore, in those receiving ACTp, an avoidance attachment style and lower number of sessions attended were predictive of poorer outcomes.

Processes and Mechanisms of Change

Extensive research has yet to be conducted on ACTp in terms of its processes and potential mediators of change. Khoury et al. (2013) conducted a meta-analysis that indicated that overall changes in mindfulness, acceptance, and compassion measures strongly predicted treatment outcomes, suggesting that acceptance/mindfulness treatments including ACTp may produce their effects by successfully altering these hypothesized mechanisms of action. In an RCT of ACTp for inpatients, Gaudiano et al. (2010) showed that changes in patients' believability of hallucinations, which was conceptualized as a proxy for cognitive defusion, statistically mediated the effects of ACT vs. treatment as usual on hallucination-related distress. Furthermore, a study combining data from two previous ACTp RCTs of inpatients with psychosis (Bach & Hayes, 2002; Gaudiano & Herbert, 2006) showed that changes in psychotic symptom believability also statistically mediated the effect that ACT vs. treatment as usual on rehospitalization rates at follow-up (Bach et al., 2013).

Research and Clinical Implications

In general, the methodological quality of the aforementioned studies of ACTp has varied, and larger samples with longer-term follow-ups are needed. In addition, information is needed comparing ACTp with other evidence-based psychosocial interventions (e.g., traditional CBT or family therapy) to better understand where the treatment might have the most significant advantages for patients. Furthermore, more research is needed on the real-world effectiveness and implementation of ACTp in typical clinical settings. Based on the evidence collected so far, ACTp appears to be a safe and efficacious treatment for patients with a range of psychotic-spectrum disorders and is one of the few treatments tested specifically for those with psychotic depression. Given its focus on acceptance, ACTp may be most appropriate and applicable for those with chronic (versus first episode) psychosis, where reducing ineffective struggle with symptoms over time may help decrease functional impairment. However, current National Institute for Health and Clinical Excellence treatment guidelines (2014) conclude that a larger body of research currently supports the efficacy of traditional CBT or family therapy for psychosis. Therefore, ACTp should be considered following a course of one of these evidence-based therapies first, if available, or based on patient preference.

Conclusions

In summary, a number of RCTs and open trials have been conducted since 2002 on ACTp. These studies generally demonstrate the safety, feasibility, and acceptability of the intervention to patients. Significant effects have been identified on positive and negative psychotic symptoms, depression, and functioning; although the magnitude of these effects has varied based on the measure used, characteristics of the sample, and selection of comparison condition. It should be noted that some of the conflicting conclusions about ACTp's effects on positive vs. negative symptoms may be largely attributable to the use of active treatment comparison conditions in some RCTs. This mirrors the equivocal results often found in RCTs of traditional CBT for psychosis when compared to other psychological therapies (Lynch et al., 2010). Most consistently, several studies have reported effects related to reduced rehospitalization rates for those receiving ACTp relative to treatment as usual alone. Furthermore, ACTp has been used in psychiatric inpatient as well as in outpatient settings, for those with first episode or early psychosis as well as those with chronic illness, and in those with major depression with psychotic features. ACTp has been delivered in group and individual formats. Although significant moderators have not been identified to date, some evidence suggests that ACTp works through reducing believability of psychotic symptoms and avoidance predicts poorer outcomes. At this time, ACTp is an evidence-based option for people with psychosis where alternative treatments (e.g., CBT for psychosis, family intervention) are not available or preferred by the patient.

DIALECTICAL BEHAVIOR THERAPY FOR BORDERLINE PERSONALITY DISORDER AND SUICIDALITY

Borderline personality disorder (BPD) is a psychological disorder first officially classified in the DSM in 1980 (Gunderson, 2009). Despite the fact that the diagnostic criteria for the disorder has not changed since the publication of DSM-III-R in 1987 (American Psychiatric Association, 1987), hundreds of scientific studies have been conducted on the disorder that have advanced our knowledge about the etiology, topography, phenomenology, associated problems, and long-term course of the disorder. Perhaps most striking is the knowledge

that what was once considered a nontreatable condition now has a number of treatments that have been found to be effective at reducing target problems.

DBT is arguably the most widely used and disseminated evidence-based treatment for BPD. DBT is a comprehensive and complex treatment designed to address a complex disorder. Although adapted for different settings and populations, "standard" outpatient DBT is a specific treatment model that includes four components, or modes, of treatment: individual therapy, skills training (usually in the form of groups), intersession phone coaching, and therapist consultation team. DBT has a stage model of treatment, which indicates that treatment should be matched to the client's level of disorder (Linehan, 1999), beginning at Stage 1 and proceeding through Stage 4. Despite the stage model that Linehan proposed, the vast majority of research on DBT's efficacy and effectiveness has been conducted on Stage 1 DBT. Stage 1 DBT is used to treat the highest level of disorder among clients, as indicated by moderate-to-severe behavioral dyscontrol. Behavior dyscontrol can be evidenced by many different topographies of behavior including suicidal behavior, NSSI, impulsive behavior, problematic substance/alcohol use, etc. The overarching goal of DBT is to develop "a life worth living."

Efficacy and Effectiveness

The first randomized controlled trial (RCT) of DBT involved 44 chronically suicidal and/or self-injuring women who met criteria for borderline personality disorder (Linehan et al., 1991). One year of DBT was compared to treatment as usual (TAU), and assessments were conducted every four months. Individuals in DBT condition had lower rates of dropout, fewer episodes of suicide attempts and nonsuicidal self-injury (then referred to as *parasuicidal acts*), and less time in ancillary psychiatric inpatient treatment, compared to individuals in the TAU condition. However, given the relatively small sample size and the lack of standardized, psychometrically validated measures for key variables at that time, more research was necessary to demonstrate the efficacy of DBT over standard care for BPD.

There have now been over 30 RCTs conducted on DBT and three meta-analytical studies that have included 5 to 18 studies (DeCou et al., 2019; Kliem et al, 2010; Panos et al., 2014). The most recent meta-analyses by DeCou and colleagues (2019) used 18 controlled trials to examine the efficacy of DBT in reducing suicidal behavior and NSSI compared to control conditions. While most of these studies included only individuals with BPD, a number were with non-BPD samples who engaged in suicidal or self-injurious behavior. This meta-analysis revealed a small difference favoring DBT over control conditions for suicidal behavior and NSSI (weighted mean effect size, $d = -.32$) and use of crisis services (weighted mean effect size, $d = -.38$). Results from the meta-analysis further indicated that DBT was not superior to control conditions in reducing suicidal ideation in the 10 studies in which it was measured, suggesting that DBT could be refined to improve its capacity to target this variable. Another meta-analysis of 16 studies (Kliem, et al., 2010) found a pre- to postintervention global effect sizes for DBT of .39.

The efficacy RCT studies have spanned several independent research groups and included both adolescent and adult samples (e.g., Linehan et al., 1993; 2015; McCauley et al., 2018; McMain et al., 2009; Mehlum et al., 2014; van den Bosch et al., 2002; Verheul et al., 2003). The most common outcome studied in DBT trials is changes in suicide attempts and self-harming behavior. The majority of RCTs of DBT for BPD have included suicidal behavior, NSSI, or substance use as an inclusion criteria for participation, which defines the study population as one that has moderate to severe behavioral dyscontrol. These research trials have also generally constricted the length of DBT treatment to one year (or six months in later trials). However, this treatment length is a somewhat arbitrary artifact of research funding limitations, and Linehan herself never thought that one year of DBT was fully sufficient at addressing all the problems for which a person with BPD might seek therapy (Linehan, 1993).

Although one-year treatment duration has been common in DBT RCTs, other research examining a six-month course of DBT has also found significant changes over time (Carter et al., 2010; Rizvi et al., 2017). For example, Rizvi and colleagues (2017) examined a six-month course of DBT delivered by graduate student trainees for 50 participants and found significant decreases in rates of suicide attempts and NSSI comparing the six months of treatment to the six months before treatment. Further, using self-report measures of psychopathology outcomes, they conducted benchmark analyses against a large-scale RCT (McMain et al., 2009) of one-year of DBT (see more details below) and found equivalent effect size magnitudes (i.e., d = .89 and 1.23 for measures of BPD symptomatology; d = .68 and .73 for global psychopathology measure).

More recent research using standardized control treatments has been less likely to find a clear superiority in favor of DBT (Clarkin et al., 2007; McMain et al., 2009). Clarkin et al. (2007) compared DBT to transference focused psychotherapy (TFP) and supportive therapy in 90 individuals with BPD and found that clients in the TFP and DBT conditions each showed significant improvements in suicidality as measured by the Overt Aggression Scale-Modified (TFP effect size r = .33; DBT effect size r = .34). McMain et al. (2009) conducted the largest RCT of DBT with 180 individuals randomized to either DBT or general psychiatric management (GPM). Both groups improved on number of suicide attempts and NSSI episodes over time (OR = .40, p < .001) but did not differ from each other (OR = .92, p = .76). Similarly, on normally distributed measures of BPD symptomatology and depression, effect size magnitudes of d = 1.13 and 1.10, respectively, indicate improvement over time but no differences between the two treatments. Data from these trials suggest that a structured treatment delivered with high treatment integrity and that targets suicidal behavior as its highest priority can yield similar results to DBT. Future research is necessary to understand what the critical and essentially unique components of DBT are and how these can be harnessed to improve outcomes.

To that end, attention has also turned to whether DBT can be broken down into its component parts (individual therapy, skills training, phone coaching, and therapist consultation team) and studied so that we can gain a better understanding of which are the necessary "ingredients" of DBT. In a landmark dismantling trial, Linehan and colleagues (2015) randomized suicidal or self-injuring people with BPD to either standard DBT, individual DBT without DBT skills training but with an activities group (DBT-I), or DBT skills training without individual therapy but with individual case management (DBT-S). Results indicated no differences between the three conditions on the occurrence of suicide attempts or NSSI (present/absent variable) or on number of suicide attempts. In terms of frequency of NSSI episodes, however, rates were significantly higher in DBT-I compared to DBT and DBT-S. Individuals in DBT-I also improved less in terms of depression and anxiety variables during the one year of treatment, but tended to "catch up" during the follow-up year. These results seem to suggest that skills training may be a particular important component of DBT and that pairing it with other types of individual therapy/case management may be efficacious.

Independent of component analysis trials, there have been many studies that have evaluated a DBT skills-only intervention (i.e., no accompanying individual DBT therapy). These studies have ranged from relatively short (8 weekly sessions; e.g., Rizvi & Steffel, 2014) to longer treatment lengths (20 weekly sessions; e.g., McMain et al., 2017) among samples of people with a wide variety of mental health problems. McMain and colleagues (2017) compared 20 weeks of DBT skills training for those with BPD to a wait-list control and showed that the individuals who received skills training exhibited greater reductions in suicidal and self-harming behaviors than those on the wait list at the 12-week follow-up, but no difference immediately posttreatment. However, individuals in the skills group condition had statistically significant differences in other variables measured at posttreatment, including BPD symptomatology (d = .32), anger (d = .80), and global symptom distress (d = .42). Similarly, Soler et al. (2009) compared 12 weeks of DBT skills training or standard group therapy for people with BPD. Suicidal and NSSI outcomes were not measured in this trial, but DBT skills training outperformed the control condition in terms of drop out, anger, depression, anxiety, and emotional instability. Studies have also examined the efficacy DBT skills training for non-BPD populations. Neasciu and colleagues (2014) compared DBT skills groups alone for individuals who had an anxiety or depression disorder with high emotion dysregulation (but not BPD) to an activities-based support group. DBT skills training outperformed the activities-based support group in reducing emotion dysregulation and anxiety, but not depression (Neasciu et al., 2014). These studies suggest that DBT skills training alone may be an efficacious intervention for BPD and related problems.

Finally, a growing body of DBT effectiveness trials (e.g., Barnicot et al., 2014; Feigenbaum et al., 2011; Goodman et al., 2016; Koons et al., 2001; Pistorello et al., 2012) examine DBT employed in "real-world settings." For example, Pistorello et al. (2012) examined DBT adapted for the context of a college counseling center compared to optimized TAU for 63 college students and found significantly greater decreases in suicidality, depression, number of NSSI events (if participant had self-injured), and BPD criteria in DBT compared to TAU. Modifications of DBT for this setting included reducing length of skills training sessions and having different attendance policies than standard DBT to account for semester breaks and summer. Feigenbaum and colleagues (2014) conducted a DBT effectiveness trial in the UK National Health Service with 42 patients randomized to receive DBT or TAU. Their results were similar to DBT efficacy trials in that both conditions demonstrated improvements over time, however, they also had notable dropout rate in that only 11 of the 26 randomized to DBT completed a year of treatment.

Despite the sheer volume of research on DBT, three methodological issues make it difficult to fully assess DBT's impact on variables of interest across studies:

1. There is no standard, empirically validated method of training DBT therapists.
2. At the moment, the measure used to determine therapist adherence to DBT (Linehan & Korslund, 2003) is unwieldy, expensive, and time-consuming. As a result, only about one-third of DBT RCTs have reported adherence scores (Miga et al., 2018).
3. Lack of long-term follow-up data has made it difficult to assess the longer-term impact of DBT on individuals with BPD.

Although some of these issues are to be expected, given the complexity of the treatment and the population, the end result leaves many unanswered questions about DBT's efficacy and what is needed to achieve the best outcomes.

Dissemination

Compared to many other evidence-based psychosocial treatments, DBT has been disseminated widely since its conception (Swenson, 2000). According to Behavioral Tech, a leading training company developed by Linehan, over 40,000 clinicians have attended a DBT workshop or training (https://behavioraltech.org/about-us/our-impact/). DBT has also been increasingly used worldwide, and not just in English-speaking countries. DBT trainings have been conducted in more than 30 countries, including Brazil, Egypt, China, and Russia (Ivanoff, 2018).

Despite these metrics of the success of DBT dissemination, there are considerable barriers to the successful implementation of DBT across settings and populations. DBT is a complex treatment developed for a complex population. It is comprised of hundreds of different strategies to employ with high-risk clients. Some studies have identified barriers to implementation in large systems. For example, Carmel, Rose, and Fruzzetti (2014) coded interviews with 19 clinicians undergoing DBT training in a large public health system and identified three thematic challenges to DBT implementation: programmatic challenges in developing and sustaining a DBT program (e.g., staff turnover rates, recruitment of appropriate clients), a lack of administrative support or organizational investment in DBT, and time commitment of providing DBT (e.g., more time spent per client in DBT, compared to other clients in the system). These themes were echoed in a qualitative interview study of administrators themselves (Herschell et al., 2009). Administrators stated that while DBT has good *face validity*, there were significant hurdles to its adoption in their setting including staff

time, turnover, tight budgets, and shifting priorities. Importantly, these problems are not necessarily specific to DBT. However, they highlight the need to have systematic plans to address them if more widespread implementation is to be achieved.

Predictors and Moderators

Very few studies have looked at predictors and moderators of treatment response in DBT. Gratz and colleagues (2020) examined whether a comorbid PTSD diagnosis predicted DBT treatment response in a sample of 56 consecutive admissions to an outpatient DBT program. They found that the 14 individuals who met criteria for PTSD at admission did not differ in rates of improvement in BPD symptomatology than the 32 individuals without PTSD. Although not a primary focus of their study, they found that older age was associated with significantly less improvement in both BPD symptom severity and emotion regulation difficulties suggesting that age may be an important predictor variable to study further. Seow et al. (2020) conducted a moderated mediation analysis with 102 individuals in a 12-week DBT program to examine whether severity of BPD symptomatology (a continuous measure, independent of diagnosis) moderated the relationship between skills use and outcomes. Their results demonstrated that pretreatment BPD symptom levels moderated the effect of skills use on posttreatment psychological distress. Specifically, in individuals with moderate to high levels of BPD symptoms, greater skills use and more positive attitudes toward skills use were linked to lower levels of psychological distress at posttreatment, whereas there was no significant relationship between skills use and posttreatment psychological distress in patients with low levels of BPD symptoms at pretreatment.

Future studies are necessary to determine who best responds to DBT in order to develop more efficient treatment recommendations. These studies should include a common set of variables (like demographic factors and BPD severity) in order to best assess these predictors.

Processes and Mechanisms of Change

Despite the presence of dozens of studies on DBT's efficacy with BPD and associated problems, there is a relative scarcity of research on process variables and mechanisms of change. However, in recent years more attention has been paid to these areas. Given the complexity of the treatment, many are eager to identify the key components of DBT that are most likely to lead to change, and thus perhaps simplify the treatment to increase its efficacy and ability to be easily disseminated.

Lynch et al. (2006) initially proposed possible mechanisms of change in DBT. Since a key tenet of DBT is that emotion dysregulation is the core to the behaviors associated with BPD, they suggested that many of their proposed mechanisms (e.g., mindfulness, chain analysis, exposure to emotion cues) are, in essence, methods to reduce the expression of ineffective action tendencies (urges) associated with emotions. Boritz et al. (2017) suggests that emotion regulation components are key mechanisms in DBT, specifically (i) increased awareness and acceptance of emotion; (ii) increased attentional control; (iii) increased ability to modulate emotion; and (iv) increased use of adaptive coping skills. However, research on these mechanisms in DBT is limited. Most studies of DBT mechanisms have been conducted on skills use and have found that increased self-reported use of skills mediates outcomes.

Neacsiu et al. (2010) combined data from three outcome trials of DBT for BPD and found that an increase in DBT skills use over time (i) fully mediated the relationship between time in treatment and decrease in likelihood of suicide attempts; (ii) partially mediated the increase in likelihood of no NSSI episodes to occur over time in treatment; and (iii) fully mediated improvements in indices of depression and anger over time. In a study of individuals who received only 20 weeks of DBT skills training, improvements in mindfulness and distress tolerance skills each independently indirectly affected the relationship between the DBT treatment and general psychopathology at posttreatment (Zeifman et al., 2020).

There is an increasing body of research indicating that mindfulness broadly (not unique to DBT) increases attentional control and reduces emotional and behavioral dysregulation (Gratz & Tull, 2010). Studies on mindfulness within DBT for BPD are limited, and often uncontrolled, but suggest that increases in mindfulness are related to decreases in BPD symptomatology (e.g., (e.g., Perroud et al., 2012; Soler et al., 2012). Carson-Wong and Rizvi (2016) developed an evaluator-rated scale of validation strategies in DBT sessions. Using that scale, they found that different validation strategies were specifically related to changes in clients' ratings of affect states during individual DBT sessions (Carson-Wong et al., 2018). Specifically, overall use of validation was not related to changes in negative affect but use of higher levels of validation strategies were. These higher levels include validation in terms of historical antecedents, current causes, and being radically genuine with the client (Linehan, 1997). These validation strategies might be considered specific to DBT, in that they had not been previously articulated as strategies to use with clients with BPD.

Conclusions

The starting point for the development of DBT was to create a treatment, with behavioral roots, to address a population previously thought untreatable. The field has come a long way in supporting that a behavioral treatment, with acceptance and dialectical strategies added, is the treatment of choice for BPD. Since the initial efficacy trial (Linehan, et al., 1991), there have been more than 30 RCTs conducted on DBT for BPD and numerous other studies on DBT for other problems and conditions (Miga et al., 2018). Together, this research suggests that DBT reduces suicide attempts, nonsuicidal self-injury episodes, and use of crisis services, including hospitalization. More research is needed to determine ways in which DBT can be more efficient and effective across different populations and settings.

MINDFULNESS AND ACCEPTANCE-BASED THERAPIES FOR EATING DISORDERS

MABTs have increasingly become one of the most frequently used treatments in clinical practice for eating disorders including anorexia nervosa (AN), bulimia nervosa (BN), and

binge eating disorder (BED) (Linardon et al., 2017). For example, in one recent study, patients with an eating disorder were more likely to report that their therapist used mindfulness techniques (77%) than CBT techniques such as food monitoring records (53%) or weekly in-session weigh-ins (39%) (Cowdrey & Waller, 2015). Despite the large clinical enthusiasm for MABTs for eating disorders, no one MABT approach stands out in terms of evidence base or clinical utilization. In fact, mindfulness-based eating awareness training (MB-EAT), ACT, and DBT, as well as integrative MABT packages, all are commonly used and have been subject of study. Of note, there is considerable overlap in the components, included in the existing treatments and the way that they are applied to eating disorder treatment with the most common components being (i) *mindful awareness*; (ii) *distress tolerance*; (iii) *emotion modulation*; and (iv) *values-based decision-making*. Accordingly, we review findings from studies of MABTs that utilize these components.

Efficacy

Preliminary evidence suggests that MABTs can be efficacious for a range of eating disorder diagnoses (Godfrey et al., 2015; Katterman et al., 2014; Linardon et al., 2017). For example, a 2017 meta-analysis identified 27 studies of MABTs for eating disorders and found statistically significant, moderate-to-large improvements in primary outcomes (i.e., global eating disorder pathology, remission, and binge eating frequency) and secondary outcomes (i.e., other cognitive symptoms of eating disorders such as weight and shape concern, depression scores, self-esteem) from pre- to posttreatment and follow-up (Linardon et al., 2017). For example, for studies that tested an MABT for BED, pre–post effect size estimates for global eating disorder psychopathology were $g = 1.18$ (95% CI [0.92, 1.44]) and for studies that tested an MABT in AN, BN, or in a transdiagnostic sample, pre–post effect size estimates were $g = 1.07$ (95% CI [0.85, 1.28]). Five distinct types of MABTs were included in this meta-analysis (e.g., dialectical behavioral therapy ($n = 14$), acceptance and commitment therapy ($n = 2$), mindfulness-based interventions ($n = 6$), compassion-focused therapy ($n = 3$), and schema therapy ($n = 2$), but no particular treatment produced a consistently larger effect size in outcome variables.

Of the 27 studies included in this meta-analysis, 13 used an RCT design. MABTs were consistently more efficacious than wait-list controls on all primary outcome variables: for example, for global eating disorder psychopathology; BED: $g = 0.92$ (95% CI [0.60, 1.25]); AN, BN, transdiagnostic sample: $g = 1.13$ (95% CI [0.61, 1.66]). MABTs were of comparable efficacy to other active comparison groups including CBT: for example, for global eating disorder psychopathology; BED: $g = 0.52$ (95% CI [–0.11, 1.16]); AN, BN, transdiagnostic sample: $g = –0.08$ (95% CI [–0.41, 0.24]). Since this 2017 meta-analysis, five additional RCTs have been published on MABTs for eating disorders. Of these, four compared an MABT to a wait-list control (Duarte et al., 2017; Pinto-Gouveia et al., 2017; Rahmani et al., 2018; Strandskov et al., 2017) and one additional study compared DBT to a CBT-informed group treatment in women with co-morbid borderline personality disorder and transdiagnostic eating pathology (Pinto-Gouveia et al., 2017). The results of these studies since the 2017 meta-analysis have broadly followed the same pattern, suggesting that MABTs are superior to wait-list controls and of comparable efficacy to standard treatment approaches.

While these results may seem promising, it is important to acknowledge that there is wide variability in rigor and design across the studies included in this meta-analysis that makes interpretation of this body of work difficult. Of the 27 studies included in the most recent meta-analysis, the majority were small, uncontrolled open trials. Only 13 studies were RCTs and, of those, 9 compared to either wait-list control (*n* = 6) or a minimally active control condition (*n* = 3). With the addition of the one additional active comparative trial since 2017, this leaves only five clinical trials that compared an MABT to an active treatment approach such as CBT (the current treatment for eating disorders with the largest evidence base). Of the five studies that compared to an active treatment, only three RCTs compared to gold-standard CBT. While each of these trials reported comparable efficacy between the MABT package tested in that trial and CBT, these trials were underpowered for comparisons of two active treatments and for tests of non-inferiority (Chen et al., 2017; Navarro-Haro et al., 2018; Wonderlich et al., 2014). For example, in the Wonderlich et al. study, 80 adults with BN were randomized to receive either CBT or integrative cognitive affective therapy, an emotion-focused MABT designed specifically for eating disorders. After 19 weeks of treatment, intent-to-treat rates for symptom remission for ICAT (37.5% at end of treatment, 32.5% at follow-up) and CBT-E (22.5% at both end of treatment and follow-up) were not significantly different, although the authors acknowledge they were underpowered to compare two active treatment approaches.

The low sample size is a concern across the range of MABTs tested for eating disorders to date. For example, the average sample size of the 13 RCTs included in the 2017 review was 58 participants, who were then split between either two or three treatment conditions. Adding to the difficulties in interpretation, the body of research as a whole has widely varied in how it was implemented (e.g., length, frequency, and number of sessions; group vs. individual) and in what specific MABT components were tested. Given that MABT treatment packages can vary widely in which treatment component they use and emphasize, we cannot assume that different treatment packages would produce the same treatment results. For example, although two of the existing RCTs that compared an MABT to CBT tested DBT (Chen et al., 2017; Navarro-Haro et al., 2018), the numerous components included in DBT (e.g., mindfulness, distress tolerance, emotion regulation, interpersonal effectiveness) and the intensive nature of the DBT treatments studied (e.g., weekly individual treatment plus weekly skills groups) limit our ability to generalize these results to other MABTs or to know which specific MABT components may be driving results.

Predictors and Moderators

The consistent finding that MABTs appear similarly effective overall compared to CBTs or other active treatment approaches supports a need to assess predictors and moderators of treatment outcomes to determine what pretreatment characteristics differentiate could be used to inform treatment matching. A recent review found that of the 39 manuscripts published to date, only four tested predictors of treatment response and only two tested moderators of response in an RCT (neither of which compared to CBT), limiting our ability to determine whether some patients may show differential improvement to CBT vs. an MABT based on the literature to date (Barney et al., 2019). Of the two moderator analyses, both showed a tendency for individuals with greater severity or length of illness to do better in the MABT condition. Although not statistically significant, Juarascio et al.'s (2013) findings showed a trend toward those with more severe eating disorder symptoms at baseline, showing greater improvements in eating disorder symptoms when they received ACT plus treatment as usual at a residential treatment facility compared to treatment as usual alone (Juarascio, 2013). Robinson and Safer (2012) found that individuals with early onset of overweight and dieting behaviors had fewer days of binge eating when treated with DBT compared to an active control condition (Robinson, 2012).

Processes and Mechanisms of Change

Despite calls for more research on mechanisms of action in eating disorder treatment research (Murphy et al., 2009), very few studies have evaluated mechanisms of action in eating disorder research as a whole (Brauhardt et al., 2014; Vall & Wade, 2015). A recent review conducted by Barney and colleagues found that this lack of mechanistic research extends to MABTs for eating disorders (Barney et al., 2019). Barney et al.'s (2019) systematic review found that of 39 manuscripts published on MABTs for BN or BED, 12 did not examine any relevant process variables, 20 examined pre–post change analyses only, five assessed for mechanisms of action by comparing change in process measure and ED symptoms through analyses such as Pearson correlations or regression, and only two used formal mediation analyses. The most frequently examined process variables were emotion regulation (*n* = 11), general mindfulness or specific mindfulness skills (*n* = 5), urges to eat in response to negative emotions (*n* = 4), and psychological flexibility (*n* = 4 studies). Pre–post change in process variables was largely consistent with hypotheses, though some mixed results were observed across studies. For example, among DBT-based studies that examined emotion regulation as a process variable, three studies found no significant pre–post changes in patients' emotion regulation following the DBT-based treatment, and the remaining studies showed variable levels of improvement ranging from small to large effect sizes. Some process variables such as psychological flexibility (in ACT-based treatments) and mindfulness (in mindfulness-based treatments) have shown greater consistency, with all studies listed in the review finding improvements in these process variables. Of the two trials that did conduct formal mediation analyses (one for an ACT-based treatment (Juarascio, 2013) and one for a mindfulness-based treatment), both did find support for improvements in psychological flexibility mediating improvement in eating disorder symptoms, provided some early support for psychological flexibility as a mechanism of action. Although simple analyses of pre–post changes in MABT constructs was more common (and results have largely been consistent with hypothesized mechanisms), inadequate study design (e.g., lack of mid-treatment assessments), inconsistency in measurement tools, and the lack of adequate comparison conditions (e.g., to test whether changes in MABT constructs also occur in CBT) limit our ability to understand mechanisms of action for existing MABTs.

Conclusions

MABTs for eating disorders are a rising area of study, and preliminary evidence suggests that MABTs produce large and clinically significant improvements in binge eating (Godfrey et al., 2015; Katterman et al., 2014). Further, MABTs have quickly become one of the most frequently used treatments in clinical practice for eating disorders, with one recent study showing that therapist are more likely to use mindfulness-based techniques than CBT-specific techniques (Cowdrey & Waller, 2015). Despite the promise of MABTs, numerous limitations in the state of the literature limit our ability to confirm the efficacy of MABTs or determine mechanisms of action and predictors/moderators of treatment outcome and further treatment trials are warranted.

ACCEPTANCE AND COMMITMENT THERAPY FOR SMOKING

Worldwide, tobacco smoking is the second leading cause of early death and disability (GBD 2015 Tobacco Collaborators, 2016), attributable to over 1 in 10 deaths (GBD 2015 Tobacco Collaborators, 2017). The current standard in smoking cessation behavioral interventions follow the US Clinical Practice Guidelines [USCPG; (Fiore et al., 2008)]. The USCPG have the following essential content for behavioral intervention: tracking smoking status, assisting in quit planning and setting a quit date, advice on FDA approved pharmacotherapy for smoking cessation, motivational interviewing to enhance motivation, cognitive behavioral skills to prevent relapse, and advice of identifying and eliciting social support for quitting (Abroms et al., 2013; Abroms et al., 2011; Fiore et al., 2000; Fiore et al., 2008). Depending on the modality of delivery, multiple meta-analyses of USCPG behavioral interventions report modest weighted average 12-month outcomes of 6–25% smoking cessation rates (Civljak et al., 2010; Lancaster & Stead, 2017; Stead et al., 2013, 2017; Webb, 2009; Whittaker et al., 2019). While these success rates are generally higher than the 4% success rate from quitting smoking on one's own (Fiore et al., 2008), there is great room for improvement.

With the aim of improving on the modest success rates of USCPG interventions, since 2004, 15 randomized clinical trials have been published that compare acceptance and commitment therapy (ACT) to USCPG interventions for tobacco smoking cessation. When applied to smoking cessation, acceptance in ACT means making room for intense physical cravings (e.g., urges to smoke), emotions (e.g., sadness that cues smoking), and thoughts (e.g., thoughts that cue smoking) while allowing these experiences to come and go. Commitment in ACT means articulating what is deeply important and meaningful to individuals – that is, their values – (e.g., caring about their health) to motivate and guide specific plans of action (e.g., stopping smoking).

Efficacy

The published randomized clinical trials comparing ACT with USCPG behavioral interventions have been conducted in four delivery modalities: group therapy, telephone coaching, website, and smartphone application. The efficacy of ACT in each of these modalities is reviewed here.

Group Therapy

Despite the numerous barriers to accessing group-delivered intervention for smoking cessation interventions, including lack of reimbursement and low patient demand (Husten, 2010), group therapy for smoking cessation remains available (Stead et al., 2017). Pilot trials have shown the promise of group-delivered (or group plus individual therapy) ACT but have been hindered by critical methodological limitations, including small sample size, quasi-experimental design, lack of a behavioral intervention control arm (e.g., comparison was medications only), and exclusion of people with substance use and psychiatric comorbidities (e.g., Brown et al., 2018; Gifford et al., 2011). Collectively, these trials provided context for a larger randomized trial of group-delivered ACT that compared five weekly 90-minute sessions of ACT to five weekly 90-minute sessions of group-delivered UCSPG skills therapy in a sample of 450 adults smoking at least 10 cigarettes per day (McClure et al., 2020). In both treatment arms, participants received eight weeks of nicotine replacement therapy. Master's level therapists delivered the interventions with a high level of adherence to their respective interventions (4.9 out of 5 in each arm). Smoking cessation rates did not differ between study arms at the main outcome of no smoking in the past 30 days (i.e., 30-day point prevalence abstinence) and at the 12-month follow-up (13.8% for ACT vs. 18.1% for USCPG; OR = .68, 95% CI [0.35, 1.27]). Taken together, the current evidence base from randomized trials suggests that group-delivered ACT is a reasonable alternative to group-delivered USCPG intervention for smoking cessation.

Telephone Coaching

Smoking cessation quitlines (QLs) have become an integral component of the public health approach to tobacco control, both in the United States and worldwide (Fiore et al., 2000; Fiore et al., 2008). In the US alone, quitlines now reach over 350,000 smokers each year (Consortium, 2017). However, their weighted average 30-day quit rate is 14% (8–20%) at 12 months postrandomization (Fiore et al., 2008; Matkin et al., 2019). An ACT approach addressed the need to improve their success rate in a pilot randomized trial (N = 121) that compared telephone therapist-delivered ACT to USCPG telephone therapist-delivered intervention, with both interventions offering five sessions [30 minutes for Call 1; 15 minutes for Calls 2–5; (Bricker, Bush et al., 2014). All participants, adults smoking at least 10 cigarettes per day, received a standard two-week course of nicotine patch or gum (participant's choice) – consistent with pharmacotherapy practices of the quitline (South Carolina State Quitline) from where participants were recruited at the time of the trial enrollment. This pilot trial showed promising results: the intent-to-treat 30-day point prevalence abstinence rates at 6 months postrandomization were 31% in ACT versus 22% in USCPG (OR = 1.5, 95% CI [0.7, 3.4]).

Website

Eleven million US smokers each year, and many millions more worldwide, use websites to help them quit smoking (Borrelli et al., 2015). Randomized trials testing websites for smoking cessation have weighted average 12-month follow-up data retention rates of 34% (range: 11–72%). The weighted-average 12-month 30-day point prevalence cessation rate for previous web-delivered intervention trials was 9% [range: 7% to 17% (Graham et al., 2016; Taylor et al., 2017)].

Two randomized trials have compared web-delivered ACT to web-delivered USCPG for smoking cessation. The first was a pilot randomized trial of 222 US adults smoking at least five cigarettes per day, comparing the ACT-based WebQuit.org website with the US National Cancer Institute's USCGP-based Smokefree.gov website (Bricker et al., 2013). No medication was provided in either arm. Results showed that more than double the fraction of participants in the ACT arm quit smoking as compared to the Smokefree arm at the three-months post randomization follow-up (23% vs. 10%; OR = 3.05; 95% CI [1.01, 9.32]). These results motivated a full-scale randomized trial comparing WebQuit.org with Smokefree.gov in a sample of 2637 adults smokers (at least five cigarettes per day) recruited from all 50 US states (Bricker et al., 2018). No medication was provided in either arm. The 12-month follow-up data retention rate was 88% (2309/2637). The 30-day point prevalence abstinence rates at the 12-month follow-up were 24% (278/1141) for WebQuit.org and 26% (305/1168) for Smokefree.gov (OR = 0.91; 95% CI [0.76, 1.10]). The difference in observed quit rates between the two trials was potentially due to the study design of the pilot (Bricker et al., 2013) vs. the full-scale trial (Bricker et al., 2018): the pilot trial had a lower retention rate (54% vs. 88%), smaller sample size (222 vs. 2637), and shorter follow-up period (3 months vs. 12 months) (Bricker et al., 2013). With a quit rate that is over two times higher than the average quit rate of web-delivered interventions (24% vs. 9%), together the two trials suggest that web-delivered ACT, in particular WebQuit, is a helpful option for people seeking online help for quitting smoking.

Smartphone Applications

Since 2012, smartphone applications for smoking cessation have been serving as digital interventions with high population-level reach (Whittaker et al., 2019). Approximately 490 English-language smoking cessation applications have now been downloaded an estimated total of 33 million times.[a] In the

United States, the reach of smoking cessation applications has been aided by the fact that, as of 2019, 81% of all adults owned smartphones – up from 35% in 2011 (Center, 2019). Despite their ubiquity, smartphone applications tested in randomized trials had six-month follow-up cessation rates ranging from 4% to 18% (Whittaker et al., 2019).

Two randomized trials have compared smartphone-delivered ACT to smartphone-delivered USCPG for smoking cessation. The first was a pilot randomized trial of 196 US adults smoking at least five cigarettes per day, comparing the ACT-based application SmartQuit with the US National Cancer Institute's USCGP-based QuitGuide application (Bricker, Mull et al., 2014). No medication was provided in either arm. On the primary outcome of 30-day point prevalence abstinence at two months post randomization, the quit rates were 13% in SmartQuit vs. 8% in QuitGuide (OR = 2.7; 95% CI [0.8–10.3]). The second was a full-scale randomized trial comparing the ACT-based application called iCanQuit with QuitGuide in a sample of 2415 adults smokers (at least five cigarettes per day) recruited from all 50 US states (Bricker, Watson, Mull et al., 2020). No medication was provided in either arm. The 12-month follow-up data retention rate was 87.2% (2107/2415). For the primary outcome of 30-day point prevalence at the 12-month follow-up, iCanQuit participants had 1.49 times higher odds of quitting smoking as compared to QuitGuide participants (28.2% [293/1040] abstinent vs. 21.1% [225/1067] abstinent; OR = 1.49; 95% CI [1.22, 1.83]). Effect sizes were very similar and statistically significant for all secondary outcomes (OR range: 1.26 to 2.20). This trial provides strong evidence that, relative to a USCPG-based smartphone application, an ACT-based smartphone application was more efficacious for quitting cigarette smoking and thus can be an impactful treatment choice.

Special Populations

Five pilot randomized trials have examined the initial efficacy of ACT for these special populations of smokers: early lapsers, young adults, mentally ill, and cancer patients. Regarding early lapsers, these are smokers who have not been able to achieve at least 72 hours of abstinence from a quit attempt and it is believed that this phenomenon is due to an inability to tolerate distress – mainly of nicotine withdrawal. Therefore, a group plus individual therapy (9 × 2-hour group and 6 × 50-minute individual sessions) treatment that compared combined gradual exposure to withdrawal-related distress with ACT skills training to standard behavioral therapy, with both arms providing 8 weeks of nicotine patch, was piloted in a randomized trial of 49 early relapsers (Brown et al., 2013). Results showed that the main effect of treatment condition was promising but not statistically significant in the 4- to 16-week follow-up period (OR = 1.83; 95% CI [0.46, 7.34]).

Regarding young adults smokers, who have the highest smoking rates of any age group, a study of 84 university student smokers compared a six-session avatar-led ACT intervention with a wait-list control, finding highly promising but not statistically significant differences at end of treatment (OR = 3.10; 95% CI [0.92, 10.41]; Karekla et al., 2020). Regarding mentally ill, who have high smoking rates, a pilot randomized

[a] April 2020 analysis by SensorTower.com of all English-language cigarette smoking cessation applications on the Google Play and Apple App Store downloaded to smartphone devices.

trial (N = 62) compared a smartphone-delivered ACT intervention tailored to the seriously mentally ill (e.g., bipolar disorder) to QuitGuide, finding highly promising but not statistically significant differences in quit rates at the 16-week follow-up (OR = 3.86; 95% CI [41, 36]; Vilardaga et al., 2019). A pilot randomized trial (N = 51) comparing WebQuit tailored to bipolar smokers to Smokefree.gov found, in both arms, identical quit rates at 4-week posttreatment follow-up (8%; OR = .96; 95% CI [0.12, 7.57]; Heffner, Kelly et al., 2020). Finally, cancer patients who smoke, up to 80% of whom continue to smoke after diagnosis, were randomized into a pilot randomized trial (N = 59) comparing a smartphone-delivered ACT intervention tailored to cancer patients to QuitGuide, finding highly promising and not significant differences in quit rates at the 8-week follow-up (OR = 5.16; 95% CI [0.71, 37.29]; Bricker, Watson, Heffner et al., 2020). Full-scale trials for all of these special populations are needed.

Dissemination

To date, there is no published research on the dissemination of efficacious ACT interventions for smoking cessation. Needed dissemination research includes testing concepts and methods for: (i) organizations and individuals to adopt ACT interventions for smoking cessation; (ii) clinicians to provide and adhere to ACT interventions for smoking cessation; (iii) evaluating the cost-effectiveness of these interventions; and (iv) maximizing population-level reach of ACT smoking cessation interventions at the lowest possible cost.

Predictors and Moderators

A minority of the randomized trials published to date have tested for baseline predictors and moderators of the effectiveness of ACT for smoking cessation. Lower baseline acceptance of cravings predicted over four times higher odds of full adherence to an ACT smoking cessation smartphone app (OR = 4.59; 95% CI [1.35, 15.54]; Zeng et al., 2016). Lower education (risk ratio [RR] = 0.492), heavier smoking (RR = 0.613), and depression (RR = 0.958) prospectively predicted lower utilization of this app (Zeng et al., 2015). Analyses from these randomized trials show no significant evidence of an interaction between treatment assignment (i.e., ACT vs. UCSPG) and these baseline characteristics: smoking history (e.g., smoked for 10 or more years; Bricker et al., 2018), gender (Bricker et al., 2018; McClure et al., 2020), age (Bricker et al., 2018), sexual orientation (i.e., LGB; Heffner, Mull et al., 2020), certain mental illnesses (i.e., bipolar, affective disorders; Heffner et al., 2018; Watson et al., 2019), and baseline acceptance of internal triggers to smoke (e.g., cravings; Bricker et al., 2018; Brown et al., 2018). By contrast, subgroup analysis of a telephone-delivered ACT intervention showed that among those scoring low on the theory-based moderator of acceptance of cravings at baseline (i.e., less willing to experience cravings; n = 57), the quit rates were 37% in ACT versus 10% in USCPG (OR = 5.3; 95% CI [1.3, 22.0]; Bricker, Bush et al., 2014). A similar result occurred in a subgroup analysis of smartphone-delivered ACT (Bricker, Mull, et al., 2014). One implication is that ACT has worked equally well for smoking cessation among these subgroups, though evidence is mixed about

whether acceptance of internal triggers moderates treatment effectiveness. Overall, the body of evidence on moderators of ACT for smoking cessation is small, with little analysis of theory-based moderators.

Processes and Mechanisms

Eleven randomized trials provide an evidence base for the mediating role of acceptance of internal triggers (e.g., cravings) in smoking cessation. Of the 11 trials, 8 showed either formal statistical mediation or higher levels of acceptance of internal triggers to smoke in the ACT intervention arm (Bricker, Bush et al., 2014; Bricker et al., 2013; Bricker, Mull, et al., 2014; Bricker et al., 2018; Brown et al., 2013; Gifford et al., 2004; Gifford et al., 2011; Vilardaga et al., 2019). In all eight trials, ACT showed more favorable smoking cessation outcomes than the USCPG comparison intervention. By contrast, the remaining three trials showed no evidence of mediation or higher acceptance of internal triggers in the ACT arm, and the cessation outcomes were similar in both arms – even though overall increases in acceptance of internal triggers predicted higher odds of smoking cessation (Brown et al., 2018; McClure et al., 2020; O'Connor et al., 2020). A process analysis of an ACT smartphone app for quitting smoking showed that tracking practice of letting urges pass (p = 0.03) and tracking ACT skill practice was predictive of smoking cessation (p = 0.01; Heffner et al., 2015). A process analysis of an ACT telephone counseling intervention found that for every one-unit increase in counselors' use of techniques for awareness and acceptance of cravings there were 45% (OR = 0.45; 95% CI [0.25, 0.80] and 52% (OR = 0.52; 95% CI [0.29, 0.92]) decreases, respectively, in the odds of the participant smoking at the next counseling session (Vilardaga et al., 2014). Together, these results have three implications:

1. Increases in acceptance of internal triggers may be an important theoretical pathway to smoking cessation.
2. ACT interventions that have higher levels of acceptance of internal triggers than comparison interventions yield higher cessation rates.
3. ACT interventions that have similar levels of acceptance of internal triggers relative to comparison interventions yield similar cessation rates.

Indeed, this latter implication may explain why the remaining three trials found similar cessation rates for ACT and the USCPG comparison interventions. For ACT intervention design, this body of evidence suggests that critical role of creating components that can impact acceptance of internal triggers to smoke. Beyond this particular process variable, the lack of smoking-specific measures of other ACT processes (e.g., cognitive defusion, committed action) currently hinder research on whether these processes mediate the effect of ACT on smoking cessation.

Conclusions

Fifteen randomized trials published over the span of 16 years (2004–2020) that have included a total of 6,991 enrolled participants show a mature and active area of research on ACT for smoking cessation. The full-scale trials published to date show that group-delivered and website-delivered ACT are solid alternatives to USCPG standard behavioral interventions for smoking cessation delivered in these same modalities. There is strong evidence that smartphone-delivered ACT is efficacious. ACT appears to be working equally well among a variety of subgroups. ACT interventions appear to be mediated through acceptance of internal triggers (e.g., cravings) to smoke.

ACCEPTANCE-BASED BEHAVIORAL TREATMENT FOR OBESITY

Over two billion adults are currently overweight, and prevalence rates are at epidemic levels in most industrialized countries. Standard behavioral treatment (SBT), if delivered intensively, produces weight losses of 8–10%, and are considered the gold standard. New approaches to weight-loss based on mindfulness and acceptance principles have been developed over the past decade. The most widely researched of these treatments is acceptance-based behavioral weight loss (ABT), which infuses behavioral treatment with mindfulness and acceptance-based strategies drawn from ACT (Hayes et al., 1999b), DBT (Linehan, 1993), and Marlatt's relapse prevention model (Marlatt & George, 1984). These strategies include values work (clarifying fundamental, personal values relevant to weight and weight control behaviors), mindful decision-making (becoming aware of, and overriding, perceptual, cognitive and affective experiences that automatically cue problematic eating and physical activity decisions), and willingness (the ability to engage in weight control behaviors even when doing so brings about a reduction in pleasure or aversive internal experiences).

Efficacy

ABT has been established as an effective treatment, capable of producing clinically significant levels of weight-loss. For instance, participants who received ABT in a 12-week open trial demonstrated 8.1% weight loss at posttreatment and maintained weight loss (an additional 2.2% loss) by six-month follow-up (Forman et al., 2009). In a rigorous randomized controlled trial, 128 overweight participants were assigned to 30 sessions of either ABT or SBT, delivered by either expert group leaders (i.e., clinical psychologists experienced in administering behavioral weight-control interventions) or novice, doctoral students. Results suggested that the advantage of ABT over SBT (10.9% vs. 8.7% at posttreatment; 9.2% vs. 7.4% at six-month follow-up) was much more pronounced for participants who received treatment delivered by experts (13.2% vs. 7.5%; 11.0% vs. 4.8%) (Forman et al., 2013). In another randomized controlled trial, 190 participants were assigned to 25 sessions over one year of either ABT or SBT. Participants in the ABT condition lost significantly more weight at posttreatment (13.3% vs. 9.8%), though the differences between conditions attenuated at one-year and two-year follow-ups (Forman et al., 2016; Forman et al., 2019). Nonetheless, a greater percentage of those in the ABT condition, compared to the SBT condition, lost 10% of their weight posttreatment (64% vs. 49%)

and at two-year follow-up (intent-to-treat 25% vs. 14%). Of note, ABT, compared to SBT, produced higher quality of life at both follow-up points, suggesting that the skills taught in ABT may have enduring benefits outside of weight loss.

Trials have also been conducted examining the efficacy of ABT amongst those with high levels of internal disinhibition (i.e., a tendency to break restraint in response to internal and external cues). Those with higher disinhibited eating demonstrate reduced weight losses in standard behavioral weight loss treatment. In an open trial, 21 individuals with high disinhibited eating who received 24 sessions of ABT over six months demonstrated surprisingly high weight losses (12.0 kg) at posttreatment and at three-month follow-up (12.1 kg; Niemeier et al., 2012).

Lillis and colleagues (2016) randomly assigned 162 individuals with high disinhibition to 32 sessions of ABT or SBT, over 12 months. Weight losses were nonsignificantly greater for the SBT at posttreatment (4.1% vs. 2.4%) but were superior for ABT at one-year follow-up (7.1 vs. 4.6 kg). In addition, both in-person and remotely delivered ABT appear to prevent weight regain in postoperative bariatric patients (Bradley et al., 2016; Bradley et al., 2017).

Two trials have examined ABT in conjunction with other intervention materials. One trial, for example, examined the efficacy of ABT paired with skills aimed at helping participants navigate the obesogenic food environment (Butryn et al., 2017). In this study, participants with overweight or obesity were randomly assigned to one of three conditions: SBT, SBT with food environment change, or ABT with food environment change. Results indicated that percent weight loss did not differ as a function of condition; percent weight loss in all conditions after 12 months was approximately 10%. In another trial, after 6 months of SBT, participants with overweight or obesity were randomly assigned to continue in the SBT condition, receive a BT intervention with an intensive focus on physical activity promotion, or receive ABT with this physical activity promotion focus (Butryn et al., 2021). At the 12- and 18-month assessments, participants displayed equivalent weight losses (i.e., approximately 12%).

Thus, overall, results support the effectiveness of ABT for weight loss. Weight losses appear to be at least equivalent to gold standard behavioral weight loss treatment. However, results are mixed with regards to whether ABT outperforms SBT. It is possible that ABT only outperforms SBT when the mindfulness- and acceptance-based components are of a sufficient intensity (i.e., not when diluted by other treatment components). A known challenge with weight-control treatments is their ability to sustain weight losses after the intervention concludes. ABT appears to offer some advantages for longer-term maintenance, but these appear modest and to attenuate over time. As such, ABT, like most treatments, most likely needs to continue in some form (e.g., weight-maintenance treatment or booster sessions) to maintain its efficacy.

Predictors and Moderators

Given ABT's focus on developing tolerance for challenging internal experiences, researchers have theorized that ABT may be especially effective for those with heightened emotional eating, mood disturbance, disinhibited eating, or susceptibility to eating cues. Forman et al. (2013), for example, found that depressive symptoms, emotional eating, disinhibited eating, and the extent to which the presence of highly palatable foods influences appetite and food desire, moderated treatment effects, such that participants with higher levels lost a greater percentage of weight if in ABT as opposed to SBT. Forman et al. (2016) also examined the potential moderating roles of depressive symptoms, disinhibited eating and the extent to which the presence of highly palatable foods influence appetite. However, interestingly, the researchers found no significant moderation effects. Instead, ABT was equivalently effective for all participants. The discrepancy between these results could be explained by the fact that the interventions had different foci. While ABT in the earlier trial emphasized willingness toward aversive states (e.g., cravings, hunger, and emotional distress), ABT in the latter trial emphasized willingness toward reductions in pleasure (e.g., loss of comfort and pleasure, and boredom). As such, it is possible that heightened emotional eating, mood disturbance, disinhibited eating, and susceptibility to eating cues are moderators of treatment effects, to the extent to which they are addressed within treatment.

Manasse et al. (2017) examined the moderating role of impulsivity, and whether it is different depending on whether participants were assigned SBT or ABT. The researchers found that inhibitory control (the ability to withhold a prepotent response) and delayed discounting (i.e., the ability to delay an immediate reward for a later, greater reward), negatively predicted weight loss in SBT, but positively predicted weight loss in the ABT condition. For instance, individuals with worse delayed discounting lost approximately 5% more weight than their better delayed discounting peers in the ABT condition. Thus, ABT may be a good match to those whose obesity is linked to impulsivity, in that the treatment enables impulsive participants to mindfully observe impulses, thus reducing automaticity, and to make decisions in line with values, as opposed to immediate desires or cravings for high-calorie foods.

Additionally, race was a moderator of treatment effect across several trials. Typically, in SBT, there is a health disparity wherein African Americans lose less weight than non-Hispanic white participants. However, ABT appears to attenuate the relationship between race and weight, wherein African Americans lose an equivalent amount of weight to non-white Hispanic participants (Butryn et al., 2017; Butryn et al., 2021; Forman et al., 2016). For instance, in one trial, African American participants receiving SBT lost about half as much weight as White participants (6.3% vs. 11.9%), as is often the case. However, those receiving a hybrid ABT displayed more similar weight losses (9.4% vs. 11.5%) (Butryn et al., 2021). While research has not yet identified mechanisms underlying this effect, one possibility is that the valued living component is especially potent for African Americans given that they report lower preexisting motivations to be thin (Vaughan et al., 2008).

Finally, the experience level of the clinicians administering the groups appears to affect treatment outcomes. Forman et al.

(2013), for example, found that the advantage of ABT was more pronounced when delivered by expert, as opposed to novice, clinicians. Further, when treatment was delivered by experts, participants in ABT lost significantly more weight at posttreatment and six-month follow-up than those in SBT. Expert status might explain why percent weight-loss in subsequent trials of ABT has differed. For example, in Forman et al. (2019) ABT was delivered by experts produced 7.5% weight-loss at one-year follow-up, whereas in Lillis et al., (2016) ABT was delivered by novices, and produced 4.1% weight-loss at one-year follow-up.

Processes and Mechanisms of Change

While a robust body of research generally supports mindfulness/acceptance-linked variables as mediators of mindfulness/acceptance-based treatments (Hayes, Pistorello, & Levin, 2012), relatively little research is available on mechanisms of action for ABT. Within this literature, researchers have not found support (Lillis et al., 2017; Niemeier et al., 2012; Schumacher et al., 2019) for mediating roles for either *general* experiential avoidance (Bond et al., 2011; Hayes, Luoma, Bond, Masuda, & Lillis, 2006) or *weight*-related willingness to experience internal experiences (Lillis & Hayes, 2007). However, some evidence supports the notion that willingness to experience internal experiences, such as urges and cravings mediates the effect of ABT. For instance, Forman et al. (2016) found that the advantage of ABT over SBT posttreatment was mediated by changes in acceptance of eating-related internal experiences from baseline to mid-treatment, and Forman et al. (2013) similarly found that changes in the eating-related acceptance mediated the advantage of ABT over SBT, but only amongst those individuals who had higher levels of emotional eating. Together, these results suggest that ABT may better target food-related experiential avoidance, as opposed to more general forms of experiential avoidance.

Mixed support has been found for values-linked mediators. Lillis et al. (2017), for example, observed greater increases in valued action in the ABT condition; however, changes in values-consistent behavior did not mediate weight-loss outcomes. On the other hand, Forman and colleagues (2016) obtained support for the mediating role of autonomous motivation, a values-linked mediator.

Conclusions

Collectively, empirical evidence indicates that ABT is efficacious for weight loss, with some research finding superiority of ABT to standard behavioral treatment, the current gold-standard treatment approach. ABT may confer some advantages for maintaining weight losses in the long-term; however, these benefits appear to attenuate over time. ABT may be more effective for people with heightened emotional eating, mood disturbance, disinhibited eating, impulsivity, or susceptibility to eating cues; however, results are mixed, and may depend on the degree to which these areas are targeted within treatment. Over several trials, ABT has been found to decrease race-based health disparities – Black Americans lose less weight than non-Hispanic White participants following SBT, but lose equivalent amounts of weight following ABT. In general, it remains unclear if mechanisms of change account for ABT's advantages over SBT, but the most support exists for increases in willingness to experience internal food-related experiences (e.g., urges and cravings to eat).

ACCEPTANCE AND COMMITMENT THERAPY FOR CHRONIC PAIN

Pain is a ubiquitous human experience – it is common across cultures, countries, genders, and the lifespan (Loeser & Melzack, 1999; Vowles et al., 2014). Chronic pain, defined as pain that persists for longer than three months (Nicholas et al., 2019), is also a common human experience (Breivik et al., 2006; Fayaz et al., 2016). The individual impact of chronic pain on daily functioning, quality of life, and productive activity is often extensive and profound (Breivik et al., 2006; Smith et al., 2001). Psychological and behavioral interventions for chronic pain have a longstanding history of effectiveness in the treatment of chronic pain and the available evidence indicates that psychological approaches are broadly effective on these outcomes (Gatchel et al., 2007; Hoffman et al., 2007; Williams et al., 2012).

The goals of ACT for chronic pain can be summarized as follows: to enable individuals to identify areas of life that have meaning even with the experience of persistent pain, to structure treatment in a manner that facilitates improved willingness to experience pain in the service of these same areas, and to improve contact with the present moment in a manner that facilitates both this willingness and awareness of opportunities to engage in meaningful activity. See McCracken and Vowles (2014), McCracken and Morley (2014), and Vowles and Thompson (2011) for extended discussions of the ACT theoretical model as it relates to chronic pain.

Efficacy

The American Psychological Association's Division of Clinical Psychology (Division 12) identifies ACT for chronic pain as having "strong" research support, the highest possible grading. Since 2016, two meta-analyses have examined the evidence of ACT for chronic pain. The first of these was an update of an 2011 meta-analysis, both of which examined ACT and mindfulness-based interventions for chronic pain (Veehof et al., 2011, 2016). The updated analysis included 25 randomized-controlled trials (RCTs) involving 1285 participants. The more recent meta-analysis included studies of ACT for chronic pain only and included 10 RCTs involving 863 participants (Hughes et al., 2017). Table 15.1 displays standard mean differences and 95% confidence intervals for both of these recent meta-analyses at post treatment and short-term follow-up (i.e., 2–6 months for Veehof et al., 2016; 3 months for Hughes et al., 2017). As displayed in Table 15.1, results were reasonably consistent across the two meta-analyses. No-to-small effects were indicated for pain intensity. Small effects were indicated for disability/functioning. Small-to-medium effects were indicated for anxiety. Medium effects were indicated for depression and pain acceptance. Only the Veehof et al. (2016) meta-analysis reported on pain interference, for which a medium-to-large effect was indicated. The results were mixed for quality of life, where effects ranged from no effect to a medium effect. Generally, good maintenance of treatment effects was indicated through follow-up.

Treatment Format and Dissemination

For chronic pain, ACT has been provided in a variety of formats, including both more traditional psychotherapy and interdisciplinary teams, as well as in individual, group, and online settings. There is evidence of a positive effect for all of

TABLE 15.1   Meta-analytic results (Standard Mean Difference, 95% CI) of ACT for chronic pain

Outcome	Veehof et al. (2016)[1]		Hughes et al. (2017)	
	Post-treatment	Follow-up (2–6 mo.)	Post-treatment	Follow-up (3 mo.)
Pain interference	.62 (.21, 1.03)	1.05 (.55, 1.56)	--	--
Disability/Functioning	.40 (.01, .79)	.39 (.11, .67)	.45 (.18, .73)	.41 (.12, .71)
Depression	.43 (.18, .68)	.50 (.19, .80)	.52 (.24, .80)[2]	.52 (.14, .90)
Anxiety	.51 (.10, .92)	.57 (.00, 1.14)	.57 (16, .98)	.32 (–.14, .79)
Quality of Life	.44 (–.05, .93)	.66 (.06, 1.26)	.05 (–.26, .36)	.26 (–.32, .85)
Pain Acceptance	--	--	.53 (.20, .85)[2]	.59 (.05, 1.13)
Pain Intensity	.24 (.06, .42)	.41 (.14, .68)	.26 (.00, .53)[2]	.29 (.00, .59)

Notes:
[1] Pooled effects for ACT and mindfulness-based studies displayed.
[2] Effect size displayed excludes statistical outlier identified by Hughes et al. (2017).

these formats, although only a few studies have performed a direct comparison of effectiveness. A recent comparative meta-analysis of ACT for chronic pain explicitly examined the relative effectiveness of unidisciplinary ACT (via clinical psychology) and interdisciplinary ACT (Vowles et al., 2020). In total, 29 studies were included, 46% of which were unidisciplinary ACT. A number of outcome domains were examined for both posttreatment and follow-ups of up to one year. Results indicated that interdisciplinary ACT had greater effect sizes for physical disability, psychosocial impact, and depression at both posttreatment and through the follow-up. The effect sizes were similar between the unidisciplinary and interdisciplinary treatment for pain intensity, pain-related anxiety, or pain acceptance. Furthermore, there was a medium relationship between treatment effectiveness and treatment duration, particularly for the psychosocial outcomes, suggesting that longer treatments were associated with greater treatment effects.

Predictors and Moderators

Predictors of treatment outcome have been examined at the level of both individual patient and trial methods. With regard to the former, few patient demographic or pain-related characteristics have been identified. For example, the three-year follow-up of Vowles et al. (2011) found no significant predictors of three-year outcomes across demographic variables (i.e., gender, age, educational achievement), pain-related characteristics (i.e., pain duration and pain intensity, pain-related medical visits), and measures baseline physical and emotional functioning (i.e., depression, physical and psychosocial disability, pain anxiety). Further, the SEM model examining outcomes across time of Vowles et al. (2014) found that pain duration, educational achievement, and age did not significantly influence outcomes. The only difference in this trial was at baseline, where females reported greater disability and depression in relation to males.

Processes and Mechanisms of Change

The studies that have specifically examined treatment processes and mechanisms for chronic pain can generally be broken down into those that have (i) examined correlations between changes in putative treatment mechanisms and treatment outcomes and (ii) those that have used other methods to examine how trajectories of change, such as within-treatment slope. With regard to correlational analyses, several studies have examined single measures of ACT mechanisms, such as pain acceptance or mindfulness, or a subset of ACT processes, such as pain acceptance and values success. In summary, the evidence suggests that changes in ACT processes are associated with chronic pain treatment outcomes of pain-related distress and disability. For example, increases in pain acceptance are reliability correlated with improvements in physical and emotional functioning through follow-ups of as long as three years (e.g., Kemani et al., 2016; Luciano et al., 2014; Vowles et al., 2011). The same is true of improvements in values success (Vowles et al., 2011; Vowles & McCracken, 2008) and psychological flexibility (Vowles & McCracken, 2010).

Two large studies have concurrently examined multiple measures associated with the ACT model, principally

pain acceptance (and engagement in valued activities, but also including aspects of mindfulness/de-centering, committed action, and self-compassion). The first was a single arm study of 384 individuals completing an interdisciplinary course of ACT for chronic pain (Scott et al., 2016). Results provided support for ACT processes in relevant measures of physical and emotional functioning in those with chronic pain, range r^2 = .07–.27, all p < .01. The second study performed a multiple-mediation analysis of pre- to posttreatment changes in multiple theorized ACT treatment processes in relation to pre-treatment to three-month follow-up changes in multiple measures of chronic pain treatment outcomes. Evidence was obtained for partial mediation at the level of most individual measures, range unstandardized B = −.01 to −3.94, all p < .001. However, pain acceptance and self-compassion, and to a smaller extent success in valued activities, were reliably significant when all potential mediators were considered collectively (Vowles et al., 2014).

Finally, a recent paper used Latent Growth Mixture Modeling (LGMM) to examine how within-treatment slope of change in valued activities was associated with outcomes at posttreatment and three-month follow-up (Vowles et al., 2019). A two-item measure of valued activities, called the Values Tracker (Pielech et al., 2016), was used weekly over a four-week interdisciplinary intervention. A single latent trajectory of positive change in valued activities was indicated across the 242 participants. Slope of change was associated with degree of improvement at posttreatment for psychosocial disability, depression, pain anxiety, and discrepancy in values importance and values success for posttreatment only. No association was indicated for physical disability.

Conclusions

Over two decades of research has examined the relevance of ACT in chronic pain. This work builds on over 50 years of evidence that psychological and behavioral approaches to chronic pain are efficacious and relevant in this area (Fordyce et al., 1973; Main et al., 2014). To date, the evidence suggests that ACT for chronic pain works reasonably well. While the majority of evidence is from shorter-term follow-ups, some longer-term evidence also exists that supports durability of treatment effects (Vowles et al., 2011). Further, the treatment processes identified in the model, most notably pain acceptance and engagement in valued activity, are reliability associated with treatment outcomes. There are several areas for improvement as well. Some of the methods of treatment trials have been problematic, particularly in relation to retention, use of active control conditions, more robust examination of treatment processes, and analysis of treatment outcomes over the longer term. Even bearing these issues in mind, however, these findings provide good support for the relevance and effect of ACT for chronic pain.

CONCLUSIONS AND RECOMMENDATIONS

Mindfulness and acceptance-based treatments (MABTs) build on traditional behavioral and cognitive therapy approaches by helping patients (1) live in and return to the present moment rather than be consumed by the past or fearful of the future; (2) utilize metacognitive skills that allow individuals to observe their internal experience for what they are rather than being caught up with them; (3) engage in present-focused, open, curious, and accepting responses to internal experiences in lieu of reactive or avoidant responses that ultimately exacerbate symptoms; and, in some cases, and/or (4) clarify and gain awareness of fundamental personal values that they want to guide their actions.

A growing body of research indicates that such treatments are efficacious in treating a wide range of mental and physical health conditions. For instance, as reviewed above, strong efficacy has been observed for MABTs in the treatment of a range of anxiety disorders, recurrent depression, psychosis, borderline personality disorder, suicidality, eating disorders, obesity, and chronic pain. MABTs for depression, psychosis, smoking cessation, and obesity have also been translated successfully into digitally delivered formats, thus increasing treatment accessibility. Moreover, for specific presentations (e.g., anxiety), MABTs offer a choice of alternative interventions, particularly for those people who show a resistance to change in traditional CBT.

However, generally speaking, there is no evidence that MABTs outperform gold-standard behavior approaches. Two exceptions may be MBCT for prevention of depressive relapse and ABT for obesity. Thus, on the whole, MABTs, are likely best conceptualized as alternative treatments to gold-standard treatments, and not as superior to them. A distinct possibility exists that MABTs confer an advantage to specific subgroups of individuals. However, existing findings are mixed and future studies should continue these investigations.

In terms of mechanisms of action of MABTs, research is inconclusive. Analyses have revealed a mediating role of acceptance of internal experiences (for treatment of anxiety, BPD and suicidality, disordered eating, obesity, smoking, and chronic pain), metacognition and depressogenic cognitions (for recurrent depression), cognitive defusion (for psychosis), and engagement in valued activities (for chronic pain). However, the specificity of these mechanisms to MABTs, as opposed to treatments more generally, is unclear. Moreover, detection of mediation does not prove that the construct in question is an activate ingredient. Dismantling trials are warranted, perhaps in the form of factorial designs that allow the efficacy of multiple treatment components to be efficiently evaluated. Identifying active ingredients will help to make MABTs more efficient and streamlined.

Some of the prominent voices in MABTs have called for doing away with the separation of MABTs from other treatments, and instead reorganizing all treatments inside a "process-based therapy" rubric (Hofmann & Hayes, 2019). The grand idea underpinning process-based therapy is to empirically identify the processes responsible for the effectiveness of treatment, and to construct a treatment based on those processes that can be flexibly applied to any case. As such, there would no longer be a need to develop a set of protocols for each specific disorder or problem. Whether such an approach will ultimately yield more flexible, efficacious, and/or disseminable treatments is as yet unknown. Regardless, however, our understanding of MABTs and their interconnections with other treatment approaches will no doubt evolve as theoretical and empirical work continues.

ABBREVIATIONS

AAQ	Acceptance and Action Questionnaire
AAQ-II	Acceptance and Action Questionnaire-II
ABT	Acceptance-based behavioral weight loss treatment
ABT/ABBT	Acceptance-based behavioral therapy
ACT	Acceptance and compassion therapy
ACTp	Acceptance and commitment therapy for psychosis
AN	Anorexia nervosa
BED	Binge eating disorder
BN	Bulimia nervosa
BPD	Borderline personality disorder
CBT	Cognitive behavioural therapy
CBT-E	Cognitive-behavioral therapy-Eating
CBTp	Cognitive behavioral therapy for psychosis
DBT	Dialectical behavior therapy
DBT-I	Dialectical behavior therapy-Individual
DBT-S	Dialectical behavior therapy-Skills training
DSM-III-R	Diagnostic and statistical manual-III-R
DSM-IV	Diagnostic and statistical manual-IV
ERP	Exposure and response prevention
GAD	Generalised anxiety disorder
GPM	General psychiatric management
HRSD	Hamilton Rating Scale for Depression
ICAT	Integrative cognitive affective therapy
LGB	Lesbian, gay, bisexual
LGMM	Latent Growth Mixture Modeling
MABTs	Mindfulness and acceptance-based treatments
mADM	Maintenance antidepressant medication
MAGT	Mindfulness and acceptance-based group therapy
MB-EAT	Mindfulness-based eating awareness training
MBCT	Mindfulness-based cognitive therapy
MBSR	Mindfulness-based stress reduction
MMB	Mindful Mood Balance
NSSI	Non-suicidal self injury
OCD	Obsessive-compulsive disorder
OR	Odds ratio
PCE	Cognitive psychoeducation program
PHQ-9	Patient Health Questionnaire-9
PMR	Progressive muscle relaxation

PRISMA	Preferred Reporting Items for Systematic Reviews and Meta-Analyses
PTSD	Post traumatic stress disorder
QLs	Quitlines
RCTs	Randomised controlled trials
RR	Risk ratio
SAD	Social anxiety disorder
SBT	Standard behavioral treatment
SCID	Structured Clinical Interview for Diagnosis
SEM	Standard error of measurement
SMD	Standard mean difference
TAU	Treatment as usual
TFP	Transference focused psychotherapy
USCPG	US clinical practice guidelines

References

Abroms, L. C., Lee Westmaas, J., Bontemps-Jones, J., Ramani, R., & Mellerson, J. (2013). A content analysis of popular smartphone apps for smoking cessation. *American Journal of Preventive Medicine, 45*(6), 732–736. https://doi.org/10.1016/j.amepre.2013.07.008

Abroms, L. C., Padmanabhan, N., Thaweethai, L., & Phillips, T. (2011). iPhone apps for smoking cessation. *American Journal of Preventive Medicine, 40*(3), 279–285. https://doi.org/10.1016/j.amepre.2010.10.032

American Psychiatric Association. (1987). *Diagnostic and statistical manual of mental disorders: DSM-III-R* (3rd. ed., rev). American Psychiatric Publishing.

Arch, J. J., Eifert, G. H., Davies, C., Plumb, J. C., Rose, R. D., & Craske, M. G. (2012). Randomized clinical trial of cognitive behavioral therapy versus acceptance and commitment therapy for the treatment of mixed anxiety disorders. *Journal of Consulting and Clinical Psychology, 80*(5), 750–765. https://doi.org/10.1037/a0028310

Arch, J. J., Wolitzky-Taylor, K. B., Eifert, G. H., & Craske, M. G. (2012). Longitudinal treatment mediation of traditional cognitive behavioral therapy and acceptance and commitment therapy for anxiety disorders. *Behaviour Research and Therapy, 50*(7–8), 469–478. https://doi.org/10.1016/j.brat.2012.04.007

Atkins, P. W., Ciarrochi, J., Gaudiano, B. A., Bricker, J. B., Donald, J., Rovner, G., Smout, M., Livheim, F., Lundgren, T., & Hayes, S. C. (2017). Departing from the essential features of a high quality systematic review of psychotherapy: A response to Öst (2014) and recommendations for improvement. *Behaviour Research and Therapy, 97*, 259–272. https://doi.org/10.1016/j.brat.2017.05.016

Aust, J., & Bradshaw, T. (2017). Mindfulness interventions for psychosis: A systematic review of the literature. *Journal of Psychiatric and Mental Health Nursing, 24*(1), 69–83. https://doi.org/10.1111/jpm.12357

Bach, P., Gaudiano, B. A., Hayes, S. C., & Herbert, J. D. (2013). Acceptance and commitment therapy for psychosis: Intent to treat, hospitalization outcome and mediation by believability. *Psychosis, 5*(2), 166–174. https://doi.org/10.1080/17522439.2012.671349

Bach, P., & Hayes, S. C. (2002). The use of acceptance and commitment therapy to prevent the rehospitalization of psychotic patients: A randomized controlled trial. *Journal of Consulting and Clinical Psychology, 70*(5), 1129–1139. https://doi.org/10.1037/0022-006X.70.5.1129

Baer, R. A., Smith, G. T., Hopkins, J., Krietemeyer, J., & Toney, L. (2006). Using self-report assessment methods to explore facets of mindfulness. *Assessment, 13*(1), 27–45. https://doi.org/10.1177/1073191105283504

Baghooli, H., Dolatshahi, B., Mohammadkhani, P., Moshtagh, N., & Naziri, G. (2014). Effectiveness of acceptance and commitment therapy in reduction of severity symptoms of patients with obsessive–compulsive disorder. *Advances in Environmental Biology*, 2519–2525.

Barney, J. L., Murray, H. B., Manasse, S. M., Dochat, C., & Juarascio, A. S. (2019). Mechanisms and moderators in mindfulness-and acceptance-based treatments for binge eating spectrum disorders: A systematic review. *European Eating Disorders Review, 27*(4), 352–380. https://doi.org/10.1002/erv.2673

Barnicot, K., Savill, M., Bhatti, N., & Priebe, S. (2014). A pragmatic randomised controlled trial of dialectical behaviour therapy: Effects on hospitalisation and post-treatment follow-up. *Psychotherapy and Psychosomatics, 83*(3), 192-193. https://doi.org/10.1159/000357365

Batink, T., Peeters, F., Geschwind, N., van Os, J., & Wichers, M. (2013). How does MBCT for depression work? Studying cognitive and affective mediation pathways. *PLoS ONE, 8*(8), e72778. https://doi.org/10.1371/journal.pone.0072778

Bluett, E. J., Homan, K. J., Morrison, K. L., Levin, M. E., & Twohig, M. P. (2014). Acceptance and commitment therapy for anxiety and OCD spectrum disorders. An empirical review. *Journal of Anxiety Disorders, 28*(6), 612–624. https://doi.org/10.1016/j.janxdis.2014.06.008

Bond, F. W., Hayes, S. C., Baer, R. A., Carpenter, K. C., Guenole, N., Orcutt, H. K., Waltz, T., & Zettle, R. D. (2011). Preliminary psychometric properties of the Acceptance and Action Questionnaire - II: A revised measure of psychological inflexibility and experiential avoidance. *Behavior Therapy, 42*(4), 676–688. https://doi.org/10.1016/j.beth.2011.03.007

Bondolfi, G., Jermann, F., der Linden, M. V., Gex-Fabry, M., Bizzini, L., Rouget, B. W., Myers-Arrazola, L., Gonzalez, C., Segal, Z., Aubry, J. M., & Bertschy, G. (2010). Depression relapse prophylaxis with mindfulness-based cognitive therapy: Replication and extension in the Swiss health care system. *Journal of Affective Disorders, 122*(3), 224–231. https://doi.org/10.1016/j.jad.2009.07.007

Boritz, T., Zeifman, R. J., & McMain, S. F. (2017). Mechanisms of change in dialectical behaviour therapy. In M. A. Swales (Ed.), *The Oxford handbook of dialectical behaviour therapy*. Oxford University Press.

Borkovec, T. D., & Costello, E. (1993). Efficacy of applied relaxation and cognitive-behavioral therapy in the treatment of generalized anxiety disorder. *Journal of Consulting and Clinical Psychology, 61*(4), 611–619. https://doi.org/10.1037//0022-006x.61.4.611

Borrelli, B., Bartlett, Y. K., Tooley, E., Armitage, C. J., & Wearden, A. (2015). Prevalence and frequency of mHealth and eHealth use among US and UK smokers and differences by motivation to quit. *Journal of Medical Internet Research, 17*(7), e164. https://doi.org/10.2196/jmir.4420

Bradley, L. E., Forman, E. M., Kerrigan, S. G., Butryn, M. L., Herbert, J. D., & Sarwer, D. B. (2016). A pilot study of an acceptance-based behavioral intervention for weight regain after bariatric surgery. *Obesity Surgery, 26*(10), 2433–2441. https://doi.org/10.1007/s11695-016-2125-0

Bradley, L. E., Forman, E. M., Kerrigan, S. G., Goldstein, S. P., Butryn, M. L., Thomas, J. G., Herbert, J. D., & Sarwer, D. B. (2017). Project HELP: A remotely delivered behavioral intervention for weight regain after bariatric surgery. *Obesity Surgery, 27*(3), 586–598. https://doi.org/10.1007/s11695-016-2337-3

Brauhardt, A., Zwaan, M. de, & Hilbert, A. (2014). The therapeutic process in psychological treatments for eating disorders: A systematic review. *International Journal of Eating Disorders, 47*(6), 565–584. https://doi.org/10.1002/eat.22287

Breivik, H., Collett, B., Ventafridda, V., Cohen, R., & Gallacher, D. (2006). Survey of chronic pain in Europe: Prevalence, impact on daily life, and treatment. *European Journal of Pain, 10*, 287–333. https://doi.org/10.1016/j.ejpain.2005.06.009

Bricker, J. B., Bush, T., Zbikowski, S. M., Mercer, L. D., & Heffner, J. L. (2014). Randomized trial of telephone-delivered acceptance and commitment therapy versus cognitive behavioral therapy for smoking cessation: A pilot study. *Nicotine & Tobacco Research, 16*(11), 1446–1454. https://doi.org/10.1093/ntr/ntu102

Bricker, J. B., Mull, K. E., Kientz, J. A., Vilardaga, R., Mercer, L. D., Akioka, K. J., & Heffner, J. L. (2014). Randomized, controlled pilot trial of a smartphone app for smoking cessation using acceptance and commitment therapy. *Drug and Alcohol Dependence, 143*, 87–94. https://doi.org/10.1016/j.drugalcdep.2014.07.006

Bricker, J.B., Mull, K.E., McClure, J.B., Watson, N.L., & Heffner, J.L. (2018). Improving quit rates of web-delivered interventions for smoking cessation: Full-scale randomized trial of WebQuit.org versus Smokefree.gov. *Addiction, 113*(5), 914-923. https://doi.org/10.1111/add.14127

Bricker, J. B., Watson, N. L., Heffner, J. L., Sullivan, B., Mull, K., Kwon, D., Westmaas, J. L., & Ostroff, J. (2020). A smartphone app designed to help cancer patients stop smoking: Results from a pilot randomized trial on feasibility, acceptability, and effectiveness. *JMIR Formative Research, 4*(1), e16652. https://doi.org/10.2196/16652

Bricker, J. B., Watson, N. L., Mull, K. E., Sullivan, B. M., & Heffner, J. L. (2020). Efficacy of smartphone applications for smoking cessation: A randomized clinical trial. *JAMA Internal Medicine*, 180(11), 1–9. https://doi.org/10.1001/jamainternmed.2020.4055

Bricker, J., Wyszynski, C., Comstock, B., & Heffner, J. L. (2013). Pilot randomized controlled trial of web-based acceptance and commitment therapy for smoking cessation. *Nicotine & Tobacco Research*, 15(10), 1756–1764. https://doi.org/10.1093/ntr/ntt056

Brown, K. W., & Ryan, R. M. (2003). The benefits of being present: Mindfulness and its role in psychological well-being. *Journal of Personality and Social Psychology*, 84(4), 822–848. https://doi.org/10.1037/0022-3514.84.4.822

Brown, R. A., Palm Reed, K. M., Bloom, E. L., Minami, H., Strong, D. R., Lejuez, C. W., Zvolensky, M. J., & Hayes, S. C. (2018). A randomized controlled trial of distress tolerance treatment for smoking cessation. *Psychology of Addictive Behaviors*, 32(4), 389–400. https://doi.org/10.1037/adb0000372

Brown, R. A., Reed, K. M. P., Bloom, E. L., Minami, H., Strong, D. R., Lejuez, C. W., Kahler, C. W., Zvolensky, M. J., Gifford, E. V., & Hayes, S. C. (2013). Development and preliminary randomized controlled trial of a distress tolerance treatment for smokers with a history of early lapse. *Nicotine & Tobacco Research*, 15(12), 2005–2015. https://doi.org/10.1093/ntr/ntt093

Butler, L., Johns, L. C., Byrne, M., Joseph, C., O'Donoghue, E., Jolley, S., Morris, E. M., & Oliver, J. E. (2016). Running acceptance and commitment therapy groups for psychosis in community settings. *Journal of Contextual Behavioral Science*, 5(1), 33–38. https://doi.org/10.1016/j.jcbs.2015.12.001

Butryn, M. L., Forman, E. M., Lowe, M. R., Gorin, A. A., Zhang, F., & Schaumberg, K. (2017). Efficacy of environmental and acceptance-based enhancements to behavioral weight loss treatment: The ENACT trial. *Obesity*, 25(5), 866–872. https://doi.org/10.1002/oby.21813

Butryn, M. L., Godfrey, K. M., Call, C. C., Forman, E. M., Zhang, F., & Volpe, S. L. (2021). Promotion of physical activity during weight loss maintenance: A randomized controlled trial. *Health Psychology*, 40(3), 178–187. https://doi.org/10.1037/hea0001043

Campbell-Sills, L., Barlow, D. H., Brown, T. A., & Hofmann, S. G. (2005). Effects of suppression and acceptance on emotional responses of individuals with anxiety and mood disorders. *Behaviour Research and Therapy*, 44(9), 1251–1263. https://doi.org/10.1016/j.brat.2005.10.001

Carmel, A., Rose, M. L., & Fruzzetti, A. E. (2014). Barriers and solutions to implementing dialectical behavior therapy in a public behavioral health system. *Administration and Policy in Mental Health and Mental Health Services Research*, 41(5), 608-614. https://doi.org/10.1007/s10488-013-0504-6

Carson-Wong, A., Hughes, C. D., & Rizvi, S. L. (2018). The effect of therapist use of validation strategies on change in client emotion in individual DBT treatment sessions. *Personality Disorders: Theory, Research, and Treatment*, 9(2), 165–171. https://doi.org/ 10.1037/per0000229

Carson-Wong, A., & Rizvi, S. (2016). Reliability and validity of the DBT-VLCS: A measure to code validation strategies in dialectical behavior therapy sessions. *Psychotherapy Research*, 26(3), 332–341. https://doi.org/10.1080/10503307.2014.966347

Carter, G. L., Willcox, C. H., Lewin, T. J., Conrad, A. M., & Bendit, N. (2010). Hunter DBT Project: Randomized controlled trial of dialectical behaviour therapy in women with borderline personality disorder. *Australian and New Zealand Journal of Psychiatry*, 44(2), 162-173. https://doi.org/10.3109/00048670903393621

Center, P. R. (2019). Internet/Broadband Fact Sheet. www.pewinternet.org/fact-sheet/internet-broadband

Chambless, D. L., & Hollon, S. D. (1998). Defining empirically supported therapies. *Journal of Consulting and Clinical Psychology*, 66(1), 7–18. https://doi.org/10.1037//0022-006X.66.1.7

Chen, E. Y., Cacioppo, J., Fettich, K., Gallop, R., McCloskey, M. S., Olino, T., & Zeffiro, T. A. (2017). An adaptive randomized trial of dialectical behavior therapy and cognitive behavior therapy for binge-eating. *Psychological Medicine*, 47(4), 703–717. https://doi.org/10.1017/S0033291716002543

Chiesa, A., & Serretti, A. (2011). Mindfulness based cognitive therapy for psychiatric disorders: A systematic review and meta-analysis. *Psychiatry Research*, 187(3), 441–453. https://doi.org/10.1016/j.psychres.2010.08.011

Civljak, M., Sheikh, A., Stead, L. F., & Car, J. (2010). Internet-based interventions for smoking cessation. *Cochrane Database of Systematic Reviews*, 9. https://doi.org/10.1002/14651858.CD007078.pub3

Clarkin, J. F., Levy, K. N., Lenzenweger, M. F., & Kernberg, O. F. (2007). Evaluating three treatments for borderline personality disorder: A multiwave study. *The American Journal of Psychiatry*, 164(6), 922–928. https://doi.org/ 10.1176/ajp.2007.164.6.922

Consortium, N. A. Q. (2017). *Results from the 2017 NAQC Annual Survey of Quitlines*. http://www.naquitline.org/?page=2017Survey

Cowdrey, N. D., & Waller, G. (2015). Are we really delivering evidence-based treatments for eating disorders? How eating-disordered patients describe their experience of cognitive behavioral therapy. *Behaviour Research and Therapy*, 75, 72–77. https://doi.org/10.1016/j.brat.2015.10.009

Cramer, H., Lauche, R., Haller, H., Langhorst, J., & Dobos, G. (2016). Mindfulness- and acceptance-based interventions for psychosis: A systematic review and meta-analysis. *Global Advances in Health and Medicine*, 5(1), 30–43. https://doi.org/10.7453/gahmj.2015.083

Craske, M. G., Niles, A. N., Burklund, L. J., Wolitzky-Taylor, K. B., Vilardaga, J. C. P., Arch, J. J., Saxbe, D. E., & Lieberman, M. D. (2014). Randomized controlled trial of cognitive behavioral therapy and acceptance and commitment therapy for social anxiety disorder: Outcomes and moderators. *Journal of Consulting and Clinical Psychology*, 82(6), 1034–1048. https://doi.org/10.1037/a0037212

Dahlin, M., Andersson, G., Magnusson, K., Johansson, T., Sjögren, J., Håkansson, A., Pettersson, M., Kadowaki, Å., Cuijpers, P., & Carlbring, P. (2016). Internet-delivered acceptance-based behaviour therapy for generalized anxiety disorder: A randomized controlled trial. *Behaviour Research and Therapy*, 77, 86–95. https://doi.org/10.1016/j.brat.2015.12.007

Dimidjian, S., Beck, A., Felder, J. N., Boggs, J. M., Gallop, R., & Segal, Z. V. (2014). Web-based mindfulness-based cognitive therapy for reducing residual depressive symptoms: An open trial and quasi-experimental comparison to propensity score matched controls. *Behaviour Research and Therapy*, 63, 83–89. https://doi.org/10.1016/j.brat.2014.09.004

Dimidjian, S., Goodman, S. H., Felder, J. N., Gallop, R., Brown, A. P., & Beck, A. (2016). Staying well during pregnancy and the postpartum: A pilot randomized trial of mindfulness-based cognitive therapy for the prevention of depressive relapse/recurrence. *Journal of Consulting and Clinical Psychology*, 84(2), 134–145. https://doi.org/10.1037/ccp0000068

Duarte, C., Pinto-Gouveia, J., & Stubbs, R. J. (2017). Compassionate attention and regulation of eating behaviour: A pilot study of a brief low-intensity intervention for binge eating. *Clinical Psychology and Psychotherapy*, 24(6), 1437–1447. https://doi.org/10.1002/cpp.2094

Dubose, A. P., Botanov, Y., & Ivanoff, A. (2019). International implementation of dialectical behaviour therapy: The challenge of training therapists across cultures. In M. A. Swales (Ed.), *The Oxford handbook of dialectical behaviour therapy* (pp. 909–930). Oxford University Press.

Eifert, G. H., & Forsyth, J. P. (2005). *Acceptance and commitment therapy for anxiety disorders: A practitioner's treatment guide to using mindfulness, acceptance, and values-based behavior change strategies*. Guilford Press.

Eifert, G. H., & Heffner, M. (2003). The effects of acceptance versus control contexts on avoidance of panic-related symptoms. *Journal of Behavior Therapy and Experimental Psychiatry*, 34(3–4), 293–312. https://doi.org/10.1016/j.jbtep.2003.11.001

Esfahani, M., Kjbaf, M. B., & Abedi, M. R. (2015). Evaluation and comparison of the effects of time perspective therapy, acceptance and commitment therapy and narrative therapy on severity of symptoms of obsessive-compulsive disorder. *Journal of the Indian Academy of Applied Psychology*, 41(3), 148–155.

Eustis, E. H., Hayes-Skelton, S. A., Roemer, L., & Orsillo, S. M. (2016). Reductions in experiential avoidance as a mediator of change in symptom outcome and quality of life in acceptance-based behavior therapy and applied relaxation for generalized anxiety disorder. *Behaviour Research and Therapy*, 87, 188–195. https://doi.org/10.1016/j.brat.2016.09.012

Evans, S., Ferrando, S., Findler, M., Stowell, C., Smart, C., & Haglin, D. (2008). Mindfulness-based cognitive therapy for generalized anxiety disorder. *Journal of Anxiety Disorders*, 22(4), 716–721. https://doi.org/10.1016/j.janxdis.2007.07.005

Fayaz, A., Croft, P., Langford, R. M., Donaldson, L. J., & Jones, G. T. (2016). Prevalence of chronic pain in the UK: A systematic review and meta-analysis of population studies. *BMJ Open*, 6, 1–12. https://doi.org/10.1136/bmjopen-2015-010364

Feigenbaum, J. D., Fonagy, P., Pilling, S., Jones, A., Wildgoose, A., & Bebbington, P. E. (2012). A real-world study of the effectiveness of DBT in the UK National Health Service. *British Journal of Clinical Psychology*, *51*(2), 121–141. https://doi.org/10.1111/j.2044-8260.2011.02017.x

Fiore, M. C., Bailey, W. C., Cohen, S. J., Dorfman, S. F., Goldstein, M. G., Gritz, E. R., Heyman, R. B., Jaén, C. R., Kotte, T. E., Lando, H. A., Mecklenburg, R. E., Mullen, P. D., Nett, L. M., Robinson, L., Stitzer, M. L., Tommasello, A. C., Villejo, L., & Wewers, M. E. (2000). *Treating tobacco use and dependence. Clinical practice guideline*. U.S. Department of Health and Human Services, Public Health Services, Rockville.

Fiore, M. C., Jaén, C. R., Baker, T. B., Bailey, W. C., Benowitz, N. L., Curry, S. J., Dorfman, S. F., Froelicher, E. S., Goldstein, M. G., Healton, C. G., Lando, H. A., Mecklenburg, R. E., Mermelstein, R. J., Mullen, P. D., Orleans, C. T., Robinson, L., Stitzer, M. L., Tommasello, A. C., Villejo, L., & Wewers, M. E. (2008). Treating tobacco use and dependence: 2008 update. In *Clinical Practice Guideline. U.S. Department of Health and Human Services, Public Health Service.*

First, M.B., Spitzer, R.L., Gibbon, M., Williams, J.B.W. (1996). *Structured Clinical Interview for DSM-IV Axis I Disorders-Patient Edition (SCID-I/P, Version 2.0)*.

Fleming, J. E., & Kocovski, N. L. (2013). *The mindfulness and acceptance workbook for social anxiety and shyness: Using acceptance and commitment therapy to free yourself from fear and reclaim your life*. New Harbinger Publications.

Foa, E. B., Kozak, M. J., Steketee, G. S., & McCarthy, P. R. (1992). Treatment of depressive and obsessive-compulsive symptoms in OCD by imipramine and behaviour therapy. *British Journal of Clinical Psychology*, *31*(3), 279–292. https://doi.org/10.1111/J.2044-8260.1992.TB00995.x

Fordyce, W E, Fowler, R. S., Lehmann, J. F., Delateur, B. J., Sand, P. L., & Trieschmann, R. B. (1973). Operant conditioning in the treatment of chronic pain. *Archives of Physical Medicine and Rehabilitation*, *54*(9), 399–408.

Forman, E. M., Butryn, M. L., Hoffman, K. L., & Herbert, J. D. (2009). An open trial of an acceptance-based behavioral intervention for weight loss. *Cognitive and Behavioral Practice*, *16*(2), 223–235. https://doi.org/10.1016/j.cbpra.2008.09.005

Forman, E. M., Butryn, M. L., Juarascio, A. S., Bradley, L. E., Lowe, M. R., Herbert, J. D., & Shaw, J. A. (2013). The mind your health project: A randomized controlled trial of an innovative behavioral treatment for obesity. *Obesity*, *21*(6), 1119–1126. https://doi.org/10.1002/oby.20169

Forman, E. M., Butryn, M. L., Manasse, S. M., Crosby, R. D., Goldstein, S. P., Wyckoff, E. P., & Thomas, J. G. (2016). Acceptance-based versus standard behavioral treatment for obesity: Results from the mind your health randomized controlled trial. *Obesity*, *24*(10), 2050–2056. https://doi.org/10.1002/oby.21601

Forman, E. M., Herbert, J. D., Moitra, E., Yeomans, P. D., & Geller, P. A. (2007). A randomized controlled effectiveness trial of acceptance and commitment therapy and cognitive therapy for anxiety and depression. *Behavior Modification*, *31*(6), 772–799. https://doi.org/10.1177/0145445507302202

Forman, E. M., Manasse, S. M., Butryn, M. L., Crosby, R. D., Dallal, D. H., & Crochiere, R. J. (2019). Long-term follow-up of the Mind Your Health Project: Acceptance-based versus standard behavioral treatment for obesity. *Obesity*, *27*(4), 565–571. https://doi.org/10.1002/OBY.22412

Forman, E. M., Shaw, J. A., Goetter, E. M., Herbert, J. D., Park, J. A., & Yuen, E. K. (2012). Long-term follow-up of a randomized controlled trial comparing acceptance and commitment therapy and standard cognitive behavior therapy for anxiety and depression. *Behavior Therapy*, *43*(4), 801–811. https://doi.org/10.1016/j.beth.2012.04.004

Forsyth, J. P., & Eifert, G. H. (2016). *The mindfulness and acceptance workbook for anxiety: A guide to breaking free from anxiety, phobias, and worry using acceptance and commitment therapy* (2nd ed.). New Harbinger Publications.

Forsyth, J. P., Eifert, G. H., & Barrios, V. (2006). Fear conditioning in an emotion regulation context: A fresh perspective on the origins of anxiety disorders. In M. G. Craske, D. Hermans, & D. Vansteenwegen (Eds.), *Fear and learning: From basic processes to clinical implications* (p. 133–153). American Psychological Association. https://doi.org/10.1037/11474-007

Gatchel, R. J., Peng, Y. B., Peters, M. L., Fuchs, P. N., & Turk, D. C. (2007). The biopsychosocial approach to chronic pain: Scientific advances and future directions. *Psychological Bulletin*, *133*, 581–624. https://doi.org/10.1037/0033-2909.133.4.581

Gaudiano, B. A. (Ed.). (2015). *Incorporating acceptance and mindfulness into the treatment of psychosis: Current trends and future directions*. Oxford University Press.

Gaudiano, B. A., Ellenberg, S., Ostrove, B., Johnson, J., Mueser, K. T., Furman, M., & Miller, I. W. (2020). Feasibility and preliminary effects of implementing acceptance and commitment therapy for inpatients with psychotic-spectrum disorders in a clinical psychiatric intensive care setting. *Journal of Cognitive Psychotherapy*, *34*(1), 80–96. https://doi.org/10.1891/0889-8391.34.1.80

Gaudiano, B. A., & Herbert, J. D. (2006). Acute treatment of inpatients with psychotic symptoms using acceptance and commitment therapy: Pilot results. *Behaviour Research and Therapy*, *44*(3), 415–437. https://doi.org/10.1016/j.brat.2005.02.007

Gaudiano, B. A., Herbert, J. D., & Hayes, S. C. (2010). Is it the symptom or the relation to it? Investigating potential mediators of change in acceptance and commitment therapy for psychosis. *Behavior Therapy*, *41*(4), 543–554. https://doi.org/10.1016/j.beth.2010.03.001

GBD 2015 Tobacco Collaborators (2016). Global, regional, and national comparative risk assessment of 79 behavioural, environmental and occupational, and metabolic risks or clusters of risks, 1990–2015: A systematic analysis for the Global Burden of Disease Study 2015. *The Lancet*, *388*(10053), 1659–1724. https://doi.org/10.1016/s0140-6736(16)31679-8

GBD 2015 Tobacco Collaborators (2017). Smoking prevalence and attributable disease burden in 195 countries and territories, 1990–2015: A systematic analysis from the Global Burden of Disease Study 2015. *The Lancet*. https://doi.org/10.1016/s0140-6736(17)30819-x

Geddes, J. R., Carney, S. M., Davies, C., Furukawa, T. A., Kupfer, D. J., Frank, E., & Goodwin, G. M. (2003). Relapse prevention with antidepressant drug treatment in depressive disorders: A systematic review. *The Lancet*, *361*(9358), 653–661. https://doi.org/10.1016/S0140-6736(03)12599-8

Geschwind, N., Peeters, F., Drukker, M., Van Os, J., & Wichers, M. (2011). Mindfulness training increases momentary positive emotions and reward experience in adults vulnerable to depression. A randomized controlled trial. *Journal of Consulting and Clinical Psychology*, *79*(5), 618–628. https://doi.org/10.1037/a0024595

Gifford, E. V., Kohlenberg, B. S., Hayes, S. C., Antonuccio, D. O., Piasecki, M. M., Rasmussen-Hall, M. L., & Palm, K. M. (2004). Acceptance-based treatment for smoking cessation. *Behavior Therapy*, *35*(4), 689–705. https://doi.org/10.1016/S0005-7894(04)80015-7

Gifford, E. V., Kohlenberg, B. S., Hayes, S. C., Pierson, H. M., Piasecki, M. P., Antonuccio, D. O., & Palm, K. M. (2011). Does acceptance and relationship focused behavior therapy contribute to bupropion outcomes? A randomized controlled trial of functional analytic psychotherapy and acceptance and commitment therapy for smoking cessation. *Behavior Therapy*, *42*(4), 700–715. https://doi.org/10.1016/j.beth.2011.03.002

Gloster, A. T., Sonntag, R., Hoyer, J., Meyer, A. H., Heinze, S., Ströhle, A., Eifert, G., & Wittchen, H.-U. (2015). Treating treatment-resistant patients with panic disorder and agoraphobia using psychotherapy: A randomized controlled switching trial. *Psychotherapy and Psychosomatics*, *84*(2), 100–109. https://doi.org/10.1159/000370162

Godfrey, K. M., Gallo, L. C., & Afari, N. (2015). Mindfulness-based interventions for binge eating: A systematic review and meta-analysis. *Journal of Behavioral Medicine*, *38*(2), 348–362. https://doi.org/10.1007/s10865-014-9610-5

Godfrin, K. A., & van Heeringen, C. (2010). The effects of mindfulness-based cognitive therapy on recurrence of depressive episodes, mental health and quality of life: A randomized controlled study. *Behaviour Research and Therapy*, *48*(8), 738–746. https://doi.org/10.1016/j.brat.2010.04.006

Goldberg, S. B., Tucker, R. P., Greene, P. A., Davidson, R. J., Kearney, D. J., & Simpson, T. L. (2019). Mindfulness-based cognitive therapy for the treatment of current depressive symptoms: A meta-analysis. *Cognitive Behaviour Therapy*, *48*(6), 445–462. https://doi.org/10.1080/16506073.2018.1556330

Goodman, M., Banthin, D., Blair, N., Mascitelli, K., Wilsnack, J., Chen, J., Messenger, J. W., Perez-Rodriquez, M. M., Triebwasser, J., Koenigsberg, H. W., Goetz, R. R., Hazlett, E. A., & New, A. S. (2016). A randomized trial of dialectical behavior therapy in high-risk suicidal veterans. *The Journal of Clinical Psychology*, *77*(12), 1591-1600. https://doi.org/10.4088/JCP.15m10235

Graham, A., Carpenter, K., Cha, S., Cole, S., Jacobs, M., Raskob, M., & Cole-Lewis, H. (2016). Systematic review and meta-analysis of internet interventions for smoking cessation among adults. *Substance Abuse and Rehabilitation, 7*, 55–69. https://doi.org/10.2147/SAR.S101660

Gratz, K. L., Berghoff, C. R., Richmond, J. R., Vidaña, A. G., & Dixon-Gordon, K. L. (2020). Examining posttraumatic stress disorder as a predictor of treatment response to dialectical behavior therapy. *Journal of Clinical Psychology, 76*(9), 1563–1574. https://doi.org/10.1002/jclp.22961

Gratz, K. L., & Tull, M. T. (2010). Emotion regulation as a mechanism of change in acceptance-and mindfulness-based treatments. In R. A. Baer (Ed.), *Assessing mindfulness and acceptance processes in clients: Illuminating the theory and practice of change* (p. 107–133). Context Press/New Harbinger Publications.

Guidi, J., Tomba, E., & Fava, G. A. (2016). The sequential integration of pharmacotherapy and psychotherapy in the treatment of major depressive disorder: A meta-analysis of the sequential model and a critical review of the literature. *The American Journal of Psychiatry, 173*(2), 128–137. https://doi.org/10.1176/appi.ajp.2015.15040476

Gunderson, J. G. (2009). Borderline personality disorder: Ontogeny of a diagnosis. *The American Journal of Psychiatry, 166*(5), 530–539. https://doi.org/10.1176/appi.ajp.2009.08121825

Hamilton, M. (1960). A rating scale for depression. *Journal of Neurology, Neurosurgery and Psychiatry, 23*, 56–62. https://doi.org/10.1136/jnnp.23.1.56

Hancock, K. M., Swain, J., Hainsworth, C. J., Dixon, A. L., Koo, S., & Munro, K. (2018). Acceptance and commitment therapy versus cognitive behavior therapy for children with anxiety: Outcomes of a randomized controlled trial. *Journal of Clinical Child & Adolescent Psychology, 47*(2), 296–311. https://doi.org/10.1080/15374416.2015.1110822

Hayes, S. C. (2004). Acceptance and commitment therapy, relational frame theory, and the third wave of behavioral and cognitive therapies. *Behavior Therapy, 35*(4), 639–665. https://doi.org/10.1016/S0005-7894(04)80013-3

Hayes, S. C., Luoma, J. B., Bond, F. W., Masuda, A., & Lillis, J. (2006). Acceptance and commitment therapy: Model, processes and outcomes. *Behaviour Research and Therapy, 44*(1), 1–25. https://doi.org/10.1016/j.brat.2005.06.006

Hayes, S. C., Pistorello, J., & Levin, M. E. (2012). Acceptance and commitment therapy as a unified model of behavior change. *The Counseling Psychologist, 40*(7), 976–1002. https://doi.org/10.1177/0011000012460836

Hayes, S. C., Strosahl, K. D., & Wilson, K. G. (2011). *Acceptance and commitment therapy: The process and practice of mindful change.* Guilford Press.

Hayes, S. C., Strosahl, K., & Wilson, K. (1999a). *Acceptance and commitment therapy: An experiential approach to behavior change.* Guilford Press.

Hayes, S. C., Strosahl, K., & Wilson, K. G. (1999b). *Acceptance and commitment therapy: Understanding and treating human suffering.* Guilford Press.

Hayes, S. C., Strosahl, K., Wilson, K. G., Bissett, R. T., Pistorello, J., Toarmino, D., Polusny, M. A., Dykstra, T. A., Batten, S. V., Bergan, J., Stewart, S. H., Zvolensky, M. J., Eifert, G. H., Bond, F. W., Forsyth, J. P., Karekla, M., & McCurry, S. M. (2004). Measuring experiential avoidance: A preliminary test of a working model. *The Psychological Record, 54*(4), 553–578. https://doi.org/10.1007/BF03395492

Hayes, S. C., Villatte, M., Levin, M., & Hildebrandt, M. (2011). Open, aware, and active: Contextual approaches as an emerging trend in the behavioral and cognitive therapies. *Annual Review of Clinical Psychology, 7*, 141–168. https://doi.org/10.1146/annurev-clinpsy-032210-104449

Hayes, S. C., Wilson, K. G., Gifford, E. V., Follette, V. M., & Strosahl, K. (1996). Experiential avoidance and behavioral disorders: A functional dimensional approach to diagnosis and treatment. *Journal of Consulting and Clinical Psychology, 64*(6), 1152–1168. https://doi.org/10.1037//0022-006x.64.6.1152

Hayes-Skelton, S. A., Roemer, L., & Orsillo, S. M. (2013). A randomized clinical trial comparing an acceptance-based behavior therapy to applied relaxation for generalized anxiety disorder. *Journal of Consulting and Clinical Psychology, 81*(5), 761–773. https://doi.org/10.1037/a0032871

Heffner, J. L., Kelly, M. M., Waxmonsky, J., Mattocks, K., Serfozo, E., Bricker, J. B., Mull, K. E., Watson, N. L., & Ostacher, M. (2020). Pilot randomized controlled trial of web-delivered acceptance and commitment therapy versus Smokefree.gov for smokers with bipolar disorder. *Nicotine & Tobacco Research, 22*(9), 1543–1552. https://doi.org/10.1093/ntr/ntz242

Heffner, J. L., Mull, K. E., Watson, N. L., McClure, J. B., & Bricker, J. B. (2018). Smokers with bipolar disorder, other affective disorders, and no mental health conditions: Comparison of baseline characteristics and success at quitting in a large 12-month behavioral intervention randomized trial. *Drug and Alcohol Dependence, 193*, 35–41. https://doi.org/10.1016/j.drugalcdep.2018.08.034

Heffner, J. L., Mull, K. E., Watson, N. L., McClure, J. B., & Bricker, J. B. (2020). Long-term smoking cessation outcomes for sexual minority vs. non-minority smokers in a large randomized, controlled trial of two web-based interventions. *Nicotine & Tobacco Research, 22*(9), 1596–1604. https://doi.org/10.1093/ntr/ntz112

Heffner, J. L., Vilardaga, R., Mercer, L. D., Kientz, J. A., & Bricker, J. B. (2015). Feature-level analysis of a novel smartphone application for smoking cessation. *The American Journal of Drug and Alcohol Abuse, 41*(1), 68–73. https://doi.org/10.3109/00952990.2014.977486

Herbert, J. D., Forman, E. M., Kaye, J. L., Gershkovich, M., Goetter, E., Yuen, E. K., Glassman, L., Goldstein, S., Hitchcock, P., & Tronieri, J. S., Berkowitz, S., & Marando-Blanck, S. (2018). Randomized controlled trial of acceptance and commitment therapy versus traditional cognitive behavior therapy for social anxiety disorder: Symptomatic and behavioral outcomes. *Journal of Contextual Behavioral Science, 9*, 88–96. https://doi.org/10.1016/j.jcbs.2018.07.008

Herschell, A. D., Kogan, J. N., Celedonia, K. L., Gavin, J. G., & Stein, B. D. (2009). Understanding community mental health administrators' perspectives on dialectical behavior therapy implementation. *Psychiatric Services, 60*(7), 989–992. https://doi.org/10.1176/ps.2009.60.7.989

Hofmann, S. G., & Asmundson, G. J. (2008). Acceptance and mindfulness-based therapy: New wave or old hat? *Clinical Psychology Review, 28*(1), 1–16. https://doi.org/10.1016/j.cpr.2007.09.003

Hofmann, S. G., & Hayes, S. C. (2019). The future of intervention science: Process-based therapy. *Clinical Psychological Science, 7*(1), 37–50. https://doi.org/10.1177/2167702618772296

Hofmann, S. G., Sawyer, A. T., Witt, A. A., & Oh, D. (2010). The effect of mindfulness-based therapy on anxiety and depression: A meta-analytic review. *Journal of Consulting and Clinical Psychology, 78*(2), 169–183. https://doi.org/10.1037/a0018555

Hollon, S. D., DeRubeis, R. J., Shelton, R. C., Amsterdam, J. D., Salomon, R. M., O'Reardon, J. P., Lovett, M. L., Young, P. R., Haman, K. L., Freeman, B. B., & Gallop, R. (2005). Prevention of relapse following cognitive therapy vs. medications in moderate to severe depression. *Archives of General Psychiatry, 62*(4), 417–422. https://doi.org/10.1001/archpsyc.62.4.417

Hughes, L. S., Clark, J., Colclough, J. A., Dale, E., & McMillan, D. (2017). Acceptance and Commitment Therapy (ACT) for chronic pain: A systematic review and meta-analysis. *Clinical Journal of Pain, 33*, 552–568. https://doi.org/10.1097/AJP.0000000000000425

Huijbers, M. J., Spinhoven, P., Spijker, J., Ruhé, H. G., van Schaik, D. J., van Oppen, P., Nolen, W. A., Ormel, J., Kuyken, W., van der Wilt, G. J., Blom, M. B., Schene, A. H., Donders, A. R., & Speckens, A. E. (2015). Adding mindfulness-based cognitive therapy to maintenance antidepressant medication for prevention of relapse/recurrence in major depressive disorder: Randomised controlled trial. *Journal of Affective Disorders, 187*, 54–61. https://doi.org/10.1016/j.jad.2015.08.023

Husten, C. G. (2010). A Call for ACTTION: Increasing access to tobacco-use treatment in our nation. *American Journal of Preventive Medicine, 38*(3), S414–S417. https://doi.org/10.1016/j.amepre.2009.12.006

Ivanoff, A., Dubose, T., Abdelkarim, A., Sher, H., Ustundag-Budak, A. M., & Henriquez, S. (2018, November 15–18). *Adopting vs. adapting DBT across cultures and diagnoses* [Conference presentation]. ABCT 52st Annual Convention, Washington D.C., United States.

Juarascio, A., Shaw, J., Forman, E., Timko, C. A., Herbert, J., Butryn, M., & Lowe, M. (2013). Acceptance and commitment therapy as a novel treatment for eating disorders: An initial test of efficacy and mediation. *Behavior Modification, 37*(4), 459–489. https://doi.org/10.1177/0145445513478633

Kabat-Zinn, J., Massion, A. O., Kristeller, J., Peterson, L. G., Fletcher, K. E., Pbert, L., Lenderking, W. R., & Santorelli, S. F. (1992). Effectiveness of a meditation-based stress reduction program in the treatment of anxiety disorders. *The American Journal of Psychiatry, 149*(7), 936–943. https://doi.org/10.1176/ajp.149.7.936

Karekla, M., Savvides, S. N., & Gloster, A. (2020). An avatar-led intervention promotes smoking cessation in young adults: A pilot randomized clinical trial. *Annals of Behavioral Medicine, 54*(10), 747–760. https://doi.org/10.1093/abm/kaaa013

Katterman, S. N., Kleinman, B. M., Hood, M. M., Nackers, L. M., & Corsica, J. A. (2014). Mindfulness meditation as an intervention for binge eating, emotional eating, and weight loss: A systematic review. *Eating Behaviours, 15*(2), 197–204. https://doi.org/10.1016/j.eatbeh.2014.01.005

Kay, S. R., Fiszbein, A., & Opler, L. A. (1987). The Positive and Negative Syndrome Scale (PANSS) for schizophrenia. *Schizophrenia Bulletin, 13*(2), 261–276. https://doi.org/10.1093/schbul/13.2.261

Keng, S.-L., Phang, C. K., & Oei, T. P. (2015). Effects of a brief mindfulness-based intervention program on psychological symptoms and well-being among medical students in Malaysia: A controlled study. *International Journal of Cognitive Therapy, 8*(4), 335–350. https://doi.org/10.1521/ijct.2015.8.4.335

Keng, S.-L., Smoski, M. J., & Robins, C. J. (2011). Effects of mindfulness on psychological health: A review of empirical studies. *Clinical Psychology Review, 31*(6), 1041–1056. https://doi.org/10.1016/j.cpr.2011.04.006

Khoury, B., Lecomte, T., Gaudiano, B. A., & Paquin, K. (2013). Mindfulness interventions for psychosis: A meta-analysis. *Schizophrenia Research, 150*(1), 176–184. https://doi.org/10.1016/j.schres.2013.07.055

Kliem, S., Kröger, C., & Kosfelder, J. (2010). Dialectical behavior therapy for borderline personality disorder. *Journal of Consulting and Clinical Psychology, 78*(6), 936–951. https://doi.org/10.1037/a0021015

Kocovski, N. L., Fleming, J. E., Blackie, R. A., MacKenzie, M. B., & Rose, A. L. (2019). Self-help for social anxiety: Randomized controlled trial comparing a mindfulness and acceptance-based approach with a control group. *Behavior Therapy, 50*(4), 696–709. https://doi.org/10.1016/j.beth.2018.10.007

Kocovski, N. L., Fleming, J. E., Hawley, L. L., Huta, V., & Antony, M. M. (2013). Mindfulness and acceptance-based group therapy versus traditional cognitive behavioral group therapy for social anxiety disorder: A randomized controlled trial. *Behaviour Research and Therapy, 51*(12), 889–898. https://doi.org/10.1016/j.brat.2013.10.007

Koons, C. R., Robins, C. J., Lindsey Tweed, J., Lynch, T. R., Gonzalez, A. M., Morse, J. Q., Bishop, G. K., Butterfield, M. I., & Bastian, L. A. (2001). Efficacy of dialectical behavior therapy in women veterans with borderline personality disorder. *Behavior Therapy, 32*(2), 371–390. https://doi.org/10.1016/S0005-7894(01)80009-5

Kroenke, K., Spitzer, R. L., & Williams, J. B. W. (2001). The PHQ-9: Validity of a brief depression severity measure. *Journal of General Internal Medicine, 16*(9), 606–613. https://doi.org/10.1046/j.1525-1497.2001.016009606.x

Kuyken, W., Byford, S., Taylor, R. S., Watkins, E., Holden, E., White, K., Barrett, B., Byng, R., Evans, A., Mullan, E., & Teasdale, J. D. (2008). Mindfulness-based cognitive therapy to prevent relapse in recurrent depression. *Journal of Consulting and Clinical Psychology, 76*(6), 966–977. https://doi.org/10.1037/a0013786

Kuyken, W., Hayes, R., Barrett, B., Byng, R., Dalgleish, T., Kessler, D., Lewis, G., Watkins, E., Brejcha, C., Cardy, J., Causley, A., Cowderoy, S., Evans, A., Gradinger, F., Kaur, S., Lanham, P., Morant, N., Richards, J., Shah, P., . . . Byford, S. (2015). Effectiveness and cost-effectiveness of mindfulness-based cognitive therapy compared with maintenance antidepressant treatment in the prevention of depressive relapse or recurrence (PREVENT): A randomised controlled trial. *The Lancet, 386*(9988), 63–73. https://doi.org/10.1016/S0140-6736(14)62222-4

Kuyken, W., Warren, F. C., Taylor, R. S., Whalley, B., Crane, C., Bondolfi, G., Hayes, R., Huijbers, M., Ma, H., Schweizer, S., Segal, Z., Speckens, A., Teasdale, J. D., Van Heeringen, K., Williams, M., Byford, S., Byng, R., & Dalgleish, T. (2016). Efficacy of mindfulness-based cognitive therapy in prevention of depressive relapse: An individual patient data meta-analysis from randomized trials. *JAMA Psychiatry, 73*(6), 565–574. https://doi.org/10.1001/jamapsychiatry.2016.0076

Kuyken, W., Watkins, E., Holden, E., White, K., Taylor, R. S., Byford, S., Evans, A., Radford, S., Teasdale, J. D., & Dalgleish, T. (2010). How does mindfulness-based cognitive therapy work? *Behaviour Research and Therapy, 48*(11), 1105–1112. https://doi.org/10.1016/j.brat.2010.08.003

Lancaster, T., & Stead, L. F. (2017). Individual behavioural counselling for smoking cessation. *Cochrane Database of Systematic Reviews, 3*(3), CD001292. https://doi.org/10.1002/14651858.CD001292.pub3

Landy, L. N., Schneider, R. L., & Arch, J. J. (2014). Acceptance and commitment therapy for the treatment of anxiety disorders: A concise review. *Current Opinion in Psychology, 2*, 70–74. https://doi.org/10.1016/J.COPSYC.2014.11.004

Lillis, J., & Hayes, S. C. (2007). Measuring avoidance and inflexibility in weight related problems. *International Journal of Behavioral Consultation and Therapy, 4*(1), 30–40. https://doi.org/10.1037/h0100829

Lillis, J., Niemeier, H. M., Thomas, J. G., Unick, J., Ross, K. M., Leahey, T. M., Kendra, K. E., Dorfman, L., & Wing, R. R. (2016). A randomized trial of an acceptance-based behavioral intervention for weight loss in people with high internal disinhibition. *Obesity, 24*(12), 2509–2514. https://doi.org/10.1002/oby.21680

Lillis, J., Thomas, J. G., Niemeier, H. M., & Wing, R. R. (2017). Exploring process variables through which acceptance-based behavioral interventions may improve weight loss maintenance. *Journal of Contextual Behavioral Science, 6*(4), 398–403. https://doi.org/10.1016/j.jcbs.2017.07.005

Linardon, J., Fairburn, C. G., Fitzsimmons-Craft, E. E., Wilfley, D. E., & Brennan, L. (2017). The empirical status of the third-wave behaviour therapies for the treatment of eating disorders: A systematic review. *Clinical Psychology Review, 58*, 125–140. https://doi.org/10.1016/j.cpr.2017.10.005

Lincoln, T. M., & Pedersen, A. (2019). An overview of the evidence for psychological interventions for psychosis: Results from meta-analyses. *Clinical Psychology in Europe, 1*(1), 1–23. https://doi.org/10.32872/cpe.v1i1.31407

Linehan, M. (1993). *Cognitive-behavioral treatment of borderline personality disorder. Diagnosis and treatment of mental disorders.* Guilford Press.

Linehan, M. M. (1997). Validation and psychotherapy. In A. C. Bohart & L. S. Greenberg (Eds.), *Empathy reconsidered: New directions in psychotherapy* (pp. 353–392). American Psychological Association.

Linehan, M. M. (1999). Development, evaluation, and dissemination of effective psychosocial treatments: Levels of disorder, stages of care, and stages of treatment research. In M. D. Glantz & C. R. Hartel (Eds.), *Drug abuse: Origins & interventions* (pp. 367–394). American Psychological Association.

Linehan, M. M., Armstrong, H. E., Suarez, A., Allmon, D., & Heard, H. L. (1991). Cognitive-behavioral treatment of chronically parasuicidal borderline patients. *Archives of General Psychiatry, 48*(12), 1060–1064. https://doi.org/10.1001/archpsyc.1991.01810360024003

Linehan, M. M., & Korslund, K. E. (2003). *Dialectical behavior therapy adherence manual.* University of Washington.

Linehan, M. M., & Wilks, C. R. (2015). The course and evolution of Dialectical Behavior Therapy. *American Journal of Psychotherapy, 69*(2), 97–110. https://doi.org/10.1176/appi.psychotherapy.2015.69.2.97

Loerinc, A. G., Meuret, A. E., Twohig, M. P., Rosenfield, D., Bluett, E. J., & Craske, M. G. (2015). Response rates for CBT for anxiety disorders: Need for standardized criteria. *Clinical Psychology Review, 42*, 72–82. https://doi.org/10.1016/j.cpr.2015.08.004

Loeser, J. D., & Melzack, R. (1999). Pain: An overview. *The Lancet, 353*, 1607–1609. https://doi.org/10.1016/S0140-6736(99)01311-2

Louise, S., Fitzpatrick, M., Strauss, C., Rossell, S. L., & Thomas, N. (2018). Mindfulness- and acceptance-based interventions for psychosis: Our current understanding and a meta-analysis. *Schizophrenia Research, 192*, 57–63. https://doi.org/10.1016/j.schres.2017.05.023

Lynch, D., Laws, K. R., & McKenna, P. J. (2010). Cognitive behavioural therapy for major psychiatric disorder: does it really work? A meta-analytical review of well-controlled trials. *Psychological Medicine, 40*(1), 9–24. https://doi.org/10.1017/S003329170900590X

Lynch, T. R., Chapman, A. L., Rosenthal, M. Z., Kuo, J. R., & Linehan, M. M. (2006). Mechanisms of change in dialectical behavior therapy: Theoretical and empirical observations. *Journal of Clinical Psychology, 62*(4), 459–480. https://doi.org/10.1002/jclp.20243

Ma, S. H., & Teasdale, J. D. (2004). Mindfulness-based cognitive therapy for depression: Replication and exploration of differential relapse prevention effects. *Journal of Consulting and Clinical Psychology, 72*(1), 31–40. https://doi.org/10.1037/0022-006X.72.1.31

Main, C. J., Keefe, F. J., Jensen, M. P., Vlaeyen, J. W. S., & Vowles, K. E. (Eds.). (2014). *Fordyce's behavioral methods for chronic pain and illness.* New York: Walters-Kluwer.

Manasse, S. M., Flack, D., Dochat, C., Zhang, F., Butryn, M. L., & Forman, E. M. (2017). Not so fast: The impact of impulsivity on weight loss varies by treatment type. *Appetite, 113*, 193–199. https://doi.org/10.1016/j.appet.2017.02.042

Marlatt, G. A., & George, W. H. (1984). Relapse prevention: Introduction and overview of the model. *British Journal of Addiction, 79*(4), 261–273. https://doi.org/10.1111/j.1360-0443.1984.tb03867.x

Martins, M. J. R. V., Castilho, P., Carvalho, C. B., Pereira, A. T., Santos, V., Gumley, A., & Macedo, A. F. de (2017). Contextual cognitive-behavioral therapies across the psychosis continuum. *European Psychologist, 22*(2), 83–100. https://doi.org/10.1027/1016-9040/a000283

Matkin, W., Ordóñez-Mena, J. M., & Hartmann-Boyce, J. (2019). Telephone counselling for smoking cessation. *Cochrane Database of Systematic Reviews, 5.* https://doi.org/10.1002/14651858.CD002850.pub4

McCauley, E., Berk, M. S., Asarnow, J. R., Adrian, M., Cohen, J., Korslund, K., Avina, C., Hughes, J., Harned, M., Gallop, R., & Linehan, M. M. (2018). Efficacy of dialectical behavior therapy for adolescents at high risk for suicide: A randomized clinical trial. *JAMA Psychiatry, 75*(8), 777-785. https://doi.org/10.1001/jamapsychiatry.2018.1109

McClure, J. B., Bricker, J., Mull, K., & Heffner, J. L. (2020). Comparative effectiveness of group-delivered acceptance and commitment therapy versus cognitive behavioral therapy for smoking cessation: A randomized controlled trial. *Nicotine & Tobacco Research, 22*(3), 354–362. https://doi.org/10.1093/ntr/nty268

McCracken, L. M., & Morley, S. (2014). The psychological flexibility model: A basis for integration and progress in psychological approaches to chronic pain management. *Journal of Pain, 15*, 221–234.

McCracken, L. M., & Vowles, K. E. (2014). Acceptance and commitment therapy and mindfulness for chronic pain: Model, process, and progress. *American Psychologist, 69*, 178–187.

McGrath, K. B., Forman, E. M., Herbert, J. D., Arch, J. J., Craske, M. G., & Eifert, G. H. (2010). Differences in therapist behavior in implementing ACT and CT for the treatment of anxiety disorders. In *The 44th Annual Convention of the Association for Behavioral and Cognitive Therapies*, San Francisco.

McHugh, R. K., Whitton, S. W., Peckham, A. D., Welge, J. A., & Otto, M. W. (2013). Patient preference for psychological vs. pharmacological treatment of psychiatric disorders: A meta-analytic review. *The Journal of Clinical Psychiatry, 74*(6), 595–602. https://doi.org/10.4088/JCP.12r07757

McMain, S. F., Guimond, T., Barnhart, R., Habinski, L., & Streiner, D. L. (2017). A randomized trial of brief dialectical behaviour therapy skills training in suicidal patients suffering from borderline disorder. *Acta Psychiatrica Scandinavica, 135*(2), 138-148. https://doi.org/10.1111/acps.12664

McMain, S. F., Links, P. S., Gnam, W. H., Guimond, T., Cardish, R. J., Korman, L., & Streiner, D. L. (2009). A randomized trial of dialectical behavior therapy versus general psychiatric management for borderline personality disorder. *The American Journal of Psychiatry, 166*(12), 1365–1374. https://doi.org/10.1176/appi.ajp.2009.09010039

McManus, F., Surawy, C., Muse, K., Vazquez-Montes, M., & Williams, J. M. G. (2012). A randomized clinical trial of mindfulness-based cognitive therapy versus unrestricted services for health anxiety (hypochondriasis). *Journal of Consulting and Clinical, 80*(5), 817–828. https://doi.org/10.1037/a0028782

Mehlum, L., Tørmoen, A. J., Ramberg, M., Haga, E., Diep, L. M., Laberg, S., Larsson, B. S., Stanley, B. H., Miller, A. L., Sund, A. M., & Grøholt, B. (2014). Dialectical behavior therapy for adolescents with repeated suicidal and self-harming behavior: A randomized trial. *Journal of the American Academy of Child & Adolescent Psychiatry, 53*(10), 1082–1091. https://doi.org/10.1016/j.jaac.2014.07.003

Miga, E. M., Neacsiu, A. D., Lungu, A., Heard, H. L., & Dimeff, L. A. (2019). Dialectical behaviour therapy from 1991–2015: What do we know about clinical efficacy and research quality?. In M. A. Swales (Ed.), *The Oxford handbook of dialectical behaviour therapy* (pp. 415–465). Oxford University Press.

Moher, D., Liberati, A., Tetzlaff, J., & Altman, D. G. (2009). Preferred Reporting Items for Systematic Reviews and Meta-Analyses: The PRISMA Statement. *PLoS Medicine, 6*(7), e1000097. https://doi.org/10.1371/journal.pmed.1000097

Murphy, R., Cooper, Z., Hollon, S. D., & Fairburn, C. G. (2009). How do psychological treatments work? Investigating mediators of change. *Behaviour Research and Therapy, 47*(1), 1–5. https://doi.org/10.1016/j.brat.2008.10.001

Najmi, S., & Wegner, D. M. (2008). The gravity of unwanted thoughts: Asymmetric priming effects in thought suppression. *Consciousness and Cognition, 17*(1), 114–124. https://doi.org/10.1016/j.concog.2007.01.006

National Institute for Health and Care Excellence (2014). *Psychosis and schizophrenia in adults: Prevention and management. Clinical Guideline (CG178).*

Navarro-Haro, M. V., Botella, C., Guillen, V., Moliner, R., Marco, H., Jorquera, M., Baños, R., & Garcia-Palacios, A. (2018). Dialectical behavior therapy in the treatment of borderline personality disorder and eating disorders comorbidity: A pilot study in a naturalistic setting. *Cognitive Therapy and Research, 42*(5), 636–649. https://doi.org/10.1007/s10608-018-9906-9

Neasciu, A. D., Rizvi, S. L., & Linehan, M. M. (2010). Dialectical behavior therapy skills use as a mediator and outcome of treatment for borderline personality disorder. *Behaviour Research and Therapy, 48*(9), 832–839. https://doi.org/10.1016/j.brat.2010.05.017

Nicholas, M., Vlaeyen, J., Rief, W., Barke, A., Aziz, Q., Benoliel, R., Cohen, M., Evers, S., Giamberardino, M. A., Goebel, A., Korwisi, B., Perrot, S., Svensson, P., Wang, S. J., Treede, R. D., & IASP Taskforce for the Classification of Chronic Pain (2019). The IASP classification of chronic pain for ICD-11: chronic primary pain. *Pain, 160*(1), 28–37. https://doi.org/10.1097/j.pain.0000000000001390

Niemeier, H. M., Leahey, T., Palm Reed, K., Brown, R. A., & Wing, R. R. (2012). An acceptance-based behavioral intervention for weight loss: A pilot study. *Behavior Therapy, 43*(2), 427–435. https://doi.org/10.1016/j.beth.2011.10.005

Niles, A. N., Wolitzky-Taylor, K. B., Arch, J. J., & Craske, M. G. (2017). Applying a novel statistical method to advance the personalized treatment of anxiety disorders: A composite moderator of comparative drop-out from CBT and ACT. *Behaviour Research and Therapy, 91*, 13–23. https://doi.org/10.1016/j.brat.2017.01.001

Nolen-Hoeksema, S., & Morrow, J. (1991). A prospective study of depression and posttraumatic stress symptoms after a natural disaster: The 1989 Loma Prieta earthquake. *Journal of Personality and Social Psychology, 61*(1), 115–121. https://doi.org/10.1037/0022-3514.61.1.115

Norton, A. R., Abbott, M. J., Norberg, M. M., & Hunt, C. (2015). A systematic review of mindfulness and acceptance-based treatments for social anxiety disorder. *Journal of Clinical Psychology, 71*(4), 283–301. https://doi.org/10.1002/jclp.22144

O'Connor, M., Whelan, R., Bricker, J., & McHugh, L. (2020). Randomized controlled trial of a smartphone application as an adjunct to acceptance and commitment therapy for smoking cessation. *Behavior Therapy, 51*(1), 162–177. https://doi.org/10.1016/j.beth.2019.06.003

Öst, L.-G. (2014). The efficacy of Acceptance and Commitment Therapy: An updated systematic review and meta-analysis. *Behaviour Research and Therapy, 61*, 105–121. https://doi.org/10.1016/j.brat.2014.07.018

Overall, J. E., & Gorham, D. R. (1962). The Brief Psychiatric Rating Scale. *Psychological Reports, 10*, 799–812. https://doi.org/10.2466/pr0.1962.10.3.799

Panos, P. T., Jackson, J. W., Hasan, O., & Panos, A. (2014). Meta-analysis and systematic review assessing the efficacy of dialectical behavior therapy (DBT). *Research on Social Work Practice, 24*(2), 213-223. https://doi.org/10.1177/1049731513503047

Perroud, N., Nicastro, R., Jermann, F., & Huguelet, P. (2012). Mindfulness skills in borderline personality disorder patients during dialectical behavior therapy: Preliminary results. *International Journal of Psychiatry in Clinical Practice, 16*(3), 189–196. https://doi.org/10.3109/13651501.2012.674531

Pielech, M., Bailey, R. W., McEntee, M. L., Ashworth, J., Levell, J., Sowden, G., & Vowles, K. E. (2016). Preliminary evaluation of the values tracker: A two-item measure of engagement in valued activities in those with chronic pain. *Behavior Modification, 40*, 239–256. https://doi.org/10.1177/0145445515616911

Pinto-Gouveia, J., Carvalho, S. A., Palmeira, L., Castilho, P., Duarte, C., Ferreira, C., Duarte, J., Cunha, M., Matos, M., & Costa, J. (2017). BEfree: A new psychological program for binge eating that integrates psychoeducation, mindfulness, and compassion. *Clinical Psychology & Psychotherapy, 24*(5), 1090–1098. https://doi.org/10.1002/cpp.2072

Pistorello, J., Fruzzetti, A. E., MacLane, C., Gallop, R., & Iverson, K. M. (2012). Dialectical behavior therapy (DBT) applied to college students: A randomized clinical trial. *Journal of Consulting and Clinical Psychology, 80*, 982-994. https://doi.org10.1037/a0029096

Rahmani, M., Omidi, A., Asemi, Z., & Akbari, H. (2018). The effect of dialectical behaviour therapy on binge eating, difficulties in emotion regulation, and BMI in overweight patients with binge-eating disorder: A randomized controlled trial. *Mental Health & Prevention, 9*, 13–18. https://doi.org/10.1016/j.mhp.2017.11.002

Ritzert, T. R., Forsyth, J. P., Sheppard, S. C., Boswell, J. F., Berghoff, C. R., & Eifert, G. H. (2016). Evaluating the effectiveness of ACT for anxiety disorders in a self-help context: Outcomes from a randomized wait-list controlled trial. *Behavior Therapy, 47*(4), 444–459. https://doi.org/10.1016/j.beth.2016.03.001

Rizvi, S. L., Hughes, C. D., Hittman, A. D., & Vieira Oliveira, P. (2017). Can trainees effectively deliver dialectical behavior therapy for individuals with borderline personality disorder? Outcomes from a training clinic. *Journal of Clinical Psychology, 73*(12), 1599–1611. https://doi.org/10.1002/jclp.22467

Rizvi, S. L., & Steffel, L. M. (2014). A pilot study of 2 brief forms of dialectical behavior therapy skills training for emotion dysregulation in college students. *Journal of American College Health, 62*(6), 434-439. https://doi.org/10.1080/07448481.2014.907298

Robinson, A. H., & Safer, D. L. (2012). Moderators of dialectical behavior therapy for binge eating disorder: Results from a randomized controlled trial. *International Journal of Eating Disorders, 45*(4), 597–602. https://doi.org/10.1002/eat.20932

Rochefort, C., Baldwin, A. S., & Chmielewski, M. (2018). Experiential avoidance: An examination of the construct validity of the AAQ-II and MEAQ. *Behavior Therapy, 49*(3), 435–449. https://doi.org/10.1016/j.beth.2017.08.008

Roemer, L., & Orsillo, S. M. (2002). Expanding our conceptualization of and treatment for generalized anxiety disorder: Integrating mindfulness/acceptance-based approaches with existing cognitive-behavioral models. *Clinical Psychology: Science and Practice, 9*(1), 54–68. https://doi.org/10.1093/clipsy/9.1.54

Roemer, L., & Orsillo, S. M. (2005). An acceptance-based behavior therapy for generalized anxiety disorder. In *Acceptance and mindfulness-based approaches to anxiety* (pp. 213–240). Springer.

Roemer, L., & Orsillo, S. M. (2008). *Mindfulness- and acceptance-based behavioral therapies in practice*. Guilford Press.

Ruiz, F. J. (2012). Acceptance and commitment therapy versus traditional cognitive behavioral therapy: A systematic review and meta-analysis of current empirical evidence. *International Journal of Psychology and Psychological Therapy, 12*(3), 333–358.

Samples, H. & Mojtabai, R. (2015). Antidepressant self-discontinuation: Results from the collaborative psychiatric epidemiology surveys. *Psychiatric Services, 66*, 455–462. https://doi.org/10.1176/appi.ps.201400021

Schumacher, L. M., Godfrey, K. M., Forman, E. M., & Butryn, M. L. (2019). Change in domain-specific but not general psychological flexibility relates to greater weight loss in acceptance-based behavioral treatment for obesity. *Journal of Contextual Behavioral Science, 12*, 59–65. https://doi.org/10.1016/j.jcbs.2019.01.008

Scott, W., Hann, K. E., & McCracken, L. M. (2016). A comprehensive examination of changes in psychological flexibility following acceptance and commitment therapy for chronic pain. *Journal of Contemporary Psychotherapy, 46*, 139–148. https://doi.org/10.1007/s10879-016-9328-5

Segal, Z. V., Bieling, P., Young, T., MacQueen, G., Cooke, R., Martin, L., Bloch, R., & Levitan, R. D. (2010). Antidepressant monotherapy vs. sequential pharmacotherapy and mindfulness-based cognitive therapy, or placebo, for relapse prophylaxis in recurrent depression. *Archives of General Psychiatry, 67*(12), 1256–1264. https://doi.org/10.1001/archgenpsychiatry.2010.168

Segal, Z. V., Dimidjian, S., Beck, A., Boggs, J. M., Vanderkruik, R., Metcalf, C. A., Gallop, R., Felder, J. N., & Levy, J. (2020). Outcomes of online mindfulness-based cognitive therapy for patients with residual depressive symptoms: A randomized clinical trial. *JAMA Psychiatry, 77*(6), 563–573. https://doi.org/10.1001/jamapsychiatry.2019.4693

Segal, Z. V., & Teasdale, J. (2018). *Mindfulness-based cognitive therapy for depression*. Guilford Publications.

Segal, Z. V., Williams, J. M. G., & Teasdale, J. D. (2013). *Mindfulness-based cognitive therapy for depression: A new approach for preventing relapse* (2nd ed.). Guilford Press.

Seow, L., Page, A. C., & Hooke, G. R. (2020). Severity of borderline personality disorder symptoms as a moderator of the association between the use of dialectical behaviour therapy skills and treatment outcomes. *Psychotherapy Research, 30*(7), 920–933. https://doi.org/10.1080/10503307.2020.1720931

Shallcross, A. J., Gross, J. J., Visvanathan, P. D., Kumar, N., Palfrey, A., Ford, B. Q., Dimidjian, S., Shirk, S., Holm-Denoma, J., Goode, K. M., Cox, E., Chaplin, W., & Mauss, I. B. (2015). Relapse prevention in major depressive disorder: Mindfulness-based cognitive therapy versus an active control condition. *Journal of Consulting and Clinical Psychology, 83*(5), 964–975. https://doi.org/10.1037/ccp0000050

Smith, B. H., Elliott, A. M., Chambers, W. A., Smith, W. C., Hannaford, P. C., & Penny, K. (2001). The impact of chronic pain in the community. *Family Practice, 18*, 292–299. https://doi.org/10.1093/fampra/18.3.292

Society of Clinical Psychology. (2016). Acceptance and commitment therapy for psychosis. Division 12 of the American Psychological Association. www.div12.org/treatment/acceptance-and-commitment-therapy-for-psychosis

Soler, J., Pascual, J. C., Tiana, T., Cebrià, A., Barrachina, J., Campins, M. J., Gich, I., Alvarez, E., & Pérez, V. (2009). Dialectical behaviour therapy skills training compared to standard group therapy in borderline personality disorder: A 3-month randomised controlled clinical trial. *Behaviour Research and Therapy, 47*(5), 353-358. https://doi.org/10.1016/j.brat.2009.01.013

Soler, J., Valdepérez, A., Feliu-Soler, A., Pascual, J. C., Portella, M. J., Martín-Blanco, A., Alvarez, E., & Pérez, V. (2012). Effects of the dialectical behavioral therapy-mindfulness module on attention in patients with borderline personality disorder. *Behaviour Research and Therapy, 50*(2), 150–157. https://doi.org/10.1016/j.brat.2011.12.002

Spidel, A., Daigneault, I., Kealy, D., & Lecomte, T. (2019). Acceptance and commitment therapy for psychosis and trauma: Investigating links between trauma severity, attachment and outcome. *Behavioural and Cognitive Psychotherapy, 47*(2), 230–243. https://doi.org/10.1017/S1352465818000413

Stead, L. F., Carroll, A. J., & Lancaster, T. (2017). Group behaviour therapy programmes for smoking cessation. *Cochrane Database of Systematic Reviews 2017, 3*. https://doi.org/10.1002/14651858.CD001007.pub3

Stead, L. F., Hartmann-Boyce, J., Perera, R., & Lancaster, T. (2013). Telephone counselling for smoking cessation. *Cochrane Database of Systematic Reviews 2013, 8*. https://doi.org/10.1002/14651858.CD002850.pub3

Strandskov, S. W., Ghaderi, A., Andersson, H., Parmskog, N., Hjort, E., Wärn, A. S., Jannert, M., & Andersson, G. (2017). Effects of tailored and ACT-influenced internet-based CBT for eating disorders and the relation between knowledge acquisition and outcome: A randomized controlled trial. *Behavior Therapy, 48*(5), 624–637. https://doi.org/10.1016/j.beth.2017.02.002

Swain, J., Hancock, K., Dixon, A., Koo, S., & Bowman, J. T. (2013). Acceptance and commitment therapy for anxious children and adolescents: Study protocol for a randomized controlled trial. *Trials, 14*, 140. https://doi.org/10.1186/1745-6215-14-140

Swain, J., Hancock, K., Hainsworth, C., & Bowman, J. (2013). Acceptance and Commitment Therapy in the treatment of anxiety: A systematic review. *Clinical Psychology Review, 33*(8), 965–978. https://doi.org/10.1016/j.cpr.2013.07.002

Swenson, C. R. (2000). How can we account for DBT's widespread popularity? *Clinical Psychology: Science and Practice, 7*(1), 87-91. https://doi.org/10.1093/clipsy.7.1.87

Taylor, G. M. J., Dalili, M. N., Semwal, M., Civljak, M., Sheikh, A., & Car, J. (2017). Internet-based interventions for smoking cessation. *Cochrane Database of Systematic Reviews 2017, 9*. https://doi.org/10.1002/14651858.CD007078.pub5

Teasdale, J. D., Moore, R. G., Hayhurst, H., Pope, M., Williams, S., & Segal, Z. V. (2002). Metacognitive awareness and prevention of relapse in depression: Empirical evidence. *Journal of Consulting and Clinical Psychology, 70*(2), 275–287. https://doi.org/10.1037//0022-006x.70.2.275

Teasdale, J. D., Segal, Z., & Williams, J. G. (1995). How does cognitive therapy prevent depressive relapse and why should attentional control (mindfulness) training help? *Behaviour Research and Therapy, 33*(1), 25–39. https://doi.org/10.1016/0005-7967(94)e0011-7

Teasdale, J. D., Segal, Z.V., Williams, J.M.G., Ridgeway, V.A., Soulsby, J.M., Lau, M.A. (2000). Prevention of relapse/recurrence in major depression by mindfulness-based cognitive therapy. *Journal of Consulting and Clinical Psychology, 68*(4), 615–623. https://doi.org/10.1037//0022-006x.68.4.615

Thomas, N. (2015). A model for the development of acceptance and mindfulness-based therapies: Preoccupation with psychotic experience as a treatment target. In B. A. Gaudiano (Ed.), *Incorporating acceptance and mindfulness into the treatment of psychosis: Current trends and future directions* (pp. 203–266). Oxford University Press.

Tonarelli, S. B., Pasillas, R., Alvarado, L., Dwivedi, A., & Cancellare, A. (2016). Acceptance and commitment therapy compared to treatment as usual in psychosis: A systematic review and meta-analysis. *Journal of Psychiatry, 19*(3), 1–5. https://doi.org/10.4172/2378-5756.1000366

Twohig, M. P., Abramowitz, J. S., Smith, B. M., Fabricant, L. E., Jacoby, R. J., Morrison, K. L., Bluett, E. J., Rueman, L., Blakely, S. M., & Ledermann, T. (2018). Adding acceptance and commitment therapy to exposure and response prevention for obsessive-compulsive disorder: A randomized controlled trial. *Behaviour Research and Therapy, 108*, 1–9. https://doi.org/10.1016/j.brat.2018.06.005

Twohig, M. P., Hayes, S. C., Plumb, J. C., Pruitt, L. D., Collins, A. B., Hazlett-Stevens, H., & Woidneck, M. R. (2010). A randomized clinical trial of acceptance and commitment therapy versus progressive relaxation training for obsessive-compulsive disorder. *Journal of Consulting and Clinical Psychology, 78*(5), 705–716. https://doi.org/10.1037/a0020508

Twohig, M. P., & Levin, M. E. (2017). Acceptance and commitment therapy as a treatment for anxiety and depression: A review. *The Psychiatric Clinics of North America, 40*(4), 751–770. https://doi.org/10.1016/j.psc.2017.08.009

Vall, E., & Wade, T. D. (2015). Predictors of treatment outcome in individuals with eating disorders: A systematic review and meta-analysis. *International Journal of Eating Disorders, 48*(7), 946–971. https://doi.org/10.1002/eat.22411

van Aubel, E., Bakker, J. M., Batink, T., Michielse, S., Goossens, L., Lange, I., Schruers, K., Lieverse, R., Marcelis, M., van Amelsvoort, T., van Os, J., Wichers, M., Vaessen, T., Reininghaus, U., & Myin-Germeys, I. (2020). Blended care in the treatment of subthreshold symptoms of depression and psychosis in emerging adults: A randomised controlled trial of Acceptance and Commitment Therapy in Daily-Life (ACT-DL). *Behaviour Research and Therapy, 128*, 103592. https://doi.org/10.1016/j.brat.2020.103592

van den Bosch, Louisa M. C., Verheul, R., Schippers, G. M., & van den Brink, W. (2002). Dialectical Behavior Therapy of borderline patients with and without substance use problems: Implementation and long-term effects. *Addictive Behaviors, 27*(6), 911–923. https://doi.org/10.1016/S0306-4603(02)00293-9

van der Velden, A. M., Kuyken, W., Wattar, U., Crane, C., Pallesen, K. J., Dahlgaard, J., Fjorback, L. O., & Piet, J. (2015). A systematic review of mechanisms of change in mindfulness-based cognitive therapy in the treatment of recurrent major depressive disorder. *Clinical Psychology Review, 37*, 26–39. https://doi.org/10.1016/j.cpr.2015.02.001

Vaughan, C. A., Sacco, W. P., & Beckstead, J. W. (2008). Racial/ethnic differences in body mass index: The roles of beliefs about thinness and dietary restriction. *Body Image, 5*(3), 291–298. https://doi.org/10.1016/j.bodyim.2008.02.004

Veehof, M. M., Oskam, M.-J., Schreurs, K. M. G., & Bohlmeijer, E. T. (2011). Acceptance-based interventions for the treatment of chronic pain: A systematic review and meta-analysis. *Pain, 152*, 533–542. https://doi.org/10.1016/j.pain.2010.11.002

Veehof, M. M., Trompetter, H. R., Bohlmeijer, E. T., & Schreurs, K. M. G. (2016). Acceptance- and mindfulness-based interventions for the treatment of chronic pain: A meta-analytic review. *Cognitive Behaviour Therapy, 45*, 1–27. https://doi.org/10.1080/16506073.2015.1098724

Verheul, R., Van Den Bosch, Louise M. C., Koeter, M. W. J., De Ridder, Maria A. J., Stijnen, T., & Van Den Brink, W. (2003). Dialectical behaviour therapy for women with borderline personality disorder: 12-month,

randomised clinical trial in the Netherlands. *The British Journal of Psychiatry, 182*(2), 135–140. https://doi.org/10.1192/bjp.182.2.135

Vilardaga, R., Heffner, J. L., Mercer, L. D., & Bricker, J. B. (2014). Do counselor techniques predict quitting during smoking cessation treatment? A component analysis of telephone-delivered acceptance and commitment therapy. *Behaviour Research and Therapy, 61*, 89–95. https://doi.org/10.1016/j.brat.2014.07.008

Vilardaga, R., Rizo, J., Palenski, P., Mannelli, P., Oliver, J. A., & McClernon, F. J. (2019). Pilot randomized controlled trial of a novel smoking cessation app designed for individuals with co-occurring tobacco dependence and serious mental illness. *Nicotine & Tobacco Research, 22*(9), 1533–1542, https://doi.org/10.1093/ntr/ntz202

Vøllestad, J., Sivertsen, B., & Nielsen, G. H. (2011). Mindfulness-based stress reduction for patients with anxiety disorders: Evaluation in a randomized controlled trial. *Behaviour Research and Therapy, 49*(4), 281–288. https://doi.org/10.1016/j.brat.2011.01.007

Vowles, K. E., Pielech, M., Edwards, K. A., McEntee, M. L., & Bailey, R. W. (2020). A comparative meta-analysis of unidisciplinary psychology and interdisciplinary treatment outcomes following Acceptance and Commitment Therapy for adults with chronic pain. *Journal of Pain, 21*, 529–545. https://doi.org/10.1016/j.jpain.2019.10.004

Wakefield, S., Roebuck, S., & Boyden, P. (2018). The evidence base of acceptance and commitment therapy (ACT) in psychosis: A systematic review. *Journal of Contextual Behavioral Science, 10*, 1–13. https://doi.org/10.1016/j.jcbs.2018.07.001

Wang, P. S., Simon, G., & Kessler, R. C. (2003). The economic burden of depression and the cost-effectiveness of treatment. *International Journal of Methods in Psychiatric Research, 12*(1), 22–33. https://doi.org/10.1002/mpr.139

Warmerdam, L., van Straten, A., Jongsma, J., Twisk, J., & Cuijpers, P. (2010). Online cognitive behavioral therapy and problem-solving therapy for depressive symptoms: Exploring mechanisms of change. *Journal of Behavior Therapy and Experimental Psychiatry, 41*(1), 64–70. https://doi.org/10.1016/j.jbtep.2009.10.003

Watson, N. L., Heffner, J. L., Mull, K. E., McClure, J. B., & Bricker, J. B. (2019). Comparing treatment acceptability and 12-month cessation rates in response to web-based smoking interventions among smokers who do and do not screen positive for affective disorders: Secondary analysis. *Journal of Medical Internet Research, 21*(6), e13500. https://doi.org/10.2196/13500

Webb, T. L. (2009). Commentary on Shahab & McEwen (2009): Understanding and preventing attrition in online smoking cessation interventions: A self-regulatory perspective. *Addiction, 104*(11), 1805–1806. https://doi.org/10.1111/j.1360-0443.2009.02751.x

Wegner, D. M. (1994). Ironic processes of mental control. *Psychological Review, 101*(1), 34–52. https://doi.org/10.1037/0033-295X.101.1.34

Wegner, D. M., & Zanakos, S. (1994). Chronic thought suppression. *Journal of Personality, 62*(4), 615–640. https://doi.org/10.1111/j.1467-6494.1994.tb00311.x

Whittaker, R., McRobbie, H., Bullen, C., Rodgers, A., Gu, Y., & Dobson, R. (2019). Mobile phone text messaging and app-based interventions for smoking cessation. *Cochrane Database of Systematic Reviews 2019, 10*. https://doi.org/10.1002/14651858.CD006611.pub5

Williams, J. M., Crane, C., Barnhofer, T., Brennan, K., Duggan, D. S., Fennell, M. J., Hackmann, A., Krusche, A., Muse, K., Von Rohr, I. R., Shah, D., Crane, R. S., Eames, C., Jones, M., Radford, S., Silverton, S., Sun, Y., Weatherley-Jones, E., Whitaker, C. J., Russell, D., & Russell, I. T. (2014). Mindfulness-based cognitive therapy for preventing relapse in recurrent depression: A randomized dismantling trial. *Journal of Consulting and Clinical Psychology, 82*(2), 275–286. https://doi.org/10.1037/a0035036

Wolgast, M. (2014). What does the Acceptance and Action Questionnaire (AAQ-II) really measure? *Behavior Therapy, 45*(6), 831–839. https://doi.org/10.1016/j.beth.2014.07.002

Wolitzky-Taylor, K. B., Arch, J. J., Rosenfield, D., & Craske, M. G. (2012). Moderators and non-specific predictors of treatment outcome for anxiety disorders: A comparison of cognitive behavioral therapy to acceptance and commitment therapy. *Journal of Consulting and Clinical Psychology, 80*(5), 786–799. https://doi.org/10.1037/a0029418

Wonderlich, S. A., Peterson, C. B., Crosby, R. D., Smith, T. L., Klein, M. H., Mitchell, J. E., & Crow, S. J. (2014). A randomized controlled comparison of integrative cognitive-affective therapy (ICAT) and enhanced cognitive-behavioral therapy (CBT-E) for bulimia nervosa. *Psychological Medicine*, *44*(3), 543–553. https://doi.org/10.1017/S0033291713001098

Wong, S. Y. S., Yip, B. H. K., Mak, W. W. S., Mercer, S., Cheung, E. Y. L., Ling, C. Y. M., Lui, W. W. S., Tang, W. K., Lo, H. H. M., Wu, J. C. Y., Lee, T. M. C., Gao, T., Griffiths, S. M., Chan, P. H. S., & Ma, H. S. W. (2016). Mindfulness-based cognitive therapy v. Group psychoeducation for people with generalised anxiety disorder randomised controlled trial. *The British Journal of Psychiatry*, *209*(1), 68–75. https://doi.org/10.1192/bjp.bp.115.166124

Wood, L., Williams, C., Billings, J., & Johnson, S. (2020). A systematic review and meta-analysis of cognitive behavioural informed psychological interventions for psychiatric inpatients with psychosis. *Schizophrenia Research*, *222*, 133–144. https://doi.org/10.1016/j.schres.2020.03.041

Yıldız, E. (2020). The effects of acceptance and commitment therapy in psychosis treatment: A systematic review of randomized controlled trials. *Perspectives in Psychiatric Care*, *56*(1), 149–167. https://doi.org/10.1111/ppc.12396

Zeifman, R. J., Boritz, T., Barnhart, R., Labrish, C., & McMain, S. F. (2020). The independent roles of mindfulness and distress tolerance in treatment outcomes in dialectical behavior therapy skills training. *Personality Disorders: Theory, Research, and Treatment*, *11*(3), 181–190. https://doi.org/10.1037/per0000368

Zeng, E. Y., Heffner, J. L., Copeland, W. K., Mull, K. E., & Bricker, J. B. (2016). Get with the program: Adherence to a smartphone app for smoking cessation. *Addictive Behaviors*, *63*, 120–124. https://doi.org/10.1016/j.addbeh.2016.07.007

Zeng, E. Y., Vilardaga, R., Heffner, J. L., Mull, K. E., & Bricker, J. B. (2015). Predictors of utilization of a novel smoking cessation smartphone app. *Telemedicine Journal and E-health*, *21*(12), 998–1004. https://doi.org/10.1089/tmj.2014.0232

ACKNOWLEDGMENT

The authors would like to thank Danielle Caby, Margaret Sala, Tetyana Yevdosyuk, and, especially, Christina Chywyl for their invaluable assistance in the preparation of this chapter.

CHAPTER 16

SYSTEMIC AND CONJOINT COUPLE AND FAMILY THERAPIES: RECENT ADVANCES AND FUTURE PROMISE

MYRNA L FRIEDLANDER, LAURIE HEATHERINGTON, AND GARY M DIAMOND

Abstract

Literature reviews and meta-analyses over the past 20 years have definitively established the efficacy of many systemic approaches to psychotherapy. Despite this important work, much remains unknown, likely due to the complexity of couple and family therapy and the heterogeneity of family structures, especially across diverse cultures. This chapter opens with a discussion of the term *systemic therapy*, which alternately refers to conjoint treatments for couples and families and to individual therapies informed by principles of systems theory. After providing a brief history of the field, we summarize representative studies of couple, family, and systemic individual therapies published between 2011 and 2018, highlighting exemplars of large-scale outcome studies and smaller-scale change process research. Based on this review, we summarize advances in knowledge and methodology since Sexton et al.'s (2013) chapter on couple and family therapy in the 6th edition of this *Handbook*. The chapter concludes with a series of change principles that cut across treatment approaches and specific recommendations for future study to advance clinical practice in a more systemically informed fashion.

OVERVIEW

INTRODUCTION

Throughout its history as a field, couple and family therapy (CFT) has played the role of a rebellious younger sibling to the more well-established field of individual psychotherapy. Conceptualizing individuals' problems systemically and contextually brought new terms, new therapeutic interventions, and new epistemologies and research models to psychotherapy.

Concerned with establishing a legitimate science of what initially was called *marital*[1] and family therapy, researchers sought to identify the best treatments for various mental, behavioral, and substance disorders. Interestingly, while early family therapies evolved in the context of specific disorders, such as schizophrenia and eating disorders, theorists viewed them as a function of interpersonal dynamics rather than resulting from disease.

Once meta-analyses of controlled studies had established the field's legitimacy (e.g. Shadish et al., 1995; Shadish & Baldwin, 2003), some CFT researchers turned their attention away from randomized clinical trials conducted in research settings. Following in the footsteps of individual therapy researchers, these investigators began testing the effectiveness of CFT in naturalistic contexts (e.g. Sexton & Turner, 2010), studying the influence of common factors (e.g. Friedlander et al., 2006) and treatment-specific change mechanisms (e.g. Christensen et al., 2005), teasing out therapist effects (e.g. Owen, Duncan et al., 2014), and collecting feedback from clients to guide treatment (e.g. Anker et al., 2009). Moving further from the medical model, researchers began developing and evaluating approaches to address family problems that carry no psychiatric diagnosis, such as acculturative stress (Negy et al., 2010), infertility (Najafi et al., 2015), child abuse and neglect (Johnson & Ketring, 2006), and young adults' unresolved anger toward their parents (G. M. Diamond et al., 2016).

All these advances notwithstanding, much remains unknown, in part due to the complexity of systems work and the heterogeneity of family structures, especially across diverse cultures (Heatherington et al., 2015). To summarize recent advances in the field and guide future study, we reviewed the systemic individual and conjoint CFT research published since Sexton et al.'s (2013) chapter in the sixth edition of this *Handbook*. We begin with a brief discussion of the term *systemic therapy*, which continue to require definitional clarity. Next, we provide an overview of the history and current state of systemic treatment and describe the parameters of the present review. After summarizing the body of systemic research published between 2011 and 2018, we discuss progress in the field since the previous *Handbook* chapter, including empirically supported principles of change, and make specific recommendations for moving the field forward substantively and methodologically.

WHAT *IS* SYSTEMIC THERAPY?

In its original and strictest sense, the term refers to models of treatment whose primary aim is to change the recursive relational dynamics in nested subsystems that sustain dysfunction (Rohrbaugh, 2014). Moreover, since all behavior is embedded in social systems that simultaneously resist and propel change, it matters less how an individual's emotional distress originated, and more how it is maintained by dysfunctional relational dynamics. The term *systemic therapy*, however, also

refers to working to reduce an individual's troubling symptoms (due to a persistent disorder like major depression or a physical condition like chronic pain) with the help of family members who see themselves as partners with the therapist rather than as clients themselves (e.g. Friedlander & Diamond, 2011). To complicate matters further, working *systemically* does not always mean seeing multiple family members conjointly; rather, individual therapy is also considered systemic when the primary interventions are intended to change the client's couple or family dynamics (McGoldrick & Carter, 2001).

The question becomes, then, what do systemic therapies have in common that distinguishes them from other therapies? After all, most psychotherapists discuss couple and family relationships with their clients. In our view, three interrelated features distinguish *systemic* therapy: (1) a conceptual formulation that specifically locates a client's problem or disorder contextually, that is, within dysfunctional familial and broader social systems (e.g. school, community, society) rather than solely within the individual; (2) the view that a person's distress is sustained by circularity (e.g. demand ↔ withdraw) in problematic relationships; and (3) a primary focus on shifting dysfunctional relations to alleviate suffering. Based on these criteria, systemic therapy typically involves working directly with couples and families. For theoretical reasons (cf. Kerr & Bowen, 1988), however, some systemic therapists work primarily with individuals but intervene in ways intended to foster systemwide change.

Simply put, there is no consensus about what is and is not systemic therapy. The term is often used interchangeably with couple and family therapy, confounding treatment *modality* with a systemic theoretical conceptualization of clients' problems. For this reason, we cast a broad net. That is, we reviewed research on individual therapies that are specifically identified as systemic, as well as conjoint couple and family treatments that focus on family relationships to enhance the health or well-being of one individual.

BRIEF HISTORY OF SYSTEMIC TREATMENTS

Early CFT pioneers disdained intrapsychic explanations of psychological disorders, preferring to locate emotional and behavioral problems *between* rather than *within* people. This perspective, based on cybernetics and general systems theory in the natural sciences (von Bertalanffy, 1950), represented a major paradigmatic shift in the mental health treatment of individuals.

Three influential theories, family systems (Bowen, 1978), structural (Minuchin, 1974), and strategic/problem focused (Watzlawick et al., 1974), dominated the field in its formative years. Common to these approaches were interventions designed to address problem-maintaining family interactions. Whereas most early theorists maintained that therapists should solely work with the whole family, others contended that systemic change can best come about by coaching individual clients how to disrupt their dysfunctional family dynamics (e.g.

---

[1] Currently, the more commonly used term is *couple* and family therapy, which includes non-married romantic partners.

Kerr & Bowen, 1988). Coaching and direct guidance also characterized various early behavioral approaches to couple (Jacobson & Margolin, 1979) and family (e.g. Patterson & Forgatch, 1985) therapies.

By the 1990s, the almost exclusive interest in family behavior was challenged by a new wave of theorizing in which emotion and cognition took center stage. Emotion was privileged by theorists whose approaches focused on addressing insecure attachments between romantic partners (Greenberg & Johnson, 1988; Johnson, 2004) and between parents and adolescents (G. S. Diamond & Siqueland, 1990). Cognition was privileged by constructivist (e.g. Sluzki, 1992; White & Epston, 1990), cognitive-behavioral (e.g. Epstein & Baucom, 2002), and solution-focused theorists (de Shazer, 1985), who contended that psychological distress is maintained not only by dysfunctional interactions but also, even largely, by how people construe their problems. Even the most behavioral of CFT theorists came to recognize that marital distress can be alleviated by helping spouses embrace acceptance rather than struggle to change one another's shortcomings (Jacobson & Christensen, 1996).

In the past 25 years, the practice of CFT has evolved considerably. Not only has basic psychological research (on effective parenting, for example) been integrated into clinical practice, but also manualized treatments have been widely disseminated (Heatherington et al., 2015). Another major trend has been the integration of different schools of CFT that once were considered theoretically incompatible (Lebow, 2014), including a meta-framework for working systemically with individuals, couples and families (Pinsof et al., 2011). As several authors recently noted, the latter trends are enhanced by the specification of change principles that cut across theoretical boundaries (e.g. Benson et al., 2012).

THE PRESENT REVIEW

To locate research published in English within the 2011–2018 time frame of this review, we began identifying systemic process and outcome studies referenced in handbooks of couple and family therapy (e.g., Gurman et al., 2011), on websites (e.g., www.sfbta.org), in meta-content reviews (e.g., Davis et al., 2012; Friedlander et al., 2016; Heatherington et al., 2015; von Sydow et al., 2010), and in quantitative meta-analyses (e.g., Friedlander et al., 2018; Pinquart et al., 2016). An electronic search was conducted within several databases using search terms like *systemic therapy/treatment, marital outcomes, couple/marital therapy* (and *intervention*), *family therapy* (and *intervention*), *couple/family process, couple/family outcome,* and so forth. Additionally, we cross-referenced articles as they were identified and visually searched the titles and abstracts of articles in 15 systemic and couple/family journals (e.g., *Family Process, Journal of Marital and Family Therapy, Contemporary Family Therapy, Couple and Family Research*).

We reviewed efficacy trials, uncontrolled naturalistic outcome studies, and studies of effective change processes. Excluded from this review were analog studies, studies of sex therapy, studies of online therapy, studies of help seeking, studies introducing new assessment tools, studies of group couple/family treatments, studies of relationship education and prevention programs, and studies of parent training for children's problems (reviewed in Chapter 18). We also excluded studies of individual youth therapy in which change in family relationships was not described as an explicit goal of treatment.

COUPLE THERAPY: DOES IT WORK?

Problems Addressed

Understandably, the primary outcome in most couple therapy studies has been relationship satisfaction, also operationalized as *relational functioning*, commitment, quality, stability (versus divorce), and adjustment. More specific relational outcomes include dyadic communication, excitement, trust, closeness or intimacy (emotional as well as sexual), cohesion, problem solving, conflict management skills, dyadic coping, certainty of commitment, and expression of affection. Research on specific couple problems includes studies of conflict resolution, caregiver empathy/support, infidelity, violence, emotional injury, and infertility. The indirect effect of couple therapy on children has also been investigated in terms of outcomes like parenting behavior and parental stress.

Many recent couple studies also aimed at improving the individual functioning of one or both partners in terms of general and specific mental health concerns, including major depression/dysthymia, obsessive compulsive disorder, post-traumatic stress/disorder (PTSD), eating disorders, childhood sexual abuse, and sexual self-esteem. Physical health concerns have also been targeted in recent studies, including smoking, substance use disorders, various cancers, neurodegenerative disease, sexual risk through transmission of HIV, and pain associated with intercourse, as well as the cost-effectiveness of couple therapy in reducing utilization of medical services.

Evidence of Efficacy and Effectiveness

Echoing Shadish and Baldwin's (2003) definitive meta-analysis of couple therapy, Lebow et al. (2012, p. 148) concluded that compared to no treatment controls, the success rates of couple therapies are "vastly superior" and comparable to the success rates of individual therapies, at roughly 70% (p. 145). Since Sexton et al.'s (2013) *Handbook* chapter, recent reviewers of the couple therapies literature have highlighted their effectiveness in alleviating couple distress (Lebow et al., 2012; Snyder & Halford, 2012), including less severe intimate partner violence (Stith et al., 2012), as well as individual distress related to alcoholism (McCrady et al., 2016; O'Farrell & Clements, 2012), drug abuse (Rowe, 2012), depression (Beach & Whisman, 2012), and psychopathology (Baucom et al., 2014).

Baucom et al. (2014) explained that the treatment of adult mental disorders in couple therapy stems from the well-established reciprocity between psychopathology and unhappy romantic relationships. In conjoint therapies, which usually involve some adaptation of cognitive-behavioral couple therapy (CBCT), improving or stabilizing the couple's relationship is seen as integral to client recovery. Even in highly satisfying relationships, the stress of a mental or substance use disorder in one member of the couple can be destabilizing (Baucom et al., 2012). Similarly, when the presenting concern involves a chronic health condition, one benefit of conjoint therapy is improved relationship functioning (Fischer et al., 2016).

In Gurman et al.'s (2011) review, only CBCT and emotionally focused couple therapy (EFCT) had been studied in randomized controlled trials (RCTs). Although recent reviewers concluded that evidence for the differential efficacy of these two approaches is inconsistent (Halford & Doss, 2016), in the seven years covered by the present review, efficacy and effectiveness research on varying models of CBCT predominate. Newer adaptations of CBCT target smoking (LaChance et al., 2015), anorexia (Bulik et al., 2012), binge eating disorder (Runfola et al., 2017), infidelity (Kröger et al., 2012), obsessive-compulsive disorder (Abramowitz et al., 2013; Belus et al., 2014), PTSD alone (Monson et al., 2012) and comorbid with alcohol use disorder (Schumm et al., 2014, 2015). In addition, cancer-related distress (Forbat et al., 2018; Heinrichs et al., 2012), neurodegenerative diseases (Ghedin et al., 2017), and genital pain (Corsini-Munt et al., 2014) have been assessed using adaptations of CBCT. EFCT has been tested for depression alone (Wittenborn et al., 2018) and in combination with antidepressant medication (Denton et al., 2012) and specifically adapted to treat posttraumatic stress disorder (PTSD) in military couples (Weissman et al., 2017), infertile couples (Najafi et al., 2015; Soltani et al., 2014), couples with a history of childhood abuse (Dalton et al., 2013), and parents raising a child with autism (Lee et al., 2017). Outcomes of other treatment models for couples have also been investigated in recent years, including cognitive existential (Couper et al., 2015), Gottman method (Garanzini et al., 2017), solution focused (Hajian & Mohammadi, 2013), systemic (Rohrbaugh et al., 2012), narrative (Seikkula et al., 2013), and time-limited psychodynamic (Balfour & Lanman, 2012) therapies.

Table 16.1 summarizes several prospective RCTs published between 2011 and 2018. The manualized treatments in these seven illustrative studies, six of which involved some form of CBCT, ranged from 4 to an average of 29 sessions. With the exception of Kröger et al.'s (2012) study of infidelity, the other six trials targeted individual problems (cancer-related distress, alcohol or substance abuse, and PTSD) in addition to the couples' relational functioning. Two investigations contrasted a manualized treatment to a wait list control (Kröger et al., 2012; Monson et al., 2012), while the cancer studies used a standard care educational control (Couper et al., 2015; Heinrichs et al., 2012; McLean et al., 2013), and the two substance use studies compared an individual, 12-step approach to a blend of individual and couple sessions (O'Farrell et al., 2017; Schumm et al., 2014).

All seven studies reported significant effects for outcomes related to individual functioning, and five of the six trials with follow-up data reported greater sustained efficacy for the couple treatment group. Whereas CBCT for infidelity (Kröger

et al., 2012) did not improve marital satisfaction, reductions were reported in the partners' depressive, anxious and PTSD-like symptoms. Similarly, couples' relationships were not significantly improved in a study targeting cancer-specific distress, possibly because the partners' pretreatment satisfaction levels were high (Heinrichs et al., 2012).

Since 2011, several follow-up investigations were published of Christensen et al.'s (2004) large-scale RCT comparing integrative behavioral couple therapy (IBCT) with traditional behavioral couple therapy (TBCT) for 134 chronically and seriously distressed married couples. A significant edge for the IBCT couples was found after two years (Baucom et al., 2011a), but the difference between therapies was negligible after the third year (Baucom et al., 2015). Although slightly more than a quarter of the couples had divorced at the five-year follow-up, this rate was lower than in most previous studies of long-term outcomes (Lebow et al., 2012). In a small subsample, the long-term divorce rate of couples with secret infidelity was significantly higher than the rates of couples (i) whose infidelity was revealed or (ii) couples who had not experienced infidelity. Notably, couples with infidelity who remained married five years post-IBCT or TBCT were similar in reported satisfaction to the couples without infidelity (Marín et al., 2014).

With respect to EFCT, follow-up assessments were conducted at four time points across 24 months (Wiebe et al., 2016, 2017). Results showed that although the level of secure attachment (the specific target of EFCT) decelerated over time, more security was associated with greater relationship satisfaction. Moreover, decreases in attachment anxiety and increases in satisfaction post-therapy, and at the two-year follow-up, were associated with couples' secure base behaviors observed during a 15-minute conflict resolution task (Wiebe et al., 2017).

Recent reviewers of the couple therapy literature concluded that effect sizes found in RCTs are consistently larger than those in effectiveness studies of routine practice (Halford et al., 2016). (See Table 16.2 for some illustrative naturalistic, uncontrolled studies.) The largest uncontrolled investigation published in recent years was a retrospective study with 877 participants in the UK who had attended at least two sessions of psychodynamic couple therapy (Hewison et al., 2016). Significant decreases were reported for both individual and couple distress, with effect sizes comparable to those found in previous RCTs, although the dropout rate was considerable. In contrast, two large-scale prospective studies, a treatment-as-usual investigation in Germany (n = 657 partners; Klann et al., 2011) and a study of 177 US military veteran couples (Doss et al., 2012) treated in five-session problem-focused communication training or an eight-session integrative, primarily behavioral therapy, found smaller effect sizes relative to RCTs, although in both studies significant individual and relational improvements were observed.

In addition to Doss et al.'s (2012) comparison of two behavioral therapies, five other studies in naturalistic settings (see Table 16.2) tested treatment as usual (Owen, Keller et al., 2014; Parker et al., 2012), integrative multisystemic therapy (Knobloch-Fedders et al., 2015), EFCT (Dalgleish et al., 2015a),

Table 16.1 Illustrative Randomized Clinical Trials of Couple Therapy (2011–2018)

Authors	Sample	Treatments	Outcomes	Follow-up	Multilevel modeling	Results
Couper et al. (2015)	62 Australian couples in which the male partner had prostate cancer	CECT (6 sessions) vs. usual medical care and information	Relationship functioning; coping; cancer distress; mental health	9 months	No	CECT was more effective than usual care at posttreatment and follow-up in terms of patient coping and relational functioning; functioning improved at follow-up, especially for younger patients. Younger partners reported better coping and less cancer-related distress. The control couples' relationship outcomes deteriorated over time.
Dalton et al. (2013)	22 Canadian couples in which the female partner had experienced childhood physical or sexual abuse	EFCT (22 couple sessions + 2 individual sessions) vs. waitlist	Relationship satisfaction; marital distress; trauma symptoms	--	No	EFCT was more effective than controls at improving relationship satisfaction; 70% of participants in the treatment group were no longer reporting clinical levels of marital distress; women's understanding of abuse changing after age 18, depression, anger/irritability related to the abuse were associated with lower relationship satisfaction at the beginning of treatment but not at the end.
Heinrichs et al. (2012)	72 German couples in which the female partner had breast or gynecological cancer	Couple skills intervention ("Side by Side") (4 sessions) vs. cancer education control	Relationship satisfaction; cancer-specific distress; posttraumatic growth; dyadic coping; communication quality	6 and 12 months	Yes	Women in skills training reported reduced fear of cancer progression, and couples reported less cancer-related avoidance, better communication skills, and more posttraumatic growth (meaning in life) posttreatment. Satisfaction was not affected, although levels were high at pre-treatment. No differences in effectiveness were found at follow-up.

(Continued)

TABLE 16.1 (CONTINUED)

Authors	Sample	Treatments	Outcomes	Follow-up	Multilevel modeling	Results
Kröger et al. (2012)	89 German couples who had or are continuing to experience infidelity	TCBT ($M = 29$ sessions) vs. waitlist	Relationship satisfaction; depression; anxiety; PTSD-like symptoms	--	Yes	TCBT reduced depression only for the unfaithful partner; for the deceived partner, TCBT was more effective in reducing PTSD-like symptoms. Trend toward improved satisfaction for the unfaithful partner, but not for the deceived partner, although anxiety was reduced for both partners.
McLean et al. (2013)	42 Canadian couples in which one partner had metastatic cancer	EFCT (8 sessions) vs. standard care	Relationship functioning; psychological symptoms; empathic caregiving; caregiver burden	3 months	Yes	Compared to standard care, EFCT improved relationship functioning and patients' experience of their caregivers' empathy at posttreatment and at follow up.
Monson et al. (2012)	40 U.S. and Canadian couples in which one partner met criteria for PTSD	CBCT vs. waitlist (15 sessions)	Relationship satisfaction; symptoms of PTSD, depression, anxiety, anger	3 months	Yes	Clinically significant improvements in satisfaction and comorbid symptom severity (PTSD, depression, anxiety, anger) were found for the treatment group at post-test and follow up.
Schumm et al. (2014)	105 U.S. women with alcohol dependence and their male partners	BCT + IBT (13 couple + 13 IBT sessions) vs. 26 IBT sessions)	Relationship satisfaction and happiness; percentage of days abstinent; adverse consequences of substance use; IPV	12 months	No	For women, BCT + IBT outperformed IBT alone in terms of abstinence, problems due to substance use, satisfaction through follow up. Women reporting high relational distress improved more in BCT. Male satisfaction and happiness were also improved for couples seen in BCT. Male- and female-initiated IPV was reduced in both treatments through follow up.

Notes. BCT = behavioral couple therapy; CBCT = cognitive-behavioral couple therapy; CECT = cognitive existential couple therapy; EFCT = emotionally focused couple therapy; IBT = individually based therapy; IPV = intimate partner violence; PTSD = post-traumatic stress disorder; TCBT = traditional couple behavior therapy.

and the Gottman method of couple therapy (Garanzini et al., 2017). Significant outcomes were observed in all six of these prospective studies, three of which reported greater relational gains with lengthier treatments (Dalgleish et al., 2015a; Garanzini et al., 2015; Knobloch-Fedders et al., 2015). Successful outcomes were also reported in terms of decreased symptoms (Parker et al., 2012) and increased functioning (Knobloch-Fedders et al., 2015) and well-being (Owen, Keller et al., 2014). In a follow-up to Dalgleish et al. (Wiebe et al., 2017; not tabled), the gains in satisfaction reported posttreatment were generally maintained through 24 months, although the rate of change decelerated with time.

Moderators of Couple Outcomes

Although many recent studies compared relational outcomes (e.g. satisfaction, commitment, distress, quality) by participants' demographic characteristics, such as gender, age, and race, relatively few of these variables were significantly associated with outcomes. The few exceptions included Doss et al. (2012), in which African American veteran couples reported comparatively more gains than Caucasian or Latino couples, and Couper et al. (2015), in which younger patients with prostate cancer and their caregivers reported more gains than their older counterparts. In fact, many studies found no gender differences in treatment gains for heterosexual couples (e.g., Hewison et al., 2016) or in comparing gay and lesbian couples (Garanzini et al, 2017). In Garanzini et al., improvements were greater for couples reporting alcohol/drug abuse and less severe physical and emotional abuse.

In Doss et al.'s (2012) veteran sample, the couples who agreed on the nature of their problems (Biesen & Doss, 2013) saw more improvements. Other studies found that the partners who benefited most from EFCT began treatment reporting greater emotional control and attachment anxiety (Dalgleish et al., 2015ab), whereas couples benefitting most from CBCT reported greater psychological distress (e.g., Doss et al., 2012; Schnaider et al., 2015). Interestingly, a recent CBCT effectiveness study in the UK found that relational distress was significantly reduced for the nonclient partners as well as for the partners with clinical levels of depression (Baucom et al., 2018, p. 275).

Other studies reported differences in outcome based on partner perspective, such as patient/caregiver (Cohen et al., 2014; Couper et al., 2015; Fredman et al., 2016; Heinrichs et al., 2012; McLean et al., 2013; O'Farrell et al., 2017), unfaithful/deceived partner (Kröger et al., 2012), and male/female initiator of violence (Rowe et al., 2011). In Couper et al. (2015), for example, male cancer patients reported better coping posttherapy, and their caregivers, especially younger ones, reported less psychological distress. In a study focusing on self-reported behavior, Fredman et al. (2016) found that one partner's high pretreatment accommodation to the other partner's PTSD, that is, changing one's behavior to minimize the partner's distress or conflict in the relationship, predicted greater satisfaction and more individual gains for both members of the couple. In a comparison of blended couple + individual sessions to couple-only therapy for women with alcohol use disorder (McCrady et al., 2016), both therapies were effective, but the blended treatment was more successful at reducing drinking among women who reported relatively more sociotropy (a tendency to please others). In Schumm et al.'s (2014) blended couple and individual, 12-step therapy for alcohol and substance use, women who began therapy with more relational distress reported significantly more posttreatment satisfaction.

Client characteristics have also been reported in terms of (1) retention in couple therapy (versus drop-out) (Fischer et al., 2017); Madsen et al., 2017; Parker et al., 2012) and (2) relational outcomes other than satisfaction, such as decreases in distrust and physical aggression (Valladares Kahn et al., 2015). In terms of long-term effectiveness, an 18-month follow-up of Doss et al.'s (2012) veteran sample showed maintenance of gains and decreased psychological distress, although no individual patient characteristics moderated these effects (Nowlan et al., 2017). At the couple level, however, a five-year follow-up of Christensen et al.'s (2004) RCT comparing IBCT and TBCT found less divorce among couples who were more committed and had lengthier marriages (Baucom et al., 2015). Notably, in the IBCT group, long-term satisfaction and less likelihood of divorce were associated with the female partner's level of desired closeness, whereas this pattern was reversed among couples in the TBCT group.

FAMILY THERAPY: DOES IT WORK?

Summarizing research between 2003 and 2010 in the sixth edition of this *Handbook*, Sexton et al. (2013) concluded that, overall, there is robust empirical support from high-quality studies for the efficacy of family-based therapies. Fifty percent of the family studies reviewed by Sexton et al. focused on five theoretical models: Multisystemic therapy (MST; Henggeler et al., 1986; 2009), functional family therapy (FFT; Sexton, 2009; Sexton & Alexander, 2002;), multidimensional family therapy (MDFT; Liddle et al., 2001, 2005), variations of cognitive-behavioral family therapy (CBT-FT; Freeman et al., 2008; Wood et al., 2006), and what Sexton et al. called *general systemic family therapy* (family members treated conjointly with an emphasis on their interactional patterns). The four theoretically specific systemic models focused on adolescents' externalizing problems (primarily delinquency and substance abuse), while the more general family therapy and CBT-based models focused on other youth problems. Sexton et al. noted that research on the specific models was of better quality than the research on general systems therapy, which tended to have mixed results. Additionally, comparisons of the four specific therapies to other treatments were largely, but not wholly, positive, although effects varied by problem type and outcome.

Reflecting on 25 years of systemic therapy research, Heatherington et al. (2015) underscored the solid evidence base for family therapies based on numerous RCTs, meta-reviews and meta-analyses. On the other hand, while the outcomes of some family approaches had been thoroughly researched, other approaches had received minimal empirical attention. Overall, family treatments for a few presenting

TABLE 16.2   Illustrative Naturalistic Effectiveness Studies of Couple Therapy (2011–2018)

Authors	Sample	Treatments	Outcomes	Process variables	Multilevel modeling	Results
Biesen & Doss (2013); Doss et al. (2012, 2015)	147–177 U.S. couples (one or both partners were veterans)	Brief problem focused and longer integrative therapy	Relationship satisfaction; therapist rated treatment success; closeness; quality of communication; psychological distress	Agreement on problems; frequency of target behaviors; therapist technique; improvement	Yes	Agreement was associated with staying in therapy and clinically significant change, but only for the brief, problem-focused group. There were no gender differences, and no treatment group differences for therapist-rated success. Both women and men made gains in satisfaction. Gains were greater for African-American than White couples. Pre-therapy levels of satisfaction accounted for gains more so than any other client characteristics. Men's gains in satisfaction and perceived communication quality slowed over time in therapy. Both partners reported more closeness and reduced distress over time in treatment. The therapists' use of integrative techniques did not predict outcome, nor did the frequency of targeted behaviors discussed in session. Early satisfaction improvement mediated later levels of psychological distress.
Burgess Moser et al. (2015); Dalgleish et al. (2015)	32 Canadian couples	EFCT	Relationship satisfaction; secure base use; support behaviors	Changes in attachment; blamer softening; working alliance; number of sessions	Yes	Clinically significant improvement in satisfaction was observed. Decreased relationship-specific anxiety and avoidance were associated with improved satisfaction, as was increased attachment security. Couples completing blamer softening reported decreased attachment anxiety. No moderator effect for dropout status was observed. The most gains in satisfaction were made by partners with more emotional control and high anxiety (but not avoidance or trust). Self-reported alliances with the therapist were generally strong (the relation of alliance to outcome was not analyzed).
Garanzini et al. (2017)	88 gay and 18 lesbian U.S. couples	GMCT	Relationship satisfaction	Time spent in therapy	No	Significant improvements were observed for both groups after the 11th session, with the most change occurring by session 3. Gains were larger for couples with addiction, minor domestic violence, and emotional abuse through humiliation and threats (rather than by isolation, coercion, controllingness, fear, or jealousy). No gay vs. lesbian differences or moderation effect for suicidality.

(Continued)

TABLE **16.2** (CONTINUED)

Authors	Sample	Treatments	Outcomes	Process variables	Multilevel modeling	Results
Knobloch- Fedders, Pinsof & Haase (2015)	125 U.S. couples	Integrative multisystemic therapy	Relationship adjustment; individual functioning	Time spent in therapy	No	Nonlinear gains in individual functioning and clinically significant gains in adjustment were observed for both men and women. Adjustment increased in the first four sessions and then stabilized. Compared to men, women reported more relationship dysfunction pre-treatment.
Owen, Duncan, et al. (2014)[1]	158 Norwegian couples	Eclectic	Relationship satisfaction; individual functioning	Working alliance	Yes	Therapist differences in client-rated alliance and therapist level of experience were uniquely associated with outcome. No outcome differences were found by therapist gender or professional discipline.
Owen, Keller et al. (2014)	30 U.S. couples	Treatment as usual	Relationship satisfaction; well being	Commitment uncertainty	Yes	Small reductions in uncertainty were associated with gains in satisfaction and well-being post-therapy. Women reported greater gains in well-being than men. No interaction between gender and change in commitment uncertainty.
Parker, Johnson & Ketring (2012)	297 U.S. couples	Treatment as usual	Symptom distress	--	No	Women's anxious attachment and men's avoidant attachment were associated with their partners' lower distress post-therapy. Among women (only), low avoidant attachment was associated with less distress post-therapy.

Notes. Studies in the same cell were based on the same sample.
[1] Secondary analysis of Anker, Owen, Duncan, & Sparks (2010). In the treatments as usual, the authors in each study described the types of interventions studied. EFCT = emotionally focused couple therapy; GMCT = Gottman method couples therapy; PDCT = psychodynamic couple therapy.

problems (youth externalizing behavior, in particular) had been much more fully developed and consequently well-studied than treatments for internalizing problems, such as anxiety and depression.

Since 2011, meta-analyses and meta-reviews have provided broad evidence of treatment efficacy. Riedinger et al., (2015), for example, found small and moderate effect sizes compared to alternative treatments and untreated controls, respectively, although the significant results were limited to the subset of studies on externalizing/substance abuse problems. Von Sydow et al.'s (2013) review of therapies for externalizing disorders that followed an explicitly systemic orientation found that of 47 international studies, 42 showed significant effects for conduct disorders, attention deficit hyperactivity disorder and substance use, with sustained results at follow-up.

The same authors' meta-analysis of studies targeting internalizing and mixed disorders (Retzlaff et al., 2013) found systemic therapy to be superior to nonsystemic control treatments and to other evidence-based treatments in 33 of 38 international studies. These general conclusions dovetail with those of meta-reviews of the evidence base for CFT for child (Carr, 2014a) and adult (Carr, 2014b) problems.

After a summary of the kinds of problems addressed in the large body of recent research on family therapy, we begin by summarizing treatment studies (2011–2018) for youth and for adults, organized by problem type (also see Table 16.3). Table 16.4 provides exemplars of randomized clinical trials (RCTs), and Table 16.5 summarizes some recent effectiveness studies of family therapy.

TABLE 16.3   Illustrative Family Therapy Outcome Studies by Targeted Problem

Disorder	Treatment	Authors	Country	N
Problems/disorders of youth				
Externalizing behaviors and substance abuse	Ecologically based family therapy (EBFT)	Bartle-Haring et al. (2018)	US	183
	Multisystemic therapy (MST)	Butler et al. (2011)	UK	108
	MST	Chapman & Shoenwald (2011)	US	1,979
	MST	Fonagy et al. (2018)	UK	684
	MST	Gervan et al. (2012)	Canada	99
	Functional family therapy (FFT)	Graham et al. 2014	Ireland	118
	Multidimensional family therapy (MDFT)	Greenbaum et al. (2015)	US	646
	MDFT	Hendricks et al. (2011)	Netherlands	109
	Brief strategic family therapy (BSFT)	Horigian, Feaster, Brincks et al. (2015)	US	480
	MDFT	Liddle et al. (2018)	US	113
	MST	Löfholm et al. (2014)	Sweden	973
	BSFT	Robbins et al. (2011)	US	481
	FFT	Rohde et al. (2014)	US	111
	MDFT	Rowe et al. (2016)	US	154
	MST	Ryan et al. (2013)	US	185
	MST	Sawyer & Borduin (2011)	US	176
	EBFT	Zhang & Sleznick (2018)	US	183
Obsessive compulsive disorder	Family-based cognitive-behavioral therapy (CBT)	Freeman et al. (2014)	US	127

(Continued)

TABLE 16.3 (CONTINUED)

Disorder	Treatment	Authors	Country	N
	Family-based exposure and response prevention	Lewin et al. (2014)	US	20
	Family-focused cognitive-behavioral therapy (FCBT)	Peris et al. (2012)	US	49
	FCBT	Piacentini et al. (2011)	US	71
	Parent-enhanced CBT	Reynolds et al. (2013)	US	50
	CBT with a parent component	Rosa-Alcázar et al. (2017)	Spain	20
	Brief family intervention to address accommodation	Thompson-Hollands et al. (2015)	US	18
Anxiety	CBT + positive family interaction therapy (PFIT)	Peris et al. (2017)	US	62
	CBT +PFIT	Piacentini et al. (2011)	US	71
	Parent-only CBT	Smith et al. (2014)	US	31
Depression and suicidality	Attachment-based family therapy (ABFT)	G.M. Diamond et al. (2016)	Israel	32
	ABFT	G.S. Diamond et al. (2012)	US	66
	Time-limited systems integrative family therapy	Garoff et al. (2012)	Finland	72
	CBT with parent sessions	Esposito-Smythers et al. (2012)	US	40
	Resourceful adolescent program for parents	Pineda & Dadds (2013)	Australia	48
	ABFT	Santens et al. (2017)	Belgium	43
Eating disorders	Family check-up	Connell et al. (2018)	US	593
	Self-harm intervention: Family therapy	Cottrell et al. (2018)	UK	852
	Partial hospitalization with parent involvement	Girz et al. (2013)	Canada	17
	Parent–child interaction therapy + emotion development module (PCIT-ED)	Luby et al. (2012)	US	54
	PCIT-ED	Luby et al. (2018)	US	229
	Family-centered partial hospitalization	Ornstein et al. (2012)	US	30
	Family-based therapy (FBT) for bulimia	Le Grange et al. (2015)	US	130
	FBT for anorexia (FBT-A)	House et al. (2012)	UK	127
	FBT-A	Le Grange et al. (2011)	US	86

(Continued)

TABLE 16.3 (CONTINUED)

Disorder	Treatment	Authors	Country	N
	FBT-A	Le Grange et al. (2014)	US	79
	FBT-A	Madden et al. (2014)	Australia	82
	Parent only FBT	Le Grange et al. (2016)	US	107
	FBT with intensive parent coaching	Lock et al. (2015)	US	45
	Adjunctive family therapy	Godart et al. (2012)	France	60
	Systemic family therapy vs. FBT	Agras et al. (2014)	US	164
	Intensive family therapy	Marzola et al. (2015)	US	74
	Enhanced CBT (CBT-E) with parents	Dalle Grave et al. (2013)	Italy	49
	CBE-E	Dalle Grave et al. (2015)	Italy	68
	Emotion-focused family therapy	LaFrance Robinson et al. (2016)	Canada	25
Family challenges				
Gang involvement	MST	Boxer et al. (2017)	US	409
Sexually transmitted infections and sexual risk in drug-involved youth	MDFT	Rowe et al. (2016)	US	154
Runaway youth	Ecologically based family therapy	Guo et al. (2016)	US	179
Asthma	Home-based family intervention for children with severe asthma	Celano et al. (2012)	US	43
Grief and bereavement	Family-focused grief therapy	Kissane et al. (2016)	US	170
	Family bereavement program	Sandler et al. (2018)	US	156
	Family-focused grief therapy	Kissane et al. (2016)	US	170
	Family bereavement program	Sandler et al. (2018)	US	156
Adult disorders				
Obsessive compulsive disorder	Nonviolent resistance intervention	Lebowitz et al. (2012)	Israel	27
	Brief family-based Intervention	Baruah et al. (2018)	India	64
Postpartum depression	Family-based therapy	Donahue et al. (2014)	US	72
	Systemic family therapy with CBT	Hou et al. (2014)	China	249
Schizophrenia	Culturally informed therapy for schizophrenia	Weisman de Mamani et al. (2014)	US	69
	Family focused treatment for adults with clinically high risk of psychosis	Miklowitz, O'Brien et al. (2014)	US	129

(Continued)

TABLE 16.3 (CONTINUED)

Disorder	Treatment	Authors	Country	N
Bipolar disorder	Family psychoeducation	Sharif et al. (2012)	Iran	70
	FFT	Miklowitz, Schneck et al. (2013)	US	40
	FFT	Miklowitz, Schneck et al. (2014)	US	145
	Psychoeducational family intervention	Fiorillo (2015)	Italy	137

Problems Addressed

Few family therapy studies target relational problems alone; rather, these problems tend to be studied along with more specific, individual outcomes, particularly disorders of children and adolescents. In recent years, the most common problems addressed in family therapy research are externalizing disorders (i.e. conduct disorder, delinquent behavior, and substance use), followed by internalizing disorders (i.e. obsessive-compulsive disorder, anxiety, depression/suicidality, and eating disorders). In recent years, several studies targeted challenging family problems, including adolescents' gang involvement (Boxer et al., 2017), sexually transmitted infections (including HIV) and risk behavior (Liddle et al., 2011), runaway youth (Guo et al., 2016), juvenile sex offenders (Rowe, 2012), and unrelenting anger toward a parent (G. M. Diamond et al., 2016).

Problems of Children and Adolescents

Externalizing Problems

Since adolescents' externalizing problems often co-occur with substance abuse, most treatments target both problems. In general, the highly studied treatments are well supported. In recent years, this conclusion has strengthened, along with the quality of studies in this area. For example, a recent meta-analysis of 19 MDFT clinical trials (van der Pol et al., 2017) showed a significant mean effect size of .24 across multiple outcome indices. A multilevel meta-analysis of 28 family treatment studies with youthful offenders (Dopp et al., 2017) reported a mean effect size of .25 for antisocial behavior, with generally long-lasting effects, and larger effect sizes for substance use outcomes as compared with changes in peer relationships. A methodologically rigorous meta-analysis (Baldwin et al., 2012) of 24 RCTs on the four most well-developed family systemic therapies for these problems (FFT, MST, MDFT, and brief strategic family therapy [BSFT; Szapocznik et al., 2012]) found significant but modest effect sizes when compared with alternative treatments (individual, group, and psychodynamic family therapy; $d = .26$) and treatment as usual (TAU; $d = .21$); effect sizes were notably larger when compared to no-treatment controls ($d = .70$).

A narrative review of the evidence for family-based treatments (Henggler & Sheidow, 2012) concluded that there is a large evidence base for the efficacy and effectiveness of MST, mixed but promising evidence for FFT, few efficacy trials but consistently positive outcomes for multidimensional foster care treatment (in which the family work is carried out with youth and their foster parents; Chamberlain, 2003), and strong, *promising* evidence for BSFT. This summary is consistent with the conclusions of other reviewers (Szapocznik et al., 2012; von Sydow et al. 2013). Of the four most well-developed treatments (FFT, MST, MDFT, BSFT), the evidence does not indicate superiority for any approach (Retzlaff et al., 2013), probably since these therapies rely on similar elements: a focus on parents/caregivers as the prime targets for immediate and sustained change, the use of behavioral and cognitive-behavioral techniques, and service delivery in the natural settings of the youth.

Regarding outcomes for drug abuse specifically, both Rowe (2012) and Hogue et al. (2014) concluded that evidence for the efficacy of some systemic treatments is quite strong. These therapies outperform most alternate treatments and are either equally efficacious or superior to individual CBT treatments, with effects lasting into young adulthood (Horigian, Feaster, Robbins et al., 2015). For marijuana abuse, studies have been replicated beyond the original development groups, as well as internationally (cf. Hendricks et al., 2011). Comparisons of family to individual CBT/CBT with motivational interviewing have been mixed, either with equivalent effects (e.g. Hendricks et al., 2011) or, in earlier studies, superiority for the family treatment (Liddle et al., 2002, 2008). On the other hand, a review by Lindström et al. (2013) concluded that compared to various controls, BSFT for adolescent drug use improved treatment retention but was not superior at reducing drug use or improving family functioning. A recent RCT (Liddle et al., 2018) demonstrated that youth with co-occurring mental health and substance use disorders can be treated equally successfully with MDFT in the home/community vs. residential treatment, challenging assumptions that adolescents who meet criteria for residential treatment can only be treated in these settings.

Notably, recent evidence indicates a cross-fertilization of treatment effects, that is, change in one domain (family functioning, youth drug use, or externalizing behavior) affecting change in other domains. This pattern has been found post-treatment as well as at follow-up. As one example, BSFT showed reduced parent alcohol use when adolescent substance was the target (Horigian, Feaster, Brincks et al., 2015). In an efficacy study of long-term effects, MST effectively addressed family dynamics as well as individual behavior (Sawyer &

TABLE 16.4 Illustrative Randomized Clinical Trials of Family Therapy (2011–2018)

Authors	Sample	Treatments	Outcomes	Follow-up	Multilevel modeling	Results
Hendriks et al., (2011)	109 Dutch adolescents with cannabis use disorder and delinquency	MDFT vs. CBT	Marijuana use, delinquent behavior, treatment response and retention	3, 6, 9, and 12 months following baseline.	No	Moderate and equivalent effects of both treatments were found for reduced marijuana use and delinquent behavior. MDFT resulted in higher retention and stronger treatment response. Adolescents with more severe problems benefitted more from MDFT. 43% of clients met criteria for treatment response at the 1-year follow-up (with no group difference).
Liddle et al. (2018)	113 US adolescents with co-occurring substance use and mental health problems (originally referred for RT)	MDFT vs. evidence-based RT	Substance use; delinquent behaviors; internalizing and externalizing symptoms	2, 4, 12, and 18 months post-baseline (see Results)	No	From baseline to 2 months, no differences were found, although youth in MDFT showed decreased internalizing symptoms; From 2–18 months, these youth retained treatment gains in substance use and delinquent behavior, while youth in RT lost gains. Gains in mental health symptoms were stable and similar across groups.
Le Grange et al. (2015)	130 US adolescents with bulimia or partial bulimia	FBT-BN vs. CBT-A	Rate of abstinence (≥ 4 weeks) from binging-purging; obsessionality; depression; % body weight; eating disorder pathology	6 and 12 months	No	FBT-BN was superior in terms of abstinence, and depression was lower at the end of treatment for the FBT-BN group. Adolescents with less family conflict fared better in FBT-BN than CBT-A.
Lewin et al. (2014)	31 US children (3 to 8 years) with OCD	Family-based E/RP vs. TAU	Obsessions/compulsions; clinician rating of illness severity; family accommodation	1 and 3 months	No	Family-based ERP had a clearly superior treatment response on a measure of obsession/compulsions (65% vs. 7% in TAU). Gains were maintained at follow-up. Gains in family accommodation and the secondary measures also favored the E-/RP group.

(Continued)

TABLE 16.4 (CONTINUED)

Authors	Sample	Treatments	Outcomes	Follow-up	Multilevel modeling	Results
Robbins et al. (2011); Horigian, Feaster, Robbins et al. (2015)	481 US adolescents with drug use and delinquency	BSFT vs. TAU	Drug use (self-reported and urine testing); treatment engagement and retention; family functioning; arrest and incarceration; externalizing behaviors (at long-term follow-up)	12 months (Robbins et al.); 3 to 7 years (Horigian et al.)	Yes	BSFT resulted in more engagement, retention, and to some degree, parent-reported family functioning. No effects on the trajectory of self-reported drug use, but youth in BSFT had less drug use during the final observation period. At the long-term follow-up, BSFT showed positive effects compared to TAU on arrests/incarceration, externalizing behaviors, but not on drug use.
Sawyer & Borduin (2011)[a]	176 US serious adolescent offenders	MST vs. individual therapy	Juvenile and adult criminal convictions (excluding traffic court); civil suits	M = 21.9 years	No	Youth in MST had significantly lower rates of arrest for felonies, misdemeanors, and involvement in civil suits (indicating less family instability). No significant differences based on race, gender, SES, number of pretreatment arrests, or arrests for violent crimes.

NOTES. [a] Follow-up from Sawyer and Borduin (1995). AFT = individual adolescent-focused therapy; CBT-A = CBT adapted for adolescents; E/RP = exposure and response prevention; FBT-BN = family-based therapy for bulimia; IT = individual therapy; MDFT = multidimensional family therapy; MST = multisystemic family therapy; RT = residential treatment; TAU = treatment as usual.

TABLE 16.5 **Illustrative Effectiveness Studies of Family Therapy (2011–2018)**

Authors	Sample	Treatments	Outcomes	Process variables	Follow-up	Multilevel modeling	Results
Asarnow et al. (2015)	45 US suicide-attempting youth (13–18 years)	SAFETY (CBT family intervention integrated with emergency services)	Suicidal behavior; youth and parent depression, hopelessness; youth social adjustment; service use and treatment satisfaction	--	3 and 6 months	No	The intervention was found to be feasible and safe, with high client satisfaction. The youth showed significant improvements on all outcomes; parental depression declined significantly. At follow-up, improvements were found for suicidal behavior, hopelessness, social adjustment, parent and youth depression. One reported suicide attempt at the 3- and one at the 6-month follow-up.
G. M. Diamond et al. (2013)	10 U.S. suicidal LGB youth (14–18 years)	ABFT-LGB	Suicidal ideation; depressive symptoms; maternal attachment–related anxiety and avoidance	--	--	No	Results showed decreased suicide ideation, depressive symptoms, decreased attachment-related anxiety and avoidance among treatment completers. The treatment was deemed feasible and acceptable.
Girz et al. (2013)	17 Canadian adolescents (M = 16 years) with various types of anorexia nervosa and bulimia	FBT in a day hospital program	Eating disorder symptoms; depression; anxiety; impact of symptoms on parents, parental self-efficacy	--	3 and 6 months	No	Results showed weight gain (for youth for whom it was a goal), decreased eating disorder symptoms, depression and anxiety; for parents, the impact of symptoms decreased and self-efficacy increased (no differences by parental role). Most psychological gains were observed between 3 and 6 months, and either maintained or continued.

(Continued)

TABLE 16.5 (CONTINUED)

Authors	Sample	Treatments	Outcomes	Process variables	Follow-up	Multilevel modeling	Results
Lebowitz et al. (2014)	10 US treatment-refusing youth (9–13 years) with severe anxiety disorder	SPACE (intervention for parents of children with anxiety disorders)	Anxiety symptoms; symptom severity; other child psychopathology; family accommodation; treatment satisfaction	--	--	No	60% of youth were treatment responders (reduced anxiety); family accommodation was reduced, child depression was marginally reduced; 70% of parents reported their child's motivation increased, as did their willingness to attend individual treatment.
Marzola et al. (2015)	74 US eating disordered adolescents (M age = 14.8 years)	IFT	Weight ≥ 95% of expected weight; eating pathology; binge-purging symptoms; treatment acceptability	Single vs. multiple family group treatment	$M = 30$ Months	No	87.8% of youth had full or partial remission; 12% had poor outcomes. No differences by treatment format (single or multiple family). No relations were found between personal characteristics and outcome. Most youth saw the treatment as useful.
LaFrance Robinson et al. (2016)	33 US parents (8 families with both parents) of adolescent and adult children (13 to 31 years) with eating disorders	EEFT	Parental self-efficacy; beliefs about children's emotions; emotional blocks; behaviors supporting the child's recovery; intentions to change or try new strategies; treatment satisfaction	--	--	No	Results showed high treatment satisfaction, increases in parental self-efficacy, attitudes and beliefs, and decrease in emotional blocks. Qualitative data showed promising parent reports of changed behaviors and intentions.

Notes. ABFT-LGB = Attachment-based family therapy for lesbian, gay, and bisexual youth; EEFT = Emotion-focused family therapy for eating disorders; Family-based ERP = Family-based exposure and response prevention; FBT = Family-based therapy; IFT = Intensive family therapy; SAFETY = Safe Alternatives for Teens and Youth; SPACE = Supportive Parenting for Anxious Childhood Emotions.

Borduin, 2011). Moreover, as shown in other studies, improvements in family functioning mediated symptom reductions in individuals. Sawyer and Borduin concluded that "positive family relations in adulthood can act as a natural social control for crime" (p. 650), possibly accounting for both the immediate and long-term effects of MST, perhaps even putting a brake on the intergenerational transmission of antisocial behavior. Indeed, secondary analyses of follow-up data from this study (Wagner et al., 2014) showed that the treatment effects on antisocial behavior spread to siblings of the originally treated youth.

Nuanced findings are typical in efficacy and effectiveness studies addressing youth externalizing behavior. That is, effects are substantial for some measures and not others, and for some follow-up periods and not others. For example, Robbins et al.'s (2011) multisite clinical trial of BSFT, which had a large and diverse community sample, found no effect over time in the trajectories of youth-reported drug use but fewer days of drug use at the final observation point, better retention and engagement in treatment, and a small improvement in family functioning. In a large study of MST for antisocial behavior (Fonagy et al., 2018), the effects of MST and management-as-usual by youth offending teams were equivalent to the benchmark in terms of the odds of youth being placed out-of-home (13% and 11%, respectively) at the 18-month follow-up period, but MST showed superior effects on some parent and youth secondary outcomes at various follow-up points. In another study, MST was superior to targeted intensive treatment-as-usual by youth offending teams in reducing offending and other antisocial behavior (reported by both youth and parents), especially at the 18-month follow-up (Butler et al., 2014).

Moderators of Outcomes for Externalizing Problems

Tests of client moderators of family treatments for these disorders include age, gender, race, ethnicity, problem severity, family constellation (two parents, single parent). Treatment factors have also been tested as moderators of efficacy or effectiveness, including length and type of treatment, such as comparing pure systemic approaches (e.g. BSFT), to more integrative models (e.g. MST and FFT), and communication patterns between therapists and parents versus between therapists and adolescents (Marchionda & Slesnick, 2013). MDFT for substance use is clearly efficacious for youth of diverse ethnicities, regardless of gender, and is particularly effective for boys, for Euro-American/non-Latinx and African-American youth (Greenbaum et al., 2015), and for youth with severe substance abuse and high levels of disruptive behavior (Welmers-van de Pol et al., 2017). With respect to MST, a meta-analysis (van der Stouwe et al., 2014) indicated greater effectiveness for youth under age 15 with more severe baseline problems, and one study (Gervan et al., 2012) found that youth improved more when their fathers participated in the treatment.

Therapist adherence to each of the four specific treatment models has shown demonstrable effects. A study comparing FFT to probation services (Sexton & Turner, 2011) found that adolescents, particularly those from the most troubled families,

with highly adherent therapists committed less crime at posttreatment and at follow-up. In an Irish study of FFT for family or school difficulties (Graham et al., 2014), families who worked with high-adherent therapists had better outcomes. Therapist adherence to BSFT predicted greater engagement and retention in therapy, as well as reduced drug use and improved family functioning (Robbins et al., 2011). In a particularly large study (429 therapists at 45 sites) of family treatment with youth at imminent risk of out-of-home placement due to criminal offenses, substance abuse, or school removal, therapist adherence to MST was associated with reduced externalizing behavior problems at one-year posttreatment, and criminal charges at four years posttreatment (Chapman & Shoenwald, 2011). Notably, adherence was higher when the therapist and caregiver had similar ethnicities, and increased adherence predicted slightly better outcomes. In MST, high caregiver reports of therapists' adherence to the treatment model were found for youth who lived at home, were engaged in school or work, and had not exhibited criminal behavior (Lofholm et al., 2014), and higher observer ratings of therapist adherence during the first month of therapy predicted subsequent decreased externalizing behavior and youth alcohol consumption at follow-up (Gillespie et al., 2017). In 218 cases of MDFT (Rowe et al., 2013), observer-rated therapist adherence predicted decreases in substance use frequency and lower rates of cannabis dependence at 12 months in a European (but not a US) sample.

Obsessive-Compulsive Disorder

Although individual CBT (Freeman et al., 2018) and psychotropic medication are effective treatments for obsessive-compulsive disorder (OCD) in children, approximately 40–50% of children either show no response or only a partial response (Peris et al., 2012; Peris & Piacentini, 2013). Due to the negative influence of family members' accommodation to OCD behaviors and the consequent disruption of family functioning, several family-inclusive treatments continue to be actively developed and tested, with strong effect sizes, not only for reducing symptoms but also for improving youth functioning (cf. Thompson-Hollands et al., 2014). For example, family CBT with children aged 8–17 found remission rates of 43%, compared to 18% in the control condition, child relaxation training/psychoeducation (Piacentini et al., 2011). In contrast to individual CBT for children, with parents attending only three sessions, large effects were found at post treatment and at follow-up for parent-enhanced CBT, in which parents attended all sessions (Reynolds et al., 2013). Even with children aged 5–8, CBT-based family treatment was significantly more effective than family relaxation training for reducing symptoms and improving child functioning (Freeman et al., 2014), as was family-based exposure and response prevention (ERP) with children aged 3–5, compared to treatment as usual (Lewin et al., 2014). On the other hand, a small clinical trial (n = 20) found no differences between CBT with a family component and parent training alone (Rosa-Alcázar et al., 2017).

The entire treatment need not be family based, as adjunctive family sessions with standard CBT tends to enhance OCD outcomes, particularly when family members' accommodation to OCD behavior is targeted (Freeman et al., 2018). One recent study, for example, showed that adding only two sessions to address family accommodation resulted in greater symptom reduction and a more rapid response than standard ERP alone (Thompson-Hollands et al., 2015). Among highly distressed families (those reporting baseline high levels of blame, conflict, and/or low cohesion), positive family interaction therapy (PFIT; Peris & Piacentini, 2013) plus CBT was found to improve family dynamics and had a 70% response rate in reducing OCD symptoms, compared to 40% in the TAU condition. Since children with highly disruptive behaviors pose a challenge to treatment engagement, providing parent management training to address the child's opposition-defiant behavior before beginning ERP showed a mean reduction of 39% in OCD symptoms in three cases, compared to three other cases in which only 10% of children improved (Sukhodolsky et al., 2013).

Researchers have also investigated treating only the parents in cases with unwilling or resistant children. A fully parent-based intervention, supportive parenting for anxious childhood emotions (SPACE; Lebowitz, 2013), involves coaching parents to reduce their accommodation behaviors and handle their children's responses more effectively by using principles of nonviolent resistance (Omer & Lebowitz, 2016). Initial findings from open trials of SPACE with 6 (Lebowitz, 2013) and 10 (Omer et al., 2014) families with difficult-to-engage children showed positive results for symptoms, parent accommodation and satisfaction.

In sum, there is strong evidence for the added value of parental/family involvement in OCD treatments for youth. Freeman et al.'s (2018) recent review of these therapies identified the PFIT approach as *probably efficacious* and other approaches to parent training as promising but *experimental*. The authors concluded that it remains to be determined how much family involvement is optimal, since researchers' use of the term *involvement* ranges from including parents as coaches or reinforcing agents to a greater inclusion of parents in both CBT and systemic intervention models.

Moderators of Outcomes for OCD

In the family CBT arm of an RCT for youth with OCD, the youth who benefited most from treatment were those from families reporting more cohesion and less parental blame and conflict (Peris et al., 2012). In terms of treatment variables, a recent meta-analysis (Rosa-Alcázar et al., 2015) found that parental involvement was a significant moderator of effect size, explaining 34% of the variance in symptom outcomes. Notably, Thompson-Hollands et al.'s (2014) meta-analysis showed superiority for treatments delivered to individual families (versus in groups) and for treatments that specifically targeted family accommodation behavior.

Emotional Regulation Problems: Anxiety

In recent years, family interventions for child anxiety disorders (generalized, social, and separation anxiety disorders) have evolved considerably, particularly aimed at improving the outcomes of individual treatments for nonresponders. Overall,

clinical trials (and reviews of trials) in which a parent component is added to individual child therapy for anxiety disorders have shown mixed findings, ranging from no benefit (cf. Thulin et al., 2014) to some benefit, especially at follow-up (Manassis et al., 2014; Smith et al., 2014; Wei & Kendall, 2014). Some reviewers (Kendall et al., 2012) concluded that with anxious parents, family CBT may result in poorer outcomes than child CBT alone. A one-stage meta-analysis (Manassis et al. 2014) of the moderating effects of more versus less (i.e. minimal) active parent involvement on children's anxiety found that active involvement with either transfer of control from therapist to parent (TC) or parent contingency management (CM) did not substantially improve posttreatment outcomes over minimal parent involvement, whereas more active involvement without TC or CM resulted in lower remission rates than child CBT with minimal involvement of parents. At the one-year follow-up, however, active parent involvement with TC or CM was superior to (a) active involvement without these features as well as (b) child CBT with minimal parent involvement.

Although parenting/family factors can contribute to the development or course of child anxiety, it has been notably difficult to demonstrate the added benefit of parent involvement in therapy. Research in this area suffers from a wide range of modes of parent involvement in treatment, the use of outcome indices that focus on child symptoms to the exclusion of family interaction variables, and a neglect of important moderators, child age, and parent anxiety disorder (Breinholst et al., 2012). It has been suggested that pretreatment assessment of relevant parent factors and investigation of targeted family interventions may improve research on child anxiety (Wei & Kendall, 2014). Indeed, recently more attention has been paid to the interpersonal dynamics surrounding family accommodation in anxiety disorder treatments, similar to the targeting of family accommodation in treatment for youth OCD (Lebowitz et al., 2016). A recent review of this literature (Norman et al., 2015) pointed to the paucity of RCTs and range of approaches for dealing with family accommodation behavior, from minimal parent involvement in treatment to (fewer) approaches that focus primarily on accommodation and the interpersonal nature of child anxiety.

For very young children, adaptations of PCIT (Eyberg & Matarazzo, 1980; McNeil & Hembree-Kigin, 2010) have yielded promising results for separation anxiety disorder, social anxiety, generalized anxiety disorder, phobias, and extreme behavioral inhibition and withdrawal (reviewed by F. Carpenter et al., 2014). These interventions target parent–child dynamics that maintain anxiety symptoms. One such model, Coaching Approach behavior and Leading by Modeling (CALM; Puliafico et al., 2013), showed preliminary evidence of efficacy in a multiple baseline study with nine children, 86% of whom no longer met criteria for an anxiety disorder at posttreatment (Comer et al., 2012).

Compared to youth OCD, the jury is still out regarding the effects of family involvement in treatments for childhood anxiety. Seasoned CBT researchers in this area (Pettit et al., 2016; Rapee, 2012; Silverman et al., 2016) concurred that the outcome data from earlier, somewhat scattershot efforts to include parents as coaches made conclusions difficult and should be replaced by more theory-driven, systemic interventions to guide decisions about when and how to institute stepped care models of clinical practice.

Depression, Self-Harm, and Suicidality

A systemic intervention for depressed and suicidal adolescents, attachment-based family therapy (ABFT; G. S. Diamond et al., 2002, 2014), demonstrated superior effectiveness compared to enhanced usual care control for reducing suicidal ideation and depressive symptoms at posttreatment and follow-up, with no moderation effect for history of sexual abuse (G. S. Diamond et al., 2012). A small, uncontrolled ABFT feasibility study in Belgium with community practitioners (Santens et al., 2017) found decreases in youth- and mother-reported depression and anxiety posttreatment. ABFT was also transported, despite some barriers, to a Norwegian clinic, showing more symptom reduction than in TAU (Israel & Diamond, 2012). Subsequently, ABFT was adapted to treat families with suicidal LGB adolescents, targeting attachment ruptures due to parental nonacceptance (G. M. Diamond et al., 2013).

Several recent investigations included parents in traditional individual therapies. In time-limited systems integrative family therapy (Byng-Hall et al.,1996), results were comparable to individual therapy alone, but better for certain clients (Garoff et al., 2012; see Moderators, below). Other trials have added family interventions to CBT, psychoeducation, and pharmacotherapy. Among youth with co-occurring depression and substance abuse, for example, Rohde et al. (2014) found that targeting the substance use first with FFT and then addressing the depression with an adolescent coping with depression course (CWD) resulted in the best substance use outcomes, compared to CWD followed by FFT or combined FFT + CWD; no differential effects were found, however, for reducing depressive symptoms. An uncontrolled pilot CBT study with a family component, Safe Alternatives for Teens and Youths (SAFETY; Asarnow et al., 2015), delivered within emergency services was found to be both feasible and safe, with significantly fewer suicide attempts and decreased ideation, hopelessness, depression, and social maladjustment at posttreatment and follow-up.

Integrating CBT with parent sessions (I-CBT) showed superior outcomes relative to enhanced TAU (Esposito-Smythers et al., 2011) for treating youth with co-occurring suicidal behavior and substance use. Whereas I-CBT is traditionally cognitive behavioral (focusing on modeling, monitoring, contingency management and affect management), another approach, the Resourceful Adolescent Parenting Program (RAP-P; Pineda & Dadds, 2013), more closely targets family functioning. Compared to routine care, RAP-P had a higher retention rate and greater reductions in psychiatric disability and suicidal behavior at posttreatment and follow-up.

Family treatments for depression are also being tested for children at various stages of development. One approach, PCIT with an emotion development module (PCIT-ED; Brinkmeyer & Eyberg, 2003), was created after being used successfully with young children who had externalizing behavior problems. A pilot study (Lenze et al., 2011) showed positive outcomes, and a small, preliminary trial (Luby et al., 2011) showed superior effects of PCIT-ED as compared with psychoeducation. Recently, a larger study comparing PCIT-ED to a wait-list control (Luby et al, 2018) supported the efficacy of this intervention for improving child functioning and reducing child depression, severity of depression and impairment, as well as parenting stress and depression, with a 96% retention rate.

In terms of adolescent self-harm, suicide attempts and ideation, reviewers noted that the most effective approaches include a focus on family interactions or nonfamilial sources of support (Brent et al., 2013). Although no randomized trial has yet demonstrated the efficacy of family therapy for self-harm (Ougrin & Asarnow, 2018), a recent review of family-based interventions for suicidal thoughts and behavior (Frey & Hunt, 2018) located 16 studies that tested 13 different interventions, three of which were judged to result in overall improvement and three in partial improvement of suicidal ideation, suicidal behavior, and/or mental health symptoms. In the UK, Self-Harm Intervention: Family Therapy (SHIFT) for 852 adolescents aged 11–17 who had self-harmed at least twice was not found to be superior to TAU in terms of adverse events or subsequent hospitalizations (Cottrell et al., 2018). The authors suggested that self-harm may be the final common pathway for a diverse set of mental health problems, necessitating an earlier, more personalized approach.

Moderators of Outcomes for Emotion Regulation Problems

In Manassis et al.'s (2014) meta-analysis, the effects of parent involvement in the child's anxiety treatment were not moderated by child age or presence of externalizing behaviors. As mentioned earlier, however, research in this area has generally neglected to account for child age and parent anxiety disorder (Breinholst et al., 2012). Regarding the treatment of depression, Garoff et al. (2012) found that limited systems integrative family therapy was particularly effective for younger children and children without a diagnosis of double depression. The Family Check-Up intervention slowed down escalating symptoms of depression in youth, but only for youth whose less severe symptoms were increasing over time, and not for youth with other symptom trajectories (Connell et al., 2018). In the SHIFT intervention for self-harming youth (Cottrell et al., 2018), adolescents from more poorly functioning families benefited most from SHIFT.

Eating Disorders

Recent reviews (Downs & Blow, 2011; Smith & Cottone, 2011) concluded that family therapy, particularly the leading systemic treatment, the Maudsley approach, also known as *family-based treatment* (FBT; Lock et al., 2001, 2013), is effective for adolescents with eating disorders. Subsequent reviewers (Jewell et al., 2016) concluded that family therapy is the strongest evidence-based treatment for anorexia, with increasing support for treating bulimia. This conclusion was supported by a meta-analysis (Couturier et al., 2013) that compared various individual therapy approaches to Maudsley-based family therapy for both disorders. Although no posttreatment differences were found, the family interventions demonstrated superior effects at follow-up. Moreover, across studies, early intervention seems to be crucial for obtaining favorable physical, psychological, and psychosocial outcomes (Treasure & Russell, 2011).

Compared to anorexia, far fewer outcome studies have been conducted for youth with bulimia, and results have generally been modest (Le Grange et al., 2015). A few studies of FBT for bulimia (FBT-BN) reported outcomes comparable to individual CBT (Murray & Le Grange, 2014). In a recent clinical trial that compared FBT-BN to CBT adapted for adolescents (CBT-A), the FBT-BN group had higher rates of abstinence from binging/purging at the end of treatment and at the 6-month (but not the 12-month) follow-up (Le Grange et al., 2015).

For anorexia, there is ample, solid evidence for the success of family-based treatments, including reductions in the frequency and duration of hospitalizations (House et al., 2012; Madden et al., 2014). Since Sexton et al.'s (2013) *Handbook* review, FBT continues to accrue strong empirical support in randomized trials. For example, an RCT comparing FBT to adolescent-focused, psychodynamically informed individual therapy, favored FBT at the 6- and 12-month follow-ups (Lock et al., 2010), but similar rates of remission were found after 2–4 years (Le Grange et al., 2014).

Due to a dearth of trained practitioners, poor access to treatment, and the common finding that nearly half of clients with anorexia are nonresponders, adaptations to FBT continue to be tested, as well as several new treatment models. Noting that late response to FBT (failure to gain 2.3 kg by week 4) diminishes recovery by 40–50%, Lock et al. (2015) tested an adapted model that included intensive parental coaching (IPC). Compared to standard FBT, IPC treatment raised the rates of full weight restoration for late responders to the same rates as early responders. Similarly, a parent-only adaptation of FBT, parent-focused treatment, was superior to standard FBT at posttreatment, although not at the 6- or 12-month follow-ups (Le Grange et al., 2016). Another family-based therapy, which includes a focus on family dynamics (versus eating symptoms), when added to outpatient TAU following hospitalization resulted in significantly better weight outcomes at the long-term (but not the short-term) follow-ups (Godart et al., 2012). Finally, an intervention called systemic family therapy (SysFT; Lock et al., 2013), which focuses more on family processes than on weight and disturbed eating, was investigated in a large controlled comparison with FBT (Agras et al., 2014). Results were equivalent for the primary outcomes, but the clients in FBT had more early weight gain, although those with severe obsessive-compulsive symptoms fared better in SysFT. In short, augmenting standard FBT appears to be effective, but current evidence for its superiority to the standard approach is mixed, depending on the follow-up period and outcome measure (Richards et al., 2018).

Among the naturalistic investigations of family interventions for anorexia, an intensive, five-day, systemic family treatment was evaluated in an archive of 74 cases, with a mean follow-up of 30 months (Marzola et al., 2015). No difference was found for treatments delivered individually versus in a family group format. Remission (on weight and eating pathology outcomes) was fully achieved by 61% of clients and partial remission by 27%, although 12% of clients had a poor response. Other researchers tested an enhanced CBT (CBT-E) for youth with anorexia (Fairburn, Cooper, & Shafran, 2013). This approach, originally devised for the treatment of BN, involves parents in traditional CBT. Results of an uncontrolled study showed that two-thirds of clients completed the 20-session treatment, making substantial changes in eating disorder pathology and weight gain, maintained over 15 months (Dalle Grave et al., 2013). These findings were substantially replicated in a different sample (Dalle Grave et al., 2015).

In yet another recent adaptation, a parent involvement component was added to partial hospitalization, with increases in parent knowledge, confidence in dealing with the eating disorder, and self-efficacy and decreases in adolescent eating disorder symptoms, anxiety, and depression (Girz et al., 2012; Ornstein et al., 2012). Finally, an emotion-focused therapy was recently adapted to the family context; this approach, which focuses on emotional processes and affect regulation as core problems, in addition to refeeding and symptom interruption, showed promising results in a small pilot investigation (LaFrance Robinson et al., 2016).

Moderators of Outcomes for Eating Disorders

Due to disparities in treatment response, the identification of significant moderators is crucial, but limited thus far. In moderator analyses of Lock et al.'s (2010) large RCT, Le Grange et al. (2012) found that at termination, clients with more severe eating disorder specific psychopathology and more eating-related obsessionality benefited more from FBT than individual, adolescent-focused treatment. At follow-up, clients with binging-purging (vs. restricting) type of anorexia who had been treated with FBT were progressing less well than clients with the restricting type. Notably, clients who gained weight early in treatment had better outcomes (Le Grange et al., 2014). In Agras et al.'s (2014) comparative study of FBT vs. SysFT, an exploratory moderator analysis suggested that clients with more severe obsessive-compulsive symptoms had greater weight gain when treated with SysFT. In FBT, results tend to be stronger for adolescents than adults, and for clients with early- versus late-onset disorders (Downs & Blow, 2011).

Across studies, better engagement in treatment and final outcomes tended to be observed among clients with anorexia who lacked co-occurring psychiatric problems, whose parents were observably high in warmth on a family interaction task (Le Grange et al., 2011) and whose mothers were observed to exhibit less expressed emotion, i.e. criticism and overinvolvement (Allan et al., 2018). Of 29 potential moderators of response to treatment for bulimia tested by Le Grange et al. (2105), the only significant variable was level of family conflict, in that less conflictual families responded better to FBT-BN.

Family Challenges

Despite the fact that therapists in community settings and private practice routinely treat relational family problems in the absence of one person's diagnosable mental or behavioral disorder, the bulk of family outcome research has traditionally been, and continues to be, focused on treating the symptoms or problematic behavior of an identified client who is seen in a conjoint context. Likely due to the medical model of diagnosing and treating individual dysfunction, grant funding is difficult to obtain for clinical trials targeting purely relational family problems. Nonetheless, researchers continue to develop and investigate conjoint treatments for families in which no one carries a behavioral or substance abuse diagnosis. Examples include studies on family interventions for grief (Kissane & Parnes, 2014) and bereavement (Sandler et al., 2018). Unfortunately, other important family difficulties, such as high-conflict divorce, while often discussed in the clinical literature, have received minimal empirical attention, if any, in terms of clinical trials.

Challenging problems tested in recent years include parenting problems with children not diagnosed with a disorder, such as an ecologically based family therapy (Guo et al., 2016) for families with runaway adolescents, and a nonviolent resistance intervention for families, including foster families, with excessively dependent, demanding and/or abusive children (Lebowitz et al., 2012; Van Holen et al., 2016). These interventions draw on classic systems theory about how attempted solutions ("trying more of the same") aggravate presenting problems, necessitating breaking the dysfunctional cycle with second-order change. Other research has been conducted for addressing child maltreatment in the context of drug abuse (Donohue et al., 2014) and for reducing the hospitalization of children with severe asthma (Celano et al., (2012).

Adult Disorders

Few systemic family interventions have been tested for adult problems, despite how stressful adults' psychiatric disorders are for children and romantic partners. The adult disorders for which systemic treatments have been studied most extensively include serious mental illness, notably schizophrenia and bipolar disorder, and substance abuse. A recent meta-analysis (Pinquart et al., 2016) of 37 clinical trials for family treatments of adults with mental disorders found a medium average effect size ($g = .51$) for systemic therapies compared to no-treatment controls and medication only; small effects were found in comparison to alternative active treatments, although the differences at follow-up tended not to be significant. Notably, dropout was less frequent among families seen in the systemic therapies than in the alternate treatments. In terms of substance abuse, an earlier comprehensive review of many RCTs and naturalistic studies (O'Farrell & Clements, 2012) concluded that family treatments are effective for motivating problem drinkers to enter treatment as well as for improving the coping of family members. Indeed, research indicates that treating adult substance use can have reverberating effects on family dynamics (O'Farrell & Clements, 2012) and youth substance use. For example, children seen in family therapy (compared to an attention control group) with their substance abusing mothers showed greater decreases in drinking and smoking tobacco and were less likely to begin using substances (Bartle-Haring et al., 2018; Zhang & Slesnick, 2018).

Recent studies have also targeted adult OCD and postpartum depression. Specifically, Baruah et al. (2018) reported that adult patients with OCD and their caregivers treated with a brief family-based intervention had less severe symptoms, less family accommodation and less expressed emotion at follow-up compared to a relaxation exercise control group. For postpartum depression, Hou et al. (2014) found that family systems therapy + CBT markedly improved mild-moderate depression and sleep quality, as compared to conventional care controls.

Serious Mental Illness

The evolution of systemic theorizing and treatments for adults with schizophrenia epitomizes the critical importance of empirical research for informing practice. Far from the early days of misguided thinking about family interactions *causing* schizophrenia, contemporary interventions are based on solid research evidence that (a) schizophrenia (and bipolar disorder) are neurocognitive disorders that exert significant stress on family (as well as individual) functioning, and (b) high levels of social interaction patterns like expressed emotion (whether in families or other living situations, such as group homes) are associated with relapse as well as rehospitalization (cf. Butzlaff & Hooley, 1998; Grácio et al., 2018).

Family psychoeducation programs have been developed and tested primarily for families in which the adult member's schizophrenia or bipolar disorder is also being treated with medication. A growing edge in treatment development and research is the application of family psychoeducation to adult depression; the first review of the evidence of its efficacy (Brady et al., 2017) is promising.

While there are variations of family psychoeducation (single family or groups of families facilitated either by a leader or by a peer), these programs share several common features: enhancing family members' knowledge and attitudes about the disorder, providing support, and addressing the family's characteristic style of interaction, intervening only as needed and in a nonblaming manner to decrease stress and improve communication and coping of all members. A variation of family psychoeducation, Family-to-Family (FTF; Lucksted et al. 2013), a 12-session, peer-driven education and support program, has also been shown to have superior (to controls) short- and longer-term benefits on distress and various indices of family functioning; these results were generalizable to families who had participated in FTF but declined to take part in the RCT (Marcus et al., 2013).

In the previous edition of this *Handbook*, Forand et al. (2013) described the efficacy estimates of family psychoeducation as compared with other psychosocial interventions for schizophrenia and bipolar disorder as "impressive" (p. 749). The scope of evidence accrued since 2011 is even more impressive, although the dissemination of family psychoeducation programs remains low, relative to their efficacy and to the need in the community. Indeed, research on effective dissemination strategies (Harvey & O'Hanlon, 2013), and on mediators and moderators, is much needed.

With respect to schizophrenia, a recent review (McFarlane, 2016) of over 100 outcome studies, 13 content reviews and several meta-analyses documented exceptionally strong evidence that family psychoeducation programs reduce relapse in schizophrenia, with more recent research demonstrating strong benefits for the first clinical episode. Moreover, promising evidence indicates that family psychoeducation may help avoid a first episode of psychosis in adults with prodromal symptoms, with effects as high as 50–60% compared to TAU.

Moreover, numerous (although not all) RCTs indicate that family psychoeducation can improve functional outcomes in the individual's physical health, social life, and employment related behavior. Current research on family psychoeducation is moving beyond basic demonstrations of efficacy to assess early intervention (Miklowitz, O'Brien et al., 2014) and to include broader outcome indices (i.e. beyond symptom reduction and relapse prevention), such as psychosocial functioning and quality of life (cf. Sharif et al., 2012; Weisman de Mamani et al., 2014).

Research on family psychoeducational interventions for bipolar disorder had a later start, but evidence for their effectiveness is substantial and accruing rapidly. In a review of 30 years of research on bipolar disorder that included eight RCTs of Family Focused Therapy (Miklowitz, 2010), Miklowitz and Chung (2016) highlighted reductions in recurrences, faster recovery from mood episodes, and reduced symptom severity in family programs compared with less intensive psychoeducation and medication alone. Patients' social functioning and relatives' perceived burden were also shown to be reduced in a large Italian, community-based study of family psychoeducation compared with a TAU control. (Fiorelli et al., 2015). Regarding moderators, families with higher levels of expressed emotion tend to benefit more from psychoeducational treatments (Miklowitz & Chung, 2016).

SYSTEMIC INDIVIDUAL THERAPIES: DO THEY WORK?

Across treatment modalities, postmodern, solution-oriented and narrative systemic therapies have been widely applied, particularly in Germany, since the 1960s (Retzlaff, 2013). Despite the widespread application, relatively few outcome investigations have been published. In a meta-content analysis of systemic therapies for adults, von Sydow et al. (2010) located only 38 controlled clinical trials published before 2009, of which only four were investigations of individual therapy.

In the 2011–2018 time frame of the present review, we located four outcome studies (published in English) of individual systemic therapy. Three of these four studies compared brief strategic therapy (BST) to other approaches. In a Polish study, Rakowska (2011) compared BST for social phobia to minimal supportive treatment ($n = 120$ outpatients). Results showed that the 10-session BST effectively reduced interpersonal sensitivity and phobic anxiety, but only for clients

without a personality disorder. In two Italian studies, (1) BST fared better than CBT at discharge and at the six-month follow-up for 60 obese inpatients with binge eating disorder (both $g = -1.09$), although no group differences emerged at discharge (Castelnuovo et al., 2011); and (2) BST + motivational interviewing did not improve biomedical or psychological outcomes over BST alone for 42 cardiac patients in a rehabilitation facility (Pietrabissa et al., 2017).

A comparison of solution-focused to psychodynamic therapy was conducted in Finland with 198 clients who had anxiety and depressive disorders (Maljanen et al., 2014). Although five symptom measures showed significant improvements for both groups after seven months, the group differences were negligible, as were differences in cost-effectiveness.

Finally, a naturalistic study (Vromans & Schweitzer, 2011) conducted in Australia compared the effectiveness of narrative therapy with 47 depressed individuals to benchmark outcomes. Results showed clinically significant reductions in depressive symptoms at posttreatment ($d = .62$) and at the three-month follow-up, with lesser gains in interpersonal relatedness.

MECHANISMS OF CHANGE: HOW DOES IT WORK?

Since Sexton et al.'s (2013) review of process research in the previous *Handbook*, an increasing number of studies have abundantly demonstrated that improved relational functioning precedes or co-occurs with targeted improvements in clients' psychological symptoms and general well-being. In addition to formal tests of mediation effects in group designs, small sample and single case studies have identified important change mechanisms within and across conjoint couple and family sessions. In the sections below, we summarize studies that examined various change mechanisms in relation to some aspect of outcome at the episode, session, or posttreatment level. (Other than where indicated, all studies described below used quantitative measures. We limited our review of qualitative studies to those in which a clinical change was described.)

Therapeutic Alliances in Systemic Therapies

As in individual psychotherapy, the most studied change process in CFT has been, and continues to be, the therapeutic alliance (Sexton et al., 2013). In addition to literature reviews (Diamond & Friedlander, 2011; Friedlander et al., 2016, 2018; Heatherington et al., 2015; Rohrbaugh, 2014) covering specific aspects of this important phenomenon, a recent meta-analysis of the association between outcome and alliance (self-reported and observed) found an overall effect size of $r = .30$, $d = .62$ in 39 independent studies (Friedlander et al., 2018). Notably, the effect sizes for couple (mean $r = .36$) and family therapy (mean $r = .25$) did not differ significantly, nor did the alliance/outcome association differ by therapist characteristics, treatment approach, or problem type. Rather, significant moderators included client age, gender, and referral source; alliance measure, type and timing of alliance assessment.

In terms of alliance type, researchers continue to find that partners' shared alliance with the therapist and/or with one another is more predictive of outcome than individual clients' alliances considered in isolation (e.g. Forsberg et al., 2014; Glebova et al., 2011; Kuhlman et al., 2013). As illustrated in several recent case studies, developing a strong within-system alliance (Artigas et al., 2017; Escudero et al., 2012) is critically important for outcome, as is addressing the experience of both members of a couple when repairing an alliance rupture with one member (Swank & Wittenborn, 2013).

Reflecting the interdependency of clients' alliances, in seven studies (six family, one couple) that identified *split* or *unbalanced* alliances, Friedlander et al.'s (2018) meta-analytic $r = .32$, $d = .67$, indicated worse outcomes when one person's alliance with the therapist was considerably stronger than that of one or more other family members. In one recent study (Bartle-Haring et al., 2012), for example, dropout from couple therapy was likely after the fourth session when the partners' self-reported alliances were notably unbalanced.

Consistent with the gender effect found in Friedlander et al.'s (2018) meta-analysis, Bartle-Haring et al. (2012) found that in couple therapy, men's alliance scores predicted outcome more so than did those of their female partners. In a study with a larger sample ($n = 195$ couples) conducted at the same training clinic, a complex relationship emerged between gender, early alliance and improvement (Glebova et al., 2011). After accounting for pretherapy level of relationship satisfaction, men's alliance perceptions assessed in session 2 predicted a change in satisfaction in session 3 for both members of the couple.

Notably, meta-analytic results showed a stronger association with outcome when the alliance was measured at multiple time points (Friedlander et al., 2018). Administering an alliance questionnaire at each session, Kuhlman et al. (2013) studied reciprocity between routinely assessed alliance perceptions and individual change over time (5–35 sessions, $m = 11$) in a sample of 29 depressed clients and their romantic partners. Covariation occurred both within and across sessions, such that "better alliance in the session is related to better well-being in the next session, and better well-being translates into a more satisfying alliance within the session in question" (Kuhlman et al., 2013, p. 9).

Recent alliance research also continues to underscore the importance of perspective in evaluating therapeutic progress. In an actor/partner evaluation of systemic TAU (Friedlander et al., 2012), for example, adolescents' alliances were associated with their own and their parents' view of therapeutic progress. On the other hand, whereas adolescents rated the family sessions as more valuable when their alliance was strong, parents rated their children's high alliance sessions as less valuable.

Alliance perspective also emerged as important in several family-based studies. In a large community sample ($n = 185$ caregivers and youth with externalizing problems), MST outcomes at termination were only associated with the therapist-caregiver bond (Glebova et al., 2018). In a Dutch MST study ($n = 89$ families; Granic et al., 2012), mothers' and therapists' alliance ratings were not correlated, but therapist-rated alliance predicted reduced maternal depression, which in turn predicted mothers' ratings of improvement in their

adolescents' externalizing behavior. In treatments for anorexia in adolescents, either observed or self-reported alliances with the therapist were associated with reduced symptoms (Isserlin & Couturier, 2012; Reinecke et al., 2016) and/or partial remission of disordered eating (Forsberg et al., 2013), whereas parent–therapist alliances predicted adolescent weight gain in some (Forsberg et al., 2014; Isserlin & Couturier, 2012), but not all (Ellison et al., 2012), studies. A unique perspective involved alliances among collaborating professionals (primary therapist, psychiatrist, nutritionist) in family-based private practice (Murray et al., 2014). Results showed that greater perceived collegiality predicted adolescent treatment completion and less disordered eating.

Within-therapist differences were found in an alliance study that compared initial BSFT sessions in four families that dropped out of treatment with four families that stayed in therapy (Sheehan & Friedlander, 2015). Compared to their work with the families that dropped out, in their initial sessions with the retained families, the therapists (a) addressed client resistance and other negative alliance behavior and (b) helped all family members to feel welcome, safe, and supported.

Collaboration, as well as therapist warmth and care emerged as critical for client engagement in interviews with parents and youthful offenders in 21 UK families receiving MST (Tighe et al., 2012). Collaboration on individualized goals developed early in treatment was also important for predicting post-therapy goal attainment in a sample of 379 Austrian and German multistressed families seen in integrated home-based therapy (Bachler et al., 2016).

Several family alliance studies highlight the critical importance of parental involvement. In an ABFT study of 10 sexual minority young adults and their non-accepting parents, follow-up interviews revealed important distinctions between cases with good versus poor alliances (Shpigel & Diamond, 2014). Only in the good alliance cases did the parents adopt family relationship building as a goal, acknowledge positive attributes of their children, and view the therapist as positive and accepting. In an ABFT study with depressed and suicidal adolescents (Feder & Diamond, 2016), parents who experienced a strong alliance with the therapist in individual sessions were more likely to display attachment-promoting behaviors in subsequent conjoint sessions with their children. Additionally, in a task analytic study of engaging reticent adolescents in the therapeutic process (Higham et al., 2012), parental support along with three therapist strategies (structuring, rolling with resistance, and understanding the adolescent's subjective experience) characterized events in which an initially disengaged adolescent became observably more involved as the session progressed.

Problematic alliances (cf. Lambert et al., 2012; Swank & Wittenborn, 2013) have been the focus of a few small sample studies in recent years. For example, among 10 Spanish families in systemic TAU, poor and deteriorating alliances with adolescents were characterized by therapists' dominant and competitive behaviors (Muñiz de la Peña et al., 2012). As another example, repair of an alliance rupture was investigated qualitatively using conversation analysis in a structural therapy session conducted by Salvador Minuchin (Muntigle & Horvath,

2016). This master therapist used a variety of alliance-focused strategies, such as "join[ing] with the family by sharing their distress," when a "disaffiliative episode" occurred at the beginning of the session (p. 102).

In another study, behavioral markers of rupture and repair were identified in a successful TAU case involving a single mother and her adolescent daughter (Escudero et al., 2012). In this study, as in two other evidence-based case studies with families at impasse (Friedlander et al., 2014; Heatherington et al., 2018), observed alliance behaviors, tracked across time, reflected clients' self-reported (a) engagement and connection with the therapist, sense of safety and within-family collaboration; (b) session impact; and (c) therapeutic progress. In all these family case studies, the therapists relied on joining/emotional connection behaviors (among other interventions) to shift the alliance from a state of discord to a state of consensus or collaboration.

Therapists' observable contributions to collaborative alliance building were also found to be important in treating 20 involuntary Portuguese families (Sotero et al., 2018). The critical interventions were aimed at facilitating engagement and a shared sense of purpose about participating together in conjoint therapy. The success of these interventions was evident in observed client behavior across time. That is, compared to the behaviors of clients in 20 voluntary families, the behaviors of family members in the involuntary group initially reflected a lack of safety and a poor within-system alliance, but by session 4 these group differences had faded (Sotero et al., 2014).

Change Processes in Couple Therapy

Relational Change Processes

Emotion focused couple therapy has been studied extensively in terms of *blamer softening*, an in-session event during which romantic partners are encouraged to express their vulnerability and unmet needs for attachment. In recent analyses of 32 Canadian couples receiving an average of 21 EFCT sessions, the occurrence of a softening event significantly predicted increases in satisfaction (Dalgleish, Johnson, Burgess Moser, Wiebe et al., 2015), not only at posttreatment but also during the session in which the softening occurred (Burgess Moser et al., 2017). Decreased attachment avoidance was also reported during these softening sessions. In a two-year follow-up, Dalgleish, Johnson, Burgess Moser, Lafontaine et al. (2015) found a weakened effect of blamer softening events on overall satisfaction for patients reporting high attachment avoidance.

Several observational studies addressed the resolution of emotional injuries in EFCT. Testing a conceptual model for promoting forgiveness and reconciliation, Zuccarini et al. (2013) identified critical elements that distinguished nine successful from nine unsuccessful therapy events. Couples whose relationship became a "potential safe haven" (p. 158) were observably more responsive and accessible to one another after having deeply explored their internal reactions to the attachment injury.

Testing a different EFCT model of forgiveness following emotional injury, Woldarsky Menses and Greenberg (2014) found that reductions in relational distress in 33 couples were uniquely associated with the injured partner's acceptance of the offending partner's expression of shame. In other samples from the same research project (McKinnon & Greenberg, 2013, 2017), expressions of vulnerability were viewed positively at the session level and predicted improved trust and resolution of unfinished business, but not overall relationship satisfaction.

Relational change mechanisms are not unique to emotion focused approaches. A recent CBCT study with veterans (Doss et al., 2015), for example, identified improvements in couples' emotional closeness as a uniquely significant mediator of effectiveness. Moreover, early improvement in relationship satisfaction predicted reduced psychological distress later in treatment. In a two-year follow-up from Christensen et al.'s (2004) RCT comparing TBCT to IBCT (with 134 couples), positive change in the quality of communication during 10-minute problem discussions was associated with continued relational improvement (Baucom, Baucom et al., 2015). Analyzing the in-session behavior of the same couples, Sevier et al. (2015) observed 1,224 therapy segments from 956 sessions. Whereas the less successful couples in both treatment groups showed a decrease over time in positive behavior and an increase in negative behavior, different behavioral trajectories emerged for the successful couples. For these couples, the increases in positive behavior observed in early TBCT sessions decreased over time, whereas the reverse pattern was observed in the IBCT sessions.

How therapists facilitate relational change was recently studied in EFCT (Furrow et al., 2012; Zuccarini et al., 2013), in treatment as usual (Margola et al., 2017), and in an experimental study comparing enactment-based to therapist-centered interventions (Butler et al., 2011). In Furrow et al.'s analyses of sessions conducted by EFCT master therapist Susan Johnson, "therapist emotional presence and a corresponding evocative vocal quality" (p. 39) seemed to facilitate deeper client experiencing in sessions with successful blamer softening. In Zuccarini et al.'s study of forgiveness, both experiential (validation and empathic processing) and systemic (reframing and restructuring interactions) interventions were effective. In Margola et al., sequential analyses showed that couples' positive coping behavior during stressful conversations was facilitated by active therapist interventions, particularly interpretation and information seeking, but hindered by therapist passivity. Finally, in Butler et al., attachment security was enhanced and maintained by enactments more so than by therapist-centered interventions in the first three of six sessions, particularly for the male partners.

Changes in Individual Members of the Couple

In several recent couple therapy studies, reduced psychological distress was found to mediate (Doss et al., 2015) or co-occur (e.g. Couper et al., 2015; Monson et al., 2012) with improvements in relationship quality. Cohen et al. (2011), for example, found that increased marital satisfaction among women with depression was mediated by positive changes in their attitudes and behaviors related to depression. In a secondary analysis of LaTaillade et al.'s (2006) study of CBCT for mildly to moderately violent couples, Hrapczynski et al. (2011) found that decreased negative attributions about the partner accompanied posttreatment increases in couple satisfaction.

Changes in individual and relational functioning do not invariably co-occur, however. Studying EFCT for 32 female survivors of child abuse and their partners, Dalton et al. (2013) found reduced couple distress posttreatment, but not reduced trauma symptoms. Investigating recently disclosed infidelity in an RCT with 89 couples, Kröger et al. (2012) found that among the deceived partners, TCBT effectively reduced individuals' PTSD-like symptoms but not their depressive symptoms. Also, relationship satisfaction was marginally improved, but only among the unfaithful partners. A naturalistic study of 125 couples seen in MST (Knobloch-Fedders et al., 2015) assessed covariation in individual functioning and relationship adjustment reported by clients before each of 8 sessions. Results showed positive changes on both variables from sessions 1 through 4, with stabilization occurring between sessions 5 and 8. In cross-lagged analyses, gender differences emerged: Significant improvements in men's individual functioning from one session to the next often preceded their reports of better relationship adjustment, but the same pattern was not found for women.

Change Processes in Family Therapy
Family Functioning

In several recent large-scale studies for youth externalizing problems, measures of family cohesion, parenting behavior, communication, and conflict were either formally tested as mediators or correlated with posttreatment outcomes. For example, in a BSFT study with 480 US adolescents and their parents (Horigan, Feaster, Brinks et al., 2015), changes in composite family functioning scores mediated reductions in parental alcohol use. In a Dutch MFT study with 256 adolescents and their families (Dekovic et al., 2012), changes in parental sense of competence predicted changes in positive discipline, which in turn predicted decreases in adolescent externalizing problems. A randomized comparison of ecologically based family therapy (EBFT), community reinforcement (CR), and motivational enhancement therapy (MET) for substance abusing runaway youth (Guo et al., 2016; Slesnick & Feng, 2016) found increased family cohesion and decreased conflict across all three treatments from baseline to 24-month follow-up. Adolescents who received EBFT demonstrated (a) more posttreatment improvement in family cohesion than did those who received CR or MET, and (b) more reduction in family conflict during treatment than those who received MET. In a UK clinical trial comparing MST to TAU (n = 108 families; Butler et al., 2011), youth delinquency and aggression declined significantly more in the MST group, although no between-treatment differences were found in the hypothesized mediators (parental supervision, warmth and communication).

Change processes have also been widely studied in family treatments for internalizing disorders. Two clinical trials targeted youth with OCD receiving either family CBT (Piacentini et al., 2011), PFIT, or TAU. Reductions in family members' accommodation to the OCD either preceded (Piacentini et al., 2011) or mediated (Peris et al., 2017) symptom

reduction. Compared to TAU, PFIT produced greater increases in family cohesion and reductions in family conflict (Peris et al., 2017). In a study for adults with OCD, brief family-based interventions were compared with a relaxation control group (Baruah et al., 2018). Results indicated that expressed emotion declined over time more so in the family treatment. In several international clinical trials targeting eating disorders, with one exception (Le Grange et al., 2012), increased parental self-efficacy occurred concurrently with improved adolescent outcomes (Robinson et al., 2013; Sadeh-Sharvit et al., 2018), decreased parental criticism (Allan et al., 2013; Darcy et al., 2013; Ellison et al., 2012), and better parental adherence to treatment objectives, such as taking control and having zero tolerance for anorectic behavior (Ellison et al., 2012).

Youth depression was targeted in a multicountry European study that compared systemic family therapy to brief individual dynamic psychotherapy (Garoff et al., 2012). Although family functioning improved in both treatments, only in the systemic group did this change predict significant reductions in symptoms. In a sample of 18 depressed and suicidal adolescents receiving ABFT, Shpigel et al. (2012) reported decreased maternal control and increased autonomy granting from sessions 1 to 4. Increases in maternal autonomy granting were associated with (a) increases in adolescents' perceptions of parental care from pre- to mid-treatment and (b) decreases in attachment-related anxiety and avoidance from pre- to three months posttreatment. Finally, decreases in adolescents' perceptions of parental control during the therapy itself were associated with reductions in their depressive symptoms up to 12 weeks posttreatment.

Beneficial changes in family functioning (e.g. perceived family burden, coping, family friction) due to family psychoeducation have also been documented (cf. Palli et al., 2015), although effectiveness rates vary across these intervention programs, populations and samples, types of family psychoeducation, and measures of family functioning. Nonetheless, McFarlane (2016) concluded that "all the efficacious family psychoeducational models reduce family expressed emotion and that doing so is directly associated with the reduction in relapse found in clinical trials" (p. 15).

In-Session Processes

Emotional processing in ABFT was the focus of three studies with 32 Israeli young adults who presented with unresolved anger toward a parent. The initial study examined the role of emotional processing during 10 weeks of either ABFT or individual emotionally focused therapy (EFT; G. M. Diamond et al., 2016). Results showed that more productive in-session emotional processing predicted greater decreases in psychological symptoms (but not other outcomes) across both approaches. In the second study, follow-up interviews were conducted with 26 of the original 32 clients (Steinmann et al., 2017). Clients in both groups attributed their treatment gains to productive emotional processing. Third, among the 15 young adults who had received ABFT, therapist interventions that promoted or curtailed productive emotional processing were examined (Tsvieli & Diamond, 2018). Results showed that productive emotional processing occurred significantly more often than chance following empty-chair interventions and when therapists focused on vulnerable emotions and unmet attachment needs. In contrast, the therapists' focus on rejecting anger led to a discontinuation of the clients' productive processing once it had begun.

Four other studies identified important therapeutic processes from observations of in-session behavior. First, in Marachionda and Slesnik's (2013) study of EBFT for substance abusing, runaway adolescents, families that completed treatment had more therapist-to-parent communication during the first session, whereas families that dropped out evidenced more therapist-to-adolescent communication. Second, based on an analysis of video recordings, Nichols and Tafuri (2013) identified 25 systemic techniques used by three expert structural therapists to challenge family members' linear thinking and promote a systemic understanding of their problems. These techniques included initiating enactments, commenting on problematic interaction patterns, and suggesting alternative ways of behaving. Third, in Orchowski's (2014) analysis of video recordings of 23 FFT cases drawn from Barrett et al.'s (2001) RCT for adolescent substance use, high proportions of therapist interventions focused on individuals, such as information seeking, and on relationships, such as reframing or diverting blame and emphasizing family connectedness, predicted increases in family functioning as reported by mothers. Fourth, Henderson et al. (2018) systematically assessed the number of family therapy techniques used during sessions of TAU for youth conduct and substance use. Greater use of these specific techniques predicted more improvement in youth-reported delinquency and externalizing behavior and marginal reductions in substance use and parent-reported behavior problems.

Finally, a few qualitative studies addressed clients' perspectives on the most helpful aspects of their experience in family therapy, both in-session and overall. Collaboration, in particular, was described as the most helpful aspect of therapy in interviews with members of 10 Norwegian families (Sundet, 2011). In another recent study, eight adolescents were interviewed several months after their participation in MST (Paradisopoulos et al., 2015). These clients attributed their sustained success to a strong therapeutic alliance, increased systemic awareness, recognition of responsibility, positive peer relations, acknowledgment and celebration of success, continued use of strategies acquired in therapy, and the identification and creation of a preferred future. In yet another qualitative study (Ripoll-Nuñez et al., 2012), clients in 11 court-referred Columbian families attributed their individual and relational gains (e.g. improved communication and perspective taking) to therapist expertise, being listened to and understood, and having experienced productive and regulated emotional family conversations.

RECENT ADVANCES IN KNOWLEDGE

Efficacy and Effectiveness

Similar to the bulk of research described in the previous *Handbook* review (Sexton et al., 2013), the objective of most recent systemic investigations has been to improve the functioning of one family member by addressing the relational functioning of the couple or family unit. Relative to the earlier review, however, a notably broader range of individual and relational problems was investigated between 2011 and 2018, with an increased number of international investigations. Moreover, CFT research, including RCTs, expanded beyond university clinics to include community agencies, residential facilities, veterans' hospitals and general medical centers, and more studies compared the effectiveness of individual CBT or psychodynamic therapy to conjoint systemic treatments. Many of these advances speak directly to what Sexton et al. called the "challenges for the next generation of CFT research and practice" (p. 628).

Notably, we located only a handful of studies of systemic individual therapies published during the 2011–2018 timeframe of the present review. This lack is in striking contrast to earlier interest in these models (Heatherington & Johnson, 2018) and to the clinical literature, which underscores the need for therapists to think systemically and contextually about psychopathology and relational problems when working exclusively with individuals.

With respect to couple therapy, researchers have continued to assess manualized treatments, not only in terms of controlled outcome studies but also in terms of treatment adherence and/or integrity. Recent naturalistic studies have used benchmarking, in which the effect sizes found in an uncontrolled study are compared with the meta-analytic effect sizes of randomized clinical trials or other uncontrolled studies. A few large-scale couple studies assessed relationship outcomes over several years. Cumulative evidence from these studies, albeit limited, suggests that differences in treatment models tend to dissipate over long periods of time, with a slim edge favoring approaches that focus on partner acceptance, understanding and emotional responsiveness.

Compared to the bulk of family intervention studies that target children's and adults' psychological disorders, increasing numbers of couple therapy studies have focused on relational concerns like infidelity, intimate partner violence, infertility and certainty of commitment. Although couple therapy research continues to be dominated by various cognitive-behavioral approaches, research on emotionally focused therapy has notably increased in recent years. In particular, the literature has burgeoned in the areas of PTSD and couple therapy for medical problems, with adaptations to address various conditions and illnesses through psychoeducation, shared decision-making, and attention to relational functioning. In addition to assessing psychosocial outcomes for the ill member of the couple, some studies also targeted the healthier partner's empathy, support, and sense of burden. When psychopathology is present, findings suggest the importance of integrating evidence-based individual therapy principles within a relational approach (Baucom et al., 2014).

In recent family therapy studies, researchers have turned their attention to new populations, for example, gang-involved youth and clinical outcomes, such as STI/HIV status and risk behavior; and unusual settings for clinical practice, like drug court and emergency services. Another trend since the last *Handbook* review is the accelerating progression of research on the most mature treatment approaches (primarily those addressing externalizing and substance use disorders of youth), including systematic implementation science research and large, hybrid efficacy/effectiveness RCTs in community settings. Regarding the latter, Bauer et al. (2015) noted that it takes 17 years on average for evidence-based practices to be incorporated into routine general practice; only about 50% of these practices are *ever* widely used in community settings (Balas & Boren, 2000). It is thus encouraging that recent work has included cost-effectiveness estimates (Goorden, Schawo et al., 2016; Goorden, Van Der Schee et al., 2016) and tests of the international transportability of controlled trials (Rigter et al., 2013).

Another trend is the increasing conceptual and technical integration of family systems dynamics into cognitive-behavioral approaches, particularly for treating OCD and child anxiety disorders and eating disorders. CFT practice and research, including studies that assess changes in family dynamics along with symptom reduction, bring together historically distinct modes of thinking about clinical improvement.

Finally, we noted an increase in interventions that specifically target a major barrier to treatment: engagement. While this barrier has long been studied in family treatments for youth externalizing disorders, engagement has recently been addressed in studies of interventions for internalizing disorders. For example, researchers have assessed strategies for engaging reluctant children with OCD and other anxiety disorders and investigated whether children who refuse individual treatment can be helped at home through caregiver training.

Cultural Factors

Recognizing that not all clients respond to treatment in the same way, recent researchers have increasingly considered how various cultural factors influence treatment effectiveness. Perhaps the most robust finding is that established, manualized couple and family treatments appear to be efficacious with diverse ethnic and racial samples. In studies conducted in North America, for example, CFT has been shown to be helpful for Latinx, African-American, Asian and other minority group clients, including low-income clients, highly religious clients, military veterans, sexual and gender minority clients, and clients coping with disabilities and serious medical conditions. Many established couple and family treatments have also been found to be efficacious in studies conducted across Europe, South America, Australia and Asia. In particular, the benefits of family psychoeducation programs for schizophrenia have been particularly well documented. Studies have tested these programs across ethnic groups in the US as well as in the UK, China, Hong Kong, India, Pakistan, Australia, Italy, Japan, Thailand, Scandinavia (McFarlane, 2016), and Iran (e.g. Rahmani et al., 2015).

With that said, few moderator studies formally examined whether specific racial or ethnic groups respond differentially to a given treatment. One study on MDFT for adolescent drug abusers found that gender and ethnicity moderated outcome (Greenbaum et al., 2015). Whereas women and Hispanics responded equally well to comparison groups, men, African

Americans and non-Hispanic European American adolescents responded better to MDFT. In a study of MST for adolescents with behavior problems and/or substance abuse, symptom severity interacted with ethnicity/race in determining degree of therapist adherence to the model and adolescents' and parents' emotional bonds with the therapist (Ryan et al., 2013).

Although many established treatments appear to be efficacious with clients from various cultural groups, many clinical researchers have adapted these treatments to be even more sensitive to, and optimally efficacious with, specific minority groups. These groups include ethnic/racial minorities (Ahmad & Reid, 2016; Weisman de Mamani et al., 2014) and sexual/gender minorities (G. M. Diamond et al., 2016; Garanzini et al., 2017; Gottman et al., 2017).

Psychological Moderators of Outcome

In addition to demographic and cultural variables, couple therapy researchers have increasingly considered psychological moderators of outcome, such as anxious and avoidant attachment, accommodating to a partner's PTSD symptoms, and having a history of childhood abuse. Researchers have also examined within-couple differences as moderators, such as similarities between partners, or their sense of "we-ness" (Rohrbaugh, 2014); greater benefits tend to be reported by couples who are more emotionally connected and committed to their relationship and who agree on the nature of their problems.

In family therapy, along with traditional demographic variables, recent moderator studies have included diagnostic variables, such as type, features (e.g. extent of obsessionality) and stage of disorder; family dynamics (extent of accommodation, blame, conflict, cohesion); and therapy processes (family members' communication patterns early in treatment, amount of parental involvement). In general, these kinds of moderating variables tend to be studied within a specific approach for treating a particular domain of problems.

Change Processes

Research on effective change mechanisms, strongly recommended in recent reviews of the systemic therapy literature, has grown due to an increased recognition of practitioners' need for more applied knowledge (Friedlander et al., 2016; Gurman, 2011; Sexton & Datchi, 2014). As noted in these reviews, the primary process variable studied in CFT continues to be the therapeutic alliance, with substantial meta-analytic evidence of its association with outcome. In recent years, increased attention has been paid to faltering and split alliances and to the question of how alliance ruptures can best be addressed therapeutically.

Treatment-specific change mechanisms have also increasingly been identified in recent years, particularly from secondary analyses of outcome studies. In couple therapy, effective emotion focused mechanisms include blamer softening and forgiveness, addressed through reframing, heightening emotional intimacy, and disclosure of attachment needs. Effective CBCT mechanisms include increasing acceptance, modifying attributions, and improving attitudes, problem solving and communication skills.

In both couple and family therapy, researchers have turned their attention to the directional influence of client improvement and relational outcomes. Whereas early family therapy studies emphasized the importance of reducing negativity and within-family blame (Sexton, 2014), in more recent investigations, change mechanisms have included emotional processing and identification of client and therapist communication patterns.

RECENT ADVANCES IN METHODOLOGY

The years 2011 to 2018 have witnessed more studies with complex quantitative designs and analyses. For example, multi-level modeling has been used to assess linear growth, that is, rates of change in process and progress variables and variability within couples and families, nested within therapists. Aside from simply reporting the significance of therapist effects, some researchers investigated the amount of variance accounted for by specific therapist characteristics, such as gender and clinical experience (Owen, Duncan et al., 2014). Similarly, multilevel modeling has been used in meta-analyses to identify the extent of variability within and across studies (e.g. Friedlander et al., 2018). Additionally, research in specific domains of family problems, particularly externalizing and substance use disorders, have used more sophisticated power analyses and meta-analyses.

Dyadic analyses have become increasingly common in the couple therapy literature in recent years, particularly the actor-partner interdependence model (Kenny & Kashy, 2010; Wittenborn et al., 2013), which allows for the identification of unidirectional and bidirectional influences of perceptions or behavior when members of a dyad are distinguishable by some characteristic, like gender. For example, when a unidirectional influence is observed in heterosexual couples, the pretreatment characteristics of female partners tends to predict the posttreatment outcomes of male partners. When bidirectional influences are observed, the characteristics of male partners also predict the outcomes of their female partners.

Additional improvements in change process research include increased testing of mediators of effectiveness, typically with multiple measures of individual and relational functioning. Indeed, family therapy research has begun to examine the ways in which family dynamics and individual symptom reduction are functionally related to each other over time. This increased attention to mediators reflects researchers' heeding the call of many previous CFT reviewers (e.g. Gurman, 2011; Heatherington et al., 2015; Sexton, 2014) to move beyond global questions ("Does model X work?") to more specific questions like, "What kinds of changes can be expected and at what point in treatment?" and "How do common and specific factors work together to bring about change?"

Since the most recent *Handbook* chapter, notably more change process research has been conducted using intensive analyses of small samples and single cases. The methods include task analyses (e.g. Furrow et al., 2012; Woolley et al., 2012) and studies that contrast change processes in successful versus unsuccessful cases (e.g. Diamond & Shpigel, 2014). In several studies, researchers used sequential analyses of observed behavior to test theorized models of client change and to understand reciprocity, that is, the extent to which therapist behavior is contingent on client antecedent behavior and vice versa (e.g. Muñiz de la Peña et al., 2012).

Qualitative methods, including discursive analyses (e.g. O'Reilly et al., 2018), are increasingly appearing in the CFT literature to provide a nuanced, verbatim understanding of conjoint therapy processes. In evidence-based case studies, excerpted dialogue is included to illustrate specific change processes in manualized therapies (Montesanto et al., 2014), in systemic TAU (Heatherington et al., 2018), and in new adaptations of well-established treatment models (Kirby et al., 2016). Qualitative methods have also been used to provide a nuanced view of phenomena traditionally studied quantitatively, such as the association between alliance-related behavior and treatment retention (Sheehan & Friedlander, 2015).

Various technological advances in recent years have allowed researchers to conduct these kinds of fine-grained analyses. These advances include computer software programs to analyze text (Rohrbaugh et al., 2012) and to track specific client and therapist behaviors in video recorded sessions (Escudero et al., 2011). In other CFT process studies, a hand-held electronic device was used to record momentary shifts in couples' perceptions during video recall sessions (L. N. Johnson et al., 2015), and fMRI scanning was used to measure changes in brain activity in response to threat versus safety cues (S. M. Johnson et al., 2013).

PRINCIPLES OF CHANGE

Given the strong evidence for the overall effectiveness of many approaches to couple and family therapy, authors have recently begun to identify transtheoretical change principles to guide practice, training, and future research. We identified a set of principles, listed below, based on the foregoing review and from other recent reviews of couple (e.g. Benson et al., 2012; Blow et al., 2009; Gurman, 2011; Lebow et al., 2012; Snyder & Halford, 2012; Sprenkle et al., 2009) and family (Friedlander et al., 2016; Lebow, 2014) intervention research.

Principles Related to Developing and Maintaining a Therapeutic Stance

- Actively *develop a warm, genuine, informal relationship* with individuals, subsystems, and the couple or family as a unit, attending closely to each client's level of safety.
- Strive to *create a balanced therapeutic alliance* with all family members; avoid split alliances by constructing a non-blaming, systemic view of the presenting problems and underlying dynamics (e.g. blame/withdraw, withdraw/withdraw) that cut across multiple concerns. Clarify each client's commitment to working toward relational improvement.
- As early as possible, *nurture a shared sense of purpose* (a common view of the problems, goals, and need for therapy) by providing opportunities for family members to listen to and

understand each other's views about what brought them to therapy.

- Help family members imagine the personal and collective benefits of solutions by *expressing optimism for the possibility of meaningful change*.

Principles Related to Facilitating Change

- Adapt evidence-based interventions to *respect clients' cultural diversity*, being mindful of (a) the influence of societal variables (culture, ethnicity, socioeconomic stress, immigration status, racism, sexism, heterosexism) on well-being and clients' responses to therapy and (b) the role of culture in family dynamics (hierarchy, power, boundaries, relations with extended family members).
- As needed, *work with individuals (or subsystems) to prepare them to collaborate* on difficult issues. Adapt cognitive, emotional, and behavioral interventions to each person's level of motivation and developmental level. For example, when a child expresses strong resistance to treatment, work with caregivers to provide at-home interventions and respond constructively to other family members' responses to this approach.
- As needed, *strengthen boundaries between people and subsystems*, particularly (a) between the couple/family unit and others, and (b) between parents and adolescent (by "rolling with resistance," presenting oneself as the adolescent's ally, supporting the adolescent's autonomy and personal goals).
- Strive to *change family members' experiences of one another*. Use enactments to assess and modify interactional dynamics, enhance safety and in-session collaboration, address attachment ruptures, teach problem solving and communication skills, and strengthen emotional connections. Facilitate the sharing of new or renewed pleasurable experiences.
- When one person is suffering from a mental or physical disorder, *involve others as a resource or support* without increasing the burden or strain of caregiving. Provide psychoeducation, encourage sharing of thoughts and feelings, and modify dysfunctional interactions that are unrelated to the disorder.
- *Help family members consider alternate, more constructive attributions* for each other's negative behaviors. In doing so, (a) strive to replace demoralization with hope by emphasizing the strengths, positive and enduring characteristics of individuals and subsystems; (b) point out the connection between clients' interaction patterns (e.g. demand-withdraw, accommodation, triangulation) and individual distress in a non-blaming way; and (c) nurture clients' willingness to take responsibility for their part in relational problems and take emotional risks with their partners or other family members.
- Directly *address dysfunctional and destructive behavior*. Pay close attention to within-system levels of power and influence to ensure safety, and intervene quickly to end hostile conflict and blaming.
- Work to *increase clients' emotional attachments* by facilitating the disclosure of emotions that a client characteristically avoids, such as fear, resentment, vulnerability, and fears of abandonment or betrayal.
- *Respond sensitively to clients who feel blamed* for their limitations; take advantage of opportunities to soften blame, so

that clients witness one another's authentic expressions of fear, vulnerability, and worry that underlie harder emotions (e.g. rejecting anger, blame and contempt) and begin to view one another with compassion.

- *Teach effective problem solving/compromise skills* through direct guidance and coaching.
- When members of a couple differ in terms of attachment insecurity, *work simultaneously to reduce hyperactivation* in the more anxious partner *and enhance emotional availability* in the more avoidant partner, without focusing too intensively on either one to the exclusion of the other.

RECOMMENDATIONS FOR FUTURE STUDY

Systemic therapies have come of age. As recommended by many previous reviewers, evidence-based treatments are now being widely disseminated internationally as well as throughout the United States. For psychotherapy research to have a significant impact on public health and policy (Kazdin & Blase, 2011), it is critical to understand the ways in which dissemination in real-world clinical settings succeeds or fails. In other words, a key question is how best to scale up complex systemic treatments for widespread use. With this point in mind, we propose the following directions for future study.

Substantive Recommendations

Notably, there is a need to *compare individual systemic therapies with conjoint treatments* for targeted problems. Practitioners are regularly faced with the question of which therapy modality to recommend to new clients who have both family and individual concerns, and the literature provides little guidance on this point. Outcome research on systemic individual therapies (solution-focused, narrative/constructivist, and strategic) has significantly dwindled, almost into nonexistence (cf. Heatherington & Johnson, 2018). Indeed, we located no research on effective change mechanisms in these approaches during the time frame of this review.

Relatedly, we recommend increased study of the *adjunctive involvement of family members* and the optimal timing for involving different constellations of clients when targeting the disorders, problems, and well-being of individuals. At what point, for example, is it most helpful to invite a partner, parent or stepparent to join the treatment? How often should family sessions be held when working with a troubled adolescent? In what clinical circumstances can outcomes be enhanced by fully involving parents in conjoint therapy sessions versus simply including them as adjunctive helpers?

More controlled tests are sorely needed to identify the most-effective *systemic interventions for parents of distressed children*. Different from parent management training, family therapy that specifically targets parental accommodation to children's symptoms, such as OCD, has shown promising results, as has couple therapy for clients whose partners are struggling with PTSD.

Similarly, it is important to investigate the benefit of *including children in the treatment of symptomatic parents*. Despite the breadth of individual and couple therapies for adults' emotional and behavioral disorders, we located few recent studies of family treatments for adult OCD, major depression, eating disorders or substance use. Clearly, children affect and are affected by their parents' dysfunction; adolescents and young adults, in particular, can be a motivating force for parental change. Of course, attention to culturally derived expectations about family relationships (such as boundaries between parents and children) are important considerations in designing these kinds of studies.

Although specific therapy models for DSM/ICD disorders continue to be developed and tested, far less attention is being paid to the kinds of *non-diagnosable family problems* that prompt people to seek help. With couples, relational outcomes other than reducing distress or enhancing satisfaction should be studied, such as certainty of commitment (Owen, Keller et al., 2014), divorce discernment (Halford et al., 2016), and effective co-parenting following separation. With families, it is essential to evaluate systemic therapies that *target various life adversities*, such as child maltreatment, separation and divorce, bereavement, incarceration, loss of income, immigration and refugee stress, and so on. Much more effectiveness research is needed with *underserved, vulnerable populations*, such as sexual/gender minority couples and families coping with multiple risk factors, such as geographical displacement and migration, chronic illness, substance dependence, poverty, and domestic violence.

Since even the most empirically supported treatments do not benefit all couples and families, increased systematic research on diverse client moderators is needed, ideally conducted in community settings. We suggest *focal, systematic testing of moderators*, including developmental (age of children, family life stage), demographic (race/ethnicity, sexual orientation, socioeconomic status), structural (e.g. one- versus two-parent; foster/adoptive families), and psychosocial variables (e.g. attachment insecurity, motivation for change, extrafamilial support, religious observance), as well as length of treatment and frequency of therapy sessions. In particular, researchers should test systemic client attributes that have substantial evidential support outside the psychotherapy literature, such as Bowen's (1978) concept differentiation of self (e.g. Skowron, 2000) and circular behavior patterns of demand-withdraw (e.g. Fournier et al., 2011).

In targeting problems for youth, *specific family functioning variables* (e.g. blame, cohesion, conflict, relational control) should be tested *as both moderators and mediators* of symptom improvement. Often, studies have supported systemic theory in terms of the contribution of family dynamics to problem maintenance and the importance of shifting dysfunctional dynamics to effect therapeutic change. An important moderating variable that has received little attention is the quality of parental relationships. For many child problems, the parenting load is high, necessitating consistency and tenacity. A strong bond between parents is most likely to facilitate symptomatic improvement in children.

To mirror the eclectic nature of contemporary systemic practice (Halford et al., 2016), we recommend continued research on *transtheoretical change processes and common factors*, such as within-couple agreement on problems (e.g. Biesen

et al., 2013) and pretherapy expectations (Friedlander et al., 2019). When relations among different common factors and clinically significant outcomes are established, researchers can begin identifying higher-order processes, such as the therapist's way of being, or "in-the-moment attitude . . . toward clients [that] provides a foundation for the therapeutic alliance" (Fife et al., 2014, p. 24).

Another promising line of research concerns the process and effectiveness of *systematic client feedback* (Pinsof et al., 2009). In conjoint therapies, questionnaires filled out by family members before or after a session can identify a split or faltering alliance as well as progress on shared treatment goals from each person's perspective. Despite the demonstrated effectiveness of routine progress monitoring (e.g. Pepping et al., 2015), little is known about *how* reviewing client feedback with family members facilitates therapist responsiveness. It has been pointed out that monitoring client feedback may be a common factor if research can identify ways in which skilled therapists take corrective action when their clients report not progressing as expected (Halford et al., 2012, p. 50).

Finally, we recommend the continued *development and testing of online interventions and technology adjuncts (monitoring, motivational, and coaching apps)* to address specific problems, such as children's OCD (Comer et al., 2017), and to enhance the quality of couples' relationships (e.g. Doss et al., 2016). The effective aspects of online programs, such as adjunctive coaching, should be identified and compared to traditional, face-to-face interventions. While telehealth is becoming routine in individual therapy, less is known about its applicability with couples and families.

Methodological Recommendations

Although naturalistic studies have far less control than RCTs over sample composition, therapist selection, and treatment adherence, *benchmark comparisons* have much value for guiding community practice. Similarly, *implementation science* research, shows great promise for addressing health disparities domestically and internationally. This approach involves community providers in all aspects of outcome evaluation, from problem identification to follow up, in order to determine what does and does not work in a specific locale for a specific population (e.g. Szapocznik et al., 2015).

To identify the most potent systemic interventions, we recommend *dismantling studies* within evidence-based approaches (Baucom & Boeding, 2013) and *single-case experiments* with repeated measures to evaluate the differential timing of theoretically critical interventions, such as blamer softening in EFCT. (See Chapter 2 for detailed accounts of these methods.) As with large group datasets, single-case experiments can be characterized as a hierarchical structure and analyzed using multilevel modeling (MLM; Moeyaert et al., 2014).

In large samples, MLM can be used to identify variables that account for differences between and within therapists, such as the therapeutic alliance (Owen, Duncan et al., 2014), and different treatment responses between and within family units. Although MLM is now commonplace in the psychotherapy literature, researchers often do not report the proportions of outcome variance at the therapist and group (couple/family) levels.

Researchers can also use MLM to investigate how a client's individual experience varies as a function of a grouping variable, such as level of stress aggregated across family members (Feaster et al., 2011). One systems-informed procedure, MLM with sequential analysis (Howe et al., 2005), specifically attends to the reciprocity and interrelatedness of data between family members (cf. L.N. Johnson, 2020).

Since the hallmark of systemic therapy is the disruption of dysfunctional reciprocity between family members (e.g. Margola et al., 2017), we recommend that researchers embrace *analyses that explicitly account for dependent data*, such as the actor-partner interdependence model (APIM; Kenny & Kashy, 2010). While the APIM has recently come into the mainstream in couple therapy, this is not the case for family therapy research. Although most APIM studies use structural equation modeling, which requires large samples, Bayesian estimation can also be used with small samples (Ozechowski, 2014).

Other systemic approaches to data analysis have yet to take hold in the CFT literature. For example, dynamic systems modeling uses cross-lagged panels to compare changes in the functioning of different dyadic subsystems within a group (e.g. mother–child, father–child, mother–father) as well as within the group as a unit (Butner et al., 2017). Other systemically informed statistical approaches include the common fate model (Ledermann & Kenny, 2012), the social relations model (Kenny, 2013), polynomial regression and response surface analysis (Kivlighan et al., 2017), and factor of curves analysis (Isiordia et al., 2017).

Finally, we recommend conducting more *small-sample process research*, including evidence-based case studies, in which systemic concepts (e.g. triangulation, within-system alliance) are identifiable in verbatim dialogue. Micro-analytic, contextualized research can also be used to examine one therapeutic process in the context of another, such as adolescents' expressions of vulnerability preceding versus following different kinds of parental behavior (Tsvieli et al., in preparation). Another methodology, task analysis, provides practical clinical maps by identifying sequences of behavior that differentiate successful from unsuccessful resolutions of common couple and family problems, such as forgiveness of emotional injury (Woldarsky Menses & Greenberg, 2014). In our view, these kinds of designs provide the most clinically rich information to guide systemic practice.

Final Thoughts

We recognize that as a research agenda, this list is daunting. Nonetheless, it is our belief that systemic and conjoint therapies will continue to attract promising new ideas and methodologies. The international expansion of systemic therapy research in recent years is particularly heartening, as is the increased attention to culturally diverse, vulnerable populations who deserve the best that our science has to offer.

Abbreviations

ABFT	attachment-based family therapy
APIM	actor-partner interdependence model
BSFT	brief strategic family therapy
BST	brief strategic therapy (BST)
CALM	Coaching Approach behavior and Leading by Modeling
CBCT	cognitive-behavioral couple therapy
CBT	cognitive behavioral therapy
CBT-A	cognitive behavioural therapy adapted for adolescents
CBT-FT	cognitive-behavioral family therapy
CFT	couple and family therapy
CM	contingency management
CR	community reinforcement
CWD	coping with depression
DSM/ICD	Diagnostic Statistical Manual/International Classification of Diseases
E-CBT	enhanced cognitive behavioural therapy
EBFT	ecologically based family therapy
EFCT	emotionally focused couple therapy
EFT	emotionally focused therapy
ERP	exposure and response prevention
FBT	family-based treatment
FBT-BN	family-based therapy for bulimia
FFT	functional family therapy
FTF	family-to-family
I-CBT	integrating CBT with parent sessions
IBCT	integrative behavioral couple therapy
IPC	intensive parental coaching
MDFT	multidimensional family therapy
MET	motivational enhancement therapy
MLM	multilevel modeling
MST	multisystemic therapy
OCD	obsessive compulsive disorder
PCIT	parent–child interaction therapy
PCIT-ED	parent–child interaction therapy with an emotion development module
PFIT	positive family interaction therapy
PTSD	post-traumatic stress disorder
RAP-P	Resourceful Adolescent Parenting Program
RCT	randomized controlled trial
SAFETY	Safe Alternatives for Teens and Youths
SHIFT	Self-Harm Intervention: Family Therapy

SPACE	supportive parenting for anxious childhood emotions
STI/HIV	sexually transmitted infections/ human immunodeficiency virus
SysFT	systemic family therapy
TAU	treatment as usual
TBCT	traditional behavioral couple therapy
TC	therapist to parent

REFERENCES

Abramowitz, J. S., Baucom, D. H., Boeding, S., Wheaton, M. G., Pukay-Martin, N. D., Fabricant, L. E., Paprocki, C., & Fischer, M. S. (2013). Treating obsessive-compulsive disorder in intimate relationships: A pilot study of couple-based cognitive-behavior therapy. *Behavior Therapy*, 44(3), 395–407. https://doi.org/10.1016/j.beth.2013.02.005

Agras, W. S., Lock, J., Brandt, H., Bryson, S. W., Dodge, E., Halmi, K. A., Jo, B., Johnson, C., Kaye, W., Wilfley, D., & Woodside, B. (2014). Comparison of 2 family therapies for anorexia nervosa: A randomized parallel trial. *JAMA Psychiatry*, 71(11), 1279–1286. https://doi.org/10.1001/jamapsychiatry.2014.1025

Allan, E., Le Grange, D., Sawyer, S. M., McLean, L. A., & Hughes, E. K. (2018). Parental expressed emotion during two forms of family-based treatment for adolescent anorexia nervosa. *European Eating Disorders Review*, 26(1), 46–52. https://doi.org/10.1002/erv.2564

Anker, M. G., Duncan, B. L., & Sparks, J. A. (2009). Using client feedback to improve couple therapy outcomes: A randomized clinical trial in a naturalistic setting. *Journal of Consulting and Clinical Psychology*, 77(4), 693–704. https://doi.org/10.1037/a0016062

Artigas, L., Mateu, C., Vilaregut, A., Feixas, G., & Escudero, V. (2017). Couple therapy for depression: Exploring how the dyadic adjustment determines the therapeutic alliance in two contrasting cases. *Contemporary Family Therapy*, 39, 195–206. https://doi.org/10.1007/s10591-017-9420-3

Asarnow, J. R., Berk, M., Hughes, J. L., & Anderson, N. L. (2015). The SAFETY program: A treatment-development trial of a cognitive-behavioral family treatment for adolescent suicide attempters. *Journal of Clinical Child and Adolescent Psychology*, 44(1), 194–203. https://doi.org/10.1080/15374416.2014.940624

Bachler, E., Frühmann, A., Bachler, H., Aas, B., Strunk, G., & Nickel, M. (2016). Differential effects of the working alliance in family therapeutic home-based treatment of multi-problem families. *Journal of Family Therapy*, 38(1), 120–148. https://doi.org/10.1111/1467-6427.12063

Balas, E. A., & Boren, S. A. (2000). Managing clinical knowledge for health care improvement. Yearbook of Medical Informatics, 1, 65–70. https://doi.org/10.1055/s-0038-1637943

Baldwin, S. A., Christian, S., Berkeljon, A., & Shadish, W. R. (2012). The effects of family therapies for adolescent delinquency and substance abuse: A meta-analysis. *Journal of Marital and Family Therapy*, 38(1), 281–304. https://doi.org/10.1111/j.1752-0606.2011.00248.x

Balfour, A., & Lanman, M. (2012). An evaluation of time-limited psychodynamic psychotherapy for couples: A pilot study. *Psychology and Psychotherapy: Theory, Research and Practice*, 85(3), 292–309. https://doi.org/10.1111/j.2044-8341.2011.02030.x

Bartle-Haring, S., Glebova, T., Gangamma, R., Grafsky, E., & Delaney, R. O. (2012). Alliance and termina¬tion status in couple therapy: A comparison of methods for assessing discrepancies. *Psychotherapy Research*, 22(5), 502–514. https://doi.org/10.1080/10503307.2012.676985

Bartle-Haring, S., Slesnick, N., & Murnan, A. (2018). Benefits to children who participate in family therapy with their substance-abusing mother. *Journal of Marital and Family Therapy*, 44(4), 671–686. https://doi.org/10.1111/jmft.12280

Barrett, H., Slesnick, N., Brody, J. L., Turner, C. W., & Peterson, T. R. (2001). Treatment outcomes for adolescent substance abuse at 4- and 7-month assessments. *Journal of Consulting and Clinical Psychology*, 69(5), 802–813. https://doi.org/10.1037/0022-006X.69.5.802

Baruah, U., Pandian, R. D., Narayanaswamy, J. C., Math, S. B., Kandavel, T., & Reddy, Y. J. (2018). A randomized controlled study of brief family-based intervention in obsessive compulsive disorder. *Journal of Affective Disorders*, 225, 137–146. https://doi.org/10.1016/j.jad.2017.08.014

Baucom, B. R., Atkins, D. C., Rowe, L. S., Doss, B. D., & Christensen, A. (2015). Prediction of treatment response at 5-year follow-up in a randomized clinical trial of behaviorally based couple therapies. *Journal of Consulting and Clinical Psychology*, 83(1), 103–114. https://doi.org/10.1037/a0038005

Baucom, D. H., Belus, J. M., Adelman, C. B., Fischer, M. S., & Paprocki, C. (2014). Couple-based interventions for psychopathology: A renewed direction for the field. *Family Process*, 53(3), 445–461. https://doi.org/10.1111/famp.12075

Baucom, D. H., & Boeding, S. (2013). The role of theory and research in the practice of cognitive-behavioral couple therapy: If you build it, they will come. *Behavior Therapy*, 44(4), 592–602. https://doi.org/10.1016/j.beth.2012.12.004

Baucom, D. H., Fischer, M. S., Worrell, M., Corrie, S., Belus, J. M., Molyva, E., & Boeding, S. E. (2018). Couple-based intervention for depression: An effectiveness study in the National Health Service in England. *Family Process*, 57(2), 275–292. https://doi.org/10.1111/famp.12332

Baucom, K. J. W., Baucom, B. R., & Christensen, A. (2015). Changes in dyadic communication during and after integrative and traditional behavioral couple therapy. *Behaviour Research and Therapy*, 65, 18–28. https://doi.org/10.1016/j.brat.2014.12.004

Baucom, K. J. W., Sevier, M., Eldridge, K. A., Doss, B. D., & Christensen, A. (2011). Observed communication in couples two years after integrative and traditional behavioral couple therapy: Outcome and link with five-year follow-up. *Journal of Consulting and Clinical Psychology*, 79(5), 565–576. https://doi.org/10.1037/a0025121

Bauer, M. S., Damschroder, L., Hagedorn, H., Smith, J., & Kilbourne, A. M. (2015). An introduction to implementation science for the non-specialist. *BMC Psychology*, 3, 32. https://doi.org/10.1186/s40359-015-0089-9

Beach, S. R., & Whisman, M. A. (2012). Affective disorders. *Journal of Marital and Family Therapy*, 38(1), 201–219. https://doi.org/10.1111/j.1752-0606.2011.00243.x

Belus, J. M., Baucom, D. H., & Abramowitz, J. S. (2014). The effect of a couple-based treatment for OCD on intimate partners. *Journal of Behavior Therapy and Experimental Psychiatry*, 45(4), 484–488. https://doi.org/10.1016/j.jbtep.2014.07.001

Bennett, K., Manassis, K., Duda, S., Bagnell, A., Bernstein, G. A., Garland, E. J., J., Miller, L. D., Newton, A., Thabane, L., & Wilansky, P. (2016). Treating child and adolescent anxiety effectively: Overview of systematic reviews. *Clinical Psychology Review*, 50, 80–94. https://doi.org/10.1016/j.cpr.2016.09.006

Benson, L. A., McGinn, M. M., & Christensen, A. (2012). Common principles of couple therapy. *Behavior Therapy*, 43(1), 25–35. https://doi.org/10.1016/j.beth.2010.12.009

Biesen, J. N., & Doss, B. D. (2013). Couples' agreement on presenting problems predicts engagement and outcomes in problem-focused couple therapy. *Journal of Family Psychology*, 27(4), 658–663. https://doi.org/10.1037/a0033422

Blow, A. J., Morrison, N. C., Tamaren, K., Wright, K., Schaafsma, M., & Nadaud, A. (2009). Change processes in couple therapy: An intensive case analysis of one couple using a common factors lens. *Journal of Marital and Family Therapy*, 35(3), 350–368. https://doi.org/10.1111/j.1752-0606.2009.00122.x

Bounoua, N., Abbott, C., Zisk, A., Herres, J., Diamond, G., & Kobak, R. (2018). Emotion regulation and spillover of interpersonal stressors to postsession insight among depressed and suicidal adolescents. *Journal of Consulting and Clinical Psychology*, 86(7), 593–603. https://doi.org/10.1037/ccp0000316

Bowen, M. (1978). *Family therapy in clinical practice*. New York: Jason Aronson.

Boxer, P., Docherty, M., Ostermann, M., Kubik, J., & Veysey, B. (2017). Effectiveness of Multisystemic Therapy for gang-involved youth offenders: One year follow-up analysis of recidivism outcomes. *Children and Youth Services Review*, 73, 107–112. https://doi.org/10.1016/j.childyouth.2016.12.008

Brady, P., Kangas, M., & McGill, K. (2017). "Family matters": A systematic review of the evidence for family psychoeducation for major depressive disorder. *Journal of Marital and Family Therapy, 43*(2), 245–263. https://doi.org/10.1111/jmft.12204

Breinholst, S., Esbjørn, B. H., Reinholdt-Dunne, M. L., & Stallard, P. (2012). CBT for the treatment of child anxiety disorders: A review of why parental involvement has not enhanced outcomes. *Journal of Anxiety Disorders, 26*(3), 416–424. https://doi.org/10.1016/j.janxdis.2011.12.014

Brinkmeyer M, & Eyberg, S.M. (2003). Parent-child interaction therapy for oppositional children. In A.E. Kazdin & J. Weisz (Eds.). *Evidence-based psychotherapies for children and adolescents.* (pp. 204–223). New York: Guilford Press.

Brown, A., Creswell, C., Barker, C., Butler, S., Cooper, P., Hobbs, C., & Thirlwall, K. (2017). Guided parent-delivered cognitive behaviour therapy for children with anxiety disorders: Outcomes at 3- to 5-year follow-up. *British Journal of Clinical Psychology, 56*(2), 149–159. https://doi.org/10.1111/bjc.12127

Bulik, C. M., Baucom, D. H., & Kirby, J. S. (2012). Treating anorexia nervosa in the couple context. *Journal of Cognitive Psychotherapy, 26*(1), 19–33. https://doi.org/10.1891/0889-8391.26.1.19

Burgess Moser, M., Johnson, S. M., Dalgleish, T. L., Lafontaine, M. F., Wiebe, S. A., & Tasca, G. A. (2016). Changes in relationship-specific attachment in emotionally focused couple therapy. *Journal of Marital and Family Therapy, 42*(2), 231–245. https://doi.org/10.1111/jmft.12139

Butler, M. H., Harper, J. M., & Mitchell, C. B. (2011). A comparison of attachment outcomes in enactment-based versus therapist-centered therapy process modalities in couple therapy. *Family Process, 50*(2), 203–220. https://doi.org/10.1111/j.1545-5300.2011.01355.x

Butler, S., Baruch, G., Hickey, N., & Fonagy, P. (2011). A randomized controlled trial of multisystemic therapy and a statutory therapeutic intervention for young offenders. *Journal of the American Academy of Child and Adolescent Psychiatry, 50*(12), 1220–1235. https://doi.org/10.1016/j.jaac.2011.09.017

Butner, J., Diets-Leben, C., Crenshaw, A., Wiltshire, T., Perry, N., Kent de Grey, R., Hogan, J. N., Smith, T. W, Baucom, K. J. W, & Baucom, B. R. W. (2017). A multivariate dynamic systems model for psychotherapy with more than one client. *Journal of Counseling Psychology, 64*(6), 616–625. https://doi.org/10.1037/cou0000238

Butzlaff, R. L., & Hooley, J. M. (1998). Expressed emotion and psychiatric relapse: A meta-analysis. *Archives of General Psychiatry, 55*(6), 547–552. https://doi.org/10.1001/archpsyc.55.6.547

Byng-Hall, J., Campbell, D., & Papadopoulos, R. (1996). *Manual: Systems integrative therapy (SIFT) – The basis for an integrative approach.* London: Tavistock Clinic.

Carpenter, A. L., Puliafico, A. C., Kurtz, S. M., Pincus, D. B., & Comer, J. S. (2014). Extending parent-child interaction therapy for early childhood internalizing problems: New advances for an overlooked population. *Clinical Child and Family Psychology Review, 17*(4), 340–356. https://doi.org/10.1007/s10567-014-0172-4

Carr, A. (2014a). The evidence base for family therapy and systemic interventions for child-focused problems. *Journal of Family Therapy, 36*(2), 107–157. https://doi.org/10.1111/1467-6427.12032

Carr, A. (2014b). The evidence base for couple therapy, family therapy and systemic interventions for adult-focused problems. *Journal of Family Therapy, 36*(2), 158–194. https://doi.org/10.1111/1467-6427.12033

Castelnuovo, G., Manzoni, G. M., Villa, V., Cesa, G. L., & Molinari, E. (2011). Brief strategic therapy vs cognitive behavioral therapy for the inpatient and telephone-based outpatient treatment of binge eating disorder: The STRATOB randomized controlled clinical trial. *Clinical Practice and Epidemiology in Mental Health, 7*, 29–37. https://doi.org/10.2174/1745017901107010029

Celano, M. P., Holsey, C. N., & Kobrynski, L. J. (2012). Home-based family intervention for low-income children with asthma: A randomized controlled pilot study. *Journal of Family Psychology, 26*(2), 171–178. https://doi.org/10.1037/a0027218

Celinska, K., Cheng, C., & Virgil, N. J. (2015). Youth and parental perspectives on the functional family therapy programme. *Journal of Family Therapy, 37*(4), 450–470. https://doi.org/10.1111/1467-6427.12051

Chamberlain, P. (2003). The Oregon multidimensional treatment foster care model: Features, outcomes, and progress in dissemination. *Cognitive and Behavioral Practice, 10*(4), 303–312. https://doi.org/10.1016/S1077-7229(03)80048-2

Chapman, J. E., & Schoenwald, S. K. (2011). Ethnic similarity, therapist adherence, and long-term multisystemic therapy outcomes. *Journal of*

Emotional and Behavioral Disorders, 19(1), 3–16. https://doi.org/10.1177/1063426610376773

Christensen, A., Atkins, D. C., Berns, S., Wheeler, J., Baucom, D. H., & Simpson, L. E. (2004). Traditional versus integrative behavioral couple therapy for significantly and chronically distressed married couples. *Journal of Consulting and Clinical Psychology, 72*(2), 176–191. https://doi.org/10.1037/0022-006X.72.2.176

Christensen, A., Doss, B. D., & Atkins, D. C. (2005). A science of couple therapy: For what should we seek empirical support? In W. M. Pinsof & J. L. Lebow, (Eds.), *Family psychology: The art of the science* (pp. 43–63). New York: Oxford University Press.

Cohen, S., O'Leary, K. D., Foran, H. M., & Kliem, S. (2014). Mechanisms of change in brief couple therapy for depression. *Behavior Therapy, 45*(3), 402–417. https://doi.org/10.1016/j.beth.2014.01.003

Collins, A. L., Love, A. W., Bloch, S., Street, A. F., Duchesne, G. M., Dunai, J., & Couper, J. W. (2013). Cognitive existential couple therapy for newly diagnosed prostate cancer patients and their partners: A descriptive pilot study. *Psycho-Oncology, 22*(2), 465–469.

Comer, J.S., Furr, J.M., Cooper-Vince, C.E., Kerns, C.E., Chan, P.T., Edson, A.L., Khanna, M., Franklin, M. E., Garcia, A. M., & Freeman, J.B. (2014). Internet-delivered, family-based treatment for early-onset OCD: A preliminary case series. *Journal of Clinical Child and Adolescent Psychology, 43*(1), 74–87. https://doi.org/10.1080/15374416.2013.855127

Comer, J. S., Furr, J. M., Kerns, C. E., Miguel, E., Coxe, S., Elkins, R. M., Carpenter, A. L., Cornacchio, D., Cooper-Vince, C. E., DeSerisy, M., Chou, T., Sanchez, A. L., Khanna, M., Franklin, M. E., Garcia, A. M., & Freeman, J. B. (2017). Internet-delivered, family-based treatment for early-onset OCD: A pilot randomized trial. *Journal of Consulting and Clinical Psychology, 85*(2), 178–186. https://doi.org/10.1037/ccp0000155

Comer, J. S., Puliafico, A. C., Aschenbrand, S. G., McKnight, K., Robin, J. A., Goldfine, M. E., & Albano, A. M. (2012). A pilot feasibility evaluation of the CALM program for anxiety disorders in early childhood. *Journal of Anxiety Disorders, 26*(1), 40–49. https://doi.org/10.1016/j.janxdis.2011.08.011

Connell, A. M., Stormshak, E., Dishion, T., Fosco, G., & Van Ryzin, M. (2018). The Family Check Up and adolescent depression: An examination of treatment responders and non-responders. *Prevention Science, 19*(Suppl 1), 16–26. https://doi.org/10.1007/s11121-015-0586-3

Corsini-Munt, S., Bergeron, S., Rosen, N. O., Mayrand, M.-H. & Delisle, I. (2014). Feasibility and preliminary effectiveness of a novel cognitive-behavioral couple therapy for provoked vestibulodynia: A pilot study. *Journal of Sexual Medicine, 11*(10), 2515–2527. https://doi.org/10.1111/jsm.12646

Cottrell, D. J., Wright-Hughes, A., Collinson, M., Boston, P., Eisler, I., Fortune, S., Graham, E. H., Green, J., House, A. O., Kerfoot, M., Owens, D. W., Saloniki, E. C., Simic, M., Lambert, F., Rothwell, J., Tubeuf, S., & Farrin, A. J. (2018). Effectiveness of systemic family therapy versus treatment as usual for young people after self-harm: A pragmatic, single phase 3, multicentre, randomised controlled trial. *The Lancet Psychiatry, 5*(3), 203–216. https://doi.org/10.1016/S2215-0366(18)30058-0

Couper, J., Collins, A., Bloch, S., Street, A., Duchesne, G., Jones, T., Olver, J., & Love, A. (2015). Cognitive existential couple therapy (CECT) in men and partners facing localised prostate cancer: A randomised controlled trial. *BJU International, 115*(Suppl 5), 35–45. https://doi.org/10.1111/bju.12991

Couturier, J., Kimber, M., & Szatmari, P. (2013). Efficacy of family-based treatment for adolescents with eating disorders: A systematic review and meta-analysis. *International Journal of Eating Disorders, 46*(1), 3–11. https://doi.org/10.1002/eat.22042

Dakof, G.A., Henderson, C.E., Rowe, C.L., Boustani, M., Greenbaum, P.E., Wang, W., Hawes, S., Linares, C., & Liddle, H.A. (2015). A randomized clinical trial of family therapy in juvenile drug court. *Journal of Family Psychology, 29*(2), 232–241. https://doi.org/10.1037/fam0000053

Dalgleish, T. L., Johnson, S. M., Burgess Moser, M., Lafontaine, M.-F., Wiebe, S. A., & Tasca, G. A. (2015). Predicting change in marital satisfaction throughout emotionally focused couple therapy. *Journal of Marital and Family Therapy, 41*(3), 276–291. https://doi.org/10.1111/jmft.12077

Dalgleish, T. L., Johnson, S. M., Burgess Moser, M., Wiebe, S. A., & Tasca, G. A. (2015). Predicting key change events in emotionally focused couple therapy. *Journal of Marital and Family Therapy, 41*(3), 260–275. https://doi.org/10.1111/jmft.12101

Dalle Grave, R., Calugi, S., Doll, H. A., & Fairburn, C. G. (2013). Enhanced cognitive behaviour therapy for adolescents with anorexia nervosa: An alternative to family therapy? *Behaviour Research and Therapy*, *51*(1), R9–R12. https://doi.org/10.1016/j.brat.2012.09.008

Dalle Grave, R., Calugi, S., Sartirana, M., & Fairburn, C. G. (2015). Transdiagnostic cognitive behaviour therapy for adolescents with an eating disorder who are not underweight. *Behaviour Research and Therapy*, *73*, 79–82. https://doi.org/10.1016/j.brat.2015.07.014

Dalton, E., Greenman, P. S., Classen, C. C., & Johnson, S. M. (2013). Nurturing connections in the aftermath of childhood trauma: A randomized controlled trial of emotionally focused couple therapy for female survivors of childhood abuse. *Couple and Family Psychology: Research and Practice*, *2*(3), 209–221. https://doi.org/10.1037/a0032772

Darcy, A. M., Bryson, S. W., Agras, W. S., Fitzpatrick, K. K., Le Grange, D., & Lock, J. (2013). Do in-vivo behaviors predict early response in family-based treatment for anorexia nervosa? *Behaviour Research and Therapy*, *51*(11), 762–766. https://doi.org/10.1016/j.brat.2013.09.003

Davis, S. D., Lebow, J. L., & Sprenkle, D. H. (2012). Common factors of change in couple therapy. *Behavior Therapy*, *43*(1), 36–48. https://doi.org/10.1016/j.beth.2011.01.009

Dattilio, F. M., Piercy, F. P., & Davis, S. D. (2014). The divide between "evidenced-based" approaches and practitioners of traditional theories of family therapy. *Journal of Marital and Family Therapy*, *40*(1), 5–16. https://doi.org/10.1111/jmft.12032

Deković, M., Asscher, J. J., Manders, W. A., Prins, P. J. M., & van der Laan, P. (2012). Within-intervention change: Mediators of intervention effects during multisystemic therapy. *Journal of Consulting and Clinical Psychology*, *80*(3), 574–587. https://doi.org/10.1037/a0028482

Denton, W. H., Wittenborn, A. K., & Golden, R. N. (2012). Augmenting antidepressant medication treatment of depressed women with emotionally focused therapy for couples: A randomized pilot study. *Journal of Marital and Family Therapy*, *38*, 23–38. https://doi.org/10.1111/j.1752-0606.2012.00291.x

De Shazer, S. (1985). *Keys to solution in brief therapy*. New York, NY: W. W. Norton.

Diamond, G. M., Diamond, G. S., Levy, S., Closs, C., Ladipo, T., & Siqueland, L. (2012). Attachment-based family therapy for suicidal lesbian, gay, and bisexual adolescents: A treatment development study and open trial with preliminary findings. *Psychotherapy*, *49*(1), 62–71. https://doi.org/10.1037/a0026247

Diamond, G.M., Shahar, B., Sabo, D. & Tsvieli, N. (2016). Attachment-based family therapy and emotion-focused therapy for unresolved anger: The role of productive emotional processing. *Psychotherapy*, *53*(1), 34–44. https://doi.org/10.1037/pst0000025

Diamond, G. M., & Shpigel, M. S. (2014). Attachment-based family therapy for lesbian and gay young adults and their persistently nonaccepting parents. *Professional Psychology: Research and Practice*, *45*(4), 258–268. https://doi.org/10.1037/a0035394

Diamond, G. S., Creed, T., Gillham, J., Gallop, R., & Hamilton, J. L. (2012). Sexual trauma history does not moderate treatment outcome in attachment-based family therapy (ABFT) for adolescents with suicide ideation. *Journal of Family Psychology*, *26*(4), 595–605. https://doi.org/10.1037/a0028414

Diamond, G. S., Reis, B. F., Diamond, G. M., Siqueland, L., & Isaacs, L. (2002). Attachment-based family therapy for depressed adolescents: A treatment development study. *Journal of the American Academy of Child and Adolescent Psychiatry*, *41*(10), 1190–1196. https://doi.org/10.1097/00004583-200210000-00008

Diamond, G. S., Siqueland, L., & Diamond, G. M. (2003). Attachment-based family therapy for depressed adolescents: Programmatic treatment development. *Clinical Child and Family Psychology Review*, *6*(2), 107–127. https://doi.org/10.1023/A:1023782510786

Donohue, B., Azrin, N. H., Bradshaw, K., Van Hasselt, V. B., Cross, C. L., Urgelles, J., Romero, V., Hill, H. H., & Allen, D. N. (2014). A controlled evaluation of family behavior therapy in concurrent child neglect and drug abuse. *Journal of Consulting and Clinical Psychology*, *82*(4), 706–720. https://doi.org/10.1037/a0036920

Dopp, A. R., Borduin, C. M., White II, Mark H., & Kuppens, S. (2017). Family-based treatments for serious juvenile offenders: A multilevel meta-analysis. *Journal of Consulting and Clinical Psychology*, *85*(4), 335–354. https://doi.org/10.1037/ccp0000183

Doss, B. D., Cicila, L. N., Georgia, E. J., Roddy, M. K., Nowlan, K. M., Benson, L. A., & Christensen, A. (2016). A randomized controlled trial of the web-based OurRelationship program: Effects on relationship and individual functioning. *Journal of Consulting and Clinical Psychology*, *84*(4), 285–296. https://doi.org/10.1037/ccp0000063

Doss, B. D., Rowe, L. S., Morrison, K. R., Libet, J., Birchler, G. R., Madsen, J. W., & McQuaid, J. R. (2012). Couple therapy for military veterans: Overall effectiveness and predictors of response. *Behavior Therapy*, *43*(1), 216–227. https://doi.org/10.1016/j.beth.2011.06.006

Downs, K. J. & Blow, A. J. (2011). A substantive & methodological review of family-based treatment for eating disorders: The last 25 years of research. *Journal of Family Therapy*, *35*(S1), 3–28. https://doi.org/10.1111/j.1467-6427.2011.00566.x

Ellison, R., Rhodes, P., Madden, S., Miskovic, J., Wallis, A., Baillie, A., Kohn, M., & Touyz, S. (2012). Do the components of manualized family-based treatment for anorexia nervosa predict weight gain? *International Journal of Eating Disorders*, *45*(4), 609–614. https://doi.org/10.1002/eat.22000

Epstein, N. B., & Baucom, D. H. (2002). *Enhanced cognitive-behavioral therapy for couples: A contextual approach*. Washington, DC: American Psychological Association. https://doi.org/10.1037/10481-000

Escudero, V., Boogmans, E., Loots, G., & Friedlander, M. L. (2012). Alliance rupture and repair in conjoint family therapy: An exploratory study. *Psychotherapy*, *49*(1), 26–37. https://doi.org/10.1037/a0026747

Escudero, V., Friedlander, M. L., & Heatherington, L. (2011). Using the e-SOFTA for video training and research on alliance-related behavior. *Psychotherapy*, *48*(2), 138–147. https://doi.org/10.1037/a0022188

Esposito-Smythers, C., Spirito, A., Kahler, C. W., Hunt, J., & Monti, P. (2011). Treatment of co-occurring substance abuse and suicidality among adolescents: A randomized trial. *Journal of Consulting and Clinical Psychology*, *79*(6), 728–739. https://doi.org/10.1037/a0026074

Eyberg, S., & Matarazzo, R. (1980). Training parents as therapists: A comparison between individual parent-child interaction training and parent group didactic training. *Journal of Clinical Psychology*, *36*(2), 492–499. https://doi.org/10.1002/jclp.6120360218

Fairburn C.G., Cooper Z., & Shafran R. (2013). Cognitive behaviour therapy for eating disorders: A "transdiagnostic" theory and treatment. *Behaviour Research and Therapy*, *41*(5), 509–528. https://doi.org/10.1016/S0005-7967(02)00088-8

Feaster, D., Brincks, A., Robbins, M., & Szapocznik, J. (2011). Multilevel models to identify contextual effects on individual group member outcomes: A family example. *Family Process*, *50*(2), 167–183. https://doi.org/10.1111/j.1545-5300.2011.01353.x

Feder, M. & Diamond, G.M. (2016). Parent-therapist alliance and parent attachment promoting behaviors in attachment-based family therapy for suicidal and depressed adolescents. *Journal of Family Therapy*, *38*(1), 82–101. https://doi.org/10.1111/1467-6427.12078

Fife, S. T., Whiting, J. B., Bradford, K., & Davis, S. (2014). The therapeutic pyramid: A common factors synthesis of techniques, alliance, and way of being. *Journal of Marital and Family Therapy*, *40*(1), 20–33. https://doi.org/10.1111/jmft.12041

Fiorillo, A., Del Vecchio, V., Luciano, M., Sampogna, G., De Rosa, C., Malangone, C., Volpe, U., Bardicchia, F., Ciampini, G., Crocamo, C., Iapichino, S., Lampis, D., Moroni, A., Orlandi, E., Piselli, M., Pompili, E., Veltro, F., Carrà, G., & Maj, M. (2015). Efficacy of psychoeducational family intervention for bipolar I disorder: A controlled, multicentric, real-world study. *Journal of Affective Disorders*, *172*, 291–299. https://doi.org/10.1016/j.jad.2014.10.021

Fischer, M. S., Baucom, D. H., & Cohen, M. J. (2016). Cognitive-behavioral couple therapies: Review of the evidence for the treatment of relationship distress, psychopathology, and chronic health conditions. *Family Process*, *55*(3), 423–442. https://doi.org/10.1111/famp.12227

Fischer, M. S., Bhatia, V., Baddeley, J. L., Al-Jabari, R., & Libet, J. (2018). Couple therapy with veterans: Early improvements and predictors of early drop-out. *Family Process*, *57*(2), 525–538. https://doi.org/10.1111/famp.12308

Fonagy, P., Butler, S., Cottrell, D., Scott, S., Pilling, S., Eisler, I., Fuggle, P., Kraam, A., Byford, S., Wason, J., Ellison, R., Simes, E., Ganguli, P., Allison, E., & Goodyer, I. M. (2018). Multisystemic therapy versus management as usual in the treatment of adolescent antisocial behaviour (START): A pragmatic, randomised controlled, superiority trial. *The Lancet Psychiatry*, *5*(2), 119–133. https://doi.org/10.1016/S2215-0366(18)30001-4

Forand, N. R., DeRubeis, R. J., & Amsterdam, J. D. (2013). Combining medication and psychotherapy in the treatment of major mental disorders. In M. J. Lambert (Ed.), *Bergin and Garfield's handbook of psychotherapy and behavior change* (6th ed., pp. 735–774). New York, NY: Wiley.

Forbat, L., Robertson, J., & McNamee, P. (2018). Couple therapy following prostate cancer surgery: A manual to guide treatment. *Journal of Family Therapy, 40*(S1), S86–S110. https://doi.org/10.1111/1467-6427.12129

Forehand, R., Jones, D. J., & Parent, J. (2013). Behavioral parenting interventions for child disruptive behaviors and anxiety: What's different and what's the same. *Clinical Psychology Review, 33*(1), 133–145. https://doi.org/10.1016/j.cpr.2012.10.010

Forsberg, S., LoTempio, E., Bryson, S., Fitzpatrick, K. K., Le Grange, D., & Lock, J. (2013). Therapeutic alliance in two treatments for adolescent anorexia nervosa. *International Journal of Eating Disorders, 46*(1), 34–38. https://doi.org/10.1002/eat.22047

Forsberg, S., LoTempio, E., Bryson, S., Fitzpatrick, K. K., Le Grange, D., & Lock, J. (2014). Parent-therapist alliance in family-based treatment for adolescents with anorexia nervosa. *European Eating Disorders Review, 22*(1), 53–58. https://doi.org/10.1002/erv.2242

Fournier, B., Brassard, A., & Shaver, P. R. (2011). Adult attachment and male aggression in couple relationships: The demand-withdraw communication pattern and relationship satisfaction as mediators., *Journal of Interpersonal Violence, 26*(10), 1982–2003. https://doi.org/10.1177/0886260510372930

Fox, S., Bibi, F., Millar, H., & Holland, A. (2017). The role of cultural factors in engagement and change in Multisystemic Therapy (MST). *Journal of Family Therapy, 39*(2), 243–263. https://doi.org/10.1111/1467-6427.12134

Fredman, S. J., Pukay-Martin, N. D., Macdonald, A., Wagner, A. C., Vorstenbosch, V., & Monson, C. M. (2016). Partner accommodation moderates treatment outcomes for couple therapy for posttraumatic stress disorder. *Journal of Consulting and Clinical Psychology, 84*(1), 79–87. https://doi.org/10.1037/ccp0000061

Freeman, J., Sapyta, J., Garcia, A., Compton, S., Khanna, M., Flessner, C., FitzGerald, D., Mauro, C., Dingfelder, R., Benito, K., Harrison, J., Curry, J., Foa, E., March, J., Moore, P., & Franklin, M. (2014). Family-based treatment of early childhood obsessive-compulsive disorder: The Pediatric Obsessive-Compulsive Disorder Treatment Study for Young Children (POTS Jr)-A randomized clinical trial. *JAMA Psychiatry, 71*(6), 689–698. https://doi.org/10.1001/jamapsychiatry.2014.170

Frey, L. M., & Hunt, Q. A. (2018). Treatments for suicidal thoughts and behavior: A review of family-based interventions. *Journal of Marital and Family Therapy, 44*(1), 107–124. https://doi.org/10.1111/jmft.12234

Friedlander, M. L., & Diamond, G. M. (2011). Couple and family therapy. In E. Altmaier & J. Hansen (Eds.), *Oxford handbook of counseling psychology* (pp. 647–675). Oxford University Press.

Friedlander, M.L., Escudero, V., Heatherington, L., & Diamond, G. M. (2011). Alliance in couple and family therapy. In J. C. Norcross (Ed.), *Psychotherapy relationships that work: Evidence-based responsiveness.* (2nd ed., pp. 92–109). Oxford University Press. https://doi.org/10.1093/acprof:oso/9780199737208.003.0004

Friedlander, M. L., Escudero, V., Horvath, A. S., Heatherington, L., Cabero, A., & Martens, M. P. (2006). System for Observing Family Therapy Alliances: A tool for research and practice. *Journal of Counseling Psychology, 53*(2), 214–225. https://doi.org/10.1037/0022-0167.53.2.214

Friedlander, M. L., Escudero, V., Welmers-van der Poll, M., & Heatherington, L. (2018). Meta-analysis of the alliance-outcome relation in couple and family therapy. *Psychotherapy, 55*(4), 356–371. https://doi.org/10.1037/pst0000161

Friedlander, M. L., Heatherington, L., & Escudero, V. (2016). Research on change mechanisms: Advances in process research. In T. Sexton & J. Lebow (Eds.), *Handbook of family therapy* (4th ed., pp. 454–467). Routledge. https://doi.org/10.4324/9780203123584-23

Friedlander, M. L., Kivlighan, D. M., Jr. & Shaffer, K. (2012). Exploring actor-partner interdependence in family therapy: Whose view (parent or adolescent) best predicts treatment progress? *Journal of Counseling Psychology, 59*(1), 168–175. https://doi.org/10.1037/a0024199

Friedlander, M. L., Lee, H. H., Shaffer, K. S., & Cabrera, P. (2014). Negotiating therapeutic alliances with a family at impasse: An evidence-based case study. *Psychotherapy, 51*(1), 41–52. https://doi.org/10.1037/a0032524

Friedlander, M. L., Muetzelfeld, H., Re, S., Colvin, K., Quinn-Nilas, C., & Smoliak, O. (2019). Introducing the Expectation and Preference Scales for Couple Therapy (EPSCT): Development, psychometric evaluation, and suggested use in practice and research. *Family Process, 58*(4), 855–872. https://doi.org/10.1111/famp.12446

Furrow, J. L., Edwards, S. A., Choi, Y., & Bradley, B. (2012). Therapist presence in emotionally focused couple therapy blamer softening events: Promoting change through emotional experience. *Journal of Marital and Family Therapy, 38*(Suppl 1), 39–49. https://doi.org/10.1111/j.1752-0606.2012.00293.x

Garanzini, S., Yee, A., Gottman, J., Gottman, J., Cole, C., Preciado, M., & Jasculca, C. (2017). Results of Gottman method couples therapy with gay and lesbian couples. *Journal of Marital and Family Therapy, 43*(4), 674–684. https://doi.org/10.1111/jmft.12276

Garoff, F. F., Heinonen, K., Pesonen, A., & Almqvist, F. (2012). Depressed youth: Treatment outcome and changes in family functioning in individual and family therapy. *Journal of Family Therapy, 34*(1), 4–23. https://doi.org/10.1111/j.1467-6427.2011.00541.x

Gervan, S., Granic, I., Solomon, T., Blokland, K., & Ferguson, B. (2012). Paternal involvement in multisystemic therapy: Effects on adolescent outcomes and maternal depression. *Journal of Adolescence, 35*(3), 743–751. https://doi.org/10.1016/j.adolescence.2011.10.009

Ghedin, S., Semi, A., Caccamo, F., Caldironi, L., Marogna, C., Piccione, F., Stabile, R., Lorio, R., & Vidotto, G. (2017). Emotionally focused couple therapy with neurodegenerative diseases: A pilot study. *American Journal of Family Therapy, 45*(1), 15–26. https://doi.org/10.1080/01926187.2016.1223562

Girz, L., Lafrance Robinson, A., Foroughe, M., Jasper, K., & Boachie, A. (2013). Adapting family-based therapy to a day hospital programme for adolescents with eating disorders: Preliminary outcomes and trajectories of change. *Journal of Family Therapy, 35*(S1), 102–120. https://doi.org/10.1111/j.1467-6427.2012.00618.x

Glebova, T., Bartle-Haring, S., Gangamma, R., Knerr, M., Delaney, R. O., Meyer, K., McDowell, T. Adkins, K. & Grafsky, E. (2011). Therapeutic alliance and progress in couple therapy: Multiple perspectives. *Journal of Family Therapy, 33*(1), 42–65. https://doi.org/10.1111/j.1467-6427.2010.00503.x

Glebova, T., Foster, S. L., Cunningham, P. B., Brennan, P. A., & Whitmore, E. A. (2018). Therapists and clients' perceptions of bonding as predictors of outcome in ultisystemic family therapy. *Family Process, 57*(4), 867–883. https://doi.org/10.1111/famp.12333

Godart, N., Berthoz, S., Curt, F., Perdereau, F., Rein, Z., Wallier, J., Horreard, A. S., Kaganski, I., Lucet, R., Atger, F., Corcos, M., Fermanian, J., Falissard, B., Flament, M., Eisler, I., & Jeammet, P. (2012). A randomized controlled trial of adjunctive family therapy and treatment as usual following inpatient treatment for anorexia nervosa adolescents. *PloS One, 7*, e28249. https://doi.org/10.1371/journal.pone.0028249

Goorden, M., Schawo, S. J., Bouwmans-Frijters, C. A., van der Schee, E., Hendriks, V. M., & Hakkaart-van Roijen, L. (2016a). The cost-effectiveness of family/family-based therapy for treatment of externalizing disorders, substance use disorders and delinquency: A systematic review. *BMC Psychiatry, 16*, 237. https://doi.org/10.1186/s12888-016-0949-8

Goorden, M., Van Der Schee, E., Hendriks, V. M., & Hakkaart-van Roijen, L. (2016b). Cost-effectiveness of multidimensional family therapy compared to cognitive behavioral therapy for adolescents with a cannabis use disorder: Data from a randomized controlled trial. *Drug and Alcohol Dependence, 162*, 154–161. https://doi.org/10.1016/j.drugalcdep.2016.03.004

Grácio, J., Gonçalves-Pereira, M., & Leff, J. (2018). Key elements of a family intervention for schizophrenia: A qualitative analysis of an RCT. *Family Process, 57*(1), 100–112. https://doi.org/10.1111/famp.12271

Graham, C., Carr, A., Rooney, B., Sexton, T., & Wilson Satterfield, L. R. (2014). Evaluation of functional family therapy in an Irish context. *Journal of Family Therapy, 36*(1), 20–38. https://doi.org/10.1111/1467-6427.12028

Granic, I., Otten, R., Blokland, K., Solomon, T., Engels, R. C. M. E., & Ferguson, B. (2012). Maternal depression mediates the link between therapeutic alliance and improvements in adolescent externalizing behavior. *Journal of Family Psychology, 26*(6), 880–885. https://doi.org/10.1037/a0030716

Greenbaum, P. E., Wang, W., Henderson, C. E., Kan, L., Hall, K., Dakof, G. A., & Liddle, H. A. (2015). Gender and ethnicity as moderators: Integrative data analysis of multidimensional family therapy randomized clinical trials. *Journal of Family Psychology, 29*(6), 919–930. https://doi.org/10.1037/fam0000127

Greenberg, L. S. (2002). *Emotion-focused therapy: Coaching clients to work through their feelings*. Washington, DC: American Psychological Association. https://doi.org/10.1037/10447-000

Greenberg, L. S., & Johnson, S. M. (1988). *Emotionally focused therapy for couples*. New York: Guilford Press.

Guo, X., Slesnick, N., & Feng, X. (2016). Changes in family relationships among substance abusing runaway adolescents: A comparison between family and individual therapies. *Journal of Marital and Family Therapy*, *42*(2), 299–312. https://doi.org/10.1111/jmft.12128

Gupta, S. K. (2011). Intention-to-treat concept: A review. *Perspectives in Clinical Research*, *2*(3), 109–112. https://doi.org/10.4103/2229-3485.83221

Gurman, A. S. (2011). Couple therapy research and the practice of couple therapy: Can we talk? *Family Process*, *50*(3), 280–292. https://doi.org/10.1111/j.1545-5300.2011.01360.x

Gurman, A. S., Lebow, J. L., & Snyder, D. K. (Eds.). (2015). *Clinical handbook of couple therapy* (5th ed.). Guilford Publications.

Hajian, A., & Mohammadi, S. (2013). The effect of training solution-focused couples therapy on dimensions of marital intimacy. *Pakistan Journal of Medical Sciences*, *29*(Suppl 1) 321–324. https://doi.org/10.12669/pjms.291(Suppl).3525

Halford, W. K., & Doss, B. D. (2016). New frontiers in the treatment of couples. *International Journal of Cognitive Therapy*, *9*(2), 124–139. https://doi.org/10.1521/ijct.2016.9.2.124

Halford, W. K., Hayes, S., Christensen, A., Lambert, M., Baucom, D. H., & Atkins, D. C. (2012). Toward making progress feedback an effective common factor in couple therapy. *Behavior Therapy*, *43*(1), 49–60. https://doi.org/10.1016/j.beth.2011.03.005

Halford, W. K., Pepping, C. A., & Petch, J. (2016). The gap between couple therapy research efficacy and practice effectiveness. *Journal of Marital and Family Therapy*, *42*(1), 32–44. https://doi.org/10.1111/jmft.12120

Harvey, C., & O'Hanlon, B. (2013). Family psycho-education for people with schizophrenia and other psychotic disorders and their families. *Australian and New Zealand Journal of Psychiatry*, *47*(6), 516–520. https://doi.org/10.1177/0004867413476754

Heatherington, L., Escudero, V., & Friedlander, M.L. (2018). Where systems theory and alliance meet: Relationship and technique in family therapy. In O. Tishby & H. Wiseman (Eds), *Developing the therapeutic relationship: Integrating case studies, research and practice* (pp. 257–288). Washington, DC: American Psychological Association. https://doi.org/10.1037/0000093-012

Heatherington, L., Friedlander, M. L., Diamond, G. M., Escudero, V., & Pinsof, W. G. (2015). 25 years of systemic therapies research: Progress and promise. *Psychotherapy Research*, *25*(3), 348–364. https://doi.org/10.1080/10503307.2014.983208

Heatherington, L. & Johnson, B. (2018). Social constructionism in couple and family therapy: Narrative, solution-focused and related approaches. In B. Friese, M. Celano, K. Deater-Deckard, E. Jouriles, & M. Whisman, (Eds.), *APA handbook of contemporary family psychology* (pp. 127–142). Washington, DC: American Psychological Association. https://doi.org/10.1037/0000099-008

Heinrichs, N., Zimmermann, T., Huber, B., Herschbach, P., Russell, D. W., & Baucom, D. H. (2012). Cancer distress reduction with a couple-based skills training: A randomized controlled trial. *Annals of Behavioral Medicine*, *43*(2), 239–252. https://doi.org/10.1007/s12160-011-9314-9

Henderson, C. E., Hogue, A., & Dauber, S. (2019). Family therapy techniques and one-year clinical outcomes among adolescents in usual care for behavior problems. *Journal of Consulting and Clinical Psychology*, *87*(3), 308–312. https://doi.org/10.1037/ccp0000376

Hendriks, V., van der Schee, E., & Blanken, P. (2011). Treatment of adolescents with a cannabis use disorder: Main findings of a randomized controlled trial comparing multidimensional family therapy and cognitive behavioral therapy in The Netherlands. *Drug and Alcohol Dependence*, *119*(1–2), 64–71. https://doi.org/10.1016/j.drugalcdep.2011.05.021

Henggeler, S. W., Schoenwald, S. K., Borduin, C. M., Rowland, M. D., & Cunningham, P. B. (2009). *Multisystemic therapy for antisocial behavior in children and adolescents*. Guilford Press.

Henggeler, S. W., & Sheidow, A. J. (2012). Empirically supported family-based treatments for conduct disorder and delinquency in adolescents. *Journal of Marital and Family Therapy*, *38*(1), 30–58. https://doi.org/10.1111/j.1752-0606.2011.00244.x

Herren, J., Freeman, J., & Garcia, A. (2016). Using family-based exposure with response prevention to treat obsessive-compulsive disorder in young children: A case study. *Journal of Clinical Psychology*, *72*(11), 1152–1161. https://doi.org/10.1002/jclp.22395

Hewison, D., Casey, P., & Mwamba, N. (2016). The effectiveness of couple therapy: Clinical outcomes in a naturalistic United Kingdom setting. *Psychotherapy*, *53*(4), 377–387. https://doi.org/10.1037/pst0000098

Higham, J., Friedlander, M. L., Escudero, V., & Diamond, G. M. (2012). Engaging reluctant adolescents in family therapy: An exploratory study of in-session processes. *Journal of Family Therapy*, *34*(1), 24–52. https://doi.org/10.1111/j.1467-6427.2011.00571.x

Hogue, A., Henderson, C. E., Ozechowski, T. J., & Robbins, M. S. (2014). Evidence base on outpatient behavioral treatments for adolescent substance use: Updates and recommendations 2007–2013. *Journal of Clinical Child and Adolescent Psychology*, *43*(5), 695–720. https://doi.org/10.1080/15374416.2014.915550

Horigian, V. E., Anderson, A. R., & Szapocznik, J. (2016). Taking brief strategic family therapy from bench to trench: Evidence generation across translational phases. *Family Process*, *55*(3), 529–542. https://doi.org/10.1111/famp.12233

Horigian, V. E., Feaster, D.J., Brincks, A., Robbins, M.S., Perez, M.A., & Szapocznik, J. (2015). The effects of Brief Strategic Family Therapy (BSFT) on parent substance use and the association between parent and adolescent substance use. *Addictive Behaviors*, *42*, 44–50. https://doi.org/10.1016/j.addbeh.2014.10.024

Horigian, V.E., Feaster, D.J., Robbins, M.S., Brincks, A.M., Ucha, J., Rohrbaugh, M. J., Shoham, V., Bachrach, K., Miller, M., Burlew, A. K., Hodgkins, C. C., Carrion, I. S., Silverstein, M., Werstlein, R., & Szapocznik, J. (2015). A cross-sectional assessment of the long term effects of Brief Strategic Family Therapy for adolescent substance use. *The American Journal on Addictions*, *24*(7), 637–645. https://doi.org/10.1111/ajad.12278

Hou, Y., Hu, P., Zhang, Y., Lu, Q., Wang, D., Yin, L., Chen, Y., & Zou, X. (2014). Cognitive behavioral therapy in combination with systemic family therapy improves mild to moderate postpartum depression. *Revista Brasileira de Psiquiatria*, *36*(1), 47–52. https://doi.org/10.1590/1516-4446-2013-1170

House, J., Schmidt, U., Craig, M., Landau, S., Simic, M., Nicholls, D., Hugo, P., Berelowitz, M., & Eisler, I. (2012). Comparison of specialist and non-specialist care pathways for adolescents with anorexia nervosa and related eating disorders. *International Journal of Eating Disorders*, *45*(8), 949–956. https://doi.org/10.1002/eat.22065

Howe, G. W., Dagne, G., & Brown, C. H. (2005). Multilevel methods for modeling observed sequences of family interaction. *Journal of Family Psychology*, *19*(1), 72–85. https://doi.org/10.1037/0893-3200.19.1.72

Isiordia, M., Conger, R., Robins, R. W., & Ferrer, E. (2017). Using the factor of curves model to evaluate associations among multiple family constructs over time. *Journal of Family Psychology*, *31*(8), 1017–1028. https://doi.org/10.1037/fam0000379

Israel, P., & Diamond, G. S. (2013). Feasibility of attachment based family therapy for depressed clinic-referred Norwegian adolescents. *Clinical Child Psychology and Psychiatry*, *18*(3), 334–350. https://doi.org/10.1177/1359104512455811

Isserlin, L., & Couturier, J. (2012). Therapeutic alliance and family-based treatment for adolescents with anorexia nervosa. *Psychotherapy*, *49*(1), 46–51. https://doi.org/10.1037/a0023905

Jacobson, N. S., & Christensen, A. (1996). *Integrative couple therapy: Promoting acceptance and change*. W. W. Norton and Co.

Jacobson, N. S., & Margolin, G. (1979). *Marital therapy: Strategies based on social learning and behavior exchange principles*. Psychology Press.

Jewell, T., Blessitt, E., Stewart, C., Simic, M., & Eisler, I. (2016). Family therapy for child and adolescent eating disorders: A critical review. *Family Process*, *55*(3), 577–594. https://doi.org/10.1111/famp.12242

Johnson, L. N., Evans, L. M., Baucom, B. R. W., & Whiting, R. B. (2020). Methods for examining mechanisms of change in systemic family therapies. In K. S. Wampler, R. B. Miller, & R. B. Seedall (Eds.), *The handbook of systemic family therapy: Volume I*. (pp. 467–489). Wiley.

Johnson, L. N., & Ketring, S. A. (2006). The therapy alliance: A moderator in therapy outcome for families dealing with child abuse and neglect. *Journal of Marital and Family Therapy*, *32*(3), 345–354. https://doi.org/10.1111/j.1752-0606.2006.tb01611.x

Johnson, L. N., Tambling, R. B., & Anderson, S. R. (2015). A video recall study of in-session changes in sentiment override. *Family Process, 54*(3), 485–497. https://doi.org/10.1111/famp.12118

Johnson, S. M. (2004). *The practice of emotionally focused couple therapy: Creating connection*. Brunner-Routledge.

Johnson, S. M., Moser, M. B., Beckes, L., Smith, A., Dalgleish, T., et al. (2013) Soothing the threatened brain: Leveraging contact comfort with emotionally focused therapy. *PLoS ONE, 8,* e79314 https://doi.org/10.1371/journal.pone.0079314

Kaslow, N. J., Broth, M. R., Smith, C. O., & Collins, M. H. (2012). Family-based interventions for child and adolescent disorders. *Journal of Marital and Family Therapy, 38*(1), 82–100. https://doi.org/10.1111/j.1752-0606.2011.00257.x

Kazdin, A.E., & Blase, S.E. (2011). Rebooting psychotherapy research and practice to reduce the burden of mental illness. *Perspectives on Psychological Science, 6*(1), 21–37. https://doi.org/10.1177/1745691610393527

Keiley, M. K., Zaremba-Morgan, A., Datubo-Brown, C., Pyle, R., & Cox, M. (2015). Multiple-family group intervention for incarcerated male adolescents who sexually offend and their families: Change in maladaptive emotion regulation predicts adaptive change in adolescent behaviors. *Journal of Marital and Family Therapy, 41*(3), 324–339. https://doi.org/10.1111/jmft.12078

Kendall, P. C., Settipani, C. A., & Cummings, C. M. (2012). No need to worry: The promising future of child anxiety research. *Journal of Clinical Child and Adolescent Psychology, 41*(1), 103–115. https://doi.org/10.1080/15374416.2012.632352

Kenny, D. A. (2013). Using the social relations model to understand relationships. In R. Erber & R. Gilmour (Eds.), *Theoretical frameworks for personal relationships* (pp. 123–140). Psychology Press.

Kenny, D.A., & Kashy, D. A. (2010). Dyadic data analysis using multilevel modeling. In J. J. Hox & J. K. Roberts (Eds.), *Handbook of advanced multilevel analysis* (pp. 335–370). Routledge.

Kerr, M. E., & Bowen, M. (1988). *Family evaluation*. W. W. Norton.

Kissane, D. W., Zaider, T. I., Li, Y., Hichenberg, S., Schuler, T., Lederberg, M., Lavelle, L., Loeb, R., & Del Gaudio, F. (2016). Randomized controlled trial of family therapy in advanced cancer continued into bereavement. *Journal of Clinical Oncology, 34*(16), 1921–1927. https://doi.org/10.1200/JCO.2015.63.0582

Kivlighan, D. J. M., Jr., Kline, K., Gelso, G. J., & Hill, C. E. (2017). Congruence and discrepancy between working alliance and real relationship: Variance decomposition and response surface analyses. *Journal of Counseling Psychology, 64*(4), 394–409. https://doi.org/10.1037/cou0000216

Klann, N., Hahlweg, K., Baucom, D. H., & Kroeger, C. (2011). The effectiveness of couple therapy in Germany: A replication study. *Journal of Marital and Family Therapy, 37*(2), 200–208. https://doi.org/10.1111/j.1752-0606.2009.00164.x

Knobloch-Fedders, L. M., Pinsof, W. M., & Haase, C. M. (2015). Treatment response in couple therapy: Relationship adjustment and individual functioning change processes. *Journal of Family Psychology, 29*(5), 657–666. https://doi.org/10.1037/fam0000131

Kröger, C., Reißner, T., Vasterling, I., Schütz, K., & Kliem, S. (2012). Therapy for couples after an affair: A randomized-controlled trial. *Behaviour Research and Therapy, 50*(12), 786–796. https://doi.org/10.1016/j.brat.2012.09.006

Kuhlman, I., Tolvanen, A., & Seikkula, J. (2013). The therapeutic alliance in couple therapy for depression: Predicting therapy progress and outcome from assessments of the alliance by the patient, the spouse, and the therapists. *Contemporary Family Therapy, 35*(1), 1–13. https://doi.org/10.1007/s10591-012-9215-5

LaChance, H., Cioe, P. A., Tooley, E., Colby, S. M., O'Farrell, T. J., & Kahler, C. W. (2015). Behavioral couples therapy for smoking cessation: A pilot randomized clinical trial. *Psychology of Addictive Behaviors, 29*(3), 643. https://doi.org/10.1037/adb0000051

LaFrance Robinson, A., Dolhanty, J., Stillar, A., Henderson, K., & Mayman, S. (2016). Emotion focused family therapy for eating disorders across the lifespan: A pilot study of a 2-day transdiagnostic intervention for parents. *Clinical Psychology and Psychotherapy, 23*(1), 14–23. https://doi.org/10.1002/cpp.1933

Lambert, J. E., Skinner, A., & Friedlander, M. L. (2012). Problematic within-family alliances in conjoint family therapy: A close look at five cases. *Journal of Marital and Family Therapy, 38*(2), 417–428. https://doi.org/10.1111/j.1752-0606.2010.00212.x

LaTaillade, J. J., Epstein, N. B., & Werlinich, C. A. (2006). Conjoint treatment of intimate partner violence: A cognitive-behavioral approach. *Journal of Cognitive Psychotherapy, 20*(4), 393–410. https://doi.org/10.1891/jcpiq-v20i4a005

Lebow, J. L. (2014). *Couple and family therapy: An integrative map of the territory*. American Psychological Association. https://doi.org/10.1037/14255-000

Lebow, J. L., Chambers, A. L., Christensen, A., & Johnson, S. M. (2012). Research on the treatment of couple distress. *Journal of Marital and Family Therapy, 38*(1), 145–168. https://doi.org/10.1111/j.1752-0606.2011.00249.x

Lebowitz, E. R. (2013). Parent-based treatment for childhood and adolescent OCD. *Journal of Obsessive-Compulsive and Related Disorders, 2*(4), 425–431. https://doi.org/10.1016/j.jocrd.2013.08.004

Lebowitz, E., Dolberger, D., Nortov, E., & Omer, H. (2012). Parent training in nonviolent resistance for adult entitled dependence. *Family Process, 51*(1), 90–106. https://doi.org/10.1111/j.1545-5300.2012.01382.x

Lebowitz, E. R., Omer, H., Hermes, H., & Scahill, L. (2014). Parent training for childhood anxiety disorders: The SPACE program. *Cognitive and Behavioral Practice, 21*(4), 456–469. https://doi.org/10.1016/j.cbpra.2013.10.004

Lebowitz, E. R., Panza, K. E., & Bloch, M. H. (2016). Family accommodation in obsessive-compulsive and anxiety disorders: A five-year update. *Expert Review of Neurotherapeutics, 16*(1), 45–53. https://doi.org/10.1586/14737175.2016.1126181

Ledermann, T., & Kenny, D. A. (2012). The common fate model for dyadic data: Variations of a theoretically important but underutilized model. *Journal of Family Psychology, 26*(1), 140–148. https://doi.org/10.1037/a0026624

Lee, N. A., Furrow, J. L., & Bradley, B. A. (2017). Emotionally focused couple therapy for parents raising a child with an autism spectrum disorder: A pilot study. *Journal of Marital and Family Therapy, 43*(4), 662–673. https://doi.org/10.1111/jmft.12225

Le Grange, D., Hoste, R. R., Lock, J., & Bryson, S. W. (2011). Parental expressed emotion of adolescents with anorexia nervosa: Outcome in family-based treatment. *International Journal of Eating Disorders, 44*(8), 731–734. https://doi.org/10.1002/eat.20877

Le Grange, D., Hughes, E. K., Court, A., Yeo, M., Crosby, R. D., & Sawyer, S. M. (2016). Randomized clinical trial of parent-focused treatment and family-based treatment for adolescent anorexia nervosa. *Journal of the American Academy of Child and Adolescent Psychiatry, 55*(8), 683–692. https://doi.org/10.1016/j.jaac.2016.05.007

Le Grange, D., Lock, J., Accurso, E. C., Agras, W. S., Darcy, A., Forsberg, S., & Bryson, S. W. (2014). Relapse from remission at two-to four-year follow-up in two treatments for adolescent anorexia nervosa. *Journal of the American Academy of Child and Adolescent Psychiatry, 53*(11), 1162–1167. https://doi.org/10.1016/j.jaac.2014.07.014

Le Grange, D., Lock, J., Agras, W. S., Bryson, S. W., & Jo, B. (2015). Randomized clinical trial of family-based treatment and cognitive-behavioral therapy for adolescent bulimia nervosa. *Journal of the American Academy of Child and Adolescent Psychiatry, 54*(11), 886–894. https://doi.org/10.1016/j.jaac.2015.08.008

Le Grange, D., Lock, J., Agras, W. S., Moye, A., Bryson, S. W., Jo, B., & Kraemer, H. C. (2012). Moderators and mediators of remission in family-based treatment and adolescent focused therapy for anorexia nervosa. *Behaviour Research and Therapy, 50*(2), 85–92. https://doi.org/10.1016/j.brat.2011.11.003

Lenze, S. N., Pautsch, J., & Luby, J. (2011). Parent-child interaction therapy emotion development: A novel treatment for depression in preschool children. *Depression and Anxiety, 28*(2), 153–159. https://doi.org/10.1002/da.20770

Levy, S. A., Russon, J., & Diamond, G. M. (2016). Attachment-based family therapy for suicidal lesbian, gay, and bisexual adolescents: A case study. *Australian and New Zealand Journal of Family Therapy, 37*(2), 190–206. https://doi.org/10.1002/anzf.1151

Lewin, A. B., Park, J. M., Jones, A. M., Crawford, E. A., De Nadai, A. S., Menzel, J., Arnold, E. B., Murphy, T. K., & Storch, E. A. (2014). Family-based exposure and response prevention therapy for preschool-aged children with obsessive-compulsive disorder: A pilot randomized controlled trial. *Behaviour Research and Therapy, 56,* 30–38. https://doi.org/10.1016/j.brat.2014.02.001

Liddle, H.A. (2016). Multidimensional family therapy: Evidence base for transdiagnostic treatment outcomes, change mechanisms, and implementation in community settings. *Family Process, 55*(3), 558–576. https://doi.org/10.1111/famp.12243

Liddle, H. A., Dakof, G. A., Parker, K., Diamond, G. S., Barrett, K., & Tejeda, M. (2001). Multidimensional family therapy for adolescent drug abuse: Results of a randomized clinical trial. *The American Journal of Drug and Alcohol Abuse*, 27(4), 651–688. https://doi.org/10.1081/ADA-100107661

Liddle, H. A., Dakof, G. A., Rowe, C. L., Henderson, C., Greenbaum, P., Wang, W., & Alberga, L. (2018). Multidimensional Family Therapy as a community-based alternative to residential treatment for adolescents with substance use and co-occurring mental health disorders. *Journal of Substance Abuse Treatment*, 90, 47–56. https://doi.org/10.1016/j.jsat.2018.04.011

Liddle, H. A., Dakof, G. A., Turner, R. M., Henderson, C. E., & Greenbaum, P. E. (2008). Treating adolescent drug abuse: A randomized trial comparing multidimensional family therapy and cognitive behavior therapy. *Addiction*, 103(10), 1660–1670. https://doi.org/10.1111/j.1360-0443.2008.02274.x

Liddle, H. A., Rodriguez, R. A., Dakof, G. A., Kanzki, E., & Marvel, F. A. (2005). Multidimensional Family Therapy: A science-based treatment for adolescent drug abuse. In J. L. Lebow (Ed.), *Handbook of clinical family therapy* (pp. 128–163). John Wiley and Sons Inc.

Lindstrøm, M., Saidj, M., Kowalski, K., Filges, T., Rasmussen, P. S., & Jørgensen, A. M. K. (2013). Brief Strategic Family Therapy (BSFT) for young people in treatment for non-opioid drug use: A systematic review. *Campbell Systematic Reviews*, 9(1), 2–95. https://doi.org/10.4073/csr.2013.7

Lock, J., Le Grange, D., Agras, W. S., & Dare, C. (2001). *Treatment manual for anorexia nervosa: A family-based approach*. Guilford Press.

Lock, J., Le Grange D., Agras, W. S., & Dare, C. (2013). *Treatment manual for anorexia nervosa: A family-based approach*. 2nd Edition. Guildford Press.

Lock, J., Le Grange, D., Agras, W. S., Fitzpatrick, K. K., Jo, B., Accurso, E., Forsberg, S., Anderson, K., Arnow, K., & Stainer, M. (2015). Can adaptive treatment improve outcomes in family-based therapy for adolescents with anorexia nervosa? Feasibility and treatment effects of a multi-site treatment study. *Behaviour Research and Therapy*, 73, 90–95. https://doi.org/10.1016/j.brat.2015.07.015

Lock, J., Le Grange, D., Agras, W. S., Moye, A., Bryson, S. W., & Jo, B. (2010). Randomized clinical trial comparing family-based treatment with adolescent-focused individual therapy for adolescents with anorexia nervosa. *Archives of General Psychiatry*, 67(10), 1025–1032. https://doi.org/10.1001/archgenpsychiatry.2010.128

Löfholm, C. A., Eichas, K., & Sundell, K. (2014). The Swedish implementation of multisystemic therapy for adolescents: Does treatment experience predict treatment adherence? *Journal of Clinical Child and Adolescent Psychology*, 43(4), 643–655. https://doi.org/10.1080/15374416.2014.883926

Luby, J. L., Barch, D. M., Whalen, D., Tillman, R., & Freedland, K. E. (2018). A randomized controlled trial of parent-child psychotherapy targeting emotion development for early childhood depression. *The American Journal of Psychiatry*, 175(11), 1102–1110. https://doi.org/10.1176/appi.ajp.2018.18030321

Luby, J., Lenze, S., & Tillman, R. (2012). A novel early intervention for preschool depression: Findings from a pilot randomized controlled trial. *Journal of Child Psychology and Psychiatry*, 53(3), 313–322. https://doi.org/10.1111/j.1469-7610.2011.02483.x

Lucksted, A., McFarlane, W., Downing, D., Dixon, L., & Adams, C. (2012). Recent developments in family psychoeducation as an evidence-based practice. *Journal of Marital and Family Therapy*, 38(1), 101–121. https://doi.org/10.1111/j.1752-0606.2011.00256.x

Lucksted, A., Medoff, D., Burland, J., Stewart, B., Fang, L. J., Brown, C., Jones, A., Lehman, A., & Dixon, L. B. (2013). Sustained outcomes of a peer-taught family education program on mental illness. *Acta Psychiatrica Scandinavica*, 127(4), 279–286. https://doi.org/10.1111/j.1600-0447.2012.01901.x

MacPherson, H. A., Leffler, J. M., & Fristad, M. A. (2014). Implementation of multi-family psychoeducational psychotherapy for childhood mood disorders in an outpatient community setting. *Journal of Marital and Family Therapy*, 40(2), 193–211. https://doi.org/10.1111/jmft.12013

Madden, S., Miskovic-Wheatley, J., Wallis, A., Kohn, M., Lock, J., Le Grange, D., Jo, B., Clarke, S., Rhodes, P., Hay, P., & Touyz, S. (2015). A randomized controlled trial of in-patient treatment for anorexia nervosa in medically unstable adolescents. *Psychological Medicine*, 45(2), 415–427. https://doi.org/10.1017/S0033291714001573

Madsen, J. W., Tomfohr-Madsen, L. M., & Doss, B. D. (2017). The impact of couple therapy on service utilization among military veterans: The moderating roles of pretreatment service utilization and premature termination. *Family Process*, 56(3), 620–635. https://doi.org/10.1111/famp.12234

Maljanen, T., Paltta, P., Härkänen, T., Virtala, E., Lindfors, O., Laaksonen, M. A., & Knekt, P. (2012). The cost-effectiveness of short-term psychodynamic psychotherapy and solution-focused therapy in the treatment of depressive and anxiety disorders during a one-year follow-up. *The Journal of Mental Health Policy and Economics*, 15(1), 13–23.

Manassis, K., Lee, T. C., Bennett, K., Zhao, X. Y., Mendlowitz, S., Duda, S., Saini, M., Wilansky, P., Baer, S., Barrett, P., Bodden, D., Cobham, V. E., Dadds, M. R., Flannery-Schroeder, E., Ginsburg, G., Heyne, D., Hudson, J. L., Kendall, P. C., Liber, J., Masia-Warner, C., . . . Wood, J. J. (2014). Types of parental involvement in CBT with anxious youth: A preliminary meta-analysis. *Journal of Consulting and Clinical Psychology*, 82(6), 1163–1172. https://doi.org/10.1037/a0036969

Marchionda, D. M., & Slesnick, N. (2013). Family therapy retention: An observation of first-session communication. *Journal of Marital and Family Therapy*, 39(1), 87–97. https://doi.org/10.1111/j.1752-0606.2011.00279.x

Marcus, S. M., Medoff, D., Fang, L. J., Weaver, J., Duan, N., Lucksted, A., & Dixon, L. B. (2013). Generalizability in the family-to-family education program randomized waitlist-control trial. *Psychiatric Services*, 64(8), 754–763. https://doi.org/10.1176/appi.ps.002912012

Margola, D., Donato, S., Accordini, M., Emery, R. E., & Snyder, D. K. (2017). Dyadic coping in couple therapy process: An exploratory study. *Family Process*, 57(2), 324–341. https://doi.org/10.1111/famp.12304

Marín, R. A., Christensen, A., & Atkins, D. C. (2014). Infidelity and behavioral couple therapy: Relationship outcomes over 5 years following therapy. *Couple and Family Psychology: Research and Practice*, 3(1), 1–12. https://doi.org/10.1037/cfp0000012

Marzola, E., Knatz, S., Murray, S. B., Rockwell, R., Boutelle, K., Eisler, I., & Kaye, W. H. (2015). Short-term intensive family therapy for adolescent eating disorders: 30-month outcome. *European Eating Disorders Review*, 23(3), 210–218. https://doi.org/10.1002/erv.2353

McCart, R. & Sheidow, A. J. (2016) Evidence-based psychosocial treatments for adolescents with disruptive behavior. *Journal of Clinical Child and Adolescent Psychology*, 45(5), 529–563. https://doi.org/10.1080/15374416.2016.1146990

McCrady, B. S., Epstein, E. E., Hallgren, K. A., Cook, S., & Jensen, N. K. (2016). Women with alcohol dependence: A randomized trial of couple versus individual plus couple therapy. *Psychology of Addictive Behaviors*, 30(3), 287–299. https://doi.org/10.1037/adb0000158

McFarlane, W. R. (2016). Family interventions for schizophrenia and the psychoses: A review. *Family Process*, 55(3), 460–482. https://doi.org/10.1111/famp.12235

McGoldrick, M., & Carter, B. (2001). Advances in coaching: Family therapy with one person. *Journal of Marital and Family Therapy*, 27(3), 281–300. https://doi.org/10.1111/j.1752-0606.2001.tb00325.x

McKinnon, J. M., & Greenberg, L. S. (2013). Revealing underlying vulnerable emotion in couple therapy: Impact on session and final outcome. *Journal of Family Therapy*, 35(3), 303–319. https://doi.org/10.1111/1467-6427.12015

McKinnon, J. M., & Greenberg, L. S. (2017). Vulnerable emotional expression in emotion focused couples therapy: Relating interactional processes to outcome. *Journal of Marital and Family Therapy*, 43(2), 198–212. https://doi.org/10.1111/jmft.12229

McLean, L. M., Walton, T., Rodin, G., Esplen, M. J., & Jones, J. M. (2013). A couple-based intervention for patients and caregivers facing end-stage cancer: Outcomes of a randomized controlled trial. *Psycho-Oncology*, 22(1), 28–38. https://doi.org/10.1002/pon.2046

McNeil, C. B., & Hembree-Kigin, T. L. (2010). *Parent-child interaction therapy*. Springer Science and Business Media. https://doi.org/10.1007/978-0-387-88639-8

Miklowitz, D. J. (2010). *Bipolar disorder: A family-focused treatment approach*. Guilford Press.

Miklowitz, D. J., & Chung, B. (2016). Family-focused therapy for bipolar disorder: Reflections on 30 years of research. *Family Process*, 55(3), 483–499. https://doi.org/10.1111/famp.12237

Miklowitz, D. J., O'Brien, M. P., Schlosser, D. A., Addington, J., Candan, K. A., Marshall, C., Domingues, I., Walsh, B. C., Zinberg, J. L., De Silva, S. D., Friedman-Yakoobian, M., & Cannon, T. D. (2014). Family-focused treatment for adolescents and young adults at high risk for psychosis: Results of a randomized trial. *Journal of the American Academy of Child and Adolescent Psychiatry*, 53(8), 848–858. https://doi.org/10.1016/j.jaac.2014.04.020

Miklowitz, D. J., Schneck, C. D., George, E. L., Taylor, D. O., Sugar, C. A., Birmaher, B., Kowatch, R. A., DelBello, M. P., & Alexson, D. A.

(2014). Pharmacotherapy and family-focused treatment for adolescents with bipolar I and II disorders: A 2-year randomized trial. *American Journal of Psychiatry*, 171(6), 658–667. https://doi.org/10.1176/appi.ajp.2014.13081130

Miklowitz, D. J., Schneck, C. D., Singh, M. K., Taylor, D. O., George, E. L., Cosgrove, V. E., Howe, M. E., Dickinson, L. M., Garber, J., & Chang, K. D. (2013). Early intervention for symptomatic youth at risk for bipolar disorder: A randomized trial of family-focused therapy. *Journal of the American Academy of Child and Adolescent Psychiatry*, 52(2), 121–131. https://doi.org/10.1016/j.jaac.2012.10.007

Minuchin, S. (1974). *Families and family therapy*. Harvard University Press.

Moeyaert, M., Ferron, J., Beretvas, S., & Van den Noortgate, W. (2014). From a single-level analysis to a multilevel analysis of single-subject experimental data. *Journal of School Psychology*, 52(2), 191–211. https://doi.org/10.1016/j.jsp.2013.11.003

Monson, C. M., Fredman, S. J., Macdonald, A., Pukay-Martin, N. D., Resick, P. A., & Schnurr, P. P. (2012). Effect of cognitive-behavioral couple therapy for PTSD: A randomized controlled trial. *JAMA: Journal of the American Medical Association*, 308(7), 700–709. https://doi.org/10.1001/jama.2012.9307

Montesano, A., Feixas, G., Muñoz, D., & Compañ, V. (2014). Systemic couple therapy for dysthymia. *Psychotherapy*, 51(1), 30–40. https://doi.org/10.1037/a0033814

Muñiz de la Peña, C., Friedlander, M. L., Escudero, V., & Heatherington, L. (2012). How do therapists ally with adolescents in family therapy? An examination of relational control communication in early sessions. *Journal of Counseling Psychology*, 59(3), 339–351. https://doi.org/10.1037/a0028063

Muntigl, P., & Horvath, A. O. (2016). A conversation analytic study of building and repairing the alliance in family therapy. *Journal of Family Therapy*, 38(1), 102–119. https://doi.org/10.1111/1467-6427.12109

Murray, S. B., Griffiths, S., & Le Grange, D. (2014). The role of collegial alliance in family-based treatment of adolescent anorexia nervosa: A pilot study. *International Journal of Eating Disorders*, 47(4), 418–421. https://doi.org/10.1002/eat.22230

Murray, S. B., & Le Grange, D. (2014). Family therapy for adolescent eating disorders: An update. *Current Psychiatry Reports*, 16(5), 447. https://doi.org/10.1007/s11920-014-0447-y

Murray, S. B., Thornton, C., & Wallis, A. (2012). A thorn in the side of evidence-based treatment for adolescent anorexia nervosa. *Australian and New Zealand Journal of Psychiatry*, 46(11), 1026–1028. https://doi.org/10.1177/0004867412455231

Najafi, M., Soleimani, A., Ahmadi, K., Javidi, N., Hoseni, E., & Pirjavid, F. (2015). The study of the effectiveness of couple emotionally focused therapy (EFT) on increasing marital adjustment and improving the physical and psychological health of the infertile couples. *Iranian Journal of Obstetrics, Gynecology and Infertility*, 17(133), 8–21.

Negy, C., Hammons, M.E., Reig-Ferrer, A., & Carper, T.M. (2010). The importance of addressing acculturative stress in marital therapy with Hispanic immigrant women. *International Journal of Clinical and Health Psychology*, 10(1), 5–21.

Nichols, M., & Tafuri, S. (2013). Techniques of structural family assessment: A qualitative analysis of how experts promote a systemic perspective. *Family Process*, 52(2), 207–215. https://doi.org/10.1111/famp.12025

Niño, A., Kissil, K., & Davey, M. P. (2016). Strategies used by foreign-born family therapists to connect across cultural differences: A thematic analysis. *Journal of Marital and Family Therapy*, 42(1), 123–138. https://doi.org/10.1111/jmft.12115

Norman, K. R., Silverman, W. K., & Lebowitz, E. R. (2015). Family accommodation of child and adolescent anxiety: Mechanisms, assessment, and treatment. *Journal of Child and Adolescent Psychiatric Nursing*, 28(3), 131–140. https://doi.org/10.1111/jcap.12116

Nowlan, K. M., Georgia, E. J., & Doss, B. D. (2017). Long-term effectiveness of treatment-as-usual couple therapy for military veterans. *Behavior Therapy*, 48(6), 847–859. https://doi.org/10.1016/j.beth.2017.05.007

O'Farrell, T. J., & Clements, K. (2012). Review of outcome research on marital and family therapy in treatment for alcoholism. *Journal of Marital and Family Therapy*, 38(1), 122–144. https://doi.org/10.1111/j.1752-0606.2011.00242.x

O'Farrell, T. J., Schumm, J. A., Murphy, M. M., & Muchowski, P. M. (2017). A randomized clinical trial of behavioral couples therapy versus individually-based treatment for drug-abusing women. *Journal of Consulting and Clinical Psychology*, 85(4), 309–322. https://doi.org/10.1037/ccp0000185

Omer, H., & Lebowitz, E. R. (2016). Nonviolent resistance: Helping caregivers reduce problematic behaviors in children and adolescents. *Journal of Marital and Family Therapy*, 42(4), 688–700. https://doi.org/10.1111/jmft.12168

O'Reilly, M., Kiyimba, N., & Lester, J. N. (2018). Discursive psychology as a method of analysis for the study of couple and family therapy. *Journal of Marital and Family Therapy*, 44(3), 409–425. https://doi.org/10.1111/jmft.12288

Ornstein, R. M., Lane-Loney, S. E., & Hollenbeak, C. S. (2012). Clinical outcomes of a novel, family-centered partial hospitalization program for young patients with eating disorders. *Eating and Weight Disorders – Studies on Anorexia, Bulimia and Obesity*, 17, e170–e177. https://doi.org/10.1007/BF03325344

Ougrin, D., & Asarnow, J. R. (2018). The end of family therapy for self-harm, or a new beginning? *The Lancet Psychiatry*, 5(3), 188–189. https://doi.org/10.1016/S2215-0366(18)30043-9

Owen, J., Duncan, B., Reese, R. J., Anker, M., & Sparks, J. (2014). Accounting for therapist variability in couple therapy outcomes: What really matters. *Journal of Sex and Marital Therapy*, 40(6), 488–502. https://doi.org/10.1080/0092623X.2013.772552

Owen, J., Keller, B., Shuck, B., Luebcke, B., Knopp, K., & Rhoades, G. K. (2014). An initial examination of commitment uncertainty in couple therapy. *Couple and Family Psychology: Research and Practice*, 3(4), 232–238. https://doi.org/10.1037/cfp0000030

Ozechowski, T. J. (2014). Empirical Bayes MCMC estimation for modeling treatment processes, mechanisms of change, and clinical outcomes in small samples. *Journal of Consulting and Clinical Psychology*, 82(5), 854–867. https://doi.org/10.1037/a0035889

Paradisopoulos, D., Pote, H., Fox, S., & Kaur, P. (2015). Developing a model of sustained change following multisystemic therapy: Young people's perspectives. *Journal of Family Therapy*, 37(4), 471–491. https://doi.org/10.1111/1467-6427.12070

Parker, M., Johnson, L.N., & Ketring, S.A. (2012). Adult attachment and symptom distress: A dyadic analysis of couples in therapy. *Journal of Family Therapy*, 34(3), 321–344. https://doi.org/10.1111/j.1467-6427.2012.00598.x

Patterson, G. R., & Forgatch, M. S. (1985). Therapist behavior as a determinant for client noncompliance: A paradox for the behavior modifier. *Journal of Consulting and Clinical Psychology*, 53(6), 846–851. https://doi.org/10.1037/0022-006X.53.6.846

Pepping, C. A., Halford, W. K., & Doss, B. D. (2015). Can we predict failure in couple therapy early enough to enhance outcome? *Behaviour Research and Therapy*, 65, 60–66. https://doi.org/10.1016/j.brat.2014.12.015

Peris, T. S., & Miklowitz, D. J. (2015). Parental expressed emotion and youth psychopathology: New directions for an old construct. *Child Psychiatry and Human Development*, 46(6), 863–873. https://doi.org/10.1007/s10578-014-0526-7

Peris, T. S., & Piacentini, J. (2013). Optimizing treatment for complex cases of childhood obsessive compulsive disorder: A preliminary trial. *Journal of Clinical Child and Adolescent Psychology*, 42(1), 1–8. https://doi.org/10.1080/15374416.2012.673162

Peris, T. S., Rozenman, M. S., Sugar, C. A., McCracken, J. T., & Piacentini, J. (2017). Targeted family intervention for complex cases of pediatric obsessive-compulsive disorder: A randomized controlled trial. *Journal of the American Academy of Child and Adolescent Psychiatry*, 56(12), 1034–1042. https://doi.org/10.1016/j.jaac.2017.10.008

Peris, T. S., Sugar, C.A., R. Bergman, L., Chang, S., Langley, A., & Piacentini, J. (2012). Family factors predict treatment outcome for pediatric obsessive-compulsive disorder. *Journal of Consulting and Clinical Psychology*, 80(2), 255–263. https://doi.org/10.1037/a0027084

Pettit, J. W., Silverman, W. K., Rey, Y., Marin, C., & Jaccard, J. (2016). Moving to second-stage treatments faster: Identifying mid-treatment tailoring variables for youth with anxiety disorders. *Journal of Clinical Child and Adolescent Psychology*, 45(4), 457–468. https://doi.org/10.1080/15374416.2015.1038824

Piacentini, J., Bergman, R. L., Chang, S., Langley, A., Peris, T., Wood, J. J., & McCracken, J. (2011). Controlled comparison of family cognitive behavioral therapy and psychoeducation/relaxation training for child obsessive-compulsive disorder. *Journal of the American Academy of Child and Adolescent Psychiatry*, 50(11), 1149–1161. https://doi.org/10.1016/j.jaac.2011.08.003

Pietrabissa, G., Manzoni, G. M., Rossi, A., & Castelnuovo, G. (2017). The MOTIV-HEART study: A prospective, randomized, single-blind pilot study of brief strategic therapy and motivational interviewing among cardiac rehabilitation patients. *Frontiers in Psychology, 8*, 83. https://doi.org/10.3389/fpsyg.2017.00083

Pineda, J., & Dadds, M. R. (2013). Family intervention for adolescents with suicidal behavior: A randomized controlled trial and mediation analysis. *Journal of the American Academy of Child and Adolescent Psychiatry, 52*(8), 851–862. https://doi.org/10.1016/j.jaac.2013.05.015

Pinquart, M., Oslejsek, B., & Teubert, D. (2016). Efficacy of systemic therapy on adults with mental disorders: A meta-analysis. *Psychotherapy Research, 26*(2), 241–257. https://doi.org/10.1080/10503307.2014.935830

Pinsof, W., Breunlin, D. C, Russell, W. P., & Lebow, J. (2011). Integrative problem-centered metaframeworks therapy II: Planning, conversing, and reading feedback. *Family Process, 50*(3), 314–336. https://doi.org/10.1111/j.1545-5300.2011.01361.x

Pinsof, W. M., Zinbarg, R. E., Lebow, J. L., Knobloch-Fedders, L. M., Durbin, E., Chambers, A., Latta, T., Karam, E., Goldsmith, J., & Friedman, G. (2009). Laying the foundation for progress research in family, couple, and individual therapy: The development and psychometric features of the initial systemic therapy inventory of change. *Psychotherapy Research, 19*(2), 143–156. https://doi.org/10.1080/10503300802669973

Puliafico, A. C., Comer, J. S., & Albano, A. M. (2013). Coaching approach behavior and leading by modeling: Rationale, principles, and a session-by-session description of the CALM program for early childhood anxiety. *Cognitive and Behavioral Practice, 20*(4), 517–528. https://doi.org/10.1016/j.cbpra.2012.05.002

Rapee, R. M. (2012). Family factors in the development and management of anxiety disorders. *Clinical Child and Family Psychology Review, 15*(1), 69–80. https://doi.org/10.1007/s10567-011-0106-3

Retzlaff, R. (2013). Development of family therapy and systemic therapy in Germany. *Contemporary Family Therapy, 35*(2), 349–363. https://doi.org/10.1007/s10591-013-9267-1

Retzlaff, R., von Sydow, K., Beher, S., Haun, M. W., & Schweitzer, J. (2013). The efficacy of systemic therapy for internalizing and other disorders of childhood and adolescence: A systematic review of 38 randomized trials. *Family Process, 52*(4), 619–652. https://doi.org/10.1111/famp.12041

Reynolds, S. A., Clark, S., Smith, H., Langdon, P. E., Payne, R., Bowers, G., Norton, E., & McIlwham, H. (2013). Randomized controlled trial of parent-enhanced CBT compared with individual CBT for obsessive-compulsive disorder in young people. *Journal of Consulting and Clinical Psychology, 81*(6), 1021–1026. https://doi.org/10.1037/a0034429

Rice, S., Halperin, S., Blaikie, S., Monson, K., Stefaniak, R., Phelan, M., & Davey, C. (2018). Integrating family work into the treatment of young people with severe and complex depression: A developmentally focused model. *Early Intervention in Psychiatry, 12*(2), 258–266. https://doi.org/10.1111/eip.12383

Richards, I. L., Subar, A., Touyz, S., & Rhodes, P. (2018). Augmentative approaches in family-based treatment for adolescents with restrictive eating disorders: A systematic review. *European Eating Disorders Review, 26*(2), 92–111. https://doi.org/10.1002/erv.2577

Riedinger, V., Pinquart, M., & Teubert, D. (2015). Effects of systemic therapy on mental health of children and adolescents: A meta-analysis. *Journal of Clinical Child and Adolescent Psychology, 46*(6), 880–894. https://doi.org/10.1080/15374416.2015.1063427

Rienecke, R. D., & Ebeling, M. (2019). Desired weight and treatment outcome among adolescents in a novel family-based partial hospitalization program. *Psychiatry Research, 273*, 149–152. https://doi.org/10.1016/j.psychres.2019.01.028

Rienecke, R. D., Richmond, R., & Lebow, J. (2016). Therapeutic alliance, expressed emotion, and treatment outcome for anorexia nervosa in a family-based partial hospitalization program. *Eating Behaviors, 22*, 124–128. https://doi.org/10.1016/j.eatbeh.2016.06.017

Rigter, H., Henderson, C. E., Pelc, I., Tossmann, P., Phan, O., Hendriks, V., Schaub, M., & Rowe, C. L. (2013). Multidimensional family therapy lowers the rate of cannabis dependence in adolescents: A randomised controlled trial in Western European outpatient settings. *Drug and Alcohol Dependence, 130*(1–3), 85–93. https://doi.org/10.1016/j.drugalcdep.2012.10.013

Ripoll, N. K., Villar, G. C. F., & Villar, C. E. (2012). Therapeutic change in Colombian families dealing with violence: Therapists, clients, and referring systems in conversation. *Journal of Marital and Family Therapy, 38*(Suppl 1), 168–186. https://doi.org/10.1111/j.1752-0606.2012.00297.x

Robbins, M. S., Feaster, D. J., Horigian, V., Rohrbaugh, M. J., Shoham, V., Bachrach, K., Miller, M., Burlew, K. A., Hodgkins, C., Carrion, I., Vandermark, N., Schindler, E., Werstlein, R., & Szapocznik, J. (2011). Results of a multi-site randomized trial comparing brief strategic family therapy and treatment as usual for drug using adolescents. *Journal of Consulting and Clinical Psychology, 79*(6), 713–727. https://doi.org/10.1037/a0025477

Robinson, A. L., Dolhanty, J., & Greenberg, L. (2015). Emotion-focused family therapy for eating disorders in children and adolescents. *Clinical Psychology and Psychotherapy, 22*(1), 75–82. https://doi.org/10.1002/cpp.1861

Robinson, A. L., Strahan, E., Girz, L., Wilson, A., & Boachie, A. (2013). 'I know I can help you': Parental self-efficacy predicts adolescent outcomes in family-based therapy for eating disorders. *European Eating Disorders Review, 21*(2), 108–114. https://doi.org/10.1002/erv.2180

Rohde, P., Waldron, H. B., Turner, C. W., Brody, J., & Jorgensen, J. (2014). Sequenced versus coordinated treatment for adolescents with comorbid depressive and substance use disorders. *Journal of Consulting and Clinical Psychology, 82*(2), 342–348. https://doi.org/10.1037/a0035808

Rohrbaugh, M. J. (2014). Old wine in new bottles: Decanting systemic family process research in the era of evidence based practice. *Family Process, 53*(3), 434–444. https://doi.org/10.1111/famp.12079

Rohrbaugh, M. J., Shoham, V., Skoyen, J. A., Jensen, M., & Mehl, M. R. (2012). We-talk, communal coping, and cessation success in a couple-focused intervention for health-compromised smokers. *Family Process, 51*(1), 107–121. https://doi.org/10.1111/j.1545-5300.2012.01388.x

Rosa-Alcázar, A. I., Iniesta-Sepúlveda, M., Storch, E. A., Rosa-Alcázar, Á., Parada-Navas, J. L., & Rodríguez, J. O. (2017). A preliminary study of cognitive-behavioral family-based treatment versus parent training for young children with obsessive-compulsive disorder. *Journal of Affective Disorders, 208*, 265–271. https://doi.org/10.1016/j.jad.2016.09.060

Rowe, C. L. (2012). Family therapy for drug abuse: Review and updates 2003-2010. *Journal of Marital and Family Therapy, 38*(1), 59–81. https://doi.org/10.1111/j.1752-0606.2011.00280.x

Rowe, C., Ablerga, L, Dakof, G.A., Henderson, C.E., Ungaro, R., & Liddle, H.A. (2016). Family-based HIV and sexually transmitted infection risk reduction for drug-involved young offenders: 42-month outcomes. *Family Process, 55*(2), 305–320. https://doi.org/10.1111/famp.12206

Rowe, L. S., Doss, B. D., Hsueh, A. C., Libet, J., & Mitchell, A. E. (2011). Coexisting difficulties and couple therapy outcomes: Psychopathology and intimate partner violence. *Journal of Family Psychology, 25*(3), 455–458. https://doi.org/10.1037/a0023696

Ryan, S. R., Cunningham, P. B., Foster, S. L., Brennan, P. A., Brock, R. L., & Whitmore, E. (2013). Predictors of therapist adherence and emotional bond in multisystemic therapy: Testing ethnicity as a moderator. *Journal of Child and Family Studies, 22*(1), 122–136. https://doi.org/10.1007/s10826-012-9638-5

Runfola, C. D., Kirby, J. S., Baucom, D. H., Fischer, M. S., Baucom, B. R., Matherne, C. E., Pental, K. Z., & Bulik, C. M. (2018). A pilot open trial of UNITE-BED: A couple-based intervention for binge-eating disorder. *International Journal of Eating Disorders, 51*(9), 1107–1112. https://doi.org/10.1002/eat.22919

Sadeh-Sharvit, S., Arnow, K. D., Osipov, L., Lock, J. D., Jo, B., Pajarito, S., Brandt, H., Dodge, E., Halmi, K. A., Johnson, C., Kaye, W., Wilfley, D., & Agras, W. S. (2018). Are parental self-efficacy and family flexibility mediators of treatment for anorexia nervosa? *International Journal of Eating Disorders, 51*(3), 275–280. https://doi.org/10.1002/eat.22826

Sandler, I., Gunn, H., Mazza, G., Tein, J. Y., Wolchik, S., Kim, H., Ayers, T., & Porter, M. (2018). Three perspectives on mental health problems of young adults and their parents at a 15-year follow-up of the family bereavement program. *Journal of Consulting and Clinical Psychology, 86*(10), 845–855. https://doi.org/10.1037/ccp0000327

Santens, T., Levy, S. A., Diamond, G. S., Braet, C., Vyvey, M., Heylboeck, E., & Bosmans, G. (2017). Exploring acceptability and feasibility of evidence-based practice in child welfare settings: A pilot study with attachment-based family therapy. *Psychologica Belgica, 57*(1), 43–58. https://doi.org/10.5334/pb.338

Sayegh, C. S., Hall-Clark, B. N., McDaniel, D. D., Halliday-Boykins, C. A., Cunningham, P. B. & Huey Jr., S. J. (2019). A preliminary investigation of ethnic differences in resistance in Multisystemic Therapy. *Journal of*

Clinical Child and Adolescent Psychology, 48(Suppl 1), S13–S23. https://doi.org/10.1080/15374416.2016.1157754

Sawyer, A. M., & Borduin, C. M. (2011). Effects of multisystemic therapy through midlife: A 21.9-year follow-up to a randomized clinical trial with serious and violent juvenile offenders. *Journal of Consulting and Clinical Psychology, 79*(5), 643–652. https://doi.org/10.1037/a0024862

Schumm, J. A., Monson, C. M., O'Farrell, T. J., Gustin, N. G., & Chard, K. M. (2015). Couple treatment for alcohol use disorder and posttraumatic stress disorder: Pilot results from US military veterans and their partners. *Journal of Traumatic Stress, 28*(3), 247–252. https://doi.org/10.1002/jts.22007

Schumm, J. A., O'Farrell, T. J., Kahler, C. W., Murphy, M. M., & Muchowski, P. (2014). A randomized clinical trial of behavioral couples therapy versus individually based treatment for women with alcohol dependence. *Journal of Consulting and Clinical Psychology, 82*(6), 993–1005. https://doi.org/10.1037/a0037497

Seikkula, J., Aaltonen, J., Kalla, O., Saarinen, P., & & Tolvanen, A. (2013). Couple therapy for depression in a naturalistic setting in Finland: A 2-year randomized trial. *Journal of Family Therapy, 35*(3), 281–302. https://doi.org/10.1111/j.1467-6427.2012.00592.x

Sexton, T. L., & Datchi, C. (2014). The development and evolution of family therapy research: Its impact on practice, current status, and future directions. *Family Process, 53*(3), 415–433. https://doi.org/10.1111/famp.12084

Sexton, T. L., Datchi-Phillips, C., Evans, L. E., LaFollette, J., & Wright, L. (2013). The effectiveness of couple and family therapy interventions. In M. Lambert (Ed.), *Bergin and Garfield's handbook of psychotherapy and behavior change* (6th ed., pp. 587–640). Wiley.

Sexton, T., Gordon, K. C., Gurman, A., Lebow, J., Holtzworth-Munroe, A. M. Y., & Johnson, S. (2011). Guidelines for classifying evidence-based treatments in couple and family therapy. *Family Process, 50*(3), 377–392. https://doi.org/10.1111/j.1545-5300.2011.01363.x

Sexton, T., & Turner, C. W. (2011). The effectiveness of functional family therapy for youth with behavioral problems in a community practice setting. *Couple and Family Psychology: Research and Practice, 1*(S), 3–15. https://doi.org/10.1037/2160-4096.1.S.3

Shadish, W. R., & Baldwin, S. A. (2003). Meta-analysis of MFT interventions. *Journal of Marital and Family Therapy, 29*(4), 547–570. https://doi.org/10.1111/j.1752-0606.2003.tb01694.x

Shadish, W. R., Ragsdale, K., Glaser, R. R., & Montgomery, L. M. (1995). The efficacy and effectiveness of marital and family therapy: A perspective from meta-analysis. *Journal of Marital and Family Therapy, 21*(4), 345–360. https://doi.org/10.1111/j.1752-0606.1995.tb00170.x

Sharif, F., Shaygan, M., & Mani, A. (2012). Effect of a psycho-educational intervention for family members on caregiver burdens and psychiatric symptoms in patients with schizophrenia in Shiraz, Iran. *BMC Psychiatry, 12*(1), 1–9.

Sheehan, A. S., & Friedlander, M. L. (2015). Therapeutic alliance and retention in brief strategic family therapy: A mixed-methods study. *Journal of Marital and Family Therapy, 41*(4), 415–427. https://doi.org/10.1111/jmft.12113

Shnaider, P., Pukay-Martin, N. D., Sharma, S., Jenzer, T., Fredman, S. J., Macdonald, A., & Monson, C. M. (2015). A preliminary examination of the effects of pretreatment relationship satisfaction on treatment outcomes in cognitive-behavioral conjoint therapy for PTSD. *Couple and Family Psychology: Research and Practice, 4*(4), 229–238. https://doi.org/10.1037/cfp0000050

Shoham, V., & Rohrbaugh, M. J. (2010). Mediators and moderators of brief strategic family therapy (BSFT) for adolescent drug use: Final report. National Institute on Drug Abuse, award 1-RO1- DA117539-01

Shpigel, M. & Diamond, G.M. (2014). Good versus poor therapeutic alliances with non- accepting parents of same-sex oriented adolescents and young adults: A qualitative study. *Psychotherapy Research, 24*(3), 376–391. https://doi.org/10.1080/10503307.2013.856043

Shpigel, M., Diamond, G. M., & Diamond, G. S. (2012). Changes in parenting behaviors in attachment-based family therapy. *Journal of Marital and Family Therapy, 38*(Suppl 1), 271–283. https://doi.org/10.1111/j.1752-0606.2012.00295.x

Silverman, W. K., Pettit, J. W., & Lebowitz, E. R. (2016). Stepping toward making less more for concerning anxiety in children and adolescents. *Clinical*

Psychology: Science and Practice, 23(3), 234–238. https://doi.org/10.1111/cpsp.12158

Skowron, E. A. (2000). The role of differentiation of self in marital adjustment. *Journal of Counseling Psychology, 47*(2), 229–237. https://doi.org/10.1037/0022-0167.47.2.229

Sluzki, C. E. (1992). Transformations: A blueprint for narrative changes in therapy. *Family Process, 31*(3), 217–230. https://doi.org/10.1111/j.1545-5300.1992.00217.x

Smith, A., & Cook-Cottone, C. (2011). A review of family therapy as an effective intervention for anorexia nervosa in adolescents. *Journal of Clinical Psychology in Medical Settings, 18*(4), 323–334. https://doi.org/10.1007/s10880-011-9262-3

Smith, A. M., Flannery-Schroeder, E. C., Gorman, K. S., & Cook, N. (2014). Parent cognitive-behavioral intervention for the treatment of childhood anxiety disorders: A pilot study. *Behaviour Research and Therapy, 61*, 156–161. https://doi.org/10.1016/j.brat.2014.08.010

Snyder, D. K., & Halford, W. K. (2012). Evidence-based couple therapy: Current status and future directions. *Journal of Family Therapy, 34*(3), 229–249. https://doi.org/10.1111/j.1467-6427.2012.00599.x

Sotero, L., Cunha, D., Da Silva, J. T., Escudero, V., & Relvas, A. P. (2018). Building alliances with (in)voluntary clients: A study focused on therapists' observable behaviors. *Family Process, 56*(4), 819–834. https://doi.org/10.1111/famp.12265

Sotero, L., Major, S., Escudero, V., & Relvas, A. P. (2014). The therapeutic alliance with involuntary clients: How does it work? *Journal of Family Therapy, 38*(1), 36–58. https://doi.org/10.1111/1467-6427.12046

Soltani, M., Shairi, M. R., Roshan, R., & Rahimi, C. R. (2014). The impact of emotionally focused therapy on emotional distress in infertile couples. *International Journal of Fertility and Sterility, 7*(4), 337–344.

Sprenkle, D. H. (2012). Intervention research in couple and family therapy: A methodological and substantive review and an introduction to the special issue. *Journal of Marital and Family Therapy, 38*(1), 3–29. https://doi.org/10.1111/j.1752-0606.2011.00271.x

Sprenkle, D. H., Davis, S. D., & Lebow, J. L. (2009). *Common factors in couple and family therapy: The overlooked foundation for effective practice.* Guilford Press.

Steinmann, R., Gat, I., Nir-Gottlieb, O., Shahar, B., & Diamond, G.M. (2017). Attachment-based family therapy and emotion-focused therapy for unresolved anger: Qualitative analysis of treatment outcome and change processes. *Psychotherapy, 54*(3), 281–291. https://doi.org/10.1037/pst0000116

Stith, S. M., McCollum, E. E., Amanor-Boadu, Y., & Smith, D. (2012). Systemic perspectives on intimate partner violence treatment. *Journal of Marital and Family Therapy, 38*(1), 220–240. https://doi.org/10.1111/j.1752-0606.2011.00245.x

Sukhodolsky, D. G., Gorman, B. S., Scahill, L., Findley, D., & McGuire, J. (2013). Exposure and response prevention with or without parent management training for children with obsessive-compulsive disorder complicated by disruptive behavior: A multiple-baseline across-responses design study. *Journal of Anxiety Disorders, 27*(3), 298–305. https://doi.org/10.1016/j.janxdis.2013.01.005

Sundet, R. (2011). Collaboration: Family and therapist perspectives of helpful therapy. *Journal of Marital and Family Therapy, 37*(2), 236–249. https://doi.org/10.1111/j.1752-0606.2009.00157.x

Swank, L. E., & Wittenborn, A. K. (2013). Repairing alliance ruptures in emotionally focused couple therapy: A preliminary task analysis. *American Journal of Family Therapy, 41*(5), 389–402. https://doi.org/10.1080/01926187.2012.726595

Szapocznik, J., Muir, J. A., Duff, J. H., Schwartz, S. J., & Brown, C. H. (2015). Brief strategic family therapy: Implementing evidence-based models in community settings. *Psychotherapy Research, 25*(1), 121–133. https://doi.org/10.1080/10503307.2013.856044

Szapocznik, J., Schwartz, S. J., Muir, J. A., & Brown, C. H. (2012). Brief strategic family therapy: An intervention to reduce adolescent risk behavior. *Couple and Family Psychology: Research and Practice, 1*(2), 134–145. https://doi.org/10.1037/a0029002

Thirlwall, K., Cooper, P., & Creswell, C. (2017). Guided parent-delivered cognitive behavioral therapy for childhood anxiety: Predictors of treatment response. *Journal of Anxiety Disorders, 45*, 43–48. https://doi.org/10.1016/j.janxdis.2016.11.003

Thirlwall, K., Cooper, P. J., Karalus, J., Voysey, M., Willetts, L., & Creswell, C. (2013). Treatment of child anxiety disorders via guided parent-delivered cognitive-behavioural therapy: Randomised controlled trial. *The British Journal of Psychiatry*, *203*(6), 436–444. https://doi.org/10.1192/bjp.bp.113.126698

Thompson-Hollands, J., Abramovitch, A., Tompson, M. C., & Barlow, D. H. (2015). A randomized clinical trial of a brief family intervention to reduce accommodation in obsessive-compulsive disorder: A preliminary study. *Behavior Therapy*, *46*(2), 218–229. https://doi.org/10.1016/j.beth.2014.11.001

Thompson-Hollands, J., Edson, A., Tompson, M. C., & Comer, J. S. (2014). Family involvement in the psychological treatment of obsessive-compulsive disorder: A meta-analysis. *Journal of Family Psychology*, *28*(3), 287–298. https://doi.org/10.1037/a0036709

Thulin, U., Svirsky, L., Serlachius, E., Andersson, G., & Öst, L. G. (2014). The effect of parent involvement in the treatment of anxiety disorders in children: A meta-analysis. *Cognitive Behaviour Therapy*, *43*, 185–200. https://doi.org/10.1080/16506073.2014.923928

Tighe, A., Pistrang, N., Casdagli, L., Baruch, G., & Butler, S. (2012). Multisystemic therapy for young offenders: Families' experiences of therapeutic processes and outcomes. *Journal of Family Psychology*, *26*(2), 187–197. https://doi.org/10.1037/a0027120

Treasure, J., & Russell, G. (2011). The case for early intervention in anorexia nervosa: Theoretical exploration of maintaining factors. *The British Journal of Psychiatry*, *199*(1), 5–7. https://doi.org/10.1192/bjp.bp.110.087585

Tsvieli, N., & Diamond, G. M. (2018). Therapist interventions and emotional processing in attachment-based family therapy for unresolved anger. *Psychotherapy*, *55*(3), 289–297. https://doi.org/10.1037/pst0000158

van der Pol, T. M., Hoeve, M., Noom, M. J., Stams, G. J. J., Doreleijers, T. A., van Domburgh, L., & Vermeiren, R. R. (2017). Research review: The effectiveness of multidimensional family therapy in treating adolescents with multiple behavior problems-A meta-analysis. *Journal of Child Psychology and Psychiatry*, *58*(5), 532–545. https://doi.org/10.1111/jcpp.12685

van der Stouwe, T., Asscher, J. J., Stams, G. J. J., Deković, M., & van der Laan, P. H. (2014). The effectiveness of multisystemic therapy (MST): A meta-analysis. *Clinical Psychology Review*, *34*(6), 468–481. https://doi.org/10.1016/j.cpr.2014.06.006

von Sydow, K., Beher, S., Schweitzer, J., & Retzlaff, R. (2010). The efficacy of systemic therapy with adult patients: A meta-content analysis of 38 randomized controlled trials. *Family Process*, *49*(4), 457–485. https://doi.org/10.1111/j.1545-5300.2010.01334.x

von Sydow, K., Retzlaff, R., Beher, S., Haun, M. W., & Schweitzer, J. (2013). The efficacy of systemic therapy for childhood and adolescent externalizing disorders: A systematic review of 47 RCTs. *Family Process*, *52*(4), 576–618. https://doi.org/10.1111/famp.12047

Valladares Kahn, S., Epstein, N. B., & Kivlighan Jr, D. M. (2015). Couple therapy for partner aggression: Effects on individual and relational well-being. *Journal of Couple and Relationship Therapy*, *14*(2), 95–115. https://doi.org/10.1080/15332691.2014.966879

von Bertalanffy, L. (1950). The theory of open systems in physics and biology. *Science*, *111*(2872), 23–29. https://doi.org/10.1126/science.111.2872.23

Vromans, L. P., & Schweitzer, R. D. (2011). Narrative therapy for adults with major depressive disorder: Improved symptom and interpersonal outcomes. *Psychotherapy Research*, *21*(1), 4–15. https://doi.org/10.1080/10503301003591792

Wagner, D. V., Borduin, C. M., Sawyer, A. M., & Dopp, A. R. (2014). Long-term prevention of criminality in siblings of serious and violent juvenile offenders: A 25-year follow-up to a randomized clinical trial of multisystemic therapy. *Journal of Consulting and Clinical Psychology*, *82*(3), 492–499. https://doi.org/10.1037/a0035624

Watzlawick, W., Weakland, J. H., & Fisch, R. (1974). *Change: Principles of problem formation and problem resolution*. W. W. Norton.

Wei, C., & Kendall, P. C. (2014). Parental involvement: Contribution to childhood anxiety and its treatment. *Clinical Child and Family Psychology Review*, *17*(4), 319–339. https://doi.org/10.1007/s10567-014-0170-6

Weisman de Mamani, A., Weintraub, M. J., Gurak, K., & Maura, J. (2014). A randomized clinical trial to test the efficacy of a family-focused, culturally informed therapy for schizophrenia. *Journal of Family Psychology*, *28*(6), 800–810. https://doi.org/10.1037/fam0000021

Weissman, N., Batten, S. V., Rheem, K. D., Wiebe, S. A., Pasillas, R. M., Potts, W., Barone, M., Brown, C.H., & Dixon, L. B. (2017). The effectiveness of emotionally focused couples therapy with veterans with PTSD: A pilot study. *Journal of Couple and Relationship Therapy*, *17*(1), 25–41. https://doi.org/10.1080/15332691.2017.1285261

Welmers-van de Poll, M. J., Roest, J. J., Van der Stouwe, T., Van den Akker, A. L., Stams, G. J. J. M., Escudero, V., Overbeek, G. J., & De Swart, J. J. W. (2018). Alliance and treatment outcome in family-involved treatment for youth problems: A three-level meta-analysis. *Clinical Child and Family Psychology Review*, *21*(2), 146–170. https://doi.org/10.1007/s10567-017-0249-y

Wiebe, S. A., Johnson, S. M., Burgess Moser, M., Dalgleish, T. L., & Tasca, G. A. (2016). Predicting follow-up outcomes in emotionally focused couple therapy: The role of change in trust, relationship-specific attachment, and emotional engagement. *Journal of Marital and Family Therapy*, *43*(2), 213–226. https://doi.org/10.1111/jmft.12199

Wiebe, S. A., Johnson, S. M., Lafontaine, M. F., Burgess Moser, M., Dalgleish, T. L., & Tasca, G. A. (2017). Two-year follow-up outcomes in emotionally focused couple therapy: An investigation of relationship satisfaction and attachment trajectories. *Journal of Marital and Family Therapy*, *43*(2), 227–244. https://doi.org/10.1111/jmft.12206

Wittenborn, A. K., Dolbin-MacNab, M. L., Keiley, M. K. (2013). Dyadic research in marriage and family therapy: Methodological considerations. *Journal of Marital and Family Therapy*, *39*(1), 5–16. https://doi.org/10.1111/j.1752-0606.2012.00306.x

Wittenborn, A. K., Liu, T., Ridenour, T. A., Lachmar, E. M., Mitchell, E. A., & Seedall, R. B. (2019). Randomized controlled trial of emotionally focused couple therapy compared to treatment as usual for depression: Outcomes and mechanisms of change. *Journal of Marital and Family Therapy*, *45*(3), 395–409. https://doi.org/10.1111/jmft.12350

Woldarsky Meneses, C., & Greenberg, L. S. (2014). Interpersonal forgiveness in emotion-focused couples' therapy: Relating process to outcome. *Journal of Marital and Family Therapy*, *40*(1), 49–67. https://doi.org/10.1111/j.1752-0606.2012.00330.x

Wood, J. J., Piacentini, J. C., Southam-Gerow, M., Chu, B. C., & Sigman, M. (2006). Family cognitive behavioral therapy for child anxiety disorders. *Journal of the American Academy of Child and Adolescent Psychiatry*, *45*(3), 314–321. https://doi.org/10.1097/01.chi.0000196425.88341.b0

Woolley, S. R., Wampler, K. S., & Davis, S. D. (2012). Enactments in couple therapy: Identifying therapist interventions associated with positive change. *Journal of Family Therapy*, *34*(3), 284–305. https://doi.org/10.1111/j.1467-6427.2011.00577.x

Yon, K., Malik, R., Mandin, P., & Midgley, N. (2017). Challenging core cultural beliefs and maintaining the therapeutic alliance: A qualitative study. *Journal of Family Therapy*, *40*(2), 180–200. https://doi.org/10.1111/1467-6427.12158

Zhang, J., & Slesnick, N. (2018). The effects of a family systems intervention on co-occurring internalizing and externalizing behaviors of children with substance abusing mothers: A latent transition analysis. *Journal of Marital and Family Therapy*, *44*(4), 687–701. https://doi.org/10.1111/jmft.12277

Zuccarini, D., Johnson, S. M., Dalgleish, T. L., & Makinen, J. A. (2013). Forgiveness and reconciliation in emotionally focused therapy for couples: The client change process and therapist interventions. *Journal of Marital and Family Therapy*, *39*(2), 148–162. https://doi.org/10.1111/j.1752-0606.2012.00287.x

CHAPTER 17

EFFICACY OF SMALL GROUP TREATMENTS: FOUNDATION FOR EVIDENCE-BASED PRACTICE

GARY M BURLINGAME AND BERNHARD STRAUSS

Abstract

In this third update chapter reviewing the small group treatment literature, we first summarize our conceptualizations and then review the evidence for efficacy and effectiveness of small group treatments. We start with comparisons of group versus individual, studies using group as primary (mood disorders, anxiety disorders) and studies, where group served as an adjunct to other treatments (i.e., eating disorders, substance related disorders, posttraumatic stress disorders). Applications of group within medical settings (breast cancer and pain) and in populations with severe mental illnesses (schizophrenia, personality disorders) follow. The specific progress since our last chapter relates to the fact that 10 meta-analyses provide the basis for this review summarizing 329 randomized clinical trials comprising almost 27,000 patients. Cohesion and alliance as process measures and predictors of outcome are described with recent meta-analytic support. Research on attachment issues in group psychotherapy and the use of online groups are presented as promising developments. With a summary of research related to measurement-based care and feedback, the chapter ends with conclusions and recommendations how to become an evidence-based group practitioner.

OVERVIEW

GENERAL INTRODUCTION TO LITERATURE OF SMALL GROUP TREATMENTS

This is our third update chapter in the Bergin and Garfield *Handbook* that reviews the small group treatment literature and a few notable events have taken place since our last chapter was published that have changed the zeitgeist. Perhaps the most significant event in North America was that group psychology and group psychotherapy was recognized as a specialty by the American Psychological Association (APA) in 2018. Recognized specialties are "defined areas of psychological practice which requires advanced knowledge and skills acquired through an organized sequence of education and training" (APA, 2007). In short, the empirical, theoretical, and clinical literature on small group treatments has now been evaluated by independent scholars and deemed to be sufficiently mature to support it as an independent specialty. Group treatment joins both established (clinical psychology, counseling psychology) and more recent (sleep) specialties recognized by APA and those of us that identify with this specialty feel a greater pressure to carefully document evidence-based practice guidelines that can guide both clinical practice and training programs. Indeed, information from our last chapter played a significant role in the evidentiary base of the APA specialty application and our previous chapter is now reproduced on the American Group Psychotherapy Association (AGPA) evidence-based practice website along with brief summaries of group treatment efficacy for nine common psychiatric disorders (APA, 2007).

A major aim in our last two versions of this chapter (Burlingame et al., 2004, 2013) was to provide the best evidence-based recommendations identifying effective group protocols designed to treat specific patient populations. The majority of contemporary group treatments are guided by these group protocols and many have been submitted to rigorous empirical scrutiny. The typical research study identifies a particular disorder and then articulates specific group interventions that are proposed to lead to desired effects (e.g., reduction in depression). The bulk of our past chapters summarized evidence on group interventions for specific patient populations leading to over 650 scholarly paper citations in Google Scholar; most cite our evidenced-based recommendations. Given this citation pattern we continue to focus heavily on the outcomes of group treatment for psychiatric disorders.

We found the same investigator pattern that we reported on in our 2013 chapter. More specifically, the majority of the randomized clinical trials (RCTs) summarized in the current chapter appear to be conducted by investigators who are specialists in either a particular psychiatric or medical disorder (e.g., depression) or theoretical orientation (cognitive-behavioral therapy; CBT) with the research being an extension of one or both of these identities. Stated differently, being a group clinician or specialist in group dynamics does not seem to be a core part of the identity of the investigators producing recent group treatment research. This creates an interesting and troubling disconnect from group research that was produced by investigators who held group treatment as a major part of their professional identity summarized in our 2004 chapter. More specifically, earlier group researchers were more conversant with the group dynamic and process literature and built these properties into their group protocols. Interestingly, as the rigor of the group treatment outcome research increases (e.g., manualized protocols, powered studies, fidelity checks, random assignment, etc.), we know less about group dynamics and processes.

In our first chapter (2004), we gave attention to well-known group properties organized by group, interpersonal, leader, and individual member domains that had been programmatically studied both in North American and European labs. We highlighted singular studies that had explored group development, Yalom's therapeutic factors and members' interpersonal styles that account for treatment outcome variance not explained by the specific protocol guiding treatment. We also made measurement recommendations for common belonging and acceptance factors (e.g., cohesion and climate) as well as common interpersonal work factors (e.g., group and member working alliance). Our 2013 chapter provided a model of evidence-based group structure (anatomy) and processes (physiology) that predict patient outcomes. We based it on Berne's analogy "that knowledge of group dynamics for a group leader is as essential as knowledge of physiology for a physian. Living organisms are composed of anatomical and physiological functions" (Burlingame et. al., 2013; p. 667). For instance, we reviewed evidence-based group dynamic factors under the control of a leader (composition, member selection, pregroup preparation, and early group structure) as well as emergent factors (development, subgroups and norms) that predicted successful group treatment. We also reviewed evidence-based group treatment processes and mechansims of change (interpersonal feedback, self-disclosure, cohesion-climate, and therapeutic factors) that predict member improvement. We ended with a high-level review of AGPA's 10 practice guidelines to provide an overall structure for group clinicians. We urge both researchers and clinicians alike to become familiar with this part of the evidence-based group literature which is relevant for today's small group treatments.

The state of the current literature and our own appreciation of the group dynamic literature led us to continue to include empirical research on these topics. However, rather than repeat group dynamic and process models and measures we've already presented, we elected to highlight promising developments that tap patient characteristics, selected group processes and the use of measures discussed in previous chapters that are now being used to impact group treatment in real-time. We end with a discussion of evidence-based group practitioner characteristics using the most recent advances in clinical and empirical literature: *practice-based group treatment*.

CONCEPTUALIZING SMALL GROUP TREATMENTS

In past chapters we used a model that identified the main sources that empirically explain patient improvement in group treatment. This model has spawned new research and evidence-based summaries regarding five sources that explain patient improvement in small group treatment, so we briefly review its main features. The first source – *formal change theory* – captures the mechanisms of change in a group protocol and overlaps with the theoretical orientation guiding psychotherapy groups (e.g., psychodynamic, interpersonal, cognitive-behavioral, humanistic). However, there is considerable group treatment research that assesses the effectiveness of support, skill training, and psycho-educational groups that are independent of theoretical orientation. The second source – *principles of small group process*—reflects group mechanisms of change that have been empirically linked to outcome. A key variable under this source is the multiperson therapeutic environment of the group format, which has been shown to be a reliable and *independent* predictor of improvement beyond the formal change theory guiding treatment. A third source – the *patient* – includes characteristics related to the disorder being treated (e.g., pretreatment severity of depressive symptoms) and *group format* characteristics that predict improvement or deterioration (e.g., attachment style, maturity of interpersonal relations). The fourth source – *group structural factors* – reflects logistical features of the group such as dose (number and length of sessions), intensity of sessions (weekly, monthly, and

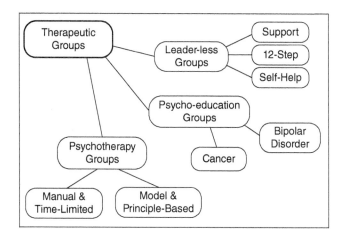

FIGURE 17.1 Conceptual framework for organizing group treatments.

bimonthly), group size, setting, and cultural factors that have been linked to treatment outcome. The final source – *group leader* – is responsible for integrating and balancing the preceding four sources. In short, the group format comprises multiple interactive sources of change, adding a higher level of complexity than one finds in the individual treatment literature.

Type of small group treatment adds another level of complexity to understanding treatment outcome and group process research. To simplify this complexity, we offer Figure 17.1 as a conceptual framework to organize the major types of therapeutic groups appearing in the treatment literature. It is a modified version of Barlow's (2013) group typology found in *Specialty Competencies in Group Psychology*. Therapeutic group treatments can be divided into three major types – *leaderless, psycho-educational,* and *psychotherapy*. The primary goal of *leaderless groups* is to support individuals suffering from a common challenge and these groups can be organized into two overlapping subtypes – self-help or mutual support and 12-step. The ubiquity of support groups is demonstrated by a simple online search that reveals an endless supply of face-to-face and online groups that address a myriad of life challenges (medical illness, parenting) and interests. In fact, the US government sponsors a health finder website (https://healthfinder.gov/FindServices/SearchContext.aspx?topic = 833) to identify local support groups that have appeared for a similar purpose (www.meetup.com). Given the ubiquity of these group treatments, it's unfortunate that they've received little empirical attention unless used as a comparison condition for active group treatment. 12-step groups are the best-known leaderless group treatments originating with alcohol anonymous – AA, formed in 1935. They follow a structured session format that is often absent in support groups and have received ample empirical attention as a stand-alone treatment for addictive disorders (e.g., Bekkering et al., 2016; McKellar et al., 2009). Given our focus on leader-led group treatments, research on support and 12-step groups is only included when contrasted with active leader-led group treatment (e.g., Lo Coco et al., 2019).

Psycho-education groups are the second major type of therapeutic group formats, and their primary goal is to provide information and skill training to help patients manage their illness. These group treatments operate in a similar manner to

disease management treatment protocols in medicine for chronic medical conditions. For example, in diabetes a better understanding of the physiological properties associated with managing blood sugar (A1C versus real-time glucose level) and behavioral changes (diet and exercise) is associated with better outcomes. The same principles are true for psycho-educational group treatments that are designed to treat chronic mental health conditions (e.g., bipolar and schizophrenia) by disseminating disease management and lifestyle information as well as training in behavioral skills. *Psychotherapy* groups are the final type and these are divided into two subtypes: manualized and model-guided groups. Manualized group treatments are typically time-limited upon a specific theoretical orientation (e.g., cognitive behavioral therapy, or CBT) having both whole-group and session-by-session goals. Treatment fidelity ratings are easier to obtain with these group treatments since there are clear session goals and interventions. Model-based group treatments are less structured than manualized protocols with principal-based interventions (e.g., acceptance and commitment therapy, or ACT) that are tailored to individual members as well as the developmental stage of the group-as-whole. As will become evident, the pattern of group type use varies by patient population and, in some cases, there is a sufficient number of studies to assess for differential outcomes.

CHAPTER ORGANIZATION AND REVIEW APPROACH

In our last review, we included studies from virtually every continent and the same is true for this update. The typical group format continues to be time-limited (10 to 20 sessions) and of a diagnostically homogenous composition. The efficacy literature is presented first and remains the bulk of this chapter. The studies reviewed in the efficacy section were located through a computer search of PsycInfo, MEDLINE, Web of Science, and Cochrane Central Register of Controlled Trials (CENTRAL) using the search terms group psychotherapy, intervention, counseling, treatment, setting, format, dynamics, and therapy producing approximately 49,000 unduplicated abstracts. We then eliminated abstracts that had been previously reviewed in 11 meta-analyses produced by our collaborative team effort (see below); this led to 1860 unique papers. Each was screened for an in-depth review using the following criteria: published between January 2010 and October 2018; group therapy was the primary mode of intervention; clinical populations; randomized clinical trials (RCTs) or effectiveness studies; and methodologically rigorous. Topics with sufficient research (> 5 studies) were supplemented with meta-analytic findings when available.

We've added new material to our group efficacy section based on conclusions from our last chapter. More specifically, in our last chapter we noted a large increase in the number and quality of studies leading to greater confidence in our evidence-based treatment recommendations. However, we also realized the limitations of our narrative review conclusions so we undertook a series of meta-analyses of small group treatment outcome literature by psychiatric disorder including only rigorous randomized clinical trials – RCTs. These meta-analyses used a common code book to enable comparisons across disorders and we registered our meta-analysis procedure (registration ID: CRD42013004419). Our goal of limiting studies to RCTs was to provide a quantitative index of efficacy of small group treatments by psychiatric disorder. In addition to team members from our longstanding US and German cooperation (Burlingame & Strauss labs), we also enlisted collaborators from Canada, Italy, and the United States who had particular expertise or interest in a specific psychiatric disorder. This cooperation led to 11 meta-analyses: 5 focusing on anxiety (social anxiety, Barkowski et al., 2016; panic, Schwartze et al., 2017; obsessive-compulsive, Schwartze et al., 2016; post-traumatic stress, Schwartze et al., 2019; and combined Barkowski et al., 2020); 2 focusing on serious mental illness (schizophrenia, Burlingame et al., 2020; borderline personality disorder, McLaughlin et al., 2019); 1 each focusing on eating disorders (Grenon et al., 2017), substance use disorders (Lo Coco et al., 2019), mood disorders (Janis et al., 2021), and investigations comparing individual and group treatment in the same study (Burlingame et al., 2016). In a previous chapter, we presented the results from our first collaborative meta-analysis focusing on inpatient group treatment (Kösters et al., 2006) showing positive effects, despite some heterogeneity. Most of these meta-analyses began by summarizing treatment recommendations using well-known international practice guidelines. They concluded by comparing meta-analytic findings with practice guideline recommendations and, where appropriate, pointed out agreement and possible practice guideline changes.

Finally, in past chapters we've noted intriguing moderators of group outcome, but these were typically based on a single study. To provide a more robust test of moderators from past chapters, each meta-analysis tested a common set of moderators using the following domains: study (year and country of publication, language, attrition, Cochrane Risk of Bias), leader (professional vs. student, level of training, single vs. co-led), patients (recruited vs. referred, age, percent of female), groups (patients per group, number of sessions, session length, composition, process assessed), treatment (theoretical orientation, total dose in minutes, setting, manualized, fidelity checks). Significant moderators identified by each meta-analysis are discussed as they relate to specific clinical populations.

Each efficacy section of the current chapter begins with a brief summary of the conclusions from our last chapter, clinical considerations and practice guideline recommendations from the American Psychiatric Association and National Institute for Health and Care Excellence (NICE) for each disorder. Next, efficacy findings from the aforementioned meta-analyses (including moderators) along with findings from recent studies published since the meta-analysis are summarized. Using this cumulative empirical foundation, treatment recommendation and possible revisions to extant practice guidelines are offered. As in our last chapter, small group efficacy findings are organized by five sections: (a) studies comparing the differential efficacy of the group versus individual formats; (b) disorders where group is the *primary* or sole treatment (major depression,

bipolar, social phobia, panic, and obsessive compulsive); (c) disorders where group is an adjunctive to other treatments (eating disorders, substance and posttraumatic stress disorders); (d) groups offered in hospital/medical settings (cancer and pain/somatoform); (e) groups for severe mental illness (schizophrenia and personality disorders). We end this section with general conclusions around efficacy.

The second major section describes promising developments in the literature including both treatment (e.g., online groups) and patient characteristics (attachment style) reflecting limited research on member characteristics since our 2013 chapter. However, each meta-analysis tested 17 moderators including patient, group, treatment and leader characteristics and significant interactions are noted. We then summarize findings from a meta-analysis on the most studied group process variable (cohesion) and its predictive relationship to treatment outcome. A major shift has occurred since our last chapter when it comes to measure-informed treatment. Several randomized clinical trials have now been conducted using measures we reviewed in past chapters and findings from these are integrated along with clinical and research recommendations. We end with an update on the framework from our last chapter – practice-based group treatment (PBGT) – to illustrate how one might integrate the findings from the chapter to empirically guide group practice.

EVIDENCE FOR EFFICACY

Our primary goal in this section is to offer evidence-based recommendations for clinical practice using randomized clinical trials that control for a host of confounds evident in effectiveness studies. In doing so, we summarize the aggregate Hedges's g in three tables that appear later in this chapter (Tables 17.1, 17.2, and 17.5) from each of the aforementioned meta-analyses. Each meta-analysis focused on group treatment protocols designed to treat patients diagnosed with a specific diagnosis; however, studies typically assessed change with several outcome measures. In order to arrive at more clinically meaningful efficacy conclusions, we relied on an approach used in our last chapter where study outcomes were categorized by the targeted effects. More specifically, each meta-analysis classified all study measures into one of two categories: primary and secondary outcomes. For example, in the depression meta-analysis, measures that assessed depressive symptoms were categorized as primary outcomes and those assessing other constructs such as wellbeing, quality of life and anxiety were classified as secondary. When possible, we used the investigator's classification of outcomes, but when these were unavailable, independent ratings using an interrater reliability criterion (commonly $r = .80$) were employed. In general, each meta-analysis provided three efficacy estimates (Hedges's g) using: (a) all outcome measures, that were then disaggregated into (b) primary or disorder targeted outcomes and (c) secondary outcome measures.

The studies listed in Tables 17.1, 17.2, and 17.5 use a common organization, which we set out here in advance and can be used as a reference point when each table is reported. The first column identifies each meta-analysis with a number connected to a citation at the bottom of each table. The next column identifies the focus of the meta-analysis, which is typically a specific psychiatric disorder. This is followed by the number of studies (comparisons) and total sample size for the intervention and control comparisons. We then report on only the primary outcomes assessed in each meta-analysis, which typically uses pre- to postimprovement. The main comparisons follow along with the number of studies supporting each comparison and the average Hedges's *g*. The final columns summarize key group treatment characteristics including the most frequently tested theoretical orientations, median number of sessions and duration in minutes, frequency of sessions, and the median size of the group. The goal of each meta-analysis was to provide conclusions that target the primary treatment outcomes by disorder. The reader is encouraged to consult individual meta-analyses that provide far more detail on patients, treatments, settings as well as effects on secondary outcomes and rates of acceptance, dropout, improvement and recovery.

Group versus Individual

We've been following the discussion on the differential effectiveness of individual versus group treatment outcomes in the literature for nearly 40 years. Proponents for each format provide both clinical and empirical evidence to support their position, and we've carefully documented these arguments in previous chapters. Metrics used by proponents of group treatment include equivalent outcomes, cost-savings associated with multiperson treatment and, the advantages of peer-support from individuals suffering from similar clinical symptoms. Metrics used by proponents of individual treatment include studies where outcomes favor the individual format as well as data showing client preference for individual treatment through higher treatment acceptance and attrition rates compared to the group format. As will become evident in subsequent sections, practice guidelines are often silent on format when making treatment recommendations or use a handful of dated studies to support or reject group as a recommended treatment.

In our chapter in the previous edition, we noted an increase in disorder specific meta-analyses that conducted subgroup format contrasts along with 23 new studies that directly tested differences in format outcomes. We concluded that there was sufficient evidence to embrace a no difference conclusion for mood, panic, personality, eating, and schizophrenia disorders, but we qualified this conclusion by noting empirical evidence to the contrary. The picture was mixed for social phobia, posttraumatic stress disorder (PTSD) and obsessive-compulsive disorder (OCD). We noted a significant limitation in format conclusions since most meta-analyses rely on between-study rather than within-study effect sizes to compare individual and group formats. Within-study comparisons are drawn from the same study where group and individual treatments are simultaneously offered, while between-study comparisons are findings from studies that test either the group or individual treatment and then pool results in a format subgroup analysis.

It is a well-accepted methodological fact (Shadish and Sweeney, 1991) that within-study comparisons rule out a host of between-study confounds (differences in treatment, patients, therapists, settings, number of sessions, etc.) and lead to stronger conclusions. However, we have documented that over 85% of the studies included in 14 disorder-specific meta-analyses testing format outcome differences used between-study comparisons (Burlingame et al., 2016). Thus, even though there is an increase in the number of meta-analyses testing format differences, conclusions are suspect, since between-study comparisons are the principal source of data. In our last chapter we also document a second methodological problem in some of the published within-study format comparisons – unequal treatments. More specifically, even when individual and group treatments are contrasted within the same study, we found a sizable number of studies where there was nonequivalence between individual and group treatments (dose and orientation) and patient assignment introducing ambiguity into comparative outcome conclusions. Stated differently, if format differences were found, we cannot rule out that these differences might be due to the confound of nonequivalence in treatments (dose and orientation) offered and/or patients assigned.

To directly address these methodological challenges, we conducted a meta-analysis to test for outcome differences between individual and group treatments contrasted in the same study over a 25-year time span. We included any psychiatric disorder and studies where identical treatments, patients and doses were used as well as studies where one or more of these factors was nonidentical. Anxiety and mood disorder studies were most prevalent (*n* = 16 and 13, respectively), followed by patients being treated for substance (9), medical (9) and eating (6) disorders. Group treatments were primarily outpatient (80%), time-limited (92%), homogenous in composition (82%), and co-led (73%). Treatment orientations were heavily weighted toward CBT (66%) with an equivalent number of studies using cognitive, psychodynamic, interpersonal, and support treatments, with most guided by a manual (80%).

Primary outcomes were reported in 68 studies, and no differences were found between formats (Table 17.1). A comparison of 46 identical treatment studies and 21 nonidentical treatment studies both produced equivalent outcomes. The average power to detect differences, if present, was high (0.92, range 0.77–1.00) suggesting a high degree of confidence in the equivalent outcome conclusion. While there were no outcome differences for both identical and nonidentical treatment comparisons, the between-study effect size heterogeneity was twice as high in the nonidentical analysis. A moderator analysis to explore the heterogeneity between nonidentical treatment comparisons showed that investigator allegiance explained between-study effect size differences. Investigators with an allegiance to a group format produced an average effect size favoring group treatments (*g* = 0.11) while those favoring individual therapy had effect sizes with a similar bias (*g* = -0.21). Nearly half of the studies reported short-term (6 months or less) follow-up and a third long-term (7–30 months), and results from both follow-up periods supported outcome equivalence. Finally, a moderator analysis of format differences by diagnosis also supported equivalence.

TABLE 17.1 Summary of Group as Primary Meta-analytic Findings

Study	Disorder	Studies (comparisons) included	N_I	N_C	(Primary) outcome	Comparison (k)	g & p	Typical group method(s)	Median: sessions, session length, sessions per week, size)
1	Individual vs. Group RCTs	68 (70)	3098	2660	Target symptoms for anxiety, mood, substance, medical, eating disorders			CBT, BT, CT, PT, IPT, ST	15 - 100/56 -1 - 7
						All Individual vs group (64)	−0.03 ns		
						Identical (46)	−0.01 ns		
						Nonidentical (21)	−0.06 ns		
2	MDD	35 (47)	1561	1357	Depression			CBT, CT, DBT, BT, IT, ST	10 – 90-1 - 8
						WLC (10)	1.10***		
						TAU (11)	0.69***		
						Pharmacotherapy (7)	0.08 ns		
3	Bipolar	7	480	407	Bipolar symptoms			PE	21 – 90-1 - 10
4	Social Anxiety	36 (43)	1187	984	Social anxiety symptoms (avoidance, anxiety)			CBT, BT (Exposure)	12 – 120 – 1 - 6
						TAU (4)	0.44*		
						WLC (28)	0.84 ***		

(Continued)

TABLE 17.1 (CONTINUED)

Study	Disorder	Studies (comparisons) included	N_I	N_C	(Primary) outcome	Comparison (k)	g & p	Typical group method(s)	Median: sessions, session length, sessions per week, size
5	Panic Disorder	15 (19)	213	181	Panic frequency, different Anxiety scales	Active Tx (15)	0.15 ns	CBT including education, cognitive restructuring, exposure, relaxation/breathing	10 – 90 – 1 - 6
						No-treatment control	1.078 (***)		
						Alternative treatment	0.178 ns		
6	OCD	12 (16)	377	455	Y-BOCS	Wait-list control (4)	0.971 (***)	CBT including psychoeducation, cognitive techniques, exposure, relapse prevention	12 – 120 – 1 - 7
						Individual psychotherapy	–0.243 ns		
						pharmacotherapy	0.183 ns		
						Common factor control	0.049 ns		

Note. IVG = individual versus group comparisons; MDD = major depressive disorder; OCD = obsessive compulsive disorder; BT = behavor therapy; CBT = cognitive; BT = behavioral therapy; CT = cognitive therapy; PT = psychodynamic therapy; IPT = interpersonal therapy; ST = supportive therapy; IT = integrative treatment, DBT = dialectical behavior therapy, PE = psycho-education.
Study: 1 Burlingame et al., 2016; 2. Janis et al 2021; 3. Barkowski et al., 2016; 4 Schwartze et al., 2017; 5. Schwartze et al., 2016
* $p < .05$, ** $p < .01$, *** $p < .001$, ns = not significant

Given the limited information on patient format preference (Swift & Callahan, 2009), we tested for differences between format on rates of treatment acceptance, dropout, improvement and remission. In our past reviews we noted comments from study authors that raised a concern that patients might prefer individual over group treatment. However, these comments are anecdotal, often appearing in the discussion section with little to no data. Thus, we empirically tested for differences in acceptance and dropout rates and found no differences in rates of acceptance ($n = 14$) or dropout ($n = 52$); this equivalence held when only identical treatments were examined. Additionally, no between study effect size heterogeneity was found for either acceptance or dropout strengthening our confidence in the equivalence conclusion. Format equivalence was also found in posttreatment rates of diagnosis remission using primary outcome measures ($n = 11$) which was supported at short-term follow up ($n = 6$) and with identical treatment contrasts ($n = 12$). Finally, rates of individual member improvement also produced format equivalence ($n = 15$) which was supported at short-term follow-up ($n = 6$) and with identical treatment contrasts ($n = 12$).

The clinical implication of these findings is clear – *"when identical treatments, patients and doses are compared, individual and group formats produce statistically indistinguishable outcomes"* (Burlingame et al., 2016; p. 457). The equivalent rates of acceptance, attrition, improvement, and recovery provide further support for the feasibility of group treatment and directly address clinical concerns regarding patient preference. The authors work in clinical settings and are well-acquainted with patient preferences and concerns about group treatment. These concerns are real and we suggest that clinicians respond to them with an explanation grounded in science. This may be enough for some patients while others may need pregroup induction and still others may decline. The bottom-line is that the empirical evidence for format equivalence has never been stronger and this finding needs to find its way into clinical practice when patients are presented with group treatment options at intake. This seems particularly important for service delivery systems that have treatment access challenges or are experiencing other treatment restrictions due to high-demand on clinical services.

This meta-analysis also helps us understand past mixed findings that have introduced ambiguity into format outcome conclusions. More specifically, the moderator analysis of nonidentical studies suggests that allegiance effects may explain why some studies find differences between formats that favor both individual and group treatment. It's interesting that allegiance appears as a significant moderator only in the nonidentical treatment studies which tended to be less rigorous leading to a greater chance of confounds. These findings suggest that clinical practice and practice guidelines might best be calibrated by findings from identical treatment randomized clinical trials. Stated differently, practice guideline revisions should explicitly consider the evidence for both individual and group treatments and use only those studies that have been shown not to be affected by allegiance; that is, those having identical treatments, patients, and doses.

Group as Primary

In our previous chapters, we recognized that group treatment is often treated as a firstline intervention. For instance, in university counseling centers that produce a significant portion of the group therapy literature, group therapy is the first line recommended treatment at intake (Burlingame et al., 2016). Clinical indictions that fall under the group as primary include several mood and anxiety disorders.

Mood Disorders

Mood disorders, including major depressive (MDD) and bipolar (BD) disorders, are some of the most common psychiatric conditions, with 12-month prevalence estimates of 7% and 0.7% in the United States respectively (APA, 2013). Between the two disorders (MDD and BD), they account for nearly half (47.5%) of worldwide estimates of years lived with a disability (Whiteford et al., 2013). Thus, identifying evidence for efficacious treatments for these mood disorders is paramount in reducing impairment worldwide.

Major Depressive Disorder – MDD. When we look at some of the symptom features of MDD – hopelessness, lack of energy/interest, withdrawal/isolation – and consider referring a prospective patient to group treatment they raise understandable clinical obstacles regarding the acceptance and attendance. While the aforementioned meta-analysis on group versus individual treatment comparisons found no differences in acceptance, attendance and dropout rates, it's important to remember that these findings were drawn from controlled trials. The controlled conditions of a randomized trial often differ dramatically from the day-to-day challenges faced in clinical practices where client preferences often drive treatment referral (Swift & Callahan, 2009). Nevertheless, the interpersonal environment inherent in group treatments may provide an immediate antidote to some depression symptoms – for example, withdrawal/isolation – a point that might be emphasized during an intake and referral session.

Practice guidelines (PGs) for MDD recommend cognitive behavioral therapy (CBT) as a gold-standard treatment since it has the most supporting evidence. While the APA and NICE guidelines do not differ by the setting of care, they do differ on format recommendations. APA notes that group treatment has comparatively less evidence than individual, but also point out that available evidence for group CBT (GCBT) is promising. On the other hand, NICE notes that GCBT effects are diminished when compared to individual treatment. Mindfulness-based cognitive therapy (MBCT) is a third-wave CBT treatment designed to be delivered in a group format. Its primary aim is to change the way depression-prone individuals relate to their negative thoughts (Segal et al., 2013). MBCT is recommended by both group and individual PGs for the maintenance phase of MDD. Interpersonal therapy (IPT) for MDD focuses on treating the client's symptoms stemming from maladaptive interaction styles. It is recommended by both PGs for individual delivery; group IPT for MDD is less enthusiastically endorsed, with NICE silent on group format and APA noting comparatively less evidence relative to individual IPT.

In 2004, we stated that cognitive-behavioral group therapy (CBGT) had convincing randomized clinical trial (RCT) support and in 2013 we reported on 10 new studies that had extended these findings. Two meta-analyses found that group therapy produced large effects (d = 1.03 to 1.10) compared to untreated controls. CBGT was the primary model (n = 8) tested in the new studies using closed group treatments, lasting 10–12 sessions. CBGT was applied to treatment-resistant medication patients showing superiority over control conditions on measures of depression. Two research teams each produced three studies exploring how changes in depression might be associated with improvement in quality of life and cognition and found no evidence for parallel change. Thus, quality of life did not appear to be an epiphenomenon of depression and the cognitive component of CBGT was not supported as the change agent suggesting other mechanisms of action might explain improvement (common factors).

Recent Meta-Analytic Support. To address PG concerns regarding the amount of evidence available testing the efficacy of group treatment for MDD we conducted a meta-analysis comprising 35 randomized control trials that produced 47 comparisons (Janis et al., 2021). Only one of these studies was included in our 2013 chapter. Together, the studies included 2918 individuals (1,561 group, 1,357 comparison) with 14 waitlist control (WLC) comparisons (N = 557), 19 treatment-as-usual (TAU) comparisons (N = 1,847), and 14 comparisons to medication condition (N = 783). These comparison conditions addressed the question: *How effective is active group treatment when compared to no-treatment, standard treatments and medication alone?*

The studies included a wide array of group models (Table 17.1) with the most frequent comparison testing CBT (14), MBCT (6), and psycho-educational (PE, 66). When group treatment was compared to WLC on depression symptoms, the pre-to-post effect was significant, large (g = 1.10) and heterogenous (I^2 = 79.7%). However, when a single outlier was removed, the effect on depression was still significant and large (g = 0.86), but heterogeneity was no longer significant. Clients in group treatments were 6.8 times more likely to be classified as improved compared to individuals receiving no treatment, and this effect had no heterogeneity. There was no indication of publication bias and attrition rates were nonsignificant indicating that client dropout rates did not differ between the group and no-treatment condition. Overall, group therapy produced significantly better outcomes than WLC conditions across all outcomes, depression specific outcomes, and recovery rates. These results provide strong support for the improvement associated with group treatment when compared to individuals receiving no treatment.

A second comparison addressed group treatment compared to treatment as usual (TAU) with some studies regulating the TAU and others leaving this up to participants to procure. The majority of studies (8/12) tested the additive power of group treatment (active control + group) beyond standard care. When group treatment was compared to TAU on depression symptoms, the pre-post treatment effect was moderate to large (g = 0.71) and when a single outlier was removed, the effect on depression was significant and

moderate (g = 0.50) but heterogeneity remained significant. Group treatment continued to produce superior outcomes at short-term follow-up (6 months or less) but it was not significantly better than TAU at long-term outcome (7–24 months). Clients in group treatments were 5.3 times more likely to be classified as improved compared to individuals receiving TAU but this effect was heterogeneous. There was no indication of publication bias and there were no differences in effects when study regulated AC was compared with patient procured TAU.

The final analysis involved seven comparisons between active group treatment and patients receiving anti-depressant medication alone. When group treatment was compared to medication only on depression symptoms, the pre-post treatment effect was small and nonsignificant (g = 0.08) although heterogeneity was significant (I^2 = 69.9%). Recovery and attrition rate comparisons were also nonsignificant with no heterogeneity. Overall, these results indicate that group therapy produces effects that are equivalent to medication alone.

In summary, the meta-analysis findings confirm and strengthen conclusions from past reviews and meta-analyses. There is strong evidence that group treatment provides large benefits when contrasted with no-treatment controls. CBGT continues to dominate with the largest number of studies but more recently, promising evidence supporting MBCT and PE group treatments is growing across WLC and TAU comparisons. Improvement in depression symptoms and recovery rates for group treatment and medication alone appear to be equivalent although the number of studies supporting this conclusion is smaller (7). Finally, none of the 17 moderators tested were found to explain variability in outcomes. When the findings from the meta-analysis comparing outcomes for individual versus group format (Burlingame et al., 2016) are combined with Janis et al (2019), there appears to be sufficient support to recommend CBGT in PGs and promising support for MBCT. More group treatment research is needed on group IPT and PE.

Bipolar Disorder – BD. Bipolar disorder is typically classified into one or two types. Bipolar 1 requires at least one manic episode with/without MDD while bipolar 2 requires one hypomanic and one MDD episode. Group treatment may play an important role with BD since medication compliance is a critical success factor in reducing the frequency and intensity of symptom recurrence. More specifically, the role of peer-pressure in group treatment may be more influential in medication compliance than professional advice. Practice guidelines for BD emphasize the important of psycho-education – PE aimed at "illness awareness, treatment compliance, early detection of prodromal symptoms and recurrences, and lifestyle regularity" (Colom et al., 2003, p. 403). While PE is a recommended psychosocial treatment in APA and NICE practice guidelines, APA is silent on format and NICE recommends against PE in a group format. CBT and interpersonal therapy – IPT for bipolar disorder is recommended in all formats by NICE, and again, APA is silent on format.

In 2013, we reported on seven new studies that focused on BD but only two used a randomized clinical trial – RCT design. Most (5) tested PE but there was little coherence in outcomes assessed across study, group length varied from 4 to 21 sessions, and patients varied from mild euthymic to acute symptoms requiring hospitalization. We cautioned against over-interpreting these findings and focused on the two RCTs that tested PE documenting reduced hospitalizations, fewer manic episodes, less intense symptoms, and more medication management visits for up to five years. We concluded by stating that the "two RCTs underscore the relapse prevention potential of PE, but additional rigorous research is needed before we can move our evaluation from promising to efficacious (p. 647)."

Recent Meta-Analytic Support. To address the limited evidence, we conducted a meta-analysis consisting of seven randomized control trials (Table 17.1). One of these studies was included in our 2013 chapter. Studies in the meta-analysis included 887 individuals (480 group, 407 comparison) with six TAU comparisons that resulted in a significant medium improvement ($g = 0.69$) with significant heterogeneity ($I^2 = 82.1\%$. However, when comparisons were limited to primary measures of bipolar disorder, the sample dropped to 467 individuals and the effect of PE was moderate ($g = 0.44$) with nonsignificant heterogeneity (Table 17.1). Long-term follow-up showed that this effect was maintained and there was no indication of publication bias, differences in rates of attrition or moderators that might explain outcomes. Overall, group therapy produced significantly better outcomes than TAU conditions on bipolar specific outcomes. These results provide stronger support for the improvement associated with group treatment when compared to individuals receiving TAU than in our previous review. The PG recommendation against group PE (NICE) is not supported by our findings although the number of studies, while double from our last review, is still small. The evidence supports group PE as a promising treatment for PG inclusion.

Anxiety Disorders

Besides depression, anxiety disorders are among the most prevalent mental disorders with an estimated one-year prevalence between 8.3% and 11.6% in a community sample (Baxter et al., 2013). As in our earlier reviews, we discriminate the existing evidence between social anxiety disorders and panic disorder. In addition, a recent meta-analysis combined all studies we found related to social anxiety and panic and also included generalized anxiety disorder (Barkowski et al., 2020).

Social Anxiety Disorders (SAD). Although the specific characteristics of SAD seem to conflict with the group treatment environment (i.e., groups elicit anxiety and are therefore avoided), there are clinical reasons that groups settings might constitute an especially suitable therapeutic format for this disorder. From a cognitive-behavioral point of view, the group environment offers a unique exposure opportunity to social situations while providing a secure context at the same time. The availability of role models that are perceived to be more similar (e.g., other patients) may make vicarious learning more powerful with SAD. Moreover, immediate feedback from other group members provide another source of influence to correct irrational beliefs about social behavior. Furthermore, socially anxious patients might especially benefit from the sense of belonging and self-validation that well-functioning groups elicit composed of people struggling with similar problems. From a more interpersonal and psychodynamic perspective, group formats present an opportunity to explore a wider range of interpersonal behavior patterns and to work with similar internal and interpersonal conflicts across participants.

Related to efficacy/effectiveness, in 2004 we stated compelling evidence for the efficacy of a single CBT developed by Heimberg and Becker (2002), which together with two similar group treatment approaches (Clark & Wells, 1995; Rapee & Heimberg, 1997) were the focus of 28 outcome studies summarized in 2013. The typical group was closed, comprised 5–10 patients treated in weekly sessions of varying duration (90 to 240 min.). Patients were between 30 and 40 years old with equal gender representation. The approaches mentioned have gained widespread acceptance as the gold standard group treatment for SAD (Hofmann & Bögels, 2006). We also included a meta-analysis (Powers et al., 2008) summarizing a portion of these studies that estimated identical effectiveness for group ($d = 0.68$) and individual treatments ($d = 0.69$).

Recent Meta-Analytic Support. Barkowski et al. (2016) covered 36 randomised-controlled group therapy studies including 2171 patients (Table 17.1). Five of these studies were included in our 2013 chapter. The included studies reported on 50 different comparisons of a group psychotherapy to a comparison group. The majority ($k = 31$) followed a cognitive-behavioral approach usually incorporating exposure, cognitive restructuring and homework assignment. Some group treatments added supplemental components such as social skills training, attention retraining or imagery. Most of these treatments (13) were guided by the treatment protocol developed by Heimberg and colleagues. Exposure and cognitive therapy alone were provided by seven and two studies, respectively. Other treatment approaches were interpersonal, psychodynamic, and social skills training.

The typical treatment structure comprised weekly 2- to 2.5-hour group sessions for 12 weeks, treating six patients per group. Some of the studies tested a shorter version of eight sessions and one study used a two-week intensive protocol. On average, the percentage of male and female patients was evenly distributed and the distribution of mean age across all studies showed a median age of 34. The largest group of comparisons were wait list control groups ($k = 23$), other studies involved common factor control groups, TAU, pharmacotherapy and individual psychotherapy. Usual comorbidities were other anxiety or mood disorders. Seven studies reported on comorbid avoidant personality disorder and seven on comorbid substance abuse. All but two studies reported outcomes assessing the specific symptomatology of SAD. A total of 25 studies included measurements assessing general psychopathology, and 50% of the studies included data on remission, response or both. A total of eight studies gave information on follow-up outcome (usually short-term).

The meta-analysis confirmed conclusions from former reviews. Since the available studies mainly used cognitive-behavioral approaches, quantitative analyses were carried out for CBT. Medium to large positive effects emerged for wait list-controlled trials for specific symptomatology (g = 0.84) and general psychopathology (g = 0.62). Group psychotherapy was also superior to common factor control conditions in alleviating symptoms of SAD, but not in improving general psychopathology. No differences appeared for direct comparisons of group psychotherapy and individual psychotherapy or pharmacotherapy and, none of the moderators tested were found to be significant. Hence, group psychotherapy for SAD is an efficacious treatment, equivalent to other treatment formats.

In a parallel search, we found 13 randomized controlled trials including *N* = 490 *children and adolescents*. Random effects meta-analyses revealed a large, significant effect of GCBT compared to no-treatment control groups (g = 1.25). Compared to common factor control groups, a large but non-significant effect but with considerable heterogeneity emerged (g = 1.14).

Recent publications related to group treatment of SAD clearly reveal an increased use of *mindfulness-based stress reduction (MBSR)*, commonly compared with CBT (e.g., Jazaieri et al., 2018; Kocovski et al., 2013, 2015; Stefan et al., 2018). In recent studies focusing on MBSR, Goldin et al. (2016), Thurston et al. (2017), and Butler et al. (2018) showed similar effects for MBSR and CBT in reduction of symptoms, self-efficacy, self-views, emotional clarity, attention to emotions and other outcomes. CBT revealed greater decreases for subtle avoidance behaviors compared to MBSR. The authors document similar change trajectories for social anxiety, reappraisal, and mindfulness, but different trajectories for disputing anxious thoughts and feeling (greater increases in CBT) or acceptance of anxiety and success (greater increases in MBSR). Changes in reappraisal were more predictive for symptom changes in CBT, whereas increases in mindful attitudes and disputing anxious feelings as well as the working alliance (Jazaieri et al., 2018) predicted symptom decrease in MBSR. These findings suggest different temporal dynamics and change mechanisms for the two approaches that lead to similar effects. These findings partially replicate the results of an earlier study that indicated different mechanisms of change (Kocovski et al., 2015).

As in our former reviews, it can be shown that the evidence for the efficacy of group therapy (CBT and recently also MBSR) for SAD is broad and solid. Accordingly, our recommendation is that group psychotherapy be added to the NICE guidelines (NICE, 2014) and be considered for other PGs.

Panic Disorder. Panic disorder, often associated with agoraphobia, is one of the disorders for which practice guidelines recommend pharmacotherapy or CBT. CBT has been tested in numerous studies focusing on individual therapy. In the last edition of this chapter, we noted CBGT as an effective model for treating panic disorder in group format with Barlow & Craske's treatment being the dominant model (Barlow & Craske, 1994) together with Clark's cognitive therapy (Clark, 1986). Most of the studies revealed high effect sizes (related to measures of general anxiety, panic, depression, or functioning), the primary focus across several studies was the clinical application and refinement of the two models. Feelings of shame and stigma may be reduced by meeting

others with similar experiences, feedback could encourage change and help to compare and contrast appraisals.

Recent Meta-Analytic Support. The effects of CBGT were confirmed in a recent meta-analysis comprising RCTs of group treatments for panic disorder which found 15 eligible studies (14 used CBT; Schwartze et al., 2017). Three of these studies were included in the 2013 edition of this chapter. The 864 patients included in the meta-analysis had a mean age of 37 years (SD = 4.4), 70% were female with 19 comparisons. Primary outcomes were panic assessments, secondary outcomes were agoraphobia, depression, and general anxiety symptoms.

Group CBT protocols usually involve multiple components such as (a) education regarding the etiology and maintenance of panic disorder, (b) cognitive restructuring (identification and modification of panic-related cognitions), (c) exposure to external situations (in vivo exposure) or internal bodily sensations (interoceptive exposure) related to the fear response, (d) relaxation training and/or breathing retraining (i.e. diaphragmatic breathing). Only one study applied group therapy based on a cognitive approach (Beck et al., 1994). However, treatment components in this approach were similar to CBT protocols but without exposure.

Treatment was usually delivered in group formats with PD patients only; two studies used mixed anxiety disorder group treatments. Ten studies compared the effects of group therapy to a wait-list control group, and one study used a minimal contact control condition. Six studies compared group therapy to an alternative PD treatment (individual therapy, pharmacotherapy, relaxation, or physical exercise). The typical group treatment used 90-minute sessions, contained 4–9 members and lasted between 8–14 sessions.

The results of the meta-analysis (Table 17.1) reveal large effects for group CBT showing a significant reduction of panic and agoraphobia symptoms when compared to no-treatment controls (g = 1.08). No significant differences were found in studies comparing group psychotherapy with alternative (including individual) treatments (g = 0.18). Short-term follow-up results (≤ 6 months) were reported in three studies. One study reported long-term follow-up and this study (Roberge et al., 2008) provided posttreatment data on the primary outcome and general anxiety favoring group treatment over individual therapy. However, while group treatment improvement was maintained at one- and two-year follow-up, individual therapy produced greater gains for depression at both follow-up time points.

When symptom remission was examined, 78% of PD patients were panic-free after group psychotherapy, compared to 33% in the wait-list control condition. However, 78% of PD patients in alternative treatment conditions and 47% in other active treatment conditions were panic-free. The panic-free rate after group therapy reported in our study was comparable to rates reported in other studies on individual psychotherapy. The average dropout rate for group psychotherapy was 15%, a rate that is similar to the dropout rate of 19.7% reported in a meta-analysis of 669 psychotherapy studies by Swift and Greenberg (2012) that were predominantly individual. Finally, no significant moderators of treatment outcome were found.

One study that was not included in the meta-analysis compared individually based CBT (considered as TAU) with mindful-based group therapy (MBGT) in a Swedish sample comprising 215 patients with a broad range of psychiatric disorders including panic (Sundquist et al., 2017). The study showed no differences between the treatments related to a reduction of psychiatric symptoms. Expectedly, the MGBT group treatment showed larger changes in a mindful attention awareness scale.

Based on the literature, the evidence supporting CBT group treatment appear to be robust. Despite the overall effect of group treatments on panic/agoraphobia symptoms, some clinical guidelines do not specifically recommend group treatment (e.g., APA 2009a; NICE 2019).

Combined Anxiety Disorders. As mentioned above, we performed an additional meta-analysis comprising 57 studies (76 comparisons), including 3,656 participants suffering from social anxiety disorder, panic disorder, or generalized anxiety disorder (GAD). Eight of these studies were included in our 2013 chapter. Overall, we found large effect sizes ($g = 0.92$) for comparisons of group therapy with no-treatment controls and no significant difference when group treatments were compared to individual psychotherapy ($g = 0.24$) or pharmacotherapy ($g = -0.05$). Finally, allegiance to a particular treatment was found to be significantly related to outcome; studies without the allegiance outcome had higher effect sizes. Overall, these findings for the effectiveness of group treatment are in contrast with the fact that group treatments do not play a significant role in anxiety disorder related practice guidelines. In fact, they are usually recommended only in cases where individual therapy is unavailable (Bandelow et al., 2014; NICE, 2013).

Obsessive-Compulsive Disorder (OCD). The group format can provide benefits for OCD patients in addition to that of individual therapy. Particularly, group treatments can foster a sense of belonging and the experience that others have similar problems. Participants can encourage, motivate, and problem-solve with each other and have the opportunity to compare and contrast their appraisals (Whittal & McLean, 2002).

In the last edition of the *Handbook*, we stated that ample evidence existed for the efficacy of CBGT which commonly includes exposure and response prevention (ERP) when it is compared to waitlist control. A meta-analytic review of 13 studies (Jonsson & Hougaard, 2009) produced an average effect size of 1.1 on the Y-BOCS for both approaches (CBGT and ERP) when compared to wait-list controls. Compared to several other disorders, the common use of the Yale-Brown Obsessive Compulsive Scale (Y-BOCS) in OCD research facilitates direct effect size comparisons.

Recent Meta-Analytic Support. Schwartze et al. (2016) identified 12 studies (including 16 comparisons) comprising 832 patients (Table 17.1). None of these studies were included in our 2013 chapter, and no moderator analyses were performed. Interventions most commonly administered were complex CBT ($k = 13$), exposure with response prevention alone ($k = 2$), and cognitive therapy ($k = 1$). The group treatments usually lasted 12 sessions (of 120 min.) and comprised 5–12 patients. Effect size estimates reveal that group psychotherapy is highly effective for improving obsessive-compulsive symptoms (Y-BOCS) in comparison to wait-list control groups (Hedges's $g = 0.97$). No significant differences in efficacy were found between group psychotherapy and active treatment control groups, such as individual psychotherapy (Hedges's $g = -0.23$), pharmacotherapy (Hedges's $g = 0.18$, or common factor control groups (Hedges's $g = 0.05$). A similar trend could be shown for secondary outcomes (depression, anxiety). No differences could be shown for comparisons of individual and group psychotherapy during follow-up (five studies).

Based on these stable results, recent studies have extended the support of CBT for OCD patients in other cultures (e.g., Safak et al., 2014), and in OCD patients with medical problems such as multiple sclerosis (Sayyah et al., 2016). One Norwegian study has also shown stability in the treatment effects reflected in YBOCS, anxiety and depression measures over 8 years (Sunde et al., 2017). Key et al. (2017) tested the effect of a mindfulness-based cognitive therapy as an augment to CBT group treatment and demonstrated an additional reduction of OCD, anxiety and depressive symptoms as well as obsessive beliefs. Futhermore, the recent literature reflects an increasing number of studies of family based CBGT for pediatric OCD cases, all indicating positive effects (Conelea et al., 2017; Schuberth et al., 2018; Selles et al., 2018).

In conclusion, our meta-analysis and recent studies provide strong evidence for CBGT for adult patients suffering from OCD. Long-term improvement is promising (Sunde et al., 2017), but more high-quality studies are needed to strengthen the evidence and allow for moderator analyses.

Group as Adjunct

Disorders that fall under group as adjunct reflect treatment regimens that include multiple simultaneous treatments. These multiple treatments may be present due to the complexity of the clinical indication that requires different professionals (e.g., eating disorder are often treated by a team including a mental health therapist, nutrition, physician, etc.). Other disorders involve mental health practitioners who are focusing on different aspects of the symptom presentation (e.g., substance-related groups treating psychiatric and addiction symptoms).

Eating Disorders

Clinically, group treatment of ED creates the opportunity to address interpersonal problems, perfectionism, and mood intolerance (Fairburn, 2008) facilitated by cohesion, peer feedback and safe expression of emotions (Yalom & Leszcz, 2005). While anorexia nervosa (AN) is both rare and rarely investigated (McIntosh et al., 2005), we observed in our last chapter that group therapy research on *bulimia nervosa* (BN) and *binge-eating disorder* (BED) had burgeoned. We found strong evidence for the effectiveness of CBGT on eating disorder symptoms (symptoms and frequency of bingeing and purging – BAP) and patient functioning.

In comparative studies of BN, condition equivalence was the rule regardless of the posttreatment outcome measure. Follow-up studies provided evidence for maintenance of benefits from CBGT for BN. Most research focused on BED with CBGT as the dominant model and when CBGT was compared with IPT, psychodynamic, and nondirective group treatments, equivalent effects on BAP were the common findings.

Recent Meta-Analytic Support. Grenon et al. (2017) conducted a meta-analysis on group approaches with eating disorders with BN and BED being the predominant presentation (*n* = 10 and 19, respectively). They summarized 27 RCTs with 31 comparisons (19 group vs. wait list, 12 group vs. active treatment; Table 17.2). Eleven of these studies were included in the 2013 edition of this chapter, and no moderator analyses were conducted due to limited sample size. Active treatment comparisons included individual CBT, supportive group nondirective, individual CBT+IPT, behavioral weight loss, and self-help (see also Grenon et al., 2019).

On average, abstinence group treatment was favored over WLC. Stated differently, group patients were five times more likely to be abstinent than WLCs at posttreatment (5.82 for BED, 2.53 for BD). Reduced frequency of bingeing and purging favored group treatment over WLC with a large effect (*g* = 0.70). After removing an outlier, a similar pattern favoring group treatment was found on ED-related psychopathology (e.g., eating attitudes, *g* = 0.49) as well as on secondary outcomes (depression and self-concept).

Comparisons of group and other treatments did not reveal statistically significant differences in abstinence rates, BAP frequency, and ED-related psychopathology. Three of the studies compared individual and group psychotherapy with no significant differences. The effects of group treatment did not differ from other treatments effects at short- and long-term follow-up. Comparisons between CBT and other treatments were small and should be interpreted with caution since limited comparisons were available. In a later publication (Grenon et al., 2019), the number of RCTs was increased to 35 with 54 direct comparisons. Eleven of these studies were included in our 2013 chapter. Again, there was an advantage over wait-list controls and no differences could be found between CBT and other active treatments.

Two recent studies not included in the above meta-analyses focused on BED and provide the first evidence for the effectiveness of dialectical behavior therapy – DBT – which incorporates a group treatment component. Rahmani et al. (2018) used an RCT to compare DBT group with WLC and found a significant reduction in BMI, binge-eating symptoms and improved emotion regulation. A second pilot study tested a cognitive-behavioral body image exposure therapy with BED reported improvement on body image, eating symptoms, depression and self-esteem (Lewer et al., 2017).

While the NICE guidelines recommend Group-CBT for BED (NICE, 2017), the very recent (2019) guidelines of the German AWMF (Arbeitsgemeinschaft Wissenschaftlich-medizinischer Fachgesellschaften = Association of Scientific Medical Societies) does not explicitly mention group treatment approaches (Association of Scientific Medical Societies, 2019).

Substance-Related Disorders

The World Health Organization describes the disease burden of drug and alcohol issues to be 5.4% worldwide (WHO, 2014). A number of psychosocial interventions for substance use disorders (SUD) in adults have demonstrated effectiveness, including coping skills training, relapse prevention, contingency management, motivational interviewing, behavioral couple therapy and motivational enhancement therapy. Most of these SUD-specific treatments are provided in a group format and have received widespread clinical acceptance in the last decades (Wendt & Gone, 2017). Reasons for the clinical predominance of group therapy are the increased focus on cost containment as well as the influence of mutual support group treatments such as Alcoholics Anonymous, Cocaine Anonymous, and Twelve-Step Facilitation Therapy in treatment programs for substance use.

In our first review of group treatment studies on substance-related disorders (Burlingame et al., 2004) we saw limited support for the effectiveness of group format. In the following review (Burlingame et al., 2013), we found more rigorous, though heterogeneous studies, both related to the programs as well as the specific populations (e.g., veterans). Most produced positive results compared to *no treatment*, and when specific group treatment programs were compared to control conditions, effect sizes were small to moderate. In summary, we concluded that "groups for substance abuse (and comorbid disorders) post moderate positive effects for both adolescents and adults with minor differences in effectiveness between specific formal change theories" (p. 651).

Recent Meta-Analytic Support. We recently published a meta-analysis of RCTs focusing on substance abuse disorders – SUDs in adults (Lo Coco et al., 2019) to provide a summary of group therapy efficacy for SUDs in adults. All available RCTs comparing group treatments for SUDs to no treatment, individual therapy, and other active treatment were included with tobacco/nicotine dependence excluded. The majority of studies recruited individuals without a psychiatric disorder.

These criteria led to 33 studies comprising 34 comparisons with 9 studies comparing group treatment to no treatment controls, 7 comparing group to individual therapy and 18 comparing group treatment to other treatments (e.g., Twelve-Steps, TAU). One study was included in our 2013 chapter and limited data did not support moderator analyses. Treatments included CBT, behavioral, mindfulness, DBT and integrative treatments (Table 17.2). Significant and small effects were found on abstinence in each comparison (*g* = 0.28 to 34; Table 17.2) and there was no heterogeneity for the no treatment and individual therapy conditions.

There was no significant effect on frequency of substance use with other treatments but group treatment outperformed individual therapy with moderate effects. A small effect was found when group was compared to no-treatment on SUD symptoms and a significant medium effect on general psychopathology when group treatment was compared to no treatment (*g* = 0.29). However, the effects of individual therapy and other treatments were small and nonsignificant (*p* < 0.07). Attrition in group treatment (32%) and control comparisons

TABLE 17.2 Summary of Group as Adjunct Meta-analytic Findings

Study	Disorder	Studies (comparisons) included	N_I	N_C	(Primary) outcome	Comparison (k)	g (p)	Typical group method(s)	Median: sessions, session length, sessions per week, size)
1	Eating disorders (BED, BN, EDNOS)	27 (31)	1132	963	Abstinence from BAP, frequency / Binge eating/purging, ED symptoms	Wait list	RR 5.51, 0.79***, 0.49***	CBT, IPT, DBT	15 – 90 – 1 – 8
						Active controls	RR 1.20, 0.24 ns, 0.12 ns		
2	Substance use disorder	33 (34)	2103	1848	Abstinence	No-treatment control	0.28	CBT (21)	12 – 90 – 1 – 8
						Individual therapy	0.34		
					Frequency of use	Other active treatments	0.29		
						Individual therapy	0.52		
						Other active treatments	0.01		
					SUD symptoms	No-treatment control	0.29		
						Individual therapy	0.06		
						Other active treatments	0.07		
					Mental state	No-treatment control			
						Individual therapy			
						Other active treatments			
3	PTSD	20 (21)	170	1074	PTSD Symptoms	No treatment	0.70 (***)	CBT (15)	15 – 95 – 1 – 7
						Active treatment	–0.02 ns		

Note. DBT = dialectical behavior therapy, STEPPS = systems for training emotional predictability & problem solving, ACT = acceptance commitment therapy, PD = psychodynamic therapy, IT = interpersonal therapy, SF = schema focused therapy, emotional intelligence therapy
Study: 1. Grenon et al. 2017; 2 Lo Coco et al., 2017; 3 Schwartze et al., 2019
* p < .05, ** p < .01, *** p < .001, ns = not significant

was comparable. Follow-up was typically assessed within 12 months of treatment completion. Improvement on the primary outcome of abstinence for group treatment showed an increase over time when compared with no treatment. However, it decreased when group treatment was compared with individual and other treatments. Unfortunately, the number of studies reporting follow-up for the other outcomes categories was too small to produce reliable results.

Despite widespread implementation of group therapy for SUDs, the evidence for effectiveness is limited. Results (Lo Coco et al., 2019) indicate that the pooled effect sizes for short-term efficacy is significant, but small on the primary outcome of abstinence in each comparison. Collectively, these findings provide some evidence for the efficacy of group treatment which is consistent with our reviews in 2004 and 2013. Greater confidence in this conclusion comes from the sensitivity analyses and low heterogeneity. While positive, further research is needed to determine the influence of sociodemographic, psychiatric, and general medical characteristics as well as patient preferences on treatment attrition and outcome (Sofin et al., 2017). Group treatment studies with long-term prospective designs are needed since one-third to one-half of individuals with SUDs achieve remission over a 17-year follow-up period (Fleury et al., 2016).

Posttraumatic Stress Disorder (PTSD)

Group treatment is one of the most common treatment modalities for posttraumatic stress disorder (PTSD, Shea et al., 2009). It is assumed that the group format involves a number of mechanisms that offer benefit beyond the individual therapy format such as mutual support, interpersonal feedback, or altruism (Yalom & Leszcz, 2005). Especially in PTSD, group therapy offers unique advantages to redevelop trusting relationships and interpersonal safety. Working with others that share similar problems can normalize trauma responses which, in turn, decrease shame and stigma. Group support and understanding may counteract isolation and alienation, which are prominent in PTSD patients (Shea et al., 2009; Sloan et al., 2012).

In our 2013 review, we highlighted research on four approaches (support/process-oriented, psychodynamic, CBGT, integrated models) that varied in methodological rigor. Uncontrolled studies dominated the literature and most studies featured CBGT. CBGT methodological rigor was high with some studies being state-of-the-art. However, populations were heterogeneous (female CSA survivors, male veterans with chronic PTSD). Together, these studies provided strong evidence for the effectiveness of a group format on trauma symptoms, depression and remission of PTSD. Secondary outcomes (anger, dissociation, anxiety, guilt) also improved. We stated that integrated models (e.g., simultaneously treating both PTSD and substance use) showed promise for the treatment of trauma and related conditions. Unfortunately, we found little research to support this finding in recent years.

Although the group format is used widely for PTSD, it is not recommended in current treatment guidelines (e.g.,

American Psychiatric Association [APA], 2009b; Department of Veterans Affairs/Department of Defense [VA/DoD], 2017; National Institute for Health and Clinical Excellence [NICE], 2018). Stated differently, most PGs are based on few published randomized controlled trials (RCTs) and may need to be updated with more current meta-analytic findings.

Recent Meta-Analytic Support. APA and NICE recommendations set the context for a meta-analysis (Schwartze et al., 2019) summarizing the efficacy of group treatments for PTSD using 20 studies and 21 comparisons (Table 17.2). Two of these studies were included in our 2013 chapter. The mean age of the 2244 individuals was 40 years; 52% were females. Three-quarters of the studies tested a form of CBT although the protocols varied widely in structure, content, and length. Five trials focused on PTSD with a comorbid disorder, three on enhancing affect regulation using skills training and psychoeducation, and another trial focused on trauma-related nightmares. Six CBT studies included a near common protocol composed of psychoeducation, exposure, cognitive restructuring, skills training, and relaxation techniques. The remaining five studies focused on psychodynamic, IPT, resilience-oriented, and cognitive therapies.

Studies also differed in their population characteristics (e.g., trauma type, comorbidity, severity of PTSD, personal background of participants) and type of comparisons with 12 studies having no-treatment, 6 with WLC, 3 with minimal contact, and 3 studies with concurrent treatment control groups. In the remaining 8 studies, comparisons were with active treatment including TAU (i.e., sleep and nightmare management, SUD treatment), common factor control (i.e., supportive group therapy/present-centered therapy, applied muscle relaxation, education group), and individual therapy. Follow-up data were reported in 11 studies with assessment time points ranging from 1 to 12 months after treatment termination.

Group treatment produced more improvement (Table 17.2) when compared with a no-treatment condition ($g = 0.70$) and similar results were reported on secondary outcomes (anxiety or depression). Remission rate was higher in the group treatment (70% and 56% for ITT) versus no treatment (34% and 29% for ITT). There were no significant differences on primary and secondary outcomes when group treatment was compared to active treatment. Three studies compared group therapy with supportive or present-centered therapy and no differences in treatment efficacy on PTSD symptoms were found. However, while supportive or present-centered therapy was originally designed to control for non-specific factors (Schnurr et al., 2003), recent discussions have classified it as a bona fide treatment for patients suffering from PTSD because of its use of specific therapeutic ingredients based on psychological principles (e.g., Frost et al., 2014).

A key difference in group treatment protocols is their emphasis on reintegrating the traumatic experience into treatment. Trauma-focused group treatments integrate memories of the trauma and try to modify the meaning of the trauma. Non-trauma-focused group treatments focus on the current impact of trauma on daily life as well as maladaptive patterns resulting from the traumatic experience (Shea et al., 2009). The meta-analysis included 8 trials testing non-trauma-focused group treatments and 13 trials testing trauma-focused protocols. No differences in outcomes were found for group treatments that had or did not have a trauma focus on PTSD symptoms or dropout. Moderator analyses confirmed gender (smaller effect sizes for males) and trauma type (smaller effect sizes in combat trauma samples compared to interpersonal/mixed trauma) as significant in explaining differences in PTSD treatment effects.

Finally, two studies published since this meta-analysis are noteworthy. One reflects an increased interest in group treatment effectiveness studies for traumatized children and adolescents (e.g., Auslander et al., 2017) and a second focuses on the growing interest in group MBSR with promising trends (e.g., Bremner et al., 2017) on PTSD symptoms.

Collectively, our conclusion is that there is sufficient evidence to declare group psychotherapy as an efficacious treatment for PTSD. While results are promising for psychodynamic, interpersonal group therapy and non-exposure-based CBT treatments, there is significant support for exposure-based CBT evidence by medium to large effect sizes. Five studies conducted by different research teams showed that exposure-based group CBT consistently proved to be more beneficial than no treatment. Furthermore, positive effects were independently replicated on different populations. Therefore, we consider exposure-based CBGT as efficacious and consideration should be given to including it within practice guidelines.

Group within Medical Settings

Our last review on *Groups within Medical Settings* included efficacy studies on group treatments for patients with breast cancer, somatoform, and pain disorders. However, during the last decade, we found evidence for interest in other medical clinical indications. Group treatment approaches for individuals with obesity have a long tradition and continue to be studied, but there was an insufficient number of high-quality studies to support a substantive review. Nevertheless, we note weight reduction groups for adults (e.g., Latner et al., 2013; Vesco et al., 2014) and children and adolescents that have shown promising results (e.g., Santiprabhob et al., 2014). Other medical conditions appearing since our last review include patients with neurological conditions (e.g., epilepsy or dementia). Overall, we expect future research on these and other group treatments within other medical settings to increase in the future due to economic and efficacy reasons. However, we restrict our review to breast cancer and pain given the number of recent studies.

Breast Cancer

Cancer is one of the most common causes of death and is often accompanied with a variety of psychological problems justifying psycho-oncological/psychotherapeutic treatment. Breast cancer is the most common oncological disease among women, with 268,600 new cases in 2018 in the US and 562,568 new cases in Europe (cf. cancernet.com). Interestingly, while the incidence of cancer is increasing, the mortality rates are decreasing. For instance, the number of long-term breast cancer survivors has reached a very high level (e.g., 90% five-year survival rate), which – from a psychological perspective – creates new psycho-oncological problems, such as fear of future progression or simply living with a history of cancer.

In our last review, we identified 23 new studies comprising supportive-expressive group therapy (SEGT), CBT, psychoeducational group (PEG) treatments, and some mixed approaches. Most studies were RCTs, and the most reliable effect across all three treatments was improvement in emotional distress. Members in CBGT and SEGT were better able to cope with their illness, while those is SEGT had better life adjustment. In contrast to earlier studies, no support for group treatments extending the life of the patient was found in any study. The most recent Cochrane review (Mustafa et al., 2013) summarized studies with 1378 women with metastatic breast cancer also showing positive effects for CBT and SEGT.

We found 28 studies published since our last review, which are summarized in Table 17.3, including mixed samples (e.g., males with prostate or bladder cancer). The trend toward greater methodological rigor has continued with a high proportion of RCTs, although some research still fits the pilot or feasibility study framework. Interestingly, a few studies mentioned in our last chapter generated long-term follow-up or secondary analyses. For example, Phillips et al. (2011) led to follow-up analyses by Stagl and colleagues (Stagl, Antoni et al., 2015; Stagl, Bouchard et al., 2015; Stagl, Lechner et al., 2015), and Antoni et al. (2006), in an RCT comparing CB stress management vs. psychoeducation generating an 11-year follow-up (Antoni et al., 2016). In general, follow-up studies showed continued benefits (e.g., reduced cortisol, depression, and mortality) relative to controls.

CBGT/Stress Management Groups. The largest number of studies published since our last review (10) used either *CBT or stress management* protocols producing improvement on emotional distress, depression, anxiety and dysfunctional fear of progression with increased resilience (Sabariego et al., 2011). A large study on weight loss in cancer patients (ENERGY trial, Rock et al., 2013, 2015) found CBT produced more weight loss than controls. Two studies compared format effectiveness. Naumann et al. (2012) found an individual exercise and counseling program to be more effective than group exercise and counseling, but Rissanen et al. (2014, 2015) found no format differences in stress and fatigue reduction, although there was better attendance for individual stress management (91% vs. 54%).

Support Groups. Two studies evaluated *support groups*. One reported positive effect related to cognitive function, body image, future perspectives and fatigue (Björneklett, Lindemalm, Ojutkangas et al., 2012; 2013b). A second study found positive effects on knowledge, fatalism, fear and social connection with telephone support groups (Heiney et al., 2012).

Psychoeducational (PE) Groups. PE group formats still play an important role in the group treatment for breast

TABLE 17.3 Group Within Medical Settings: (Breast) Cancer and Pain

	Study Characteristics					Sample Characteristics				
									Range average	
Study	%RCT	%ITT	%Attr	Follow-up	A	C	age	% Females	Effects related to different outcome criteria
Breast Cancer										
CBT groups and stress management Antoni et al. 2016, Stagl et al. 2015 a,b,c, Phillips et al. 2011 (all related to Antoni et al. 2006); Manne et al. (2016; 2017), Merckaert et al. (2016), Loprinzi et al (2011), Naumann et al. (2012), Pelekasis et al. (2016), Rissanen et al., (2014, 2015), Rock et al. (2013, 2015), Sabariego et al. (2011)	100	8 v 13	8–58 (11 yrs)	6–24 mo. (Antoni et al., 2006: 15 yrs).	12–334	12–348	49–61	100 (exception: Sabariego et al., 2011: 85.6%)	Anxiety (4) Depressive symptoms (3) Distress (2) QoL (2) Perceived stress (2) Weight/BMI (2) Gene expression (1) Mortality (1) Use of skills (1) Well-being (1) Quality of sleep (1) Costs (1) Fear of progression (1)
Support Groups: Björneklett, Lindemalm, Ojutkangas et al., 2012; Björneklett, Lindemalm, Rosenblad et al., 2012; 2013a,b), Heiney et al. (2012)	100	50	5–13 (6.5 yrs: 28%)	16 w.–12 mo. (+ 6.5 yrs)	92–178	93–175	56–58	100	Anxiety/Fear (2) QoL (1) Fatigue (1) Knowledge (1) Social connection (1) Fatalism/Future perspectives (1) Cognitive function (1)

(Continued)

TABLE 17.3 (Continued)

	Study Characteristics				Sample Characteristics				
Study	%RCT	%ITT	%Attr	Follow-up	A	C	Range average age	% Females	Effects related to different outcome criteria
Psychoeducation Boesen et al. 2011; Bredal et al (2014); Causarano et al. (2015); Simoncini et al. (2017); Jones et al. (2013); Ramos et al. (2018)	100	33	4–29	0–12 m.	21–216	20–226	49–50	100	Self efficacy (1) Sartisfaction (1) Knowledge (1) Posttraumatic growth (1) Anxiety (1) Hopelessness (1) Decisional conflicts (1) QoL (1) Adherence (1)
Mindfulness-based and other third-wave approaches Carlson et al. (2015, 2016); Cerezo et al. (2014); Freeman et al. (2015); van der Spek, Vos et al. (2017); van der Spek, Willemsen (2017): Victorson et al. (2017); Zhang et al. (2017); Monti et al. (2013); Schellekens et al. (2017, related to Carlson et al. 2013)	100	50	3–45	4 w.–12 mo.	24–134	19–118	40–75	100 (exceptions: van der Spek, Vos et al., 2017: Viktorson et al., 2017)	Stress (5) Mood (4) QoL (3) Anxiety (2) Personal relations (2) Posttraumatic growth (1) Well-being (1) Happiness (1) Optimism (1) Resilience (1) Fatigue (1) Sleep (1) Cognitive functions (1) Personal growth (1) Fighting spirit (1) Posttraumatic growth (1)

TABLE 17.3 (CONTINUED)

	Study Characteristics				Sample Characteristics				
Study	%RCT	%ITT	%Attr	Follow-up	A	C	Range average age	% Females	Effects related to different outcome criteria

Pain

Fibromyalgia Bourgault, et al. (2015), Martins, et al. (2014); Olsson et al. (2012); Parra-Delgado & Latorre-Postigo (2013); Thieme et al. (2016); Wicksell et al. (2013); Torres et al. (2018); Vallejo et al. (2015); Castel et al. (2012)	100	55	0–35	0–12 mo.	12–43	15–30	39–53	58–100	Pain relief (5) Pain-related functioning (3) QoL (3) Depression (3) Pain disability (2) Self-efficacy (2) Anxiety (2) Blood pressure (1) Distress (1)
Chronic pain Garland & Howard (2013); Gebler & Maercker (2014); Gustavsson & von Koch (2017); Harris et al. (2017); Inoue et al. (2014); Kemani et al. (2015); Kjeldgaard et al. (2014); Knox et al. (2014); Lamb et al. (2010); Lamb et al. (2012); Le Borgne et al. (2016); Linden et al. (2014); Marques et al. (2014); Mehlsen et al. (2017); Morone et al. (2016); Sleptsova et al. (2013)	85	66	5–53	0–9yrs (Md = 6 mo.)	7–403	7–300	38–74	65	Pain relief (10) Pain disability (6) Mood (3) Self-efficacy (2) Analgesics usage (1) Catastrophizing thought (1) Distress (1) Functional components of pain (1) Anxiety (1) Attentional bias (1)
Specific pain Bergeron et al., (2016); Brotto et al. (2015); Helminen et al. (2015); Lomholt, et al. (2015); Vitiello et al. (2013)	100	80	0–33	2–12 mo.	9–122	10–123	12–73	85	Pain relief (2) QoL (1) Adaptive cognitions (1) Well-being (1)

cancer with six new studies identified. In some, PE and TAU support group formats were equally effective (Boesen et al., 2011; Bredal et al., 2014), while others found PE producing improvement in posttraumatic growth (Ramos et al., 2018), knowledge about the disease/treatment (Jones et al., 2013) and decisional conflict (Causarano et al., 2015). Simoncini et al. (2017) demonstrated equivalent effects for individual and group PE on treatment adherence, quality of life (QoL) and anxiety, although group treatment was more time-efficient.

Mindfulness-Based: MB and Third-Wave Approaches. Group treatments increasingly used *MB and third-wave* protocols. The eight studies in Table 17.3 primarily applied these to breast cancer showing positive effects of mindfulness, imagery and meaning. The YOGA group formats showed improvement on stress symptoms, mood, QoL, anxiety, personal relations, and post traumatic growth. Only two of the studies went beyond efficacy analyses with one (Schellekens et al., 2017) identifying social support as a mediator for cancer recovery and a second finding working alliance and engagement predicting outcome in CBT couple group treatments (Manne et al., 2017).

As evident in the effects depicted in Table 17.3, the outcomes studied are very different since our last review focusing on posttraumatic growth, optimism, and resilience. This outcome heterogeneity hampers strong narrative conclusions compared to our last review. CBGT, support, and PE group treatments still play a significant role in the most recent literature. However, supportive-expressive group treatments have fallen away and have been replaced by MB and third-wave interventions.

Pain

We previously focused on somatoform disorders, but the limited studies and changes in diagnostic criteria – somatoform has been replaced with somatic symptom disorders – do not support summarizing research for this diagnosis. Thus, we focus solely on pain, a field that has produced a large number of studies since our last review (Table 17.3).

The immense costs of pain treatment coupled with the high risk of pain medication addiction may be fueling the increase in RCTs on non-pharmacological treatments, including group therapy. We previously concluded that CBGT was effective in reducing pain intensity and pain-related psychological symptoms, as well as increasing quality of life. CBGT research has continued with heterogeneous pain conditions including chronic back pain with positive effects on pain intensity, functional impairment, depression, and anxiety. A recent meta-analysis (Niknejad et al., 2018) of 22 studies summarizing the effectiveness of psychological interventions for chronic pain in older adults (mean age = 71.9 yrs.) found treatment format as the only significant moderator of pain outcomes; group treatment produced more favorable effects. In our search, we located 32 new group treatment studies since our 2013 review treating pain in all age groups that can be classified into three categories: fibromyalgia, chronic pain including low back pain, and specific pain.

Fibromyalgia. The group treatment studies (9) focusing on *fibromyalgia* tested CBGT, operational behavior therapy (OBT), ACT, self-management training, MB and Music Imagery. With the exception of the MB intervention (Parra-Delgado & Latorre-Postigo, 2013), group treatments outperformed controls (mostly WLC) on pain reduction. Group treatments also outperformed controls on function, anxiety and depression, self-efficacy, and pain-related disability in some studies (Bourgault et al., 2015; Martins et al., 2014; Olsson et al., 2012; Thieme et al., 2016; Torres et al., 2018; Wicksell et al., 2013). A CBT study (Vallejo et al., 2015) compared face-to-face with internet-based (iCBT) therapy and found equivalent improvement on psychological distress and coping, although iCBT showed greater improvement in self-efficacy. A single study compared CBGT with CBGT plus hypnosis, finding the latter more effective (Castel et al., 2012).

Chronic Pain. CBGT continues to be a dominant approach with improvement in coping with pain and reduced pain-related disability. However, there are more mixed findings in recent studies than we previously reported. CBGT continues to outperform controls (e.g., physical therapy, health education) in several studies (Knox et al., 2014, Le Borgne et al., 2016; Inoue et al., 2014; Linden et al., 2014; Morone et al., 2016; Thorn et al., 2018). However, in others CBGT shows superior pain-related outcomes, but no differences on general psychopathology (e.g., Linden et al., 2014). Still others found CBGT equivalent to controls in pain reduction but better on secondary outcomes (anxiety, depression; e.g., Taylor et al., 2016). Five studies found CBGT to be equivalent to active group and control conditions (Harris et al., 2017; Kjeldgaard et al., 2014; Marques et al., 2014; Mehlsen et al., 2017; Sleptsova et al., 2013). Thus, CBGT findings, while positive, are clearly more mixed since our last review.

Third-wave approaches (ACT, MB) along with meditation, produced positive effects on attentional bias (Garland & Howard, 2013) and other pain outcomes (Zgierska et al., 2016). Interestingly, greater improvement was found when an existential component was added to CBGT compared to CBGT alone (Gebler & Maerker, 2014). When ACT was compared to applied relaxation (AR, Kemani et al., 2015), ACT showed greater pre- to posttreatment pain improvement but AR produced the same improvement by six-month follow-up.

Two studies from our last review (Gustavsson et al., 2010; Lamb et al., 2010) generated follow-up assessments. The first study reported on a nine-year follow-up of multicomponent group treatment intervention that continued to show group patients having less pain-related disability, pain intensity, and analgesics use than individually administered physical therapy (Gustavsson & Koch, 2017). A second study reported on a three-year follow-up of CBGT for chronic pain, demonstrating that pre–post outcome improvements were maintained (Lamb et al., 2012).

Specific Pain. CBGT to manage intercourse pain (dyspareunia) was compared with medication and waitlist (Bergeron et al., 2016; Brotto et al., 2015) with mixed findings.

CBGT was more effective than medication but equivalent to the WLC. Further conflicting results were found for CBGT and arthritis pain. Positive effects were found for adolescents suffering from juvenile arthritis (CBGT vs. wait-list; Lomholt et al., 2015), but two studies with adults suffering from knee arthritis pain showed no difference between CBGT and a psychoeducational intervention (Vitiello et al., 2013). In a third study, CBGT produced greater effects on well-being but equivalence on pain intensity (compared to ordinary GP treatment; Helminen et al., 2015).

Taken together, CBGT as a gold-standard group treatment for pain is only partially supported by the most recent evidence. The conflicting evidence may be indicative of the need to improve psychological group treatment of pain. It might also suggest the importance of pain treatment including multiple components. For example, in individual treatment of pain, exposure has been shown to be a promising alternative to CBT (Glombiewski et al., 2018) and the mixed findings for group treatment, coupled with the positive findings for multi-component group treatment, is promising. Finally, the large number of recent studies justify a meta-analytic review to test alternative combinations and define new research and treatment directions.

Groups for Severe Mental Illness

Once again, we found group treatments being heavily relied on for patients diagnosed with severe mental illness. As we've stated in previous chapters, these disorders typically consume far more mental health resources due to their chronicity and symptom severity increases, often leading to rehospitalization. Some disorders include disease management groups intended to increase medication and treatment compliance (e.g., schizophrenia), while other disorders have groups that focus on multiple psychosocial targets (e.g., personality disorders)

Schizophrenia

Schizophrenia is a biologically based disorder leading to the primary practice guideline of antipsychotic medications (APA – Lehman et al., 2010; NICE 2014). Given the significant functional impairment associated with this disorder, a number of psychosocial treatments have been studied including family interventions, social skills training, psychoeducation, assertive community treatment, supported employment/vocational rehabilitation, and psychotherapy with CBT being the predominant model studied. These psychosocial treatments are often tailored to individual patients but some are offered in a group format. Practice guideline endorsement of these psychosocial treatments are mixed. CBT and family therapy are recommended in APA and NICE practice guidelines; however, both recommend that CBT be delivered in an individual format while NICE endorses multifamily group (MFG) treatment. Social skill therapy (SST) and psychoeducation are endorsed by APA but NICE questions the value of SST.

In our last review, we concluded that group treatment for patients diagnosed with schizophrenia had good-to-excellent empirical support. CBT targeting schizophrenia-specific symptoms had the highest number of new studies (11) with the

majority (80%) being RCTs that compared CBT with standard care. Symptom distress change was mixed, but there was more uniform improvement on self-esteem, social anxiety, coping, functioning, and quality-of-life outcomes. Multifamily group (MFG) treatments target medication compliance, psychoeducation and problem solving and five RCTs with TAU comparisons found support for decreased rehospitalization, improved family functioning, but there was comparable symptom distress change. Traditional social skills training (SST) targets behavioral deficits in social skills and interpersonal functioning. They have recently been combined with CBT with improved social and living skill outcomes. Psycho-education group (PEG) treatments disseminate disease management information and a small number of studies (4) showed limited improvement in patient functioning, symptom distress and rehospitalization.

Recent Meta-Analytic Support. In an effort to address the mismatch between the empirical literature and practice guidelines, Burlingame et al. (2020) conducted a meta-analysis spanning nearly 30 years (1990–2018) of research on group treatment for patients diagnosed with schizophrenia (Table 17.4). Group treatments having five or more studies were included: CBT, MFG, SST, PEG, cognitive remediation (CR), and meta-cognitive training (MCT). The latter two did not appear in our last review and reflect relatively new treatments. CR is a behavioral treatment targeting improved attention, memory, and executive functioning and MCT targets thoughts patterns (e.g., jumping to conclusions) associated with schizophrenia. The meta-analysis was limited to randomized clinical trials with contrasts to active treatment – TAU or passive controls (WLC, attention). To limit random heterogeneity, studies were only included if the two most frequently used schizophrenia measures were included in the study – Brief Psychiatric Rating Scale (BPRS; Overall & Gorham, 1962) and Positive and Negative Syndrome Scale (PANSS; Kay et al., 1987). Two additional outcome domains were assessed: (a) treatment-specific assessed outcomes (e.g., CR expects an increase in executive functioning and SST attempts to reduce social skills deficits) and (b) general functioning.

Contrasts were based on 60 treatment comparisons from 52 studies that included 4156 individuals. Six of these studies were included in our 2013 chapter. The average patient was a 34-year-old male (63%) and treated in an outpatient clinic. The typical group had 18 biweekly 75-minute sessions comprised of 7 members with a 12% attrition rate and the groups were evenly split between patients with homogeneous (e.g., first episode) and heterogeneous diagnoses (e.g., schizophrenia and schizoaffective). Most groups (79%) followed a manual but only a third (38%) had adherence checks.

Group Treatment Efficacy on Schizophrenia Outcomes.
Four treatments (SST, MFG, CR & PEG) posted significant improvement over TAU and passive controls (Table 17.4). SST posted the highest level of improvement on schizophrenia outcomes with a moderate effect. While this provides clear and compelling evidence for the efficacy of SST, a cautionary note is found in the significant heterogeneity (75%) of effects across

TABLE 17.4 Summary of Meta-Analyses for Severe Mental Illness

Study	Disorder	Studies (comparisons) included	N_I	N_C	(Primary) outcome	Comparison (k)	g (p)	Typical group method(s)	Median: sessions, session length, sessions per week, size)
1	Schizophrenia	52 (60)	2303	1840	SZ = PANSS, BPRS	Active – TAU and passive – WLC		CR, SST, MCT, MFG, CBT, IPT, PE	18 – 75- 2 – 7
						CR (17)	0.31**		
						SST (11)	0.53***		
						PE (8)	0.29*		
						MCT (6)	0.16 ns		
						MFG (5)	0.39*		
						CBT (5)	0.08 ns		
						IPT (3)	0.24 ns		
2	BPD	24	813	792	BPD symptoms	TAU (13)	0.72***	DBT, ACT, STEPPS, PD, IT, SFT, EIT	28 – 120 – 1 – 7
						TAU compr (5)	0.47*		
						Adjunct (6)	1.13***		
					Suicidality/Parasuicidality	TAU (19)	0.46***		
						TAU compr (14)	0.44***		
						Adjunct (4)	0.65 ns		

Note. ACT = acceptance commitment therapy, CBT = cognitive behavioral therapy, CR = cognitive remediation, DBT = dialectical behavior therapy, EIT = emotional intelligence therapy, IT = interpersonal therapy, IPT = integrated psychological therapy, MCT = meta-cognitive therapy, MFG = multifamily group, PD = psychodynamic therapy, PE = psycho-educational, SFT = schema focused therapy, SST = social skills therapy, STEPPS = systems for training emotional predictability & problem solving

Study: 1 Burlingame et al. 2020; 2 McLaughlin et al. (2019)

* $p < .05$, ** $p < .01$, *** $p < .001$, ns = not significant

the 11 studies. CR was the most frequently studied treatment producing a significant small-to-moderate effect size. However, unlike SST, there was no heterogeneity (1%) across the 17 studies examined, suggesting a stable effect. Both PEG and MFG group treatments produced significant, but small effects. While the PEG effect size was larger than MFG, the high and significant heterogeneity (83%) across the 5 studies examined weaken our confidence in the average effect. Interestingly, there was no heterogeneity found in the MFG effect size, increasing our confidence in this estimate.

We find these significant findings intriguing on a few fronts. First, both NICE and APA practice guidelines question the value of group SST. However, the APA guidelines are based on 1970s–1980s research and there is less clarity on the research that leads to the NICE guideline. The meta-analytic findings clearly support the efficacy of SST as a recommended group treatment. However, the heterogeneity in SST effects suggest that improvement may vary by model, setting, or some other unknown variable raising caution around generalizability. Given the large number of studies and low heterogeneity, our confidence in the efficacy of CR remains high as a recommended group treatment. The effects for MFG and PEG are similar to CR, supporting them as recommended treatments, but, the evidentiary basis is smaller for both and the heterogeneity in MFG effect sizes raises the same caution noted for SST group treatments. Nonetheless, we believe there is sufficient evidence to reconsider practice guideline recommendations when it comes to these four group treatments.

Three treatments – CBT, MCT and IPT – produced effects that were not significant (Table 17.4), leading us to conclude that they are ineffective in changing schizophrenic symptoms when assessed by the BPRS and PANNS given the most recent evidence although improvement was noted in other symptom domains. The CBT finding matches past meta-analytic findings (Velthorst et al., 2015) although the findings disagree with three CBT meta-analyses (Barrowclough et al., 2006; Hazell et al., 2016; Wykes et al., 2008). However, a careful analysis reveals virtually no study overlap and since comparisons are limited by measure (PANSS & BPRS) and control groups differences, our current conclusion is that CBT delivered in a group format may be ineffective in changing positive and negative symptoms of schizophrenia. The absence of CBT effect size heterogeneity strengthens this conclusion but, the small number of controlled CBT studies clearly calls for further research with a larger sample size. MCT effects were also not significant on changing positive and negative symptoms of schizophrenia, and this finding agrees with a MCT meta-analysis (van Oosterhout et al., 2016). Moreover, the addition of four unique group treatment studies and the absence of heterogeneity increases confidence in the ineffective conclusion. Finally, the jury is out on IPT effectiveness given the small number of controlled trials, which are undoubtedly due to the measure and control group limitations of the meta-analysis.

Treatment-Specific Improvement. A second finding from the Burlingame et al. (2020) meta-analysis was that improvement in treatment specific outcomes predicted improvement in schizophrenia outcomes. More specifically, the question posed by the meta-analysis was: If CR produced better outcomes for a group member's executive functioning – a treatment-specific outcome – would there be a parallel increase in the improvement on schizophrenia outcomes? This question was tested using 41 studies that assessed treatment-specific outcomes. A meta-regression analysis found that treatment-specific outcomes explained 16% of improvement on schizophrenia outcomes. Stated differently, as CR, MCT, PE and SST group treatments had their intended effect, there was a small but significant amount of variance in schizophrenia outcomes explained. This finding is important in that it supports the importance of monitoring treatment-specific outcomes for individual group members. It also provides indirect support for the underlying mechanism of change in these four treatments. An even more intriguing meta-regression finding was that treatment specific outcomes explained 44% of the general functioning outcomes. However, both meta-regression findings disappeared at follow up, which may be explained by a smaller sample size or the durability of the effect. Finally, moderator analyses showed that group leaders with more training (doctoral versus masters) as well as group treatments having a higher dose (more sessions) were associated with more improvement in treatment specific outcomes.

Personality Disorders

Borderline personality disorder – BPD is one of the most commonly treated personality disorders in clinical practice and practice guidelines from the American Psychiatric Association indicate the primary treatment should be psychotherapy complemented by symptom-targeted pharmacotherapy (Oldham et al., 2010). Group treatment may be a uniquely suited format for treating BPD. For instance, it provides members with an opportunity to practice skills (e.g., emotional regulation in dialectical behavior therapy: DBT) in an interpersonal environment which approximates real life more closely than individual therapy. In addition, the peer support provided by group members and leaders may improve motivation and treatment compliance (Linehan, 2014). Patients diagnosed with BPD are prone to distrust and see others as having negative intentions and the initial trust built through therapist interactions followed by social relationships in the group setting provides a reality check on these tendencies. Indeed, some have suggested that group treatment promotes change in attachment patterns (Marmarosh, 2014) through the social environment created by the group format (Bateman & Fonagy, 2016). There are disadvantages to group format, including the potential for intense affect, fears of abandonment and, distorted interpersonal relationships that come with BPD (Yalom & Leszcz, 2005).

In our last review, we noted that dialectal behavior therapy had received the most empirical attention through its 2.5 hour/weekly, 12-month skills group treatment that complements individual therapy and telephone coaching. We noted the consistent positive effects in reducing suicidal ideation and self-harm from meta-analytic reviews (Kliem et al., 2010) and promising evidence from RCTs supporting its efficacy, even when comorbid substance use was present. Unfortunately, a dismantling study (Koerner & Linehan, 2000) did not support the group format component of DBT and we suggested further research testing the independent effects of the skills-group treatment. The Systems Training for Emotional Predictability and Problem Solving (STEPPS) is a less time consuming (20-week) group treatment protocol that emphasizes emotional and behavior management and four trials had shown promising results. Several day-treatment programs had also shown encouraging results including the 18-month Mentalization-Based Day Treatment (MBDT; Bateman & Fonagy, 1999) that lowered emergency room visits and admissions relative to TAU. We reviewed six less rigorous studies testing traditional day-treatment programs that include cognitive, dynamic and process group treatment and found improvement in symptoms, hospitalization rates and social functioning. Finally, research on inpatient programs that integrate 6–18 months of inpatient and outpatient care showed that they outperformed TAU on measures of symptoms and functioning but also had a very high rate of dropout (47%).

Recent Meta-Analytic Support. McLaughlin and colleagues (2019) conducted a meta-analysis of 24 studies with 1595 participants which included all of the treatments examined in our last review. Eleven of these studies were included in our 2013 chapter. All the studies were randomized controlled trials comparing group treatment for BPD against TAU where group treatment was the primary therapeutic intervention. Two primary outcomes were assessed: BPD symptoms derived from diagnostic criteria and suicidality/parasuicidality. The average patient was a 31-year-old female (88%) treated in an outpatient setting (75%) with DBT (58%) who was taking medication (71%) and also receiving individual therapy or case management. The typical group had seven members and two leaders and met for 28 two-hour weekly sessions following a manual with adherence checks (71%). The three primary comparisons included TAU, comprehensive TAU where group treatment was part of a comprehensive treatment program (e.g., DBT), and adjunct where group treatment (e.g., ACT) was added to an existing treatment of medication and individual therapy.

Large effects (Table 17.4) were found for BPD symptoms when group treatment was contrasted against all TAU conditions with high heterogeneity. When treatment subtypes were contrasted, statistically significant differences were found. Comprehensive treatment programs (e.g., DBT) fell into the moderate range while group treatment as adjunct posted large effects. A second significant moderator was group size; as it increased, member improvement decreased. A moderator analysis comparing DBT against all other treatments (ACT, STEPPS, PD, IPT, SFT, EIT) revealed no reliable difference although descriptive results favored ACT and SFT. Moderate effects were found on the suicidality and parasuicidality outcomes when group treatment was compared to all TAU conditions. Unlike the BPD symptoms analysis, other treatments (ACT, psychodynamic) produced more improvement than DBT but the number of studies makes this finding tentative. Like BPD symptoms, larger group size was associated with less improvement. Finally, when secondary outcomes were examined, group treatments posted a significant moderate effect for the anxiety and depression measures compared to all TAU conditions. No differences between group treatment and TAU were found on hospitalization and attrition rates with 27% of patients prematurely leaving treatment.

The results of the McLaughlin et al. (2019) meta-analysis provide strong empirical support for the effectiveness of group treatment in all forms for reducing BPD symptoms. The fact that the DBT effect size replicate past meta-analytic estimates on BPD symptoms (Cristea et al., 2017) increases confidence in these findings. In general, theoretical orientation did not explain improvement on BPD symptoms and the descriptive differences that favored other treatments (e.g., ACT) over DBT are limited by small sample sizes. Further confidence in McLaughlin and colleagues' findings is found in the replication of the DBT effect size on suicidality/parasuicidality (Stoffers et al., 2012). Type of TAU (psychotherapy versus case/clinical management) did not produce different effect sizes suggesting a benefit for adding group treatment, irrespective of the type of standard care offered. Our general conclusion is that outpatient BPD group treatment produces reliable improvement with DBT having the strongest empirical support. There is an insufficient number of studies to make reliable conclusions for non-DBT outpatient (DBT, ACT, STEPPS, PD, IPT, SFT, EIT), day-treatment, and inpatient group treatments; future research is encouraged. While Mentalization-Based Day Treatment (MBDT; Bateman & Fonagy, 1999) appeared in our earlier review, recent research (Edel et al., 2017; Phillips et al., 2018) did not meet the RCT standard set by McLaughlin et al. (2019) making definitive conclusions illusive.

PROMISING DEVELOPMENTS IN SMALL GROUP TREATMENT OUTCOME

As in our previous chapters, we noticed several pockets of new research that we considered promising. These areas parallel research topics found in the individual therapy literature. For instance, attachment theory has a long history in understanding an individual personality and differential response to treatment. In our 2013 chapter we noted individuals who were at the forefront of applying attachment style to group treatment (e.g., Tasca). A new group of individuals have joined these pioneers (Marmarosh, Maxwell, etc.) strengthing and extending past findings. As we write this chapter, the world is experiencing a COVID-19 pandemic and the social distancing required by this disorder have led to a reliance on telehealth. We note the additional work investigating on-line groups and raise questions about "what's next."

Attachment Style

Among the dynamics and personal characteristics that patients and therapists bring into a group, attachment styles and representations, based on the individual´s attachment history, have been highlighted in recent years (cf. Marmarosh, Markin & Spiegel, 2013, see also Marmarosh, 2017; Tasca et al., 2013). Since it is well known that attachment plays an important role in the prediction of outcome and process in individual therapy (e.g., Bernecker et al., 2017; Levy et al., 2018), attachment issues have finally found empirical attention in group research. Recently, conceptual developments that integrate attachment theory into group therapy approaches have appeared: Mentalization-Based

Group Treatment (MBGT, Karterud, 2015) or Focused Brief Group Therapy (FBGT, Whittingham, 2017).

Several authors have reflected on the meaning of the group (Smith et al., 1999) and its leader (Leszcz, 2017) as a secure base or safe haven. Accordingly, in a group-related model of psychological change Mikulincer and Shaver (2017) postulate that "repeated interactions with responsive and supportive leaders and cohesive groups beneficially alter a person´s attachment patterns and psychological functioning" (p. 161). There is evidence that specific moments in a group treatment can activate the attachment system of group members (e.g., situations of separation).

While Mikulincer and Shaver´s (2017) assumption is mainly based on findings from social/organizational psychology, there is increasing research showing positive changes in attachment related to group psychotherapy (Keating et al., 2014; Kinley & Reyno, 2013; Kirchmann et al., 2012; Tasca et al., 2006). Maxwell et al. (2014) demonstrated that positive changes in attachment were related with an improvement in interpersonal problems and depressive symptoms. Clinically, Marmarosh and Tasca (2013) articulate how attachment theory can be applied to group treatment by fostering the secure base in the group through cohesion, enabling members to regulate emotions, leading to better reflective functioning and relationships.

Empirically, it has been shown that attachment dimensions (commonly anxiety and avoidance) are important predictors for the process and outcome in group psychotherapy, both on an individual level as well as on an aggregated level. Tasca and colleagues have explored these questions primarily in group treatments for patients with eating disorders (BED). For example, anxious members do better in group therapies fostering cohesion (Tasca et al., 2006), whereas avoidant members have greater rates of dropping out (Tasca et al., 2004, 2006), repelled by the pressures to be more intimate in the group setting (Illing et al., 2011). Gallagher et al. (2014) found an increase in group cohesion in both high and low attachment anxiety conditions, but also that attachment anxiety at baseline acted as a moderator between growth in cohesion and outcome. More specifically, increase in cohesion was associated with improved binge eating symptoms only for patients with high attachment anxiety scores. Fox and colleagues (2021) found that compassion-focused group treatments positively impacted attachment anxiety.

Kivlighan et al. (2012) used an actor-partner interdependence model (APIM) to explore the relationship between members' attachment anxiety and avoidance and their perceptions of the group climate. They showed that aggregated perceptions of attachment anxiety and avoidance were negatively related to a member´s perception of engagement (measured with the GCQ), but positively related to the perception of the group climate. Such complex analyses could be of clinical relevance with respect to group treatment selection and composition. In a more recent study, Kivlighan, Lo Coco, Gullo et al. (2017) studied individual members´ attachment and the attachment of the other group members in a sample of 201 members of 20 different groups and related attachment to GQ scales. They showed that attachment heterogeneity in a group setting

was connected to the perception of members´ stronger bonding relationships and lower negative relationships. Positive bonding increased when a patient with high avoidance was added to a group treatment with patients who are low in attachment avoidance. Finally, group members reported weaker negative relationships when their attachment anxiety or avoidance became higher or lower than the average attachment anxiety or avoidance of the other members.

In summary, an increasing number of studies indicate the relevance of attachment for group psychotherapy. Group leaders might consider if their specific group treatment might: (a) interact with their members attachment style – e.g., anxious or avoidant attachment, (b) explain drop out or willingness to engage in the groups' climate, (c) moderate the cohesion-outcome relationship discussed below, or (d) be useful in member selection and group composition. Clearly, the theoretical and empirical literature on attachment in group treatment is still embryonic. However, the increase in the number of studies addressing this patient characteristic and its clinical relevance is hard to ignore. We look forward to both greater conceptual development and empirical support on this topic in future research.

Online Groups

In 2013, we observed that there was an increase in "evaluating the augmentation of existing group treatments through technology, that is, online modes of delivery" (p. 666). First attempts at studying applications of group treatment from an asynchronous (e.g., internet forum proving contact to a therapist) and synchronous online contact (e.g., real time) were appearing in the literature and we described them as promising. However, the situation has changed remarkably (e.g., Arnberg et al., 2014).

Asynchronous Group Applications

Moderated forums and discussion groups are common components of internet treatment programs that have been designed for a variety of disorders; for example, anxiety disorders (Titov et al., 2010); bipolar disorders (Gliddon et al., 2019; Lauder et al., 2015); depressive symptoms or disorders (Griffiths et al., 2012; Kordy et al., 2016); eating disorders (Jacobi et al., 2012; Kass et al., 2014); and cancer (Melton et al., 2017). Most studies we found using asynchronous group treatments tested the efficacy of the internet program within RCTs (e.g., Lauder et al., 2015) or evaluated the users´ satisfaction (e.g., Moessner & Bauer, 2012). Although the general and specific effectiveness of the programs is usually confirmed, the studies do not allow us to tease out the specific role of the group element. We found a single study assessing an internet program for eating disorder risk prevention where guided discussion groups had an effect on outcome compared to the same program with no discussion groups (Kass et al., 2014).

Synchronous Online Groups

These online interventions have gained importance and group elements consist of chat rooms/groups where participants meet each other and the therapist. We found seven RCTs with larger samples dealing with a variety of clinical problems (eating disorders, depression, ADHD, cancer, social anxiety disorder, and being victim of family violence). Most studies confirm the benefits of the internet program including the group component when compared to wait-list or TAU conditions (e.g., Crisp et al., 2014; van der Zanden et al., 2012), while others indicate format equivalence when compared to asynchronous (or nonvirtual) group treatments (see above; Pettersson et al., 2017; Schulz et al., 2016). Users commonly reflect a high degree of satisfaction and indicate that the online group was an important source to increase coping (Hopf et al., 2013; Stephen et al., 2013).

Internet-based (group) programs are seen as less stigmatizing, specifically appropriate for specific users. For instance, young people and those with limited access to psychosocial support find these interventions to be more economic. Schulz et al. (2016) found that the average amount of therapist weekly time per participant was reduced by 71% compared to traditional CBGT and internet group treatments for social anxiety disorders. Tate et al. (2017) demonstrated in an RCT that a four-month hybrid internet weight loss program with monthly face-to-face large-group meetings was equally effective to traditional group meetings and that the online interventions increased the cost-effectiveness.

In summary, we detected an increase of studies using internet-based technology both, for providing forums and discussion (asynchronous) group settings as well as synchronous online interventions for a wide range of disorders. As in individual psychotherapy, the development of internet-based online group treatments has made considerable progress reflecting the fact that new technologies allow these interventions to reach a much wider range of patients than face-to-face encounters.

SMALL GROUP PROCESS

In past chapters, we have: (a) provided recommended measures of group process, (b) presented a conceptual model to explicate the complexity of therapeutic processes in small groups, and (c) reviewed new measures intended to psychometrically tease apart the complexity of small group treatment processes. In our last review, we summarized the empirical evidence that supported cohesion as the best predictor of outcome in small group treatment. However, a limitation of this research was that it only assessed two of the three group structural relationships – member-to-member and member-to-group. As noted below, the most recent research on cohesion continues this pattern. However, a small and growing number of studies have begun to test the member-to-leader predictive relationship with outcome. We briefly summarize this research and make clinical and empirical recommendations.

Cohesion as a Predictor of Outcome

In our chapter in the last edition of this *Handbook*, we reported on a meta-analysis (Burlingame et al., 2011) of 40 studies published between 1969 and 2009 that tested the predictive relationship of cohesion and treatment outcome in group treatment. A significant weighted-average correlation ($r = .25$)

was found based on more than 3,300 group members, and we concluded that "cohesion predicts outcome across the most common theoretical orientations and that the size of this relationship varies by measure" (Burlingame et al., 2013; p. 671). This meta-analysis also found five moderators that explained variability in the size of the cohesion-outcome relationship. While cohesion is statistically significant across all theoretical orientations, it is most strongly correlated in interpersonal models, followed by psychodynamic and CBT. Higher cohesion–outcome correlations were found for leaders who emphasized member-to-member interaction, group treatments lasting more than 12 sessions, moderately sized groups (5–9 members), and groups composed of younger members.

This meta-analysis was recently updated (Burlingame, McClendon et al., 2018) with 55 studies and more than 6,000 group members returning a similar significant weighted average correlation between cohesion and outcome: $r = .26$ (95% CI = .20, .31), a moderate effect ($d = 0.56$) with high heterogeneity (79.3%). There was no evidence of publication or outlier bias. Interestingly, 73% of the newly published studies (2010–2018) reported a significant cohesion-outcome relationship compared to 43% of the older studies. This suggests greater empirical support for cohesion's moderating effect on member improvement in recently published evidence-based group protocols that focused on specific patient populations.

The high level of heterogeneity was explored with the moderators used in the previous meta-analysis. Two previous moderators fell away (group size, member age), three were replicated (theoretical orientation, member-to-member interaction, and number of sessions) and three new moderators (leader interventions, type of outcome measure, and group) were added. Once again, higher cohesion-outcome correlations were produced by interpersonal models ($r = .48$), followed by psychodynamic ($r = .27$) and CBT ($r = .22$). However, two additional theoretical orientations posted significant relationships including supportive and eclectic ($r = .22$ each). We believe that cohesion has sufficient empirical support to be considered an evidence-based relationship factor for five orientations; interpersonal, psychodynamic, CBT, supportive, and eclectic. Further replications included higher cohesion-outcome correlations for leaders who emphasized member-to-member interaction and number of sessions. However, unlike the previous meta-analysis, dose produced a more refined statistically significant pattern. More specifically, groups with 20 or more sessions posted the highest relationship ($r = .41$), followed by those with 13–19 sessions ($r = .27$), and 12 or fewer sessions ($r = .21$).

One of the new moderators tested cohesion as a therapeutic strategy. We hypothesized that studies where cohesion was focused on as a group intervention ($n = 6$) should produce a higher cohesion–outcome relationship compared to studies that did not ($n = 47$) and statistical support was found for this relationship ($r = .40$ and .22, respectively). Higher correlations were found when interpersonal and self-esteem outcome measures were used but the cohesion–outcome relationship for general psychiatric and depression symptoms was nearly identical to the overall estimate ($r = .25$). Finally, analogue group treatments (volunteer and task groups) produced higher correlations (*r* = .58 and *r* = .56, respectively) than psychoeducation, therapy, or support groups (*r* = .22, *r* = .24, and *r* = .25, respectively) but the former reflected only two studies, making it difficult to arrive at definitive conclusions.

One of the limitations we've noted in past meta-analytic findings (Burlingame et al., 2011; Burlingame, McClendon et al., 2018) is the single point-in-time assessment of cohesion and outcome. With the application of continuous monitoring of outcome and process systems found in measurement-based care models described below, a small but growing number of studies assess both outcome and the therapeutic relationship on a session by session basis. We located eight studies (Burlingame, McClendon et al., 2018) Gallagher et al., 2014; Hornsey et al., 2012; Illing et al., 2011; Lo Coco et al., 2012; Norton & Kazantzis, 2016; Obeid et al., 2018; Tasca et al., 2013), and all but one found a significant slope change for cohesion. Unfortunately, most studies only assessed outcome on a pre–post basis, but the few studies that assessed outcome continuously (Burlingame, McClendon et al., 2018; Obeid et al., 2018) report significant correlations between cohesion and outcome (*r* = .19 to .21) that fall within the confidence interval of the above meta-analyses. Thus, it appears that point-in-time and continuous measurement both support the cohesion–outcome relationship.

Alliance as a Predictor of Outcome

There are very few published studies that simultaneously assess the therapeutic relationship with measures that tap all three structural components – member-to-member, member-to-group, and member-to-leader. Those that do report a common latent factor (e.g., Johnson et al., 2005) with both shared and unique variance. We simply need more research on the correlations of these three structural components to tease apart the shared and unique effect that each has with treatment outcome. Such research would be critical to the clinical implementation of the measurement-based care models reviewed below that provide feedback to the therapist on therapeutic relationship deterioration and failure. However, we first focus on the few studies since our last review that examine member-to-leader relationship – typically using alliance measures from the individual therapy literature.

In an early study, Abouguendia et al. (2004) used a four-item survey to assess the working relationship between 139 group members and their leader who delivered either interpretive or supportive group therapy for complicated grief (Piper et al., 2001) reporting a significant relationship between alliance and outcome (*r* = .34 to .36). They also assessed patient expectancies using three individualized treatment objectives and found that pretreatment expectancies mediated alliance–outcome relationship. A subsequent secondary analysis of the same data (Joyce et al., 2007) revealed that both alliance and cohesion were consistent predictors of treatment outcome. These intriguing findings spurred new research since our last review that used standardized measures of alliance and expectancies.

Tsai et al. (2014) used standardized measures of expectancies (Outcome Expectancy Scale; Ogrodniczuk & Sochting, 2010), alliance (Working Alliance Inventory; Horvath & Greenberg, 1989), and outcome measures tapping depression, anxiety, and interpersonal problems in a study of 80 outpatients receiving treatment in group CBT for depression. They found that positive pretreatment expectancies were associated with higher early treatment alliance but not mid-treatment alliance. In secondary analysis of Tsai et al.'s study that controlled for intragroup dependency, Visla et al. (2018) found a bidirectional relationship between outcome expectancies and alliance. The authors state, "Higher baseline outcome expectations related to better early to mid-treatment alliance, which, in turn, related to lower posttreatment depression" (p. 450) and that "Better early alliance related to higher subsequent outcome expectations, which in turn related to fewer posttreatment interpersonal problems" (p. 451).

These bidirectional findings, if replicated, have promising clinical implications. Realistic pretreatment expectations may lead to the ability to establish a strong and productive therapeutic relationship. On the other hand, an alliance rupture with the therapist may lower a patient's faith in the therapy working, lowering expectancies underscoring the importance of continuous monitoring reviewed below. We urge more research on the interaction between the therapeutic relationship and patient expectancies using more sophisticated mediation analyses to tease apart direct and indirect effects. We also remind future researchers that in our last chapter we reviewed the clinical outcome results (CORE; MacKenzie & Dies, 1982) battery revised by an international taskforce of American Group Psychotherapy Association (Burlingame et al., 2006; Strauss et al., 2008) that includes two additional instruments assessing expectancies in group treatment.

The remaining studies assessing the alliance in group treatment produced mixed findings. A secondary analysis (Mortberg, 2014) of data from a randomized controlled trial of group and individual CBT for social phobia (Mortberg et al., 2007) reported a nonsignificant alliance–outcome relationship in patients receiving individual compared to group therapy. Tasca et al. (2016) found that improvement in alliance for eating disorder patients receiving emotionally focused group therapy predicted improvement in binge eating outcomes. However, improvement in the binge eating outcome was not associated with improvement in alliance, suggesting a uni- rather than bidirectional relationship.

Finally, Ruglass and colleagues (2012) studied the alliance–outcome relationship in a secondary data analysis from a controlled trial that compared an evidence-based CBT group intervention (Seeking Safety) against a psycho-educational control group (Hien et al., 2009). Patients included 223 women suffering from comorbid posttraumatic stress disorder – PTSD and substance use disorders and outcome assessed symptoms from both disorders. The alliance (Revised Helping Alliance Questionnaire II; Luborsky et al., 1996) predicted improvement on PTSD outcomes and group attendance but was not related to substance use outcomes.

In a recent meta-analysis from our labs, articles describing the relation between member-leader alliance and outcome published between 1969 and 2019 were analyzed (Alldredge et al., 2021). The 29 studies in this meta-analysis included 3,628 patients producing a weighted average correlation between alliance and outcme of *r* = .17 (*p* < .001) with a corresponding effect size of *d* = 0.34. The alliance–outcome association was moderated by the treatment orientation (lower correlation in CBT than other group treatments) and the reporting perspective (higher correlation for patient reported than mixed or observer reported alliance).

MEASUREMENT-BASED CARE (MBC)

Group leaders are faced with the nearly impossible task of managing the simultaneous treatment of 8–10 members. In past chapters, we encouraged group leaders to use measures to supplement their clinical judgment when they select group members, track small group processes such as cohesion to predict potential dropouts and assess each member symptomatic improvement. In 2013, we reviewed the CORE-R battery disseminated by the American Group Psychotherapy Association as one evidenced-based resource that contains selection, process and outcome measure recommendations. These recommendations fit the broader rubric of MBC systems that is gaining traction in the empirical literature and clinical practice. We made these recommendations knowing that routine outcome monitoring – ROM systems – have been present in practice guidelines as an evidence-based intervention for the past 15–20 years.

ROM systems are web-based or stand-alone systems that establish baseline psychiatric distress with an outcome measure administered at the first session. Patient progress is tracked using the same outcome measure typically administered before each treatment session. Progress feedback is provided to the therapist before subsequent sessions using *change alerts* that indicate if reliable improvement or deterioration has occurred since intake. Some ROM systems provide *status alerts* that compare a patient's current distress to norms signaling if a patient is experiencing clinical or nonclinical levels of distress. A few ROM systems offer *progress alerts* that use a patient's temporal pattern of change and compared it to normative change trajectories to determine if a patient is on-track (OT) or not-on-track (NOT) for a successful treatment outcome (Burlingame, Whitcomb et al., 2018).

In a special issue of *Psychotherapy*, Wampold (2015) declared that ROM systems had "come of age" (p. 458) given the empirical evidence that ROM feedback leads to reduced treatment failures and improved outcomes. Indeed, Krageloh and colleagues' (2015) review of 25 studies testing the effect of ROM systems found larger effects for ROM studies that included all three types of alerts (change, status and progress). A problem with Wampold's declaration that ROM has come of age is the lack of studies testing ROM systems in group treatments. The ROM train left the station nearly two decades ago and group treatment was left on the platform. Evidence for this assertion lies in the fact that none of Krageloh et al.'s 25 studies tested group treatment. However, progress has been made in the last decade.

Results from Randomized Clinical Trials of Testing MBC in Group Treatment

ROM systems assume that the patient change information provided by ROM systems is unavailable to therapists. Chapman and colleagues (2012) tested this assumption in group treatment by comparing the accuracy of therapist predictions of change alerts (improved, deteriorated, or no change) with actual *change alerts* using the OQ-45 (Lambert, 2015). Ten group leaders at a university counseling center (5) or state psychiatric hospital (5) rated 64 group members who were participating in 12-session groups at the third, sixth, and ninth group session using change alerts (improved, deteriorated, or no change). Leader generated change predictions were then compared to actual change alerts from the OQ-45 and no relationship was found. Similar independence was found on leader ratings of the therapeutic relationship compared to member self-report. Chapman et al. (2012) concluded that the patient change information provided by ROM systems is unavailable to group therapists, supporting the importance of both outcome and relationship measure feedback in group therapy.

We located two nonrandom cohort studies of ROM feedback in group treatment. These studies initially measured a cohort group with an outcome measure to establish a TAU baseline without providing any feedback to therapists or patients. Therapists in a subsequent cohort group were provided feedback on different patients using the same outcome measure. The outcomes of these two non-equivalent cohort groups were then compared. Unfortunately, the two nonrandom cohort group studies produced mixed findings. Newnham et al. (2010) compared 461 inpatient and day-treatment patients treated with a 10-day CBT group with 408 patients who received *progress alert* feedback on the fifth day of CBT group treatment and found that NOT feedback patients showed greater improvement. Koementas-de Vos et al., (2018) compared a 132-member cohort group of outpatients receiving CBT or interpersonal group therapy that varied between 6–24 sessions with a 137-member cohort group who received *change alert* feedback and found no differences in outcome between the two groups. Differences in measures, settings, and alert as well as nonrandom assignment and a low NOT base rate (4%) in the second study all are plausible explanations of the mixed findings. Fortunately, greater rigor and clarity exist from more controlled studies.

We located five randomized clinical trials – RCTs, testing the effect of ROM systems with group treatment; the first three tested the same ROM system. Schuman et al. (2015) tested *progress alert* feedback with 263 soldiers receiving five-session groups. The 8–12 members in each group were randomly assigned to the feedback and no-feedback condition and 40% of cases had at least one NOT alert. A small significant improvement effect ($d = 0.28$) was found for progress alert feedback. Slone et al. (2015) tested *progress alert* feedback on 84 students receiving 10-session group treatments at a university counseling center. Unlike Schuman et al., groups rather than members were randomly assigned to a feedback or control condition and group leaders were encouraged to use the feedback to enhance client scores. Less than 5% of the cases had a least one NOT alert and a moderate significant improvement effect ($d = 0.41$) was found supporting progress feedback. Davidsen et al. (2017) tested *progress alert* feedback with 159 eating disordered patients receiving 20–25 sessions of group treatment along with individual sessions with a physician, dietician, physiotherapist, and social worker over 10–14 months.

Both outcome and therapeutic relationship was provided, and 65% of the cases alerted at least once; no effect for feedback was found on either primary or secondary measures. The authors suggest the highly structured treatment and presence of other treatments as explanations for the null effect.

Two RCTs tested two different ROM systems. Wise and Streiner (2018) tested *progress alert* feedback with 161 patients in an intensive outpatient program who received three hours/day of process, CBT, and skill training group treatment (9 hours/week). Each group contained 8–12 members who were randomly assigned to the feedback or no-feedback condition and 39% of cases had at least one NOT alert. No effect was found on four outcomes measures or on measures of therapeutic alliance and client satisfaction. Burlingame, Whitcombe et al. (2018) held *progress alert* feedback constant and tested whether feedback on therapeutic relationship would enable a group leader to reverse relationship deterioration (*change alert*) and relationship failure (*status alerts*). A total of 432 members were assigned to 58 semester-long groups held at three university counseling centers, and 35% of the cases alerted at least once. Groups rather than members were randomly assigned, and both *change and status alerts* were associated with improvement on subscales that assessed positive bond and positive work facets of the therapeutic relationship. No effects were found on the subscale that assessed alliance ruptures.

It's important to note that feedback in group treatment is in an embryonic stage, with only five RCTs compared to the dozens that exist for individual therapy, so our conclusions are tentative. Three different ROM systems were tested, one received no support, one with mixed support, and one with support from a single study leading to an overall pattern of mixed findings. However, the two studies reporting no support (Davidsen et al., 2017; Wise & Streiner, 2018) had more difficult patient populations served by intensive outpatient programs, and patients received multiple treatments. Those that found support had patients with less distress and group as their primary treatment. Thus, outcome and relationship feedback may be more promising when patients are less distressed and when group is their primary treatment. We have two studies that provide support for outcome feedback and one that provides support for therapeutic relationship feedback. Clearly, more research is needed on both fronts, with less-distressed populations receiving a single group as their primary treatment and with more difficult patient populations receiving multiple simultaneous treatments.

CONCLUSIONS AND RECOMMENDATIONS

We end our journey by initially looking back to the efficacy conclusions we made in our 2013 chapter. This provides us with the context for comparing how the literature has grown in establishing the empirical foundation for small group treatments. Indeed, we believe this foundation is sufficiently robust that it can support revisions to evidence-based group treatment (EBGT) and have recommended practice guideline revisions for practitioners. We also note promising developments using the categories of the model we introduced in our 2004 chapter that explain why group treatment may be effective. As

in previous editions, we offer seven recommendations that we believe will improve future research on small group treatment and end with what we now believe it takes to become an evidence-based group practitioner.

Efficacy of Group Treatment

In our last edition, our conclusions were based on over 250 studies testing group treatments with 12 disorders/patient populations. We noted greater rigor in methodology increasing our confidence in effectiveness and efficacy conclusions. We reported good-to-excellent evidence for most disorders (panic, social phobia, OCD, eating disorders, substance abuse, trauma related disorders, breast cancer, schizophrenia, and personality disorders) and promising evidence for others (mood, pain/somatoform, inpatient). We noted the dominance of CBT for some disorders but also found evidence for clinician choice with other disorders. Convincing evidence was provided for format equivalence and cost-effectiveness data showed that group treatment had a distinct fiscal advantage over individual treatment.

This review provides a stronger evidentiary foundation than our last review. It is built on 10 group-specific meta-analysis (Tables 17.1, 17.2, and 17.5) that use within-study contrasts, ruling out a host of confounds found in past reviews and meta-analyses that typically make format conclusions using between-study contrasts. The 10 meta-analyses summarize findings from 329 randomized clinical trials (370 contrasts) that treated nearly 27,000 patients, making it the largest empirical summary of group treatment efficacy. These meta-analyses used a registered methodology and included the most rigorous published studies testing the efficacy of group treatment against no-treatment and active treatment controls. The cancer and pain research summarized in Table 17.3 add more than 40 additional studies yielding a total sample of over 370 studies. By comparison, this review not only has more studies but they are far more rigorous than those included in our last chapter.

Table 17.5 summarizes the primary outcome effects from the disorder-specific meta-analyses described in this chapter. The first two columns delineate the disorder and the number of comparisons used to compare group treatments against no-treatment (WLC) and other active treatment control conditions; in general, the larger the number the more reliable the estimate. The next column is the effect on the primary outcome measure targeting key symptoms (e.g., MDD = depression) and all eight disorders making comparisons with no treatment produce significant improvement with seven of the eight posting large effects. Indeed, the only disorder posting a small effect is group treatment for substance use disorders. It should be noted that the values we include in this column may be lower than reported as the main effect in the meta-analyses because we elected to list the effect size where outliers were eliminated which typically reduced heterogeneity providing a more reliable efficacy estimate. The fourth column directly assesses the reliability of the effect size by indicating if significant heterogeneity exists. When there is none, we indicate this by a bold **N**, which means we place greater confidence in the effect size estimate. Finally, the fifth column records rate estimates of patients who no longer met diagnosis after treatment.

TABLE 17.5 High-Level Summary of Group Meta-Analyses for Multiple Disorders

Disorder	Wait-list pre–post comparison	Wait list control – WLC Heterogeneity Y/N	Wait list pre–post recovery rate – RR	Active control pre–post comparison	Active control comparison Heterogeneity	Active control pre–post recovery rate – RR
MDD	$g = .86*$ $(k = 10)$	N**	6.8	$g = .69$ $(k = 12)$, $.08$ $(k = 7)$ (AC+, M)	Y	5.28
Bipolar				$g = .44$ $(k = 6)$ (AC+)	N	
SAD	$g = .84$ $(k = 25)$	N		$g = .06$ $(k = 15)$ (CF, M, I)	Y	
Panic	$g = 1.08$ $(k = 9)$	N		$g = .18$ $(k = 6)$	Y	
OCD	$g = .97$ $(k = 4)$	N		$g = -.02$ $(k = 9)$ (I,M,CF)	N	
PTSD	$g = .70$ $(k = 13)$	Y	2.02 $(k = 5)$	$g = -.02$ $(k = 8)$ (AC)	N	.79 $(k = 2)$
Combined Anxiety	$g = 1.02$ $(k = 45)$	Y		$g = .15$ $(k = 26)$ (I, M, CF)	Y	
Eating disorders	$g = .70$ $(k = 13)$	N	5.51[a]	$g = .24$ $(k = 8)$ (AC)	Y	1.20
Substance	$g = .28$[a] $(k = 8)$	N		$g = .29$[a] $(k = 15)$ (AC+)	Y	
Schizophrenia				CR+: $g = .31$ $(k = 17)$ SST+: $g = .53$ $(k = 11)$ PE+: $g = .29$ $(k = 8)$ MFG+: $g = .39$ $(k = 5)$	N Y Y N	
BPD				$g = .72$ (6) (AC+)	Y	

Note. AC = Active treatment control, + = indicates group has been added to an existing active treatment, BPD = borderline personality disorder, k = # of comparisons, CF = common factor, M = medication, MDD = Major depressive disorder, I = individual, OCD = obsessive compulsive disorder, SAD = social anxiety disorder, Y = significant.
[a] Abstinence from binge eating/purging or substance use.
* $p < .05$.
** $p > .05$ or no significant heterogeneity.

The empirically supported message from over 125 randomized clinical trials is that group treatment produces large effects when compared to no-treatment across common mood and anxiety disorders. Further, 75% of the disorders listed in Table 17.5 yielding no-treatment comparisons (MDD, SAD, panic, OCD, eating, and substance disorders) have effect sizes with no heterogeneity and should be considered reliable estimates of group treatment effect. With scarce mental health resources producing limited access to individual treatment, these results provide an empirically supported treatment option. Group treatment should be considered an efficacious and viable option for many anxiety and mood disorders. Indeed, these findings suggest that putting a potential patient on a waitlist (i.e., no treatment) when they could be efficaciously treated in group format raises an important ethical issue; are we withholding an empirically supported treatment? Practice guidelines that do not consider group treatment for these disorders may be negligent when viewed from the patient perspective since available recovery rates show that two to seven times more patients improve with group versus no treatment. We wondered why group treatment was being neglected in current practice guidelines. Could it reflect an anachronistic bias? An apprehension or anxiety about leading group treatments? We've documented in earlier chapters that 75% of the APA approved clinical psychology programs do not require group training. Could this neglect be due to a lack of knowledge?

The second half of Table 17.5 compares the same empirically supported group treatment protocols against active treatments that often-included individual, medication and common factor treatment control groups. Contrasts typically took two forms; those where group treatment were added to an existing treatment indicated by a + (i.e., active treatment vs. group + active treatment), and those where group treatment was directly compared to an active treatment condition (active treatment vs. group). Four clear messages emerge:

1. All eight effect sizes for group treatment impact when added (+) to treatment-as-usual produced significant improvement.
2. All seven effect sizes when group treatment was directly contrasted with active treatment show no reliable differences.
3. Group treatment outperformed common factor controls in two of the three meta-analyses.
4. While heterogeneity was higher than WLC contrasts, four disorders (bipolar, OCD, PTSD, and schizophrenia) have group treatment protocols that produced reliable improvement over active treatment controls without heterogeneity.

These are remarkable findings since two of these disorders (bipolar and schizophrenia) are with chronic populations that are difficult to treat and most active treatment contrasts employed evidence-based treatments (e.g., individual, medication treatments).

Collectively, the WLC and active treatment comparisons provide the strongest argument for including group as a treatment option in practice guidelines in our near 40 years of reviewing group literature. Moreover, the effect sizes correspond with clinical practice, with small improvements seen with chronic and difficult disorders (BPD, schizophrenia, substance) and larger effects with common anxiety and mood disorders. When one couples these findings with the large number of studies supporting format equivalence reviewed above (Burlingame et al., 2016), a compelling argument emerges for the use of evidence-based group protocols, particularly in systems of care where resources are stretched or scarce.

We recognize that group treatment is a more complex treatment than individual treatment from a delivery context. However, when delivered by trained therapists it is a triple E treatment (Yalom & Leszcz, 2020). That is, it is *effective* when compared to no treatment, it is *equivalent* to other bona fide treatments including the individual format, and it is more *efficient* in therapist time and cost when compared to individual therapy. Of course, the efficiency argument is a double-edged sword from the patient perspective; it is more time consuming and logistically less flexible. Indeed, we've shown in an RCT that having a group treatment infrastructure (e.g., group coordinator and group consultant) improves group outcomes but also extracts a toll on resources (Burlingame et al., 2002). Thus, our view is that robust group treatment programs are more easily implemented in agency or institutional settings than in private practice.

Promising Developments

In our last review, we highlighted developments in each of the categories of our model that empirically explain group outcomes. More specifically, in: (a) *formal change theory* – we noted integrated treatment protocols that strategically blend multiple formal change theories; (b) *group structure* – we noted heterogenous composition strategies: (c) *patient characteristics* – we noted attachment style research; (d) *small group process* – attempts to integrate relationship constructs, such as the Group Questionnaire (GQ); and (e) *leader* – we described an increase use of online group treatments.

In this review, from a *formal change theory* perspective we noted an increase in group third wave treatments such as MBSR and ACT for several disorders. Two promising integrative approaches have been developed since our last chapter, although both need more research. Whittingham (2015) developed an eight-session manualized focused brief group therapy (FGBT) that combines elements derived from Yalom and Leszcz (2005) process groups and attachment theory. FGBT uses the Inventory of Interpersonal Problems (IIP; Horowitz et al., 2000) to determine the interpersonal pattern of group members, wedding group and individual interpersonal goals. FGBT can be seen as an example of a standardized short term group manual that could find a broad dissemination within student counseling centers; however, we could find no other models that fit the dissemination phenomenon found in the individual therapy literature. A second integrative approach that combines psychodynamic, interpersonal and attachment theory is group psychodynamic-interpersonal psychotherapy (GPIP; Tasca et al., 2006), which has shown promising outcomes in studies of patients with binge-eating disorders and perfectionism (Hewitt et al., 2015; Ivanova et al., 2015).

Both models can be viewed as *trans-diagnostic groups* that are more common in the psychodynamic field. A remarkable manualized *trans-diagnostic group* approach focuses on mixed group treatments composed of patients with anxiety, mood, or personality disorders (Lorentzen et al., 2013). Lorentzen and colleagues assessed the efficacy of this group format in an RCT that compared short- and long-term group analysis (STG vs. LTG) in a Norwegian sample (*n* = 167). One of the major findings was greater effectiveness of LTG for patients with comorbid personality pathology. Interestingly, patients without comorbid personality pathology did not show any additional gain from LTG compared to STG (Lorentzen et al., 2015). Additional findings support the above conclusions of the relationship between alliance and cohesion with outcome as well as more complex patterns of change (e.g., Fjeldstad et al., 2017; Lorentzen et al., 2018). Additional and promising psychodynamic group research can be found for mentalization approaches within a day treatment setting (Brand et al., 2016).

Our update on *patient characteristics* continues to focus on *attachment*. We agree with Marmarosh (2014) that the most recent group research has the potential to move the field forward. Indeed, the studies we reviewed above lead us to believe that the literature has left its embryonic stage and moved to a more mature status. Our update on *leader characteristics* also continues to focus on *online groups*. The research on these group treatments has continued to proliferate – as has the use of the internet and social media in general. Indeed, individual therapy apps have proliferated since our past review and we see online group treatments offering an opportunity to reach patients in need of psychosocial support, but have difficulties in accessing professional help due to geographical, social or psychological reasons.

Apart from studies related to alliance and cohesion, we were not able to detect any specific trends in *group process research*, although we identify a variety of innovative approaches relating to content (e.g., alliance rupture repairs, Lo Coco et al., 2019) and methodology (e.g., actor–partner interdependence analysis, the analysis of trajectories and multilevel group phenomena or the application of the social relations models to understand dyadic perceptions within groups; Christensen & Feeney, 2016; Frankfurt et al., 2016; Kivlighan & Kivlighan, 2016; Kivlighan, Lo Coco, Oieni et al., 2017). These trends, along with group treatments research on *training* (Barlow, 2013; Strauss et al., 2012) and *adverse effects* (Schneibel et al., 2017), are promising harbingers of a complex and rich future for the group outcome literature.

Recommendations for the Small Group Process

The therapeutic relationship may be the best predictor of outcome in group treatment. The cohesion-outcome relationship is robust across five cohesion measures (Group Climate Questionnaire, Mackenzie, 1983; Cohesion Scale, Gross, 1957; Group Cohesion, Piper et al., 1983; Group Atmosphere Scale, Silbergeld et al., 1975; Therapeutic Factors Inventory – Cohesion Subscale, Lese and MacNair-Semands, 2000), clinical setting (inpatient and outpatient), theoretical orientation (interpersonal, psychodynamic, CBT, supportive, and eclectic)

and diagnostic classification (Axis I, II, and V codes). There continues to be a lack of distinction in the empirical findings when group members rate the two of the three relationship structures; member–member and member–group. Nonetheless, measures tapping both relationship structures produce equivalent correlations with treatment outcome. Accordingly, practitioners should consider routinely monitoring member perceptions and include interventions designed to enhance the therapeutic relationship (cf. Burlingame et al., 2002).

In our past chapters, we've called for outcome researchers to add group process measures and the bulk of alliance research reflects this practice. Indeed, this practice has advanced our understanding of the therapeutic relationship–outcome link beyond studies reviewed in past chapters. However, we also note that the most clinically promising findings emerged from the single study that was specifically designed to test the interactive relationship between expectancy, alliance and outcome (Tsai et al., 2014). All but one of the five secondary analyses report a significant relationship between alliance and outcome. The replication across secondary analysis studies, along with the intriguing bidirectional relationship reported above, underscore the importance of the third structural component of the group therapeutic relationship – member-to-leader.

Based on these general conclusions, we offer the following selection of recommendations for future research on small group treatment:

1. Despite the significant advances in studies reflecting the efficacy of group treatment, there is still a need for replications across other clinical populations.
2. Future studies should also focus on other theoretical orientations that play an important role in individual psychotherapy (e.g., psychodynamic or systemic approaches), but are rarely investigated in a group setting, at least under controlled and methodologically rigorous conditions (Strauss, 2017).
3. There is a specific need for more systematic studies on the effects of small groups within medical settings (e.g., related to neurological disorders, obesity, specific crises related to chronic diseases, and their treatment), including the consideration of physiological parameters. A recent promising meta-analysis (Shields et al., 2020) showed that psychological interventions in general can have positive effects on immune system functions such as cytokines, and that interventions that included a group component even enhanced immune functions more greatly than those without a group component.
4. We decided to restrict our systematic review and our meta-analyses to RCTs and did not report effectiveness studies that nevertheless would be of equal importance. In fact, we did not report on studies that tested the effectiveness of group treatment delivered in routine clinical practice. Since there is a clear progress in the attraction of groups for practitioners (sometimes even supported by political programs as for example in Germany), systematic studies of group practice would be helpful. These could be based on practice-research networks (PRNs) that still are uncommon in the group world. Reliable effectiveness studies

could help to support health organizations and institutions providing practice guidelines to consider group treatment as an important alternative to individual psychotherapy.

5. We described several fields in this chapter as promising: feedback in group treatment, online groups, attachment as an important moderator. These definitely need more systematic research to leave the "embryonic state."

6. The group literature needs more research dealing with special needs and modifications of group programs, depending on cultural diversity and ethnic minorities.

7. Finally, as we stated in the 2004 and 2013 editions of this *Handbook*, there is still a lack of process studies and studies focusing on principles of change. Accordingly, the knowledge about these principles is restricted to alliance and cohesion as empirically supported relationship variables (Castonguay et al., 2019). There is a need for studies extending the view on the complex interplay of process variables such as relationship, expectancy, and outcome using innovative methodological approaches and research designs.

Becoming an Evidence-Based Group Practitioner

We ended our last review with a caricature from a 2008 special issue of the *Journal of Clinical Psychology* on evidence-based group treatment. The caricature described an evidence-based group clinician (Burlingame & Beecher, 2008) being guided by: (a) an empirically supported group protocol; (b) empirically supported practice guidelines (Klein, 2008; Leszcz & Kobos 2008; (c) practice-based assessment to guide practice; and (d) multicultural competence. The bulk of this chapter provides updated evidence on efficacious group protocols for mood and anxiety disorders, medical populations, seriously mentally ill and several promising new clinical indications. As we've stated above, the evidence has never been stronger, so there is no longer any reason to run a group "by the seat of your pants." Our overriding message is for practitioners to use an evidence-based group treatment – EBGT.

While AGPA's practice guidelines are adequate, we believe there have been sufficient empirical advances over the 10+ years since they've been released to warrant an update. There is much more to effective group treatment than simply applying an EST to a group of patients with the same disorder. The recognition of group treatment by APA as an accredited specialty sets a professional standard for the training needed to effectively conduct small group treatments. Several training tracks are available to acquire the group competencies (Barlow, 2013) that are essential for delivering effective group treatment. Both the APA (e.g., predoctoral, internship and postdoctoral) and AGPA model (certified group psychotherapist) offer training programs.

There has been a quantum leap in the empirical support of practice-based assessment since our last review. Promising evidence is now available on the impact of tracking patient outcomes and key moderators of improvement (therapeutic relationship) in group treatment. The advent of new group-based process and outcome tracking systems is a clarion call to revise the AGPA CORE Battery (Burlingame et al., 2006; Strauss et al., 2008) described in our previous-edition chapter.

Finally, advances in multicultural competences is mixed. Positive advances include the continuation of cultural adaptations of group treatment protocols initially tested in North America and Europe to other cultures. Unfortunately, we found a paucity of research that specifically focused on diversity and multicultural competence. This needs immediate attention. As you can see, promising advances in the past decade in all four areas and encourage group leaders to inform their practice with these four bodies of evidence.

ABBREVIATIONS

AA	Alcoholics Anonymous
AC	Active control
ACT	Acceptance and commitment therapy
AGPA	American Group Psychotherapy Association
AN	Anorexia nervosa
APA	American Psychological Association
APIM	Actor-partner interdependence model
BAP	Bingeing and purging
BD	Bipolar disorder
BED	Binge-eating disorder
BN	Bulimia nervosa
BPD	Borderline personality disorder
CBGT	Cognitive-behavioral group therapy
CBT	Cognitive-behavioral therapy
CR	Cognitive remediation
CSA	Child sexual abuse
DBT	Dialectical behavior therapy
EBGT	Evidence-based group treatment
ED	Eating disorders
EIT	Emotional intelligence therapy
ERP	Exposure and response prevention
FGBT	Focused brief group therapy
GAD	Generalised anxiety disorder
GCBT	Group cognitive behavioral therapy
iCBT	internet-based cognitive-behavioral therapy
IPT	Interpersonal therapy
MBC	Measurement-based care
MBGT	Mindfulness-based group therapy
MBSR	Mindfulness-based stress reduction
MCBT	Mindfulness-based cognitive therapy
MCT	Meta-cognitive training
MDD	Major depressive disorder
MFG	Multi-family group

NICE	National Institute for Health and Care Excellence
NOT	Not-on-track
OBT	Operational behavior therapy
OCD	Obsessive compulsive disorder
OT	On-track
PBGT	Practice-based group treatment
PD	Personality disorder
PE	Psycho-educational
PEG	Psycho-educational group
PGs	Practice guidelines
PRNs	Practice research networks
PTSD	Posttraumatic stress disorder
QoL	Quality of life
RCT	Randomized clinical trial
ROM	Routine outcome monitoring
SAD	Social anxiety disorder
SEGT	Supportive-expressive group therapy
SST	Social skill therapy
STEPPS	Systems training for emotional predictability and problem solving
SUD	Substance use disorders
TAU	Treatment-as-usual
WLC	Wait-list control
Y-BOCS	Yale-Brown Obsessive Compulsive Scale

REFERENCES

Abouguendia, M., Joyce, A. S., Piper, W. E., & Ogrodniczuk, J. S. (2004). Allicance as a mediator of expectancy effects in short-term group psychotherapy. *Group Dynamics: Theory, Research, and Practice, 8*(1), 3–12. https://doi.org/10.1037/1089-2699.8.1.3

Alldredge, C. T., Burlingame, G. M., Yang, C., & Rosendahl, J. (2021). Alliance in group therapy: A meta-analysis. *Group Dynamics: Theory, Research, and Practice, 25*(1), 13–28. https://doi.org/10.1037/gdn0000135

American Psychiatric Association. (2007). *Practice guideline for the treatment of patients with obsessive-compulsive disorder.* Arlington, VA: American Psychiatric Association. Retrieved from http//www.psych.org/psych_pract/treatg/pg/ prac_ guide.cfm

American Psychiatric Association. (2009a). *Practice guideline for the treatment of patients with panic disorder* (2nd ed.). American Psychiatric Association. Retrieved from https://psychiatryonline.org/pb/assets/raw/sitewide/practice_guidelines/guidelines/panicdisorder.pdf

American Psychiatric Association. (2009b). Guideline watch (March 2009): Practice guideline for the treatment of patients with acute stress disorder and posttraumatic stress disorder. American Psychiatric Association. Retrieved from https://psychiatryonline.org/pb/assets/raw/sitewide/practice_guidelines/guidelines/acutestressdisorderptsd-watch.pdf

American Psychiatric Association. (2013). *Diagnostic and statistical manual of mental disorders: DSM-5.* Arlington, VA. https://doi.org/10.1176/appi.books.9780890425596

Antoni, M. H., Bouchard, L. C., Jacobs, J. M., Lechner, S. C., Jutagir, D. R., Gudenkauf, L. M., Carver, C. S., Lutgendorf, S., Cole, S. W., Lippman, M., & Blomberg, B. B. (2016). Stress management, leukocyte transcriptional changes and breast cancer recurrence in a randomized trial: An exploratory analysis. *Psychoneuroendocrinology, 74,* 269–277. https://doi.org/10.1016/j.psyneuen.2016.09.012

Antoni, M. H., Lechner, S. C., Kazi, A., Wimberly, S. R., Sifre, T., Urcuyo, K. R., Phillips, K., Glück, S., & Carver, C. S. (2006). How stress management improves quality of life after treatment for breast cancer. *Journal of Consulting and Clinical Psychology, 74*(6), 1143–1152. https://doi.org/10.1037/0022-006X.74.6.1143

Arnberg, F. K., Linton, S. J., Hultcrantz, M., Heintz, E., & Jonsson, U. (2014). Internet-delivered psychological treatments for mood and anxiety disorders: A systematic review of their efficacy, safety, and cost-effectiveness. *PLoS ONE, 9,* e98118. https://doi.org/10.1371/journal.pone.0098118

Association of Scientific Medical Societies (2019). Diagnosis and treatment of eating disorders. Retrieved from https://www.awmf.org/leitlinien/detail/ll/051-026.html

Auslander, W., McGinnis, H., Tlapek, S., Smith, P., Foster, A., E. & Dunn, J. (2017). Adaptation and implementation of a trauma-focused cognitive behavioral intervention for girls in child welfare. *American Journal of Orthopsychiatry, 87*(3), 206–215. https://doi.org/10.1037/ort0000233

Bandelow, B., Lichte, T., Rudolf, S., Wiltink, J., & Beutel, E. M. (2014). The diagnosis and treatment recommendations for anxiety disorders. *Deutsches Ärzteblatt International, 111,* 473–480. https://doi.org/10.3238/arztebl.2014.0473

Barkowski, S., Schwartze, D., Strauss, B., Burlingame, G. M., Barth, J., & Rosendahl, J. (2016). Efficacy of group psychotherapy for social anxiety disorder: A meta-analysis of randomized-controlled trials. *Journal of Anxiety Disorders, 39,* 44–64. https://doi.org/10.1016/j.janxdis.2016.02.005

Barkowski, S., Schwartze, D., Strauss, B., Burlingame, G., & Rosendahl, J. (2020). Efficacy of group psychotherapy for anxiety disorders: A systematic review and meta-analysis. *Psychotherapy Research, 30,* 965–982. https://doi.org/10.1080/10503307.2020.1729440

Barlow, D. H., & Craske, M. G. (1994). *Mastery of your anxiety and panic II.* Albany, NY: Graywind.

Barlow, S. H. (2013). *Specialty competencies in group psychology.* New York, NY: Oxford University Press.

Barrowclough, C., Haddock, G., Lobban, F., Siddle, R., Roberts, C., & Gregg, L. (2006). Group cognitive-behavioural therapy for schizophrenia. Randomised controlled trial. *The British Journal of Psychiatry 189,* 527–532. https://doi.org/10.1192/bjp.bp.106.021386

Bateman, A., & Fonagy, P. (1999). Effectiveness of partial hospitalization in the treatment of borderline personality disorder: A randomized controlled trial. *The American Journal of Psychiatry, 156*(10), 1563–1569. https://doi.org/10.1176/ajp.156.10.1563

Bateman, A., & Fonagy, P. (2016). *Mentalization-based treatment for personality disorders: A practical guide.* New York, NY, US: Oxford University Press. https://doi.org/10.1093/med:psych/9780199680375.001.0001

Baxter, A. J., Scott, K. M., Vos, T., & Whiteford, H. A. (2013). Global prevalence of anxiety disorders: A systematic review and meta-regression. *Psychological Medicine, 43*(5), 897–910. https://doi.org/10.1017/S003329171200147X

Beck, J. G., Stanley, M. A., Baldwin, L. E., Deagle, E. A., & Averill, P. M. (1994). Comparison of cognitive therapy and relaxation training for panic disorder. *Journal of Consulting and Clinical Psychology, 62*(4), 818–826. https://doi.org/10.1037/0022-006X.62.4.818

Bekkering, G. E., Mariën, D., Parylo, O., & Hannes, K. (2016). The effectiveness of self-help groups for adolescent substance misuse: A systematic review. *Journal of Child & Adolescent Substance Abuse, 25*(3), 229–244. https://doi.org/10.1080/1067828X.2014.981772

Bergeron, S., Khalifé, S., Dupuis, M. J., & McDuff, P. (2016). A randomized clinical trial comparing group cognitive–behavioral therapy and a topical steroid for women with dyspareunia. *Journal of Consulting and Clinical Psychology, 84*(3), 259–268. https://doi.org/10.1037/ccp0000072

Bernecker, S. L., Banschback, K., Santorelli, G. D., & Constantino, M. J. (2017). A web-disseminated self-help and peer support program could fill gaps in mental health care: Lessons from a consumer survey. *Journal of Medical Internet Research, 4*(1), e5. https://doi.org/10.2196/mental.4751

Björneklett, H. G., Lindemalm, C., Ojutkangas, M. L., Berglund, A., Letocha, H., Strang, P., & Bergkvist, L. (2012). A randomized controlled trial of a support group intervention on the quality of life and fatigue in women after primary treatment for early breast cancer. *Supportive Care in Cancer, 20*(12), 3325–3334. https://doi.org/10.1007/s00520-012-1480-1

Björneklett, H. G., Lindemalm, C., Rosenblad, A., Ojutkangas, M., Letocha, H., Strang, P., & Bergkvist, L. (2012). A randomised controlled trial of support group intervention after breast cancer treatment: Results on anxiety and depression. *Acta Oncologica*, *51*(2), 198–207. https://doi.org/10.3109/0284186X.2011.610352

Björneklett, H. G., Rosenblad, A., Lindemalm, C., Ojutkangas, M. L., Letocha, H., Strang, P., & Bergkvist, L. (2013a). A randomized controlled trial of support group intervention after breast cancer treatment: Results on sick leave, health care utilization and health economy. *Acta Oncologica*, *52*(1), 38–47. https://doi.org/10.3109/0284186X.2012.734921

Björneklett, H. G., Rosenblad, A., Lindemalm, C., Ojutkangas, M., Letocha, H., Strang, P., & Bergkvist, L. (2013b). Long-term follow-up of a randomized stud of support group intervention in women with primary breast cancer. *Journal of Psychosomatic Research*, *74*(4), 346–353. https://doi.org/10.1016/j.jpsychores.2012.11.005

Boesen, E. H., Karlsen, R., Christensen, J., Paaschburg, B., Nielsen, D., Bloch, I. S., Christiansen, B., Jacobsen, K., & Johansen, C. (2011). Psychosocial group intervention for patients with primary breast cancer: A randomised trial. *European Journal of Cancer*, *47*(9), 1363–1372. https://doi.org/10.1016/j.ejca.2011.01.002

Bourgault, P., Lacasse, A., Marchand, S., Courtemanche-Harel, R., Charest, J., Gaumond, I., Barcellos de Souza, J., & Choinière, M. (2015). Multicomponent tnterdisciplinary group tntervention for self-management of fibromyalgia: A mixed-methods randomized controlled trial. *PLoS ONE*, *10*, e0126324. https://doi.org/10.1371/journal.pone.0126324

Brand, T., Hecke, D., Rietz, C., & Schultz-Venrath, U. (2016). Therapieeffekte mentalisierungsbasierter und psychodynamischer Gruppenpsychotherapie in einer randomisierten Tagesklinik-Studie. *Gruppenpsychother. Gruppendynamik*, *52*, 156–174.

Bredal, I. S., Kåresen, R., Smeby, N. A., Espe, R., Sørensen, E. M., Amundsen, M., Aas, H., & Ekeberg, Ø. (2014). Effects of a psychoeducational versus a support group intervention in patients with early-stage breast cancer: Results of a randomized controlled trial. *Cancer Nursing*, *37*, 198–207. https://doi.org/10.1097/NCC.0b013e31829879a3

Bremner, J. D., Mishra, S., Campanella, C., Shah, M., Kasher, N., Evans, S., Fani, N., Shah, A. J., Reiff, C., Davis, L. L., Vaccarino, V., & Carmody, J. (2017). A pilot study of the effects of mindfulness-based stress reduction on post-traumatic stress disorder symptoms and brain response to traumatic reminders of combat in Operation Enduring Freedom/Operation Iraqi Freedom combat veterans with post-traumatic stress disorder. *Frontiers in Psychiatry*, *8*, 157. https://doi.org/10.3389/fpsyt.2017.00157

Brotto, L. A., Basson, R., Smith, K. B., Driscoll, M., & Sadownik, L. (2015). Mindfulness-based group therapy for women with provoked vestibulodynia. *Mindfulness*, *6*(3), 417–432. https://doi.org/10.1007/s12671-013-0273-z

Burlingame, G., Beacher, M. (2008). New directions and resources in group psychotherapy. *Journal of Clinical Psychology: In Session*, *64*(11), 1197–1205. https://doi.org/10.1002/jclp.20534

Burlingame, G. M., Earnshaw, D., Hoag, M., Barlow, S. H., Richardson, E. J., Donnell A. J., Villani, J. (2002). A systematic program to enhance clinician group skills in an inpatient psychiatric hospital. *International Journal of Group Psychotherapy*, *52*(4), 555–587. https://doi.org/10.1521/ijgp.52.4.555.45523

Burlingame, G. M., MacKenzie, K. R., & Strauss, B. (2004). Small-group treatment: Evidence for effectiveness and mechanisms of change. In M. J. Lambert (Ed.), *Bergin & Garfield's handbook of psychotherapy and behavior change* (5th ed., pp. 647–696). Hoboken, NJ: Wiley.

Burlingame, G. M., McClendon, D. T., & Alonso, J. (2011). Cohesion in group therapy. *Psychotherapy*, *48*(1), 34–42. https://doi.org/10.1037/a0022063

Burlingame, G. M., McClendon, D. T., & Yang, C. (2018a). Cohesion in group therapy: A meta-analysis. *Psychotherapy*, *55*(4), 384–398. https://doi.org/10.1037/pst0000173

Burlingame, G. M., Seebeck, J. D., Janis, R. A., Whitcomb, K. E., Barkowski, S., Rosendahl, J., & Strauss, B. (2016). Outcome differences between individual and group formats when identical and nonidentical treatments, patients, and doses are compared: A 25-year meta-analytic perspective. *Psychotherapy*, *53*(4), 446–461. https://doi.org/10.1037/pst0000090

Burlingame, G. M., Strauss, B., & Joyce, A. S. (2013). Change mechanisms and effectiveness of small-group treatments. In M. J. Lambert (Ed.), *Bergin & Garfield's handbook of psychotherapy and behavior change* (6th ed., pp. 640–673).

Burlingame, G. M., Strauss, B., Joyce, A., MacNair-Semands, R., MacKenzie, K. R., Ogrodniczuk, J., & Taylor, S. M. (2006). *CORE Battery-Revised: An assessment tool kit for promoting optimal group selection, process and outcome.* New York, NY: American Group Psychotherapy Association.

Burlingame, G. M., Svien, H., Hoppe, L., Hunt, I., & Rosendahl, J. (2020). Group therapy for schizophrenia: A meta-analysis. *Psychotherapy*, *57*(2), 219–236. https://doi.org/10.1037/pst0000293

Burlingame, G. M., Whitcomb, K. E., Woodland, S. C., Olsen, J. A., Beecher, M., & Gleave, R. (2018b). The effects of relationship and progress feedback in group psychotherapy using the Group Questionnaire and Outcome Questionnaire–45: A randomized clinical trial. *Psychotherapy*, *55*(2), 116–131. https://doi.org/10.1037/pst0000133

Butler, R. M., Boden, M. T., Olino, T. M., Morrison, A. S., Goldin, P. R., Gross, J. J., & Heimberg, R. G. (2018). Emotional clarity and attention to emotions in cognitive behavioral group therapy and mindfulness-based stress reduction for social anxiety disorder. *Journal of Anxiety Disorders*, *55*, 31–38. https://doi.org/10.1016/j.janxdis.2018.03.003

Carlson, L. E., Beattie, T. L., Giese-Davis, J., Faris, P., Tamagawa, R., Fick, L. J., Degelman, E. S., & Speca, M. (2015). Mindfulness-based cancer recovery and supportive-expressive therapy maintain telomere length relative to controls in distressed breast cancer survivors. *Cancer*, *121*(3), 476–484. https://doi.org/10.1002/cncr.29063

Carlson, L. E., Doll, R., Stephen, J., Faris, P., Tamagawa, R., Drysdale, E., et al. (2013). Randomized controlled trial of mindfulness-based cancer recovery versus supportive expressive group therapy for distressed survivors of breast cancer (MINDSET). *Journal of Clinical Oncology*, *31*, 3119–3126. https://doi.org/10.1200/JCO.2012.47.5210

Carlson, L. E., Tamagawa, R., Stephen, J., Drysdale, E., Zhong, L., Speca, M. (2016). Randomized-controlled trial of mindfulness-based cancer recovery versus supportive expressive group therapy among distressed breast cancer survivors (MINDSET): Long-term follow-up results. *Psycho-Oncology*, *25*(7), 750–759. https://doi.org/10.1002/pon.4150

Castel, A., Cascón, R., Padrol, A., Sala, J., & Rull, M. (2012). Multicomponent cognitive-behavioral group therapy with hypnosis for the treatment of fibromyalgia: Long-term outcome. *The Journal of Pain*, *13*(3), 255–265. https://doi.org/10.1016/j.jpain.2011.11.005

Castonguay, L.G., Constantino, M., Beutler, L.E. (2019). *Principles of change – How psychotherapists implement research in practice.* New York: Oxford University Press.

Causarano, N., Platt, J., Baxter, N. N., Bagher, S., Jones, J. M., Metcalfe, K. A., Hofer, S. O., O'Neill, A. C., Cheng, T., Starenkyj, E., & Zhong, T. (2015). Pre-consultation educational group intervention to improve shared decision-making for postmastectomy breast reconstruction: A pilot randomized controlled trial. *Supportive Care in Cancer*, *23*(5), 1365–1375. https://doi.org/10.1007/s00520-014-2479-6

Cerezo, M. V., Ortiz-Tallo, M., Cardenal, V., & de la Torre-Luque, A. (2014). Positive psychology group intervention for breast cancer patients: A randomised trial. *Psychological Reports: Disability & Trauma*, *115*(1), 44–64. https://doi.org/10.2466/15.20.PR0.115c17z7

Chapman, C. L., Burlingame, G. M., Gleave, R., Rees, F., Beecher, M., & Porter, G. S. (2012). Clinical prediction in group psychotherapy. *Psychotherapy Research*, *22*(6), 673–681. https://doi.org/10.1080/10503307.2012.702512

Christensen, P. N., & Feeney, M. E. (2016). Using the social relations model to understand dyadic perceptions within group therapy. *Group Dynamics: Theory, Research, and Practice*, *20*(3), 196–208. https://doi.org/10.1037/gdn0000051

Clark, D. M. (1986). A cognitive approach to panic. *Behaviour Research and Therapy*, *24*(4), 461–470. https://doi.org/10.1016/0005-7967(86)90011-2

Clark, D. M., & Wells, A. (1995). A cognitive model of social phobia. In R. G. Heimberg (Ed.), *Social phobia: Diagnosis, assessment, and treatment* (pp. 69–93). Guilford Press.

Colom, F., Vieta, E., Martinez-Arán, A., Reinares, M., Goikolea, J. M., Benabarre, A., Torrent, C., Comes, M., Corbella, B., Parramon, G., & Corominas, J. (2003). A randomized trial on the efficacy of group psychoeducation in the prophylaxis of recurrences in bipolar patients whose disease is in remission. *Archives of General Psychiatry*, *60*(4), 402–407. https://doi.org/10.1001/archpsyc.60.4.402

Conelea, C. A., Selles, R. R., Benito, K. G., Walther, M. M., Machan, J. T., Garcia, A. M., Sapyta, J., Morris, S., Franklin, M., & Freeman, J. B. (2017). Secondary outcomes from the pediatric obsessive compulsive disorder treatment study II. *Journal of Psychiatric Research, 92,* 94–100. https://doi.org/10.1016/j.jpsychires.2017.04.001

Crisp, D., Griffiths, K., Mackinnon, A., Bennett, K., & Christensen, H. (2014). An online intervention for reducing depressive symptoms: Secondary benefits for self-esteem, empowerment and quality of life. *Psychiatry Research. 216*(1), 60–66. https://doi.org/10.1016/j.psychres.2014.01.041

Cristea I. A., Gentili C., Cotet C. D., Palomba D., Barbui C., & Cuijpers P. (2017). Efficacy of psychotherapies for borderline personality disorder: A systematic review and meta-analysis. *JAMA Psychiatry, 74*(4), 319–328. https://doi.org/10.1001/jamapsychiatry.2016.4287

Davidsen, A. H., Poulsen, S., Lindschou, J., Winkel, P., Tróndarson, M. F., Waaddegaard, M., & Lau, M. (2017). Feedback in group psychotherapy for eating disorders: A randomized clinical trial. *Journal of Consulting and Clinical Psychology, 85*(5), 484–494. https://doi.org/10.1037/ccp0000173

Department of Veterans Affairs (2017). Management of posttraumatic stress disorder and acute stress reaction. *VA/DOD Clinical Practice Guidelines.* Retrieved from https://www.healthquality.va.gov/guidelines/MH/ptsd/

Edel, M., Raaff, V., Dimaggio, G., Buchheim, A., & Brüne, M. (2017). Exploring the effectiveness of combined mentalization-based group therapy and dialectical behaviour therapy for inpatients with borderline personality disorder – A pilot study. *British Journal of Clinical Psychology, 56*(1), 1–15. https://doi.org/10.1111/bjc.12123

Fairburn, C. G. (2008). Inpatient, day patient and two forms of outpatient CBT-E. In C. G. Fairburn (Ed.), *Cognitive behavior therapy and eating disorders* (pp. 231–244). New York: Guilford Press.

Fjeldstad, A., Høglend, P., & Lorentzen, S. (2017). Patterns of change in interpersonal problems during and after short-term and long-term psychodynamic group therapy: A randomized clinical trial. *Psychotherapy Research, 27*(3), 350–361. http://dx.doi.org/10.1080/10503307.2015.1102357

Fox, J., Cattani, K., & Burlingame, G. M. (2021). Compassion focused therapy in a university counseling and psychological services center: A feasibility trial of a new standardized group manual. *Psychotherapy Research, 31*(4), 419–431. https://doi.org/10.1080/10503307.2020.1783708

Fleury, M.-J., Djouini, A., Huỳnh, C., Tremblay, J., Ferland, F., Ménard, J.-M., & Belleville, G. (2016). Remission from substance use disorders: A systematic review and meta-analysis. *Drug and Alcohol Dependence, 168,* 293–306. https://doi.org/10.1016/j.drugalcdep.2016.08.625

Frankfurt, S., Frazier, P., Syed, S., & Jung, K. R. (2016). Using group-based trajectory and growth mixture modeling to identify classes of change trajectories. *The Counseling Psychologist, 44*(5), 622–660. doi: 10.1177/0011000016658097

Freeman, L. W., White, R., Ratcliff, C. G., Sutton, S., Stewart, M., Palmer, J. L., Link, J., & Cohen, L. (2015). A randomized trial comparing live and telemedicine deliveries of an imagery-based behavioral intervention for breast cancer survivors: Reducing symptoms and barriers to care. *Psycho-Oncology, 24,* 910–918. https://doi.org/10.1002/pon.3656

Frost, N. D., Laska, K. M., & Wampold, B. E. (2014). The evidence for present-center therapy as a treatment for posttraumatic stress disorder. *Journal of Traumatic Stress, 27*(1), 1–8. https://doi.org/10.1002/jts.21881

Gallagher, M. E., Tasca, G. A., Ritchie, K., Balfour, L., & Bissada, H. (2014). Attachment anxiety moderates the relationship between growth in group cohesion and treatment outcomes in group psychodynamic interpersonal psychotherapy for women with binge eating disorder. *Group Dynamics: Theory, Research, and Practice, 18*(1), 38–52. https://doi.org/10.1037/a0034760

Garland, E. L., & Howard, M. O. (2013). Mindfulness-oriented recovery enhancement reduces pain attentional bias in chronic pain patients. *Psychotherapy and Psychosomatics, 82*(5), 311–318. https://doi.org/10.1159/000348868

Gebler, F. A., & Maercker, A. (2014). Effects of including an existential perspective in a cognitive-behavioral group program for chronic pain: A clinical trial with 6 months follow-up. *The Humanistic Psychologist, 42*(2), 155–171. https://doi.org/10.1080/08873267.2013.865188

Gliddon, E., Cosgrove, V., Berk, L., Lauder, S., Mohebbi, M., Grimm, D., Dodd, S., Coulson, C., Raju, K., Suppes, T., & Berk, M. (2019). A randomized controlled trial of MoodSwings 2.0: An internet-based self-management program for bipolar disorder. *Bipolar Disorders, 21*(1), 28–39. https://doi.org/10.1111/bdi.12669

Glombiewski, J. A., Holzapfel, S., Riecke, J., de Jong, J., Lemmer, G., & Rief, W. (2018). Exposure and CBT for chronic back pain: An RCT on differential

efficacy and optimal length of treatment. *Journal of Consulting Clinical Psychology 86*(6), 533–545. https://doi.org/10.1037/ccp0000298

Goldin, P. R., Morrison, A., Jazaieri, H., Brozovich, F., Heimberg, R., & Gross, J. J. (2016). Group CBT versus MBSR for social anxiety disorder: A randomized controlled trial. *Journal of Consulting and Clinical Psychology, 84*(5), 427–437. https://doi.org/10.1037/ccp0000092

Grenon, R., Carlucci, S., Brugnera, A., Schwartze, D., Hammond, N., Ivanova, I., Mcquaid, N., Proulx, G., & Tasca, G. A. (2019). Psychotherapy for eating disorders: A meta-analysis of direct comparisons. *Psychotherapy Research, 29*(7), 833–845. https://doi.org/10.1080/10503307.2018.1489162

Grenon, R., Schwartze, D., Hammond, N., Ivanova, I., Mcquaid, N., Proulx, G., & Tasca, G. A. (2017). Group psychotherapy for eating disorders: A meta-analysis. *International Journal of Eating Disorders, 50*(9), 997–1013. https://doi.org/10.1002/eat.22744

Griffiths, K. M., Mackinnon, A. J., Crisp, D. A., Christensen, H., Bennett, K., & Farrer, L. (2012). The effectiveness of an online support groups for members of the community with depression: A randomised controlled trial. *PLoS ONE, 7,* e53244. https://doi.org/10.1371/journal.pone.0053244

Gross, E. F. (1957). *An empirical study of the concepts of cohesiveness and compatibility.* Honors thesis, Harvard University.

Gustavsson, C., Denison, E., & von Koch, L. (2010). Self-management of persistent neck pain: A randomized controlled trial of a multi-component group intervention in primary health care. *European Journal of Pain, 14*(6), 630.e1–630.e11. https://doi.org/10.1016/j.ejpain.2009.10.004

Gustavsson, C., & von Koch, L. (2017). A 9-year follow-up of a self-management group intervention for persistent neck pain in primary health care: A randomized controlled trial. *Journal of Pain Research, 10,* 53–64. https://doi.org/10.2147/JPR.S125074

Harris, A., Moe, T. F., Eriksen, H. R., Tangen, T., Lie, S. A., Tveito, T. H., & Reme, S. E. (2017). Brief intervention, physical exercise and cognitive behavioural group therapy for patients with chronic low back pain (The CINS trial). *European Journal of Pain, 21*(8), 1397–1407. https://doi.org/10.1002/ejp.1041

Hazell, C. M., Hayward, M., Cavanagh, K., & Strauss, C. (2016). A systematic review and meta-analysis of low intensity CBT for psychosis. *Clinical Psychology Review, 45,* 183–192. https://doi.org/10.1016/j.cpr.2016.03.004

Heimberg, R. G., & Becker, R. E. (2002). *Cognitive-behavioral group therapy for social phobia: Basic mechanisms and clinical strategies.* New York, NY: Guilford Press.

Heiney, S. P., Underwood, S. M., Tavakoli, A., Adams, S. A., Wells, L. M., & Bryant, L. H. (2012). Randomized trial of therapeutic group by teleconference: African American women with breast cancer. *Cancer, 118*(15), 3822–3832. https://doi.org/10.1002/cncr.26676

Helminen, E. E., Sinikallio, S. H., Valjakka, A. L., Väisänen-Rouvali, R. H., & Arokoski, J. P. (2015). Effectiveness of a cognitive–behavioural group intervention for knee osteoarthritis pain: A randomized controlled trial. *Clinical Rehabilitation, 29*(9), 868–881. https://doi.org/10.1177/0269215514558567

Hewitt, P. L., Mikail, S. F., Flett, G. L., Tasca, G. A., Flynn, C. A., Deng, X., Kaldas, J. & Chen. C. (2015). Psychodynamic/interpersonal group psychotherapy for perfectionism: Evaluating the effectiveness of a short-term treatment. *Psychotherapy, 52*(2), 205–217. http://dx.doi.org/10.1037/pst0000016

Hien, D. A., Wells, E. A., Jiang, H., Suarez-Morales, L., Campbell, A. N., Cohen, L. R., Miele, G. M., Killeen, T., Brigham, G. S., Zhang, Y., Hansen, C., Hodgkins, C., Hatch-Maillette, M., Brown, C., Kulaga, A., Kristman-Valente, A., Chu, M., Sage, R., Robinson, J. A., . . . Nunes, E. V. (2009). Multisite randomized trial of behavioral interventions for women with co-occuring PTSD and substance use disorders. *Journal of Consulting and Clinical Psychology, 77*(4), 607–619. https://doi.org/10.1037/a0016227

Hofmann, S. G., & Bögels, S. M. (2006). Recent advances in the treatment of social phobia: Introduction to the special issue. *Journal of Cognitive Psychotherapy, 20*(1), 3–5. https://doi.org/10.1891/jcop.20.1.3

Hopf, R. B., Grange, D. L., Moessner, M., & Bauer, S. (2013). Internet-based chat support groups for parents in family-based treatment for adolescent eating disorders: A pilot study. *European Eating Disorders Review, 21*(3), 215–223. https://doi.org/10.1002/erv.2196

Hornsey, M. J., Olsen, S., Barlow, F. K., & Oei, T. P. S. (2012). Testing a single-item visual analogue scale as a proxy for cohesiveness in group psychotherapy. *Group Dynamics: Theory, Research, and Practice, 16*(1), 80–90. https://doi.org/10.1037/a0024545

Horowitz, L. M., Alden, L. E., Wiggins, J. S., & Pincus, A. L. (2000). *Inventory of Interpersonal Problems (IIP)—Manual*. San Antonio, TX: The Psychological Corporation.

Horvath, A. O., & Greenberg, L. S. (1989). Development and validation of the Working Alliance Inventory. *Journal of Counseling Psychology, 36*(2), 223–233. https://doi.org/10.1037/0022-0167.36.2.223

Illing, V., Tasca, G. A., Balfour, L., & Bissada, H. (2011). Attachment dimensions and group climate growth in a sample of women seeking treatment for eating disorders. *Psychiatry, 74*(3), 255–269. https://doi.org/10.1521/psyc.2011.74.3.255

Inoue, M., Inoue, S., Ikemoto, T., Arai, Y. C. P., Nakata, M., Miyazaki, A., Nishihara, M., Kawai, T., Hatakeyama, N., Yamaguchi, S., Shimo, K., Miyagawa, H., Hasegawa, T., Sakurai, H., Hasegawa, Y., Ohmichi, Y., & Ushida, T. (2014). The efficacy of a multidisciplinary group program for patients with refractory chronic pain. *Pain Research and Management, 19*(6), 302–308. https://doi.org/10.1155/2014/728063

Ivanova, I. V., Tasca, G. A., Hammond, N., Balfour, L., Ritchie, K., Koszycki, D., & Bissada, H. (2015). Negative affect mediates the relationship between interpersonal problems and binge-eating disorder symptoms and psychopathology in a clinical sample: A test of the interpersonal model. *European Eating Disorders Review, 23*(2), 133–138. https://doi-org.erl.lib.byu.edu/10.1002/erv.2344

Jacobi, C., Völker, U., Trockel, M. T., & Taylor, C. B. (2012). Effects of an Internet-based intervention for subthreshold eating disorders: A randomized controlled trial. *Behaviour Research and Therapy, 50*(2), 93–99. https://doi.org/10.1016/j.brat.2011.09.013

Janis, R. A., Burlingame, G. M., Svien, H., Jensen, J., & Lundgreen R. (2021). Group therapy for mood disorders: A meta-analysis. *Psychotherapy Research, 31*(3), 647–474. https://doi.org/10.1080/10503307.2020.1817603

Jazaieri, H., Goldin, P. R., & Gross, J. J. (2018). The role of working alliance in CBT and MBSR for social anxiety disorder. *Mindfulness, 9*(5), 1381–1389. https://doi.org/10.1007/s12671-017-0877-9

Johnson, J. E., Burlingame, G. M., Olsen, J. A., Davies, D. R., & Gleave, R. L., (2005). Group climate, cohesion, alliance, and empathy in group psychotherapy: Multilevel structural equation models. *Journal of Counseling Psychology, 52*(3), 310–321. https://doi.org/10.1037/0022-0167.52.3.310

Jones, J. M., Cheng, T., Jackman, M., Walton, T., Haines, S., Rodin, G., & Catton, P. (2013). Getting back on track: Evaluation of a brief group psychoeducation intervention for women completing primary treatment for breast cancer. *Psycho-Oncology, 22*(1), 117–124. https://doi.org/10.1002/pon.2060

Jónsson, H., & Hougaard, E. (2009). Group cognitive behavioural therapy for obsessive–compulsive disorder: A systematic review and meta-analysis. *Acta Psychiatrica Scandinavica, 119*(2), 98–106. https://doi.org/10.1111/j.1600-0447.2008.01270.x

Joyce, A. S., Piper, W. E., & Ogrodniczuk, J. S. (2007). Therapeutic alliance and cohesion variables as predictors of outcome in short-term group psychotherapy. *International Journal of Group Psychotherapy, 57*(3), 269–296. https://doi.org/10.1521/ijgp.2007.57.3.269

Karterud, S. (2015). *Mentalization-based group therapy (MBT-G): A theoretical, clinical, and research manual*. OUP Oxford. https://doi.org/10.1093/med:psych/9780198753742.001.0001

Kass, A. E., Trockel, M., Safer, D. L., Sinton, M. M., Cunning, D., Rizk, M. T., Genkin, B. H., Weisman, H. L., Bailey, J. O., Jacobi, C., Wilfley, D. E., & Taylor, C. B. (2014). Internet-based preventive intervention for reducing eating disorder risk: A randomized controlled trial comparing guided with unguided self-help. *Behaviour Research and Therapy, 63*, 90–98. https://doi.org/10.1016/j.brat.2014.09.010

Kay, S. R., Fiszbein, A., & Opler, L. A. (1987). The positive and negative syndrome scale (PANSS) for schizophrenia. *Schizophrenia Bulletin, 13*, 261–276. https://doi.org/10.1093/schbul/13.2.261

Keating, L., Tasca, G. A., Gick, M., Ritchie, K., Balfour, L., & Bissada, H. (2014). Change in attachment to the therapy group generalizes to change in individual attachment among women with binge eating disorder. *Psychotherapy, 51*(1), 78–87. https://doi.org/10.1037/a0031099

Kemani, M. K., Olsson, G. L., Lekander, M., Hesser, H., Andersson, E., & Wicksell, R. K. (2015). Efficacy and cost-effectiveness of acceptance and commitment therapy and applied relaxation for longstanding pain.

The Clinical Journal of Pain, 31(11), 1004–1016. https://doi.org/10.1097/AJP.0000000000000203

Key, B. L., Rowa, K., Bieling, P., McCabe, R., & Pawluk, E. J. (2017). Mindfulness-based cognitive therapy as an augmentation treatment for obsessive–compulsive disorder. *Clinical Psychology & Psychotherapy, 24*(5), 1109–1120. https://doi.org/10.1002/cpp.2076

Kinley, J. L., & Reyno, S. M. (2013). Attachment style changes following intensive short-term group psychotherapy. *International Journal of Group Psychotherapy, 63*(1), 53–75. https://doi.org/10.1521/ijgp.2013.63.1.53

Kirchmann, H., Steyer, R., Mayer, A., Joraschky, P., Schreiber-Willnow, K., & Strauss, B. (2012). Effects of adult inpatient group psychotherapy on attachment characteristics: An observational study comparing routine care to an untreated comparison group. *Psychotherapy Research, 22*(1), 95–114. https://doi.org/10.1080/10503307.2011.626807

Kivlighan, D. M., Jr, Coco, G. L., & Gullo, S. (2012). Attachment anxiety and avoidance and perceptions of group climate: An actor-partner interdependence analysis. *Journal of Counseling Psychology, 59*(4), 518–527. https://doi.org/10.1037/a0030173

Kivlighan, D. M. III, & Kivlighan, D. M., Jr. (2016). Examining between-leader and within-leader processes in group therapy. *Group Dynamics: Theory, Research, and Practice, 20*(3), 144–164. https://doi.org/10.1037/gdn0000050

Kivlighan, D. M., Jr., Lo Coco, G., Gullo, S., Pazzagli, C., & Mazzeschi, C. (2017). Attachment anxiety and attachment avoidance: Members' attachment fit with their group and group relationships. *International Journal of Group Psychotherapy, 67*(2), 223–239. https://doi.org/10.1080/00207284.2016.1260464

Kivlighan, D. M., Jr., Lo Coco, G., Oieni, V., Gullo, S., Pazzagli, C., & Mazzeschi, C. (2017). All bonds are not the same: A response surface analysis of the perceptions of positive bonding relationships in therapy groups. *Group Dynamics: Theory, Research, and Practice, 21*(3), 159–177. https://doi.org/10.1037/gdn0000071

Kjeldgaard, D., Forchhammer, H. B., Teasdale, T. W., & Jensen, R. H. (2014). Cognitive behavioural treatment for the chronic post-traumatic headache patient: A randomized controlled trial. *The Journal of Headache and Pain, 15*, 81. https://doi.org/10.1186/1129-2377-15-81

Klein, R. H. (2008). Toward the establishment of evidence-based practices in group psychotherapy. *International Journal of Group Psychotherapy, 58*(4), 441–454. https://doi.org/10.1521/ijgp.2008.58.4.441

Kliem, S., Kröger, C., & Kosfelder, J. (2010). Dialectical behavior therapy for borderline personality disorder: A meta-analysis using mixed-effects modeling. *Journal of Consulting and Clinical Psychology, 78*(6), 936–951. https://doi.org/10.1037/a0021015

Knox, C. R., Lall, R., Hansen, Z., & Lamb, S. E. (2014). Treatment compliance and effectiveness of a cognitive behavioural intervention for low back pain: A complier average effect approach to the BeST data set. *BMC Musculoskeletal Disorders, 15*, 17. https://doi.org/10.1186/1471-2474-15-17

Kocovski, N. L., Fleming, J. E., Hawley, L. L., Ho, M. H. R., & Antony, M. M. (2015). Mindfulness and acceptance-based group therapy and traditional cognitive behavioral group therapy for social anxiety disorder: Mechanisms of change. *Behaviour Research and Therapy, 70*, 11–22. https://doi.org/10.1016/j.brat.2015.04.005

Kocovski, N. L., Fleming, J. E., Hawley, L. L., Huta, V., & Antony, M. M. (2013). Mindfulness and acceptance-based group therapy versus traditional cognitive behavioral group therapy for social anxiety disorder: A randomized controlled trial. *Behaviour Research and Therapy, 51*(12), 889–898. https://doi.org/10.1016/j.brat.2013.10.007

Koementas-de Vos, M. M. W., Nugter, M. A., Engelsbel, F., & De Jong, K. (2018). Does progress feedback enhance the outcome of group psychotherapy? *Psychotherapy, 55*(2), 151–163. https://doi.org/10.1037/pst0000164

Koerner, K., Linehan, M., M. (2000). Research on dialectical behavior therapy for patients with borderline personality disorder. *Psychiatric Clinics of North America, 23*(1), 151–167. https://doi.org/10.1016/S0193-953X(05)70149-0

Kordy, H., Wolf, M., Aulich, K., Bürgy, M., Hegerl, U., Hüsing, J., Puschner, B., Rummel-Kluge, C., Vedder, H., & Backenstrass, M. (2016). Internet-delivered disease management for recurrent depression: A multicenter randomized controlled trial. *Psychotherapy and Psychosomatics, 85*(2), 91–98. https://doi.org/10.1159/000441951

Kösters, M., Burlingame, G. M., Nachtigall, C., & Strauss, B. (2006). A meta-analytic review of the effectiveness of inpatient group psychotherapy. *Group Dynamics: Theory, Research and Practice, 10*(2), 146–163. https://doi.org/10.1037/1089-2699.10.2.146

Krägeloh, C. U., Czuba, K. J., Billington, D. R., Kersten, P., & Siegert, R. J. (2015). Using feedback from patient-reported outcome measures in mental health services: A scoping study and typology. *Psychiatric Services, 66*(3), 224–241. https://doi.org/10.1176/appi.ps.201400141

Lamb, S. E., Hansen, Z., Lall, R., Castelnuovo, E., Withers, E. J., Nichols, V., Potter, R., Underwood, M. R., & Back Skills Training Trial investigators. (2010). Group cognitive behavioural treatment for low-back pain in primary care: A randomised controlled trial and cost-effectiveness analysis. *The Lancet, 375*(9718), 916–923. https://doi.org/10.1016/S0140-6736(09)62164-4

Lamb, S. E., Mistry, D., Lall, R., Hansen, Z., Evans, D., Withers, E. J., Underwood, M. R., & Back Skills Training Trial Group. (2012). Group cognitive behavioural interventions for low back pain in primary care: Extended follow-up of the Back Skills Training Trial (ISRCTN54717854). *Pain, 153*(2), 494–501. https://doi.org/10.1016/j.pain.2011.11.016

Lambert, M. J. (2015). Progress feedback and the OQ-system: The past and the future. *Psychotherapy, 52*(4), 381–390. https://doi.org/10.1037/pst0000027

Latner, J. D., Ciao, A. C., Wendicke, A. U., Murakami, J. M., & Durso, L. E. (2013). Community-based behavioral weight-loss treatment: Long-term maintenance of weight loss, physiological, and psychological outcomes. *Behaviour Research and Therapy, 51*(8), 451–459. https://doi.org/10.1016/j.brat.2013.04.009

Lauder, S., Chester, A., Castle, D., Dodd, S., Gliddon, E., Berk, L., Chamberlain, J.A., Klein, B., Gilbert, M., Austin, D.W., & Berk, M. (2015). A randomized head to head trial of MoodSwings.net.au: An internet based self-help program for bipolar disorder. *Journal of Affective Disorders, 171*, 13–21. https://doi.org/10.1016/j.jad.2014.08.008

Le Borgne, M., Boudoukha, A. H., Petit, A., & Roquelaure, Y. (2016). Évaluation de l'efficacité d'une thérapie comportementale et cognitive (TCC) de groupe auprès de patients souffrant de lombalgies chroniques liées au travail. *Journal de Thérapie Comportementale et Cognitive, 26*(3), 131–138. https://doi.org/10.1016/j.jtcc.2016.06.007

Lehman, A. F., Liebermann, J. A., Dixon, L. B., McGlashan, T. H., Miller, A. L., Perkins, D. O., & Kreyenbuhl, J. (2010). *Practice guidelines for the treatment of patients with schizophrenia* (2nd ed.). Washington, DC: American Psychiatric Publishing.

Lese, K. P., & MacNair-Semands, R. R. (2000). The Therapeutic Factors Inventory: Development of a scale. *Group, 24*(4), 303–317. https://doi.org/10.1023/A:1026616626780

Leszcz, M. (2017). How understanding attachment enhances group therapist effectiveness. *International Journal of Group Psychotherapy, 67*(2), 280–287. https://doi.org/10.1080/00207284.2016.1273745

Leszcz, M., & Kobos, J. C. (2008). Evidence-based group psychotherapy: Using AGPA's practice guidelines to enhance clinical effectiveness. *Journal of Clinical Psychology, 64*(11), 1238–1260. doi: 10.1002/jclp.20531

Levy, K. N., Kivity, Y., Johnson B. N., & Gooch, C. V. (2018). Adult attachment as a predictor and moderator of psychotherapy outcome: A meta-analysis. *Journal of Clinical Psychology, 74*(11), 1997–2013. https://doi.org/10.1002/jclp.22685

Lewer, M., Kosfelder, J., Michalak, J., Schroeder, D., Nasrawi, N., & Vocks, S. (2017). Effects of a cognitive-behavioral exposure-based body image therapy for overweight females with binge eating disorder: A pilot study. *Journal of Eating Disorders, 5*, 43. https://doi.org/10.1186/s40337-017-0174-y

Linden, M., Scherbe, S., & Cicholas, B. (2014). Randomized controlled trial on the effectiveness of cognitive behavior group therapy in chronic back pain patients. *Journal of Back and Musculoskeletal Rehabilitation, 27*(4), 563–568. https://doi.org/10.3233/BMR-140518

Linehan, M. , M., (2014). *DBT training manual.* New York, NY: The Guilford Press.

Lo Coco, G., Gullo, S., & Kivlighan, D. M., Jr. (2012). Examining patients' and other group members' agreement about their alliance to the group as a whole and changes in patient symptoms using response surface analysis. *Journal of Counseling Psychology, 59*(2), 197–207. https://doi.org/10.1037/a0027560

Lo Coco, G., Melchiori, F., Oieni, V., Infurna, M. R., Strauss, B., Schwartze, D., Rosendahl, J., & Gullo, S. (2019). Group treatment for substance use disorder in adults: A systematic review and meta-analysis of randomized-controlled trials. *Journal of Substance Abuse Treatment, 99*, 104–116. https://doi.org/10.1016/j.jsat.2019.01.016

Lomholt, J. J., Thastum, M., Christensen, A. E., Leegaard, A., & Herlin, T. (2015). Cognitive behavioral group intervention for pain and well-being in children with juvenile idiopathic arthritis: A study of feasibility and preliminary efficacy. *Pediatric Rheumatology Online Journal, 13*, 35. https://doi.org/10.1186/s12969-015-0032-x

Loprinzi, C. E., Prasad, K., Schroeder, D. R., & Sood, A. (2011). Stress Management and Resilience Training (SMART) program to decrease stress and enhance resilience among breast cancer survivors: A pilot randomized clinical trial. *Clinical Breast Cancer, 11*(6), 364–368. https://doi.org/10.1016/j.clbc.2011.06.008

Lorentzen, S., Ruud, T., Fjeldstad, A., & Høglend, P. A. (2013). Comparison of a short- and long-term group psychotherapy: Randomised clinical trial. *The British Journal of Psychiatry, 203*, 280–287. https://doi.org/10.1192/bjp.bp.112.113688

Lorentzen, S., Ruud, T., Fjeldstad, A., & Høglend, P. A. (2015). Personality disorder moderates outcome in short- and long-term group analytic psychotherapy: A randomized clinical trial. *British Journal of Clinical Psychology, 54*, 129–146. https://doi.org/10.1111/bjc.12065

Lorentzen, S., Strauss, B., & Altmann, U. (2018). Process-outcome relationships in short- and long-term psychodynamic group psychotherapy: Results from a randomized clinical trial. *Group Dynamics: Theory, Research, and Practice, 22*(2), 93–107. https://doi.org/10.1037/gdn0000084

Luborsky, L, Barber, J. P., Siqueland, L., Johnson, S., Najavitas, L. M., Frank, A., & Daley, D. (1996). The revised helping alliance questionnaire (HAq-II): Psychometric properties. *Journal of Psychotherapy Practice and Research, 5*(3), 260–271. https://doi.org/10.1037/t07504-000

MacKenzie, K. R. (1983). The clinical application of a group climate measure. In R. R. Dies & K. R. MacKenzie (Eds.), *Advances in group psychotherapy: Integrating research and practice* (pp. 159–170). Madison, CT: International Universities Press.

MacKenzie, K. R., & Dies, R. R. (1982). *CORE battery: Clinical outcome results.* New York, NY: American Group Psychotherapy.

Manne, S. L., Kashy, D., Siegel, S. D., & Heckman, C. J. (2017). Group therapy processes and treatment outcomes in 2 couple-focused group interventions for breast cancer patients. *Psycho-Oncology, 26*(12), 2175–2185. https://doi.org/10.1002/pon.4323

Manne, S. L., Siegel, S. D., Heckman, C. J., & Kashy, D. A. (2016). A randomized clinical trial of a supportive versus a skill-based couple-focused group intervention for breast cancer patients. *Journal of Consulting and Clinical Psychology, 84*(8), 668–681. https://doi.org/10.1037/ccp0000110

Marques, A. P., Magalhães, M. O., Comachio, J., Muto, L. H. A., e Silva, A. C., Almeida, G. P. L., Franca, F. J. R., Ramos, L. A. V. & Burke, T. N. (2014). FRI0561–HPR Effect of cognitive behavioral therapy and exercise versus supervised exercise program in patients with chronic nonspecific low back pain: A randomized controlled. *Annals of the Rheumatic Diseases, 73*(Suppl 2), 1198–1198. https://doi.org/10.1136/annrheumdis-2014-eular.3670

Marmarosh, C. L. (2014). Empirical research on attachment in group psychotherapy: Moving the field forward. *Psychotherapy, 51*(1), 88–92. https://doi.org/10.1037/a0032523

Marmarosh, C. L. (2017). Attachment in group psychotherapy: Bridging theories, research, and clinical techniques. *International Journal of Group Psychotherapy, 67*(2), 157–160. https://doi.org/10.1080/00207284.2016.1267573

Marmarosh, C. L., Markin, R. D., & Spiegel, E. B. (2013). *Attachment in group psychotherapy.* Washington, DC, US: American Psychological Association. https://doi.org/10.1037/14186-000

Marmarosh, C. L., & Tasca, G. A. (2013). Adult attachment anxiety: Using group therapy to promote change. *Journal of Clinical Psychology, 69*(11), 1172–1182. https://doi.org/10.1002/jclp.22044

Martins, M. R. I., Gritti, C. C., dos Santos Junior, R., de Araújo, M. C. L., Dias, L. C., Foss, M. H. D. A. A., de Andrade, L. B., & Rocha, C. E. D. A. A. (2014). Randomized controlled trial of a therapeutic intervention group in patients with fibromyalgia syndrome. *Revista Brasileira de Reumatologia (English Edition), 54*, 179–184. https://doi.org/10.1016/j.rbre.2013.10.002

Maxwell, H., Tasca, G. A., Ritchie, K., Balfour, L., & Bissada, H. (2014). Change in attachment insecurity is related to improved outcomes 1–year post group therapy in women with binge eating disorder. *Psychotherapy, 51*(1), 57–65. https://doi.org/10.1037/a0031100

McIntosh, V. V., Jordan, J., Carter, F. A., Luty, S. E., (2005). Three psychotherapies for anorexia nervosa: A randomized, controlled trial. *The American*

Journal of Psychiatry 162(4), 741–747. https://doi.org/10.1176/appi. ajp.162.4.741

McKellar, J. D., Harris, A. H., & Moos, R. H. (2009). Patients' abstinence status affects the benefits of 12-step self-help group participation on substance use disorder outcomes. *Drug and Alcohol Dependence, 99*(1–3), 115–122. https://doi.org/10.1016/j.drugalcdep.2008.07.005

McLaughlin, S. P. B., Barkowski, S., Burlingame, G. M., Strauss, B., & Rosendahl, J. (2019). Group psychotherapy for borderline personality disorder: A meta-analysis of randomized-controlled trials. *Psychotherapy, 56*(2), 260–273. https://doi.org/10.1037/pst0000211

Mehlsen, M., Hegaard, L., Ørnbøl, E., Jensen, J. S., Fink, P., & Frostholm, L. (2017). The effect of a lay-led, group-based self-management program for patients with chronic pain: A randomized controlled trial of the Danish version of the Chronic Pain Self-Management Programme. *Pain, 158*(8), 1437–1445. https://doi.org/10.1097/j.pain.0000000000000931

Melton, L., Brewer, B., Kolva, E., Joshi, T., & Bunch, M. (2017). Increasing access to care for young adults with cancer: Results of a quality-improvement project using a novel telemedicine approach to supportive group psychotherapy. *Palliative & Supportive Care, 15*(2), 176–180. https://doi.org/10.1017/S1478951516000572

Merckaert, I., Lewis, F., Delevallez, F., Caillier, M., Delvaux, N., Libert, Y., Liénard, A., Nogaret, J., Slachmuylder, J., & Razavi, D. (2016). Régulation émotionnelle au début de la période de rémission dans le cadre du cancer du sein: Impact d'une intervention de groupe à composantes multiples. IXe congrès de l'AFPSA De l'expertise scientifique à l'expertise profane... (14-16 Décembre 2016: Lyon)

Mikulincer, M., & Shaver, P. R. (2017). Augmenting the sense of attachment security in group contexts: The effects of a responsive leader and a cohesive group. *International Journal of Group Psychotherapy, 67*(2), 161–175. https://doi.org/10.1080/00207284.2016.1260462

Moessner, M., & Bauer, S. (2012). Online counselling for eating disorders: Reaching an underserved population? *Journal of Mental Health, 21*(4), 336–345. https://doi.org/10.3109/09638237.2011.643512

Monti, D. A., Kash, K. M., Kunkel, E. J., Moss, A., Mathews, M., Brainard, G., Anne, R., Leiby, B. E., Pequinot, E., & Newberg, A. B. (2013). Psychosocial benefits of a novel mindfulness intervention versus standard support in distressed women with breast cancer. *Psycho-Oncology, 22*(11), 2565–2575. https://doi.org/10.1002/pon.3320

Morone, N. E., Greco, C. M., Moore, C. G., Rollman, B. L., Lane, B., Morrow, L. A., Glynn, N. W., & Weiner, D. K. (2016). A mind-body program for older adults with chronic low back pain: A randomized clinical trial. *JAMA Internal Medicine, 176*(3), 329–337. https://doi.org/10.1001/jamainternmed.2015.8033

Mörtberg, E. (2014). Working alliance in individual and group cognitive therapy for social anxiety disorder. *Psychiatry Research, 220*(1–2), 716–718. https://doi.org/10.1016/j.psychres.2014.07.004

Mörtberg, E., Clark, D. M., Sundin, O., & Aberg, Wistedt, A., (2007). Intensive group cognitive treatment and individual cognitive therapy vs. treatment as usual in social phobia: A randomized controlled trial. *Acta Psychiatrica Scandinavica, 115*(2), 142–154. https://doi.org/10.1111/j.1600-0447.2006.00839.x

Mustafa, M., Carson-Stevens, A., Gillespie, D., & Edwards, A. G. (2013). Psychological interventions for women with metastatic breast cancer. *Cochrane Database of Systematic Reviews, 6*, 1–71. https://doi.org/10.1002/14651858.CD004253.pub4

National Institute for Health and Care Excellence. (2013). *Social anxiety disorder: Recognition, assessment and treatment.* (NICE Clinical Guideline 159). NICE, 2014. https://www.nice.org.uk/guidance/cg159/resources/social-anxiety-disorder-recognition-assessment-and-treatment-pdf-35109639699397.

National Institute for Health and Care Excellence (2014). *Psychosis and schizophrenia in adults: Prevention and management.* London, UK: NICE.

National Institute for Health and Care Excellence (2017). Eating disorders: Recognition and treatment. Retrieved from https://www.nice.org.uk/guidance/ng69/chapter/Recommendations#treating-binge-eating-disorer

National Institute for Health and Care Excellence (2018). Post traumatic stress disorder. Nice Guidline NG116. Retrieved from https://www.nice.org.uk/guidance/ng116

National Institute for Health and Care Excellence. (2019). *Generalised anxiety disorder and panic disorder in adults: Management.* (NICE Clinical Guideline 113). Update 2019; NICE, 2019. https://www.nice.org.uk/guidance/cg113

Naumann, F., Munro, A., Martin, E., Magrani, P., Buchan, J., Smith, C., Piggott, B., & Philpott, M. (2012). An individual-based versus group-based exercise and counselling intervention for improving quality of life in breast cancer survivors. A feasibility and efficacy study. *Psycho-Oncology, 21*(10), 1136–1139. https://doi.org/10.1002/pon.2015

Newnham, E. A., Hooke, G. R., & Page, A. C. (2010). Progress monitoring and feedback in psychiatric care reduces depressive symptoms. *Journal of Affective Disorders, 127*(1–3), 139–146. https://doi.org/10.1016/j.jad.2010.05.003

Niknejad, B., Bolier, R., Henderson, C. R., Delgado, D., Kozlov, E., Löckenhoff, C. E., & Reid, M. C. (2018). Association between psychological interventions and chronic pain outcomes in older adults: A systematic review and meta-analysis. *JAMA Internal Medicine, 178*(6), 830–839. https://doi.org/10.1001/jamainternmed.2018.0756

Norton, P. J., & Kazantzis, N. (2016). Dynamic relationships of therapist alliance and group cohesion in transdiagnostic group CBT for anxiety disorders. *Journal of Consulting and Clinical Psychology, 84*(2), 146–155. https://doi.org/10.1037/ccp0000062

Obeid, N., Carlucci, S., Brugnera, A., Compare, A., Proulx, G., Bissada, H., & Tasca, G. A. (2018). Reciprocal influence of distress and group therapeutic factors in day treatment for eating disorders: A progress and process monitoring study. *Psychotherapy, 55*(2), 170–178. https://doi.org/10.1037/pst0000138

Ogrodniczuk, J. S., & Sochting, I. (2010). *Outcome expectancy scale.* The University of British Columbia.

Oldham, J., Gabbard, G., Goin, M., Gunderson, J., Soloff, P., Spiegel, D., & Phillips, K. (2010). *Practice guidelines for the treatment of patients with borderline personality disorder.* Arlington, VA: American Psychiatric Association.

Olsson, G. L., Kemani, M., Jensen, K., Kosek, E., Kadetoff, D., Sorjonen, K., Ingvar, M., & Wicksell, R. (2012). Acceptance and commitment therapy for fibromyalgia: A randomized controlled trial. *Scandinavian Journal of Pain, 3*(3), 183–183. https://doi.org/10.1016/j.sjpain.2012.05.027

Overall, J. E., & Gorham, D. R. (1962). The brief psychiatric rating scale. *Psychological Reports, 10*(3), 799–812. https://doi.org/10.2466/pr0.1962.10.3.799

Parra-Delgado, M., & Latorre-Postigo, J. M. (2013). Effectiveness of mindfulness-based cognitive therapy in the treatment of fibromyalgia: A randomised trial. *Cognitive Therapy and Research, 37*(5), 1015–1026. https://doi.org/10.1007/s10608-013-9538-z

Pelekasis, P., Zisi, G., Koumarianou, A., Marioli, A., Chrousos, G., Syrigos, K., & Darviri, C. (2016). Forming a stress management and health promotion program for women undergoing chemotherapy for breast cancer: A pilot randomized controlled trial. *Integrative Cancer Therapies, 15*(2), 165–174. https://doi.org/10.1177/1534735415598225

Pettersson, R., Söderström, S., Edlund-Söderström, K., & Nilsson, K. W. (2017). Internet-based cognitive behavioral therapy for adults with ADHD in outpatient psychiatric care: A randomized trial. *Journal of Attention Disorders, 21*(6), 508–521. https://doi.org/10.1177/1087054714539998

Phillips, B., Wennberg, P., Konradsson, P., & Franck, J. (2018). Mentalization-based treatment for concurrent borderline personality disorder and substance use disorder: A randomized controlled feasibility study. *European Addiction Research, 24*(1), 1–8. https://doi.org/10.1159/000485564

Phillips, K. M., Antoni, M. H., Carver, C. S., Lechner, S. C., Penedo, F. J., McCullough, M. E., Gluck, S., Derhagopian, R. P., & Blomberg, B. B. (2011). Stress management skills and reductions in serum cortisol across the year after surgery for non-metastatic breast cancer. *Cognitive Therapy and Research, 35*(6), 595–600. https://doi.org/10.1007/s10608-011-9398-3

Piper, W. E., Marrache, M., Lacroix, R., Richardsen, A. M., & Jones, B. D. (1983). Cohesion as a basic bond in groups. *Human Relations, 36*(2), 93–108. https://doi.org/10.1177/001872678303600201

Piper, W. E., McCallum, M., Joyce, A. S., Rosie, J. S., & Ogrodniczuk, J. S. (2001). Patient personality and time-limited group psychotherapy for complicated grief. *International Journal of Group Psychotherapy, 51*(4), 525–552. https://doi.org/10.1521/ijgp.51.4.525.51307

Powers, M. B., Sigmarsson, S. R., & Emmelkamp, P. M. G. (2008). A meta-analytic review of psychological treatments for social anxiety disorder.

International Journal of Cognitive Therapy, *1*(2), 94–113. https://doi.org/10.1521/ijct.2008.1.2.94

Rahmani, M., Omidi, A., Asemi, Z., & Akbari, H. (2018). The effect of dialectical behaviour therapy on binge eating, difficulties in emotion regulation and BMI in overweight patients with binge-eating disorder: A randomized controlled trial. *Mental Health & Prevention*, *9*, 13–18. https://doi.org/10.1016/j.mhp.2017.11.002

Ramos, C., Costa, P. A., Rudnicki, T., Marôco, A. L., Leal, I., Guimarães, R., Fougo, J. L., & Tedeschi, R. G. (2018). The effectiveness of a group intervention to facilitate posttraumatic growth among women with breast cancer. *Psycho-Oncology*, *27*(1), 258–264. https://doi.org/10.1002/pon.4501

Rapee, R. M., & Heimberg, R. G. (1997). A cognitive-behavioral model of anxiety in social phobia. *Behaviour Research and Therapy*, *35*(8), 741–756. https://doi.org/10.1016/S0005-7967(97)00022-3

Rissanen, R., Arving, C., Ahlgren, J., & Nordin, K. (2014). Group versus individual stress management intervention in breast cancer patients for fatigue and emotional reactivity: a randomised intervention study. *Acta Oncologica*, *53*(9), 1221–1229. https://doi.org/10.3109/0284186X.2014.923935

Rissanen, R., Nordin, K., Ahlgren, J., & Arving, C. (2015). A stepped care stress management intervention on cancer-related traumatic stress symptoms among breast cancer patients – a randomized study in group vs. individual setting. *Psycho-Oncology*, *24*(9), 1028–1035. https://doi.org/10.1002/pon.3763

Roberge, P., Marchand, A., Reinharz, D., & Savard, P. (2008). Cognitive-behavioral treatment for panic disorder with agoraphobia: A randomized, controlled trial and cost-effectiveness analysis. *Behavior Modification*, *32*(3), 333–351. https://doi.org/10.1177/0145445507309025

Rock, C. L., Byers, T. E., Colditz, G. A., Demark-Wahnefried, W., Ganz, P. A., Wolin, K. Y., Elias, A., Krontiras, H., Liu, J., Naughton, M., Pakiz, B., Parker, B. A., Sedjo, R. L., Wyatt, H., & Exercise and Nutrition to Enhance Recovery and Good Health for You (ENERGY) Trial Group (2013). Reducing breast cancer recurrence with weight loss, a vanguard trial: the Exercise and Nutrition to Enhance Recovery and Good Health for You (ENERGY) trial. *Contemporary Clinical Trials*, *34*(2), 282–295. https://doi.org/10.1016/j.cct.2012.12.003

Rock, C. L., Flatt, S. W., Byers, T. E., Colditz, G. A., Demark-Wahnefried, W., Ganz, P. A., Wolin, K. Y., Elias, A., Krontiras, H., Liu, J., Naughton, M., Pakiz, B., Parker, B. A., Sedjo, R. L., & Wyatt, H. (2015). Results of the Exercise and Nutrition to Enhance Recovery and Good Health for You (ENERGY) trial: A behavioral weight loss intervention in overweight or obese breast cancer survivors. *Journal of Clinical Oncology*, *33*(28), 3169–3176. https://doi.org/10.1200/JCO.2015.61.1095

Ruglass, L. M., Miele, G. M., Hien, D. A., Campbell, A. N. C., Hu, M.-C., Caldeira, N., Jiang, H., Litt, L., Killeen, T., Hatch-Maillette, M., Najavits, L., Brown, C., Robinson, J. A., Brigham, G. S., & Nunes, E. V. (2012). Helping alliance, retention, and treatment outcomes: A secondary analysis from the NIDA clinical trials network women and trauma study. *Substance Use & Misuse*, *47*(6), 695–707. https://doi.org/10.3109/10826084.2012.659789

Sabariego, C., Brach, M., Herschbach, P., Berg, P., & Stucki, G. (2011). Cost-effectiveness of cognitive-behavioral group therapy for dysfunctional fear of progression in cancer patients. *The European Journal of Health Economics*, *12*(5), 489–497. https://doi.org/10.1007/s10198-010-0266-y

Şafak, Y., Karadere, M. E., Özdel, K., Özcan, T., Türkçapar, M. H., Kuru, E., & Yücens, B. (2014). Obsesif kompülsif bozuklukta bilişsel davranışçı grup psikoterapisinin etkinliğinin değerlendirilmesi. *Turk Psikiyatri Derg*, *25*(4), 225–233.

Santiprabhob, J., Leewanun, C., Limprayoon, K., Kiattisakthavee, P., Wongarn, R., Aanpreung, P., & Likitmaskul, S. (2014). Outcomes of group-based treatment program with parental involvement for the management of childhood and adolescent obesity. *Patient Education and Counseling*, *97*(1), 67–74. https://doi.org/10.1016/j.pec.2014.07.002

Sayyah, M., Bagheri, M., Karimi, N., & Ghasemzadeh, A. (2016). The effectiveness of group cognitive behavioral therapy in treating obsessive-compulsive disorder in women with multiple sclerosis (MS): A randomized double-blind controlled trial. *Electron Physician*, *8*(4), 2243–2248. https://doi.org/10.19082/2243

Schellekens, M. P., Tamagawa, R., Labelle, L. E., Speca, M., Stephen, J., Drysdale, E., Sample, S., Pickering, B., Dirkse, D., Savage, L. L., &

Carlson, L. E. (2017). Mindfulness-Based Cancer Recovery (MBCR) versus Supportive Expressive Group Therapy (SET) for distressed breast cancer survivors: Evaluating mindfulness and social support as mediators. *Journal of Behavioral Medicine*, *40*(3), 414–422. https://doi.org/10.1007/s10865-016-9799-6

Schneibel, R., Wilbertz, G., Scholz, C., Becker, M., Brakemeier, E. L., Bschor, T., Zobel, I., & Schmoll, D. (2017). Adverse events of group psychotherapy in the in-patient setting—results of a naturalistic trial. *Acta Psychiatrica Scandinavica*, *136*, 247–258. https://doi.org/10.1111/acps.12747

Schuberth, D. A., Selles, R. R., & Stewart, S. E. (2018). Coercive and disruptive behaviors mediate group cognitive-behavioral therapy response in pediatric obsessive-compulsive disorder. *Comprehensive Psychiatry*, *86*, 74–81. https://doi.org/10.1016/j.comppsych.2018.07.012

Schuman, D. L., Slone, N. C., Reese, R. J., & Duncan, B. (2015). Efficacy of client feedback in group psychotherapy with soldiers referred for substance abuse treatment. *Psychotherapy Research*, *25*(4), 396–407. https://doi.org/10.1080/10503307.2014.900875

Schnurr, P. P., Friedman, M. J., & Foy, D. W. (2003). Randomized trial of trauma-focused group therapy for posttraumatic stress disorder. *Archive of General Psychiatry*, *60*(5), 481–489. https://doi.org/10.1001/archpsyc.60.5.481

Schulz, A., Stolz, T., Vincent, A., Krieger, T., Andersson, G., & Berger, T. (2016). A sorrow shared is a sorrow halved? A three-arm randomized controlled trial comparing internet-based clinician-guided individual versus group treatment for social anxiety disorder. *Behaviour Research and Therapy*, *84*, 14–26. https://doi.org/10.1016/j.brat.2016.07.001

Schwartze, D., Barkowski, S., Burlingame, G. M., Strauss, B., & Rosendahl, J. (2016). Efficacy of group psychotherapy for obsessive-compulsive disorder: A meta-analysis of randomized controlled trials. *Journal of Obsessive-Compulsive and Related Disorders*, *10*, 49–61. https://doi.org/10.1016/j.jocrd.2016.05.001

Schwartze, D., Barkowski, S., Strauss, B., Burlingame, G. M., Barth, J., & Rosendahl, J. (2017). Efficacy of group psychotherapy for panic disorder: Meta-analysis of randomized, controlled trials. *Group Dynamics: Theory, Research, and Practice*, *21*(2), 77–93. https://doi.org/10.1037/gdn0000064

Schwartze, D., Barkowski, S., Strauss, B., Knaevelsrud, C., & Rosendahl, J. (2019). Efficacy of group psychotherapy for posttraumatic stress disorder: Systematic review and meta-analysis of randomized controlled trials. *Psychotherapy Research*, *29*(4), 415–431. https://doi.org/10.1080/10503307.2017.1405168

Segal, Z. V., Williams, J. M. G., & Teasdale, J. D. (2013). *Mindfulness-based cognitive therapy for depression* (2nd ed.). New York, NY: Guilford Press.

Selles, R. R., Belschner, L., Negreiros, J., Lin, S., Schuberth, D., McKenney, K., Gregorowski, N., Simpson, A., Bliss, A., & Stewart, S. E. (2018). Group family-based cognitive behavioral therapy for pediatric obsessive compulsive disorder: Global outcomes and predictors of improvement. *Psychiatry Research*, *260*, 116–122. https://doi.org/10.1016/j.psychres.2017.11.041

Shadish, W. R. & Sweeney, R. B. (1991). Mediators and moderators in meta-analysis: There's a reason we don't let dodo birds tell us which psychotherapies should have prizes. *Journal of Consulting and Clinical Psychology*, *59*(6), 883–893. https://doi.org/10.1037/0022-006X.59.6.883

Shea, M. T., McDevitt-Murphy, M., Ready, D. J., & Schnurr, P. P. (2009). Group therapy. In E. B. Foa, T. M. Keane, M. J. Friedman, & J. A. Cohen (Eds.), *Effective treatments for PTSD: Practice guidelines from the International Society for Traumatic Stress Studies* (pp. 306–326). New York, NY, US: Guilford Press.

Shields, G.S., Spahr, C.M., Slavich, G.M. (2020). Psychosocial interventions and immune system function: A systematic review and meta-analysis of randomized controlled trials. *JAMA Psychiatry*, *77*(10), 1031–1043. https://doi.org/10.1001/jamapsychiatry.2020.0431

Silbergeld, S., Koenig, G. R., Manderscheid, R. W., Meeker, B. F., & Hornung, C. A. (1975). Assessment of environment-therapy systems: The Group Atmosphere Scale. *Journal of Consulting and Clinical Psychology*, *43*(4), 460–469. https://doi.org/10.1037/h0076897

Simoncini, M. C., Santoro, L., Baggi, F., Teixeira, L. F. N., Marotta, M. S., Sandrin, F., Bonacossa, E., Lani, G., Massaro, M. A., Mattia, I., & Berrocal, C. (2017). Can group education improve adherence and enhance breast cancer rehabilitation after axillary dissection? A randomized clinical trial. *Journal of Evidence-Based Psychotherapies*, *17*(2), 1–22. https://doi.org/10.24193/jebp.2017.2.1

Sleptsova, M., Wössmer, B., Grossman, P., & Langewitz, W. (2013). Culturally sensitive group therapy for Turkish patients suffering from chronic pain: A randomised controlled intervention trial. *Swiss Medicine Weekly, 143.* https://doi.org/10.4414/smw.2013.13875

Sloan, D. M., Bovin, M. J., & Schnurr, P. P. (2012). Review of group treatment for PTSD. *The Journal of Rehabilitation Research and Development, 49*(5), 689–702. https://doi.org/10.1682/JRRD.2011.07.0123

Slone, N. C., Reese, R. J., Mathews-Duvall, S., & Kodet, J. (2015). Evaluating the efficacy of client feedback in group psychotherapy. *Group Dynamics: Theory, Research, and Practice, 19*(2), 122–136. https://doi.org/10.1037/gdn0000026

Smith, E. R., Murphy, J., & Coats, S. (1999). Attachment to groups: Theory and management. *Journal of Personality and Social Psychology, 77*(1), 94–110. https://doi.org/10.1037/0022-3514.77.1.94

Sofin, Y., Danker-Hopfe, H., Gooren, T., & Neu, P. (2017). Predicting inpatient detoxification outcome of alcohol and drug dependent patients: The influence of sociodemographic environment, motivation, impulsivity, and medical comorbidities. *Journal of Addiction, 2017,* 1–11. https://doi.org/10.1155/2017/6415831

Stagl, J. M., Antoni, M. H., Lechner, S. C., Bouchard, L. C., Blomberg, B. B., Glück, S., Derhagopian, R. P., & Carver, C. S. (2015). Randomized controlled trial of cognitive behavioral stress management in breast cancer: A brief report of effects on 5-year depressive symptoms. *Health Psychology, 34*(2), 176–180. https://doi.org/10.1037/hea0000125

Stagl, J. M., Bouchard, L. C., Lechner, S. C., Blomberg, B. B., Gudenkauf, L. M., Jutagir, D. R., Glück, S., Derhagopian, R. P., Carver, C. S., & Antoni, M. H. (2015). Long-term psychological benefits of cognitive-behavioral stress management for women with breast cancer: 11-year follow-up of a randomized controlled trial. *Cancer, 121*(11), 1873–1881. https://doi.org/10.1002/cncr.29076

Stagl, J. M., Lechner, S. C., Carver, C. S., Bouchard, L. C., Gudenkauf, L. M., Jutagir, D. R., Diaz, A., Yu, Q., Blomberg, B. B., Ironson, G., Glück, S., & Antoni, M. H. (2015). A randomized controlled trial of cognitive-behavioral stress management in breast cancer: Survival and recurrence at 11-year follow-up. *Breast Cancer Research and Treatment, 154,* 319–328. https://doi.org/10.1007/s10549-015-3626-6

Ştefan, C. A., Căpraru, C., & Szilágyi, M. (2018). Investigating effects and mechanisms of a mindfulness-based stress reduction intervention in a sample of college students at risk for social anxiety. *Mindfulness, 9*(5), 1509–1521. https://doi.org/10.1007/s12671-018-0899-y

Stephen, J., Rojubally, A., MacGregor, K., McLeod, D., Speca, M., Taylor-Brown, J., Fergus, K., Collie, K., Turner, J., Sellick, S., Mackenzie, G. (2013). Evaluation of CancerChatCanada: A program of online support for Canadians affected by cancer. *Current Oncology, 20*(1), 39–47. https://doi.org/10.3747/co.20.1210

Stoffers, J. M., Völlm, B. A., Rücker, G., Timmer, A., Huband, N., & Lieb, K. (2012). Psychological therapies for people with borderline personality disorder. *Cochrane Database of Systematic Reviews, 8,* CD005652.

Strauss, B. (2017). Psychodynamic group psychotherapy – Effects and side-effects. *Psychodynamic Psychotherapy, 16,* 73–84.

Strauss, B., Burlingame, G. M., & Bormann, B. (2008). Using the CORE-R battery in group psychotherapy. *Journal of Clinical Psychology, 64*(11), 1225-1237. https://doi.org/10.1002/jclp.20535

Strauss, B., Schreiber-Willnow, K., Kruse, J., Schattenburg, L., Seidler, K. P., Fischer, T., Papenhausen, R., Möller, E., Dobersch, J., Wünsch-Leiteritz, A., Huber, T., Kriebel, R., Liebler, A., Mattke, D., Weber, R., & Bormann, B. (2012). Training background, everyday practice, and training needs of group therapists working in inpatient psychotherapy—Results of a survey. *Zeitschrift fur Psychosomatische Medizin und Psychotherapie, 58*(4), 394–408. https://doi.org/10.13109/zptm.2012.58.4.394

Sunde, T., Walseth, L. T., Himle, J. A., Vogel, P. A., Launes, G., Haaland, V. Ø., Hoffart, A., Johnson, S. U., & Haaland, Å. T. (2017). A long-term follow-up of group behavioral therapy for obsessive-compulsive disorder in a general outpatient clinic in Norway. *Journal of Obsessive-Compulsive and Related Disorders, 14,* 59–64. https://doi.org/10.1016/j.jocrd.2017.06.002

Sundquist, J., Palmér, K., Johansson, L. M., & Sundquist, K. (2017). The effect of mindfulness group therapy on a broad range of psychiatric symptoms: A randomised controlled trial in primary health care. *European Psychiatry, 43,* 19–27. https://doi.org/10.1016/j.eurpsy.2017.01.328

Swift, J. K., & Callahan, J. L. (2009). The impact of client treatment preferences on outcome: A meta-analysis. *Journal of Clinical Psychology, 65*(4), 368–381. https://doi.org/10.1002/jclp.20553

Swift, J. K., & Greenberg, R. P. (2012). Premature discontinuation in adult psychotherapy: A meta-analysis. *Journal of Consulting and Clinical Psychology, 80*(4), 547–559. https://doi.org/10.1037/a0028226

Tasca, G. A., Compare, A., Zarbo, C., & Brugnera, A. (2016). Therapeutic alliance and binge-eating outcomes in a group therapy context. *Journal of Counseling Psychology, 63*(4), 443–451. https://doi.org/10.1037/cou0000159

Tasca, G. A., Ritchie, K., Conrad, G., Balfour, L., Gayton, J., Lybanon, V., & Bissada, H., (2006). Attachment scales predict outcome in a randomized controlled trial of two group therapies for binge eating disorder: An aptitude by treatment interaction. *Psychotherapy Research, 16*(1), 106–121. https://doi.org/10.1080/10503300500090928

Tasca, G. A., Ritchie, K., Demidenko, N., Balfour, L., Krysanski, V., Weekes, K., Barber, A., Keating, L., & Bissada, H. (2013). Matching women with binge eating disorder to group treatment based on attachment anxiety: outcomes and moderating effects. *Psychotherapy Research, 23*(3), 301–314. https://doi.org/10.1080/10503307.2012.717309

Tasca, G. A., Taylor, D., Ritchie, K., & Balfour, L. (2004). Attachment predicts treatment completion in an eating disorders partial hospital program among women with anorexia nervosa. *Journal of Personality Assessment, 83*(3), 201–212. https://doi.org/10.1207/s15327752jpa8303_04

Tate, D. F., Valle, C. G., Crane, M. M., Nezami, B. T., Samuel-Hodge, C. D., Hatley, K. E., Diamond, M., & Polzien, K. (2017). Randomized trial comparing group size of periodic in-person sessions in a remotely delivered weight loss intervention. *International Journal of Behavioral Nutrition and Physical Activity, 14*(1), 144. https://doi.org/10.1186/s12966-017-0599-3

Taylor, S. J., Carnes, D., Homer, K., Kahan, B. C., Hounsome, N., Eldridge, S., Spencer, A., Pincus, T., Rahman, A., & Underwood, M. (2016). Novel three-day, community-based, nonpharmacological group intervention for chronic musculoskeletal pain (COPERS): A randomised clinical trial. *PLoS Medicine, 13,* e1002040. https://doi.org/10.1371/journal.pmed.1002040

Thieme, K., Turk, D. C., Gracely, R. H., & Flor, H. (2016). Differential psychophysiological effects of operant and cognitive behavioural treatments in women with fibromyalgia. *European Journal of Pain, 20*(9), 1478–1489. https://doi.org/10.1002/ejp.872

Thorn, B. E., Eyer, J. C., Van Dyke, B. P., Torres, C. A., Burns, J. W., Kim, M., Newman, A. K., Campbell, L. C., Anderson, B., Block, P. R., Bobrow, B. J., Brooks, R., Burton, T. T., Cheavens, J. S., DeMonte, C. M., DeMonte, W. D., Edwards, C. S., Jeong, M., Mulla, M. M., . . . Tucker, D. H. (2018). Literacy-adapted cognitive behavioral therapy versus education for chronic pain at low-income clinics: A randomized controlled trial. *Annals of Internal Medicine, 168*(7), 471–480. https://doi.org/10.7326/M17-0972

Thurston, M. D., Goldin, P., Heimberg, R., & Gross, J. J. (2017). Self-views in social anxiety disorder: The impact of CBT versus MBSR. *Journal of Anxiety Disorders, 47,* 83–90. https://doi.org/10.1016/j.janxdis.2017.01.001

Titov, N., Andrews, G., Johnston, L., Robinson, E., & Spence, J. (2010). Transdiagnostic internet treatment for anxiety disorders: A randomized controlled trial. *Behaviour Research and Therapy, 48*(9), 890–899. https://doi.org/10.1016/j.brat.2010.05.014

Torres, E., Pedersen, I. N., & Pérez-Fernández, J. I. (2018). Randomized trial of a Group Music and Imagery Method (GrpMI) for women with fibromyalgia. *Journal of Music Therapy, 55*(2), 186–220. https://doi.org/10.1093/jmt/thy005

Tsai, M., Ogrodniczuk, J. S., Sochting, I., & Mirmiran, J. (2014). Forecasting success: Patients' expectations for improvement and their relations to baseline, process and outcome variables in group cognitive–behavioural therapy for depression. *Clinical Psychology & Psychotherapy, 21*(2), 97–107. https://doi.org/10.1002/cpp.1831

van der Spek, N., Vos, J., van Uden-Kraan, C. F., Breibart, W., Cuijpers, P., Holtmaat, K., Witte, B. I., Tollenaar, R. A. E. M., & Verdonck-de Leeuw, I. M. (2017). Efficacy of meaning-centered group psychotherapy for cancer survivors: A randomized controlled trial. *Psychological Medicine, 47*(11), 1990–2001. https://doi.org/10.1017/S0033291717000447

van der Spek, N., Willemsen, V., Knipscheer-Kuipers, K., Verdonck-de Leeuw, I., Breibart, W. S., & Poppito, S. R. (2017). *Behandelprotocol zingevingsgerichte groepstherapie voor mensen met kanker: Handleiding voor therapeuten.* Springer.

van der Zanden, R., Kramer, J., Gerrits, R., & Cuijpers, P. (2012). Effectiveness of an online group course for depression in adolescents and young adults: A randomized trial. *Journal of Medical Internet Research*, *14*(3), e86. https://doi.org/10.2196/jmir.2033

van Oosterhout, B., Smit, F., Krabbendam, L., Castelein, S., Staring, A. B., & van der Gaag, M., (2016). Metacognitive training for schizophrenia spectrum patients: A meta-analysis on outcome studies. *Psychological Medicine* *46*(1), 47–57. https://doi.org/10.1017/S0033291715001105

Vallejo, M. A., Ortega, J., Rivera, J., Comeche, M. I., & Vallejo-Slocker, L. (2015). Internet versus face-to-face group cognitive-behavioral therapy for fibromyalgia: A randomized control trial. *Journal of Psychiatric Research*, *68*, 106–113. https://doi.org/10.1016/j.jpsychires.2015.06.006

Velthorst, E., Koeter, M., Van Der Gaag, M., Nieman, D. H., Fett, A. K., Smit, F., Staring, A. B., Meijer, C., & De Haan, L. (2015). Adapted cognitive–behavioural therapy required for targeting negative symptoms in schizophrenia: Meta-analysis and meta-regression. *Psychological Medicine*, *45*(3), 453–465. https://doi.org/10.1017/S0033291714001147

Vesco, K. K., Karanja, N., King, J. C., Gillman, M. W., Leo, M. C., Perrin, N., McEvoy, C. T., Eckhardt, C. L., Smith, S, & Stevens, V. J. (2014). Efficacy of a group-based dietary intervention for limiting gestational weight gain among obese women: A randomized trial. *Obesity*, *22*(9), 1989–1996. https://doi.org/10.1002/oby.20831

Victorson, D., Hankin, V., Burns, J., Weiland, R., Maletich, C., Sufrin, N., Schuette, S., Gutierrez, B., & Brendler, C. (2017). Feasibility, acceptability, and preliminary psychological benefits of mindfulness meditation training in a sample of men diagnosed with prostate cancer on active surveillance: Results from a randomized controlled pilot study. *Psycho-Oncology*, *26*, 1155–1163. https://doi.org/10.1002/pon.4135

Vîslă A., Constantino, M. J., Newkirk, K., Ogrodniczuk, J. S., & Sochting, I. (2018). The relation between outcome expectation, therapeutic alliance, and outcome among depressed patients in group cognitive-behavioral therapy. *Psychotherapy Research*, *28*(3), 446–456. https://doi.org/10.1080/10503307.2016.1218089

Vitiello, M. V., McCurry, S. M., Shortreed, S. M., Balderson, B. H., Baker, L. D., Keefe, F. J., Rybarczyk, B. D., & Von Korff, M. (2013). Cognitive-behavioral treatment for comorbid insomnia and osteoarthritis pain in primary care: The lifestyles randomized controlled trial. *Journal of the American Geriatrics Society*, *61*(6), 947–956. https://doi.org/10.1111/jgs.12275

Wampold, B. E. (2015). Routine outcome monitoring: Coming of age - With the usual developmental challenges. *Psychotherapy*, *52*(4), 458–462. https://doi.org/10.1037/pst0000037

Wendt, D. C., & Gone, J. P. (2017). Group therapy for substance use disorders: A survey of clinician practices. *Journal of Groups in Addiction & Recovery*, *12*(4), 243–259. https://doi.org/10.1080/1556035X.2017.1348280

Whiteford, H. A., Degenhardt, L., Rehm, J., Baxter, A. J., Ferrari, A. J., & Erskine, H. E. (2013). Global burden of disease attributable to mental and substance use disorders: Findings from the Global Burden of Disease Study 2010. *The Lancet*, *382* (9904), 1575-1586. https://doi.org/10.1016/S0140-6736(13)61611–6

Whittal, M. L., & McLean, P. D. (2002). Group CBT of OCD. In R. O. Frost & G. Steketee (Eds.), *Cognitive treatment of obsessive-compulsive disorder: Theory and treatment* (pp. 417–433). New York: Elsevier. https://doi.org/10.1016/B978-008043410-0/50028-3

Whittingham, M. (2015). Focused brief group therapy. In E. S. Neukrug (Eds.), *The SAGE encyclopedia of theory in counseling and psychotherapy* (pp. 419–423). SAGE Publishing.

Whittingham, M. (2017). Attachment and interpersonal theory and group therapy: Two sides of the same coin. *International Journal of Group Psychotherapy*, *67*(2), 276–279. https://doi.org/10.1080/00207284.2016.1260463

Wicksell, R. K., Kemani, M., Jensen, K., Kosek, E., Kadetoff, D., Sorjonen, K., Ingvar, M., & Olsson, G. L. (2013). Acceptance and commitment therapy for fibromyalgia: A randomized controlled trial. *European Journal of Pain*, *17*(4), 599–611. https://doi.org/10.1002/j.1532-2149.2012.00224.x

Wise, E. A., & Streiner, D. L. (2018). Routine outcome monitoring and feedback in an intensive outpatient program. *Practice Innovations*, *3*(2), 69–83. https://doi.org/10.1037/pri0000064

World Health Organization. (2014). *Global status report on alcohol and health 2014*. Retrieved from https://www.who.int/substance_abuse/publications/alcohol_2014/en/

Wykes, T., Steel, C., Everitt, B., & Tarrier, N. (2008). Cognitive behavior therapy for schizophrenia: Effect sizes, clinical models, and methodological rigor. *Schizophrenia Bulletin*, *34*(3), 523–537. https://doi.org/10.1093/schbul/sbm114

Yalom, I. D., & Leszcz, M. (2005). *The theory and practice of group psychotherapy*. New York: Basic Books.

Yalom, I. D., & Leszcz, M. (2020). *The theory and practice of group psychotherapy* (5th ed.). Basic Books.

Zgierska, A. E., Burzinski, C. A., Cox, J., Kloke, J., Stegner, A., Cook, D. B., Singles, J., Mirgain, S., Coe, C. L., & Bačkonja, M. (2016). Mindfulness meditation and cognitive behavioral therapy intervention reduces pain severity and sensitivity in opioid-treated chronic low back pain: Pilot findings from a randomized controlled trial. *Pain Medicine*, *17*(10), 1865–1881. https://doi.org/10.1093/pm/pnw006

Zhang, J., Zhou, Y., Feng, Z., Fan, Y., Zeng, G., & Wei, L. (2017). Randomized controlled trial of mindfulness-based stress reduction (MBSR) on posttraumatic growth of Chinese breast cancer survivors. *Psychology, Health & Medicine*, *22*(1), 94–109. https://doi.org/10.1080/13548506.2016.1146405

PSYCHOTHERAPY FOR CHILDREN AND ADOLESCENTS: FROM EFFICACY TO EFFECTIVENESS, SCALING, AND PERSONALIZING

MEI YI NG, JESSICA L SCHLEIDER, RACHEL L HORN, AND JOHN R WEISZ

Abstract

Although youth and adult psychotherapy draw on shared theories and methods, they differ in important ways. In this chapter, we highlight these differences and summarize the results of meta-analyses that take stock of nearly six decades of youth psychotherapy outcome research. We trace the evolution of criteria for identifying evidence-based psychotherapies (EBPs), update and organize the growing list of EBPs identified to treat a range of youth problem areas, and review research addressing how, for whom, and under what conditions these EBPs work, including associations with parenting, family involvement, and youth age that are especially pertinent in therapy with youths. Later sections of this chapter cover emerging research to expand the reach of psychotherapy, to maximize its effectiveness in everyday settings, and to tailor treatments for individual youths. We describe efforts to disseminate and implement EBPs by changing service systems; repackaging treatments for clinical, school, primary care, and summer camp settings; and creating single-session and digital versions. In addition, we discuss broad shifts in understanding, assessing, and treating psychopathology – including the development of testable methods for personalizing psychotherapy – and how these changes may advance psychotherapy with youths and families. We conclude by summarizing significant advances, highlighting issues that still need to be addressed, and offering our perspectives on where the field of youth psychotherapy is headed.

OVERVIEW

INTRODUCTION

Efforts to help young people deal with emotional and behavioral difficulties are probably as old as parenthood, but formal guidance on how to help also has deep historical roots. Models, precepts, and strategies have been derived from ancient religious teachings (e.g., biblical instructions not to spare the rod), from Greek philosophers (e.g., Plato's argument that education should involve teaching children to *desire* the right things), and from a broad array of prominent literary figures. Diverse philosophical and cultural forces have played important roles, but the notion that offering psychological help might become a professional specialty emerged about a century ago, influenced in part by Sigmund Freud (1856–1939), then by his daughter Anna (1895–1982); her work as an analyst specializing in children and adolescents helped make youth psychotherapy a specialty. The subsequent expansion of that specialty was fueled by models and methods very different from psychoanalysis. Early work by Mary Cover Jones (1924a, b) using direct conditioning and modeling to reduce young children's fears helped launch a *behavioral therapy (BT)* revolution. Later, cognitive approaches pioneered by Aaron Beck (e.g., Beck, 1970), and others (e.g., Meichenbaum & Goodman, 1971) helped to launch *cognitive-behavioral therapy (CBT)* for children and adolescents (herein referred to collectively as *youths*). By the late 20th century, youth psychotherapy had diversified so dramatically that 551 different named youth therapies had been identified (Kazdin, 2000).

Overview of This Chapter

Although youth and adult psychotherapy share a common ancestry and draw on some of the same theories and methods, they differ in important ways. Hence, treatment developers have created separate therapies specifically designed for young people – albeit often derived partly from adult treatments – and separate bodies of research assessing youth and adult psychotherapies have built up over the decades. We begin this chapter by highlighting some ways that psychotherapy with youths differs from psychotherapy with adults and then taking stock of the treatment outcome literature on youth psychotherapy. In this first section, we include findings from meta-analyses of youth psychotherapy that emerged after we wrote our review in the previous edition of this *Handbook* (see Weisz, Ng et al., 2013). Next, we describe evidence-based psychotherapies (EBPs) and note how criteria for identifying youth EBPs have evolved since the previous edition of this chapter. We also provide an updated list of EBPs for a range of problems experienced by youths, based on a series of systematic reviews published by the Society of Clinical Child and Adolescent Psychology, American Psychological Association (APA) Division 53, within the last few years. Then we review research addressing how, for whom, and under what conditions EBPs work for young people, focusing on findings from recent meta-analytic and systematic reviews. The aforementioned sections are primarily concerned with research assessing youth psychotherapy outcomes, predictors, mediators, and moderators using established methods employed for the past several decades.

The second half of this chapter covers emerging research to expand the reach of EBPs, improve their effectiveness under everyday conditions encountered by youths, and tailor them to the unique needs of individual youths and families. Disseminating treatments to the youths and families who need them, and implementing those treatments in various settings, has become a prominent focus of youth psychotherapy researchers, especially in the past decade. We devote the next section to their efforts. Finally, we describe major shifts in understanding, assessing, and treating psychopathology. These shifts have included the development of testable methods for personalizing psychotherapy, and they illustrate the emerging future of youth psychotherapy research. We conclude by summarizing significant advances, highlighting issues that still need to be addressed, and offering our perspectives on where the field of youth psychotherapy is headed.

The Distinctive Character of Psychotherapy with Youths

Youth psychotherapy differs from adult psychotherapy in several ways that present both challenges and opportunities for therapists working with youths and families. One difference relates to the initiation of and motivation for treatment. Treatment referrals for young people are usually made by parents, often prompted by teachers or other adults. Adults initiate the youth therapy, arrange payment, and identify referral concerns and treatment goals. Young people participate as the clients or patients, but they may exert less influence than the adults, and the different parties to the process may not agree on what the therapy is for. In one study, when clinically referred children and their parents separately identified the problems for which the child needed help, 63% of the parent–child pairs did not agree on even a single problem (Yeh & Weisz, 2001). Another study (Hawley & Weisz, 2003) investigated youth, parent, and therapist views on the problems to be addressed in outpatient therapy, and found that three-quarters of the triads did not reach consensus on a single problem; where there was some agreement, therapists agreed more with parents than with their young patients. Given these circumstances, young people often begin therapy less motivated than the adults involved and the adults who seek out therapy for themselves. Thus, a challenge for the youth therapist is to build rapport and a strong therapeutic alliance with a young person who never sought therapy in the first place.

Youth and adult psychotherapy also differ in the sources of information needed by and available to therapists for planning and monitoring treatment. Youth therapists ideally collect information from their young clients as well as adults in their client's life – parents especially, and teachers when possible. These different informants tend to show low to modest agreement in what they report (Achenbach et al., 1987; De Los Reyes, 2011; De Los Reyes et al., 2010; Richters, 1992).

Disagreements may arise in part because of differences in developmental level (e.g., limitations in young people's self-awareness or expressive language) or in opportunities to observe (adults cannot observe their children in all settings or observe their children's thoughts and emotions). Parents' reports on their children's behavior may also be affected by parents' own life stresses, mental health problems, or undetected agendas (e.g., low problem levels reported by those who fear child protective services; see Kazdin & Weisz, 1998). Adults' reports may also reflect the values, beliefs, practices, and ideals of their cultural reference group (see Weisz et al., 1997). Because youth therapy involves multiple stakeholders and informants who are at different developmental levels and have different perspectives, motivations, ideals, and goals, it can be more complicated to ascertain treatment needs, monitor treatment progress, and assess treatment outcomes for youths than for adults in individual therapy.

Youth and adult therapy also differ in patient agency. Children and adolescents, much more than adults, are captives of environments constructed by others; they live in family, neighborhood, and school contexts they did not choose and over which they have limited control. In many cases, the pathology being treated may reside less in the youth than in a harmful environment the youth can neither escape from nor alter significantly. The impact of such factors as who lives in the home, how these individuals interact, what resources they have, and whether outside agencies (e.g., child welfare or law enforcement) are involved may limit the impact of individual interventions that focus only on the youth. This reality has heightened attention to approaches that blend individual with environmental intervention, and strategies for extending treatment into the ecosystem of the youth and family (see, e.g., Buchannan et al., 2017; Henggeler & Schaeffer, 2017; Schoenwald et al., 1998; Weisz, Ugueto, et al., 2013).

On a more optimistic note, the same factors that increase the complexity of therapy with youths may also present opportunities that are less available in adult therapy. For example, multiple informants may give the therapist an especially rich picture of the youth's strengths and difficulties, and how these may vary by context. Moreover, supportive adults in the youth's life (e.g., parents, other relatives, coaches, teachers, school counselors) can serve as allies and change agents. Within some treatment approaches (e.g., Multisystemic Therapy), therapists work with one or more of these adults to extend interventions into the real-world contexts of the youth's everyday life.

Research on the Effects of Youth Psychotherapy

Although we have noted key differences between youth psychotherapy and adult psychotherapy, we can trace the rise of contemporary research in both areas to highly critical reviews published almost 70 years ago. These include reviews of (primarily) adult therapy findings (Eysenck, 1952) and (primarily) youth therapy findings (Levitt, 1957, 1963), which reached a

similar conclusion; rates of improvement were about the same whether people received treatment or not. That conclusion was discouraging, but the studies reviewed were not consistently rigorous or well-designed, and researchers began upgrading their methods to clarify the picture.

Over the decades since, research assessing treatment effects has grown increasingly rigorous and precise, with a clear shift from studies of unspecified psychotherapy for poorly specified youth problems to tests of specific treatments targeting specific problems and disorders, with clear documentation of the treatment procedures, typically provided in manuals. The number of well-controlled studies of such well-specified psychotherapies for young people now exceeds 500 published reports (see examples in Weisz & Kazdin, 2017; Weisz, Kuppens et al., 2017). Some of these studies have used multiple baseline designs, ABAB reversal designs, and various single-subject approaches (see Barlow et al., 2009; Kazdin, 2011). There are valuable meta-analyses of the resulting findings, particularly for youth disruptive behavior (Chen & Ma, 2007), autism spectrum disorders (Campbell, 2003), and social skill deficits (Mathur et al., 1998). However, the most widely accepted study design bearing on youth psychotherapy outcomes is the randomized controlled trial (RCT), and meta-analyses of RCT findings represent the highest level of evidence in evidence-based medicine guidelines (e.g., OCEBM Levels of Evidence Working group, 2011).

In light of these advances, most youth psychotherapy meta-analyses have focused on the rapidly expanding body of evidence from RCTs. Five such meta-analyses, spanning an especially broad array of youth treatments for different problems and disorders, were conducted first by Casey and Berman (1985; 75 studies of children aged 12 years and younger), then by Weisz and colleagues (1987; 108 studies of youths aged 4–18), Kazdin and colleagues (1990; 223 studies of youths aged 4–18), Weisz and colleagues (1995; 150 studies of youths aged 2–18), and most recently by Weisz, Kuppens, and colleagues (2017; 447 studies of youths aged 4–18). The metric of treatment benefit in the studies encompassed within these meta-analyses is the *effect size* – the standardized mean difference between randomly assigned treatment and control groups on clinical outcome measures at posttreatment, and sometimes later follow-up. The mean posttreatment effect size across the five meta-analyses has ranged roughly from medium to large, based on Cohen's (1988) benchmarks (small = 0.2, medium = 0.5, large = 0.8). The means are shown in Figure 18.1. As the figure shows, the effects of youth psychotherapy overlap substantially with effects in meta-analyses of mainly adult psychotherapy (e.g., Smith & Glass, 1977; Shapiro & Shapiro, 1982; see Chapter 5 in this volume).

The adult therapy meta-analyses shown in Figure 18.1 are rather dated, but they are included because they focused – like the youth meta-analyses in Figure 18.1 – on a broad array of treated problems and treatment methods. In years since the early 1980s, meta-analyses of adult psychotherapy trials have been more narrowly focused, often addressing only one target problem (e.g., major depressive disorder) or one treatment

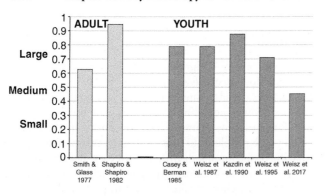

FIGURE 18.1 Mean psychotherapy effect sizes reported in five meta-analyses of youth psychotherapy RCTs (shown in dark gray) and two meta-analyses of mainly adult RCTs (shown in light gray).

approach (e.g., CBT). Many of these more focused adult meta-analyses have shown mean effect sizes roughly within the range of the two shown in Figure 18.1. For example, Cuijpers et al. (2019) and Mohr et al. (2014), examining trials encompassing a range of treatment methods for adult depression, found mean effect sizes of 0.70 and 0.54, respectively; and Cuijpers et al. (2014) found a mean effect size of 0.84 in a meta-analysis encompassing multiple methods of treatment for adult GAD. Readers seeking to make additional comparisons can find mean effect sizes from 24 focused meta-analyses of adult psychotherapy for depression, anxiety, obsessive-compulsive disorder (OCD), post-traumatic stress disorder (PTSD), bipolar disorder, and psychotic disorders, in Cuijpers (2019).

The youth psychotherapy trend across decades in Figure 18.1 suggests the possibility of a decline in mean effect size over time. The question of whether the potency of therapies is changing over time is an important one that warrants close attention because it indicates how successful we have been as a field in using the scientific method to strengthen interventions over time. To address that question, we recently completed a meta-analysis of trends over time in the magnitude of treatment benefit as indicated by study effect sizes across the decades (Weisz et al., 2019). Our search identified 453 RCTs spanning 53 years (1963–2016) and involving more than 30,000 youths (mean age 4–18 years). We examined change over time in mean effect size for four clusters of studies – that is, those focused on treatment of anxiety, depression, ADHD, and conduct problems. We found that mean effect sizes increased nonsignificantly for anxiety and decreased nonsignificantly for ADHD, but disappointingly the means decreased significantly over time for depression and for conduct problems. We analyzed various study characteristics as potential moderators of outcome, searching for artifactual explanations (e.g., differences in the rigor of the studies conducted over time), but found little basis for qualifying these downward trends. The findings suggest that new treatment approaches may be needed, especially for depression and conduct problems. Concerns about youth depression treatment, in particular, are underscored by the consistently modest effect sizes found in two focused meta-analyses of youth depression

treatment (Eckshtain et al., 2020; Weisz et al., 2006) and in our 2017 comprehensive meta-analysis (Weisz, Kuppens, et al., 2017). Furthermore, in our recent meta-analysis (Cuijpers et al., 2020) of 366 trials comparing the effects of psychotherapies for depression across the lifespan, mean treatment effects in children ($g = 0.35$) and adolescents ($g = 0.55$) were significantly lower than those in young adults ($g = 0.98$) and middle-aged adults ($g = 0.77$).

The numerous smaller meta-analyses of youth psychotherapy that have been published since the 1980s reflect the maturation of the field over the past half-century – problems and theoretical orientations have been increasingly differentiated, each has amassed a sizeable evidence base, and meta-analysts have addressed increasingly specific questions within their specialty. Nevertheless, the findings of the broad-based meta-analyses reviewed here illustrate how synthesizing a large body of evidence spanning multiple decades and encompassing a range of problems can illuminate areas of concern, highlight questions for the field, and suggest directions for future research.

EVIDENCE-BASED PSYCHOTHERAPIES FOR YOUTHS

The specialization of youth psychotherapy research was driven in part by a movement to identify therapies as evidence-based. After the broad-based meta-analyses of the 1980s and 1990s demonstrated that psychotherapy was generally helpful, researchers focused their efforts on demonstrating which specific therapies were helpful for which problems. One prominent effort was spearheaded by the Society of Clinical Psychology, APA Division 12, which convened the Task Force on Promotion and Dissemination of Psychological Procedures (1995) to devise ways to educate psychologists, third party payors (e.g., insurance companies, government agencies), and the general public about effective therapies. The task force specified criteria for empirically validated treatments and provided examples of therapies meeting those criteria in their 1995 report. This work spurred further efforts to refine the criteria and expand the search for therapies meeting these criteria (Chambless et al., 1996, 1998; Kendall, 1998), as well as a change in terminology to empirically supported therapies (Chambless & Hollon, 1998) to reflect the incomplete, ongoing process of validating treatments. Although different terms have been used, we use EBPs as a general term to refer to psychological interventions with empirically demonstrated benefits in this chapter, consistent with recent usage in youth psychotherapy research (e.g., Southam-Gerow & Prinstein, 2014; Weisz & Kazdin, 2017).

Identifying Youth Evidence-Based Psychotherapies

Among the most influential works on identifying EBPs for youth are a series of special issues and reviews published in the *Journal of Clinical Child and Adolescent Psychology* (*JCCAP*), the flagship journal of the Society of Clinical Child and Adolescent Psychology, APA Division 53. These works track the exponential growth of youth psychotherapy outcome research, the increasingly elaborate evaluation criteria, and the evolution of related terminology.

The first such special issue on *Empirically Supported Psychosocial Interventions for Children*, edited by Christopher Lonigan, Jean Elbert, and Suzanne Bennett Johnson, was published in 1998 in *JCCAP*, then known as *Journal of Clinical Child Psychology*. The editors adapted earlier criteria developed by the Task Force on Promotion and Dissemination of Psychological Procedures (1995) and by Chambless et al. (1996) for two levels of evidence: *well-established* treatments required more stringent criteria (e.g., demonstrated efficacy compared to alternative treatment or placebo in at least two good group-design experiments by different research teams or in more than nine single-case experiments), and *probably efficacious* treatments had more relaxed criteria (e.g., demonstrated efficacy compared to no-treatment control in at least two group-design experiments, or compared to alternative treatment or placebo in at least two group-design experiments by the same research team, or in more than three single-case experiments). These criteria were applied to systematic reviews of outcome studies on five common problems for which children and adolescents receive treatment – depression, anxiety, and phobias; disruptive behavior; attention-deficit hyperactivity disorder (ADHD); and autism.

The second special issue on *Evidence-based Psychosocial Treatments for Children and Adolescents*, edited by Wendy Silverman and Stephen Hinshaw (2008), was published a decade later in *JCCAP*. The editors explained that the addition of adolescent(s) in the special issue title, journal name, and division name reflected the inclusion of both children and adolescents in the work of Division 53; and the change in terminology to *evidence-based* was intended to maintain consistency with terms used by the APA and the medical field, and to increase the accessibility of literature on EBPs to the layperson and professionals outside psychology. Drawing from recommendations published since the first special issue (e.g., Chambless & Hollon, 1998), Silverman and Hinshaw modified the criteria for well-established and probably efficacious treatments (e.g., demonstrated equivalence to established treatments in two sufficiently powered group-design experiments qualified for well-established status), and added two lower levels of evidence: *possibly efficacious* treatments (i.e., demonstrated efficacy in at least one good study in the absence of contradictory findings), and *experimental* treatments (i.e., untested in studies meeting criteria). They also broadened the scope of the second special issue to encompass nine target problems – trauma exposure, OCD, adolescent eating disorders and problems, and adolescent substance use, in addition to the five covered in the first special issue – and one special population, ethnic minority youth.

Rather than publish a third special issue after another decade, *JCCAP* editor, Mitchell Prinstein, and newly appointed associate editor, Michael Southam-Gerow, announced in their January 2014 editorial that they would publish a new feature in regular issues, known as an *Evidence Base Update*, to keep pace with the burgeoning literature. The editors further revised the criteria to be used for identifying youth EBPs, explicitly distinguishing *methods criteria* (i.e., RCT, treatment manuals or equivalent, population with clear inclusion criteria treated for specified problem, reliable and valid outcome assessment, appropriate data analysis and sufficient sample size) from *evidence criteria* (i.e., number of studies of a certain type showing a specific pattern of results). Although both kinds of criteria were already included in the previous special issues, giving explicit instructions on how to factor them in determining a treatment's level of evidence increases transparency, and likely reliability, in evaluating treatments. Notably, the editors included a fifth level of evidence – treatments of *questionable efficacy* – to classify treatments tested in good group-design experiments and found to produce no benefit compared to another treatment or control group. Finally, the editors instructed reviewers to classify "treatment families" (i.e., treatments utilizing common principles and techniques, e.g., behavioral parent training) rather than brand-name therapies (i.e., a treatment protocol by a specific developer, e.g., The Incredible Years).

At least 23 *Evidence Base Updates* have since been published (as of June 2019). The reviewers were tasked not only with reviewing new literature but also with reevaluating prior literature using the new criteria (Prinstein & Southam-Gerow, 2014). These reviews covered 14 target problems, including five new areas – bipolar spectrum disorders, body-focused repetitive behavior disorders, self-injurious thoughts and behaviors, elimination disorders, and obesity (see next section, Current Status of Youth EBPs, and Table 18.1) – plus two multiple-problem topics on interventions for minority youth (Pina et al., 2019) and strategies to improve engagement (Becker et al., 2018). This new format of identifying youth EBPs has broadened the scope of reviews and reduced the interval between reviews (from 10 years to roughly four years).

Current Status of Youth Evidence-Based Psychotherapies

In this section, we summarize the findings of the *JCCAP* Evidence Base Updates. We focus on treatments that the latest reviews have established as EBPs (i.e., in the well-established or probably efficacious levels) and highlight major changes in the level of empirical support for treatments reviewed in the second special issue (Silverman & Hinshaw, 2008), which was a focus of our previous chapter. In Table 18.1, we have compiled the treatments accorded EBP status for the 14 target problems in the *JCCAP Evidence Base Updates* (for a full list of all treatments assigned to the five levels of evidence, see Table 18.2 in the Supplemental Materials section at the end of this chapter.) A layperson summary of results from each Evidence Base Update can be found on the Division 53 web-based resource (effectivechildtherapy.org).

Autism Spectrum Disorder

As part of their review of therapies for children with autism spectrum disorder (ASD) aged five years or younger, Smith and Iadarola (2015) conceptualized interventions along several dimensions. For example, they categorized therapies by scope, whereby comprehensive treatments addressed all needs over hundreds or thousands of intervention hours and focused ones addressed fewer needs over 50 hours or less; and by theoretical principle, whereby treatments belong under applied behavior

TABLE 18.1   Youth Psychotherapies Classified Well-Established or Probably Efficacious for 14 Target Problems, Adapted from *Evidence Base Updates* in the *Journal of Clinical Child and Adolescent Psychology*

Target problem	Level 1: Well-established treatments	Level 2: Probably efficacious treatments
Autism spectrum disorder (Smith & Iadarola, 2015)	• ABA–individual, comprehensive • ABA + DSP–teacher-implemented, focused	• ABA–individual, focused for augmentative and alternative communication • ABA + DSP–individual, focused • DSP–focused parent training
Bipolar spectrum disorders (Fristad & MacPherson, 2014)	• None	• Family psychoeducation + skill building
Depression (Weersing et al., 2017)	• CBT–group (adolescents) • CBT–individual (adolescents) • IPT–individual (adolescents)	• IPT–group (adolescents)
Anxiety		
Youth (Higa-McMillan et al., 2016)	• CBT [a] • CBT with parents [b] • CBT + medication [b] • Education • Exposure • Modeling	• Family psychoeducation • Relaxation • Assertiveness training • Attention control [c] • CBT for child and parent • Cultural storytelling • Hypnosis • Stress inoculation
Early childhood (Comer et al., 2019)	• CBT–family-based	• CBT–parent group • CBT–parent group + CBT–child group
Trauma exposure (Dorsey et al., 2017)	• CBT–individual + parent involvement • CBT–individual • CBT–group	• CBT–group + parent involvement • EMDR
Obsessive-compulsive disorder (Freeman et al., 2018)	• CBT–family focused • CBT (young children) [d]	• CBT–individual • CBT–non face-to-face • CBT–technology-based delivery [d] • CBT + positive family interaction [d]
Body-focused repetitive disorders (Woods & Houghton, 2016)	• None	• BT–individual for thumb sucking
Self-injurious thoughts and behaviors (Glenn et al., 2019)	• DBT for deliberate self-harm and suicide attempt	• DBT for NSSI • CBT–individual + family for suicide attempt • Integrated family therapy for suicide attempt • IPT–individual for suicide ideation • Psychodynamic therapy – individual + family for deliberate self-harm • Parent training for self-injurious thoughts and behaviors

(Continued)

TABLE 18.1 (CONTINUED)

Target problem	Level 1: Well-established treatments	Level 2: Probably efficacious treatments
Attention-deficit hyperactivity disorder (Evans et al., 2018)	• Behavioral parent training (preschool, elementary) • Behavioral classroom management (preschool, elementary) • Behavioral peer intervention (elementary) • Combined behavior management interventions (preschool, elementary) • Organization training (elementary, adolescents)	• Combined training interventions – extensive practice and feedback
Disruptive Behavior		
Child (Kaminski & Claussen, 2016)	• BT–parent group • BT–parent individual with child participation	• BT–parent group + BT–child group • BT–parent group with child participation + family problem-solving training • BT–parent group with child participation • BT–parent individual • BT–parent individual with child participation + BT–child individual with parent participation + teacher training • BT–parent self-directed • BT–child group • BT–child group + teacher training • BT–child individual • BT–child individual with parent participation • Parent-focused therapy–group • Child-centered play–group • Child-centered play–individual
Adolescent[e] (McCart & Sheidow, 2016)	• Combined BT, CBT, & family therapy - Multisystemic Therapy (JJ) - Treatment Foster Care Oregon Therapy (JJ)	• CBT - Aggression Replacement Training + Positive Peer Culture (JJ) - Solution-Focused Group Program (JJ) • Combined BT, CBT, & family therapy - Multisystemic Therapy (non-JJ) - Functional Family Therapy (JJ)
Youth illegal sexual behaviors (Dopp, et al. 2017)	• None	• Multisystemic Therapy for problem sexual behaviors
Substance use (Hogue et al., 2014)	• CBT–individual • CBT–group • FBT–ecological • MET/CBT • MET/CBT + FBT–behavioral	• FBT–behavioral • MI/MET • FBT–ecological + contingency management • MET/CBT + FBT–behavioral + contingency management • MET/CBT + contingency management
Eating disorders (Lock, 2015)	• Family therapy–behavioral for anorexia nervosa	• Family therapy–systemic for anorexia nervosa • Insight-oriented psychotherapy–individual for anorexia nervosa

(Continued)

TABLE **18.1** (CONTINUED)

Target problem	Level 1: Well-established treatments	Level 2: Probably efficacious treatments
Overweight and obesity (Altman & Wilfley, 2015)	• Family-based behavioral treatment (children) • Parent-only behavioral treatment (children)	• None
Elimination disorders (Shepard et al., 2017)	• Urine alarm therapy for enuresis • Dry-bed training for enuresis	• Full spectrum home therapy for enuresis • Biofeedback for encopresis • Enhanced toilet training for encopresis

Note: ABA = applied behavior analysis; CBT = cognitive-behavioral therapy; DBT = dialectical behavior therapy; DSP = developmental social-pragmatic; EMDR = eye movement desensitization and processing; FBT = family-based therapy; IPT = interpersonal psychotherapy; JJ = juvenile-justice involved; MET = motivational enhancement therapy; non-JJ = not juvenile-justice involved; NSSI = nonsuicidal self-injury.
[a] Well-established based on symptom outcome, also well-established based on functional outcome.
[b] Well-established based on symptom outcome, but probably efficacious based on functional outcome.
[c] Possibly efficacious based on symptom outcome, but questionable efficacy based on functional outcome.
[d] These treatments are organized according to a new framework by Freeman et al. (2018).
[e] In this review, some treatment families appear in multiple levels of evidence because McCart and Sheidow (2016) assigned different "brand-name" therapies within the same treatment family to different levels; these brand-name therapies are listed for the first two levels of evidence and omitted from the other levels for brevity.

analysis (ABA), the developmental social-pragmatic (DSP) model, or both. Smith and Iadarola contrasted the ABA view of ASD as a learning difficulty that may be manifested in a range of abilities, and that can be treated with operant conditioning techniques such as reinforcing adaptive behaviors, with the DSP view of difficulty in joint engagement with others as a central deficit of ASD, thus, treatment involves promoting caregiver responsiveness (e.g., imitating the child) to improve social communication and interaction. Smith and Iadarola identified five EBPs:

1. Individual, comprehensive ABA (e.g., Lovaas's model of early intensive behavioral intervention, Smith, 2010), which kept its well-established status since the previous review by Rogers and Vismara (2008)
2. Teacher-implemented, focused ABA + DSP (e.g., Goods et al., 2013), newly classified as well-established
3. Individual, focused ABA for augmentative and alternative communication (e.g., Bondy & Frost, 2001)
4. Individual, focused ABA + DSP (e.g., Kasari et al., 2006)
5. Focused DSP parent training (Casenhiser et al., 2013) – all new entries to the probably efficacious level

Bipolar Spectrum Disorders

Fristad and MacPherson (2014) reviewed psychosocial interventions for bipolar spectrum disorders among youths, noting that these interventions serve an important adjunctive function to medication by improving families' ability to cope with symptoms and prevent relapse. They identified one EBP and accorded it probably efficacious status: family psychoeducation plus skill building, which involves working with single or multiple families to improve their understanding of the youth's symptoms, typical course, and treatment options; and to foster their use of skills (e.g., problem solving, communication,

medication adherence, CBT strategies) to manage symptoms (see Fristad et al., 2011; Miklowitz et al., 2004).

Depression

Similar to David-Ferdon and Kaslow's (2008) review, Weersing and colleagues' (2017) *Evidence Base Update* evaluated treatments separately for children and for adolescents with depression; however, they applied stricter inclusion criteria to the studies they reviewed (e.g., youths needed to meet diagnostic criteria, clinical cutoffs, or be identified by mental health professionals). Consequently, no EBPs were identified for depressed children by Weersing et al., although David-Ferdon and Kaslow had previously classified CBT and BT as probably efficacious treatments for children. Stricter criteria notwithstanding, Weersing et al. identified four EBPs for depressed adolescents: individual CBT, group CBT, and individual IPT – all currently well-established treatments and previously evaluated as well-established or probably efficacious – and finally, group IPT, newly elevated to probably efficacious status. For adolescents, CBT includes components such as scheduling pleasant activities, identifying and modifying negative cognitions, relaxation training, and practicing problem solving (e.g., Clarke & DeBar, 2010), whereas IPT focuses on interpersonal issues common among adolescents (e.g., changes in the parent–teen relationship, role transitions) and helps the adolescent develop skills (e.g., constructive communication) to address these relationship difficulties (Mufson et al., 1993).

Anxiety

Two *Evidence Base Updates* on anxiety were published – one dedicated to reviewing 50 years of anxiety treatment research among youths of all ages (Higa-McMillan et al., 2016), and another documenting the relatively new area of early childhood anxiety and related problems (e.g., behavioral inhibition, traumatic stress) among youths aged seven or younger, which had minimal overlap (three studies) with the first update (Comer et al., 2019).

Higa-McMillan and colleagues (2016) evaluated treatment effects separately on symptoms and functioning. Four treatments achieved EBP status for both symptom and functional outcomes: CBT alone, with parents (e.g., parent training, psychoeducation), or with medication (see, e.g., Kendall et al., 2017); and exposure – often considered the core ingredient of CBT for anxiety and does not include modification of anxious thoughts. Ten other treatments were assigned EBP status based on symptom outcomes only (most were not assessed on functioning), including some related to CBT (e.g., modeling, family psychoeducation, relaxation) and others unrelated such as cultural storytelling (Malgady et al., 2010) and hypnosis (Stanton, 1994).

Similarly, Comer and colleagues (2019) identified three EBPs, all CBT with similar content delivered in various modalities: family-based (i.e., individual parent–child dyad or parent only sessions, e.g., Hirshfeld-Becker et al., 2010), group parent, and group parent plus group child. All three involved child exposure – in-session or facilitated by parents outside of the session – and many addressed parent overprotection and accommodation of child anxiety (see later section, Family Attitudes and Involvement), the parent–child relationship, and parents' own anxiety.

Both reviews elevated CBT to well-established status from the probably efficacious designation given by Silverman, Pina, et al. (2008), and both highlighted exposure as a common element in the most efficacious treatments. Notably, the EBPs for young children with anxiety and related problems all involve substantial parent involvement, with some treatments involving only parents, whereas many of those for youth in general do not.

Trauma Exposure

In their review of psychosocial treatments for youths experiencing mental health symptoms related to trauma exposure, Dorsey and colleagues (2017) identified five EBPs. Three CBT modalities (individual, individual with parent involvement, and group) were designated as well-established treatments and one CBT modality (group with parent involvement) was designated as a probably efficacious treatment. Brand-name protocols of individual and group CBT were previously identified by Silverman, Ortiz, et al. (2008) as EBPs for trauma. However, eye movement desensitization and reprocessing (EMDR) is newly established as an EBP, accorded probably efficacious status by Dorsey et al. CBT for trauma in youth involves safety planning to reduce future risk of trauma exposure and core components of CBT for anxiety, which may be incorporated during the writing and reading of a trauma narrative (e.g., describing the traumatic experience as a form of exposure, identifying and modifying self-blaming thoughts within the narrative); some protocols involve preparing the parent to hear the narrative and praise the youth for their courage to confront their trauma (e.g., Trauma-Focused CBT, Cohen et al., 2010), whereas protocols addressing trauma due to parental physical

abuse involve changing parenting behaviors to prevent future abuse (e.g., parent–child CBT, Runyon et al., 2004). EMDR incorporates many core components of CBT while providing simultaneous bilateral sensory input to produce eye movement (e.g., Farkas et al., 2010), leading Dorsey and colleagues to call for further research to examine whether EMDR-specific elements produce incremental benefit.

Obsessive-Compulsive Disorder

Freeman and colleagues (2014; 2018) authored two *Evidence Base Updates* on psychosocial treatments for youth OCD; we summarize their 2018 findings as their conclusion in this review considered both the earlier- and later-reviewed evidence. Barrett and colleagues' (2008) review identified a single EBP for youth OCD – individual exposure-based CBT, similar to CBT for youth anxiety but often including ritual response prevention. Freeman et al. (2018) retained individual CBT as a probably efficacious treatment and designated CBT in non–face-to-face (e.g., via phone, webcam) and family-focused formats as probably efficacious and well-established treatments, respectively. They also noted that subsequent studies had predominantly tested variations of CBT with different aims: to establish efficacy in new populations (e.g., young children), to improve efficacy (e.g., augmenting with positive family interaction), or to increase transportability (e.g., via technology). Hence, they also organized treatments according to a new framework that considered study aim. We have reported their findings under both traditional and new frameworks in Table 18.1.

Body-Focused Repetitive Disorders

Woods and Houghton (2016) reviewed the evidence on psychosocial treatments for five body-focused repetitive behaviors including trichotillomania (i.e., hair pulling), excoriation (i.e., skin picking), nail biting, cheek biting, and thumb sucking. They found one EBP – individual BT for thumb sucking, which they assessed as probably efficacious. The authors included treatments based on learning principles within BT, including aversive conditioning, stimulus control, reinforcement, social support, and training in becoming aware of the behavior and generating an incompatible response (e.g., Habit Reversal Training, Azrin & Nunn, 1973). For the other four disorders, the only treatments assessed as possibly efficacious or experimental were behavioral or cognitive behavioral, leading the authors to conclude that the evidence base (albeit limited) points to BT as the current standard of care for body-focused repetitive disorders in youths.

Self-Injurious Thoughts and Behaviors

Glenn and colleagues (2015; 2019) authored two *Evidence Base Updates* on psychosocial treatments of self-injurious thoughts and behaviors among youths. We summarize their 2019 findings, which accounted for evidence in both reviews. They identified six EBPs:

1. Dialectical behavior therapy (DBT) for adolescents, which includes individual therapy, multifamily groups to learn skills such as distress tolerance and mindfulness, coaching

via telephone, and treatment team consultation meetings (Rathus & Miller, 2014)

2. Individual CBT plus family component (e.g., Esposito-Smythers et al., 2011)
3. Individual psychodynamic therapy plus family component, which seeks to improve the youth's understanding of how behaviors, thoughts, and feelings are interconnected (Rossouw & Fonagy, 2012)
4. Integrated family therapy, comprising elements of CBT, DBT, family therapy, and social-ecological theory (Asarnow et al., 2015)
5. Individual IPT for adolescents (Mufson et al., 1993)
6. Parent training, which includes psychoeducation and skill-building for resolving family conflict (Pineda & Dadds, 2013).

Noting that the level of evidence differed by outcome (e.g., suicide ideation, nonsuicidal self-injury), Glenn et al. accorded both well-established and probably efficacious status to DBT and probably efficacious status to the other five treatments.

Attention-Deficit Hyperactivity Disorder

Evans and colleagues (2014; 2018) authored two *Evidence Base Updates* on psychosocial treatments for youth ADHD, following Pelham and Fabiano's (2008) review. We summarize their 2018 findings, which incorporate all prior evidence. Evans et al. (2018) identified six EBPs, including the three behavioral interventions previously accorded well-established status by Pelham and Fabiano in which adaptive behaviors are increased and maladaptive ones are decreased via contingencies (e.g., selective attention, time-out) applied by parents (e.g., Defiant Children, Barkley, 1997), by school staff in classrooms (e.g., Mikami et al., 2012), or by parents or staff in recreational or social settings (e.g., Summer Treatment Program, Pelham et al., 2017, see also later section, Summer Camp Settings) – and a fourth EBP comprising some combination thereof. They reviewed sufficient literature for various age groups to determine that these behavioral interventions meet well-established criteria for elementary school-age children and mostly for preschoolers as well, but not yet for adolescents. Fortunately, Evans et al. (2018) found evidence that early adolescents benefit from the two EBPs established after Pelham and Fabiano's review: organization training, which builds skills in organizing school materials (e.g., Langberg et al., 2012), and combined training interventions which involve extensive practice of, and feedback on, skills relevant to adaptive functioning plus other interventions, for example, organization training plus study and interpersonal skills groups (e.g., Challenging Horizons Program, Evans et al., 2016).

Disruptive Behavior

Eyberg and colleagues (2008) identified 16 EBPs for disruptive behavior – the largest number of EBPs for any disorder category. Subsequently, *JCCAP* published three separate reviews of psychosocial treatments for children (Kaminski & Claussen, 2017), adolescents who did not engage in sexual offending (McCart &

Sheidow, 2016), and youths who engaged in illegal sexual behaviors (Dopp et al., 2017). Separate reviews were justified by the extensive evidence base addressing each population of disruptive youths and by developmental differences in the types of problematic behaviors (e.g., mild oppositional behavior in children v. aggressive or law-breaking behavior in adolescents) and intervention targets (e.g., primarily parenting behavior for children v. parenting and multiple systems for adolescents; see McCart & Sheidow, 2016).

Kaminski and Clausen (2017) organized the treatments for disruptive children into six broad categories based on primary recipient and theoretical orientation; treatments from four of these categories emerged as EBPs:

1. *Parent BT*. Parent BT teaches parents skills to manage child behavior (similar to behavioral parent training for ADHD) and also build a positive parent–child relationship (e.g., Parent Management Training Oregon, Forgatch & Gerwitz, 2017).
2. *Child BT*. Child BT teaches children social skills by helping them to understand their emotions and social situations and how to respond appropriately (e.g., Problem Solving Skills Training, Kazdin, 2017).
3. *Parent-focused therapy*. The aim is to improve parents' emotion awareness and regulation, attitudes about their child, or boundaries in the family (e.g., Havighurst et al., 2013).
4. *Child-centered play therapy*. This therapy provides a supportive relationship to the child to facilitate exploration of negative emotions (e.g., Meany-Whalen et al., 2014).

Parent BT was the only category with well-established treatments, though there were also BT treatments at the probably efficacious and possibly efficacious levels depending on the modality (i.e., group, individual, or self-directed) and whether it was a standalone treatment or had added components (e.g., child participation, child BT, teacher training; see Supplemental Materials).

McCart and Sheidow (2016) evaluated evidence of treatment benefit separately for three subgroups of disruptive adolescents with differing needs: those involved in the juvenile justice system (likely needing high-intensity treatment), those not justice-involved, and those primarily disruptive in school. They also categorized treatments for disruptive adolescents by theoretical orientation (e.g., BT/parenting skills, CBT, family therapy, psychodynamic therapy, and combinations thereof), but assigned brand-name treatments rather than treatment families into the five evidence levels.

As a result, they identified five brand-name EBPs for justice-involved adolescents: (a) Multisystemic Therapy (MST; Henggeler & Schaeffer, 2017) and (b) Treatment Foster Care Oregon (TFCO, formerly known as Multidimensional Treatment Foster Care; Buchanan et al., 2017) were designated well-established treatments; also, (c) Functional Family Therapy (FFT; Waldron et al., 2017), (d) Aggression Replacement Training + Positive Peer Culture (Gibbs et al., 1995), and (e) Solution-Focused Group Program (Shin, 2009) were designated probably efficacious status. MST was also accorded probably efficacious status for treating non-justice-involved adolescents – this was the sole EBP identified for this subgroup, and no EBP was identified for adolescents who were primarily disruptive in school. MST, TFCO, and FFT were categorized as involving combined BT, CBT, and family therapy, whereas the other two EBPs were categorized as CBT. The combined treatments not only blend coaching in parenting skills with CBT strategies for parent and adolescent but also target the adolescent's family relationships and multiple other systems (e.g., peer, school, community, legal, child welfare) and are often delivered in home or community settings.

Finally, Dopp and colleagues (2017) identified only one EBP for youth illegal sexual behaviors, which they accorded probably efficacious status – MST adapted for problem sexual behaviors (Borduin & Munschy, 2014).

The identification of parent BT, youth BT/CBT, and the combined BT-CBT-family therapy as EBPs is consistent with Eyberg et al.'s review, whereas the parent-focused and child-centered approaches have been newly identified as EBPs – but only for disruptive children. It is noteworthy that despite the large evidence base of parent BT for child disruptive behavior, no parent BT treatments emerged as EBPs for adolescent disruptive behavior. Moreover, youth BT/CBT treatments were designated as EBPs for child and adolescent disruptive behaviors, but only as an experimental treatment for youth sexual offending. Overall, the three reviews underscore the need to consider both developmental stage and nature of problem behaviors when treating disruptive youths.

Substance Use

Hogue and colleagues (2014; 2018) authored two *Evidence Base Updates* on psychosocial treatments for adolescent substance use (e.g., alcohol, cannabis, and other drugs, not including nicotine). Their 2018 review, which considered both the earlier- and later-reviewed evidence, identified 10 EBPs, of which five are standalone treatments:

1. Individual CBT.
2. Group CBT, which uses cognitive modification and coping behaviors to avoid substance use (Waldron & Kaminer, 2004).
3. Ecological family-based treatment, which targets multiple systems adolescents interact with and includes some brand-name EBPs (i.e., FFT, MST) for adolescent disruptive behavior.
4. Behavioral family-based treatment, which identifies and modifies the antecedents and consequences of substance use in the family context to reduce substance use (Bry, 1988).
5. Motivational interviewing, which employs conversational techniques to strengthen the youth's commitment to change their substance use behavior (e.g., Motivational Enhancement Therapy, Miller & Rollnick, 1991).

The first three treatments remain well-established, and the fourth remains probably efficacious, since the previous review by Waldron and Turner (2008), whereas motivational interviewing is newly established as probably efficacious by Hogue et al. The remaining five EBPs are integrated treatments combining one or more of the standalone treatments with other components (see Table 18.1).

Eating Disorders

Lock (2015) reviewed the evidence on psychosocial treatments for four eating disorders: anorexia nervosa, bulimia nervosa, binge eating disorder, and avoidant restrictive food intake disorder (ARFID). He identified three EBPs for anorexia: (a) family therapy with a behavioral focus, which supports parents to restore the youth's weight by managing the youth's eating behaviors and energy expenditure (e.g., the Maudsley model, Dare & Eisley, 1997); (b) family therapy with a focus on the family system, which targets family dynamics that may be related to the disorder (e.g., Selvini-Palazzoli & Viaro, 1988); and (c) individual insight-oriented psychotherapy, which uses self-psychology and cognitive therapy to improve the youth's self-worth and self-regulation (Fitzpatrick et al., 2010). The first EBP retains its well-established status from the previous review by Keel and Haedt (2008) and the latter two are newly classified as probably efficacious by Lock. Unfortunately, no EBPs were identified for bulimia and binge eating disorder (though possibly efficacious treatments were identified, see Supplemental Materials), and no treatment studies of ARFID meeting criteria at any level were located by Lock.

Overweight and Obesity

In their review of psychosocial interventions for overweight and obese youths, Altman and Wilfley (2015) focused on multicomponent treatments, citing lack of support for single-component treatments. They noted that all multicomponent treatments may include some combination of diet change, physical activity modification, behavioral techniques, or family involvement, but differ as to which components are combined, and the nature and extent of each component. They identified two EBPs, classifying both as well-established treatments for children (albeit not for adolescents): (a) family-based behavioral treatment, which sets behavior and weight loss goals for both youths and parents (e.g., Epstein et al., 1990); and (b) parent-only behavioral treatment, which involves direct intervention with parents only to engage them as change agents (e.g., Apter et al., 1998).

Elimination Disorders

Shepard and colleagues (2017) reviewed psychosocial treatments for two elimination disorders in youths: nocturnal enuresis and encopresis. They identified three EBPs for nocturnal enuresis:

1. *Urine alarm therapy.* This is a well-established treatment in which sensors in the youth's clothing or mattress pad activate an alarm upon detecting the first drop of urine, thereby conditioning the youth to awaken when they sense a full bladder (Houts, 2010).
2. *Dry-bed training.* This second well-established treatment combines the urine alarm with operant conditioning strategies

such as positive practice (e.g., sitting at the toilet regardless of the urge to urinate, Azrin et al., 1974).

3. *Full-spectrum home therapy.* This is a probably efficacious, less burdensome version of dry-bed training plus relapse prevention (Houts, 2008).

For encopresis, Shepard et al. identified two EBPs, both probably efficacious treatments:

1. *Biofeedback.* Electrodes or balloons are placed at the anus, allowing youths to monitor, and subsequently improve control of, their anorectal muscle contractions (for a review, see Coulter et al., 2002).
2. *Enhanced toilet training.* This involves behavioral modification and education about breathing and muscle functions to facilitate bowel movements (for a review, see Mellon, 2012).

Progress Summary in the Identification of Youth Evidence-Based Psychotherapies

Psychotherapies that meet rigorous standards for evidence-based status are available for all 14 target problems reviewed in *JCCAP* over the past five years – nearly three times the number of target problems reviewed in their first youth EBP special issue (Lonigan et al., 1998). Furthermore, multiple EBPs were identified for all but two problems (bipolar spectrum disorders and body-focused repetitive disorders), and many therapies previously classified as probably efficacious in the second youth EBP special issue (Silverman & Hinshaw, 2008) are now classified as well-established.

How Does Youth Psychotherapy Work, with Whom, and under What Conditions?

Besides developing psychotherapies and testing whether they work, researchers have also sought to understand how (i.e., through what processes and mechanisms), with whom (i.e., for which subpopulations of youth), and under what conditions therapies work. This research can contribute to the field in several ways. First, identifying change processes (i.e., what the therapist or client does during or as a result of sessions) and change mechanisms (i.e., client characteristics and skills generalized beyond treatment sessions) can guide efforts to intensify their activation, thereby strengthening the potency of therapies (Doss et al., 2004). Second, an understanding of how youth and family characteristics relate to treatment outcome can inform efforts to set realistic treatment expectations and select the optimal treatment. In particular, the unique role of age and parent involvement in psychotherapy with minors warrants clinicians' attention. Indeed, several *Evidence Base Updates* reviewed in the previous section have explicitly categorized treatments by youth age and presence or type of parent involvement, sometimes finding different levels of evidentiary support for the same type of treatment depending on these characteristics. Third, delineating the conditions under which treatment

gains are maximized can inform their implementation in the everyday settings where youths and families receive services. Accordingly, we review findings on how well EBPs work under clinically representative conditions, compared to therapy as it is usually carried out in clinical settings. Throughout this section, we focus on mediators, moderators, or predictors of outcome found across multiple target problems or across studies aggregated in systematic or meta-analytic reviews. A comprehensive review of moderators, predictors, or mediators of outcome, many of which are problem- and treatment-specific, is beyond the scope of this chapter. We refer interested readers to the *Evidence Base Updates* and to reviews elsewhere (Maric et al., 2015; Weersing & Weisz, 2002) and our chapter from the previous edition of this *Handbook* (Weisz, Ng et al., 2013).

Do Putative Change Processes and Mechanisms Explain Youth Treatment Outcomes?

Cognitions and parenting practices are putative change mechanisms of multiple youth EBPs, and therapeutic alliance is a putative change process common to all therapies. We summarize research assessing whether these three commonly assessed constructs mediate or predict youth therapy outcomes.

Youth and Family Cognitions

Given that CBT is the most common treatment family among the EBPs for youth emotional disorders and problems, cognitions are among the most frequently assessed putative mediators. A number of studies have tested whether therapy works by changing negative, maladaptive, or irrational thoughts as prescribed by the CBT theoretical model.

In the previous edition, we noted that several RCTs of CBT for depressed youths have documented pessimistic/less optimistic explanatory style (Jaycox et al., 1994; Yu & Seligman, 2002), negative automatic thoughts (Kaufman et al., 2005; Stice et al., 2010), and dysfunctional attitudes (Ackerson et al., 1998) as treatment mediators, but that findings were mixed across studies or between measures within studies. Further support for cognitive change as a mediator of depressive symptoms comes from RCTs testing family-based CBT for youths *without* major depressive disorder. Depressive symptom outcomes among offspring of parents with a history of major depression (Compas et al., 2010), and among children with bipolar disorder (MacPherson et al, 2016) were mediated, respectively, by secondary control coping, emphasizing youths' use of cognitive strategies to adapt to stressful situations, and interestingly, *family* positive reframing. According to MacPherson and colleagues, cognitive strategies may be difficult for younger children with severe mood symptoms and neural dysfunction typical of pediatric bipolar disorder to implement on their own, but may be more feasibly initiated and encouraged by parents.

We also previously described RCT findings that anxiety treatment outcomes were mediated by anxious self-statements, alone or relative to positive self-statements, though not by depressive or positive self-statements (Kendall & Treadwell; 2007; Lau et al., 2010; Treadwell & Kendall, 1996), and also by self-perceived ability of youths to cope with feared situations (Lau et al., 2010). Since then, other RCTs have generated findings that both support and contradict cognitive mediators of CBT for youth anxiety. Youth coping ability, as perceived by youths themselves and their parents, emerged as a mediator in the Child and Adolescent Anxiety Multimodal Study (CAMS; Walkup et al., 2008), not only for CBT but also for pharmacotherapy with selective serotonin reuptake inhibitor (SSRI) and for combined CBT–SSRI combination treatment (Kendall et al., 2016). Moreover, self-reported frequency of cognitive coping (i.e., positive cognitive restructuring, distraction strategies) and perceived control over anxiety-related situations mediated symptom reduction in another CBT trial for anxious youths, although change in perceived control was also mediated by symptom reduction (Hogendoorn et al., 2014). On the other hand, anxious self-statements were not replicated as a mediator in CAMS (Kendall et al., 2016). Similarly, negative cognitions including both anxious (i.e., threat) and depressive (i.e., failure) content did not mediate outcomes in the other trial (Hogendoorn et al., 2014); surprisingly, positive cognitions did, in contrast to previous research (Kendall & Treadwell; 2007; Treadwell & Kendall, 1996).

Overall, there is a small, but growing body of research documenting cognitive variables as treatment mediators among youths with depression, anxiety, and bipolar disorder. However, conflicting findings and variation in study and measure characteristics, including cognitive measure, youth age, treatment format, and timepoints assessed, make it difficult to draw clear conclusions about cognitions as mediators. It also bears mentioning that only one-third of these mediation studies (i.e., Compas et al., 2010; Hogendoorn et al., 2014; Kendall et al., 2016; Stice et al., 2010) assessed whether cognitive changes predicted subsequent symptom improvement – a necessary condition for change mechanism status (Kazdin, 2007). Clearly, more studies assessing cognitive variables as mediators are needed, especially those utilizing multiple measurement timepoints and analytic approaches that allow temporal ordering of cognitive change and symptom improvement to be assessed.

Parenting Practices

Many of the youth EBPs aim to reduce youth problematic behaviors by improving parent or caregiver practices. Providing parents with skills to effectively manage youth behavior is the primary objective of behavioral parenting training/parent BT for child ADHD and disruptive behavior, and one of the targets of family-based treatments for adolescent disruptive behavior and illegal sexual offending, as well as for other problems (e.g., substance use, bipolar disorder).

In our previous chapter, we had commented on the especially rich literature assessing mediators of EBPs for disruptive behavior problems. Different treatment developer teams converged on the finding that parenting practices mediated outcomes (e.g., Eddy & Chamberlain, 2000; Beauchaine et al., 2005), although some parenting measures were not significant mediators (e.g., Henggeler et al., 2009). A sizable body of research on EBPs for disruptive behavior has accumulated to

allow a more fine-grained analysis of whether mediation by parenting practices may be associated with study and measure characteristics. In their review of 25 RCTs of behavioral parent training (including family-based treatments) assessing parenting behaviors as mediators of externalizing behavior problems, Forehand and colleagues (2014) found that 45% of mediation tests were significant. They reported that larger proportions of significant tests came from studies of younger children (mean age < 10 years old), studies of at-risk youth (v. clinic-referred), or studies that were less rigorous (i.e., combined parenting with other variables or did not demonstrate temporal precedence of the mediator variable). The authors explained these findings partly by noting the potentially greater malleability of both parenting practices and youth behavior problems for children who are younger or experiencing milder problems. More intriguing were the differences among categories of parenting behaviors – Forehand et al. documented that only 10% of mediation tests were significant for monitoring/supervision (e.g., greater awareness of youth activity/ location), over one-quarter for negative parenting (e.g., less criticism), roughly one-half each for positive parenting (e.g., more praise) and for discipline (e.g., more consistent), and a striking 90% for composite measures of two or more categories. They interpreted the robust mediation findings with composite measures as stemming from the additive or interactive effects of multiple categories of parenting on changing youth behavior, and the weak findings with monitoring/supervision as resulting from the small number of studies with adolescent samples, for whom this parenting practice would be most relevant.

Parenting practices have also been investigated as mediators of EBPs for ADHD, but this literature is much smaller. Previously, we described results from the Multimodal Treatment Study of Children with ADHD (MTA; MTA Cooperative Group, 1999) showing that improvement in discipline, but not in positive involvement or deficient monitoring by parents, mediated the effects of combined behavior management interventions (including behavioral parent training) plus stimulant medication on child social skills. Of note, parent discipline was improved by behavior management without medication, but was *not* associated with improved child outcomes. Another study of a behavioral peer intervention that involved coaching parents to facilitate appropriate social behavior among their children with ADHD found that increased facilitation of child engagement in peer activities and decreased criticism by parents, respectively, mediated child social functioning outcomes (Mikami et al., 2010). However, the authors reported that mediation by each of these parenting behaviors only held for one of several outcome measures used within the study, and that other parenting behaviors, including feedback given to correct their child's playgroup behavior, praise and warmth toward the child, or hosting of playdates, did not mediate any outcome.

Parenting practices have begun to be examined as treatment mediators in other youth problem areas. At least two RCTs have found support for parenting mediators of adolescent substance use outcomes (Black & Chung, 2014). In one trial (Henderson et al., 2009), parent monitoring of adolescents' activities and peers mediated the effects of an ecological family-based treatment on abstinence, albeit not on frequency of substance use, prompting the authors to speculate that monitoring may serve to prevent substance use among adolescents but not reduce it among those continuing to use substances. In the other trial (Winters et al., 2012, 2014), a composite measure of positive parenting, discipline, and monitoring mediated the effects of motivational interviewing plus parent session on substance use frequency at a subsequent (one-year), but not concurrent (six-month) follow-up assessment. Pediatric bipolar disorder is another problem that may be ameliorated to some extent by change in parenting practices. A composite measure of parents' self-perceived skills in managing their child's behavior and efficacy in coping with the disorder mediated the effects of family-based CBT on children's manic symptoms and global functioning (MacPherson et al., 2016).

In sum, there is a burgeoning evidence base supporting parenting practices as treatment mediators for child disruptive behavior problems, and modest empirical support of parenting mediators for adolescent disruptive behavior and substance use, and for child ADHD and bipolar disorder. Moreover, the majority of the studies (roughly two-thirds of those reviewed by Forehand et al., 2014 as well as Henderson et al., 2009, Mikami et al., 2010, Winters et al. 2014) assessed whether change in parenting prospectively predicted improvement in outcome. However, the impact of parenting may depend on study and measure characteristics as highlighted by Forehand and colleagues (2014), who caution against applying conclusions from at-risk, younger children to clinically referred, older youths and call for more research on parental monitoring/supervision in particular.

Therapeutic Alliance

Therapeutic alliance and relationship variables are widely regarded as common factors contributing to successful outcomes across treatment families and formats. Recent meta-analyses of the alliance–outcome association in youth psychotherapy studies report mean correlations ranging from 0.19 in analyses of prospective associations (Karver et al., 2018) to 0.29 in analyses of self-report alliance measures obtained from adolescents (mean age 12–19 years) (Murphy & Hutton, 2018). Including only prospective associations minimizes the confound from the impact of early treatment gains on later alliance, therefore the estimate by Karver and colleagues more closely approximates the effects of alliance on outcome. Nevertheless, both these estimates are closer to the mean correlation of 0.28 based on a much larger pool of adult psychotherapy studies (Horvath et al., 2011) and appear larger than the estimate of 0.14 from an earlier meta-analysis of youth psychotherapy studies (McLeod, 2011) cited in our previous chapter. Possible explanations for the smaller association estimated by McLeod include the inclusion of more family-based and systemic therapies and of service utilization outcomes, which were associated with smaller effect sizes (Karver et al., 2018; McLeod, 2011). In Karver and colleagues' recent meta-analysis, alliance–outcome associations were larger in non-RCTs (v. RCTs), treatments of internalizing disorders (and likely externalizing disorders as well, v. substance use and eating disorders), behavioral (v. mixed behavioral and nonbehavioral) treatments, and outpatient (v. inpatient) settings. They reported no significant differences in associations by informant or alliance type (i.e., parent–therapist alliance v. youth–therapist alliance) – a notable null finding given parents' critical role in initiating therapy and facilitating their child's and their own continued engagement.

Meta-analyses converge on a small-to-medium alliance–outcome association in youth psychotherapy studies, with findings depending on study design, target problem, and treatment characteristics. Although the link between alliance and outcome is clear, the link between treatment and alliance is not. Few studies have examined alliance as a mediator of the relationship between treatment condition or therapist behaviors and outcome (Karver et al., 2018), and few intervention studies targeting engagement have even measured therapeutic alliance or relationship as an outcome (Becker et al., 2018). Further research is needed to address the questions of how much therapist behaviors or interventions can modify the therapeutic alliance or relationship in psychotherapy with youths and families.

Challenges and Opportunities in Research on Change Processes and Mechanisms

Cognitions, parenting practices, and therapeutic alliance are among the most thoroughly studied and best-supported mediators and predictors of treatment outcome across youth psychotherapies. In addition, there are increased efforts to examine whether change in these variables temporally precedes outcomes, in line with Kazdin's (2007) recommendations. New study designs and analytical methods have been developed to investigate putative change mechanisms and processes more rigorously (Carper et al., 2018).

Ideally, such new studies should be guided by existing research, but several challenges make it difficult to draw specific conclusions. Few RCTs have tested cognitive mediators for any target problem and parenting mediators for problems other than disruptive behavior. Even the relatively large pool of disruptive behavior studies is greatly reduced once divided up by candidate moderators – any study design, participant, treatment, or measure characteristic, or combination thereof. The small number of studies, with heterogeneous characteristics, compounded by the tendency for mediation studies to be underpowered (Kraemer et al., 2002), makes it difficult to draw conclusions from the mixed mediation findings generated for nearly every target problem. Are the mixed findings a result of random variation around a true population mediation effect of zero, with larger mediation outliers oversampled due to publication bias? Is there a true nonzero mediation effect in the population that is sometimes undetected due to low power? Or does the presence and size of the mediation effect systematically vary by moderators? These are important and intriguing questions for the field.

Forehand and colleagues' (2014) review had started to answer some of these questions by documenting proportions of mediation tests that were significant and comparing these proportions across potential moderators, but they acknowledge that simple vote counts are not an ideal way to reach conclusions.

Another option is to apply the criteria for empirically supported therapies (see Chambless & Hollon, 1998; Southam-Gerow & Prinstein, 2014) in order to give greater weight to mediators identified by independent research teams in RCTs with an alternative treatment or placebo control, and with fewer contradictory findings, which we undertook in our own review of mediators in youth depression psychotherapies (Ng et al., 2020). One of the most promising ways to integrate mixed findings from small, heterogeneous studies is to conduct meta-analytic structural equation modeling (MASEM; Cheung & Hafdahl, 2016) or individual participant data (IPD) meta-analysis (Cooper & Patall, 2009), which can synthesize findings from study-level (e.g., correlations, means, standard deviations) or raw data without requiring the study authors to conduct mediation tests. This approach has several advantages including boosting power by combining samples; quantifying the mediation effect, examining how it varies as a function of moderators, and estimating the impact of publication bias; and greatly expanding the number and representativeness of study samples.

Do Youth and Family Characteristics Predict or Moderate Youth Treatment Response?

Some of the most commonly assessed participant characteristics in youth treatment studies include race and ethnicity, age, family attitudes and involvement, and comorbidities. We summarize research assessing whether these characteristics moderate or predict outcomes.

Race and Ethnicity

Following Huey and Polo's (2008) review of EBPs for racial and ethnic minority youth in the *JCCAP* second special issue, which found no well-established treatments, Pina and colleagues (2019) reviewed a study sample twice as large and identified four well-established treatments: CBT for Hispanic/Latino youth with anxiety, MST for disruptive behavior in African American youth, family therapy for disruptive behavior in Hispanic/Latino youth, and family therapy for substance use in Hispanic/Latino youth. Labeled as probably efficacious were IPT for Hispanic/Latino youth with depression, CBT for African American youth with disruptive behavior, and resilient peer treatment for African American youth with trauma and stress. Despite this progress, minority representation remains lacking: no studies identified in either review included an adequate sample of Native American youth, and the sole probably efficacious treatment for Asian American youths in the 2008 review was dropped to experimental status in the 2019 update due to small sample size (Rowland et al., 2005).

The findings on ethnicity as a moderator of treatment outcome were mixed. Pina and colleagues (2019) reported that the majority of studies testing EBPs did not find that ethnicity significantly moderated treatment effect, but almost all found that minority ethnicity was associated with poorer outcomes. Hispanic/Latino youths with anxiety (Walkup et al., 2008), African American boys with aggression/disruptive behavior (Lochman & Wells, 2002), and minority youths with substance use problems (Slesnick et al., 2013), among others, all experienced poorer treatment response than their European American

peers. The only exception to this pattern: African American youths who received MST experienced faster recovery over hospitalization but European American youths did not (Huey et al., 2004).

Age

Meta-analyses have repeatedly shown that age moderates treatment outcomes across youth psychopathologies. A meta-analysis (Comer et al., 2013) of psychosocial treatment for early childhood (eight years or younger, mean age = 4.7 years) disruptive behavior problems found a larger effect for behavioral treatments than nonbehavioral treatments, and for older children than younger children. Additional investigation is needed to assess whether factors such as willingness to engage in treatment, cognitive abilities, or symptom severity and presentation vary systematically with age in a way that explains the increase in treatment response. The same relationship was found in a meta-analysis (Gutermann et al., 2016) of PTSD in youths and young adults (25 years or younger, mean age = 12.6 years). In this meta-analysis, studies that assessed young adults reported greater treatment effect sizes than studies reporting on youths: moderator analyses found that age moderated effect sizes in the pooled analysis ($B = 0.04$, $p = .02$), including RCTs and studies comparing interventions with active controls or usual care. The authors offered several interpretations: the demands of PTSD treatment may exceed the cognitive abilities of younger trauma survivors, greater trauma severity in older subjects may allow for larger improvements to occur, or PTSD assessments for youth may not adequately capture youths' symptoms and subsequent progress; further research is needed before drawing conclusions about the causes of reduced treatment benefit for traumatized youth. In contrast, the opposite relationship has been observed by Turner and colleagues (2018) in their review of CBT for OCD: older youths benefitted less from CBT than their younger counterparts.

Whether age is more consistently associated with increased or decreased benefit, if a pattern exists at all, remains to be seen – the role of age has been insufficiently explored for many other treatments and disorders. For example, Weersing and colleagues' (2017) Evidence Base Update of youth depression treatments found only one study (Curry et al., 2006) meeting their inclusion criteria that explored the potential moderating role of age, which reported that treatment effects diminished with age within their adolescent sample. However, Nilsen et al.'s (2013) review of youth anxiety and depression treatment noted that the majority of studies did not find age to be a significant moderator.

Family Attitudes and Involvement

Parents, guardians, and other caregivers (abbreviated here as *parents*) play a unique role in youth mental health and psychopathology due to the dependent nature of youth. Family can influence youth mental health outcomes through direct involvement in treatment or through their attitudes and behaviors at home. Although moderators such as age may have different effects by context, family measures appear to have a fairly consistent influence in psychotherapy: when parents are actively involved in their child's treatment or positively endorse the treatment, the treatment benefit tends to be larger.

In Gutermann and colleagues' (2016) meta-analysis of PTSD treatment, significantly larger effect sizes were observed for youth treatments that incorporated parents (g = 1.01) compared to those that exclusively worked with the youth (g = 0.81). Hendriks and colleagues (2015) reviewed meta-analyses and reviews of childhood aggression treatment research studies and found five studies that assessed parent involvement as a moderator. Three of these studies (Epstein et al., 2015; Battagliese et al., 2015; Farmer et al., 2002) reported that parent-focused treatment, alone or in addition to youth-focused treatment, had better outcomes than youth-focused treatment alone; however, the other two studies (Bakker et al., 2017; Lundahl et al., 2006) found no effect for parent involvement. Parent involvement may interact with other characteristics such as age to influence treatment outcomes. As noted in an earlier section (Current Status of Youth EBPs), parents play a central role in all EBPs identified for young children with anxiety and related problems (Comer et al., 2019) but are involved in just one of many EBPs for older children and adolescents (Higa-McMillan et al., 2016).

One important exception to this pattern, a situation where well-meaning family behaviors reduce treatment benefit rather than enhancing it, is family accommodation. *Family accommodation* broadly refers to the ways in which family members of an individual with a mental disorder alter their behavior to help the individual avoid distress associated with their symptoms (Calvocoressi et al., 1995). For youths with OCD, family accommodation frequently includes providing reassurance, participating in the youth's rituals, and helping the youth avoid situations that trigger symptoms (Calvocoressi et al., 1999). Though these behaviors are generally well-intentioned and enacted to minimize distress when it arises, they do not reduce symptoms or improve the youth's well-being in the long-term. Turner and colleagues' (2018) review of youth OCD treatment found that the effect of CBT was moderated by family accommodation, such that higher reported family accommodation was associated with poorer outcomes in therapy. This finding suggested that addressing parental accommodation would be one way of improving treatment outcomes – consistent with Comer and colleagues (2019) observation that many EBPs for young children included such content.

Comorbidities

Much like age, the presence of co-occurring disorders frequently relates to treatment benefit during therapy, but the direction of the association is inconsistent. In McGuire and colleagues' (2015) meta-analysis of youth OCD treatment, the presence of co-occurring anxiety disorders was associated with larger effect sizes for CBT, but this relationship was not present when serotonin reuptake inhibitors were used instead of CBT. Turner and colleagues' (2018) meta-analysis of OCD treatment also found a relationship between comorbidities and treatment outcomes, reporting that comorbid tics were associated with reduced response to an SSRI, and that depressive

symptoms and any comorbid psychiatric disorder predicted greater OCD symptom severity after CBT. This conflicting evidence may indicate that different comorbidities with OCD had different effects on the treatment response, such that the report of any comorbidity captured disorders that impaired treatment response, or the CBT that targeted OCD may have reduced anxiety as well, which improved both OCD symptoms and overall functioning. These explanations and other possible causal mechanisms have yet to be explored.

Nilsen and colleagues' (2013) systematic review of youth anxiety and depression treatment found mixed reports on the effects of comorbidities. Although a number of studies (e.g., Jayson et al., 1998; Manassis et al., 2002) reported that comorbidities had no effect on treatment outcomes, two studies showed comorbid anxiety disorders predicted poorer outcomes (Brent et al., 1998; Rohde et al., 2001), and a third found that anxiety predicted greater improvement (Young et al., 2006). Lundkvist-Houndoumadi and colleagues' (2014) review of CBT for youth anxiety also found that non-anxiety comorbidities (i.e. mood disorders, ADHD) were associated with greater anxiety severity at posttreatment but not reduced improvement over the course of treatment. These findings are not contradictory if one considers the higher starting point associated with comorbidities: the same amount of improvement results in a poorer outcome when the baseline problem severity is higher. Nilsen and colleagues also reported on two instances of comorbid anxiety as a moderator of depression outcome: the benefit of CBT over nondirective supportive therapy was enhanced by comorbid anxiety (Brent et al., 1998), and the benefit of IPT for adolescents compared to treatment as usual was greater in the presence of comorbid panic disorder but no other anxiety disorders (Young et al., 2006).

Lewey and colleagues (2018) considered comorbidities in their meta-analysis of EMDR and trauma-focused CBT for adolescents. They found that overall treatment effects were small, but there was a greater decline in post-traumatic stress symptoms for subjects with comorbid diagnoses (Lewey et al., 2018). Riosa et al. (2011) specifically investigated psychosocial interventions for youths with comorbidities. They contrasted youths whose comorbidities were of the same type as the target problem, such that problems were all internalizing or all externalizing (e.g., a youth treated for depression who also has anxiety) with those whose comorbidities included a mix of internalizing and externalizing conditions (e.g., a youth treated for depression who also has conduct problems). Their analysis demonstrated that greater treatment effect sizes were observed when the comorbidities were more similar to the target problem; this finding was expected, given the greater symptom overlap between similar conditions.

Challenges and Opportunities in Research on Moderators and Predictors

Pina and colleagues' (2019) *Evidence Base Update* on psychotherapy for ethnic minority youth indicates noteworthy progress in addressing mental health for these populations, increasing from zero well-established treatments in 2008 to four in 2019. However, the authors are very forward about the persistent problems in this field. As previously noted, all of the well-established treatments were rated as such for African American or Hispanic/Latino youths – in contrast, there were no studies identified that contained a substantial enough Native American sample to even consider an experimental treatment. Advancing mental health care for ethnic minority youths requires research to expand to more populations than have been previously explored. Additionally, investigating moderators that may be disproportionately present in or even exclusive to ethnic minority youth is vital to improving treatment outcomes. Finally, the identification of well-established treatments for these youths is an excellent first step, but this proof of efficacy does not translate to feasibility for widespread implementation. More work is needed to make these programs widely available and accessible to the youths who need them.

The widespread findings that age and comorbidities affect youth treatment benefit reflect major challenges in addressing youth mental health. The extensive evidence for age as a moderator across multiple disorders and treatments may be attributable to the pace of development through childhood and adolescence. Rapid developmental advances can make it difficult to develop widely effective interventions because the abilities and needs of disordered youth vary more from year to year than those of adults with similar conditions. Age-related differences in treatment outcome may be better addressed by taking into consideration the developmental mechanisms involved in the onset of psychopathology versus optimal functioning in the design or even the timing of treatments – however, available interventions informed by developmental psychopathology are rare (Cicchetti & Toth, 2017). Fortunately, clinical scientists have made greater headway in improving treatment outcomes for youths with comorbidities through the development of transdiagnostic and modular treatments that facilitate targeting similar mechanisms underlying multiple concerns and combining elements from EBPs designed for different problems (see later section, "Repackaging EBPs for Flexibility and Accessibility").

The literature on the family's influence on treatment outcomes suggests that incorporating some elements of psychoeducation or treatment for guardians is likely to be useful for improving youth outcomes across diagnoses. Parent-inclusive treatments may be able to modify family accommodation and attitudes toward treatment in addition to providing psychoeducation. This research into the benefits of engaging family members positively in treatment also highlights the importance of having supportive caregivers for improving youth mental health. Although connecting children with loving families generally goes beyond the scope of clinical scientists and practitioners, it is vital to consider the role of family in light of the disproportionate rates of psychological disorders among youths in foster care compared to the general population (Turney & Wilderman, 2016). Among the EBPs discussed earlier, one (TFCO, Buchanan et al., 2017) places delinquent youths in foster care as part of their treatment – both the foster family and the family of origin are engaged to support these youths with the goals of symptom reduction but also family reunification and improved youth welfare.

How Well Does Youth Psychotherapy Work under Clinically Representative Conditions?

The preceding section documents the remarkable progress made in developing and identifying EBPs for a variety of problems in young people – but how well do these therapies work under real-world clinical conditions, where youths are clinically referred for treatment rather than recruited, therapists are clinical practitioners rather than research staff, and therapy takes place within clinical service rather than laboratory settings? Unfortunately, research indicates that when EBPs move from the research labs where they were developed toward clinically representative conditions (e.g., Curtis et al., 2004, Dodge, 2009, Southam-Gerow et al., 2010), treatment benefit drops – a phenomenon that we have termed the *implementation cliff* (Weisz et al., 2014). Challenges that are common under clinically representative conditions (e.g., youth comorbidities that would exclude them from many RCTs, parent stress leading to treatment dropout, time constraints of practitioners with full caseloads, lack of organizational support for adoption of new practices) may all contribute to the implementation cliff (see Weisz, Ugueto et al., 2013).

A related question is whether youth EBPs actually work better than usual clinical care. Two meta-analyses sought to answer this important question. A primary objective of building and testing new treatments is to improve on the youth outcomes current practices produce. Thus, these two meta-analyses included only RCTs that had directly compared EBPs to usual clinical care; understandably, the studies involved more clinically representative conditions than typical RCTs, including more clinically referred youths, treatment by clinical practitioners, and treatment done in clinical service settings. The two meta-analyses (Weisz et al., 2006; Weisz, Kuppens, et al., 2013) included 32 and 52 RCTs, respectively. In both meta-analyses, the EBPs significantly outperformed usual care. However, the magnitude of the benefit, compared to usual care, was markedly lower than in RCTs generally; the mean effect sizes of 0.29 and 0.30, in the 2006 and 2013 meta-analyses respectively, corresponded to a probability of only 0.58 (slightly more than chance at 0.50) that the average youth in the evidence-based treatment group would be better off after treatment than the average youth in the usual care group. Another concern was the finding in the 2013 meta-analysis that EBPs did not significantly outperform usual care among studies using clinically referred youths, or youths impaired enough to meet criteria for a formal diagnosis. This is bad news, because these are two groups for whom treatment success should have especially high priority. These findings suggest a need for treatment development focused on building interventions that can function well with clinically referred young people, and that can produce markedly greater improvement than usual clinical care.

DISSEMINATION AND IMPLEMENTATION OF YOUTH PSYCHOTHERAPY

Even more sobering than the findings that EBPs may not perform as well as expected under the usual conditions that youths seek treatment is the fact that up to 80% of youths with mental health needs go without specialist mental health services (Cummings et al., 2013; Merikangas et al., 2011). Even among those who do access care, many receive treatment that is not evidence-based; rather, youths tend to receive a wide range of clinician-preferred treatments lacking research support (Williams & Beidas, 2019), often delivered in an unstructured manner unlikely to reduce clients' distress (Garland et al., 2013). Further, the structure of existing treatments may limit families' abilities to complete the treatments they begin. Mental health interventions are generally designed for delivery in physical clinics, in a one-to-one format, and by highly trained professionals – and they are costly in both time and money, spanning many sessions across multiple weeks (tested youth psychosocial therapies average 16 sessions; Weisz, Kuppens et al., 2017). Thus, many youths who access mental health treatment drop out prematurely, completing just over three therapy sessions on average (Harpaz-Rotem et al., 2004).

Together, these challenges have spurred the growth of dissemination and implementation (DI) science and practice in order to spread EBPs to those who can benefit from them, and to integrate them into specific settings effectively, as an increasingly prominent branch of youth psychotherapy research (see Weisz et al., 2014). One focus of DI science involves rebooting youth mental health interventions – that is, building more *potent*, *accessible*, and *sustainable* treatments and service delivery systems (Kazdin & Blase, 2011). Efforts toward this goal include system-level, *whole-service* transformation initiatives; efforts to repackage EBPs, improving their flexibility and fit within both clinical and nontraditional settings (e.g., schools and pediatric clinics); the creation of brief single-session interventions, built for scalability; and the proliferation of digital health interventions. These innovations suggest promising, potentially complementary paths forward toward more accessible, effective supports for youth emotional and behavioral problems.

Whole-Service Initiatives

One approach to improving the accessibility and potency of services involves a comprehensive, systems-level approach, termed *whole-service initiatives*, which are initiatives designed to shift the *structures* underlying youth-directed systems of specialty mental health care. One recent example of such a *whole-service* effort is the Children's and Young People's Improving Access to Psychological Therapies (CYP IAPT) program, initiated in the United Kingdom in 2011 by the Department of Health (https://cypiapt.com) and modeled after the original IAPT program, which targeted adults. CYP IAPT aims to improve youths' and families' access to EBPs – and, to ensure the program's acceptability, seek youth and family participation in all aspects of care, service delivery, and design. CYP IAPT addresses the full range of mental health difficulties presenting in community-based child and adolescent mental health services (CAMHS) throughout England. The program capitalized on preexisting CAMHS partnerships between public commissioners of mental health services and the country's National Health Service (NHS), along with local authorities and voluntary sector service providers. CYP IAPT involves mandatory routine outcome monitoring (ROM) measures of user participation, which are standardized questionnaires before each

treatment session to gauge the youth client's problem severity, their sense of progress toward treatment goals, and the degree to which their expectancies around treatment are being met. Moreover, the CYP IAPT initiative supports therapist training in evidence-based intervention modalities, with a focus on low-intensity and principle-guided treatments.

Evidence supports strong acceptability and effectiveness for CYP IAPT. Based on a rapid internal audit of over 350 CAMHS clinicians across 12 agencies (Edbrooke-Childs et al., 2015), the percentage of community-based clinical cases closed out of mutual agreement (versus premature termination) increased by 75% in the years following initiation of CYP IAPT; the number of weeks between referral and first appointment declined by 10 weeks (from 16.6 to 6.6); and well over half of surveyed clinicians reported "often" or "always" using outcome data to inform clinical practice. Further, youth who participated in focus groups spoke to feelings of empowerment and control resulting from their personal involvement in their own mental health treatment. The replicability of programs like CYP IAPT outside of England is unclear, given significant cross-national differences in healthcare policy, resource allocation toward youth mental health services, and government control over mental health service structures (and relatedly, unification versus fragmentation in within-country healthcare systems). Nonetheless, the CYP IAPT program suggests a promising path forward, in cases where unified, systems-level change is a feasible goal.

Repackaging Evidence-Based Psychotherapies for Flexibility and Accessibility

Here, we review research to improve the flexibility and accessibility of EBPs for youth in clinical, school, primary care, and summer camp settings.

Clinical Settings

Historically, the complexity and number of EBP manuals has constrained their uptake in clinical settings. For instance, the vast number of focal treatments – each targeting isolated clinical problems (despite the prevalence of comorbidity among youths presenting for clinical services), and each requiring specific training to administer (despite overlap across manuals) – directly undermines dissemination efforts. A generation of clinic-based treatments have emerged to better address the need for flexible, simple, multiproblem treatments – and to consider these needs from the earliest stages of program design. Examples include transdiagnostic and modular treatments, each of which is described in detail below.

Unlike focal, single-diagnosis protocols, *transdiagnostic treatments* target overlapping features thought to underlie multiple disorders and presenting problems – especially those that show high levels of comorbidity (e.g., depression and anxiety disorders). Advances in understandings of affective neuroscience and latent structures of youth psychopathology have catalyzed the design of protocols designed for flexible application for clients presenting with a range of symptoms sharing common etiology (Craske et al., 2009; Farchione et al., 2012). Evidence has supported the promise of transdiagnostic psychotherapies for alleviating psychopathology in youths (Ehrenreich et al., 2009; Weersing et al., 2012). For example, the Unified Protocol for Transdiagnostic Treatment of Emotional Disorders in Children (UP-C) and Adolescents (UP-A) target vulnerabilities such as high negative emotionality and emotion regulation deficits that are common across youth depressive and anxiety disorders. UP-A outperformed a wait-list control in reducing adolescent anxiety and depressive symptoms (Ehrenreich-May et al., 2017) and UP-C performed as well as or better than focal treatments in reducing anxiety in youth (Kennedy et al., 2019).

Unlike traditional treatment manuals, which involve multiple sessions designed for sequential administration, *modular treatments* allow clinicians the flexibility to individualize treatment. More specifically, clinicians are guided to administer various modules – commonly used elements of evidence-based treatments for youth internalizing and externalizing problems (Chorpita & Daleiden, 2009) – deemed most appropriate for a given case and sequenced as needed based on presenting concerns. The term *modular* is sometimes used interchangeably with *transdiagnostic*, but these terms are distinct. To qualify as modular, treatments must be sectioned into stand-alone, self-contained units (modules), and each module must have unique goals and be compatible with other modules to enable multiple logical combinations (Boustani et al., 2017). Modules tend to include at least four sections:

1. An introduction to the new skill, including psychoeducation on its utility and application
2. Instructions as to how and when to deploy the skill
3. In-session skill rehearsal or practice
4. Assignment of out-of-session homework to practice the skill in everyday life

A given module may focus on any component of evidence-based therapy, from *relaxation* to *problem-solving* to *behavioral activation* – and modules may be administered in an order deemed ideal for a given client, according to their problems and needs.

Modular approaches have shown considerable promise in outpatient clinical settings. In a large randomized trial, children who received Modular Approach to Therapy for Children (MATCH; Chorpita & Weisz, 2005) experienced significantly faster improvement relative to children who received traditional, manualized treatments (Weisz et al., 2012). Children who received MATCH also had significantly fewer diagnoses at posttest relative to children who received usual care, and these group differences persisted through 12-month follow-up (Chorpita et al., 2013). Moreover, clinicians expressed greater satisfaction with modular treatment relative to manualized interventions and usual care (Chorpita et al., 2015). In a more recent study, children who received modular therapy experienced significantly faster improvement in symptoms and functional impairment compared to children who received community-implemented, focal EBPs (Chorpita et al., 2017).

School Settings

Schools are frequently identified as an ideal venue for mental health service expansion, as schools offer less stigmatizing and more accessible environments than specialty outpatient clinics (Stiffman et al, 2010). However, school settings confer special challenges to implementing EBPs. School mental health (SMH) providers have high caseloads that limit treatment time with individual students, receive little training in EBPs, and report low administrative support and competing responsibilities as barriers to delivering manualized treatments to students (George et al., 2013). More broadly, SMH care in the US is fragmented across disciplines and typically viewed as disconnected from the broader mission of schools to promote academic achievement, disincentivizing top-down investment in school-based mental health services (Fazel et al., 2014; Rones & Hoagwood, 2000).

To address these complexities, researchers have increasingly focused on interventions that can support over-burdened SMH providers to deploy research-based approaches that fit students' diverse mental health needs (Weisz, Bearman, et al., 2017). As one example, the Brief Intervention for School Clinicians (BRISC) is a brief, evidence-based, flexible mental health intervention designed to fit the school context while maintaining a clear treatment structure (Lyon et al., 2015), including shorter (20- to 30-minute) session lengths to fit within school schedules and a focus on a limited number of therapeutic skills, minimizing training burden. Early findings suggest that BRISC increases intervention efficiency (over half of students completed treatment within four sessions) and improves students' proactive coping and overall social-emotional functioning. Several other modular therapies have been evaluated in school settings, and a recent systematic review found these approaches to be highly acceptable to stakeholders and potentially efficacious in reducing youth symptoms, particularly depression and anxiety (Kininger et al., 2018). However, evidence remains inconclusive regarding the sustainability of these treatments – that is, whether SMH providers continue to implement them with fidelity after formal research projects end.

In addition to training and implementation support focused on use of flexible, evidence-based components, consultation with school-based providers has also supported the use of computerized measurement feedback systems (MFSs) that keep SMH clinicians on track and support implementation of mental health interventions with adherence (Lyon et al., 2016). Research is currently focused on the ways in which an SMH-specific MFS may be useful to clinicians in delivering evidence-based practices (Lyon et al., 2016).

Primary Care Settings

A vast majority of US youth visit primary care practitioners (PCPs) at least annually (Kolko & Perrin, 2014). As such, integrated primary medical-mental health services – that is, the provision of mental health assessment and treatment in primary care settings – may facilitate the identification of youths with mental health needs and improve their engagement with treatment (Asarnow & Miranda, 2014). Evidence suggests the utility of integrated primary–mental health care for adults: co-locating primary and behavioral health clinics, including mental health specialists as staff on primary care teams, and streamlining mental health screening and referral channels have all yielded higher rates of mental health-care engagement and improved clinical outcomes among adults (Archer et al., 2012). Support is now accumulating for such approaches in pediatric settings. A recent meta-analysis evaluated 31 RCTs comparing integrated, primary medical-mental health-care approaches with usual pediatric primary care (Asarnow et al., 2015). Overall, primary care-based treatments produced significantly greater youth symptom reductions than did usual primary care ($d = 0.42$), with a 66% probability that a randomly selected youth would experience better outcomes after receiving an integrated behavioral health intervention than a randomly selected youth receiving usual care. Importantly, all treatment trials in the meta-analysis utilized mental health interventions with empirical support – such as primary care-based CBT for youth internalizing distress (Clarke et al., 2005; Richardson et al., 2014), behavior parent training for child conduct problems (Lavigne et al., 2008; Reid, et al., 2013), or motivational interviewing for adolescent substance use (D'Amico et al., 2008; Audrain-McGovern et al., 2011). Settings in which interventions were delivered within a system of collaborative care – a team-based approach in which PCPs, care managers, and mental health specialists work jointly to assess, treat, and monitor youth patients – yielded especially strong meta-analytic effects ($d = 0.63$). Although additional research is needed to assess the long-term sustainability and effectiveness of integrated care efforts for youths, results underscore the benefits of this approach, and highlight primary care as a promising setting from which to increase youths' and families' mental health service access.

Summer Camp Settings

Redesigning youth mental health interventions to resemble traditional summer camps offers another opportunity to improve treatment engagement and efficiency, with the added benefit of normalizing treatment and reaching youth unlikely to access support in more traditional settings. Over 30 clinical trials have supported the efficacy of the contingency management- and parent training-based Summer Treatment Program (STP) for youth with ADHD (see earlier section, "Current Status of Youth Evidence-Based Psychotherapies"), oppositional behaviors, and conduct problems (see Fabiano et al., 2014, for a review). For instance, STP campers participate in group-based social skills training as part of morning meetings, where specific social skills are introduced (e.g., prosocial behaviors linked to communication, participation, validation, and cooperation). Counselors then track and grant "points" or rewards for campers' displays of these skills throughout each day, providing consistent reinforcement for positive behavior change.

Additional camp-based approaches targeting anxiety-related disorders have also shown promise. One example is the Child Anxiety Multi-Day Program (CAMP), a one-week, exposure-based program for girls with separation anxiety disorder (SAD) (Santucci & Ehrenreich-May, 2013). CAMP begins as a day camp and ends with a therapeutic sleepover, creating built-in graded exposures from children's engagement in normative – yet increasingly difficult – camp-like activities. CAMP has significantly reduced both separately anxiety symptoms and functional impairment in girls with SAD relative to a wait-list control (Santucci & Ehrenreich-May, 2013). Other camp-based programs include Brave Buddies, a therapeutic summer program for the treatment of selective mutism (Kurtz, 2009), and Emotion Detectives, a preventative camp-based intervention that teaches emotion-focused skills for coping with anxiety and depression (Ehrenreich-May & Bilek, 2011). In addition to their efficacy, these treatments have yielded high levels of acceptability and satisfaction among parents and children alike, suggesting their goodness-of-fit within the mental health-care ecosystem – at least for some subset of youths in need. Additionally, high levels of treatment satisfaction have been reported by both parents and children (Ehrenreich-May & Bilek, 2011; Santucci & Ehrenreich-May, 2013).

Novel Directions in Building Accessible Interventions

Two new directions with the potential to greatly expand the accessibility of interventions include brief single-session interventions and digital health interventions. We review work in these areas and selected examples in this section.

Single-Session Interventions

In addition to altering systems of care and adapting psychotherapies to fit specific settings, novel work points to innovative strategies that may augment efforts to expand accessible treatment options for youth. As one example, research on brief interventions – more specifically, single-session interventions (SSIs) – may offer a promising path toward improving scalability, cost-effectiveness, and completion rates for youth mental health services. Evidence from social psychology, educational psychology, and public health suggests that SSIs – particularly, theoretically precise, mechanism-targeted programs – can strengthen academic, interpersonal, and physical health outcomes in youth (Aronson et al., 2009; Eaton, et al., 2012; Yeager et al., 2016). Literature also supports the utility of SSIs for reducing and preventing psychopathology in youth, from anxiety and fears (Simon et al., 2019) and oppositional behaviors (Mejia et al., 2015) to depressive symptoms (Schleider & Weisz, 2018; Schleider et al., 2020). In a meta-analysis of 50 randomized clinical trials (Schleider & Weisz, 2017a; $N = 10,508$ youths), SSIs for youth psychological problems demonstrated a significant positive effect ($g = 0.32$). This effect did not differ when comparing treatments (i.e., trials for youths with psychiatric diagnoses) to preventive interventions, suggesting SSIs' capacity to benefit youth with low, moderate, and even severe symptoms. Further, significant effects emerged even for self-administered (e.g., computerized) SSIs completed without a therapist ($g = 0.32$). Numerically, SSIs' overall effects are slightly smaller than those for traditional, multi-session youth psychotherapy (Weisz, Kuppens et al., 2017; mean $g = 0.46$ for treatments lasting 16 sessions, on average). However, their brevity and accessibility – especially self-administered SSIs – suggests their potential to exert scalable benefits.

Further research is needed to determine the full extent of SSIs' promise (see Schleider & Weisz, 2017b, for a review). SSIs have been most effective in reducing youth anxiety and conduct problems, whereas SSIs targeting youth depression have shown nonsignificant overall effects (Schleider & Weisz, 2017a; however, studies of SSIs that have reduced adolescent depressive symptoms have been published subsequent to this meta-analysis: e.g., Schleider & Weisz, 2018; Schleider et al., 2020). Separately, SSIs' effects have generally waned over time, with effects dropping considerably (to mean *g* = 0.07) after three-month follow-up (Schleider & Weisz, 2017b). SSI trials have also relied largely on youth self-report outcome measures, and some have used weak metrics for clinical significance of SSIs' effects (e.g., outcomes in an RCT of a disordered eating SSI included body satisfaction and dietary restraint but not BMI changes or DSM-5 eating disorder symptoms; Diedrichs et al., 2015). Further, two-thirds of the SSI studies used no-treatment or wait-list controls. More rigorous, longer-term trials of SSIs targeting depression and associated problems are important next steps.

Notably, SSIs in the aforementioned meta-analysis with highly specific intervention targets (i.e., those designed to shift well-defined beliefs or behaviors) were more effective than those without specific targets. For instance, one of the best-studied mental health SSIs is One-Session Treatment for Specific Phobia (OST; Davis, Ollendick, & Ost, 2012). OST is built on graded exposure, widely viewed as an active ingredient in EBPs for anxiety (Chorpita & Daleiden, 2009; see also earlier section, Current Status of Youth EBPs). Research on OST strongly suggests the potency of targeting maladaptive avoidance via exposure in treating specific phobias (Ollendick & Davis, 2013). Other promising, mechanism-targeted SSIs for youth mental health problems are deliverable without clinician involvement and outside of clinical settings. Thirty-minute computer-based interventions instilling "growth mindsets" of personality (the belief that personal attributes, including shyness, sadness, and social skills, can change) have prevented or reduced depressive symptoms (Miu & Yeager, 2015; Schleider et al., 2020) in community samples of high school students; they have also strengthened perceived control and reduced internalizing problems in high-symptom early adolescents (Schleider & Weisz, 2018). The growth mindset SSI is thought to target "keystone beliefs" for adolescents (Yeager & Walton, 2011): a type of cognition that may be especially relevant to adaptive stress-coping for adolescents undergoing socially challenging transitions (i.e., starting middle or high school). By focusing on a single, empirically identified takeaway message (or intervention target) – and by delivering that message in a nonstigmatizing manner that encourages autonomy (by virtue of being self-administered) – this variety of SSI may relay a memorable and relevant message to reducing adolescent internalizing distress.

Digital Health Interventions

Researchers have proposed that fast-growing technological innovations introduce unprecedented opportunities to improve the efficiency, reach, personalization, and appeal of mental health treatments – especially for "digital native" children and adolescents (Fairburn & Patel, 2017; Hollis et al., 2017). These digital health interventions (DHIs), including remotely delivered therapies (e.g., computer-based and phone/text-based treatment), smartphone apps, and wearable technologies, are thought to capitalize on the ubiquitous role of digital media in young people's daily lives.

However, the effectiveness of DHIs in reducing the overall burden of mental illness has progressed slowly at best (Hollis et al., 2017; Wykes & Brown, 2016). The empirical picture is especially mixed with respect to DHIs for youths. A recent overview of systematic reviews observed that the overall effect sizes for youth mental health DHIs were medium-to-large for anxiety symptoms and small-to-medium for depressive symptoms when compared to wait-list control conditions – but these effect sizes diminished to small and nonsignificant levels, overall (*d* < .20), when compared to active (but nontherapeutic) comparison conditions (Hollis et al., 2017; Pennant et al., 2015). A recent meta-analysis suggested that some degree of human guidance in youth-focused DHIs may help augment their effects (Hollis et al., 2017). For instance, DHIs that include a component of engagement monitoring or follow-up calls from teachers or health professionals are frequently present in effective DHIs. However, as discussed in the previous section, some fully self-administered, computer-based SSIs have significantly reduced depressive symptoms in youth (Miu & Yeager, 2015; Schleider & Weisz, 2018; Schleider et al., 2020). Further research is needed to ascertain when, to what degree, and for whom human guidance is needed to facilitate symptom change. Notably, the overall quality of clinical research on youth-directed DHIs has been low, characterized by heterogeneity in methodology, intervention content, and dose; unblinded outcome assessment; short-term follow-ups; and poor specification of human support (Hollis et al., 2017).

Despite these challenges to interpreting the extant literature, there is growing consensus about an especially critical limitation of youth-directed DHIs: high attrition rates for DHIs, both within and outside of formal clinical trials (Scholten & Granic, 2019; Välimäki et al., 2017). Meta-analytic evidence suggests that 70% of participants complete 75% of mental health DHIs with 4 to 10 modules (Karyotaki et al., 2015), and attrition is consistently higher among youths than adults (Välimäki et al., 2017). One solution may involve designing DHIs that may confer clinical benefit after just one module or contact, as in SSIs. But a broader solution will likely require a user-centered approach to DHI design. At present, few DHIs approximate the level of attractiveness and interactivity to which young digital natives are accustomed (Scholten & Granic, 2019). Indeed, most DHIs that have shown efficacy in clinical trials – such as MoodGym, Camp Cope-A-Lot, and BRAVE (see Stiles-Shields et al., 2016, for a review) – are manualized CBT converted to a digital format, with limited flexibility or interactivity. These DHIs may be effective when completed in full (e.g., in a well-monitored RCT); however, in real-world contexts, low engagement and premature attrition may be the rule rather than the exception.

One example of an evidence-based DHI that successfully incorporated a user-centered design is the SPARX program, which teaches CBT skills through an interactive video game (Merry et al., 2012). In SPARX's fantasy world, the youth – assigned an avatar – proceeds through various quests involving application of various cognitive-behavioral skills. For instance, in a quest that teaches cognitive restructuring, the user must shoot down gloomy negative automatic thoughts (GNATS) by correctly categorizing those thoughts as errors in thinking. In a randomized noninferiority trial, SPARX produced significantly higher remission rates versus treatment-as-usual among adolescents seeking help for depressive symptoms (Merry et al., 2012). DHIs designed with similar levels of interactivity, consistent with what digital natives expect from interactive media, may help mitigate the high-attrition concern within youth-directed DHIs and maximize their potential to reduce the overall burden of youth psychopathology.

SHIFTS IN UNDERSTANDING, ASSESSING, AND TREATING YOUTH PSYCHOPATHOLOGY

Several related theoretical and methodological developments also have the potential to reduce youth mental health burden. Although these developments have generated limited empirical evidence directly applicable to youth psychotherapies, we view them as promising future directions for moving youth psychotherapy research forward. First, new approaches to classifying mental health problems have emerged as alternatives to the traditional diagnostic categories. Each approach holds the potential to characterize each youth's mental health problems in a more precise, valid manner by considering multiple dimensions of psychopathology. Second, mobile technologies and quantitative methods have advanced tremendously over the past decade. These advances serve as tools to collect detailed information about individual youths over time and to process these data for clinical applications tailored to their needs. Third, the precision medicine initiative has been launched to advance the assessment and treatment of various health conditions by accounting for individual differences in the factors that drive those conditions. This initiative marks a shift from developing and improving treatments to produce the best outcome for *all youths on average* to generating strategies that personalize treatments to produce the best outcome *for each individual youth*. All three developments are consistent with an increasing emphasis on idiographic research – the in-depth study of the individual (see, e.g., Schork 2015) – and may produce innovative solutions to intervene in a more targeted, potent manner.

Dimensional Conceptualizations of Psychopathology

Official diagnostic nosologies such as the DSM promote categorical disease-like definitions of mental illness. Categorical nosologies have guided both the development of youth treatments (i.e., treatments tend to target individual categorical diagnoses) and assessment of their effects (i.e., presence versus absence of diagnosis or clinically elevated symptoms at post-treatment). Although categorical nosologies have been useful in certain respects, including early treatment development, their utility is limited by the mixed evidence for the reliability of disorder categories, high levels of comorbidity, and substantial within-diagnosis heterogeneity (Essau et al, 2018 Kessler et al., 2005; Regier et al., 2013). Thus, alternative approaches to

conceptualizing and measuring youth psychopathology have emerged, including process-based, latent variable, and data-driven approaches. These approaches are based on dimensional rather than categorical understandings of psychopathology and may suggest ways to build better-targeted, more personalized interventions for diverse youth problem types. Below, we summarize notable innovations in this domain: process-based taxonomies such as the Research Domain Criteria framework; model-based, latent-variable based taxonomies, such as the hierarchical taxonomy of psychopathology; and a dynamic-systems, network approach to psychopathology.

Process-Based Approach

To better identify and integrate understandings of biological, genetic, and physiological processes into the etiology of mental disorders, the US National Institute of Mental Health (NIMH) initiated the Research Domain Criteria project (RDoC; Insel et al., 2010). The RDoC framework is not a diagnostic classification system; rather, it is conceptualized as a long-term program of scientific research that may ultimately inform the development of such a system (Lilienfeld & Treadway, 2016). More specifically, RDoC proposes a matrix to guide psychological and neuroscientific research. The matrix outlines the domains thought to constitute core psychological processes underlying human emotions and behavior; it also identifies how processes in each domain may be measured at different units of analysis, from basic and biological (cellular) to subjective (self-report).

There are six currently identified domains:

1. *Negative valence systems* enable responses to aversive stimuli such as fear, anxiety, or loss.
2. *Positive valence systems* enable responses to positive stimuli such as reward seeking and habit learning.
3. *Cognitive systems* enable basic processes such as attention, perception, and memory.
4. *Systems for social processes* enable interpersonal processes such as attachment and social communication.
5. *Arousal and regulatory systems* enable homeostatic systems such as circadian rhythms and sleep-wakefulness.
6. *Sensorimotor systems* enable motor actions and patterns. Each domain may be evaluated across seven units of analysis: genes, molecules, cells, circuits, physiology, behavior, and self-report.

Ultimately, the matrix is meant to guide research on how processes in these basic domains of functioning shape human behavior and outcomes – as well as whether, and to what degree, disruptions in various processes influence maladaptive outcomes (i.e. psychopathology, dimensionally defined).

RDoC shifts the focus from traditional diagnostic categories to continuous dysregulations in underlying neurobiological systems (First, 2012). Thus, it creates the potential for a classificatory framework that conceptualizes psychopathology based on bottom-up processes rather than top-down, descriptive categories. Notably, RDoC has received criticism for its overreliance on biology: indeed, RDoC's matrix rests on the assumption that mental disorders may be conceptualized as disorders of brain circuitry and that these dysfunctions are quantifiable via clinical neuroscience tools such as electrophysiology and functional neuroimaging (First, 2012). Further, psychological, developmental, and sociocultural variables are currently omitted from the research matrix. The National Institute of Mental Health released a Note on its most recent RDoC matrix stating the importance of considering developmental and environmental factors in RDoC-guided research, including questions worthy of investigation in future work (NIMH, 2019; www.nimh.nih.gov/research/research-funded-by-nimh/rdoc/developmental-and-environmental-aspects.shtml). Further, review articles have proposed ways in which the RDoC framework may dovetail with basic research on developmental psychopathology (Franklin et al., 2015; Lebowitz et al., 2018; Mittal & Wakschlag, 2017). However, the goal of applying RDoC to developing process-based, targeted, and developmentally sensitive treatments for youth mental health difficulties remains largely aspirational.

Latent Variable Approach

Traditional psychiatric nosologies define mental disorders as distinct categories, yet evidence suggests that disorders lie on a continuum with normality and are highly comorbid with one another. Latent-variable approaches to psychopathology propose that this comorbidity in fact reflects underlying, higher-order dimensions (or spectra) of psychopathology (Eaton, 2015). As such, conceptualizations of psychopathology's structure that rely on these underlying dimensions may better align nosology with evidence. Latent variable approaches to psychopathology are not new: Achenbach's pioneering work suggested that children's symptoms and behaviors tended to converge broadly in two fundamental internalizing and externalizing dimensions (Achenbach & Edelbrock, 1978, 1984).

More recent work suggests that a larger number of spectra may provide more complete explanations for psychopathology and comorbidity in youths and in adults (Eaton et al., 2012; Hankin et al., 2017; Hankin, 2019). One prominent example is the Hierarchical Taxonomy of Psychopathology, or 'HiTOP' (Kotov et al., 2017; renaissance.stonybrookmedicine.edu/HITOP). In contrast to RDoC, HiTOP is a phenotypic, data-driven model and does not directly incorporate etiology. The HiTOP system includes five hierarchically structured levels: (a) signs and behaviors that organize into symptom components (e.g., insomnia) and maladaptive traits (e.g., emotional lability); (b) dimensional syndromes characterized by clusters of symptoms; (c) groups of similar syndromes termed subfactors (e.g., the distress subfactor includes depression, generalized anxiety, and posttraumatic stress); (d) spectra, such as an internalizing dimension that consists of distress, fear, eating pathology, and sexual problems; and (e) an aggregate super-spectra, representing a general factor for psychopathology (p-factor). Within the HiTOP system, any number of dimensions may be included, allowing for varying levels of model parsimony, depending on a model's purpose (e.g., comprehensive, individual assessment versus epidemiological research). Further, dimensions at different levels correlate with distinct risk factors and outcomes – broader spectra have shown links

to family history of psychopathology and childhood adversity (Caspi et al., 2014; Martel et al., 2017), whereas narrower dimensions show stronger associations to academic achievement and executive functions (Patalay et al., 2015; Waldman et al., 2016) – suggesting clinical utility to a multilevel, dimensional structure. HiTOP's applications to the assessment of youth psychopathology have yet to be formalized; for instance, a neurodevelopmental disorder dimension has been proposed but is still undergoing factor analytic examination (Michelini et al., 2019). However, its potential remains for informing a more parsimonious, maximally informative "roadmap" for assessing and treating dimensions of difficulties rather than disorders in youth.

Network Approach

The network perspective to psychopathology is another data-driven approach to understanding psychopathology that has gained considerable momentum in recent years (Borsboom, 2017; McNally, 2018). Rather than focus on underlying dimensions or disease entities, it conceptualizes psychopathology as a complex network of directly associated, often reinforcing individual symptoms. Risk factors (e.g., genetic disposition, environmental stressors) are proposed to "activate" individual symptoms, which, in turn, trigger other symptoms, initiating a cascade of effects that may eventually settle into a state of mutual reinforcement, even after the removal of the precipitating stressor (Borsboom, 2017). Although a majority of network analyses to date have been cross-sectional, and therefore cannot support the causal interpretations that are central to network theory, cross-sectional networks remain a useful means of exploring patterns of comorbidity across individuals (Bos et al., 2017). Under this interpretation, what may be considered "disorders" are in fact groups or clusters of symptoms that are strongly associated with one another – eliminating the need for disorder categories or dimensions and providing novel, dynamic-systems explanations for both psychiatric comorbidity and within-disorder variability. Critically, the model's focus on individual symptoms allows researchers to quantify the importance of each specific symptom within the context of the overall network (e.g., by quantifying its "centrality" among other presenting symptoms). As such, the network approach may provide a more detailed and nuanced description of the structure of psychopathology at the symptom-level.

For instance, a network analysis in a large, diverse sample of adolescents identified self-hatred, loneliness, sadness, and pessimism as the most central symptoms of adolescent depression (Mullarkey et al., 2019); a separate study focused on a community adolescent sample observed that these same symptoms, more than any other individual depressive symptoms, were most strongly linked to adolescent life satisfaction (Mullarkey et al., 2018). Limited work focused on adolescents (and virtually none on children) has been conducted using the network approach, and moving ahead, it will be essential to assess whether these findings converge across diverse samples, using a diversity of symptom measures, before making strong claims or suggesting implications for clinical treatment (Vazire, 2018). Replication efforts are especially critical given recent challenges to the replicability of symptom networks (Forbes et al., 2017); however, re-analyses of the same data suggest that networks are indeed replicable (Borsboom et al., 2017). If evidence accumulates that further suggests the promise of networks to replicate, and for specific network parameters (e.g., symptom central-ity) to predict clinically important outcomes over time, it will be of great value to test such parameters as potential targets for precise interventions focused on youths' most central symptoms of psychopathology.

Mobile Technologies and Machine Learning Methods

In our earlier section (DHIs), we discussed how digital tech-nology provides alternative formats to deliver interventions to youths (e.g., computer-based interventions). Mobile technolo-gies, including smartphones, smartwatches, and activity track-ers (e.g., FitBits), also facilitate data collection as people go about their everyday lives. Consequently, mobile technologies have accelerated the development of quantitative methods to analyze these data, including machine learning to detect pat-terns in big data. Mobile technologies and quantitative meth-ods, separately and combined, have the potential to become very scalable, powerful tools for collecting and analyzing data needed to personalize mental health interventions, especially for young people.

Smartphones and Wearable Technology

The ubiquity, acceptability, and capacity of mobile devices to collect multiple types and large amounts of data frequently, even continuously, position them as ideal data collection tools. This is especially true for young people – nearly all (95%) US adolescents aged 13–17 reported owning or having access at home to a smartphone (i.e., mobile phone with apps serving various functions) in 2018; smartphone ownership remains consistently high (93%–97%) among youths across all socio-economic levels (Anderson & Jiang, 2018). In contrast, fewer (88%) adolescents in the same study reported owning or hav-ing home access to a computer, especially those from lower socioeconomic levels (75%–78%). Moreover, smartphones and other mobile devices (e.g., mobile phones) have been used successfully in research with youths aged seven or older, including those with various mental and physical health prob-lems (Heron et al., 2017; Wen et al., 2017). Consumer-grade wearables (e.g., FitBits), although less commonly used by youths, are starting to be used in pilot research with youths and have shown good acceptability and convergent validity with research-grade devices (e.g., actigraphs; Bagot et al., 2018).

Mobile technologies facilitate the assessment of youths' experiences in real time as they go about their daily lives by col-lecting two types of data. Active data requires user participation, for example, self-report of mood, events, or behavior when prompted (e.g., by text messages); whereas passive data involves unobtrusive sensing of real-world behavior (e.g., geolocation) and technology-mediated behavior (e.g., social media use; Aung et al., 2017; Onnela & Rauch, 2016). Wearables can measure physiological (e.g., heart rate) in addition to behavioral data (e.g., physical activity). Although there is a long tradition of collecting active data and some types of passive data from youths as part of *ecological momentary assessment* (EMA; Shiffman et al., 2008), research applying EMA to psychological interven-tion is still in its infancy – especially for youths (Heron et al., 2017). Few consumer mental health apps are based on research evidence and emphasize confidentiality (Radovic et al., 2016); moreover, EBP content is sparse and EMA is infrequently used in such apps (Bry et al., 2018).

One promising effort utilizing EMA to tailor an EBP and improve its efficacy is an adjunctive smartphone app and clini-cian portal designed to enhance brief in-person CBT for anx-ious youths (Silk et al., 2020). Designed to be used with an eight-session protocol of Coping Cat, SmartCAT 2.0 includes a gamified, user-centered experience (e.g., games designed to reinforce skills, digital points and trophies for skills practice) and a secure platform for therapists to assign and monitor youths' skills practice and to exchange text messages, photos, or videos (Pramana et al., 2018). A unique feature of SmartCAT that leverages smartphone functions and EMA principles is the skills coach, which guides youths to complete an exposure using their own personalized coping and problem-solving plan, which can be youth-initiated, scheduled to launch at specified times, or programmed to activate in locations where the youth usually feels anxious using "geofencing" (i.e., the phone's GPS function automatically detects when the youth enters a virtual boundary of a real location marked out in advance by the therapist and family). An open trial indicated strong ratings of usability and satisfaction by youths, parents, and therapists; frequent usage by youths between sessions; improvement in most skills targeted by SmartCAT; and a higher than expected remission rate (67%) for this CBT pro-tocol (Silk et al., 2019).

Smartphones may be further leveraged for therapeutic applications when combined with machine learning techniques (elaborated in the next section). There is growing interest among researchers to develop apps to detect or even prospec-tively *predict* vulnerable mental health states, such as heightened suicide and self-harm risk, a mood episode, substance use relapse, or a psychotic episode to inform prevention and early intervention efforts (e.g., Aung et al., 2017). In particular, apps that rely mostly on passive data generated from naturalistic smartphone use would impose minimal burden on the user and thus be more sustainable. Furthermore, these apps may obtain clinically important information that users are unable to report – an advantage for youths who may lack the cognitive capacity, emotional awareness, or vocabulary to articulate dis-tressing thoughts and feelings. Efforts are underway to identify which types of data are associated with clinical measures and how to translate them into clinically meaningful information for adults (e.g., Or, Torous, & Onnela, 2017; Or, Torous, Simms, et al., 2017), but at least one research team has created this type of app with plans to test it with adolescents (Lind et al., 2018).

With this new direction come new challenges. For exam-ple, using mobile technologies for mental health raises a host of ethical issues, especially when the users are minors. App developers, and the researchers and clinicians who use these apps, will need to decide how to address risk states or other situations that would call for immediate action or mandated reporting in a clinical context. Maintaining the privacy and confidentiality of these sensitive data may also be challenging. In addition to app developers employing measures to keep the data securely stored and transmitted, youths may need to be taught the reasons and strategies for keeping their data secure, given the potential for mobile devices to be lost, stolen, hacked, and accessed by peers or family members. In addition, there are questions about the role that parents should play. Would requiring parent consent reduce access to apps that could possibly be beneficial to youth? For example, youths may not want to inform parents that they are engaging in substance use or other risk behaviors for which they want to access digital mental health services. If parents are aware of their children's app use, to what extent should they monitor it, keeping both safety and privacy in mind? Longer-term considerations include potential harms of keeping smartphones on at all times (e.g., to facilitate continuous passive data collection), missed opportunities to learn important skills (e.g., self-monitoring) taken over by an app, as well as financial considerations for families and clinicians in using these apps. An online community of researchers (thecore.ucsd.edu) has formed to discuss these ethical issues; ongoing consultations with various stakeholders will become increasingly important.

Machine Learning

One can imagine that the average smartphone user is continually generating a lot of data (e.g., screen time, call and text logs, voice characteristics, GPS location, physical activity, photos, and videos). Huge volumes of different varieties of data produced at high velocity become what has been referred to as *big data* (Laney, 2001). Machine learning (ML) techniques are critical in making sense of big data because they can identify patterns in large quantities of multidimensional data without specific hypotheses, thereby allowing the extraction of meaningful information. ML is also pervasive in everyday applications, such as the email spam filter. Because there is no way to code the correct label (spam or not spam) for every possible message, algorithms are trained on example messages, implemented to sort new mail, and designed to become more accurate when the user provides feedback by moving mislabeled emails to the correct box. Machine learning is fundamentally different from traditional statistical techniques because of its ability to advance without explicit human instruction (Bishop, 2006): when building a regression model without ML, the final equation includes all and only predictors and interaction terms specified in the input. On the other hand, ML can identify clusters based on interacting predictors or even drop parameters from the final model when they do not meaningfully contribute to prediction. Various types of ML techniques have been used in mental health research (see Dwyer et al., 2018). Here, we describe two that have been used in youth psychotherapy research.

Model-based random forest is one ML technique that has been used to identify predictors of treatment response. This technique relies on tree-based algorithms: the most basic prediction model – in this case, the intercept predicting treatment outcome – is split into nodes along the most statistically significant effect modifier (here, a moderator) when one or more variables predict differences in outcome. The splitting process is repeated until there is no longer predictor-related variability,

which results in subgroup-specific prediction models. The *forest* is generated by repeatedly constructing tree models using different samples of the data and moderators, and a predetermined variable (for our purposes, treatment group) is the first split in every tree for the model-based forest. Model-based random forests can provide, among other data, treatment benefit predictions for an individual and relative modifier effects at the forest level, allowing a researcher to determine which modifiers are especially relevant for predicting treatment benefit (Seibold et al., 2018).

Support vector machine (SVM) is another ML technique that has been utilized in youth psychotherapy research. SVM is used for data classification problems, where the goal is to predict which group (i.e., treatment responder or nonresponder, patient with or without comorbidities) a data point belongs to as accurately as possible, while taking care to avoid overfitting the sample data at the expense of generalization. The graphs and plots commonly shown in publications include two dimensions and are therefore displayed on the *X–Y* plane. For a categorization problem in two-dimensional space, groups are defined by a line passing through this plane, and the line is oriented to maximize the correct classification of data points. SVM performs this same task on a much larger scale: it operates in massive multidimensional space and divides this space into categories using hyperplanes (Gholami & Fakhari, 2017).

It is important to recognize that ML techniques are susceptible to some of the same limitations as traditional methods, including issues relating to statistical power, erroneous conclusions to hypothesis tests, and incomplete or inaccurate data. However, the aforementioned benefits of ML make these methods well worth the additional complexity: as big data becomes more prevalent, the ability to process massive amounts of information without the bias of preexisting hypotheses can enhance our understanding of treatment moderators and individual treatment benefit.

Precision Medicine and Personalized Mental Health Intervention

The advances we described in the conceptualization of psychopathology and in the collection and analysis of detailed behavioral data to make individual predictions may support a shift toward precision medicine – or, in youth mental psychotherapy, personalized intervention: evidence-guided tailoring of EBPs to serve an individual's needs (Ng & Weisz, 2016; National Institute of Mental Health, 2015). Notably, personalized intervention for youth mental health problems differs from precision medicine for physical conditions, which involve personalized prescribing of drugs to individuals based on tests of genetic or biological mechanisms underlying the condition. Although there are recent calls to incorporate digital phenotyping—moment-by-moment quantification of individual behavior measured by smartphones—into precision medicine (see Onnela & Rauch, 2016), the biomarker-based subgroup approach remains predominant, and evidence for this approach is scarce in psychopathology (Insel & Cuthbert, 2015). Consequently, a plethora of alternative approaches to personalizing interventions for mental health challenges have been developed (see Ng and Weisz, 2016, 2017, for comprehensive reviews). These approaches include MFS and modular therapies, both discussed in an earlier section (DI of Youth Psychotherapy). Briefly, MFSs facilitate routine monitoring of week-to-week fluctuations in youths' symptoms to inform clinical decision-making (Kelley & Bickman, 2009), and modular therapies enable session-by-session selection of specific modules to address each youth's most problematic symptoms or hindrances to treatment progress (Chorpita & Weisz, 2009; Weisz et al., 2012). In this section, we focus on three other approaches with active ongoing research efforts: treatment selection, treatment sequencing and combination, and treatment tailoring based on intensive assessment of the individual.

Treatment Selection

Researchers are exploring ways to improve psychotherapy outcomes by identifying the most beneficial treatment for each individual client – even if that treatment is not the most beneficial, or is equally beneficial compared with another treatment, for the average patient in RCTs. Several research teams have applied machine learning methods to clinical characteristics or demographics to generate individualized metrics, which quantify the expected benefit of a treatment or the relative benefit of one treatment over another for each patient. Unlike conventional moderator and predictor findings, individualized metrics generate predictions that integrate multiple, even conflicting, associations between various characteristics a patient may possess, and therefore could greatly simplify clinical decision-making. Here we focus on treatment selection research with youths (for a comprehensive review of treatment selection methods; see Chapter 20).

Probability of treatment benefit (PTB; Lindhiem et al., 2012) is an individualized metric that reports the likelihood of a patient improving with a particular treatment based on one baseline variable. Initial problem severity (as mild, moderate, or severe) is the only baseline metric currently published in PTB, but the framework could be extended to other measures. When considering treatment for a new patient, a clinician can determine the patient's problem severity via psychometric tests and use that information to determine their likelihood of benefitting. The PTB was developed using a treatment study of youth conduct problems (Kolko et al., 2009) and has also been used by Beidas and colleagues (2014) to analyze data from the CAMS dataset, revealing comparable outcomes for CBT, SSRI (sertraline), and the CBT–SSRI combination treatment for youths with mild baseline anxiety. In contrast, the likelihood of a normal-range outcome for youths with initially severe anxiety varied dramatically by treatment: 48% for CBT, 27% for SSRI, and 62% for the combination. Selecting a treatment by incorporating PTB with patient values and preferences has also been explored: Lindhiem and colleagues (2018) developed an interactive decision support tool that integrates these factors to generate a treatment recommendation. Although the tool was well-received by parent and youth participants, this pilot included only a small sample ($n = 9$) and there was no investigation into whether this tool improved patient outcomes, so additional testing should be conducted before wide-scale implementation is considered.

Foster and colleagues (2019) used model-based random forest (described earlier in this chapter) to calculate patient-specific treatment benefit. They developed this individualized metric by analyzing data from the Treatment for Adolescents Depression Study (TADS; March et al., 2004). The patient-specific predictions consistently reflected the findings from the original TADS analysis: SSRI (fluoxetine) was superior to CBT and combination treatment was superior to either treatment alone. However, the magnitude of the increased benefit associated with the superior treatment varied in relation to some of the effect modifiers. Baseline depression severity predicted the magnitude of the difference between SSRI and CBT and between combination treatment and SSRI; greater severity heightened the benefit of SSRI relative to CBT but lessened the relative benefit of combination treatment over SSRI. For the difference between combination treatment and SSRI, the superiority of combination treatment was heightened for adolescents with higher expectations for treatment and reduced for those with a history of trauma.

Individualized treatment assignment research follows two distinct paths. Methods like the PTB are straightforward to calculate, easy to implement in clinical practice, and intelligible to patients and their families, as suggested by the findings of Lindhiem and colleagues' (2018) in relation to their decision support system. However, their ease of use sacrifices complex prediction: they only account for one modifying variable, potentially overshadowing other relevant factors. In contrast, metrics like patient-specific treatment effects (Foster et al., 2019) require more advanced statistics to compute. Their increased complexity reduces accessibility for patients and clinicians but improves treatment assignment by including multiple predictors. Future individualized metrics research should aim to bridge this divide – perhaps through an interactive software – by accounting for complex inputs without becoming burdensome or impractical in practice.

Treatment Sequencing and Combination

Selecting a treatment is only the first step in personalizing intervention. If the client does not respond well, therapists are often faced with the decision of whether, or when, to switch to a different treatment, intensify the initial treatment, or combine it with another treatment to elicit a better response. Sequential, multiple assignment, randomized trials (SMARTs) were designed to generate evidence to inform these kinds of decisions by assigning individuals at least twice to treatment conditions, first randomizing them to alternative treatments and then assessing response, thereafter, assigning them to the same treatment or a different, intensified, or combined treatment depending partly on how they respond to the first treatment (Lei et al, 2012). There are at least 22 SMARTs in various stages of completion, and 14 of these focus on children or adolescents (including transitional age youths 18–25 years) who are experiencing or at risk for a range of target problems, including autism, ADHD, conduct problems, depression, suicide, substance use, and obesity (see https://methodology.psu.edu/ra/adap-inter/projects).

One SMART that clearly illustrates how this design contributes to clinical decisions about sequencing or combining treatments was conducted by Pelham and colleagues (2016). Children with ADHD were randomized first to low-dose behavioral intervention (parent training and classroom intervention) or low-dose stimulant medication (methylphenidate), and then assessed after eight weeks and monthly thereafter as needed; responders continued their assigned treatment and nonresponders were re-randomized to a higher-dose of their assigned treatment or combined behavioral–medication treatment. This study showed not only that starting with behavioral intervention was more efficacious than starting with medication, but that nonresponders who first started behavioral intervention and then added medication did the best, and those who started with medication and then added behavioral intervention did the worst (Pelham et al., 2016). This finding is striking, considering that an influential multisite RCT (non-SMART) reported that combined behavioral–medication treatment outperformed either treatment alone (MTA Cooperative Group, 1999). The SMART study suggests that the most efficacious and efficient strategy may be to start with behavioral intervention first, and if that does not work, to add medication, rather than to apply the reverse sequence or to start both concurrently. Another SMART demonstrates how this design informs clinical decisions about when to switch treatments, with its finding that assessing response to IPT and switching nonresponders to higher-intensity IPT or combination IPT–SSRI (fluoxetine) was more efficacious when done at the four-week timepoint instead of the eight-week timepoint (Gunlicks-Stoessel et al., 2019).

Even SMARTs that show no main effect of treatment, sequence, or timepoint may yield valuable information. For example, clinicians may employ any of the tested treatments or sequences, depending on accessibility in local contexts (Fatori et al., 2018), they may choose treatments that better engage families (Naar-King et al., 2016), or they may consider baseline characteristics such as age that have moderated outcomes (Naar et al., 2019). However, due to lack of independent replication and power to detect differences among multiple subdivisions of the sample, SMART investigators (e.g., Gunlicks-Stoessel et al., 2019) have suggested that their findings be considered preliminary.

Treatment Tailoring Based on Intensive Assessment of the Individual

Central to personalized intervention is the idea that clinically relevant differences in individual characteristics, contexts, and psychopathology may not be optimally captured by traditional group designs such as RCTs, which usually assess participants several times from baseline through post-treatment or follow-up in the lab. Hence, researchers are advocating for intensive research designs that involve daily or more frequent assessment of individuals, with or without repeated assignment of intervention, and exploit mobile technologies to collect active or passive data in real-time, real-world contexts. These designs may be accompanied by advanced quantitative methods designed to understand how the variables of interest (e.g., intervention, outcome, mechanisms) relate to one another over time within each person, and how these relations may be moderated by stable individual differences or fluctuating conditions.

One line of research aims to develop just-in-time-adaptive interventions (JITAIs)–apps programmed to provide the optimal type and dose of intervention (e.g., activity suggestions) at the right time (e.g., during a risk state or when someone is receptive) by adapting to a person's changing internal state and external environment (Nahum-Shani et al., 2018). Micro-randomized trials (MRTs; Klasnja et al., 2015) are a novel group experimental design that has been proposed to build the evidence base needed to design JITAIs. MRTs randomly assign intervention components at multiple possible decision points, possibly hundreds or thousands of times, to learn not only *what* intervention component is most effective and *for whom* (by studying stable moderators), but also *when* it is most effective (by studying time-varying moderators). There are at least six MRTs underway, one of which targets adolescents and transitional age youths at risk for substance use disorders (see https://www.methodology.psu.edu/ra/adap-inter/mrt-projects/). Recognizing that engagement is critical to the success of a JITAI – perhaps especially for young people, who less frequently initiate treatment on their own – the investigators are first conducting an MRT to identify the most effective engagement strategies (e.g., aquarium theme, games, points, fish trivia, inspirational messages, funny gifs, life insights, reminder notifications) for this target population (Rabbi et al., 2017).

As with other group experiments, MRTs are intended to test intervention and moderation effects *averaged across individuals*, and to allow inference about these effects in the population or some subpopulation (The Penn State Methodology Center, 2020). In contrast, idiographic designs such as N-of-1 trials are intended to test these effects or other relevant variable relationships *within a specific individual*, and to allow inference about these effects in that individual—although results aggregated across multiple individuals may also yield clinical insights about the subpopulation or population to which these individuals belong (Schork, 2015). Personalized intervention informed by an idiographic, intensive research design has produced promising results in adults (Fisher et al., 2019) and is discussed further in Chapter 20.

Conclusions and Recommendations

We conclude this chapter by summarizing and reflecting on the knowledge gained about child and adolescent psychotherapy over the past half-century and offering our recommendations on opportunities that researchers can take to move the field forward.

What Have We Learned About Psychotherapy for Children and Adolescents?

Researchers have accomplished a great deal in developing, testing, and identifying therapies that work for a broad range of youth mental health problems. The current emphasis on treatment families indicates that multiple protocols utilizing similar psychological principles and practice elements have been tested in RCTs, reflecting the increasing maturity of the field. Moreover, mediation studies have generated support for the theoretical models of two of the most well-studied youth EBPs, CBT and behavioral parent training (and related treatments), though consistent therapeutic alliance–outcome associations point to the importance of this common factor alongside theory-specific putative change mechanisms and processes for youth outcomes.

The outcome literature has expanded substantially within many target problems, warranting separate reviews, or separate classifications within the same review, for different subpopulations of youths. Notably, differences emerged in the number and type of EBPs identified for younger children versus older children or adolescents for several problems (i.e., depression, anxiety, ADHD, disruptive behavior, overweight and obesity), pointing to a lack of EBPs for some youths (e.g., no EBPs for depressed children and for obese adolescents) and the differential impact of parent and systems involvement across ages and target problems. Together with the meta-analytic findings demonstrating age and family variables as common treatment moderators, the EBP reviews suggest that the youth's age and the family's involvement are key considerations in youth psychotherapy research and practice. However, many challenges remain: mixed findings for moderators and the dearth of EBP findings for Native American and Asian American youths illustrate areas in need of further study. Additionally, many potential moderators remain inadequately investigated, including those most relevant to ethnic minority youths. The literature suggests that change processes and mechanisms may also differ across subgroups, but true moderation effects are difficult to distinguish from random variation when the study pool and participant samples are small. Future researchers may be better equipped to explore these factors via machine learning, big data, and newer meta-analytic approaches.

Meta-analyses indicate that the potential of psychotherapy to alleviate youth psychopathology has yet to be fully realized – due in part to challenges associated with implementing lab-tested EBPs in everyday clinical contexts, as well as an imperfect understanding of psychopathology and the multitude of youth and family characteristics that impact treatment response. Thus, although young people now have multiple therapeutic options for most mental health problems, and many of these options may prove helpful on average, clinical scientists need to find ways to boost the level of benefit for each youth, and particularly when EBPs are delivered within the real-world conditions of everyday clinical care. Moreover, the benefit that therapies can provide needs to be made available to more young people – a goal that may be achievable by reconceptualizing what therapy can look like and delivering it in scalable ways (Kazdin et al., 2018).

Fortunately, researchers are actively working to disseminate EBPs more widely and implement them effectively in clinical practice settings. Related efforts have included collaboration with various stakeholders involved with youth mental health and well-being, including governments, mental health and primary care clinic systems, and schools, whose participation are critical to the adoption and sustainability of new practices. Researchers have also devised creative ways to reach and retain the youths and families who need them, as well as the therapists who need to deliver them – for example, by repackaging EBPs in a highly engaging summer camp or computer game format, in a low-burden single-session format, or as part of modular and transdiagnostic protocols that facilitate therapist decision-making and

flexible, targeted treatment of multiple problems common within and across youths. Development and evaluation of DI approaches have accelerated over the past decade (see Williams & Beidas, 2019). DI science has become, and will continue to be, a major emphasis within youth psychotherapy research.

New directions in improving mental health outcomes by personalizing youth psychotherapy have emerged. A nascent literature is demonstrating that there are optimal ways to select, sequence, combine, time, and deliver interventions to maximize therapeutic benefit to each individual, supported by innovations in the conceptualization of psychopathology, in mobile technologies, and in quantitative methods and research design. Although empirical findings on personalizing psychotherapies for youth are currently limited (see Ng & Weisz, 2016, 2017), we expect more findings to accumulate in the near future as part of a broader, growing movement drawing on expertise from the clinical sciences, statistics, computer science, and engineering to improve human health in increasingly precise ways (see md2k.org).

How Can We Move Youth Psychotherapy Research Forward?

Our aim for this chapter was to provide a comprehensive review of modern youth psychotherapy: its distinctive features relative to adult psychotherapy, the evolution of the literature in recent years, and the emerging effort to understand treatment in greater detail, including the mechanisms of change and the specific populations and contexts in which treatment is effective. The field is clearly making great progress, from the increase in the number of evidence-based practices to the incorporation of new technologies into research and intervention. Despite this progress, there are still many aspects of youth psychotherapy research and practice that require additional support. We recommend that youth psychotherapy researchers take advantage of the following opportunities for growth.

Moving forward, it is vital that evidence-based practices be established for minority youths. There are only four well-established EBPs for ethnic minority youths; while it is very possible that some interventions that are well-established with predominantly Caucasian samples are also highly effective for ethnic minority youths, research with large minority samples is needed before conclusions can be drawn. Native American youths have been particularly neglected in psychotherapy research. In addition to reduced life expectancy and greater incidence of physical health conditions, the suicide rate is unusually high for Native American youths (Abbasi, 2018), and they are significantly more likely to experience multiple adverse childhood experiences, which are associated with mental health disturbances (Kenney & Singh, 2016). This evidence for great need contrasts sharply with the broader treatment literature: in their efforts to identify EBPs for ethnic minority youths, neither Huey and Polo (2008) nor Pina and colleagues (2019) could identify any treatments for Native American youths. More concerning, however, is that neither found any studies with a sufficiently large Native American population that met inclusion criteria. Though null research findings would be disappointing, the complete absence of literature is an entirely different problem.

This problem is not limited to ethnic minorities. At present, there are no currently established EBPs for sexual or gender minority youths. It is vital that effective interventions be identified for these youths, given the abundance of literature suggesting that they face ongoing mental health difficulties – for example, elevated rates of victimization, substance use, and suicidality are reported for lesbian, gay, and bisexual high school students (Zaza et al., 2016). In addition, Toomey and colleagues (2018) reported that in a national survey of adolescents aged 11–19, transgender, nonbinary, and gender-questioning youths were significantly more likely to report at least one past suicide attempt (subgroup estimates ranged from 27.9% to 50.8%) than their cisgender peers (17.6% of females, 9.8% of males). There is a multitude of evidence to suggest that biological or social interventions not directly targeting mental health may be associated with a lower incidence of mental illness in these populations (e.g., Walls et al., 2008; de Vries et al., 2011; Durwood et al., 2017), but this fact does not eliminate the need to identify the most beneficial psychosocial or pharmaceutical interventions for these youths. With so much evidence that minority youth populations have an urgent need for effective psychological interventions, it is imperative that researchers identify relevant EBPs.

In addition to expanding EBPs, increasing data-sharing practices and standardizing predictors can close the gaps in our existing literature. Much clinical research is not sufficiently powered to detect subgroup differences (Brookes et al., 2004) or mediators (Kraemer et al., 2002). Meta-analyses thus suffer doubly: not all studies test the same predictors as moderators, and even those that do may not use the same measures for a given construct. For example, one research team might ask for youth or parent report of ethnicity, while another might only ask if the youth is white or nonwhite, Hispanic or non-Hispanic. Often, meta-analysts are forced to collapse categories within a potential moderator to accommodate larger numbers of studies, which limits their ability to examine subgroup differences at a level that would be more clinically meaningful. Much like the standards developed for attaining EBP status, clear guidelines for data collection would allow for better comparison across trials. This would enable meta-analyses to accurately consider within-study findings of moderator analyses. Relatedly, greater use of services like Open Science Framework (OSF; see Foster & Deardorff, 2017) or the NIMH's National Data Archive (NDA) will allow researchers to access more data and reevaluate past trials with new statistical methods. Increased access to raw data or summary statistics will also greatly facilitate MASEM and IPD meta-analysis, the approaches we believe can help consolidate findings on putative mediators from decades of youth psychotherapy RCTs (Ng et al., 2020).

Youth psychotherapy research has generated plenty of useful information, but – as we have discussed – there is still much work to be done. There are a number of valuable findings reviewed in this chapter that require follow-through in research or practice. The implementation cliff, off which the efficacy of treatment falls when the intervention transitions from RCTs into clinically representative conditions, is a well-documented problem that results from both shortcomings of our treatment protocols (e.g., the inability to address multiple disorders) and real-world barriers to treatment access/adherence (e.g., the inability to consistently transport a child to and from treatment each week). Despite these issues, new RCTs frequently do not take place under clinically representative conditions, and there has not been adequate research to test supports against the institutional and familial obstacles to treatment.

Researchers have opened up a number of exciting avenues recently, and supporting ongoing work in these areas is of the utmost importance. Coincidentally, many of these research developments may help rectify issues like the implementation cliff that have been long recognized but rarely addressed. Short interventions, like BRISC in schools, and SSIs, may help circumvent these problems, but further implementation research is vital. Digital interventions likewise have great potential for minimizing barriers to treatment completion but are not yet sufficiently developed. SMART and JITAIs will inevitably prove themselves valuable for making intervention more effective and efficient, but they too are still in development.

Stated briefly, the companion themes of youth psychotherapy research going forward should be expansion and enrichment. The EBP movement has led to the identification of effective and potentially effective treatments for a variety of disorders and problems, but this work has not yet fully considered the range of youths who could benefit from it most. Major obstacles to treatment implementation and utilization have been identified, but supports for overcoming these barriers to care in the community remain understudied. The new intervention frameworks and methods show great potential for developing treatments that are more personalizable, affordable, and/or effective than their predecessors, yet the research on almost all of these methods is still in its infancy. Youth psychotherapy researchers have made significant progress in recent years—there is great progress yet to be made by expanding their work.

A remarkably rich mix of challenges and opportunities coexist in the field of youth psychotherapy today. Talented clinical scientists are stepping up to these challenges and working with colleagues in other fields, practitioners, and multiple stakeholders invested in youth mental health to strengthen and broaden access to therapies for maximum real-world impact. Their combined efforts hold the promise of increasingly potent intervention that offers genuine benefit to children, adolescents, and their families.

ABBREVIATIONS

ABA	Applied Behavior Analysis
ABAB	Single case design
ADHD	Attention deficit hyperactivity disorder
APA	American Psychological Association
ARFID	Avoidant restrictive food intake disorder
BMI	Body Mass Index
BRISC	Brief Intervention for School Clinicians
BT	Behavior therapy
CAMHS	Child and adolescent mental health services

CAMP	Child Anxiety Multi-Day Program
CAMS	Child and Adolescent Anxiety Multimodal Study
CBT	Cognitive behavioral therapy
CYP IAPT	Children's and Young People's Improving Access to Psychological Therapies
DBT	Dialectical behavior therapy
DHIs	Digital health interventions
DSP	Developmental social-pragmatic model
EBPs	Evidence-based psychotherapies
EMA	Ecological momentary assessment
EMDR	Eye movement desensitization and reprocessing
FFT	Functional family therapy
GAD	generalized anxiety disorder
GNATS	gloomy negative automatic thoughts
HiTOP	Hierarchical Taxonomy of Psychopathology
IPD	Individual participant data
IPT	Interpersonal psychotherapy
JCCAP	Journal of Clinical Child and Adolescent Psychology
JITAIs	just-in-time-adaptive interventions
MASEM	Meta-analytic structural equation modeling
MATCH	Modular Approach to Therapy for Children
MFSs	Measurement feedback systems
ML	Machine learning
MRTs	microrandomized trials
MST	Multisystemic Therapy
MTA	Multimodal Treatment Study of Children with ADHD
NDA	National Data Archive
OCD	obsessive compulsive disorder
OCEBM	Oxford Centre for Evidence-Based Medicine
PCPs	primary care practitioners
PTB	probability of treatment benefit
PTSD	Post-traumatic stress disorder
RCT	randomized controlled trial
RDoC	Research Domain Criteria
SAD	separation anxiety disorder
SMARTs	sequential, multiple assignment, randomized trials
SMH	school mental health
SPARX	online e-therapy tool

SSIs	single-session interventions
SSRI	selective serotonin reuptake inhibitor
STP	Summer Treatment Program
SVM	support vector machine
TADS	Treatment for Adolescent Depression Study
TFCO	Treatment Foster Care Oregon
UP-A	Unified Protocol for Transdiagnostic Treatment of Emotional Disorders in Adolescents
UP-C	Unified Protocol for Transdiagnostic Treatment of Emotional Disorders in Children (UP-C)

REFERENCES

Abbasi, J. (2018). Why are American Indians dying young? *JAMA, 319*(2), 109–111. https://doi.org/10.1001/jama.2017.10122

Achenbach, T. M., & Edelbrock, C. S. (1978). The classification of child psychopathology: A review and analysis of empirical efforts. *Psychological Bulletin, 85*(6), 1275–1301 https://doi.org/10.1037/0033-2909.85.6.1275

Achenbach, T. M., & Edelbrock, C. S. (1984). Psychopathology of childhood. *Annual Review of Psychology, 35*(1), 227–256. https://doi.org/10.1146/annurev.ps.35.020184.001303

Achenbach, T. M., McConaughy, S. H., & Howell, C.T. (1987). Child/adolescent behavioral and emotional problems: Implications of cross-informant correlations for situational specificity. *Psychological Bulletin, 101*(2), 213–232. https://doi.org/10.1037/0033-2909.101.2.213

Ackerson, J., Scogin, F., McKendree-Smith, N., & Lyman, R. D. (1998). Cognitive bibliotherapy for mild and moderate adolescent depressive symptomatology. *Journal of Consulting and Clinical Psychology, 66*(4), 685–690. https://doi.org/10.1037/0022-006X.66.4.685

Addington, J., Liu, L., Buchy, L., Cadenhead, K. S., Cannon, T. D., Cornblatt, B. A., Perkins, D. O., Seidman, L. J., Tsuang, M. T., Walker, E. F., Woods, S. W., Bearden, C. E., Mathalon, D. H., & McGlashan, T. H. (2015). North American Prodrome Longitudinal Study (NAPLS 2): The Prodromal Symptoms. *The Journal of Nervous and Mental Disease, 203*(5), 328–335. https://doi.org/10.1097/NMD.0000000000000290

Altman, M., & Wilfley, D. E. (2015). Evidence update on the treatment of overweight and obesity in children and adolescents. *Journal of Clinical Child & Adolescent Psychology, 44*(4), 521–537. https://doi.org/10.1080/15374416.2014.963854

Anderson, M., & Jiang, J. (2018, May 31). *Teens, social media & technology 2018.* Pew Research Center. https://www.pewresearch.org/internet/2018/05/31/teens-social-media-technology-2018/

Apter, A., Fainaru, M., Golan, M., & Weizman, A. (1998). Parents as the exclusive agents of change in the treatment of childhood obesity. *The American Journal of Clinical Nutrition, 67*(6), 1130–1135. https://doi.org/10.1093/ajcn/67.6.1130

Archer, J., Bower, P., Gilbody, S., Lovell, K., Richards, D., Gask, L., Dickens, C., & Coventry, P. (2012). Collaborative care for depression and anxiety problems. *Cochrane Database of Systematic Reviews, 10*, CD006525. https://doi.org/10.1002/14651858.CD006525.pub2

Aronson, J., Cohen, G., McCloskey, W., Montrosse, B., Lewis, K., & Mooney, K., (2009). Reducing stereotype threat in classrooms: A review of social-psychological intervention studies on improving the achievement of Black students. Washington, DC: U.S. Department of Education, Institute of Education Sciences, National Center for Education Evaluation and Regional Assistance.

Asarnow, J. R., Berk, M., Hughes, J. L., & Anderson, N. L. (2015). The SAFETY Program: A treatment-development trial of a cognitive-behavioral family treatment for adolescent suicide attempters. *Journal of Clinical Child & Adolescent Psychology, 44*(1), 194–203. https://doi.org/10.1080/15374416.2014.940624

Asarnow, J. R., & Miranda, J. (2014). Improving care for depression and suicide risk in adolescents: Innovative strategies for bringing treatments to community settings. *Annual Review of Clinical Psychology*, 10, 275–303. https://doi.org/10.1146/annurev-clinpsy-032813-153742

Asarnow, J. R., Rozenman, M., Wiblin, J., & Zeltzer, L. (2015). Integrated medical-behavioral care compared with usual primary care for child and adolescent behavioral health: A meta-analysis. *JAMA Pediatrics*, 169(10), 929–937. https://doi.org/10.1001/jamapediatrics.2015.1141

Audrain-McGovern, J., Stevens, S., Murray, P. J., Kinsman, S., Zuckoff, A., Pletcher, J., Moss, D., Baumritter, A., Kalkhuis-Beam, S., Carlson, E., Rodriguez, D., & Wileyto, E. P. (2011). The efficacy of motivational interviewing versus brief advice for adolescent smoking behavior change. *Pediatrics*, 128(1), e101–e111. https://doi.org/10.1542/peds.2010-2174

Aung, M. H., Matthews, M., & Choudhury, T. (2017). Sensing behavioral symptoms of mental health and delivering personalized interventions using mobile technologies. *Depression and Anxiety*, 34(7), 603–609. https://doi.org/10.1002/da.22646

Azrin, N. H., Nunn, R. G., & Frantz-Renshaw, S. (1982). Habit reversal vs. negative practice treatment of self-destructive oral habits (biting, chewing or licking of the lips, cheeks, tongue or palate). *Journal of Behavior Therapy and Experimental Psychiatry*, 13(1), 49–54. https://doi.org/10.1016/0005-7916(82)90035-0

Azrin, N. H., Sneed, T. J., & Foxx, R. M. (1974). Dry-bed training: Rapid elimination of childhood enuresis. *Behaviour Research and Therapy*, 12(3), 147–156. https://doi.org/10.1016/0005-7967(74)90111-9

Bagot, K. S., Matthews, S. A., Mason, M., M. Squeglia, Lindsay, Fowler, J., Gray, K., Herting, M., May, A., Colrain, I., Godino, J., Tapert, S., Brown, S., & Patrick, K. (2018). Current, future and potential use of mobile and wearable technologies and social media data in the ABCD study to increase understanding of contributors to child health. *Developmental Cognitive Neuroscience*, 32, 121–129. https://doi.org/10.1016/j.dcn.2018.03.008

Bakker, M. J., Greven, C. U., Buitelaar, J. K., Glennon, J. C., (2017). Practitioner review: Psychological treatments for children and adolescents with conduct disorder problems - A systematic review and meta-analysis. *Journal of Child Psychology and Psychiatry*, 58(1), 4–18. https://doi.org/10.1111/jcpp.12590

Barkley, R. A. (1997). *Defiant children: A clinician's manual for assessment and parent training*. New York, NY: Guilford.

Barlow, D. H., Nock, M. K., & Hersen, M. (2009). *Single case experimental designs: Strategies for studying behavior change* (3rd ed.). Boston, MA: Allyn & Bacon.

Barrett, P. M., Farrell, L., Pina, A. A., Peris, T. S., & Piacentini, J. (2008). Evidence-based psychosocial treatments for child and adolescent obsessive-compulsive disorders. *Journal of Child and Adolescent Clinical Psychology*, 37(1), 131–155. https://doi.org/10.1080/15374410701817956

Battagliese, G., Caccetta, M., Luppino, O. I., Baglioni, C., Cardi, V., Mancini, F., Buonanno, C., (2015). Cognitive-behavioral therapy for externalizing disorders: A meta-analysis of treatment effectiveness. *Behaviour Research and Therapy*, 75, 60–71. https://doi.org/10.1016/j.brat.2015.10.008

Beauchaine, T. P., Webster-Stratton, C., & Reid, M. J. (2005). Mediators, moderators, and predictors of 1–year outcomes among children treated for early-onset conduct problems: A latent growth curve analysis. *Journal of Consulting and Clinical Psychology*, 73(3), 371–388. https://doi.org/10.1037/0022-006X.73.3.371

Beck, A. T. (1970). Cognitive therapy: Nature and relation to behavior therapy. *Behavior Therapy*, 1(2), 184–200. https://doi.org/10.1016/S0005-7894(70)80030-2

Becker, K. D., Boustani, M., Gellatly, R., & Chorpita, B. F. (2018). Forty years of engagement research in children's mental health services: Multidimensional measurement and practice elements. *Journal of Clinical Child & Adolescent Psychology*, 47(1), 1–23. https://doi.org/10.1080/15374416.2017.1326121

Beidas, R. S., Lindhiem, O., Brodman, D. M., Swan, A., Carper, M., Cummings, C., Kendall, P. C., Albano, A. M., Rynn, M., Piacentini, J., McCracken, J., Compton, S. N., March, J., Walkup, J., Ginsburg, G., Keeton, C. P., Birmaher, B., Sakolsky, D., & Sherrill, J. (2014). A probabilistic and individualized approach for predicting treatment gains: An extension and application to anxiety disordered youth. *Behavior Therapy*, 45(1), 126–136. https://doi.org/10.1016/j.beth.2013.05.001

Bickman, L., Kelley, S. D., Breda, C., de Andrade, A. R., & Riemer, M. (2011). Effects of routine feedback to clinicians on mental health outcomes

of youths: Results of a randomized trial. *Psychiatric Services*, 62(12), 1423–1429. https://doi.org/10.1176/appi.ps.002052011

Black, J. J., & Chung, T. (2014). Mechanisms of change in adolescent substance use treatment: How does treatment work? *Substance Abuse*, 35(4), 344–351. https://doi.org/10.1080/08897077.2014.925029

Bondy, A., & Frost, L. (2001). The picture exchange communication system. *Behavior Modification*, 25(5), 725–744. https://doi.org/10.1177/0145445501255004

Borduin, C. M., & Munschy, R. M. (2014). *Multisystemic therapy for youths with problem sexual behaviors*. Unpublished manuscript, Department of Psychological Sciences, University of Missouri.

Borsboom, D. (2017). A network theory of mental disorders. *World Psychiatry*, 16(1), 5–13. https://doi.org/10.1002/wps.20375

Borsboom, D., Fried, E. I., Epskamp, S., Waldorp, L. J., van Borkulo, C. D., van der Maas, H. L. J., & Cramer, A. O. J. (2017). False alarm? A comprehensive reanalysis of "Evidence that psychopathology symptom networks have limited replicability" by Forbes, Wright, Markon, and Krueger (2017). *Journal of Abnormal Psychology*, 126(7), 989–999. https://doi.org/10.1037/abn0000306

Bos, F. M., Snippe, E., de Vos, S., Hartmann, J. A., Simons, C. J., van der Krieke, L., de Jonge, P., & Wichers, M. (2017). Can we jump from cross-sectional to dynamic interpretations of networks? Implications for the network perspective in psychiatry. *Psychotherapy and Psychosomatics*, 86(3), 175–177. https://doi.org/10.1159/000453583

Boustani, M. M., Gellatly, R., Westman, J. G., & Chorpita, B. F. (2017). Advances in cognitive behavioral treatment design: Time for a glossary. *The Behavior Therapist*, 40, 199–207.

Brent, Kolko, Birmaher, Baugher, Bridge, Roth, & Holder. (1998). Predictors of treatment efficacy in a clinical trial of three psychosocial treatments for adolescent depression. *Journal of the American Academy of Child & Adolescent Psychiatry*, 37(9), 906–914. https://doi.org/10.1097/00004583-199809000-00010

Bry, B. H. (1988). Family-based approaches to reducing adolescent substance use: Theories, techniques and findings. In E. R. Rahdert & J. Grabowski (Eds.), *Adolescent drug abuse: Analyses of treatment research* (pp. 39–68). Rockville, MD: DHHS. https://doi.org/10.1037/e468212004-001

Bry, L. J., Chou, T., Miguel, E., & Comer, J. S. (2018). Consumer smartphone apps marketed for child and adolescent anxiety: A systematic review and content analysis. *Behavior Therapy*, 49(2), 249–261. https://doi.org/10.1016/j.beth.2017.07.008

Buchannan, R., Chamberlain, P., & Smith, D. K. (2017). Treatment foster care for adolescents: Research and implementation. In J. R. Weisz & A. E. Kazdin (Eds.), *Evidence-based psychotherapies for children and adolescents*, (3rd ed., pp. 177–196). New York, NY: Guilford Press.

Calvocoressi, L., Lewis, B., Harris, M., Trufan, S. J., Goodman, W. K., McDougle, C. J., & Price, L. H. (1995). Family accommodation in obsessive-compulsive disorder. *The American Journal of Psychiatry*, 152(3), 441–443. https://doi.org/10.1176/ajp.152.3.441

Calvocoressi, L. M., Mazure, C. V., Kasl, S. J., Skolnick, J. L., Fisk, D. H., Vegso, S., Van Noppen, B., & Price, L. (1999). Family accommodation of obsessive-compulsive symptoms: Instrument development and assessment of family behavior. *The Journal of Nervous & Mental Disease*, 187(10), 636–642. https://doi.org/10.1097/00005053-199910000-00008

Campbell, J. M. (2003). Efficacy of behavioral interventions for reducing problem behavior in persons with autism: A quantitative synthesis of single-subject research. *Research in Developmental Disabilities*, 24(2), 120–138. https://doi.org/10.1016/S0891-4222(03)00014-3

Carper, M. M., Makover, H. B., & Kendall, P. C. (2018). Future directions for the examination of mediators of treatment outcomes in youth. *Journal of Clinical Child & Adolescent Psychology*, 47(2), 345–356. https://doi.org/10.1080/15374416.2017.1359786

Casenhiser, D. M., Shanker, S. G., & Stieben, J. (2013). Learning through interaction in children with autism: Preliminary data from a social-communication-based intervention. *Autism*, 17(2), 220–241. https://doi.org/10.1177/1362361311422052

Casey, R. J., & Berman, J. S. (1985). The outcome of psychotherapy with children. *Psychological Bulletin*, 98(2), 388–400. https://doi.org/10.1037/0033-2909.98.2.388

Caspi, A., Houts, R. M., Belsky, D. W., Goldman-Mellor, S. J., Harrington, H., Israel, S., Meier, M. H., Ramrakha, S., Shalev, I., Poulton, R., & Moffitt,

T. E. (2014). The p factor: one general psychopathology factor in the structure of psychiatric disorders? *Clinical Psychological Science, 2*(2), 119–137. https://doi.org/10.1177/2167702613497473

Chambless, D. L., Baker, M. J., Baucom, D. H., Beutler, L. E., Calhoun, K. S., Crits-Christoph, P., Daiuto, A., DeRubeis, R., Detweiler, J., Haaga, D. A. F., Bennett Johnson, S., McCurry, S., Mueser, K. T., Pope, K. S., Sanderson, W. S., Shoham, V., Stickle, T., Williams, D. A. & Woody, S.R. (1998). Update on empirically validated therapies II. *Clinical Psychologist, 51*(1), 3–16. https://doi.org/10.1037/e619622010-001

Chambless, D. L. & Hollon, S. D. (1998). Defining empirically supported therapies. *Journal of Consulting and Clinical Psychology, 66*(1), 7–18. https://doi.org/10.1037/0022-006X.66.1.7

Chambless, D. L., Sanderson, W. C., Shoham, V., Johnson, S. B., Pope, K. S., Crits-Christoph, P., Baker, M., Johnson, B., Woody, S. R., Sue, S., Beutler, L., Williams, D. A., & McCurry, S. (1996). An update on empirically validated therapies. *The Clinical Psychologist, 9*, 5–18. https://doi.org/10.1037/e555332011-003

Chen, C., & Ma, H. (2007). Effects of treatment on disruptive behaviors: A quantitative synthesis of single-subject researches using the PEM approach. *The Behavior Analyst Today, 8*(4), 380–397. https://doi.org/10.1037/h0100629

Cheung, M. W.-L., & Hafdahl, A. R. (2016). Special issue on meta-analytic structural equation modeling: Introduction from the Guest Editors. *Research Synthesis Methods, 7*, 112–120. https://doi.org/10.1002/jrsm.1212

Chorpita, B.F., & Daleiden, E.L. (2009). Mapping evidence-based treatments for children and adolescents: Application of the distillation and matching model to 615 treatments from 322 randomized trials. *Journal of Consulting and Clinical Psychology, 77*(3), 566–579. https://doi.org/10.1037/a0014565

Chorpita, B. F., Daleiden, E. L., Park, A. L., Ward, A. M., Levy, M. C., Cromley, T., Chiu, A. W., Letamendi, A. M., Tsai, K. H., & Krull, J. L. (2017). Child STEPs in California: A cluster randomized effectiveness trial comparing modular treatment with community implemented treatment for youth with anxiety, depression, conduct problems, or traumatic stress. *Journal of Consulting and Clinical Psychology, 85*(1), 13–25. https://doi.org/10.1037/ccp0000133

Chorpita, B. F., Park, A., Tsai, K., Korathu-Larson, P., Higa-McMillan, C. K., Nakamura, B. J., Weisz, J. R., & Krull, J. (2015). Balancing effectiveness with responsiveness: Therapist satisfaction across different treatment designs in the Child STEPs randomized effectiveness trial. *Journal of Consulting and Clinical Psychology, 83*(4), 709–718. https://doi.org/10.1037/a0039301

Chorpita, B. F., Weisz, J. R., Daleiden, E. L., Schoenwald, S. K., Palinkas, L. A., Miranda, J., Higa-McMillan, C. K., Nakamura, B. J., Austin, A. A., Borntrager, C. F., Ward, A., Wells, K. C., Gibbons, R. D., & Research Network on Youth Mental Health (2013). Long-term outcomes for the Child STEPs randomized effectiveness trial: A comparison of modular and standard treatment designs with usual care. *Journal of Consulting and Clinical Psychology, 81*(6), 999–1009 https://doi.org/10.1037/a0034200

Chung, Y., Addington, J., Bearden, C., Cadenhead, K., Cornblatt, B., Mathalon, D., McGlashan, T., Perkins, D., Seidman, L. J., Tsuang, M., Walker, E., Woods, S. W., McEwen, S., van Erp, T. G. M., Cannon, T., North American Prodrome Longitudinal Study (NAPLS) Consortium and the Pediatric Imaging, Neurocognition, and Genetics (PING) Study Consortium (2018). Use of machine learning to determine deviance in neuroanatomical maturity associated with future psychosis in youths at clinically high risk. *JAMA Psychiatry, 75*(9), 960–968. https://doi.org/10.1001/jamapsychiatry.2018.1543

Cicchetti, D., & Toth, S. (2017) Using the science of developmental psychopathology to inform child and adolescent psychotherapy. In J. Weisz & A. Kazdin (Eds.), *Evidence-based psychotherapies for children and adolescents* (3rd ed). New York: Guilford Press.

Clarke, G., Debar, L., Lynch, F., Powell, J., Gale, J., O'Connor, E., Ludman, E., Bush, T., Lin, E. H., Von Korff, M., & Hertert, S. (2005). A randomized effectiveness trial of brief cognitive-behavioral therapy for depressed adolescents receiving antidepressant medication. *Journal of the American Academy of Child & Adolescent Psychiatry, 44*(9), 888–898. https://doi.org/10.1016/S0890-8567(09)62194-8

Clarke, G. N., & DeBar, L. L. (2010). Group cognitive behavioral treatment for adolescent depression. In J. R. Weisz & A. E. Kazdin (Eds.), *Evidence-based psychotherapies for children and adolescents* (2nd ed., pp. 110–125). New York, NY: Guilford Press

Cohen, J. (1988). *Statistical power analysis for the behavioral sciences* (2nd ed.). Hillsdale, NJ: Lawrence Erlbaum Associates.

Cohen, J. A., Mannarino, A. P., & Deblinger, E. (2010). Trauma-focused cognitive-behavioral therapy for traumatized children. In J. R. Weisz & A. E. Kazdin (Eds.), *Evidence-based psychotherapies for children and adolescents*, (2nd ed., pp. 295–311). New York, NY: Guilford Press. https://doi.org/10.1037/e606702009-001

Cohen, Z., Kim, T., Van, H., Dekker, J., & Driessen, E. (2020). A demonstration of a multi-method variable selection approach for treatment selection: Recommending cognitive-behavioral versus psychodynamic therapy for mild to moderate adult depression. *Psychotherapy Research, 30*(2), 137–150. https://doi.org/10.1080/10503307.2018.1563312

Comer, J. S., Chow, C., Chan, P. T., Cooper-Vince, C., & Wilson, L. A. (2013). Psychosocial treatment efficacy for disruptive behavior problems in very young children: A meta-analytic examination. *Journal of the American Academy of Child & Adolescent Psychiatry, 52*(1), 26–36. https://doi.org/10.1016/j.jaac.2012.10.001

Comer, J. S., Hong, N., Poznanski, B., Silva, K., & Wilson, M. (2019). Evidence base update on the treatment of early childhood anxiety and related problems. *Journal of Clinical Child & Adolescent Psychology, 48*(1), 1–15 https://doi.org/10.1080/15374416.2018.1534208

Compas, B. E., Champion, J. E., Forehand, R., Cole, D. A., Reeslund, K. L., Fear, J., Hardcastle, E. J., Keller, G., Rakow, A., Garai, E., Merchant, M. J., & Roberts, L. (2010). Coping and parenting: Mediators of 12–month outcomes of a family group cognitive-behavioral preventive intervention with families of depressed parents. *Journal of Consulting and Clinical Psychology, 78*(5), 623–634. https://doi.org/10.1037/a0020459

Cooper, H., & Patall, E.A. (2009). The relative benefits of meta-analysis conducted with individual participant data versus aggregated data. *Psychological Methods, 14*(2), 165–176. https://doi.org/10.1037/a0015565

Coulter, I. D., Favreau, J. T., Hardy, M. L., Morton, S. C., Roth, E. A., & Shekelle, P. (2002). Biofeedback interventions for gastrointestinal conditions: A Systematic Review. *Alternative Therapies in Health and Medicine, 8*(3), 76–83.

Craske, M. G., Rose, R. D., Lang, A., Welch, S. S., Campbell-Sills, L., Sullivan, G., Sherbourne, C., Bystritsky, A., Stein, M. B., & Roy-Byrne, P. P. (2009). Computer-assisted delivery of cognitive behavioral therapy for anxiety disorders in primary-care settings. *Depression and Anxiety, 26*(3), 235–242. https://doi.org/10.1002/da.20542

Cuijpers, P. (2019). Targets and outcomes of psychotherapies for mental disorders: An overview. *World Psychiatry, 18*(3), 276–285. https://doi.org/10.1002/wps.20661

Cuijpers, P., Karyotaki, E., Eckshtain, D., Ng, M. Y., Corteselli, K., Noma, H., Quero, S., & Weisz, J. R. (2020). Psychotherapy for depression across different age groups: A meta-analysis. *JAMA Psychiatry, 77*(7), 694–702. https://doi.org/10.1001/jamapsychiatry.2020.0164

Cuijpers, P., Karyotaki, E., Reijnders, M., & Ebert, D. D. (2019). Was Eysenck right after all? A reassessment of the effects of psychotherapy for adult depression. *Epidemiological Psychiatric Science, 28*(1), 21–31. https://doi.org/10.1017/S2045796018000057

Cuijpers, P., Sijbrandij, M., Koole, S., Huibers, M., Berking, M., & Andersson, G. (2014). Psychological treatment of generalized anxiety disorder: A meta-analysis. *Clinical Psychology Review, 34*(2), 130–140. https://doi.org/10.1016/j.cpr.2014.01.002

Cummings, J. R., Wen, H., & Druss, B. G. (2013). Improving access to mental health services for youth in the United States. *JAMA, 309*(6), 553–554. https://doi.org/10.1001/jama.2013.437

Curtis, N. M., Ronan, K. R., & Borduin, C. M. (2004). Multisystemic intervention: A meta-analysis of outcome studies. *Journal of Family Psychology, 18*(3), 411–419. https://doi.org/10.1037/0893-3200.18.3.411

Dare, C., & Eisler, I. (1997). Family therapy for anorexia nervosa. In D. M. Garner & P. Garfinkel (Eds.), *Handbook of treatment for eating disorders* (pp. 307–324). New York, NY: Guilford.

D'Amico, E. J., Miles, J. N., Stern, S. A., & Meredith, L. S. (2008). Brief motivational interviewing for teens at risk of substance use consequences: A randomized pilot study in a primary care clinic. *Journal of Substance Abuse Treatment, 35*(1), 53–61. https://doi.org/10.1016/j.jsat.2007.08.008

David-Ferdon, C., & Kaslow, N. J. (2008). Evidence-based psychosocial treatments for child and adolescent depression. *Journal of Child and Adolescent Clinical Psychology, 37*(1), 62–104. https://doi.org/10.1080/15374410701817865

Davis, T. E., Ollendick, T. H., & Öst, L. G. (2012). *Intensive one-session treatment of specific phobias.* New York: Springer. https://doi.org/10.1007/978-1-4614-3253-1

De Los Reyes, A. (2011). Special section: More than measurement error: Discovering meaning behind informant discrepancies in clinical assessments of children and adolescents. *Journal of Clinical Child and Adolescent Psychology, 40*(1), 1–9. https://doi.org/10.1080/15374416.2011.533405

De Los Reyes, A., Goodman, K. L., Kliewer, W., & Reid-Quiñones, K. (2010). The longitudinal consistency of mother-child reporting discrepancies of parental monitoring and their ability to predict child delinquent behaviors two years later. *Journal of Youth and Adolescence, 39*, 1417–1430. https://doi.org/10.1007/s10964-009-9496-7

De Vries, A., Steensma, T., Doreleijers, T., & Cohen-Kettenis, P. (2011). Puberty suppression in adolescents with gender identity disorder: A prospective follow-up study. *Journal of Sexual Medicine, 8*(8), 2276–2283. https://doi.org/10.1111/j.1743-6109.2010.01943.x

Diedrichs, P. C., Atkinson, M. J., Steer, R. J., Garbett, K. M., Rumsey, N., & Halliwell, E. (2015). Effectiveness of a brief school-based body image intervention 'Dove Confident Me: Single Session' when delivered by teachers and researchers: Results from a cluster randomised controlled trial. *Behaviour Research and Therapy, 74*, 94–104. https://doi.org/10.1016/j.brat.2015.09.004

Dodge, K. (2009). Community intervention and public policy in the prevention of antisocial behavior. *Journal of Child Psychology and Psychiatry, 50*(1–2), 194–200. https://doi.org/10.1111/j.1469-7610.2008.01985.x

Dopp, A. R., Borduin, C. M., Rothman, D. B., & Letourneau, E. J. (2017). Evidence-based treatments for youths who engage in illegal sexual behaviors. *Journal of Clinical Child & Adolescent Psychology, 46*(5), 631–645. https://doi.org/10.1080/15374416.2016.1261714

Dorsey, S., McLaughlin, K. A., Kerns, S. E., Harrison, J. P., Lambert, H. K., Briggs, E. C., Revillion Cox, J., & Amaya-Jackson, L. (2017). Evidence base update for psychosocial treatments for children and adolescents exposed to traumatic events. *Journal of Clinical Child & Adolescent Psychology, 46*(3), 303–330. https://doi.org/10.1080/15374416.2016.1220309

Doss, B. D. (2004). Changing the way we study change in psychotherapy. *Clinical Psychology: Science and Practice, 11*(4), 368–386. https://doi.org/10.1093/clipsy.bph094

Durwood, L., McLaughlin, K. A., & Olson, K. R. (2017). Mental health and self-worth in socially transitioned transgender youth. *Journal of the American Academy of Child and Adolescent Psychiatry, 56*(2), 116–123.e2. https://doi.org/10.1016/j.jaac.2016.10.016

Dwyer, D. B., Falkai, P., & Koutsouleris, N. (2018). Machine learning approaches for clinical psychology and psychiatry. *Annual Review of Clinical Psychology, 14*, 91–118. https://doi.org/10.1146/annurev-clinpsy-032816-045037

Eaton, N. (2015). Latent variable and network models of comorbidity: Toward an empirically derived nosology. *Social Psychiatry and Psychiatric Epidemiology, 50*(6), 845–849. https://doi.org/10.1007/s00127-015-1012-7

Eaton, N. R., Keyes, K. M., Krueger, R. F., Balsis, S., Skodol, A. E., Markon, K. E., Grant, B. F., & Hasin, D. S. (2012). An invariant dimensional liability model of gender differences in mental disorder prevalence: Evidence from a national sample. *Journal of Abnormal Psychology, 121*(1), 282–288. https://doi.org/10.1037/a0024780

Eckshtain, D., Kuppens, S., Ugueto, A., Ng, M.Y., Vaughn-Coaxum, R., Corteselli, K., & Weisz, J.R. (2020). Meta-analysis: 13–year follow-up of psychotherapy effects on youth depression. *Journal of the American Academy of Child and Adolescent Psychiatry, 59*(1), 45–63. https://doi.org/10.1016/j.jaac.2019.04.002

Edbrooke-Childs, J., O'Herlihy, A., Wolpert, M., Pugh, K., & Fonagy, P. (2015). *Children and young people's improving access to psychological therapies: Rapid internal audit national report.* Evidence-Based Practice Unit, Anna Freud Centre/University College London.

Eddy, J. M., & Chamberlain, P. (2000). Family management and deviant peer association as mediators of the impact of treatment condition on youth antisocial behavior. *Journal of Consulting and Clinical Psychology, 68*(5), 857. https://doi.org/10.1037/0022-006X.68.5.857

Edgcomb, J., & Zima, B. (2018). Medication adherence among children and adolescents with severe mental illness: A systematic review and meta-analysis. *Journal of Child and Adolescent Psychopharmacology, 28*(8), 58–520. https://doi.org/10.1089/cap.2018.0040

Ehrenreich, J. T., Goldstein, C. R., Wright, L. R., & Barlow, D. H. (2009). Development of a unified protocol for the treatment of emotional disorders in youth. *Child & Family Behavior Therapy, 31*(1), 20–37. https://doi.org/10.1080/07317100802701228

Ehrenreich-May, J., & Bilek, E. L. (2011). Universal prevention of anxiety and depression in a recreational camp setting: An initial open trial. *Child & Youth Care Forum, 40*(6), 435–455. https://doi.org/10.1007/s10566-011-9148-4

Ehrenreich-May, J., Rosenfield, D., Queen, A. H., Kennedy, S. M., Remmes, C. S., & Barlow, D. H. (2017). An initial waitlist-controlled trial of the unified protocol for the treatment of emotional disorders in adolescents. *Journal of Anxiety Disorders, 46*, 46–55. https://doi.org/10.1016/j.janxdis.2016.10.006

Epstein, L. H., Valoski, A., Wing, R. R., & McCurley, J. (1990). Ten-year follow-up of behavioral, family-based treatment for obese children. *Journal of the American Medical Association, 264*(19), 2519–2523. https://doi.org/10.1001/jama.1990.03450190051027

Epstein, R. A., Fonnesbeck, C., Potter, S., Rizzone, K. H., & McPheeters, M. (2015). Psychosocial interventions for child disruptive behaviors: A meta-analysis. *Pediatrics, 136*(5), 947–960. https://doi.org/10.1542/peds.2015-2577

Esposito-Smythers, C., Spirito, A., Kahler, C. W., Hunt, J., & Monti, P. (2011). Treatment of co-occurring substance abuse and suicidality among adolescents: A randomized trial. *Journal of Consulting and Clinical Psychology, 79*(6), 728–739 https://doi.org/10.1037/a0026074

Essau, C. A., Lewinsohn, P. M., Lim, J. X., Moon-ho, R. H., & Rohde, P. (2018). Incidence, recurrence and comorbidity of anxiety disorders in four major developmental stages. *Journal of Affective Disorders, 228*, 248–253. https://doi.org/10.1016/j.jad.2017.12.014

Evans, S. W., Langberg, J. M., Schultz, B. K., Vaughn, A., Altaye, M., Marshall, S. A., & Zoromski, A. K. (2016). Evaluation of a school-based treatment program for young adolescents with ADHD. *Journal of Consulting and Clinical Psychology, 84*(1), 15–30. https://doi.org/10.1037/ccp0000057

Evans, S. W., Owens, J. S., Wymbs, B. T., & Ray, A. R. (2018). Evidence-based psychosocial treatments for children and adolescents with attention deficit/hyperactivity disorder. *Journal of Clinical Child & Adolescent Psychology, 47*(2), 157–198. https://doi.org/10.1080/15374416.2017.1390757

Evans, S. W., Schultz, B. K., DeMars, C. E., & Davis, H. (2011). Effectiveness of the Challenging Horizons After-School Program for young adolescents with ADHD. *Behavior Therapy, 42*(3), 462–474. https://doi.org/10.1016/j.beth.2010.11.008

Eyberg, S. M., Nelson, M. M., & Boggs, S. R. (2008). Evidence-based psychosocial treatments for children and adolescents with disruptive behavior. *Journal of Child and Adolescent Clinical Psychology, 37*(1), 215–237. https://doi.org/10.1080/15374410701820117

Eysenck H.J. (1952). The effects of psychotherapy: An evaluation. *Journal of Consulting and Clinical Psychology, 16*(5), 319–324. https://doi.org/10.1037/h0063633

Fabiano, G. A., Schatz, N. K., & Pelham, W. E. (2014). Summer treatment programs for youth with ADHD. *Child and Adolescent Psychiatric Clinics of North America, 23*(4), 757–773. https://doi.org/10.1016/j.chc.2014.05.012

Fairburn, C. G., & Patel, V. (2017). The impact of digital technology on psychological treatments and their dissemination. *Behaviour Research and Therapy, 88*, 19–25. https://doi.org/10.1016/j.brat.2016.08.012

Farchione, T. J., Fairholme, C. P., Ellard, K. K., Boisseau, C. L., Thompson-Hollands, J., Carl, J. R., Gallagher, M. W., & Barlow, D. H. (2012). Unified protocol for transdiagnostic treatment of emotional disorders: A randomized controlled trial. *Behavior Therapy, 43*(3), 666–678. https://doi.org/10.1016/j.beth.2012.01.001

Farkas, L., Cyr, M., Lebeau, T.M., & Lemay, J. (2010). Effectiveness of MASTR/EMDR therapy for traumatized adolescents. *Journal of Child & Adolescent Trauma, 3*(2), 125–142. https://doi.org/10.1080/19361521003761325

Farmer, E.M.Z., Compton, S.N., Bums, B.J., & Robertson, E. (2002). Review of the evidence base for treatment of childhood psychopathology: Externalizing disorders. *Journal of Consulting and Clinical Psychology, 70*(6), 1267–1302. https://doi.org/10.1037/0022-006X.70.6.1267

Fatori, D., de Bragança Pereira, C. A., Asbahr, F. R., Requena, G., Alvarenga, P. G., De Mathis, M. A., Rohde, L. A., Leckman, J. F., March, J. S., Polanczyk, G. V., Miguel, E. C., & Shavitt, R. G. (2018). Adaptive treatment strategies for children and adolescents with Obsessive-Compulsive Disorder: A sequential multiple assignment randomized trial. *Journal of Anxiety Disorders, 58*, 42–50. https://doi.org/10.1016/j.janxdis.2018.07.002

Fazel, M., Hoagwood, K., Stephan, S., & Ford, T. (2014). Mental health interventions in schools in high-income countries. *The Lancet Psychiatry, 1*(5), 377–387. https://doi.org/10.1016/S2215-0366(14)70312-8

Fedewa, Ahn, Reese, Suarez, Macquoid, Davis, & Prout. (2016). Does psychotherapy work with school-aged youth? A meta-analytic examination of moderator variables that influence therapeutic outcomes. *Journal of School Psychology, 56*, 59–87. https://doi.org/10.1016/j.jsp.2016.03.001

First, M. B. (2012). The National Institute of Mental Health Research Domain Criteria (RDoC) project: moving towards a neuroscience-based diagnostic classification in psychiatry. In K. Kendler & J. Parnas (Eds.), *Philosophical issues in psychiatry II: Nosology* (pp. 12–18). Oxford University Press. https://doi.org/10.1093/med/9780199642205.003.0003

Fisher, A. J., Bosley, H. G., Fernandez, K. C., Reeves, J. W., Soyster, P. D., Diamond, A. E., & Barkin, J. (2019). Open trial of a personalized modular treatment for mood and anxiety. *Behavior Research and Therapy, 116*, 69–79. https://doi.org/10.1016/j.brat.2019.01.010

Fitzpatrick, K. K., Moye, A., Hoste, R., Lock, J., & Le Grange, D. (2010). Adolescent focused therapy for adolescent anorexia nervosa. *Journal of Contemporary Psychotherapy, 40*, 31–39. https://doi.org/10.1007/s10879-009-9123-7

Forbes, M. K., Wright, A. G., Markon, K. E., & Krueger, R. F. (2017). Evidence that psychopathology symptom networks have limited replicability. *Journal of Abnormal Psychology, 126*(7), 969–988. https://doi.org/10.1037/abn0000276

Forehand, R., Lafko, N., Parent, J., & Burt, K. B. (2014). Is parenting the mediator of change in behavioral parent training for externalizing problems of youth? *Clinical Psychology Review, 34*(8), 608–619. https://doi.org/10.1016/j.cpr.2014.10.001

Forgatch, M. S., & Gewirtz, A. H. (2017). The evolution of the Oregon Model of parent management training: An intervention for adolescent antisocial behavior in children and adolescents. In J. R. Weisz & A. E. Kazdin (Eds.), *Evidence-based psychotherapies for children and adolescents* (3rd ed., pp. 85–102). New York, NY: Guilford Press.

Foster, E. D., & Deardorff, A. (2017). Open Science Framework (OSF). *Journal of the Medical Library Association: JMLA, 105*(2), 203–206. https://doi.org/10.5195/JMLA.2017.88

Foster, S., Mohler-Kuo, M., Tay, L., Hothorn, T., & Seibold, H. (2019). Estimating patient-specific treatment advantages in the 'Treatment for Adolescents with Depression Study'. *Journal of Psychiatric Research, 112*, 61–70. https://doi.org/10.1016/j.jpsychires.2019.02.021

Franklin, J. C., Jamieson, J. P., Glenn, C. R., & Nock, M. K. (2015). How developmental psychopathology theory and research can inform the research domain criteria (RDoC) project. *Journal of Clinical Child & Adolescent Psychology, 44*(2), 280–290. https://doi.org/10.1080/15374416.2013.873981

Freeman, J., Benito, K., Herren, J., Kemp, J., Sung, J., Georgiadis, C., Arora, A., Walther, M., & Garcia, A. (2018). Evidence base update of psychosocial treatments for pediatric obsessive-compulsive disorder: Evaluating, improving, and transporting what works. *Journal of Clinical Child & Adolescent Psychology, 47*(5), 669–698. https://doi.org/10.1080/15374416.2018.1496443

Freeman, J., Garcia, A., Frank, H., Benito, K., Conelea, C., Walther, M., & Edmunds, J. (2014). Evidence base update for psychosocial treatments for pediatric obsessive-compulsive disorder. *Journal of Clinical Child & Adolescent Psychology, 43*(1), 7–26. https://doi.org/10.1080/15374416.2013.804386

Fristad, M. A., Goldberg-Arnold, J. S., & Leffler, J. M. (2011). *Psychotherapy for children with bipolar and depressive disorders.* New York, NY: Guilford

Fristad, M. A., & MacPherson, H. A. (2014). Evidence-based psychosocial treatments for child and adolescent bipolar spectrum disorders. *Journal of Clinical Child & Adolescent Psychology, 43*(3), 339–355. https://doi.org/10.1080/15374416.2013.822309

Garland, A. F., Haine-Schlagel, R., Brookman-Frazee, L., Baker-Ericzen, M., Trask, E., & Fawley-King, K. (2013). Improving community-based mental health care for children: Translating knowledge into action. *Administration and Policy in Mental Health and Mental Health Services Research, 40*, 6–22. https://doi.org/10.1007/s10488-012-0450-8

George, M., Taylor, L., Schmidt, S. C., & Weist, M. D. (2013). A review of school mental health programs in SAMHSA's national registry of evidence-based programs and practices. *Psychiatric Services, 64*(5), 483–486. https://doi.org/10.1176/appi.ps.000502012

Gholami, R., & Fakhari, N. (2017). Support vector machine: Principles, parameters, and applications. In P. Samui, S. S. Roy, & V. E. Balas (Eds.), *Handbook of neural computation.* Elsevier Science. https://doi.org/10.1016/B978-0-12-811318-9.00027-2

Gibbs, J. C., Potter, G. B., & Goldstein, A. P. (1995). *The EQUIP Program: Teaching youth to think and act responsibly through a peer-helping approach.* Champaign, IL: Research Press.

Glenn, C. R., Esposito, E. C., Porter, A. C., & Robinson, D. J. (2019). Evidence base update of psychosocial treatments for self-injurious thoughts and behaviors in youth. *Journal of Clinical Child & Adolescent Psychology, 48*(3), 357–392. https://doi.org/10.1080/15374416.2019.1591281

Glenn, C. R., Franklin, J. C., & Nock, M. K. (2015). Evidence-based psychosocial treatments for self-injurious thoughts and behaviors in youth. *Journal of Clinical Child & Adolescent Psychology, 44*(1), 1–29. https://doi.org/10.1080/15374416.2014.945211

Goods, K. S., Ishijima, E., Chang, Y.-C., & Kasari, C. (2013). Preschool based JASPER intervention in minimally verbal children with autism: Pilot RCT. *Journal of Autism and Developmental Disorders, 43*, 1050–1056 https://doi.org/10.1007/s10803-012-1644-3

Gunlicks-Stoessel, M., Mufson, L., Bernstein, G., Westervelt, A., Reigstad, K., Klimes-Dougan, B., Cullen, K., Murray, A., & Vock, D. (2019). Critical decision points for augmenting interpersonal psychotherapy for depressed adolescents: A pilot sequential multiple assignment randomized trial. *Journal of the American Academy of Child & Adolescent Psychiatry, 58*(1), 80–91. https://doi.org/10.1016/j.jaac.2018.06.032

Gunlicks-Stoessel, M., Mufson, L., Westervelt, A., Almirall, D., & Murphy, S. (2016). A pilot SMART for developing an adaptive treatment strategy for adolescent depression. *Journal of Clinical Child & Adolescent Psychology, 45*(4), 480–494. https://doi.org/10.1080/15374416.2015.1015133

Gutermann, J., Schreiber, F., Matulis, S., Schwartzkopff, L., Deppe, J., & Steil, R. (2016). Psychological treatments for symptoms of posttraumatic stress disorder in children, adolescents, and young adults: A meta-analysis. *Clinical Child and Family Psychology Review, 19*(2), 77–93. https://doi.org/10.1007/s10567-016-0202-5

Hankin, B. L. (2019). A choose your own adventure story: Conceptualizing depression in children and adolescents from traditional DSM and alternative latent dimensional approaches. *Behaviour Research and Therapy, 118*, 94–100. https://doi.org/10.1016/j.brat.2019.04.006

Hankin, B. L., Davis, E. P., Snyder, H., Young, J. F., Glynn, L. M., & Sandman, C. A. (2017). Temperament factors and dimensional, latent bifactor models of child psychopathology: Transdiagnostic and specific associations in two youth samples. *Psychiatry Research, 252*, 139–146. https://doi.org/10.1016/j.psychres.2017.02.061

Harpaz-Rotem, I., Leslie, D., & Rosenheck, R. A. (2004). Treatment retention among children entering a new episode of mental health care. *Psychiatric Services, 55*(9), 1022–1028. https://doi.org/10.1176/appi.ps.55.9.1022

Hawley, K. M., & Weisz, J. R. (2003). Child, parent, and therapist (dis)agreement on target problems in outpatient therapy: The therapist's dilemma and its implications. *Journal of Consulting and Clinical Psychology, 71*(1), 62–70. https://doi.org/10.1037/0022-006X.71.1.62

Havighurst, S. S., Wilson, K. R., Harley, A. E., Kehoe, C., Efron, D., & Prior, M. R. (2013). "Tuning into kids": Reducing young children's behavior problems using an emotion coaching parenting program. *Child Psychiatry and Human Development, 44*(2), 247–264. https://doi.org/10.1007/s10578-012-0322-1

Hendriks, A. M., Bartels, M., Colins, O. F., & Finkenauer, C. (2018). Childhood aggression: A synthesis of reviews and meta-analyses to reveal patterns and opportunities for prevention and intervention strategies. *Neuroscience and Biobehavioral Reviews, 91*, 278–291. https://doi.org/10.1016/j.neubiorev.2018.03.021

Henggeler, S. W., Letourneau, E. J., Chapman, J. E., Borduin, C. M., Schewe, P. A., & McCart, M. R. (2009). Mediators of change for multisystemic therapy with juvenile sexual offenders. *Journal of Consulting and Clinical Psychology, 77*(3), 451–462. https://doi.org/10.1037/a0013971

Henggeler, S. W., & Schaeffer, C. (2017). Treating serious antisocial behavior using Multisystemic Therapy. In J. R. Weisz & A. E. Kazdin (Eds.), *Evidence-based psychotherapies for children and adolescents* (3rd ed., pp. 197–214). New York, NY: Guilford Press.

Heron, K. E., Everhart, R. S., McHale, S. M., & Smyth, J. M. (2017). Using mobile-technology-based ecological momentary assessment (EMA)

methods with youth: A systematic review and recommendations. *Journal of Pediatric Psychology, 42*(10), 1087–1107. https://doi.org/10.1093/jpepsy/jsx078

Higa-Mcmillan, C., Francis, S., Rith-Najarian, L., & Chorpita, B. (2015). Evidence base update: 50 years of research on treatment for child and adolescent anxiety. *Journal of Clinical Child & Adolescent Psychology, 45*(2), 1–23. https://doi.org/10.1080/15374416.2015.1046177

Hirshfeld-Becker, D. R., Masek, B., Henin, A., Blakely, L. R., Pollock-Wurman, R. A., McQuade, J., DePetrillo, L., Briesch, J., Ollendick, T. H., Rosenbaum, J. F., & Biederman, J. (2010). Cognitive behavioral therapy for 4- to 7-year-old children with anxiety disorders: A randomized clinical trial. *Journal of Consulting and Clinical Psychology, 78*(4), 498–510 https://doi.org/10.1037/a0019055

Hogendoorn, S. M., Prins, P. J., Boer, F., Vervoort, L., Wolters, L. H., Moorlag, H., Nauta, M. H., Garst, H., Hartman, C. A., & de Haan, E. (2014). Mediators of cognitive behavioral therapy for anxiety-disordered children and adolescents: Cognition, perceived control, and coping. *Journal of Clinical Child & Adolescent Psychology, 43*(3), 486–500. https://doi.org/10.1080/15374416.2013.807736

Hogue, A., Henderson, C. E., Ozechowski, T. J., & Robbins, M. S. (2014). Evidence base on outpatient behavioral treatments for adolescent substance use: Updates and recommendations 2007–2013. *Journal of Clinical Child & Adolescent Psychology, 43*(5), 695–720. https://doi.org/10.1080/15374416.2014.915550

Hollis, C., Falconer, C. J., Martin, J. L., Whittington, C., Stockton, S., Glazebrook, C., & Davies, E. B. (2017). Annual research review: Digital health interventions for children and young people with mental health problems-A systematic and meta-review. *Journal of Child Psychology and Psychiatry, 58,* 474–503. https://doi.org/10.1111/jcpp.12663

Horvath, A. O., Del Re, A. C., Flückiger, C., & Symonds, D. (2011). Alliance in individual therapy. *Psychotherapy, 48*(1), 9–16. https://doi.org/10.1037/a0022186

Houts, A.C. (2008). Parent guide to enuresis treatment [PDF file]. http://drhouts.com/pdfs/100_PARENT_GUIDE_6th_Ed_2008.pdf

Houts, A. C. (2010). Behavioral treatment for enuresis. In J. R. Weisz & A. E. Kazdin (Eds.), *Evidence-based psychotherapies for children and adolescents* (2nd ed., pp. 359–374). New York: Guilford.

Huey, S. J., Henggeler, S. W., Rowland, M. D., Halliday-Boykins, C. A., Cunningham, P. B., Pickrel, S. G., & Edwards, J. (2004). Multisystemic therapy effects on attempted suicide by youths presenting psychiatric emergencies. *Journal of the American Academy of Child & Adolescent Psychiatry, 43*(2), 183–190. https://doi.org/10.1097/00004583-200402000-00014

Huey Jr., S. J., & Polo, A. J. (2008). Evidence-based psychosocial treatments for ethnic minority youth. *Journal of Clinical Child and Adolescent Psychology, 37*(1), 262–301. https://doi.org/10.1080/15374410701820174

Insel, T., Cuthbert, B., Garvey, M., Heinssen, R., Pine, D. S., Quinn, K., Sanislow, C., & Wang, P. (2010). Research domain criteria (RDoC): Toward a new classification framework for research on mental disorders. *American Journal of Psychiatry, 167*(7), 748–751. https://doi.org/10.1176/appi.ajp.2010.09091379

Insel, T. R., & Cuthbert, B. N. (2015). Brain disorders? Precisely. *Science, 348*(6234), 499–500. https://doi.org/10.1126/science.aab2358

Jayson D, Wood A, Kroll L, Fraser J, Harrington R (1998) Which depressed patients respond to cognitive-behavioral treatment? *Journal of the American Academy of Child & Adolescent Psychiatry, 37*(1), 35–39. https://doi.org/10.1097/00004583-199801000-00014

Jaycox, L., Reivich, K., Gillham, J. E. & Seligman, M. E. P. (1994). Prevention of depressive symptoms in school children. *Behavioral Research and Therapy, 32*(8), 801–816. https://doi.org/10.1016/0005-7967(94)90160-0

Jernigan, T. L., Brown, T. T., Jr, Hagler, D. J., Jr, Akshoomoff, N., Bartsch, H., Newman, E., Thompson, W. K., Bloss, C. S., Murray, S. S., Schork, N., Kennedy, D. N., Kuperman, J. M., McCabe, C., Chung, Y., Libiger, O., Maddox, M., Casey, B. J., Chang, L., Ernst, T. M., Frazier, J. A., ... Pediatric Imaging, Neurocognition and Genetics Study (2015). *The Pediatric Imaging, Neurocognition, and Genetics (PING) data repository*. NeuroImage, 124(Pt B), 1149–1154. https://doi.org/10.1016/j.neuroimage.2015.04.057

Johnson, B.T. (2012). Meta-analysis of single-session behavioral interventions to prevent sexually transmitted infections: Implications for bundling prevention packages. *American Journal of Public Health, 102,* e34–e44. https://doi.org/10.2105/AJPH.2012.300968

Kaminski, J. W., & Claussen, A. H. (2017). Evidence base update for psychosocial treatments for disruptive behaviors in children. *Journal of Clinical Child & Adolescent Psychology, 46*(4), 477–499. https://doi.org/10.1080/15374416.2017.1310044

Karyotaki, E., Kleiboer, A., Smit, F., Turner, D. T., Pastor, A. M., Andersson, G., Berger, T., Botella, C., Breton, J. M., Carlbring, P., Christensen, H., de Graaf, E., Griffiths, K., Donker, T., Farrer, L., Huibers, M. J., Lenndin, J., Mackinnon, A., Meyer, B., Moritz, S., ... Cuijpers, P. (2015). Predictors of treatment dropout in self-guided web-based interventions for depression: An 'individual patient data' meta-analysis. *Psychological Medicine, 45*(13), 2717–2726. https://doi.org/10.1017/S0033291715000665

Kasari, C., Freeman, S., & Paparella, T. (2006). Joint attention and symbolic play in young children with autism: A randomized controlled intervention study. *Journal of Child Psychology and Psychiatry, 47,* 611–620. https://doi.org/10.1111/j.1469-7610.2005.01567.x

Kaufman, N. K., Rohde, P., Seeley, J. R., Clarke, G. N., & Stice, E. (2005). Potential mediators of cognitive-behavioral therapy for adolescents with co-morbid major depression and conduct disorder. *Journal of Consulting and Clinical Psychology, 73*(1), 38–46. https://doi.org/10.1037/0022-006X.73.1.38

Kazdin, A. E. (2000). *Psychotherapy for children and adolescent: Directions for Research.* New York, NY: Oxford University Press. https://doi.org/10.1093/med:psych/9780195126181.001.0001

Kazdin, A. E. (2007). Mediators and mechanisms of change in psychotherapy research. *Annual Review of Clinical Psychology, 3,* 1–27. https://doi.org/10.1146/annurev.clinpsy.3.022806.091432

Kazdin, A. E. (2011). *Single-case research designs: Methods for clinical and applied settings.* Oxford, UK: Oxford University Press.

Kazdin, A. E. (2017). Parent management training and problem-solving skills training for child and adolescent conduct problems. In J. R. Weisz & A. E. Kazdin (Eds.), *Evidence-based psychotherapies for children and adolescents* (3rd ed., pp. 142–158). New York, NY: Guilford Press.

Kazdin, A. (2018). *Innovations in psychosocial interventions and their delivery: Leveraging cutting-edge science to improve the world's mental health.* Oxford: Oxford University Press USA - OSO. https://doi.org/10.1093/med-psych/9780190463281.001.0001

Kazdin, A. E., Bass, D., Ayers, W. A., & Rodgers, A. (1990). Empirical and clinical focus of child and adolescent psychotherapy research. *Journal of Consulting & Clinical Psychology, 58*(6), 729–740. https://doi.org/10.1037/0022-006X.58.6.729

Kazdin, A. E., & Weisz, J. R. (1998). Identifying and developing empirically supported child and adolescent treatments. *Journal of Consulting and Clinical Psychology, 66*(1), 19–36. https://doi.org/10.1037/0022-006X.66.1.19

Keel, P. K., & Haedt, A. (2008). Evidence-based psychosocial treatments for eating problems and eating disorders. *Journal of Child and Adolescent Clinical Psychology, 37*(1), 39–61. https://doi.org/10.1080/15374410701817832

Kelley, S. D., & Bickman, L. (2009). Beyond outcomes monitoring: Measurement feedback systems (MFS) in child and adolescent clinical practice. *Current Opinion in Psychiatry, 22*(4), 363–368. https://doi.org/10.1097/YCO.0b013e32832c9162

Kendall, P. C. (1998). Empirically supported psychological therapies [Special section]. *Journal of Consulting and Clinical Psychology, 66*(1), 3–167. https://doi.org/10.1037/0022-006X.66.1.3

Kendall, P. C., Crawford, E. A., Kagan, E. R., Furr, J. M., & Podell, J. L. (2017). Child-focused treatment for anxiety. In J. R. Weisz & A. E. Kazdin (Eds.), *Evidence-based psychotherapies for children and adolescents* (3rd ed., pp. 17–34). New York, NY: Guilford Press.

Kendall, P. C., Cummings, C. M., Villabø, M. A., Narayanan, M. K., Treadwell, K., Birmaher, B., Compton, S., Piacentini, J., Sherrill, J., Walkup, J., Gosch, E., Keeton, C., Ginsburg, G., Suveg, C., & Albano, A. M. (2016). Mediators of change in the Child/Adolescent Anxiety Multimodal Treatment Study. *Journal of Consulting and Clinical Psychology, 84*(1), 1–14. https://doi.org/10.1037/a0039773

Kendall, P. C., & Treadwell, K. H. (2007). The role of self-statements as a mediator in treatment for youth with anxiety disorders. *Journal of Consulting and Clinical Psychology, 75*(3), 380–389. https://doi.org/10.1037/0022-006X.75.3.380

Kennedy, S. M., Bilek, E. L., & Ehrenreich-May, J. (2019). A randomized controlled pilot trial of the unified protocol for transdiagnostic treatment of emotional disorders in children. *Behavior Modification, 43*(3), 330–360 https://doi.org/10.1177/0145445517753940

Kenney, M., & Singh, G. (2016). Adverse childhood experiences among American Indian/Alaska native children: The 2011–2012 National Survey of Children's Health. *Scientifica, 2016*, 1–14. https://doi.org/10.1155/2016/7424239

Kessler, R. C., Berglund, P., Demler, O., Jin, R., Merikangas, K. R., & Walters, E. E. (2005). Lifetime prevalence and age-of-onset distributions of DSM-IV disorders in the National Comorbidity Survey Replication. *Archives of General Psychiatry, 62*(6), 593–602. https://doi.org/10.1001/archpsyc.62.6.593

Kim, J.-W., Sharma, V., & Ryan, N. D. (2015). Predicting methylphenidate response in ADHD using machine learning approaches. *International Journal of Neuropsychopharmacology, 18*(11), 1–7. https://doi.org/10.1093/ijnp/pyv052

Kininger, R. L., O'Dell, S. M., & Schultz, B. K. (2018). The feasibility and effectiveness of school-based modular therapy: A systematic literature review. *School Mental Health, 10*, 339–351. https://doi.org/10.1007/s12310-018-9270-7

Klasnja, P., Hekler, E. B., Shiffman, S., Boruvka, A., Almirall, D., Tewari, A., & Murphy, S. A. (2015). Microrandomized trials: An experimental design for developing just-in-time adaptive interventions. *Health Psychology, 34*(Suppl), 1220–1228. https://doi.org/10.1037/hea0000305

Kolko, D. J., Dorn, L. D., Bukstein, O. G., Pardini, D., Holden, E. A., & Hart, J. (2009). Community vs. clinic-based modular treatment of children with early-onset ODD or CD: A clinical trial with 3–year follow-up. *Journal of Abnormal Child Psychology, 37*(5), 591–609. https://doi.org/10.1007/s10802-009-9303-7

Kolko, D.J., & Perrin, E (2014). The integration of behavioral health interventions in children's health care: Services, science, and suggestions. *Journal of Clinical Child and Adolescent Psychology, 43*(2), 216–228. https://doi.org/10.1080/15374416.2013.862804

Kurtz, S. (2009). *Camp Brave Buddies, 2009: Summer day camp for children with selective mutism.* Unpublished treatment manual.

Laney, D. (2001). 3–D data management: Controlling data volume, velocity and variety. Application Delivery Strategies by META Group Inc. http://blogs.gartner.com/doug-laney/files/2012/01/ad949-3D-Data-Management-Controlling-Data Volume-Velocity-and-Variety.pdf

Lau, W.-Y., Chan, C. K.-Y., Li, J. C.-H., & Au, T. K.-F. (2010*).* Effectiveness of group cognitive-behavioral treatment for childhood anxiety in community clinics. *Behaviour Research and Therapy, 48*(11), 1067–1077. https://doi.org/10.1016/j.brat.2010.07.007

Lebowitz, E. R., Gee, D. G., Pine, D. S., & Silverman, W. K. (2018). Implications of the Research Domain Criteria project for childhood anxiety and its disorders. *Clinical Psychology Review, 64*, 99–109. https://doi.org/10.1016/j.cpr.2018.01.005

Lei, H., Nahum-Shani, I., Lynch, K., Oslin, D., & Murphy, S. A. (2012). A "SMART" design for building individualized treatment sequences. *Annual Review of Clinical Psychology, 8*, 21–48. https://doi.org/10.1146/annurev-clinpsy-032511-143152

Levitt, E. E. (1957). The results of psychotherapy with children: An evaluation. *Journal of Consulting Psychology, 21*(3), 189–196. https://doi.org/10.1037/h0039957

Levitt, E. E. (1963). Psychotherapy with children: A further evaluation. *Behaviour Research and Therapy, 1*(1), 45–51. https://doi.org/10.1016/0005-7967(63)90007-X

Lewey, J. H., Smith, C. L., Burcham, B., Saunders, N. L., Elfallal, D., & O'Toole, S. K. (2018). Comparing the effectiveness of EMDR and TF-CBT for children and adolescents: A meta-analysis. *Journal of Child & Adolescent Trauma, 11*(4), 457–472. https://doi.org/10.1007/s40653-018-0212-1

Lilienfeld, S. O., & Treadway, M. T. (2016). Clashing diagnostic approaches: DSM-ICD versus RDoC. *Annual Review of Clinical Psychology, 12*, 435–463. https://doi.org/10.1146/annurev-clinpsy-021815-093122

Lind, M. N., Byrne, M. L., Wicks, G., Smidt, A. M., & Allen, N. B. (2018). The Effortless Assessment of Risk States (EARS) tool: An interpersonal approach to mobile sensing. *JMIR Mental Health, 5*(3), e10334. https://doi.org/10.2196/10334

Lindhiem, O., Kolko, D. J., & Cheng, Y. (2012). Predicting psychotherapy benefit: A probabilistic and individualized approach. *Behavior Therapy, 43*(2), 381–392. https://doi.org/10.1016/j.beth.2011.08.004

Lochman, J. E., & Wells, K. C. (2002). Contextual social-cognitive mediators and child outcome: A test of the theoretical model in the Coping Power Program. *Development and Psychopathology, 14*(4), 945–967. https://doi.org/10.1017/S0954579402004157

Lock, J. (2015). An update on evidence-based psychosocial treatments for eating disorders in children and adolescents. *Journal of Clinical Child & Adolescent Psychology, 44*(5), 707–721. https://doi.org/10.1080/15374416.2014.971458

Lonigan, C. J., Elbert, J. C., & Johnson, S. B. (1998). Empirically supported psychosocial interventions for children: An overview. *Journal of Clinical Child Psychology, 27*(2), 138–145. https://doi.org/10.1207/s15374424jccp2702_1

Lundahl, B., Risser, H.J., & Lovejoy, M.C., (2006). A meta-analysis of parent training: Moderators and follow-up effects. *Clinical Psychology Review, 26*(1), 86–104. https://doi.org/10.1016/j.cpr.2005.07.004

Lundkvist-Houndoumadi, I., Hougaard, E., & Thastum, M. (2014). Pre-treatment child and family characteristics as predictors of outcome in cognitive behavioural therapy for youth anxiety disorders. *Nordic Journal of Psychiatry, 68*(8), 524–535. https://doi.org/10.3109/08039488.2014.903295

Lyon, A. R., Bruns, E. J., Ludwig, K., Vander Stoep, A., Pullmann, M. D., Dorsey, S., Eaton, J., Hendrix, E., & McCauley, E. (2015). The Brief Intervention for School Clinicians (BRISC): A mixed-methods evaluation of feasibility, acceptability, and contextual appropriateness. *School Mental Health, 7*, 273–286. https://doi.org/10.1007/s12310-015-9153-0

Lyon, A. R., Lewis, C. C., Boyd, M. R., Hendrix, E., & Liu, F. (2016). Capabilities and characteristics of digital measurement feedback systems: Results from a comprehensive review. *Administration and Policy in Mental Health and Mental Health Services Research, 43*, 441–466. https://doi.org/10.1007/s10488-016-0719-4

MacPherson, H. A., Weinstein, S. M., Henry, D. B., & West, A. E. (2016). Mediators in the randomized trial of child- and family-focused cognitive-behavioral therapy for pediatric bipolar disorder. *Behaviour Research and Therapy, 85*, 60–71. https://doi.org/10.1016/j.brat.2016.08.014

Manassis, K., Mendlowitz, S. L., Scapillato, D., Avery, D., Fiksenbaum, L., Freire, M., Monga, S., & Owens, M. (2002) Group and individual cognitive-behavioral therapy for childhood anxiety disorders: A randomized trial. *Journal of the American Academy of Child & Adolescent Psychiatry, 41*(12), 1423–1430. https://doi.org/10.1097/00004583-200212000-00013

March, J., Silva, S., Petrycki, S., Curry, J., Wells, K., Fairbank, J., Burns, B., Domino, M., McNulty, S., Vitiello, B., Severe, J., & Treatment for Adolescents with Depression Study (TADS) Team. (2004). Fluoxetine, cognitive-behavioral therapy, and their combination for adolescents with depression: Treatment for Adolescents with Depression Study (TADS) randomized controlled trial. *JAMA 292* (7), 807–820. https://doi.org/10.1001/jama.292.7.807

Maric, M., Prins, P. J. M., & Ollendick, T. H., *Moderators and mediators of youth treatment outcomes* (2015). New York: Oxford University Press. https://doi.org/10.1093/med:psych/9780199360345.001.0001

Martel, M. M., Pan, P. M., Hoffmann, M. S., Gadelha, A., do Rosário, M. C., Mari, J. J., Manfro, G. G., Miguel, E. C., Paus, T., Bressan, R. A., Rohde, L. A., & Salum, G. A. (2017). A general psychopathology factor (P factor) in children: Structural model analysis and external validation through familial risk and child global executive function. *Journal of Abnormal Psychology, 126*(1), 137–148. https://doi.org/10.1037/abn0000205

Mathur, S. R., Kavale, K. A., Quinn, M. M., Forness, S. R., & Rutherford, R. B., Jr. (1998). Social skills interventions with students with emotional and behavioral problems: A quantitative synthesis of single-subject research. *Behavioral Disorders, 23*(3), 193–201. https://doi.org/10.1177/019874299802300306

McCart, M. R., & Sheidow, A. J. (2016). Evidence-based psychosocial treatments for adolescents with disruptive behavior. *Journal of Clinical Child & Adolescent Psychology, 45*(5), 529–563. https://doi.org/10.1080/15374416.2016.1146990

McGuire, J., Piacentini, J., Lewin, A., Brennan, E., Murphy, T., & Storch, E. (2015). A meta-analysis of cognitive behavior therapy and medication for child obsessive-compulsive disorder: Moderators of treatment efficacy, response, and remission. *Depression and Anxiety, 32*(8), 580–593. https://doi.org/10.1002/da.22389

McLeod, B. D. (2011). Relation of the alliance with outcomes in youth psychotherapy: A meta-analysis. *Clinical Psychology Review, 31*(4), 603–616. https://doi.org/10.1016/j.cpr.2011.02.001

McNally, R. J. (2019). The network takeover reaches psychopathology. *Behavioral and Brain Sciences, 42*, e15. https://doi.org/10.1017/S0140525X18001073

Meany-Walen, K. K., Bratton, S. C., & Kottman, T. (2014). Effects of Adlerian play therapy on reducing students' disruptive behaviors. *Journal of Counseling & Development, 92*, 47–56. https://doi.org/10.1002/j.1556-6676.2014.00129.x

Mellon, M. W. (2012). Encopresis. In P. Sturmey & M. Hersen (Eds.), *Handbook of evidence-based practice in clinical psychology, volume 1: Child and adolescent disorders* (pp. 361–388). Hoboken, NJ: Wiley.

Meichenbaum, D., & Goodman, S. (1971). Training impulsive children to talk to themselves: A means of developing self-control. *Journal of Abnormal Psychology, 77(2)*, 115–126. https://doi.org/10.1037/h0030773

Merikangas, K. R., He, J. P., Burstein, M., Swanson, S. A., Avenevoli, S., Cui, L., Benjet, C., Georgiades, K., & Swendsen, J. (2010). Lifetime prevalence of mental disorders in US adolescents: Results from the National Comorbidity Survey Replication-Adolescent Supplement (NCS-A). *Journal of the American Academy of Child & Adolescent Psychiatry, 49(10)*, 980–989. https://doi.org/10.1016/j.jaac.2010.05.017

Merry, S. N., Stasiak, K., Shepherd, M., Frampton, C., Fleming, T., & Lucassen, M. F. (2012). The effectiveness of SPARX, a computerised self-help intervention for adolescents seeking help for depression: Randomised controlled non-inferiority trial. *British Medical Journal, 344*, e2598. https://doi.org/10.1136/bmj.e2598

Michelini, G., Barch, D. M., Tian, Y., Watson, D., Klein, D. N., & Kotov, R. (2019). Delineating and validating higher-order dimensions of psychopathology in the Adolescent Brain Cognitive Development (ABCD) study. bioRxiv, 548057. https://doi.org/10.1038/s41398-019-0593-4

Mikami, A. Y., Griggs, M. S., Lerner, M. D., Emeh, C. C., Reuland, M. M., Jack, A., & Anthony, M. R. (2012). A randomized trial of a classroom intervention to increase peers' social inclusion of children with attention-deficit hyperactivity disorder. *Journal of Consulting and Clinical Psychology, 81(1)*, 100–112. https://doi.org/10.1037/a0029654

Mikami, A. Y., Lerner, M. D., Griggs, M. S., McGrath, A., & Calhoun, C. D. (2010). Parental influence on children with attention-deficit/hyperactivity disorder: II. Results of a pilot intervention training parents as friendship coaches for children. *Journal of Abnormal Child Psychology, 38(6)*, 737–749. https://doi.org/10.1007/s10802-010-9403-4

Miklowitz, D. J., George, E. L., Axelson, D. A., Kim, E. Y., Birmaher, B., Schneck, C., Beresford, C., Craighead, W. E., & Brent, D. A. (2004). Family-focused treatment for adolescents with bipolar disorder. *Journal of Affective Disorders, 82*, S113–S128. https://doi.org/10.1016/j.jad.2004.05.020

Miller, W. R., & Rollnick, S. (1991). *Motivational interviewing: Preparing people to change addictive behaviors,* New York: Guilford.

Mittal, V. A., & Wakschlag, L. S. (2017). Research Domain Criteria (RDoC) grows up: Strengthening neurodevelopmental investigation within the RDoC framework. *Journal of Affective Disorders, 216*, 30–35. https://doi.org/10.1016/j.jad.2016.12.011

Miu, A. S., & Yeager, D. S. (2015). Preventing symptoms of depression by teaching adolescents that people can change: Effects of a brief incremental theory of personality intervention at 9–month follow-up. *Clinical Psychological Science, 3(5)*, 726–743. https://doi.org/10.1177/2167702614548317

Mohr, D. C., Ho, J., Hart, T. L., Baron, K. G., Berendsen, M., Beckner, V., Cai, X., Cuijpers, P., Spring, B., Kinsinger, S. W., Schroder, K. E., & Duffecy, J. (2014). Control condition design and implementation features in controlled trials: A meta-analysis of trials evaluating psychotherapy for depression. *Translational Behavioral Medicine, 4(4)*, 407–423. https://doi.org/10.1007/s13142-014-0262-3

MTA Cooperative Group. (1999). A 14–month randomized clinical trial of treatment strategies for attention-deficit/hyperactivity disorder. *Archives of General Psychiatry, 56(12)*, 1073–1086. https://doi.org/10.1001/archpsyc.56.12.1073

Mufson, L., Moreau, D., Weissman, M. M., & Klerman, G. (1993). *Interpersonal Psychotherapy for Depressed Adolescents.* New York, NY: Guilford Press.

Mullarkey, M. C., Marchetti, I., & Beevers, C. G. (2019). Using network analysis to identify central symptoms of adolescent depression. *Journal of Clinical Child & Adolescent Psychology, 48(4)*, 656–668. https://doi.org/10.1080/15374416.2018.1437735

Mullarkey, M. C., Marchetti, I., Bluth, K., Carlson, C. L., & Beevers, C. G. (2018). Symptom centrality, not severity or endorsement rate, identifies adolescent depression symptoms most strongly associated with life satisfaction. *PsyArXiv.* https://doi.org/10.31234/osf.io/79hcj

Murphy, R., & Hutton, P. (2018). Practitioner review: Therapist variability, patient-reported therapeutic alliance, and clinical outcomes in adolescents undergoing mental health treatment- A systematic review and meta-analysis. *Journal of Child Psychology and Psychiatry, 59(1)*, 5–19. https://doi.org/10.1111/jcpp.12767

Naar, S., Ellis, D., Idalski Carcone, A., Jacques-Tiura, A. J., Cunningham, P., Templin, T., Hartlieb, K. B., & Jen, K. L. (2019). Outcomes from a sequential multiple assignment randomized trial of weight loss strategies for African American adolescents with obesity. *Annals of Behavioral Medicine, 53(10)*, 928–938. https://doi.org/10.1093/abm/kaz003

Naar-King, S., Ellis, D. A., Idalski Carcone, A., Templin, T., Jacques-Tiura, A. J., Brogan Hartlieb, K., Cunningham, P., & Jen, K. L. C. (2016). Sequential multiple assignment randomized trial (SMART) to construct weight loss interventions for African American adolescents. *Journal of Clinical Child & Adolescent Psychology, 45(4)*, 428–441. https://doi.org/10.1080/15374416.2014.971459

Nahum-Shani, I., Smith, S. N., Spring, B. J., Collins, L. M., Witkiewitz, K., Tewari, A., & Murphy, S. A. (2017). Just-in-time adaptive interventions (JITAIs) in mobile health: Key components and design principles for ongoing health behavior support. *Annals of Behavioral Medicine, 52(6)*, 446–462. https://doi.org/10.1007/s12160-016-9830-8

Ng, M. Y., DiVasto, K. A., Cootner, S., Gonzalez, N., & Weisz, J. R. (2020). What do 30 years of randomized trials tell us about how psychotherapy improves youth depression? A systematic review of candidate mediators. *Clinical Psychology: Science and Practice. Advance online publication.* https://doi.org/10.1111/cpsp.12367

Ng, M. Y., & Weisz, J. (2016). Annual research review: Building a science of personalized intervention for youth mental health. *Journal of Child Psychology and Psychiatry, 57(3)*, 216–236. https://doi.org/10.1111/jcpp.12470

Ng, M. Y., & Weisz, J. R. (2017). Personalizing evidence-based psychotherapy for children and adolescents in clinical care. In J. R. Weisz & A. E. Kazdin, (Eds), *Evidence-based psychotherapies for children and adolescents* (3rd ed., pp. 501–519). New York: Guilford.

Nilsen, T., Eisemann, S., & Kvernmo, M. (2013). Predictors and moderators of outcome in child and adolescent anxiety and depression: A systematic review of psychological treatment studies. *European Child & Adolescent Psychiatry, 22(2)*, 69–87. https://doi.org/10.1007/s00787-012-0316-3

OCEBM Levels of Evidence Working Group. (2011). The Oxford 2011 levels of evidence. http://www.cebm.net/index.aspx?o=5653

Ollendick, T. H., & Davis III, T. E. (2013). One-session treatment for specific phobias: a review of Öst's single-session exposure with children and adolescents. *Cognitive Behaviour Therapy, 42(4)*, 275–283. https://doi.org/10.1080/16506073.2013.773062

Onnela, J. P., & Rauch, S. L. (2016). Harnessing smartphone-based digital phenotyping to enhance behavioral and mental health. *Neuropsychopharmacology, 41(7)*, 1691. https://doi.org/10.1038/npp.2016.7

Or, F., Torous, J., & Onnela, J. P. (2017). High potential but limited evidence: Using voice data from smartphones to monitor and diagnose mood disorders. *Psychiatric Rehabilitation Journal, 40(3)*, 320. https://doi.org/10.1037/prj0000279

Or, F., Torous, J., Simms, J., & Onnela, J. P. (2017) Smartphone applications for monitoring mood disorders: A systematic review. Manuscript submitted for publication.

Patalay, P., Fonagy, P., Deighton, J., Belsky, J., Vostanis, P., & Wolpert, M. (2015). A general psychopathology factor in early adolescence. *The British Journal of Psychiatry, 207(1)*, 15–22. https://doi.org/10.1192/bjp.bp.114.149591

Pelham, W. E., Gnagy, E. M., Greiner, A. R., Fabiano, G. A., Waschbusch, D. A., & Coles, E. K. (2017). Summer treatment program for attention-deficit/hyperactivity disorder. In J. R. Weisz & A. E. Kazdin (Eds.), *Evidence-based psychotherapies for children and adolescents* (3rd ed., pp. 215–232). New York, NY: Guilford Press.

Pelham, W. E., & Fabiano, G. A. (2008). Evidence-based psychosocial treatments for attention-deficit/hyperactivity disorder. *Journal of Clinical Child and Adolescent Psychology, 37(1)*, 184–214. https://doi.org/10.1080/15374410701818681

Pelham Jr, W. E., Fabiano, G. A., Waxmonsky, J. G., Greiner, A. R., Gnagy, E. M., Pelham III, W. E., Coxe, S., Verley, J., Bhatia, I., Hart, K., Karch, K., Konijnendijk, E., Tresco, K., Nahum-Shani, I., & Murphy, S. A. (2016). Treatment sequencing for childhood ADHD: A multiple-randomization study of adaptive medication and behavioral interventions. *Journal of*

Clinical Child & Adolescent Psychology, 45(4), 396–415. https://doi.org/10.1080/15374416.2015.1105138

Pennant, M. E., Loucas, C. E., Whittington, C., Creswell, C., Fonagy, P., Fuggle, P., Kelvin, R., Naqvi, S., Stockton, S., Kendall, T., & Expert Advisory Group (2015). Computerised therapies for anxiety and depression in children and young people: A systematic review and meta-analysis. *Behaviour Research and Therapy, 67*, 1–18. https://doi.org/10.1016/j.brat.2015.01.009

Pina, A. A., Polo, A. J., & Huey, S. J. (2019). Evidence-based psychosocial interventions for ethnic minority youth: The 10–year update. *Journal of Clinical Child & Adolescent Psychology, 48*(2), 179–202. https://doi.org/10.1080/15374416.2019.1567350

Pineda, J., & Dadds, M. R. (2013). Family intervention for adolescents with suicidal behavior: A randomized controlled trial and mediation analysis. *Journal of the American Academy of Child and Adolescent Psychiatry, 52*(8), 851–862 https://doi.org/10.1016/j.jaac.2013.05.015

Pramana, G., Parmanto, B., Lomas, D., Lindhiem, O., Kendall, P. C., & Silk, J. S. (2018). Using mobile health gamification to facilitate cognitive behavioral therapy skills practice in child anxiety treatment: Open clinical trial. *JMIR Serious Games, 6*(2), e9. https://doi.org/10.2196/games.8902

Rabbi, M., Philyaw-Kotov, M., Lee, J., Mansour, A., Dent, L., Wang, X., Cunningham, R., Bonar, E., Nahum-Shani, I., Klasnja, P., Walton, M., & Murphy, S. (2017, September). SARA: A mobile app to engage users in health data collection. In *Proceedings of the 2017 ACM International Joint Conference on Pervasive and Ubiquitous Computing and Proceedings of the 2017 ACM International Symposium on Wearable Computers* (pp. 781–789). ACM.

Radovic, A., Vona, P. L., Santostefano, A. M., Ciaravino, S., Miller, E., & Stein, B. D. (2016). Smartphone applications for mental health. *Cyberpsychology, Behavior, and Social Networking, 19*(7), 465–470 https://doi.org/10.1089/cyber.2015.0619

Rathus, J. H., & Miller, A. L. (2014). *Dialectical behavior therapy skills manual for adolescents.* New York, NY: The Guilford Press.

Regier, D. A., Narrow, W. E., Clarke, D. E., Kraemer, H. C., Kuramoto, S. J., Kuhl, E. A., & Kupfer, D. J. (2013). DSM-5 field trials in the United States and Canada, Part II: Test-retest reliability of selected categorical diagnoses. *The American Journal of Psychiatry, 170*(1), 59–70. https://doi.org/10.1176/appi.ajp.2012.12070999

Richardson, L. P., Ludman, E., McCauley, E., Lindenbaum, J., Larison, C., Zhou, C., Clarke, G., Brent, D., & Katon, W. (2014). Collaborative care for adolescents with depression in primary care: A randomized clinical trial. *JAMA, 312*(8), 809–816. https://doi.org/10.1001/jama.2014.9259

Richters, J. E. (1992). Depressed mothers as informants about their children: A critical review of the evidence for distortion. *Psychological Bulletin, 112*(3), 485–499. https://doi.org/10.1037/0033-2909.112.3.485

Riosa, P. B., McArthur, B. A., & Preyde, M. (2011). Effectiveness of psychosocial intervention for children and adolescents with comorbid problems: A systematic review. *Child and Adolescent Mental Health, 16*(4), 177–185. https://doi.org/10.1111/j.1475-3588.2011.00609.x

Rohde, P., Clarke, G. N., Lewinsohn, P. M., Seeley, J. R., & Kaufman, N. K. (2001). Impact of comorbidity on a cognitive-behavioral group treatment for adolescent depression. *Journal of the American Academy of Child & Adolescent Psychiatry, 40*(7), 795–802. https://doi.org/10.1097/00004583-200107000-00014

Rogers, S. J., & Vismara, L.A. (2008). Evidence-based comprehensive treatments for early autism. *Journal of Child and Adolescent Clinical Psychology, 37*(1), 8–38. https://doi.org/10.1080/15374410701817808

Rones, M., & Hoagwood, K. (2000). School-based mental health services: A research review. *Clinical Child and Family Psychology Review, 3*, 223–241. https://doi.org/10.1023/A:1026425104386

Rossouw, T. I., & Fonagy, P. (2012). Mentalization-based treatment for self-harm in adolescents: A randomized controlled trial. *Journal of the American Academy of Child and Adolescent Psychiatry, 51*(12), 1304–1313. https://doi.org/10.1016/j.jaac.2012.09.018

Rowland, M. D., Halliday-Boykins, C. A., Henggeler, S. W., Cunningham, P. B., Lee, T. G., Kruesi, M. J., & Shapiro, S. B. (2005). A randomized trial of multisystemic therapy with Hawaii's Felix Class youths. *Journal of Emotional and Behavioral Disorders, 13*(1), 13–23. https://doi.org/10.1177/10634266050130010201

Runyon, M. K., Ryan, E., Kolar, R., & Deblinger, E. (2004). An overview of child physical abuse: Developing an integrated parent-child cognitive-behavioral treatment approach. *Trauma, Violence, & Abuse, 5*(1), 65–85 https://doi.org/10.1177/1524838003259323

Santucci, L. C., & Ehrenreich-May, J. (2013). A randomized controlled trial of the Child Anxiety Multi-Day Program (CAMP) for separation anxiety disorder. *Child Psychiatry & Human Development, 44*, 439–451. https://doi.org/10.1007/s10578-012-0338-6

Schleider, J.L., Burnette, J.L., Widman, L., Hoyt, C.L., & Prinstein, M.J. (2020). Randomized trial of a single-session growth mindset intervention for rural adolescents' internalizing and externalizing problems. *Journal of Clinical Child and Adolescent Psychology, 49*(5), 660–672. https://doi.org/10.1080/15374416.2019.1622123

Schleider, J.L., & Weisz, J.R. (2017a). Little treatments, promising effects? Meta-analysis of single-session interventions for youth psychiatric problems. *Journal of the American Academy of Child & Adolescent Psychiatry, 56*(2), 107–115. https://doi.org/10.1016/j.jaac.2016.11.007

Schleider, J. L., & Weisz, J. R. (2017b). Can less be more? The promise (and perils) of single-session youth mental health interventions. *The Behavior Therapist, 40*, 256–261.

Schleider, J. L., & Weisz, J. R. (2018). A single-session growth mindset intervention for adolescent anxiety and depression: 9-month outcomes of a randomized trial. *Journal of Child Psychology and Psychiatry, 59*, 160–170. https://doi.org/10.1111/jcpp.12811

Scholten, H., & Granic, I. (2019). Use of the principles of design thinking to address limitations of digital mental health interventions for youth. *Journal of Medical Internet Research, 21*(1), e11528. https://doi.org/10.2196/11528

Schork, N. J. (2015). Personalized medicine: Time for one-person trials. *Nature News, 520*(7549), 609–611. https://doi.org/10.1038/520609a

Seibold, H., Zeileis, A., Hothorn, T., 2018. Individual treatment effect prediction for amyotrophic lateral sclerosis patients. *Statistical Methods in Medical Research, 27*(10), 3104–3125. https://doi.org/10.1177/0962280217693034

Selvini-Palazzoli, M., & Viaro, M. (1988). The anorectic process in the family: A six-stage model as a guide for individual therapy. *Family Process, 27*(2), 129–148. https://doi.org/10.1111/j.1545-5300.1988.00129.x

Shapiro, D.A., & Shapiro, D. (1982). Meta-analysis of comparative therapy outcome studies: A replication and refinement. *Psychological Bulletin, 92*(3), 581–604. https://doi.org/10.1037/0033-2909.92.3.581

Shepard, J. A., Poler Jr, J. E., & Grabman, J. H. (2017). Evidence-based psychosocial treatments for pediatric elimination disorders. *Journal of Clinical Child & Adolescent Psychology, 46*(6), 767–797. https://doi.org/10.1080/15374416.2016.1247356

Shiffman, S., Stone, A. A., & Hufford, M. R. (2008). Ecological momentary assessment. *Annual Review in Clinical Psychology, 4*, 1–32. https://doi.org/10.1146/annurev.clinpsy.3.022806.091415

Shin, S.-K. (2009). Effects of a solution-focused program on the reduction of aggressiveness and the improvement of social readjustment for Korean youth probationers. *Journal of Social Service Research, 35*(3), 274–284. https://doi.org/10.1080/01488370902901079

Silk, J. S., Pramana, G., Sequeira, S. L., Lindhiem, O., Kendall, P. C., Rosen, D., & Parmanto, B. (2020). Using a smartphone app and clinician portal to enhance brief cognitive behavioral therapy for childhood anxiety disorders. *Behavior Therapy, 51*(1), 69–84. https://doi.org/10.1016/j.beth.2019.05.002

Silverman, W. K., & Hinshaw, S. P. (2008). The second special issue on evidence-based psychosocial treatments for children and adolescents: A 10–year update. *Journal of Child and Adolescent Clinical Psychology, 37*(1), 1–7. https://doi.org/10.1080/15374410701817725

Silverman, W. K., Ortiz, C. D., Viswesvaran, C., Burns, B. J., Kolko, D. J., Putman, F. W., & Amaya-Jackson, L. (2008). Evidence-based psychosocial treatments for children and adolescents exposed to traumatic events. *Journal of Child and Adolescent Clinical Psychology, 37*(1), 156–183. https://doi.org/10.1080/15374410701818293

Silverman, W. K., Pina, A. A., & Viswesvaran, C. (2008). Evidence-based psychosocial treatments for phobic and anxiety disorders in children and adolescents. *Journal of Child and Adolescent Clinical Psychology, 37*(1), 105–130. https://doi.org/10.1080/15374410701817907

Simon, E., Driessen, S., Lambert, A., & Muris, P. (2019). Challenging anxious cognitions or accepting them? Exploring the efficacy of the cognitive elements of cognitive behaviour therapy and acceptance and commitment therapy in the reduction of children's fear of the dark. *International Journal of Psychology, 55*(1), 90–97. https://doi.org/10.1002/ijop.12540

Slesnick, N., Erdem, G., Bartle-Haring, S., & Brigham, G. S. (2013). Intervention with substance-abusing runaway adolescents and their families: Results of a randomized clinical trial. *Journal of Consulting and Clinical Psychology*, *81*(4), 600–614. https://doi.org/10.1037/a0033463

Smith, M. L., & Glass, G.V. (1977). Meta-analysis of psychotherapy outcome studies. *American Psychologist*, *32*(9), 752–760. https://doi.org/10.1037/0003-066X.32.9.752

Smith, T. (2010). Early and intensive behavioral intervention in autism. In J. R. Weisz & A. E. Kazdin (Eds.), *Evidence-based psychotherapies for children and adolescents*, (2nd ed., pp. 312–326). New York, NY: Guilford Press.

Smith, T., & Iadarola, S. (2015). Evidence base update for autism spectrum disorder. *Journal of Clinical Child & Adolescent Psychology*, *44*(6), 897–922. https://doi.org/10.1080/15374416.2015.1077448

Southam-Gerow, M. A., & Prinstein, M. J. (2014). Evidence base updates: The evolution of the evaluation of psychological treatments for children and adolescents. *Journal of Clinical Child and Adolescent Psychology*, *43*(1), 1–6. https://doi.org/10.1080/15374416.2013.855128

Southam-Gerow, M. A., Weisz, J. R., Chu, B. C., McLeod, B. D., Gordis, E. B., & Connor-Smith, J. K. (2010). Does CBT for youth anxiety outperform usual care in community clinics?: An initial effectiveness test. *Journal of the American Academy of Child & Adolescent Psychiatry*, *49*(10), 1043–1052. https://doi.org/10.1016/j.jaac.2010.06.009

Squeglia, L., Ball, T., Jacobus, J., Brumback, T., Mckenna, B., Nguyen-Louie, T., Sorg, S. F., Paulus, M. P., & Tapert, S. F. (2017). Neural predictors of initiating alcohol use during adolescence. *The American Journal of Psychiatry*, *174*(2), 172–185. https://doi.org/10.1176/appi.ajp.2016.15121587

Stanton, H. E. (1994). Self-hypnosis. *Contemporary Hypnosis*, *11*, 14–18.

Stice, E., Rohde, P., Seeley, J. R., & Gau, J. M. (2010). Testing mediators of intervention effects in randomized controlled trials: An evaluation of three depression prevention programs. *Journal of Consulting and Clinical Psychology*, *78*(2), 273–280. https://doi.org/10.1037/a0018396

Stiffman, A. R., Stelk, W., Horwitz, S. M., Evans, M. E., Outlaw, F. H., & Atkins, M. (2010). A public health approach to children's mental health services: Possible solutions to current service inadequacies. *Administration and Policy in Mental Health and Mental Health Services Research*, *37*, 120–124. https://doi.org/10.1007/s10488-009-0259-2

Stiles-Shields, C., Ho, J., & Mohr, D. C. (2016). A review of design characteristics of cognitive behavioral therapy-informed behavioral intervention technologies for youth with depression and anxiety. *Digital Health*, *2*, 2055207616675706. https://doi.org/10.1177/2055207616675706

The Penn State Methodology Center. (2020, May 7). *Micro-randomized trial FAQ.* https://www.methodology.psu.edu/ra/adap-inter/faq/

Toomey, R. B., Syvertsen, A. K., & Shramko, M. (2018). Transgender adolescent suicide behavior. *Pediatrics*, *142*(4). https://doi.org/10.1542/peds.2017-4218

Treadwell, K. H., & Kendall, P. C. (1996). Self-talk in youth with anxiety disorders: States of mind, content specificity. *Journal of Consulting and Clinical Psychology*, *64*(5), 941–950. https://doi.org/10.1037/0022-006X.64.5.941

Turner, C., O'Gorman, B., Nair, A., & O'Kearney, R. (2018). Moderators and predictors of response to cognitive behaviour therapy for pediatric obsessive-compulsive disorder: A systematic review. *Psychiatry Research*, *261*, 50–60. https://doi.org/10.1016/j.psychres.2017.12.034

Välimäki, M., Anttila, K., Anttila, M., & Lahti, M. (2017). Web-based interventions supporting adolescents and young people with depressive symptoms: Systematic review and meta-analysis. *JMIR mHealth and uHealth*, *5*(12), e180. https://doi.org/10.2196/mhealth.8624

Vazire, S. (2018). Implications of the credibility revolution for productivity, creativity, and progress. *Perspectives on Psychological Science*, *13*(4), 411–417. https://doi.org/10.1177/1745691617751884

Waldman, I. D., Poore, H. E., van Hulle, C., Rathouz, P. J., & Lahey, B. B. (2016). External validity of a hierarchical dimensional model of child and adolescent psychopathology: Tests using confirmatory factor analyses and multivariate behavior genetic analyses. *Journal of Abnormal Psychology*, *125*(8), 1053–1066. https://doi.org/10.1037/abn0000183

Waldron, H. B., Brody, J. L., & Hops, H. (2017). Functional family therapy for adolescent substance use disorders. In J. R. Weisz & A. E. Kazdin (Eds.), *Evidence-based psychotherapies for children and adolescents* (3rd ed., pp. 342–358). New York, NY: Guilford Press.

Waldron, H. B., & Kaminer, Y. (2004). On the learning curve: The emerging evidence supporting cognitive-behavioral therapies for adolescent substance abuse. *Addiction*, *99*(Suppl. 2), 93–105. https://doi.org/10.1111/j.1360-0443.2004.00857.x

Waldron, H. B., & Turner, C. W. (2008). Evidence-based psychosocial treatments for adolescent substance abuse. *Journal of Child and Adolescent Clinical Psychology*, *37*(1), 238–261. https://doi.org/10.1080/15374410701820133

Walkup, J. T., Albano, A. M., Piacentini, J., Birmaher, B., Compton, S. N., Sherrill, J. T., Ginsburg, G. S., Rynn, M. A., McCracken, J., Waslick, B., Iyengar, S., March, J. S., & Kendall, P. C. (2008). Cognitive behavioral therapy, sertraline, or a combination in childhood anxiety. *The New England Journal of Medicine*, *359*, 2753–2766. https://doi.org/10.1056/NEJMoa0804633

Walls, N. E., Freedenthal, S., & Wisneski, H. (2008). Suicidal ideation and attempts among sexual minority youths receiving social services. *Social Work*, *53*(1), 21–29. https://doi.org/10.1093/sw/53.1.21

Weersing, V. R., Jeffreys, M., Do, M. C. T., Schwartz, K. T., & Bolano, C. (2017). Evidence base update of psychosocial treatments for child and adolescent depression. *Journal of Clinical Child & Adolescent Psychology*, *46*(1), 11–43. https://doi.org/10.1080/15374416.2016.1220310

Weersing, V. R., Rozenman, M. S., Maher-Bridge, M., & Campo, J. V. (2012). Anxiety, depression, and somatic distress: Developing a transdiagnostic internalizing toolbox for pediatric practice. *Cognitive and Behavioral Practice*, *19*(1), 68–82. https://doi.org/10.1016/j.cbpra.2011.06.002

Weisz, J., Bearman, S. K., Santucci, L. C., & Jensen-Doss, A. (2017). Initial test of a principle-guided approach to transdiagnostic psychotherapy with children and adolescents. *Journal of Clinical Child & Adolescent Psychology*, *46*(1), 44–58. https://doi.org/10.1080/15374416.2016.1163708

Weisz, J. R., Chorpita, B. F., Palinkas, L. A., Schoenwald, S. K., Miranda, J., Bearman, S. K., Daleiden, E. L., Ugueto, A. M., Ho, A., Martin, J., Gray, J., Alleyne, A., Langer, D. A., Southam-Gerow, M. A., Gibbons, R. D., & Research Network on Youth Mental Health. (2012). Testing standard and modular designs for psychotherapy treating depression, anxiety, and conduct problems in youth: A randomized effectiveness trial. *Archives of General Psychiatry*, *69*(3), 274–282. https://doi.org/10.1001/archgenpsychiatry.2011.147

Weisz, J. R., Jensen-Doss, A., & Hawley, K. M. (2006). Evidence-based youth psychotherapies versus usual clinical care: A meta-analysis of direct comparisons. *American Psychologist*, *61*(7), 671–689. https://doi.org/10.1037/0003-066X.61.7.671

Weisz, J. R., & Kazdin, A. E. (Eds.). (2017). *Evidence-based psychotherapies for children and adolescents* (3rd ed.). New York, NY: Guilford Press.

Weisz, J.R., Kuppens, S., Eckshtain, D., Ugueto, A.M., Hawley, K.M., & Jensen-Doss, A. (2013). Performance of evidence-based youth psychotherapies compared with usual clinical care: A multilevel meta-analysis. *JAMA Psychiatry*, *70*(7), 750–761. https://doi.org/10.1001/jamapsychiatry.2013.1176

Weisz, J.R., Kuppens, S., Ng, M.Y., Eckshtain, D., Ugueto, A.M., Vaughn-Coaxum, R., Jensen-Doss, A., Hawley, K.M., Krumholz, L.S., Chu, B.C., Weersing, V.R., & Fordwood, S.R. (2017). What five decades of research tells us about the effects of youth psychological therapy: A multilevel meta-analysis and implications for science and practice. *American Psychologist*, *72*(2), 79–117. https://doi.org/10.1037/a0040360

Weisz, J.R., Kuppens, S., Ng, M.Y., Vaughn-Coaxum, R.A., Ugueto, A.M., Eckshtain, D., & Corteselli, K.A. (2019). Are psychotherapies for young people growing stronger? Tracking trends over time for youth anxiety, depression, ADHD, and conduct problems. *Perspectives on Psychological Science*, *14* (2), 216–237. https://doi.org/10.1177/1745691618805436

Weisz, J. R., McCarty, C. A., Eastman, K. L., Suwanlert, S., & Chaiyasit, W. (1997). Developmental psychopathology and culture: Ten lessons from Thailand. In S. S. Luthar, J. Burack, D. Cicchetti, & J. R. Weisz (Eds.), *Developmental psychopathology: Perspectives on adjustment, risk, and disorder* (pp. 568–592). Cambridge, England: Cambridge University Press.

Weisz, J. R., McCarty, C. A., & Valeri, S. M. (2006). Effects of psychotherapy for depression in children and adolescents: A meta-analysis. *Psychological Bulletin*, *132*(1), 132–149. https://doi.org/10.1037/0033-2909.132.1.132

Weisz, J. R., Ng, M. Y., & Bearman, S. K. (2014). Odd couple? Reenvisioning the relation between science and practice in the dissemination-implementation era. *Clinical Psychological Science*, *2*(1), 58–74. https://doi.org/10.1177/2167702613501307

Weisz, J.R., Ng, M.Y., Rutt, C., Lau, N., & Masland, S. (2013). Psychotherapy for children and adolescents. In M. J. Lambert (Ed.), *Bergin and Garfield's handbook of psychotherapy and behavior change* (6th ed., pp. 541–586). Hoboken, NJ: Wiley.

Weisz, J.R., Ugueto, A.M., Cheron, D.M., & Herren, J. (2013). Evidence-based youth psychotherapy in the mental health ecosystem. *Journal of Clinical Child and Adolescent Psychology, 42*(2), 274–286. https://doi.org/10.1080/15374416.2013.764824

Weisz, J. R., Weiss, B., Alicke, M. D., & Klotz, M. L. (1987). Effectiveness of psychotherapy with children and adolescents: A meta-analysis for clinicians. *Journal of Consulting & Clinical Psychology, 55*(4), 542–549. https://doi.org/10.1037/0022-006X.55.4.542

Weisz, J. R., Weiss, B., Han, S.S., Granger, D. A., & Morton, T. (1995). Effects of psychotherapy with children and adolescents revisited: A meta-analysis of treatment outcome studies. *Psychological Bulletin, 117*(3), 450–468. https://doi.org/10.1037/0033-2909.117.3.450

Wen, C. K. F., Schneider, S., Stone, A. A., & Spruijt-Metz, D. (2017). Compliance with mobile ecological momentary assessment protocols in children and adolescents: A systematic review and meta-analysis. *Journal of Medical Internet Research, 19*(4). https://doi.org/10.2196/jmir.6641

Williams, N. J., & Beidas, R. S. (2019). The state of implementation science in child psychology and psychiatry: A review and suggestions to advance the field. *Journal of Child Psychology and Psychiatry, 60*(4), 430–450 https://doi.org/10.1111/jcpp.12960

Winters, K. C., Fahnhorst, T., Botzet, A., Lee, S., & Lalone, B. (2012). Brief intervention for drug-abusing adolescents in a school setting: Outcomes and mediating factors. *Journal of Substance Abuse Treatment, 42*(3), 279–288. https://doi.org/10.1016/j.jsat.2011.08.005

Winters, K. C., Lee, S., Botzet, A., Fahnhorst, T., & Nicholson, A. (2014). One-year outcomes and mediators of a brief intervention for drug abusing adolescents. *Psychology of Addictive Behaviors, 28*(2), 464–474. https://doi.org/10.1037/a0035041

Woods, D.W., & Houghton, D.C. (2016). Evidence-based psychosocial treatments for pediatric body-focused repetitive behavior disorders, *Journal of Clinical Child & Adolescent Psychology, 45*(3), 227–240. https://doi.org/10.1080/15374416.2015.1055860

Wykes, T., & Brown, M. (2016). Over promised, over-sold and underperforming?-e-health in mental health. *Journal of Mental Health, 25*(1), 1–4. https://doi.org/10.3109/09638237.2015.1124406

Yeager, D. S., Lee, H. Y., & Jamieson, J. P. (2016). How to improve adolescent stress responses insights from integrating implicit theories of personality and biopsychosocial models. *Psychological Science, 27*(8), 1078–1091. https://doi.org/10.1177/0956797616649604

Yeager, D. S., & Walton, G. M. (2011). Social-psychological interventions in education: They're not magic. *Review of Educational Research, 81*(2), 267–301. https://doi.org/10.3102/0034654311405999

Yeh, M., & Weisz, J. R. (2001). Why are we here at the clinic? Parent-child (dis)agreement on referral problems. *Journal of Consulting and Clinical Psychology, 69*(6), 1018–1025. https://doi.org/10.1037/0022-006X.69.6.1018

Young, J. F., Mufson, L., Davies, M. (2006). Impact of comorbid anxiety in an effectiveness study of interpersonal psychotherapy for depressed adolescents. *Journal of the American Academy of Child & Adolescent Psychiatry 45*(8), 904–912. https://doi.org/10.1097/01.chi.0000222791.23927.5f

Yu, D. L., & Seligman, M. E. P. (2002). Preventing depressive symptoms in Chinese children. *Prevention and Treatment, 5*(1), 9. https://doi.org/10.1037/1522-3736.5.1.59a

Zaza, S., Kann, L., & Barrios, L. (2016). Lesbian, gay, and bisexual adolescents: Population estimate and prevalence of health behaviors. *JAMA, 316*(22), 2355–2356. https://doi.org/10.1001/jama.2016.11683

Supplemental Materials

Table 18.2 lists youth psychotherapies classified into five levels of empirical support for 14 target problems.

TABLE 18.2 Youth Psychotherapies Classified into Five Levels of Empirical Support for 14 Target Problems, Adapted from Evidence Base Updates in the *Journal of Clinical Child and Adolescent Psychology*

Target problem	Level 1: Well-established treatments	Level 2: Probably efficacious treatments	Level 3: Possibly efficacious treatments	Level 4: Experimental treatments	Level 5: Treatments of questionable efficacy
Autism spectrum disorder (Smith & Iadarola, 2015)	ABA–Individual, comprehensive ABA + DSP–Teacher-implemented, focused	ABA–Individual, focused for augmentative and alternative communication ABA + DSP–Individual, focused DSP-Focused parent training	ABA + DSP–Individual, comprehensive ABA–classrooms, comprehensive ABA–focused for spoken communication ABA–parent-training, focused DSP–Teacher-implemented, focused	ABA + DSP classrooms, –comprehensive ABA+ DSP– Parent training, focused	None
Bipolar spectrum disorders (Fristad & MacPherson, 2014)	None	Family psychoeducation + skill building	CBT	DBT Interpersonal & social rhythm therapy	None
Depression (Weersing et al., 2017)	CBT–Group (adolescents) CBT–Individual (adolescents) IPT–Individual (adolescents)	IPT–Group (adolescents)	CBT–Technology-assisted (children) CBT–Group (children) BT (children) CBT–Bibliotherapy (adolescents) Family-Based Intervention (adolescents)	CBT–Individual (children) Psychodynamic therapy (children) Family-based intervention (children) CBT–Technology-assisted (adolescents)	None

(Continued)

TABLE 18.2 (CONTINUED)

Target problem	Level 1: Well-established treatments	Level 2: Probably efficacious treatments	Level 3: Possibly efficacious treatments	Level 4: Experimental treatments	Level 5: Treatments of questionable efficacy
Anxiety Youth (Higa-McMillan et al., 2016)	CBT [a] CBT with parents [b] CBT + medication [b] Education Exposure Modeling	Family psychoeducation Relaxation Assertiveness training Attention control [c] CBT for child and parent Cultural storytelling Hypnosis Stress inoculation	Contingency management Group therapy	Biofeedback CBT with parents only Play therapy Psychodynamic therapy Rational emotive therapy Social skills	Assessment/monitoring Attachment theory Client-centered therapy EMDR Peer pairing Psychoeducation Relationship counseling Teacher psychotherapy
Early childhood (Comer et al., 2019)	CBT–Family-Based	CBT–Parent group CBT–Parent group + CBT–Child group	None	Play Therapy Attachment-Based Therapy	Relaxation training
Trauma exposure (Dorsey et al., 2017)	CBT–Individual + parent involvement CBT–Individual CBT–Group	CBT–Group + parent involvement EMDR	Integrated Therapy for Complex Trauma–Individual Mind-Body Skills–Group	Client-Centered Play Therapy–Individual Mind-Body Skills–Individual Psychoanalysis–Individual	Creative expressive + CBT–Group
Obsessive-compulsive disorder (Freeman et al., 2018)	CBT–Family focused CBT (young children) [d]	CBT–Individual CBT–Not face-to-face CBT–Technology-based delivery [d] CBT + Positive family interaction [d]	CBT–Family focused group CBT–Non-family focused group Effectiveness treatment studies [d] CBT–Intensive delivery [d]	Acceptance and commitment therapy [d] Attachment-based therapy CBT for co-occurring PANS/PANDAS [d] CBT + cognitive bias modification of interpretation [d] CBT–Self-help studies [d] CBT + Parent training [d] CBT for co-occurring externalizing disorders [d]	None

(Continued)

TABLE 18.2 (CONTINUED)

Target problem	Level 1: Well-established treatments	Level 2: Probably efficacious treatments	Level 3: Possibly efficacious treatments	Level 4: Experimental treatments	Level 5: Treatments of questionable efficacy
Body-focused repetitive disorders (Woods & Houghton, 2016)	None	BT–Individual for thumb sucking	BT–Individual for trichotillomania	CBT–Individual for trichotillomania BT–Individual or excoriation, nail biting, & check biting CBT–Multicomponent for nail biting	Massed negative practice for trichotillomania
Self-injurious thoughts and behaviors (Glenn et al., 2019)	DBT for deliberate self-harm & suicide attempt	DBT for NSSI CBT–Individual + family for suicide attempt Integrated family therapy for suicide attempt IPT–Individual for suicide ideation Psychodynamic therapy – Individual + family for deliberate self-harm Parent training for self-injurious thoughts and behaviors	Multiple systems therapy for suicide attempt	CBT–Individual for suicide attempt & suicide ideation CBT –Individual + family for suicide ideation Psychodynamic therapy – Family-based for suicide ideation & suicide attempt Integrated family therapy for NSSI Family therapy for suicidal ideation & deliberate self-harm Multiple systems therapy for suicidal ideation Brief family-based therapy for suicide attempt, suicide ideation, & deliberate self-harm Support-based therapy for suicide ideation Brief skills training for NSSI, suicide attempt, & suicide ideation MI for suicide ideation Resource interventions for deliberate self-harm & suicide ideation	Eclectic group therapy for deliberate self-harm & suicide ideation Support-based therapy for suicide attempt Resource intervention for suicide attempt

(Continued)

Table 18.2 (Continued)

Target problem	Level 1: Well-established treatments	Level 2: Probably efficacious treatments	Level 3: Possibly efficacious treatments	Level 4: Experimental treatments	Level 5: Treatments of questionable efficacy
Attention-deficit hyperactivity disorder (Evans et al., 2018)	Behavioral parent training (preschool, elementary) Behavioral classroom management (preschool, elementary) Behavioral peer intervention (elementary) Combined behavior management interventions (preschool, elementary) Organization training (elementary, adolescents)	Combined training interventions–extensive practice & feedback	Behavioral parent training (adolescents) Neurofeedback training (elementary)	Cognitive training (elementary) Combined training interventions–Limited practice & feedback Behavioral parent training– Modified for specific populations (elementary)	Social skills training (elementary) Physical activity (elementary) Omega 3/6 supplements (adolescents)
Disruptive behavior Child (Kaminski & Claussen, 2016)	BT–Parent group BT–Parent individual with child participation	BT–Parent group + BT–child group BT–Parent group with child participation + family problem-solving training BT–Parent group with child participation BT–Parent individual BT–Parent individual with child participation + Teacher training BT–Child individual with parent participation + Teacher training BT–Parent self-directed BT–Child group BT–Child group + Teacher training BT–Child individual BT–Child individual with parent participation Parent-focused therapy–group Child-centered play-group Child-centered play-individual	BT–Parent group + BT– Parent individual with child participation + BT–Child group + BT–Child INDIVIDUAL BT–Parent group + Parent-focused therapy BT–Parent group + teacher training + BT–Child group BT–Parent group + teacher training BT–Parent individual with child participation + Addressing parental mental health needs BT–Child group + BT–Child individual Teacher training	Family problem-solving training	None

(Continued)

TABLE 18.2 (CONTINUED)

Target problem	Level 1: Well-established treatments	Level 2: Probably efficacious treatments	Level 3: Possibly efficacious treatments	Level 4: Experimental treatments	Level 5: Treatments of questionable efficacy
Adolescent [e] (McCart & Sheidow, 2016)	Combined BT, CBT, & family therapy - Multisystemic therapy (JJ) - Treatment foster care Oregon therapy (JJ)	CBT —Aggression replacement training + Positive peer culture (JJ) - Solution-focused group program (JJ) Combined BT, CBT, & family therapy - Multisystemic therapy (non-JJ) - Functional family therapy (JJ)	BT or parenting skills (non-JJ) CBT (JJ) Combined BT and CBT (non-JJ)	BT or parenting skills (non-JJ) CBT (SCH, JJ, non-JJ) Family therapy (non-JJ) Mentoring (SCH) Combined BT and CBT (JJ, non-JJ) Combined CBT and mindfulness (non-JJ) Combined BT and attachment-based therapy (JJ, non-JJ) Combined family therapy and emotionally focused approaches (JJ) Combined BT, CBT, and family therapy (JJ, non-JJ) Combined BT, CBT, and wraparound (JJ)	BT or parenting skills (JJ, non-JJ) CBT (JJ, non-JJ) Psychodynamic therapy (non-JJ) Combined BT and CBT (JJ, non-JJ) Combined humanistic, bibliotherapy, psychodynamic therapy, and CBT (SCH)
Youth illegal sexual behaviors (Dopp, et al. 2017)	None	Multisystemic therapy for problem sexual behaviors	None	CBT Behavioral management through adventure	None
Substance use (Hogue et al., 2014)	CBT–Individual CBT–Group FBT–Ecological MET/CBT MET/ CBT + FBT–Behavioral	FBT–Behavioral MI/MET FBT–Ecological + Contingency management MET/CBT + FBT–Behavioral + Contingency management MET/CBT + Contingency management	DC/12	None	None

(Continued)

Table 18.2 (Continued)

Target problem	Level 1: Well-established treatments	Level 2: Probably efficacious treatments	Level 3: Possibly efficacious treatments	Level 4: Experimental treatments	Level 5: Treatments of questionable efficacy
Eating disorders (Lock, 2015)	Family Therapy–Behavioral for anorexia nervosa	Family therapy–Systemic for anorexia nervosa Insight-oriented psychotherapy–Individual for anorexia nervosa	Family therapy–Behavioral for bulimia CBT–Guided self-help for bulimia CBT–Individual for bulimia CBT–Internet-facilitated self-help for binge eating	CBT–Broad, individual for anorexia nervosa Cognitive training– Individual for anorexia nervosa CBT–Individual for bulimia Supportive psychotherapy –Individual for anorexia nervosa IPT–Individual for binge eating DBT–Individual for binge eating DBT–Family for binge eating	None
Overweight and obesity (Altman & Wilfley, 2015)	Family-based behavioral treatment (children) Parent-only behavioral treatment (children)	None	Family-based behavioral treatment–parent only (adolescents) Behavioral weight loss treatment with family involvement (toddlers, children, adolescents) Family-based behavioral treatment–guided self help	Appetite awareness training Regulation of cues treatment	None
Elimination disorders (Shepard et al., 2017)	Urine alarm therapy for enuresis Dry-bed training for enuresis	Full spectrum home therapy for enuresis Biofeedback-enhanced toilet training for encopresis	Lifting for enuresis	None	Hypnotherapy for enuresis Retention control training for enuresis

Note: ABA = applied behavior analysis; BT = behavior therapy; CBT = cognitive-behavioral therapy; DBT = dialectical behavior therapy; DC/12 = drug counseling/12 step; DSP = developmental social-pragmatic; EMDR = eye movement desensitization and processing; FBT = family-based therapy; IPT = interpersonal psychotherapy; JJ = juvenile-justice involved; MET = motivational enhancement therapy; MI = motivational interviewing; non-JJ = not juvenile-justice involved; NSSI = nonsuicidal self-injury; PANDAS = pediatric autoimmune neuropsychiatric disorders associated with streptococcal infections; PANS = pediatric acute-onset neuropsychiatric syndrome; SCH = school disruption.

a   Well-established based on symptom outcome, also well-established based on functional outcome.

b   Well-established based on symptom outcome, but probably efficacious based on functional outcome.

c   Possibly efficacious based on symptom outcome, but questionable efficacy based on functional outcome.

d   These treatments are organized according to a new framework by Freeman et al. (2018).

e   In this review, some treatment families appear in multiple levels of evidence because McCart and Sheidow (2016) assigned different "brand-name" therapies within the same treatment family to different levels; these brand-name therapies are listed for the first two levels of evidence and omitted from the other levels for brevity.

INCREASING PRECISION AND SCALE IN THE PSYCHOLOGICAL THERAPIES

•

CHAPTER 19

Personalized Treatment Approaches

Zachary D Cohen, Jaime Delgadillo, and Robert J DeRubeis

Abstract

In the modern history of psychotherapy, understanding the individual patient and how to optimize treatment for each individual has been an important challenge. For the therapist, personalization often has meant deciding which treatments to offer based on clinical assessment and formulation, or deciding moment-to-moment what techniques to employ, given what has been happening in therapy with the patient, informed by a particular theoretical framework, or based on clinical judgment. Efforts to improve outcomes through treatment personalization based on expert clinical assessments and psychological theory have been largely unfruitful, despite their intuitive appeal. Furthermore, numerous studies over 50 years have highlighted the limitations of clinical judgment, making a compelling case for the use of data-driven, actuarial methods to enhance treatment decisions. New statistical approaches, including machine learning, have propelled advancements in our ability to develop data-derived decision aids that can be tested and easily disseminated. Personalization can take several forms, including determining the appropriate level of care or treatment package, selecting and ordering of treatment components or modules, identifying therapeutic targets, or matching patients to specific therapists. This chapter reviews the evidence for different forms of treatment personalization, from intuitive and theory-based approaches to contemporary data-driven approaches. After summarizing the limitations of the current field, the chapter concludes with a discussion of what the future could hold.

Overview

Introduction: The Personalized Treatment Imperative

People respond differently to psychotherapy, even if they present with similar problems and are treated by the same therapist with similar methods (Kiesler, 1966). This phenomenon is often called the *heterogeneity of treatment effect* (Varadhan et al., 2013). Empirical studies highlighting the prognostic value of individual differences were conducted early in the 20th century (e.g., Strupp, 1964), spurring many psychotherapists to argue for the need to personalize and adjust interventions with regard to features other than diagnosis (Garfield, 1996). This view has been ubiquitous in clinical psychology for many decades, and has its corollary in Gordon Paul's classic question to the field: "*What* treatment, by *whom*, is most effective for *this* individual with *that* specific problem, and under *which* set of circumstances?" (Paul, 1967, p. 111). Accordingly, psychotherapists have been attempting to deliver personalized therapy for decades, but there is tremendous diversity in the approaches they have used. Recent efforts to personalize treatment across mental health have focused on selecting the optimal psychotherapy for an individual among the available evidence-based approaches (Cohen & DeRubeis, 2018). In this chapter, we present a review of several approaches to personalization and propose conceptual frameworks aimed at helping readers (i) to understand; (ii) to categorize; and (iii) to appraise the methodological rigor of these different approaches. Strengths and weaknesses of different approaches will be illustrated using examples from the literature. Overall, this chapter aims to survey the landscape of personalization from a historical and methodological perspective, clarifying key concepts, and concluding with a consideration of future research directions that promise to enhance the precision and effectiveness of personalization.

This is an auspicious moment in the evolution of personalization in psychotherapy. The increasing emphasis on evidence-based psychological treatments, combined with rapid developments in statistical methodologies and the availability of datasets that can take advantage of these developments, are driving a proliferation of research programs that are giving rise to a new field of precision mental health care. As investigators begin to implement more complex methodologies, they discover a multitude of additional hurdles that must be surmounted in order for their contributions to be ready to be used by the clinicians and patients who might benefit from them. In this chapter, we will examine a variety of questions and methods that come into play in research on, and in the implementation of, personalized treatment approaches. Along the way we propose a lexicon that we hope will organize and clarify the many conceptual and methodological distinctions that abound in this work, and we will present examples of research and implementation efforts that can serve as springboards for programs going forward.

The chapter is organized in six parts. The second section introduces a framework that comprehensively maps out the various approaches to personalization seen in the psychotherapy literature. This framework offers a taxonomy of distinctive dimensions of personalization and serves to organize a discussion of the variety of traditions and methods in this area. In the third section, we describe historical efforts to characterize or systematize the personalization of psychotherapy. The fourth section provides a description of contemporary innovations, focusing on data-driven algorithms, and highlighting promising lines of research and cutting-edge demonstrations. In the fifth section we discuss relevant methodological and statistical issues. In the sixth section, we describe key challenges that must be addressed if research on personalization is to play a major role in how psychotherapy is practiced. We end with suggestions for how these barriers can be overcome, and a discussion of future directions.

A CONCEPTUAL FRAMEWORK FOR PERSONALIZED PSYCHOTHERAPY

The framework in Figure 19.1 depicts, as dimensions, fundamental ways in which approaches to personalization differ from each other. This is proposed as an organizing framework

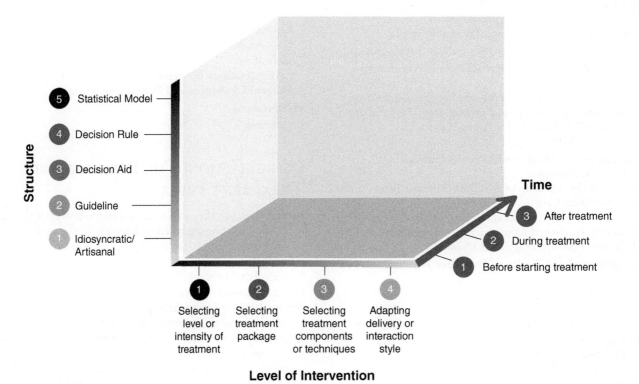

FIGURE 19.1   Three dimensions of personalization (3DP).

to understand and catalog the variety of ways in which personalized therapy has been pursued and promoted. The framework, called the *Three Dimensions of Personalization (3DP)*, enables us to describe the types of decisions that can be made to personalize treatment, the timing of these decisions, and the methods used to inform such decisions. Multiple combinations of features across these three dimensions are possible, thus enabling psychotherapy researchers to derive a highly specific taxonomy of features that characterizes current approaches to personalization. In what follows, we will unpack these concepts and offer some illustrative examples.

The *Time* dimension characterizes the stage at which personalization decisions are made along a patient's treatment pathway. This could be before the start of treatment (Time 1, or 3DP:T1), across the course of treatment (3DP:T2), or after treatment has ended (3DP:T3) (e.g., relapse prevention). The *Level of Intervention* dimension describes the level of specificity of treatment decisions, pertaining to macro-level decisions (e.g., high intensity versus low intensity interventions; or which treatment modality to offer, such as cognitive behavioral therapy [CBT] or psychodynamic psychotherapy) and micro-level decisions (*which* specific treatment techniques and *how* they should be delivered).

The *Structure* dimension characterizes the *method* of personalization, and the extent to which such a method is formalized or standardized. For simplicity, we locate these various approaches along a continuum from less structured to highly structured methods. At the less formal end of the continuum, *idiosyncratic* or *artisanal* approaches (Structure 1, or 3DP:S1) privilege a clinician's experience, intuition, and judgment. Because the artisanal (Perlis, 2016) method of decision-making is highly variable from clinician to clinician, it is therefore less formalized and more difficult to replicate. Even if an expert clinician made consistently effective intuitive decisions that resulted in good treatment outcomes, such a method would not be easily accessible to other clinicians, unless it was somehow formalized and structured.

Along the *Structure* dimension, we also find *guidelines* (3DP:S2), which – in the field of psychotherapy – are usually developed by expert panels who survey and synthesize the current scientific evidence or consensus regarding best practices. According to the Institute of Medicine, clinical practice guidelines are systematically developed statements to help clinicians and patients make health care decisions under specific clinical circumstances (Field & Lohr, 1990). However, this assistance often takes a more narrative form, and many clinical practice guidelines are neither sufficiently structured nor intended to provide definitive answers or fixed protocols for clinicians to follow. More structure is offered by standardized *decision aids* (3DP:S3), which are defined as interventions that support clinicians and patients by making their decisions explicit, by providing information regarding options and associated benefits and harms, and by helping to align decisions with personal values (Stacey et al., 2017). As described in the development of the International Patient Decision Aids Standards checklist (Elwyn et al., 2006), decision aids can take the form of things like leaflets or videos that provide information about the available treatments, or they can be delivered as *algorithmic* tools

such as interactive, rule- or tree-based decision aids. This illustrates that the labels along the *Structure* dimension are not all mutually exclusive categories, but instead function more as a spectrum of increasing specificity. Examples of this overlap are that many guidelines (3DP:S2) include decision-aids (3DP:S3), that a decision-rule (3DP:S4) is a special type of a decision-aid, and that some decision-rules are informed by statistical models (3DP:S5).

The final two categories along the *Structure* dimension both rely on algorithms to generate information for use in clinical decision-making. Algorithms lend standardization to the decision-making process, and their outputs (often a recommendation or prediction) are intended to be clear and precise. Thus, *algorithmic* approaches to personalization are highly formalized and structured, offering a greater degree of reproducibility. The defining feature of an algorithm is that it has clearly operationalized inputs and outputs, and a fixed, reproducible process for translating the inputs into the outputs.

One category of algorithms comprises *decision rules or decision trees* (3DP:S4), which can take the form of decision flow diagrams. When these are based on empirical data and research, they can be considered *data-informed*. However, it is important to highlight that the term algorithm, ubiquitous in the medical decision-making literature, should not be assumed to indicate that a model is data-informed, data-driven, or derived from a statistical model. *Data-driven* models are those in which the relationships instantiated in the model attempt to represent, quantitatively, relationships that exist in the data from which they were derived (these distinctions are addressed in the subsequent section).

At the apex of the *Structure* dimension are algorithmic personalization approaches based on *statistical models* (3DP:S5). If well-developed, data-driven statistical models have the potential to improve the accuracy and effectiveness of clinical decision-making. Although statistical models need not be derived from data (nor do they always aim to model real relationships), only data-driven statistical models will be discussed in this chapter.

The *Structure* dimension is closely related to the sources of information that clinicians use to personalize treatment. These sources can include their clinical experience and intuition, available theories, empirical evidence, or quantitative data-driven models (see Figure 19.2 later in the chapter for more on sources of information).

The landscape of personalized psychotherapy approaches contains a wide variety of different combinations of features of the three dimensions of personalization. For example, there are algorithmic statistical models designed to make decisions about which treatment package to offer a patient before the start of treatment (3DP:S5-L2-T1); decision aids based on theoretical models for choosing treatment strategies during treatment (3DP:S3-L3-T2); and algorithmic decision rules, designed to offer relapse prevention support in a targeted way, that identify patients at high risk of relapse after therapy (3DP:S4-L3-T3). This framework allows for the classification of a great diversity of approaches to personalization. In the next section, we will refer to the 3DP framework

Developmental continuum of personalized treatment models

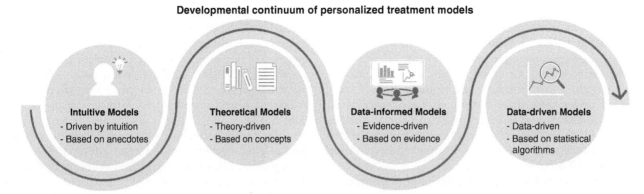

FIGURE 19.2 Sources of information along a developmental continuum of personalized treatment approaches.

as we provide examples of early approaches to psychotherapy personalization.

INTUITIVE AND THEORETICAL APPROACHES TO PSYCHOTHERAPY PERSONALIZATION

Our historical overview of personalization approaches begins with a discussion of less formalized, *intuitive* approaches. This is followed by a discussion of *theoretical* approaches, which vary in their level of structure, and which typically have emerged from intuitive models as they become formalized and, in many cases, subjected to empirical tests.

Intuitive Approaches to Psychotherapy Personalization

Personalized psychotherapy has its roots in intuitive and theoretical models. *Idiosyncratic eclecticism* is an artisanal approach wherein therapists select treatment strategies and concepts based on their subjective appeal or their familiarity (Wheeler, 1993). Such an approach is underpinned by the belief that tacit, informal and intuitive clinical impressions are the most valid inputs available for guiding clinical decisions. Proponents of this approach in health care have argued that expert practitioners have an ability to know intuitively what will be the most effective way to intervene at any decision point in therapy (e.g., Benner & Tanner, 1987; Schon, 1984; Welsh & Lyons, 2001).

A common thread across these approaches is the notion that different patients, even if they share a diagnosis and other clinical features, require different therapeutic strategies. Also central to these approaches is the belief that, because patients' needs and goals change over time, therapists must tailor their approach to each patient, and to changes in a patient's needs and circumstances. Given that a therapist may draw upon an extensive array of techniques, a rationale is required to decide which techniques to apply for each case and at what specific point in time.

Despite its commonsense appeal, the wisdom of relying *solely* on clinical judgment is strongly questioned by a large body of accumulated evidence over the last 50 years. Authors of narrative reviews (Bell & Mellor, 2009; Dawes et al., 1989, 1993; Garb, 2005; Grove & Meehl, 1996; Meehl, 1954; Sawyer, 1966) and meta-analyses (Ægisdóttir et al., 2006; Grove et al., 2000) converge on the observation that clinical judgment and clinicians' prognostic assessments are highly variable and error-prone, are influenced by known biases (e.g., confirmation bias), and tend to be outperformed by formal/actuarial methods, such as those based on data-driven statistical models and decision rules. It therefore behooves clinicians to look for guidance from tools or systems beyond their own clinical judgment when making important treatment decisions (Magnavita & Lilienfeld, 2016).

Still, evidence-based tools are not widely accepted or used in routine psychotherapy practice (Gaudiano et al., 2011). Moreover, the influence of therapists' personality and epistemological beliefs, as well as their training and supervision experiences have been widely documented as determinants of their preferences for therapeutic orientations and selection of techniques (e.g., Arthur, 2001). Paradoxically, while the therapist may have the intention to personalize therapy according to the patient's features, the process itself is likely influenced by a therapist's own features (e.g., personality, philosophical ideas, adherence to clinical intuition as a privileged source of information) and idiosyncratic circumstances (e.g., relationships with peers, the influence of particular supervisor). Therefore, idiosyncratic eclecticism fails to customize therapy for individuals based on formal theoretical models or data-driven models, instead privileging the therapist's attitudes, beliefs, and preferences. This approach can also result in an unsystematic treatment process that is difficult to replicate and can impede therapists' ability to develop competence in any one approach or technique, which necessarily requires systematic repetition. Idiosyncratic eclecticism also makes it difficult to form an objective view about the effects of techniques, as it avoids the consistent application of an intervention and systematic observation of its effects across cases that would inform future decisions. Despite these shortcomings, eclecticism is frequently advocated in counseling and psychotherapy training courses (Wheeler, 1993) and is prominently endorsed in surveys of practicing therapists and psychologists (Norcross, 2005; Norcross & Prochaska, 1988).

The *pluralistic approach*, a close cousin of idiosyncratic eclecticism, acknowledges the idiosyncratic nature of clinicians' judgments and instead advocates that decisions should be guided less by therapists' judgments and more by patients' needs, wants, and preferences (Cooper & McLeod, 2011). Therapists are thus encouraged to decide on the tasks of therapy based on collaborative discussions about patients' idiosyncratic goals and preferences about the style (e.g., more vs. less directive) and focus (e.g., past vs. present; building on strengths vs. addressing weaknesses) of therapy. In one version of this approach, the therapist relies on a structured inventory of preferences called the *Therapy Personalization Form* (TPF) to guide conversations about the initial selection of treatment strategy and style (Bowens & Cooper, 2012). Subsequent adaptations of therapy are accomplished by the completion and discussion of the TPF at regular review points. Compared to idiosyncratic eclecticism, the pluralistic approach is more systematic and mindful of research evidence (cf. Ong et al., 2020). However, it still relies mainly on clinical opinions and indirect evidence to guide its treatment selection method. For instance, the TPF approach was developed through a series of qualitative investigations of therapists' experiences of therapeutic dilemmas, and from the documentation of therapists' opinions about how to respond to patients' needs (Bowens & Cooper, 2012). To date, there is no evidence that personalization via TPF leads to superior treatment outcomes, relative to a standardized psychological treatment approach.

Theoretical Approaches to Psychotherapy Personalization

Toward the middle of the *Structure* dimension (Figure 19.1), we can find more systematic approaches that are guided by formal clinical assessment and theory. For example, Lazarus' multimodal therapy approach (2005) advocates the structured assessment of seven discrete and interactive modalities: behavior, affect, sensation, imagery, cognition, interpersonal relationships, and drugs/biology (BASIC ID), from which the therapist develops a BASIC ID profile. The profile, which informs a conceptualization of how these modalities interact to cause distress or dysfunction, serves as a formal blueprint to guide the selection of techniques to rectify problems in one or more domains. Furthermore, the sequence of techniques to be used is matched to the BASIC ID blueprint, which usually starts with one modality and moves sequentially to other modalities. Multimodal therapy is an example of *systematic technical eclecticism*, which is informed primarily by theory (in particular social-cognitive learning theory) but which also advocates techniques that are empirically supported. Notwithstanding its intuitive appeal, clinical parsimony, and the fact that it is premised on empirically supported theories, there is not a single experimental comparison of multimodal therapy versus inactive or active control conditions.

Another example of systematic technical eclecticism can be found in Beutler's *systematic treatment selection* (STS) approach (Beutler et al., 2005). In it, standardized questionnaires are used to assess four domains: functional impairment, coping style, reactance/resistance, and distress or emotional arousal. The resulting profile is used as a decision aid (3DP:S3) to prescribe specific techniques that are believed to be the most appropriate for a patient with that profile. An assessment of functional impairment is used to determine the intensity (e.g., frequency/duration of sessions, combination of group, individual, pharmacological interventions) of treatment. The assessment of coping style (internalizing vs. externalizing style) informs the selection of techniques (3DP:L3) that emphasize insight and activation of emotions (for internalizers) versus those that focus on practical skill-building and systematic feedback (for externalizers). Patients are also assessed according to reactance/resistance, which in turn guides the therapist to adopt a less directive approach for highly resistant patients and a more directive approach for those who are less resistant (3DP:L4). Finally, the patient's level of distress or emotional arousal is monitored to guide the selection of techniques that may serve to optimally modulate emotions. For example, strategies to promote cognitive dissonance may be selected in cases where blunted affect may interfere with motivation and engagement, whereas for patients with highly aroused emotions strategies might aim to contain and soothe their distress.

Integrative Approaches

Integrative approaches are said to emerge in two ways: through the theoretical integration of two or more approaches or through the assimilation of other approaches into one's practice over time (Cooper & McLeod, 2011). Some examples of theoretical integration include cognitive analytic therapy (Ryle et al., 1990) and cognitive behavioral analysis system of psychotherapy (CBASP, McCullough Jr, 2003), both of which draw from cognitive and psychodynamic theories. Similarly, both dialectic behavioral therapy (DBT), which was developed by Linehan to treat suicidal patients (1993), and mindfulness-based cognitive therapy (MBCT), which was developed by Segal, Williams and Teasdale (2001) as a relapse prevention strategy for individuals with major depressive disorder (MDD), demonstrate the gradual assimilation of meditation practices and emotion regulation strategies into a CBT framework. Integrative approaches do not always emerge with the explicit goal to personalize treatment for individuals, but the personalization imperative is often implicit in the rationale for theoretical or technical integration. The above cited therapies, for example, were born of the authors' dissatisfaction with then-current approaches and their apparent lack of efficacy/effectiveness with specific hard to treat groups: patients with chronic affective disorders, suicidality, and severe interpersonal difficulties. Thus, integrative treatments are often claimed to be well-suited for specific subgroups of the clinical population, such as those with dysthymia (CBASP), recurrent depression (MBCT), or borderline personality disorder and suicidality

(DBT). In this way, integrative approaches often coalesce into standardized interventions, which are then selected for subgroups of patients who are assumed to be well-matched to the intervention, thus blending into the *theoretical* approach to personalization. Many of these formalized integrative treatments have been evaluated in RCTs and are now evidence-based interventions for specific patient populations (e.g., Piet & Hougaard, 2011).

Matching Treatments to Disorders

Indeed, one of the most prominent ways to approach the "what works for whom" question is to prescribe therapies that have empirical support for the treatment of specific clinical problems and populations. The vast majority of research regarding treatment selection over the past half-century has taken the form of identifying the best mapping of disorders to treatment packages, many of which were developed for specific disorders or patient populations. For example, prolonged exposure (PE) was developed by Foa to treat patients with post-traumatic stress disorder (PTSD; Foa & Rothbaum, 1998). Largely founded on the controlled trials and meta-analytic evidence base, the disorder-matching approach has yielded different frameworks for treatment selection, where personalization mostly involves matching an evidence-based therapy to the patient's principal presenting problem or diagnosis. When algorithmic, this information can be used in a decision rule (e.g., if borderline personality disorder with suicidality, provide DBT; if PTSD, provide prolonged exposure; if obsessive-compulsive disorder [OCD], provide exposure and response prevention, etc.). If not a formal algorithm, as is often the case in guidelines, this information can take the form of a decision aid. Typically, the therapist and patient collaborate in reviewing initial diagnostic assessment results, they identify the principal problem(s), and this guides the selection of a disorder-specific treatment package or series of modules (i.e., discrete treatment tasks for the target problems).

This approach is endorsed by authoritative guidelines such as those published by the American Psychological Association's task force on the promotion and dissemination of psychological procedures (Chambless & Hollon, 1998; Chambless & Ollendick, 2001; Tolin et al., 2015), the UK National Institute for Health and Care Excellence (National Collaborating Centre for Mental Health [NCCMH], 2011), the Canadian Psychological Association (2012), and the Royal Australian and New Zealand College of Psychiatrists (Malhi et al., 2015). Such guidelines commonly advocate the prescription of first-line or empirically supported therapies, followed by "probably efficacious" treatments as second-line options when first-line treatments are ineffective, unavailable, or unacceptable to the individual. Criteria that must be met to be considered an empirically supported therapy usually include support by at least two well-conducted experimental studies, ideally carried out by different research groups, in clearly specified clinical samples, targeting specific outcome domains and supported by standardized treatment manuals (Chambless & Hollon, 1998; Tolin et al., 2015).

Guidelines cited above have produced diagnostic treatment matching systems for a range of common mental disorders such as depression, generalized anxiety disorder, obsessive-compulsive disorder, social anxiety disorder, specific phobias, panic disorder, substance use disorders, eating disorders, and other conditions. The integrative therapy approach described above has also tended to become assimilated into this algorithmic diagnosis-based treatment matching scheme. For example, MBCT has been recommended as a relapse prevention intervention, specifically for patients with recurrent major depression in remission who have experienced at least three previous episodes (Piet & Hougaard, 2011). In another example, DBT has been recommended to reduce the risk of self-harm in patients with borderline personality disorder, within a structured program including individual therapy, group-based skills training and access to support between sessions (NCCMH, 2009).

Notwithstanding its prominence in current practice guidelines, the disorder-matching approach faces a practical challenge from the proliferation of different treatment approaches, which has resulted in an abundance of evidence-based interventions for many of the common mental disorders. For example, prolonged exposure, cognitive-processing therapy (CPT), trauma-focused CBT, and eye movement desensitization and reprocessing (EMDR) are all evidence-based interventions for PTSD, and a variety of pharmacological and psychological interventions, including CBT, behavioral activation, interpersonal therapy (IPT), psychodynamic therapy, and emotion-focused therapy, are considered evidence-based treatments for depression. The disorder-matching treatment selection scheme has also been criticized on philosophical and methodological grounds. Some fundamental questions about the empirically supported therapy paradigm and approach to treatment selection concern the issues of generalizability, heterogeneity and diagnostic specificity. Given the rigorous selection criteria imposed in RCTs to safeguard internal validity, trial participants may not be representative of ordinary treatment-seeking samples in routine care. For example, people with certain comorbidities (e.g., substance use disorders, personality disorders, chronic illnesses) are often excluded, and the limited representation of people from minority racial and ethnic groups or disadvantaged socioeconomic backgrounds may limit the generalizability of the results of some RCTs to routine care settings (Henrich et al., 2010). This matter is accentuated by evidence that these very sources of heterogeneity (e.g., comorbidity) are known to be common. For example, Kessler et al. (2005) reported that only 50% of people with diagnosed mental disorders in an epidemiological survey met criteria for a single disorder, with the rest meeting criteria for two or more comorbid disorders. Furthermore, these sources of heterogeneity are relevant to patients' prognoses. For instance, systematic reviews indicate that comorbid personality disorders (Newton-Howes et al., 2014), comorbid chronic illnesses (Dickens et al., 2013), and socioeconomic deprivation (Finegan et al., 2018) are associated with poorer psychological treatment outcomes. This evidence partly supports Garfield's (1996) argument that overly focusing on diagnosis as a privileged criterion for treatment selection minimizes the influence of other sources of information that may be highly relevant to the outcome of a given treatment. Wampold and Imel (2015) argue that the many RCTs that generally find equivalent effects when comparing alternative forms of psychological treatment challenge the predominance of diagnostic classification as the sole criteria for treatment selection. While some have interpreted this latter observation as evidence that all *bona fide* therapies work through common factors, it is also plausible that different treatment techniques or packages work differentially for patients with specific attributes that may be unrelated to diagnosis (e.g., coping style and reactance, as described earlier). These differential response phenomena are known as aptitude-by-treatment interactions (ATI, Cronbach, 1957; Cronbach & Snow, 1977). Insofar as these phenomena are present, our ability to understand what works for whom will be limited by recruiting homogeneous samples, focusing primarily on diagnosis, and examining clinical effects at an aggregated level.

Other Theory-Based Approaches to Treatment Selection and Adaptation

A common way in which psychotherapy researchers have sought to identify the treatments that are most effective for specific patients has been through the development of theory-driven treatment matching approaches. A citation classic in this literature is Project MATCH, a large (N = 1726) RCT designed to test *a priori* matching hypotheses about subgroups of patients with alcohol use problems who might respond differentially to three treatments: CBT, motivational enhancement therapy, and 12-step facilitation (Project MATCH Research Group, 1997). The results offered partial support for 4 out of 20 theoretically informed client characteristics (psychiatric severity, anger, support for drinking, and alcohol dependence). However, the significance of interaction effects varied across assessment time-points and the authors concluded that treatment matching did not substantially improve patient outcomes (Project MATCH Research Group, 1998).

In the area of depression treatment, Miller et al. (2005) randomly assigned N = 121 patients to receive either their matched or nonmatched treatment across four conditions: (1) pharmacotherapy; (2) combined pharmacotherapy and cognitive therapy; (3) combined pharmacotherapy and family therapy; and (4) a combination of all three treatments. The personalization algorithm took the form of a decision rule that used specific cutoffs on self-report questionnaires and an interviewer-rated scale collected pretreatment to indicate both the optimal level of care *and* treatment type (3DP:S4-L1+L2-T1). This matching system was constructed based on a deficit remediation theoretical model that hypothesized that patients with deficits in a specific area (cognitive distortions, family impairment) would benefit most from a treatment that directly addressed those deficits. The findings were mixed: adequately matched patients had better treatment outcomes compared to mismatched patients on some measures (Hamilton Rating Scale for Depression change, % improved) but not others (Beck Depression Inventory; suicidal ideation; symptom

remission). Cheavens et al. (2012) provide another example of a similar approach to personalization based on the capitalization versus compensation model. Patients (N = 34) were assessed on therapy skill use across four domains (behavioral, cognitive, interpersonal, and mindfulness) using a semi-structured interview at baseline. A panel of evaluators and supervisors made consensus determinations about each patient's two relative strength domains and two relative deficit domains, and the patients were then randomized to receive the two modules that could capitalize on their existing strengths (capitalization), or to receive the two modules that could remediate their skill deficits (compensation). Their comparison of these two theory-based personalization approaches for selecting technique-focused modules (3DP:S4-L3-T1) found evidence for early and sustained advantages in depression symptom reductions for those in the approach based on capitalization (Cheavens et al., 2012).

In another prospective trial, Watzke et al. (2010) randomized individuals (N = 291) initiating inpatient psychotherapy (either CBT or psychodynamic therapy) to either theoretically informed systematic treatment selection (distinct from Beutler's STS described earlier) or to random allocation. Treatment matching in the experimental group was carried out by multidisciplinary team consensus, using a theoretical model whereby patients' goals, diagnoses, and other factors (preference, motivation, cognitive and interpersonal deficits, etc.) determined which treatment package they received (3DP:S3-L2-T1). Goals that were related to insight and emotion tended to favor a match with psychodynamic therapy, whereas goals that related to coping and behavior change favored a match with CBT. Patients with an anxiety disorder, eating disorder or PTSD, as well those with a low level of cognitive reflection were also mostly matched with CBT. The main results found no general effect of systematic treatment selection, although secondary analyses suggested that, within those who received psychodynamic therapy, matched cases had better long-term outcomes than randomized cases.

Overall, *theoretical* models of treatment matching such as those described above have tended to yield mixed and inconclusive findings, which reflects the pattern observed for the vast number of aptitude-by-treatment interaction studies conducted over the last four decades (Dance & Neufeld, 1988; Smith & Sechrest, 1991; Snow, 1991). Such mixed and unreplicated findings could be related to methodological limitations such as small sample sizes and the predominant testing of single-moderator hypotheses. Recent studies have been moving toward data-driven multivariable approaches, where the combined influence of multiple attributes is examined in order to identify cases that respond differentially to alternative forms of treatment. These approaches will be covered in more detail in the subsequent sections of this chapter.

Another approach to personalization involves the adaptation of standard treatments with the goal of increasing their acceptability or effectiveness. Some have proposed that effective treatment adaptation can be achieved by expert psychotherapists using their clinical judgment and clinical case formulations (Betan & Binder, 2010; Eells et al., 2005; Persons, 1991; Smits et al., 2019). However, there is little experimental support for the supposed advantage of treatment adaptation guided by clinical intuition over standardized and protocol-driven interventions. Compared to intuitive models, theoretical models for treatment adaptation have gained some empirical support. According to psychological theory, therapy is more likely to be acceptable and effective if the rationale, concepts and delivery are reasonably well-aligned to a patient's worldview and culture (Cloitre et al., 2020). Significant meta-analytic support for this claim exists (Benish et al., 2011; Chowdhary et al., 2014; Hall et al., 2016). One such meta-analysis by Soto and colleagues (2018) examined 99 studies ($N = 13,813$) and found that culturally adapted interventions resulted in better treatment outcomes compared to standard interventions. In these studies, the most frequent adaptations involved providing treatment in the patient's preferred language, explicit mention of cultural content/values in treatment, and matching patients with therapists of a similar ethnic background. However, meta-analytic evidence regarding the impact of such adaptation is mixed (Captari et al., 2018; Cuijpers, Karyotaki, Reijnders, Purgato et al., 2018). For example, a meta-analysis by Cabral and Smith (2011) found almost no benefit to matching clients with therapists based on race or ethnicity.

Another theory in psychotherapy is that collaboration and the therapeutic alliance can be enhanced by accommodating a patient's preferences, thus resulting in better treatment adherence and therapeutic outcomes. A meta-analysis of 29 randomized clinical trials ($N = 5294$) found that providing patients with their preferred psychosocial mental health treatment was associated with lower dropout and greater alliance scores, but not associated with depression and anxiety outcomes, remission, global outcomes, attendance, or treatment satisfaction (Windle et al., 2019). Patients' expectations and preferences for a particular treatment approach could, in turn, be influenced by their interaction with the therapist, or through preparatory interventions such as role inductions and motivational interviewing (Ogrodniczuk et al., 2005; Walitzer et al., 1999). The conceptual and statistical challenges that can arise when investigating patient preference in the context of randomized clinical trials require careful consideration (Gemmell & Dunn, 2011; Walter et al., 2017). Although preference accommodation at the level of selecting interventions seems to be supported by empirical research (Zoellner et al., 2019), the benefits of accommodating preferences about therapy style and techniques require further empirical investigation through comparisons against standardized treatment models with or without adequate preparatory strategies.

Summary: The Road to Precision Starts with Trial and Error

In this section, we have endeavored to present a historical overview of intuitive and theoretical approaches developed with the aim to personalize and ultimately improve the effectiveness of psychotherapy. Rather than an exhaustive review of studies, we have chosen to provide a developmental perspective on the evolution of concepts, methods and trends in the field, supported by a selection of illustrative examples. The personalization imperative has often been approached from an intuitive perspective, based on the notion that clinical expertise is sufficient to meet the needs of patients encountered in practice. Yet, evidence collected over 50 years convincingly demonstrates that clinical judgment is highly variable and error-prone. Nevertheless, clinical observation and speculation have paved the way for the development of theories that generate formal hypotheses about what works for whom and thus are more amenable to validation through experimental tests. In recent decades, the advent of empirically supported treatments and the growth of the clinical trials literature has led to the development of theoretical approaches for treatment selection. Today, the most common forms of treatment selection applied in routine care clinical practice rely on guidelines based on the empirically supported therapy literature and disorder-matching. Other theoretical approaches that aim to reconcile personalization with current clinical practice guidelines have focused on ways to adapt empirically supported therapies to the features of individual patients. Of these approaches, cultural adaptation has accrued the most empirical support. Overall, intuition and theory have paved the way for the development of more structured and precise *algorithmic* approaches, which are the focus of the remaining sections of this chapter. This historical development, moving from intuitive toward theoretical, data-informed and data-driven approaches, is represented in Figure 19.2.

CONTEMPORARY APPLICATIONS OF PERSONALIZATION IN PSYCHOTHERAPY

Data-driven approaches to personalization are a recent development in the field of psychotherapy. The basic premise of data-driven treatment personalization is relatively simple and theoretically sound: if you can predict something relevant about a treatment decision that contains uncertainty, this information could be used to increase the likelihood of making better decisions, which should improve outcomes in the aggregate. These approaches, which are the foundation for the highly structured approaches from the upper end of the *Structure* continuum depicted in Figure 19.1, have several distinctive features: they are developed using observed data (e.g., outcomes from psychotherapy patients); they are developed using statistical analyses; and their outputs (e.g., treatment recommendations or prognostic information) are generated by an algorithm. As such, the decisions that are guided by data-driven approaches are highly standardized, and therefore reproducible, in contrast to decisions derived from intuitive approaches. In this section, we will describe several data-driven approaches, organized according to the *Level of Intervention* domain outlined in Figure 19.1, which aim to inform decisions about how to personalize care by selecting the right treatment intensity, package, or component, or by adjusting therapy delivery or interaction style.

Selecting the Intensity of Psychotherapeutic Interventions in Stratified Care

Across medicine, it is common for interventions to vary in their level of intensity and cost. For example, distinctions are made between primary care (routine interventions), secondary care (specialist interventions), and tertiary or hospital-based care (more invasive or costly interventions). Similarly, a specific treatment modality can vary in intensity. For example, in pharmacotherapy, a single medicine can be prescribed or it can be augmented or combined with other medicines. In psychotherapy as well, intensity can vary from lower to higher intensity interventions. Low intensity interventions are often provided for less severe or non-chronic cases of common mental disorders (NCCMH, 2011). These interventions include brief (i.e., eight or fewer sessions), low-cost, psycho-educational interventions such a computerized CBT, bibliotherapy, and group-based treatments. Such interventions have garnered considerable empirical support in the treatment of depression and anxiety disorders (Coull & Morris, 2011). In contrast, high intensity interventions include empirically supported individual psychotherapies such as those described earlier in this chapter (e.g., CBT, IPT, EMDR, PE, CPT etc.), as well as combination treatments – psychotherapy plus pharmacotherapy – which can be twice as lengthy and costly as low intensity treatment options. Given some evidence that low and high intensity psychological interventions can be equally effective *on average* (e.g., internet-based vs. face-to-face CBT; Carlbring et al., 2018), stepped care has been recommended in clinical guidelines as a cost-effective way to provide low and high intensity treatments in a sequential way (NCCMH, 2011). Stepped care has a well-established evidence base (Firth et al., 2015), and it is a standard strategy for mental health care delivery in countries like the United Kingdom (Clark, 2018).

Recent work has highlighted how the identification of different patient subgroups could inform comparisons of therapies of different strengths. Building on work in which they had proposed the *patient response profiles* framework (DeRubeis, Gelfand et al., 2014), Gelfand and colleagues presented simulations that demonstrate how, depending on the mix of patient types, a comparison between a stronger and a weaker treatment can either reflect the actual difference in strength or can make it appear that there is little if any difference between the two treatments (Gelfand et al., under review). Their analysis highlights the importance of identifying, in advance if possible, those who are as likely to benefit from a less intensive treatment as from a stronger treatment, and those for whom a greater benefit is expected in the stronger treatment. Recent work has extended these concepts to comparisons of diagnosis-specific and transdiagnostic interventions (Dalgleish et al., 2020).

In recent years, researchers have developed data-driven models to identify different phenotypes or subgroups of patients with specific characteristics who may vary in their need for higher intensity treatments for their depression or anxiety. In a large (N = 16,636) naturalistic cohort study of patients who accessed stepped care interventions, Saunders et al. (2016) applied latent cluster analysis to identify eight subgroups of patients who shared similar pretreatment clinical and demographic features. The authors found that patients classified into three of the profiles tended to have a higher probability of depression symptom recovery in high intensity relative to low intensity treatments, whereas those in the other five profiles did not. Using data from an independent sample of 44,905 patients, Saunders et al. (2020) replicated many of these findings using a latent variable mixture modeling approach that leveraged the eight profiles previously identified in Saunders et al. (2016). In addition to observing that a subset of the profiles were associated with differential outcomes between low and high intensity therapies, they examined differences in outcome between different types of high intensity therapies (CBT and Counseling) and identified profiles that were associated with differential likelihood of reliable recovery in one specific intervention versus the other.

Delgadillo and colleagues (2016), applying bootstrapped logistic regression methods to data obtained from a stepped care psychological treatment service, identified robust predictors of depression treatment outcomes. Based on the regression weights associated with these predictors, they developed the Leeds Risk Index (LRI), which classifies patients as having low, moderate or high predicted risk of enduring depression symptoms after treatment. In a prospective field-test of the index, therapists used the LRI to guide the assignment of patients (N = 157) to either low or high intensity treatments (Delgadillo, Appleby et al., 2020). The pattern of outcomes in this uncontrolled open trial of LRI-informed allocation was favorable in comparison to a case-control matched sample drawn from archival clinical records that had undergone stepped care.

Recent studies have applied penalized regression approaches to develop prognostic indices, which combine pretreatment patient features in a way that can help rank cases according to their expected outcomes (e.g., a continuum ranging from excellent to poor predicted treatment response). Using data (N = 622) from a three-arm randomized controlled trial (treatment as usual [TAU] vs. brief therapy vs. CBT), Lorenzo-Luaces et al. (2017) combined several pretreatment patient characteristics using a regularized regression equation (bootstrapped LASSO technique) to develop a depression prognostic index. Using this index, they observed that the 75% of patients with the best prognoses responded similarly to all treatments. However, among the 25% of cases with poorer prognoses, recovery rates were substantially higher in the CBT condition (60%) than in TAU (39%) or brief therapy (44%). Using a similar modeling approach in a naturalistic cohort study (N = 1512) of stepped care treatments, Delgadillo et al. (2017) developed a depression prognostic index which was used to classify cases into two groups: complex cases (28% of cases with the poorest expected prognosis) and standard cases (the majority). Using a split-halves cross-validation procedure, they observed that complex cases in the test sample had higher depression recovery rates when they were assigned directly to high intensity therapy rather than starting with low intensity psychological interventions. This advantage was large and statistically significant for the complex cases, whereas it was small and non-significant for the standard cases.

The algorithm developed by Delgadillo et al. (2017) has been implemented in a large (N = 951) multiservice cluster randomized trial (Delgadillo et al., under review), making it the first prospective test of the utility of a data-driven treatment recommendation algorithm for stratification in psychotherapy. Depression recovery rates were higher in patients whose assignment was informed by the algorithm's recommendation, relative to the patients who were allocated according to usual stepped care. The findings from this study are encouraging regarding the potential for the development, implementation, and dissemination of data-driven treatment selection approaches.

Selecting Treatment Packages

Systematic reviews of evidence-based interventions within specific patient populations have generally supported the conclusion that the *average* treatment effects of most evidence-based interventions are not different from one another. For example, Cuijpers and colleagues (2020) conducted a network meta-analysis to examine 101 studies of treatments for depression, comprising 11,910 patients, and found no difference in rates of response or remission between patients who received antidepressants or psychotherapy. However, they also found significant heterogeneity of observed treatment responses, reflecting the fact that some patients show significant improvement whereas others evidence little-to-no improvement, or even deterioration. Thus, one of the most basic and essential questions that precision medicine approaches can answer in mental health is *which* of the available evidence-based treatment packages is likely to result in the best outcome for a given individual (3DP:L2). This is the core question for personalized treatment selection (Cohen & DeRubeis, 2018).

Several data-driven approaches to treatment selection have been described in the literature. What most of these approaches have in common is the goal of generating an index of the expected differential magnitude – or likelihood – of response between two (or more) available treatment packages. All of these approaches use statistical modeling to capture the collective predictive signal from multiple pretreatment variables. If this signal is strong enough, the index derived from it can be used to inform, for each new patient, a treatment recommendation. It is understood that, for many patients, even a powerful model will predict little if any differential benefit from one treatment versus another. But a powerful model will be able to inform treatment decisions in such a way that substantially better outcomes are achieved, in the aggregate, relative to random assignment (or one of the other comparisons described below in the next section) (Kapelner et al., 2021).

One of these approaches, proposed by DeRubeis, Cohen and colleagues (2014), yields for any individual a *Personalized Advantage Index* (PAI), which is a signed score that indicates which of two interventions is expected to result in a better outcome. The magnitude of the index reflects the strength of the expectation. DeRubeis, Cohen et al. (2014) first demonstrated the PAI approach using data from a randomized comparison of CBT versus pharmacotherapy (paroxetine) in outpatients with major depressive disorder. Numerous studies and research groups have applied variations of this PAI approach to examine if subgroups of patients can be identified who respond differentially to: CBT vs. interpersonal psychotherapy (Huibers et al., 2015; van Bronswijk, Bruijniks et al., 2020; van Bronswijk et al., 2019); trauma-focused CBT vs. EMDR (Deisenhofer et al., 2018); prolonged exposure vs. cognitive processing therapy (Keefe et al., 2018); group CBT vs. transdiagnostic group CBT (Eskildsen et al., 2020); group CBT vs. a group integrative positive psychological intervention (Lopez-Gomez et al., 2019); CBT vs. CBT with exposure and emotion-focused elements (Friedl, Berger, et al., 2020); usual face-to-face CBT vs. blended face-to-face plus internet CBT (Friedl, Krieger, et al., 2020); CBT vs. psychodynamic therapy (Cohen et al., 2020; Schwartz et al., 2020); CBT vs. counselling for depression (Delgadillo & Gonzalez Salas Duhne, 2020); ADM (sertraline) vs. placebo (Webb, Trivedi et al., 2019); continuation-phase cognitive therapy vs. antidepressant medication (fluoxetine, Vittengl et al., 2017); and DBT vs. general psychiatric management (Keefe et al., 2020).

Other approaches have been used to develop data-driven treatment selection models. Nearest neighbors modeling (Lutz et al., 2006) identifies, for each treatment, a subset of patients who are most similar to a given index patient on a set of variables (i.e., the index patient's "nearest neighbors"). The recommendation for the index patient is derived by calculating the difference in average outcome scores observed in one treatment versus the other, among the index patient's nearest neighbors. Other methods with similar goals are described by Kraemer (2013) – the M* approach, implemented by Wallace et al. (2013) and Petkova et al.'s (2017) composite moderator approach, as demonstrated by Cloitre and colleagues (2016) as well as in a recent tutorial (Petkova et al., 2019).

An index of predicted differential benefit can also be derived from two (or more) separate prognostic models, each of which is constructed using only data from patients who were treated with one of the interventions (e.g., Deisenhofer et al., 2018; Delgadillo & Gonzalez Salas Duhne, 2020; Furukawa, Debray et al., 2020; Kessler et al., 2017). The difference between the patient's predicted outcome in each treatment forms the basis for the treatment recommendation.

Other approaches for predicting differential benefit exist. Methodological development in statistical prediction algorithms is ongoing, and the application of novel approaches such as the super learner ensemble machine learning method (van der Laan et al., 2007) promises to provide increasingly powerful predictive information to support treatment personalization. When more than two options are under consideration, the statistical and practical complexity of treatment selection increases. For examples of such developments, see Zilcha-Mano et al. (2016) and Furukawa, Debray et al. (2020).

Selecting Treatment Components or Techniques

Another approach to psychotherapy personalization involves the selection of treatment components or techniques in a way that would maximize improvement for patients with specific features (3DP:L3). Developing such a system, and defining an explicit decision-making process to select the type and sequence of treatment components, has been the aim of recent investigations. The advent of modular psychotherapies, such as the unified protocol (Barlow et al., 2017) and MATCH (Chorpita & Daleiden, 2009), presents a novel opportunity to formalize this approach, wherein a therapist constructs a modular treatment package that is meant to address a patient's principal symptoms and concerns. In the context of psychotherapy, Chorpita et al. (2005) defined modularity as breaking up complex activities into self-contained, smaller units that can function independently while also working together as part of a package.

For psychological treatments that can be modularized, two goals of personalized mental health research are to attempt to predict *which* components are going to be most important for an individual to receive, and to predict the optimal *order* in which components should be delivered. Importantly, this approach to personalization does not require that the treatment components themselves be altered. Individually constructed modular treatments could maximize efficiency by ensuring that patients are provided with only the specific components they need, and could increase adherence by minimizing the likelihood of patients receiving irrelevant or contraindicated interventions. These aims are relevant for both face-to-face psychotherapy as well as technology-based interventions. They are especially relevant in the context of transdiagnostic treatments, and when creating treatment plans for patients with significant comorbidity who present with a variety of potential targets. Another attractive feature of this internal personalization approach is that, unlike selecting between therapeutic modalities that would likely be delivered by different providers, this approach allows the therapist to personalize treatment themselves, as opposed to (for example) having to refer their client to another provider.

Theory-based approaches for personalizing treatment by determining which treatment components to deliver have often failed to outperform non-personalized interventions. For example, Moritz et al. (2016) assessed patients with OCD ($N = 89$) on 14 different cognitive biases and dysfunctional coping styles and then randomized the patients to receive either the full version of a self-help metacognitive bibliotherapy or an individually adapted version that only included the specific chapters theoretically indicated to address their endorsed target areas. The authors found that this algorithmic approach to personalization (3DP:S4-L3-T1) did not outperform simple provision of the entire manual (Moritz et al., 2016). Another example of a theory-based approach is "The Toolbox," a web-based self-guided app recommendation service in which users could select one or more "well-being categories" and then one or more goals, and then would be provided with a selection of what were determined to be relevant apps and tools to browse and download (3DP:S4-L3-T1). The personalized recommendation algorithm was developed through a participatory design approach with young people and mental health professionals based on a theory of change and theories of reasoned and planned behavior (Antezana et al., 2015). Bidargaddi and colleagues (2017) evaluated this non-data-driven approach to personalization in a randomized trial that compared it against a four-week wait-list control and found no benefit on the primary outcome.

In contrast to many theory-based approaches, randomized comparisons of data-informed personalized modular psychotherapy against usual-care conditions have often reported favorable results (e.g., Chorpita et al., 2017; Weisz et al., 2012). In a sample of youths, Weisz and colleagues (2012) evaluated a data-informed personalized modular treatment (MATCH) that comprised procedures from each of three separate standard interventions for depression, anxiety, and conduct disorder. The RCT ($N = 174$) compared MATCH against standardized treatment (one of three manualized interventions) and a usual-care control arm and found that the modular condition was associated with superior outcomes relative to standardized treatment and usual-care.

Mohr et al. (2019) provide an example of a data-driven approach to recommending treatment components (3DP:L3). The algorithm was developed in a large training sample ($N > 100,000$) primarily by modeling associations between client characteristics and differential engagement with the modules. The authors noted that the decision not to use differential change in clients' symptoms was largely driven by data availability (Personal Communication, Mohr & Schueller, 11/13/2019). However, given the high rate of dropout often observed in digital mental health (Cuijpers et al., 2019), maximizing engagement is a sensible goal. In their factorial RCT ($N = 301$), Mohr et al. (2019) reported that, relative to those who received no recommendations, those who received the weekly personalized recommendations evidenced greater engagement and larger improvements in depression, but not anxiety, symptoms. Unfortunately, given the lack of a control comparison (e.g., sham recommendations), the possibility remains that, instead of being due to the personalized nature of the recommendations, the improved outcomes were simply the result of receiving reminders to download and use the apps, and that non-personalized recommendations might have worked just as well (or better).

The personalization discussed so far has relied on *nomothetic* statistical approaches, which trade on similarities and differences between individuals. In nomothetic personalization, predictions of response to specific treatment strategies are made for individuals using data from a reference group of cases treated in the past and who have features that are similar to the target patients. *Idiographic* approaches (Fisher & Bosley, 2020; Fisher et al., 2018; Wright & Woods, 2020), on the other hand, focus on within-person patterns, rather than patterns that are observed across individuals. The construction of these person-specific statistical models requires intensive longitudinal measurement. A model developed from an individual's own data can then be used to inform decisions about specific treatment strategies for that individual (Fernandez et al., 2017; Rubel et al., 2018).

For example, Fisher et al. (2019) developed personalized treatment plans for 40 CBT patients who had completed daily symptom measures over a one-month pre-treatment period, using ecological momentary assessments. Patients' symptom profiles were examined using person-specific factor-analytic (P-technique) and dynamic factor modeling techniques, and this information guided the construction of individualized treatment plans which drew upon modules from the Unified

Protocol for transdiagnostic treatment of emotional disorders (Barlow et al., 2011). The authors reported large pre–post treatment effect sizes ($g = 1.86$ in the intention-to-treat analysis) for this individualized treatment approach, although – as the authors note – these findings are from a small ($N = 32$ completers) uncontrolled open trial.

Nuances in the methodology of this interesting trial can help illustrate some of the complexity in the personalization literature that motivated our creation of the frameworks described in Figures 19.1–19.3. The trial (Fisher et al., 2019) was split into two phases that demonstrate different ways in which data-driven approaches can inform treatment selection. For one phase, an expert panel of clinicians met to discuss each patient's ideographic modeling results and develop the personalized treatment plans (Figure 19.3, process #5). For another phase, a dynamic assessment and treatment algorithm (Fernandez et al., 2017) automatically translated each patient's ideographic modeling results into a personalized treatment plan (see Figure 19.3, process #6) using an item-module matching matrix. Of interest is that this matrix was constructed based on a predominantly theory-driven match between the different symptoms and CBT strategies in the modules believed to target such symptoms, instead of, for example, on empirical evidence of whether each module of the Unified Protocol (or the technique it contained) had been shown to impact one or more of the target symptoms (i.e., data-informed), or an actual quantification of the magnitude of the effect of each module on the targets (i.e., data-driven). Thus, the second personalization approach described by Fisher et al. (2019) is a statistical model (3DP:S5-L3-T1) that illustrates a blend of a data-driven approach (the ideographic modeling component) with a theoretical approach (the item-module matching matrix). These idiographic methods and related process-based therapies (e.g., Hofmann & Hayes, 2019) are promising new approaches for advancing data-driven psychotherapy personalization.

Adjusting Psychotherapy As It Unfolds

Another important way in which personalization approaches differ concerns *when* the personalization scheme is applied (the Time dimension of Figure 19.1). Thus far, we have focused on the decisions that are made prior to the initiation of treatment (3DP:T1). When decisions are made, instead, dynamically over the course of treatment, one can refer to this as *adjusting treatment* (3DP:T2). Much of this growing literature focuses on adaptive treatment strategies such as just-in-time adaptive interventions (JITAI), which have the goal of delivering specific components of an intervention package at the optimal time for each individual (Nahum-Shani et al., 2015, 2018). These approaches have great potential for personalizing treatment, especially in the context of digital interventions (Goldstein et al., 2017) and digital phenotyping of mobile devices (Bae et al., 2018).

One foundational practice that can support treatment adjustment is routine outcome monitoring, whereby a client's symptoms are tracked over time using validated psychometric measures (Lambert et al., 2018). Routine outcome monitoring

is used in *feedback-informed treatment*, in which the clinician is notified as to whether the patient is "on track" or "not on track," a categorization that relies on a comparison of a patient's progress against expected progress, based on available normative data from clinical samples. Numerous systematic reviews and meta-analyses demonstrate that dynamically adjusting the treatment plan and approach using feedback-informed treatment leads to improved psychotherapy outcomes. A detailed review of the empirical support for feedback-informed treatment is found in Chapter 4 of this *Handbook*.

Another way in which time-varying prediction approaches can be used to improve patient outcomes is by identifying when a patient is at a high risk for dropout, so that interventions to increase the likelihood of retention can be initiated (Lutz et al., 2019, 2020). For example, Forsell et al. (2019) constructed predictive models using only longitudinal symptom data from a large naturalistic sample ($N > 5000$) of patients in a 12-week program of therapist guided internet-delivered CBT for depression, panic, or social anxiety. They found that sufficiently accurate predictions (which they defined as a balanced accuracy of 65%) could be generated starting halfway through treatment. Lorimer and colleagues (2020) demonstrated how risk of relapse could be dynamically predicted across the 12-month period following successful acute treatment using a multivariable ensemble machine learning approach.

Levin and colleagues (2018) evaluated a data-informed (but not data-driven) personalized psychotherapy in a small RCT ($N = 69$) that compared four weeks of digital acceptance and commitment therapy (ACT) with skill coaching that was tailored based on ecological momentary assessment (EMA) against random skill coaching or no skill coaching. All participants completed EMA, and participants in both skills conditions were blinded to allocation. Those in the tailored condition received the ACT skill component linked to the highest-rated problem (where the linking was based on both theory and observed associations, derived from an earlier pilot study, between specific skill coaching sessions and specific outcome variables). Although the authors acknowledged that the study was underpowered to detect differences between the active conditions, they found that the personalized just-in-time adaptive intervention (3DP:S5-L4-T2) led to significant improvements in a variety of outcomes, relative to the random coaching and control conditions.

Smyth and Heron (2016) provide a clear example of the potential of data-informed decision-rules for personalizing treatment that occurs dynamically across treatment (3DP:S4-L4-T2). Participants ($N = 90$) were randomized to one of three conditions in which they completed EMA about stress and mood 3X-per-day: EMA-only, EMA plus tailored recommendations about micro-interventions for responding to stress and negative mood, or EMA plus semi-random reminders about using randomly selected micro-interventions. In the tailored condition, recommendations were provided when a participant's EMA indicated moderately-high or high stress or negative affect (based on >= 1 SD above their person-centered mean, which was determined based on a two-day lead-in where they only completed EMA). The specific intervention recommendations were based on participants' symptom reports in the EMA. Relative to the comparison conditions, the data-informed JITAI resulted in lower self-reported negative affect, fewer reported stressful events, lower cortisol levels, better sleep quality, and lower levels of potentially problematic health behaviors (e.g., alcohol consumption).

METHODOLOGICAL AND STATISTICAL ISSUES FOR PERSONALIZED PSYCHOTHERAPY

All models are wrong, but some are useful.
– Famous aphorism on statistical modeling coined by
George Box (Box & Draper, 1987)

The decision to implement a new approach for personalizing treatment that deviates from current evidence-based practices should be informed by evidence of its utility. A savvy consumer of the constantly evolving field of personalized mental health care will want to know how to evaluate the literature critically. In general, there are several stages in the development and validation of data-driven personalization models (Delgadillo & Lutz, 2020). Early stages involve the construction and testing of a clinical prediction model that is intended to inform decision-making. More advanced stages involve case studies of implementation, prospective field-tests (e.g., Delgadillo, Appleby et al., 2020), and clinical trials of the resulting decision support systems in clinical practice (e.g., Lutz et al., 2021). A personalization system must first be constructed in order for it to be evaluated, and it must be described in sufficient detail if it is to be implemented by those who did not develop it. In the following, we address these three features of personalization systems. We begin with considerations relevant to the evaluation of such systems, as understanding how an approach has been subjected to empirical tests and what is known about the value it can provide is, we believe, of utmost importance to the general consumer of research on personalization. Although it can be helpful to know and understand how an approach was developed, it is not required for an independent evaluation of its utility.

The following high-level overview of model construction and evaluation builds upon decades of work by groups across medicine and statistics. More extensive discussion and guidelines for prediction model development and validation are provided by the "Transparent Reporting of a multivariable prediction model for Individual Prognosis or Diagnosis" (TRIPOD) system (Collins et al., 2015; Moons et al., 2015). The PROGRESS (PROGnosis RESearch Strategy) group has provided recommendations for predictive modeling in health care research (Hemingway et al., 2013; Hingorani et al., 2013; Riley et al., 2013; Steyerberg et al., 2013). The Predictive Approaches to Treatment effect Heterogeneity (PATH) Statement gives specific guidance for using predictive modeling

of heterogeneity of treatment effects to inform clinical practice (Kent, Paulus et al., 2020; Kent, Van Klaveren et al., 2020). Wherever possible, we will refer the reader to these and other resources for more comprehensive discussions of relevant issues (e.g., Riley, van der Windt et al., 2019; Steyerberg, 2019).

Evaluation

In this section, we review the variety of approaches that can be used to evaluate psychotherapy personalization systems and the data-driven prediction models on which they are sometimes based. We will discuss contemporary methods for the evaluation of approaches used to select treatment packages as well as those used to tailor treatment.

Evaluating the Performance of Data-Driven Models

A statistical model developed in a given dataset (often called a *training sample*) should be evaluated using held-out data to estimate key performance measures, such as accuracy, for the predictions (Jacobucci et al., 2020). Held-out data can also be used to gain insight into the potential utility of the recommendations that can be derived from a predictive model. When an external data-source is unavailable for use as a held-out test-sample, internal validation, via techniques such as cross-validation or bootstrapping, should be performed to generate an estimate of the model's ability to provide accurate and precise predictions in a new sample (Steyerberg et al., 2001). The split halves approach should be avoided (Steyerberg & Harrell, 2016). Cross-validation methods can also be used internally during model construction, such as when selecting variables or tuning model hyperparameters. When estimates of a model's performance are derived from internal validation, failure to incorporate in the cross-validation all the steps needed to generate the model will lead to biased (overoptimistic) estimates of model performance (Steyerberg et al., 2003). The steps include variable selection, imputation of missing data, and weight setting. Even when all pertinent procedures have been included during cross-validation, the estimate of model accuracy can still be biased if the training sample is small (Varoquaux, 2018).

A variety of factors must be considered when estimating the sample sizes needed to develop (Riley, Snell et al., 2019a, 2019b; van Smeden et al., 2019) and validate (Archer et al., 2020) prediction models. Riley and colleagues (2020) provide comprehensive guidance on sample size issues, including an R package that implements their recommended procedure.

The generalizability of a model's predictions will likely be limited if it is applied in new cases or services that differ considerably to those used to train the model. It cannot be known with certainty, in advance, what characteristics of patients, treatments, or providers will affect generalizability, so the best we can do is to apply our knowledge of the domains and adjust our expectations of the utility of the model in the test sample accordingly. For example, it would be unsurprising if a model developed in a study of university counseling patients generalized poorly to an inpatient care population. Prospective randomized experiments that use the same assessment and treatment procedures as were used to develop the model avoid many of the limitations encountered in tests that use preexisting data or data from contexts that differ from the model's development. We refer to this as *context specificity*: a prediction model is only expected to generalize to new samples that are sufficiently similar (e.g., in their features and treatment context).

An important aspect of the development and evaluation of statistical models for treatment personalization is *calibration*, which refers to the extent to which a model's predictions align with the true observed values (Alba et al., 2017; Steyerberg et al., 2010). Van Calster and colleagues (2019) highlight the potential dangers of – as well as advice on how to avoid – poorly calibrated predictive models in clinical decision-making. Huang and colleagues (2020) provide an extensive tutorial aimed at clinical researchers, complete with R code demonstrating calibration of predictive models for treatment personalization.

Another way in which prediction performance can be evaluated is through prospective designs. For example, Symons and colleagues (2020) developed a set of multivariable prediction models using data from patients (N = 1016) who had received a CBT-based intervention for alcohol dependence. They then generated prospective predictions for 220 new patients using these models and compared them against predictions made by 10 clinical psychologists, and observed superior accuracy and calibration for the model-based predictions.

In summary, numerous methodological choices can affect the performance and clinical utility of prediction models. Ideally, clinical prediction models are constructed using sample sizes large enough to provide adequate power, missing data are addressed properly, internal and external cross-validation methods are used appropriately, and evaluations of generalizability are conducted on independent test samples.

Evaluating the Potential Clinical Utility of Treatment Personalization Approaches

When a treatment personalization approach relies on a prediction model, accurate and precise predictions can reasonably be assumed to be a necessary condition for the success of the system, but they should not be assumed to be sufficient. Thus, although it is important to use data and procedures that maximize the chance of obtaining a valid estimate of a prediction model's performance (e.g., accuracy), the question that will reveal the real-world utility of a model in a given context is: "Can the application of this treatment personalization approach, informed by the model's predictions, improve patients' outcomes, relative to the way in which the relevant decisions are currently made?" Answering that question requires the consideration of a multitude of factors beyond predictive accuracy.

Figure 19.3 depicts a variety of ways in which decision-making processes can translate information about the patient into specific treatment-relevant decisions. The first column of *The Information-to-Decision Translational Framework* aligns with the *Structure* dimension of the 3DP framework (see Figure 19.1). The second and third columns describe the

outputs, which can be quantitative (e.g., predicted post-treatment symptom score) or qualitative (e.g., "psychotherapy is the optimal treatment for this client"). The fourth column (human filter) illustrates that information from a treatment personalization approach either leads directly to changes in the intervention for the client (i.e., without review by a human, as in #4 and #6), or is used by the clinician, client, or both in the form of a shared decision-making process to determine how to personalize treatment. Tests of treatment personalization systems that employ a human filter must be able to account for the fact that patients or clinicians can override the recommendation, thus affecting the extent to which the evaluation still reflects the quality of the quantitative or qualitative information that was generated.

Kraepelien and colleagues' (2019) study of a personalization approach highlights this issue. The authors describe how, after generating the personalized treatment plan, "The therapist would then present the patient with two recommended problem areas to work with, but the patient had the final word and could change to the two preferred problem areas of his or her choice. There was no measure of how often the patient chose to focus on other problem areas than the recommended" (Kraepelien et al., 2019, p. 3). As the patients were allowed to disregard the recommendations, and because there was no record of how frequently this occurred, a post-hoc analysis exploring the outcomes for the subset of patients who decided to follow the recommendations was not possible.

Figure 19.3 was created to be illustrative, and thus does not provide a comprehensive mapping of all possible scenarios. For example, Figure 19.3's process #5 does not capture perfectly the first approach used by Fisher and colleagues (2019) that was described earlier in this chapter, in which quantitative outputs generated by statistical models were sent directly to an expert panel of clinicians who then developed the personalized treatment plan (without the quantitative outputs first being translated into an explicit recommendation).

The three conceptual frameworks illustrated in Figures 19.1–19.3 can be used together to describe, organize, and critique a variety of approaches to personalization in the psychotherapy literature. However, none of these frameworks address the "How well does it work?" question. It is to this important issue – evaluation – that we now turn.

Evaluating Treatment Selection Approaches in Real-World Settings

Having already reviewed methods for quantifying prediction model accuracy, we will now focus on the more holistic evaluation of personalization *systems*. Approaches that provide inferential statistics about the expected performance of data-driven treatment selection rules are an active area of research (Kapelner et al., 2021; Luedtke & van der Laan, 2016a; Luedtke & van der Laan, 2017). Comparisons of outcomes for patients assigned to their model-predicted optimal treatment versus those assigned to their nonoptimal treatment, or those assigned randomly, can indicate whether there is signal in the set of predictions that rises above the noise. However, the effect size associated with the first comparison (optimal vs. nonoptimal) is unlikely to reflect any real-world scenario,

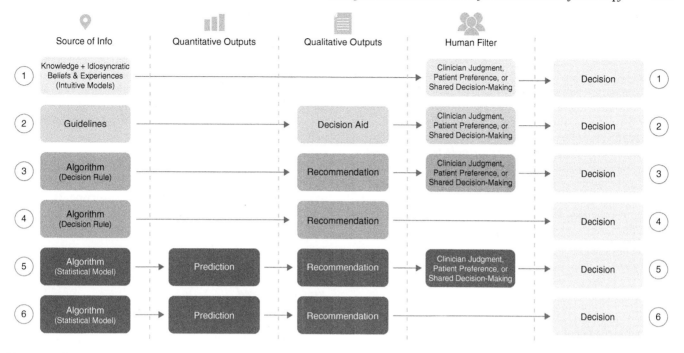

FIGURE 19.3   The Information-to-decision translational framework

CC BY 4.0 Zachary Cohen, Jaime Delgadillo, Robert DeRubeis, & Jenny Xin

given that it is difficult to imagine a clinician intentionally allocating all of their patients to their contra-indicated treatment. And although the comparison of optimal vs. random is reasonable and informative, it still might provide a biased estimate of the potential real-world impact of a personalization approach, insofar as current practice (e.g., allocation-as-usual) deviates from randomness (or quasi-randomness). A more clinically relevant question is whether the recommendations derived from the model outperform typical or state-of-the-art methods that are in place for the decision of interest.

One way to address this question is through the collection of relevant baseline data (e.g., patient preference or clinician judgment) for secondary data analysis in the context of prospective randomized clinical trials. For example, a recent study by van Bronswijk, Lemmens et al. (2020) used an RCT of cognitive therapy vs. interpersonal therapy to compare model-based treatment recommendations against therapists' recommendations (recorded prior to randomization), which were based on case presentations of diagnostic workups. Model-based recommendations outperformed clinicians' recommendations. The authors also found evidence that patients who were randomized to the treatment recommended by the clinicians had worse outcomes than those randomized to the treatment identified by clinicians as nonpreferred, providing further caution against relying on intuitive treatment selection approaches.

Clinically relevant tests of model-driven personalization regimes are provided by prospective trials in which patients are randomized to receive treatment personalized based on the output of an algorithm (#6, Figure 19.3) or to treatment determined by means other than the application of the algorithm, such as *patient preference*, *clinician judgment*, or *shared*

decision-making (Figure 19.3, process #1), which is often described as *allocation-as-usual*.

It is understood that when an algorithm is disseminated, those using it will often allow input, after the fact, from the patient and clinician, in ways that could either enhance or detract from its utility. However, a test of a data-driven algorithm can be confounded if its application allows for a reversal of its recommendation by the clinician or patient. Likewise, the comparison condition can be contaminated if clinicians or clients in that condition are provided with information derived from the model. Further, differences in hope or expectancy can arise when the patient or clinician thinks they are working together on a treatment plan that has been "personalized" for that patient. Alternatively, they might be suspicious of a process whereby treatment is automatically selected by the algorithm without their input. Methods that can control for these potential confounds include incorporating patient preference as a feature in the statistical model or investigating separately the outcomes of patients whose recommended personalization was reversed by clinician judgment. Regarding personalization placebo effects, participants could be blinded as to whether they had been randomized to the personalized condition, or a double-blind could be implemented by providing clinicians in the control condition with fake (e.g., random) treatment recommendations.

If an unconfounded application of randomization is not possible (#6, Figure 19.3), an alternative experimental condition is for the recommendation from the algorithm to inform the clinician's decision or a decision that is shared between the clinician and the client (#5, Figure 19.3). An advantage of this algorithm-informed selection process is that it reflects how algorithms are most likely to be implemented in practice.

A limitation is that the utility, or accuracy, of the algorithm cannot be estimated independent of the input from the clinician and client. Relative to algorithm-based treatment selection, deviations from the algorithm's recommendation due to clinical judgment or patient influence could result in either improvements or worsening of patient outcomes. To the extent that a model's recommendation is not followed in the model-*informed* condition, the researcher cannot fully evaluate how well patients would have fared if their treatment had followed the model-derived plan. When departures from the model-derived recommendation are allowed, the number of reversals needs to be documented in order to elucidate the extent to which the experimental condition has been contaminated, and to permit secondary analyses of patients for whom the recommendations were and were not followed.

Evaluating Approaches to Tailoring Psychotherapy

When evaluating personalized psychotherapy that takes the form of selecting treatment components (3DP:L3) or adapting delivery style (3DP:L4), there are also several important methodological choices that must be made in relation to the control or comparison conditions. In order to address the specific question of the effectiveness of the personalization component itself, the personalized psychotherapy could be compared against a version of the same psychotherapy that lacks personalization, contains pseudo-personalization, uses randomized personalization, or that uses a comparable real-world approach to personalization (e.g., comparing data-driven selection of treatment components against patient preference-based selection of treatment components). The methods of blinding (if any) the researcher decides to employ in any of the above comparisons can have a significant impact on the interpretation of the study results. For any of the randomized comparisons discussed in this section, randomization could occur at the level of the patient, the clinician, or at the level of a clinic or hospital.

More complex trial designs can allow for compelling evaluations of different aspects of personalized psychotherapy. A study by Schulte et al. (1992) provides perhaps the best example of how the *personalization* in a psychotherapy personalization system can be evaluated. Phobic patients ($N = 120$) were randomly assigned to one of three conditions: (i) standardized *in vivo* exposure therapy, (ii) personalized treatment in which the therapist used their case conceptualization to design a specific treatment plan for their patient that could use all therapeutic methods commonly employed in behavior therapy and cognitive therapy, or (iii) a yoked control group, in which each patient's treatment followed a manual that was created based on the treatment records of a specific patient in the personalized treatment condition with whom they were paired. A highly clinically relevant question – "Does this personalized therapy outperform standard evidence-based treatment?"– can be answered through the comparison of the standardized and personalized conditions. This contrast, however, does not allow for a pure evaluation of the personalization itself, due to differences in technique use (e.g., those in the standardized

condition received more in vivo exposure and less cognitive methods) and treatment duration (patients in the personalized therapy received, on average, six more sessions) that arose due to the flexibility in the personalized therapy. The comparison of the yoked condition against personalized therapy controls for these differences in technique and duration, thus allowing for the evaluation of the more scientifically interesting question: "What is the specific value of the *personalization* in this individually tailored psychotherapy?" Schulte et al. (1992) found that standardized exposure therapy outperformed personalized therapy (comparison 1). They also found that the clinical decision-making that had guided the personalization had no impact on patient outcomes (comparison 2). To truly learn the value of psychotherapy personalization, more studies that allow for these nuanced comparisons (e.g., Kerns et al., 2014) are needed.

How Personalization Approaches Are Defined and Presented

Personalization systems need to be clearly defined, reproducible, and trainable. These requirements are similar to what is required for the evaluation of a structured psychotherapy, which would be unlikely to have a meaningful real-world impact in clinical settings if new practitioners could not be trained in its delivery. Similarly, warning flags should be raised if the description of the system through which personalization occurs is insufficiently detailed, or if the description reveals that the process would be unlikely to be replicable or trainable. Bonnett et al. (2019) discussed four different models of how clinical prediction models can be presented in order to serve as practical decision tools for clinicians. These models differ in complexity and sophistication; from simple point-scoring systems to determine if a patient's profile surpasses the threshold for a specific clinical decision, to fully computerized interfaces that automate complex statistical algorithms using a user-friendly input device. All of these options have advantages and disadvantages, and the choice of interface broadly depends on the clinical setting and the complexity of the underlying algorithm.

Berger et al. (2014) provide an example of a well-defined, replicable, data-informed approach to personalization. Patients with social anxiety, generalized anxiety, or panic were randomized to wait-list control, disorder-specific, or individually tailored internet-based guided self-help, where the intervention was tailored based on a series of pretreatment assessments (3DP:S4-L3-T1). Patients who were in the disorder-specific condition received only the content for their principal diagnosis as determined by a diagnostic interview, whereas patients who were in the individually tailored condition received content specific to any problem area in which they scored at least 1.5 standard deviations higher than the normal population mean on the disorder-specific measure. In an example of a clearly defined data-informed approach, Delgadillo, Appleby et al. (2020) developed a data-driven decision algorithm called the Leeds Risk Index, which enables clinicians to easily implement a regression-based scoring system to decide which patients with common mental disorders should be offered low intensity guided self-help or high intensity psychotherapies. This method is highly standardized and guided by a simple visual diagram that fits with the definition of a "nomogram" as described by Bonnett et al. (2019).

Constructing Data-Driven Personalized Treatment Decision Support Systems

Having already covered the ways in which information (i.e., a prediction or recommendation) from a treatment personalization approach could be used and evaluated, as well as the ways in which the translation of these outputs (regardless of their quality) can be influenced by the decision-making process, we now turn to the process of constructing the data-driven statistical models on which the most powerful treatment personalization approaches will be based. The various decisions that must be made throughout the stages of model development matter. Different researchers using the same data can draw very different conclusions about how to personalize treatment, as demonstrated in a recent "crowd-sourced" analysis in which 12 research teams analyzed the same EMA dataset to select treatment targets (Bastiaansen et al., 2020). For historical perspectives on approaches to building statistical models for treatment selection in psychotherapy, see recent reviews by Cohen and DeRubeis (2018) and Cohen et al. (2019).

Sample Considerations

The limited sample sizes available in randomized clinical trials are often insufficient to adequately power the evaluation of prescriptive models. Luedtke and colleagues' (2019) simulations suggest that, in order to have adequate statistical power to develop and evaluate models and to detect clinically significant marginal improvements associated with treatment selection, at least 300 patients per treatment arm are needed. Lorenzo-Luaces et al. (2020) reviewed personalized medicine studies comparing CBT to other treatments for depression and identified 19 published multivariable prediction models, none of which met Luedtke and colleagues' sample size recommendation. As a solution to the sample size issues discussed throughout this chapter, Kessler and colleagues (2019) proposed that researchers first begin by developing models using a large observational (non-randomized) datasets. Archival data will often lack the richness of datasets from RCTs, and such samples rarely provide the tight control over treatment parameters and assessment that is afforded by RCTs. Thus, the authors proposed an iterative process, whereby models developed in observational samples are subsequently examined in RCT datasets, and then tested prospectively in experimental studies. Delgadillo and Lutz (2020) described a similar development pathway where clinical prediction models are initially trained in large ($N > 1000$) observational datasets using an external cross-validation design, and then are prospectively tested in field tests (e.g., small-scale prospective studies), randomized controlled trials, and then in implementation case studies that examine their effectiveness in routine care.

Supervised versus Unsupervised Learning Approaches

One important initial decision when creating a data-driven personalization system is whether to apply a *supervised* or *unsupervised* modeling approach, the goals of which can differ. Supervised learning approaches aim to predict an outcome based on a number of inputs, whereas unsupervised approaches aim to model associations or patterns among a set of inputs, without the involvement of a specified outcome measure (Hastie et al., 2009).

A typical use-case for unsupervised approaches in treatment personalization is when information about patients is used to generate categories or dimensions, typically without the use of information about the treatment(s) received or outcomes observed during treatment. Associations with outcomes are examined only after the data-driven categories or dimensions are created. Common types of unsupervised approaches involve *clustering* and *dimensionality reduction*. Dimensionality reduction approaches include principal components analysis and exploratory or confirmatory factor analysis. Worked examples of clustering approaches that can inform psychotherapy treatment selection can be seen for latent profile analysis (Saunders et al., 2016), latent variable mixture modeling (Saunders et al., 2020), and agglomerative hierarchical and *k*-means cluster analysis (Deckersbach et al., 2016).

A wide variety of supervised learning approaches have been applied in mental health predictive modeling (see the previous section), ranging from classic ordinary least squares linear regression to nonparametric machine learning approaches, including random forests and Bayesian additive regression trees. The majority of the data-driven efforts we have described in this chapter aim to take advantage of associations between patient characteristics that can be ascertained prior to selecting a treatment (3DP:T1) and the primary outcomes resulting from the treatments under consideration (e.g., symptom reduction). Supervised learning approaches can also be employed to predict secondary outcomes (e.g., treatment dropout; Lutz et al., 2018) that are presumed to be related to the outcome of interest (e.g., symptom response). When selecting secondary outcomes as targets for supervised personalization models, it is sensible to leverage presumed mediators of change. For example, in face-to-face therapy, common targets include attendance (e.g., Davis et al., 2020), engagement with the procedures of the therapy, homework compliance, or measures of the therapeutic alliance (e.g., Rubel et al., 2020). If there is a strong link between a presumed mediator and the outcome of interest, a model that predicts patients' scores on the mediator will tend also to predict outcome.

Prognostic and Prescriptive Modeling

The PROGRESS Group defined a prognostic factor as "any measure that, among people with a given health condition (that is, a start point), is associated with a subsequent clinical outcome (an endpoint)" (Hemingway et al., 2013). Models comprising prognostic variables (Steyerberg et al., 2013) can be contrasted with those that include prescriptive variables (also known as moderators or effect modifiers), which affect the direction or strength of the differences in outcome between two or more treatments (Baron & Kenny, 1986). A prescriptive variable is one that interacts with the treatment variable to predict differential response between treatments, and thus is informative for treatment selection models. See Cohen et al. (2019) for a comprehensive discussion of prognostic and prescriptive variables. For the purpose of this chapter, we will define prognostic models as any models that are constructed in a way that aims to predict an outcome of interest for a specific population, but without including treatment-moderator interaction terms. For example, a model that is constructed using only data from clients with depression who have been treated with psychodynamic therapy would be prognostic, because there is no way to know whether the predictive relationships instantiated in the model are identical to or different from those that would be observed had the same or similar individuals from the same population been treated with CBT, or medication, or had they received no treatment at all. Similarly, a model constructed using a mixed sample of individuals with depression, some of whom were treated with psychodynamic therapy, others of whom were treated with medication, would be classified as prognostic if information about *which* treatment each individual received was not available to the model, because there would be no explicit mechanism to capture differential response. Although this chapter is mostly focused on prognostic models of treatment response, another relevant form of prognostic modeling is risk-prediction (e.g., Ebert et al., 2019), which can be used to identify individuals at risk for developing problems or disorders (e.g., Kiekens et al., 2019; King et al., 2008).

The distinction between prognostic and prescriptive clinical prediction models takes on special importance in the arena of personalization. A systematic review of methods for regression-based clinical prediction modeling by Rekkas and colleagues (2020) described three categories: risk-based methods (prognostic factors only), optimal treatment regime methods (treatment effect modifiers or prescriptive factors), and treatment effect modeling methods (which can include both prognostic and prescriptive factors). The goal of a treatment personalization approach (see Figure 19.1, *Level of Intervention* and *Timing* dimensions) can inform the decision of which modeling technique to use. For example, efforts to ensure that clients are initially triaged to the appropriate *level* of care are often amenable to prognostic modeling approaches (discussed in the previous section; see also Cohen & DeRubeis, 2018), whereas efforts to select treatment packages are often well-served by prescriptive modeling approaches.

Variable Selection

An important step of the *feature engineering* phase of constructing data-driven statistical models is the selection of *which* variables to include in the model. Different approaches applied to the same dataset can generate conflicting information about variable importance (Cohen et al., 2020). Repeated failures to identify any single predictive variable with large enough effects

to guide treatment personalization (Cuijpers, Karyotaki, Reijnders, & Huibers, 2018; Simon & Perlis, 2010) reflect the need for multivariable approaches that can take into account the cumulative signal from multiple predictive factors (see Cohen & DeRubeis [2018] for a discussion of this issue). The selection process can itself have multiple stages, which can be guided by practical, theoretical, or empirical considerations. Methods have been developed specifically for selecting variables in the context of treatment personalization (Bossuyt & Parvin, 2015; Janes et al., 2011). As part of the STRengthening Analytical Thinking for Observational Studies (STRATOS) initiative, Sauerbrei and colleagues (2020) published an extensive review of variable selection in which they summarize strengths and weaknesses of different approaches. They conclude that there is insufficient evidence to strongly recommend any single approach to variable selection, and that more research comparing different techniques is needed. Feature selection should incorporate cross-validation procedures that aim to select variables that are more likely to generalize to new samples and that are not overly influenced by overfitting (Rodriguez et al., 2009).

Machine Learning

Although the exact definition of machine learning remains elusive, this family of modeling approaches comprises methods that learn automatically from data, often flexibly capturing nonlinear associations and higher-order interactions. Uses of statistical modeling to draw conclusions from data can be broadly described as either serving the goal of explanation/inference (which seeks to extract information about the nature of relations between variables) or prediction (Shmueli, 2010). Breiman (2001) described these, respectively, as "The Data Modeling Culture" and "The Algorithmic Modeling Culture." The latter approach is most often associated with machine learning. Arnold and colleagues (2020) discuss the implications of the differences between prediction and "causal explanation" on the use of machine learning methods. As a comprehensive discussion of machine learning is beyond the scope of this chapter, we refer the interested reader to several recent reviews, which can provide: a broad background on machine learning in clinical psychology (Coutanche & Hallion, 2019; Dwyer et al., 2018); a more quantitative review of machine learning-based prediction for mental health outcomes (Salazar de Pablo et al., 2021); and a review specifically focused on machine learning in psychotherapy research (Aafjes-van Doorn et al., 2020).

Machine-learning algorithms have gained widespread popularity in the mental health treatment outcome prediction literature (Lee et al., 2018). Novel modeling approaches have been developed that focus specifically on interactions and are thus well-suited to treatment selection (e.g., qualitative interaction trees; Dusseldorp & Van Mechelen, 2014). See Kapelner et al. (2021) for an extensive discussion of recent developments in statistical modeling. In mental health prediction, several studies have reported superior predictive performance of machine learning over classic regression (Kessler et al., 2016;

Rosellini et al., 2018; Wardenaar et al., 2014; Webb, Cohen et al., 2019; c.f., Symons et al., 2020). Vollmer and colleagues (2020) set forth a helpful series of 20 critical questions (focused on six areas: inception, study, statistical methods, reproducibility, impact evaluation, and implementation) for all stakeholders involved in health-focused machine-learning efforts that aim to "provide a framework for research groups to inform the design, conduct, and reporting; for editors and peer reviewers to evaluate contributions to the literature; and for patients, clinicians, and policy makers to critically appraise where new findings may deliver patient benefit" (Vollmer et al., 2020). Although machine-learning approaches like neural networks, deep learning, boosting, support vector machines, and random forests – collectively called pure prediction algorithms by Efron (2020) – can result in improved predictive performance, key questions remain about when and how they can best be implemented (see the limitations section for further discussion).

Selecting a specific model or modeling approach to use can be challenging, especially given the abundance of publications in this space (Adibi et al., 2020). One way to inform this decision is to construct multiple predictive models in a sample using different approaches and then compare their performance using cross-validation, bootstrapping, or a held-out test sample (e.g., Delgadillo, Rubel, & Barkham, 2020; Hilbert et al., 2020; Webb, Cohen et al., 2019). A more advanced approach is to develop an ensemble in which multiple models are combined to optimize performance. An example of an ensemble machine-learning approach is "super learning" (van der Laan et al., 2007), which uses cross-validation to select weights for a set of algorithms, and can also be used to construct ensembles for dynamic treatment regimes (Luedtke & van der Laan, 2016b). After constructing the ensemble approach, the fit of the individual models can be compared against the ensemble. For two examples using the SuperLearner package in R (Polley et al., 2016), see Rosellini et al. (2018) and Webb, Cohen et al. (2019).

Novel Research Designs for Constructing Data-Driven Personalized Treatments

Novel trial designs such as balanced fractional factorial trials (e.g., Watkins et al., 2016) and sequential multiple assignment randomized trials (SMART; e.g., Southward & Sauer-Zavala, 2020) are promising complements to more data-analytic ideographic (e.g., Altman et al., 2020) and nomothetic (e.g., Pearson et al., 2019) approaches to understanding the links between specific psychotherapy techniques and outcomes, and individual differences in response to different therapeutic elements. Clinical trials based on these new paradigms have the potential to help overcome some of the main barriers to understanding how and for whom treatments work, such as the sample size constraints that hampered the field's ability to draw meaningful conclusions from the dismantling or component trial literature (Cuijpers et al., 2017). In the context of digital therapeutics, these highly efficient experimental designs can facilitate the rapid development and evaluation of scalable personalized treatments (Uwatoko et al., 2018).

CHALLENGES: ANALYTIC, METHODOLOGICAL, AND STATISTICAL PROBLEMS WITH THE EXISTING LITERATURE ON PERSONALIZED PSYCHOTHERAPY

Personalized and precision approaches have garnered significant enthusiasm in mental health (Hollon et al., 2019; Holmes et al., 2018) and medicine more broadly (Collins & Varmus, 2015). Unfortunately, many – but not all – of these approaches have failed to live up to their promise (Joyner & Paneth, 2019; Prasad et al., 2016; Senn, 2018; Wilkinson et al., 2020). If personalized and precision mental health are going to make meaningful impacts on real-world patient care, the methodological rigor of the development, reporting, and evaluation of these approaches must be improved.

Defining and Reporting Personalization Systems

Sufficient detail must be provided to allow a proper evaluation of a system for personalizing treatment. Multiple reviews suggest that this essential criterion is not being met. Using the TRIPOD checklist, Heus and colleagues (2018) reviewed publications reporting multivariable prediction models in top journals across 37 clinical domains. They identified 170 models and found that over 80% of the models were lacking key information, such as model specification or performance. These findings are reflected in the psychotherapy personalization literature as well. For example, consider Johansson et al.'s (2012) description of a personalization approach from their small RCT ($N = 40$ vs. 39) comparing standardized vs. individually tailored digital CBT: "An individualized treatment plan was prepared for each participant randomized to the tailored treatment. The treatment plans were formed by discussion in the research group and were mainly based on the SCID interview and results from self-report measures" (Johansson et al., 2012, p. 5). Not only is this description of the personalization insufficiently detailed to allow a reader to implement or evaluate the approach, but it also reveals levels of clinical judgment and flexibility that greatly decrease the likelihood that the approach could be replicated or disseminated. Similar issues regarding detail or flexibility can be seen across the literature on personalized therapy (Berger et al., 2017; Carlbring et al., 2011; Evers et al., 2014; Kraepelien et al., 2018, 2019; van Beugen et al., 2016).

Current Limitations of Machine Learning

The marriage of machine learning and precision medicine has also come under recent scrutiny (Wilkinson et al., 2020). Substantial evidence suggests that machine learning approaches should not be assumed to be a panacea, and that their use should be justified through comparisons against more simple methods of constructing clinical prediction models. A multitude of primary analyses as well as meta-analyses have reported similar performance for logistic regression and machine learning in prediction across a variety of domains including: diabetes (Lynam et al., 2020), chronic diseases (Nusinovici et al., 2020), traumatic brain injury (Gravesteijn et al., 2020), heart failure (Desai et al., 2020), and psychological treatments for depression and anxiety (Bone et al., 2021). Some studies have found evidence for improvements in accuracy when using machine learning approaches (relative to logistic regression) with more complex data (e.g., rich EMR-based information; Desai et al., 2020). One complicating feature of the literature comparing machine-learning to non-machine-learning approaches is the inconsistency with which several of the most commonly used modeling techniques are classified. For example, Dwyer et al. (2018) describe penalized regression approaches (such as lasso, ridge, and elastic net regression) as machine learning. However, a recent systematic review of clinical prediction models (Christodoulou et al., 2019) that reported no advantage of machine learning over logistic regression categorized penalized regressions under the umbrella of logistic regression. Instead of relying on blanket statements about the benefits (or lack thereof) of machine learning, contextualized comparisons of specific approaches should be pursued.

Evaluation

Rigorous evaluation of personalized treatment approaches and the clinical prediction models on which they are sometimes based is essential (Hingorani et al., 2013; Pencina et al., 2020). Accordingly, it is alarming that, regarding the proliferation of clinical prediction models across the medical literature, including mental health, only a small proportion have been subjected to external validation (Collins et al., 2014; Siontis et al., 2015). For example, a systematic review of clinical prediction models in patients with chronic obstructive pulmonary disease identified 408 published models, less than 10% of which had been externally validated (Bellou et al., 2019). Low frequency of external validation has also been noted in systematic reviews of clinical prediction models in breast cancer (29%; Phung et al., 2019), cardiovascular disease risk (36%; Damen et al., 2016) and outcomes (17%; Wessler et al., 2015), preeclampsia (6%; De Kat et al., 2019), contrast-induced acute kidney injury (9%; Allen et al., 2017), and colorectal cancer (He et al., 2019). Wynants and colleagues' (2020) "living systematic review" (Macdonald et al., 2020) identified 145 prediction models for COVID-19, and concluded that "proposed models are poorly reported, at high risk of bias, and their reported performance is probably optimistic. Hence, we do not recommend any of these reported prediction models for use in current practice" (Wynants et al., 2020, p. 2). The importance of proper external validation can be seen in Gupta and colleagues' (2020) prospective evaluation of 22 published prediction models for COVID-19. They found, using decision curve analysis, that not a single multivariable model evidenced consistently higher net benefit for clinical deterioration or mortality than applying a rubric based on a single indicator (i.e., admission oxygen saturation on room air as a predictor of clinical deterioration; patient age for mortality) to stratify treatment, across a range of threshold probabilities. In summary, although well-established clinical prediction models in medicine do exist (e.g., Han et al., 2014;

Hippisley-Cox et al., 2008; Maeda et al., 2019), the vast majority have either been poorly constructed, inadequately described, or insufficiently validated, and when evaluated, their clinical utility has often been negligible.

A recent systematic review and meta-analysis of precision psychiatry identified 584 studies in which prediction models (diagnostic, prognostic, or prescriptive) had been developed, only 10.4% and 4.6% of which reported having conducted proper internal and external validation, respectively (Salazar de Pablo et al., 2021). External cross-validation of the performance of predictive treatment selection models in psychotherapy has been exceedingly rare, perhaps in part due to the lack of overlap between variables across studies. One of the only attempts at cross-trial prediction of psychotherapy outcomes that used randomized data revealed significant reductions in the estimated advantage of treatment selection: van Bronswijk, Bruijniks et al. (2020) developed a model in an RCT comparing CBT and IPT, and found that the effect size estimate (generated via internal cross-validation) of receiving the model-indicated treatment shrank by 77% when that model was used to predict outcomes in a dataset from a second RCT of the same two treatments. However, there are examples of studies using naturalistic data that provide evidence for the generalizability of clinical prediction models in external test samples (e.g., Delgadillo & Gonzalez Salas Duhne, 2020; Delgadillo et al., 2017; Schwartz et al., 2020), some of which report impressive prediction accuracy in external samples from different psychological services that were not used to train the prediction model (Bone et al., 2021).

Much of the published literature on the prospective evaluation of personalized approaches to psychological interventions involves clinical trials that were designed to test the effectiveness of the intervention package and not the specific benefit of personalization. Myriad trials have compared personalized or tailored approaches to usual-care or control conditions (e.g., Buhrman et al., 2015; Carlbring et al., 2011; Chorpita et al., 2017; Day et al., 2013; Hallgren et al., 2015; Karyotaki et al., 2019; Nordgren et al., 2014; Silfvernagel et al., 2012, 2018; Strandskov et al., 2017; Twomey et al., 2017; van Beugen et al., 2016; Weisel et al., 2019). However, because these studies lacked analogous non-personalized comparisons, there is no way to know how much, if any, of the advantages for the personalized interventions (for those that reported them) was due to the fact that they were tailored to the patients. These trials, while useful for understanding whether the interventions themselves are more effective than the conditions with which they are compared, fail to provide evidence for the *specific* value of personalization. When a personalized psychotherapy is compared to a non-personalized variant, reduced effect sizes for specific tests of personalization should be expected (relative to comparisons against control comparisons); thus, larger samples will be required to adequately power these trials.

When the specific effects of personalization have been properly evaluated in randomized comparisons of personalized treatments against equivalent standard or static interventions (such tests are rare to begin with), the results have been mixed. Such comparisons, when based on non-data-driven approaches, have often found that treatment personalization failed to improve outcomes (e.g., Batterham et al., 2018; Johansson et al., 2012; Kerns et al., 2014; Moritz et al., 2016) (cf. Cheavens et al., 2012; Miller et al., 2005).

A Cautionary Example from Personalized Pharmacotherapy

Recent findings from the pharmacotherapy research literature also underscore the importance of evaluating personalized treatment approaches. Even before the recent focus on precision psychiatry (e.g., pharmacogenetic and biomarker approaches to medication selection), guidelines existed describing how to personalize treatment to a patient. For example, when an inadequate response was observed to a given antidepressant, changing the dosage of the medication, augmenting the medication with a second one, or switching to a different class of antidepressants were (and still are) widely accepted "best practices." As we have seen in other contexts, *best* does not necessarily mean "validated," or even "tested." In comparisons of the effects of switching classes versus switching within the same class of antidepressants, some have found small or inconsistent increments of response or remission (Papakostas & Fava, 2008), and others have reported no advantage of switching at all (Bschor & Baethge, 2010; Rush et al., 2006; Souery et al., 2011). In regard to dosage adjustment as a way to optimize treatment response, a meta-analysis by Furukawa, Salanti, and colleagues (2020) of 123 RCTs comprising 30K participants found no evidence of efficacy benefit of dose adjustment beyond the minimum licensed dose for SSRIs, venlafaxine, or mirtazapine. That these widely used and profession-endorsed methods of personalizing pharmacotherapy (Bauer et al., 2007) lack consistent supportive evidence of efficacy (c.f., Trivedi et al., 2004) highlights the importance of rigorous evaluation of personalized treatment approaches in mental health, including in psychotherapy.

CONCLUSIONS

An Evolutionary Perspective

Over 50 years have passed since Gordon Paul's call for more personalized approaches to psychotherapy, based on an understanding of *what works for whom* (Paul, 1967). Since then, numerous approaches to personalization have emerged. In this chapter, we have attempted to examine these approaches from a historical and conceptual perspective. We have described this literature as gradually evolving from idiosyncratic approaches that are informed by clinical intuition towards algorithmic approaches that are informed by empirical data. Evolution is characterized by the diversification of species, by haphazard mutations in their traits, and by the persistence or decline of traits through natural selection. As such, we have observed a similar process along the history of personalized psychotherapy: intuitions bred theories; theories bred data; and data gave rise to statistical algorithms (Figure 19.2). Today, the field of psychotherapy finds itself crossing paths with the fields of big data, predictive analytics,

machine learning, and artificial intelligence. Along this evolutionary pathway we find a richly diverse ecosystem of personalization.

Some approaches have been highly influential and persistent, such as the disorder-specific treatment selection approach that is widely adopted in contemporary clinical guidelines for evidence-based treatment. Others have failed to become mainstream practice or have fallen out of favor over time. This can be seen as a form of natural selection in the field of psychotherapy personalization. We have offered a taxonomy of features that can help characterize these diverse approaches, along the dimensions of *Structure, Level of Intervention* and *Time* (see Figure 19.1; 3DP: The Three Dimensions of Personalization). More recent approaches are characterized by greater complexity and sophistication, leveraging advances in methodology and data science. Despite this progress, we cannot yet confidently assert that recent data-driven approaches to personalization are more clinically effective. The evidence on data-driven approaches is still embryonic and we do not yet have the clinical trials or meta-analytic evidence needed to clearly demonstrate their advantage over standardized (e.g., generic, not explicitly personalized) psychotherapy. Taking a historical view, formalized approaches to personalization in psychotherapy are still in their early days. Despite the numerous studies cited in this chapter, the status of the evidence-base as a whole should be viewed as preliminary, with more research needed prior to clinical implications being derived with confidence. Nevertheless, data-driven approaches are emerging at a rapid pace and are likely to lead to future breakthroughs in our ability to improve the effectiveness of psychological care.

Current Challenges and Future Directions

The progress of this field, to some extent, will depend on a concerted effort by psychotherapy researchers, in collaboration with their colleagues in statistics and other areas, to overcome some of the methodological limitations that we have outlined in this chapter. Furthermore, the advent of data-driven decision tools also raises important questions related to the ethical implementation of such technologies in routine care.

Methodological Issues

In our view, researchers' enthusiasm for new technologies (e.g., new data collection techniques such as ecological momentary assessments; computerized treatment modules; network modeling; machine learning analyses) has often taken precedence over basic aspects of methodological rigor. Methodological issues that have been neglected in this literature include the following:

- A lack of attention to statistical power considerations, exemplified by the development of clinical prediction models in inadequately small samples.
- A lack of attention to the problem of overfitting, exemplified by statistical models that are tested within the same sample used to construct the model without protective measures such as cross-validation, resampling or regularization techniques.

- A lack of attention to generalizability issues, exemplified by the predominance of prediction and personalization algorithms that are tested without the use of an external test sample.
- Poor specification and description of personalization models (e.g., their development and implementation), which limits the possibility of independent replication by other independent scientists.
- A lack of preregistration and other open-science best-practices in secondary data-analytic personalization efforts.
- The development of overly complex "black box" models, exemplified by complicated treatment selection and prediction methods that are not easily explainable to therapists or patients, thus potentially limiting their implementation in clinical practice.
- A scarcity of personalization models or tools that are designed using data from typical clinical populations, exemplified by models built on efficacy trials data which may not necessarily generalize to ordinary healthcare samples. Also lacking are prediction models constructed and evaluated using so-called non-WEIRD samples (western, educated, industrialized, rich and democratic).
- A scarcity of prospective tests of personalization methods, and particularly tests using rigorous experimental designs such as randomized clinical trials of personalization methods that are specified *a priori*.

Implementation Issues

As reliable evidence for the value of personalized approaches accumulates, the field will need to turn to issues of dissemination and implementation. Some relevant questions in this regard are the following:

- How common is bias in data-driven algorithms? What are the causes of biased algorithms and what can be done to detect and mitigate their impact? The consequences of biased algorithms include predictions that are less accurate for underrepresented minority populations, and unfair resource allocation, as when certain groups are denied equitable access to treatments from which they could benefit (Obermeyer et al., 2019).
- Do clinicians trust data-driven algorithms? How can they be effectively trained to use such algorithms? Would they follow an algorithm when their clinical intuition conflicts with its recommendation? Are some clinicians more likely to use algorithms compared to others? Which clinical decisions are better left to algorithms and which are better left to clinical experience?
- How do patients feel about the use of algorithms to inform their treatment? Is it necessary for patients to understand how these algorithms work? What if the patient's preferences are at odds with the recommendations from an algorithm?
- What role can industry play in the future of personalized psychotherapy? How can artificial intelligence and decision support tools for psychotherapy be implemented at scale? What are the implications for confidentiality and data protection?

What are the implications for data sharing and open science? What are the implications for the ethical governance and regulation of future artificial intelligence devices?
- What are the implications for the training of new generations of psychotherapists? What skills and knowledge will new psychotherapists need to acquire in order to understand and use data-driven personalization methods (Lutz et al., 2020)?

Recent evidence suggests that although progress is being made on some of the issues in reporting and statistical methodology described in this chapter (Najafabadi et al., 2020), significant work remains. Recent developments described in this chapter provide reasons to be optimistic. Prospective demonstrations of improved outcomes achieved through data-driven personalization have begun to emerge (Lutz et al., 2021; Delgadillo et al., under review). It is likely that, in the not-so-distant future, data-driven decision support tools will be part of the arsenal of tools available to psychotherapists.

ABBREVIATIONS

3DP	Three Dimensions of Personalization
ACT	acceptance and commitment therapy
ATI	aptitude-by-treatment interactions
BASIC ID	behavior, affect, sensation, imagery, cognition, interpersonal relationships, and drug/biology
CBASP	cognitive behavioral analysis system of psychotherapy
CBT	cognitive behavioral therapy
CPT	cognitive-processing therapy
DBT	dialectic behavioral therapy
EMA	ecological momentary assessment
EMDR	eye movement desensitization and reprocessing
EMR	electronic medical records
IPT	interpersonal therapy
LASSO	least absolute shrinkage and selection operator
LRI	Leeds Risk Index
MBCT	mindfulness-based cognitive therapy
MDD	major depressive disorder
NCCMH	National Collaborating Centre for Mental Health
OCD	obsessive-compulsive disorder
PAI	personalized advantage index
PATH	predictive approaches to treatment effect heterogeneity
PE	prolonged exposure
PROGRESS	PROGnosis RESearch Strategy

PTSD	post-traumatic stress disorder
RCT	randomized clinical trial
SMART	sequential multiple assignment randomized trials
STRATOS	STRengthening Analytical Thinking for Observational Studies
STS	systematic treatment selection
TAU	treatment as usual
TPF	Therapy Personalization Form
TRIPOD	Transparent Reporting of a multivariable prediction model for Individual Prognosis or Diagnosis
WEIRD	western, educated, industrialized, rich and democratic

REFERENCES

Aafjes-van Doorn, K., Kamsteeg, C., Bate, J., & Aafjes, M. (2020). A scoping review of machine learning in psychotherapy research. *Psychotherapy Research*, *31*(1), 92–116. https://doi.org/10.1080/10503307.2020.1808729

Adibi, A., Sadatsafavi, M., & Ioannidis, J. P. (2020). Validation and utility testing of clinical prediction models: Time to change the approach. *Journal of the American Medical Association*, *324*(3), 234–236. https://doi.org/10.1001/jama.2020.1230

Ægisdóttir, S., White, M. J., Spengler, P. M., Maugherman, A. S., Anderson, L. A., Cook, R. S., Nichols, C. N., Lampropoulos, G. K., Walker, B. S., & Cohen, G. (2006). The meta-analysis of clinical judgment project: Fifty-six years of accumulated research on clinical versus statistical prediction. *The Counseling Psychologist*, *34*(3), 341–382. https://doi.org/10.1177/0011000005285875

Alba, A. C., Agoritsas, T., Walsh, M., Hanna, S., Iorio, A., Devereaux, P. J., McGinn, T., & Guyatt, G. (2017). Discrimination and calibration of clinical prediction models: Users' guides to the medical literature. *Journal of the American Medical Association*, *318*(14), 1377–1384. https://doi.org/10.1001/jama.2017.12126

Allen, D. W., Ma, B., Leung, K. C., Graham, M. M., Pannu, N., Traboulsi, M., Goodhart, D., Knudtson, M. L., & James, M. T. (2017). Risk prediction models for contrast-induced acute kidney injury accompanying cardiac catheterization: Systematic review and meta-analysis. *Canadian Journal of Cardiology*, *33*(6), 724–736. https://doi.org/10.1016/j.cjca.2017.01.018

Altman, A. D., Shapiro, L. A., & Fisher, A. J. (2020). Why does therapy work? An idiographic approach to explore mechanisms of change over the course of psychotherapy using digital assessments. *Frontiers in Psychology*, *11*, 782. https://doi.org/10.3389/fpsyg.2020.00782

Antezana, G., Bidargaddi, N., Blake, V., Schrader, G., Kaambwa, B., Quinn, S., Orlowski, S., Winsall, M., & Battersby, M. (2015). Development of an online well-being intervention for young people: An evaluation protocol. *JMIR Research Protocols*, *4*(2), e48. https://doi.org/10.2196/resprot.4098

Archer, L., Snell, K. I. E., Ensor, J., Hudda, M. T., Collins, G. S., & Riley, R. D. (2020). Minimum sample size for external validation of a clinical prediction model with a continuous outcome. *Statistics in Medicine*. *40*(1), 133–146. https://doi.org/10.1002/sim.8766

Arnold, K. F., Davies, V., de Kamps, M., Tennant, P. W., Mbotwa, J., & Gilthorpe, M. S. (2020). Reflections on modern methods: Generalized linear models for prognosis and intervention—Theory, practice and implications for machine learning. *International Journal of Epidemiology*, *49*(6), 2074–2082. https://doi.org/10.1093/ije/dyaa049

Arthur, A. R. (2001). Personality, epistemology and psychotherapists' choice of theoretical model: A review and analysis. *European Journal of Psychotherapy, Counselling & Health*, *4*(1), 45–64. https://doi.org/10.1080/13642530110040082

Bae, S., Chung, T., Ferreira, D., Dey, A. K., & Suffoletto, B. (2018). Mobile phone sensors and supervised machine learning to identify alcohol use events in young adults: Implications for just-in-time adaptive interventions. *Addictive Behaviors*, *83*, 42–47. https://doi.org/10.1016/j.addbeh.2017.11.039

Barlow, D. H., Farchione, T. J., Bullis, J. R., Gallagher, M. W., Murray-Latin, H., Sauer-Zavala, S., Bentley, K. H., Thompson-Hollands, J., Conklin, L. R., Boswell, J. F., Ametaj, A., Carl, J. R., Boettcher, H. T., & Cassiello-Robbins, C. (2017). The unified protocol for transdiagnostic treatment of emotional disorders compared with diagnosis-specific protocols for anxiety disorders: A randomized clinical trial. *JAMA Psychiatry*, *74*(9), 875–884. https://doi.org/10.1001/jamapsychiatry.2017.2164

Barlow, D. H., Farchione, T. J., Fairholme, C., Ellard, K., Boisseau, C., Allen, L., & Ehrenreich-May, J. (2011). *The unified protocol for transdiagnostic treatment of emotional disorders: Therapist guide*. Oxford University Press.

Baron, R. M., & Kenny, D. A. (1986). The moderator-mediator variable distinction in social psychological research: Conceptual, strategic, and statistical considerations. *Journal of Personality and Social Psychology*, *51*(6), 1173–1182. https://doi.org/10.1037//0022-3514.51.6.1173

Bastiaansen, J. A., Kunkels, Y. K., Blaauw, F. J., Boker, S. M., Ceulemans, E., Chen, M., Chow, S. M., de Jonge, P., Emerencia, A. C., Epskamp, S., Fisher, A. J., Hamaker, E. L., Kuppens, P., Lutz, W., Meyer, M. J., Moulder, R., Oravecz, Z., Riese, H., Rubel, J., Ryan, . . . Bringmann, L. F. (2020). Time to get personal? The impact of researchers choices on the selection of treatment targets using the experience sampling methodology. *Journal of Psychosomatic Research*, *137*, 110211. https://doi.org/10.1016/j.jpsychores.2020.110211

Batterham, P. J., Calear, A. L., Farrer, L., McCallum, S. M., & Cheng, V. W. S. (2018). FitMindKit: Randomised controlled trial of an automatically tailored online program for mood, anxiety, substance use and suicidality. *Internet Interventions*, *12*, 91–99. https://doi.org/10.1016/j.invent.2017.08.002

Bauer, M., Bschor, T., Pfennig, A., Whybrow, P. C., Angst, J., Versiani, M., Möller, H.-J., Disorders, W. T. F. o. U. D., Bauer, M., & Bschor, T. (2007). World Federation of Societies of Biological Psychiatry (WFSBP) guidelines for biological treatment of unipolar depressive disorders in primary care. *The World Journal of Biological Psychiatry*, *8*(2), 67–104. https://doi.org/10.1080/15622970701227829

Bell, I., & Mellor, D. (2009). Clinical judgements: Research and practice. *Australian Psychologist*, *44*(2), 112–121. https://doi.org/10.1080/00050060802550023

Bellou, V., Belbasis, L., Konstantinidis, A. K., Tzoulaki, I., & Evangelou, E. (2019). Prognostic models for outcome prediction in patients with chronic obstructive pulmonary disease: Systematic review and critical appraisal. *British Medical Journal*, *367*, l5358. https://doi.org/10.1136/bmj.l5358

Benish, S. G., Quintana, S., & Wampold, B. E. (2011). Culturally adapted psychotherapy and the legitimacy of myth: A direct-comparison meta-analysis. *Journal of Counseling Psychology*, *58*(3), 279–289. https://doi.org/10.1037/a0023626

Benner, P., & Tanner, C. (1987). How expert nurses use intuition. *The American Journal of Nursing*, *87*(1), 23–34.

Berger, T., Boettcher, J., & Caspar, F. (2014). Internet-based guided self-help for several anxiety disorders: A randomized controlled trial comparing a tailored with a standardized disorder-specific approach. *Psychotherapy*, *51*(2), 207–219. https://doi.org/10.1037/a0032527

Berger, T., Urech, A., Krieger, T., Stolz, T., Schulz, A., Vincent, A., Moser, C. T., Moritz, S., & Meyer, B. (2017). Effects of a transdiagnostic unguided Internet intervention ('velibra') for anxiety disorders in primary care: Results of a randomized controlled trial. *Psychological Medicine*, *47*(1), 67–80. https://doi.org/10.1017/S0033291716002270

Betan, E. J., & Binder, J. L. (2010). Clinical expertise in psychotherapy: How expert therapists use theory in generating case conceptualizations and interventions. *Journal of Contemporary Psychotherapy*, *40*(3), 141–152. https://doi.org/10.1007/s10879-010-9138-0

Beutler, L. E., Consoli, A. J., & Lane, G. (2005). Systematic treatment selection and prescriptive psychotherapy: An integrative eclectic approach. In J. C. Norcross & M. R. Goldfried (Eds.), *Handbook of psychotherapy integration* (2nd ed., pp. 121–143).

Bidargaddi, N., Musiat, P., Winsall, M., Vogl, G., Blake, V., Quinn, S., Orlowski, S., Antezana, G., & Schrader, G. (2017). Efficacy of a web-based guided recommendation service for a curated list of readily available mental health and well-being mobile apps for young people:

Randomized controlled trial. *Journal of Medical Internet Research, 19*(5), e141. https://doi.org/10.2196/jmir.6775

Bone, C., Simmonds-Buckley, M., Thwaites, R., Sandford, D., Merzhvynska, M., Rubel, J., Deisenhofer, A-K., Lutz, W., & Delgadillo, J. (2021). Dynamic prediction of psychological treatment outcomes using routinely collected symptom data. *The Lancet Digital Health, 3*(4), e231–e240. https://doi.org/10.1016/S2589-7500(21)000-2

Bonnett, L. J., Snell, K. I., Collins, G. S., & Riley, R. D. (2019). Guide to presenting clinical prediction models for use in clinical settings. *British Medical Journal, 365*, 1737. https://doi.org/10.1136/bmj.l737

Bossuyt, P. M., & Parvin, T. (2015). Evaluating biomarkers for guiding treatment decisions. *eJIFCC, 26*(1), 63–70. https://www.ncbi.nlm.nih.gov/pubmed/27683482

Bowens, M., & Cooper, M. (2012). Development of a client feedback tool: A qualitative study of therapists' experiences of using the Therapy Personalisation Forms. *European Journal of Psychotherapy & Counselling, 14*(1), 47–62. https://doi.org/10.1080/13642537.2012.652392

Box, G. E., & Draper, N. R. (1987). *Empirical model-building and response surfaces.* John Wiley & Sons.

Breiman, L. (2001). Statistical modeling: The two cultures (with comments and a rejoinder by the author). *Statistical Science, 16*(3), 199–231. https://projecteuclid.org/euclid.ss/1009213726

Bschor, T., & Baethge, C. (2010). No evidence for switching the antidepressant: Systematic review and meta-analysis of RCTs of a common therapeutic strategy. *Acta Psychiatrica Scandinavica, 121*(3), 174–179. https://doi.org/10.1111/j.1600-0447.2009.01458.x

Buhrman, M., Syk, M., Burvall, O., Hartig, T., Gordh, T., & Andersson, G. (2015). Individualized guided internet-delivered cognitive-behavior therapy for chronic pain patients with comorbid depression and anxiety. *The Clinical Journal of Pain, 31*(6), 504–516. https://doi.org/10.1097/AJP.0000000000000176

Cabral, R. R., & Smith, T. B. (2011). Racial/ethnic matching of clients and therapists in mental health services: A meta-analytic review of preferences, perceptions, and outcomes. *Journal of Counseling Psychology, 58*(4), 537–554. https://doi.org/10.1037/a0025266

Canadian Psychological Association. (2012). Evidence-based practice of psychological treatments: A Canadian perspective. *Canada: CPA task force on evidence-based practice of psychological treatments.*

Captari, L. E., Hook, J. N., Hoyt, W., Davis, D. E., McElroy-Heltzel, S. E., & Worthington Jr, E. L. (2018). Integrating clients' religion and spirituality within psychotherapy: A comprehensive meta-analysis. *Journal of Clinical Psychology, 74*(11), 1938–1951. https://doi.org/10.1002/jclp.22681

Carlbring, P., Andersson, G., Cuijpers, P., Riper, H., & Hedman-Lagerlöf, E. (2018). Internet-based vs. face-to-face cognitive behavior therapy for psychiatric and somatic disorders: An updated systematic review and meta-analysis. *Cognitive Behaviour Therapy, 47*(1), 1–18. https://doi.org/10.1080/16506073.2017.1401115

Carlbring, P., Maurin, L., Torngren, C., Linna, E., Eriksson, T., Sparthan, E., Straat, M., Marquez von Hage, C., Bergman-Nordgren, L., & Andersson, G. (2011). Individually-tailored, internet-based treatment for anxiety disorders: A randomized controlled trial. *Behaviour Research and Therapy, 49*(1), 18–24. https://doi.org/10.1016/j.brat.2010.10.002

Chambless, D. L., & Hollon, S. D. (1998). Defining empirically supported therapies. *Journal of Consulting and Clinical Psychology, 66*(1), 7–18. https://doi.org/10.1037//0022-006x.66.1.7

Chambless, D. L., & Ollendick, T. H. (2001). Empirically supported psychological interventions: Controversies and evidence. *Annual Review Psychology, 52*(1), 685–716. https://doi.org/10.1146/annurev.psych.52.1.685

Cheavens, J. S., Strunk, D. R., Lazarus, S. A., & Goldstein, L. A. (2012). The compensation and capitalization models: A test of two approaches to individualizing the treatment of depression. *Behaviour Research and Therapy, 50*(11), 699–706. https://doi.org/10.1016/j.brat.2012.08.002

Chorpita, B. F., & Daleiden, E. L. (2009). Mapping evidence-based treatments for children and adolescents: Application of the distillation and matching model to 615 treatments from 322 randomized trials. *Journal of Consulting and Clinical Psychology, 77*(3), 566–579. https://doi.org/10.1037/a0014565

Chorpita, B. F., Daleiden, E. L., Park, A. L., Ward, A. M., Levy, M. C., Cromley, T., Chiu, A. W., Letamendi, A. M., Tsai, K. H., & Krull, J. L. (2017). Child STEPs in California: A cluster randomized effectiveness trial comparing modular treatment with community implemented treatment for youth

with anxiety, depression, conduct problems, or traumatic stress. *Journal of Consulting and Clinical Psychology, 85*(1), 13–25. https://doi.org/10.1037/ccp0000133

Chorpita, B. F., Daleiden, E. L., & Weisz, J. R. (2005). Modularity in the design and application of therapeutic interventions. *Applied and Preventive Psychology, 11*(3), 141–156. https://doi.org/10.1016/j.appsy.2005.05.002

Chowdhary, N., Jotheeswaran, A. T., Nadkarni, A., Hollon, S. D., King, M., Jordans, M. J., Rahman, A., Verdeli, H., Araya, R., & Patel, V. (2014). The methods and outcomes of cultural adaptations of psychological treatments for depressive disorders: A systematic review. *Psychological Medicine, 44*(6), 1131–1146. https://doi.org/10.1017/S0033291713001785

Christodoulou, E., Ma, J., Collins, G. S., Steyerberg, E. W., Verbakel, J. Y., & Van Calster, B. (2019). A systematic review shows no performance benefit of machine learning over logistic regression for clinical prediction models. *Journal of Clinical Epidemiology, 110*, 12–22. https://doi.org/10.1016/j.jclinepi.2019.02.004

Clark, D. M. (2018). Realizing the mass public benefit of evidence-based psychological therapies: The IAPT program. *Annual Review of Clinical Psychology, 14*, 159–183. https://doi.org/10.1146/annurev-clinpsy-050817-084833

Cloitre, M., Cohen, Z. D., & Schnyder, U. (2020). Building a science of personalized interventions for PTSD. In D. Forbes, J. I. Bisson, C. M. Monson, & L. Berliner (Eds.), *Effective treatments for PTSD: Practice guidelines from the International Society for Traumatic Stress Studies* (3rd ed., pp. 451–468). Guilford Publications.

Cloitre, M., Petkova, E., Su, Z., & Weiss, B. (2016). Patient characteristics as a moderator of post-traumatic stress disorder treatment outcome: Combining symptom burden and strengths. *BJPsych Open, 2*(2), 101–106. https://doi.org/10.1192/bjpo.bp.115.000745

Cohen, Z. D., Ashar, Y. K., & DeRubeis, D. J. (2019). Moving beyond "one size fits all". In S. Dimidjian (Ed.), *Evidence-based practice in action: Bridging clinical science and intervention* (pp. 111–132). Guilford Press.

Cohen, Z. D., & DeRubeis, R. J. (2018). Treatment selection in depression. *Annual Review of Clinical Psychology, 14*, 209–236. https://doi.org/10.1146/annurev-clinpsy-050817-084746

Cohen, Z. D., Kim, T. T., Van, H. L., Dekker, J. J. M., & Driessen, E. (2020). A demonstration of a multi-method variable selection approach for treatment selection: Recommending cognitive-behavioral versus psychodynamic therapy for mild to moderate adult depression. *Psychotherapy Research, 30*(2), 137–150. https://doi.org/10.1080/10503307.2018.1563312

Collins, F. S., & Varmus, H. (2015). A new initiative on precision medicine. *New England Journal of Medicine, 372*(9), 793–795. https://doi.org/10.1056/NEJMp1500523

Collins, G. S., de Groot, J. A., Dutton, S., Omar, O., Shanyinde, M., Tajar, A., Voysey, M., Wharton, R., Yu, L.-M., & Moons, K. G. (2014). External validation of multivariable prediction models: A systematic review of methodological conduct and reporting. *BMC Medical Research Methodology, 14*(1), 40. https://doi.org/10.1186/1471-2288-14-40

Collins, G. S., Reitsma, J. B., Altman, D. G., & Moons, K. G. (2015). Transparent reporting of a multivariable prediction model for individual prognosis or diagnosis (TRIPOD): The TRIPOD Statement. *Circulation, 131*(2), 211–219. https://doi.org//10.1161/CIRCULATIONAHA.114.014508

Cooper, M., & McLeod, J. (2011). Person-centered therapy: A pluralistic perspective. *Person-Centered & Experiential Psychotherapies, 10*(3), 210–223. https://doi.org/10.1080/14779757.2011.599517

Coull, G., & Morris, P. (2011). The clinical effectiveness of CBT-based guided self-help interventions for anxiety and depressive disorders: A systematic review. *Psychological Medicine, 41*(11), 2239–2252. https://doi.org/10.1017/S0033291711000900

Coutanche, M. N., & Hallion, L. S. (2019). Machine learning for clinical psychology and clinical neuroscience. In A. G. C. Wright & M. N. Hallquist (Eds.), *The Cambridge handbook of research methods in clinical psychology* (pp. 467–482). Cambridge University Press. https://doi.org/10.1017/9781316995808

Cronbach, L. J. (1957). The two disciplines of scientific psychology. *American Psychologist, 12*(11), 671–684. https://doi.org/10.1037/h0043943

Cronbach, L. J., & Snow, R. E. (1977). *Aptitudes and instructional methods: A handbook for research on interactions.* Irvington.

Cuijpers, P., Cristea, I. A., Karyotaki, E., Reijnders, M., & Hollon, S. D. (2019). Component studies of psychological treatments of adult depression: A systematic review and meta-analysis. *Psychotherapy Research, 29*(1), 15–29. https://doi.org/10.1080/10503307.2017.1395922

Cuijpers, P., Karyotaki, E., Reijnders, M., & Huibers, M. J. H. (2018). Who benefits from psychotherapies for adult depression? A meta-analytic update of the evidence. *Cognitive Behaviour Therapy, 47*(2), 91–106. https://doi.org/10.1080/16506073.2017.1420098

Cuijpers, P., Karyotaki, E., Reijnders, M., Purgato, M., & Barbui, C. (2018). Psychotherapies for depression in low- and middle-income countries: A meta-analysis. *World Psychiatry, 17*(1), 90–101. https://doi.org/10.1002/wps.20493

Cuijpers, P., Noma, H., Karyotaki, E., Cipriani, A., & Furukawa, T. A. (2019). Effectiveness and acceptability of cognitive behavior therapy delivery formats in adults with depression: A network meta-analysis. *JAMA Psychiatry, 76*(7), 700–707. https://doi.org/10.1001/jamapsychiatry.2019.0268

Cuijpers, P., Noma, H., Karyotaki, E., Vinkers, C. H., Cipriani, A., & Furukawa, T. A. (2020). A network meta-analysis of the effects of psychotherapies, pharmacotherapies and their combination in the treatment of adult depression. *World Psychiatry, 19*(1), 92–107. https://doi.org/10.1002/wps.20701

Dalgleish, T., Black, M., Johnston, D., & Bevan, A. (2020). Transdiagnostic approaches to mental health problems: Current status and future directions. *Journal of Consulting and Clinical Psychology, 88*(3), 179–195. https://doi.org/10.1037/ccp0000482

Damen, J. A., Hooft, L., Schuit, E., Debray, T. P., Collins, G. S., Tzoulaki, I., Lassale, C. M., Siontis, G. C., Chiocchia, V., & Roberts, C. (2016). Prediction models for cardiovascular disease risk in the general population: Systematic review. *British Medical Journal, 353*, i2416. https://doi.org/10.1136/bmj.i2416

Dance, K. A., & Neufeld, R. W. (1988). Aptitude-treatment interaction research in the clinical setting: A review of attempts to dispel the" patient uniformity" myth. *Psychological Bulletin, 104*(2), 192–213. https://doi.org/10.1037/0033-2909.104.2.192

Davis, A., Smith, T., Talbot, J., Eldridge, C., & Betts, D. (2020). Predicting patient engagement in IAPT services: A statistical analysis of electronic health records. *Evidence Based Mental Health, 23*(1), 8–14. https://doi.org/10.1136/ebmental-2019-300133

Dawes, R. M., Faust, D., & Meehl, P. E. (1989). Clinical versus actuarial judgment. *Science, 243*(4899), 1668–1674. https://doi.org/10.1126/science.2648573

Dawes, R. M., Faust, D., & Meehl, P. E. (1993). Statistical prediction versus clinical prediction: Improving what works. In G. Keren & C. Lewis (Eds.), *A handbook for data analysis in the behavioral sciences: Methodological issues* (pp. 351–367). Lawrence Erlbaum Associates.

Day, V., McGrath, P. J., & Wojtowicz, M. (2013). Internet-based guided self-help for university students with anxiety, depression and stress: A randomized controlled clinical trial. *Behaviour Research and Therapy, 51*(7), 344–351. https://doi.org/10.1016/j.brat.2013.03.003

De Kat, A. C., Hirst, J., Woodward, M., Kennedy, S., & Peters, S. A. (2019). Prediction models for preeclampsia: A systematic review. *Pregnancy Hypertension, 16*, 48–66. https://doi.org/10.1016/j.preghy.2019.03.005

Deckersbach, T., Peters, A. T., Sylvia, L. G., Gold, A. K., da Silva Magalhaes, P. V., Henry, D. B., Frank, E., Otto, M. W., Berk, M., & Dougherty, D. D. (2016). A cluster analytic approach to identifying predictors and moderators of psychosocial treatment for bipolar depression: Results from STEP-BD. *Journal of Affective Disorders, 203*, 152–157. https://doi.org/10.1016/j.jad.2016.03.064

Deisenhofer, A. K., Delgadillo, J., Rubel, J. A., Bohnke, J. R., Zimmermann, D., Schwartz, B., & Lutz, W. (2018). Individual treatment selection for patients with posttraumatic stress disorder. *Depression and Anxiety, 35*(6), 541–550. https://doi.org/10.1002/da.22755

Delgadillo, J., Ali, S., Fleck, K., Agnew, C., Southgate, A., Parkhouse, L., Cohen, Z. D., DeRubeis, R. J., and Barkham, M. (under review). StratCare: A pragmatic, multi-site, single-blind, cluster randomised controlled trial of stratified care for depression.

Delgadillo, J., Appleby, S., Booth, S., Burnett, G., Carey, A., Edmeade, L., Green, S., Griffin, P., Johnson, E., Jones, R., Parker, P., Reeves-McLaren, L., & Lutz, W. (2020). The Leeds Risk Index: Field-Test of a stratified psychological treatment selection algorithm. *Psychotherapy and Psychosomatics, 89*(3), 189–190. https://doi.org/10.1159/000505193

Delgadillo, J., & Gonzalez Salas Duhne, P. (2020). Targeted prescription of cognitive-behavioral therapy versus person-centered counseling for depression using a machine learning approach. *Journal of Consulting and Clinical Psychology, 88*(1), 14–24. https://doi.org/10.1037/ccp0000476

Delgadillo, J., Huey, D., Bennett, H., & McMillan, D. (2017). Case complexity as a guide for psychological treatment selection. *Journal of Consulting and Clinical Psychology, 85*(9), 835–853. https://doi.org/10.1037/ccp0000231

Delgadillo, J., & Lutz, W. (2020). A development pathway towards precision mental health care. *JAMA Psychiatry, 77*(9), 889–890. https://doi.org/10.1001/jamapsychiatry.2020.1048

Delgadillo, J., Moreea, O., & Lutz, W. (2016). Different people respond differently to therapy: A demonstration using patient profiling and risk stratification. *Behaviour Research and Therapy, 79*, 15–22. https://doi.org/10.1016/j.brat.2016.02.003

Delgadillo, J., Rubel, J., & Barkham, M. (2020). Towards personalized allocation of patients to therapists. *Journal of Consulting and Clinical Psychology, 88*(9), 799–808. https://doi.org/10.1037/ccp0000507

DeRubeis, R. J., Cohen, Z. D., Forand, N. R., Fournier, J. C., Gelfand, L. A., & Lorenzo-Luaces, L. (2014). The Personalized Advantage Index: Translating research on prediction into individualized treatment recommendations. A demonstration. *PLOS One, 9*(1), e83875. https://doi.org/10.1371/journal.pone.0083875

DeRubeis, R. J., Gelfand, L. A., German, R. E., Fournier, J. C., & Forand, N. R. (2014). Understanding processes of change: How some patients reveal more than others – and some groups of therapists less – about what matters in psychotherapy. *Psychotherapy Research, 24*(3), 419–428. https://doi.org/10.1080/10503307.2013.838654

Desai, R. J., Wang, S. V., Vaduganathan, M., Evers, T., & Schneeweiss, S. (2020). Comparison of machine learning methods with traditional models for use of administrative claims with electronic medical records to predict heart failure outcomes. *JAMA Network Open, 3*(1), e1918962-e1918962. https://doi.org/10.1001/jamanetworkopen.2019.18962

Dickens, C., Cherrington, A., Adeyemi, I., Roughley, K., Bower, P., Garrett, C., Bundy, C., & Coventry, P. (2013). Characteristics of psychological interventions that improve depression in people with coronary heart disease: A systematic review and meta-regression. *Psychosomatic Medicine, 75*(2), 211–221. https://doi.org/10.1097/PSY.0b013e31827ac009

Dusseldorp, E., & Van Mechelen, I. (2014). Qualitative interaction trees: A tool to identify qualitative treatment-subgroup interactions. *Statistics in Medicine, 33*(2), 219–237. https://doi.org/10.1002/sim.5933

Dwyer, D. B., Falkai, P., & Koutsouleris, N. (2018). Machine learning approaches for clinical psychology and psychiatry. *Annual Review of Clinical Psychology, 14*, 91–118. https://doi.org/10.1146/annurev-clinpsy-032816-045037

Ebert, D. D., Buntrock, C., Mortier, P., Auerbach, R., Weisel, K. K., Kessler, R. C., Cuijpers, P., Green, J. G., Kiekens, G., Nock, M. K., Demyttenaere, K., & Bruffaerts, R. (2019). Prediction of major depressive disorder onset in college students. *Depression and Anxiety, 36*(4), 294–304. https://doi.org/10.1002/da.22867

Eells, T. D., Lombart, K. G., Kendjelic, E. M., Turner, L. C., & Lucas, C. P. (2005). The quality of psychotherapy case formulations: A comparison of expert, experienced, and novice cognitive-behavioral and psychodynamic therapists. *Journal of Consulting and Clinical Psychology, 73*(4), 579–589. https://doi.org/10.1037/0022-006X.73.4.579

Efron, B. (2020). Prediction, estimation, and attribution. *Journal of the American Statistical Association, 115*(530), 636–655. https://doi.org/10.1080/01621459.2020.1762613

Elwyn, G., O'Connor, A., Stacey, D., Volk, R., Edwards, A., Coulter, A., Thomson, R., Barratt, A., Barry, M., Bernstein, S., Butow, P., Clarke, A., Entwistle, V., Feldman-Stewart, D., Holmes-Rovner, M., Llewellyn-Thomas, H., Moumjid, N., Mulley, A., Ruland, C., . . . Whelan, T. (2006). Developing a quality criteria framework for patient decision aids: Online international Delphi consensus process. *British Medical Journal, 333*(7565), 417. https://doi.org/10.1136/bmj.38926.629329.AE

Eskildsen, A., Reinholt, N., van Bronswijk, S., Brund, R. B. K., Christensen, A. B., Hvenegaard, M., Arendt, M., Alrø, A., Poulsen, S., Rosenberg, N. K., Huibers, M. J. H., & Arnfred, S. (2020). Personalized psychotherapy for outpatients with major depression and anxiety disorders: Transdiagnostic versus diagnosis-specific group cognitive behavioural therapy. *Cognitive Therapy and Research, 44*(5), 988–1001. https://doi.org/10.1007/s10608-020-10116-1

Evers, A. W., Gieler, U., Hasenbring, M. I., & van Middendorp, H. (2014). Incorporating biopsychosocial characteristics into personalized healthcare: A clinical approach. *Psychotherapy and Psychosomatics, 83*(3), 148–157. https://doi.org/10.1159/000358309

Fernandez, K. C., Fisher, A. J., & Chi, C. (2017). Development and initial implementation of the Dynamic Assessment Treatment Algorithm (DATA). *PLOS One, 12*(6), e0178806. https://doi.org/10.1371/journal.pone.0178806

Field, M. J., & Lohr, K. N. (1990). *Clinical practice guidelines. Directions for a new program.* National Academy Press.

Finegan, M., Firth, N., Wojnarowski, C., & Delgadillo, J. (2018). Associations between socioeconomic status and psychological therapy outcomes: A systematic review and meta-analysis. *Depression and Anxiety, 35*(6), 560–573. https://doi.org/10.1002/da.22765

Firth, N., Barkham, M., & Kellett, S. (2015). The clinical effectiveness of stepped care systems for depression in working age adults: A systematic review. *Journal of Affective Disorders, 170*, 119–130. https://doi.org/10.1016/j.jad.2014.08.030

Fisher, A. J., & Bosley, H. G. (2020). Identifying the presence and timing of discrete mood states prior to therapy. *Behaviour Research and Therapy, 128*, 103596. https://doi.org/10.1016/j.brat.2020.103596

Fisher, A. J., Bosley, H. G., Fernandez, K. C., Reeves, J. W., Soyster, P. D., Diamond, A. E., & Barkin, J. (2019). Open trial of a personalized modular treatment for mood and anxiety. *Behaviour Research and Therapy, 116*, 69–79. https://doi.org/10.1016/j.brat.2019.01.010

Fisher, A. J., Medaglia, J. D., & Jeronimus, B. F. (2018). Lack of group-to-individual generalizability is a threat to human subjects research. *Proceedings of the National Academy of Sciences, 115*(27), E6106–E6115. https://doi.org/10.1073/pnas.1711978115

Foa, E. B., & Rothbaum, B. O. (1998). *Treatment manuals for practitioners. Treating the trauma of rape: Cognitive-behavioral therapy for PTSD.* Guilford Press. https://doi.org/10.1080/10503309123313332731

Forsell, E., Isacsson, N., Blom, K., Jernelöv, S., Ben Abdesslem, F., Lindefors, N., Boman, M., & Kaldo, V. (2019). Predicting treatment failure in regular care internet-delivered cognitive behavior therapy for depression and anxiety using only weekly symptom measures. *Journal of Consulting and Clinical Psychology, 88*(4), 311–321. https://doi.org/10.1037/ccp0000462

Friedl, N., Krieger, T., Chevreul, K., Hazo, J. B., Holtzmann, J., Hoogendoorn, M., Kleiboer, A., Mathiasen, K., Urech, A., & Riper, H. (2020). Using the personalized advantage index for individual treatment allocation to blended treatment or treatment as usual for depression in secondary care. *Journal of Clinical Medicine, 9*(2), 490. https://doi.org/10.3390/jcm9020490

Furukawa, T. A., Debray, T. P. A., Akechi, T., Yamada, M., Kato, T., Seo, M., & Efthimiou, O. (2020). Can personalized treatment prediction improve the outcomes, compared with the group average approach, in a randomized trial? Developing and validating a multivariable prediction model in a pragmatic megatrial of acute treatment for major depression. *Journal of Affective Disorders, 274*, 690–697. https://doi.org/10.1016/j.jad.2020.05.141

Furukawa, T. A., Salanti, G., Cowen, P. J., Leucht, S., & Cipriani, A. (2020). No benefit from flexible titration above minimum licensed dose in prescribing antidepressants for major depression: Systematic review. *Acta Psychiatrica Scandinavica, 141*(5), 401–409. https://doi.org/10.1111/acps.13145

Garb, H. N. (2005). Clinical judgment and decision making. *Annual Review of Clinical Psychology, 1*, 67–89. https://doi.org/10.1146/annurev.clinpsy.1.102803.143810

Garfield, S. L. (1996). Some problems associated with "validated" forms of psychotherapy. *Clinical psychology: Science and practice, 3*(3), 218–229. https://doi.org/10.1111/j.1468-2850.1996.tb00073.x

Gaudiano, B. A., Brown, L. A., & Miller, I. W. (2011). Let your intuition be your guide? Individual differences in the evidence-based practice attitudes of psychotherapists. *Journal of Evaluation in Clinical Practice, 17*(4), 628–634. https://doi.org/10.1111/j.1365-2753.2010.01508.x

Gelfand, L. A., Lorenzo-Luaces, L., & DeRubeis, R. J. (*under review*). Effects of patient response pattern distributions on comparisons of psychosocial treatments for major depressive disorder.

Gemmell, I., & Dunn, G. (2011). The statistical pitfalls of the partially randomized preference design in non-blinded trials of psychological interventions. *International Journal of Methods in Psychiatric Research, 20*(1), 1–9. https://doi.org/10.1002/mpr.326

Goldstein, S. P., Evans, B. C., Flack, D., Juarascio, A., Manasse, S., Zhang, F., & Forman, E. M. (2017). Return of the JITAI: Applying a just-in-time adaptive intervention framework to the development of m-health solutions for addictive behaviors. *International Journal of Behavioral Medicine, 24*(5), 673–682. https://doi.org/10.1007/s12529-016-9627-y

Gravesteijn, B. Y., Nieboer, D., Ercole, A., Lingsma, H. F., Nelson, D., Van Calster, B., Steyerberg, E. W., & collaborators, C.-T. (2020). Machine learning algorithms performed no better than regression models for prognostication in traumatic brain injury. *Journal of Clinical Epidemiology, 122*, 95–107. https://doi.org/10.1016/j.jclinepi.2020.03.005

Grove, W. M., & Meehl, P. E. (1996). Comparative efficiency of informal (subjective, impressionistic) and formal (mechanical, algorithmic) prediction procedures: The clinical–statistical controversy. *Psychology, Public Policy, and Law, 2*(2), 293–323. https://doi.org/https://doi.org/10.1037/1076-8971.2.2.293

Grove, W. M., Zald, D. H., Lebow, B. S., Snitz, B. E., & Nelson, C. (2000). Clinical versus mechanical prediction: A meta-analysis. *Psychological Assessment, 12*(1), 19–30. https://www.ncbi.nlm.nih.gov/pubmed/10752360

Gupta, R. K., Marks, M., Samuels, T. H. A., Luintel, A., Rampling, T., Chowdhury, H., Quartagno, M., Nair, A., Lipman, M., Abubakar, I., van Smeden, M., Wong, W. K., Williams, B., Noursadeghi, M., & Group, U. C.-R. (2020). Systematic evaluation and external validation of 22 prognostic models among hospitalised adults with COVID-19: An observational cohort study. *European Respiratory Journal, 56*, 2003498. https://doi.org/10.1183/13993003.03498-2020

Hall, G. C., Ibaraki, A. Y., Huang, E. R., Marti, C. N., & Stice, E. (2016). A meta-analysis of cultural adaptations of psychological interventions. *Behavior Therapy, 47*(6), 993–1014. https://doi.org/10.1016/j.beth.2016.09.005

Hallgren, M., Kraepelien, M., Lindefors, N., Zeebari, Z., Kaldo, V., & Forsell, Y. (2015). Physical exercise and internet-based cognitive–behavioural therapy in the treatment of depression: Randomised controlled trial. *The British Journal of Psychiatry, 207*(3), 227–234. https://doi.org/10.1192/bjp.bp.114.160101

Han, J., King, N. K., Neilson, S. J., Gandhi, M. P., & Ng, I. (2014). External validation of the CRASH and IMPACT prognostic models in severe traumatic brain injury. *Journal of Neurotrauma, 31*(13), 1146–1152. https://doi.org/10.1089/neu.2013.3003

Hastie, T., Tibshirani, R., & Friedman, J. (2009). *The Elements of Statistical Learning* (2nd ed.). Springer.

He, Y., Ong, Y., Li, X., Din, F. V., Brown, E., Timofeeva, M., Wang, Z., Farrington, S. M., Campbell, H., & Dunlop, M. G. (2019). Performance of prediction models on survival outcomes of colorectal cancer with surgical resection: A systematic review and meta-analysis. *Surgical Oncology, 29*, 196–202. https://doi.org/10.1016/j.suronc.2019.05.014

Hemingway, H., Croft, P., Perel, P., Hayden, J. A., Abrams, K., Timmis, A., Briggs, A., Udumyan, R., Moons, K. G., Steyerberg, E. W., Roberts, I., Schroter, S., Altman, D. G., Riley, R. D., & Group, P. (2013). Prognosis research strategy (PROGRESS) 1: A framework for researching clinical outcomes. *British Medical Journal, 346*, e5595. https://doi.org/10.1136/bmj.e5595

Henrich, J., Heine, S. J., & Norenzayan, A. (2010). The weirdest people in the world? *Behavioral and Brain Sciences, 33*(2–3), 61–83. https://doi.org/10.1017/S0140525X0999152X

Heus, P., Damen, J., Pajouheshnia, R., Scholten, R., Reitsma, J. B., Collins, G. S., Altman, D. G., Moons, K. G. M., & Hooft, L. (2018). Poor reporting of multivariable prediction model studies: Towards a targeted implementation strategy of the TRIPOD statement. *BMC Medicine, 16*(1), 120. https://doi.org/10.1186/s12916-018-1099-2

Hilbert, K., Kunas, S. L., Lueken, U., Kathmann, N., Fydrich, T., & Fehm, L. (2020). Predicting cognitive behavioral therapy outcome in the outpatient sector based on clinical routine data: A machine learning approach. *Behaviour Research and Therapy, 124*, 103530. https://doi.org/10.1016/j.brat.2019.103530

Hingorani, A. D., Windt, D. A., Riley, R. D., Abrams, K., Moons, K. G., Steyerberg, E. W., Schroter, S., Sauerbrei, W., Altman, D. G., Hemingway, H., & Group, P. (2013). Prognosis research strategy (PROGRESS) 4:

Stratified medicine research. *British Medical Journal, 346*, e5793. https://doi.org/10.1136/bmj.e5793

Hippisley-Cox, J., Coupland, C., Vinogradova, Y., Robson, J., Minhas, R., Sheikh, A., & Brindle, P. (2008). Predicting cardiovascular risk in England and Wales: Prospective derivation and validation of QRISK2. *British Medical Journal, 336*(7659), 1475–1482. https://doi.org/10.1136/bmj.39609.449676.25

Hofmann, S. G., & Hayes, S. C. (2019). The future of intervention Sscience: Process-based therapy. *Clinical Psychological Science, 7*(1), 37–50. https://doi.org/10.1177/2167702618772296

Hollon, S. D., Cohen, Z. D., Singla, D. R., & Andrews, P. W. (2019). Recent developments in the treatment of depression. *Behavior Therapy, 50*(2), 257–269. https://doi.org/10.1016/j.beth.2019.01.002

Holmes, E. A., Ghaderi, A., Harmer, C. J., Ramchandani, P. G., Cuijpers, P., Morrison, A. P., Roiser, J. P., Bockting, C. L. H., O'Connor, R. C., Shafran, R., Moulds, M. L., & Craske, M. G. (2018). The Lancet Psychiatry Commission on psychological treatments research in tomorrow's science. *Lancet Psychiatry, 5*(3), 237–286. https://doi.org/10.1016/S2215-0366(17)30513-8

Huang, Y., Li, W., Macheret, F., Gabriel, R. A., & Ohno-Machado, L. (2020). A tutorial on calibration measurements and calibration models for clinical prediction models. *Journal of the American Medical Informatics Association, 27*(4), 621–633. https://doi.org/10.1093/jamia/ocz228

Huibers, M. J., Cohen, Z. D., Lemmens, L. H., Arntz, A., Peeters, F. P., Cuijpers, P., & DeRubeis, R. J. (2015). Predicting optimal outcomes in cognitive therapy or interpersonal psychotherapy for depressed individuals using the personalized advantage index approach. *PLOS One, 10*(11), e0140771. https://doi.org/10.1371/journal.pone.0140771

Jacobucci, R., Littlefield, A. K., Millner, A. J., Kleiman, E. M., & Steinley, D. (2020). Pairing machine learning and clinical psychology: How you evaluate predictive performance matters. https://doi.org/10.31234/osf.io/2yber

Janes, H., Pepe, M. S., Bossuyt, P. M., & Barlow, W. E. (2011). Measuring the performance of markers for guiding treatment decisions. *Annals of Internal Medicine, 154*(4), 253–259. https://doi.org/10.7326/0003-4819-154-4-201102150-00006

Johansson, R., Sjoberg, E., Sjogren, M., Johnsson, E., Carlbring, P., Andersson, T., Rousseau, A., & Andersson, G. (2012). Tailored vs. standardized internet-based cognitive behavior therapy for depression and comorbid symptoms: Arandomized controlled trial. *PLOS One, 7*(5), e36905. https://doi.org/10.1371/journal.pone.0036905

Joyner, M. J., & Paneth, N. (2019). Promises, promises, and precision medicine. *Journal of Clinical Investigation, 129*(3), 946–948. https://doi.org/10.1172/JCI126119

Kapelner, A., Bleich, J., Levine, A., Cohen, Z. D., DeRubeis, R. J., & Berk, R. (2021). Evaluating the effectiveness of personalized medicine with software. *Frontiers in Big Data, 4*(8). https://doi.org/10.3389/fdata.2021.572532

Karyotaki, E., Klein, A. M., Riper, H., Wit, L., Krijnen, L., Bol, E., Bolinski, F., Burger, S., Ebert, D. D., Auerbach, R. P., Kessler, R. C., Bruffaerts, R., Batelaan, N., van der Heijde, C. M., Vonk, P., Kleiboer, A., Wiers, R. W., & Cuijpers, P. (2019). Examining the effectiveness of a web-based intervention for symptoms of depression and anxiety in college students: Study protocol of a randomised controlled trial. *BMJ Open, 9*(5), e028739. https://doi.org/10.1136/bmjopen-2018-028739

Keefe, J. R., Kim, T. T., DeRubeis, R. J., Streiner, D. L., Links, P. S., & McMain, S. F. (2020). Treatment selection in borderline personality disorder between dialectical behavior therapy and psychodynamic psychiatric management. *Psychological Medicine*, 1–9. https://doi.org/10.1017/S0033291720000550

Keefe, J. R., Wiltsey Stirman, S., Cohen, Z. D., DeRubeis, R. J., Smith, B. N., & Resick, P. A. (2018). In rape trauma PTSD, patient characteristics indicate which trauma-focused treatment they are most likely to complete. *Depression and Anxiety, 35*(4), 330–338. https://doi.org/10.1002/da.22731

Kent, D. M., Paulus, J. K., Van Klaveren, D., D'Agostino, R., Goodman, S., Hayward, R., Ioannidis, J. P., Patrick-Lake, B., Morton, S., & Pencina, M. (2020). The predictive approaches to treatment effect heterogeneity (PATH) statement. *Annals of Internal Medicine, 172*(1), 35–45. https://doi.org/10.7326/M18-3667

Kent, D. M., Van Klaveren, D., Paulus, J. K., D'Agostino, R., Goodman, S., Hayward, R., Ioannidis, J. P., Patrick-Lake, B., Morton, S., & Pencina, M. (2020). The Predictive Approaches to Treatment effect Heterogeneity (PATH) statement: Explanation and elaboration. *Annals of Internal Medicine, 172*(1), W1–W25. https://doi.org/10.7326/M18-3668

Kerns, R. D., Burns, J. W., Shulman, M., Jensen, M. P., Nielson, W. R., Czlapinski, R., Dallas, M. I., Chatkoff, D., Sellinger, J., & Heapy, A. (2014). Can we improve cognitive–behavioral therapy for chronic back pain treatment engagement and adherence? A controlled trial of tailored versus standard therapy. *Health Psychology, 33*(9), 938.

Kessler, R. C., Bossarte, R. M., Luedtke, A., Zaslavsky, A. M., & Zubizarreta, J. R. (2019). Machine learning methods for developing precision treatment rules with observational data. *Behaviour Research and Therapy, 120*, 103412. https://doi.org/10.1016/j.brat.2019.103412

Kessler, R. C., Chiu, W. T., Demler, O., Merikangas, K. R., & Walters, E. E. (2005). Prevalence, severity, and comorbidity of 12-month DSM-IV disorders in the National Comorbidity Survey Replication. *Archives of General Psychiatry, 62*(6), 617–627. https://doi.org/10.1001/archpsyc.62.6.617

Kessler, R. C., van Loo, H. M., Wardenaar, K. J., Bossarte, R. M., Brenner, L. A., Cai, T., Ebert, D. D., Hwang, I., Li, J., de Jonge, P., Nierenberg, A. A., Petukhova, M. V., Rosellini, A. J., Sampson, N. A., Schoevers, R. A., Wilcox, M. A., & Zaslavsky, A. M. (2016). Testing a machine-learning algorithm to predict the persistence and severity of major depressive disorder from baseline self-reports. *Molecular Psychiatry, 21*(10), 1366–1371. https://doi.org/10.1038/mp.2015.198

Kessler, R. C., van Loo, H. M., Wardenaar, K. J., Bossarte, R. M., Brenner, L. A., Ebert, D. D., de Jonge, P., Nierenberg, A. A., Rosellini, A. J., Sampson, N. A., Schoevers, R. A., Wilcox, M. A., & Zaslavsky, A. M. (2017). Using patient self-reports to study heterogeneity of treatment effects in major depressive disorder. *Epidemiology and Psychiatric Sciences, 26*(1), 22–36. https://doi.org/10.1017/S2045796016000020

Kiekens, G., Hasking, P., Claes, L., Boyes, M., Mortier, P., Auerbach, R., Cuijpers, P., Demyttenaere, K., Green, J., & Kessler, R. (2019). Predicting the incidence of non-suicidal self-injury in college students. *European psychiatry, 59*, 44–51. https://doi.org/10.1016/j.eurpsy.2019.04.002

Kiesler, D. J. (1966). Some myths of psychotherapy research and the search for a paradigm. *Psychological Bulletin, 65*(2), 110–136. https://doi.org/10.1037/h0022911

King, M., Walker, C., Levy, G., Bottomley, C., Royston, P., Weich, S., Bellon-Saameno, J. A., Moreno, B., Svab, I., Rotar, D., Rifel, J., Maaroos, H. I., Aluoja, A., Kalda, R., Neeleman, J., Geerlings, M. I., Xavier, M., Carraca, I., Goncalves-Pereira, M., Vicente, B., Saldivia, S., Melipillan, R., Torres-Gonzalez, F., & Nazareth, I. (2008). Development and validation of an international risk prediction algorithm for episodes of major depression in general practice attendees: The PredictD study. *Archives of General Psychiatry, 65*(12), 1368–1376. https://doi.org/10.1001/archpsyc.65.12.1368

Kraemer, H. C. (2013). Discovering, comparing, and combining moderators of treatment on outcome after randomized clinical trials: A parametric approach. *Statistics in Medicine, 32*(11), 1964–1973. https://doi.org/10.1002/sim.5734

Kraepelien, M., Forsell, E., Karin, E., Johansson, R., Lindefors, N., & Kaldo, V. (2018). Comparing individually tailored to disorder-specific internet-based cognitive–behavioural therapy: Benchmarking study. *BJPsych Open, 4*(4), 282–284. https://doi.org/10.1192/bjo.2018.41

Kraepelien, M., Svanborg, C., Lallerstedt, L., Sennerstam, V., Lindefors, N., & Kaldo, V. (2019). Individually tailored internet treatment in routine care: A feasibility study. *Internet Interventions, 18*, 100263. https://doi.org/10.1016/j.invent.2019.100263

Lambert, M. J., Whipple, J. L., & Kleinstäuber, M. (2018). Collecting and delivering progress feedback: A meta-analysis of routine outcome monitoring. *Psychotherapy, 55*(4), 520–537. https://doi.org/10.1037/pst0000167

Lazarus, A. A. (2005). Multimodal therapy. In J. C. Norcross & M. R. Goldfried (Eds.), *Handbook of psychotherapy integration* (2nd ed., pp. 105–120).

Lee, Y., Ragguett, R. M., Mansur, R. B., Boutilier, J. J., Rosenblat, J. D., Trevizol, A., Brietzke, E., Lin, K., Pan, Z., Subramaniapillai, M., Chan, T. C. Y., Fus, D., Park, C., Musial, N., Zuckerman, H., Chen, V. C., Ho, R.,

Rong, C., & McIntyre, R. S. (2018). Applications of machine learning algorithms to predict therapeutic outcomes in depression: A meta-analysis and systematic review. *Journal of Affective Disorders, 241*, 519–532. https://doi.org/10.1016/j.jad.2018.08.073

Levin, M. E., Haeger, J., & Cruz, R. A. (2018). Tailoring acceptance and commitment therapy skill coaching in the moment through smartphones: Results from a randomized controlled trial. *Mindfulness, 10*(4), 689–699. https://doi.org/10.1007/s12671-018-1004-2

Linehan, M. (1993). *Cognitive-behavioral treatment of borderline personality disorder.* Guilford Press.

Lopez-Gomez, I., Lorenzo-Luaces, L., Chaves, C., Hervas, G., DeRubeis, R. J., & Vazquez, C. (2019). Predicting optimal interventions for clinical depression: Moderators of outcomes in a positive psychological intervention vs. cognitive-behavioral therapy. *General Hospital Psychiatry, 61*, 104–110. https://doi.org/10.1016/j.genhosppsych.2019.07.004

Lorenzo-Luaces, L., DeRubeis, R. J., van Straten, A., & Tiemens, B. (2017). A prognostic index (PI) as a moderator of outcomes in the treatment of depression: A proof of concept combining multiple variables to inform risk-stratified stepped care models. *Journal of Affective Disorders, 213*, 78–85. https://doi.org/10.1016/j.jad.2017.02.010

Lorenzo-Luaces, L., Peipert, A., De Jesús Romero, R., Rutter, L. A., & Rodriguez-Quintana, N. (2020). Personalized medicine and cognitive behavioral therapies for depression: Small effects, big problems, and bigger data. *International Journal of Cognitive Therapy.* https://doi.org/https://doi.org/10.1007/s41811-020-00094-3

Lorimer, B., Delgadillo, J., Kellett, S., & Lawrence, J. (2020). Dynamic prediction and identification of cases at risk of relapse following completion of low-intensity cognitive behavioural therapy. *Psychotherapy Research, 31*(1), 1–14. https://doi.org/10.1080/10503307.2020.1733127

Luedtke, A., Sadikova, E., & Kessler, R. C. (2019). Sample size requirements for multivariate models to predict between-patient differences in best treatments of major depressive disorder. *Clinical Psychological Science, 7*(3), 445–461. https://doi.org/https://doi.org/10.1177/2167702618815466

Luedtke, A. R., & van der Laan, M. J. (2016a). Statistical inference for the mean outcome under a possibly non-unique optimal treatment strategy. *Annals of Statistics, 44*(2), 713–742. https://doi.org/10.1214/15-AOS1384

Luedtke, A. R., & van der Laan, M. J. (2016b). Super-learning of an optimal dynamic treatment rule. *International Journal of Biostatistics, 12*(1), 305–332. https://doi.org/10.1515/ijb-2015-0052

Luedtke, A. R., & van der Laan, M. J. (2017). Evaluating the impact of treating the optimal subgroup. *Statistical Methods in Medical Research, 26*(4), 1630–1640. https://doi.org/10.1177/0962280217708664

Lutz, W., Deisenhofer, A.-K., Rubel, J., Bennemann, B., Giesemann, J., Poster, K., & Schwartz, B. (2021). Prospective evaluation of a clinical decision support system in psychological therapy. *Journal of Consulting and Clinical Psychology, in press,* https://doi.org/10.1037/ccp0000642.

Lutz, W., Rubel, J. A., Schwartz, B., Schilling, V., & Deisenhofer, A.-K. (2019). Towards integrating personalized feedback research into clinical practice: Development of the Trier Treatment Navigator (TTN). *Behaviour Research and Therapy, 120*, 103438. https://doi.org/10.1016/j.brat.2019.103438

Lutz, W., Saunders, S. M., Leon, S. C., Martinovich, Z., Kosfelder, J., Schulte, D., Grawe, K., & Tholen, S. (2006). Empirically and clinically useful decision making in psychotherapy: Differential predictions with treatment response models. *Psychological Assessment, 18*(2), 133–141. https://doi.org/10.1037/1040-3590.18.2.133

Lutz, W., Schwartz, B., Gomez Penedo, M. J., Boyle, K., & Deisenhofer, A.-K. (2020). Working towards the development and implementation of precision mental healthcare: An example. *Administration and Policy in Mental Health, 47*(5), 856–861. https://doi.org/10.1007/s10488-020-01053-y

Lutz, W., Schwartz, B., Hofmann, S. G., Fisher, A. J., Husen, K., & Rubel, J. A. (2018). Using network analysis for the prediction of treatment dropout in patients with mood and anxiety disorders: A methodological proof-of-concept study. *Scientific Reports, 8*(1), 1–9. https://doi.org/10.1038/s41598-018-25953-0

Lynam, A. L., Dennis, J. M., Owen, K. R., Oram, R. A., Jones, A. G., Shields, B. M., & Ferrat, L. A. (2020). Logistic regression has similar performance to optimised machine learning algorithms in a clinical setting: Application to the discrimination between type 1 and type 2 diabetes in young

adults. *Diagnostic and Prognostic Research, 4*, 6. https://doi.org/10.1186/s41512-020-00075-2

Macdonald, H., Loder, E., & Abbasi, K. (2020). Living systematic reviews at The BMJ. *British Medical Journal, 370*, m2925. https://doi.org/10.1136/bmj.m2925

Maeda, Y., Ichikawa, R., Misawa, J., Shibuya, A., Hishiki, T., Maeda, T., Yoshino, A., & Kondo, Y. (2019). External validation of the TRISS, CRASH, and IMPACT prognostic models in severe traumatic brain injury in Japan. *PLOS One, 14*(8), e0221791. https://doi.org/10.1371/journal.pone.0221791

Magnavita, J. J., & Lilienfeld, S. O. (2016). Clinical expertise and decision making: An overview of bias in clinical practice. In J. J. Magnavita (Ed.), *Clinical decision making in mental health practice* (pp. 23–60). American Psychological Association. https://doi.org/10.1037/14711-002

Malhi, G. S., Bassett, D., Boyce, P., Bryant, R., Fitzgerald, P. B., Fritz, K., Hopwood, M., Lyndon, B., Mulder, R., Murray, G., Porter, R., & Singh, A. B. (2015). Royal Australian and New Zealand College of Psychiatrists clinical practice guidelines for mood disorders. *Australian and New Zealand Journal of Psychiatry, 49*(12), 1087–1206. https://doi.org/10.1177/0004867415617657

McCullough Jr, J. P. (2003). *Treatment for chronic depression: Cognitive behavioral analysis system of psychotherapy (CBASP)* (Vol. 13). Educational Publishing Foundation.

Meehl, P. E. (1954). *Clinical versus statistical prediction: A theoretical analysis and a review of the evidence.* University of Minnesota Press. https://doi.org/http://dx.doi.org/10.1037/11281-000

Miller, I. W., Keitner, G. I., Ryan, C. E., Solomon, D. A., Cardemil, E. V., & Beevers, C. G. (2005). Treatment matching in the posthospital care of depressed patients. *American Journal of Psychiatry, 162*(11), 2131-2138. https://doi.org/10.1176/appi.ajp.162.11.2131

Mohr, D. C., Schueller, S. M., Tomasino, K. N., Kaiser, S. M., Alam, N., Karr, C., Vergara, J. L., Gray, E. L., Kwasny, M. J., & Lattie, E. G. (2019). Comparison of the effects of coaching and receipt of app recommendations on depression, anxiety, and engagement in the IntelliCare platform: Factorial randomized controlled trial. *Journal of Medical Internet Research, 21*(8), e13609. https://doi.org/10.2196/13609

Moons, K. G., Altman, D. G., Reitsma, J. B., Ioannidis, J. P., Macaskill, P., Steyerberg, E. W., Vickers, A. J., Ransohoff, D. F., & Collins, G. S. (2015). Transparent Reporting of a multivariable prediction model for Individual Prognosis or Diagnosis (TRIPOD): Explanation and elaboration. *Annals of Internal Medicine, 162*(1), W1-W73. https://doi.org/10.7326/M14-0698

Moritz, S., Stepulovs, O., Schröder, J., Hottenrott, B., Meyer, B., & Hauschildt, M. (2016). Is the whole less than the sum of its parts? Full versus individually adapted metacognitive self-help for obsessive-compulsive disorder: A randomized controlled trial. *Journal of Obsessive-Compulsive and Related Disorders, 9*, 107–115. https://doi.org/10.1016/j.jocrd.2016.04.001

Nahum-Shani, I., Hekler, E. B., & Spruijt-Metz, D. (2015). Building health behavior models to guide the development of just-in-time adaptive interventions: A pragmatic framework. *Health Psychology, 34*(S), 1209-1219. https://doi.org/10.1037/hea0000306

Nahum-Shani, I., Smith, S. N., Spring, B. J., Collins, L. M., Witkiewitz, K., Tewari, A., & Murphy, S. A. (2018). Just-in-time adaptive interventions (JITAIs) in mobile health: Key components and design principles for ongoing health behavior support. *Annals of Behavioral Medicine, 52*(6), 446–462. https://doi.org/10.1007/s12160-016-9830-8

Najafabadi, A. H. Z., Ramspek, C. L., Dekker, F. W., Heus, P., Hooft, L., Moons, K. G., Peul, W. C., Collins, G. S., Steyerberg, E. W., & van Diepen, M. (2020). TRIPOD statement: A preliminary pre-post analysis of reporting and methods of prediction models. *BMJ Open, 10*(9), e041537. https://doi.org/10.1136/bmjopen-2020-041537

National Collaborating Centre for Mental Health. (2009). *Borderline personality disorder: Treatment and management.* British Psychological Society.

National Collaborating Centre for Mental Health. (2011). *Common mental health disorders: Identification and pathways to care* (Vol. 123). RCPsych Publications.

Newton-Howes, G., Tyrer, P., Johnson, T., Mulder, R., Kool, S., Dekker, J., & Schoevers, R. (2014). Influence of personality on the outcome of treatment in depression: Systematic review and meta-analysis. *Journal of Personality Disorders, 28*(4), 577–593. https://doi.org/10.1521/pedi_2013_27_070

Norcross, J. C. (2005). A primer on psychotherapy integration. In J. C. Norcross & M. R. Goldfried (Eds.), *Handbook of psychotherapy integration* (2nd ed., pp. 3–23). Oxford University Press. https://doi.org/10.1093/med:psych/9780195165791.003.0001

Norcross, J. C., & Prochaska, J. O. (1988). A study of eclectic (and integrative) views revisited. *Professional Psychology: Research and Practice, 19*(2), 170–174. https://doi.org/10.1037/0735-7028.19.2.170

Nordgren, L. B., Hedman, E., Etienne, J., Bodin, J., Kadowaki, A., Eriksson, S., Lindkvist, E., Andersson, G., & Carlbring, P. (2014). Effectiveness and cost-effectiveness of individually tailored internet-delivered cognitive behavior therapy for anxiety disorders in a primary care population: A randomized controlled trial. *Behaviour Research and Therapy, 59*, 1–11. https://doi.org/10.1016/j.brat.2014.05.007

Nusinovici, S., Tham, Y. C., Chak Yan, M. Y., Wei Ting, D. S., Li, J., Sabanayagam, C., Wong, T. Y., & Cheng, C. Y. (2020). Logistic regression was as good as machine learning for predicting major chronic diseases. *Journal of Clinical Epidemiology, 122*, 56–69. https://doi.org/10.1016/j.jclinepi.2020.03.002

Obermeyer, Z., Powers, B., Vogeli, C., & Mullainathan, S. (2019). Dissecting racial bias in an algorithm used to manage the health of populations. *Science, 366*(6464), 447. https://doi.org/10.1126/science.aax2342

Ogrodniczuk, J. S., Joyce, A. S., & Piper, W. E. (2005). Strategies for reducing patient-initiated premature termination of psychotherapy. *Harvard Review of Psychiatry, 13*(2), 57–70. https://doi.org/10.1080/10673220590956429

Ong, W. T., Murphy, D., & Joseph, S. (2020). Unnecessary and incompatible: A critical response to Cooper and McLeod's conceptualization of a pluralistic framework for person-centered therapy. *Person-Centered & Experiential Psychotherapies, 19*(2), 168–182. https://doi.org/10.1080/14779757.2020.1717987

Papakostas, G. I., & Fava, M. (2008). Predictors, moderators, and mediators (correlates) of treatment outcome in major depressive disorder. *Dialogues in Clinical Neuroscience, 10*(4), 439–451. https://doi.org/10.31887/DCNS.2008.10.4/gipapakostas

Paul, G. L. (1967). Strategy of outcome research in psychotherapy. *Journal of Consulting Psychology, 31*(2), 109–118. https://doi.org/10.1037/h0024436

Pearson, R., Pisner, D., Meyer, B., Shumake, J., & Beevers, C. G. (2019). A machine learning ensemble to predict treatment outcomes following an Internet intervention for depression. *Psychological Medicine, 49*(14), 2330–2341. https://doi.org/10.1017/S003329171800315X

Pencina, M. J., Goldstein, B. A., & D'Agostino, R. B. (2020). Prediction models-development, evaluation, and clinical application. *New England Journal of Medicine, 382*(17), 1583–1586. https://doi.org/10.1056/NEJMp2000589

Perlis, R. H. (2016). Abandoning personalization to get to precision in the pharmacotherapy of depression. *World Psychiatry, 15*(3), 228–235. https://doi.org/10.1002/wps.20345

Persons, J. B. (1991). Psychotherapy outcome studies do not accurately represent current models of psychotherapy: A proposed remedy. *American Psychologist, 46*(2), 99–106. https://doi.org/10.1037/0003-066X.46.2.99

Petkova, E., Park, H., Ciarleglio, A., Todd Ogden, R., & Tarpey, T. (2019). Optimising treatment decision rules through generated effect modifiers: A precision medicine tutorial. *BJPsych Open, 6*(1), e2. https://doi.org/10.1192/bjo.2019.85

Petkova, E., Tarpey, T., Su, Z., & Ogden, R. T. (2017). Generated effect modifiers (GEM's) in randomized clinical trials. *Biostatistics, 18*(1), 105–118. https://doi.org/10.1093/biostatistics/kxw035

Phung, M. T., Tin, S. T., & Elwood, J. M. (2019). Prognostic models for breast cancer: A systematic review. *BMC Cancer, 19*(1), 230. https://doi.org/10.1186/s12885-019-5442-6

Piet, J., & Hougaard, E. (2011). The effect of mindfulness-based cognitive therapy for prevention of relapse in recurrent major depressive disorder: A systematic review and meta-analysis. *Clinical Psychology Review, 31*(6), 1032–1040. https://doi.org/10.1016/j.cpr.2011.05.002

Prasad, V., Fojo, T., & Brada, M. (2016). Precision oncology: Origins, optimism, and potential. *Lancet Oncology, 17*(2), e81–e86. https://doi.org/10.1016/S1470-2045(15)00620-8

Project MATCH Research Group. (1997). Matching alcoholism treatments to client heterogeneity: Project MATCH posttreatment drinking outcomes. *Journal of Studies on Alcohol, 58*(1), 7–29. https://www.ncbi.nlm.nih.gov/pubmed/8979210

Project MATCH Research Group. (1998). Matching patients with alcohol disorders to treatments: Clinical implications from Project MATCH. *Journal of Mental Health, 7*(6), 589–602. https://doi.org/10.1080/09638239817743

Rekkas, A., Paulus, J. K., Raman, G., Wong, J. B., Steyerberg, E. W., Rijnbeek, P. R., Kent, D. M., & van Klaveren, D. (2020). Predictive approaches to heterogeneous treatment effects: A scoping review. *BMC Medical Research Methodology, 20*(1), 264. https://doi.org/10.1186/s12874-020-01145-1

Riley, R. D., Ensor, J., Snell, K. I. E., Harrell, F. E., Jr., Martin, G. P., Reitsma, J. B., Moons, K. G. M., Collins, G., & van Smeden, M. (2020). Calculating the sample size required for developing a clinical prediction model. *British Medical Journal, 368*, m441. https://doi.org/10.1136/bmj.m441

Riley, R. D., Hayden, J. A., Steyerberg, E. W., Moons, K. G., Abrams, K., Kyzas, P. A., Malats, N., Briggs, A., Schroter, S., Altman, D. G., Hemingway, H., & Group, P. (2013). Prognosis Research Strategy (PROGRESS) 2: Prognostic factor research. *PLOS Medicine, 10*(2), e1001380. https://doi.org/10.1371/journal.pmed.1001380

Riley, R. D., Snell, K. I., Ensor, J., Burke, D. L., Harrell Jr, F. E., Moons, K. G., & Collins, G. S. (2019a). Minimum sample size for developing a multivariable prediction model: Part I–Continuous outcomes. *Statistics in Medicine, 38*(7), 1262–1275.

Riley, R. D., Snell, K. I., Ensor, J., Burke, D. L., Harrell Jr, F. E., Moons, K. G., & Collins, G. S. (2019b). Minimum sample size for developing a multivariable prediction model: PART II-binary and time-to-event outcomes. *Statistics in Medicine, 38*(7), 1276–1296. https://doi.org/10.1002/sim.7993

Riley, R. D., van der Windt, D., Croft, P., & Moons, K. G. (2019). *Prognosis research in healthcare: Concepts, methods, and impact.* Oxford University Press.

Rodriguez, J. D., Perez, A., & Lozano, J. A. (2009). Sensitivity analysis of k-fold cross validation in prediction error estimation. *IEEE Transactions on Pattern Analysis and Machine Intelligence, 32*(3), 569–575. https://doi.org/10.1109/TPAMI.2009.187.

Rosellini, A. J., Dussaillant, F., Zubizarreta, J. R., Kessler, R. C., & Rose, S. (2018). Predicting posttraumatic stress disorder following a natural disaster. *Journal of Psychiatric Research, 96*, 15–22. https://doi.org/10.1016/j.jpsychires.2017.09.010

Rubel, J. A., Fisher, A. J., Husen, K., & Lutz, W. (2018). Translating person-specific network models into personalized treatments: Development and demonstration of the Dynamic Assessment Treatment Algorithm for Individual Networks (DATA-IN). *Psychotherapy and Psychosomatics, 87*(4), 249–251. https://doi.org/10.1159/000487769

Rubel, J. A., Zilcha-Mano, S., Giesemann, J., Prinz, J., & Lutz, W. (2020). Predicting personalized process-outcome associations in psychotherapy using machine learning approaches-A demonstration. *Psychotherapy Research, 30*(3), 300–309. https://doi.org/10.1080/10503307.2019.1597994

Rush, A. J., Trivedi, M. H., Wisniewski, S. R., Stewart, J. W., Nierenberg, A. A., Thase, M. E., Ritz, L., Biggs, M. M., Warden, D., Luther, J. F., Shores-Wilson, K., Niederehe, G., Fava, M., & Team, S. D. S. (2006). Bupropion-SR, sertraline, or venlafaxine-XR after failure of SSRIs for depression. *New England Journal of Medicine, 354*(12), 1231–1242. https://doi.org/10.1056/NEJMoa052963

Ryle, A., Poynton, A. M., & Brockman, B. J. (1990). *Cognitive-analytic therapy: Active participation in change: A new integration in brief psychotherapy.* John Wiley & Sons.

Salazar de Pablo, G., Studerus, E., Vaquerizo-Serrano, J., Irving, J., Catalan, A., Oliver, D., Baldwin, H., Danese, A., Fazel, S., Steyerberg, E. W., Stahl, D., & Fusar-Poli, P. (2021). Implementing precision psychiatry: A systematic review of individualized prediction models for clinical practice. *Schizophrenia Bulletin, 47*(2), 284–297. https://doi.org/10.1093/schbul/sbaa120

Sauerbrei, W., Perperoglou, A., Schmid, M., Abrahamowicz, M., Becher, H., Binder, H., Dunkler, D., Harrell, F. E., Jr., Royston, P., Heinze, G., & For TG2 of the STRATOS Initiative (2020). State of the art in selection of variables and functional forms in multivariable analysis-outstanding issues. *Diagnostic and Prognostic Research, 4*, 3. https://doi.org/10.1186/s41512-020-00074-3

Saunders, R., Buckman, J. E. J., & Pilling, S. (2020). Latent variable mixture modelling and individual treatment prediction. *Behaviour Research and Therapy, 124*, 103505. https://doi.org/10.1016/j.brat.2019.103505

Saunders, R., Cape, J., Fearon, P., & Pilling, S. (2016). Predicting treatment outcome in psychological treatment services by identifying latent profiles of patients. *Journal of Affective Disorders, 197*, 107–115. https://doi.org/10.1016/j.jad.2016.03.011

Sawyer, J. (1966). Measurement and prediction, clinical and statistical. *Psychological Bulletin, 66*(3), 178–200. https://doi.org/10.1037/h0023624

Schon, D. A. (1984). *The reflective practitioner: How professionals think in action* (Vol. 5126). Basic Books.

Schulte, D., Künzel, R., Pepping, G., & Schulte-Bahrenberg, T. (1992). Tailor-made versus standardized therapy of phobic patients. *Advances in Behaviour Research and Therapy, 14*(2), 67–92. https://doi.org/10.1016/0146-6402(92)90001-5

Schwartz, B., Cohen, Z. D., Rubel, J. A., Zimmermann, D., Wittmann, W. W., & Lutz, W. (2020). Personalized treatment selection in routine care: Integrating machine learning and statistical algorithms to recommend cognitive behavioral or psychodynamic therapy. *Psychotherapy Research, 31*(1), 1–19. https://doi.org/10.1080/10503307.2020.1769219

Segal, Z. V., Williams, J. M. G., & Teasdale, J. D. (2001). *Mindfulness-based cognitive therapy for depression: A new approach to preventing relapse*. Guilford Publications.

Senn, S. (2018). Statistical pitfalls of personalized medicine. *Nature, 563*(7733), 619–621. https://doi.org/10.1038/d41586-018-07535-2

Shmueli, G. (2010). To explain or to predict? *Statistical Science, 25*(3), 289–310. https://doi.org/10.1214/10-STS330

Silfvernagel, K., Carlbring, P., Kabo, J., Edstrom, S., Eriksson, J., Manson, L., & Andersson, G. (2012). Individually tailored internet-based treatment for young adults and adults with panic attacks: Randomized controlled trial. *Journal of Medical Internet Research, 14*(3), e65. https://doi.org/10.2196/jmir.1853

Silfvernagel, K., Westlinder, A., Andersson, S., Bergman, K., Diaz Hernandez, R., Fallhagen, L., Lundqvist, I., Masri, N., Viberg, L., Forsberg, M. L., Lind, M., Berger, T., Carlbring, P., & Andersson, G. (2018). Individually tailored internet-based cognitive behaviour therapy for older adults with anxiety and depression: A randomised controlled trial. *Cognitive Behaviour Therapy, 47*(4), 286–300. https://doi.org/10.1080/16506073.2017.1388276

Simon, G. E., & Perlis, R. H. (2010). Personalized medicine for depression: Can we match patients with treatments? *The American Journal of Psychiatry, 167*(12), 1445–1455. https://doi.org/10.1176/appi.ajp.2010.09111680

Siontis, G. C., Tzoulaki, I., Castaldi, P. J., & Ioannidis, J. P. (2015). External validation of new risk prediction models is infrequent and reveals worse prognostic discrimination. *Journal of Clinical Epidemiology, 68*(1), 25–34. https://doi.org/10.1016/j.jclinepi.2014.09.007

Smith, B., & Sechrest, L. (1991). Treatment of aptitude X treatment interactions. *Journal of Consulting and Clinical Psychology, 59*(2), 233–244. https://doi.org/10.1037//0022-006x.59.2.233

Smits, J. A., Powers, M. B., & Otto, M. W. (2019). *Personalized exposure therapy: A person-centered transdiagnostic approach*. Oxford University Press.

Smyth, J. M., & Heron, K. E. (2016). Is providing mobile interventions "just-in-time" helpful? An experimental proof of concept study of just-in-time intervention for stress management. *2016 IEEE Wireless Health*, 1–7. https://doi.org/doi: 10.1109/WH.2016.7764561

Snow, R. E. (1991). Aptitude-treatment interaction as a framework for research on individual differences in psychotherapy. *Journal of Consulting and Clinical Psychology, 59*(2), 205–216. https://doi.org/10.1037/0022-006X.59.2.205

Soto, A., Smith, T. B., Griner, D., Domenech Rodriguez, M., & Bernal, G. (2018). Cultural adaptations and therapist multicultural competence: Two meta-analytic reviews. *Journal of Clinical Psychology, 74*(11), 1907–1923. https://doi.org/10.1002/jclp.22679

Souery, D., Serretti, A., Calati, R., Oswald, P., Massat, I., Konstantinidis, A., Linotte, S., Bollen, J., Demyttenaere, K., Kasper, S., Lecrubier, Y., Montgomery, S., Zohar, J., & Mendlewicz, J. (2011). Switching antidepressant class does not improve response or remission in treatment-resistant depression. *Journal of Clinical Psychopharmacology, 31*(4), 512–516. https://doi.org/10.1097/JCP.0b013e3182228619

Stacey, D., Legare, F., Lewis, K., Barry, M. J., Bennett, C. L., Eden, K. B., Holmes-Rovner, M., Llewellyn-Thomas, H., Lyddiatt, A., Thomson, R., & Trevena, L. (2017). Decision aids for people facing health treatment or screening decisions. *Cochrane Database of Systematic Reviews, 4*(4), CD001431. https://doi.org/10.1002/14651858.CD001431.pub5

Steyerberg, E. W. (2019). *Clinical prediction models*. Springer.

Steyerberg, E. W., Bleeker, S. E., Moll, H. A., Grobbee, D. E., & Moons, K. G. M. (2003). Internal and external validation of predictive models: A simulation study of bias and precision in small samples. *Journal of Clinical Epidemiology, 56*(5), 441–447. https://doi.org/10.1016/s0895-4356(03)00047-7

Steyerberg, E. W., & Harrell, F. E., Jr. (2016). Prediction models need appropriate internal, internal-external, and external validation. *Journal of Clinical Epidemiology, 69*, 245–247. https://doi.org/10.1016/j.jclinepi.2015.04.005

Steyerberg, E. W., Harrell, F. E., Borsboom, G. J. J. M., Eijkemans, M. J. C., Vergouwe, Y., & Habbema, J. D. F. (2001). Internal validation of predictive models. *Journal of Clinical Epidemiology, 54*(8), 774–781. https://doi.org/10.1016/s0895-4356(01)00341-9

Steyerberg, E. W., Moons, K. G., van der Windt, D. A., Hayden, J. A., Perel, P., Schroter, S., Riley, R. D., Hemingway, H., Altman, D. G., & Group, P. (2013). Prognosis Research Strategy (PROGRESS) 3: Prognostic model research. *PLOS Medicine, 10*(2), e1001381. https://doi.org/10.1371/journal.pmed.1001381

Steyerberg, E. W., Vickers, A. J., Cook, N. R., Gerds, T., Gonen, M., Obuchowski, N., Pencina, M. J., & Kattan, M. W. (2010). Assessing the performance of prediction models: A framework for traditional and novel measures. *Epidemiology, 21*(1), 128–138. https://doi.org/10.1097/EDE.0b013e3181c30fb2

Strandskov, S. W., Ghaderi, A., Andersson, H., Parmskog, N., Hjort, E., Warn, A. S., Jannert, M., & Andersson, G. (2017). Effects of tailored and ACT-influenced Internet-based CBT for eating disorders and the relation between knowledge acquisition and outcome: A randomized controlled trial. *Behavior Therapy, 48*(5), 624–637. https://doi.org/10.1016/j.beth.2017.02.002

Strupp, H. H. (1964). *A bibliography of research in psychotherapy*. Psychotherapy Research Project, Department of Psychiatry, University of North Carolina School of Medicine.

Symons, M., Feeney, G. F. X., Gallagher, M. R., Young, R. M., & Connor, J. P. (2020). Predicting alcohol dependence treatment outcomes: A prospective comparative study of clinical psychologists versus 'trained' machine learning models. *Addiction, 115*(11), 2164–2175. https://doi.org/10.1111/add.15038

Tolin, D. F., McKay, D., Forman, E. M., Klonsky, E. D., & Thombs, B. D. (2015). Empirically supported treatment: Recommendations for a new model. *Clinical Psychology: Science and Practice, 22*(4), 317–338. https://doi.org/10.1111/cpsp.12122

Trivedi, M. H., Rush, A. J., Crismon, M. L., Kashner, T. M., Toprac, M. G., Carmody, T. J., Key, T., Biggs, M. M., Shores-Wilson, K., Witte, B., Suppes, T., Miller, A. L., Altshuler, K. Z., & Shon, S. P. (2004). Clinical results for patients with major depressive disorder in the Texas Medication Algorithm Project. *Archives of General Psychiatry, 61*(7), 669–680. https://doi.org/10.1001/archpsyc.61.7.669

Twomey, C., O'Reilly, G., & Meyer, B. (2017). Effectiveness of an individually-tailored computerised CBT programme (Deprexis) for depression: A meta-analysis. *Psychiatry Research, 256*, 371–377. https://doi.org/10.1016/j.psychres.2017.06.081

Uwatoko, T., Luo, Y., Sakata, M., Kobayashi, D., Sakagami, Y., Takemoto, K., Collins, L. M., Watkins, E., Hollon, S. D., Wason, J., Noma, H., Horikoshi, M., Kawamura, T., Iwami, T., & Furukawa, T. A. (2018). Healthy Campus Trial: A multiphase optimization strategy (MOST) fully factorial trial to optimize the smartphone cognitive behavioral therapy (CBT) app for mental health promotion among university students: Study protocol for a randomized controlled trial. *Trials, 19*(1), 353. https://doi.org/10.1186/s13063-018-2719-z

van Beugen, S., Ferwerda, M., Spillekom-van Koulil, S., Smit, J. V., Zeeuwen-Franssen, M. E., Kroft, E. B., de Jong, E. M., Otero, M. E., Donders, A. R., van de Kerkhof, P. C., van Middendorp, H., & Evers, A. W. (2016). Tailored therapist-guided internet-based cognitive behavioral treatment for psoriasis: A randomized controlled trial. *Psychotherapy Psychosomatics, 85*(5), 297–307. https://doi.org/10.1159/000447267

van Bronswijk, S. C., Bruijniks, S. J., Lorenzo-Luaces, L., Derubeis, R. J., Lemmens, L. H., Peeters, F. P., & Huibers, M. J. (2020). Cross-trial prediction in psychotherapy: External validation of the Personalized Advantage Index using machine learning in two Dutch randomized trials comparing CBT versus IPT for depression. *Psychotherapy Research, 31*(1), 1–14. https://doi.org/10.1080/10503307.2020.1823029

van Bronswijk, S. C., DeRubeis, R. J., Lemmens, L., Peeters, F., Keefe, J. R., Cohen, Z. D., & Huibers, M. J. H. (2019). Precision medicine for long-term depression outcomes using the Personalized Advantage Index approach: Cognitive therapy or interpersonal psychotherapy? *Psychological Medicine*, 1–11. https://doi.org/10.1017/S0033291719003192

van Bronswijk, S. C., Lemmens, L. H., Huibers, M. J., & Peeters, F. P. (2020). Selecting the optimal treatment for a depressed individual: Clinical judgment or statistical prediction? *Journal of Affective Disorders, 279*, 149–157. https://doi.org/10.1016/j.jad.2020.09.135

van Calster, B., Wynants, L., Timmerman, D., Steyerberg, E. W., & Collins, G. S. (2019). Predictive analytics in health care: How can we know it works? *Journal of the American Medical Informatics Association, 26*(12), 1651–1654. https://doi.org/10.1093/jamia/ocz130

van der Laan, M. J., Polley, E. C., & Hubbard, A. E. (2007). Super learner. *Statistical Applications in Genetics and Molecular Biology, 6*(1), 25. https://doi.org/10.2202/1544-6115.1309

van Smeden, M., Moons, K. G., de Groot, J. A., Collins, G. S., Altman, D. G., Eijkemans, M. J., & Reitsma, J. B. (2019). Sample size for binary logistic prediction models: Beyond events per variable criteria. *Statistical Methods in Medical Research, 28*(8), 2455–2474. https://doi.org/10.1177/0962280218784726

Varadhan, R., Segal, J. B., Boyd, C. M., Wu, A. W., & Weiss, C. O. (2013). A framework for the analysis of heterogeneity of treatment effect in patient-centered outcomes research. *Journal of Clinical Epidemiology, 66*(8), 818–825. https://doi.org/10.1016/j.jclinepi.2013.02.009

Varoquaux, G. (2018). Cross-validation failure: Small sample sizes lead to large error bars. *NeuroImage, 180*(Pt A), 68–77. https://doi.org/10.1016/j.neuroimage.2017.06.061

Vittengl, J. R., Anna Clark, L., Thase, M. E., & Jarrett, R. B. (2017). Initial Steps to inform selection of continuation cognitive therapy or fluoxetine for higher risk responders to cognitive therapy for recurrent major depressive disorder. *Psychiatry Research, 253*, 174–181. https://doi.org/10.1016/j.psychres.2017.03.032

Vollmer, S., Mateen, B. A., Bohner, G., Kiraly, F. J., Ghani, R., Jonsson, P., Cumbers, S., Jonas, A., McAllister, K. S. L., Myles, P., Granger, D., Birse, M., Branson, R., Moons, K. G. M., Collins, G. S., Ioannidis, J. P. A., Holmes, C., & Hemingway, H. (2020). Machine learning and artificial intelligence research for patient benefit: 20 critical questions on transparency, replicability, ethics, and effectiveness. *British Medical Journal, 368*, l6927. https://doi.org/10.1136/bmj.l6927

Walitzer, K. S., Dermen, K. H., & Connors, G. J. (1999). Strategies for preparing clients for treatment: A review. *Behavior Modification, 23*(1), 129–151. https://doi.org/10.1177/0145445599231006

Wallace, M. L., Frank, E., & Kraemer, H. C. (2013). A novel approach for developing and interpreting treatment moderator profiles in randomized clinical trials. *JAMA Psychiatry, 70*(11), 1241–1247. https://doi.org/10.1001/jamapsychiatry.2013.1960

Walter, S., Turner, R., Macaskill, P., McCaffery, K., & Irwig, L. (2017). Beyond the treatment effect: Evaluating the effects of patient preferences in randomised trials. *Statistical Methods in Medical Research, 26*(1), 489–507. https://doi.org/10.1177/0962280214550516

Wampold, B. E., & Imel, Z. E. (2015). *The great psychotherapy debate: The evidence for what makes psychotherapy work*. Routledge.

Wardenaar, K. J., van Loo, H. M., Cai, T., Fava, M., Gruber, M. J., Li, J., de Jonge, P., Nierenberg, A. A., Petukhova, M. V., Rose, S., Sampson, N. A., Schoevers, R. A., Wilcox, M. A., Alonso, J., Bromet, E. J., Bunting, B., Florescu, S. E., Fukao, A., Gureje, O., . . . Kessler, R. C. (2014). The effects of co-morbidity in defining major depression subtypes associated with long-term course and severity. *Psychological Medicine, 44*(15), 3289–3302. https://doi.org/10.1017/S0033291714000993

Watzke, B., Ruddel, H., Jurgensen, R., Koch, U., Kriston, L., Grothgar, B., & Schulz, H. (2010). Effectiveness of systematic treatment selection for psychodynamic and cognitive-behavioural therapy: Randomised controlled trial in routine mental healthcare. *The British Journal of Psychiatry, 197*(2), 96–105. https://doi.org/10.1192/bjp.bp.109.072835

Webb, C. A., Cohen, Z. D., Beard, C., Forgeard, M., Peckham, A. D., & Björgvinsson, T. (2019). Personalized prognostic prediction of treatment outcome for depressed patients in a naturalistic psychiatric hospital setting: A comparison of machine learning approaches. *Journal of Consulting and Clinical Psychology, 88*(1), 25. https://doi.org/10.1037/ccp0000451

Webb, C. A., Trivedi, M. H., Cohen, Z. D., Dillon, D. G., Fournier, J. C., Goer, F., Fava, M., McGrath, P. J., Weissman, M., Parsey, R., Adams, P., Trombello, J. M., Cooper, C., Deldin, P., Oquendo, M. A., McInnis, M. G., Huys, Q., Bruder, G., Kurian, B. T., Jha, M., DeRubeis, R. J., & Pizzagalli, D. A. (2019). Personalized prediction of antidepressant v. placebo response: Evidence from the EMBARC study. *Psychological Medicine, 49*(7), 1118–1127. https://doi.org/10.1017/S0033291718001708

Weisel, K. K., Zarski, A. C., Berger, T., Krieger, T., Schaub, M. P., Moser, C. T., Berking, M., Dey, M., Botella, C., Banos, R., Herrero, R., Etchemendy, E., Riper, H., Cuijpers, P., Bolinski, F., Kleiboer, A., Gorlich, D., Beecham, J., Jacobi, C., & Ebert, D. D. (2019). Efficacy and cost-effectiveness of guided and unguided internet- and mobile-based indicated transdiagnostic prevention of depression and anxiety (ICare Prevent): A three-armed randomized controlled trial in four European countries. *Internet Interventions, 16*, 52–64. https://doi.org/10.1016/j.invent.2018.04.002

Weisz, J. R., Chorpita, B. F., Palinkas, L. A., Schoenwald, S. K., Miranda, J., Bearman, S. K., Daleiden, E. L., Ugueto, A. M., Ho, A., Martin, J., Gray, J., Alleyne, A., Langer, D. A., Southam-Gerow, M. A., Gibbons, R. D., & the Research Network on Youth Mental Health (2012). Testing standard and modular designs for psychotherapy treating depression, anxiety, and conduct problems in youth: A randomized effectiveness trial. *Archives of General Psychiatry, 69*(3), 274–282. https://doi.org/10.1001/archgenpsychiatry.2011.147

Welsh, I., & Lyons, C. M. (2001). Evidence-based care and the case for intuition and tacit knowledge in clinical assessment and decision making in mental health nursing practice: An empirical contribution to the debate. *Journal of Psychiatric and Mental Health Nursing, 8*(4), 299–305. https://doi.org/10.1046/j.1365-2850.2001.00386.x

Wessler, B. S., Lai YH, L., Kramer, W., Cangelosi, M., Raman, G., Lutz, J. S., & Kent, D. M. (2015). Clinical prediction models for cardiovascular disease: Tufts predictive analytics and comparative effectiveness clinical prediction model database. *Circulation: Cardiovascular Quality and Outcomes, 8*(4), 368–375. https://doi.org/10.1161/CIRCOUTCOMES.115.001693

Wheeler, S. (1993). Reservations about eclectic and integrative approaches to counselling. In W. Dryden (Ed.), *Questions and answers on counselling in action* (pp. 86–89). Sage Publications.

Wilkinson, J., Arnold, K. F., Murray, E. J., van Smeden, M., Carr, K., Sippy, R., de Kamps, M., Beam, A., Konigorski, S., & Lippert, C. (2020). Time to reality check the promises of machine learning-powered precision medicine. *The Lancet Digital Health, 2*(12), e677–e680. https://doi.org/10.1016/S2589-7500(20)30200-4

Windle, E., Tee, H., Sabitova, A., Jovanovic, N., Priebe, S., & Carr, C. (2019). Association of patient treatment preference with dropout and clinical outcomes in adult psychosocial mental health interventions: A systematic review and meta-analysis. *JAMA Psychiatry, 77*(3), 294-302. https://doi.org/10.1001/jamapsychiatry.2019.3750

Wright, A. G. C., & Woods, W. C. (2020). Personalized models of psychopathology. *Annual Review of Clinical Psychology, 16*, 49–74. https://doi.org/10.1146/annurev-clinpsy-102419-125032

Wynants, L., Van Calster, B., Collins, G. S., Riley, R. D., Heinze, G., Schuit, E., Bonten, M. M. J., Damen, J. A. A., Debray, T. P. A., De Vos, M., Dhiman, P., Haller, M. C., Harhay, M. O., Henckaerts, L., Kreuzberger, N., Lohman, A., Luijken, K., Ma, J., Andaur, C. L., . . . van Smeden, M. (2020). Prediction models for diagnosis and prognosis of Covid-19 infection: Systematic review and critical appraisal. *British Medical Journal, 369*, m1328. https://doi.org/10.1136/bmj.m1328

Zilcha-Mano, S., Keefe, J. R., Chui, H., Rubin, A., Barrett, M. S., & Barber, J. P. (2016). Reducing dropout in treatment for depression: Translating dropout predictors into individualized treatment recommendations. *Journal of Clinical Psychiatry, 77*(12), e1584-e1590. https://doi.org/10.4088/JCP.15m10081

Zoellner, L. A., Roy-Byrne, P. P., Mavissakalian, M., & Feeny, N. C. (2019). Doubly randomized preference trial of prolonged exposure versus sertraline for treatment of PTSD. *The American Journal of Psychiatry, 176*(4), 287–296. https://doi.org/10.1176/appi.ajp.2018.17090995

CHAPTER **20**

Combining Psychotherapy and Medications: It's All About the Squids and the Sea Bass (at Least for Nonpsychotic Patients)

STEVEN D HOLLON, PAUL W ANDREWS, MATTHEW C KELLER, DAISY R SINGLA, MARTA M MASLEJ, AND BENOIT H MULSANT

Abstract

The empirically supported psychotherapies (ESTs) can be as efficacious as medications (on average) in the treatment of the various nonpsychotic disorders, whereas medications form the core of treatment for the psychotic disorders with psychotherapy serving as an adjunct at best. Psychotherapy and medications likely work through different mechanisms and the two are often combined, although there may be reasons to be cautious in that regard, at least for the nonpsychotic disorders. There are emerging indications that adding medication may interfere with the long-term enduring effects that at least some types of psychotherapy possess and even worse that medications may have an iatrogenic effect of their own that worsens the course of the underlying disorder. We may have little choice but to medicate with the psychoses, but for the nonpsychotic disorders, such choice may exist and be to the benefit of the majority of patients.

OVERVIEW

INTRODUCTION

The various empirically supported psychotherapies (EST) can be as efficacious as medications (on average) in the treatment of the various nonpsychotic disorders and at least some appear to have an enduring effect that medications simply lack, whereas medications form the core of treatment for the psychotic disorders with psychotherapy serving as an adjunct at best. Psychotherapy and medications likely work through different mechanisms and the two are often combined, although, as we describe below, there may be reasons to be cautious in that regard, at least for the nonpsychotic disorders. There are emerging indications that adding medication may interfere with the long-term enduring effects that at least some types of psychotherapy possess and even worse that medications may have an iatrogenic effect of their own that worsens the course of the underlying disorder. We may have little choice but to medicate with the psychoses, but for the nonpsychotic disorders, such choice may exist for the majority of patients.

In this chapter we draw on evolutionary biology and evolutionary genetics to make sense out of these broad trends. We ask six questions:

With respect to the nonpsychotic disorders:

1. Is psychotherapy truly superior to medications in the treatment of the nonpsychotic disorders, and if so, why?
2. Is it ever advantageous to add medications in combination for such patients?

With respect to the psychotic disorders:

3. Is it truly advantageous to add psychotherapy to medications in the treatment of the psychotic disorders?
4. Is psychotherapy ever sufficient on its own?

With respect to both sets of disorders:

5. Do medications worsen the course of the underlying disorder?
6. Can preventive interventions forestall risk for initial onset of the various disorders?

EVOLUTIONARY BIOLOGY AND EVOLUTIONARY GENETICS

Not all forms of distress necessarily represent *diseases* or *disorders* but may instead be adaptations that evolved to serve a function in our ancestral past. As such they may represent reactive defenses to a variety of environmental challenges. For example, fever is an adaptation that evolved to combat infections (Shephard et al., 2016), nausea to expel ingested toxins (Treisman, 1977), and pain to protect against further tissue damage (Sneddon et al, 2014). Such adaptations, although often unpleasant to experience, are responses to environment challenges (internal or external) and not the pathologies themselves.

Similarly, depression and anxiety also may represent adaptations that evolved to serve a function. Since the most common nonpsychotic "disorders" largely revolve around these and similar types of affective distress, it may be unwise to assume that they represent dysfunction when they may in fact be "species-typical" responses to specific kinds of environmental threats. The adaptive value of anxiety is readily accepted and easily understood; it serves to protect the organism from external threat by promoting avoidance of dangerous situations. Depression is less readily accepted as an evolved adaptation despite the fact that grief (largely homologous with depression) is almost universally distributed across the species. Depressive symptoms often emerge following important life stressors or events, such as major loss or reversal, suggesting

that depression, like anxiety, may be a response to environmental circumstances (Keller et al., 2007). The adaptive value of this response may be to keep the person focused on the cause of that distress until it can be resolved (Andrews & Thompson, 2009). Reactions disproportionate to the situation may reflect a breakdown in the mechanism that evolved to serve that function, but symptoms alone are not necessarily an indication of "disorder" or "disease."

Most single-gene (Mendelian) disorders are both extremely rare and highly dysfunctional; whether an individual will reproduce depends upon whether it is dominant or recessive and the age of manifestation (see Table 20.1 adapted from Keller & Miller, 2006). Serious mental illnesses (SMIs) like schizophrenia and bipolar I disorder (highlighted in Table 20.1) tend to be intermediate between the Mendelian disorders and the less severe but more common mental "disorders" like anxiety and unipolar depression in terms of both heritability and prevalence. In general, the psychotic disorders tend to be more severe and have a more profound effect on reproductive fitness, especially the schizophrenias and especially then for males (Power et al., 2013). (People with bipolar disorder do not appear to be disadvantaged when it comes to the capacity to form relations or produce offspring but do have the highest rate of divorce of any of the psychiatric disorders.) At this time, psychotic disorders are best treated with medications and likely represent breakdowns in one or more evolved adaptations; these are true "diseases" (aka "disorders") in which something in the brain is not working right. They may or may not represent points of rarity; schizophrenia may be on the same continuum as schizotypal personality disorder and creativity, but in terms of its impact on function and reproduction, it truly is an SMI. Bipolar disorder may or may not be related to unipolar depression (it shares many genes and has a preponderance of unipolar relatives), but it is far less common and far more heritable. It also is more likely to involve psychosis and is evenly divided across the genders whereas unipolar depression is twice as common in women than in men. We are less certain that bipolar disorder represents a true malfunction in the brain than the schizophrenias, but more certain than we are than with any but the most severe psychotic unipolar depressions. We note that heritability is not destiny; the odds that someone with an identical twin who has been manifestly psychotic will themselves have a psychotic episode is only slightly above 50%, up to 50 times higher than the 1–2% base rate in the general population, but nothing approaching the quasi-certainty for the Mendelian disorders.

What we think this means is that adding medications to the ESTs for the more common nonpsychotic "disorders" should be approached with caution. We put "disorders" in quotes because from an evolutionary perspective there is nothing disordered about an evolved adaptation that is doing what it was designed to do. The common nonpsychotic "disorders" typically revolve around negative affective states associated with a "whole body response" (physiology, cognition, and behavior) that operates in an integrated fashion to provide the organism with its best

TABLE 20.1 Comparisons of frequencies: Examples of Mendelian disorders and common mental disorders

Disorder	Genetics or heritability (h^2)	Lifetime prevalence (Female/Male Ratio)
Mendelian Disorders	Mutations	
Dyskeratosis congenita	Recessive	.001% (1:1)
Granulomatous disease type 1	Recessive	.001% (1:1)
Juvenile onset Parkinson's	Recessive	.001% (3:2)
Apert's syndrome	Dominant	.001% (1:1)
Achondroplastic dwarfism	Dominant	.003% (1:1)
Severe Mental Disorders		
Autism	$h^2 \cong .90$	2% (1:5)
Schizophrenia	$h^2 \cong .80$	1% (1:1)
Bipolar disorder	$h^2 \cong .80$	1% (1:1)
Common Mental Disorders		
Unipolar depression	$h^2 \cong .45$	16% (2:1)
Specific phobia	$h^2 \cong .40$	7% (2:1)
Panic disorder[1]	$h^2 \cong .40$	5% (2:1)
SAD[2]	$h^2 \cong .35$	12% (1:1)
GAD[3]	$h^2 \cong .30$	6% (2:1)
PTSD[4]	$h^2 \cong .30$	7% (2:1)
OCD	$h^2 \cong .45$	2% (2:1)

Note: Data obtained from Online Mendelian Inheritance of Man (2006) for Mendelian disorders and the National Institute of Mental Health (1998) for serious and common mental disorders. When best estimates were unavailable, we used the average of the reported estimates.
[1] Heritability and prevalence data from Na et al., 2011.
[2] Heritability and prevalence data from Stein et al., 2017.
[3] Heritability and prevalence data derived from Davies et al. 2015.
[4] Heritability and prevalence data from Norrholm & Ressler 2009.
Key: GAD: generalized anxiety disorder; OCD: obsessive-compulsive disorder; PTSD: post-traumatic stress disorder; SAD: social anxiety disorder

chance of dealing with the situation by which it was elicited (see Sneddon et al., 2014, with respect to pain and Tooby & Cosmides, 1990, with respect to affect). Anxiety helps us to avoid imminent threats (Bateson et al, 2011; Nesse, 2019); depression redirects energy to rumination (an intense and persistent style of thinking) in response to (or in anticipation of) potential loss; and anger helps us avoid exploitation (Sell et al., 2009). These patterns are anything but random and any instance of nonrandom organization in a biological system requires an explanation. Natural selection is the one organizing principle that provides an explanation for nonrandom organization and it is reasonable to assume that such coordinated but differentiated proclivities evolved to provide the differential responses needed to deal with different kinds of stressors (Andrews et al., 2002; Andrews et al., 2020; Tooby et al., 2003). The majority of individuals with common mental "disorders" may be experiencing distress as a consequence of the operation of evolved adaptations that might be better facilitated than suppressed. We spend the rest of the chapter describing "disorders" and "diseases," nonpsychotic and psychotic, in keeping with our point, but first we illustrate the potential risks of simply "medicating" an evolved adaptation.

It's All About the Squids and the Sea Bass

Any organism has to navigate two often competing goals in order to contribute to the propagation of its genes; it must get lunch without becoming something else's lunch, unless you are a male praying mantis, in which case you propagate your genes by letting your girlfriend bite your head off for her lunch (Brown & Barry, 2016). Affects play an organizing function in terms of readying the physical structure of the body for action. (Not all evolutionary theorists ascribe a causal motivational role to affect; LeDoux (2019) regards affect as an epiphenomenon that plays no organizing or motivating role, but he still talks about survival behaviors that subserve the same functions.) The more complex the central nervous system, the more complex and plastic those actions can be, and the greater role higher information processing centers play in that regard. In humans and most, if not all, vertebrates, the central nervous system is divided into two competing systems: the *behavioral facilitation system* (BFS) that propels you toward appetitive pursuits like food or reproduction and the *behavioral inhibition system* (BIS) that propels (or keeps) you away from danger (Gray, 1990). Positive affects largely coordinate the drive for appetitive rewards and negative affects largely coordinate avoidance of, or movement away from, danger. Given that becoming lunch forestalls any opportunity to lunch in the future, avoiding risk usually trumps appetitive pursuits.

Squid live in the oceans in great numbers and sea bass feed on squid. As far as we can tell, squids prefer not to be eaten, and when a sea bass comes too near the squids engage in evasive maneuvers that reduce their risk. There is a question as to whether squids feel pain and if so, whether pain increases their chances of survival. In an ingenious study, Crook and colleagues subjected pairs of squids to the surgical removal of one of their arms (one under anesthesia and the other not) and two others were left uninjured (one anesthetized and the other not) (Crook et al., 2014). Six hours later, after the effects of the anesthesia had worn off, quartets of squid (one from each cell of the 2×2 design) were then placed in a tank with a hungry sea bass. By the time the squids were placed in the tank, human observers could detect no difference in swimming behaviors of the squids as a function of whether they had been subjected to the surgery – but the sea bass could. The sea bass selectively targeted the injured squids (as predators tend to do) and moved through an attack sequence from orientation to pursuit to attack to capture as shown in the top half of Figure 20.1. The squids, on the other hand, responded with a sequence of their own, moving from primary defense (avoiding detection via blending into the background – in effect, hiding in plain sight) to secondary defenses that involved evasive maneuvers, culminating in the use of an escape jet and discharge of ink into the water, as depicted in the bottom half of that same figure. The "alert distance" is the point at which the squids switch from primary to secondary defenses. What the investigators observed was that the squid that had been operated on without anesthesia began to shift from primary to secondary evasive maneuvers sooner

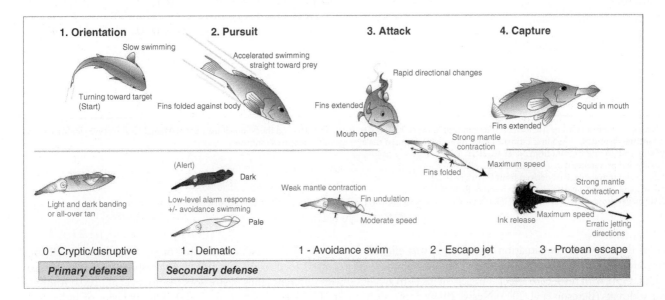

FIGURE 20.1 It's All About the Squids and the Sea Bass (Pain as an Evolved Adaptation)

Top: Four stages of predator behavior. *Orientation* is the change in direction toward a squid from an ongoing swimming trajectory and the distance from fish to squid is the "start-distance" of the predation attempt. *Pursuit* is an accelerated approach toward a squid, with the fish's fins folded. *Attack* is close-proximity "grappling," with the fish's mouth open and fins extended to facilitate rapid directional changes. *Capture* is any part of the squid's body in the mouth of the fish. Bottom: Defensive responses of squid to the fish. *Primary defense* (avoiding detection via crypsis) escalates to secondary defenses once the squid is alerted. Crypsis – chromatophore patterns of disruptive banding – occurs often during early encounter stages; it received an escalation score of 0. Distance between squid and fish at the first secondary defensive behavior is the "alert distance." *Secondary defenses* were scored based on their typical progression. Deimatic chromatophore displays that distract or startle a predator were scored 1, as were slow avoidance swimming evoked by distant threat. Escape jetting without inking was scored 2. Ink release, combined with erratic escape jetting, was scored 3. The highest score was recorded for each encounter.

Adapted with permission from Crook, R. J., Dickson, K., Hanlon, R. T., & Walters, E. T. (2014). Nociceptive sensitization reduces predation risk. *Current Biology*, 24(10), 1121–1125.

(they lengthened their "alert distance") than the squid that had not been injured (whether anesthetized or not), but that the squid that had been operated on under anesthesia did not start evading any sooner than the uninjured squid and were the ones most likely to be eaten. Being injured increased the risk of predation (both groups of injured squid were more likely to be eaten than those that were not) but being injured and not feeling the pain was worse; those squid who were injured under anesthesia did not start their evasive maneuvers any sooner than the squid who were uninjured and were the ones most likely to be caught. The moral of the story is that to be forewarned is to be forearmed [or in the case of the squid "seven-armed" (plus two longer tentacles) but with compensatory behaviors]. The inference is that the experience of pain even hours earlier altered the timing of onset of the propensity to evade.

Affects as Evolved Adaptations

We make this point because the common mental "disorders" largely involve aversive affective experiences that serve to coordinate "whole body" responses that culminate in behaviors that (at least in our ancestral past) likely served to increase adaptive fitness. To the extent that aversive affects still serve such a function, it may not be wise to simply "anesthetize" the distress. Psychiatric medications are particularly good at reducing affective distress in nonpsychotic patients; whether that is good for the patient depends on what role that distress plays in coordinating a response to the life problems that they evolved to address. With psychotic disorders we have few alternatives; the costs of an untreated episode of psychosis can be very high. Patients with a history of psychotic mania have the highest divorce rate associated with any major mental disorder and patients with a history of schizophrenia are less likely to have a spouse from whom to get divorced (especially if male). But for patients with nonpsychotic disorders for whom other alternatives exist, the question can be raised as to whether there are nonpharmacological alternatives that reduce distress in a fashion that furthers the adaptation that aversive affect evolved to serve. That question is especially relevant if those alternatives can reduce future risk. That is the question we address throughout the remainder of the chapter.

We focus on two sets of nonpsychotic "disorders," the mood disorders and the anxiety disorders, the two most prevalent forms of psychopathology, and two sets of psychotic disorders, the schizophrenias and the bipolar disorders, next to autism the most heritable of the psychiatric disorders. The two sets of nonpsychotic disorders can each be treated with psychotherapy alone, medications alone, or a combination of the two, whereas the two sets of psychotic disorders are almost always treated with medications, with psychotherapy sometimes added as an adjunct. We spend the most time on the mood disorders (especially unipolar depression) in part because those are the disorders that we know best and in part because those are the disorders that have been most often studied with respect to treatment combinations. That also is because most of what we know about any possible enduring effects of psychotherapy comes from that literature and also because one particular class of medications, the selective serotonin reuptake

inhibitors (SSRIs), now account for the bulk of the prescriptions written for any of the nonpsychotic disorders, anxiety included. If medications raise evolutionary concerns, unipolar depression is the place to begin.

NONPSYCHOTIC "DISORDERS"

The nonpsychotic disorders largely revolve around negative affects like depression and anxiety and it is axiomatic in evolutionary biology that the different negative affects motivate and coordinate different "whole-body" responses in response to different challenges that maximized the likelihood of passing on the organism's gene line in our ancestral past. To the extent that this is true then any intervention that facilitates the functions that those adaptations evolved to serve is likely to be preferred over those that simply anesthetize the distress. As Nesse (2019) opines in the title of his recent treatise on evolutionary psychiatry, there may be "good reasons for bad feelings." Our basic premise is that psychotherapy typically advances those evolved functions whereas psychiatric medications simply anesthetize the distress. The evolutionary anthropologists Syme and Hagen (2019) make a similar distinction (arrived at independently) between what they call the highly heritable low prevalence developmental disorders [autism (with its early onset) and the schizophrenias and bipolar I disorder (with adolescent onset or later)] and the modestly heritable but highly prevalent aversive but adaptive nonpsychotic disorders (especially depression and anxiety), as well as further distinguishing disorders of aging (senescence and dementia) and environmental mismatch (attention deficit hyperactivity disorder).

Mood "Disorders"
Prevalence and Heritability

Unipolar depression is the single most prevalent of the psychiatric "disorders." Major depressive disorder (MDD: its most severe diagnostic category) has a lifetime prevalence of 16%, with women showing nearly twice the rates of men (20%/12%) based on retrospective epidemiology surveys (Kessler, Berglund et al., 2005). Estimates based on prospective cohort samples followed from birth suggest an even higher prevalence, with up to 50% of the cohort having one or more diagnosable depressions by the time they are in their mid-30s, with women again nearly doubling the rates observed for men (Monroe et al., 2019). Given that the largest of the cohort samples has only reached its mid-30s, there is considerable time for those who have not yet been depressed to experience episodes of their own. Moreover, as shown in Figure 20.2, the majority of the additional cases are individuals with clear external precipitants (major life events) and few if any subsequent recurrences. The authors call them "depression possible" as distinguished from the other set of individuals who are likely to have repeated episodes even in the absence of obvious precipitants that they label "recurrence prone." From an evolutionary perspective it seems likely "depression possible" is "species typical" and reflects a normal reaction to an abnormal situation (Wakefield, 1992). First-episode patients are rare in

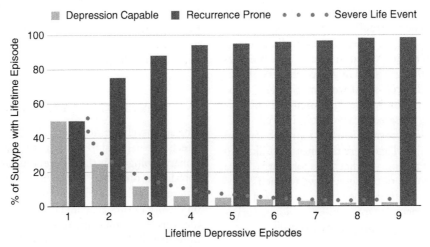

FIGURE 20.2 The decreasing association between severe life events and successive recurrences as explained by the dual pathway models.

The progressive changes are portrayed in the composition of depression capable versus recurrence prone subtypes as the number of lifetime episodes increases. The weakening association of severe life events with recurrences is depicted by the dotted line for severe life events that accompanies the diminishing representation of the depression capable subtype as the number of lifetime episodes increases.

Reprinted with permission from Monroe, S. M., Anderson, S. F., & Harkness, K. L. (2019). Life stress and major depression: The mysteries of recurrences. *Psychological Review, 126*(6), 791–816.

clinical settings (unless chronic) and it is likely that much of the clinical literature is based on people who are "recurrence prone," perhaps as a consequence of some prior diathesis that makes them particularly susceptible to becoming depressed when experiencing less extreme events.

Age of Onset and Gender Disparity

Depression prior to puberty is relatively rare and usually transient. The real explosion in incidence takes place in early adolescence; that is when the nearly 2-to-1 ratios of women to men first emerge and that disparity subsequently stays constant across the lifespan (Hankin & Abramson, 2001). No one knows for sure why the incidence of depression explodes during early adolescence or why women exhibit nearly twice the incidence shown by men, but the timing and the gender disparity are certain to attract the attention of evolutionary biologists. Most diseases kill you in the first year of life or in your dotage; there are few highly prevalent diseases or disorders that first emerge during adolescence when our evolutionary ancestors started to form families and take on adult responsibilities. Moreover, the gender disparity that emerges (and is not found in bipolar disorders) strongly suggests that unipolar depression is an adaptation that evolved to serve a function and that function was particularly pressing in young adolescent females.

Is Depression an Evolved Adaptation?

Two other "affective" syndromes that are related to clinical depression may provide some insight as to what function(s) (if any) it evolved to serve. Both inflammation and starvation share many features with clinical depression, and its

prototypic melancholic subtype in particular. Both share with melancholic depression a general sense of lassitude, low mood, and a loss of interest in hedonic pursuits, but here the similarities end. As shown in Figure 20.3, when fighting off an infection, energy is diverted away from hedonic pursuits and toward immune system functions, whereas in starvation, energy is diverted away from the immune system and other functions and toward the maintenance of vital body organs (and foraging) (Andrews et al., 2015). No one needs to reproduce when they are fighting off an infection or when they are starving, and growth is not at a premium in either; there is time for each later when the crisis has been surmounted. The other process that energy is directed away from is cognition; the brain is a very energy-expensive organ and you do not need to think that clearly when you are sick or all that often when you are wasting away (other than about food). These energy transfers are coordinated by serotonin, an evolutionary ancient neurotransmitter that is the proximal target of all current antidepressant medications (ADMs) other than bupropion (Andrews et al., 2015).

The cortex is the recipient of that energy transfer when someone is clinically depressed (labeled melancholia in the figure in keeping with Hippocrates' original theory) and rumination is the consequence. As shown in Figure 20.4, when someone has melancholia and the raphe nucleus fires (the location of all the cell bodies in the brain that use serotonin as a neurotransmitter), it projects to the amygdala (causing attention to be focused on the current problem), the hippocampus (causing working memory to be devoted to the problem), the lateral prefrontal cortex (minimizing distraction and facilitating problem-solving), the nucleus accumbens (decreasing

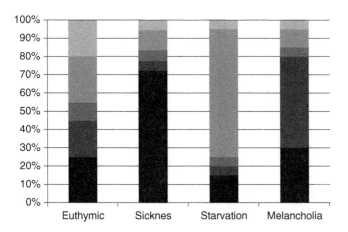

FIGURE 20.3 Graphical representation of how depressed organisms make different adaptive trade-offs in allocating limited energetic resources:

The numbers are hypothetical and illustrative. Relative to normal baseline: infection involves upregulated immune function, while growth and reproduction are downregulated. In starvation, a higher proportion of energetic reserves are devoted to maintenance, while growth, reproduction, and immune functions are suppressed. Melancholia involves an increase in cognition and possibly immune function, while growth and reproduction are down regulated.

Reprinted with permission from Andrews, P. W., Bharwani, A., Lee, K. R., Fox, M., & Thomson, J. A. Jr. (2015). Is serotonin an upper or a downer? The evolution of the serotonergic system and its role in depression and the antidepressant response. *Neuroscience and Biobehavioral Reviews, 51,* 164-188.

interest in hedonic pursuits), and the hypothalamus (slowing growth, reproduction, and physical activity). In essence, when someone becomes clinically depressed, their energy is directed to the cortex in a manner that sustains cognition and it is serotonin that coordinates. That suggests an adaptation that evolved to respond to some ancestral threat.

Why is so much energy transferred to cognition when someone is depressed? Andrews and Thomson (2009) suggest that this is so that they can solve complex social problems. In our ancestral past, ostracism from the social group was tantamount to a death sentence, especially for a young mother caring for a child. Primates live in social groups and survival depends on staying in the good graces of the rest of the troop. If a breach arose, it would be imperative to fix it so as to not be forced to leave. Without the support and protection of the social group one would likely starve or become something else's lunch (there are other predators in the world besides sea bass). Primates are contentious creatures, however, and although they evolved to live in social groups, problems do arise. If an interpersonal problem does arise, it is likely to be complicated and to require attention to redress. Women ruminate more than men even when not depressed and becoming depressed increases rates of rumination in either gender (Nolen-Hoeksema, 2012). The analytical rumination

hypothesis (ARH) suggests that energy is directed toward the brain when there is a complex problem to be solved and that the increase in rumination, often presumed to be just a "symptom" of depression, is in fact an evolved adaptation that functions to facilitate resolution of that complex (often interpersonal) problem. This resolution reduces the risk for social ostracism and increases the odds of survival for the individual and (if female) any offspring in her care (Andrews & Thomson, 2009). Not all problems are necessarily social in nature, but the same proclivities that help one think through affiliative issues can help resolutions in the achievement domain as well.

Rumination has gotten a bad name among clinicians, but it is clinicians who have made it so. Most dictionaries define rumination as "thinking deeply about a topic" whereas medical dictionaries typically add qualifiers like "obsessively" or "unproductively." In the cognition literature, there are two basic modes of thinking; Type 1 is fast and intuitive, whereas Type 2 is slow and reasoned (Evans & Stanovich, 2013; see also Kahneman, 2011). When paired with a negative emotion like fear or anger, Type 1 thinking helps you respond rapidly to an imminent threat ("false alarms" are common but less likely to be fatal than "false negatives" when the coiled figure on the ground turns out to be a poisonous snake) but requires little in the way of energy expenditure (Bodenhausen, Sheppard, & Kramer, 1994). Happiness also promotes Type 1 thinking, possibly because happiness signals that things are good and further processing is not necessary. Type 2 thinking is energetically expensive because it requires holding information in short-term memory so that the problem can be considered from multiple perspectives. The preponderance of the evidence suggests that humans (laboratory animals too) tend to switch to the more energetically expensive Type 2 thinking when there is a complex problem to be solved that does not benefit from an intuitive Type 1 processing response (Andrews et al., 2015, 2020).

Pharmacotherapy for Depression

There are four major classes of ADMs and a handful of others that do not fit into those major classes. The monoamine oxidase inhibitors (MAOIs) are the oldest (and possibly the most powerful), but also the most difficult to manage because they require specific dietary restrictions (foods high in tyramine like red wine and aged cheese) and avoidance of some over-the-counter medications least they trigger a potentially life-threatening hypertensive crisis. MAOIs work by inhibiting monoamine oxidase, the enzyme that breaks down biogenetic amines in the neuron. Monoamine oxidase is bound to the outer membrane of the mitochondria, the "blast furnaces" found within each cell that generate much of the energy used by the body. The importance of this proximity will be addressed.

The tricyclic antidepressants (TCAs) were developed about the same time as the MAOIs and are nearly as powerful but also problematic. The problems with the TCAs are two-fold; they are unpleasant to take (they blur your vision and

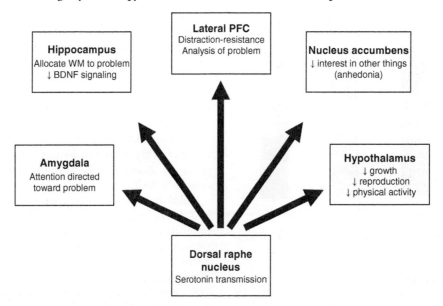

FIGURE 20.4 Serotonin evolved to regulate energy to keep organism focused on solving the problem at hand (analytic rumination) rather than using resources for growth and pursuit of rewards.

The main projection regions for elevated serotonin transmission in rodent models of melancholia and the hypothesized effects on symptoms in humans. Increased serotonin transmission coordinates multiple processes that promote sustained processing of the problem that triggered the episode: (1) Transmission to the amygdala directs attention to the problem that triggered the episode. (2) Transmission to the hippocampus promotes changes in synaptic plasticity involved in allocating working memory to the triggering problem and reduces BDNF signaling. (3) Transmission to the lateral PFC is involved in processing of the problem and promoting the resistance to distracting stimuli. (4) Transmission to the nucleus accumbens produces anhedonia that reduces the interest in attending to alternative stimuli. (5) Transmission to the hypothalamus downregulates other energetically expensive processes (growth and reproduction) that could draw limited resources away from processing of the problem, which probably contributes to many psychomotor symptoms (e.g., reduced eating and sexual activity, social withdrawal, lethargy).

Reprinted with permission from Andrews, P. W., Bharwani, A., Lee, K. R., Fox, M., & Thomson, J. A. Jr. (2015). Is serotonin an upper or a downer? The evolution of the serotonergic system and its role in depression and the antidepressant response. *Neuroscience and Biobehavioral Reviews, 51*, 164–188.

make your mouth dry) and they are lethal in overdose (as little as a two-week supply can kill someone). Since few patients are seen on a weekly basis after the first few weeks, sending a depressed (and often suicidal) patient home with more than a week's supply of TCAs is tantamount to sending someone home with a loaded gun. About 13.8% of intentional self-poisonings with TCAs result in death, a mortality rate nearly 30 times that for the SSRIs (Hawton et al., 2010). TCAs also impair higher-order cognition, particularly in older patients. Unlike the MAOIs that work in the presynaptic neuron to inhibit degradation, the TCAs (and most other types of ADMs including the SSRIs) work primarily by blocking reuptake into the presynaptic neuron. Whereas the MAOIs block the oxidation of all three biogenic amines implicated in depression (including dopamine), the TCAs block reuptake of only two (norepinephrine and serotonin). Norepinephrine in the brain is largely concentrated in neurons that have their cell bodies in the locus coeruleus and that play a major role in activating the "fight/flight" BIS stress response.

It became apparent by the early 1970s that serotonin was a major modulator for the other biogenic amines, especially dopamine that largely regulates BAS approach behaviors for appetitive stimuli and norepinephrine that largely regulates BIS escape/avoidance behaviors from aversive stimuli. With that recognition, the search was on for medications that were

selective to serotonin alone. Fluoxetine was the first of the SSRIs to hit the market and it revolutionized the treatment of depression in the United States and around the world. It was not because SSRIs are more powerful than either MAOIs or TCAs (if anything, they are a little less efficacious), but they are considerably safer (at least in the short run) and, unlike the benzodiazepines that were at that time widely prescribed for anxiety disorders, not addictive (at least in the conventional sense). As a consequence, primary care physicians were comfortable prescribing SSRIs rather than referring depressed patients on to psychiatrists for more difficult-to-manage ADMs like the MAOIs or the TCAs. Most people have a general practitioner or internist; few have psychiatrists or psychotherapists unless they are following up on a referral. Prior to the 1990s, nearly twice as many depressed patients were treated with psychotherapy as with medications; over the next two decades, those percentages completely reversed (Marcus & Olfson, 2010; Olfson et al., 2002). The ADMs are now the second most widely prescribed type of medications worldwide, trailing only the statins that are used to treat high cholesterol.

By the end of the 1990s, it became apparent that not everyone responded to medications like the SSRIs that targeted only a single neurotransmitter and a novel class of medications was developed that targeted norepinephrine as well as serotonin, the serotonin-norepinephrine reuptake inhibitors (SNRIs). The hope was that they would be more efficacious than the SSRIs, but that was realized to only a very modest extent, although some patients will respond to the one who will not respond to the other. SNRIs are more lethal in overdose than the SSRIs (because of their noradrenergic effects) but are far less lethal than the older TCAs (Hawton et al., 2010).

There are several other types of ADMs that do not fit into one of these four classes and although each has its indications, they are used far less often than the SSRIs or SNRIs. Bupropion affects norepinephrine and dopamine but not serotonin and that means that it does not produce the anorgasmia or decrease in libido caused by the SSRIs. Some psychiatrists refer to bupropion as the "party drug" for precisely that reason. It also helps people stop smoking, likely because it offsets the dopamine deficiency triggered by nicotine withdrawal. Mirtazapine has both serotonergic and some noradrenergic properties but is relatively safe in overdose. It also tends to be sedating which can be helpful if a patient is having trouble with insomnia. The problem with mirtazapine is that it tends to increase appetite (carbohydrates especially) and leads to weight gain; few young women with access to the internet will take the medication even if prescribed. Nefazadone is a serotonin antagonist and reuptake inhibitor with some weak effects on norepinephrine and dopamine. It is not a particularly potent antidepressant and it is rarely used nowadays because it can cause liver failure. However, it was the ADM used in the trial that produced the largest advantage for combined treatment in the literature in a study focused on the treatment of chronic depression (Keller et al., 2000). The pharmaceutical company that markets nefazadone funded the trial in hopes of finding a market niche for its otherwise underperforming ADM.

Most psychiatrists nowadays typically start patients on an SSRI and move next to an SNRI if the patient does not respond. They use TCAs only if they must and they rarely use MAOIs. Most research psychiatrists "dose to remission," raising the dose to the maximally tolerated dose and augmenting or switching as indicated across all major classes (or single variants) until the patient is fully asymptomatic. About a third of all patients with MDD will remit on their first ADM, whereas that proportion can be doubled within a year with the kind of aggressive progression just described (Rush et al., 2006). Most primary care providers are reluctant to prescribe any ADMs other than the SSRIs or SNRIs or to dose them aggressively (most ADMs have a dose-response curve such that at least some patients will need higher doses to remit). This means is that the majority of patients put on ADMs by their primary care providers get better (response) but do not get fully well (remission). This is highly problematic but predictable.

Psychosocial Treatments for Depression

There are four major psychosocial treatments for depression that have met with particular success when compared to medications and a fifth that evidenced some success in an initial trial but did not fare well in a subsequent effort at replication. Cognitive therapy was the first of the psychosocial interventions to be shown to be at least as efficacious as ADMs (Rush

et al., 1977) and superior to placebo among patients with more severe (DeRubeis et al., 2005) or atypical depressions (Jarrett et al., 1999). It also appears to have an enduring effect that reduces rates of relapse by more than half following treatment termination relative to ADM (Hollon, DeRubeis et al., 2005). This is one of the more robust effects in the psychosocial literature and has been essentially replicated in seven of the eight relevant trials (Cuijpers et al., 2013). Despite its name, cognitive therapy is a cognitive-behavioral intervention (hence we will abbreviate as CBT until we get to the anxiety disorders for which separate cognitive behavioral and cognitive therapies have been contrasted) in which patients are encouraged to use their own behaviors and reasoning skills to test the accuracy of their beliefs. As author PWA has pointed out, it depends heavily on the patient being able to think carefully about their problems and that is something that they could not do if they were dealing with a "broken brain" (Andrews et al., 2020). Interpersonal problems are often dealt with and the core beliefs addressed are as likely to involve lovability as competence. As might be expected from an evolutionary perspective, symptom clusters differ as a function of the triggering event: death of a loved one and romantic breakups are marked by high levels of sadness, anhedonia, appetite loss, and (for romantic breakups) guilt, whereas chronic stress and (to a lesser extent) failure are associated with fatigue and hypersomnia but less sadness, anhedonia, and appetite loss (Keller et al., 2007).

Behavioral activation (BA) involves encouraging patients to resume normal levels of activity in the face of their depressions (most people treat depression like the flu and do less) and to pursue potential sources of gratification whether they feel like it or not (and especially if they are dissuaded by potential risks). BA shares many of its behavioral strategies with CBT but pays no attention to the content of beliefs. It too compares favorably to ADM, with each being superior to pill-placebo among patients with more severe depressions (Dimidjian et al., 2006). It also appears to have an enduring effect (albeit tested only once) that cuts risk for relapse by half relative to prior ADM (Dobson et al., 2008). Although it does not address cognition directly, it does facilitate problem solving, albeit in an "act first and do not overthink it" fashion.

Problem-solving therapy (PST) is the third major cognitive-behavioral intervention that has been shown to be as efficacious as medications and to have a specific effect relative to placebo in one trial in primary care (Mynors-Wallis et al., 1995). It also enhanced the efficacy of medications when added in combination in a second trial in primary care (Mynors-Wallis et al., 2000). It has not been as extensively tested as CBT or even BA but appears to help offset the decline in executive functions among the elderly (Areán et al., 1993).

Interpersonal psychotherapy (IPT) is the other major intervention (along with CBT and the newer BA the best established of the ESTs) that has been shown to be as efficacious as ADM among patients with more severe depression and to have a specific effect relative to pill-placebo in the NIMH Treatment of Depression Collaborative Research Program (TDCRP: Elkin et al., 1989; 1995). Unlike CBT or BA, it has not been adequately tested with respect to enduring effects; no such evidence was found in the follow-up to the TDCRP, but the test was less than ideal for a number of methodological reasons (Shea et al., 1992). Another more recent trial found that it did not differ from prior CBT in terms of rate of relapse following treatment termination, but it was not clear how powerfully each EST was implemented in what was essentially an effectiveness trial (Lemmens et al., 2020). IPT explicitly eschews childhood reconstruction or generation of a transference neurosis, strategies that form the core of the more conventional dynamic approach from which it sprang, but even more traditional approaches have shown some promise; a short-term dynamic psychotherapy called supportive-expressive psychotherapy was as efficacious as ADM (although neither exceeded pill-placebo) in one trial (Barber et al., 2012), and in another 18 months of psychoanalytic psychotherapy was no more efficacious but more enduring than treatment as usual (including ADM) (Fonagy et al., 2015).

A fifth intervention called the cognitive-behavioral-analysis system of psychotherapy (CBASP) evidenced a particularly large advantage (a 25% increment) for combined treatment over either monotherapy (nefazadone) in a sample selected on the basis of chronicity (Keller et al., 2000) but did not fare all that well in replication (Kocsis et al., 2009). Enthusiasm has clearly waned for this approach, although our own sense is that this was premature. Chronic depression is known to be prognostic of poor response and the subsequent Kocsis trial was less a replication than an even more stringent test in a sample of patients who did not respond to an adequate trial of ADM that most other interventions would have had trouble passing. The field can be fickle at times and CBASP presents some interesting features that might well enhance the effects of medication in a chronic population. We know little about possible enduring effects for CBASP.

The bottom line is that virtually every type of psychosocial intervention seems to work (patients do better on any intervention than in its absence), although none appears to be clearly superior to the other with respect to acute response (American Psychological Association, 2019). This may be in large part because depression is quite responsive to nonspecific effects; a meta-analytic comparison that apportioned the amount of variance accounted for across no treatment, nonspecific controls, or active interventions found that about a third of the change observed across the course of treatment would have happened in its absence (spontaneous remission), half could be attributed to nonspecific processes mobilized by any treatment, and only about a sixth was a consequence of the kinds of specific factors mobilized by the "name brand" treatments just described (Cuijpers et al., 2012). Specificity of acute response appears to be largely moderated by severity; ADM does not separate from pill-placebo among the half or more of patients with less severe MDD (Fournier et al., 2010) and the only times in which an EST has ever beaten a nonspecific control has been among patients with more severe depressions (Driessen et al., 2010). Some other nonpsychotic disorders are not so responsive to nonspecific effects, but with respect to unipolar depression it appears that among those who are less severe *anything works better than nothing and nothing works better*

than anything else. It is only among patients with more severe depressions that specific effects emerge and that seems to be true both for psychotherapy and for medication.

Not everyone agrees that severity moderates the specificity of "true-drug" response relative to pill-placebo but those studies that disagree typically rely on data from industry-funded trials that screen out patients with less severe MDD and use "placebo washouts" to screen out patients who are particularly likely to respond to nonspecific factors prior to randomization (Furukawa et al., 2018; Gibbons et al., 2012; Rabinowitz et al., 2016). Such design features increase the likelihood of finding main effects for medications among patients with more severe depressions but greatly reduce the likelihood of detecting severity by treatment interactions by restricting the range of severity sampled. Fournier and colleagues sampled placebo-controlled comparisons between psychotherapy and medications that included the full range of MDD severity and eschewed placebo washouts. Kirsch (2019) cites a still unpublished Independent Patient Data Meta-analysis (IPDMA) conducted by Stone and colleagues at the Food and Drug Administration (FDA) that summarizes data on over 70,000 patients across more than 200 trials that shows a clear severity by treatment interaction despite these methodological constraints. This study will likely be the last word in this debate.

Adding Medications Enhances Acute Response (a Little)

Given how responsive unipolar depression is to nonspecific effects, it is not surprising that while combined treatment tends to be somewhat more effective than either monotherapy alone, the increments are not all that large (increments of 10–25% with effect sizes on the order of d = .31–.35: Cuijpers, Dekker et al., 2009; Cuijpers, van Straten et al., 2009). A recent network meta-analysis based on 101 studies including nearly 12,000 patients found that combined treatment enhanced response to either monotherapy by about 25% (RR = 1.27 relative to psychotherapy alone and RR = 1.25 relative to ADM alone) with negligible differences between the two (RR = 0.97) (Cuijpers et al., 2020). Both combined treatment (COM) (RR = 1.23) and psychotherapy alone (RR = 1.17) were more acceptable than ADM alone. The active pharmacological agent appears to account for about a quarter of that increment relative to pill-placebo; that implies that the larger portion is attributable to nonspecific factors (hopes and expectations) involved in bringing another modality on board (Cuijpers et al., 2010). What also is not clear is if these increments are a consequence of an additive or synergistic effect for any given patient or just more fortuitous matching of the optimal treatment to a given patient (Hollon, Jarrett et al., 2005). In a reanalysis of an earlier trial that focused solely on patients with more severe MDD, DeRubeis et al. (2005) found that about 30% of patients would have done better on ADM than with CBT and another 30% would have done better with CBT than on ADM (DeRubeis, Cohen et al., 2014). Had patients been assigned to their optimal condition instead of being randomized, outcomes would have improved across the full sample by as much as the drug-placebo difference in FDA trials (ES = 0.31) and twice that size for specific responders (ES = 0.58) (Turner et al., 2008).

Different Strokes for Different Folks

It remains to be seen whether such findings will replicate in other samples. That depends on the extent to which different patients respond differentially to psychotherapy versus medications and whether those differences (if they do exist) can be detected. Cohen and DeRubeis (2018) describe the application of even more powerful detection methods based on machine learning than the purely regression-based approach that they used in the study just described that give reason to be optimistic (see Chapter 19). Application of such strategies should allow us to determine the extent to which the rather modest but robust advantage evident for combined treatment is a consequence of better matching of treatments to patients (which could mean that no single individual does better in combined treatment than they do on their optimal modality) or some additional additive or synergistic effect (most or all benefit to a greater extent from the combination).

Figure 20.5 highlights these possibilities (adapted from DeRubeis, Gelfand et al., 2014). The process starts by measuring a set of baseline characteristics chosen to represent an array of indices that are easily assessed, like demographics and history of illness, and (if possible) somewhat more difficult to assess characteristics that are expected (on the basis of theory) or have been found (in past research) to be predictive of response in one or both modalities. Patients are then randomized to the respective treatments and prognostic indices are generated for each. Prognostic indices are simply algorithms generated (in this case via machine learning) to predict response in each of the respective modalities. As shown in Figure 20.5, if patients are plotted with respect to their score on each prognostic index, two clinically useful properties can be derived. Where a patient sits with respect to the diagonal (from lower left to upper right) indicates their general prognosis (how responsive they are to treatment on average) and how far they sit off the diagonal indicates the specificity of that response (with direction indicating the optimal intervention). If different patients did not respond differentially to different treatments, then everyone would sit tightly on the diagonal and what specific monotherapy someone got would not matter. Nonetheless, some or all might still show a differential response to the combination that cannot be accounted for by distance off the diagonal and if so, that increment would have to reflect an additive or synergistic effect of combining treatment that goes beyond simple optimization. If all of the advantage observed for combined treatment can be accounted for by distance off the diagonal (specificity of response) then the reason it works better than one or both of the monotherapies is simply because it ensures that all patients get their optimal intervention. Adding a third combined treatment condition and generating three sets of prognostic indices can play this process out. Such a visual depiction would require three dimensions and yield a cubic structure that would show at a glance the extent to which optimization versus additivity or synergy determined the advantage. This is important

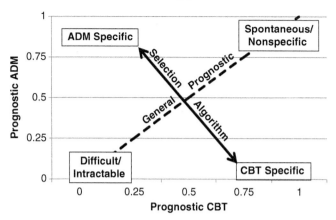

General Prognostic: Ave Prog Indices/Selection Algorithm: Diff Prog Indices

FIGURE 20.5 Prognostic indices and selection algorithm.

Machine learning can be used to generate prognostic indices for two or more interventions that can then be used to identify a general prognostic index that indicates how likely a given patient is to respond to either treatment and a selection algorithm [aka precision treatment rule (PTR)] that can be used to specify the optimal treatment for a given patient (distance from the general prognostic diagonal). Any population will consist of four general types of patients: *difficult/intractable* patients unlikely to respond to either intervention; *CBT specific* patients more likely to respond to CBT than to ADM; *ADM specific* patients more likely to respond to ADM than to CBT; and *spontaneous/nonspecific* patients likely to respond to either modality for nonspecific reasons including those who spontaneously remit.

Adapted with permission from DeRubeis, R. J., Gelfand, L. A., German, R. E., Fournier, J. C., & Forand, N. R. (2014). Understanding processes of change: How some patients reveal more than others—and some groups of therapists less—about what matters in psychotherapy. *Psychotherapy Research, 24,* 419–428.

because combined treatment is always more expensive than either single modality both in terms of costs and potential risks. It is likely better to start with one treatment than with two and to add the other only when we must, but better still to know in advance who is likely to need both.

Making Tests of Mediation More Precise

Moderation always implies differential mediation, and if different patients respond differentially to different treatments then those patients must be following different causal processes (Kazdin, 2007). Whether those processes are different in quality or quantity is likely related to whether the advantage comes from better optimization (the more it does, the more different patients are adhering to different mechanisms) or from additivity or synergism (a larger "dose" of the same mechanism in the case of the former and a true interaction between different mechanisms in the latter). Detecting moderation allows for tests of *moderated mediation* by means of including patient-by-mediator interactions based on the prognostic algorithms generated in Figure 20.5 to the tests of mediation as depicted in Figure 20.6. This allows for a more precise test of mediation since it specifies who should adhere to each mechanism rather than mixing those who do and do not (Preacher et al., 2007).

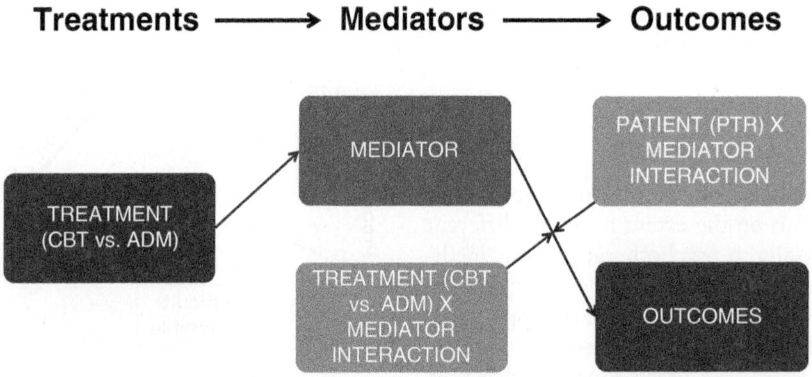

Treatments ⟶ **Mediators** ⟶ **Outcomes**

FIGURE 20.6 *Moderated mediation: Precision treatment rules (PTRs) to enhance the precision of tests of mediation.*

Only those patients who show a specific response to a given intervention are adhering to mechanisms specific to that intervention, but most tests of mediation fail to specify which patients in the larger sample ought to show such specificity of response. This has the effect of watering down tests of mediation since the magnitude of the effect to be detected will be diluted by inclusion of patients who do not adhere to that mechanism. This can be dealt with by including interactions between the selection algorithms generated [aka precision treatment rules (PTRs)] and the purported mediators in the tests of mediation. Similarly, whereas change in mediators can drive change in outcomes for some patients, change in outcomes can drive change in mediators in others (reverse causality). This can be dealt with by including treatment by mediator interactions in the tests of mediation. Both are instances of moderated mediation, and inclusion of each can make the tests of mediation more precise and likely to detect causality.

Adapted with permission from Hollon, S. D., DeRubeis, R. J., & Evans, M. D. (1987). Causal mediation of change in treatment for depression: Discriminating between nonspecificity and noncausality. *Psychological Bulletin, 102*(1), 139–149.

Adding Medications Enhances Acute Effects (for Some)

Combined effects may be highly moderated. A recent trial both points to the role of moderation and raises concerns about the possible unintended effects of combined treatment. In that study, 452 depressed outpatients meeting criteria for MDD were randomized to either ADM alone or in combination with CBT (COM) (Hollon, DeRubeis et al., 2014). Patients were first treated for up to 18 months to the point of remission (defined as four weeks of minimal symptoms) then continued in treatment to the point of recovery (six months without relapse). Patients who relapsed during continuation were brought back to remission as often as necessary and then continued in treatment for up to 42 months (from initial randomization) to the point of recovery. As shown in Figure 20.7, patients treated with COM showed a modest but hardly remarkable 10% increment over ADM alone in overall rates of recovery. In point of fact, that increment was wholly attributable to the third of the sample that was not chronic but more severe, for whom the increment was in the order of 30%. The third of the sample that was chronic did not benefit from adding CBT and the third of the sample that was neither chronic nor severe did not need it. That is the essence of moderation.

But Adding Medications May Interfere with CBT's Enduring Effects

The problem was that adding ADM in combination appeared to wipe out any enduring effect for CBT, even among those nonchronic patients with more severe depressions who actually benefited from the combination (DeRubeis et al., 2020). Whereas CBT typically cuts risk for relapse by more than half relative to ADM following treatment termination, a robust

effect found in seven of eight relevant trials (Cuijpers et al., 2013), maintaining recovered patients on ADM reduced risk for recurrence but prior exposure to CBT did not. This despite the fact that two earlier trials with extended follow-ups found that prior exposure to CBT alone reduced risk for recurrence relative to withdrawal from ADM among recovered patients after a year of continuation medication (Dobson et al., 2008; Hollon, DeRubeis et al., 2005). Three earlier trials involving combined treatment in much smaller samples showed decidedly mixed results; one found an enduring effect for prior COM (Evans et al., 1992) whereas another did not despite finding such an effect for CBT alone (Simons et al., 1986) and a third was too muddled to draw conclusions (Blackburn et al., 1986). It would be premature to conclude that adding ADM in combination interferes with CBT's enduring effect, but the best available evidence at this time suggests that it might be the case. As we discuss in the section on panic disorder, this is not the first study to find such an effect. The issue needs to be resolved on empirical grounds, but we are no longer as comfortable concluding that combinations retain the benefits of each of the monotherapies as we have asserted in the past (Hollon, Jarrett et al., 2005).

Are Antidepressant Medications Iatrogenic?

Even more problematic is the possibility that ADMs have an iatrogenic effect that suppresses symptoms by means of working through a mechanism that prolongs or worsens the underlying episode. Many believe that ADMs work by virtue of correcting a deficit in neurotransmitter levels in the synapse but, in fact, no such deficit appears to exist. It is not possible to measure serotonin levels in the brain in an intact human being without harm, so Barton and colleagues inserted a catheter into the jugular vein (the most proximal downstream measure

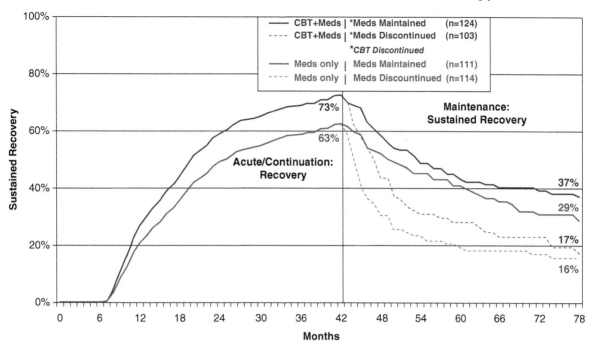

FIGURE 20.7 Sustained Recovery as a Function of Treatment Condition

The *x*-axis represents time, in months, from random assignment through acute and continuation treatment to the second randomization to be maintained on or withdrawn from medications. The *y*-axis represents the estimated recovery (acute/continuation) to sustained recovery rates across the three-year mainte-nance period. The beginning points for the CBT and ADM conditions from phase 1 reflect the percentage of patients with these conditions who met recovery criteria during phase 1. Sustained recovery was estimated as a function of phase 1 and phase 2 treatment conditions. CBT+Meds: combination cognitive behavior therapy and antidepressant medication during phase 1; Meds only: antidepressant medication alone during phase 1.

Adapted with permission from Hollon, S. D., DeRubeis, R. J., Fawcett, J., Amsterdam, J. D., Shelton, R. C., Zajecka, J., Young, P.R., & Gallop, R. (2014). Effect of cognitive therapy with antidepressant medications vs antidepressants alone on the rate of recovery in major depressive disorder: A randomized clinical trial. JAMA Psychiatry, 71(10), 1157–1164; and DeRubeis, R. J., Zajecka, J., Shelton, R. C., Amsterdam, J. D., Fawcett, J., Xu, C., Young, P. R., Gallop, R., & Hollon, S. D. (2020). Prevention of recurrence after recovery from a major depressive episode with antidepressant medication alone or in combination with cognitive behavior therapy: Phase 2 of a 2-phase randomized clinical trial. *JAMA Psychiatry*, 77(3), 237–245.

of blood flow from the brain) to measure levels of its principal metabolite 5-HIAA (Barton et al., 2008). What they found was that 5-HIAA levels were elevated in unmedicated depressed patients relative to healthy controls and that these elevations normalized with SSRI treatment, something that the authors noted went against the prevailing wisdom. It is well established that all serotonergic ADMs have their proximal effect by increasing levels of extracellular serotonin (non-serotonergic ADMs do the same to other neurotransmitters). How can it be that medications that increase extracellular serotonin (up to four times what is found in nature) can reduce depressive symptoms if serotonin levels are already elevated?

As shown by Barton and colleagues and depicted in Figure 20.8, there may be no functional deficit in serotonin or serotonin transmission in depression, since synaptic serotonin levels are lower in nondepressed controls (A) than they are in unmedicated depression (B) (Andrews et al., 2015). All ADMs increase the amount of neurotransmitter in the synapse at least initially; monoamine oxidase inhibitors (MAOIs) inhibit degradation in the presynaptic neuron whereas all the others all block reuptake by transporters of one or more of the biogenic amines. Either mechanism has the effect of producing a short-lived increment in the

neurotransmitter in the synapse (C). However, as those amounts rise to levels not seen in nature, homeostatic regula-tory mechanisms kick in bringing those levels back to base-line (synthesis shuts down in the presynaptic neuron and sensitivity is reduced in the post-synaptic neuron) (D). The upshot is that ADMs increase the amount of extracellular neurotransmitter only long enough to cause homeostatic reg-ulatory mechanisms to turn the system back down. This is not unique to ADMs, as most psychoactive medications work by virtue of triggering a counter response from homeostatic regulatory mechanisms (Hyman & Nestler, 1996). Metaphorically, this is analogous to holding a match up to a thermostat to turn a furnace down, although in this metaphor the match stays lit and the furnace stays off for as long as the medications stay in the system.

It may not be nice to fool Mother Nature. As shown in Figure 20.9, Andrews and colleagues (2011) speculate that essentially "hijacking" the underlying homeostatic mechanisms that regulate the biogenic amine neurotransmitter systems cre-ates a counterforce that they call *oppositional perturbation* that is like a coiled spring ready to recoil back to its previous position once the medications are taken away. Evolutionary biology is sometimes faulted (unfairly) for not generating testable

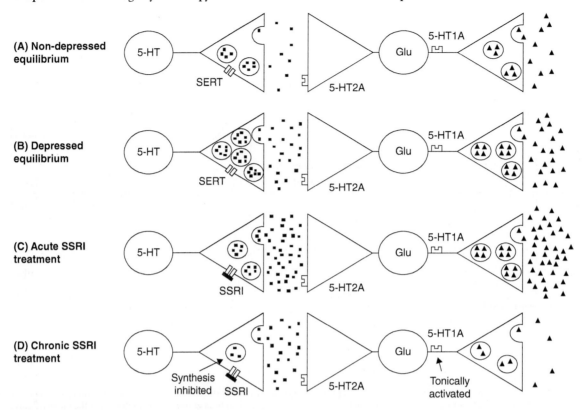

FIGURE 20.8 Hypothetical serotonin and glutamate patterns in projection regions.

(A) Nondepressed equilibrium: homeostatic mechanisms regulate equilibrium between serotonin levels and subsequent glutamate activity; (B) depressed equilibrium: serotonin transmission is elevated (due to activation of the dorsal raphe nucleus under stress) leading to greater glutamate activation; (C) acute SSRI treatment: the initial effect of SSRI treatment is to increase extracellular serotonin (via blocking reuptake through the serotonin transporter), which, in turn, drives even greater glutamate activation; (D) chronic SSRI treatment: leads to down-regulation of excess glutamate activity via activation of homeostatic mechanisms (inhibition of serotonin synthesis and tonic activation of the 5-HT$_{1A}$ heteroreceptor) in a manner analogous to holding a match up to a thermostat to turn down a furnace. It is homeostatic response (driven by elevating the level of serotonin) that reduces glutamatergic activity and produces the antidepressant response.

Reprinted with permission from Andrews, P. W., Bharwani, A., Lee, K. R., Fox, M., & Thomson, J. A. Jr. (2015). Is serotonin an upper or a downer? The evolution of the serotonergic system and its role in depression and the antidepressant response. *Neuroscience and Biobehavioral Reviews, 51*, 164–188.

hypotheses, but that is not the case in this instance as the likelihood of relapse following discontinuation should be a function of the extent of oppositional perturbation produced by a given class of medications. It turns out that that is exactly what was found in a meta-analysis author PWA conducted of the various discontinuation trials (Andrews et al., 2012). As shown in Figure 20.10, patients who remit on pill-placebo are only half as likely to relapse following discontinuation as patients who remit on SSRIs that perturb only serotonin. Risk for relapse goes up even further for the SNRIs and TCAs that also perturb norepinephrine in addition to serotonin. Risk of relapse is highest of all for the MAOIs that perturb all three major biogenic amines (including dopamine). There is a striking correspondence between degree of perturbation and risk of relapse following discontinuation, as evolutionary theory would predict. Score one for Mother Nature.

Combine Treatments at Your (Patient's) Peril

The bottom line is that while combined treatment is more efficacious than either monotherapy alone in terms of acute response, that increment may be limited to a subset of the population and come at the price of interfering with any enduring effect that the psychosocial intervention might otherwise possess. More problematic still is the possibility that ADMs may have an iatrogenic effect of their own that prolongs the life of the underlying episode, making relapse virtually inevitable at any point the medications are withdrawn. Primary care physicians with no particular training in psychiatric diagnostics now write the vast majority of prescriptions for ADMs. It is likely that they are both medicating patients who do not need to be medicated (the "depression possible") and under treating those who do (best clinical psychiatric practice calls for dosing to remission and switching or augment patients who are better but still not fully well). There has been a marked increase in the number of patients medicated in the last quarter century in the United States and most of that increase is attributable to patients with less severe distress being put on medications by their primary care physicians (Olfson et al., 2019). This concern is exacerbated by the fact that most primary care physicians have little or no training in psychiatric diagnoses but are comfortable prescribing SSRIs (Mojtabai & Olfson, 2011). It is not clear that these patients need to be on medications in the

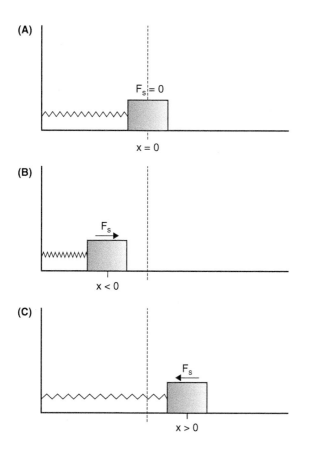

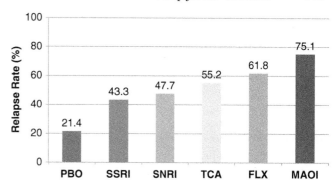

FIGURE 20.10 Risk of relapse following medication discontinuation.

The extent to which a given medication class perturbs the underlying neurotransmitter systems as assessed in rodents predicts the likelihood of relapse following medication withdrawal in humans. After discontinuation, all ADMs have at least twice the risk of relapse as pill-placebo. PBO: placebo; SSRI: selective serotonin reuptake inhibitor; SNRI: serotonin-norepinephrine reuptake inhibitor; TCA: tricyclic antidepressant; FLX: fluoxetine; MAOI: monoamine oxidase inhibitor.

Adapted with permission from Andrews, P. W., Thomson, J. A. Jr., Amstadter, A., & Neale, M. C. (2012). Primum non-nocere: an evolutionary analysis of whether antidepressants do more harm than good. *Frontiers in Psychology, 3*, 117.

FIGURE 20.9 What happens when ADMs are discontinued?

Like a spring, synaptic serotonin has an equilibrium level (Panel A). When one takes an antidepressant (Panel B), the drug perturbs the system from equilibrium. Just as a spring resists a perturbation by producing an opposing force (F_s), the brain produces an opposing force (proportional to the strength of the drug) that attempts to bring synaptic serotonin back to equilibrium. When the drug is discontinued (Panel C), the oppositional force causes an overshoot that is proportional to the strength of the drug.

Adapted from Andrews, P. W., Kornstein, S., Halberstadt, L., Gardner, C., & Neale, M. C. (2011). Blue again: Perturbational effects of antidepressants suggest monoaminergic homeostasis in major depression. *Frontiers in Psychology, 2*, 159.

first place (psychiatrists are less likely to medicate patients with less severe depressions than general practitioners) but if medications do produce oppositional perturbation then it is likely that these patients will have trouble coming off without experiencing a "relapse" no matter how long they are kept on "maintenance" medications (since the never remit) that will lead to them being put back on. If so, then the SSRIs may represent the ultimate "better built mousetrap" for the pharmaceutical industry in that they create a need for ongoing medication treatment that does not itself exist in nature. Aldous Huxley would be proud.

Finally, there are indications that medications may increase the risk of "all-cause" mortality; serotonin plays a central role in the way that energy is deployed throughout the body and the brain (recall that monoamine oxidase is found on the outer membranes of mitochondria, the "blast furnaces" for the brain) and the consequences of its perturbation may go well beyond the simple regulation of affective states. A recent meta-analysis of long-term naturalistic studies found that being on an ADM was associated with a 30% increment in "all-cause" mortality among patients free from heart disease (serotonergic ADMs are mildly protective for the latter), regardless of medication class (Maslej et al., 2017). Controlling for premedication depression levels increased the mortality estimates; that would not have been the case had the finding been purely artifactual. While we do not want to over-interpret purely longitudinal data, these findings do give pause, since they suggest that a widely prescribed class of medication may have deleterious effects over the long term about which most prescribing clinicians are unaware.

Some patients who will not respond to psychotherapy will respond to ADM and you must get a patient well to keep them well (DeRubeis, Cohen et al., 2014). That being said, until we can specify just who those patients are, our sense is that ADMs should only be added in the absence of a response in adequate trials of at least one EST. This is quite different than what we would have said a little more than a decade ago when we suggested that combined treatment retained the specific benefits of each monotherapy with no downside other than increased cost (Hollon, Jarrett et al., 2005). However, recent findings since that time suggest that it may be wise to start with psychotherapy and add medications in combination only when we must. Available evidence suggests that there are some patients for whom medications work better than psychotherapy, and for at least some of those patients staying on medications might work better than coming off; that appears to be the case for patients with depressions superimposed on Axis 2 personality disorders (Fournier et al., 2008). But there is little evidence that that is true for patients with chronic depression (Hollon, DeRubeis et al., 2014), among the patients for whom combined treatment is commonly recommended (American Psychiatric Association, 2010a; American Psychological Association, 2019; NICE, 2018). It will be important to differentiate between patient characteristics that truly moderate differential response (point to who will show a specific advantage) versus those purely prognostic indices that only predict poorer response regardless of the nature of the intervention (see Fournier et al., 2009).

Prevention of Initial Onset

Finally, there are indications that at least some psychosocial interventions along the lines of the ones just described can forestall the onset of depression. Garber and colleagues found that a cognitive behavioral preventive intervention forestalled onsets in at-risk adolescents as long as their parents were not currently depressed (Garber et al., 2009) and that this preventive effect lasted across the course of adolescence (Brent et al., 2015). Similarly, skills-training programs based on CBT and IPT, respectively, provided as part of an ongoing "wellness" class in a universal (not selected for being at elevated risk) sample of adolescents, reduced symptom levels relative to a no-intervention control. The greatest effects were evident for those with the highest depression scores at baseline; the effects were further moderated by achievement (biggest effects for CBT) versus affiliative (biggest effects for IPT) orientations (Horowitz et al., 2007). It appears that psychosocial interventions can be used to forestall depression in adolescents.

Summary

Regarding the first question that we formulated at the beginning of the chapter, psychosocial interventions can be as efficacious as medication treatment with respect to acute response. Those that have been adequately tested appear to have an enduring effect that medications simply lack. Regarding the second question raised, combined treatment can enhance the efficacy of acute response relative to either monotherapy, but that effect is small, heavily moderated (only found in a subset of the patients) and may interfere with any enduring effect that the psychosocial intervention may possess. Regarding the fifth question, there is reason to think that ADMs may have an iatrogenic effect that prolongs the life of the underlying episode (and possibly worsens the course of the underlying disorder); and regarding our sixth and final question raised, psychosocial interventions can be used to forestall onsets in at-risk adolescents. Those ESTs that best address the functions that depression evolved to serve compare favorably to ADMs that suppress distress but risk prolonging the life of the episode.

Anxiety "Disorders"

Prevalence and Heritability

The anxiety disorders are even more prevalent in aggregate than the mood disorders with up to 31.9% of adults meeting criteria for one or more anxiety disorders and women showing higher rates than men (38.0%/26.1%) (Harvard Medical School, 2007). The different disorders show different rates of prevalence and prevalence-by-gender ranging from specific phobia (12.5%: 15.8%/8.9%), social anxiety disorder (12.1%: 13.0%/11.1%), childhood/adult separation disorder (9.2%: 10.8%/7.2%), panic disorder (4.7%: 6.2%/3.1%), agoraphobia without panic (1.3%: 1.6%/1.1%), generalized anxiety disorder (5.7%: 7.1%/4.2%), posttraumatic stress disorder (6.8%: 9.7%/3.6%), and obsessive-compulsive disorder (2.3%: 3.1%/1.6%). Heritability for each is modest at best, ranging from .30 to .50 across the different diagnostic subcategories.

Age of Onset and Gender Disparities

What gets counted as an anxiety disorder changes over time (PTSD is now classified as a stress disorder and OCD is classified separately) and there are indications that the anxiety disorders and mood disorders share a common set of genes (Kendler et al., 1987). Most of the anxiety disorders (social anxiety is an exception) are about twice as common in women as in men and each can be as adequately treated with psychotherapy as with medications, with the former more enduring. Onset is earlier than for the mood disorders, often prior to puberty.

Pharmacotherapy for Anxiety

The anxiolytics were once the medication of choice for the treatment of the anxiety disorders (and the most commonly prescribed of the psychiatric medications) but they are highly addictive, and their effects tend to fade over time such that they have been supplanted by the SSRIs (NICE, 2011a). As with the mood disorders, the SSRIs are symptom-suppressive but stop working once they are discontinued. Again, as with the mood disorders, there are indications that adding medication to psychotherapy may interfere with any enduring effects that the latter might possess (Forand et al., 2013). Although the field is becoming transdiagnostic, the relevant treatment literature tends to focus more on discrete diagnostic categories, and we structure the discussion to follow in that fashion.

Specific Phobias

Phobic disorders tend to be more situational than temporal; people with phobias typically feel distress only when confronted by (or thinking about) the object or situation that they fear, but that propensity tends to be stable over time in the absence of treatment. They are somewhat less likely to impair function than some of the other anxiety disorders (Kessler, Chiu et al., 2005), but often go untreated and tend to persist over time (Stinson et al., 2007). The relative stability of specific fears and phobias over time was a puzzle for early Pavlovian conditioning models because they should have extinguished over subsequent encounters, as they typically do in laboratory studies. The reason is that phobic individuals become quite adept at escaping from or better still avoiding such encounters. No exposure means that there is no extinction.

There is clear evidence that humans are "prepared" to learn to fear stimuli that represented dangers in our evolutionary past (Öhman & Mineka, 2001). Falls in bathtubs are commonplace but there are no reported instances of "bathtub phobias" as might be expected by simple conditioning models. Poisonous snakes and spiders would have represented real risks in our evolutionary past and fears of such organisms are readily acquired even among young infants (Öhman & Mineka, 2003). Curiously, gender disparities are greater for snake and spider phobias (up to four times greater in women than they are in men) than they are for other specific phobias such as injections or heights (Fredrikson et al., 1996). Why this should be is not clear, although women were more likely to be exposed to such dangers during foraging (gathering roots and vegetables) and would have greater need for vigilance during childcare (young children tend to explore their environs) than men; moreover, infants and young children rarely survived their mother's death in ancestral times so the fitness cost to the gene line of being bitten by a poisonous snake or spider would be greater for women than for men (Buss, 2008).

As for the other anxiety disorders, the older anxiolytics were once the treatment of choice but have been largely supplanted by the newer SSRIs. That being said, most specific phobias are so readily treated by exposure-based behavioral interventions (sometimes targeting beliefs that overestimate the danger) that medication treatment is rarely necessary. D-cycloserine and glucocorticoids have been used in some research studies to enhance in-vivo exposure in the treatment of specific phobias (Eaton et al., 2018), but appear to have little added benefit when the behavioral intervention is adequately implemented and are rarely used in practice (Hofmann et al, 2013). Exposure treatment can either be fast (direct exposure to the feared stimulus) or slow (moving up a graded hierarchy of increasingly anxiety-provoking stimuli) and each is comparably efficacious.

Most phobic reactions involve sympathetic arousal (the physiological manifestation of the "flight/fight" reaction) in the presence of the feared stimulus. In the second half of the last century that was often treated via systematic desensitization – a combination of relaxation training with a very gradual exposure to anxiety eliciting cues. Systematic desensitization was based on the notion that pairing the feared stimulus [the conditioned stimulus (CS)] with the unconditioned response (anxiety) would strengthen the bond between the two, but that was in fact a misunderstanding of classical (aka Pavlovian) conditioning. Simply presenting the CS in the absence of the truly dangerous (or evolutionarily prepared) unconditioned stimulus (UCS) should be sufficient to bring about the extinction of the fear response. That is the basis for exposure (plus response prevention to ensure that the patient does not "escape") and it works extremely well (Davis et al., 2009), often in as little as a single session across a variety of different specific phobias, including small animal phobias (Öst et al., 1991; 1997; 2001).

Blood-needle-injury phobia is the one outlier among the specific phobias in that the initial sympathetic arousal is followed by a parasympathetic response in which blood pressure drops rapidly and the patient often faints (Öst, 1992). As opposed to the other specific phobias in which relaxation can but does not need to be used to reduce arousal in the presence of the phobic cue, in blood-needle-injury phobia, it often is helpful to get the patient aroused or angry (anything to drive the blood pressure up) before exposure to the specific problematic cues or situations, an approach referred to as applied tension (Öst & Sterner, 1987). Although trials are few, the approach appears to be specifically efficacious (Simon et al., 2009).

Panic Disorder and Agoraphobia

Panic disorder involves the sudden overwhelming experience of fear that seems to arise unbidden and can lead to the agoraphobic avoidance of situations in which help could not be obtained if such an attack were to occur (American Psychiatric Association, 2013). Biological models view panic as the consequence of a propensity for the locus coeruleus (the collection of cell bodies for all neurons that use norepinephrine as a neurotransmitter that underlies the stress response) to discharge spontaneously. These models imply treatment with medications will be needed for an indefinite period of time. Behavior theory views panic as a conditioned response to internal sensations that is best extinguished via repeated exposure to interoceptive cues. Cognitive theory posits that people experience panic attacks when they misinterpret benign bodily sensations as signs of impending physical or mental catastrophe (Beck & Emery, 1985; Clark, 1986). These catastrophic cognitions are seen as the necessary and sufficient cause of panic attacks (precursor to agoraphobia) and their disconfirmation is the primary treatment goal. An evolutionary perspective on panic suggests that it is an adaptation that evolved to facilitate escape in dangerous situations that is sometimes triggered in the absence of risk (Nesse, 1987).

As is the case for unipolar depression, panic disorder can be treated with either psychotherapy (Hofman & Smits, 2008) or medications (Batelaan et al., 2012). The cognitive and behavioral therapies have an enduring effect that medications simply lack and are listed as the treatment of choice for panic by NICE (2011a). Combining psychotherapy with medications produces modest increments in acute response (1.16 times relative to psychotherapy alone and 1.24 times relative to ADM alone) (Furukawa et al., 2006). However, just as with unipolar depression, there are indications that adding ADM may interfere with whatever enduring effects CBT (or other psychosocial interventions) may possess.

Three studies indicate that CBT has an enduring effect in the treatment of panic disorder, including two that suggest that ADM may interfere with that effect when added in combination. In the first, Clark and colleagues found cognitive therapy (CT) focused on the disconfirmation of catastrophic misinterpretations to be superior to either imipramine ADM alone or with applied relaxation, with both superior in turn to a waitlist control (Clark et al., 1994). Nearly 90% of the patients treated with CT were panic-free after three months of treatment versus only about 50% of the patients in the other two treatments and virtually none of the patients assigned to the waitlist. CT also produced greater change in catastrophic cognitions than did either of the other conditions in a manner suggestive of mediation. Medications were continued for another six months and then withdrawn with patients in the psychosocial conditions receiving only a limited number of booster sessions between months three and six. All patients were then followed across the next nine months. Only 5% of the patients previously treated with CT subsequently relapsed, compared with 40% of patients withdrawn from ADM. Patients who had the fewest catastrophic cognitions at end of treatment were the least likely to relapse following treatment termination. This suggests that CT not only has an enduring effect similar to that for unipolar depression but also that it is mediated by change in cognition as specified by theory. The approach is so powerful that a handful of sessions can be sufficient (Clark et al., 1999).

The second study illustrates our concern regarding possible interference effects of ADMs. Barlow and colleagues conducted a multisite placebo-controlled trial in which patients with panic disorder (with or without agoraphobia) were randomly assigned to three months of weekly acute treatment followed by six months of monthly maintenance treatment with either CBT or imipramine alone or in combination (Barlow et al., 2000). The study also included a cell in which CBT was combined with pill-placebo. Each monotherapy was superior to pill-placebo and combined treatment was superior to either monotherapy by the end of maintenance treatment. Imipramine produced the highest rates of response among treatment completers, but CBT was more enduring. As shown in Figure 20.11, patients who responded to CBT were less likely to relapse following treatment termination than patients who responded to imipramine. Adding medications to CBT appeared to interfere with its enduring effect, as patients in the condition combining CBT and active medications were more likely to relapse after treatment termination than patients treated with CBT alone. By contrast, patients in the placebo combination were no more likely to relapse than patients treated with CBT alone. This means that the mechanism by which ADM interfered with CBT's enduring effect was pharmacological and not psychological.

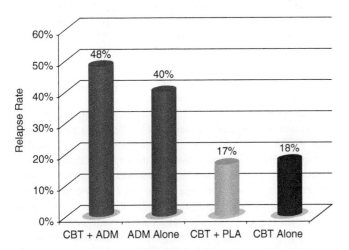

FIGURE 20.11 Adding active medications undercuts cognitive behavior therapy's (CBT's) enduring effect.

Patients with panic disorder treatment to remission with cognitive behavior therapy (CBT) alone were more than half as likely to relapse following treatment termination than patients treated to remission with imipramine antidepressant medication (ADM alone). Adding active medication in combination eliminated any enduring effect that CBT otherwise possessed and turned it into expensive pharmacotherapy (CBT + ADM). This interference effect was clearly pharmacological rather than psychological in nature, since CBT retained its enduring effect even after adding an inert pill-placebo such that patients believed they were taking an active medication (CBT + PLA).

Adapted with permission from Barlow, D. H., Gorman, J. M., Shear, M. K., & Woods, S. W. (2000). Cognitive-behavioral therapy, imipramine, or their combination for panic disorder: A randomized controlled trial. *JAMA, 283*(19), 2529–2536.

A third earlier trial also provided evidence of interference but likely via a different mechanism. Marks and colleagues randomized patients to either exposure or relaxation crossed with alprazolam (a high potency benzodiazepines with a short half-life) or pill-placebo and found a main effect for exposure and an interaction favoring alprazolam (Marks et al., 1993). However, the exposure patients treated with active medication were more likely to relapse following discontinuation than exposure patients treated with placebo. Due to its very short half-life, it is notoriously hard to withdraw patients from alprazolam, which we suspect played a role in driving relapse among prior exposure patients. It is unclear whether the underlying mechanism was a failure to form synaptic connections (as we think is what is going on in unipolar depression) or something else such as state-dependent learning or attribution of change to medication treatment, but something untoward was clearly going on.

The bottom line is that panic disorder is best treated with a cognitive or cognitive-behavioral intervention that involves interoceptive exposure and disconfirming beliefs. Doing so in combination with ADMs or anxiolytics interferes with whatever enduring effect that psychotherapies may have for reasons that may vary across medication class. That is not to say that there may not be some patients who simply do not respond to psychosocial interventions; for those patients, medications might be necessary (you have to get somebody better to keep them better). If such patients do exist (and it remains to be seen if they do) then it also is likely that they will need to stay on maintenance medications to forestall the return of symptoms. The optimal strategy would appear to be to start panic patients on one form of exposure-based intervention (cognitive or cognitive- behavioral) and add medications only for those patients who do not respond.

Agoraphobia is more complicated still and is likely to require considerable effort to get a patient to venture away from home in the absence of their "safe person." Most instances of agoraphobia start with panic attacks and then move on to progressively greater avoidance until the patient becomes largely homebound, by which point the panic attacks largely abate. It is highly likely that they will start again once the patient begins to venture back out into the world. Although there is reason to think that being on SSRIs may facilitate willingness to undertake such "risks," they likely will interfere with consolidation of learning that might otherwise endure.

Social Anxiety Disorder (SAD)

SAD involves an undue fear of evaluation by others and the desire to avoid situations in which scrutiny is anticipated (American Psychiatric Association, 2013). It is a surprisingly common (12.6% lifetime prevalence) and can have quite a disruptive effect on functioning and quality of life (Kessler, Berglund et al., 2005). A recent genome-wide association study (GWAS) could account for about 12% of the heritability on the basis of the single nucleotide polymorphisms (SNPs) identified with a significant negative correlation with extroversion but little overlap with neuroticism (Stein et al., 2017). SAD is the one type of anxiety that is not differentially distributed as a function of gender (McLean et al., 2011). Why that should be is not clear, but the lack of differential must have some evolutionary significance, perhaps preserving reproductive fitness among males in the face of aggressive competitors. SAD tends to follow a chronic course if left untreated and considerably impairs both social and vocational pursuits (Grant et al., 2005).

SAD can be treated with either psychotherapy or medications and the two are often combined although explicit tests of such combinations are few. It is common practice for patients to be allowed to enter purely psychotherapy trials on stable doses of medications (something that is rarely done in the depression literature). In earlier decades, most patients were medicated with benzodiazepines or MAOIs (in the case of stage fright), but the SSRIs now predominate.

Psychotherapy too has undergone something of a transition. Behavioral and cognitive-behavioral interventions used to involve some combination of exposure plus social skills training and were usually conducted in groups so as to facilitate each (Heimberg et al., 1995). The model underlying this approach posited that classically conditioned anxiety interfered with the development or deployment of social skills. Although beliefs were addressed to some extent, change was largely presumed to come from the extinction of conditioned fear and the acquisition of social skills that were acquired and practiced in a group CBT setting. Although the approach addresses both cognition and behavior, it places a heavier emphasis on the latter (as tends to be the case in the United States). Moreover, as is typically the case for approaches emerging from a more behavioral tradition, cognitions tend to be treated as if they were covert behaviors (self-statements) that are replaced based on repetition (like habits) as opposed to idiosyncratic beliefs that need to be explored and are best changed by evidential disconfirmation.

Clark and Wells (1995) made a major theoretical revision in this model based on discussions with their clients and their experimental psychopathology studies. What they learned is that clients often go into social situations overly concerned that they would do something to embarrass and humiliate themselves in front of the other(s). As a consequence, they focus more intently on their own behavior in social interactions than they do on the other person. Their impression of how they are coming across tends to be unduly negative and they engage in a coordinated set of "safety behaviors" (hand over mouth or monitoring what they say as they say it) as a defense. Although intended to protect them from ridicule, these behaviors have the perverse effect of making them seem disinterested and aloof. Where Clark and Wells differed most from the more structured CBT approach developed by Heimberg and colleagues is that they were concerned with the idiosyncratic meanings that each patient brought to interpersonal interactions. Their patients all followed the same process; they focused more on themselves than they did on the other person and engaged in "safety behaviors" to protect themselves from embarrassment that made them seem less engaged, but what they thought they had to protect themselves from varied across patients. It was their personal meanings that had to be understood and deconstructed.

Armed with this information, Clark and Wells built an intervention that first mapped the idiosyncratic beliefs that patients had regarding interpersonal interactions and the "safety behaviors" that they used to protect themselves from humiliation and then asked them to have a brief conversation with someone they had never met, both with and without their safety behaviors, videotaping both encounters. Patients typically found that quite intimidating but even more illuminating; in most instances, it was clear even to them that they came across as more spontaneous and interested when they dropped their safety behaviors. Therapy would then proceed to a series of behavioral experiments (usually outside of the office and accompanied by the therapist who would first model the more "relaxed" behavior) that would culminate in a series of "catastrophic experiments" in which first the therapist and then the client would commit intentional "faux pas" just so they could observe the reactions of other people. In most instances, nobody noticed and, almost invariably, if someone did notice, they did not care.

We provided a more extended discussion of the Clark and Wells model because of its apparent superiority over other closely related (and largely successful with respect to acute and enduring effects) approaches. Individual CT á la Clark and Wells was superior to group CBT in terms of both acute response and across a six-month follow-up in a German trial (Stangier et al., 2003) and superior to either group CBT or treatment as usual (including medications) in another trial conducted in Sweden (Mörtberg et al., 2007) with gains maintained across five years (Mörtberg et al., 2011). Individual CT also was superior to either fluoxetine or pill-placebo in the first of two English studies (Clark et al., 2003) and superior to exposure plus response prevention in a second (Clark et al., 2006). A recent multisite German trial found CT superior to IPT at each of two different sites including one with an allegiance to IPT (Stangier et al., 2011) and a second multi-site German trial found it superior to dynamic psychotherapy (Leichsenring et al., 2013). Cognitive change appears to mediate the effects of treatment, as specified by theory (Hoffart et al., 2009). Our predilection is to prefer the more cognitive approach that addresses the idiosyncratic meaning system of the individual client over the more structured cognitive behavioral ones that are less individualized, and the existing data appear to be consistent with that predilection. Nonetheless, it is clear that group CBT is both specific and enduring. We will be curious to see if adding SSRIs interferes with the enduring effect for each and predict that it will.

A network meta-analysis involving 101 trials and over 13,000 patients found that both medications and psychotherapy were efficacious in treating SAD relative to no treatment controls (Mayo-Wilson et al., 2014). Such comparisons establish efficacy (that the treatment works better than its absence) but not necessarily specificity (that it has an active mechanism that goes beyond the generic benefits of simply going into treatment) or superiority (that it works better than other active interventions) (Hollon, Areán et al., 2014). Indirect comparisons indicated that CBT (broadly defined) was superior to psychodynamic psychotherapy, IPT, mindfulness, and supportive psychotherapy. Among the different medication classes, MAOIs had the largest effect (SMD = −1.01), with benzodiazepines (SMD = −0.96) and SSRIs close behind (SMD = –0.91). Combined treatment produced the largest differential effect of all (SMD = –1.30), but that effect was based on only five trials. Clark and Wells' version of individual cognitive therapy (CT) generated the single largest effect for psychotherapy alone (SMD = –1.56) relative to group CBT *á la* Heimberg (SMD = –0.80), which did produce the largest effect observed in that literature when combined with the MAOI phenelzine (SMD = –1.69). Individual CT *á la* Clark and Wells has not been combined with ADM but did as well when provided alone.

Although this network meta-analysis did not assess relapse rates following the end of treatment (few of the studies reported treatment-free follow-ups), it did note that most patients who respond to SSRIs relapse within a few months of being taken off medications (Montgomery et al., 2005; Stein et al., 2002). The effects of group CBT or individual CT usually are well maintained at follow-up (Haug et al., 2003) and patients often make further gains after treatment ends (Mörtberg et al., 2011). That would appear to be similar to what we find in depression; ADM is efficacious in suppressing symptoms as long as it is taken but symptoms tend to return when it is discontinued. Given that social anxiety tends to be even more chronic (as opposed to episodic) than depression, it would not be surprising if the differential between nonenduring medications versus enduring psychotherapies might be even larger than it is for depression. Long-term enduring effects have not been studied as extensively in social anxiety as they have in depression, but to the extent that they have, the results are strikingly similar, regardless of psychotherapy type or medication class [exposure vs. SSRI in Haug et al., 2003; group CBT vs. MAOI in Liebowitz et al., 1999 and Praško et al., 2006; individual CT (a specific type of CBT) vs. SSRIs in Clark et al., 2003 and Mörtberg et al., 2007]. For example, although medication treatment was somewhat more efficacious than group CBT in the trial by Heimberg and colleagues, 50% of the MAOI responders relapsed when medications were taken away as compared to only 17% of the patients treated with group CBT (Liebowitz et al., 1999). With respect to our first question, it appears that either psychotherapy (at least the cognitive and behavioral therapies) or medications (antidepressants or benzodiazepines) are specifically efficacious with respect to the reduction of acute symptoms but that those same cognitive and behavioral interventions have an enduring effect that medications simply lack.

Our second question has to do with whether adding the two in combination is beneficial, and again, as is the case for depression, that appears to depend on whether we are concerned with maximizing acute response or extending long-term gain. Combined treatment typically outperforms either monotherapy in terms of acute response (Bernik et al., 2018; Blanco et al., 2010; Blomhoff et al., 2001; Knijnik et al., 2008; see Davidson et al., 2004 for an exception) but is associated with higher rates of deterioration (likely equivalent to relapse in a mostly chronic disorder) following treatment termination in the two studies that have compared prior combined treatment to prior CBT alone (Haug et al., 2003; Praško et al, 2006). This is not compelling evidence (more studies especially with the more efficacious group CBT and the even more efficacious individual CT are needed) but it is consistent

with the notion that adding ADM may interfere with any enduring effect that group CBT or individual CT may possess.

Generalized Anxiety Disorder (GAD)

Generalized anxiety disorder is marked by persistent or chronic worry and tension; it essentially represents a relatively constant state of vigilance. As currently defined (the diagnosis has been narrowed in recent years) it is not all that prevalent (5.7%: 7.1%/4.2%) and only modestly heritable (h^2 = 0.32) (Keller & Miller, 2006). Like most of the other anxiety disorders (other than SAD), it is twice as prevalent in women as men.

The evolutionary advantages of such vigilance are evident even if it undermines quality of life, much as it is better to have a smoke alarm go off when there is no fire than to have it fail to go off when there is (Nesse, 2019). Male rhesus monkeys leave their natal troop in adolescence and must be accepted by another troop to find a mate; those that are more vigilant and less prone to annoy their elders (more internalizing than externalizing) are allowed up to an extra year before they are driven off, doubling their chances of survival (Suomi, 2006).

GAD can be at least as adequately treated with psychotherapy as with medications and again there are indications of enduring effects that medications lack. Benzodiazepines induce dependence and lose potency with prolonged use and antidepressants are purely palliative and do nothing to reduce future risk (NICE, 2011a). According to NICE, traditional forms of psychotherapy have been unimpressive the few times that they have been tested (NICE, 2011a), whereas CBT is both efficacious and specific for GAD. Comparisons to no treatment generate large effects (0.87) and effects in comparisons to nonspecific controls are at least moderate (0.57) in size (Mitte, 2005). CBT is one of two psychosocial interventions (along with the more purely behavioral applied relaxation) recommended as a first-line treatment for GAD by the NICE guidelines (NICE, 2011b). The cognitive and behavioral interventions appear to be at least as efficacious as medications and quite possibly longer lasting, although direct comparisons are few and discontinuation designs have yet to be implemented. CBT is not addictive like benzodiazepines and free from the adverse effects of ADMs. There are few comparisons of combined treatment to either monotherapy. Power and colleagues found CBT plus diazepam superior to diazepam alone but not to CBT alone or in combination with pill-placebo (Power et al., 1990). A six-month follow-up indicated that CBT (with or without diazepam or placebo) was superior to diazepam alone with no indication of any interference effect. A naturalistic study found no differences among brief dynamic psychotherapy versus medications (benzodiazepines) alone or in combination (Ferrero et al., 2007).

That being said, CBT has evolved to a considerable extent over recent decades and has become increasingly cognitive in nature, in a manner that reflects the newfound focus on worry. With the change in emphasis in the disorder from arousal to worry, Ladouceur and colleagues dropped relaxation training entirely to focus more intensively on purely cognitive targets like intolerance of uncertainty and cognitive avoidance (Ladouceur et al., 1999). This more intensive cognitive intervention was superior to a minimal treatment control with gains sustained over a one-year follow-up regardless of whether it was provided in an individual (Ladouceur et al., 2000) or group format (Dugas et al., 2003). Even more recent trials suggest that this more intensive cognitive approach and a more recent focus on beliefs about uncontrollability may be superior to and longer lasting than more purely behavioral approaches (Dugas et al., 2010; Wells et al., 2010).

Posttraumatic Stress Disorder (PTSD)

PTSD involves a common set of symptoms (re-experiencing, avoidance, and hyperarousal) as a consequence of disparate trauma (such as rape, combat, accidents, and the like). PTSD was first recognized as a coherent "disorder" in the 1980s. It is both modestly prevalent (6.8%: 9.7%/3.6%) and modestly heritable ($h^2 = 0.30$) in a manner that suggests that exposure to trauma is necessary but not sufficient (Keller & Miller, 2006). As for most of the other anxiety disorders, PTSD is more prevalent in women than in men, but that likely is at least partly accounted for by the gender disparity in sexual assault. Occupation related traumas such as army, police, fireman, and medics are more prevalent in males. This reflects the fact that the different genders are exposed to different types of risk. The modest heritability may be related to who develops the syndrome among those exposed to traumatic life events. Only about one trauma survivor in five goes on to develop PTSD and among those survivors with an identical twin, hippocampal volume is already reduced in the co-twin who was not exposed to traumatic event (Gilbertson et al., 2002). This suggests that reduced hippocampal volume may predate and increase risk for the development of PTSD following exposure to trauma and is not a consequence of exposure to the trauma itself.

Those individuals exposed to trauma who are least capable of processing the experience at the time and who subsequently try hardest not to think about the event appear to be the ones most likely to develop PTSD in its aftermath and the most effective treatments all involve some kind of reliving of the experience (American Psychological Association, 2017). More purely behavioral approaches like prolonged exposure (PE) involve repeated verbal and imaginal recreations of the event(s) and presume an underlying extinction/habituation mechanism (Foa & Rothbaum, 1998). PE was the first of the successful psychosocial interventions, but it can be excruciating to go through, and attrition rates are high. Cognitive processing therapy (CPT) is a more benign approach in which patients write out a description of what took place and then read it back to themselves aloud, often in the presence of a therapist (Resick & Schnicke, 1992). It can be as efficacious as PE but is not so difficult to endure and attrition rates tend to be lower. Cognitive therapy (CT) is more benign still; patients are asked to relive the event only two or three times (Ehlers & Clark, 2000). The first reliving is intended to identify the meaning of the event and its impact on patients' beliefs about themselves. These beliefs are then subjected to empirical scrutiny and tested, as would be the case for any other disorder using this approach. Additional exposures are used only to ensure that the patient can relive the experience without undue distress and to identify classically conditioned triggers to the recollection process. As for CPT, CT appears to be at least as efficacious as PE, but with lower rates of attrition still.

PTSD is not only disconcerting to the individual afflicted, but it also can have a negative impact on that person's relationships. An approach has been developed called cognitive-behavioral conjoint therapy (CBCT) that brings the life partner in as well in an attempt to deal with the kinds of problems that often develop in intimate relationships as a consequence of PTSD (Monson & Fredman, 2012). Other than a single RCT, support for this approach has largely rested on uncontrolled designs that suggested improvements in patient- and partner-rated PTSD symptoms and affective distress, with findings on relationship satisfaction and partner accommodation somewhat more mixed (Liebman et al., 2020).

None of these approaches are all that widely practiced, since many therapists are as avoidant as their patients about reliving the traumatic event(s). Publication of the 2017 guideline by the American Psychological Association elicited over 43,000 signatures on a petition to rescind and the guideline has been called a "tragedy" by a pair of leading psychotherapy researchers for allegedly devaluing the therapeutic relationship (Norcross & Wampold, 2019). Noting the superiority of approaches that involve reliving in no way devalues the relationship since a therapist always is involved. There is a fourth exposure-based approach called Eye Movement Desensitization and Reprocessing (EMDR) therapy that was roundly dismissed by academics (initially) but found widespread acceptance in the clinical practice community. As it was originally practiced, EMDR involved having the therapist wave his or her finger back and forth in front of the patient's eyes as the patient recounted the traumatic event. The intervention was first developed by a practicing clinician and propagated via paid workshops rather than formal academic papers and the scientific community largely dismissed its underlying theoretical rationale (neural reprogramming). In point of fact, EMDR actually works fairly well (it fell just short of being recommended in the APA guideline largely on a technicality) and its underlying theoretical rationale is not all that far off the mark; anything that distracts the patient during the reliving helps to degrade memory reconsolidation and making eye-movements during recall seems to work particularly well (van den Hout et al., 2012). Our own sense is that reliving the traumatic event is the key therapeutic process and that anything that helps a therapist overcome his or her own reluctance to do so works to the benefit of both patient and therapist.

PTSD symptoms do respond to the same types of medications as the other nonpsychotic mood and anxiety disorders, but once again those effects are largely symptom-suppressive and dissipate once the medications are taken away. For example, van der Kolk and colleagues found either EMDR or an SSRI (fluoxetine) superior to pill-placebo in terms of producing acute response, but relapse was far more frequent following medication discontinuation (van der Kolk et al., 2007). Combinatorial studies are few and largely inconclusive so that it is hard to know if adding ADM interferes with any enduring effect that psychotherapy may possess. What does seem to be the case is that relapse is relatively rare following the reliving; patients can encounter new trauma, but according to the same experts who developed some of the exposure interventions, the symptoms from an adequately treated trauma do not appear to return (Hollon, 2019). We find this so surprising that we await empirical confirmation, but if true, it may be because the symptoms that define the disorder are a consequence of trying not to think about the event (which may itself be a consequence of having trouble processing it at the time).

It is noteworthy that critical incident stress debriefing (CISD) not only *does not* prevent PTSD (van Emmerik et al., 2002) but also may increase its likelihood (Arnold et al., 2002). This is one of the few psychosocial interventions that actually appears to have an iatrogenic effect (Dimidjian & Hollon, 2010). The brain is wired to be especially alert to potential dangers and efforts to suppress thinking about threats (past or future) are unlikely to succeed for long. Reliving the experience is not the end of the therapeutic process (the meaning still needs to be processed and life must go on) but it is usually the end of the flashbacks and nightmares (at least with respect to that specific traumatic event). Whether adding medications would impede the process remains to be determined but given what we have seen with the other mood and anxiety disorders, we suspect that medications would relieve distress for only so long as they are taken and might interfere with reliving's enduring effects.

Obsessive-Compulsive Disorder

Obsessive-compulsive disorder (OCD) is characterized by recurrent intrusive thoughts (obsessions) followed by attempts to prevent the dreaded outcome suggested by the obsessions through carrying out repetitive ritualistic behavioral or mental acts (compulsions). The compulsions relieve the anxiety generated by the obsessions but only temporarily; in effect, reducing the anxiety reinforces the compulsions via operant mechanisms while the compulsions themselves serve as "safety behaviors" that keep the individual from learning that the feared actions or their consequences will not occur. OCD often starts in childhood or adolescence and tends to follow a chronic if somewhat episodic course with exacerbations during periods of stress (American Psychiatric Association, 2013). It is relatively rare for a nonpsychotic disorder with a prevalence of 1–3% and is one of the most impairing of the nonpsychotic disorders (Kessler, Chiu, et al., 2005). Heritability is modest (h^2 = 0.29) and about half of that liability is shared with the other anxiety disorders (Paul, 2010).

Exposure plus response prevention (ERP) is the oldest and best established of the psychosocial interventions for OCD and has been found to be superior to its absence (efficacy) and nonspecific controls (specificity) in dozens of trials (American Psychiatric Association, 2007; NICE, 2005). It has been found to be superior to ADMs in a direct comparison (Foa et al., 2005) and to enhance ADM's efficacy when added in combination (Tenneij et al., 2005). Most critically, ERP appears to have an enduring effect not found for ADM following treatment termination (Simpson et al., 2004). This is an impressive record.

That being said, recent ERP protocols often include discussion of the patient's OCD-related beliefs along with the evidential disconfirmation provided by exposure assignments and often incorporate behavioral experiments in an explicit effort to test beliefs (McMillan & Lee, 2010). In effect, what was originally a largely behavioral intervention has morphed into one that is somewhat cognitive behavioral in nature. Some now conceptualize the differences between ERP and CBT as largely a matter of emphasis (Abramowitz et al., 2005).

Contemporary cognitive theory has taken this process further and now emphasizes what it means to the patient to have the intrusive cognition rather than the content of the obsession itself (Rachman, 2003). For example, the fact that a young mother has intrusive thoughts that she might kill her infant is not inherently problematic in itself unless she further assumes that this means that she really does want to kill her child or that she is a bad mother for having such thoughts. In most instances, it is the problematic interpretation underlying the intrusion that leads to the distress (and subsequent ritualistic undoing); one of personal responsibility in the sense of being a danger to oneself or others for failing to engage in the compulsion (Salkovskis, 1999).

Given this formulation, the newer cognitive approach (integrative cognitive therapy) seeks to identify and change the interpretation of the intrusion rather than to dispute its accuracy (as in conventional CBT) or to simply extinguish the anxiety that it generates (as in ERP). It employs a process of guided discovery to help the patient construct an alternative formulation to the obsessive concern ("It is not that I want to hurt my child but rather that I worry about what it means that I have that thought") and then run a series of experiments to test the competing formulations. Exposure and response prevention are still used but represent only one of several strategies designed to test the accuracy of the underlying beliefs. Integrative cognitive therapy is similar to cognitive therapy for depression or social anxiety in that it focuses on identifying and changing the client's idiosyncratic beliefs (personal meaning system) often via behavioral means.

All three approaches compare favorably to medication treatment (de Haan et al., 1997; Foa et al., 2005; Jaurrieta et al., 2008; Sousa et al., 2006; van Balkom et al., 1998) although only ERP has been tested in a design capable of detecting enduring effects (Simpson et al., 2004). What remains unclear is whether adding ADM to these psychosocial interventions interferes with any enduring effects.

Prevention of Initial Onset

Given that at least the cognitive and behavioral interventions have enduring effects not found for medications, we would have anticipated that efforts would have been made to forestall initial onsets. As previously noted, some care might need to be exercised in that regard with respect to trauma, since there are indications that too early interventions might actually be iatrogenic, but it is likely that trauma is an anomaly in that regard. CBT is efficacious in the treatment of a variety of anxiety disorders prior to puberty, but bona fide prevention trials are hard to find. That may be a function of the early onset for the anxiety disorders.

Summary

Regarding the first question raised in the introduction with respect to the anxiety disorders, psychotherapy tends to outperform ADM in the reduction of acute distress and often has an enduring effect that medications simply lack. With respect to the second question, there also are indications that, as with depression, adding medications may interfere with any enduring effects that psychotherapy may possess. The SSRIs have largely supplanted the benzodiazepines as the medication of choice for the anxiety disorders, largely because they are safer to use and less addictive (in the classical sense), but the overall picture with respect to combining drugs and psychotherapy is remarkably similar to what it is for depression, although no particular moderator effect relative to severity has been established (or even explored). With respect to our fifth question, it is not clear that medications worsen the course of the underlying disorder, but it also is not clear that anyone has ever looked. With respect to our sixth and final question, it also is not clear whether early intervention can forestall the initial onset of the disorder(s), although again it is not clear that anyone has ever tried. Given the enduring effects of some of the psychosocial interventions, it might be worth a try.

PSYCHOTIC DISORDERS

The psychotic disorders are marked by low prevalence and high heritability. Whereas the "species typical" nonpsychotic disorders (depression and anxiety) appear to be evolved adaptations that increase the fitness of the gene line, the psychotic disorders tend to be highly disabling and to reduce Darwinian fitness (Keller, 2018). The question, then, is why such deleterious genes are not removed via purifying effects of natural selection, and the likely answers involve balance selection (some subset of the problematic genes confers a selective advantage in terms of increased creativity) and especially mutation-selection-drift (mutations occur at a high enough rate to balance out the purifying effects of selection). The bottom line for is that the psychotic disorders likely do reflect true "diseases" rather than evolved adaptations and, as described below, are best treated by pharmacological or somatic means with psychotherapies adjunctive at best.

The Schizophrenias
Prevalence and Heritability
The schizophrenias are relatively rare (1–2% of the population) and highly heritable ($h^2 \cong 0.80$) (Sullivan & Allen, 2004). Having a first-degree relative with schizophrenia increases risk tenfold and having an identical twin with the disorder pushes the risk to over 50% (Lichtenstein et al., 2006). The fact that identical twins are only concordant for the disorder about half the time suggests that genes are necessary but not sufficient and leaves some hope for prevention. Large sample GWAS studies indicate that many genes contribute risk for the disorder but that the effect for each is minuscule and that there is overlap in the genes causal to schizophrenia and those involved in bipolar disorder (Allardyce et al., 2018).

Age of Onset and Gender Disparity
The typical age of onset for the schizophrenias is in mid-to-late adolescence or early adulthood and somewhat later in women than in men (Hafner et al., 1994). Childhood onset is relatively rare, but home movies suggest subtle behavioral anomalies are evident in early childhood for at least some who go on to develop the disorder (Ellison et al., 1998). Unlike most nonpsychotic "disorders," the schizophrenias are evenly distributed across the genders, although males tend to be more severely afflicted and show evidence of reduced fecundity (Power et al., 2013). There is variability in long-term prognosis; about a third of first-episode patients make a relatively full recovery, about a third show clear signs of the disorder but function to some extent, and a third remain markedly impaired and dysfunctional. Good premorbid adjustment, rapid onset, affective distress, and positive symptoms all predict better prognosis (NICE, 2014b).

Pharmacotherapy
Antipsychotic medications represent the core of the treatment of the schizophrenias and the first- and second-generation antipsychotics are the most effective tools for suppressing psychotic symptoms (American Psychiatric Association, 2020; NICE, 2009). However, up to a third of all patients will show poor initial response and another third will continue to experience symptoms even on medications (Lehman et al., 2004). Life expectancy is reduced by about a decade, partly as a consequence of diseases related to obesity and life-style risk factors like smoking and inactivity that may be either disease- or medication-related (Joukamaa et al., 2006). There are indications that long-term prognosis is better in low- and middle-income countries where antipsychotic medications are less likely to be used. Whether that reflects an iatrogenic effect of medications or a greater acceptance of residual symptoms in those cultures is unclear. Whitaker (2010) argued for the former in a controversial treatise that pointed out that there was little evidence that prevalence, prognosis, and rates of disability had improved with the advent of the psychiatric medications and if anything had gotten worse. Introduction of the psychiatric medications has been credited with allowing more patients to function outside of inpatient settings than otherwise would have been the case, but that coincided with the move toward deinstitutionalization and better care in the community (Hollon & Beck, 1978). It remains unclear whether antipsychotic medications prevent long-term deterioration in the course of the disorder or merely suppress symptoms at the expense of impeding recovery and increasing all-cause mortality. In this context, it remains unclear whether some patients are better served by riding out their initial psychotic decompensation in the context of a therapeutic community sans medications (Bola et al., 2006). However, this approach is not feasible for patients presenting with severe symptoms associated with inability to function, suicidality, or potential violence.

Psychotherapy
One of the authors (SDH) trained on the first edition of the *Handbook* and contributed the chapter on drugs and psychotherapy to the second as his first professional publication

(Hollon & Beck, 1978). That earlier chapter found only a handful of RCTs that compared psychotherapy alone (usually either dynamic or nonspecific) to medications and in none of those trials did psychotherapy alone fare as well as medication monotherapy. Behavior therapy has been used from time to time but usually in an effort to control specific symptoms in the context of token economies (Liberman, 1972). Beck's first CT publication was a case study of a patient suffering from paranoid schizophrenia (Beck, 1952) but he moved on to the treatment of depression and the anxiety disorders over the following half-century (Beck, 2005). Interest in CT in the treatment of schizophrenia was rekindled in the 1990s as several disparate groups rediscovered Beck's earlier work and he convened an annual conference in 1999 on its treatment that alternated between the US and the UK in subsequent years (Hollon, 2021). A handful of studies suggest that CT can reduce the degree of belief in delusional thinking in unmedicated patients, but those trials are few in number and largely focused on first episode or good prognosis patients. Not all patients need to stay on medications forever; about 30% were doing well off medications in a 10-year follow-up (Wils et al., 2017). However, there is no clear evidence that psychotherapy of any kind contributes to that capacity.

Psychotherapy in Combination with Pharmacotherapy

A variety of adjunctive psychosocial treatments have been developed to enhance the effectiveness of medications or to relieve chronic medication-resistant symptoms and efforts are being made to use psychosocial treatments to delay medication use for early episode psychosis. None of these approaches has been all that successful and the treatment of schizophrenia lags behind that of the nonpsychotic "disorders." Clinical practice guidelines for the treatment of the schizophrenias recommend a number of different types of psychosocial interventions intended to preserve functioning and adjustment in the community (American Psychiatric Association, 2020). Coordinated specialty care (CSC) programs that incorporate family involvement, resiliency training, supported employment and education, and individualized medication treatment are recommended for people going through their first episode of psychosis. Psychoeducation regarding differential diagnosis, risks of untreated illness, treatment options, and benefits and risks of treatment generally are recommended for all. Supported employment services are often required to provide assistance searching for and maintaining competitive employment along with job training and embedded along with job support and mental health treatment (Frederick & VanderWeele, 2019). Assertive community treatment (ACT) is a multidisciplinary team-based approach that is intended to coordinate a range of services to forestall homelessness and legal and financial difficulties (McDonagh et al., 2017). Cognitive remediation is one of the most useful and most effective psychosocial interventions for the schizophrenias (Bowie et al., 2020). Self-management skills and recovery-focused interventions are used to recognize signs of relapse, develop a relapse prevention plan, and enhance coping skills to address persistent problems and improve quality of life and social and occupational functioning (Grady & Gough, 2014). Most such efforts are intended to forestall deterioration and reflect the overall severity and functional impairment that is inherent in the disorder.

Formal psychotherapies are often used adjunctively but rarely tested. CT and family-focused therapy are two exceptions. As previously noted, Beck's early work was "rediscovered" by clinicians in the UK and extended by several disparate groups in consultation with him. Implicit in this approach is the notion that delusions represent an attempt to make sense out of troublesome or puzzling experiences and that persons with schizophrenia are not impervious to evidence or reason (Beck & Rector, 2000). Over 30 trials conducted over the next decade largely in the UK found a moderate-sized effect with d's ranging from .35 to .45 on both positive and negative symptoms (Wykes et al., 2008). This work led to CT being recommended as an adjunct to medications by guidelines in both the UK (NICE, 2014b) and the US (American Psychiatric Association, 2020), although it is practiced far more often in the former than in the latter. In the US, Beck and colleagues have focused more on helping low-functioning patients with chronic schizophrenia and neurocognitive impairment reconnect with life. Beck and colleagues shifted the emphasis from the predominantly symptom-oriented approach that typifies the UK protocols to a more person-oriented approach that highlights the interests and strengths of each patient. Treatment is focused on identifying and promoting goals that improve the quality of life and facilitate reintegration into society via addressing "defeatist" beliefs that exacerbate the impact of neurocognitive impairment (Grant & Beck, 2009). The approach is explicitly recovery-oriented and treats functional outcomes as the primary target rather than an exclusive focus on symptom change. The addition of this recovery-oriented approach to CT produced meaningful improvements in functional outcomes relative to standard treatment including medication and supportive counseling across 18 months of treatment in a controlled trial (Grant et al., 2012).

Family-focused treatment (FFT) is predicated on the notion that expressed emotionality (criticism especially) within the family increases risk for relapse (Vaughn & Leff, 1976). FFT focuses on efforts to work with family members to improve their communication skills and reduce criticisms (implied or explicit) of the afflicted individual. Several trials have indicated that adding FFT to medication treatment reduces risk for relapse by as much as continuing medication alone does relative to pill-placebo (Goldstein & Miklowitz, 1995). Not all patients who experience a psychotic break live with their families, but the success of FFT in reducing subsequent risk suggests a prophylactic effect that raises the prospect of primary prevention. This is an issue to which we return below.

Prevention of Initial Onset

Despite the fact that heritability is high for the schizophrenias ($h^2 \cong .80$), the fact that concordance between identical twins is only a little more than 50/50 suggests that primary prevention might be possible. It is likely that genetic liability is necessary but far from sufficient to ensure onset. It is not clear that psychosocial interventions can forestall risk, but one place to start might be to look for general life-skills that help young people navigate adolescence, akin to what is done in depression. Also, likely to be of use are FFTs that can be applied to high-risk families with histories of disorder. In a recent trial, adolescents and young adults at elevated risk for schizophrenia on the basis of prodromal signs or genetic risk showed greater improvement in positive symptoms if randomized to 18 sessions of FFT versus 3 sessions of enhanced care (Miklowitz et al., 2014). Only about 20% of the participants were on antipsychotic medications at the start of the trial. Six of the 102 participants randomized progressed to full-blown psychotic episodes over the course of the trial; none were on medications at the time and only one was in the FFT condition. A meta-analysis of four trials in a similar at-risk population found that CT reduced positive symptoms by about a third of a standard deviation and cut risk for transition to full-blown psychosis by half relative to supportive psychotherapy (Stafford et al., 2013). Such efforts are preliminary, but given the detrimental impact of the disorder, anything that can be done to stop the first episode would be a real boon.

Summary

The basic thesis of this chapter is that psychotherapy is at least as efficacious and more enduring than ADM in the treatment of the less-severe nonpsychotic "disorders," but that medications (or somatic treatments) are required in the treatment of the inherently more severe psychotic disorders. That is certainly the case for the schizophrenias, although it may not be the case for all individuals at risk who have yet to have their initial episode or first episodes of psychosis. The schizophrenias are relatively rare and highly heritable and (at least at this time) clearly better treated with medications than with psychotherapy. The answer to question #3 that we raised in the beginning of the chapter (whether psychotherapy alone was sufficient) is that while psychosocial interventions have an adjunctive role to play, they are clearly not the primary intervention and unlikely to be used alone (at least for the vast majority of patients). What we think this means is that the schizophrenias represent a true "disease" in the evolutionary sense and not an evolved adaptation. With respect to question #4, there are indications that psychotherapy might be sufficient on its own if introduced early enough for patients at lower risk, but this work remains promissory at best and needs to be replicated. With respect to our question #5, it remains unclear whether medications worsen the course of the underlying disorder, but there is reason to believe that they might and that randomized longitudinal trials are needed to determine whether that is the case. With respect to our question #6, there are promising but still preliminary indications that preventive interventions can be used to forestall initial onset. Nothing would be more important to pursue. We turn next to the bipolar disorders, the other major low prevalence/high heritability SMI for which medications are primary and psychotherapy is adjunctive at best.

Bipolar Disorder
Prevalence and Heritability

Like the schizophrenias, bipolar I disorder (defined by one or more manic episodes) is relatively rare (1% of the population) and highly heritable ($h^2 \cong .65-.80$) (Barnett & Smoller, 2009). Inclusion of bipolar II and cyclothymia (neither psychotic) brings the prevalence up to nearly 4% (Kessler, Berglund, et al., 2005), and there is reason to think that a subset of the patients diagnosed with unipolar depression are really "hidden bipolars" who seek treatment for their depressions but are happy with their hypomania (Angst 2008). As for the schizophrenias, risk for someone with an identical twin who has expressed the disorder is only slightly more than half. This suggests that genes are necessary but not sufficient.

Age of Onset and Gender Disparity

About half of all instances of bipolar disorder have their initial onset during adolescence (and a very few in childhood) (American Psychiatric Association, 2010b). As opposed to unipolar depression, bipolar disorders are evenly divided across the genders. The combination of low prevalence, high heritability, and lack of gender disparity suggests that bipolar disorder may be more an aberration in an evolved mechanism (a disease) than an evolved adaptation in itself. This is in marked in contrast with unipolar "disorder."

Pharmacotherapy

Patients with bipolar I disorder (mania) are encouraged to get on a mood stabilizer (lithium or an anticonvulsant) and to stay on that regime for the rest of their lives (American Psychiatric Association, 2010b). The atypical antipsychotics can used for the prophylaxis of episodes, but they are better used to stabilize an acute manic episode (NICE, 2014a). Depressive episodes can be treated with ADMs, but those patients should be protected by a mood stabilizer so as not to trigger a manic episode (Goldberg, 2003). Patients with bipolar II (hypomania) often go unmedicated (other than for their depressive episodes); increased energy and high spirits are often valued by the patient and can enhance the quality of life.

Psychotherapy

In an earlier review, Scott (1995) noted that up until that time, no RCT had ever examined the efficacy of psychotherapy alone in the treatment of bipolar I (psychotic mania). So far as we know, that is still the case 35 years later. Early efforts to treat manic-depressive disorder with dynamic psychotherapy were largely unsuccessful and efforts to apply psychosocial interventions to the treatment of bipolar disorder were restricted to examining its role as an adjunct to medication treatment. One of the authors (SDH) was involved in two disastrous attempts to wean "bipolar" patients off of medications in the mid-1970s; in both instances, there were questions about whether the patients were truly bipolar when they were put on medications. Each went into fully manic episodes within weeks of being taken off of their lithium and both required subsequent hospitalizations to bring the episode back under control.

That is not to say that patients who never go beyond hypomania (bipolar II) necessarily need to be medicated; in fact, given the propensity for ADMs to drive manic episodes in patients in the bipolar spectrum, such patients might be better off treated with psychotherapy alone. As Angst (2008) points out, that is likely already the case, since such patients are far more likely to seek treatment for their depressive episodes than for their hypomania. Angst refers to such patients as "hidden bipolars" and, given the unreliability of the diagnosis of bipolar II, such patients are more likely to be screened into trials for unipolar "disorders" than bipolar disorders. That being said, studies evaluating the efficacy of psychotherapy alone in the treatment of bipolar II are few in number and only modestly promising (see for example Swartz et al., 2018).

Psychotherapy in Combination with Pharmacotherapy

A recent network analysis across 39 relevant RCTs including bipolar I and bipolar II patients found that adding any of several skills-based psychotherapies to standard pharmacotherapy cut risk for recurrence by nearly half [odds ratio (OR) = .56] (Miklowitz et al., 2020). CT (SMD = –0.32) and with less certainty family or conjoint therapy and IPT (SMD = –0.46 each) were associated with stabilizing depressive symptoms. Those same three interventions were associated with significantly improved outcomes with respect to mania (all SMDs –0.31 to –0.35) relative to treatment as usual including standard pharmacotherapy. This is impressive evidence for the value of adding a psychosocial intervention to medications as an adjunct. Although differences exist across the different interventions, virtually all try to regularize sleep and behavioral routines (Hollon & Ponniah, 2014). Psychoeducation (PE) in which patients are trained to identify prodromal indices and seek prompt treatment (usually a medication adjustment) has been found to reduce risk for mania (but not depression) relative to treatment as usual (Perry et al., 1999). IPT extended to provide order in daily life and to help maintain affective stability (renamed Interpersonal Social Rhythm Therapy or IPSRT), was found to extend time between episodes in medicated patients (Frank et al., 2005). FFT for schizophrenia has been adapted to the treatment of the bipolar disorders and (like IPSRT), has been found to both reduce acute distress and to prevent subsequent episodes (Miklowitz et al., 2000; Miklowitz et al., 2003). CT performed slightly but not significantly less well than IPSRT and FFT in the Systematic Treatment Enhancement Program for Bipolar Disorder (STEP-BD) trial (Miklowitz et al., 2007). An earlier trial in the UK evidenced a preventive effect for CT (Lam et al., 2003) that extended over a two-year follow-up (Lam et al., 2005), but those findings were not replicated in a larger multi-site trial (Scott et al., 2006). We are not sure the Scott trial should be the last word on efficacy of CT for bipolar depression (large multisite trials are where good interventions go to die) but that study has cooled interest in the approach.

Prevention of Initial Onset

Given the modest success of FFT in delaying or preventing the onset of psychosis in at-risk adolescents and its corollary success in reducing acute distress and preventing subsequent episodes in adolescents and adults who have already expressed the disorder, FFT would appear to be a likely candidate to test with respect to the prevention of initial episodes of bipolar disorder (Miklowitz & Chang, 2008). A subsequent comparison among high-risk children and adolescents found that FFT produced a more rapid recovery from initial mood symptoms and a more favorable trajectory over the subsequent year than an educational control (Miklowitz et al., 2013). This work is promising but has not yet been fully realized. As for the schizophrenias, any intervention that can prevent or even delay initial onsets is likely to have greater benefit across the lifespan than subsequent treatment interventions once the actual disorder has been expressed.

Summary

It is striking that the psychosocial interventions that are at least as efficacious and longer lasting than medications for unipolar depression are only adjunctive at best to pharmacotherapy for bipolar I. There is little evidence that any psychosocial intervention is efficacious in the treatment of an existing manic episode and very modest evidence that they do anything to forestall their onset. They are somewhat more efficacious in treating or even preventing the depressive episodes but not so much as in unipolar depressions of comparable severity. This is somewhat of a puzzle since the depressions that occur in bipolar I disorder are symptomatically similar to (although more likely to be psychotic than) unipolar depressions. This leads us to think that there is something profoundly different between the two polarities. As was the case for the schizophrenias, we suspect that bipolar I disorder represents a "true" disease, a breakdown in an evolved adaptation, and not simply an evolved adaptation in and of itself.

CONCLUSIONS

We return to our original organizing principle: disorders that are highly prevalent but only modestly heritable (such as unipolar depression and the anxiety disorders) are likely to be evolved adaptations that respond better to psychosocial interventions that facilitate the functions these adaptations evolved to serve than to medications that merely anesthetize the distress by suppressing symptoms. Disorders that are low in prevalence but highly heritable, like the schizophrenias and bipolar 1 (psychotic mania), likely represent diseases that are best treated (at least at this time) with medications, alone or in combination with psychotherapy.

The field has been aware of the differential treatment response for quite some time, but the notion that differences in heritability and prevalence might reflect different evolutionary processes is relatively unique and would not have occurred had clinical theorists not been influenced by evolutionary biology and genetics. The implication is that when evolved adaptations lead to consequences that produce distress in the service of motivating a coordinated response that addresses the specific challenge, it is best to treat them with interventions that further the functions that they evolved to serve, likely psychosocial interventions that improve interpersonal or problem-solving skills. Such skills may well prove useful to those who suffer from low prevalence but highly heritable diseases (the psychotic disorders) but something more in terms of pharmacological or somatic treatment is likely to be needed with the psychosocial intervention an adjunct at best. Even within the nonpsychotic "disorders" there may be some individuals who will only respond to medications and those individuals may be well advised to stay on maintenance medications for the rest of their lives, but the available evidence suggests that psychosocial treatments that advance the functions that negative affects evolved to serve are preferable for most nonpsychotic patients.

ABBREVIATIONS

5-HIAA	5-Hydroxyindoleacetic acid
ACT	assertive community treatment
ADM	antidepressant medications
APA	American Psychological Association
ARH	analytical rumination hypothesis
BA	behavioural activation
CBASP	cognitive behavioral-analysis system of psychotherapy
CBT	cognitive behavioural therapy
CS	conditioned stimulus
CT	cognitive therapy
EMDR	Eye Movement Desensitization and Reprocessing
ERP	exposure plus response prevention
ES	effect size
EST	empirically supported treatment
FDA	Food and Drug Administration
FFT	family-focused treatment
GAD	generalized anxiety disorder
IPDMA	Individual Participant Data Meta-analysis
IPSRT	Interpersonal Social Rhythm Therapy
IPT	interpersonal psychotherapy
MAOI	monoamine oxidase inhibitors

MDD	major depressive disorder
NICE	National Institute for Health and Clinical Excellence
NIMH TDCRP	National Institute for Mental Health – Treatment of Depression Collaborative Research Project
OCD	Obsessive compulsive disorder
OR	odds ratio
PE	psychoeducation
PST	problem solving therapy
PTSD	post-traumatic stress disorder
RR	relative risk
SAD	social anxiety disorder
SMD	standardized mean difference
SNPs	single nucleotide polymorphisms
SNRI	serotonin-norepinephrine reuptake inhibitor
SSRI	selective serotonin reuptake inhibitor
STEP-BD	systematic treatment enhancement program for bipolar disorder
TCA	tricyclic antidepressants

REFERENCES

Abramowitz, J. S., Taylor, S., & McKay, D. (2005). Potentials and limitations of cognitive treatments for obsessive-compulsive disorder. *Cognitive Behavior Therapy, 34*, 140–147. www.tandf.co.uk/journals/titles/16506073.asp

Allardyce, J., Leonenko, G., Hamshere, M., Pardiñas, A. F., Forty, L., Knott, S., Gordon-Smith, K., Porteous, D. J., Haywood, C., Di Florio, A., Jones, L., McIntosh, A. M., Owen, M. J., Holman, P., Walters, J. T. R., Craddock, N., Joenes, I., O'Donovan, M. C., & Escott-Price, V. (2018). Association between schizophrenia-related polygenic liability and the occurrence and level of mood-incongruent psychotic symptoms in bipolar disorder. *JAMA Psychiatry, 75*(1), 28–35. https://doi.org/10.1001/jamapsychiatry.2017.3485

American Psychiatric Association. (2007). Practice guideline for the treatment of patients with obsessive-compulsive disorders. *The American Journal of Psychiatry, 164*(Suppl. 7), 1–53. http://ajp.psychiatryonline.org

American Psychiatric Association. (2010a). *Practice guideline for the treatment of patients with major depressive disorder* (3rd ed.) American Psychiatric Press.

American Psychiatric Association. (2010b). *Practice guideline for the treatment of patients with bipolar disorder* (2nd ed.) American Psychiatric Press.

American Psychiatric Association. (2013). *Diagnostic and statistical manual of mental disorders (5th ed: DSM-5).* American Psychiatric Association.

American Psychiatric Association. (2020). *Practice guideline for the treatment of patients with schizophrenia* (3rd ed.) American Psychiatric Press.

American Psychological Association. (2017). *Clinical practice guidelines for the treatment of PTSD.* APA Press. www.apa.org/ptsd-guideline/

American Psychological Association. (2019). *Clinical practice guidelines for the treatment of depression across three age cohorts.* APA Press. https://www.apa.org/depression-guideline/guideline.pdf

Andrews, P. W., Bharwani, A., Lee, K. R., Fox, M., & Thomson, J. A. Jr. (2015). Is serotonin an upper or a downer? The evolution of the serotonergic system and its role in depression and the antidepressant response. *Neuroscience and Biobehavioral Reviews*, *51*, 164-188. https://doi.org/10.1016/j.neubiorev.2015.01.018

Andrews, P. W., Gangestad, S. W., & Matthews, D. (2002). Adaptationism, exaptationism, and evolutionary behavioral science. *Behavioral and Brain Sciences*, *25*, 534–553. https://doi.org/10.1017/S0140525X02000092

Andrews, P. W., Kornstein, S., Halberstadt, L., Gardner, C., & Neale, M. C. (2011). Blue again: Perturbational effects of antidepressants suggest monoaminergic homeostasis in major depression. *Frontiers in Psychology*, *2*, 159. https://doi.org/10.3389/fpsyg.2011.00159

Andrews, P. W., Maslej, M. M., Thomson, J. A., Jr., & Hollon, S. D. (2020). Disordered doctors or reasoning rats? Testing adaptationist and disorder hypotheses for melancholic depression and their relevance for clinical psychology. *Clinical Psychology Review*, *82*. https://doi.org/10.1016/j.cpr.2020.101927

Andrews, P. W., & Thomson, J. A., Jr. (2009). The bright side of being blue: Depression as an adaptation for analyzing complex problems. *Psychological Review*, *116*(3), 620–654. https://doi.org/10.1037/a0016242

Andrews, P. W., Thomson, J. A. Jr., Amstadter, A., & Neale, M. C. (2012). Primum non-nocere: An evolutionary analysis of whether antidepressants do more harm than good. *Frontiers in Psychology*, *3*, 117. https://doi.org/10.3389/fpsyg.2012.00117

Angst, J. (2008). Bipolar disorder – methodological problems and future perspectives. *Dialogues in Clinical Neuroscience*, *10*(2), 129–139. https://doi.org/10.31887/DCNS.2008.10.2/jangst

Areán, P. A., Perri, M. G., Nezu, A. M., Schein, R. L., Christopher, F., & Joseph, T. X. (1993). Comparative effectiveness of social problem-solving therapy and reminiscence therapy as treatments for depression in older adults. *Journal of Consulting and Clinical Psychology*, *61*(6), 1003–1010. https://doi.org/10.1037/0022-006X.61.6.1003

Barber, J. P., Barrett, M. S., Gallop, R., Rynn, M.A., & Rickels, K. (2012). Short-term dynamic psychotherapy versus pharmacotherapy for major depressive disorder: A randomized placebo-controlled trial. *Journal of Clinical Psychiatry*, *73*(1), 67–73. https://doi.org/10.4088/JCP.11m06831

Barlow, D. H., Gorman, J. M., Shear, M. K., & Woods, S. W. (2000). Cognitive-behavioral therapy, imipramine, or their combination for panic disorder: A randomized controlled trial. *JAMA*, *283*(19), 2529–2536. https://doi.org/10.1001/jama.283.19.2529

Barnett, J. H., & Smoller, J. W. (2009). The genetics of bipolar disorder. *Neuroscience*, *164*(1), 331–343. https://doi.org/10.1016/j.neuroscience.2009.03.080

Barton, D. A., Esler, M. D., Dawood, T., Lambert, E. A., Haikerwal, D., Brenchley, C., Socratous, F., Hastings, J., Guo, L., Wiesner, G., Kye, D. M., Bayles. R-. Schlaich, M. P., & Lambert, G. W. (2008). Elevated brain serotonin turnover in patients with depression. *Archives of General Psychiatry*, *65*, 38–46. https://doi.org/10.1001/archgenpsychiatry.2007.11

Batelaan, N. M., van Balkom, A. J. L. M., & Stein, D. J. (2012). Evidence-based pharmacotherapy of panic disorder: An update. *The International Journal of Neuropsychopharmacology*, *15*(3), 403–415. https://doi.org/10.1017/S1461145711000800

Bateson, M., Brilot, B., & Nettle, D. (2011). Anxiety: An evolutionary approach. *Canadian Journal of Psychiatry*, *56*(12), 707–715. http://dx.doi.org/10.1177/070674371105601202

Beck, A. T. (1952). Successful outpatient psychotherapy of a chronic schizophrenic with a delusion based on borrowed guilt. *Psychiatry*, *15*(3), 205–212. https://doi.org/10.1080/00332747.1952.11022883

Beck, A. T. (2005). The current state of cognitive therapy: A 40-year retrospective. *Archives of General Psychiatry*, *62*(9), 953–959. https://doi.org/10.1001/archpsyc.62.9.953

Beck, A. T., & Emery, G. (1985). *Anxiety disorders and phobias: A cognitive perspective*. Basic Books.

Beck, A. T., & Rector, N. (2005). Cognitive approaches to schizophrenia: Theory and therapy. *Annual Review of Clinical Psychology*, *1*, 577–606. https://doi.org/10.1146/annurev.clinpsy.1.102803.144205

Bernik, M., Corregiari, F., Savoia, M. G., de Barros Neto, T. P., Pinheiro, C., & Neto, F. L. (2018). Concomitant treatment with sertraline and social skills training improves social skills acquisition in social anxiety disorder: A double-blind, randomized controlled trial. *PloS ONE*, *13*(10), e0205809. https://doi.org/10.1371/ journal.pone.0205809

Blackburn, I. M., Eunson, K. M., & Bishop, S. (1986). A two-year naturalistic follow-up of depressed patients treated with cognitive therapy, pharmacotherapy and a combination of both. *Journal of Affective Disorders*, *10*(1), 67–75. https://doi.org/10.1016/0165-0327(86)90050-9

Blanco, C., Heimberg, R. G., Schneier, F. R., Fresco, D. M., Chen, H., Turk, C. L., Vermes, D., Erwin, B. A., Schmidt, A. B., Juster, H. R., Campeas, R., & Liebowitz, M. R. (2010). A placebo-controlled trial of phenelzine, cognitive behavioral group therapy, and their combination for social anxiety disorder. *Archives of General Psychiatry*, *67*(3), 286–295. https://doi.org/10.1001/archgenpsychiatry.2010.11

Blomhoff, S., Haug, T. T., Hellström, K., Holme, I., Humble, M., Madsbu, H. P., & Wold, J. E. (2001). Randomised controlled general practice trial of sertraline, exposure therapy and combined treatment in generalised social phobia. *The British Journal of Psychiatry*, *179*(1), 23–30. https://doi.org/10.1192/bjp.179.1.23

Bodenhausen, G. V., Sheppard, L. A., & Kramer, G. P. (1994). Negative affect and social judgment: The differential impact of anger and sadness. *European Journal of Social Psychology*, *24*(1), 45–62. https://doi.org/10.1002/ejsp.2420240104

Bola, J. R. (2006). Medication-free research in early episode schizophrenia: Evidence of long-term harm? *Schizophrenia Bulletin*, *32*(2), 288–296. https://doi.org/10.1093/schbul/sbj019

Bowie, C. R., Bell, M. D., Fiszdon, J. M., Johannesen, J. K., Lindenmayer, J. P., McGurk, S. R., Medalia, A. A., Penadés, R., Saperstein, A. M., Twamley, E. W., Ueland, T., & Wykes, T. (2020). Cognitive remediation for schizophrenia: An expert working group white paper on core techniques. *Schizophrenia Research*, *215*, 49–53. https://doi.org/10.1016/j.schres.2019.10.047.

Brent, D.A., Brunwasser, S.M., Hollon, S.D., Weersing, V.R., Clarke, G.N., Dickerson, J.F. Beardslee, W.R., Gladstone, T.R., Porta, G., Lynch, F.L., Iyengar, S., & Garber, J. (2015). Prevention of depression in at-risk adolescents: Impact of a cognitive behavioral prevention program on depressive episodes, depression-free days, and developmental competence 6 years after the intervention. *JAMA Psychiatry*, *72*(11), 1110–1118. http://doi:10.1001/jamapsychiatry.2015.1559

Brown, W. D., & Barry, K. L. (2016). Sexual cannibalism increases male material investment in offspring: Quantifying terminal reproductive effort in a praying mantis. *Proceedings of the Royal Society B: Biological Sciences*, *283*(1833), 20160656. https://doi.org/10.1098/rspb.2016.0656

Buss, D. M. (2008). *Evolutionary psychology: The new science of the mind*. Allyn & Bacon.

Clark, D. M. (1986). A cognitive approach to panic. *Behaviour Research and Therapy*, *24*(4), 461–470. https://doi.org/10.1016/0005-7967(86)90011-2

Clark, D. M., Ehlers, A., Hackmann, A., McManus, F., Fennell, M., Grey, N., Waddington, L., & Wild, J. (2006). Cognitive therapy versus exposure and applied relaxation in social phobia: A randomized controlled trial. *Journal of Consulting and Clinical Psychology*, *74*(3), 568–578. https://doi.org/10.1037/0022-006X.74.3.568

Clark, D. M., Ehlers, A., McManus, F., Hackmann, A., Fennell, M. J. V., Campbell, H., Flower, T., Davenport, C., & Louis, B. (2003). Cognitive therapy versus fluoxetine in generalized social phobia: A randomized placebo-controlled trial. *Journal of Consulting and Clinical Psychology*, *71*(6), 1058–1067. https://doi.org/10.1037/0022-006X.71.6.1058

Clark, D. M., Salkovskis, P. M., Hackmann, A., Middleton, H., Anastasiades, P., & Gelder, M. (1994). A comparison of cognitive therapy, applied relaxation and imipramine in the treatment of panic disorder. *British Journal of Psychiatry*, *164*(6), 759–769. https://doi.org/10.1192/bjp.164.6.759

Clark, D. M., Salkovskis, P. M., Hackmann, A., Wells, A., Ludgate, J., & Gelder, M. (1999). Brief cognitive therapy for panic disorder: A randomized controlled trial. *Journal of Consulting and Clinical Psychology*, *67*(4), 583–589. https://doi.org/10.1037/0022-006X.67.4.583

Clark, D. M. & Wells, A. (1995). A cognitive model of social phobia. In R. G. Heimberg, M. Liebowitz, D. Hope, & F. Schneier (Eds.), *Social phobia: Diagnosis, assessment, and treatment* (pp. 69–93). Guilford Press.

Cohen, Z. D., & DeRubeis, R. J. (2018). Treatment selection in depression. *Annual Review of Clinical Psychology*, *14*, 209–236. https://doi.org/10.1146/annurev-clinpsy-050817-084746

Crook, R. J., Dickson, K., Hanlon, R. T., & Walters, E. T. (2014). Nociceptive sensitization reduces predation risk. *Current Biology*, *24*(10), 1121–1125. https://doi.org/10.1016/j.cub.2014.03.043

Cuijpers, P., Dekker, J., Hollon, S. D., & Andersson, G. (2009). Adding psychotherapy to pharmacotherapy in the treatment of depressive disorders in adults: A meta-analysis. *Journal of Clinical Psychiatry, 70*(9), 1219–1229. https://doi.org/10.4088/jcp.09r05021

Cuijpers, P., Driessen, E., Hollon, S. D., van Oppen, P., Barth, J., & Andersson, G. (2012). The efficacy of non-directive supportive therapy for adult depression: A meta-analysis. *Clinical Psychology Review, 32*(4), 280–291. https://doi.org/10.1016/j.cpr.2012.01.003

Cuijpers, P., Hollon, S. D., van Straten, A., Bockting, C., Berking, M., & Andersson, G. (2013). Does cognitive behavior therapy have an enduring effect that is superior to keeping patients on continuation pharmacotherapy? *BMJ Open, 3*(4), e002542. https://doi.org/10.1136/bmjopen-2012-002542

Cuijpers, P., Noma, H., Karyotaki, E., Vinkers, C. H., Cipriani, A., & Furukawa, T. A. (2020). A network meta-analysis of the effects of psychotherapies, pharmacotherapies and their combination in the treatment of adult depression. *World Psychiatry, 19*(1), 92–107. https://doi.org/10.1002/wps.20701

Cuijpers, P., van Straten, A., Hollon, S. D., & Andersson, G. (2010). The contribution of active medication to combined treatments of psychotherapy and pharmacotherapy for adult depression: A meta-analysis. *Acta Psychiatrica Scandinavica, 121*(6), 415–423. https://doi.org/10.1111/j.1600-0447.2009.01513.x

Cuijpers, P., van Straten, A., Warmerdam, L., & Andersson, G. (2009). Psychological treatment versus combined treatment of depression: A meta-analysis. *Depression & Anxiety, 26*(3), 279–288. https://doi.org/10.1002/da.20519

Davidson, J. R. T., Foa, E. B., Huppert, J. D., Keefe, F. J., Franklin, M. E., Compton, J., Zhao, N., Connor, K. M., Lynch, T. R., & Gadde, K. M. (2004). Fluoxetine, comprehensive cognitive behavioral therapy, and placebo in generalized social phobia. *Archives of General Psychiatry, 61*(10), 1005–1013. http://doi.org/10.1001/archpsyc.61.10.1005

Davies, G., Armstrong, N., Bis, J. C., Bressler, J., Chouraki, V., Giddaluru, S., Hofer, E., Ibrahim-Verbaas, C. A., Kirin, M., Lahti, J., van der Lee, S. J., Le Hellard, S., Liu, T., Marioni, R. E., Oldmeadow, C., Postmus, I., Smith, A. V., Smith, J. A., Thalamuthu, A., Thomson, R., . . . Deary, I. J. (2015). Genetic contributions to variation in general cognitive function: a meta-analysis of genome-wide association studies in the CHARGE consortium (N=53949). *Molecular Psychiatry, 20*(2), 183–192. https://doi.org/10.1038/mp.2014.188

Davis, T. E., III, Ollendick, T. H., & Öst, L.-G. (2009). Intensive treatment of specific phobias in children and adolescents. *Cognitive and Behavioral Practice, 16*, 294–303. https://doi.org/10.1016/j.cbpra.2008.12.008

de Haan, E., van Oppen, P., van Balkom, A. J. Spinhoven, P., Hoogduin, K. A. L., & van Dyck, R. (1997). Prediction of outcome and early vs. late improvement in OCD patients treated with cognitive behaviour therapy and pharmacotherapy. *Acta Psychiatrica Scandinavica, 96*, 354–361. https://doi.org/10.1111/j.1600-0447.1997.tb09929.x

DeRubeis, R. J., Cohen, Z. D., Forand, N. R., Fournier, J. C., Gelfand, L. A., Lorenzo-Luaces, L. (2014). The Personalized Advantage Index: Translating research on prediction into individualized treatment recommendations. A demonstration. *PLoS One, 9*(1), e83875. https://doi.org/10.1371/journal.pone.0083875

DeRubeis, R. J., Gelfand, L. A., German, R. E., Fournier, J. C., & Forand, N. R. (2014). Understanding processes of change: How some patients reveal more than others—and some groups of therapists less—about what matters in psychotherapy. *Psychotherapy Research, 24*, 419–428. https://doi.org/10.1080/10503307.2013.838654

DeRubeis, R. J., Hollon, S. D., Amsterdam, J. D., Shelton, R. C., Young, P. R., Salomon, R. M., O'Peardon, J. P., Lovett, M. L., Gladis, M. M., Brown, L., & Gallop, R. (2005). Cognitive therapy vs. medications in the treatment of moderate to severe depression. *Archives of General Psychiatry, 62*(4), 409–416. https://doi.org/10.1001/archpsyc.62.4.409

DeRubeis, R. J., Zajecka, J., Shelton, R. C., Amsterdam, J. D., Fawcett, J., Xu, C., Young, P. R., Gallop, R., & Hollon, S. D. (2020). Prevention of recurrence after recovery from a major depressive episode with antidepressant medication alone or in combination with cognitive behavior therapy: Phase 2 of a 2-phase randomized clinical trial. *JAMA Psychiatry, 77*(3), 237–245. https://doi.org/10.1001/jamapsychiatry.2019.3900

Dimidjian, S., & Hollon, S. D. (2010). How would you know if psychotherapy was harmful? *American Psychologist, 65*, 21–33. https://doi.org/10.1037/a0017299

Dimidjian, S., Hollon, S. D., Dobson, K. S., Schmaling, K. B., Kohlenberg, R. J., Addis, M. E., Gallop, R., McGlinchey, J. B., Markley, D. K., Gollan, J. K., Atkins, D. C., Dunner, D. L., & Jacobson, N. S. (2006). Behavioral activation, cognitive therapy, and antidepressant medication in the acute treatment of major depression. *Journal of Consulting and Clinical Psychology, 74*, 658–670. https://doi.org/10.1037/0022-006X.74.4.658

Dobson, K. S., Hollon, S. D., Dimidjian, S., Schmaling, K. B., Kohlenberg, R. J., Gallop, R. J., Rizvi, S. L., Gollan, J. K., Dunner, D. L., & Jacobson, N. S. (2008). Randomized trial of behavioral activation, cognitive therapy, and antidepressant medication in the prevention of relapse and recurrence in major depression. *Journal of Consulting and Clinical Psychology. 76*(3), 468–477. https://doi.org/10.1037/0022-006X.76.3.468

Driessen, E., Cuijpers, P., Hollon, S. D., & Dekker, J. J. M. (2010). Does pretreatment severity moderate the efficacy of psychological treatment of adult outpatient depression? A meta-analysis. *Journal of Consulting and Clinical Psychology, 78*(5), 668–680. http://doi.org/10.1037/a0020570

Dugas, M.J., Brillon, P., Savard, P., Turcotte, J., Gaudet, A., Ladouceur, R., Leblanc, R., & Gervais, N. J. (2010). A randomized clinical trial of cognitive-behavioral therapy and applied relaxation for adults with generalized anxiety disorder. *Behavior Therapy, 41*(1), 46–58. https://doi.org/10.1016/j.beth.2008.12.004

Dugas, M. J., Ladouceur, R., Léger, E., Freeston, M., H., Langlois, F., Provencher, M. D., & Boisvert, J. (2003). Group cognitive–behavioral therapy for generalized anxiety disorder: Treatment outcome and long-term follow-up. *Journal of Consulting and Clinical Psychology, 71*(4), 821–825. http://doi.org/10.1037/0022-006X.71.4.821

Eaton, W. W., Bienvenu, O. J., & Miloyan, B. (2018). Specific phobias. *Lancet Psychiatry, 5*(8), 678–686. https://doi.10.1016/S2215-0366(18)30169-X

Ehlers, A., & Clark, D. M. (2000). A cognitive model of posttraumatic stress disorder. *Behaviour Research and Therapy, 38*(4), 319–345. https://doi.org/10.1016/S0005-7967(99)00123-0

Elkin, I., Gibbons, R.D., Shea, M.T., Sotsky, S.M., Watkins, J.T., Pilkonis, P.A., & Hedeker, D. (1995). Initial severity and differential treatment outcome in the National Institute of Mental Health Treatment of Depression Collaborative Research Program. *Journal of Consulting and Clinical Psychology, 63*(5), 841–847. https://doi.org/10.1037/0022-006X.63.5.841

Elkin, I., Shea, M. T., Watkins, J. T., Imber, S.D., Sotsky, S. M., Collins, J. F., Glass, D. R., Pilkonis, P. A., Leber, W. R., Docherty, J. P., Fiester, S. J., & Parloff, M. B. (1989). National Institute of Mental Health Treatment of Depression Collaborative Research Program: General effectiveness of treatments. *Archives of General Psychiatry, 46*(11), 971–982. https://doi.org/10.1001/archpsyc.1989.01810110013002

Ellison, Z., van Oz, J., & Murray, R. (1998). Special feature: Childhood personality characteristics of schizophrenia: Manifestations of, or risk factors for, the disorder? *Journal of Personality Disorders, 12*(3), 247–261. https://doi.org/10.1521/pedi.1998.12.3.247

Evans, J. St. B. T., & Stanovich, K. E. (2013). Dual-Process theories of higher cognition: Advancing the debate. *Perspectives on Psychological Science, 8*(3), 223–241. https://doi.org/10.1177/1745691612460685

Evans, M. D., Hollon, S. D., DeRubeis, R. J., Piasecki, J. M., Grove, W. M., Garvey, M. J., & Tuason, V. B. (1992). Differential relapse following cognitive therapy and pharmacotherapy for depression. *Archives of General Psychiatry, 49*(10), 802–808. https://doi.org/10.1001/archpsyc.1992.01820100046009

Ferrero, A., Pierò, A., Fassina, S., Massola, T., Lanteri, A., Daga, G. A., & Fassino, S. (2007). A 12-month comparison of brief psychodynamic psychotherapy and pharmacotherapy treatment in subjects with generalised anxiety disorders in a community setting. *European Psychiatry, 22*(8), 530–539. https://doi.org/10.1016/j.eurpsy.2007.07.004

Foa, E. B., Liebowitz, M. R., Kozak, M. J., Davies, S., Campeas, R., Franklin, M. E., Huppert, J. D., Kjernisted, K., Rowan, V., Schmidt, A. B., Simpson, H. B., & Tu, X. (2005). Randomized, placebo-controlled trial of exposure and ritual prevention, clomipramine, and their combination in the treatment of obsessive-compulsive disorder. *The American Journal of Psychiatry, 162*(1), 151–161. https://doi.org/10.1176/appi.ajp.162.1.151

Foa, E., & Rothbaum, B. A. (1998). *Treating the trauma of rape: Cognitive-behavioral therapy for PTSD*. Guilford.

Fonagy, P., Rost, F., Carlyle, J. A., McPherson, S., Thomas, R., Pasco Fearon, R. M., Goldberg, D., & Taylor, D. (2015). Pragmatic randomized controlled trial of long-term psychoanalytic psychotherapy for treatment-resistant depression: The Tavistock Adult Depression Study (TADS). *World Psychiatry, 14*(3), 312–321. https://doi.org/10.1002/wps.20267

Forand, N. R., DeRubeis, R. J., & Amsterdam, J. D. (2013). Combining medication and psychotherapy in the treatment of major mental disorders. In M. J. Lambert (Ed.), *Garfield and Bergin's handbook of psychotherapy and behavior change* (6th ed., pp. 735–774). John Wiley & Sons, Inc.

Fournier, J. C., DeRubeis, R. J., Hollon, S. D., Dimidjian, S., Amsterdam, J. D., Shelton, R. C., & Fawcett, J. (2010). Antidepressant drug effects and depression severity: A patient-level meta-analysis. *JAMA, 303*(1), 47–53. https://doi.org/10.1001/jama.2009.1943

Fournier, J. C., DeRubeis, R. J., Shelton, R. C., Gallop, R., Amsterdam, J. D., & Hollon, S. D. (2008). Antidepressant medications versus cognitive therapy in depressed patients with or without personality disorder. *The British Journal of Psychiatry, 192*(2), 124–129. http://doi.org/10.1192/bjp.bp.107.037234

Fournier, J. C., DeRubeis, R. J., Shelton, R. C., Hollon, S. D., Amsterdam, J. D., & Gallop, R. (2009). Prediction of response to medication and cognitive therapy in the treatment of moderate to severe depression. *Journal of Consulting and Clinical Psychology, 77*(4), 775–787. https://doi.org/10.1037/a0015401

Frank, E., Kupfer D. J, Thase, M. E., Mallinger, A. G., Swartz, H. A., Fagiolini, A. M., Grochocinski, V., Houck, P., Scott, J., Thompsonn, W., & Monk, T. (2005). Two-year outcomes for interpersonal and social rhythm therapy in individuals with bipolar I disorder. *Archives of General Psychiatry, 62*(9), 996–1004. https://doi.org/10.1001/archpsyc.62.9.996

Frederick, D. E., & VanderWeele, T. J. (2019). Supported employment: Meta-analysis and review of randomized controlled trials of individual placement and support. *PloS ONE, 14*(2), e0212208. https://doi.org/10.1371/journal.pone.0212208

Fredrikson, M., Annas, P., Fischer, H., & Wik, G. (1996). Gender and age differences in the prevalence of specific fears and phobias. *Behaviour Research and Therapy, 34*(1), 33–39. https://doi.org/10.1016/0005-7967(95)00048-3

Furukawa, T. A., Maruo, K., Noma, H., Tanaka, S., Imai, H., Shinohara, K., Yamawaki, S., Levine, S. Z., Goldberg, Y., Leucht, S., & Cipriani, A. (2018). Initial severity of major depression and efficacy of new generation antidepressants: Individual participant data meta-analysis. *Acta Psychiatrica Scandinavia, 137*(6), 450–458. https://doi.org/10.1111/acps.12886

Furukawa, T. A., Watanabe, N., & Churchill, R. (2006). Psychotherapy plus antidepressant for panic disorder with or without agoraphobia: Systematic review. *The British Journal of Psychiatry, 188*(4), 305–312. https://doi.org/10.1192/bjp.188.4.305

Garber, J., Clarke, G. N., Weersing, V. R., Beardslee, W. R., Brent, D. A., Gladstone, T. R. G., DeBar, L. L., Lynch, F. L., D'Angelo, E., Hollon, S. D., Shamseddeen, W., & Iyengar, S. (2009). Prevention of depression in at-risk adolescents: A randomized controlled trial. *JAMA, 301*(21), 2215–2224. http://doi.org/10.1001/jama.2009.788

Gibbons, R. D., Hur, K., Brown, C. H., Davis, J. M., & Mann, J. J. (2012). Benefits from antidepressants: Synthesis of 6-week patient-level outcomes from double-blind placebo-controlled randomized trials of fluoxetine and venlafaxine. *Archives of General Psychiatry, 69*(6), 572–579. http://doi.org/10.1001/archgenpsychiatry.2011.2044

Gilbertson, M. W., Shenton, M. E., Ciszewski, A., Kasai, K., Lasko, N. B., Orr, S. P., & Pittman, R. K. (2002). Smaller hippocampal volume predicts pathologic vulnerability to psychological trauma. *Nature Neuroscience, 5*(11), 1242–1247. https://doi.org/10.1038/nn958

Goldberg, J. F. (2003). When do antidepressants worsen the course of bipolar disorder? *Journal of Psychiatric Practice, 9*(3), 181–194. https://journals.lww.com/practicalpsychiatry/toc/2003/05000

Goldstein, M. J., & Miklowitz, D. J. (1995). The effectiveness of psychoeducational family therapy in the treatment of schizophrenic disorders. *Journal of Marital and Family Therapy, 21*(4), 361–376. https://doi.org/10.1111/j.1752-0606.1995.tb00171.x

Grady, P. A., & Gough, L. L. (2014). Self-management: A comprehensive approach to management of chronic conditions. *American Journal of Public Health, 104*(8), e25–e31. https://doi.org/10.2105/AJPH.2014.302041

Grant, B. F., Hasin, D. S., Blanco, C., Stinson F. S., Chou, S. P., Goldstein, R. B., Rise, B., Dawson, D. A., Smith, S., Saha, T. D., & Huang, B. (2005). The epidemiology of social anxiety disorder in the United States: Results from the National Epidemiologic Survey on Alcohol and Related Conditions. *Journal of Clinical Psychiatry, 66*(11), 1351–1361. https://doi.org/10.4088/JCP.v66n1102

Grant, P. M., & Beck, A. T. (2009). Defeatist beliefs as a mediator of cognitive impairment, negative symptoms, and functioning in schizophrenia. *Schizophrenia Bulletin, 35*(4), 798–806. https://doi.org/10.1093/schbul/sbn008

Grant, P. M., Huh, G. A., Perivoliotis, D., Stolar, N. M., & Beck, A. T. (2012). Randomized trial to evaluate the efficacy of cognitive therapy for low-functioning patients with schizophrenia. *Archives of General Psychiatry, 69*(2), 121–127. https://doi.org/10.1001/archgenpsychiatry.2011.129

Gray, J. A. (1990). Brain systems that mediate both emotion and cognition. *Cognition and Emotion, 4*(3), 269–288. https://doi.org/10.1080/02699939008410799

Hafner, H., Maurer, K., Loffler, W., & Reicher-Rössler, A. (1994). The epidemiology of early schizophrenia: Influence of age and gender on onset and early course. *The British Journal of Psychiatry, 164*(S23), 29–38. https://doi.org/10.1192/S0007125000292714

Hankin, B. L., & Abramson, L. Y. (2001). Development of gender differences in depression: An elaborated cognitive vulnerability-transactional stress theory. *Psychological Bulletin, 127*(6), 773–796. https://doi.org/10.1037//0033-2909.127.6.773

Hawton, K., Bergen, H., Simkin, S., Cooper, J., Waters, K., Gunnell, D., & Kapur, N. (2010). Toxicity of antidepressants: Rates of suicide relative to prescribing and non-fatal overdose. *The British Journal of Psychiatry, 196*(5), 354–358. https://doi.org/10.1192/bjp.bp.109.070219

Harvard Medical School (2007). National comorbidity survey (NCS). www.hcp.med.harvard.edu/ncu/index.php. Data table 1: Lifetime prevalence DSM-IV/WHM-CIDI disorders by sex and cohort.

Haug, T. T., Blomhoff, S., Hellstrøm, K., Holme, I., Humble, M., Madsbu, H. P., & Wold, J. E. (2003). Exposure therapy and sertraline in social phobia: I-year follow-up of a randomised controlled trial. *The British Journal of Psychiatry, 182*(4), 312–318. https://doi.org/10.1192/bjp.182.4.312

Heimberg, R. G., Liebowitz, M., Hope, D., & Schneier, F. (1995). *Social phobia: Diagnosis, assessment, and treatment*. Guilford Press.

Hoffart, A., Borge, F. M., Sexton, H., & Clark, D. M. (2009). Change processes in residential cognitive and interpersonal therapy for social phobia: A process outcome study. *Behavior Therapy, 40*(1), 10–22. https://doi.org/10.1016/j.beth.2007.12.003

Hofmann, S. G., & Smits, J. A. J. (2008). Cognitive-behavioral therapy for adult anxiety disorders: A meta-analysis of randomized placebo-controlled trials. *The Journal of Clinical Psychiatry, 69*(4), 621–632. https://doi:10.4088/jcp.v69n0415

Hofmann, S. G., Smits, J. A. J., Rosenfield, D., Simon, N., Otto, M. W., Meuret, A. E., Marques, L., Fang, A., Tart, C., & Pollack, M. H. (2013). D-Cycloserine as an augmentation strategy with cognitive-behavioral therapy for social anxiety disorder. *The American Journal of Psychiatry, 170*(7), 751–758. https://doi.org/10.1176/appi.ajp.2013.12070974

Hollon, S. D. (2019). Treatment of depression versus treatment of PTSD: A commentary. *The American Journal of Psychiatry, 176*(4), 259–261. https://doi.org/10.1176/appi.ajp.2019.19020173

Hollon, S. D. (2021). Aaron Beck and the history of cognitive therapy: A tale of two cities (and one Institute). In W. Pickren (Ed.), *Oxford research encyclopedia of history of psychology*. Oxford University Press.

Hollon, S. D., Areán, P. A., Craske, M. G., Crawford, K. A., Kivlahan, D. R., Magnavita, J. J., Ollendick, T. H., Sexton, T. L., Spring, B., Bufka, L. F., Galper, D. G., & Kurtzman, H. (2014). Development of clinical practice guidelines. *Annual Review of Clinical Psychology, 10*, 213–241. https://doi.org/10.1146/annurev-clinpsy-050212-185529

Hollon, S. D., & Beck, A. T. (1978). Psychotherapy and drug therapy: Comparisons and combinations. In S. L. Garfield & A. E. Bergin (Eds.), *Handbook of psychotherapy and behavior change: An empirical analysis* (2nd ed., pp. 437–490). Wiley.

Hollon, S. D., DeRubeis, R. J., & Evans, M. D. (1987). Causal mediation of change in treatment for depression: Discriminating between nonspecificity and noncausality. *Psychological Bulletin, 102*(1), 139–149. https://doi.org/10.1037/0033-2909.102.1.139

Hollon, S. D., DeRubeis, R. J., Fawcett, J., Amsterdam, J. D., Shelton, R. C., Zajecka, J., Young, P. R., & Gallop, R. (2014). Effect of cognitive therapy with antidepressant medications vs antidepressants alone on the rate of recovery in major depressive disorder: A randomized clinical trial. *JAMA Psychiatry, 71*(10), 1157–1164. https://doi.org/10.1001/jamapsychiatry.2014.1054

Hollon, S. D., DeRubeis, R. J., Shelton, R. C., Amsterdam, J. D., Salomon, R. M., O'Reardon, J. P., Lovett, M. L., Young, P. R., Haman, K. L., Freeman, B. B., & Gallop, R. (2005). Prevention of relapse following cognitive therapy versus medications in moderate to severe depression. *Archives of General Psychiatry, 62*(4), 417–422. https://doi.org/10.1001/archpsyc.62.4.417

Hollon, S. D., Jarrett, R. B., Nierenberg, A. A., Thase, M. E., Trivedi, M., & Rush, A. J. (2005). Psychotherapy and medication in the treatment of adult and geriatric depression: Which monotherapy or combined treatment? *Journal of Clinical Psychiatry, 66*(4), 455–468. https://doi.org/10.4088/JCP.v66n0408

Hollon, S. D., & Ponniah, K. (2010). A review of empirically supported psychological therapies for mood disorders in adults. *Depression and Anxiety, 27*(10), 891–932. https://doi.org/10.1002/da.20741

Horowitz, J. L., Garber, J., Siesla, J. A., Young, J. F., & Mufson, L. (2007). Prevention of depressive symptoms in adolescents: A randomized trial of cognitive–behavioral and interpersonal prevention programs. *Journal of Consulting and Clinical Psychology, 75*(5), 693–607. http://doi.org/10.1037/0022-006X.75.5.693

Hyman, S. E., & Nestler, E. J. (1996). Initiation and adaptation: A paradigm for understanding psychotropic drug action. *American Journal of Psychiatry, 153*(2), 151–162. https://psycnet.apa.org/doi/10.1176/ajp.153.2.151

Jarrett, R. B., Schaffer, M., McIntire, D., Witt-Browder, A., Kraft, D., & Risser, R. C. (1999). Treatment of atypical depression with cognitive therapy or phenelzine: A double blind, placebo-controlled trial. *Archives of General Psychiatry, 56*(5), 431–437. https://doi.org/10.1001/archpsyc.56.5.431

Jaurrieta, N., Jimenez-Murcia, S., Menchón, J. M., del Pino Alonso, M., Segalàs, C., Álvarez- Moya, E. M., Labad, J., Granero, R., & Vallejo, J. (2008). Individual versus group cognitive-behavioral treatment for obsessive-compulsive disorder: A controlled pilot study. *Psychotherapy Research, 18*(5), 604–614. https://doi.org/10.1080/10503300802192141

Joukamaa, M., Heliövaara, M., Knekt, P., Aromaa, A., Raitasalo, R., & Lehtinen, V. (2006). Schizophrenia, neuroleptic medication and mortality. *The British Journal of Psychiatry, 188*(2), 122–127. https://doi.org/10.1192/bjp.188.2.122

Kahneman, D. (2011). *Thinking, fast and slow.* Farrar, Straus and Giroux.

Kazdin, A. E. (2007). Mediators and mechanisms of change in psychotherapy research. *Annual Review of Clinical Psychology, 3*, 1–27. https://doi.org/10.1146/annurev.clinpsy.3.022806.091432

Keller, M. B., McCullough, J. P., Klein, D. N., Arnow, B., Dunner, D. L., Gelenberg, A. J., Markowitz, J. C., Nemeroff, C. B., Russell, J. M., Thase, M. E., Trivedi, M. H., & Zajecka, J. (2000). A comparison of nefazodone, the cognitive behavioral-analysis system of psychotherapy, and their combination for the treatment of chronic depression. *New England Journal of Medicine, 342*(20), 1462–1470. https://doi.org/10.1056/NEJM200005183422001

Keller, M. C. (2018). Evolutionary perspectives on genetic and environmental risk factors for psychiatric disorders. *Annual Review of Clinical Psychology, 14*, 471–493. https://doi.org/10.1146/annurev-clinpsy-050817-084854

Keller, M. C., & Miller, G. (2006). Resolving the paradox of common, harmful, heritable mental disorders: Which evolutionary genetic models work best? *Behavioral and Brain Sciences, 29*, 385–452.

Keller, M. C., Neale, M. C., & Kendler, K. S. (2007). Association of different adverse life events with distinct patterns of depressive symptoms. *The American Journal of Psychiatry, 164*(10), 1521–1529. https://doi.org/10.1176/appi.ajp.2007.06091564

Kendler, K. S., Heath, A. C., Martin, N. G., & Eaves, L. J. (1987). Symptoms of anxiety and symptoms of depression: Same genes, different environments? *Archives of General Psychiatry, 44*(5), 451–457. https://doi.org/10.1001/archpsyc.1987.01800170073010

Kessler, R. C., Berglund P., Demler, O., Jin, R., Merikangas, M. R., & Walters, E. E. (2005). Lifetime prevalence and age-of-onset distributions of DSM-IV disorders in the National Comorbidity Replication Study. *Archives of General Psychiatry, 62*(6), 593–602. https://doi.org/10.1001/archpsyc.62.6.593

Kessler, R. C., Chiu, W. T., Demler, O., Merikangas, K. R., & Walters, E. E. (2005). Prevalence, severity, and comorbidity of 12-month DSM-IV disorders in the National Comorbidity Survey Replication. *Archives of General Psychiatry, 62*(6), 617–627. https://doi.org/10.1001/archpsyc.62.6.617

Kirsch, I. (2019). Placebo effects in the treatment of depression and anxiety. *Frontiers in Psychiatry, 10*, 407. https://doi.org/10.3389/fpsyt.2019.00407

Knijnik, D. Z., Blanco, C., Salum, G. A., Moraes, C. U., Mombach, C., Almeida, E., Pereira, M., Strapasson, A., Manfro, G. G., & Eizirik, C. L. (2008). A pilot study of clonazepam versus psychodynamic group therapy plus clonazepam in the treatment of generalized social anxiety disorder. *European Psychiatry, 23*(8), 567–574. https://doi.org/10.1016/j.eurpsy.2008.05.004

Kocsis, J. H., Gelenberg, A. J., Rothbaum, B. O., Klein, D. N., Trivedi, M. H., Manber, R., Keller, M. B., Leon, A. C., Wisniewski, S. R., Arnow, B. A., Markowitz, J. C., & Thase, M. E. (2009). Cognitive behavioral analysis system of psychotherapy and brief supportive psychotherapy for augmentation of antidepressant nonresponse in chronic depression: The REVAMP Trial. *Archives of General Psychiatry, 66*(11), 1178–1188. https://doi.org/10.1001/archgenpsychiatry.2009.144

Ladouceur, R., Dugas, M. J., Freeston, M. H., Leger, E., Gagnon, F., & Thibodeau, N. (2000). Efficacy of a cognitive-behavioral treatment for generalized anxiety disorder: Evaluation in a controlled clinical trial. *Journal of Consulting and Clinical Psychology, 68*(6), 957–964. https://doi.org/10.1037//0022-006x.68.6.957

Ladouceur, R., Dugas, M. J., Freeston, M. H., Rhéaume, J., Blais, F., Boisvert, J.-M., Gagnon, F., & Thibodeau, N. (1999). Specificity of generalized anxiety disorder symptoms and processes. *Behavior Therapy, 30*(2), 191–207. https://doi.org/10.1016/S0005-7894(99)80003-3

Lam, D. H., Hayward, P., Watkins, E. R., Wright, K., & Sham, P. (2005). Relapse prevention in patients with bipolar disorder: Cognitive therapy outcome after 2 years. *The American Journal of Psychiatry, 162*(2), 324–329. https://doi.org/10.1176/appi.ajp.162.2.324

Lam, D. H., Watkins, E. R., Hayward, P., Bright, J., Wright, K., Kerr, N., Parr-Davis, G., & Sham, P. (2003). A randomized controlled study of cognitive therapy for relapse prevention for bipolar affective disorder: Outcome of the first year. *Archives of General Psychiatry, 60*(2), 145–152. https://doi.org/10.1001/archpsyc.60.2.145

LeDoux, J. (2019). *The deep history of ourselves: The four-billion-year story of how we got conscious brains.* Viking.

Lehman, A. F., Lieberman, J. A., Dixon, L. B., McGlashan, T. H., Miller, A. L., Perkins, D. O., Kreyenbuhl, J., McIntyre, J. S., Charles, S. C., Altshuler, K., Cook, I., Cross, C. D., Mellman, L., Moench, L. A., Norquist, G., Twemlow, S. W., Woods, S., Yager, J., Hafter Gray, S., . . . Regier, D. (2004). Practice guideline for the treatment of patients with schizophrenia (2nd ed.) *The American Journal of Psychiatry, 161*(2 Suppl), i-iv+1–56.

Liebman, R. E., Whitfield, K. M., Sijercic, I., Ennis, N., & Monson, C. M. (2020). Harnessing the healing power of relationships in trauma recovery: A systematic review of cognitive-behavioral conjoint therapy for PTSD. *Current Treatment Options in Psychiatry, 7*, 203–220. https://doi.org/10.1007/s40501-020-00211-1

Leichsenring, F., Salzer, S., Beutel, M. E., Herpertz, S., Hiller, W., Hoyer, J., Huesing, J., Joraschky, P., Nolting, B., Poehlmann, K., Ritter, V., Stangier, U., Strauss, B., Stuhldreher, N., Tefikow, S., Teismann, T., Willutzki, U., Wiltink, J., & Leibing, E. (2013). Psychodynamic therapy and cognitive-behavioral therapy in social anxiety disorder: A multicenter randomized controlled trial. *The American Journal of Psychiatry, 170*(7), 759–767. https://doi.org/10.1176/appi.ajp.2013.12081125

Lemmens, L. H. J. M., van Bronswijk, S. C., Peeters, F. P. M. L., Arntz, A., Roefs, A., Hollon, S. D., DeRubeis, R. J., & Huibers, M. J. H. (2020). Interpersonal psychotherapy versus cognitive therapy for depression: How they work, how long, and for whom – Key findings from an RCT. *American Journal of Psychotherapy, 73*(1), 8–14. https://doi.org/10.1176/appi.psychotherapy.20190030

Liberman, R. P. (1972). Behavioral modification of schizophrenia: A review. *Schizophrenia Bulletin, 1*(6), 37–48. https://doi.org/10.1093/schbul/1.6.37

Lichtenstein, P., Björk, C., Hultman, C. M., Scolnick, E., Sklar, P., & Sullivan, P. F. (2006). Recurrence risks for schizophrenia in a Swedish national cohort. *Psychological Medicine, 36*(10), 1417–1425. https://doi.org/10.1017/S0033291706008385

Liebowitz, M. R., Heimberg, R. G., Schneier, F. R., Hope, D. A., & Davies, S. (1999). Cognitive-behavioral group therapy versus phenelzine in social phobia: Long-term outcome. *Depression and Anxiety, 10*(3), 89–98. https://doi.org/10.1002/(SICI)1520-6394(1999)10:3%3C89::AID-DA1%3E3.0.CO;2-5

Marcus, S. C., & Olfson, M. (2010). National trends in the treatment for depression from 1998 to 2007. *Archives of General Psychiatry, 67*(12), 1265–1273. https://doi.org/10.1001/archgenpsychiatry.2010.151

Marks, I. M., Swinson, R. P., Başoğlu, M., Kuch, K., Noshirvani, H., O'Sullivan, G., Lelliott, P. T., Kirby, M., McNamee, G., Sengun, S., & Wickwire, K. (1993). Alprazolam and exposure alone and combined in panic disorder with agoraphobia. A controlled study in London and Toronto. *The British Journal of Psychiatry, 162*, 776–787. https://doi:10.1192/BJP.162.6.776

Maslej, M. M., Bolker, B. M., Russell, M. J., Eaton, K., Durisko, Z., Hollon, S. D., Swanson, G. M., Thomson, J. A., Mulsant, B. H., & Andrews, P. W. (2017). The mortality and myocardial effects of antidepressants are moderated by preexisting cardiovascular disease: A meta-analysis. *Psychotherapy and Psychosomatics, 86*(5), 268–282. https://doi.org/10.1159/000477940

Mayo-Wilson, E., Dias, S., Mavranezouli, I., Kew, K., Clark, D. M., Ades, A. E., & Pilling, S. (2014). Psychological and pharmacological interventions for social anxiety disorder in adults: A systematic review and network meta-analysis. *Lancet Psychiatry, 1*(5), 368–376. https://doi.org/10.1016/S2215-0366(14)70329-3

McDonagh, M. S., Dana, T., Selph, S., Devine, E. B., Cantor, C., Bougatsos, C., Blazina, I., Grusing, S., Fu, R., Kopelovich, S. L., Monroe-DeVita, M. Haupt, D. W. (2017). Treatments for schizophrenia in adults: A systematic review. Comparative effectiveness review No. 198. (Prepared by the Pacific Northwest Evidence-based Practice Center under Contract No. 290-2015-00009-I.) AHRQ Publication No. 17(18) –EHC031-EF. Rockville, MD, Agency for Healthcare Research and Quality. https://effectivehealthcare.ahrq.gov/topics/ schizophrenia-adult/research-2017.

McLean, C. P., Asnaani, A., Litz, B. T., & Hofmann, S. G. (2011). Gender differences in anxiety disorders: Prevalence, course of illness, comorbidity and burden of illness. *Journal of Psychiatric Research, 45*(8), 1027–1035. https://doi.org/10.1016/j.jpsychires.2011.03.006

McMillan, D., & Lee, R. (2010). A systematic review of behavioral experiments vs exposure alone in the treatment of anxiety disorders: A case of exposure while wearing the emperor's new clothes? *Clinical Psychology Review, 30*(5), 467–478. https://doi.org/10.1016/j.cpr.2010.01.003

Miklowitz, D. J., & Chang, K. D. (2008). Prevention of bipolar disorder in at-risk children: Theoretical assumptions and empirical foundations. *Development and Psychopathology, 20*(3), 881–897. https://doi.org/10.1017%2FS0954579408000424

Miklowitz, D. J., Efthimiou, O., Furukawa, T. A., Scott, J., McLaren, R., Geddes, J. R., Cipriani, A. (2020). Adjunctive psychotherapy for bipolar disorder: A systematic review and component network meta-analysis. *JAMA Psychiatry*. Published online October 14, 2020. https://doi.org/10.1001/jamapsychiatry.2020.2993

Miklowitz, D. J., George, E. L., Richards, J. A., Simoneau, T. L., & Suddath, R. L. (2003). A randomized study of family-focused psychoeducation and pharmacotherapy in the outpatient management of bipolar disorder. *Archives of General Psychiatry, 60*(9), 904–912. https://doi.org/10.1001/archpsyc.60.9.904

Miklowitz, D. J., O'Brien, M. P., Schlosser, D. A., Addington, J., Candan, K. A., Marshall, C., Domingues, I., Walsh, B. C., Zinberg, J. L., de Silva, S. D., Friedman-Yakoobian, M., & Cannon, T. D. (2014). Family focused treatment for adolescents and young adults at high risk for psychosis: Results of a randomized trial. *Journal of the American Academy of Child and Adolescent Psychiatry, 53*(8), 848–858. https://doi.org/10.1016/j.jaac.2014.04.020

Miklowitz DJ, Otto MW, Frank E, Reilly-Harrington, N. A., Wisniewski, S. R., Kogan, J. N., Nierenberg, A. A., Calabrese, J. R., Marangell, L. B., Gyulai, L., Araga, M., Gonzalez, J. M., Shirley, E. R., Thase, M. E., & Sachs, G. S. (2007). Psychosocial treatments for bipolar disorder: A 1-year randomized trial from the Systematic Treatment Enhancement Program. *Archives of General Psychiatry, 64*(4), 419–427. https://doi.org/10.1001/archpsyc.64.4.419

Miklowitz, D. J., Schneck, C. D., Walshaw, P. D., Singh, M. K., Garrett, A., Sugar, C., & (2013). Early intervention for symptomatic youth at risk for bipolar disorder: A randomized trial of family-focused therapy. *Journal of the American Academy of Child and Adolescent Psychiatry, 52*(2), 121–131. https://doi.org/10.1016/j.jaac.2012.10.007

Miklowitz, D. J., Simoneau, T. L., George, E. L., Richards, J. A., Kalbag, A., Sachs-Ericsson, N., & Suddath, R. (2000). Family-focused treatment of bipolar disorder: One-year effects of psychoeducational program in conjunction with pharmacotherapy. *Biological Psychiatry, 48*, 582–592. https://doi:10.1016/S0006-3223(00)00931-8

Mitte, K. (2005). Meta-analysis of cognitive–behavioral treatments for generalized anxiety disorder: A comparison with pharmacotherapy. *Psychological Bulletin, 131*(5), 785–795. https://doi.org/10.1037/0033-2909.131.5.785

Monroe, S. M., Anderson, S. F., & Harkness, K. L. (2019). Life stress and major depression: The mysteries of recurrences. *Psychological Review, 126*(6), 791–816. https://doi.org/10.1037/rev0000157

Monson, C. M., & Fredman, S. J. (2012). *Cognitive-behavioral conjoint therapy for PTSD: Harnessing the healing power of relationships*. Guilford Press.

Montgomery, S. A., Nil, R., Dürr-Pal, N., Loft, H., & Boulenger, J. P. (2005). A 24-week randomized, double-blind, placebo-controlled study of escitalopram for the prevention of generalized social anxiety disorder. *Journal of Clinical Psychiatry, 66*(10), 1270–1278. https://doi.org/10.4088/jcp.v66n1009

Mörtberg, E., Clark, D. M., & Bejerot, S. (2011). Intensive group cognitive therapy and individual cognitive therapy for social phobia: Sustained improvement at 5-year follow-up. *Journal of Anxiety Disorders, 25*(8), 994–1000. https://doi.org/10.1016/j.janxdis.2011.06.007

Mörtberg, E., Clark, D. M., Sundin, O., & Åberg Wistedt, A. (2007). Intensive group cognitive treatment and individual cognitive therapy vs. treatment as usual in social phobia: A randomized controlled trial. *Acta Psychiatrica Scandinavia, 115*(2), 142–154. http://doi.org/10.111/j.1600-0447.2006.00839.x

Mojtabai, R., & Olfson, M. (2011). Proportion of antidepressants prescribed without a psychiatric diagnosis is growing. *Health Affairs, 30*(8), 1434–1442. https://doi.org/10.1377/hlthaff.2010.1024

Mynors-Wallis, L. M., Gath, D. H., Day, A., & Baker, F. (2000). Randomised controlled trial of problem-solving treatment, antidepressant medication, and combined treatment for major depression in primary care. *British Medical Journal, 320*, 26–30. https://doi.org/10.1136/bmj.320.7226.26

Mynors-Wallis, L. M., Gath, D. H., Lloyd-Thomas, A. R., & Tomlinson, D. (1995). Randomised controlled trial comparing problem solving treatment with amitriptyline and placebo for major depression in primary care. *British Medical Journal, 310*, 441–445. https://doi.org/10.1136/bmj.310.6977.441

Na, H. R., Kang, E. H., Lee, J. H., & Yu, B. H. (2011). The genetic basis of panic disorder. *Journal of Korean Medical Science, 26*(6), 701–710. https://doi.org/10.3346/jkms.2011.26.6.701

National Institute for Health and Clinical Excellence (NICE, 2005). *Obsessive-compulsive disorder: Core interventions in the treatment of obsessive-compulsive disorder and body dysmorphic disorder*. Clinical Guideline (CG) 31. www.nice.org.uk/CG31

National Institute for Health and Clinical Excellence (NICE, 2009). *Schizophrenia: Core interventions in the treatment and management of schizophrenia in in adults in primary and secondary care*. CG82. www.nice.org.uk/CG82

National Institute for Health and Clinical Excellence. (NICE, 2011a). *Generalized anxiety disorder and panic disorder in adults: Management*. CG 113. www.nice.org.uk/CG113

National Institute for Health and Clinical Excellence (NICE, 2011b). *Common mental health disorders: Identification and pathways to care*. CG123. www.nice.org.uk/CG1123

National Institute for Health and Clinical Excellence (NICE, 2014a). *Bipolar disorder: Assessment and management*. CG185. www.nice.org/uk/CG185

National Institute for Health and Clinical Excellence (NICE, 2014b). *Psychosis and schizophrenia in adults: Treatment and management (updated edition)*. CG178. www.nice.org.uk/guidance/cg178

National Institute for Health and Clinical Excellence (NICE, 2018). Depression in adults: Treatment and management (draft for second consultation). London, UK, National Collaborating Centre for Mental Health, 2014.

National Institute of Mental Health (1998). Genetics and mental disorders: Report of the National Institute of Mental Health's Genetic Workgroup. NIH Publication No. 98-4268.

Nesse, R. M. (1987). An evolutionary perspective on panic disorder and agoraphobia. *Ethology and Sociobiology, 8,* 73S–83S. https://doi:10.1016/0162-3095(87)90020-3

Nesse, R. M. (2019). *Good reasons for bad feelings: Insights from the frontier of evolutionary psychiatry.* Dutton.

Nolen-Hoeksema, S. (2012). Emotion regulation and psychopathology: The role of gender. *Annual Review of Clinical Psychology, 8,* 161–187. https://doi.org/10.1146/annurev-clinpsy-032511-143109

Norcross, J. C., & Wampold, B. E. (2019). Relationships and responsiveness in the psychological treatment of trauma: The tragedy of the APA Clinical Practice Guideline. *Psychotherapy, 56*(3), 391–399. https://doi.org/10.1037/pst0000228

Norrholm, S. D., & Ressler, K. J. (2009). Genetics of anxiety and trauma-related disorders. *Neuroscience, 164*(1), 272–287. https://doi.org/10.1016/j.neuroscience.2009.06.036

Öhman, A., & Mineka, S. (2001). Fear, phobias and preparedness: Toward an evolved module of fear and fear learning. *Psychological Review, 108*(3), 483–522. https://psycnet.apa.org/doi/10.1037/0033-295X.108.3.483

Öhman, A., & Mineka, S. (2003). The malicious serpent: Snakes as a prototypical stimulus for an evolved module of fear. *Current Directions in Psychological Science, 12,* 5–8. https://doi.org/10.1111%2F1467-8721.01211

Olfson, M., Marcus, S. C., Druss, B., & Pincus, H. A. (2002). National trends in the outpatient treatment of depression. *The American Journal of Psychiatry, 159*(11), 1914–1920. https://doi.org/10.1176/appi.ajp.159.11.1914

Olfson, M., Wang, S., Wall, M., Marcus, S. C., & Blanco, C. (2019). Trends in serious psychological distress and outpatient mental health care of US adults. *JAMA Psychiatry, 76*(2), 152–161. https://doi.org/10.1001/jamapsychiatry.2018.3550

Online Mendelian Inheritance of Man (OMIM). McKusick-Nathans Institute for Genetic Medicine, Johns Hopkins University (Baltimore, MD) and National Center for Biotechnology Information, National Library of Medicine (Bethesda, MD), April 10, 2006. World Wide Web URL: http://www.ncbi.nlm.nih.gov/omim/

Öst, L.-G. (1992). Blood and injection phobia: Background and cognitive, physiological, and behavioral variable. *Journal of Abnormal Psychology, 101*(1), 68–74. https://doi.org/10.1037//0021-843x.101.1.68

Öst, L.-G., Alm, T., Brandberg, M., & Breitholtz, E. (2001). One vs. five sessions of exposure and five sessions of cognitive therapy in the treatment of claustrophobia. *Behaviour Research and Therapy, 39*(2), 167–183. https://doi.org/10.1016/S0005-7967(99)00176-X

Öst, L.-G., Brandberg, M., & Alm, T. (1997). One versus five sessions of exposure in the treatment of flying phobia. *Behaviour Research and Therapy, 35*(11), 987–996. https://doi.org/10.1016/S0005-7967(97)00077-6

Öst, L.-G., Salkovskis, P., & Hellström, K. (1991). One-session therapist directed exposure vs. self-exposure in the treatment of spider phobia. *Behavior Therapy, 22*(3), 407–422. https://doi.org/10.1016/S0005-7894(05)80374-0

Öst, L.-G., & Sterner, U. (1987). Applied tension: A specific behavioral method for the treatment of blood phobia. *Behavioural Research and Therapy, 25*(1), 25–29. https://doi.org/10.1016/0005-7967(87)90111-2

Paul, D. L. (2010). The genetics of obsessive-compulsive disorder: A review. *Dialogues in Clinical Neuroscience, 12*(2), 149-163. https://dx.doi.org/10.31887/DCNS.2010.12.2/dpauls

Perry, A., Tarrier, N., Morriss, R., McCarthy, E., & Limb, K. (1999). Randomised controlled trial of efficacy of teaching patients with bipolar disorder to identify early symptoms of relapse and obtain treatment. *British Medical Journal, 318,* 149–153. https://doi.org/10.1136/bmj.318.7177.149

Power, K. G, Simpson, R. J., Swanson, V., & Wallace, L. A. (1990). A controlled comparison of cognitive-behaviour therapy, diazepam, and placebo, alone and in combination, for the treatment of generalised anxiety disorder. *Journal of Anxiety Disorders, 4*(4), 267–292. https://doi.org/10.1016/0887-6185(90)90026-6

Power, R. A., Kyaga, S., Uher, R., MacCabe, J. H., Langstrom, N., Landen, M., McGuffin, P., Lewis, C. M., Lichtenstein, P., & Svensson, A. C. (2013). Fecundity of patients with schizophrenia, autism, bipolar disorder, depression, anorexia nervosa, or substance abuse vs their unaffected siblings. *JAMA Psychiatry, 70*(1), 22–30. https://doi.org/10.1001/jamapsychiatry.2013.268

Praško, J., Dockery, C., Horáček, J., Houbová, P., Kosová, J., Klaschka, J., Pašková, B., Prašková, H., Seifertová, D., Záleský, R., & Höschl, C. (2006). Moclobemide and cognitive behavioral therapy in the treatment of social phobia. A six-month controlled study and 24 months follow up. *Neuro Endocrinology Letters, 27*(4), 473–481. https://www.nel.edu/userfiles/articlesnew/NEL270406A20.pdf

Preacher, K. J., Rucker, D. D., & Hayes, A. F. (2007). Addressing moderated mediation hypotheses: Theory, methods, and prescriptions. *Multivariate Behavioral Research. 42*(1), 185–227. https://doi.org/10.1080/00273170701341316

Rabinowitz, J., Werbeloff, N., Mandel, F. S., Menard, F., Marangell, L., & Kapur, S. (2016). Initial depression severity and response to antidepressants v. placebo: Patient-level data analysis from 34 randomised controlled trials. *The British Journal of Psychiatry, 209*(5), 427–428. http://doi.org/10.1192/bjp.bp.115.173906

Rachman, S. J. (2003). *The treatment of obsessions.* Oxford University Press.

Resick, P. A., & Schnicke, M. K. (1992). Cognitive processing therapy for sexual assault victims. *Journal of Consulting and Clinical Psychology, 60*(5), 748–756. https://psycnet.apa.org/doi/10.1037/0022-006X.60.5.748

Rush, A. J., Beck, A. T., Kovacs, M., & Hollon, S. D. (1977). Comparative efficacy of cognitive therapy and pharmacotherapy in the treatment of depressed outpatients. *Cognitive Therapy and Research, 1,* 17–37. https://doi.org/10.1007/BF01173502

Rush, A. J., Trivedi, M. H., Wisniewski, S. R., Nierenberg, A. A., Stewart, J. W., Warden, D., Niederehe, G., Thase, M. E., Lavori, P. W., Lebowitz, B. D., McGrath, P. J., Rosenbaum, J. F., Sackeim, H. A., Kupfer, D. J., Luther, J., & Fava, M. (2006). Acute and longer-term outcomes in depressed outpatients requiring one or several treatment steps: A STAR*D report. *The American Journal of Psychiatry, 163*(11), 1905–1917. https://ajp.psychiatryonline.org/doi/full/10.1176/ajp.2006.163.11.1905

Salkovskis, P. M. (1999). Understanding and treating obsessive-compulsive disorder. *Behaviour Research and Therapy, 37*(Suppl. 1), S29–S52.

Scott, J. (1995). Psychotherapy for bipolar disorder. *The British Journal of Psychiatry, 167*(5), 581–588. https://doi.org/10.1192/bjp.167.5.581

Scott, J., Paykel, E., Morriss, R., Bentall, R., Kinderman, P., Johnson, T., Abbott, R., & Hayhurst, H. (2006). Cognitive-behavioural therapy for severe and recurrent bipolar disorders. *The British Journal of Psychiatry, 188*(4), 313–320. https://doi.org/10.1192/bjp.188.4.313

Sell, A., Tooby, J., & Cosmides, L. (2009). Formidability and the logic of human anger. *Proceedings of the National Academy of Science (PNAS), 106*(35), 15073–15078. https://doi.org/10.1073/pnas.0904312106

Shea, M. T., Elkin, I., Imber, S. D., Sotsky, S. M., Watkins, J. T., Collins, J. F., Pilkonis, P. A., Beckham, E., Glass, D. R., Dolan, R. T., & Parloff, M. B. (1992). Course of depressive symptoms over follow-up: Findings from the National Institute of Mental Health Treatment of Depression Collaborative Research Program. *Archives of General Psychiatry, 49*(10), 782–787. https://doi.org/10.1001/archpsyc.1992.01820100026006

Shephard, A. M., Bharwani, A., Durisko, Z., & Andrews, P. W. (2016). Reverse engineering the febrile system. *The Quarterly Review of Biology, 91*(4), 419–457. https://doi.org/10.1086/689482

Simon, E., Meuret, A., & Ritz, T. (2009). Treatments for blood-injection-injury phobia: A critical review of the current evidence. *Journal of Psychiatric Research, 43*(15), 1235–1242. https://doi.org/10.1016/j.jpsychires.2009.04.008

Simons, A. D., Murphy, G. E., Levine, J. E., & Wetzel, R. D. (1986). Cognitive therapy and pharmacotherapy for depression: Sustained improvement over one year. *Archives of General Psychiatry, 43*(1), 43–49. https://doi.org/10.1001/archpsyc.1986.01800010045006

Simpson, H. B., Liebowitz, M. R., Foa, E. B., Kozak, M. J., Schmidt, A. B., Rowan, V., Petkova, E., Kjernisted, K., Huppert, J. D., Franklin, M. E., Davies, S. O., & Campeas, R. (2004). Post-treatment effects of exposure therapy and clomipramine in obsessive-compulsive disorder. *Depression and Anxiety, 19*(4), 225–233. https://doi.org/10.1002/da.20003

Sneddon, L. U., Elwood, R. W., Adamo, S. A., & Leach, M. C. (2014). Defining and assessing animal pain. *Animal Behaviour, 97*, 201–212. https://doi.org/10.1016/j.anbehav.2014.09.007

Sousa, M. B., Isolan, L. R., Oliveira, R. R., Manfro, G. G., & Cordioli, A. V. (2006). A randomized clinical trial of cognitive-behavioral group therapy and sertraline in the treatment of obsessive-compulsive disorder. *Journal of Clinical Psychiatry, 67*(7), 1133–1139. https://doi:10.4088/JCP.V67N0717

Stafford, M. R, Jackson, H., Mayo-Wilson, E., Morrison, A. P., & Kendall, T. (2013). Early interventions to prevent psychosis: Systematic review and meta-analysis. *BMJ, 346*, f185. https://doi.org/10.1136/bmj.f185

Stangier, U., Heidenreich, T., Peitz, M., Lauterbach, W., & Clark, D. M. (2003). Cognitive therapy for social phobia: Individual versus group treatment. *Behaviour Research and Therapy, 41*(9), 991–1007. https://doi.org/10.1016/S0005-7967(02)00176-6

Stangier, U., Schramm, E., Heidenreich, T., Berger, M., & Clark, D. M. (2011). Cognitive therapy vs interpersonal psychotherapy in social anxiety disorder: A randomized controlled trial. *Archives of General Psychiatry, 68*(7), 692–700. https://doi.org/10.1001/archgenpsychiatry.2011.67

Stein, D. J., Versiani, M., Hair, T., & Kumar, R. (2002). Efficacy of paroxetine for relapse prevention in social anxiety disorder: A 24-week study. *Archives of General Psychiatry, 59*(12), 1111–1118. https://doi.org/10.1001/archpsyc.59.12.1111

Stein, M. B., Chen, C.-Y., Jain, S., Jensen, K. P., He, F., Heeringa, S. G., Kessler, R. C., Maihofer, A., Nock, M. K., Ripke, S., Sun, X., Thomas, M. L., Ursano, R. J., Smoller, J. W., & Gelernter, J. (2017). Genetic risk variants for social anxiety. *American Journal of Medical Genetics Part B Neuropsychiatric Genetics, 174*(2), 120–131. https://doi.org/10.1002/ajmg.b.32520

Stinson, F. S., Dawson, D. A., Chou, S. P., Smith, S., Goldstein, R. B., Ruan, W. J., & Grant, B. F. (2007). The epidemiology of DSM-IV specific phobia in the USA: Results from the National Epidemiologic Survey on Alcohol and Related Conditions. *Psychological Medicine, 37*(7), 1047–1059. https://doi.org/10.1017/s0033291707000086

Suomi, S. J. (2006). Risk, resilience, and gene x environment interactions in rhesus monkeys. *Annals of the New York Academy of Sciences, 1994*, 52–62. https://doi.org/10.1196/annals.1376.006

Sullivan, R. J., & Allen, J. S. (2004). Natural selection and schizophrenia. *Behavioral and Brain Sciences, 27*(6), 865–866. https://doi.org/10.1017/S0140525X04330190

Swartz, H. A., Rucci, P., Thase, M. E., Wallace, M., Carretta, E., Celedonia, K. L., & Frank, E. (2018). Psychotherapy alone and combined with medication as treatments for bipolar II depression: A randomized controlled trial. *Journal of Clinical Psychiatry, 79*(2), 16m11027. https://doi.org/10.4088/JCP.16m11027

Syme, K. L., & Hagen, E. H. (2020). Mental health is biological health: Why tackling "diseases of the mind" is an imperative for biological anthropology in the 21ˢᵗ century. *Yearbook of physical anthropology, 171*(Suppl 70), 87–117. https://doi:10.1002/ajpa.23965

Tenneij, N. H., van Megen, H. J. G. M., Denys, D. A. J. P., & Westenberg, H. G. M. (2005). Behavior therapy augments response of patients with obsessive-compulsive disorder responding to drug treatment. *Journal of Clinical Psychiatry, 66*(9), 1169–1175. https://research.vu.nl/ws/files/2114880/tenneij

Tooby, J., & Cosmides, L. (1990). The past explains the present: Emotional adaptations and the structure of ancestral environments. *Ethology and Sociobiology, 11*(4-5), 375–424. https://doi.org/10.1016/0162-3095(90)90017-Z

Tooby, J., Cosmides, L., & Barrett, H. C. (2003). The second law of thermodynamics is the first law of psychology: Evolutionary developmental psychopathology and the theory of tandem, coordinated inheritances: Comment on Lickliter and Honeycutt. *Psychological Bulletin, 129*(6), 858–865. https://doi.org/10.1037/0033-2909.129.6.858

Treisman, M. (1977). Motion sickness: An evolutionary hypothesis. *Science, 197*(4302), 493–495. https://doi.org/10.1126/science.301659

Turner, E. H., Matthews, A. M., Linardatos, E., Tell, R. A., & Rosenthal, R. (2008). Selective publication of antidepressant trials and its influence on apparent efficacy. *New England Journal of Medicine, 358*, 252–260. https://doi.org/10.1056/NEJMsa065779

van Balkom, A. J. L. M., de Haan, E., van Oppen, P. Spinhoven, P., Hoogduin, K. A., & van Dyck, R. (1998). Cognitive and behavioral therapies alone versus in combination with fluvoxamine in the treatment of obsessive-compulsive disorder. *The Journal of Nervous and Mental Disease, 186*(8), 492–499. https://research.vumc.nl/en/publications/cognitive-and-behavioral-therapies-alone

van den Hout, M. A., Rijkeboer, M. M., Engelhard, I. M., Klugkist, I., Hornsveld, H., Toffolo, M. J. B., & Cath, D. C. (2012). Tones inferior to eye movements in the EMDR treatment of PTSD. *Behaviour Research and Therapy, 50*(5), 275–279. https://doi.org/10.1016/j.brat.2012.02.001

van der Kolk, B. A., Spinazzola, J., Blaustein, M. E., Hopper, J. W., Hopper, E. K., Korn, D. L., & Simpson, W. B. (2007). A randomized clinical trial of eye movement desensitization and reprocessing (EMDR), fluoxetine, and pill placebo in the treatment of posttraumatic stress disorder: Treatment effects and long-term maintenance. *Journal of Clinical Psychiatry, 68*, 37–46. https://doi:10.4088/JCP.V68N0105

van Emmerik, A. A. P., Kamphuis, J. H., Hulsbosch, A. M., & Emmelkamp, P. M. G. (2002). Single session debriefing after psychological trauma: A meta-analysis. *The Lancet, 360*(9335), 766–771. https://doi.org/10.1016/S0140-6736(02)09897-5

Vaughn, C. E., & Leff, J. P. (1976). The influence of family and social factors on the course of psychiatric illness: A comparison of schizophrenia and depressed neurotic patients. *The British Journal of Psychiatry, 129*(2), 125–137. https://doi.org/10.1192/bjp.129.2.125

Wakefield, J. C. (1992). Disorder as harmful dysfunction: A conceptual critique of DSM-III-R's definition of mental disorder. *Psychological Review, 99*(2), 232–247. https://psycnet.apa.org/doi/10.1037/0033-295X.99.2.232

Wells, A., Welford, M., King, P., Papageorgiou, Wisely, J., & Mendel, E. (2010). A pilot randomized trial of metacognitive therapy vs applied relaxation in the treatment of adults with generalized anxiety disorder. *Behaviour Research and Therapy, 48*(5), 429–434. https://doi.org/10.1016/j.brat.2009.11.013

Whitaker, R. (2010). *Anatomy of an epidemic: Magic bullets, psychiatric drugs, and the astonishing rise of mental illness in America*. Crown Publishers.

Wils, R. S., Gotfredsen, D. R., Hjorthøj, C., Austin, S. F., Albert, N., Secher, R. G., Elgaard Thorup. A. A., Mors, O., & Nordentoft, M. (2017). Antipsychotic medication and remission of psychotic symptoms 10 years after a first-episode psychosis. *Schizophrenia Research, 182*, 42–48. https://doi.org/10.1016/j.schres.2016.10.030

Wykes, T., Steel, C., Everitt, B., & Tarrier, N. (2008). Cognitive behavior therapy for schizophrenia: Effect sizes, clinical models, and methodological rigor. *Schizophrenia Bulletin, 34*(3), 523–537. https://doi.org/10.1093/schbul/sbm114

CHAPTER 21

INTERNET APPROACHES TO PSYCHOTHERAPY: EMPIRICAL FINDINGS AND FUTURE DIRECTIONS

GERHARD ANDERSSON AND THOMAS BERGER

Abstract

During the last 20 years, many internet-delivered psychological treatments have been developed and tested for a wide range of clinical problems. Therapist-guided internet treatments are effective in controlled trials and meta-analyses on mood and anxiety disorders, but also for several health problems and transdiagnostic problems (e.g., procrastination). Controlled trials indicate that guided internet-treatments can be as effective as face-to-face treatments, that they lead to sustained improvements, work in clinically representative conditions, and are cost-effective. Less is known about moderators and mediators of change. Therapist-supported internet interventions are most likely more effective than self-guided treatments, and the alliance between therapists and patients also seems to play a role in therapy outcomes. Internet interventions hold promise as a way to increase access to evidence-based psychological treatments, and psychotherapists will likely use internet interventions as complements to face-to-face therapy in the future.

OVERVIEW

INTRODUCTION

Much has changed in the world since the first edition of this handbook (Bergin & Garfield, 1971). One significant change in society has been the introduction of information technology and, in particular, the internet (Krotoski, 2013). Both in terms of communication and access to information, the internet has arguably changed our lives and not only in the Western parts of the world but increasingly in all continents. In addition to being a way to communicate and search for information, modern information technology has also opened up new ways to experience the world in the form of games, virtual reality (VR), and perhaps new ways to form and maintain social relations in various social networks. This information technology revolution has also influenced psychotherapy research and practice. The literature on internet-delivered psychological treatments has snowballed over recent years. As we will show in this chapter, the efficacy and effectiveness of this novel treatment format has been demonstrated in many randomized controlled trials, systematic reviews, and meta-analyses for a wide range of clinical problems.

Internet-delivered treatments offer many potential benefits, such as providing broader and easier access to treatments affordably and conveniently. However, there are also concerns, for example, about confidentiality, privacy, reliability of the technology, and also whether a therapeutic alliance can develop in internet-based therapies (Berger, 2017; Rochlen, Zack, & Speyer, 2004). Negative attitudes of health care professionals toward internet-delivered interventions seem to be common (Schroeder et al., 2017), and the lack of acceptance of this new treatment format by health-care professionals was highlighted as the most critical barrier to the implementation of internet-delivered interventions into routine care (Topooco et al., 2017). Indeed, and despite the extensive body of research and potential benefits of internet-delivered interventions, the actual use and implementation of internet-delivered treatments into routine care lags behind the possibilities and remains a challenge (Vis et al., 2018).

As we write this chapter, the world is still in the middle of the coronavirus pandemic. Therapists and mental health service providers have been forced to either pause therapy or provide therapy at a distance such as via video-conferencing psychotherapy. Suddenly even therapists who would never have tried without having been forced to find a solution, have begun using new technologies. Anecdotally, many of these therapists tell us that therapy at a distance works surprisingly well. Accordingly, it has been argued that the current "black swan" moment – an unforeseen event that changes everything - will soon lead to a shift in mental health care provision toward internet-delivered therapy and care (Wind et al., 2020).

While the future will show whether the coronavirus pandemic will provide internet-delivered therapies with a sustained impetus, this chapter focusses on current evidence for internet-delivered treatment. As already mentioned, there is now a large body of research on internet interventions. It is important to note that the internet can be involved in many aspects of the treatment process that are not covered in this chapter, such as searching for treatment alternatives, checking out a specific therapist, completing online assessments instead of paper and pencil tests, getting feedback on progress, as well as the measurement of therapy outcomes. Also, not covered here are VR exposures, attention training programs, serious games, and various other components that can be part of the treatment being delivered from a distance using the internet (Andersson, 2015). Besides these specific applications, there are various forms of internet-delivered treatments. Before presenting the empirical evidence, we will first define and distinguish various types of internet approaches to psychotherapy.

TYPES OF INTERNET APPROACHES TO PSYCHOTHERAPY

Defining internet-delivered psychological treatments can be difficult as the internet can be used for various types of activities, such as communicating with the client, and providing information (Barak et al., 2009). Moreover, many terms have been used to describe therapeutic activities conducted via the internet, such as e-therapy, cybertherapy, online therapy,

e-mental health, computer-mediated interventions, or web-based treatments. Generally, internet approaches to psychotherapy can be divided according to various criteria, such as (a) therapist involvement, (b) communication mode, (c) therapeutic approach and content, and (d) combination with in-person therapy.

Therapist Involvement

A first possible distinction of internet-delivered treatments relates to the amount and intensity of therapist contact and support provided during treatment. There are: (a) online therapies such as email, chat or video-conferencing therapies, in which the internet is used as a communication medium between the therapist and the patient; (b) web-based (unguided) self-help programs that only use the internet to provide information and that do not include any contact with a therapist during treatment; and (c) internet-based guided self-help approaches, in which the presentation of a web-based self-help program is combined with regular, often weekly, therapist contact.

Communication Mode

A second distinction relates to the communication mode used between therapists and patients in treatment formats that include contact with a therapist. Modes of communication in online therapies using the internet as a communication medium include: (a) text-based and asynchronous communication (i.e., email therapy); (b) text-based and almost real-time communication (i.e., chat therapy); and (c) audio- or video-based real-time communication.

Therapeutic Approach and Content

Internet-delivered treatments differ concerning therapeutic approach and content on which a treatment is based. The majority of research and implementations have focused on internet-delivered cognitive behavioral therapy (ICBT). However, there are studies on interventions following psychodynamic principles (Andersson, Paxling et al., 2012), interpersonal psychotherapy (Donker et al., 2013), integrative approaches (Meyer et al., 2009) and different forms of CBT such as acceptance and commitment therapy (Lappalainen et al., 2014).

In terms of content, the web-based self-help programs used in guided and unguided treatments often comprise self-help texts that can be of similar length as self-help books. The text can be supplemented by figures, pictures, film, and interactive graphs. Moreover, there are examples of self-help materials that are available for listening as an option for the client (i.e., like an audiobook) (Klein et al., 2011). The contents of a typical internet treatment comprise separate chapters/modules/lessons (different terms are used). As most internet interventions have been based on CBT, a typical treatment program would comprise five key components: (a) information and psychoeducation; (b) introduction to concepts and making your own formulation including rationale for the whole treatment; (c) information regarding specific treatment components such as working with thoughts, registrations sheets and homework assignments; (d) further modules that follow the previous steps, for example, exposure instructions and rationale for each technique to be tested; and (e) summary and advice on relapse (Andersson, 2015).

In terms of length, the programs tend to mimic manualized treatments but are often a bit shorter. For example, an internet depression program might last 8 weeks (Andersson et al., 2005), even if a program for social anxiety disorder used in clinical practice was extended to 15 weeks (El Alaoui et al., 2015). There are also examples of shorter programs, for example, five weeks for specific phobia (Andersson, Waara, et al.,

2013). An example of a screenshot of a treatment program is provided in Figure 21.1.

Combination with In-Person Therapy

Internet-based interventions can be delivered entirely via the internet, or they can be blended with conventional face-to-face sessions. Most of the research on internet interventions has focused on treatments that are delivered entirely via the internet. However, there is a growing literature with large trials on blended treatments (Kleiboer et al., 2016), and some

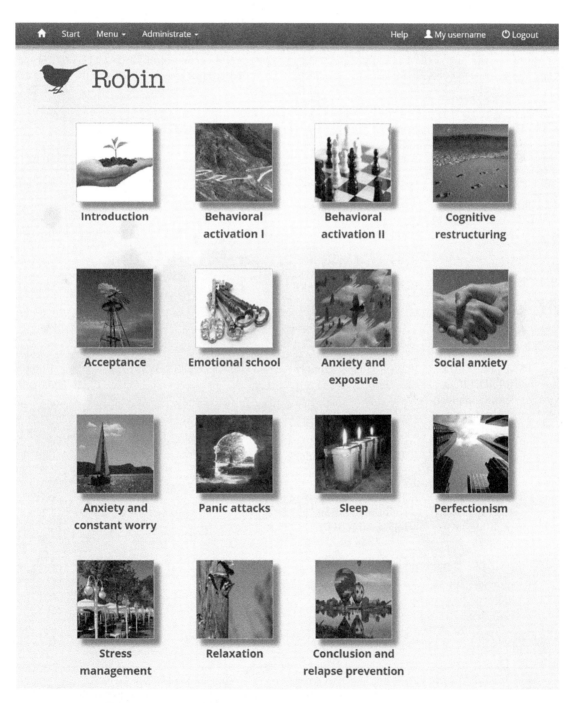

FIGURE 21.1 Screenshot of Iterapi program landing page

results are suggesting that therapist time can be substantially reduced without any loss of efficacy when adding internet-based treatment modules (Thase et al., 2018). The term *blended treatment* can include any possible combination of regular face-to-face treatments and web-based interventions (Erbe et al., 2017). For instance, treatment components of a web-delivered intervention may be integrated intensively and used during the face-to-face treatment or may rather be used as an adjunctive intervention (Berger et al., 2018).

EMPIRICAL FINDINGS

While internet interventions have existed for only about 20 years and therefore might be expected to have a limited evidence-base, this is not the case as there is a large number of controlled trials and at least 300 RCTs for a range of client

conditions and disorders. The approach taken here is to cover a majority of the topics and, where possible, refer to systematic reviews and meta-analyses. As can be seen from the overview of the evidence below, the main bulk of research has been on internet-based guided and unguided self-help approaches. Thus, most interventions with empirical evidence include a web-based self-help program and a supportive therapist. There are far fewer controlled trials of online therapies such as chat-, email-, and video-conferencing therapies, using the internet only as a communication medium.

Research Findings on Anxiety and Related Disorders

An overview of the evidence for anxiety disorders and related disorders is presented in Table 21.1. A Cochrane Review that included studies treating adults with social anxiety disorder,

TABLE 21.1 Recent Meta-Analyses of Internet Interventions for Anxiety Disorders

Meta-analysis	Condition(s)	Treatment	Comparisons	$N_{studies}$ ($N_{subjects}$)	Hedges' g (95% CI)
Andrews et al. (2018)	SAD	ICBT + clinical support	WLC	11 (950)	0.92 (0.76, 1.08)
	PD	ICBT + clinical support	WLC/IC	12 (584)	1.31 (0.85, 1.76)
	GAD	ICBT + clinical support	WLC	9 (1103)	0.70 (0.39, 1.01)
Carlbring et al. (2018)	SAD	ICBT + clinical support	F2F	3 (261)	0.16 (−0.16, 0.47)
	PD	ICBT + clinical support	F2F	3 (248)	−0.05 (-0.30, 0.20)
Kampmann et al. (2016)	SAD	ICBT/IPT + clinical support (five studies/ conditions on unguided ICBT)	WLC	16 (1274)	0.84 (0.72, 0.97)
Olthuis et al. (2016)	SAD, PD, GAD, PTSD, OCD, specific phobia, multiple anxiety disorders	ICBT + clinical support	WLC/IC/ODG F2F	30 (2147) 7 (450)	1.06 (0.82, 1.29) −0.06 (−0.37, 0.25)
Richards et al., (2015)	GAD	ICBT/IPDT/mindfulness + clinical support	WLC	8 (570)	0.91 (0.56, 1.25)
Romijn et al. (2019)	SAD, PD, GAD, specific phobia, multiple anxiety disorders	ICBT + clinical support (4 studies/conditions on unguided ICBT)	WLC	41 (2920)	0.72 (0.60, 0.83)
	SAD, PD, specific phobia, multiple anxiety disorders	ICBT + clinical support	F2F	12 (788)	0.12 (−0.02, 0.26)
Sijbrandij et al. (2016)	PTSD	ICBT + clinical support	WL/SC/TAU	12 (1306)	0.71 (0.49, 0.93)

Note: SAD = social anxiety disorder; PD = panic disorder with or without agoraphobia; GAD = generalized anxiety disorder; PTSD = post-traumatic stress disorder; OCD = obsessive compulsive disorder; ICBT = internet-based cognitive behavioral therapy; IPT = interpersonal psychotherapy; IPDT = internet-based psychodynamic treatment ; F2F = face-to-face therapy; WLC = wait-list control; IC = information control; ODG = online discussion group; SC = supportive counselling; TAU = treatment as usual panic disorder, agoraphobia, generalized anxiety disorder, specific phobia, post-traumatic stress disorder and obsessive compulsive disorder showed between-group effect sizes (ES) of Hedges' $g = 1.06$ (30 studies; $N = 2147$ participants) in the comparison of guided self-help treatments with wait list, information, or discussion group only control groups, and between-group ESs of $g = 0.06$ comparing guided ICBT with face-to-face CBT (7 studies; $N = 450$) at posttreatment on disorder-specific anxiety symptoms (Olthuis et al., 2016). A more recent meta-analysis found a nonsignificant between-group effect of $g = 0.12$ (in favor of internet-based interventions) in 12 studies ($N = 788$) comparing internet-based treatment with face-to-face treatment (Romijn et al., 2019).

Concerning specific disorders and starting with *social anxiety disorder* (previously referred to as social phobia), a meta-analysis comparing guided and unguided self-help treatments with wait-list control groups in 16 trials ($N = 1274$) reported an average between-group ES of $g = 0.84$ (Kampmann et al., 2016). Another meta-analysis, including studies comparing internet-based guided treatment with face-to-face therapy, showed nonsignificant between-group effects of $g = 0.16$ in favor of internet-based interventions (three studies, $N = 261$; (Carlbring et al., 2018).

Social anxiety disorder is one of the clinical fields where research on Internet-based treatments has been most extensive during the last decade, with randomized controlled trials not only on ICBT but also on psychodynamic internet treatment (Johansson et al., 2017), interpersonal psychotherapy in a self-help format (Dagöö et al., 2014), and acceptance-oriented CBT (Gershkovich et al., 2017). Furthermore, ICBT has been tested in a group treatment format (Schulz et al., 2016) and delivered via a mobile application (Stolz et al., 2018). All these approaches and formats achieved effects similar to those reported in the meta-analyses mentioned above. Similar effects have also been found in applications for younger adults (Kahlke et al., 2019; Tillfors et al., 2011). Furthermore, effectiveness trials showed large within-groups ESs in patients undergoing routine care (El Alaoui et al., 2015; Nordgreen et al., 2018). In addition, there are studies on long-term outcomes that we will cover later.

With regard to *panic disorder, with or without agoraphobia*, there are controlled trials conducted in at least eight countries. To our knowledge, there has been no focused study on therapeutic orientations other than CBT. One meta-analysis on guided ICBT showed a between-group ES against waiting list or information control groups at post-treatment of $g = 1.31$, based on 12 trials ($N = 584$; (Andrews et al., 2018). Another meta-analysis only including trials comparing guided ICBT with face-to-face CBT found a nonsignificant average between-group ES of $g = 0.06$ (Carlbring et al., 2018); three studies, $N = 248$. Furthermore, the effectiveness of guided ICBT has also been shown when delivered within routine psychiatric care, with pre- to posttreatment ESs of $g = 1.1$ ($N = 570$ patients; Hedman, Ljótsson, et al., 2013). ICBT has also shown to be effective for children with the caveat that panic disorder was one of several conditions included (Jolstedt et al., 2018). In this study, children aged 8–12 years with a diagnosis of principal anxiety disorder were randomized either to guided ICBT ($n = 66$) or internet-delivered child-directed play ($n =$

65). The clinician-assessed severity rating of the principal anxiety disorder improved significantly after the 12-week treatment in both groups. However, greater improvement was seen with ICBT than with the active control, with a between-group ES of $d = 0.77$ (Jolstedt et al., 2018). Older clients have not been the topic of separate trials on panic disorder but have been included in transdiagnostic studies and shown to be effective with large within-group ESs (Dear et al., 2015; Titov et al., 2016).

Concerning *generalized anxiety disorder*, a meta-analysis comparing internet-based guided treatment with waiting list control groups reported an average between-group ES at post-treatment of $g = 0.91$ based on eight studies ($N = 570$; (Richards et al., 2015). This meta-analysis also included a trial on psychodynamic internet treatment (Andersson, Paxling, et al., 2012) and a mindfulness-based intervention (Boettcher et al., 2014). Another meta-analysis with slightly different studies found a similar result ($g = 0.70$ based on 9 studies; $N = 1103$ participants; Andrews et al., 2018). To our knowledge, there are no studies focused on children and adolescents, but large within-group ESs for older adults have been reported (Titov et al., 2016). The effectiveness of guided ICBT in routine practice has also been shown, with pre- to posttreatment ESs of $d = 0.91$ ($N = 588$ patients; Mewton et al., 2012). GAD has been a common condition in trials on transdiagnostic ICBT, which we will cover separately.

Although *posttraumatic stress disorder (PTSD)* has been assigned to the Trauma and Stressor-related Disorders category in the *DSM-5* (American Psychiatric Association, 2013), we address the condition here. There are trials on different forms of ICBT, including a treatment protocol called Interapy, which was one of the first internet-delivered treatments (Lange et al., 2000). In Interapy, individuals are asked to describe details of the trauma in writing (imaginal exposure), to reappraise the trauma (cognitive restructuring), and to perform a social sharing and farewell ritual. In a meta-analysis that also includes guided ICBT that more closely resembles regular face-to-face CBT, an average between-group ES at posttreatment of $g = 0.71$ has been reported (Sijbrandij et al., 2016). This meta-analysis was based on 12 studies ($N = 1139$) and compared ICBT with wait-list control groups, treatment as usual, or supportive counseling. There is also an effectiveness study showing large within-group ESs, specifically for Interapy in routine practice (Ruwaard et al., 2012). There are no controlled studies on other treatment forms than CBT, except for a study on internet-delivered computerized cognitive and affective remediation training (Fonzo et al., 2019). Furthermore, trauma-related studies have been published for specific target groups, with one example being a trial on women who had experienced traumatic childbirth (Nieminen et al., 2016).

Obsessive-compulsive disorder (OCD) is no longer categorized as an anxiety disorder in the DSM V (American Psychiatric Association, 2013) but, as with PTSD, we will address the disorder here given the overlap with anxiety disorders. In a meta-analysis comparing guided ICBT with wait-list control groups, between-group ESs of $g = 0.85$ were reported, based on four trials ($N = 238$; Pozza et al., 2016). There are also a few reports showing large pre- to post effects in regular clinical settings (Klein et al., 2011). Interestingly, there is one trial on the combination of d-cycloserine and ICBT (Andersson et al., 2015), suggesting that ICBT lends itself to translational research combining pharmacological and psychological interventions. There is also a trial on OCD in adolescents and children involving support from parents in the treatment showing promising between-group ESs of $d = 0.69$ on the primary assessor-blinded OCD measure in comparison with a wait-list control group (Lenhard et al., 2017). On a related note, there is a study on body dysmorphic disorder showing large between-group ESs of $d = 0.95$ in the comparison of ICBT with supportive therapy delivered online (Enander et al., 2016).

There are only a few studies on *specific phobia*, but two small trials have directly compared one-session live exposure treatment against therapist-guided ICBT for spider phobia (Andersson et al., 2009) and snake phobia (Andersson, Waara, et al., 2013). Both studies indicated equivalence and large within-group ESs but were too small to allow any conclusions. There is also a small trial on flight phobia showing large effects of guided and unguided ICBT against a waiting-list condition (Campos et al., 2019). In addition, pilot studies on specific phobia in children with parent involvement (Vigerland et al., 2013) and an open study on dental phobia have been conducted, all showing large within-group ESs (Shahnavaz et al., 2018).

Overall, more and larger studies are needed in the field of ICBT for specific phobia. A promising development here is internet-based treatments in virtual reality. Given technological advances and cost reductions, VR can now be delivered as part of an ICBT program (e.g., with therapist contact and outcome measures delivered via the internet and the treatment presented in a smartphone application) (Lindner et al., 2017). In a recent trial, 193 individuals with acrophobia symptoms and access to a smartphone were randomized to either self-guided app-based virtual-reality CBT using low-cost (cardboard) VR goggles or a waiting-list control group. Results showed a significant reduction of acrophobia symptoms at posttreatment for the VR app compared with the controls (Donker et al., 2019).

Severe health anxiety, also referred to as illness anxiety disorder (previously known as hypochondriasis), is characterized by excessive concern about having or developing a serious, undiagnosed general medical disease (American Psychiatric Association, 2013). There are controlled efficacy trials from Sweden. For instance, in the comparison of guided ICBT with an attention control condition, large between-group ESs of $d = 1.52$–1.62 on health anxiety measures were reported (Hedman et al., 2011). In a trial on illness anxiety disorder and somatic symptom disorder conducted in Australia, guided ICBT was compared with an active control group who received anxiety psychoeducation, clinical support, and monitoring. Results showed large between-group effects of $d = 1.39$ on the primary health anxiety measure (Newby et al., 2018). There are no effectiveness trials or published comparisons against face-to-face treatment.

In sum, internet-delivered psychological treatments have been developed and tested for most anxiety disorders. There is strong evidence of effects for some conditions (e.g., social anxiety disorder), but also a need for more research on disorders such as specific phobia. In some conditions, such as social anxiety disorder and panic disorder, controlled trials indicate that guided treatments can be as effective as face-to-face treatments. Furthermore, trials on internet interventions based on approaches other than ICBT, such as a psychodynamic approach, interpersonal psychotherapy, and mindfulness and acceptance-oriented approaches, also show promise.

Research Findings on Mood Disorders

Major depression and *depressive symptoms* have been the focus of a large number of controlled studies. Some of the largest psychotherapy trials have been on ICBT for depression, which included more than 1000 participants (Klein et al., 2016). We present an overview of meta-analyses in Table 21.2. For depressive symptoms, there is a large literature on unguided internet interventions, including an individual patient-level meta-analysis (IPDMA) reporting an average between-group ES of $g = 0.33$ in comparison with waiting-list, care-as-usual, and attention control groups in 16 studies (Karyotaki et al., 2017). Almost the same pooled ES of $g = 0.36$ for unguided interventions was found in the meta-analysis of Richards and Richardson (2012), which reported an average between groups ES of $g = 0.56$ for both unguided and guided interventions (see Table 21.2).

Many studies have included therapist-support ranging from minor support (asynchronous email 10 minutes per week) to scheduled real-time chat sessions (Topooco et al., 2018). In the meta-analysis of Richards and Richardson (2012), therapist-guided interventions showed ESs of $g = 0.78$ in comparison with wait-list and care-as-usual control groups. Königbauer et al. (2017) report a between-groups ES of $g = 0.90$ for guided self-help interventions in 10 studies, including participants fulfilling the diagnostic criteria of major depressive disorder or dysthymia. In a meta-analysis comprising four studies ($N = 261$) that only included trials comparing internet-based with face-to-face therapy, results showed nonsignificant between-group effects of $g = 0.16$ in favor of internet-based interventions (Carlbring et al., 2018).

In the field of internet-based depression treatment, there is also a large depression trial on online CBT delivered in real-time via text chats (Kessler et al., 2009). In this multicenter trial, 297 individuals with a confirmed diagnosis of depression were randomly assigned to therapist-delivered chat therapy in addition to usual care or usual care from their general practitioner. The primary outcome was recovery from depression at four months. Results showed that 38% of the patients in the chat therapy group recovered from depression versus 24% in the control group at four months (odds ratio 2.39).

Individualized email therapy has been compared with a guided self-help approach, both based on CBT, for individuals with major depression (Vernmark et al., 2010). Results showed significant symptom reductions in both treatment groups with moderate to large ESs in comparison with a waiting list control group. Overall, these findings indicated that both guided self-help and individualized email therapy can be effective. Moreover, there is a systematic review, but no meta-analysis, on video-conferencing psychotherapy for depression (Berryhill et al., 2019). In this review, which also included some studies targeting

TABLE 21.2 Recent Meta-Analyses of Internet Interventions for Depressive Symptoms and Disorders

Meta-analysis	Condition(s)	Treatment	Comparisons	$N_{studies}$ ($N_{subjects}$)	Hedges' g (95% CI)
Andrews et al. (2018)	MDD/Dys/Depressive Symptoms	ICBT/IPDT + clinical support (4 studies/conditions without clinical support)	WLC/IC/CAU	32 (5642)	0.67 (0.51, 0.81)
Carlbring et al. (2018)	Depressive Symptoms	ICBT/iACT + clinical support	F2F	4 (261)	0.16 (-0.16, 0.47)
Karyotaki et al. (2017)	Depressive Symptoms	ICBT without clinical support	WLC/CAU/attention placebo	16 (4590)	0.33 (0.19, 0.46)
Königbauer et al. (2018)	MDD/Dys	ICBT + clinical support/email therapy	WLC	10 (N/A)	0.90 (0.73, 1.07)
Richards et al., (2012)	MDD/Dys/Depressive Symptoms	ICBT with and without clinical support/ chat, email therapy; IPST/structured writing intervention	WLC/CAU	19 (2996)	0.56 (0.41, 0.71)

Note: MDD = major depressive disorder; Dys = dysthymia; ICBT = internet-based cognitive behavioral therapy; IPT = interpersonal psychotherapy; IPDT = internet-based psychodynamic treatment ; IACT = internet-based acceptance and commitment therapy; IPST = internet-based problem-solving therapy; F2F = face-to-face therapy; WLC = wait-list control; IC = information control; CAU = care as usual anxiety disorders, most of the 13 randomized controlled trials reported no statistical differences between video-conferencing psychotherapy and in-person therapy, and significant reductions in depressive symptoms with within-group ESs ranging from medium to very large (Berryhill et al., 2019).

Effectiveness studies have also shown large within-group ESs for guided self-help in routine practice (Ruwaard et al., 2012). The most studied psychotherapy form for depression is CBT (Webb et al., 2017). However, there are internet trials on acceptance and commitment therapy (Lappalainen et al., 2014), problem-solving therapy (Warmerdam et al., 2010), behavioral activation (Carlbring et al., 2013), psychodynamic treatment (Johansson et al., 2012), interpersonal psychotherapy (Donker et al., 2013), and transdiagnostic and tailored CBT-oriented interventions (see Research Findings on Transdiagnostic Interventions below). The studies on these treatments showed the same pattern of results as ICBT, with medium-to-large effects for therapist-guided and small-to-medium effects for unguided interventions.

There are programs for specific groups such as older adults showing large within-group ESs (Titov et al., 2015). Furthermore, there are trials on *postpartum* and *antenatal depression* (e.g., O'Mahen et al., 2014). A meta-analysis showed medium-to-large between-group ESs of $g = 0.63$ on depressive symptoms based on eight trials in the comparison of guided self-help versus wait-list and usual care controls (Lau et al., 2017). There is also not much research on *bipolar disorder* to date (Hidalgo-Mazzei et al., 2015), but a recent controlled trial showed promising results (Gliddon et al., 2019).

Some controlled studies have investigated comorbid depression as an outcome in patients with *neurological* or *somatic disorders* such as *epilepsy*, *multiple sclerosis*, and *diabetes*. In a trial investigating unguided ICBT in patients with epilepsy, a neurological disorder that is often accompanied by comorbid depression, Schroeder et al. (2014) observed a small-to-medium ES in depression symptoms ($d = 0.29$) and in fatigue ($d = 0.32$). In another trial with patients with multiple sclerosis, an inflammatory, demyelinating neurodegenerative disease of the central nervous system that often involves depressive symptoms, patients receiving unguided ICBT experienced a significant decline in depressive symptoms and motor fatigue with medium ESs ($d = 0.52$ and $d = 0.46$, respectively), compared with usual care (Fischer et al., 2015). Another trial examined the efficacy of guided ICBT for patients with diabetes and comorbid depressive symptoms. In comparison with a brief online unguided psychoeducation program for depression, participants receiving guided ICBT showed significantly less depressive symptom severity at posttreatment ($d = 0.89$; Nobis et al., 2015).

In summary, a large number of controlled trials have demonstrated the efficacy of internet interventions for major depression and depressive symptoms. Meta-analyses report small-to-medium effect sizes for unguided self-help treatments, and medium-to-large effect sizes when delivered as guided interventions, both compared with wait-list or usual-care control groups. As in other conditions, most studies were on ICBT. However, controlled trials on other therapeutic approaches, such as psychodynamic treatment, interpersonal psychotherapy, problem-solving therapy, behavioral activation, and acceptance and commitment therapy showed the same pattern of results as ICBT. Some trials are indicating that guided internet interventions and face-to-face treatments produce equivalent overall effects. However, more studies, preferably with larger sample sizes, are needed to establish the equivalence of the two treatment formats.

Research Findings on Transdiagnostic Interventions

Given the substantial overlap between anxiety and mood disorders programs, studies have tested transdiagnostic internet intervention approaches. Here we present findings on mindfulness-based online interventions, as well as on combined results for tailoring and unified treatments. With regard to mindfulness, controlled trials have been summarized in a meta-analysis (Sevilla-Llewellyn-Jones et al., 2018). The authors included 12 controlled studies and found that internet-based mindfulness interventions were effective in reducing depression in their total clinical sample ($d = 0.61$), which was also the case in a subgroup with anxiety disorders ($d = 0.65$), but not in a subgroup with depression ($d = 0.21$).

With regard to tailoring, treatment modules are selected based on information from questionnaires, clinical interviews, and preferences. Tailored ICBT sometimes includes fixed treatment modules and then optional or selected modules; for example, introduction and closure/end may be fixed whereas working with stress, anxiety, mood, relaxation, social anxiety, etc. can be selected (Carlbring et al., 2010). In contrast, unified treatments, informed by the work of Barlow (Barlow et al., 2004), involve a core set of CBT techniques that are transdiagnostic in nature (e.g., working with dysfunctional thoughts) (Titov et al., 2010). In some transdiagnostic ICBT treatments, there are also optional additional modules making the difference between tailored and transdiagnostic/unified treatment smaller (Berger et al., 2014). A meta-analysis of tailored and transdiagnostic ICBT treatments based on 19 controlled trials found large between-group effects on anxiety outcomes ($g = 0.82$) and depression outcomes ($g = 0.79$) in comparison with wait-list control groups, but no difference between the two approaches (Păsărelu et al., 2017). The exception was a larger effect of transdiagnostic ICBT on quality of life measures. In sum, there is evidence to suggest that transdiagnostic and tailored ICBT and possibly mindfulness are effective in treating symptoms of anxiety and depression.

Research Findings on Somatic Disorders, Insomnia, Addictions, Eating Disorders, and Stress

As with anxiety and mood disorders, there is a vast literature on *somatic disorders* and *problems* (Mehta et al., 2019) and this field is growing rapidly, putting our review at risk of missing studies or not fully representing conditions for which there are few studies and no systematic reviews. Examples include conditions like *Parkinson's disease* (Kraepelien et al., 2015) and *chronic fatigue* (Janse et al., 2018), for which there is much less work than for problems such as *chronic pain*. In Table 21.3, we limit the number of conditions to the ones for which there are available focused meta-analyses. We refer to other conditions as well in the text.

Controlled studies (Buhrman et al., 2004), comparisons against face-to-face treatment (de Boer et al., 2014), effectiveness studies (Dear et al., 2018), and meta-analyses (Buhrman et al., 2016) have been reported with regards to *chronic pain* and *headache*, the latter being one of the first somatic conditions for which an internet treatment was developed and tested (Ström et al., 2000). Based on 22 studies ($N = 5642$), Buhrman et al. (2016) reported an average between-group ES of $g = 0.39$ for guided and unguided ICBT, as well as internet-based acceptance and commitment therapy (ACT) versus waiting-list, treatment as usual, and active controls. In line with face-to-face treatment, the observed effects tend to be small-to-medium, with notable exceptions such as studies on *fibromyalgia* showing large effects (Hedman-Lagerlöf et al., 2018).

Tinnitus, dizziness, and *hearing disorders* have been the topic of much research, and in particular tinnitus (constant ringing or buzzing in the ear), for which many trials have been conducted (Andersson et al., 2002). A recent meta-analysis reported the reduction of tinnitus distress compared with both waiting list ($g = 0.59$) and active controls ($g = 0.32$; Beukes et al., 2019). ICBT and face-to-face group CBT were also compared in one study of chronic tinnitus, and no significant difference was found (Jasper et al., 2014). There is also evidence for the effectiveness of ICBT in clinical settings (Kaldo-Sandstrom et al., 2004). Some studies have also been carried out on hearing loss and dizziness, showing small to moderate effects (Beukes et al., 2019). One example is a trial on acceptance-oriented ICBT for persons with hearing loss and psychological distress (Molander et al., 2018).

Cancer is a heterogeneous topic, not only with respect to various forms of the disease, but also in terms of different interventions and forms of support that have been investigated. Here we focus on psychological treatments such as ICBT, for which only a few controlled studies have been reported and no large-scale meta-analysis has been conducted. However, separate studies and reviews have focused on factors associated with cancer such as fatigue (Abrahams et al., 2017) and insomnia (Zachariae et al., 2018). In the trial conducted by Abrahams et al. (2017), 122 disease-free severely fatigued survivors of breast cancer, were randomly allocated to guided ICBT or care as usual. The ICBT group reported significantly lower fatigue scores at six months with large between-group ESs ($d = 1.0$). Zachariae et al. (2018) found large ESs ($d = 1.17$) of an unguided

TABLE 21.3   Recent Meta-Analyses of Internet Interventions for Somatic Disorders, Insomnia, Addictions, and Stress

Meta-analysis	Condition(s)	Treatment	Comparisons	$N_{studies}$ ($N_{subjects}$)	Hedges' g (95% CI)
Buhrman et al. (2016)	Chronic pain and headache	ICBT/ACT+ clinical support (5 studies without clinical support)	WLC/TAU/ AC/F2F	22 (5642)	0.39 (0.20, 0.56)
Beukes et al. (2019)	Tinnitus and hearing loss	ICBT/iACT + clinical support	WLC/AC/F2F	15 (1811)	0.59 (0.29, 0.90)
Zachariae et al., (2016)	Insomnia	ICBT with ($n = 6$) and without ($n = 5$) clinical support	WLC/AC	11 (1460)	1.09 (0.74, 1.45)
Riper et al. (2014)	Alcohol Misuse	ICBT, PNF, MI with and without support	WLC/Alcohol brochure	23 (5612)	0.20 (0.13, 0.27)
Boumparis et al. (2017)	Illicit Substance Misuse	ICBT, MI, CRA with and without support	WLC/TAU/AC	17 (2836)	0.31 (0.23, 0.39)
Heber et al. (2017)	Stress	Stress management, mindfulness, problem solving, emotion regulation with ($n = 10$) and without ($n = 16$) clinical support	WLC/NT/ attention placebo	26 (4226)	0.43 (0.31, 0.54)

Note: ICBT = internet-based cognitive behavioral therapy; ACT = acceptance and commitment therapy; PNF = personalized normative feedback; MI = motivational interviewing; CRA = community reinforcement approach; WLC = wait-list control; TAU = care as usual; AC = active controls; F2F = face-to-face treatment; NT = no treatment

ICBT program on insomnia in breast cancer survivors in comparison with wait-list control group. In another trial, 129 newly diagnosed patients with cancer were randomly assigned to guided ICBT or a care-as-usual control group (Urech et al., 2018). ICBT was effective in significantly improving quality of life and reducing distress, but not in changing anxiety or depression (Urech et al., 2018).

Irritable bowel syndrome (IBS) is a common pain-related condition. To our knowledge, trials have been conducted in Sweden (Ljótsson, Hedman, et al., 2011) and the United States (Hunt et al., 2009). The interventions have mainly been focused on exposure, but since components of mindfulness were included, the Swedish program has sometimes been wrongly categorized as a mindfulness treatment. Controlled efficacy trials (Ljótsson, Hedman, et al., 2011) and effectiveness trials (Ljótsson, Andersson, et al., 2011) have been published showing moderate to large between-group ESs on primary IBS-symptoms in comparison with wait-list control groups (e.g., $d = 0.77$; Ljótsson, Andersson, et al., 2011). Furthermore, a medium between-group effect was found for guided ICBT for adolescents (13–17 years of age) in comparison with a wait-list control group (Bonnert et al., 2017).

Cardiovascular disease is a significant challenge for health care, and psychological distress, including symptoms of depression, are common (Cohen et al., 2015). Research on internet interventions in this field has so far been limited to a few trials. Findings have been mixed, with some studies showing nonexistent or small effects (Norlund et al., 2018) and a few more promising on depression outcomes (Johansson et al., 2019). In their systematic review of internet-delivered self-management programs for patients with coronary heart disease, Palacios et al. (2017) found seven trials ($N = 1321$) and a considerable heterogeneity between studies in terms of the intervention content, outcomes measured, study quality, and outcome. They concluded that more well-designed randomized controlled trials are needed.

There are several trials and programs for *insomnia*, with the first being published on a Swedish program (Ström et al., 2004), which has subsequently been replicated by different research groups in, for example, the United States (Ritterband, Thorndike, Gonder-Frederick, et al., 2009), the Netherlands (Luik et al., 2019), and Switzerland (Krieger, Urech, et al., 2019). As shown in Table 21.3, a meta-analysis reported an average between-group ES of $g = 1.09$ concerning insomnia severity for guided and unguided ICBT in comparison with mainly wait-list control groups based on 11 studies ($N = 1460$; Zachariae et al., 2016). In addition to these studies, there is evidence that guided ICBT can be as effective as group-delivered face-to-face CBT, with large ESs in both treatment conditions (Blom et al., 2015). Furthermore, there is initial evidence that ICBT for insomnia also works in routine practice (Elison et al., 2017).

Internet interventions, often informed by CBT and motivational interviewing, have also been developed and tested for addictions including *smoking* (Taylor et al., 2017), *alcohol* (Hoch et al., 2016), *cannabis* (Boumparis et al., 2019), and other *illicit drugs* such as opioids (Boumparis et al., 2017). There are also programs and trials on pathological gambling (Carlbring & Smit, 2008). In addition to controlled trials, implementation studies and patient-level meta-analyses have been conducted (Riper et al., 2018). From these meta-analyses, it can be concluded that internet interventions are effective in achieving positive behavioral change through reducing problematic behaviors (Chebli et al., 2016). However, the ESs in comparison with waiting lists tend to be small to moderate (see Table 21.3).

A systematic review of internet-based interventions for *eating disorders* in adults identified eight randomized controlled trials with a total of 609 participants (Dolemeyer et al., 2013). Seven of the eight studies were based on CBT, and they were found to be beneficial in comparison with waiting-list control groups with small-to-moderate ESs ranging between $d = 0.20$ and $d = 0.52$ on primary outcome measures such as binge episodes and purging. In a direct comparison of guided ICBT with individual face-to-face CBT for full or subsyndromal binge eating disorder, ICBT was inferior in reducing the number of days with objective binge eating episodes and eating disorder psychopathology with small-to-medium ESs ranging between $g = 0.22$ and $g = 0.41$ (de Zwaan et al., 2017). Thus, face-to-face treatment may be the better treatment option for binge eating disorder.

Interestingly, quite a few trials on prevention of eating disorders have been conducted with internet-based treatments (Winzelberg et al., 2000). In their meta-analysis, Loucas et al. (2014) identified 13 studies using ICBT, and they reported small reductions in eating disorder psychopathology, weight concern, and drive for thinness with ESs of around $g = 0.30$ in comparison with wait-list control groups.

Based on the promising results of an early trial (Zetterqvist et al., 2003), several studies have been conducted on stress management. A recent meta-analysis included 23 trials, showing a small-to-medium between-group ES ($g = 0.43$; Heber et al., 2017; see Table 21.3). However, as is often the case, guided interventions ($g = 0.64$) were found to be significantly better than unguided internet treatments ($g = 0.33$), which indicates that stress is a problem for which guidance makes a difference. Effects were also moderated by the theoretical orientation of the interventions with CBT and ACT being more effective than other interventions. In this literature, there are also studies on subgroups such as middle managers (Persson Asplund et al., 2018), employees (Heber et al., 2016), and students (Hintz et al., 2015). Importantly, however, we could not find any direct comparisons between face-to-face and internet-delivered stress management. In addition, there are too few studies and many uncertainties with regard to effectiveness to ascertain that data collected in regular practice show similar findings to those observed in research trials (Frazier et al., 2015).

In sum, the literature on somatic disorders, insomnia, addictions, eating disorders, and stress is growing rapidly. The current findings suggest that internet interventions can be effective for these major health problems. In some conditions such as addictions, eating disorders, and some of the somatic disorders, the ESs in comparison with wait-list or usual-care control groups are small-to-medium, but from a public health point of view, this may warrant large-scale implementation of internet interventions. In other somatic conditions such as tinnitus and irritable bowel syndrome and stress management,

ESs for guided internet interventions are medium-to-large. Moreover, meta-analyses show large ESs for guided internet-based CBT for insomnia.

Other Clinically Relevant Problems and Conditions

Probably because internet interventions are both easier to develop and test in controlled trials, there are several programs of studies on different clinically relevant conditions for which there is often limited research for traditional psychological treatments (Andersson, Titov, et al., 2018). Here we cover interventions on (1) maladaptive perfectionism, (2) increased self-criticism, (3) procrastination, (4) loneliness, (5) complicated grief, and (6) sexual problems:

1. *Maladaptive perfectionism.* A program for maladaptive perfectionism has been developed and tested in a trial involving 156 participants (Rozental, Shafran, et al., 2017). Typical of ICBT studies, the perfectionism treatment included psychoeducation, a cognitive-behavioral conceptualization of maintaining factors, and exercises regarding cost-benefit analyses, value clarification, behavioral experiments, identifying maladaptive beliefs, graded exposure, implementing problem-solving techniques, relapse prevention, and self-compassion. Results on the primary outcome at posttreatment showed moderate-to-large between-group ESs ($d = 0.68–1.00$).
2. *Self-criticism and lack of self-compassion.* The related concepts of *self-criticism* and a *lack of self-compassion* were the focus of a trial with 122 participants, in which the efficacy of an online version of a compassion-focused treatment was compared with care as usual (Krieger, Reber, et al., 2019). Results on self-reported depressive, anxiety, and distress symptoms, as well as self-compassion, showed moderate-to-large between-group ESs ($d = 0.79–1.21$).
3. *Procrastination.* An online program for procrastination was tested in a trial that included 150 participants who were randomized to guided self-help, unguided self-help, or to a wait-list control group (Rozental, Forsell, et al., 2015). Results at posttreatment showed a moderate between-group ES against the wait list for the main outcome with the guided treatment (Cohen's $d = 0.70$) and unguided treatment ($d = 0.50$), yielding largely the same outcome with no significant difference between the two active treatments.
4. *Loneliness.* Käll, Jägholm, et al. (2020) developed and tested an online program for the transdiagnostic problem of loneliness. The eight-week program contained elements specific for loneliness, such as psychoeducation, as well as more generic elements such as challenging of dysfunctional thoughts and beliefs, strategies to reduce rumination, behavioral experiments and behavioral activation. The trial included 73 participants who were randomized to treatment or a waiting list. The between-group ES on the primary outcome at posttreatment was $d = 0.77$. Further work on the development of ICBT for loneliness has recently been conducted (Käll, Shafran, et al., 2020).

5. *Complicated grief.* This problem has been studied both in association with trauma (Lange et al., 2000) and as a separate condition. A program based on writing assignments (45-minute writing assignments twice a week over five weeks) was tested in a trial with 55 participants randomized to treatment or waiting list (Wagner et al., 2006). The results showed large between-group effects on measures of intrusion ($d = 1.20$) and avoidance ($d = 1.06$). It is important to note that not all studies have yielded such large effects on measures of grief following bereavement (van der Houwen et al., 2010).
6. *Sexual problems.* Studies on sexual problems include research related to erectile dysfunction (Andersson et al., 2011), sexual problems following cancer treatment (Schover et al., 2012), and sexual related health issues in men (van Lankveld et al., 2009) and women (van Lankveld, 2016). No meta-analysis has been reported, and outcomes vary in trials with between-group ESs ranging from small to large. The list of conditions related to men's and women's health also includes studies on urinary incontinence (Sjöström et al., 2013), premenstrual dysphoric disorder (Weise et al., 2019), menopause symptoms (Lindh-Åstrand et al., 2015), and infertility distress (Haemmerli et al., 2010).

   Although most studies on sexual problems have been focused on individual clients, there have been exceptions, such as studies involving parents in the treatment of children with anxiety (Vigerland et al., 2016) and couples therapy for distressed couples (Doss et al., 2016). Moreover, while still at an early stage there are studies on caregivers (Meichsner et al., 2019), significant others of persons with problem gambling (Magnusson et al., 2019), and programs to reduce intimate partner violence (Hesser et al., 2017).

In summary, multiple health and psychological problems have been the focus of internet treatment research, and the consistent picture that emerges is that most programs and studies tend to generate outcomes in line with what to expect from regular psychological treatments. At this point in time, however, the literature is scattered and more research activity is needed. It should also be noted that while not the focus of this chapter, there are a large number of interventions (mainly smartphone applications) that are not evidence-based and not even tested in feasibility studies.

Effectiveness and Cost-Effectiveness

The development of interventions often begins with research studies conducted in specialist settings and universities. However, following initial evidence, the question becomes whether the interventions work in real-world settings and situations that clinicians encounter in their daily routine practice. There is now an increasing number of effectiveness studies on internet-delivered interventions, and some of these studies have been mentioned in the sections above. Findings on the effectiveness of internet interventions in routine practice were summarized in an initial review in which four controlled trials and eight open studies were included (combined $N = 3,888$; Andersson & Hedman, 2013). They found effectiveness studies on ICBT for panic disorder, social anxiety disorder, generalized anxiety disorder, posttraumatic stress disorder, depression, tinnitus, and irritable bowel syndrome. All these studies showed moderate-to-large within-group ESs ranging from $d = 0.56$ in an effectiveness study on ICBT for tinnitus (Kaldo-Sandstrom et al., 2004) to $d = 2.50$ in a study on ICBT for panic disorder (Bergström et al., 2009). Much more work has been reported since then, with large effectiveness studies such as the evaluation of a national e-mental health service in Australia, in which within-group ESs between $d = 0.70$ and $d = 2.40$ were reported for patients suffering from various common mental disorders (Titov et al., 2017).

The literature on the cost-effectiveness of internet interventions for mental health problems has mainly concerned ICBT. In one review, Donker et al. (2015) identified nine studies that contained analyses related to societal outcomes. These outcomes include direct and indirect costs such as health sector costs, other sector costs, patient/family costs, and productivity losses. Findings showed that guided internet interventions were likely to be more cost-effective than control conditions such as wait-list control groups and group treatments. However, a more recent patient-level analysis including 1426 participants from five studies could not conclude that guided internet-based interventions for depression were cost-effective compared to care-as-usual and wait-list controls from a societal perspective (Kolovos et al., 2018). Clearly, more research is needed on the cost-effectiveness of internet-based treatments.

Long-Term Outcomes

Although several trials on internet interventions have reported follow-up data to one-year, no systematic review has been conducted on their findings. However, a review on longer follow-ups has recently been published (Andersson, Rozental et al., 2018). Based on 902 participants, the review involved 14 studies that reported follow-up data at least two years after treatment completion, with an average follow-up period of three years. Long-term outcome studies on panic disorder, social anxiety disorder, generalized anxiety disorder, depression, mixed anxiety and depression, obsessive-compulsive disorder, pathological gambling, stress, and chronic fatigue were included. The pre- to follow-up within-group ES was Hedge's $g = 1.52$. While this large effect is in line with short-term outcomes, it must be interpreted with caution, given the small number of studies, the uncontrolled nature of the effects, and uncertainties regarding the naturalistic course of some conditions. It should also be mentioned that there are few face-to-face trials with longer follow-ups than one-year, making comparisons difficult.

Negative Outcomes and Null Effects

There is increasing literature on negative effects and null effects of internet interventions (Rozental et al., 2014), with negative effects being reported in clinical trials, as well as being the focus of separate research efforts. One example of a large-scale investigation of negative effects was an individual patient meta-analysis (IPDMA) on a large data set of individual controlled trials on ICBT for anxiety, depression, and some other disorders and problems (Rozental, Magnusson, et al., 2017). Based on data from 29 trials ($N = 2,866$), the authors reported deterioration rates of 5.8% in treatment conditions and 17.4% in the control conditions. Using a smaller sample ($N = 558$) and content analysis of actual client reports, Rozental, Boettcher, et al. (2015) found that the reported negative effects (9.3% of the sample) could be categorized as patient-related negative effects, such as greater awareness of the condition and feeling worse during treatment, and treatment-related negative effects such as problems with the format and technology of internet interventions.

The same IPDMA data set (Rozental et al., 2019) was used to derive estimates of null effects of ICBT, arguably a neglected factor in psychotherapy research. Focusing on the participants who had received treatment, the authors reported that 26.8% could be classified as nonresponders according to the reliable change index. Taken together, current empirical findings suggest that a small proportion of clients deteriorate and approximately 25% show nonresponse. Arguably, internet intervention research may help us obtain better estimates of improvement, nonresponse, and deterioration given the larger data sets it can collect and the relative ease of its implementation.

Role of the Therapists, Therapist Effects, and the Therapeutic Alliance

An important line of research on internet interventions has focused on the degree of support and guidance required during the self-help treatments in order to be effective (Berger, Hämmerli, et al., 2011). The current literature suggests that unguided internet interventions with no human support at any stage (including no initial intake interview) tend to be associated with high dropout rates (Melville et al., 2010), lower adherence (Christensen et al., 2009), and possibly also lower effects (Karyotaki et al., 2017), even for clients who manage to complete a treatment without any support (Andersson, 2016). Therapist-supported internet interventions are, however, most likely not associated with higher dropout rates compared with regular face-to-face psychotherapy (van Ballegooijen et al., 2014). There are examples of programs that have included support on request (Berger, Caspar, et al., 2011; Hadjistavropoulos et al., 2017), or automated messages (Titov et al., 2013), that have generated large treatment effects. However, these successful unguided treatments also tend to include a backup and possibilities for clients to contact the clinicians when needed.

Many clients and practicing therapists prefer to have contact during a treatment (Berger, Hämmerli, et al., 2011), and there is a growing literature on therapist factors that can have an impact on a client's improvement, especially concerning comorbid symptoms not directly targeted by a disorder-specific treatment program (Almlöv et al., 2009). Even if the support given in internet treatments tends to be more in the form of encouragement and about the homework and tasks presented in the treatment, there are several tasks that can be important to manage when supporting a client. For example, in one study on generalized anxiety disorder, permissive therapist behaviors in relation to deadlines were associated with poorer outcomes

(Paxling et al., 2013). By contrast, in another investigation on depression behaviors, affirmations, encouragement and self-disclosure were all associated with better outcomes (Holländare et al., 2016). In another study of depression, therapist behaviors (e.g., administrative statements and task prompting) were associated with lower symptom improvement at posttreatment (Schneider et al., 2016). These three studies suggest that the supporting therapist can have an impact on the outcomes of internet treatments. Subsequent development in this area has focused on improving the categorization of therapist behaviors and treatment fidelity (Hadjistavropoulos et al., 2018) and on predicting treatment outcome based on therapeutic email conversations (Hoogendoorn et al., 2017).

The role of the therapist–client relationship has been the topic of numerous studies (see Chapters 7 and 8), and the therapeutic alliance has also been investigated in studies on internet interventions (Berger, 2017). Most of the research has been on the patient-rated alliance using measures such as the Working Alliance Inventory (Horvath & Greenberg, 1989). Reviews concluded that independent of communication modalities (e.g., email, videoconferencing), diagnostic groups and amount of contact between clients and therapists, client-rated alliance scores were high, roughly equivalent to alliance ratings found in studies on face-to-face therapy (Berger, 2017; Pihlaja et al., 2018). Furthermore, a recent correlational meta-analysis revealed a moderate overall association between the working alliance and treatment outcome of $r = 0.25$ across 18 studies (Probst et al., 2019). In one study, alliance ratings were obtained before, during, and after internet treatment for anxiety disorders, and the findings showed that alliance rating increased during treatment (Bergman Nordgren et al., 2013). This suggests that clients have a clear perception of a present therapist and that ratings of tasks, goals, and the bond are sensitive to change. There are, however, to our knowledge, no studies on ruptures in alliance in internet treatments, and future research should also identify unique characteristics of the therapeutic alliance in the different treatment formats (Berger, 2017).

In sum, therapist-supported internet interventions are most likely more effective than self-guided treatments. How the therapist behaves in the communication with the client makes a difference, and the well-studied phenomenon of the working alliance can be observed in internet interventions as well.

Qualitative Studies

There is an increasing number of qualitative studies on internet interventions, often including open-ended interview questions and research methods such as grounded theory (Glaser & Strauss, 1967). To our knowledge, there few systematic meta-synthesis of this literature, but a review of qualitative studies of computerized interventions has been published (Knowles et al., 2014). Qualitative studies can add valuable information that are more likely to be missed by structured questionnaires and interviews. An example is a study in which 12 participants in a trial, selected according to a maximum variation strategy with regard to treatment outcome, were interviewed six months after treatment completion (Bendelin et al., 2011). Transcribed interviews were analyzed using qualitative methods with components of both thematic analysis and grounded theory. The authors discerned three distinct change processes relating to how participants had experienced and worked with the internet treatments: (a) readers, (b) strivers, and (c) doers. The somewhat-unexpected finding was that there were participants who read and took part in the program while not engaging in homework assignments (e.g., readers). They were also more disappointed and did not benefit from the treatment.

Another way to use qualitative methodology is to conduct studies before testing the interventions in controlled trials, one example being a study on experiences of an internet-based support and coaching model for adolescents and young adults with ADHD and autism spectrum disorder (Sehlin et al., 2018). We recommend that researchers in the field of internet interventions, and indeed in the broader field of psychotherapy as well, consider qualitative research as part of their treatment research programs.

Level of Technologization

Internet-delivered interventions have used more or less advanced technologies. Virtual-reality treatments were initially only possible to deliver in lab settings (Côté & Bouchard, 2008). However, as already mentioned, given the expansion of low-cost equipment, it is now possible to conduct studies on home-based VR programs that can be combined with internet programs and outcome assessments (Lindner et al., 2017). Furthermore, although still experimental, there are more and more programs using conversational agents or chatbots. Conversational agents, such as Siri (Apple) and Alexa (Amazon), are computer programs designed to respond to users in natural language. In a recent study, it was demonstrated that a text-based conversational agent, mimicking a therapeutic dialogue, could significantly reduce symptoms of depression and anxiety among a nonclinical college student population, compared to an information-only control group (Fitzpatrick et al., 2017). Serious games, which are computer games designed for a primary purpose other than pure entertainment and which add fun and competition to serious tasks, are another example of a treatment format the requires advanced programming (Mohr et al., 2013). In particular, for children and adolescents, serious games can be a way to make treatment more appealing (Merry et al., 2012).

KNOWLEDGE GAPS

Predictors, Moderators, and Mediators of Outcome

As with psychotherapy research in general, the search for moderators and mediators of treatment outcome has been the topic of much internet intervention research. The literature is scattered with a few consistent findings, but several topics, such as the role of therapists and therapeutic alliance (see above), have been investigated. Here we will comment on some additional research.

An important topic is the role of demographics as predictors of outcome in internet interventions, which have been studied extensively with few consistent findings across trials. One reason could be that the inclusion and exclusion criteria in trials mean that the possible predictors of outcome are not included. Examples include being able to use a computer and read, and also participants with either too severe or too mild problems. Occasionally, significant demographic predictors of outcome have been reported (Hedman et al., 2012). The previously mentioned patient-level meta-analysis (Andersson et al., 2019) showed that higher symptom severity on the primary outcome measure at baseline (odds ratio [OR] = 1.36) and being female (OR = 2.22) increased the odds of responding to treatment. Having an anxiety disorder was found to decrease the response to treatment (OR = 0.51). In another IPDMA study with 2705 participants focusing on dropout from depression treatment, the authors found that male gender (relative risk, RR = 1.08), lower educational level (RR = 1.26) and co-morbid anxiety symptoms (RR = 1.18) significantly increased the risk of dropping out (Karyotaki et al., 2015). These are promising findings as previous studies on predictors of outcome often have included much smaller samples.

A series of studies has investigated the role of cognitive function as predictors of outcome in internet interventions. Tests of executive function have been collected in association with clinical trials. Whereas most studies have shown no effects (Andersson et al., 2008; Lindner et al., 2016), one study found a negative association between perseverative errors and negative treatment outcomes in a study on ICBT for older adults (Silfvernagel et al., 2018).

Another variable that has been investigated is the role of genes. This research has been a fruitful collaboration across disciplines, and for example, genes have been extensively investigated in connection with psychiatric disorders such as 5-HTTLPR, a gene that codes for the serotonin transporter. To date, no clear associations have been established in research (Andersson, Rück, et al., 2013; Hedman et al., 2012), but separate processes such as exposure may be more linked to genetic profile (Lonsdorf et al., 2010).

A final example of research on predictors of outcome concerns brain imaging. One study on social anxiety disorder showed neural correlates of change following ICBT and bias modification training online (Månsson et al., 2013). A subsequent study reported structural changes (Månsson et al., 2017; Månsson et al., 2016) and, using machine learning, it was possible to predict responder status at a one-year follow-up (Månsson et al., 2015). There are also studies on depression showing changes in brain function following ICBT for depression (Tiger et al., 2014), and also one study in which brain morphology at baseline could predict outcome of ICBT for depression (Webb et al., 2018).

The research on predictors of outcome has been based on data collected either before treatment starts or early ratings of therapeutic alliance and treatment credibility. However, in order to study mechanisms of change, measures need to be collected during a treatment (Kazdin, 2007). This is often a time-consuming task in psychotherapy research. In internet interventions, weekly measures can be embedded in the treatment delivery without taking time from a session or requiring

therapist motivation to collect the data, which then can be used for statistical analyses (Hesser, 2015). There are some process studies in which weekly measures have been used to investigate mediators of outcome in internet interventions. In a study on health anxiety in which both mediators and health anxiety were measured weekly throughout the treatment, results showed that reduced perceived risk of disease, less attention to bodily symptoms, and reduced intolerance of uncertainty significantly mediated improvement (Hedman, Andersson, et al., 2013). There are other studies on mediators of change (van Luenen et al., 2019), but still few in which the timeline of mediation occurring before change has been considered when planning data collection.

Outcome Measures

Most research on internet interventions, and indeed psychotherapy in general, rely on self-report measures of symptoms and problems, sometimes complemented by structured interviews measuring similar constructs (e.g., psychiatric diagnoses). There is, however, some research on other outcome variables, and we will give three examples here:

1. *The role of knowledge and knowledge acquisition in internet interventions.* Research on this concept has clear links with face-to-face research on memory of therapy and ways to improve memory of therapy components (Harvey et al., 2014). In one study on social anxiety disorder, a knowledge test was administered before and after the intervention, and results showed improved knowledge when considering certainty of knowledge (Andersson, Carlbring, et al., 2012). Similar improvements were found in a study on eating disorders (Strandskov et al., 2017) and adolescent depression (Berg et al., 2019). Following this work, studies on ways to improve learning and knowledge acquisition in internet interventions are in progress.

2. *Cognitive tests of selective information processing.* There are a few studies here as well, but one example is a study in which a test of future-directed thinking was administered before and after depression treatment showing statistically significant improvements (Andersson, Sarkohi, et al., 2013). Most of the research in this domain has been in studies on bias modification training in which tests like the dot probe task have been included (Boettcher et al., 2013) as part of the intervention. Another example is a test of positive imagery (Blackwell et al., 2015).

3. *Ecological momentary assessment (EMA) often via smartphones.* This third example study (see Areán et al., 2016) provides still different outcome and process measures. There are also examples of studies incorporating sensors of heart rate and activity monitoring (Mohr et al., 2017). Research in this field is in its early phase (Colombo et al., 2019), but can be informative to predict outcome (Mikus et al., 2018) and could also be used as outcomes.

In sum, internet intervention research may allow new ways to collect data and also facilitates broadening of what data to collect in psychotherapy research.

LIMITATIONS, FUTURE DIRECTIONS, AND CONCLUDING COMMENTS

Limitations

We will start by mentioning some limitations of this chapter and the research covered. As stated, this is a rapidly growing field. A first problem is the quality of the research that varies considerably. On the one hand, the field is full of controlled trials, often being the largest trials ever for a particular problem. However, it is also the case that many studies are published that have not been registered or planned in great detail, with a new phenomenon that could be named pilot RCTs. In other words, relative to regular therapy research, it is so much easier to get participants and run trials that the phase of open pilot studies becomes less needed when a controlled study adds the same and more information. Another related possible limitation is that the field of internet interventions is mostly driven by data rather than by a theoretical understanding of what makes therapy work. As Ritterband and colleagues already mentioned more than a decade ago: The field needs a model to help (a) describe and explain how behaviors change, and symptoms improve through the use of internet interventions; (b) guide intervention development and facilitate testing of the intervention; and (c) firmly establish this method of treatment with a theoretical foundation (Ritterband, Thorndike, Cox et al., 2009). Since then, few researchers have made any serious attempts to delineate mechanisms that are unique to internet interventions (Mohr et al., 2013; Ritterband, Thorndike, Cox et al., 2009; Schueller et al., 2017). Related to this is the fact that questions such as whether internet interventions work and whether they work equally well as face-to-face treatments were in the foreground of research on internet interventions. While now moving on from an outcome to a process and process-outcome research phase, research should also be designed to understand better specific processes of change in internet interventions, such as specific characteristics of the online relationship between patients and therapists (Berger, 2017).

Future Directions

As with all future predictions, there are many possibilities but also uncertainties. First, we believe that there will be technological advancements. One example is already here in the form of embodied conversational agents (ECAs) that are computer-generated characters that simulate key properties of human face-to-face conversation (Provoost et al., 2017). We expect this to be a topic for research (Ly et al., 2017), but we cannot know if ECAs will be able to replace therapists or what the added value might be in relation to text-based support that is generally provided in guided internet interventions. Another technical advancement is how large data sets can be used with the help of machine learning. This will possibly facilitate the search for outcome predictors (Lenhard et al., 2018).

A second development is the translation and cultural adaption of intervention programs into different languages. There are several examples of internet treatment programs that have been translated and culturally adapted for non-Western languages; for example, Arabic (Wagner et al., 2012), Kurdish (Nygren et al., 2019), and Chinese (Choi et al., 2012; Kishimoto et al., 2016). Future programs and studies will most likely expand on this with the possibilities of world trials being close at hand (Gentile et al., 2019). In this respect, it may also be possible to help clients in countries for which there is a lack of services (Munoz, 2010). Here we also expect treatment programs to become more sophisticated in terms of translation and adaption (Salamanca-Sanabria et al., 2019), which not only concern language but may also pertain to other aspects such as gender and sexual orientation.

Another prediction is that information technology at large and in particular evidence-based internet interventions will be used as part of clinical services and not only as alternatives or complements (Fairburn & Patel, 2017). It is also possible that internet interventions will be used in training of psychologists and psychotherapists. There is a growing literature on blended treatments that we commented on earlier, but there is also evidence to suggest that stakeholders might prefer blended treatment over internet interventions for more severe problems (Topooco et al., 2017). Related to this is the concept of stepped care in which a client who does not respond is stepped up to the next level of care. There is some work carried out on internet interventions as part of a stepped-care model (Haug et al., 2015). However, it could also be that triage and careful selection of treatment formats may be an alternative route, given the finding that internet interventions can result in similar outcomes as face-to-face therapy (Carlbring et al., 2018).

A further prediction is that programs and studies will focus on more severe and chronic conditions, as is already the case in some studies (Meyer et al., 2015), and that treatment of longer duration than a few months will be studied. This could be in the form of blended internet and face-to-face interventions for conditions like borderline personality disorder (Klein et al., 2018) and psychotic disorders (Ruegg et al., 2018; Westermann et al., 2020).

A final prediction for the future is that there will be more large trials using factorial designs (Kelders et al., 2015). The factorial experiment is an efficient and economical way of studying the individual and combined effects of sets of intervention components (Collins et al., 2014). However, factorial designs are still rare in psychotherapy research. Also, because in traditional psychotherapy, it is challenging to demarcate treatment components from each other clearly and to avoid an unwanted drift of therapists from the treatment protocol. With the advent of internet-delivered treatments, the possibility to successfully realize factorial designs has improved because in this new treatment format, the intervention content can be standardized, and treatment integrity (the degree to which an intervention is implemented as intended) can be controlled. Furthermore, Internet studies make it possible to generate large enough samples to conduct factorial trials to investigate mechanisms of change and to isolate treatment components (Watkins et al., 2016).

Concluding Comments

We conclude by stating that internet interventions research has been one of the most rapid developments in the psychotherapy field ever seen. Over a period of 20 years, a vast number of treatments have been developed and tested, and in many cases, large effects have been observed (Andersson, 2018). It could even be described as a revolution in treatment research. It may very well be that we face a situation in which there is more empirical support for internet interventions than for regular face-to-face psychotherapy for some disorders and conditions. However, there is still room for improvement as few treatment programs have been implemented, change mechanisms are largely unknown, some programs and procedures have failed to generate good effects and also been associated with large dropout rates, and much of the research has been on educated clients in Western countries. This is not unique for internet interventions, but there is a need for broader recruitment and focus on clients with fewer resources. In spite of these problems, however, internet interventions are most likely here to stay and will hopefully increase client access to evidence-based psychological treatments.

ABBREVIATIONS

ACT	acceptance and commitment therapy
ADHD	attention deficit hyperactivity disorder
CBT	cognitive behavioral therapy
ECA	embodied conversational agents
EMA	ecological momentary assessment
ES	effect sizes
GAD	general anxiety disorder
IBS	irritable bowel syndrome
ICBT	internet-delivered cognitive behavioral therapy
IPDMA	individual patient data meta-analysis
OCD	obsessive-compulsive disorder
PTSD	posttraumatic stress disorder
RCT	randomized controlled trial

REFERENCES

Abrahams, H. J. G., Gielissen, M. F. M., Donders, R. R. T., Goedendorp, M. M., van der Wouw, A. J., Verhagen, C., & Knoop, H. (2017). The efficacy of Internet-based cognitive behavioral therapy for severely fatigued survivors of breast cancer compared with care as usual: A randomized controlled trial. *Cancer, 123*(19), 3825–3834. https://doi.org/10.1002/cncr.30815

Almlöv, J., Carlbring, P., Berger, T., Cuijpers, P., & Andersson, G. (2009). Therapist factors in Internet-delivered CBT for major depressive disorder. *Cognitive Behaviour Therapy, 38*(4), 247–254. https://doi.org/10.1080/16506070903116935

American Psychiatric Association. (2013). *Diagnostic and statistical manual of mental disorders. DSM-5.* Washington: American Psychiatric Press. https://doi.org/10.1176/appi.books.9780890425596

Andersson, E., Hedman, E., Enander, J., Radu Djurfeldt, D., Ljótsson, B., Cervenka, S., Isung, J., Svanborg, C., Mataix-Cols, D., Kaldo, V., Andersson, G., Lindefors, N., & Rück, C. (2015). D-cycloserine vs placebo as adjunct to cognitive behavioral therapy for obsessive-compulsive disorder and interaction with antidepressants: A randomized clinical trial. *JAMA Psychiatry, 72*(7), 659–667. https://doi.org/10.1001/jamapsychiatry.2015.0546

Andersson, E., Rück, C., Lavebratt, C., Hedman, E., Schalling, M., Lindefors, N., Eriksson, E., Carlbring, P., Andersson, G., & Furmark, T. (2013).

Genetic polymorphisms in monoamine systems and outcome of cognitive behavior therapy for social anxiety disorder. *PloS One, 8*, e79015. https://doi.org/10.1371/journal.pone.0079015

Andersson, E., Walén, C., Hallberg, J., Paxling, B., Dahlin, M., Almlöv, J., Kallström, R., Wijma, K., Carlbring, P., & Andersson, G. (2011). A randomized controlled trial of guided Internet-delivered cognitive behavioral therapy for erectile dysfunction. *Journal of Sexual Medicine, 8*(10), 2800–2809. https://doi.org/10.1111/j.1743-6109.2011.02391.x

Andersson, G. (2015). *The internet and CBT: A clinical guide.* Boca Raton: CRC Press. https://doi.org/10.1201/b13645

Andersson, G. (2016). Internet-delivered psychological treatments. *Annual Review of Clinical Psychology, 12*, 157–179. https://doi.org/10.1146/annurev-clinpsy-021815-093006

Andersson, G. (2018). Internet interventions: past, present and future. *Internet Interventions, 12*, 181–188. https://doi.org/10.1016/j.invent.2018.03.008

Andersson, G., Bergström, J., Holländare, F., Carlbring, P., Kaldo, V., & Ekselius, L. (2005). Internet-based self-help for depression: A randomised controlled trial. *The British Journal of Psychiatry, 187*, 456–461. https://doi.org/10.1192/bjp.187.5.456

Andersson, G., Carlbring, P., Furmark, T., & on behalf of the SOFIE Research Group. (2012a). Therapist experience and knowledge acquisition in Internet-delivered CBT for social anxiety disorder: A randomized controlled trial. *PloS One, 7*(5), e37411. https://doi.org/10.1371/journal.pone.0037411

Andersson, G., Carlbring, P., & Grimlund, A. (2008). Predicting treatment outcome in Internet versus face to face treatment of panic disorder. *Computers in Human Behavior, 24*(5), 1790–1801. https://doi.org/10.1016/j.chb.2008.02.003

Andersson, G., Carlbring, P., & Rozental, A. (2019). Response and remission rates in internet-based cognitive behavior therapy: An individual patient data meta-analysis. *Frontiers in Psychiatry, 10*, 749. https://doi.org/10.3389/fpsyt.2019.00749

Andersson, G., & Hedman, E. (2013). Effectiveness of guided Internet-delivered cognitive behaviour therapy in regular clinical settings. *Verhaltenstherapie, 23*, 140–148. https://doi.org/10.1159/000354779

Andersson, G., Paxling, B., Roch-Norlund, P., Östman, G., Norgren, A., Almlöv, J., Georén, L., Breitholtz, E., Dahlin, M., Cuijpers, P., Carlbring, P., & Silverberg, F. (2012). Internet-based psychodynamic vs. cognitive behavioural guided self-help for generalized anxiety disorder: A randomised controlled trial. *Psychotherapy and Psychosomatics, 81*(6), 344355. https://doi.org/10.1159/000339371

Andersson, G., Rozental, A., Shafran, R., & Carlbring, P. (2018). Long-term effects of internet-supported cognitive behavior therapy. *Expert Review of Neurotherapeutics, 18*(1), 21–28. https://doi.org/10.1080/14737175.2018.1400381

Andersson, G., Sarkohi, A., Karlsson, J., Bjärehed, J., & Hesser, H. (2013b). Effects of two forms of internet-delivered cognitive behaviour therapy on future thinking. *Cognitive Therapy and Research, 37*(1), 29–34. https://doi.org/10.1007/s10608-012-9442-y

Andersson, G., Strömgren, T., Ström, L., & Lyttkens, L. (2002). Randomised controlled trial of internet based cognitive behavior therapy for distress associated with tinnitus. *Psychosomatic Medicine, 64*(5), 810–816. https://doi.org/10.1097/00006842-200209000-00014

Andersson, G., Titov, N., Dear, B. F., Rozental, A., & Carlbring, P. (2018). Internet-delivered psychological treatments: From innovation to implementation. *World Psychiatry, 18*(1), 20–28. https://doi.org/10.1002/wps.20610

Andersson, G., Waara, J., Jonsson, U., Malmaeus, F., Carlbring, P., & Öst, L.-G. (2009). Internet-based self-help vs. one-session exposure in the treatment of spider phobia: A randomized controlled trial. *Cognitive Behaviour Therapy, 38*(2), 114120. https://doi.org/10.1080/16506070902931326

Andersson, G., Waara, J., Jonsson, U., Malmaeus, F., Carlbring, P., & Öst, L.-G. (2013). Internet-based vs. one-session exposure treatment of snake phobia: A randomized controlled trial. *Cognitive Behaviour Therapy, 42*(4), 284291. https://doi.org/10.1080/16506073.2013.844202

Andrews, G., Basu, A., Cuijpers, P., Craske, M. G., McEvoy, P., English, C. L., & Newby, J. M. (2018). Computer therapy for the anxiety and depression disorders is effective, acceptable and practical health care: An updated meta-analysis. *Journal of Anxiety Disorders, 55*, 70–78. https://doi.org/10.1016/j.janxdis.2018.01.001

Areán, P. A., Ly, K. H., & Andersson, G. (2016). Mobile technology for mental health assessment. *Dialogues in Clinical Neuroscience, 18*(2), 163–169.

Barak, A., Klein, B., & Proudfoot, J. G. (2009). Defining Internet-supported therapeutic interventions. *Annals of Behavioral Medicine, 38*(1), 417. https://doi.org/10.1007/s12160-009-9130-7

Barlow, D. H., Allen, L. B., & Choate, M. L. (2004). Toward a unified treatment for emotional disorders. *Behavior Therapy, 35*(2), 205–230. https://doi.org/10.1016/S0005-7894(04)80036-4

Bendelin, N., Hesser, H., Dahl, J., Carlbring, P., Zetterqvist Nelson, K., & Andersson, G. (2011). Experiences of guided Internet-based cognitive-behavioural treatment for depression: A qualitative study *BMC Psychiatry, 11*, 107. https://doi.org/10.1186/1471-244X-11-107

Berg, M., Rozental, A., Johansson, S., Liljethörn, l., Radvogin, E., Topooco, N., & Andersson, G. (2019). The role of knowledge in Internet-based cognitive behavioural therapy for adolescent depression: Results from a randomised controlled study. *Internet Interventions, 15*, 10–17. https://doi.org/10.1016/j.invent.2018.10.001

Berger, T. (2017). The therapeutic alliance in internet interventions: A narrative review and suggestions for future research. *Psychotherapy Research, 27*(5), 511–524. https://doi.org/10.1080/10503307.2015.1119908

Berger, T., Boettcher, J., & Caspar, F. (2014). Internet-based guided self-help for several anxiety disorders: A randomized controlled trial comparing a tailored with a standardized disorder-specific approach. *Psychotherapy, 51*(2), 207–219. https://doi.org/10.1037/a0032527

Berger, T., Caspar, F., Richardson, R., Kneubühler, B., Sutter, D., & Andersson, G. (2011). Internet-based treatment of social phobia: A randomized controlled trial comparing unguided with two types of guided self-help. *Behaviour Research and Therapy, 49*(3), 158–169. https://doi.org/10.1016/j.brat.2010.12.007

Berger, T., Hämmerli, K., Gubser, N., Andersson, G., & Caspar, F. (2011). Internet-based treatment of depression: A randomized controlled trial comparing guided with unguided self-help. *Cognitive Behaviour Therapy, 40*(4), 251–266. https://doi.org/10.1080/16506073.2011.616531

Berger, T., Krieger, T., Sude, K., Meyer, B., & Maercker, A. (2018). Evaluating an e-mental health program ("deprexis") as adjunctive treatment tool in psychotherapy for depression: Results of a pragmatic randomized controlled trial. *Journal of Affective Disorders, 227*, 455–462. https://doi.org/10.1016/j.jad.2017.11.021

Bergman Nordgren, L., Carlbring, P., Linna, E., & Andersson, G. (2013). Role of the working alliance on treatment outcome in tailored internet-based cognitive behavioural therapy for anxiety disorders: randomized controlled pilot trial. *JMIR Research Protocols, 2*(1), e4. https://doi.org/10.2196/resprot.2292

Bergström, J., Andersson, G., Karlsson, A., Andreewitch, S., Rück, C., Carlbring, P., & Lindefors, N. (2009). An open study of the effectiveness of internet treatment for panic disorder delivered in a psychiatric setting. *Nordic Journal of Psychiatry, 63*(1), 4450. https://doi.org/10.1080/08039480802191132

Berryhill, M. B., Culmer, N., Williams, N., Halli-Tierney, A., Betancourt, A., Roberts, H., & King, M. (2019). Videoconferencing psychotherapy and depression: A systematic review. *Telemedicine Journal and e-Health, 25*(6), 435–446. https://doi.org/10.1089/tmj.2018.0058

Beukes, E. W., Manchaiah, V., Allen, P. M., Baguley, D. M., & Andersson, G. (2019). Internet-based interventions for adults with hearing loss, tinnitus, and vestibular disorders: A systematic review and meta-analysis. *Trends in Hearing, 23*, 2331216519851749. https://doi.org/10.1177/2331216519851749

Blackwell, S. E., Browning, M., Mathews, A., Pictet, A., Welch, J., Davies, J., Watson, P., Geddes, J. R., & Holmes, E. A. (2015). Positive imagery-based cognitive bias modification as a web-based treatment tool for depressed adults: A randomized controlled trial. *Clinical Psychological Science, 3*(1), 91–111. https://doi.org/10.1177/2167702614560746

Blom, K., Tarkian Tillgren, H., Wiklund, T., Danlycke, E., Forssén, M., Söderström, A., Johansson, R., Hesser, H., Jernelöv, S., Lindefors, N., Andersson, G., & Kaldo, V. (2015). Internet vs. group cognitive behavior therapy for insomnia: A randomized controlled non-inferiority trial. *Behaviour Research and Therapy, 70*, 47–55. https://doi.org/10.1016/j.brat.2015.05.002

Boettcher, J., Leek, L., Matson, L., Holmes, E. A., Browning, M., MacLeod, C., Andersson, G., & Carlbring, P. (2013). Internet-based attention modification for social anxiety: A randomised controlled comparison of training towards negative and training towards positive cues. *PloS One, 8*, e71760. https://doi.org/10.1371/journal.pone.0071760

Bonnert, M., Olén, O., Lalouni, M., Benninga, M. A., Bottai, M., Engelbrektsson, J., Hedman, E., Lenhard, F., Melin, B., Simrén, M., Vigerland, S., Serlachius, E., & Ljótsson, B. (2017). Internet-delivered cognitive behavior therapy for adolescents with irritable bowel syndrome: A randomized controlled trial. *American Journal of Gastroenterology, 112*(1), 152–162. https://doi.org/10.1038/ajg.2016.503

Boumparis, N., Karyotaki, E., Schaub, M. P., Cuijpers, P., & Riper, H. (2017). Internet interventions for adult illicit substance users: A meta-analysis. *Addiction, 112*(9), 1521–1532. https://doi.org/10.1111/add.13819

Boumparis, N., Loheide-Niesmann, L., Blankers, M., Ebert, D. D., Korf, D., Schaub, M. P., Spijkerman, R., Tait, R. J., & Riper, H. (2019). Short- and long-term effects of digital prevention and treatment interventions for cannabis use reduction: A systematic review and meta-analysis. *Drug and Alcohol Dependence, 200*, 82–94. https://doi.org/10.1016/j.drugalcdep.2019.03.016

Buhrman, M., Fältenhag, S., Ström, L., & Andersson, G. (2004). Controlled trial of Internet-based treatment with telephone support for chronic back pain. *Pain, 111*(3), 368–377. https://doi.org/10.1016/j.pain.2004.07.021

Buhrman, M., Gordh, T., & Andersson, G. (2016). Internet interventions for chronic pain including headache: A systematic review. *Internet Interventions, 4*(1), 17–34. https://doi.org/10.1016/j.invent.2015.12.001

Campos, D., Bretón-López, J., Botella, C., Mira, A., Castilla, D., Mor, S., Baños, R., & Quero, S. (2019). Efficacy of an internet-based exposure treatment for flying phobia (NO-FEAR Airlines) with and without therapist guidance: a randomized controlled trial. *BMC Psychiatry, 19*(1), 86. https://doi.org/10.1186/s12888-019-2060-4

Carlbring, P., Andersson, G., Cuijpers, P., Riper, H., & Hedman-Lagerlöf, E. (2018). Internet-based vs. face-to-face cognitive behavior therapy for psychiatric and somatic disorders: An updated systematic review and meta-analysis. *Cognitive Behaviour Therapy, 47*(1), 1–18. https://doi.org/10.1080/16506073.2017.1401115

Carlbring, P., Hägglund, M., Luthström, A., Dahlin, M., Kadowaki, Å., Vernmark, K., & Andersson, G. (2013). Internet-based behavioral activation and acceptance-based treatment for depression: A randomized controlled trial. *Journal of Affective Disorders, 148*(2–3), 331–337. https://doi.org/10.1016/j.jad.2012.12.020

Carlbring, P., Maurin, L., Törngren, C., Linna, E., Eriksson, T., Sparthan, E., Strååt, M., Marquez von Hage, C., Bergman-Nordgren, L., & Andersson, G. (2010). Individually tailored internet-based treatment for anxiety disorders: a randomized controlled trial. *Behaviour Research and Therapy, 49*(1), 18–24. https://doi.org/10.1016/j.brat.2010.10.002

Carlbring, P., & Smit, F. (2008). Randomized trial of Internet-delivered self-help with telephone support for pathological gamblers. *Journal of Consulting and Clinical Psychology, 76*(6), 1090–1094. https://doi.org/10.1037/a0013603

Chebli, J. L., Blaszczynski, A., & Gainsbury, S. M. (2016). Internet-based Interventions for addictive behaviours: A systematic review. *Journal of Gambling Studies, 32*(4), 1279–1304. https://doi.org/10.1007/s10899-016-9599-5

Choi, I., Zou, J., Titov, N., Dear, B. F., Li, S., Johnston, L., Andrews, G., & Hunt, C. (2012). Culturally attuned Internet treatment for depression amongst Chinese Australians: A randomised controlled trial. *Journal of Affective Disorders, 136*(3), 459–468. https://doi.org/10.1016/j.jad.2011.11.003

Christensen, H., Griffiths, K. M., & Farrer, L. (2009). Adherence in internet interventions for anxiety and depression. *Journal of Medical Internet Research, 11*(2), e13. https://doi.org/10.2196/jmir.1194

Cohen, B. E., Edmondson, D., & Kronish, I. M. (2015). State of the art review: Depression, stress, anxiety, and cardiovascular disease. *American Journal of Hypertension, 28*(11), 1295–1302. https://doi.org/10.1093/ajh/hpv047

Collins, L. M., Dziak, J. J., Kugler, K. C., & Trail, J. B. (2014). Factorial experiments: Efficient tools for evaluation of intervention components. *American Journal of Preventive Medicine, 47*(4), 498–504. https://doi.org/10.1016/j.amepre.2014.06.021

Colombo, D., Fernández-Álvarez, J., Patané, A., Semonella, M., Kwiatkowska, M., García-Palacios, A., Cipresso, P., Riva, G., & Botella, C. (2019). Current state and future directions of technology-based ecological momentary assessment and intervention for major depressive disorder: A systematic review. *Journal of Clinical Medicine, 8*(4), 465. https://doi.org/10.3390/jcm8040465

Côté, S., & Bouchard, S. (2008). Virtual reality exposure for phobias: A critical review. *Journal of Cyber Therapy & Rehabilitation, 1*(1), 75–91.

Dagöö, J., Asplund, R. P., Bsenko, H. A., Hjerling, S., Holmberg, A., Westh, S., Öberg, L., Ljótsson, B., Carlbring, P., Furmark, T., & Andersson, G. (2014). Cognitive behavior therapy versus interpersonal psychotherapy for social anxiety disorder delivered via smartphone and computer: A randomized controlled trial. *Journal of Anxiety Disorders, 28*(4), 410–417. https://doi.org/10.1016/j.janxdis.2014.02.003

de Boer, M. J., Versteegen, G. J., Vermeulen, K. M., Sanderman, R., & Struys, M. M. (2014). A randomized controlled trial of an Internet-based cognitive-behavioural intervention for non-specific chronic pain: An effectiveness and cost-effectiveness study. *European Journal of Pain 18*(10), 1440–1451. https://doi.org/10.1002/ejp.509

de Zwaan, M., Herpertz, S., Zipfel, S., Svaldi, J., Friederich, H. C., Schmidt, F., Mayr, A., Lam, T., Schade-Brittinger, C., & Hilbert, A. (2017). Effect of Internet-based guided self-help vs individual face-to-face treatment on full or subsyndromal binge eating disorder in overweight or obese patients: The INTERBED randomized clinical trial. *JAMA Psychiatry, 74*(10), 987–995. https://doi.org/10.1001/jamapsychiatry.2017.2150

Dear, B. F., Courtney, C., Khor, K. E., McDonald, S., Ricciardi, T., Gandy, M., Fogliati, V. J., & Titov, N. (2018). The pain course: Exploring the feasibility of an Internet-delivered pain management program when offered by a tertiary pain management service. *Clinical Journal of Pain, 34*(6), 505–514. https://doi.org/10.1097/AJP.0000000000000565

Dear, B. F., Zou, J. B., Ali, S., Lorian, C. N., Johnston, L., Sheehan, J., Staples, L. G., Gandy, M., Fogliati, V. J., Klein, B., & Titov, N. (2015). Clinical and cost-effectiveness of therapist-guided internet-delivered cognitive behavior therapy for older adults with symptoms of anxiety: A randomized controlled trial. *Behavior Therapy, 46*(2), 206–217. https://doi.org/10.1016/j.beth.2014.09.007

Dolemeyer, R., Tietjen, A., Kersting, A., & Wagner, B. (2013). Internet-based interventions for eating disorders in adults: a systematic review. *BMC Psychiatry, 13*, 207. https://doi.org/10.1186/1471-244X-13-207

Donker, T., Bennett, K., Bennett, A., Mackinnon, A., van Straten, A., Cuijpers, P., Christensen, H., & Griffiths, K. M. (2013). Internet-delivered interpersonal psychotherapy versus internet-delivered cognitive behavioral therapy for adults with depressive symptoms: randomized controlled noninferiority trial. *Journal of Medical Internet Research, 15*(5), e82. https://doi.org/10.2196/jmir.2307

Donker, T., Blankers, M., Hedman, E., Ljótsson, B., Petrie, K., & Christensen, H. (2015). Economic evaluations of Internet interventions for mental health: a systematic review. *Psychological Medicine, 45*(16), 3357–3376. https://doi.org/10.1017/S0033291715001427

Donker, T., Cornelisz, I., van Klaveren, C., van Straten, A., Carlbring, P., Cuijpers, P., & van Gelder, J. L. (2019). Effectiveness of self-guided app-based virtual reality cognitive behavior therapy for acrophobia: A randomized clinical trial. *JAMA Psychiatry, 76*(7), 682–690. https://doi.org/10.1001/jamapsychiatry.2019.0219

Doss, B. D., Cicila, L. N., Georgia, E. J., Roddy, M. K., Nowlan, K. M., Benson, L. A., & Christensen, A. (2016). A randomized controlled trial of the web-based OurRelationship Program: Effects on relationship and individual functioning. *Journal of Consulting and Clinical Psychology, 84*(4), 285–296. https://doi.org/10.1037/ccp0000063

El Alaoui, S., Hedman, E., Kaldo, V., Hesser, H., Kraepelien, M., Andersson, E., Rück, C., Andersson, G., Ljótsson, B., & Lindefors, N. (2015). Effectiveness of internet-based cognitive behavior therapy for social anxiety disorder in clinical psychiatry. *Journal of Consulting and Clinical Psychology, 83*(5), 902–914. https://doi.org/10.1037/a0039198

Elison, S., Ward, J., Williams, C., Espie, C., Davies, G., Dugdale, S., Ragan, K., Chisnall, L., Lidbetter, N., & Smith, K. (2017). Feasibility of a UK community-based, eTherapy mental health service in Greater Manchester: repeated-measures and between-groups study of 'Living Life to the Full Interactive', 'Sleepio' and 'Breaking Free Online' at 'Self Help Services'. *BMJ Open, 7*(7), e016392. https://doi.org/10.1136/bmjopen-2017-016392

Enander, J., Andersson, E., Mataix-Cols, D., Lichtenstein, L., Alström, K., Andersson, G., Ljótsson, & Rück, C. (2016). Therapist guided internet based cognitive behavioural therapy for body dysmorphic disorder: single blind randomised controlled trial. *British Medical Journal, 352*, i241. https://doi.org/10.1136/bmj.i241

Erbe, D., Eichert, H. C., Riper, H., & Ebert, D. D. (2017). Blending face-to-face and internet-based interventions for the treatment of mental disorders in adults: Systematic review. *Journal of Medical Internet Research, 19*(9), e306. https://doi.org/10.2196/jmir.6588

Fairburn, C. G., & Patel, V. (2017). The impact of digital technology on psychological treatments and their dissemination. *Behaviour Research and Therapy, 88*, 19–25. https://doi.org/10.1016/j.brat.2016.08.012

Fischer, A., Schröder, J., Vettorazzi, E., Wolf, O. T., Pöttgen, J., Lau, S., Heesen, C., Moritz, S., & Gold, S. M. (2015). An online programme to reduce depression in patients with multiple sclerosis: A randomised controlled trial. *The Lancet Psychiatry, 2*(3), 217–223. https://doi.org/10.1016/S2215-0366(14)00049-2

Fitzpatrick, K. K., Darcy, A., & Vierhile, M. (2017). Delivering cognitive behavior therapy to young adults with symptoms of depression and anxiety using a fully automated conversational agent (Woebot): A randomized controlled trial. *JMIR Mental Health, 4*(2), e19. https://doi.org/10.2196/mental.7785

Fonzo, G. A., Fine, N. B., Wright, R. N., Achituv, M., Zaiko, Y. V., Merin, O., Shalev, A. Y., & Etkin, A. (2019). Internet-delivered computerized cognitive & affective remediation training for the treatment of acute and chronic posttraumatic stress disorder: Two randomized clinical trials. *Journal of Psychiatric Research, 115*, 82–89. https://doi.org/10.1016/j.jpsychires.2019.05.007

Frazier, P., Meredith, L., Greer, C., Paulsen, J. A., Howard, K., Dietz, L. R., & Qin, K. (2015). Randomized controlled trial evaluating the effectiveness of a web-based stress management program among community college students. *Anxiety, Stress, and Coping, 28*(5), 576–586. https://doi.org/10.1080/10615806.2014.987666

Gentile, A. J., La Lima, C., Flygare, O., Enander, J., Wilhelm, S., Mataix-Cols, D., & Ruck, C. (2019). Internet-based, therapist-guided, cognitive-behavioural therapy for body dysmorphic disorder with global eligibility for inclusion: an uncontrolled pilot study. *BMJ Open, 9*(3), e024693. https://doi.org/10.1136/bmjopen-2018-024693

Gershkovich, M., Herbert, J. D., Forman, E. M., Schumacher, L. M., & Fischer, L. E. (2017). Internet-delivered acceptance-based cognitive-behavioral intervention for social anxiety disorder with and without therapist support: A randomized trial. *Behavior Modification, 41*(5), 583–608. https://doi.org/10.1177/0145445517694457

Glaser, B. G., & Strauss, A. L. (1967). *The discovery of grounded theory: Strategies for qualitative research.* New York: Aldine. https://doi.org/10.1097/00006199-196807000-00014

Gliddon, E., Cosgrove, V., Berk, L., Lauder, S., Mohebbi, M., Grimm, D., Dodd, S., Coulson, C., Raju, K., Suppes, T., & Berk, M. (2019). A randomized controlled trial of MoodSwings 2.0: An internet-based self-management program for bipolar disorder. *Bipolar Disorders, 21*(1), 28–39. https://doi.org/10.1111/bdi.12669

Hadjistavropoulos, H. D., Schneider, L. H., Edmonds, M., Karin, E., Nugent, M. N., Dirkse, D., Dear, B. F., & Titov, N. (2017). Randomized controlled trial of internet-delivered cognitive behaviour therapy comparing standard weekly versus optional weekly therapist support. *Journal of Anxiety Disorders, 52*, 15–24. https://doi.org/10.1016/j.janxdis.2017.09.006

Hadjistavropoulos, H. D., Schneider, L. H., Klassen, K., Dear, B. F., & Titov, N. (2018). Development and evaluation of a scale assessing therapist fidelity to guidelines for delivering therapist-assisted internet-delivered cognitive behaviour therapy. *Cognitive Behaviour Therapy, 47*(6), 447–461. https://doi.org/10.1080/16506073.2018.1457079

Haemmerli, K., Znoj, H., & Berger, T. (2010). Internet-based support for infertile patients: A randomized controlled study. *Journal of Behavioral Medicine, 33*(2), 135–146. https://doi.org/10.1007/s10865-009-9243-2

Harvey, A. G., Lee, J., Williams, J., Hollon, S. D., Walker, M. P., Thompson, M. A., & Smith, R. (2014). Improving outcome of psychosocial treatments by enhancing memory and learning. *Perspectives on Psychological Science, 9*(2), 161–179. https://doi.org/10.1177/1745691614521781

Haug, T., Nordgreen, T., Öst, L.-G., Kvale, G., Tangen, T., Andersson, G., Carlbring, P., Heiervang, E. R., & Havik, O. E. (2015). Stepped care versus face-to-face cognitive behavior therapy for panic disorder and social anxiety disorder: Predictors and moderators of outcome. *Behaviour Research and Therapy, 71*, 76–89. https://doi.org/10.1016/j.brat.2015.06.002

Heber, E., Ebert, D. D., Lehr, D., Cuijpers, P., Berking, M., Nobis, S., & Riper, H. (2017). The benefit of web- and computer-based interventions for stress: A systematic review and meta-analysis. *Journal of Medical Internet Research, 19*(2), e32. https://doi.org/10.2196/jmir.5774

Heber, E., Lehr, D., Ebert, D. D., Berking, M., & Riper, H. (2016). Web-based and mobile stress management intervention for employees: A randomized controlled trial. *Journal of Medical Internet Research, 18*(1), e21. https://doi.org/10.2196/jmir.5112

Hedman, E., Andersson, E., Andersson, G., Lindefors, N., Lekander, M., Rück, C., & Ljótsson, B. (2013). Mediators in Internet-based cognitive behavior therapy for severe health anxiety. *PloS One, 8*, e77752. https://doi.org/10.1371/journal.pone.0077752

Hedman, E., Andersson, E., Ljótsson, B., Andersson, G., Andersson, E. M., Schalling, M., Lindefors, N., & Rück, C. (2012). Clinical and genetic outcome determinants of Internet- and group-based cognitive behavior therapy for social anxiety disorder. *Acta Psychiatrica Scandinavica, 126*(2), 126–136. https://doi.org/10.1111/j.1600-0447.2012.01834.x

Hedman, E., Andersson, G., Ljótsson, B., Andersson, E., Rück, C., Asmundson, G. J. G., & Lindefors, N. (2011). Internet-based cognitive-behavioural therapy for severe health anxiety: Randomised controlled trial. *The British Journal of Psychiatry, 198*(3), 230–236. https://doi.org/10.1192/bjp.bp.110.086843

Hedman, E., Ljótsson, B., Rück, C., Bergström, J., Andersson, G., Kaldo, V., Jansson, L., Andersson, E., Andersson, E., Blom, K., El Alaoui, S., Falk, L., Ivarsson, J., Nasri, B., Rydh, S., & Lindefors, N. (2013). Effectiveness of internet-based cognitive behaviour therapy for panic disorder in routine psychiatric care. *Acta Psychiatrica Scandinavica, 128*(6), 457–467. https://doi.org/10.1111/acps.12079

Hedman-Lagerlöf, M., Hedman-Lagerlöf, E., Axelsson, E., Ljotsson, B., Engelbrektsson, J., Hultkrantz, S., Lundbäck, K., Björkander, D., Wicksell, R. K., Flink, I., & Andersson, E. (2018). Internet-delivered exposure therapy for fibromyalgia: A randomized controlled trial. *Clinical Journal of Pain, 34*(6), 532–542. https://doi.org/10.1097/AJP.0000000000000566

Hesser, H. (2015). Modeling individual differences in randomized experiments using growth models: Recommendations for design, statistical analysis and reporting of results of internet interventions. *Internet Interventions, 2*(2), 110–120. https://doi.org/10.1016/j.invent.2015.02.003

Hesser, H., Axelsson, S., Bäcke, V., Engstrand, J., Gustafsson, T., Holmgren, E., Jeppsson, U., Pollack, M., Nordén, K., Rosenqvist, D., & Andersson, G. (2017). Preventing intimate partner violence via the Internet: A randomized controlled trial of emotion-regulation and conflict-management training for individuals with aggression problems. *Clinical Psychology & Psychotherapy, 24*(5), 1163–1177. https://doi.org/10.1002/cpp.2082

Hidalgo-Mazzei, D., Mateu, A., Reinares, M., Matic, A., Vieta, E., & Colom, F. (2015). Internet-based psychological interventions for bipolar disorder: Review of the present and insights into the future. *Journal of Affective Disorders, 188*, 1–13. https://doi.org/10.1016/j.jad.2015.08.005

Hintz, S., Frazier, P. A., & Meredith, L. (2015). Evaluating an online stress management intervention for college students. *Journal of Counseling Psychology, 62*(2), 137–147. https://doi.org/10.1037/cou0000014

Hoch, E., Preuss, U. W., Ferri, M., & Simon, R. (2016). Digital interventions for problematic cannabis users in non-clinical Settings: Findings from a systematic review and meta-analysis. *European Addiction Research, 22*(5), 233–242. https://doi.org/10.1159/000445716

Holländare, F., Gustafsson, S. A., Berglind, M., Grape, F., Carlbring, P., Andersson, G., Hadjistavropoulos, H. D., & Tillfors, M. (2016). Therapist behaviours in internet-based cognitive behaviour therapy (ICBT) for depressive symptoms. *Internet Interventions, 3*, 1–7. https://doi.org/10.1016/j.invent.2015.11.002

Hoogendoorn, M., Berger, T., Schulz, A., Stolz, T., & Szolovits, P. (2017). Predicting social anxiety treatment outcome based on therapeutic email conversations. *IEEE Journal of Biomedical and Health Informatics, 21*(5), 1449–1459. https://doi.org/10.1109/JBHI.2016.2601123

Horvath, A. O., & Greenberg, L. S. (1989). The development and validation of the Working Alliance Inventory. *Journal of Counseling Psychology, 36*(2), 223–233. https://doi.org/10.1037/0022-0167.36.2.223

Hunt, M. G., Moshier, S., & Milonova, M. (2009). Brief cognitive-behavioral internet therapy for irritable bowel syndrome. *Behaviour Research and Therapy, 47*(9), 797–802. https://doi.org/10.1016/j.brat.2009.05.002

Janse, A., Worm-Smeitink, M., Bleijenberg, G., Donders, R., & Knoop, H. (2018). Efficacy of web-based cognitive-behavioural therapy for chronic fatigue syndrome: randomised controlled trial. *The British Journal of Psychiatry, 212*(2), 112–118. https://doi.org/10.1192/bjp.2017.22

Johansson, P., Westas, M., Andersson, G., Alehagen, U., Broström, A., Jaarsma, T., Mourad, G., & Lundgren, J. (2019). An internet-based cognitive behavioral therapy program adapted to patients with cardiovascular disease and depression: Randomized controlled trial. *JMIR Mental Health, 6*(10), e14648. https://doi.org/10.2196/14648

Johansson, R., Ekbladh, S., Hebert, A., Lindström, M., Möller, S., Petitt, E., Poysti, S., Larsson, M. H., Rousseau, A., Carlbring, P., Cuijpers, P., & Andersson, G. (2012). Psychodynamic guided self-help for adult depression through the internet: a randomised controlled trial. *PloS One, 7*, e38021. https://doi.org/10.1371/journal.pone.0038021

Johansson, R., Hesslow, T., Ljótsson, B., Jansson, A., Jonsson, L., Färdig, S., Karlsson, J., Hesser, H., Frederick, R. J., Lilliengren, P., Carlbring, P., & Andersson, G. (2017). Internet-based affect-focused psychodynamic therapy for social anxiety disorder: A randomized controlled trial with 2-year follow-up. *Psychotherapy, 54*(4), 351–360. https://doi.org/10.1037/pst0000147

Jolstedt, M., Wahlund, T., Lenhard, F., Ljótsson, B., Mataix-Cols, D., Nord, M., Öst, L-G., Högström, J., Serlachius, E., & Vigerland (2018). Efficacy and cost-effectiveness of therapist-guided internet cognitive behavioural therapy for paediatric anxiety disorders: a single-centre, single-blind, randomised controlled trial. *The Lancet Child & Adolescent Health, 2*(11), 792–801. https://doi.org/10.1016/S2352-4642(18)30275-X

Kahlke, F., Berger, T., Schulz, A., Baumeister, H., Berking, M., Auerbach, R. P., Bruffaerts, R., Cuijpers, P., Kessler, R. C., & Ebert, D. D. (2019). Efficacy of an unguided internet-based self-help intervention for social anxiety disorder in university students: A randomized controlled trial. *International Journal of Methods in Psychiatric Research, 28*(2), e1766. https://doi.org/10.1002/mpr.1766

Kaldo-Sandstrom, V., Larsen, H. C., & Andersson, G. (2004). Internet-based cognitive-behavioral self-help treatment of tinnitus: Clinical effectiveness and predictors of outcome. *American Journal of Audiology, 13*(2), 185–192. https://doi.org/10.1044/1059-0889(2004/023)

Käll, A., Jägholm, S., Hesser, H., Andersson, F., Mathaldi, A., Tiger Norkvist, B., Shafran, R., & Andersson, G. (2020). Internet-based cognitive behavior therapy for loneliness: A pilot randomized controlled trial. *Behavior Therapy, 51*(1), 5468. https://doi.org/10.1016/j.beth.2019.05.001

Käll, A., Shafran, R., Lindegaard , T., Bennett, S., Cooper, Z., Coughtrey, A., & Andersson, G. (2020). A common elements approach to the development of a modular cognitive behavioural theory for chronic loneliness. *Journal of Consulting and Clinical Psychology, 88*(3), 269–282. https://doi.org/10.1037/ccp0000454

Kampmann, I. L., Emmelkamp, P. M., & Morina, N. (2016). Meta-analysis of technology-assisted interventions for social anxiety disorder. *Journal of Anxiety Disorders, 42*, 71–84. https://doi.org/10.1016/j.janxdis.2016.06.007

Karyotaki, E., Kleiboer, A., Smit, F., Turner, D. T., Pastor, A. M., Andersson, G., Berger, T., Botella, C., Breton, J. M., Carlbring, P., Christensen, H., de Graaf, E., Griffiths, K., Donker, T., Farrer, L., Huibers, M. J., Lenndin, J., Mackinnon, A., Meyer, B., Moritz, S., . . . Cuijpers, P. (2015). Predictors of treatment dropout in self-guided web-based interventions for depression: An "individual patient data" meta-analysis. *Psychological Medicine, 45*(13), 2717–2726. https://doi.org/10.1017/S0033291715000665

Karyotaki, E., Riper, H., Twisk, J., Hoogendoorn, A., Kleiboer, A., Mira, A., Mackinnon, A., Meyer, B., Botella, C., Littlewood, E., Andersson, G., Christensen, H., Klein, J. P., Schröder, J., Bretón-López, J., Scheider, J., Griffiths, K., Farrer, L., Huibers, M. J., Phillips, R., . . . Cuijpers, P. (2017). Efficacy of self-guided internet-based cognitive behavioral therapy in the treatment of depressive symptoms: A meta-analysis of individual participant data. *JAMA Psychiatry, 74*(4), 351–359. https://doi.org/10.1001/jamapsychiatry.2017.0044

Kazdin, A. E. (2007). Mediators and mechanisms of change in psychotherapy research. *Annual Review of Clinical Psychology, 3*, 1–27. https://doi.org/10.1146/annurev.clinpsy.3.022806.091432

Kelders, S. M., Bohlmeijer, E. T., Pots, W. T., & van Gemert-Pijnen, J. E. (2015). Comparing human and automated support for depression: Fractional factorial randomized controlled trial. *Behaviour Research and Therapy, 72*, 72–80. https://doi.org/10.1016/j.brat.2015.06.014

Kessler, D., Lewis, G., Kaur, S., Wiles, N., King, M., Weich, S., Sharp, D. J., Araya, R., Hollinghurst, S., & Peters, T. J. (2009). Therapist-delivered internet psychotherapy for depression in primary care: a randomised controlled trial. *The Lancet, 374*(9690), 628–634. https://doi.org/10.1016/S0140-6736(09)61257-5

Kishimoto, T., Krieger, T., Berger, T., Qian, M., Chen, H., & Yang, Y. (2016). Internet-based cognitive behavioral therapy for social anxiety with and without guidance compared to a wait list in China: A propensity score study. *Psychotherapy and Psychosomatics, 85*(5), 317–319. https://doi.org/10.1159/000446584

Kleiboer, A., Smit, J., Bosmans, J., Ruwaard, J., Andersson, G., Topooco, N., Berger, T., Krieger, T., Botella, C., Baños, R., Chevreul, K., Araya, R., Cerga-Pashoja, A., Cieślak, R., Rogala, A., Vis, C., Draisma, S., van Schaik, A., Kemmeren, L., Ebert, D., . . . Riper, H. (2016). European comparative effectiveness research on blended depression treatment versus treatment-as-usual (E-COMPARED): Study protocol of a randomized controlled non-inferiority trial in eight European countries. *Trials, 17*, 387. https://doi.org/10.1186/s13063-016-1511-1

Klein, B., Meyer, D., Austin, D. W., & Kyrios, M. (2011). Anxiety online: A virtual clinic: Preliminary outcomes following completion of five fully automated treatment programs for anxiety disorders and symptoms. *Journal of Medical Internet Research, 13*, e89. https://doi.org/10.2196/jmir.1918

Klein, J. P., Berger, T., Schröder, J., Späth, C., Meyer, B., Caspar, F., Lutz, W., Arndt, A., Greiner, W., Gräfe, V., Hautzinger, M., Fuhr, K., Rose, M., Nolte, S., Löwe, B., Anderssoni, G., Vettorazzi, E., Moritz, S., & Hohagen, F. (2016). Effects of a psychological internet intervention in the treatment of mild to moderate depressive symptoms: Results of the EVIDENT study, a randomised controlled trial. *Psychotherapy and Psychosomatics, 85*(4), 218–228. https://doi.org/10.1159/000445355

Klein, J. P., Hauer, A., Berger, T., Fassbinder, E., Schweiger, U., & Jacob, G. (2018). Protocol for the REVISIT-BPD trial, a tandomized controlled trial testing the effectiveness of an internet-based self-management intervention in the treatment of borderline personality disorder (BPD). *Frontiers in Psychiatry, 9*, 439. https://doi.org/10.3389/fpsyt.2018.00439

Knowles, S. E., Toms, G., Sanders, C., Bee, P., Lovell, K., Rennick-Egglestone, S., Coyle, D., Kennedy, C. M., Littlewood, E., Kessler, D., Gilbody, S., & Bower, P. (2014). Qualitative meta-synthesis of user experience of computerised therapy for depression and anxiety. *Plos One, 9*, e84323. https://doi.org/10.1371/journal.pone.0084323

Kolovos, S., van Dongen, J. M., Riper, H., Buntrock, C., Cuijpers, P., Ebert, D. D., Geraedts, A. S., Kenter, R. M., Nobis, S., Smith, A., Warmerdam, L., Hayden, J. A., van Tulder, M. W., & Bosmans, J. E. (2018). Cost effectiveness of guided Internet-based interventions for depression in comparison with control conditions: An individual-participant data meta-analysis. *Depression and Anxiety, 35*(3), 209–219. https://doi.org/10.1002/da.22714

Königbauer, J., Letsch, J., Doebler, P., Ebert, D., & Baumeister, H. (2017). Internet- and mobile-based depression interventions for people with diagnosed depression: A systematic review and meta-analysis. *Journal of Affective Disorders, 223*, 28–40. https://doi.org/10.1016/j.jad.2017.07.021

Kraepelien, M., Svenningsson, P., Lindefors, N., & Kaldo, V. (2015). Internet-based cognitive behavioral therapy for depression and anxiety in Parkinson's disease - A pilot study. *Internet Interventions, 2*(1), 1–6. https://doi.org/10.1016/j.invent.2014.11.006

Krieger, T., Reber, F., von Glutz, B., Urech, A., Moser, C. T., Schulz, A., & Berger, T. (2019). An internet-based compassion-focused intervention for increased self-criticism: A randomized controlled trial. *Behavior Therapy, 50*(2), 430–445. https://doi.org/10.1016/j.beth.2018.08.003

Krieger, T., Urech, A., Duss, S. B., Blättler, L., Schmitt, W., Gast, H., Bassetti, C., & Berger, T. (2019). A randomized controlled trial comparing guided internet-based multi-component treatment and internet-based guided sleep restriction treatment to care as usual in insomnia. *Sleep Medicine, 62*, 43–52. https://doi.org/10.1016/j.sleep.2019.01.045

Krotoski, A. (2013). *Untangling the web. What the internet is doing to you.* London: Guardian books.

Lange, A., Schrieken, B., van den Ven, J.-P., Bredweg, B., Emmelkamp, P. M. G., van der Kolk, J., Lydsdottir, L., Massaro, M., & Reuvers, A. (2000). "Interapy": The effects of a short protocolled treatment of posttraumatic stress and pathological grief through the Internet. *Behavioural and Cognitive Psychotherapy, 28*(2), 175–192. https://doi.org/10.1017/S1352465800001089

Lappalainen, P., Granlund, A., Siltanen, S., Ahonen, S., Vitikainen, M., Tolvanen, A., & Lappalainen, R. (2014). ACT Internet-based vs face-to-face? A randomized controlled trial of two ways to deliver Acceptance and Commitment Therapy for depressive symptoms: An 18-month follow-up. *Behaviour Research and Therapy, 61*, 43–54. https://doi.org/10.1016/j.brat.2014.07.006

Lau, Y., Htun, T. P., Wong, S. N., Tam, W. S. W., & Klainin-Yobas, P. (2017). Therapist-supported internet-based cognitive behavior therapy for stress, anxiety, and depressive symptoms among postpartum women: A systematic review and meta-analysis. *Journal of Medical Internet Research, 19*(4), e138. https://doi.org/10.2196/jmir.6712

Lenhard, F., Andersson, E., Mataix-Cols, D., Rück, C., Vigerland, S., Högström, J., Hillborg, M., Brander, G., Ljungström, M., Ljótsson, B., & Serlachius, E. (2017). Therapist-guided, internet-delivered cognitive-behavioral therapy for adolescents with obsessive-compulsive disorder: A randomized controlled trial. *Journal of the American Academy of Child and Adolescent Psychiatry, 56*(1), 10-19.e12. https://doi.org/10.1016/j.jaac.2016.09.515

Lenhard, F., Sauer, S., Andersson, E., Månsson, K., Mataix-Cols, D., Rück, C., & Serlachius, E. (2018). Prediction of outcome in internet-delivered cognitive behaviour therapy for paediatric obsessive-compulsive disorder: A machine learning approach. *International Journal of Methods in Psychiatric Research, 27*(1), e1576. https://doi.org/10.1002/mpr.1576

Lindh-Åstrand, L., Spetz Holm, A.-C., Sydsjö, G., Andersson, G., Carlbring, P., & Nedstrand, E. (2015). Internet-delivered applied relaxation for vasomotor symptoms in postmenopausal women: Lessons from a failed trial. *Maturitas, 80*(4), 432–434. https://doi.org/10.1016/j.maturitas.2015.01.010

Lindner, P., Carlbring, P., Flodman, E., Hebert, A., Poysti, S., Hagkvist, F., Johansson, R., Zetterqvist Westin, V., Berger, T., & Andersson, G. (2016). Does cognitive flexibility predict treatment gains in Internet-delivered psychological treatment of social anxiety disorder, depression, or tinnitus? *PeerJ, 4*, e1934. https://doi.org/10.7717/peerj.1934

Lindner, P., Miloff, A., Hamilton, W., Reuterskiöld, L., Andersson, G., Powers, M., & Carlbring, P. (2017). Creating state of the art, next-generation Virtual Reality exposure therapies for anxiety disorders using consumer hardware platforms: Design considerations and future direction. *Cognitive Behaviour Therapy, 46*(5), 404420. https://doi.org/10.1080/16506073.2017.1280843

Ljótsson, B., Andersson, G., Andersson, E., Hedman, E., Lindfors, P., Andréewitch, S., Rück, C., & Lindefors, N. (2011). Acceptability, effectiveness, and cost-effectiveness of internet-based exposure treatment for irritable bowel syndrome in a clinical sample: A randomized controlled trial. *BMC Gastroenterology, 11*, 110. https://doi.org/10.1186/1471–230X-11–110

Ljótsson, B., Hedman, E., Andersson, E., Hesser, H., Lindfors, P., Hursti, T., Rydh, S., Rück, C., Lindefors, N., & Andersson, G. (2011). Internet-delivered exposure based treatment vs. stress management for irritable bowel syndrome: A randomized trial. *American Journal of Gastroenterology, 106*(8), 1481–1491. https://doi.org/10.1038/ajg.2011.139

Lonsdorf, T. B., Rück, C., Bergström, J., Öhman, A., Andersson, G., Lindefors, N., & Schalling, M. (2010). The COMTval158met polymorphism is associated with symptom relief during exposure-based cognitive-behavioral treatment in panic disorder. *BMC Psychiatry, 10*, 99. https://doi.org/10.1186/1471–244X-10-99

Loucas, C. E., Fairburn, C. G., Whittington, C., Pennant, M. E., Stockton, S., & Kendall, T. (2014). E-therapy in the treatment and prevention of eating disorders: A systematic review and meta-analysis. *Behaviour Research and Therapy, 63*, 122–131. https://doi.org/10.1016/j.brat.2014.09.011

Luik, A. I., van der Zweerde, T., van Straten, A., & Lancee, J. (2019). Digital delivery of cognitive behavioral therapy for insomnia. *Current Psychiatry Reports, 21*, 50. https://doi.org/10.1007/s11920-019-1041-0

Ly, K. H., Ly, A.-M., & Andersson, G. (2017). A fully automated conversational agent for promoting mental well-being: A pilot RCT using mixed methods. *Internet Interventions, 10*, 39–46. https://doi.org/10.1016/j.invent.2017.10.002

Magnusson, K., Nilsson, A., Andersson, G., Hellner, C., & Carlbring, P. (2019). Internet-delivered cognitive-behavioral therapy for significant others of treatment-refusing problem gamblers: A randomized wait-list controlled wait-list trial. *Journal of Consulting and Clinical Psychology, 87*(9), 802–814. https://doi.org/10.1037/ccp0000425

Månsson, K. N. T., Carlbring, P., Frick, A., Engman, A., Olsson, C. J., Bodlund, O., Furmark, T., & Andersson, G. (2013). Altered neural correlates of affective processing after internet-delivered cognitive behavior therapy for social anxiety disorder. *Psychiatry Research: Neuroimaging, 214*(3), 229–237. https://doi.org/10.1016/j.pscychresns.2013.08.012

Månsson, K. N. T., Frick, A., Boraxbekk, C.-J., Marquand, A. F., Williams, S. C. R., Carlbring, P., Andersson, G., & Furmark, T. (2015). Predicting long-term outcome of Internet-delivered cognitive behavior therapy for social anxiety disorder using fMRI and support vector machine learning. *Translational Psychiatry, 5*(3), e530. https://doi.org/10.1038/tp.2015.22

Månsson, K. N. T., Salami, A., Carlbring, P., Boraxbekk, C.-J., Andersson, G., & Furmark, T. (2017). Structural but not functional neuroplasticity one year after effective cognitive behaviour therapy for social anxiety disorders. *Behavioural Brain Research, 318*, 45–51. https://doi.org/10.1016/j.bbr.2016.11.018

Månsson, K. N. T., Salami, A., Frick, A., Carlbring, P., Andersson, G., Furmark, T., & Boraxbekk, C.-J. (2016). Neuroplasticity in response to cognitive behavior therapy for social anxiety disorder. *Translational Psychiatry, 6*(2), e727. https://doi.org/10.1038/tp.2015.218

Mehta, S., Peynenburg, V. A., & Hadjistavropoulos, H. D. (2019). Internet-delivered cognitive behaviour therapy for chronic health conditions: A systematic review and meta-analysis. *Journal of Behavioral Medicine, 42*(2), 169–187. https://doi.org/10.1007/s10865-018-9984-x

Meichsner, F., Theurer, C., & Wilz, G. (2019). Acceptance and treatment effects of an internet-delivered cognitive-behavioral intervention for family caregivers of people with dementia: A randomized-controlled trial. *Journal of Clinical Psychology, 75*(4), 594613. https://doi.org/10.1002/jclp.22739

Melville, K. M., Casey, L. M., & Kavanagh, D. J. (2010). Dropout from Internet-based treatment for psychological disorders. *British Journal of Clinical Psychology, 49*(4), 455–471. https://doi.org/10.1348/014466509X472138

Merry, S. N., Stasiak, K., Shepherd, M., Frampton, C., Fleming, T., & Lucassen, M. F. (2012). The effectiveness of SPARX, a computerised self help intervention for adolescents seeking help for depression: Randomised controlled non-inferiority trial. *British Medical Journal, 344*, e2598. https://doi.org/10.1136/bmj.e2598

Mewton, L., Wong, N., & Andrews, G. (2012). The effectiveness of internet cognitive behavioural therapy for generalized anxiety disorder in clinical practice. *Depression and Anxiety, 29*(10), 843–849. https://doi.org/10.1002/da.21995

Meyer, B., Berger, T., Caspar, F., Beevers, C. G., Andersson, G., & Weiss, M. (2009). Effectiveness of a novel integrative online treatment for depression (Deprexis): Randomized controlled trial. *Journal of Medical Internet Research, 11* (2), e15. https://doi.org/10.2196/jmir.1151

Meyer, B., Bierbrodt, J., Schröder, J., Berger, T., Beevers, C. G., Weiss, M., Jacob, G., Späth, C., Andersoon, G., Lutz, W., Hautzinger, M., Löwe, B., Rose, M., Hohagen, F., Casper, F., Greiner, W., Moritz, S., & Klein, J. P. (2015). Effects of an internet intervention (Deprexis) on severe depression symptoms: Randomized controlled trial. *Internet Interventions, 2*(1), 48–59. https://doi.org/10.1016/j.invent.2014.12.003

Mikus, A., Hoogendoorn, M., Rocha, A., Gama, J., Ruwaard, J., & Riper, H. (2018). Predicting short term mood developments among depressed patients using adherence and ecological momentary assessment data. *Internet Interventions, 12*, 105–110. https://doi.org/10.1016/j.invent.2017.10.001

Mohr, D. C., Burns, M. N., Schueller, S. M., Clarke, G., & Klinkman, M. (2013). Behavioral intervention technologies: Evidence review and recommendations for future research in mental health. *General Hospital Psychiatry, 35*(4), 332–338. https://doi.org/10.1016/j.genhosppsych.2013.03.008

Mohr, D. C., Zhang, M., & Schueller, S. M. (2017). Personal sensing: Understanding mental health using ubiquitous sensors and machine learning. *Annual Review of Clinical Psychology, 13*, 23–47. https://doi.org/10.1146/annurev-clinpsy-032816-044949

Molander, P., Hesser, H., Weineland, S., Bergwall, K., Buck, S., Jäder-Malmlöf, J., Lantz, H., Lunner, T., & Andersson, G. (2018). Internet-based Acceptance and Commitment Therapy for psychological distress experienced by people with hearing problems: A pilot randomized controlled trial. *Cognitive Behaviour Therapy, 47*(2), 169–184. https://doi.org/10.1080/16506073.2017.1365929

Munoz, R. F. (2010). Using evidence-based internet interventions to reduce health disparities worldwide. *Journal of Medical Internet Research, 12*(5), e60. https://doi.org/10.2196/jmir.1463

Newby, J. M., Smith, J., Uppal, S., Mason, E., Mahoney, A. E. J., & Andrews, G. (2018). Internet-based cognitive behavioral therapy versus psychoeducation control for illness anxiety disorder and somatic symptom disorder: A randomized controlled trial. *Journal of Consulting and Clinical Psychology, 86*(1), 89–98. https://doi.org/10.1037/ccp0000248

Nieminen, K., Berg, I., Frankenstein, K., Viita, L., Larsson, K., Persson, U., Spånberger, L., Wretman, A., Silfvernagel, K., Andersson, G., & Wijma, K. (2016). Internet-delivered cognitive behaviour therapy of posttraumatic stress symptoms following childbirth - A randomized controlled trial. *Cognitive Behaviour Therapy, 45*(4), 287–306. https://doi.org/10.1080/16506073.2016.1169626

Nobis, S., Lehr, D., Ebert, D. D., Baumeister, H., Snoek, F., Riper, H., & Berking, M. (2015). Efficacy of a web-based intervention with mobile phone support in treating depressive symptoms in adults with type 1 and type 2 diabetes: A randomized controlled trial. *Diabetes Care, 38*(5), 776–783. https://doi.org/10.2337/dc14-1728

Nordgreen, T., Gjestad, R., Andersson, G., Carlbring, P., & Havik, O. E. (2018). The effectiveness of guided internet-based cognitive behaviour therapy for social anxiety disorder in a routine care setting. *Internet Interventions, 13*, 2429. https://doi.org/10.1016/j.invent.2018.05.003

Norlund, F., Wallin, E., Olsson, E. M. G., Wallert, J., Burell, G., von Essen, L., & Held, C. (2018). Internet-based cognitive behavioral therapy for symptoms of depression and anxiety among patients with a recent myocardial infarction: The U-CARE heart randomized controlled trial. *Journal of Medical Internet Research, 20*(3), e88. https://doi.org/10.2196/jmir.9710

Nygren, T., Brohede, D., Koshnawa, K., Osmana, S. S., Johansson, R., & Andersson, G. (2019). Internet-based treatment of depressive symptoms in a Kurdish population: A randomized controlled trial. *Journal of Clinical Psychology, 75*(6), 985–998. https://doi.org/10.1002/jclp.22753

Olthuis, J. V., Watt, M. C., Bailey, K., Hayden, J. A., & Stewart, S. H. (2016). Therapist-supported internet cognitive behavioural therapy for anxiety disorders in adults. *The Cochrane Database of Systematic Reviews, 3*(3), Cd011565. https://doi.org/10.1002/14651858.CD011565.pub2

O'Mahen, H. A., Richards, D. A., Woodford, J., Wilkinson, E., McGinley, J., Taylor, R. S., & Warren, F. C. (2014). Netmums: A phase II randomized controlled trial of a guided Internet behavioural activation treatment for postpartum depression. *Psychological Medicine, 44*(8), 1675–1689. https://doi.org/10.1017/S0033291713002092

Palacios, J., Lee, G. A., Duaso, M., Clifton, A., Norman, I. J., Richards, D., & Barley, E. A. (2017). Internet-delivered self-management support for improving coronary heart disease and self-management-related outcomes: A systematic review. *Journal of Cardiovascular Nursing, 32*(4), E9–E23. https://doi.org/10.1097/JCN.0000000000000392

Pǎsǎrelu, C., Andersson, G., Bergman Nordgren, L., & Dobrean, A. (2017). Internet-delivered transdiagnostic and tailored cognitive behavioral therapy for anxiety and depression: A systematic review and meta-analysis. *Cognitive Behaviour Therapy, 46*(1), 1–28. https://doi.org/10.1080/16506073.2016.1231219

Paxling, B., Lundgren, S., Norman, A., Almlöv, J., Carlbring, P., Cuijpers, P., & Andersson, G. (2013). Therapist behaviours in internet-delivered cognitive behaviour therapy: Analyses of e-mail correspondence in the treatment of generalized anxiety disorder. *Behavioural and Cognitive Psychotherapy, 41*(3), 280–289. https://doi.org/10.1017/S1352465812000240

Persson Asplund, R., Dagöö, J., Fjellström, I., Niemi, L., Hansson, K., Zeraati, F., Zeraati, F., Ziuzina, M., Geraedts, A., Ljótsson, B., Carlbring, P., & Andersson, G. (2018). Internet-based stress management for distressed managers: Results from a randomised controlled trial. *Occupational and Environmental Medicine, 75*(2), 105–113. https://doi.org/10.1136/oemed-2017-104458

Pihlaja, S., Stenberg, J. H., Joutsenniemi, K., Mehik, H., Ritola, V., & Joffe, G. (2018). Therapeutic alliance in guided internet therapy programs for depression and anxiety disorders - A systematic review. *Internet Interventions, 11*, 1–10. https://doi.org/10.1016/j.invent.2017.11.005

Pozza, A., Andersson, G., & Dèttore, D. (2016). Therapist-guided internet-based cognitive-behavioural therapy for adult obsessive-compulsive disorder: A meta-analysis. *European Psychiatry, 33*(Suppl.), S276–S277. https://doi.org/10.1016/j.eurpsy.2016.01.737

Probst, G. H., Berger, T., & Flückiger, C. (2019). The alliance-outcome relation in internet-based interventions for psychological disorders: A correlational meta-analysis. *Verhaltenstherapie*, https://doi.org/10.1159/000503432

Provoost, S., Lau, H. M., Ruwaard, J., & Riper, H. (2017). Embodied conversational agents in clinical psychology: A scoping review. *Journal of Medical Internet Research, 19*(5), e151. https://doi.org/10.2196/jmir.6553

Richards, D., & Richardson, T. (2012). Computer-based psychological treatments for depression: A systematic review and meta-analysis. *Clinical Psychology Review, 32*(4), 329–342. https://doi.org/10.1016/j.cpr.2012.02.004

Richards, D., Richardson, T., Timulak, L., & McElvaney, J. (2015). The efficacy of internet-delivered treatment for generalized anxiety disorder: A systematic review and meta-analysis. *Internet Interventions, 2*(3), 272–282. https://doi.org/10.1016/j.invent.2015.07.003

Riper, H., Hoogendoorn, A., Cuijpers, P., Karyotaki, E., Boumparis, N., Mira, A., Andersson, G., Berman, A. H., Bertholet, N., Bischof, G., Blankers, M., Boon, B., Boß, L., Brendryen, H., Cunningham, J., Ebert, D., Hansen, A., Hester, R., Khadjesari, Z., Kramer, J., . . . Smit, J. H. (2018). Effectiveness and treatment moderators of internet interventions for adult problem drinking: An individual patient data meta-analysis of 19 randomised controlled trials. *Plos Medicine, 15*, e1002714. https://doi.org/10.1371/journal.pmed.1002714

Ritterband, L. M., Thorndike, F. P., Cox, D. J., Kovatchev, B. P., & Gonder-Frederick, L. A. (2009). A behavior change model for internet interventions. *Annals of Behavioral Medicine, 38*(1), 18–27. https://doi.org/10.1007/s12160-009-9133-4

Ritterband, L. M., Thorndike, F. P., Gonder-Frederick, L. A., Magee, J. C., Bailey, E. T., Saylor, D. K., & Morin, C. M. (2009). Efficacy of an Internet-based behavioral intervention for adults with insomnia. *Archives of General Psychiatry, 66*(7), 692–698. https://doi.org/10.1001/archgenpsychiatry.2009.66

Romijn, G., Batelaan, N., Kok, R., Koning, J., van Balkom, A., Titov, N., & Riper, H. (2019). Internet-delivered cognitive behavioral therapy for anxiety disorders in open community versus clinical service recruitment: Meta-analysis. *Journal Medical Internet Research, 21*(4), e11706. https://doi.org/10.2196/11706

Rozental, A., Andersson, G., Boettcher, J., Ebert, D., Cuijpers, P., Knaevelsrud, C., Ljótsson, B., Kaldo, V., Titov, N., & Carlbring, P. (2014). Consensus statement on defining and measuring negative effects of Internet interventions. *Internet Interventions, 1*(1), 12–19. https://doi.org/10.1016/j.invent.2014.02.001

Rozental, A., Andersson, G., & Carlbring, P. (2019). In the absence of effects: An individual patient data meta-analysis of non-response and its predictors in internet-based cognitive behavior therapy. *Frontiers in Psychology, 10*, 589. https://doi.org/10.3389/fpsyg.2019.00589

Rozental, A., Boettcher, J., Andersson, G., Schmidt, B., & Carlbring, P. (2015). Negative effects of Internet interventions: A qualitative content analysis of patients' experiences with treatments delivered online. *Cognitive Behaviour Therapy, 44*(3), 223–236. https://doi.org/10.1080/16506073.2015.1008033

Rozental, A., Forsell, E., Svensson, A., Andersson, G., & Carlbring, P. (2015). Internet-based cognitive behavior therapy for procrastination: A randomized controlled trial. *Journal of Consulting and Clinical Psychology, 83*(4), 808–824. https://doi.org/10.1037/ccp0000023

Rozental, A., Magnusson, K., Boettcher, J., Andersson, G., & Carlbring, P. (2017). For better or worse: An individual patient data meta-analysis of deterioration among participants receiving Internet-based cognitive behavior therapy. *Journal of Consulting and Clinical Psychology, 85*(2), 160–177. https://doi.org/10.1037/ccp0000158

Rozental, A., Shafran, R., Wade, T., Egan, S., Nordgren, L. B., Carlbring, P., Landström, A., Roos, S., Skoglund, M., Thelander, E., Trosell, L., Örtenholm, A., & Andersson, G. (2017). A randomized controlled trial of Internet-based cognitive behavior therapy for perfectionism including an investigation of outcome predictors. *Behaviour Research and Therapy, 95*, 79–86. https://doi.org/10.1016/j.brat.2017.05.015

Ruegg, N., Moritz, S., Berger, T., Ludtke, T., & Westermann, S. (2018). An internet-based intervention for people with psychosis (EviBaS): Study protocol for a randomized controlled trial. *BMC Psychiatry, 18*(1), 102. https://doi.org/10.1186/s12888-018-1644-8

Ruwaard, J., Lange, A., Schrieken, B., Dolan, C. V., & Emmelkamp, P. (2012). The effectiveness of online cognitive behavioral treatment in routine clinical practice. *PloS One, 7*(7), e40089. https://doi.org/10.1371/journal.pone.0040089

Salamanca-Sanabria, A., Richards, D., & Timulak, L. (2019). Adapting an internet-delivered intervention for depression for a Colombian college student population: An illustration of an integrative empirical approach. *Internet Interventions, 15*, 76–86. https://doi.org/10.1016/j.invent.2018.11.005

Schneider, L. H., Hadjistavropoulos, H. D., & Faller, Y. N. (2016). Internet-delivered cognitive behaviour therapy for depressive symptoms: An exploratory examination of therapist behaviours and their relationship to outcome and therapeutic alliance. *Behavioural and Cognitive Psychotherapy, 44*(6), 625–639. https://doi.org/10.1017/S1352465816000254

Schover, L. R., Canada, A. L., Yuan, Y., Sui, D., Neese, L., Jenkins, R., & Rhodes, M. M. (2012). A randomized trial of internet-based versus traditional sexual counseling for couples after localized prostate cancer treatment. *Cancer, 118*(2), 500–509. https://doi.org/10.1002/cncr.26308

Schröder, J., Bruckner, K., Fischer, A., Lindenau, M., Kother, U., Vettorazzi, E., & Moritz, S. (2014). Efficacy of a psychological online intervention for depression in people with epilepsy: A randomized controlled trial. *Epilepsia, 55*(12), 2069–2076. https://doi.org/10.1111/epi.12833

Schulz, A., Stolz, T., Vincent, A., Krieger, T., Andersson, G., & Berger, T. (2016). A sorrow shared is a sorrow halved? A three-arm randomized controlled trial comparing internet-based individually versus group-guided self-help treatment for social anxiety disorder. *Behaviour Research and Therapy, 84*, 1426. https://doi.org/10.1016/j.brat.2016.07.001

Sehlin, H., Ahlström, B. H., Andersson, G., & Wentz, E. (2018). Experiences of an internet-based support and coaching model for adolescents and young adults with ADHD and autism spectrum disorders - a qualitative study. *BMC Psychiatry, 18*, 15. https://doi.org/10.1186/s12888-018-1599-9

Sevilla-Llewellyn-Jones, J., Santesteban-Echarri, O., Pryor, I., McGorry, P., & Alvarez-Jimenez, M. (2018). Web-based mindfulness interventions for mental health treatment: Systematic review and meta-analysis. *JMIR Mental Health, 5*(3), e10278. https://doi.org/10.2196/10278

Shahnavaz, S., Hedman-Lagerlof, E., Hasselblad, T., Reuterskiold, L., Kaldo, V., & Dahllof, G. (2018). Internet-based cognitive behavioral therapy for children and adolescents with dental anxiety: Open trial. *Journal of Medical Internet Research, 20*(1), e12. https://doi.org/10.2196/jmir.7803

Sijbrandij, M., Kunovski, I., & Cuijpers, P. (2016). Effectiveness of internet-delivered cognitive behavioral therapy for posttraumatic stress disorder: A systematic review and meta-analysis. *Depression and Anxiety, 33*(9), 783–791. https://doi.org/10.1002/da.22533

Silfvernagel, K., Westlinder, A., Andersson, S., Bergman, K., Diaz Hernandez, R., Fallhagen, L., Lundqvist, I., Masri, N., Viberg, L., Forsberg, M. L., Lind, M., Berger, T., Carlbring, P., & Andersson, G. (2018). Individually tailored internet-based cognitive behaviour therapy for older adults with anxiety and depression: A randomised controlled trial. *Cognitive Behaviour Therapy, 47*(4), 286–300. https://doi.org/10.1080/16506073.2017.1388276

Sjöstrom, M., Umefjord, G., Stenlund, H., Carlbring, P., Andersson, G., & Samuelsson, E. (2013). Internet-based treatment of stress urinary incontinence: A randomised controlled study with focus on pelvic floor muscle training. *British Journal of Urology International, 112*(3), 362–372. https://doi.org/10.1111/j.1464-410X.2012.11713.x

Stolz, T., Schulz, A., Krieger, T., Vincent, A., Urech, A., Moser, C., Westermann, S., & Berger, T. (2018). A mobile app for social anxiety disorder: A three-arm randomized controlled trial comparing mobile and PC-based guided self-help interventions. *Journal of Consulting and Clinical Psychology, 86*(6), 493–504. https://doi.org/10.1037/ccp0000301

Strandskov, S. W., Ghaderi, A., Andersson, H., Parmskog, N., Hjort, E., Svanberg Wärn, A., Jannert, M., & Andersson, G. (2017). Effects of tailored and ACT-Influenced Internet-based CBT for eating disorders and the relation between knowledge acquisition and outcome: A randomized controlled trial. *Behavior Therapy, 48*(5), 624637. https://doi.org/10.1016/j.beth.2017.02.002

Ström, L., Pettersson, R., & Andersson, G. (2000). A controlled trial of self-help treatment of recurrent headache conducted via the internet. *Journal of Consulting and Clinical Psychology*, 68(4), 722–727. https://doi.org/10.1037/0022-006X.68.4.722

Ström, L., Pettersson, R., & Andersson, G. (2004). Internet-based treatment for insomnia: A controlled evaluation. *Journal of Consulting and Clinical Psychology*, 72(1), 113–120. https://doi.org/10.1037/0022-006X.72.1.113

Taylor, G. M. J., Dalili, M. N., Semwal, M., Civljak, M., Sheikh, A., & Car, J. (2017). Internet-based interventions for smoking cessation. *The Cochrane Database of Systematic Reviews*, 9(9), CD007078. https://doi.org/10.1002/14651858.CD007078.pub5

Thase, M. E., Wright, J. H., Eells, T. D., Barrett, M. S., Wisniewski, S. R., Balasubramani, G. K., McCrone, P., & Brown, G. K. (2018). Improving the efficiency of psychotherapy for depression: Computer-assisted versus standard CBT. *The American Journal of Psychiatry*, 175(3), 242–250. https://doi.org/10.1176/appi.ajp.2017.17010089

Tiger, M., Rück, C., Forsberg, A., Varrone, A., Lindefors, N., Halldin, C., Farde, L., & Lundberg, J. (2014). Reduced 5-HT(1B) receptor binding in the dorsal brain stem after cognitive behavioural therapy of major depressive disorder. *Psychiatry Research*, 223(2), 164170. https://doi.org/10.1016/j.pscychresns.2014.05.011

Tillfors, M., Andersson, G., Ekselius, L., Furmark, T., Lewenhaupt, S., Karlsson, A., & Carlbring, P. (2011). A randomized trial of Internet delivered treatment for social anxiety disorder in high school students. *Cognitive Behaviour Therapy*, 40(2), 147–157. https://doi.org/10.1080/16506073.2011.555486

Titov, N., Andrews, G., Johnston, L., Robinson, E., & Spence, J. (2010). Transdiagnostic Internet treatment for anxiety disorders: A randomized controlled trial. *Behaviour Research and Therapy*, 48(9), 890–899. https://doi.org/10.1016/j.brat.2010.05.014

Titov, N., Dear, B. F., Ali, S., Zou, J. B., Lorian, C. N., Johnston, L., Terides, M. D., Kayrouz, R., Klein, B., Gandy, M., & Fogliati, V. J. (2015). Clinical and cost-effectiveness of therapist-guided internet-delivered cognitive behavior therapy for older adults with symptoms of depression: a randomized controlled trial. *Behavior Therapy*, 46(2), 193–205. https://doi.org/10.1016/j.beth.2014.09.008

Titov, N., Dear, B. F., Johnston, L., Lorian, C., Zou, J., Wootton, B., Spence, J., McEvoy, P. M., & Rapee, R. M. (2013). Improving adherence and clinical outcomes in self-guided internet treatment for anxiety and depression: randomised controlled trial. *PloS One*, 8, e62873. https://doi.org/10.1371/journal.pone.0062873

Titov, N., Dear, B. F., Staples, L., Bennett-Levy, J., Klein, B., Rapee, R. M., Andersson, G., Purtell, C., Bezuidenhout, G., & Nielssen, O. B. (2017). The first 30 months of the MindSpot Clinic: Evaluation of a national e-mental health service against project objectives. *Australian and New Zealand Journal of Psychiatry*, 51(12), 1227–1239. https://doi.org/10.1177/0004867416671598

Titov, N., Fogliati, V. J., Staples, L. G., Gandy, M., Johnston, L., Wootton, B., Nielssen, O., & Dear, B. F. (2016). Treating anxiety and depression in older adults: randomised controlled trial comparing guided v. self-guided internet-delivered cognitive-behavioural therapy. *BJPsych Open*, 2(1), 50–58. https://doi.org/10.1192/bjpo.bp.115.002139

Topooco, N., Berg, M., Johansson, S., Liljethörn, L., Radvogin, E., Vlaescu, G., Nordgren, L. B., Zetterqvist, M., & Andersson, G. (2018). Chat- and internet-based cognitive-behavioural therapy in treatment of adolescent depression: randomised controlled trial. *BJPsych Open*, 4(4), 199–207. https://doi.org/10.1192/bjo.2018.18

Topooco, N., Riper, H., Araya, R., Berking, M., Brunn, M., Chevreul, K., Cieslak, R., Ebert, D. D., Etchmendy, E., Herrero, R., Kleiboer, A., Krieger, T., García-Palacios, A., Cerga-Pashoja, A., Smoktunowicz, E., Urech, A., Vis, C., Andersson, G., On behalf of the E-COMPARED consortium. (2017). Attitudes towards digital treatment for depression: A European stakeholder survey. *Internet Interventions*, 8, 1–9. https://doi.org/10.1016/j.invent.2017.01.001

Urech, C., Grossert, A., Alder, J., Scherer, S., Handschin, B., Kasenda, B., Borislavova, B., Degen, S., Erb, J., Faessler, A., Gattlen, L., Schibli, S., Werndli, C., Gaab, J., Berger, T., Zumbrunn, T., & Hess, V. (2018). Web-based stress management for newly diagnosed patients with cancer (STREAM): A randomized, wait-list controlled intervention study.

Journal of Clinical Oncology, 36(8), 780–788. https://doi.org/10.1200/JCO.2017.74.8491

van Ballegooijen, W., Cuijpers, P., van Straten, A., Karyotaki, E., Andersson, G., Smit, J. H., & Riper, H. (2014). Adherence to Internet-based and face-to-face cognitive behavioural therapy for depression: A meta-analysis. *PloS One*, 9, e100674. https://doi.org/10.1371/journal.pone.0100674

van der Houwen, K., Schut, H., van den Bout, J., Stroebe, M., & Stroebe, W. (2010). The efficacy of a brief internet-based self-help intervention for the bereaved. *Behaviour Research and Therapy*, 48(5), 359–367. https://doi.org/10.1016/j.brat.2009.12.009

van Lankveld, J. (2016). Internet-based interventions for women's sexual dysfunction. *Current Sexual Health Reports*, 8, 136–143. https://doi.org/10.1007/s11930-016-0087-9

van Lankveld, J. J., Leusink, P., van Diest, S., Gijs, L., & Slob, A. K. (2009). Internet-based brief sex therapy for heterosexual men with sexual dysfunctions: a randomized controlled pilot trial. *Journal of Sexual Medicine*, 6(8), 22242236. https://doi.org/10.1111/j.1743-6109.2009.01321.x

van Luenen, S., Kraaij, V., Spinhoven, P., Wilderjans, T. F., & Garnefski, N. (2019). Exploring mediators of a guided web-based self-help intervention for people with HIV and depressive symptoms: Randomized controlled trial. *JMIR Mental Health*, 6(8), e12711. https://doi.org/10.2196/12711

Vernmark, K., Lenndin, J., Bjärehed, J., Carlsson, M., Karlsson, J., Öberg, J., Carlbring, P., Eriksson, T., & Andersson, G. (2010). Internet administered guided self-help versus individualized e-mail therapy: A randomized trial of two versions of CBT for major depression. *Behaviour Research and Therapy*, 48(5), 368–376. https://doi.org/10.1016/j.brat.2010.01.005

Vigerland, S., Ljótsson, B., Thulin, U., Öst, L.-G., Andersson, G., & Serlachius, E. (2016). Internet-delivered cognitive behavioral therapy for children with anxiety disorders: A randomized controlled trial. *Behaviour Research and Therapy*, 76, 47–56. https://doi.org/10.1016/j.brat.2015.11.006

Vigerland, S., Thulin, U., Svirsky, L., Öst, L.-G., Ljótsson, B., Lindefors, N., Andersson, G., & Serlachius, E. (2013). Internet-delivered CBT for children with specific phobia: A pilot study. *Cognitive Behaviour Therapy*, 42(4), 303–314. https://doi.org/10.1080/16506073.2013.844201

Wagner, B., Knaevelsrud, C., & Maercker, A. (2006). Internet-based cognitive-behavioral therapy for complicated grief: A randomized controlled trial. *Death Studies*, 30(5), 429–453. https://doi.org/10.1080/07481180600614385

Wagner, B., Schulz, W., & Knaevelsrud, C. (2012). Efficacy of an Internet-based intervention for posttraumatic stress disorder in Iraq: a pilot study. *Psychiatry Research*, 195(1–2), 85-88. https://doi.org/10.1016/j.psychres.2011.07.026

Warmerdam, L., van Straten, A., Jongsma, J., Twisk, J., & Cuijpers, P. (2010). Online cognitive behavioral therapy and problem-solving therapy for depressive symptoms: Exploring mechanisms of change. *Journal of Behavior Therapy and Experimental Psychiatry*, 41(1), 6470. https://doi.org/10.1016/j.jbtep.2009.10.003

Watkins, E., Newbold, A., Tester-Jones, M., Javaid, M., Cadman, J., Collins, L. M., Graham, J., & Mostazir, M. (2016). Implementing multifactorial psychotherapy research in online virtual environments (IMPROVE-2): study protocol for a phase III trial of the MOST randomized component selection method for internet cognitive-behavioural therapy for depression. *BMC Psychiatry*, 16, 345. https://doi.org/10.1186/s12888-016-1054-8

Webb, C. A., Olson, E. A., Killgore, W. D. S., Pizzagalli, D. A., Rauch, S. L., & Rosso, I. M. (2018). Rostral anterior cingulate cortex morphology predicts treatment response to internet-based cognitive behavioral therapy for depression. *Biological Psychiatry. Cognitive Neuroscience and Neuroimaging*, 3(3), 255–262. https://doi.org/10.1016/j.bpsc.2017.08.005

Webb, C. A., Rosso, I. M., & Rauch, S. L. (2017). Internet-based cognitive-behavioral therapy for depression: Current progress and future directions. *Harvard Review of Psychiatry*, 25(3), 114122. https://doi.org/10.1097/HRP.0000000000000139

Weise, C., Kaiser, G., Janda, C., Kues, J., Andersson, G., Strahler, J., & Kleinstäuber, M. (2019). Internet-based cognitive-behavioural intervention for women with premenstrual dysphoric disorder: A randomised controlled trial. *Psychotherapy and Psychosomatics*, 88(1), 16–29. https://doi.org/10.1159/000496237

Westermann, S., Rüegg, N., Lüdtke, T., Moritz, S., & Berger, T. (2020). Internet-based self-help for psychosis: Findings from a randomized controlled trial. *Journal of Consulting and Clinical Psychology*, *88*(10), 937–950. https://doi.org/10.1037/ccp0000602

Winzelberg, A. J., Eppstien, D., Eldredge, K. L., Wilfley, D., Dasmahapatra, R., Dev, P., & Taylor, C. B. (2000). Effectiveness of an internet-based program for reducing risk factors for eating disorders. *Journal of Consulting and Clinical Psychology*, *68*(2), 346–350. https://doi.org/10.1037/0022-006X.68.2.346

Zachariae, R., Amidi, A., Damholdt, M. F., Clausen, C. D. R., Dahlgaard, J., Lord, H., Thorndike, F. P., & Ritterband, L. M. (2018). Internet-delivered cognitive-behavioral therapy for insomnia in breast cancer survivors: A randomized controlled trial. *Journal of the National Cancer Institute*, *110*(8), 880–887. https://doi.org/10.1093/jnci/djx293

Zachariae, R., Lyby, M. S., Ritterband, L. M., & O'Toole, M. S. (2016). Efficacy of internet-delivered cognitive-behavioral therapy for insomnia - A systematic review and meta-analysis of randomized controlled trials. *Sleep Medicine Reviews*, *30*, 1–10. https://doi.org/10.1016/j.smrv.2015.10.004

Zetterqvist, K., Maanmies, J., Ström, L., & Andersson, G. (2003). Randomized controlled trial of internet-based stress management. *Cognitive Behaviour Therapy*, *32*(3), 151–160. https://doi.org/10.1080/16506070302316s

CHAPTER 22

EXTENDING THE SCALABILITY AND REACH OF PSYCHOSOCIAL INTERVENTIONS

ALAN E KAZDIN

Abstract

This chapter focuses on the treatment gap, which refers to the discrepancy in the proportion of the population in need of services and the proportion that receives them. Currently, in the United States (and worldwide), most individuals in need of mental health services receive no treatment. Although there are many barriers, a key barrier is the dominant model of delivering psychosocial interventions. The model includes one-to-one, in-person treatment, with a trained mental health professional, provided in a clinical setting (e.g., clinic, private practice office, health-care facility). That model greatly limits the scale and reach of psychosocial interventions. The chapter discusses delivery models that would permit reaching more individuals in need, highlights criteria for developing such models, and illustrates novel models already available. The models include task shifting, best-buy interventions, disruptive innovations, and several others. These models encompass interventions that include but also depart from the usual forms of intervention that currently dominate psychosocial treatment research. A critical if not arguably the most important challenge of psychosocial intervention research is to reach individuals in need with the many excellent evidence-based interventions and with evidence-based models of delivery.

INTRODUCTION

Psychological treatment research has advanced enormously, as illustrated in many ways. First, the development and delineation of evidence-based treatments have progressed such that there is now a long list of interventions with multiple controlled trials and meta-analyses that support their efficacy. These include a broad set of cognitive behavioral interventions, more traditional treatments (e.g., psychodynamic therapies, humanistic therapy, variations of family therapy), and many others (e.g., Kazdin 2018; Society of Clinical Psychology, 2018; Substance Abuse and Mental Health Services Administration [SAMHSA], 2017b).[1] Second, advances have emerged in the

---

[1] Prior to 2018 SAMHSA included a National Registry of Evidence-based Programs and Practices (NREPP) and listed over 400 evidence-based psychosocial interventions (SAMHSA, 2017b). In April of 2018, this was discontinued and replaced by the Evidence-Based Practices Resource Center with a goal of providing "communities, clinicians, policy makers, and others in the field with the information and tools they need to incorporate evidence-based practices into their communities or clinical settings" (online).

individualization or personalization of treatment. Rather than looking at broad moderators, new methods are available to personalize treatment more narrowly by using machine learning and multivariate prediction and multiple regression models to optimize the match between clients and the treatments from which they are likely to profit (e.g., Cohen & DeRubeis, 2018; Kessler, 2018, chapter 20 this volume). Third, the study of neurological processes and biomarkers of psychotherapy outcome has accelerated greatly (e.g., Lueken & Hahn, 2016; Marwood et al., 2018). Fine-grained assessments elaborate change processes and relate these to core features of clinical dysfunction. Fourth, transtreatments and modular treatments have been developed (Barlow et al., 2018; Greeson, Garland, & Black, 2014; Murray & Dorsey, 2013; Murray et al., 2014). *Transtreatments* are interventions that can be applied across many different disorders. Modular treatments consist of units or components of treatment that are selectively deployed in any given case to match the clinical problem(s) the client brings to treatment. Both of these include core components that can be applied broadly to diverse clinical problems (e.g., variations of depression and anxiety). Fifth, technology is playing an increasing role in treatment delivery and assessment of patient status in real time. Among the many examples, online computer programs, applications (apps), virtual reality, and socially assistive robots are increasingly used as stand-alone interventions or as complements to existing treatment (e.g., Ebert et al., 2018; Fairburn & Patel, 2017; Lui et al., 2017; Scassellati et al., 2018). Finally, treatment dissemination has flourished. Increasingly researchers have focused on ways of extending treatment to clinical practice, evaluating methods of accomplishing that, and focusing on large-scale extensions (e.g., Clark, 2018; Elkin et al., 2017; Finley et al., 2015). My points merely sample key lines of work. The overall point is that psychological treatment research continues to advance along several fronts and to extend these advances to clinical services and for children, adolescents, and adults.

Treatment-related areas of research have progressed in many ways as well. First, in research there has been a move away from traditional categorical diagnosis as characterized by the *International Statistical Classification of Diseases and Related Health Problems* (World Health Organization [WHO], 2010) and the *Diagnostic and Statistical Manual of Mental Disorders* (American Psychiatric Association, 2013). Current attention in research focuses on fundamental psychological, biological, and social processes that underlie, span, and delineate disorders (e.g., Lindenmayer, 2018; Stoyanov, Correia, & Cuthbert, 2019).

Second, and related, many neurological processes and genetic influences that underlie them are known now to be common to many psychiatric disorders (e.g., Dedic et al., 2018; Gandal et al., 2018). Psychiatric disorders have been reconsidered by some as brain disorders or brain-circuit disorders (e.g., Insel & Cuthbert, 2015). Other factors are emerging as central

to mental disorders (e.g., microbiota, immune system) (e.g., Cenit et al., 2017; Rieder et al., 2017).

Third, well recognized now is that disorders are intricately connected. This includes the comorbidity of mental disorders (e.g., anxiety and depression) and comorbidity of mental disorders and physical disorders (e.g., anxiety and depression comorbid with a variety of physical conditions such as asthma, hypertension, obesity, and diseases of the digestive system) (e.g., Berginк et al., 2018; Buist-Bouman et al., 2005; Essau et al., 2018; Patalay & Hardman, 2019). This too has advanced the focus on underpinnings, commonalities, and antecedents of psychiatric disorders.

Fourth and most relevant to the present chapter is recognition of the incidence and prevalence of mental disorders worldwide. Mental disorders are pervasive and have enormous impact on individuals, families, and society. For example, depression is the leading cause of disability worldwide, with an estimated 4.4% of the world's population (approximately 322 million people) living with the disorder (WHO, 2017). By itself this is astounding, but perhaps more so by noting that depression is only one of many psychiatric disorders and sources of psychological impairment. As with my prior comments on treatment advances, so too many additional advances might be sampled related to the conceptualization and evaluation of the prevalence of mental disorder – with a few of them highlighted above because of their implications for treatment. The pervasiveness of mental disorders poses enormous challenges for providing services.

This chapter examines what can be done to reach people experiencing psychological problems and who are not receiving services. The term *psychological problems* includes mental illnesses that meet formal (well-specified) criteria of psychiatric disorder, but also subclinical dysfunction that falls below that bar, as well as any fact of affect, cognition, and behavior that impairs functioning in daily life. The focus is on *psychosocial interventions*, a broad term that allows me to cover a range of novel interventions that can address those clinical problems.

Psychotherapy is a large set of interventions within that broad domain and is included in this chapter. The chapter begins with a discussion of the scope of psychological problems and the paucity of interventions that are provided to reach people in need. These topics set the stage for novel lines of treatment delivery to supplement the dominant model of providing psychotherapy.[2] In addition, recommendations are made to develop and evaluate interventions and models of delivery that can begin to reach the majority of individuals in need of services but who receive none.

---

[2] The focus of the chapter is on treatment. Prevention is relevant and no less important but raises a broader and different set of issues and there for is beyond the scope of the chapter.

TREATMENT GAP

Overview of the Problem

The availability of evidence-based treatments for a variety of clinical problems and prevalence of many disorders in varying degrees raises the obvious challenge, namely, ensuring that the treatments reach people in need of services. The *treatment gap* refers to the difference in the proportion of people who have disorders or a specific disorder (prevalence) and the proportion of those individuals who receive care (Kohn et al., 2004; Patel et al., 2010). In the context of mental health, considerable evidence has addressed and documented the gap among different samples globally, for various disorders, age groups, and time periods (e.g., Andrade et al., 2014; Becker & Kleinman, 2013; Merikangas et al., 2011; Steel et al., 2014; Whiteford et al., 2013).

In the United States, millions of children, adolescents, and adults experience significant mental health problems and receive no help whatsoever. For example, from reports of the National Comorbidity Study, we have learned that 26% of the US population meet criteria for a psychiatric disorder within the past 12 months (Kessler et al., 1994; Kessler, Chiu, et al., 2005). This increases to 46% of the population over the course of life (Kessler, Berglund et al., 2005). For ease of computation, consider that approximately 25% of the US population experience a psychiatric disorder during a given year and 50% in their lifetime. From a US population of approximately 330 million (August 2020, www.census.gov/popclock), this translates to approximately 83 million and 165 million people, respectively. Important to add is that the estimates may be conservative; some disorders (e.g., schizophrenia) as well as subsyndromal (subclinical) disorders often are omitted from surveys of prevalence. Moreover, some evidence points to increases in the rates of disorders in the past 10–20 years (e.g., Martins et al., 2017; Twenge et al., 2018).

Separate lines of research have addressed the extent to which individuals in need of services receive them. In the US, approximately 70% of people in need of services do not receive any services (Kessler et al., 2005). Ethnic minority groups (e.g., African, Hispanic, and Native Americans) have much less access to care than do European Americans (e.g., Alegria et al., 2008, 2010; McGuire & Miranda, 2008). For example, African Americans are less likely to have access to services than are European Americans (12.5% vs. 25.4%), and Hispanic Americans are less likely to have adequate care than are European Americans (10.7% versus 22.7%; Wells et al., 2001). The lack of available services for most people and systematic disparities among those services underlie the importance of delivering services in ways that can reach many more people as well as can target special groups.

The problem of high prevalence rates and a gap in the proportion that receives treatment has been studied internationally. The WHO Mental Health Survey Consortium (2004) provided extensive data on the treatment gap from surveys of over 60,000 adults in 14 countries in the Americas, Europe, Middle East, Africa, and Asia. The proportion of respondents who received treatment for emotional or substance-use disorders during the previous 12 months ranged from a low of 0.8% (Nigeria) to a high of 15.3% (United States). These percentages refer to those who received treatment among those in need. These numbers convey that the vast majority (99.2% and 84.7%, respectively (by subtracting the above percentages from 100%) of individuals in need did not receive treatment.

Another recent review conveyed the treatment gap in relation to depression across 21 countries (Thornicroft et al., 2017). In high-income countries, one in five (20%) individuals with depression received minimally adequate treatment. In low-middle-income countries, 1 in 27 (3.7%) received treatment for depression. Overall, among many countries, disorders, time frames, and measures the conclusion remains that most people with a diagnosable psychiatric condition do not receive treatment.

Among the small minority of individuals who do receive services, what exactly do they receive? In the WHO study, receiving services was based on asking respondents if they ever had any contact from a long list of caregivers either as an outpatient or inpatient for problems with emotions, nerves, mental health, or use of alcohol or drugs. Included were mental health professionals (e.g., psychiatrist, psychologist), general medical or other professionals (e.g., general practitioner, occupational therapist), religious counselors (e.g., minister, sheikh), and traditional healers (e.g., herbalist, spiritualist). The list varied among countries depending on local circumstances where types of healers may vary. The precise service provided by these individuals was not identified. Also, the duration of the intervention was not known, but receiving services required at least one contact. Thus, when we say that 15% of individuals received treatment, information is ambiguous and could be one contact with someone who has had no training in mental health.

In the US, the National Comorbidity Survey-Replication study also has provided data on who receives treatment as well as some further information about the nature of that treatment (Wang, Lane et al., 2005). Over 9,000 individuals with psychiatric disorders answered questions about their treatment that included who the service provider was (e.g., psychiatric, family physical, social worker, spiritual advisor, and others) and the type of treatment they received (e.g., self-help group, medication, hospital admission). The study evaluated whether individuals received any treatment and, if so, if this was minimally adequate, which was defined as receiving an intervention (e.g., medication, psychotherapy) that followed evidence-based guidelines for the specific disorder and included multiple contacts (rather than only one visit) (see Wang et al., 2002 for elaboration). For individuals with a psychiatric disorder, 21.5% received treatment from a mental health specialist; 41.7% received treatment if this is expanded to include contact with any health-care person, in addition to those trained in mental health. For individuals who did not meet criteria for disorder (subsyndromal disorder), 4.4% received treatment from a mental health specialist and 10.1%

received treatment if this is expanded to include any contact. Overall, across the entire sample, only 32.7% were classified as receiving at least minimally adequate treatment. The investigators concluded that only one third of treatments provided met minimal standards of adequacy based on evidence-based treatment guidelines.

Key points summarize the state of the treatment gap. First, most individuals with mental disorders do not receive treatment, and that applies to the US and other countries. There is no single summary percentage one can provide because of variation among studies in the disorders that are included (e.g., subsyndromal disorders, substance use and abuse, personality disorders); what counts as treatment; the list of who is included as potential service providers (e.g., mental health professional, religious leader); and the ethnicity, culture, and country of the sample. And yet, through it all, it is clear that we are not providing treatment to the large majority of people in need of services.

Second, when treatment is provided, it includes a variety of interventions administered by mental health professionals, health-care professionals in other areas (e.g., general practitioners), and by others (e.g., religious leaders, healers). This care usually refers to some contact. Yet that contact is not necessarily formalized psychological treatment or medication.

Third and related, evidence-based treatments are used infrequently for mental disorders for the proportionately few individuals who receive care. Epidemiological surveys have not been designed to probe in depth precisely what the interventions are, how long they are administered, and whether the persons administering the treatment are trained in use of the treatment. Yet, we know from other sources as well that evidence-based treatments are not being used for mental and substance use disorders as a general rule (Institute of Medicine [IOM], 2001, 2006; National Academies of Science, Engineering, and Medicine [NAS], 2018). The goals for individual patients and service providers are not just to receive and provide any treatment but, rather, to receive and provide the best treatments and specifically those that have an evidence base. In addition to ensuring that the most well-supported interventions are provided to those who seek and receive treatment, we need to extend these treatments to the much larger group of people in need who receive no services at all.

Barriers to Seeking and Receiving Treatment Services

There are, of course, many reasons why most people in need of psychological services receive no treatment. To begin, receiving services for psychological dysfunction encompasses several steps:

1. Experience symptoms or some form of dysfunction.
2. Identify those as symptoms or something in need of help.
3. Decide whether action is needed to do something about the symptoms.
4. Identify the options for intervention (e.g., a psychosocial treatment, medication, or something else).

5. Seek and actually obtain treatment if that is the option selected.
6. Begin the treatment.
7. Remain in treatment as needed, and with people who have recurrent disorders beginning the process anew when symptoms return.

These seem like a natural flow of steps, and once one is started, the rest of the steps should unfold. Yet, multiple obstacles at each step can impede or prevent the individual from moving forward and receiving care (Jorm, 2012). When the process does unfold, there are remarkable delays. From identifying the problem through help seeking, usually many years (~8 years) have elapsed (Thompson et al., 2008; Wang, Berglund et al., 2005). And for many people, even beginning the process is not perceived as worthwhile. Indeed, a survey in six European countries indicated that one third of individuals believed that professional mental health care is worse than or equal to no help at all for mental disorders (ten Have et al., 2010).

The obstacles that impede or prohibit a person from moving forward in the sequence and receiving care have been well described (Andrade et al., 2014; Corrigan et al., 2014; Hinshaw & Stier, 2008). The obstacles often are referred to as *barriers to care* or *barriers to treatment*. Two broad categories are often defined based on the source of the barrier: system-level factors (e.g., financial costs, whether a service is available, and policy issues) and attitudinal factors (e.g., stigma, mental health literacy, views that treatment will not be of much help). I have summarized key barriers in Table 22.1 to recognize that any new treatments or models of delivery will continue to have limited reach if these barriers are not surmounted or bypassed in some way.

DOMINANT MODEL OF TREATMENT DELIVERY

Overview

There is one barrier I did not list (Table 22.1), namely, how psychotherapies are delivered. I refer to this barrier or impediment as the *dominant model of treatment delivery* (i.e., the most common way psychological interventions are provided to individuals who seek treatment). It is critical to distinguish a treatment or intervention technique from how that treatment is delivered. The distinction is easily conveyed in multiple contexts. For example, in our daily lives, reminders (the intervention) of what we hope to do in a given day or week can be delivered to us in many ways, including smartphone or smartwatch alerts, calendar reminders, a physically printed to-do list (how quaint), and verbal appeals from loving partner. These many ways are the means or models of delivery. In the context of physical health care, some vaccines (the intervention) can be provided by injection, nasal spray, orally, or a needle-free patch (the models of delivery). In the context of mental health care, so too can we distinguish the intervention (e.g., cognitive behavioral therapy) from the models of delivery (e.g., via a live therapist, smartphone app, or the web).

TABLE 22.1 Barriers to Mental Health Care

Barrier type	Brief description
System factors	
Cost of mental health services	Treatment is not affordable because services are not covered by insurance of the client, not completely covered, or the out-of-pocket costs are too expensive. The complexity of understanding what is and is not covered or negotiating all of this (reimbursement forms, appealing after a claim has been refused) can be daunting.
Policy and legal constraints	Government policies (e.g., federal, state, province) as well as third-party payers may restrict what conditions can be treated and reimbursed or for how long treatment can be provided (e.g., number of sessions, days) and still be reimbursed. These constraints also include limited financial resources as a matter of budgets, policy, or law that provides too few services and therefore less accessible services.
Too few providers to deliver services	Mental health professionals are not available in sufficient numbers to provide services to meet the need. This is a worldwide problem in developing (low- and middle-income) and developed (higher income) countries as well. In the US, trained professionals are insufficient in number to treat all those in need and are concentrated in urban areas. Too few meet the ethnic demographic of the nation or focus on clinical problems for which the need is the great.
Attitudinal factors	
Stigma	Stigma refers to negative beliefs and practices by a group about a condition—in this case mental disorders. Concerns among potential clients or consumers of treatment with being labeled (diagnosed) with a mental disorder or by being associated with treatment for a mental disorder. Stigma can lead to genuine discriminatory practices and domains of rejection (e.g., employment, promotion). Also, individuals may view their own dysfunction with stigma (self-stigma), which can interfere with identifying themselves as having a mental disorder and seeking treatment.
Mental health literacy	Information individuals have and what they know about mental disorders, whether one has symptoms or a disorder that warrants treatment, what the options are for treatment, and how to pursue those options and obtain treatment.
Cultural and ethnic influences	Individuals of cultural and ethnic minorities have less access to services for health care in general, including mental health care. Views about whether psychological problems warrant treatment, entry into any health-care service, or seeking treatment can vary widely. Some problems (e.g., anxiety, depression) may not be seen as a reason to seek treatment or to be involved with a health care system. This is not the same as mental health literacy, which is more about knowing, but rather is more firmly rooted in cultural practices and beliefs.

In relation to various forms of traditional, cognitive behavioral, and other psychotherapies, the dominant model of delivery has three interrelated characteristics:

1. Treatment sessions are provided in person and one-to-one with a client (individual, couple, family).
2. Treatment is administered by a highly trained (e.g., master's or doctoral level) mental health professional.
3. Sessions are held at a clinic, private office, or health-care facility.

To be sure, there are changes (e.g., as in the use of technology), as I mention shortly. Even so, in research and clinical practice, the model continues to rule. We are familiar with the term *treatment as usual*, to refer to the practices that are routinely used in a clinical service. Not yet coined is *treatment delivery model as usual*, which I am referring to as the dominant model as a less-cumbersome term.

This model of delivery has strong historical connections to medicine, and in that context is referred to as the *physician's practice model* (Christensen et al., 2009). Indeed, historically many psychological techniques (e.g., Mesmerism, hypnosis, psychoanalysis) that have played pivotal roles in the development of contemporary psychosocial therapies were provided by physicians (e.g., Anton Mesmer, James Braid, and Sigmund Freud, respectively) and followed the usual medical practice model of seeing the doctor for individual sessions, although the setting occasionally included house calls rather than a clinical setting or a private office (e.g., Breuer & Freud, 1957).

Conceptually, treatments have varied tremendously over the years. Pioneers of treatment techniques illustrate this nicely. Examples that occupy special places in the history of the development of psychosocial therapies include pioneers such as Carl Rogers (1902–1987; client-centered psychotherapy), Albert Ellis (1913–2007; rational emotive behavior therapy), Andrew Salter (1914–1996; conditioned reflex therapy), Joseph Wolpe (1915–1997; systematic desensitization), Aaron Beck (1921– ; cognitive therapy for depression), and Arnold Lazarus (1932–2013; multimodal therapy). Each of these pioneers provided a new conceptual view of treatment, different procedures from what had been used by others, and, in varying degrees, connected the conceptual view and treatment techniques they proposed (see Kazdin, 1978).

With remarkable changes in treatment technique, the dominant model of delivery has changed very little. Indeed, if one examines the continued flow of creative interventions (e.g., dialectical behavior therapy, acceptance and commitment therapy, interpersonal psychotherapy, multisystemic therapy) and current randomized trials that are produced, the dominant model of delivery has continued (in-person, one-to-one sessions with a mental health professional, and a special setting), with notable exceptions and promising leads highlighted later. This model applies to evidence-based as well as non-evidence-based interventions and treatments as usual. This dominant model has been enduring, is in demand, and can deliver many interventions effectively, but consider the limitations.

Limitations of the Model in Reaching People

The dominant model limits the degree to which treatment can be extended to reach many individuals in need (Fairburn & Patel, 2014; Kazdin & Blase, 2011). Consider just one facet of the model, namely, the model's reliance on mental-health professionals. In the United States, for example, there are too few trained mental health professionals (Health Resources and Services Administration, 2010; Hoge et al., 2007; SAMHSA, 2013) and the proportion of professionals to clients in need is projected to become much worse through 2025 (NAS, 2017).

Perhaps the obvious solution is the one to pursue (i.e., we just need to recruit and train many more mental health professionals). Having more mental health professionals might be valuable but cannot be expected by itself to have significant impact on reaching the millions of people in need. Moreover, there are huge restrictions in the geographical distribution, interests, and composition of the professional workforce. Let us consider these, in turn.

First, in the US, mental health professionals are concentrated in highly populated, affluent urban areas and in cities with major universities (Health Resources and Services Administration, 2010). All of the states in the US include rural areas where the concentration of people to square miles of land is low (www.hrsa.gov/ruralhealth/aboutus/definition.html). For these areas and small towns more generally, very few and more commonly no mental health professionals may be available.

Second, most mental health professionals do not provide care to populations and clinical problems for which there is an especially great demand (children and adolescents, the elderly, ethnic and minority group members, single-parents, victims of violence, and individuals with intellectual disabilities, of lower income, or living in rural areas). For example, most psychiatric disorders have their onset in childhood and adolescence, but most individuals in the mental health professions are trained in the treatment of adults. At the other end of the age spectrum, the proportion of elderly individuals is expanding rapidly in the US (and worldwide) and are increasingly underserved in mental (and physical) health services (Andreas et al., 2017; IOM, 2011a, 2012). As with the case of children and adults, too few mental health professionals are trained to provide services to the elderly.

Finally, disproportionately few mental health professionals reflect the cultural and ethnic characteristics of those in need of care. Individuals do not necessarily have to be treated by persons of the same ethnic and cultural group with which they identify. Yet matching the diversity of the population in need of treatment has direct implications for clients seeking, remaining in, and profiting from treatment (e.g., Griner & Smith, 2006; Kim et al., 2005; Zane et al., 2005).

For the above reasons, expanding the workforce to deliver treatment with the usual, in-person, one-to-one model of care, with a trained mental health professional may not have major impact on reaching the vast number of people in need of services. The increased person power is not likely to provide treatments where they are needed, for the problems that are needed, and attract the cultural and ethnic mix of clientele that are essential. Professional organizations and funding agencies that provide support for trainees can incentivize professional development in areas of need (e.g., training in rural psychology, mental health services for special groups). Also, we would never want to turn down more resources to provide services. It is just that as a solution to the problem of increasing the scale of interventions, increasing more of what we are doing now in relation to the model of delivery will not suffice in closing the treatment gap.

Another feature of the dominant model raises similar concerns in reaching individuals in need. Usually, clients are required to go to a special setting (e.g., clinic, private office, hospital), and that is a constraint, too. Settings where services are provided are not readily available for most individuals. And going to a setting raises a host of other barriers that are both system issues (e.g., transportation) and attitudinal issues (e.g., stigma).

One-to-one, in-person therapy is referred to here as the dominant model because clinical practice, graduate school training, clinical program accreditation, pre- and postdoctoral internships, and research on psychosocial interventions draw heavily on this model. The dominant model has benefits that are already well known, not the least of which is serving as the main platform for developing evidence-based interventions and for administering the treatments in clinical work. None my comments detract from these remarkable benefits. And for individuals who have access to that model, there may be little need to provide new ways of delivering treatment. My focus pertains to what would be needed to reach the unserved majority of individuals.

EXTENDING THE DOMINANT MODEL TO REACH MORE PERSONS IN NEED

Extensions of the dominant model have altered how treatments are administered in an effort to surmount barriers and obstacles to delivery. Perhaps the greatest extension is related to the use of technology to deliver treatment. I will mention technology later because so many of the options are novel and arguably more than extensions of the dominant model. Apart from the use of technology, I highlight a few of these extensions in the dominant model of delivery because they are important in their own right and also set the stage for the other models that a provide a greater leap in the efforts to scale treatments. The extensions I highlight next in many ways serve as the middle ground between the dominant model and more distinct departures of models of extending care. What I refer to as extensions and illustrate here and the novel models highlighted in a subsequent section both reflect a recognition of the failure of treatment as usually delivered to reach most people in need.

Engaging Clients in Therapy

Although the dominant model is limited in the number of individuals in need of treatment who can be reached, much can be done to extend the reach of that model. Among the issues is that many individuals who do have access do not seek treatment, and among those who do enter treatment, the dropout rates often are high (20–60%; see Becker et al., 2018; Roseborough et al., 2016; Swift & Greenberg, 2012). One area of research to address the matter focuses on engagement of clients. Engagement refers to attending treatment, being committed to treatment, remaining in treatment, and engaging in the prescribed practices (Constantino et al., 2010; Mitchell & Selmes, 2007).

A comprehensive review of 40 years of research of engagement research focused on utilization and participation in child mental health services (Becker et al., 2018). Engagement encompassed several domains of participation in treatment, including the relationship with the therapist, expectancies for change, attendance, understanding the treatment, and adhering to tasks in and outside of treatment. Interventions were evaluated in relation to engagement in the treatment process (coding different facets of engagement I mentioned) rather than clinical outcomes (e.g., symptom reduction, prosocial functioning). The review identified multiple strategies (e.g., appointment reminders, psychoeducation, goal setting, motivational interviewing) among studies that encompassed many treatment settings, types of treatments, and clinical problems. Typically, strategies to enhance engagement were part of intervention packages that did not permit isolation of specific components that accounted for the effects. Even so, some of the strategies emerged as increasing engagement in the treatment process because they were included in studies where engagement was the highest. Accessibility promotion, which used strategies to convey that services are convenient and that made them accessible (e.g., via on-site childcare, taxi vouchers, and bus tokens) was among the highest-impact strategy to improve engagement. Additional elements that were most frequently drawn on to improve engagement were assessment of the client's strengths and needs, psychoeducation, focus on barriers to treatment, and goal setting.

The engagement research raises a critically important issue that has been applied to the dominant model (and could be applied elsewhere). Given the dominant model, can we systematically bring more people into the model and retain them to reap the benefits of therapy? Although the model may be limited and more mental health professionals are invariably needed, are we optimizing use of the model? Current research suggests that there are evidence-based methods for engaging persons in treatment and that would be important to draw on to optimize the reach of the dominant model.

Large-Scale Dissemination of Treatment

Dissemination of treatment usually refers to closing the research–practice gap, that is, extending treatments developed in research to clinical practice. Typically, the issue is not one of scaling treatment to increase the number of people who provide or receive services, but rather improving the services that are provided. In some cases, services are improved and at the same time extended broadly to reach more people in need.

A model that addresses both the research–practice and treatment gaps is the program referred to as Improving Access to Psychological Therapies (IAPT). This is a large-scale program in England designed to greatly increase the availability of effective psychological treatment for depression and anxiety (Clark, 2011, 2012, 2018). Begun in 2008, this government-based program within the English National Health Service includes plans to recruit and train therapists. The program was successful in training therapists, in treating a large number of patients (> 3,500 in the first year), and in demonstrating improvements in patient outcomes, as reflected in reductions in depression and anxiety. In subsequent years, the program was extended, and within three years, 95% of the services that provided care were participating in the program. Over 3,600 new therapists had been recruited. Services saw approximately 310,000 and 399,000 patients by the end of years 1 and 2, respectively, per year, with the goal of scaling up to 900,000 per year. In a recent report, IAPT services have been extended to 960,000 patients per year, a figure that reflects approximately 16% of the community prevalence of depression and anxiety disorders (Clark, 2018). The program has been established in all (209) services in the local health regions in England.

Improvements in clinical outcomes were documented early in the program. Moreover, data showed that thousands of patients (> 13,000) were no longer receiving sick pay and/or state benefits. Thus, treatment was shown to have paid for itself (and more) in terms of government savings. The program continues with further government funding, improvements and extensions in training, extensions in the clinical problems and client populations treated (e.g., children, elderly persons), the use of additional interventions (e.g., mindfulness), and delivery treatment via the internet (Clark, 2018).

Several facets of the program, including recruitment of therapists, implementation of assessments, and monitoring and supervision of treatment, are all part of the success. At a broader scale, this is a model that reflects a partnership involving central government support and the collaboration of services and disciplines (e.g., psychology and economics from the beginning). Especially striking is the evidence that shows the impact of the program on domains that include but go beyond clinical outcomes, such as penetration (extensions) of the treatment to the population in need and the economic costs and benefits. In other words, the utility and benefits of the program can be seen and conveyed to diverse parties in concrete ways. The program is one of few dissemination efforts showing large-scale extension of treatment to not only train therapists in place already but also recruit new therapists and services that extend the reach of treatment (see Clark, 2018).

There are other efforts to train practitioners in evidence-based interventions and to do so on a large scale, as for example in large federal government organizations (Veterans Health Administration), private health-care systems in the US (Kaiser Permanente Health Care System), and local communities (e.g., Karlin et al., 2019; Karlin & Cross 2014; Stuart, Schultz, & Ashen, 2018). Programs of dissemination usually focus on ensuring that existing clinicians are using the best evidence-based practices (to bridge the research-practice gap) rather than to increase the number of providers and significantly increase the proportion of individuals in need who receive treatment (treatment gap). The IAPT example nicely blurs that distinction by encompassing both.

Reconceptualizing How Treatments Are Developed

The usual way we develop psychosocial treatments is to begin with a focus on a clinical disorder, a model or theory of how that disorder emerges, how treatment can address key components of the disorder, and what we might draw from the human and nonhuman animal research (e.g., extinction, fear conditioning, learned helplessness) in the way of principles or techniques. We then begin tests of treatment procedures derived from these sources under well-controlled conditions. These steps exemplify many of the virtues of good science (e.g., developing a conceptual model, testing under carefully controlled conditions, evaluating process and outcome). A difficulty emerges when one wishes to generalize and extend the finding to applied settings, in this case clinical practice. The highly controlled conditions of research (e.g., including recruitment of cases, often with strict inclusion and exclusion criteria) make perfect sense in the treatment trials but may limit extending treatments to practice and broader-scale application.

Researchers have increasingly argued for considering how treatment will be used and how it might be extended on a larger scale at the point of designing treatment (e.g., Fixsen et al., 2009; Lyon & Koerner, 2016; Weisz et al., 2015). In the context of policy development, the term *strategic science* has been used to delineate consideration at the outset what is needed in the research to optimize ultimate utilization and adoption. This approach has been extended to improve the impact of treatments in the context of eating disorders (Brownell & Roberto, 2015; Roberto & Brownell, 2017). In the context of psychotherapy, a similar approach has been suggested.

For example, in one model of treatment development, several dimensions were proposed to be considered from the very outset, that is, when the technique is being developed (Lyon & Koerner, 2016). The dimensions include:

- *Learnability*. Provide clinicians with opportunities to quickly learn to use the treatments.
- *Efficiency*. Attend to the time, effort, and cost of using the treatment.
- *Memorability*. Ensure that critical elements of treatment can be remembered and successfully applied without added supports.
- *Error avoidance and recovery*. Facilitate recovery from errors or misapplications of treatment.
- *Acceptability/satisfaction*. Ensure that the interventions are viewed as acceptable to clinicians.
- *Low cognitive load*. Keep the interventions simple.
- *Exploiting natural constraints*. Make sure the interventions will fit the contexts in which they will be used.

The approach using these dimensions begins with the problem we are trying to solve, namely to develop treatment that can be readily extended to clinical practice and/or to be delivered in various settings and through various service providers outset. These dimensions are relevant if treatment is to be used by a wider range of providers (e.g., lay individuals, individuals from non–mental health professions). Many evidence-based treatments are already available. For such treatments, the value may come from considering how the treatments vary on critical dimensions and whether that facilitates disseminating the treatments more broadly to include but to go beyond applications in the dominant model.

Integrated Care: Primary Care and Behavioral Health

Traditionally, the care of physical health is handled in primary care facilities that are devoted exclusively to medical concerns. This traditional care often is described as *fractionated* because services address only a segment or fraction of the needs of individuals. Integrated care is a model of bringing together multiple resources to address the range of physical, mental health, and substance use problems one may experience, including mental health problems and life style (e.g., diet, exercise, cigarette smoking and in this sense is opposite from fractionated care (see SAMHSA, 2017a).[3] Although the

---

[3] There are many different terms that are used for or overlap with integrated care. An early effort to codify these, identified 52 terms that are used, and that was over two decades ago (Leathard, 1994). Sample terms to describe the approach to care include interprofessional, interdisciplinary, multidisciplinary, interagency, cross agency, partnerships, and many more. *Patient-centered medical homes* is frequently used as a term in contemporary work (e.g., Kazak et al., 2017). Not all terms are interchangeable and even when the same term is used (e.g., integrated care), there are many models and variations in part based on precisely what services are offered and for what populations. Amid the diversity, the model of care includes several common characteristics: *comprehensive care:* Among multiple disciplines to help with the range of medical and psychological, services; *patient-centered:* Emphasis on the whole person and partnering both with the individual and family and integration of culture, values, and preferences of the patient; *coordinated care:* Linking, managing transitions between types of care and settings if needed; *accessible services:* Facilitating receipt of services with shorter wait times, easier access to contract of the team; and *quality and safety:* Commitment to using evidence-based practices, shared decision-making with patients and families, measuring patient experiences (Agency for Healthcare Research and Quality, 2017).

concept of integration of services is not new (e.g., Starfield, 1992; WHO, 2001b), there has been renewed attention in the importance of integration and accelerated efforts to facilitate the changes in health-care delivery (Crowley & Kirschner, 2015; Kazak et al., 2017).

The rationale for integration of services is based on multiple considerations:

- Mental and physical health problems go together (e.g., Lehman & Dixon, 2016; SAMHSA, 2017a). Scott et al., 2016); a mental health problem is likely to be associated with a physical health problem and vice versa.
- When individuals with mental disorders do go for treatment, they are likely to go to a primary care (e.g., internal medicine) service. A significant proportion of these patient visits (30–40%) are for the treatment of a mental disorder (Ansseau et al., 2004; Wittchen et al., 2003).
- The barriers (e.g., stigma of going to a mental health service) can be reduced by integrating care of multiple types in a primary care facility that people are more likely to attend.
- While receiving care for physical health, assessments can identify psychiatric problems (e.g., risk of suicide) that otherwise would be neglected (Lanzillo et al., 2019).
- The critical role of behavioral health (e.g., life-style practices, management of stress) can be more readily addressed as part of physical and mental health care when this is integrated into a single setting.

Integration provides greater opportunity to reach a segment of the population that seeks physical health care and, in the process, will have access to mental health care as well. Of course, there are many challenges. Many people do not seek or obtain physical health care. And, in relation to mental health, too few professionals are available to treat the vast majority in need whether in integrated care or clinical practice. Also, integrated care still has conceptual and implementation challenges in light of the different professions involved, how to foster their seamless collaboration, how information is collected and managed, how costs are shared and billed, and broadly how the baton is passed from one type of care to other types of care within the setting (Ahgren & Axelsson, 2011; Crowley & Kirschner, 2015). Among the main challenge is the wide range of patients and patient needs that might need to be served in a given setting as reflected in diverse types of physical disorders (e.g., emergency, acute and chronic disorders), mental disorders (e.g., eating disorders, depression, substance abuse), and behavioral health needs (e.g., antismoking, diet and exercise for special populations). Overall, integrated care is clearly a positive move in extending treatment and in ways that reduce some barriers of seeking and obtaining mental health services. Integrated care usually includes components of the dominant model of delivering psychological treatment (e.g., meeting with a trained professional, going to a special setting), but the research and context make this very different and provide an important extension of that model. It will be important to see empirical evaluations of the extent to which the model and its many variations reduce the treatment gap and achieve therapeutic changes.

General Comments

Engaging clients in therapy, disseminating treatment on a large scale, developing treatments initially so they can reach clinicians and more people in need, and utilizing integrated care are four illustrations of efforts to extend psychotherapy and the dominant model of delivery. There are others that might be cited as well, such as the use of technology and the increased use of lay counselors to deliver treatment. I will return to both of these because they blend into novel models in diverse ways.

There may well be an overall zeitgeist in treatment delivery that recognizes the importance of and need to go well beyond what we have been doing traditionally, given what we know now about the scope of psychological problems that impair functioning. Indeed, the need to move to additional models of delivery has spanned decades (e.g., Christensen et al., 1978; Collins et al., 2013; Ryder, 1988). The novel models I discuss later are in keeping with the zeitgeist but reflect many advances in health care and other domains. The models often include different ways of extending treatment and different interventions from those that we usually conceive of as psychological treatment.

KEY CHARACTERISTICS OF SCALABLE MODELS

Before highlighting models of treatment delivery, it is useful to step back a bit. What is the problem we are trying to address and indeed solve? That problem is to reach people in need of services with effective interventions and who are unserved or underserved by current treatments, that is, we wish to narrow the treatment gap. With that in mind, we can ask the more specific question, what are the key characteristics of models of delivery needed to reach that goal? These characteristics are different from those outlined on characteristics of treatment (e.g., learnability, memorability) that focused on treatment techniques and what might make them more readily extended to practice. More broadly, characteristics we would want in the models of delivery can be identified. Table 22.2 summarizes several characteristics that ought to guide our development of interventions and focus our attention on delivery of the interventions.

Scalability is clearly a place to begin in pondering what characteristics models of delivery ought to include. To begin, the model of delivery ought to able to reach very large numbers of individuals in need. We are not necessarily talking about the intervention itself (e.g., cognitive behavioral therapy), but rather whether it can be delivered in such a way to make it not a boutique intervention for the very special few who have access.

Reach as a criterion overlaps with but is distinguishable from scalability. Many groups are especially excluded from treatment and for a variety of reasons. In the US, as I mentioned, these include children and adolescents, the elderly, ethnic and minority group members, single parents, victims of violence, and individuals with intellectual disabilities, of lower income, or living in rural areas. Members of these groups are

TABLE 22.2   Key Characteristics of Models of Treatment Delivery to Reach People in Need of Services

Characteristic	Definition
Scalability	The capacity of the intervention to be applied in a way that reaches a large number of people
Reach	Capacity to extend treatment to individuals not usually served or well served by the traditional dominant service delivery model
Affordability	Relatively low cost compared to the usual model that relies on individual treatment by highly trained (Master's, doctoral degree) professionals
Expansion of the nonprofessional work force	Increase the number of providers who can deliver interventions
Expansion of settings where interventions are provided	Bring interventions to locales and everyday settings where people in need are likely to participate or attend already
Feasibility	Ensure the interventions can be implemented and adapted to varied local conditions to reach diverse groups in need
Flexibility	Ensure that there are options and choices because no one model of delivery is likely to have the reach needed
Acceptability of the model of delivery	The intervention must be acceptable to potential consumers of treatment and those who provide treatment. Acceptability refers to refers to judgments by laypersons, clients, and others of whether the intervention procedures are appropriate, fair, and reasonable for the problem that is to be treated. The extension here is that the model of delivery must be acceptable and is separate from the acceptability of the intervention.

even less likely to receive treatment than are individuals with none of these characteristics. Scaling treatments so that more people receive them does not necessarily handle disparities in treatment. We could be scaling up to reach more of the people (e.g., majority group members, living in urban areas); that would address one problem (making treatment available to more people) but perpetuate another problem (neglecting the same groups we are neglecting now). Reach extends the criterion of scalability to ensure that those groups least likely to receive care are specifically targeted by our models of delivery. This criterion addresses health-care disparities.

Affordability is important because cost is a major and multifaceted barrier to receiving or providing care. On the receiving side, cost of individual sessions (without insurance and even with insurance) can stop people from seeking or remaining in a treatment that is otherwise available. Even when people believe they have coverage, insurance claims for mental health services are often rejected, and that can deter seeking further treatment (e.g., Chedekel, 2016). Apart from affordability from the perspective of the client, there is the other side, namely, affordability from the standpoint of those who fund or provide deliver services (e., federal and state governments in the US). Of course, demonstrations that service delivery costs can be recovered, as in the IAPT example (Clark, 2018), serve as a model.

Expansion of the nonprofessional workforce obviously can increase the reach of treatment. I mentioned earlier that the administration of treatment by trained mental health professionals as part of the dominant model of delivering treatment

can limit reaching many people in need. The number of professionals, where they are located (urban areas), the restricted range of what they treat in relation to need, and the paucity of a diverse ethnic and cultural diversity all are limits in relation to reaching people. The obvious question, of course, is who else but highly trained mental professionals can administer psychological treatments for significant mental health problems? As I will address later, evidence supports the notion that individuals without an advanced degree or training in psychology, psychiatry, or social work can effectively administer treatment. Sufficient to emphasize here, highly trained mental health professionals are not always and perhaps not even usually necessary to administer psychosocial interventions effectively. A model of delivery that permits treatment to be effectively administered by lay individuals would help close the treatment gap. A step toward that on the treatment side has been to simplify treatment by placing treatment into trainable modules so it can be more readily administered by individuals with little or no advanced training in the mental health professions (e.g., Barlow et al., 2018; Bolton et al., 2014; Patel et al., 2010, 2011, 2016). In any case, one characteristic we probably want of novel models of treatment delivery is that there are more people available to provide services.

Expansion of the settings where interventions are provided addresses another limitation of the dominant model of delivering therapy. Currently, most evidence-based interventions require individuals to go to a clinic, hospital, or private practice office. That raises physical obstacles (e.g., transportation, location) and may heighten attitudinal obstacles (e.g., stigma) and thwart engagement in the therapy process (Becker et al., 2018). Those obstacles aside, the current physical settings would not be able to accommodate treatment that was scaled to reach large numbers and those in special areas (e.g., inner city, rural areas) where few facilities and services tend to be available. Of course, the use of technology (e.g., internet, apps) moves treatment out of physical locales and brings treatment to people's homes. The integration of mental health services in settings where physical health care is provided (integrated care) might bring more people into mental health services. Yet other locations to which people have access could be used to provide services too (e.g., schools, shopping centers, urgicare centers), with examples discussed later.

Feasibility has to do more with practical features of the delivery model. In fact, can the model be implemented, given the circumstances of the local conditions? These conditions may include physical characteristics or infrastructure (e.g., access to computers or any health-care facilities), but also to cultural and ethnic beliefs. That is, a very scalable treatment in principle might still not be scalable in practice because delivery is not likely to occur or be subscribed to in light of beliefs, cultural practices, or views of symptoms and treatment by various groups. The intervention and model of delivery must be practical and likely to be subscribed to. And there are examples available in non-Western cultures. Texting, for example, can be a highly feasible intervention in cultures where there are remote rural areas and no landlines, but cellular phones are very prevalent (e.g., Lester et al., 2010).

Flexibility is important in developing novel models of delivery. One of the problems with the dominant model that I did not emphasize is that for most therapists and clients, it is not just the dominant model; it is the only model. To reach people in need, it would be valuable to have multiple delivery models as options so that a given intervention (e.g., cognitive behavioral therapy, graduated exposure, mindfulness) could be provided in multiple ways. Flexibility could mean how a given model is applied but also choice among models that vary on accessibility and acceptability. Flexibility and choice of models may be the best way to ensure that groups with the greatest health-care disparities receive services.

The final characteristic is referred to as *acceptability of the model of delivery*. Acceptability has to do with consumer views of how appropriate, suitable, and reasonable the treatment or model of delivery is, i.e., the means or procedures rather than the outcomes.[4] For many people an intervention requiring one

to visit a place labeled as a clinic and see a therapist is less acceptable than an intervention where one can work via a video chat service (e.g., Skype or FaceTime or the equivalent) from one's own home. Overall, we not only need interventions that are acceptable but also acceptable models of delivery. Flexibility of the intervention is relevant here because multiple models are needed precisely because acceptability is likely to vary for different group of individuals and as well within groups.

Some general points should be raised about the characteristics of models of delivery to be considered when developing interventions. First, the characteristics I mention might be considered as a guide rather than a comprehensive list. Second, the characteristics overlap but are different enough (e.g., scalability and reach) to make them worth distinguishing. Third, characteristics are each a matter of degree. Models of delivering treatment could vary on a continuum for each characteristic. Fourth, no one model is likely to address each or even most of the characteristics very well. Multiple models of delivery are needed so that treatment can reach many people and in different ways, depending on barriers, acceptability, affordability, and other characteristics of both the interventions and the way they are provided.

NOVEL MODELS OF TREATMENT DELIVERY

Multiple models have emerged from global health care, business, economics, and the media—all well outside of traditional psychological and psychiatric care (see Kazdin, 2018). Table 22.3 provides several models of delivery and their key characteristics. I highlight three examples to convey different ways in which treatments can reach large numbers of individuals. The models I illustrate have evidence that they can deliver treatments in ways that are effective.

Task Shifting

Task shifting is a method to strengthen and expand the health-care workforce by redistributing the tasks of delivering services to a broad range of individuals with less training and fewer qualifications than traditional workers (e.g., doctors, nurses) (see WHO, 2008).[5] This redistribution allows an increase in the total number of health workers (e.g., nonprofessionals, lay individuals) to scale up the scope of providing services. The concept and practices of task shifting are not new and currently are in place in many developed countries (e.g., Australia, England, United States) where nurses, nurse assistants, and pharmacologists provide services once reserved for doctors. Also, community health workers, a term defined long before task shifting was developed, have provided specific health services (e.g., birthing, neonatal care, immunization) in developing and developed countries and with demonstrated efficacy (e.g., Bang et al., 2005; Greenwood et al., 1989).

---

[4] Acceptability has been evaluated extensively in the context of evaluating various treatment options such as psychotherapy, medications, and behavior-change interventions (e.g., Carter, 2007; Kaltenthaler et al., 2008). In this context, acceptability influences the likelihood that clients will continue in or drop out of the intervention, whether clients carry out the procedures prescribed during the intervention, and whether professionals (e.g., educators, therapists) actually use the procedure correctly (e.g., Allinder & Oats, 1997; Arndorfer et al., 1999; Kazdin et al., 1997). We know there are cultural and ethnic differences in seeking treatment, utilizing clinical services, and treatment preferences (Boothe et al., 2005; Miranda et al., 2005). It is likely that acceptability is influenced by each of these. Thus, acceptability is not a property or characteristic of treatment per se, but a characteristic in the context of ethnic and cultural perspectives in relation to that treatment.

[5] *Task sharing* is also used. Task shifting and sharing both involve distributing the tasks normally provided by health professionals to lay individuals or at least sharing those. For present purposes, I will refer to *task shifting* to encompass both of these to make the points.

TABLE 22.3   Novel Models of Delivering Treatment

Model	Key characteristic	Examples	Sample references & illustrations
Task shifting (and sharing)	Expanding the workforce by using lay individuals to administer interventions that otherwise might be delivered by health professionals.	Used worldwide for treatment and prevention of HIV/AIDS. Recently extended to mental health service delivery.	WHO (2008) Fulton et al. (2011)
Disruptive innovations	A process in which services or products that are expensive, complicated, and difficult to deliver move in novel ways to alter these characteristics. In health care, services are brought to people more than bringing people to the services.	The delivery of health screening and treatment in shopping malls, drug stores, and grocery stores. Use of smartphones, apps, tablets to assess and deliver mental health interventions.	C.M. Christensen et al. (2009) Rotheram-Boris et al. (2012)
Interventions in everyday (unconventional settings)	Expansion of health care beyond clinics and traditional settings to places that people normally attend for other reasons. Overlaps with disruptive innovation but comes from different tradition and draws on different settings (e.g., schools, work place, churches, hair salons, barber shops).	Delivery of health screening and education messages in hair salons, mental health clinic in Walmart.	Linnan et al. (2014) Luque et al. (2014)
Best-buy interventions	Interventions selected based on their cost-effectiveness, affordability, feasibility for the setting (e.g., country, city), and other criteria. Conceived as an economic tool to help countries select among evidence-based strategies to have impact, where impact is quantified (estimated) for different strategies.	To reduce use of tobacco use, raising taxes, protecting people from cigarette smoke, warning about the dangers of smoking, and enforcing bans.	Chisholm et al. (2007) WHO (2011a)
Fostering lifestyle changes	A range of behaviors individuals can engage in that are known to have impact on physical and / or mental health including controlling diet, exercising, meditation, and interacting with nature.	Exercise has broad impact on health and physical health.	Deslandes et al. (2009) Walsh (2011)
Social media	Use of widely available material that includes social networking (e.g., Facebook, Twitter, texting, YouTube, Skype) that bring people together in novel ways and to present information, to obtain assessment, and to provide feedback or delivery of interventions. Interventions can be brought to people where ever they are through these media connections.	Writing regularly as part of blogging to draw on many evidence-based expressive writing interventions; meeting with a therapist or support group in a virtual social world.	Baker & Moore (2008) Gorini et al. 2008)

(Continued)

Tᴀʙʟᴇ 22.3 (Cᴏɴᴛɪɴᴜᴇᴅ)

Model	Key characteristic	Examples	Sample references & illustrations
Entertainment-education	Use of television or radio to deliver health-care messages and to model health-promoting behaviors. A culturally sensitive long-running series (e.g., TV series) in which different characters take on different roles, deal with the challenges related to the focus of the intervention, and model adaptive strategies.	Early application focused on reducing the birthrate and use of birth control in Mexico.	Singhal & Rogers (1999) Singhal et al. (2004)
Socially assistive robots	Robots that interact with humans in some way. They are able to provide education, feedback, coach patients through activities and tasks, and provide companionship.	Provide companionship with the elderly to reduce loneliness, depression, social isolation, and cognitive impairment	Bemelmans et al. (2012) Rabbitt et al. (2015)
Social network interventions	Delineation of networks and using the networks to spread information or an intervention through individuals varying in degrees of separation from key individuals in that network	Use of peer groups to influence substance use and cigarette smoking.	Christakis & Fowler (2009) Valente (2010)

Task shifting emerged from global health initiatives, particularly in developing countries. These initiatives focused on treating and preventing infectious (e.g., malaria, HIV/AIDS, tuberculosis) and noncommunicable disease (e.g., cardiovascular disease, diabetes, cancer, respiratory disease) and improving living conditions and education (e.g., IOM, 2010, 2011b; United Nations, 2000; WHO, 2011a). These initiatives provide an important context because they contended with key challenges of meeting health-care needs in many cultures, under a variety of conditions (e.g., enormous resource constraints, geographical obstacles), and where people in need of services were not receiving them. Key strategies to address the problems included reorganizing and decentralizing health services to accommodate the limited traditional resources and infrastructure (e.g., medical personnel, hospitals). Most task-shifting applications have focused on physical health in developing countries (e.g., Ethiopia, Haiti, Malawi, and Namibia) where shortages of human resources and the burden of illness (e.g., HIV/AIDS) are acute. Empirical evaluations have shown that task shifting can rapidly increase access to services, reach large numbers of individuals in need, yield good health outcomes, and has high levels of patient and lay counselor satisfaction (WHO, 2008).

Task shifting has been extended to mental health problems because of its ability to be scaled up to provide services to individuals who otherwise do not have access to care and its adaptability to diverse countries, cultures, and local conditions. An exemplary application of task shifting in mental health was

a randomized controlled trial of treatment of anxiety and depression in India (Patelet al., 2010, 2011). Twenty-four public and private facilities (including more than 2,700 individuals with depression or anxiety) received a stepped-care intervention beginning with psychoeducation and then interpersonal psychotherapy, as needed and as administered by lay counselors. The lay counselors had no health background and underwent a structured two-month training course. Medication was available as was specialist attention (health professional) for suicidal patients. At 6 and 12 months after treatment, the intervention group had higher rates of recovery than did a treatment-as-usual control group administered by a primary health-care worker, as well as lower severity symptom scores, lower disability, fewer planned or attempted suicides, and fewer days of lost work. Overall, the study showed that lay counselors could be trained to administer interventions with fidelity and that their interventions reduced the rates of disorder in a large sample. This is an excellent example of extending evidence-based treatments developed in controlled research settings to community applications but with a change in the model of delivery of those treatments. An evidence-based intervention, interpersonal psychotherapy, constituted one of the treatments, but the novelty was in the model of delivery that allowed the intervention to reach many more people than typically is the case in the dominant model where a mental health professional delivers the intervention.

Beyond the prior example, task shifting now has been evaluated in several controlled trials for the treatment of autism spectrum disorder, depression, anxiety, eating disorders, trauma, schizophrenia, and alcohol abuse, in which evidence-based treatments are administered by lay individuals (e.g., Balaji et al., 2012; Bolton et al., 2014; Divan et al., 2019; Kilpela et al., 2014; Nadkarni, et al., 2016; Patel et al., 2016; Rahman et al., 2008, 2016). These demonstrations not only establish the clinical utility of task shifting but add to the evidence that lay counselors can deliver evidence-based interventions and achieve favorable treatment outcomes (e.g., Barnett et al., 2018; Kohrt et al., 2018; Singla et al., 2017). Moreover, studies evaluated outcomes on a larger-than-usual scale for psychological intervention studies, evaluated and monitored treatment fidelity, and included follow-up, among other features.

As any single model of delivering treatment, task shifting has its own unique challenges. Among them is the two-fold task of obtaining personnel. The first of these tasks is to recruit the individuals who will deliver treatment. This is easier in most circumstances than obtaining trained mental health professionals, but still can be an issue depending on the scope and scale of the treatment that is to be delivered and other potential constraints (e.g., applications in multiple rural settings). The second personnel challenge is obtaining sufficient trainers to develop the skills in those who provide direct treatment. In some of the physical health task-shifting work, administration of treatment (e.g., medication) was more straightforward than administration of psychotherapy. These challenges do not at all detract from the contributions of task shifting. Moreover, many of the concerns I highlight here in passing have been addressed empirically in early applications of task shifting (WHO, 2008). Also, guidelines for training lay therapists are available, based on experiences and empirical evaluations across multiple countries (Caulfield et al., 2019).

Best-Buy Interventions

Economics of physical health care have added to the impetus to identify novel models of providing services for physical and mental health care. A survey of world business leaders by the World Economic Forum indicated that chronic disease (e.g., cardiovascular disease, cancer) is a major threat to economic growth globally (Bloom et al., 2011; WHO, 2011b). Disability and mortality exert economic impact not only on individuals, families, and households, but also on industries and societies through consumption of health-care services, loss of income, reduced productivity, and capital expenditures that could otherwise support public and private investment. Best-buy interventions have emerged from this context to designate interventions for physical illnesses, particularly the control of chronic diseases globally (IOM, 2010).

Best buy refers to an intervention for which "there is compelling evidence that is not only highly cost effective, but is also feasible, low-cost (affordable), and appropriate to implement within the constraints of a local health system" (WHO, 2011a, p. 2). Best buy also considers features such as appropriateness for the setting (e.g., culture, resources), capacity of the health system to deliver a given intervention to the targeted population, technical complexity of the intervention (e.g., level of training that might be required), and acceptability based on cultural, religious, and social norms.

Identifying best buys was conceived as an economic tool to help countries evaluate how to achieve a given amount of change, given the number of individuals in need of the intervention, the potential savings of those changes, and the cost differences of alternative strategies (e.g., Chisholm et al., 2007; Chisholm & Saxena, 2012; WHO, 2011b). For example, in one analysis, four criteria (health impact, cost-effectiveness, cost of implementation, and feasibility of scaling up) were used to identify best-buy interventions that would have significant public health impact on noncommunicable diseases including cardiovascular disease, cancers, diabetes, and chronic lung disease (WHO, 2011a). Best buys for cardiovascular disease and diabetes were counseling, multi-drug therapy, and aspirin. These were selected in light of the reduction of disease burden and very low cost. The example is not necessarily one that applies to all locales. Best-buy interventions can differ for a given disorder and country, given variation in the health-care resources, infrastructure, and distribution of the population (e.g., very sparsely populated areas).

Best-buy interventions for physical diseases often focus on domains of functioning that overlap with and are part of behavior, lifestyle, and mental health, as reflected in substance use and abuse (e.g., alcohol and tobacco). For example, for alcohol use, best-buy interventions include enhanced taxation of alcoholic beverages and comprehensive bans on advertising and marketing, based on their favorable cost-effectiveness, affordability overall, and feasibility. Intervening on excessive alcohol use itself was identified as a best buy for reducing the incidence of cardiovascular diseases and cancers, and with impact likely to extend to other burdensome conditions (e.g., cirrhosis of the liver, depression, and traffic injuries and deaths; WHO, 2011a). More explicit designations of best buys have been identified for select mental disorders. For example, for clinical depression, generically produced antidepressant medication, brief psychotherapy, and treating depression in primary care qualified as best buys (Chisholm et al., 2007). For psychoses, treating people with antipsychotic drugs and with psychosocial support are regarded as best buys.

Best-buy interventions are based on estimates of utilization and impact, relying on mathematical models (e.g., Chisolm et al., 2007). Empirical tests of the models are then conducted to ensure that well-intended, feasible, and scalable interventions yield the intended outcomes. As in any large-scale intervention, sustaining the integrity of the intervention can be a challenge. Yet, some best-buy interventions (e.g., selective taxes, bans on advertising to reduce substance use and abuse) differ from the usual psychological interventions and do not require compliance by clients in the same way as psychosocial treatments usually do and do not require adherence to a specific treatment protocols by therapists. There is evidence from research as well as large-scale reports that taxes can be effective in changing health-related behaviors (see Desmond-Hellmann, 2016). Of course, taxes and advertising have their own problems (e.g., black market sales that are not taxed, advertising not reaching the target population, adverse public reaction to control in this fashion), but these different problems are precisely the reasons why we need multiple models of delivering interventions. No single model or small set of models is likely to reach the vast majority in need of services and we would want models with different benefits as well as liabilities.

Disruptive Innovations

Disruptive technology or disruptive innovations emerged from business rather than health care (Bower & Christensen, 1995; Christensen, 2003; Christensen et al., 2009). The concept pertains to a change in a product or service that is not a linear, evolutionary, or incremental step. Rather the product or service often provides a disruptive, disjunctive, or qualitative leap and develops or extends a market that is not otherwise being served.

Disruptive innovation theory refers to the process by which products or services that are complicated, expensive, and less affordable move to novel delivery models and products that change these characteristics. The concept of disruptive innovation is much less familiar but the many innovative products and services that illustrate its application are part of our daily lives. Examples include innovations in manufacturing (e.g., interchangeable parts, assembly line car production), business (e.g., smartphones, smartwatches, tablets), consumer purchasing (e.g., via credit cards, smartphones, PayPal, drone delivery of packages), social networking (e.g., Facebook, Twitter, LinkedIn), and health care (e.g., home pregnancy tests, medical robotics, urgicare, and walk-in and minute clinics) (see Christensen et al., 2009). These innovations often provide simpler, less expensive, or more convenient solutions to problems and often can be scaled to reach people who would not otherwise have access.

Telemedicine, which refers to the use of communication and information technology to extend the reach of medical practice, is one example of a disruptive innovation that has changed how and where some patients receive medical care (e.g., Roine et al., 2001). Telemedicine in the form we know has been use for many decades but can be traced to earlier times (e.g., ancient Greece; Bashshur & Shannon, 2009). At the same time, leaps in both hardware and software have extended the range of remote current applications, as illustrated by the development of diverse specialty areas (e.g., telepsychiatry, telesurgery, teleopthamology, teleaudiology, teleneurology) (e.g., Dorsey et al., 2018; Hilty et al., 2018; Lee & Lee, 2018; Martini et al., 2013). (Teleproctology has emerged recently but is a little behind the other areas [Pulles et al., 2017].)

Other disruptive innovations in health care have utilized nonmedical settings, such as drug stores and shopping malls to provide a range of services to measure blood pressure or cholesterol, treat various illnesses (e.g., allergies, pinkeye, strep throat) and skin conditions (e.g., cold sores, minor burns, wart removal), and provide vaccines (e.g., flu shots). Many of these settings improve access to care and are increasingly expanding the range of physical and mental conditions that are included. Patient referrals can be made if the tests reveal the need for further diagnostic work or intervention.

Disruptive innovations can provide accessible ways of delivering mental health interventions (see Rotheram-Borus et al., 2012). Many interventions have already extended to mental health care through the use of smartphones, tablets, apps, websites, and video conferencing (e.g., Backhaus et al.,

2012; Barak et al., 2008; Bennett-Levy, 2010; Parikh & Huniewicz, 2015; Price et al., 2014). For example, smartphones and tablets provide opportunities for assessing psychological states and bringing interventions to individuals in their everyday lives. The assessment can provide feedback in real time that can activate treatment from one's communication device, as exemplified in the use of biofeedback (e.g., Pallavicini et al., 2009; Zhang et al., 2010). Sensors that monitor heart or breathing rate and provide information immediately (e.g., in color or graphical display) can prompt the use of relaxation and other self-management techniques (e.g., RelaxLine, 2010; StressEraserPro, 2020). Other sensors are designed to assess and track emotions, followed by interventions to promote mental health and well-being (e.g., Sentio Solutions, 2018). Apps for smartphones, smartwatches, and tablets are constantly emerging and now allow assessment, feedback, and applications of interventions that can change mental health care. Smart clothing that tracks a variety of biological measures, used more commonly in relation to exercise and athletics, has now found its way into assessment and treatment feedback loops in physical and mental health care (e.g., Chen et al., 2016; Witte & Zarnekow, 2019).[6]

Online delivery of treatment is a disruptive intervention that extends of the dominant model of therapy. For example, multiple options are available online for the treatment of anxiety and depression (e.g., Spek et al., 2007 Spijkerman et al., 2016). These programs often include the same core cognitive behavioral treatment sessions as used with in-person treatment (e.g., scheduling of positive activities, identifying and challenging cognitive distortions) and are divided into sessions (with video clips describing key information and assigned homework) that patients can complete from home. There are now scores of other evidence-based self-help psychosocial interventions for a range of psychological problems (Bennett-Levy et al., 2010; Harwood & L'Abate, 2010; Karyotaki et al., 2017; Pearcy et al., 2016). These interventions can leap over many of the usual barriers of receiving treatment and expand on the dominant model of in-person, individual psychotherapy at a clinic.

Technology-based psychosocial interventions vary in the extent to which they utilize facets of the dominant model. For example, some web-based treatments are administered one-to-one by a mental health professional but do not require the client to go to a clinic. Others are based on self-help and may involve no therapist at all. And still others use lay counselors with back-up by mental health professional as needed. All variations can contribute to extending treatment to those who otherwise would not receive services. Yet, we still need more demonstrations that technology in fact can and does reach large numbers of individuals, and in the process has impact. The evidence base for a given intervention (e.g., cognitive behavioral therapy) cannot be assumed to apply when the

---

[6] I mention examples of technology that are commercial projects. The list is arbitrary from an unlimited set of resources. I am not endorsing any product mentioned in this chapter and I have no connection, financial or otherwise, to those that are mentioned here.

model of delivery changes from the one(s) in which the original evidence was established.

Such extensions are evident. For example, in one demonstration, cognitive behavioral treatment was provided on line as a course (Titov et al., 2015). Support was provided by a trained therapist by phone or email on a weekly basis. A total of 1,471 individuals completed treatment (out of 2,049 who enrolled). Even with the use of a trained therapists (one feature of the dominant treatment model), the application was conducted on a relatively large scale (mean therapist time per case was 112 minutes). The results indicated improvements on multiple outcome measures with the level of improvements comparable to those achieved with in-person cognitive behavioral therapy as established in other studies. The scale of delivery, feasibility, and patient satisfaction were all promising. However, this was not a controlled trial and focused on pre-to-post changes of the one (large) group that received treatment.

An example of a very large-scale application and controlled trial consisted of a web-based intervention for smoking cessation (Muñoz et al., 2016). The program was available in two languages (Spanish and English) and was visited by over 290,000 individuals from 168 countries. Data reported for over 7,000 participants revealed smoking quit rates ranging from 39% to 50% at different points of assessment up to an 18-month follow-up. This program advanced the notion of Massive Open Online Interventions (MOOI) to resemble the model (Massive Open Online Courses, MOOC) in education. MOOI can make interventions available to reach individuals on a large scale, as demonstrated in the context of cigarette smoking. In our work with treatment of children, we have established the efficacy of a parenting intervention for children referred for aggressive and antisocial behavior using the dominant model of treatment delivery and then with online treatment, all evaluated in multiple randomized controlled trials (see Kazdin, 2017b). The program was extended in the MOOC format to help parents with childrearing challenges more generally and has reached approximately 60,000 parents (as of November 2019; Kazdin, 2017a). This latter application has not been evaluated in controlled studies, and hence merely conveys the reach of that format.

As I noted, technology has many forms and formats. It is useful to consider technology at an early stage, even though facets (e.g., telepsychiatry) are not new. And yet, other technologies with some use in both mental and physical health care (e.g., social robotics) are rather unfamiliar (see Broadbent, 2017; Rabbitt et al., 2015). The broad term *technology* is not very informative in light of the diversity of interventions and models of delivery that it encompasses. Even so, many of the interventions comprising this rubric share a number of strengths, limitations, and potential (e.g., Aboujaoude et al., 2015; Bennett & Glasgow, 2009). The potential is the ability to provide mental health care to children, adolescents, and older individuals – groups especially unlikely to receive services (see Jones, 2014; Lane et al., 2016).

As it relates to the focus of this chapter, there are relatively few applications of technology demonstrating that interventions can be scaled to reach large numbers and produce significant (statistically, clinically) outcomes. In general, the development and application of technology-based interventions might well be scalable and for diverse populations. Evidence for many applications might well be on the horizon, but there has been cogent concern voiced that the contribution of the use of technology might be oversold at this time or at least until better scaling with outcome evidence are forthcoming (e.g., Bauer & Mossner, 2013; Donker et al., 2013; Tomlinson et al., 2012).

In addition, technologies, bring their own set of limitations related to adoption, including acceptability of the public in the context of treatment, maintaining participation in a program that may not be or seem individualized, and access to the internet where that is needed. Interestingly, the utility and adoption of technology (by clinical services, therapists, and clients) may well improve in the next decade as a function of cohort effects. Younger age individuals are increasingly at home with technology and social media, and young children routinely chat with relatives via smartphones and Skype. Indeed, it is not so surprising to learn that a 9-month-old infant accidentally rented a car online (Kim, 2015). Also, in some settings (e.g., colleges and universities), mental health services often cannot meet the demands, and technology-based services might be especially viable (Auerbach et al., 2016; Prince, 2015). The overall point is clear. Technology is central to our everyday lives and awaits newborns as they enter the world. (Actually, there are many apps parents can use to monitor and bond with the fetus so the fetus can begin exposure to technology even earlier.) How technology is viewed and accessed may well change as many people are connected to the web or some smart device most of the time. Clarification of what is and is not evidence-based will be needed.

If technology as a means of providing mental health services takes the route of other disruptive innovations, the landscape of treatment may change considerably. When disruptive innovations first emerge (e.g., personal computer, cell phone), they do not compete head-to-head with the traditional product (e.g., mainframe computer, centralized computers in industry and on campuses, landline phones, pay phones). Over time, the innovation may begin to compete and take over as the product develops and the use expands. The expansions include greater convenience, ease of use, and portability in relation to original products. Perhaps innovative treatment delivery models that are disruptive including those involving technology will have a similar course.

General Comments

I have illustrated a few of the models as part of the longer list (in Table 22.3). A few clarifications are critical. To begin, I do not wish to imply that the list is exhaustive. I have drawn on models usually considered outside the traditions the mental health professions (e.g., public health, business), but that can be used to delivery mental health related interventions. Other models within and out of the mental health professions could have been included. For example, community mental health represents a model of care with an extensive history and tradition within psychology (Sarason, 1974). Moreover, with increased attention to crises in world mental health, community-based interventions have played a major role in low- and middle-income countries where mental health services are administered in the home, school, and refugee camps (e.g., Barnett et al., 2017; Kohrt et al., 2018; Singla et al., 2017). Such services might be part of extending treatment to everyday settings, which I list as a separate model (Table 22.3). Yet, community mental health has its own set of guiding principles and practices.

Second, how the models are labeled and listed can be defended because of different traditions but still overlap in practice. For example, task-shifting practices are usually conducted in everyday settings, which I include as a separate model. Yet, task shifting now has its own literature with multiple controlled mental health intervention studies, and delineating that model by itself helps bring these into focus (e.g., Javadi et al., 2017). How the models are parsed and labeled and the complete range of models that might be listed and mobilized to close the treatment gap are slightly beyond the goals of this chapter. Indeed, ideally this chapter would spawn additional models and combinations. More, different, and more scalable models of treatment are needed in comparison to what dominates mental health care at present in low-, middle-, and high-income countries.

In illustrating novel models, three points are important to underscore:

1. *In suggesting novel models, this is not a call to eliminate or reduce the dominant model.* That point will be clear later in the discussion of the need for multiple models, but is important to state explicitly. This chapter is about what more is needed and how to expand our delivery models to close the treatment gap.
2. *The priority is still to focus on evidence-based treatments.* The focus on models as a way to deliver such treatments does not move away from or abandon evidence.
3. *Models too must be evidence based.* That is, it must be shown that they can deliver an intervention and generate outcome data from controlled trials attesting to the models. The models I have illustrated meet this latter criterion, as do each of those in Table 22.3, but in varying degrees. [7]

My illustrations convey that novel models of delivery have been applied and raise the prospect of providing evidence-based interventions on a large scale. Some of the models make clear the distinction between treatment technique (the procedures or means of altering a clinical problem) from the model of delivery (how that technique is dispensed or provided). Task shifting is one example where evidence-based treatments (e.g., cognitive behavioral therapy, interpersonal psychotherapy), well established in the dominant model of delivering therapy, is delivered by lay individuals. In other models, the distinction between technique and delivery is blurred. For example, best-buy interventions can be well outside the usual psychosocial techniques

(e.g., changes in taxes, advertising) and are delivered in ways well outside of traditional treatment (e.g., laws, social policy).

Many of the models have emerged and been applied to physical health (e.g., chronic and infectious disease) but prompted extensions to mental health for a few key reasons. First, global health initiatives to address physical health-care services revealed gaps in mental health services (IOM, 2010; WHO, 2011b). In addition, many barriers for delivering care for physical health care to large swaths of individuals in need, particularly in developing countries, were recognized to be similar to the barriers of providing mental health care (Lancet Global Mental Health Group, 2007; Sharan et al., 2009). Consequently, models for delivering treatment proved to be applicable to both mental and physical health services. As highlighted with best-buy interventions, an intervention with a primary target of reducing one type of dysfunction (e.g., substance use and abuse) may have direct consequences on other types of dysfunction (e.g., physical disease and mortality).

Second, it has become increasingly clear that mental and physical health are inextricably intertwined, with bidirectional, reciprocal, and comorbid relations. Indeed, a variety of common influences promote both physical and mental illness. Some of the more familiar culprits include inflammation and stress, but there are now many others, including air pollutants and particulates (e.g., Bakian et al., 2015; Lim et al., 2012), breastfeeding practices (e.g., Krol et al., 2014; Oddy et al., 2010), microbiota in our guts (e.g., Kleiman et al., 2015; Nowakowski et al., 2016), and mitochondrial abnormalities (e.g., Rezin et al., 2009; Rossignol & Frye, 2015), to mention a few. In addition, psychological factors (e.g., depression) can directly influence the course of physical diseases (e.g., heart disease, HIV by decreasing medication adherence). Finally, micronutrients, now investigated in multiple trials, can effect significant change in physical and psychiatric disorders (Kaplan et al., 2015; Rucklidge & Kaplan, 2013). More generally, reducing the burdens of physical health cannot neglect mental health, as reflected in the oft-cited statement, there is "no health without mental health" (Prince et al., 2007, p. 859; WHO, 2005, p. 11). In any case, models of delivering treatments can apply to both physical and mental health, and several treatments may be expected to have impact on both as well.

The move to integrated-health care that provides physical and mental health-care services in the same facility further acknowledges the benefits of treating both in juxtaposition (e.g., Collins et al., 2013; Crowley & Kirschner, 2015; Richardson et al., 2005). Integration provides greater opportunity to reach a segment of the population that seeks physical health care and consequently also will have access to mental health care. Of course, there are many who do not seek or obtain physical health care. However, the key point is to have multiple models of delivering mental health services to capture an increasing portion of the individuals who otherwise receive no services. Integrated care does not have to be the solution but could be a significant part of multiple strategies.

The models I have illustrated and otherwise listed add to the dominant model and increase the likelihood of

[7] In the table, social networking, socially assistive robots, as models of delivery, have evidence in their behalf but not as extensive as other models (e.g., task shifting, Entertainment Education; see Kazdin, 2018).

reaching more people who are not being served but who need mental health care. Those who are unserved within a country or among different countries are heterogeneous in culture, ethnicity, geography, resources, infrastructure for providing and receiving care, and many other characteristics that can influence treatment delivery. The cultural sensitivity issue warrants further comment. Many of the evidence-based treatments have been developed, evaluated, and implemented largely in Western cultures and could readily vary in applicability and effectiveness among diverse cultures. It is true that many of these treatments do not vary in effectiveness across the few ethnic cultural groups (out of thousands internationally) to which they have been extended (e.g., Miranda et al., 2005). In addition, many treatments have been developed based on considering cultural and ethnic issues at the outset (see Koslofsky & Domenech Rodríguez, 2017). Models also must ensure that they are accessible, accessed, and acceptable to diverse groups.

The novel models I have mentioned begin with a multicultural and indeed global perspective and as part of that are designed to accommodate local conditions including what is feasible, not just economically, but what is acceptable to those who would be the recipients of intervention. For example, in task shifting lay members of the communities in which treatment is provided are directly involved in delivery of the care. Thus, one is delivering and receiving interventions among one's peers of the same culture, ethnicity, and traditions. In best-buy interventions, precisely what interventions are likely to be appropriate is determined by local conditions and resources (e.g., government, political, likely impact) and in that sense also are compatible with the culture and society. A seemingly great best-buy intervention (e.g., taxes, advertising, medication) might not fit at all for a given country and culture, not just for feasibility or relevance but because one or more of these is not an acceptable way of exerting influence effectively in that culture. More broadly, any one model will have its own set of limitations and will miss key segments of the population in need of services. But multiple models, particularly those that begin with what characteristics are needed to provide treatment on a large scale, are likely to have the needed impact.

MULTIPLE MODELS ARE NEEDED

A diverse set of models is needed to address the challenge of closing or significantly reducing the treatment gap to ensure those least likely to receive care are appropriately and effectively included, and that the burdens of mental illness are reduced. If we want to reach people in need, first and foremost, we need models that can be scaled up to connect with the enormous numbers who currently are unserved. Yet even if any particular model could be scaled up, its inherent features probably will cause it to omit some segment of the population in need or to be deemed unacceptable to a population it could reach. That is why we want multiple models to deliver psychosocial interventions.

Figure 22.1 provides pictorial illustration of what we are trying to accomplish and how multiple models play a critical role.

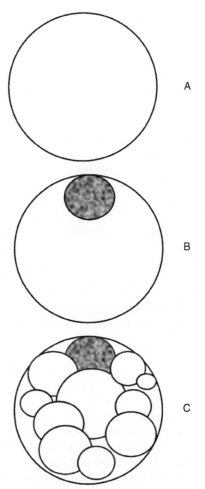

FIGURE 22.1 Representation of the Role of Multiple Models for Reaching Individuals in Need of Services

Notes. The upper circle or pie (A) is intended to represent all those individuals in need of psychological services. The middle circle (B) consists of all persons in need of services but with a small shaded portion (not intended to represent the scale) who receives the dominant model of psychotherapy. The lower circle (C) includes multiple models. Each model is represented by a circle and serves (provides intervention for) some segment of the population in need. The multiple circles obviously serve many more individuals in need of services. They also overlap (spill on to each other) a bit, because for any single group that needs to be reached, more than one model is likely to be needed. Actually, C should have many overlapping models that would have even more overlap and more options. Finally, note there are still spaces in C not covered by one of the models. The reality may be that even with multiple models, some individuals in need of care will be missed. This means only that the goals to develop the models cannot be static and new options will invariably be welcome and necessary. The models listed in Table 22.3 are designed to reach a greater proportion of individuals in need. More models may well be developed beyond those I have highlighted.

Consider the top portion of the figure (A) to represent all individuals in need of mental health services. This would include individuals with clinical dysfunction, subclinical disorders, and others who are impaired in some way due to some facet of their emotional, cognitive, behavioral, or social functioning (e.g., stress and distress, loneliness, suicidality) that somehow is not covered by the previous categories.

The middle portion of the figure (B) shows a small circle (a very small subgroup) covering up part of the larger circle.

That circle represents the small portion of individuals in need of services who do receive treatment and receive that through the dominant model of individual (or small unit such as couple, family, group) therapy. An obvious feature of B is that most individuals in need of treatment (A portion) still are not receiving interventions. As I have shown at the beginning of the chapter, B is primarily where we are now. This chapter is about the bottom portion (C) where each circle represents a model of intervention delivery.

A few features of the C portion are noteworthy. First, the various models of delivery (each model is a circle within the larger circle) overlap with one another, i.e., occupy the same space in some places. This is an important feature because one model will have inherent limitations (e.g., vary in feasibility or acceptability to a given constituency) and perhaps not even reach those who are especially neglected by current services.

Second, the dominant model of administering treatment (shaded circle from B and also now in C) is still present. There is nothing in this chapter to suggest eliminating that model. Lamentably, the dominant model (or any single model) by itself has very little impact on reducing the burdens of mental illness on any scale but may reach a small portion (of the pie, A in the figure) who need care.

Third, the figure (C) conveys that even with multiple overlapping models, there are still spaces in the larger circle that are that are not covered. These spaces reflect people in need of treatment who will still receive none. Even with many models and overlap, we cannot be assured we will reach everyone in need. Consider what a remarkable accomplishment a simple reversal of the following statistic would be. Currently approximately 70% of individuals in the US in need of mental health services receive nothing! What an accomplishment it would be to deploy multiple models of delivery so that 70% received an evidence-based intervention! Of course, we would like the percentage to be much higher, but the bar is so low now that reaching most people in need and achieving 70% would be a virtual revolution in mental health care. The point is to recognize that we will be less than perfect in reaching everyone. But we could do vastly better as we approach the goal of reaching most and almost all individuals in need of services. Multiple models are available that make that feasible. Moreover, if the goal of reaching most people in need were more explicitly embraced, no doubt other models and variations would emerge.

I have presented models as a way of addressing the treatment gap. The models could also be applied to prevention. I was not able to take up that facet. Yet, a critical feature related to both treatment and prevention would be to improve the base level of physical and mental health that could reduce the incidence of disorders or simply increase the ability to manage the slings and arrows of life that often precipitate disorders. There are many intervention opportunities that do not involve traditional psychotherapy techniques. Examples include fostering widespread opportunities for exercise (e.g., at school and workplace) and the use of social networks to promote behavioral health (e.g., National Physical Activity Plan Alliance, 2016; Perkins, Subramanian, & Christakis, 2015).

RECOMMENDATIONS AND PRIORITIES FOR RESEARCH

Recommendations for next steps for research begin with considering overarching questions of this chapter.

1. Are we closing the treatment gap? That is, are proportionately more people in need of services receiving them?
2. Are we reaching subpopulations within the culture that are the least likely to receive care?
3. When interventions are scaled up to reach more people and special populations, do we achieve outcomes that significantly improve their functioning?

These questions and the many ways of addressing them are separate from the usual psychotherapy agenda, focus, and publications on the topic of evidence-based treatment. They are also questions that require collaborations with individuals from multiple disciplines. For example, when mental health professionals and psychotherapy researchers think about assessment, the focus typically is on the process and outcomes in a given study. These are obviously important; I am suggesting a very different focus, level of analysis, and additional assessment that permit empirically based responses to the questions. More outcome studies that are relatively small scale in highly controlled settings, more uses of transtreatments and modular treatments, more meta-analyses of everything, more efforts to ensure that therapists in practice are using evidence-based treatments, and more research on moderators, mediators, and mechanisms and new ways to search for them, are among the common topics for which more research is needed. I am not challenging these per se. I am noting that psychotherapy research addressing these now very traditional foci leaves largely untouched the three questions I have noted.

One can move to more concrete levels with recommendations. First, one path of least resistance would be to pair psychotherapy researchers with those who develop technology-based versions of treatment. Technological applications of treatments (e.g., apps as one example) continue to proliferate, and controlled trials cannot begin to keep up with the pace. Thus, many if not most of such treatments are not evaluated empirically. Yet, many of these can reach people in need. Consequently, this might be a useful path to begin to identify scalable interventions. We do need the demonstration projects (small scale randomized controlled trials like those we currently do very well), but also the move to evaluation when the intervention is scaled. We want to go beyond discussion sections in research reports, merely saying that this or that intervention has potential to be scaled. At some point, and I am arguing for *now*, we want direct tests of scaling to address the treatment gap.

Second, special attention might be accorded in those populations least likely to receive treatment. Can we reach these individuals, provide acceptable treatment, and achieve important treatment outcomes? There are many research studies focusing on outreach and to different populations. For such studies, the next step is scaling to reach more of those special populations. As with many areas I have addressed, psychotherapy research has initial leads and evidence. The move to scaling is not trivial, and in the process, the evidence may not apply. That is, the means of delivery might well alter the efficacy of a given technique, and that must be evaluated empirically. Perhaps in some areas of psychotherapy research, the move to scalable interventions that are then evaluated is not such a leap.

Third, low-cost interventions might be a high-priority research focus. Low-cost interventions (e.g., national or local campaigns, advertisements, medical or psychological services in drug stores or in the workplace) might be feasible in extending treatment on a large scale. Low cost does not necessarily mean less effective than higher-cost interventions, but even if it did there might be benefits for modest improvements among the many who currently receive no treatment.

The cost of the interventions raises broad issues related to implementation of both models and interventions. For example, *stepped care* is a term frequently used in the context of interventions and in both physical and mental health care. Stepped care is the notion that less intensive, less costly, and more readily applicable interventions are the place to begin, and one moves to more aggressive, costly, and specialized interventions only when needed. The concept has been around for some time and continues to be advocated as a model for providing psychological interventions (e.g., Clark, 2011; Draper & O'Donohue, 2011; Haaga, 2000; Newman & Howard, 1986). Stepped care involves dual considerations of not only the intervention technique but also the model of delivery, because models can vary considerably in effort and cost. More research on stepped care, what are the steps, and decision-making about how to implement both stepped-care treatments and models, could provide the basis for scaling interventions.

Finally, assessment and monitoring warrant special attention as part of the research agenda. Whether we are closing the treatment gap and having impact with novel models are empirical questions. Connecting treatment to national surveillance would be important to measure the penetration of treatments in the populations of interest (e.g., to close the treatment gap) as well as the impact on the burden of mental illness. In the US, for example, many national programs (e.g., Zero suicide, Winnable Battles, Healthy People 2020) have had large-scale assessments in place to evaluate impact on mental and physical health.

A concrete example related to the treatment gap is nicely illustrated in the context of cigarette smoking where researchers have developed an index referred to as the Reach Ratio (Baskerville et al., 2016; Campbell et al., 2014). The index calculates the proportion of individuals in a given subgroup (e.g., men, women; but any subgroup) who receive or are reached by treatment in proportion to the distribution of that group in the overall population with the problem. Thus, a ratio of 1.0 would mean that the intervention is reaching that subgroup in proportion to the extent to which that group shows the problem in the population (prevalence). Disparities in delivery of the intervention would be below that number and show that the reach of treatment is much less than the proportion of individuals overall with the problem. That measure focuses on disparities rather than scalability but illustrates the broader point. We would want much more attention to indices of scalability

and reach to show that models we are using reach people not otherwise receiving services and that clinical outcomes were achieved.

There are many questions to address about what, where, to whom, and how to ensure the treatment gap is reduced and at what cost. It is important to keep in mind that scaling up treatment for mental disorders can product huge savings (see Chisholm et al., 2016; Clark, 2018). Even if the savings were not evident, one would want to argue the importance of disability and impairment as critical personal and social issues. Of course, moral and legal issues might be raised (e.g., withholding effective treatments from most people in need when treatments are available, systematically excluding special groups whom we know are the least likely to receive services). Yet, the goal of the chapter was to convey some of the options (models) for reaching people in need and underscoring the evidence for both interventions and models of delivery to accomplish that.

I have highlighted some of the key areas of research. Perhaps the initial priority is recognizing the treatment gap, seeking evidence-based solutions that could be deployed to reduce that gap, and evaluating outcomes among those who have reached by treatment. These priorities and challenges are inherently collaborative endeavors. They involve the health-care professions as well as law, policy, government agencies, and business and industry that delineate what services are reimbursed. Collaborations invariably occur but perhaps more organizational leadership is needed. For example, in academia, there are programs or institutes in a given university separately for neuroscience, nanotechnology, and biomedical engineering (e.g., Sharp et al., 2016). Each area spans multiple disciplines and departments that come together for common goals, methods, and interests. Something like these programs or institutes may be needed that draws colleagues, methods, and perspectives from many different sciences, professions, and services with the goal of reducing the treatment gap for mental and physical health.

SUMMARY AND CONCLUSIONS

Psychotherapy research has advanced remarkably and along several fronts. One of the main advances has been the development of evidence-based treatments. There are now scores of such treatments as applied the many different disorders. Enormous attention has been given to dissemination of treatment to services and settings where these techniques can be used. Dissemination has been designed primarily to close the research-practice gap, i.e., ensuring that treatments demonstrated to be effective in the context of clinical research are in use in clinical practice. Occasionally dissemination programs also extend treatment to people who otherwise might not be treated (e.g., IAPT program I have discussed). This chapter focused on a gap that has received considerably less attention in the psychosocial intervention literature, namely, the treatment-gap, i.e., the difference in the proportion of individuals in need of services and those who receive them. Most individuals in need of treatment in the US and worldwide do not receive any treatment, much less one of those designated as evidence based.

There are many different reasons people do not receive care including barriers such as costs of treatment, accessibility of services near where many patients live, stigma, and several others. One barrier to treatment has been the traditional and still dominant method of delivering services. The vast majority of psychological treatments, evidence based or not, are delivered in a model that includes: (a) treatment sessions that provided in person and one-to-one with a client (individual, couple, family, group); (b) treatment administered by a highly trained (e.g., master's or doctoral level) mental health professional; and (c) sessions held at a clinic, private office, or health-care facility. To be sure, there are departures from this model, especially perhaps with several innovations that rely on technology (e.g., online, self-help, and apps). Yet, interventions delivered via the dominant model are not likely to reach many people.

Novel models are needed that can be scaled up to reach a large number of people and to reach diverse of individuals who are among the most likely to receive few or no services. Models are available, and these are not abstract conceptual models with potential. Many have been tested (e.g., task shifting, best buy, Entertainment Education, use of lay counselors), have been shown to be viable means that can: deliver evidence-based interventions, reach large numbers, and extend to individuals (e.g., in rural areas) with lack of access to traditional services. It is important to reiterate that multiple models are needed to provide the coverage (Figure 22.1) to optimize the number of people we reach and to provide options and choices as to how they receive care.

Research on clinical trials within psychology and psychiatry has been and continue to be remarkable. We have a constant stream of excellent outcome studies, and from them interventions that continue can be shown to improve people's lives (or at least to yield significant effect sizes). Yet, a critical priority is missing, namely, ensuring that they can reach people in need. Dissemination to practice is important (research-practice gap) and exemplary programs (e.g., IAPT) have scaled up interventions as part of dissemination efforts. Apart from remarkable exceptions, addressing the research-practice gap does not address the treatment gap.

I have identified a few research priorities. However, at this stage I believe it is more productive to make very clear the questions the research priorities ought to address. I noted three questions:

1. Are we closing the treatment gap?
2. Are we reaching populations within the culture that are the least likely to receive care?
3. When interventions are scaled up to reach more people and special populations, do we achieve outcomes that significantly improve their functioning?

These have not been the usual questions to guide psychosocial intervention research.

At this point, we can say, based on empirical evidence, that the majority of people in need of treatment services receive nothing (i.e., no treatment). In many controlled trials of psychotherapy, the control or comparison group for the intervention the investigator wishes to evaluate is treatment as usual, that is, the service routinely provided at a given clinic. There is no criticism here of such trials except to underscore that treatment as usual for those who need care is no treatment and not even wait-list control. Both evidence-based interventions and evidence-based models of delivery are now available to ensure or at least greatly increase the likelihood that the majority of people in need of services receive treatment, and an evidence-based treatment at that.

ABBREVIATIONS

IAPT	Improving Access to Psychological Therapies
IOM	Institute of Medicine
MOOC	Massive Open Online Courses
MOOI	Massive Open Online Interventions
NAS	National Academies of Science, Engineering, and Medicine
SAMHSA	Substance Abuse and Mental Health Services Administration
WHO	World Health Organization

REFERENCES

Aboujaoude, E., Salame, W., & Naim, L. (2015). Telemental health: A status update. *World Psychiatry*, 14(2), 223–230. https://doi.org/10.1002/wps.20218

Agency for Healthcare Research and Quality (AHRQ) (2017). Patient-centered Medical Home Resource Center. Available at https://pcmh.ahrq.gov/page/defining-pcmh

Ahgren, B., & Axelsson, R. (2011). A decade of integration and collaboration: The development of integrated health care in Sweden 2000–2010. *International Journal of Integrated Care*, 11(5) (Special 10th Anniversary Edition). https://doi.org/10.5334/ijic.566

Alegría, M., Chatterji, P., Wells, K., Cao, Z., Chen, C. N., Takeuchi, D., Jackson, J., & Meng, X. L. (2008). Disparity in depression treatment among racial and ethnic minority populations in the United States. *Psychiatric Services*, 59(11), 1264–1272. https://doi.org/10.1176/ps.2008.59.11.1264

Alegría, M., Vallas, M., & Pumariega, A. J. (2010). Racial and ethnic disparities in pediatric mental health. *Child and Adolescent Psychiatric Clinics of North America*, 19(4), 759–774. https://doi.org/10.1016/j.chc.2010.07.001

Allinder, R.M., & Oats, R.G. (1997). Effects of acceptability on teachers' implementation of curriculum-based measurement and student achievement in mathematics computation. *Remedial and Special Education*, 18(2), 113–120. https://doi.org/10.1177/074193259701800205

American Psychiatric Association (2013). *Diagnostic and statistical manual of mental disorders* (5th ed.). Arlington, VA: American Psychiatric Publishing. https://doi.org/10.1176/appi.books.9780890425596

Andrade, L.H., Alonso, J., Mneimneh, Z., Wells, J.E., Al-Hamzawi, A., Borges, G., Bromet, E., Bruffaerts, R., de Girolamo, G., de Graaf, R., Florescu, S., Gureje, O., Hinkov, H. R., Hu, C., Huang, Y., Hwang, I., Jin, R., Karam, E. G., Kovess-Masfety, V., Levinson, D., ... Kessler, R.C. (2014). Barriers to mental health treatment: Results from the WHO World Mental Health Surveys. *Psychological Medicine*, 44(6), 1303–1317. https://doi.org/10.1017/S0033291713001943

Andreas, S., Schulz, H., Volkert, J., Dehoust, M., Sehner, S., Suling, A., Ausín, B., Canuto, A., Crawford, M., Da Ronch, C., Grassi, L., Hershkovitz, Y., Muñoz, M., Quirk, A., Rotenstein, O., Santos-Olmo, A. B., Shalev, A., Strehle, J., Weber, K., Wegscheider, K., ... Härter, M. (2017). Prevalence of mental disorders in elderly people: The European MentDis_ICF65+ study. *The British Journal of Psychiatry*, *210*(2), 125–131. https://doi.org/10.1192/bjp.bp.115.180463

Ansseau, M., Dierick, M., Buntinkx, F., Cnockaert, P., De Smedt, J., Van Den Haute, M., & Vander Mijnsbrugge, D. (2004). High prevalence of mental disorders in primary care. *Journal of Affective Disorders*, *78*(1), 49–55. https://doi.org/10.1016/S0165-0327(02)00219-7

Arndorfer, R.E., Allen. K.D., & Aljazireh, L. (1999). Behavioral health needs in pediatric medicine and the acceptability of behavioral solutions: Implications for behavioral psychologists. *Behavior Therapy*, *30*(1), 137–148. https://doi.org/10.1016/S0005-7894(99)80050-1

Auerbach, R. P., Alonso, J., Axinn, W. G., Cuijpers, P., Ebert, D. D., Green, J. G., Hwang, I., Kessler, R. C., Liu, H., Mortier, P., Nock, M. K., Pinder-Amaker, S., Sampson, N. A., Aguilar-Gaxiola, S., Al-Hamzawi, A., Andrade, L. H., Benjet, C., Caldas-de-Almeida, J. M., Demyttenaere, K., Florescu, S., ... Bruffaerts, R. (2016). Mental disorders among college students in the World Health Organization World Mental Health Surveys. *Psychological Medicine*, *46*(14), 2955–2970. https://doi.org/10.1017/S0033291716001665

Backhaus, A., Agha, Z., Maglione, M.L., Repp, A., Ross, B., Zuest, D., Rice-Thorp, N. M., Lohr, J, & Thorp, S.R. (2012). Videoconferencing psychotherapy: A systematic review. *Psychological Services*, *9*(2), 111–131. https://doi.org/10.1037/a0027924

Baker, J.R., & Moore, S.M. (2008). Blogging as a social tool: A psychosocial examination of the effects of blogging. *Cyberpsychology & Behavior*, *11*(6), 747–749. https://doi.org/10.1089/cpb.2008.0053

Bakian, A.V., Huber, R.S., Coon, H., Gray, D., Wilson, P., McMahon, W.M., & Renshaw, P.F. (2015). Acute air pollution exposure and risk of suicide completion. *American Journal of Epidemiology*, *181*(5), 295–303. https://doi.org/10.1093/aje/kwu341

Balaji, M., Chatterjee, S., Koschorke, M., Rangaswamy, T., Chavan, A., Dabholkar, H., Dakshin, L., Kumar, P., John, S., Thornicroft, G., & Patel, V. (2012). The development of a lay health worker delivered collaborative community based intervention for people with schizophrenia in India. *BioMed Central Health Services Research*, *12*. (Online at www.biomedcentral.com/1472-6963/12/42/)

Bang, A.T., Reddy, H.M., Deshmukh, M.D., Baitule, S.B., & Bang, R.A. (2005). Neonatal and infant mortality in the 10 years (1993–2003) of the Gadchiroli field trial: Effect of home-based neonatal care. *Journal of Perinatology*, *25*, S92–S107. https://doi.org/10.1038/sj.jp.7211277

Barak, A., Hen, L., Boniel-Nissim, M., & Shapira, N. (2008). A comprehensive review and a meta-analysis of the effectiveness of internet-based psychotherapeutic interventions. *Journal of Technology in Human Services*, *26*(2–4), 109–160. https://doi.org/10.1080/15228830802094429

Barlow, D. H., Farchione, T. J., Sauer-Zavala, S., Latin, H. M., Ellard, K. K., Bullis, J. R., Bentley, K. H., Boettcher, H. T., & Cassiello-Robbins, C. (2018). *Unified protocol for transdiagnostic treatment of emotional disorders: Therapist guide*. (2nd ed.). New York: Oxford University Press. https://doi.org/10.1093/med-psych/9780190685973.001.0001

Barnett, M. L., Gonzalez, A., Miranda, J., Chavira, D. A., & Lau, A. S. (2018). Mobilizing community health workers to address mental health disparities for underserved populations: A systematic review. *Administration and Policy in Mental Health and Mental Health Services Research*, *45*, 195–211. https://doi.org/10.1007/s10488-017-0815-0

Bashshur, R., & Shannon, G. W. (2009). *History of telemedicine: Evolution, context, and transformation*. New Rochelle, NY: Mary Ann Liebert.

Baskerville, N. B., Hayward, L., Brown, K. S., Hammond, D., Kennedy, R. D., & Campbell, H. S. (2015). Impact of Canadian tobacco packaging policy on quitline reach and reach equity. *Preventive Medicine*, *81*, 243–250. https://doi.org/10.1016/j.ypmed.2015.09.010

Bauer, S., & Moessner, M. (2013). Harnessing the power of technology for the treatment and prevention of eating disorders. *International Journal of Eating Disorders*, *46*(5), 508–515. https://doi.org/10.1002/eat.22109

Becker, A. E., & Kleinman, A. (2013). Mental health and the global agenda. *New England Journal of Medicine*, 369, 66–73. https://doi.org/10.1056/NEJMra1110827

Becker, K. D., Boustani, M., Gellatly, R., & Chorpita, B. F. (2018). Forty years of engagement research in children's mental health services: Multidimensional measurement and practice elements. *Journal of Clinical Child & Adolescent Psychology*, *47*(1), 1–23. https://doi.org/10.1080/15374416.2017.1326121

Bemelmans, R., Gelderblom, G.J., Jonker, P., & De Witte, L. (2012). Socially assistive robots in elderly care: A systematic review into effects and effectiveness. *Journal of the American Medical Directors Association*, *13*(2), 114–120. https://doi.org/10.1016/j.jamda.2010.10.002

Bennett, C.G., & Glasgow. R.E. (2009). The delivery of public health interventions via the internet: Actualizing their potential. *Annual Review of Public Health*, *30*, 273–292. https://doi.org/10.1146/annurev.publhealth.031308.100235

Bennett-Levy, J., Richards, D. A., Farrand, P., Christensen, H., Griffiths, K. M., Kavanagh, D. J., Klein, B., Lau, M. A., Proudfoot, J., Ritterband, L., White, J., & Williams, C. (Eds.). (2010). *Oxford guide to low intensity CBT interventions*. Oxford, UK: Oxford University Press.

Bergink, V., Pop, V. J. M., Nielsen, P. R., Agerbo, E., Munk-Olsen, T., & Liu, X. (2018). Comorbidity of autoimmune thyroid disorders and psychiatric disorders during the postpartum period: A Danish nationwide register-based cohort study. *Psychological Medicine*, *48*(8), 1291–1298. https://doi.org/10.1017/S0033291717002732

Bloom, D.E., Cafiero, E.T., Jané-Llopis, E., Abrahams-Gessel, S., Bloom, L.R., Fathima, S., Feigl, A.B., Gaziano, T., Mowafi, M., Pandya, A., Prettner, K., Rosenberg, L., Seligman, B., Stein, A.Z., & Weinstein, C. (2011). *The global economic burden of noncommunicable diseases*. Geneva: World Economic Forum. (available at www.weforum.org/EconomicsOfNCD)

Bolton, P., Lee, C., Haroz, E. E., Murray, L., Dorsey, S., Robinson, C., Ugueto, A. M., & Bass, J. (2014). A transdiagnostic community-based mental health treatment for comorbid disorders: Development and outcomes of a randomized controlled trial among Burmese refugees in Thailand. *PLoS Medicine*, *11*, e1001757. https://doi.org/10.1371/journal.pmed.1001757

Boothe, J., Borrego, J., Jr., Hill, C., & Anhalt, K. (2005). Treatment acceptability and treatment compliance in ethnic minority populations. In C.L. Frisby & C.R. Reynolds (Eds.), *Comprehensive handbook of multicultural school psychology* (pp. 945–972). Hoboken, NJ: John Wiley & Sons.

Bower, J.L., & Christensen, C.M. (1995). Disruptive technologies: Catching the wave. *Harvard Business Review*, January-February, 43–53.

Breuer, J., & Freud, S. (1957). *Studies in hysteria*. New York: Basic Books.

Broadbent, E. (2017). Interactions with robots: The truths we reveal about ourselves. *Annual Review of Psychology*, *68*, 627–652. https://doi.org/10.1146/annurev-psych-010416-043958

Brownell, K.D., & Roberto, C.A., (2017) Strategic science with policy impact. *The Lancet*, *385*(9986), 2445–2446. https://doi.org/10.1016/S0140-6736(14)62397-7

Buck, J., Manges, K., & Kaboli, P. (2016). Asynchronous teleneurology: A systematic review of electronic provider-to-provider communications (P3.400). *Neurology*, *86*(16 Supplement), P3–400.

Buist-Bouwman, M.A., de Graaf, R., Vollebergh, W. A. M., & Ormel, J. (2005). Comorbidity of physical and mental disorders and the effect on work-loss days. *Acta Psychiatrica Scandinavica*, *111*(6), 436–443. https://doi.org/10.1111/j.1600-0447.2005.00513.x

Campbell, H. S., Baskerville, N. B., Hayward, L. M., Brown, K. S., & Ossip, D. J. (2014). The reach ratio—A new indicator for comparing quitline reach into smoking subgroups. *Nicotine & Tobacco Research*, *16*(4), 491–495. https://doi.org/10.1093/ntr/ntt192

Carter, S. L. (2007). Review of recent treatment acceptability research. *Education and Training in Developmental Disabilities*, *42*(3), 301–316.

Caulfield, A., Vatansever, E.., Lambert, G., & Van Bortel, T. (2019). WHO guidance on mental health training: A systematic review of the progress for non-specialist health workers. *BMJ Open*, *9*, e024059. https://doi.org/10.1136/bmjopen-2018-024059

Cenit, M. C., Sanz, Y., & Codoñer-Franch, P. (2017). Influence of gut microbiota on neuropsychiatric disorders. *World Journal of Gastroenterology*, *23*(30), 5486–5498. https://doi.org/10.3748/wjg.v23.i30.5486

Chedekel, L. (2016) Report: Private insurers deny more claims for mental health care. *The Connecticut. Health I-Team*, online at http://c-hit.org/2016/05/12/report-private-insurers-deny-more-claims-for-mental-health-care/

Chen, M., Ma, Y., Song, J., Lai, C. F., & Hu, B. (2016). Smart clothing: Connecting human with clouds and big data for sustainable health monitoring. *Mobile Networks and Applications*, *21*, 825–845. https://doi.org/10.1007/s11036-016-0745-1

Chisholm, D., Lund, C., & Saxena, S. (2007). Cost of scaling up mental health-care in low- and middle-income countries. *The British Journal of Psychiatry*, *191*(6), 528–535. https://doi.org/10.1192/bjp.bp.107.038463

Chisholm, D., & Saxena, S. (2012). Cost effectiveness of strategies to combat neuropsychiatric conditions in sub-Saharan Africa and South East Asia: Mathematical modelling study. *British Medical Journal, 344*, e609. https://doi.org/10.1136/bmj.e609

Chisholm, D., Sweeny, K., Sheehan, P., Rasmussen, B., Smit, F., Cuijpers, P., & Saxena, S. (2016). Scaling-up treatment of depression and anxiety: A global return on investment analysis. *The Lancet Psychiatry, 3*(5), 415–424. https://doi.org/10.1016/S2215-0366(16)30024-4

Christakis, N.A., & Fowler, J.H. (2009). *Connected: The surprising power of our social networks and how they shape our lives.* New York: Little, Brown.

Christensen, A., Miller, W.R., & Muñoz, R.F. (1978). Paraprofessionals, partners, peers, paraphernalia, and print: Expanding mental health service delivery. *Professional Psychology. 9*(2), 249–270. https://doi.org/10.1037/0735-7028.9.2.249

Christensen, C.M. (2003). *The innovator's solution: Creating and sustaining successful growth.* Boston, MA: Harvard Business School.

Christensen, C.M., Grossman, J.H., & Hwang, J. (2009). *The innovator's prescription: A disruptive solution for health care.* New York: McGraw Hill.

Clark, D. M. (2011). Implementing NICE guidelines for the psychological treatment of depression and anxiety disorders: The IAPT experience. *International Review of Psychiatry, 23*(4), 318–327. https://doi.org/10.3109/09540261.2011.606803

Clark, D. M. (2012). The English Improving Access to Psychological Therapies (IAPT) Program. In McHugh & D.H. Barlow (Eds.). *Dissemination and implementation of evidence-based psychological interventions* (pp. 61–77). New York: Oxford University Press.

Clark, D.M. (2018). Realizing the mass public benefit of evidence-based psychological therapies: The IAPT program. *Annual Review of Clinical Psychology, 14*, 159–183. https://doi.org/10.1146/annurev-clinpsy-050817-084833

Cohen, Z. D., & DeRubeis, R. J. (2018). Treatment selection in depression. *Annual Review of Clinical Psychology, 14*, 209–236. https://doi.org/10.1146/annurev-clinpsy-050817-084746

Collins, P.Y., Insel, T.R., Chockalingam, A., Daar, A., & Maddox, Y.T. (2013). Grand challenges in global mental health: Integration in research, policy, and practice. *PLoS Medicine, 10*(4), e1001434. https://doi.org/10.1371/journal.pmed.1001434

Constantino, M. J., Castonguay, L. G., Zack, S. E., & DeGeorge, J. (2010). Engagement in psychotherapy: Factors contributing to the facilitation, demise, and restoration of the therapeutic alliance. In D. Castro-Blanco & M. S. Karver (Eds.), *Elusive alliance: Treatment engagement strategies with high-risk adolescents* (pp. 21–57). Washington, D. C.; American Psychological Association. https://doi.org/10.1037/12139-001

Corrigan, P.W., Druss, B. G., & Perlick, D. A. (2014). The impact of mental illness stigma on seeking and participating in mental health care. *Psychological Science in the Public Interest, 15*(2), 37–70. https://doi.org/10.1177/1529100614531398

Crowley, R. A., & Kirschner, N. (2015). The integration of care for mental health, substance abuse, and other behavioral health conditions into primary care: Executive summary of an American College of Physicians position paper. *Annals of Internal Medicine, 163*(4), 298–299. https://doi.org/10.7326/M15-0510

Dedic, N., Pöhlmann, M. L., Richter, J. S., Mehta, D., Czamara, D., Metzger, M. W., Dine, J., Bedenk, B. T., Hartmann, J., Wagner, K. V., Jurik, A., Almli, L. M., Lori, A., Moosmang, S., Hofmann, F., Wotjak, C. T., Rammes, G., Eder, M., Chen, A., Ressler, K. J., . . . Deussing, J. M. (2018). Cross-disorder risk gene CACNA1C differentially modulates susceptibility to psychiatric disorders during development and adulthood. *Molecular Psychiatry, 23*, 533. https://doi.org/10.1038/mp.2017.133

Deslandes, A., Moraes, H., Ferreira, C., Veiga, H., Silveira, H., Mouta, R., Pompeu, F. A., Coutinho, E. S., &Laks, J. (2009). Exercise and mental health: Many reasons to move. *Neuropsychobiology, 59*(4), 191–198. https://doi.org/10.1159/000223730

Desmond-Hellmann, S. (2016). *What if? A letter from the CEO of the Bill and Melinda Gates Foundation.* Available on line from the Foundation at http://www.gatesfoundation.org/2016/ceo-letter?wt.mc_id=05_25_2016_02_ceoletter16_gf-pgoogle_&wt.tsrc=gfpgoogle

Divan, G., Vajaratkar, V., Cardozo, P., Huzurbazar, S., Verma, M., Howarth, E., Emsley, R., Taylor, C., Patel, V., & Green, J. (2019). The feasibility and effectiveness of PASS plus, a lay health worker delivered comprehensive intervention for autism spectrum disorders: Pilot RCT in a rural low and middle income country setting. *Autism Research, 12*(2), 328–339. https://doi.org/10.1002/aur.1978

Donker, T., Petrie, K., Proudfoot, J., Clarke, J., Birch, M. R., & Christensen, H. (2013). Smartphones for smarter delivery of mental health programs: A systematic review. *Journal of Medical Internet Research, 15*(11), e247. https://doi.org/10.2196/jmir.2791

Dorsey, E. R., Glidden, A. M., Holloway, M. R., Birbeck, G. L., & Schwamm, L. H. (2018). Teleneurology and mobile technologies: The future of neurological care. *Nature Reviews Neurology, 14*, 285. https://doi.org/10.1038/nrneurol.2018.31

Draper, C., & O'Donohue, W. (Eds.) (2011). *Stepped care and e-health: Practical applications to behavioral disorders.* New York: Springer Science + Business Media, LLC. https://doi.org/10.1007/978-1-4419-6510-3

Ebert, D. D., Van Daele, T., Nordgreen, T., Karekla, M., Compare, A., Zarbo, C., Brugnera, A., Øverland, S., Trebbi, G., Jensen, K. L., Kaehlke, F., Baumeister, H., & Taylor, J. (2018). Internet-and mobile-based psychological interventions: Applications, efficacy, and potential for improving mental health. *European Psychologist, 23*, 167–187. https://doi.org/10.1027/1016-9040/a000318

Elkin, T. D., Sarver, D. E., Wong Sarver, N., Young, J., & Buttross, S. (2017). Future directions for the implementation and dissemination of statewide developmental-behavioral pediatric integrated health care. *Journal of Clinical Child & Adolescent Psychology, 46*(4), 619–630. https://doi.org/10.1080/15374416.2016.1152551

Essau, C. A., Lewinsohn, P. M., Lim, J. X., Moon-ho, R. H., & Rohde, P. (2018). Incidence, recurrence and comorbidity of anxiety disorders in four major developmental stages. *Journal of Affective Disorders, 228*, 248–253. https://doi.org/10.1016/j.jad.2017.12.014

Fairburn, C. G., & Patel, V. (2014). The global dissemination of psychological treatments: A road map for research and practice. *The American Journal of Psychiatry, 171*(5), 495–498. https://doi.org/10.1176/appi.ajp.2013.13111546

Fairburn, C. G., & Patel, V. (2017). The impact of digital technology on psychological treatments and their dissemination. *Behaviour Research and Therapy, 88*, 19–25. https://doi.org/10.1016/j.brat.2016.08.012

Finley, E. P., Garcia, H. A., Ketchum, N. S., McGeary, D. D., McGeary, C. A., Stirman, S. W., & Peterson, A. L. (2015). Utilization of evidence-based psychotherapies in Veterans Affairs posttraumatic stress disorder outpatient clinics. *Psychological Services, 12*(1), 73–82. https://doi.org/10.1037/ser0000014

Fixsen, D. L., Blase, K. A., Naoom, S. F., & Wallace, F. (2009). Core implementation components. *Research on Social Work Practice, 19*(5), 531–540. https://doi.org/10.1177/1049731509335549

Fulton, B. D., Scheffler, R. M., Sparkes, S. P., Auh, E. Y., Vujicic, M., & Soucat, A. (2011). Health workforce skill mix and task shifting in low income countries: A review of recent evidence. *Human Resources for Health, 9*, 1. https://doi.org/10.1186/1478-4491-9-1

Gandal, M. J., Haney, J. R., Parikshak, N. N., Leppa, V., Ramaswami, G., Hartl, C., Schork, A. J., Appadurai, V., Buil, A., Werge, T. M., Liu, C., White, K. P., CommonMind Consortium, PsychENCODE Consortium, iPSYCH-BROAD Working Group, Horvath, S., & Geschwind, D. H. (2018). Shared molecular neuropathology across major psychiatric disorders parallels polygenic overlap. *Science, 359*(6376), 693–697. https://doi.org/10.1126/science.aad6469

Gorini, A., Gaggioli, A., Vigba, C., & Riva, G. (2008). A second life for ehealth: Prospects for use of 3–D virtual worlds in clinical psychology. *Journal of Medical Internet Research, 10*(3). https://doi.org/10.2196/jmir.1029

Greenwood, B.M., Greenwood, A.M., Snow, R.W., Byass, P., Bennett, S., & Hatib-N'Jie, A.B. (1989). The effects of malaria chemoprophylaxis given by traditional birth attendants on the course and outcome of pregnancy. *Transactions of the Royal Society of Tropical Medicine and Hygiene Journal, 83*(5), 589–594. https://doi.org/10.1016/0035-9203(89)90362-3

Greeson, J., Garland, E.L., & Black, D. (2014). A transtherapeutic approach for transdiagnostic mental processes. In Le, A., Ngnoumen, C.T., & Langer, E.J. (Eds.). *The Wiley Blackwell handbook of mindfulness* (pp. 533–562). New York: John Wiley & Sons. https://doi.org/10.1002/9781118294895

Griner, D., & Smith, T. B. (2006). Culturally adapted mental health intervention: A meta-analytic review. *Psychotherapy: Theory, Research, Practice, Training, 43*(4), 531–548. https://doi.org/10.1037/0033-3204.43.4.531

Haaga, D. A. F. (2000). Introduction to the special section on stepped-care models in psychotherapy. *Journal of Consulting and Clinical Psychology*, *68*(4), 547–548. https://doi.org/10.1037/0022-006X.68.4.547

Harwood, T.M., & L'Abate, L. (2010). *Self-help in mental health: A critical review*. New York: Springer. https://doi.org/10.1007/978-1-4419-1099-8

Health Resources and Services Administration. (2010). *Health professional shortage areas: Mental health designated populations*. Rural Assistance Center. Retrieved from www.raconline.org/ maps/mapfiles/hpsa_mental.png

Hilty, D. M., Rabinowitz, T., McCarron, R. M., Katzelnick, D. J., Chang, T., Bauer, A. M., & Fortney, J. (2018). An update on telepsychiatry and how it can leverage collaborative, stepped, and integrated services to primary care. *Psychosomatics*, *59*(3), 227–250. https://doi.org/10.1016/j.psym.2017.12.005

Hinshaw, S. P., & Stier, A. (2008). Stigma as related to mental disorders. *Annual Review of Clinical Psychology*, *4*, 367–393. https://doi.org/10.1146/annurev.clinpsy.4.022007.141245

Hoge, M.A., Morris, J.A., Daniels, A.S., Stuart, G.W., Huey, L.Y., & Adams, N. (2007). *An action plan for behavioral health workforce development*. Washington, DC: Department of Health and Human Services.

Insel, T.R., & Cuthbert, B.M. (2015). Brain disorders? Precisely. *Science*, *348* (6234), 499–500. https://doi.org/10.1126/science.aab2358

Institute of Medicine. (2001). *Crossing the quality chasm: A new health system for the 21st century*. Washington, DC: National Academies Press.

Institute of Medicine. (2006), *Improving the quality of care for mental and substance use conditions*. Washington, DC: National Academies Press.

Institute of Medicine. (2010). *Promoting cardiovascular health in the developing world: A critical challenge to achieve global health*. Washington, DC: National Academies Press.

Institute of Medicine. (2011a). *Child and adolescent health and health care quality: Measuring what matters*. Washington, DC: National Academies Press.

Institute of Medicine. (2011b). *Country-level decision making for control of chronic diseases*. Washington, DC: National Academy Press.

Institute of Medicine. (2012). *The mental health and substance use workforce for older adults: In whose hands?* Washington, DC: National Academies Press.

Javadi, D., Feldhaus, I., Mancuso, A., & Ghaffar, A. (2017). Applying systems thinking to task shifting for mental health using lay providers: A review of the evidence. *Global Mental Health*, *4*, e14. https://doi.org/10.1017/gmh.2017.15

Jones, D.J. (Ed.) (2014). Special section: Technology and children's mental health. *Journal of Clinical Child and Adolescent Psychology*, *43*(1), 63–142. https://doi.org/10.1080/15374416.2013.859082

Jorm, A.F. 2012. Mental health literacy: Empowering the community to take action for better mental health. *American Psychologist*, *67*(3), 231–243. https://doi.org/10.1037/a0025957

Kaltenthaler, E., Sutcliffe, P., Parry, G., Beverley, C., Rees, A., & Ferriter, M. (2008). The acceptability to patients of computerized cognitive behaviour therapy for depression: A systematic review. *Psychological Medicine*, *38*(11), 1521–1530. https://doi.org/10.1017/S0033291707002607

Kaplan, B.J. Rucklidge, J.J., Romijn, A., & McLeod, K. (2015). The emerging field of nutritional mental health: Inflammation, the microbiome, oxidative stress, and mitochondrial function. *Clinical Psychological Science*, *3*(6), 964–980. https://doi.org/10.1177/2167702614555413

Karlin, B. E., Brown, G. K., Jager-Hyman, S., Green, K. L., Wong, M., Lee, D. S., Bertagnolli, A., & Ross, T. B. (2019). Dissemination and implementation of cognitive behavioral therapy for depression in the Kaiser Permanente Health Care System: Evaluation of initial training and clinical outcomes. *Behavior Therapy*, *50*(2), 446–458. https://doi.org/10.1016/j.beth.2018.08.002

Karlin, B. E., & Cross, G. (2014). From the laboratory to the therapy room: National dissemination and implementation of evidence-based psychotherapies in the US Department of Veterans Affairs Health Care System. *American Psychologist*, *69*(1), 19–33. https://doi.org/10.1037/a0033888

Karyotaki, E., Riper, H., Twisk, J., Hoogendoorn, A., Kleiboer, A., Mira, A., Mackinnon, A., Meyer, B., Botella, C., Littlewood, E., Andersson, G., Christensen, H., Klein, J. P., Schröder, J., Bretón-López, J., Scheider, J., Griffiths, K., Farrer, L., Huibers, M. J., Phillips, R., ... Cuijpers, P. (2017). Efficacy of self-guided internet-based cognitive behavioral therapy in the treatment of depressive symptoms: A meta-analysis of individual participant data. *JAMA Psychiatry*, *74*(4), 351–359. https://doi.org/10.1001/jamapsychiatry.2017.0044

Kazak, A.E., Nash, J.M., Hiroto, K., & Kaslow, N.J. (2017). Psychologists in patient-centered medical homes (PCMHs): Roles, evidence, opportunities, and challenges. *American Psychologist*, *72*(1), 1–12. https://doi.org/10.1037/a0040382

Kazdin, A.E. (1978). *History of behavior modification: Experimental foundations of contemporary research*. Baltimore: University Park Press. (Sponsored by the National Academy of Sciences.)

Kazdin, A.E. (2017a). *Everyday parenting: The ABCs of child rearing*. On-line course (free). New Haven, CT and Mountain View, CA: Yale University and Coursera. at https://www.coursera.org/learn/everyday-parenting

Kazdin, A.E. (2017b). Parent management training and problem-solving skills training for child and adolescent conduct problems. In J.R. Weisz & A.E. Kazdin (Eds.). *Evidence-based psychotherapies for children and adolescents* (3rd ed., pp. 142–158). New York: Guilford Press.

Kazdin, A.E. (2018). *Innovations in psychosocial interventions and their delivery: Leveraging cutting-edge science to improve the world's mental health*. New York: Oxford University Press. https://doi.org/10.1093/med-psych/9780190463281.001.0001

Kazdin, A.E., & Blase, S.L. (2011). Rebooting psychotherapy research and practice to reduce the burden of mental illness. *Perspectives on Psychological Science*, *6*(1), 21–37. https://doi.org/10.1177/1745691610393527

Kazdin, A.E., Holland, L., & Crowley, M. (1997). Family experience of barriers to treatment and premature termination from child therapy. *Journal of Consulting and Clinical Psychology*, *65*(3), 453–463. https://doi.org/10.1037/0022-006X.65.3.453

Kessler, R.C. (2018). The potential of predictive analytics to provide clinical decision support in depression treatment planning. *Current Opinion in Psychiatry*, *31*(1), 32–39. https://doi.org/10.1097/YCO.0000000000000377

Kessler, R.C., Berglund, P., Demler, O., Jin, R., Merikangas, K. R., & Walters, E. E. (2005). Lifetime prevalence and age-of-onset distributions of DSM-IV disorders in the National Comorbidity Survey Replication. *Archives of General Psychiatry*, *62*(6), 593–602. https://doi.org/10.1001/archpsyc.62.6.593

Kessler, R.C., Chiu, W. T., Demler, O., & Walters, E. E. (2005). Prevalence, severity, and comorbidity of 12–month DSM-IV disorders in the National Comorbidity Survey Replication. *Archives of General Psychiatry*, *62*(6), 617–627. https://doi.org/10.1001/archpsyc.62.6.617

Kessler, R.C., Demler, O., Frank, R.G., Olfson, M., Pincus, H.A., Walters, E.E., Wang, P., Wells, K. B., & Zaslavsky, A.M. (2005). Prevalence and treatment of mental disorders, 1990 to 2003. *New England Journal of Medicine*, *352*, 2515–2523. https://doi.org/10.1056/NEJMsa043266

Kessler, R.C., McGonagle, K.A., Zhao, S., Nelson, C.B., Hughes, M., Eshleman, S., Wittchen, H. U., & Kendler, K.S. (1994). Lifetime and 12–month prevalence of DSM-III-R psychiatric disorders in the United States: Results from the National Comorbidity Survey. *Archives of General Psychiatry*, *51*(1), 8–9. https://doi.org/10.1001/archpsyc.1994.03950010008002

Kilpela, L.S., Hill, K., Kelly, M.C., Elmquist, J., Ottoson, P., Keith, D., Hildebrandt, T., & Becker, C.B. (2014). Reducing eating disorder risk factors: A controlled investigation of a blended task-shifting/train-the-trainer approach to dissemination and implementation. *Behaviour Research and Therapy*, *63*, 70–82. https://doi.org/10.1016/j.brat.2014.09.005

Kim, B. S., Ng, G. F., & Ahn, A. J. (2005). Effects of client expectation for counseling success, client-counselor worldview match, and client adherence to Asian and European American cultural values on counseling process with Asian Americans. *Journal of Counseling Psychology*, *52*(1), 67-76. https://doi.org/10.1037/0022-0167.52.1.67–76

Kim, S. (2015, April). Priceline acknowledges baby as 'unusual' purchaser of $516 car rental. *ABC News, Good Morning America*. Available online at https://gma.yahoo.com/priceline-acknowledges-baby-unusual-purchaser-516-car-rental-201043173--abc-news-personal-finance.html

Kleiman, S.C., Watson, H.J., Bulik-Sullivan, E.C., Huh, E.Y., Tarantino, L.M., Bulik, C.M., & Carroll, I.M. (2015). The intestinal microbiota in acute anorexia nervosa and during renourishment: Relationship to depression, anxiety, and eating disorder psychopathology. *Psychosomatic Medicine*, *77*(9), 969–981. https://doi.org/10.1097/PSY.0000000000000247

Kohn, R., Saxena, S., Levav, I., & Saraceno, B. (2004). The treatment gap in mental health care. *Bulletin of the World Health Organization*, *82*, 858–866.

Kohrt, B., Asher, L., Bhardwaj, A., Fazel, M., Jordans, M., Mutamba, B., Nadkarni, A., Pedersen, G. A., Singla, D. R., & Patel, V. (2018). The role of communities in mental health care in low-and middle-income countries: A meta-review of components and competencies. *International Journal of Environmental Research and Public Health, 15*(6), 1279. https://doi.org/10.3390/ijerph15061279

Koslofsky, S., & Domenech Rodríguez, M. M. (2017). Cultural adaptations to psychotherapy: Real-world applications. *Clinical Case Studies, 16*(1), 3–8. https://doi.org/10.1177/1534650116668273

Krol, K.M., Rajhans, P., Missana, M., & Grossmann, T. (2014). Duration of exclusive breastfeeding is associated with differences in infants' brain responses to emotional body expressions. *Frontiers in Behavioral Neuroscience, 8*, 459. https://doi.org/10.3389/fnbeh.2014.00459

Lancet Global Mental Health Group. (2007). Scale up services for mental disorders: A call for action. *The Lancet, 370*(9594), 1241–1252. https://doi.org/10.1016/S0140-6736(07)61242-2

Lane, G. W., Noronha, D., Rivera, A., Craig, K., Yee, C., Mills, B., & Villanueva, E. (2016). Effectiveness of a social robot, "Paro," in a VA long-term care setting. *Psychological Services, 13*(3), 292. https://doi.org/10.1037/ser0000080

Lanzillo, E.C., Horowitz, L.M., Wharff, E.A., Sheftall, A.H., Pao, M., & Bridge, J.A. (2019). The importance of screening preteens for suicide risk in the emergency department. *Hospital Pediatrics, 9*(4), 305–307. https://doi.org/10.1542/hpeds.2018-0154

Leathard, A. (Ed.) (1994). *Going inter-professional: Working together for health and welfare.* London: Routledge.

Lee, J. Y., & Lee, S. W. H. (2018). Telemedicine cost–effectiveness for diabetes management: A systematic review. *Diabetes Technology & Therapeutics, 20*(7), 492–500. https://doi.org/10.1089/dia.2018.0098

Lehman, A. F., & Dixon, L. (Eds.). (2016). *Double jeopardy: Chronic mental illness and substance use disorders.* London: Routledge. https://doi.org/10.4324/9781315534770

Lim, Y.H., Kim, H., Kim, J.H., Bae, S., Park, H.Y., & Hong, Y.C. (2012). Air pollution and symptoms of depression in elderly adults. *Environmental Health Perspectives, 120*(7), 1023–1028. https://doi.org/10.1289/ehp.1104100

Lindenmayer, J. P. (2018). The NIMH Research Domain Criteria initiative and comorbidity in schizophrenia: Research implications. *Psychiatric Annals, 48*(12), 547–551. https://doi.org/10.3928/00485713-20181108-01

Linnan, L.A., Kim, A.E., Wasilewski, Y., Lee, A.M., Yang, J., & Solomon, F. (2001). Working with licensed cosmetologists to promote health: Results from the North Carolina BEAUTY and Health pilot study. *Preventive Medicine, 33*(6), 606–612. https://doi.org/10.1006/pmed.2001.0933

Lueken, U., & Hahn, T. (2016). Functional neuroimaging of psychotherapeutic processes in anxiety and depression: From mechanisms to predictions. *Current Opinion in Psychiatry, 29*(1), 25–31. https://doi.org/10.1097/YCO.0000000000000218

Lui, J.H., Marcus, D.K., & Barry, C.T. (2017). Evidence-based apps? A review of mental health mobile applications in a psychotherapy context. *Professional Psychology: Research and Practice, 48*(3), 199. https://doi.org/10.1037/pro0000122

Luque, J.S., Ross, L., & Gwede, C.K. (2014). Qualitative systematic review of barber-administered health education, promotion, screening and outreach programs in African-American communities. *Journal of Community Health, 39*, 181–90. https://doi.org/10.1007/s10900-013-9744-3

Lyon, A.R., & Koerner, K. (2016). User-centered design for psychosocial intervention development and implementation. *Clinical Psychology: Science and Practice, 23*(2), 180–200. https://doi.org/10.1111/cpsp.12154

Martini, M.G., Hewage, C.T., Nasralla, M.M., Smith, R., Jourdan, I., & Rockall, T. (2013, July). 3-D robotic tele-surgery and training over next generation wireless networks. In *Engineering in Medicine and Biology Society (EMBC), 2013 35th Annual International Conference of the IEEE* (pp. 6244–6247). https://doi.org/10.1109/EMBC.2013.6610980

Martins, S.S., Sarvet, A., Santaella-Tenorio, J., Saha, T., Grant, B.F., & Hasin, D.S. (2017). Changes in US lifetime heroin use and heroin use disorder: Prevalence from the 2001–2002 to 2012–2013 National Epidemiologic Survey on Alcohol and Related Conditions. *JAMA Psychiatry, 74*(5), 445–455. https://doi.org/10.1001/jamapsychiatry.2017.0113

Marwood, L., Wise, T., Perkins, A. M., & Cleare, A. J. (2018). Meta-analyses of the neural mechanisms and predictors of response to psychotherapy in depression and anxiety. *Neuroscience and Biobehavioral Reviews, 95*, 61–72. https://doi.org/10.1016/j.neubiorev.2018.09.022

McGuire, T.G., & Miranda, J. (2008). New evidence regarding racial and ethnic disparities in mental health: Policy implications. *Health Affairs, 27*(2), 393–403. https://doi.org/10.1377/hlthaff.27.2.393

Merikangas, K.R., He, J. P., Burstein, M., Swendsen, J., Avenevoli, S., Case, B., Georgiades, K., Heaton, L., Swanson, S., & Olfson, M. (2011). Service utilization for lifetime mental disorders in US adolescents: Results of the National Comorbidity Survey–Adolescent Supplement (NCS-A). *Journal of the American Academy of Child & Adolescent Psychiatry, 50*(1), 32–45. https://doi.org/10.1016/j.jaac.2010.10.006

Miranda, J., Bernal, G., Lau, A.S., Kohn, L., Hwang, W.C., & LaFromboise, T. (2005). State of the science on psychosocial interventions for ethnic minorities. *Annual Review of Clinical Psychology, 1*, 113–142. https://doi.org/10.1146/annurev.clinpsy.1.102803.143822

Mitchell, A.J., & Selmes, T. (2007). Why don't patients attend their appointments? Maintaining engagement with psychiatric services. *Advances in Psychiatric Treatment, 13*(6), 423–434. https://doi.org/10.1192/apt.bp.106.003202

Muñoz, R.F., Bunge, E.L., Chen, K., Schueller, S.M., Bravin, J.I., Shaughnessy, E.A., & Pérez-Stable, E.J. (2016). Massive open online interventions (MOOIs): A novel model for delivering behavioral health services worldwide. *Clinical Psychological Science, 4*(2), 194–205. https://doi.org/10.1177/2167702615583840

Murray, L.K. & Dorsey, S. (2013). *Common Elements Treatment Approach (CETA): Counselor manual* (Thailand version). Bloomberg School of Public Health: Johns Hopkins University.

Murray, L.K., Dorsey, S., Haroz, E., Lee, C., Alsiary, M. M., Haydary, A., Weiss, W. M., & Bolton, P. (2014). A common elements treatment approach for adult mental health problems in low-and middle-income countries. *Cognitive and Behavioral Practice, 21*(2), 111–123. https://doi.org/10.1016/j.cbpra.2013.06.005

Nadkarni, A., Weobong, B., Weiss, H.A., McCambridge, J., Bhat, B., Katti, B., Murthy, P., King, M., McDaid, D., Park, A. L., Wilson, G. T., Kirkwood, B., Fairburn, C. G., Velleman, R., & Patel, V. (2017). Counselling for Alcohol Problems (CAP), a lay counsellor-delivered brief psychological treatment for harmful drinking in men, in primary care in India: A randomised controlled trial. *The Lancet, 389*(10065), 186–195. https://doi.org/10.1016/S0140-6736(16)31590-2

National Academies of Sciences, Engineering, and Medicine. (2017). *Making eye health a population health imperative: Vision for tomorrow.* Washington, DC: National Academies Press.

National Academies of Sciences, Engineering, and Medicine. (2018). *Crossing the global quality chasm: Improving health care worldwide.* National Academies Press.

National Physical Activity Plan Alliance (2016). *US national physical activity plan.* Columbia, SC: http://physicalactivityplan.org/index.html

Newman, F.L., & Howard, K.I. (1986). Therapeutic effort, treatment outcome, and national health policy. *American Psychologist, 41*(2), 181–187. https://doi.org/10.1037/0003-066X.41.2.181

Nowakowski, M. E., McCabe, R., Rowa, K., Pellizzari, J., Surette, M., Moayyedi, P., & Anglin, R. (2016). The gut microbiome: Potential innovations for the understanding and treatment of psychopathology. *Canadian Psychology, 57*(2), 67–75. https://doi.org/10.1037/cap0000038

Oddy, W.H., Kendall, G.E., Li, J., Jacoby, P., Robinson, M., de Klerk, N.H., Silburn, S. R., Zubrick, S. R., Landau, L. I., & Stanley, F.J. (2010). The long-term effects of breastfeeding on child and adolescent mental health: A pregnancy cohort study followed for 14 years. *Journal of Pediatrics, 156*(4), 568–574. https://doi.org/10.1016/j.jpeds.2009.10.020

Pallavicini, F., Algeri, D., Repetto, C., Gorini, A., & Giuseppe Riva, G. (2009). Biofeedback, virtual reality and mobile phones in the treatment of Generalized Anxiety Disorder (GAD): A phase-2 controlled clinical trial. *Journal of CyberTherapy & Rehabilitation, 2*(4), 315–327.

Parikh, S. V., & Huniewicz, P. (2015). E-health: An overview of the uses of the Internet, social media, apps, and websites for mood disorders. *Current Opinion in Psychiatry, 28*(1), 13–17. https://doi.org/10.1097/YCO.0000000000000123

Patalay, P., & Hardman, C. A. (2019). Comorbidity, codevelopment, and temporal associations between body mass index and internalizing symptoms from early childhood to adolescence. *JAMA Psychiatry.* https://doi.org/10.1001/jamapsychiatry.2019.0169

Patel, V., Maj, M., Flisher, A. J., Silva, M. J., Koschorke, M., Prince, M., & WPA Zonal and Member Society Representatives. (2010). Reducing the treatment gap for mental disorders: A WPA survey. *World Psychiatry, 9*(3), 169–176. https://doi.org/10.1002/j.2051-5545.2010.tb00305.x

Patel, V., Weiss, H.A., Chowdhary, N., Naik, S., Pednekar, S., Chatterjee, S., Bhat, B., Araya, R., King, M., Simon, G., Verdeli, H., & Kirkwood, B.R. (2011). Lay health worker led intervention for depressive and anxiety disorders in India: Impact on clinical and disability outcomes over 12 months. *The British Journal of Psychiatry, 199*(6), 459–466. https://doi.org/10.1192/bjp.bp.111.092155

Patel, V., Weiss, H.A., Chowdhary, N., Naik, S., Pednekar, S., Chatterjee, S., De Silva, M. J., Bhat, B., Araya, R., King, M., Simon, G., Verdeli, H., & Kirkwood, B.R. (2010). Effectiveness of an intervention led by lay health counsellors for depressive and anxiety disorders in primary care in Goa, India (MANAS): A cluster randomised controlled trial. *Lancet, 376*(9758), 2086–2095. https://doi.org/10.1016/S0140-6736(10)61508-5

Patel, V., Weobong, B., Weiss, H. A., Anand, A., Bhat, B., Katti, B., Dimidjian, S., Araya, R., Hollon, S. D., King, M., Vijayakumar, L., Park, A-La, McDaid, D., Wilson, T., Velleman, R, Kirkwood, B. R., & Fairburn, C.G. (2016). The Healthy Activity Program (HAP), A lay counsellor-delivered brief psychological treatment for severe depression, in primary care in India: A randomised controlled trial. *The Lancet, 389*(10065), 176–185. https://doi.org/10.1016/S0140-6736(16)31589-6

Pearcy, C. P., Anderson, R. A., Egan, S. J., & Rees, C. S. (2016). A systematic review and meta-analysis of self-help therapeutic interventions for obsessive–compulsive disorder: Is therapeutic contact key to overall improvement? *Journal of Behavior Therapy and Experimental Psychiatry, 51*, 74–83. https://doi.org/10.1016/j.jbtep.2015.12.007

Perkins, J.M., Subramanian, S.V., & Christakis, N.A. (2015). Social networks and health: A systematic review of sociocentric network studies in low- and middle-income countries. *Social Science & Medicine, 125*, 60–78. https://doi.org/10.1016/j.socscimed.2014.08.019

Price, M., Yuen, E. K., Goetter, E. M., Herbert, J. D., Forman, E. M., Acierno, R., & Ruggiero, K. J. (2014). mHealth: A mechanism to deliver more accessible, more effective mental health care. *Clinical Psychology & Psychotherapy, 21*(5), 427–436. https://doi.org/10.1002/cpp.1855

Prince, J.P. (2015). University student counseling and mental health in the United States: Trends and challenges. *Mental Health & Prevention, 3*(1–2), 5–10. https://doi.org/10.1016/j.mhp.2015.03.001

Prince, M., Patel, V., Saxena, S., Maj, M., Maselko, J., Phillips, M.R., & Rahman, A. (2007). No health without mental health. *The Lancet, 370*(9590), 859–877. https://doi.org/10.1016/S0140-6736(07)61238-0

Pulles, R.L., Urquizo, M.C, & Carrera, A. (2017). The present situation of e-health and mHealth in Ecuador. *Latin American Journal of Telehealth, 4*(3), 261–267.

Rabbitt, S.M., Kazdin, A.E., & Scassellati, B. (2015). Integrating socially assistive robotics into mental healthcare interventions: Applications and recommendations for expanded use. *Clinical Psychology Review, 35*, 35–46. https://doi.org/10.1016/j.cpr.2014.07.001

Rahman, A., Hamdani, S.U., Awan, N.R., Bryant, R.A., Dawson, K.S., Khan, M.F., Azeemi, M. M., Akhtar, P., Nazir, H., Chiumento, A., Sijbrandij, M., Wang, D., Farooq, S., & van Ommeren M. (2016). Effect of a multicomponent behavioral intervention in adults impaired by psychological distress in a conflict-affected area of Pakistan: A randomized clinical trial. *JAMA, 316*(24), 2609–2617. https://doi.org/10.1001/jama.2016.17165

Rahman, A., Malik, A., Sikander, S., Roberts, C., & Creed, F. (2008). Cognitive behaviour therapy-based intervention by community health workers for mothers with depression and their infants in rural Pakistan: A cluster-randomised controlled trial, *The Lancet, 372*(9642), 902–909. https://doi.org/10.1016/S0140-6736(08)61400-2

RelaxLine (2010). *Bellybio interactive breathing*. Retrieved from http://itunes.apple.com/us/app/bellybio-interactive-breathing/id353763955?mt=8

Rezin, G.T., Amboni, G., Zugno, A.I., Quevedo, J., & Streck, E.L. (2009). Mitochondrial dysfunction and psychiatric disorders. *Neurochemical Research, 34*, 1021–1029. https://doi.org/10.1007/s11064-008-9865-8

Richardson, C.R., Faulkner, G., McDevitt, J., Skrinar, G. S., Hutchinson, D. S., & Piette, J. D. (2005). Integrating physical activity into mental health services for persons with serious mental illness. *Psychiatric Services, 56*(3), 324–331. https://doi.org/10.1176/appi.ps.56.3.324

Rieder, R., Wisniewski, P. J., Alderman, B. L., & Campbell, S. C. (2017). Microbes and mental health: A review. *Brain, Behavior, and Immunity, 66*, 9–17. https://doi.org/10.1016/j.bbi.2017.01.016

Roberto, C. A., & Brownell, K. D. (2017). Strategic science for eating disorders research and policy impact. *International Journal of Eating Disorders, 50*(3), 312–314. https://doi.org/10.1002/eat.22678

Roine, R., Ohinmaa, A., & Hailey, D. (2001). Assessing telemedicine: A systematic review of the literature. *Canadian Medical Association Journal, 165*(6), 765–771.

Roseborough, D. J., McLeod, J. T., & Wright, F. I. (2016). Attrition in psychotherapy: A survival analysis. *Research on Social Work Practice, 26*(7), 803–815. https://doi.org/10.1177/1049731515569073

Rossignol, D.A., & Frye, R.E. (2015). Mitochondrial dysfunction in psychiatric disorders. In A. Dietrich-Muszalska, V., Chauhan, & S. Grignon (Eds.), *Studies on psychiatric disorders* (pp. 231–244). New York: Springer. https://doi.org/10.1007/978-1-4939-0440-2_12

Rotheram-Borus, M.J., Swendeman, D., & Chorpita, B.F. (2012). Disruptive innovations for designing and diffusing evidence-based interventions. *American Psychologist, 67*(6), 463–476. https://doi.org/10.1037/a0028180

Rucklidge, J. J., & Kaplan, B. J. (2013). Broad-spectrum micronutrient formulas for the treatment of psychiatric symptoms: A systematic review. *Expert Review of Neurotherapeutics, 13*(1), 49–73. https://doi.org/10.1586/ern.12.143

Ryder, D. (1988). Minimal intervention: A little quality for a lot of quantity. *Behaviour Change, 5*(3), 100–107. https://doi.org/10.1017/S081348390000797X

Sarason, I. (1974). *The psychological sense of community: Prospects for a Community Psychology*. San Francisco, CA: Jossey-Bass.

Scassellati, B., Boccanfuso, L., Huang, C. M., Mademtzi, M., Qin, M., Salomons, N., Ventola, P., & Shic, F. (2018). Improving social skills in children with ASD using a long-term, in-home social robot. *Science Robotics, 3*(21), eaat7544. https://doi.org/10.1126/scirobotics.aat7544

Scott, K. M., Lim, C., Al-Hamzawi, A., Alonso, J., Bruffaerts, R., Caldas-de-Almeida, J.M., Florescu, S., de Girolamo, G., Hu, C., de Jonge, P., Kawakami, N., Medina-Mora, M. E., Moskalewicz, J., Navarro-Mateu, F., O'Neill, S., Piazza, M., Posada-Villa, J., Torres, Y., & Kessler, R. C. (2016). Association of mental disorders with subsequent chronic physical conditions: World mental health surveys from 17 countries. *JAMA Psychiatry, 73*(2), 150–158. https://doi.org/10.1001/jamapsychiatry.2015.2688

Sentio Solutions (2018). *Feel*. San Francisco: CA. https://www.myfeel.co/how-it-works Inc.

Sharan, P., Gallo, C., Gureje, O., Lamberte, E., Mari, J.J., Mazzotti, G., Patel, V., Swartz, L., Olifson, S., Levav, I., de Francisco, A., Saxena, S., & World Health Organization-Global Forum for Health Research - Mental Health Research Mapping Project Group (2009). Mental health research priorities in low- and middle-income countries of Africa, Asia, Latin America and the Caribbean. *The British Journal of Psychiatry, 195*(4), 354–363. https://doi.org/10.1192/bjp.bp.108.050187

Sharp, P., Jacks, T., & Hockfield, S. (2016). Capitalizing on convergence for health care. *Science, 352*(6293), 1522–1523. https://doi.org/10.1126/science.aag2350

Singhal, A., Cody, M.J., Rogers, E.M., & Sabido, M. (Eds.). (2003). *Entertainment-education and social change: History, research, and practice*. Mahwah, NJ: Lawrence Erlbaum. https://doi.org/10.4324/9781410609595

Singhal, A. & Rogers, E.M. (1999). *Entertainment-education: A communication strategy for social change*. Mahwah, NJ: Lawrence Erlbaum.

Singla, D. R., Kohrt, B. A., Murray, L. K., Anand, A., Chorpita, B. F., & Patel, V. (2017). Psychological treatments for the world: Lessons from low- and middle-income countries. *Annual Review of Clinical Psychology, 13*, 149–181. https://doi.org/10.1146/annurev-clinpsy-032816-045217

Society of Clinical Psychology, American Psychological Association (March, 2018). *Psychological treatments*. Available on line at https://www.div12.org/treatments/

Spek, V., Cuijpers, P.I.M., Nyklícek, I., Riper, H., Keyzer, J., & Pop, V. (2007). Internet-based cognitive behaviour therapy for symptoms of depression and anxiety: A meta-analysis. *Psychological Medicine, 37*(3), 319–328. https://doi.org/10.1017/S0033291706008944

Spijkerman, M. P. J., Pots, W. T. M., & Bohlmeijer, E. T. (2016). Effectiveness of online mindfulness-based interventions in improving mental health:

A review and meta-analysis of randomised controlled trials. *Clinical Psychology Review, 45*, 102–114. https://doi.org/10.1016/j.cpr.2016.03.009

Starfield, B. (1992). *Primary care: Concept, evaluation, and policy.* New York: Oxford University Press.

Steel, Z., Marnane, C., Iranpour, C., Chey, T., Jackson, J. W., Patel, V., & Silove, D. (2014). The global prevalence of common mental disorders: A systematic review and meta-analysis 1980–2013. *International Journal of Epidemiology, 43*(2), 476–493. https://doi.org/10.1093/ije/dyu038

Stoyanov, D., Correia, D.T., & Cuthbert, B.N. (2019). The Research Domain Criteria (RDoC) and the historical roots of psychopathology: A viewpoint. *European Psychiatry, 57*, 58–60. https://doi.org/10.1016/j.eurpsy.2018.11.007

StressEraserPro. (2020). *StressEraser Pro.* National Centre Stress management in Netherland. http://www.stresseraserpro.com/home

Stuart, S., Schultz, J., & Ashen, C. (2018). A new community-based model for training in evidence-based psychotherapy practice. *Community Mental Health Journal, 54*, 912. https://doi.org/10.1007/s10597-017-0220-x

Substance Abuse and Mental Health Services Administration (2013). *Report to Congress on the Nation's Substance Abuse and Mental Health Workforce Issues.* Rockville, MD: SAMHSA. Available on line at https://store.samhsa.gov/shin/content/PEP13-RTC-BHWORK/PEP13-RTC-BHWORK.pdfhttps://store.samhsa.gov/shin/content/PEP13-RTC-BHWORK/PEP13-RTC-BHWORK.pdf

Substance Abuse and Mental Health Services Administration (2017a). *Center for Integrated Health Solutions: Rockville, MD: SAMHSA.* Retrieved from https://www.integration.samhsa.gov/search?q=what+is+integrated+care

Substance Abuse and Mental Health Services Administration (2017b). *National registry of evidence-based programs and practices.* Rockville, MD: SAMHSA. Accessed on line (January 2017) (see Footnote 1 of this chapter)

Swift, J. K., & Greenberg, R. P. (2012). Premature discontinuation in adult psychotherapy: A meta-analysis. *Journal of Consulting and Clinical Psychology, 80*(4), 547–559. https://doi.org/10.1037/a0028226

ten Have, M., de Graaf, R., Ormel, J., Vilagut, G., Kovess, V., Alonso, J., & ESEMeD/MHEDEA 2000 Investigators. (2010). Are attitudes towards mental health help-seeking associated with service use? Results from the European Study of Epidemiology of Mental Disorders. *Social Psychiatry and Psychiatric Epidemiology, 45*, 153–163. https://doi.org/10.1007/s00127-009-0050-4

Thompson, A., Issakidis, C., & Hunt, C. (2008). Delay to seek treatment for anxiety and mood disorders in an Australian clinical sample. *Behaviour Change, 25*(2), 71–78. https://doi.org/10.1375/bech.25.2.71

Thornicroft, G., Chatterji, S., Evans-Lacko, S., Gruber, M., Sampson, N., Aguilar-Gaxiola, S., Al-Hamzawi, A., Alonso, J., Andrade, L., Borges, G., Bruffaerts, R., Bunting, B., de Almeida, J. M., Florescu, S., de Girolamo, G., Gureje, O., Haro, J. M., He, Y., Hinkov, H., Karam, E., . . . Kessler, R. C. (2017). Undertreatment of people with major depressive disorder in 21 countries. *The British Journal of Psychiatry, 210*(2), 119–124. https://doi.org/10.1192/bjp.bp.116.188078

Titov, N., Dear, B. F., Staples, L.G., Bennett-Levy, J., Klein, B., Rapee, R.M., Shann, C., Richards, D., Andersson, G., Ritterband, L., Purtell, C., Bezuidenhout, G.,Johnston, L., & Nielssen, O.B. (2015). MindSpot clinic: An accessible, efficient, and effective online treatment service for anxiety and depression. *Psychiatric Services, 66*(10), 1043–1050. https://doi.org/10.1176/appi.ps.201400477

Tomlinson, M., Rotheram-Borus, M.J., Swartz, L., & Tsai, A.C. (2013) Scaling up mHealth: Where is the evidence? *PLoS Med 10*(2), e1001382. https://doi.org/10.1371/journal.pmed.1001382

Twenge, J. M., Joiner, T. E., Rogers, M. L., & Martin, G. N. (2018). Increases in depressive symptoms, suicide-related outcomes, and suicide rates among US adolescents after 2010 and links to increased new media screen time. *Clinical Psychological Science, 6*(1), 3–17. https://doi.org/10.1177/2167702617723376

United Nations (2000, September). *Resolution adopted by the General Assembly: United Nations Millennium Declaration.* Available online at www.un.org/millennium/declaration/ares552e.pdf

Valente, T.W. (2010). *Social networks and health: Models, methods, and applications.* New York: Oxford University Press. https://doi.org/10.1093/acprof:oso/9780195301014.001.0001

Walsh, R. (2011). Lifestyle and mental health. *American Psychologist, 66*(7), 579–592. https://doi.org/10.1037/a0021769

Wang, P.S., Berglund, P., Olfson, M., Pincus, H.A., Wells, K.B., & Kessler, R.C. (2005). Failure and delay in initial treatment contact after first onset of mental disorders in the National Comorbidity Survey Replication. *Archives of General Psychiatry, 62*(6), 603–613. https://doi.org/10.1001/archpsyc.62.6.603

Wang, P.S., Demler, O., & Kessler, R.C. (2002). Adequacy of treatment for serious mental illness in the United States. *American Journal of Public Health, 92*(1), 92–98. https://doi.org/10.2105/AJPH.92.1.92

Wang, P.S., Lane, M., Olfson, M., Pincus, H.A., Wells, K. B., & Kessler, R. C. (2005). Twelve-month use of mental health services in the United States: Results from the National Comorbidity Survey Replication. *Archives of General Psychiatry, 62*(6), 629–640. https://doi.org/10.1001/archpsyc.62.6.629

Weisz, J.R., Krumholz, L.S., Santucci, L., Thomassin, K., & Ng, M.Y. (2015). Shrinking the gap between research and practice: Tailoring and testing youth psychotherapies in clinical care contexts. *Annual Review of Clinical Psychology, 11*, 139–163. https://doi.org/10.1146/annurev-clinpsy-032814-112820

Wells, K., Klap, R., Koike, A., & Sherbourne, C. (2001). Ethnic disparities in unmet need for alcoholism, drug abuse, and mental health care. *The American Journal of Psychiatry, 158*(12), 2027–2032. https://doi.org/10.1176/appi.ajp.158.12.2027

Whiteford, H. A., Degenhardt, L., Rehm, J., Baxter, A. J., Ferrari, A. J., Erskine, H. E., Charlson, F. J., Norman, R. E., Flaxman, A. D., Johns, N., Burstein, R., Murray, C. J., & Vos, T. (2013). Global burden of disease attributable to mental and substance use disorders: Findings from the Global Burden of Disease Study 2010. *The Lancet, 382*(9904), 1575–1586. https://doi.org/10.1016/S0140-6736(13)61611-6

Wittchen, H. U., Mühlig, S., & Beesdo, K. (2003). Mental disorders in primary care. *Dialogues in Clinical Neuroscience, 5*(2), 115–128.

Witte, A. K., & Zarnekow, R. (2019, January). Transforming personal healthcare through technology-A systematic literature review of wearable sensors for medical application. *In Proceedings of the 52nd Hawaii International Conference on System Sciences*, 3848–3857. https://doi.org/10.24251/HICSS.2019.466

World Health Organization (2001a). *International Classification of Functioning, Disability and Health* (ICF). Geneva: WHO.

World Health Organization. (2001b). *The World Health Report 2001: Mental health: New understanding, new hope.* Geneva: WHO.

World Health Organization (2005). *Mental health: Facing the challenges, building solutions.* Copenhagen, Denmark: WHO Regional Office for Europe.

World Health Organization (2008). *Task shifting: Global recommendations and guidelines.* Geneva: WHO.

World Health Organization (2010). *International classification of diseases-10* (4th ed.). Geneva: WHO.

World Health Organization (2011a). *Prevention and control of NCDS: Summary.* First Global Ministerial Conference on Healthy Lifestyles and Noncommunicable Disease Control. Moscow.

World Health Organization (2011b). *Scaling up action against non-communicable diseases: How much will it cost?* Geneva: WHO.

World Health Organization. (2017). *Depression and other common mental disorders: Global health estimates* (No. WHO/MSD/MER/2017.2). World Health Organization.

World Mental Health Survey Consortium (2004). Prevalence, severity, and unmet need for treatment of mental disorders in the World Health Organization World Mental Health Surveys. *JAMA, 291*(21), 2581–2590. https://doi.org/10.1001/jama.291.21.2581

Zane, N., Sue, S., Chang, J., Huang, L., Huang, J., Lowe, S., Srinivasan, S., Chun, K., Kurasaki, K., & Lee, E. (2005). Beyond ethnic match: Effects of client-therapist cognitive match in problem perception, coping orientation, and therapy goals on treatment outcomes. *Journal of Community Psychology, 33*(5), 569–585. https://doi.org/10.1002/jcop.20067

Zhang, Z., Wu, H., Wang, W., & Wang, B. (2010). A smartphone based respiratory biofeedback system. *Biomedical Engineering and Informatics (BMEI), 3rd International Conference Proceedings, 2*, 717–720. https://doi.org/10.1109/BMEI.2010.5640072

TOWARDS THE FUTURE

●

IV

TOWARDS THE FUTURE

CHAPTER 23

Epilogue: Prevalent Themes, Predictions, and Recommendations

Louis G Castonguay, Catherine F Eubanks, Shigeru Iwakabe, Mariane Krause, Andrew C Page, Sigal Zilcha-Mano, Wolfgang Lutz, and Michael Barkham

Abstract

In this concluding chapter, we identify some of the most prevalent themes that cut across the previous chapters. We also make predictions and recommendations about future studies in psychotherapy. Among these recommendations are "old" issues that have not received much attention in recent years. Also highlighted are emerging themes that may or may not be adopted by diverse stakeholders in the field of mental health. The chapter ends with broad recommendations regarding interventions and methods that, based on current empirical evidence, should be promoted in practice, training, and policy guidelines.

Overview

Where Are We, and Where Are We Likely to Go?
   Psychotherapy Outcome
   Routine Outcome Monitoring and Clinical
      Feedback System
   Client Predictors and Moderators
   Process
   Therapist Effects
Where Else Should We Go?
   Training
   Deterioration and Negative Processes
   Nonsymptomatic Outcomes
   Integrative Approaches and Practices
   "Old" Methods
   Statistical and Technological Advances
Will They Stay or Will They Go?
What Should Have More Impact?
Abbreviations
References

Based on a review of the previous chapters of this *Handbook*, as well as the authors' own perspectives, this concluding chapter offers a synopsis of current trends in psychotherapy research as well as an agenda for future studies – those that are most likely to be prominent, some that should be strongly encouraged, and others that may or may not be fruitful pathways to knowledge and action.

Where Are We, and Where Are We Likely to Go?

Following are some themes that have been prominent in recent years and that are likely to be of particularly high heuristic value for future research.

Psychotherapy Outcome

Over the last decade, the evidence for the efficacy and effectiveness of psychotherapy has been solidified – showing that a large number of clients benefit from it, with a substantial percentage of them achieving clinically significant change (Chapter 5). During the same period of time, many studies have provided additional support for psychotherapy in routine practice across diverse clinical settings in different regions of the world (Chapter 6). Put simply, psychotherapy, as it is conducted in the real world, works. Interestingly, however, research also shows that the rate of change varies across clients, which should guard against the adoption of a fixed number of sessions to guide the delivery of treatments, both in naturalistic and randomized clinical trial (RCT) settings (Chapter 5).

In addition, recent findings have further confirmed that four major theoretical orientations – dynamic (Chapter 12), humanistic-experiential (Chapter 13), cognitive behavioral (CBT; Chapters 14 and 15), and systemic therapies (Chapter 16) – can be viewed as evidence-based treatments for a diversity of clinical problems. With regard to depression and anxiety disorders, research indicates that psychological therapies can be at least as effective as medication in terms of treatment response, with some treatment packages (in particular CBT) having demonstrated better long-term impact than pharmacological treatments (Chapter 20). In the treatment of psychotic problems (i.e., schizophrenia and bipolar disorders), a considerable number of studies have provided support for the role of psychosocial therapies (CBT, interpersonal therapy, family or conjoint therapy) as an adjunct to medication (Chapter 20).

Comparisons of psychosocial therapies have continued to reveal small differences between them in terms of outcome, and when such differences are observed, they tend to consistently favor CBT over other approaches (Chapter 5). Such consistent small effects should be recognized (rather than being swept under the rug of an overgeneralizing "Dodo verdict" assumption of equivalence), as they can potentially have a large impact on efforts to disseminate evidence-based practice at scale. Yet, the fact that several types of treatment have been shown to be efficacious provides the field with a range of options in its efforts to address clients' various preferences and treatment responses (Chapter 5).

Evidence has also accumulated about the positive effect of psychotherapy, again with a range of clinical problems, when delivered in groups (Chapter 17), via the internet (Chapter 21), as well as when provided to children and adolescents (Chapter 18). Research has also demonstrated that psychotherapy can be conducted in ways that can be better attuned the needs and resources of diverse populations, as cultural adapted treatments have been found to be more effective than non-adapted treatments (Chapter 5).

It is worth nothing that the level of support for psychotherapy outcome has relied on a large number of meta-analyses and network meta-analyses (Chapters 2 and 5) that have been conducted since the last edition of this *Handbook*, including several for the current edition (Chapters 12, 13, and 17). Despite such support, however, the previous chapters have identified many avenues in need of further investigations. Some of these are aimed at improving the assessment of psychotherapy, such as conducting long-term and repeated follow-up assessments of outcome, as well as assessing cost-effectiveness (Chapter 5). Others are focused on ways that could improve psychotherapy across its various approaches or modalities, including the integration of findings from psychopathology and basic sciences, augmentation current treatments with additional interventions, and the modification the frequency or duration of sessions.

Although major orientations and modalities rest on solid empirical grounds, many lines of new research have been recommended in each of the specific chapter addressing them. Major themes that cut across these lines include: investigating and/or improving treatments for specific populations (e.g., ethnic, sexual, and gender minorities, depressed youth, anorexia nervosa in adults) and clinical problems (e.g., humanistic-experiential therapy for anxiety disorders, psychodynamic therapy for treatment resistant depression, internet treatment for severe and chronic difficulties such as borderline personality disorder); improving and testing specific approaches of a particular orientation (e.g., systemic individual therapy, CBT group therapy for depression);

comparing treatment approaches within orientations (e.g., CBT vs. CBT-Enhanced for eating disorders, humanistic-experiential treatments that are more vs. less process guided); and comparing treatment orientations or modalities (e.g., acceptance and commitment therapy vs. family therapy for psychosis, internet therapy vs. face-to-face therapy, long-term impact of CBT vs. combination of CBT and pharmacotherapy for depression and anxiety disorders).

The importance of conducting more research on the implementation, dissemination, and impact of evidence-based treatments in naturalistic settings (effectiveness studies) has also been emphasized in several chapters. Furthermore, what is likely to receive more empirical attention is the scaling up of effective treatments. We predict that in the next decade a substantial number of studies will be conducted on a variety of ways to deliver psychotherapy (e.g., technologically-based treatments, low cost and/or intensity interventions, provision of services by paraprofessionals) to address what Kazdin refers to as the "treatment gap" – the marked disproportion between the number of individuals in the world who are in need of mental health care and the number of individuals who receive it (Chapter 22). Transdiagnostic and modular treatments, which have been developed in part to facilitate dissemination of evidence-based interventions in real-world settings, have gained interest in recent years and are also likely to be the object of further investigations across theoretical orientations and clinical populations (Chapters 12, 18, and 19).

Importantly, the beneficial impact of therapy has been documented via qualitative studies in terms that are not captured by symptom change, such as "narrative identity repair" (e.g., coming to terms with aversive experiences, acquiring new sources of meaning; Chapter 11). To further advance the contribution and recognition of qualitative methodologies, more emphasis and efforts have been recommended toward the: (1) replication and expansion of current qualitative outcome findings for a diversity of theoretical orientations and cultures; (2) integration of results of qualitative research, via systematic review and qualitative meta-analyses; (3) comparison of quantitative and qualitative findings across different forms of treatment; and (4) combination of qualitative and quantitative methods in study designs (Chapters 3 and 11). We also believe that efforts to integrate and synthesize quantitative and qualitative results related to a diversity of topics should be reinforced through funding, hiring, and promotion practices. Considering the wealth of research available and rapidly accumulating, such efforts could help the field process what we know and what we do not know and thus move forward rather than constantly reinventing the wheel.

Routine Outcome Monitoring and Clinical Feedback System

Routine outcome monitoring (ROM), and the psychometrically based clinical feedback system (CFS) associated with it, is an established evidence-based practice that has been implemented in diverse clinical settings via a myriad of measurement systems (Chapter 4). This practice is unique in its seamless integration of outcome and process, where the tracking of client change and provision of immediate and actional information is aimed at facilitating decision-making throughout therapy, which in turn is aimed at enhancing client change.

From its beginning in the late 1980s, as a way to complement the predominant focus on treatment with a focus on patients, research on the effectiveness of ROM/CFS has accelerated over the last 20 years – as conveyed by the compilation of nine meta-analyses, six of them having emerged since the last edition of this *Handbook*. This is not counting the explosion of research that has been conducted in routine clinical settings based on the adoption of ROM/CFS (Chapter 6).

Mostly conducted on individual therapy for adults, research on the effectiveness of ROM/CFS has been expanded to group therapy (Chapter 17), youth treatment (Chapter 18), and supervision (Chapter 10). The focus of ROM/CFS systems has also been broadened, from the reduction of deterioration and the enhancement of the general effectiveness of therapy, to the amelioration of premature termination and self-harm. Routine measurement systems have also been developed to address specific clinical populations (e.g., college students) and to assess process variables (e.g., alliance).

While we predict that ROM/CFS is here to stay, more research needs to be conducted on their adoption and repeated use throughout treatment, validation across cultures, languages, clinical populations and settings, as well as expansion of clinically relevant constructs to assess. Future research should also attempt to understand the mechanisms of change underlying its effectiveness, such as how it allows therapists to be more attuned to particular needs of a client, including family (Chapter 16). In addition, ROM should be conducted regularly (e.g., on a monthly basis via Ecological Momentary Assessment technology) during long-term follow-up in order to assess maintenance or improvement of therapeutic gain, as well as relapse (Chapter 5). Importantly, attempts to improve the development, implementation, and clinical utility (including at an organizational level) of ROM/CFS should rely on recent and future qualitative studies (Chapter 11).

Client Predictors and Moderators

Over the last decade, considerable attention has been given to identifying characteristics of clients who are more or less likely to benefit from therapy (predictors) and those who are more or less likely to benefit from one type of therapy than another (moderators). Still, in many chapters covering specific treatment orientations and modalities, authors noted the need for even more research on predictors and moderators. A top priority is diversity, including variables related to race/ethnic, cultural, social/economic, sexual, and gender minorities. While recent investigations have been reported on such crucial issues throughout this edition of the handbook, no chapter has concluded that sufficient emphasis has be given to understanding and being optimally responsive to the needs, resources, and strengths associated with various identities and social realities (e.g., clients living in economically deprived areas). We hope that findings and recommendations provided in this current edition will serve as a bridge from decades of sparse empirical attention to a wealth of information, the breath of depth of it to be captured in a specific chapter of the next edition.

In addition to diversity, Chapter 7 addresses a wide range of client characteristics that have been examined (including via recent meta-analyses) and/or deserve further investigations. These include: age, religiosity/spirituality, initial severity, comorbidity, expectations, preferences, credibility, locus of control, coping style, alexithymia, psychological mindedness, perfectionism/self-criticism, motivation, stage of change, problem assimilation, reactance, interpersonal problems, attachment style, and social support. Complementing the assessment of client characteristics at an individual level, recent advances in statistical analyses (e.g., growth mixture modeling) have identified, at pretreatment, subgroups of clients who are likely to have different patterns of change during therapy (Chapters 2 and 4).

Developments in research methods and statistics (e.g., large data sets, machine learning) have opened up new directions to identify optimal treatments for particular clients, not only in terms of therapeutic approaches (e.g., dialectic behavior therapy vs. general psychiatric management) and modalities (e.g., psychosocial therapy [CBT] vs. pharmacotherapy), but also with regard to level of care (e.g., high vs. low intensity), type and sequence of components prescribed in a specific treatment package (e.g., modular psychotherapies), and adjustment of interventions during treatment (e.g., via clinical feedback provided by routine outcome measurement) (see Chapter 19, as well as Chapters 4, 5, 18, and 20). We believe these data-driven efforts toward personalized treatments will generate more research, not only in terms of moderators of outcome but also in terms of moderators of mechanisms of change (Chapters 12 and 20).

Process

The time when one could lament that the process of change has been ignored by psychotherapy researchers, or some fragments of them, is long gone. Studies attempting to understand what has taken place during treatment that might explain how therapy works have been reported in all the chapters on specific approaches and modalities covered in this *Handbook*. In addition, four chapters have presented recent quantitative or qualitative individual studies, systematic reviews, and/or meta-analyses on a range of process variables that cut across different forms of psychotherapy or that are assumed to be unique to particular treatments (Chapters 6, 7, 8, and 11). The process variable that has received the most attention is the therapeutic alliance, not only in terms of number of studies (in different approaches and treatment modalities) but also with respect to the sophisticated methods and statistical analyses that have been used in its investigation. Recent studies have not only highlighted the direct and indirect relationship between alliance and outcome, but also the complex nature of this relationship based on different patterns or episodes during treatment, convergence and discrepancy between client and therapist perceptions from session to session, client and therapist interdependent measurement of both the alliance and the outcome, and various links between alliance and other therapeutic variables. In addition, recent studies have provided supportive evidence for the causal role of the alliance on client improvement.

There are, however, many questions related to the alliance that deserve attention from future research. While there has been an increased recognition by therapists of diverse orientations that alliance ruptures do occur during treatment and that interventions have been developed to attempt to address them, more needs to be known. As recommended in Chapter 12, we predict that particular emphasis will be given to defining and measuring more accurately such ruptures, identifying what leads to them (including how therapists contribute to them), assessing their impact on outcome, testing and improving interventions to repair them, figuring out how best to train therapists in recognizing and effectively attending to them, as well as understanding how the resolution of ruptures can lead to therapeutic change. Although the alliance has been reliably predictive of outcome, considerations of measurement issues might allow future studies to more accurately reveal the part of the outcome variance it explains, such as assessing it at least four times during treatment (Chapter 8) and developing measures that lead to less positively skewed responses (i.e., high alliance scores; Chapter 2). In addition to regarding the alliance as a treatment predictor, future studies should consider alliance as an outcome (e.g., as a measure of treatment engagement), and thus investigate process variables that may have a positive or negative impact on the alliance (e.g., techniques; Chapter 18).

Other than the alliance, several relational variables have been investigated, including the real relationship, empathy, positive regard, genuineness, dyadic congruence, synchronicity, and interpersonal complementarity. In addition, many client (e.g., emotional and narrative processing, cognitions and metacognitions, cognitive defusion in psychotic clients [believability of hallucinations], insight/self-understanding, acceptance of internal experience, engagement, resistance, interpersonal impact/behavior, parenting practices in youth treatment), therapist (e.g., skills and interventions, treatment adherence and competence, countertransference, interpersonal impact/behavior, self-disclosure/immediacy, emotional expression, multicultural competence and orientation [i.e., therapist's humility, comfort, and attention to cultural opportunities], flexibility/responsivity, therapist support in internet treatment), and treatment variables (e.g., number of sessions, setting) have been examined. Future studies on the nature and impact of these variables (and for that matter, the alliance) should attempt to: (1) examine whether the association between process and outcome takes place at the client level, therapist level, or both (using multilevel modeling analyses); (2) explore whether such an association is more likely to be a cause or an effect (e.g., via the correlation between the process variable and following change, or within-client analyses on repeated assessments of process and outcome); (3) investigate the variations, linear or not, and fluctuations of such association during therapy (e.g., via the repeated assessment of process [including therapist interventions] at different phases of treatment, of outcome trajectory throughout treatment, as well as of significant events and sudden gains or losses at any point in treatment); (4) assess the moderating role of client, therapist, clinic/setting, and supervisor characteristics, as well as process variables on such associations (e.g., the effect of interactions between technique and relationship variables); (5) examine the dyadic processes intrinsic to the client [individual, couple, family, or group] and therapist experience of process and outcome variables (e.g., via actor-partner interdependence model); (6) identify which process variables

are mediators/mechanisms of change (e.g., changes in the client that are produced by the treatment and are explaining improvement); (7) determine which factors are triggering such mediators/mechanisms of change; (8) explore whether these mediators/mechanisms of change, or any relationship between process variables and outcome, are specific to one approach, common to a number of them (i.e., "faux unique"), or contrary to theory driven assumptions; (9) examine potential overlaps in process variables to determine shared variances as well as unique contribution of each variable in accounting for change; and (10) conduct qualitative – or mixed quantitative and qualitative – analyses of process variables and their impact during session, postsession, and posttreatment (via methods presented in Chapters 3, 11, and 13).

As for the alliance, specific directions for future research have been recommended for many of these process variables, such as investigating therapist adherence outside of RCT settings, where the high level of control on the use of techniques may prevent a fair assessment of their helpfulness (Chapter 2); assessing the "intuitive relationship" between competence and outcome by unpacking the impact of specific components of competency under particular treatment conditions (Chapter 12); improving our definition and measurement of insight/self-understanding and engagement to more accurately understand their impact (Chapters 7, 8, and 12); investigating cognitive variables as mediators of change in youth treatment (Chapter 18); examining client resistance and therapist interventions to address it in different approaches, including CBT (Chapters 7, 8); further exploring how therapists can facilitate productive emotional and narrative processes in humanistic-experiential therapy and, no doubt, in other treatments (Chapter 13); discovering and confirming ways by which client and therapist differences manifest themselves in and impact the process of change (Chapter 11); and understanding in what context, with whom, and how therapists can foster client change by expressing their own emotions, working with client hostility, and promoting their autonomy (Chapter 7). Considering their conceptual and clinical importance, the field should also address the relative paucity of empirical attention that has been paid to therapist countertransference, flexibility and responsiveness, and multicultural orientation (Chapter 7), as well as to process variables in group therapy other than cohesion (Chapter 17).

Therapist Effects

Also complementing the long-standing focus on treatment approaches has been the examination of the therapist in accounting for change. Like patient-focused research, empirical work on therapist effects gained traction approximately 20 years ago and can now be viewed as a zeitgeist in psychotherapy research. Based on the use of multilevel modeling analyses, the current state of knowledge suggests that therapist differential effectiveness explains a meaningful part of the outcome variance, and that the magnitude of therapist effects is higher in naturalistic (approximately 6%) compared to controlled settings (approximately 3%), as well as with more severe clients (Chapters 5 and 9). Therapist effects have also been demonstrated with specific populations, including race/ethnic minority clients, race/ethnicity and gender intersectionality (white men, white women, women of color, and men of color), and clients with mild-to-moderate symptom levels (Chapters 5, 6, and 9). Recent studies also suggest that some therapists are more effective than others in maintaining session attendance, preventing drop out, facilitating early changes, and fostering the effectiveness of ROM/CFS (Chapters 6 and 9). Despite these advances, much more effort should be made toward estimating therapist effects in RCTs and particular attention should be given to these effects in studies (RCT or not) that involve a large sample of therapists and a large sample of clients per therapist (Chapters 2 and 9). More research is also needed to determine whether therapist effects are generic or specific; that is, whether more effective therapists are better than others with most clinical problems or whether some therapists are more effective than most clinicians but only for particular types of difficulties (Chapter 9). Relatedly, efforts have begun to investigate whether matching specific groups of therapist and specific groups of clients can lead to improvement of outcome (Chapter 5). These data-driven efforts, like those mentioned earlier with regard to personalized treatments, reflect the current movement toward precision medicine.

A much greater emphasis has been placed, over the last 10 years or so, on explaining therapist effects. Several variables have been investigated, such as therapist contribution to the alliance, facilitative interpersonal skills, Rogerian attitudes, professional humility, attachment style, and interpersonal motivation (Chapters 5 and 9). While some of these factors have generated more robust support than others, much more research is needed to better define, more regularly assess, more broadly explore, and more firmly demonstrate what makes some therapists consistently more effective than others, and what make some therapists work better with some clients than with others.

WHERE ELSE SHOULD WE GO?

Below are some themes – mostly "old" ones – that have been more or less neglected in recent years but that might have high heuristic value for future research.

Training

Even before psychotherapy became a part of established professional disciplines (e.g., clinical and counseling psychology, psychiatry, social work program), training was deemed as a necessary condition for practice – in the early days of the talking cure, all had to be trained (at least via a personal analysis) to be recognized as a psychoanalyst – all except Freud, that is! Yet, this ubiquitous and continuous requirement has been the object of limited empirical attention. This is one glaring example of the discrepancy between what is of primary interest to most researchers and what is crucial to all practitioners' professional lives. There have been studies on clinicians' development (Orlinsksy & Rønnestad, 2005) and training experience (Messina et al., 2017). Empirical investigations have also been conducted on learning of a number of specific interventions and skills (such as helping skills, empathy, self-awareness, self-disclosure and immediacy, theory-specific techniques, cultural knowledge, awareness, and skills), as well as on supervision (Chapter 10). However, whether these experiences, learning, and the supervision process are related to clinical performance and/or client outcome deserves more empirical attention. Furthermore, studies that have investigated the link between the level of or time in training and a client's improvement have led to mixed if not humbling findings (Chapters 6, 9, and 10), indicating the need to better understand and improve how we teach psychotherapy. Research, including in group therapy (Chapter 17), is needed to figure out what components, methods, and models of training are helpful; what competencies and skills should be acquired; when (learning sequence) and from whom (including trainer and supervisor effects) these should be learned; as well as how to improve training by integrating and fostering cultural issues. This type of research is not only likely to strengthen science and practice connections, but to better prepare and guide clinicians in their provision of care.

Deterioration and Negative Processes

The fact that a substantial number of clients get worse during or as a result of psychotherapy is nothing new. Findings about deterioration were published by Allen Bergin in the 1960s (see Lambert et al., 2010) and lengthily described in the first edition of this *Handbook*. However, while some pioneers of our field, most noticeably Hans Strupp (see Moras et al., 2010), have helped process researchers to keep their eyes on negative or hindering events (e.g., Safran & Muran, 2000), deterioration has been largely off the radar of outcome researchers for decades (Barlow, 2010). Fortunately, the work of Lambert (a colleague of Bergin) on routine outcome measuring (see Ogles & Hayes, 2010), along with Lilienfeld's (2007) paper on potentially harmful treatments, served as catalysts for the more widespread attention currently paid to deterioration and factors that can lead to it. Nonetheless, more quantitative and qualitative studies remain needed to identify and address process and outcome warning signals, and directions for future research can be found in many chapters of this *Handbook* (Chapters 4, 5, 6, 9, 11, 14, 17, and 21). Such studies have a unique potential toward enhancing the view of research as clinically pertinent knowledge – if not only by increasing practitioners' awareness of their first duty and their ability to fulfill its daunting nature: First do no harm.

Nonsymptomatic Outcomes

For most outcome researchers, symptomatic changes, positive and negative, have been the primary markers of psychotherapy effectiveness or lack of thereof. Clinicians' goals and assessment of their work, however, are rarely restricted to decrease of distress and impairment. This is not new. From the beginning, insight-oriented therapies have been focused on change in personality, both from a clinical and an empirical perspective. For example, as part of one of the earliest research programs in psychotherapy, Carl Rogers and his colleagues measured how therapy can lead to less discrepancy between who clients want to be and who they are (see Elliott & Farber, 2010). Such an "old" construct is reflecting a psychological health perspective that is consistent with targets of change that are now being recommended by researchers, such as quality of life (Chapters 4 and 5), and acquisition of new knowledge and skills (Chapters 11 and 21). Interestingly, these targets may be convergent with the current interest of other stakeholders in mental health care. In a recent study, one of the topics for future research most frequently suggested by both clinicians and administrators involved in a practice research network was "client ongoing psychological functioning/life satisfaction" (Youn et al., 2019). Pushing further along a positive mental health perspective, we recommend that future research pay more attention to the assessment of potential effects of psychotherapy that have been identified in qualitative analyses of humanistic-experiential treatments (Chapter 13). Regrouped in three main categories (*appreciating experiences of self*; *appreciating experience of self in relationship to others*; and *changed view of self/others*), such effects may capture complex and meaningful changes that both therapists and clients prize in successful therapy – irrespective of the approach used.

Integrative Approaches and Practices

More than 40 years ago, Sol Garfield and his colleague Richard Kurtz created shock waves in the field by reporting that a large number of clinicians surveyed in the US defined themselves as eclectic (see Beutler & Simons, 2010). Several surveys conducted since then indicate that, at least in the US, integrative therapy has been the modal orientation espoused by respondents (Norcross & Alexander, 2019). There is, unfortunately, no correspondence between this clinical reality and the agenda of most outcome researchers – such a gap, in our opinion, needs to be addressed if researchers hope to have their work viewed as being more representative and relevant by full time clinicians. One way that integration has so far been studied is via the investigation of "formal" integrative approaches, such as cognitive behavioral analysis system of psychotherapy (see Boswell et al., 2019 for a review). New developments and future directions of research have been presented by researchers in this *Handbook* (Chapters 8, 12, 14, 16, and 17) and elsewhere (Norcross & Goldfried, 2019) with regard to the investigation of integrative approaches, and their comparison with pure-form treatments.

In addition to these top-down suggestions, we recommend the development of bottom-up-based research programs which, in line with Garfield's contribution, would seek to give voice to clinicians. With the quantitative and qualitative methods that we now have, however, such programs could go beyond general surveys by involving the report, observation, and intensive analysis of specific interventions as they occur in practice. With routine outcome measurement easily available, highly effective clinicians could be identified and invited to participate in collaborative investigations. Having already been done with one clinician (Hansen et al., 2015), this process could be expanded in the context of agencies and/or practice research networks (through procedures approved by clinicians, administrators, professional boards of research ethics) to larger samples of therapists. The examination of both process and outcome would likely help delineate when, how, and with whom effective therapists

combine techniques from different approaches, as well as draw on principles of change that are common across multiple approaches (Goldfried, 1980). This could then serve as the basis of marker-responsive intervention protocols (Constantino et al., 2013) that could later be tested with large samples of clinicians – thereby closing clinical and empirical loops, from the observations of current practice, the planned efforts to improve such practice in clinical routine, to the testing of these efforts (Chapter 6). Such a bottom-up strategy could help the field move beyond the traditional translation of knowledge (knowledge created in controlled environments by scholars who see few clients, which is then imported to naturalistic environments) toward the creation of new landscapes of knowledge and action via the collaboration of stakeholders working in the same environment (Castonguay, 2011).

"Old" Methods

As noted in Chapter 13, a range of research methodologies are required in order to better understand and improve psychotherapy, especially if our investigations are to be broadened with respect to diversity and worldwide populations. These methodologies should include ones that have been developed many moons ago but have receded with the ascension of the RCT as the gold standard for sanctioning scientifically supported practice. Case studies, for example, which have been crucial for the development of insight and behavioral change-oriented approaches, are the focus of renewed interest and have been promoted as a methodology to provide evidence of efficacy, as well as to build and refine theories of psychotherapy (Chapters 3 and 13). Several methods for single-case and small samples that have passed the test of time, such as task analyses, sequential analyses, and single experimental case designs, have been giving (or reissuing) a strong vote of confidence for their ability to examine relationships between various process and outcome variables (Chapters 13 and 16). At the group level, the recent use of a classic multiple baseline design (Muran et al., 2018) should also inspire future research, as a way to assess the additive effect of specific interventions via between-group and within-client analyses aimed at controlling for client variables, therapist variables, and their interaction (Chapter 12).

Qualitative analyses are yet another set of empirical tools that have a long history in psychotherapy. In the 1980s, for example, they were central to a variety of methods aimed at providing contextual and sequential descriptions of complex episodes and patterns of change (see Greenberg & Pinsoff, 1986). Predicted to reduce the gap between research and practice within a decade, these methods were then promoted as a possible "paradigm shift in psychotherapy process research, bringing it closer to the clinical method" (Elliott, 1983, p. 47). Although they have shaped the development of humanistic-experiential approaches (Chapter 13), qualitative analyses have not gained as much traction in other orientations. Echoing calls made in the current *Handbook* (Chapters 16, 21), we believe that the time is ripe for rigorous qualitative methods (e.g., grounded theory) to be used more broadly. On their own, or alongside quantitative findings, these methods are fruitful strategies to discover, clarify, and confirm client and therapist experiences (e.g., helpful and hindering aspects, significant events), which in turn can help us refine our conceptual models, improve our awareness of the complexity of therapeutic interactions, and implement timely and responsive technical and/or relational interventions in the appropriate context (Chapters 3 and 11). The decision to devote two chapters to qualitative methods in the current edition of this *Handbook* is both a reflection of their increasing contribution to the scientific basis of psychotherapy (in terms of number and methodological integrity) and an effort to push against the field's tendency to privilege quantitative investigations and neglect the value of qualitative research. Using Elliott's (1983) evocative words, we do indeed believe that these methods have potential to make the "researcher-therapist boundary more permeable" (albeit a few years later than he hoped for), not only by addressing issues that are crucial to clinicians but by doing so in ways that are consistent with how they seek to understand the process of change.

The 1980s also saw meta-analysis take center stage. As previously mentioned, researchers have substantially relied on this method to assess the efficacy of psychotherapy. The same is now true for process variables (Chapters 7, 8, and 12). We expect more meta-analyses (and network analyses) to be conducted, accounting for recent developments and innovations (Chapter 4), as well as further use with qualitative studies (Chapters 3 and 11). Yet, we do not believe that the field should rely exclusively on these methods, considering the limitations typically associated with them such as the aggregation of studies of various levels of quality (Chapters 2, and 5). In fact, arguments have been made to promote single RCTs (especially with non-CBT treatments) of high quality as a guiding resource for future update of practice policies (Chapter 5). One feature suggested for such high-quality RCTs is the use of CBT as a comparator (instead of wait list, placebo, or other control conditions) to assess whether promising approaches can match or surpass the effectiveness of the most established treatment. Finally, two chapters in this *Handbook* remind the field of the foundational importance of measurement and promote "old" methods to improve its precision and effective use, such as item response theory and individualized measures of client problems or treatment goals (Chapters 2 and 4).

Statistical and Technological Advances

There has been an explosion of new methods over the last two decades. We have already mentioned a number of statistical ones in the paragraphs above, such as growth mixture modeling, machine learning, multilevel modeling, mediator analyses, actor–partner interdependence models, and within-client analyses. We predict that these will be adopted more broadly, along with others that are aimed at assessing more precisely psychopathology and treatment responses, as well as approximating the dyadic and causal relationships among multiple variables involved in the process of change; for example, longitudinal multitrait-multimethod, individual networks of symptom, truth and bias model, polynomial regression

response surface analysis, social relations model, instrumental variables method, lagged multilevel and cross-lagged path models, latent-growth curve and latent change score modeling (Chapters 2, 4, 6, 7, 8, 16, 17, and 18). At the same time, the lure of such methods and the temptation to examine complex relationship with them should not let researchers ignore warnings about their potential flaws (Chapters 13 and 19), reminders about paramount issues of measurement and power (Chapters 2, 4, 5, 7, and 19), as well as the wisdom of being guided by sound theory and empirical evidence (Chapter 2).

A number of sophisticated technologies have also begun to be used in psychotherapy research, and their implementations for both empirical and clinical purposes are sure to increase. Attuned to the way of life of "digital natives" (Chapter 18), some of them allow for the longitudinal, immediate, and valid collection of day-to-day, moment-to-moment data. They can also foster the dissemination of mental health interventions – including to underserved populations and patients with severe mental illness such as psychosis. Among these technological advances are tools (e.g., smart phones, wearables) used for ecological momentary assessment and passive or personal sensing (to monitor physiological reactions, behaviors, cognitions, emotions, symptoms, location, movement, light, sound, etc.) and software for automated analyses of text, speech, and language processing (Chapters 2, 4, 15, 16,18, and 21). Recently developed technologies also involve ecological momentary interventions (e.g., Smith & Juarascio, 2019).

WILL THEY STAY OR WILL THEY GO?

A number of themes, most of them "newcomers," that have recently received considerable attention may, or may not, reveal themselves to be fruitful heuristics for future research. We briefly mention a few here, representing different dimensions of mental health care: therapist, therapist–client interaction, organizational, and professional.

Based on the science of expertise, *deliberate practice* involves the repeated rehearsal of specific tasks that are tailored to an individual's training needs, challenge the trainee to work beyond their comfort zone, foster mental representations of effective task performance, and allow the trainee to receive immediate feedback (Ericsson et al., 1993). Considering the less than convincing evidence to support current methods of training, there has been a lot of enthusiasm (in terms of books, videos, and workshops) for recent efforts to incorporate deliberate practice into psychotherapy training (Rousmaniere, 2016). As reviewed in Chapter 10, various forms of deliberate practice have also been the object of empirical investigations, which have landed promising support. Questions about the dissemination and generalizability of deliberate practice, however, are fair game; for example, how well do deliberate practice efforts operationalize the construct? (see Ericsson & Harwell, 2019). Will deliberate practice exercises be perceived as too anxiety provoking, burdensome, and/or "artificial," by trainees and supervisors? Will it enhance or interfere with therapists' attention and response to the subtle and complex fluctuations of interpersonal dynamics at the heart of psychotherapy?

Cutting-edge studies aimed at capturing aspects of these dynamics have measured various dimensions of *synchronicity* between client and therapist. Such studies are likely to improve our theoretical models, not only about the process of change and its interactive nature, but about patterns (dysfunctional and adaptive) of interpersonal relationships in general. However, the focus of some of these studies (e.g., movement, heart rate) and the methodologies they involve raise questions about whether their findings will lead to actionable and retainable interventions that can improve change. As noted in Chapter 7, it is also not clear whether synchronicity is a cause or an effect of good relational process and whether therapists can learn to increase it.

A few steps removed from the therapist and client relationship are *organizational variables* that are parts of the framework within which therapy is conducted. Recent studies on center and neighborhood effects, for example, have suggested that where clients receive treatment and where they live make a difference (Chapter 6). While they can improve our understanding of the impact, of lack of thereof, of current psychosocial therapies, one can question whether these findings will stimulate more ambitious studies and new forms of engagement outside the "therapy box." Even if future research confirms that these are robust and meaningful contributors of outcome variance, will it be too much of a challenge to investigate bidirectional questions about moderators and mediators; for example, under what circumstances or with what life experience or training can therapists work responsively and effectively with individuals from socially deprived areas? Do the challenges and stressors of poverty, and/or some therapists' failures to appreciate and understand these stressors, explain why some treatment formats are linked to premature termination? Are these realities going to force stakeholders to examine how and by whom psychotherapy is offered and delivered to meet the particular needs of communities and/or underserved populations? Will these findings encourage the same stakeholders to demonstrate that psychotherapy can be part of social efforts to decrease inequities?

Throughout this *Handbook*, repeated calls for *collaboration among stakeholders* have been made to accelerate the advancement of the field. Such collaboration has been advocated between researchers of different orientations to design valid comparison trials (Chapters 12 and 13) and to develop fair practice guidelines based on empirical evidence (Chapter 13); between clinicians, researchers, and administrators to conduct scientifically rigorous and clinically helpful studies (Chapter 6); between mental health professionals, scientists from diverse domains, governments and policy makers, as well as representatives of care systems, public health, schools, technology industry, and business – let alone *consumers of care* – in order to identify, disseminate, assess, and reimburse effective treatments (Chapters 3, 11, 14, 18, 19, and 22); and between researchers to standardize data collection, share data, recruit larger samples, as well as to enhance commitment to different facets of open-science practices (Chapter 2, 3, 18, and 19). Beyond calls for action, there is evidence that partnerships can be created and that lessons can be derived from them to foster new ones (Chapter 6). But while pulling together diverse sources of knowledge and expertise is feasible and has its benefits, it remains to be seen whether the obstacles and challenges involved (prime among them being the lack of time and incentives) will prevent such efforts from being generalizable to various settings and, as importantly, to be sustainable. An obvious question is whether such collaboration can be maintained without external funding? A much bolder question is whether such collaboration should take place with funding? It may well be that fruits of a collaboration between clinician and researchers, for example, will be more retainable if they have been seeded and harvested as an intrinsic part of day-to-day functioning, rather than being the results of externally driven opportunities to get funding without intention, plan, or effort to maintain improvement of a care system.

WHAT SHOULD HAVE MORE IMPACT?

Most of the previous chapters have derived a host of specific clinical, training, and policy-making implications from the research they reviewed. We encourage readers to examine all of them, even those that have emerged from domains outside of their conceptual or methodological preferences. The same way that some variables that are assumed to be unique to one orientation have been shown to predict change in other approaches, recommendations voiced within one particular avenue of knowledge and action may open up new ways of thinking and doing across others. Here, as an end point to this *Handbook*, we want to offer broader implications, that we hope will have an impact on the field of psychotherapy at large. These implications have one thing in common: They are all based on laments about the lack of a fair recognition of the robust scientific foundations of a particular orientation, modality, or type of research. Based on the findings reviewed in this volume, we think that these complaints are justified. As such, we recommend that training, practice, and policies guidelines across the world promote the acquisition and implementation of interventions and knowledge based on the following:

- *The systemic approach*, the "rebellious younger sibling to the more well-established field of individual psychotherapy" (Chapter 16, p. 545), which offers constructs to describe and interventions to address complex dysfunctional patterns of interpersonal interactions, familial, and social.
- *The humanistic orientation*, the third force in psychology, which has fueled the growth of some professional disciplines (e.g., counseling psychology) but has yet to be fully integrated (even conditionally accepted!) within others (e.g., clinical psychology).
- *The psychodynamic approach*, which, despite being the source of concepts and interventions adopted, consciously or not, by many evidence-based treatments (Chapter 12), is still viewed by too many as not being empirically supported – a remanence of the false assumption that theories linked to Freud are not falsifiable, and thus not scientific.
- *Group therapy*, the imperative value of which has been symbolized as a "triple E treatment" (Chapter 17): Effective,

Equivalent to other empirically supported treatments, and Efficient in terms of cost of mental health service.

- *Qualitative analyses*, which, based on rich epistemological perspectives and well-defined methodologies, can increase the breadth and depth of our understanding of the context, experience, and conduct of psychotherapy.
- *Process research*, which can identify factors that are link to outcome, including various ways by which therapists and clients can best collaborate to foster therapeutic growth across and within particular orientations. These are not new ideas, having been voiced in more eloquent ways by numerous scholars since process research began – 80 years ago (see Elliott and Farber, 2010). However, the depth and breadth of empirical knowledge about what facilitates change – and what interferes with or inhibits change – should receive more recognition in policies aimed at enhancing clinical, training, and dissemination efforts.
- *Practice-based evidence* (including patient focused research and practice-research networks), as a source of empirical support for the effectiveness of psychotherapy as practiced in clinical routine, as well as a conduit for the contribution of clinicians in the prioritizing, designing, implementing, and disseminating of research.

It is also unfortunate, in our view, that CBT treatments (across its different "waves") have failed to be systematically and extensively taught and implemented in some regions of the world. Trainees, clinicians, and researchers who ignore or dismiss the empirical support of CBT for a wide range of clinical problems, clinical populations, and treatment modalities are depriving themselves of a rich, valid, and helpful source of knowledge toward understanding and reducing human suffering.

We also point out that our recommendations should not be misconstrued as an encouragement to contain the advancement of research and practice within distinct frameworks or paradigms. As previously mentioned, integrative approaches (derived from a top-down and bottom-up approaches) deserve more recognition and research attention.

The approaches and methods above should be relied on more fully and consistently in our effort to improve the scientific basis of psychotherapy, as well as its practice and training. Needless to say, this should not come at the expense of paying the attention that is due to other methodological and theoretical contributions, some of them having already been recognized in training, practice, and policies guidelines. For example, we think that it is important for the field to conduct more high-quality RCTs not only to provide additional support to the value and impact of therapy, but in order to sharpen and increase the range of options from which we can assign the most appropriate therapies to particular patients (Chapter 5).

Ultimately, we believe that fruitful progress in our scientific and clinical endeavors to develop the most effective and personally responsive psychosocial therapies will be enhanced by validating and learning from multiple theoretical and methodological approaches, and by fostering collaboration between many stakeholders in the field of mental health.

ABBREVIATIONS

CBT	cognitive behavioral therapy
CFS	clinical feedback system
RCT	randomized clinical trial
ROM	routine outcome monitoring

REFERENCES

Barlow, D. H. (2010). Negative effects from psychological treatments: A perspective. *American Psychologist, 65*(1), 13–20. https://doi.org/10.1037/a0015643

Beutler, L. E., & Simons, A. D. (2010). Sol L. Garfield: A pioneer in bringing science to clinical psychology. In L. G. Castonguay, J. C. Muran, L., Angus, J. H. Hayes, N. Ladany & T. Anderson. (Eds.), *Bringing psychotherapy research to life: Understanding change through the work of leading clinical researchers* (pp. 309–317). Washington, DC: American Psychological Association Press.

Borkovec, T. D. (1994). Between-group therapy outcome design: Design and methodology. In L. S. Onken & J. D. Blaine (Eds.), *NIDA Research Monograph No. 137* (pp. 249–289). Rockville, MD: National Institute on Drug Abuse.

Boswell, J. F., Newman, M. G., & McGinn, L. K (2019). Outcome research on psychotherapy integration. In J. C. Norcross & M. R. Goldfried (Eds.), *Handbook of psychotherapy integration* (3rd ed., pp. 405–431). New York: Oxford University Press.

Castonguay, L. G. (2011). Psychotherapy, psychopathology, research and practice: Pathways of connections and integration. *Psychotherapy Research, 21*, 125–140. https://doi.org/10.1080/10503307.2011.563250

Constantino, M. J., Boswell, J. F., Bernecker, S. L., & Castonguay, L. G. (2013). Context-responsive integration as a framework for unified psychotherapy and clinical science: Conceptual and empirical considerations. *Journal of Unified Psychotherapy and Clinical Science, 2*, 1–20.

Elliott, R. (1983). Fitting process research to the practicing psychotherapist. *Psychotherapy: Theory, Research & Practice, 20*(1), 47–55. https://doi.org/10.1037/h0088478

Elliott, R., & Farber, B.A. (2010). Carl Rogers: Idealistic pragmatist and psychotherapy research pioneer. In L. G. Castonguay, J. C. Muran, L. Angus, J. A. Hayes, N. Ladany, & T. Anderson (Eds.), *Bringing psychotherapy research to life: Understanding change through the work of leading clinical researchers* (pp. 17–27). Washington, DC: American Psychological Association Press.

Ericsson, K.A., & Harwell, K.W. (2019) Deliberate practice and proposed limits on the effects of practice on the acquisition of expert performance: Why the original definition matters and recommendations for future research. *Frontiers in Psychology, 10*, 2396. https://doi.org/10.3389/fpsyg.2019.02396

Ericsson, K. A., Krampe, R. T., & Tesch-Römer, C. (1993). The role of deliberate practice in the acquisition of expert performance. *Psychological Review, 100*, 363. https://doi.org/10.1037/0033-295X.100.3.363

Goldfried, M. R. (1980). Toward the delineation of therapeutic change principles. *American Psychologist, 35*, 991–999. http://dx.doi.org/10.1037/0003-066X.35.11.991

Greenberg, L. S., & Pinsof. W. M. (Eds.) (1986). *The psychotherapeuric process: A research handbook*. New York: Guilford.

Hansen, B. P., Lambert, M. J., & Vlass, E. N. (2015). Sudden gains and losses in the clients of a "supershrink": 10 case studies. *Pragmatic Case Studies in Psychotherapy, 11*(3), Article 1, 154–201. http://pcsp.libraries.rutgers.edu

Lambert, M. J., Gurman, A. S., & Richards, S. (2010). Allen Bergin: Consummate scholar and charter member of the Society for Psychotherapy Research. In L. G. Castonguay, J. C. Muran, L. Angus, J. A. Hayes, N. Ladany, & T. Anderson (Eds.), *Bringing psychotherapy research to life: Understanding change through the work of leading clinical researchers* (pp. 101–111). Washington, DC: American Psychological Association Press.

Lilienfeld, S. O. (2007). Psychological treatments that cause harm. *Perspectives on Psychological Science, 2*, 53–70. https://doi.org/10.1111/j.1745-6916.2007.00029.x

Messina, I., Gelo, O., Sambin, M., Bianco, F., Mosconi, A., Fenelli, A., Curto, M., Gullo, S., & Orlinsky, D. (2018). Trainees' self-evaluation of their development as psychotherapists: An Italian contribution to an international collaborative study on psychotherapy training. *Clinical Psychology and Psychotherapy*, 25, 338–347. https://doi.org/10.1002/cpp.2165

Moras, K., Anderson, T., & Piper, W. E. (2010). Hans Strupp: A founder's contributions to a scientific basis for psychotherapy. In L. G. Castonguay, J. C. Muran, L. Angus, J. A. Hayes, N. Ladany, & T. Anderson (Eds.), *Bringing psychotherapy research to life: Understanding change through the work of leading clinical researchers* (pp. 51–61). Washington, DC: American Psychological Association Press.

Muran, J. C., Safran, J. D., Eubanks, C. F., & Gorman, B. S. (2018). The effect of an alliance-focused training on cognitive-behavioral therapy for personality disorders. *Journal of Consulting & Clinical Psychology*, 86, 384–397. https://doi.org/10.1037/ccp0000284

Norcross, J. C., & Alexander, E. F. (2019). A primer on psychotherapy integration. In J. C. Norcross & M. R. Goldfried (Eds.), *Handbook of psychotherapy integration* (3rd ed., pp. 3–27). New York: Oxford University Press.

Norcross J. C. & Goldfried, M. R. (Eds) *Handbook of psychotherapy integration* (3rd ed.). New York: Oxford University Press.

Ogles, B. M., & Hayes, J. A. (2010). Michael J. Lambert: Building confidence in psychotherapy. In L. G. Castonguay, J. C. Muran, L. Angus, J. A. Hayes, N. Ladany, & T. Anderson (Eds.), *Bringing psychotherapy research to life: Understanding change through the work of leading clinical researchers* (pp. 141–151). Washington, DC: American Psychological Association Press.

Orlinsky, D. E., & Rønnestad, M. H. (2005). *How psychotherapists develop: A study of therapeutic work and professional growth*. Washington, DC: American Psychological Association.

Rousmaniere, T. G. (2016). *Deliberate practice for psychotherapists: A guide to improving clinical effectiveness*. Routledge Press (Taylor & Francis).

Safran, J. D., & Muran, J. C. (2000). *Negotiating the therapeutic alliance: A relational treatment guide*. Guilford Press.

Smith, K. E., & Juarascio, A. (2019). From ecological momentary assessment (EMA) to ecological momentary intervention (EMI): Past and future directions for ambulatory assessment and interventions in eating disorders. *Current Psychiatry Reports*, 21, 53. https://doi.org/10.1007/s11920-019-1046-8

Youn, S., Xiao, H., McAleavey, A. A., Scofield, B. E., Pedersen, T. R., Castonguay, L. G., Hayes, J. A., & Locke, B. D. (2019). Assessing and investigating clinicians' research interests: Lessons on expanding practices and data collection in a large practice research network. *Psychotherapy*, 56(1), 67–82. https://doi.org/10.1037/pst0000192

Appendix

TABLE OF CONTENTS FOR ALL CHAPTERS AND EDITIONS OVER THE LAST 50 YEARS

As a special feature of this anniversary issue, we include an appendix comprising both a recognition of and tribute to each contributing author to the seven editions of the *Handbook*. The table sets out a schematic summary of chapter titles, authors, as well as sections from all editions.

We hope this table will provide readers, particularly those wishing to gain a sense of the history of the *Handbook*, with an additional overview of the common themes and traditions as well as changes in key areas in the field of psychotherapy research over the last 50 years.

Michael Barkham, Wolfgang Lutz, & Louis G Castonguay

Editions

1e	2e	3e	4e	5e	6e	7e
Theory, methodology, and experimentation	**Basic methodology and orientation**	**Historical, methodological, and conceptual foundations**	**Historical, methodological, ethical, and conceptual foundations**	**Historical, methodological, ethical, and conceptual foundations**	**Historical, methodological, and conceptual foundations**	**History and methods**
Some historical and conceptual perspectives on psychotherapy and behavior change (*Urban & Ford*)	Psychotherapy research and practice: An overview (*Strupp*)	Introduction and historical overview (*Garfield & Bergin*)	Introduction and historical overview (*Garfield & Bergin*)	Introduction and historical overview (*Lambert, Bergin, & Garfield*)	Introduction and historical overview (*Lambert*)	Traditions and new beginnings: Historical and current perspectives on research in psychotherapy and behavior change (*Lutz, Castonguay, Lambert, & Barkham*)
Experimental designs in psychotherapy research (*Kiesler*)	Experimental designs in psychotherapy research (*Gottman & Markman*)	Research designs and methodology (*Kazdin*)	Methodology, design, and evaluation in psychotherapy research (*Kazdin*)	Methodology, design, and evaluation in psychotherapy research (*Kendall, Holmbeck, & Verduin*)	Methodology, design, and evaluation in psychotherapy research (*Comer & Kendall*)	Methodological foundations and innovations in quantitative psychotherapy research (*Baldwin & Goldberg*)
The application of psychophysiological methods to the study of psychotherapy and behavior modification (*Lang*)	Psychobiological foundations of psychotherapy and behavior change (*Schwartz*)	Social psychological approaches to psychotherapy and behavior change (*Brehm & Smith*)	Assessing psychotherapy outcomes and processes (*Lambert & Hill*)	Theoretical challenges to therapy practice and research: The constraint of naturalism (*Slife*)	Qualitative research: Methods and contributions (*McLeod*)	The conceptualization, design, and evaluation of qualitative methods in research on psychotherapy (*Levitt, McLeod, & Stiles*)
Laboratory interview research as an analogue to treatment (*Heller*)	Social psychological approach to psychotherapy research (*Strong*)	Developmental perspectives on psychotherapy and behavior change (*Achenbach*)	The NIMH treatment of depression collaborative research program: Where we began and where we are (*Elkin*)	Methodological issues in studying psychotherapy processes and outcomes (*Hill & Lambert*)	Practice-oriented research: Approaches and applications (*Castonguay, Barkham, Lutz, & McAleavey*)	—
Social psychological approaches to psychotherapy research (*Goldstein & Simonson*)	—	—	—	—	Measuring change in psychotherapy research (*Ogles*)	—
Clinical innovation in research and practice (*Lazarus & Davison*)	—	—	—	—		

Note: †H. M. Levitt; ††E. E. Levitt; * D. A. Shapiro; ** A. K. Shapiro

Analysis of client-centered, psychoanalytic, eclectic, and related therapies	Evaluation of process and outcome in psychotherapy and behavior change	Evaluation of process and outcome in psychotherapy and behavior change	Evaluating the ingredients of therapeutic efficacy	Evaluating the ingredients of therapeutic efficacy	Evaluating the ingredients of therapeutic efficacy	Measuring and evidencing change in efficacy and practice-based research
The evaluation of therapeutic outcomes (*Bergin*)	The evaluation of therapeutic outcomes (*Bergin & Lambert*)	The effectiveness of psychotherapy (*Lambert, Shapiro*, & Bergin*)	The effectiveness of psychotherapy (*Lambert & Bergin*)	The efficacy and effectiveness of psychotherapy (*Lambert & Ogles*)	The efficacy and effectiveness of psychotherapy (*Lambert*)	Measuring, predicting, and tracking change in psychotherapy (*Lutz, de Jong, Rubel, & Delgadillo*)
Research on client variables in psychotherapy (*Garfield*)	Research on client variables in psychotherapy (*Garfield*)	Research on client variables in psychotherapy (*Garfield*)	Research on client variables in psychotherapy (*Garfield*)	The influence of client variables on psychotherapy (*Clarkin & Levy*)	The client in psychotherapy (*Bohart & Wade*)	The efficacy and effectiveness of psychological therapies (*Barkham & Lambert*)
Research on certain therapist interpersonal skills in relation to process and outcome (*Truax & Mitchell*)	Research on therapist variables in relation to process and outcome (*Parloff, Waskow, & Wolfe*)	Research on therapist variables in psychotherapy (*Beutler, Crago, & Arizmendi*)	Therapist variables (*Beutler, Machado, & Neufeldt*)	Therapist variables (*Beutler, Malik, Alimohamed, Harwood, Talebi, Noble, & Wong*)	Therapist effects: Findings and methods (*Baldwin & Imel*)	Practice-based evidence –findings from routine clinical settings (*Castonguay, Barkham, Youn, & Page*)
						Therapeutic ingredients
Content analysis studies of psychotherapy: 1954 through 1968 (*Marsden*)	The relation of process to outcome in psychotherapy (*Orlinsky & Howard*)	Process and outcome in psychotherapy (*Orlinsky & Howard*)	Process and outcome in psychotherapy – Noch einmal (*Orlinsky, Grawe, & Parks*)	Fifty years of psychotherapy process-outcome research: Continuity and change (*Orlinsky, Rønnestad, & Willutzki*)	Psychotherapy process-outcome research (*Crits-Christoph, Connolly Gibbons, & Mukherjee*)	Patient, therapist, and relational factors (*Constantino, Boswell, & Coyne*)
Quantitative research on psychoanalytic therapy (*Luborsky & Spence*)	Quantitative research on psychoanalytic therapy (*Luborsky & Spence*)	–	–	–	–	Psychotherapy process – outcome research: Advances in understanding causal connections (*Crits-Christoph & Connolly Gibbons*)
Placebo effects in medicine, psychotherapy, and psychoanalysis (*Shapiro***)	Placebo effects in medical and psychological therapies (*Shapiro** & Morris*)					Therapist effects: History, methods, magnitude, and characteristics of effective therapists (*Wampold & Owen*)
Research on psychotherapy with children (*Levitt†**)	Research on psychotherapy with children (*Barrett, Hampe, & Miller*)					Training and supervision in psychotherapy: What we know and where we need to go (*Knox & Hill*)
Psychotherapy and ataraxic drugs (*May*)	Psychotherapy and drug therapy: Comparisons and combinations (*Hollon & Beck*)					Qualitative research: contributions to psychotherapy practice, theory and policy (*McLeod, Stiles, & Levitt†*)

Note: †H. M. Levitt; ††E. E. Levitt; * D. A. Shapiro; ** A. K. Shapiro

Editions

1e	2e	3e	4e	5e	6e	7e
Analysis of behavioral therapies	**Analyses of developments in the behavior therapies**	**Behavioral & cognitive therapies**	**Major approaches**	**Major approaches**	**Major approaches**	**Therapeutic approaches and formats**
Counterconditioning and related methods (*Eysenck & Beech*)	Behavioral psychotherapy of adult neurosis (*Marks*)	Behavior therapy with adults (*Emmelkamp*)	Behavior therapy with adults (*Emmelkamp*)	Behavior therapy with adults (*Emmelkamp*)	Behavior therapy with adults (*Emmelkamp*)	Research on dynamic therapies (*Barber, Muran, McCarthy, Keefe, & Zilcha-Mano*)
The operant approach in behavior therapy (*Krasner*)	The application of operant techniques in treatment, rehabilitation and education (*Kazdin*)	Research on cognitive therapies (*Hollon & Beck*)	Cognitive and cognitive behavioral therapies (*Hollon & Beck*)	Cognitive and cognitive behavioral therapies (*Hollon & Beck*)	Cognitive and cognitive behavioral therapies (*Hollon & Beck*)	Research on humanistic-experiential psychotherapies: Updated review (*Elliott, Watson, Timulak, & Sharbanee*)
Psychotherapy based on modeling principles (*Bandura*)	Behavior therapy with children (*Ross*)	Behavioral medicine and health psychology (*Pomerleau & Rodin*)	Psychodynamic approaches (*Henry, Strupp, Schacht, & Gaston*)	Research on experiential psychotherapies (*Elliott, Greenberg, & Lietaer*)	Research on dynamic therapies (*Barber, Muran, McCarthy, & Keefe*)	Cognitive, behavioral, and cognitive behavioral therapy (First and second waves) (*Newman, Agras, Haaga, & Jarrett*)
The nature of learning in traditional and behavioral psychotherapy (*Murray & Jacobson*)	Psychological modeling: Theory and practice (*Rosenthal & Bandura*)	—	Research on experiential psychotherapies (*Greenberg, Elliott, & Lietaer*)	—	Research on humanistic-experiential psychotherapies (*Elliott, Greenberg, Watson, Timulak, & Freire*)	Mindfulness and acceptance-based treatments (*Forman, Arch, Bricker, Gaudiano, Juarascio, Rizvi, Segal, & Vowles*)
Therapeutic approaches to the home, family, school, group, organization, and community	**Learning, cognitive, and self-control processes in psychotherapy and behavior change**	**Child and family therapies**	**Research on applications in special groups and settings**	**Research on applications in special groups and settings**	**Research on applications in special groups and settings**	Systemic and conjoint couple and family therapies: Recent advances and future promise (*Friedlander, Heatherington, & Diamond*)
Behavioral intervention procedures in the classroom and in the home (*Patterson*)	Cognition and learning in traditional and behavioral psychotherapy (*Murray & Jacobson*)	Behavior therapy with children and adolescents (*Ollendick*)	Psychotherapy for children and adolescents (*Kazdin*)	Psychotherapy for children and adolescents (*Kazdin*)	Psychotherapy for children and adolescents (*Weisz, Ng, Rutt, Lau, & Masland*)	Efficacy of small group treatments: Foundation for evidence-based practice (*Burlingame & Strauss*)
Evaluative research and community mental health (*Roen*)	Cognitive and self-control therapies (*Mahoney & Arnkoff*)	Research on marital and family therapies (*Gurman, Kniskern, & Pinsof*)	The process and outcome of marital and family therapy: Research review and evaluation (*Alexander, Holtzworth-Munroe, & Jameson*)	Levels of evidence for the models and mechanisms of therapeutic change in family and couple therapy (*Sexton, Alexander, & Mease*)	The effectiveness of couple and family-based clinical interventions (*Sexton, Datchi, Evans, LaFollette, & Wright*)	Psychotherapy for children and adolescents: From efficacy to effectiveness, scaling, and personalizing (*Ng, Schleider, Horn, & Weisz*)

Note: †H. M. Levitt; ††E. E. Levitt; * D. A. Shapiro; ** A. K. Shapiro

	Editions						
	1e	**2e**	**3e**	**4e**	**5e**	**6e**	**7e**
	Empirical research in group psychotherapy (*Bednar & Lawlis*)	**Appraisals of group and innovative approaches in psychotherapy and behavior change**	**Special topics**	Experiential group research (*Bednar & Kaul*)	Small-group treatment: Evidence for effectiveness and mechanisms of change (*Burlingame, MacKenzie & Strauss*)	Change mechanisms and effectiveness of small group treatments (*Burlingame, Strauss, & Joyce*)	**Increasing precision and scale in the psychological therapies**
	The effects of human relations training (*Gibb*)	Research on brief and crisis-oriented psychotherapies (*Butcher & Koss*)	Research on brief psychotherapy (*Koss & Butcher*)	Research on brief psychotherapy (*Koss & Shiang*)	Health psychology (*Creer, Holroyd, Glasgow, & Smith*)	Behavioral medicine and clinical health psychology (*Smith & Williams*)	Personalized treatment approaches (*Cohen, Delgadillo, & DeRubeis*)
	Research on educational and vocational counseling (*Myers*)	Experiential group research: Current perspectives (*Bednar & Kaul*)	Research on group and related therapies (*Kaul & Bednar*)	Behavioral medicine and health psychology (*Blanchard*)	Combining psychotherapy and psychopharmacology for treatment of mental disorders (*Thase & Jindal*)	Combining medication and psychotherapy in the treatment of major mental disorders (*Forand, DeRubeis, & Amsterdam*)	Combining psychotherapy and medications: It's all about the squids and sea bass (at least for nonpsychotic patients) (*Hollon, Andrews, Keller, Singla, Maslej, & Mulsant*)
	—	Research on marital and family therapy: Progress, perspective, and prospect (*Gurman & Kniskern*)	Research on educational and vocational counseling (*Myers*)	Medication and psychotherapy (*Klerman, Weissman, Markowitz, Glick, Wilner, Mason, & Shear*)	Research on psychotherapy with culturally diverse populations (*Zane, Hall, Sue, Young, & Nunez*)	Training and supervision in psychotherapy (*Hill & Knox*)	Internet approaches to psychotherapy: Empirical findings and future directions (*Andersson & Berger*)
	—	Research on psychotherapy and behavior change with the disadvantaged (*Lorion*)	Research on psychotherapy with the disadvantaged (*Lorion & Felner*)	Research on psychotherapy with culturally diverse populations (*Sue, Zane, & Young*)	Overview, trends, and future issues (*Lambert, Garfield, & Bergin*)	—	Extending the scalability and reach of psychosocial interventions (*Kazdin*)
	—	—	Drugs and psychotherapy (*Klerman*)	—	—	—	—
	Evaluating the training of therapists	**Evaluating the training of therapists**	**Evaluating the training of therapists**	**Summation**	—	—	**Toward the future**
	Research on the teaching and learning of psychotherapeutic skills (*Matarazzo*)	Research on the teaching and learning of psychotherapeutic skills (*Matarazzo*)	Research on the teaching and learning of psychotherapeutic skills (*Matarazzo & Patterson*)	Overview, trends, and future issues (*Bergin & Garfield*)	—	—	Epilogue: Prevalent themes, predictions, and recommendations (*Castonguay, Eubanks, Iwakabe, Krause, Page, Zilcha-Mano, Lutz, & Barkham*)

Note: †H. M. Levitt; ††E. E. Levitt; * D. A. Shapiro; ** A. K. Shapiro

AUTHOR INDEX

SUBJECT INDEX

Page numbers in *italics* indicate tables and figures.

pharmacotherapy effectiveness comparison, 142–143, 711–713, 714–720, *715–719*
psychodynamic therapy for, 147–148, 150
psychoeducation for, 147
psychosocial treatment overview, 713–714
treatment effects, 139–141, *140*, 147–150, *149*
Mood stabilizers, 729
MOOI (Massive Open Online Interventions), 778
Motivation
as outcome factor, 238–239
patterns of, 403
of therapist, *229*, 238–239, *317*, 318
Motivational enhancement therapy (MET), 281, 485
Motivational interviewing (MI). *See also* Humanistic-experiential psychotherapies
about, 422, *423*
empirical findings, 281, 484, 485–486, 489, 635
humanistic-experiential psychotherapy comparison, 449
internet-delivered, 748
MST. *See* Multisystemic therapy
MTMM (multi-trait-multi-method), 93
Multicultural competence (MCC), of therapist, 167–168, *246*, 248–249, 615
Multicultural orientation (MCO), 249
Multidimensional family therapy (MDFT), 545, *548*, *550*, *552*, 556
Multidimensional symptom scales, 92
Multidimensional Treatment Foster Care, 634
Multilevel and mixed models, 100–101, 105, 110
Multilevel models (MLMs)
EMA studies and, 102
historical context, 298–299
power issues and, 304
quantitative analysis and, 30–31
of therapeutic effects, 266–267, 287, 298–299, 302–307, *303*
Multilevel vector-autoregressive model (ML-VAR), 102
Multimodal therapy approach, 677
Multiple baseline designs, 36
Multiple clinics, effectiveness of, 198–200
Multiple imputation (MI) model, 98
Multiple sclerosis, 746
Multisystemic therapy (MST)
about: introduction, 545
change processes and, 564
empirical findings, *548*, *550*, 551, *553*, 556, 634–635
therapeutic alliance effects and, 562
Multi-trait-multi-method (MTMM), 93
Multivariate Imputation by Chained Equations (MICE), 98
Multivariate models, 36
Muthen-Roy model, 101

N

Naltrexone, 275, 281
Narrative analysis, 58, *59*, 61–62
Narrative case studies, 66
Narrative identity, 366
Narrative processes and assimilations, 52, 446–448, 449–450
Narrative therapy, 561
Narrative way of knowing, 52
National Comorbidity Study, 765
National Comorbidity Survey-Replication study, 765–766
National Data Archive (NDA), 653
National Institute for Health and Care Excellence, 678
National Institute of Health, 68, 91
National Institute of Mental Health (NIMH)
process-based approach to mental disorders, 646–647
Research Domain Criteria (RDoC), 91
Treatment of Depression Collaborative Research Program (TDCRP), 8–9, 25, 197, 304–305, 714
Native American clients, 652, 765
Naturalistic datasets, 35

Natural selection, 707
Nearest-neighbor approach, 116
Nearest neighbors (NN), 57–58
Nefazadone, 713
Negative affects, 709
Negative directional bias, 110
Negative outcomes, 367, 797
Neighborhood effects, 211
Nested data, 98, 100
Network approach to psychopathology, 647–648
Network meta-analysis (NMA), 137
Network models, 102–103
Neural reprogramming, 725
Neurofeedback, 104
Neuroscience, of depression, 475
Next-turn proof procedure, 63
NICE guidelines
for depression, 199
for general anxiety disorders, 724
on schizophrenia treatment, 728
on supportive therapy for psychosis, 437
NIHM. *See* National Institute of Mental Health
Nocebo effect, 141
Nocturnal enuresis, 635–636
Nodes, 102
Nomothetic personalization, 683–684
Nonattendance, 200
Nondirective relationship control condition, 422, *423*, 449, 450
Noninferiority trials, 24–25
Nonlinear interaction, 106
Nonlinear processes, 109–110
Nonprofessional workforce expansion, 772, *772*, 773–776
Nonrandomized trials, 23
Nonstochastic methods, 97
Nonsymptomatic outcomes, 797–798
Norepinephrine, 712
No-show appointments, 200
Nosology, 91
Not on track (NOT), 106, 112
No-treatment control design, 23, 141–142
Novice therapists, defined, 328. *See also* Training, of novice therapists

O

Obesity, 525–527, *632*, 635, *670*
Object relations, 398, 403
Observational process studies, 27–29
Observer-rated measures, 22
Obsessive-compulsive disorder (OCD)
in adolescents, *548–549*
CBT for, 476–477, 478, 556–557, 633, 726, 743–744
cognitive therapy for, 726
empirical findings, 150–152, 154, *155*
epidemiology, 720, 726
exposure therapies for, 510, 556–557, 594, 633, 726
family therapy for, *548–550*, *552*, 556–557, 560, 564
group treatments for, *589*, 594, *612*
internet-delivered treatments for, 743–744
mindfulness and acceptance-based treatments for, 508, 510
pharmacotherapy effectiveness comparison, 478, 726
youth evidence-based psychotherapies for, *630*, 633, *666*
One-Session Treatment for Specific Phobia (OST), 645
Online narratives and videos, 370
Online therapy. *See* Internet-delivered treatments
Ontology, defined, 53
on track (OT; responding to treatment as expected), 106, 112
Open science, 39, 43
Open Science Framework (OSF), 653
Opioid use disorder, 488, 748
Oppositional perturbation, 718
OQ-45 (Change in Outcome Questionnaire-45), *164*

OQ Analyst System, 112–114
Ordinal interaction, 106
Organizational obstacles, 114
Organization training, 634
Ostracism, 711
Outcome expectations, of therapist, 234, 245
Outcome measures. *See* Change measurement and modeling
Outcome-oriented case studies, 66
Outcome Questionnaire (OQ-45), 93
Outcome research, 4, 8–9. *See also* Cost-effectiveness,-benefit, and-utility studies; Efficacy and effectiveness; Meta-analysis; Patient factors; Randomized controlled trials; Relational process factors; Therapist factors
Overly nurturant interpersonal style, 208
Oxytocin saliva samples, 104

P

Pain management, 527–528, *527*, *601*, 602–603, 707, *708*, 747, *747*
Panic disorder (PD). *See also* Anxiety disorders
CBT for, 476, 477, 478, 743, 750
comorbid conditions, 233
empirical findings, 150–152, 153–154, *155*, 273
epidemiology, 720
as evolved adaptation, 721
exposure therapy for, 477
group therapy for, *589*, 593–594, *612*
internet-delivered treatments for, 743, 744
mindfulness and acceptance-based treatments for, 510
pharmacotherapy effectiveness comparison, 478, 721–722, *722*
Panic-focused psychodynamic psychotherapy (PFPP), 153–154, 273, 282
Paradigm approach, 52–55
Parent behavioral training, 634, 635
Parent–child interaction therapy + emotion development module (PCIT-ED), *549*, 557, 558
Parent contingency management (CM), 557
Parent-enhanced CBT, *549*
Parent-focused therapy, 634
Parenting practices, 637–638
Parkinson's disease, 746–747
Partial hospitalization, *549*
Pathological gambling, 748, 749
Patient factors, 225–245
about: abstract and introduction, 225–226
about: overview, 227, *228–230*
about: summary and future directions, 252–253
beliefs and preferences, *228–229*, 230–231, 234–236, 275
change process and, 404
contributions to therapy process, *230*, 242–245
demographics and, 227–232, *228*
diagnostic comorbidity, *228*, 233–234
interpersonal, *230*, 241–242
intrapsychic, *229*, 236–241
mental health, *228–229*, 232–234
as predictor of change, 105, *105*
preferences, *229*, 230–231, 235–236
severity of problem, *228*, 232–233
in therapeutic alliance, 398
treatment credibility, *229*, 235
treatment expectations, *228*, 234–235
Patient Health Questionnaire-9 (PHQ-9), 158, 172
Patient Reported Outcome Measurement Information System (PROMIS®), 89, 99
Patient response profiles framework, 681
Patient to therapist ratio (PTR), 318
Pausing Inventory Categorization System (PICS), 370
PBE. *See* Practice-based evidence
PCIT-ED (parent–child interaction therapy + emotion development module), *549*, 557, 558
PD. *See* Panic disorder
PDT. *See* Psychodynamic therapy
PE. *See* Psychoeducation
Perfectionism, as outcome factor, *229*, 238

PDT process research on, 397–402
power negotiations, 354
practice-based evidence on, 200–203, 207–208, 209
process-outcome effect of, 269–272, 288
psychodynamic therapy and, 397–402, 406–407
qualitative research on, 353–355
relationship factors overlapping with, 271
ruptures in, 271, 399–402
similarities and differences accounts, 146–147, *146*
split or unbalanced, 562
in systemic therapy, 561–563
treatment package efficacy evaluation, 30–31
youth psychotherapy change process and, 638
Therapist effects, 297–326
about: abstract and introduction, 297–298
about: future directions, 320–321, 795–797
about: historical context, 298–300
on attendance, 196
in clinical trials, 304–307, *305*
continuing education and, 320, 321
cultural diversity and cultural competence and, 162, 195, 318–319, 320
defined, 300–302, *301*
on dropout, 196
efficacy and, 146–147, *146*, 161–163, 176
estimating methods, 302–304, *303*
exemplary study, in naturalistic setting, 307–308, *308*
with internet-delivered treatment, 750–751
interpretation of, in naturalistic settings, 308–309, *309*
magnitude of, 304–309
meta-analysis, 305–306, *306*, 308
in naturalistic settings, 307–309, 320
in particular client populations, 194–195
practice-based evidence on, 194–196
process-outcome research and, 337
in randomized controlled studies, 305–307, *306*, 320
as ratio of variances, 301–302
therapist level predictors, 309–320, *311. See also* Therapist level predictors
therapist uniformity assumption, 299–300
training and, 320, 321
treatment package efficacy evaluation, 25–26
Therapist factors, 245–250
about: abstract and introduction, 225–226, 245, *246*, 311
about: future directions, 253
about: summary, 252
countertransference, *246*, 248
emotional expression, *246*, 248
flexibility, *246*, 249, 250
immediacy, 247–248
interpersonal impacts and behaviors, 245–247, *246*
multicultural competence, 167–168, *246*, 248–249, 615
multicultural orientation, *246*, 249
outcome expectations, 245, *246*
as predictor of change, 105, *105*
responsivity, *246*, 249–250
self-disclosure, 247–248
in therapeutic alliance, 398–399
therapist competence, 277, 282–284
Therapist level predictors
attitudes toward practice, 313–316, *314–316*, 320
cultural competence as, 318–319, 320
disaggregation of patient and therapist contributions, 310–311, 316–318, *317*
interpretation of evidence, 319–320
multilevel models for, 309–311
personality of therapist, 313–316, *314–316*
practice features, 313–316, *314–316*
professional practice characteristics, 313, *313*, 357
relative effectiveness within therapists, 318–319, *318*
study review, 311–319
therapist demographics and experience, 312–313, *312*

therapist skill measurement outside of therapy, 319, *321*
Therapists. *See also* Therapeutic alliance; Therapist effects; Therapist factors; Therapist level predictors
accuracy of interpretations, 284
adherence research on, 277
personal development of, 357–358
professional development of, 313, *313*, 357–358. *See also* Training, of novice therapists
Therapist self-disclosure (TSD), 247–248
Therapy Personalization Form (TPF), 677
Therapy-related interpersonal behavior (TRIB), 319–320
Theta score, 99
"Third wave" behavioral treatments, 508. *See also* Mindfulness and acceptance-based treatments
Three Dimensions of Personalization (3DP), *674*, 675–676, 677
Time-limited dynamic psychotherapy (TLDP), 244
Time series panel analysis (TSPA), 102
Tinnitus, 747, *747*, 750
Tobacco use. *See* Smoking cessation
Toilet training (enhanced), 636
"The Toolbox," 683
Top-down processes, 475
Total effect, 29
Traditional behavioral couple therapy (TBCT), 542, *544*
Training, of novice therapists, 327–349
about: abstract and introduction, 327–329
about: historical context, 329–331
about: summary and future directions, 339–340, 797
behavioral therapy training, 335–336, 345
bibliotraining, 336
CBT training, 335–336
cultural competence training, 336
definitions, 328
deliberate practice and, 336–337
as delivery limitation, 768, 769–770
didactic-experiential training, 336
dream work, 336
empathy/facilitative conditions/alliance training, 334
empirical findings, 211–212, 356, 357
experiential psychotherapy training, 335
feedback, 336
helping skills training, 329–334, 335, 344–345
humanistic-experiential psychotherapy training, 336, 451
other theoretically-specific training, 336
psychodynamic/interpersonal psychotherapy training, 335, 336
self-awareness training, 334–335
self-training, 336
sequence of training, 339
supervision, 313, *313*, 327–328, 336–337, 340–344, 345
theoretical orientation training, 356
as therapist effect, 313, *313*
time (experience) effects, 337–338
trainer effects, 339
Transdiagnostic treatments, 642–643
Transferability, 76
Transference, 282, 360, 403
Transference-focused therapy (TFP), 156, 282, 284, 491, 518
Transformational outcome narratives, 366
Transient side-effects, 367
Transparent Reporting of a multivariable prediction model for Individual Prognosis or Diagnosis (TRIPOD) system, 685
Transtreatments, 764
Trauma-and stressor-related disorders. *See also* Posttraumatic stress disorder
CBT for, 154, 633
client-lived experience of diagnosis, 355
cost-effectiveness of psychotherapy, 157

empirical findings, 150–152, 154, *155*, 356–357
humanistic-experiential psychotherapies for, *430*, 444, 449
practice-based evidence on, 206
psychodynamic therapy for, 391–394, *392–393*
youth evidence-based psychotherapies for, *630*, 633, *666*
Trauma-focused CBT, 154, 633
Treatment-as-usual control condition, 24, 141–142
Treatment credibility, 235
Treatment diffusion, 27
Treatment dosage (dose-effect), 95–96, 163–165, *164*, 177
Treatment expectations, 234–235
Treatment for Adolescents Depression Study (TADS), 650
Treatment Foster Care Oregon (TFCO), 634–635
Treatment gap, 227, 765–766, 771–773, 779, 781–783
Treatment of Depression Collaborative Research Program (TDCRP), 8–9, 25, 197, 304–305, 714
Treatment preferences, 235–236
Treatment-resistant depression, 174
Tricyclic antidepressants (TCAs), 711, 712, 718
Trim-and-fill analyses, 38
Trustworthiness, 70
Truth and bias model, 110
12-step facilitation, 281, 485, 487, 491
Two-chair dialogue task, 444
Type I and II error rates, 32

U
Unfinished business, 444
Unidimensional/disorder-specific scales, 92
Unified Protocol for Transdiagnostic Treatment of Emotional Disorders in Children (UP-C) and Adolescents (UP-A), 643
Unit creation, 61–62
Unsupervised learning approaches, 689
Urine alarm therapy, 635
US Clinical Practice Guidelines (USCPG), 522–523, 524–525
US National Institute of Health, 67, 68

V
Validity, 21
Vanderbilt I study, 364–365
Vanderbilt Psychotherapy Process Scale (VPPS), 397
Variability in process data, 28
Variable selection, 106
Virtual reality treatments, 744, 751
Visual analog scales, 107
Voices, assimilated, 360–361
VPPS (Vanderbilt Psychotherapy Process Scale), 397

W
WAI-SR, 100
Wait-list control design, 141–142
Ward method, 67
Ways of knowing, 52
Ways of Responding (WOR), 279
Wearable technology, 104, 648–649
Web-based smoking cessation treatments, 778
Web-delivered treatments. *See* Internet-delivered treatments
WebQuit.org, 523
Websites, 523. *See also* Internet-delivered treatments
Weight loss, 525
Whole-service initiatives, 642
WHO Mental Health Survey Consortium (2004), 765
Within-cluster relationships, 30–31
Within-group effect sizes, 93
Within-patient variations, 108–110
WOR (Ways of Responding), 279
Working Alliance Inventory (WAI), 397
World Economic Forum, 776